# Geographica

## WORLD ATLAS & ENCYCLOPEDIA

# Geographica

## WORLD ATLAS & ENCYCLOPEDIA

h.f.ullmann

Information in this edition:

The figures quoted in the statistics for the various countries are taken from a variety of sources: population figures are based on numbers quoted by the United Nations, economic data are taken either from World Bank statistics or the "CIA World Fact Book". The sizes of countries, their geography and social conditions are based on the "CIA World Fact Book" and information from the German Foreign Office. The publishers have made every effort to ensure that such information has been thoroughly researched.

In endeavouring for uniformity and comparability of economic data, the figures given consistently refer to Gross National Income (GNI) per capita, calculated by the Atlas method. This value has been expressed as Gross National Product in the past (changing in 1999). It refers not to total earnings of the country or region itself (Gross Domestic Product) but to those of the people living in the region and obtaining an income from economic activity. Both GNI and GDP, however, refer to market prices including taxes on goods (production taxes and import duties) but not including any subsidies or aid. The actual details of the calculation can nevertheless vary enormously since they may be based on floating currency rates for the US dollar (used as standard in this book), on a specific and abstract dollar value or on the actual purchasing power of the local currency.

| | |
|---|---|
| **Publisher:** | Gordon Cheers |
| **Associate publisher:** | Margaret Olds |
| **Managing editors:** | Philippe Sandall (text) |
| | Valerie Marlborough (maps) |
| **Editors:** | Scott Forbes |
| | Sue Grose-Hodge |
| | Gillian Hewitt |
| | Siobhan O'Connor |
| | Sarah Shrubb |
| | Carolyn Beaumont |
| | Anna Cheifetz |
| | Clare Double |
| | Kate Etherington |
| | Denise Imwold |
| | Heather Jackson |
| | Oliver Rennert |
| **Map editors:** | Janet Parker |
| | Fran Church |
| | Heather Martin |
| | Marlene Meynert |
| | Jan Watson |
| **Chief designer:** | Clare Forte |
| **Senior designer:** | Robert Taylor |
| **Production designers:** | Deborah Clarke |
| | Max Peatman |
| | James Young |
| **Cartographic manager:** | Graham Keane |
| **Senior cartographer:** | Andrew Dunlop |
| **Cartographers:** | Weimin Gu |
| | Paul McDonald |
| | David Morris |
| | Melissa O'Brien |
| | Clare Varney |
| **Consultant for water areas:** | Tony Davidson |
| **Thematic maps:** | John Frith |
| **Contour shading:** | John Gittoes |
| | Oliver Rennert |
| | Ray Sims |
| **Researchers:** | Derek Barton |
| | Claudia Zipfel |
| **Gazetteer:** | Valerie Marlborough |
| | Heather Jackson |
| | Janet Parker |
| | Dee Rogers |
| | Clare Double |
| **Typesetting:** | Dee Rogers |
| **Photo research:** | Gordon Cheers |
| **Photo library:** | Susan Page |
| **Production managers:** | Linda Watchorn |
| | Angela Alegounarias |
| **Publishing coordinator:** | Sarah Sherlock |
| **Publishing assistants:** | Olivia Kleindienst |
| | Anabel Pandiela |

**Layout (pages 105–461) and update of this edition:**
Martin Sulzer-Reichel,
Agents–Producers–Editors Int'l,
Richmond, VA

This edition published by arrangement with Random House Australia Pty Ltd.

Photos © Random House Australia Pty Ltd 1999
  from the Random House Photo Library, apart from the following:
pages 6 and 7 top left and bottom right, page 8 center and top right © Anglo-Australian Observatory (photograph by David Malin);
page 7 top right © Anglo-Australian Observatory/Royal Observatory Edinburgh (photograph from UK Schmidt plates by David Malin);
page 13 © 1999 by Fred Espenak;
pages 4, 5, 6 (bottom), page 8 (left), pages 9, 10, 12, 15, 17 courtesy of NASA
page III and cover courtesy of NASA Goddard Space Flight Center, A. F. Hasler, K. Palaniappan, H. Pierce, M. Manyin
© Sipa Press, Paris: pages 150 top (Thuan), 174 bottom (Abd Rabbo), 237 top right (Adenis), page 322 right (José Nicolas), page 332 bottom (Witt), page 335 top (Chalasani), page 343 top (Boigey);
© Laif, Cologne: pages 169 top right (Celentano), page 251 top (Zanettini), 444 (Kristensen)
© action press, Hamburg: pages 232–33 (Scanpix), 235 bottom (Lehtikuva)
© Bodil Sunde, Oslo: page 232 bottom right
© Look, Munich: pages 238, 238/39 (both: Wohner), 247 center, 392 (both: Heeb)
© ArchiTektur Bilderservice Kandula, Witten: page 248
© Tandem Verlag GmbH: page 249 top (Bednorz), 394 (Beans)
© Institut für Auslandsbeziehungen, Stuttgart: page 333

Text © Random House Australia Pty Ltd 1999

**Copyright © 2008 for this updated edition:**
**Tandem Verlag GmbH**
**h.f.ullmann is an imprint of Tandem Verlag GmbH**

Project management for this updated edition: Anke Moritz
Overall responsibility for production: h.f.ullmann publishing, Potsdam, Germany

Special edition

Printed in Singapore

ISBN 978-3-8331-5945-9

10 9 8 7 6 5 4 3 2
X IX VIII VII VI V

If you would like to be informed about forthcoming h.f.ullmann titles, you can request our newsletter by visiting our website (**www.ullmann-publishing.com**) or by emailing us at: newsletter@ullmann-publishing.com.
h.f.ullmann, Birkenstraße 10, 14469 Potsdam, Germany

**page V:** A Parisian sidewalk café, France
**page XII:** A farm at the foot of Mount Giestoso, Minho, Portugal
**pages XIV–XV:** View from Plaka towards the hill Lykavittos in Athens, Greece
**pages XXII–1:** Tongariro, volcano and crater, New Zealand
**pages 52–53:** An Aboriginal man fishing with spears in wetlands in the Northern Territory, Australia
**pages 98–99:** The countryside near Yangshuo in Guangxi Zhuangzu Zizhiqu Province, China
**pages 106–07:** A village on the Sepik River, Papua New Guinea
**pages 142–43:** Terrassed hills looking towards the Himalayas, Nepal
**pages 226–27:** The village Trebarwith Strand on the north coast of Carnwall, United Kingdom
**pages 310–11:** Rhinoceroses and calves in the waters of the Luangwa River in Zambia
**pages 374–75:** Grand Canyon, Arizona, USA
**pages 432–33:** Autumn colors in Tierra del Fuego, Argentina
**pages 462–63:** Polar bears in Arctic Siberia
**pages 472–73:** A whale shark in California waters
**pages 480–81:** Melting water in the Sharkiphu River Valley, Nepal

# Consultants and Contributors

## GENERAL EDITOR

Professor Ray Hudson BA, PhD, DSc
(University of Bristol), DSc (Honoris Causa, University
of Roskilde); Department of Geography, University of
Durham

## CONSULTANTS

Professor Tom McKnight BA, MA, PhD (University
of Wisconsin); Professor Emeritus of Geography,
University of California, Los Angeles

Professor Joan Clemons PhD (University of
Minnesota); Visiting Professor, Graduate School
of Education and Information Studies, University
of California, Los Angeles

Professor John Overton MA, PhD (Cambridge);
Professor, Institute of Development Studies, School
of Global Studies, Massey University

Professor Toru Taniuchi BA, MSc, DSc, (University
of Tokyo); Professor of Human Geography,
University of Tokyo, Japan

Professor Bruce Thom BA, PhD (Louisiana State
University), FIAG; Emeritus Professor of Geography,
University of Sydney, Visiting Professor of Geography,
University of New South Wales,

Professor William Wonders BA (Hons), MA, PhD
(University of Toronto), Fil.Dr.h.c. (Uppsala);
University Professor and Professor Emeritus of
Geography, University of Alberta

## CONTRIBUTORS
### Part 1 Planet Earth

Professor Bruce Thom BA, PhD (Louisiana State
University), F.I.A.G.

Dr John O'Byrne BSc, PhD (University of Sydney)
Dr Noel de Souza BSc (Hons), MSc., Doctorat de
Specialité (University of Paris)

Dr Ron Horvath BA, MA, PhD (University of
California, Los Angeles)

Dr Scott Mooney BSc (Hons), PhD (University of
New South Wales

### Part 2 People and Society

Dr Ron Brunton BA, MA, PhD (La Trobe
University)

Associate Professor Sybil Jack MA, BLitt (Oxon),
DipEd (University of New England)

Dr Ron Horvath BA, MA, PhD (University of
California, Los Angeles)

Tess Rod BA (Hons), MA, BComm

Roger Sandall BA, MA (Columbia University)

### Part 3 Regions of the World

Professor Bruce Thom BA, PhD (Louisiana State
University), F.I.A.G.

Roger Sandall BA, MA (Columbia University)

Dr Noel de Souza BSc (Hons), MSc, Doctorat de
Specialité (University of Paris)

Robert Coupe MA, DipEd

## CARTOGRAPHIC CONSULTANTS

Henk Brolsma, Associateship in Land Surveying;
Australian Antarctic Division, Tasmania,
Australia
*Antarctica*

Dr John Cornell BA, PhD (University of London)
*Papua New Guinea, Pacific Islands, Island
Nations and Dependencies*

Tony Davidson
*Europe, Russian Federation, former Soviet Republics*

Dr Noel de Souza BSc (Hons), MSc, Doctorat de
Specialité (University of Paris)
*India, Sri Lanka, Nepal, Bangladesh, Bhutan,
Pakistan*

Dr Joan Hardjono BA, LittB, PhD (University of New
England); Padjadjaran State University, Bandung,
Indonesia
*Indonesia, Malaysia, Singapore*

Dr Philip Hirsch BA, PhD
*Thailand, Laos, Myanmar, Cambodia, Vietnam,
Philippines*

Professor Naftali Kadmon BA, MSc, PhD (University
of Wales); Professor Emeritus, The Hebrew University
of Jerusalem, Israel
*Israel, Turkey, Iran, Cyprus, Afghanistan*

Gerry Leitner
*South America, Central America*

Dr Zhilin Li BEng, PhD (University of Glasgow)
Assistant Professor, The Hong Kong Polytechnic
University, Hong Kong
*China*

Professor Tanga Munkhtsetseg; International Relations
Institute, Ulan Bator, Mongolia
*Mongolia*

Chonghyon Paku MA BSc; Baito-Bunka University,
Tokyo, Japan
*Korea*

Karen Puklowski NZCD/Survey; Massey University,
New Zealand
*New Zealand*

Professor Chris Rogerson BSc (Hons), MSc, PhD
(Queens), FSAGS; University of Witwatersrand,
Johannesburg, South Africa
*Subsaharan Africa*

Dr Nasser Salma PhD (University of Washington,
Seattle); Associate Professor, King Saud University,
Riyadh, Saudi Arabia
*Arabic speaking countries of the Middle East
and Saharan Africa*

Brian Stokes BBus (Tourism), AssDipCart
*Australia*

Professor Toru Taniuchi BA, MSc, DSc (University
of Tokyo); Professor of Human Geography,
University of Tokyo, Japan
*Japan*

Glenn Toldi BSc, DipCart&GIS
*United States of America, Canada*

Lillian Wonders BA, MA
*Canada*

# Content

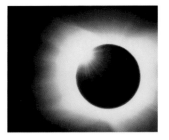

HOW THIS BOOK WORKS       X
FOREWORD                  XIII
INTRODUCTION              XIV

## PART 1

### Planet Earth       1

#### EARTH IN SPACE       2

Origins of the Universe • Galaxies • Stars • The Solar System • Planet Earth • The Moon • Space Exploration

#### EARTH AS A BIOPHYSICAL SYSTEM       18

Evolution of the Earth • Movement of Plates • Rocks • Landforms • Climate • The Water Cycle • Oceanography • Plants and Animals • Earth's Biosphere • Soils

#### EARTH AS A HOME FOR HUMANS       40

Land Resources • Ocean Resources • Commerce • Population and Health • Natural Hazards

## PART 2

### People and Society       52

Human Evolution • The First Modern Humans • Human Migrations • Languages and Writing • The Rise of Agriculture • Emerging Civilizations • The Impact of Civilization • From City-States to Empires • Religions of the World • Traders and Travelers • Explorers and Settlers • The Industrial World • The Nation-State • International Organizations • Globalization

#### TIMELINES OF WORLD HISTORY       86

## PART 3

### Regions of the World       98

### OCEANIA       106

New Zealand • Australia • Tuvalu • Samoa • Tonga • Papua New Guinea • Solomon Islands •

# Content

Vanuatu • Fiji • Palau • Micronesia • Marshall Islands • Kiribati • Nauru

*Dependencies and Territories: American Samoa, Ashmore and Cartier Islands, Baker and Howland Islands, Cook Islands, French Polynesia, Guam, Jarvis Island, Johnston Atoll, Kingman Reef, Cocos (Keeling) Islands, Coral Sea Islands, Midway Islands, New Caledonia, Niue, Northern Mariana Islands, Norfolk Island, Palmyra Atoll, Pitcairn Islands, Tokelau, Wake Island, Wallis and Futuna Islands, Christmas Island*

MAPS OF OCEANIA     128

## ASIA AND THE MIDDLE EAST     142

Indonesia • East Timor • Philippines • Brunei • Singapore • Malaysia • Cambodia • Vietnam • Laos • Thailand • Myanmar (Burma) • China • Taiwan • North Korea • South Korea • Japan • Sri Lanka • Maldives • India • Bangladesh • Bhutan • Nepal • Pakistan • Saudi Arabia • Yemen • Oman • United Arab Emirates • Kuwait • Qatar • Bahrain • Israel • Jordan • Lebanon • Syria • Iraq • Iran • Afghanistan • Kazakhstan • Uzbekistan • Mongolia • Kyrgyzstan • Turkmenistan • Tajikistan • Armenia • Azerbaijan • Georgia • Turkey • Cyprus

*Dependencies and Territories: Gaza Strip, West Bank, British Indian Ocean Territory, Paracel Islands, Spratly Islands*

MAPS OF ASIA AND THE MIDDLE EAST     194

## EUROPE AND THE RUSSIAN FEDERATION     226

Iceland • Norway • Sweden • Denmark • Finland • Estonia • Latvia • Lithuania • Germany • Netherlands • Belgium • Luxembourg • France • Monaco • Switzerland • Liechtenstein • Austria • Portugal • Andorra • Spain • Italy • San Marino •

# Content

Vatican City • Malta • Slovenia • Croatia • Bosnia and Herzegovina • Macedonia • Serbia • Kosovo • Montenegro • Hungary • Albania • Romania • Bulgaria • Greece • Czech Republic • Slovakia • Poland • Belarus • Ukraine • Moldova • Russian Federation • United Kingdom • Ireland

*Dependencies: Faeroe Islands, Gibraltar, Guernsey, The Isle of Man, Jersey, Svalbard*

**MAPS OF EUROPE AND THE RUSSIAN FEDERATION**     280

## AFRICA     310

Morocco • Algeria • Tunisia • Libya • Egypt • Mauritania • Cape Verde • Senegal • Gambia • Guinea-Bissau • Guinea • Sierra Leone • Liberia • Côte d'Ivoire • Mali • Burkina Faso • Ghana • Togo • Benin • Niger • Chad • Nigeria • Cameroon • Central African Republic • Equatorial Guinea • São Tomé and Príncipe • Gabon • Congo • Democratic Republic of the Congo • Angola • Sudan • Eritrea • Ethiopia • Djibouti • Somalia • Uganda • Kenya • Tanzania • Rwanda • Burundi • Zambia • Malawi • Mozambique • Zimbabwe • Botswana • Swaziland • Lesotho • Namibia • South Africa • Comoros • Seychelles • Madagascar • Mauritius

*Dependencies and Territories: Mayotte, Réunion, Western Sahara, St Helena*

**MAPS OF AFRICA**     356

## NORTH AND CENTRAL AMERICA     374

Canada • United States of America • Bahamas • Cuba • Jamaica • Haiti • Dominican Republic • St Kitts and Nevis • Antigua and Barbuda • Dominica • St Lucia • St Vincent and the Grenadines • Barbados • Grenada • Trinidad and Tobago • Mexico • Guatamala • Belize • Honduras • El Salvador • Nicaragua • Costa Rica • Panama

# Content

*Dependencies and Territories: Virgin Islands of the United States, Anguilla, Aruba, Bermuda, British Virgin Islands, Cayman Islands, Greenland, Guadeloupe, Jan Mayen, Martinique, Montserrat, Navassa, Netherlands Antilles, Puerto Rico, St Pierre and Miquelon, Turks and Caicos Islands*

**MAPS OF NORTH AND
CENTRAL AMERICA**     **406**

**SOUTH AMERICA**     **432**

Colombia • Venezuela • Guyana • Ecuador • Suriname • Brazil • Peru • Bolivia • Chile • Argentina • Uruguay • Paraguay

*Dependencies and Territories: Falkland Islands, French Guiana, South Georgia and the South Sandwich Islands*

**MAPS OF SOUTH AMERICA**     **446**

**THE POLAR REGIONS**     **462**

Antarctica • Arctic

*Dependencies and Territories: Bouvet Island, French Southern and Antarctic Lands, Heard and MacDonald Islands, Peter I Island*

**MAPS OF THE POLAR
REGIONS**     **470**

**THE OCEANS**     **472**

**MAPS OF THE OCEANS**     **476**

**PART 4**

**Gazetteer**     **480**

# How This Book Works

*Geographica* is an authoritative, comprehensive and fully illustrated reference guide to the world. With maps, photographs, illustrations and text, *Geographica* will carry readers on a journey from outer space and Earth's place in the universe to the nations and cities, towns and even villages on the furthermost parts of the globe. An expert team of geographers, historians, anthropologists, astronomers, writers, editors and cartographers have worked together to create this reference.

The first part of the book is organized in topics which are each presented on a double-page spread for easy access to information. The text has been written by leading experts in their fields. The very best photographs have been

chosen, and illustrations and thematic maps have been specially commissioned to complement the text. Many of the double-page spreads contain a feature box which looks at one aspect of the topic on the spreads in detail.

*Geographica* then moves on to the core of the book; this contains maps and detailed text on the world's 193 nations which are members of the United Nations and 65 dependencies and overseas territories. The world has been divided into major continents or regions (Oceania, Asia and the Middle East, Europe and the Russian Federation, Africa, North America and Central America, South America, Polar Regions, and Oceans). Each region starts with an introductory essay on the

region in general and then moves on to entries for every country, territory or dependency. The country entries feature informative descriptions of the nation and its people, physical features and land use, culture, and economy and resources. Each country entry includes a locator map, the national flag, a locator globe, and a Fact File. Entries for the major nations also include a historical timeline. The entries for the dependencies and territories follow the country entries.

The Fact Files contain a wealth of carefully researched information for quick access to each nation's key indicators, such as form of government, infant mortality, literacy, ethnic diversity, religions and economy, as well as basic data

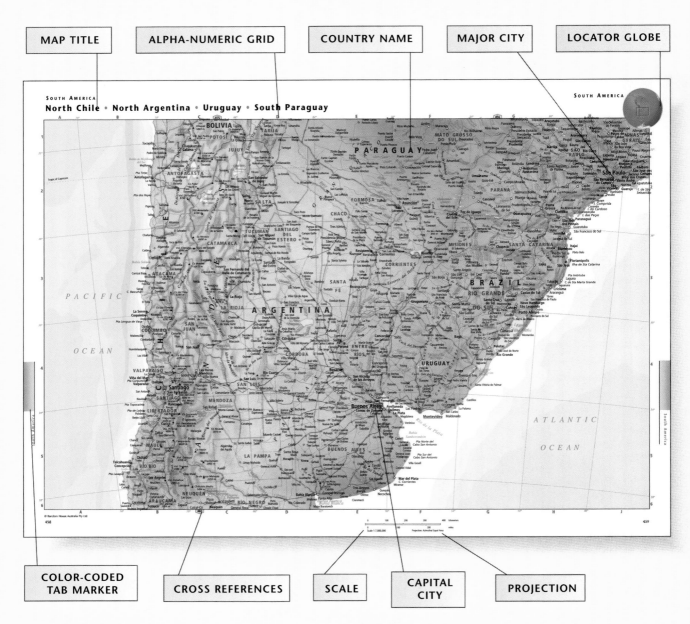

**MAP TITLE** · **ALPHA-NUMERIC GRID** · **COUNTRY NAME** · **MAJOR CITY** · **LOCATOR GLOBE**

**COLOR-CODED TAB MARKER** · **CROSS REFERENCES** · **SCALE** · **CAPITAL CITY** · **PROJECTION**

# Legend

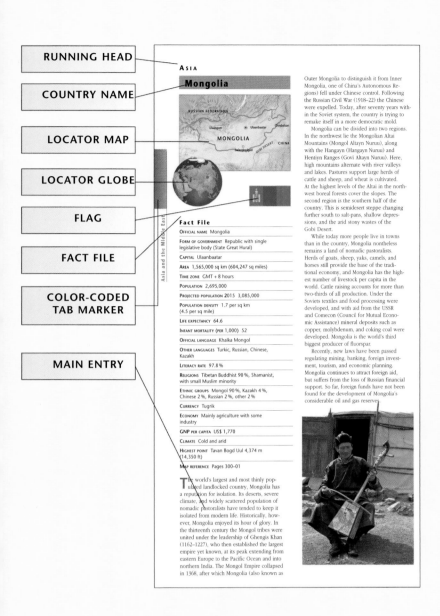

| | |
|---|---|
| **RUNNING HEAD** | ASIA |
| **COUNTRY NAME** | **Mongolia** |
| **LOCATOR MAP** | |
| **LOCATOR GLOBE** | |
| **FLAG** | |
| **FACT FILE** | |
| **COLOR-CODED TAB MARKER** | |
| **MAIN ENTRY** | |

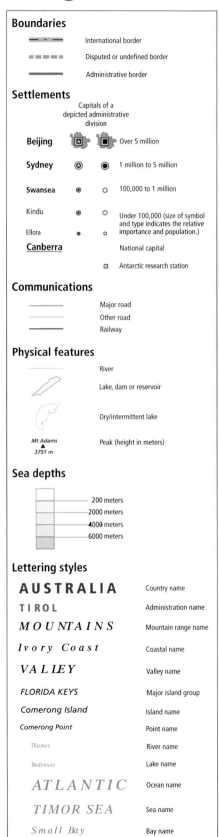

Outer Mongolia to distinguish it from Inner Mongolia, one of China's Autonomous Regions) fell under Chinese control. Following the Russian Civil War (1918–22) the Chinese were expelled. Today, after seventy years within the Soviet system, the country is trying to remake itself in a more democratic mold.

Mongolia can be divided into two regions. In the northwest lie the Mongolian Altai Mountains (Mongol Altayn Nuruu), along with the Hangayn (Hangayn Nuruu) and Hentiyn Ranges (Govĭ Altayn Nuruu). Here, high mountains alternate with river valleys and lakes. Pastures support large herds of cattle and sheep, and wheat is cultivated. At the highest levels of the Altai in the northwest boreal forests cover the slopes. The second region is the southern half of the country. This is semidesert steppe changing further south to salt-pans, shallow depressions, and the arid stony wastes of the Gobi Desert.

While today more people live in towns than in the country, Mongolia nonetheless remains a land of nomadic pastoralists. Herds of goats, sheep, yaks, camels, and horses still provide the base of the traditional economy, and Mongolia has the highest number of livestock per capita in the world. Cattle raising accounts for more than two-thirds of all production. Under the Soviets textiles and food processing were developed, and with aid from the USSR and Comecon (Council for Mutual Economic Assistance) mineral deposits such as copper, molybdenum, and coking coal were developed. Mongolia is the world's third biggest producer of fluorspar.

Recently, new laws have been passed regulating mining, banking, foreign investment, tourism, and economic planning. Mongolia continues to attract foreign aid, but suffers from the loss of Russian financial support. So far, foreign funds have not been found for the development of Mongolia's considerable oil and gas reserves.

The world's largest and most thinly populated landlocked country, Mongolia has a reputation for isolation. Its deserts, severe climate, and widely scattered population of nomadic pastoralists have tended to keep it isolated from modern life. Historically, however, Mongolia enjoyed its hour of glory. In the thirteenth century the Mongol tribes were united under the leadership of Ghengis Khan (1162–1227), who then established the largest empire yet known, at its peak extending from eastern Europe to the Pacific Ocean and into northern India. The Mongol Empire collapsed in 1368, after which Mongolia (also known as

---

## Legend

### Boundaries

International border

Disputed or undefined border

Administrative border

### Settlements

Capitals of a depicted administrative division

| | | |
|---|---|---|
| **Beijing** | | Over 5 million |
| **Sydney** | | 1 million to 5 million |
| **Swansea** | | 100,000 to 1 million |
| **Kindu** | | Under 100,000 (size of symbol and type indicates the relative importance and population.) |
| **Ellora** | | |
| <u>Canberra</u> | | National capital |
| | | Antarctic research station |

### Communications

Major road

Other road

Railway

### Physical features

River

Lake, dam or reservoir

Dry/intermittent lake

Mt Adams
▲
3751 m

Peak (height in meters)

### Sea depths

200 meters
2000 meters
4000 meters
6000 meters

### Lettering styles

| | |
|---|---|
| **AUSTRALIA** | Country name |
| **TIROL** | Administration name |
| *MOUNTAINS* | Mountain range name |
| *Ivory Coast* | Coastal name |
| *VALLEY* | Valley name |
| *FLORIDA KEYS* | Major island group |
| *Comerong Island* | Island name |
| *Comerong Point* | Point name |
| *Thames* | River name |
| *Bodensee* | Lake name |
| *ATLANTIC* | Ocean name |
| *TIMOR SEA* | Sea name |
| *Small Bay* | Bay name |

---

including offical name, population, language, currency, and climate. All figures are the latest available and have been drawn from internationally recognized sources. Economic data are taken either from World Bank statistics or the *CIA World Fact Book.* Geographic data comes from the *CIA World Fact Book* or the German Foreign office

Regional maps are at the end of each section for ease of reference. Physical and political maps for each region are followed by more detailed mapping. Editorial policy on the spelling of place names was decided after researching a wide number of sources. The cartographic and editorial team used the *US Board of Geographic Names* database as a guide, and a team of international cartographic experts was consulted on maps for every region. Our

editorial policy has been to use English for the names of countries (e.g., France), international bodies of water (e.g., Pacific Ocean, Black Sea) and regional features that cross international borders (e.g., Carpathian Mountains). Local name forms have been used for all other names, but for capital cities and for some major cities and features, the English name is also provided in brackets. These English names are cross-referenced in the gazetteer, which includes all names on the physical and political maps, as well as the regional maps.

Recent name changes and boundary changes are shown on the maps. The contour shading used on the maps is based on a combination of altitude and vegetation and provides an idea of how the area would appear from space.

# Foreword

Geographica should be seen as a pathway for a journey of each reader's discovery of the world. Our journey commences with the origin of the universe and the birth of Earth, the planet of life. Land, water and the atmosphere provide sustenance for complex evolving life forms, culminating in the arrival of those dominant creatures, humans. Geological history, influenced by ever-changing natural forces, gradually turns into documented human history. Then our journey leads us into an understanding of how Earth has been transformed by the actions of countless millions of humans and their immediate ancestors over the past million years or so.

Geographica is about a world that has, and will continue to be, changed. It is designed to be a substantial reference of world information. Original maps convey a vast amount of place-names and boundaries, many of which have changed with the course of history. Timelines describe events that have influenced how humans relate to their environment and to each other. Fact Files for each country offer readers comprehensive descriptions of national identities as they have emerged in recent times, many of which are still undergoing change. A number of essays are used to highlight key characteristics of the way landscapes have evolved and how humans relate to each other.

These features are documented by new maps on a world scale and also on national scales.

The journey Geographica offers readers is the exploration of a world often ravaged by war, pestilence, human suffering, and the degradation of the environment. But it is also a world where we can conquer great challenges, discover the unknown, and improve the quality of life of many people through the better use of natural and human resources. The future always holds great uncertainty; yet knowledge of the past and present geographical and historical conditions of our planet can only strengthen our ability to plan for a peaceful and ecologically sustainable world in which we and the generations to come can lead fulfilling lives.

This volume represents the combined efforts of many people. As geographers, cartographers, historians, illustrators and editors we seek to offer our readers a substantial educational experience—a journey into the past and an appreciation of the present as it has evolved.

**Professor BRUCE G. THOM**
**BA, PhD (Louisiana State University), FIAG**

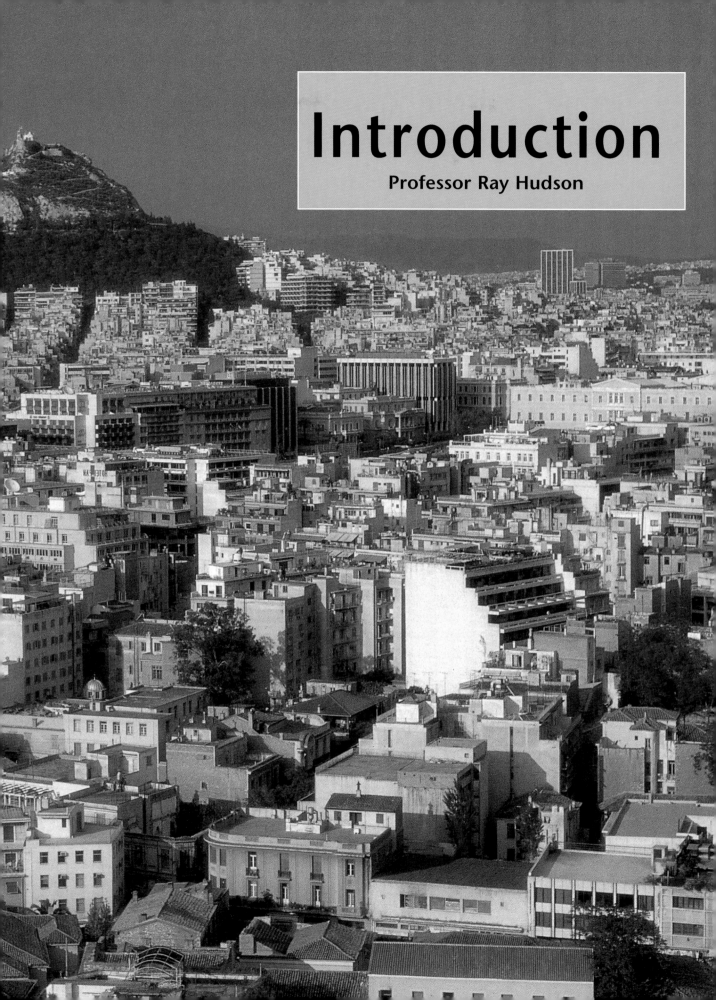

# Introduction

**Professor Ray Hudson**

# Europe and the Russian Federation: The Changing Scene

*The Mediterranean area is the birthplace of the ancient Greek and Roman civilizations. The Acropolis in Athens (above) bears the ruins of buildings from around 400 BC. Carcassone Castle, France (opposite), is an excellent example of medieval fortification.*

If you look at Earth on a globe, the extent of the roughly triangular landmass covered by Europe and the Russian Federation is staggering—an enormous swathe of land extending almost around the world and from around 35° north of the equator to well into the Arctic Circle.

On two and a half sides, this large triangle is bounded by seas and oceans. This gives an initial indication of one of the many problems of defining precisely where the boundaries of Europe and the Russian Federation lie—many of the islands (of which arguably the most significant are those that make up the United Kingdom and the Republic of Ireland) lie off the coasts of Europe and the Federation. Furthermore, some European countries continue to have overseas territories that are colonies or dependencies, legacies of former empires, and a few have offshore islands that are an integral part of the national state—the Azores and Canary Islands in the Atlantic Ocean, parts of the territories of Portugal and Spain respectively, for example.

There are fairly clear physical boundaries to continental mainland Europe to the west (the Atlantic Ocean), to the north (the Arctic Ocean) and to the south (the Mediterranean Sea), although the southern boundary is less clear-cut around the eastern extremities of the Mediterranean Sea. Turkey, for example, is a member of NATO (the North Atlantic Treaty Organization) but is not generally regarded as a part of Europe.

In the same way, the Russian Federation has clear physical boundaries to the north, east and south, but at its western edge the European landmass slides into the Asian landmass without a precise border. Often the range of the Ural Mountains is taken as the boundary between European Russia to the west and the vast Siberian Plain and Asia to the east. In other respects, however, the boundary between Europe and Asia is more of a political and cultural divide than one that can be defined unambiguously by topography and physical geography.

## THE NATURAL ENVIRONMENT

The natural environment of Europe and the Russian Federation is extremely diverse, as variations in latitude, longitude, and altitude combine to produce a great range of climatic and physical conditions and corresponding flora and fauna. Some of these environments have offered attractive possibilities for human settlement, influencing early patterns of habitation and also migration; others are harsh and unwelcoming, and have proved difficult to colonize even with the help of developments in contemporary technology.

The legacies of geology offer great opportunities in some parts of Europe and the Russian Federation, which have rich deposits of carboniferous and metallic minerals. Historically, these resources have been critical in influencing the pattern of economic development within these areas.

## CLIMATE

Europe and the Russian Federation exhibit a vast latitudinal and longitudinal spread that is reflected in great climatic variation. The landmass extends almost around the globe, from a little more than 20°W at the westernmost tip of Ireland (though the western tip of Greenland is more than 70°W) all the way east (to around 170°E at the tip of the Bering Strait, which separates Asia from Alaska).

From its southernmost point, just below 35°N on the Greek island of Crete (although the Canary Islands lie not far north of the Tropic of Cancer in the Atlantic Ocean, just off the west African coast) Europe stretches northwards above the Arctic Circle, to North Cape in Norway. Much of Russia also lies well north of the Arctic Circle, extending almost to Alaska. Land in these latitudes is typically tundra, with the soil frozen for much of the year (permafrost) and a very short growing season.

The mean January temperature is below 0°C (32°F) over much of central, eastern and northern Europe and much of the Russian Federation; in inland Siberia it even falls below –50°C (–58°F). Few people live in these harsh environments.

In contrast, much of western and southern Europe has a more temperate climate and supports larger populations, though heavy urbanization means that distributions are uneven. The moderation of climatic extremes is especially noticeable in the west of the continent. Here, the effects of the Atlantic Ocean and the Gulf Stream soften the climatic extremes found in the continental interior in areas of eastern Europe and the Russian Federation. Mean July temperatures rarely exceed 30°C (86°F) even in the southernmost parts of Europe, but often exceed 20°C (68°F) over much of the inland continental areas of the Russian Federation. Given the longitudinal extent of Europe and the Russian Federation, the climatic contrast between maritime and inland continental areas is extremely pronounced.

The climate in the southern areas of Europe, around the Mediterranean Sea, is warm temperate with mild, wet winters and hot, dry summers—the classic Mediterranean climate in which much of European civilization and culture first took root during the classical Greek and Roman periods of history.

This broad climatic pattern generated by latitudinal and longitudinal variation is further complicated by altitudinal variation which adds another layer of complexity to the pattern of climatic variation.

## LANDFORMS

The landscape of much of the area, and of Europe in particular, is the product of past (but in geological time, fairly recent) periods of orogenesis—when upward movements of the Earth's crust formed mountain ranges—especially during the Alpine period. Major mountain ranges stretch from the Iberian Peninsula through the Massif Central of France to the French, Swiss, Italian and Austrian Alps, to the Dynaric Alps and Apennines on either side of the Adriatic Sea in Italy and the former Yugoslavia respectively, and as far east as the Carpathian Alps, mainly in the eastern part of Romania. Most of Europe's major rivers, including the Danube, Rhine, Rhone, Loire and Po, originate in

these upland areas and drain to the various seas surrounding the continent.

To the southeast, the Caucasus form a land boundary on the bridge of land separating the Black Sea and the Caspian Sea, between Armenia and Azerbaijan and Turkey and Iran to their southeast. In the northwest, much of Scandinavia is also mountainous. A large part of these mountainous areas have been glaciated and processes of glaciation are ongoing.

To the north of the main mountain regions, most of Europe and the Russian Federation comprise the north European and Siberian plains. While some major rivers, such as the Ob and Yenisei, drain from the Siberian Plain to the Arctic Ocean, much of the drainage of the plain is to inland seas and lakes. The Volga River, for example, drains into the Caspian Sea, and other rivers drain into the Aral and Black Seas. The plains are periodically interrupted by ranges of mountain (such as the Urals) and by lower lying hills, bounded to the south by the hill and mountain ranges of Iran, Afghanistan, China and Mongolia.

In the far east, the Siberian Plain gradually rises in elevation and eventually gives way to the Verkoyhansk and then the Kolyma Mountains before the Russian Federation finally reaches its eastern boundaries in the Bering Sea and the Sea of Okhotsk.

Much of these plains was formed by various types of glacial deposits. In the north, much of Finland and southern Scandinavia also exhibit considerable evidence of glacial erosion, as in the numerous lakes of Finland.

## VEGETATION

Much of Europe is forested, especially in the higher regions. The natural vegetation of the vast majority of Europe and a fair part of the

Russian Federation is a mixture of broad-leafed deciduous and coniferous forest. Deciduous trees are generally more prevalent in the milder and wetter temperate areas, with conifers found further north in the colder regions; where the climate becomes too harsh for trees, tundra is dominant.

Around the Mediterranean region, evergreen trees and shrubs are the most common form of vegetation. As rainfall decreases with increasing distance eastwards, however, forested areas give way to steppe grassland. Within the milder temperate and Mediterranean areas, increasing altitude produces the same changes in vegetation as increasing latitude.

## ENVIRONMENTAL TRANSFORMATION

While forest is the natural vegetation of much of Europe and Russia, the majority of this, especially in Europe, has been cleared for agriculture and other uses. Manufacturing industry, mining, and the expansion of cities and towns have all dramatically changed the landscape, and advances in technology have also allowed us to exploit the resources offered by the natural environment. Indeed, much of what is often thought of as the natural landscape is in fact a social product—the result of extended interactions between people and the environment. This process of environmental transformation has a very long history—it started when people first began to make the transition from peripatetic hunter-gatherers to become sedentary agriculturalists and farmers, establishing communities and settlements.

It is only in the last two or three hundred years, however, that dramatic technological advances in agriculture, combined with the developments of the Industrial Revolution, have allowed people to radically alter the natural environment in Europe. Irrigation and artificial

fertilizers have permitted agriculture to flourish in formerly uncultivable regions, and the gradual process of removing natural vegetation and adding chemicals to the soil has altered the natural balance which had evolved over thousands of years.

While large-scale environmental processes remain beyond human control, the capacity to alter environmental conditions on a local or regional scale and to overcome environmental constraints has increased greatly in modern time, especially in wealthier countries. Such transformations have become integral to the development of industrial capitalism in Europe. One spectacular example of this is the reclamation of the Dutch polders and the subsequent development of intensive commercial glasshouse agriculture on this land which used to be part of the sea. Conquering nature was also an important preoccupation in the communist former USSR (Union of Soviet Socialist Republics), where it was seen as proof of the capacity of state socialism to triumph over a hostile environment for the collective good.

Thus in a whole variety of ways, and for a variety of motives, people have learned to modify their local environments so that they can live more comfortably, so that plants can be cultivated and animals reared.

It is also worth remembering, however, that human efforts to transform the natural environment and improve material living standards in turn have their own impact on the environment. One of the most spectacular—and unwanted—examples of this is the dramatic shrinkage of the inland Aral Sea in Kazakhstan in the Russian Federation. Another is the extensive soil erosion induced by large-scale agriculture in formerly fertile natural grassland transformed to cereal and cotton-growing areas. Manmade disasters

can also have a devastating environmental impact—radioactive waste and smoke from the 1986 fire at the Chernobyl nuclear reactor, in Ukraine, spread widely over much of Russia and Europe as a result of westerly winds.

In addition, other human activities in the countries of Europe and the Russian Federation are a major contributing force to processes such as global warming which threatens possible climatic change and rising sea levels. Low-lying coastal areas and those that have been reclaimed from the sea (like the polders of the Netherlands) are particularly vulnerable to such changes.

## A CHANGING
## POLITICAL-ECONOMIC MAP

For much of their history, the lands of Europe and the Russian Federation have been the arena for a succession of migrations and movements of people. As they gradually became settled, people sought to establish the boundaries of their own territories and armed conflict and wars became almost endemic as different groups sought to expand their territory, or to protect it from others seeking to take it from them. Empires were built, then declined within Europe—from the Roman to the Austro-Hungarian.

For several hundred years, this ebb and flow of political fortunes as an assortment of emperors, kings, queens and princes fought to consolidate and increase their territory, was accompanied by economic stagnation as European economies were predominantly organized around various forms of subsistence agriculture.

*The church of Sveti Jovan Bogoslov Kaneo, on the shores of Ohrid Lake, Macedonia (right). Blaenau Ffestiniog in Wales, where the houses are dwarfed by the slate mine workings (above).*

### THE GROWTH OF EMPIRES

Towards the end of the fifteenth century, a number of European states began to explore the possibilities of creating empires outside Europe. This added a new dimension to the political struggle between states, and a new source of economic dynamism, as new subtropical and tropical crops and products began to arrive in Europe.

A number of European states sought to establish new empires in the "New World", and there was much competition between the British, Dutch, French, Portuguese and Spanish. By the nineteenth century, however, Britain had emerged as the dominant power (despite the loss of its colonies in North America). Trade began to allow the accumulation of capital and, in due course, that capital was channelled into economic development within Europe.

The agricultural and industrial revolutions gave considerable impetus to the economies of the leading European states, as industrial capitalism became established first in Britain and then in Belgium, Germany, France and other continental European countries. This diffusion was an uneven process, however, and many areas of Europe and Russia were virtually untouched by these new developments, remaining locked in a pre-industrial and pre-capitalist world until well into the twentieth century.

The rise of industrial powers within Europe increased the pressure among them to create empires. New colonies would provide European countries with cheap food and raw materials while also creating a new market, beyond the national markets, for the sale of industrial goods made in Europe. In the latter part of the nineteenth century European countries such as Belgium and Germany joined in the race to establish their own foreign empires. At the same time the struggle for supremacy within Europe intensified, as larger modern national states became established. This process of state building often led to people of different nations becoming citizens of the same state. People and places moved between states as national boundaries shifted (for example, Alsace and Lorraine moved between France and Germany on an almost regular basis). This process of economic and territorial competition finally culminated in the appalling destruction of the First World War, and the postwar settlement led to the creation of completely new states in the Baltic and the Balkans as the old Austro-Hungarian Empire was dismantled.

There followed a period of deep economic recession and dislocation, part of a wider global slump. This helped produce a resurgence of nationalist sentiment, most infamously in Germany, with the rise of fascism and its concepts of racial supremacy and *lebensraum* (living space), which were used to justify ethnic cleansing and territorial aggrandizement. Other parts of Europe followed a different path—most notably Russia. Here the October 1917 Revolution established a communist government and presaged the emergence of the USSR, dominated by Russia, in 1922. In 1939, the growing ambitions of fascist Germany culminated in the outbreak of the

Second World War, leading to further devastation and carnage in Europe.

## AFTER THE SECOND WORLD WAR

The immediate postwar period was to reshape the map of Europe for the next fifty or so years—in ways that had global implications—until the de facto collapse of socialism in Europe in 1989 and the formal break-up of the USSR in 1991. At the end of the Second World War, the USSR occupied most of eastern Europe. The partitioning of Berlin between East and West in 1948 and the creation of two Germanies (the Federal Republic of Germany and the German Democratic Republic) confirmed that postwar Europe would be divided into two ideologically opposed blocs, a capitalist West and communist East. The "Cold War" had descended on Europe.

In 1949 NATO was established as a common defense organization in the west. The USSR developed a series of buffer satellite states between itself and Western Europe, and became the center of both economic (COMECON) and defense (the Warsaw Pact) alliances. In these ways, the USSR sought to prevent the spread of capitalism into the East and to limit the ambitions of the USA, with which it vied to become the dominant global power.

There were also significant moves to redraw the political map within Western Europe—in large part stimulated by a wish to avoid future European wars—by creating new supranational institutions. Thus in 1951 the European Coal and Steel Community (the ECSC) was established with the signing of the Treaty of Paris by Belgium, France, Germany, Italy, Luxembourg and the Netherlands. This sought to guarantee the future peace of Europe by inextricably binding together the coal and steel industries of France and Germany, then seen as the key to the capacity to wage war. Plans for a greater degree of political unification and the creation of a common European Defense Force foundered.

In response, the six signatories of the Treaty of Paris then signed the Treaty of Rome (in 1957) creating the European Economic Community (EEC). The aim of the EEC was to promote democratic political systems and economic growth and the free movement of capital and labor within the territory of the member countries. This posed problems for those Western European states that had not signed the Treaty of Rome. In 1960 Austria, Denmark, Portugal, Norway, Sweden, Switzerland and the United Kingdom signed the Stockholm Convention, which established the European Free Trade Area (EFTA). This effectively divided Western Europe into two free trade areas, EFTA and the EEC. Much of the next thirty or so years witnessed a redefinition of the boundaries between these two groupings.

In the late 1950s and 1960s the countries of the EEC enjoyed sustained high rates of economic growth—so much so that they drew in migrant workers from Mediterranean Europe and North Africa as a way of avoiding labor shortages. Other Western European countries began to gaze with envious eyes at the economic growth rates of the six signatories to the Treaty of Rome, and to consider whether their interests would not be better served by joining the EEC.

In 1973 Denmark, Ireland, and the UK became members of the EEC, significantly shifting the balance between it and EFTA.

In the 1960s and 1970s, the EEC concluded a series of trade treaties with a number of southern European, Mediterranean and North African states and former colonies in other regions of the developing world. These trade and aid agreements tied these countries closely into the EEC's economy in various ways—as markets for their agricultural produce and migrant workers and as suppliers of technology, especially that needed for industrial development.

Several of the southern European states actively sought full membership of the EEC but failed to meet a key condition for entry to the club—Greece, Portugal and Spain had dictatorial rather than democratic political systems. With a return to democracy in the mid-1970s in these countries, however, the way was clear for full membership—Greece joined the EEC in 1981, Portugal and Spain in 1986. The reunification of the two Germanies in 1990 further enlarged the European Community, while in 1995 Austria, Finland and Sweden also joined. The EEC now had 15 members.

There are strong pressures for further expansion, predominantly south and east, with Cyprus, the Czech Republic, Estonia, Hungary, Poland and Slovenia signing on in 2004. Thus former members of COMECON became members of the European Union following the breakup of the USSR and the emergence of the looser federation of the Commonwealth of Independent States (CIS) in 1991.

This is seen as a way of underwriting capitalism and democracy throughout Eastern Europe in the twenty-first century, much as the Mediterranean enlargement of the 1980s was seen as a way of underpinning democracy and ensuring the end of dictatorships in Greece, Portugal and Spain.

At the same time as extending territorially, there have also been processes of deepening integration, leading to a transition from the EEC to the European Union following the 1992 Maastricht Treaty. There have been significant moves to complete the Single European Market and towards economic and monetary union, with eleven of the member states signing up to a common currency (the Euro) from 1 January 1999 (the non-participants are Denmark, Greece, Sweden and the UK).

There has been a complex process of political change throughout Europe since the 1950s, with tendencies towards the creation and collapse of supranational organizations. Of particular significance has been the collapse of the former USSR and, related to this, of the federal Yugoslav Republic. Here, ethnic and religious tensions which had been kept in check for many decades were suddenly released with devastating and tragic consequences. Much of the Balkans and many of the republics in the southeastern European part of the Commonwealth of Independent States erupted into violence as a range of national groups sought to secure their own territorial states. They often pursued this goal using savage military force and ethnic cleansing on a scale not seen in Europe since the horrors of the Holocaust in the 1930s.

At the the beginning of the twenty-first century, as at the start of the twentieth century, much of Europe has again been engulfed in war, centered on the Balkans. Unlike the early years of the last century, however, developments in the global media now ensure that individuals worldwide are kept informed of events in the European arena as televisions broadcast pictures (transmitted in real time) of the damage wrought by missile attacks and "smart" bombs, and of refugees forced to flee their homes under threat of death.

## ECONOMIC DIVERSITY: VARIETIES OF CAPITALISM

With the formal dissolution of the USSR in 1991, the economic landscape was no longer one of competition between capitalism and socialism but rather one of competition between varieties of capitalism found over Europe and the Russian Federation.

One immediate consequence of the collapse of socialism was to increase poverty and inequality within this new shared space. Attempts to establish thriving capitalist economies over much of Eastern Europe and Russia and its republics failed initially, as the cultural and institutional requirements for such a change were simply not present. Moreover, the social welfare supports of the former socialist system were swept away.

Economic transition was reasonably smooth in the more economically advanced countries of the former COMECON in which forms of private property ownership had survived in the socialist period or emerged well before 1989 (in the Czech Republic, Hungary and Poland).

Elsewhere, however, economies simply collapsed, while in Russia and several of the other member states of the Commonwealth of Independent States, black markets, gangsterism and crim-

inal capitalism of a sort associated with the Mafia became the norm. Where economic collapse went hand-in-hand with the devastation of war and forced population movements, problems of poverty, ill health and death became even more acute.

In contrast, over much of the European Union, economic fortunes have become more assured and lifestyles correspondingly more comfortable. There are differences in the forms of capitalism (for example, Germany and Sweden remain much more committed to corporatist approaches, the UK to a neo-liberal market approach), but even these differences have been reduced by the need to conform to the criteria for entry to the European Monetary Union. This is not to deny that considerable inequalities remain within the European Union—at national, regional and local scales and between people—but these are insignificant compared with the situation in much of Eastern Europe, Russia and the rest of the CIS.

There are marked variations in population densities within the European Union, with people heavily clustered in urban areas, which typically rely on service-based economies. There are similar variations in output and income per capita and also in the sectoral structure of economies, with the more developed and affluent regions generally relying less upon agriculture and more upon advanced services. National economies vary greatly in size and structure, but the pattern and variation at subnational scales is more complex still.

The scope of welfare state provision has certainly been reduced over much of Western Europe, often as a direct response to the need to meet the fiscal and macroeconomic requirements for entry to the European Monetary Union. Nevertheless, the welfare net still remains in place to an extent no longer found over much of

the remainder of Russia and the CIS and parts of southern and eastern Europe.

This provision, along with the perception of more and better job opportunities in the West, has encouraged fears of floods of economic migrants (as opposed to political refugees) from Eastern Europe and the Russian Federation (as well as possibly from North Africa). One consequence of this has been concern about both immigration polices into the European Union and

the status of individuals of varied ethnic origins who have lived in Europe for decades, after arriving as temporary migrant workers, but who still lack citizenship rights.

We began with a question—where is Europe? However, more important questions to consider for the future are perhaps who are Europeans now, what does it mean to be European, and what are the rights and responsibilities of each putative European citizen?

*The mild climate of Madeira makes these Portuguese islands a popular resort all year round (left). An aerial view of the old city of Salzburg (top) on the south bank of the Salzach River, in Austria. Dubrovnik (above), in Croatia, is another city that retains its Old Town charm; here the Franciscan belltower is featured.*

## Part 1

# Planet Earth

# Earth in Space

*Humans have always been fascinated by Earth's place in the universe. Earth (above) is just one of many planets, moons, asteroids and comets that form our solar system. We still have much to learn about how the solar system formed, and to predict about how it will end. An artist's impression of the surface of Earth (right) shows the land and water that cover its crust.*

Ideas on the origin of Earth, other planets, the Sun and stars can be traced to the time of classical Greece. They range from an Earth-centered universe to one where the position of this tiny, life-generating planet is placed in a context of an expanding universe populated by billions of stars, with an unknown number of planets similar to ours in composition and structure.

It was late in the eighteenth century that the great early geologist James Hutton (1726–97), a Scot, captured in a few poignant words the vastness and the immensity of time over which Earth, the Sun, the solar system, the galaxies, and the universe have evolved. He noted that there is "no vestige of a beginning, no prospect of an end". This phrase challenged the established thinking of a very limited time for the creation of the natural world and opened up a new era of geological and cosmological thought.

We live on a planet that is circling a single star of apparently limitless energy. Yet we now know that the engine of nuclear heat driving the Sun has a birth and a stable phase, and, as it runs short of hydrogen fuel, will go through enormous cataclysms. This process will absorb the Sun's dependent planets, and eventually lead to its own slow "death".

Our views of Earth as part of the universe have varied over time. New concepts and theories, such as Einstein's general theory of relativity, have offered scientists different perspectives on the origin of the universe and all matter. New technologies ranging from telescopes to satellites have opened up vast vistas within and beyond our solar system. Now available to scientists are tools to measure the composition and structure of matter racing through space. We understand much better the characteristics of various forces at work, such as those driving the expansion of the universe, the clustering of stars, the condensation of gases, the orbits of planets, and the movement of meteorites.

The Big-Bang model for the universe is based on a number of observations. It is not speculation. Yet, as a model of how the universe evolved, it has been modified by cosmologists and scientists over time. New observations should lead to further changes as we continue to explore whether there is enough matter and energy in the universe to slow and stop the expansion started 10 billion or 15 billion years ago.

As gases condensed to form stars, there was a distinct tendency for these stars to cluster. The Milky Way Galaxy is an example of a large spiral galaxy or cluster of stars composed of a thin, circular disk surrounding a central bulge. Interestingly, new technologies show that many galaxies, including the Milky Way, have more mass than can readily be seen. There also appears to exist at the core of some galaxies a central powerhouse generating narrow jets of high-energy particles streaming outwards. Only more observations and theorizing will help us understand the significance of these phenomena.

Yet it is the stars themselves which offer so many clues to the origin of the universe and, ultimately, ourselves. They vary widely in size, color, and temperature. Stars are powered by nuclear reactions whereby hydrogen is fused to helium. We now possess knowledge of sequences through which stars may change from one state to another. Our Sun is no exception and can be seen as representative of an average star in the Milky Way Galaxy. It generates light and heat, which are transmitted through space to help transform life on the surface of one of its planets, Earth.

Radiometric dating of ancient rocks on Earth and its moon give some clue as to the age of the solar system—about 5 billion years. Cooling and consolidation under gravity of interstellar gases and dust created the Sun and progressively hardened objects accreted and condensed to form the eight planets and their moons. Early in the period of planet formation, the sweeping up of solar system debris led to bombardment of planet and moon surfaces, a phenomenon dramatically depicted today by photographs of the cratered surface of Earth's moon.

The Sun is the ultimate source of energy for life processes on planet Earth. As the Sun formed, it captured most matter in the Solar system, leaving only 0.1 percent to form the planets, their moons, asteroids, comets and dust. The Sun possessed sufficient mass to generate electromagnetic or radiant energy at various wavelengths. The hot Sun mostly radiates shorter wavelength energy, especially at visible wavelengths. There are also large sunspots caused by magnetic storms on the Sun's surface. They can be observed as visible dark patches and as areas of X-ray activity ejecting electrically charged particles, the solar wind. Sunspot activity is not constant but is cyclic in behavior. When these particles meet the Earth's atmosphere dramatic visual displays occur, especially in polar latitudes. Whether sunspots influence the weather is uncertain.

The spinning Earth orbits the Sun in a distance of approximately 150 million km (93 million miles). Energy is received at a more or less constant rate, but is distributed unevenly because of the tilt of Earth's axis, yielding seasonal changes in temperature away from the equator. Yet Earth possesses its own heat engine: radioactive processes within its core help generate gases into the atmosphere and drive movements of its crustal plates. The presence of different gases, including water vapor, has provided that vital mixture of substances from which life has evolved, as well as the thin protective envelope high in oxygen and nitrogen which forms the atmosphere.

Thus spaceship Earth, spinning systematically around the Sun, receiving heat, generating gases and driving its crust into mountains, offers various life forms an environment for evolution. Over time these environments change. Ultimately the future of the planet itself is tied to that of its solar system and its Sun.

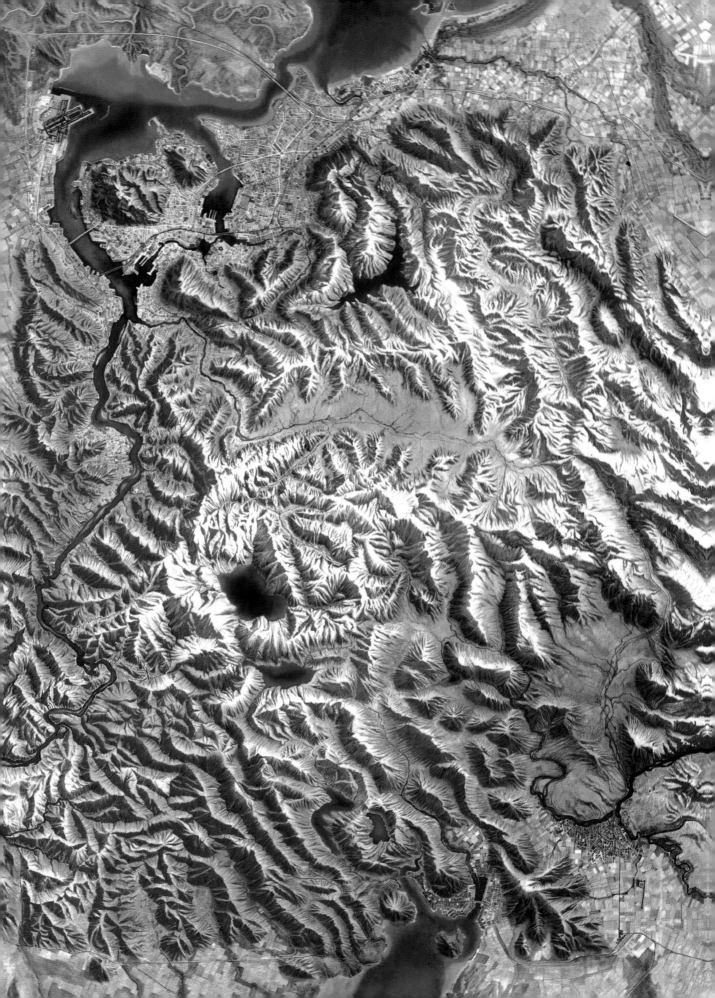

# ORIGINS OF THE UNIVERSE

When we look out across the universe, we look back in time. Light traveling from distant galaxies, speeding across 300,000 km (186,000 miles) every second, has taken billions of years to reach Earth. We see the most distant galaxies across billions of light years, as those galaxies were when the universe was younger.

What is the universe really like? The modern view of the origins and future of the universe is based on the idea of a Big Bang that marked the beginning of the ongoing expansion of the universe. The popular view of the Big Bang, however, imagines galaxies flying away from one another out into empty space after a massive explosion. This naturally leads to questions about what happened before the Big Bang, and where it occurred. However, these questions arise from a misunderstanding of the Big Bang concept. Galaxies do not fly away from each other through space; rather, space itself expands, carrying the galaxies with it. The Big Bang was not an explosion *in* space, but an explosion *of* space and time. All of space and time arose in the Big Bang. There was no time before the Big Bang, and all of space was involved.

## A brief history of the universe

Ten to fifteen billion years ago, the universe of space and time began, as a hugely hot cauldron of energy governed by physical laws that we do not yet understand. Within a tiny fraction of a second the expansion had moderated the conditions to a point from which (we believe) our current understanding of physical laws can begin to describe what happened. The universe was expanding and cooling, but there may also have been a brief spurt of dramatic inflation in size—this is critical to understanding today's universe. If this sudden growth spurt *did* occur, then the part of the universe that telescopes can survey today was merely a tiny fraction of the total.

After no more than 10 millionths of a second, the universe had become a sea of high energy radiation—gamma ray photons characteristic of a temperature well over 1 trillion degrees. At such energy, photons can produce a pair of particles, a matter particle and its anti-matter partner, which exist fleetingly before annihilating each other in a flash of gamma ray radiation.

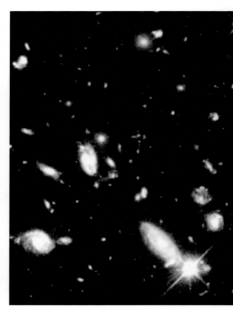

As the universe continued to expand, the photons dropped in energy as the temperature fell. Particle production ended, first for the heavy particles and then for the light ones. Most of the particle and anti-particle pairs were annihilated, leaving only a small residue—the protons, neutrons, and electrons that we know today.

As the temperature dropped further, some of these particles combined to build simple atomic nuclei. Within half an hour this phase was over, and, for the next few hundred thousand years, the universe was an expanding gas of light nuclei and electrons in a sea of photons. It was an opaque fog until continued cooling allowed the atomic nuclei to capture electrons and form atoms of simple elements, mostly hydrogen and helium. Without the free electrons to scatter them, the photons streamed freely through space and the fog cleared.

Matter was then free to respond to the influence of gravity alone. The first generations of individual stars formed from small knots in larger gas clouds that became whole galaxies of stars. The galaxies formed into clusters and superclusters that are still scattered throughout the universe today.

## Are we sure of this picture?

This view of the universe is rather different from earlier versions. Ancient Egyptian cosmology featured the sky goddess Nut arched over Earth, with the sun god Ra traveling across the sky every day. Greek thinkers removed gods from their cosmology, and constructed their world view largely on philosophical grounds. A more scientific approach to cosmology

began to emerge after Copernicus, in the sixteenth century, discovered that it was the Earth that traveled around the Sun. The current view is the latest step in scientific cosmology, but can we be sure that the modern picture will not also be superseded?

Three important observations form the basis of the Big Bang model. The first emerged early in the twentieth century, when observations revealed the expansion of the universe. This fits into Einstein's theory of General Relativity, which describes the nature of space and time. The second key observation is recent measurements of the abundance of light elements, especially helium, in the universe. These observations agree with the amount that the Big Bang model predicts to have been formed in its first few minutes.

Perhaps the most compelling plank supporting the Big Bang concept was the discovery in 1965 of cosmic background radiation—an all-pervasive glow coming from all parts of the sky. It is our view of radiation from the era when the universe became transparent. It is the glow of the Big Bang itself, cooled by the universe's expansion.

Recent years have been exciting in cosmology, because new observations have begun to allow us to choose between variations of the basic Big Bang cosmology and some alternative concepts to the Big Bang itself. In particular, the Cosmic Background Explorer (COBE) satellite

*After about two minutes the temperature had dropped below 1 billion degrees—low enough for nuclear reactions to build some of the light elements, especially helium.*

*In its first seconds, the universe was a dynamic soup of gamma ray photons and particles such as protons and electrons, which are the building blocks of atoms.*

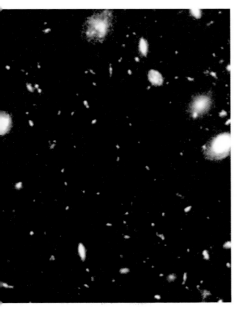

*Far left: This Hubble telescope image shows a large galaxy. Its gravitational force is so strong it can bend light, changing what we see from Earth. The blue images are one galaxy, not scattered objects. Center: Each speck of light in this Hubble Deep Field picture is a distant galaxy. Above: These quasar images show events that happened more than a billion years ago.*

## Gravitational lenses

In recent years astronomers have discovered a new way in which to probe further into the universe and at the same time seek out dark matter closer to home. Einstein's theory of General Relativity predicted that the straight line path of light across the universe is affected by gravity. This was first observed in 1919, when light from stars was observed to be minutely deflected as it passed the Sun.

Recent observations have revealed the gravitational effect of whole galaxies and even clusters of galaxies, which can act as a lens to bend and focus light coming from more distant galaxies. Although the images produced by these gravitational lenses are distorted, they do enable us to study light from galaxies that would otherwise be far beyond the reach of our telescopes.

This gravitational lensing has also been seen—on a smaller scale—when the light of distant stars brightens briefly; this is because of gravitational lensing caused by an intervening object. Knowing this allows us to study the lensing objects that are part of the halo of dark matter believed to encircle our galaxy. What is this dark matter? It seems that gravitational lensing may be able to tell us.

revealed the incredible smoothness of the cosmic background radiation, in all directions, challenging us to explain how the clumpy distribution of galaxies we see today could have had time to develop. Exactly how much time has passed in building this pattern remains uncertain, since astronomers are only now beginning to agree on just how fast the universe is expanding. This is a time of dramatic developments in cosmology.

### Will the expansion continue?

Will the universe go on expanding until all the stars have died? The force of gravity governs the fate of the universe, so the question becomes: is there enough matter and energy in the universe to slow and stop the expansion? In mapping the distribution of matter, it is now clear that there is more matter out there than is apparent. This "dark matter" must surround many galaxies, including the Milky Way, to explain the motions of stars within them. There is more in clusters of galaxies, helping to hold them together.

Studies are seeking further evidence of this matter, trying to determine what it is: small dark planets, star-sized bodies, or something less familiar.

Adding all this together, normal forms of matter appear to account for less than 10 percent of the matter needed to halt universal expansion. But many cosmologists think that less than 10 percent is quite close to 100 percent in this instance. Moreover, there are theoretical reasons for thinking the universe may in fact be on that balance point between eternal expansion and ultimate halt and collapse. It may be that most of the matter in the universe is in forms as yet unseen.

The history of the Sun and Earth play only a small part in this picture. Born long after the Big Bang, both will die long before the universe changes much from the way it looks today.

*One of the galaxies that formed over 10 billion years ago was the Milky Way. A mere 4.6 billion years ago the Sun was born within it.*

*Tiny bumps in the density of matter in the early universe grew, under the influence of gravity, to form the galaxies and clusters of galaxies that we see today.*

*After several hundred thousand years, at a temperature of around 3000 °C (5450 °F), the electrons were captured by atoms and the universe suddenly became transparent.*

# GALAXIES

Many people today are city dwellers whose view of the night sky is hindered by the bright lights of the modern world. When we are fortunate enough to look at the night sky from a dark place, we see thousands of stars and the faint starry band of the Milky Way meandering across the sky. We now know that this is an insider's view of the vast collection of more than 100 billion stars we call the Milky Way Galaxy.

A dark sky will also reveal the Andromeda Galaxy, an even larger star system lying beyond the boundaries of the Milky Way. Both are members of the small cluster of galaxies called the Local Group, which lies on the edge of a supercluster of galaxies. Beyond lies the vast expanse of the universe—countless more distant galaxies.

## The Milky Way

In 1785, William Herschel, the astronomer who discovered Uranus, counted stars in various directions across the sky and decided that the Sun lay near the center of a flattened disk of stars. In 1917, Harlow Shapley studied the distribution of globular clusters—clusters of hundreds of thousands of stars—and concluded that they clustered around the center of the galaxy in the direction of the constellation of Sagittarius. Herschel had been deceived by the clouds of dust which are scattered through the Milky Way and which obscure our view of more distant stars.

The modern view reveals the Milky Way to be a large spiral galaxy composed of a thin circular disk surrounding a central bulge, with a halo of stars and globular

clusters. Light would take about 100,000 years to speed across the disk: a distance of 100,000 light years. Traveling as fast as the fastest spacecraft, a trip across the galaxy would take well over a billion years! The Sun lies in the disk, some 28,000 light years from the center, completing an orbit around the central bulge every 240 million years.

Around 95 percent of the visible mass of the galaxy is composed of stars, in particular the vast mass of faint Sun-like stars that contribute the yellowish background glow of the disk and bulge. Despite their vast numbers, the distances between the stars are immense, compared with their sizes. The nearest stars to the Sun are 4.3 light years away (40 trillion km; 25 trillion miles). Traveling on the fastest spacecraft, this trip would take some 60,000 years.

The heart of the galaxy is a mystery being slowly unveiled by observations using radio and infrared telescopes which can pierce the veil of dust which hides it from our eyes. Astronomers suspect that it harbors a black hole with the mass of more than a million suns.

The remaining mass we see in the galaxy is the thin interstellar medium of gas and dust lying between the stars. Most of this is compacted into dense, cold clouds of gas laced with traces of dust.

*This spiral galaxy, above, has two prominent arms, showing red patches of ionized hydrogen where stars have formed. A barred spiral galaxy, right, showing the yellow color of old stars at its nucleus, with young, blue stars in its arms.*

The Milky Way system originated in a vast condensation of gas, which began to form stars within a billion years of the Big Bang. Early generations of stars in this cloud included those that form the halo of stars and globular clusters surrounding the galaxy. Successive generations of stars had orbits much closer to the thin disk we see today. When the Sun was formed 4.6 billion years ago, the galaxy was already middle aged, and would have looked much as it does today.

New stars are still being born from clouds of gas. While they live, these beacons and their gaseous birthplaces trace out the

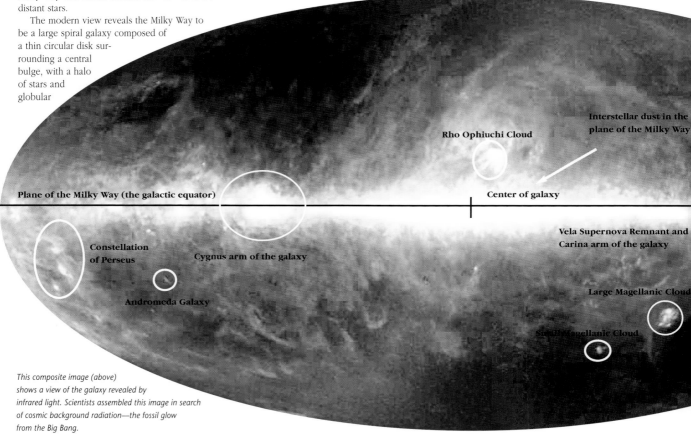

Interstellar dust in the plane of the Milky Way

Rho Ophiuchi Cloud

Center of galaxy

Plane of the Milky Way (the galactic equator)

Vela Supernova Remnant and Carina arm of the galaxy

Constellation of Perseus

Cygnus arm of the galaxy

Large Magellanic Cloud

Andromeda Galaxy

Small Magellanic Cloud

*This composite image (above) shows a view of the galaxy revealed by infrared light. Scientists assembled this image in search of cosmic background radiation—the fossil glow from the Big Bang.*

spiral arms within the background glow of the disk.

Individual stars will live and die, but the Milky Way will probably continue to look much as it does today for billions of years, until stars such as the Sun are long dead.

### Other galaxies

The existence of galaxies other than the Milky Way was long suspected, but only became accepted in the 1920s, when Edwin Hubble measured the distance to some nearby galaxies. We classify galaxies according to their overall appearance, since only in the nearest ones can even the brightest stars be discerned individually.

Most familiar are the spiral galaxies like the Milky Way. Photos of these galaxies reveal that they are in beautiful spiral patterns, traced out by bright stars and gas, hiding the fainter background glow of the disk in which they lie. The spiral patterns range from loosely wound S-shapes to arms so tightly wound that the spiral cannot be

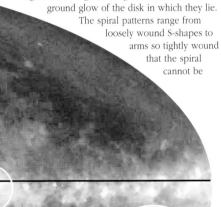

**Orion Nebula**

**Constellation of Orion**

discerned. The Milky Way falls midway in this range. Some spirals have a distinct bar across the nucleus from which the spiral arms trail.

Other galaxies show no apparent structure beyond a smooth spherical or elliptical shape. Unlike the spirals, these elliptical galaxies usually lack any significant signs of recent star formation or the gas to promote it. Giants of this class are rare, but are the most massive galaxies known. On the other end of the scale, faint dwarf ellipticals, little larger than a globular star cluster, are probably the most common type of galaxy.

Perhaps a quarter of all galaxies are classified as irregular because they do not fit neatly into either of these categories. They are typically faint, but with a mix of old and young stars, gas, and dust.

Many galaxies, including the Milky Way, show signs of more mass than can readily be seen. Some galaxies hide another enigma—a central powerhouse at their core that generates narrow jets of high-energy particles streaming outward. These active galaxies are believed to be powered by matter swirling around a massive black hole. It may be that many large galaxies have a central black hole with a mass equal to millions of suns, but in most of them, as in the Milky Way, this lies dormant unless brought to life by an inflow of gas.

### Clusters of galaxies

Galaxies, like some stars within galaxies, tend to exist in clusters. The Milky Way's Local Group is a small cluster, with 30 or so members, most of them small elliptical or irregular galaxies. The nearest large cluster of galaxies is the Virgo cluster, with some 2,500 members, lying about 60 million light years away. The Virgo cluster is a major component of the Local Supercluster.

Compared with the amount of space between the stars, galaxies in these clusters are relatively close together. As a result of this proximity, they sometimes run into one another, causing cosmic fireworks. The stars within the galaxies almost never collide, but the tenuous interstellar clouds crash together and form new stars, changing the appearance of the galaxy and possibly triggering the nuclear powerhouse into activity.

*Some of the bright galaxies of the Virgo cluster, top. Above: This galaxy, Centaurus A, features an unusual obscuring dust cloud and is a powerful source of radio, X- and gamma rays.*

### Exploring space

Before the telescope, astronomy consisted largely of measuring and predicting the positions of stars and planets observed by eye. In 1609 a revolution began, when Galileo Galilei used a telescope to reveal mountains on the Moon, Jupiter's moons, and countless stars in the Milky Way. Despite these amazing discoveries, however, for the next 250 years astronomy was predominantly devoted to measuring positions and cataloging.

Almost 150 years ago, the first identification of a chemical element in the Sun was made using a spectrograph, which separates sunlight into its component colors. This marked the start of our ability to deduce the composition of the stars. The science of astrophysics was born.

Today, spectrographs are used on optical telescopes hundreds of times the size of Galileo's first instruments. One of these, the Hubble Space Telescope, views the sky from above the distorting effect of Earth's atmosphere. Optical telescopes joined by radio telescopes on the ground and in space can be used to form large radio arrays. Other observatories in space search for sources of infrared and ultraviolet light, X-rays, and gamma rays.

# STARS

When we look at the stars in the night sky, it is easy to understand how people in ancient times imagined them to be flickering lights attached to the dark vault of the sky. It was not until 1838 that the first stellar distance was measured and the enormous distances of the stars from Earth and from each other were confirmed.

The first half of the twentieth century saw the development of the physics necessary to understand the composition and structure of the stars and the sources of nuclear energy that power them. As a result, astronomers today have an extensive understanding of the stars and the way they have evolved.

## Types of star

While stars vary widely in size, color, and temperature, they are all essentially vast balls of hot gas powered by nuclear reactions deep in their cores. For most of the life of a star, these reactions fuse hydrogen into helium. Late in its life, a star leaves behind this main sequence phase and develops into a giant, converting helium into carbon and heavier elements. In both processes, a small fraction of the matter is converted into energy. The temperatures that are required in a star's core in order to achieve this are measured in tens of millions of degrees.

The main factor determining the characteristics of a main sequence star is its mass—how much matter it contains. Stars range in mass from less than one-tenth of the Sun's mass to perhaps more than 50 times its mass. At the top end of the range are the rare massive stars, which are a few times the size of the Sun but radiate hundreds of thousands of times more energy from their blue-white surfaces. The Sun itself has a slightly yellow color to its 6,000 °C (10,800 °F) surface. A less massive main sequence star will be somewhat smaller than the Sun, perhaps less than 1 percent as bright, with a cooler, red hue. Red dwarfs of this sort can only be seen from relatively nearby, but are the most common stars in the galaxy.

At the end of their main sequence lifetimes, stars swell to become giants and supergiants. The largest of these are cool red stars, which are more than a thousand times larger and a million times brighter than the Sun. Many of the giants will end their days as white dwarfs only as big as Earth—the faint glowing embers of old stars.

## The nearest star

The Sun, which is the only star that we can readily see as anything other than a point of light, is representative of an average star in the Milky Way. Its surface displays a cycle of activity that

This globular cluster—47 Tucanae, above—is an enormous group of stars formed early in the life of the Milky Way Galaxy; it contains some of the oldest known stars. One hundred and eighty years ago, the massive star Eta Carinae experienced an outburst which created the lobes of gas now surrounding it, right.

is roughly 11 years long. The most obvious manifestations of the cycle are sunspots, the number of which rises and falls during the course of the cycle. Sunspots are often larger than Earth, and are relatively dark in appearance because magnetic effects make them slightly cooler than their surroundings. They are also centers of other activity—powerful solar flares, for instance, which last for a few minutes, glowing brightly and pouring hot gas into space. This gas is channeled by the solar magnetic field and sometimes strikes Earth, causing intense auroral displays near the poles and disrupting radio communication and, sometimes, electrical power systems.

The sudden outburst of a flare punctuates a more general outflow from the Sun's hot outer atmosphere, known as the corona. This solar wind is relatively mild when compared with the massive outflows from certain other stars. While the Sun will lose little mass through the solar wind during the course of its life, larger stars can blow away a sizeable proportion of their mass in this way.

Observations reveal that some other stars have cycles of activity that resemble those of the Sun. Although we are unable to see sunspots on their surfaces, we can detect the slight changes in brightness that accompany changes in activity.

The Sun's magnetism arises from the flow of electrical currents within its outer layers, but most of its material is packed closer to the core, where the energy is generated. In recent

*Star birth begins deep in a tenuous cloud of interstellar gas and dust. Perhaps triggered by the birth or death of stars nearby, the cloud begins to collapse.*

*This pillar of gas, left, contains cool hydrogen gas and dust and can incubate new stars. It is a part of the Eagle Nebula, a star-forming region 7,000 light years away. The Trifid Nebula, above, contains hot young stars which cause the gas to emit red light, and cooler gas and dust reflecting blue light.*

*As the gas falls in under the force of gravity, it heats up, becoming a protostar, glowing warmly with infrared light through an obscuring cocoon of gas and dust.*

*A star like the Sun takes millions of years to form. It then embarks on the main part of its existence, living for 10 billion years as a stable main sequence star.*

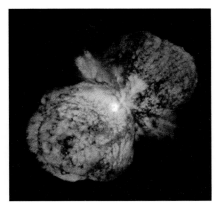

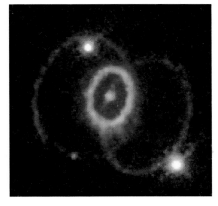

*Left: These rings of glowing gas surround an exploded star which was first observed in 1987—a supernova. It is 169,000 light years away in the Large Magellanic Cloud, a nearby galaxy visible from the southern hemisphere.*

years, astronomers have begun to probe beneath the surface of the Sun using a technique called helioseismology. This is helping to clarify our picture of the Sun's structure.

### The life of a star

A constant battle takes place between gravity, which is attempting to pull a star inward, and the pressure of hot gas pushing outward. The battle starts when gravity begins to collapse a small part of an interstellar gas cloud. As the cloud falls in, the temperature at its core increases, and eventually hydrogen begins to fuse together to form helium. The collapse slows as the growing pressure of the hot gas resists the gravitational force. Finally the collapse comes to a halt; the protostar has become a stable main sequence star.

A star such as the Sun will remain balanced in this state for around 10 billion years, constantly converting hydrogen to helium at its core and by degrees growing a little bigger and a little brighter. The Sun is currently about halfway through its main sequence phase.

In approximately 5 billion years, after it has circled the center of the galaxy some 20 more times, the Sun will begin to grow quite rapidly. By the time it has doubled in size, the oceans on Earth will have completely boiled away. Eventually, the Sun will become a red giant, perhaps 100 times larger and 1,000 times

brighter than it is at the moment. It will envelop Mercury, Venus, and Earth, evaporating Earth's atmosphere and eventually causing the planet to spiral inward to oblivion.

Cooler, lower-mass stars will follow much the same path, but over spans of time so long that not even the oldest of them has yet had time to complete its sedate main sequence life. In contrast, massive stars consume their nuclear fuel at a prodigious rate and become red giants in a matter of only a few million years.

Once it has become a red giant, the Sun will begin to fuse helium to carbon in its core. However, this new energy source will only delay the inevitable victory of gravity. Within about a billion years the Sun will peel off its outer layers to reveal a white dwarf remnant that will cool slowly, over billions more years.

Stars that begin life larger than about eight times the mass of the Sun will blow away much of their mass during the course of their lives, but will still end up too large to survive as white dwarfs. Instead, they blow up in brilliant supernova explosions, leaving neutron stars or black holes to mark their passing.

### After a supernova

Massive stars die spectacularly in a supernova explosion. If the remnant after the explosion is less than about three times the mass of the Sun, a neutron star will result. Despite the intense force of gravity, the neutrons making up much of the star refuse to collapse any further than a dense ball 20 km (12 miles) across. Neutron stars are sometimes seen as pulsing sources of radiation—they are then called pulsars.

If the remnant of the star contains more than three solar masses of material, the strength of the gravitational force cannot be resisted, and the collapse produces a black hole. Not even light can escape from within a black hole. Any matter that falls within the boundary of a black hole is lost from view.

The importance of black holes and neutron stars to astronomy lies more in what happens in the intense gravitational field around them than in what is inside them. Gas falls onto black holes or neutron stars with tremendous energy, producing intense radiation. The largest black holes are believed to be millions of times the mass of the Sun, and reside in the nuclei of active galaxies. They are the powerhouses of these beacons that shine across the universe.

*The Sun will live on as a white dwarf for billions of years, slowly fading from view, with little or no nuclear fusion to slow the cooling.*

*After perhaps 1 billion years as a giant, the Sun will eject its outer layers to form a short-lived planetary nebula surrounding the cooling core.*

*About 10 billion years after it formed, the Sun will run short of hydrogen fuel in its core, but it will actually increase its energy output and swell to become a red giant.*

# THE SOLAR SYSTEM

Among more than 200 billion stars in the Milky Way Galaxy, one is unique. It is the Sun—the only star that we know has a planetary system, including at least one planet which can support life as we know it. That planet is Earth, of course, although Mars may also be a candidate.

Until recently, the Sun's family was the only planetary system we knew of, but evidence that large planets circle several Sun-like stars is now accumulating. In time, observations may reveal that they also have Earth-sized planets.

## The solar system's formation

A little less than 5 billion years ago, the Sun was formed in a cloud of interstellar gas. The infant Sun was surrounded by a cooling disk of gas and dust—the solar nebula—where knots of material were forming, colliding, breaking, and merging. The larger objects, called planetesimals, grew by accreting smaller particles, until a few proto-planets dominated. The protoplanets from the warm inner parts of the disk became the small rocky planets. Further out, in a cooler region where ices of water, ammonia, and methane could condense, the giant planets formed. These planets grew in mass more rapidly, forming deep atmospheres around rocky cores. The giant planets copied the Sun's accretion disk in miniature to create their moons.

As the Sun settled into its present stable state, the pressure of radiation and the gas of the solar

wind streaming outward blew away the remains of the solar nebula. The newborn planets swept up the larger debris. In the process they were subjected to an intense bombardment, evidence of which we see in the craters on the rocky surfaces of the inner solar system and the icy surfaces of the moons of the outer solar system.

The solar system today has been largely swept clean of the debris of its formation. It is dominated by the Sun, at its center, which constitutes almost 99.9 percent of the solar system's mass. Most of the remainder is contained in the two giant planets Jupiter and Saturn, while Earth represents less than 0.0003 percent of the Sun's mass.

The region of space inhabited by the planets is a flat plane centered on the Sun and about 15 billion km (just under 10 billion miles) across. This is almost 50 times the span of Earth's orbit. Vast as this sounds, it is only 0.02 percent of the distance to the nearest star! The great void of interplanetary space is sparsely populated by debris orbiting the distant Sun, ranging in size from particles of dust to rocky asteroids and icy comets—these may be tens or even hundreds of kilometers across.

## The family of planets

The inner rocky planets and asteroids and Earth's Moon share a common heritage, yet visits by spacecraft have revealed their histories to be quite different. The smaller ones, Mercury and the Moon, are geologically dead worlds retaining little or no atmosphere. Mars has had more geological activity and features Olympus Mons, the solar system's largest volcano. The larger inner planets, Venus and Earth, are similar in size but differ geologically. Both show evidence of volcanic activity, but Earth's activity includes moving plates of rock causing active mountain building; this has not occurred on Venus.

The common thread in the surface histories of the rocky planets is the heavy bombardment they underwent early in their existence. Occasional impacts still occur, as was dramatically illustrated in 1994 when Comet Shoemaker-Levy 9 broke

Above: An image of the Sun taken using the red light of hydrogen, showing a loop of gas, called a prominence, erupting from the solar surface.

into fragments and crashed into Jupiter.

Of the inner planets, Venus, Earth, and Mars have significant atmospheres, although these are only thin veneers over their rocky surfaces. The atmospheres of Venus and Mars today are mostly carbon dioxide. Earth's atmosphere is unique in having only traces of carbon dioxide in an atmosphere consisting mainly of nitrogen and oxygen. A combination of oceans of liquid water, an active geological history and abundant plant life has stripped the atmosphere of much of its carbon dioxide, and released oxygen.

In stark contrast, the faces presented by the giant outer planets, Jupiter and Saturn, are clouds of ammonia compounds and water in layers riding high in deep atmospheres. These gaseous envelopes are believed to surround a mantle of liquid metallic hydrogen overlying a rocky core. The clouds are split into bands by high-speed winds circulating in regular patterns within the atmosphere. They are punctuated now and then by cyclonic storms, the best known being Jupiter's Great Red Spot, which has survived for at least 300 years.

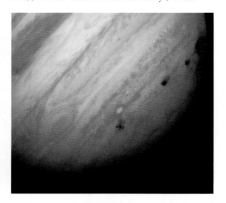

The asteroid Ida, top, seen by the Galileo spacecraft; a tiny moon can be seen to the right. Comet West displays its tails across the sky, above. Above right: Jupiter, showing the short-lived scars of the impact of Comet Shoemaker-Levy 9. Right: The planets' relative distances from the Sun (see box opposite).

*Above: The Sun's family is comprised of eight major planets and many smaller moons and asteroids (not to scale).*

The smaller, colder giants, Uranus and Neptune, have few atmospheric features, and their blue–green coloring results from methane in the atmosphere. Their atmospheres overlie an icy core of water, methane, ammonia, and rock.

The giant planets all have large moons in orbit around them which were formed in their surrounding nebulae, plus smaller objects that are probably captured asteroids. The largest moons, Jupiter's Ganymede and Saturn's Titan, are larger than the planet Mercury. Most of the moons have thick, icy crusts pitted with craters that date from the heavy bombardment which scarred the inner planets. The one exception is Jupiter's large inner moon Io, which has a surface covered in sulfur-rich rock. Io is locked in a gravitational embrace with Jupiter and its neighboring moons, Europa and Ganymede, which causes heating and results in it being the most volcanically active place in the solar system.

All four giant planets have systems of thin rings orbiting over their equators. Saturn's famous rings are by far the most substantial, but none of the rings is solid. They are composed of icy particles that range in size from tiny specks to blocks as large as houses, and their orbits are shepherded by the gravitational influences of nearby moons. Pluto is a dwarf planet. Until 2006 it was classified as the ninth and furthest planet of the solar system.

## What the future holds

As in the past, the future of the solar system will be dominated by the evolution of the Sun. About 5 billion years from now, the Sun will suddenly increase in size and brightness, ultimately encompassing most of the inner planets, causing their orbits to decay and the planets to spiral into the Sun. The outer planets and their moons will be subjected to 1,000 times the current energy output from the Sun; this will melt icy surfaces and alter their atmospheres. Within a few hundred million years the Sun will decrease in size to become a white dwarf, only feebly illuminating the remains of its family.

## Planetary facts

**Mercury**
Diameter: 4,878 km (3,031 miles)
Average distance from Sun: 0.4 AU*
Known moons: None

**Venus**
Diameter: 12,104 km (7,521 miles)
Average distance from Sun: 0.7 AU*
Known moons: None

**Earth**
Diameter: 12,756 km (7,925 miles)
Average distance from Sun: 1.0 AU*
Known moons: 1

**Mars**
Diameter: 6,787 km (4,217 miles)
Average distance from Sun: 1.5 AU*
Known moons: 2

**Jupiter**
Diameter: 143,800 km (89,400 miles)
Average distance from Sun: 5.2 AU*
Known moons: 16

**Saturn**
Diameter: 120,660 km (75,000 miles)
Average distance from Sun: 9.5 AU*
Known moons: 18

**Uranus**
Diameter: 51,120 km (31,765 miles)
Average distance from Sun: 19.2 AU*
Known moons: 17

**Neptune**
Diameter: 49,500 km (30,760 miles)
Average distance from Sun: 30.1 AU*
Known moons: 8

*AU stands for astronomical unit: an AU is the average distance between Earth and the Sun—about 150 million km (93 million miles).

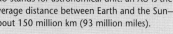

# PLANET EARTH

All the planets in the solar system lie in almost the same plane. This reflects their common origin in the disk surrounding the infant Sun. In contrast to the planets, the dwarf planet Pluto wanders far from this disk, indicating a history we can only suspect, but clearly one that differs considerably from those of the planets. Earth is a better-behaved member of the Sun's family but, like the rest of the planets, it has its own particular characteristics and history.

## Earth's motion

The orbits of all the planets around the Sun are elliptical, but, like those of most of the planets, Earth's orbit is quite close to circular. The distance between Earth and the Sun varies between 147 and 152 million km (92 and 95 million miles), known as 1.0 AU (astronomical unit). The point of closest approach occurs on 2 January each year, during the southern hemisphere's summer. It is a common misconception that the small change in distance produces the Earth's seasons.

Apart from its revolution around the Sun, Earth also spins around a rotation axis which passes through the north and south geographic poles. Seen from above the north pole, Earth spins on its axis in a counterclockwise direction, and it circles the Sun in the same counterclockwise

direction. Most of the other planets and major moons behave in the same way, which again points to their having common origins.

Earth travels around its orbit at 30 km per second (18 miles per second). At this speed, it takes 365.25 days to complete one circuit—that period defines our calendar year. The period of a day is defined by the rotation of Earth on its axis relative to the stars—once every 23 hours and 56 minutes. In that time, however, Earth has also advanced 2.6 million km (1.6 million miles) along its curving orbit, so it has to turn a little further to rotate once relative to the Sun. This takes about 4 extra minutes, and makes the time from midday one day to midday the next exactly 24 hours.

## Changing seasons

The Earth's axis is tilted relative to the plane of its orbit by 23.5°. This axis remains pointed in the same orientation relative to the stars as Earth circles the Sun. As a result, Earth's northern hemisphere is tilted more directly toward the Sun in the middle of the calendar year.

From the ground, the Sun then appears higher in the sky and the direct sunlight leads to warmer weather—the northern summer. At the same time, the southern hemisphere has a more oblique view of the Sun, resulting in cooler winter weather. The situation is reversed six months later when Earth is on the opposite side of its orbit.

The direction of Earth's axis is not strictly fixed, but swings around in a circuit lasting 26,000 years. As a result of this precession, our seasons today would seem out of step to the ancient Egyptians, who lived some 5,000 years ago. Their seasons would have differed by around two months from ours, Earth's rotation axis having changed its direction somewhat since that time.

Other effects also operate over periods of tens of thousands of years to slightly change Earth's tilt and how close Earth gets to the Sun. Acting together, these effects produce changes in the amount of heat Earth receives from the Sun, and

these changes may significantly affect Earth's climate. There is some evidence that these changes result in periodic ice ages, but the concept remains controversial. Links between the Sun's 11-year sunspot numbers cycle and the Earth's climate also remain speculative.

## The largest rocky planet

The Earth is a ball of rock 12,756 km (7,925 miles) in diameter at the equator, but its rotation causes it to be slightly flattened at the poles. It is the largest of the rocky planets in the solar system and, as a result of its bulk, it retains a hot interior; the

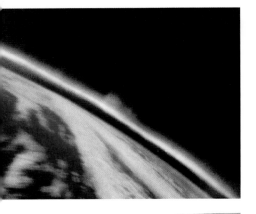

*The Earth is surrounded by a protective magnetic envelope called the magnetosphere (in blue and brown, above). Some charged particles from the Sun (red arrows) tend to be channeled down onto the Earth's poles where they cause the air to glow as an aurora, as seen from a space shuttle (top).*

## Magnetic reversals

When molten lava from a volcano cools and solidifies, it captures the orientation and strength of the Earth's magnetic field at that time and place. This built-in compass needle has proved a powerful tool for studying the gradual drift of Earth's continents. It has also revealed periods, usually spaced by a few hundred thousand years, when Earth's magnetic field has briefly disappeared. Within a geological instant of only about 5,000 years, the field shrinks to zero and then reappears with magnetic north and south swapped. The magnetic imprint of this swapping is found in alternating bands of rocks along mid-oceanic ridges. Each band is made of rocks formed around the same time, and with the same magnetic signature. This provides dramatic confirmation of the pic-

ture of continents drifting apart with new crust forming between them. The origin of this change in magnetic directions lies in the electrical dynamo working in Earth's outer core to create the field. How it happens so quickly and why the interval is so irregular remain unknown.

How this change would affect those migratory animals that seem to use the direction of the magnetic field to navigate on their journeys, we do not know. And what if we lost the protective cloak of the Earth's magnetosphere? Cosmic ray particles from the Sun and interstellar space that are normally deflected or trapped by the magnetosphere would reach the surface of Earth. This would cause dramatically higher rates of genetic damage to animals and plants and lead to mutations and perhaps extinctions.

temperature may reach 6,000 °C (10,830 °F) at the core—as hot as the surface of the Sun.

The core is a mix of metallic nickel and iron split into a solid inner core and an outer fluid zone which reaches halfway to the surface. Enclosing the outer core is Earth's mantle. The dense rocks in this zone flow, over geologic time, under the intense heat and pressure. Overlying the mantle, Earth's crust is a skin of lightweight rocks: a mere 60 km (36 miles) deep at its thickest.

Its inner heat makes Earth one of the most seismically active objects within the solar system. On the surface, it causes volcanic activity, and at greater depth, it drives the separate plates of the crust into motion. This motion—folding the rocks of the crust—creates mountain ranges. At the perimeters of the plates, new crust is created or old crust destroyed. Atmospheric forces such as wind and water flow also reshape Earth's surface, by eroding rock and depositing weathered material to form new sedimentary rock strata.

All these processes together act to renew the planet's surface over hundreds of millions of years, removing or altering the ancient impact scarring that can be seen on the surfaces of so many other objects in the solar system. Only a few recent impact craters are visible, providing hints of Earth's turbulent early history.

### Earth's atmosphere

Earth is surrounded by a thin atmospheric envelope which tapers off into space and is all

*Right, top: A total solar eclipse occurs when the Moon passes in front of the Sun and obscures it. As the Sun is finally eclipsed, rays of sunlight filtering through the hills and valleys on the Moon's edge create an effect known as Baily's beads, center. Right, bottom: A lunar eclipse—the Moon darkens as it passes through the Earth's shadow.*

but gone 100 km (62 miles) above the surface. This envelope maintains the surface at a higher temperature than it would otherwise be, permitting oceans of liquid water on the surface. The atmosphere is a unique mixture of nitrogen and oxygen, with only traces of carbon dioxide and other gases, and is certainly not Earth's primeval atmosphere. Oxygen only began to build up when primitive forms of life developed photosynthesis. Oxygen reacts to form ozone, which protects the surface of the planet from intense ultraviolet radiation. Life has crafted the environment of the blue planet to suit itself.

Above the atmosphere lies the protective cocoon of the magnetosphere—the domain of Earth's magnetic field. While most of the particles flowing from the Sun are deflected by the magnetosphere, some become ensnared and are channeled onto the north and south poles, forming the glowing aurorae.

The magnetic field originates in electrical currents within Earth's outer fluid core, and its axis is at a slightly different angle from the planet's rotation axis. As a result, Earth's magnetic and rotation poles are not quite the same, creating a difference between magnetic north, as measured by a compass, and "true" north.

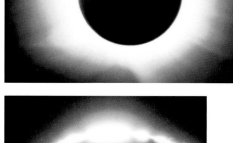

# THE MOON

Alight in the darkness of night, the Moon was considered a deity in many ancient cultures and has provided humans with their calendar. The 29½ days it takes to go through its cycle of phases is close to the length of a month, the word "month" coming from the word "moon".

Galileo's telescopic observations in 1609 of mountains on the Moon played an important part in showing people that the Moon and planets were worlds something like Earth. But the greatest step in this process was the series of six Apollo landings on the Moon between 1969 and 1972. So far, the Moon is the only other world that humans have visited.

## Phases of the Moon

The Moon orbits Earth in just under 27½ days relative to the stars. Earth moves appreciably along its curving path around the Sun in that time, however, so the Moon needs to travel for two more days to get back to the same position relative to the Sun and Earth and complete its cycle of phases. At the same time, the Moon is rotating on its own axis, but the strong gravitational pull of Earth has

locked these two motions together. As a result, the Moon always presents the same familiar face to us on Earth: apart from a little around the edges, we never see the "far side" of the Moon. It also means that a "day" on the Moon is two weeks long!

Half of the Moon is always lit by the Sun, and the amount of that sunny half we can see from Earth depends on where the Moon is in its orbit. If it lies directly sunward of the Earth, the Moon's night side (not the far side) is presented to our view. It appears dark and invisible when it is near the Sun in the sky. This is New Moon. Over the following days the sunlight begins to illuminate one edge of the visible face and the Moon appears as a crescent shape in the twilight sky. The crescent expands through First Quarter and on to Full Moon, when the fully illuminated disk is opposite the Sun in the sky. Over the following two weeks the sunlit portion of the disk shrinks back through Third Quarter towards New Moon.

## Solar and lunar eclipses

The Moon's orbit is tilted by just over 5° to the plane of Earth's orbit. As a result, the New Moon usually passes close to the Sun in the sky, but does not cross it.

About twice a year, however, the orbital angles converge—the Sun and Moon line up and the Moon's shadow is cast towards Earth. Sometimes the shadow only just reaches Earth, as a dark spot no more than 270 km (170 miles) across. As Earth turns underneath it, the spot draws a thin line of darkness across the globe.

The Earth-bound observer sited somewhere along the total eclipse track sees the Moon as just big enough to cover the disk of the much larger but more distant Sun. Day turns to night for a few minutes as the solar disk is covered, revealing the faint glow of the surrounding corona.

*The Moon orbits Earth once a month, above, as the Earth itself orbits the Sun. We only see one face of the Moon, but how much is lit by sunlight depends on the Moon's position in its orbit. The lower illustrations show the Moon's changing phases as we see them, corresponding to the Moon's position in the upper illustration.*

Observers usually find the few minutes of a total solar eclipse a remarkable experience, and some have felt compelled to travel around the world, chasing further opportunities to see one.

A wider swath of Earth's surface lies off the track of totality, and sees the Sun only partly eclipsed. Also, about half the time, the shadow falls short of Earth, causing the Moon to appear too small to cover the Sun in the sky; this is called an annular eclipse, and it lacks the darkness and magic of a total eclipse.

When the situation of Earth and the Moon are reversed, the Full Moon can be eclipsed by Earth's shadow. Sky watchers on the whole night side of Earth will see the Moon darken for several hours as it traverses Earth's wide shadow. The effect is somewhat less dramatic than a solar eclipse, but more commonly seen.

## The motions of the tides

The most obvious effect of the Moon on Earth is the tides. These alterations in sea level twice a day are caused by the gravitational pull of the Moon on water and on Earth itself.

The water on the side of Earth nearest the Moon feels a stronger force from the Moon than does the center of Earth, which is itself more

*Tides in the oceans, and even in the rocks of the Earth's surface, are caused by the changing gravitational pull of the Sun and Moon as the Moon circles the Earth. High tides as Earth faces the Moon, top, and low tides in the same places when the Moon has moved, above.*

strongly attracted than water on the side away from the Moon. This results in water accumulating in two high tides: one on the side of Earth facing the Moon, and one on the far side. In between these regions of high tide are regions of low tide, where the water level is at its lowest. Tide heights vary greatly because of local effects, but they can range as high as 10 m (33 ft) in some locations. Tides of a few centimeters are also raised in the rocky crust of Earth itself.

But tidal forces have even more profound consequences. The Earth's rotation slows by 0.0023 seconds per century. This makes a day now four hours longer than a day was when the first complex life forms arose in Earth's oceans. The same effect on the smaller Moon has already slowed its rotation to make its "day" equal its orbital period. Tidal forces are also causing the Moon to recede from Earth by about 4 cm (1¹⁄₂ in) a year. As a result, solar eclipses will eventually all be annular, because the Moon will be too far away to ever fully cover the Sun's disk.

### Lunar history

The origin of the Moon has long been a subject of debate, but current theory imagines a collision over 4 billion years ago between the infant Earth and another planetesimal as large as Mars. Some of the lighter debris then collected in orbit around Earth to become the Moon.

Both Earth and the Moon were subjected to intense bombardment early in their histories, as the solar system was swept clear of most of the debris of its formation. On the Moon, the last stages of this cosmic storm are still recorded in the bright highland areas of the surface, which are covered with impact craters. Other areas suffered large impacts late in the bombardment; these gouged enormous basins in the surface. Many of the basins on the side nearest Earth were soon flooded by dark lava flows from within the Moon. Rocks brought back to Earth by Apollo astronauts reveal that the youngest of these maria (singular mare, Latin for "sea") is over 3 billion years old, despite being marked by relatively few craters.

Since that time, the Moon has cooled to inactivity, with only occasional impacts changing the scene. The last large impact occurred perhaps 100 million years ago, creating the crater Tycho and splashing debris across the surface.

A new generation of spacecraft has recently begun to build on the legacy of the Apollo missions, by studying the Moon again. The most exciting finding from these recent studies has been the apparent discovery of water ice on the Moon's cold crater floors. These crater floors are shielded from the glare of radiation from the Sun, which bombards the rest of the surface unhindered by any atmosphere.

### Man on the Moon

Man's first step on the Moon was taken on July 20, 1969, during the US Apollo XI mission, and was watched by millions around the world as it was broadcast live on television.

The excitement this event generated may seem extraordinary now, but man seems to have always dreamt of walking on the Moon.

Since that first landing, when Buzz Aldrin and Neil Armstrong both stepped onto the Moon, there have been six other Apollo Moon missions, all between 1969 and 1972. One was aborted, but on each of the others, two more astronauts walked on the surface of the Moon.

*Below: Buzz Aldrin taking a historic step on the Moon, watched by millions of television viewers on 20 July 1969. Bottom: Earthrise—taken from Apollo 11, this picture shows the Earth coming up over the Moon's horizon.*

# SPACE EXPLORATION

O ur view of the solar system and the wider universe has improved dramatically in recent years. The exploration of the solar system by robot probes has revolutionized our perspective on the planets and their moons. Closer to home, telescopes in Earth orbit have studied the universe using ultraviolet, X-ray and gamma-ray radiation which is invisible from the ground. Arrays of radio telescopes, including one in space, probe the radio universe at finer resolution than any single optical telescope can achieve. On the ground, optical astronomers are building a new generation of larger telescopes which will probe the visible universe more deeply than ever before, and scan the infrared radiation coming from the sky to study regions hidden from visible light.

## Exploring the solar system

The space age began with the beeping voice of Sputnik 1 circling Earth in 1957. In retrospect, it seems a small step, but Sputnik led to a series of Soviet Luna and American Pioneer and Ranger spacecraft over the next few years; they sped past the Moon or deliberately crashed into it.

The exploration of the planets began with attempts to reach Venus and Mars in the early 1960s. In 1973, the US Mariner 10 spacecraft successfully flew past Venus and then continued to Mercury, where it captured what are still the only close-up images we have of the surface of that planet. The surface of Venus is hidden by perpetual clouds, but in 1975 the Soviet Venera 9 and 10 landers returned images of a rocky, desolate surface. More recently, radar maps of the surface have been produced by the Pioneer Venus and Magellan spacecraft.

While the Soviets explored Venus, the Americans were visiting Mars. In 1976, the Viking 1 and 2 orbiters arrived to map the surface from space for several years, while their accompanying landers studied two sites on the surface and tested, unsuccessfully, for evidence of life. This exploration of the surface was not resumed for another 21 years until, in 1997, the Mars Pathfinder landed, with its rover Sojourner. The exploration of Mars continues today with renewed vigor.

The exploration of the giant outer planets began in 1972 with the launch of Pioneer 10, followed soon after by Pioneer 11. They returned the first stunning images of Jupiter's colorful clouds and the surfaces of its major moons. Pioneer 11 continued on to a repeat performance at Saturn in 1979. By that time a new generation of explorers, Voyager 1 and 2, had already reached Jupiter. Both journeyed on to Saturn, and Voyager 2 then made a foray to the realms of Uranus and Neptune. All four of these interplanetary explorers are still journeying outward, reaching in different directions towards the edge of the Sun's domain. Meanwhile, the exploration of the giant planets continues, with the Galileo spacecraft surveying Jupiter and Cassini orbiting Saturn since July 9, 2004.

While the outer reaches of the solar system were being explored, objects closer to home were also under investigation. Comets, asteroids and the Moon have all recently been explored.

## Humans in space

The exploration of the solar system by robot spacecraft has been paralleled by a program of human spaceflight closer to Earth. It began in 1961, four years after Sputnik 1, with the flight of Yuri Gagarin in a Vostok spacecraft. The Soviets continued with the Voskhod and Soyuz programs. After being beaten into orbit, the US rapidly developed the techniques of working in space in the Mercury and Gemini programs, with the ultimate goal of satisfying President John F. Kennedy's challenge of landing a man on the moon before the end of the 1960s.

A lunar landing was the objective of the Apollo program. It began disastrously with a fire in early 1967 which killed three astronauts. The first piloted mission was Apollo 7 in 1968, followed in rapid

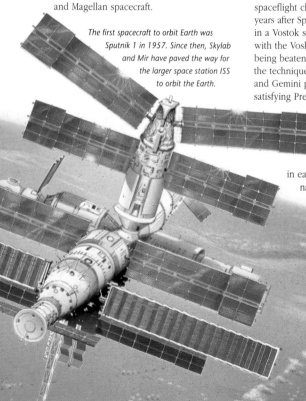

*The first spacecraft to orbit Earth was Sputnik 1 in 1957. Since then, Skylab and Mir have paved the way for the larger space station ISS to orbit the Earth.*

## Planetary science spacecraft

**PAST MISSIONS**

**Mariner 9** (1971, NASA)
The first spacecraft to orbit Mars. Carried out detailed photography of the surface and of Phobos and Deimos, Mars' two moons.

**Apollo 11, 12, 14, 15, 16, 17** (1969–72, NASA)
Manned landings on the Moon and sample returns.

**Pioneer 10** (1973, NASA)
First spacecraft to fly by Jupiter. Now about 12 billion km (6.6 billion miles) from the Sun (2006).

**Pioneer 11** (1974–79, NASA)
Followed Pioneer 10 in 1974; first probe to study Saturn (1979). The mission was terminated in 1995.

**Mariner 10** (1974–75)
Used Venus as a gravity assist to Mercury; returned the first close-up images of the atmosphere of Venus in ultraviolet; made three flybys of Mercury.

**Venera 9** (1975, USSR)
Landed on Venus, returned pictures of the surface.

**Pioneer Venus** (1978, NASA)
An orbiter and four atmospheric probes; made the first high-quality map of the surface of Venus.

**Viking 1** (1976, NASA)
Probe in Martian orbit and lander set down on the western slopes of Chryse Planitia; returned images and searched for Martian microorganisms.

**Viking 2** (1976, NASA)
Arrived in Martian orbit a month after Viking 1:

succession by Apollo 8, 9, and 10, which tested the equipment needed for the landing. On July 20, 1969, the program reached its culmination, with the landing of the Apollo 11 lunar module Eagle on the dusty floor of the Moon's Sea of Tranquillity. Soon afterward, Neil Armstrong became the first human to set foot on the Moon.

The Apollo program continued through five more successful landings, returning 382 kg (844 lb) of lunar rock and soil, plus photographs and other data which have shaped our current understanding of the history of the Moon.

The 1970s were the in-between years of US manned space activities: between the Apollo program and the advent of the reusable space shuttle. In 1981 the much-delayed space shuttle Columbia was launched for the first time, and a schedule of regular launches has continued since then, but with a break of more than two years after the loss of all seven crew members in the Challenger accident in 1986.

The Soviet human spaceflight program concentrated on learning how to cope with long periods in space aboard the Salyut and Mir space stations. The US program featured Skylab in the early 1970s and then lapsed until US and international astronauts began to visit Mir during the 1990s. Since November 2000, lander touched down in Utopia Planitia; same tasks as Viking 1, plus seismometer.

**Magellan** (1989, NASA)
Mapped 98 percent of the surface of Venus at better than 300 m (1,000 ft), and obtained comprehensive gravity-field map for 95 percent of the planet.

**Galileo** (1989–2003, NASA)
While in transit to Jupiter, returned the first resolved images of two asteroids (951 Gaspra and 243 Ida), plus pictures of the impact of Comet SL9 on Jupiter (1994). Disintegrated in Jupiter's dense atmosphere. Atmospheric probe has studied Jupiter's upper atmosphere. Mission hampered by antenna problems.

**Stardust** (1999–2006, NASA)
Launched on February 7, 1999, Stardust flew within 236 km (147 miles) of Comet Wild 2 in January 2004 and collected particles from its tail before it returned to Earth in January 2006.

**ONGOING MISSIONS**

**Voyager 1** (1977– , NASA)
Flew past Jupiter (1979) and Saturn (1980). In 2007, the craft was 15.2 billion km (9.4 billion miles) away from the sun.

**Voyager 2** (1977– , NASA)
Launched just before Voyager 1, Voyager 2 flew by Jupiter (1979), Saturn (1981), Uranus (1986), and Neptune (1989). In 2006, the craft was about 12 billion km (7.3 billion miles) from Earth.

**Ulysses** (1990– , ESA/NASA)
Launched to investigate the Sun's polar regions. Gravity boost from Jupiter in 1992 took it out of the plane in which the planets orbit and over the Sun's south, then north, poles.

**SOHO** (1996– , ESA/NASA)
Solar Heliospheric Observatory (for studying the Sun and its structure), in solar orbit 1.5 million km (1 million miles) from Earth.

**Mars Surveyor Program** (1996– , NASA)
Mars Global Surveyor is the first mission of a 10-year program of robotic exploration of Mars. It entered polar orbit in September 1997 and is mapping surface topography and distribution of minerals, and monitoring global weather.

**Cassini** (1997– , ESA/NASA)
Consists of an orbiter to study Saturn's clouds and a probe to land on Titan, Saturn's largest moon. Used gravity to assist flybys of Venus, Earth, and Jupiter; arrived at Saturn in 2004.

**Spirit and Opportunity** (2003– , NASA)
Two probes designed for studying the geology of Mars, where they landed in 2004.

**Mars Express** (2003– , ESA)
European mission to completely map the planet Mars and study its surface and atmosphere, that landed in 2003.

**New Horizons** (2006– , NASA)
Launched in 2006 to visit the dwarf planet Pluto.

*Bottom left: As part of the Pathfinder mission, the unmanned Sojourner rover took X-ray measurements of Martian rocks. Below: The nucleus of Halley's comet, taken by Giotto spacecraft in 1986. Bottom right: astronauts carrying out repairs on the Hubble Space Telescope, 1993.*

experiments with long-term human presence in space are conducted on the international space station ISS, in preparation for possible manned missions to Mars.

## Exploring the universe

One function of an orbiting space station is to serve as an astronomical observing platform. However, most astronomical observations from within Earth's orbit are performed by unmanned telescope observatories controlled from the ground. The best known is the Hubble Space Telescope (HST), a 2.4 m (95 in) aperture telescope which offers views of unprecedented sharpness in infrared, visible, and ultraviolet light. It orbits at a height of about 600 km (375 miles) above the Earth's surface—well above the blurring effects of Earth's atmosphere.

Equally important is the range of astronomical satellites studying other radiation from space. Satellites such as the International Ultraviolet Explorer (IUE) and the InfraRed Astronomical Satellite (IRAS) have made major contributions in the past. More recently, the Cosmic Background Explorer (COBE) has probed the glow of the Big Bang, while satellites such as BeppoSAX have hunted down elusive sources of energetic gamma-ray bursts. The Japanese Halca satellite is a radio telescope which observes the sky in conjunction with Earth-bound telescopes to create a radio telescope thousands of kilometers across. The Solar Heliospheric Observer (SOHO) observes the Sun from a point 1.5 million km (1 million miles) closer to the Sun than Earth.

## Search for life

One of the reasons for exploring the solar system is to search for life beyond Earth. The desolate surfaces of Mercury, Venus, and the Moon are not promising sites. Mars, historically the most popular source of alien neighbors, remains a far more likely candidate after the discoveries of the space age. Although the surface is cold and dry today, evidence indicates it was once warmer and water flowed on it. The Viking landers searched for life in 1976 without success. There is no evidence yet that life ever arose on Mars.

The Galileo mission to Jupiter has enlivened speculation that Europa (right) may have a warm ocean of water under its icy crust. Perhaps life could arise there. Cassini also examines Saturn's moon, Titan, and may show whether it has lakes or oceans of carbon compounds where some sort of life might have appeared.

Life elsewhere in the solar system is likely to be primitive, but its discovery may be within reach of interplanetary spacecraft from Earth.

The search for life among the stars is far more difficult. Current efforts are directed at listening with radio telescopes for signals from distant civilizations. This project is known as SETI—the Search for Extra-Terrestrial Intelligence.

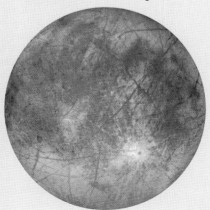

# Earth as a biophysical system

*The plants and animals we know today—such as this Chinstrap Penguin in Antarctica, above— have evolved over thousands of years to adapt to their surroundings. Opposite: Volcanoes, such as this one in New Zealand, can provide geologists with clues to the puzzle of Earth's history.*

There are many factors that make Earth a unique planet. Its atmosphere, oceans, moving plates, escaping gases, diverse life forms, soils, and the presence of humans all contribute to a distinctive biophysical system. Above all else, it is the dynamic, ever-changing ways in which the air, land, and oceans interact that create particular landscapes available for human use and abuse. From the equator to the poles, from mountains to the depths of ocean basins, plants and animals go through their life cycles nurtured by the climates and the nutrients in soils and waters.

Yet what we observe today has not always been present. The world humans inhabit has been transformed not once, but many times since the hard, rocky crusts of continents and the watery masses of oceans first formed, around 4 billion years ago.

Charles Darwin was one of many scientists who conceptualized patterns of evolution. Organisms did not immediately find their place in the world, he proposed; rather, there were countless histories of evolving life for the different plants and animals that have occupied space on land or in the sea over geological time. These patterns of evolution were not uniform. Past life histories show punctuated successions of periods dominated by particular organisms, followed by extensive extinctions of various species. The cause and meaning of such changes are often a mystery and remain to be explained.

It is very difficult to unravel Earth's history. Geologists and paleontologists are like detectives. They are required to piece together fragmentary evidence using their imagination, and their sense of adventure and curiosity, exploring the world and discovering for themselves what has happened in the past. Some geologists, such as Charles Lyell, have had the ability to synthesize masses of information and develop generalized histories from field observations and interpretations. Increasingly, new technologies, including the capacity to calculate accurately the age of rocks using radiometric dating methods, have opened new vistas of thought, allowing the testing of theories such as that of continental drift.

Discoveries of magnetic reversals in rocks on the floor of oceans, the volcanic character of mid-oceanic ridges, and the age of oceanic basalts covered by a veneer of geologically young sediment, have contributed to our understanding of the processes of sea-floor spreading and hence to the development of plate tectonic theory. This was one of the most remarkable scientific advances of the twentieth century. It formalized the grand dreams of those who could see evidence for the validity of continental drift theory in the rock record and in the distribution of plants and animals. Yet, for decades, these geologists and biologists were not able to convince the skeptics, because they had no mechanism to explain the movement of the relatively light continental crust over vast distances. New

technologies in ocean research changed all that; with plate tectonics, it is possible to explain much more satisfactorily the formation of mountains, as well as the distribution of earthquakes, volcanoes and many life forms.

Plants and animals, or biota, occur in particular groups, reflecting their adaptation to each other and to the environment. Interaction of biota with climatic, soil, landform, and other conditions has been the subject of much ecological discovery. Competition and predation are just two of the ways in which species function—on a range of scales from microorganisms in the soil to whales at sea. On land and in the ocean, there are clear regional groupings of biota which contribute to the differences between places. But even these differences are not static—they too are subject to change.

Changes in climate, for instance, whether it be over millions of years or tens of years, require organisms to adjust. On a global scale, it is possible to document periods of Earth cooling and the consequent expansion of ice sheets and falls in sea level. Vast areas of Europe and North America were under 1 km (0.6 mile) of ice as little as 15,000 years ago. Yet Earth warmed, and the glaciers retreated. Today, these areas are home to millions of people.

Rising sea levels flooded continental shelves and river valleys, creating new habitats for plants and animals; in the fertile deltaic plains of many countries, for instance. Such changes have taken place many times over the past 2 million years, the so-called Quaternary period of Earth's history. Understanding why these and other, smaller-scale climatic fluctuations such as the El Niño phenomenon occur is still the subject of much scientific debate.

Against the background of natural variability in climate, another factor comes into play—the impact of humans disturbing the chemistry of the atmosphere and inducing global warming, or the greenhouse effect.

Plants, animals, and human productivity are highly dependent on the state of soils. Continental rocks are of varied chemical composition; on exposure to the atmosphere, they disintegrate or weather into different mixtures of mineral matter combined with decayed matter from plants and animals. The close inter-relationship between soils and climate, vegetation, landforms, and rock type is well known, and this knowledge has helped us develop crops which can be grown successfully in different soils. Again, however, we are confronted with lands that become transformed as soils are overused and exploited, losing their productive capacity and causing populations to decline and migrate.

Landscapes derived from the changing yet distinctive combinations of these biophysical factors constitute part of the human inheritance. Increasingly, we are recognizing our responsibility towards the management or stewardship of this heritage.

# EVOLUTION OF THE EARTH

Earth is believed to have developed, along with the rest of the solar system, some 4,500 to 5,000 million years ago, when whirling dust aggregated to form the Sun and the planets. In the process, Earth may have attracted a primordial gaseous atmosphere around itself. The planet was then dominated by volcanic eruptions pouring out gases, including water vapor, onto its surface.

These gases gave rise to Earth's present atmosphere. As Earth's surface cooled, the water vapor condensed to form oceans. The oxygen content of the atmosphere was built up through photosynthesis by primitive life forms. Earth's plant life, through photosynthesis, gives off oxygen, which is then available to help sustain animals, including humans.

Earth's average density is about 5.5 g/cu cm (3.2 oz/cu in), but this is not uniformly distributed. Earth is formed of concentric layers, the innermost layers having the greatest densities. The density of Earth's crust is only about 2.7 g/cu cm (1.6 oz/cu in), about half its average density; the highest densities (around 12.5 g/cu cm—7.2 oz/ cu in) lie at the planet's core, which is believed to consist of iron and nickel, both of which are dense materials.

## The surface of Earth

When compared to its diameter, Earth's crust is very thin—only 5 to 40 km (3 to 25 miles). Much of Earth's surface is covered by water bodies, such as oceans, inland seas, lakes, and rivers, and these constitute the hydrosphere. The atmosphere and the hydrosphere together sustain plants and animals, which form the biosphere.

Earth's crust is cool on the surface, with temperatures in most cases not exceeding 30 °C (86 °F), but its deepest parts have temperatures as high as 1,100 °C (2,010 °F). The material of which the crust is composed can be divided into light continental material and heavier oceanic material. Light continental material has a density of 2.7 gm/cu cm (1.6 oz/cu in), and is often granitic. Heavier oceanic material has a density of 3.0 gm/cu cm (1.7 oz/cu in), and is mostly basaltic.

The thickness of Earth's crust varies widely; it is much thicker under the continents (an average of 40 km [25 miles]) and much thinner under the oceans (an average of 5 km [3 miles]). The crust is thickest below young, folded mountains such as the Alps and the Himalayas. In places such as these, it can be as thick as 64 km (40 miles).

## Below Earth's crust

Below Earth's surface lie the mantle and the core. The mantle is a thick, mostly solid layer. It is about 2,895 km (1,800 miles) thick, with temperatures ranging from 1,100 °–3,600 °C (2,010 °–6,510 °F). The upper mantle is about 670 km (420 miles) thick and contains pockets of molten material. In some places, this molten material finds its way to Earth's surface through fractures, causing volcanic eruptions such as those along the mid-oceanic ridges or in isolated hot spots. A feature of the upper mantle is the low-velocity zone, as defined by the decrease in seismic waves penetrating through the Earth. The rock here is near or at its melting point, and

*The core of Earth is made of solid iron, and has a temperature of 4,000 °C (7,230 °F). This is surrounded by liquid iron, and it is this layer that generates Earth's magnetic field. Above this is the mantle, made of rocks. This is topped by Earth's crust, which is made of lighter rocks.*

**Crust**

**Mantle**

**Outer Core**

**Inner Core**

forms material known as "hot slush", which is capable of motion or flow. It is a mobile layer, over which crustal plates can move. In contrast to this, the much thicker lower mantle (2,230 km; 1,385 miles) is entirely solid.

Earth's core is divided into an outer liquid core (2,250 km; 1,400 miles thick) and an inner solid core (1,255 km; 780 miles thick). The outer core has temperatures ranging between 3,600 °C (6,510 °F) and 4,200 °C (7,590 °C). Its liquid nature has been deduced from earthquake information.

Earthquakes transmit seismic P- and S-waves. S-waves cannot pass through liquid layers and are therefore deflected from Earth's core. In contrast, P-waves, which can be transmitted through liquids, pass through the liquid outer layer and eventually emerge on the other side of Earth.

## Above Earth's surface

Earth's present atmosphere and water make it unique amongst the other planets of the solar system. The atmosphere, however, has undergone many changes in its long history. If Earth still had an atmosphere of primordial gases, that atmosphere would resemble the gaseous mix which occurs elsewhere in the solar system. This mixture contains an abundance of hydrogen and helium, as well as of carbon.

These gases, however, occur in very small amounts in Earth's present atmosphere. It is very likely that those primordial gases were lost from Earth's atmosphere and that a secondary atmosphere developed around the planet from gases emitted by volcanoes and produced by chemical and biological processes.

It is significant that the elements which form Earth's atmosphere are also found in its crust and thus an exchange between the two can take place. For example, carbon occurs in carbon dioxide in the atmosphere and in the oceans, in calcium carbonate in limestones, and in organic compounds in plant and animal life. Both carbon dioxide and oxygen form part of the cyclic process that involves photosynthesis by plants and respiration by animals. Oxygen was actually absent or present only in very small

*Active volcanoes, such as Volcan de Pacaya, in Guatemala (left) generally occur along fault lines between plates or along mid-oceanic ridges. Molten lava bursts through the Earth's crust and flows downwards, sometimes causing great loss of life and the destruction of entire towns.*

amounts in Earth's early atmosphere, but became abundant much later. The abundance of plant life that had developed by about 400 million years ago must have boosted oxygen supplies to their current level in Earth's atmosphere. It now seems that oxygen levels which could sustain animal life may possibly have existed as early as some 700 million years ago.

The atmosphere, which rises above Earth's surface to 100 km (60 miles), is mainly made up of nitrogen (78 percent) and oxygen (21 percent), with the remaining 1 percent made up of small quantities of carbon dioxide (0.04 percent), hydrogen, water vapor, and various other gases such as argon. The atmosphere has a layered structure: the densest layers lie close to Earth's surface and the atmosphere becomes more and more rarefied as one moves upwards.

The layer of most concern to us is the troposphere. It is about 12 km (7.5 miles) thick, and contains 75 percent of all the atmospheric gases, including those essential for life. It is within this layer that all our weather occurs. The temperature falls as one rises in this layer.

The stratosphere lies above the troposphere and is about 40 km (25 miles) thick. It contains a narrow layer of ozone molecules. This ozone layer protects life on Earth by shielding it from harmful ultraviolet radiation from the Sun. This ozone layer is under threat from the emission of chemicals produced by human activities—especially chlorofluorocarbons (CFCs), which have been used in aerosol cans and refrigerators. When chlorine is released from CFCs, it rises to the ozone layer and destroys ozone molecules.

In 1985, a large hole (7.7 million square km; 3 million square miles) was discovered in the ozone layer over Antarctica. The depletion of ozone in the area where the hole is has been linked to the increase in skin cancers, especially in Australia. Damage to the ozone layer implies that human impact reaches out 15 to 55 km (9 to 35 miles) into the atmosphere. Worldwide concern about ozone depletion has led to government action; there are now international agreements relating to phasing out the use of CFCs.

## Human contribution to Earth's evolution

The changes in the composition of Earth's atmosphere, and the damage to the ozone layer, vividly demonstrate that since the advent of industrialization, humans have had considerable impact on Earth's environment and, as a consequence, on its biosphere. Many of these adverse effects were not foreseen.

It is becoming increasingly clear that human behavior can have far-reaching consequences; not only on our own local environment, but on the entire evolution of Earth. Therefore, all proposed industrial, agricultural, and other developments need to be carefully evaluated in terms of their impact on the environment before they are approved and implemented.

The gaseous mix of the troposphere has also been inadvertently altered by humans, particularly since the acceleration of industrialization in the nineteenth century. The principal change is the increase of carbon dioxide due to emissions from the burning of fossil fuels (coal, natural gas, and petroleum) by factories, power plants, railway engines, and automobiles.

Although carbon dioxide forms only about 0.04 percent of Earth's atmosphere, it is a critical component because, along with the other greenhouse gases, it acts as a blanket, trapping some of the heat of the Earth that would otherwise escape into space.

The emission of carbon dioxide and other gases (methane, nitrous oxide, and ozone) is believed to have caused global warming—the greenhouse effect. Global temperatures have risen by 0.3°C to 0.6°C (32.5°F to 33.1°F) since the mid-nineteenth century and, at the current rate of increase of greenhouse gases,

this figure could double by the middle of the twenty-first century. Some predictions place the increase at between 1.5°C (34.7°F) and 5.5°C (41.9°F).

The weather patterns in the world have shown great disturbance in recent decades, according to some observers. This also is being attributed to the greenhouse effect. If global warming continues, it could result in the melting of polar ice sheets and the consequent rising of sea levels, which in turn would seriously threaten low-lying areas, including quite a number of major coastal cities.

*The troposphere is the layer of the atmosphere where life exists. The stratosphere is the next layer. The ozone layer, which absorbs most of the Sun's harmful ultraviolet rays, is in the stratosphere. The next layer is the mesosphere. The thermosphere is the outer layer of our atmosphere. Gases are very thin here, and this is where auroras and meteors are seen. The red line shows the decreases and increases in temperature through each layer of the atmosphere.*

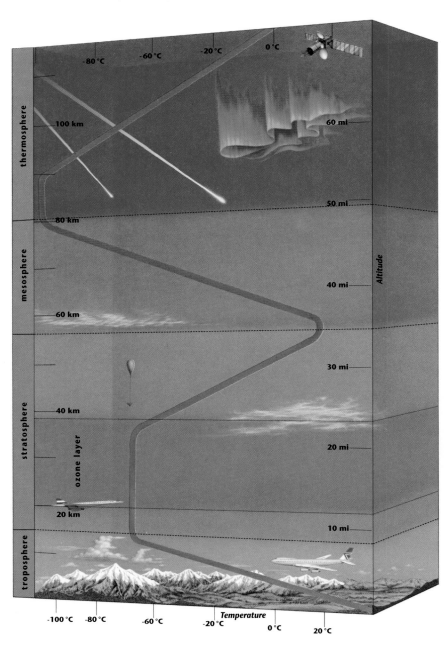

# MOVEMENT OF PLATES

E arth is a dynamic planet, and forces within it are continuously active. Continents and oceans have changed in position and shape over time. Earthquakes and other evidence prove that Earth's crust, which is a solid and rigid layer, is broken up into parts called lithospheric or tectonic plates. Plate boundaries coincide with major earthquake zones, many of which also have volcanic chains along them. Seven major plates (Pacific, North American, South American, Eurasian, African, Indo-Australian, and Antarctic), and perhaps twice as many minor plates, have been identified.

Over many millions of years, crustal plates have moved considerably. They have separated (divergent plates), giving rise to oceans, collided (convergent plates), forming the world's highest mountains and the deep oceanic trenches, and slid past each other along fault lines. Thus Earth's crust has spread at divergent plate boundaries and contracted at convergent plate boundaries.

## Divergent plate boundaries

In the middle of the Atlantic and Indian oceans, and in the eastern part of the Pacific Ocean, long rifts exist where molten material has risen to form undersea chains of volcanoes. This molten material originates from magma pockets within Earth's upper mantle, and crystallizes as basalt on cooling. These oceanic volcanic chains, called mid-oceanic ridges, form an interlinked system about 60,000 km (37,300 miles) long. In some places, the volcanoes have erupted above the water level, forming islands such as Iceland and the Azores.

Mid-oceanic ridges are not continuous features, but are fractured at several places, with parts being offset by transform faults. Shallow-focus earthquakes, recorded by sensitive instruments, occur frequently along mid-oceanic ridges.

Each time a new series of volcanic eruptions takes place, the existing ridge is split in two and the parts are pushed apart, spreading the sea floor. The corresponding parts of the early ridges are now far apart, on opposite sides of the current mid-oceanic ridge. The separated bands can be identified on the basis of their recorded magnetic directions and age. When the basaltic bands crystallized, Earth's magnetic direction at the time of formation was imprinted in them. Such data proves that Earth's magnetic direction has reversed many times during geological history.

Sea-floor spreading is believed to have produced the Atlantic and Indian oceans, and to have enlarged the Pacific Ocean. Plates move very slowly—on average, only about 2–5 cm ($^3/_4$–2 inches) per year—with the spreading of the Atlantic Ocean having taken about 65 million years. Some plates are separating much more quickly—the Nazca and Pacific plates move at about 18 cm (7 inches) per year.

Compared with the continental crust, which is more than 1,000 million years old, most of the oceanic crust (at less than 65 million years old) is geologically very young, the youngest parts being those that lie along the mid-oceanic ridges.

The Red Sea is an example of new sea-floor spreading, whilst the elongated Great Rift Valley in Africa, which extends for more than 2,890 km (1,800 miles), possibly represents new continental rifting and splitting. There are several centers of volcanic eruptions along the Rift Valley; to the north and south of Lake Kivu, for example.

## Convergent plate boundaries

Crustal plates may split and diverge on one side, and collide with other plates on the opposite side, giving rise to volcanic chains and oceanic ridges.

Earth's crust is made up of rigid tectonic plates. Their movement, over millions of years, has determined the structure of our continents and oceans, the formation of mountains and volcanoes, and the distribution of earthquakes.

When plates collide, one plate slides under the other one in a process called subduction, the subducted plate being pushed deep into Earth's mantle. As a result of subduction, collision zones are marked by deep focus earthquakes, such as have occurred in recent times in Japan, Iran and Afghanistan. Subducted plates are dragged deep into the Earth, where they melt. This molten material later rises to form volcanoes.

The deep oceanic trenches lying parallel to the volcanic island arcs, which formed as a result of oceanic-to-oceanic plate collisions, are the deepest features on Earth's surface, ranging from 7,000 to 11,000 m (23,000 to 36,000 ft) deep. The Marianas Trench in the West Pacific is nearly 11,000 m (more than 35,000 ft) deep. There are several trenches in the western Pacific, along the coasts of Japan and the Philippines.

Where continental and oceanic plates collide, the continental plate is crumpled and the oceanic plate buckles downward deep into Earth, where it melts and mixes with the molten material inside the Earth. Lavas from this mixed molten material are lighter in density and color than oceanic basalt. The rock formed is andesite and it is found along

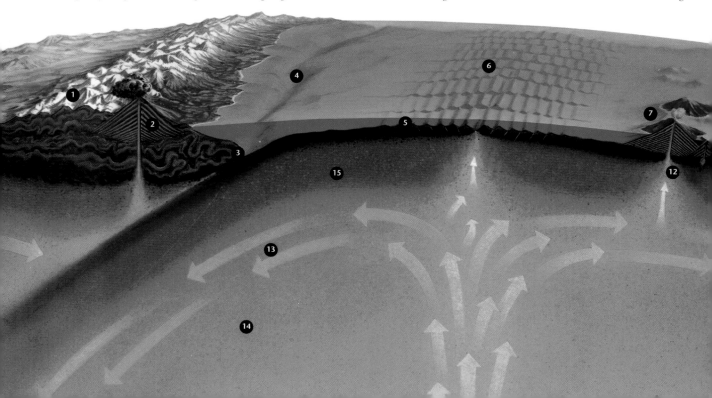

*A panoramic view of the Himalayas, the world's highest mountain range (left). The Himalayas are actually made up of three ranges, formed at different times. The koala (below), unique to Australia, may be an animal that became isolated after the break-up of the supercontinent Gondwanaland.*

a long chain around the Pacific Ocean. Several plates have collided with the Pacific Plate, giving rise to folded mountain chains, including the Cascade Range in the western USA, and the Andes in South America. This circum-Pacific zone is often referred to as the "Ring of Fire" because of the presence of active volcanoes.

Continent-to-continent plate collisions result in the formation of mountain ranges such as the European Alps and the Himalayas, in Asia. The process gives rise to crustal thickening.

The stupendous Himalayan range arose when the Indo-Australian Plate collided with the Eurasian Plate. The Eurasian Plate rode over the Indian side, pushing up huge sedimentary strata from the then-existing sea into great mountain folds, some of which were thrust towards the south and almost overturned.

Three parallel ranges were formed in successive geological epochs. The southernmost chain is the lowest, ranging from 900 to 1,200 m (2,950 to 3,935 ft) in height, whilst the middle chain rises 2,000 to 4,500 m (6,560 to 14,765 ft). The chain of highest elevation, lying in the north, has the world's highest peaks (topped by Mount Everest, at 8,848 m [29,028 ft]), which are about 8,500 m (27,885 ft) in height. Its average altitude is 6,000 m (19,685 ft). It adjoins the high Tibetan Plateau, which has an average altitude of 4,000 m (13,125 ft).

### Transform fault boundaries

The third type of plate boundary involves two plates sliding past each other along a fault line. There is no collision or separation involved, but earthquakes result from the movement of these plates. The best-known example of this is the San Andreas Fault in California, which has been associated with major earthquakes in San Francisco and Los Angeles. Along that fault line, the Pacific Plate is sliding northwards in relation to the adjacent North American Plate.

### Continental drift

It was in 1922 that Alfred Wegener first expounded his theory that the continents had drifted to their present positions. His hypothesis centered on the close jigsaw fit of Africa and South America. The English philosopher and essayist Francis Bacon had drawn attention to this much earlier, as did Snider-Pellegrini in 1858, who pointed to the similarities in the characteristics of plant fossils in coal deposits found in both continents.

Wegener marshalled evidence to show that the fit involved the juxtaposition of river valleys, mountain chains, and similar rock formations and mineral deposits. Those rock formations contained similar fossils. Wegener hypothesized that all the continents once formed a single landmass, which he named Pangaea, and which, he claimed, began breaking up in the Carboniferous Period (divided into the Pennsylvanian and Mississipian epochs in the United States) about 300 million years ago. That split first resulted in two continents: a

northern one called Laurasia and a southern one called Gondwanaland. The various supposed parts of the southern continent (South America, Africa, India, Australia, and Antarctica) showed a much better geological fit than did the supposed parts of the northern one.

Wegener's theory was based on the premise that the light continents floated on a denser underlying crust, and that these continents thus drifted to their present positions. The absence of an acceptable mechanism for drifting was used as an argument against Wegener's ideas—it was thought physically impossible that the solid continents could have moved through an underlying rigid, denser layer.

Nevertheless, many scientists were inclined to accept that the continents had moved to their present positions because there was mounting geological evidence, such as that marshalled by Alex du Toit of South Africa, which proved similarities in areas which had been said to have once been joined together.

During the past 50 years, modern technology has provided much new information about the sea floors. In particular, evidence has emerged leading to the acceptance of sea-floor spreading. This, in turn, has led to the development of plate tectonics, which may be considered an update of Wegener's ideas about continental movement. As a result, his main ideas about the original juxtaposition of the continents have now been largely vindicated.

*The processes and results of plate movement:*
*1. Fold mountains  2. Active volcano  3. Subduction zone*
*4. Subduction trench  5. Spreading sea-floor  6. Mid-oceanic ridge  7. Hot spot island chain (volcanic)*
*8. Oceanic crust  9. Colliding plates form mountain chain*
*10. Fold mountains  11. Rift valley  12. Hot spot*
*13. Magma (convection currents)*
*14. Asthenosphere*
*15. Lithosphere*

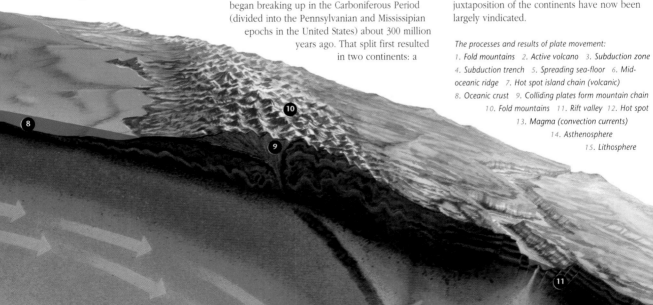

# ROCKS

Earth's crust consists of rocks. These rocks combine a variety of minerals that may or may not be crystalline, and which can form in several ways. Igneous rocks are made of crystalline minerals which originate during the cooling of molten material called magma. In contrast, sedimentary rocks result from the compaction or consolidation of loosened minerals, rock fragments, and plant and animal matter. Metamorphic rocks are formed when existing rocks are altered through pressure and temperature—they result either from compaction under pressure or from partial remelting, when new minerals can be formed from crystallization.

## Minerals

Minerals are inorganic substances with defined chemical and atomic structures. When magmas cool, minerals crystallize. Each mineral exhibits its own unique crystalline shape. Minerals can also originate in the breakdown of pre-existing minerals, as in the case of clays, or from the reconstitution of existing materials, as in the case of metamorphic rocks.

A common mineral is quartz (an oxide of silica), which occurs as large crystals in some rocks and as sand on sea shores. It is a light-colored mineral. Other light-colored minerals include felspars, which are silicates combining silica, aluminum, potassium, sodium, and calcium. These light-colored minerals are commonly found in rocks of light density, such as granite. Dark-colored silicates, which are combinations of silica, magnesium, and iron (pyroxenes, amphiboles, olivine, and dark micas), predominate in dark-colored rocks such as basalt.

## Igneous rocks

When molten material lying deep within Earth's crust cools, minerals form large crystals, because of slow cooling, producing plutonic igneous rocks. The most common plutonic rock is granite, which is also the rock that is most widespread in the continental crust. Granite is light colored and low in density because it contains silica and felspars.

When magma is extruded onto the Earth's surface as lava, faster cooling takes place, resulting in smaller crystals, even glass. The most common volcanic rock is basalt, which is dark colored and dense because of dark-colored minerals such as biotite, pyroxenes, amphiboles, and olivine. The ocean floors are largely made up of basalt.

Large pockets of magma inside the crust give rise to large rock bodies called batholiths, which are mostly made of granite and are often found in great mountain ranges. Smaller igneous intrusions may form in cracks and joints in other rocks. When these intrusions cut through sedimentary strata, they are called dikes; intrusions between the bedding planes of strata are known as sills.

The vapors emanating from igneous intrusions often crystallize in neighboring rocks as valuable minerals—gold, silver, copper, lead, and zinc. Such deposits are found in recent geological formations such as those around the Pacific "Ring of Fire," as well as in more ancient rocks such as those near the Kalgoorlie goldfields of Western Australia. A rare igneous rock called kimberlite, which occurs in pipe-like shapes, contains diamond deposits such as those found in South Africa.

## Sedimentary rocks

Sedimentary rocks can be made up of either organic or inorganic particles. Organic sediments are the remains of plants and animals—one example of a sedimentary rock made up of plant remains is coal. Large deposits of limestone are mostly the result of the precipitation of calcium carbonate, but can also be the result of the agglomeration, or clustering, of sea shell fragments and the building of coral reefs. Inorganic sedimentary rocks include those made up of sand (sandstone), clays (shale), or pebbles cemented together (conglomerate).

Sedimentary strata deposited in large basins like the sea sometimes become exposed through vertical uplift, in which case the strata may remain horizontal. When strata are folded in the process of mountain formation, however, they form complex structures such as anticlines (dome-shaped folds) and synclines (basin-shaped folds). Anticlines have often become reservoirs for petroleum, while basin-type structures can often contain artesian water.

Several valuable minerals are found in sedimentary rocks: iron ores; oxides of aluminum (bauxite); and manganese. Coal deposits are sedimentary accumulations of transformed ancient forests. Building materials such as sandstones and materials for producing cement and fertilizers also come from sedimentary rocks.

## Metamorphic rocks

When sedimentary rocks are subjected to high pressure they alter to become metamorphic rocks. Thus shale is converted to the more solid slate, sandstone to the very hard rock called quartzite and limestone to the crystallized rock known as marble. The presence of chemical impurities in limestone can result in marbles of a variety of colors and patterns.

When sedimentary and igneous rocks are subjected to high pressure as well

| Era | Major geological events | Period | Millions of years ago |
|---|---|---|---|
| **CENOZOIC** | • Ice age<br>• First humans | Quaternary | |
| | | | 1.6 |
| | • Rockies, Alps and Himalayas begin to form<br>• First hominids | Tertiary | |
| | | | 65 |
| **MESOZOIC** | • First flowering plants<br>• Extinction of giant reptiles | Cretaceous | |
| | | | 145 |
| | • Pangaea splits into Gondwanaland and Laurasia<br>• First birds and mammals | Jurassic | |
| | | | 208 |
| | • First dinosaurs<br>• Supercontinent of Pangaea in existence | Triassic | 245 |
| **PALEOZOIC** | • First amphibians | Permian | 288 |
| | • Extensive forests, which later formed coal deposits | Carboniferous | |
| | | | 360 |
| | | Devonian | 408 |
| | • First land plants | Silurian | 438 |
| | | Ordovician | |
| | | | 506 |
| | • Age of the trilobites, the first complex animals, which had hard shells and were marine | Cambrian | 570 |
| **PRE-CAMBRIAN** | • Oldest rocks on Earth's crust identified<br>• First life forms: single cell forms like bacteria and algae<br>• Continents and oceans formed<br>• Extensive sedimentary rocks like iron ore deposits were laid down | | 4560 |

*The Grand Canyon, USA (right), with a color-coded strip added (see geological time scale, left) to illustrate the geological history of the area. The diagram shows geological eras from the origin of Earth (4,560 million years ago) until the Cenozoic Era, which began 65 million years ago.*

*An area of the East Sussex, United Kingdom coast known as the Seven Sisters (far left) consists primarily of limestone, a sedimentary rock. The banded boulders (left) in the Canadian Rockies, and the Waitomo Caves in the North Island, New Zealand (below) are also limestone; its appearance depends on the depositional environment in which it formed.*

as high temperature, partial melting can take place. This partially remelted material gives rise to crystalline metamorphic rocks called schist and gneiss. Gneiss resembles granite in appearance, but it generally has a layered structure. Schists are made of platy minerals, including micas.

Large igneous intrusions often change the rocks into which they intrude to metamorphic rocks through the effects of the heat and the gases that they carry. Batholiths, the largest igneous intrusions, have created metamorphic aureoles in contact zones such as are found in the Alps.

Two important building materials, slate and marble, are metamorphic rocks. Other commercially valuable metamorphic mineral deposits include talc (used for cosmetics) and graphite (used for making pencils).

### The rock cycle

In recent years, the concept of the rock cycle has proven useful. It represents the continuous recycling of rock materials and their conversion into different rock types, and helps link the various kinds of rocks found on Earth's surface.

When igneous rocks are exposed on the surface of Earth, they become weathered. Solar radiation, running water, ice, wind, and waves all weather rocks mechanically. Water acidified through the absorption of carbon dioxide and organic acids weathers rocks chemically. Over a long period, mechanical and chemical weathering produces pebbles, sands, and clays, which often consolidate into sedimentary rocks.

When these rocks are then dragged deep into Earth's crust by the process of plate subduction, they enter zones of very high pressure and temperature, resulting in partial melting and producing crystalline metamorphic rocks. If the rocks are carried still deeper into the Earth, however, where the

temperatures are high enough to melt the rocks completely, a new magma is formed. This new magma may either crystallize deep inside Earth and form new plutonic igneous rocks, or be extruded as volcanic lavas.

Where volcanoes have erupted along zones of plate subduction, a rock named andesite has formed from lavas; this rock is a mixture of dark- and light-colored minerals, as it reflects the mixing of light continental and dark oceanic materials.

# LANDFORMS

Earth's surface is constantly being transformed by falling rain, glaciers, rivers, underground water, wind, and waves. These constantly erode the land, transporting debris and depositing it elsewhere. The land is moulded into new forms through erosion, and new landforms are also created by the deposition of eroded debris.

Rainfall and water flow in creeks and rivers are the main agents of landform creation in humid areas; glaciers are the most important agents at high latitudes and in mountainous areas of heavy snowfall; and wind is important in arid areas.

### Landforms of erosion

Glaciers, rivers, winds, and waves are powerful erosive agents. Glaciers pluck pieces of rock from valley sides, rivers carry rock fragments along in their current, and winds lift and transport particles of dust. Air and water velocities determine the erosive force of winds and rivers, and the rock fragments they carry with them make these agents additionally abrasive.

Rock fragments embedded in glaciers scour rock surfaces on the glacier's floor and sides; sand and gravel in fast-flowing rivers erode their floors and banks; and wind-borne sand blasts rock surfaces, creating intricate structures. Platforms, caves, and cliffs are formed by the action of waves carrying sand, pebbles and boulders and beating them against rocky coasts.

Rivers in mountainous areas flow rapidly because of steep slope gradients. Such streams may be highly erosive, and may cut their channels vertically, producing V-shaped valley profiles.

Glaciers are made of solid ice, and result from the compaction of snow. Some of the longest

*The following features are those typically found in glacial areas, showing the close interconnection between current landforms and past glaciers:* 1. *Cirque basin* 2. *Hanging valley in a glacial trough* 3. *Outwash plain from glacial meltwater* 4. *Terminal moraine of a valley glacier* 5. *Lateral moraine* 6. *Medial moraine* 7. *Ground moraine* 8. *Arête or sharp-crested ridge* 9. *Horn or sharp peak*

glaciers remaining, at 39 to 73 km (24 to 46 miles) in length, are found in the Karakoram ranges in the Himalayas. Although they generally move very slowly (2 to 3 cm [3/4 to 1 1/4 inches] per day), glaciers are powerful eroders, and can move 4 to 5 m (13 to 16 1/2 ft) a day.

Glaciers typically create U-shaped valleys called troughs. Glaciers at the head of sloping valleys give rise to basin-shaped features known as cirques. When cirques from two opposing sides meet through erosion, a pass, or col, is formed. Between glacial valleys, sharp ridges, known as arêtes, develop. At the top of glacial mountains, arêtes meet at sharp peaks called horns, such as those on the Matterhorn and Mt Everest.

Where glaciers have disappeared, troughs are exposed, along with tributary glacial valleys, and these form hanging valleys perched above scarps. They often have streams cascading over them as waterfalls, and are often used as sites for the generation of hydroelectric power.

Depending on their velocity, winds can lift loose rock particles or soils. Generally speaking, the wind transports particles which are dry and not protected by plant cover—so wind action is mostly restricted to arid and semiarid regions, and some coastal areas. Strong winds can scoop out hollows in loose, dry soil. This process is known as deflation, and the hollows formed are called blowouts. These can range in diameter from about a meter to a kilometer or more.

When waves approach a coastline made up of headlands and bays, they gather around the headlands and spread out in the bays. Wave energy becomes concentrated on the headlands, where the steady pounding carves platforms and cliffs. In bays, by contrast, wave energy is dissipated, and the waves deposit sand and other detritus. These may also be transported along the shore, depending on the angle of the coast in relation to the direction of the waves.

Rock debris—such as loose, unsupported material and waterlogged soil—tends to move down hill slopes through the action of gravity.

Slow movements known as soil creep are often imperceptible, and are indicated only by the changed position of fixed objects—trees, fences, and houses. The shaking of sloping ground by earthquakes can trigger a more rapid movement of loose materials. Fast movements such as landslides (or snow avalanches) tend to occur after heavy rains (or snowfalls) on steep slopes. In contrast to landslides, slumps are formed when slopes slip in a backward rotation, a phenomenon sometimes found in waterlogged soils.

### Transportation and deposition of rock debris

The debris resulting from erosion is transported by glaciers, rivers, winds, and waves. A glacier carries assorted rock debris (boulders, pebbles, or finer materials) on or beneath its solid surface.

As a glacier moves, it plucks rocks from the valley walls, and the rock debris falls along the sides of the glacier to form what are known as lateral moraines. When two glaciers meet and coalesce, two lateral moraines join in the center of the new, larger glacier, forming a medial moraine.

As mountain glaciers reach lower, warmer levels, they melt and drop their debris, which forms terminal moraines. The resulting meltwater carries a fine glacial flour, which may be spread as a vast depositional plain. Rich soils have

An aerial view of a braided river channel showing the build up of sediment on the river bed (far left), and a coastline dramatically eroded by wave action (left). The cirque (below) shows typically steep walls—carved by the movement of glacial ice—and a flat floor.

developed in such plains in both northern Europe and the northern United States.

The amount of rock particle rivers and winds carry is determined by velocity; in general, larger particle sizes need greater velocities. At lower speeds, rivers deposit their sediment load, which then forms fertile alluvial flats and broad alluvial plains. These areas may be periodically inundated by floods. Much of the sediment carried by rivers in flood is deposited at the coast as deltas. Several major rivers carry high sediment loads—the Huang River in China carries more than one and a half million tonnes annually.

### Wind

Other landforms result from wind. Strong winds can lift and carry sands, while lighter winds lift and carry silts and clays. High winds rework sand masses into dunes of various types, depending on sand availability and wind direction. Sand dunes in deserts include crescent-

shaped barchans, which have gentle windward slopes and abrupt leeward slopes—the crescent's horns point downwind. Silt-sized particles are transported by the wind to form thick, fertile deposits known as loess. Extensive deposits of loess are found on the edges of some deserts and in areas once glaciated (northern China and the Mississippi Valley, for instance).

### Waves

Waves tend to approach a beach perpendicularly. The movement of the wave as it runs onto the beach is known as swash; the water, or backwash, then returns to the sea. Swash and backwash move sand along beaches, which contributes to

littoral or longshore drift (when waves approach the beach at an angle). Along coastal plains, waves tend to build sand barriers by the shore. Lagoons develop behind these barriers, which are connected to the sea by tidal inlets. These lagoons can later fill with sediment, a stage in the gradual seaward extension of the coastal plain. The sea-level rise, on the other hand, along with storm wave erosion, can drive the sand barriers landward.

During the next several decades, because of global warming, the sea level may rise at rates up to 10 cm (4 inches) per year. This would cause the loss of sand barriers and adjacent lagoons and wetlands, and the loss of some islands on coral reefs.

# CLIMATE

Just as weather is the day-to-day condition of the atmosphere, climate consists of the long-term average of weather conditions, including seasonal and year-to-year variability, and extremes. Many distinctive climatic types can be identified. These vary with regard to incoming solar radiation, temperature, wind, precipitation (rainfall and snowfall), evaporation, storms (type, frequency and magnitude), and seasonal patterns.

## Solar radiation

Solar radiation (insolation) is received unequally in different parts of Earth. The equatorial belt receives strong solar radiation uniformly throughout the year, whilst places close to the poles, in contrast, have great differences between summer and winter solar radiation; perpetual ice climates exist at the poles. Along the equator, the lands are warm throughout the year, but, in the latitudes further away from the equator, seasonal variations become more discernible, with marked differences in the temperate zone.

## General atmospheric circulation

The large amount of heat received at the equator means that air becomes heated and expands, and this air rises and flows towards the poles. Some of this air flows back to the equator in the form of trade winds as part of the Hadley Cell circulation. Flowing from the east, these winds are called easterlies. The subtropical belt (up to about 30° latitude), is the zone of large high-pressure cells from which winds move through more temperate latitudes towards the poles. Cold, dense air from the poles flows, as polar fronts, back through these latitudes towards the equator. These fronts clash with tropical air masses in the temperate

zones, giving give rise to cyclones (low-pressure cells), which bring inclement weather and rainy days. Such weather conditions are more common in the northern hemisphere, where there are extensive landmasses. In the southern hemisphere, in contrast, there are more extensive oceans. In that belt, between 40° latitude and Antarctica, a westerly wind blows eastward along an almost unbroken stretch of seas throughout the year.

## Climatic types

Of the several proposed climatic classifications, the best known is that devised by Köppen, who divided climates broadly into five classes: A, B, C, D, and E. The humid climates are A, C, and D, with A being the warmest and lying in the tropics, C being found in the warm temperate regions, and D covering cold climates with regular winter snowfall. Arid climates, both tropical and temperate, are classed as B climates. Ice sheets are represented by E climates.

## Humid tropical climates (A)

Type A climates are found between 25°N and 25°S latitudes. These humid tropical climates receive abundant rainfall and have year-round high temperatures, with the areas further away from the equator having hot summers and mild winters.

These areas favor the abundant growth of vegetation, particularly rainforest. This climatic belt has extensive agriculture and often large populations. Heavy rainfall and high temperatures, however, leach soils of their valuable nutrients, which is detrimental for agriculture.

A typical A climate is the tropical monsoon climate that is found in Southeast Asia. It is characterized by a distinct season of heavy rainfall,

*Monsoon flooding in Vietnam (above). Monsoons are usually annual events, and deliver 85% of East Asia's annual rainfall, but can also cause devastation to low-lying areas.*

preceded and followed by dry months; for example, large parts of India and Southeast Asia receive most of their rain between June and September, while March to May are typically dry months. Along the west coast of India, annual rainfall can be as high as 25,400 to 28,800 mm (9,900 to 1,123 inches).

## Desert climates (B)

Deserts are found in subtropical and temperate zones, and are classified by Köppen as B-type climates. Being areas of low rainfall, deserts have either few plants, or only small plants that are particularly well suited to dry environments.

Hot deserts lie in the subtropics—in the belt extending from North Africa (the Sahara Desert) and the Middle East to northwestern India (the Thar Desert)—and in the Central Australian Desert. These deserts have high daily temperature ranges; it can be very hot during the day and quite cool at night. The Gobi Desert, which lies in central Asia, is the best-known cold desert.

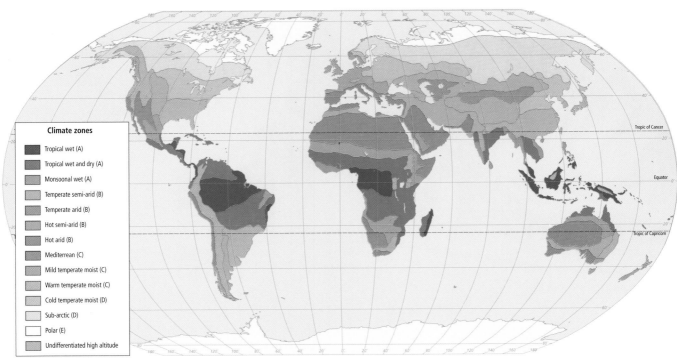

**Climate zones**

- Tropical wet (A)
- Tropical wet and dry (A)
- Monsoonal wet (A)
- Temperate semi-arid (B)
- Temperate arid (B)
- Hot semi-arid (B)
- Hot arid (B)
- Mediterrean (C)
- Mild temperate moist (C)
- Warm temperate moist (C)
- Cold temperate moist (D)
- Sub-arctic (D)
- Polar (E)
- Undifferentiated high altitude

Projection: Robinson  Equatorial Scale approx 1:110 million

## Humid temperate climates (C)

Type C climates lie between latitudes of 25° and 45°. They have marked seasonal variations, with temperature differences between summer and winter being quite large. The Mediterranean climate is a good example of a B climate; summer temperatures can on occasions soar to the mid-40s (110°F) in southern Greece and Italy, while winter temperatures can fall to 10°C (50°F). The Mediterranean climate is characterized by cold, wet winters and hot, dry summers.

The temperate zone close to the tropics (25° to 35° latitudes) is warm. It is now common to find that belt referred to as the subtropics. The subtropical areas lying along the eastern sides of the continents are particularly warm, as they receive the warm easterly tropical winds, and warm ocean currents flow along their coasts. This east coast climate is found in southeast China, eastern Australia and South America.

In contrast, the westerlies in the higher latitudes (35° to 60° latitudes) give rise to a cooler west coast climate. Year-round rainfall and adequate temperatures promote the growth of forests in both east and west coast climates.

Grasslands generally occur in the continental interiors of C climate areas, where annual rainfall is moderate (300 to 400 mm; 12 to 16 in), and water in the soil is not abundant. These areas lie in the rainshadows of major mountain ranges. Seasonal temperature ranges are usually sizeable.

## Cold temperate climates (D)

Moving into the temperate zone close to the poles, temperatures fall because there is reduced solar radiation. This is exacerbated by cold polar winds.

Polar winds are easterlies, although their directions can be variable in temperate latitudes. Such type D climates lie between 45° and 65° latitudes, and are only significant in the northern hemisphere—the equivalent belt in the southern hemisphere is mostly covered by the oceans.

The taiga climate is a good example of this climate; lying close to the Arctic polar region, the area is characterized by abundant snowfall and unique woodlands. Temperatures in winter commonly fall to -30°C (-22°F), and in some places can go as low as -40°C (-40°F). During midsummer, however, temperatures can rise to around 15°C (60°F) or higher.

## Ice climates (E)

E-type climates are found between 65° and 90° latitudes, the principal examples being Antarctica and Greenland. These ice sheets cover about 10 percent of Earth's surface, and form an essential part of the system which regulates the global atmospheric circulation. These areas are subject to long periods of darkness, and temperatures rise above freezing level for only 2 to 4 months a year.

If global warming reduces the extent of these ice sheets, climatic conditions in the world will alter: ice melting would contribute to rises in sea level, with adverse effects on low-lying areas.

## The El Niño phenomenon

Deviations from normal temperature patterns of the waters in the southern Pacific Ocean, between Australia and South America, result in the phenomenon called El Niño. Under normal conditions, eastern trade winds blow across the Pacific. These drive the sun-warmed surface water from the central Pacific to the coast off northern Australia. When clouds form above this area of warm water and move over Indonesia, Papua New Guinea, and Australia they bring rain with them.

Every two to seven years, however, this pattern is interrupted by the El Niño event. During El Niño, the Pacific Ocean off Australia does not warm as much as it normally does. Instead, it becomes warmer right up to the coast of Peru in South America. At the same time, the easterly trade winds that blow across the Pacific reverse their direction. This causes high-pressure systems to build up to the north of and across the Australian continent, preventing moist tropical air reaching the continent. These conditions in turn result in storms, and in rain falling in the eastern Pacific Ocean and in South America instead of in Australia, Papua New Guinea, and Indonesia, which then suffer drought conditions.

While the effects of El Niño are sometimes weak, at other times they are very strong. During a severe El Niño period, extreme drought conditions prevail, as in 1982–83 and 1997–98. In contrast, heavy rainfall and flooding occurred in parts of North and South America. In 1997, there were severe storms and floods in Mexico and further north along the west coast of the United States.

The converse of the El Niño effect is the La Niña effect, which is an exaggeration of normal conditions. This takes place when trade winds blow strongly and consistently across the Pacific towards Australia. This pushes the warm waters from the central Pacific, off the northern Australian coast, to build up into a mass that is bigger than normal. Thus, much more cloud develops than usual, and this brings considerably more rain to Australia and neighboring countries.

# THE WATER CYCLE

Earth, in contrast to all the other planets in the solar system, has an abundant supply of water. Much of this, of course, lies in the oceans and seas (more than 97 percent), and is saline. The polar ice caps lock up slightly more than 2 percent of the remaining water, leaving less than 1 percent of fresh water to sustain life on Earth. Human needs are met by the water from rainfall, rivers, and underground supplies (plus a small amount from desalination plants).

Water falls as rain and snow, and flows as rivers and glaciers before ultimately reaching the sea. It also sinks into the ground to form underground water reservoirs, to emerge as springs or to seep into river water. Fresh supplies of water are continuously needed and nature provides this supply through the water cycle.

## How the water cycle works

Solar energy evaporates exposed water from seas, lakes, rivers, and wet soils; the majority of this evaporation takes place over the seas. Water is also released into the atmosphere by plants through photosynthesis. During this process, known as evapotranspiration, water vapor rises into the atmosphere.

Clouds form when air becomes saturated with water vapor. The two major types of cloud formations are a stratified or layered gray cloud called stratus, and a billowing white or dark gray cloud called cumulus. Nimbostratus clouds and cumulonimbus clouds are the cloud types that are associated with rainy weather; nimbostratus clouds will bring steady rain, and cumulonimbus clouds will bring stormy weather.

Precipitation as rain, snow, or hail ensures that water returns to Earth's surface in a fresh form. Some of this rain, however, falls into the seas and is not accessible to humans. When rain falls, it either washes down hill slopes or seeps underground; when snow and hail melt, this water may also sink into the ground.

Rainfall also replenishes river water supplies, as does underground water. Snowfall may consolidate into glaciers and ice sheets which, when they melt, release their water into the ground, into streams, or into the seas.

### Water in river courses

Rivers pass through several phases on their journey from hilly and mountainous areas to the seas and oceans. In their early phases—that is, close to their sources in the hills and mountains—they have steep slope gradients and, therefore, move with high velocities. They carry rock fragments and have high erosive force.

In these areas, the energy from streams provides the potential for hydroelectric development. This potential has been harnessed in many places, such as in the foothills of the Himalayas in Nepal.

On flat plains, rivers tend to wind their way in meandering courses. Here, the water flow has now lost most of its erosive capacity. Massive clay deposits may also give rise to fertile alluvial plains. During times of heavy rainfall, flooding can take place, and this is a serious issue along some of the major rivers of the world, such as the Mississippi in the United States, the Yangtze in China, and the Ganges in India.

*The Arrigetch peaks and glacier, in Alaska (above). Water is released as steam into the atmosphere from electric power plants (right). A hot water artesian bore (far right).*

### Human interference in the water cycle

There has been considerable human interference in the water cycle throughout recorded history, but far more so since the beginning of the twentieth century. For centuries, humans have built dams across rivers to store water, which is then used for irrigation, or for domestic or industrial water supply. Dams have also been built to control river flooding, such as across the Huang River in China, and to produce electricity.

The Aswan Dam across the Nile provides arid Egypt with essential water. The two highest dams in the world, more than 300 m (985 ft) in height, have been built across the Vakhsh River in Tajikistan. The dam with by far the largest reservoir capacity—2,700 million cubic meters (3,530 million cubic yards)—is the Owen Falls Dam, across the Nile, in Uganda.

Hydroelectric power is generated in several parts of the world, such as at Itaipu, across the Parana River, in Brazil—this dam can generate

12,600 megawatts of power. The building of dams in areas prone to earthquakes, such as Japan, however, causes great concern because of the potential for serious damage.

Water is necessary for agriculture, industry, and domestic use. Agriculture depends on rainfall, as well as on irrigation from stored water. The provision of water for domestic use—particularly the need for clean drinking water—has become very important with the spread of urbanization. Reservoirs are often built to ensure urban water supplies and water is purified before being channelled to consumers.

The discharge of industrial, agricultural, and domestic effluents into streams and lakes (especially in the twentieth century) has reduced water quality and damaged aquatic life. These effluents include metallic substances. One of the most dramatic examples has been the discharge of mercury into rivers in Japan. This mercury has now entered the food chain through fish, creating serious health problems. The discharge of pesticides has also

## Artesian wells

When rain falls, some of it sinks into the ground and is held in the soil—this water is known as ground water. A layer under the ground becomes saturated with this seeped water; the surface of this layer is called the water table. Wells are mostly dug to tap water in the water table. There is another way, however, that water can seep under the ground to form water reservoirs. Some types of rock are porous, and this allows them to hold water; water can move through such permeable rock.

Sandstone is a permeable rock. If a sandstone bed is dipping at an angle, rainwater can penetrate the exposed part of the rock and travel along the stratum into the ground. The water will be retained by the sandstone layer if the rocks above and below it are impermeable. If this water reservoir lies well below the ground, it is held under pressure; if a well is bored to the reservoir, the water will gush out under this pressure. These reservoirs are called artesian wells. The permeable strata that carry the water are called

aquifers; the impermeable layers which lie above and below the aquifers are known as aquicludes.

Artesian waters are important where rainfall is low and water supplies uncertain. Overuse of artesian water can result in the ground sinking, and if the reservoir is close to the sea, excessive removal of water can allow saline water to penetrate the reservoir, reducing water quality.

been detrimental to aquatic life, and excessive use of fertilizers, along with salts released into rivers and lakes by poor land use practices, have also altered the ecological balance.

Changes in air quality brought about by humans have also affected the water cycle. The use of fossil fuels to generate electricity and power transport has resulted in substantial sulfur dioxide and nitrogen oxide emissions. When these gases and water react, sulfuric and nitric acids are produced. These pollutants are present in clouds and fog, and fall with rain and snow as acid rain. A pH value of 5 in water is acidic enough to damage aquatic life.

This acid rain phenomenon is most likely to occur in dense industrial centers such as those in the United States, Canada, and Europe. The problem, however, is not confined to these areas, as winds blow polluting gases over long distances. Acids can become concentrated in still waters and threaten aquatic life. The entire ecology of affected lakes, including the natural food chains, can be very seriously harmed.

*The water cycle (below): the sun heats water, which evaporates and rises into the atmosphere as water vapor, only to fall again later as rain and snow. The rain and snow then concentrate in rivers, or flow as ground water to the sea.*

# OCEANOGRAPHY

Earth is the only planet of the solar system with seas and oceans, and these cover more than 70 percent of its surface. The oceans lie in large and deep basins in Earth's crust. The seas, however, spread to the margins of the continents, drowning their shelves. The melting of the ice sheets following the end of the last ice age (about 15,000 years ago) resulted in a rise in sea levels and thus an increased area covered by seas.

## Ocean currents

The waters of the oceans are in constant motion. This motion takes the form of ocean currents. These currents move at an average of 8 km (5 miles) per hour, and redistribute heat energy, thus influencing climate. Winds are the most important originators of ocean currents in the upper layers of the seas: they produce a frictional drag on the water which pushes it along.

As water is a fluid, it is subject to the Coriolis effect (caused by Earth's rotation)—that is, currents tend to move towards the right in the northern hemisphere and towards the left in the southern hemisphere. The resulting deflection is 45° to that of the direction of the wind. In the deeper parts of the oceans, it is water density that produces

ocean currents. Water density depends upon two factors: temperature and salinity. The colder the water is, the denser it is; and the higher the salinity, the higher the density. The circulation which results from temperature and salinity difference is referred to as thermo-haline circulation.

There are broadly two types of ocean current: warm currents, which originate in tropical areas; and cold currents, which originate in polar areas. Warm currents are mostly located in the upper 100 m (330 ft) of the seas. Cold currents, on the other hand, are often encountered at greater depths. They move more slowly because of the overlying pressure exerted by surface water. The exchange of heat energy occurs as equatorial currents move towards the poles and polar currents move towards the equator. This exchange moderates Earth's heat patterns, preventing the equatorial belt becoming unbearably hot and the waters in the temperate zone becoming much colder than they are today.

Ocean water temperatures are a major influence on climatic conditions; warm currents bring warmth to the coastlines along which they flow and, likewise, cold currents reduce temperatures in the lands along which they flow.

### Warm tropical ocean currents

Winds blowing westward along the equatorial belt generate west-flowing ocean currents called equatorial currents. When water from the equatorial currents piles up against land, the current reverses its direction and flows eastward, resulting in equatorial counter currents.

Equatorial currents turn towards the right in the northern hemisphere and towards the left in the southern hemisphere as a result of the

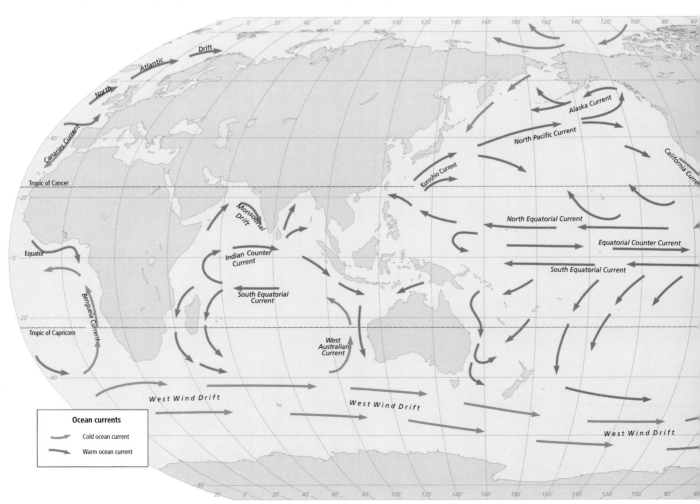

Ocean currents
— Cold ocean current
— Warm ocean current

Projection: Robinson    Equatorial Scale approx 1:110 milliom

*A sea whip in the warm waters of the Indian Ocean (far left). Coral islands (left) are at risk if sea levels rise because of the greenhouse effect. Polar bears in Arctic Siberia (below) survive on the ice floes, which are broken off icebergs by strong currents and winds. The southern right whale (far below) feeds off aquatic life that thrives in the nutrient-rich Antarctic waters, which are now threatened by ozone depletion.*

Coriolis effect, and because of that motion, they develop into huge, circular, whorl-like rotating systems. These systems are known as gyres. Gyres rotate in a clockwise direction in the northern hemisphere and an anticlockwise direction in the southern hemisphere.

The distribution of the continental landmasses influences the size and shape of these gyres. There are major gyres in the northern and southern Atlantic and Pacific oceans, and in the southern Indian Ocean. There is also a gyre in the northern Indian Ocean, but it is restricted by the landmasses surrounding it, and so is much smaller.

Gyres carry warm equatorial water into the temperate zone. These currents carry about 25 percent of all the heat that moves polewards from the equator. In the North Atlantic, the Gulf Stream or North Atlantic Drift, which flows from the Gulf of Mexico towards Western Europe, warms the seas around those countries, making their climates warmer. Thus London (51°32'N) is warmer than New York, even though New York lies at a much lower latitude (40°43'N), because of this warming effect.

The Japan Current, flowing from Southeast Asia, warms the eastern coasts of China and Japan. The west coast of Japan, on the other hand, is cooled by cold currents originating in northern areas. The magnitude of large ocean currents is demonstrated by the enormous amount of water they can carry—for example, the Gulf Stream carries more than 50 million cubic meters (65.5 million cubic yards) per second.

The build-up of warm waters can have significant effects on climate. For example, tropical cyclones or hurricanes or typhoons develop in the areas of warm water in Southeast Asia. These can have devastating effects on those areas.

Also, temperature changes in the waters of the South Pacific Ocean provide indications of the El Niño and La Niña weather disturbances. The onset of El Niño is heralded by unusually high water temperatures in the central Pacific, with the warm water spreading across to South America.

### Cold polar currents

Cold ocean currents originate in polar regions. They flow deep in the oceans and only surface through upwelling—when winds blowing from the land drive warm surface water back out into the ocean. Cold water then rises to the surface.

Two well-known upwelling sites, both on the western sides of continents, are the Humboldt or Peru Current along the coast of South America and the Benguela Current in southern Africa. Their nutrient-laden waters are rich breeding grounds for fish.

Two important cold currents flowing on the eastern sides of continents are the Kamchatka Current, which flows alongside Siberia and Japan, and the Labrador Current, which flows along the east coasts of Canada and the United States.

### Icebergs and ice floes

Seas in the polar zones can freeze, forming pack ice that covers the sea surface. If subjected to strong currents or winds, this pack ice can break into pieces, called floes. Ice broken from ice sheets can also be seen floating in the seas as icebergs. Ice floes are mostly less than 5 m (16¹/₂ ft) thick—much thinner than icebergs.

Icebergs can be very thick indeed—up to hundreds of meters in thickness—but only about one-sixth of an iceberg floats above water. The rest of it remains submerged or hidden below the water. This makes icebergs a major navigational hazard. There are always likely to be icebergs in the North Atlantic; they originate from the Greenland ice sheet and its glaciers.

### The Antarctic zone

The waters around Antarctica flow in an unbroken band around the globe because there are no land areas to obstruct them. The West Wind Drift, as the winds blowing incessantly from the west to the east are called, results in some of the world's most turbulent seas. The seas in latitudes between 40°S and 60°S have been referred to as the "Roaring Forties," the "Furious Fifties," and the "Screaming Sixties."

In the Southern Ocean around Antarctica, between the latitudes 50°S and 60°S, cold currents interact with the warm currents coming from the tropics. The cold, nutrient-rich waters are driven upwards by this convergence, becoming the breeding ground for abundant oceanic life. These waters are thus a vital component of the food chain which depends upon that aquatic life.

*(map labels:)* Gulf Stream · Tropic of Cancer · Equator · Tropic of Capricorn · Peru (Humboldt) Current · Brazil Current

# PLANTS AND ANIMALS

Earth is about 4,500 million years old. After about 1,000 million years, most of the basic metabolic processes on which modern life depends were in place. The first eukaryote cells (cells that were capable of resisting oxidation) appeared about 1,500 million years ago. After about 4,000 million years, multicellular animals and plants appear in the fossil record. In the past 600 million years, life has exploded into a vast array of forms, but many of the animals and plants we are familiar with are relatively recent arrivals.

To deduce the history of Earth's life forms (collectively known as biota), and the prevailing environmental conditions, scientists primarily rely on physical evidence: the character of rocks or the fossils contained within them. Increasingly, however, biochemical evidence is also used.

## The first life forms

Life is defined as a self-contained system of molecules that can duplicate itself from generation to generation. In Earth's early history, the elements that make up the vast majority of living tissues (hydrogen, carbon, oxygen, and nitrogen) were available in some form, and energy was abundant. Also, the concentration of

atmospheric oxygen was low, which probably allowed a period of chemical evolution before the development of life. The earliest life forms may have resembled the bacteria-like organisms that exist today in hot springs associated with volcanic activity.

The first bacteria-like microfossils are dated at 3,500 million years old. Stromatolites, fossilized mats of cyanobacteria (a bacteria secreted by blue-green algae), first appear in the fossil record at about this time. These are the dominant fossils found in rocks older than about 550 million years. Between about 3,500 and 1,500 million years ago, cyanobacteria and blue-green algae were probably the main forms of life. Importantly, they slowly contributed oxygen to the atmosphere.

The build-up of free oxygen, hazardous to most life forms, may have stimulated the development of organisms with more complex cellular organisation (the eukaryotes) about 1,500 million years ago. The eukaryotes could reproduce sexually, thus allowing evolution-

*Stromatolites in Hamelin Pool, Shark Bay, Western Australia.*

ary change. They generated more oxygen and eventually (by about 1,300 million years ago) an ozone shield—this is probably what enabled further biotic evolution.

The earliest fossil record of protozoans, which are animals and so derive their energy from ingesting other organisms, is from about 800 million years ago. By about 680 million years ago, the protozoa were a highly diverse and complex range of multicellular animals—mostly coral- or worm-like life forms.

### Invertebrates and vertebrates

During the late Proterozoic or early Paleozoic Era, the principal groups (or phyla) of invertebrates appeared. Trilobites were probably the dominant form of marine life during the Cambrian Period. The seas teemed with a huge diversity of animals, including a group with an elongated support structure, a central nerve cord, and a blood circulatory system—members of the phylum to which humans belong, the Chordata.

A major extinction event ended the Cambrian Period. The Ordovician Period (500 to 435 million years ago) is characterized by another increase in species diversity. The fossil record is dominated by marine invertebrates, but vertebrates also appear. The primitive jawless fish of 485 million years ago are the first ancestors of all advanced life forms: fish, amphibians, reptiles, birds, and mammals. Another major extinction event ended this period.

### From ocean to land

The first land plants—probably similar to modern liverworts, hornworts, and mosses— seem to have arisen about 450 million years ago. The move onto land was a significant evolutionary step; life on land was very different, demanding innovation and evolutionary change.

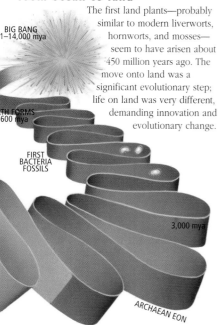

BIG BANG
1–14,000 mya

TH FORMS
600 mya

FIRST
BACTERIA
FOSSILS

3,000 mya

ARCHAEAN EON

CENOZOIC ERA

65 mya

2 mya

During the Silurian Period (435 to 395 million years ago), algae diversified and all the major fish groups appear. Fossils of vascular plants (with specialized systems for moving nutrients, liquids, and so on) are found at about 430 million years ago. *Cooksonia*, a small moss-like plant common at this time, may have resulted in two distinct lines of evolution, one leading to all other higher plants. Floras of the late Silurian to early Devonian time are very similar worldwide, and may constitute evidence that the supercontinent Pangaea existed then.

During the mid-Devonian Period (395 to 345 million years ago), plants underwent a remarkable diversification, resulting in the development of Devonian "forests," which included giant clubmosses (lepidodendrons) and horsetails (calamites). The fossil record of the amphibians also begins here—animals were moving onto land—and the first fern-like foliage and gymnosperms appeared. The late Devonian was also marked by a mass extinction event.

Fossils from the Carboniferous Period (345 to 280 million years ago) suggest that the clubmoss forests teemed with spiders, scorpions, and centipedes. Amphibians gave rise to the first reptiles about 300 million years ago—vertebrates were no longer dependent on returning to water to reproduce. A trend towards an ice age occurred in the late Carboniferous Period, leading to low-diversity flora dominated by primitive seed ferns.

The Permian Period (280 to 245 million years ago) is dominated by the fossil remains of primitive members of the conifer line. By this period, reptiles with skeletal features characteristic of mammals were present.

### The Age of Reptiles

The largest mass extinction event on record marked the end of the Permian Period. During the Mesozoic Era (245 to 65 million years ago), the "Age of Reptiles," flowering plants, dominated by cycads and gymnosperms early on, developed. Birds and mammals also appeared.

During the Triassic Period (245 to 200 million years ago), mammals, lizards, and dinosaurs appear in the fossil record. Some long-established reptiles were replaced by new groups, including the turtles, crocodilians, dinosaurs, and pterosaurs. Dinosaurs date from early in the Triassic Period. From about 220 million years ago they dominated land habitats—for almost 160 million years. Mammals (initially small, perhaps nocturnal, shrew-like creatures) appear to have arisen from mammal-like reptiles. There was another mass extinction event (about 200 million years ago) in the late Triassic Period. Frogs and toads may have appeared around this time.

Pangaea began to break up during the Jurassic Period (200 to 145 million years ago). Ocean currents and the global climate were altered. The position of the continents and the break-up sequence determined the migration routes available and, therefore, the interrelation or common features of the plants and animals that we now see in the modern world.

Jurassic rocks include Earth's earliest fossils of flies, mosquitoes, wasps, bees, and ants; modern types of marine crustaceans were abundant. It was also a critical point in the evolution of birds, which evolved either from the dinosaurs or from an earlier group of reptiles. The Archaeopteryx, which existed about 150 million years ago, is perhaps the most famous early bird-like animal.

The early Cretaceous Period (145 to 65 million years ago) had a cosmopolitan flora. The first record of bats appears at this time. From about 80 million years ago, gymnosperms and angiosperms expanded at the expense of cycads and ferns. Mammals were also becoming dominant.

The Cretaceous Period also saw the apparent rise of the monotreme and marsupials and placentals, and the first predatory mammals. The diversification and spread of angiosperms provided the impetus for the co-evolution of animals.

### The Age of Mammals

A great extinction event occurred at the end of the Cretaceous Period, causing the demise of the dinosaurs and the loss of about 25 percent of all known animal families. This change marks the beginning of the Cenozoic Era (65 million years ago to the present). This era saw the formation of the famous mountain systems of the world, the movement of the continents to their present positions, and a cooling trend that culminated in the ice ages of the Quaternary Period.

After dinosaurs died out, mammals quickly expanded into newly vacated habitats and roles, adapting and diversifying. Eventually, the warm-blooded animals came to dominate, so the Cenozoic Era is often called the "Age of Mammals." Late in the era, humans finally appear.

The Tertiary Period (65 to 1.8 million years ago) saw major new groups developing within pre-established plant families. Grasses appeared (about 50 million years ago), expanding particularly in the Miocene Period. The development of grasslands resulted eventually in a proliferation of grazing mammals. Hoofed, placental herbivores are first recorded as fossils 85 million years ago. The first horses appeared about 55 million years ago. A similar explosion in small rodents also occurred from about 40 million years ago.

Although birds have been essentially modern since the start of the Cenozoic Era, the first songbirds seem to appear at about 55 million years ago; all the major bird groups of the modern world had evolved by 50 million years ago. At about the same time (mid-Eocene Period), the carnivorous mammals split into two major lines: the dogs and the cats, basically. The first toothed whales are from the Oligocene epoch and the first plankton-feeding whales are from the Miocene.

The first primates seem to date from the end of the Cretaceous Period, though it seems that both monkeys and apes did not separate from earlier groups until the Oligocene epoch. The oldest biped yet found—usually taken as the start of the hominids—is from about 4.4 million years ago.

Nearly 2.5 million years ago, stone tool users— the hallmark of our own genus, Homo—seem to have arisen. Homo erectus, dating from about 1.8 million years ago, migrated from Africa as far as China and Southeast Asia. Our species, Homo sapiens, seems to have evolved in Africa within the past 200,000 years and to have migrated out of that continent only during the past 100,000 years.

# EARTH'S BIOSPHERE

The biosphere is the zone where all living organisms on Earth are found. It includes parts of the lithosphere (Earth's crust and mantle), the hydrosphere (all the waters on Earth), and the atmosphere. The term "biosphere" can also refer collectively to all Earth's living organisms.

Imagine a sort of biological spectrum, arranged from the simple to the complex; it would start with subatomic particles, then move through atoms, molecules, compounds, protoplasm, cells, tissues, organs, organ systems, organisms, populations, communities, and ecosystems, to, eventually, the biosphere. Each stage represents another level of organization, and each level implies new attributes and different properties.

"Population" refers to a group of organisms of a particular kind that form a breeding unit. Not all individuals of a kind (or species) can mix—for example, due to geographic isolation—so a population is the functional group that is capable of breeding. A "community" is all the populations of plants, animals, bacteria, and fungi that live in an environment and interact with one another. Populations within a community are linked by their interaction and effects on each other, and by their responses to the environment they share.

"Ecosystem" is a shortening of "ecological system," the concept that the living (biotic) community and the non-living (abiotic) environment are a functioning, integrated system. An ecosystem involves transfer and circulation of materials and energy between living and non-living systems. There is almost infinite variety in the magnitude of ecosystems, from a global ecosystem that encompasses the entire biosphere to the ecosystem of a fallen log or of the underside of a rock, or even of a drop of water.

Environmental conditions influence the distribution of individual organisms. Limiting factors may be physical (such as temperature and moisture availability) or biotic (such as competition, predation, and the presence of suitable food or other resources). A limiting factor is anything that tends to make it more difficult for an organism to grow, live, or reproduce—that makes some aspect of physiology or behavior less efficient and therefore less competitive.

The distribution of organisms is strongly influenced by the fact that each kind can tolerate only a certain set of conditions. For many organisms, distribution is critically associated with, or determined by, relationships with other organisms. A community of organisms is thus likely to include a loose collection of populations with similar environmental requirements, and possibly another, tighter, collection of organisms that are dependent in some way on each other.

Due to genetic variation, individuals within a population have a range of tolerances around their ecological optimum, but beyond a particular tolerance limit, the species is unable to live. Importantly, this spread means a group may be able to cope with environmental change. A species must be able to complete all phases of its life cycle in a given region if it is to persist for a prolonged period, and different species vary in their tolerance of environmental factors.

## The major biomes

Communities are strongly linked to their physical environment or habitat; this habitat is also modified by its communities. Since climate, soils, and biotic factors vary around the world, communities are bound to change. Vegetation is often the most visible aspect of communities, so they are often classified on the basis of vegetation. Communities recognized by their vegetation structure are termed "associations" or "formations;" when the definition also implies the consideration of animal communities, the term "biome" is used.

A biome is a grouping of communities or ecosystems that have similar appearances or structures (physiognomy). As physiognomy generally reflects the environment, the environmental characteristics of a specific biome on one continent will be similar to that same biome on any other. Furthermore, widely separated biomes are likely to include unrelated animals with a similar role and possibly similar morphology (form and structure), due to convergent evolution (animals evolving separately, but having similar characteristics).

At the global level, a number of distinctive features are generally recognized. There are several forest biomes, ranging in diversity and ecological complexity from tropical rainforest to the coniferous high-latitude forests of the northern hemisphere. In regions with seasonal contrasts in rainfall, trees become more widely spaced, species less diverse, and savanna grasses more characteristic of grassland areas develop. Other grassland biomes occur in temperate climates. Shrublands are dominated by shortish, scraggly trees or tall bushes, and may have an understorey of grasses.

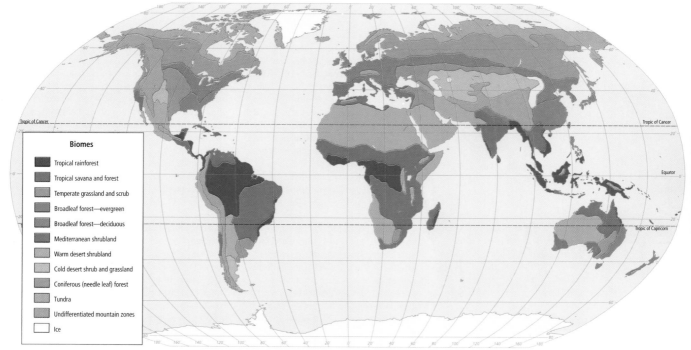

**Biomes**

- Tropical rainforest
- Tropical savana and forest
- Temperate grassland and scrub
- Broadleaf forest—evergreen
- Broadleaf forest—deciduous
- Mediterranean shrubland
- Warm desert shrubland
- Cold desert shrub and grassland
- Coniferous (needle leaf) forest
- Tundra
- Undifferentiated mountain zones
- Ice

Projection: Robinson    Equatorial Scale approx 1:110 million

*These monkeys have adapted to life in the trees in Lombok, Indonesia (left). They find their food there, sleep there, and can move quickly through the branches at considerable heights from the ground. The Weddell seal in Antarctica (below) has few predators, and finds plenty of food in the nutrient-rich waters of the Ross Sea.*

*A frill-necked lizard from Australia (left) is well adapted to live in its dry environment, and giraffes in Tanzania (above) fill the large herbivore ecological niche of their environment.*

In drier climates, scrub vegetation may be quite scattered and small in size.

The boundaries of Earth's biomes are rather blurred and maps can only show approximate distributions. Human activity has greatly disturbed natural ecosystems, often leaving mere remnants of once-vast areas of forest or grassland.

## Energy in the biosphere

Most life on Earth is supported by the continuous flow of energy from the Sun into the biosphere. A tiny proportion of this radiant energy is used by plants, which are then able to maintain the biomass and the vital processes of the entire biosphere. Energy is eventually converted to heat and lost from the system.

Plants are capable of capturing and storing energy from sunlight. In the process called photosynthesis, plants absorb the radiant energy of the Sun and transform it into the energy of chemical bonds. The energy left after that used for the vital processes of the plant may accumulate as organic matter, and is available for harvest by animals and decomposition by bacteria and fungi.

As only plants can trap solar energy, their productivity determines the energy limits of the entire biosphere, and the total size of all consumer populations, including humans. The amount of this leftover energy is highest in regions with optimum conditions for plant growth.

On land, productivity is controlled primarily by water availability; in aquatic environments, nutrient availability is crucial. The most productive regions are found at the interface between the land and the sea. Generally, terrestrial communities are much more productive than aquatic systems.

The energy stored by plants as organic matter sustains other organisms. This transfer of energy, as food, from plants to herbivores, and from herbivores to carnivores, is a food chain. At each level of a food chain, a large amount of energy is degraded into heat and other forms of non-recoverable energy, so there is a steep decrease in productivity for each step up the sequence of the food chain. Correlated with this is usually a decrease in the number of organisms, and thus a decrease in total biomass.

## The ecological niche

An ecological niche is the role that an organism plays in the ecosystem. Whereas habitat is the physical position of the organism, the ecological niche represents its functional position. For example, within grasslands, the kangaroo in Australia occupies the same niche as the bison in North America. They have the same role—large herbivores. Natural selection has often resulted in organisms adapting to their role, which means that the morphology of an animal can often be a good indicator of its niche.

Species vary in the breadth of their niche—some are specialists, others are generalists. Specialists are usually more efficient in the use of resources, due to adaptation, but they are also more vulnerable to change.

Importantly, two species with similar ecological requirements cannot occupy the same niche within an environment. This principle, called competitive exclusion, means that cohabiting organisms either use different resources, behave in such a way that resources are shared, or exist in a variable environment that favors each species alternately. Species that do have similar niches must compete for resources.

Specialization reduces this competition and, given time, adaptation to this new role may result in an altered morphology. Competitive exclusion is thus an extremely important evolutionary force.

*The diagram below illustrates the food chain in the tundra. At the top of the chain is the wolf, who has no predators. At the bottom is the vegetation. In between are insects, small mammals (such as lemmings, ground squirrels, and Arctic hares) and birds, followed by other larger mammals such as caribou and Arctic foxes.*

# SOILS

Soil formation is a very complex process. It involves the interaction of climate, type of rock, topography and biota (the total plant and animal life of a region). These factors operate over time, and the amount of time required for soil formation varies substantially from place to place—some soils and their associated weathered products have been forming for millions of years. Soils are formed from weathered materials, usually with the addition of organic matter. The disintegration or weathering of rocks is the result of both physical and chemical processes. Physical weathering breaks rocks down into fragments, while chemical weathering leads to the transformation of rock minerals into products of different composition.

## Climate and soils

Weathering products are largely determined by climatic conditions. Mechanical weathering is particularly powerful in drier environments; in hot deserts, the heating of rocks induces expansion and subsequent breakdown of exposed surfaces; freezing has a similar effect. Salt crystallization in crevices mechanically disintegrates rocks. Root growth also leads to mechanical dislodgment.

In wet climates, moisture helps remove particles from exposed rocks, and provides a means by which minerals in those rocks can be attacked chemically to form clay minerals. Pure water is not a significant chemical agent; but the presence of dissolved carbon dioxide and complex organic substances in soil waters generates a chemical environment able to decompose, remove and redeposit rock (clay-rich) materials and salts.

Hot wet climates, plus the opportunity for plants to grow on stable surfaces for long periods

of time, leads to extensive decomposition of rocks. In humid tropical climates, mineral decomposition results in the formation of oxides of aluminum and iron-producing red soils, sometimes cemented into a brick-like substance known as laterite. Such soils are much less fertile than those formed under somewhat drier grassland climates, where organic (or humic) matter and calcium-rich salts accumulate into a nutrient-rich soil capable of growing crops such as wheat and barley.

## Rock type and soils

Within one climate area, soil type can vary as a result of the weathering of rocks of different mineral composition. Granites, basalts, quartz-rich sandstones and limestones are common rock types containing distinctive minerals. Chemical decomposition of these rocks over time will yield soils with different types and quantities of clays, varying amounts of precipitated salts, and different degrees of water retention and mobility (due to the existence of pore spaces and the capacity of minerals to absorb moisture).

Similar rock types in contrasting climate zones may also produce different soils. For instance, different rates and intensities of weathering can yield dark, organic-rich soils in grassland areas, underlain by basalt, whereas basalt soils in tropical areas are likely to be red and iron-rich.

## Soil processes

The essence of soil formation is the breakdown and mobilization of mineral and organic matter in the presence of water. Living and dead organisms, both microscopic and larger (such as earthworms), assist in this process. The result is the formation of layers, or horizons. Each horizon has distinctive

color, grain size (texture), chemical composition, organic matter content and pore space size (porosity). In some soils, binding agents such as organic colloids or iron oxides harden the layers. Over time, these layers may thicken, depending on slope position and the rate of landscape removal or deposition. Ground water movements can lead to precipitation of salts in soil layers, or even on the surface, leading to reduced soil productivity, as in lands bordering the Aral Sea.

Well-structured soils generally display "A," "B" and "C" horizons; A and B horizons are the real soil layers, known as the solum, while the C horizon consists of the weathered parent rock. The A horizon—the exposed soil—is often dark at the top because of the accumulation of organic material. A horizons are subject to leaching (eluviation). Leached material is transported to the B horizon, where it is deposited (illuviation); some B horizons are poor in organic material. Eluviation is assisted by the organic acids produced by decaying vegetation.

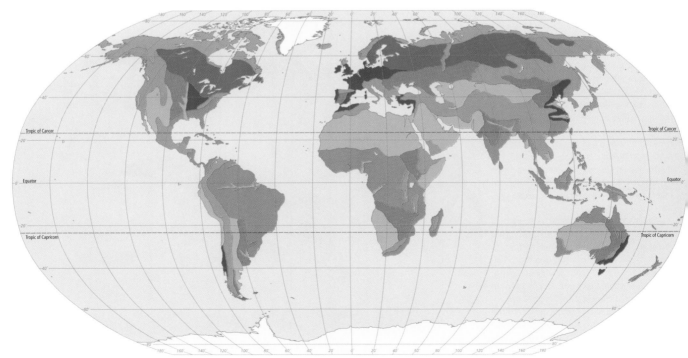

*Layers of soil are exposed in this weathered escarpment, Australia (far left); parched, eroded ground leaves trees unable to tap into food and water in the soil, Papua New Guinea (left); this plant from the desert of Angola and Namibia has adapted to life in desert soil.*

## Soil nutrients

Soil texture and composition influence plant growth and therefore the suitability of a soil for agricultural use. Chemical and organic materials form colloids. Colloids are negatively charged, and attract plant nutrients such as calcium, magnesium, and potassium, which are positive ions (or cations). These nutrients are essential to the existence of all life on Earth.

Gray sandy soils of temperate regions are generally acidic; these soils are not rich in plant nutrients such as calcium and potassium, but this can be corrected by adding lime and fertilizers. On the other hand, some dry desert soils, which often contain mineral accumulations such as calcium carbonate and salts, are alkaline. Whilst many such soils have excessive salt levels, some are quite fertile and, irrigated, can be used for agriculture.

## Soil types

Many attempts have been made to classify soils. Properties such as color, texture, composition, horizon thickness and porosity are used to define soil types. But even locally there can be considerable variation in soil type, given changes in elevation, slope angle, rock type and vegetation. In mountainous or hilly areas, for example, many different soil types may exist within short distances over a range of altitudes and slope positions.

At the global scale, soil types largely reflect climatic conditions. However, the history of a land surface may also be significant. The "fresh" deposits of recently deglaciated places in North America and Europe contain relatively poorly leached minerals, contrasting markedly with ancient unglaciated tropical plateaus, from which nutrient-rich minerals have long been removed.

Any world map of soil types must be a broad generalization. Iron-rich weathered soils can occur in areas where past climates have had a significant effect (for instance, southwest Western Australia). Alluvial soils, on the other hand, are constantly forming and reforming as new sediments are deposited in flood plains. Yet soils in both areas may be extremely rich in nutrients and thus of great agricultural significance. By way of contrast, the sparsity of moisture and biota in desert regions, or the presence of ice on the ground, will greatly inhibit soil development.

*A soil section, showing horizons enriched by organic matter (A1), and leached of humus and minerals (A2). A horizon of accumulation (B) contains mineral matter leached from above. The bedrock (D) is decomposed into a weathered horizon (C).*

### Soil zones

- Warm to cool temperate forest soils, moderately to highly leached, moderate to low in mineral bases and organic material, well developed horizons [Alfisols, Gray-brown podzolics].
- Cool temperate forest soils with highly leached upper profile, acidic accumulation of humus, iron and aluminum in illuvial horizon [Spodosols, Podzols].
- Grassland soils of subhumid and semiarid areas, often mixed with shrubs, organic-rich in upper profile in more moist regions, also rich in mineral bases, fertile [Mollisols, Chernozems, Vertisols].
- Latosolic soils of tropical and subtropical climates with forest and/or savanna cover; highly to moderately leached profile, low in mineral bases but high in oxides [Ultisols, Oxisols, Red Podzolics, Laterites—some relic of past climates].
- Desert soils of arid areas with little soil profile development and very low organic material but may contain abundant salts [Aridisols].
- Alluvial soils in all climates especially in deltas, subject to frequent flooding and new deposition of river silt, fertile (only major areas shown) [Entisols].
- Tundra soils in subpolar areas with permanently frozen subsoils; subject to mass movement on slopes (solifluction) [Inceptisols].
- Mountainous areas: soils are typically shallow and stony and highly variable in profile and thickness depending on climate and slope position; includes localized areas of fertile soils especially in mountain basins and near volcanoes.
- Ice sheets

# Earth as a Home for Humans

*All humans live by exploiting Earth's natural resources, whether by small-scale fishing in Malawi (above) or employing modern farming techniques to farm cattle in Australia (opposite).*

As humans, we dominate our planet. There are very few places where our impact is not felt. Even the atmosphere has now been altered by gases produced by humans, and some of these—such as chloroflurocarbons (CFCs)—are the result of chemical processes alien to natural systems. Many who travel or work at sea are aware of human debris in our waters. Lakes are drying up and are often heavily polluted, as are rivers. Much of the forests and grasslands of Earth have been disturbed. Over the past 200 to 300 years, in particular, we have transformed this planet in ways which at times enhance our welfare, but at others threaten the existence of societies.

As the human race evolved, so did its capacity to utilize natural resources. The mineral uranium was of little use to societies for much of human history, but, from the end of the Second World War, its value as a destructive force and as a source of power has grown immensely. In contrast, the fertile soils of river floodplains and deltas have long been utilized in some areas, and civilizations such as those of Egypt have depended upon their richness. But as a resource, soils need nourishment. Without appropriate care, their ability to maintain the levels of productivity necessary for agriculture will decline. History is full of accounts of battles waged to maintain social structures and population levels in the face of soil degradation. On the other hand, other societies, such as in China, Japan, and Western Europe, have carefully nurtured their soil resources.

For the early humans, the vast forests of Earth were largely avoided. There is some evidence that forests displaced human activities during the period of global warming immediately following the Ice Age in Europe. Progressively, however, forests in tropical, temperate and high latitude areas have been removed or exploited to create new land uses. Today, fires sweep across vast areas of Amazonian and Indonesian rainforests as more timber is removed and land is cleared for cattle grazing and crops.

Marine life has long provided food for humans. Fishing in shallow waters using primitive lines and spears has developed into sophisticated technologies enabling large ships to roam the oceans capturing fish over a vast range of depths. Fears of exploitation and the reduction of stocks to levels at which particular species will not survive have resulted in international agreements on resource use, although the effectiveness of these agreements is in question, with countries such as Japan and Norway still actively hunting whales, for example. Other forms of more sustainable fishing have been developed to feed societies which are heavily dependent upon food from the sea. This includes various forms of aquaculture at sea, in sheltered bays, and on reclaimed land.

Pressures placed on natural resources are closely linked to population growth. One of the most amazing and environmentally significant aspects of the twentieth cen-

tury has been the rate of increase in population. With over 6.5 billion people alive at the moment and perhaps close to 10 billion by the year 2050, it is no wonder that environmental managers, planners, and scientists are deeply worried about the consequences. Also, population increases are not distributed evenly across the world; it is often in developing countries already suffering from depleted resources that the impacts of many new mouths to feed will be most harshly felt. The effective and equitable distribution of food to those in need will become increasingly important. Unfortunately, major health problems also arise in countries where food supplies are threatened. The impact of poverty and disease, and the capacity of international aid and economic organizations to support developing countries, create further uncertainties in a world beset with environmental and other problems.

Higher standards of living using available natural resources have been made possible through human inventions, including those designed to increase food production and to resist the ravages of pests and diseases in plants and animals. Many areas of high population have benefited from the so-called "green" revolution, but the ability of pathogens and parasites to undergo genetic change and therefore develop resistance to controls reminds us of the need for constant vigilance and research. Undertaking this research and acting on knowledge gained from other countries remain issues of global concern.

What has changed dramatically in recent years is the ability of individuals and groups to communicate quickly across vast distances. In one sense, space has "shrunk". Geographical isolation—such as that imposed by mountain ranges—no longer impedes the information flow; in the past, such barriers meant that separate languages developed in Papua New Guinea (for instance) in regions which, although physically close, were separated by their inaccessibility. Today, satellite television communications, electronic mail facilitated by fiber optic networks, and 24-hours-a-day business transactions are part of a global economic system which enables information to flow within and between nations.

The ability of societies to respond to natural hazards is another issue of great concern to international aid agencies and governments. Natural hazards may be insidious (droughts) or virtually instantaneous (earthquakes). Great loss of life and property can ensue; the impacts do not respect national economic strength (for example, the number of deaths as a result of tornadoes in the United States). Yet some areas are subject to frequent disasters of a scale which disturbs the economy. Floods in Bangladesh are of this category. Greenhouse-effect-induced rises in the sea level are another more insidious hazard which potentially threatens the futures of coral island nations such as the Maldives in the Indian Ocean.

# LAND RESOURCES

Humans meet their principal needs—for water, minerals, and plants—from the land. Inorganic resources include minerals, water, and various elements in soils, whilst organic or biotic resources include plant and animal life. Fossil fuels (coal, petroleum, and natural gas) are of biotic origin. Both mineral and biotic resources are unequally distributed throughout the world—while some countries have abundant plant and water resources, others do not.

The presence or absence of water is often reflected in population densities, with high rainfall areas generally attracting, and being able to support, greater concentrations of people. China, for example, lacks water in its western half, but has a water surplus in its eastern half, and this is reflected in its population distribution.

Mineral resources are also very unevenly distributed. Some countries possess abundant reserves of certain minerals (such as petroleum in the Middle East), and others have gold reserves (Russia and South Africa).

The fact that resources are unequally distributed means that countries must trade what they have for what they need. The highly industrialized countries of Western Europe and Japan, for instance, import raw materials to run their industries. Also, many countries depend upon fossil fuel imports for their energy supplies.

## Climate

Climate can be considered a resource because agriculture is so highly dependent on climate. The world's industries and urban centers are mostly located where there is a favorable climate—in areas which have comfortable temperature ranges and adequate rainfall.

Agricultural products can, generally, only be grown economically in suitable climatic conditions. Since the middle of the nineteenth century, plantations in the tropics have produced sugar, tea, coffee, and rubber for international consumption—these areas have been exploited for the production of crops that do not grow elsewhere and are much in demand. Likewise, wheat and other cereals are produced in temperate climates and exported internationally.

## Landforms

Human settlement concentrates along river plains and deltas because of fertile soils and available water. In Japan, flat land is prized because of its

A beef cattle feedlot in California, USA (above). This is a method of intensive agriculture; less land is needed per head of cattle, but cattle lead a more restricted existence.

scarcity. In some places, such as in Japan and on the island of Java in Indonesia, hillsides have been terraced for agriculture. In Europe and North America, deposits of sediment, encrusted with ice age glaciations, form fertile plains.

## Agriculture

A long-established agricultural practice is "slash-and-burn." This involves clearing a forest patch, then burning to fertilize the soils; cultivation only

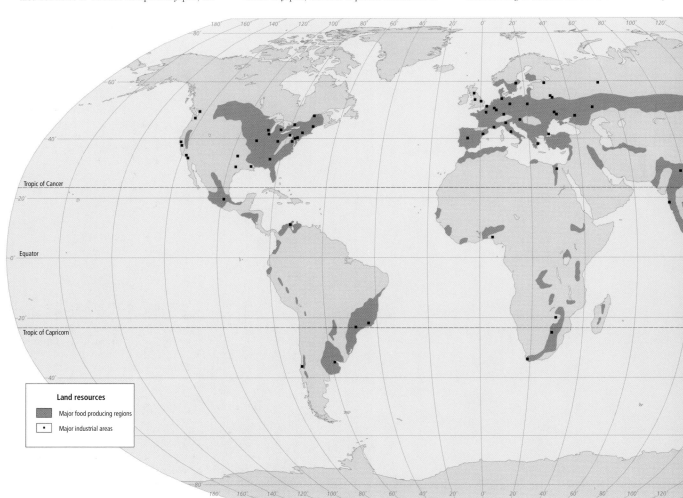

**Land resources**

■ Major food producing regions

▪ Major industrial areas

Projection: Robinson    Equatorial Scale approx 1:155 million

*Vast wheatfields like these in Saskatchewan, Canada (left) and the "Super Pit" in Kalgoorlie, Australia (below) both show human interference with the environment, and depend on high levels of mechanization. Near Beijing, China (bottom), people still use donkeys to plow—a pre-industrial farming method still practiced in less developed countries.*

lasts a few seasons as the soils become depleted of nutrients. The exhausted patches are then abandoned and a new patch of forest is cleared. Secondary forests grow in these abandoned sites and, after some years, the reafforested areas can be used again. This rotating system can only support small numbers of people. It is not suitable for the type of food production that is needed for large, or growing, populations.

The development of grain farming, some 10,000 years ago, ensured food production for large populations. It led to sedentary settlements and, ultimately, to some of the great ancient civilizations such as

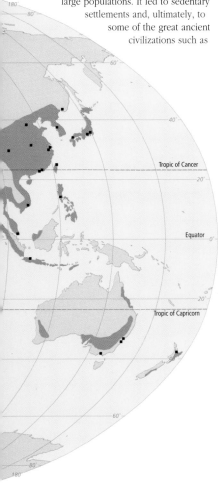

Egypt, northern China, and the Indus Valley. Since the nineteenth century, agriculture has seen the development of mechanization, the use of fertilizers and pesticides, and improved varieties of both plant and animal species. These new developments paralleled the great milestones in industrialization, such as the invention of steam engines, the internal combustion engine, electric power and, more recently, the silicon chip.

The population explosion in several developing countries within the past 50 years greatly increased their demand for food, and it became necessary to increase crop yields per unit of land. This ushered in the so-called Green Revolution, which involved using high-yielding seeds, fertilizers, and pesticides. Although these products increased grain output, the increase has been at some environmental and social cost.

Brazil is a good example of changing uses of the land. Before becoming a colony, its agriculture was of the slash-and-burn type practiced by forest Indians. Colonialism brought in plantation agriculture. The development of coffee plantations boosted Brazil's economy. Great increases in population have placed pressure on its once largely untapped resource, the Amazon rainforest. Large tracts of the Amazon are being transformed by people wishing to establish farms; forests are being burnt down to clear land for agriculture. Large areas are also being cleared to raise beef cattle for export; this also, of course, results in the large-scale loss of forests.

Tropical rainforest clearance cannot easily be reversed. Currently, more than 10 million hectares (24.7 million acres) of forests are being lost each year. These large-scale clearances have adverse effects globally—they accelerate global warming and its effects on climate.

## Minerals

Minerals supply the raw materials for several major industries: for the extraction of metals (primarily iron); for fuels such as uranium, coal, and petroleum; and for manufacturing fertilizers and cement. Minerals are valuable resources because they only occur in some places and are finite in nature: once extracted, they cannot be renewed. Minerals are very important for sustaining modern civilization and, as standards of living continue to rise

on a global scale, so too does the demand for minerals. In fact, more minerals have been mined in the twentieth century than in all previous centuries combined. As demand for minerals increases and they become more scarce, their strategic importance to industry—including, especially, the defence industry—also increases, placing even greater strain on already vulnerable finite resources.

The principal metal in demand is iron for making steel; steel forms the basis of much of the world's manufacturing, and every major industrial country produces steel. Other important metals include aluminum, copper, lead, and zinc.

Coal, petroleum, and natural gas provide energy supplies, and, in recent decades, uranium has provided the basis for nuclear energy. Coal is used for electricity generation and in the manufacture of steel. The ever-growing use of automobiles ensures continuing demand for petroleum, while natural gas is being used extensively for heating. Nuclear energy is currently the subject of much controversy because of dangers associated with nuclear power generation, the problems of nuclear waste disposal, and the potential for using nuclear materials from such plants for nuclear weapons.

The greatly increased use of minerals by the developed countries, and the increasing use by newly industrializing countries, has led to concerns about there being adequate mineral supplies for the future. Substitution of new materials for metals and the search for new or renewable energy sources—such as solar power or wind generation—are amongst the developments aimed at conserving our mineral resources.

# OCEAN RESOURCES

The oceans, covering more than 70 percent of Earth's surface, are the source of enormous amounts of valuable resources. These broadly fall into two main categories: marine life and minerals. Marine life can be divided into pelagic forms and benthic forms. Pelagic forms move about in the waters—these resources include fish and marine mammals. Benthic forms, which live on the sea floor, include corals, molluscs, and crustaceans. There are also marine plants such as kelp that are harvested and used by humans.

The oceans also contain mineral deposits, including petroleum and gas, and mineral nodules. These resources are generally more difficult and expensive to obtain than marine life, but they are of great economic importance.

Within the past 50 years, modern technology has meant that detailed mapping of the oceans has become possible. Recent studies of the oceans, using this technology, have revealed some well-defined physiographic patterns: close to the land lie continental shelves which often end in steep continental slopes; these are followed, further from the shore, by gently sloping features called continental rises, which end in deep ocean basins; and the latter are intersected by mid-oceanic ridges. There are different marine resources commonly found in the different zones where these physiographic features are found.

Many nations, realizing the potential riches of the oceans, have declared resource boundaries under the United Nations' Law of the Sea Convention. Territorial seas are normally set at 12 nautical miles (22 km) from the coast, whilst exclusive economic zones extend to 200 nautical miles (370 km). These mostly include the resource-rich continental shelves.

Continental shelves, however, can vary in width from 110 to 170 nautical miles (200 to 320 km); the shelves in the Atlantic Ocean and the Gulf of Mexico are exceptional in being up to 260 nautical miles (480 km) wide. A nation can legitimately claim all its adjacent continental shelf, even if that shelf extends beyond 200 nautical miles (370 km), as is the case with the United States and Australia. As a result of this law, some small island nations, such as in those in the South Pacific, have maritime claims that far exceed their land areas.

## Fishing

Fishing is the most important resource-gathering activity from the seas. In recent decades, however, overfishing of the seas has reached, in some places, crisis proportions. For example, the North Pacific haddock catch dwindled in 1974 to less than 10 percent of what it had been a decade earlier, and the once highly productive cod fishing industry in Canada, employing an estimated 40,000 people, collapsed in 1992.

Several nations grant licenses to foreign fishing fleets to fish in their waters, and this can exacerbate the situation, as has been the case with the southern bluefin tuna from the waters of Australia, New Zealand, and the Southern Ocean. Overfishing is threatening the very existence of this tuna species; the numbers of this species have fallen, it is estimated, to just 2 to 5 percent of its original population.

Until recently, whales were one of the most threatened species of marine life, but a huge international outcry against whale hunting has resulted in most whaling nations giving up whaling altogether and international agreements for whale protection being enacted. The outcry was

Brightly colored fishing boats docked at Nha Trang, Vietnam (above). During the late twentieth century, fishing has been affected by changes in technology and by ocean pollution.

generated not only as a result of concern for preservation of whale species, but also because of the horrific nature of the hunting itself.

By the time that whale protection measures were agreed upon, however, several species—including the bowhead, gray and right whale species—had been hunted almost to extinction.

An extensive whale sanctuary in the Southern Ocean now covers the territory of more than 90 percent of the world's whale population. Japan and Norway, however, continue to hunt whales. Japan justifies its whaling operations on the grounds of scientific research, but this explanation is not generally accepted by conservation groups, many of which continue to campaign against all forms of whale hunting.

## Coastal fishing

Seas close to shore are usually rich in a wide variety of marine organisms, and have traditionally been fishing grounds for coast-dwelling commun-

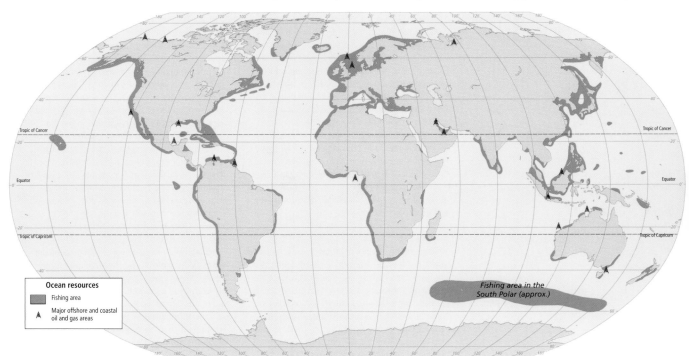

### Ocean resources

- ▓ Fishing area
- ▲ Major offshore and coastal oil and gas areas

Fishing area in the South Polar (approx.)

Tropic of Cancer · Equator · Tropic of Capricorn

Projection: Robinson   Equatorial Scale approx 1:155 million

ities. These are also the areas, not surprisingly, where shellfish farming, aquaculture (fish farming), and salt extraction have, more recently, been widely undertaken.

Kelp, which is rich in both potash and iodine, is another product harvested from the seas in coastal areas. It is used for both food and fertilizer.

Fish breeding and shellfish farming, such as oyster breeding, are carried out close to the land. Aquaculture can provide reliable and convenient fish supplies, in contrast to fishing—it is no longer possible to depend upon the ever-dwindling supplies from the seas. Fish farming has been practiced for a long time—the breeding of fish in freshwater lakes in China, for instance, has been carried out for a great many years.

Modern aquaculture is a high-technology industry, as it requires meticulous monitoring of water conditions (such as salinity, oxygen levels, and water temperature) and nutrition. Only a limited number of species—salmon in the Outer Hebrides of Great Britain, for example—are being farmed at present.

In the Inland Sea of Japan, an arm of the sea has been completely cut off by metal nets, thus creating a confined space in which fish can be bred. In Japan particularly, seaweed is another important product of aquaculture.

Coastal countries that do not have sufficient supplies of fresh water can extract fresh water from sea water. However, the capital equipment required to establish these desalination plants is costly. There are several such plants for producing fresh water from salt water in the oil-rich countries bordering the Persian–Arabic Gulf—Kuwait, for instance, has desalination plants.

## Continental shelves
These shallow, gently sloping features range in depth between 120 and 180 m (400 to 600 ft). When surface sea water is blown away from the land by offshore winds, colder nutrient-rich water rises to the surface. Where such waters are sunlit—these are known as epipelagic or euphotic zones—they make excellent breeding grounds for the minute marine organisms known as plankton. Plankton are tiny plant (phytoplankton) and animal (zooplankton) organisms that provide nutrition for other larger marine organisms.

Although sunlight can penetrate as far as 1,000 m (3,300 ft) below the ocean surface, photosynthesis can only take place in depths of up to 200 m (660 ft). As a result, phytoplankton can only survive within this shallow layer of ocean water. Small zooplankton feed on the phytoplankton in this layer and they, in turn, are preyed upon by larger organisms such as anchovies and squid. Larger fish such as tuna feed on the smaller marine life, only to be, in turn, consumed by still larger fish. This marine food chain extends even beyond the seas, to the seabirds which are the predators of fish.

The cold and extremely nutrient-rich waters in the continental shelves surrounding Antarctica are the breeding ground for small crustaceans known as krill. Species including seals and whales, as well as penguins, feed on krill.

In recent decades, rich petroleum and natural gas deposits have been discovered in the continental shelves. The petroleum deposits originated from the debris of marine organisms in oxygen-free shelf bottoms millions of years ago. Amongst the well-known deposits that are currently being exploited are those in the North Sea, the Gulf of Mexico, and off the city of Bombay on India's west coast.

Improvements in drilling technology have enabled exploration in ever-deeper seas; drilling for natural gas deposits is currently being carried out at depths of more than 1,700 m (5,600 ft) in the Marlim field, off Brazil.

## Ocean basins
The ocean basins are made up of large, flat areas called abyssal plains. These abyssal plains lie at depths of about 4,000 m (15,000 ft). In these dark and cold areas, temperatures are low, perhaps only 4 °C (40 °F), compared with around 20 °C (68 °F) at the ocean surface.

These deep ocean basins lack plankton and are, therefore, not rich in marine life. Large parts of these plains, however, are covered with minerals, the most important of which are manganese nodules in the Pacific, Atlantic and southern Indian oceans. These nodules could be exploited at depths of up to 5,000 m (16,500 ft) using technology that has already been developed, but this is currently not economically viable.

The ocean basins are intersected by mid-oceanic ridges, which are formed by volcanic eruptions. The sea water and sediments around them often contain concentrations of zinc, lead, copper, silver, and gold. While these minerals are of considerable economic value and, therefore, importance, no method has yet been devised to extract them economically.

## Ocean pollution
The seas have, unfortunately, long been considered convenient dumping grounds for waste—anything from urban sewage to nuclear materials. Chemicals from factories, fertilizers and pesticides from agricultural areas, and oil slicks from ships are also being released, often illegally, into the seas. Ballast water taken on by large ships on one side of the world is released on the other, with all its attendant marine organisms thus finding their way into other environments. The effects of such pollution are quite severe already in some areas, particularly in the semi-enclosed waters of the Mediterranean Sea.

Pollution threatens the existence of marine life, and thus, because marine ecological systems are entwined with land-based ecological systems, it will eventually affect life on land, including human life. There are more immediate effects, too, in some cases: dangerous oil spills such as that from the Exxon Valdez in Alaska threaten the livelihood of the nearby fishing communities who depend on the sea for their economic existence. Fishing communities in the Gulf of Mexico have also experienced this threat following oil spills from offshore petroleum wells.

# COMMERCE

The movement of goods and services from place to place has long been a characteristic of human endeavour. The exchange of products, information and ideas within an economic system extends beyond subsistence societies, and into the "global village" of today. The scale of transactions has changed, though—it now ranges from village or tribal bartering to the almost instantaneous transfer of vast sums of money on the international foreign exchange market. The size and bulk of trade also varies with the commodity, and there are great contrasts—camel trains range across deserts and huge bulk carriers roam the oceans.

Trade is the transport and/or communication of commodities from place to place, and is generally measured in terms of the monetary value of the items moved. Until the advent of steam-driven trains and ships and the extensive use of iron and steel for the manufacture of such carriers, the time taken and capacity to move large volumes of materials was limited. These technological limitations helped determine what could be traded, and what could be traded economically.

The volume and scope of trade, the movement of people, and the flow of information increased enormously in the nineteenth century, and will continue to do so. The effects of the increasing numbers of roads, cars, and trucks since the Second World War, for example, are so all-encompassing that it is difficult for many people to imagine life without these relatively recent transportation innovations. Add to these changes the enormous advances in electronic communication technology, and it is easy to see why today's modern suburbanites have become almost completely dependent upon their cars and their electronic communication devices.

The communication of information (ideas, images, audio signals, and written texts), especially as it converges with computer technology to produce information technology (IT), is undergoing another technological revolution. Information technology, combined with cable, satellite, optical fiber, and other technologies, can now transmit digitized information (including money) over cyberspace from one part of the globe to another instantaneously, and with potentially staggering effects. Entire national economic systems can suffer very quickly as a result of currency crises facilitated by the use of such technologies—this happened in parts of Asia during 1997 and 1998.

## International trade imbalances

To appreciate the effects of recent changes in transportation and communication technology on trade, it is useful to compare trade between highly industrialized nations (such as the United Kingdom) and other parts of the world in the 1950s with that today.

An international division of labor existed then. Some countries produced manufactured goods in factories, using a highly skilled and well-paid labor force. These goods were traded for primary commodities (coffee and gold, for instance), which were produced by poorly paid and relatively unskilled labor. This unbalanced market system generated an unequal exchange: wealth

accumulated in the industrialized areas, leading to unprecedented levels of development, while the other regions remained underdeveloped, largely because of these trade imbalances. That is, the Western world became richer and the Third World remained underdeveloped and poor.

## Recent developments

In the 1960s, manufacturing jobs began to move to selected sites in the so-called developing countries, resulting in deindustrialization in the center, and selective industrialization in the periphery, of the global economy. The textile industry was an early industrial sector to move to the periphery, so some "banana" republics became "pajama" republics. The term "newly industrialized nation" applied to former peripheral nations such as Singapore, South Korea, Mexico, and a dozen or so other countries that were undergoing sustained, rapid growth in manufacturing.

The term "economic tiger" also arose, to describe the performance of some countries in the Pacific Rim. Their economies grew faster than those of the USA or Europe during the 1980s and early 1990s, but as those economies were export-oriented, they suffered greatly as a result of the withdrawal of foreign funds after 1987.

International commerce is led by the wealthy economies; it increasingly involves service industries based on innovation and technology—finance, insurance, transport, marketing and information flow. Trade in raw materials, including those from countries heavily dependent on agriculture or mining, today accounts for little more than 20 percent of total world trade.

*Satellite receiving dishes like this one (left) are more common now, as international trade becomes increasingly dependent on satellite communications.*

Container ships like the Katie (left) transport all manner of goods worldwide today. Increased freeway traffic (in San Diego, California, US, below) and the pollution it causes are a result of increased technology use in many countries. Simpler forms of transport, such as those that are used in Agra, India (bottom), are still used in developing countries.

Manufactured goods are now produced and supplied by a range of developed and developing countries with former closed economies—China, for instance, is becoming more market-oriented and is contributing significantly to world trade.

## Multinationals and trade blocs

Another major trend is the spread of multinationals in an ever-widening global process. This is occurring in a number of fields that are engaged in world trade. This process is epitomized by the internationalization of stock markets—they operate around the clock and now even penetrate countries such as Russia.

A further feature of world commerce has been the emergence of powerful trade groups or blocs. These represent collections of countries which, as groups, have accepted rules and regulations that permit a freer exchange of goods and services between the countries in the group. Three main trade blocs are the European Union (EU), the signatories to the North American Free Trade Agreement (NAFTA), and the Association of South-East Asian Nations (ASEAN). The release of a single currency, the Euro, in parts of the EU in 1999 signalled another major development in the concept of trade between and within blocs.

## Adverse effects of the global economy

Despite the benefits which have arisen from the growth and development of international trade, there are many areas where market liberalization and the availability of funds for investment and growth have created problems.

The replacement of subsistence agriculture by a limited range of "cash" crops is one. This change has placed many societies at the mercy of declines in commodity prices, or the failure of the crop itself, due to climatic or other factors.

The need for capital has raised debt levels in countries such as Thailand, Mexico, and Indonesia to amounts which, at times of crisis, may induce political and social instability. International funding agencies such as the International Monetary Fund (IMF) and the World Bank, as well as aid agencies operating through the United Nations (UN), have become critical in sustaining these economies in the face of changes in technology and the global marketplace, which they may not have survived or been able to exploit.

## "E" stands for "electronic"

E-mail and e-commerce (electronic mail and electronic commerce) are still quite new to many, but they represent changes in the way business and communication are conducted, worldwide, that will soon affect everyone.

E-mail allows people to write messages on their computer screens and then, via a phone connection, and for the cost of only a local telephone call, send those messages instantaneously to any person (or group of people) who has the equipment to receive them. It is therefore cheaper (and, of course, faster!) than mailing a letter, cheaper than faxing written material overseas, and cheaper than telephoning overseas—and it is user-friendly.

E-commerce means the buying and selling of goods and services via the Internet. It is even newer than e-mail, and has not yet won the acceptance that e-mail has. There are issues—credit card security (the majority of purchases made on the Internet are made by credit card), censorship and copyright, to mention just three—that are as yet unresolved. These issues are particularly difficult as the Internet does not reside in any country; it exists only in "cyberspace",

and it is not clear who has jurisdiction to regulate behavior on it, nor how, in practical terms, such regulation could effectively occur.

The attractions of e-commerce are many: the buyer can, from home, view and compare a range of alternative products; there are web sites that specialize in comparison shopping, so the purchaser can find very low prices for some products; and consumers can buy products that are not available locally at all. The sorts of things that are succeeding in this brave new market range from groceries to clothes, books and compact discs, computers, airplane tickets and shares.

In October 2006, a Forrester Research report was published which claimed that non-travel online retail revenues will top the quarter-trillion-dollar mark by 2011. Currently, in the US alone there are at least eight million active web shopping households. Today, e-commerce encompasses a wide range of business activities, from e-banking to offshore manufacturing to e-logistics. There is no end in sight for the ever growing importance of e-commerce and the dependence of modern industries on electronically enabled business processes.

# POPULATION AND HEALTH

The growth of the human population in just the last 50 years has been staggering. In 1950, the global population was 2.5 billion, and it is currently 6.5 billion. It is projected that 8.5 billion people will live on the planet in 2025 and perhaps 10 billion people by 2050. If you are 30 years of age or less by the year 2000 and living in a developed country, according to current life expectancy figures, you will probably live through the final exponential surge in the human population—it is estimated that the total number of people may start to decline in the second half of the twenty-first century.

Exponential growth refers to the doubling of a population over a given time period. The growth of the human population is of deep concern, as 6.5 billion people at current levels of resource consumption and waste generation are already causing major environmental problems.

## Factors causing population growth

How is the growth in population explained? Demographers and population geographers generally begin explaining world population growth by discussing its two immediate causes: increased fertility and changes in mortality. Fertility refers to the number of children born to women of childbearing age. Mortality refers to various aspects of death, including how long people tend to live (life expectancy) and the causes of death (viruses, cancers, accidents, etc.).

Other factors that play a part in any explanation of population growth include the level of economic development of a given place, the availability of birth control, and the way people in different societies think about children.

Before the Industrial Revolution, the world's population grew slowly or did not grow at all. Although fertility was high in pre-modern societies—women commonly gave birth to between 8 and 12 children—mortality was also high. One out of four children died before reaching its first birthday (infant mortality) and perhaps another one out of five died before reaching 5 years of age (child mortality). Infectious diseases and poor diet were the major causes of high mortality, including infant and child mortality.

Why was the fertility rate so high then? If a family wanted or needed six children, mortality rates alone would require them to have ten or more. Families required the children for agricultural and domestic labor, and as a source of support when a parent grew old—children were the only pension fund available.

The early exponential growth of population resulted from a substantial improvement in the health of populations, especially with respect to control of infectious diseases and the improvement of nutrition, both of which reduced the mortality rate without a corresponding decline in the fertility rate. Infant and child mortality plummeted, and population growth surged.

As economic and social development moved into a more advanced stage, the economic meaning of children also changed. As children began attending school, they were no longer available for labor, and children became an expense rather than an asset. Raising a child today in a developed country may now cost between $US 250,000 and $US 750,000. Thus, fertility rates have declined with advanced development because of the increased survival rates of children (increased health) and because parents become economically poorer by having many children (though not necessarily socially poorer) today, as against the past, when children labored for their parents for a substantial portion of their lives.

The advent of modern birth control has also played an important role in the decline of fertility. Most, if not all, developed countries have fertility rates below that required for maintaining current levels of population; immigration is the major factor responsible for continued population growth within developed countries.

## Life expectancy—the individual

Looking at changes in health in greater depth, the health of a population has three components: mortality, morbidity (sickness), and disability. Life

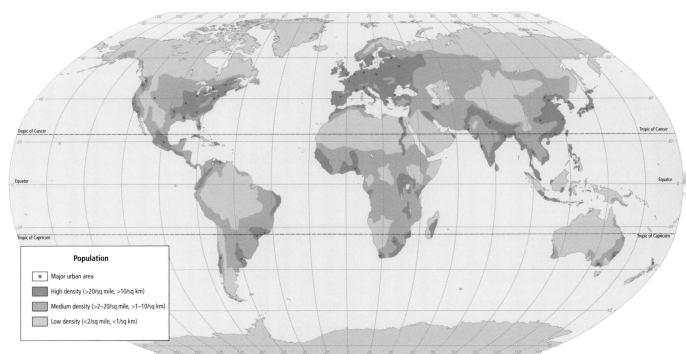

### Population

- Major urban area
- High density (>20/sq mile, >10/sq km)
- Medium density (>2–20/sq mile, >1–10/sq km)
- Low density (<2/sq mile, <1/sq km)

Projection: Robinson   Equatorial Scale approx 1:110 million

*Exponential population growth occurs when rising prosperity coincides with high fertility rates, as in Bangladesh (above). Communities in Zimbabwe (above right) work to improve their health, while some countries such as India (right) continue to suffer low life expectancy.*

expectancy is commonly accepted in demography and development studies as a good general index of the health of a population. In fact, many see life expectancy as the single best index of the development of a nation or population, but it is important to remember that life expectancy specifically measures only the effects of mortality changes; it does not relate to the sickness and disability aspect of human health.

Life expectancy was generally low before the Industrial Revolution. If life expectancy is expressed in terms of years a population as a whole lives, then life expectancy was low (between 45 and 55 years), mainly because of the prevalence of infectious diseases (measles, pneumonia, polio, and malaria, for instance), poor nutrition, lack of family planning, and the like.

Substantial advances in the reduction of a range of infectious diseases, coupled with improvement in nutrition, represent what the United Nations Children's Fund describes in their annual publication *The Progress of Nations* as simply that—the progress of nations. Life expectancy increases by 10 to 15 years because of these improvements to health.

Further increases in life expectancy—when compared with, say, life expectancy in the late 1960s and into the 1970s—are the result of advances in the reduction of death due to degenerative diseases (strokes, cancers, and heart attacks, for example) and the greater emphasis on improving lifestyle—a healthy diet, regular exercise and a reduction in smoking.

For a few nations, life expectancy is slightly more than 81 years at present. On the global scale, life expectancy at birth was 46 years in 1950, 64 years in the late 1990s, and is projected to be 77 years in the year 2050.

### Life expectancy—the global view

Considerable regional diversity in the causes of population growth and life expectancy is evident in the early 2000s. Generally speaking, North America, Australia and Europe have high life expectancy and have internal growth rates below population replacement; South America and East and Southeast Asia are not far behind; and Africa south of the Sahara has low life expectancy, but population growth remains explosively high.

Many of the countries in the former communist world are experiencing deterioration in health, and life expectancy is actually declining in some of those nations, including Russia. It is interesting to compare the two most populous nations, China and India. Changes to population growth and life expectancy in China resemble those in other East and Southeast Asian nations, whereas India continues to have a very high growth rate and a moderately low life expectancy.

### The future for life expectancy

Is there a limit to life expectancy? This is a most controversial topic about which there is no agreement. Under natural conditions, all life forms have a limit, called senescence: the point where an organism simply wears out. For the human population, senescence was believed to be roughly 85 years; however, a few population

### Famine

Famine can be defined as a high degree of lack of food within a population, and it often goes along with widespread mortality. Malnutrition, on the other hand, refers to levels of nourishment that are below those needed to maintain health, and can apply to a whole population or part of a population.

Both are thought to be results of population pressure —the pressure that builds, in developing countries particularly, between the size of the population and the economic resources (especially food) of the country. Falling living standards can be an early sign, in countries with rapidly growing populations, of this pressure. Many societies have suffered famines; in modern times, famine has most often affected societies in Africa.

The links between famine and malnutrition and mortality and fertility now seem not nearly as clear as may previously have been thought. Investigations into mortality in developing countries have found that it is the combination of malnourishment and infectious disease that is responsible for high mortality among infants and children, not simply lack of food.

It seems that populations are able to maintain their rates of fertility despite quite large reductions in nutritional levels—metabolic rates actually appear to readjust.

groups live into the low 90s. Genetic and other medical research, however, may well change the upper limit of life expectancy during the first half of the twenty-first century.

Of course, all of this optimistically assumes that improvements in health will continue. It remains to be seen whether or not the impact of diseases such as AIDS will retard or even reverse the historical improvement in human health, the resistance of some forms of bacteria to antibiotics, in particular, will give rise to deaths from diseases or infections previously thought to be under control, and whether the advances that come through medical research will be affordable to a sizeable proportion of the world's population.

# NATURAL HAZARDS

Natural events which cause damage and loss of life are classified as natural hazards. These hazards are generally unpredictable—they strike suddenly and can therefore leave the affected populations traumatized. Natural hazards can result from movements taking place inside the Earth or on its surface, or in its atmosphere.

Movements within the Earth result in volcanic eruptions and earthquakes. Changing weather conditions generate wind storms, cyclones, tornadoes, heavy rainfall, and snowfall, as well as lightning strikes, which can trigger forest fires. River floods and tsunamis can cause loss of life and serious damage to property.

## Earthquakes

Plate collision along the Japanese archipelago makes that area vulnerable to earthquakes and to tsunamis generated by earthquakes on the ocean floor. Plates sliding past each other can also cause earthquakes, such as along the San Andreas Fault in California, where earthquakes have occurred in San Francisco and in Los Angeles.

Earthquakes strike suddenly, and if they are of high intensity, buildings can be toppled and life and property lost. The famous San Francisco earthquake of 1906 was devastating to that city and its people—hundreds of buildings were destroyed and the resulting fires swept through the city center, leaving about 3,000 people dead and many thousands more homeless.

An intense earthquake in 1995 toppled and wrecked the tall buildings and infrastructure of Kobe, in Japan, killing more than 6,000 of its inhabitants and injuring more than 35,000 others. The worst scenarios involve earthquakes located close to inhabited areas, notably cities.

On the Richter scale, earthquakes are serious when they exceed a magnitude of 4, cause damage when they exceed 5 and are intensely destructive when they are between 7 and 8.6. Although more than a million earthquakes occur every year, most of these are of low magnitude, and cause no loss of life or damage to property. High-intensity earthquakes, on the other hand, are capable of causing great damage and therefore receive the most publicity, particularly when they are centered on densely populated areas.

## Tsunamis

Earthquakes taking place on the sea bed can trigger tsunamis (tidal waves) which, on reaching land, can assume enormous proportions and result in great damage. Such waves may be less than 1 m (3 ft) in height where they begin, in the deep oceans, but they can reach the enormous heights of more than 30 m (100 ft) as they approach land, and they cause devastation to low-lying areas. Worse still, within seconds, more than one such giant tidal wave can strike.

In 1983, a tsunami resulted in the deaths of 30,000 people in Japan. On 17 July 1998, a tsunami struck the northern coast of Papua New Guinea, killing around 4,000 people.

In December 2004, one of the worst tsunamis ever recorded occurred in the Indian Ocean. It claimed around 227,000 lives, most of them Indonesian.

## Volcanoes

Volcanic eruptions are common along certain paths, which are also seismic zones. Here, crustal plates separate and collide. Volcanoes erupt where molten material (magma) accumulates just below Earth's surface and then rises to the surface. A volcanic explosion ejects ash and superheated steam into the atmosphere and cascades very hot lava along the sides of the volcanic cones. Volcanic eruptions are another natural disaster that can be devastating to life and property.

In AD 79, lava and ash destroyed the ancient city of Pompeii in southern Italy when Mt Vesuvius erupted. Mt Pelée, in Martinique, erupted in 1902, destroying the city of St Pierre and killing most of its inhabitants. Mt Pinatubo, in the Philippines, erupted in 1991, ejecting steam, ash, and lava, and threatened hundreds of thousands of people just 27 km (17 miles) away in Angeles; its ash even blanketed parts of Manila. Volcanic eruptions are also common in Bali and Java (Indonesia).

Volcanic eruptions are rated on the Volcanic Explosivity Index. The Krakatoa eruption of 1883 in Indonesia, one of the most spectacular on record, is rated at 6. No recorded eruption has

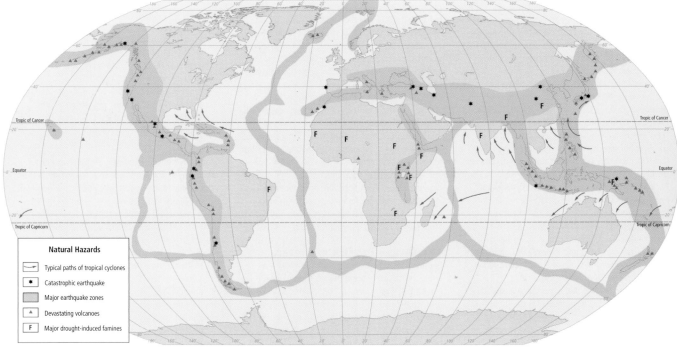

**Natural Hazards**

| | |
|---|---|
| ⊂⊃ | Typical paths of tropical cyclones |
| ✳ | Catastrophic earthquake |
| ▨ | Major earthquake zones |
| ▲ | Devastating volcanoes |
| F | Major drought-induced famines |

Projection: Robinson   Equatorial Scale approx 1:155 million

Tropic of Cancer

Equator

Tropic of Capricorn

Wildfires (bushfires, far left) consume large tracts of forest in many countries every year. Often lives are also lost, and millions of dollars worth of property is destroyed. Mt Pinatubo in the Philippines erupted in 1991 (left), causing widespread damage with devastating mud slides which swamped a large area including the town of Lahar (bottom). Drought (below) is a more predictable natural hazard.

reached 8, which is the highest possible rating. The Krakatoa eruption was heard more than 4,500 km (2,800 miles) away; it generated tsunamis, and more than 30,000 people are believed to have perished as a result.

## Tropical cyclones and tornadoes

Tropical cyclones, known as typhoons in East Asia and hurricanes in the Caribbean, are also very destructive atmospheric hazards. Tropical cyclones are whirling, low-pressure vortices that can be up to 500 km (310 miles) in diameter and have wind speeds reaching more than 200 km (125 miles) per hour. They can pick up trees, rooftops, light boats, and planes and destroy them. This flying debris is enormously dangerous to people, too.

In coastal areas, large waves, or surges, which sweep the land may be generated, resulting in considerable damage. These cyclones have a calm center, called the "eye" of the cyclone; when the eye passes over an area there is a period of calm, after which the storm returns in all its fury, but with the winds now reversed in direction.

The coastal areas of Southeast and East Asia, the Bay of Bengal, the Pacific Ocean west of Mexico, the Caribbean and Florida, plus island groups of the Pacific Ocean such as Fiji, and northern Australia, are amongst the areas most prone to tropical cyclones.

Cyclones have struck with great fury along the coast of Bangladesh, a small country which mostly consists of the combined deltas of the Ganges and Brahmaputra rivers. That low-lying deltaic area is particularly vulnerable to the surges which cyclones can generate. This has resulted, on several occasions, in considerable loss of life and damage to property.

In contrast to tropical cyclones, tornadoes are small low-pressure cells, not more than 0.5 km (3/10 mile) across. They are, however, very intense, and their wind speeds can exceed 400 km (250 miles) per hour. They thus have the potential to inflict sudden and serious damage. Their vortices become vividly visible as they whip up soil and other debris. The most damaging tornadoes occur in the central parts of the United States, although mini-versions are also found in parts of eastern Australia.

## River floods

River floods are a common hazard in floodplains. Spectacular floods, covering thousands of square kilometers, often occur over the immense plains of the major rivers of China, India, and Bangladesh. These areas are often densely populated because of the fertile soils and abundant water supplies.

The Huang River in China flows along a course which is elevated over the surrounding plains; this is because levees have naturally built up on its sides. These levees have been further reinforced by human action. The bursting of the levees in 1887 inundated more than 130,000 sq km (50,000 sq miles) and resulted in a million deaths.

In the case of the Ganges River in India and Bangladesh, the deforestation in the Himalayas has resulted, at times, in water from heavy rainfall and snowmelt rushing onto the vast plains through which the Ganges runs and flooding them. In 1988, 90 percent of Bangladesh lay under water when the Ganges flooded.

Floods regularly bring human and economic disasters to many parts of the world—in 1998 alone, 250 million people were affected by the flooding of the Yangtze River in China—and dams and irrigation networks have been built across many flood-prone rivers in an attempt to mitigate and control flood damage.

## Wildfires

Wildfires or bushfires strike when forests are dry. These fires can cause serious damage and result in significant air pollution. The 1997 wildfires in the tropical forests of Sumatra, Indonesia, for instance, released a dense pall of smoke over a large area, including parts of Malaysia and Singapore. These fires were lit by humans clearing land for agriculture or woodchipping. Normally, rains ensure that wildfires are temporary, and restricted to a small area. In Sumatra, however, the prolonged drought, blamed on the El Niño effect, resulted in the uncontrollable spread of the wildfires.

The naturally occurring eucalypt forests of Australia and the eucalypt forest plantations of California are also particularly prone to wildfires, as the volatile oil the eucalypts contain makes them highly flammable. Every year, wildfires wipe out large areas of these forests and damage human settlements or property in the process.

Remote sensing, using satellites and highly sophisticated monitoring techniques, is now being used to track possible natural disasters. It provides data to ground centers about the development of tropical cyclones, the spreading of flood waters from rivers, and the build-up of lava in volcanoes. Such advance warning systems have already helped save lives and limit damage.

## Part 2

# People
## and Society

# The Changing Scene

*Human societies have changed more during the 20th century than in any previous one, but mechanized facilities are not yet available to all—no running water for these Indian women in Varanasi, opposite. Conversely, highly sophisticated cultures developed thousands of years ago without modern conveniences, leaving treasures such as this floor mosaic, above, from Cyprus.*

Today's global pattern of peoples and nations rests on a long process of social evolution, going back about 2 million years. It was then that humanity began to clearly distinguish itself as something special on the planet—and unlike the great apes—by physical and mental changes such as a fully upright way of walking, and much bigger brains than the apes possessed. Then, some time in the past 40,000 years, the great evolutionary breakthrough occurred: a fully developed capacity for language, an ability to create new tools for new purposes, and a talent for forward planning. Previously nomadic, hunting wild animals and foraging for seeds and fruits, humans now chose to live a more settled existence. People began to live in regular campsites and used shelters they made themselves. In some places they dug pits for food storage, and had well-built, regularly used fireplaces as far back as 20,000 years ago. Art and religion also appeared, with remarkable cave paintings and evidence of ritual associated with the burial of the dead.

It is thought that *Homo sapiens sapiens* (the technical name for modern humans) originated in Africa. From there waves of migration carried people to every corner of Earth: to distant Australia perhaps 50,000 years ago, to North America across a land bridge (where the Bering Strait is now) perhaps 20,000 years ago. As they moved, they took their languages with them, and when they settled, their languages continued to evolve, many soon becoming mutually unintelligible. Then, around 10,000 years ago came a major development—the rise of agriculture and permanent settlements. In Turkey and Iraq, in China, and in Mexico, farmers began to grow wheat and barley, or rice, or maize. At around the same time, the first farm animals were domesticated: pigs and cattle, goats and sheep, and llamas in South America.

Permanent farming settlements transformed human life economically, and on this foundation civilizations arose in different parts of the world. In Egypt and Iraq, in China and India, in Mexico and Peru, some towns became cities, with centralized political systems, strong rulers, and monumental buildings. The buildings were often religious temples associated with a class of priests, and in Egypt they were tombs for divine kings, built to preserve their bodies and effects for the afterlife. These social and political developments were accompanied by equally significant developments in science and technology.

The Stone Age, which for millions of years had provided stone implements for hunters, and then stone adzes and reaping blades for the first farmers, came to an end. First bronze was invented, then people found out how to make iron—by 500 BC, iron tools and weapons were spread throughout Europe and Asia. Metals and metallurgical science gave those who had them a huge military advantage over those who did not, as did the wheel, when it appeared around 3,500 BC. Horses harnessed to chariots changed the nature of warfare in ancient times.

War and conquest were normal conditions of life. Other things being equal, victory went to those whose weapons were most advanced. Some dominant cities developed into empires, subjecting other cultures to their rule. The Roman Empire, at its height, included large areas of Europe,

North Africa, and the Middle East. By 206 BC, China was united under the Qin Dynasty, while by AD 1,520 the Incas controlled some 2,000 miles (3,330 km) of territory west of the Andes in South America. The military advantages of steel weapons and guns were demonstrated by the easy victories of Cortez over the Aztecs (1521) and Pizarro over the Incas (1533) against vastly greater numbers of ill-equipped Amerindian forces. The consequences of empire were that the knowledge, ideas, religion, technology and language of the dominant civilization were spread far and wide. Trade, both private and state-sponsored, also played a major role in this. The Han Empire in China (206 BC to AD 220), for instance, traded its silks with the Syrians of the Roman Empire far to the west. Arab trade spread round the Indian Ocean, and by AD 1200 had reached as far east as Java.

The spread of the main world religions has also been of major importance in the last two thousand years. These religions have been responsible for the most enduring examples of the art, literature, and architecture of civilization. A major distinction can be made between proselytizing religions, which actively seek to convert people to their beliefs (such as Chistianity, Islam, and Buddhism) and those which do not, such as Hinduism and Judaism. The world's three major religions are Christianity (33.1 percent), Islam (20.3 percent), and Hinduism (13.3 percent), the first two being derived from early Judaism (0.2 percent).

In the past 200 years, industrialization has been the biggest force for social change. Beginning in England with textile manufacturing in the 1780s, then progressing to manufacturing based on iron and steel in the nineteenth century, industrialization now combines science with technology in an unending cycle of invention and discovery. What began in Europe has now spread to every country in the world. Industry, which takes raw materials and then turns them into products to be traded, has provided millions of jobs for peasants who would otherwise be tied to the land. But in order to take those jobs they have moved into the cities. Urbanization has created huge concentrations of people in Asia and in South America, and while raising incomes, it has brought social problems too.

Political changes have come thick and fast. The nation-state arose as a political movement in Europe in the nineteenth century, where it superseded an earlier pattern of city-states such as Venice, Antwerp and Amsterdam. After the Second World War it spread through Asia and Africa during the process of decolonization, and since 1989 it has disrupted the domains of the former Soviet Union. Endemic conflicts born of nationalism continue to plague troublespots in Africa, Indo-China, the Balkans, and the Middle East. However, there has been at the same time a balancing move toward large, over-arching international organizations. The European Union steadily moves toward greater political and economic unity. Meanwhile, the United Nations, its resources and abilities increasingly overstretched, its goals more honored in the breach than in the observance, endeavors to keep international peace.

# HUMAN EVOLUTION

The oldest primate fossils found in Africa and Asia date from between 45 and 50 million years ago. Around 15 million years ago, Asian and African hominoids (the earliest known ancestors of both humans and apes) diverged. The African hominoids adapted to woodland and savanna habitats and developed the ability to walk on two legs, while the Asian hominoids continued their tree-climbing existence. Although the fossil record is incomplete, a later divergence probably occurred among African hominoids between gorillas and the common ancestors of humans and chimpanzees.

### Early hominids
The first hominids (the earliest ancestors of modern human beings not also related to modern great apes) developed about 5 to 6 million years ago. During the earliest phases of their evolution, hominids underwent anatomical changes that resulted in an erect posture, allowing them to walk habitually on two legs.

Other changes included the reduction of canine teeth and the development of a comparatively vertical face. Features that are widely accepted as hominid hallmarks, such as a larger brain and the capacity for cultural life (indicated by stone or bone tools), appeared later.

The earliest hominid fossils have been found in southern and eastern Africa. The Olduvai Gorge in the Great Rift Valley of

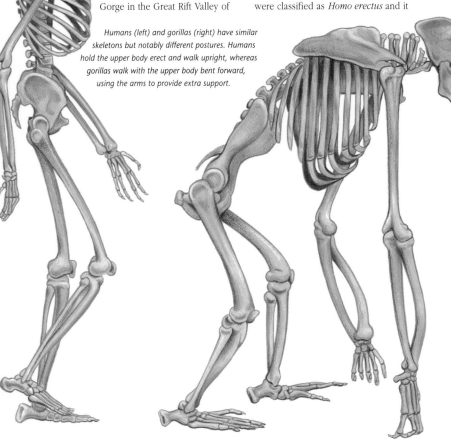

*Humans (left) and gorillas (right) have similar skeletons but notably different postures. Humans hold the upper body erect and walk upright, whereas gorillas walk with the upper body bent forward, using the arms to provide extra support.*

Tanzania has proved to be a rich source. In the 1930s, the anthropologist Louis Leakey began excavations there, and in the ensuing years he and others found a large number of hominid fossils and stone tools. The most famous find occurred in 1959 when his wife Mary uncovered a hominid fossil she called *Zinjanthropus*, believed to be 1,750,000 years old. Most scholars now believe that *Zinjanthropus* is an example of *Australopithecus* (specifically *Australopithecus boisei*), the earliest group of hominids yet found.

### Handy man
Other hominid fossils found at Olduvai Gorge were more clearly identifiable as members of our own genus, *Homo*. These hominids were tool users and have been classified as *Homo habilis* ("handy man"). Tools similar to those found at Olduvai have been found at sites elsewhere in Africa and dated at between 1,800,000 and 2,340,000 years old.

Fossils of species that are more recognizably like ourselves have also been found in Africa and dated at about 1.9 million years ago. The best example is a nearly complete 1.6-million-year-old skeleton found in northern Kenya and known as Turkana Boy. The boy died in adolescence, but, had he lived to maturity, he would have been tall (about 1.8 m [6 ft]), with long, slender limbs, and well adapted to living on the open savanna.

Turkana Boy and other similar fossils found in Africa were originally thought to resemble specimens discovered in Java and China. All were classified as *Homo erectus* and it

was believed that *Homo erectus* had evolved in Africa and then migrated to Asia about 1 million years ago. Discoveries in China in the past decade, however, together with the application of more sophisticated dating methods to previously excavated Asian sites, have pushed back the date of the first appearance of early hominids in Asia to about 2 million years ago. Hominid fossils found in Longgupo Cave in Sichuan province in China, dated at around 1.9 million years old, more closely resemble the earlier hominid species *Homo habilis*. This suggests a much earlier migration out of Africa. As a result, some scholars now believe that *Homo erectus* evolved independently in Asia and was not an African species. African hominid fossils of a more modern appearance, such as Turkana Boy, are now classified as a separate species, *Homo ergaster*.

Although there are a number of early hominid sites in Europe, they have yielded few fossils. Sites containing tools have been dated at around 1 million years old, with the earliest being about 1.5 million years old. Until recently, some of these were classified as *Homo erectus* sites. Since this species is now considered to be an Asian evolutionary sideline, however, the fossil record is being reassessed. In 1994, excavations in northern Spain produced numerous simple stone tools and some hominid fossils subsequently classified as a separate species, *Homo heidelbergensis*. This find has been dated at more than 780,000 years old and may provide evidence for the European ancestors of the Neanderthals.

### Archaic *Homo sapiens*
The earliest archaeological discoveries made in Europe were fossils of archaic *Homo sapiens*. The fossils were named Neanderthals, after the Neander Valley near Düsseldorf in Germany, where they were first discovered in 1865. This find caused widespread excitement as it was the first discovery of an extinct ancestor of modern humans. Since then, numerous Neanderthal sites have been found throughout Europe and the Middle East. The Neanderthals are generally considered to be a subspecies of *Homo sapiens*, known as *Homo sapiens neanderthalensis*. However, some scholars believe that the Neanderthals' less evolved physical characteristics and less sophisticated technology indicate that they were a separate species, *Homo neanderthalensis*.

The Neanderthals lived in Europe and Western Asia approximately 35,000 to 130,000 years ago, overlapping with the modern human species (*Homo sapiens sapiens*). They had larger brain cases and smaller back teeth than earlier populations, but differed from modern humans in their receding forehead and large, protruding face with front teeth and forward-projecting jaw. The Neanderthals had a relatively short, bulky stature and considerable strength, and showed evidence of complex cultural traits and social organization. For example, they used planning and cooperation to hunt large mammals. They also buried their dead and seem to have had some knowledge of art, demonstrating a capacity for symbolic behavior. Their vocal apparatus and neurological structure provide indirect evidence that they may also have developed speech.

Neanderthals disappear from the archaeological record around 40,000 years ago in the Middle East and about 35,000 years ago in Europe. It may be that they slowly evolved into modern humans, contributing to the gene pool of the present-day inhabitants of Europe and the Middle East. However, many scholars now think that they were gradually overwhelmed and replaced by incoming populations of a more advanced species classified as *Homo sapiens sapiens*, or modern humans.

### Out of Africa

The early history of modern humans is still uncertain, as the fossil record is far from complete. Some scholars argue that *Homo sapiens sapiens* developed independently, in a number of different geographical locations. Others consider that what is popularly called the "out of Africa" theory better reflects what is now known about the process of evolution. This proposes that modern human populations are all descended from a single ancestral population that emerged at one location between 150,000 and 100,000 years ago. Increasing archaeological evidence suggests that the place of origin of modern humans was somewhere in Africa. From this homeland, *Homo sapiens sapiens* migrated northward into Europe some 40,000 to 100,000 years ago, and then spread throughout the world, gradually replacing more archaic populations wherever they encountered them.

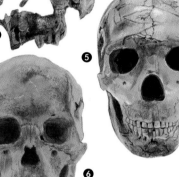

Human fossil skulls: 1. *Australopithecus boisei* 2. *Homo habilis* 3. *Homo ergaster* 4. *Homo erectus* 5. *Homo sapiens neanderthalensis* 6. *Homo sapiens sapiens*. Note the gradual disappearance of the thick brow ridges, and the growth of the cranium—indicative of increasing brain capacity and intelligence.

## The classification of primate fossils

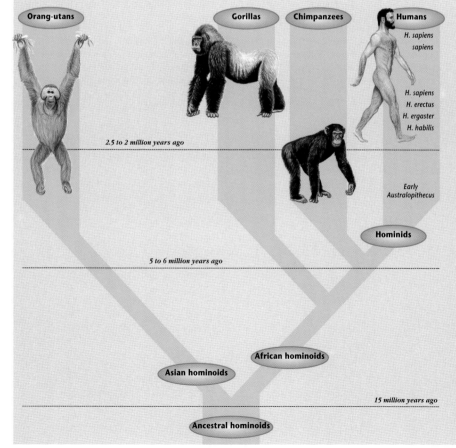

Orang-utans

Gorillas  Chimpanzees  Humans

H. sapiens sapiens

H. sapiens
H. erectus
H. ergaster
H. habilis

2.5 to 2 million years ago

Early Australopithecus

Hominids

5 to 6 million years ago

African hominoids

Asian hominoids

15 million years ago

Ancestral hominoids

In 1735, the Swedish naturalist Carl Linnaeus caused a public outcry when he classified human beings as part of the animal kingdom. Today, however, his taxonomy—which has been extensively revised and expanded—is the accepted way of classifying all forms of plant and animal life.

The human species, *Homo sapiens sapiens*, belongs to the genus *Homo* (which includes our hominid ancestors) in the family *Hominidae* (which includes the apes). This family is in turn part of the Primate order. The relationship between humans, apes, and early hominid fossils is problematic. Recent studies by molecular biologists have shown that there is a much closer genetic link between humans and the African great apes (especially chimpanzees) than might have been predicted from comparing their anatomies. This has led some taxonomists to place humans, gorillas, and chimpanzees in one family, *Hominidae*, and Asian apes such as the orang-utan in another, *Pongidae*.

The currently accepted classification of hominid fossils establishes a chronology for modern humans from the development of the first australopithecine species (appearing around 5 million years ago), to early *Homo* species such as *Homo habilis* and *Homo erectus* (from around 2 million years ago), through to later *Homo* species (around 1 million years ago) and archaic *Homo sapiens* such as the Neanderthals (about 130,000 years ago). Both the classification and the chronology are likely to be revised as new fossil discoveries are made.

# THE FIRST MODERN HUMANS

The success of modern humans, *Homo sapiens sapiens*, in colonizing Earth's landmasses owes much to the evolutionary changes that occurred in the physical form and mental capacity of hominids. Although the basic hominid anatomy changed little, the features that distinguished hominids from other hominoids, such as their erect posture, ability to walk habitually on two legs, vertical face, smaller teeth and enlarged brain, were refined in each successive species and subspecies. By far the most significant change, and the one that signaled the emergence of *Homo sapiens sapiens*, was the progressive enlargement of the brain, which was out of all proportion to changes in body size. In absolute terms, the average brain capacity of modern humans is three times that of the great apes.

Increased brain capacity allowed *Homo sapiens sapiens* to develop greater intelligence and problem-solving capabilities. This led to the appearance of tools as well as speech and language (although full language capacity emerged less than 40,000 years ago). It also enabled modern humans to develop strategies for coping with harsh environments, such as camp fires, clothing, natural food storage facilities, and primitive cooking methods. Further intellectual development resulted in a flourishing cultural life and increased capacity for social organization, which in turn stimulated the growth of civilizations and led to the evolution of modern society.

## Making and using tools

Many people believe that it is the presence of tools that distinguishes early humans (*Homo* spp.) from other hominids, but a number of other animals also make and use tools. Chimpanzees, for instance, have demonstrated an ability to make and use tools for digging for food. More specifically, some scholars have argued that it is the power and complexity of human tool assemblages that distinguishes humans. However, the simplicity of the tool assemblages of archaic humans and certain hunter-gatherers of the recent past makes this explanation inadequate. What *is* unique about human tool making and tool use is that the tools were made for particular purposes. Moreover, they were constantly improved and adapted for new purposes, to the extent that tools eventually pervaded all aspects of human life. This is not the case among chimpanzees.

The first hominid fossils associated with hand-made tools were those of *Homo habilis*, found at Olduvai Gorge in Tanzania, and dated at about 2 million years old. Tools have been found in older East African sites, but without any fossil remains. Although earlier hominid species knew how to make and use tools, it was probably only with the emergence of the genus *Homo* that tools became part of daily life.

The early *Homo habilis* tools were crude, stone hand-axes. Unsurprisingly, stone and some bone tools dominate the archaeological record. Tools made of perishable materials such as wood are found occasionally at waterlogged, frozen, or arid sites, but such finds are rare. From about one million years ago, tool assemblages became more specialized, but it is only in the past 40,000 years that there has been a proliferation of designs.

The simplicity of early tools clearly indicates that hominids obtained their food by foraging and scavenging. The traditional view that the hunting of animals accompanied and influenced the evolutionary development of modern humans has been reassessed in the light of this evidence. Regular

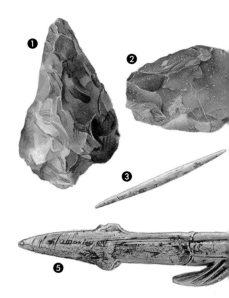

hunting, particularly the killing of large mammals, probably began later. Far more important at this stage in the evolution of modern humans was the development of an ability to plan ahead. Although this would become essential for organizing hunts, it was also required at an earlier stage to enable humans to forage for food and store supplies for lean times.

## Art and cooking skills

There seems to have been a watershed in the development of modern humans around 40,000 years ago. This is reflected in a dramatic world-

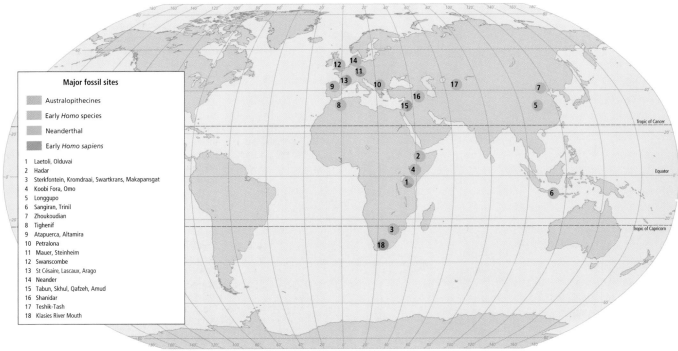

### Major fossil sites

- Australopithecines
- Early *Homo* species
- Neanderthal
- Early *Homo sapiens*

1 Laetoli, Olduvai
2 Hadar
3 Sterkfontein, Kromdraai, Swartkrans, Makapansgat
4 Koobi Fora, Omo
5 Longgupo
6 Sangiran, Trinil
7 Zhoukoudian
8 Tighenif
9 Atapuerca, Altamira
10 Petralona
11 Mauer, Steinheim
12 Swanscombe
13 St Césaire, Lascaux, Arago
14 Neander
15 Tabun, Skhul, Qafzeh, Amud
16 Shanidar
17 Teshik-Tash
18 Klasies River Mouth

Projection: Robinson   Equatorial Scale approx 1:155 million

Many people believe that the invention and use of tools distinguished the early humans from other hominids. The development of human technology is reflected in these tools (below):

1. Scraper from Swanscombe, England; 300,000–200,000 BP
2. Sidescraper from Le Moustier, France; 70,000–35,000 BP
3. Bone point from Aurignac, France, 35,000–23,000 BP
4. Bifacial stone knife from Solutré, France; 20,000–17,000 BP
5. Bone harpoon from Le Morin, France, 16,000–8,000 BP

❹

## The art of early hunter–gatherers

wide change in the archaeological evidence. Not only did tool assemblages become more sophisticated, but art, in the form of jewellery, figurines, paintings, and engravings (often depicting hunting scenes), also become prevalent. The widespread use of raw materials that could only have been obtained from distant sources suggests that trade networks had expanded. Camp sites show evidence of more settled living, including artificial shelters, food storage pits, and well-built, regularly used fireplaces. Burial sites become more elaborate, containing ornaments and other cultural objects. The disposal of the dead clearly involved some form of ritual, reflecting metaphysical concerns and symbolic behavior.

There also appears to have been a "culinary revolution," with stone knives being used to cut up food. This allowed for more thorough cooking, which may in turn have resulted in changes in the cranial structure of humans, as large teeth would no longer have been necessary for tearing raw or partially roasted meat.

These cultural and physical changes occurred during the last ice age, which culminated about 15,000 to 20,000 years ago, when glaciers covered large areas of the world. Successful strategies developed by modern humans to cope with the deteriorating climate gave them a clear advantage over more archaic forms of *Homo sapiens*. Despite the spread of hostile environments during the ice age, *Homo sapiens sapiens* succeeded in colonizing the world far more rapidly and extensively than earlier hominid migrants.

Colonization on the scale undertaken by *Homo sapiens sapiens* required all of the species' new-found technical and social skills. Its success depended not just on tools and an ability to plan ahead, but also on the existence of extensive social structures which could provide the support and cooperation necessary for the completion of long, hazardous journeys into unknown lands.

Art is widely believed to have originated during the last ice age and appears to have flourished mainly in Europe and the southern hemisphere (southern Africa and Australia). Little has been found at ice-age sites in North Africa, China, or elsewhere in Asia. This does not mean, however, that art did not exist in these areas—it may simply be that the forms of artistic expression were more temporary or that the materials used did not survive.

Ice-age art is linked with major innovations in tool technology, including well-crafted and highly efficient blades, and hafted spears. With the rapid evolution of hunting techniques, obtaining food would no longer have been as difficult and, consequently, more effort could be expended on the development of art, language, and spiritual interests. No record remains of stories, songs, or dances of these pre-literate cultures, nor of artworks made out of perishable materials. The art that has survived can be divided into two main types: moveable objects and rock art.

Moveable objects comprise small figures or decorated weapons made of stone, bone, antler, ivory, or clay, which were sometimes placed in graves to accompany the deceased in the afterlife. Rock art, such as engravings and paintings, is often found in caves. While drawings of human figures have been found, most rock art depicts game animals such as bison, mammoths, deer, and bears, which were important sources of food, clothing, tools, weapons, and ornaments. Outstanding examples of cave art were discovered in the nineteenth century at Altamira in northern Spain and at Lascaux in southwestern France.

*This ancient cave painting (above) was found in Rhodes-Matapos National Park in Zimbabwe, Africa. Fertility figures, such as the 20,000-year-old Willendorf Venus from Austria (left), are among the earliest indications of a human concern with rituals and symbols.*

# HUMAN MIGRATIONS

Recent research undertaken on fossil and genetic evidence suggests that hominids migrated "out of Africa" on many occasions, probably beginning with *Homo erectus*, *Homo habilis*, or the taller and more slender *Homo ergaster* more than 2 million years ago. Changes in the climate may have been a major factor in these early migrations. One theory suggests that between 2 million and 3 million years ago, a widespread drop in temperature led to the replacement of the tropical woodlands in eastern Africa by savanna grassland. This change in vegetation favored the *Homo* species over the australopithecines. With their larger brains, more generalized diets, and greater tool-using ability, the *Homo* species adapted more readily to the open terrain and soon began to roam widely. Initially, they probably followed the land mammals on which they scavenged, as the animals moved north and east following the expansion of the grasslands.

To date, early *Homo* sites have been discovered at several Asian sites in the Republic of Georgia, in China, and on the island of Java in Indonesia. Early humans did not make an appearance in Europe until some time later (around 1 to 1.5 million years ago), and this region remained sparsely populated until 500,000 years ago.

During their migrations, early *Homo* species would have crossed various land bridges that appeared during the recurring ice ages of the past 2 million years. However, to explain the presence of 800,000-year-old stone tools on the Indonesian island of Flores, which would have remained at least 20 km (12 miles) offshore even at the height of the ice ages, scientists have tentatively suggested that *Homo erectus* made use of simple vessels such as bamboo rafts to cross short stretches of sea.

## Migrations by modern humans

Compared with the migrations made by archaic populations, the spread of modern humans during the last 100,000 years occurred remarkably rapidly. Furthermore, *Homo sapiens sapiens* ventured much farther than earlier hominids, eventually reaching the Americas and Australia. These more extensive migrations were made possible by this species' greater adaptability and by the exposure of numerous land bridges during the last ice age.

Scientists are still debating when and how the Americas were colonized, although it is generally accepted that hunting groups crossed into Alaska via a land bridge in the Bering Strait. This could have occurred either between 63,000 and 45,000 years ago or between 35,000 and 10,000 years ago. Although some argue that the earlier crossing is more likely because the Alaskan ice sheet would not have been as extensive as during the later period, the earliest reliable dates for archaeological sites in North America are no more than 20,000 years old. Consequently, the more widely held view is that the crossing occurred between 12,000 and 20,000 years ago, with people gradually drifting south down the continent. Recent evidence suggests that Monte Verde in southern Chile may have been settled as early as 12,500 years ago.

The question of whether there was one or more crossings is also unresolved. Some researchers believe that genetic variations among the indigenous peoples of the Americas are so great that they suggest three or four waves of migration. A more recent assessment cautiously suggests that there were no more than two waves—one arriving about 20,000 to 25,000 years ago and the other around 11,300 years ago. These early settlers were probably of more diverse origins than previously

thought, and some may even have arrived by sea rather than across the land bridge.

Debates of a similar nature surround the colonization of Australia. The earliest direct evidence of humans is about 40,000 years old (claims that various artifacts and sites in the Northern Territory date from around 60,000 years ago have not been confirmed). Since some of these sites are in the south of the continent, dates of up to 50,000 to 60,000 years ago for the initial arrival of humans from Southeast Asia have been proposed to allow for the settlement of large areas of the continent by 40,000 years ago. The absence of Asian fauna in Australia indicates that there must

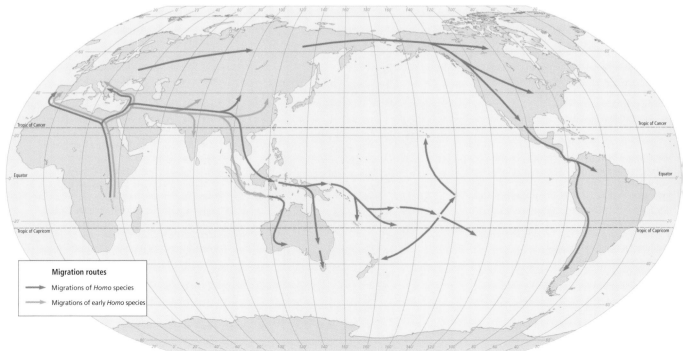

Migration routes

→ Migrations of *Homo* species

→ Migrations of early *Homo* species

Projection: Robinson   Equatorial Scale approx 1:155 million

have been a substantial stretch of sea between the two continents for millions of years.

## Colonizing the Pacific

The islands along the western rim of the Pacific were probably colonized around the same time as Australia and New Guinea, when sea levels were sufficiently low for them to be linked to the Asian mainland. Of course, *Homo erectus* may also have occupied these islands while they were linked to the mainland during earlier periods of glaciation, but the earliest signs of human occupation in Japan have been dated at around 30,000 years ago. Based on the evidence currently available, it appears that other islands on the western Pacific rim, such as most of the Philippines, were probably occupied 10,000 to 15,000 years later.

By the time European explorers reached the Pacific region in the early sixteenth century, virtually every inhabitable island was populated. Exactly when and how all the islands of the Pacific were first settled, however, is not entirely clear. The archaeological evidence is still meager, and there is considerable speculation about early migrations.

Not long after the Second World War, in an attempt to prove that the population of the Polynesian islands originated in South America, the Norwegian ethnologist and adventurer Thor Heyerdahl and his small crew sailed from the Pacific coast of South America to Polynesia on a balsa raft named *Kon-Tiki*. Although Heyerdahl showed that such a voyage was possible, most scholars still believe that the great bulk of linguistic and botanical evidence suggests that the populations originally came from Southeast Asia rather than South America.

The Pacific Islands are customarily divided into three ethnogeographic areas: Melanesia, Micronesia, and Polynesia. Melanesia includes the predominantly dark-skinned peoples of New Guinea, the Bismarck Archipelago, the Solomons,

Vanuatu, New Caledonia, and Fiji. Micronesia comprises the very small islands and atolls in the northern Pacific, including the Marianas, Carolines, and Marshalls. Polynesia forms a large triangle in the eastern Pacific, from Hawaii in the north, to New Zealand in the south, and Easter Island in the east. Despite these classifications, however, archaeological evidence, linguistic studies, and blood group analyses all suggest similar origins for the people of the three areas. The physical and cultural differences between modern-day peoples may result from the fact that the islands were occupied by successive waves of migrants.

## The Lapita people

The earliest dates for settlement of the Pacific Islands in Micronesia and Polynesia go back no further than the second millennium BC. As they moved eastward, these early settlers took with them a well-developed agricultural tradition based on taro, yams, and pigs. This agricultural

tradition was associated with a coarse, finely decorated pottery known as Lapita ware. By studying the distribution of this pottery, archaeologists have been able to trace the movement of this people across the Pacific.

One theory suggests that the Lapita people began to make their way eastward from eastern Indonesia or the Philippines about 4,000 years ago and then spread farther eastward through New Guinea to the southwestern Pacific. It is thought that they may have been forced to keep moving as a result of pressure from incoming groups of rice-growers. As they moved, they gradually developed distinctive Polynesian characteristics, which included complex hierarchical social, political, and religious systems.

The last region of the Pacific to be settled by Polynesians was New Zealand. Colonists probably arrived there by canoe from the Hawaiian islands some time around AD 1,000, although many scholars now favor a date closer to AD 750.

# LANGUAGES AND WRITING

As with many other questions about human evolution, there is still no consensus about the origin of speech and language. A number of scholars have suggested that art and language must be closely intertwined because they both require the ability to understand abstract ideas and symbolic concepts and to share these understandings with others as part of a cultural system. According to this theory, fully fledged languages would not have existed before the appearance of art—which first emerged about 40,000 years ago. If this argument is correct, archaic *Homo sapiens* such as the Neanderthals, who coexisted for some time with *Homo sapiens sapiens* and also created primitive art, would have possessed some form of language. Certainly, no one doubts that the Neanderthals were able to communicate with each other, although changes to the brain and facial structure would have meant the linguistic ability of *Homo sapiens sapiens* was markedly superior.

The complexity of human language and speech is dependent on a number of neural and anatomical mechanisms found only in *Homo sapiens sapiens*. These include a vocal tract that permits a wide range of speech sounds, areas of the brain that control and interpret these sounds, and an efficient memory that can use past experiences as a guide to the future. Although scientists believe that earlier hominid species were able to communicate both vocally and by gestures (just as animals do), their use of words, concepts, and sentence construction (syntax) would have been limited. Even chimpanzees can be taught to use words when placed in a human-like environment, yet they never progress beyond the vocabulary or grammatical ability of an average three-year-old child.

Humans alone are able to talk to each other, rather than just transmit words.

Although fully fledged linguistic ability would have been found only among *Homo sapiens sapiens*, it is still possible that language of some sort existed among the first anatomically modern humans in East Africa as early as 130,000 years ago. Some scientists even argue that *Homo habilis* may have been able to communicate vocally, albeit in a much simpler fashion. In other words, early humans may have had speech, but not a complete language.

Further evidence that early hominids were able to communicate verbally has recently emerged from what may at first seem an unlikely source: scientific research into the evolution of dogs. Studies in molecular biology suggest that wolves evolved into domestic animals more than 130,000 years ago, and wolf bones have even been found with 400,000-year-old hominid bones. These facts suggest that the association between humans and canines goes back a very long time. Some scientists now think that the domestication of canines had a profound effect on human evolution. The close association with dogs would have made it less crucial for early hominids to have a keen sense of smell that would alert them to other hominids or animal predators. In turn, this would have allowed the development of the facial and cranial modifications necessary for speech.

## Languages of the world

Thousands of languages are spoken in the world today. Populations that share similar cultures and live only a short distance apart may still speak languages that are quite distinct and not readily understood by neighboring populations.

For example, the inhabitants of New Guinea and adjacent islands speak approximately 1,000 different languages, or about one-fifth of the world's total.

At the same time, similarities exist between languages used in different parts of the world, which suggests that they developed from a common source. Scholars group such languages in families on the basis of similarities in vocabulary, sound systems, and grammar. English, for example, is part of the Indo-European family, which includes languages of antiquity, such as Sanskrit and classical Greek, as well as contemporary languages in both Asia and Europe, such as Hindi and Russian. Other geographically dispersed language families are Malayo-Polynesian (also known

| The world's major languages | |
|---|---|
| **Language** | **Speakers (millions)** |
| **Mandarin (Chinese)** | 873 |
| **Spanish** | 322 |
| **English** | 309 |
| **Arabic** | 206 |
| **Hindi** | 181 |
| **Portuguese** | 177.5 |
| **Bengali** | 171 |
| **Russian** | 145 |
| **Japanese** | 122 |
| **German** | 95.4 |
| **Wu (Chinese)** | 77.2 |
| **Javanese** | 75.5 |

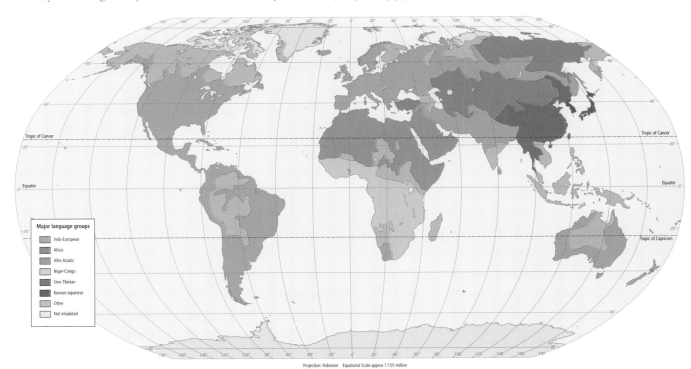

Major language groups
- Indo-European
- Altaic
- Afro-Asiatic
- Niger-Congo
- Sino-Tibetan
- Korean-Japanese
- Other
- Not inhabited

Projection: Robinson   Equatorial Scale approx 1:155 million

*As a result of geographical isolation, the Papuan tribes that gather at traditional sing-sing ceremonies (left) may speak many different languages. Egyptian hieroglyphs (bottom) are a form of pictorial writing, whereas the Latin script on this tablet from the Coliseum (below) illustrates alphabetic writing.*

as Austronesian), which includes Hawaiian, Javanese, and the languages of Madagascar, and Uralic, which includes Finnish, Hungarian, and the Samoyed language of Northern Siberia.

The first languages were disseminated in a number of ways. The most obvious was migration. As they spread out across the globe, early peoples carried their languages into uninhabited territory. Languages would also have spread as a result of contact between different peoples. For example, the invention and adoption of food production would have encouraged agricultural peoples to migrate into territory occupied by hunter–gatherers, who may then have adopted both the cultivation techniques and language of the immigrants.

A third form of language dissemination involves the replacement of an existing language by one spoken by a dominant group. The development of complex societies allowed incoming minorities with some form of centralized organization to dominate larger populations, who, in many cases, subsequently adopted the language of the elite. For example, the adoption of the Chinese language family in southern China in historical times occurred as a result of the military expansion of the Chinese empire.

### The origins of writing

Writing is thought to have arisen around 5,000 to 6,000 years ago in Sumeria (southern Mesopotamia), and to have appeared shortly afterward in widely separate parts of the world, including Egypt (3000 BC), the Indus Valley (2500 BC), and China (2000 BC). Writing may have spread from Sumeria to the Indus and probably also to Egypt, but it was almost certainly independently invented in both China and, later, Mesoamerica, where it first appeared in the third century AD. Writing was unknown elsewhere in the Americas, even in the highly developed Inca civilization of the central Andes which flourished in the fifteenth century.

Scholars usually distinguish three broad kinds of writing systems, although in practice some

systems combine elements of more than one kind. They are known as logographic, syllabic, and alphabetic writing.

In logographic writing, separate symbols are used to represent single words. This can complicate the representation of even simple statements. Because most of the symbols in logographic writing have, or originally had, a pictorial basis, it is believed that this is the earliest form of writing. Examples of logographic writing include early Sumerian cuneiform, Egyptian hieroglyphs, and modern Chinese characters.

In syllabic writing, symbols represent syllables. Examples of this type include later Sumerian cuneiform and the remarkable Cherokee syllabary developed by a Native American called Sequoyah in Arkansas in the early nineteenth century.

The third, and now most common, form of writing is alphabetic, in which symbols represent units of sound, or phonemes. Widespread alphabetic systems include Arabic, Roman (which is

used for English and most other European languages), and Cyrillic (used for Russian and some other Slavic languages).

It has been suggested that these three types of writing reflect an evolutionary progression, from logographic to alphabetic; however, most scholars now regard this view as too simplistic. For instance, in a number of writing systems, logographic elements have been adopted, discarded, and then reintroduced.

The development of writing is closely associated with the rise of hierarchical societies. Literacy contributed to the formation of more complex state structures and bureaucratic institutions. In its early stages, it was often closely linked to religious activities and authorities. In Sumeria, for instance, the recording of economic transactions was controlled by religious officialdom. Writing also arose as a religious practice in Mesoamerica, remaining the preserve of the elite until the Spanish conquest in the sixteenth century.

# THE RISE OF AGRICULTURE

Humanity's transition from a mobile life of hunting and gathering to a sedentary farming lifestyle in settled communities was not a sudden "revolution". It took place by degrees, with the dependence on cultivation increasing slowly as selective breeding modified wild plant species. Nevertheless, in terms of the prehistory of modern humans (100,000 years or so), the emergence of full-scale agriculture, which includes the development of both plant cultivation and animal husbandry, was relatively rapid.

It is probable that the cultivation of plants developed independently in a number of different regions, including the Fertile Crescent (a region stretching from present-day central Turkey southeastward through Iraq to the Persian Gulf), China, Mesoamerica (roughly

## Foods and their origins

Most agricultural products were native to one part of the world and then spread gradually to other regions. The following list shows the origins of selected foods.

| | |
|---|---|
| wheat | Fertile Crescent |
| potatoes | Central Andes |
| rice | China |
| maize | Mesoamerica |
| sugar | New Guinea |
| coffee | Ethiopia |
| tea | China |
| apples | Western Europe |
| oranges | Southeast Asia |
| sheep | Fertile Crescent |
| turkey | Mexico |

present-day Mexico and Guatemala), and the Central Andes. Some scholars suggest that food production also originated in other centers such as New Guinea and West Africa.

Plant cultivation first occurred in the Fertile Crescent, where evidence for the domestication of grains such as wheat and barley, and other foods such as pulses and olives, begins to make an appearance in the archaeological record around 11,000 years ago. Flax was also cultivated as a source of fiber for making cloth. Although much of this area was then, as it is now, rocky and rather arid, the fertility of the river floodplains probably encouraged an increasing reliance on cultivation. In the region between the Tigris and Euphrates rivers in present-day Iraq, the development of canal-based irrigation allowed farming centers to flourish. From there, agricultural methods spread throughout the Mediterranean, across the Balkans, and along the Danube River into central Europe. By 7,000 years ago, farming was also firmly established in Egypt's Nile Valley.

Recent archaeological finds have indicated that plant cultivation may have begun in Asia not long after it began in the Fertile Crescent. For example, it is possible that rice was cultivated along the middle Yangtze of central China as early as 9,500 years ago. In northern China, there is evidence that millet and rapeseed were grown around the same time. Farming practices spread along the fertile floodplains of Chinese rivers, where many early sites have been found. At about the same time, local people also began to domesticate animals, including pigs, cattle, sheep, dogs, and chickens.

Food production may have arisen independently in at least two parts of the Americas. One of these

is the Peruvian Andes, where beans were cultivated perhaps as early as 7,000 years ago. At around the same time, people in Mesoamerica also started to grow beans, together with squash and pumpkins. Maize, which became the most important staple, may not have been cultivated until more than a thousand years later. The early archaeological record is sparse in South America, but it appears that plants such as manioc, amaranths, peanuts, potatoes, cotton, and chili peppers were slowly domesticated in different parts of the continent.

Agriculture may have begun earlier in New Guinea. In the island's central highlands, archaeologists have discovered evidence of irrigation ditches in areas of swamp which date from around 9,000 years ago. They remain uncertain about the types of crops grown there, although taro and other native noncereal plants are likely candidates.

### The domestication of animals

Although the dog was domesticated somewhat earlier, the process of rearing animals for food—and later for clothing and as draft and pack animals—began at around the same time as plant cultivation. Many animals hunted by humans were unsuitable for breeding as a result of such factors as their diet, growth rate, ability to breed in captivity, or behavioral disposition. Domestication therefore had to proceed by trial and error, and gradually it modified many species.

Some animals, such as the wild pig and the auroch (a large, long-horned wild ox), were distributed over a wide area of Europe and Asia, and were probably domesticated independently in a number of places. Others, such as goats and sheep,

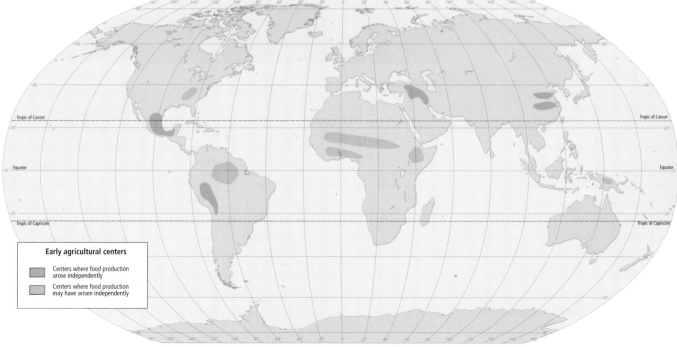

**Early agricultural centers**

Centers where food production arose independently

Centers where food production may have arisen independently

Projection: Robinson   Equatorial Scale approx 1:155 million

Food production began independently in China when rice was cultivated about 9,000 years ago in the valley of the Yangtze River. From there, rice cultivation spread throughout Southeast Asia, reaching Indonesia (left) about 4,000 years ago. The shift from hunting-gathering to agriculture resulted in the development of new technologies, including animal-driven pulley systems like the one on this well in Egypt (below).

were confined largely to the Middle East and western Asia, and were later introduced into Europe. The people of the Andes domesticated llamas for use as pack animals and guinea pigs for food. The earliest evidence for the domestication of cats has been found in Greece. Cats were subsequently domesticated in many areas, usually to protect grain stores from rodents.

## Why choose agriculture?

Not all communities switched to agriculture as soon as they came into contact with it. Many early peoples remained dependent on food collecting and hunting, and hunter-gatherer societies continue to exist to this day. These communities may modify their environment—for example, by burning vegetation to encourage growth that attracts game—and some also undertake minimal husbanding of plant resources, such as replanting rootstock cuttings and protecting fruit-bearing trees. But despite this and the fact that they may have often come into contact with people practicing agriculture, they have chosen not to switch to a sedentary lifestyle based on farming.

The reason for this is that subsisting as a hunter-gatherer usually requires less work than subsisting as a farmer. As long as population densities remain low, a food-collecting lifestyle can be more attractive and efficient, and provide a more balanced and diverse diet. In fact, scientists find it hard to explain why certain populations ever became totally dependent on farming. However, once the switch had been made, the demographic and social consequences of an agricultural lifestyle would have made it difficult to reverse the trend.

## The consequences of agriculture

Agriculture transformed both human societies and landscapes. The need to make cultivation more efficient encouraged rapid technological innova-

tions. The use of clay, which was already known in pre-agricultural times, became widespread and people began to make large receptacles for food and water. In turn, these receptacles transformed diets, as grains and pulses could be soaked and boiled, making them easier to eat and digest. Other innovations that emerged in agricultural societies were metalworking, the wheel (which improved the making of pots and stimulated progress in transport), and the use of sails on boats. Small copper objects have been found at early agricultural sites in the Middle East, but extensive metalworking and purification techniques were not developed until a few thousand years later.

Early agricultural societies were based on small village communities. As the range of domesticated plants and animals grew, the village economies became increasingly diverse and food production techniques improved. These developments enabled communities to create surpluses which could be used to support full-time craftspeople. Specialization led to internal barter and to trade with other communities. Items and commodities that were found or produced in only certain localities were traded over considerable distances. Social divisions also increased and, in many areas, complex hierarchies, headed by hereditary leaders, came into existence. In some societies, elite classes emerged who were able to devote their time to religious, cultural, and military pursuits while living off the surplus produced by subordinate groups.

## Agriculture and demographics

Some scholars believe that population growth encouraged the adoption of agriculture, while others think that it was agriculture that triggered an increase in population. Although there is no firm demographic evidence to decide the question, archaeological research suggests that the number and size of settlements usually increased following the appearance of food production in a region.

Despite the attractions of new technologies, many communities, including the San of the Kalahari Desert in southwestern Africa, rejected agriculture and continue to follow a hunting-gathering lifestyle to this day (above right).

The rapid expansion of agriculture affected the environment, in some cases quite catastrophically. For example, archaeologists have found that the barren landscape of modern Greece is the result of more than 5,000 years of farming, during which deforestation and land clearance led to the loss of topsoil and severe soil erosion.

# EMERGING CIVILIZATIONS

The first civilizations arose on the fertile alluvial basins of major rivers such as the Tigris-Euphrates in Iraq, the Nile in Egypt, the Indus in Pakistan, and the Yellow (Huang Ho) in China. These regions shared many common features, including arid environments that made agricultural communities dependent on irrigation, and readily available supplies of raw materials such as stone, metal, and wood. The Tigris-Euphrates, Nile, and Indus regions were probably linked by trade well before the appearance of the early cities, but Chinese civilization developed in relative isolation.

## The first urban societies

Cities emerged in all four regions during the third millennium BC as villages and towns slowly grew into cities with large public buildings and developed specialized and well-organized production and trade, forms of writing, hierarchical social structures, and centralized political systems. This process of evolution varied, although the cultural attributes of emerging cities were similar.

In most cases, cities arose following the emergence of a social elite. As a class or family became dominant, it usually sought to create a power base in one region. This power base attracted immigrants and businesses, resulting in the rapid growth of the urban community. Scholars have suggested various reasons for the emergence of social elites. Some propose that the

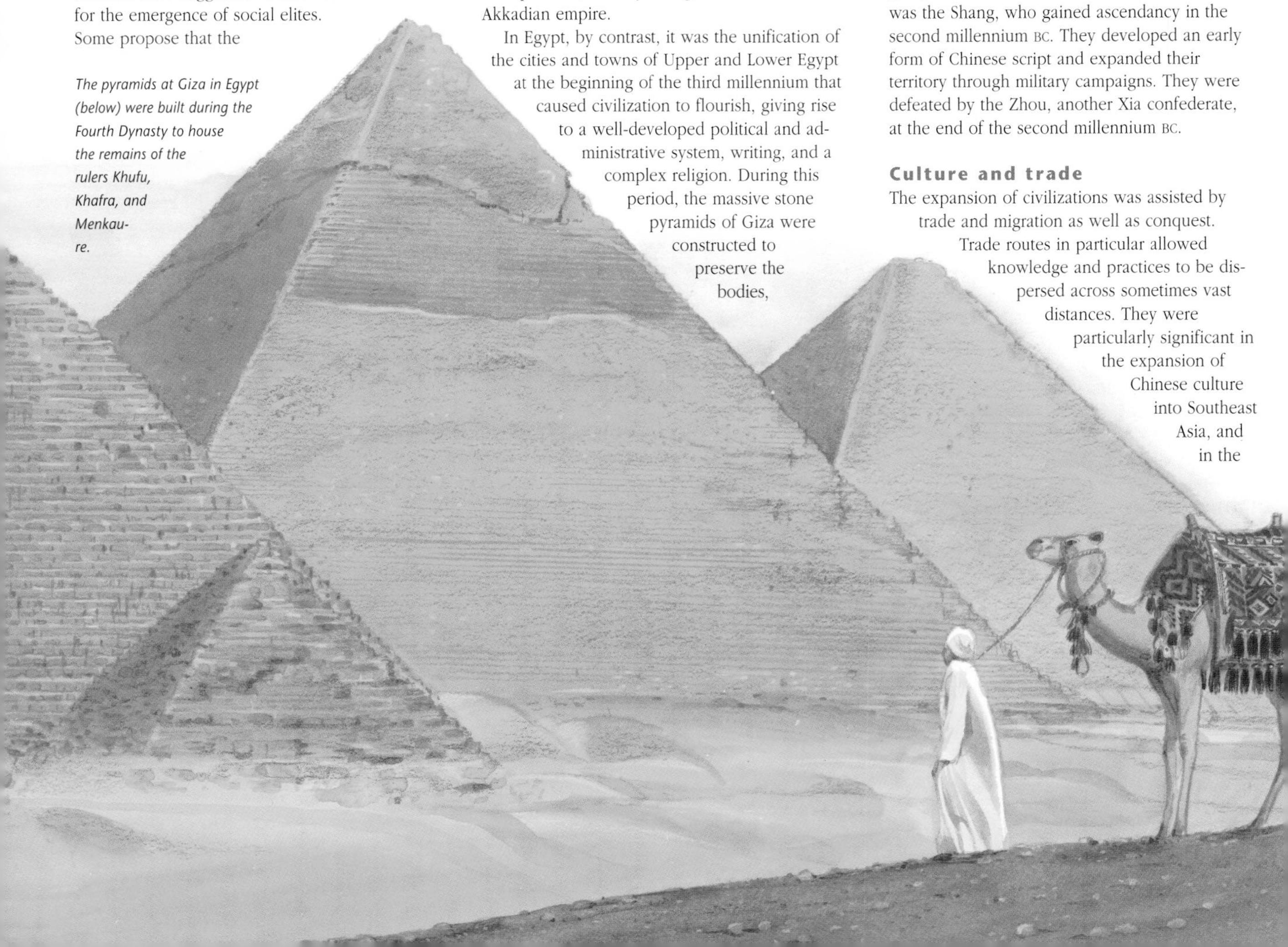

*The pyramids at Giza in Egypt (below) were built during the Fourth Dynasty to house the remains of the rulers Khufu, Khafra, and Menkaure.*

construction and maintenance of the large-scale irrigation works needed to support a growing population would have required considerable organization and encouraged the development of a managerial class. Others emphasize the role of specialized production and trade in creating a dominant commercial class. Another explanation is the growing influence of warfare: as settlements were overrun by invading peoples, their inhabitants were often forced to become the subjects of their conquerors. It was probably a combination of all these factors that led to the development of the first "upper classes" and the first sophisticated urban societies.

## Cradles of civilization

In the region between the Tigris and Euphrates rivers known as Mesopotamia, farming gradually became more productive, canals were built, large temple platforms (called ziggurats) were erected, and the cuneiform script was simplified and standardized. Crafts, such as pottery and metalwork, became more specialized and production more organized, leading to greater social divisions in society. The city-states had their own monarchs, and were often heavily fortified. Their ascendancy came to an end, however, around 2350 BC, when Sargon, a military ruler from Agade in central Mesopotamia, forcibly amalgamated them into the Akkadian empire.

In Egypt, by contrast, it was the unification of the cities and towns of Upper and Lower Egypt at the beginning of the third millennium that caused civilization to flourish, giving rise to a well-developed political and administrative system, writing, and a complex religion. During this period, the massive stone pyramids of Giza were constructed to preserve the bodies,

knowledge, and wealth of the Egyptian kings in the afterlife. The pyramids also symbolized the structure of Egyptian society, with the god-king at the apex, officials in the middle levels, and the mass of the population at the bottom.

The emergence of the Indus civilization was marked by the appearance of distinctive artistic styles in pottery, copper, and bronze (a copper-tin alloy). These objects were traded with nomadic pastoral peoples who, in turn, transported the merchandise into central Asia and along the coast of the Arabian Sea. Around 2400 BC, the different cultural traditions of the Indus merged into one, called Harappa by archaeologists after the first city to be excavated in this region. Harappa culture had writing, a form of centralized control for administration and commerce, and large buildings made out of baked brick. In contrast to other early civilizations, however, Harappan society does not seem to have included a priest-king class, nor did its spread depend on military conquest.

In China, it is likely that villages merged to form states in several areas, but legend and archaeological evidence locate the first civilization, that of the Xia, in the middle and lower valleys of the Yellow River, from about the end of the third millennium BC. Texts written much later suggest that the Xia united a number of groups in a loose confederation. One of these was the Shang, who gained ascendancy in the second millennium BC. They developed an early form of Chinese script and expanded their territory through military campaigns. They were defeated by the Zhou, another Xia confederate, at the end of the second millennium BC.

## Culture and trade

The expansion of civilizations was assisted by trade and migration as well as conquest. Trade routes in particular allowed knowledge and practices to be dispersed across sometimes vast distances. They were particularly significant in the expansion of Chinese culture into Southeast Asia, and in the

These bas-reliefs (left), which date from about 500 BC, decorate the walls of the ancient Mesopotamian city of Persepolis. Greek city-states such as Athens (bottom) emerged around 750 BC. At that time, Teotihuacán (below) in Mesoamerica was one of the largest cities in the world.

spread of Egyptian and Middle Eastern traditions as far as North Africa, southern Asia, and Europe.

The first major European civilization emerged in Crete at the end of the third millennium BC. The Minoans, whose powerful navy controlled the Aegean Sea for much of the second millennium BC, constructed large cities centered on elaborate palaces including those at Knossos, Malia, and Phaistos. Later, urban societies also sprang up on the Greek mainland, the most notable being the Mycenean civilization, which came to prominence during the late second millennium BC. Classical Greek civilization emerged during the first millennium BC in a number of self-governing cities such as Athens and Sparta. These urban societies were distinguished by the formal constitutions that directed their political life and by the increasing power held by the male citizenry at the expense of a centralized leadership.

Civilizations also developed independently, but much later, among the agricultural communities of Mesoamerica and the central Andes. Mesoamerican civilizations emerged during the first millennium BC. The most important was that of the Maya, who developed a form of writing around AD 300. The Maya maintained commercial ties to city-states developing elsewhere in the region. One of these, Teotihuacán, in central Mexico, was an important trade center with a population that peaked at more than 100,000 around AD 600. During the same period, several interrelated civilizations existed in the central Andes, with territories that are now in present-day Peru and Bolivia. These societies created monumental buildings and elaborate crafts, but left no evidence of any written languages.

## The meaning of "civilization"

In eighteenth-century Europe, "civilization" meant cultural refinement—the opposite of barbarism. Nineteenth-century social philosophers found this meaning too restrictive, so they used the term in the plural sense to refer to large-scale societies. This usage is followed by present-day sociologists and anthropologists.

Human societies can be classified in terms of their size and complexity. Small-scale or tribal societies comprise small bands loosely coordinated by kinship relations. These groups often live together at permanent settlements, although some may be nomadic. Medium-sized communities are usually made up of clusters of villages or small towns united under some form of confederation or chiefdom. In large-scale societies, at least some of the inhabitants live in large urban societies which are linked by a network of social, economic, and cultural ties, and normally unified under a centralized political organization.

Early Mesopotamian artworks such as this ivory carving often include portraits of members of the ruling elite.

# THE IMPACT OF CIVILIZATION

The main impetus for rapid progress over the past few thousand years was the development of large-scale urban societies. Their benefits in enriching human experience through technological innovation, scientific knowledge, and diversity in social life appear obvious. Certain consequences of civilization were less benign, however. These include the increasing destructiveness of warfare, the spread of disease, and the life-long bondage imposed on certain classes of people.

## Innovation and adaptation

Many thousands of years elapsed between the development of specialized stone and bone tool assemblages and the beginnings of food production. After the adoption of agriculture and a sedentary lifestyle, however, the widespread diffusion of the latest innovations occurred remarkably rapidly. This was partly due to the obvious usefulness of the technology. Many inventions were developed in one location and then rapidly dispersed because of their immediate utility. The wheel, for example, appears to have been invented near the Black Sea around 3400 BC, and within a few hundred years, it was being used throughout Europe and Asia.

Another reason for the exponential growth of technology was that new inventions were rapidly adapted to diverse local needs. For example, shortly after the emergence of the wheel, innovations based on this technology—such as pulleys, water wheels, and windmills—appeared and then spread quickly along ever-expanding trade routes.

Some innovations, however, did not travel as extensively as may be expected. For example, the wheel was probably also invented independently in Mesoamerica, where it was used in children's toys, but it was never adopted for transportation in this region due to the lack of draft animals. Nor did the wheel spread from Mesoamerica to South America, even though the people of the Andes had the Americas' only beast of burden— the llama—and despite the fact that technologies such as metallurgy had already spread northward from the Andes to Mesoamerica.

## Technology and warfare

New technologies led to the expansion of production and, consequently, an increase in the size of urban populations. As cities grew in size, conflict over land with neighboring agricultural and pastoral peoples often led to warfare. In turn, this stimulated the manufacture of weaponry.

Early weapons were made of bronze, but by the beginning of the first millennium BC, iron weapons were being widely produced in the Fertile Crescent, and smelting techniques, which produced an early form of steel, were already well understood there. By 500 BC, iron tools and weapons were widespread throughout Europe and Asia. However, ironworking did not appear in the Americas until after the Spanish conquests of the sixteenth century. The devastating effectiveness of steel weaponry was demonstrated by the Spanish conquest of the Incas. In 1532, the conquistador Pizzaro, with an army of only 168 soldiers, was able to defeat the Inca army of more than 80,000 soldiers and capture their emperor Atahualpa.

Monuments to royalty, such as the massive temple of Abu Simbel in Egypt (above) built during the reign of Ramses II (1279–1213 BC), reflect both the development of technology and the emergence of complex social hierarchies.

The Spanish soldiers had chain mail, helmets, steel swords, lances, daggers, and horses, whereas the Inca army was protected by quilted padding, armed with blunt clubs, and traveled on foot.

## Science and disease

Although many advances in the domestication of plants and animals and in technology were the result of accidental discoveries or trial and error, written records indicate that early civilizations were making careful observations of natural phenomena. For example, the Maya developed a calendar based on the solar year and lunar month, and could predict eclipses—a feat that required advanced mathematical skills. The Egyptians acquired considerable medical knowledge and surgical skills. Among the sophisticated techniques they developed was the practice of trepanation. This involved the cutting of bone in the skull to relieve pressure on the brain resulting from a skull fracture, or to treat headaches or epilepsy.

A sedentary lifestyle enabled ailing individuals to receive better care than

*Invented in western Asia, the wheel was rapidly adapted to create devices such as the water wheel (below). As a result of their preference for cooler climates, llamas (left) never spread northward to Mesoamerica. Sophisticated soceieties such as that of the Maya (bottom) thus remained without pack animals.*

they would receive if they remained nomadic. However, large concentrations of people living in close proximity to domestic animals and (initially, at least) dependent on a relatively limited range of foods created the perfect environment for the spread of disease. When human populations are small and move frequently, the opportunities for parasitic infections to spread are limited. Urban lifestyles, in contrast, with their permanent housing and large refuse dumps, attract disease-carrying vermin and insects, and allow parasites to spread more quickly. Land clearance, irrigation, and the use of natural fertilizers would also have encouraged certain diseases in sedentary communities, particularly where diets were deficient and the population less resilient. Even more significant was the domestication of animals. Today, people associate animals with diseases such as rabies, anthrax, and parasitic worms, but domestic animals were also the original source of infections that are now commonly transmitted by humans, such as smallpox, measles, and influenza.

The spread of disease was encouraged by trade, migration, and conquest. For example, bubonic plague is thought to have been restricted to Asia until it was spread to other parts of the world by traders. When it reached Europe in the mid-fourteenth century, it wiped out one quarter of the population. Diseases carried by conquering armies were often more destructive than their military campaigns. For example, in 1520, the Spaniards under Cortés inadvertently brought smallpox to the Aztecs, causing a massive epidemic that killed more than half the population and led to the demise of the empire.

*As civilizations grew and technology spread, warfare, as depicted in this bas-relief from Nineveh in Assyria, became more sophisticated and more commonplace.*

## Social hierarchies

The increasing division of labor and the steady enhancement of specialized skills in urban communities led to the development of ever-more sophisticated social hierarchies. People directly involved in food production—the commoners— were often obliged to provide tribute payments to a centralized authority. This did not necessarily mean that commoners were physically separated from the elite—in many early cities, they lived in close proximity to each other and even shared in decision-making. But as urban populations increased and relationships became more complex, so the social distinctions became more marked.

In China, for instance, the Shang, and later the Zhou, administered a feudal system of vassal states. Members of the royal clan, and others who assisted the king, were granted fiefdoms over parts of the kingdom. Below these nobles and loyal administrators were the farmers from whose ranks the soldiers were recruited. At the lowest end of the social scale were the slaves, who were usually nomadic pastoralists captured by the ruling elite. This pattern of enslaving captives was common in these evolving nation-states, probably because mass production and large-scale public works provided many uses for slaves in menial occupations.

## Domestic horses

Today's domestic horses are descended from wild species native to southern Russia. Horses were first domesticated there around 4000 BC— much later than most other domestic animals— and before long had become the principal means of transportation throughout much of Asia and Europe. Horses transformed warfare, providing formidable military advantages when yoked to battle chariots or ridden. At the same time, however, they transmitted several diseases to humans, including tetanus and the common cold.

*Mongolian horses are the only surviving relatives of the species from which all domestic horses are descended.*

# FROM CITY-STATES TO EMPIRES

There is no doubt that warfare was a part of human experience long before historical records were kept—even the small-scale societies of Melanesia that existed at the time of the first European contact were involved in frequent and violent tribal conflicts. However, the scale, range, and destructiveness of war increased significantly with the development of the first states. High population density, advances in transport and weapons technology, centralized decision-making, and a new fervor among troops willing to die for a powerful leader allowed extensive resources to be mobilized for warfare. This in turn meant that military engagements could take place much farther from home. Whereas war had previously involved only the annexation of adjacent territories from enemies who had either been chased away, killed, or enslaved, now they could lead to the amalgamation of entire societies into larger political units. Furthermore, the subjugated peoples could be forced to pay tribute, thereby increasing the ruler's resources for further campaigns. In this way, empires were born.

The rise of empires greatly enhanced the diffusion of knowledge, ideas, technology, languages, and cultural traditions. It also expanded trade links and imposed administrative and political unity on previously dispersed communities, laying the foundations for future nation-states.

There are three broad reasons why rulers of small city-states and medium-sized kingdoms ventured into empire-building. One was to create alliances that would provide protection against an external threat—the formation of the Chinese Empire is a good example of this. Another reason was to subdue a persistent enemy—this is why Alexander the Great began his conquests. The third was to acquire control over desired commodities, trade routes, and other resources—Roman expansion can be explained in this way. All three reasons influenced most expansionist ambitions, but one tended to be more dominant than the others in the building of individual empires.

## The threat from the north

By the third century BC, the Zhou kingdom of northeastern China was breaking up, having been weakened by years of attacks perpetrated by warring tribal peoples to the north and northwest. Following the collapse of the kingdom, wars broke out between rival states and various alliances were formed and severed. Eventually, one of the Zhou vassal states, the Qin (221–206), gained ascendancy and brought the other states under their control. They then set about uniting the states into a single Chinese empire. The principle objective of this policy was to secure Qin territory against the foreign invaders that had plagued the Zhou. To ensure the protection of the empire, the Qin began to construct an enormous physical barrier to invasion by linking defensive structures originally built during the Zhou period. The Great Wall, as this barrier came to be known, would eventually stretch 3,000 km (1,860 miles) across northern China. The Qin also built an extensive network of highways and canals to improve communications throughout their empire.

Following the death of the first emperor, the Qin Empire was taken over by the Han in 206 BC. The Han expanded their empire further south beyond the floodplains of the Yellow (Huang Ho) and Yangtze rivers, and also defeated tribes to the west. This helped silk merchants to create a new trade route through central Asia which eventually extended all the way to Europe.

## Alexander the Great

The rise of the Persian Empire in the sixth century BC posed a significant threat to Greek city-states such as Athens and Sparta. They responded by forming strategic alliances, which they managed to maintain long enough to defeat the Persians during the following century. However, subsequent disputes between the cities allowed Philip II of Macedon to take advantage of their disunity and unite Greece with Macedonia in 338 BC. In the following year, Philip declared war on Persia to revenge the Persian devastation of Greece, but before the war could begin he was assassinated.

Philip was succeeded by his son, Alexander, who realized his father's plans to crush Greece's formidable enemy. He successfully engaged the Persian army in Turkey and the eastern Mediterranean, moved westward to Egypt where he founded the city of Alexandria, and finally crushed the Persians in a decisive battle at Gaugamela in Mesopotamia in 331 BC. His conquests continued to the Indus River before he turned back, only to die suddenly at the age of 33 in Mesopotamia in 323 BC. Alexander's vast empire was divided up between his generals, and, without a strong leader, it soon disintegrated, although the kingdoms of Egypt, Persia, and Macedonia persisted.

Despite his short reign, Alexander left a long-lasting legacy. His decision to take scholars and scientists on his campaigns ensured that Greek learning, language, and cultural traditions were disseminated widely. He founded a number of Hellenic cities with Greeks and Macedonians, the most notable being Alexandria, which became a renowned center of learning.

Although the Greek city-states had previously established trade centers throughout the northern Mediterranean, they had largely left the southern shore to the Phoenicians. Alexander's conquests extended Hellenistic influence into North Africa and the Middle East. In this way, Alexander imposed a cultural unity on the Mediterranean region which stimulated trade and learning and which later played a significant part in the advancement of the Roman Empire.

## The Roman Empire

In the seventh century BC, Rome was one of several small towns in the Tiber Valley that were situated on a strategically important road leading to saltworks at the mouth of the Tiber River. During the following two centuries, Rome gained control of neighboring territories, including the valuable saltworks, and became a potent force in local politics and commerce. Like other Mediterranean cities in that era, Rome was strongly influenced by Greek culture, but it never came under Greek control.

In the fifth century BC, Rome became a republic ruled by a Senate formed by an aristocratic clique. From that time, Rome gradually expanded its territory to encompass the whole of the Italic peninsula—while Alexander was conquering Persia, Rome was winning decisive battles for the control of southern Italy.

Success in southern Italy encouraged the Romans to seize Sicily, which was then under the

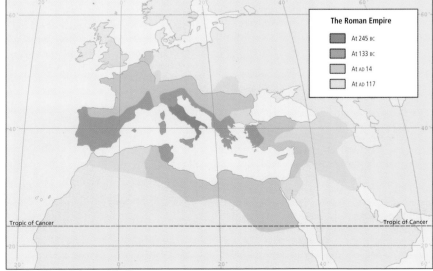

The Roman Empire

At 245 BC

At 133 BC

At AD 14

At AD 117

Tropic of Cancer

Tropic of Cancer

Projection: Robinson   Scale approx 1:40 million

*This map (left) shows the gradual expansion of the Roman Empire, which reached its greatest extent during the reign of Trajan (AD 98–117). Construction of the Great Wall of China (right) began during the Qin Empire (221– 206 BC). Extensive sections of the wall were rebuilt during the 15th and 16th centuries.*

influence of the North African city of Carthage. Over the next 100 years, the Romans fought three major wars—known as the Punic Wars—against Carthage to gain control of the western Mediterranean. By the end of the Third Punic War (146 BC), Carthage had been completely destroyed and Rome had emerged as by far the strongest force in the region. The empire subsequently extended eastward to Greece and the Middle East, where it benefited greatly from Greek advances in art, learning, and technology. Later still, the empire expanded to include large areas of present-day France, Germany, and England, spreading Hellenic culture and Roman political and social institutions across most of Europe.

*During the first century bc, the Roman Empire expanded rapidly. Under Pompey, Roman armies seized parts of the Middle East, including Syria (above) in 64 BC in the west, Julius Caesar (above right) led the conquest of Gaul in 58–50 BC. Both generals subsequently laid claim to the title of emperor. Victory in a short civil war allowed Caesar to begin his reign in 48 BC.*

# RELIGIONS OF THE WORLD

Religions are a feature of almost all of the world's cultures. They have been the inspiration for much of the world's great art, music, architecture, and literature, but also the source of longstanding disputes and local, regional, and international conflicts.

The tenets and forms of religious belief vary widely. While most religions involve the worship of a deity or deities, supreme beings play only a minor role in some faiths such as Theravada Buddhism. Nor do all religions have practices, core doctrines, and moral codes that are common to every follower. For example, while Hinduism retains a self-identity developed historically through confrontation with other religious traditions such as Buddhism, Islam, and Christianity, it remains extremely diverse internally.

The great majority of the world's religions evolved among particular peoples who had no interest in attracting converts. Few tribal peoples, for instance, would attempt to persuade their neighbors to adopt their religious beliefs and practices. Similarly, some prominent religions such as Hinduism and Judaism make no effort to seek converts. However, religion is frequently the cause of great social conflict, particularly where two or more proselytizing religions are in competition. Even within religions that have a core doctrine, comparatively minor differences of faith or practice can cause bitter divisions—past tensions between Christian denominations are a good example of this. Frequently, religious conflicts are aggravated by historical factors and by the extent to which religious divisions are overlaid by other divisions, such as language, ethnicity, and class.

## World religions

One-third of the world's population identify themselves as Christians, with about half belonging to the Roman Catholic Church. The next largest religious group is Islam, which includes more than one-fifth of the world's population. These two major faiths are monotheistic—that is, they are based on the belief that there is only one God—and both developed out of Judaism. Hinduism, a non-proselytizing religion followed by almost 13 percent of the world's population, is the third largest faith. Buddhism, which is the third largest proselytizing religion, has approximately 325 million adherents.

Judaism was originally the tribal religion of a people who traced themselves back to Abraham. Abraham is said to have migrated with his clan from the city of Ur in Mesopotamia to Canaan in the eastern Mediterranean. His descendants moved to Egypt, where they were later enslaved, and were

then led back to Canaan by Moses around 1200 BC. Although Judaism has a comparatively small number of contemporary adherents (around 14 million), it is significant both for its role in the development of Christianity and Islam and for its continuing influence on cultural and historical events.

Christianity originated as a movement within Judaism. Fundamental to its doctrine is the belief that Jesus Christ was the Messiah prophesied in the Old Testament. After Christ's crucifixion, Christian doctrines were disseminated throughout the Mediterranean by the apostles and by missionaries, the most prominent of whom was Saint Paul (also known as Saul of Tarsus). Christianity then spread throughout the Roman Empire, first among Jewish communities and then into the general population.

Ethnic religions 4.0%
Sikhs 0.4%
Judaism 0.3%
Christianity 33.0%
Islam 19.6%
Other 4.7%
Buddhism 6.0%
Chinese folk religions 6.2%
Hinduism 12.8%
No religion 13.0%

*This pie chart shows the percentages of the world's population belonging to the major religions. Despite their small number, the Jews (above right) have had a major influence on history, culture, and other religions.*

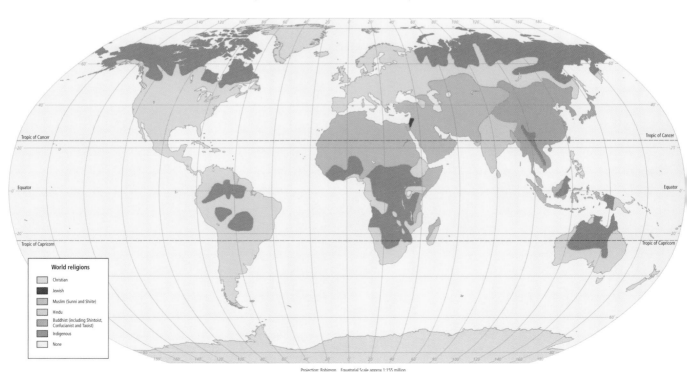

**World religions**
- Christian
- Jewish
- Muslim (Sunni and Shiite)
- Hindu
- Buddhist (including Shintoist, Confucianist and Taoist)
- Indigenous
- None

Projection: Robinson   Equatorial Scale approx 1:155 million

*Christianity spread rapidly through Europe after the fall of the Roman Empire; churches can be found all over Britain (left). Tibetan Buddhism (below) is based on a tradition called Tantric Buddhism which emerged in India in the seventh century AD. Islam spread to Southeast Asia along trade routes, reaching Malaysia (below left) in the fourteenth century.*

Early persecution of Christians by the Romans gave way to tolerance early in the fourth century AD when the emperor Constantine converted and Christianity became the official state religion. Christianity continued to spread after the fall of the empire in the fifth century, reaching most of Europe by the end of the first millennium. Later, particularly during the era of European expansion in the fifteenth and sixteenth centuries, missionary activity disseminated Christianity to other parts of the world. Over the centuries, theological disputes have resulted in major schisms, out of which have grown the Orthodox, Catholic, Protestant, and other traditions.

Islam was founded early in the seventh century AD by Muhammad, a merchant from the prosperous Arabian city of Mecca. Muhammad had contact with both Jewish and Christian communities, and he came to regard the Judaeo-Christian prophets, including Christ, as forerunners of Islam. After receiving revelations about the worship of one God (Allah), Muhammad began to preach against the polytheistic practices of his home city. Persecution then forced him and his followers to flee to Medina. This migration (Hegira), which took place in AD 622, marks the beginning of the Muslim calendar. By the time of his death in AD 632, Muhammad had become the political and spiritual leader of much of Arabia. After his death, Muslims expanded their territory beyond the Arabian peninsula. At its peak, the Arab Empire stretched from Spain and Morocco in the west to Afghanistan and central Asia in the east, but the Islamic religion was carried even farther into Asia and Africa by Muslim traders.

### Eastern deities

Hinduism has its roots in Vedism, the religion of the Indo-European peoples who inhabited northern India during the second millennium BC. The religion's sacred texts are the Vedas which explore humankind's place in the cosmos and describe the roles played by various gods in the functioning of the universe. During the first millennium AD, cults associated with two of these deities, Vishnu and Shiva, spread throughout the continent. Hinduism has a large and faithful following among the diverse peoples of the Indian subcontinent, but it has relatively few adherents elsewhere, except among the descendants of Indian emigrants. This is in part due to its non-proselytizing nature.

Like Christianity and Islam, Buddhism, the third major proselytizing religion, is also based on the religious enlightenment experienced by one man. However, it has much earlier origins. According to tradition, Siddhartha Gautama lived in northeastern India in the sixth century BC, and was reared in the royal household. In his adulthood, Siddhartha is said to have sought enlightenment, which he achieved through a night of meditation, thereby becoming the Buddha or Awakened One. For 45 years he traveled India as an itinerant teacher while formalizing his religious precepts. His teachings spread into southern Asia, where the first Buddhist tradition, the Theravada (meaning "doctrine of the elders"), still prevails in Sri Lanka, Myanmar, Cambodia, Laos, and Thailand. However, it retains few followers in India. Buddhism also spread to the east (Tibet, China, and Japan), where the second tradition, Mahayana (meaning "great vehicle") Buddhism, emerged in the second century BC. A more liberal tradition, Mahayana is said to express greater compassion and social concern than the more aloof Theravada Buddhism.

## What is religion?

Scholars have found it extremely difficult to come up with a definition that will allow a clear-cut distinction between religious and non-religious phenomena. In broad terms, religion covers the beliefs and associated practices that focus on the relationship between humans and the supernatural, represented by a god or gods. These beliefs and practices address the ultimate questions of human existence, providing a sense of meaning and purpose to life. Frequently, they also create a feeling of fellowship and community with others who share the same beliefs and practices.

Approached in these terms, religions or religious activity can be found in all, or nearly all, eras and places, although the emphasis placed on religion by particular communities may vary greatly. Scholars have sometimes been surprised to discover that certain tribal or peasant peoples, who might have been assumed to be preoccupied with religion, are in fact relatively indifferent to it.

Religious practices may also have their origins in the need to regulate or control communities. Religion may enforce "taboo" or unacceptable behavior in order to preserve a peaceful and sustainable society.

# TRADERS AND TRAVELERS

Humans moved from place to place either individually or in groups long before written records existed. The earliest records show they were impelled by a desire to occupy more fertile areas, by a desire for booty, by an urge to trade, by religious piety which took them on pilgrimages, by a thirst for knowledge, and sometimes by the fear of invasion.

Before the Christian era, Buddhism led monks from the East to travel to India to visit sites where Gautama had been. Nearly 2,000 years later, Ibn Battuta, an Islamic qadi (religious judge), after setting out in AD 1325 to go to Mecca, as all good Mohammedans sought to do, found that he could not rest until he had visited every Muslim state in Asia, Africa, and Europe. Although on his return to Fez, the sultan's court was incredulous at Battuta's stories, they were written down, and in such ways knowledge of the world was spread.

## The spread and decline of empires

The growth of empires fostered trade and treaties, both with neighbors and with more distant powers. The Han Empire in China, for example, traded with Phoenicians, Carthaginians, Syrians, and the Roman Empire in silks, iron, furs, glass, and other exotic goods. Merchants also brought back knowledge—in the first century AD, a Greek navigator wrote of the Indian Ocean, where Hindu traders competed with merchants from the Red Sea and Arabs dealing in wax and ivory, rhinoceros horns, tortoiseshell, and palm oil.

However, nomads were always pressing at the frontiers of such empires, seeking to loot and ransack. Loose confederations of "barbarians"—as the civilized empires considered them—hungry for plunder, breached the defences. The Roman

Empire bought their "barbarians" off for a time by settling some on the borders, as confederates, to keep out other tribes, but eventually pressures caused the empire's defences to tumble. In AD 410, Rome itself was overrun.

The influx of mixed Germanic tribes was precipitated by the driving force of the Huns, who, according to the Goths, were the offspring of witches and evil spirits. No one knows where they originated. From the Carpathian mountains, however, they moved into the Mediterranean region and, by AD 450, under Attila, were poised to crush and drive out the Goths. Then their alliances crumbled, and they disappeared from Europe as quickly as they had come.

Instead, waves of Ostrogoths, Visigoths, Franks, and Saxons arrived and settled in England, France, Spain, Italy, and parts of North Africa, mixing with the local inhabitants, quarrelling amongst themselves and moving on to settle in new areas.

## The Arab Empire

While Western Europe was fragmented and trade was declining, in the East, the Byzantine Empire remained the bulwark of Christianity against the rising Arab Empire. Mohammed's followers were spurred on by the idea of jihad, or holy war, which combined religion with military exploits. After taking Syria and Egypt, they swept along the North African coast, took the Maghrib, and crossed into Spain. They attacked Byzantium by sea and blockaded Constantinople between AD 673 and 678. In the eighth century, the caliphs of Damascus and Baghdad ruled an empire that stretched from Persia to Morocco.

The Arabs were also starting to dominate Africa by the eighth century. The peoples of the plateau

between the Niger and the Benin had mined and used gold and copper, and later iron, long before Christ. Exotic archaeological finds and the presence of Asian food plants clearly show that trade began early in these areas. Tribal organization became more sophisticated, in order to control and tax trade and the trade routes. By the eighth century, empires such as Ghana had emerged. The Arabs had been pushing their way down the east coast of Africa well before Mohammed. They visited trading posts such as Sofala and dealt with the inland kingdoms, exchanging exotic goods for gold. After AD 700, they began colonizing the coast, establishing settlements such as Mogadishu and Mombasa. They also moved south across the Sahara, and established Arabic kingdoms.

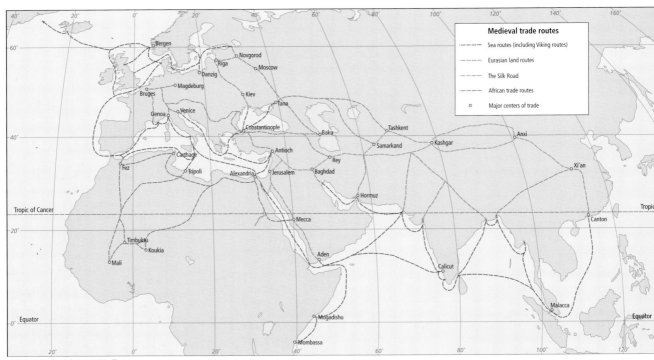

**Medieval trade routes**

- – – – Sea routes (including Viking routes)
- – – – Eurasian land routes
- – – – The Silk Road
- – – – African trade routes
- ○ Major centers of trade

Projection: Robinson   Scale approx 1:70 million

Viking graves in Denmark (far left) are a reminder of the early European territorial wars. Khiva (left) was a trading post on the trade route between East and West. Zanzibar (below), an island south of Mombasa, was for many years the center of the slave trade in Africa. Venice today (bottom) is not the major trading power it was in the thirteenth century.

The Arabs next pushed east across the Indian Ocean, carrying Islam to India and overwhelming the Hindu trading colonies of Sumatra, Java, and Borneo, and eventually acquiring a firm footing in Canton and other major Chinese cities.

### The Chinese Empire
In the period after the Han, successive empires had been established in China, some ruled by nomad invaders. The Tang had subdued their neighbors and ruled from Korea to the frontiers of Persia. They had also established extensive links with the West. When Canton was sacked in 879, the slaughtered included large numbers of Nestorian Christians, Arabs, Jews, and Zoroastrians.

### Western Europe
In the eighth century, driven by population pressure, Viking settlers from Scandinavia set out along the inland rivers to Constantinople to fight for the emperor, and by sea in longboats to prey upon the coasts of Northern Europe. Sturdy fighters and skilled sailors, the Vikings explored the western routes via Iceland and Greenland towards the American continent, perhaps even landing there. In time, they settled—in Scotland, Ireland, northern England, and Normandy—and turned to trading.

After the spread of the Arab Empire had been halted in the West by the battle of Poitiers in 732, a new and fragile balance of power saw trade reviving in Western Europe. In 1095, the West felt strong enough to challenge Islam for possession of Jerusalem, and two centuries of Crusades (religious wars) began. The Crusades, however, did not hinder the growing trade in the Mediterranean.

Merchants sought protection behind city walls and, by the twelfth century, fought for the right to govern themselves as independent communities. In Italy, luxury goods brought overland from the mythic Eastern lands of India and Cathay could now be imported from the Near Eastern ports. Genoa, Florence, and Venice became the starting point for travelers and pilgrims going to Jerusalem.

In the north, cities along the great rivers and the Baltic coasts joined in a federation called the Hanse to strengthen their power and regulate trade in the fish and forest products they exported.

Even so, it was the Arabs who could move freely and upon whose knowledge the West relied—few Western merchants traveled to Asia.

### The Mongols
Paradoxically, it was the Mongols who reopened the great land trade routes to the West and enabled Western merchants and missionaries to visit the East. The nomads who inhabited the great steppes were united by Genghis Khan in the first part of the thirteenth century into a powerful empire, with its capital at Korokaras. The Mongol hordes provided an extremely effective army, whose tactics left all who faced it outmatched—so much so that that it was seen as an instrument of divine will and punishment. They annexed Russia, ravaged Hungary, overwhelmed China, and set up the Mongol Empire. This empire was ruled in Marco Polo's time by Kublai Khan, whose ambitions stretched to conquering Java and Japan. In 1258,

the Mongols defeated the Turks and took Iraq and Persia. They controlled communications between these centers and enticed or forced skilled workers and traders to live with them.

It was only when the Mongols were eventually converted to Islam and became more sedentary that the Ottoman Turks were able to retake the Arab Empire and once again cut off Western travelers from land routes to India and China.

### Marco Polo

Marco Polo, a thirteenth-century Venetian, is possibly the most famous of early Western travelers. His journey to the Mongol Empire followed a long trading journey that his father and his uncle had made. He learnt Mongolian, and for many years served as an official for the emperor Kublai Khan. His account of his travels, which he dictated while in prison after having been captured by the Genoese, was the major source of Western knowledge of the Far East until the nineteenth century.

# EXPLORERS AND SETTLERS

Carrying goods by water may have been cheap in the days of the great empires, but it was fraught with difficulties. Sailing out of sight of land required astronomical and mathematical skills, and sophisticated instruments. The combination of wind, tide, and current with a difficult and rocky shore could be a lethal one.

At the height of the era of world exploration, no one ruled the seas, and pirates were a constant threat. Many of the most honored explorers, such as Vasco da Gama, Alfonso de Albuquerque, and Francis Drake, were also pirates. Seaborne empires such as that of Sri Vijaya had existed before, but during this time, the European empires were unparalleled in their domination of the oceans.

## Early explorers

The disruption of overland trade that occurred as a result of the Turks taking Constantinople in 1453 stimulated the search for sea routes to the East. Portugal had long been pushing down the western coast of Africa, albeit slowly, and had established a military hold on that coast which excluded traders from other countries. In 1488, Bartholomew Diaz reached the Cape of Good Hope.

Many had sailed west from Europe by this time, and all had been lost. But in 1492, Christopher Columbus found a route and, upon his return, brought the unexpected news of "unknown lands" which were not part of Asia. However, the eastward passage was still of more immediate promise, and in 1497, Vasco da Gama, with the help of an Arab pilot, penetrated the Arab-dominated Indian Ocean.

In an epic voyage that took from 1519 to 1522, Ferdinand Magellan, sailing westward, showed that the world was indeed round. French, Dutch,

and English explorers and seafarers were soon blocking the Spanish and Portuguese attempts to monopolize these trading routes.

## Southeast Asia

In Asia, trade was the primary objective of exploration. The existing highly developed, wealthy, sophisticated empires were largely invulnerable. However, Portuguese merchants, in well-armed ships, and protected by forts and royal fleets, did succeed in competing with the established Arab merchants.

In 1500, the Portuguese obtained trading rights on the west coast of India. In 1510, they settled in Malacca, the great emporium from which ships went to Borneo, Ternate, Tidore, and Amboina, and eventually to China and Japan. About 1565, the Spanish established an alternative route, with ships regularly crossing the Pacific to the Philippines. As the market for spices became saturated, trade in gold, ivory, silks, Indian cotton textiles, Chinese porcelain, tea, and coffee developed. By 1600, the Dutch and English East India companies had entered the competition, and eventually the Dutch controlled most of the spice trade from Batavia.

For more than two centuries, the costs of governing a distant state restricted colonization. In India, for instance, the British East India Company hesitated to assume direct rule until pushed by French competition. Only in the nineteenth century did direct rule become common.

## South and Central America

The discovery of gold, silver, pearls, and industrial raw materials made the Americas attractive to the Europeans. The conquest of the Aztec and Inca empires enabled Spain to establish its rule

from the Caribbean to Mexico, Peru, and Chile, while the Portuguese colonized Brazil. A steady trickle of fortune hunters from Spanish dominions in Europe took over the land and its inhabitants, causing an economic and cultural transformation. Despite the humanitarian protests of missionaries, exploitation of local labor, plus epidemics and diseases brought by the Europeans resulted in up to 95 percent of the indigenous population dying.

African slaves were imported to work the mines whose silver had such profound effects on sixteenth-century Europe. Sugar, cotton, and tobacco production also required intensive labor, and so the slave trade grew. Hides, indigo, cochineal, forest products, dyes, and drugs also went east in return for manufactured metals, guns, and

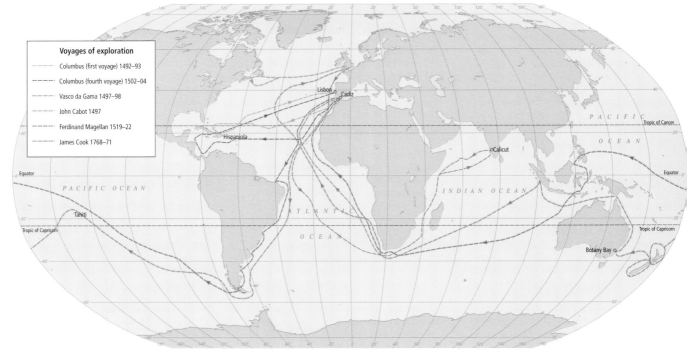

**Voyages of exploration**

- - - - - Columbus (first voyage) 1492–93
- – – – Columbus (fourth voyage) 1502–04
- ——— Vasco da Gama 1497–98
- ——— John Cabot 1497
- ——— Ferdinand Magellan 1519–22
- ——— James Cook 1768–71

Projection: Robinson   Equatorial Scale approx 1:110 million

*Workers in Cochin, India (left) still deal in spices—here, turmeric. This Dutch map of the East Indies (below) is from the early colonial days. A replica of Captain Cook's Endeavour (bottom) reminds us of the vessels sailed during the age of exploration. Machu Picchu, in Peru (bottom left), is a moving record of a long-dead civilization.*

textiles. By the seventeenth century, the Dutch, English and French were also involved.

### North America

The temperate areas of North America, already inhabited by Native American Indians, were initially less interesting to the European states. Cod fishing off Newfoundland did not need shore settlements. The French, Dutch, and English, however, all eventually established east coast settlements, from the early seventeenth century. There was royal supervision, but no state financing of these colonies. Each of the colonies had its own government, constitution, and purpose. Many were established as a refuge from religious persecution, and sought self-sufficiency. Staple exports were hard to find, migrants hard to entice, and transportation of convicts was an unsatisfactory solution. So total populations remained low.

Southern colonies such as Virginia grew tobacco and, later, cotton, and increasingly used slave labor. The other colonies supplied basic foodstuffs to the Caribbean. In the eighteenth century, sugar, cotton, and tobacco still dominated as exports. Migration was becoming more attractive, though, as the economic revolution in Europe displaced laborers. The wars of independence opened the United States to migrants from all over Europe, and as the numbers of migrants grew, settlers moved west. In the nineteenth century, this trickle became a flood.

### Growth of a world system

European exploration established a worldwide network—regular long-distance trading voyages took up to two years or more, so exploiting the new discoveries required some form of settlement. Europeans established trading posts wherever they went. They also soon required more capital, bigger ships, and new forms of organization. Shipyards alone required the kind of complex organization that was soon used in the factories of the Industrial Revolution. European merchants became global carriers, meeting local requirements

and introducing new commodities—horses and cotton to America; maize and turkeys to Europe.

Australasia was the last area to be drawn into this global network. In 1787, the British government chose Australia as a destination for convicts; the plan included the colonies being self-supporting. Initially, there was little but timber to offer world trade, and Europeans struggled to adapt the livestock and crops they brought with them to local conditions. Eventually, minerals were discovered as the interior of Australia was explored, wool became a staple, and convict transportation was replaced by free migration.

Ecologically, the world has been transformed by exploration and its consequences—and not always for the better. In many places, the indigenous population has been largely swept aside through disease, displacement, and massacre, and survives today only as a small minority.

As worldwide trading routes developed, so too did the movement of people attracted by the prospect of personal betterment. In the nineteenth and twentieth centuries, population pressure and sometimes persecution in the homeland pushed millions, mainly young males, to move to new countries. The Scots and Irish went to the United States and Australia; Jews left Eastern Europe for Israel, Britain, and America; Indian workers settled in South Africa, the South Pacific

islands, and East Africa; and Chinese laborers went to the goldfields in America, Australia, and elsewhere. Cultures have become mixed and modified as people intermarried and adapted to new conditions.

### The world is round

On September 20, 1519, the *Trinidad, San Antonio, Victoria, Concepción,* and *Santiago,* under the command of Ferdinand Magellan, set out to travel west from Spain and return from the east. News of the terrors and dangers of the journey—the empty Pacific, the difficulties of finding water and victuals, the strange cultures of the natives—only served to increase Western fascination with new horizons.

Magellan himself died en route in 1521, and it was del Cano who brought the single surviving ship back to Spain in September 1522. The expedition members had suffered mutiny and desertion, disease and famine, attacks by natives, involvement in local wars, and the treachery of supposed allies. They had proven that the Spice Islands could be reached by sailing west, but concluded that the length of the voyage made it uneconomic.

# THE INDUSTRIAL WORLD

Modern industrial societies were born in the eighteenth century, when an expanding workforce and rapid developments in technology resulted in the transformation of the social and economic structure of British society. Over the past 200 years, industrialization has spread to other parts of the globe, distributing the commercial benefits of technology and improving the lifestyles of many, but also creating social and political problems, particularly in urban areas.

## Preindustrial Britain

The Industrial Revolution began in Great Britain in the second half of the eighteenth century. Several factors made Britain ripe for industrial development. Improvements in agricultural methods during the first half of the century had reduced the number of workers required to produce sufficient food for the population, making agricultural laborers available for industrial production. At the same time, wealth for investment had accumulated to a considerable degree, and much of it was concentrated in the hands of commercially minded individuals. A growing class of artisans and practical scientists possessed a high level of expertise in technologies, such as machinery, that could be readily applied to production processes. Continuing improvements in inland transportation, particularly river, canal, and road transport, allowed the rapid distribution of goods. Finally, Britain's growing empire provided it with access to vast overseas markets.

## The Industrial Revolution

The first phase of the Industrial Revolution took place between the 1780s and 1830s, and was based on the early mechanization of production

processes. The new industrial system focused on textiles (especially cotton) and textile machinery, and employed waterpower as its principal source of energy. It centered on the city of Manchester, in northern England. Here, in 1780, Richard Arkwright, inventor of the water-powered spinning frame, opened the largest factory yet built, employing 600 workers. Britain's position as head of the world's largest empire gave it a massive advantage in the textile trade; it could ensure a plentiful and cheap supply of cotton from the slave-labor-based plantations in the American South, and its powerful navy could protect its trade.

This first phase of industrial development was limited in two senses: it was narrowly focused (upon the textile industry), and it applied existing knowledge and skills rather than transforming the country's technological base. It was, however, revolutionary in that new economic relationships were forged between people, a new system of production was created, and a new society and historical epoch emerged.

## The evolution and spread of industry

The second phase of the Industrial Revolution occurred between the 1840s and 1880s, and was revolutionary in technological terms. Iron and steel manufacture in factories powered by steam engines represented a major innovation. When this technology was used to develop railroads and steamships, the country entered a new phase of production and transport. Britain became "the workshop of the world", supplying the materials for a remarkable burst of railroad-building activity in Europe and in former colonies of European nations. Factories now employed thousands of

workers, rather than hundreds. The effects of this iron-and-steel-based Industrial Revolution on Britain were much more pronounced than were those of its predecessor. The employment generated was considerably greater, wages and living standards increased significantly, and British exports, which included foreign investments in railroads, rose phenomenally.

The revolution soon spread, with Germany and the USA among the first nations to industrialize on a large scale. Railroads helped achieve the integration of nation-states in Europe and opened up the Americas, as well as new colonies elsewhere. In the USA, the expansion and settlement of the frontier beyond the Mississippi River is closely associated with the penetration of the new railroads, the "Iron Horse".

Industrial centers
- Major industrial center
- Country borders in 1914

A steam train (above) and a textile mill (below) are potent symbols of early industrializaion. The Firth of Forth bridge (left) is more recent—a marvel of Victorian engineering. In countries such as India (bottom), modern technologies are replacing those of earlier times.

## Modern industrialization

The third phase of the Industrial Revolution began in the last decades of the nineteenth century up to the First World War. Advances in electrical and heavy engineering and industry, and the exploitation of steel alloys and heavy chemicals allowed warfare on an unprecedented scale. New factory systems combined electricity with power tools, overhead cranes, and more durable materials. Giant firms, cartels, and monopolies became the leading commercial organizations, and the ownership of capital rapidly became concentrated. The map on the left shows major European industrial centers at the time of the war. Germany and the USA had already began to rival the United Kingdom for industrial supremacy. At the same time, other nations, including Switzerland and the Netherlands, industrialized. Soon, Europeans introduced industrial practices to other parts of the world.

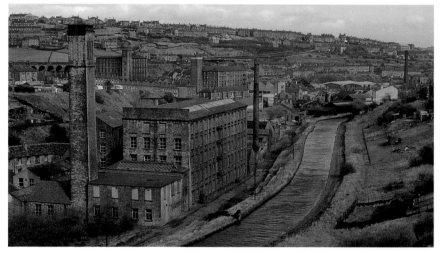

The Industrial Revolution continues to this day with the industrialization in the last few decades of nations like China, Korea, Singapore, Mexico, Brazil, and Thailand. This process has created a somewhat artificial but widely adopted distinction between "developed" countries—those which are industrialized—and "developing" countries, which still depend largely on agriculture.

## The consequences of industrialization

The application of industrial technology to an economy generally results in a population shift from rural to urban areas, as agricultural employment dwindles and people move to cities to work in industries and services. This process is known as urbanization. In the nineteenth century, the population of London, for example, rose from about 1 million in 1800 to almost 7 million in 1900.

While new industries raised living standards for many, the urban poor suffered overcrowding, poor sanitation, and pollution. There are many parallels between the social conditions in nineteenth-century United Kingdom cities and those in newly industrialized cities today. For example, the rapid expansion of an urban area such as Mexico City,

which has grown from 3 million inhabitants in 1950 to about 19.2 million today, has resulted in acute social problems—water shortages, severe air pollution, and a chronic lack of adequate housing.

Recently, the industrialization of certain developing countries has had an interesting effect on the economies of the world's first industrial nations. Newly industrialized nations, particularly in Southeast Asia, have attracted manufacturing investment from the older developed countries; to such an extent that there has actually been a decline in manufacturing jobs—a deindustrialization process—in the countries where the first and second phases of the Industrial Revolution initially occurred. The United Kingdom, Germany, and the USA have all deindustrialized to some extent.

But today's era of industrialization differs significantly from its earlier phases. Owing to new forms of technology, particularly in transport and communications, the contemporary industrial system extends to all corners of the globe, and encompasses most commodities. The Industrial Revolution has now entered its worldwide phase, integrating selected localities as workshops of emerging global factories.

# THE NATION-STATE

The world's nation-states, as represented today by the lines on a political map of the world, evolved over the past 500 years. Sixteenth-century Europe, for example, consisted of approximately 1,500 politically independent units. Yet by the start of the twentieth century, the continent was made up of only 20 nation-states. Since then, nation-states have flourished—today there are 193 nations and 65 territories on the political map of the world. New supranational groups emerging at the end of the twentieth century have led many commentators to question the ability of nation-states to solve problems within their own borders and deal with the powerful forces operating at a regional or worldwide level.

## From city-state to nation-state

Before the appearance of the nation-state in Europe, city-states such as Venice, Antwerp, and Amsterdam occupied center stage in politics and economics. For much of the seventeenth and eighteenth centuries, Amsterdam was the control

center for local, regional, and even worldwide affairs. The creation of the first nation-states, or more accurately, territorial nation-states, occurred during the 1770s and 1780s.

The catalyst was competitive rivalry between Amsterdam, England, and France. The incorporation of national territory was a new feature of the political landscape, and it gave nation-states major economic and military advantages over city states. In economic terms, for example, the nation-state could profit from its national market for goods. In military terms, it could more readily raise an army from its citizenry.

What do we mean by the term nation-state? It is useful to think of a nation-state as a combination of three elements: nation (ethnicity), state (the institutionalized regime of power), and territory (the spatially bounded area of state control).

A nation is a group of people who believe that they are an ethnic community with deep historical roots and the right to their own sovereign state. Nationalism is the cause through which such groups claim their right to be a sovereign power within a particular territory. Nationalism has its origins in the convergence of capitalism with print technology in the sixteenth century. The creation of separate vernacular print communities led to the decline of Latin as a lingua franca, and played a critical role in forming national identities.

Although ethnic identity was a significant factor in the formation of many nation-states, nations

*The city-state of Venice (left) was an important trading center from the tenth century onward. Today it forms part of a modern nation-state, the republic of Italy. These Dutch-style buildings in Suriname (below) hint at the nation's past history when it was part of the Dutch colonial empire.*

seldom consist of a single ethnic group. Indeed, such entities are extremely rare, Iceland being one of very few contemporary examples. A survey of 164 nations in 1984 counted 589 ethnic groups, an average of more than three ethnic groups per nation. A major role of mass education has been to integrate diverse ethnic groups and regional minorities into a single community, often called the "melting-pot approach" to nation-building.

The second element of a nation-state, the state, refers to the institutions of political power within a country. These include its legislature, judiciary, political parties, and security forces. State power is organized into a wide variety of regimes, including constitutional monarchies, republics, theocracies, and totalitarian dictatorships. In the 1990s, three out of five states in the world were democracies—this is a historic high.

The third element that is used to define a nation is its territory, the physical area over which it has control. This area is normally marked out by geographical boundaries. Nation-state territories have typically been viewed as economic, political, social, and cultural containers that are largely sovereign and entitled to be free from outside interference. However, disputes over boundaries and national sovereignty have led to a number of major conflicts, particularly during the years of the twentieth century.

## The rise of the nation-state

The process of dividing the world outside Europe into nation-states occurred largely in the context of the empires that the major colonizers—Spain, Portugal, The Netherlands, France, and the United Kingdom—had built during the previous four centuries. Most of the border lines on the contempor-

*Internal conflicts between groups who consider themselves to be of a separate nation can lead to a state fragmenting into smaller ones, as in the former Yugoslavia (right). Indian Sikhs on parade (below right): the world's largest democracy is home to a wide range of ethnic groups.*

ary political map of the world have their origins in two major phases of decolonization.

The first phase unfolded over the half-century following the American War of Independence in 1776. About 100 colonies combined to form the current nation-states in the Americas. Little further decolonization occurred for more than a century, until around the time of the Second World War. Notable exceptions were the British settler colonies of Canada, Australia, and South Africa. The second major phase of decolonization began after the Second World War, when "the winds of change" blew through Africa, South and Southeast Asia, and islands in the Caribbean and the Pacific and Indian Oceans. This resulted in the formation of another approximately 110 nation-states.

Nation-states continued to be created in the 1990s—15 nations were created as a result of the break-up of the Soviet Union in 1991, for example. Eritrea, Slovenia, Croatia, and Macedonia became independent in 1991, as did the Czech Republic, Slovakia, and Namibia in 1994. The final outcome of the break-up of Yugoslavia is still uncertain. Internal ethnic tension in some areas has grown enormously, and ethnic-based nationalist movements continue to emerge. This kind of conflict is currently the most common—of the 89 armed conflicts that occurred between 1989 and 1992, only 3 were between nations.

At the same time, in Europe, where the nation-state first began, the European Union, a supra-

national regional state, continues to transform the European political landscape. Most of Western Europe has now been combined within the European Union, while a number of other European states have applied for admission and await entry. Some commentators see the European Union as the beginning of the end of the territorial nation-state as we have known it; it has undoubtedly changed long-held ideas on what makes a nation.

**New European democracies**

- New European democracies
- Existing democracies
- International border

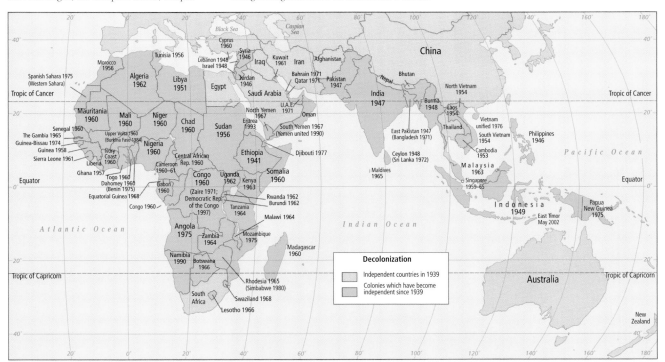

**Decolonization**

- Independent countries in 1939
- Colonies which have become independent since 1939

# INTERNATIONAL ORGANIZATIONS

During the second half of the twentieth century, international organizations, including intergovernmental and nongovernmental bodies, have grown significantly in both number and stature. Today, there are about 500 intergovernmental organizations, such as the United Nations (UN) and the International Monetary Fund (IMF), and approximately 5,000 nongovernmental organizations (NGOs), including the Red Cross and Amnesty International. That represents roughly five times the number that were active at the end of the Second World War.

International organizations form an important part of the social glue that binds the nations and peoples of the world together. They create a set of rules, norms, and procedures—encapsulated in international law, particularly in the form of treaties and conventions signed by nation-states—that define the expected conduct of participants in the international community.

## United Nations

The largest and most influential intergovernmental organization is the United Nations. Its predecessor was the League of Nations, which was founded at the end of the First World War, in an attempt to prevent further international conflict. Based in Geneva, the League gradually expanded its membership and became a focus for growing numbers of nongovernmental bodies. However, the refusal of the United States to ratify the League's covenant, and the League's inability to prevent expansion by Germany, Italy, and Japan in the 1930s led to its ceasing operations during the Second World War.

The United Nations (UN) was established in San Francisco in 1946, and now has its headquarters in New York. As with the League of Nations, the main motivation for the creation of the UN was collective security. Sixty years later, the membership of the UN has grown to 192, and only the Vatican City and a small number of territories (including French Polynesia and the Channel Islands) are not formal member states.

On the world stage, the UN is critically important, but relatively weak and often controversial. At times it has appeared to be an impotent and ineffective institution that more resembles a debating society for the superpowers, their client states, and major power blocs than anything remotely like a "world government".

It is, of course, important to remember that the UN is not a world government, in that its member states remain independent and sovereign entities. Furthermore, most of the member states clearly have an ambivalent attitude towards the organization. For example, the Norwegians are strong supporters of the UN, but refuse to accept UN

*Refugees in the Sudan (below) and the young Somali girl (left) are likely to receive assistance from international organizations—via UN peacekeeping forces.*

directives on whaling. The USA frequently seeks UN support for military intervention abroad, but constantly defers payment of its UN dues. Resulting financial difficulties hamper UN operations. Even after the Cold War, when it seemed to have grown enormously in importance and stature, the UN operated on about the same budget as the Tokyo fire department.

During the half-century following the establishment of the UN, other collective issues, including environmental, economic, and legal issues, have been placed under the umbrella of the intergovernmental system. For example, the World Bank and the International Monetary Fund (IMF) have become responsible for managing a wide variety of international economic issues: the IMF coordinates international currency exchange and the balance of international payments, and the World Bank borrows the savings of rich nations and lends them to poor nations under conditions not available on the private capital markets.

## Nongovernmental organizations

Nongovernmental organizations (NGOs) are private organizations that are today regarded as legitimate players on the world stage alongside nation-states and intergovernmental organizations. Generally, however, NGOs have significantly less power and far fewer financial resources.

Most NGOs are primarily concerned with the empowerment of marginal and impoverished sectors of the world's population through increasing those people's participation in resolving their own problems. NGOs tend to focus upon specific issues. For example, Greenpeace raises awareness of environmental issues, Planned Parenthood campaigns for reproductive rights and family planning, groups such as the International Federation of the Red Cross and the Red Crescent Societies provide disaster relief, and Médecins Sans Frontières provides medical care.

## International organizations and human rights

Human rights is one highly significant area where international organizations have created the emerging rules, norms, and legal instruments that link nations and their citizens together in an embryonic worldwide system. Human rights are the laws, customs, and practices that have evolved to protect people, minorities, groups, and races from oppressive rulers and governments.

Before the Second World War, international human rights issues were restricted to matters such as slavery or armed conflict, and discussions about human rights (and recognition of them) took place mainly within the borders of particular nation-states. A turning point in the history of human rights occurred on December 10, 1948, when the Universal Declaration of Human Rights was adopted by the General Assembly of the UN without a dissenting vote.

Over the next half-century, major advances were made. Most significantly, a series of international covenants was drafted and adopted by the

*A land rights protest in Australia (above). International human rights organizations are increasingly exerting pressure on governments to recognize indigenous peoples' rights.*

UN and subsequently ratified by individual nation-states. Once ratified by a nation-state, the human rights legislation was usually incorporated within the state's own legal system.

Although the UN has been prominent in human rights legislation, private individuals and nongovernmental organizations such as Amnesty International have frequently provided the political pressure that has persuaded intergovernmental and national agencies to act. Often, though, such action has been taken only reluctantly and retrospectively. The fact that countless millions of people have suffered (and many still do) terrible violations of their rights as human beings, even since the Declaration of Human Rights, is something of an indictment of the Declaration and of the UN's ability and will to enforce it. Most observers still regard the Declaration of Human Rights as inadequate and in need of enforcement. Its emergence, and the opportunity it created to bring such issues to world attention, are one positive result of the growth in importance of international organizations. While this has certainly produced a world that is better than it was, it is still by no means all that it could be.

Again, the ambivalent attitudes of nation-states to international organizations is a significant factor, affecting their ability to function effectively. For example, when concerns about human rights in Afghanistan were raised by the UN and NGO representatives in 1998, the ruling Taliban militia asked the organizations to leave the country. Yet, when it appeared that Iran may have been ready to invade Afghanistan to protect some of its own citizens, the Taliban sought support from the UN to keep Iran out. At the beginning of the twenty-first century, the idea of setting up global governance is still on the world's agenda, but only just.

## THE UNITED NATIONS SYSTEM

**International Court of Justice**

**Secretariat**

┌─**Trusteeship Council**

**General Assembly** ───── └─**Security Council**
*Committees*

*Peacekeeping Operations*
*International Tribunals*
*Military Staff Committees*
*Standing Committees*

**Economic and Social Council (ECOSOC)**

### UN Programs:

| | |
|---|---|
| **INSTRAW** | UN International Research and Training Institute for the Advancement of Women |
| **ITC** | International Trade Center |
| **UNCHS** | UN Center for Human Habitats |
| **UNCTAD** | UN Conference on Trade and Development |
| **UNDCP** | UN Drug Control Program |
| **UNDP** | UN Development Program |
| **UNEP** | UN Environment Program |
| **UNFPA** | UN Fund for Population Activities |
| **UNHCF** | UN High Commission for Refugees |
| **UNICEF** | UN Children's Emergency Fund |
| **UNIFEM** | UN Development Fund for Women |
| **UNITAR** | UN Institute for Training and Research* |
| **UNU** | UN University |
| **WFC** | World Food Council |
| **WFP** | World Food Program |

*Functional Commissions*

*Regional Commissions*

*Standing Committees*

*Expert Bodies*

### Specialized Agencies:

| | |
|---|---|
| **FAO** | Food and Agriculture Organization, Rome |
| **ICAO** | International Civil Aviation Organization, Montreal |
| **IFAD** | International Fund for Agricultural Development, Rome |
| **ILO** | International Labor Organization, Geneva |
| **IMF** | International Monetary Fund, Washington |
| **IMO** | International Maritime Organization, London |
| **ITU** | International Telecommunications Union, Geneva |
| **UNESCO** | UN Educational, Scientific, and Cultural Organization, Paris |
| **UNIDO** | UN Industrial Development Organization, Vienna |
| **UPU** | Universal Postal Union, Berne |
| **WHO** | World Health Organization, Geneva |
| **WIPO** | World Intellectual Property Organization, Geneva |
| **WMO** | World Meteorological Association, Geneva |
| **WTO** | World Trade Organization, Geneva* |

### World Bank Group, Washington

| | |
|---|---|
| **IBRD** | International Bank for Reconstruction and Development |
| **IDA** | International Development Association |
| **IFC** | International Finance Corporation |
| **MIGA** | Multilateral Investment Guarantee Agency |

*\* Does not report to ECOSOC*

# GLOBALIZATION

Globalization refers to a change of scale in human processes and activities which has occurred during the last quarter of a century—one in which the nation-state is giving way, in many fields, to global organizations. Until recently, it was generally felt that human and environmental affairs could and should be conducted at a national level. Nation-states were, in principle at least, sovereign or independent units. Of course, nation-states had relations with one another, and these were referred to as international, as in the terms "international trade" and "international relations". In the 1990s, however, "international" and "internationalization" have been increasingly replaced by "global" and "globalization", as national boundaries have begun to seem less significant in economic, political, cultural, and environmental terms.

## The global economy

Transnational corporations—companies that operate in a large number of countries—are the movers and shakers of the modern global economy. Among the firms with operations that are nearly worldwide are Exxon and Royal Dutch Shell in petroleum; McDonalds, Seagrams, Sara Lee, Nabisco and Nestlé in food and beverages; BMW, Ford, Volkswagen, and General Motors in automobiles; and Mitsubishi and Mitsui in banking, manufacturing, and trade.

Although few (if any) companies can be described as truly global at this time—most still focus on certain markets and report to shareholders in their home country—the term "global" is commonly used in business circles to identify a level of operations that many companies hope to attain in the not-too-distant future. This would involve a truly international workforce, shareholders in a number of nation-states, and products that are sold in all markets.

The flow of money from country to country is also encouraging the surge in economic globalization. National boundaries are no barrier to the movement of funds; thanks to modern telecommunications and computer technology, funds can now be rapidly transferred to any part of the globe. Such transactions have, it now appears, created a much more volatile and less secure world. In 2008, within a matter of weeks, a recession triggered by problems in the real estate market and banking system in the United States led to worldwide economic crisis.

The phenomenal growth of the Internet has created opportunities for even small companies to operate at a global level. By selling goods via the World Wide Web, a firm can now compete in markets where it could not previously have established a presence, whether for geographical, political, or financial reasons. Governments are struggling to cope with the implications of this for the regulation of trade within their countries. How, for example, do they impose sales taxes on goods or services that are purchased in the virtual market of cyberspace?

Many commentators assert that globalization will transform the world economy in the twenty-first century, leaving no national products, no national corporations, no national industries, and no national economies. To succeed in the global marketplace, countries will have to depend entirely on the skills of their inhabitants, and will have to deal with powerful external forces that could create an ever-widening gulf between skilled, globally aware citizens and a growing unskilled, out-of-touch underclass.

## World politics

The globalization of politics has resulted in the decline of the nation-state and the growth of international organizations. Although they remain the principal players on the world political stage, nation-states now appear less independent and less sovereign than they used to. One response to this has been to look to international organizations such as the United Nations to assume some of the roles previously played by nation-states.

Perhaps the most significant political event in the 1990s was the end of the Cold War. During the Cold War (1946–91), most nation-states belonged to one of three geopolitical worlds: the First World, consisting of developed capitalist nations, and dominated by the USA; the Second World, consisting of developed communist nations, and dominated by the Soviet Union; and the Third World, consisting of developing nations that were in theory not aligned with either of the superpowers. The demise of the Cold War brought an end to these divisions, and created a geopolitical situation no longer driven by the rivalry of two opposing superpowers.

Some commentators believe that this has created a vacuum, where no effectively organized power system exists. In the past, when major geopolitical shifts occurred, one dominant power was typically replaced by another: Great Britain (as the United Kingdom was known) replaced Amsterdam, and the USA later replaced the United Kingdom. Globalization has produced a world so complex and integrated that it no longer seems possible for a single nation-state to play the dominant role that these nations once played. The growing emphasis on and allocation of power to international organizations can be seen as an attempt to fill this power vacuum.

## The global village

Discussions of the globalization of culture often begin with the expression "global village", a term coined in the 1960s by Marshall McLuhan, an American commentator. He believed that television would replace the printed word as the primary medium of wider social integration, eventually uniting the people of the world through their collective participation in media events. In the 1990s, events such as the Gulf War, the annual Academy Awards, the death of an English princess, and certain sporting competitions were watched on television by people in almost all the world's countries—an audience of between 1 and 2 billion people.

*Dealings on the Tokyo Stock Exchange (right) can affect the economy of many other countries; financial centers such as Chicago (below) are experiencing the globalization of trade.*

The fact that a rapidly growing number of people are involved in maintaining the global village raises a number of questions. For instance, will globalization mean an inevitable cultural homogenization? Opinion is sharply divided on this question. A great deal of evidence supports the view that a global culture is developing. On the other hand, powerful movements which actively resist this cultural homogenization have also emerged—militant Islamic, Hindu, and Zionist organizations, for example.

One issue that has played a major role in raising awareness of the ways in which we truly are a global community is the environment. The first Earth Day in 1970 marked the beginning of mass awareness of the global significance of environ-mental issues. Over the next three decades, evidence of the extent of degradation of Earth's natural environment caused by human activity has mounted. This has forced governments and individuals to examine their impact on the natural world, and has encouraged political cooperation at a global level to effect change.

A series of international environmental forums have been held, including Stockholm (1972), the Earth Summit at Rio de Janeiro (1992), the Population Conference at Cairo (1994), and the Convention on Climate Change in Kyoto (1997). All stressed the worldwide and interconnected nature of the growing environmental crisis. The Earth Summit was attended by an unprecedented 130 heads of state, 1,500 nongovernmental organizations, and 7,000 accredited journalists. However, despite the willingness of many nations to discuss these issues globally, the desire or ability to act locally may be absent.

The slogan "Think globally, act locally" has been widely employed to express the scale shift involved in this transformation of economics, politics, culture, and nature—from what used to be thought local or national concepts to what are now recognized as (or have become) international, global concerns. Globalization may prove to be the key change in the twenty-first century.

*Advertising signs in this village in Peru (below) are an example of the penetration of multi-national corporations into a developing country.*

# Oceania and Antarctica

# Asia and the Middle East

**1.8 MILLION BP** Hominids of *Homo erectus* species living in Java, Indonesia

Skull of *Homo erectus*

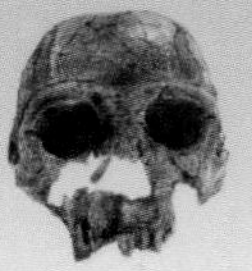

**130,000 BP** *Homo neanderthalensis* (Neanderthals) living in western Asia; they have social organization and hunt using strategy and cooperation

**1.9 MILLION BP** Modern hominids resembling *Homo habilis* living in caves in Sichuan Province, China

**800,000 BP** *Homo erectus* using simple rafts on Indonesian island of Flores

**460,000 BP** Earliest known controlled use of fire at Zhoukoudian Cave, China

**90,000 BP** *Homo sapiens sapiens* present at several sites in Israel

# Europe and the Russian Federation

**780,000 BP** Tool-using hominids living in northern Spain. Classified as *Homo heidelbergensis*, they may have been the ancestors of Neanderthals

**130,000 BP** Emergence of *Homo neanderthalensis* (Neanderthals); they have social organization and hunt using strategy and cooperation

**1.5 MILLION BP** Hominids arrive from Africa

**500,000 BP** Archaic *Homo sapiens* appears in Europe

**100,000 BP** Neanderthals burying their dead; possibly using burial rituals and decorating graves

# Africa

**4.0 MILLION BP** Earliest recognizable hominid (form of human), *Australopithecus ramidus*, living in southern and eastern Africa

**3.0 MILLION BP** Hominids living in caves in southern Africa feeding on plants and animals

**2.3 MILLION BP** Emergence of *Homo habilis* in East Africa, a hominid associated with first use of crude stone tools

**1.5 MILLION BP** Hominids spread northward, crossing Sahara Desert region at time of abundant vegetation

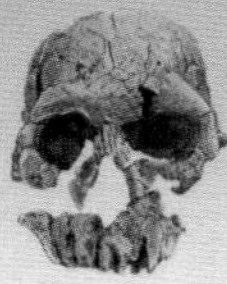

Skull of *Homo ergaster*

**150,000–100,000 BP** Modern humans, *Homo sapiens sapiens*, appear in various parts of Africa and begin to migrate northward

**5.0 MILLION BP** The southern ape (Australopithecine) family splits into three branches, which will slowly evolve into gorillas, chimpanzees, and humans

**3.5 MILLION BP** Footprints left at Laetoli, Tanzania, by *Australopithecus afarensis*, a hominid that walks upright

**1.9 MILLION BP** Hominids of more modern appearance, *Homo ergaster*, appear in Africa, probably evolving from *Homo habilis*

**800,000 BP** Archaic *Homo sapiens* evolves in Africa

**200,000 BP** Anatomically modern humans, distinguished by larger brain and use of more sophisticated tools, inhabit a number of cave sites in southern Africa

# North and Central America

# South America

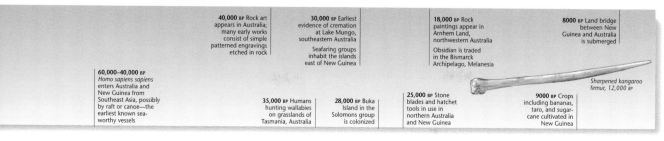

**40,000 BP** Rock art appears in Australia; many early works consist of simple patterned engravings etched in rock

**30,000 BP** Earliest evidence of cremation at Lake Mungo, southeastern Australia

Seafaring groups inhabit the islands east of New Guinea

**18,000 BP** Rock paintings appear in Arnhem Land, northwestern Australia

Obsidian is traded in the Bismarck Archipelago, Melanesia

**8000 BP** Land bridge between New Guinea and Australia is submerged

*Sharpened kangaroo femur, 12,000 BP*

**60,000–40,000 BP** *Homo sapiens sapiens* enters Australia and New Guinea from Southeast Asia, possibly by raft or canoe—the earliest known seaworthy vessels

**35,000 BP** Humans hunting wallabies on grasslands of Tasmania, Australia

**28,000 BP** Buka Island in the Solomons group is colonized

**25,000 BP** Stone blades and hatchet tools in use in northern Australia and New Guinea

**9000 BP** Crops including bananas, taro, and sugarcane cultivated in New Guinea

---

**68,000 BP** *Homo sapiens sapiens* living in parts of China

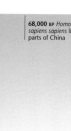

*Neanderthal skull*

**20,000 BP** Modern humans (*Homo sapiens sapiens*) migrate across Eurasia as far as Siberia

**11,000 BP** Cultivation of domesticated grains such as wheat and barley in the Fertile Crescent

**9,500 BP** Evidence of rice cultivation in central China

**9,000 BP** Crops including sesame and eggplant are cultivated in the Indus Valley

Pigs domesticated in Anatolia, Turkey

**40,000 BP** Neanderthals disappear from the fossil record in western Asia

**12,000 BP** Dogs domesticated in southwestern Asia

*Jomon pot, 12,500–9,500 BP*

**12,500 BP** Jomon people of Japan produce the world's first clay vessels

**10,000 BP** Cattle domesticated in Anatolia, in present-day Turkey

**8,500 BP** Smelting of copper, gold, and lead in southwestern Asia

**7,500 BP** Pottery is produced in China

---

**50,000 BP** Simple engravings carved on cave walls in eastern Europe

**35,000 BP** Neanderthals disappear from the fossil record, perhaps displaced by *Homo sapiens sapiens*

Appearance of Cro-Magnon peoples, noted for their use of bone tools and sewn hides

*Austrian fertility figure, 20,000 BP*

**15,000 BP** First evidence of use of watercraft in the Mediterranean

**14,000 BP** Elaborate huts of interlocked mammoth bones built to provide shelter during winter at Mezhirich, Ukraine

**8,000 BP** Permanent farming settlements established in southeastern Europe

*idescraper tool rom France, 0,000–35,000 BP*

**40,000 BP** *Homo sapiens sapiens* arrives from Africa, bringing more sophisticated tools and skills

**32,000 BP** First cave art appears in southwestern France and northern Spain

**15,000–12,000 BP** Magdalenian phase, during which most of the best-known cave art is produced, including the galleries of Lascaux, France, and Altamira, Spain

**10,500 BP** Beginning of colonization of Mediterranean islands, which takes 4,000 years

---

**23,000 BP** Rock paintings on inland shelters show ceremonial dancers and herds of game animals, including antelope

**9000 BP** Pottery containers in use in settled areas of the Nile Valley, Egypt

**25,000 BP** Paintings on rock slabs made by Stone Age hunter-gatherers in Namibia show animals such as elephants and giraffes

**12,000 BP** Rock carvings in the Sahara Desert, in present-day Algeria, depict North African aurochs

**8000 BP** Crops including figs and chufa are cultivated in the Nile Valley, Egypt

*Skull of Homo sapiens sapiens*

---

**12,000 BP** Date of earliest reliable evidence of human habitation of North America, found at sites in Alaska

**11 000 BP** Numerous human settlements appear across present-day United States

Humans hunt mammoths at Clovis, New Mexico

Dogs domesticated

*North American Clovis point tool, c. 11,500 BP*

**35,000–12,000 BP** *Homo sapiens sapiens* enters North America across Bering Strait land bridge between Asia and present-day Alaska, and spreads southward

**14,500 BP** Disputed date for evidence of human habitation at Meadowcroft Shelter in southwestern Pennsylvania; site includes firepits, stone tools, and plaited basketry

**10,000 BP** Hunters use trenches to trap and kill bison at Casper, Wyoming

**9,000 BP** Native peoples of Mesoamerica begin to collect plants more intensively, perhaps beginning domestication

---

**12,500 BP** Humans inhabiting Monte Verde in southern Chile; evidence includes stone tools, animal skins on poles, and plant remains

**12,000 BP** Well-organized hunter-gatherers living in the cold high-altitude puna grasslands of modern-day Peru, feeding on plants and vicuñas (a relative of the llama)

**8,500 BP** Beans and chili peppers cultivated in central Andes

*Monte Verde hut, 12,500 BP*

**25,000 BP** Disputed date for evidence of human habitation of eastern South America, including Pedra Furada in Brazil

**11,000 BP** Humans inhabit Cueva Fell, Tierra del Fuego, southern Chile

**10,000 BP** Potatoes cultivated in the Andes of present-day Bolivia

## Oceania and Antarctica

**4000 BC** Pig husbandry and vegetable growing (mainly taro) in mainland New Guinea

Forest cleared on the Bismarck Archipelago to increase agricultural production

**3600 BC** Simple pottery is made on Vanimo coast of northern New Guinea

*Lapita pottery, c. 1100 BC*

**1500 BC** Fiji is settled by Lapita people

**4500–4000 BC** People living on High Cliffy Island off Western Australia build stone structures as dwellings or for ceremonial purposes

**3500 BC** Giant clam-shell adzes in use in Sepik-Ramu basin of New Guinea

**2500 BC** "Saltwater" people of the Kimberley Coast region of northwestern Australia use fire-hardened spears for fishing

**1600 BC** Austronesian colonization of New Guinea and the Bismarck Archipelago followed by emergence of Lapita culture, named for its distinctive pottery bearing complex geometric designs

**1200 BC** Lapita people colonize New Caledonia, Tonga, Samoa

## Asia and the Middle East

**4200 BC** Copper and bronze being worked in Mesopotamia

**3500 BC** Small cities based on earlier farming communities appear in Sumer, the southern part of Mesopotamia

**3000 BC** Sumerians develop a writing system consisting of pictograms pressed in clay tablets; they also develop the first wheeled vehicles

People from southern Asia (Austronesians) begin expansion south and east into the Philippines, eastern Indonesia, and New Guinea

**2400 BC** Harappa civilization merges diverse cultures in the Indus Valley; Harappan building methods involve use of bricks and architectural planning

**1800 BC** Indo-Europeans spread to the Middle East and eastern Mediterranean

**1500 BC** The Aryans, an Indo-European people, migrate from central Asia to northern India

**1290 BC** Traditional date for Moses lead the Hebrews from slavery in Egypt bac to tribal lands in Canaan (Palestine)

**5000 BC** First settlements appear in Mesopotamia, the fertile area between the Tigris and Euphrates rivers

**4000 BC** Sailing ships in use in Mesopotamia

**2600 BC** Writing system based on pictograms in use in China

**2200 BC** Semites migrate from Arabia to Mesopotamia and found Babylonian and Assyrian kingdoms

**1595 BC** The Hittites, a powerful Indo-European people from Hattusas in present-day Turkey, sack Babylon; by 1500 BC they control all of Asia Minor

## Europe and the Russian Federation

**4000 BC** Farming reaches northern Europe

Horses domesticated in the Ukraine; they become the main means of transport throughout Europe and Asia and confer major advantages in battle

**2500 BC** Rise of Minoan civilization—Europe's first—on the island of Crete and in surrounding Aegean region

Dolmen, large standing stones usually topped by a horizontal stone, are erected in Scandinavia

**1800 BC** Stone circle at Stonehenge, Wiltshire, England, completed; work may have started as early as 3500 BC

**1600–1500 BC** Minoan centers destroyed by invaders or earthquakes

Rise of Mycenaean civilization on Greek mainland

**5000 BC** Earliest evidence of burials in Scandinavia

Land bridge between Britain and Europe submerged by rising sea levels

Copper in use in south-eastern Europe

*Poulnabrone tomb, Ireland, 3000 BC*

**1650 BC** Writing systems known as Linear A and Linear B in use in Crete and mainland Greece; Linear A is a Minoan script, whereas Linear B constitutes an early form of Mycenaean Greek

**1250–1200 BC** Mycenean centers destroyed by conflict or earthquakes

## Africa

**4000 BC** People living in central Sudan in loosely organized communities, tending cattle, sheep, and goats as well as continuing to hunt and fish

Copper smelting in Egypt

**3000 BC** Donkeys used for farming in the Nile Valley

First scientific astronomy observations in Egypt and Babylonia

Yams and palm oil domesticated in tropical West Africa

Beginning of Bantu expansion from West Africa into Congo Basin

**2650 BC** Nile Valley civilization flourishes; pyramids constructed during this period are the most elaborate burial tomb structures to date

**2000 BC** Kingdom of Kush established in middle Nile Valley

Invention of the water wheel in Egypt

**1333–1323 BC** Tutankhamun reigns as Pharaoh of Egypt, coming to the throne at age nine and ruling from Memphis near Cairo with the help of regent, Ay

**5000 BC** Growth of Nubian settlement in the Nile Valley; agricultural methods begin to spread southward

**2200 BC** Ducks and geese domesticated in Egypt

**1500 BC** Trade routes between North Africa and the rest of Africa are disrupted by the spread of the Sahara Desert

Egyptians conquer Kush

**1290 BC** Rock temples of Abu Simbel built in Egypt by Rameses

## North and Central America

**3500 BC** Bison hunted on the Great Plains

Beginning of classic period of Northwest Coast culture of Pacific Northwest, characterized by lavish ceremonies and ornate woodwork

Turkeys domesticated in Mesoamerica

**1200 BC** Olmec civilization spreads throughout much of Mesoamerica; it lasts for 900 years

**5000 BC** Caribbean islands colonized by people arriving in dugout canoes from the Yucatán Peninsula, present-day Mexico

Plants such as squash, amaranth, chili, and gourds cultivated in Tehuacán Valley, Mesoamerica

Gill-net fishing practiced in Pacific Northwest

**2500 BC** Squash cultivated in eastern North America, as well as sumpweed, goosefoot, and sunflowers, whose large seeds are stored as winter food

Simple pottery appears in North America

*Olmec head*

**1300 BC** People in south-eastern North America, in the area known as the lower Mississippi, build major earthworks such as those found at Poverty Point in Louisiana

## South America

**3500 BC** Valdivia culture begins to develop in the Andes (in present-day Ecuador); it is characterized by a complex social culture and village life

Manioc (cassava) and potato cultivated in many parts of the Andes and Amazonia

**2500 BC** Elaborate temples and mounds constructed in Peruvian highlands

**1200 BC** Terracing used to increase agricultural output in Andes

**3000 BC** Cotton grown at Valdivia centers of Ancon and Huaca Prieta in coastal valleys of present-day Peru; mound architecture built at nearby sites such as El Paraiso

Valdivia culture produces incised ceramics at Puerto Horniga

Squash, capsicum, and peppers grown in Peruvian Andes

**5000 BC** In the central Andes, beans are cultivated

**4000 BC** Llamas, alpacas, and guinea pigs domesticated in Peru

**1800 BC** Huge ceremonial complexes built in coastal valleys of Peru at sites including Casma Valley

**1000** BC Settlement of southern Mariana islands of Micronesia

**500** BC A distinctive Polynesian culture emerges in islands of southwestern Pacific

**528** BC Buddhism begins under Siddhartha (Gautama Buddha) in Benares, India, and later spreads to Sri Lanka, Myanmar, Laos, Thailand, and other parts of southern Asia

*Bronze vessel from China*

**331** BC Alexander the Great conquers the Persian Empire, winning a decisive battle at Gaugamela, Mesopotamia

**112** BC Development of the Silk Road as a trading route between China and the West

**1020** BC Israelites establish a kingdom in Palestine

**221–211** BC Shih Huang orders construction of Great Wall of China to protect Qin Empire against nomadic tribes of northern steppes

**400** BC Cast iron in use in China

c. **5** BC Birth of Jesus Christ in Bethlehem

**800** BC Etruscans settle in central-western Italy between the Arno and Tiber rivers

Phoenician colonies established in Spain, Sardinia, and Sicily

**620** BC Roman alphabet, derived from Etruscan, in use

**336** BC Alexander the Great succeeds father Philip II as ruler of Macedonia; he soon tightens control of Greek city-states and expands Macedonian Empire into Asia

**218–201** BC Hannibal crosses the Alps to invade Italy from the north, beginning the Second Punic War

**146** BC Rome emerges victorious from Third Punic War

**776** BC The Olympic Games, a combination of religious festival and athletic contest, first held in Delphi and Olympia, Greece

**750** BC Rise of Greek city-states including Athens, Corinth, Sparta, and Thebes

Etruscan alphabet in use

Work begins on the Acropolis, Athens

**600–400** BC Growth of Celtic warrior societies; major centers include Hunsrück-Eifel region of Germany and Champagne district of France

c. **350–322** BC Aristotle writes his major works, advancing the idea that Earth is the center of the universe around which other planets revolve

**290** BC Romans take control of central Italy

**264–241** BC First Punic War between Rome and Carthage initiates long battle for dominance of Mediterranean

**51** BC Julius Caesar conquers Celtic tribes of Gaul as far as the Rhine; he reaches Britain in 55 BC, but Romans do not occupy the country until 43 AD

**750** BC Kingdom of Kush-Meroë conquers Egypt and rules until 670 BC

Phoenicians colonize coast of North Africa

*Gold sheath from Kush-Meroë Kingdom*

**480** BC City of Carthage flourishes and holds sway over the western Mediterranean

**275** BC The first lighthouse to use reflected light from a fire to warn sea traffic of danger is built at Alexandria in Eygpt

**200** BC Paper made from papyrus in use in Egypt is used all over the western world

**1000** BC Bantu expansion reaches Rift Valley

Kush becomes independent

**300** BC African rice is grown in the Niger delta

**146** BC Carthage destroyed by Roman army at end of Third Punic War

**1000** BC Agriculture, in the form of the cultivation of maize, established in south-western North America

**650** BC Appearance of Zapotec hieroglyphs, the earliest form of Mesoamerican writing

**500** BC Adena people of midwestern North America build mounds for ceremonial purposes

Monte Albán, in Mexico's southern highlands, becomes capital city of Zapotec culture; it thrives for about 1,200 years

**300** BC The pyramids of the sun temple in Teotihuacan, Mexico, are completed

Hohokam, Mogollon, and Anasazi peoples inhabit southern North America; the Anasazi occupy villages built beneath overhanging cliffs in and around Chaco Canyon, New Mexico

**600** BC Team games played with a rubber ball on ball courts in San Lorenzo and La Venta in present-day Mexico; the games may have involved human sacrifices

**200** BC In north-eastern North America, Hopewell culture begins to take over from Adena; the Hopewell become the region's first farmers

**900** BC Carving of Tello Obelisk, an ornate granite monolith from Chavín de Huántar, one of the most remarkable artefacts of Chavín culture

*Tello Obelisk, 900 BC*

**200** BC Rise of Nasca culture in Peru, noted for its immense geometric figures etched into the ground and only visible from the air; the patterns may mark the sun's passage at solstice

**1000** BC The Chavín culture begins to flourish in northern Andes

**750** BC Gold mining taking place in central Andes

## Oceania and Antarctica

AD 186 One of the world's most violent volcanic eruptions occurs at Mt Taupo, New Zealand, destroying surrounding forests over a radius of 75 km (47 miles)

*Fishhook from Marquesas Islands*

AD 0 Marquesas Islands colonized

AD 500 Polynesian settlers reach Hawaii and Easter Island

## Asia and the Middle East

AD 220 Demise of Han Empire in China

AD 527–565 Byzantine Empire (359–1453) reaches its zenith under Justinian I

*Stone sculpture, Gupta dynasty*

c. AD 30 Crucifixion of Jesus Christ in Jerusalem

AD 319–450 Gupta dynasty flourishes in India

c. AD 500 Buddhism and Confucianism introduced to Japan from China

AD 622 Followers of Mohammed (570–632), founder of Islam, flee to Medina to escape persecution; this event denotes the start of the Muslim calendar

## Europe and the Russian Federation

AD 117 Roman Empire reaches its greatest extent under Trajan; in Britain, the northern boundary is later marked by Hadrian's Wall (built AD 122)

AD 330 Roman Emperor Constantine I converts to Christianity, which subsequently becomes the Empire's official religion

AD 450 Germanic tribes from northern Europe, such as the Angles, Jutes, and Saxons, begin to settle in England

AD 476 Western Roman Empire comes to an end when Romulus Augustus is ousted by Goths

AD 79 The cities of Pompeii and Herculaneum, Italy, are destroyed by the eruption of Mt Vesuvius

AD 140 The Greek astronomer Ptolemy publishes his *Almagest*, an encyclopaedia of scientific information, including his theory that Earth is the center of the universe

AD 443 Attila leads Huns and other barbarian tribes into western Europe; he is turned back in 450 at Châlons by a coalition of Franks and Visigoths led by Aetius

AD 452 Venice founded by refugees from central Europe fleeing the attacks of Attila the Hun

## Africa

c. AD 350 Aksum converts to Christianity; the empire extends inland

c. AD 570 Nubian kingdom converts to Christianity

AD 0–100 Kingdom of Aksum in present-day Ethiopia becomes a major trading center; elaborate temples and palaces are constructed

*Pillar at Aksum*

AD 400–500 Bantu people migrate to southern Africa seeking land for grazing sheep and cattle and planting crops; they soon displace Khoisan hunter-gatherers

AD 634 Arabs begin to colonize North Africa

## North and Central America

c. AD 200 Pyramid of the Sun is built at Teotihuacán in eastern Mexico

AD 426 Mayan dynasty of 16 kings founded at Copán in present-day Honduras

AD 700 Start of the Pueblo period in southwestern North America; native peoples including Hopi and Zuni live in villages built mainly of adobe

AD 250 Start of the Classic phase of Mayan civilization; growth of Mayan city-states on Yucatán Peninsula (Mexico) and in present-day Guatemala

*Jade ritual offering, Copán dynasty*

AD 100 Mayan hieroglyphic writing comes into use

AD 550–800 Mayan civilization reaches its zenith

## South America

AD 200–600 Moche civilization of Peru produces highly decorated ceramic pots and murals for public buildings; the Pyramid of the Sun in Moche Valley is the region's largest adobe structure

AD 700 Sicán culture flourishes in the Batán Grande area of Peru's northern coast; the capital city includes 12 adobe pyramids and tombs for leaders

*Moche ear ornament*

AD 100 Tiwanaku and Wari develop as principal urban centers of southern-central Andes

AD 500 Wari becomes major Andean city with strong administrative structures, large buildings, and highly developed crafts, including ceramics

AD **800** Fishhooks in use along the southeast coast of Australia, similar to those found in New Guinea

AD **900–1000** Polynesians first reach New Zealand islands and settle

Gigantic stone statues are erected on Easter Island

Pitcairn Islands are colonized by Polynesians

*Easter Island statue*

**1300** Chatham Islands, 800 km (500 miles) east of New Zealand, become the last Pacific islands to be colonized by Polynesian settlers

---

AD **868** The first woodblock-printed book, *The Diamond Sutra*, appears in China

**1000** Chinese scientists invent gunpowder

**1038** Seljuk Turks start Turkish Muslim dynasty; by 1071, it controls Asia Minor

**1096–99** First Crusaders temporarily wrest Jerusalem from Arab control

**1189** Third Crusade led by Richard I of England and Philippe II of France leads to truce with Arabs

**1275–92** Italian merchant Marco Polo resident at court of Mongol emperor Kublai Khan in China

**1369** Mongol leader Tamerlane assumes leadership of Samarkand; he later extends his empire into Persia and India

AD **960** Beginning of Song Dynasty in China, which will last until 1279; it adopts Neo-Confucianism as official philosophy

**1048** First movable type in use in China, consisting of clay characters in an iron frame

**1100** Chinese invent the magnetic compass

**1147–49** Second Crusade ends in failure to recapture Holy Land

**1192** Yoritomo becomes first Shogun (commander-in-chief) of Japan, initiating the so-called Kamakura period, which is dominated by Samurai and lasts until 1333

**1368** After a century of Mongol rule, the Ming dynasty takes power in China, initiating a 300-year period of isolation during which art and culture flourish

---

AD **711** Moors invade Spain, bringing Islamic influence to Europe

AD **800** Charlemagne crowned Holy Roman Emperor in Rome by Pope Leo III

Viking people of Scandinavia begin to explore and plunder the European coastline; they eventually colonize Iceland and parts of Britain and set up trading posts in eastern Europe

**1232** Pope Gregory IX establishes the Inquisition, a special court set up at Toulouse, France, to investigate heresies against the Catholic Church

**1280** Windmills in use in western Europe

**1300** The Renaissance begins in Italy and spreads throughout Europe

**1337** Start of the Hundred Years War between England and France

AD **771** Charlemagne becomes king of the Franks; he soon expands Frankish Empire in central Europe

**1066** Norman king William I (Conqueror) invades England and commissions Domesday Book to assess the wealth of the country; population estimated at around 2 million

**1326** Gunpowder being used in cannons

**1346** Black Death (bubonic plague) spreads from Asia Minor to Italy and from there to the rest of Europe; 25 percent of the European population die within five years

---

AD **800** Rise of the Kingdom of Ghana in West Africa, which lasts until 1050

c. **1000** Growth of urban centers in southern Africa; craftworks are traded widely

Rise of kingdoms of Yoruba in present-day Nigeria

Rise of empire of Great Zimbabwe in East Africa, which flourishes until 1400

**1100** Different language groups begin to emerge, including the Xhosa and the Zulu

**1150** Emergence of Hausa city-states in present-day Nigeria

**1300** Emergence of the Benin Empire of Nigeria, West Africa

Construction of royal court at Great Zimbabwe

**1340** Empire of Songhai, a strong trading state in present-day Mali, founded on Niger River

AD **900** Trading routes established between East and West Africa as well as across the Sahara

**1050** Tokolor people of Senegal, West Africa, become the first group south of the Sahara to follow Islam

**1062** Almoravid Muslim sect takes control of Morocco, establishing its capital at Marrakesh

**1130** Almohad Muslim sect rises up against corrupt Almoravids, taking control of North Africa and ruling until 1212

**1200** Mali Empire, in present-day Ghana, establishes Muslim rule in West Africa; it lasts 200 years

**1312–37** Mali Empire reaches its zenith

**1350** Complex irrigation methods in use in East African Rift Valley

---

AD **980** Viking outlaw Erik the Red establishes settlement in Greenland; population of settlement may have reached 5,000, but it is eventually abandoned in 15th century when climate becomes colder

**1000** Viking explorers land on various parts of American coast including Baffin Island, Labrador, and Newfoundland (possibly the place known as Vinland in Norse legends)

Toltecs of Tula (in present-day Hidalgo, Mexico) found an empire which flourishes for next 200 years

**1200** Several tribes, including the Mexica, migrate to the Valley of Mexico, leading to the foundation of Aztec civilization; they begin terracing mountain slopes for food cultivation

**1250** Emerald Mound, a huge ceremonial site near Natchez Trace Parkway, Mississippi, in use

c. **1300** Drought in southwestern USA forces Anasazi and other native peoples to abandon homelands

AD **800** Native Americans living in present-day Illinois start to abandon hunter-gatherer way of life in favor of agriculture; maize becomes a major crop

Mayan population of Copán Valley reaches 20,000

**1150** Growth of communities in present-day Alabama, Georgia, and Oklahoma; they produce many decorated ceremonial objects

**1325** Aztecs establish their capital of Tenochtitlán, which grows into a major city with 250,000 inhabitants; it later becomes Mexico City

---

AD **800** Machu Picchu, a site of religious and symbolic importance for the Inca people, is built in the mountains above the Urubamba Valley in Peru

**1200** Cuzco becomes capital of Inca civilization; Inca cultivate mountainous areas with irrigation canals in order to feed a growing population

AD **725** Tiwanaku becomes a major Moche population center with up to 50,000 inhabitants

AD **850** Chimiú people found Chimor Empire and build capital of Chan Chan in the Moche valley; by 1100 it has a population of 8,000

*Inca ceramic plate*

**1250** Emergence of Killke style of ceramics in the Cuzco area; this will later become the distinctive style of the Inca civilization

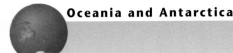

# 1400 to 1699

## Oceania and Antarctica

**c. 1500** Moas hunted to extinction in New Zealand

*Moa*

**1400** Traders and fishing vessels from the islands of present-day Indonesia visit the north coast of Australia

Temple city of Nan Madol in use off the island of Temwen, Micronesia; built of stone on artificial islands, it is only accessible by boat

## Asia and the Middle East

*Ottoman Constantinople*

**1453** Constantinople falls to the Ottoman Turks

**1526** Mogul Empire founded when Babar invades Hindustan and conquers all of northern India; for 200 years the empire is well administered, centralized, and prosperous

**1543** Shipwrecked Portuguese traders become the first Europeans to visit Japan; they introduce the first firearms to the country

**1405** Death of Tamerlane

**1498** Portuguese sailor Vasco da Gama reaches the Malabar coast in India after sailing round the Cape of Good Hope

**1502** Founding of Safavid dynasty in Persia by Ismail, who proclaims himself shah; the dynasty lasts until 1736

**1534** Ottoman Turks invade Mesopotamia taking Tabriz and Baghdad

## Europe and the Russian Federation

**1450** Beginning of Little Ice Age which brings harsh winters, wet summers, and food shortages to Europe for next 400 years

Johannes Gutenberg builds the first printing press

**1455** Gutenberg prints the Mazarin Bible at Mainz, Germany

**1492** Spanish expel Moors from Granada, their last stronghold in Spain

**1538** Flemish geographer Gerardus Mercator uses the name "America" on maps for the first time

**1543** Nicholas Copernicus proposes that Earth revolves around the Sun, challenging the traditional Ptolemaic view that the opposite was true

**1517** Reformation begins when German priest Martin Luther nails 95 theses challenging the power of the Catholic Church to a church door in Wittenberg; the movement soon spreads throughout Europe

**1400** Leprosy eradicated in most parts of Europe due to improved diet and sanitation

**1453** End of the Hundred Years War between England and France

**1478** Queen Isabella of Spain sets up Spanish Inquisition to investigate heretical activities

**1546** Mercator declares that Earth has a magnetic pole

## Africa

**1415** Portuguese explore North and West African coast in caravels, a new kind of sturdy sailing vessel, capturing Ceuta under Henry the Navigator

**1464** Songhai secedes from Mali; in 1468, it captures Timbuktu

**1486** Portuguese reach Angola on the West African coast

**1500** Rise of the Bornu Empire in northern Nigeria following Kanem Empire's demise; it reaches its zenith at end of century

**1450** Rise of empires of Congo and Ndongo in central Africa (present-day Congo and Democratic Republic of the Congo)

State of Bono in West Africa becomes an important gold-mining center

**1471** Portuguese establish forts on West African coast and begin trading in gold

**1488** First Portuguese vessels arrive at the Cape of Good Hope

**1517** Ottoman Turks take control of Egypt after defeating the Mamelukes (Muslim slave soldiers) and rule for the next 250 years

**1400–1500** Rise of Nyoro kingdom in present-day Uganda

## North and Central America

*Aztec mask*

**c. 1450** Pueblo farmers of southwestern North America trade with plains-hunters of the north, exchanging corn, cotton goods, and pottery for buffalo meat and hides

**1492** Italian seafarer Christopher Columbus reaches the Caribbean and discovers Watling Island, Cuba, and Haiti

**1497** John Cabot and son Sebastian explore the east coast of North America

**1524** Italian navigator Giovanni da Verrazzano explores northeast coast of North America

Spanish conquer Mayan lands

**1540–42** Spanish explorer Francisco Coronado explores southwestern North America

**1500** Aztec Empire at its height

**1519** Spanish conquistador Hernán Cortéz meets Aztec ruler Montezuma II at Tenochtitlán, Mexico; two years later, he seizes the city and Montezuma

**1400** End of the early Aztec phase sees widespread use of chinampas, swamplands reclaimed for agricultural plantations

**c. 1460** Mississippian Native American societies living along river valleys of eastern North America increasingly dependent on agriculture; they build large earthen mound structures for religious ceremonies

**1494** Treaty of Tordesillas divides the New World between Spain and Portugal; the treaty is rejected by other European maritime powers

**1539** Spanish explorer Hernando de Soto reaches Florida and travels up the Mississippi River

## South America

**1438** Pachacuti becomes Inca leader and begins expanding empire

*Gold Inca beaker, 1500s*

**1499** Amerigo Vespucci sails from Spain to South America

**1516** Spanish explorer Juan Díaz de Solis becomes the first European to land in present-day Argentina; he is killed by Querandi indians

**1525** Civil war breaks out in Inca Empire between north led by Atahualpa and south led by his brother Huáscar

**1545** Spanish discover silver at Potosí in central Andes, starting a rush to exploit this valuable resource

**1400** Rise of Inca Empire known as Tawantinsuyu; Incas develop building techniques of great precision and begin to construct an extensive road system

**1450** Incas conquer Chimú state in Peru

**1500** Pedro Alvarez Cabral discovers Brazil and claims it for Portugal

**1521** Spanish explore northern coast of South America and start a colony in what becomes Venezuela

**1532** Spanish conquistador Francisco Pizarro imprisons Inca emperor Atahualpa; despite an enormous ransom being paid, Atahualpa is executed

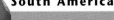

**1568** Spanish sailors visit the Solomon Islands

**1595** Spanish sailor Mendaña de Neyra discovers and names the Marquesas Islands, which now are part of French Polynesia

**1606** Dutchman Willem Janszon lands on north coast of Australia

Spanish navigator Luis Vaez de Torres sails through the strait that subsequently bears his name without realizing that a continent lies to his south

**1616** Dutch sea captain Dirck Hartog lands on the west coast of Australia

Dutch navigators Willem Schouten and Jakob le Maire visit Tonga

**1642–43** Dutch navigator Abel Tasman lands on Van Diemen's Land (now Tasmania), claiming possession for the Netherlands; he then discovers the west coast of New Zealand and sights the eastern islands of Fiji and Tongatapu in the Tongan group

**1644** Tasman charts part of the coastline of northern and western Australia

**1688** English adventurer William Dampier spends two months on the west coast of Australia

**1699** Dampier returns to explore the west coast of Australia; unimpressed, he sails north for New Guinea

---

**1568** Akbar, greatest of the Moghuls and grandson of the empire's founder Babar, conquers Chitor in Rajasthan, quells the Rajput princes, and takes control of the region

**1580** Unification of Japan under Oda Nobunaga

**1597** Dutch establish trading post at Batavia (Jakarta) in Dutch East Indies

**1600** British East India Company established to develop trade in Asia and challenge the trading empires of the Portuguese and Spanish; similar trading companies subsequently set up by Dutch (1602) and French (1604)

**1603** Tokugawa Shogunate begins rule in Japan, continuing until 1867

**1623** At trading center of Ambon, Dutch behead British traders accused of plotting to take over the Dutch fortress; incident creates friction between trading powers

**1632–43** Taj Mahal, a white marble mausoleum, built at Agra, India, by Emperor Shah Jehan in memory of his wife Mumtaz Mahal

**1639** English colonists settle at Madras in India

**1643** First French missionaries arrive in Vietnam

**1644** The Manchus, a people from Manchuria, invade China from northwest and establish Qing dynasty, bringing peace and prosperity

**1674** Dutch traders help local Muslim leader, Amangkurat I, head of the kingdom of Maturam, Indonesia, to suppress rebellion; in return, Dutch gain possession of parts of central Java

**1683** China seizes Formosa

---

**1569** Mercator produces *Cosmographia*, which includes the first navigational maps of the world

**1571** Battle of Lepanto halts maritime expansion of Ottoman Empire

**1572** In France, 10 years of religious conflict climax in St Bartholomew's Day Massacre of 3,000 Huguenots (Protestants) in Paris; many Huguenots seek refuge in England

**1588** Spanish Armada, Philip II of Spain's invasion force against England, is defeated by Sir Francis Drake in the English Channel

**1603** King James VI of Scotland becomes James I of England

**1609** Mathematician-astronomer Galileo Galilei improves the recently invented telescope and describes Jupiter's satellites

Johannes Kepler announces his laws of planetary motion

**1618** Start of Thirty Years War between Protestant powers—England, Holland, Scandinavia, and German states—and Spain and the Habsburg Empire

**1643** Barometer invented by Italian scientist Evangelista Torricelli

**1642–48** English Civil War leads to execution of Charles I

**1665** The Great Plague of London takes 70,000 lives between July and October; the following year much of the city is destroyed by a fire lasting from February 2 to 9

**1661** Ottoman Turks invade Transylvania and Hungary

**1682** Edmond Halley identifies a bright comet and correctly predicts that it will reappear in 1758 and approximately every 77 years thereafter

**1675** Greenwich Observatory established by English astronomer Edmond Halley

**1699** Under Treaty of Carlowitz, defeated Turks forced to cede most of Balkans to Austrian Habsburgs

---

*Yoruba sculpture*

**1591** Morocco defeats Songhai, bringing the empire to an end

**1600** Oyo Empire becomes one of the most successful of the Yoruba states after the leader Orompoto uses proceeds of trade to build a large army

**1613** Portuguese priest and explorer Pedro Paez discovers the source of the Blue Nile: Lake Tana in Tanzania

**1619** First slaves from West Africa shipped to Virginia, North America, by Dutch traders

**1626** French establish settlements on Madagascar but island does not become a colony until 1896

**1637** French establish military base in Senegal, West Africa

**1652** Dutch East India Company establishes garrison at site of modern-day Cape Town

**1657** First Dutch settlers take up land grants at Liesbeeck River near Cape Town

First slaves brought to the Cape from India, Indonesia, and West Africa by Dutch

**1660** Rise of Bambara kingdoms of Segu and Kaarta on the Niger River; by 1670 they have replaced the Mandingo Empire

**1670** Rise of Ashanti Empire in West Africa in modern-day Ghana; by early eighteenth century its rulers are supplying slaves to Dutch and British traders

---

**1583** The English found a colony at St Johns, Newfoundland

**1584** Sir Walter Raleigh claims Virginia on east coast of North America for England; attempts to form a permanent settlement fail

**1605** Port Royal in Nova Scotia becomes the first French settlement in North America

**1607** Jamestown, Virginia, becomes first permanent English settlement in North America

**1619** The first slaves from West Africa are sold in Virginia, North America, by Dutch traders

**1620** The Pilgrim Fathers leave Plymouth, England, and cross the Atlantic to the New World in the *Mayflower*

**1624** The Dutch establish a settlement at New Netherlands, North America

**1642** The French establish site of Montréal on the St Lawrence seaway

**1663** The North American French colonies form a Province by amalgamating as New France, with Québec as the capital

**1670** Hudson's Bay Company founded in London by English and French merchants seeking to establish fur trade in the Hudson Bay region of northeastern Canada

**1682** René La Salle explores the Mississippi River and claims Louisiana for France

---

**1553** First settlements of Santiago del Estero and Tucumán in Argentina founded by Spanish arriving from Peru in search of gold and silver

**1567** Two million South American Indians die from typhoid fever introduced by Spanish soldiers

**1573** Córdoba and Mendoza grow as part of trade routes between Chile and Argentina

**1580** Spanish colonists establish settlement at Buenos Aires on La Plata estuary

**1616** Dutch navigator Willem Schouten sights Cape Horn, the tip of South America

**1620** Expansion of silver mining at Potosí, Bolivia

**1624** Dutch seize Brazilian territory of Bahia; they later take control of the rich sugar-producing area of Pernambuco (1630–54)

**1630** Portuguese begin to import large numbers of slaves from Africa to work on sugar plantations of northeastern Brazil, displacing native populations

*Ankle fetter used to secure slaves*

**1695** Large gold deposits discovered in central Brazil, in the area now known as Minas Gerais, triggering an influx of prospectors

## Oceania and Antarctica

Captain James Cook, 1728–79

**1765** British explorer John Byron sails through the Pacific while searching for the "Great South Land," and visits numerous islands including the Gilbert Islands

**1788** First Fleet under Captain Arthur Phillip arrives at Botany Bay to found a British penal colony; disappointed with Botany Bay, Phillip establishes the colony at Port Jackson

**1722** Dutch explorer Jacob Roggeveen explores the Pacific, visiting Samoa and Easter Island as well as Makatea, Bora-Bora, and Maupiti

**1766–69** Comte Louis Antoine de Bougainville, scientist and navigator, travels widely throughout the Pacific, visiting Tahiti, the New Hebrides, New Britain, and New Guinea

**1770** After visiting Tahiti and New Zealand, English navigator Captain James Cook charts the east coast of Australia and lands at Botany Bay

**1793** First free British settlers arrive in New South Wales, Australia

## Asia and the Middle East

**1715** Chinese conquer Mongolia and Turkestan

**1755** The Nawab of Bengal occupies Calcutta, taking many British prisoners, some of whom die in the "Black Hole," a small room used as a jail; British, led by Robert Clive, retake Calcutta

**1761** British capture of Pondicherry marks the end of French colonial power in India

British East India Company coat of arms

**1707** Mt Fuji, Japan's biggest volcano, erupts

**1730** An earthquake on the island of Hokkaido, Japan, causes the deaths of 137,000 people

**1740** British East India Company takes over Mogul land

Dutch and British armies oust Portuguese spice traders and establish ports at Madras, Bombay, and Calcutta

**1769** Severe famines in Bengal lead to rural depopulation for more than 20 years

**1771** Political crisis of the "Tay Son Rebellion" in Vietnam under which the old Confucian order is threatened by reforms inspired by Western ideas

## Europe and the Russian Federation

**1707** Act of Union unites Scotland and England as Great Britain

**1725** John Harrison, English clockmaker, invents a device for measuring longitude at sea and on land

**1755** Lisbon is destroyed by a major earthquake; it is the first earthquake to be studied by scientists

**1769** After several years of development, Scotsman James Watt invents the double-acting rotary steam engine which is introduced to textile mills and other factories

**1701–14** War of Spanish Succession

**1713** Peace of Unsikaupunki ends the Great Northern War between Sweden and Russia; after more than 350 years of allegiance to Sweden, Finland comes under Russian control (until 1721)

**1735** Swedish naturalist Carl Linnaeus publishes *Systema Naturae*, a system for classifying plants and animals; his basic hierarchy is still in use

**1760** Rise of Amsterdam as world's major economic center

**1781** German-born English astronomer Sir William Herschel discovers the planet Uranus; Herschel's studies form the basis of modern astronomy

**1789** The French Revolution begins with the storming of the Bastille and lasts for 10 years

## Africa

**1757** Sultan Muhammad ibn Abd Allah brings peace and stability to Morocco after a period of unrest and economic decline

**1779** Sporadic warfare breaks out in south between Dutch and British colonists and indigenous Xhosa people; the conflict lasts for the next 100 years

**1787** British set up a colony at Sierra Leone, West Africa

**1790** In present-day northern Nigeria, the Islamic Fulani people from Senegal wage a holy war (jihad) against the Hausa kings

**1713** Native Khoikhoi pastoralists of South Africa replaced by "trekboer" settler farmers in search of grazing land; huge numbers of native Khoisan people die in smallpox epidemic

South African San or Bushman

**1760** Slaves are traded in increasing numbers in what is now Gabon, West Africa, often in exchange for European goods such as guns, textiles, and rum

**1795** British occupy Cape Town, a vital supply post on Britain's expanding trade routes prior to opening of the Suez canal; British settlers arrive in increasing numbers

Scottish explorer Mungo Park reaches the Niger River

## North and Central America

**1740–48** War between Britain and France over North America

**1763** Peace of Paris treaty ending Seven Years War in Europe awards Canada to Britain

**1775** Beginning of American War of Independence (to 1783); the following year the 13 American colonies adopt the Declaration of Independence, thereby founding the USA

**1787** Delegates at a national constitutional convention—the "Founding Fathers"—create the US Constitution

**1789–93** Alexander Mackenzie explores northwestern North America, crossing over the Rockies to reach the Pacific Ocean

**1720** Spanish soldiers invade Texas

**1752** American scientist and diplomat Benjamin Franklin proves that lightning is an electrical discharge and invents the lightning conductor

**1770–72** British adventurer Samuel Hearne explores territories to the northwest of Hudson Bay in northern Canada

**1791** Canada is divided into French- and English-speaking territories by the Constitutions Act

**1793** Eli Whitney invents the cotton gin, a mechanical threshing machine

## South America

**1770–80** Improved navigational methods strengthen links between Europe and Latin America, creating opportunities for economic growth

**1790** Native people and imported Africans used as slaves on plantations in Brazil; many die from European diseases

**1700** Bourbon Spain establishes the Viceroyalty of New Grenada in central and South America; Peru is forced to release control of Guayaquil in modern-day Ecuador

**1743** Charles-Marie de la Condamine, a French scientist given the task of measuring a degree of longitude on the equator, takes measurements in Ecuador and then explores the Amazon, bringing back samples of the rubber tree and platinum

**1780** Tupac Amaru II leads an unsuccessful revolt by native people against Spanish rule in Peru

**1799–1804** German scientist Alexander von Humboldt explores central and South America

**1803** British penal settlements founded in Hobart and Port Arthur in Tasmania

**1837** Frenchman Lieutenant Jules Dumont d'Urville discovers Joinville Island, off Antarctica

**1840** The Treaty of Waitangi gives Britain sovereignty over New Zealand but also gives Maori people sovereignty over their lands (as well as British citizenship), creating conflicting expectations

**1861** Thomas Mort builds the first refrigeration unit for the transportation of meat in Sydney, Australia

Gold Rush in New Zealand

**1895** Norwegian whaler Henryk Johan Bull becomes the first person to land on the Antarctic continent at what is now Cape Adare

Beginning of severe droughts in Australia which last for the next seven years

**1820** Russian naval officer Captain Fabian von Bellingshausen is possibly the first person to see Antarctica

**1839–43** British explorers Ross and Crozier map the coast of Antarctica in the *Erebus* and the *Terror*; two volcanoes are later named after the ships

**1851** Beginning of the Australian Gold Rush

**1868** Transportation of convicted criminals from Britain to Australia ends with the arrival of the last convict ship in Western Australia

**1893** New Zealand becomes the first country in the world to give the vote to women

---

**1800** British East India Company trading in China; British smuggle opium into China to offset other exports and Opium War breaks out when Chinese object

**1842** Treaty of Nanjing ends first Opium War; China cedes Hong Kong to Britain

**1850** Failure of monsoon rains in northern India causes famine lasting more than 30 years

**1883** Krakatau, Indonesia, erupts, killing 36,000 people; the explosion is heard up to 3,650 km (1,400 miles) away

**1894–95** Sino-Japanese War breaks out over Korea—Japan emerges victorious and annexes Formosa

**1880s** Indian Nationalist Movement, including Indian National Congress, campaigns for an end to British rule

**1815** The largest volcanic eruption ever, at Tambora, Indonesia, kills at least 10,000 people; more than 80,000 later die of starvation and disease resulting from climatic effects of eruption

**1857** The Indian Revolt against heavy taxes results in considerable loss of British and Indian lives; it is ruthlessly suppressed

**1876** Queen Victoria becomes Empress of India

**1887–88** Huang (Yellow) River in China floods, killing 1 million people

**1891** A severe earthquake in Japan kills up to 10,000 people

---

**1804** After conquering much of western Europe, including the Netherlands, Switzerland, and northern Italy, Napoleon crowns himself emperor of France

**1834** British mathematician Charles Babbage invents the "analytical machine," forerunner of the computer

**1848** Revolutions occur in various parts of Europe, including Germany, France, Austria, and Italy

**1859** Publication of Charles Darwin's *The Origin of Species*, which expounds the theory of natural selection

**1871** Unification of Germany under Emperor William I

*Charles Darwin, 1809–82*

**1835** French mathematician Gaspard de Coriolis describes how winds and ocean currents are deflected clockwise around high-pressure systems in northern hemisphere and anti-clockwise in southern hemisphere

Halley's comet reappears, as he had predicted

**1850** Karl Marx, a German economist living in London, publishes *The Communist Manifesto*

French physician Louis Pasteur advances a theory that germs cause disease

**1861** Italy becomes a single state under King Victor Emmanuel II of Sardinia after Giuseppe Garibaldi and his "red shirts" defeat Bourbon troops

**1899** French meteorologist Teisserenc de Bort discovers that temperature stops decreasing at around 10 km (6 miles) above sea level; this leads to discovery of atmospheric layers

**1815** Napoleon defeated by British army at Waterloo

---

**c.1800** Zulu nation founded in what is now Kwazulu-Natal, South Africa, forcing Shoshangane clan into Swaziland and Mzilikazi clan into Zimbabwe

**1853** Scottish explorer and missionary David Livingstone begins his exploration of central Africa

**1860** Laborers from India are imported by Natal farmers to work on farms and plantations

**1870** Gold and diamonds discovered in South Africa

**1884–85** Conference held in Berlin divides up remaining African territories between Germany, France, and Britain

**1899** Start of the Second Boer War between British and Afrikaners (Boers)

Gold-mining industry in South Africa employs 110,000 workers; almost 100,000 are African laborers

**1861** British occupy Lagos in Nigeria

**1871** US journalist Henry Morton Stanley locates Livingstone, who has mapped the river systems of central Africa and traced the source of the Zambeze

**1836–38** 10,000 Boer (Dutch) settlers unhappy with British rule in the Cape set out on Great Trek to seek new territories in Natal and Orange River region

**1858** English explorers John Speke and Richard Burton discover Lake Victoria; Speke later discovers the source of the Nile

**1869** The Suez Canal opens, allowing a much reduced voyage time between the Mediterranean Sea and the Indian Ocean

**1880–81** British attempts to bring the Boer republics (of Orange Free State and Transvaal) into a federation fail when the Boers defeat the British in the First Boer War

**1830–48** France conquers Algeria

---

**1803** Napoleon sells almost 3 million sq km (900,000 sq miles) of southern central North America to the USA in a deal known as the Louisiana Purchase

**1813** Mexico declares its independence

**1837** Samuel Morse demonstrates the electric telegraph in New York

**1861–65** American Civil War between the North and the South caused by disputes over political and economic issues, including the abolition of slavery

**1876** Scots-born American Alexander Graham Bell invents the telephone

**1886** The trans-continental Canadian Pacific Railway is completed

**1804–05** US army officers Meriwether Lewis and William Clark explore the Missouri River, cross the Rocky Mountains, and reach the Pacific Ocean

**1824** The Erie Canal opens, creating a navigational route between the Great Lakes and the Atlantic Ocean

**1848** As a result of victory over Mexico, the USA gains vast areas of western and southern North America

Discovery of gold in California causes an influx of prospectors in the first Gold Rush

*Gold nugget*

**1867** USA purchases Alaska from Russia

**1879** Thomas Edison invents electric lighting

**1898** Spanish-American War ends with Cuba becoming independent and the USA gaining Puerto Rico, Guam, and the Philippines

---

**1808** Prince John, royal ruler of Portugal, is forced to flee from Portugal and declares Rio de Janeiro capital of the worldwide Portuguese Empire; he returns to Portugal in 1821

**1824** Simón Bolívar wins a victory over Spanish troops at Ayacucho, Peru, ending Spanish control in South America

**1866** San Roque Dam built on the Paraná River, Argentina, to supply hydroelectric power and water for irrigation

**1879** Population of Gran Chaco region of Argentina grows rapidly as a result of the expansion of the beef industry, with large numbers of immigrants arriving from Europe

**1880** Japanese immigrants begin to settle in southeastern Brazil to profit from rapid growth of coffee plantations

**1889** Brazil becomes a republic

**1822** Prince John's son Pedro declares Brazil's independence and is crowned Emperor

**1830** Argentina lays claim to Islas Malvinas (the Falkland Islands); three years later, Britain occupies the islands

**1870** Rubber production soars in the Amazon area of Brazil, attracting migrants from the eastern seaboard and from Europe

**1879–83** Pacific War between Chile, Peru, and Bolivia over nitrate deposits results in Chile taking territory in southern Peru

**1888** Brazil abolishes slavery: 750,000 people are freed

**1816** Argentina declares independence from Spain

## Oceania and Antarctica

**1901–04** British navy captain Robert Scott undertakes the first inland exploration of Antarctica

**1907** Englishman Ernest Shackleton, a member of Scott's earlier expedition, reaches the South Magnetic Pole in Antarctica

**1914–18** 330,000 Australians and 100,000 New Zealanders travel overseas to fight in the First World War

**1928** Australian aviator Bert Hinkler arrives at Darwin, Australia, after a 15-day flight from Croydon, England, via Rome, Egypt, India, Malaya, and Java

**1939** Australia and New Zealand send troops to support Britain in the Second World War; hundreds of thousands fight in Europe and the Pacific

**1947** New Zealand's parliament adopts the Statute of Westminster (1931) which gives it formal independence from the UK

**1901** Federation of the six Australian colonies results in the formation of the Commonwealth of Australia

**1911** Norwegian explorer Roald Amundsen and his team become the first to reach the South Pole on December 11; just over one month later a British expedition under Captain Scott accomplishes the same feat, but the team perishes on the return journey

First World War digger's hat

**1919** Influenza pandemic leaves thousands of Australians dead

**1930** The Depression hits Australia and New Zealand

Amy Johnson arrives at Darwin, Australia, having flown solo from London, UK; she fails by only 4 days to beat Hinkler's record

**1942** Japanese troops occupy New Guinea

Japanese submarines enter Sydney Harbour, Australia

## Asia and the Middle East

**1907** France seizes Lao territories east of the Mekong River; formerly under control of Thailand, they include much of present-day Cambodia, Laos, and Vietnam

**1934** Mao Ze Dong leads the Long March of the Communist revolutionaries across China

**1945** First atomic bombs dropped on Japanese cities of Hiroshima and Nagasaki by USA, bringing the war in the Pacific to an end

**1946** Start of war in Indochina between French colonial power and Vietnamese nationalists led by Ho Chi Minh (to 1954)

Mao Ze Dong, 1893–1976

**1900** In Peking (Beijing), the Boxer Rebellion of Chinese nationalists against foreign interests is put down by British and Russian forces

**1911** Rebels proclaim Chinese republic under Sun Yat-sen; last Chinese Emperor Pu Yi relinquishes throne in the following year

**1927–28** Civil War in China between the Communist party and the Kuomintang (Nationalist Party) under Chiang Kai-Shek; Nationalists take Beijing

**1948** State of Israel proclaimed following partition of Palestine

**1947** India gains independence and is partitioned, with Pakistan becoming separate Muslim state

**1949** Communist party takes control of China

## Europe and the Russian Federation

**1914** Assassination of Archduke Francis-Ferdinand at Sarajevo in Bosnia triggers the First World War between Germany, Austria-Hungary, and the Ottoman Empire on one side, and Britain, France, and Russia on the other; more than 8 million soldiers die

**1917** The second Russian Revolution takes place in March and Russian royal family killed; in October, the Bolsheviks seize power

**1928** The world's first antibiotic, penicillin, is discovered by Scottish scientist Alexander Fleming

**1936–39** Spanish Civil War between Nationalists and Republicans results in General Franco becoming Nationalist head of state of the Falangist (Fascist) government

**1945** Second World War ends in Europe (8 May) and the Pacific (2 September); the death toll includes more than 14 million soldiers and about 27 million civilians

**1905** Bloody suppression of riots in St Petersburg leads to the first Russian Revolution

**1916** German-born physicist Albert Einstein publishes his General Theory of Relativity, which suggests that the universe is expanding

**1918–19** Influenza pandemic leaves millions of Europeans dead and kills up to 40 million worldwide

**1933** Adolf Hitler becomes Chancellor of Germany; his National Socialist Party ends democratic rule

**1939** Germany invades Poland, starting the Second World War

## Africa

**1907** Mahatma Gandhi campaigns in South Africa for civil rights of ethnic Indian population

**1931** South Africa granted independence by Britain as a member of the Commonwealth

**1949–50** Racial apartheid becomes the official policy of the National Party government of South Africa

**1912** The African National Congress (ANC) founded in South Africa by a small group of educated black Africans seeking political rights

African National Congress flag

**1935** Seeking to expand its African territories, Italy invades Ethiopia, capturing Addis Ababa in 1936; Haile Selassie flees until British troops restore him to office during Second World War

**1902** Britain emerges victorious from Second Boer War

## North and Central America

**1903** First successful flights in heavier-than-air machines made by brothers Orville and Wilbur Wright at Kitty Hawk, North Carolina

**1917** United States enters First World War

**1927** Charles Lindbergh makes the first nonstop solo flight across the Atlantic Ocean from Roosevelt Field, New York, to Le Bourget near Paris

**1941** Japanese attack on US naval base at Pearl Harbor, Oahu Island, Hawaii, brings USA into the Second World War; during the war, the USA loses 292,000 troops, Canada 43,000

**1948** Universal Declaration of Human Rights adopted by General Assembly of UN in New York; it sets out minimum standards of civil and political rights to which all people are entitled

Wright brothers' Flyer III, 1905

**1902** Mt Pelée, Martinique, erupts, killing 20,000 and burying the town of St Pierre

**1906** San Francisco is devastated by a major earthquake measuring 8.3 on the Richter scale

**1918** Influenza pandemic begins in North America; it eventually kills up to 40 million worldwide

**1929** The Wall Street Crash of October 24 causes widespread financial instability; it is followed by the Great Depression which spreads worldwide

**1945** Founding charter of United Nations (UN) signed by 51 nations in San Francisco

## South America

**1930s** Huge population growth and urbanization occurs, particularly in Argentina and Uruguay, chiefly as a result of large-scale immigration

**1942** Brazil supports Allies in Second World War and sends 25,000 troops to fight in Italy

**1946** Juan Perón becomes President of Argentina with backing of both army and labor unions

**1914** First World War initially disrupts Latin American trade, but for some countries this is followed by an export-led boom which lasts until the Depression

**1932–35** Paraguay defeats Bolivia in war over Chaco region; final settlement negotiated in 1938 awards Chaco territory to Paraguay

**1944** A massive earthquake kills 5,000 people in the Andean San Juan province of Argentina

**1951** Australia, New Zealand, and the USA sign the ANZUS defence treaty; the signatories agree to offer mutual support in the event of an attack on any of the other parties

*Antarctic penguin*

**1960** Swiss diver Jacques Piccard and the US navy's Donald Walsh explore the Mariana Trench in the Pacific Ocean to a depth of 11,000 m (36,089 feet)—the lowest known point on the ocean floor

**1975** Papua New Guinea becomes independent

Thousands of refugees from Vietnam, Laos, and Cambodia, many of them ethnic Chinese, begin to flee to Australia by boat

**1985** New Zealand's anti-nuclear policy sours relations with traditional allies France and the United States

**1996–97** Despite worldwide protests, France concludes a series of nuclear weapon tests on Muraroa Atoll in the South Pacific before agreeing to sign the UN Test Ban Treaty

**1959** Antarctic Treaty bans military activity in Antarctica; signatories also agree to suspend territorial claims

**1974** Cyclone Tracy destroys Darwin in northern Australia

**1979** Scientists discover a hole in the ozone layer above Antarctica

---

**1953** Mt Everest is climbed for the first time by New Zealand explorer Edmund Hillary and Sherpa Tenzing Norgay

**1959** China suppresses revolt in Tibet; Tibet's spiritual leader, the Dalai Lama, flees to India

**1975** Vietnam War ends with the fall of Saigon after the withdrawal of US troops

**1995** A massive earthquake lasting less than a minute kills 5,000 people in Kobe, Japan, and causes massive disruption to transport and industry

**1950** Korean War begins when North Korean communist troops invade South Korea; the war lasts until 1953, with US troops fighting on the South Korean side

*Potala Palace, Tibet*

**1957** Vietnam War starts when North Vietnamese (Viet Cong) attack South Vietnamese

**1965** US troops based in South Vietnam committed to aid South Vietnamese forces

**1976** An earthquake in Tangshan near Beijing, China, kills more than 200,000 people and injures another 150,000

**1991** Mt Pinatubo in the Philippines erupts killing 30 people and leaving 10,000 homeless

Following Iraq's occupation of the oil-rich state of Kuwait, US combines with the UK, France, and other allies to defeat Iraq in the Gulf War

**2003** The United States and the UK are leading a coalition of 32 countries attack Iraq without sanction by the UN Security Council and topple the regime of Saddam Hussein. They hand nominal control over to a council in June 2004; first democratic elections are supposed to be held in early 2005

---

**1961** Russian cosmonaut Yuri Gagarin becomes the first man in space and the first to orbit Earth

Berlin Wall erected by the East German government to stop citizens escaping to the West

**1974** Turkish troops invade northern Cyprus following the overthrow of the island's president, Greek Archbishop Makarios; fighting between Greek and Turkish Cypriots results in the creation of a neutral corridor across the island

**1989** Collapse of Communism in the Soviet Union and Eastern Europe: Russian leader Mikhail Gorbachev and US President George Bush declare the end of the Cold War, and the Berlin Wall is dismantled

**1991** Civil War in former Yugoslavia between Croatia and Bosnia; UN sends peacekeeping forces

Collapse of the Soviet Union

**1967** A military junta seizes power in Greece overthrowing the government led by King Constantin II. Georgios Papadopoulos heads the junta and is elected president in 1973

**1984** HIV, the virus that causes AIDS and has already taken the lives of millions worldwide, is identified by Luc Montaigner at the Institut Pasteur, Paris

**1986** An accident at the Chernobyl nuclear power station in the Ukraine contaminates a huge area and spreads fallout across Europe

Russia launches Mir, an Earth-orbiting space station

**1995** Talks at Dayton, Ohio, USA, aimed at ending conflict in Bosnia, lead to a peace agreement; hostilities are gradually halted

**1957** The space age starts with the launching by Russia of Sputnik I, a satellite capable of orbiting Earth

*Sputnik 1, 1957*

---

**1956** Egypt closes Suez Canal; British, French, and Israeli troops invade to reopen it but UN intervenes to halt fighting

Independence of Morocco, Tunisia, and Sudan recognized by France

**1960** Massacre of 67 anti-apartheid demonstrators at Sharpeville, Johannesburg, South Africa

**1962** Nelson Mandela and other members of ANC imprisoned in South Africa

Algerian war of independence ends French rule

**1976** Young blacks protesting against compulsory Afrikaans language lessons are gunned down by police at Soweto, Johannesburg, South Africa

**1993** Civil war in Rwanda between Hutu and Tutsi people results in the slaughter of hundreds of thousands of Tutsi

**1994** Global population problems discussed at World Population Conference, Cairo, Egypt

Nelson Mandela elected President in first nonracial, democratic general election in South Africa

**1953** Military coup in Egypt ends monarchy of King Farouk and imposes republic

**1961** South Africa becomes a republic; sanctions imposed by several countries in response to apartheid policies

**1964** Former British colony of Rhodesia (now Zimbabwe) declares independence

**1967** Civil war in Nigeria; Biafra secedes until 1970

World's first heart transplant carried out in Cape Town by Dr Christiaan Barnard

**1977** Commencement of civil war and famine in Ethiopia, which lead to thousands of deaths

**1990** ANC leader Nelson Mandela freed from prison in South Africa; the following year, apartheid is abolished

---

**1961** US President John F. Kennedy backs an invasion of communist Cuba by exiled Cubans but fails to send US troops; Fidel Castro's forces easily repulse the attack at the Bay of Pigs

**1968** Martin Luther King and Robert Kennedy assassinated

**1974** US Space probe Mariner 10 sends back the first close-up pictures of the rings surrounding the planets Mercury and Venus

**1981** First flight of the space shuttle *Columbia*

First case of AIDS recognized

**1989** US invades Panama

*Space shuttle*

**2001** On September 11, terrorists of the Al-Qaida movement fly planes into the World Trade Center in New York and the Pentagon in Virginia. Around 3,000 people are killed

**1969** US astronauts Neil Armstrong and Buzz Aldrin make first landing on the moon from the spaceship *Apollo 11*

**1982** A volcanic eruption at El Chichón, Mexico causes the deaths of 3,500 people and blackens the sky for almost two days

**2009** On January 20, 2009, Barack Obama is the first African American to be sworn in as president of the United States

**1963** Assassination of President John F. Kennedy

**1980** Eruption of Mt St Helens, Washington State, USA—one of the largest in modern times

---

**1960** In Santiago, Chile, 5,000 people are killed by an earthquake

**1970** Salvador Allende of Chile becomes the world's first freely elected Marxist president

**1973** Allende is deposed and killed in a military coup led by General Augusto Pinochet

**1982–83** The century's most severe episode of the El Niño effect: Chile experiences record rainfall

**1992** Global environmental problems debated at first Earth Summit in Rio de Janiero, Brazil

Alberto Fujimori, President of Peru, suspends parliament claiming corruption among government officials; a new constitution is approved in 1993

**1955** General strike in Argentina; Perón and wife Eva sent into exile

**1973–76** Perón returns to Argentina and is re-elected, but dies in 1974; his third wife Isobel governs until Army chiefs arrest her; thousands subsequently killed by "security forces"

**1982** Argentina invades Falkland Islands; Britain uses military force to retake the islands by 14 June

**1988** General Pinochet's rule in Chile rejected by large majority in plebiscite

## Part 3

# Regions of the World

# World regions: The Changing Scene

*Culture is one way of defining world regions: the Middle East and Central Asia, for example, have a broadly Islamic culture in common (above). North America stretches from Canada (opposite) to Mexico and can be defined by its geographical, as well as its cultural, boundaries.*

Geographers, in their attempt to subdivide Earth's land surface into coherent areas, developed the concept of regions. Regions can be delineated within continents or within countries, depending at what scale study is being conducted.

Regions are parts of the world that have some degree of similarity in one or more characteristics, such as physiography, climate, culture, or economy. For example, a Himalayan region can be based on physiography, a Saharan region determined by its desert climate, a Confucian East Asia region determined by a dominant culture, and a European Economic Community region defined by countries linked by economic cooperation. In this atlas, however, much larger regions have been identified.

Regions, under whatever criteria they are defined, must be geographically contiguous. Countries adjacent to each other often share a major characteristic. Thus, the countries of Southeast Asia have a tropical, humid climate which ensures the growing of tropical crops such as tropical fruits, tea, coffee, and rubber. In contrast, several Middle Eastern countries have arid climates which inhibit large scale agriculture. Southeast Asia and the Middle East can be considered as regions where climate is one of the distinguishing characteristics.

In other cases, culture may be an important criterion for defining a region. The Middle East, besides being climatically different from other parts of Asia, also differs culturally. North and Central America have considerable cultural and economic differences that justify their being differentiated. This is also true for Africa, North Africa differing in several aspects from the countries south of the Sahara.

Very often a number of small countries lying close to each other may share one or more characteristics. This is the case with the small island nations of the Pacific. They can then be said to lie within an identifiable region or sub-region. On the other hand, some large countries, such as the Russian Federation have sufficient climatic and cultural diversity within their borders for sub-regions to be identified.

The naming and defining of continents was the first attempt to mark out large regions on the map of the world. Because the continents were named and defined by Europeans, the perspectives used were European. For example, some names came from ancient Greece where the lands lying to its east were named Asia and the lands to its west were called Europe. Because of the European perspective, it became customary to refer to the eastern lands close to Europe as the Near East, the lands lying far to the east as the Far East, and the lands in between as the Middle East.

Europe and Asia are geographically contiguous, forming the Eurasian landmass, but there are sufficient differences between them for them to be identifiable as two separate continents. This traditional separation is largely based on cultural and historical factors, the lines dividing the two continents being accepted by convention.

Africa, the two American continents, Australia, and Antarctica are easily defined because of their separation from other landmasses. Australia, New Zealand, and several Pacific islands are customarily included in a large region known as Oceania that includes a variety of climates, economies, and cultures. The only factor that gives Oceania its coherence is that these lands form a large cluster in the Central and South Pacific Ocean.

Regions or sub-regions can be identified within most of the world's continents. For instance, the large continent of Asia contains areas with distinctive characteristics that allow them to be considered as regions. Asia has been customarily subdivided into East Asia, Southeast Asia, South Asia (the Indian subcontinent), West Asia (the Middle East), Central Asia, and North Asia (Siberia). Monsoon Asia (or Asia-Pacific), a larger region, defined on the basis of climate, stretches across East, Southeast, and South Asia. Monsoon Asia is humid, extremely populous, and has extensive agriculture. Central Asia and the Middle East, on the other hand, are more arid, less populated, and have limited scope for agriculture, except where irrigated water is available.

Europe was within the last half century politically divided into Eastern and Western Europe. This ideological divide resulted in contrasting economic systems, the residual effects of which can still be seen. On economic grounds, Eastern and Western Europe can be considered as sub-regions. Climate can be used to differentiate Mediterranean Europe from lands north of the Alps.

In this atlas, the world has been divided up in seven regions, which are identical to the continents and some of which are split up into subregions: Oceania; Asia and the Middle East, consisting of the subregions Southeast Asia, East Asia, Indian Subcontinent, and the Middle East; Europe with its subregions Northern, Central, Southwestern, Southeastern, and Eastern Europe, as well as the British Isles; Africa, divided into Northern, Western, Central, Eastern, and Southern Africa; North and Central America with the additional subregion of the Caribbean; South America; and the Polar Regions.

Information is provided on each region in a systematic way, recognizing that for some areas and countries data is relatively sparse and incomplete. The descriptions of each area have been organized into sections in order to show difference and similarities as well as highlight those factors responsible for natural, economic, and social conditions.

ARCTIC OCEAN

Spitsbergen

Greenland
(Kalaallit Nunaat)

Severnaya
Zemlya

Ostrov
Kotel'nyy

GREENLAND
SEA

Nordkapp

Novaya
Zemlya

KARSKOYE
MORE

MORE
LAPTEVYKH

Poluostrov Taymyr

Ozero
Taymyr

Severo-Sibirskaya Nizmennost'

NORWEGIAN
SEA

BARENTS
SEA

Arctic Circle

Iceland

Scandinavia

Gulf of Bothnia

BALTIC SEA

Onezhskoye
Ozero

Ladozhskoye
Ozero

North European Plain

Zapando
Sibirskaya
Ravnina

Ural'skiy Khrebet

Ob'

Yenisey

Sredne-
Sibirskoye
Ploskogor'ye

Yeniseyskiy Kryazh

Lena

Verkhoyanskiy Khrebet

Khrebet Cherskogo

British
Isles

NORTH
SEA

Rhine

Dnepro

Volga

Carpathian Mts.

SEA OF
AZOV

ARAL
SEA

Balqash
Köli

Mongol Altayn Nuruu

Ozero
Baykal

Stanovoy Khrebet

OKHOTSKO-
MORE

Ostrov
Sakhalin

Amur

Ku

Bay of
Biscay

ALPS

Pyrenees

Apennines

BLACK SEA

Gora El'brus
5641 m

CASPIAN
SEA

Amu Darya

Syrdar'ya

Tian Shan

Kunlun Shan

Gobi

Da Hinggan Ling

SEA OF
JAPAN

Hokkaidō

Iberian
Peninsula

Balkan
Pen.

MEDITERRANEAN SEA

Tigris

Euphrates

Dasht e Kavir

Hindu Kush

Pamirs

Huang

Honshū

Strait of Gibraltar

ATLAS MTS

SAHARA

Libyan Des.

L. Nasser

Nile

An Nafūd
Desert

Persian Gulf

Kuh e Hazaran

Thar
Desert

HIMALAYA

Mt Everest
8848 m

Chang

YELLOW
SEA

EAST CHINA
SEA

Kyūshū

Nansei - shotō

Tropic of Cancer

SAHEL

RED SEA

Arabian
Peninsula

Ar Rub' al Khālī

ARABIAN
SEA

Deccan

Eastern Ghats

Ganga
(Ganges)

Western Ghats

Bay of
Bengal

Mekong

Hainan

Taiwan

Luzon

Philippines

PHILIPPINE
SEA

Lac Tchad
(Lake Chad)

Gulf of Aden

Ethiopian
Highlands

Horn of
Africa

ANDAMAN
SEA

Cape
Comorin

Sri Lanka

SOUTH
CHINA
SEA

SULU
SEA

Mindanao

Lake
Volta

Niger

Gulf of
Guinea

Equator

Congo
Basin

Great Rift Valley

Lake
Victoria

Kilimanjaro 5895 m

Malay
Peninsula

Sumatera
(Sumatra)

Borneo

Sulawesi
(Celebes)

CELEBES
SEA

MOLUCCA SEA

Jazirah
Doberai

Pk Jaya 5030 m

New
Guinea

BISMARCK
SEA

Congo

L. Tanganyika

JAVA SEA

BANDA SEA

ARAFURA SEA

Cape
York
Pen.

Great Barrier

GREAT DIVIDING RANGE

St Helena

Zambezi

Lake
Kariba

Limpopo

Namib Desert

Mozambique Channel

Madagascar

Mauritius

INDIAN OCEAN

TIMOR SEA

Arnhem
Land

Kimberley
Plateau

Barkly Tableland

Tropic of Capricorn

Kalahari
Dessert

Drakensberg

Great Sandy
Desert

Great Victoria
Desert

Nullarbor Plain

Simpson Desert

Eyre
Pen.

Great
Australian
Bight

Tasr

SOUTH

ATLANTIC

OCEAN

Îles
Crozet

Îles de Kerguélen

Antarctic Circle

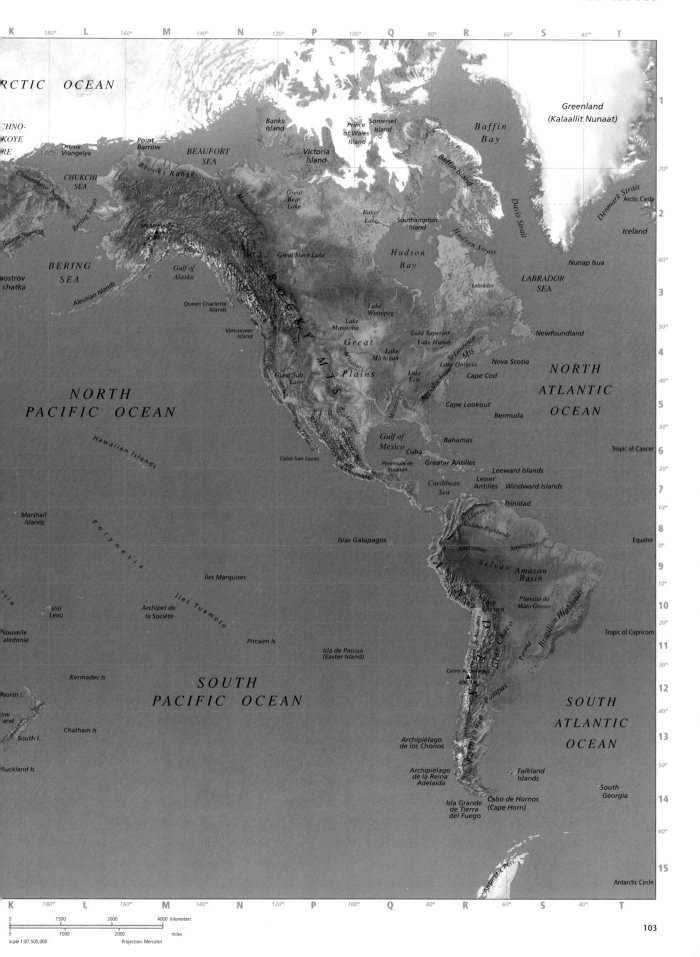

Scale 1:87,500,000    Projection: Mercator

# The World: Political

ARCTIC OCEAN

SVALBARD (Nor.)

Novaya
Zemlya

Novosibirskiye
Ostrova

JAN MAYEN
(Nor.)

BARENTS
SEA

Arctic Circle

CELAND

FAEROE IS
(Den.)

SWEDEN

FINLAND

R U S S I A N

OKHOTSKO
MORE

NORWAY

Helsinki

Oslo

Stockholm

Tallinn

ESTONIA

Riga

F E D E R A T I O N

Ostrov
Sakhalin

UNITED
KINGDOM

DENMARK
København

LITHUANIA
Vilnius

LATVIA

Minsk

Moskva

ISLE OF MAN (U.K.)

Dublin

ISLE OF MAN
(U.K.)

Amsterdam

NETH.

Berlin

POLAND

BELARUS

Astana

Ulaanbaatar

IRELAND

London

BELG.

GERMANY

Warszawa

Kyyiv

KAZAKHSTAN

MONGOLIA

Beijing

P'yŏngyang

CHANNEL ISLANDS (U.K.)

Paris

Luxembourg

LUX.

LIECH.

CZECH REP.
Praha
Wien
Bratislava

SLOVAKIA

MOLDOVA

UKRAINE

NORTH KOREA

Bishkek

KYRGYZSTAN

Sŏul

FRANCE

Bern

SWITZ.

SLOV.

HUNG.
Budapest

AUST.

Chișinău

București

GEORGIA

T'bilisi

UZBEKISTAN

Toshkent

TAJIKISTAN

SOUTH KOREA

JAPAN

Tōkyō

ANDORRA

Ljubljana

Zagreb

CROAT.

ROMANIA

ARM.

AZER.

Baki

TURKMENISTAN

Dushanbe

C H I N A

PORTUGAL

Madrid

Roma

Sarajevo

BOS. H.

SERB.

MONT.

KOSOVO

Sofiya

BULGARIA

Ankara

Yerevan

Ashgabat

Kābol

Islāmābād

Lisboa

SPAIN

ITALY

Tiranë

ALBANIA

Skopje

MACE.

GREECE

TURKEY

Tehrān

AFGHANISTAN

PAKISTAN

New
Delhi

NEPAL

Kathmandu

BHUTAN

Thimphu

TAIWAN

Madeira
(Port.)

Rabat

Alger

Tūnis

MALTA
Valletta

Athína

CYPRUS

SYRIA

IRAQ

I R A N

Dimashq

Baghdād

Al Kuwayt

KUWAIT

BAHRAIN

Al Manāmah

Ad Dawhah

QATAR

Abū Zaby

U.A.E.

Masqaţ

OMAN

Dhaka

BANGLADESH

I N D I A

MYANMAR

Hà Nôi

LAOS

Viangchan

VIETNAM

GIBRALTAR (U.K.)

Islas
Canarias
(Sp.)

MOROCCO

W. SAHARA

ALGERIA

TUNISIA

Ţarābulus

LIBYA

EGYPT

Al Qāhirah

LEBANON

Bayrūt

Yerushalayim

ISRAEL

JORDAN

Ammān

Ar Riyāḑ

SAUDI ARABIA

Bay of
Bengal

Yangon

THAILAND

Krung Thep

CAMBODIA

Manila

PHILIPPINES

GUAM (U.S.A.)

NORT
MARI.
(U.

Tropic of Cancer

MAURITANIA

Nouakchott

MALI

NIGER

CHAD

Al Khartūm

SUDAN

Asmara

ERITREA

YEMEN

Şan'a'

Suquţrá
(Yemen)

ARABIAN SEA

DJIBOUTI

Djibouti

SRI LANKA

Colombo

MALDIVES

Male

Phnum Pénh

Bandar Seri
Begawan

BRUNEI

Koror

PALAU

MIC

SENEGAL

Dakar

GAMBIA

GUINEA-
BISSAU

Bamako

Niamey

BURKINA
FASO

Ouagadougou

Ndjamena

NIGERIA

Abuja

C.A.R.

Bangui

ETHIOPIA

Ādīs Ābeba

MALAYSIA

Kuala Lumpur

SINGAPORE

GUINEA

Conakry

SIERRA
LEONE

Freetown

CÔTE
D'IVOIRE

GHANA

TOGO

BENIN

Porto-Novo

CAMEROON

Yaoundé

Lomé

SOMALIA

Muqdisho

Equator

LIBERIA

Monrovia

Yamoussoukro

Accra

Malabalo

EQ. GUINEA

Libreville

GABON

DEM. REP.

Kampala

UGANDA

RWANDA

Kigali

KENYA

Nairobi

CHAGOS
Archipelago

INDONESIA

Jakarta

EAST TIMOR

PAPUA NEW G

Port Moresby

SÃO TOMÉ & PRÍNCIPE

CONGO

Brazzaville

OF THE CONGO

Bujumbura

BURUNDI

TANZANIA

Dodoma

Victoria

SEYCHELLES

BRITISH INDIAN
OCEAN TERRITORY
(U.K.)

Kinshasa

Luanda

ANGOLA

ZAMBIA

Lusaka

MALAWI

Lilongwe

Moroni

COMOROS

MAYOTTE
(Fr.)

Antananarivo

COCOS (KEELING)
ISLANDS (Aust.)

CHRISTMAS
ISLAND (Aust.)

I N D I A N   O C E A N

ASHMORE & CARTIER ISLANDS
ISLANDS (Aust.)

A U S T R A L I A

ASCENSION
ISLAND (ST HELENA)

ST HELENA
(U.K.)

NAMIBIA

Windhoek

BOTSWANA

Gaborone

ZIMBABWE

Harare

MOZAMBIQUE

Maputo

SWAZILAND

Mbabane

MAURITIUS

Port Louis

RÉUNION
(Fr.)

MADAGASCAR

Tropic of Capricorn

Pretoria

Bloemfontein

Maseru

LESOTHO

SOUTH AFRICA

CORAL
ISLA
(Aus

Cape Town

Île Amsterdam
(Fr.)

Ca

TA

TRISTAN DA
CUNHA
(U.K.)

Tasmania

SOUTH
ATLANTIC OCEAN

FRENCH SOUTHERN &
ANTARCTIC ISLANDS (Fr.)

Prince Edward Is
(S. Africa)

Îles Crozet
(Fr.)

Îles de Kerguélen
(Fr.)

HEARD & McDONALD
ISLANDS (Aust.)

Mac

BOUVERT ISLAND
(Nor.)

S O U T H E R N   O C E A N

A N T A R C T I C A

Antarctic Circle

Scale: 1:87,500,000        Projection: Mercator

# Oceania

Oceania is the name given to a group of islands spread over 8.5 million sq km (3.3 million sq miles) in the Pacific Ocean, the majority of which lie in the southern hemisphere. The islands range in size from the large island continent of Australia, through medium-sized nations such as Papua New Guinea and New Zealand, to much smaller countries, such as Vanuatu and Tonga.

On cultural grounds, the islands can be divided into four groups. The first, Micronesia, lies east of the Philippines and includes the Federated States of Micronesia, Palau, the Marshall Islands, Nauru, and the USA dependencies of Guam and the Northern Mariana Islands. Melanesia, the second group, lies east of Indonesia and Australia, and includes Papua New Guinea, the Solomon Islands, Vanuatu, Fiji, Tonga, Tuvalu, and Samoa and the dependencies of New Caledonia (France) and American Samoa. Polynesia, the third, lies in the center of the Pacific Ocean, and includes Kiribati, French Polynesia, and the dependencies of Niue, the Cook Islands (NZ), the Pitcairn Islands (UK), and Hawaii (part of the USA). The fourth group comprises Australia and New Zealand. Unlike the other groups, these islands have indigenous populations, but the majority of the population are people who have migrated from Europe over the last two centuries. Australian dependencies include Norfolk Island in the Pacific Ocean and the Cocos (Keeling) and Christmas Islands in the Indian Ocean.

## Physical features

Physiographically, the islands of Oceania can be classed into four categories. First there is Australia, situated in the middle of the Indo-Australian Plate, where there was no mountain building during the Tertiary geological era. Australia's eastern high-lands, the eroded remnants of old mountains, are a series of elevated plateaus; the western half of the country is an ancient eroded plateau linked to the east by vast sedimentary basins.

In the second category are the islands lying along the collision boundaries between crustal plates. In the South Pacific, New Zealand, Papua New Guinea, the Solomon Islands, and Fiji are within the collision zone between the Indo-Australian and the Pacific plates. In the North Pacific, the Mariana Islands lie along the collision boundary of the Eurasian and Pacific plates. These collisions have produced folded mountain ranges. New Zealand and Papua New Guinea have young mountain ranges, some peaks exceeding 3,000 m (10,000 ft).

The third category includes volcanic islands such as Fiji, which rise from the floor of the Pacific Ocean basin. Much smaller than the countries in the second category, they are mostly made up of high mountains, with some low-lying fringes along the coastlines, including coral reefs.

Finally, there are coral islands and atolls, such as Tuvalu. Atolls form low-lying circular coral reefs which enclose lagoons. The atolls typically develop around submerged volcanic cones. In some places, such as in Guam, coral islands have been raised by crustal movements.

## Climate and vegetation

Oceania can be divided into two climatic zones: temperate and tropical. A large part of Australia and all of New Zealand lie in the temperate zone, while most of the island countries of the Pacific are tropical. Persistent trade winds dominate much of Oceania, and tropical cyclones often cause considerable damage.

Large parts of Australia are arid or semiarid. Humid zones are found along most of the east coast and Tasmania, and in part of the northern coast during summer. Most of New Zealand, Papua New Guinea and most of the islands in the Pacific are humid. However, droughts associated with the El Niño phenomenon have been frequent in recent decades in northern Australia and Papua New Guinea.

Rainforests, both tropical and temperate, occur in all the humid regions of Oceania—Australia and the larger and high (mostly volcanic) islands. However, deforestation has taken place in several places, such as parts of eastern Australia, Tasmania, New Zealand, and the Solomon Islands.

*The kangaroo, probably Australia's most well known native animal. While some such animals are threatened with extinction, kangaroos are in fact regarded as pests by many.*

Isolation has been a major factor in the development of unique species of animals, birds, and plants in the Pacific islands. The spread of human habitation and hunting has seriously affected native animals, especially in Australia—several species are extinct or endangered.

## Population

In 2005 the population of Oceania totaled 33.4 million. Australia and New Zealand accounted for 24.4 million people and Papua New Guinea for 6.1 million people. The remaining 2.9 million inhabitants are scattered on many small islands over a large area. Life expectancy for the area as a whole is 72.6 years for males and 77.9 for females. The annual population growth rate averages 1.2 percent but this varies widely, with 1 percent for Australia, 0.9 percent for New Zealand, 2 percent for Papua New Guinea, and 1.9 percent for Melanesia. Rates of urbanization vary widely too, being 91.6 percent for Australia and New Zealand and 13.2 percent for Papua New Guinea.

## Agriculture

Agriculture in Oceania can be divided into three kinds: labor-intensive subsistence agriculture, which occurs in most of the tropical islands of the Pacific; plantation crops, which are cultivated in the medium-sized tropical islands; and capital-intensive agriculture, which is found in Australia and New Zealand.

Subsistence agriculture in the Pacific islands consists of short-life items such as cassava, taro, yams, breadfruit, and sweet potatoes. Bananas and papayas are the most commonly grown fruits. Coconut palms grow on almost all the islands, and are a source of fresh food. Oil is extracted from the dried coconut meat (copra). Copra is exported from countries such as Vanuatu and Samoa. Cash crops, often a legacy of colonial times, are also important in some of the Pacific nations—sugar in Fiji and cocoa in Vanuatu.

Fishing is important for the majority of Pacific islands, as their economic zones extend to the 200 nautical mile limit—a large area compared to the size of many of the islands. Several islands have granted fishing licenses to Japanese, South Korean, and Taiwanese companies.

*Palms in the Finke Valley, central Australia (left), and forests edging Lake Matheson in southern New Zealand (above). The New Ireland coast (right), and a young girl in traditional dress and face paint (above right), both in Papua New Guinea.*

## Industrialization

Australia and New Zealand both have modern diversified economies with well-established infrastructures. Australia is particularly well favored as it has rich mineral deposits and energy sources. Manufacturing, including food processing, makes an important contribution to the economy of these two Pacific nations.

In contrast, the other islands of the Pacific are not industrially developed. Papua New Guinea, is rich in minerals such as copper and gold, and has recently discovered natural gas fields. There are nickel deposits in New Caledonia and gold in Fiji, both of which are exported rather than used in local industries.

Many islands in the Pacific have few resources; some have insufficient land for their people and a number lack adequate supplies of drinking water. This shortage of natural resources, coupled with poor infrastructures, has impeded industrial development. Industry in most of the islands is limited to food processing.

Tourism has become an important source of revenue for much of Oceania. Australia and New Zealand offer tourists modern amenities and facilities, while the beautiful scenery of tropical Pacific Islands like Fiji, Tahiti, Vanuatu, and the Northern Mariana Islands attract visitors.

## Languages

Culturally, Oceania can be divided into two major groups: the predominantly European settlements of Australia and New Zealand, and Melanesia, Polynesia, and Micronesia, which have been long settled by Oceanic peoples. New Caledonia is partially settled by Europeans.

During the colonial era, the entire region came under European influence. This resulted in English and French becoming important languages, depending on the colonial powers (Britain, America, and France). English is the official language of New Zealand, Australia, Papua New Guinea, the Solomon Islands, Vanuatu, and Fiji. French is spoken in New Caledonia and French Polynesia. On several of the Pacific islands, particularly Papua New Guinea and Vanuatu, pidgin is a common lingua franca.

In Australia, only remnants of the numerous Aboriginal languages that were spoken in the continent before European settlement still exist. Several of these languages are found in the Northern Territory and the northern part of Western Australia (the Kimberleys), where Walmadjeri is becoming a common language among several Aboriginal tribes. In New Zealand, which has a significant Maori population, the Maori language is widely spoken.

Numerous languages are found in Melanesia, Polynesia, and Micronesia. In Papua New Guinea, hundreds of languages are spoken, Austronesian languages being spoken along the coastline and Papuan languages in the highlands. Austronesian languages such as Fijian in Fiji and Tahitian, Tongan, and Samoan in Polynesia are widespread.

## Boundary disputes and wars

The whole region was affected by the Japanese invasion during World War II, and was the site of many important battles. No significant boundary disputes exist in the region. In recent decades, boundaries have been drawn up for Oceanic economic zones. However, there have been civil disturbances in Fiji, the Solomon Islands, and New Caledonia—in Fiji and on the Solomon Islands due to the struggle for a less racially biased government in the years since their independence, and in New Caledonia related to the wish of some people to become independent from France.

### Nations

| | |
|---|---|
| Australia | PAGE 110 |
| Fiji | PAGE 111 |
| Kiribati | PAGE 112 |
| Marshall Islands | PAGE 112 |
| Micronesia | PAGE 113 |
| Nauru | PAGE 114 |
| New Zealand | PAGE 114 |
| Palau | PAGE 116 |
| Papua New Guinea | PAGE 116 |
| Samoa | PAGE 117 |
| Solomon Islands | PAGE 118 |
| Tonga | PAGE 119 |
| Tuvalu | PAGE 119 |
| Vanuatu | PAGE 120 |

### Dependencies & territories

| | |
|---|---|
| American Samoa | PAGE 121 |
| Ashmore and Cartier Islands | PAGE 121 |
| Baker and Howland Islands | PAGE 121 |
| Christmas Island | PAGE 127 |
| Cocos (Keeling) Islands | PAGE 123 |
| Cook Islands | PAGE 121 |
| Coral Sea Islands | PAGE 124 |
| French Polynesia | PAGE 122 |
| Guam | PAGE 122 |
| Jarvis Island | PAGE 122 |
| Johnston Atoll | PAGE 123 |
| Kingman Reef | PAGE 123 |
| Midway Islands | PAGE 124 |
| New Caledonia | PAGE 124 |
| Niue | PAGE 124 |
| Norfolk Island | PAGE 125 |
| Northern Mariana Islands | PAGE 125 |
| Palmyra Atoll | PAGE 126 |
| Pitcairn Islands | PAGE 126 |
| Tokelau | PAGE 126 |
| Wake Island | PAGE 126 |
| Wallis and Futuna Islands | PAGE 127 |

# Oceania

New Zealand · · · · · · 110

Australia · · · · · · · · 111

Tuvalu · · · · · · · · 113

Samoa · · · · · · · · 113

Tonga · · · · · · · · 114

Papua New Guinea · · · 115

Solomon Islands · · · · 115

Vanuatu · · · · · · · 116

Fiji · · · · · · · · · 117

Palau · · · · · · · · 117

Micronesia · · · · · · 118

Marshall Islands · · · · 119

Kiribati · · · · · · · 119

Nauru · · · · · · · · 120

Dependencies · · · · · 121

## New Zealand

**NEW ZEALAND**

### OVERSEAS TERRITORIES

Cook Islands

Niue

Tokelau

## Fact File

| | |
|---|---|
| OFFICIAL NAME | New Zealand |
| FORM OF GOVERNMENT | Monarchy with single legislative body (House of Representatives) |
| CAPITAL | Wellington |
| AREA | 268,680 sq km (103,737 sq miles) |
| TIME ZONE | GMT + 12 hours |
| POPULATION | 4,173,000 |
| PROJECTED POPULATION 2015 | 4,457,000 |
| POPULATION DENSITY | 15.5 per sq km (40.2 per sq mile) |
| LIFE EXPECTANCY | 80.2 |
| INFANT MORTALITY (PER 1,000) | 5 |
| OFFICIAL LANGUAGES | English, Maori, sign language |
| LITERACY RATE | 99% |
| RELIGIONS | Anglican 14.9%, Roman Catholic 12.4%, Presbyterian 10.9%, other Christian 15.3%, other 20.5%, unaffiliated 26% |
| ETHNIC GROUPS | European 69.8%, Maori 7.9%, other (including Samoan, Tongan, Cook Islander, Asian) 22.3% |
| CURRENCY | New Zealand dollar |
| ECONOMY | Services 69.2%, industry 26%, agriculture 4.8% |
| GNI PER CAPITA | US$ 28,780 |
| CLIMATE | Temperate: warmer in north, colder in south and wetter in west |
| HIGHEST POINT | Mt Cook 3,764 m (12,349 ft) |
| MAP REFERENCE | Pages 132–33 |

Mountainous, partly volcanic, and situated approximately 1,600 km (1,000 miles) southeast of Australia, New Zealand is the biggest of the island groups that constitute Oceania. It consists of two main islands, which are separated by Cook Strait, as well as several smaller islands, and three small territories in the Pacific Ocean. The country's temperate climate has wide regional variations, the northern part of the North Island being subtropical while in the southern extremity of the South Island winter snow is common.

New Zealand has a liberal and progressive political history, pioneering votes for women in 1893, introducing a welfare state including a health service in 1938, and having a creditable record in ethnic relations.

The first people to arrive in the country were the Polynesian ancestors of the Maori around 750 to 1,000 years ago. In 1642 the Dutch explorer Abel Tasman was probably the first European to sight the islands, and in 1769

Captain James Cook was the first to land on them. The period that followed was characterized by settlement by whalers and sealers, and by Maori tribal warfare using modern firearms. This conflict came to an end when the Maori chiefs ceded sovereignty to the British Crown in the Treaty of Waitangi, which was signed on 6 February 1840. This day is still celebrated annually as the "Waitangi Day", New Zealand's national holiday.

After this date systematic and mostly peaceful colonization took place. By the 1860s, however, conflicts arose between settlers and Maori over land rights, especially in the North Island, eventually giving rise to outright war. When hostilities came to an end in 1872 the outcome in terms of landholding was decidedly in the settlers' favor. In recent years claims for compensation to Maori have become a major political issue. Aotearoa, which means "Land of the Long White Cloud", is the Maori name for New Zealand.

Geologically, New Zealand is a relatively young country. The Southern Alps in the South Island emerged from the sea in the course of the past 10 to 15 million years, while the volcanic action that shaped much of North Island occurred between 1 and 4 million years ago. The comparatively low ranges on North Island are formed from folded sedimentary rocks with higher volcanic peaks. Overlaying these rocks in the center of the North Island is a plateau of lava, pumice, and volcanic tuff. Minor earthquakes are common in New Zealand, and there are many areas of volcanic and geothermal activity on the North Island. Three volcanoes dominate the central plateau (Ruapehu being the most active of them) while Lake Taupo, the country's largest natural lake, occupies an ancient crater. In the South Island the Southern Alps form a northeast-southwest oriented ice-capped central massif with Mt Cook at its center. Glaciers descend the flanks of this massif and on the rainy western side forested slopes fall steeply to the sea. On the east, broad outwash fans lead to the much drier, treeless lowlands of the Canterbury Plains. The rugged, forested coastline of the South Island's far southwest, deeply indented with fiords, comprises Fiordland, the country's largest national park.

Few landscapes have been as extensively transformed by humans as that of New Zealand. From 1850 to 1950 vast areas of forest in the North Island were cleared, leaving steep, bare hills which were sown with grass for grazing herds of sheep. Erosion is now a serious problem in many of these areas. Rich pastures produced by year-round rain made agriculture the original foundation of the economy. The

## Timeline

| | | | | | | | | |
|---|---|---|---|---|---|---|---|---|
| **c. 1500–1600** Maori build many *pa*, earthwork forts, to protect communities, and settle Chatham Islands | **1642–43** Abel Tasman explores coasts of the islands for Dutch East India Co. Does not land and recommends no action be taken | **1835** Britain establishes a protectorate over New Zealand | **1852** European population 28,000, including 15,000 colonists brought in by New Zealand Co (founded 1838) | **1853** New Zealand granted self-government; first provincial super-intendents and councils are elected | **1860** Maori Wars between Maori and British over land; Maori resistance worn down after defeat at Te Ranga | **1900** Maori population down to 40,000 due to disease and warfare; European population about 1 million | **1931** Country's worst earthquake hits Hawke Bay, killing more than 250 people and devastating cities of Napier and Hastings |
| **c. AD 900** Polynesians reach New Zealand islands and settle, founding *Aotearoa*— Land of the Long White Cloud | **c. 1500–1600** Moas, large flightless birds, hunted to extinction; Maori live off seals, fish, root fern, and cultivate kumera, taro | **1769** Captain James Cook sails around both islands and claims them for Britain; Maori population 100,000 | **1791** Traders from Sydney begin sealing and whaling, some settling in Bay of Islands | **1840** Treaty of Waitangi gives Britain sovereignty over New Zealand and Maori sovereignty over their lands | **1860** Gold rush in Otago brings European and Asian immigrants; another rush occurs in Canterbury in 1864 | **1881** Refrigeration allows export of dairy produce and meat to European markets, helping to overcome economic depression | **1914** New Zealand troops join Australians in support of Allies; in 1915 they help establish ANZAC legend in landings at Gallipoli |

*The kea, the world's only alpine parrot, is widespread on the South Island of New Zealand (above); Snowcapped Mt Taranaki on the North Island (right).*

export of frozen mutton to Britain began as early as 1881, and New Zealand is still one of the world's main exporters of wool, cheese, butter, and meat. While in earlier years these product were distributed primarily to Great Britain, today they are exported to Australia, the USA, Japan, and other parts of Asia. Since 1984 successive governments have sought to reorient the largely agrarian economy towards a more industrialized, open economy that is better positioned to compete globally. This was part of a wider attempt at economic reform which aimed to reduce the role of the state and increase that played by private enterprise.

New Zealand has only limited petroleum resources, though it does produce natural gas—almost a third of which is used to make synthetic petrol. There are large reserves of coal. The most important source of domestic energy is hydroelectric power, easily generated because of the favorable rainfall and terrain. This has allowed the development of aluminum production using imported bauxite. In recent years, new products have been developed for new international markets. One of these is kiwifruit, the main fresh fruit export in 1996; new varieties of high-quality apples are currently a leading export. A minor feature of the rural scene only twenty years ago, vineyards are now widespread, Marlborough, Hawke Bay, and Gisborne are some of the outstanding main wine-producing regions. Forest products play a vital economic role. Radiata pine, the main commercial timber, is grown in vast state pine forests. Cutting rights to parts of these areas have been sold and the industry as a whole widely privatized.

New Zealand's varied natural scenery, combining quiet harbors and sunlit beaches, with volcanoes, lakes, alpine snowfields and fiords, draws more than 2 million visitors per year. As a dollar-earner tourism is second only to primary industry.

| | 1950s Postwar boom leads to migration from rural areas to the cities by Maori | 1985 David Lange's Labour Government bans nuclear-powered and nuclear-missile carrying ships from New Zealand ports |
|---|---|---|
| 1939–45 New Zealand supports Allies in Europe, also raising a Third Division to aid US forces in the Pacific and defend their own country | 1975 Maori protests culminate in a Land March from the far north to Wellington | 2005 In New Zealand, sign language becomes the third official language |

## Australia

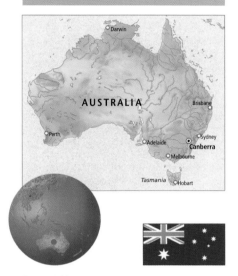

### Fact File

**OFFICIAL NAME** Commonwealth of Australia

**FORM OF GOVERNMENT** Federal constitutional monarchy with two legislative bodies (Senate and House of Representatives)

**CAPITAL** Canberra

**AREA** 7,686,850 sq km (2,967,893 sq miles)

**TIME ZONE** GMT + 8–10 hours

**POPULATION** 20,601,000

**PROJECTED POPULATION 2015** 22,397,000

**POPULATION DENSITY** 2.7 per sq km (6.9 per sq mile)

**LIFE EXPECTANCY** 80.7

**INFANT MORTALITY (PER 1,000)** 4.5

**OFFICIAL LANGUAGE** English

**OTHER LANGUAGES** Indigenous languages (e. g. Aranda, Warlpiri, Pitjantjatjara, Tiwi), Italian, Greek

**LITERACY RATE** 99 %

**RELIGIONS** Roman Catholic 26.4 %, Anglican 20.5 %, other Christian 20.5 %, other 17.3 %, none 15.3 %

**ETHNIC GROUPS** European 92 %, Asian 7 %, other (including Aboriginals) 1%

**CURRENCY** Australian dollar

**ECONOMY** Services 70.6 %, industry 26.4 %, agriculture 3 %

**GNI PER CAPITA** US$ 35,960

**CLIMATE** Hot and arid in center; tropical in north with one wet season (November to March); temperate in southeast and along southern coasts

**HIGHEST POINT** Mt Kosciuszko 2,229 m (7,313 ft)

**MAP REFERENCE** Pages 134–35

Australia is both the world's smallest continental landmass and the sixth-largest country. Most of it consists of low plateaus, and almost one-third is desert. First occupied about 40,000 to 50,000 years ago by peoples from Asia (the ancestors of today's Aboriginals), Australia was visited by Dutch explorers in the seventeenth century, including Abel Tasman in 1642 and 1644, and by the Englishman William Dampier in 1688 and 1699. After being claimed for Britain by Captain James Cook in 1770, a penal colony was established by the British in what is now Sydney in 1788. Some 160,000 convicts arrived before "transportation" from Britain was phased out in the nineteenth century. By then many free settlers had also arrived, and the gold rushes of the 1850s attracted still more people. With both wool and wheat exports providing economic security, the settler population sought greater independence from Britain, and a measure of self-government was granted in 1850. In 1901 the six states formed themselves into the Commonwealth of Australia, and in the 100 years since federation the country has become a successful, prosperous modern democracy. Current concerns include the consequences of economic dependence on Asian markets at a time of recession, demands for the frank acknowledgment of the history of Aboriginal displacement and dispossession, and whether there should be a republican government.

The Western Plateau constitutes the western half of the Australian continent. Made of ancient rocks, the plateau rises near the west coast—the iron-rich Hamersley Range representing its highest elevation in the northwest—and then falls eastward toward the center of the continent. The arid landscape alternates between worn-down ridges and plains, and depressions containing sandy deserts and salt lakes. There is

little surface water. The flatness of the plateau is interrupted by the MacDonnell and Musgrave mountain ranges in the center of the continent and the Kimberley and Arnhem Land plateaus in the north. Sheep and cattle are raised on large holdings in parts of this region.

The Central Lowlands forming the Great Artesian Basin, and river systems including the Carpentaria, Eyre, and Murray basins constitute a nearly continuous expanse of lowland that runs north to south. The river systems feed into Lake Eyre, the Bulloo system, or the Darling River. While the Murray Basin is the smallest of the three, its rivers—the Murray and its tributary the Darling—are Australia's longest and most important. Artesian bores make cattle and sheep

raising possible through much of the semiarid Central Lowlands.

The Eastern Highlands (known as the Great Dividing Range) and the relatively narrow eastern coastal plain constitute Australia's third main geographic region. This has the greatest relief, the heaviest rainfall, the most abundant and varied vegetation, and accordingly the densest human settlement. A notable feature of the eastern marine environment is the Great Barrier Reef. The world's most expansive coral reef complex, it lies off the northeast coast, stretching some 2,500 km (1,550 miles) from the Tropic of Capricorn to Papua New Guinea. A major tourist attraction, with over 400 types of coral and 1,500 species of fish, it is today protected as the Great Barrier Reef Marine Park.

The island of Tasmania, to the southeast of mainland Australia, has spectacular mountain wilderness areas and more than thirty percent of the state is protected World Heritage areas, national parks, and reserves.

Australian plant and animal life is quite distinctive. The most common trees are the gums (*Eucalyptus*) and wattles (*Acacia*). Highly adaptable, *Eucalyptus* varieties range from the tall flooded gum, found on the fringes of rainforests, to the mallee which grows on dry plains. Most native mammals are marsupials, and include kangaroos, koalas, wombats, and possums. Australia's monotremes—the platypus

*Finke Gorge National Park in the Northern Territory (above). The Apostles, Port Campbell National Park, Victoria (right). Women at Maketti Fou Market in Samoa (right page).*

and the echidna—which both lay eggs and suckle their young, are unique in all the world. There are also about 400 species of reptile and some 700 species of bird. Australia's vulnerability to introduced plant and animal species was dramatically shown by the spread of prickly pear, which took over vast areas of rural New South Wales and Queensland in the 1920s, and the plagues of rabbits that devastated pastures for a century until the 1960s. Both scourges have been tamed by biological controls.

Once heavily dependent on the pastoral industry—nearly one-third of Australia is still used for grazing sheep—the nation's economy is now more diversified, with an important manufacturing sector. Australia is also rich in mineral resources, the leading export earners being iron ore from Western Australia and coking coal from Queensland and New South Wales. In addition bauxite is mined in the Northern Territory and Queensland.

In recent years Australia has produced more than one-third of the world's diamonds, fourteen percent of its lead, and eleven percent of its uranium and zinc. Because commodities account for more than eighty percent of exports, changing commodity prices have severe economic effects. The current high prices of natural resources are responsible for Australia's steady economic growth since 2002. The government has been encouraging increased exports of manufactured goods—cars are being exported to the Gulf States, for example—but international competition is intense. The 1998 Asian economic downturn affected the tourist industry, which was the largest single foreign exchange earner, with 12.8 percent of the total.

## STATES

**New South Wales** • Sydney
**Queensland** • Brisbane
**South Australia** • Adelaide
**Tasmania** • Hobart
**Victoria** • Melbourne
**Western Australia** • Perth

## TERRITORIES

**Australian Capital Territory** • Canberra
**Northern Territory** • Darwin

## OVERSEAS TERRITORIES

**Ashmore and Cartier Islands**
**Christmas Island**
**Cocos (Keeling) Island**
**Coral Sea Islands**
**Heard and McDonald Islands**
**Norfolk Island**

| Timeline | c. 15,000 BP Rock art paintings created in shelters and caves of northwest Australia | c. 13,000 BP People of robust appearance with thick skulls and large jaws living at Kow Swamp, Murray Valley, Victoria | 1606 Dutch navigator Willem Jansz, first European to set foot in Australia, lands on Cape York Peninsula | 1770 James Cook explores the east coast of Australia and the New Zealand islands, claiming both for Great Britain | 1813 First European crossing of the Blue Mountains, west of Sydney, opens up inland plains to pastoralists | 1851 Gold discoveries first in New South Wales and then Victoria; gold rushes generate wealth and population increase | 1868 Transportation of convicts abolished; last ship lands in Fremantle, WA | 1919 More than 6,000 people die in the worst 'flu epidemic in New South Wales history |
|---|---|---|---|---|---|---|---|---|
| c. 40,000 BP First Australians arrive in log canoes or sail boats from southeast Asia | c. 25,000 BP Earliest evidence of cremation, Lake Mungo, New South Wales | c. 6000–5000 BC Dingoes brought to Australia, probably domesticated dogs belonging to people migrating from southeast Asia | 1642 Dutch navigator Abel Tasman lands in Van Diemen's Land (now Tasmania), taking possession for Holland | 1788 First Fleet under Captain Arthur Phillip arrives; penal colony set up in Port Jackson. Aboriginal population c. 750,000 | 1829 Charles Sturt explores the Darling River system and later travels inland to disprove the myth of an inland sea | 1855–56 Augustus Charles Gregory makes first west-to-east land crossing of the continent | 1914–18 Australia sends 417,000 troops to fight in First World War; 54,000 killed in battle and 155,000 wounded | 1933 Aboriginal population reduced to 66,000 as a result of suppression and disease |

# Tuvalu

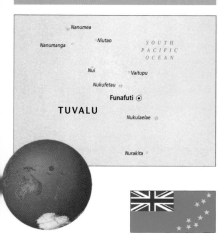

## Fact File

OFFICIAL NAME Tuvalu

FORM OF GOVERNMENT Constitutional monarchy with single legislative body (Parliament)

CAPITAL Funafuti

AREA 26 sq km (10 sq miles)

TIME ZONE GMT + 12 hours

POPULATION 12,200

PROJECTED POPULATION 2015 14,500

POPULATION DENSITY 469.2 per sq km (1,220 per sq mile)

LIFE EXPECTANCY 69

INFANT MORTALITY (PER 1,000) 19

OFFICIAL LANGUAGES Tuvaluan, English

LITERACY RATE not available

RELIGIONS Church of Tuvalu (Congregationalist) 97 %, Seventh-Day Adventist 1.4 %, Baha'i 1 %, other 0.6 %

ETHNIC GROUPS Polynesian 96 %, other 4 %

CURRENCY Tuvaluan dollar, Australian dollar

ECONOMY Services 56.2 %, industry 27.2 %, agriculture 16.6 %

GNI PER CAPITA US$ 2,100

CLIMATE Tropical, moderated by trade winds

HIGHEST POINT Unnamed location on Niulakita 4.6 m (15 ft)

MAP REFERENCE Page 139

Tuvalu is a tiny Pacific island state which holds the distinction of having the world's smallest economy. It consists of five coral atolls and four reef islands, none of which is more than 5 m (15 ft) above sea level, about midway

between Hawaii and Australia. Formerly known as the Ellice Islands (and once part of the British colony of the Gilbert and Ellice Islands), they were first populated by Polynesian migrants from Samoa and Tonga some time in the fourteenth century—the language used today is a Polynesian-Samoan dialect. Though the islands were sighted by the Spanish in the sixteenth century, further European contact did not take place until the eighteenth century, and it was not until 1826 that the whole group was finally discovered and mapped. In the 1860s labor recruiters known as "blackbirders" became active, either inveigling or abducting islanders for work on Fijian and Australian sugar plantations (the population fell from 20,000 in 1850 to 3,000 in 1880).

The abuses of the labor trade led the British government to annex the islands as a protectorate in 1892. Though brought together as a single administrative unit, the Micronesian Gilbertese and the Polynesian Tuvaluans were not comfortable with this arrangement, and in 1978 Tuvalu became an independent state closely linked with Britain.

Tuvalu's chain of coral islands is 579 km (360 miles) long, consisting north to south of the islands of Nanumea, Niutao, Nanumanga, Nui, Vaitupu, Nukufetau, Funafuti (the capital), Nukulaelae, and Niulakita. There are no streams or rivers on any of the islands, and groundwater is not drinkable. All water needs must be met by catchment systems with storage facilities. Although the soil is of poor quality, subsistence farming supports about seventy percent of the population. The limited range of food crops that can be cultivated, such as taro. must be grown in special pits dug out of the coral. Although the islands support no export crop other than coconuts, the area of the maritime Exclusive Economic Zone is 1.2 million sq km (500,000 sq miles). The rich fishing grounds within this zone are a source of revenue from license fees paid by fishing fleets for example from Korea and the USA. Too small, remote, and lacking in amenities to be able to establish a tourist industry, government revenues come mainly from the sale of stamps and coins and from remittances: large numbers of Tuvalu men live and work abroad, some as seamen and others mining phosphate on Nauru. The value of imports exceeds exports by 200 to 1. Substantial income is generated by an international trust fund established in 1987 by Australia, New Zealand, and the United Kingdom, which is also supported by Japan and South Korea.

# Samoa

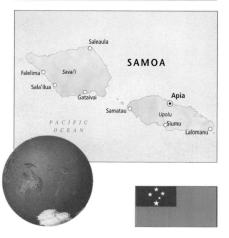

## Fact File

OFFICIAL NAME Independent State of Samoa

FORM OF GOVERNMENT Constitutional monarchy with single legislative body (Legislative Assembly)

CAPITAL Apia

AREA 2,860 sq km (1,104 sq miles)

TIME ZONE GMT – 11 hours

POPULATION 217,000

PROJECTED POPULATION 2015 198,000

POPULATION DENSITY 75.9 per sq km (196.6 per sq mile)

LIFE EXPECTANCY 71.6

INFANT MORTALITY (PER 1,000) 25

OFFICIAL LANGUAGES Samoan, English

LITERACY RATE 99.7 %

RELIGIONS Christian 98 % (50 % associated with London Missionary Society), other 2 %

ETHNIC GROUPS Samoan 92.6 %, mixed Polynesian-European 7 %, European 0.4 %

CURRENCY Tala

ECONOMY Industry 58.4 %, services 30.2 %, agriculture 11.4 %

GNI PER CAPITA US$ 2,430

CLIMATE Tropical, wet season from December to April followed by a cooler dry season from May to November

HIGHEST POINT Mauga Silisili 1,857 m (6,089 ft)

MAP REFERENCE Pages 136, 141

The Samoan islands lie in the South Pacific about midway between Hawaii and New Zealand. Consisting of the two big islands of Savai'i and Upolu, plus seven small islands and a number of islets, Samoa is a larger island group with a much greater population than American Samoa, which lies further east, but has a more uncertain economic future.

Believed to have been originally settled by Tongans around 1000 BC, the islands of Samoa were first visited by Europeans when the French explorer Louis Antoine de Bougainville arrived in 1766. A mission was established in 1835 by the London Missionary Society. In the late nineteenth

| 1941 Australia's involvement in Second World War dominated by entry of Japanese after Pearl Harbor | 1967 Referendum accords citizenship to Aboriginal people for the first time by a vote of 90.8 percent of the population | 1991–92 Severe drought associated with El Niño climate pattern affects eastern Australia |
| --- | --- | --- |
| 1949 Construction of Snowy Mountain's hydroelectric scheme, Australia's largest (completed in 1972) | 1974 Cyclone Tracy destroys most of Darwin, Northern Territory | 1992 High Court ruling (Mabo) that Australia was not "empty" when Europeans arrived allows native title claims to proceed |

ETHNIC GROUPS Polynesian 98%, European 2%

CURRENCY Pa'anga

ECONOMY Services 57%, agriculture 25%,
industry 18%

GNI PER CAPITA US$ 2.320

CLIMATE Tropical, moderated by trade winds;
wettest period December to March

HIGHEST POINT Mt Kao 1,033 m (3,389 ft)

MAP REFERENCE Pages 136, 141

The Polynesian kingdom of Tonga consists of an archipelago of 170 islands (36 of them inhabited) northeast of New Zealand in the South Pacific. Samoa lies to the north and Fiji to the west. Inhabited since about 1000 BC, they were named the "Friendly Isles" by Captain James Cook when he visited them in the 1770s. When Wesleyan missionaries arrived in the 1820s the people quickly began to adopt Christianity. In 1900, after Germany made colonial moves toward the islands, the King of Tonga signed a Treaty of Friendship and Protection with Britain.

Tonga was never fully colonized, and its people see themselves and their royal family as unique in the Pacific. A monarchy in which the king and a small group of hereditary nobles have a permanent majority in the Legislative Assembly, Tonga is now experiencing growing demands for a more democratic form of government. Although politicians of the newly established Pro-Democracy Movement have been harrassed for sedition and defamation there are signs the king may be ready for change: in 1995 he announced that it would only be a matter of time before a fully elected government was created.

North to south Tonga's three main groups of islands are Vava'u, Ha'apai, and Tongatapu, the archipelago dividing into two parallel belts of islands. In the east there are low, fertile coralline-limestone formations. In the west the terrain is higher and volcanic, the island of Kao, north of Tofua, rising to 1,033 m (3,389 ft). Mountainous landscapes of volcanic rock are found on the Vava'u group and one island in the Ha'apai group. In 1995 a new volcanic island which had emerged from the sea was discovered in the Ha'apai group. About 25 percent of Tonga's land area is arable, but surface water is rare on the coral islands.

Most of the people of Tonga live by subsistence farming, the main food crops being yams, taro, and cassava. Two-thirds of exports come from coconuts, bananas, and vanilla beans, other cash crops being pumpkin, fruits and vegetables, cocoa, coffee, ginger, and black pepper. Despite the high level of agricultural activity a good deal of food has to be imported, most of it coming from New Zealand. In the early 1990s the economy continued to grow, largely because of a rise in pumpkin exports, increased foreign aid, and a number of construction projects. Tourism is now the main source of hard currency earnings, but Tonga remains dependent on sizeable aid funds, plus remittances from its many citizens who live and work in New Zealand, Australia, and the USA.

century control of the islands was contested by three colonial powers—Britain, Germany, and the USA—Germany taking control for a short period from 1899. After the First World War the islands were administered by New Zealand. In 1962 Samoa regained full independence and signed a friendship treaty with New Zealand. Samoa is a society in which chiefly rank plays an important part, matai (men who head extended families) having a good deal more power, prestige, and authority than commoners. This system has delayed the introduction of full democracy. In 1991 the first direct elections under a universal franchise were held, but only matai were allowed to be candidates.

The larger islands of Samoa are volcanic, Savai'i experiencing major eruptions in 1902 and 1911. The interiors of Savai'i and Upolu are broadly similar; their mountainous central regions are densely forested and cut by a number of fast-flowing rivers. Major streams include the Sili and Faleata on Savai'i, and the Vaisigano on Upolu. Narrow coastal plains lie between the highlands and the sea; coral reefs lie offshore. Other than arable land (nineteen percent), the only natural resources are hardwood forests and fish. Yams, breadfruit, banana, and papaya are grown for food, and cocoa, taro, and coconuts (for oil, copra, and cream) are cultivated for export.

With assistance from the United Nations, fishing has also become a significant export industry. Reforestation programs have been introduced with the aim of keeping timber exports at a sustainable level. Power for industry—a Japanese automobile parts factory opened in 1991—is mainly provided by hydroelectricity.

The economy depends heavily on remittances from Samoans working overseas and on foreign aid to support a level of imports that significantly exceeds export earnings. Tourism has become the most important growth industry. Many of the more than 100,000 visitors per year come to see the house that was once lived in by the Scottish writer Robert Louis Stevenson. It is now the official residence of the Samoan Head of State.

## Tonga

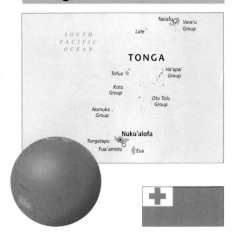

## Fact File

OFFICIAL NAME Kingdom of Tonga

FORM OF GOVERNMENT Constitutional monarchy with single legislative body (Legislative Assembly)

CAPITAL Nuku'alofa

AREA 748 sq km (289 sq miles)

TIME ZONE GMT + 12 hours

POPULATION 119,000

PROJECTED POPULATION 2015 134,000

POPULATION DENSITY 159.1 per sq km
(411.8 per sq mile)

LIFE EXPECTANCY 70.4

INFANT MORTALITY (PER 1,000) 11.9

OFFICIAL LANGUAGES Tongan, English

LITERACY RATE 98.9%

RELIGIONS Protestant 60% (including Free Wesleyan 43%, other 17%), Roman Catholic 16%, Mormon 12%, other 2%

# Papua New Guinea

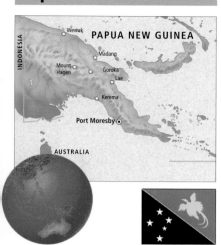

## Fact File

OFFICIAL NAME  Independent State of Papua New Guinea

FORM OF GOVERNMENT  Constitutional monarchy with single legislative body (National Parliament or House of Assembly)

CAPITAL  Port Moresby

AREA  462,840 sq km (178,703 sq miles)

TIME ZONE  GMT + 10 hours

POPULATION  5,392,000

PROJECTED POPULATION 2015  7,319,000

POPULATION DENSITY  12.8 per sq km (30.2 per sq mile)

LIFE EXPECTANCY  66

INFANT MORTALITY (PER 1,000)  46.7

OFFICIAL LANGUAGES  English, Pidgin, Motu

OTHER LANGUAGES  Approximately 820 indigenous languages

LITERACY RATE  57.3 %

RELIGIONS  Roman Catholic 22 %, Lutheran 16 %; Presbyterian, Methodist, London Missionary Society 8 %; Anglican 5 %; Evangelical Alliance 4 %; other protestant 11 %, indigenous beliefs 34 %,

ETHNIC GROUPS  New Guinea Papuan 84 %; Polynesian, Chinese, European and other 16 %

CURRENCY  Kina

ECONOMY  Industry 37.3 %, agriculture 34 %, services 28.7 %

GNI PER CAPITA  US$ 850

CLIMATE  Tropical, with wet season December to March

HIGHEST POINT  Mt Wilhelm 4,509 m (14,793 ft)

MAP REFERENCE  Page 140

Papua New Guinea consists of the eastern half of the large island of New Guinea, the 600 or so smaller islands of the Bismarck Archipelago, and the island Bougainville in the west. It lies north of northeastern Australia, just south of the equator. The largely rural population of "mainland" Papua New Guinea is made up of hundreds of distinct tribal groups, speaking more than 820 different languages. They can be broadly divided into the lowlanders of the coast and the more isolated highlanders of the mountainous interior. The main island was named New Guinea in 1545 by a Spanish explorer who thought its people resembled those of the African Guinea coast. During the last two centuries the Netherlands, Germany, Japan, and Australia have controlled parts of it at different times. The western half—West Irian (Irian Jaya)—is now part of Indonesia; the eastern half, most recently administered by Australia, became fully independent as Papua New Guinea in 1975. Australia's relationship remains close, and it contributes twenty percent of the state budget.

A cordillera of rugged mountains runs down the main island. Covered with tropical forest, these mountains have an average elevation of between 2,500 m and 4,600 m (8,000 ft and 15,000 ft). In high and isolated valleys there are settlements where people live by cultivating traditional garden crops such as sweet potato, sugar cane, bananas, maize, and cassava. Pigs are raised, but are eaten mainly at ceremonies for status and ritual purposes. Taro is a staple food of the villagers in the lowlands, where yams and sago are also grown. Most of the soil is heavily leached, and fertile only in lowland areas and upland basins. On the southwestern coast the Fly River forms a vast swampy delta plain that is one of the world's biggest wetlands. The other major islands further east (New Ireland, New Britain, Manus, and Bougainville) are mainly of volcanic origin and are generally ringed by coral reefs. Nearly three-quarters of the land area of Papua New Guinea is covered with dense rainforest.

The country does have a variety of natural resources but rugged terrain and the high cost of infrastructure make their extraction difficult. Much travel and transport is only possible by air. While most people live by subsistence agriculture, copper and gold account for about sixty percent of export earnings. The main cash crops are coffee, cocoa, coconuts, palm kernels, tea, and rubber. Timber from the forests is also important. The government is looking to petroleum and mineral exports to drive its program of economic development, but there are social and political obstacles to be overcome. Corruption is endemic, tribal and criminal violence are high, and what was once the world's biggest copper mine—Panguna on Bougainville—has been closed for years. The Bougainville people are culturally kin to the people of the Solomons and strongly resent their domination by Papua New Guinea. Grievances over their share of the proceeds from the mine and compensation have become a demand for independence. After eruptions of violence in the 1990s, however, the government managed to consolidate the situation since 2001.

*A Samoan church with a Mediterranean influence (left page). Mudmen at Mt Hagen, in the Papua New Guinea highlands (right).*

# Solomon Islands

## Fact File

OFFICIAL NAME  Solomon Islands

FORM OF GOVERNMENT  Constitutional monarchy with single legislative body (National Parliament)

CAPITAL  Honiara

AREA  28,450 sq km (10,985 sq miles)

TIME ZONE  GMT + 11 hours

POPULATION  581,000

PROJECTED POPULATION 2015  589,000

POPULATION DENSITY  20.4 per sq km (52.9 per sq mile)

LIFE EXPECTANCY  73.4

INFANT MORTALITY (PER 1,000)  19.7

OFFICIAL LANGUAGE  English

OTHER LANGUAGES  Pidgin, approximately 80 different indigenous languages

LITERACY RATE  62 %

RELIGIONS  Protestant 77 % (including Anglican 32.8 %, Evangelical 17 %, Seventh Day Adventist 11.2 %), Roman Catholic 19 %, not specified 4 %

ETHNIC GROUPS  Melanesian 94.5 %, Polynesian 3 %, Micronesian 1.2 %, European 0.7 %, other 0.6 %

CURRENCY  Soloman Islands dollar

ECONOMY  Services 47 %, agriculture 42 %, industry 11 %

GNI PER CAPITA  US$ 730

CLIMATE  Tropical, most rain falling November to April

HIGHEST POINT  Mt Makarakomburu 2,447 m (8,126 ft)

MAP REFERENCE  Pages 140, 141

Oceania

GNI PER CAPITA  US$ 1,840

CLIMATE  Tropical, moderated by trade winds

HIGHEST POINT  Mt Tabwemasana 1,877 m (6,152 ft)

MAP REFERENCE  Pages 136, 141

Vanuatu is an archipelago in the South Pacific consisting of thirteen large islands and seventy islets. Part of Melanesia, it lies northeast of New Caledonia and west of Fiji. Inhabited since 5000 BC, it was first visited by Europeans when the Portuguese arrived in 1606. After Captain Cook explored the islands in 1774 he named them the New Hebrides, and they were jointly administered by France and Britain from 1887. In the late 1800s labor recruiters inveigled and sometimes kidnapped islanders for work on sugar plantations in Australia and Fiji. Aside from this, the islands remained isolated until the Second World War, when Espíritu Santo and Port Vila became major US military bases in the Pacific. In 1980 the archipelago became independent under the name Vanuatu. Since then, after surviving a secession attempt by a francophone movement on the island of Espíritu Santo, the country has had a volatile but democratic political life. Vanuatu is populated almost entirely by ethnic Melanesians speaking 110 distinct languages—the world's highest per capita density of language forms. The lingua franca is a form of pidgin known as Bislama.

Most of the islands are mountainous and volcanic in origin, with coral beaches and offshore reefs. The interior is forested, with limited land for coastal cultivation. Some 75 percent of the people live by subsistence farming, growing taro, yams, sweet potatoes, bananas, and cassava for food, as well as cash crops such as coconuts, cocoa, and coffee. Fishing is also important. Unlike most South Pacific islands, beef raising is of economic significance, livestock numbering some 130,000 head of cattle. Meat canning is an industry. Frozen beef and fish are exported. Other exports include copra, shells, coffee, and cocoa. Mineral deposits are negligible. Recently the government has emphasized tourist development (tourism is now the second largest earner of foreign exchange after copra), offshore banking, and foreign investment, advertising Vanuatu's potential as a finance center and tax haven. There is a "flag of convenience" shipping registry of some sixty ships from twenty countries.

The Solomon Islands lie in the western Pacific, northeast of Australia. Inhabited by Melanesian people since about 1000 BC, they consist of two chains of islands running southeast of Bougainville. They were named by the Spanish navigator Alvaro de Mendana, who visited them in 1568 and thought he had found "the riches of Solomon." Twenty years later he returned and established a small, short-lived colony on the Santa Cruz Islands. Outside contacts were few in the ensuing centuries. In the 1870s and 1880s labor recruiters called "blackbirders" were busy inveigling islanders into working on Australian sugar plantations and their unsavory activities led Britain to establish a protectorate over the Southern Solomons in 1893.

In the Second World War the Solomons were occupied by the Japanese. The battle for Guadalcanal saw fierce fighting between Japanese and US forces, the islands overall being the scene of several major Allied naval and military victories. In recent years relations with Papua New Guinea have been strained because of the Solomon Islands' support for secessionists on Bougainville and the rebels of the Bougainville Revolutionary Army. Although Bougainville is geographically and ethnically a part of the Solomon Islands group, it has been treated politically as a part of Papua New Guinea for more than one hundred years.

Geologically, the islands represent a part of the submerged outermost crustal fold of the ancient Australian continent. Their interiors are rugged and mountainous. The six main islands—Guadalcanal, Malaita, New Georgia, Makira (formerly San Cristobal), Santa Isabel, and Choiseul—are all of volcanic origin, and have densely forested ranges with steep-sided river valleys. Around the coasts are narrow plains where most of the population live as subsistence farmers growing beans, coconuts, palm kernels, rice, potatoes, and vegetables. Palm oil, cocoa and copra are leading agricultural exports, and tuna fish is the single biggest earner. Forestry is an important industry but the unsustainable level of timber extraction is an environmental concern. The islands are rich in undeveloped mineral resources such as lead, zinc, nickel, gold, bauxite, and phosphate—significant phosphate deposits are being mined on Bellona Island. The government is nearly insolvent and depends on foreign aid; another problem is the high population growth rate.

## Vanuatu

## Fact File

OFFICIAL NAME  Republic of Vanuatu

FORM OF GOVERNMENT  Republic with single legislative body (Parliament)

CAPITAL  Port Vila

AREA  12,200 sq km (4,710 sq miles)

TIME ZONE  GMT + 11 hours

POPULATION  215,000

PROJECTED POPULATION 2015  270,000

POPULATION DENSITY  17.6 per sq km (45.6 per sq mile)

LIFE EXPECTANCY  63.6

INFANT MORTALITY (PER 1,000)  50.8

OFFICIAL LANGUAGES  English, French

OTHER LANGUAGES  Bislama (ni-Vanuatu-pidgin), about 110 Melanesian languages

LITERACY RATE  74 %

RELIGIONS  Presbyterian 31.4 %, Anglican 13.4 %, Catholic 13.1 %, Seventh-Day Adventist 10.8 %, other Christian 13.8, indigenous beliefs 5.6 %, other 11.9 %

ETHNIC GROUPS  Ni-Vanuatu 98.5 %, other 1.5 %

CURRENCY  Vatu

ECONOMY  Services 62 %, agriculture 26 %, industry 12 %

# Fiji

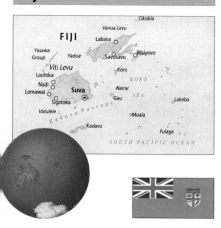

## Fact File

**OFFICIAL NAME** Republic of Fiji

**FORM OF GOVERNMENT** Republic with two legislative bodies (Senate and House of Representatives)

**CAPITAL** Suva

**AREA** 18,270 sq km (7,054 sq miles)

**TIME ZONE** GMT + 12 hours

**POPULATION** 932,000

**PROJECTED POPULATION 2015** 874,000

**POPULATION DENSITY** 51 per sq km (132.1 per sq mile)

**LIFE EXPECTANCY** 70.4

**INFANT MORTALITY (PER 1,000)** 11.9

**OFFICIAL LANGUAGE** English

**OTHER LANGUAGES** Fijian, Hindustani

**LITERACY RATE** 93.7 %

**RELIGIONS** Christian 53 % (including Methodist 34.5 %, Roman Catholic 7.2 %), Hindu 34 %, Muslim 7 %, other 6 %

**ETHNIC GROUPS** Fijian 54.8 %, Indian 37.4 %, other (including European, other Pacific Islanders, Chinese) 7.8 %

**CURRENCY** Fiji dollar

**ECONOMY** Services 77.6 %, industry 13.5 %, agriculture 8.9 %,

**GNI PER CAPITA** US$ 3,800

*A coastal village in the Solomon Islands, with some Second World War pontoons (left page top). The Parliament House buildings in Suva, Fiji (above). Fruit and vegetables for sale at Port Vila Market, Vanuatu (below).*

**CLIMATE** Tropical, with wet season November to April

**HIGHEST POINT** Mt Tomanivi 1,324 m (4,344 ft)

**MAP REFERENCE** Pages 137, 141

Fiji consists of an archipelago of more than 800 islands and islets, 110 of them inhabited, located about two-thirds of the way from Hawaii to New Zealand. Lying on the air route from Australia to the west coast of the USA, Fiji is well served by flights, and is attracting an increasing number of tourists. Originally inhabited by Melanesian islanders organized into a number of tribes, the islands were visited by Dutch explorers in 1643, and from 1800 attracted growing numbers of traders, along with missionaries who converted the people to Christianity. A period of intense tribal warfare was brought to an end when the paramount chief ceded sovereignty to the British in 1874. Five years later, in 1879, the British began bringing in Indian laborers for the purpose of sugar production; by the time Fiji obtained its independence in 1970 their descendants outnumbered the country's ethnic Fijians.

Racial divisions have caused tension and instability, as for many years the Indian immigrants were treated as second-class citizens, despite their vital role in the sugar industry. A coup in 1987, led by a Fijian army officer against a democratically elected government in which Indians were the majority, led to a new constitution in 1990 which was racially weighted to ensure permanent indigenous Fijian rule. Many Indian-Fijians emigrated as a result. In May 1999, the Indian leader of the Fijian Labor Party, Mahandra Chaudrey, was democratically elected Prime Minister. After a coup in May 2000, new elections were held in 2001 and the winner, Laisenia Qarase, was re-elected in May 2006, but ousted in December of the same year by a military coup.

The main islands are of volcanic origin. About seventy percent of the population live on the two biggest—Viti Levu and Vanua Levu. These have a sharp and rugged relief, rising to Mt Tomanivi on Viti Levu. The islands lie in a cyclone path (Cyclone Kina caused much damage in 1993) and trade winds bring heavy rain to their eastern sides. Dense tropical forest covers the higher slopes. Sugarcane is grown on the fertile coastal plains, sugar exports and tourism with 400,000 visitors per year being Fiji's main sources of foreign exchange. Fiji has one of the most developed of the Pacific island economies, producing (as well as sugar) copra, gold, silver, clothing, and timber.

# Palau

## Fact File

**OFFICIAL NAME** Republic of Palau

**FORM OF GOVERNMENT** Republic in free association with the USA; two legislative bodies (Senate and House of Delegates)

**CAPITAL** Koror

**AREA** 458 sq km (177 sq miles)

**TIME ZONE** GMT + 10 hours

**POPULATION** 21,100

**PROJECTED POPULATION 2015** 21,000

**POPULATION DENSITY** 46.1 per sq km (119.2 per sq mile)

**LIFE EXPECTANCY** 71

**INFANT MORTALITY (PER 1,000)** 13.7

**OFFICIAL LANGUAGES** Palauan, English

**OTHER LANGUAGES** Sonsoral, Angaur, Japanese, Tobi

**LITERACY RATE** 92 %

**RELIGIONS** Roman Catholic 41.6 %, Protestant 23.3 %, indigenous Modekngei religion 8.8 %, other 26.3 %

**ETHNIC GROUPS** Palauan (mixed Polynesian, Melanesian, Malayan) 69.9 %, Filipino 15.3 %, Chinese 4.9 %, other 9.9 %

**CURRENCY** US dollar

**ECONOMY** Services 81.8 %, industry 12 %, agriculture 6.2 %

**GNI PER CAPITA** US$ 8,210

**CLIMATE** Tropical, with wet season May to November

**HIGHEST POINT** Mt Ngerchelchauus 242 m (794 ft)

**MAP REFERENCE** Page 138

Palau consists of several groups of islands in the northwest Pacific, about 750 km (450 miles) east of the Philippine island of Mindanao. The westernmost of the Micronesian Caroline chain, and settled by Southeast Asian migrants from about 1000 BC, the islands have in the past 100 years been successively occupied and controlled by Spain, Germany, Japan, and the USA. After Spain's defeat in the 1898 Spanish-American War they were sold to

Germany. Japan seized and held the islands
from the outbreak of the First World War until
the Second World War, when Japanese and
US forces fought for control over them. In 1978
Palau rejected incorporation into the neighboring Federated States of Micronesia (a union
of the rest of the Caroline Islands); in 1981 it
adopted a constitution banning nuclear weapons
and military bases in the area; and in 1982 it
entered into a Compact of Free Association with
the USA which contained military provisions in
conflict with its constitution. After a lengthy political stalemate, in 1993 voters finally approved
the Compact, which provides US$ 500 million
in aid over fifteen years in exchange for the right
of the USA to maintain military facilities there.
In 1994 Palau became the 185th member of
the UN, and in 1995 it joined the South
Pacific Forum.

Palau, an archipelago of six separate
groups of islands, consists of 26 islands and
over 300 islets. The terrain varies from the
mountainous main island of Babelthuap to low
coral islands usually fringed by reefs. Natural
resources consist of forests, minerals (including
gold), marine products, and deep-seabed
minerals. The rural people live by subsistence
agriculture, growing coconuts, cassava, and
sweet potatoes (though the rugged terrain of the
larger islands makes farming difficult), and by
fishing. Industries include tourism, craft items
made from shell, wood, and pearls, and some
commercial fishing. Exports include trochus
shell, tuna, copra, and handicrafts. The government is the main employer, and relies heavily
on aid from the USA. As a result, the population
has a per capita income five times that of the
Philippines.

## Micronesia

## Fact File

**OFFICIAL NAME** Federated States of Micronesia

**FORM OF GOVERNMENT** Federal Republic in free
association with the USA; single legislative body
(Congress)

**CAPITAL** Palikir

**AREA** 702 sq km (271 sq miles)

**TIME ZONE** GMT + 9–10 hours

**POPULATION** 107,000

**PROJECTED POPULATION 2015** 116,000

**POPULATION DENSITY** 152.4 per sq km
(394.8 per sq mile)

**LIFE EXPECTANCY** 70.7

**INFANT MORTALITY (PER 1,000)** 23

**OFFICIAL LANGUAGE** English

**OTHER LANGUAGES** Micronesian and Polynesian
languages

**LITERACY RATE** 89 %

**RELIGIONS** Roman Catholic 50 %, Protestant 47 %,
other and none 3 %

**ETHNIC GROUPS** Micronesian and Polynesian

**CURRENCY** US dollar

**ECONOMY** Services 55.9 %, agriculture 28.9 %,
industry 15.2 %

**GNI PER CAPITA** US$ 2,470

**CLIMATE** Tropical. Heavy rainfall year-round
and occasional typhoons

**HIGHEST POINT** Totolom 791 m (2,595 ft)

**MAP REFERENCE** Page 138

The Federated States of Micronesia consist
of four states—Yap, Chuuk (Truk), Pohnpei,
and Kosrae—made up of four island groups
spread out across 3,200 km (2,000 miles) of
ocean. Formerly known as the Caroline Islands,
they are located in the northern Pacific about
halfway between Australia and Japan. They
are populated by Micronesian and Polynesian
peoples divided into nine separate ethnic groups.

First settled around 1000 BC, the islands were
visited by Spanish seafarers in 1565 and were
annexed by Spain in 1874. In 1899 Spain sold
them to Germany, and at the beginning of the
First World War Japan took posession of them.
After Japan's defeat in the Second World War,
the USA took over the administration of the
islands. US control ended in 1986 when the
Federated States of Micronesia and the USA
signed a fifteen-year Compact of Free Association that is currently renegotiated. This granted
internal self-government, with the USA retaining responsibility for the country's defense.

During the course of the Second World
War Chuuk was one of Japan's most important
bases in the Pacific Ocean. Tourists now come
to the island to scuba dive among the numerous
wartime wrecks in the lagoon.

The 607 widely scattered islands of Micronesia
vary geologically from high and mountainous
terrain to low coral atolls. Most of the islands
are volcanic in origin, and the hot, rainy climate
produces lush vegetation and tropical rainforest.
Volcanic outcrops occur on Pohnpei, Kosrae,
and Chuuk. Some of the atolls lack any surface
water. Droughts occur frequently on Chuuk, often
leading to water rationing. In 1992 emergency
supplies of water had to be brought from Guam
to Chuuk by the US Navy.

Subsistence fishing and farming occupies
the majority of the population, with farmers
growing tropical fruits and vegetables, coconuts,
cassava (tapioca), sweet potatoes, and black
pepper, and raising pigs and chickens. Fish,
bananas, and black pepper are exported,
and as a result of attempts at economic
diversification a clothing industry has been
developed.

Aside from deposits of high-grade phosphate
the islands have few mineral resources. Imports
exceed exports by a ratio of more than four to
one, and the country as a whole depends
heavily on financial aid from the USA. There
is some potential for tourism—with their rich
marine life the islands are a prime destination
for scuba divers—but poor infrastructure
and the country's remoteness hinder further
development.

*Some of the islands of Palau, seen from the air (top).*
*Mangroves in Micronesia (above). An aerial view of*
*some of the Marshall Islands (right).*

# Marshall Islands

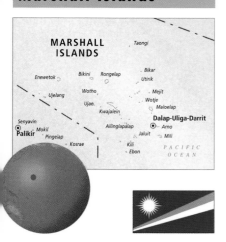

## Fact File

OFFICIAL NAME  Republic of the Marshall Islands

FORM OF GOVERNMENT  Republic in free association with the USA; one legislative body (Nitijela)

CAPITAL  Dalap-Uliga-Darrit

AREA  181 sq km (70 sq miles)

TIME ZONE  GMT + 12 hours

POPULATION  63,000

PROJECTED POPULATION 2015  70,000

POPULATION DENSITY  348.1 per sq km (900 per sq mile)

LIFE EXPECTANCY  70.9

INFANT MORTALITY (PER 1,000)  26.4

OFFICIAL LANGUAGE  English

OTHER LANGUAGES  Marshallese, Japanese

LITERACY RATE  93.7 %

RELIGIONS  Protestant 89.1 %, Roman Catholic 8.4 %, other 2.5 %

ETHNIC GROUPS  Micronesian 97 %, other 3 %

CURRENCY  US dollar

ECONOMY  Services 53.4, agriculture 31.7 %, industry 14.9 %

GNI PER CAPITA  US$ 3,070

CLIMATE  Tropical, with wet season May to November

HIGHEST POINT  Unnamed location on Likiep 10 m (33 ft)

MAP REFERENCE  Pages 138–39

A group of 31 coral atolls, five islands, and 1,152 islets, the Republic of the Marshall Islands is situated in the northern Pacific about halfway between Hawaii and Papua New Guinea. Settled around 2000 BC, the islands were visited by Spanish seafarers in 1529, and since 1874 have been successively under Spanish, German, Japanese, and US control. In 1986 they entered into a Compact of Free Association with the US. During the years after the Second World War the Marshalls became known as the location where the USA carried out nuclear bomb tests (on Bikini and Enewetak Atolls between 1946 and 1958). Claims for compensation by those affected or displaced by the tests have been settled in recent years, an award of US$ 40 million to 1,150 Marshall Islanders being made by the Nuclear Claims Tribunal in 1995. Cleanup work to remove residual radiation from Bikini Lagoon continues.

The terrain consists of low coral limestone and sand islands. Two archipelagoes of islands run roughly parallel northeast to southwest, the easternmost chain being a continuation of the Gilbert Islands of western Kiribati. Originating as coral reefs formed upon the rims of submerged volcanoes, each of the main islands encloses a lagoon. Bordering the cyclone belt, and nowhere higher than 10 m (30 ft) above sea level, they are vulnerable to storms and tidal waves. In June 1994 a tidal wave swept over the capital on Majuro Atoll.

On the outlying atolls a typical Pacific island subsistence economy survives, centered on agriculture and fishing. Small farms produce commercial crops such as coconuts, tomatoes, melons, and breadfruit, and a handful of cattle ranches supplies the domestic meat market. Industry consists of handicrafts, fish processing, and copra production, and the main exports are tuna, copra, and coconut oil products. About ten percent of the population is employed in the tourist industry (visitors come from Japan and the USA), now the main source of foreign exchange. Imports are eleven times export rates, all fuel must be imported, and the country as a whole is heavily dependent on aid from the US plus income from the US leasing of Kwajalein Atoll for missile testing. With US grants scaled back since 2001, every economic activity helping the country is being explored.

# Kiribati

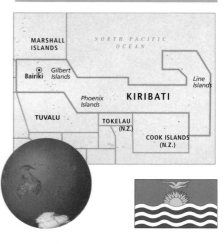

## Fact File

OFFICIAL NAME  Republic of Kiribati

FORM OF GOVERNMENT  Republic with single legislative body (National Assembly)

CAPITAL  Bairiki

AREA  810 sq km (277 sq miles)

TIME ZONE  GMT +12/11 hours

POPULATION  110,000

PROJECTED POPULATION 2015  130,000

POPULATION DENSITY  135.8 per sq km (397 per sq mile)

LIFE EXPECTANCY  62.9

INFANT MORTALITY (PER 1,000)  44.7

OFFICIAL LANGUAGE  English

OTHER LANGUAGE  Gilbertese

LITERACY RATE  90 %

RELIGIONS  Roman Catholic 52 %, Protestant (Congregational) 40 %, other (including Seventh-Day Adventist, Baha'i, Church of God, Mormon) 8 %

ETHNIC GROUPS  Micronesian 98.5 %, Polynesian, Chinese, European 1.5 %

CURRENCY  Australian dollar

ECONOMY  Services 65.3 %, industry 32 %, agriculture 2.7 %

GNI PER CAPITA  US$ 1,170

CLIMATE  Tropical, moderated by trade winds

HIGHEST POINT  Unnamed location on Banaba Island 81 m (266 ft)

MAP REFERENCE  Page 139

The Republic of Kiribati (pronounced Kiribass) consists of 33 scattered coral atolls in three separate groups in the mid-Pacific, plus the volcanic island, Banaba. The three groups are the seventeen former Gilbert Islands in the west, the eight Phoenix Islands, and the eight Line Islands.

Banaba Island has provided the region with the most income. It is one of three great phosphate rock islands in the Pacific Ocean, the others being Nauru and Makatea. The people of Kiribati are Micronesian, though the Banabans pride themselves on being ethnically distinct.

Kiritimati Island (also known as Christmas Island), one of the Line Islands, was the site of

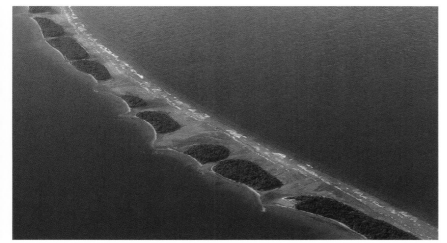

the first British nuclear tests in the Pacific in 1957, but is now a favored location for tourist development. For Kiribati as a whole, it is difficult to see what else besides tourism can be developed as a national source of income—it is classified by the United Nations as a Least Developed Country. The phosphate deposits on Banaba had been exhausted by the time of independence in 1979. Copra (68 percent), seaweed (sixteen percent) and fish (fifteen percent) are now the main exports. A basic subsistence economy still flourishes, with small farms and gardens producing taro, breadfruit, and sweet potatoes. Kiribati imports little food but it depends heavily on foreign aid, largely from the UK and Japan. Aid has been 25 to fifty percent of gross domestic product in recent years.

Though Kiribati is a democracy, the political parties continue to be strongly influenced by a traditional chief system and have little formal organization. A major difficulty for Kiribati today is the problem of environmental degradation from the overpopulation of Tarawa, the island capital to which many Kiribati have migrated because of the lack of job opportunities elsewhere.

*Huts on a coconut plantation in Kiribati (above). Phosphate mine on Nauru (below). Pristine waters off the Cook Islands (right page).*

## Nauru

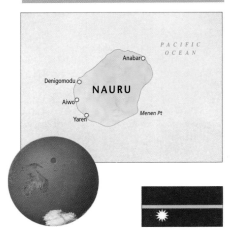

### Fact File

| | |
|---|---|
| **OFFICIAL NAME** | Republic of Nauru |
| **FORM OF GOVERNMENT** | Republic with single legislative body (Parliament) |
| **CAPITAL** | None; government offices in Yaren |
| **AREA** | 21 sq km (8.1 sq miles) |
| **TIME ZONE** | GMT + 12 hours |
| **POPULATION** | 13,800 |
| **PROJECTED POPULATION 2015** | 15,000 |
| **POPULATION DENSITY** | 657.1 per sq km (1,703.7 per sq mile) |
| **LIFE EXPECTANCY** | 63.8 |
| **INFANT MORTALITY (PER 1,000)** | 9.4 |
| **OFFICIAL LANGUAGE** | Nauruan |
| **OTHER LANGUAGE** | English |
| **LITERACY RATE** | not available |
| **RELIGIONS** | Protestant 66 %, Roman Catholic 33 % |
| **ETHNIC GROUPS** | Nauruan 58 %, other Pacific Islander 26 %, Chinese 8 %, European 8 % |
| **CURRENCY** | Australian dollar |

| | |
|---|---|
| **ECONOMY** | Phosphate mining, financial services, coconut production |
| **GNI PER CAPITA** | not available |
| **CLIMATE** | Tropical, with wet season November to February |
| **HIGHEST POINT** | Unnamed location 61 m (200 ft) |
| **MAP REFERENCE** | Pages 138–39 |

Nauru is a tiny island in the Pacific 3,000 km (2,000 miles) northeast of Australia. It is the world's smallest republic and, because of the wealth of its phosphate deposits, Nauruans enjoyed one of the highest per capita incomes in the Third World. The phosphate deposits have been depleted, however, and the government has spent the country's income as well as the money that had been saved. As a consequence, the country is on the brink of bankruptcy and it is hard to get reliable data on its economy.

Although little is known of the original Polynesian inhabitants of the island, it was first visited by Europeans when a British ship stopped there in 1798. Clan warfare among the Polynesians became widespread in the 1870s, leading the Germans (who then controlled the Marshall Islands, and whose traders were active on Nauru) to incorporate it into their administration in 1888. Phosphate mining by both a German and a British company began in 1906. After the First World War the administration of Nauru passed to Australia and independence was granted in 1968. In 1970 Australia, New Zealand, and Great Britain relinquished their joint control of the phosphate industry to a Nauruan governmental agency, the Nauru Phosphate Corporation.

The island is a 21 sq km (8.1 sq mile) raised coral reef with a central plateau. This plateau consists of phosphate beds created by seabird droppings over the course of many centuries. It is encircled by a fertile belt of semicultivated land where most of the people live. A ring road forms a continuous strip settlement around the coastal perimeter, where houses and other buildings occupy the only habitable land. After more than ninety years of continual phosphate mining, much of the rest of the island—in effect a largely worked-out quarry—has an aspect of lunar desolation. The climate is hot and humid, but because clouds sometimes miss the small island, years can pass without any rainfall at all. What little vegetation there is consists of coconut palms, breadfruit trees, and scrub.

About eighty percent of the island is now uninhabitable and uncultivable, and as a result all food, fuel, manufactured goods, building materials, and machinery are imported. The high proportion of processed foods in the inhabitants' diet has led to widespread obesity, and approximately one-third of the people suffer from non-insulin-dependent diabetes. Although many Nauruans live in traditional houses, they tend to spend their considerable incomes on luxury cars and electrical goods. Much phosphate income has been invested in trust funds to serve the country's long-term needs, but not all the investments have been wise and since 1990 dividends have fallen sharply.

# Dependencies and Territories

## American Samoa

### Fact File

**OFFICIAL NAME** Territory of American Samoa

**FORM OF GOVERNMENT** Unincorporated and unorganized territory of the USA

**CAPITAL** Pago Pago

**AREA** 199 sq km (77 sq miles)

**TIME ZONE** GMT – 11 hours

**POPULATION** 57,500

**LIFE EXPECTANCY** 76.5

**INFANT MORTALITY (PER 1,000)** 8.7

**LITERACY RATE** 97%

**CURRENCY** US dollar

**ECONOMY** Fishing 34%, government 33%, other 33%

**CLIMATE** Tropical; wet season November to April

**MAP REFERENCE** Pages 136, 141

Consisting of aroup of five volcanic islands and two atolls in the South Pacific located about midway between Hawaii and New Zealand, American Samoa has been settled by Polynesian peoples since about 800 BC. The first European contact was made by the Dutch in 1722. British missionaries were active in the region from 1830 onwards. In 1872 the USA won exclusive rights from the High Chief to use Pago Pago as a strategic base for the American fleet. Pago Pago has one of the best natural deepwater harbors in the region, sheltered by surrounding mountains from rough seas and high winds. About ninety percent of trade is with the USA, which heavily subsidizes the economy. Tuna fishing, processing, and export are the foundation of private sector economic activity.

## Ashmore and Cartier Islands

### Fact File

**OFFICIAL NAME** Territory of Ashmore and Cartier Islands

**FORM OF GOVERNMENT** External territory of Australia

**CAPITAL** None; administered from Canberra

**AREA** 5 sq km (2 sq miles)

**TIME ZONE** GMT + 8 hours

**POPULATION** No permanent population

**CLIMATE** Tropical

**MAP REFERENCE** Page 134

Uninhabited islands in the Indian Ocean northwest of Australia, Ashmore and Cartier Islands are at no point higher than 3 m (10 ft) above sea level. The terrain consists of sand and coral. The islands are surrounded by reefs and shoals that can pose a maritime hazard. The Australian government monitors the state of the Ashmore Reef National Nature Reserve by regularly sending experts. The defense of the islands is also in the hands of the Australian government and the Royal Australian Navy and Air Force make visits from time to time.

## Baker and Howland Islands

### Fact File

**OFFICIAL NAME** Baker and Howland Islands

**FORM OF GOVERNMENT** Unincorporated territory of the USA

**CAPITAL** None; administered from Washington DC

**AREA** 3 sq km (1.2 sq miles)

**TIME ZONE** GMT – 10 hours

**POPULATION** No permanent population

**CLIMATE** Hot, dry, and windy

**MAP REFERENCE** Page 139

Baker Island is an uninhabited atoll in the North Pacific, midway between Hawaii and Australia. The terrain consists of a low coral island surrounded by a narrow reef. The island's climate is equatorial with little rainfall, constant wind, and burning sun. Used by the US military during the Second World War, it is now primarily a nesting habitat for seabirds and marine wildlife. Howland Island is an uninhabited atoll nearby. Another low coral island surrounded by a narrow reef, it has no supply of fresh water. Entry to Baker and Howland Islands, a National Wildlife Refuge run by the US Department of the Interior, is prohibited except by special-use permit.

## Cook Islands

### Fact File

**OFFICIAL NAME** Cook Islands

**FORM OF GOVERNMENT** Self-governing in free association with New Zealand

**CAPITAL** Avarua

**AREA** 240 sq km (93 sq miles)

**TIME ZONE** GMT – 10 hours

**POPULATION** 21,900

**LIFE EXPECTANCY** not available

**INFANT MORTALITY** not available

**LITERACY RATE** 95%

**CURRENCY** New Zealand dollar

**ECONOMY** Services 75.3%, agriculture 15.1%, industry 9.6%

**CLIMATE** Tropical, moderated by trade winds

**MAP REFERENCE** Pages 136–37, 139

About 3,500 km (2,175 miles) northeast of New Zealand, the Cook Islands consist of 24 widely separated coral atolls in the north, and hilly, volcanic islands in the south. The Polynesian inhabitants are believed to have settled the islands around AD 500 to 800. They were visited by the Spanish in 1595; explored by Captain James Cook in 1773 and 1777; Christianized by British missionaries after 1821; and annexed to New Zealand in 1901. Since independence in 1965 the islands have been self-governing in free association with New Zealand. They have a fully responsible government, with elections every five years to a 25-member parliament, based on full adult suffrage. The climate is tropical with plentiful rainfall. Agriculture provides the economic base, and the main export earners are fruit, copra, and clothing. Marine culture has recently led to the production of black pearls and trochus shell. Financial services are available. New Zealand is both the main trading partner (taking 96 percent of exports) and the source of substantial aid. In the course of recent years, tourism has been expanding.

# French Polynesia

## Fact File

| | |
|---|---|
| OFFICIAL NAME | Territory of French Polynesia |
| FORM OF GOVERNMENT | Overseas territory of France |
| CAPITAL | Papeete |
| AREA | 4,167 sq km (1,609 sq miles) |
| TIME ZONE | GMT – 10 hours |
| POPULATION | 283,000 |
| LIFE EXPECTANCY | 76.5 |
| INFANT MORTALITY (PER 1,000) | 7.7 |
| LITERACY RATE | 98 % |
| CURRENCY | CFP (Comptoirs Français du Pacifique) franc |
| ECONOMY | Services 77.9 %, industry 19 %, agriculture 3.1 % |
| CLIMATE | Tropical |
| MAP REFERENCE | Page 137 |

French Polynesia comprises five archipelagoes in the South Pacific, midway between Australia and South America, scattered over an area of ocean as large as Europe. They include the Society Islands (Archipel de la Société), the Marquesas (Îles Marquises), the Tubuai Islands, and the Tuamotus (Archipel des Tuamotu). The Polynesian inhabitants first settled the islands about 2,000 years ago. European contact dates from 1767. The conversion of the islanders to Christianity began in 1797 and after three years of armed resistance the chiefs of Tahiti accepted French colonial control in 1843. The islands send two deputies and a senator to the French Assembly in Paris, and since 1984 have had a local territorial assembly as well. Famous for providing the artist Gauguin with his best-known subjects, French Polynesia has been in

the news more recently as a site for French nuclear testing on the atoll of Mururoa. This ceased in 1995. Large military expenditures over the preceding thirty years have provided the islands with employment, high wages, and improved infrastructure, and resulted in seventy percent of the population moving to live on Tahiti. Tourism now accounts for twenty percent of the gross domestic product, and cultured pearls are the main export.

Uninhabited Clipperton Island, a coral atoll in the Pacific Ocean west of Mexico, is administered by France from French Polynesia.

# Guam

## Fact File

| | |
|---|---|
| OFFICIAL NAME | Territory of Guam |
| FORM OF GOVERNMENT | Organized, unincorporated territory of the USA |
| CAPITAL | Agana |
| AREA | 541 sq km (209 sq miles) |
| TIME ZONE | GMT + 10 hours |
| POPULATION | 176,000 |
| LIFE EXPECTANCY | 78.9 |
| INFANT MORTALITY (PER 1,000) | 6.6 |
| LITERACY RATE | 99 % |
| CURRENCY | US dollar |
| ECONOMY | Services 78 %, industry 15 %, agriculture 7 % |
| CLIMATE | Tropical, moderated by trade winds; wet season July to October |
| MAP REFERENCE | Page 138 |

The largest and most southerly of the Mariana Islands in the northwest Pacific, Guam lies about 2,000 km (1,200 miles) due east of Manila

in the Philippines. Originally settled by Malay-Filipino peoples around 1500 BC, Guam was mapped by Ferdinand Magellan in 1521, claimed by Spain from 1565, and since Spain's defeat in the Spanish-American War in 1899 has been administered by the USA. Of volcanic origin, Guam consists of a relatively flat coralline limestone plateau (which is the source of most fresh water for the island), with steep coastal cliffs and narrow coastal plains in the north, low-rising hills in the center, and mountains in the south. About half its population are Chamorro, of mixed Indonesian, Spanish, and Filipino descent. The island is of great strategic importance to the USA and about one-third of its land is occupied by American naval and airforce facilities. This has resulted in a high standard of living, and there are concerns about the unemployment that is likely to follow the planned closing of four naval installations. As a Pacific tourist destination Guam is second only to Hawaii.

# Jarvis Island

## Fact File

| | |
|---|---|
| OFFICIAL NAME | Jarvis Island |
| FORM OF GOVERNMENT | Unincorporated territory of the USA |
| CAPITAL | None; administered from Washington DC |
| AREA | 4.5 sq km (1.7 sq miles) |
| TIME ZONE | GMT – 10 hours |
| POPULATION | No permanent population |
| CLIMATE | Hot, dry, and windy |
| MAP REFERENCE | Page 139 |

Oceania

An uninhabited island in the South Pacific, Jarvis Island lies about midway between Hawaii and the Cook Islands. A sandy coral islet with a fringing reef, it has a tropical climate with little rain and no fresh water. Guano deposits were worked until late in the nineteenth century, and Millersville settlement on the west of the island was used as a weather station from 1935 until the Second World War. Ground cover consists of sparse bunch grass, prostrate vines, and low-growing shrubs. The island is mainly a nesting place for seabirds and marine wildlife. Entry is by special-use permit only.

## Johnston Atoll

### Fact File

| | |
|---|---|
| OFFICIAL NAME | Johnston Atoll |
| FORM OF GOVERNMENT | Unincorporated territory of the USA |
| CAPITAL | None; administered from Washington DC |
| AREA | 2.8 sq km (1.1 sq miles) |
| TIME ZONE | GMT – 10 hours |
| POPULATION | No permanent population |
| ECONOMY | US military base |
| CLIMATE | Hot, dry, and windy |
| MAP REFERENCE | Page 139 |

This remote coral atoll consisting of two islets, Johnston Island and Sand Island, lies in the North Pacific about one-third of the way between Hawaii and the Marshall Islands. The atoll is 5 m (16 ft) above sea level at its highest point and has a dry tropical climate, northeast trade winds ensuring little seasonal temperature variation.

Mined during the nineteenth century for its extensive guano deposits, the atoll is now home to approximately 1,200 US military personnel. It was formerly used as a nuclear weapons testing site. The territory is administered by the US Defense Nuclear Agency. The incineration plant for chemical warfare agents on Johnston Island was removed completely by 2004.

## Kingman Reef

### Fact File

| | |
|---|---|
| OFFICIAL NAME | Kingman Reef |
| FORM OF GOVERNMENT | Unincorporated territory of the USA |
| CAPITAL | None; administered from Washington DC |
| AREA | 1 sq km (0.4 sq miles) |
| TIME ZONE | GMT – 10 hours |
| POPULATION | No permanent population |
| CLIMATE | Tropical, moderated by sea breezes |
| MAP REFERENCE | Page 139 |

A barren triangular-shaped reef in the North Pacific, Kingman Reef is about halfway between Hawaii and American Samoa. No more than 1 m (3 ft) above sea level, and awash most of the time, the reef is a maritime hazard. Although no economic activity takes place and the reef is uninhabited, the deep interior lagoon was used as a halfway station between Hawaii and American Samoa when Pan American Airways used flying boats in the Pacific in 1937 and 1938. While there is no land flora, the reef is rich in marine life. It is administered by the US Navy.

## Cocos (Keeling) Islands

### Fact File

| | |
|---|---|
| OFFICIAL NAME | Territory of Cocos (Keeling) Islands |
| FORM OF GOVERNMENT | External territory of Australia |
| CAPITAL | West Island |
| AREA | 14 sq km (5.4 sq miles) |
| TIME ZONE | GMT + 7 hours |
| POPULATION | 600 |
| LIFE EXPECTANCY | Not available |
| INFANT MORTALITY (PER 1,000) | Not available |
| LITERACY RATE | Not available |
| CURRENCY | Australian dollar |
| ECONOMY | Coconut and copra production |
| CLIMATE | Tropical, moderated by trade winds |
| MAP REFERENCE | Page 134 |

The Cocos (Keeling) Islands are a group of 27 coral atolls in the Indian Ocean midway between Australia and Sri Lanka. When discovered in 1609 by the East India Company's Captain William Keeling they were uninhabited. In 1827 the Scot John Clunies-Ross brought some Malays with him and established a settlement. The inhabited islands today are Home Island, where the Cocos Malays live, and West Island, with a small European community. The group has been administered

*The peaks of Anau and Nunue Bora Bora, French Polynesia (left page bottom). Bora Bora resort and lagoon on the Society Islands (above center). Looking out over the city and bay, Guam (below).*

directly by the Australian government since a referendum in 1984. Coconuts are the sole cash crop, copra and fresh coconuts the major export earners. Though local gardens and fishing make a contribution, additional food and other necessities must come from Australia.

## Coral Sea Islands

### Fact File

OFFICIAL NAME  Coral Sea Islands Territory

FORM OF GOVERNMENT  External territory of Australia

CAPITAL  None; administered from Canberra

AREA  3 sq km (1.2 sq miles)

TIME ZONE  GMT + 10 hours

POPULATION  No permanent population

CLIMATE  Tropical

MAP REFERENCE  Page 135

These uninhabited sandy islands and coral reefs are located in the Coral Sea northeast of Australia's Great Barrier Reef. The numerous small islands and reefs are scattered over a sea area of about 1 million sq km (386,000 sq miles), with Willis Islets the most important. Nowhere more than 6 m (20 ft) above sea level, the area is an important nesting area for seabirds and turtles. There are no permanent freshwater resources and the islands are occasionally subject to cyclones. Although there are no indigenous inhabitants, three meteorologists are stationed there. Defense is the responsibility of Australia, the islets being regularly visited by the Royal Australian Navy. Australia controls the activities of visitors.

## Midway Islands

### Fact File

OFFICIAL NAME  Midway Islands

FORM OF GOVERNMENT  Unincorporated territory of the USA

CAPITAL  None; administered from Washington DC

AREA  5.2 sq km (1.9 sq miles)

TIME ZONE  GMT – 10 hours

POPULATION  No permanent population

ECONOMY  US military base

CLIMATE  Tropical, moderated by sea breezes

MAP REFERENCE  Page 139

The two Midway Islands constitute part of an atoll in the northern Pacific at the extreme western end of the Hawaiian chain, 1,931 km (1,200 miles) northwest of Hawaii. Their name derives from their position midway along the old shipping route from California to Japan.

The atoll is almost completely flat, and none of the land is higher than 4 m (13 ft) above sea level. During the Second World War it was the scene of a major battle between Japan and the USA, and afterward it was used as a naval airbase, which was closed down in 1993. Today, it is a wildlife refuge and currently is the nesting area of the world's largest Laysan albatross colony. From 1996 until 2001 the refuge was open to the public, but it is currently closed for an unspecified period of time.

## New Caledonia

### Fact File

OFFICIAL NAME  Territory of New Caledonia and Dependencies

FORM OF GOVERNMENT  Overseas territory of France

CAPITAL  Nouméa

AREA  19,060 sq km (7,359 sq miles)

TIME ZONE  GMT + 11 hours

POPULATION  225,000

LIFE EXPECTANCY  74.8

INFANT MORTALITY (PER 1,000)  7.2

LITERACY RATE  96.2 %

CURRENCY  CFP (Comptoirs Français du Pacifique) franc

ECONOMY  Services 76 %, agriculture 15 %, industry 9 %

CLIMATE  Tropical, moderated by trade winds

MAP REFERENCE  Pages 136, 141

New Caledonia is a group of islands 1,500 km (900 miles) off the northeast coast of Australia. Rich in minerals, and with more than fourty percent of the world's known nickel resources, it is France's largest overseas territory. First populated by indigenous Kanaks (who call the land Kanaky) around 4000 BC, the islands were visited by the Spanish in the sixteenth and seventeenth centuries, were named by Captain James Cook in 1774, and were used as a penal settlement by France between 1853 and 1897. By the end of the nineteenth century French settlers owned more than ninety percent of the land. Dissatisfaction with their situation led to violent resistance from the Kanaks during the 1970s and 1980s, but more recently they have come to accept French rule. The Kanaks now represent only 43 percent of the population, while 37 percent are of European descent. The main island, Grand Terre, consists of coastal plains with a mountainous interior. Only a small amount of land is suitable for cultivation. New Caledonia's prosperity is almost entirely dependent on nickel production, so the economy is at the mercy of varying world demand. Tourism from France, Japan, and Australia is also important.

## Niue

### Fact File

OFFICIAL NAME  Niue

FORM OF GOVERNMENT  Self-governing territory in free association with New Zealand

CAPITAL  Alofi

AREA  260 sq km (100 sq miles)

TIME ZONE  GMT – 11 hours

| | |
|---|---|
| POPULATION | 1,400 |
| LIFE EXPECTANCY | Not available |
| INFANT MORTALITY (PER 1,000) | Not available |
| LITERACY RATE | 95 % |
| CURRENCY | New Zealand dollar |
| ECONOMY | Services 49.5 %, industry 26.9 %, agriculture 23.6 % |
| CLIMATE | Tropical, moderated by trade winds |
| MAP REFERENCE | Pages 132, 136 |

Niue is one of the world's biggest coral atolls, lying about 700 km (400 miles) east of Tonga in the South Pacific. The terrain consists of a central limestone plateau with steep cliffs around the coast; the highest point is 68 m (223 ft). The economy is heavily dependent on aid from the New Zealand government. Most of the inhabitants live by subsistence farming. Light industry consists of processing passionfruit, lime oil, honey, and coconut cream. The sale of postage stamps and tourism are also a source of foreign currency. Remittances from family members living overseas supplement domestic income: lack of employment opportunities on the island means that five out of six of the people of Niue live and work in New Zealand.

## Northern Mariana Islands

### Fact File

| | |
|---|---|
| OFFICIAL NAME | Commonwealth of the Northern Mariana Islands |
| FORM OF GOVERNMENT | Territory of the USA; commonwealth in political union with the USA |
| CAPITAL | Saipan |
| AREA | 477 sq km (184 sq miles) |
| TIME ZONE | GMT + 10 hours |
| POPULATION | 86,600 |
| LIFE EXPECTANCY | 76.5 |
| INFANT MORTALITY (PER 1,000) | 6.7 |
| LITERACY RATE | 97 % |
| CURRENCY | US dollar |
| ECONOMY | Tourism, industry, agriculture |
| CLIMATE | Tropical, moderated by trade winds |
| MAP REFERENCE | Page 138 |

These islands are located in the North Pacific about three-quarters of the way between Hawaii and the Philippines. Unlike the nearby Caroline Islands, the Northern Marianas chose not to seek independence in 1987, preferring to remain part of the USA. There are fourteen main islands including Saipan, Rota, and Tinian. The southern islands are limestone with level terraces and fringing coral reefs; the northern

islands are volcanic, with active volcanoes on Pagan and Agrihan. There is little seasonal variation in the tropical marine climate, as the temperature is moderated by northeast trade winds. The people of the islands belong to a variety of ethnic groups and include Chamorros (mixed Indonesian, Spanish, and Filipino), Micronesians, Japanese, Chinese, and Koreans. The economy is substantially supported by the USA. Tourism is a fast-growing source of income, employing increasing numbers of the workforce and bringing in most revenue. Cattle ranches produce beef, and small farms produce coconuts, breadfruit, tomatoes, and melons. Industry consists of handicrafts, light manufacturing, and garment production.

## Norfolk Island

### Fact File

| | |
|---|---|
| OFFICIAL NAME | Territory of Norfolk Island |
| FORM OF GOVERNMENT | External territory of Australia |

*An aerial view of Amadee Island, New Caledonia (left page). Clear blue waters form an inlet on the South Pacific island of Niue (top). Historic colonial buildings and ruins on Norfolk Island (above).*

| | |
|---|---|
| CAPITAL | Kingston |
| AREA | 35 sq km (14 sq miles) |
| TIME ZONE | GMT + 11.5 hours |
| POPULATION | 2,100 |
| LIFE EXPECTANCY | Not available |
| INFANT MORTALITY (PER 1,000) | Not available |
| LITERACY RATE | Not available |
| CURRENCY | Australian dollar |
| ECONOMY | Tourism, agriculture |
| CLIMATE | Subtropical |
| MAP REFERENCE | Pages 133, 136 |

Some 1,400 km (850 miles) east of Australia, Norfolk Island is inhabited by descendants of the famous mutineers from HMS *Bounty*. Of volcanic origin, the island was uninhabited when discovered by Captain James Cook in 1774. After serving as a penal settlement in Australia's early history it became a refuge for the entire population of the Pitcairn Islands' *Bounty* mutiny survivors, who were resettled there in 1856. (Some later returned to live on Pitcairn Island.) The present inhabitants speak a mixture of

nineteenth century English, Gaelic, and Old Tahitian. They enjoy a degree of autonomy and have rejected proposals to become a part of the Australian state. While there is no income tax, the government raises revenue from customs duty, liquor sales, a public works levy, financial institutions levy, and departure fees. Tourism is the main activity, the island receiving around 30,000 visitors each year.

## Palmyra Atoll

### Fact File

OFFICIAL NAME  Palmyra Atoll

FORM OF GOVERNMENT  Incorporated territory of the USA

CAPITAL  None; administered from Washington DC

AREA  12 sq km (4.6 sq miles)

TIME ZONE  GMT – 10 hours

POPULATION  No permanent population

CLIMATE  Tropical

MAP REFERENCE  Page 139

A privately owned uninhabited atoll in the northern Pacific, Palmyra Atoll lies about halfway between Hawaii and Samoa. At no point more than 2 m (6 ft) above sea level, the atoll consists of about fifty islets covered with dense vegetation, coconut palms, and balsa-like trees that grow up to 30 m (100 ft) tall. A number of roads and causeways were built during the Second World War, but they are now overgrown and unserviceable, as is the airstrip. In 2001, the atoll and a 12 mile wide area of sea around it was declared a nature conservancy area. There are plans to turn the atoll into a "get away from it all" tourist complex.

## Pitcairn Islands

### Fact File

OFFICIAL NAME  Pitcairn, Henderson, Ducie, and Oeno Islands

FORM OF GOVERNMENT  Overseas territory of the United Kingdom

CAPITAL  Adamstown

AREA  47 sq km (18 sq miles)

TIME ZONE  GMT – 8.5 hours

POPULATION  48

LIFE EXPECTANCY  Not available

INFANT MORTALITY (PER 1,000)  Not available

LITERACY RATE  Not available

CURRENCY  New Zealand dollar

ECONOMY  Fishing, agriculture, services

CLIMATE  Tropical, with rainy season from November to March

MAP REFERENCE  Page 137

The Pitcairn Islands are located in the South Pacific about midway between Peru and New Zealand. They have a rugged volcanic formation, cliffs along a rocky coast, and a tropical, hot, and humid climate. The islands are the United Kingdom's most isolated dependency. Uninhabited when they were discovered by Europeans, they were used as a refuge by the mutineers from HMS *Bounty* in 1790, some of whose descendants still live there speaking a part-Tahitian, part-English dialect. They exist by fishing and subsistence farming. The fertile valley soils produce fruits and vegetables including citrus, sugarcane, watermelons, bananas, yams, and beans. Barter is an important economic activity. The main source of revenue is the sale of postage stamps and handicrafts to passing ships.

## Tokelau

### Fact File

OFFICIAL NAME  Tokelau

FORM OF GOVERNMENT  Territory of New Zealand

CAPITAL  None; administrative center on each atoll

AREA  10 sq km (3.9 sq miles)

TIME ZONE  GMT – 11 hours

POPULATION  1,430

LIFE EXPECTANCY  Not available

INFANT MORTALITY (PER 1,000)  Not available

LITERACY RATE  Not available

CURRENCY  New Zealand dollar

ECONOMY  Agriculture, industry

CLIMATE  Tropical, moderated by trade winds April to November

MAP REFERENCE  Page 139

Tokelau is a small group of islands in the southern Pacific about midway between Hawaii and New Zealand. The islands consist of low coral atolls, none of the atolls rises higher than 5 m (16 ft) above sea level enclosing large lagoons. Situated in the Pacific typhoon belt (a cyclone in 1990 destroyed a great deal of Tokelau's infrastructure), they have a tropical climate moderated by trade winds. There are limited natural resources, and subsistence farmers grow coconuts, breadfruit, papaya, and bananas. Small-scale industry produces copra, woodwork, plaited craft goods, stamps, and coins. An anticipated tuna cannery is expected to help sustain the economy, and it is hoped that a catamaran link between the various atolls will boost tourism. Aid from New Zealand is the main source of revenue and money remitted by relatives who live and work in New Zealand is a vital source of domestic income.

## Wake Island

### Fact File

OFFICIAL NAME  Wake Island

FORM OF GOVERNMENT  Unincorporated territory of the USA

CAPITAL  None; administered from Washington DC

AREA  6.5 sq km (2.5 sq miles)

TIME ZONE GMT + 12 hours

POPULATION No permanent population

ECONOMY US military base

CLIMATE Tropical

MAP REFERENCE Page 138

Wake Island is located in the North Pacific about two-thirds of the way between Hawaii and the Northern Mariana Islands. It consists of three tiny coral islets linked by causeways around a lagoon. The islets are built on fragments of the rim of an extinct underwater volcano, the lagoon being the former crater. With no indigenous inhabitants or economic activity, the 300 or so US military personnel stationed on Wake Island provide help in the case of emergency landings by aircraft on transpacific flights.

# Wallis and Futuna Islands

## Fact File

OFFICIAL NAME Territory of the Wallis and Futuna Islands

FORM OF GOVERNMENT Overseas territory of France

CAPITAL Mata Utu

AREA 274 sq km (106 sq miles)

TIME ZONE GMT + 12 hours

POPULATION 16,400

LIFE EXPECTANCY Not available

INFANT MORTALITY (PER 1,000) Not available

LITERACY RATE 50 %

CURRENCY CFP (Comptoirs Français du Pacifique) franc

ECONOMY Agriculture, fishing

CLIMATE Tropical, with wet season November to April

MAP REFERENCE Page 139

This group comprises three main islands—Futuna, Alofi and Wallis (Uvea)—and twenty islets, located west of Samoa and northeast of Fiji. They are of volcanic origin, with low hills rising to 765 m (2,510 ft) at Mt Singavi. All the main islands have fringing reefs. In the hot wet season from November to April 2,500–3,000 mm (100–120 in) of rain may fall. This rain, combined with deforestation (timber is used locally for fuel), has eroded the terrain of Futuna. The people live by subsistence farming. Exports are negligible and French aid is essential to the islands. First settled perhaps 2,000 years ago, and visited by the Dutch in 1616, the islands became a French protectorate in 1886. In a referendum on independence in 1959 they chose to become a French Overseas Territory. There is no independence movement.

## The problem of coral bleaching

Coral reefs constitute one of the Earth's great diverse ecosystems. They are made of limestone formed by millions of tiny marine animals and can only live in tropical seas within a narrow range of physical and chemical conditions. Coral reefs generally form only when winter water temperatures exceed 18 °C (64 °F) and when light levels are high. Coral is found in the rock record in the form of fossils dating back to the Paleozoic Era. However, although coral has survived this long, it is not immune to the impact of human activities.

In recent years scientists have become interested in the apparent link between the death of large tracts of coral in the Pacific and Caribbean regions and global warming. The greenhouse effect—a result of changes in the amounts of carbon dioxide and other gases in the atmosphere since the industrial revolution—is the cause of this global warming. Satellite data from the US National Oceano-graphic and Atmospheric Administration show a warming trend in sea-surface temperatures since 1982. In some areas, such as along the Great Barrier Reef in Australia, a combination of higher than usual summer temperatures and the run-off from floods (which reduces salinity) appears to be damaging the coral. As the essential conditions required for the maintenance of a healthy reef system are disrupted, the coral formations turn white.

What will happen to coral reefs in the future? Are the bleaching episodes observed in recent years in so many tropical areas really due to global warming or are there other causes? Predictions that ocean surface temperatures in the tropics may rise by up to 5 °C (41°F) in the 21st century are no longer considered fantasy. If this happens, it could greatly disturb even resilient ecosystems, such as coral reefs, and reduce the Earth's biodiversity as well as the ability of societies to live and work in these areas.

# Christmas Island

## Fact File

OFFICIAL NAME Territory of Christmas Island

FORM OF GOVERNMENT External territory of Australia

CAPITAL The Settlement

AREA 135 sq km (52 sq miles)

TIME ZONE GMT + 7 hours

POPULATION 1,400

LIFE EXPECTANCY Not available

INFANT MORTALITY (PER 1,000) Not available

LITERACY RATE Not available

CURRENCY Australian dollar

ECONOMY Mining, tourism

CLIMATE Tropical, moderated by trade winds

MAP REFERENCE Page 134

A small island in the Indian Ocean, Christmas Island is about 300 km (200 miles) south of Java. Coastal cliffs rise steeply to a central plateau. Formerly uninhabited, Chinese and Malayan labor was brought in to mine the island's rich phosphate deposits in the 1890s, and from 1900 the people enjoyed an economic boom. The mine now operates under strict environmental controls to preserve remaining rainforest. After heavy Australian government investment in infrastructure, a hotel complex was opened in 1993.

*Coconuts are piled on a beach in the Pacific Islands (left page bottom). Bananas are grown on Tokelau (bottom).*

# Oceania: Physical

© Random House Australia Pty Ltd

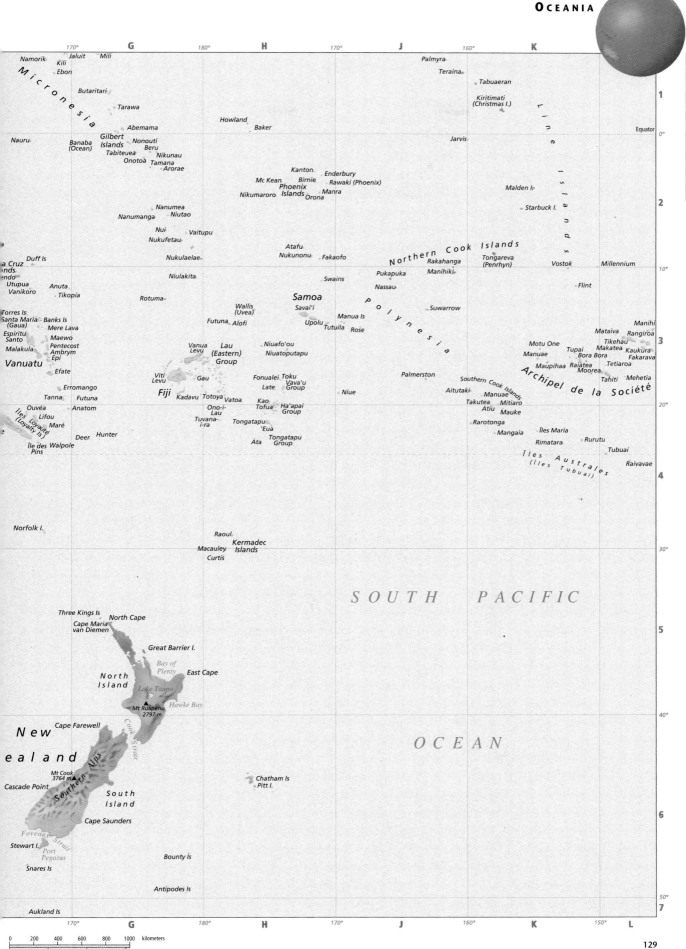

Scale 1:25,000,000    Projection: Mercator

0   200   400   600   800   1000   kilometers

0   200   400   600   miles

# Oceania: Political

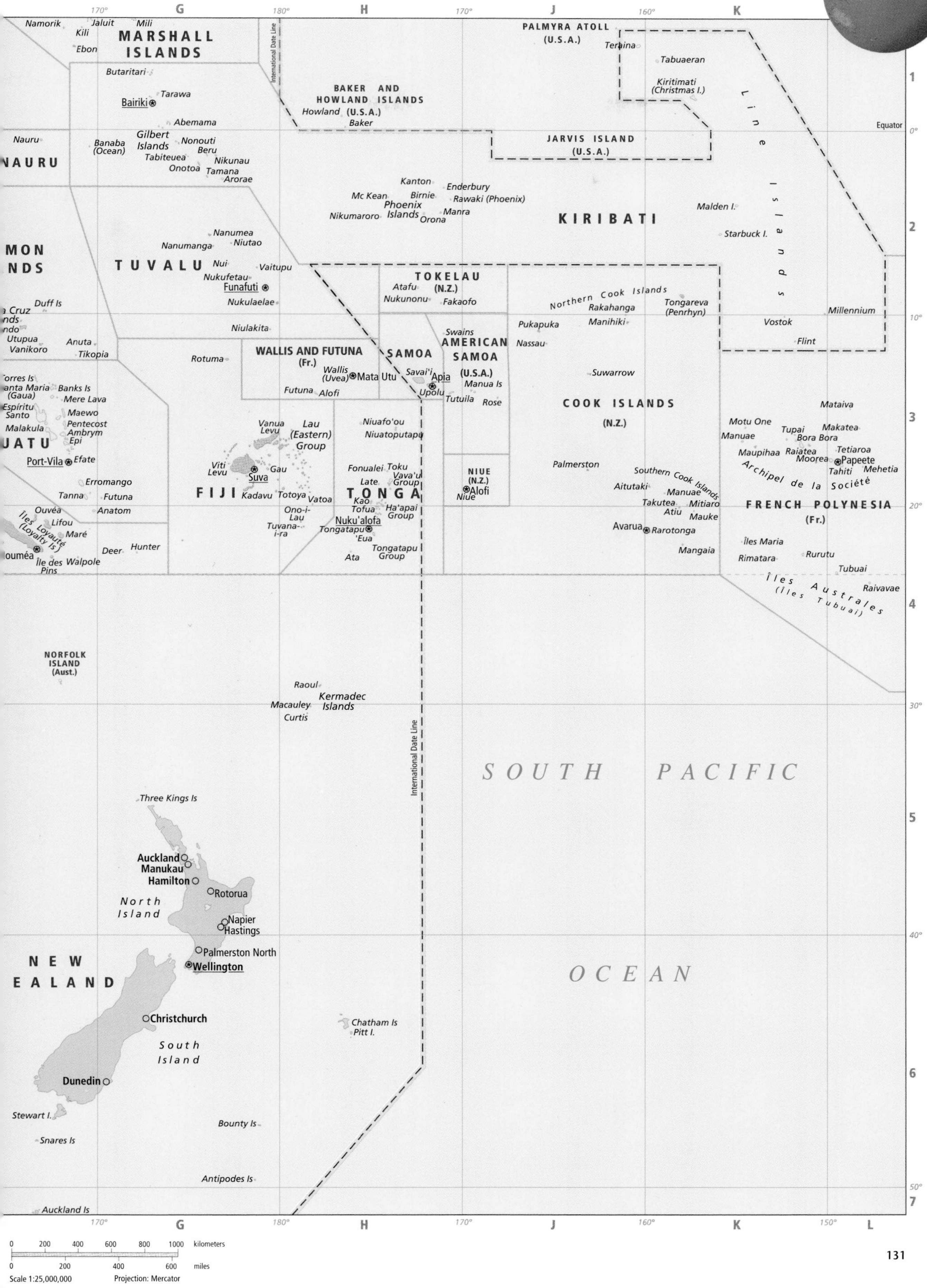

Oceania

International Date Line

**MARSHALL ISLANDS**

Namorik
Jaluit
Kili
Mili
Ebon
Butaritari
Bairiki
Tarawa
Abemama

PALMYRA ATOLL
(U.S.A.)
Teraina
Tabuaeran
Kiritimati
(Christmas I.)

BAKER AND
HOWLAND ISLANDS
Howland (U.S.A.)
Baker

Nauru
Banaba
(Ocean)
Gilbert
Islands
Nonouti
Beru
Nikunau
Tabiteuea
Onotoa
Tamana
Arorae

JARVIS ISLAND
(U.S.A.)

Equator

**NAURU**

Kanton
Enderbury
Mc Kean
Birnie
Rawaki (Phoenix)
**Phoenix
Islands**
Nikumaroro
Manra
Orona

**K I R I B A T I**

Malden I.
Starbuck I.

**SOLOMON
ISLANDS**

Duff Is

Nanumea
Niutao
Nanumanga
Nui
Vaitupu
Nukufetau
**T U V A L U**
Funafuti
Nukulaelae

**TOKELAU
(N.Z.)**
Atafu
Nukunonu
Fakaofo

Northern Cook Islands
Rakahanga
Tongareva
(Penrhyn)

Vostok
Millennium

Line Islands

Flint

a Cruz
nds
ndo
Utupua
Vanikoro

Anuta
Tikopia

Niulakita

**WALLIS AND FUTUNA
(Fr.)**
Rotuma
Wallis
(Uvea) Mata Utu
Futuna
Alofi

Swains
**SAMOA**
Savai'i Apia
Upolu

**AMERICAN
SAMOA
(U.S.A.)**
Manua Is
Tutuila
Rose

Pukapuka
Nassau
Manihiki
Suwarrow

Motu One
Mataiva
Manuae
Tupai
Makatea
Maupihaa
Raiatea
Tetiaroa
Moorea
Papeete
Archipel de la Société
Tahiti Mehetia

Torres Is
anta Maria
(Gaua)
Banks Is
Espiritu
Santo
Mere Lava
Maewo
Malakula
Pentecost
Ambrym
Epi

**UATU**
Port-Vila Efate

Vanua
Levu
**Lau
(Eastern)
Group**

Niuafo'ou
Niuatoputapu

**COOK ISLANDS
(N.Z.)**

Palmerston

Erromango

Tanna
Futuna
Anatom

Viti
Levu
Suva
Gau
Kadavu
**FIJI**
Totoya
Ono-i-
Lau
Vatoa
Tuvana-
i-ra

Fonualei Toku
Late
Vava'u
Group
Kao
Tofua
**T O N G A**
Ha'apai
Group
Ata
Tongatapu
Group
'Eua
Nuku'alofa
Tongatapu

**NIUE
(N.Z.)**
Alofi
Niue

Southern Cook Islands
Aitutaki
Manuae
Takutea
Mitiaro
Atiu
Mauke
Avarua Rarotonga
Mangaia

**FRENCH POLYNESIA
(Fr.)**
Îles Maria
Rimatara
Rururu
Tubuai
Raivavae

Îles Australes
(Îles Tubuai)

Ouvéa
Lifou
Îles Loyauté
(Loyalty Is)
Maré
oumea
Île des
Pins
Deer
Walpole
Hunter

**NORFOLK
ISLAND
(Aust.)**

Raoul
Macauley
**Kermadec
Islands**
Curtis

International Date Line

**S O U T H    P A C I F I C**

Three Kings Is

Auckland
Manukau
Hamilton
Rotorua

**N o r t h
I s l a n d**

Napier
Hastings

Palmerston North
Wellington

**N E W
EALAND**

Christchurch

Chatham Is
Pitt I.

**O C E A N**

**S o u t h
I s l a n d**

Dunedin

Stewart I.

Snares Is

Bounty Is

Antipodes Is

Auckland Is

0   200   400   600   800   1000   kilometers
0   200   400   600   miles
Scale 1:25,000,000      Projection: Mercator

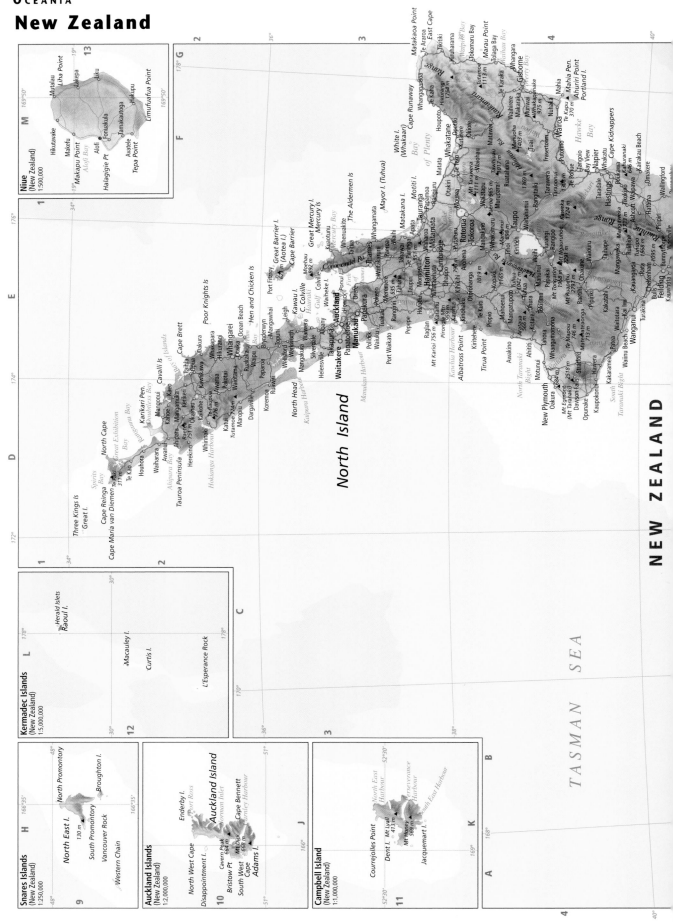

Niue
(New Zealand)
1:500,000

Snares Islands
(New Zealand)
1:250,000

Kermadec Islands
(New Zealand)
1:5,000,000

Auckland Islands
(New Zealand)
1:2,000,000

Campbell Island
(New Zealand)
1:1,000,000

North Island

NEW ZEALAND

TASMAN SEA

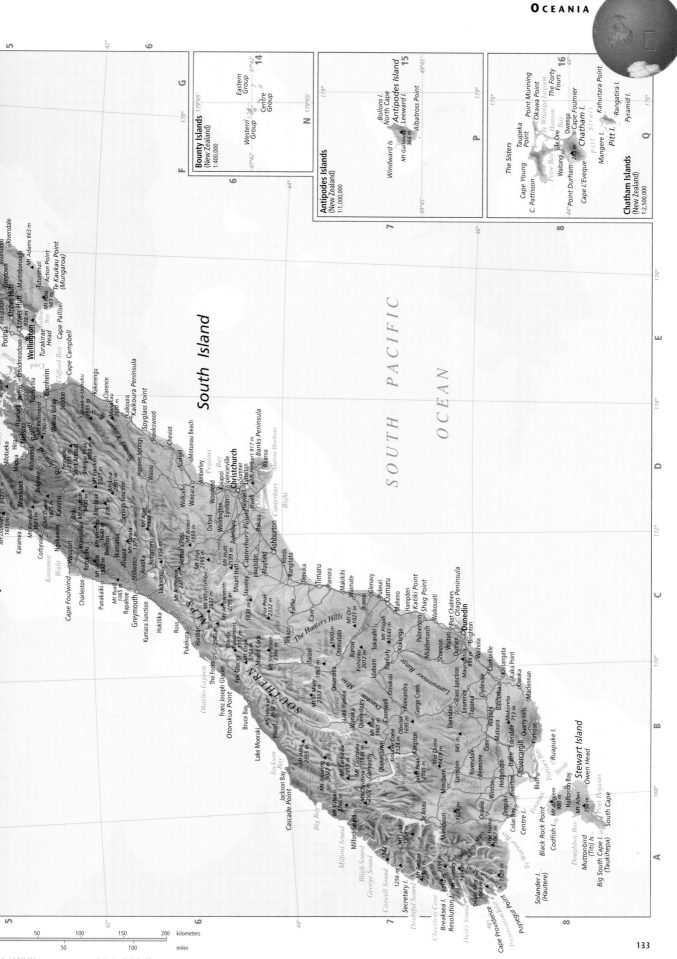

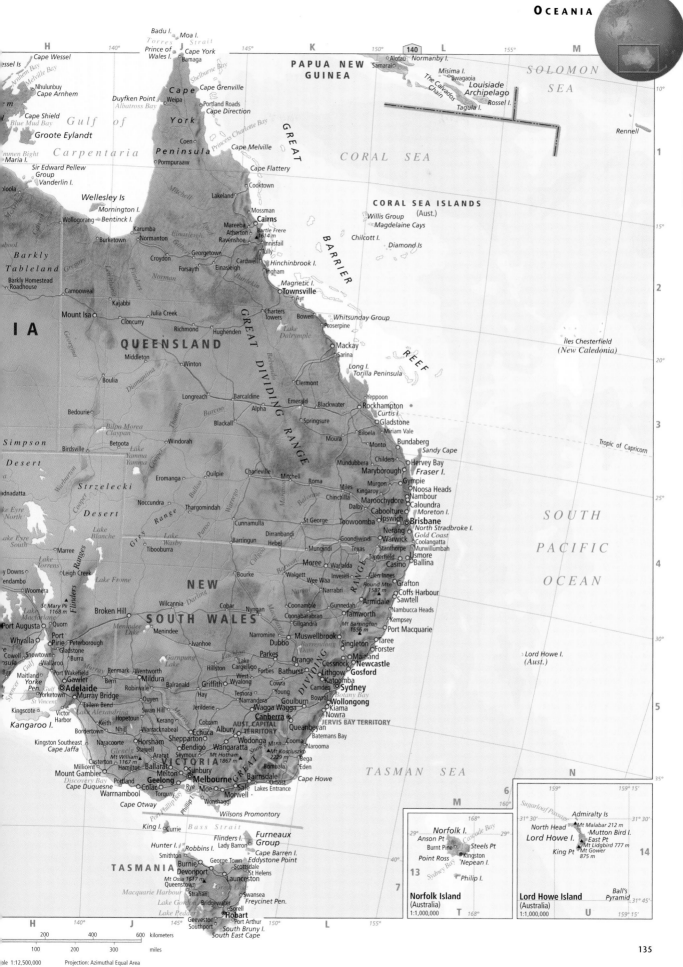

Oceania

H · 140° · J · 145° · K · 150° · [140] · L · 155° · M

Cape Wessel
*essel Is*
*Arnhem Bay*
Nhulunbuy
Cape Arnhem
*m*
Cape Shield
*Blue Mud Bay*
Groote Eylandt
*Gulf of*
*Carpentaria*
*Maria I.*
Sir Edward Pellew
Group
Vanderlin I.
*oola*
Wellesley Is
Mornington I.
Wollogorang  Bentinck I.

Badu I.  Moa I.
*Torres Strait*
Prince of
Wales I.  Cape York
Bamaga
Cape Grenville
Weipa
*Cape Direction*
Portland Roads
*Cape*
*York*
*Princess Charlotte Bay*
*Peninsula*
Coen
Pormpuraaw
Cape Melville
Cape Flattery

PAPUA NEW
GUINEA
Alotau  Normanby I.
Samarai
Misima I.
Bwagaoia
*The Calvados Chain*
Louisiade
Archipelago
Tagula I.  Rossel I.

*SOLOMON*
*SEA*

Rennell

CORAL  SEA

*10°*

*1*

CORAL SEA ISLANDS
(Aust.)
Willis Group
Magdelaine Cays
Chilcott I.
Diamond Is

*15°*

Cooktown
Lakeland
Mossman
*GREAT*
Mareeba  Cairns
Atherton  Bartle Frere
Ravenshoe  1614 m
Innisfail
Tully
Cardwell
Hinchinbrook I.
Ingham
Magnetic I.
Townsville
Ayr
*BARRIER*

Barkly
Tableland
Barkly Homestead
Roadhouse
Camooweal
Mount Isa
Burketown
Karumba
Normanton
Croydon
Forsayth
Georgetown
Einasleigh
*Einasleigh*
*Gilbert*
*Mitchell*
Charters
Towers
Bowen
Proserpine
*Whitsunday Group*

*Barkly*
*Norman*
*Flinders*
Kajabbi
Julia Creek
Cloncurry
Richmond
Hughenden
*REEF*

*IA*
QUEENSLAND
*GREAT DIVIDING RANGE*
Middleton
Winton
Boulia
*Diamantina*
Longreach
Barcaldine
*Thomson*
Clermont
Emerald
Blackwater
Mackay
Sarina
Long I.
Torilla Peninsula

*2*

Íles Chesterfield
(New Caledonia)

*20°*

Bedourie
*Barcoo*
Blackall
Alpha
Springsure
Moura
Yeppoon
Rockhampton
Gladstone
Curtis I.
Miriam Vale

SOUTH

Birdsville
Windorah
Betoota
*Bilpa Morea*
*Claypan*
*Lake*
*Yamma Yamma*
Eromanga
Quilpie
Charleville
Mitchell
Roma
Miles
Kingaroy
Chinchilla
Dalby
Monto
Biloela
Bundaberg
*Sandy Cape*
Childers
Hervey Bay
Maryborough
Fraser I.
Gympie
Murgon
Nambour
Maroochydore
Caloundra
Moreton I.
Caboolture

PACIFIC

*Tropic of Capricorn*

*25°*

*Simpson*
*Desert*
*odnadatta*
*Strzelecki*
*Desert*
*ke Eyre*
*North*
*Lake Eyre*
*South*
Marree
*Cooper*
Noccundra
Thargomindah
Cunnamulla
*Warrego*
St George
Dirranbandi
Hebel
Goondiwindi
Texas
Stanthorpe
Warwick
Ipswich  Brisbane
Toowoomba  North Stradbroke I.
Nerang  Gold Coast
Coolangatta
Murwillumbah
Lismore
Tenterfield  Ballina
Casino

SOUTH
PACIFIC
OCEAN

*Simpson*
*y Downs*
*endambo*
Woomera
*Lake*
*Torrens*
*Lake Frome*
Marree
Leigh Creek
*St Mary Pk*
*1168 m*
*Flinders Ranges*
Broken Hill
Wilcannia
*Darling*
Bourke
Walgett
Moree
Warialda
Inverell
Glen Innes
Round Mtn
1582 m
Grafton
Coffs Harbour
Sawtell

*4*

Lord Howe I.
(Aust.)

*30°*

Port Augusta
Quorn
Whyalla
*Cowell*
*Snowtown*
Port
Pirie  Peterborough
*Gladstone*
Burra
*nsula*
*Maitland*
*Yorke*
*Pen.*
Port Wakefield
Gawler
*St Vincent*
Adelaide
Murray Bridge
*Lake*
*Macfarlane*
Menindee
*Menindee*
*Lake*
Ivanhoe
NEW
SOUTH WALES
Cobar
Nyngan
Coonamble
Coonabarabran
Gilgandra
Narromine
Dubbo
*Macquarie*
*Bogan*
Narrabri
Wee Waa
Gunnedah
Tamworth
Armidale
Nambucca Heads
Kempsey
Port Macquarie
Mt Barrington
1556 m
Taree
Forster

*RANGE*
Whyalla
*Spencer*
*Gulf*
Kingscote
*Kangaroo I.*
Kingston Southeast
Cape Jaffa
*Lake*
*Gairdner*
Wentworth
Renmark
Berri
Mildura
Balranald
Robinvale
*Murray*
Hillston
*Lachlan*
Lake
Cargelligo
West
Wyalong
Forbes
Parkes
Orange
Bathurst
Lithgow
Cessnock
Maitland
Newcastle
Gosford
Katoomba
Singleton
Muswellbrook
*Burrendong*
*Dam*

*5*

Whyalla
Cowell
*Maitland*
Port Wakefield
*Yorketown*
*St Vincent*
*Gulf*
Victor
Harbor
*Lake Alexandrina*
Tailem Bend
Keith
Bordertown
Naracoorte
Kingston Southeast
Cape Jaffa
Millicent
Mount Gambier
*Discovery Bay*
Cape Duquesne
Warrnambool
Cape Otway
Swan Hill
Kerang
Cohuna
Echuca
Shepparton
Benalla
Wangaratta
Wodonga
Albury
Wagga Wagga
Young
Cowra
Temora
Narrandera
Jerilderie
Deniliquin
Hay
Griffith
Leeton
Cootamundra
Gundagai
Goulburn
Yass
Cooma
Bombala
Eden
Cape Howe
Camden
Sydney
Wollongong
Kiama
Nowra
Queanbeyan
Canberra
AUST. CAPITAL
TERRITORY
Batemans Bay
Bega
JERVIS BAY TERRITORY
Bowral

Nhill
Warracknabeal
Horsham
Stawell
Ararat
Mt William
1167 m
Hamilton
Casterton
Portland
VICTORIA
Mt Hotham
1867 m
Mt Kosciuszko
2229 m
*Snowy Mtns*
Cooma
Orbost
Lakes Entrance
Bairnsdale
Sale
Moe
Morwell
Wonthaggi

*GREAT*

*TASMAN  SEA*

*35°*

Seymour
Bendigo
Ballarat
Sunbury
Melton
Geelong
Colac
Torquay
Rye
*Port Phillip Bay*
Melbourne
*Phillip I.*
*Wilsons Promontory*

*N*

*6*

Warrnambool

*7*

King I.
Currie
Hunter I.
Smithton
Robbins I.
*Bass  Strait*
Flinders I.
Lady Barron
Furneaux
Group
Cape Barren I.
Eddystone Point
George Town
Scottsdale
St Helens

TASMANIA
Burnie
Devonport
Mt Ossa 1617 m
Queenstown
*Macquarie Harbour*
Strahan
Launceston
Swansea
Freycinet Pen.
*Lake Gordon*
Bridgewater
Sorell
*Lake Pedder*
Geeveston
Southport
Hobart
Port Arthur
South Bruny I.
South East Cape

H · 140° · J · 145° · L · 150° · 155°

M · 160° · N · 165°

U

*29°*
Norfolk I.
Anson Pt
Burnt Pine
Point Ross
*Cascade Bay*
Steels Pt
Kingston
Nepean I.
Philip I.

*13*

Norfolk Island
(Australia)
1:1,000,000

*159° · 159° 15'*
*Sugarloaf Passage*
Admiralty Is
North Head  Mt Malabar 212 m
Mutton Bird I.
Lord Howe I.  East Pt
Mt Lidgbird 777 m
King Pt  Mt Gower
875 m
*31° 30'*
*Ball's*
*Pyramid*
*31° 45'*

*14*

Lord Howe Island
(Australia)
1:1,000,000

*159° 15'*

Scale 1:12,500,000     Projection: Azimuthal Equal Area

0  200  400  600  kilometers
0  100  200  300  miles

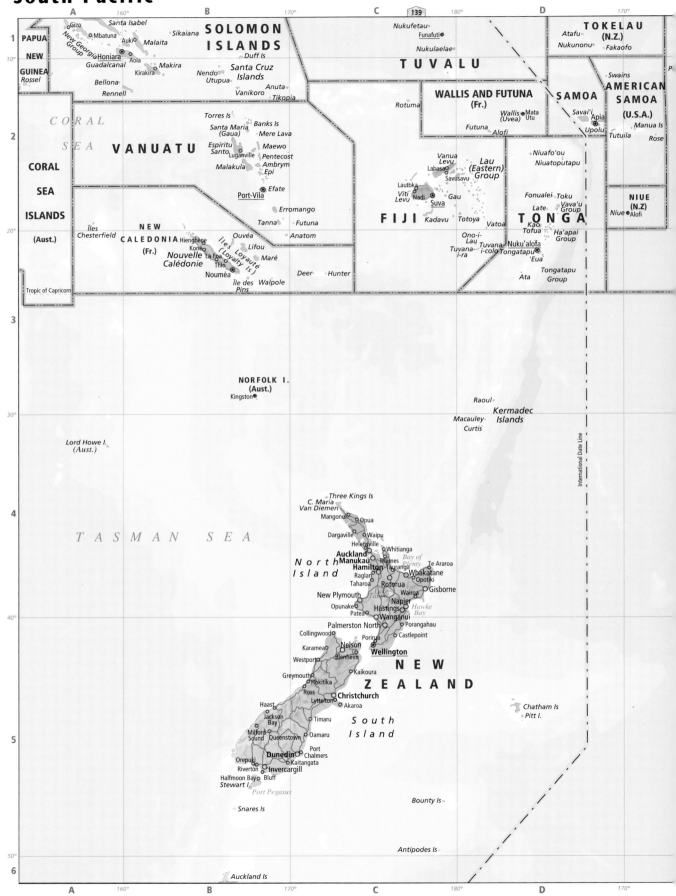

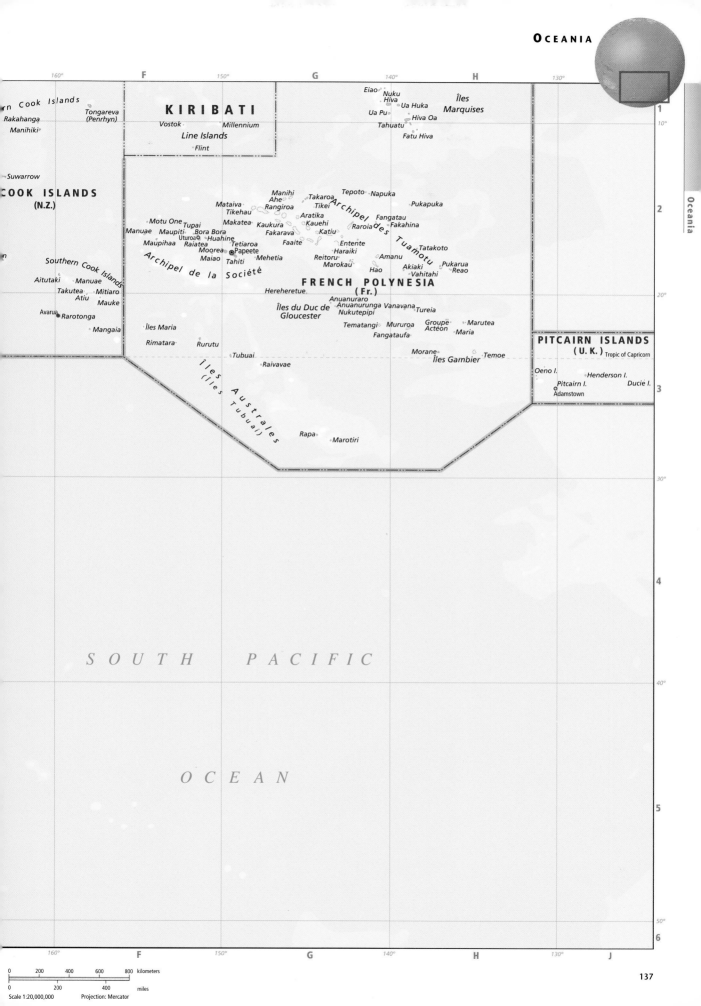

160° F 150° G 140° H 130°

**KIRIBATI**

rn Cook Islands
Tongareva (Penrhyn)
Rakahanga
Manihiki

Vostok
Millennium
Line Islands
Flint

Eiao
Nuku
Hiva
Ua Huka
Ua Pu
Hiva Oa
Tahuatu
Fatu Hiva
Îles Marquises

1
10°

Suwarrow

**COOK ISLANDS**
**(N.Z.)**

Manihi
Ahe
Mataiva
Rangiroa
Tikehau
Makatea
Motu One
Tupai
Manuae
Maupiti
Bora Bora
Maupihaa
Uturoa
Huahine
Raiatea
Maiao
Moorea
Papeete
Tetiaroa
Maiao
Tahiti
Mehetia

Takaroa
Tepoto
Napuka
Tikei
Aratika
Kauehi
Kaukura
Katiu
Fakarava
Faaite
Haraiki
Reitoru
Marokau
Hao

Pukapuka
Fangatau
Fakahina
Raroia
Tatakoto
Entente
Amanu
Akiaki
Vahitahi
Pukarua
Reao

Archipel des Tuamotu

2
20°

Southern Cook Islands
Aitutaki
Manuae
Takutea
Mitiaro
Atiu
Mauke
Avarua
Rarotonga
Mangaia

Archipel de la Société

**FRENCH POLYNESIA**
**(Fr.)**

Hereheretue

Îles Maria
Rimatara
Rurutu
Tubuai
Raivavae

Îles Australes
(Îles Tubuai)

Anuanuraro
Anuanurunga
Nukutepipi
Îles du Duc de
Gloucester
Tematangi
Fangataufa
Mururoa
Vanavana
Vavavana
Tureia
Groupe
Actéon
Maria
Marutea

Morane
Îles Gambier
Temoe

**PITCAIRN ISLANDS**
**( U. K. )**  Tropic of Capricorn

Oeno I.
Pitcairn I.
Adamstown
Henderson I.
Ducie I.

3

Rapa
Marotiri

30°

*S O U T H    P A C I F I C*

4
40°

*O C E A N*

5
50°

6

160° F 150° G 140° H 130° J

0  200  400  600  800  kilometers
0  200  400  miles
Scale 1:20,000,000  Projection: Mercator

# North Pacific

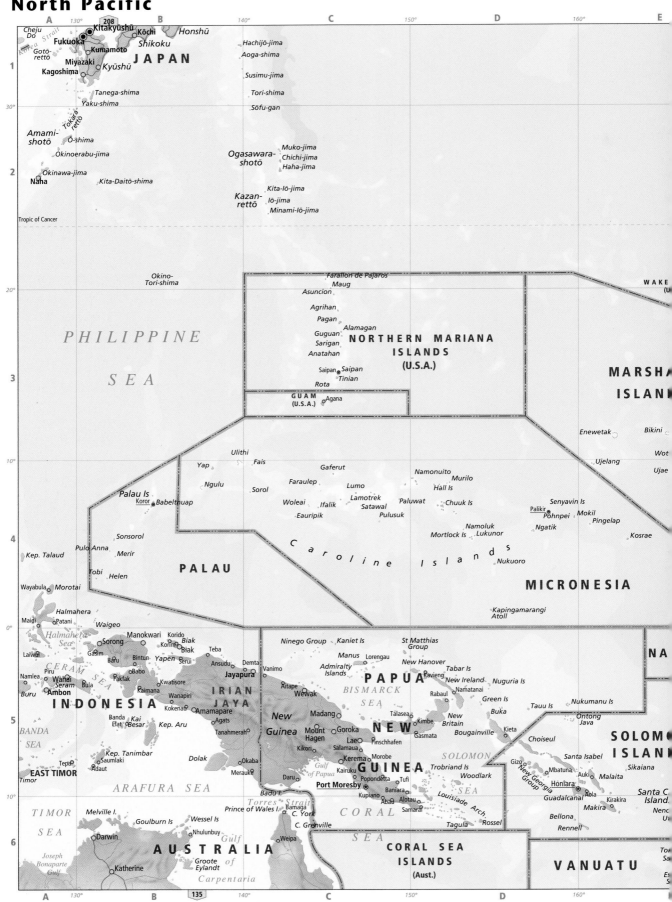

208

**Kitakyūshū**
Cheju Do
**Fukuoka** ○ Kōchi     Honshū
Gotō-rettō     **Kumamoto**     Shikoku
**Miyazaki**     **Kyūshū**
**Kagoshima**
**JAPAN**
Hachijō-jima
Aoga-shima
Susimu-jima
Tanega-shima
Yaku-shima     Tori-shima
Sōfu-gan
30°

Amami-shotō
Ō-shima
Okinoerabu-jima
Tokara-rettō
Ogasawara-shotō     Muko-jima
Chichi-jima
Haha-jima
Okinawa-jima
**Naha**     Kita-Daitō-shima
Kazan-rettō     Kita-Iō-jima
Iō-jima
Minami-Iō-jima
Tropic of Cancer

Okino-Tori-shima
20°     Farallon de Pajaros     WAKE
Maug     (U...
Asuncion
Agrihan
Pagan
**PHILIPPINE**     Guguan     Alamagan
Sarigan     **NORTHERN MARIANA**
Anatahan     **ISLANDS**     **MARSHA...**
**(U.S.A.)**     **ISLAN...**
Saipan • Saipan
**SEA**     Tinian
Rota
GUAM
(U.S.A.)  • Agana
Enewetak     Bikini
Ulithi
10°     Yap     Fais     Wot...
Ngulu     Sorol     Gaferut     Ujelang
Ujae
Faraulep     Lumo     Namonuito     Murilo
Palau Is     Woleai     Ifalik     Lamotrek     Hall Is
Koror     Babelthuap     Eauripik     Satawal     Paluwat     Chuuk Is     Senyavin Is
Pulusuk     Palikir     Mokil
Sonsorol     Namoluk     Pohnpei     Pingelap
Pulo Anna     Merir     Mortlock Is     Lukunor     Ngatik
Kep. Talaud     **PALAU**     Caroline     Islands     Kosrae
Tobi     Helen     Nukuoro
Wayabula • Morotai     **MICRONESIA**
Maidi     Halmahera
Patani     Waigeo     Kapingamarangi
Halmahera     Manokwari     Korido     Atoll
Laiwui     Sea     Sorong     Korim     Biak     Ninego Group     Kaniet Is     St Matthias     NA...
Gasim     Bintun     Biak     Manus     Group
Namlea     Piru     Baru     Yapen     Teba     Lorengau     New Hanover
Buru     Wahai     Pakfak     Ansudu     Admiralty     Kavieng     Tabar Is
Seram     Bula     Kwatisore     Demta     Islands     New Ireland     Nuguria Is
**Ambon**     Kaimana     Serui     Vanimo     **PAPUA**     Rabaul     Green Is
Wanapiri     **Jayapura**     Aitape     BISMARCK     Namatanai     Tauu Is     Nukumanu Is
**INDONESIA**     Kokenau     Wewak     SEA     New     Buka     Ontong
**IRIAN**     Madang     Talasea     Britain     Java
Banda     Kai     **JAYA**     Kimbe     Bougainville     Kieta     **SOLOM...**
Elat     Besar     Amamapare     New     Gasmata     Kita     **ISLAN...**
Agats     Guinea     Mount     Goroka     **NEW**     Finschhafen     Choiseul
**BANDA**     Hagen     Lae     SOLOMON     Gizo     Santa Isabel
**SEA**     Kep. Tanimbar     Tanahmerah     Kikori     Salamaua     Morobe     Sikaiana
Saumlaki     Dolak     Okaba     Kerema     Trobriand Is     Honiara     Auki     Malaita
Tepa     Adaut     Merauke     **GUINEA**     Woodlark     Mbatuna     Rola
**EAST TIMOR**     Daru     Kupiano     Popondetta • Tufi     SEA     Guadalcanal     Kirakira
Timor     Badu I.     **Port Moresby**     Baniara     Makira     Santa C...
Abau     Alotau     Louisiade     Island     Ne...
**TIMOR**     Prince of Wales I.     Bamaga     Kupiano     Samarai     Arch.     Bellona     U...
Melville I.     Wessel Is     C. York     **CORAL**     Tagula     Rossel     Rennell
**SEA**     Goulburn Is     Nhulunbuy     C. Grenville
Gulf     **AUSTRALIA**     Weipa     **SEA**     **CORAL SEA**
**Darwin**     Groote     of     **ISLANDS**     **VANUATU**
Joseph     Eylandt     **(Aust.)**
Bonaparte     **Katherine**     Carpentaria
Gulf

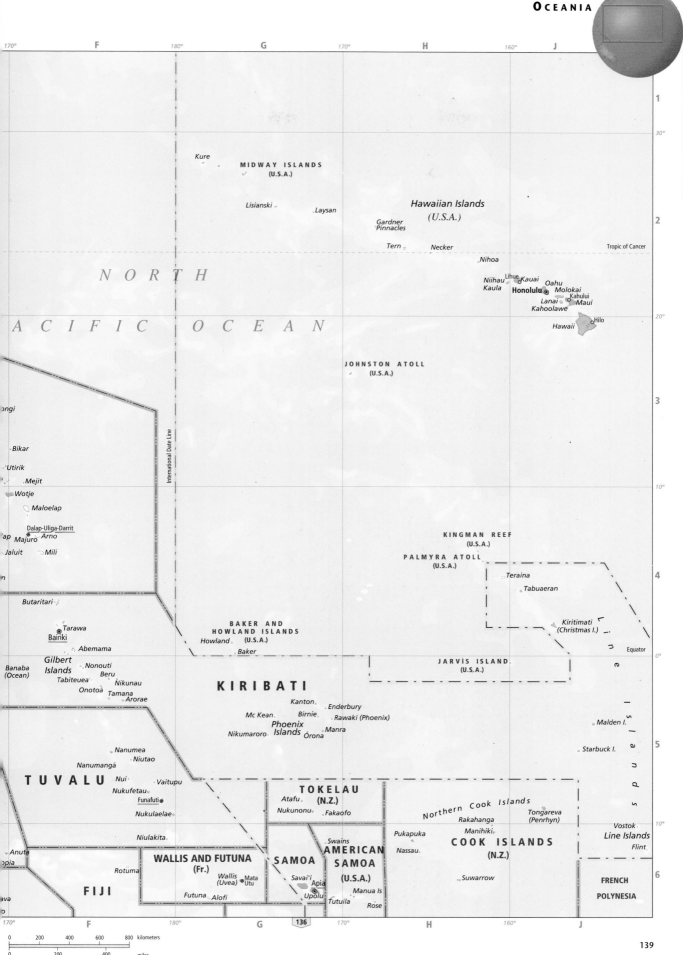

170°  F  180°  G  170°  H  160°  J

1

30°

*Kure*  MIDWAY ISLANDS  (U.S.A.)

Hawaiian Islands
(U.S.A.)

2

*Lisianski*  *Laysan*  *Gardner*
*Pinnacles*

*Tern*  *Necker*  Tropic of Cancer

*Nihoa*

*Niihau* *Lihue* *Kauai*  *Oahu*
*Kaula*  **Honolulu**  *Molokai*
*Kahului*
*Lanai* *Maui*
*Kahoolawe*

N O R T H

20°

P A C I F I C   O C E A N  *Hawaii* *Hilo*

JOHNSTON ATOLL
(U.S.A.)

3

*ongi*

*Bikar*

*Utirik*

*Mejit*

10°

*Wotje*

*Maloelap*

International Date Line

Dalap-Uliga-Darrit
*ap* *Majuro* *Arno*
*Jaluit* *Mili*

KINGMAN REEF
(U.S.A.)

PALMYRA ATOLL
(U.S.A.)

*Teraina*

4

*Tabuaeran*

*Butaritari*

*Tarawa*  BAKER AND
*Bairiki*  HOWLAND ISLANDS  *Kiritimati*
*Abemama*  *Howland*  (U.S.A.)  (Christmas I.)

*Howland*

*Baker*  Equator

*Banaba*  *Gilbert*  *Nonouti*  JARVIS ISLAND
*(Ocean)*  *Islands*  *Beru*  (U.S.A.)

*Tabiteuea*  *Nikunau*

*Onotoa* *Tamana*

*Arorae*  K I R I B A T I

*Kanton*

*Malden I.*

*Mc Kean.*  *Birnie*  *Enderbury*
*Rawaki (Phoenix)*

*Phoenix*  *Manra*

*Nikumaroro*  *Islands*  *Orona*

*Starbuck I.*

*Nanumea*

*Niutao*

*Nanumangä*

*Nui*  *Vaitupu*

T U V A L U  TOKELAU
(N.Z.)

*Atafu*  Northern Cook Islands  *Tongareva*
(Penrhyn)

*Nukufetau*

*Funafuti*  *Nukunonu*
*Fakaofo*  *Rakahanga*

*Nukulaelae*  *Pukapuka*  *Manihiki*

10°

*Niulakita*  *Nassau*  COOK ISLANDS
(N.Z.)

*Swains*

*Anuta*  WALLIS AND FUTUNA  SAMOA  AMERICAN
*(Fr.)*  SAMOA
*opia*  (U.S.A.)

*Rotuma*  *Wallis*  *Savai'i*  *Suwarrow*
*(Uvea)* *Mata*
*Utu*  *Apia*

*ava*  *Futuna*  *Upolu*  FRENCH
FIJI  *Alofi*  *Manua Is*
*Tutuila*  POLYNESIA
*Rose*

170°  F  180°  G  170°  H  160°  J

*Vostok*

Line Islands

*Flint*

L
i
n
e

I
s
l
a
n
d
s

0  200  400  600  800 kilometers

0  200  400  miles

Scale 1:20,000,000  Projection: Mercator

# Papua New Guinea

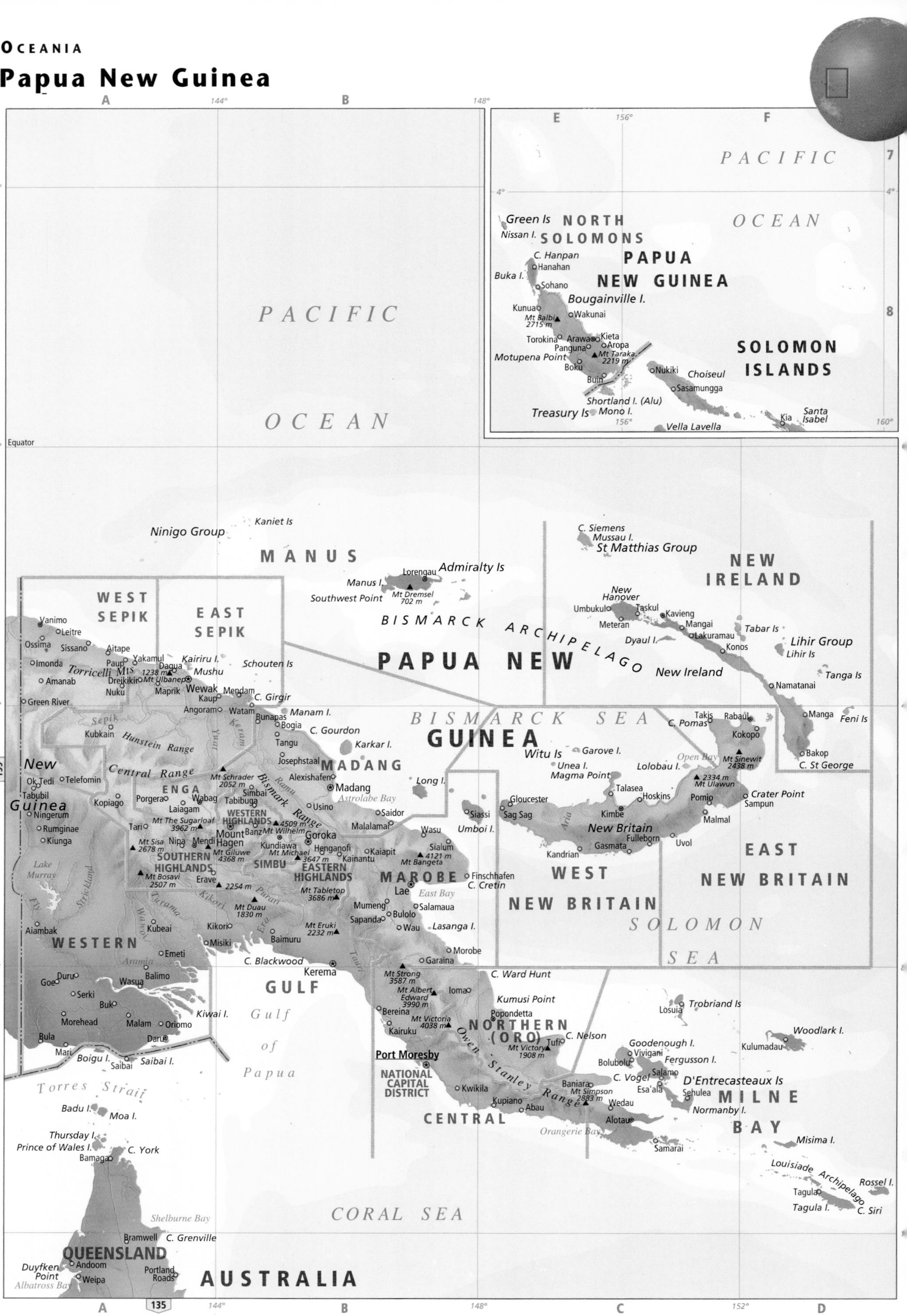

Oceania

**E** · 156° · **F**

*PACIFIC*

7

*OCEAN*

4°

**Green Is** · **N O R T H**
*Nissan I.* · **S O L O M O N S**
C. Hanpan · **PAPUA**
Buka I. · Hanahan · **NEW GUINEA**
Kunua · Sohano
Mt Balbi ▲ · Wakunai · **Bougainville I.**
2715 m
Torokina · Kieta · **SOLOMON**
Panguna · Aropa · **ISLANDS**
Arawa
Motupena Point · ▲ Mt Taraka
Boku · 2219 m
Buin · Nukiki · Choiseul
Shortland I. (Alu) · Sasamungga
**Treasury Is** · Mono I. · Kia · Santa
156° · Isabel
Vella Lavella · 160°

8

**A** · 144° · **B** · 148°

*PACIFIC*

1

Equator · 0°

*OCEAN*

2

**Kaniet Is**
*Ninigo Group* · **M A N U S**
Manus I. · Lorengau · **Admiralty Is**
Southwest Point · Mt Dremsel
702 m

**C. Siemens**
Mussau I.
**St Matthias Group** · **NEW**
**IRELAND**
New
Hanover
Umbukul · Taskul · Kavieng
Meteran · Mangai
Dyaul I. · Lakuramau · **Tabar Is**
Konos · **Lihir Group**
Lihir Is
*Tanga Is*
Namatanai

**B I S M A R C K   A R C H I P E L A G O**

**PAPUA NEW**

3

*Vanimo* · **WEST** · **EAST**
*Leitre* · **SEPIK** · **SEPIK**
Ossima · Sissano · Aitape
Imonda · Yakamul · Kairiru I.
Daqua · Mushu · *Schouten Is*
Amanab · Drejkikir · Mt Ulbaneg
Nuku · Maprik · Wewak
Green River · Mendam
Angoram · C. Girgir
*Sepik* · Watam · Manam I.
Bunapas · Bogia
Kubkain · *Hunstein Range* · Tangu · C. Gourdon
*Karkar I.*
Josephstaal · **MADANG**
*New* · **ENGA** · Alexishafen
Ok Tedi · Telefomin · *Central Range* · Usino · Madang
*Guinea* · Porgera · Wabag · *Astrolabe Bay*
Ningerum · Kopiago · Laiagam · Tabibuga
Rumginae · Tari · Mt The Sugarloaf · **WESTERN** · Mt Schrader
Kiunga · 3962 m · **HIGHLANDS** · 2052 m
Mt Sisa · Nipa · Mt Wilhelm · Banz
2678 m · Mendi · Mt Giluwe · 4509 m · **Goroka**
4368 m · Kundiawa · Henganofi
*Lake* · **SOUTHERN** · **SIMBU** · Mt Michael
*Murray* · **HIGHLANDS** · 3647 m · Kainantu
Mt Bosavi · Erave · **EASTERN**
2507 m · 2254 m · Mt Tabletop · **HIGHLANDS**
3686 m · **MOROBE**
Mt Duau · Mumeng
Kubeai · 1830 m · Bulolo
**WESTERN** · Kikori · Mt Eruki · Wau
Misiki · 2232 m
Aiambak · Baimuru · Morobe
Goe · Duru · Balimo · C. Blackwood · Garaina
Serki · Wasua · Kerema · Mt Strong
Buk · **GULF** · 3587 m
Morehead · Malam · Oriomo · *Gulf* · Mt Albert
Bula · Kiwai I. · *of* · Edward · Ioma
Mari · Daru · *Papua* · 3990 m
Boigu I. · Bereina
Saibai · Kairuku · Mt Victoria
*Torres Strait* · 4038 m
Badu I. · **Port Moresby**
Moa I. · **NATIONAL**
*Thursday I.* · **CAPITAL**
*Prince of Wales I.* · **DISTRICT**
Bamaga · C. York · Kwikila
**CENTRAL**
Kupiano

**PAPUA NEW GUINEA**

**B I S M A R C K   S E A**

**GUINEA**

Witu Is · Garove I.
Unea I. · **New**
Magma Point · Takis · Rabaul
C. Pomas · Kokopo
Lolobau I. · *Open Bay* · Mt Sinewit
▲ 2438 m
▲ 2334 m · C. St George
Gloucester · Talasea · Mt Ulawun
Siassi · Hoskins · Pomio · Crater Point
Sag Sag · Kimbe · Sampun
Umboi I. · **New Britain** · Malmal
Wasu · Kandrian · Gasmata · Uvol
Sialum · Fulleborn
Saidor · Kaiapit · 4121 m
Malalamai · Kainantu · **WEST** · **EAST**
Long I. · **NEW BRITAIN** · **NEW BRITAIN**
Finschhafen
Lae · C. Cretin · *SOLOMON*
*East Bay* · **NEW BRITAIN**
Salamaua · Lasanga I. · *SEA*
Sapanda

Manga · Feni Is

4°

199

4

*New*
*Guinea*
Mt Hagen
Mount · 3962 m · Simbai

C. Ward Hunt
Kumusi Point · **Trobriand Is**
Popondetta · Losuia
**NORTHERN** · C. Nelson
**(ORO)** · Tufi · Goodenough I.
Mt Victory · Vivigani · Woodlark I.
1908 m · Fergusson I.
Bolubolu · Kulumadau
C. Vogel · Salamo
Baniara · Esa'ala · **MILNE**
Mt Simpson · Schulea
2883 m · Wedau · Normanby I. · **BAY**
Alotau · Misima I.
Samarai
*Orangerie Bay* · Tagula
Abau · *Louisiade Archipelago*
Tagula I. · Rossel I.
C. Siri

5

*Shelburne Bay*

Bramwell · C. Grenville

**QUEENSLAND**
Duyfken · Andoom · **AUSTRALIA**
Point · Weipa · Portland
*Albatross Bay* · Roads

12°

6

**A** · 135° · **B** · 144° · **C** · 148° · 152° · **D**

*CORAL SEA*

© Random House Australia Pty Ltd

kilometers · 0 · 100 · 200 · 300 · 400
miles · 0 · 100 · 200
Scale 1:7,000,000 · Projection: Mercator

# Islands of the Pacific

SOLOMON ISLANDS
Scale 1: 8,500,000

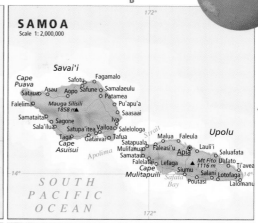

SAMOA
Scale 1: 2,000,000

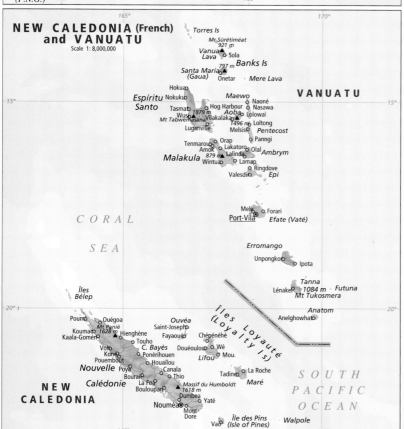

NEW CALEDONIA (French) and VANUATU
Scale 1: 8,000,000

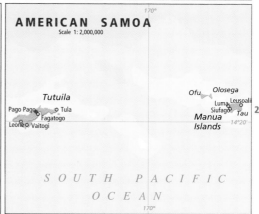

AMERICAN SAMOA
Scale 1: 2,000,000

VAVA'U GROUP (Tonga)
Scale 1: 1,000,000

FIJI
Scale 1: 7,000,000

TONGATAPU GROUP (Tonga)
Scale 1: 1,000,000

# Asia

Asia, the largest continent, covers 43.6 million sq km (16.8 million sq miles), about one-third of the world's land surface. Its western boundaries are the Ural Mountains, the Ural River, the Caspian and Black seas and the Dardanelles Straits, which separate Europe from Asia. The Red Sea and the Suez Canal separate Asia from Africa. Indonesia is the southeasternmost country of Asia.

Asia is traditionally divided into East, Southeast, South, the Indian subcontinent, Central, and North Asia (Siberia, which is part of the Russian Federation, is included with Europe). The Middle East is discussed on the following pages.

Southeast Asia contains the archipelagic nations of Indonesia, Malaysia, East Timor, and the Philippines, as well as Singapore, Brunei, Laos, Vietnam, Cambodia, Thailand, and Myanmar (Burma). China, Japan, North and South Korea, and Taiwan comprise East Asia. The Indian subcontinent includes India, Pakistan, Bangladesh and Sri Lanka; Nepal and Bhutan in the Himalayas; and the coral island archipelago of the Maldives. Central and West Asia include the former Soviet republics of Kazakhstan, Uzbekistan, Kyrgyzistan, Tajikistan, Turkmenistan, Azerbaijan, and Armenia as well as Mongolia and mountainous Afghanistan.

## Physical features

Asia is a very geologically active continent. Large areas are covered by mountain and volcanic chains—the world's highest mountain range (the Himalayas), the Indonesian volcanic arc, and the volcanic chains of Japan and the Philippines. Asia also contains some parts of the world's most ancient (Pre-Cambrian) formations, in the Indian and Arabian Peninsulas and in Siberia.

Mountain ranges, plateaus, and basins lie within Asia's heartland. The world's highest plateau is in Tibet, averaging 4,000 m (13,000 ft) in altitude, and is bounded to the south by the Himalayas, to

the north by the Kunlun Range, and to the west by the Karakoram Range. Further north, the Tarim and Dzungarian basins lie close to sea level, while the Turfan Depression is 142 m (470 ft) below it.

Numerous streams and nineteen major rivers, ranging from 2,500 to 5,500 km (1,500 and 3,400 miles) in length, flow in Asia. These include the Yangtze and Huang Rivers in China, the Indus and Ganges Rivers of the Indian subcontinent and the Mekong River on the Indochinese Peninsula.

## Climate and vegetation

Asia can be broadly divided into a humid monsoon belt in South, Southeast, and East Asia and an arid to semiarid zone, in Central Asia.

During summer, the monsoons blow north, toward the continental margins, while in winter they reverse direction and blow toward the south. Some East Asian areas receive rainfall from both monsoons. The Himalayan Range and adjacent mountain ranges concentrate summer rainfall in parts of South and Southeast Asia. Hot, humid climates prevail in South and Southeast Asia while cold climates, with snowfall during winter, are found in more northern parts (the Himalayas and the mountain ranges in Central Asia). The Plateau of Tibet has an extremely cold climate.

Tropical rainforests once covered large parts of South and Southeast Asia, but are now being cleared for agriculture and logging, especially of hardwoods. This threatens the plant and animal diversity of these forests, which is very high.

Broad-leaf evergreen forests cover parts of subtropical East Asia. There are deciduous forests further north in cool, temperate climates, and boreal forests where the winters are cold. The Plateau of Tibet is an almost treeless tundra, with mosses, grasses, lichens, and a few small shrubs.

Grasslands cover areas in the rainshadow belts where rainfall is limited: tropical grasslands in the Deccan Plateau in India and the Khorat Plateau in Thailand, and temperate grasslands (steppes) in the semiarid parts of Central Asia.

Central Asia is predominantly arid to semiarid, with warm summers and winters where the temperature can fall below freezing. The Gobi Desert, the coldest dry desert, lies in this region.

*Terraced fields in India (left), a carved entrance in Bali (top), and a curious monkey in Indonesia (above) demonstrate the variety of landform zones and land uses in Asia.*

## Population

Asia's vast population (3.94 billion inhabitants, as of 2005, representing some 60.5 percent of the world's people) is predominantly found in the monsoon belt. The population explosion within the last fifty years (some countries experienced a three-fold increase during this period) is the result of advances in agriculture and improved medical facilities. During this period, life expectancies improved throughout Asia. Life expectancy is currently highest in East Asia (72.1 years for males and 76.3 years for females) and lowest in South Asia (63.1 years for males and 66.1 years for females). The high population growth rate has subsided, being currently 0.5 percent in East Asia to 1.5 on the Indian subcontinent.

Population indicators for the most developed Asian countries are similar to those for many Western countries: low population growth rates and high life expectancies characterize the more industrialized nations such as Japan and Singapore. High growth rates and much lower life expectancies, however, are found in the least developed countries, such as Bangladesh and Nepal. These characteristics reflect the enormous differences in standards of living between the most and least developed countries in Asia. Urbanization is highest in the most developed areas, but despite having a number of large cities and growing urbanization, Asia still has a low urban population—39.9 percent.

Industrialization in most Asian countries has, as elsewhere, centered on major urban areas. Labor from rural areas has drifted to urban centers in search of employment. The ensuing urban population explosion has put pressure on infrastructure, and given rise to problems such as the growth of slum dwellings, traffic congestion, and air and water pollution.

## Agriculture

A high proportion of Asia's population lives on the alluvial plains of rivers (and their deltas) of the monsoon belt, and is engaged in agriculture.

The monsoon belt is noted for its intensive rice and wheat farming. The population explosion created enormous demand for food. The area under cultivation was expanded through deforestation and by farming marginal areas, such as the borders of deserts, but the Green Revolution was more successful: high-yielding seeds, fertilizers and pesticides often tripled grain yields. However, environmental problems, caused by the chemicals used and by invasions of insects, have raised a number of concerns. In semiarid Central Asia, wheat farming and animal rearing are the main forms of agriculture. With irrigation, cotton is now successfully grown in several places.

## Industrialization

By the 1980s, several East Asian countries had developed industrialized economies, largely dependent on imported raw materials, particularly minerals and energy supplies. Manufacturing in Asia ranges from labor-intensive industries such as clothing in the less developed economies to electronics, computers, and motor vehicles in the more developed ones. Japan, the world's second-largest economy, manufactures electronic goods, steel, motor vehicles and ships. Japan's approach has been imitated by South Korea, Hong Kong and Singapore, which have all rapidly industrialized. Thailand, Malaysia, the Philippines, and Indonesia have followed suit.

China and India initially aimed at agricultural and industrial self-sufficiency to support their enormous populations. They possess huge agricultural sectors, but their exports have shifted progressively to industrial products. They have considerable scientific expertise—in nuclear and space technology and satellite launching services (China), and computer programming (India).

The Central Asian nations, following the breakup of the former Soviet Union, are making a slow and painful transition from a state-controlled to a free market economy. There is, as yet, limited industrialization in the countries of Central Asia. Kazakhstan produces metals and chemicals and Azerbaijan, which is rich in petroleum deposits and may establish petroleum-based industries, currently manufactures mining equipment.

*The Flaming Cliffs in Mongolia's arid Gobi Desert, Central Asia (above). This Vietnamese woman (below) is carrying wood from her home in the hills to sell.*

## Languages

Many languages, belonging to several language families, are spoken in Asia. Chinese Mandarin, Cantonese, and Wu are the most widely spoken in East Asia. Japanese is increasingly important. In Southeast Asia, Indonesian and Malaysian predominate, while languages of the Chinese-Tibetan family, such as Burmese and Thai, are spoken in the mainland belt. South Asia has two major language families: Indo-Aryan in the north, of which Hindi and Urdu are the most widespread, and Dravidian, which includes Tamil, in the southern areas. In Central Asia, Ural-Altaic languages, several of which are related to Turkish, are mainly used.

Russian is widely spoken in the former Soviet republics, and of the colonial languages, only English is still important, and continues to spread.

## Boundary disputes and wars

Armed conflicts continued after the Second World War in Asia, especially during the decolonization phase. Wars resulted in the division of both Korea and Vietnam into two nations: communist North and democratic South. The Vietnam war ended in 1975, when the country reunified. North and South Korea remain technically at war.

Following the division of British India into India and Pakistan in 1947, there was armed conflict over the divided Himalayan state of Jammu and Kashmir; this issue is still unresolved. War between India and Pakistan resulted in 1971 in the creation of the Bangladesh. Armed conflicts along the disputed boundaries of China have taken place between China and India along the Himalayas, between China and Russia along the Amur River, and between China and Vietnam along their common border. Indonesia incorporated the former Portuguese colony of now independent East Timor. The ownership of the Spratly Islands in the South China Sea is causing tension between China, Malaysia, Philippines, Vietnam, and Taiwan. The "War on Terror" in Afghanistan and Iraq has dominated affairs throughout the region since late 2001.

## Nations

| | |
|---|---|
| Afghanistan | PAGE 184 |
| Armenia | PAGE 188 |
| Azerbaijan | PAGE 189 |
| Bangladesh | PAGE 170 |
| Bhutan | PAGE 171 |
| Brunei | PAGE 150 |
| Cambodia | PAGE 152 |
| China | PAGE 158 |
| East Timor | PAGE 148 |
| Georgia | PAGE 190 |
| India | PAGE 168 |
| Indonesia | PAGE 148 |
| Japan | PAGE 164 |
| Kazakhstan | PAGE 184 |
| Kyrgystan | PAGE 186 |
| Laos | PAGE 154 |
| Malaysia | PAGE 151 |
| Maldives | PAGE 167 |
| Mongolia | PAGE 186 |
| Myanmar (Burma) | PAGE 157 |
| Nepal | PAGE 172 |
| North Korea | PAGE 162 |
| Pakistan | PAGE 173 |
| Philippines | PAGE 149 |
| Singapore | PAGE 150 |
| South Korea | PAGE 163 |
| Sri Lanka | PAGE 166 |
| Taiwan | PAGE 162 |
| Tajikistan | PAGE 188 |
| Thailand | PAGE 156 |
| Turkmenistan | PAGE 187 |
| Uzbekistan | PAGE 185 |
| Vietnam | PAGE 153 |

## Dependencies & territories

| | |
|---|---|
| British Indian Ocean Territory | PAGE 193 |
| Paracel Islands | PAGE 193 |
| Spratly Islands | PAGE 193 |

# The Middle East

The term "Middle East" applies to the belt of countries in Southwest Asia that lies between Afghanistan and Turkey. It stretches southward to include the Arabian Peninsula. The Middle East is characterized by its arid climate, its petroleum riches, and the prevalence of Islam as its predominant religion. The Middle East forms a strategic belt between the dynamic developing industrial countries of Asia and the long-developed countries of Europe.

The countries of Iran, Iraq, Syria, Turkey, and Cyprus form the northern belt, while toward their south lie Lebanon, Israel, Jordan and the states of the Arabian Peninsula. Saudi Arabia occupies a large part of the peninsula; Oman and Yemen share the southern part of the peninsula and the United Arab Emirates, Bahrain, Qatar, and Kuwait lie along the Arabian (also known as Persian) Gulf.

Afghanistan lies in the area where the Middle East, South Asia, and Central Asia meet. The North African nations of Egypt, Sudan, and Libya are also sometimes considered part of the Middle East, for linguistic and cultural reasons.

## Physical features

The collision of the Iranian and Arabian tectonic plates with the Eurasian Plate resulted in the mountain ranges that run from Turkey to Iran. The belt between Turkey and Iran is characterized by elongated mountain ranges such as the Zagros and Alborz ranges in Iran and the Pontic and Taurus Mountains in Turkey. These ranges form part of the extensive Alpine-Himalayan Mountain Range system that was formed during the Tertiary geological period. This area is prone to earthquakes, of which there have been several in recent decades. There are plateaus in both Turkey (Anatolian Plateau) and Iran.

In contrast to the geologically active Tertiary mountain belt, the Arabian Plateau is part of an ancient and geologically stable shield.

*Jumeura Mosque, Dubai, in the United Arab Emirates (below left). Shiraz-style grapevines with clay supports in Iran (right). These ancient ruins at Buṣrá ash Shām, in Syria (right page, bottom), remind us how long human civilization has existed in this area.*

## Climate and vegetation

The Middle East is predominantly arid to semi-arid, except for the areas that adjoin the Mediterranean, Aegean, Black and Caspian Seas. The region is characterized by high temperatures, especially in the Arabian, Syrian and Iranian deserts. In contrast, winter temperatures close to freezing point occur in the highlands and snow falls in some of the higher mountainous areas. There are great seasonal temperature differences on the plateaus, as shown by Tehrān and Ankara, which reach temperatures of about 30 °C (85 °F) in summer and fall as low as freezing point in winter.

The region receives little annual rainfall, except for winter rain in the areas bordering the Mediterranean, and there is a serious shortage of fresh water in the Gulf area. Vegetation in this region is dominated by thorny scrubland.

The Euphrates and Tigris are the largest rivers in the Middle East. Several short rivers flow into the Mediterranean, Black, and Caspian Seas.

## Population

The population of the region is about 306 million (2005). Life expectancies have improved in recent years and now stand at 67.5 years for males and 72 years for females. The population growth rate is moderate, at 1.8 percent. Urbanization has been increasing steadily during recent decades and now stands at 65.5 percent; this reflects the decreasing importance of agriculture and pastoralism in the economies of these countries. In several countries, particularly in the Gulf States, petroleum has indirectly assisted the growth of urbanization as oil-generated revenues have been invested in urban areas and projects.

## Agriculture

Because of the arid climate, only a small part of the region can support agriculture.

The Euphrates and Tigris Rivers, with their alluvial plains and extensive irrigation, are significant agricultural areas, but their rising salinity levels constitute a major problem. The region has a great need for irrigation—Syria, for example, has built the Euphrates Dam to irrigate the northeastern part of the country. Israel has also developed areas of intensive irrigation-based agriculture.

Wheat, barley, and rice are the major cereals. Important cash crops include tobacco, sugarcane, cotton, fruits and tea. Dates are a common fruit and are cultivated in oasis areas. Livestock mostly consists of camels, sheep, and goats; herds of goats have been blamed for stripping the ground bare of vegetation, which has resulted in soil erosion and the acceleration of desertification in some areas.

Agriculture based on growing olives, grapes, citrus fruits and apples is found in the Mediterranean coastal areas.

Fishing is important in several places, including the Black and Caspian seas.

*The birthplace of Aphrodite in Cyprus (far left). Traditional trading dhows in Doha, Qatar (left). Women in the Gaza Strip demonstrate for the release of Palestinian prisoners (below). International fast food in Dubai (above)*

## Industrialization

Petroleum reserves are the region's most abundant resource. Oil-rich Saudi Arabia, Iran, Iraq, Kuwait, and the United Arab Emirates have economies predominantly based on petroleum exports, which makes them vulnerable to fluctuations in the price of petroleum. Petroleum prices escalated during the mid to late 1970s, but since then prices have fallen considerably. Oil wealth has facilitated the import of foodstuffs, manufactured goods, and luxury items, and has been also used for military purchases and development.

The hot, arid areas of the region are largely unsuited to the establishment of industries. The lack of fresh water is so severe in the Gulf region that desalinization plants have been set up to produce potable water. Oil-based electricity is generated in the oil-rich countries, and coal-based electricity is widely used in Turkey. Hydroelectric power is produced in Syria and Turkey.

Industries that use local materials, such as food processing, petroleum refining, and petrochemical industries, have been developed in some places. Some light consumer-based industries, including textiles, footwear, cigarettes, and paper, have also been established. The countries of the eastern Mediterranean are comparatively more industrialized than the rest of the region, but frequent conflicts with neighboring countries in the area have hampered their ability to maintain production.

## Languages

Three language families—the Indo-European, Turkic, and Semitic—are found in the Middle East. The Indo-European languages represented include Persian, Pashto, Kurdish, Armenian, and Baluchi. Turkish and Azerbaijani are Turkic languages, and Arabic and Hebrew are Semitic.

## Boundary disputes and wars

The region has experienced several conflicts and wars within the last fifty years. The Israeli-Arab conflict has been the most prominent and is yet to be resolved. Lebanon was drawn into the conflict, which adversely affected its economy.

Iraq's attempt to conquer the Arab-speaking region of southwestern Iran lasted for years, and

drained both Iraq and Iran of resources. Iraq's conquest of Kuwait, the subsequent Gulf War, the ousting of Saddam Hussein and the attempt to install a democratic regime in 2003/04 mainly by a coalition of the United States and Great Britain have seriously affected Iraq's economy.

The Kurdish-speaking area, shared by Turkey, Iraq, and Iran, has also been involved in armed conflict, in its attempt to secure independence.

The Turkish conquest of the northern, Turkish-speaking part of Cyprus has strained relations between Greece and Turkey.

## Nations

|  | |
|---|---|
| Bahrain | PAGE 178 |
| Cyprus | PAGE 191 |
| Iran | PAGE 183 |
| Iraq | PAGE 182 |
| Israel | PAGE 179 |
| Jordan | PAGE 180 |
| Kuwait | PAGE 177 |
| Lebanon | PAGE 180 |
| Oman | PAGE 175 |
| Qatar | PAGE 177 |
| Saudi Arabia | PAGE 174 |
| Syria | PAGE 181 |
| Turkey | PAGE 190 |
| United Arab Emirates | PAGE 176 |
| Yemen | PAGE 175 |

## Autonomous regions

|  | |
|---|---|
| Gaza Strip | PAGE 192 |
| West Bank | PAGE 193 |

## Southeast Asia

Indonesia · · · · · · · · · 148
East Timor · · · · · · · · · 148
Philippines · · · · · · · · 149
Brunei, Singapore · · · 150
Malaysia · · · · · · · · · · 151
Cambodia · · · · · · · · 152
Vietnam · · · · · · · · · · 153
Laos · · · · · · · · · · · · · 154
Thailand · · · · · · · · · · 156
Myanmar (Burma) · · · 157

## Indonesia

### Fact File

OFFICIAL NAME  Republic of Indonesia

FORM OF GOVERNMENT  Republic with single legislative body (House of Representatives)

CAPITAL  Jakarta

AREA  1,919,440 sq km (741,096 sq miles)

TIME ZONE  GMT +7–9 hours

POPULATION  238,000,000

PROJECTED POPULATION 2015  251,000,000

POPULATION DENSITY  124 per sq km (321.1 per sq mile)

LIFE EXPECTANCY  70.5

INFANT MORTALITY (PER 1,000)  31

OFFICIAL LANGUAGE  Bahasa Indonesia

OTHER LANGUAGES  English, Dutch, indigenous languages

LITERACY RATE  90.4 %

RELIGIONS  Muslim 86.1 %, Christian 8.7 %, Hindu 1.8 %, Buddhist 1 %, other 2.4 %

ETHNIC GROUPS  Javanese 40.6 %, Sundanese 15 %, Minangkabau 2.7 %, other 41.7 %

CURRENCY  Rupiah

ECONOMY  Industry 46.7 %, services 39.4 %, agriculture 13.9 %

GNI PER CAPITA  US$ 1,650

CLIMATE  Tropical, with wet season December to March (except in Moluccas where wet season is June to September)

HIGHEST POINT  Puncak Jaya 5,030 m (16,502 ft)

MAP REFERENCE  Pages 198–99, 200–01

After 30 years of economic progress, the collapse of the economy in 1998 triggered an outbreak of violent protest against the government. A change of leadership followed in 1999, and promises of new and more open elections. Nevertheless, long-suppressed class, ethnic, and religious conflicts have been unleashed. Guerrilla groups fought against the national unity imposed on the numerous Indonesian islands by Jakarta's urban elite, but a historic agreement was reached in 2005, followed by democratic elections in 2006.

The 13,677 islands of the world's largest archipelago (6,000 of them inhabited) rest on the platform of two continental shelves. The southern chain of islands, from Sumatra to Timor, including Borneo, form part of the Sunda shelf, a largely submerged extension of the Asian continent. The northern Moluccas and New Guinea rest on the Sahul shelf, a northern extension of the Australian continent. Between the shelves, Sulawesi and the southern Moluccas form the island summits of suboceanic mountain ranges flanked by sea trenches 4,500 m (14,800 ft) deep. All Indonesia's main islands are mountainous: Sumatra, Java, and the Lesser Sunda Islands (Nusa Tengara) form an arc containing 200 volcanoes, many of which are active—Krakatoa (Pulau Rakata) among them.

In Sumatra, along with 10 active volcanoes there are a number of crater lakes, such as Lake Toba, at an altitude of 900 m (2,953 ft). Much of the island was once forested but over-cutting of timber in the lowlands means that native forest is now restricted to reserves and national parks. Isolated mountain forests remain in remote areas. The heavily populated island of Java has a long range containing 50 active volcanoes and 17 that are only recently dormant.

Throughout the archipelago many coasts are lined with mangrove swamps, notably in eastern Sumatra and southern Kalimantan. Several of the islands are of great beauty: tourism, not only to Bali, has been a major activity in recent years.

Indonesia's complex and varied population, and its four major religions—Islam, Hinduism, Christianity, and Buddhism—reflect the country's varied history. Hinduism was the first major religious influence 2,000 years ago, followed by Buddhism in the seventh century AD. Hindu-Buddhist religious authority began to decline with the collapse of the Majapahit Empire in the fourteenth century, and the arrival of Arab traders from the west gradually established Islam as the dominant religion.

Under Dutch colonial rule from 1608, the islands were from 1830 subject to a severe regime known as the Culture System. This involved the forced cultivation of commercial crops for export and resulted in a distortion of the traditional economy. Indonesia fell to the Japanese in the Second World War. After 1945 Indonesia became independent.

About 18 percent of Indonesia's land area is permanently cultivated. Most people live by agriculture, growing rice, maize, cassava, and sweet potato. There are also extensive plantations producing rubber, palm oil, sugarcane, coffee, and tea. The last 30 years have seen an intensive state-directed drive toward industrialization, based on abundant natural resources: oil, natural gas, timber, metals, and coal. Prosperity was initially tied to oil exports, but now the economy's growth depends on the continuing expansion of non-oil exports.

## East Timor

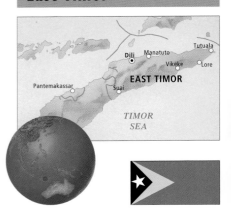

### Fact File

OFFICIAL NAME  Democratic Republic of Timor-Leste

FORM OF GOVERNMENT  Republic with one legislative body

CAPITAL  Dili

AREA  15,007 sq km (5,794 sq miles)

TIME ZONE  GMT + 9 hours

POPULATION  1,109,000

PROJECTED POPULATION 2015  1,504,000

POPULATION DENSITY  73.9 per sq km (191.4 per sq mile)

LIFE EXPECTANCY  66.9

INFANT MORTALITY (PER 1,000)  42

OFFICIAL LANGUAGES  Portuguese, Tetum

OTHER LANGUAGES  English, Bahasa Indonesia, Galole, Mambae, Kemak, and 12 other indigenous languages

LITERACY RATE  58.6 %

RELIGIONS  Roman Catholic 98 %, Protestant 1 %, Muslim 1 %

ETHNIC GROUPS  Timoran 78 %, Indonesian 20 %, Chinese 2 %

CURRENCY  U.S. Dollar

ECONOMY  Services 55 %, agriculture 32.2 %, industry 12.8 %

GNI PER CAPITA  US$ 1,510

CLIMATE  Tropical, with wet season December to March

HIGHEST POINT  Tata Mailau 2,963 m (9,717 ft)

MAP REFERENCE  198

First settled by the Portuguese in 1520, the eastern part of the island of Timor was annexed by Indonesia in 1976. In 1999, the UN intervened and formed a transitional administration providing the country with its governance that communicates directly with the East Timorese to ensure their participation in the administration. The economy of the mountainous country is based on agricultural produce, pearls, and fishing.

# Philippines

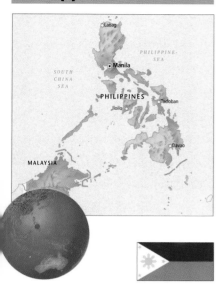

## Fact File

**OFFICIAL NAME** Republic of the Philippines

**FORM OF GOVERNMENT** Republic with two legislative bodies (Senate and House of Representatives)

**CAPITAL** Manila

**AREA** 300,000 sq km (115,830 sq miles)

**TIME ZONE** GMT +8 hours

**POPULATION** 92,681,000

**PROJECTED POPULATION 2015** 101,090,000

**POPULATION DENSITY** 308.9 per sq km (800.1 per sq mile)

**LIFE EXPECTANCY** 70.8

**INFANT MORTALITY (PER 1,000)** 21.5

**OFFICIAL LANGUAGE** Filipino (Tagalog)

**OTHER LANGUAGES** English, more than 80 indigenous languages

**LITERACY RATE** 92.6%

**RELIGIONS** Roman Catholic 80.9%, Protestant 11.6%, Muslim 5%, Buddhist and other 2.5%

**ETHNIC GROUPS** Malay 95,5%, Chinese 1.5%, other 3%

**CURRENCY** Philippine peso

**ECONOMY** Services 54.8%, industry 31.4%, agriculture 13.8%

**GNI PER CAPITA** US$ 1,620

**CLIMATE** Tropical, with wet season June to November

**HIGHEST POINT** Mt Apo 2,954 m (9,692 ft)

**MAP REFERENCE** Page 204

The Philippines present a combination that is unique in Asia. The people are Malayo-Polynesian; the majority of the population is Roman Catholic; English is the only common language in a country that has 87 native tongues; nearly four centuries of Spanish colonialism have left a flavor of Latin America; and 100 years of US influence (following the Spanish-American War in 1898) mean that the Philippines is also somewhat Americanized.

Long ago, and before the Spaniard explorer Ferdinand Magellan arrived from across the Pacific on his round-the-world voyage in 1521, Islam had reached the southern island of Mindanao. It is still the religion of a substantial minority in that part of the country. The Spanish then imposed whatever unity the archipelago can be said to have (there are 7,107 islands), building haciendas and sugar plantations on its main islands. Administered by the USA from 1898, the Philippines was occupied by the Japanese during the Second World War, was governed by the corrupt Marcos regime from 1965 to 1986—when a widespread popular rebellion finally forced him into exile—and faced a wide range of insurgencies over more than 40 years. The first insurgents were communist; more recently they have often been members of the Islamic Moro Liberation Front. However, after major successes in capturing or killing key terrorists in 2006/2007, a peace accord has been reached with one group and a cease-fire with others.

There are three main island groupings within the archipelago: the Luzon group, the Visayan group, and the Mindanao and Sulu Islands. Luzon to the north and Mindanao to the south are the two biggest islands and together they constitute two-thirds of the country's total land area.

All the main islands have a rugged mountainous and volcanic topography with narrow coastal belts, a north–south alignment of upland ridges, and rivers that drain northwards. North of Manila Bay, and stretching to the shores of the Lingayan Gulf, is Luzon's heavily populated central plain. This is an important rice-producing area. Beyond hills to the northeast lies the fertile valley of the Cagayan River. Irrigated rice terraces, constructed by the Igorot people, rise up the mountain slopes of northern Luzon. The peninsulas of southeastern Luzon contain a number of volcanoes. The highest peak in the Philippines, Mt Apo (2,954 m, 9,693 ft), is on Mindanao.

Government investment and a range of tax concessions have been tried to encourage industrial development. Mixing agriculture and light industry, the Philippine economy has been growing at a steady rate in recent years, without approaching the dynamic performance of other countries in the region.

While rice is the Philippines' main food crop, maize is the staple on the islands of Cebu, Leyte, and Negros, reflecting the country's old connection with Spanish America.

The country is well supplied with mineral resources, and nickel, tin, copper, zinc, and lead are processed in smelting and refining facilities. The Philippines is also the world's biggest supplier of refractory chrome, and the second biggest user of geothermal power after the USA. Foreign investment became sluggish as a consequence of the 1998 regional economic slowdown. Persistent weaknesses include rudimentary infrastructure, power failures, low savings rates, and a foreign debt of US$ 72 billion.

*Borobudur, the world's largest Buddhist monument, was built in the ninth century BC on the island of Java (left page, top). A coral reef in the Philippines (bottom left). The so-called "Chocolate Hills" in Bohol in the Philippines (top right).*

# Brunei

## Fact File

**OFFICIAL NAME** State of Brunei Darussalam

**FORM OF GOVERNMENT** Sultanate with advisory council of Cabinet Ministers

**CAPITAL** Bandar Seri Begawan

**AREA** 5,770 sq km (2,228 sq miles)

**TIME ZONE** GMT +8 hours

**POPULATION** 381,000

**PROJECTED POPULATION 2015** 453,000

**POPULATION DENSITY** 66 per sq km (171 per sq mile)

**LIFE EXPECTANCY** 75.5

**INFANT MORTALITY (PER 1,000)** 12.7

**OFFICIAL LANGUAGES** English, Malay

**OTHER LANGUAGE** Chinese, Iban

**LITERACY RATE** 92.7 %

**RELIGIONS** Muslim 67 %, Buddhism 13 %, Christian 10 %, indigenous beliefs and other 10 %

**ETHNIC GROUPS** Malay 67 %, Chinese 15 %, indigenous 6 %, other 12 %

**CURRENCY** Bruneian dollar

**ECONOMY** Industry 71.6 %, services 27.5 %, agriculture 0.9 %

**GNI PER CAPITA** US$ 26,930

**CLIMATE** Tropical

**HIGHEST POINT** Gunong Pagon 1,850 m (6,070 ft)

**MAP REFERENCE** Page 201

Oil was discovered in the sultanate of Brunei in 1929. By the time it became independent on 1 January 1984 this small country on the north coast of Borneo was already prosperous. Today its oil revenues have made Brunei's sultan perhaps the richest man in the world, and given its people one of the highest per capita incomes in Asia. There is no income tax, the government subsidizes food and housing, and provides free medical care. The downside is that all government employees (two-thirds of the workforce) are banned from political activity, and the Sultan of Brunei rules by decree. Some nongovernmental political groupings have been allowed but the sultan remains firmly in control. There is disquiet among Bruneians over the rising number of

resident foreigners, as demand for both skilled and unskilled labor brings contract workers in from outside.

Brunei consists of two semi-enclaves on the northwest coast of Borneo which are bordered by the Malaysian state of Sarawak. They are separated by a few kilometers of coastline where the Limbang River enters Brunei Bay. The topography in both areas consists of hills bordering a narrow, swampy coastal plain. More than two-thirds of the country is tropical forest.

Brunei is almost entirely supported by exports of oil and natural gas. Petroleum revenues account for more than 50 percent of gross domestic product. Production is carried out by Brunei Shell Petroleum in which the government holds a 50 percent stake. Most crude oil is exported to Japan, South Korea and the USA. Liquefied natural gas is produced in one of the world's biggest plants, at Lumut in Malaysia, and is sold to power and gas companies in Tokyo and Osaka. About 80 percent of Brunei's food is imported, but there has been a push to achieve agricultural self-sufficiency. Small farms grow rice, fruit, and vegetables. The government Forestry Department, which controls all forest reserves, is expanding into value-added activities such as furniture production.

*Fair in Bandar Seri Begawan, Brunei (above). A view of Singapore's central business district (below). Street vendor with customers in Malaysia (right page bottom).*

# Singapore

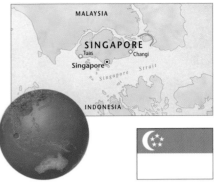

## Fact File

**OFFICIAL NAME** Republic of Singapore

**FORM OF GOVERNMENT** Republic with single legislative body (Parliament)

**CAPITAL** Singapore

**AREA** 693 sq km (267.6 sq miles)

**TIME ZONE** GMT + 8 hours

**POPULATION** 4,608,000

**PROJECTED POPULATION 2015** 4,809,000

**POPULATION DENSITY** 6,649.4 per sq km (17,219.7 per sq mile)

**LIFE EXPECTANCY** 81.9

**INFANT MORTALITY (PER 1,000)** 2.3

**OFFICIAL LANGUAGES** Malay, Chinese, Tamil, English

**LITERACY RATE** 92.5 %

**RELIGIONS** Buddhist and Taoist 51 %, Muslim 15 %, Christian 15 %, Hindu 4 %, other 15 %

**ETHNIC GROUPS** Chinese 76.8 %, Malay 13.9 %, Indian 7.9 %, other 1.4 %

**CURRENCY** Singapore dollar

**ECONOMY** Services 68.8 %, industry 31.2 %, agriculture 0 %

**GNI PER CAPITA** US$ 32,470

**CLIMATE** Tropical

**HIGHEST POINT** Bukit Timah 166 m (545 ft)

**MAP REFERENCE** Page 200

Amuddy, mangrove-swampy islet nobody wanted in 1819, Singapore is now a leading Asian city-state with one of the highest standards of living in the world. This was achieved without any resources beyond the skills and commitment of its citizens and the economic vision of its leadership. Standing at the southern extremity of the Malay Peninsula, Singapore was established as a free-trading port and settlement early in the nineteenth century by the English colonial administrator Sir Stamford Raffles. Without customs tariffs or other restrictions it drew numbers of Chinese immigrants, and after the opening of the Suez Canal played a leading role in the growing trade in Malaysian rubber and tin.

After the Second World War, during which it was occupied by the Japanese, it reverted to its former status as a British crown colony. In 1963 it became part of Malaysia, but, after two years, tensions between Chinese Singapore and the Malay leadership in Kuala Lumpur led Malaysia to force the island to go it alone. Under Lee Kuan Yew, prime minister for 31 years until 1990, a strategy of high-tech industrialization enabled the economy to grow at a rate of 7 percent a year. However, freedom of speech is constrained, political debate limited, and both public behavior and private life are watched closely (chewing gum is forbidden, and vandalism punished by caning).

Singapore Island is largely low-lying, with a hilly center. With limited natural freshwater resources, water is brought from the Malaysian mainland nearby. Reservoirs on high ground hold water for the city's use. Urban development has accelerated deforestation and swamp and land reclamation: 5 percent of the land is forested, and 4 percent is arable. In addition to the main island of Singapore there are 57 smaller islands lying within its territorial waters, many of them in the Strait of Singapore, which opens from the busy seaway of the Strait of Malacca. Between the main island and the Malaysian mainland is the narrow channel of the Johore Strait. A causeway across this strait links Malaysia to Singapore.

While the foundation of its economic growth was the export of manufactured goods, the government has in recent years promoted Singapore as a financial services and banking center, using the latest information technology. In 1995 this sector led economic growth. Singapore is a world leader in biotechnology. Rising labor costs threaten the country's competitiveness today, but its government hopes to offset this by increasing productivity and improving infrastructure. Because of the reduced growth rate accompanying the Asian economic downturn, major infrastructural development has taken place since 1998: an additional section for Changi International Airport, extensions to the mass rapid transit system, and a deep-tunnel sewerage project to dispose of wastes. In applied technology, per capita output, investment, and industrial harmony, Singapore possesses many of the attributes of a large modern country.

# Malaysia

## Fact File

**OFFICIAL NAME** Malaysia

**FORM OF GOVERNMENT** Federal constitutional monarchy with two legislative bodies (Senate and House of Representatives)

**CAPITAL** Kuala Lumpur

**AREA** 329,750 sq km (127,316 sq miles)

**TIME ZONE** GMT + 8 hours

**POPULATION** 25,274,000

**PROJECTED POPULATION 2015** 30,047,000

**POPULATION DENSITY** 76.6 per sq km (198.5 per sq mile)

**LIFE EXPECTANCY** 73

**INFANT MORTALITY (PER 1,000)** 16.4

**OFFICIAL LANGUAGE** Malay (Bahasa Malaysia)

**OTHER LANGUAGES** Austronesian languages, Aslian, Chinese languages, Tamil, English

**LITERACY RATE** 88.7 %

**RELIGIONS** Muslim 60.4 %, Buddhist 19.2 %, Christian 9.1 %, Hindu 6.3 %, Confucian and Taoist 2.8 %, other 2.2 %

**ETHNIC GROUPS** Malay 50.4 %, Chinese 23.7 %, Bumiputera 11 %, Indian 7.1 %, other 7.8 %

**CURRENCY** Ringgit (Malaysian dollar)

**ECONOMY** Industry 45.3 %, services 44.8 %, agriculture 9.9 %

**GNI PER CAPITA** US$ 6,540

**CLIMATE** Tropical, with northeast monsoon October to February and southwest monsoon May to September

**HIGHEST POINT** Gunung Kinabalu 4,100 m (13,450 ft)

**MAP REFERENCE** Pages 200–01

Malaysia consists of the southern part of the Malay Peninsula, with Thailand to its north, plus the regions of Sarawak and Sabah in northern Borneo. Like Singapore, which lies at the southern tip of the Malay Peninsula, Malaysia has enjoyed an impressive record of economic growth in recent times, although it suffered severely during the 1998 and 2001/2002 economic crises.

In the fifteenth century a part of Malaysia was famous as the Kingdom of Malacca (now Melaka), a state that became powerful through its control of local sea routes and shipping. In 1414 the ruler of Malacca adopted Islam, which is still the religion of Malaysia today. Seized by the Portuguese to serve as a base for the lucrative spice trade in 1511, and held by the Dutch from 1641, Malacca was captured by the British in 1795.

In 1819, the British took control of Singapore, as well, and in 1867 they established the Straits Settlements, which consisted of Penang Island (Pinang) in the northeast, Malacca, and Singapore, as a crown colony.

During the Second World War Malaysia was occupied by the Japanese. In 1945, Great Britain resumed control over what was then called Malaya, but an alliance led by Tunku Abdul Rahman finally gained Malaysia's independence from the British. A guerrilla war then broke out, led by communists who were sympathetic to the Chinese Revolution. This insurgency was defeated after a four-year military campaign, after which the country evolved into the modern state it is today.

Ethnic tensions continue to exist, principally between the Malays, who are the most

numerous group, and the Chinese, who are smaller in number but considerably more prosperous. There were riots between the Malays and Chinese in 1969 with heavy loss of life. The many "affirmative action" provisions that are now in place to open opportunities for Malays at the expense of Chinese and Indians are strongly resented by the latter groups. There are also a number of unresolved territorial disputes with neighboring states—Sabah in Borneo, for example, being claimed by the Philippines.

Fold mountains aligned on a north-south axis dominate the Malay Peninsula. There are seven or eight distinct chains of mountains, many of which have exposed granite cores. Climbing to 2,189 m (7,181 ft) at Gunung Tahan, the main range divides the narrow coastal belt to the east from the fertile alluvial plains in the west. To the south lies poorly drained lowland, marked by isolated hills, some of which rise to over 1,060 m (3,500 ft). Several smaller rivers have also contributed to the margin of lowland around the peninsular coasts.

About 2,000 km (1,250 miles) east of the Malay Peninsula, northern Borneo has a mangrove-fringed coastal plain about 65 km (40 miles) wide, rising behind to hill country averaging 300 m (1,000 ft) in height. This ascends through various secondary ranges to the mountainous main interior range. The granite peak of Gunung Kinabalu, the highest mountain in Southeast Asia, rises from the northern end of this range in Sabah, towering above Kinabalu National Park. Dense rainforest in Sarawak and Sabah support a great diversity of plants and animals.

With a mixture of private enterprise and public management, the Malaysian economy grew nine percent annually in 1988–1995 and five to six percent since 2003. Substantial inroads are being made towards the reduction of poverty, and real wages are rising. New light industries including electronics are playing an important role in this development: Malaysia is the world's biggest producer of disk drives. Heavy industry has also grown, not least thanks to the export of Malaysia's "national car", the Proton.

The traditional mainstays of the economy, however, remain rice, rubber, palm oil, and tin—Malaysia being the world's foremost producer of palm oil and tin. Rice, however, is becoming a problem. Subsistence farming has regularly failed to ensure self-sufficiency in food, and rice production does not meet demand. The main industries on the peninsula are rubber and palm oil processing and manufacturing, light industry, electronics, tin mining, smelting, logging, and timber processing. The main activities on Sabah and Sarawak are logging, petroleum production, and the processing of agricultural products. Malaysia exports more tropical timber than any other country, and the tribal people of Sarawak have been campaigning against the scale of logging on their land. The Asian economic downturn in 1997–1998 and in 2001–2002 saw a depreciation of the Malaysian currency and a marked slowing of the growth of their economy.

# Cambodia

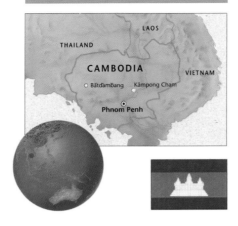

## Fact File

| | |
|---|---|
| OFFICIAL NAME | Kingdom of Cambodia |
| FORM OF GOVERNMENT | Constitutional monarchy with single legislative body (National Assembly) |
| CAPITAL | Phnom Penh |
| AREA | 181,040 sq km (69,900 sq miles) |
| TIME ZONE | GMT +7 hours |
| POPULATION | 14,242,000 |
| PROJECTED POPULATION 2015 | 16,641,000 |
| POPULATION DENSITY | 78.7 per sq km (203.7 per sq mile) |
| LIFE EXPECTANCY | 61.7 |
| INFANT MORTALITY (PER 1,000) | 56.6 |
| OFFICIAL LANGUAGE | Khmer |
| OTHER LANGUAGES | French, Vietnamese, Chinese |
| LITERACY RATE | 73.6 % |
| RELIGIONS | Theravada Buddhism 95 %, other 5 % |
| ETHNIC GROUPS | Khmer 90 %, Vietnamese 5 %, Chinese 1 %, other 4 % |
| CURRENCY | Riel |
| ECONOMY | Services 43 %, agriculture 31 %, industry 26 % |
| GNI PER CAPITA | US$ 540 |
| CLIMATE | Tropical, with wet season May to November |
| HIGHEST POINT | Phnum Aôral 1,810 m (5,938 ft) |
| MAP REFERENCE | Page 203 |

The Southeast Asian country of Cambodia is famous both culturally and politically. At Angkor Wat and Angkor Thom it has the world's largest group of religious buildings, a priceless relic of the Hindu Khmer Empire (AD 802 to 1432). It also saw an outbreak of communist fanaticism in the 1970s in which over 2 million people died. Under French rule for almost a century from 1863, Cambodia won independence in 1954. In the late 1950s and during the 1960s there was a short period of relative stability in which the country developed its agricultural resources and rubber plantations and managed to achieve self-sufficiency in food.

Years of internal political struggles, in combination with Cambodia's involvement in the Vietnam War, led to a takeover by the Communist Khmer Rouge under the leadership of Pol Pot in 1975. With the aim of creating a classless agrarian society, money and private property were abolished, the professional classes were murdered (anyone with glasses was considered intellectual, and therefore at risk), and townspeople were brutally moved into the countryside and left to fend for themselves. Half a million refugees fled to Thailand, and between one eighth and one quarter of the entire population died. The regime fell in 1978 and Pol Pot went into hiding, but civil war continued for some years; Pol Pot died in 1998 without ever having to face trial for the atrocities that were committed under his direction. A devastated and desperately poor nation,

## Vietnam

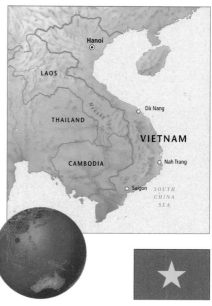

stripped of what little economic infrastructure and trained personnel it once had, Cambodia is still in the process of putting itself together again.

The country's heartland consists of a wide basin drained by the Mekong River. In the center of this lies the Tonlé Sap (Great Lake), surrounded by a broad plain. When the rain is meager and the Mekong is low—from November to June—the lake drains south toward the sea. But during the rainy season when the Mekong is high—from July to October—the flow reverses, and the lake doubles its area to become the largest freshwater lake in Southeast Asia. The wealth of the fabled "gentle kingdom" of Cambodia consists of fish from the lake and rice from the flooded lowlands, a year-round water supply being provided by an extensive system of irrigation channels and reservoirs. Directly south of the lake, the Cardamom (Chuŏr Phnum Kravan) and Elephant (Chuŏr Phnum Dămrek) Mountains look out over a narrow coastal plain.

Reconstructing the Cambodian economy is bringing almost as many costs as benefits. Tropical rainforest timber, especially teak and rosewood, is Cambodia's most important resource. For twenty years it was sold in huge quantities by all the various factions in order to finance their war efforts. Now indiscriminate tree-felling is a major environmental problem. A 1992 moratorium on logging is largely being ignored, and gems are another resource but strip mining is causing habitat loss, and the destruction of mangrove swamps is threatening the sustainability of fisheries. Starting from a very low base, growth was strong in the early 1990s, but a lack of skills at all levels of administration and management, as well as the rampaging corruption, is slowing progress.

*Angkor Wat is the largest of the many temples built by the Khmer people in Cambodia about 1,000 years ago (above).*
*Rice paddies in east Malaysia (left page).*

## Regional conflicts

**1946** Vietnam: Return of French after Second World War. Outbreak of First Indochina War.
**1954** Vietnam: Defeat of French at Dien Bien Phu. Division of Vietnam into North supported by USSR and South supported by USA.
**1960** Vietnam: Communists in South initiate guerrilla war as Viet Cong.
**1961** Vietnam: USA sends "military advisers" to South Vietnam to fight Viet Cong.
**1964** US Congress approves war with Vietnam. US bombs Vietnamese sanctuaries in Laos, plus Ho Chi Minh Trail—north-south supply route.
**1965** Vietnam: Arrival of first US combat troops. Start of intense US bombing of North Vietnam which continues until 1968.
**1970** Right-wing coup in Cambodia deposes Prince Sihanouk. In exile Sihanouk forms movement backed by communist Khmer Rouge.
**1974** Cambodia: Sihanouk and Khmer Rouge capture Phnom Penh. Thousands die as revolutionary programs are enforced (1975).
**1975** Vietnam: Fall of Saigon. North Vietnamese and Viet Cong take power in South. Laos: Communist Pathet Lao seize power.
**1976** Cambodia: Sihanouk resigns—all power held by Pol Pot, leader of the Khmer Rouge.
**1978** Vietnam invades Cambodia.
**1979** Vietnam captures Phnom Penh. Pol Pot flees, responsible for over 2 million deaths.
**1989** Vietnamese troops leave Cambodia.
**1991** Cambodia: Sihanouk again head of state. Flight of Khmer Rouge officials.
**1992** Vietnam: Foreign investment permitted; Communist Party monopoly unchanged.
**1993** Cambodia: UN-supervized elections. Departure of UN peace mission.
**1995** Normalization of US-Vietnam relations.
**1997** Cambodia: Violent coup restores power to communists under Hun Sen.
**1998** Cambodia: Pol Pot dies.
**2002** East Timor gains independence.
**2006** Military coup overturns civil government in Thailand.

### Fact File

**OFFICIAL NAME** Socialist Republic of Vietnam

**FORM OF GOVERNMENT** Communist state with single legislative body (National Assembly)

**CAPITAL** Hanoi

**AREA** 329,560 sq km (127,243 sq miles)

**TIME ZONE** GMT +7 hours

**POPULATION** 86,117,000

**PROJECTED POPULATION 2015** 96,467,000

**POPULATION DENSITY** 261.3 per sq km (676.8 per sq mile)

**LIFE EXPECTANCY** 71.3

**INFANT MORTALITY (PER 1,000)** 23.6

**OFFICIAL LANGUAGE** Vietnamese

**OTHER LANGUAGES** Chinese, French, English, Khmer, indigenous languages

**LITERACY RATE** 90.3 %

**RELIGIONS** Buddhist 9.3 %, Roman Catholic 6.7 %, other (Taoist, Islam and indigenous beliefs) 3.2 %, none 80.6 %

**ETHNIC GROUPS** Kinh (Viet) 86.2 %, Tay 1.9 %, Thai 1.7 %, Muong 1.5 %, Khome 1.4 %, Hoa 1.1 %, Nun 1.1 %, Hmong 1 %, others 4.1 %

**CURRENCY** Dong

**ECONOMY** Industry 42.3 %, services 38.2 %, agriculture 19.5 %

**GNI PER CAPITA** US$ 790

**CLIMATE** Tropical in south, subtropical in north; wet season May to October

**HIGHEST POINT** Fan Si Pan 3,143 m (10,312 ft)

**MAP REFERENCE** Page 203

Vietnam is located on the eastern side of the Indochinese Peninsula. A long, narrow strip of country lying between two major river systems, Vietnam bears the scars of one of the longest and most devastating wars of the second half of the

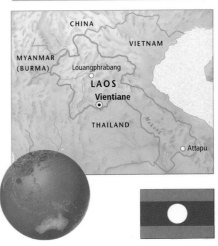

# Laos

twentieth century. Historically, it was under Chinese domination for more than a thousand years, achieving a degree of independence in AD 939. Christian missionary activity began in the seventeenth century and it was a French colony from 1883. During the Second World War, a communist-led resistance movement fought the Japanese, and later fought the returning French, defeating them decisively in 1954. The country was divided into two mutually hostile regimes, with a communist government in the North and a French- and later US-backed government in the South. The North initiated twenty years of insurgency and then full-scale war (the North backed by the USSR, the South by the USA with up to 500,000 troops), eventually winning in 1975 and establishing the Socialist Republic of Vietnam.

About 66 percent of Vietnam's land area is dominated by the heavily forested terrain of the Annam Highlands (or Chaîne Annamitique). The crest of this range mainly follows the western border with Laos in the north and with Cambodia to the south. At either end of the country are intensively cultivated and densely populated river deltas—the Red River Delta in the north, which is also fed by waters from the valley of the Da, and the Mekong Delta in the south. Both are major rice-growing areas. Rice is the main staple and export crop, Vietnam being the world's third-largest exporter. Other food crops include sweet potato and cassava. On the mountain slopes of the Annam Highlands, tea, coffee, and rubber plantations have been established.

Most mineral resources are located in the north and include anthracite and lignite. Coal is the main export item and is the principal energy source.

After 10 years during which a typical communist command economy was imposed, along with collectivized agriculture, the government changed direction. In 1986 the more liberal *doi moi* ("renovation") policy was introduced. Investment was welcomed from outside, and during the period 1990 to 1995 real growth averaged more than 8 percent annually, a number sought to be equalled in 2007–2012. Vastly growing exports and Vietnam's joining of the WTO in 2007 are expected to further boost its economic growth.

Foreign capital contributed to a boom in commercial construction, and there was strong growth in services and industrial output. Crude oil remains the country's largest single export, now amounting to a quarter of exports overall, slightly more than manufactures. But progress is handicapped by a continuing strong commitment to state direction and bureaucratic controls. Banking reform is needed and administrative and legal barriers delay investment. A new constitution of 1992 limits the influence of the Communist Party and liberalizes the economy and politics. The human rights situation has since improved but the still powerful CPV continues to curtail civil rights.

## Fact File

**OFFICIAL NAME** Lao People's Democratic Republic

**FORM OF GOVERNMENT** Communist state with single legislative body (National Assembly)

**CAPITAL** Vientiane

**AREA** 236,800 sq km (91,428 sq miles)

**TIME ZONE** GMT +7 hours

**POPULATION** 6,678,000

**PROJECTED POPULATION 2015** 6,699,000

**POPULATION DENSITY** 28.2 per sq km (73 per sq mile)

**LIFE EXPECTANCY** 56.3

**INFANT MORTALITY (PER 1,000)** 79.6

**OFFICIAL LANGUAGE** Lao

**OTHER LANGUAGES** French, Chinese, Vietnamese

**LITERACY RATE** 68.7 %

**RELIGIONS** Buddhist 65 %, animist and other 35 %

**ETHNIC GROUPS** Lao Loum (lowland) 68 %, Lao Theung (upland) 22 %, Lao Soung (highland) 9 %, ethnic Vietnamese and Chinese 1 %

CURRENCY Kip

ECONOMY Agriculture 41.3 %, industry 32.2 %, services 26.5 %

GNI PER CAPITA US$ 580

CLIMATE Tropical monsoonal, with wet season May to October

HIGHEST POINT Phou Bia 2,817 m (9,242 ft)

MAP REFERENCE Pages 202–03

Laos is the only landlocked country in Southeast Asia. It also has one of the last official communist regimes, and is the poorest state in the region. Once the home of the fourteenth century kingdom of Lan Xang (the Million Elephant Kingdom), Laos became a French protectorate in 1893. Independent in 1953, it was fought over by royalists, communists, and conservatives from 1964 onward. It was used as a military supply route by the North Vietnamese during the Vietnam War and was heavily bombed with defoliants by the USA in the late 1960s. In 1975 it fell into the hands of the communist Pathet Lao who established a one-party state. Although the leadership has for economic reasons relaxed its doctrinal grip—the 1978 collectivization of agriculture was reversed in 1990—many hill-tribe people, such as the Hmong, remain alienated from the regime. Some continue guerrilla resistance, while others live in exile in Thailand. A new constitution in 1991 confirmed the monopoly of the communist Lao People's Revolutionary Party.

From the mountains in the northwest and the Plateau de Xiangkhoang, the country extends southeast, following the line of the Anamitique Range. A number of rivers cross the country westward from this range to the Mekong River which forms the western border, among them the Banghiang, the Noi, and the Theun. The fertile Mekong floodplains in the west provide the only generally cultivable lowland. Despite deforestation and erosion, forest still covers 55 percent of the country.

Most of the Laotian people are engaged in subsistence agriculture. In addition to the staple, rice, other crops which are grown include maize, vegetables, tobacco, coffee, and cotton. Opium poppies and cannabis are grown illegally: Laos is the world's third-largest opium producer.

The policy of privatization and decentralization that was adopted in 1986 has produced growth averaging 7.5 percent annually since 1988. Textile and garment manufacture was established, as well as motorcycle assembly. The country's primitive infrastructure is a major handicap to continued growth. Laos has no railroads, its roads are inadequate, and its telecommunications severely limited.

While the country is still heavily influenced by Vietnam, it has experienced substantial growth, especially since the United Stated lifted their twenty-year trade embargo in 1995 and Laos joined the ASEAN in 1997.

*A fisherman casting his net from a basket boat in Vietnam (left page top). Women at a market in Hanoi (left page above). Vietnamese farmers working in the rice fields (left page below). View of the Mekong plain (above right).*

## Indochina

The term Indochina indicates that cultural influences from India and China are intermingled throughout this region. Also once known as French Indochina, it consists of the three states of Vietnam, Laos, and Cambodia, all of which were formerly associated with France in a political group known as the French Union. Despite the fact that the French exercised political control over their countries from the late nineteenth century, the Vietnamese, Cambodian, and Laotian royal houses continued to exercise wide authority. The Japanese occupied Indochina during the Second World War, but interfered little in the existing colonial arrangements; only after 1945 did the military turmoil begin which was to convulse the region.

In 1945, following the withdrawal of the Japanese, the Vietnamese communist nationalist leader Ho Chi Minh proclaimed the Democratic Republic of Vietnam. The returning French attempted to hold their colonial possession together, but soon the protracted guerrilla struggle that became known as the First Indochina War broke out. The forces in the North received support from the Chinese. In 1954 after the siege of Dien Bien Phu, both France and China agreed to a ceasefire. North Vietnam and South Vietnam were divided along the 17th parallel, and France had to withdraw from the region and recognize the independence of its former colonies Vietnam, Laos, and Cambodia.

During the 1960s North Vietnamese attempts to infiltrate and subvert the southern area led to the Second Indochina War, also know as the Vietnam War. This period saw increasing United States military involvement in the defense of South Vietnam. The US gave strong support to the South Vietnamese government and in 1961 the US commenced sending military advisers. The US actively entered the Vietnam War in 1964. Fighting continued until the Paris ceasefire of 1973, and Saigon was ultimately captured by the North Vietnmese in 1975.

Between 1954 and 1975 about 1,000,000 North Vietnamese soliders, 200,000 South Vietnamese soldiers and 500,000 civilians were killed. Between 1961 and 1975 about 56,500 US soldiers were killed. In 1976 the Socialist Republic of Vietnam was established. This period also saw the rise and fall of the Khmer Rouge regime in Cambodia, and was followed by a Vietnamese invasion of Cambodia in 1978. Before withdrawing from Cambodia Vietnam installed in power the Communist Khmer People's Revolutionary Party (now the Cambodian People's Party) whose domination of the political system, reinforced by a violent coup in 1997, is a source of international concern.

Today several boundary disputes exist between the three countries of Indochina. In addition to Vietnam's claims to various islands in the South China Sea, sections of the boundary between Cambodia and Vietnam are in dispute, and the maritime boundary between these countries is not defined. Similar boundary disputes also exist between Laos and Thailand.

# Thailand

## Fact File

**OFFICIAL NAME** Kingdom of Thailand

**FORM OF GOVERNMENT** Constitutional monarchy with two legislative bodies (Senate and House of Representatives)

**CAPITAL** Bangkok

**AREA** 514,000 sq km (198,455 sq miles)

**TIME ZONE** GMT +7 hours

**POPULATION** 65,493,000

**PROJECTED POPULATION 2015** 66,763,000

**POPULATION DENSITY** 127.4 per sq km (330 per sq mile)

**LIFE EXPECTANCY** 72.8

**INFANT MORTALITY (PER 1,000)** 18.2

**OFFICIAL LANGUAGE** Thai

**OTHER LANGUAGES** Chinese, Malay, English

**LITERACY RATE** 92.6 %

**RELIGIONS** Buddhist 94.6 %, Muslim 4.6 %, Christian 0.7 %, other 0.1 %

**ETHNIC GROUPS** Thai (Siamese, Shan, Lao) 75 %, Chinese 14 %, other 11 %

**CURRENCY** Baht

**ECONOMY** Services 44,7 %, industry 43.9 %, agriculture 11.4 %

**GNI PER CAPITA** US$ 3,400

**CLIMATE** Tropical, with wet season June to October, cool season November to February, hot season March to May

**HIGHEST POINT** Doi Inthanon 2,576 m (8,451 ft)

**MAP REFERENCE** Pages 202–03

Lying between Burma, Laos, and Cambodia, Thailand has a system of "semi-democracy" that has somehow preserved it from the misfortunes of its neighbors. Known as Siam until 1939, it was the home of the Buddhist kingdom of Ayutthaya from the fourteenth to the eigh-

teenth centuries, during which time the monarch came to be regarded as a sort of god-king, and a bureaucratic administration system was developed. The Chakkri Dynasty was founded in 1782 at Bangkok, and in the late nineteenth century its representatives ushered Siam into the modern age: treaties with the West were signed, slavery abolished, and study abroad encouraged. The king acquiesced in a bloodless coup which set up a constitutional monarchy in 1932. Since then civilian and military governments have alternated, climaxing in the events of 1992, when violent demonstrations against another military general taking over the government led the king to intervene, and the constitution was amended. The prime minister now has to be an elected member of parliament. The military continues to play an important part in both political and industrial life, as proved in its 2006 coup.

Thailand can be divided into four regions. To the north there are forested mountain ranges which are the southernmost extension of the Himalayas. The rich intermontane valleys of the Rivers Ping, Yom, Wang, and Nan support intensive agriculture and the forests produce teak and other valuable timbers. The forests provide a home for many hill tribes who live by the alternating cultivation of dry rice and opium poppies. In the northeast lies the Khorat Plateau, a region of poor soils sparsely vegetated with savanna woodlands where crops of rice and cassava are grown. The third region is the central plains—Thailand's rice bowl—with vistas of rice fields, canals, rivers, and villages on stilts. The mountainous southern provinces on the Malay Peninsula are dominated by tropical rainforest. The hills produce tin ore and plantation rubber and the picturesque islands off the west coast draw tourists.

Agriculture is still the main employer, although its economic importance is declining. Rice is the principal crop and Thailand is still one of the world's leading exporters. Other crops include sugar, maize, rubber, manioc, pineapples, and seafoods. Mineral resources include tin ore, lead, tungsten, lignite, gypsum, tantalum, fluorite, and gemstones. Thailand is the world's second largest

producer of tungsten, and the third largest tin producer. Tourism is the largest single source of foreign exchange, the development of resorts on the coast along the Andaman Sea having been a major success.

The development of urban manufacturing industry, involving the export of high-technology goods, has been the most significant feature of the economy in recent years. This and the development of the service sector have fueled a growth rate of 9 percent since 1989. Thailand's domestic savings rate of 35 percent is a leading source of capital, but the country has also received substantial investment from overseas. Beginning in 1997, Thailand was the first country in the region to be affected by a range of problems associated with the Asian economic downturn, but it since has recovered with growth rates between six and seven percent in recent years.

# Myanmar (Burma)

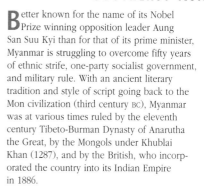

## Fact File

**OFFICIAL NAME** Union of Myanmar (Burma)

**FORM OF GOVERNMENT** Military regime; legislative body (People's Assembly) has never convened since military takeover in 1988

**CAPITAL** Yangon (Rangoon)

**AREA** 678,500 sq km (261,969 sq miles)

**TIME ZONE** GMT + 6.5 hours

**POPULATION** 47,758,000

**PROJECTED POPULATION 2015** 51,998,000

**POPULATION DENSITY** 70.4 per sq km (182.3 per sq mile)

**LIFE EXPECTANCY** 62.9

**INFANT MORTALITY (PER 1,000)** 49.1

**OFFICIAL LANGUAGE** Burmese

**OTHER LANGUAGES** Indigenous languages (Shan, Kachin, Karen), English

**LITERACY RATE** 89.9 %

**RELIGIONS** Buddhist 89 %, Christian 4 % (Baptist 3 %, Roman Catholic 1 %), Muslim 4 %, other 3 %

**ETHNIC GROUPS** Burman 68 %, Shan 9 %, Karen 7 %, Rakhine 4 %, Chinese 3 %, Mon 2 %, other 7 %

**CURRENCY** Kyat

**ECONOMY** Agriculture 50 %, services 32.4 %, industry 17.6 %

**GNI PER CAPITA** not available (less than US$ 935)

**CLIMATE** Tropical monsoon; dry zone around Mandalay; moderate temperature on Shan Plateau

**HIGHEST POINT** Hkakabo Razi 5,881 m (19,294 ft)

**MAP REFERENCE** Pages 202, 205

*Ruins of a Thai Buddhist temple (left page bottom). Landscape near Chiang Mai, in Thailand (top center). Two hill tribe women from the mountains of northern Thailand (above). Buddhist temple ruins at Pagan in Myanmar (bottom).*

Better known for the name of its Nobel Prize winning opposition leader Aung San Suu Kyi than for that of its prime minister, Myanmar is struggling to overcome fifty years of ethnic strife, one-party socialist government, and military rule. With an ancient literary tradition and style of script going back to the Mon civilization (third century BC), Myanmar was at various times ruled by the eleventh century Tibeto-Burman Dynasty of Anarutha the Great, by the Mongols under Khublai Khan (1287), and by the British, who incorporated the country into its Indian Empire in 1886.

After the country gained independence from Great Britain in 1948, General Ne Win's Burmese Socialist Program Party swiftly abolished all private enterprise and private trade, nationalized industry, and placed the country under military control. Within a short time, one of the region's richest countries had become an impoverished backwater. For decades, a substantial portion of the government's energy and 35 percent of its budget has been directed towards efforts to suppress ethnic insurgent movements led by Karens, Shans, Kachins, Mons, and others. In order to fund their resistance, these groups grew opium poppies, a traditional crop, which has led to the country becoming one of the world's largest opium producers.

Situated on the Bay of Bengal between Bangladesh and Thailand, Myanmar consists of central lowlands, where 75 percent of the population lives, enclosed by mountains to the north, bordering China, and west, bordering India, and the Shan Plateau to the east forming a frontier with Laos. The western mountains run southwest along the Indian border and form a series of forested ridges, ending in the Arakan Yoma Range (Pegu Yoma). From the mountains in the north the Irawaddy River flows south 2,100 km (1,300 miles), passing the ancient city of Mandalay and the capital of Yangon (Rangoon) on its way to the Andaman Sea. While the coast has a wet climate, the inner region, sheltered from the seasonal monsoon, has an annual rainfall of less than 100 cm (40 in). Here, in narrow valleys, small-scale irrigation supports such crops as rice, sugarcane, cotton, and jute.

Myanmar is quite rich in natural resources, having fertile soils and good fisheries, along with teak, gems, and natural gas and oil. Recently there has been some liberalization of the economy, most notably of small scale enterprise. Twenty-five percent, however, remains under state control, and the key industries—in energy, heavy industry, and foreign trade—consist of twenty military-run enterprises. A recent boom in trade with China has filled the north with Chinese goods and foreign visitors. Economic weaknesses include a shortage of both skilled labor, and trained managers and technicians. Price controls have led to an economy that is permeated by the black market. Published estimates of Myanmar's foreign trade are therefore greatly understated.

## East Asia

China · · · · · · · · · · 158
Taiwan · · · · · · · · · 162

North Korea · · · · · · 162
South Korea · · · · · · 163
Japan · · · · · · · · · · 164

## China

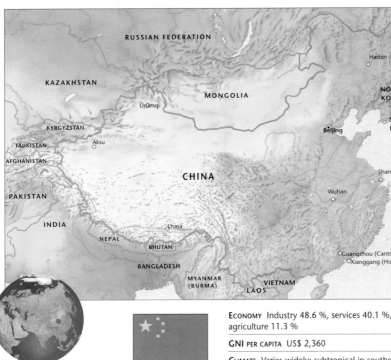

### Fact File

OFFICIAL NAME People's Republic of China

FORM OF GOVERNMENT Communist republic with single legislative body (National People's Congress)

CAPITAL Beijing

AREA 9,596,960 sq km (3,705,386 sq miles)

TIME ZONE GMT + 8 hours

POPULATION 1,330,044,000

PROJECTED POPULATION 2015 1,388,600,000

POPULATION DENSITY 138.6 per sq km (358.9 per sq mile)

LIFE EXPECTANCY 73.2

INFANT MORTALITY (PER 1,000) 21.2

OFFICIAL LANGUAGE Mandarin Chinese

OTHER LANGUAGES Yue (Cantonese), Wu (Shanghaiese), Minbei (Fuzhou), Minnan (Hokkien), other minority languages (Tibetan, Uyguran, Mongolian)

LITERACY RATE 90.9 %

RELIGIONS Officially atheist; traditionally Confucian, Taoist, Buddhist; small Muslim and Christian minorities

ETHNIC GROUPS Han Chinese 92 %, other (including Zhuang, Uygur, Hui, Yi, Tibetan, Miao, Manchu, Mongol, Buyi, Korean) 8 %

CURRENCY Yuan

ECONOMY Industry 48.6 %, services 40.1 %, agriculture 11.3 %

GNI PER CAPITA US$ 2,360

CLIMATE Varies widely: subtropical in southeast; temperate in east; cold and arid on southwestern Tibetan plateau; arid in northern deserts; cold temperate in northeast

HIGHEST POINT Mt Everest 8,848 m (29,028 ft)

MAP REFERENCE Pages 205, 206, 210–11, 212–13, 214–15

Although it is the third largest country in the world, and the most populous, China today remains something of an enigma to much of the rest of the world: it has an increasingly capitalistic economy, but political control remains solidly in the hands of an old-style Communist Party leadership. There is a great deal riding on how successfully this "socialist market economy" works. With a civilization extending back more than 5,000 years, China's history has tended to combine long periods of dynastic stability with shorter periods of sudden and dramatic change. Approximately in the last hundred years China has once again gone through a series of convulsive social, political, and economic transformations. Once isolated, agrarian, and indifferent to other societies and cultures, China's future is now that of a modern industrial nation trading with much of the world. Politically it remains a one-party state. The political reforms that would be necessary to bring about greater democracy are widely discussed in western media, as are civil liberties and human rights issues, but they are not yet on the agenda of China itself.

### Physical features and land use

China can be divided into three major geographic regions: the mountains to the west, including the vast Plateau of Tibet; the series of deserts and desert basins starting in the northwest with the Tarim Basin and the Taklimakan Desert, reaching across the Nei Mongol Plateau (Nei Mongol Gaoyuan) to Manchuria (Taklimakan Shamo) in the northeast; and the largely low-lying eastern region consisting of the valleys and floodplains of the Chang Jiang (Yangtze) and Huang (Yellow) Rivers, extending to the coastal plains including the Pearl River in the south.

The melting snows of the Plateau of Tibet feed several major rivers—the Brahmaputra, flowing south to India, the Salween (Nu) of Myanmar (Burma), and the Mekong which skirts Laos and Thailand before passing through Cambodia and reaching the sea in Vietnam. In addition, the plateau is the source of both the Huang (Yellow), and the mighty Chang Jiang (Yangtze), China's two main rivers, both of which drain into the East China Sea. The Plateau of Tibet, some parts of which are permanently covered in snow, is the highest region in the world, averaging about 4,900 m (16,000 ft), with ranges rising from 6,100 to 7,300 m (20,000 to 24,000 ft). It is bounded to the north by the Kunlun Shan Range, and to the south along the borders of India, Nepal, and Bhutan by the mountain system of the Himalayas. The plateau is a harsh environment, hostile to human settlement, and most of the plateau's 2 million inhabitants live in the southern region. The Himalayan ranges also have great political significance. They form a massive rampart along China's southwestern frontier, and for centuries they have provided a natural defensive barrier against the west. This is one of the reasons China is unwilling to allow the pressure for Tibetan independence to take it beyond the status of an "autonomous region".

The second geographic region of China stretches from the Tarim Basin and Dzungarian Basin (Junggar Pendi) in the northwest, past the southern fringes of the Gobi Desert to Northern Manchuria. For the most part it is too arid and cold for agriculture. Here, pastoralists such as the Uighurs of Xinjiang keep sheep, goats, and herds of horses. However, some oasis crops are grown around the rim of the Taklimakan Desert, and there are small farming settlements in the Gansu corridor to the north of the Qilian Mountains. The Turfan Depression (Turpan Pendi) (both the lowest and the hottest place in China at 154 m [505 ft] below sea level) lies northeast of the Tarim Basin. East of the Gobi Desert lies the agricultural area of the Manchurian Plain, where coarse grains and soy beans are cultivated. In Northern Manchuria the growing season is extremely short: only ninety days a year are frost free.

The eastern region of central China is where two-thirds of the country's people live. This was the cradle of Chinese civilization. On the region's fertile alluvial plains the most distinctive features of China's economic and social life developed—intensive irrigated agriculture and the Chinese peasant family. Known as "China's Sorrow," the Huang (Yellow) River makes its way across the North China Plain. For hundreds of years it caused repeated, serious flooding, with enormous loss of life, but today modern flood-control schemes have reduced this danger.

Further south, near the Chang Jiang (Yangtze) delta, the plain changes into a landscape characterized by large lakes and intricate networks of canals, many of them centuries old. The Chang Jiang is China's largest and most important river, and much of it is navigable, providing an essential transportation route. When the river level is high, vessels of 10,000 tonnes may reach Wuhan, and 1,000-tonne barges can reach Chongqing in Sichuan. What is called the "Red Basin" of Sichuan is a fertile and highly productive area far up the Chang Jiang, separated from the lower valley by steep-sided gorges. It is intensively cultivated, and the landscape is dominated by rice fields arranged in terraces extending up the hill-sides. Summer weather in the central valley of the Chang Jiang is hot and humid, with temperatures at Nanjing reaching 44 °C (111 °F).

A distinctive landscape in southern China (famous for centuries as an inspiration for Chinese landscape painters) is found in northeastern Guizhou Province, where limestone spires and pinnacles rise above small, intensively cultivated plains. This heavily eroded area is marked by sink-holes, caverns, and underground streams. In the coastal lowlands of Guangdong Province, in the far south, the climate is tropical and farmers enjoy a year-round growing season. On Hainan Island, flanking the Gulf of Tongking, it is possible to culti-vate three crops of rice per year. Other crops grown in the south include sugar, bananas, and tropical fruits. During the summer, cyclones and typhoons frequently strike the southeast coast.

*Threshing rice after harvesting (below). Buddhist prayer flags in the Potala Palace, in Lhasa, Tibet (above right). The countryside near Yangshuo in Guangxi Zhuangzu Zizhiqu Province (below right).*

### Early history

Civilization arose along the borders of the North China Plain. Here, about 1700 BC, the Shang Dynasty originated in the Huang Valley. Noted for their craftsmanship in bronze, along with important achievements as the use of the wheel, the calendar, and a form of writing, the Shang Dynasty lasted until 1122 BC. The next dynasty, the Zhou, lasted several centuries. It was in this time that the teachings of the philosopher-teacher Confucius (551–479 BC) originated, which provided a pattern for Chinese society for centuries to come. Iron casting, metal coinage, and silk were also introduced at this time. During the short-lived Qin Dynasty (221–206 BC) a ruler arose named Qin Shihuang. He unified the nation, began the fortification of China's northern boundary with the Great Wall, and established the civil service. He was buried at Lintong with an army of 6,000 terracotta warriors which are still standing and continue to be a major tourist attraction.

In 206 BC the Han Dynasty was begun. During the four centuries of the Han, the Chinese invented paper and the seismograph,

steel was first made, Buddhism was introduced from India, and the boundaries of China were extended nearly to their present limits. Under the Sui (AD 581–618) a large part of the Grand Canal linking the north with the Chang Valley was built. During the 300 years of the Tang Dynasty which followed, China became the world's most extensive empire. Paper money was adopted, block printing was invented, and priceless ceramic vases were produced. In these centuries and those of the Song Dynasty (AD 960–1269), China's popula-tion, threatened by incursions of nomads from the north, began to concentrate in the warmer, more productive south. By the thirteenth cen-tury most people lived in the south, including the Chang Valley. The Song Dynasty is some-times regarded as China's Golden Age. Trade with other nations expanded, and Chinese shipping took porcelain and silk to the East Indies, India, and Africa.

Northern invaders ended the Song Dynasty. By 1223 Ghengis Khan's Mongols held control over much of the north, and in 1260 Kublai Khan proclaimed himself emperor, with Beijing as his capital. Unified by the conquests of the

Mongol tribes, by 1300 the empire reached from Kiev to the Persian Gulf, and from Burma to Korea. Muslims, Christians, and Armenians all came to China at this time— among them possibly the Italian Marco Polo, who claimed in his writings that he served under Kublai Khan.

After the Mongols were overthrown, Chinese rule was re-established under the Ming Dynasty in 1368, and the Great Wall was restored and extended to its present length of 6,400 km (4,000 miles). During the three centuries of Ming rule numerous palaces were built, including the Imperial Palace at Beijing, and Chinese ships explored as far afield as the Red Sea. It was during this period that the first Christian missions began to appear in China: the Jesuits established themselves with the Portuguese at Macao in the sixteenth century.

Chinese civilization's main features, however, had been laid down in the time of the Han, Tang, and Song. During the rule of those dynasties Confucianism became the pervasive social ethic, which placed great value on the subordination of the individual to both family and state. In addition, porcelain manufacture and silk production reached a rare perfection; and various inventions were made which found their way to the West, most notably that of gunpowder and of paper. Despite the development of large cities and the growth of an educated bureaucratic elite, Chinese society remained largely agricultural, and its economic base depended on the productivity of the rural peasantry.

The Qing Dynasty (1683–1912) represented a return to power of northern people, the Manchus, descendants of the Mongols. Aggressive at first, seizing Taiwan and garrisoning Tibet, by the nineteenth century the Qing government had become weak. Famine and unrest had made the country vulnerable to external forces,and by the century's end China had been divided into spheres of influence among the major Western powers, a disintegration hastened by

peasant uprisings (the Taiping Rebellion of 1850–64) and military defeats (the Sino-Japanese War of 1894–95). In 1912 the last of China's emperors abdicated and a republic was proclaimed.

## Modern history

Political and military disorder prevailed during the next forty years. At first the country was fought over by rival warlords. Two hostile competing political movements offered solutions to this chaos—the Kuomintang (or Chinese National Party), and the Communist Party (founded in 1921)—but neither was able to assert overall control. Then in 1931 Japan seized Manchuria, and in 1937 war broke out between China and Japan. During this time the communists sharpened their military and political skills. Mao Zedong gained the support of the peasantry and demonstrated it could succeed at guerrilla warfare. Hostilities between the Kuomintang and the communists temporarily ceased in order to defeat Japan, but once this was achieved, in 1945, a civil war broke out that would claim over 12 million lives. Victory went to the communists, and the People's Republic of China was proclaimed in October 1949.

Mass starvation, malnutrition, and disease were brought under control in the inital years of communist rule and land reform was begun. As part of a planned economy the rural popula-tion was organized into 50,000 communes—units which farmed the land collectively. Communes also had responsibility for rural industries, schools, and clinics. During these years morale and dedication were high. Many of the former

middle class suffered grave priva-tions in "re-education camps", but living stan-dards improved for the majority, and corruption and bureaucratic sloth were not major problems.

Mao Zedong, however, was determined to push radical programs of industrialization and political change. In 1958 the "Great Leap Forward" initiative tried to industrialize the country using the organization of the communes, and to increase steel production by using backyard furnaces. It was a disaster of colossal proportions. Between 1959 and 1961, failed economic policies led to widespread famine, disease, and attempted rebellion. As many as 20 million people died.

Mao increasingly suspected his associates of disloyalty, believing some wanted to take "the capitalist road". In 1966 he launched the Great Proletarian Cultural Revolution to extirpate "old thought, old culture, old customs, and old habits". China's local authorities were, in effect, put on trial, many community members were abused and tormented, and the Red Guards rampaged through numerous cities destroying property and wrecking ancient works of art.

In 1967 the army was called in to restore order. Mao's death in 1976 brought change. There was even, in 1978, a brief flirtation with free speech. Deng Xiaoping, a new leader with a different vision of Chinese communism, yet no less determined to assert his power, began the process of economic liberalization that has led to today's state-managed capitalism and rigid political regime.

Taiwan and Tibet complicate China's relations with the West. China insists that Taiwan (the Republic of China) must rejoin the main-

| **Timeline** | | **460,000 BP** Earliest claimed evidence of controlled use of fire (Zhoukoudian Cave) by *Homo erectus,* called "Peking Man" | **7500 BC** Farmers of central and southern China domesticate foxtail millet and rice | **2600 BC** Writing system based on pictograms in use— many characters similar to those still used today | | **214 BC** First part of Great Wall of China completed under Qin Dynasty to protect against Turkish and Mongol invasions | **c. 100 AD** Paper made from hemp and rags in use with solid inks in north-west China | **1213** Genghis Khan leads Mongolian invasion—up to 30 million Chinese are slaughtered |
| --- | --- | --- | --- | --- | --- | --- | --- | --- |
| | **1.9 MYA** Appearance of early hominids who closely resemble *Homo habilis* (Longgupo Cave, Sichuan Province) | **800,000 BP** Hominid *Homo erectus,* now considered to have evolved in Asia; present in China possibly 1.8 MYA | **68,000 BP** *Homo sapiens sapiens* present in China | **5500 BC** First thick clay pottery used in fishing villages along southern coastline | **800 BC** Population more than 13 million under the Chou Dynasty | **206 BC** Shi Huangdi (First Emperor) is buried with 6,000 life-size terracotta warriors at Chang-an near Xi'an | **618** Tang Dynasty sees great economic development; Grand Canal links Huang and Chang rivers (completed 1283) | **1279** The Mongols under Kublai Khan (grandson of Genghis Khan) take control of all China; Beijing now the capital |

land as a province. In the case of Tibet, it may be that the exiled but highly popular religious leader, the Dalai Lama, has awakened unrealistic hopes for political independence. Tibet itself, however, has severely suffered under the regime, and thousands of its people have been killed. China's historic use of the region as a defensive bulwark in the west makes independence unlikely. Civil rights do not exist in other parts of China, either. Law is arbitrary, and courts are often conducted by army personnel without legal training. Students demonstrating for greater democracy in Beijing in 1989 were met with tanks and hundreds were killed and injured in the well-known Tiananmen Square massacre. In 1998, an attempt to organize an independent political party was put down and its leaders jailed. While the West did not cease its criticism of China's disregard for human rights, China hoped to present itself to the world as a modern and open country in the Olympic Games of summer 2008. But activists for the liberation of Tibet as well as for the religious freedom of Muslim Chinese also tried to use the games and the publicity leading up to them to attract worldwide public attention.

## The economy

China has plentiful and diverse natural resources. Coal deposits exist in most of its twenty-two provinces, and there are seventy

*Part of the Great Wall of China (left page top).*
*Girl eating noodles (left page bottom). Downtown*
*Hong Kong, seen from the air (right). A government*
*building in Shanhaiguan (below).*

major production centers: Hebei, Shanxi, Shandong, Jilin, and Anhui are the most important. China also has deposits of iron ore and is a major producer of tungsten. Industries produce iron, steel, coal, machinery, armaments, textiles, and petroleum. The main exports are textiles, chemicals, light industrial goods, armaments, oil, and oil products. This will soon change, though, as the rapid increase in automobile use in China in the early twenty-first century has already led to a drastic increase in fuel comsumption. China is on the verge of becoming a net importer of oil, and world oil prices are rising due to this increased demand. Questions about the Chinese economy do not center on resources, skills or capacity, but instead on the ideological clash between a market-oriented economy and the rigid controls of the Communist Party.

In 1978 the leadership began moving away from Soviet-style central planning. In agriculture, household responsibility replaced collectivization and brought an immediate rise in productivity. In industry, the decision-making power of plant managers and local officials was

increased, small-scale private enterprise was allowed, and foreign investment and trade were encouraged. As a result, agricultural output doubled in the 1980s and industry made major gains. Gross domestic product has increased tenfold since 1978, and today China is the second-largest economic power after the US.

The present system, however, combines the worst of communism (bureaucracy, inertia, and corruption) and capitalism (windfall gains and high inflation). Additional difficulties arise from revenue collection of every kind; from extortion and other economic malpractices; and from inefficient state enterprises. Between 100 and 150 million rural workers are adrift between country and city. Arable land is growing scarce. Serious environmental problems exist—air pollution from the use of coal, and water pollution from industrial effluents; falling water tables and nation-wide water shortages; and the fact that less than ten percent of sewage is treated.

### PROVINCES AND CAPITALS

**Anhui** • Hefei
**Fujian** • Fuzhou
**Gansu** • Lanzhou
**Guangdong** • Guangzhou
**Guizhou** • Guiyang
**Hainan** • Haikou
**Hebei** • Shijiazhuang
**Heilongjiang** • Harbin
**Henan** • Zhengzhou
**Hubei** • Wuhan
**Hunan** • Changsha
**Jiangsu** • Nanjing
**Jiangxi** • Nanchang
**Jilin** • Changchun
**Liaoning** • Shenyang
**Qinghai** • Xining
**Shaanxi** • Xi'an
**Shandong** • Jinan
**Shanxi** • Taiyuan
**Sichuan** • Chengdu
**Yunnan** • Kunming
**Zhejiang** • Hangzhou

### AUTONOMOUS REGIONS

**Guangxi Zhuangzu** • Nanning
**Nei Monggol** • Hohhot
**Ningxia Huizu** • Yinchuan
**Tibet (Xizang)** • Lhasa
**Xinjiang Uygur** • Ürümqi

### SPECIAL ADMINISTRATIVE REGIONS

**Xianggang (Hong Kong)** • Xianggang (Hong Kong)
**Macao** • Macao

### MUNICIPALITIES

**Beijing, Shanghai, and Tianjin**

| | | | | | | |
|---|---|---|---|---|---|---|
| **1275** Marco Polo, a Venetian, supposedly visits China (until 1292) to establish trade links with the country he calls "Cathay" | **1800** British smuggle in opium; war breaks out in 1839 when Chinese object. Treaty in 1842 ends war; China cedes Hong Kong to Britain | **1900** Chinese "Boxer" rebellion in Peking (Beijing) against foreign interests put down by British and Russian forces | **1927–28** Civil War between Communist party and Kuomintang under Chiang Kai-Shek; Nationalists take Beijing | **1949** Mao Zedong proclaims People's Republic of China after a four-year civil war costing 12 million lives | **1958** "Great Leap Forward" to foster development damages economy and leads to severe food shortages; 20 million die by 1962 | **1989** Pro-democracy demonstrations crushed by the use of tanks in Tiananmen Square, Beijing, with hundreds killed |
| | | | | | | **1997** China regains control of Hong Kong, imposes 'One China, two systems' policy |
| **1644** The Manchus establish Qing Dynasty, bringing peace and prosperity; the population rises to 200 million by 1700 | **1887–88** Huang River floods killing as many as 2.5 million people. It has flooded 1,500 times in the last 3,500 years | **1911** Rebels proclaim republic—Emperor Pu Yi abdicates in 1912. In 1913 Sun Yat-sen founds Kuomintang (Nationalist Party) | **1934** Mao Zedong leads Long March of the Communists across China | **1950** China invades Tibet; the Dalai Lama, Tibet's spiritual leader, flees to India | **1979** "One-child families" policy introduced to curb population growth | **1990** Census shows that China's population exceeds 1.1 billion people |
| | | | | | | **1998** Chang Jiang River floods kill 3,000 with 250,000 homeless |
| | | | | | | **1999** New constitution introduces "rule of law" |

# Taiwan

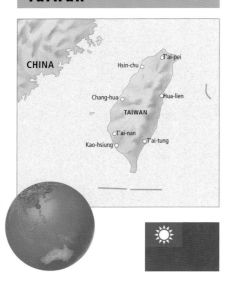

## Fact File

**OFFICIAL NAME** Republic of China

**FORM OF GOVERNMENT** Republic with two legislative bodies (National Assembly and Legislative Yuan)

**CAPITAL** T'ai-pei (Taipei)

**AREA** 35,980 sq km (13,892 sq miles)

**TIME ZONE** GMT + 8 hours

**POPULATION** 22,921,000

**PROJECTED POPULATION 2015** 23,600,000

**POPULATION DENSITY** 637 per sq km (1,649.9 per sq mile)

**LIFE EXPECTANCY** 77.8

**INFANT MORTALITY (PER 1,000)** 5.5

**OFFICIAL LANGUAGE** Mandarin Chinese

**OTHER LANGUAGES** Taiwanese, Min, Hakka, Malayo-Polynesian languages

**LITERACY RATE** 96,1 %

**RELIGIONS** Buddhist, Confucian, and Taoist 93 %; Christian 4.5 %; other 2.5 %

**ETHNIC GROUPS** Taiwanese 84 %, mainland Chinese 14 %, indigenous 2 %

**CURRENCY** New Taiwain dollar

**ECONOMY** Services 71.1 %, industry 27.5 %, agriculture 1.4 %

**GNI PER CAPITA** US$ 17,250

**CLIMATE** Tropical, with wet season May to September

**HIGHEST POINT** Yu Shan 3,997 m (13,113 ft)

**MAP REFERENCE** Page 206

Taiwan is a large island off the coast of China which, with support from the USA, has acted as a de facto independent country for the past 50 years. This is strongly opposed by China, which from the seventeenth century controlled the island and made it a Chinese province in the 1880s. However, Beijing has not had effective control of Taiwan for 100 years. It was ceded to Japan in 1895 (after Japanese victory in the Sino-Japanese War). From 1949 until the present it has been under the Nationalist Kuomintang (KMT),

who after being driven from mainland China by the communists in 1949 used Taiwan as their last refuge. Ruling dictatorially over the Taiwanese until 1987, the KMT turned the country into a political, military, and economic fortress.

Seated in the UN as the official representative of China for two decades, Taiwan was displaced in 1971, and still has a marginal status in the international community. Today, after democratic elections, multiple parties are represented in the National Assembly, and both the president and the prime minister are native-born Taiwanese.

High mountains extending the length of the island occupy the central and eastern parts of Taiwan. The mountains of the Central Range, or Taiwan Shan, are the top of a submerged mountain chain, and rise steeply up from the east coast. Lush vegetation is found through much of the interior—the poor commercial quality of most of the timber has preserved it as forest cover. Rising to altitudes of more than 3,000 m (10,000 ft), the lower slopes support evergreens such as camphor and Chinese cork oak, while further up pine, larch, and cedar dominate. Rice is grown on the well-watered lowlands of the western coastal plain. Other crops include sugarcane, sweet potatoes, tea, bananas, pineapples, and peanuts.

Economically, agriculture is now of less importance than Taiwan's thriving industrial sector. The country as a whole demonstrated an almost unprecedented growth rate of nine percent annually for three decades until 1996. During this period it was successively the world's biggest producer of television sets, watches, personal computers, and track shoes. Among Taiwan's strengths are its highly educated workforce, many US-trained, with an inside knowledge of the US market. Today the leading exports are electrical machinery, electronic products, textiles, footwear, foodstuffs, and plywood and wood products. With huge dollar reserves, Taiwan has become a major investor in China, Malaysia, and Vietnam. The Asian economic downturn in 1998 had a steadying effect. China insists upon reunification and has rejected calls for a peace summit made by the Democratic Progressive Party (DPP).

# North Korea

## The Korean War, 1950–53

Occupied by Japan from 1910 until the Second World War, in 1945 Korea found itself divided between a Soviet-controlled north and an American-controlled south, with a frontier along the 38th parallel. This de facto division of the peninsula was formalized in 1948. In June 1950 heavily armed troops and tanks from the communist People's Republic of North Korea invaded the south, precipitating three years of bitter conflict.

Authorised by a UN resolution, American and South Korean troops, supported by contingents from Britain, Canada, France, and other allies, then fought to reclaim southern territory under the UN flag. Their success soon had the North Koreans in retreat, and American seaborne landings put allied troops far behind the North Korean lines. A crisis then arose when the allied commander, General Douglas MacArthur, neared

## Fact File

**OFFICIAL NAME** Democratic People's Republic of Korea

**FORM OF GOVERNMENT** Communist state with single legislative body (Supreme People's Assembly)

**CAPITAL** P'yongyang

**AREA** 120,540 sq km (46,540 sq miles)

**TIME ZONE** GMT + 9 hours

**POPULATION** 23,479,000

**PROJECTED POPULATION 2015** 24,416,000

**POPULATION DENSITY** 194.8 per sq km (504.5 per sq mile)

**LIFE EXPECTANCY** 72.2

**INFANT MORTALITY (PER 1,000)** 21.9

**OFFICIAL LANGUAGE** Korean

**LITERACY RATE** 99 %

**RELIGIONS** Buddhist and Confucian 51 %, traditional beliefs (Shamanism, Chond-gyo) 25 %, Christian 4 %, other 20 %

**ETHNIC GROUPS** Korean 100 %

**CURRENCY** Won

**ECONOMY** Industry 43.1 %, services 33.6 %, agriculture 23.3 %

**GNI PER CAPITA** not available (less than US$ 935)

**CLIMATE** Temperate, with cold, snowy winters and warm, wet summers

**HIGHEST POINT** Mt Paektu 2,744 m (9,003 ft)

**MAP REFERENCE** Page 208

North Korea occupies the northern half of the Korean Peninsula. It is separated from South Korea along the ceasefire line that was established at the end of the Korean War (1950–53), roughly along the 38th parallel. After a period as an independent kingdom in the tenth century AD, control of Korea was disputed for hundreds of years between China and Japan, the latter seizing it as a colony in 1910. Following the Second World War it became a separate communist state and after the Korean War it developed into a rigidly closed totalitarian state system. The 50-year-long personal rule of Kim Il Sung ("Great Leader") passed by hereditary succession to his son Kim Jong Il ("Dear Leader") in 1994. The people of North Korea are classed by the state into three quasi-castes: loyal, wavering, and hostile. Membership of a caste determines whether an individual receives either education or employment. Citizens are subject to arbitrary arrest and execution for criticizing the Korean leaders or listening to foreign broadcasts. Unceasing political indoctrination takes place through the media, the workplace, the military, mass spectacles, and cultural events.

Mountains and rugged hills occupy most of the Korean Peninsula, and dominate its northern half. In the northeast the volcanic peak of Mt Paektu is surrounded by the Kaema Plateau. High forested mountains, cut by river gorges, lie along the border with Manchuria, northeast China. Other mountain chains extend north to south along the east coast. The Yalu River valley in the northwest marks the Korean-Chinese border, while to the southwest the fertile Chaeryŏng and Pyongyang plains are the main areas for agricultural activity. The principal crop is rice, followed by millet and other grains.

The North Korean economy is run according to the Stalinist model. More than 90 percent of operations are controlled by the state, agriculture is entirely collectivized, and state-owned industry produces 95 percent of all manufactured goods. Despite over 50 years of complete control by the state, the country is still not self-sufficient in food. The industrial sector produces military weapons, chemicals, minerals, along with a number of food products and textiles.

During the late 1990s the economy was in crisis: power supplies were unreliable and food shortages were causing famine in the countryside. North Korea continues to fall farther behind South Korean development and living standards. Instability in foreign affairs is caused by constant tensions with South Korea, the expulsion of UN observers from nuclear facilities, the country's possession of nuclear weapons, and underground nuclear testing carried out in 2008, exacerbated by the compelling suspicion that the country is trading with this technology, making it available to countries such as Syria.

the border of China. Hundreds of thousands of Chinese "volunteers" poured across the Yalu River into North Korea, and drove the allies far into the south once more. A counter-offensive in 1951 pushed the North Koreans and Chinese troops back to the vicinity of the 38th parallel, where an armistice took place in 1953.

After almost 40 years of tension and a series of minor military clashes a non-aggression pact was negotiated between North and South Korea in 1991. While the war resulted in North Korea becoming a rigid Stalinist state, it also ensured decades of US economic and military protection for South Korea.

For some the war is still not over: in October 1998 a 72-year-old South Korean soldier, who escaped from the north after 45 years as a prisoner-of-war, reported that 30 others like him were still being held in North Korean camps.

*Business street in Taipei (left page bottom).*
*Korean border posts on the 38th parallel (below center).*

## South Korea

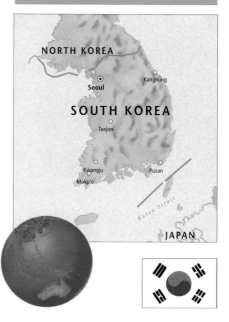

## Fact File

**OFFICIAL NAME** Republic of Korea

**FORM OF GOVERNMENT** Republic with single legislative body (National Assembly)

**CAPITAL** Seoul

**AREA** 98,480 sq km (38,023 sq miles)

**TIME ZONE** GMT +9 hours

**POPULATION** 49,233,000

**PROJECTED POPULATION 2015** 49,117,000

**POPULATION DENSITY** 499.9 per sq km (1,294.9 per sq mile)

**LIFE EXPECTANCY** 77.4

**INFANT MORTALITY (PER 1,000)** 5.9

**OFFICIAL LANGUAGE** Korean

**OTHER LANGUAGES** English, Japanese

**LITERACY RATE** 97.9 %

**RELIGIONS** Christianity 26.3 %, Buddhism 23.2 %, other 1.3 %, no religion 49.2 %

**ETHNIC GROUPS** Korean 99.9 %, Chinese 0.1 %

**CURRENCY** Won

**ECONOMY** Services 57.6 %, industry 39.4 %, agriculture 3 %

**GNI PER CAPITA** US$ 19,690

**CLIMATE** Temperate, with cold winters and hot, wet summers

**HIGHEST POINT** Halla-san 1,950 m (6,398 ft)

**MAP REFERENCE** Page 208

South Korea occupies the southern half of the Korean Peninsula. The border between South and North Korea consists of the ceasefire line established at the end of the Korean War (1950–53), roughly corresponding to the original pre-1950 border at the 38th parallel. The kingdom of Korea was dominated by either China or Japan for many centuries and finally annexed by Japan in 1910. After Japan's defeat at the

Asia and the Middle East

## Japan

end of the Second World War, Korea was divided between a northern Soviet zone of influence, and a southern zone under US control. These zones soon became separate political entities. In 1950 communist North Korea invaded South Korea, and though the war ended in a stalemate in 1953, bitter hostility between north and south endures to the present day, with covert operations continuing.

In the 40-year period following 1953, both Koreas diverged socially, politically, and economically. South Korea, after a few years under the authoritarian rule of its first president, established constitutional liberalism in the Second Republic of 1960. From then until his assassination in 1979 it was under the elected presidency of General Park Chung Hee, who laid the basis for the economic success of the modern South Korean state with a combination of state planning and free-market incentives.

While questionable practices flourished at the top (two former presidents have been jailed) the country achieved a remarkable record of growth. Only 40 years ago its standard of living was much the same as the poorer countries of Africa. Today its gross domestic product per capita is seven times India's, thirteen times North Korea's, and on a par with some economies of the European Union. Regionally, its technological and scientific prowess is second only to Japan's.

More than 80 percent of South Korea's terrain is mountainous. Along the eastern side of the country the Tabaek-Sanmaek Mountains descend north to southwest. The Han and Naktong Rivers

drain from these mountains through low-lying plains—the Han to the northwest, the Naktong to the south. Densely populated and intensively farmed, these plains cover 15 percent of South Korea's total land area. Rice, a staple crop in which the country is almost self-sufficient, is grown on family-owned farms. Other food crops include barley and fruit such as apples, grapes, peaches, nectarines, and plums. Silk and tobacco are produced for the export market.

About two-thirds of South Korea is forested. As many as 3,000 small islands lie off the west and south coasts, including Cheju which has South Korea's highest peak, the extinct volcano Halla-san at 1,950 m (6,398 ft).

There is little at the high-tech end of modern industry that South Korea does not manufacture and sell. It produces electronic equipment, machinery, ships, and automobiles. Textiles, an early item in its drive for export success, remain significant, along with clothing, food processing, chemicals, and steel. Real gross domestic product grew by an average of ten percent from 1986 to 1991, then tapered off. With the downturn in the Asian economies in 1998 the economy shrank for the first time in years, but the country won praise from the IMF (International Monetary Fund) for acting promptly in order to wipe out billions in bad bank loans and purge companies that were unviable.

*A broad avenue in Seoul, South Korea (above). Rural scenery in South Korea (below). A traditional house in rural Japan (right page top). The Ginza district in Tokyo, Japan (left).*

### Fact File

**OFFICIAL NAME** Japan

**FORM OF GOVERNMENT** Constitutional monarchy with two legislative bodies (House of Councillors and House of Representatives)

**CAPITAL** Tokyo

**AREA** 377,835 sq km (145,882 sq miles)

**TIME ZONE** GMT +9 hours

**POPULATION** 127,288,000

**PROJECTED POPULATION 2015** 126,607,000

**POPULATION DENSITY** 336.9 per sq km (872.5 per sq mile)

**LIFE EXPECTANCY** 82.1

**INFANT MORTALITY (PER 1,000)** 2.8

**OFFICIAL LANGUAGE** Japanese

**LITERACY RATE** 99 %

**RELIGIONS** Shinto and Buddhist 84 %, other (including Christian 0.7 %) 16 %

**ETHNIC GROUPS** Japanese 98.5 %, Korean 0.5 %, Chinese 0.4 %, other 0.6 %

**CURRENCY** Yen

**ECONOMY** Services 72 %, industry 26.5 %, agriculture 1.5 %

**GNI PER CAPITA** US$ 37,670

**CLIMATE** Ranges from cold temperate in north to subtropical in south; wet season June to July

### Timeline

| | 660 BC Legendary leader Jimmu Tenno is Japan's first emperor and founds imperial dynasty which still holds office today | AD 200 In the Yayoi peri (until c. AD 700) ric grown in irrigated fie and people live in villa protected by moats a wooden palisa |
|---|---|---|
| **4500 BC** Islands of Japan inhabited by peoples from Asia. They are later known as Jomon after their pottery | **c. 1500 BC** Rice is introduced from China and cultivated in the islands for the first time | **400 BC** Wet rice farming introduce from Korean penin intensive agricultur enables larger pop ulation to survive |

**HIGHEST POINT** Fuji-san (Mt Fuji) 3,776 m (12,388 ft)

**MAP REFERENCE** Pages 208–09

Mainly mountainous, with intensively cultivated coastal plains, the archipelago of Japan lies off the east Asian coast close to Korea and China. By the early 1990s it had become an industrial and trading colossus second only to the USA. But cracks in the country's apparently impregnable economic facade began to appear in 1998 as the yen slid steadily against the dollar. The nation's vast scientific and technological resources, its highly educated personnel, and its substantial trade surpluses mean that it is better placed than most countries to cope with this and other problems.

## History

First populated by migrants from mainland Asia, by the fifth century AD Japan was controlled by a number of clans. During the next 300 years several features of Chinese civilization were introduced, including Buddhism, Chinese script, and methods of administration, while cities modeled on those of the Tang Dynasty were built at Nara (AD 710) and Kyoto (AD 794). Centralized government, however, failed to eventuate and the clan basis of society prevailed. From the twelfth century until the rise of the Tokugawas, power was held by rival groups of feudal lords, or shoguns, and the emperor was a largely symbolic figure. Lasting from 1192 to 1867, the shogun era fostered an ethical code known as bushido (the path of the warrior, or samurai) that stressed loyalty, frugality, and courage.

Until 1945 Japan remained unconquered. Two Mongol fleets sent to invade the country were destroyed by typhoons in 1274 and 1281, founding the legend of a kamikaze or "divine wind" sent to protect "the land of the Gods". From 1603 a form of semi-centralized feudal rule was imposed by the ruling shogunate, the Tokugawas. Under this family, some 250 daimyo (or "great names") ran their own estates watched by state inspectors and a network of spies. Western influence appeared briefly in 1542, when missionaries arrived from Macao bringing clocks, carpets, guns, and Christianity. The reaction of the Tokugawas was to close the door: from 1639 Japan's citizens were not allowed to travel abroad, and trading contacts were limited to a single Dutch settlement at Nagasaki.

This ended in 1853 when Commodore Perry of the US Navy brought a squadron of warships into Yokohama Harbor, demanding that the country's ports be opened to Western trade. The now weak Tokugawa shogunate collapsed, imperial rule was resumed under the Meiji Restoration, and within 50 years Japan had become westernized and a rising industrial force. Victories in wars with China (1894–95) and Russia (1904–05) led to the seizure of Taiwan and Korea. Expanding imperial ambi-

tions led later to the invasion of China, and eventually, in 1941, to an attack on Hawaii and Japan's entry into the Second World War. Allied victory in 1945 was followed by the introduction of a liberal, US-imposed democratic constitution which has since guided the nation's development.

## Physical features and land use

Four large islands, so closely grouped that bridges and a tunnel now connect them, make up 98 percent of Japan's territory. They occupy a highly unstable zone on the earth's crust, and earthquakes and volcanic eruptions are frequent: 140,000 died in the 1923 earthquake which hit Yokohama and part of Tokyo; 6,000 died in the Kobe earthquake of January 1995. Folding and faulting has produced a mosaic of landforms throughout Japan, mountains and hills alternating with small basins and coastal plains. Inland there are several calderas and volcanic cones, the most famous being Fuji-san (3,776 m; 12,388 ft), the highest mountain in Japan, which last erupted in 1707.

Hokkaido, the northernmost of the main islands, is the most rural and traditional. Japan's biggest and most productive farming region, it has a climate similar to the US midwest—which may be why American advisors established wheat farming there in the 1860s. Hokkaido now produces more than half of Japan's grains. Southwest of Hokkaido lies the island of Honshu, where the Japanese Alps provide spectacular scenery. The Kanto Plain where Tokyo stands is the largest of various small alluvial plains, their soils enriched by centuries of careful cultivation. Today the conurbation this plain supports is Japan's most heavily industrialized and densely populated region. From southwestern Honshu across the two southern islands of Shikoku and Kyushu a complex of mountain peaks and undulating uplands stretches down to the Ryukyu Islands (Nansei-Shotō), which includes Okinawa, before extending south toward Taiwan.

## Economy

Japan's economy is notable for government-industry cooperation, a motivated population with a strong work ethic, high educational levels, and a mastery of high technology. These factors combined with a small defense allocation (one percent of gross domestic product) have made it one of the most powerful economies in the industrialized world. Japan is one of the world's largest and most advanced producers of steel and non-ferrous metallurgy, heavy electrical equipment, construction and mining equipment, motor vehicles and parts, communications and electronic equipment, machine tools, automated production systems, railroad rolling stock, ships, chemicals, textiles, and processed foods. Industry depends heavily on imported raw materials and fuel. The small agricultural sector is highly protected and subsidized; its crop yields are among the world's highest. Self-sufficient in rice, Japan imports about fifty percent of its other grain needs. After decades of spectacular growth, the late 1990s saw a marked contraction. In 2000/2001, efforts to revive economic growth were hampered by the slow US, European, and Asian economies. After 2002, growth improved. Japan's huge government debt—176% of its GDP—and the aging of the population are two major longterm problems.

| 550 Buddhism introduced from China | 1281 Mongol conqueror Kublai Khan's invasion plans fail when his fleet is destroyed by a typhoon | 1600 Honshu, Shikoku, and Kyushu united under the Tokugawa shogunate which rules for more than 250 years | 1730 An earthquake on the island of Hokkaido causes the deaths of 137,000 people | 1883 Tsunami kills 30,000 people. Three years later a tsunami occurs off Honshu and kills 28,000 people | 1945 USA drops atomic bombs, destroying Hiroshima and Nagasaki. Second World War ends | 1994 Population of Tokyo-Yokohama exceeds 8 million | 2003 For the first time since World War II, Japan deploys military troops overseas, in Iraq |
|---|---|---|---|---|---|---|---|
| 300 Large-scale immigration from the Asian continent until around 750 leads to a big increase in the population | 794 Japanese capital moves from Nara, the eastern end of the Tang Silk Road trade route, to Heian (called later Kyoto) until 1185 | 1543 Portuguese sailors visit islands of southern Kyushu, making Europe aware of the wealth of the Japanese islands | 1707 Mt Fuji, Japan's biggest volcano, erupts | 1875 Population reaches more than 35 million; Tokyo 1 million by end of the century | 1923 The Great Kanto earthquake, fires, and tsunamis destroy much of Tokyo-Yokohama and kill more than 140,000 people | 1964 Shinkansen high-speed "bullet train" links Tokyo and Kyoto traveling at speeds of 210 km (130 miles) an hour | 1995 Earthquake destroys much of Kobe city and kills 6,000 people |

## Indian subcontinent

| | |
|---|---|
| Sri Lanka | 166 |
| Maldives | 167 |
| India | 167 |
| Bangladesh | 170 |
| Bhutan | 171 |
| Nepal | 172 |
| Pakistan | 173 |

## Sri Lanka

HIGHEST POINT  Mt Pidurutalagala 2,524 m (8,281 ft)

MAP REFERENCE  Page 216–17

### Fact File

OFFICIAL NAME  Democratic Socialist Republic of Sri Lanka

FORM OF GOVERNMENT  Republic with single legislative body (Parliament)

CAPITAL  Colombo (Sri Jayawardanapura-Kotte)

AREA  65,610 sq km (25,332 sq miles)

TIME ZONE  GMT + 5.5 hours

POPULATION  21,129,000

PROJECTED POPULATION 2015  19,960,000

POPULATION DENSITY  322 per sq km (834.1 per sq mile)

LIFE EXPECTANCY  75

INFANT MORTALITY (PER 1,000)  19

OFFICIAL LANGUAGES  Sinhala, Tamil

OTHER LANGUAGES  Malayan, English

LITERACY RATE  90.7 %

RELIGIONS  Buddhist 69.1 %, Muslim 7.6 %, Hindu 7.1 %, Christian 6.2 %, other 10 %

ETHNIC GROUPS  Sinhalese 73.8 %, Tamil 8.5 %, Sri Lankan Moor 7.2 %, other 10.5 %

CURRENCY  Sri Lankan rupee

ECONOMY  Services 56.5 %, industry 26.9 %, agriculture 16.6 %

GNI PER CAPITA  US$ 1,540

CLIMATE  Tropical; southwest wetter with most rain falling April to June and October to November; northeast drier with most rain falling December to February

Sri Lanka is a large, scenically dramatic island off India's southeast coast, and was known as Ceylon until 1972. It has a mountainous center, and a string of coral islets called "Adam's Bridge" link it to India in the northwest. Over the last 50 years the country has suffered intermittent strife. For over 1,000 years a minority of Hindu Tamils in the north and a majority of Sinhalese elsewhere have lived side by side. From the sixteenth century successive European nations—the Portuguese, the Dutch, and the British—visited and left their ethnic mark. Britain controlled the whole island from 1815, and brought in large numbers of additional Tamil plantation workers from south India later that century.

When Sri Lanka gained its independence in 1948 the majority Sinhalese stripped 800,000 Tamils of citizenship and the right to vote, and made Sinhala the country's sole official language. From that point onwards there has been civil unrest and from 1983 there has been civil war. The Tamil demand for an autonomous northern state has been complicated by separate leftist insurrections by radical Sinhalese seeking to overthrow the government. From 2002 to 2008, a ceasefire negotiated by Norway was in place. On May 17, 2009, the Tamil separatist movement (Tamil Tigers) conceded its defeat. On May 18, their leader was killed, likely putting an end to the bloody civil war. At the same time, the myriad of political parties and movements bring discord into political discourse, and the approximately 90,000 lives lost in the course of the conflict will make reconciliation and a new beginning difficult.

With high mountains, intermontane plateaus, and steep river gorges, the rugged terrain of the central uplands dominates the island. Much of this higher ground is devoted to growing tea on large plantations. Overall, 37 percent of the country supports tropical vegetation and open woodland. Though it has been reduced by deforestation, rainforest still covers the wettest areas. The fertile, rice-growing northern plains are bordered to the southeast by the Mahaweli River.

Among Sri Lanka's mineral resources are a variety of precious and semi-precious stones including sapphire, ruby, tourmaline, and topaz. Also mined are graphite, mineral sands, and phosphates. About 43 percent of the workforce is engaged in agriculture, the main subsistence crop being rice—although production falls considerably short of the country's requirements. Fruit, vegetables, and spices are grown as staples as well as for export and Sri Lanka is one of the world's main exporters of tea. But today industry, dominated by the manufacture of clothing and expanding in special Export Processing Zones, has overtaken agriculture as the principal source of export earnings. The extent to which Sri Lanka's future prospects will be improved by the new political situation is not yet clear. Currently the country is still saddled with an uncertain economic climate that deters tourism and discourages foreign investors.

# Maldives

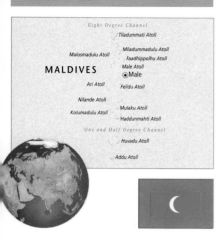

today the people are mainly Sunni Muslims and there are 689 mosques. For the next 800 years the islands were ruled as a Muslim sultanate, though there was a brief period, between 1558 and 1573, of Portuguese control from Goa. The British established a protectorate in 1887, the islands achieved independence in 1965, and the sultan was deposed in 1968. Since then, political power has been concentrated in the hands of a few influential families. Widespread riots in 2004 and 2005 weakened the government and finally led to democratic elections in 2008. The new president established a foundation funded by revenue from tourism, intended to finance the purchase of land in case the effects of global warming make the Maldives, which are barely above sea level, uninhabitable. Under consideration are areas in India, Sri Lanka, and Australia.

The atolls of the Maldives are coral reefs which have grown up around the peaks of a submerged volcanic mountain range. None of them rise more than 1.8 m (6 ft) and 80 percent of the entire country is less than 1 m (3 ft) above sea level. There is serious concern that if the greenhouse effect causes a rise in sea levels, some may be submerged. Apart from that, the islands lose their natural protection due to the depletion of the reef—coral lime is often used as building material.

Food crops include coconuts, bananas, mangoes, sweet potatoes, and spices. Agriculture plays a role in the economy, though constrained by the small amount of cultivable land, and most staple foods must be imported. In the lagoons and the open sea fish are plentiful. Bonito and tuna are leading exports, fishing being the second leading growth sector of the economy. Manufacturing, consisting mainly of garment production, boat building, and handicrafts, accounts for 15 percent of gross domestic product. Since the 1980s tourism has been the leading growth sector, and now accounts for more than 60 percent of foreign exchange receipts. At present more than 90 percent of tax revenue comes from import duties and tourism-related taxes.

## Fact File

OFFICIAL NAME  Republic of the Maldives

FORM OF GOVERNMENT  Republic with single legislative body (Citizens Council)

CAPITAL  Male

AREA  300 sq km (116 sq miles)

TIME ZONE  GMT + 5 hours

POPULATION  379,000

PROJECTED POPULATION 2015  353,000

POPULATION DENSITY  1,263.3 per sq km (3,267.2 per sq mile)

LIFE EXPECTANCY  65.1

INFANT MORTALITY (PER 1,000)  51.6

OFFICIAL LANGUAGE  Divehi

OTHER LANGUAGES  Arabic, English, Hindi

LITERACY RATE  96.3 %

RELIGIONS  Predominantly Sunni Muslim

ETHNIC GROUPS  Sinhalese, Dravidian, Arab, African

CURRENCY  Rufiyaa

ECONOMY  Services 77 %, agriculture 16 %, industry 7 %

GNI PER CAPITA  US$ 3,200

CLIMATE  Tropical, with wet season May to August

HIGHEST POINT  Unnamed location on Wilingili 2.4 m (7.9 ft)

MAP REFERENCE  Page 216

The Maldive Archipelago consists of an 800 km (500 mile) string of nearly 2,000 islands and atolls (202 of them inhabited) southwest of India's southern tip, Cape Comorin. Made up of tiny islets ringed by white sands and clear blue lagoons, they have recently been developed as tourist resorts and receive up to 300,000 visitors each year. Long ago, their first visitors were probably Dravidians from southern India, in around 400 BC. Centuries later, the islands seem to have been taken over by people from Sri Lanka—Divehi, the national language, is a form of Sinhalese, one of the official languages on Sri Lanka. In 1153 the king of the Maldives ordered his subjects to adopt Islam in place of Buddhism:

# India

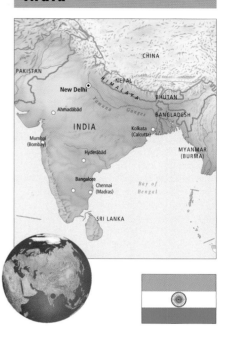

## Fact File

OFFICIAL NAME  Republic of India

FORM OF GOVERNMENT  Federal republic with two legislative bodies (Council of States and People's Assembly)

CAPITAL  New Delhi

AREA  3,287,590 sq km (1,269,338 sq miles)

TIME ZONE  GMT + 5.5 hours

POPULATION  1,147,996,000

PROJECTED POPULATION 2015  1,302,535,000

POPULATION DENSITY  349.2 per sq km (904.4 per sq mile)

LIFE EXPECTANCY  69.3

INFANT MORTALITY (PER 1,000)  32.3

OFFICIAL LANGUAGES  Hindi, Bengali, Telugu, Marathi, Tamil, Urdu, Gujarati, Malayalam, Kannada, Oriya, Punjabi, Assamese, Kashmiri, Sindhi, Sanskrit, English

OTHER LANGUAGES  Hindustani, about 700 indigenous languages

LITERACY RATE  61 %

RELIGIONS  Hindu 80.5 %, Muslim 13.4 %, Christian 2.3 %, Sikh 1.9 %, Buddhist 0.7 %, Jain 0.5 %, other 0.7 %

ETHNIC GROUPS  Indo-Aryan 72 %, Dravidian 25 %, Mongoloid and other 3 %

CURRENCY  Indian rupee

ECONOMY  Services 52.9 %, industry 29.4 %, agriculture 17.7 %

GNI PER CAPITA  US$ 950

*Tea pickers on a tea estate in the highlands of Sri Lanka (left page top). The facade of a Hindu temple in Sri Lanka (left page bottom). One of the many palm-fringed beaches in the Maldives (below).*

CLIMATE Tropical in south, temperate in north;
monsoons June to September

HIGHEST POINT Kanchenjunga 8,598 m (28,208 ft)

MAP REFERENCE Pages 216–17, 218–19

India is the world's largest democracy, and
one of the oldest and most successful in
Asia. It is also the world's second most populous country, encompassing a great variety
of peoples, several major religious groupings,
and more than 700 languages. In the fifty plus
years since it gained independence from Britain
in 1947, India has on the whole managed
humanely and responsibly where other
countries in the region have become totalitarian, or succumbed to military rule.

There are, however, major conflicts—
there have been three wars with neighboring
Pakistan alone. The dispute with Pakistan over
the territory of Kashmir remains unresolved. The
caste system produces endemic injustice. Millions
of its citizens live in desperate poverty. But
Indians can change their government democratically by going to the polls, and the lot of most
people has slowly but steadily improved. After
a long period of state regulation of industry,
significant barriers that hinder outside investment, and a maze of protectionist controls, the
country is beginning to open its economy to
the outside world. Population growth, however,
at a rate of more than 1.5 percent on a base of
almost 1.2 billion people, tends to cancel out
much of the potential benefit from the nation's
gains.

### Physical features and land use

North to south, India can be divided into three
main regions: the Himalayas and their foothills;
the Indo-Gangetic Plain; and the Deccan
Plateau. From the northernmost border, the
heavily glaciated terrain of the Himalayas—the
world's highest mountains—cover 15 percent
of the total surface area. The name itself comes
from the Nepalese *him* ("snows") and *alya*
("home of"), the mountains being revered as
the home of the gods. They rise to elevations
of over 7,000 m (23,000 ft) in the Ladakh and
Karakoram ranges. The western highlands
towards the Karakorams are harsh, dry, and
inhabited only by small communities of herds-
people. At lower altitudes alpine meadows are
grazed by the sheep of migratory pastoralists
who arrive in the summer with their flocks.
Lower still, rice terraces and orchards are
found in the Vale of Kashmir.

The eastern highlands of northern Assam
are markedly different. They are much wetter—
this is where rhododendrons and magnolias
grow wild and where terraced hills support
buckwheat, barley, and rice. The climate of
the high plateau of Meghalaya, separated from
the Himalayas by the valley of the Brahmaputra River, is damp and cool. On its southern
flanks Cherrapunji has one of the world's highest rainfalls, averaging 10,798 mm (421.1 in)
per year.

South of the northern mountains lie the terai
or foothill plains; still further south the main
plains region of India stretches from the western
coastal lowlands, in a northern arc past the Thar

Desert and down the Gangetic Plain to the
mouth of the Hooghly River on the Bay of
Bengal. In the northwest—the Punjab and
Haryana—farmers grow winter wheat, summer
rice, cotton, and sugarcane, with sorghum in
the drier areas. On the lowlands of the central
part of Uttar Pradesh millet and sorghum
are preferred to wheat and rice. Jute is cultivated where the Ganges enters the distribu-

| Timeline | | | 530 BC First invasion by Persians (Iranians) who sieze Gandhara (now Afghanistan) and parts of Punjab | 326 BC Alexander the Great invades India near the Indus River (now Pakistan) but is unable to sustain the colony when attacked | 300 AD Gupta Dynasty begins. Separate kingdoms allowed to prosper within the Gupta Empire for 200 years | 1497 Vasco da Gama reaches trading port of Calicut; Portuguese later establish trading supremacy in Indian Ocean | 1526 Babar conquers northern India, establishing Mogul Empire. Empire prospers for 200 years | 1632 Taj Mahal built at Agra by Emperor Shah Jehan in memory of his wife Mumtaz Mahal (completed 1643) |
|---|---|---|---|---|---|---|---|---|
| | c. 3500 BC First civilizations in Indus Valley (now Pakistan)—planting crops and domesticating sheep, cattle, and goats | 2600 BC Dravidian peoples develop cities of Harappa and Mohenjo Daro in Indus Valley | 1500 BC Aryan tribes from central Asia force Dravidians southward. Aryans plant wheat and barley, and introduce caste system | c. 500 BC Buddhism becomes widely accepted over the next 300 years but Hinduism eventually predominates | 320 BC Maurya Dynasty (until c. 185 BC) rules an empire covering almost all India from a base at Patna | 1200 Delhi Sultanate brings Muslim rule to India, destroying many Hindu temples and building great mosques in their place | 1555 Emperor Akbar the Great, regarded as the greatest of the Moguls, subdues Rajput princes to control India | |

## STATES AND CAPITALS

**Andhra Pradesh** • Hyderabad
**Arunachal Pradesh** • Itanagar
**Assam** • Dispur
**Bihar** • Patna
**Goa** • Panaji
**Gujarat** • Gandhinagar
**Haryana** • Chandigarh
**Himachal Pradesh** • Simla
**Jammu and Kashmir** • Srinagar (summer)
Jammu (winter)
**Karnataka** • Bangalore
**Kerala** • Trivandrum
**Madhya Pradesh** • Bhopal
**Maharashtra** • Mumbai (Bombay)
**Manipur** • Imphal
**Meghalaya** • Shillong
**Mizoram** • Aizawl
**Nagaland** • Kohima
**Orissa** • Bhubaneswar
**Punjab** • Chandigarh
**Rajastan** • Jaipur
**Sikkim** • Gangtok
**Tamil Nadu** • Chennai (Madras)
**Tripura** • Agartala
**Uttar Pradesh** • Lucknow
**West Bengal** • Kolkata (Calcutta)

## UNION TERRITORIES

**Andaman and Nicobar Islands** • Port Blair
**Chandigarh** • Chandigarh
**Dadra and Nagar Haveli** • Silvassa
**Daman and Diu** • Daman
**Delhi** • Delhi
**Lakshadweep** • Kavaratti
**Pondicherry** • Pondicherry

tary system of the delta, while mangrove swamps line the marine margins of the delta itself.

The Thar Desert in the northwest contains a broad area of dunes in Rajasthan; southwest of this lie the cotton-growing lands of Gujarat, which includes the low peninsular plateau of Kathiawar between the Gulf of Khambhat and the Gulf of Khachchh, not far from the Pakistan border. The Vindya Range east of the Gulf of Khambhat separates the Indo-Gangetic Plain from peninsular India and the Deccan Plateau. This plateau contains some of the world's oldest rocks, large tracts being covered with later basalt flows. The western edge of the plateau is defined by the mountain chain of the Western Ghats. At the foot of these mountains lies a coastal plain with coconut groves, fishing villages, rice fields, and tapioca plantations. On the plateau itself the main crops are millet and pulses.

### History

Of India's various civilizations, the earliest developed in the Indus Valley (c. 2600 BC) and in the Ganges Valley (c. 1500 BC). At this time the subcontinent was mainly peopled by ethnic Dravidians. It is thought that the Indus civilization succumbed to an invasion of Sanskrit-speaking Aryan peoples who introduced the caste system, a scheme of social division that is fundamental in Indian life. Another important early civilization was the Maurya, which under Ashoka, who reigned

*Women washing clothes beside the Ganges in Varanasi (left page bottom left). Drying chilis in Rajasthan (left page bottom right). The Taj Mahal near Agra (top center). The severe poverty of innumerable people such as those here in the streets of Varanasi is one of the major problems in India (above).*

from 273 to 232 BC, came to dominate the subcontinent. Later, a succession of Arab, Turkish, and Mongol influences led to the founding of the Mogul Empire in 1526, which under Akbar (1542–1605) was extended throughout most of northern India and part of the Deccan. It was during the time of Mogul rule that the Taj Mahal was built by Shah Jahan.

The British effectively controlled India from 1805, introducing a civil service and a code of law during the nineteenth century which have profoundly shaped the nation since that time. With the advent of independence in 1947, the division between Hindus and Muslims resulted in the violent and tumultuous partition of the country into India and Pakistan. This first major division to split the country indicates that the most serious rifts within Indian society tend to be religious. In recent years the Sikhs of the Punjab have also been agitating for independence.

### Economy

Once essentially rural, India's economy is now a mix of village farming, modern agriculture, handicrafts, a variety of modern industries, and innumerable support services. During the 1980s economic growth allowed a marked increase in real per capita private consumption. Since 1991 production, trade, and investment reforms have provided new opportunities for Indian business and some 200 million middle-class consumers. Among the nation's strengths is a home market of some 1,100 million, along with a workforce that includes many who are highly skilled, including those trained in high-tech areas such as computer programming.

The textile sector is highly efficient. There has been a massive rise in foreign investment as the country has been opened up to foreign competition. The downside of this situation includes a sizeable budget deficit along with high defense spending (including that for nuclear weapons) because of the continuing conflict with Pakistan. Other negative features include an absence of even elementary social services, poor roads, inadequate port facilities, and an antiquated telecommunications system.

| | | | | | | | | |
|---|---|---|---|---|---|---|---|---|
| **1769** Severe famines in Bengal lead to rural depopulation for more than 20 years | **1857** Indian Revolt against heavy taxes results in considerable loss of British and Indian lives. It is ruthlessly suppressed | **1876** Queen Victoria becomes Empress of India | **1883** Commission on famine recommends building irrigation canals to supply water from Himalayas to grain-producing areas | **1943** Severe food shortages in Bengal made worse by the army using scarce supplies results in loss of many lives | **1965** Border war with Pakistan over Kashmir | **1998** India tests nuclear weapons, followed by Pakistan; tension over Kashmir issue continues | **2004** A tidal wave caused by an earthquake on the sea bed claims around 19,000 lives |
| **1740** East India Co (founded 1600) takes over Mogul land. Dutch, British establish ports at Madras, Bombay, Calcutta | **1800** East India Co trades between Britain, Europe, China. India produces raw materials for British factories | **1850** Failure of monsoon rains causes famines in northern India for more than 30 years | **1880s** Indian Nationalist Movement begins pressure for an end to British rule; violent attacks by extremists | **1921** After more than 12 million deaths in flu epidemic of 1918–19 India's population surges; by 1921 it passes 250 million | **1947** India gains independence. Pakistan becomes a separate Muslim state (East and West). India takes over Kashmir | **1971** East Pakistan becomes independent country of Bangladesh; India's population reaches 500 million | **2001, 2002** Severe terrorist attacks are blamed on Pakistan and lead India and Pakistan to the brink of a nuclear war |

# Bangladesh

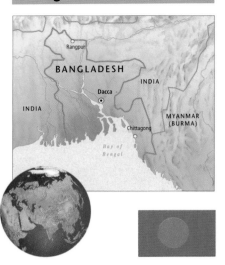

## Fact File

**OFFICIAL NAME** People's Republic of Bangladesh

**FORM OF GOVERNMENT** Republic with single legislative body (National Parliament)

**CAPITAL** Dacca

**AREA** 144,000 sq km (55,598 sq miles)

**TIME ZONE** GMT + 6 hours

**POPULATION** 153,547,000

**PROJECTED POPULATION 2015** 180,114,000

**POPULATION DENSITY** 1066.3 per sq km (2,761.7 per sq mile)

**LIFE EXPECTANCY** 63.2

**INFANT MORTALITY (PER 1,000)** 57.5

**OFFICIAL LANGUAGE** Bangla

**OTHER LANGUAGES** Other Indo-Aryan as well as Tibeto-Burmese languages, Munda, Mon-Khmer-languages, English

**LITERACY RATE** 43.1 %

**RELIGIONS** Muslim 83 %, Hindu 16 %, other (mainly Buddhist, Christian) 1 %

**ETHNIC GROUPS** Bengali 98 %, Biharis and tribal peoples 2 %

**CURRENCY** Taka

**ECONOMY** Services 52.3 %, industry 28.7 %, agriculture 19 %

**GNI PER CAPITA** US$ 470

**CLIMATE** Tropical, with three seasons: cool, dry winter (October to March); hot, humid summer (March to June); and cool, wet monsoon (June to October)

**HIGHEST POINT** Mt Keokradong 1,230 m (4,035 ft)

**MAP REFERENCE** Page 219

Known for tropical cyclones and endemic poverty, the small and densely populated country of Bangladesh lies north of the Bay of Bengal. Most of its frontier is with India and it has a short border with Myanmar (Burma) in the southeast. The name Bangladesh means "the land of the Bengalis", a

people who have contributed a great deal to Indian history. Once a part of the Mauryan Empire of the fourth century BC, Bengal has been mainly Muslim since the thirteenth century, though during its more recent history its Muslim people have often been ruled by Hindu overlords. At the time of the partition of India in 1947, this situation led to the founding of East Pakistan, the oriental wing of the Muslim state that was set up following independence from Britain. In 1971 resentment of the power and privileges accorded to West Pakistan resulted in East Pakistan breaking away and forming the independent state of Bangladesh. Since then its history has been one of political coups, dissolved parliaments and civil unrest, compounded by recurring natural disasters. In 1991 the worst cyclone in memory killed over 140,000 people.

Bangladesh is low and flat, its physiography determined by three navigable rivers—the Ganges (Padma), Brahmaputra (Jamuna) and the smaller Meghna. At their confluence they form the biggest delta in the world. The western part of this delta, which is over the border in India, is somewhat higher, and is less subject to flooding. What is called the "active delta"

*Bangladeshi women doing agricultural work (top). Bus station in Dacca, Bangladesh (above). The Taksang monastery in Bhutan (right page bottom).*

lies in Bangladesh and this region is frequently flooded. During monsoons the water rises as much as 6 m (18 ft) above sea level, submerging two-thirds of the country, and the delta's changing channels are also hazardous to life, health, and property. However, the floods are also beneficial in that they renew soil fertility with silt, some of it washed down from as far away as Tibet. Whole new islands are formed by alluvial deposition, and the highly fertile silt can yield as many as three rice crops a year. The far southeastern region of Chittagong has the only high country in Bangladesh, with forested ridges and rubber plantations.

Bangladesh is a major recipient of international aid. Disbursements of aid are currently running at more than 1,000 times the annual value of foreign investment. Despite the efforts of the international community, however, it remains one of the world's poorest and least developed nations. Rice is the main crop in the country's basically agrarian economy, followed by jute, tea, and sugarcane. Bangladesh is the world's largest supplier of high quality jute. About half the crop is exported in its raw form and the rest is processed for export as hessian, sacking, and carpet backing. A modern paper industry utilizes bamboo from the hills. Other industries include textiles, fertilizer, glass, iron and steel, sugar, cement, and aluminum. Fishing, in the wide net of freshwater rivers and lakes as well as in the Bay of Bengal, is also economically important. An important source of foreign currencies are the money transfers of the many Bangladeshis working abroad. They send substantial amounts to support their families at home. However, there are a number of serious impediments to further progress. They include frequent cyclones and floods, inefficient state-owned enterprises, a labor force growing (as a consequence of a steady population growth) faster than it can be absorbed by agriculture alone, the desolate infrastructure and delays in developing energy resources such as natural gas, which is the only fuel that is gained in any amount worth mentioning. A program intended to achieve a higher liberalization of the economy has been introduced; however, corruption and the meddling and interfering of the military as well as the inertia of political forces have made it hard to bring the program to fruition.

## Issues in Bangladesh

After 15 years of military rule multi-party politics returned to Bangladesh in 1990, and the country's first woman prime minister, Begum Khaleda Zia, leader of the Bangladesh Nationalist Party (BNP), was elected in 1991. However, in the same year the authority of the president was severely curtailed and political factionalism divides the nation. Bangladesh remains politically unstable.

There are few major differences in the national policies of the political parties and the antagonism between them appears to be fuelled largely by the dislike of the country's prominent female politicians for each other (the opposition Awami League is also led by a woman). Despite the fact that women are heading the political system, women in Bangladesh face discrimination in health care, education, and employment. In addition, dowry related violence against women does occur.

Religious divides exist, as elsewhere in the region. Tension between Bangladesh's Hindus and the Muslim majority is a problem, and Buddhist tribes in the southeast are agitating for autonomous rule. Relations with neighboring India are also strained, although in 1996 the countries signed a treaty agreeing to share resources after an Indian dam on the Ganges River reduced water available for irrigation in Bangladesh.

An exodus of refugees from Myanmar (Burma)—as many as 200,000 by early 1992—also stretches Bangladesh's scarce resources.

International aid finances 90 percent of state capital spending and an economic liberalization program has been introduced.

# Bhutan

## Fact File

**OFFICIAL NAME** Kingdom of Bhutan

**FORM OF GOVERNMENT** Monarchy with single legislative body (National Assembly)

**CAPITAL** Thimphu

**AREA** 47,000 sq km (18,147 sq miles)

**TIME ZONE** GMT + 5.5 hours

**POPULATION** 682,000

**PROJECTED POPULATION 2015** 737,000

**POPULATION DENSITY** 14.5 per sq km (37.6 per sq mile)

**LIFE EXPECTANCY** 65.5

**INFANT MORTALITY (PER 1,000)** 51.9

**OFFICIAL LANGUAGE** Dzongkha

**OTHER LANGUAGES** Tibeto-Burmanese (among them Bumthangkha, Sarchopkha, Tsangla) and Indo-Aryan languages (including Nepalese)

**LITERACY RATE** 47 %

**RELIGIONS** Lamaistic Buddhism 75 %, Hinduism 25 %

**ETHNIC GROUPS** Bhote (Tibetan) 50 %, ethnic Nepalese 35 %, indigenous or migrant tribes 15 %

**CURRENCY** Ngultrum

**ECONOMY** Services 38.1 %, industry 37.2 %, agriculture 24.7 %

**GNI PER CAPITA** US$ 1,770

**CLIMATE** Tropical on southern plains; cool winters and hot summers in central valleys; cold winters and cool summers in mountains

**HIGHEST POINT** Kula Kangri 7,553 m (24,780 ft)

**MAP REFERENCE** Page 219

A tiny landlocked kingdom nestling in the Himalayas between India and Tibet, Bhutan is difficult to visit, and remains largely closed to the outside world. It is the world's most "rural" country, with less than six percent of its population living in towns and over ninety percent dependent on agriculture to make their living. Despite its isolation and apparent tranquillity, the country is torn by fierce, long-standing ethnic tensions which its absolute monarch does little to mitigate. Bhutan's longest-resident ethnic group consists of the Tibetans who probably migrated there 1,000 years ago. Early in the twentieth century, in order to end continual fighting between rival warlords in the area, the British administration in neighboring India established a hereditary monarch in Bhutan, the "Dragon King", in 1907.

The monarch is head of both the state and the government. Though the last king, Jigme Singye Wangchuck, was a modernizer and intent on changing Bhutan's feudal ways, his emphasis on a sense of national identity founded on the language, laws, and dress of his own Drukpa group has stirred up bitter opposition among the resident Hindu Nepalese in southern Bhutan. Many have been deported, and others have fled

to refugee camps in southeast Nepal. Dzongkha, which has been proclaimed the official language of the country, is the natural language of only sixteen percent of Bhutan citizens. In March 2005, a new draft constitution was unveiled, introducing major democratic reforms. A national referendum for its approval should occur in 2008. In December 2006, the king abdicated the throne to his son to give him experience as head of state before the democratic transition.

There are three main regions distinguished largely by altitude—the Great Himalayas, crowned by enormous peaks along the border with Tibet; the slopes and fertile valleys of the Lesser Himalayas, which are divided by the Wong, Sankosh, Tongsa and Manas Rivers; and the Duars Plain which opens out towards India from the foothills of the mountains. The central uplands and foothills are cultivated with food staples including maize, wheat, barley, and potatoes. This area supports the greatest portion of the population. Below this the Duars Plain falls away into broad tracts of semitropical forest, savanna, and bamboo jungle. Forests still cover nearly 75 percent of Bhutan's land area, and timber is both exported to India and used in Bhutan itself as fuel.

Almost all trade is with India. As an export, timber is outweighed in importance by cement. Other revenue-earning activities include a limited tourist industry geared at upscale, environmentally conscientious tourists, as well as the sale of stamps. Bhutan has tremendous hydropower potential, but most manufacturing is of the cottage-industry type. Development projects such as road construction rely to a large extent on Indian migrant labor. Though stabilized at a low level (the economy is one of the world's smallest and poorest) the country's balance of payments is strong, with comfortable reserves.

*Mt Everest and surrounding peaks in Nepal (below). Villagers on a suspension bridge in northern Pakistan (right page top). The road between Quetta in Pakistan and the border with Iran (right page bottom).*

# Nepal

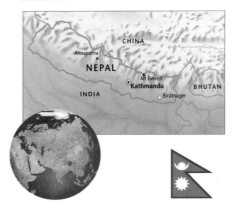

## Fact File

| | |
|---|---|
| **OFFICIAL NAME** | Nepal |
| **FORM OF GOVERNMENT** | Federal republic |
| **CAPITAL** | Kathmandu |
| **AREA** | 140,800 sq km (54,363 sq miles) |
| **TIME ZONE** | GMT + 5.5 hours |
| **POPULATION** | 29,519,000 |
| **PROJECTED POPULATION 2015** | 32,843,000 |
| **POPULATION DENSITY** | 209.7 per sq km (543 per sq mile) |
| **LIFE EXPECTANCY** | 60.9 |
| **INFANT MORTALITY (PER 1,000)** | 62 |
| **OFFICIAL LANGUAGE** | Nepali |
| **OTHER LANGUAGES** | Indo-Aryan languages (among them Maithili and Bihari), Tibeto-Burmese languages (including Tamang, Newari) |
| **LITERACY RATE** | 48.6 % |
| **RELIGIONS** | Hindu 80.6 %, Buddhist 10.7 %, Muslim 4.2 %, other 4.5 % |
| **ETHNIC GROUPS** | Chhettri 15.5 %, Brahman-Hill 12.5 %, Magar 7 %, Tharu 6.6 %, Tamang 5.5 %, |

Newar 5.4 %, Kami 3.9 %, Yadav 3.9 %, other 39.7 %

| | |
|---|---|
| **CURRENCY** | Nepalese rupee |
| **ECONOMY** | Services 42 %, agriculture 38 %, industry 20 % |
| **GNI PER CAPITA** | US$ 340 |
| **CLIMATE** | Subtropical in south, with wet season July to October; cold and snowy in north, wetter in east |
| **HIGHEST POINT** | Mt Everest 8,848 m (29,028 ft) |
| **MAP REFERENCE** | Pages 218–19 |

The birthplace of the Buddha in c. 568 BC, Nepal is a small landlocked republic on the southern slopes of the Himalayas. It is surrounded by India to the west, south, and east, and has a border with China (Tibet) to the north. Tourists coming to trek in the mountains and climb the peaks contribute to national income, but Nepal remains one of the world's poorest countries. Historically, it was influenced both by the Buddhist/Mongol culture of Tibet and by the Hindu/Indian culture of the subcontinent. The royal family ruled from 1769 until 2007. During British colonial rule in India a British resident was installed to provide "guidance" in foreign affairs. In 1959 the country's first elections were held (the Nepali Congress party winning), but in 1960 the king suspended the constitution, and no further elections were held until 1992. In the late 1990s a parliamentary impasse existed: neither the Nepali Congress nor the United Marxist-Leninist (UML) parties had a clear majority. After the 2002 massacre of the king and nine of his family members, his brother and successor tried to introduce a more liberal system. Continuing insurgency led to the dissolution of the parliament, and in November 2006, a peace accord was reached and the Maoists were admitted to parliament. In 2008, the constituent assembly declared Nepal a republic.

The mountainous heart of Nepal, consisting of the towering Himalayas (including the highest and third-highest peaks in the world, Mt Everest and Kanchenjunga) and the lower Siwalik Range to the south, covers three-quarters of the country. Three main river systems cut the Himalayas, the Karnali (feeding the Ganges), the Gandak, and the Kosi. Kathmandu stands among fruit trees and rice fields typical of Nepal's densely populated uplands. Further south, on the Terai/Ganges Plain, farming settlements grow rice, wheat, maize, sugarcane, and jute which are the country's economic maintstay.

Some ninety percent of Nepalis live by subsistence farming, and many do not live well: more than forty percent of Nepal's citizens are undernourished. Most industry is concerned with the processing of jute, sugarcane, tobacco, and grain. Recently textile and carpet production has expanded and now provides 85 percent of foreign exchange earnings. The country has limitless hydropower resources. Electricity could be sold to Indian industry south of the border, and various schemes have been proposed, but environmental considerations weigh against them. Restructuring is needed. International aid funds 62 percent of Nepal's development budget and 34 percent of total government expenditures.

# Pakistan

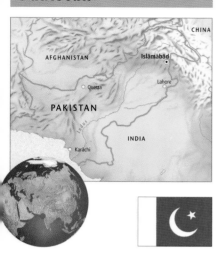

## Fact File

**OFFICIAL NAME** Islamic Republic of Pakistan

**FORM OF GOVERNMENT** Republic with two legislative bodies (Senate and National Assembly)

**CAPITAL** Islāmābād

**AREA** 803,940 sq km (310,401 sq miles)

**TIME ZONE** GMT + 5 hours

**POPULATION** 167,762,000

**PROJECTED POPULATION 2015** 190,659,000

**POPULATION DENSITY** 208.7 per sq km (540.5 per sq mile)

**LIFE EXPECTANCY** 64.1

**INFANT MORTALITY (PER 1,000)** 67

**OFFICIAL LANGUAGE** Urdu

**OTHER LANGUAGES** Punjabi, Sindhi, Urdu, Pashto, Baluchi, Brahvi, English

**LITERACY RATE** 49.9 %

**RELIGIONS** Muslim 97 % (Sunni 77 %, Shi'a 20 %), other (Christian, Hindu) 3 %

**ETHNIC GROUPS** Punjabi 50 %, Sindhi 15 %, Pashtun (Pathan) 15 %, Mohajir (Indian immigrants and their descendants) 8 %, Baloch 5 %, other 7 %

**CURRENCY** Pakistani rupee

**ECONOMY** Services 53.7 %, industry 26.8 %, agriculture 19.5 %

**GNI PER CAPITA** US$ 870

**CLIMATE** Mainly arid; temperate in northwest, cold and snowy in mountains

**HIGHEST POINT** K2 8,611 m (28,251 ft)

**MAP REFERENCE** Page 221

Pakistan occupies the valley of the Indus and its tributaries in the northwest of the Indian subcontinent. Its most sensitive political frontiers are with India to the east and Afghanistan to the west. It has shorter borders with Iran and China.

A part of India until 1947, Pakistan shares with it a history of early civilizations, migrations, and invasions—farmers in the Indus Valley were already using elaborate irrigation works by the second millennium BC. At the time of partition in

1947, Pakistan was two widely separated territories (West and East Pakistan). A dispute over Kashmir has poisoned relations with India since that time. In 1971 East Pakistan achieved independence as Bangladesh. In that year the populist leader Ali Bhutto assumed power in Pakistan, and in 1973 announced a program of "Islamic socialism" under which banks, insurance companies, heavy industry, and even education were nationalized. Since 1977, when he was overthrown by General Zia ul-Haq (and subsequently executed), military and civilian rule have alternated, accompanied by varying degrees of violence and disorder.

Although 97 percent of Pakistan's population is Muslim, there is a wide range of ethnic groupings, languages, and conflicts. The main linguistic separation is between Iranian languages such as Baluchi and Pashto on one hand, and the Indo-Aryan languages of Punjabi, Sindhi, and Urdu on the other. Each of Pakistan's minorities has its own particular concerns. In the northwest of the country the Pathans want to join their kinsmen over the Afghan frontier. The Urdu-speaking

Mohajirs migrated by the millions from India at the time of partition and make up the majority of the population in Karachi and Hyderabad. They resent Punjabi domination and the rule of the old land-owning elite.

The whole of Pakistan is drained by the Indus River. Rising in the Great Highlands of the north it flows southwest, joined by tributaries such as the Jhelum, Chenab, Beas, Ravi, and Sutlej, and forms a fertile and densely populated floodplain in the east of the country before spilling into the Arabian Sea. The waters of this basin feed into one of the largest irrigation systems in the world, the total area being 13 million hectares (32 million acres). Two constructions, one at Tarbela on the Indus, and the other at Mangla on the Jhelum, are among the world's biggest earth- and rock-filled dams. West of the Indus delta is an ascending landscape of alternating ridges and arid basins, some containing salt marshes like the Hamun-i-Mashkel. In the extreme northwest are the Great Highlands, with the Khyber Pass on the frontier with Afghanistan to the west and the spectacular peaks of the Karakoram and Pamirs to the east. Along with Nanga Parbat, these include the second highest mountain in the world—K2, Mt Godwin Austen (8,611 m; 28,251 ft) on the border of Tibet.

Irrigation agriculture combined with the new plant varieties that were introduced as part of the "green revolution" during the 1970s produces abundant cotton, wheat, rice, and sugarcane. Fruit and vegetables are also grown widely, while opium poppies and cannabis are illegally cultivated to supply the international drug trade. Despite the fact that almost half the population work on the land, agriculture now accounts for less than a quarter of the national income.

Karachi is a considerable manufacturing center for the production of textiles, as is Lahore. Other industries produce a wide variety of petroleum products, construction materials, foodstuffs, and paper products. The country has large reserves of unused minerals: copper, bauxite, phosphates, and manganese. However, Pakistan also faces a range of problems. The country's economy is dependent on the highly competitive textile sector, there is a chronic trade deficit and debt burden, and much of the nation's revenue goes into funding massive defense spending on items such as nuclear weaponry and the army.

## Middle East

Saudi Arabia · · · · · · 174
Yemen · · · · · · · · · 175
Oman · · · · · · · · · · 175
United Arab
  Emirates · · · · · · · 176
Kuwait · · · · · · · · · 177
Qatar · · · · · · · · · 177
Bahrain · · · · · · · · 178
Israel · · · · · · · · · 179
Jordan · · · · · · · · 180
Lebanon · · · · · · · 180
Syria · · · · · · · · · 181
Iraq · · · · · · · · · · 182
Iran · · · · · · · · · · 183

## Saudi Arabia

### Fact File

**OFFICIAL NAME** Kingdom of Saudi Arabia

**FORM OF GOVERNMENT** Monarchy with advisory Consultative Council

**CAPITAL** Ar Riyadh (Riyadh)

**AREA** 1,960,582 sq km (756,981 sq miles)

**TIME ZONE** GMT + 3 hours

**POPULATION** 28,161,000

**PROJECTED POPULATION 2015** 29,265,000

**POPULATION DENSITY** 14.4 per sq km (37.2 per sq mile)

**LIFE EXPECTANCY** 76.1

**INFANT MORTALITY (PER 1,000)** 12

**OFFICIAL LANGUAGE** Arabic

**OTHER LANGUAGE** English

**LITERACY RATE** 78.8 %

**RELIGIONS** Sunni Muslim 85 %, Shi'a Muslim 15 %

**ETHNIC GROUPS** Arab 90 %, mixed African-Asian 10 %

**CURRENCY** Saudi riyal

**ECONOMY** Industry 65.9 %, services 31.1 %, agriculture 3 %

**GNI PER CAPITA** US$ 15,440

**CLIMATE** Mainly hot and arid; some areas rainless for years

**HIGHEST POINT** Jabal Sawdā' 3,133 m (10,279 ft)

**MAP REFERENCE** Pages 220–21

Saudi Arabia occupies the majority of the Arabian Peninsula and covers an area about the size of western Europe. With one-quarter of the world's petroleum reserves, it supplies several major industrial nations with oil. Its role as the custodian of Islam's most holy places, Mecca (Makkah) and Medina (Al Madīnah), is an equally important feature of this country. Aloof from international affairs for many years, Saudis steeled themselves to fight Iraq (which they had earlier supported) in 1990–91. The 500,000 Western troops who entered the country (considered by many to be a profanation of Muslim land) were seen by Saudis as both necessary and unwelcome. The war highlighted tensions in a society which remains largely feudal in terms of politics (192 people were beheaded in 1995), yet because of its oil cannot entirely escape the influence of the modern world.

Mecca was Muhammad's birth-place (c. 570) and Medina (al Madīnah) the place where Islam was born. In the eighteenth century the Sa'ud Bedouins adopted a severe branch of Islam—the Wahhabi Movement. With its austere criminal code, this was established by the Saudis throughout their country early in the twentieth century. During the 1930s most Saudis were still living traditional desert lives, but this changed dramatically when oil was found near Riyadh in 1937. The lavish spending for which the royal family was known in the 1960s and 1970s ended with the sharp drop in oil prices of the 1980s. In the 1990s, this started to have effects on society as a whole. People who were content to live

under absolute monarchic rule with prodigious benefits increasingly began to question the balance of power. Per capita income fell from $17,000 in 1981 to $10,430 in 2004, but has since started rising again.

A range of mountains extends northwest to southeast, parallel to the Red Sea, arising to 3,133 m (10,279 ft) at Jabal Sawdā in the southwest, which is Saudi Arabia's highest peak. The Asir Highlands in this southwestern corner is the only region that receives reliable rainfall. Benefiting from the monsoon, the slopes are terraced to grow grain and fruit trees. Further east, separated from the mountains by a wide stretch of basaltic lava, is the high central desert plateau of Najd. The eastern border of this region is a vast arc of sandy desert, broadening into the two dune-wastes of Arabia: An Nafūd in the north, and Ar Rub' al Khāli, or "Empty Quarter", to the south—the latter being the world's largest expanse of sand. Some Bedouin nomads still live here as traders and herdsmen. Over 95 percent of Saudi Arabia is arid or semiarid desert.

Petroleum accounts for 75 percent of budget revenue, 35 percent of gross domestic product, and ninety percent of export earnings. Saudi Arabia has the largest known reserves of petroleum in the world (26 percent of the proven total), is the single largest exporter of petroleum, and has taken full advantage of this by developing world-class associated industries. For more than a decade, however, expenditures have outstripped income. The government plans to restrain public spending and encourage more non-oil exports. As many as 4 million foreign workers are employed in Saudi Arabia, and the 2 million pilgrims who come to make the traditional pilgrimage to Mecca each year also contribute largely to national income.

*Pilgrims in Mecca (left). Saudis at a market wearing traditional dress (above). A Yemeni desert town (right page).*

# Yemen

## Fact File

**OFFICIAL NAME** Republic of Yemen

**FORM OF GOVERNMENT** Republic with single legislative body (House of Representatives)

**CAPITAL** San'ā'

**AREA** 527,970 sq km (203,849 sq miles)

**TIME ZONE** GMT + 3 hours

**POPULATION** 23,013,000

**PROJECTED POPULATION 2015** 28,288,000

**POPULATION DENSITY** 43.6 per sq km (112.9 per sq mile)

**LIFE EXPECTANCY** 62.9

**INFANT MORTALITY (PER 1,000)** 56.3

**OFFICIAL LANGUAGE** Arabic

**OTHER LANGUAGES** South Arab languages (e. g. Soqutri)

**LITERACY RATE** 50.2 %

**RELIGIONS** Muslim: predominantly Sunni in the south, Shi'ite majority in the north

**ETHNIC GROUPS** Predominantly Arab; small mixed African-Arab and Indian minorities

**CURRENCY** Yemeni rial

**ECONOMY** Services 46.2 %, industry 41.5 %, agriculture 12.3 %

**GNI PER CAPITA** US$ 870

**CLIMATE** Mainly arid; humid in southwest and cooler in western highlands; drier in east

**HIGHEST POINT** Jabal an-Nabi Shu'ayb 3,760 m (12,336 ft)

**MAP REFERENCE** Page 220

Yemen occupies the southwestern corner of the Arabian Peninsula. Although its people have been Muslim for centuries it has deeply divided political allegiances and was two separate countries until 1990. North Yemen became independent of the Ottoman Empire in 1918, and in 1962 the Yemen Arab Republic (YAR) was proclaimed. The politics of the YAR tended to be conservative and Islamic. South Yemen came under British influence in 1839 and Aden became a vital port on the sea route to India. In 1967 the British withdrew from the region, and in 1969 the People's Democratic Republic of Yemen was proclaimed—the only Marxist state in the Arab world.

The north and south had been mutually hostile since independence, but a turning point came with the Soviet collapse in 1989. Having lost USSR support, South Yemen sought political union with the YAR. In 1990 the two countries became the Republic of Yemen. In 1994 an assassination attempt on a northern politician led to civil war and the south's attempted secession. An uneasy peace prevails.

The narrow Red Sea coastal plain of Tihāma, extending south from Saudi Arabia, is generally barren: here, cotton-growing predominates. From the coast the land rises steeply to a comparatively fertile and well-cultivated interior. Around San'ā' vines are cultivated and a variety of fruit crops are grown. The mountains overlooking San'ā' rise to Jabal an-Nabi Shu'ayb, the highest point on the Arabian Peninsula. From these heights a number of rivers drain east toward the Ar Rub' al Khālī (Empty Quarter) where they disappear into the sands. Along the coast of the Gulf of Aden a sandy plain rises inland to the rugged Yemen Plateau, which to the north slopes down to the uninhabited wastes of the Rub al-Khali. In this region ten percent of the mainly rural population are nomadic.

Despite oil and gas reserves, Yemen is weak economically. In the Gulf War of 1990–91 Yemen supported Iraq. As punishment, Saudi Arabia and Kuwait expelled hundreds of thousands of Yemeni workers. Their remittances ceased and they became a huge burden on the economy. The government then abandoned agricultural subsidies and farmers stopped growing food and export crops. Instead they planted a shrub called qat—a stimulant used by Yemenis that has no export value. High inflation and political conflicts make it difficult to implement long-range economic policies and reforms.

# Oman

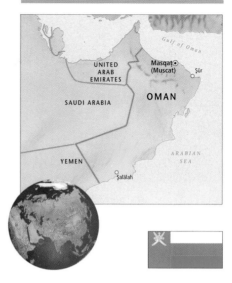

## Fact File

**OFFICIAL NAME** Sultanate of Oman

**FORM OF GOVERNMENT** Monarchy with advisory Consultative Council

**CAPITAL** Masqaṭ (Muscat)

**AREA** 212,460 sq km (82,031 sq miles)

**TIME ZONE** GMT + 4 hours

**POPULATION** 3,312,000

**PROJECTED POPULATION 2015** 3,051,000

**POPULATION DENSITY** 15.6 per sq km (40.4 per sq mile)

**LIFE EXPECTANCY** 73.9

**INFANT MORTALITY (PER 1,000)** 17.5

**OFFICIAL LANGUAGE** Arabic

**OTHER LANGUAGES** Baluchu, Farsi (Persian), Urdu, English

**LITERACY RATE** 81.4 %

**RELIGIONS** Ibadhi Muslim 75 %, Sunni Muslim, Shi'a Muslim and Hindu 25 %

**ETHNIC GROUPS** Mainly Arab with Baluchi, Indian, Pakistani, Sri Lankan, Bangladeshi, African minorities

**CURRENCY** Omani rial

**ECONOMY** Services 59.5 %, industry 38.3 %, agriculture 2.2 %

**GNI PER CAPITA** US$ 11,120

**CLIMATE** Mainly hot and arid; light rains in south June to September

**HIGHEST POINT** Jabal Ash Shām 2,980 m (9,777 ft)

**MAP REFERENCE** Pages 220–21

Oman is the third-largest country in the Arabian Peninsula. Situated on the peninsula's eastern corner, it looks across the Arabian Sea toward Baluchistan and India—in fact Baluchis form a small but significant part of the population. A small, separate, and highly strategic piece of Oman's territory is the tip of the Musandam Peninsula, com-

manding the entrance to the Strait of Hormuz. The Omani capital of Masqaṭ (Muscat) was a trading center for hundreds of years, dhows sailing to India in one direction and down the African coast to Zanzibar in the other. Zanzibar itself was an Omani conquest, and in the 1960s, when it became part of Tanzania, many Arab Zanzibaris came to Oman. From 1798 Oman had strong ties with the British, and it became a British protectorate. Full independence came in 1971.

Sultan Qabus Ibn Sa'id rules his country as an absolute monarch, advised by a majlis ash shura ("consultative council"), but in the late 1990s the country was moving towards a constitutional government. In the late 1960s Oman faced a leftist rebellion in the western province of Dhofur, encouraged and supported by the People's Republic of Yemen across the border. This was defeated in 1975. Since then, with the country enjoying the prosperity of its oil and natural gas (huge additional reserves were discovered in 1991), peace has reigned.

In the north the limestone Hajar Mountains overlook the fertile coastal plain of al-Batinah. Most of Oman's population lives along the alluvial al-Batinah strip, where date gardens stretch for more than 250 km (155 miles). The Jabal Akhdar ridge is the highest part of the Hajar Range, rising to 3,107 m (10,193 ft). Soils in the upland region are poor: herders use the area for running camels, sheep, and goats. Wadis cutting the Jabal Akhdar ridge, underground canals, and wells provide a certain amount of irrigation. North of the Ẓufār (Dhofar) uplands in the southwest the desert meets the sandy wastes of the Saudi Arabian Ar Rub' al Khāli (or "Empty Quarter").

Rural Omanis live by subsistence agriculture, growing dates, limes, bananas, alfalfa, and vegetables. Pastoralists keep camels, cattle, sheep, and goats. The smaller urban population, however, including a considerable number of guest workers, depends on imported food. The national economy as a whole is dominated by the oil industry: petroleum accounts for nearly ninety percent of export earnings, about 75 percent of government revenues, and roughly forty percent of gross domestic product. Oman has proved oil reserves of 4.7 billion barrels, which are equal to almost twenty year's supply at the present rate of extraction.

# United Arab Emirates

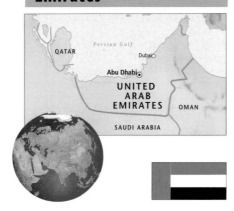

## Fact File

**OFFICIAL NAME** United Arab Emirates

**FORM OF GOVERNMENT** Federation of Emirates with one advisory body (Federal National Council)

**CAPITAL** Abu Dhabi

**AREA** 82,880 sq km (32,000 sq miles)

**TIME ZONE** GMT + 4 hours

**POPULATION** 4,621,000

**PROJECTED POPULATION 2015** 5,263,000

**POPULATION DENSITY** 55.8 per sq km (144.4 per sq mile)

**LIFE EXPECTANCY** 75.9

**INFANT MORTALITY (PER 1,000)** 13.1

**OFFICIAL LANGUAGE** Arabic

**OTHER LANGUAGES** Hindi, Urdu, Farsi (Persian), English

**LITERACY RATE** 77.9 %

**RELIGIONS** Muslim 96 % (Shi'a 16 %); Christian, Hindu, other 4 %

**ETHNIC GROUPS** Emirati 19 %, other Arab and Iranian 23 %, South Asian 50 %, other expatriates 8 % (only 20 % of population are citizens)

**CURRENCY** Emirian dirham

**ECONOMY** Industry 59.3 %, services 38.9 %, agriculture 1.8 %

**GNI PER CAPITA** not available (more than US$ 11,456)

**CLIMATE** Mainly arid; cooler in eastern mountains

**HIGHEST POINT** Jabal Yibir 1,527 m (5,010 ft)

**MAP REFERENCE** Pages 220–21

People in the seven small principalities that form the United Arab Emirates lived for centuries as seagoing traders on the shores of the Persian Gulf. When piracy became a nuisance in 1820, Britain entered into truces with the local emirs to end attacks on shipping, and established a protectorate in the region. Soon the principalities were known as the Trucial States. In 1971 they became independent and formed the federation of sheikdoms now known as the United Arab Emirates (UAE). They are situated along the southern coast of the Persian Gulf between the Qatar Peninsula to the west and the Straits of Hormuz, and share borders with Qatar, Saudi Arabia, and Oman.

Abū Zaby (Abu Dhabi) is more than six times the size of all the other states put together, has the biggest population, and is the main oil producer. In the form of federal funds, it contributes to development projects in the poorer states. The port in Dubayy (Dubai) is one of the world's largest maritime facilities, and has attracted companies from 58 countries active in the petroleum industry, trading, and financial services. A major economic contribution has been made by expatriates who flocked to the country during the 1970s' oil boom—only twenty percent of UAE citizens are native born. Whether this workforce can now be 'Emiratized' is a concern, as is the growth of Islamic fundamentalism among the young. In world affairs the UAE is a force for moderation in the Arab world. It maintains close links with the UK and USA.

The Gulf coast features saline marshes merging inland with barren desert plains. In the east there is a range of steep mountains. These are an extension of Oman's Hajar Mountains, running northward along the Musandam Peninsula. The sheikhdom of Al Fujayrah looks out from this peninsula onto the Gulf of Oman, and contains the only highland expanse. Less than l.2 percent of UAE land is arable, and most vegetation is sparse and scrubby. Virtually all agricultural activity is found in the emirates of Sharjah, Ras al Khaimana, Ajman, and Fujairah, where oasis date palms grow. Government incentives, however, plus irrigation works, have increased the number of farmers fourfold in recent years. While much food is imported, self-sufficiency in wheat is still a target.

Once an impoverished region of small desert sheikhdoms, the UAE has since 1973 been transformed into a modern state with a high standard of living. Oil and gas production is the largest economic sector, accounting for 89 percent of export revenue. Though in the short term the fortunes of the economy fluctuate with the price of gas and oil, at the present level of production oil reserves should last more than 100 years. Increased privatization is being encouraged by the government, and service industries are being developed. Although the UAE is much stronger economically than most of the Gulf States, a number of weaknesses remain. While the largest solar-powered water-production plant in the Gulf region is at Taweela, industrial development is likely to be limited by the fact that water will always be in short supply. There is a lack of skilled labor. Most raw materials and foodstuffs have to be imported.

# Kuwait

## Fact File

**OFFICIAL NAME** State of Kuwait

**FORM OF GOVERNMENT** Emirate (hereditary monarchy) with single legislative body (National Assembly)

**CAPITAL** Al Kuwayt (Kuwait)

**AREA** 17,820 sq km (6,880 sq miles)

**TIME ZONE** GMT + 3 hours

**POPULATION** 2,597,000

**PROJECTED POPULATION 2015** 3,378,000

**POPULATION DENSITY** 145.7 per sq km (377.5 per sq mile)

**LIFE EXPECTANCY** 77.5

**INFANT MORTALITY (PER 1,000)** 9.2

**OFFICIAL LANGUAGE** Arabic

**OTHER LANGUAGE** English

**LITERACY RATE** 93.3 %

**RELIGIONS** Muslim 85 % (of which Sunni 70 %, Shi'a 30 %), other (including Christian, Hindu, Parsi) 15 %

**ETHNIC GROUPS** Kuwaiti 45 %, other Arab 35 %, South Asian 9 %, Iranian 4 %, other 7 %

**CURRENCY** Kuwaiti dinar

**ECONOMY** Services 51.5 %, industry 48.1 %, agriculture 0.4 %

**GNI PER CAPITA** US$ 31,640

**CLIMATE** Arid; cool winters and hot, humid summers

**HIGHEST POINT** Ash Shakayah 290 m (951 ft)

**MAP REFERENCE** Page 220

The Arab emirate of Kuwait lies in the northwest corner of the Persian Gulf, dwarfed by its neighbors Iraq, Iran, and Saudi Arabia. Beneath its surface lie huge oil reserves. It was settled by wandering Arab peoples in the eighteenth century. When Germany and Turkey were eyeing Kuwait possessively in the nineteenth century it formed a defensive alliance with Great Britain, becoming a British protectorate in 1914. In 1961, when it gained independence, Kuwait was claimed by Iraq.

A constitution was inaugurated by the as Sabah ruling family in 1962. Whenever the National Assembly has been critical, however, it has been suspended. In 1990, Iraq invaded. The Kuwaitis endured six months of brutality and the destruction of the city of Kuwait before a US-led international coalition expelled the Iraqis in 1991. During the occupation 400,000 residents fled the country; 200,000 Palestinian migrant workers were not allowed to return, as the Palestinian Liberation Organization had supported Iraq. The destruction of Kuwaiti oil wells by Iraq and deliberate oil-spills in the Gulf have caused environmental costs still difficult to assess. The damage done in the Third Gulf War in 2003 was much less severe.

Kuwait consists of an undulating sandy plateau which rises westward to an elevation of about 300 m (1,000 ft) on the Iraq-Saudi Arabia border. Along the border the plateau is cut to a depth of 45 m (150 ft) by the Wādī al Bāţin. In the northeast there are a few salt marshes and in the northwest is the Jal az-Zawr escarpment. Vegetation is mostly limited to salt-tolerant plants along the coast, though in modern urban areas green spaces have been produced by irrigating imported soil. The territory of Kuwait also includes nine islands, of which Bubiyan is the largest.

Kuwait owns ten percent of the world's proven crude oil reserves. Its petroleum sector currently accounts for nearly half of gross domestic product, ninety percent of export revenues, and seventy percent of government income. With the exception of fish, Kuwait depends almost wholly on food imports, though hothouses and hydroponics produce some fruit and vegetables. About 75 percent of potable water must be distilled or imported. The shortage of water constrains industrial activities, which at present include petrochemical production, food processing, desalination, construction materials, and salt. The World Bank has urged the government to push ahead with privatization, including in the oil industry.

# Qatar

## Fact File

**OFFICIAL NAME** State of Qatar

**FORM OF GOVERNMENT** Monarchy with Advisory Consultative Council

**CAPITAL** Ad Dawḥah (Doha)

**AREA** 11,437 sq km (4,416 sq miles)

**TIME ZONE** GMT + 3 hours

**POPULATION** 929,000

**PROJECTED POPULATION 2015** 966,000

**POPULATION DENSITY** 81.2 per sq km (210.4 per sq mile)

**LIFE EXPECTANCY** 74.4

**INFANT MORTALITY (PER 1,000)** 16.9

**OFFICIAL LANGUAGE** Arabic

**OTHER LANGUAGES** Urdu, Farsi (Persian), English

**LITERACY RATE** 89 %

**RELIGIONS** Muslim 77.5 %, Christian 8.5 %, other 14 %

**ETHNIC GROUPS** Arab 40 %, Pakistani 18 %, Indian 18 %, Iranian 10 %, other 14 %

**CURRENCY** Qatari rial

**ECONOMY** Industry 71.2 %, services 28.7 %, agriculture 0.1 %

**GNI PER CAPITA** not available (one of the world's highest)

**CLIMATE** Hot and arid; humid in summer

**HIGHEST POINT** Qurayn Aba al Bawl 103 m (338 ft)

**MAP REFERENCE** Page 220

Qatar is a small, wealthy emirate in the Persian Gulf. In 1971 it chose not to join the neighboring United Arab Emirates as a member state, but to go it alone. Recently it has continued to act with independence, signing a security pact with the USA in 1995 involving the stationing of 2,000 US troops, while simultaneously challenging the Gulf Cooperation Council's policy on Iraq. During the 2003 war againt Iraq led by the United States, the United Kingdom and their allies, the military headquarter was located in Doha. The peninsula it occupies, projecting north from the southern shore of the Persian Gulf near Bahrain,

*A village in the Oman mountains, surrounded by terraced cultivation (left page above). Kuwait City, the capital of Kuwait (below).*

consists of flat and semiarid desert. Most of its population are guest workers from the Indian subcontinent, Iran, and North Africa.

Qatar was ruled for centuries by the Khalifah dynasty. A rift in dynastic affairs opened in 1783, war with Bahrain followed in 1867, and then the British intervened to set up a separate emirate under the ath Thani family. Qatar became a full British protectorate in 1916. At this time it was occupied by nomadic Bedouin wandering the peninsula with their herds of goats and camels. Oil production, which commenced in 1949, changed everything and now almost ninety percent of the people live in the capital city of Ad Dawḥah (Doha) or its suburbs. The northern parts of Qatar are dotted with abandoned villages.

A bloodless palace coup in 1995 saw the present emir displace his father, a move that was accepted without fuss. The emir of Qatar rules as an absolute monarch. He occupies the office of prime minister and he appoints his own cabinet. He is advised by a partially elected thirty-member majlis ash shura (consultative council). From time to time there are calls for democratic reforms from prominent citizens.

The Qatar Peninsula is mainly low-lying except for a few hills in the west of the country at Jabal Dukhān (the Dukhan Heights) and some low cliffs in the northeast. Sandy desert, salt flats, and barren plains cut by shallow wadis (creek beds) occupy 95 percent of its land area. There is little rainfall aside from occasional winter showers. As a result of the shortage of fresh water Qatar is dependent on large-scale desalinization facilities. Summers are usually hot and humid; winter nights can be cool and chilly. Drought-resistant plant life is mainly found in the south. However, by tapping groundwater supplies, Qatar is now able to cultivate most of its own vegetables.

Crude oil production and refining is by far the most important industry. Oil accounts for more than thirty percent of gross domestic product, about 75 percent of export earnings, and seventy percent of government revenues. Reserves of 15.2 billion barrels should ensure continued output at present levels for at least another hundred years. Oil has given Qatar a per capita gross domestic product that exceeds most of the leading western European industrial economies. Long-term goals include the development of offshore wells and economic diversification.

## Bahrain

### Fact File

**OFFICIAL NAME** Kingdom of Bahrain

**FORM OF GOVERNMENT** Constitutional monarchy

**CAPITAL** Al Manāmah (Manama)

**AREA** 665 sq km (257 sq miles)

**TIME ZONE** GMT + 3 hours

**POPULATION** 718,000

**PROJECTED POPULATION 2015** 857,000

**POPULATION DENSITY** 1,079.7 per sq km (2,793.8 per sq mile)

**LIFE EXPECTANCY** 74.9

**INFANT MORTALITY (PER 1,000)** 15.6

**OFFICIAL LANGUAGE** Arabic

**OTHER LANGUAGES** English, Farsi (Persian), Urdu

**LITERACY RATE** 86.5 %

**RELIGIONS** Muslim 81.2 %, Christian 9 %, other 9.8 %

**ETHNIC GROUPS** Bahraini 62 %, Asian 13 %, other Arab 10 %, Iranian 8 %, other 7 %

**CURRENCY** Bahraini dinar

**ECONOMY** Services 56 %, industry 43.6 %, agriculture 0.4 %

**GNI PER CAPITA** US$ 19,350

**CLIMATE** Mainly arid, with mild winters and hot, humid summers

**HIGHEST POINT** Jabal ad Dukhān 122 m (400 ft)

**MAP REFERENCE** Page 220

The State of Bahrain is a cluster of 35 small, low-lying islands located in the Persian Gulf, just 28 km (17 miles) from the west coast of the Qatar Peninsula. The islands were once the heart of the ancient Dilmun civilization and have been a trading center for more than 4,000 years. Bahrain was the first of the Gulf States to export oil, soon after reserves were discovered in 1932. A 25 km (16 mile) causeway links the main island to Saudi Arabia.

After the collapse of Beirut in Lebanon in the 1970s, which previously had been the region's main commercial center, Bahrain began to provide banking and financial services, at the same time increasing its transport and communication facilities. When the elected assembly was dissolved in 1975 and the country reverted to traditional authoritarian rule, there was growing unrest among the fundamentalist Shi'ite Muslim majority. Encouraged in their resistance by Iran, the Shi'ites resent their low status under Bahrain's Sunni Muslim ruling family. In the opinion of Shi'ite fundamentalists this family is unacceptable for a number of reasons: It belongs to a branch of Islam they regard as oppressive, it is liberal and modernizing in its economic policies, and it is a supporter of US policy. US military air bases on Bahrain were essential strategic assets during the 1990–91 Gulf War.

Consisting of barren rock, sandy plains, and salt marshes, the landscape of Bahrain is low-lying desert for the most part, rising to a low central escarpment. Winters are dry and mild, summers hot and humid. There are no natural freshwater resources. All the country's water needs must be met by groundwater from springs and from desalinated sea water. Imported soil has been used to create several small fertile areas, and domestic agricultural production is actually capable of meeting local demand for fruit and vegetables. However, the degradation of the existing arable land is an environmental concern, along with damage to coastlines, coral reefs, and sea life resulting from spills of oil and oil-tanker discharges.

Waning oil production since the 1970s has forced Bahrain to diversify its economy. Since the opening of the causeway linking the country to Saudi Arabia in 1986 there has been a boom in weekend tourism, with visitors pouring in from the Gulf States. Bahrain is now the Arab world's most important banking center, and numerous multinational firms with business in the Gulf have offices in the country. Ship repairs are also undertaken in Bahrain. Petroleum production and processing account for approximately eighty percent of export receipts. Natural gas has assumed greater importance, and is used to supply local industries, including an aluminum smelting plant. However, unemployment among the young, especially among the Shi'ite majority, is a cause of social unrest and continuing economic concern.

# Israel

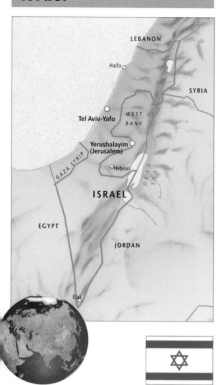

## Fact File

**OFFICIAL NAME** State of Israel

**FORM OF GOVERNMENT** Republic with single legislative body (Knesset)

**CAPITAL** Jerusalem

**AREA** 20,770 sq km (8,019 sq miles)

**TIME ZONE** GMT + 2 hours

**POPULATION** 7,112,000

**PROJECTED POPULATION 2015** 7,797,000

**POPULATION DENSITY** 342.4 per sq km (886.9 per sq mile)

**LIFE EXPECTANCY** 80.6

**INFANT MORTALITY (PER 1,000)** 4.3

**OFFICIAL LANGUAGES** Hebrew, Arabic

**OTHER LANGUAGES** Yiddish, English, French, German, Hungarian, Romanian, Russian, Spanish

**LITERACY RATE** 97.1 %

**RELIGIONS** Jewish 76.4 %, Muslim 16 %, Christian 2.1 %, Druze 1.6 %, other 3.9 %

**ETHNIC GROUPS** Jewish 76.4 %, Arab 22.6 %, other 1 %

**CURRENCY** Shekel

**ECONOMY** Services 67.1 %, industry 30.2 %, agriculture 2.7 %

**GNI PER CAPITA** US$ 21,900

**CLIMATE** Temperate along coast, hot and dry in south and east

**HIGHEST POINT** Har Meron 1,208 m (3,963 ft)

**MAP REFERENCE** Page 225

Created as a Jewish homeland in 1948, Israel is a small country with an illustrious past that involves three of the world's great religions, and an uncertain future. For fifty years, through a succession of wars with hostile Arab neighbors, a secular, democratic political system has managed to constrain strong religious tendencies deeply rooted in the past. Key events in the Jewish history of the region are: first, the occupation of the land by the twelve tribes of Israelites 4,000 years ago; second, the scattering (or "diaspora") of the one surviving tribe, the Jews, following a failed revolt against Rome in AD 138; third, the rise of Zionism in the nineteenth century advocating a Jewish homeland in Palestine as a solution to centuries of exile and persecution; fourth, the Holocaust, which reinforced arguments for territorial independence; and fifth, the proclamation of the State of Israel in May 1948, leading to the emigration of many Palestinian Arabs. Since then there has been continual strife between the new state and its neighbors. Israel's subsequent seizure and occupation of additional territories (see entries for Gaza Strip and West Bank) has been bitterly resisted by their Arab inhabitants. This conflict has intensified as Jewish religious fundamentalists continue to expand their settlements in contested areas. After the country signed a peace treaty with Egypt in 1979 and especially while Prime Minister Yitzhak Rabin conducted a policy of appeasement with Jordan and the Palestinians until he was murdered in 1995 by a Jewish extremist, the peace process made quite some progress and the foundation of an independent Palestinian state is also the declared goal of the international community. However, ongoing acts of terrorism by Arab fanatics as well as the very harsh politic of the State of Israel in its pursuit of domestic security continue to pose a severe threat to the peace process.

Geographically, Israel consists of four main regions: the Mediterranean coastal plain of Sharon, irrigated by the Qishon, Soreq, and Sarida Rivers; the rolling hills extending from Galilee in the north to Judea in the center; the Jordan-Red Sea section of the Rift Valley running north to south the full length of the eastern frontier from the Golan Heights to the Gulf of Aqaba; and the great southern wedge of desert plateau called the Negev (Ha Negev), which makes up about half of Israel's total land area. With irrigation, the Mediterranean coastal plain is fertile fruit-growing country. In the drier southern stretches its dunes have been stabilized with grass and tamarisk and reclaimed for pasture. The northern hill country around Galilee has good rainfall and a rich black soil weathered from basalt. Here and around Judea, pine and eucalyptus trees have been planted to anchor the soil and retain water. The Valley of Jezreel ('Emeq Yizre'el), lying between Galilee and Samaria to the south, has deep alluvial soils which are intensively tilled for market gardening. The Jordan-Western Negev Scheme—the most ambitious of Israel's various irrigation projects—diverts water from the upper Jordan and other sources through a series of culverts and canals south to the Negev. The desert is widely covered with blown sand and loess, but tomatoes and grapes grow well when supplied with water.

Israel has the most industrialized economy in the region. Iron is smelted at Haifa and there are steel foundries at Acre. Chemical manufacturing takes place at Haifa and in plants by the Dead Sea. A national electricity grid provides power to widely dispersed towns where factories produce textiles, ceramics, and other products. In the Negev south of Beersheba new settlements mine oil, copper, and phosphates, the factories using potash and salt from the Dead Sea. Israel is largely self-sufficient in food production except for grains. Diamonds, high-technology equipment, and agricultural products are leading exports. About half the government's external debt is owed to the USA, its main source of aid. To earn foreign exchange the government has been targeting high-tech international market niches such as medical scanning equipment. Matters of continuing economic concern include the high level of unemployment following large-scale immigration from the former USSR, and the need to import strategically important raw materials.

*A spice seller in a Bahrain market (left page top).
The Old City of Yerushalayim (Jerusalem) from the
Mount of Olives, with the golden dome of the
al Aqsa Mosque (below).*

Asia and the Middle East

# Jordan

## Fact File

**OFFICIAL NAME** Hashemite Kingdom of Jordan

**FORM OF GOVERNMENT** Constitutional monarchy with two legislative bodies (House of Notables and House of Representatives)

**CAPITAL** 'Ammān

**AREA** 92,300 sq km (35,637 sq miles)

**TIME ZONE** GMT + 2 hours

**POPULATION** 6,199,000

**PROJECTED POPULATION 2015** 6,923,000

**POPULATION DENSITY** 67.2 per sq km (173.9 per sq mile)

**LIFE EXPECTANCY** 78.7

**INFANT MORTALITY (PER 1,000)** 15.6

**OFFICIAL LANGUAGE** Arabic

**OTHER LANGUAGE** English

**LITERACY RATE** 89.9 %

**RELIGIONS** Sunni Muslim 92 %, Christian 6 %, other 2 %

**ETHNIC GROUPS** Arab 98 %, Circassian 1 %, Armenian 1 %

**CURRENCY** Jordanian dinar

**ECONOMY** Services 86.2 %, industry 10.3 %, agriculture 3.5 %

**GNI PER CAPITA** US$ 2,850

**CLIMATE** Mainly arid, but northwest temperate with cool, wet winters and hot, dry summers

**HIGHEST POINT** Jabal Ramm 1,754 m (5,755 ft)

**MAP REFERENCE** Page 225

The small Arab kingdom of Jordan, rich in historic associations and sites, lies between Saudi Arabia, Israel, and Syria, and also shares a border with Iraq. It has to deal with Israel on the one hand and with Israel's various Arab antagonists on the other, while accommodating huge numbers of refugees. After the Ottoman Turks were driven out during the First World War the British installed the Hashemite monarchy in 1921. In 1946 Jordan became independent, and King Hussein reigned from 1952 until his death in 1999.

Governing Jordan has not been easy, many problems being connected with what is known as the West Bank. As a result of the Six Day War in 1967, the territory west of the Jordan River, and formerly part of Jordan, came under Israeli control. This area, containing both Jerusalem and much of Jordan's most fruitful land, remains a trouble spot. With emigré Palestinians using Jordan as a base for guerrilla activities (they were expelled in 1970–71), through two Gulf Wars in which Jordan was sympathetic to Iraq (its major supplier of oil), and with the recent expansion of Israeli settlements in the area, the West Bank became impossible to regain or to administer. In 1988 Jordan ceded it to the PLO.

The Red Sea-Jordan section of the Rift Valley forms the country's western border. It contains the Jordan River valley, the Dead Sea (the lowest point on the earth's surface, at 400 m/1,312 ft below sea level), the Sea of Galilee, and Wadī al Arabah. Parts of the Jordan Valley and the highlands east of the Rift Valley are irrigated, making arable farming possible. Crops include vegetables, olives, and fruit. Eighty percent of Jordan's land area is desert. In the north it merges with the Syrian Desert and in the south with the deserts of Saudi Arabia. Less than 0.5 percent of the country is forested, mainly in the east. Vegetation ranges from Mediterranean plants in the mountains to grass, sagebrush and shrubs in the steppe country.

Jordan has poor water, oil, and coal supplies. In the late 1970s and early 1980s it received substantial Arab aid and the economy grew at more than ten percent a year. In the late 1980s reductions in aid and in worker remittances slowed and imports outstripped exports. In 1991 the Second Gulf War overwhelmed the country. Worker remittances came to a halt, trade contracted, and additional refugees arrived, further straining resources. Recovery since that time has been uneven. Poverty, debt, and unemployment are continuing problems.

*One of the many rock-cut facades in the ancient city of Petra in Jordan (below). Byblos Harbor in Lebanon (right page bottom). Krac des Chevaliers in Syria, a French Crusader castle built in the twelfth century (right page top).*

# Lebanon

## Fact File

**OFFICIAL NAME** Republic of Lebanon

**FORM OF GOVERNMENT** Republic with single legislative body (National Assembly)

**CAPITAL** Beirut

**AREA** 10,400 sq km (4,015 sq miles)

**TIME ZONE** GMT + 2 hours

**POPULATION** 3,972,000

**PROJECTED POPULATION 2015** 4,431,000

**POPULATION DENSITY** 381.9 per sq km (989.3 per sq mile)

**LIFE EXPECTANCY** 73.4

**INFANT MORTALITY (PER 1,000)** 22.6

**OFFICIAL LANGUAGE** Arabic

**OTHER LANGUAGES** Armenian, Kurdish, French, English

**LITERACY RATE** 87.4 %

**RELIGIONS** Muslim 60 %, Christian 39 %, other 1 %

**ETHNIC GROUPS** Arab 95 %, Armenian 4 %, other 1 %

**CURRENCY** Lebanese pound

**ECONOMY** Services 75.9 %, industry 19 %, agriculture 5.1 %

**GNI PER CAPITA** US$ 5,770

**CLIMATE** Temperate, with short mild, wet winters and long, hot, dry summers. In winter rainfall in mountains often turns to snow

**HIGHEST POINT** Qurnat as Sawdā' 3,088 m (10,131 ft)

**MAP REFERENCE** Page 225

Lebanon, a small country on the eastern shore of the Mediterranean Sea, consists of the region that was once known as the Levant. It has a history that goes back at least 5,000 years. First settled by the Phoenicians around 3000 BC, it saw Alexander the Great (356–323 BC) conquer the Phoenician city of Tyre, and it later became part of the Roman Empire. Early in the seventh century AD Maronite Christians (named after Maro, a Syrian monk who was the sect's founder) settled in northern Lebanon; later, Druze Arabs, who are aligned with Shi'ite Islam, settled in the south of the country, and Sunni Muslims came to the coastal towns. From the eleventh to the thirteenth century the region was a center of confrontation between Western Christians and Muslims during the Crusades. It then became part of the Muslim Mameluke Empire. In 1516 the Ottoman Turks took control of the country, their rule finally ending with conquest by the British and French during the First World War.

From 1920, following the withdrawal of Turkish forces, a French administration sought to balance the interests of the country's various religious groups. During this period Beirut, which already had a cosmopolitan air, took on a distinctly French flavor. The city became both a center of international commerce and a playground of the rich. The country gained independence in 1946. Deep and persistent tensions between Muslim and various non-Muslim sections of the population led to an outbreak of guerrilla war in 1975. For the next fifteen years much of the country was devasted by civil war, and much of its urban infrastructure was destroyed.

From the narrow coastal plain along the Mediterranean, where crops are grown with the aid of irrigation, the land rises eastward to form the Lebanon Mountains (Jabal Lubnān). Running from north to south, these cover about thirty percent of Lebanon's land area. Between the harsh slopes of this range and the Anti-Lebanon Chain (Jabal ash Sharqī) that borders Syria lies the fertile el Beqaa Valley which is another agricultural area. This is traversed by the River Litani on its journey south, before emptying into the Mediterranean Sea above Şūr (the ancient city of Tyre).

Decades of fighting have left the Lebanese economy in ruins and there is a severe housing shortage. Tourism, which was once an important source of revenue, is beginning to revive with the rebuilding of the once-popular Corniche seafront area at Beirut. Since the decline of industry as a result of the war, agriculture has come to play a more important role: crops include apples, citrus fruits, bananas, carrots, grapes, tomatoes, and olives. Opium poppies and cannabis are illegally produced for export. Traditional areas of activity in the past were banking, food processing, textiles, cement, oil refining, and chemicals. The country now depends heavily on foreign aid.

## Syria

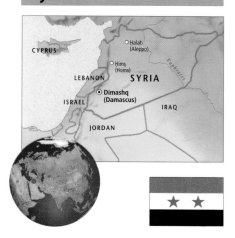

### Fact File

| | |
|---|---|
| **OFFICIAL NAME** | Syrian Arab Republic |
| **FORM OF GOVERNMENT** | Republic with single legislative body (People's Council) |
| **CAPITAL** | Dimashq (Damascus) |
| **AREA** | 185,180 sq km (71,498 sq miles) |
| **TIME ZONE** | GMT + 2 hours |
| **POPULATION** | 19,748,000 |
| **PROJECTED POPULATION 2015** | 23,510,000 |
| **POPULATION DENSITY** | 106.6 per sq km (276.2 per sq mile) |
| **LIFE EXPECTANCY** | 70.9 |
| **INFANT MORTALITY (PER 1,000)** | 26.8 |
| **OFFICIAL LANGUAGE** | Arabic |
| **OTHER LANGUAGES** | Kurdish, Armenian, Aramaic, Karbadian |
| **LITERACY RATE** | 79.6 % |
| **RELIGIONS** | Sunni Muslim 74 %, other Muslim sects 16 %, Christian 10 %; tiny Jewish communities |
| **ETHNIC GROUPS** | Arab 90.3 %, Kurd, Armenian, other 9.7 % |
| **CURRENCY** | Syrian pound |
| **ECONOMY** | Services 66.3 %, agriculture 19.2 %, industry 14.5 % |
| **GNI PER CAPITA** | US$ 1,760 |
| **CLIMATE** | Temperate, with mild, wet winters and dry, hot summers; arid in interior |
| **HIGHEST POINT** | Jabal ash Shaykh 2,814 m (9,232 ft) |
| **MAP REFERENCE** | Pages 200, 225 |

**S**yria is in the eastern Mediterranean, with Iraq and Turkey to the east and north and Lebanon, Israel and Jordan to the west and south. Throughout history it has played a key role in the region. Over the years Egyptians, Hittites, Persians, Greeks, and Romans came and went. Converted to Islam when overrun by the Arabs in 634, the Syrians' capital Damascus became a major center during the Umayyad Dynasty. Crusaders seized much of Syria in the twelfth century, but were ousted by the Kurdish general Saladin. Under French control from 1920, Syria became independent in 1946. After various military coups and counter-coups the Ba'ath Party seized power in 1963, and from 1971 until his death in 2000 party leader Hafez al-Assad has ruled Syria with an iron fist. A member of the minority Alawite religious sect, he has faced resistance from other Muslims, notably the Sunni majority. But when the Sunni Muslim Brotherhood rose against Damascus in 1992 their revolt was crushed, with up to 20,000 deaths. Following the Second Gulf War in 1991 Syria received huge amounts of aid as a result of its unexpected support for the coalition against Iraq. As a member of the Security Council, however, it sternly opposed the Third Gulf War in 2003.

Syria's Mediterranean coast, well-watered from subterranean sources, is one of the country's most fertile, intensively farmed, and densely populated regions. Inland is the Ghab Depression, a rift valley flanked by two mountain ranges. Here the Orontes ('Āṣī) River flows through gorges and wide valleys. To the south, the Heights of Hermon rise above the eastern slopes of the Anti-Lebanon Range (Jabal ash Sharqī). Snowmelt from the range provides water for Damascus. Inland lies the Syrian Desert (Bādiyat ash Shām), crossed by the Euphrates River (Firat Nehri). Oil was discovered along the Euphrates in the 1980s. Power from the Euphrates barrage produces seventy percent of Syria's electricity.

Under the socialist Ba'ath Party most industry is government controlled. The main industries are textiles, food processing, beverages, tobacco, phosphate rock mining, petroleum, and cement. Oil, textiles, cotton, and agricultural produce are the main exports. The country has many weak government-owned firms and low productivity. Oil production has begun to ebb and unemployment is expected to rise as the more than sixty percent of the population that is under twenty years old enters the labor force. Syria's Gulf War aid windfall of $5 billion has been spent.

# Iraq

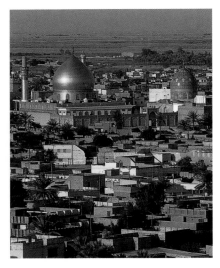

*View across the rooftops of Sāmarrā', Iraq, to the River Tigris (left). A portion of the facade of the Imam Mosque in Eşfahan, Iran (right page bottom).*

## Fact File

**OFFICIAL NAME** Republic of Iraq

**FORM OF GOVERNMENT** Republic in transition with interim government

**CAPITAL** Baghdād

**AREA** 437,072 sq km (168,753 sq miles)

**TIME ZONE** GMT + 3 hours

**POPULATION** 28,221,000

**PROJECTED POPULATION 2015** 34,947,000

**POPULATION DENSITY** 64.6 per sq km (167.2 per sq mile)

**LIFE EXPECTANCY** 69.6

**INFANT MORTALITY (PER 1,000)** 46.4

**OFFICIAL LANGUAGE** Arabic

**OTHER LANGUAGES** Aramaic, Azerbaijani

**LITERACY RATE** 74.1 %

**RELIGIONS** Muslim 97 % (Shi'a 60 %–65 %, Sunni 32 %–37 %), Christian or other 3 %

**ETHNIC GROUPS** Arab 75 %–80 %, Kurd 15 %–20 %, other (including Turkoman, Assyrian) 5 %

**CURRENCY** Iraqi dinar

**ECONOMY** Industry 68 %, services 27 %, agriculture 5 %

**GNI PER CAPITA** not available (estimated middle income between US$ 935 and 3,705)

**CLIMATE** Mainly arid, with cold winters and hot summers; winter snows in northern mountains

**HIGHEST POINT** Kūh-e Hājī Ebrāhīm 3,600 m (11,811 ft)

**MAP REFERENCE** Page 220

If any country has the right to call itself the cradle of Western civilization it is Iraq. The first city-states in the region date from nearly 3500 BC. The land "between the waters" of the Tigris and the Euphrates Rivers (the meaning of the old name Mesopotamia) has seen many empires come and go. Babylon defeated its old rival Assyria here in 612 BC, and in the seventh century BC the territory was seized by the Persians; Baghdad became the greatest commercial and cultural center of the Muslim world. The Persians held Iraq until they were conquered by Alexander the Great in 334 BC.

Part of the Ottoman Empire from 1534 to 1918, Iraq became independent in 1932.

Modern Iraq has been involved in three major conflicts in the space of twenty years: the First Gulf War between Iraq and Iran, 1980–88; the Second Gulf War in which it invaded Kuwait, 1990–91; and finally the Third Gulf War in 2003 that achieved the downfall of Saddam Hussein's regime, but has so far failed to install a stable, democratic form of government.

After the days of the early Mesopotamian empires, the Arab peoples brought Islam to Iraq in the seventh century AD. Like Iran, Iraq has a majority of Shi'ite Muslims. Unlike Iran, the ruling elite in Iraq are Sunni Muslims who fear their own Shi'ites are secretly loyal to Iran. This underlies the tension within Iraqi society and was the reason for the very restrictive politics of Saddam Hussein. The situation of the Kurds relates to an ethnic rather than a religious division. Distrusted and persecuted in every land in which they live (Turkey, Iran, Iraq, Syria, and Armenia) Iraq's Kurds were assaulted by Baghdad with chemical weapons in the 1980s.

In the far northeast Iraq shares part of the Zagros Mountains (Kūhhā-ye Zāgròs) with Iran. In the west its territory includes a piece of the Syrian Desert. The rest of the country falls into two broad physiographic categories—the lowland desert to the west which makes up nearly forty percent of the total land area; and the Tigris-Euphrates basin known formerly as Mesopotamia. Here the two rivers flow southeast roughly parallel, before meeting in a vast swamp on their way to the Persian Gulf. In this swamp live communities of Marsh Arabs, Shi'ite Muslims targeted by the leadership in Baghdad after an attempted rebellion following the Second Gulf War. Most Iraqi agricultural activity takes place in the alluvial Tigris-Euphrates plain, where one-third of the farms are irrigated. Vegetables and cereals are the most important crops. In addition to the rice grown in warmer lowland areas, wheat and barley are cultivated in the temperate country near the Zagros Mountains. Exports have fallen sharply, but in better times Iraq's date crop met eighty percent of world demand.

Three wars—the second followed by international embargoes designed to force acceptance of UN inspection of weapons of mass destruction—and the civil war following the US invasion of 2003 have severely damaged the Iraqi economy. It was formerly dominated by the oil sector, but today oil exports are probably no more than ten percent of their former level. Agricultural development has been hampered by labor shortages, salinization of the land, and the dislocation caused by earlier land reform and collectivization programs. Due to civil strife and enormous numbers of people fleeing their home, living standards continue to deteriorate. It remains to be seen whether the efforts of the interim government, which works closely with the US- and UK-led forces, will manage to establish peace and promote economic development, but prospects seem dark.

## Middle East conflicts

**1964** Iran: Ayatollah Khomeini exiled for criticism of Shah's secular state.

**1967** Israel: Six Day War with Arab states; seizes the Gaza Strip, Sinai, the Golan Heights, and the West Bank of the Jordan River.

**1972** Iraq: Nationalization of western-owned Iraq Petroleum Company.

**1973** Egypt and Syria join in attack on Israel.

**1979** Israel: Peace Treaty signed with Egypt. Iraq: Saddam Hussein takes over. Iran: Fall of the Shah. Ayatollah Khomeini returns from exile. Iran declared an Islamic Republic.

**1980** Iraqi invasion starts Iran–Iraq War.

**1988** Iran: US naval ship shoots down Iranian airliner, 290 killed. End of Iran-Iraq Gulf War. Iraqi troops use chemical weapons on Kurds.

**1990** Iraq invades and annexes Kuwait.

**1991** Western allies with UN mandate liberate Kuwait. UN demands Iraq accept weapons monitoring and destroy weapons of mass destruction.

**1993** Israel: PLO recognizes Israel in return for Palestinian autonomy in Gaza Strip and Jericho.

**1994** Iraq recognizes Kuwaiti sovereignty.

**1995** Israel: Palestinian autonomy extended to much of West Bank. PM Rabin assassinated.

**1997** UN charges Iraqi officials with blocking weapons inspections. Iran: Mohammed Khatami becomes president.

**1998** Iraq: Obstruction of UN weapons inspectors and fear of Iraq's biological weapons program leads to heavy bombing by US and UK.

**2003** Iraq: Saddam Hussein's regime is overthrown by US and UK forces and a small coalition; severe international criticism.

**2005** Iraq: Democratic elections and constitutional negotiations. Lebanon: Withdrawal of Syrian troops after 30 years.

**2006** Lebanon: Invasion by Israeli troops seeking to eliminate Hizbollah guerillas.

**2006** Iraq: Saddam is tried and hanged.

**2008/2009** Israel responds to Hamas rocket attacks with air strikes and ground assaults in the Gaza Strip.

# Iran

## Fact File

**OFFICIAL NAME** Islamic Republic of Iran

**FORM OF GOVERNMENT** Theocratic republic with single legislative body (Islamic Consultative Assembly)

**Capital** Tehrān

**AREA** 1,648,000 sq km (636,293 sq miles)

**TIME ZONE** GMT + 3.5 hours

**POPULATION** 65,875,000

**PROJECTED POPULATION 2015** 79,379,000

**POPULATION DENSITY** 40 per sq km (103.5 per sq mile)

**LIFE EXPECTANCY** 70.9

**INFANT MORTALITY (PER 1,000)** 36.9

**OFFICIAL LANGUAGE** Farsi (Persian)

**OTHER LANGUAGES** Turkic, Kurdish, Luri, Baloch, Azerbaijanian, Arabic, Armenian

**LITERACY RATE** 77 %

**RELIGIONS** Shi'a Muslim 89 %, Sunni Muslim 9 %, other (including Zoroastrian, Jewish, Christian, and Baha'i) 2 %

**ETHNIC GROUPS** Persian 51 %, Azeri 24 %, Gilaki and Mazandarani 8 %, Kurd 7 %, Arab 3 %, Lur 2 %, Baloch 2 %, Turkmen 2 %, other 1 %

**CURRENCY** Rial

**ECONOMY** Services 46.4 %, industry 42.9 %, agriculture 10.7 %

**GNI PER CAPITA** US$ 3,470

**CLIMATE** Mainly arid, temperate in far north; cold winters and hot summers

**HIGHEST POINT** Qolleh-ye Damāvand 5,671 m (18,605 ft)

**MAP REFERENCE** Pages 220–21, 222

Iran is one of the largest of the Persian Gulf States. It has borders with ten other countries in the region including Afghanistan, Pakistan, and Turkey. Now the home of the world's largest theocracy, and the main center for militant Shi'a Islam, Persia (as it was formerly known) has seen the rise and fall of a number of civilizations, including those of the Medes, Persians, Greeks, and Parthians. In the seventh century it was overrun by an invasion of Arabs who introduced Islam, a religion which under the Safavids in 1502 became the Shi'ite form of the faith that prevails today. Oil was discovered in Iran in 1908. From that time on Persia (retitled in the 1920s by a Shah who adopted the name Iran because it meant "Aryan") became of growing interest to the great powers, and the requirements of international oil companies began to figure in Iranian life.

After the Second World War the Iranians found the corrupt and despotic rule of Shah Reza Pahlavi intolerable, and in 1979 he was overthrown in the first national revolution to be led by Islamic fundamentalists. This event has had profound effects and repercussions throughout the Muslim world. Iran's subsequent support for Islamic radicalism abroad soon led to strained relations with Central Asian, Middle Eastern, and North African nations, as well as the USA. After Iran's economic difficulties and isolation had caused a general relaxation both in the domestic regime and in its external affairs for a while, this trend was reversed when the ultraconservative layman Ahmadinejad came to power in 2005.

The entire central region of Iran is dominated by a high, arid plateau (average elevation 1,200 m; 3,937 ft), most of it salt desert, containing the Dasht-e Lūt (Great Sand Desert) and the Dasht-e-Kavīr (Great Salt Desert). Mountain ranges surround the plateau: the volcanic Elburz Range (Reshteh-ye Kūhhā-ye Alborz) along the Caspian Sea; the Khorasan and Baluchestan Ranges in the east and southeast; and the Zagros Mountains (Kūhhā-ye Zāgros) inland from the Persian Gulf.

The most productive parts of Iran, and the most heavily populated, lie on its periphery. In the north are the fisheries, tea gardens, and rice fields of the Caspian shore. In Khuzestan to the south there are sugar plantations and oilfields—a prime target of the Iraqis when they invaded in 1980 at the start of the eight-year Iran-Iraq War. Westward lie the wheatfields of Azarbaijan, while to the east are the fruit groves of the oases of Kavir in Kavir (Dasht-e Kavīr) and Lut in Lut Desert (Dasht-e Lūt).

Approximately eight percent of Iran's land is arable, and eleven percent of it is forested, mostly in the provinces of Gilan and Mazandaran which border the Caspian Sea. The province of Tehrān, which includes the country's capital of the same name in the north, is by far the most densely populated region supporting about eighteen percent of the population.

In the years after 1945 Iran's economy became almost totally dependent on oil, and earnings from oil exports still provide 85 percent of its export revenue. But by the end of the war with Iraq (1980–88) production had fallen to just half the level of 1979. This, combined with the general fall in oil prices, and a surge in imports that began in 1989, has left Iran in severe financial difficulties, and there has been a marked decline in the general standard of living. Ideological considerations hamper effective reforms: there is a continuing struggle between the powerful religious leadership on the one hand, and reformist politicians on the other, over how to run a modern economy. The mullahs (the Islamic clergy) object to the government using borrowed money and are firmly opposed to the importation of "corrupt" Western technology.

Overall, the Iranian economy is a mix of centrally planned large-scale state enterprise; village-based agriculture producing wheat, barley, rice, sugar beet, tobacco, and pistachio nuts; and small-scale private trading and service ventures.

## Central and West Asia

Afghanistan · · · · · · · · 184
Kazakhstan · · · · · · · · 184
Uzbekistan · · · · · · · · 185
Mongolia · · · · · · · · 186
Kyrgyzstan · · · · · · · · 186
Turkmenistan · · · · · · · 187
Tadjikistan · · · · · · · · 188
Armenia · · · · · · · · · 188
Azerbaijan · · · · · · · · 189
Georgia · · · · · · · · · 190
Turkey · · · · · · · · · · 190
Cyprus · · · · · · · · · 191

Dependencies · · · · · · 192

## Afghanistan

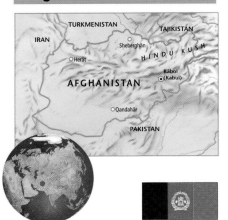

### Fact File

**OFFICIAL NAME** Islamic Republic of Afghanistan

**FORM OF GOVERNMENT** Islamic republic

**CAPITAL** Kābol (Kabul)

**AREA** 647,500 sq km (250,000 sq miles)

**TIME ZONE** GMT + 4.5 hours

**POPULATION** 32,738,000

**PROJECTED POPULATION 2015** 35,631,000

**POPULATION DENSITY** 50.6 per sq km (131 per sq mile)

**LIFE EXPECTANCY** 44.2

**INFANT MORTALITY (PER 1,000)** 154.7

**OFFICIAL LANGUAGES** Dari (Afghan Persian), Pashto

**OTHER LANGUAGES** Uzbek, Turkmen, Indi and Pamiri languages, Dravidian

**LITERACY RATE** 28.1 %

**RELIGIONS** Sunni Muslim 80 %, Shi'a Muslim 19 %, other 1 %

**ETHNIC GROUPS** Pashtun 42 %, Tajik 27 %, Hazara 9 %, Uzbek 9 %, Aimak 4 %, Turkmen 3 %, other 6 %

**CURRENCY** Afghani

**ECONOMY** Agriculture 38 %, services 38 %, industry 24 %

**GNI PER CAPITA** not available (less than US$ 935)

**CLIMATE** Mainly semiarid, but arid in southwest and cold in mountains; hot summers and cold winters

**HIGHEST POINT** Nowshak 7,485 m (24,557 ft)

**MAP REFERENCE** Page 221

Afghanistan is a landlocked country in the central part of South Asia with nearly three-quarters of its territory mountainous. It shares a western frontier with Iran, while Pakistan is across the southeastern border. Once a part of the ancient Persian Empire, Afghanistan was conquered by Alexander the Great in 328 BC. In the seventh century AD it adopted Islam. From 1953 it was closely allied with the former Soviet Union. In 1979 the Soviet government intervened to install a communist faction, and though constantly beseiged by mujahideen guerrilla fighters, maintained its military occupation until 1989. After the over-throw of the communist government in 1992 the mujahideen began fighting among themselves along ethnic lines. In 1996–2001, the Sunni Mus-lim Taliban militia, associated with the majority Pashtun, was in control of the country and imposed a strict Islamic rule. An international alliance overthrew them in late 2001 and insti-gated democratic elections in 2004 to allow the country to return to a semblance of normality.

Geographically, the country's largest area is the thinly populated central highlands. This comprises most of the Hindu Kush, the second highest range in the world. The northeast is seismically active. Much of the rest is desert or semidesert, except for a few fertile and heavily populated valleys. Most agriculture takes place on the northern plains, near the frontiers of Turkmenistan, Uzbekistan, and Tajikistan. The country's main river basins are those of the Amu Darya, Helmand, and Kābol.

Afghanistan is very poor: a list of 192 coun-tries ranked for calorie intake in 1995 placed Afghanistan 191. It depends largely on wheat farming and the raising of sheep and goats. During the Soviet occupation and the subsequent internecine conflict, one-third of the population left the country. Many have now come home to an economically devastated land. Millions of people lack food, clothing, housing, and medical care. Though data are shaky, it is likely that the country's most profitable crop is opium, Afghanistan reputedly being the world's second largest producer after Myanmar (Burma), and a major source of hashish.

## Kazakhstan

### Fact File

**OFFICIAL NAME** Republic of Kazakhstan

**FORM OF GOVERNMENT** Republic with two legislative bodies (Senate and Majilis)

**CAPITAL** Aqmola (Astana)

**AREA** 2,717,300 sq km (1,049,150 sq miles)

**TIME ZONE** GMT + 6 hours

**POPULATION** 15,341,000

**PROJECTED POPULATION 2015** 16,299,000

**POPULATION DENSITY** 5.6 per sq km (14.6 per sq mile)

**LIFE EXPECTANCY** 67.6

**INFANT MORTALITY (PER 1,000)** 26.6

**OFFICIAL LANGUAGE** Kazakh

**OTHER LANGUAGE** Russian

**LITERACY RATE** 99.5 %

**RELIGIONS** Muslim 47 %, Russian Orthodox 44 %, Protestant 2 %, other 7 %

**ETHNIC GROUPS** Kazak 53.4 %, Russian 30 %, Ukrainian 3.7 %, Uzbek 2.5 %, German 2.4 %, Tatar 1.7 %, Uygur 1.4 %, other 4.9 %

**CURRENCY** Tenge

**ECONOMY** Services 54.8 %, industry 39.4 %, agriculture 5.8 %

**GNI PER CAPITA** US$ 5,060

**CLIMATE** Mainly arid; cold winters and hot summers; cooler in north

**HIGHEST POINT** Khan Tängiri Shyngy 6,995 m
(22,949 ft)

**MAP REFERENCE** Pages 222–23

With a land area nearly as large as India,
Kazakhstan is an important member of the
newly formed Commonwealth of Independent
States (CIS). In earlier times, when it was a Soviet
Republic, authorities used the region for testing
nuclear weapons and for exiling ethnic minorities.

In the 1950s and 1960s when the Soviet "virgin
lands" project was underway, vast tracts of pasture
were sown with wheat or given over to livestock
production, and waters from rivers running into
the Aral Sea were used in irrigation schemes. As
a result, the sea shrank by seventy percent.

During the years of Soviet domination, high
levels of immigration from Russia resulted in the
Kazakhs being outnumbered. Outmigration of
Russians since 1991 and the return of many expatriates has resulted in a Kazak majority once
more, but ethnic tensions remain high.

Much of the country is tablelands—the eroded
tableland of the east featuring shallow uplands,
depressions, and lakes—and there are also several mountains ranges in the east including the
Altai Range (Mongol Altayn Nuruu). Running
from north to south, steppe country gives way to
desert or semidesert, though irrigation schemes
have made large areas productive between the
Aral Sea and Lake Balkhash (Balqash Köli).

With a climate marked by intense winter cold
and extreme summer heat, rainfall is generally
low. The lakes in the center of the country are
saline, as are the marshes in the west, and in the
central region there are few permanent rivers.
The grassy steppes of the north are the most
naturally fertile part of the country. Though the
region has traditionally been associated with
livestock rearing (Kazakhstan still supports up to
200,000 nomadic shepherds and herdsmen) the
agricultural policies of the Soviet period converted
much pasture to grain cultivation. By 1989 the
country accounted for twenty percent of the
entire cultivated area of the Soviet Union and
twelve percent of its grain output.

Other crops grown include fruits, potatoes,
vegetables, sugar beet, and cotton. High quality
wool is produced, and Kazakhstan supplies meat
to surrounding countries. Industry is based mainly
on processing raw materials: fuel, metals, textiles,
chemicals, and food. Products include rolled metals,
agricultural machinery, plastics, clothing, footwear,
paper, and cement. Well endowed with oil and gas
reserves, the country also has deposits of coal, iron
ore, bauxite, copper, nickel, tungsten, zinc, and
silver. In addition, it holds seventy percent of CIS
gold reserves. The government has been pursuing
a moderate program of reform and privatization—
investment incentives have been established, state
controls have been lifted, and assets privatized. But
government control of key industries remains extensive. Lack of pipeline transportation for oil export hinders a likely source of economic growth.

Environmental problems are extensive and
severe. Radioactive or toxic chemical sites associated with weapons development are widespread.
The drying up of the Aral Sea has left a crust of
chemical pesticides which is periodically blown
about in noxious dust storms.

# Uzbekistan

*The city of Kābol in Afghanistan, devastated by years
of warfare (left page bottom). The Tila Kara Marasa, in
Registan Square, Samarqand, Uzbekistan, built in the
seventeenth century (above).*

## Fact File

**OFFICIAL NAME** Republic of Uzbekistan

**FORM OF GOVERNMENT** Republic with single
legislative body (Supreme Assembly)

**CAPITAL** Toshkent (Tashkent)

**AREA** 447,400 sq km (172,741 sq miles)

**TIME ZONE** GMT + 6 hours

**POPULATION** 28,268,000

**PROJECTED POPULATION 2015** 30,645,000

**POPULATION DENSITY** 63.2 per sq km
(163.6 per sq mile)

**LIFE EXPECTANCY** 65.4

**INFANT MORTALITY (PER 1,000)** 67.8

**OFFICIAL LANGUAGE** Uzbek

**OTHER LANGUAGES** Russian, Tajik

**LITERACY RATE** 99.3 %

**RELIGIONS** Muslim 88 % (mostly Sunnis),
Eastern Orthodox 9 %, other 3 %

**ETHNIC GROUPS** Uzbek 80 %, Russian 5.5 %,
Tajik 5 %, Kazakh 3 %, Tatar 1.5 %, other 5 %

**CURRENCY** Som

**ECONOMY** Services 37.5 %, industry 33.1 %,
agriculture 29.4 %

**GNI PER CAPITA** US$ 730

**CLIMATE** Mainly arid, with cold winters and
long, hot summers

**HIGHEST POINT** Adelunga Toghi 4,301 m (14,111 ft)

**MAP REFERENCE** Pages 222–23

Uzbekistan stretches from the shrinking Aral
Sea to the heights of the western Pamirs.
Its main frontiers are with Kazakhstan to the
north and Turkmenistan to the south. The Uzbek
people are of Turkic origin and seem to have
taken their name from the Mongol Öz Beg Khan
(AD 1313–40), who may also have converted
them to Islam. In the fifteenth century they
moved south into their present land. The
Muslim cities of Samarqand and Bukhoro are in
Uzbekistan, Bukhoro being a major religious
center. Muslims unable to visit Mecca can
become hajis by visiting Bukhoro seven times

instead. In the former USSR the territory was the
Uzbek Soviet Socialist Republic, and Uzbek leaders
suffered much during Stalin's purges. In 1991
Uzbekistan became independent and is today
ruled by the old communist elite as a de facto
one-party state. The most populous of the Central
Asian republics, Uzbekistan also has the greatest
variety of ethnic groups. This is often a source of
conflict. The Turkish-speaking Uzbeks clash with
the Farsi-speaking Tajiks, and the Meskhetian
Turks (deported from Georgia to Central Asia by
Stalin) clash with the Uzbeks in the Fergana
Valley. In 1999/2000, the Islamic Movement tried
in vain to erect an Islamic Caliphate there.

The middle region of Uzbekistan consists
of the desert plains of the Kyzyl Kum (Peski
Kyzylkum). While some of this area supports
herders with cattle and sheep, today it is more
important for its oil and gas reserves. To the
west is the river delta formed where the
Syrdar'ya (Oxus) enters the Aral Sea, while
the Ustyurt Plateau lies in the extreme northwest.
East of the Kyzyl Kum, beyond the capital of
Toshkent and the Chatkal Mountains, is a spur
jutting into Kyrgyzstan. This contains a large part
of the fertile Fergana Basin. Uzbekistan is the
world's fourth-largest cotton producer, and the
Fergana Valley bears the environmental scars of
the fertilizers and pesticides which helped to
bring this about.

Although it grows large quantities of cotton,
Uzbekistan is unable to produce enough grain
for its own needs, importing it from Russia,
Kazakhstan, and the USA. A rethinking of the
Soviet-style economy has yet to take place.

As well as one of the world's largest gold-
mines, at Murantau, Uzbekistan has large deposits
of natural gas, petroleum, coal, and uranium.
Gas is currently used domestically, but it could
become a major export. After 1991 the government tried to strengthen the economy with subsidies and tight price controls. Inflation rose to
1,500 percent at one point and in 1995 food
rationing had to be introduced. At present, efforts
are being made to tighten monetary policies,
expand privatization, and to reduce the state's
role in the economy, as well as strengthen political and economic ties with Russia.

# Mongolia

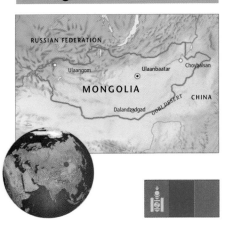

## Fact File

**OFFICIAL NAME** Mongolia

**FORM OF GOVERNMENT** Republic with single legislative body (State Great Hural)

**CAPITAL** Ulaanbaatar (Ulan Bator)

**AREA** 1,564,116 sq km (604,247 sq miles)

**TIME ZONE** GMT + 8 hours

**POPULATION** 2,996,000

**PROJECTED POPULATION 2015** 2,858,000

**POPULATION DENSITY** 1.9 per sq km (5 per sq mile)

**LIFE EXPECTANCY** 67.3

**INFANT MORTALITY (PER 1,000)** 41.2

**OFFICIAL LANGUAGE** Khalka Mongol

**OTHER LANGUAGES** Turkic, Russian, Chinese, Kazakh

**LITERACY RATE** 97.8 %

**RELIGIONS** Tibetan Buddhist 50 %, Shamanist and Christian 6 %, Muslim 4 %, none 40 %

**ETHNIC GROUPS** Mongol 94.9 %, Kazakh 5 %, other 0.1 %

**CURRENCY** Tugrik

**ECONOMY** Services 40.8 %, industry 40.4 %, agriculture 18.8 %

**GNI PER CAPITA** US$ 1,290

**CLIMATE** Cold and arid

**HIGHEST POINT** Tavan Bogd Uul 4,374 m (14,350 ft)

**MAP REFERENCE** Pages 300–01

The world's largest and most thinly populated landlocked country, Mongolia has a reputation for isolation. Its deserts, severe climate, and widely scattered population of nomadic pastoralists have tended to keep it isolated from modern life. Historically, however, Mongolia enjoyed its hour of glory. In the thirteenth century the Mongol tribes were united under the leadership of Ghengis Khan (1162–1227), who then established the largest empire yet known, at its peak extending from eastern Europe to the Pacific Ocean and into northern India. The Mongol Empire collapsed in 1368, after which Mongolia (also known as

Outer Mongolia to distinguish it from Inner Mongolia, one of China's Autonomous Regions) fell under Chinese control. Following the Russian Civil War (1918–22) the Chinese were expelled. Today, after seventy years within the Soviet system, the country is trying to remake itself in a more democratic mold.

Mongolia can be divided into two regions. In the northwest lie the Mongolian Altai Mountains (Mongol Altayn Nuruu), along with the Hangayn (Hangayn Nuruu) and Hentiyn Ranges (Govĭ Altayn Nuruu). Here, high mountains alternate with river valleys and lakes. Pastures support large herds of cattle and sheep, and wheat is cultivated. At the highest levels of the Altai in the northwest boreal forests cover the slopes. The second region is the southern half of the country. This is semidesert steppe changing further south to salt-pans, shallow depressions, and the arid stony wastes of the Gobi Desert.

While today more people live in towns than in the country, Mongolia nontheless remains a land of nomadic pastoralists. Herds of goats, sheep, yaks, camels, and horses still provide the base of the traditional economy, and Mongolia has the highest number of livestock per capita in the world. Cattle raising accounts for more than two-thirds of all production. Under the Soviets textiles and food processing were developed, and with aid from the USSR and Comecon (Council for Mutual Economic Assistance) mineral deposits such as copper, molybdenum, and coking coal were developed. Mongolia is the world's third biggest producer of fluorspar.

Recently, new laws have been passed regulating mining, banking, foreign investment, tourism, and economic planning. Mongolia continues to attract foreign aid, but suffers from the loss of Russian financial support. So far, foreign funds have not been found for the development of Mongolia's considerable oil and gas reserves.

# Kyrgysztan

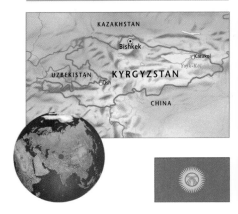

## Fact File

**OFFICIAL NAME** Kyrgyz Republic

**FORM OF GOVERNMENT** Republic with two legislative bodies (Assembly of People's Representatives and Legislative Assembly)

**CAPITAL** Bishkek

**AREA** 198,500 sq km (76,641 sq miles)

**TIME ZONE** GMT + 6 hours

**POPULATION** 5,357,000

**PROJECTED POPULATION 2015** 5,782,000

**POPULATION DENSITY** 27 per sq km (69.9 per sq mile)

**LIFE EXPECTANCY** 69.1

**INFANT MORTALITY (PER 1,000)** 32.3

**OFFICIAL LANGUAGE** Kyrghiz

**OTHER LANGUAGE** Russian

**LITERACY RATE** 98.7 %

**RELIGIONS** Muslim 75 %, Russian Orthodox 20 %, other 5 %

**ETHNIC GROUPS** Kyrghiz 64.9 %, Uzbek 13.6 %, Russian 12.5 %, Dungan 1.1 %, Ukrainian 1 %, Uygur 1 %, other 5.9 %

**CURRENCY** Som

**ECONOMY** Services 49.1 %, agriculture 30.9 %, industry 20 %

**GNI PER CAPITA** US$ 590

**CLIMATE** Subtropical in southwest, temperate in valleys, cold and snowy in mountains

**HIGHEST POINT** Pik Pobedy 7,439 m (24,406 ft)

**MAP REFERENCE** Page 223

Kyrgyzstan is a small, mountainous, landlocked country in Central Asia. China lies over the massive peaks of the Tian Shan Range along its southeast border, Kazakhstan is to the north, and Uzbekistan and Tajikistan are to the southwest. Not only is Kyrgyzstan the least urbanized of all the ex-Soviet republics, its population is growing faster in rural areas than in the towns. Native Kyrgyz are barely a majority and ethnic tension

*A Mongolian musician playing a horsehair fiddle (left). Women at the market in the town of Osh, Kyrgyzstan (right page top). Melon sellers at a market in Turkmenistan (right page bottom).*

with Uzbeks and other nationals from nearby countries is a feature of everyday life. Fierce clashes between Kyrgyz and Uzbeks took place in the border city of Osh in 1990. Historically, the once nomadic Muslim Kyrgyz pastoralists are descended from refugees of Mongolian and Turkic origin who entered the region in the thirteenth century, escaping from Mongol invaders. For a while in the eighteenth century the region came under Manchu domination, then during the nineteenth century Russia began to colonize the country. Russian immigrants took the best land, settling in the low-lying, fertile areas. For years after the country's incorporation into the Soviet Union in the 1920s, resistance was carried out by local guerrilla groups called *basmachi*. Since independence in 1991, Kyrgyzstan has pursued liberal political and economic policies, but is plagued by corruption and is faced with undemocratic developments in its government.

Geographically, Kyrgyzstan is dominated by the western end of the Tian Shan Range, which rises to Pik Pobedy (7,439 m; 24,406 ft) on the Chinese border. A large part of this mountain range is permanently snow-capped. The rest of the country is made up of a series of mountainous parallel ridges, separated by deep valleys and basins. The deep waters of Lake Ysyk-Köl are surrounded by snowy mountains in the northeast. The Fergana Valley, which is the main lowland region, lies in the southwest.

Much of the lower land is pasture for sheep, pigs, cattle, goats, horses, and yaks. Irrigated land is used to produce crops ranging from sugar beet and vegetables to rice, cotton, tobacco, grapes, and mulberry trees (for feeding silkworms). There are major salination problems caused mainly by the excessive irrigation of cotton.

Cotton, wool, and meat are the main agricultural products and exports: one of Kyrgyzstan's strengths is agricultural self-sufficiency. It has small quantities of coal, oil, gas, and the extensive snow-covered ranges ensure great hydropower potential. Energy policy aims at developing these resources in order to make the country less dependent on Russia. Following independence, Kyrgyzstan has carried out market reforms, such as an improved regulatory system and land reform, but political instability in 2005/06 has undercut the investment climate. The economy is still dominated by the state. Foreign aid plays a major role in the country's budget.

# Turkmenistan

## Fact File

| | |
|---|---|
| **OFFICIAL NAME** | Republic of Turkmenistan |
| **FORM OF GOVERNMENT** | Republic with single legislative body (Parliament) |
| **CAPITAL** | Ashgabat |
| **AREA** | 488,100 sq km (188,455 sq miles) |
| **TIME ZONE** | GMT + 5 hours |
| **POPULATION** | 5,180,000 |
| **PROJECTED POPULATION 2015** | 5,498,000 |
| **POPULATION DENSITY** | 10.6 per sq km (27.5 per sq mile) |
| **LIFE EXPECTANCY** | 68.6 |
| **INFANT MORTALITY (PER 1,000)** | 51.8 |
| **OFFICIAL LANGUAGE** | Turkmen |
| **OTHER LANGUAGES** | Russian, Uzbek |
| **LITERACY RATE** | 98.8 % |
| **RELIGIONS** | Muslim 89 %, Eastern Orthodox 9 %, unknown 2 % |
| **ETHNIC GROUPS** | Turkmen 85 %, Uzbek 5 %, Russian 4 %, other 6 % |
| **CURRENCY** | Manat |
| **ECONOMY** | Services 47.7 %, industry 40.8 %, agriculture 11.5 % |
| **GNI PER CAPITA** | not available (estimated between US$ 900 and 3,000) |
| **CLIMATE** | Mainly arid, with cold winters and hot summers |

**HIGHEST POINT** Ayrybaba 3,139 m (10,298 ft)

**MAP REFERENCE** Page 222

Turkmenistan is in southern Central Asia. From the Caspian Sea it stretches east to Afghanistan, and borders Iran to the south. Kazakhstan and Uzbekistan lie to the north. The Turkmen are probably descended from the same tribes as the Seljuk and Ottoman Turks who conquered what is now Turkey in the eleventh century. Russia annexed Turkmenistan in 1884 and began colonizing it in 1906. In 1924 it became the Turkmen Soviet Socialist Republic. Fierce local resistance to Sovietization continued into the 1930s and there were mass arrests of cultural and religious leaders. Turkmenistan declared its independence in 1991 but little has changed politically. The first secretary of the former Communist Party became president for life, elected with a 99.5 percent share of the vote. Following his death in 2006, multi-candidate elections were held in 2007, which were won by his former aide, Gurbanguly Berdimuhammedov.

More than ninety percent of the country is arid, the greater part of it being the Kara Kum Desert. Most of the Kara Kum is made up of the plains of the Krasnovodskoye Plato, but ten percent consists of huge sand dunes. In the east the Amu Darya River forms part of the Afghanistan border. This river once fed the Aral Sea but from the 1950s much of its water was diverted into the Kara Kum Canal which crosses two-thirds of the country westward to Kizyl-Arvat (Gyzlarbat). This provided irrigation for cotton, but also helped dry up the Aral Sea. To the west of the plateau the land falls to the Caspian shore.

Turkmenistan is poor, despite its natural gas and oil reserves. Half its irrigated land is planted in cotton but industrial development has been limited. Apart from Astrakhan rugs and food processing, industry is largely confined to mining sulfur and salt, and natural gas production. Through 1995 inflation soared, and falling production saw the budget shift from a surplus to a deficit. Since independence in 1991 there have been few changes in economic policy, leading to growing poverty and a shortage of basic foods. Cotton and grain harvests were disastrous in 1996 and desertification remains a serious problem. There is hope that the new government will be more open towards foreign investment.

## Armenia

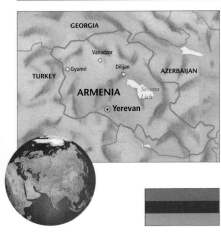

## Tajikistan

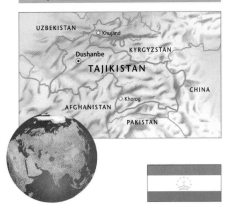

Tajikistan lies between Uzbekistan, Afghanistan, and China on the western slope of the Pamirs. It also shares a border with Kyrgyzstan to the north. The country is an irregular shape because it was carved out of the Soviet Republic of Uzbekistan on Stalin's orders in 1929. This was intended to deal with Tajik resistance to the Soviet regime, but as it left the two Tajik centers of Samarqand and Bukhoro in Uzbekistan, it merely added another grievance. The Tajiks are Persian-Iranian culturally and linguistically, not Turkic-Mongol like many other peoples of Central Asia. Immigration of both Uzbeks and Russians during the Soviet era caused further resentment. Since independence in 1991 ethnic hostility has resulted in a state of near civil war. Tens of thousands were killed and thousands more have fled to Afghanistan and Kyrgyzstan. Only in 1997 was a peace achieved. It remains a major objective to overcome the destructions of the war.

A long finger of territory in the north contains the only fertile agricultural region. This is the western end of the Fergana Valley through which the Syrdar'ya drains northwest toward the Aral Sea. Cotton is the chief crop, though cereals and fruit are also grown. The region has seen the overuse of pesticides on cotton, and the drying up of the distant Aral Sea has been aggravated by water taken for irrigation. Between this valley and one to the south drained by the Vakhsh stand the Turkestan and Gissar Ranges. This substantial physical divide also corresponds to the political divide between the Uzbek communists in the north and the Islamic secularists in the south. Most of eastern Tajikistan consists of the Pamirs, a part of the Tien Shan Range of western China.

Tajikistan has the second-lowest per capita gross domestic product of any former USSR republic, the fastest growing population, and a low standard of living. Agriculture is the most important sector and cotton the main crop. The country has limited mineral resources, including silver, gold, uranium, and tungsten. Hydropower provides energy for the manufacture of aluminum, cotton textiles and clothing, and for food processing. The economy is weak from years of conflict. Subsidies once provided by the USSR are gone, along with markets—Russia once bought Tajik uranium for its weapons program. Basic subsistence for many people depends on foreign aid. Social instability, plus the continuation of Soviet-era politicians and officials in power, has prevented economic reforms.

### Fact File

OFFICIAL NAME  Republic of Tajikistan

FORM OF GOVERNMENT  Republic with single legislative body (Supreme Assembly)

CAPITAL  Dushanbe

AREA  143,100 sq km (55,251 sq miles)

TIME ZONE  GMT + 6 hours

POPULATION  7,212,000

PROJECTED POPULATION 2015  7,703,000

POPULATION DENSITY  50.4 per sq km (130.5 per sq mile)

LIFE EXPECTANCY  65

INFANT MORTALITY (PER 1,000)  42.3

OFFICIAL LANGUAGE  Tajik

OTHER LANGUAGES  Russian, Uzbek

LITERACY RATE  99.5 %

RELIGIONS  Sunni Muslim 85 %, Shi'a Muslim 5 %, other (including Russian Orthodox) 10 %

ETHNIC GROUPS  Tajik 79.9 %, Uzbek 15.3 %, Russian 1.1 %, Kyrgyz 1.1 %, other 2.6 %

CURRENCY  Tajik ruble

ECONOMY  Services 46.2 %, industry 30.4 %, agriculture 23.4 %

GNI PER CAPITA  US$ 460

CLIMATE  Mild winters and hot summers in valleys and on plains, drier and much colder in mountains

HIGHEST POINT  Pik imeni Ismail Samani 7,495 m (24,590 ft)

MAP REFERENCE  Page 223

### Fact File

OFFICIAL NAME  Republic of Armenia

FORM OF GOVERNMENT  Republic with single legislative body (National Assembly)

CAPITAL  Yerevan

AREA  29,800 sq km (11,506 sq miles)

TIME ZONE  GMT + 4 hours

POPULATION  2,969,000

PROJECTED POPULATION 2015  2,976,000

POPULATION DENSITY  99.6 per sq km (258 per sq mile)

LIFE EXPECTANCY  72.4

INFANT MORTALITY (PER 1,000)  20.9

OFFICIAL LANGUAGE  Armenian

OTHER LANGUAGE  Russian

LITERACY RATE  99.4 %

RELIGIONS  Armenian Orthodox 94.7 %, other (Russian Orthodox, Muslim, Protestant) 5.3 %

ETHNIC GROUPS  Armenian 97.9 %, Kurd 1.3 %, Russian 0.5 %, other 0.3 %

CURRENCY  Dram

ECONOMY  Services 46.4 %, industry 36.4 %, agriculture 17.2 %

GNI PER CAPITA  US$ 2,640

CLIMATE  Mainly dry, with cold winters and warm summers; cooler in mountains

HIGHEST POINT  Aragats Lerr 4,090 m (13,419 ft)

MAP REFERENCE  Page 222

Armenia is a small, mountainous, Christian country, landlocked between hostile Muslim neighbors. To the east is Azerbaijan, and to the west is Turkey, which inflicted genocidal massacres on the Armenian people between 1894 and 1915. The legendary resting place of Noah's Ark after the Flood (its capital supposedly founded by Noah himself), Armenia had already existed as a distinct country for 1,000 years when in the fourth century AD it became the first in the world to make Christianity its state religion. The country has been fought over at various times by Romans, Persians, and Mongols. It became a Soviet Socialist Republic in 1922 and gained its independence from the Soviet Union in 1991. In 1988 there was a devastating earthquake which killed 25,000 people and destroyed power stations and other infrastructure, and in the same year conflict began over Nagorno-Karabakh, an internal Azerbaijani area largely populated by Christian Armenians which is claimed by Armenia.

The mountains of the Lesser Caucasus (Malyy Kavkaz) cover most of the country. The landscape is rugged, and includes extinct volcanoes and high lava plateaus cut with ravines. An active seismic area, the frequency of earthquakes in Armenia indicates that mountain-building is still taking place. Although the city of Ararat is in Armenia, Mt Ararat itself is across the border in Turkey. The centrally located Lake Sevan (Sevana Lich) lies nearly 2,000 m (6,000 ft) above sea level, but its use for hydropower has drained it to a point where drinking water supplies are threatened. Steppe vegetation is the main cover and drought-resistant grasses and sagebrush grow on the lower mountain slopes, where jackals, wildcats, and the occasional leopard are found.

As a Soviet Republic, Armenia developed an industrial sector, supplying machine building tools, textiles, and other manufactured goods to other republics in return for raw materials and energy. It has few natural resources, although formerly lead, copper, and zinc were mined, and there are deposits of gold and bauxite. Agriculture is an important source of income. In irrigated areas around Yerevan, crops include grapes, almonds, figs, and olives, while apples, pears, and cereals are grown on higher ground. Armenia is also known for its quality brandies and wines. Economic decline in the period from 1991 to 1994 was a direct result of the ongoing conflict over Nagorno-Karabakh. In retaliation for Armenia's military activities in the region, Turkey and Azerbaijan blockaded pipeline and railroad traffic into the country, causing chronic energy shortages. There have been improvements, but full economic recovery is unlikely before Armenia's conflict with its neighbors is settled.

*A yurt in the Pamir region of Tajikistan (left page top). View over the city of Yerevan in Armenia, with Mt Ararat in the background (below).*

# Azerbaijan

## Fact File

**OFFICIAL NAME** Republic of Azerbaijan

**FORM OF GOVERNMENT** Federal republic with single legislative body (National Assembly)

**CAPITAL** Baki (Baku)

**AREA** 86,600 sq km (33,436 sq miles)

**TIME ZONE** GMT + 4 hours

**POPULATION** 8,178,000

**PROJECTED POPULATION 2015** 9,008,000

**POPULATION DENSITY** 94.4 per sq km (244.6 per sq mile)

**LIFE EXPECTANCY** 66.3

**INFANT MORTALITY (PER 1,000)** 56.4

**OFFICIAL LANGUAGE** Azerbaijani

**OTHER LANGUAGES** Russian, Armenian

**LITERACY RATE** 98.8 %

**RELIGIONS** Muslim 93.4 %, Russian Orthodox 2.5 %, Armenian Orthodox 2.3 %, other 1.8 %

**ETHNIC GROUPS** Azeri 90.6 %, Dagestani peoples 2.2 %, Russian 1.8 %, Armenian 1.5 %, other 3.9 %

**CURRENCY** Manat

**ECONOMY** Industry 63.3 %, services 30.5 %, agriculture 6.2 %

**GNI PER CAPITA** US$ 2,550

**CLIMATE** Mainly semiarid

**HIGHEST POINT** Bazardüzü Dağ 4,466 m (14,652 ft)

**MAP REFERENCE** Page 222

Oil was being collected from the Caspian Sea near Baku at least 1,000 years ago, when the area was known as "land of eternal fire" because of burning natural gas flaming out of the ground. Today oil from Baku continues to be the mainstay of the Azerbaijani economy. The home of an independent Azeri state as early as the fourth century BC, the region later fell under the influence of Persia, then in the eleventh century Turkic-speaking people moved in and assumed control. A period of affiliation with the Soviets following the Russian Revolution led to Azerbaijan becoming a member of the Soviet Union in 1936. In 1990 it was one of the first Soviet Republics to declare independence.

Since 1988 there have been troubles with Armenia over the region of Nagorno-Karabakh in southwestern Azerbaijan. This territorial dispute (Armenia now holds twenty percent of the region, most of the people in Nagorno-Karabakh being Christian Armenians) remains a major political problem for the newly independent state.

A range of the Great Caucasus (Bol'shoy Kavkas) running at an angle toward the Caspian Sea separates Russia from Azerbaijan, and reaches almost as far as Baku. South of this range, draining out of the foothills of the Caucasus in Georgia, the Kura (Kür) River reaches a broad floodplain, some of which lies below sea level. The mountains of the Lesser Caucasus (Malyy Kavkaz) form much of Nagorno-Karabakh in the southwest and also stand between Azerbaijan and its isolated enclave-territory Naxçivan. Although a Naxçivan independence movement exists, this territory, which is surrounded by Iran and Armenia, is regarded by the government as part of the Azerbaijan state. Dry and subtropical, the lowlands experience mild winters and long, hot summers, and are frequently affected by drought. Plant cover consists of steppe grassland in the drier lowland regions, woods in the mountains, and swamps in the southeast.

Early this century Baku supplied as much as half the world's oil, but production declined steadily during the final years under Soviet control as plants became antiquated and maintenance was neglected. The 1994 ratification of a $7.5 billion deal with a consortium of Western oil companies marked a turning point, and a revival in this sector can be expected. Baku was the fifth biggest city in Soviet Russia and had a well diversified industrial sector. It is hoped the oil deal will stimulate new production of chemicals, textiles, and electrical goods.

Though Azerbaijan has only a small amount of arable land, it is a major producer of cotton, tobacco, grapes, and other fruit. Sturgeon from the Caspian was an important source of caviar but this industry is threatened by serious water pollution. One hundred years of intensive oil production, plus overuse of toxic defoliants in cotton growing, have taken a severe environmental toll. Azerbaijani scientists consider the Abseron Peninsula, where Baku stands, to be one of the most ecologically devastated areas in the world.

## Georgia

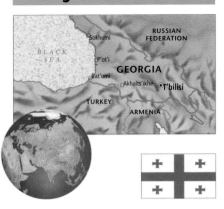

### Fact File

OFFICIAL NAME  Republic of Georgia

FORM OF GOVERNMENT  Republic with single legislative body (Parliament)

CAPITAL  T'bilisi

AREA  69,700 sq km (26,911 sq miles)

TIME ZONE  GMT + 4 hours

POPULATION  4,631,000

PROJECTED POPULATION 2015  4,188,000

POPULATION DENSITY  66.4 per sq km (172.1 per sq mile)

LIFE EXPECTANCY  76.5

INFANT MORTALITY (PER 1,000)  16.8

OFFICIAL LANGUAGE  Georgian

OTHER LANGUAGES  Russian, Armenian, Azeri, Abkhasian, Ossetian

LITERACY RATE  100 %

RELIGIONS  Christian Orthodox 83.9 %, Muslim 9.9 %, Armenian-Gregorian 3.9 %, Catholic 0.8 %, other 1.5 %

ETHNIC GROUPS  Georgian 83.8 %, Azeri 6.5 %, Armenian 5.7 %, Russian 1.5 %, other 2.5 %

CURRENCY  Lari

ECONOMY  Services 57.6 %, industry 29.3 %, agriculture 13.1 %

GNI PER CAPITA  US$ 2,120

CLIMATE  Temperate, with cool winters and hot, dry summers; subtropical on Black Sea coast

HIGHEST POINT  Gora Kazbek 5,047 m (16,558 ft)

MAP REFERENCE  Page 222

A mountainous country in the shadow of the Great Caucasus (Bol'shoy Kavkas), Georgia lies on the shore of the Black Sea between the Russian Federation and Turkey, and has borders with Armenia and Azerbaijan in the southeast. It has a long national history. The land of the Golden Fleece in Greek mythology (Colchis was today's Plain of Kolkhida) Georgia was conquered by Romans, Persians, Arabs, Tartars, and Turks before falling to the Russians around 1800. Nevertheless, it has a strong culture, with a literary tradition based on a distinctive language and alphabet.

In 1991 Georgia rushed to proclaim its independence from the crumbling Soviet Union, but the question of independence for Abkhazia and South Ossetia continues to be a source of tension, which in 2008 even culminated in military clashes between Russia and Georgia. The town of Gori is the birthplace of Georgia's most famous—and infamous—son, Josef Stalin.

Georgia has four main areas: the Great Caucasus Range (Bol'shoy Kavkas) to the north, which provides a natural boundary with Russia; the Black Sea Plain in the west, including the subtropical Kholkida lowlands; the eastern end of the Lesser Caucasus (Malyy Kavkaz) to the south, whose peaks and plateaus extend into Turkey and Armenia; and a central plateau, the Kartalinian Plain, where the capital of T'bilisi stands. Further east, the Kura (Kür) River and its tributaries drain through numerous upland valleys toward Azerbaijan and the Caspian Sea. The mountains contain extensive woodlands (nearly forty percent of the country is forested) with broadleaf beech, oak, and chestnut at lower levels, and a sparse covering of birch at higher elevations.

Georgia is an agricultural country, and the main industries are food processing and wine production. Collectivization had less impact on Georgia than elsewhere in the Soviet Union, so the recovery of its rural sector post-1991 has been fairly painless. Privately owned plots flourish, agriculture as a whole producing citrus fruits, tea (the main crop), grapes, tobacco, wheat, barley and vegetables, while perfumes are made from flowers and herbs. The Imeretia district has a flourishing silk industry. Other products from a small industrial sector include machinery, chemicals, and textiles. Manganese, copper, cobalt, and vanadium are mined. Tourism was once important, but has been damaged by civil strife. There are severe energy shortages. In the long term, hopes for Georgian economic progress hinge on re-establishing trade ties with Russia, and on international transportation (such as handling oil from Azerbaijan) through its Black Sea ports.

## Turkey

### Fact File

OFFICIAL NAME  Republic of Turkey

FORM OF GOVERNMENT  Republic with single legislative body (Grand National Assembly of Turkey)

CAPITAL  Ankara

AREA  780,580 sq km (301,382 sq miles)

TIME ZONE  GMT + 2 hours

POPULATION  71,893,000

PROJECTED POPULATION 2015  82,111,000

POPULATION DENSITY  92.1 per sq km (238.5 per sq mile)

LIFE EXPECTANCY  73.1

INFANT MORTALITY (PER 1,000)  37

OFFICIAL LANGUAGE  Turkish

OTHER LANGUAGES  Kurdish, Arabic

LITERACY RATE  87.4 %

RELIGIONS  Muslim 99.8 % (mostly Sunni), other 0.2 %

ETHNIC GROUPS  Turkish 80 %, Kurdish 20 %

CURRENCY  Turkish lira

ECONOMY  Services 62.8 %, industry 28.3 %, agriculture 8.9 %

GNI PER CAPITA  US$ 8,020

CLIMATE  Temperate, with mild, wet winters and hot, dry summers; arid in the interior

HIGHEST POINT  Ağrı Dağı (Mt Ararat) 5,166 m (16,949 ft)

MAP REFERENCE  Page 224

Asia Minor, a large mountainous plateau lying between the Black Sea and the Mediterranean, forms the main part of Turkey. A much smaller part, European Turkey or Thrace, lies across the narrow straits of the Bosphorus and the Dardanelles. Early in the twentieth century Turkey's leader Kemal Ataturk (1881–1938) attempted to create a modern Islamic state that was willing and able to be a part of Europe. At the end of the twentieth century, with Islamic fundamentalism a growing internal force and no end in sight to the repression of the Kurds, his legacy is uncertain. Since the start of negotiations in October 2005 regarding entry to the EU, inspections are taking place to ascertain whether Turkey fulfills all the preconditions of the

Copenhagen Summit. Apart from economic and
human rights questions this includes the solution
of the situation of the Turkish Kurds as well as
the status of the island of Cyprus. Turkey has
occupied the Muslim north of Cyprus since 1974,
but their claim is not recognized internationally.
The Kurds in southeastern Turkey are demanding
an independent homeland. Opposed by the state,
this conflict has resulted in an estimated 19,000
deaths so far.

Historically, Asia Minor or Anatolia was the
stage on which some famous scenes have been
enacted. The legendary city of Troy stood on
the shore of the Aegean. Ephesus and its ruins
can still be visited today. Astride the Bosphorus,
Constantinople (now Istanbul) was the capital
of the Byzantine Empire from the fourth century
AD until it fell to the Seljuk Turks in 1453.
Later, during the height of its expansion in the
sixteenth century, the empire of the Ottoman
Turks spread throughout the Middle East and
North Africa, carrying Islam through the Balkans
to Vienna. From this time the Ottoman Empire
steadily declined (becoming known as "the
sick man of Europe") until it was finally dismantled at the end of the First World War.
The boundaries of the present Turkish state
were set in 1923.

European Turkey has fertile rolling plains
surrounded by low mountains. The main feature
of the Asian provinces is the largely semiarid
Central Anatolian Plateau (1,000 to 2,000 m;
3,300 to 6,600 ft) much of which is used for
grazing sheep. On its southern flank the three
main ranges of the Taurus Mountains lie inland
from the Mediterranean coast. In addition to
timber, the uplands provide summer grazing for
the flocks of the plateau. The Pontic Mountains
stretching west to east along the Black Sea
boundary of the plateau are more densely
wooded, and have fertile plains. A number
of other ranges further east culminate in the
volcanic cone of Ağrı Dağı (Mt Ararat) (5,166 m;
16,949 ft). Important minerals found in the
thinly populated eastern regions include
chrome, copper, oil, and gold. Tobacco and
figs are grown in two fertile valleys that lead
westward down from the plateau to the Aegean
Sea. Cotton is produced on the plain near the
southern city of Adana.

The Turkish economy combines modern
industry and commerce with village agriculture
and crafts. Though still of importance, agriculture
has been overtaken by manufacturing. A busy
industrial sector produces textiles, processed
foods, steel, petroleum, construction materials,
lumber, and paper, while coal, chromite, and
copper are mined. Energy for industry comes in
part from oil that is imported, but also from
domestic coal and from the country's abundant
hydroelectric power.

During the 1980s growth averaged more than
seven percent a year. In 1994 an outbreak of
triple-digit inflation led to a period during which
public debt, money supply, and the current account deficit were simultaneously out of control.
Severe austerity measures and structural reforms
were required in order to correct the situation.
Shifting political coalitions and economic instability present a challenge for Turkey today.

## Cyprus

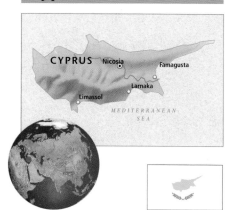

## Fact File

OFFICIAL NAME  (Greek/Turkish) Republic of Cyprus

FORM OF GOVERNMENT  Republic (in the
Commonwealth)

CAPITAL  Lefkosia (Nicosia)

AREA  9,250 sq km (3,571 sq miles)

TIME ZONE  GMT + 2 hours

POPULATION  793,000

PROJECTED POPULATION 2015  929,000

POPULATION DENSITY  85.7 per sq km (222.1 per sq mile)

LIFE EXPECTANCY  78.2

INFANT MORTALITY (PER 1,000)  6.8

OFFICIAL LANGUAGES  Greek, Turkish

OTHER LANGUAGE  English

LITERACY RATE  97.6%

RELIGIONS  Greek Orthodox 78%, Muslim 18%,
other 4%

ETHNIC GROUPS  Greek 77%, Turkish 18%, other 5%

CURRENCY  Cypriot pound, Turkish lira

ECONOMY  Services 78%, industry 19.2%,
agriculture 2.7%

GNI PER CAPITA  US$ 24,940

CLIMATE  Temperate, with cool, wet winters and
warm, dry summers

HIGHEST POINT  Olympos 1,951 m (6,404 ft)

MAP REFERENCE  Page 224

# CENTRAL AND WEST ASIA

Cyprus takes its name from "kypros," the
Greek word for copper. It was an important
metal 3,000 years ago, in classical times, and is
still exported today. Occupied by a succession
of Phoenicians, Greeks, and Romans, held from
1571 by the Turks and by the British from 1878,
Cyprus today is a deeply divided island. The
southern part forms the Republic of Cyprus
proper, where most of the population lives.
Since 1982 the northern part has consisted of
an autonomous region calling itself the Turkish
Republic of Northern Cyprus (see box). The
Greek part of the island became part of the EU
in 2004 after voting down reunification with
the Turkish north.

Along the north coast runs the long limestone
range of the Kyrenia Mountains. Just south of
this range is the fertile Mesaoria Plain between
Morphou and Ammochostos (Famagusta) where
grapes, potatoes, citrus fruits, and cereals are
grown, and the steeper land supports sheep,
goats, and cattle. In the south is the broad,
mineral-rich massif of Troödos, which mainly
contains the copper. This constitutes fifty percent
of the country's total land area and is a good
geological example of an ophiolite, a dome
of mineral-rich sub-oceanic rocks. Both major
rivers flow from this massif—the Pedieas to
Ammochostos Bay (Famagusta Bay), the Karyoti
to Morphou Bay. Nearly half the total area of
Cyprus is arable and twenty percent of this is
irrigated.

The gap between the economic fortunes
of the two parts of Cyprus continues to grow
wider. The agriculturally based Turkish north,
severely disrupted by the events of 1974, has
not recovered well, but has rather suffered
considerably from inflation. It continues to
produce some cereals, meat, fruits, and
olives.

The Greek Cypriot southern half of the
island has prospered from a greater diversity
of activities, including growing tourism,
manufacturing, as well as the income from
military installations, such as the British air
base of Akrotiri near Limassol. Manufactured
products include cigarettes, wine, clothing,
footwear, and cement.

*Walls like those of a fortress surround this church in
Georgia (left page top). Buildings carved from rock in
Cappadocia, Turkey (below).*

## The Cyprus question

The Cypriots were among the first Christians. Between 644 and 975 the island was attacked and invaded multiple times in the course of the expansion of Islam. In 1195, after the Thrid Crusade, the island was awarded to the family of Guy de Lusignan as recompensation for his loss of the crown of Jerusalem. In 1487 the island came under the tutelage of the Venetians.

In 1571 the Ottomans conquered the island and slew many of its Greek inhabitants before they settled their own countrymen there. With the decline of the Ottoman Empire in the nineteenth century, a treaty was concluded with the United Kingdom that handed control of the islands over to the British crown (in 1925 Cyprus became an official colony). Soon the Greek Cypriots started to advocate the unification of the island with Greece. This was supported by the leaders of the Greek Orthodox church who argued that eighty percent of the population wanted to

become part of the "mother country". In 1931 fighting broke out in Nicosia. After the Second World War the claim for unification was renewed. The political situation became even more explosive when another Greek group appeared who opted for the independence of the island.

In 1960 Cyprus became independent but soon new fights broke out. For ten years Greeks and Turks contested for supremacy. In 1974 Turkish troups invaded the north of the island and occupied forty percent of the island, expelling approximately 200,000 Greeks to the south. Nine years later Northern Cyprus declared its independence. It was only recognized by Turkey and is ruled by a government headed by a president. A great opportunity to reunite the two halves was voted down by the population of the Greek part of the island shortly before Greek Cyprus joined the EU in 2004; whether this will change in the near future remains doubtful.

# Dependencies and

## Gaza Strip

### Fact File

OFFICIAL NAME Gaza Strip (preferred Palestinian term, Gaza District)

FORM OF GOVERNMENT Recently vacated by Israel in favour of the Palestinian Authority; transitional government

CAPITAL Gaza

AREA 360 sq km (139 sq miles)

TIME ZONE GMT + 2 hours

POPULATION 1,537,000

LIFE EXPECTANCY 72.3

INFANT MORTALITY (PER 1,000) 21.4

LITERACY RATE 92.4 %

CURRENCY Israeli shekel

ECONOMY Services 79 %, industry 13 %, agriculture 8 % (includes West Bank)

CLIMATE Temperate. Mild winters; warm, dry summers

MAP REFERENCE Page 225

The Gaza Strip is a disputed territory on the Mediterranean with a large permanent exile population of Palestinians, most of whom are descended from those who fled Israel in 1948. Egypt lies to the south and Israel surrounds it to the east and north. Like the West Bank, the Gaza Strip has been in Israeli hands since the Six Day War of 1967. Formally incorporated into Israel in 1973, eight Israeli settlements have been built since 1967. From the time Israel assumed control, the Gaza Strip has been the scene of unrest and violence, the town of Gaza witnessing the Palestinian intifada ("uprising") in 1987–89. The accord reached between the Palestine Liberation Organization (PLO) and Israel in May 1994 gave self-rule to the Gaza Strip pending "final status" talks to take place in the future. The cycle of violence, involving Palestinian bombings in Israel and Israeli reprisals, makes a resolution of the territory's status difficult to achieve. A declaration of independence for Palestine that had been planned for May 1999 was postponed until some later date still to be defined. In 2005, Israel began evacuating settlements in Gaza, in the hope of advancing the peace process. However, the planned foundation of an independent Palestinian state remains a vague hope.

*A frontier point with UN supervision in Nicosia, Cyprus (top). A flourishing olive tree in Cyprus that is about 1,000 years old (bottom). A semi-permanent home on the West Bank, an area still in dispute (right page top).*

# Territories in Asia

## West Bank

### Fact File

**OFFICIAL NAME** West Bank

**FORM OF GOVERNMENT** Disputed by Israel and Palestinian National Authority; interim self-government administered by Palestinian Legislative Council

**CAPITAL** Jerusalem

**AREA** 5,860 sq km (2,263 sq miles)

**TIME ZONE** GMT + 2 hours

**POPULATION** 2,612,000

**LIFE EXPECTANCY** 73.7

**INFANCY MORTALITY (PER 1,000)** 18.2

**LITERACY RATE** 92.4 %

**CURRENCY** Israeli shekel, Jordanian dinar

**ECONOMY** Services 79 %, industry 13 %, agriculture 8 % (includes Gaza Strip)

**CLIMATE** Temperate, with cool to mild winters and warm to hot summers

**MAP REFERENCE** Page 225

Under a 1947 UN agreement this area on the west bank of the Jordan River was to become Palestinian when the State of Israel was formed. After the 1967 Six Day War Israel had control of a larger area than originally proposed. The building of Israeli settlements since then has been bitterly resented by the more than ninty-five percent Palestinian Arab population. The area depends on remittances from workers in Israel. Lack of jobs has also led to many working in the Gulf States. But the *intifada* in 1987–89 reduced the numbers working in Israel, and many West Bank workers were sent home following Palestinian support for Iraq in the Gulf War. Unemployment presently is about 20.3 percent. Under a 1993–95 Israeli-PLO declaration certain powers were to be transferred to a Palestinian Legislative Council, but ongoing Palestinian bombings in Israel, Israeli reprisals, and persistent Israeli settlement construction make a speedy end to strife unlikely. Whether the resumption of talks that came about as a conse-quence of heightened US pressure in 2003 will indeed lead to resolution of the remaining issues—one of them being the status of Jerusalem, claimed as capital by the Palestinians as well as by the Israelis—is highly doubtful. Corruption and scan-dals in the Palestinian leadership, their inability to keep fundamentalist terrorists at bay, the power struggle between the Fatah and the religious Hamas, as well as Israel's policy of targeting and assassinating people they deem dangerous, make peace highly elusive.

## British Indian Ocean Territory

### Fact File

**OFFICIAL NAME** British Indian Ocean Territory

**FORM OF GOVERNMENT** Overseas territory of the United Kingdom

**CAPITAL** None

**AREA** 60 sq km (23 sq miles)

**TIME ZONE** GMT + 5 hours

**POPULATION** no permanent population

**ECONOMY** Air Force base

**CLIMATE** Tropical, moderated by trade winds

**MAP REFERENCE** Page 104

Otherwise known as the Chagos Islands, and the location of the US-UK military base of Diego Garcia, the British Indian Ocean Territory is a group of 2,300 islets located about 1,600 km (1,000 miles) from southern India and 600 km (400 miles) south of the Maldives. The islets are coral atolls and once supported a few people who produced copra for export. The islets were bought for $3 million by Britain from Mauritius but have been uninhabited since the plantations were closed and the population relocated to Mauritius in 1973.

## Paracel Islands

### Fact File

**OFFICIAL NAME** Paracel Islands

**FORM OF GOVERNMENT** Disputed territory occupied by China

**CAPITAL** None

**AREA** not available

**TIME ZONE** GMT + 8 hours

**POPULATION** no permanent population; Chinese garrisons

**CLIMATE** Tropical. Prone to typhoons

**MAP REFERENCE** Page 203

Situated in the South China Sea, the Paracel Islands consist of two groups of coral atolls: the Crescent Group in the west and the Amphi-trite Group in the East. They are a collection of coral atolls about one-third of the way from central Vietnam to the northern Philippines. The Chinese have garrisoned the islands and have built port facilities and an airport on Woody Island.

## Spratly Islands

### Fact File

**OFFICIAL NAME** Spratly Islands

**FORM OF GOVERNMENT** Disputed territory claimed by China, Taiwan, Vietnam, Malaysia, and the Philippines

**CAPITAL** None

**AREA** 5 sq km (1.9 sq miles)

**TIME ZONE** GMT + 8 hours

**POPULATION** no permanent population

**CLIMATE** Tropical. Prone to typhoons

**MAP REFERENCE** Page 203

The Spratly Islands consist of a collection of reefs, islands, and atolls scattered across a large area of the South China Sea, about two-thirds of the way from southern Vietnam to the southern Philippines. Brunei has made Louisa Reef an exclusive economic zone, but has not publicly claimed the island. The islands are subject to territorial disputes because of their proximity to oil- and gas-producing sedimentary basins.

# Asia and the Middle East: Physical

ATLANTIC OCEAN

British Isles

Ireland

NORWEGIAN SEA

GREENLAND SEA

ARCTIC OCEA

Arctic Circle

Svalbard

Zemlya Frantsa-Iosifa

Galdhøpiggen 2469 m

Nordkapp

Iberian Peninsula

Scandinavia

BARENTS SEA

Novaya Zemlya

Jebel Toubkal 4165 m

Pyrenees

Massif Central

Islas Baleares

Mont Blanc 4807 m

Corse

Kol'skiy Poluostrov

Ostrov Kolguyev

Ostrov Vaygach

KARSKOYE MORE

Gydanskiy Poluostrov

Poluostr

Atlas Mountains

Grand Erg Occidental

MEDITERRANEAN SEA

TYRRHENIAN SEA

Sardegna

Appennino

North European Plain

Ural'skiy Khrebet (Ural Mountains)

Grand Erg Oriental

Sicilia

Dinara

Carpathian Mts

Zapadno

SAHARA

IONIAN SEA

Stara Planina

Hora Hoverla 2061 m

Sibirskaya

Ravnina

Tropic of Cancer

MEDITERRANEAN SEA

AEGEAN SEA

Kryms'kyy Pivostriv (Crimean Peninsula)

BLACK SEA

Sea of Azov

Caspian Depression

Mongol Altayn

Khalij Surt

Kriti

Anatolia

Mughalzhar Tauy

Aral Sea

Tavan Bogd Uul 4374 m

Libyan Desert

Cyprus

Toros Dağları

Anadolu Dağları

Gora El'brus 5641 m

Plato Ustyurt

Peski Kyzylkum

Tibesti

Western Desert

Sinā'

Jabal ash Shaykh 2814 m

Ağrı Dağrı (Mt Ararat) 5137 m

Reshteh-ye Kuhha-ye Alborz (Elburz Mts)

Balqash Köli

Tian Shan

Pic Pobedy 7439 m

Eastern Desert

Al Hijāz

Bādiyat ash Shām (Syrian Desert)

An Nafūd

Dasht-e Kavīr

Iranian Plateau

Dasht-e Lut

Pik Imeni Ismail Samani 7495 m

Tarim Pendi

Lake Nasser

RED SEA

Arabian

Peninsula

Kūhhā-ye Zāgros (Zagros Mountains)

Persian Gulf

Hindu Kush

Sulaimān Range

Helmand

K2 8611 m

Kunlun Sha

Qingzang Gaoy (Plateau of Ti

HIMALAY

Indus

Nyainge

Ar Rub'al Khālī

Gulf of Oman

Indo-Gangetic Plain

Thar Desert

Mt Everest 8848 m

75

Ethiopian Highlands

Gulf of Aden

Rann of Kachchh

Vindhya Range

Sātpura Range

Ganga (Ganges)

Mouths of the Ganges

Equator

Lake Albert

Lake Turkana

Suquţrá

ARABIAN

SEA

Godavari

Deccan

Western Ghats

Eastern Ghats

Bay of Bengal

Lake Victoria

Kirinyaga (Mt Kenya) 5199 m

Andama Islar

Lake Tanganyika

Kilimanjaro 5895 m

Cape Comorin

Sri Lanka

Nic Isl

Great Rift Valley

Seychelles

Maldives

INDIAN

OCEAN

Comoros

Madagascar

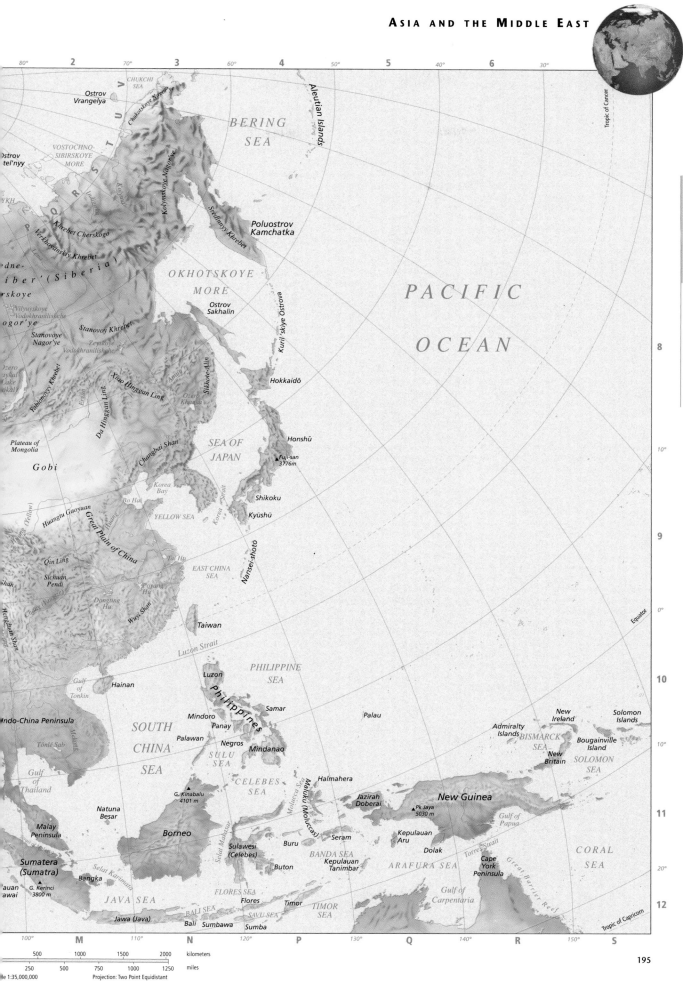

Asia and the Middle East

**Map Labels:**

CHUKCHI SEA
Ostrov Vrangelya
VOSTOCHNO-SIBIRSKOYE MORE
Ostrov ...tel'nyy
...YKH
Chukotskoye Nagor'ye
Kolymskoye Nagor'ye
Khrebet Cherskogo
Verkhoyanskiy Khrebet
...dne-...iber' (Siberia)
...rskoye
...nogor'ye
Vilyuyskoye Vodokhranilishche
Stanovoye Nagor'ye
Stanovoy Khrebet
Zeyskoye Vodokhranilishche
Ozero Baykal (Lake Baikal)
Yablonovyy Khrebet
Plateau of Mongolia
Gobi
Plateau of Mongolia
Huangtu Gaoyuan
Qin Ling
Sichuan Pendi
...shan
Hengduan Shan
Erg...
Da Hinggan Ling
Xiao Hinggan Ling
Changbai Shan
Sikhote-Alin
Amur
Ozero Khanka
Huang (Yellow)
Bo Hai
Korea Bay
Korea Strait
YELLOW SEA
Great Plain of China
Tai Hu
Chang Yiang
Dongting Hu
Poyang Hu
Wuyi Shan
EAST CHINA SEA
Nansei-shotō
Hainan
Gulf of Tonkin
Indo-China Peninsula
Tônlé Sab
Mekong
SOUTH CHINA SEA
Gulf of Thailand
Malay Peninsula
Natuna Besar
Sumatera (Sumatra)
G. Kerinci 3800 m
Bangka
...auan
...awai
Selat Karimata
JAVA SEA
BALI SEA
Jawa (Java)
Bali
Sumbawa
Borneo
G. Kinabalu 4101 m
SULU SEA
CELEBES SEA
Selat Makassar
Sulawesi (Celebes)
Buton
FLORES SEA
Flores
Sumba
SAVU SEA
Timor
TIMOR SEA

BERING SEA
Aleutian Islands
Chukotskoye Nagor'ye
Sredinnyy Khrebet
Poluostrov Kamchatka
OKHOTSKOYE MORE
Ostrov Sakhalin
Kuril'skiye Ostrova
Hokkaidō
SEA OF JAPAN
Honshū
Fuji-san 3776m
Shikoku
Kyūshū

PACIFIC OCEAN

Taiwan
Luzon Strait
Luzon
PHILIPPINE SEA
Mindoro
Panay
Palawan
Negros
Samar
Philippines
Mindanao
Halmahera
Maluku (Moluccas)
Molucca Sea
Buru
Seram
BANDA SEA
Kepulauan Tanimbar
Jazirah Doberai
Pk Jaya 5030 m
New Guinea
Kepulauan Aru
Dolak
ARAFURA SEA
Cape York Peninsula
Gulf of Carpentaria
Torres Strait
Gulf of Papua
Great Barrier Reef
CORAL SEA

Palau
Admiralty Islands
New Ireland
Solomon Islands
BISMARCK SEA
Bougainville Island
New Britain
SOLOMON SEA

Tropic of Cancer
Equator
Tropic of Capricorn

**Grid references:** 2, 3, 4, 5, 6 (top); M, N, P, Q, R, S (bottom); 8, 9, 10, 11, 12 (right); 80°, 70°, 60°, 50°, 40°, 30° (top); 100°, 110°, 120°, 130°, 140°, 150° (bottom); 10°, 0°, 10°, 20° (right)

**Scale bar:**
kilometers: 500, 1000, 1500, 2000
miles: 250, 500, 750, 1000, 1250

Scale 1:35,000,000    Projection: Two Point Equidistant

# Asia and the Middle East: Political

Asia and the Middle East

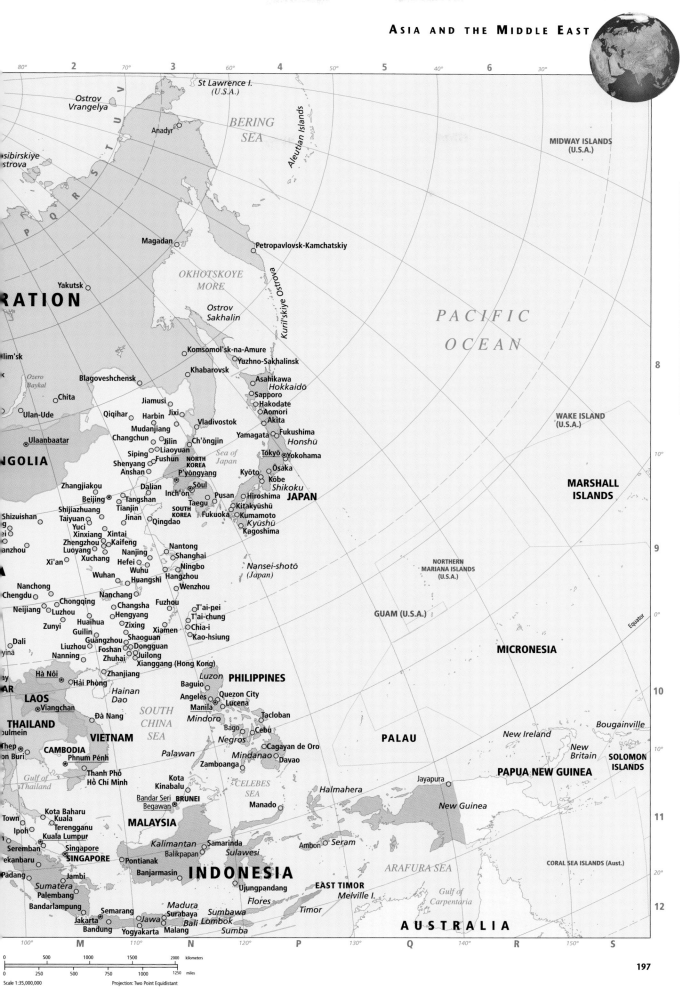

2  80°  3  70°  4  60°  5  50°  6  40°  6  30°

St Lawrence I.
(U.S.A.)

*Ostrov*
*Vrangelya*

*sibirskiye*
*strova*

BERING
SEA

Aleutian Islands

MIDWAY ISLANDS
(U.S.A.)

Anadyr

8

Magadan
Petropavlovsk-Kamchatskiy

*OKHOTSKOYE*
*MORE*

Yakutsk

RATION

*Ostrov*
*Sakhalin*

PACIFIC
OCEAN

*lim'sk*

*Ozero*
*Baykal*

Blagoveshchensk

Komsomol'sk-na-Amure

*Kuril'skiye Ostrova*

Khabarovsk

Chita

Jiamusi

Asahikawa
*Hokkaidō*
Sapporo
Hakodate
Aomori

WAKE ISLAND
(U.S.A.)

Ulan-Ude

Qiqihar   Harbin
Mudanjiang

Jixi
Vladivostok
Akita
Yamagata  Fukushima

10°

Ulaanbaatar

Changchun  Jilin
Siping   Liaoyuan

Ch'ŏngjin

*Honshū*

NGOLIA

Shenyang  Fushun
Anshan

NORTH
KOREA
P'yŏngyang

Tōkyō
Yokohama

Kyōto   Ōsaka
Sŏul         Kōbe
Inch'ŏn      *Shikoku*

MARSHALL
ISLANDS

Zhangjiakou

Dalian

*Sea of*
*Japan*

Shizuishan
g
ei

Beijing
Shijiazhuang
Taiyuan
Yuci

Tangshan
Tianjin
Jinan

Pusan
Taegu   Hiroshima   JAPAN
SOUTH   Kitakyūshū
KOREA  Fukuoka  Kumamoto
*Kyūshū*
Kagoshima

anzhou

Xinxiang  Xintai
Zhengzhou  Kaifeng
Luoyang

Qingdao

9

Xi'an   Xuchang

Nantong
Nanjing
Hefei
Shanghai

*Nansei-shotō*
*(Japan)*

NORTHERN
MARIANA ISLANDS
(U.S.A.)

Wuhan
Huangshi

Ningbo
Hangzhou
Wenzhou

A

Nanchong
Chengdu

Nanchang

Chongqing

Changsha
Hengyang

Fuzhou

GUAM (U.S.A.)

Equator   0°

Neijiang
Luzhou

T'ai-pei
T'ai-chung

Zunyi

Huaihua

Zixing

Chia-i
Xiamen   Kao-hsiung

MICRONESIA

Dali
yǐnā

Guilin
Liuzhou
Nanning

Shaoguan
Guangzhou
Foshan  Dongguan
Zhuhai  Juilong

Xianggang (Hong Kong)

10

ay
AR

Hà Nôi
Hải Phòng

Zhanjiang

*Hainan*
*Dao*

*Luzon*   PHILIPPINES

Baguio
Angeles   Quezon City
Manila   Lucena

Bougainville

New Ireland

LAOS
Viangchan

Đà Nang

*SOUTH*
*CHINA*
*SEA*

*Mindoro*

Tacloban

PALAU

New
Britain

10°

New
Ireland

SOLOMON
ISLANDS

THAILAND
oulmein

VIETNAM

Bago   Cebu
*Negros*

PAPUA NEW GUINEA

Thep
on Buri

CAMBODIA
Phnum Pénh

*Palawan*

Cagayan de Oro
*Mindanao*  Davao

Jayapura

Thanh Phố
Hồ Chí Minh

Zamboanga

*Gulf of*
*Thailand*

Kota
Kinabalu

*CELEBES*
*SEA*

*Halmahera*

*New Guinea*

11

Bandar Seri
Begawan  BRUNEI

Manado

Kota Baharu  Kuala
Ipoh   Terengganu

Kuala Lumpur

MALAYSIA

*Kalimantan*  Samarinda

Balikpapan  *Sulawesi*

Ambon   *Seram*

CORAL SEA ISLANDS (Aust.)

Town

Seremban
ekanbaru

SINGAPORE

Singapore

Pontianak

Banjarmasin

INDONESIA

*ARAFURA SEA*

20°

Padang

Jambi

*Sumatera*
Palembang

Ujungpandang
*Flores*

*Gulf of*
*Carpentaria*

Bandarlampung

Semarang

*Madura*
Surabaya
*Jawa*
Malang

*Sumbawa*
*Bali*  *Lombok*
*Sumba*

Melville I.

*Timor*

AUSTRALIA

12

Jakarta
Bandung

Yogyakarta

M  110°  N  120°  P  130°  Q  140°  R  150°  S

100°

0   500   1000   1500   2000  kilometers
0   250   500   750   1000  1250  miles

Scale 1:35,000,000   Projection: Two Point Equidistant

# East Indonesia

LABUAN
BRUNEI
Bandar Seri Begawan
Tg Baram
Lutong
Miri
Batu Niah
SARAWAK
Long Teru
Rumah Kulit
Long Murum
Longnawan
BORNEO
G. Liangpran 2240 m
G. Menyapa 2000 m
Purukcahu
Kualakurun
Benangin
KALIMANTAN
TENGAH
Pendang
Muarapayang
Palangkaraya
Amuntai
Kupangnunding
G. Serempaka 1380 m
Tanahgrogot
Jangeru
Pulangpisau
Rantau
KALIMANTAN
SELATAN
Banjarmasin
Martapura
Pagatan
Kintap
Batakan
Tg Selatan
Tg Layar

MALAYSIA
Kuala Penyu
Victoria
Beaufort
Muara
Brunei Bay
Telupid
G. Trus Madi 2649 m
Lamag
Sukau
Lahad Datu
SABAH
Pinangah
Sapulut
Kunak
Kalabakan
Tawau
P. Sebatik
Sempurna
P. Timbun Mata
Tel. Darvel
Sibutu I.
Sibutu Group
Tawitawi I.
Tapul Group
PHILIPPINES
Batulaki
Sarangani Is
Geme
Mangara
Kep. Talaud
Beo
Tahuna
Ngalipaeng
P. Sangihe
P. Siau
Ulu
P. Tahulandang
P. Biaro
P. Bangka
Ternate
P. Halmahera

CELEBES
SEA

Longbawan
G. Murud 2438 m
G. Harun 2160 m
G. Basakan 1372 m
P. Mandul
Tangung
Sesayap
Mantadau
Tarakan
G. Bakayan 1599 m
Nyurang
Tanjungselor
Tg Batu
P. Maratua
Tanjungredeb
Tintang
Barung
Pulai
G. Guguang 2467 m
G. Kemal 2053 m
Pelawanbesar
TIMUR
Sepasu
Tg Mangkalihat
Kembangjanggut
Bontang
Equator
Longiram
Samarinda
Danau Melintang
Danau Semayang
Danau Jempang
KALIMANTAN
Balikpapan
Tel. Adang
Tg Mangkalihat

Selat Makasar

Tg Dampelas
Tg Manimbaya
Donggala
Palu
Pakuli
SULAWESI (CELEBES)
Mamuju
G. Gandadiwata 3074 m
Tg Kai
Rantepao
Makale
G. Rantekombola 3455 m
Majene
Polewali
SULAWESI
Parepare
Singkang
Danau Tempe
Watampone
SELATAN
Ujungpandang (Makassar)
Maros
G. Lompobatang 2876 m
Sinjai
Bira
P. Selayar
Benteng

Tg Arus
G. Dako 2304 m
Tolitoli
Bukaan
Peg. Paleleh
Tinabogan
G. Ogoamas 2565 m
Tinombo
Sigenti
Kasimbar
Tawaeli
Toboli
Parigi
Dongala
Sedoa
Tomini
Tel. Poso
G. Katoposa 2835 m
Uekuli
Poso 2563 m
Tenamatua
Taripa
G. Kambuno 2950 m
Peg. Quarles
Wotu
Danau Matana
Palopo
Tg Bulupulu
Peg. Mekongga
Danau Towuti
G. Mekongga 2790 m
Tg Lasoni
Tg Tapaulama
Tel. Matarape
P. Manui
Kendari
Siwa
Tel. Bone
Watunea
P. Padamarang
Kolaka
Kolono
P. Wowoni
SULAWESI
TENGGARA
Daule
Tampo
Raha
P. Muna
P. Buton
Pising
Mawasangka
Tg Goram
Tg Pemali
Kep. Tukangbesi

Tg Kandi
SULAWESI UTARA
Manado
Tondano
Tel. Amurang
Tg Samia
Boroko
Kotamobagu
D. Linboto
G. Tentolomatinan 2207 m
Gorontalo
Tembito
Bilungala
Ongunoi
Marisa
G. Bulawa 1970 m
Kep. Togian
Selat Walea
Kep. Togian
Bunta
Luwuk
Teku
Tg Api
Batuhitam
G. Tumpu 2400 m
Batui
P. Peleng
Tg Santigi
Kep. Banggai
Teluk Tolo
Teluk Tomini
MOLUCCA
SEA
Menanga
P. Mangole
Auponhia
P. Taliabu
P. Sanana
Tg Waka
P. Palpetu
G. Kapalatmada 2729 m
Namlea
Bara
P. Buru
Tifu
Tg Palpetu

INDONESIA

Java Sea
Kep. Masalembu
P. Madura
Kep. Kangean
BALI SEA
Situbondo
Bondowoso
Jawa (Java)
G. Rajung 3332 m
Banyuwangi
JAWA TIMUR
Denpasar
Bali
Singaraja
Negara
Mataram
Praya
Lombok
P. Nusa Penida
G. Agung 3142 m
BALI
NUSA TENGGARA BARAT
FLORES SEA
P. Tanahjampea
P. Kalao
P. Bonerate
Asambi
P. Kalaotoa
Sumbawa Besar
G. Rinjani 3726 m
Selong
Dompu
Plampang
Sumbawa
G. Tambora 2821 m
Bima
Raba
P. Komodo
Labuhanbajo
P. Rinca
Ruteng
Reo
Tg Besi
Nebe
Ranakah 2382 m
Ende
Paga
Flores
Waikabubak
Tg Sasar
NUSA TENGGARA TIMUR
Waingapu
Sumba
Baing
G. Wanggamet 1225 m
P. Sawu
Larantuka
G. Kelimutu 1200 m
Maumere
Kep. Solor
P. Adonara
Lamakera
P. Pantar
Kep. Alor
Kalabahi
Alor
Airpanas
Hatpaas
Laliki
Arwala
P. Wetar
Selat Wetar
Lautem
Manatuto
Dili
Aileuo
G. Tata Mailau 2963 m
EAST TIMOR
Vikeke
Suai
Atambua
Pantemakassar
G. Mutis 2427 m
Kefamenanu
Soe
Barate
Timor
Kupang
Tg Ela
Tg Pukuatu
Nembrala
Roti
Selat Roti
SAVU SEA
TIMOR SEA
Baukau
Tutu
Lore

INDIAN OCEAN

116°
120°
124°

E    132°    F    136°    G    140°

1

4°

2

*PACIFIC*

*OCEAN*

Equator   0°

HALMAHERA
SEA

otai
ngeo
erebere
i

Akelamo
orolemo
atam

P. Waigeo
Rabia
Mega
Koor
Warmandi
Tg Manundi   P. Supiori
Manokwari
Korido
Korim
Tg Dadi
Ambuaki
Kaironi
Tg Memori
Namber
Biak
P. Supiori
Tg Wararisbari
P. Biak
G. Kwoka
3000 m
Sajam
G. Mebo
2940 m
P. Numfor
P. Salawati
Sorong
Germakolo
Rawas
Oransbari
Selat Yapen
Tg D'Urville
Gasim
Ransiki
P. Num
P. Yapen
Teba
Sarmi
Seget
Baru
Robooksibia
Serui
Pamdai
Maffin
Betaf
Ansudu
Atkri
Inanwatan
P. Rumberpon
Tel.
Waropen
Tg Ranbausawa
Kaptiau
Depapre
Demta
Jayapura
WEST
SEPIK
Tamulol
Tg Sabra
Tomu
P. Waar
Danau
Sentani
Vanimo
Leitre
P. Misool
Kokas
Babo
Tel. Bintuni
Tel. Cenderawasih
G. Dom
Krau
Sissano
CERAM SEA
(JCCAS)
Wahai
Tanisapata
Rufrufua
Siembra
Nabire
IRIAN JAYA
1430 m
Tariku
PEG. VAN REES
Ossima
Imonda
Aitape
Fakfak
Kwatisore
Taritatu
Amanab
Torricelli Mts
Amahai
Bula
P. Karas
Kaimana
Danau
Yamur
Wandai
G. Angemuk
3962 m
Green River
Haya
Bemu
Kilwo
Tg Marsimang
Mirobia
Tel.
Kamrau
Danau
Paniai
G. Ubia
4234 m
Wamena
Pk Trikora
4730 m
EAST
SEPIK
Sepik
Urung
P. Seram
Tg Tongerai
Enarotali
Pk Jaya
5030 m
Tembagapura
Kubkain
Kep. Gorong
Kep. Watubela
Tg Papisoi
P. Adi
Aiduna
Wanapiri
Uta
Peg.
Pk Yamin
4595 m
Pk Mandala
4700 m
New
Guinea
Kokenau
Maoke
Jayawijaya
Tabubil
Telefomin
MALUKU
Kep. Kai
Tg Borang
Amamapare
Jayawijaya
Ningerum
Rumginae
Kiunga
P. Kai Besar
Banda Elat
Dobo
Agats
Tanahmerah
Kep. Kai
Kecil
Dosi
Kep. Aru
Lake
Murray
Tg Weduar
Tg Ngoni
Mapi
Aiambak
WESTERN
Damar
Tg Laru Mat
Tg De Jongs
Digul
Fly
Strickland
Kep. Tanimbar
Tg Waarlangier
Tg Ngabordamlu
Tafermaar
P. Dolak
Pembre
Duru
Goe
Watmuri
P. Yamdena
Batkes
Kimaan
Okaba
Serki
Buk
Tepa
Latdalam
Saumlaki
Wamal
Kumbe
Morehead
ermata
Kep. Babar
Adaut
Eliase
Tg Vals
Kladar
P. Komoran
Merauke
Bula
Mari
Boigu I.

*ARAFURA SEA*

Torres   Strait

Badu I.
Moa I.
Thursday I.
Prince of Wales I.
Bamaga

5

C. Van Diemen
Dundas
Strait
Cape Wessel
Wessel
Is
Bathurst I.
Melville I.
Cobourg
Pen.
C. Cockburn
Goulburn Is
Howard
Island
Melville Bay
C. Keith
Van Diemen Gulf
C. Hotham
**AUSTRALIA**
Beagle Gulf
Darwin
Nhulunbuy

12°

6

E    132°    134    F    136°    G    140°    H

0   100   200   300   400   kilometers
0   100   200   miles
Scale 1:7,000,000     Projection: Mercator

# West Indonesia · Malaysia · Singapore

SOUTH CHINA SEA

P. Balambangan
P. Banggi
P. Malawali
*Pattan*
P. Jambongan
Kudat
Langkon
Kanibongan
Tuaran
G. Kinabalu
4101 m
Lingkabau
**Sandakan**
Tapul Group
Tawitawi I.
Kota Kinabalu
SABAH
LABUAN
Kuala Penyu
Telupid
Sukau
Lamag
Lahad Datu
BRUNEI
Victoria
Beaufort
G. Tras Madi
2649 m
Pinangah
Kunak
P. Timbun Mata
Bandar Seri
Begawan
Muara
*Brunei*
Sapulut
Kalabakan
Tawau
Sibutu I.
Sibutu Group
Tg Baram
Lutong
Miri
G. Pagon
1850 m
G. Murud
2438 m
Longbawan
G. Basakan
1372 m
P. Sebatik
Long Teru
Batu
Niah
G. Mulu
2371 m
G. Harun
2160 m
P. Mandul
Tg Kidurong
**Bintulu**
Long Murum
Tangung
Tarakan
SARAWAK
Peg. Iran
Nyurang
Tanjungselor
Tg Sirik
P. Bruit
Mukah
Tatau
G. Bakayan
1599 m
P. Batu
P. Maratua
Tg Datu
Tg Sipang
Sematan
Debak
Saratok
Kejaman
Rumah
Kulit
Longnawan
G. Kemal
2053 m
Tanjungredeb
Barung
Tg Arus
G. Dako
2304 m
**Kuching**
Bandar Sri Aman
(Simanggang)
Bau
Julau
Song
Kapit
BORNEO
G. Guguang
2467 m
Tintang
Pulai
Toliton
Tg Mangkalihat
Tinabogan
Sambas
Pemangkat
G. Niut
1701 m
G. Lawit
1767 m
G. Kerihun
1980 m
G. Liangpran
2240 m
KALIMANTAN TIMUR
G. Menyapa
2000 m
Pelawanbesar
Sepasu
Tg Dampelas
Tg Manimbaya
G. Ogoamas
2565 m
Sigenti
Tinombo
Equator
**Singkawang**
Mempawah
Ngabang
Sanggau
Sintang
Putussibau
*Danau Luar*
*Danau Sentarum*
Kembangjanggut
Longiram
Bontang
Kasimbar
SULAWESI
TENGAH
*Teluk
Tomini*
Donggala
Tawaeli
Toboli
**Pontianak**
KALIMANTAN BARAT
G. Saran
1758 m
Nangapinoh
Purukcahu
*Danau
Melintang*
*Danau
Semayang*
*Danau
Jempang*
**Samarinda**
**Palu**
Pakuli
Parigi
Sedoa
*Tel.
Poso*
Poso
Kertamulia
G. Raya
2278 m
Benangin
Muarapayang
G. Lumut
1233 m
**Balikpapan**
**SULAWESI
(CELEBES)**
Taripa
P. Padangtikar
P. Maya
Telukbatang
Sukadana
Sandai
G. Sebayan
1377 m
Peg. Schwaner
Kualakurun
KALIMANTAN TENGAH
G. Serempaka
1380 m
Tanahgrogot
*Tel. Adang*
Mamuju
G. Kambuno
2950 m
G. Gandadiwata
3074 m
Wotu
Kep. Karimata
Nangatayap
Ketapang
Tumbangsamba
Memala
Pendang
Kupangnunding
Jangeru
Rantepao
Makale
G. Bulupulu
G. Rantekombola
3455 m
Belitung
Sukaraja
Pangkalanbuun
Kumai
Palangkaraya
Sampit
Amuntai
G. Besar
1892 m
Pulangpisau
Rantau
KALIMANTAN SELATAN
Majene
Polewali
Siwa
Tanjungpandan
P. Bawal
P. Gelam
Semuda
*Danau
Sembulu*
Kotabaru
SULAWESI SELATAN
**Parepare**
Singkang
*Tel.*
Manggar
Tg Sambar
Tg Keluang
*Tel.
Kumai*
**Banjarmasin**
Martapura
Pagatan
P. Sebuku
*Danau
Tempe*
Bone
Dendang
*Tel.
Sampit*
Tg Malatayur
Tg Puting
Kintap
Semaras
P. Laut
Maros
Watampone
Batakan
Tg Selatan
Tg Layar
**Ujungpandang
(Makassar)**
G. Lompobatang
2876 m
Sinjai
Bira
INDONESIA
JAVA SEA
Kep. Masalembu
*Selat
Selayar*
Benteng
TA RAYA
a
Kep. Karimunjawa
P. Bawean
P. Selayar
Pamanukan
Subang
Indramayu
JAWA TENGAH
Tg Bugel
Keling
G. Muria
1602 m
Jepara
Kudus
Rembang
Tuban
Ketapang
P. Madura
Kep. Kangean
Bandung
Cirebon
**Pekalongan**
Blora
Bangkalan
P. Tanahjampea
Purwakarta
Tegal
**Semarang**
Wonosobo
Gresik
Pamekasan
P. Kalao
Garut
G. Careme
3078 m
Salatiga
**Surabaya**
BALI SEA
FLORES
SEA
sikmalaya
Ciamis
Purwokerto
G. Slamet
3418 m
**Surakarta (Solo)**
Madiun
Pasuruan
Situbondo
Tg Besi
Reo
Cilacap
Magelang
Kediri
Malang
G. Argopuro
3088 m
Bondowoso
Bali
Singaraja
G. Rinjani
3726 m
G. Tambora
2821 m
Bima
Raba
P. Komodo
Labuhanbajo
Ruteng
**Yogyakarta**
Ponorogo
G. Lawu
3265 m
G. Liman
2561 m
G. Kelud
3332 m
G. Raung
3332 m
Mataram
Sumbawa
Besar
Dompu
G. Ranakah
2382 m
JAWA
(JAVA)
Parangtritis
Pacitan
Blitar
G. Semeru
3676 m
Kepanjen
Jember
Banyuwangi
Selong
Praya
Plampang
P. Rinca
Flores
BARAT
YOGYAKARTA
JAWA TIMUR
P. Nusa
Barung
Negara
G. Agung
3142 m
BALI
**Denpasar**
P. Nusa
Penida
Lombok
Sumbawa
NUSA TENGGARA BARAT
Tg Sasar
Waingapu
G. Wanggamet
1225 m
Waikabubak
Sumba
NUSA TENGGARA TIMUR
Baing

P. Natuna
Besar
P. Lagong
P. Subi
P. Subi Besar
P. Panjang
P. Serasan
*Selat Serasan*
Midai
Tg Mungguresak
Paloh
Tg Datu
Tg Gunung
Tg Bangkai
Tg Putus
Peg. Hose
Peg. Muller
Peg. Sambaliung
*Selat Makasar*
Peg. Quarles
Peg. Meratus
Kep. Karimata
*Selat Karimata*

Asia and the Middle East
204
198

# Thailand · Laos · Cambodia · Vietnam

Gejiu
Wenshan
Malipo
Pingguo
Binyang
Wuming
Litang
Guiping
Teng Xian
Yunan
Sihui
Guangzhou
(Canton)
Boluo
Huizhou
Haifeng
Jiazi
Hà Giang
Jingxi
Tiandeng
Daxin
Fusui
Nanning
Heng
Lingshan
Yulin
Luchuan
Gaozhou
Rong Xian
Cenxi
Deqing
Yunfu
Zhaoqing
Foshan
Shunde
Dongguan
Taiping
Ruidong
Lufeng

2419 m
Nà Hang
Longzhou
Banli
Beiliu
Yangchun
GUANGDONG
Xinhui
Jiangmen
Zhong-
shan
Shenzhen
Danshui
Shanwei
Hàm Yên
Bắc Quang
Pingxiang
Ningming
Qinzhou
Zhanghuang
Yunkai
Dashan
Enping
Taishan
Zhuhai
Macao
Jiulong
(Kowloon)

Yên Bái
Đoan Hùng
Lang Sơn
Bắc Cạn
1312 m
Hepu
Lianjiang
Anpu
Gaozhou
Pingsha
Guanghai
Shangchuan Dao
Xianggang (Hong Kong)

CHINA

S O U T H

C H I N A

S E A

XISHA QUNDAO
(Paracel Island)
(Sovereignty disputed)

SPRATLY ISLANDS
(Sovereignty disputed)

MALAYSIA
Langkon
Tuaran
Kota Kinabalu
G. Kinabalu
4101 m

Scale 1:7,000,000          Projection: Mercator

# Philippines

PHILIPPINE

SEA

PHILIPPINES

**Batan Is**
Basco

*Babuyan Is*

*Babuyan Channel*

Mayraira Pt
Bangui
Bacarra
Laoag
Batac
Badoc
Vigan
Narvacan
Candon
Cervantes
San Fernando
Bauang
Bolinao
Cabauyan I.
Agno
Lingayen
Villasis
San Jose
Baler
San Carlos
Iba
High Peak
2037 m
Tarlac
Botolan
Capas
Mt Pinatubo
1759 m
Angeles
Gapan
San Fernando
Malolos
Olongapo
Balanga
Bagac
Mariveles
Muntinlupa
Nasugbu
Calatagan
Lobo
Golo I.
C. Calavite
Paluan
Mamburao
Mindoro
Sablayan
San Jose
Bulalacao
(San Pedro)
Busuanga I.
Coron
Ilin I.
Semirara Is
Culion I.
Coron I.

Abulog
Palaui I.
Aparri
Agbulu
Alcala
Tuao
Tuguegarao
Ilagan
Cauayan
Santiago
Bagabag
Tabuk
Lubuagan
Bontoc
Banaue
Mt Sicapoo
2048 m
Cabugao
Bangued
C. Engaño
Gonzaga

Mt Pulog
2934 m
Luzon

Tarigtig Pt
C. San Ildefonso

Baler Bay

Dingalan Bay

Polillo Is

Infanta

Lamon
Bay

Calagua Is

Labo
Daet
Mt Labo
1544 m
Calauag
Tinambac
Yog Pt
Viga
Catanduanes I.
Virac
Naga
Pili
Lagonoy
San Andres
Tabaco
Batan I.
Rapu Rapu I.
Legaspi
Donsol
Sorsogon
Bulan
Matnog

Manila
Santa Cruz
Calamba
San Pablo
Lipa
Lucena
Batangas
Calapan
Mt Halcon
2587 m
Pinamalayan
Bongabong
Romblon
Tablas I.
Mt Baco
2488 m
Calintaan
San Jose
Mandaon
Mt Guitinguitin
2050 m
Balud
Pulanduta Pt
Nabas
Pucio Pt
Kalibo
Culasi

Sibuyan I.
Ticao I.
Masbate
Mt Capotoan
850 m
Masbate I.
Placer

Biliran I.

Calbayog
Catbalogan
Samar
Taft
Borongan
Llorente
Guiuan

Naval
Carigara
San Remigio
Tacloban
Ormoc
Baybay
Leyte
Homonhon I.
Desolation Pt
Loreto
Dinagat I.
Siargao I.
Dapa
Bucas Grande I.
Cantilan
Surigao
Tandag

VISAYAN
SEA

Roxas
Daanbantayan
Bantayan
Sara
Passi
Tibiao
Panay
Bagong
Iloilo
Silay
Cadiz
Camotes Is
Sogod
Maasin
Hilongos
Pituyan
San Jose
Miagao
Bago
Bacolod
San
Carlos
Toledo
Mandaue
Lapu-Lapu
Cebu
Danao
Anini-y
Panay Gulf
Negros
Kabankalan
Cebu
Bohol
Guindulman
Sipalay
Cauayan
Dalaguete
Tagbilaran
Hinoba-an
Santander
Santa Catalina
Dumaguete
Siquijor I.
Camiguin I.
Diuta Pt
Mt Hilonghilong
2012 m
Tolong Bay
Siaton

Siargao I.

Bucas Grande I.

Nelyan Pt
Linapacan I.
Iloc I.
El Nido
Batas I.
Maytiguid I.
Cuyo Is
Taytay
Dumaran I.
Boayan I.
Bacao
Caruray
Roxas
Cleopatra Needle
1593 m
Bacungan
Anepahan
Puerto Princesa
Long Pt
Panagtaran Pt
Victoria Peak
1709 m
Aborlan
Quezon
Rasa I.
Palawan
Mt Mantalingajan
2073 m
Brooke's Point
Rio Tuba
San Antonio
Bay
C. Buliluyan
Pandanan I.
Bugsuk I.
Balabac
Balabac I.

SULU SEA

Siaton
Dapitan
Balingoan
Balingasag
Butuan
Bayugan
Dipolog
Oroquieta
El Salvador
Gingoog
Lianga
Sindangan
Mt Jimenez
2425 m
Malindang
Cagayan de Oro
Hinatuan
Malaybalay
Sanco Pt
Ozamiz
Iligan
Bislig
Panganuran
Iligan
Bay
Marawi
Mindanao
Liloy
Kalatungan
Mts
2865 m
Valencia
Cateel
Siocon
Pagadian
Kabasalan
Ipil
Monkeyo
Baganga
Tungawan
Margosatubig
Parang
Midsayap
Kibawe
Tagum
Caraga
Sibuco
Bolong
Olutanga I.
Cotabato
Pikit
Mabini
Mt Apo
2954 m
Samal I.
Davao
Zamboanga
Sacol I.
Moro Gulf
Kidapawan
Digos
Mati
Isabela
Lamitan
Linao Pt
Tacurong
Lamigan Pt
Maluso
Basilan I.
1011 m
Lebak
Norala
Koronadal
Davao
Gulf
Patikul
Jolo
Jolo I.
Surallah
Malita
C. San Augustin
Tapul I.
Kiamba
Mt Matutum
2295 m
General Santos
(Dadiangas)
Tapul Group
Siasi
Glan
Tawitawi I.
Batulaki
Sarangani I.

SULU
ARCHIPELAGO

CELEBES

SEA

Geme
Beo
Kep. Talaud
Mangaran

Tahuna
P. Sangihe

SOUTH

CHINA

SEA

Palawan Passage

Honda Bay

Island Bay

Imuruan Bay
Ulugan
Bay

P. Balambangan
P. Banggi
Kudat
P. Malawali
Tel. Paitan
P. Jambongan
Langkon
Kanibongan
Tuaran
G. Kinabalu
4101 m
Lingkabau
Sandakan
SABAH
Telupid
Lamag
Sukau
Kota Kinabalu
Beaufort
G. Trus Madi
2649 m
Kinabatangan
Lahad Datu
Kuala Penyu
Victoria
Muara
Brunei
Bay
Bandar Seri
Begawan
BRUNEI
Pinangah
MALAYSIA
Kunak
P. Timbun
Mata
Kalabakan
Tawau
Semporna
Sibutu I.
Sibutu Group
G. Murud
2160 m
G. Mulu
Longbawan
G. Basakan
1372 m
P. Sebatik
Sesayap
P. Mandul

INDONESIA

© Random House Australia Pty Ltd

204

kilometers 0    100    200    300    4
miles  0    100    200
Scale 1:7,000,000
Projection: Mercator

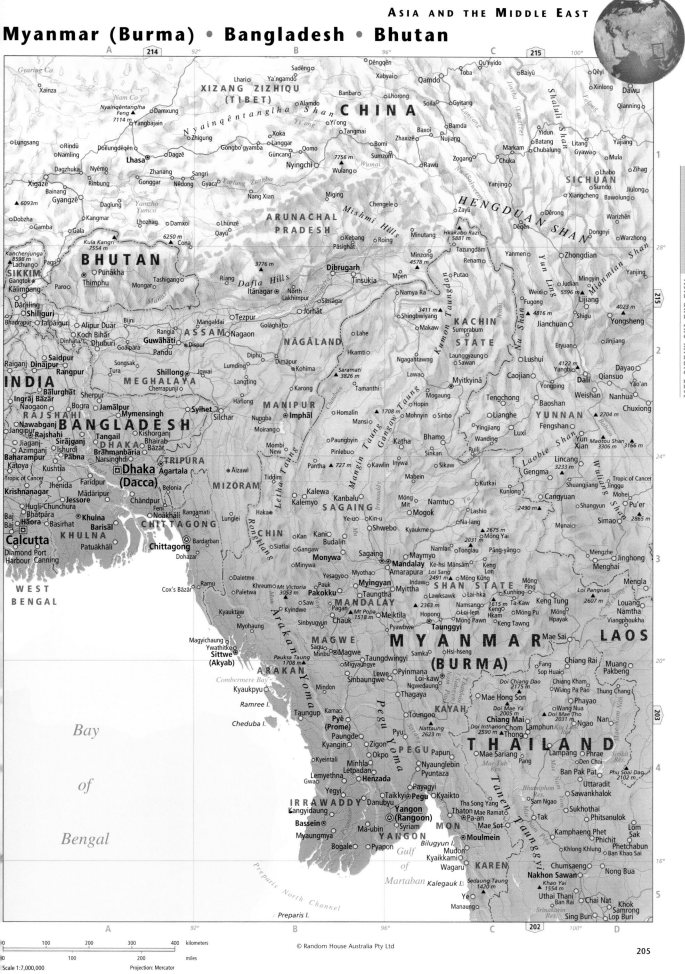

# Myanmar (Burma) • Bangladesh • Bhutan

Gyaring Co
Xainza
Lungsang
Namling
Rindü
Dagzhuka
Nyêmo
Xigazê
Bainang
Gyangzê
6093m
Dobzha
Gamba
Kanchenjunga
8598 m
Lachung
Pagri
SIKKIM
Gangtok
Kālimpang
Darjiling
Shiliguri
Bhadrapur Jalpaiguri
Raiganj Dinajpur
INDIA
Bālurghāt
Ingrāj Bāzār
Naogaon
RAJSHAHI
Nawabganj
Jangipur
Jiaganj
Azimganj
Baharampur
Katoya
Kushtia
Jhenida
Krishnanagar
Hugli-Chunchura
Baj
Bhātpāra
Bāj
Haora
Basirhat
Calcutta
Diamond Port
Harbour
Canning

WEST
BENGAL

Bay
of
Bengal

Nam Co
Nyainqêntanglha
Feng
7114 m
Damxung
Yangbajain
Zhigung
Lhasa
Zhanang
Nêdong
Gyaca
Sangri
Rinbung
Gonggar
Daglung
Kangmar
Yamzho
Yumco
Lhozhag
Damxoi
Gala
Kula Kangri
7554 m
BHUTAN
Punākha
Thimphu
Paro
Mongar
Tashigang
Koch Bihār
Dhuburi
Goalpāra
Rangia
Mangaldai
Tezpur
Tura
Songsak
Shillong
MEGHALAYA
Cherrapunji
Sylhet
Silchar
Hāflong
Jowai
Karong
Langting
Lumding
Dimāpur
Kohima
Imphāl
MANIPUR
Moirang
Mombi
New

XIZANG ZIZHIQU
(TIBET)
Nyainqêntanglha Shan
Gongbo'gyamba
Güncang
Qomo
Xoka
Langgar
Yi'ong
7756 m
Sumzom
Wulang
Nyingchi
Chengele
Minutang
ARUNACHAL
PRADESH
Kebang
Roing
Pāsighāt
3776 m
Itānagar
Riang
Dafla Hills
North
Lakhimpur
Dibrugarh
Tinsukia
Namya Ra
Jorhāt
Golāghāt
Shingbwiyang
3411 m
Nagaon
ASSAM
Dispur
Diphu
NĀGĀLAND
Hkamti
Saramati
3826 m
Tamanthi
Homalin
Mansi
Paungbyin
Pinlebu
Pantha
727 m
Kalewa
Tiddim
Haka
Siatlai
Gangaw
CHIN
Kan
Kani
Kanbalu
Budalin
Minywa
Monywa
Yesagyo
Myothao
Pauk
Saw

Sadêng
Ya'ngamdo
Dêngqên
Lhario
Xabyai
Banbar
Lhorong
Soila
Gyitang
Qamdo
Qu'nyido
Toba
Baiyü
Qêyi
Xinlong
Dāwu

CHINA

Bomi
Tangmai
Baxoi
Zhaxizê
Nujiang
Zogang
Markam
Zayü
Renam
HENGDUAN SHAN
Bamda
Rawu
Yanjing
Hkakabo Razi
5881 m
Tazungdām
Minzong
4578 m
Putao
Weixi
Fugong
4816 m
Judian
5596 m
Mingyin
Lijiang
4023 m
SICHUAN
Xiangcheng
Sumdo
Bawolung
Dêrong
Warizhên
Dongnyi
Warzhong
Zhongdian
Mianmian Shan
Yanji
Yongsheng
Yao'an
Chuxiong

KACHIN
STATE
Sumprabum
Makaw
Ngagahtawng
Sawan
Launggyaung
Lawa
Myitkyinā
Mogaung
Hopin
Mohnyin
Sinbo
Kawlin
Inywa
Sikaw
Kutkai
Mong
Mit
Namtu
Mogok
Kyaukme
Na-lang
Mabein
Nu Shan
Yun Ling
Caojian
4122 m
Yongping
Lushui
Eryuan
Jianchuan
Shigu
Jinjiang
Dayao
Qiansuo
Nanhua
Baoshan
Tengchong
Lianghe
Yingjiang
Luxi
Wanding
Ruili
Laobie Shan
Gengma
Lincang
3233 m
Shuangjiang
2490 m
Cangyuan
Jinggu
Shangyun
2704 m
YUNNAN
Dali
Weishan
Fengshan
Maotou Shan
3306 m
3166 m
Tropic of Cancer
Mohei
Pu'er
Simao
2865 m
Jingdong
Menghai
Mengzhe
Jinghong
Mengla
Loi Pangnao
2607 m
Louang
Namtha
Viangphoukha

SAGAING
Shwebo
Ye-u
Kin-u
Sagaing
Mandalay
Amarapura
Myingyan
Pakokku
Pagan
Meiktila
Taungtha
Myittha
Indaw
Namlan
Tonglau
Pāng-yang
2675 m
Mong Yai
2031 m
Loi Sang
2491 m
Mong Küng
2363 m
Lawksawk
Namsang
Hopong
Mong Pawn
Keng Tawng
SHAN STATE
Ke-hsi Mānsām
Lai-hka
Loi-lem
1615 m
Ta-Kaw
Mong Pu
Mong Hpayak
Keng Lon
Kunhing
Mong
Ping
Mengzhe
Kunlong
Loi-kaw
Keng
Hkam
Keng Tung
Mong Yawng

MANDALAY
Mt Popa
1518 m
Chauk
Sinbyugyun
Kyaukpadaung
Pyawbwe
Taunggyi
Hsi-hseng
Mawkmai
Samka
Loikaw

MAGWE
Magwe
Minbu
Sagu
Migyaungye
Taungdwingyi
Pyinmana
Ngwedaung
Sinbaungwe
Thagaya
KAYAH
Mae Sai
Fang
Sop Huai
Chiang Rai
Muang
Pakbeng
Doi Chiang Dao
2175 m
Chiang Kham
Wiang Pa Pao
Thung Chang
Mae Hong Son
Phayao
Doi Mae Ya
2005 m
Wang Nua
Ngao
Nan
Doi Mae Tho
2031 m

LAOS

ARAKAN
Arakan Yoma
Magyichaung
Ywathitke
Sittwe
(Akyab)
Pauksa Taung
1708 m
Mindon
Lewe
Loi-kaw
Mt Victoria
3053 m
Kama
Kyindwe
Pauksa
Combermere Bay
Kyaukpyu
Ramree I.
Cheduba I.
Taungup
Pyè
(Prome)
Paungde
Kyangin
Kyeintali
Minhla
Gwa
Okpo
Zigon
Papun
Nyaunglebin
Pyuntaza
Lemyethna
Yegyi
Letpadan
Henzada
Payagyi
Kyangidaung
Danubyu
Taikkyi
Pegu
Kyaikto
Bassein
Ma-ubin
Yangon
(Rangoon)
Syriam
Pa-an
Myaungmya
Bogale
Pyapon
MON
Bilugyun I.
Moulmein
Mudon
Kyaikkami
Wagaru
Gulf
of
Martaban
Kalegauk I.
Ye
Manaung

M Y A N M A R
(BURMA)

PEGU
Pegu Yoma
PEGU

IRRAWADDY
YANGON

Chiang Mai
Lamphun
Chom
Thong
Doi Inthanon
2590 m
Mae Sariang
Pang
Mae Tub
Res.
THAILAND
Mae Ramat
Mae Sot
Tak
Lampang
Phrae
Den Chai
Uttaradit
Sawankhalok
Sukhothai
Phitsanulok
Ban Pak Pat
Phu Soai Dao
2102 m
Lom
Sak
Kamphaeng Phet
Phichit
Phetchabun
Ban Khao Sai
Khlong Khlung
KAREN
Tanen Taunggyi
Nakhon Sawan
Chumsaeng
Nong Bua
Khao Yai
1554 m
Srinakarin
Res.
Sedaung Taung
1420 m
Uthai Thani
Ban Rai
Chai Nat
Khok
Samrong
Lop Buri
Sing Buri

0   100   200   300   400 kilometers
0      100        200 miles
Scale 1:7,000,000
Projection: Mercator

# Southeast China

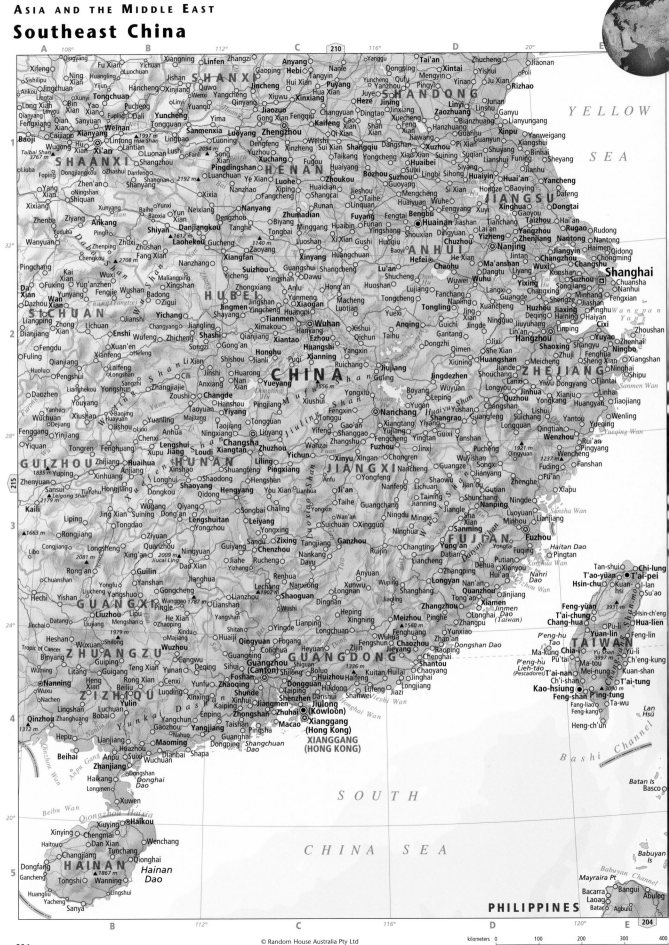

YELLOW

SEA

CHINA

SOUTH

CHINA SEA

PHILIPPINES

Hainan
Dao

TAIWAN

Bashi Channel

© Random House Australia Pty Ltd

kilometers 0    100    200    300    400

miles 0    100    200

Scale 1:7,000,000      Projection: Equidistant Conic

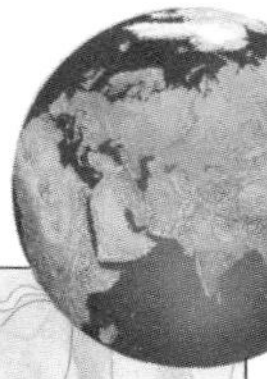

# Xianggang (Hong Kong) and Guangdong, China

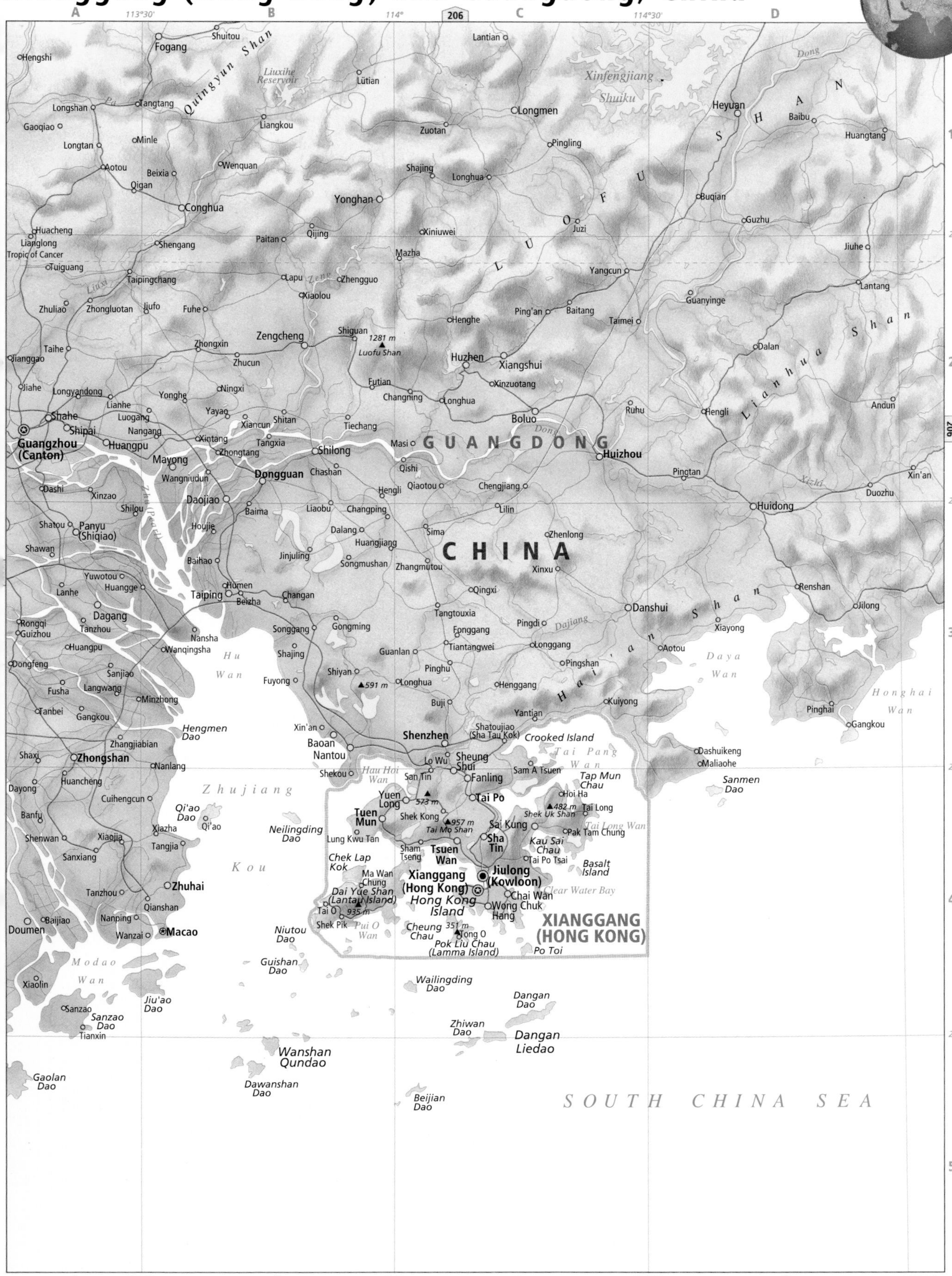

Hengshi
Fogang
Shuitou
Quingyun Shan
Liuxihe Reservoir
Lütian
Lantian
Xinfengjiang Shuiku
Dong
Heyuan
Baibu
Huangtang

Longshan
Tangtang
Liangkou
Zuotan
Longmen
Pingling
Buqian
Guzhu

Gaoqiao
Minle
Wenquan
Shajing
Longhua
Jiuhe

Longtan
Beixia
Yonghan
Yangcun
Lantang

Aotou
Qigan
Conghua
Xiniuwei
Juzi
Guanyinge

Huacheng
Shengang
Paitan
Qijing
Mazha
Ping'an
Baitang
Taimei
Dalan

Lianglong
Tropic of Cancer
Taipingchang
Lapu
Zhengguo
Henghe
Xiangshui
Ruhu
Hengli

Tuiguang
Xiaolou
Shiguan
Huzhen
Xinzuotang
Andun

Zhuliao
Zhongluotan
Jiufo
Fuhe
1281 m
Luofu Shan
Futian
Longhua
Boluo
Pingtan

Qianggao
Taihe
Zengcheng
Zhongxin
Zhucun
Changning
Dong
Huizhou
Huidong
Xin'an

Jiahe
Longyandong
Lianhe
Yonghe
Xiancun
Shitan
Tiechang
Masi
GUANGDONG
Duozhu

Shahe
Luogang
Nangang
Xintang
Zhongtang
Tangxia
Shilong
Qishi
Qiaotou
Chengjiang
Lilin
Pingtan

Guangzhou (Canton)
Shipai
Huangpu
Mayong
Dongguan
Chashan
Hengli
Liaobu
Changping
Sima
Zhenlong
Danshui
Xiayong
Renshan

Dashi
Xinzao
Shilou
Daojiao
Baima
Dalang
Huangjiang
CHINA
Xinxu
Pingdi
Jilong

Shatou
Panyu (Shiqiao)
Houjie
Jinjuling
Songmushan
Zhangmutou
Qingxi
Tangtouxia
Fonggang
Longgang
Aotou

Shawan
Yuwotou
Huangge
Baihao
Changan
Gongming
Tiantangwei
Pingshan

Ronggi
Lanhe
Taiping
Humen
Beizha
Songgang
Shajing
Guanlan
Pinghu
Henggang
Kuiyong
Pinghai
Honghai Wan

Guizhou
Dagang
Tanzhou
Wanqingsha
Hu Wan
Shiyan
591 m
Longhua
Buji
Yantian
Daya Wan
Gangkou

Dongfeng
Huangpu
Sanjiao
Nansha
Fuyong
Shatoujiao (Sha Tau Kok)

Fusha
Langwang
Hengmen Dao
Xin'an
Baoan
Nantou
Lo Wu
Sheung Shui
Sam A Tsuen
Dashuikeng
Maliaohe
Sanmen Dao

Tanbei
Gangkou
Zhangjiabian
Shenzhen
Shekou
San Tin
Fanling
Crooked Island
Tap Mun Chau

Shaxi
Nanlang
Zhuhiang
Hau Hoi Wan
Yuen Long
573 m
Tai Po
Hoi Ha
Tai Long

Zhongshan
Huancheng
Cuihengcun
Qi'ao Dao
Qi'ao
Neilingding Dao
Tuen Mun
Shek Kong
957 m
Tai Mo Shan
Sha Tin
Shek Uk Shan 482 m
Pak Tam Chung

Dayong
Banfu
Xiaojia
Xiazha
Tangjia
Kou
Lung Kwu Tan
Tsuen Wan
Sai Kung
Kau Sai Chau
Tai Po Tsai
Basalt Island

Shenwan
Sanxiang
Chek Lap Kok
Ma Wan
Chung
Xianggang (Hong Kong)
Sham Tseng
Jiulong (Kowloon)
Chai Wan
Clear Water Bay

Tanzhou
Qianshan
Zhuhai
Niutou Dao
Dai Yue Shan (Lantau Island)
Hong Kong Island
Wong Chuk Hang
XIANGGANG (HONG KONG)

Baijiao
Nanping
Wanzai
Macao
Tai O
935 m
Shek Pik
Pui O Wan
Cheung Chau
351 m
Tong O
Po Toi

Doumen
Guishan Dao
Pok Liu Chau (Lamma Island)

Modao Wan
Wailingding Dao
Dangan Dao

Xiaolin
Jiu'ao Dao
Zhiwan Dao
Dangan Liedao

Sanzao
Sanzao Dao
Tianxin

Gaolan Dao
Wanshan Qundao
Dawanshan Dao
Beijian Dao
SOUTH CHINA SEA

Liuotuan
Zengcheng
Lianhua Shan
Hai'an Shan
Yizui
Luo Fu Shan
Guanyinge

Scale 1:900,000
Projection: Equidistant Conic
0  25  50 kilometers
0  20  miles

# Japan • Korea

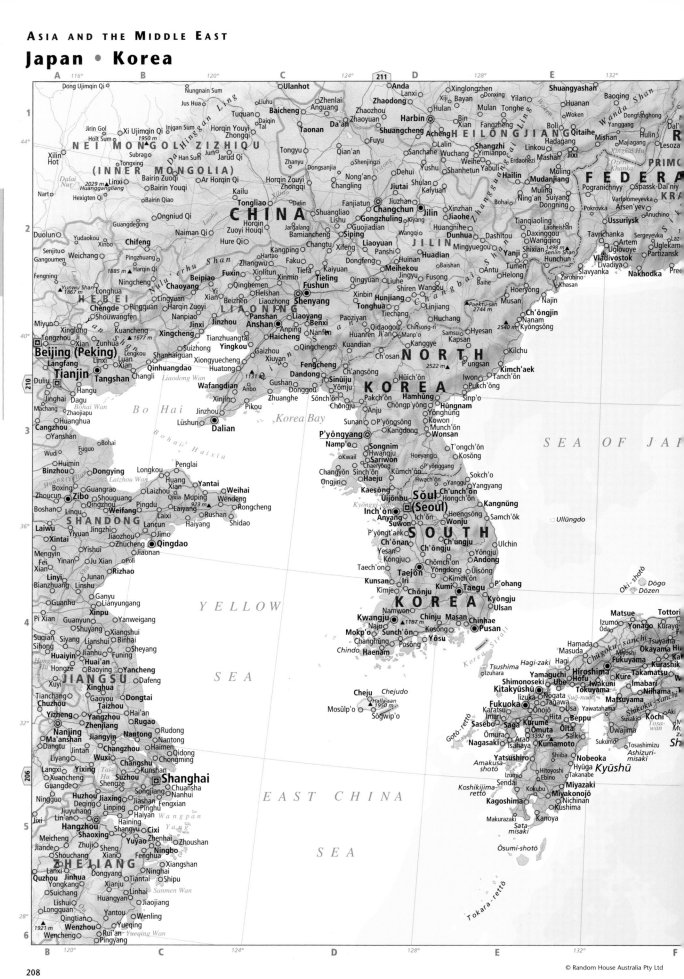

Asia and the Middle East

210

206

208

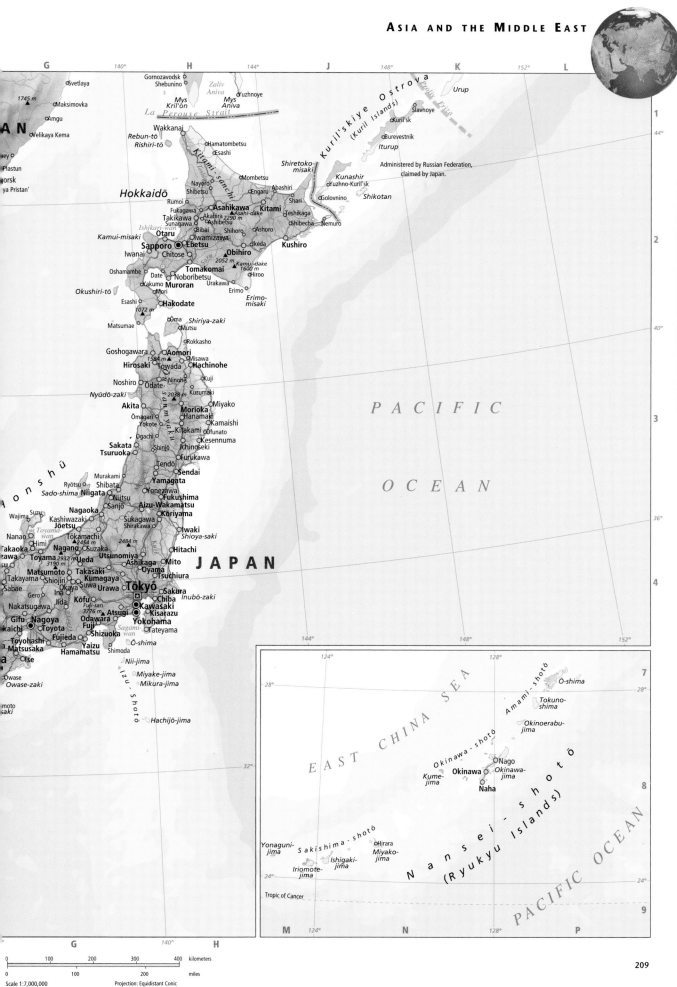

G    140°    H    144°    J    148°    K    152°    L

Svetlaya
1745 m
Maksimovka
Amgu
Velikaya Kema
key
Plastun
vorsk
ya Pristan'

Gornozavodsk
Shebunino
Mys
Kril'ón
Zaliv
Aniva
Mys
Aniva
Yuzhnoye
Urup
Pacific
Frísa
La Perouse Strait
Kuril'skiye Ostrova
(Kuril Islands)
Slavnoye
Kuril'sk
Burevestnik
Iturup

Wakkanai
Rebun-tō
Rishiri-tō
Hamatombetsu
Esashi
Hokkaidō
Nayoro
Shibetsu
Rumoi
Fukagawa
Takikawa
Sunagawa
Bibai
Asahikawa
Asahi-dake
Akabira 2290 m
Ashibetsu
Kamui-misaki
Otaru
Iwamizawa
Sapporo Ebetsu
Iwanai
Chitose
Oshamambe
Date
Yakumo
Mori
Okushiri-tō
Esashi
1072 m
Matsumae
Ōma
Mutsu
Shiriya-zaki
Rokkasho
Goshogawara
Hirosaki
Towada
Misawa
Hachinohe
Noshiro
Ōdate
Ninohe
Kuji
Kuzumaki
Akita
2038 m
Miyako
Ōmagari
Morioka
Hanamaki
Kamaishi
Yokote
Ōfunato
Ogachi
Kitakami
Kesennuma
Shinjō
Ichinoseki
Sakata
Tendō
Furukawa
Tsuruoka
Murakami
Yamagata
Ryōtsu
Shibata
Sendai
Sado-shima
Niigata
Yonezawa
Niitsu
Fukushima
Nagaoka
Sanjō
Aizu-Wakamatsu
Kashiwazaki
Sukagawa
Kōriyama
Jōetsu
Shirakawa
Iwaki
2454 m
Shioya-zaki
Suzaka
Hitachi
Nagano
Utsunomiya
JAPAN
Ueda
Ashikaga
Mito
Takasaki
Oyama
Tsuchiura
Matsumoto
Kumagaya
Shiojiri
Okaya
Urawa
Suwa
Tōkyō
Sakura
Inubō-zaki
Kōfu
Chiba
Fuji-san
Kawasaki
Atsugi
Kisarazu
Odawara
Fuji
Yokohama
Shizuoka
Tateyama
Yaizu
Fujieda
Ō-shima
Hamamatsu
Shimoda
Nii-jima
Miyake-jima
Mikura-jima
Hachijō-jima

Shiretoko-misaki
Mombetsu
Abashiri
Shari
Teshikaga
Shibecha
Engaru
Golovnino
Nemuro
Ashoro
Shihoro
Ikeda
Kushiro
Obihiro
Kamui-dake
2052 m
1600 m
Hiroo
Erimo
Erimo-misaki
Tomakomai
Noboribetsu
Muroran
Urakawa
Hakodate
Honshū
Kitami
Kunashir
Yuzhno-Kuril'sk
Shikotan
Administered by Russian Federation,
claimed by Japan.

Aomori
1584 m

Takaoka
Toyama 2932 m
3190 m

PACIFIC

OCEAN

Scale 1:7,000,000
Projection: Equidistant Conic

0   100   200   300   400   kilometers
0   100   200   miles

EAST CHINA SEA
Amami-shotō
Ō-shima
Tokuno-shima
Okinoerabu-jima
Okinawa-shotō
Nago
Okinawa
Okinawa-jima
Naha
Nansei-shotō
(Ryukyu Islands)
Yonaguni-jima
Sakishima-shotō
Hirara
Miyako-jima
Ishigaki-jima
Iriomote-jima
Kume-jima
PACIFIC OCEAN
Tropic of Cancer

# Northeast China · Mongolia

# Northwest China • East Kazakhstan • Mongolia

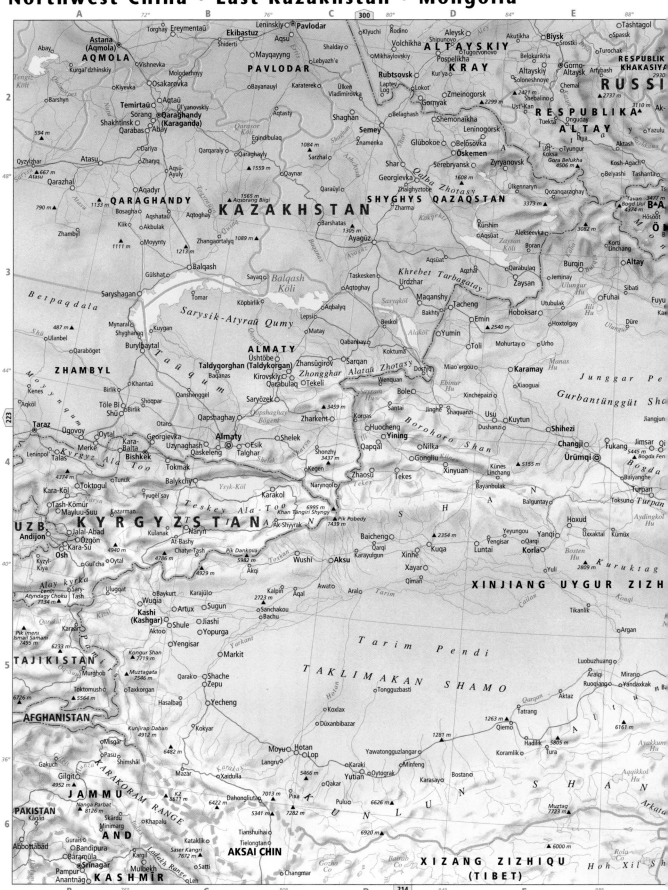

Asia and the Middle East

© Random House Australia Pty Ltd

Scale 1:7,000,000
Projection: Equidistant Conic

0    100    200    300    400 kilometers
0         100         200 miles

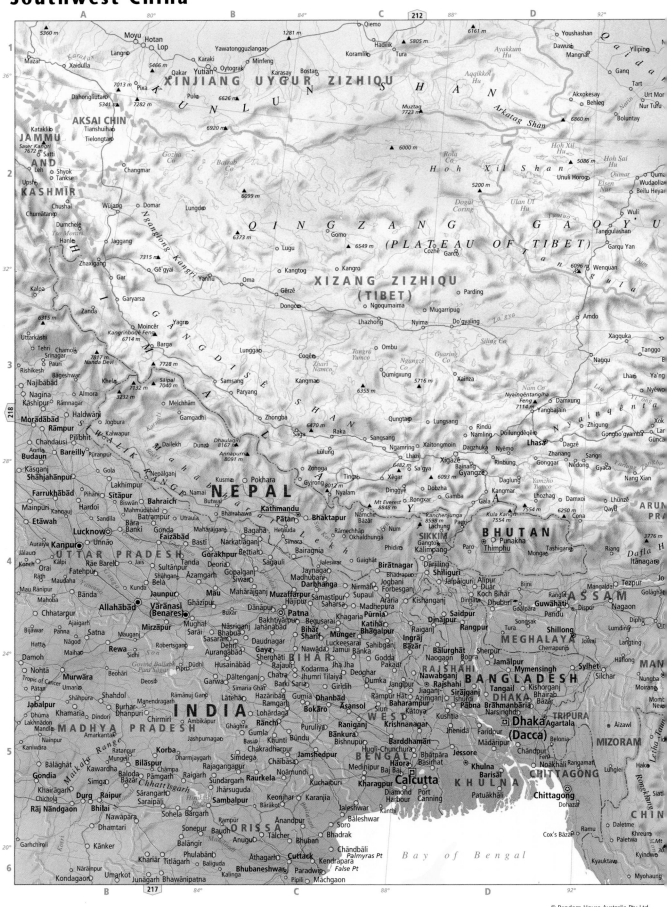

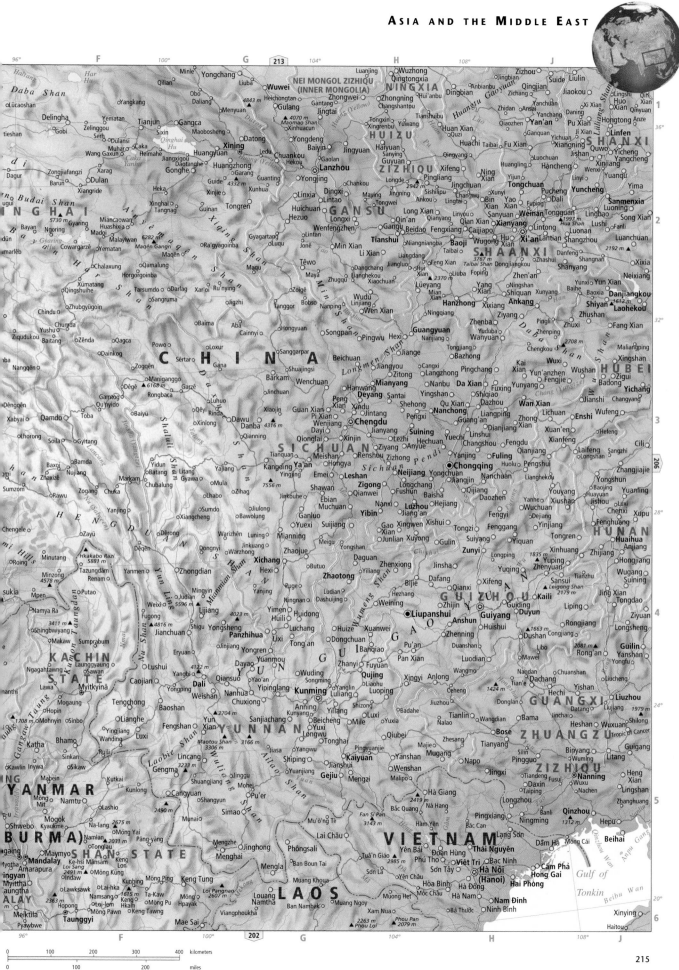

Scale 1:7,000,000          Projection: Equidistant Conic

# South India • Sri Lanka

© Random House Australia Pty Ltd

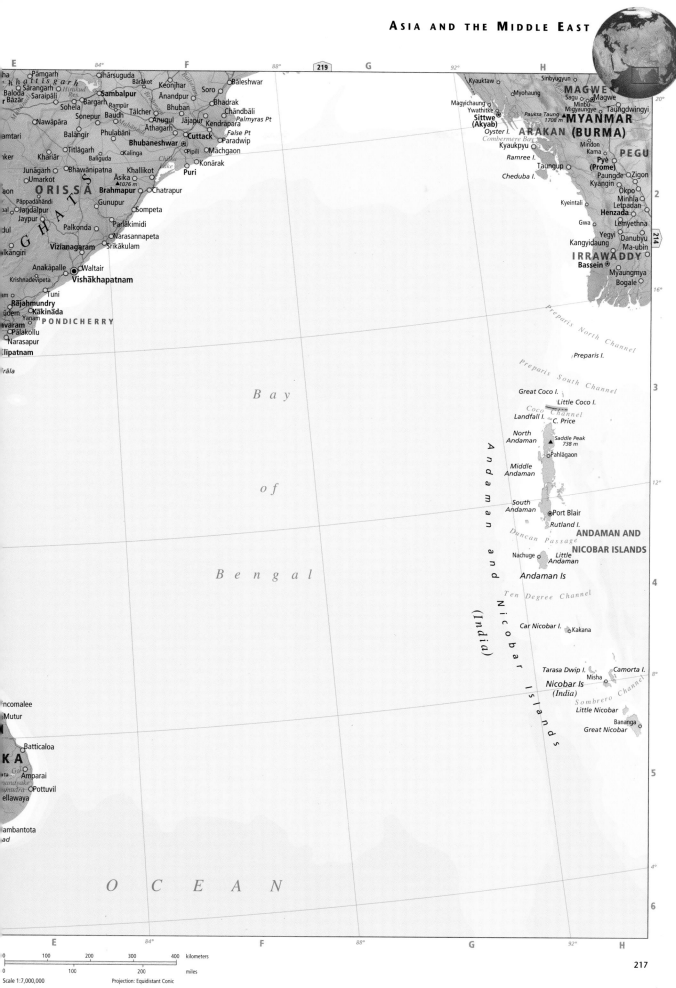

E     84°     F     88°     G     92°     H

~hhattisgarh
Baloda
r Bāzār    Sārangarh    Jhārsuguda
Pāmgarh
Saraipāli    Hirakud    Keonjhar    Soro    Bāleshwar
Res.
Sohela    Sambalpur    Barkot
Nawāpāra    Bargarh    Rampur    Ānandpur    Bhadrak
Sonepur    Baudh    Tālcher    Bhuban    Chāndbāli
Phulabāni    Anugul    Palmyras Pt
Balāngir    Āthagarh    Jājapur    Kendrāpara
Titlāgarh    Bhubaneshwar    Cuttack    Paradwip
Khariār    Baliguda    Kalinga    Pipili    False Pt
Bhawānipatna    Khallikot    Māchgaon
ORISSA
Junāgarh    Āsika    Konārak
Umarkot    Brahmapur    Chatrapur    Puri
Pāppadāhandi    1076 m
Jaypur    Gunupur
Jagdālpur    Parlākimidi
Palkonda
GHATS    Sompeta
alkāngiri    Vizianagaram    Narasannapeta
dul    Anakāpalle    Srikākulam
Krishnadevipeta    Waltair
Vishākhapatnam
Tuni
am    Rājahmundry
üdem    Kākināda
avaram    Yanam
PONDICHERRY
Pālakollu
Narasapur
lipatnam
rāla

Bay

of

Bengal

A
n
d
a
m
a
n
 
a
n
d
 
N
i
c
o
b
a
r
 
I
s
l
a
n
d
s
 
(India)

O   C   E   A   N

ncomalee
Mutur
Batticaloa
KA
ata    Amparai
nandyak
pmudra    Pottuvil
ellawaya

ambantota
ad

Kyauktaw    Sinbyugyun
MAGWE
Myohaung    Sagu    Minbu    Magwe
Magyichaung    Ywathitke    Minbu    Taungdwingyi
Ywathitke    Migyaungye
Sittwe    Pauksa Taung    MYANMAR
(Akyab)    Oyster I.    1708 m
Kyaukpyu    ARAKAN (BURMA)
Combermere Bay    Mindon
Ramree I.    Kama    PEGU
Taungup    Pyè
Cheduba I.    (Prome)
Paungde
Kyangin    Zigon
Kyeintali    Okpo
Minhla
Letpadan
Gwa    Henzada
Yegyi    Lemyethna
Kangyidaung    Danubyu
Ma-ubin
IRRAWADDY
Bassein
Myaungmya
Myaungmya
Bogale

Preparis North Channel

Preparis I.

Preparis South Channel

Great Coco I.
Little Coco I.
Coco Channel
Landfall I.    C. Price
North    Saddle Peak
Andaman    738 m
Pahlāgaon
Middle
Andaman
South
Andaman    Port Blair
Rutland I.
ANDAMAN AND
NICOBAR ISLANDS
Nachuge    Little
Andaman
Andaman Is

Ten Degree Channel

Car Nicobar I.    Kakana

Tarasa Dwip I.    Camorta I.
Misha
Nicobar Is
(India)
Sombrero Channel
Little Nicobar
Bananga
Great Nicobar

Duncan Passage

E     84°     F     88°     G     92°     H

0    100    200    300    400   kilometers
0    100    200   miles
Scale 1:7,000,000      Projection: Equidistant Conic

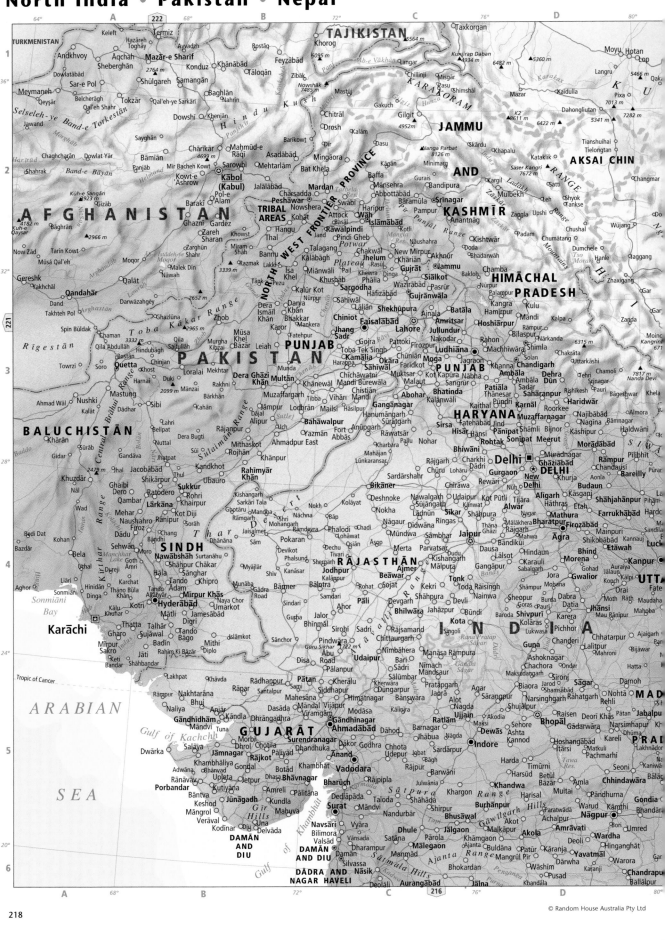

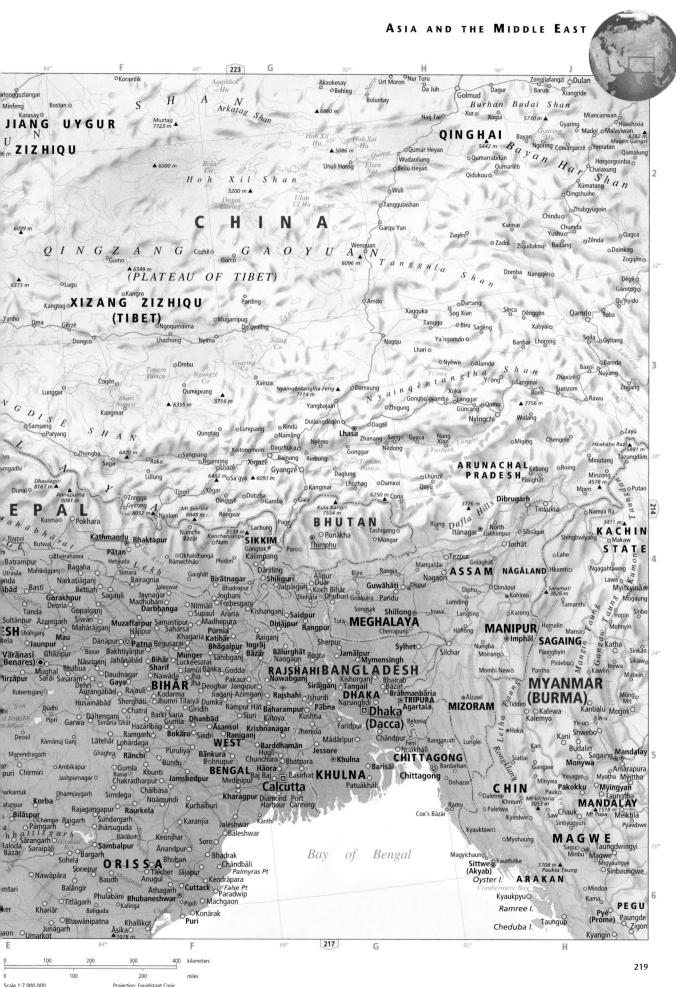

# CHINA

## QINGHAI

### JIANG UYGUR
ZIZHIQU

### QINGZANG GAOYUAN
(PLATEAU OF TIBET)

### XIZANG ZIZHIQU
(TIBET)

Koramlik
Minfeng
Karasay
Bostan
Muztag 7723 m
Aqqikkol Hu
Arkatag Shan
6860 m
Akkokesay
Behleg
Boluntay
Urt Moron
Nur Turu
Da Juh
Nur Moron
Golmud
Zongjiafangzi
Barun
Dulan
Xiangtou
Naij Tal
Burhan Budai Shan
Miancaowan
Xur
Xugui
5730 m
Gyaring
Madoi
Huashixia
Malayiwan
6282 m
Maqên Gangri

Hoh Xil Hu
6000 m
Rola Co
Cozhê
Garco
Hoh Sai Hu
5086 m
Uuli Horog
Qumar Heyan
Wudaoliang
Beilu Heyan
Qumarrbdun
Bayan
5442 m
Ngoring Hu
Gyaring Hu
Cowargarzê
Yematan
Horgorgoinba
Chalaxung
Qamalung

6099 m
Dogai Coring
5200 m
Ulan Ul Hu
Tuotuo
Wuli
Tanggulashan
Garqu Yan
Zaqên
Zadoi
Ziqudukou
Kaimar
Yushu
Chumda
Baitang
Zênda
Dainkog
Zogqên

6373 m
Lugu
6549 m
Gomo
Wenquan
6096 m
Tanggula Shan
Domba
Nanggên
Dêgê
Gamtog
Qu'nyido

Kangtog
Kangro
Parding
Amdo
Dartang
Xagquka
Sog Xian
Sêrca
Dênggên
Qamdo
Toba

Yanhu
Oma
Gêrzê
Ngoqumaima
Mugarripu
Do'gyaling
Zagya
Xaggu
Tanggo
Biru
Sadêng
Xabyai
Soila
Gyitang

Dongco
Lhazhong
Nyima
Siling Co
Nagqu
Ya'ngamdo
Banbar
Lhorong

Tangra Yumco
Ombu
Gyaring Co
Lhari
Nyêwo
Alamdo
Zhaxize
Zogang

Coqên
Ngangzê Co
Qumigxung
Nam Co
Damxung
Nyingêntanglha Shan
Yi'ong
Tangmai
Bomi
Sumzom
Rawu
Zayü

Lunggar
Zhari Namco
5716 m
6355 m
Nyainqêntanglha Feng 7114 m
Yangbajain
Zhugin
Gongbo'gyamba
Güncang
7756 m
Hkakabo Razi 5881 m

Samsang
Paryang
Zhongba
6470 m
Raka
Sangsang
Ngamring
Rindü
Namling
Nyêmo
LHASA
Zhanang
Sangri
Gyaca
Nang Xian
Langbo
Yarlung
Miging
Chengele
Tazungdam
Putao

Zhongba
Saga
Lülung
Lhazê
Xaitongmoin
Dazhuka
Bainang
Rinbung
XIGAZÊ
Nyingchi
Wulang
Minutang
Minzong
4578 m
Mpen
Namya Ra

Dhaulagiri 8167 m
Annapurna 8091 m
Zongga
Gyirong
6482 m
Sa'gya
6093 m
GYANGZÊ
Doilungdêqên
Dagzê
Gonggar
Nêdong
Kangma
Daglung
6250 m
Lhozhag
Damxoi
Lhünzê
Qayü
Cona
3776 m
Riang
Dafla Hills
3411 m
Dibrugarh
Tinsukia

### ARUNACHAL PRADESH

Dunai
Kusma
Pokhara
Mt Everest 8848 m
8012 m
Nyalam
Nāmche Bāzār
Kanchenjunga 8598 m
Lachung
Num
Pagri
Gala
Kula Kangri 7554 m
Kebang
Roing
Pasighat
Kangtog
North Lakhimpur
Sibsagar
Shingbwiyang
Makaw
Ngagahtawng
Lawa

### EPAL
### NEPAL

### SIKKIM
### BHUTAN
### KACHIN STATE

Bhairahawa
Butwal
Kathmandu
Bhaktapur
Pātan
Hetauda
Simara
Bairagnia
Okhaldhunga
Rāmechhāp
Phidim
Gangtok
Kālimpong
Paroo
Thimphu
Punākha
Tashigang
Mongar
Itānagar
Tezpur
Jorhat
Lahe
Myitkyinā
Mogaung
Hopin
Sinbo

Batrampur
Namai
Mahārājganj
Bagaha
Bettiah
Narkatiāganj
Simra
Jaleswar
Gaighāt
Birātnagar
Dārjiling
Shiliguri
Jalpaiguri
Alipur Duār
Bijni
Koch Bihar
Dinhata
Dhuburi
Rangia
Guwāhāti
Pandu
Goalpara
Songsak
Dispur
Mangaldai
Golāghāt
Nagaon
Diphu
Dimāpur
Kohima
Saramati 3826 m
Karong
Lumding
Homalin
Tamanthi
Mansi
Katha
Sinkan
Sikaw
Mabein

### ASSAM
### NĀGĀLAND
### MANIPUR
### SAGAING

Gorakhpur
Deoria
Sultānpur
Āzamgarh
Tanda
Gopalganj
Bhairawa
Siwan
Chapra
Muzaffarpur
Samastipur
Hājipur
Darbhanga
Madhubani
Supaul
Araria
Nirmāli
Forbesganj
Kishanganj
Saidpur
Dinājpur
Raiganj
Tura
Cherrapunji
Shillong
Jowai
Hāflong
Nungba
Paungbyin
Pinlebu
Mombi New
Imphal
Moirang
Tiddim
Kalewa
Mawlaik
Kani
Kawlin
Inywa
Wuntho

### MEGHALAYA

ESH
shāhganj
Mau
Jaunpur
Ghāzipur
Danāpur
PATNA
Begusarai
Khagaria
Katihar
Pūrnia
Balurghāt
Bogra
Naogaon
Jamālpur
Sherpur
Mymensingh
Sylhet
Silchar
Mombi New
Haka
Aizawl

Vārānasi (Benares)
Mughal Sarāi
Bhabua
Buxar
Bakhtiyārpur
Jahānābād
Nāsriganj
Bihār Sharif
Munger
Bhāgalpur
Ingraj Bāzār
Jamūi Bānka
Sāhibganj
Godda
Pakaur
Dumka
Nawabganj
Rajshahi
Sirājganj
Tangail
Brāhmanbāria
Agartala
Narsinghdi

### RAJSHAHI
### BANGLADESH
### TRIPURA
### MIZORAM
### MYANMAR (BURMA)

Mirzāpur
Daudnagar
Dehri
Aurangābād
Nawāda
Jha
Deoghar
Jangipur
Baharampur
Ishurdi
Pābna
Kushtia
Faridpur
DHAKA
Dhaka (Dacca)
Belonia
Rangamati
Siatlai
Gangaw
Kalemyo
Shwebo
Monywa

### BIHAR

Husainābād
Sherghāti
Gaya
Rajauli
Kodarma
Barki Saria
Jhumri Tilaiyā
Giridih
Rāmpur Hāt
Suri
Kātoya
Krishnanagar
Jhenida
Mādāripur
Jessore
Noākhāli
Feni
Noākhāli
Lunglei
Gangaw
Pauk
Ye-u
Kani
Budalin
Sagaing
Mandalay

Robertsganj
Dūdhi
Pipri
Garwa
Dāltenganj
Chatra
Hazāribāg
Simaria Ghāt
Ramgarh
Bokāro
Sindri
Dhanbād
Āsansol
Rānigani
Barddhamān
Chunchura
Hāora
Baj Baj
Basirhat
KHULNA
Barisāl
Barguna
Gangaw
Daletme
Khreum
Mt Victoria 3053 m
Paletwa
Pauk
Chauk
Mt Popa 1518 m
Pakokku
Myingyan
Amarapura
Myotha
Myittha
Meiktila
Pyawbwe

### WEST BENGAL

Deosil
Manendragarh
Ambikāpur
Jashpurnagar
Gumla
Basia
Khunti
Ranchi
Bundu
Bānkura
Bishnupur
Bhatpara
Khulna
Chittagong
Dohazar
Ramu
Cox's Bāzār
Kyauktaw
Minbya
Myohaung
Magyichaung
Sittwe (Akyab)
Ywathitke
Pakkoku

### CHIN
### MANDALAY

kantak
Chirmiri
Korba
Bilāspur
Champa
Raigarh
Sarangarh
Rajagangapur
Sundargarh
Jhārsuguda
Simdega
Noāmundi
Chāibāsa
Jamshedpur
Medinīpur
Kharagpur
Diamond Harbour
Canning
Kānthi
Baleshwar
Daletme
Kindwe
Saw
Kyindwe
Sinbyugyun
Sagu
Minbu
Magwe
Taungdwingyi

### MAGWE

Baloda
Sāngarh
Saraipāli
Sambalpur
Bargarh
Bhuban
Chāndbāli
Bhadrak
Keonjhar
Ānandpur
Soro
Karanjia
Jaleshwar
Bārākot
False Pt
Paradwip
Māchgaon
Pauksa Taung
1708 m
Minbu
Migyaungye
Sinbaungwe

### ORISSA
### ARAKAN
### PEGU

Khariār
Nawāpāra
Sohela
Sonepur
Balāngir
Baudh
Anugul
Talcher
Dhenkānāl
Jājapur
Kendrāpāra
Pipili
Konārak
Puri
Kyaukpyu
Ramree I.
Cheduba I.
Mindon
Kama
Pyè (Prome)
Paungde
Zigon
Kyangin

Umarkot
Khalliāt
Kalingā
Āsika
1076 m
Junāgarh
Bhawānipatna
Phulbāni
Bhubaneshwar
Cuttack
Kalinga
False Pt
Taungup
Combermere Bay
Oyster I.
Kyaukpyu

Chhattīsgarh
Titlāgarh
Baliguda
Titlāgarh

## Bay of Bengal

## KHULNA
## CHITTAGONG

Calcutta

Scale 1:7,000,000
Projection: Equidistant Conic

0 100 200 300 400 kilometers
0 100 200 miles

# Middle East

# Kazakhstan • Central Asian Republics

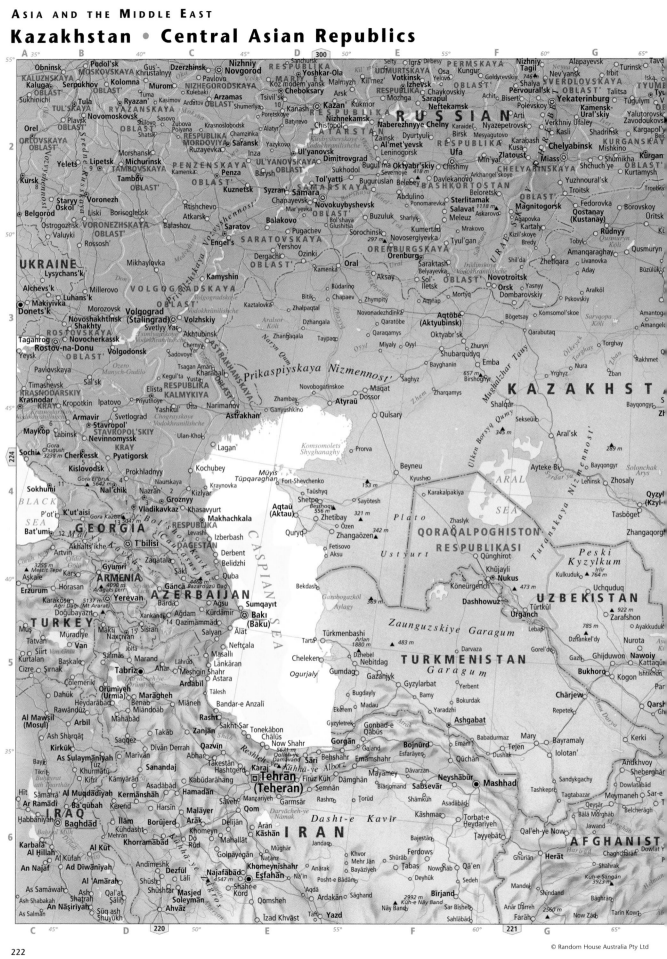

© Random House Australia Pty Ltd

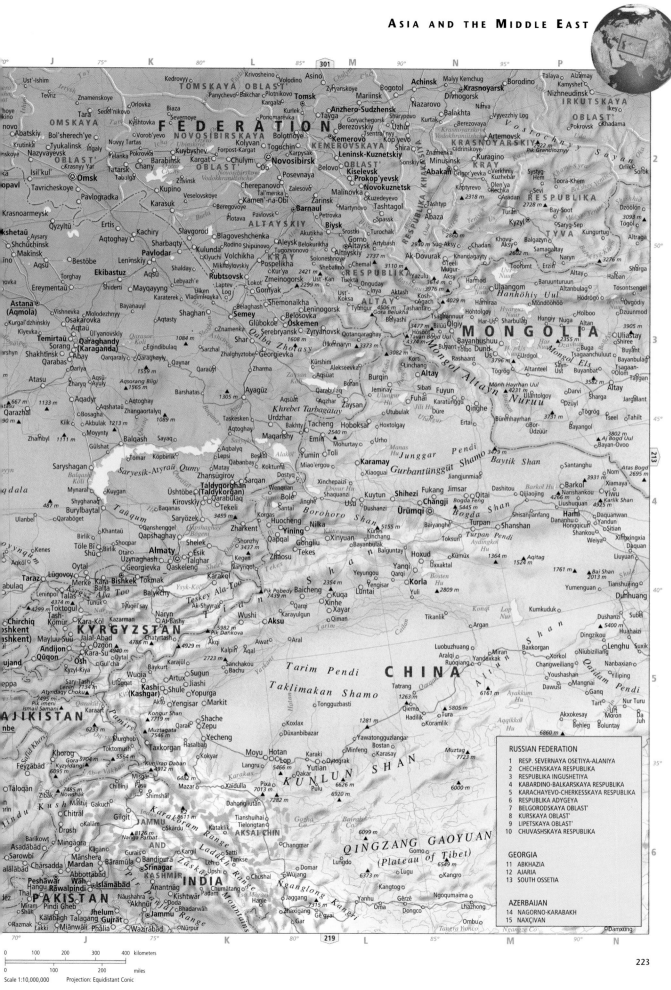

RUSSIAN FEDERATION
1 RESP. SEVERNAYA OSETIYA-ALANIYA
2 CHECHENSKAYA RESPUBLIKA
3 REPUBLIKA INGUSHETIYA
4 KABARDINO-BALKARSKAYA RESPUBLIKA
5 KARACHAYEVO-CHERKESSKAYA RESPUBLIKA
6 RESPUBLIKA ADYGEYA
7 BELGORODSKAYA OBLAST'
8 KURSKAYA OBLAST'
9 LIPETSKAYA OBLAST'
10 CHUVASHSKAYA RESPUBLIKA

GEORGIA
11 ABKHAZIA
12 AJARIA
13 SOUTH OSSETIA

AZERBAIJAN
14 NAGORNO-KARABAKH
15 NAXCIVAN

0   100   200   300   400 kilometers
0        100        200 miles
Scale 1:10,000,000   Projection: Equidistant Conic

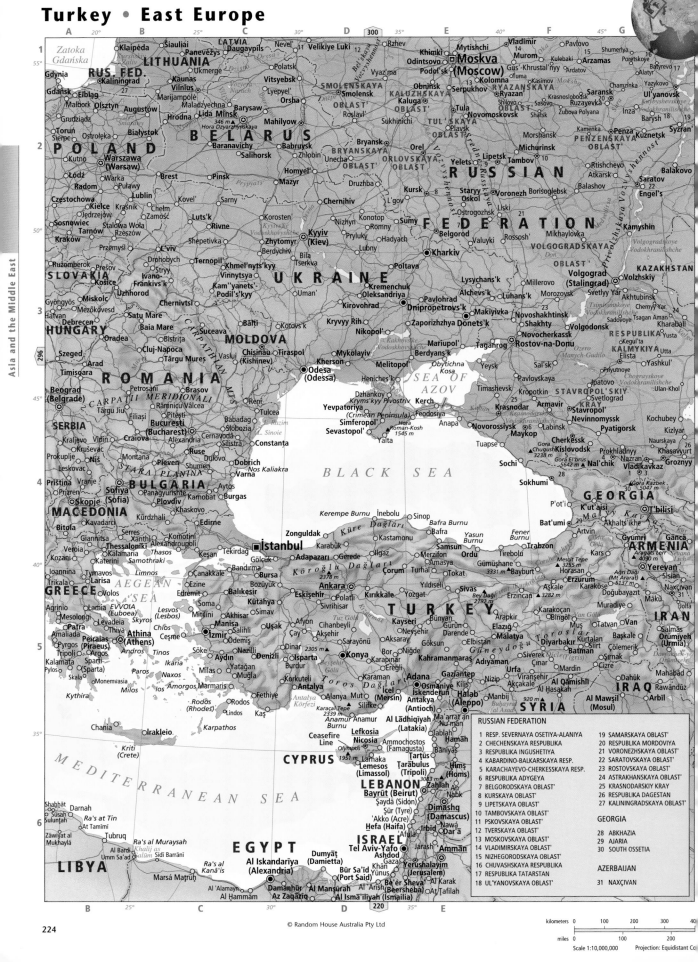

RUSSIAN FEDERATION

| | |
|---|---|
| 1 RESP. SEVERNAYA OSETIYA-ALANIYA | 19 SAMARSKAYA OBLAST' |
| 2 CHECHENSKAYA RESPUBLIKA | 20 REPUBLIKA MORDOVIYA |
| 3 REPUBLIKA INGUSHETIYA | 21 VORONEZHSKAYA OBLAST' |
| 4 KABARDINO-BALKARSKAYA RESP. | 22 SARATOVSKAYA OBLAST' |
| 5 KARACHAYEVO-CHERKESSKAYA RESP. | 23 ROSTOVSKAYA OBLAST' |
| 6 RESPUBLIKA ADYGEYA | 24 ASTRAKHANSKAYA OBLAST' |
| 7 BELGORODSKAYA OBLAST' | 25 KRASNODARSKIY KRAY |
| 8 KURSKAYA OBLAST' | 26 REPUBLIKA DAGESTAN |
| 9 LIPETSKAYA OBLAST' | 27 KALININGRADSKAYA OBLAST' |
| 10 TAMBOVSKAYA OBLAST' | |
| 11 PSKOVSKAYA OBLAST' | GEORGIA |
| 12 TVERSKAYA OBLAST' | |
| 13 MOSKOVSKAYA OBLAST' | 28 ABKHAZIA |
| 14 VLADIMIRSKAYA OBLAST' | 29 AJARIA |
| 15 NIZHEGORODSKAYA OBLAST' | 30 SOUTH OSSETIA |
| 16 CHUVASHSKAYA RESPUBLIKA | |
| 17 RESPUBLIKA TATARSTAN | AZERBAIJAN |
| 18 UL'YANOVSKAYA OBLAST' | 31 NAXÇIVAN |

kilometers 0    100    200    300    40

miles 0    100    200

Scale 1:10,000,000    Projection: Equidistant Co

MEDITERRANEAN

SEA

© Random House Australia Pty Ltd

Scale 1:3,500,000
Projection: Equidistant Conic

100
50
100
200 kilometers
miles

# Europe and the Russian Federation

Covering 10.5 million sq km (4 million sq miles), Europe is the second smallest continent in the world. It is part of the Eurasian landmass and its conventional separation from Asia is therefore more cultural than physical. The Ural Mountains and Ural River, the Caspian and Red Seas, and the Dardanelles Straits separate Europe from Asia and, to the south, the Mediterranean Sea separates it from Africa.

The countries of Europe can be divided into three groups: Western Europe, Eastern Europe (most countries of which came under the influence of the former Soviet Union), and the countries that emerged from the break-up of the former Soviet Union. Each of these groups can be distinguished by the history of its political systems.

Western Europe includes Andorra, Austria, Belgium, Denmark, Finland, France, Germany, Greece, Iceland, Ireland, Italy, Liechtenstein, Luxembourg, Malta, Monaco, the Netherlands, Norway, Portugal, San Marino, Spain, Sweden, Switzerland, the United Kingdom and Vatican City. There are also several dependencies: Guernsey, Jersey, the Isle of Man, and Gibraltar are dependencies of the United Kingdom, the Faeroe Islands of Denmark and Svalbard of Norway.

The nations of Eastern Europe are Poland, Hungary, the Czech Republic, Slovakia, Bulgaria, Romania, Albania, as well as former Yugoslavia—now Slovenia, Croatia, Bosnia and Herzegovina, Macedonia, Serbia, Montenegro, and Kosovo.

When the former Soviet Union broke up, several new nations emerged in Europe and Asia; the European nations consist of the Russian Federation, Ukraine, Belarus, Latvia, Lithuania, Estonia, and Moldova.

During the last 500 years, Europe has exerted a strong influence on the rest of the world through colonialism. Several Western European countries were colonial powers and their languages have become international; European sciences, laws, and arts have spread around the globe. European companies developed commercial agriculture, mining, and manufacturing in their colonies. The colonial powers promoted European migration to the Americas, Australia, and New Zealand—Europeans are now the dominant people there. Many Europeans also migrated to South Africa.

## Physical features

The elongated Tertiary Period mountain chain that stretches between the Alps in France and the Carpathians in Romania, rising 3,000 to 4,500 m (10,000 to 15,000 ft), is a prominent feature in Europe. In contrast, there are geologically old and worn-down mountains in Scandinavia and northern Britain. Glacial carving, including sharp-peaked mountains (such as the Matterhorn) and flat-bottomed, steep-sided glacial valleys as in Switzerland, is found in most European mountainous areas. Along the Scandinavian coasts there are fiords, which are glacial valleys drowned by the sea. There are extensive plains in Central and Eastern Europe and France. Europe is well watered by a large number of rivers—the Volga, the Danube, the Rhône, and the Rhine. Many of these rivers are navigable far inland and are interconnected in places by canals.

## Climate and vegetation

Although much of Europe can be described as humid temperate, significant climatic differences exist within its borders. The climates of Western Europe are moderated by the Atlantic Ocean, which is warmed by the waters of the Gulf Stream.

In contrast, the winter temperatures in continental Russia are below freezing.

The northernmost parts of Europe are treeless, with very cold winters and mild summers. Further south is the taiga, with broad-leaf deciduous and needle-leaf coniferous trees covering large tracts of land, particularly in Russia.

Cool, humid temperate climates stretch along the coast of the Atlantic Ocean between northern Spain and Norway, including Iceland. This area is characterized by mixed forests, but most of the original trees have been cleared. Some forests, like the Black Forest, have been harmed by acid rain.

Further inland, Central and Eastern Europe experience more extreme temperature ranges. There is a semiarid belt in the south, and forests are found in the wetter and higher areas. The drier regions with less reliable rainfall, such as the Ukraine and southwestern Russia, are characterized by extensive steppes of short grasses.

The southern Mediterranean belt experiences hot, dry summers and cool, wet winters. Forests and scrub cover large areas.

## Population

The population of Europe in 2005 (including the Russian Federation) totaled 731 million. The relatively high standards of living in most European nations are reflected in life expectancies of 70.5 years for males and 78.8 years for females. Population numbers are stable, with a near zero growth rate. The Russian Federation alone has 144.0 million people; its life expectancies are 59.0 years for males and 72.6 years for females.

There has been significant urbanization in Europe since the nineteenth century, and this accelerated following the Second World War. Currently 73.3 percent of the population lives in cities and towns (83.5 percent in northern Europe and 66.1 percent in southern Europe); the figure for the Russian Federation is 73.3 percent.

## Agriculture

Europe has a well-developed agricultural economy based on a wide range of food and animal products. Farming is more advanced in Western Europe, in terms of technology and organization, than in the former communist countries of Eastern Europe, which experimented with collectivized agriculture for several decades. Farm size varies considerably, but pressure to create larger farm units is changing the agricultural landscape.

Within Europe's cool, humid zone, mixed farming (grain growing and livestock rearing) is widespread. Wheat, barley, and rye are the main grains, and sheep and cattle the main livestock. Dairy farming is important in some of the cool countries such as the Netherlands and Denmark. Apples and pears are significant fruits.

Southern Europe, with its warm, dry summers and mild winters, is suited to growing grapes, citrus fruits, and olives. Irrigation is extensively used in parts of the Mediterranean areas for growing rice, for example.

There is extensive fishing in the Atlantic Ocean and in both the Mediterranean and Black Seas.

*A valley (with vineyards) in Switzerland (below), and a beech forest in Germany (right), both in Western Europe.*

## Industrialization

Europe was the first part of the world to become industrialized, and through scientific innovation and extensive use of technology, remains one of the world's most developed regions. British and French industries, in particular, benefited from raw materials supplied by their colonies; the colonies in turn provided markets for manufactured goods.

Manufacturing in Europe ranges from the processing of agricultural raw materials, as in the production of wine and olive oil, and the manufacturing of basic industrial items such as steel, petroleum refining, chemicals, fertilizers and cement, to the production of highly sophisticated items like cars, ships, aircraft, and electronic goods.

While European industries largely import the minerals they require, there are some significant mineral deposits in the region: coal (in several places), petroleum (in the North Sea and Eastern Europe), and iron ore (in Ukraine and Russia). The Russian Federation exports natural gas by pipeline to several European countries, and it is also a major producer of gold.

Considerable damage was done to industry and infrastructure during both world wars, particularly the second, but Europe rebuilt. Western Europe prospered, with large-scale restructuring and industrialization, while communist-controlled Eastern Europe lagged behind. These nations are now joining the market economy, but it will take time for them to catch up. Currently some East European nations are economically stagnant, and the Russian Federation, facing economic collapse, needs foreign aid to restructure its economy.

Industrialization and urbanization have taken their toll on the environment. Air pollution, acid rain, and river-water pollution are common. Sulfur dioxide levels have been reduced thanks to international cooperation, but emission of nitrogen oxides remains high, and global warming is considered to be one of the most important ecological issues. The Mediterranean, Black and Baltic Seas have been badly affected by the discharge of waste products.

## Languages

Europe has a large number of languages, most of them belonging to the three major Indo-European language family groups: the Latin-based or Romance languages, the Germanic, and the Slavic.

## Nations

| | | | |
|---|---|---|---|
| Albania | PAGE 263 | Monaco | PAGE 246 |
| Andorra | PAGE 251 | Montenegro | PAGE 261 |
| Austria | PAGE 248 | Netherlands | PAGE 240 |
| Belarus | PAGE 268 | Norway | PAGE 230 |
| Belgium | PAGE 241 | Poland | PAGE 267 |
| Bosnia and Herzegovina | PAGE 259 | Portugal | PAGE 250 |
| Bulgaria | PAGE 264 | Romania | PAGE 263 |
| Croatia | PAGE 258 | Russian Federation | PAGE 271 |
| Czech Republic | PAGE 266 | San Marino | PAGE 256 |
| Denmark | PAGE 233 | Serbia | PAGE 260 |
| Estonia | PAGE 235 | Slovakia | PAGE 267 |
| Finland | PAGE 234 | Slovenia | PAGE 258 |
| France | PAGE 243 | Spain | PAGE 252 |
| Germany | PAGE 238 | Sweden | PAGE 231 |
| Greece | PAGE 265 | Switzerland | PAGE 246 |
| Hungary | PAGE 262 | Ukraine | PAGE 269 |
| Iceland | PAGE 230 | United Kingdom | PAGE 274 |
| Ireland | PAGE 277 | Vatican City | PAGE 256 |
| Italy | PAGE 254 | | |
| Kosovo | PAGE 261 | | |
| Latvia | PAGE 236 | | |
| Liechtenstein | PAGE 248 | | |

### Dependencies

| | | | |
|---|---|---|---|
| Lithuania | PAGE 237 | Faeroe Islands | PAGE 278 |
| Luxembourg | PAGE 243 | Gibraltar | PAGE 278 |
| Macedonia | PAGE 260 | Guernsey | PAGE 278 |
| Malta | PAGE 257 | The Isle of Man | PAGE 279 |
| Moldova | PAGE 270 | Jersey | PAGE 279 |
| | | Svalbard | PAGE 279 |

The Latin-based languages include Spanish, Italian, French, Portuguese, and Romanian. The Germanic languages comprise English, German, Dutch, Danish, Swedish, and Norwegian. Latvian and Lithuanian are distinct Baltic languages. Celtic languages (Irish and Scottish Gaelic, Welsh) are spoken by minorities in the British Isles and also in France (Breton). The main Slavic languages are Russian, Ukrainian, Belarusian, Polish, Czech, Slovak, and Bulgarian, while another group (Serbo-Croatian, Slovene, and Macedonian) is found in the Balkans.

Other languages include Greek, Albanian, and Turkish, which are spoken in parts of the Balkans; Finnish in Scandinavia; and Basque and Catalan in Spain and France.

While most European nations have a dominant language, there are some exceptions. Switzerland has French, German, and Italian-speaking zones, and Belgium is divided into Flemish and French-speaking areas. There are German-speaking areas in Hungary, the Czech Republic, Poland, and France, and there are Russian-speaking minorities in all the former Soviet Union nations.

### Boundary disputes and wars

The First and Second World Wars both began as boundary disputes between European countries before engulfing most of the continent. The domination of Eastern Europe by the powerful former Soviet Union resulted in a political, ideological, and military "iron curtain" dividing the continent until the early 1990s. Currently most of Europe's national boundaries are accepted, with some exceptions. The break-up of Yugoslavia resulted in ethnic wars which sought to redraw the existing boundaries; this was notable in the division of Bosnia and Herzegovina. The current division of Cyprus into Greek and Turkish areas is a source of friction between those countries. Spain's claim to British-held Gibraltar is another contested issue, though otherwise these countries remain friendly.

Several separatist movements exist, for example the Basque and Catalan regions (Spain) and Corsica (France).

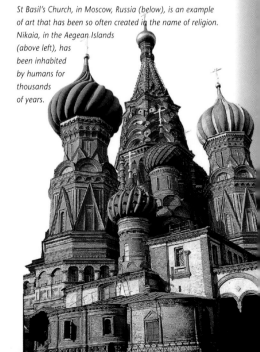

*St Basil's Church, in Moscow, Russia (below), is an example of art that has been so often created in the name of religion. Nikaia, in the Aegean Islands (above left), has been inhabited by humans for thousands of years.*

## Northern Europe

| | |
|---|---|
| Iceland | 230 |
| Norway | 230 |
| Sweden | 231 |
| Denmark | 233 |
| Finland | 234 |
| Estonia | 235 |
| Latvia | 236 |
| Lithuania | 237 |

## Iceland

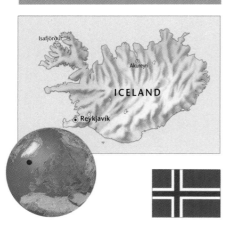

### Fact File

OFFICIAL NAME  Republic of Iceland

FORM OF GOVERNMENT  Republic with single legislative body (Parliament)

CAPITAL  Reykjavík

AREA  103,000 sq km (39,768 sq miles)

TIME ZONE  GMT

POPULATION  304,000

PROJECTED POPULATION 2015  320,000

POPULATION DENSITY  3 per sq km (7.6 per sq mile)

LIFE EXPECTANCY  80.6

INFANT MORTALITY (PER 1,000)  3.3

OFFICIAL LANGUAGE  Icelandic

LITERACY RATE  99 %

RELIGIONS  Lutheran 85.5 %, other Protestant 6.3 %, Roman Catholic 2.0 %, other 3.8 %, none 2.4 %

ETHNIC GROUPS  Icelandic 94 %; others including Danish, American, British, Norwegian, German 6 %

CURRENCY  Króna

ECONOMY  Services 69.1 %, industry 25.7 %, agriculture 5.2 %

GNI PER CAPITA  US$ 54,100

CLIMATE  Cool temperate, with cool, windy winters and mild, wet summers

HIGHEST POINT  Hvannadalshnukur 2,119 m (6,952 ft)

MAP REFERENCE  Page 284

True to its name, one-tenth of the total area of the island of Iceland, in the north Atlantic Ocean, is covered in icefields and glaciers. The human occupation of this island, which lies just south of the Arctic Circle, dates back to the late ninth century AD when Norwegian Vikings settled there. In the thirteenth century the Icelanders submitted to Norwegian rule and a century and a half later, when the Norwegian and Danish monarchies were combined, they came under Danish control. In 1918 Iceland was granted its independence, but still owed allegiance to the Danish monarch. In 1944, as the result of a referendum, Iceland chose to become a republic.

In 1972, because of its economic dependence on the surrounding seas, Iceland, without consultation with other nations, more than quadrupled the extent of its territorial waters from twelve to fifty nautical miles. Three years later it extended them to 200 nautical miles, a provocative move that brought condemnation, particularly from Britain, and gave rise to serious aggression at sea between Icelandic and British fishing vessels. After long and tense negotiations Britain was later granted some degree of access to the disputed waters.

In addition to icefields and glaciers, Iceland's spectacularly rugged and volcanic landscape includes hot springs, sulphur beds, geysers, lava fields, deep rocky canyons, and plummeting waterfalls. There are numerous small freshwater lakes and 200 volcanoes, many of which are active. Earth tremors, and occasionally larger quakes, are a frequent feature.

The interior of the island consists mainly of an elevated plateau of basalt, interspersed with occasional high peaks. There are small areas of forest and very little arable land. In the north, however, there are extensive grasslands where a small number of sheep, cattle, and horses can graze. More than ninety percent of the population lives in towns and cities around the coast, mainly in the southwest corner near Reykjavík.

Deep-sea fishing is the backbone of Iceland's economy, with fish and associated products constituting more than two-thirds of the country's exports. Apart from fish processing, aluminum smelting from imported bauxite and cement manufacture are growing industries. All of Iceland's domestic and industrial electricity needs are met by locally generated power from hydroelectric or geothermal plants. About one in four Icelanders is employed in manufacturing and processing industries. Iceland attracts about 150,000 tourists a year, more than half its permanent population, making tourism an important income-earner.

The people of Iceland enjoy a very high standard of living. Their economy is robust but is susceptible to variations in international fish prices. The country's free healthcare system has contributed to a life expectancy that is among the highest in the world.

*Feda on Feda Fiord, Kvinestal, Norway (right page top). High plateau country, dotted with tiny lakes, in Norway (bottom center).*

## Norway

### Fact File

OFFICIAL NAME  Kingdom of Norway

FORM OF GOVERNMENT  Constitutional monarchy with single legislative body (Parliament)

CAPITAL  Oslo

AREA  324,220 sq km (125,181 sq miles)

TIME ZONE  GMT + 1 hour

POPULATION  4,644,000

PROJECTED POPULATION 2015  4,932,000

POPULATION DENSITY  14.3 per sq km (37.1 per sq mile)

LIFE EXPECTANCY  79.8

INFANT MORTALITY (PER 1,000)  3.6

OFFICIAL LANGUAGE  Norwegian

OTHER LANGUAGES  Sami (Lapp), Finnish

## Sweden

**LITERACY RATE** 100 %

**RELIGIONS** Lutheran 85.7 %; other (including Baptist, Pentecostalist, Methodist and Roman Catholic) 14.3 %

**ETHNIC GROUPS** Norwegian 96.6 %, Danish 0.4 %, British 0.3 %, Swedish 0.3 %, other (including Lapps) 2.4%

**CURRENCY** Norwegian krone

**ECONOMY** Services 54.7 %, industry 42.9 %, agriculture 2.4 %

**GNI PER CAPITA** US$ 76,450

**CLIMATE** Cold in north and inland, temperate and wet on coast

**HIGHEST POINT** Glittertind 2,469 m (8,101 ft)

**MAP REFERENCE** Pages 284–85, 286

Norway's long, narrow landmass wraps around the western part of Sweden and the north of Finland and shares a land border with the north-west tip of the Russian Federation. Its rugged western coastline is washed by the North Sea in the south and the Norwegian Sea further north. Its northern tip juts into the Arctic Ocean, making it the northernmost part of Europe. To the south the Skagerrak Strait separates it from the northern tip of Denmark. Like the Swedes and Danes, modern Norwegians are descendents of the Vikings,

Teutonic peoples who settled the area and, from the ninth to the eleventh centuries AD, raided and conquered lands to the north, east, and west. In the fourteenth century Denmark, Sweden, and Norway came under Danish rule. Although Sweden became independent in the sixteenth century, Norwegians remained subject to the Danes. In 1815, at the end of the Napoleonic Wars, in which Denmark sided with France, control of Norway was transferred to the Swedish crown. The modern Norwegian state dates from 1905, when the country declared its independence. Norway remained neutral in the First World War and was not attacked. However, Nazi forces invaded in 1940 and, despite spirited resistance, subdued the country. Norway joined the NATO alliance in 1949, and in 1994, as already in 1972, attempted to join the European Union, a move that was thwarted when the option was defeated at a referendum. Norway is a parliamentary democracy with a monarch as the titular head of state.

Norway's more than 21,000 km (13,000 miles) of coast is punctuated by deep fiords. Most of the country consists of mountains with deep valleys formed by ancient glaciers. There are also vast areas of high plateaus. More than one-quarter of the land surface is forested, mainly with conifers, and there are many lakes. The population is centered in the lowlands on the southern coasts and in the southeast. Only a tiny proportion of the land area is suitable for cultivation and agriculture is limited mainly to areas around lakes.

Norway has large oil and gas reserves in the North Sea and produces more oil and gas than any other European country. Its electricity, produced mainly from hydroelectric plants, is used largely to power industry. Key industries include pulp and paper manufacture, shipbuilding, and aluminum production. Fishing and fish farming are also major industries and farmed salmon is a main export.

### OVERSEAS TERRITORIES

**Bouvet Island**
**Jan Mayen**
**Peter Island**
**Svalbard**

### Fact File

**OFFICIAL NAME** Kingdom of Sweden

**FORM OF GOVERNMENT** Constitutional monarchy with single legislative body (Parliament = Riksdag)

**CAPITAL** Stockholm

**AREA** 449,964 sq km (173,731 sq miles)

**TIME ZONE** GMT + 1 hour

**POPULATION** 9,045,000

**PROJECTED POPULATION 2015** 9,440,000

**POPULATION DENSITY** 20.1 per sq km (52.1 per sq mile)

**LIFE EXPECTANCY** 80.7

**INFANT MORTALITY (PER 1,000)** 2.8

**OFFICIAL LANGUAGE** Swedish

**OTHER LANGUAGES** Lapp, Finnish

**LITERACY RATE** 99 %

**RELIGIONS** Lutheran 87 %, other (including Catholic and Pentecostal) 13 %

**ETHNIC GROUPS** Swedish 91 %, others include Lapp, Finnish, Yugoslav, Danish, Norwegian, Greek, Turkish 9 %

**CURRENCY** Swedish krona

**ECONOMY** Services 69.8 %, industry 28.9%, agriculture 1.3 %

**GNI PER CAPITA** US$ 46,060

**CLIMATE** Temperate in the south, with cold winters and mild summers; subpolar in the north, with severe winters

**HIGHEST POINT** Kebnekaise 2,111 m (6,926 ft)

**MAP REFERENCE** Pages 284–85

The fourth largest country in Europe, Sweden shares the Scandinavian Peninsula with Norway, which sits between it and the North

Europe and the Russian Federation

## PROVINCES

Älvsborg • Blekinge • Gävleborg
Göteborg and Bohus • Gotland
Halland • Jämtland • Jönköping
Kalmar • Kopparberg • Kristianstad
Kronoberg • Malmöhus • Norrbotten
Örebro • Östergötland • Skaraborg
Södermanland • Stockholm • Uppsala
Värmland • Västerbotten
Västernorrland • Västmanland

Atlantic Ocean. To the northeast Sweden shares a border with Finland, and its eastern coastline is separated from the west coast of Finland by the Gulf of Bothnia. Its southern shores are washed by the Baltic Sea, and south of the land border with Norway the Kattegat Strait divides it from the northern tip of Denmark. Close to Sweden's southeast tip are Gotland and Öland, the largest of many islands dotted around the Swedish coastline.

By the seventh century AD, Teutonic tribes from the south had occupied much of central Sweden, and between the ninth and the eleventh centuries Swedes took part in Viking raids deep into Russia and south to the Black Sea. Over the following five centuries Sweden and Denmark vied for Scandinavian supremacy. Both Sweden and Norway came under the Danish crown in 1397, but fifty years later the Swedes rebelled and elected their own king. The accession to the Swedish throne in 1523 of Gustav I ended Danish claims to all but the south of Sweden. During the next 200 years Sweden became one of the most powerful states in Europe, annexing parts of Estonia, Finland, and Poland, driving the Danes out of southern Sweden, and playing a crucial role in curbing Habsburg expansion in northern Europe. At the beginning of the eighteenth century, however, a coalition of Russia, Poland, and Denmark forced Sweden to relinquish its Baltic possessions.

At the end of the Napoleonic wars, in 1815, Norway was ceded to Sweden, a union that lasted until 1905. In the mid-nineteenth century the beginnings of parliamentary democracy were introduced in Sweden with the establishment of a two-chamber parliament, although suffrage was limited largely to landowners and industrialists. Universal adult suffrage was introduced in 1919.

Sweden remained neutral in both the First and the Second World Wars. Following the Second World War it tried unsuccessfully to form a military alliance with Denmark and Norway. When these nations joined NATO Sweden did not follow, fearing closer ties with the West might damage its relations with the Soviet Union, and give it an excuse to absorb Finland into the Soviet bloc. Since then, although maintaining a high level of defence preparedness, it has kept its distance from NATO and maintained its reputation for neutrality, for playing an active role in international affairs, and as a negotiator in international disputes.

During the 1960s and early 1970s the Social Democrats, who had laid the foundations of a welfare state since 1932, held the majority of seats in the Riksdag and were able to govern alone. They then inaugurated the more radical socialist policies which came to define modern Swedish politics. Welfare services were extended, and "the Swedish Way" was seen by socialists as a model for the rest of Europe. After 1982 Olof Palme's government introduced what it called a middle way between capitalism and communism, with annual levies on profits and wages which went into "wage-earner funds" used to buy stock in private firms for the benefit of labor. Palme was assassinated in mysterious circumstances in Stockholm in 1986. By then the economic costs of the welfare state were becoming evident. The country had almost zero economic growth, and was becoming less competitive in world markets.

From the late 1970s domestic policy discussion has been less along socialist/capitalist lines and more concerned with ecological issues. Sweden has taken the lead in a number of environmental debates, and has been the venue of influential conferences devoted to such matters as global warming and greenhouse gases. An

application for EC (now EU) membership was lodged in 1992. In 1995 it was admitted to the European Union. Sweden is a constitutional monarchy with a single-chamber parliament that is elected every three years.

### Physical features and land use

Northeastern Sweden is a region of low plateaus that drop away to a coastal plain along the Gulf of Bothnia, but rise to the Kjólen Mountains along the Norwegian border. Most of the country's more than 95,000 lakes are in this mountainous region. Shaped by ancient glaciers, many of the lakes are in the upper valleys of the numerous rivers that flow east to the Gulf of Bothnia. They are the source of most of Sweden's hydroelectricity, which is gradually replacing nuclear energy as the main means of power generation. The mountains are heavily forested. Despite extensive land clearing for agriculture in the south, well over half the country remains forested, with spruce, pine and birch among the most prominent trees.

Central Sweden is a lowland area that stretches between Stockholm in the east and the country's

*Stadshuset in Stockholm, Sweden (above). Rows of holiday chalets and small boats in Smøgen, Sweden (left). Early summer foliage in a birch forest (below). Cafés along the harbor in Copenhagen, Denmark (right page).*

second largest city, Göteborg, in the southwest. Four large lakes—the only remnants of a strait that once joined the Baltic to the Kattegat Strait—cover much of this region, the most heavily populated part of the country. The rich soils around these lakes support much of Sweden's agricultural produce, which includes cereals and vegetables and fodder crops for large herds of cattle. Dairy farming is the main form of agriculture, and Sweden is self-sufficient in dairy products.

South of the lakes is a low, largely infertile plateau and further south, stretching to the tip of the peninsula and across to the island of Gotland, is a rich plain—the most intensively cultivated part of the country. Significant areas of woodland still survive here, dotted between stretches of farming and grazing land.

Although it lacks oil and coal reserves, Sweden is rich in mineral resources, most of which are concentrated in the northeast. These include iron ore, zinc, lead, copper, and silver, and almost one-sixth of the world's known reserves of uranium.

## Industry, commerce, and culture

Sweden's vast forests are the basis for timber and paper manufacturing industries that form almost one-fifth of the country's exports. Machines, cars, trucks, aircraft, chemical and electrical goods, and communication equipment are among the chief manufacturing industries, based in the central region and Malmö in the southwest.

Apart from the Saami people (Lapps) in the far north of the country, Sweden is ethnically and culturally quite homogeneous. Despite there being a relatively high rate of unemployment, its citizens enjoy one of the highest standards of living in Europe and an extensive range of government-provided social services. Sweden also boasts one of Europe's highest rates of female participation throughout its workforce.

# Denmark

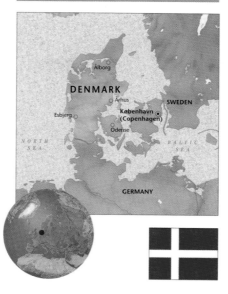

## Fact File

| | |
|---|---|
| OFFICIAL NAME | Kingdom of Denmark |
| FORM OF GOVERNMENT | Constitutional monarchy with one legislative body (Parliament) |
| CAPITAL | Copenhagen (København) |
| AREA | 43,094 sq km (16,629 sq miles) |
| TIME ZONE | GMT + 1 hour |
| POPULATION | 5,485,000 |
| PROJECTED POPULATION 2015 | 5,510,000 |
| POPULATION DENSITY | 127.3 per sq km (329.8 per sq mile) |
| LIFE EXPECTANCY | 78.1 |
| INFANT MORTALITY (PER 1,000) | 4.4 |
| OFFICIAL LANGUAGE | Danish |
| OTHER LANGUAGES | Faroese, Greenlandic, German |
| LITERACY RATE | 99 % |
| RELIGIONS | Lutheran 95 %, other Protestant and Roman Catholic 3 %, Muslim 2 % |
| ETHNIC GROUPS | Danish 97.1 %, German 1.6 %, Turkish 0.5 %, Swedish 0.4 %, British 0.2 %, other 0.2 % |
| CURRENCY | Danish krone |
| ECONOMY | Services 72.4 %, industry 26.1 %, agriculture 1.5 % |
| GNI PER CAPITA | US$ 54,910 |
| CLIMATE | Temperate, with cold, wet winters and mild summers |
| HIGHEST POINT | Yding Skovhoj 173 m (568 ft) |
| MAP REFERENCE | Page 286 |

Denmark is both the smallest and the southernmost of the Scandinavian countries. Most of its land area consists of the Jutland Peninsula, which pushes northward from the northwestern tip of Germany. The North Sea washes Denmark's western coast, the Skagerrak Strait lies to the north separating it from the southern coast of Norway, and the Kattegat Strait separates it from the southwestern tip of Sweden. The Baltic Sea is to the east and here, stretching almost as far as the southwestern tip of Sweden, is an archipelago of more than 400 islands. The largest of these islands is Sjaelland, on which is situated the Danish capital, Copenhagen.

Like the inhabitants of Sweden and Norway, modern Danes are descended from Viking invaders who from the fifth century AD moved northward into Scandinavia and then outward to other parts of western and eastern Europe. For much of its history, Denmark was the dominant country in Scandinavia. At the end of the fourteenth century, Norway and Sweden, as well as Iceland, were united under the Danish crown. The Swedes elected their own monarch fifty years later, but Norway continued to be part of Denmark for more than 400 years—until 1815, when the Congress of Vienna awarded it to Sweden in retaliation for Denmark having supported Napoleon Bonaparte. Despite its neutrality, Denmark was

## Scandinavia

Today the term Scandinavia is often understood to refer only to Norway and Sweden, which both occupy the Scandinavian Peninsula, and the more southerly peninsula and islands that make up Denmark. Many people, however, would also include Finland, Iceland, and the Faeroe Islands, which are possessions of Denmark. These countries are also collectively referred to as the Nordic countries, or Norden.

Culturally, geographically, and geologically, the countries of Scandinavia have much in common and the whole region forms a distinctive part of Europe. All of them lie close to the Arctic Circle and share a cold, moist, and often harsh climate, which is mitigated in parts of Scandinavia by the effect of the Gulf Stream. All five countries have a high degree of ethnic and religious homogeneity. Lutheran is the overwhelmingly predominant religion in every part of Scandinavia. The languages of four of the countries are closely related, but Finnish is entirely different and is more closely related to the Estonian language. Historical links are also very strong and during the fifteenth century the countries were united under Danish rule. For five centuries, until 1809, Finland was under Swedish control and Swedish was the language of its ruling classes. For almost a century, until 1905, Norway was ruled by Sweden, and Iceland only gained its independence as late as 1944, after almost five and a half centuries of Danish rule and domination.

Greenland has been part of Denmark since the early eighteenth century. Situated to the west of Iceland, it is ethnically distinct and geographically closer to North America. Although it was granted home rule in 1979 its inhabitants are still Danish citizens and Denmark still controls Greenland's foreign affairs.

Despite climatic difficulties, Scandinavian economies have traditionally depended heavily on agriculture and fishing. The improvements in agricultural techniques and technologies that flowed from the Industrial Revolution were slow to be implemented in Scandinavia and until late in the nineteenth century the region remained economically stagnant. In recent years, however, there have been significant technological innovations and increasing industrialization and Scandinavians now enjoy some of the highest standards of living in Europe.

invaded by Germany during 1940. Liberated by British forces in 1945, Denmark joined the NATO alliance following the war, and in 1973 became a member of the European Union. Denmark is a constitutional monarchy, with a hereditary monarch. Its single-house parliament, which is headed by a prime minister, is elected every four years.

Almost the whole of Denmark is low-lying and its surface is covered in many places by rocky glacial debris, most prominently in the undulating mass of moraine that runs down the center of the Jutland Peninsula. This divides the peninsula into two distinct regions. To the west is a sandy landscape with extensive dunes and lagoons along the North Sea coast. To the east lies a loam plain, which extends across the islands of the archipelago, as far as the Baltic coast. This fertile region supports significant crops of barley, wheat, and sugar beet and a thriving livestock and dairying industry. Fishing, which is still a leading Danish industry, is based for the most part on the extensive, shallow lagoons that lie along the western coastline of Jutland.

As well as constituting a significant proportion of the country's exports, Denmark's agricultural and fishing produce also provide the raw materials for food processsing industries, which are a major source of employment. Other significant industries, for which Denmark imports most of the raw materials, are iron and metal working, machinery manufacturing, and furniture making. While its unemployment rate was high during much of the 1990s, it is around 3.8 % today. The Danes generally enjoy a high standard of living. An extensive social security system means that serious poverty is comparatively rare throughout the country.

### OVERSEAS TERRITORIES

**Faeroe Islands**
**Greenland**

# Finland

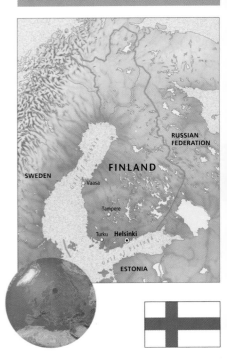

## Fact File

**OFFICIAL NAME** Republic of Finland

**FORM OF GOVERNMENT** Republic with single legislative body (Parliament)

**CAPITAL** Helsinki

**AREA** 338,145 sq km (130,558 sq miles)

**TIME ZONE** GMT + 2 hours

**POPULATION** 5,245,000

**PROJECTED POPULATION 2015** 5,384,000

**POPULATION DENSITY** 15.5 per sq km (40.2 per sq mile)

**LIFE EXPECTANCY** 78.8

**INFANT MORTALITY (PER 1,000)** 3.5

**OFFICIAL LANGUAGES** Finnish, Swedish

**OTHER LANGUAGES** Russian, Lapp

**LITERACY RATE** 100 %

**RELIGIONS** Lutheran 84.2 %, Greek Orthodox 1.1 %, none 13.5 %, other 1.2 %

**ETHNIC GROUPS** Finnish 93.4 %, Swedish 5.7 %, others (including Russian, Roma, Sami) 0.9 %

**CURRENCY** Euro

**ECONOMY** Services 65.6 %, industry 31.8 %, agriculture 2.6 %

**GNI PER CAPITA** US$ 44,400

**CLIMATE** Mainly cold temperate, but polar in arctic regions

**HIGHEST POINT** Haltiatunturi 1,328 m (4,357 ft)

**MAP REFERENCE** Pages 284–85, 287

Except for a small section of Norway which cuts it off from the Arctic Ocean, Finland is the most northerly country in continental Europe. As well as its northern boundary with Norway, Finland borders northern Sweden to the west and the Russian Federation in the east. In the south, the Gulf

of Finland, the easternmost part of the Baltic Sea, separates it from Estonia, and on the west the Gulf of Bothnia, a northern inlet of the Baltic, sits between it and southern Sweden.

Modern Finland has its roots in a seventh century AD invasion by tribes from the Volga. They displaced the Lapps, Asiatic people who had lived in the area for centuries, and drove them north. Only about 2,500 Lapps, or Sami, who have their own culture and language, now survive in the north, tending reindeer herds. Viking incursions followed and in the twelfth century Swedes invaded Finland, bringing Christianity. Finland remained under Swedish control for the next 650 years, until 1809, when the Russians took over. Swedish influence is still evident in the country's significant Swedish-speaking minority, and the fact that some towns have both Finnish and Swedish names. A relatively benign Russian rule allowed considerable freedoms and encouraged a resurgence of the Finnish language, which had largely fallen into disuse. A more oppressive regime towards the end of the century fanned Finnish nationalism, and at the time of the Russian Revolution in 1917 the country seized its independence.

Finland's harsh climate and the ruggedness of its northern regions means that most of its people live in the more moderate south. Much of the land consists of flat expanses of granite rock, the legacy of extensive glaciation. Remnants of an ancient mountain range, rising in places to more than 1,000 m (3,300 ft), exist in Lapland, the northern part of the country. There are more than 60,000 substantial lakes throughout Finland, mainly in the south, and tens of thousands of smaller ones. Forests, mainly of pine, birch, and spruce cover more than half the land area, contributing to the country's heavy reliance on timber-related industries, including wood processing, pulp, and papermaking.

Less than one-tenth of Finland's land is arable and agricultural production, which includes cereals, potatoes and sugar beet, is confined to the summer months, when the country is not snowbound.

In the 1980s living standards in Finland rose markedly, rivaling those of Sweden, although they fell back in the recession of the early 1990s. The country has an effective government-sponsored health system and the population is one of the most literate and highly educated in the world.

## Estonia

### Fact File

**OFFICIAL NAME** Republic of Estonia

**FORM OF GOVERNMENT** Republic with single legislative body (Parliament)

**CAPITAL** Tallinn

**AREA** 45,226 sq km (17,395 sq miles)

**TIME ZONE** GMT + 2 hours

**POPULATION** 1,308,000

**PROJECTED POPULATION 2015** 1,300,000

**POPULATION DENSITY** 28.9 per sq km (75.2 per sq mile)

**LIFE EXPECTANCY** 72.6

**INFANT MORTALITY (PER 1,000)** 7.5

**OFFICIAL LANGUAGE** Estonian

**OTHER LANGUAGES** Latvian, Lithuanian, Russian

**LITERACY RATE** 99.8 %

**RELIGIONS** Lutheran 13.6 %; Russian Orthodox 12.8 %, other Christian 1.4 %, unaffiliated 34.1 %, other 38.1 %

**ETHNIC GROUPS** Estonian 67.9 %, Russian 25.6 %, Ukrainian 2.1 %, Belarusian 1.3 %, other 3.1 %

**CURRENCY** Kroon

**ECONOMY** Services 68.5 %, industry 28.5 %, agriculture 3 %

**GNI PER CAPITA** US$ 13,200

**CLIMATE** Cool temperate; cold winters and mild summers

**HIGHEST POINT** Mt Munamagi 318 m (1,043 ft)

**MAP REFERENCE** Page 287

It has been claimed that Estonia's flag, consisting of a blue, a black, and a white horizontal bar, represents the country's blue skies, black soils, and snowy winters. This, the smallest and least populous of the three Baltic countries, contains more than 1,500 lakes within its borders and its land area includes more than 800 islands in the Baltic Sea and the Gulf of Finland. The largest of the lakes, Lake Peipus, is in the far east of the country and forms most of its border with Russia.

Russia has been the dominant power in Estonia's recent history and the large ethnic Russian minority bears witness to this. From the thirteenth until the eighteenth century the Estonians were ruled by outsiders, first the Germans and then the Swedes. In 1721 Russia assumed control and ruled the country for almost 200 years. Occupied by Germany during the First World War, Estonia declared its independence in 1918. This was achieved

*The medieval rooftops of Tallinn, the capital of Estonia (above). Savonlinna, a city on the Finnish Seenplatte, in the foreground the fortress Olavinlinna (below). The harbor of Stockholm, Sweden (left page).*

in 1920 when, after an armed struggle, Russia formally recognized the small country. It was a short-lived victory, however. During World War II Estonia was overrun first by the Russians and then by the Germans. In 1944 it was returned to the Soviets and remained part of the USSR until it declared itself independent in August 1991, following Lithuania's example of the previous year. Since 2004 Estonia has been a member of the EU.

Most of Estonia is low-lying and flat or gently undulating. Large areas of land are barren and stony, a legacy of the glaciers that once covered much of the landscape. There are extensive woodlands which supply the raw materials for the country's important timber and woodworking industries. Engineering and textile manufacture are also significant. Despite its black soils, little of the land is arable and the main agricultural industries are dairying and livestock raising, especially pig farming. Mineral resources are meager, though extensive deposits of shale are used in the production of gas and chemical products.

Compared with other former Soviet republics, the people of Estonia enjoy a high standard of living. The economy, after declining for some years following independence, has improved steadily as increasing trade with Western countries has shielded Estonia from some of the effects of the declining Russian economy.

*Strollers in Tallinn, the capital of Estonia, which is the country's main port (below center). The Latvian capital Riga (right page bottom). More than 60% of the Latvian population lives in cities. The rooftops of a town in Latvia (right). The picturesque castle of Trakai in Lithuania (right page top).*

## The Baltic States

The nations of Estonia, Latvia, and Lithuania, on the eastern edge of the Baltic Sea, are collectively known as the Baltic States. Similar in their physical environments and sharing a common history of almost uninterrupted Russian domination from the eighteenth century until they achieved independence in 1991, the three countries have quite distinct ethnic and linguistic identities, as well as diverse earlier histories.

The ethnic composition of Estonia and Latvia reflects the long period of Russian rule, with native Estonians and Latvians comprising under two-thirds of their respective populations, the rest being made up mainly of ethnic Russians and immigrants from other former Soviet countries. Lithuania is more ethnically homogeneous. In all three countries, however, more than nine out of ten people claim the native language as their own. Latvian and Lithuanian are both Indo-European languages, but Estonian is more closely related to Finnish. The strong German influence on both Estonian and Latvian culture is manifested in the dominance of the Lutheran religion in those countries, while the predominance of Catholics in Lithuania stems from that country's past links with Poland. In the fifteenth century Lithuania was a major European power, whose territories took in parts of Belarus and Ukraine and stretched from the Baltic to the Black Seas. In the sixteenth century it merged with Poland and the countries remained united for more than 200 years. Estonia and Latvia, on the other hand, were never great powers, enduring about 1,000 years of foreign domination before gaining their independence.

Near the end of the First World War in 1918 the Baltic States became independent, but in 1940 they were incorporated into the Soviet

Union and occupied by Soviet troops, a move that was sanctioned by the Germans but never recognized by the United States, even following the war. A deliberate policy of Russification took place during the 1950s. This resulted in massive immigration, often of manual workers, from Russia and the forced emigration of many highly qualified native Baltic peoples to other parts of the Soviet Union. Despite this, nationalistic aspirations in the region remained undiminished and after an attempted coup against Soviet leader Mikhail Gorbachev in 1991, the Baltic States declared and were granted their independence. Soon after, they became members of the United Nations, and in 2004 they joined the EU.

## Latvia

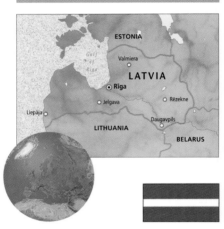

### Fact File

**OFFICIAL NAME** Republic of Latvia

**FORM OF GOVERNMENT** Republic with single legislative body (Parliament)

**CAPITAL** Riga

**AREA** 64,589 sq km (24,749 sq miles)

**TIME ZONE** GMT + 2 hours

**POPULATION** 2,245,000

**PROJECTED POPULATION 2015** 2,189,000

**POPULATION DENSITY** 34.8 per sq km (90.7 per sq mile)

**LIFE EXPECTANCY** 71.9

**INFANT MORTALITY (PER 1,000)** 9

**OFFICIAL LANGUAGE** Latvian

**OTHER LANGUAGES** Russian

**LITERACY RATE** 99.7%

**RELIGIONS** Mainly Lutheran with Russian Orthodox and Roman Catholic minorities

**ETHNIC GROUPS** Latvian 58%, Russian 30%, Belarusian 4%, Ukrainian 3%, Polish 3%, Lithuanian 1%, other 1%

**CURRENCY** Lats

ECONOMY Services 74.7 %, industry 22 %, agriculture 3.3 %

GNI PER CAPITA US$ 9,930

CLIMATE Temperate; cold, wet winters, mild summers

HIGHEST POINT Gaizinkalns 312 m (1,024 ft)

MAP REFERENCE Page 287

Latvia lies between its sister Baltic republics of Estonia to the north and Lithuania to the south, its coastline along the Baltic Sea indented by the Gulf of Riga. To the east and southeast respectively it shares borders with the Russian Federation and Belarus. Like Estonia and Lithuania, Latvia has been controlled by foreign powers for most of its history. For more than 1,000 years its inhabitants, the Letts, have been ruled successively by Germans, Poles, Swedes, and finally Russians. In 1991 Latvia declared its independence from the Soviet Union. It is now a multi-party parliamentary democracy with an elected president as head of state. The Communist Party of Latvia has been banned.

The country is mostly flat with hillier land in the east. There are large areas of bogs and swamps and about forty percent of the land is woodland or forest, in which oak and pine predominate. Small farms account for most agriculture, which is mainly dairy farming and cattle raising. Some grain and vegetable crops are also grown. Forestry and fishing, which were important in earlier times, have enjoyed a resurgence in recent years.

Latvia is the most heavily industrialized of the Baltic States. It has few mineral resources and imports the raw materials needed for its industries—the manufacture of electrical goods, shipbuilding, and train and vehicle making. It relies on its former ruler for energy supplies and much of the Russian Federation's oil and gas exports pass through the Latvian port of Venspils. Air and water pollution from industrial wastes is a matter of concern.

Latvia's economy was severely affected in 1995 by bank failures and financial scandals, and its dependence on Russia limits its development. Latvians have a reasonable standard of living, although discrepancies in wealth are marked.

# Lithuania

## Fact File

OFFICIAL NAME Republic of Lithuania

FORM OF GOVERNMENT Republic with single legislative body (Parliament)

CAPITAL Vilnius

AREA 65,200 sq km (25,174 sq miles)

TIME ZONE GMT + 2 hours

POPULATION 3,565,000

PROJECTED POPULATION 2015 3,263,000

POPULATION DENSITY 54.7 per sq km (141.6 per sq mile)

LIFE EXPECTANCY 74.7

INFANT MORTALITY (PER 1,000) 6.6

OFFICIAL LANGUAGE Lithuanian

OTHER LANGUAGES Russian, Polish, Belarusian

LITERACY RATE 99.6 %

RELIGIONS Roman Catholic 79 %; Russian Orthodox 4.1 %, Protestant 1.9 %, other or unspecified 5.5 %, none 9.5 %

ETHNIC GROUPS Lithuanian 83.4 %, Polish 6.7 %, Russian 6.3 %, other 3.6 %

CURRENCY Litas

ECONOMY Services 61.4 %, industry 33.3 %, agriculture 5.3 %

GNI PER CAPITA US$ 9,920

CLIMATE Temperate; cold winters and mild summers

HIGHEST POINT Mt Juozapine 292 m (958 ft)

MAP REFERENCE Pages 287, 289

The largest of the Baltic states, Lithuania has borders with Latvia to the north, Belarus to the east and southeast, Poland to the south, and the Russian Federation—the enclave Kaliningrad—to the southwest. The Baltic Sea lies to its west. In the thirteenth century, Lithuania was united under a Christian king, in the sixteenth century it merged with Poland, then in 1795 it came under Russian control. Occupied by Germany in the First World War, Lithuania became independent in 1918. It became part of the Soviet Union in 1940 and was then invaded by Germany. When Soviet armies arrived in 1944, over 200,000 people, more than three-quarters of them Jews, had perished. In 1991 the country declared its independence from the Soviet Union. It is now a multi-party democracy with a president as head of state and a prime minister as head of government. Like the other Baltic states it is also a member of the UN and the EU since 2004.

Most of Lithuania consists of a relatively fertile plain with extensive marshlands and forests. Many marshes have been reclaimed for growing cereal and vegetable crops. Sand dunes predominate along the Baltic coast and there is a range of hills dotted with more than 3,000 lakes in the southeast. Numerous rivers traverse the landscape.

Machine manufacturing, petroleum refining, shipbuilding, and food processing are some of Lithuania's key industries, but they have resulted in soil and groundwater contamination. The country has few natural resources and depends on Russia for oil and most of the raw materials needed for its industries. The main forms of agriculture are dairy farming and pig and cattle raising. Foreign government and business support have helped form a free market economy, though foreign investment declined in 2006.

## Central Europe

Germany · · · · · · · · 238
Netherlands · · · · · · 240
Belgium · · · · · · · · 241
Luxembourg · · · · · 243
France · · · · · · · · 243
Monaco · · · · · · · · 246
Switzerland · · · · · · 246
Liechtenstein · · · · · 248
Austria · · · · · · · · 248

## Germany

### STATES

**Baden-Württemberg • Bavaria • Berlin Brandenburg • Bremen • Hamburg Hesse • Lower Saxony • Mecklenburg-West Pomerania • North Rhine-Westphalia Rhineland-Palatinate • Saarland • Saxony Saxony-Anhalt • Schleswig-Holstein Thuringia (Thüringen)**

*Norman Foster's new dome of the Reichstag, Berlin (below left). The gable of the Hamlin Leisthaus (below right). View from Philosophenweg onto Heidelberg with Alte Brücke and castle (above center). Neuschwanstein in Bavaria, built by Ludwig II, late-nineteenth century (right page bottom).*

### Fact File

OFFICIAL NAME Federal Republic of Germany

FORM OF GOVERNMENT Federal republic with two legislative bodies (Federal Council and Federal Assembly)

CAPITAL Berlin

AREA 357,021 sq km (137,846 sq miles)

TIME ZONE GMT + 1 hour

POPULATION 82,370,000

PROJECTED POPULATION 2015 81,825,000

POPULATION DENSITY 230.7 per sq km (597.6 per sq mile)

LIFE EXPECTANCY 79.1

INFANT MORTALITY (PER 1,000) 4

OFFICIAL LANGUAGE German

OTHER LANGUAGES Turkish, Italian, Greek, Dutch, Spanish, Danish, Frisian, Sorbian

LITERACY RATE 99%

RELIGIONS Protestant 34%, Roman Catholic 34%, Muslim 4%, unaffiliated or other 28%

ETHNIC GROUPS German 91.5%, Turkish 2.4%, Croatian, Bosnian and Serb 2%, Italian 1%, other 3.1%

CURRENCY Euro

ECONOMY Services 70.2%, industry 29%, agriculture 0.8%

GNI PER CAPITA US$ 38,860

CLIMATE Temperate, with cool, wet winters (colder in east and south) and mild summers

HIGHEST POINT Zugspitze 2,962 m (9,718 ft)

MAP REFERENCE Pages 288–89

Landlocked except for two stretches of coast along the North and Baltic Seas, Germany shares land borders with nine countries. Poland is located to the east; the Czech Republic to the southeast; Austria and Switzerland to the south; France to the southwest; and Luxembourg, Belgium and the Netherlands to the west. Germany's coastlines are separated by the Jutland Peninsula, at the southern end of which Germany borders Denmark.

### History

The area currently occupied by Germany was roughly defined in the tenth century AD when Duke Conrad became king of the German-speaking eastern part of the Frankish Empire, which had been established several centuries earlier by Charlemagne and had dissolved into several parts after his death. Several kings

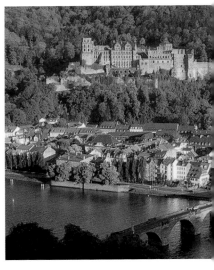

brought about substantial changes in the territory of the German Empire. Especially during the reign of the Saxon Emperor Otto I (AD 936–973), Germany's territory was extended eastward. In 1273, however, the accession of the Austrian Rudolf of Habsburg to the throne ushered in a long period of Austrian domination. The rise of Protestantism under Martin Luther during the sixteenth and seventeenth centuries as well as the Counter-Reformation of the Catholic Church flamed nationalist as well as religious passions and fueled several insurgencies, unrests and wars, such as the peasants' revolt in 1524, which were savagely suppressed. At the same time the territorial princes used the unrests to lead campaigns to enlarge their spheres of influence and their territories. The climax of this century of wars was the Thirty Years War of 1618–48 in which, amid wholesale devastation, German states achieved the right to religious, if not political, autonomy and the emperor lost his de facto dominance over the empire.

Austria, home of the Habsburg dynasty of emperors and up until that time the leading power, was substantially weakened by the long years of war and this encouraged individual German states such as Saxony, Hanover, Bavaria, and Brandenburg/Prussia to increase their power. During the eighteenth century, under the leadership of Frederick II the Great, Prussia developed into a major European power, gaining control of much of present-day Poland, formerly ruled by Austria. At the end of the eighteenth century, Napoleon's armies overran both Austria and Prussia, which effectively brought the German Empire to an end in 1806. After Napoleon's defeat in 1815 Prussia became the dominant force in a German Confederation, a loose union of German princedoms. This confederation, however, was still nominally under Austrian—the emperor's—control. In 1866, under the leadership of Otto von Bismarck, the Prussians defeated the Austrian Habsburgs, driving them out of Germany. Bismarck was also instrumental in bringing about the Franco-Prussian War of 1870–71. The Prussian victory, which culminated in the coronation of Wilhelm I of

Prussia as German emperor in Versailles, consolidated Prussia as the leading European power and brought northern and southern Germany together to form a unified German Empire (Reich). Now the king of Prussia was emperor of Germany as well.

Germany's expansionist ambitions and its aggressive arms build-up during the last years of the nineteenth century in combination with the manifold rivalries between the various European powers led to international tensions that finally erupted in the First World War. At the end of the war, in 1918, Germany found itself along with its allies Austria and Turkey, defeated and its emperor, Wilhelm II, in exile. All other German kings and princes were forced to abdicate as well. In 1919, the Weimar Republic, with a president and legislature elected by universal suffrage, ruling a German territory that was substantially smaller than the pre-war state had been. However, popular resentment was fanned by the loss of German territory and the harsh regime of reparations that were imposed by the Treaty of Versailles. This resentment was exacerbated by a high rate of unemployment, soaring inflation in the 1920s and the onset of serious economic depression at the end of the decade. Extremist groupings to the left and right of the political spectrum thrived and battled over their ideological differences in bloody street fights. In 1933 Adolf Hitler was elected chancellor as head of the National Socialist (Nazi) Party (NSDAP), promising to return the country to its former level of influence and power. The "Führer" soon eliminated all democratic organs, ruthlessly pursued his goals and cruelly suppressed any opposition. Eventually, Hitler plunged Europe into the Second World War when he invaded Poland in September 1939. Especially the Jews suffered from his reign of terror: More than six million Jewish people troughout Europe were murdered and maltreated in concentration and labor camps before the war ended in 1945.

At the end of the war a defeated and devastated Germany was divided into two principal zones, the western half administered by Britain, France, and the United States, and the eastern part under Soviet control (Poland and the Soviet Union had first incorporated large parts of eastern Prussia into their territories). In 1949 this resulted in the creation of two separate states: the Federal Republic of Germany in the west, under a democratically elected government and firmly embedded in the western alliances; and the Democratic Republic of Germany under a central, Soviet-dominated communist government in the east. Thus divided, the two Germanies became a focal point for Cold War tensions in Europe over the next 40 years. Control of the city of Berlin, in East German territory, was divided between the two countries. East Berlin was sealed off when communist authorities constructed a wall between the two parts of the city in 1961.

As the Soviet Union faltered in the late 1980s, waves of unrest in East Germany led to the collapse of its government and the reunification of the whole country in October 1990, with Berlin as its capital. In December, elections including the entire country were held. Germany's political system is based on the 1949 West German constitution, which stipulates a parliament elected by universal suffrage for a four-year term with a president, elected by both houses of the parliament for a five-year term, as titular head of state.

### Physical features and land use

Germany is divided into many different landforms. The southern part of the country is generally mountainous and heavily forested. In the southwestern region east of the Rhine River which forms the border with France, is the vast expanse of rugged wooded peaks that constitute the Black Forest, an extension of Switzerland's Jura Mountains. Further east the thickly wooded Bavarian Plateau rises out of the Danube Valley, leading to the spectacular peaks of the Alps along the border between Austria and Germany in the far southeast.

The central part of Germany is also a highland area, part of a chain of mountains and hills that extends from France as far east as the Carpathians. These, too, are heavily wooded, particularly in the more mountainous regions. The valleys are often fertile and undulating and extensively planted with crops and vines. The highest and most rugged peaks are found in the Harz Mountains in the north of these central uplands. In the northern part of the central uplands, where the country slopes toward the northern plain, there are areas of fertile soil that support crops such as wheat, barley, and sugar beet.

Northern Germany is an extensive lowland plain that covers about one-third of the country's area. Part of the North European Plain that stretches eastward into Russia, it is a region of fertile pasture and croplands, sandy heaths and stretches of marshland. A network of northward-flowing rivers, most notably the Elbe and its tributaries, drains this northern plain.

About one-third of German land is cultivated. Cereal crops are widely grown, as well as beets and potatoes. Large areas are used as pastures. Especially in the Hallertau region hops is grown for the German beers that are famous throughout the world. Vineyards are most widespread in the valleys of the Rhine and Mosel Rivers. Especially in the south, along the shores of the Bodensee (or Lake of Constance) which lies between Germany, Switzerland and Austria, fruit is cultivated wherever the climate will allow it. Cattle and pigs are the principal livestock and are concentrated mainly on the northern plain and in the foothills of the Alps.

### Industry, commerce, and culture

Manufacturing industry, centered largely in the Ruhr Valley but also in such cities as Frankfurt, Stuttgart, Munich, Hannover, Hamburg, and Berlin among many others, is the main strength of the German economy. Coal is the only mineral resource of which Germany has large reserves, although its importance has declined in recent decades as oil has replaced it as the primary industrial fuel. Iron and steel production support well-developed machine manufacturing and other metal industries. Cement, chemical, automobile, and electronic industries are also significant.

Unification has resulted in the juxtaposition of one of the world's most developed and efficient industrial economies with one that was mostly uncompetitive and outmoded in its methods and equipment. As a result, Germany has suffered considerable economic and social disruption as the more affluent western part of the country has had to subsidize attempts to improve conditions in the east. There is still a noticeable discrepancy between standards of living in east and west, and wages in the east are considerably lower. The move to a market economy in the former East Germany, with its emphasis on greater efficiency, has created high levels of unemployment. Under the former communist regime unemployment was virtually non-existent.

# Netherlands

## Fact File

**OFFICIAL NAME** Kingdom of the Netherlands

**FORM OF GOVERNMENT** Constitutional monarchy with two legislative bodies (First Chamber and Second Chamber)

**CAPITAL** Amsterdam; The Hague is the seat of government

**AREA** 41,526 sq km (16,033 sq miles)

**TIME ZONE** GMT + 1 hour

**POPULATION** 16,645,000

**PROJECTED POPULATION 2015** 16,625,000

**POPULATION DENSITY** 400.8 per sq km (1,038.2 per sq mile)

**LIFE EXPECTANCY** 79.3

**INFANT MORTALITY (PER 1,000)** 4.8

**OFFICIAL LANGUAGE** Dutch

**OTHER LANGUAGES** Frisian

**LITERACY RATE** 99 %

**RELIGIONS** Roman Catholic 31 %, Protestant 20 %, Muslim 5.5 %, other 2.5 %, none 41 %

**ETHNIC GROUPS** Dutch 83 %, other (including Turkish, Moroccan, Surinamese, Indonesian) 17 %

**CURRENCY** Euro

**ECONOMY** Services 73.7 %, industry 24.1 %, agriculture 2.2 %

**GNI PER CAPITA** US$ 45,820

**CLIMATE** Temperate, with cool winters and mild summers

**HIGHEST POINT** Mt Vaalserberg 321 m (1,053 ft)

**MAP REFERENCE** Page 288

Situated in northwestern Europe, with a western and northern coastline on the North Sea, the Netherlands is bordered by Germany to its east and Belgium to its south. About half the area of this low-lying nation is below sea level and the country is saved from inundation only by a series of coastal dikes and sand dunes, heavily planted with marram grass to prevent erosion, and a com-

plex network of canals and waterways, into which excess water is pumped from low-lying areas and then carried to the rivers that flow to the coast. For centuries the Dutch have been engaged in battle with the sea, and have gradually reclaimed huge amounts of land from it. In the last century more than 3,000 sq km (1,160 sq miles) of land were added. The most spectacular reclamation was the Zuiderzee project that began in 1920 and was completed almost 50 years later. Several polders were created in the former bay, the largest of them being Flevoland and the Noordoostpolder. The newly gained areas are important for settling and economy. They substantially relieve the agglomerations in the south of the country.

In the first century BC the Germanic peoples of the Low Countries, which include present-day Belgium and Luxembourg, were colonized by Roman armies. From the fifth century AD the region came under the successive control of Frankish, Burgundian, Austrian, and finally, in the fifteenth century, Spanish rulers. In 1568, William of Orange, outraged by Spain's suppression of a spreading Protestant movement, led a revolt. In 1581 the seven northern provinces of the Low Countries declared their independence as the United Provinces of the Netherlands.

This set the scene for the consolidation and expansion of Dutch power throughout the seventeenth century. Trading posts and colonies were established in the East Indies (now Indonesia), the Caribbean (the Antilles), Africa, and South and North America. This period also saw the emergence of the Netherlands as a great maritime nation and a blossoming of Dutch art, literature, and scientific achievements.

The French, under Napoleon, invaded in 1794. After the defeat of France, the Congress of Vienna united the Netherlands, Belgium, and Luxembourg under a Dutch monarch in 1814. Belgium declared itself independent in 1831 and Luxembourg was granted autonomy in 1848. In 1848 a new constitution was introduced reducing the power of the monarch and

investing greater authority in the Estates-General, as the parliament is still called. This laid the groundwork for the later emergence of a parliamentary democracy under a monarch with strictly formalized and limited powers.

The Netherlands remained neutral in the First World War and its neutrality was respected by both sides. In the Second World War it was overrun by Nazi forces in 1940, in blatant breach of interntional law. Its East Indies colonies were invaded by Japan. At the end of the war, the Netherlands began an armed conflict with rebel forces in its East Indies colony. It finally granted them independence, as the Republic of Indonesia, in 1949. Suriname, in South America, became independent in 1975, leaving the Antilles and Aruba as the Netherlands' only overseas territories.

After the Second World War the Netherlands joined the NATO alliance and became one of the founder members of the European Economic Community, later the European Community and then the European Union. In 1992

the Treaty on European Union, the Maastricht Treaty, was signed in the southern Dutch city of Maastricht.

## Physical features and land use

Almost all of the Netherlands is flat and much of the landscape is covered by small farming plots, intensively cultivated and surrounded by ditches or canals. Dotting the landscape are windmills which for centuries have been used to drain the land. These are now largely picturesque as they have been supplanted by motor pumps. Much of this land is dedicated to horticulture, especially the growing of tulips and other bulb plants, often in tandem with vegetable produce.

Cattle farming and dairying, the country's main forms of agriculture, are strongest in the northwest, in the provinces of North Holland and Friesland, on either side of the Ijsselmeer, the area of the Zuiderzee project. The Ijsselmeer is an expanse of fresh water, separated from the salt water of the Waddenzee by a dike that is 32 km (20 miles) long. This lies between the northwest coast and a succession of accumulations of sand which are known as the West Frisian Islands. On the land side, streets are built on the dike.

Further south, near the coast, is a succession of densely populated urban areas that include Amsterdam and the other major Dutch cities, including Rotterdam, one of the world's largest ports. Together with other important cities such as Haarlem, The Hague, Utrecht, Delft, and Leyden, the main centers Amsterdam and Rotterdam form an extended agglomeration, called the Randstad Holland. Just south of this urban conglomeration, the major rivers that flow into the Netherlands—among them the Rhine from Germany and the Schelde and the Meuse from Belgium—share a common delta area. The only relief from flat land is in the

### OVERSEAS TERRITORIES

**Aruba**
**Netherlands Antilles**

far southeast, where a range of hills rises in places to about 100 m (300 ft).

## Industry and commerce

Concentrated in the heavily populated urban southwest, manufacturing industry employs about one in five members of the workforce. Food processing, chemical and electrical machinery manufacture, metal, engineering, electronic products, and petroleum refining are major industries. Natural gas is the country's principal natural resource, and there are extensive reserves in the north.

Most Dutch people enjoy an affluent lifestyle, although some groups of immigrants on the fringes of the cities live in conspicuous poverty. Social services are well developed and the country has one of the best state-funded healthcare systems in the world.

*Houses and houseboats along one of Amsterdam's canals (left page top). Spreading fields of bulbs in the Netherlands (bottom). Renaissance buildings in Antwerp, Belgium (below).*

# Belgium

## Fact File

| | |
|---|---|
| OFFICIAL NAME | Kingdom of Belgium |
| FORM OF GOVERNMENT | Federal constitutional monarchy with two legislative bodies (Senate and Chamber of Deputies) |
| CAPITAL | Brussels |
| AREA | 30,528 sq km (11,780 sq miles) |
| TIME ZONE | GMT + 1 hour |
| POPULATION | 10,404,000 |
| PROJECTED POPULATION 2015 | 10,613,000 |
| POPULATION DENSITY | 340.8 per sq km (883.2 per sq mile) |
| LIFE EXPECTANCY | 79.1 |
| INFANT MORTALITY (PER 1,000) | 4.5 |
| OFFICIAL LANGUAGES | French, Dutch, German |
| LITERACY RATE | 99 % |
| RELIGIONS | Roman Catholic 75 %, Protestant or other 25 % |
| ETHNIC GROUPS | Flemish 58 %, Walloon 31 %, mixed and other 11 % |
| CURRENCY | Euro |
| ECONOMY | Services 74.4 %, industry 24.5 %, agriculture 1.1 % |
| GNI PER CAPITA | US$ 40,710 |
| CLIMATE | Temperate, with mild, wet winters and cool summers |
| HIGHEST POINT | Mt Botrange 694 m (2,277 ft) |
| MAP REFERENCE | Pages 288, 291 |

This small, densely populated country has a 60 km (40 mile) coastline on the North Sea and is bounded by France to the west and south, Luxembourg at its southeastern corner, Germany to the east, and the Netherlands to the north. Its name derives from the Belgae, the Gallic race that occupied the area when invading Roman armies arrived in the first century BC. Over more than 2,000 years the region has been dominated by a succession of foreign powers, which explains Belgium's linguistic diversity. From the eighteenth century, Belgium was ruled by Austria, France,

contribution to the economy is not significant. Sugar beet, potatoes, wheat, and barley are the main crops and livestock consists largely of pigs and cattle.

Belgium is a heavily industrialized country and its population is highly urbanized. Except for coal, it is poor in natural resources and relies heavily on imported raw materials to fuel its industries. Almost all the industrial centers are in the Flemish area in the north of the country. Antwerp, Europe's third-largest port and the most populous city in Belgium handles the largest part of the country's imports and exports, and it is the center of numerous heavy industries including petroleum refining, plastics, petrochemicals, and heavy machinery manufacture. The manufacture of textiles is particularly associated with the cities of Ghent and Bruges. Iron and steel making, food processing, and glass manufacture are some of the other important industries.

Many of the major industrial centers are connected by a network of canals, along which barges transport cargo. One of the most celebrated of these is the Albert Canal, which links Liège with Antwerp.

While heavy industry has contributed significantly to Belgium's export earnings, it has had a decidedly negative impact on the environment. The Meuse River, which is a major source of drinking water, has been severely polluted by industrial wastes and fertilizers. The acid rain that falls on Belgium and its neighboring countries has been attributed largely to the air pollution that is caused by Belgian industry.

Approximately seventy-five percent of the population are Roman Catholic. There also are Protestant congregations as well as quite a number of Jews. Economic growth dropped sharply between 2001 and 2003 because of the global economic slowdown, and it recovered only moderately in 2004–2006.

*The historic city of Bruges in Belgium (above left). Cows grazing in the Belgian countryside (below left). La Roque Gageac, a picturesque town on the slopes of the Dordogne Valley in France (below).*

then the Netherlands. In 1830 the Belgians declared their independence and installed Leopold I, a relative of the future English Queen Victoria, as their king. Today the country is a parliamentary democracy with a monarch as head of state.

Belgium's population is divided into two main groups. The larger group, the Flemings, lives mostly in the north of the country and speaks Flemish, which is closely related to Dutch. The south is inhabited by the French-speaking Walloons. There is also a German-speaking community to the east of the city of Liège. Brussels, the capital, is officially bilingual. It is the headquarters of the European Union and the North Atlantic Treaty Organization, NATO. Due to the large variety of organizations headquartered here, Brussels is occasionally called the secret capital of Europe. It is one of the most important service centers of Western Europe and is also the home of many banking and insurance firms.

Inland of the beaches and sand dunes along the North Sea lies a narrow strip of drained, reclaimed marshland, interspersed with dikes and traversed by canals. This region gives way to a central, fertile low-lying plain that rises to a low plateau north of the Meuse-Sambre river system. South of these rivers lie Belgium's uplands. In this rugged, sparsely populated area there are a number of mountain ranges, the most extensive of which is the Ardennes. This heavily wooded high plateau of sandstone and shale is punctuated by flat-topped peaks and cut by deep chasms and valleys. Forestry is the main industry in this southern region, where oak and beech trees predominate. Coal mining, once important around the city of Charleroi in the south of Belgium, is now declining.

Belgium's agriculture is centered on its rich northern plain, where crops are secondary to livestock rearing. Although about half the land area has been cleared for agriculture, its

# Luxembourg

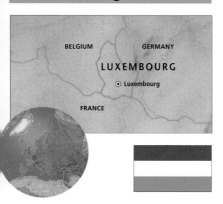

## Fact File

**OFFICIAL NAME** Grand Duchy of Luxembourg

**FORM OF GOVERNMENT** Constitutional monarchy with single legislative body (Chamber of Deputies)

**CAPITAL** Luxembourg

**AREA** 2,586 sq km (998 sq miles)

**TIME ZONE** GMT + 1 hour

**POPULATION** 486,000

**PROJECTED POPULATION 2015** 510,000

**POPULATION DENSITY** 187.9 per sq km (487 per sq mile)

**LIFE EXPECTANCY** 79.2

**INFANT MORTALITY (PER 1,000)** 4.6

**OFFICIAL LANGUAGE** Luxembourgish

**OTHER LANGUAGES** French, German

**LITERACY RATE** 100 %

**RELIGIONS** Roman Catholic 87 %, Protestant, Jewish and Muslim 13 %

**ETHNIC GROUPS** Luxembourger 70 %, other 30 % (mainly French, Portuguese, Belgian, German, Italian, Duch, Spanish and others)

**CURRENCY** Euro

**ECONOMY** Services 86 %, industry 13 %, agriculture 1 %

**GNI PER CAPITA** US$ 75,880

**CLIMATE** Temperate, with cool winters and mild summers

**HIGHEST POINT** Burgplatz 559 m (1,834 ft)

**MAP REFERENCE** Page 291

The Grand Duchy of Luxembourg is one of the smallest countries in Europe. Situated in northern Europe, it shares borders with Belgium to the west and France to the south. Three connecting rivers—the Our, Sûre, and the Moselle—separate it from Germany to the east. Part of the Holy Roman Empire from the tenth century AD, Luxembourg became an independent duchy in 1354, one of hundreds of such states in medieval Europe. It is the only one to survive today as an independent nation. Throughout the intervening centuries, Luxembourg has come under Austrian, Spanish, French, and Dutch rule. In 1830 part of the duchy was taken over by Belgium when that country split from the Netherlands. Luxembourg separated from the Netherlands in 1890. Germany occupied Luxembourg during both world wars and annexed it in 1942. After the Second World War it became a founding member of NATO and in 1957 joined the European Economic Community. It has been a keen advocate of European cooperation and was the first country, in 1991, to ratify the Maastricht Treaty. Luxembourg is a constitutional monarchy, with the Grand Duke as head of state, and a prime minister as head of an elected 21-member Council of State. The country's official language, Luxembourgish, is a dialect of the German language and strongly influenced by French. In schools, both German and French are taught, the latter being the main language in the higher grades.

The northern part of Luxembourg is called the Oesling. Covering about one-third of the country's total area, it is part of the densely forested Ardennes mountain range. Numerous river valleys dissect this northern region and deer and wild boar abound. It is a rugged, picturesque area but has poor soils. In contrast, the southern two-thirds, known as the Gutland or Bon Pays (meaning good land), consists of plains and undulating hills covered with rich soils and extensive pastureland. The Gutland area is still strongly agricultural. Wheat, barley, potatoes, and grapes are the principal crops and more than 15 million litres of dry white wine is produced, most of which is consumed locally.

Iron ore deposits in the south of the country contributed to the development of a thriving iron and steel industry. These deposits are now less abundant and industries such as food processing, chemical manufacturing and tire making now rival steel in importance. A growing service sector, especially in banking, has become increasingly central to the country's prosperity.

The people of Luxembourg are among the most affluent in the world. Unemployment is low and salaries, especially among urban workers, are high.

# France

## Fact File

**OFFICIAL NAME** French Republic

**FORM OF GOVERNMENT** Republic with two legislative bodies (Senate and National Assembly)

**CAPITAL** Paris

**AREA** 547,030 sq km (211,208 sq miles)

**TIME ZONE** GMT + 1 hour

**POPULATION** 60,876,000

**PROJECTED POPULATION 2015** 63,746,000

**POPULATION DENSITY** 111.3 per sq km (288.2 per sq mile)

**LIFE EXPECTANCY** 80.9

**INFANT MORTALITY (PER 1,000)** 3.4

**OFFICIAL LANGUAGE** French

**OTHER LANGUAGES** Alsatian, Basque, Breton, German, Catalan, Corsican, Flemish, Occitan, overseas: Patois

**LITERACY RATE** 99 %

**RELIGIONS** Roman Catholic 83–88 %, Muslim 5–10 %, Protestant 2 %, Jewish 1 %, unaffiliated 4 %

**ETHNIC GROUPS** French 95 %; others, including Algerian, Portuguese, Moroccan, Italian, and Spanish 5 %

**CURRENCY** Euro

**ECONOMY** Services 76.7 %, industry 21 %, agriculture 2.3 %

**GNI PER CAPITA** US$ 38,500

**CLIMATE** Temperate, with cool winters and mild summers; warmer on the Mediterranean coast

**HIGHEST POINT** Mont Blanc 4,807 m (15,771 ft)

**MAP REFERENCE** Pages 290–91

Situated at the west of continental Europe, France roughly resembles a hexagon and has three long stretches of coastline. To the north the English Channel separates it from the southern coast of England (the Channel Tunnel now links the two), to the west it faces the Bay of Biscay, and its southern shores are

Europe and the Russian Federation

on the Mediterranean Sea. To the northeast and east, it shares borders with Belgium, Luxembourg, Germany, Switzerland, and Italy, and in the far southwest the Pyrenees Mountains separate it from Spain. South-east of the mainland, in the Mediterranean, is the French island of Corsica.

## History

A political entity roughly equivalent to the area of present-day France was first established in AD 843, when the Treaty of Verdun divided the enormous Frankish Empire, which had reached its high point under Charlemagne, between Charlemagne's three grandsons. These divisions corresponded approximately to what are now France, Germany, and Italy. Charles the Bald thus became king of Francia Occidentalis. His Carolingian Dynasty lasted only until 987, when territorial fighting between feudal lords led to the election of Hugh Capet, who controlled the region around Paris, as king. The Capetian Dynasty lasted for almost 350 years, during which time it consolidated its power and extended its territory. When the crown passed to Philip VI, the first of the Valois rulers, in 1328, France was a great European power, although much of its present territory was in the hands of the English, who also laid claim to sovereignty over all of France. In 1338 there began a series of wars which later became known as the Hundred Years War. Despite a major French defeat at Agincourt in 1415, these conflicts eventually led to the expulsion of the English from nearly all of France by the middle of the fifteenth century.

In the second half of the sixteenth century, France was wracked by religious wars between

Catholics and Protestants (Huguenots). These finally ended in 1598 with the accession of the first Bourbon king, the Protestant-turned-Catholic Henry of Navarre. Under the Bourbons, and especially under the 72-year reign of Louis XIV that ended in 1715, the monarchy reigned supreme and France acquired colonies in places as far afield as India, North America, and the Caribbean. Under royal patronage, French literature, art, and music flourished, and the royal court in Versailles was the most opulent in Europe and became a role model for basically every European prince. Such immense luxury, however was only possible due to ruthless exploitation of the Sun King's subjects. After his death, weak leadership, extremely high taxation and a series of debilitating wars during the eighteenth century led to the popular unrest that culminated in the French Revolution of 1789, which overthrew the monarchy and deposed the nobility but soon collapsed into a period of anarchy and savagery. The rise of Napoleon Bonaparte restored some stability and he conquered large parts of Europe between 1799 and 1814, only to lose it again. He was ultimately defeated in 1815 at the Battle of Waterloo, in Belgium, and sentenced to exile on St Helena Island where he died in 1821.

Napoleon's defeat ushered in a period of political instability that saw first the restoration of the monarchy, which was twice overthrown in revolutions (1830 and 1848), then the installation of Napoleon's nephew, Louis-Napoleon, first as president of a republic and then as the Emperor Napoleon III. The defeat of France in the Franco-Prussian War of 1870–71 led to a new republic and a period of relative stability in which France acquired new colonies in Africa and Indochina.

During the twentieth century France suffered grievously in both world wars. In the trench warfare of the First World War, almost a million and a half French lives were lost and the northwest of the country was devastated. In the Second World War northern France was occupied by German forces and the south was administered from Vichy by a pro-Nazi collaborationist government led by Maréchal Pétain.

Political instability continued after the Second World War, as France unsuccessfully waged a war against insurgents in Indochina and as unrest in French-controlled Algeria threatened to bring down the government. In 1957 France's Second World War hero, Charles de Gaulle, was invited to assume power, under a constitution that greatly

*A cheese shop in Paris (left). The Arc de Triomphe, built by Emperor Napoleon I, is one of the landmarks of the French capital Paris (above center).*

increased the powers of the president. This constitution has since undergone a number of revisions, the latest being in 2000. The French president, who controls defense and finance, is elected by universal suffrage for a five-year term. There are two houses of parliament, the National Assembly and the Senate. The representatives in the National Assembly, who hold legislative authority, are elected every five years, while one-third of the Senate, with an advisory role, are chosen at three-year intervals.

## Physical features and land use

Much of France is low-lying with almost two-thirds of its land at an elevation of less than 250 m (800 ft). These lowland regions, interspersed with a number of hilly areas, stretch from the Belgian and German borders across the north to the rugged Breton Peninsula in the west, and inland to the Pyrenees in the southwest. Further east, along the Mediterranean coast and hemmed in by mountains, is the low-lying region of western Provence in the Rhône Delta. Except for the far northeast, which forms part of the Flanders Plain, most of these lowland areas comprise the basins of France's four main rivers and their tributaries. In the north, the Seine flows northwest through Paris and the surrounding Île-de-France to the English Channel. France's longest river, the Loire, flows north through the central region, then westward to the Atlantic Ocean. Further south the Garonne, which rises in the Pyrenees, drains much of southwest France on its way to the Atlantic near Bordeaux; and in the east the Rhône, rising in Switzerland, flows west to Lyon where, fed by the Saône from the north, it courses due south to the Mediterranean.

| **Timeline** | | 15,000–10,000 BP Cave paintings at sites such as Lascaux and Pech Merle depicting bulls, mammoths, horses, and humans | 400 BC Franks and Visigoths move east into Gaul, defeating the Romans | AD 987 Hugh Capet becomes the first of the Capetian kings to rule all France | 1337–1453 France and England fight the Hundred Years war; despite English victories at Crécy and Agincourt the French triumph | 1562–98 Wars of religion between Catholics and Huguenots (Protestants) | 1789 The storming of the Bastille by the Paris mob marks the start of the French Revolution | 1799 Napoleon Bonaparte seizes power; first as consul and later as Emperor of France |
|---|---|---|---|---|---|---|---|---|
| 35,000 BP Neanderthal people lived in caves, sometimes burying dead using decorated tombstones | 30,000–20,000 BP Cro-Magnon population in the southwest spreads out to northern and eastern regions | 600 BC Greek merchants establish Massilia (later Marseilles) as a port on the Mediterranean coast | 59–50 BC Roman legions led by Julius Caesar occupy the entire area of Gaul (France) | 1309–77 The papacy moves from Rome to Avignon in southern France | 1643 Religious persecution causes 200,000 Huguenots to flee, resulting in economic decline | 1792 First French Republic established; Louis XVI executed (1793) | 1814–15 Napoleon exiled to St Helena after losing Battle of Waterloo; monarchy restored under Louis XVIII |

In the center and south of the country a vast central plateau, the Massif Central, covers almost a sixth of the total land area. Much of its landscape is rugged, characterized by granite outcrops, extinct volcanic peaks, and deep gorges. At its highest point, it reaches almost 1,900 m (6,000 ft). East of the Massif Central, separated from it by the Rhône Valley, are the Alps, which form the border with Italy and extend to the coast in the southeast corner of the country. North of the Alps, the Jura, characterized by high limestone cliffs, separate France from Switzerland and further north, the heavily forested Vosges Mountains fringe the Rhine Valley near the German border. In the far southwest the Pyrenees, which rival the Alps in rugged splendor but are less accessible, stand between France and Spain.

## Industry, commerce, and agriculture

Second only to the USA as an exporter of agricultural produce, France produces a wide range of food, although most farms are relatively small and thus specialized on a smaller range of products. Over half the land area is cultivated, mainly in the low-lying regions, the most abundant crops being wheat, maize, barley, and sugar beet. Vast areas, especially in the Burgundy and Champagne regions in the central north, around Bordeaux in the southwest and the Rhône Valley in the south, are devoted to viticulture. France is Europe's second largest wine producer. Along the Mediterranean coast mainly fruit, olives and flowers are cultivated. Extensive fields devoted to perfume and healing plants such as the lavender grown in many parts of Provence constitute one of the specialties

of the region. The Atlantic coast with its mild climate is used to cultivate special crops.

After Germany, France is the largest industrial power in Europe, and until recently many of its industries were state-owned. Paris, Lille, Nantes, and Strasbourg in the north, Lyon and Grenoble in the center, and Marseilles and Toulouse in the south are among the major manufacturing centers. The main industries include steelmaking, car, aircraft, and weapons manufacture, oil refining, machine making, textiles, and chemicals. The large woods are used for lumbering, the production of paper and furniture, as well as cork and diverse resins. The production of food and stimulants such as spirits is another important area. Mineral resources are not abundant, though there are reserves of iron ore, zinc, and uranium. Most of France's electricity, almost eighty percent, is generated by state-owned nuclear plants.

On average, the French enjoy a high standard of living, but there are considerable disparities between rich and poor, with considerable wealth concentrated in the area around Paris and parts of southern France. In recent years, especially, the relatively dismal economic outlook for young

people of immigrant backgrounds has led to riots and severe public unrest, especially in the greater Paris region.

### REGIONS

Alsace • Aquitaine • Auvergne • Basse-Normandie • Bourgogne • Bretagne • Centre • Champagne-Ardenne • Corse • Franche-Comté • Haute-Normandie • Île-de-France • Languedoc-Roussillon • Limousin • Lorraine • Midi-Pyrénées • Nord-Pas-de-Calais • Pays de la Loire • Picardie • Poitou-Charentes • Provence-Alpes-Côte d'Azur • Rhônes-Alpes

### OVERSEAS TERRITORIES

French Guiana • French Polynesia • French Southern and Arctic Lands • Guadeloupe • Martinique • Mayotte • New Caledonia • Réunion • St Pierre and Miquelon • Wallis and Futuna Islands

## The European Union

On 1 January 1999 eleven European countries adopted a new and common currency—the Euro. This momentous step marked the climax of a movement for closer European integration which had begun in 1957. In March of that year Belgium, France, the Federal Republic of Germany, Italy, Luxembourg, and the Netherlands signed a treaty which proposed the gradual integration of their economies in the European Economic Community (EEC, later called the European Community or EC). They planned to gradually eliminate restrictive quotas and import duties between member nations to allow the free movement of persons and capital within their common boundaries. It was hoped the larger market that resulted would promote greater productivity, higher standards of living and, most of all, eliminate European wars.

The success of the Community led to a number of additional countries seeking membership. Others, however, objected to the surrender of sovereignty that was entailed: at first Britain, along with the Scandinavian nations, Switzerland, Austria, and Portugal, formed their own—though not very successful—free-trade area (known as the outer seven or EFTA) instead. Nor were the policies of the EEC uniformly successful: the Common Agricultural Policy, for example, led to the overproduction of butter, wine, and sugar in member countries. However, although

national referenda on membership and treaty ratification have not been without a degree of controversy, most of the countries in Europe have now decided that the benefits of being a member of the EC outweigh the costs, and by 1997 all of the following states belonged: Austria, Belgium, Denmark, Finland, France, Germany, Greece, Ireland, Italy, Luxembourg, the Netherlands, Portugal, Spain, Sweden, and the UK. In 2004 ten more countries have joined the Union: Estonia, Latvia, Lithuania, Poland, the Czech Republic, Slovakia, Slovenia, Hungary, Malta and Cyprus (the Greek part of the island), and Bulgaria and Romania have followed suit in 2007.

With the ratification of the Maastricht Treaty in 1992 which prepared the way for monetary union and the Euro, the EEC and its associated bodies became formally known as the European Union (EU). An important feature of monetary union has been the establishment of an independent European Central Bank (ECB). This bank has as its main goal "price stability", a term meaning inflation of less than two percent per year. Since 2001, thirteen EU-countries have introduced the new currency. The UK, Denmark, and Sweden decided not to do so. New members must have adopted the Exchange Rate Mechanism and satisfy other criteria for two years before they may introduce the Euro.

| | | | | | | | |
|---|---|---|---|---|---|---|---|
| **1848** Riots in Paris, with street fighting between the army and mobs of hungry, unemployed workers | **1889** The Eiffel Tower, an iron structure designed by Gustave Alexandre Eiffel for the Exhibition of the same year, built in Paris | **1914** First World War starts: Allies create the Western Front in north France to stop German advance; deadlock lasts three and a half years—1,357,800 French casualties | **1944** Allied troops reach Paris; General de Gaulle returns from exile in England to form a provisional government | **1960** Rapid rise in immigration from ex-colonial territories in North Africa and the Caribbean brings concern over jobs; also first nuclear tests | **1978** The disaster of the tanker ship *Amoco Cadiz* on the French Atlantic coast causes an environmental catastrophe | **1994** Railway tunnel under English Channel connects France and the United Kingdom; idea first proposed in 1802 by Mathieu to Napoleon |

| | | | | | | |
|---|---|---|---|---|---|---|
| **1870–71** France loses Franco-Prussian War; Alsace and Lorraine ceded to Germany | **1918** First World War ends with Treaty of Versailles under which Alsace and Lorraine are returned to France by Germany | **1939** Start of Second World War and subsequent German invasion of France leads to occupation of Paris (1940) | **1957** France joins other European nations in forming the European Common Market by signing the Treaty of Rome | **1968** Student protests lead to a general strike over educational policies and political dissatisfaction; General de Gaulle resigns | **2003** First purely EU peace corps led by French soldiers is sent by the EU to the civil war regions of the Democratic Republic of Congo |

# Monaco

## Fact File

**OFFICIAL NAME** Principality of Monaco

**FORM OF GOVERNMENT** Constitutional monarchy with single legislative body (National Council)

**CAPITAL** Monaco

**AREA** 1.95 sq km (0.7 sq miles)

**TIME ZONE** GMT + 1 hour

**POPULATION** 32,800

**PROJECTED POPULATION 2015** 33,000

**POPULATION DENSITY** 16,820.5 per sq km (46,857.1 per sq mile)

**LIFE EXPECTANCY** 80

**INFANT MORTALITY (PER 1,000)** 5.2

**OFFICIAL LANGUAGE** French

**OTHER LANGUAGES** Italian, English, Monégasque

**LITERACY RATE** 99 %

**RELIGIONS** Roman Catholic 90 %, other 10 %

**ETHNIC GROUPS** French 47 %, Monégasque 16 %, Italian 16 %, other 21 %

**CURRENCY** Euro

**ECONOMY** Services 95.1 %, industry 4,9 % agriculture 0 %

**GNI PER CAPITA** not available (more than US$ 11,455)

**CLIMATE** Temperate, with mild, wet winters and hot, dry summers

**HIGHEST POINT** Mt Agel 140 m (459 ft)

**MAP REFERENCE** Page 291

Monaco, the world's smallest independent nation after the Vatican City, sits on the Mediterranean coast in the far southeast corner of France. Except for its coastline, it is completely surrounded by French territory. In the thirteenth century the Genoese built a fortress there and in 1297 members of the Grimaldi family of Genoa established themselves as rulers. Grimaldi princes retained control for almost 500 years, until 1792, when an uprising deposed the reigning prince and declared the state a republic. France annexed Monaco the following year but in 1815, after the Congress of Vienna, it was placed under the protection of Sardinia. France annexed most of Monaco, including Menton, in 1848. In 1861, the Grimaldis were restored as rulers of less than half their former territory, governing under French protection. In 1911 democratic government was introduced by Prince Albert of Monaco. An 18-member National Council is elected every five years, but the head of government is selected by the monarch from a list drawn up by the French government. The present monarch, Prince Albert II, is a descendant of the Grimaldis. His father, Rainier III, achieved fame in 1956 for his marriage to the American film actress Grace Kelly.

Occupying the lower slopes of the Maritime Alps, Monaco is hilly and rugged. It is densely populated, mainly by foreign nationals. In the southwest is the industrial district of Fontvieille, which consists partly of land reclaimed from the sea. Further east is the old town of Monaco-Ville, where the royal palace is situated. La Condamine, the banking, commercial, and fashionable residential center, overlooks a sheltered harbor. Northeast of La Condamine is Monte Carlo, with its casino, luxury hotels, and apartment blocks.

Apart from pharmaceutical, food processing, and other light industries in Fontvieille, Monaco thrives on its attractions as a tourist haven. The major drawing card is the state-run casino, from which the citizens of Monaco are banned. Until 1962, Monaco's status as a tax haven attracted many wealthy French businesses. The people of Monaco still pay no income tax, but foreigners now do, though at quite favorable rates.

*View of Monte Carlo, Monaco (below). An alpine vegetable farm in Switzerland (above center). View of Zürich, Switzerland (right page below). The Wetterhorn Mountain near Grindelwald in the Bernese Oberland, Switzerland (right page bottom).*

# Switzerland

## Fact File

**OFFICIAL NAME** Swiss Confederation

**FORM OF GOVERNMENT** Federal republic with two legislative bodies (Council of States and National Council)

**CAPITAL** Berne

**AREA** 41,290 sq km (15,942 sq miles)

**TIME ZONE** GMT + 1 hour

**POPULATION** 7,582,000

**PROJECTED POPULATION 2015** 7,699,000

**POPULATION DENSITY** 183.6 per sq km (475.6 per sq mile)

**LIFE EXPECTANCY** 80.7

**INFANT MORTALITY (PER 1,000)** 4.2

**OFFICIAL LANGUAGES** German, French, Italian, Romansch

**OTHER LANGUAGES** Spanish

**LITERACY RATE** 99 %

**RELIGIONS** Roman Catholic 41.8 %, Protestant 35.3 %, Muslim 4.3 %, Orthodox 1.8 %, other 16.8 %

**ETHNIC GROUPS** German-speaking Swiss 65 %, French-speaking Swiss 18 %, Italian-speaking Swiss 10 %, Romansch 1 %, other 6 %

**Currency** Swiss franc

**Economy** Services 64.5 %, industry 34.0 %, agriculture 1.5 %

**GNI per capita** US$ 59,880

**Climate** Temperate, varying with altitude; generally cold winters and warm, wet summers

**Highest point** Dufourspitze 4,634 m (15,203 ft)

**Map reference** Pages 288, 291, 294

A landlocked country in central Europe, Switzerland shares borders with Italy to its south and southeast, France to its west, Germany to its north, and Austria and Liechtenstein to its east. This small nation has enjoyed a generally peaceful independence for more than 450 years, despite the conflicts that have often raged around it. Modern Switzerland dates back to the late thirteenth century when three German districts, or cantons, combined to form a federation. A century later other cantons had joined the federation, which survived as a unit despite linguistic differences and often intense and violent conflicts between Catholics and emerging Protestant groups. Although part of the Holy Roman Empire, and effectively under Habsburg domination, the Swiss cantons remained neutral during the Thirty Years War of 1618–48, at the end of which they were formally granted independence. In 1798 French revolutionary armies invaded Switzerland and declared it to be a centralized Helvetic Republic, named after Helvetia, the Roman province that had existed there in Roman times. In 1815, after the defeat of Napoleon, the Congress of Vienna declared Switzerland to be independent once more, as well as permanently neutral, and added two more cantons—Valais and the previously separate republic of Geneva.

The country has maintained this military neutrality ever since and its stance has been respected by its neighbors throughout numerous conflicts, including the First and Second World Wars. Religious tensions flared briefly in 1847, when the Catholic cantons seceded. The following year, however, a new constitution, inspired by that of the United States, re-established the former federation and defined Switzerland as a republic with a strong central government but with considerable powers still vested in individual cantons. In 1874 a new constitution was adopted which essentially confirmed this division of power. Switzerland's central government, which controls foreign policy, railway and postal services, and the mint, consists of an elected bicameral parliament, with a president and vice president elected by the Federal Assembly from among the members of the Federal Council for a one-year term. Women were granted the vote only in 1971, and in the Appenzell canton only in 1990.

### Physical features and land use

Mountains dominate the Swiss landscape making it Europe's most mountainous country. They cover seven-tenths of the land area. The rest of the country consists of an elevated central plateau on which the majority of the population lives and which is the center of the country's agricultural, industrial, and economic activity. This area is bordered by a number of large lakes and drained by the River Aare, which rises in Lake Neuchâtel and flows northward into the Rhine, which constitutes Switzerland's border with Germany and part of Austria. Lake Neuchâtel is overlooked by the lightly wooded Jura Mountains, which separate Switzerland from France. More than half of Switzerland is covered by the peaks and glaciers of the Alps, which sweep across the south of the country. The most spectacular sections are in the Pennine Alps along the southwestern frontier with Italy. Both the Rhône and the Rhine Rivers originate in this alpine region and drain it in opposite directions, flowing respectively through the two largest lakes in the country, which are Lake Geneva in the far southwest, and Lake Constance in the far northeast.

About one-quarter of Switzerland consists of forests, which are found mainly in the valleys and on the lower slopes. Cypresses and figs are prominent among the tree species. About one-tenth of the land is arable. Crop cultivation is concentrated in the area immediately to the east and southeast of the Jura and in the valleys of the Rhône and Rhine Rivers. Wheat, potatoes, and sugar beet are the main crops. The principal agricultural activity, however, is dairy farming, although pig raising is also significant. Switzerland produces less than half its food needs.

Switzerland is not well endowed with mineral resources. Most of the country's electricity is generated by hydropower, but a significant amount is provided by the country's five nuclear power plants. A sixth nuclear plant was planned but was cancelled in the aftermath of the Chernobyl disaster in Ukraine in 1986.

### Industry, commerce, and culture

Switzerland has for centuries been a world leader in the production of precision instruments such as clocks and watches. Other industries which are vital to the country's prosperity include heavy engineering, textile manufacture, clothing, chemicals and food processing. Swiss chocolate, sought after the world over because of its high quality, is also a major contributor to the national economy. Tourism, centered mainly on the Alps, attracts more than 13.8 million visitors annually.

Banking is highly developed and is one of the country's key industries. Switzerland attracts almost half the world's foreign investment capital and is the base of numerous multinational companies.

Although the country is divided geographically among its predominantly German-, Italian- and French-speaking populations, Switzerland is now a unified nation and its people have a strong sense of common purpose. This is attributable in large measure to Switzerland's status as one of the world's most stable and prosperous countries, with a very high per capita income.

Europe and the Russian Federation

# Liechtenstein

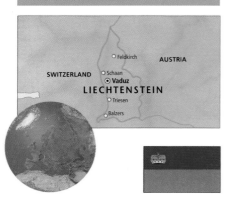

## Fact File

**OFFICIAL NAME** Principality of Liechtenstein

**FORM OF GOVERNMENT** Constitutional monarchy with single legislative body (Parliament)

**CAPITAL** Vaduz

**AREA** 160 sq km (62 sq miles)

**TIME ZONE** GMT + 1 hour

**POPULATION** 34,500

**PROJECTED POPULATION 2015** 38,000

**POPULATION DENSITY** 215.6 per sq km (556.5 per sq mile)

**LIFE EXPECTANCY** 80

**INFANT MORTALITY (PER 1,000)** 4.5

**OFFICIAL LANGUAGE** German

**LITERACY RATE** 100 %

**RELIGIONS** Roman Catholic 76.2 %, Protestant 7.0 %, other 6.2 %, unknown 10.6 %

**ETHNIC GROUPS** Alemannic 86 %, Italian, Turkish and other 14 %

**CURRENCY** Swiss franc

**ECONOMY** Services 55 %, industry 39 %, agriculture 6 %

**GNI PER CAPITA** not available (considered to be the world's highest)

**CLIMATE** Temperate, with cold, wet winters and mild, humid summers

**HIGHEST POINT** Grauspitz 2,599 m (8,527 ft)

**MAP REFERENCE** Page 288

This small Central European country sits high in the Alps. To the west the Rhine River forms a border with Switzerland, with which Liechtenstein has political ties and whose currency it shares. Austria lies to the east and south. The country takes its name from the Austrian Liechtenstein family which, in 1699 and 1713, acquired two fiefdoms and formed them into the principality. It later came under French and then German influence. In 1866 it achieved independence, and two years later declared itself permanently neutral, a position it has since maintained. In all subsequent European wars, Liechtenstein has remained unmolested. Its head of state is an hereditary monarch who appoints a government on the recommendation of an elected parliament. Elections are held every four years and there is universal adult suffrage, although women have had the vote only since 1984.

The Rhine is the source of Liechtenstein's agricultural strength. Its floodplain, once marshy, has been drained and reclaimed for agricultural and pastoral use. The capital sits on a plateau overlooking the undulating expanses of the Rhine Valley. The slopes of the Rhatikon alpine range rise to impressive peaks in the south. From the southern highlands, the Samina River flows northward through the center of the country. Thick forests—of beech, maple, and ash—cover much of the mountain region.

The main agricultural industries are cattle, sheep, and pig raising, and some vegetables and cereal crops are grown. There is little heavy industry but prominent among light industries are textile and ceramic goods and the manufacture of electronic equipment. There are no mineral resources, and Liechtenstein imports all its fuel and raw materials. A major source of revenue is the sale of postage stamps. More than half the country's residents are foreign nationals, largely attracted by the country's low rates of taxation and its banking laws, which ensure great secrecy. The population's living standard is very high and the unemployment rate around 1.3 percent. The organization of health care is closely linked to the adjacent Swiss cantons.

# Austria

## Fact File

**OFFICIAL NAME** Republic of Austria

**FORM OF GOVERNMENT** Federal republic with two legislative bodies (Federal Council and National Council)

**CAPITAL** Vienna (Wien)

**AREA** 83,870 sq km (32,382 sq miles)

**TIME ZONE** GMT + 1 hour

**POPULATION** 8,206,000

**PROJECTED POPULATION 2015** 8,514,000

**POPULATION DENSITY** 97.8 per sq km (253.4 per sq mile)

**LIFE EXPECTANCY** 79.4

**INFANT MORTALITY (PER 1,000)** 4.5

**OFFICIAL LANGUAGE** German

**LITERACY RATE** 98 %

**RELIGIONS** Roman Catholic 73.6 %, Protestant 4.7 %, Muslim 4.2 %, other 5.5 %, none 12.0 %

**ETHNIC GROUPS** Austrian 91.1 %, Croatian, Slovene, Bosnian, Serb 4.0 %, Turkish 1.6 %, German 0.9 %, other 2.4 %

**CURRENCY** Euro

**ECONOMY** Services 68 %, industry 30.3 %, agriculture 1.7 %

**GNI PER CAPITA** US$ 42,700

**CLIMATE** Temperate with cold winters and mild to warm summers; colder in mountains

**HIGHEST POINT** Grossglockner 3,797 m (12,457 ft)

**MAP REFERENCE** Page 294

The present borders of this landlocked Central European country date back to the Treaty of Versailles of 1919, which presided over the dismantling of the Austro-Hungarian Empire. Germany lies directly to the north of Austria's narrow western boundary, Switzerland and Liechtenstein to its west, and Italy to its south. At its wider eastern end Slovenia lies to the south, Hungary and Slovakia to the east, and the Czech Republic to the north.

Austria's history for most of the last seven hundred years is bound up with the fortunes of the archdukes and later emperors of the Habsburg family who ruled it, and at times

much of the rest of Europe, from 1278 until the First World War. Roman conquest of most of present-day Austria was followed in the fourth and fifth centuries AD by invasions by Germanic and Celtic tribes and by the Franks under Charlemagne during the eighth century. The land fell to the King of Bohemia in 1252, only to be wrested from him by Rudolf of Habsburg just 26 years later. Rudolf called himself archduke and declared the title hereditary.

From then until the sixteenth century the Habsburg Empire expanded until it dominated much of Europe, including Spain (as well as its American colonies), part of Italy, the Netherlands, and Burgundy. Charles V, 1520–58, proudly stated that he ruled an empire in which the sun never set. During the sixteenth century Hungary and Bohemia came under Habsburg rule, and a Turkish siege of Vienna was repulsed.

Catholic Austria's forced capitulation to German Protestantism at the end of the Thirty Years War saw Austria take second place to France as the leading European power. However, it remained a significant force with dominion over much of Europe, despite its loss of control over Spain in the early eighteenth century, a debilitating War of Succession between 1740 and 1748, and defeat by Prussian forces in 1763.

Napoleon's victory at the Battle of Austerlitz was a low point for Austria, but upon Napoleon's defeat in 1814 Austria emerged as leader of a new German Confederation. Following the Austro-Prussian War of 1866, Austria and Hungary were combined under Habsburg rule to form the Austro-Hungarian Empire. However, it also meant that Austria lost its dominance in Germany to Prussia and ended up not being part of the German Empire that was created in 1871. The Austrian annexation of Bosnia and Herzegovina in 1908 created the circumstances which culminated in the assassination of the

*Landscape Liechtenstein, in the background Vaduz Palace (left page bottom). Belvedere Palace in Vienna, one of the political and cultural metropolises in Europe (above). Winter in Zell am See, Austria (right).*

heir to the Austro-Hungarian throne in Sarajevo in 1914 and the outbreak of the First World War. When the empire ended after the war, the Habsburgs were expelled and Austria became a republic bounded by its present borders.

Annexed by Nazi Germany in 1938 under the Austrian-born Adolf Hitler, Austria was part of the Third Reich until occupied by Allied forces in 1945. The Allies did not withdraw until 1955, when Austria was recognized internationally as an independent, democratic, and permanently neutral state. Today Austria is governed by a bicameral parliament elected for four-year terms. The president, whose role is essentially ceremonial, is directly elected for a six-year term.

### Physical features and land use

Almost two-thirds of Austria consists of the Alps, which sweep west to east across the country in a succession of ranges almost as far as Vienna. Much of the alpine area is characterized by snowfields, glaciers, and snowy peaks. About one-third of the country's population lives in the valleys between the ranges. Many passes such as the Brenner or Timmelsjoch have allowed people to traverse the mountain ranges of the

Alps since antiquity. To the north of the Alps, the lower, heavily forested mountains of the Bohemian Massif, which cover about one-tenth of the land area, extend across the borders of the Czech Republic and Slovakia. Lowland areas lie along the eastern end of the Alps extending into Hungary, and in the Danube Valley in the north. Most of Austria's main transport routes traverse this northern "corridor," which links Germany with Vienna and countries farther east.

Almost all the arable land is in the northeast, and is divided between pasture and croplands. Root crops, such as potatoes and cereals, are the principal crops. There are also extensive vineyards which supply a significant wine industry. The main livestock are cattle and pigs.

### Industry, commerce, and culture

Austria is not rich in mineral resources, although it has some reserves of oil, iron ore, brown coal, and magnesite—a major resource in chemical industries. It imports most of the raw materials it needs for the manufacturing industries that form the backbone of its economy. More than seventy percent of electricity is generated hydroelectrically. Iron and steel-making are the principal heavy industries and are large export earners. Aluminum, chemicals, and food processing are also significant. Tourism, based largely on the many alpine ski resorts, but also on the cultural attractions of such cities as Vienna and Salzburg, contributes greatly to the country's economic well-being. There are more than 30 million visitors each year.

Austrians are generally conservative in their social attitudes and financial habits. They are savers rather than spenders or investors and the country has a high proportion of its wealth in savings deposits. Much of the country's industry, including iron and steel, and energy production is nationalized and there is a well-developed system of state social services. Most Austrians enjoy a comfortable lifestyle, exceptions being the many refugees from the former Yugoslav republics who have entered the country during the 1990s.

## Southwestern Europe

Portugal · · · · · · · · · 250
Andorra · · · · · · · · · 251
Spain · · · · · · · · · · 252
Italy · · · · · · · · · · 254
San Marino · · · · · · · 256
Vatican City · · · · · · 256
Malta · · · · · · · · · · 257

## Portugal

### Fact File

**OFFICIAL NAME** Portuguese Republic

**FORM OF GOVERNMENT** Republic with single legislative body (Assembly of the Republic)

**CAPITAL** Lisbon

**AREA** 92,391 sq km (35,672 sq miles)

**TIME ZONE** GMT

**POPULATION** 10,677,000

**PROJECTED POPULATION 2015** 10,805,000

**POPULATION DENSITY** 115.6 per sq km (299.3 per sq mile)

**LIFE EXPECTANCY** 78

**INFANT MORTALITY (PER 1,000)** 4.9

**OFFICIAL LANGUAGE** Portuguese

**LITERACY RATE** 93.3 %

**RELIGIONS** Roman Catholic 84.5 %, Protestant 2.2 %, other 0.3 %, unknown 9.1 %, none 3.9 %

**ETHNIC GROUPS** Mainly Portuguese with a small minority of immigrants from former colonies

**CURRENCY** Euro

**ECONOMY** Services 66.5 %, industry 25.4 %, agriculture 8.1 %

**GNI PER CAPITA** US$ 18,950

**CLIMATE** Temperate; cool and rainy in north, warm and dry in south

**HIGHEST POINT** Ponta de Pico in the Azores 2,351 m (7,713 ft); Serra de Estrela on the mainland, 1,993 m (6,539 ft)

**MAP REFERENCE** Page 292

Situated at the western edge of the Iberian Peninsula, Portugal is shaped somewhat like a long, narrow rectangle. It has a long Atlantic coastline bordering its western edge, and a much shorter one at its southern extremity. Spain surrounds it on the other two sides.

From the second century BC until the fifth century AD, Portugal was part of the Roman Empire. As the empire collapsed the territory suffered a series of invasions—by Germanic tribes, Visigoths, and in the eighth century by Muslim Moors from northern Africa. The Moors were finally expelled by Christian invaders from Burgundy during the twelfth century and a Burgundian line of monarchs was established. An abortive Castilian attempt to seize the crown in the fourteenth century saw a new dynasty installed under John of Aviz, who reigned as John I. His son, Prince Henry the Navigator, encouraged widespread exploration and the establishment of a vast empire, with colonies in Africa, South America, India, and Southeast Asia. The invasion of Portugal by the Spanish in 1581, even though they were expelled 60 years later, heralded the decline in Portugal's influence. A French invasion in 1807 was reversed three years later when the British expelled the invaders in 1811.

During the nineteenth century widespread poverty and growing resentment at the power of the monarchy culminated in the 1910 revolution, in which the monarchy was overthrown. An army coup in 1926 installed Olivier Salazar as a right-wing dictator. He remained in power until 1968, but his successor, Marcello Caetano, was overthrown by a left-wing army coup in 1974, which eventually led to democratic elections in 1976. Portugal is now a democratic republic with a popularly elected president as head of state, and became a member of the European Union in 1985.

Portugal is divided fairly evenly into its wetter northern and more arid southern regions by the River Tagus. This river flows west into the country from Spain and then takes a southwesterly course toward the Atlantic, entering it at Lisbon (Lisboa). Highland forested areas dominate the north. The highest mountains are in the far north, especially in the east. Here the landscape is characterized by high plateaus punctuated by deep gorges and river valleys, which gradually descend to the western coastal plain. In these mountains are thick forests of both conifers and deciduous trees. South of the Douro River the landscape becomes less rugged and the slopes more gentle until they reach the plain around the Tagus. South of the Tagus, the country is mainly flat or undulating. In the Tagus Valley and further south are forests of cork oaks, the bark of which is used to produce cork for wine or for flooring. In the Algarve, in the far south, a range of hills runs across the country from the Spanish border to its southwestern tip.

Portugal has two self-governing regions in the Atlantic: the nine volcanic islands that constitute the Azores and the volcanic archipelago of two inhabited and two groups of

*Farm buildings at the foot of Mt Giestoso in Minho Province, Portugal (left). The village of Ponte da Lima surrounded by terraced fields in Andrao, Portugal (right page bottom). The church S. Martín de la Cortinada in the Ordino Valley, Andorra (right page top).*

## Portuguese products

Portugal is famous for two products, cork and port. Before modern plastics were invented cork had no equal as a strong, lightweight, buoyant, impermeable, and elastic material. It is the bark of the cork oak, found in Portugal, Spain and the Mediterranean region. Cork was formerly used for lifebelts and floats on fishing nets, and is only slowly being replaced as a stopper for wine bottles by plastics. Its impermeability makes it also an increasingly sought-after raw material for the production of shoe soles. Portugal produces more cork than the rest of the world combined.

The bark is first harvested when a tree is about twenty years old, supplies being taken at subsequent ten-year intervals. The cork is removed by making cuts in the bark using a curved knife. The pieces are soaked in water, scraped, washed, and dried.

Port is a dark red, full-bodied fortified wine named after the town of Porto, from which it has been exported for many years. No one variety of grape is used. The wine's distinctiveness comes from the climate and soil of the mountainous Alto Douro region of north Portugal, and from the methods of cultivation and wine-making used in its production. Especially British capital contributed to the port industry, and the UK was for many years the main destination for the finished product.

uninhabited islets that make up Madeira. Portugal returned its last territory, Macau, to China in 1999.

By Western European standards Portugal remains a highly rural society, with agriculture and fishing still employing a significant number of the country's workforce. Many farms, especially the smaller ones that predominate in the north, continue to use traditional methods. Cereals and vegetables are widely cultivated, and wine production, especially port wine from the Douro Valley, is the major agricultural activity. Manufacturing is growing in importance, much of it concerned with processing the country's agricultural products. Paper—based in recent years on fast-growing eucalyptis trees—and cork manufacture, and texiles and footwear, are among the significant industries. Tourism, especially in the warm, southern Algarve region, has greatly expanded, leading to rapid building development and considerable attendant environmental degradation.

# Andorra

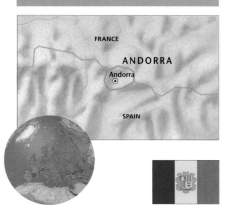

## Fact File

**OFFICIAL NAME** Principality of Andorra

**FORM OF GOVERNMENT** Co-principality with single legislative body (General Council of the Valleys)

**CAPITAL** Andorra la Vella

**AREA** 468 sq km (174 sq miles)

**TIME ZONE** GMT + 1 hour

**POPULATION** 72,400

**PROJECTED POPULATION 2015** 75,000

**POPULATION DENSITY** 154.7 per sq km (416.1 per sq mile)

**LIFE EXPECTANCY** 83.5

**INFANT MORTALITY (PER 1,000)** 4.0

**OFFICIAL LANGUAGE** Catalan

**OTHER LANGUAGES** French, Spanish, Portuguese

**LITERACY RATE** 100 %

**RELIGIONS** Roman Catholic predominant

**ETHNIC GROUPS** Spanish 43 %, Andorran 33 %, Portuguese 11 %, French 7 %, other 6 %

**CURRENCY** Euro

**ECONOMY** Tourism, tobacco production, financial services

**GNI PER CAPITA** US$ 23,950

**CLIMATE** Temperate; snowy winter, warm summers

**HIGHEST POINT** Coma Pedrosa 2,946 m (9,665 ft)

**MAP REFERENCE** Page 293

The tiny landlocked principality of Andorra sits high in the Pyrenees, between France and Spain. From 1278 Andorra's government was shared between France and Spain. For 300 years it was jointly administered by the Bishop of Urgel in Spain and the Count of Foix in France. In the sixteenth century sovereignty passed to the French king and, after the French Revolution of 1789, to the French head of state. Today the Bishop of Urgel and the French president are official chiefs of state. Since 1993, however, when the first democratic elections were held, authority has been vested in a 28-member General Council of the Valleys. France and Spain are responsible for its defence, and both have a representative on the General Council.

Andorra is mountainous with spectacular peaks. The country is snow-covered for six months in winter, but summers are warm and dry. Two south-flowing branches of the River Valira—the Valira del Nord and the Valira d'Orient—flow through a series of valleys and gorges between ranges. They join in the center of the country and flow as one stream into Spain. The Valira is a major source of hydroelectric power.

About one third of the population are citizens of Andorra: the rest are foreign residents, mainly French and Spanish. Almost two-thirds of the population live in the capital and the cities of Les Escaldes and Encamp. Tourism is the mainstay of the economy, and every year there are more than 12 million visitors, mainly skiers. Goods are duty-free in Andorra. This acts as a magnet to tourists and is vital to the economy, as is the sale of hydroelectricity to neighboring Catalonia. Banking services are significant, but there is little secondary industry, apart from cigarette and cigar making. As well as tobacco, some fruit, vegetables, and other crops are grown on the tiny amount of land that can be cultivated. Many of the village-dwellers are small farmers. Their sheep, cattle, and goats graze in the upland meadows during summer.

# Spain

## Fact File

**OFFICIAL NAME**  Kingdom of Spain

**FORM OF GOVERNMENT**  Constitutional monarchy with two legislative bodies (Senate and Congress of Deputies)

**CAPITAL**  Madrid

**AREA**  504,782 sq km (194,897 sq miles)

**TIME ZONE**  GMT + 1 hour

**POPULATION**  40,491,000

**PROJECTED POPULATION 2015**  46,000,000

**POPULATION DENSITY**  80.2 per sq km (207.8 per sq mile)

**LIFE EXPECTANCY**  79.9

**INFANT MORTALITY (PER 1,000)**  4.3

**OFFICIAL LANGUAGE**  Spanish (Castilian)

**OTHER LANGUAGES**  Catalan, Galician, Basque

**LITERACY RATE**  97.9 %

**RELIGIONS**  Roman Catholic 94 %, other 6 %

**ETHNIC GROUPS**  Castilian Spanish 72 %, Catalan 16 %, Galician 8 %, Basque 2 %, other 2 %

**CURRENCY**  Euro

**ECONOMY**  Services 66.6 %, industry 29.8 %, agriculture 3.6 %

**GNI PER CAPITA**  US$ 29,450

**CLIMATE**  Temperate, with mild, wet winters and hot, dry summers; cooler and wetter in northwest

**HIGHEST POINT**  Mulhacén (in continental Spain) 3,478 m (11,411 ft), Pico del Teide (on Tenerife, Canary Islands) 3718 m (12,269 ft)

**MAP REFERENCE**  Pages 292–93

**MAP REFERENCE**  Pages 292–93

Spain occupies the bulk of the Iberian Peninsula at the southwestern tip of Europe. It shares land borders with Portugal to the west, France to the north, and the tiny principality of Andorra, perched high in the Pyrenees on the border with France. To the west and south Spain has short stretches of coastline along the Atlantic Ocean, and to the north a long coast on the Bay of Biscay. Its southern tip is separated from Morocco by the narrow Strait of Gibraltar and its southeastern and eastern coastlines are on the western edge of the Mediterranean Sea.

The Iberian Peninsula had already experienced a long history of human habitation at the end of the third century BC, when the Romans subdued the Celts, Iberians, and Basques who lived there. The region remained a Roman colony until the Visigoths invaded early in the fifth century AD. Over the next three centuries the region became Christianized, but in AD 711 an invasion from Morocco in the south established what would become a flourishing Islamic civilization that lasted for six centuries. In the ninth century Christian invaders from the north gained control of Catalonia in the northeast, thus beginning a slow process of reconquest. By the early thirteenth century, the Moors only retained control of Granada in the south.

The marriage of Ferdinand II of Aragon and Isabella I of Castile in 1469 brought together the two most powerful states on the peninsula, and in 1492, when the Moors were finally expelled from Granada, Spain became a unified country under Catholic rule. Thus began a century of Spanish exploration and conquest in which Spain acquired colonies in Central and South America, as well as the Philippines in Southeast Asia. The Spanish also ruled a large part of Western Europe, including Portugal, the Netherlands, Austria, and parts of Italy.

The beginning of Spain's decline from being a dominant power in the world to a state of secondary importance can be traced to 1588, when Philip II sent his mighty armada of 130 ships in an abortive attempt to invade Protestant England. This defeat by the English spelled the end of Spain's maritime dominance. By 1714 Spain had lost all its European possessions and by 1826 it had been forced to surrender all its American colonies except Cuba and Puerto Rico.

*A small farm in the province of Navarra (below). Fertile countryside in Catalonia (right).*

| Timeline | | | | | | | |
|---|---|---|---|---|---|---|---|
| | **10,000 BC** Images of bison painted on the walls of a deep cave at Altamira, northern Spain, probably used for ceremonies | **3200 BC** Larger communities develop around southern and southwestern Spain and Portugal, such as Los Millares, Almeria | **1000 BC** Phoenician traders from eastern Mediterranean begin to colonize southern and eastern coasts of Spain | **218 BC** After defeat of Carthaginians in the Second Punic War, Spain slowly becomes part of the Roman Empire | **AD 711** Moors invade from North Africa bringing Islam and building palaces and mosques | | **1469** Marriage of Ferdinand of Aragon and Isabella of Castile brings together both kingdoms—almost all of modern Spain |
| **780,000 BP** Stone tools used by hominids in northern Spain; classified as *Homo heidelbergensis* | **280,000 BP** Caves inhabited by *Homo sapiens* at Atapuerca, Burgos, northern Spain, as well as Torralba and Ambrona | **5500 BC** Sheep and wheat grown by early farmers along the western Mediterranean | **3000 BC** Iberian people, including Gauls and Basques, move in from the north to found towns on Iberian Peninsula | **400 BC** Carthaginians of North Africa take over much of Spain | **AD 476** Romans rename peninsula Hispania; lose control to Germanic tribes who occupy whole territory by 573 | **962–1212** Christians push back Moors; Moors confined to Granada | **1492** Columbus sails on first voyage in the service of Ferdinand and Isabella; Spanish take last Moorish stronghold, Granada |

French revolutionary forces invaded Spain in 1794. They were defeated in 1814 and the Spanish Bourbon monarchy was restored. During the nineteenth and much of the twentieth century Spain has been destabilized by political turmoil and a series of military revolts and wars. Quarrels about the succession to the crown led to the removal of Isabella II from the throne in 1868, the declaration of a republic in 1873, and a military uprising in 1874 that restored the monarchy. In 1898 Spain and the United States fought a war at the end of which a defeated Spain was forced to cede its colonies of Cuba, Puerto Rico, and the Philippines to its adversary.

Spain remained neutral in both world wars, but was wracked by a bitter civil war from 1936 to 1939. Universal adult suffrage was introduced in 1931 and in 1936 the election of a Republican government with socialist leanings prompted an army officer, Francisco Franco, to lead a revolt against the government. With the support of right-wing Spanish forces and of Fascist Italy and Nazi Germany, and after the loss of 750,000 Spanish lives, Franco's forces were eventually victorious and Franco was installed as head of state. His dictatorial regime lasted until his death in 1975. Almost immediately the monarchy was restored and in June 1977 the first parliamentary elections since 1936 were held. In December 1978 a referendum approved a new constitution in which Spain was declared a parliamentary democracy with a monarch as head of state. There are two houses of parliament, both elected by universal adult suffrage for maximum terms of four years.

## Physical features and land use

More than half Spain's land area is occupied by a central plateau, the Meseta, which has an average elevation of 700 m (2,300 ft). Much of the Meseta is harsh and barren. It is surrounded by mountain ranges to the north, northeast, south, and southwest, and is traversed by a low mountain range, the Sistema Central. The plateau is drained by three rivers—the Douro to the north of the Sistema Central, and the Tagus and Guadiana to its south—all of these rivers flow westward to the Atlantic.

In the far northeast of the country, between the Sistema Ibérico (a range that fringes the Meseta on the northeast and the Pyrenees to the north) is an extensive lowland area through which the Ebro River, which rises in the Basque country, flows south to the Mediterranean. In the southwest of Spain, beyond the Sierra Morena Range at the Meseta's southwestern edge, the Guadalquivir River drains another extensive low-lying region. In the far southeast is a coastal range, the Sistema Pinibético, which contains the snow-covered peaks of the Sierra Nevada, including the country's highest mountain, Mulhacén.

*The Ramblas in Barcelona (above). Storks are among the many bird species found in southern Spain (right).*

About one-tenth of Spain is heavily forested. Most of the forests are in the north and northwest, where the weather is wetter and more humid than in the center and south. Beech and oak predominate. Despite the fact that much of the country is arid and covered with low-growing scrub and water is a scarce resource, crops are widely grown. The most productive areas are in the north of the country, especially in the valley of the Ebro. There are significant crops of cereals, vegetables, fruits, and olives.

Spain is one of Europe's main producers of wine and there are 1.2 million hectares (3.0 million acres) of vineyards, mainly in the south and east. About one-fifth of Spain is pastureland, though cattle and dairying are largely confined to the north and pig farming to the southwest. Sheep are widespread on the Meseta, while goats graze in many of the more barren regions.

## Industry and commerce

Although Spain has a wide range of mineral resources, it is not rich in any of them and imports the oil and gas needed to fuel its industries. These industries are concentrated towards the north, mainly around the major cities of Madrid and Barcelona. Spain is a major manufacturer of motor vehicles and a number of multinational companies have car manufacturing plants in parts of northern and central Spain. Steelmaking and shipbuilding are among the most significant heavy industries. There are important shipyards at Barcelona, on the Mediterranean coast, La Coruña in the far northwest, and Cádiz in the southwest. Chemical manufacture and fishing are also major industries. Spain has one of the world's largest

fishing fleets, although its activities have been curtailed in recent years by European Union restrictions in response to serious fish stock depletions. About one in ten of Spain's workers are employed in the tourist industry.

While Spain is still a predominantly Catholic country, the influence of the Church has waned in recent years. This is reflected in the fact that Spain has one of the lowest birth rates in Europe, though divorce is still relatively rare. Most Spaniards enjoy a relatively high standard of living, and while high unemployment was a problem around 2000, it has decreased to about 8 percent.

### REGIONS

**Andalusia • Aragon • Asturias Baleares • Basque Country Canary Islands • Cantabria Castilla-La Mancha • Castilla y León Catalonia • Ceuta and Melilla Extremadura • Galicia • La Rioja Madrid • Murcia • Navarra • Valencia**

**1516** King Charles I, grandson of Ferdinand and Isabella, is first Habsburg to rule Spain; becomes Holy Roman Emperor in 1519

**1808** French invade Spain; Spanish resistance grows, French expelled in Peninsular War with the help of Great Britain (1814)

**1931** King Alfonso XIII flees after elections show preference for a republic; Spain briefly a democracy—deep political divisions

**1960s** Rapid industrialization, expansion of economy and growth in tourist resort development along Mediterranean

**1973** Basque separatists (ETA) assassinate Prime Minister Carrero Blanco in Madrid

**1976** Government under Prime Minister Suarez liberalizes politics, permits new parties to participate in elections (1977)

**1986** Prime Minister González embarks on more economic development; Spain joins European Community (EC)

**2004** A bloody attack by al-Qaida on two local trains in Madrid claims several hundred lives

**1556** Charles's son becomes King Philip II; height of Spanish Empire in Americas, Europe, and Africa

**1820** Spanish troops refuse to sail to reconquer American colonies; revolt spreads, crushed with help of French troops

**1860** Population begins to decline for almost a century due to emigration

**1936–38** Spanish Civil War; victorious Nationalists under General Franco enter Madrid in 1939

**1970** Population grows following industrialization. More than 1 million immigrants in 10 years, almost half illegal

**1975** On the death of Franco, Spain adopts political reform agenda despite accession of Juan Carlos (grandson of Alfonso XIII) as king

**1980** The 2.5 million Basque people of northern Spain are granted limited autonomy

**1995** Population more than 39 million; Spain lifts passport controls with EC nations

# Italy

## Fact file

**OFFICIAL NAME** Italian Republic

**FORM OF GOVERNMENT** Republic with two legislative bodies (Senate and Chamber of Deputies)

**CAPITAL** Rome

**AREA** 301,230 sq km (116,305 sq miles)

**TIME ZONE** GMT + 1 hour

**POPULATION** 58,145,000

**PROJECTED POPULATION 2015** 59,001,000

**POPULATION DENSITY** 193 per sq km (499.9 per sq mile)

**LIFE EXPECTANCY** 80.1

**INFANT MORTALITY (PER 1,000)** 5.6

**OFFICIAL LANGUAGE** Italian

**OTHER LANGUAGES** German, French, Slovenian

**LITERACY RATE** 98.4 %

**RELIGIONS** Roman Catholic 90 %, other 10 %

**ETHNIC GROUPS** Mainly Italian (including Sardinians and Romansh people, German speaking South Tyroleans and Franco-Provençales)

**CURRENCY** Euro

**ECONOMY** Services 69.2 %, industry 28.9 %, agriculture 1.9 %

**GNI PER CAPITA** US$ 33,540

**CLIMATE** Temperate; north has cool, wet winters and warm, dry summers; south has mild winters and hot, dry summers

**HIGHEST POINT** Mont Blanc 4,807 m (15,771 ft)

**MAP REFERENCE** Pages 294–95

Situated in southern central Europe, the Italian mainland consists of a long peninsula that juts out into the Mediterranean Sea. Shaped roughly like a long, high-heeled boot, this land mass is bordered to the north by Switzerland and Austria, to the west by France, and to the east by Slovenia. At the southwestern tip of the peninsula, the narrow Strait of Messina separates the toe of the boot from the large Italian island of Sicily, while further west in the Mediterranean, separated from the mainland by the Tyrrhenian Sea and sitting just south of the French island of Corsica, is the island of Sardinia, also part of Italy. About 70 other small islands, scattered mainly around the coasts of Sicily and Sardinia and off the western coast of the mainland, make up the rest of present-day Italy. The peninsula's eastern coastline is washed by the waters of the Adriatic Sea, across which lies the coast of Croatia.

## History

Italy's capital, Rome, situated in central western Italy, was for 800 years, from about 400 BC, the hub of the mighty Roman Empire. At the height of their powers in the first and second centuries AD the Romans controlled the whole of the Italian Peninsula and vast swathes of Europe. Their empire stretched as far as Britain in the north, the Iberian Peninsula in the west, into Egypt in North Africa and eastward as far as the Persian Gulf. Italy became Christianized after the conversion of the Roman Emperor Constantine in AD 313. The sacking of Rome by the Visigoths in AD 410 precipitated a series of subsequent invasions which resulted, over the centuries, in the fragmentation of Italy into a number of states ruled by different powers. For some time all of Italy came under the control of the eastern Roman Empire, based in Constantinople. The Franks, under Charlemagne, gained control of much of northern Italy at the end of the eighth century AD, and in the eleventh century the Normans invaded Sicily, which led to the creation of a kingdom based around the southern city of Naples.

In the later Middle Ages a number of powerful city-states emerged in central and northern Italy, the most notable being Florence, Pisa, Venice, and Genoa. From the fourteenth century, these states, especially Florence, promoted a great cultural revival which involved a blossoming of artistic, musical, literary, and scientific activity. This revival, which gradually spread through most of Europe, is now known as the Renaissance.

France, Spain, and Austria vied for domination of different parts of Italy between the fifteenth and the eighteenth centuries. Most of Italy fell to Napoleon's armies in 1796–97, but after his downfall in 1815 Italy was again fragmented, with Austria the dominant power in the north. A series of uprisings during the 1820s and 1830s gave rise to the movement known as the Risorgimento (resurrection), which eventually led to the total unification of Italy and the installation of Victor Emmanuel II, the King of Sardinia, as King of Italy in 1861. During the next half-century Italy acquired a number of overseas territories including Eritrea, part of Somalia, and some Greek islands.

Although officially allied to Germany, Italy at first remained neutral in the First World War and later joined the Allied side. In 1919 Benito Mussolini, a former socialist, founded the Fascist Party as a bulwark against communism. In 1922 he seized power, setting up a dictatorship. Embarking on a policy of foreign conquest, Italy invaded Ethiopia in 1935. Fascist Italy joined the side of Nazi Germany in the Second World War but in 1943 it was invaded by Allied troops and subsequently declared war on its former German ally. Dismissed from the Italian government, Mussolini was installed by Germany as head of a puppet government in northern Italy but he was captured and executed by partisans in 1945.

After the war, Italy was stripped of its foreign territories. A referendum in 1946 resulted in the abolition of the monarchy and the establishment of a democratic republic. Since then, government in Italy has been wracked by instability as changing allegiances and coalitions have created a succession of short-lived governments. In 1993 a referendum approved a plan to simplify Italy's complex electoral system. Since 1994 three-quarters of the members of Italy's two houses of parliament have been elected by a simple majority of votes, while the rest are elected by proportional representation. The president, whose duties are largely ceremonial, is elected for a seven-year term. Both houses are elected for a maximum of five years.

| Timeline | | | | | | |
|---|---|---|---|---|---|---|
| | **6th century BC** Under rule of Etruscan kings Rome grows from village to wealthy city | **476** Germanic leader Odoacer defeats last Roman Emperor; ends dominance of western sector of Roman Empire | **962** Otto the Great crowned Emperor of the Holy Roman Empire | **c. 1300** Renaissance begins. Interest flourishes in arts, sciences, and literature as well as philosophy, politics, and religion | **1519** King Charles I of Spain becomes Holy Roman Emperor. Seizes much of Italy including Rome and Milan from France | **1796** Napoleon Bonaparte invades north Italy, setting up independent republics. Interest in Italian independence grows |
| **900 BC** Etruscan civilization founded between Arno and Tiber Rivers by people arriving from the east; lasts till c. 200 BC | **568 BC** Langobardi (Lombards) seize much of northern Italy from Roman Empire | **AD 79** Mt Vesuvius near Naples erupts, buries city of Pompeii in lava and ash, and Herculaneum under mud | **800** Pope Leo III crowns Charlemagne Emperor of the Romans | **1000** Rise of city-states such as Florence, Venice, Genoa, and Pisa which have strong commercial and cultural identities | **1345** Black Death, bubonic plague, kills more than one-quarter of the population | **1663** Volcano Mt Etna erupts destroying much of the town of Catania, north-east Sicily |

## Physical features and land use

Most of Italy is mountainous, with a central range, the Appenines, sweeping down the length of the peninsula and extending into Sicily, where the still-active volcanic peak of Mount Etna soars to a height of 3,323 m (10,902 ft) above sea level. Further north, near Naples, the active Mount Vesuvius offers evidence of the volcanic origins of Italy's mountains. The Appenines, which are rich in limestone, reach heights of almost 3,000 m (10,000 ft) in the Gran Sasso Range, east of Rome. The slopes of the Appenines are covered with thin soils, which in some places provide reasonable pasture. In the valleys there are some extensive stretches of arable land. At the far northwestern tip of the Italian Peninsula the Appenines merge with the Alps, which are generally higher than the Appenines and which arch right across the north of Italy, forming natural boundaries with the countries of Switzerland, Austria, and France. In the southern extremities of the Alps are a series of large, spectacular lakes which include the much visited Lago Maggiore, Lago di Como, and Lago di Garda. These lakes and the rivers that feed into them are the source of the hydroelectricity which supplies about half the electricity needs of industrialized northern Italy.

In the northeast of the country, enclosed by the Alps to the north and the west and the Appenines to the south, and stretching eastwards as far as the Adriatic coast, is the country's largest lowland region, known as the Plain of Lombardy. Drained by the River Po, which flows from west to east across the widest part of the country, this area is the most fertile as well as the most heavily industrialized and populous part of Italy. About two-fifths of Italy's crops are grown here. Agri-

The Forum Romanum, once the centerpiece of the Roman Empire, Rome (above left). Fishing boats in the harbor of Camogli in Liguria, northern Italy (above right). The Tower of Pisa (below right). The rooftops of Florence, including the cathedral, seen from Piazzale Michelangelo (below left).

culture is also extensive on the coastal plains on each side of the Appenines. Farms are mainly small. Crops include potatoes, wheat, maize, olives, and other vegetables as well as a wide range of citrus and stone fruits. Italy produces more wine than any other country and there are extensive vineyards, most particularly in the Chianti region in Tuscany. Sheep, pigs, and cattle are the principal livestock.

## Industry, commerce, and culture

Apart from marble in the south, for which it is famous, and some oil deposits in Sicily, Italy is not well endowed with mineral resources and imports most of the energy needed by its highly developed industrial sector. This is concentrated overwhelmingly in the north of the country—although Naples, Bari, and Taranto in the south and Rome in the center have a certain amount of heavy industry— and is based around such cities as Milan, Turin, and Genoa. The building of cars, aircraft, and other transport equipment are major industries, as are tool, textile, clothing, and chemical manufacture.

Italy's manufacturing sector, which was heavily subsidized by the state, developed largely in the half-century since the Second World War, before

which the economy was based predominantly on agriculture. It now employs about a fifth of the country's workforce. Tourism is an important source of income, with about 36 million people visiting Italy every year.

There is a great divide in Italy between the high living standards of the industrialized, affluent north and the much lower living standards of the largely undeveloped south, especially in Calabria in the far south. In the south unemployment is chronically high, investment is hard to attract, poverty is widespread, and for many people crime offers the best means of survival.

### REGIONS

Abruzzi • Basilicata • Calabria
Campania • Emilia-Romagna
Friuli-Venezia Giulia • Lazio • Liguria
Lombardy • Marche • Molise
Piedmont • Puglia • Sardinia
Sicily • Trentino-Alto Adige • Tuscany
Umbria • Valle d'Aosta • Veneto

| 1814 Napoleon defeated by European powers; under Congress of Vienna most of Italy returns to Austrian rule | 1861 King Victor Emmanuel announces Kingdom of Italy to include entire peninsula except Rome, Venice, and San Marino | 1908 Earthquake in Messina, Sicily, kills 120,000 people | 1922 Mussolini becomes leader and the Fascist movement grows | 1940 Italy's forces defeated in Eritrea, Ethiopia, and Greece; Mussolini overthrown, but reinstalled by Germans | 1960s Rapid postwar industrialization brings prosperity to northern cities but the south remains largely agricultural and poor | 1980 Earthquake in southern Italy kills more than 4,500 and leaves 400,000 homeless |

| 1858 French troops help Kingdom of Sardinia to push back Austrian troops, regaining most of northern Italy | 1860 Garibaldi's redshirts regain control of Sicily; eventually they take all southern Italy, including Naples | 1915 Italy joins Allies in First World War | 1939 Start of Second World War; Italy enters on Germany's side nine months later, soon after the fall of France, in June 1940 | 1943 Allies invade Italy; Italian prime minister signs armistice with Allies; Italy declares war on Germany | 1997 Earthquake in central Italy causes severe damage in St Francis' Dome in Assisi with its famous Giotto frescoes. Already in 2002 restoration of the paintings is completed | 2003 Despite massive opposition from the public, the Italian government sends 3,000 troops to Iraq |

# San Marino

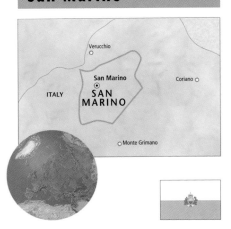

## Fact File

**OFFICIAL NAME** Republic of San Marino

**FORM OF GOVERNMENT** Republic with single legislative body (Great and General Council)

**CAPITAL** San Marino

**AREA** 61 sq km (24 sq miles)

**TIME ZONE** GMT + 1 hour

**POPULATION** 30,000

**PROJECTED POPULATION 2015** 32,000

**POPULATION DENSITY** 491.8 per sq km (1,250 per sq mile)

**LIFE EXPECTANCY** 81.9

**INFANT MORTALITY (PER 1,000)** 5.4

**OFFICIAL LANGUAGE** Italian

**LITERACY RATE** 96%

**RELIGIONS** Roman Catholic 95%, other 5%

**ETHNIC GROUPS** Sanmarinesi 87%, Italian 12%, other 1%

**CURRENCY** Euro

**ECONOMY** Services 58%, industry 40%, agriculture 2%

**GNI PER CAPITA** US$ 45,130

**CLIMATE** Temperate, with mild winters and warm summers

**HIGHEST POINT** Monte Titano 739 m (2,425 ft)

**MAP REFERENCE** Page 294

Completely surrounded by Italian territory, most of the tiny state of San Marino sits on the slopes of Mount Titano in the Appenine Mountains, 20 km (12 miles) inland from the city of Rimini on the Adriatic coast of northern Italy. The republic takes its name from St Marinus who, so legend has it, arrived there with a group of followers in the fourth century AD and established a settlement. This makes it arguably the world's oldest surviving republic. Records of its existence can be traced back to the twelfth century. It became one of the many mini-states on the Italian Peninsula and was accorded papal recognition in 1631. The Sanmarinesi, as its inhabitants are known, offered refuge to Giuseppe Garibaldi when he passed through

*Square in San Marino with the old governmental building (above). St Peter's Square in Vatican City, seen from the roof of the basilica (below). One of Malta's megalithic temples, built more than 5,000 years ago (right page bottom).*

in 1849, pursued by his enemies. However, when the newly unified state of Italy was declared in 1861 the Sanmarinesi declined to join. San Marino fought with Italy in the First World War. In the Second World War it began by supporting Fascist Italy but later changed sides and was invaded by Germany. San Marino is a democratic republic with elections held every five years. Two Capitani regenti who are elected by the parliament and are in office for six months serve as heads of state. There is a single legislative body that consists of sixty members.

This picturesque little country is centered on the fortified medieval town of San Marino, where most of the population lives. On the lower slopes, beneath the rugged limestone peak, are thick forests, expanses of pasture-land and a string of ancient villages. Almost one-fifth of the land is used for agriculture. Cereals, olives, and vines are cultivated and sheep and goats are raised. Cheeses and wine are its principal agricultural products.

Since 1862 San Marino has had a friendship and cooperation treaty with Italy. It also shares its currency—since 2001 the Euro according to the Maastricht Treaty—and enjoys a standard of living roughly equivalent to that of its neighbor. About one in five Sanmarinesi workers are in the tourism industry, which caters to more than 2 million visitors each year, although many do not stay overnight but rather stay on the Adriatic Sea and take excursions into the ancient republic. Winemaking, textiles, and ceramics are significant industries. Even more important is the sale of the country's distinctive postage stamps, which are sought by collectors and account for up to ten percent of the country's revenues.

# Vatican City

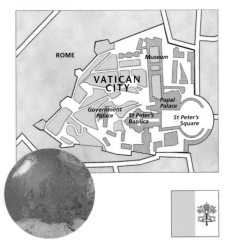

## Fact File

**OFFICIAL NAME** State of the Vatican City (The Holy See)

**FORM OF GOVERNMENT** Absolute elected monarchy with single legislative body (Pontifical Commission)

**CAPITAL** Vatican City

**AREA** 0.44 sq km (0.16 sq miles)

**TIME ZONE** GMT + 1 hour

**POPULATION** 820

**PROJECTED POPULATION 2015** 800

**POPULATION DENSITY** 1,863.6 per sq km (5,125 per sq mile)

**LIFE EXPECTANCY** Not available

**INFANT MORTALITY (PER 1,000)** Not available

**OFFICIAL LANGUAGES** Italian, Latin

**LITERACY RATE** 100%

**RELIGION** Roman Catholic 100%

**ETHNIC GROUPS** International

**CURRENCY** Euro

**ECONOMY** Services 100%

**GNI PER CAPITA** Not available

**CLIMATE** Temperate, with mild winters and hot summers

HIGHEST POINT Unnamed location 75 m (246 ft)

MAP REFERENCE Page 295

Occupying a hill in the city of Rome on the western bank of the Tiber, and including the pope's summer residence at Castel Gandolfo southeast of Rome, and ten churches throughout Rome as well, Vatican City is the world's smallest state, and probably its most homogeneous. Its population is 100 percent Catholic, and it is the home of the pope, the spiritual head of the Roman Catholic Church, and several hundred clergy and Catholic lay people, all employees of the Vatican.

Vatican City is all that remains of the former Papal States, which from the fourteenth to the nineteenth centuries expanded from a palace on the present site to cover an area—with changing borders—of almost 45,000 sq km (17,000 sq miles) which was a large part of mainland Italy. During the Risorgimento ("resurrection"), which resulted in the unification of Italy in the 1860s, most of this area was absorbed into the new Italian state headed by King Victor Emmanuael II. From 1870 until 1929, neither the Church nor successive Italian governments recognized each other's sovereignty over the area, which the Church refused to relinquish to the state. In 1929, however, Pope Leo XI and Mussolini concluded an agreement—the Lateran Treaty—under which the independence of the Vatican City State, and the pope's temporal sovereignty over it, was recognized in return for the Church's recognition of the kingdom of Italy. Under this treaty, Catholicism was also recognized as the state religion of Italy.

This provision, along with a number of other privileges enjoyed by the Church in Italy, was removed under a subsequent Church-state agreement, known as a "concordat", signed in 1984. Vatican City now has diplomatic relations with more than 100 countries, although it is the only remaining independent country not represented in the United Nations. It has the pope as its head of state, while responsibility for administration of the area is vested in a Commission of Cardinals. The roles of secretary of state, chief of staff, and foreign minister are filled by senior members of the clergy.

Surrounded by medieval walls, Vatican City contains the huge St Peter's Basilica, built between 1506 and 1626 by a number of architects, including Michelangelo and Bernini. Pilgrims come to visit the basilica in vast numbers throughout the year, but particularly to celebrate Christmas and Easter. Visitors also come to see the richly endowed Vatican Museums, which include the renowned Sistine Chapel (the personal chapel of the popes) in the Vatican Palace. Parklands cover most of Vatican City.

Vatican City has its own radio station, publishes a daily newspaper, and issues its own stamps and coins. It also has an army—the 100-strong Swiss Guard—which is responsible for maintaining security. Vatican state finances depend on voluntary contributions, interest on extensive investments, and on the income derived from millions of tourists.

## Malta

### Fact File

OFFICIAL NAME Republic of Malta

FORM OF GOVERNMENT Republic with single legislative body (House of Representatives)

CAPITAL Valletta

AREA 320 sq km (124 sq miles)

TIME ZONE GMT + 1 hour

POPULATION 404,000

PROJECTED POPULATION 2015 420,000

POPULATION DENSITY 1,262.5 per sq km (3,258.1 per sq mile)

LIFE EXPECTANCY 79.3

INFANT MORTALITY (PER 1,000) 3.8

OFFICIAL LANGUAGES Maltese, English

LITERACY RATE 92.8%

RELIGIONS Roman Catholic 98%, other 2%

ETHNIC GROUPS Maltese (mixture of Arab, Sicilian, French, Spanish, Italian and British)

CURRENCY Euro

ECONOMY Services 74.9%, industry 22.3%, agriculture 2.8%

GNI PER CAPITA US$ 15,310

CLIMATE Temperate, with mild, wet winters and hot, dry summers

HIGHEST POINT Dingli Cliffs 245 m (804 ft)

MAP REFERENCE Pages 361, 362

The Republic of Malta consists of an archipelago of three inhabited islands—Malta, Gozo, and Comino—and three tiny uninhabited islands, which are little more than rocky outcrops. They are situated in the center of the Mediterranean Sea 93 km (58 miles) south of Sicily. Malta is the largest and most populous of the islands. It contains the capital, Valletta, the country's fifth largest city, picturesquely situated on a promontory between two harbors, and the four larger cities of Birkirkara, Qormi, Hamrun, and Sliema. Successive civilizations have recognized the importance of Malta's position and the advantages of its many harbors. It was occupied successively by the Phoenicians, the Greeks, and the Romans. In the ninth century AD, when it was part of the Byzantine Empire, it was conquered by Arabs but fell two centuries later to Sicily and then in 1282 to Spain. In 1530 the Spanish king gave Malta to the Knights of St John, a religious order, which built and fortified the town of Valletta and occupied the island of Malta until it was seized by Napoleon in 1798. Britain took the island in 1800 and held it until 1947, when the country was granted self-government as a parliamentary democracy. In 1964 Malta gained full independence. In 1987 Malta created a new constitution that declared its political neutrality, a feature not affected by its entry into the EU in 2004.

The three inhabited islands are mostly flat—although the island of Malta is undulating in places—with spectacular rocky coastlines. There is little natural vegetation and there are no forests or major rivers. Low rainfall, poor drainage, a limestone base and a hot climate all contribute to the paucity of the islands' shallow soils, which, however, support a range of cereal and vegetable crops as well as substantial vineyards.

Apart from limestone for building, Malta has virtually no mineral resources and is heavily dependent on imported materials. It has no natural sources of energy and produces only one-fifth of its population's food needs. Tourism is the mainstay of the economy. Every year about a million visitors, mainly from the United Kingdom, arrive to enjoy its beaches, its historic towns, and its rugged scenery. Ship repairs and clothing and textile manufacture are other significant industries. The average income is low by Western standards and Maltese residents are among the least affluent of Western Europeans.

## Southeastern Europe

Slovenia, Croatia · · · · · · 258
Bosnia and Herzegovina 259
Macedonia · · · · · · · · 260
Serbia · · · · · · · · 260
Kosovo · · · · · · · · · 261
Montenegro · · · · · · · 261
Hungary · · · · · · · · 262
Albania · · · · · · · · 263
Romania · · · · · · · · 263
Bulgaria · · · · · · · · 264
Greece · · · · · · · · · 265

## Slovenia

### Fact File

OFFICIAL NAME  Republic of Slovenia

FORM OF GOVERNMENT  Republic with two legislative bodies (National Assembly and National Council)

CAPITAL  Ljubljana

AREA  20,273 sq km (7,827 sq miles)

TIME ZONE  GMT + 1 hour

POPULATION  2,008,000

PROJECTED POPULATION 2015  1,992,000

POPULATION DENSITY  99 per sq km (256.5 per sq mile)

LIFE EXPECTANCY  76.7

INFANT MORTALITY (PER 1,000)  4.3

OFFICIAL LANGUAGE  Slovenian

OTHER LANGUAGES  Serbian, Croatian, Hungarian, Italian

LITERACY RATE  99.7 %

RELIGIONS  Roman Catholic 57.8 %, Muslim 2.4 %, Orthodox 2.3 %, other 27.4 %, none 10.1

ETHNIC GROUPS  Slovene 83.1 %, Serbian 2.0 %, Croatian 1.8 %, Bosnian 1.1 %, other 12.0 %

CURRENCY  Euro

ECONOMY  Services 63.5 %, industry 34.4 %, agriculture 2.1 %

GNI PER CAPITA  US$ 20,960

CLIMATE  Temperate, with colder winters and hotter summers inland

HIGHEST POINT  Mt Triglav 2,864 m (9,396 ft)

MAP REFERENCE  Page 294

This former Yugoslav republic shares borders with Italy to the west, Austria to the north, Hungary to the east, and Croatia to the south. The port of Koper on Slovenia's short coastline on the Gulf of Venice is an important transit point for products from Austria and much of Central Europe. First settled by Slavic peoples in the sixth century AD, Slovenia became a Hungarian province in the eleventh century. Austria gained control of the region in the sixteenth century, and Slovenia was later absorbed into the Austro-Hungarian Empire. At the end of the First World War it became part of the Kingdom of the Croats, Serbs, and Slovenes, which in 1929 became Yugoslavia. Like the rest of Yugoslavia, it was occupied by Axis powers during the Second World War. In 1991 it became the first Yugoslav republic to declare its independence. This prompted a military response from the Yugoslav army, which, however, withdrew its forces after a ten-day conflict. According to its constitution of 1991, Slovenia is a democratic republic with a directly elected president and a prime minister as head of the government. Since 2004 it has been a member of the EU.

Slovenia is mountainous, with the highest and most spectacular regions in the Slovenian Alps near the border with Austria in the northwest. Almost half the land is densely forested. There are areas of lowland in the west near the coast and much of the center and east of the country consists of undulating plains. The most fertile region is in the east, where the Drava River flows southward across the Pannonian Plain into Croatia.

Slovenia's tourist industry, based on its alpine scenery and its coastal beaches, remains important, although it has been adversely affected by conflicts in the region. A large part of the workforce is employed in mining and manufacturing industries. Metallurgy and heavy machine manufacture, including trucks and cars, are prominent among these. Textile manufacture is also widespread. The main mineral resource is coal and there are large mercury deposits in the northwest. Dairy farming and pig raising are the main agricultural activities. Slovenia's nuclear power plant, which supplies one-third of the country's electricity, is a cause of some international tension, especially with Austria.

## Croatia

### Fact File

OFFICIAL NAME  Republic of Croatia

FORM OF GOVERNMENT  Republic with two legislative bodies (House of Districts and House of Assembly)

CAPITAL  Zagreb

AREA  56,542 sq km (21,831 sq miles)

TIME ZONE  GMT + 1 hour

POPULATION  4,492,000

PROJECTED POPULATION 2015  4,455,000

POPULATION DENSITY  79.4 per sq km (205.8 per sq mile)

LIFE EXPECTANCY  75.1

INFANT MORTALITY (PER 1,000)  6.5

OFFICIAL LANGUAGE  Croatian

OTHER LANGUAGES  Serbian, languages of the minorities

LITERACY RATE  98.1 %

RELIGIONS  Catholic 87.8 %, Orthodox 4.4 %, Muslim 1.3 %, other 6.5 %

ETHNIC GROUPS  Croat 89.6 %, Serb 4.5 %, other (including Bosnian, Hungarian, Slovenian) 5.9 %

*Lake Bled in Slovenia (left page). Dubrovnik old town in Croatia that was heavily damaged during the Serbian-Croat War (right).*

**CURRENCY** Kuna

**ECONOMY** Services 61.2 %, industry 31.6 %, agriculture 7.2 %

**GNI PER CAPITA** US$ 10,460

**CLIMATE** Temperate; cold winters and warm summers inland, cooler and more temperate along coast

**HIGHEST POINT** Dinara 1,830 m (6,004 ft)

**MAP REFERENCE** Pages 294, 296

Croatia wraps around the northern and western extremities of Bosnia and Herzegovina, allowing its neighbor a tiny 20 km (12 mile) toehold south of its almost 600 km (375 mile) stretch of coastline on the Adriatic Sea. It also shares borders with Slovenia to the northwest, Hungary to the northeast, and Serbia to the east. The state of Croatia emerged in the ninth century AD, peopled by Slavic immigrants from present-day Ukraine. In 1091 it was invaded by Hungary with which it remained united until 1526 when most of the country came under the rule of the Ottoman Turks. In 1699 the Turks were driven out by the Austrian Habsburgs. Once again Croatia came under Hungarian rule, but with its own monarch. In 1867 Croatia became part of the Austro-Hungarian Empire. In 1918 it declared its independence and joined with its neighboring states to form the Kingdom of Serbs, Croats, and Slovenes—the precursor of the state of Yugoslavia. Serbian domination of the new country provoked agitation by Croation separatists, and in 1939 this led to Croatia's being declared a self-governing region within Yugoslavia. During the Second World War, the invading Axis powers proclaimed Croatia an independent state and installed a Fascist government intent on eliminating Serbs, Jews, and all political oppostion. At the war's end, Croatia once again became a republic in the reformed state of Yugoslavia. In 1991, after a referendum, Croatia declared its independence and was then plunged into civil war as Croatian Serbs, supported by the Yugoslav army, sought to incorporate Croatia into a "Greater Serbia." The war ended officially in 1992, but hostilities between Serbs and Croats continued until 1995.

Along Croatia's spectacular Dalmatian coast are scattered about 600 small rocky islands, many of them former alpine peaks, isolated by rises in sea level. Further inland in the north, the Pannonian Plain, traversed by the Drava, Danube, and Sava Rivers, is a fertile region centered around Zagreb, which is the hub of the country's agricultural production. A little more than one-fifth of the land is devoted to agriculture and about one-fifth of the population is directly involved in agricultural production. Cereal crops, fruit, and tobacco are widely grown and sheep are raised. Timber is a significant resource, and reserves of minerals, coal and iron are mined. Civil and other regional wars in the 1990s have seriously impeded Croatia's transition to a market economy and cut industrial production. The tourist industry, once of great economic significance, had largely ceased to exist in the early 1990s. However, following huge efforts to eliminate the destructions of war it is on the rise again.

# Bosnia and Herzegovina

## Fact File

**OFFICIAL NAME** Republic of Bosnia and Herzegovina

**FORM OF GOVERNMENT** Federal republic with two legislative bodies (Chamber of Municipalities and Chamber of Citizens)

**CAPITAL** Sarajevo

**AREA** 51,129 sq km (19,781 sq miles)

**TIME ZONE** GMT + 1 hour

**POPULATION** 4,590,000

**PROJECTED POPULATION 2015** 3,899,000

**POPULATION DENSITY** 89.8 per sq km (232 per sq mile)

**LIFE EXPECTANCY** 78.3

**INFANT MORTALITY (PER 1,000)** 9.3

**OFFICIAL LANGUAGES** Bosnian, Serbian, Croatian

**LITERACY RATE** 94.7 %

**RELIGIONS** Muslim 40 %, Orthodox 31 %, Roman Catholic 15 %, Protestant 4 %, other 10 %

**ETHNIC GROUPS** Bosnian 48.0 %, Serb 37.1 %, Croat 14.3 %, other 0.6 %

**CURRENCY** Konvertibilna marka (BAM)

**ECONOMY** Services 66 %, industry 23.8 %, agriculture 10.2 %

**GNI PER CAPITA** US$ 3,580

**CLIMATE** Cold winters and warm summers; cooler in the north and southern mountains

**HIGHEST POINT** Mt Maglic 2,386 m (7,828 ft)

**MAP REFERENCE** Pages 294, 296

The federation of Bosnia and Herzegovina has a mere 20 km (12 miles) of coast at its southern tip on the Adriatic. It borders Croatia to the north and west, and shares a border to the east with Serbia and with Montenegro. Serbs first settled in Bosnia in the seventh century AD. In the twelfth century the country came under Hungarian control, and Ottoman Turks conquered it two centuries later. It was ceded to the Austro-Hungarian Empire in 1908, and in 1918 became part of the Kingdom of Serbs, Croats, and Slovenes, which was later renamed Yugoslavia.

The republic was formed in 1994 when, after several years of fighting sparked by the breaking up of Yugoslavia in 1991, Bosnian Croats and Muslims (called Bosniaks) agreed to joint control of the region. Fighting went on for a further 18 months as Bosnian Serbs, backed by Serbia, sought to have a portion of the country incorporated into Serbia. The war came to an uneasy end in 1995 when Serbia abandoned its claims on Bosnian territory. Now named Bosnia and Herzegovina, the country is divided for purposes of administration almost equally between the Muslim-Croat Federation and the Bosnian Serbs.

Much of the land is mountainous and the south consists largely of a harsh limestone plateau. About a quarter of the land, especially in the mountains, is covered in forests of pine and beech. Before the economy collapsed, forestry products were a major source of earnings. Most agriculture is centered in the fertile valley of the Sava River, which forms the border with Croatia. Crops include grapes, other fruit, and cereals. Sheep raising is also significant.

In 2006, a value-added tax (VAT) was introduced and has developed into a significant source of revenues for all layers of government. Bosnia and Herzegovina joined the Central European Free Trade Agreement since 2006. The country still receives substantial reconstruction assistance and humanitarian aid from the international community.

# Macedonia

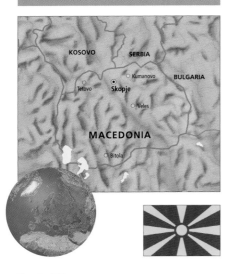

## Fact File

OFFICIAL NAME  Former Yugoslav Republic of Macedonia

FORM OF GOVERNMENT  Republic with single legislative body (Assembly)

CAPITAL  Skopje

AREA  25,333 sq km (9,781 sq miles)

TIME ZONE  GMT + 1 hour

POPULATION  2,061,000

PROJECTED POPULATION 2015  2,037,000

POPULATION DENSITY  81.4 per sq km (280.1 per sq mile)

LIFE EXPECTANCY  74.5

INFANT MORTALITY (PER 1,000)  9.3

OFFICIAL LANGUAGE  Macedonian

OTHER LANGUAGES  Albanian, Turkish, Serbian, Croatian

LITERACY RATE  96.1 %

RELIGIONS  Macedonian Orthodox 64.7 %, Muslim 33.3 %, other Christian 0.4 %, other 1.6 %

ETHNIC GROUPS  Macedonian 64.2 %, Albanian 25.2 %, Turkish 3.9 %, Roma 2.7 %, Serb 1.8 %, other 2.2 %

CURRENCY  Denar

ECONOMY  Services 59.9 %, industry 28.2 %, agriculture 11.9 %

GNI PER CAPITA  US$ 3,460

CLIMATE  Temperate, with cold winters and hot summers

HIGHEST POINT  Mt Korab 2,753 m (9,032 ft)

MAP REFERENCE  Pages 296–97, 298

This small, landlocked Balkan country in south-eastern Europe is bordered by Serbia and the Kosovo to the north, Bulgaria to the east, Greece to the south, and Albania to the west. During the third century BC Macedonia was the heart of the Greek Empire. It later became a Roman province, but from the fourth century AD it was invaded numerous times. In the fourteenth century it came under Ottoman control. As the Ottoman Empire declined in the nineteenth century, Bulgaria, Greece, and Serbia contended for control of Macedonia and by the First World War it had been divided between them. Present-day

Macedonia is essentially the region that was in Serbian hands at the end of the First World War. Macedonia was then incorporated into the Kingdom of Serbs, Croats, and Slovenes, which in 1929 became the Republic of Yugoslavia. In 1946 it became an autonomous republic within Yugoslavia. In 1991 Macedonia withdrew from Yugoslavia and it is now a multi-party democracy, governed by a legislative body with 120 elected members and a directly elected president. Tensions with neighbors remain high. Macedonia is also the name of a Greek province. This is why the official name of the country is "Former Yugoslav Republic of Macedonia".

Macedonia is largely isolated from its neighbors by mountains. Mountain ranges separate it from Greece in the south and the Korab Mountains in the west lie along the Albanian and Serbian borders. Much of the country is a plateau more than 2,000 m (6,500 ft) above sea level. The River Vadar rises in the northwest. It flows north, almost to the Yugoslavian border, then continues on a southeasterly course through the center of the country and into Greece.

One-quarter of the land is used for agriculture. Crops include cereals, fruits, vegetables, and cotton, and sheep and cattle are raised extensively. The country is self-sufficient in food and, thanks to its coal resources, in energy. Manufacturing industries have suffered since independence, partly because of trade embargoes imposed by Greece. Macedonia is the least developed of the former Yugoslav republics and is suffering a declining standard of living.

# Serbia

## Fact File

OFFICIAL NAME  Republic of Serbia

FORM OF GOVERNMENT  Republic

CAPITAL  Belgrade

AREA  77,848 sq km (30,057 sq miles)

TIME ZONE  GMT + 1 hour

POPULATION  8,033,000

PROJECTED POPULATION 2015  8,000,000

POPULATION DENSITY  103.7 per sq km (267.3 per sq mile)

LIFE EXPECTANCY  75.3

INFANT MORTALITY (PER 1,000)  not available

OFFICIAL LANGUAGE  Serbian

OTHER LANGUAGES  Albanian, Croatian, Hungarian, Romanian, Slovak, Ukrainian

LITERACY RATE  96.4 %

RELIGIONS  Serbian Orthodox 85 %, Catholic 5.5 %, Protestant 1.1 %, others 8.4 %

ETHNIC GROUPS  Serbs 82.9 %, Hungarian 3.9 %, Bosniaks 1.8 %, Roma 1.4 %, other 10 %

CURRENCY  Dinar

ECONOMY  Services 63.5 %, industry 24.2 %, agriculture 12.3 %

GNI PER CAPITA  US$ 6,100

CLIMATE  Temperate, with cold winters and hot summers

HIGHEST POINT  Gusam 2,539 m (8,330 ft)

MAP REFERENCE  Page 296

Since its separation from Montenegro in 2006, Serbia is an entirely landlocked country, and it shares borders with nine countries. These are Bosnia and Herzegovina, Croatia, Hungary, Romania, Bulgaria, Macedonia, Albania, the Kosovo, and Montenegro. Serbia is all that remains of the former federation after five of the originally six constituent republics—Slovenia, Croatia, Bosnia and Herzegovina, Macedonia, and Montenegro—have seceded since the early 1990s.

Yugoslavia came into existence in December 1918 as a combination of Serbia and Montenegro together with several regions (including Slovenia, Croatia, and Bosnia and Herzegovina) that had been under Austro-Hungarian control. Serbia had become formally independent in 1878, bringing to an end between four and five centuries of almost continuous Ottoman rule. The new country was originally called the Kingdom of Serbs, Croats, and Slovenes, but the name Yugoslavia was adopted in 1929. During the Second World War Yugoslavia was invaded by Germany and Italy, and the country was further devastated by civil war. More than a million Yugoslavs perished during this time. At the end of the war a communist government led by Marshal Tito (Josip Broz), came to power, that remained independent of the Soviet Union. After Tito died in 1980, ethnic tensions began to emerge, and in 1991 Croatia and Slovenia seceded, followed by Macedonia and Bosnia and Herzegovina. The ensuing four years of bitter ethnic-based conflict was officially ended in November 1995. In the Kosovo province, mainly inhabited by Muslim Albanians, the ethnic conflicts persisted. In 1999 an international alliance and NATO reacted to massive actions of the Serbian army by bombing Yugoslavia. An international peacekeeping force led by Russia and the USA was installed in Kosovo in 2000. In the fall of 2000, elections brought reformers into power, and in March 2003 a new constitution replaced the federal republic by the union of two states, Serbia and Montenegro. Each had their

Europe and the Russian Federation

own president and parliament, but there was also one president heading the entire country as chief of state and leader of the government. At a referendum in spring of 2006, the people of Montenegro voted for their independence, and on June 3 the union split into two separate countries. A new constitution was accepted in October 2006, maintaining Kosovo as an integral part of the Serb nation. That province, however, declared its independence from Serbia on 17 February 2008.

Serbia is largely flat. However, the heavily forested Balkan Mountains separate it from Bulgaria and stretch across much of southern and central Serbia and into Bosnia and Herzegovina. In the north of the country, and covering most of the province of Vojvodina, is the fertile Pannonian Plain. A number of rivers including the Sava, the Tisza, and the Danube traverse it.

Agricultural produce is centered on the northern plain, which supports substantial crops of grain and vegetables as well as livestock and poultry. Serbia has considerable reserves of coal and petroleum and is largely self-sufficient in fuel. Most of these resources are in the northern province of Vojvodina. Mining and heavy machine manufacture are major contributors to the country's economy, which remains seriously destabilized by years of warfare and the consequent disruption of trade links. Unemployment remains a serious problem, but the real GDP growth rate for 2005 was 5.9 percent, excluding Kosovo.

# Kosovo

## Fact File

**OFFICIAL NAME** Republic of Kosovo

**FORM OF GOVERNMENT** Republic

**CAPITAL** Priština

**AREA** 10 877 sq km (4,200 sq miles)

**TIME ZONE** GMT + 1 hour

**POPULATION** 2,127,000

**PROJECTED POPULATION 2015** not available

**POPULATION DENSITY** 195.6 per sq km (506.4 per sq mile)

**LIFE EXPECTANCY** 69

**INFANT MORTALITY (PER 1,000)** not available

**OFFICIAL LANGUAGE** Albanian, Serbian

**OTHER LANGUAGES** Bosnian, Romanian, Turkish

**LITERACY RATE** not available

**RELIGIONS** Muslim, Serbian Orthodox, Catholic

**ETHNIC GROUPS** Albanian 88 %, Serb 7 %, other (Bosnian, Ashkali, Roma, Turks, Ashkali) 5 %

**CURRENCY** Euro

**ECONOMY** Services 60 %, industry 20 %, agriculture 20 %

**GNI PER CAPITA** US$ 1800

**CLIMATE** Temperate, with cold winters and hot summers

**HIGHEST POINT** Daravica 2,656 m (8,714 ft)

**MAP REFERENCE** Page 296

This very young country has common borders with Serbia, Macedonia, Albania, and Montenegro. While still a Serbian province mainly inhabited by Albanians it was known as Kosmet, a compound word consisting of Kosovo and Metohija, the two regions that form today's Kosovo. To the Serbs, the dissolution of the Kosovo meant the loss of the very heart of their national identity. Indeed, the name of the region refers to the Kosovo Polje, Field of the Blackbirds, which is located not far from its capital, Priština. This was the center of the Serbian Empire that had forced the Byzantine emperor to recognize its autonomy after the Fourth Crusade of 1204-1205. Only in 1371 did the Ottomans managed to weaken the Serbs in the Battle of the Maritza and then defeat them decisively in the Battle of Kosovo Field, in which King Lazar as well as Sultan Murad I were mortally wounded. It took one last campaign in 1459 to 1461 to completely subdue Serbia and turn it into a Turkish province. The Battle of Kosovo Field became mythicized in Serbian historiography, and there is probably no other event in Serbian history that was more formative for the Serbian national awareness. Even though the Field of Blackbirds was abandoned after the battle and later settled and farmed by Muslim Albanians, the Serbs retained their strong emotional ties to the region.

After the First Balkan War of 1912, Kosovo was integrated into Serbia and finally into Yugoslavia. In 1974, the Yugoslav constitution made the region, which had already been granted autonomy, an autonomous province within Serbia. After the autonomy was revoked in 1989, the fight about the status of the province became increasingly violent on both sides. Finally, the international community and NATO started bombing the remainder of Yugoslavia in 1999 and put Kosovo under UN protection (UNMIK). The inability of the Serbs and the Kosovars to find a solution despite years of negotiations finally led to the declaration of independence of Kosovo, which was immediately recognized by the USA and shortly thereafter by the other G7 countries, as well as the majority of Western Europe. Other countries such as Spain, Russia, and Serbia declared the act illegial, and while the Serbian government does not hold defacto power in the Kosovo, the Kosovar administration fails to control the Serb-dominated north.

Political instability goes hand in hand with a difficult economic situation. Even though the province, always a poor one, has made a strong recovery recently, it still depends on the financial support of Kosovars abroad—mainly in Germany and Switzerland—whose contributions represent about thirty percent of Kosovo's GDP. The BNI lies sixty percent below that of Albania, and over forty percent of the population is unemployed, eking out an existence by subsistence farming. The natural resources—lignite, magnesium, lead, zinc, nickel, chrome, aluminium, and various construction materials—are unused for lack of investments to replace old, Soviet-era machinery.

# Montenegro

## Fact File

**OFFICIAL NAME** Republic of Montenegro

**FORM OF GOVERNMENT** Republic

**CAPITAL** Podgorica

**AREA** 14,026 sq km (5,470 sq miles)

**TIME ZONE** GMT + 1 hour

**POPULATION** 678,000

**PROJECTED POPULATION 2015** 604,000

**POPULATION DENSITY** 48.3 per sq km (123.9 per sq mile)

**LIFE EXPECTANCY** 74.5

**INFANT MORTALITY (PER 1,000)** 22.3

**OFFICIAL LANGUAGE** Serbian

**OTHER LANGUAGES** Albanian, Bosnian, Croatian

**LITERACY RATE** not available

**RELIGIONS** Orthodox, Muslim, Roman Catholic

**ETHNIC GROUPS** Montenegrin 43 %, Serbian 32 %, Bosnian 8 %, Albanian 5 %, other (Muslims, Croats, Roma) 12 %

**CURRENCY** Euro

**ECONOMY** not available

**GNI PER CAPITA** US$ 5,180

**CLIMATE** Temperate, cold winters and warm summers inland, cooler and more temperate along the coast

**HIGHEST POINT** Bobotov Kuk 2,522 m (8,274 ft)

**MAP REFERENCE** Page 296

At its southwestern edge, Montenegro has a notable strip of coastline on the Adriatic Sea. To the west, the north, and the south, it borders on Croatia, Bosnia and Herzegovina, Serbia, the Kosovo, and Albania. The name of Montenegro (or Crna Gora), "Black Mountain," has been in use since the fifteenth century, when the House of Crnojevic ruled the principality of Zeta. In 1516, the secular prince of Zeta abdicated in favor of Archbishop Vasilje, and from the sixteenth to nineteenth centuries, Montenegro maintained its character as a theocracy as well as its independence from the Ottoman Empire. After it had been transformed into a secular principality in 1852 (the ruling bishop had married and left the priesthood), some of the Montenegrins voted to become a part of the Kingdom of Serbs, Croats, and Slovenes after World War I. This step was fervently opposed by others, who fought against this union until the rebellion was finally suppressed in 1924. Later, after the Second World War, during which the area was occupied first by the Italians and then by the Germans, it became a constituent republic of the reconstructed Yugoslavia. When Yugoslavia was racked by civil wars after Tito's death in 1980 and the four other Yugoslav republics of Slovenia, Croatia, Bosnia and Herzegovina, as well as Macedonia declared their independence in the course of the last decade of the twentieth century, Montenegro remained loosely associated with Serbia, initially as the Federal Republic of Yugoslavia, later called the Republic of Serbia and Montenegro. Only three years after this federation was formed, a referendum was held on May 21, 2006, and a little more than 55% of those who voted were in favor of separation from Serbia. The independence of the country was declared on June 3, 2006. Montenegro became a member of the United Nations on June 28, 2006, and is currently in the process of applying for acceptance into other organizations such as NATO, the European Union, the World Trade Organization, the World Bank, and the European Bank for Reconstruction and Development.

Apart from its coastline and a narrow plain that extends along it, only about 4 kilometers (2.5 miles) wide, Montenegro consists largely of rugged limestone mountains and high plateaus. In fact, much of the country is covered by the bare limestone ridges of the Dinaric Alps, with an average elevation of about 1,000 meters (3,281 feet) above sea level, which run from Slovenia south into Albania.

The key industries of the country—aluminum and steel production, coal mining, forestry, and the generation of electricity—have been mostly privatized, and its economy has been stabilized. Montenegro experienced one of the highest hyperinflations in history—3 million percent in January 1994—and had become one of the poorest countries in Europe, with the majority of its people living below the poverty line. However, the first steps toward severing ties with Serbia in 1997 and an emphasis on attracting direct foreign investment have helped instigate economic growth.

# Hungary

## Fact File

**OFFICIAL NAME** Republic of Hungary

**FORM OF GOVERNMENT** Republic with single legislative body (National Assembly)

**CAPITAL** Budapest

**AREA** 93,030 sq km (35,919 sq miles)

**TIME ZONE** GMT + 1 hour

**POPULATION** 9,931,000

**PROJECTED POPULATION 2015** 9,783,000

**POPULATION DENSITY** 106.8 per sq km (276.5 per sq mile)

**LIFE EXPECTANCY** 73.2

**INFANT MORTALITY (PER 1,000)** 8

**OFFICIAL LANGUAGE** Hungarian

**OTHER LANGUAGES** Romany, German, Croatian, Slovakian, Romanian

**LITERACY RATE** 99.4 %

**RELIGIONS** Roman Catholic 51.9 %, Calvinist 15.9 %, Lutheran 3.0 %, other 14.7 %, unaffiliated 14.5 %

**ETHNIC GROUPS** Hungarian 92.2 %, Roma 1.9 %, other 5.9 %

**CURRENCY** Forint

**ECONOMY** Services 65.7 %, industry 31.5 %, agriculture 2.8 %

**GNI PER CAPITA** US$ 11,570

**CLIMATE** Temperate; cold, wet winters and warm summers

**HIGHEST POINT** Mt Kékes 1,014 m (3,327 ft)

**MAP REFERENCE** Pages 289, 294, 296

A landlocked Central European country, Hungary shares borders with Serbia to the south, Croatia and Slovenia to the southwest, Austria to the west, Slovakia to the north, Ukraine to the northeast and Romania to the southeast. Modern Hungary had its beginnings in the eighth century AD, when the area was settled by the Magyars, nomadic tribes from the central Volga. Their kingdom thrived and expanded. In the sixteenth century the Turks seized the central part of Hungary and the northern and western sections of the country accepted Austrian Habsburg

rule rather than submit to Turkish domination. In 1699 the Turks were driven out and the entire country came under Habsburg rule. Continuing unrest and the defeat of Austria by the Prussians in 1866 culminated in the establishment of Austria-Hungary as a dual monarchy in 1867. The defeat of Austria-Hungary in 1918 was followed by the establishment of the Hungarian nation, but with two-thirds of its former territory and almost sixty percent of its former population ceded to surrounding states. In the Second World War Hungary sided with Germany against the Soviet Union and was finally occupied by Soviet forces as they pushed southward in 1945. In 1948 communists again seized control with Soviet support, beginning 42 years of Soviet domination. A popular anti-communist uprising in 1956 was brutally suppressed by the Soviet Union. As the Soviet Union began to collapse a new constitution in 1989 set the scene for Hungary's first multi-party elections in 1990.

Hungary is drained by two southward-flowing rivers, the Danube and the Tisza. These two rivers traverse the Great Hungarian Plain, which occupies most of the eastern part of the country and more than half the total land area. West of the Danube a line of hills and mountains runs northeast from Lake Balaton, which covers an area of 370 sq km (140 sq miles), to the Slovakian border, where it joins the Carpathian Mountains. Northwest of these hills the Little Hungarian Plain extends to the westward-flowing Danube, which here separates Hungary from Slovakia. While most of the low-lying areas have long been cleared of trees, some of the forested areas still survive in the hills and mountains.

Most of the two plains areas are fertile agricultural country, although there are dry sandy expanses, as well as marshlands that are home to a rich variety of waterbirds. More than seventy percent of Hungary's agricultural land is devoted to crops, the most important of which are maize, wheat, sugar beet, and sunflowers. Of the rest, more than four-fifths are meadows and pasturelands and the rest are orchards and vineyards. Pigs and poultry are the most extensively farmed livestock.

Except for natural gas, bauxite, and lignite—a low quality coal that provides much of the country's energy—Hungary is poorly endowed with mineral resources. It imports most of the raw materials for its now largely privatized industries, among which iron and steel production and the manufacture of fertilizers, pharmaceuticals, and cement are prominent. Most of these industries are located in the north and are centered mainly around the capital, Budapest, and Miskolc, which is the second-largest city and is situated in the far northeast. Aluminum, using local bauxite, is manufactured north of Lake Balaton.

Hungarians enjoy a reasonable standard of living by the standards of former communist countries, though it still compares unfavorably with that in most Western countries. Pollution of air, soil, and water is a major problem and almost half the population lives in seriously affected areas.

## Romania

## Albania

### Fact File

**OFFICIAL NAME** Republic of Albania

**FORM OF GOVERNMENT** Republic with single legislative body (National Assembly)

**CAPITAL** Tiranë

**AREA** 28,748 sq km (11,100 sq miles)

**TIME ZONE** GMT + 1 hour

**POPULATION** 3,620,000

**PROJECTED POPULATION 2015** 3,346,000

**POPULATION DENSITY** 125.9 per sq km (326.1 per sq mile)

**LIFE EXPECTANCY** 77.8

**INFANT MORTALITY (PER 1,000)** 19.3

**OFFICIAL LANGUAGE** Albanian

**OTHER LANGUAGES** Greek, Macedonian

**LITERACY RATE** 98.7 %

**RELIGIONS** Muslim 70 %, Albanian Orthodox 20 %, Roman Catholic 10 %

**ETHNIC GROUPS** Albanian 95 %, Greek 3 %, other 2 %

**CURRENCY** Lek

*The fourteenth-century citadel of Gjirokastër in Albania (above).*

**ECONOMY** Services 58.7 %, agriculture 21.2 %, industry 20.1 %

**GNI PER CAPITA** US$ 3,290

**CLIMATE** Mild temperate with cold, wet winters and warm, dry summers; colder in mountains

**HIGHEST POINT** Maja e Korabit 2,753 m (9,032 ft)

**MAP REFERENCE** Pages 296–97

Albania shares borders with Greece to the southeast and Macedonia to the east. Serbia, the Kosovo, and Montenegro wrap around the northern part of the country. At its western edge it has a coastline 362 km (225 miles) long along the Adriatic Sea. For 500 years until 1912, when it became independent, Albania was part of the Ottoman Empire, and a large majority of the population is Muslim. In 1912 it declared its independence and in 1939 Albania was invaded by Italy. After the Second World War the country came into the Soviet sphere of influence. From 1946 until 1992 Albania was part of the Soviet bloc, although it often adopted policies independent of, and sometimes at odds with, the Moscow line. When the European communist system unraveled in the early 1990s Albania, in 1992, was the last country in Europe to abandon a communist regime.

Except for a narrow strip of plains along its coastline, Albania is hilly and mountainous. Most Albanian people eke out an existence through farming on the plains, which contain the only cultivable land. Even here, much of the country is marshy and difficult to access. Corn, wheat, barley, and fruits are among the main crops. Little is exported because transport methods are primitive. In most areas people use horse- or mule-drawn vehicles. Mountains cover seven-tenths of the country. In the north are the Albanian Alps, and there are highlands in the center and south. Numerous rivers, notably the Drin in the north, and the Vijose in the south, flow to the coast from the highlands. Albania has significant reserves of natural resources such as petroleum, iron, and other mineral ores, plus natural gas, but most remain undeveloped.

The mountainous landscape makes land access difficult, and marshes restrict access to much of the coast. Rail links are few and there are no railway lines to neighboring countries. This has contributed to Albania's relative cultural and linguistic distinctness. Despite its conversion to free market ideals, Albania has failed to emerge from the cycle of poverty, continuing food shortages, and violence, fed to a large extent by the flood of refugees from the troubles in former Yugoslavia.

### Fact File

**OFFICIAL NAME** Romania

**FORM OF GOVERNMENT** Republic with two legislative bodies (Senate and House of Deputies)

**CAPITAL** Bucharest

**AREA** 237,500 sq km (91,699 sq miles)

**TIME ZONE** GMT + 2 hours

**POPULATION** 22,247,000

**PROJECTED POPULATION 2015** 20,598,000

**POPULATION DENSITY** 93.7 per sq km (242.6 per sq mile)

**LIFE EXPECTANCY** 72.2

**INFANT MORTALITY (PER 1,000)** 23.7

**OFFICIAL LANGUAGE** Romanian

**OTHER LANGUAGES** Hungarian, German, Romany

**LITERACY RATE** 97.3 %

**RELIGIONS** Orthodox 86.8 %, Protestant 7.5 %, Roman Catholic 4.7 %, other 1.0 %

**ETHNIC GROUPS** Romanian 89.5 %, Hungarian 6.6 %, Roma 2.5 %, other 1.4 %

**CURRENCY** Leu

**ECONOMY** Services 56.5 %, industry 35.6 %, agriculture 7.9 %

**GNI PER CAPITA** US$ 6,150

**CLIMATE** Temperate; cold winters and warm, wet summers; cooler in Carpathian Mountains

**HIGHEST POINT** Moldoveanu 2,544 m (8,346 ft)

**MAP REFERENCE** Page 296

Except for its Black Sea coast, Romania is landlocked—by Ukraine to the north, Moldova to the northeast, Hungary to the west, Serbia to the southwest, and Bulgaria to the south. From the sixth century AD the country was often invaded. From the ninth to the eleventh centuries Magyars occupied part of Transylvania and between the fourteenth and sixteenth centuries Walachia, Moldova, and Transylvania formed part of the Ottoman Empire. At the end of the First World War, Bessarabia—most of present-day Moldova—Transylvania and Bukovina were restored to Romania. Much of this land was lost during the Second World War when Romania, which sided with Nazi Germany, came under Soviet control.

During Nicolai Ceausescu's oppressive regime, beginning in 1967, Romania distanced itself from the Soviets. In 1989 a popular uprising saw Ceausescu arrested and executed. Romania is now ruled by an elected parliament headed by a president. In 2007, it became a member of the EU.

The Carpathian Mountains curve through the center of the country, dividing the timbered uplands of Transylvania from the Danube Plain. The southern part of the range, the Transylvanian Alps, contains the highest peaks and the most rugged scenery. The fertile eastern plain is crossed by many tributaries of the Danube. To the east, around the Danube Delta, the land is marshy and dotted with numerous lakes and lagoons.

There has been a shift towards heavy industries since the 1970s but agriculture is still economically important. Maize, wheat, vegetables, and grapes for wine are the main crops and sheep and pigs the main livestock. Romania is rich in coal, natural gas, iron ore, and petroleum. Most of the raw materials for the country's industries are imported. Prominent industries include chemical and metal processing and machine manufacturing. Lumbering has depleted much of the country's forest and industry has caused widespread pollution. Moves to a market economy have been slow and Romania's standard of living remains relatively low.

# Bulgaria

## Fact File

**OFFICIAL NAME** Republic of Bulgaria

**FORM OF GOVERNMENT** Republic with single legislative body (National Assembly)

**CAPITAL** Sofia

**AREA** 110,910 sq km (42,822 sq miles)

**TIME ZONE** GMT + 2 hours

**POPULATION** 7,263,000

**PROJECTED POPULATION 2015** 7,180,000

**POPULATION DENSITY** 65.5 per sq km (169.6 per sq mile)

**LIFE EXPECTANCY** 72.8

**INFANT MORTALITY (PER 1,000)** 18.5

**OFFICIAL LANGUAGE** Bulgarian

**OTHER LANGUAGES** Turkish, Romany

**LITERACY RATE** 98.2 %

**RELIGIONS** Bulgarian Orthodox 82.6 %, Muslim 12.2 %, other Christian 1.2 %, other 4.0 %

**ETHNIC GROUPS** Bulgarian 83.9 %, Turkish 9.4 %, Roma 4.7 %, other 2.0 %

**CURRENCY** Lev

**ECONOMY** Services 61.4 %, industry 32.3 %, agriculture 6.3 %

**GNI PER CAPITA** US$ 4,590

**CLIMATE** Temperate, with cold, wet winters and hot, dry summers

**HIGHEST POINT** Mt Musala 2,925 m (9,596 ft)

**MAP REFERENCE** Pages 296–97

Bulgaria is situated on the east of the Balkan Peninsula with a coastline along the Black Sea. To the west it shares borders with Serbia as well as Macedonia. Turkey lies to its southeast, and Greece to its southwest. In the north the River Danube forms most of the border between Bulgaria and Romania.

Modern Bulgarians are descendants of the Bulgars, who arrived from north of the Danube in the late seventh century AD and established dominance over the Slavic races that had settled the area over the previous two centuries. The Christian religion, which is still dominant in the country, was established in the ninth century. A century of Byzantine domination in the eleventh and twelfth centuries was followed by a period of independence. In 1396 Turkish armies invaded and Bulgaria was then dominated for five centuries by the Turks until Russian intervention ended Ottoman rule in 1878. Full independence, however, did not come until 1908, when Prince Ferdinand of Saxe-Coburg, the elected ruler of Bulgaria, assumed the title of Tsar.

Bulgaria sided with the losing sides in both the First and Second World Wars, and as a result its boundaries changed several times as territories were ceded to it or confiscated. Its present boundaries were established by a 1947 treaty. From then until the fall of the Soviet Union in the early 1990s, Bulgaria remained one of the most loyal of Soviet satellites. A new constitution came into force in 1991, and in the following year the first free elections were held. In 2004, the country joined NATO, and in 2007 it became a member of the EU.

The country's landscape is defined by three ranges of mountains and two extensive expanses of lowland. The Danube Valley is the country's richest agricultural area, producing significant yields of wheat, maize, and other cereal crops. The Balkan Mountains, running east-west across much of central Bulgaria, reach heights of up to 2,000 m (6,500 ft). They divide the Danube Valley from the southern lowlands, where tobacco and grapes are among the principal crops in the fertile valleys around the Maritsa River. The vineyards in this region produce some of southern Europe's finest wines. In the southwest the Rhodopi Massif, which contains the country's loftiest peak, forms the mountainous border with Greece.

More than six million tourists, attracted to its Black Sea coastline, come to Bulgaria each year and contribute significantly to its economy. Most of the country's export earnings stem from its machinery and other manufacturing industries. While there have been tentative moves towards the establishment of a free market economy, high inflation, foreign debt, and worker unrest have contributed to a far from robust short-term economic outlook.

*The Transylvanian Alps in Romania (above left). Alexander Nevsky Cathedral in Sofia, Bulgaria (below left). The city of Athens, the capital of Greece (right page).*

# Greece

## Fact File

**OFFICIAL NAME** Hellenic Republic

**FORM OF GOVERNMENT** Republic with single legislative body (Chamber of Deputies)

**CAPITAL** Athens

**AREA** 131,940 sq km (50,942 sq miles)

**TIME ZONE** GMT + 2 hours

**POPULATION** 10,723,000

**PROJECTED POPULATION 2015** 11,273,000

**POPULATION DENSITY** 81.3 per sq km (210.5 per sq mile)

**LIFE EXPECTANCY** 79.5

**INFANT MORTALITY (PER 1,000)** 5.3

**OFFICIAL LANGUAGE** Greek

**OTHER LANGUAGES** Albanian, Macedonian, Turkish, Romanian

**LITERACY RATE** 96 %

**RELIGIONS** Greek Orthodox 98 %, Muslim 1.3 %, other 0.7 %

**ETHNIC GROUPS** Greek 98 %, other 2 %

**CURRENCY** Euro

**ECONOMY** Services 71.6 %, industry 24.8 %, agriculture 3.6 %

**GNI PER CAPITA** US$ 29,630

**CLIMATE** Temperate, with mild, wet winters and hot, dry summers

**HIGHEST POINT** Mt Olympus 2,917 m (9,570 ft)

**MAP REFERENCE** Page 297

Mainland Greece occupies the southernmost part of the Balkan Peninsula. The western shores of this peninsula are washed by the Ionian Sea, while on the east the Aegean Sea lies between it and Turkey. In the north, Greece shares borders with Albania, and to the northeast with Macedonia and Bulgaria. In its far northeast corner there is a short border with Turkey. Dotted all over the Aegean Sea and also in the Ionian Sea are more than 1,500 Greek islands, only about ten percent of which are inhabited. South of the mainland, in the Mediterranean Sea, is the large island of Crete.

It was in Crete that the seeds of Greek civilization were sown. For more than 2,000 years, from about 3500 BC, the Minoan civilization grew and flourished here. In about the sixteenth century BC it spread to Mycenae, in the Peloponnese Peninsula. In the fifth century BC Athens emerged as the center of Greek culture. It developed rich traditions in literature, theater, philosophy and politics which established the values on which most modern Western civilizations are based. In the fourth century BC, under Alexander the Great, a vast Greek Empire spread across Asia as far as India and southward as far as Alexandria in Egypt. Subsumed into the Roman Empire by the beginning of the second century BC, Greece eventually came under Byzantine rule, where it remained until the fall of Constantinople in AD 1204. After a quick succession of foreign rulers, the Ottoman Turks conquered Greece towards the end of the fourteenth century. Modern Greece dates back to 1832, when the country emerged from almost 400 years of Turkish domination and established a monarchy.

In 1941 Greece was overrun, in the face of fierce resistance, by German and Italian troops. It was liberated during 1944 by British and Greek forces, but almost immediately the country was plunged into civil war as monarchists and communists fought for supremacy. This destructive and debilitating struggle finally ended in 1949 with a victory by the monarchists. However, a military coup in 1967 resulted in the monarchy being expelled and a republic being established under an oppressive dictatorship. This regime fell in 1974 after an abortive attempt to invade Cyprus. In 1975, civilian government was restored and Greece became a democratic republic with a president elected for a five-year term, and a single-chamber parliament headed by a prime minister elected every four years. Its political system soon proved stable enough that Greece was admitted as the tenth member of the EC in 1981 and adopted the Euro in 2001.

Most of mainland Greece is mountainous, being dominated by the Pindos Mountains, an extension of the Dinaric Alps that extend southeastward throughout the peninsula from the Albanian border. The mountains that form Crete and the island of Rhodes, near the southwestern tip of Turkey, were once part of the same range. In the northeast the Rhodope Mountains form a natural border with Bulgaria. The only extensive low-lying areas are the northern plain, which extends from the Maritsa River on the Turkish border across the northern Aegean region to the Greek province of Macedonia, and the plain of Thessaly in the central eastern mainland. Much of the Greek landscape, including that of many of the islands, is sparsely vegetated and has a rugged, rocky grandeur that, together with its warm climate, its beaches, and its rich historic heritage, attracts more than 12 million foreign visitors every year.

Despite its generally poor soils, Greece is heavily dependent on agriculture, which still employs about one-quarter of the workforce, largely on relatively small and inefficient farms. Wheat, olives, tobacco, and citrus and other fruits are among the main crops, and olives, particularly, are a major export item. Sheep and pigs are the principal livestock and are widely raised on the mainland and on Crete. Greece is almost self-sufficient in food production.

Not well endowed with mineral resources, Greece needs to import most of the raw materials for its industries, the majority of which are centered on Athens, though the area around Salonica in the northeast is also heavily industrialized. Food processing based on local agricultural production is important, as are textile manufacture and chemical processing. The tourist industry has helped the development of many local small-scale enterprises in such areas as ceramics, crafts, and textiles.

## Eastern Europe

Czech Republic · · · · · 266
Slovakia · · · · · · · · · 267
Poland · · · · · · · · · · 267
Belarus · · · · · · · · · 268
Ukraine · · · · · · · · · 269
Moldova · · · · · · · · · 270
Russian Federation · · · 271

## Czech Republic

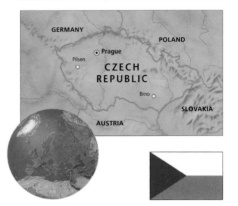

### Fact File

OFFICIAL NAME Czech Republic

FORM OF GOVERNMENT Republic with two legislative bodies (Senate and Chamber of Deputies)

CAPITAL Prague

AREA 78,866 sq km (30,450 sq miles)

TIME ZONE GMT + 1 hour

POPULATION 10,221,000

PROJECTED POPULATION 2015 10,129,000

POPULATION DENSITY 129.6 per sq km (335.7 per sq mile)

LIFE EXPECTANCY 76.6

INFANT MORTALITY (PER 1,000) 3.8

OFFICIAL LANGUAGE Czech

OTHER LANGUAGES Slovak, German, Polish

LITERACY RATE 99 %

RELIGIONS Roman Catholic 26.8 %, Protestant 2.1 %, other 3.3 %, unspecified 8.8 %, unaffiliated 59.0 %

ETHNIC GROUPS Czech 90.4 %, Moravian 3.7 %, Slovak 1.9 %, other 4.0 %

CURRENCY Koruna

ECONOMY Services 58.8 %, industry 38.4 %, agriculture 2.8 %

GNI PER CAPITA US$ 14,450

CLIMATE Temperate, with cold winters and mild, wet summers

HIGHEST POINT Mt Snezka 1,602 m (5,256 ft)

MAP REFERENCE Pages 288–89

*The Bohemian city of Český Krumlov in the Czech Republic (right). The city of Trenčín in Slovakia (right page top).*

A landlocked country in Central Europe, until 1993 the Czech Republic was linked to Slovakia, its neighbor to the southeast, from which it is separated by the Carpathian Mountains. The Czech Republic consists mainly of the ancient provinces of Bohemia in the west and Moravia in the east as well as part of the province of Silesia, but most of it now forms a portion of Poland.

Czechoslovakia came into existence in 1918 with the collapse of the Austro-Hungarian Empire at the close of the First World War. The Czechs and the Slovaks had been under one rule since 1471, and since 1526 had been under Austrian domination. Germany occupied Czech territory in 1939, establishing a protectorate of Bohemia-Moravia and setting up a separate state in Slovakia. In 1948 the communists came to power and the country, once again united, came under Soviet influence. Nationalist fervor was never far below the surface and in 1968 caused a movement for democracy. The "Prague Spring," led by Alexander Dubcek, was put down by an invasion of Soviet forces. In 1989 a popular movement led to a transition to a democratic state. Tensions between Czechs and the minority Slovaks led to a peaceful separation of the two states on 1 January 1993.

Bohemia consists largely of gentle hills and plateaus. Low ranges of mountains surround the province to the north, west, and south and the central plateau is traversed by the Elbe and Vltava Rivers, which merge and flow into Germany. Most of the country's agriculture is centered on this river system and much of its produce, including wheat, barley, and potatoes, is transported along these waterways. Bohemia and Moravia are separated by a plateau known as the Moravian Heights. While Moravia is hillier than Bohemia, the center of the province, around Brno, consists of an extensive low plain. Winters are colder and rainfall is heavier in Moravia than in Bohemia. Although not richly endowed with natural resources, reserves of black coal and iron ore have aided the development of iron and steelmaking as the country's major industries. Other important industries include clothing and car manufacture. Bohemian glass is famous worldwide. Industrial production, however, has fallen in the 1990s as the country moves toward a free market economy. Tourism has made up for some of this fall-off.

### Czech conflict

The country formerly known as Czechoslovakia was at the center of successive conflicts in the twentieth century. It contains a volatile mixture of ethnic and political differences, and in the past fell victim to German and Soviet totalitarian regimes. Hitler used the disaffection of the German minority in the Sudetenland as an excuse for invading Czechoslovakia in 1938. An insecure period of democracy after 1945 (marred by the expulsion of the still-resident German population) was followed by a communist takeover under Soviet auspices in 1948. In 1968 an effort to democratize the system led by Alexander Dubcek was crushed by Soviet tanks. Along with other parts of Eastern Europe it won independence from communist control in 1989, and since 2004 has been a member of the EU—but these developments have been accompanied by the rise of ethnic separatism, and claims by former German citizens for restitution of property seized at the time of their expulsion after the Second World War. On 1 January 1993 the Czechs separated from the Slovaks in the "velvet divorce", and two republics—the Czech "western" and the Slovak "eastern"—came into existence. Under the presidency of the internationally renowned playwright Vaclav Havel (1993–2003), a wholesale dismantling of state economic controls and structures then took place. However, the government which undertook these extensive reforms collapsed amid scandal and economic chaos at the end of 1997.

# Slovakia

## Fact File

**OFFICIAL NAME** Slovak Republic

**FORM OF GOVERNMENT** Republic with single legislative body (National Parliament)

**CAPITAL** Bratislava

**AREA** 48,845 sq km (18,859 sq miles)

**TIME ZONE** GMT + 1 hour

**POPULATION** 5,455,000

**PROJECTED POPULATION 2015** 5,392,000

**POPULATION DENSITY** 111.7 per sq km (289.3 per sq mile)

**LIFE EXPECTANCY** 75.2

**INFANT MORTALITY (PER 1,000)** 7

**OFFICIAL LANGUAGE** Slovak

**OTHER LANGUAGES** Hungarian, Czech

**LITERACY RATE** 99.6 %

**RELIGIONS** Roman Catholic 68.9 %, Protestant 10.8 %, Greek Catholic 4.1 %, other 3.2 %, none 13.0 %

**ETHNIC GROUPS** Slovak 85.8 %, Hungarian 9.7 %, Roma 1.7 %, Ruthenian/Ukrainian 1.0 %, other 1.8 %

**CURRENCY** Koruna

**ECONOMY** Services 63.9 %, industry 33.5 %, agriculture 2.6 %

**GNI PER CAPITA** US$ 11,730

**CLIMATE** Temperate, with cold winters and warm, wet summers

**HIGHEST POINT** Gerlachovka 2,655 m (8,711 ft)

**MAP REFERENCE** Page 289

This small Central European country is bordered by Poland to the north, the Czech Republic to the northwest, Austria to the west, Hungary to the south, and Ukraine to the east. It is the smaller, less populous, and less industrially developed part of the former state of Czechoslovakia, which split peacefully in 1993 to form the two separate nations of Slovakia and the Czech Republic.

Ethnically distinct from their former compatriots, the Slovaks had lived for ten centuries under continuous Hungarian domination when in 1918 they merged with the Czechs to form a new, independent nation. At the beginning of the Second World War, Czechoslovakia was invaded by Germany and the Germans installed a pro-Fascist government in Slovakia. Soviet troops restored the pre-war status quo in 1945 and communists seized power in 1948, making the country effectively a Soviet satellite. In 1968 Soviet forces invaded to put down an attempt to establish democracy under the leadership of Czechoslovakia's First Secretary, Alexander Dubcek, a Slovak. Twenty-one years later a revival of nationalism and a weakened Soviet Union led to a successful declaration of independence and the establishment of democratic government. Since its separation from the Czech Republic, Slovakia has been governed by a single-chamber parliament whose 150 members, or deputies, are elected for a four-year term.

Except for lowland areas in the south and southeast, most of the country is ruggedly mountainous, with extensive forests and tracts of pastureland. In the north of the country the high Carpathian Mountains extend along the Polish border, and further south the Tatra Mountains, an offshoot of the Carpathians and the Slovakian Ore Mountains, run parallel across the center of the country. Ski resorts in the Tatra Mountains attract large numbers of tourists. The Danube, which forms part of the border with Hungary, flows through an extensive fertile plain. Most of Slovakia's agriculture, which employs not quite six percent of the workforce, is centered here and in the lowland area further to the east. Wheat and potatoes are the principal crops, and sheep, cattle, and pigs are widely raised.

Slovakia is poorly endowed with mineral resources. There are significant deposits of lignite, but most of it is poor in quality. Industries, which employ about one in three workers, are centered mainly around the cities of Bratislava in the southwest and Kosice in the southeast. Significant industries are iron and steelmaking, and car and clothing manufacture. The move from a centrally controlled to a privatized market economy has proceeded fitfully, and the country has suffered economically from the loss of subsidies that it used to receive from the Czech Republic.

# Poland

## Fact File

**OFFICIAL NAME** Republic of Poland

**FORM OF GOVERNMENT** Republic with two legislative bodies (Senate and Parliament or Sejm)

**CAPITAL** Warsaw

**AREA** 312,685 sq km (120,727 sq miles)

**TIME ZONE** GMT + 1 hour

**POPULATION** 38,501,000

**PROJECTED POPULATION 2015** 37,580,000

**POPULATION DENSITY** 123.1 per sq km (318.9 per sq mile)

**LIFE EXPECTANCY** 75.4

**INFANT MORTALITY (PER 1,000)** 6.9

**OFFICIAL LANGUAGE** Polish

**LITERACY RATE** 99.8 %

**RELIGIONS** Catholic 89.8 %, Eastern Orthodox 1.3 %, other 0.6 %, unspecified 8.3 %

**ETHNIC GROUPS** Polish 96.7 %, German 0.4 %, Belarusian 0.1 %, Ukrainian 0.1 %, other 2.7 %

**CURRENCY** Zloty

**ECONOMY** Services 64.4 %, industry 31.6 %, agriculture 4 %

**GNI PER CAPITA** US$ 9,840

**CLIMATE** Temperate, with cold winters and warm, wet summers

**HIGHEST POINT** Rysy 2,499 m (8,199 ft)

**MAP REFERENCE** Page 289

Situated in northern Central Europe, Poland has a northern coastline on the Baltic Sea and shares land borders with seven countries. To the west the Oder River forms part of the border with Germany, while to the southwest the Sudeten Mountains separate it from the Czech Republic. The Carpathian Mountains form a natural boundary with Slovakia in the south. Ukraine and Belarus lie to the east, Lithuania is to the northeast, and a part of the Russian Federation is adjacent to Poland's northern coastline.

In the seventh and eighth centuries AD, Slavic peoples originally from the south of Europe—known as Polanie, or plain-dwellers—occupied most of Poland. In the tenth century their king was converted to Christianity, beginning a strong tradition of Catholicism that has survived to the present, despite attempts by post-war communist governments to suppress it. During the course of the next two centuries, invaders from Prussia divided up the country, which was reunited in the fourteenth century.

Poland retained its independence and at times even extended its power during the following two centuries, but again came under Prussian and Austrian control in the late eighteenth century. The nation regained its independence in 1918 with the defeat of Austria and Germany in the First World War. Early in the Second World War, Poland was attacked and overrun by Germany and then Russia, which divided the country between them until June 1941, when the Germans took full control. After the war Poland's borders shifted to the west, as portions of what was formerly Germany was ceded to Poland, and as the Soviets were granted control of substantial territories in the east. Under these arrangements Poland suffered a net loss of both territory and population. From that point on until 1989 Poland was effectively a vassal state of its much larger neighbor, the Soviet Union.

Growing civil unrest during the 1980s culminated in a series of strikes in a range of industries, organized by the trade union Solidarity. In 1989 the besieged government capitulated and allowed Solidarity to contest the government elections, which Solidarity won decisively. The first entirely free elections were held in 1991 and Lech Walesa, the leader of Solidarity, became Poland's first president. It is now a democratic republic with a directly elected president and a multi-party system. In 2004 it became a member of the EU.

Except for the mountain ranges in the south and southwest, most of Poland is low-lying, forming part of the North European Plain. The landscape is drained by numerous rivers, the most significant of which is the Vistula, which originates in the Carpathian Mountains and flows through the center of the country, through Warsaw, and on to the Baltic Sea near the industrial city of Gdansk. Most of this plain is fertile land covered with rich loess soil which supports a range of cereal and vegetable crops, in which Poland is almost self-sufficient, and livestock, the most important of which are cattle and pigs. In the northeast the country is more undulating, and much of northern Poland is dotted with extensive lakes. Towards the Baltic coast a range of hills known as the Baltic Heights slope down to a sandy coastal plain.

Agriculture, which once employed more than half of Poland's workforce, still accounts for just over 16 percent of it. The post-war years saw a rapid expansion of heavy industries, which now include shipbuilding, based in Gdansk, and steel and cement manufacture based around the mining centers in the south. Many industrial activities are associated with Poland's rich coal reserves, and coal is used to generate more than half the country's electricity. Reliance on this form of fuel has resulted in serious air pollution and acid rain. Other mineral resources include natural gas, iron ore, and salt, on which important chemical industries are based.

Poland has been more successful than many former communist states in converting to a privatized economy. While many Poles have prospered from a growing number of entrepreneurial opportunities, however, others have seen their incomes substantially lowered. Unemployment remains comparatively high (14.9 percent in 2007).

*The rooftops of Gdansk in northern Poland, a major port and birthplace of the trade union Solidarity (below). An oil well in a village in Belarus (right page top). Yalta and the crowded promenade on the Black Sea, Ukraine (right page bottom).*

# Belarus

## Fact File

| | |
|---|---|
| OFFICIAL NAME | Republic of Belarus |
| FORM OF GOVERNMENT | Republic with single legislative body (Supreme Soviet) |
| CAPITAL | Minsk |
| AREA | 207,600 sq km (80,154 sq miles) |
| TIME ZONE | GMT + 2 hours |
| POPULATION | 9,686,000 |
| PROJECTED POPULATION 2015 | 9,260,000 |
| POPULATION DENSITY | 46.7 per sq km (120.8 per sq mile) |
| LIFE EXPECTANCY | 70.3 |
| INFANT MORTALITY (PER 1,000) | 6.5 |
| OFFICIAL LANGUAGE | Belarusian |
| OTHER LANGUAGES | Russian, languages of the minorities |
| LITERACY RATE | 99.6 % |
| RELIGIONS | Eastern Orthodox 80 %, other (including Roman Catholic and small Muslim and Jewish communities) 20 % |
| ETHNIC GROUPS | Belarusian 81.2 %, Russian 11.4 %, Polish 3.9 %, Ukrainian 2.4 %, other 1.1 % |
| CURRENCY | Belarusian ruble |
| ECONOMY | Services 50.6 %, industry 40.6 %, agriculture 8.8 % |
| GNI PER CAPITA | US$ 4,220 |
| CLIMATE | Temperate, with cold winters and mild, wet summers |
| HIGHEST POINT | Mt Dzyarzhynskaya 346 m (1,135 ft) |
| MAP REFERENCE | Pages 287, 299, 300 |

Until 1991, when it declared its independence of the disintegrating Soviet Union, Belarus was known as the Byelorussian (which means "White Russian") Soviet Socialist Republic. Throughout its extensive and troubled history, Belarus has been dominated, invaded, and sometimes devastated by a succession of foreign powers. Initally settled by Slavic tribes in the sixth century AD, the country came under the control of Kiev in the ninth century. Three centuries later it was conquered by invading armies from neighboring Lithuania and in the sixteenth century, with the merging of Lithuania and Poland, Polish

influences were also dominant. During the course of the eighteenth century the region came under Russian control and even today Belarus is economically dependent on its huge and powerful eastern neighbor.

Belarus was ravaged in the First and Second World Wars. The German invasion of 1941 saw the deaths of 1.3 million people and the virtual annihilation of the country's Jewish population. Many of Belarus's buildings were reduced to rubble and its capital, Minsk, was razed. Further devastation, in the form of nuclear contamination, occurred in 1986 after the Chernobyl disaster in Ukraine, its neighbor to the south. Much of the farming land in the southern part of Belarus remains contaminated by fallout from the accident and is unsafe for cultivation.

The country is generally low-lying, the landscape varying from sandy hills in the north to swampy areas in the south, many of which have been drained and their rich soils cultivated. There are about 11,000 lakes and the country is traversed by numerous rivers, which complement the extensive road and railway networks as a major means of transportation. Forests and woodland cover about thirty percent of the country and almost half the land area is devoted to agriculture, the main crops being barley, rye, potatoes, sugar beet, and flax. There are large numbers of livestock, and dairy and pig farming are important industries.

Belarus is relatively poor in natural resources although it has significant reserves of peat and rock salt and small reserves of coal. It is deeply in debt to the Russian Federation and relies on Russia for the electricity needed to power its industries, which include vast petrochemical plants and truck manufacturing.

Strikes and industrial and political unrest have been a significant feature of Belarusian life during its short period as an independent nation, sometimes aggravated by the inability of the government to pay many of its workers. A controversial treaty signed with Russia in 1996 resulted in a substantial merging of aspects of the economy with that of its large neighbor. This was seen by many as a sign of a progressive whittling away of the country's independence.

# Ukraine

## Fact File

**OFFICIAL NAME** Ukraine

**FORM OF GOVERNMENT** Republic with single legislative body (Supreme Council)

**CAPITAL** Kiev

**AREA** 603,700 sq km (233,089 sq miles)

**TIME ZONE** GMT + 2 hours

**POPULATION** 45,994,000

**PROJECTED POPULATION 2015** 43,428,000

**POPULATION DENSITY** 76.2 per sq km (197.3 per sq mile)

**LIFE EXPECTANCY** 68.1

**INFANT MORTALITY (PER 1,000)** 9.2

**OFFICIAL LANGUAGE** Ukrainian

**OTHER LANGUAGES** Russian, Romanian, Hungarian, Polish

**LITERACY RATE** 99.4 %

**RELIGIONS** Orthodox 44 %, Ukrainian Catholic 6 %, other (including Protestants, Jews and Muslims) 12 %, none 38 %

**ETHNIC GROUPS** Ukrainian 77.8 %, Russian 17.3 %, other 4.9 %

**CURRENCY** Hryvna

**ECONOMY** Services 58.6 %, Industry 32.3 %, agriculture 9.1 %

**GNI PER CAPITA** US$ 2,550

**CLIMATE** Temperate, with cold winters and mild summers; warmer on Black Sea coast

**HIGHEST POINT** Hora Hoverla 2,061 m (6,762 ft)

**MAP REFERENCE** Pages 289, 298

Ukraine, formerly part of the USSR, has a southern coastline on the Black Sea and on the almost landlocked Sea of Azov. Surrounding it are seven other countries. From southeast across its northern border to south-west, they are the Russian Federation, Belarus, Poland, Slovakia, Hungary, Romania, and Moldova. The Ukrainian capital, Kiev, has existed since the ninth century AD, when a Viking tribe established a center there. A century later it was a powerful force in Eastern Europe. It was overrun by Mongols in the thirteenth century and then came under Polish control. In the seventeenth century the eastern part of Ukraine fell to the Russians, who eventually absorbed the whole of the country into their empire. Despite attempts to establish a separate state after the 1917 Revolution, invading Soviet armies subdued Ukraine in 1920. During the 1930s more than 3 million Ukrainians perished in a famine and another 6 million died in the Nazi occupation during the Second World War. After the war, part of western Ukraine that was under Polish occupation was returned, as was the Crimea, and Ukraine assumed its present boundaries under Soviet domination. Ukraine declared its independence in 1991 as the Soviet Union began to break up, although it retained close ties with Russia, and the question of just how close this relationship should be remains one of the most virulent issues in Ukrainian politics. It is now a democratic republic, with a directly elected president as head of state.

Formerly referred to as "the granary of the Soviet Union", most of Ukraine consists of fertile black-soil plains that produce an abundance of wheat and other cereal grains as well as vegetables, fruits, and fodder crops. Much of the country's agricultural output remains affected by the widespread contamination caused by the nuclear accident at Chernobyl in 1986.

There are mountainous areas in the southwest, where the Carpathian Mountains sweep down from Poland, and in the Crimean Peninsula in the far south. The Dnieper River flows through the heart of the country and empties into the Black Sea. In its northern plain there are large stretches of marshland and many forest-rimmed lakes. In the south, bordering the Black Sea, much of the landscape is a semiarid, treeless plain.

Coal is Ukraine's most abundant and heavily exploited mineral resource. There are also significant reserves of natural gas, uranium, and oil, though the latter remains largely unexploited. Steel production, machine building, engineering, and chemical processing are the main industries. These industries are centered around the large cities and coalfields in the east of the country. In the post-Soviet era, the Ukrainian economy has suffered periods of extremely high inflation and growth has been hampered by a largely conservative legislature that has resisted many attempts at reform. There is widespread poverty, exacerbated by a declining healthcare system.

Europe and the Russian Federation

# Moldova

## Fact File

**OFFICIAL NAME** Republic of Moldova

**FORM OF GOVERNMENT** Republic with single legislative body (Parliament)

**CAPITAL** Chisinau

**AREA** 33,843 sq km (13,067 sq miles)

**TIME ZONE** GMT + 2 hours

**POPULATION** 4,324,000

**PROJECTED POPULATION** 2015 3,645,000

**POPULATION DENSITY** 127.8 per sq km (330.9 per sq mile)

**LIFE EXPECTANCY** 70.5

**INFANT MORTALITY (PER 1,000)** 13.5

**OFFICIAL LANGUAGE** Moldovan

**OTHER LANGUAGES** Russian, Gagauz (Turkish dialect)

**LITERACY RATE** 99.1 %

**RELIGIONS** Eastern Orthodox 98.0 %, Jewish 1.5 %, Baptist and other 0.5 %

**ETHNIC GROUPS** Moldovan/Romanian 78.2 %, Ukrainian 8.4 %, Russian 5.8 %, Gagauz 4.4 %, Bulgarian 1.9 %, other 1.3 %

**CURRENCY** Leu

**ECONOMY** Services 60.5 %, industry 21,7 % agriculture 17.8 %

**GNI PER CAPITA** US$ 1,260

**CLIMATE** Temperate, with mild winters and warm summers

**HIGHEST POINT** Mt Balaneshty 430 m (1,411 ft)

**MAP REFERENCE** Page 296

Moldova is a small, landlocked country in southeastern Europe near the northern shores of the Black Sea. To the west the Prut River separates Moldova from Romania. Otherwise, it is completely enclosed by Ukrainian territory. Bessarabia—the section between the Prut and Dniester Rivers—which comprises almost all of present-day Moldova, was under Ottoman rule until 1812, when it passed to Russian control. With the collapse of the Russian Empire after the First World War, Bessarabia merged in 1918 with Romania, with which it is ethnically and linguistically almost identical.

## The Commonwealth of Independent States

The Commonwealth of Independent States (CIS) is a loose confederation of twelve former Soviet republics that was created after the breakdown of the Soviet Union in 1991. The idea for the formation of the commonwealth was agreed to at a meeting of the presidents of Russia, Belarus, and Ukraine in Minsk, capital of Belarus, in early December 1991 and was ratified at Alma-Ata in Kazakhstan by eleven of the former Soviet republics on 21 December. Georgia and the three Baltic states of Estonia, Latvia, and Lithuania declined to join; Georgia became a member in 1993 but withdrew in 2006. Turkmenistan also discontinued its permanent membership in 2005 and is now an associate member. Not surprisingly, Russia assumed the status of dominant member of the group, taking control of all former Soviet embassies and consulates and occupying the former Soviet Union's seat on the United Nations Security Council. Minsk was designated as the administrative center of the new commonwealth, which was more of an alliance than a state entity. According to the agreement, the political independence of each state was guaranteed in return for a commitment to some economic and defence cooperation.

The commonwealth remains a tenuous confederation and there are many areas of dispute between its constituent members. There is natural suspicion that the Russian Federation seeks to impose its political will on the other members, which was strengthened in 1996 when the Russian parliament, or Duma, passed a non-binding resolution in favor of reinstating the former Soviet Union. Difficult economic conditions throughout the former Soviet Union have led to increasing support for a return to the previous status quo.

The part of Moldova east of the Dniester remained under Russian control. As a result of the Nazi-Soviet Pact of 1940 Romania was forced to cede Bessarabia. Most of it was combined with a narrow strip of the Ukraine east of the Dniester to form the new state of Moldova. The remaining parts were incorporated into Ukraine.

After the Second World War, Moldova became a Soviet republic and systematic attempts were made to suppress all links with Romania. Large numbers of ethnic Romanians were forcibly removed to other countries in the Soviet Union, and Russian and Ukrainian immigration was fostered. Independence came in 1991 as the Soviet Union crumbled, but tensions between the predominantly Russian population in the region lying to the east of the Dniester, who wished to declare a separate republic, and the ethnic Romanians, who sought closer ties or even reunification, with Romania, resulted in violent clashes. In 1992, a joint Russian-Moldovan peacekeeping force was instituted to help restore order, although ethnic tensions persist. In 1994 a constitution was adopted that defined the country as a democratic republic. Moldova is the poorest nation in Europe and was the first former Soviet state to elect a communist president in 2001.

Most of the countryside of Moldova is lowlying but hilly steppe country. It is eroded by rivers and the landscape is cut by numerous deep valleys and gorges. Thick forests grow on many of the hillsides and most of the country is covered with thick, black, fertile soils. This fertile land, combined with a temperate climate, short winters and high summer rainfall, made Moldova one of the foremost producers of food in the former Soviet Union.

Agriculture remains the main element in the Moldovan economy. Vegetables, sunflower seeds, tobacco, wheat, and maize are the principal crops, as well as grapes, which contribute to a thriving winemaking and exporting industry. Cattle and pig raising are also widespread.

The country has minimal reserves of mineral resources and depends upon Russian imports for all its oil, gas, and coal supplies. Electricity, too, is mainly imported and due to the outdated electrical grid power shortages occur quite frequently. Industries include machine manufacturing and food processing.

# Russian Federation

## Fact file

**OFFICIAL NAME** Russian Federation

**FORM OF GOVERNMENT** Federal republic with two legislative bodies (Federation Council and State Duma)

**CAPITAL** Moscow

**AREA** 17,075,200 sq km (6,592,735 sq miles)

**TIME ZONE** GMT + 3–13 hours

**POPULATION** 140,702,000

**PROJECTED POPULATION 2015** 136,479,000

**POPULATION DENSITY** 8.2 per sq km (21.3 per sq mile)

**LIFE EXPECTANCY** 65.9

**INFANT MORTALITY (PER 1,000)** 10.8

**OFFICIAL LANGUAGE** Russian

**OTHER LANGUAGES** More than 100 minority languages

**LITERACY RATE** 99.4 %

**RELIGIONS** Russian Orthodox 15–20 %, Muslim 10–15 %, other Christian 2 %, other and large number of non-practicing believers and non-believers 73 %

**ETHNIC GROUPS** Russian 79.8 %, Tatar 3.8 %, Ukrainian 2.0 %, Bashkir 1.2 %, Chuvash 1.1 %, other 12.1 %

**CURRENCY** Ruble

**ECONOMY** Services 56.2 %, industry 39.1 %, agriculture 4.7 %

**GNI PER CAPITA** US$ 7,560

**CLIMATE** Warm and dry in far south; cold temperate (long, cold winters and short, mild summers) in most inland areas; polar in far north

**HIGHEST POINT** Mt Elbrus 5,633 m (18,481 ft)

**MAP REFERENCE** Pages 299, 300–01

*Oktober Square with the Palace of the Republic in Minsk, capital of Belarus (left page). The gilded domes and turrets of Pushkin Palace in Moscow (above right). A river winding through fertile farming country in Russia (below right).*

Sprawling across the easternmost part of northern Europe and occupying the whole of northern Asia, the Russian Federation, often called simply Russia, is the largest country in the world—it is almost twice the size of the United States—and it has the sixth largest population. Its 21 republics cover three-quarters of the area of what was for almost 70 years (until it collapsed in 1991) the Union of Soviet Socialist Republics (USSR).

The Russian Federation has long coastlines along the Arctic Ocean in the north and along the Pacific Ocean in the east. Its southeastern coastline is on the Sea of Japan and north of this the Kamchatka Peninsula encloses the Sea of Okhotsk. In its far southwestern corner there is a short stretch of coast along the Caspian Sea; a little further north, it briefly borders the Black Sea; and in the northwest, near St Petersburg, it touches on the eastern tip of the Gulf of Finland. Its mainland has borders with twelve other countries. In the far southeast it borders the northeast tip of North Korea. In the south it borders China in two places: to the east and the west of its long border with Mongolia. The western half of its southern border is with the former Soviet republic of Kazakhstan. To the

west of the Caspian Sea are Azerbaijan and Georgia, and north of the Black Sea are Ukraine, Belarus, Latvia, and Estonia. Northeast of the Gulf of Finland is a border with Finland and at its very northwest tip the Russian Federation borders on a tiny part of Norway. Further west, tucked in between Lithuania and Poland, and with a coast on the Baltic Sea, is another small area of Russian territory, centered on the coastal city of Kaliningrad.

## History

Until the sixth century AD, almost all of what is now Russia was inhabited only by nomadic tribes of Finnic and Slavic origin. In the sixth century peoples from what are now Iran and Turkey settled the part of southwestern Russia between the Carpathian Mountains and the Volga River, establishing a capital on the Caspian Sea. They in turn were overrun by Viking invaders and traders who spread southward along river routes from the Baltic Sea. One tradition has it that modern Russia dates back to the establishment of a dynasty by the Viking Rurik at Novgorod in AD 862. Soon after, however, the center of power moved farther southwest, to Kiev in present-day Ukraine, and a unified confederation known as Kievan Rus emerged. In the tenth century the leader

Vladimir was converted to Christianity. Over the next two centuries a Russian culture based on the traditions of Orthodox Christianity developed, but in the thirteenth century Kievan Rus fell to invaders from Mongolia and the confederation broke down into a number of dukedoms, under Mongol domination. The Muscovite dukes emerged as the most powerful, mainly through their role as tribute collectors for the Mongols. Opposition to Mongol rule gathered strength during the fourteenth century and in the fifteenth century the Muscovite Duke Ivan III finally expelled the Mongols. His grandson, Ivan IV, known as "The Terrible," was the first to declare himself "Tsar of all the Russians". Under his oppressive rule, which lasted from 1533 to 1584, the power of princes and landowners (known as "boyars") was broken and the Muscovite state spread eastward across the Urals and into what is now Siberia.

After Ivan's death, a series of internal disputes culminated in Polish invasion in 1609 and, after the ousting of the Poles in 1612, the emergence of the first Romanov tsar, Mikhail, in 1613. Under his grandson, Peter I (known as "The Great"), who ruled from 1696 to 1725, the country was renamed "Russia", and a new capital was established at St Petersburg. Territories along the Baltic were acquired from Sweden, and Western European ideas, technology, and styles of dress and other fashions were embraced. During the eighteenth and nineteenth centuries Russia extended its borders south and east into Asia.

The defeat of Napoleon's invading armies in 1812 confirmed Russia's status as a great power, but the country remained socially and industrially backward in comparison with Western Europe. A feudal system, under which peasants were bonded to landlords, remained until 1861, when

Tsar Alexander II abolished serfdom. Alexander's political and social reforms earned him powerful enemies and led to his assassination in 1881. The oppressive rule of his successor, Alexander III, spawned the formation of the Marxist Russian Social Democratic Party in 1898, under the leadership of Vladimir Ilich Ulyanov, who called himself Lenin. Civil unrest intensified following Russia's defeat in its war with Japan in 1904–05, forcing Tsar Nicholas II to establish a parliament, known as the Duma, elected by a very limited suffrage, and to institute some civil liberty reforms.

These reforms, however, failed to stem the revolutionary tide, which was further strengthened by the reverses and heavy loss of life in the First World War. In February 1917 rioting and strikes broke out in the capital, St Petersburg. There was a massive defection of Russian troops, and Tsar Nicholas II abdicated, leading to the decisive revolution of October 1917, in which the All-Russian Communist Party emerged as the ruling force with Lenin as dictatorial leader. Four years of civil war ensued until the communists fully took control. In December 1922, Russia, with Moscow as its capital, became the dominant power in the newly formed Union of Soviet Socialist Republics, having seized Georgia, Armenia, and Azerbaijan and established its ascendancy in Ukraine and central Asia.

Following Lenin's death in 1924, there was a bitter factional struggle for power. By 1929 Joseph Vissarionovich Dzhugashvili, who called himself Stalin, "Man of Steel", was the undisputed leader and remained in power until he died in 1953. Under his regime, agriculture was collectivized, industry expanded, and brutal labor camps were established in Siberia for those suspected of espousing dissident ideas. Political rivals and enemies, whether real or imagined, were routinely eliminated in a series of ruthless purges. In one purge in 1929–30, hundreds of thousands of peasants who opposed farm collectivization were either murdered or sent away to remote, desolate parts of the country. Farm collectivization led to immense agricultural disruption and resulted in famine in the early 1930s in which many thousands of people died.

Russia and the rest of the Soviet Union suffered terribly during the Second World War. At first allied with Germany in 1939 and 1940 the Soviet Union seized territory in Poland and Romania, and annexed the Baltic republics of Estonia, Latvia, and Lithuania. In 1941, Hitler's troops suddenly invaded the Soviet Union, and in the occupation and struggles that ensued in the following four years an estimated 20 million Soviet citizens were killed.

At the end of the war, the regions that were occupied by Soviet forces—most of Eastern Europe—came under Soviet domination. This gave rise to a forty-year period of international tension as the Soviet Union and the United States assumed the mantles of mutually distrustful, competing superpowers, each building up an arsenal of ever more potentially destructive nuclear weapons. During the premiership of Stalin's successor, Nikita Khrushchev, the Soviet Union and its satellites entered into a defense treaty, the Warsaw Pact, to oppose the Western NATO alliance. Nuclear war seemed a real danger in 1962, when a Soviet attempt to place nuclear weapons on Cuba was met by a United States blockade. Khrushchev's humiliating backdown in this crisis, as well as a serious rift between Russia and communist China, led to his removal from office the next year and his replacement by Leonid Brezhnev.

The Brezhnev era lasted until 1982, and during this time Soviet-Western relations fluctuated. Periods of relaxation, which became known as "détente", alternated with times of renewed suspicion and hostility. Despite this, and despite the USSR's invasions of Czechoslovakia in 1968 and Afghanistan in December 1979, genuine agreements about arms reduction were achieved. During the brief premierships of Brezhnev's two immediate successors, East-West relations soured again. However, in 1985, the accession to the leadership of Mikhail Gorbachev led to an era of greater trust as well as to a less dictatorial and more open style of political leadership, and the first tentative moves toward a loosening of government controls over the economy. The terms *glasnost,* meaning "openness", and *perestroika*, meaning "restructuring", were used widely at this time in reference to Gorbachev's reforms.

Growing social unrest, deteriorating economic conditions, and a resurgence of nationalism in a number of Soviet republics created immense strains in the Soviet Union. An attempted coup by communist conservatives took place in 1991 but was put down, largely through the heroic opposition of Boris Yeltsin, who emerged as the de facto leader of the country, enjoying widespread popular support.

Against Gorbachev's wishes, the Soviet Union was officially dissolved in December 1991 and replaced by the Commonwealth of Independent States (CIS; see box on page 270). Gorbachev then resigned as president and Yeltsin assumed control. Yeltsin's leadership was confirmed in a national referendum that was held in 1993 and, despite a poor economic situation and widespread hardship as well as serious misgivings about his health, Yeltsin was reelected president in 1996. In the parliamentary, or Duma, elec-

**Timeline**

| AD 300 Spread of peoples including Huns, Goths, and Magyars into forests west of the Ural Mountains | AD 830 Scandinavian merchants establish new base in the Volga region, close to present-day Ryazan | 1237 Russia becomes part of Mongol Empire until late 1400s, extending the empire's boundaries to Arctic, Baltic and Pacific | 1547 Ivan IV, known as "the Terrible", is crowned tsar and takes the title for all Russia | 1613 Mikhail IV is the first Romanov tsar; his family rules until the murder of Nicholas II in 1918 | 1703 Peter the Great opens Russia to Western ideas. Builds St Petersburg on the Baltic Sea, making it the capital in 1712 |
|---|---|---|---|---|---|
| 20,000 BP Huts made from mammoth bones covered in animal skins at Mezhirich in Ukraine region | 4000 BC Horses domesticated on the steppes, first mainly as draft animals but later (2000 BC) as fast transport in warfare | AD 770 Germanic traders and soldiers from Baltic move into Volga region previously occupied by Finnic and Slavic groups | AD 882 Scandinavian groups capture Kiev; Russia takes its name from Kievan Rus, term given by Slavic groups to the Black Sea area | 1318 Mongols appoint Yuri of Moscow Crown Prince; he makes Moscow an important center and later the capital of Russia | 1697 First recorded eruption of Klyuchevskaya Volcano in Kamchatka, Siberia | 1725 Catherine the Great becomes Empress. Encourages Western ideas in arts and education. Most Russians impoverishe |

tions, however, conservative nationalists, some of them stridently anti-Western, received widespread support.

A new constitution adopted in 1993 established a two-chambered Federal Assembly, headed by a prime minister, who is appointed by the president. The president is popularly elected for a five-year term and has considerable independent powers, including the right to dissolve parliament.

## Physical features and land use

Stretching all the way from the Arctic Ocean in the north to the border with Kazakhstan in the south, the Ural Mountains separate European Russia in the west from the vast Siberian Plain to the east. European Russia, where most of the population lives and where the bulk of Russian industry and agriculture is located, consists mainly of a huge fertile plain, the East Europe Plain, which has an average elevation of 170 m (550 ft) but rises to a maximum of 400 m (1,300 ft). In the far southwest, the Caucasus Mountains form a natural boundary with Georgia and Azerbaijan, and there are upland areas in the far north near the border with Finland. In the western part of the plain are the Valdai Hills, in which the Volga and Dnieper Rivers have their source.

Most of Russia's agriculture is concentrated in the south of the plain, as the harsh climates further north are not conducive to growing crops or raising livestock. Less than one-tenth of Russia's land area is under cultivation. Cereals are the main crops, although in most years the country produces only about half the grain it requires. The rest has to be imported. Livestock raising, most commonly poultry, cattle and dairy farming, is also based mainly in the west.

To the east of the Ural Mountains, the Siberian Plain is largely desolate, treeless, and flat. Central Siberia, to the east of the Yenisey River, is a region of plateaus that range from between 450 and 900 m (1,500 and 3,000 ft) in height and rise in the south to a series of mountain ranges that border Mongolia and China. Lowlands flank these plateaus to the north and east. East of the Lena River the country rises again toward the rugged and mountainous east coast. South of the Bering Sea, the Kamchatka Peninsula and the Kuril Islands form part of the Pacific "Ring of Fire". This is an area of considerable geothermal activity and there are about thirty active volcanoes.

The landscape of northern Russia is mainly arctic tundra—a treeless expanse which remains frozen throughout the year. Tundra vegetation consists of sedges, grasses, mosses, lichens, and ground-hugging plants. Further south, and in the southwest, the landscape varies between tracts of semidesert and expanses of forest, largely conifers, known as the taiga.

## Industry, commerce, and culture

Russia, and especially Siberia, has abundant mineral resources. These contributed greatly to the country's rapid transformation during the Soviet period from a predominantly agricultural economy to one that was heavily industrialized. These mineral resources underpin the federation's present reliance on heavy industry and provide important mining exports. They include coal, petroleum, natural gas, iron ore, bauxite, copper, lead, zinc, and gold and other precious metals. Steelmaking, the manufacture of agricultural machinery, chemicals, textiles, and food processing are among the principal industries, centered on such large cities to the west of the Ural Mountains as Moscow, St Petersburg, Novgorod, and Volgograd, but also in a number of cities in Siberia such as Yekaterinburg and Novosibirsk.

The country's move toward a market economy has been fraught with difficulties and has been accompanied by a marked increase in social and financial inequalities as a new class of rich entrepreneurs has emerged. The majority of Russians live in relative poverty, victims of steeply rising prices and severe shortages of food and other basic consumer items. Corruption and crime have also increased significantly and a number of the leaders of organized crime are among the richest citizens in the nation. These conditions were aggravated by a virtual collapse of the Russian economy in 1998 and continuing political uncertainty based on serious doubts about the health and capacity of the president, Boris Yeltsin. His successor in 1999, Vladimir Putin, took a stronger line but earned harsh international criticism regarding both his actions against Chechnya fighting for its

*Shoppers in Arbat Street, a prosperous part of Moscow (left page top). Fishing through a hole in the ice, using large nets, in Siberia (above). St Petersburg, once the capital of Russia, seen from across the misty Neva River (below).*

independence as well as against democratic institutions including freedom of the press.

Russia has contributed much to literature, music, and the performing arts, especially in the nineteenth century. Writers such as Ivan Sergeevich Turgenev prepared the way for other giants of literature like Leo Tolstoy and Fyodor Mikhailovich Dostoyevsky. Among composers, Pyotr Ilyich Tchaikovsky and Igor Stravinsky established Russia's place in musical history. The Imperial Russian Ballet was founded in 1735, and Russian ballet has become internationally renowned for its choreography and dancers like Anna Pavlova and Rudolf Nureyev.

Europe and the Russian Federation

| 1773–74 The Peasants Revolt sweeps across Russia from the Urals to the Volga but is put down by troops | 1890 Migration of large numbers of people from eastern Russia to Siberia and Asia lasts for around 10 years | 1917 Revolution puts Bolsheviks in power after storming of the Winter Palace, at St Petersburg | 1918 Tsar Nicholas II and family are shot, allegedly at the hands of the Bolsheviks; Moscow again capital of Russia | 1928 First Five-Year Plan introduced to further centralize the economy and increase industrial and agricultural production | 1935 Great Purge by Stalin's secret police takes many lives; millions starve in a famine partly caused by farm collectivization | 1956 Bezymianny Volcano in Kamchatka, Siberia, erupts leaving ash 50 cm (20 in) deep 10 km (6 miles) from volcano | 1985 Gorbachev heads Communist Party; pursues policies of *perestroika* ("economic restructuring") and *glasnost* ("openness") |
| 1812 Napoleon's invasion of Russia defeated. Most of the 500,000 French forces die or are captured | 1891 Construction of the Trans-Siberian Railroad from Moscow to Vladivostok begins. Not completed until 1916 | 1914 Germany declares war on Russia and for three years Russia sides with Allies | 1918–20 Communists victorious in a civil war with the anti-communist White Russians | 1929 Stalin becomes undisputed leader and rules USSR for more than 20 years until his death in 1953 | 1941 Russia sides with Allies in Second World War after Germany invades USSR and is defeated in the Battle of Stalingrad (1943) | 1986 Chernobyl nuclear reactor in Ukraine explodes; cancers from radiation kill up to 40,000 worldwide | 2002 In the Rome Declaration Russia becomes a partner with equal rights in the NATO |

## The British Isles

United Kingdom (Great Britain and Northern Ireland) · 274
Ireland · · · · · · · · · · 277
Dependencies · · · · · 278

## United Kingdom

Outer Hebrids
Shetland Islands
SCOTLAND
NORTH SEA
Edinburgh
Glasgow
NORTHERN IRELAND
Belfast
Newcastle upon Tyne
UNITED KINGDOM
IRELAND
IRISH SEA
Liverpool
Manchester
Leeds
ENGLAND
WALES
Cardiff
Oxford
London
Southampton
Plymouth
English Channel

### Fact File

**OFFICIAL NAME** United Kingdom of Great Britain and Northern Ireland

**FORM OF GOVERNMENT** Constitutional monarchy with two legislative houses (House of Lords and House of Commons)

**CAPITAL** London

**AREA** 244,820 sq km (94,525 sq miles)

**TIME ZONE** GMT

**POPULATION** 60,944,000

**PROJECTED POPULATION 2015** 62,787,000

**POPULATION DENSITY** 248.9 per sq km (644.7 per sq mile)

**LIFE EXPECTANCY** 78.9

**INFANT MORTALITY (PER 1,000)** 4.9

**OFFICIAL LANGUAGE** English

**OTHER LANGUAGES** Welsh, Scots Gaelic, Manx, Cornish

**LITERACY RATE** 99%

**RELIGIONS** Christian (Anglican, Roman Catholic, Presbyterian and Methodist) 71.6%, Muslim 2.7%, Hindu 1.0%, other 1.6%, none 23.1%

**ETHNIC GROUPS** Indigenous (English 83.6%, Scottish 8.6%, Welsh 4.9%, Northern Irish 2.9%) 91.2%, Irish 2.9%, African 2.0%, Indian 1.8%, other 2.1%

**CURRENCY** Pound sterling

**ECONOMY** Services 75.7%, industry 23.4%, agriculture 0.9%

**GNI PER CAPITA** US$ 42,740

**CLIMATE** Temperate, with cool winters and mild summers; generally wetter and warmer in the west, and cooler in the north

**HIGHEST POINT** Ben Nevis 1,343 m (4,406 ft)

**MAP REFERENCE** Pages 302–03

Lying just north of the westernmost edge of continental Europe, the United Kingdom consists of the large island of Great Britain, the far northeast corner of the island of Ireland, which sits across the Irish Sea to the west, and several hundred small islands scattered around the British coast. The United Kingdom is separated by the English Channel from the north coast of France which, at its nearest point, is no more than 32 km (20 miles) away, and a rail tunnel under the Channel now links England and France. England, in the south and southwest, occupies the greatest part of the island. Scotland is to the north, and Wales in the west juts out into the Irish Sea. The long eastern coast of Great Britain faces the North Sea; its western coastline is on the Atlantic Ocean and the Irish Sea.

### History

Thanks partly to the natural protection offered by surrounding waters, but also to its maritime supremacy in certain periods of history and to a degree of good fortune in others, Britain is unique among major European nations in that it has escaped foreign invasion for almost 1,000 years. When William, Duke of Normandy led his successful invasion in 1066, it was the culmination of a long series of incursions that the island kingdom had suffered since the first invasion by the Romans in the first century AD.

Within 60 years of their arrival in Britain in AD 55, the Romans had established control over England and Wales and later introduced Christianity. When they finally withdrew at the beginning of the fifth century, the Britons eventually fell prey to Germanic tribes from Scandinavia and the Low Countries. By the eighth century most of Britain, except the far west and the north, had succumbed and the country was divided into a number of Anglo-Saxon kingdoms.

Viking attacks from Norway and Denmark occurred during the course of the eighth and ninth centuries, with Danish invaders controlling much of north and northeast England by the late ninth century. United under the kings of Wessex by the middle of the tenth century, England again fell to Danish control early in the eleventh century. When Edward the Confessor came to the throne in 1042, he presided over a unified, but fractious, kingdom. On his death in 1066 both his brother-in-law, Harold, and his cousin, William of Normandy, claimed the throne. William was victorious at the Battle of Hastings and was crowned on Christmas Day 1066.

The feudal system of government developed by William the Conqueror gave significant power to the nobles. Under Henry II, the first Plantagenet king, power became more centralized in the crown. This and increasing civil unrest during the reign of John, led to a revolt by nobles, who in 1215 forced the king to sign the Magna Carta, a document limiting royal power and enshrining basic civil rights. This in turn gave rise to the development of a more consultative style of government, and, by the late thirteenth century, to the establishment of a House of Commons with powers to raise taxes.

Under Edward I (1272–1307) Wales was brought under English control, much of Ireland was subjugated, and a portion of Scotland was conquered. In 1314, however, at the Battle of

### Timeline

| | | | | | | | |
|---|---|---|---|---|---|---|---|
| **4000 BC** Tribes from various parts of Europe arrive; they farm and live in villages, burying their dead in earth mounds | **43 BC–AD 446** Roman occupation of Britain brings wealth, military skills, and Christianity; Hadrian's Wall built AD 120 | **1066** Norman invasion. William I's *Domesday Book* assesses Britain's wealth and estimates population about 2 million | **1300** Population reaches 5 million after expanding rapidly as a result of more efficient farming methods | **1536** Parliament formally makes Wales part of English territory | **1664–66** Great Plague kills more than 75,000 of London's population of around 450,000, then spreads to other parts of the country | **1801** Act of Union extended to join Ireland to United Kingdom |
| **200,000 BC** Hominids living in southeastern Britain use stone tools and hunt animals | **12,000 BC** Paleolithic hunters carve mammal bones at Cresswell Crags, Derbyshire; one shows a dancing man, others, animal heads | **3300 BC** Construction of a large stone circle begins: Stonehenge completed 1800 BC | **AD 410** Anglo-Saxons settle in south England destroying remains of Roman culture; later, Danish Vikings settle in north and east | **1489** Enclosure of common land forces many people off the land, causing rebellions and rural depopulation | **1500** Little ice age of cold winters and wet summers (which continues until 1700) causes crop failures across the country | **1707** Act of Union between England and Scotland creates United Kingdom of Great Britain | **1750** Use of iron grows rapidly; machines for spinning and weaving invented in late 1700s, accelerating Industrial Revolution |

Bannockburn, the English were driven out of Scotland. Between 1338 and 1453, in a series of devastating wars known as the Hundred Years War, England lost all its French territories. This led to a further 30 years of civil war, known as the Wars of the Roses, which culminated in the accession to the throne of Henry VII, the first of the Tudor monarchs, in 1485.

The Tudor dynasty lasted until 1603, and during this time, especially during the reign of Elizabeth I (1558–1603), England became a leading power in the world, enjoying a golden age in which colonies were established in North America, British navigators sailed to remote corners of the globe, and there was a notable flowering of English theater, first and foremost thanks to William Shakespeare. During the reign of Elizabeth's father, King Henry VIII, Protestantism, in the form of the Church of England, had been established in England.

When Elizabeth died without an heir, James VI of Scotland, the first Stuart king, succeeded her, combining the two kingdoms and reigning as James I of England. Attempts by his son, Charles I, to curb the powers of parliament led to the outbreak of civil war in 1642. With the victory of the parliamentary armies, led by Oliver Cromwell, in 1646, the monarchy was abolished and a commonwealth, virtually a military dictatorship, set up under Cromwell. The Commonwealth did not long survive the death of Cromwell and in 1660 Charles II was installed as king. When his brother, the Catholic James II, attempted to restore Catholic domination, however, he was ousted and his Protestant daughter, Mary, and her Dutch husband, William of Orange, accepted the crown in 1689. In the same year, parliament enacted legislation barring Catholics from the throne. In 1690, at the Battle of the Boyne, their armies defeated a Catholic uprising in Ireland. In 1707 an Act of Union between the Scottish and English parliaments formally joined the two countries. Scottish rebellions against British rule were finally put down in 1746, when Charles Edward Stuart (Bonnie Prince Charlie) was defeated in the Battle of Culloden.

Under the Hanoverian monarchs, the first of whom, George I, accepted the throne in 1814 as King of Great Britain and Ireland, greater power devolved to the parliament. In 1721, Sir Hugh Walpole became the first prime minister to head a ministry that exercised executive power with the sanction of parliament. The eighteenth century, too, was a period of great expansion of British power that saw the acquisitions of British colonies in India and Canada and the exploration and colonization of Australia. A major setback was the loss of the American colonies in 1776. The military defeat of Irish rebels in 1798 led to an Act of Union that formally joined the two countries, the UK and Ireland, in 1801. Defeat of Bonaparte at Waterloo in 1815 confirmed Britain as the world's leading power.

The nineteenth century was a time of further expansion and consolidation of Britain's influence and power. By the end of Queen Victoria's 64-year reign in 1901, Britain's colonies extended throughout much of the world, including large parts of Africa, although by then Australia, New Zealand, and Canada had gained their independence and demands for Irish independence were growing. During the century a number of Reform Bills brought in significant democratic reforms and the Industrial Revolution resulted in increasing industrialization, urban growth, and a slowly rising standard of living.

Three-quarters of a million British soldiers were killed during the First World War, which also left the country considerably weakened economically. This situation was exacerbated by the Great Depression. After a protracted and bitter struggle, Ireland, with the exception of the provinces of Northern Ireland, became independent in 1922 and British troops faced growing unrest in India and parts of the Middle East. Following the Second World War, in which British cities, especially London, were subjected to sustained German bombardment from the air, Britain endured almost a decade of austerity.

India gained its independence in 1947, and in 1956 Britain suffered a humiliating defeat in its armed attempt to prevent Egypt's nationalization of the Suez Canal. In 1982 Britain was again at war, this time against Argentina, which attempted to seize the Falkland Islands. In a two-week conflict, Britain repulsed the Argentines with the loss of 255 British lives. In recent years bitter violence between Catholics and Protestants in Northern Ireland has been a major preoccupation of British governments. Since 1995, however, there have been developments, including the Belfast Treaty of 1998, which established the Northern Ireland Assembly. Although it has been suspended multiple times, it was restored on 8 May 2007.

Britain, as a member of the European Union and a signatory of the Maastricht Treaty, is a significant force in Europe as it moves closer to political and economic integration. It is one of the world's most stable multi-party democracies in spite of ongoing debate about the role and viability of the monarchy and of its unelected, and largely hereditary, upper house of parliament, the House of Lords, which is in the process of reform. Power resides in the House of Commons, which is elected by universal adult suffrage for terms of five years.

### Physical features and land use

The United Kingdom has a considerable variety of landscapes, ranging from craggy mountain ranges and tranquil upland lakes in the north, to gently rolling hills and green plains that are characteristic of the south and southeast. The majority of the mountain ranges are very old, geologically speaking.

Scotland is the most mountainous part of the country. Mainland Scotland has three main regions: the Highlands in the north, the Southern Uplands near the border with England, and in between the flatter, though often hilly, Central

*Scotney Castle in Kent, southeastern England (left page). A tile-hung house in a village in southern England (right). Ebbw Valley British Steel tinplate mill in the town of Ebbw Vale, south Wales (far right).*

Europe and the Russian Federation

| | | | | | | | | |
|---|---|---|---|---|---|---|---|---|
| **1825** World's first public railway opens between Stockton and Darlington, starting a worldwide boom in railway construction | **1845–46** Potato crop failure causes Great Famine in Ireland; millions die or emigrate to England, USA, Canada, Australia | **1914–18** First World War against Germany causes the loss of more than 900,000 British Empire lives | | **1930s** Unemployment rises to 3 million; some relief provided by economic progress in manufacturing industries | **1945** Churchill loses election to Labour Party's Attlee who begins a program of reconstruction, reform, and nationalization | **1967** Britain fails to join the EC; membership not achieved until 1973; sterling devalued | **1994** Passenger train services through the fixed-link railway tunnel under the English Channel link France and the UK | **2005** Several attacks by Islamic extremists on the London underground claim 56 lives and injured around 700 |
| | **1837** Queen Victoria crowned. Rule lasts until 1901, coincides with period of great wealth and growth of British Empire | **1901** The population of Britain reaches 42 million after rapid population growth in the second half of the nineteenth century | | **1920** Northern Ireland separates from the rest of Ireland and remains part of the United Kingdom; the Irish Free State (southern Ireland) is set up in 1921 | **1939–45** Cities across Britain bombed during Second World War— widespread damage and the loss of thousands of lives | **1957** Extensive postwar migration from Commonwealth regions such as Pakistan, India, and West Indies | **1975** Offshore North Sea oilfields begin operation, boosting the UK economy; Britain becomes self-sufficient in oil | **1999** Scotland and Wales elect regional parliaments as part of the devolution program |

## CONSTITUENT COUNTRIES

England • London
Scotland • Edinburgh
Northern Ireland • Belfast
Wales • Cardiff

## OVERSEAS TERRITORIES

Anguilla
Bermuda
British Indian Ocean Territory
British Virgin Islands
Cayman Islands
Falkland Islands
Gibraltar
Guernsey
Isle of Man
Jersey
Montserrat
Pitcairn Islands
St Helena
South Georgia and the South Sandwich islands
Turks and Caicos islands

Lowlands. It also has several groups of offshore islands: the Shetlands in the far north, the Orkneys off the northeastern tip of the mainland, and the Inner and Outer Hebrides off the northwestern coast. The most rugged country is in the north, where two granite ranges, the North West Highlands and the Grampians, dominate the scene. In the northwest the mountains are cut by deep glaciated valleys and the coastline is rocky and deeply indented. South and east of the Great Glen, which contains the famous Loch Ness, are the Grampians, where Britain's highest peaks are found. Here, the country is generally less harsh, and there are stretches of sheep-grazing land and forested slopes where there are herds of deer. East of the Grampians is a rich agricultural lowland area that stretches in an arc from near Inverness around to Aberdeen.

Scotland's two largest cities, Glasgow and Edinburgh, lie in the Central Lowlands, the most populous region and Scotland's industrial heart. The Central Lowlands contain several ranges of undulating hills and are drained by the eastward-flowing Tay and Forth Rivers and the westward-flowing Clyde. The area east of Edinburgh is prime country, both for stock raising and crop cultivation. The Southern Uplands, gentler and less lofty than their northern counterparts, are characterized by hills, moorlands, and picturesque valleys, and in the valley of the Tweed and its tributaries are large areas of sheltered farmland. The Cheviot Hills in the south form a natural border with England.

Beginning just south of the Cheviot Hills and running southward as far as north Derbyshire are the Pennine Mountains, a predominantly limestone range of hills, plateaus, expanses of moorlands, and soft, green valleys, which are often referred to as the Dales. West of the Pennines, and separated from it by the valley of the Eden River, are the Cumbrian Mountains, a region of craggy peaks with many lakes. This

is England's famous Lake District. To the east of the Pennines are the elevated expanses of the North York Moors.

South of the Pennines, beginning around the fertile valleys of the Trent and Avon Rivers, the countryside becomes flatter and gently undulating, reaching its lowest point in the marshy fen country north of Cambridge. Numerous ranges of hills provide relief from the generally rolling countryside. The most notable hills are the Cotswolds in the central southwest, where England's longest river, the Thames, begins its course eastward across the country, passing through London and out to the North Sea.

Wales, which juts out into the Irish Sea to the west of England, is more mountainous, its center dominated by the Cambrian Mountains, in which the Severn, Britain's second longest river, arises. Mount Snowdon, in Snowdonia, a large national park in northern Wales, rises to 1,085 m (3,559 ft) and is the highest peak in England and Wales.

Northern Ireland is flat for the most part, but to the north of Belfast is the Antrim Plateau, whose basalt cliffs provide some of the country's most arresting coastal scenery.

### Industry, commerce, agriculture, and culture

Crop cultivation in Britain is concentrated mainly in the east and southeast of the country. Wheat is the principal crop, though potatoes and fruits are widely cultivated. Pasturelands are more common in the west and southwest, where sheep and cattle raising and dairy farming predominate. Although the United Kingdom exports much of its produce, it still imports about one-third of its food needs.

The United Kingdom has traditionally relied on coal for its energy resources, and there are still adequate reserves. However, the replacement of most coal-fired power stations with gas-powered facilities in recent years has resulted in the near closure of the coal-mining industry. The country also has a number of nuclear power stations which are a continuing subject of controversy. Oil and gas reserves in the North Sea are a major source of revenue, and have helped to make the country self-sufficient in energy.

Manufacturing was once the mainstay of the British economy, with a large proportion of heavy industry centered on industrial cities in the Midlands such as Birmingham, Manchester, and Liverpool. Food processing, machinery, and textile manufacture are still among the principal manufacturing industries. Motor vehicle and aircraft manufacture are long-established core industries, although much of the motor vehicle industry is now owned by foreign companies. Most of the raw materials needed to supply Britain's industries have to be imported from other countries.

Apart from the ethnic and cultural minorities found in Wales and Scotland, Britain's population is relatively homogeneous. Since the 1950s, however, large numbers of immigrants from former British colonies in the Caribbean, Asia (especially India and Pakistan), and Africa have changed the racial composition, most notably in inner-city areas, where the majority of ethnic minorities have congregated. Despite certain tensions, these immigrants are now generally accepted as an integral, if still relatively disadvantaged, part of British society.

Britain's economy is one of the most developed in Western Europe and its people enjoy a high standard of living, although there are considerable variations in levels of affluence. Universal free education and health systems are maintained by the state, although some social services and the value of pensions, including those for the elderly, have been sharply cut back in recent years.

*A unionist mural in Belfast, Northern Ireland (above).*
*A cobbled shopping street in Dublin, Ireland (below).*

# Ireland

brought Christianity to Ireland in AD 432, and to this day Catholicism remains the dominant religion. From the eighth century AD Viking raiders attacked the coasts and settled some coastal regions, but they were finally repulsed in 1014. During the twelfth century, the pope, Adrian IV, ceded the entire island to the English crown, but another five centuries were to pass before local opposition was finally subjugated. From 1846 to 1851 disease destroyed the Irish staple crop, potatoes, leading to famine and more than a million deaths. Roughly half the population emigrated at this time, mainly to the USA.

Although the Irish were granted a degree of autonomy in the eighteenth century, opposition to British rule festered throughout the nineteenth century, leading to the unsuccessful Easter Rebellion of 1916 and the eventual granting of home rule to most of the island, as the Irish Free State, in 1921. In 1949 the Republic of Ireland was declared and formal ties with the British crown were severed. Today Ireland is a parliamentary democracy, with a popularly elected president as head of state and two houses of parliament.

Most of the landscape consists of a low-lying limestone plain, with undulating hills and areas of

fertile soils. Small lakes and peat bogs abound throughout the countryside. Mountain ranges run along much of the coast, creating some of Europe's most spectacular coastal scenery, especially in the southwest. The most significant ranges are the Wicklow Mountains in the southeast and Macgillicuddy's Reeks in the far southwest. The Shannon, the country's longest river, rises in the Iron Mountains not far from the Northern Ireland border. It drains the central plain and flows through a number of Ireland's largest lakes.

Traditionally an agricultural country, Ireland now relies mainly on manufacturing and processing industries for its present, relatively healthy, economic strength. The country joined the European Community in 1973. Four in ten members of the population live in urban areas. Clothing, pharmaceuticals, and the manufacture of heavy machinery contribute largely to Ireland's export earnings and tourism is also significant. Approximately 8 million people visit Ireland every year. About one in eight workers is still involved in agriculture, mainly in livestock raising and dairying, but also in cultivating crops such as potatoes, barley, and wheat. The country has reserves of natural gas, oil and peat.

## Fact File

**OFFICIAL NAME** Ireland, Eire

**FORM OF GOVERNMENT** Republic with two legislative bodies (Senate and House of Representatives)

**CAPITAL** Dublin

**AREA** 70,280 sq km (27,135 sq miles)

**TIME ZONE** GMT

**POPULATION** 4,156,000

**PROJECTED POPULATION 2015** 4,805,000

**POPULATION DENSITY** 59.1 per sq km (153.2 per sq mile)

**LIFE EXPECTANCY** 78.1

**INFANT MORTALITY (PER 1,000)** 5.1

**OFFICIAL LANGUAGES** Irish Gaelic, English

**LITERACY RATE** 99.0 %

**RELIGIONS** Roman Catholic 88.4 %, Anglican 3.0 %, other Christian 1.6 %, other 3.5 %, none 3.5 %

**ETHNIC GROUPS** Irish 94 %, English minority

**CURRENCY** Euro

**ECONOMY** Services 49 %, industry 46 %, agriculture 5 %

**GNI PER CAPITA** US$ 48,140

**CLIMATE** Temperate, with cool, wet winters and mild summers; wetter in the west

**HIGHEST POINT** Carrauntoohil 1,041 m (3,415 ft)

**MAP REFERENCE** Pages 303, 309

Situated in the northern Atlantic Ocean and separated from the British mainland to the east by the Irish Sea, the republic of Ireland covers more than three-quarters of the island of Ireland. The northeast corner comprises the six counties that form Northern Ireland, which is part of the United Kingdom.

In the fourth century BC, Gaelic-speaking invaders conquered the island and established a Celtic civilization. Tradition has it that St Patrick

## The Troubles in Northern Ireland

Ever since Britain's granting of independence to the Irish Free State in 1921, Northern Ireland has been a troubled province, a place where terrorism and sectarian strife have been the norm. The arrangements for the government of Northern Ireland created bitter resentment among its minority Catholic population. Northern Ireland was granted self-government, with its own parliament in Belfast, but maintaining strong links with the British government in London. The government ruled blatantly in favor of the Protestant majority, excluding Catholics from positions of authority or influence. Catholics moved in great numbers from the country to Belfast and other cities in order to find work, almost invariably in menial jobs in shipbuilding, textile, and other industries.

The Irish Republican Army (IRA), which had used guerrilla tactics against the British during Ireland's struggle for independence, became a threat to the stability of Northern Ireland, carrying out sporadic attacks on Protestant targets. When in 1948 the Irish Free State, as Ireland was then called, left the British Commonwealth and became the Republic of Ireland, battle lines became marked. The IRA began to campaign aggressively for Northern Ireland to be absorbed into the republic and for a breaking of ties with Britain, but for the next two decades it made little progress in the face of Northern Ireland's largely apathetic Catholic population.

However, as discrimination, especially in housing and employment, continued in Northern Ireland, Catholics grew increasingly militant, and in the late 1960s waged a widespread campaign for increased civil rights. Their demonstrations provoked counter-demonstrations by militant Protestants and a 30-year period of violent sectarian clashes was launched. The situation was aggravated by the arrival of British troops,

ostensibly to maintain the peace. They were soon perceived by Catholics to be acting in the interests of the Protestants, especially after 1972, when they opened fire on Catholic demonstrators in Londonderry, killing 13 of them. In March 1972, in the wake of this incident, the British government suspended the parliament in Belfast and instituted direct rule for the province from London, a move that antagonized people on both sides of the struggle.

The desire of one section of the IRA to abandon violence led to a split in 1969. A wing of the IRA—the Provisionals, or Provos—consisting mainly of younger members, remained committed to terrorism and during the 1970s and 1980s carried out repeated bombings, murders, and kidnappings of both civilians and British army personnel, not only in Ireland, but also on the British mainland. Protestants in Northern Ireland responded in kind. From the early 1970s until the mid-1990s more than 3,000 people died in the conflict, and many more were wounded. The most prominent victim was Earl Mountbatten, who was assassinated in the Irish Republic in 1979. Northern Ireland towns and cities were divided into Catholic and Protestant zones, and an atmosphere of fear and distrust prevailed.

Any possibility of a negotiated peace was thwarted by the determination of successive British governments not to recognize or to have discussions with the IRA. This situation changed in 1994, when the Provisional IRA suspended its terrorist campaign and talks, at first in secret, but later open, were held in London. The talks broke down in 1996 when the Provisional IRA revoked its cease-fire and continued its attacks. The Belfast or Good Friday Agreement of 1998 led to the establishment of a Northern Irish Assembly, which was dissolved in 2000 due to a flare of violence but resinstated in 2007.

Europe and the Russian Federation

## Dependencies in Europe

### Faeroe Islands

 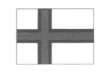

#### Fact file

OFFICIAL NAME  Faeroe Islands

FORM OF GOVERNMENT  Self-governing overseas administrative division of Denmark

CAPITAL  Torshavn

AREA  1,400 sq km (541 sq miles)

TIME ZONE  GMT

POPULATION  48,700

LIFE EXPECTANCY  79.3

INFANT MORTALITY (PER 1,000)  6.5

LITERACY RATE  Not available

CURRENCY  Danish krone

ECONOMY  Services 62 %, agriculture 27 %, industry 11 %

CLIMATE  Mild winters, cool summers; foggy and windy

MAP REFERENCE  Page 302

The Faeroes are an archipelago of 22 islands in the north Atlantic Ocean between Scotland and Iceland, eighteen of which are inhabited. Though part of Danish territory, the Faeroes have enjoyed a high degree of autonomy since 1948. They have their own parliament, elected for four-year terms. In the eleventh century these islands came under Norwegian control, but when the crowns of Norway and Denmark combined in the fourteenth century, Denmark became the dominant power. Since 1709 the islands have been administered by Denmark. The Faeroes, formed from volcanic lava, are rocky, with spectacular cliffs along the coasts. Sheep raising has been the economic mainstay, though recently fishing has supplanted it in importance. Despite international criticism, the Faeroese continue whaling.

### Gibraltar

#### Fact file

OFFICIAL NAME  Gibraltar

FORM OF GOVERNMENT  Self-governing overseas territory of the United Kingdom

CAPITAL  Gibraltar

AREA  6.5 sq km (2.5 sq miles)

TIME ZONE  GMT + 1 hour

POPULATION  28,000

LIFE EXPECTANCY  80.1

INFANT MORTALITY (PER 1,000)  4.9

LITERACY RATE  Above 80 %

CURRENCY  Gibraltar pound

ECONOMY  Financial services, tourism, manufacturing, horticulture

CLIMATE  Temperate; mild winters and warm summers

MAP REFERENCE  Page 292

Jutting into the Strait of Gibraltar at the southwest tip of Spain, Gibraltar sits at the entrance to the Mediterranean Sea. Spain's capture of Gibraltar in 1462 ended seven centuries of Moorish rule. Seized by the British and Dutch in 1704, it was ceded to Britain in 1713 and, despite subsequent Spanish attempts to take it back, it has remained in British hands ever since. Spain and Britain still dispute possession of "The Rock". In two referendums in 1967 and 2002 an overwhelming majority of the inhabitants voted for staying with the UK. Gibraltar has its own elected parliament and is virtually autonomous. Britain maintained a military garrison until 1991, then handed over control to the local regiment. Gibraltar consists of a high rocky mountain, joined to the Spanish mainland by a sandy plain. Tourism is highly important for its economy.

### Guernsey

#### Fact File

OFFICIAL NAME  Bailiwick of Guernsey

FORM OF GOVERNMENT  British crown dependency

CAPITAL  St Peter Port

AREA  63 sq km (24 sq miles)

TIME ZONE  GMT

POPULATION  65,700

LIFE EXPECTANCY  80.7

INFANT MORTALITY (PER 1,000)  4.5

LITERACY RATE  Not available

CURRENCY  Guernsey pound

ECONOMY  Services 87 %, industry 10 %, agriculture 3 %

CLIMATE  Temperate; mild winters and cool summers

MAP REFERENCE  Page 304

Guernsey, the second largest of the Channel Islands, lies in the English Channel 50 km (30 miles) to the west of France. Though it is a British dependency, it is effectively self-governing, and administers all the other Channel Islands bar Jersey. During the Second World War they were the only region of Britain to be occupied by German troops. Picturesque scenery, a gentle climate, and the relaxed lifestyle of its inhabitants make tourism an economic mainstay. Market gardening is also important and the island is famed for its distinctive cattle. Immigration is strictly controlled.

## Jersey

### Fact File

**OFFICIAL NAME** Bailiwick of Jersey

**FORM OF GOVERNMENT** British crown overseas

**CAPITAL** St Helier

**AREA** 117 sq km (45 sq miles)

**TIME ZONE** GMT

**POPULATION** 91,500

**LIFE EXPECTANCY** 79.7

**INFANT MORTALITY (PER 1,000)** 5

**LITERACY RATE** Not available

**CURRENCY** Jersey pound

**ECONOMY** Services 97 %, industry 2 %, agriculture 1 %

**CLIMATE** Temperate; mild winters and cool summers

**MAP REFERENCE** Page 290

Jersey, the largest and most populous of the Channel Islands, lies in the English Channel, 20 km (12 miles) from the west coast of the Cherbourg Peninsula in northern France. Said to be the sunniest part of the British Isles, it is noted for its superb beaches. These account for the booming tourist industry which, along with financial services, has in recent years supplanted agriculture as the mainstay of the economy.

Jersey is a dependency of the British crown, but it has its own legislature and a tax regime that is entirely independent and whose low rates attract many foreign businesses. Jersey cattle are among the most important exports,

and flower cultivation is also a significant source of income.

## Svalbard

### Fact File

**OFFICIAL NAME** Svalbard

**FORM OF GOVERNMENT** Territory of Norway

**CAPITAL** Longyearbyen

**AREA** 62,049 sq km (23,957 sq miles)

**TIME ZONE** GMT + 1 hour

**POPULATION** 2,200

**LIFE EXPECTANCY** Not available

**INFANT MORTALITY (PER 1,000)** Not available

**LITERACY RATE** Not available

**CURRENCY** Norwegian krone

**ECONOMY** Mainly coal mining, some tourism

**CLIMATE** Polar, moderated by Gulf Stream ocean current; cold winters and cool summers

**MAP REFERENCE** Page 300

Situated in the Arctic Ocean about 650 km (400 miles) north of Norway, Svalbard consists of nine bleak, rocky, and icy islands. From Viking times until the sixteenth century, these islands remained unknown. Recently they have served as a base for Arctic explorers. Svalbard's coal reserves have been mined by a number of nations under Norway's supervision. Now, only Norway and Russia mine the much depleted deposits. Vegetation on the islands is restricted to mosses, lichens, and a few hardy, low-growing plants. Visitors are attracted by the many migratory birds.

## The Isle of Man

### Fact File

**OFFICIAL NAME** The Isle of Man

**FORM OF GOVERNMENT** British crown dependency

**CAPITAL** Douglas

**AREA** 588 sq km (227 sq miles)

**TIME ZONE** GMT

**POPULATION** 76,200

**LIFE EXPECTANCY** 78.8

**INFANT MORTALITY (PER 1,000)** 5.6

**LITERACY RATE** Not available

**CURRENCY** Manx pound

**ECONOMY** Services 86 %, industry 13 %, agriculture 1 %

**CLIMATE** Temperate; cool, wet winters and mild summers

**MAP REFERENCE** Page 306

The Isle of Man is situated in the Irish Sea between the west coast of England and Northern Ireland, and just south of Galloway in Scotland. At its southern tip is a tiny uninhabited island, the Calf of Man, which is a nature reserve. Two regions of uplands in the center of the main island are divided by a valley extending from Douglas, on the east coast, to Peel, on the west.

The Isle of Man is a dependency of the British crown, but has its own legislature, legal system, and taxation system. Traditionally agriculture and fishing have been the main sources of income, but it now depends mainly on tourism and financial and business services. Although English is the main language, the local Gaelic language—known as Manx—was almost defunct, but serious efforts are being made to reestablish it as a widely spoken language that is taught in schools.

*St Peter Port, in Guernsey (left page left). A seaside town on the Isle of Man (left page right). A skidoo and sleds on Svalbard (top). The castle of Montorgueil on Jersey (right).*

## The Channel Islands

The Channel Islands lie in the English Channel between 15 and 50 km (10 and 30 miles) off the coast of Normandy in northern France. As well as the two largest islands of Jersey and Guernsey, there are the smaller islands of Sark and Alderney and a number of even smaller islands. In all, the Channel Islands cover an area of only 200 sq km (80 sq miles).

Since the Norman invasion of England in 1066, these islands have been dependencies of the British crown and are the only part of the Duchy of Normandy to have been retained by Britain after 1204.

Both Jersey and Guernsey have separate legislatures and their own taxation systems, independent of Britain. While English is the most widely spoken language, French is also common and it is the official language of the Jersey legislature. The majority of the place names on Jersey are French.

Especially during the summer, both English and French tourists flock to these islands, and tourism, along with financial services, is now the mainstay of the islands' economies. The residents of the islands enjoy a high standard of living, maintained by strictly enforced residential controls.

# Europe: Physical

Europe and the Russian Federation

ATLANTIC
OCEAN

NORWEGIAN SEA

Iceland
Hekla
1491 m
Hvannadalshnúkur
2119 m

Arctic Circle

Vesterålen
Lofoten
Halti
1328 m
Kebnekaise
2111 m

Scandinavia

Faeroe
Islands

Shetland
Islands

Rockall

Hebrides
Cape
Wrath

Orkney
Islands

Galdhøpiggen
2469 m

British
Isles

Ben Nevis
1343 m
Grampian
Mountains

NORTH SEA

Vänern

Gotland

Öland
BALTIC SEA

Skagerrak

Kattegat

Jylland

Carrauntoohil
1041 m
Mizen
Head

Lough
Neagh

Shannon

IRISH
SEA
Snowdon
1085 m

Pennines

Trent

St George's
Channel

CELTIC SEA

Bornholm

Ostfriesische Inseln

North

Land's End

English Channel
Strait of Dover

Channel
Islands

Seine

Marne

Botrange 694 m

Ardennes

Meuse

Moselle

Taunus

Harz

Erzgebirge
Sudety

Praděd
1492 m

Rhein

Gerlachovský Štít
2655 m

Loire

Cher

Vosges

Jura

Schwarzwald

Donau

Inn

Zugspitze
2962 m

Bay
of
Biscay

Cabo
Fisterra

Garonne

Dordogne

Massif
Central

Lac Léman
Matterhorn
4478 m
Mont Blanc
4807 m

Monte
Rosa
4634 m

Großglockner
3797 m

Dolomiti

Triglav
2863 m

Balaton

Plain of
Hungary

Minho

Cordillera Cantábrica

PYRENEES

Cévennes

Duero

Pico de
Aneto
3404 m

Golfe
du Lion

LIGURIAN
SEA

ALPS

APPENNINO

Dinara

1522 m

Iberian

Peninsula

Ebro

Tajo

Corse

ADRIATIC SEA

Korab
2764 m

Cabo de
São Vicente

Sierra Morena
Guadalquivir

Islas Baleares
Menorca

Eivissa
Mallorca

Strait of Bonifacio

Sardegna

Golfo di
Taranto

Oros Oly
2917

Golfo
de Cádiz

Golfo de
Valencia

TYRRHENIAN
SEA

Pindos

Ionioi Nisoi

Pelopo

Sierra Nevada
Mulhacén
3481 m

Strait of
Gibraltar

MEDITERRANEAN

Strait of Sicily

Sicília
Monte Etna
3323 m

Cap
Bon

Malta

IONIAN SEA

ATLAS MOUNTAINS

Jebel
Toubkal
4165 m

Jabal ash Sha'nabī
1544 m

SEA

Shaṭṭ al Jarīd

BARENTS SEA

Ostrov Kolguyev

Kol'skiy Poluostrov

BELOYE MORE

Cheshskaya Guba

Timanskiy Kryazh

Severnaya Dvina

Onezhskoye Ozero

Ladozhskoye Ozero

Ozero Il'men

Rybinskoye Vodokhranilishche

Gor'kovskoye Vodokhranilishche

Kamskoye Vodokhranilishche

Kuybyshevskoye Vodokhranilishche

U R A L ' S K I Y   K H R E B E T   ( U R A L   M O U N T A I N S )

Z a p a d n o   S i b i r s k a y a   R a v n i n a

Ob'

Irtysh

Ozero Chany

Ob'

Izhma

Pechora

Vychegda

Ishim

Tobol

Russian Plain

Srednerusskaya Vozvyshennost'

Privolzhskaya Vozvyshennost'

Volga

Don

Dnieper

Dniester

Kakhovs'ke Vodoskhovyshche

Volgogradskoye Vodokhranilishche

Tsimlyanskoye Vodokhranilishche

Ozero Manych-Gudilo

Caspian Depression

Ural

Zhayyq

Mughalzhar Tauy

Syrdar'ya

Esil

Tengiz Köli

Balqash Köli

ARAL SEA

Peski Kyzylkum

Plato Ustyurt

Amu Darya

Zaunguzskiye Garagum

CASPIAN SEA

SEA OF AZOV

Kuban

Kryms'kyy Pivostriv (Crimean Pen.)

BLACK SEA

Gora El'brus 5642 m ▲

BOL'SHOY KAVKAZ

Gora Kazbek 5047 m ▲

Bazardüzü Dag 4466 m ▲

Aragats Lerr 4090 m ▲

Ağri Dağı (Mt Ararat) 5137 m ▲

Van Gölü

Daryācheh-ye Orūmīyeh

Reshteh-ye Kūhhā-ye Alborz (Elburz Mountains)

Qolleh-ye Damāvand 5671 m

Dasht-e Kavīr

Dasht-e Lūt

Iranian Plateau

MARMARA DENIZI

A n a t o l i a

Tuz Gölü

Toros Dağları (Taurus Mountains)

Antalya Körfezi

Kızılırmak

K ū h h ā - y e   Z ā g r o s   ( Z a g r o s   M o u n t a i n s )

Euphrates

Tigris

Persian Gulf

Strait of Hormuz

Rodos

Dodekanisos

Cyprus

Olympos 1951 m ▲

Qurnat as Sawdā' 3088 m ▲

Jabal ash Shaykh 2814 m ▲

B ā d i y a t   a s h   S h ā m   (Syrian Desert)

150   300   450   600   750 kilometers

150   300   450 miles

ale 1:15,000,000   Projection: Conic Equidistant

# Europe: Political

**RUSSIAN FEDERATION**

**KAZAKHSTAN**

**UZBEKISTAN**

**TURKMENISTAN**

**IRAN**

**TURKEY**

**SYRIA**

**IRAQ**

**CYPRUS**

**GEORGIA**

**AZERBAIJAN**

**ARMENIA**

**AFGHANISTAN**

**ISRAEL**   **JORDAN**   **SAUDI ARABIA**   **KUWAIT**   **OMAN**   **U.A.E.**

**BLACK SEA**

*CASPIAN SEA*

Kolpashevo · Anzhero-Sudzhensk · Tomsk · Kemerovo · Leninsk-Kuznetskiy · Novosibirsk · Barnaul · Biysk · Rubtsovsk

Nizhnevartovsk · Surgut · Igrim · Nyagan' · Inta · Nar'yan Mar · Pechora · Ukhta · Mezen'

Tatarsk · Omsk · Nazyvayevsk · Ishim · Tyumen' · Serov · Kurgan · Kamensk-Ural'skiy · Nizhniy Tagil · Yekaterinburg · Pervoural'sk · Chelyabinsk · Zlatoust

Severodvinsk · Arkhangel'sk · Kem' · Monchegorsk · Apatity · Kandalaksha · Murmansk

Syktyvkar · Kotlas · Solikamsk · Berezniki · Perm' · Votkinsk · Izhevsk · Sarapul

Medvezh'yegorsk · Petrozavodsk · Vologda · Cherepovets · Kostroma · Yaroslavl' · Rybinsk · Ivanovo

Sankt-Peterburg · Kolpino · Novgorod · Tver' · Sergiyev Posad · Velikiye Luki · Obninsk · Kolomna · Ryazan' · Murom

Vyatka · Naberezhnyye Chelny · Ufa · Magnitogorsk · Kazan' · Cheboksary · Nizhniy Novgorod · Arzamas · Al'met'yevsk · Sterlitamak · Salavat · Orsk

Moskva · Smolensk · Kaluga · Tula · Novomoskovsk · Ul'yanovsk · Saransk · Penza · Syzran' · Tol'yatti · Samara · Novokuybyshevsk · Sol'-Iletsk · Orenburg · Dimitrovgrad

Bryansk · Orel · Kursk · Lipetsk · Tambov · Saratov · Engel's · Balakovo

Chernihiv · Sumy · Belgorod · Voronezh · Volzhskiy · Vologograd

Kyyiv · Kharkiv · Poltava · Kremenchuk · Luhans'k · Astrakhan'

Dniprodzerzhyns'k · Donets'k · Makiyivka · Rostov-na-Donu · Taganrog · Zaporizhzhya · Mariupol'

Kirovohrad · Kryvyy Rih · Mykolayiv · Kherson · Melitopol' · Krasnodar · Armavir · Stavropol'

Bălţi · MOLDOVA · Chişinău · Odesa · Simferopol' · Novorossiysk · Maykop · Cherkessk · Nal'chik · Groznyy · Vladikavkaz · Makhachkala

Braila · Sevastopol' · Sochi

Constanţa · Varna · Burgas · agora

Rodos

URKAINE · RUS · Homyel'

**Scale 1:15,000,000**   Projection: Conic Equidistant

0  150  300  450  600  750  kilometers

0  150  300  450  miles

Europe and the Russian Federation

© Random House Australia Pty Ltd

Scale 1:3,500,000     Projection: Equidistant Conic

0   50   100   200 kilometers
0   50   100 miles

Europe and the Russian Federation

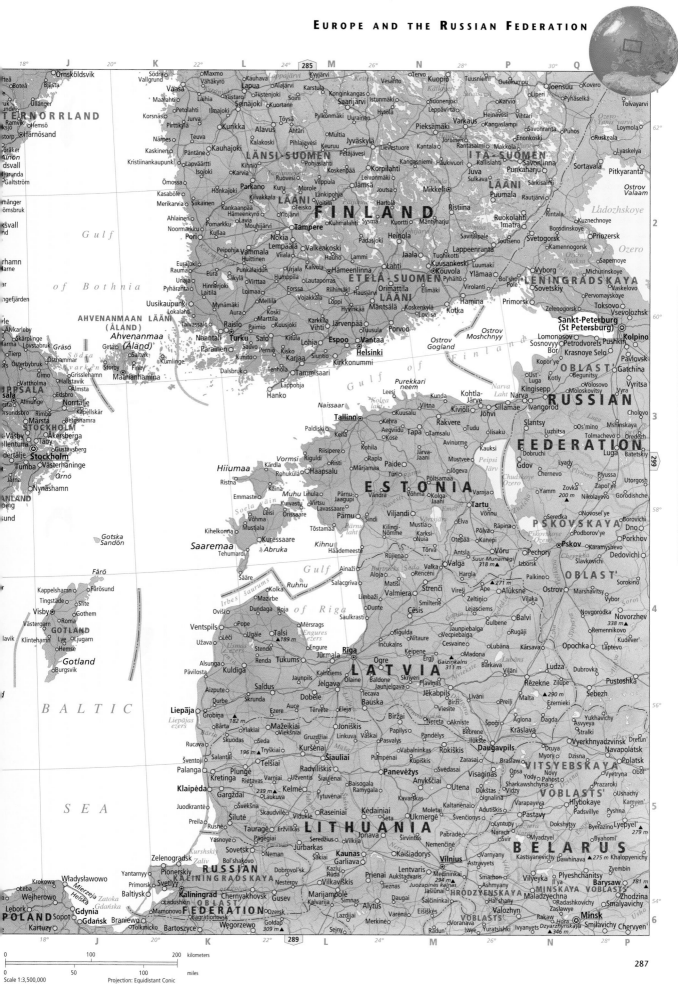

**FINLAND**

LÄNSI-SUOMEN LÄÄNI

ITÄ-SUOMEN LÄÄNI

ETELÄ-SUOMEN LÄÄNI

AHVENANMAAN LÄÄNI (ÅLAND)

Ahvenanmaa (Åland)

Helsinki

Tampere

Turku

Espoo

Vantaa

Sankt-Peterburg (St Petersburg)

**RUSSIAN FEDERATION**

LENINGRADSKAYA OBLAST'

PSKOVSKAYA OBLAST'

KALININGRADSKAYA OBLAST'

Kaliningrad

**ESTONIA**

Tallinn

Tartu

Pärnu

Narva

**LATVIA**

Riga

Liepāja

Ventspils

Jūrmala

Daugavpils

**LITHUANIA**

Vilnius

Kaunas

Klaipėda

Panevėžys

Šiauliai

**BELARUS**

Minsk

VITSYEBSKAYA VOBLASTS'

HRODZYENSKAYA VOBLASTS'

MINSKAYA VOBLASTS'

**POLAND**

Gdańsk

Gdynia

**SWEDEN**

Stockholm

GOTLAND

Gotland

Öland

*Gulf of Bothnia*

*BALTIC SEA*

*Gulf of Finland*

*Gulf of Riga*

TERNORRLAND

0 100 200 kilometers

0 50 100 miles

Scale 1:3,500,000    Projection: Equidistant Conic

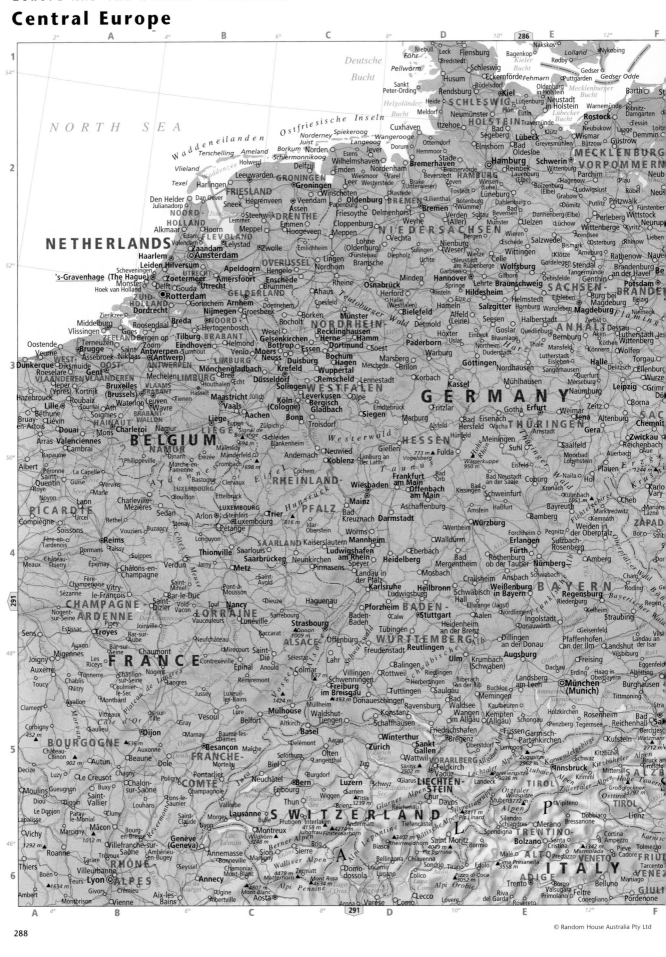

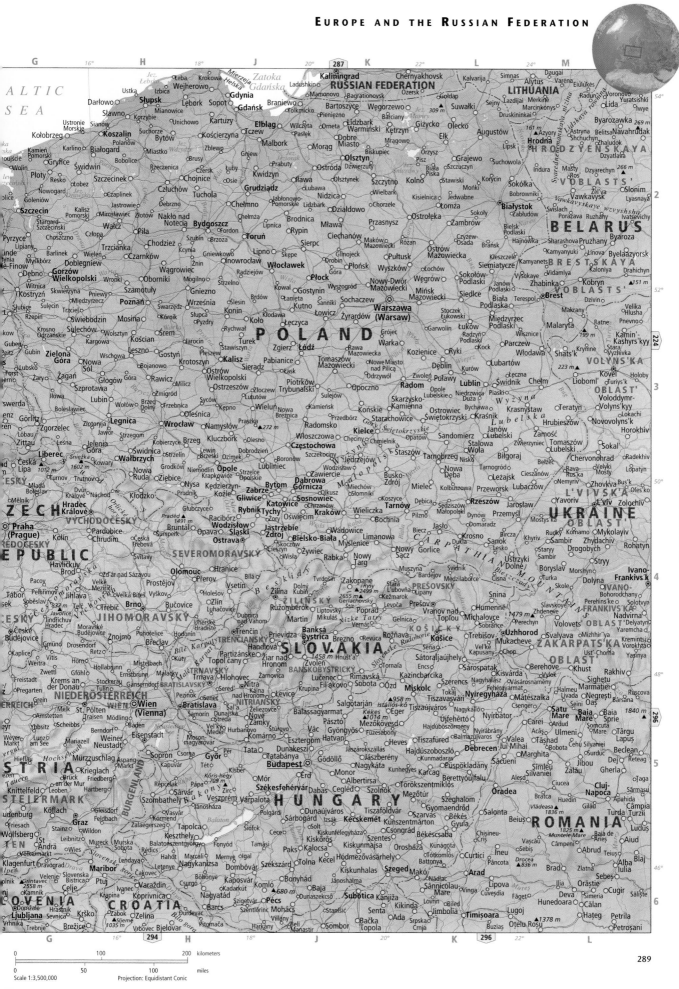

289

Scale 1:3,500,000
Projection: Equidistant Conic

0     100     200 kilometers
0    50    100 miles

# France · Switzerland

291

Scale 1:3,500,000   Projection: Equidistant Conic

100   200 kilometers
50   100 miles

# Spain • Portugal

© Random House Australia Pty Ltd

**FRANCE**

Mimizan, Pissos, Casteljaloux, Aiguillon, Nérac, Agen, Caussade, Najac, Naucelle, Millau, 1567 m, Uzès, Avignon

Sabres, Labrit, Houeillès, Condom, Montech, Montauban, Cordes-sur-Ciel, Carmaux, Ganges, Sommières, Nîmes, PROVENCE-ALPES-CÔTE-D'AZUR

Morcenx, Roquefort, Moissac, Albi, Camarès, Le Caylar, Lodève, Arles, Martigues, Aix-en-Provence

Mont-de-Marsan, Gaillac, Lacaune, Bédarieux, Montpellier, Sète, Saintes-Maries-de-la-Mer, Marseille

AQUITAINE, Bayonne, Tartas, Mugron, Riscle, Armagnac, MIDI-PYRÉNÉES, Castres, Saint-Pons-de-Thomières, Pézenas, Agde, Cap Croisette

Biarritz, Orthez, Garlin, Lombez, Auch, Gimont, Colomiers, Toulouse, Montagne Noire 1210 m, Béziers, Cap d'Agde

Cambo-les-Bains, Saint-Palais, Pau, Tarbes, Castelnau-Magnoac, Carbonne, Castelnaudary, Carcassonne, Narbonne, LANGUEDOC-ROUSSILLON, Golfe du Lion

PAÍS VASCO, Donostia-San Sebastián, Saint-Jean-Pied-de-Port, Lourdes, Montréjeau, Saint-Girons, Pamiers, Foix, Quillan, Sigean, Étang de Bages

Pamplona, Oloron-Sainte-Marie, Larun, Urdos, Pic d'Anie 2504 m, Vignemale 3298 m, Salau, Pic de Saint-Barthélemy 2348 m, Tuchan, Estagel, Étang de Leucate

ANDORRA, Andorra la Vella, Pic d'Estats 3145 m, Prades, Perpignan, Port-Vendres, Cabo de Creus

Pico de Aneto 3404 m, Mont-Louis, Pic du Canigou 2784 m, Figueres, Golfo de Roses

La Seu d'Urgell, Puigcerdà, Camprodon, Ripoll, Banyoles, La Escala

CATALUÑA, Berga, Puig-reig, Torelló, Vic, Girona, Palafrugell, Palamós, San Feliú de Guixols, Costa Brava

Manresa, Granollers, Calella, Ossa de Mar

Montserrat 1236 m, Terrassa, Mataró, Santa Coloma de Gramanet, Badalona

Tàrrega, Igualada, Sabadell, Barcelona, L'Hospitalet de Llobregat

**SPAIN**

**MEDITERRANEAN SEA**

Islas Baleares (Balearic Islands), Cabo de Caballería, Menorca, Ciudadela, Cabo de Formentor, El Toro 350 m, Mahón, Cabo Dartuch

Pollença, Alcúdia, Puig Major 1445 m, Sóller, Inca, Artà, Manacor, Porto Cristo

Banyalbufar, Andratx, Palma de Mallorca, Santanyí, Mallorca, ISLAS BALEARES

Sa Dragonera, Cabo de Salinas, Cabrera

Eivissa (Ibiza), San Juan Bautista, Punta Grossa, Islas Baleares

San Antonio Abad, 475 m, Eivissa (Ibiza), Formentera

Golfo de Valencia

**VALENCIA**

**ALGERIA**

Dellys, Azeffoun, Azazga, Alger (Algiers), El Harrach, Tizi Ouzou, Lakhdaria, Bou Ismaïl, Tipasa, Larba, Bouira, 2309 m, Cherchell, Blida, Médéa, Bïr Ghbalou, Sour el Ghozlane, 'Aïn Defla, El Affroun, Khemis Miliana, Berrouaghia, Bougzoul, M'Sila

Ténès, Chlef, Bou Kadir, Theniet el Had, Chahbounia, 'Aïn el Hadjel, Sidi Lakhdar, Sidi Ali, Oued Rhiou, Ksar el Boukhari

Mostaganem, Arzew, Relizane, Tissemsilt, Rahouia, Mehdia, 'Aïn Oussera, Zenzach, Bou Saâda

Oran, Sig, Mohammadia, Mascara, Tiaret, Sougueur, Ksar Chellala

'Aïn Temouchent, Beni-Saf, Cap des Trois Fourches, Isla del Alborán, Cabo de Gata

0    100    200 kilometers
0  50  100 miles
Scale 1:3,500,000    Projection: Equidistant Conic

Europe and the Russian Federation

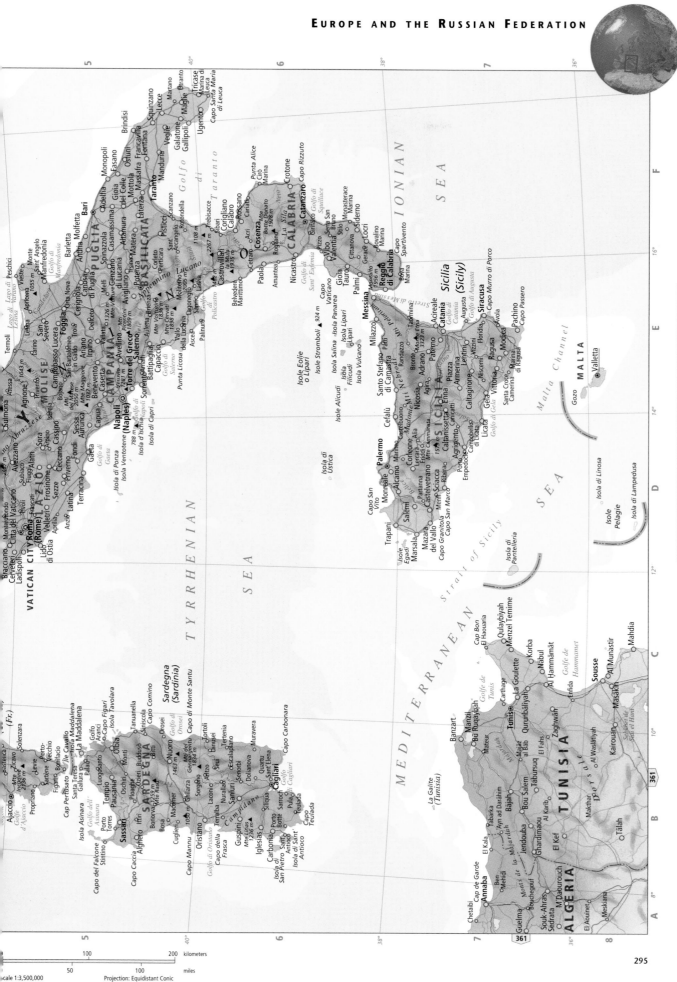

Scale 1:3,500,000          Projection: Equidistant Conic

# Southeast Europe

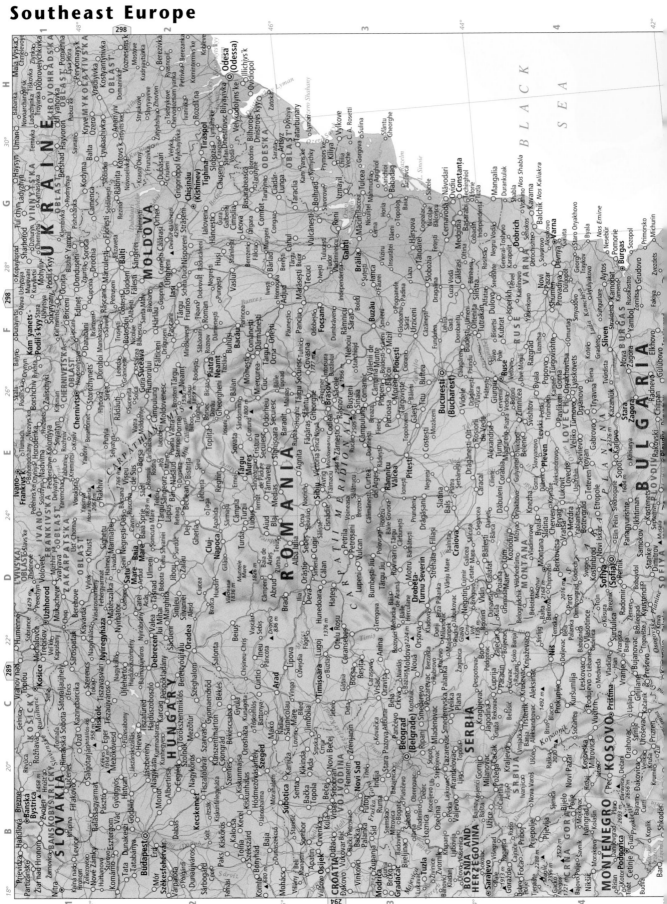

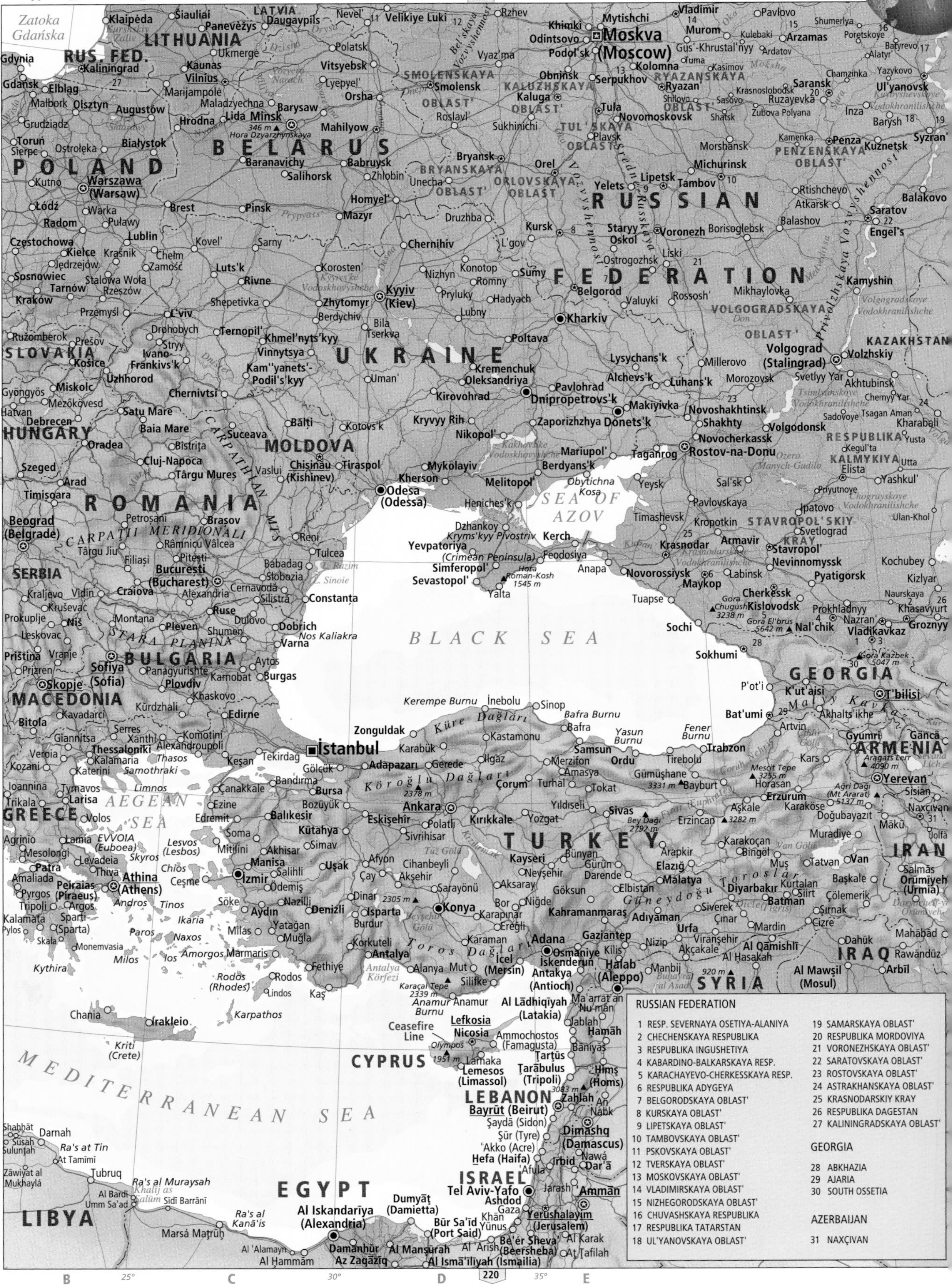

Europe and the Russian Federation

**Seas and bodies of water:** Zatoka Gdańska, SEA OF AZOV, BLACK SEA, AEGEAN SEA, MEDITERRANEAN SEA

**Countries and regions:** LITHUANIA, RUS. FED., BELARUS, POLAND, RUSSIAN FEDERATION, SLOVAKIA, HUNGARY, UKRAINE, MOLDOVA, ROMANIA, SERBIA, BULGARIA, MACEDONIA, GREECE, TURKEY, GEORGIA, ARMENIA, IRAN, IRAQ, SYRIA, LEBANON, CYPRUS, ISRAEL, EGYPT, LIBYA, KAZAKHSTAN, RESPUBLIKA KALMYKIYA

### RUSSIAN FEDERATION

| | |
|---|---|
| 1 RESP. SEVERNAYA OSETIYA-ALANIYA | 19 SAMARSKAYA OBLAST' |
| 2 CHECHENSKAYA RESPUBLIKA | 20 RESPUBLIKA MORDOVIYA |
| 3 RESPUBLIKA INGUSHETIYA | 21 VORONEZHSKAYA OBLAST' |
| 4 KABARDINO-BALKARSKAYA RESP. | 22 SARATOVSKAYA OBLAST' |
| 5 KARACHAYEVO-CHERKESSKAYA RESP. | 23 ROSTOVSKAYA OBLAST' |
| 6 RESPUBLIKA ADYGEYA | 24 ASTRAKHANSKAYA OBLAST' |
| 7 BELGORODSKAYA OBLAST' | 25 KRASNODARSKIY KRAY |
| 8 KURSKAYA OBLAST' | 26 RESPUBLIKA DAGESTAN |
| 9 LIPETSKAYA OBLAST' | 27 KALININGRADSKAYA OBLAST' |
| 10 TAMBOVSKAYA OBLAST' | |
| 11 PSKOVSKAYA OBLAST' | **GEORGIA** |
| 12 TVERSKAYA OBLAST' | |
| 13 MOSKOVSKAYA OBLAST' | 28 ABKHAZIA |
| 14 VLADIMIRSKAYA OBLAST' | 29 AJARIA |
| 15 NIZHEGORODSKAYA OBLAST' | 30 SOUTH OSSETIA |
| 16 CHUVASHSKAYA RESPUBLIKA | |
| 17 RESPUBLIKA TATARSTAN | **AZERBAIJAN** |
| 18 UL'YANOVSKAYA OBLAST' | 31 NAXÇIVAN |

298

© Random House Australia Pty Ltd

kilometers 0   100   200   300

miles 0   100   200

Scale 1:10,000,000   Projection: Equidistant C[...]

# West Russian Federation

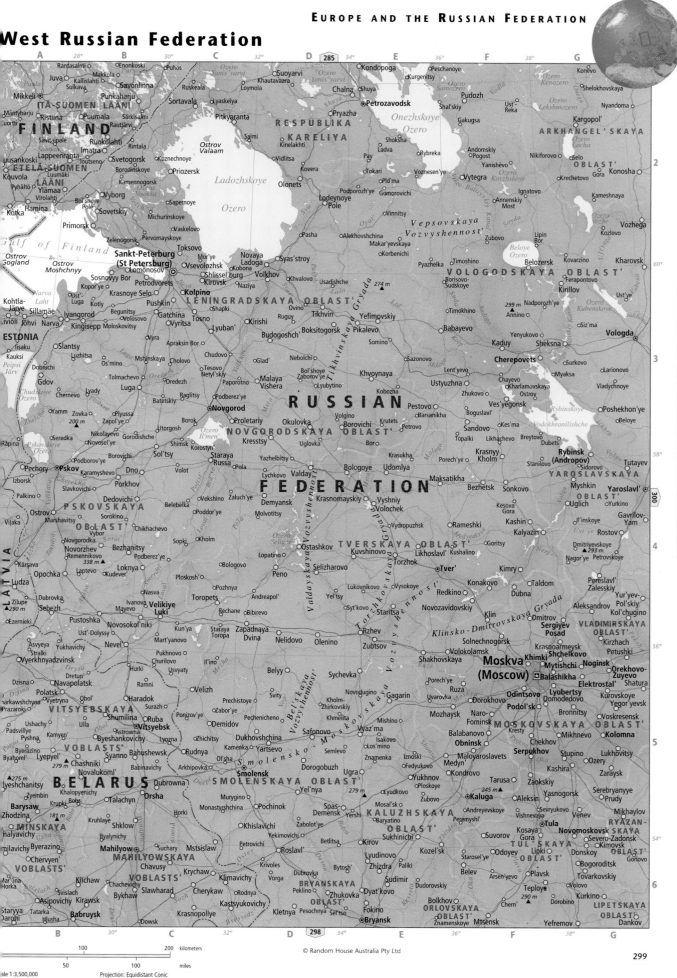

Scale 1:3,500,000

Projection: Equidistant Conic

# Russian Federation and Surrounding Countries

410

Europe and the Russian Federation

**RUSSIAN FEDERATION**
1 RESPUBLIKA DAGESTAN
2 RESPUBLIKA INGUSHETIYA
3 CHECHENSKAYA RESPUBLIKA
4 RESP. SEVERNAYA OSETIYA-ALANIYA
5 KABARDINO-BALKARSKAYA RESPUBLIKA
6 KARACHAYEVO-CHERKESSKAYA RESPUBLIKA
7 RESPUBLIKA ADYGEYA
8 RESPUBLIKA KALMYKIYA
9 RESPUBLIKA MORDOVIYA
10 CHUVASHSKAYA RESPUBLIKA
11 RESPUBLIKA TATARSTAN
12 RESPUBLIKA MARIY EL
13 UDMURTSKAYA RESPUBLIKA
14 RESPUBLIKA BASHKORTOSTAN

**GEORGIA**
15 ABKHAZIA
16 AJARIA
17 SOUTH OSSETIA

**AZERBAIJAN**
18 NAGORNO-KARABAKH
19 NAXÇIVAN

213    208

0    200    400    600    800 kilometers
0    200    400    miles
Scale 1:20,000,000    Projection: Equidistant Conic

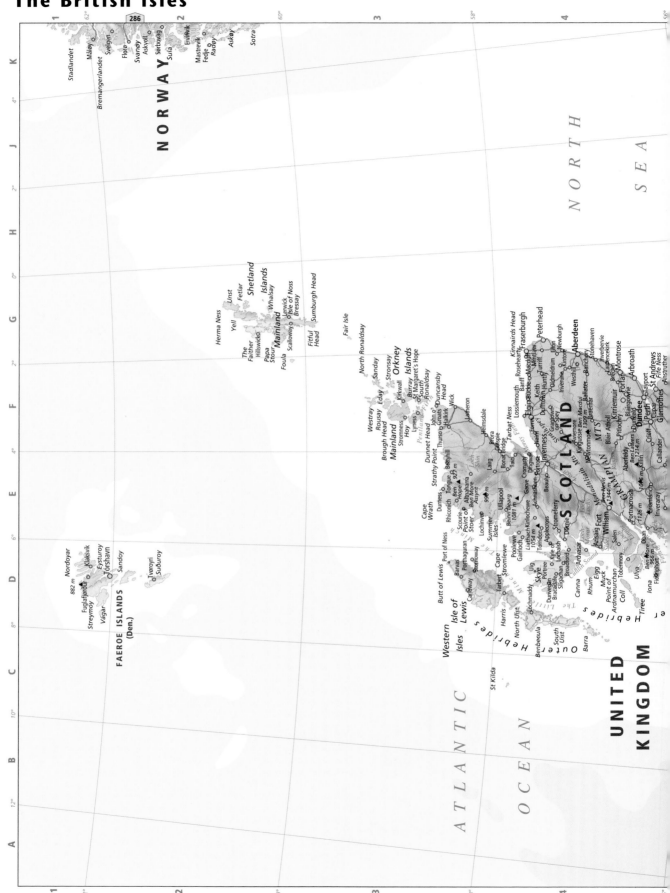

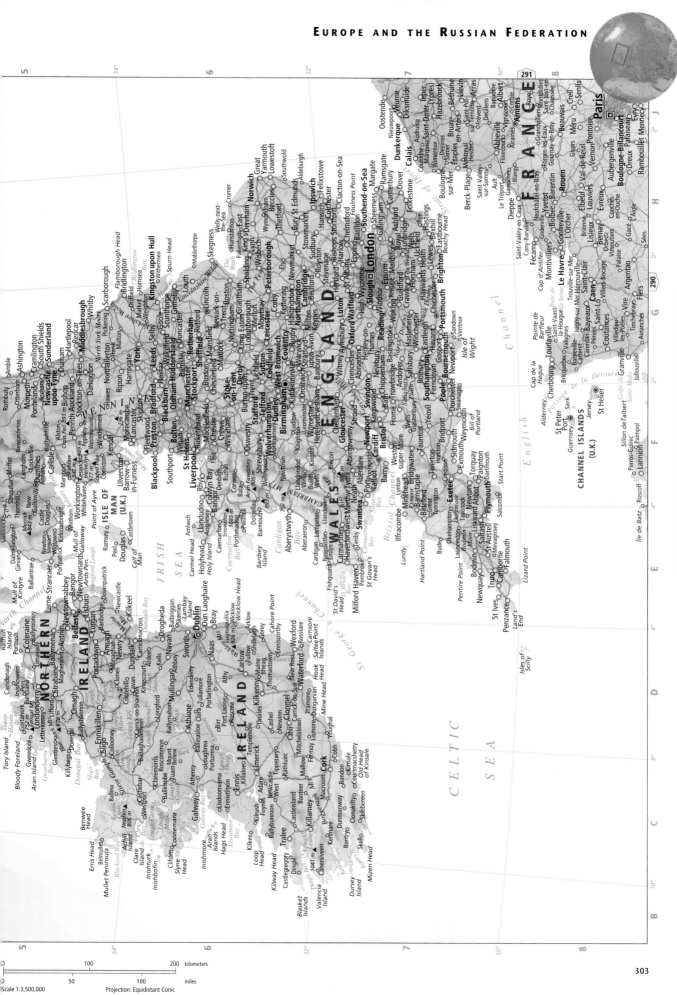

Scale 1:3,500,000          Projection: Equidistant Conic

0     50     100     miles

0     100     200     kilometers

# South England • Wales

**Welsh Unitary Authorities**

43 NEATH PORT TALBOT
44 BRIDGEND
45 RHONDDA CYNON TAFF
46 MERTHYR TYDFIL
47 CAERPHILLY
48 CARDIFF
49 VALE OF GLAMORGAN
50 BLAENAU GWENT
51 TORFAEN
52 NEWPORT
53 MONMOUTHSHIRE
54 WREXHAM
55 FLINTSHIRE

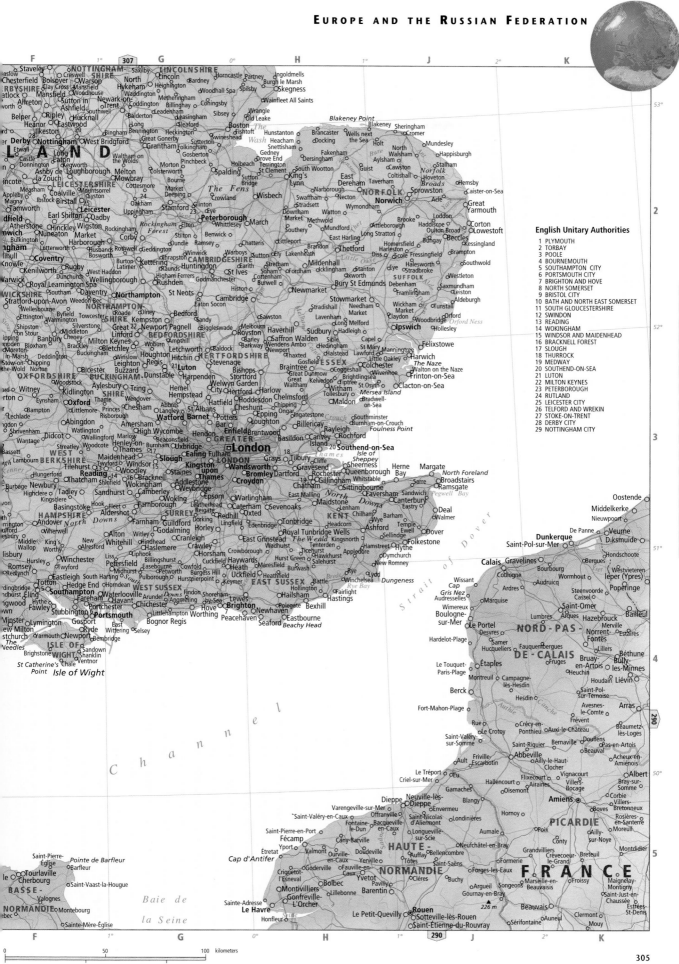

**English Unitary Authorities**

1 PLYMOUTH
2 TORBAY
3 POOLE
4 BOURNEMOUTH
5 SOUTHAMPTON CITY
6 PORTSMOUTH CITY
7 BRIGHTON AND HOVE
8 NORTH SOMERSET
9 BRISTOL CITY
10 BATH AND NORTH EAST SOMERSET
11 SOUTH GLOUCESTERSHIRE
12 SWINDON
13 READING
14 WOKINGHAM
15 WINDSOR AND MAIDENHEAD
16 BRACKNELL FOREST
17 SLOUGH
18 THURROCK
19 MEDWAY
20 SOUTHEND-ON-SEA
21 LUTON
22 MILTON KEYNES
23 PETERBOROUGH
24 RUTLAND
25 LEICESTER CITY
26 TELFORD AND WREKIN
27 STOKE-ON-TRENT
28 DERBY CITY
29 NOTTINGHAM CITY

Scale 1:1,500,000

Projection: Equidistant Conic

0          50          100 kilometers

0     25     50 miles

© Random House Australia Pty Ltd

**English Unitary Authorities**

23 PETERBOROUGH
24 RUTLAND
25 LEICESTER CITY
26 TELFORD AND WREKIN
27 STOKE-ON-TRENT
28 DERBY CITY
29 NOTTINGHAM CITY
30 NORTH EAST LINCOLNSHIRE
31 KINGSTON UPON HULL
32 NORTH LINCOLNSHIRE
33 HALTON
34 WARRINGTON
35 BLACKBURN WITH DARWEN
36 BLACKPOOL
37 YORK CITY
38 DARLINGTON
39 HARTLEPOOL
40 STOCKTON-ON-TEES
41 MIDDLESBROUGH
42 REDCAR AND CLEVELAND

**Welsh Unitary Authorities**

54 WREXHAM
55 FLINTSHIRE

NORTH SEA

Farne Island
Lindisfarne
Bamburgh
North Sunderland
Beadnell Bay
Embleton
Boulmer
Lesbury
Warkworth
Amble
Togston
Ulgham
Longhorsley
Ashington
Lynemouth
Newbiggin-by-the-sea
Bedlington
Blyth
Cramlington
Whitley Bay
Seaton
North Tynemouth
Shields South Shields
Gateshead
TYNE & WEAR
Sunderland
Washington
Houghton-le-Spring
Chester-le-Street
Durham
Peterlee
Trimdon Hartlepool
Ferryhill 39 Tees Bay
Shildon Billingham
Newton Stockton Redcar Saltburn-by-the-Sea
Aycliffe on-Tees 42 Loftus
Darlington 40 Thornaby Guisborough
38 on Tees Sandsend
Scotch Corner Stokesley Castleton Whitby
Crathorne Sleights
Catterick Egton Robin Hood's
North York Bay
NORTH Northallerton Hackness
Leeming Bar Kirkbymoorside Wrelton Scalby Scarborough
Bedale Rosedale Helmsley Seamer
Thirsk Abbey Pickering Filey
YORKSHIRE Topcliffe Filey Head
Ripon Coxwold Malton Hunmanby
Boroughbridge Easingwold North Flamborough
Ripley Norton Grimston Bempton Flamborough Head
Knaresborough Stillington Wharram Bridlington
Harrogate Haxby Fridaythorpe le Street Langtoft Bridlington
Wetherby York Driffield Bay
Spofforth 37 Stamford EAST RIDING Skipsea
Horsforth Bridge OF YORKSHIRE
Leeds Tadcaster Boston Spa Holme upon Pocklington Brandesburton
Pudsey Garforth Spalding Moor Market Leven Hornsea
Morley Castleford Selby Bubwith Weighton Beverley
Pontefract Howden Tunstall
Wakefield Knottingley South Cave 31 Bilton Withernsea
Darton Elmsall Goole Snaith Brough Kingston Anlaby
Barnsley South Askern Thorne Scunthorpe Barton-upon-Hull Patrington
Bentley Crowle 32 upon-Humber Easington
Doncaster Immingham Spurn Head
Rossington Epworth Brigg Grimsby
Maltby Kirton Caistor Cleethorpes
Blyton in Lindsey 30 Tetney
Gainsborough North
Market Binbrook Somercotes
Rasen Louth
Saxilby Manby Mablethorpe
Punholme Maltby Sutton on Sea
LINCOLNSHIRE Wragby le Marsh
Lincoln Horncastle Alford Ingoldmells
North Bardney Partney Burgh le Marsh
Hykeham Woodhall Spa Spilsby Skegness
Waddington Coningsby Wainfleet All Saints
Metheringham Billinghay
Southwell Coddington Sibsey Wrangle
Newark- Leadenham Old Leake
on-Trent Long Sleaford Boston The
Bennington Heckington Wash
West Bridgford Great Gonerby Swineshead Hunstanton Blakeney Point
Grantham Sutterton Heacham Brancaster Blakeney Sheringham
Waltham on Folkingham Gosberton Docking Wells next Holt Cromer
the Wolds Morton Pinchbeck Gedney the Sea Mundesley
Castle Pinchbeck Holbeach Drove End Dersingham North Walsham Happisburgh
Donnington Bourne Spalding Terrington Fakenham Guist Aylsham
Ashby de Melton Cottesmore Sutton St Clement Snettisham Hemsby
la Zouch Mowbray Market South Wootton East Taverham Caister-on-Sea
Coalville Mountsorrel Deeping King's Dereham Norfolk
LEICESTERSHIRE Oakham Crowland Wisbech Lynn Swaffham Necton Sprowston
Syston 24 Stamford The Fens Stradsett Watton Norwich Acle
Ibstock Birstall Glinton Narborough NORFOLK Great
Earl 23 Eye Downham Wymondham Brooke Yarmouth
Shilton Leicester Oadby Uppingham Peterborough Whittlesey March Market Methwold Loddon Corton
Hinckley Wigston Rockingham Elton Southery Mundford Haddiscoe Lowestoft
Market Corby Stilton Benwick Long Attleborough Bungay Beccles
Harborough Oundle Ramsey CAMBRIDGESHIRE Chatteris Littleport East Harling Stratton Oulton Broad Kessingland
Homersfield

Scale 1:1,500,000    Projection: Equidistant Conic

kilometers
0   50   100
miles
0   25   50

# Scotland

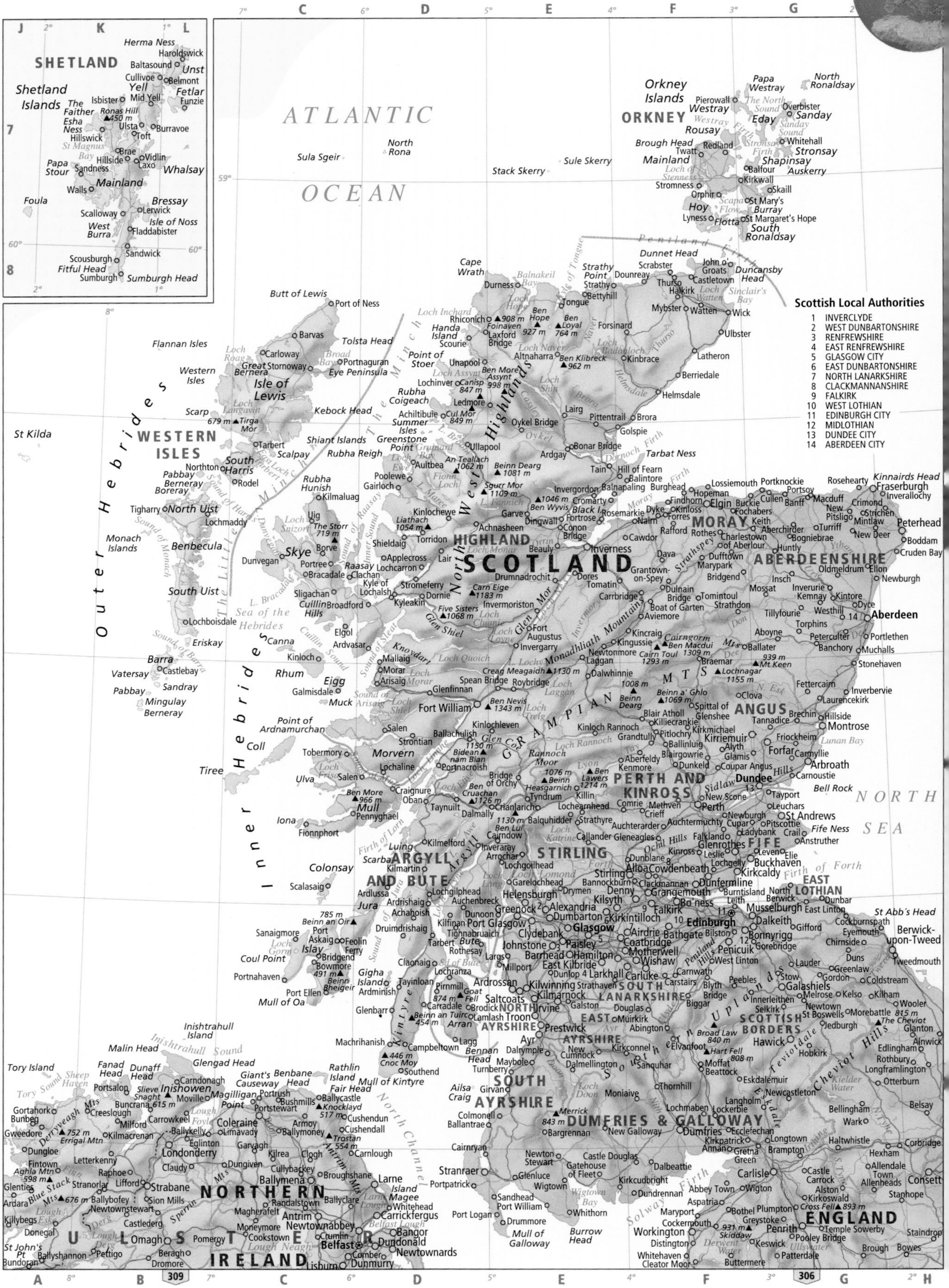

Europe and the Russian Federation

## Scottish Local Authorities

1. INVERCLYDE
2. WEST DUNBARTONSHIRE
3. RENFREWSHIRE
4. EAST RENFREWSHIRE
5. GLASGOW CITY
6. EAST DUNBARTONSHIRE
7. NORTH LANARKSHIRE
8. CLACKMANNANSHIRE
9. FALKIRK
10. WEST LOTHIAN
11. EDINBURGH CITY
12. MIDLOTHIAN
13. DUNDEE CITY
14. ABERDEEN CITY

**SHETLAND**

Shetland Islands

Herma Ness, Haroldswick, Baltasound, Unst, Cullivoe, Belmont, Fetlar, Yell, Mid Yell, Funzie, The Faither, Isbister, Ronas Hill 450 m, Esha Ness, Ulsta, Toft, Burravoe, Hillswick, Hillside, Brae, Vidlin, Laxo, Whalsay, Papa Stour, Sandness, Mainland, Walls, Foula, Scalloway, Lerwick, Bressay, West Burra, Isle of Noss, Fladdabister, Scousburgh, Sandwick, Fitful Head, Sumburgh, Sumburgh Head

**ORKNEY**

Orkney Islands

Papa Westray, North Ronaldsay, Westray, Pierowall, Rousay, Eday, Sanday, Brough Head, Redland, Twatt, Whitehall, Stronsay, Mainland, Shapinsay, Auskerry, Stromness, Orphir, Kirkwall, Scapa Flow, St Mary's, Burray, Hoy, Lyness, Flotta, South Ronaldsay, St Margaret's Hope

**ATLANTIC OCEAN**

Sula Sgeir, North Rona, Stack Skerry, Sule Skerry, St Kilda

**SCOTLAND**

**HIGHLAND**, **MORAY**, **ABERDEENSHIRE**, **ANGUS**, **PERTH AND KINROSS**, **STIRLING**, **FIFE**, **EAST LOTHIAN**, **ARGYLL AND BUTE**, **SOUTH LANARKSHIRE**, **NORTH AYRSHIRE**, **EAST AYRSHIRE**, **SOUTH AYRSHIRE**, **SCOTTISH BORDERS**, **DUMFRIES & GALLOWAY**

West Highlands, Grampian Mts, Monadhliath Mountains, Cairngorm Mts, North West Highlands

**WESTERN ISLES**, Outer Hebrides, Inner Hebrides, Isle of Lewis, North Uist, South Uist, Benbecula, Barra, Skye, Rhum, Eigg, Muck, Coll, Tiree, Mull, Iona, Colonsay, Jura, Islay, Arran, Bute

Ben Nevis 1343 m, Ben Macdui 1309 m, Cairngorm, Cairn Toul 1293 m, Ben Lawers 1214 m, Ben More 998 m

**NORTHERN IRELAND**, ULSTER, Londonderry, Belfast, Antrim

**ENGLAND**

**NORTH SEA**

© Random House Australia Pty Ltd

kilometers 0 — 50

miles 0 — 25 — 50

Scale 1:2,000,000

Projection: Equidistant Conic

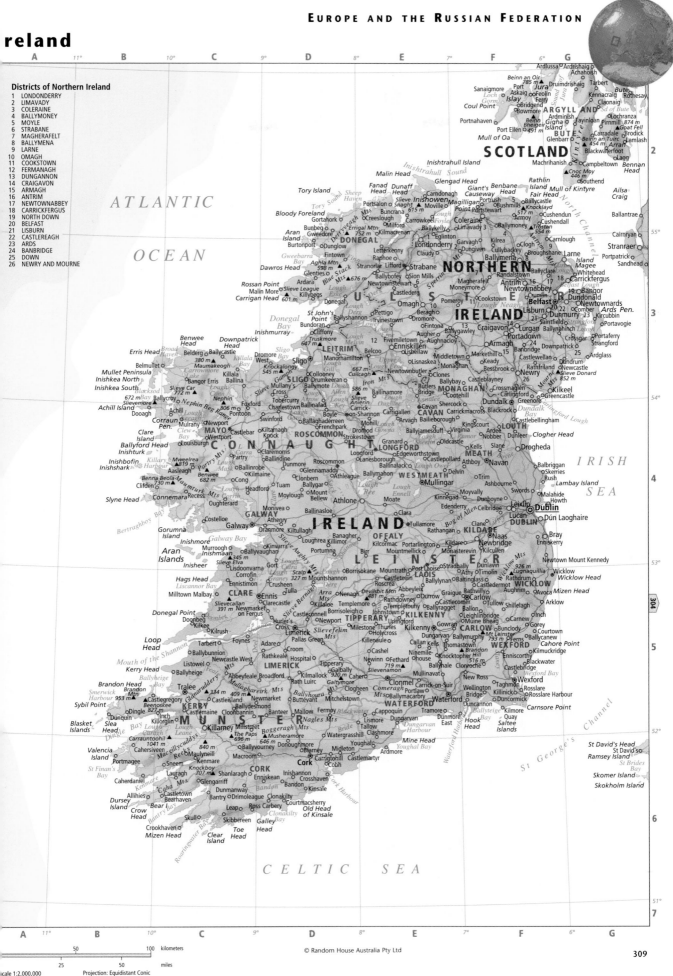

# Africa

Africa, the world's second-largest continent, covers 30.3 million sq km (11.6 million sq miles). It is separated from Europe by the Mediterranean Sea and from Asia by the Red Sea and the Suez Canal. It is bounded by the Atlantic Ocean to the west and the Indian Ocean to the east.

Africa can be broadly divided in two based on culture and to some extent climate: North Africa, and Africa south of the Sahara. Arid North Africa includes Morocco, Western Sahara, Algeria, Tunisia, Libya, and Egypt, all of which are climatically and culturally akin to the Middle East.

South of them a semiarid zone stretches across Mauritania, Mali, Niger, Chad, Sudan, Ethiopia, and Somalia. Humid tropical Africa includes Guinea, Guinea-Bissau, Sierra Leone, Liberia, Côte d'Ivoire, Ghana, Togo, Benin, Nigeria, Cameroon, the Central African Republic, Gabon, Congo, the Democratic Republic of the Congo (formerly Zaire), Uganda, Kenya, Tanzania, Angola, Zambia, Malawi, Zimbabwe, and Mozambique. Southern Africa includes large regions of semiarid and arid land. Namibia is largely desert and there are extensive arid areas in Botswana and South Africa.

## Physical features

Africa consists of a number of plateaus, dissected in the east by the Rift Valley. Volcanic eruptions and elongated lakes and valleys are found along this rift. The Atlas Mountains in the northwest of the continent are the only geologically recent mountains in Africa.

Africa has several long rivers. The Nile, around 6,693 km (4,160 miles) long, arises in the Kenyan highlands, flows north and disgorges in the Mediterranean. The basins of the Congo (around 4,630 km [2,880 miles] long), the Zambeze (around 2,735 km [1,700 miles] long) and the Niger (around 4,100 km [2,150 miles]) cover vast areas.

## Climate and vegetation

Africa is a continent of climatic contrasts. Arid North Africa contains the world's largest hot desert, the Sahara. Drought- and fire-resistant shrubs and grasses are found there. To its north lie narrow zones along the Mediterranean coast with cool, wet winters and hot, dry summers.

On the southern border of the Sahara lies the Sahel, consisting of thorny woodlands and grasslands with scattered trees. Rainfall is gen-

erally low and variable. The area is prone to severe droughts, such as those in the 1980s in Ethiopia and in the 1990s in Somalia. Injudicious cattle herding and grain farming contributed to desertification.

In central and west Africa, equatorial and tropical conditions prevail, with annual rainfall exceeding 1,270 mm (50 in). Forests and woodlands cover large areas. The forests are layered—shrubs and mosses at lower layers and large tree canopies at higher layers. Each layer possesses abundant and distinct wildlife. East Africa has a monsoon climate, and its forests are less dense. In areas of lesser rainfall (less than 380 mm [15 in]), thorny woodlands and grasslands occur. The forests of Africa harbor chimpanzees and gorillas, and their bird life is profuse.

The vegetation of the semiarid lands of the southernmost part of Africa, notably around the borders of the Kalahari Desert, consists of thorny scrub and grasslands. A greater variety of plants occurs in the wetter coastal and upland areas of the southeast parts of South Africa.

Africa's savannas possess among the richest and most diverse animal populations of the world. Zebras, antelopes, giraffes, elephants, rhinoceros, and wildebeest roam in herds, preyed upon by carnivores such as lions, tigers, leopards, hyenas, jackals, and foxes. Bird life includes ostriches and raptors such as eagles and hawks.

Large-scale hunting of wildlife, begun during the colonial era, has had a major impact on Africa's animals. The most notable example has been the quest for ivory—world bans on the trading of ivory have reduced the threat to elephant populations. Other threatened species are white and black rhinoceros, the pygmy hippopotamus, the black wildebeest and some types of zebra.

Islands off the African coast also have their distinct (and distinctive) plant and animal species, notably the lemurs in Madagascar, and the seas are also rich in animal life, including whales, seals, dugongs, and manatees.

*Zebras (left) and elephants (top) are among the most beloved of African animals. These Sudanese people (center) are migrating to Egypt in search of work.*

## Population

From being the apparent origin of the human species, Africa's population has grown to 922 million people (2007). The high rate of population increase between 1985 and 1990 of three percent per annum put pressure on resources and food supplies; currently the growth rate has fallen to 2.3 percent. Life expectancies are low in comparison with other continents: 51.7 years for males and 53.8 years for females.

In arid North Africa, populations are concentrated along the Mediterranean. In Egypt, ninety percent of the country's people live along the banks of the Nile River and on its delta. In humid tropical Africa, populations are more dispersed.

A lack of employment in rural areas during the twentieth century has caused a drift to the cities, resulting in fringe urban settlements with poor facilities. In 2005, an estimated 39.7 percent of Africa's people lived in urban areas.

## Agriculture

More than sixty percent of Africa's people depend upon agriculture for their livelihood. Farming is mostly of the subsistence variety—the Hausa people in the west African savannas grow grains and herd animals, and the Tuareg people in the Sahara practice pastoralism, for example.

Rice, maize, and wheat are grown in several parts of Africa, either where rainfall is adequate or through the use of irrigation (in Egypt and Nigeria). Fruits and vegetables are also grown: bananas and mangoes in humid tropical areas, date palms in arid areas, and citrus fruits, grapes, and olives in areas with a Mediterranean climate.

Plantation agriculture and large-scale farming were established by Europeans in tropical humid

Africa and southern Africa. The plantations provide some countries with their main export earnings—tea and coffee in Burundi and Rwanda, peanuts in Senegal, and tobacco in Malawi.

Prolonged droughts in several parts of Africa, especially in the semiarid Sahel, have severely affected food production. Agricultural production has also been disrupted by civil wars and wars between neighboring countries.

In the countries of the Gulf of Guinea, tropical forests are logged for valuable timbers including mahogany, but forest depletion destroys animal habitats and may affect the global climate.

## Industrialization

Mineral-rich Africa exports most of the minerals it extracts. Algeria, Libya, and Nigeria are major petroleum producers, and oil is also found in Angola, Benin, Guinea-Bissau, and Egypt; natural gas occurs in Algeria, Libya, and Egypt. A rich metallic ore belt extending from central to southern Africa contains copper, zinc, and lead in the Democratic Republic of the Congo and Zambia, iron ore in South Africa and Zimbabwe, nickel in Botswana and South Africa, and manganese in South Africa. South Africa is a major gold and platinum producer. Diamonds are mined in Namibia, South Africa, the Democratic Republic of the Congo, and Angola. Uranium is found in the Central African Republic.

Several African countries obtain more than half their export earnings from a single commodity: Libya, Nigeria, Gabon, Angola, and Egypt from petroleum; Guinea from bauxite. Even South Africa, with its diversified economy, depends on gold for forty percent of its export earnings.

Despite the continent's natural resources, there are no developed countries in Africa. A large proportion of African countries have low indicators for nutrition, education, health, and life expectancy. The United Nations designates these as the world's least developed nations. Several countries, such as Somalia and the Sudan, are not self-sufficient in food production and have during drought and war desperately needed food and aid.

Relatively few African countries have developed significant manufacturing industries. The major exception is South Africa, which now exports machinery and other equipment. During the years of apartheid, however, their racially-based separate development policy created a wide gulf in living standards between the majority black and minority white populations, which will still take considerable time to bridge. Egypt and Kenya produce textiles, processed foods, and cement.

## Languages

A large number of languages are spoken in Africa, but many, such as Tigre and Chadic in northeast Africa and Berber in North Africa, are restricted to small tribal groups. Zulu is spoken by a large group in South Africa. Arabic is the main language of North Africa and the adjoining countries just south of the Sahara. Some languages are widely used, such as Swahili in east Africa and Hausa in west Africa. Malagasy, spoken in Madagascar, is related to Southeast Asian languages.

*This traditionally costumed dancer from Malawi (above right) entertains at both funerals and more cheerful festivities.*

During the colonial period, several European languages became official languages in various parts of Africa, and French, Portuguese, and English are still spoken over large areas. These languages allow communication between tribal groups which speak different languages.

### Boundary disputes and wars

From the sixteenth century onward, Africa was overrun by colonial powers including France, Britain, Portugal, Spain, and Germany. The colonists had great impact in the areas of language, law, and education. The current borders of the nations of Africa were determined during colonial times, too, and often cut across tribal areas, separating members of the same ethnic groups while bringing together traditionally antagonistic tribes: The Somalis for instance found themselves in Somalia, Kenya, and Ethiopia.

Following decolonization, several tribal conflicts have erupted, such as the genocide of Tutsis by the Hutus in Rwanda in 1994. Nigeria had a lengthy period of insurrection when its southern part seceded to form the short-lived Republic of Biafra. A similar conflict rages in southern and western Sudan. These internal conflicts and military coups have inhibited development in large areas of Africa—the civil war in the Democratic Republic of the Congo between 1999 and 2003 killed approximately 2.5 million people; war-torn Somalia has, at present, no effective central government; and Zulu demands for greater autonomy are causing tension in South Africa.

## Nations

| | |
|---|---|
| Algeria | PAGE 314 |
| Angola | PAGE 335 |
| Benin | PAGE 327 |
| Botswana | PAGE 347 |
| Burkina Faso | PAGE 325 |
| Burundi | PAGE 343 |
| Cameroon | PAGE 330 |
| Cape Verde | PAGE 318 |
| Central African Republic | PAGE 331 |
| Chad | PAGE 328 |
| Comoros | PAGE 351 |
| Congo | PAGE 333 |
| Congo, Democratic Republic of | PAGE 334 |
| Côte d'Ivoire | PAGE 323 |
| Djibouti | PAGE 338 |
| Egypt | PAGE 316 |
| Equatorial Guinea | PAGE 331 |
| Eritrea | PAGE 336 |
| Ethiopia | PAGE 338 |
| Gabon | PAGE 333 |
| Gambia | PAGE 320 |
| Ghana | PAGE 325 |
| Guinea | PAGE 321 |
| Guinea-Bissau | PAGE 321 |
| Kenya | PAGE 340 |
| Lesotho | PAGE 349 |
| Liberia | PAGE 323 |
| Libya | PAGE 316 |
| Madagascar | PAGE 353 |
| Malawi | PAGE 344 |
| Mali | PAGE 324 |
| Mauritania | PAGE 318 |
| Mauritius | PAGE 353 |
| Morocco | PAGE 314 |
| Mozambique | PAGE 345 |
| Namibia | PAGE 349 |
| Niger | PAGE 327 |
| Nigeria | PAGE 329 |
| Rwanda | PAGE 342 |
| São Tomé and Príncipe | PAGE 332 |
| Senegal | PAGE 319 |
| Seychelles | PAGE 351 |
| Sierra Leone | PAGE 322 |
| Somalia | PAGE 339 |
| South Africa | PAGE 350 |
| Sudan | PAGE 336 |
| Swaziland | PAGE 348 |
| Tanzania | PAGE 341 |
| Togo | PAGE 326 |
| Tunisia | PAGE 315 |
| Uganda | PAGE 340 |
| Zambia | PAGE 344 |
| Zimbabwe | PAGE 346 |

## Dependencies & territories

| | |
|---|---|
| Mayotte | PAGE 354 |
| Réunion | PAGE 355 |
| St Helena | PAGE 355 |
| Western Sahara | PAGE 354 |

## Autonomous communities

| | |
|---|---|
| Ceuta and Melilla | PAGE 355 |
| Canary Islands | PAGE 355 |
| Madeira | PAGE 355 |

# North Africa

| | |
|---|---|
| Morocco | 314 |
| Algeria | 314 |
| Tunisia | 315 |
| Libya | 316 |
| Egypt | 316 |

## Morocco

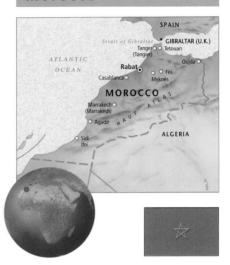

### Fact File

**OFFICIAL NAME** Kingdom of Morocco

**FORM OF GOVERNMENT** Constitutional monarchy with single legislative body (Chamber of Representatives)

**CAPITAL** Rabat

**AREA** 446,550 sq km (172,413 sq miles)

**TIME ZONE** GMT

**POPULATION** 34,343,000

**PROJECTED POPULATION 2015** 34,330,000

**POPULATION DENSITY** 76.9 per sq km (199.2 per sq mile)

**LIFE EXPECTANCY** 71.5

**INFANT MORTALITY (PER 1,000)** 38.2

**OFFICIAL LANGUAGE** Arabic

**OTHER LANGUAGES** Berber languages (Tachelhit, Tamzight, Tarifit, etc.), French, Spanish

**LITERACY RATE** 52.3 %

**RELIGIONS** Muslim 98.7 %, Christian 1.1 %, Jewish 0.2 %

**ETHNIC GROUPS** Arab-Berber 99.1 %, Jewish 0.2 %, other 0.7 %

**CURRENCY** Moroccan dirham

**ECONOMY** Services 47.7 %, industry 37.9 %, agriculture 14.4 %

**GNI PER CAPITA** US$ 2,250

**CLIMATE** Temperate along northern coast, arid in south, cooler in mountains

**HIGHEST POINT** Jebel Toubkal 4,165 m (13,665 ft)

**MAP REFERENCE** Pages 360–61

Morocco's earliest inhabitants were the Berbers, who still live in the country today. At one time under Carthaginian rule, and then a part of the Roman Empire, the Berbers were overrun by Arabs in the seventh century AD and converted to Islam. The country's name derives from the Arabic al-maghrib al-aqsa ("the farthest west"), and because of the protective barrier of the Atlas Mountains, Morocco has always been less a part of the Arab world than the other North African states. Under political pressure from Spain and France during the nineteenth century, Morocco became a French protectorate in 1912. About 35 percent of the people live in the highlands and are Berber-speaking, while the Arab majority live in the lowlands.

Under the rule of King Hassan II (1961–99) and since of his son Mohammed VI, Morocco has followed generally pro-Western policies. Hassan's popularity at home owed a good deal to Morocco's disputed territorial claim to the phosphate-rich resources of Western Sahara across the southern border. A costly armed struggle with the Polisario Front guerrilla movement of Western Sahara led to a ceasefire in 1992, by which time 170,000 of the native-born Sahrawis of the region had become refugees in Algeria. Sovereignty is still unresolved and a UN-organized referendum on its final status has been repeatedly postponed .

More than one-third of Morocco is mountainous. Three parallel ranges of the Atlas Mountains run southwest to northeast, where a plateau stretches toward the Algerian border. Most of the people living in the mountains are peasant cultivators and nomadic herders. Modern economic development is found mainly on the Atlantic plains and the plateaus—the fertile Moulouyan, Rharb, Sous, and High (Haut) Atlas plains constituting virtually all of Morocco's cultivable land. In the Rharb and Rif regions extensive areas are covered with cork oak, while on the northern slopes there are forests of evergreen oak and cedar. Wildlife includes Cuvier's gazelle, the Barbary macaque, and the mouflon (a wild sheep), while desert animals such as the fennec fox live in the south.

In 1995 Morocco suffered its worst drought in 30 years. This seriously affected agriculture, which produces about one-third of Morocco's exports and employs about half the workforce. Irrigation is essential over most of the country, the chief crops being barley and wheat along with citrus fruit, potatoes, and other vegetables. Dates are grown in desert oases. Along the Atlantic coast fishing plays a major role. The country's natural resources are still largely undeveloped. It has coal, iron ore, and zinc, along with the world's largest reserves of phosphates. Debt servicing, unemployment, the high rate of population increase, as well as the unresolved territorial claim to Western Sahara are all long-term problems.

## Algeria

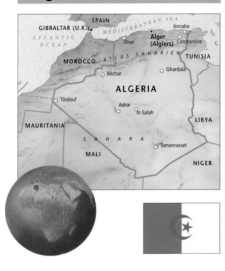

### Fact File

**OFFICIAL NAME** People's Democratic Republic of Algeria

**FORM OF GOVERNMENT** Republic with single legislative body (National People's Assembly), but currently governed by military-backed council

**CAPITAL** Alger (Algiers)

**AREA** 2,381,740 sq km (919,590 sq miles)

**TIME ZONE** GMT

**POPULATION** 33,770,000

**PROJECTED POPULATION 2015** 38,088,000

**POPULATION DENSITY** 14.2 per sq km (36.7 per sq mile)

**LIFE EXPECTANCY** 73.8

**INFANT MORTALITY (PER 1,000)** 28.8

**OFFICIAL LANGUAGE** Arabic

**OTHER LANGUAGES** French, Berber languages (Tamazight, Kabyl)

**LITERACY RATE** 69.9 %

**RELIGIONS** Sunni Muslim 99 %; Christian, Jewish 1 %

**ETHNIC GROUPS** Arab-Berber 99 %, European 1 %

**CURRENCY** Algerian dinar

**ECONOMY** Industry 61.4 %, services 30.4 %, agriculture 8.2 %

**GNI PER CAPITA** US$ 3,620

**CLIMATE** Mild temperate in north, with cool, wet winters and hot, dry summers; arid in south

**HIGHEST POINT** Mt Tahat 2,918 m (9,573 ft)

**MAP REFERENCE** Pages 360–61

The largest state in the north of Africa, Algeria was once a province of the Roman Empire known as Numidia, and since early times it has been the home of nomadic Berber peoples. Arabs came to the region during the seventh century, bringing Islam, and in the sixteenth century Algeria was incorporated into the Ottoman Empire. From the sixteenth to the nineteenth centuries Algeria posed a significant threat to all who used the nearby regions of the Mediterranean Sea. The pirates of what was at that time called the Barbary

Africa

GNI PER CAPITA US$ 3,200

CLIMATE Temperate in north, with mild, rainy winters and hot, dry summers; desert in south

HIGHEST POINT Jabal ash Sha'nabī 1,544 m (5,065 ft)

MAP REFERENCE Page 361

*A water seller in Morocco (left page). The Algerian town of Ghardaïa lies at the eastern end of the Grand Erg Occidental, on the fringe of the Sahara Desert (above). Workmen renovating a building in Tunisia (below).*

Coast made a lucrative living by trading in slaves and by attacking passing shipping. A French colony from 1848, Algeria won its independence in 1962 after eight years of bitter war. Thirty years of peace followed, but after 1992 the country was torn by violence. The ruthless civil conflict between the government and the Islamic Salvation Front (FIS) cost tens of thousands their lives and kept flaring up after elections 1999 and 2004.

More than ninety percent of Algeria's people live on the narrow, fertile, discontinuous coastal strip on the Mediterranean. One-third of the population lives by farming, and it is here that most of the country's arable land is found—only three percent of the whole country. Inland, and to the south, are the Maritime Atlas Mountains. Their northern slopes have a relatively reliable rainfall and support a shrinking forest of pines, cedars, evergreens, and cork oaks. A high plateau about 250 km (150 miles) wide lies between the coastal range and the Atlas Saharien Mountains. Beyond these, all the way to the boundaries of Mali and Niger, stretches the sandy, rocky waste of the Sahara Desert, dotted here and there with small oasis settlements.

As much as 85 percent of Algeria's land area is desert. In many parts of the country rain almost never falls and the summer heat is intense. Along the Mediterranean coast, however, while the summers are hot and dry the winters are wet. Wildlife on the inland plateaus includes wild boar and gazelle; in the desert there are small mammals such as the jerboa and the Saharan hare.

Oil and natural gas are the foundation of Algeria's economy and over the years revenue from these sources has encouraged a wide range of industrial development. From the late 1960s, the country's economy was run as a centrally controlled state system along Soviet lines. This began to change following 1989 with the introduction of market mechanisms. The farming region along the northern coast produces wheat, barley, oats, grapes, and olives, and supplies a wide variety of early fruit and vegetables to markets in Europe.

## Tunisia

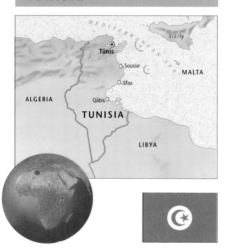

## Fact File

OFFICIAL NAME Republic of Tunisia

FORM OF GOVERNMENT Republic with single legislative body (Chamber of Deputies)

CAPITAL Tūnis

AREA 163,610 sq km (63,170 sq miles)

TIME ZONE GMT + 1 hour

POPULATION 10,384,000

PROJECTED POPULATION 2015 11,204,000

POPULATION DENSITY 63.5 per sq km (164.4 per sq mile)

LIFE EXPECTANCY 75.6

INFANT MORTALITY (PER 1,000) 23.4

OFFICIAL LANGUAGE Arabic

OTHER LANGUAGES French, Berber languages

LITERACY RATE 74.3 %

RELIGIONS Muslim 98 %, Christian 1 %, Jewish 1 %

ETHNIC GROUPS Arab-Berber 98 %, European 1 %, Jewish and other 1 %

CURRENCY Dinar

ECONOMY Services 62.8 %, industry 25.7 % agriculture 11.5 %

Tunisia has a long history. Located in North Africa, across from Sicily, it was founded by Phoenician sailors 3,000 years ago, became famous as the Carthage of Queen Dido, and fell to the Romans in 146 BC. Arab conquest brought Islam to the region in the seventh century AD.

In modern times control of Tunisia was disputed by Italy, England, and France before it became a French protectorate in 1883. Ruled since independence in 1956 as a de facto one-party state, Tunisia held its first multi-party elections in 1994 (the government claiming 99.9 percent of the vote). Tunisia is a relatively prosperous country, strongly influenced by French and European culture, with a record of modest but steady economic growth. While Islamic fundamentalism is on the rise, women are treated with greater equality in Tunisia than elsewhere in the Arab world.

The eastern end of the Atlas Mountains juts across the border from Algeria in the north. A mountainous plateau called the Dorsale extends northeast sloping down to the coastal plains. Parallel to the Mediterranean Sea in the extreme northwest, the Kroumirie Mountains, covered with cork oaks, shelter the fertile valley of the Majardah River as it flows down from the Dorsale. Harnessed for hydroelectric power, this enters the sea near Tūnis across broad alluvial lowlands used for growing a wide variety of crops, some extensively irrigated, including wheat and barley, olives, sugar beet, citrus fruits, grapes, and vegetables. South of the mountains a dry expanse of plateau-steppe gives way to a series of salt lakes, the largest, Shaṭṭ al Jarīd, extending halfway across the country. The large remaining area to the south is desert.

Tunisia has a diverse economy. Agriculture is the main employer, but in recent years it has declined in importance as a revenue earner relative to mineral and petroleum exports. Most industrial production is based on agricultural and mining products. Real growth averaged five percent from 2003 to 2005, with moderate inflation. Growth in tourism has been a key factor. Since the 1960s Tunisia has been a popular destination for European tourists, drawn by winter sunshine, beaches, and Roman remains. In recent years, however, tourism slacked somewhat, especially due to the activities of Islamic militants. Tunisia tries to reduce its trade barrieers with the EU to boost its economic growth.

# Libya

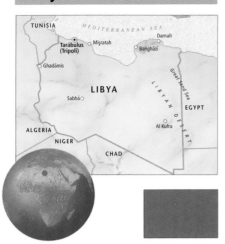

## Fact File

**OFFICIAL NAME** Socialist People's Libyan Arab Jamahiriya

**FORM OF GOVERNMENT** Republic with single legislative body (General People's Congress)

**CAPITAL** Tarābulus (Tripoli)

**AREA** 1,759,540 sq km (679,358 sq miles)

**TIME ZONE** GMT + 2 hours

**POPULATION** 6,174,000

**PROJECTED POPULATION 2015** 7,129,000

**POPULATION DENSITY** 3.5 per sq km (9.1 per sq mile)

**LIFE EXPECTANCY** 77.1

**INFANT MORTALITY (PER 1,000)** 21.9

**OFFICIAL LANGUAGE** Arabic

**OTHER LANGUAGES** Berber and Nilo-Saharan languages, Italian, English

**LITERACY RATE** 82.6 %

**RELIGIONS** Sunni Muslim 97 %, other 3 %

**ETHNIC GROUPS** Berber and Arab 97 %; other (including Greek, Maltese, Italian, Egyptian, Pakistani, Turkish, Indian, Tunisian) 3 %

**CURRENCY** Libyan dinar

**ECONOMY** Industry 83 %, services 14.9 %, agriculture 2.1 %

**GNI PER CAPITA** US$ 9,010

**CLIMATE** Mainly arid; temperate along coast

**HIGHEST POINT** Bikubiti 2,285 m (7,497 ft)

**MAP REFERENCE** Page 362

First settled by the Greeks, and once part of the empire of Alexander the Great, Libya was ruled by the Romans for 500 years. Later, in AD 642, the region was conquered by the Arabs, and later still became part of the Ottoman Empire. It was occu-

pied by Italy in 1911, and the years 1938 to 1939 saw Mussolini bring in 30,000 Italians to farm the Jefra Plain. Libya became independent in 1951. Since 1969, when he seized power, it has been a one-party socialist state ruled dictatorially by Colonel Muammar al Gaddafi. In 1992–99 the country suffered UN sanctions due to his support of terrorist cells.

The arid Saharan Plateau takes up a vast 93 percent of Libya's land area. The great expanse of the Sahara gives way to a fertile coastal strip along the Mediterranean coast, where the majority of the population lives, though only one percent of the total land area is arable. Tripoli stands on the Jefra Plain, Libya's most productive farming area. Cereals, particularly barley, are the most important crop. Sorghum is grown in the Fezzan to the south; wheat, tobacco, and olives are produced in the north; and dates and figs are cultivated at a few scattered oases in the desert. Predominantly low-lying, the desert terrain rises southward to Bikubiti in the Tibesti Range on the border with Chad. The country is without lakes or perennial rivers, and artesian wells supply nearly two-thirds of its water.

Oil provides almost all export earnings and about one-third of the gross domestic product. Though Libya's per capita gross domestic product is usually Africa's highest, the people suffer from periodic shortages of basic goods and foodstuffs caused by import restrictions. The largely state-controlled industrial sector (almost all the oil companies were nationalized in 1973) suffers from overstaffing and other constraints. However, oil revenues have enabled important state initiatives to be undertaken: the Great Manmade River Project being built to bring water from large aquifers under the Sahara to the coastal cities is one of the world's largest water development projects.

# Egypt

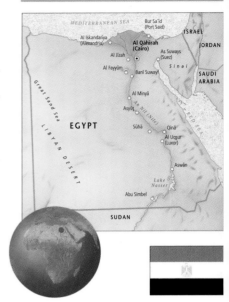

## Fact File

**OFFICIAL NAME** Arab Republic of Egypt

**FORM OF GOVERNMENT** Republic with two legislative bodies (Advisory Council and People's Assembly)

**CAPITAL** Al Qāhirah (Cairo)

**AREA** 1,001,450 sq km (386,660 sq miles)

**TIME ZONE** GMT + 2 hours

**POPULATION** 81,714,000

**PROJECTED POPULATION 2015** 86,219,000

**POPULATION DENSITY** 81.6 per sq km (211.3 per sq mile)

**LIFE EXPECTANCY** 71.9

**INFANT MORTALITY (PER 1,000)** 28.4

**OFFICIAL LANGUAGE** Arabic

**OTHER LANGUAGES** Nubian and Berber languages, English, French

**LITERACY RATE** 71.4 %

**RELIGIONS** Muslim (mostly Sunni) 90 %, Christian (Coptic) 9 %, other Christian 1 %

**ETHNIC GROUPS** Egyptian 98 %; Berber, Nubian, Bedouin 1 %; Greek, Armenian, other European 1 %

**CURRENCY** Egyptian pound

**ECONOMY** Services 45.1 %, industry 41.1 %, agriculture 13.8 %

**GDP PER CAPITA** US$ 1,580

**CLIMATE** Mainly arid; mild winters, hot, dry summers

**HIGHEST POINT** Jabal Kātrīna 2,629 m (8,625 ft)

**MAP REFERENCE** Pages 362–63

## Timeline

| | | | | | |
|---|---|---|---|---|---|
| **c. 2650 BC** The first pyramids are built during a 500-year period of peace and prosperity under the Old Kingdom | **1497–26 BC** King Thutmose III's reign marks height of Empire; buildings include Temple of Amon at Karnak | **332 BC** Egypt becomes part of Alexander the Great's empire; he builds the city of Alexandria on the Mediterranean coast | **AD 642** Egypt comes under the control of Muslim Arabs from the regions to the east | **1798** Napoleon conquers Egypt and leaves French troops in control of the country | **1801** British and Ottoman troops expel French occupation forces from Egypt |
| **c. 3600 BC** Agriculture begins in alluvial soils deposited in the Nile Valley; irrigation used for growing fruit and vegetables | **c. 3100 BC** King Menes founds first dynasty to rule nation; civilization begins with uniting of Upper and Lower regions in Nile Valley | **1991 BC** Egypt's power expands—King Amenemhet I and his successors conquer Nubia and trade with Syria and Palestine | **1153 BC** Assassination of Ramses III; Egyptian power declines as a result of corruption and feuding between priests and kings | **31 BC** Rome takes control of Egypt when Mark Antony and Cleopatra's navy is defeated by Octavian's fleet at Battle of Actium | **1517** Ottoman Turks defeat the Mamelukes (Turks, Mongols, and Circassians) and rule for the next 250 years |

Egypt is sometimes known as "the gift of the Nile" (An Nīl) because the waters of this famous river have always been the lifeblood of the country. Every year until the Aswan High Dam was built, the Nile would flood, spreading fertile silt across the floor of the valley. It was in the Nile Valley that Egyptian civilization began, 6,000 years ago, and the country was the first to have a society organized along political lines. The Great Pyramid itself, still one of the largest structures in the world, was built 5,000 years ago. Since then innumerable rulers and conquerors have come and gone—Persians, Greeks, and Romans being followed by the seventh-century conquests of Mohammed's followers and the conversion of the region to Islam. During the nineteenth century, after the construction of the Suez Canal in 1869, Egypt came increasingly under the influence of the French and the British. Britain made it a protectorate from 1914 to 1922. It was not until 1952 that Egypt became an independent republic.

## Physical features and land use

Egypt is defined by the valley of the Nile and the spreading deserts on either side. The Nile rises at Lake Victoria, further south, and enters the country across the southern border, from Sudan. It first fills huge Lake Nasser, formed by the Aswan High Dam, which was completed in 1965. It then makes an eastward bend near Luxor before flowing steadily north. At Cairo the river fans out into a broad delta before entering the Mediterranean. The area north of Cairo is often known as Lower Egypt and the area south of Cairo as Upper Egypt.

Although the lands of the valley and the delta constitute only three percent of Egypt's total land area, this is where 99 percent of the people live and where nearly all agricultural activity takes place. West of the Nile, extending to the Libyan border, lies the Western (or Libyan) Desert. This arid limestone region consists of low valleys and scarps, and in the north contains a large area below sea level called the Qattara Depression. Scattered across the desert are isolated fertile oases where date palms grow. It is hoped to increase the agricultural production of these oases by using deep artesian bores.

Between the Nile and the Red Sea is the Eastern (or Arabian) Desert. Here, grasses, tamarisks, and mimosas grow, providing desert nomads with feed for their sheep, camels, and goats. Between the Gulf of Suez and the border with Israel is the almost uninhabited triangular limestone plateau of the Sinai Peninsula. Egypt's highest peak, Jabal Kātrīnā, is found in Sinai's mountainous south.

## People and culture

While there are significant cultural differences between the ninety percent of the population who are Hamitic and the Afro-Nubian peoples of the Upper Nile near Sudan, Egypt has a long tradition of ethnic and religious tolerance. In Cairo and Alexandria there have always been sizeable colonies of Greeks and Armenians, and although most Jews have now left for Israel, there is still a small Jewish community in Cairo. The small number of desert Bedouin divide into two main groups. In the southern part of the Eastern Desert live the Arabdah and Bisharin (Hamitic Beja), while Saadi and Murabatin (of Arab and Berber ancestry) are found throughout the Western Desert.

Ancient Egypt's art, architecture, pyramids and tombs are among the treasures of civilization. Evidence from tombs shows that even at the time of the first recorded dynasty, about 4400 BC, furniture inlaid with ivory and ebony was being made, along with alabaster vessels and fine work in copper and gold. In the pyramid-building period between 3700 BC and 2500 BC the Great Pyramid of Cheops was erected, a project thought to have occupied 100,000 men for twenty years. The pyramids were themselves immense tombs, containing chambers in which dead kings were buried, supplied with all they might need—food, clothing, and furniture—in the afterlife. It is not known when exactly Christianity began in Egypt, but it was very early, around AD 40. The new faith was readily accepted since the hope of a future life coincided with the views of the Egyptians themselves.

Today about eight to ten percent of the people are Coptic Christians. The Copts claim to have received the gospel directly from St Mark, the first bishop of Alexandria. Their community has always valued education highly, and has contributed many figures to Egyptian public life. About ninety percent of the population are Muslim, mainly Sunni.

With the rise of Islamic fundamentalism, the most bitter conflict within Egypt is between the modernizing political elite and the fundamentalist Moslem Brotherhood. The latter is held responsible for terrorist activities, but today seems to be under control. Arabic is the official language, but several other languages are used by ethnic minorities, from Hamito-Sudanic among the Nubians to the Berber-related language of the Siwah tribe east of the Qattara Depression.

## Economy and resources

Food crops have been grown in the fertile soils of the Nile floodplain and delta for many thousands of years. But a population of more than 81 million, increasing by almost 1.4 million per year, is placing considerable pressure on Egypt's agricultural resources. In addition, salination of land below the High Aswan Dam, land lost to growing urbanization, and desertification as a result of wind-blown sand, are all reducing the amount of arable land. Today much of Egypt's food is imported.

In manufacturing, textiles are by far the largest industry, and include spinning, weaving, and the dyeing and printing of cotton, wool, silk, and synthetic-fiber materials. Along with finished textiles, raw cotton remains one of the main exports, only exceeded in value by petroleum and, recently, natural gas. There are plans to restore the Suez Canal's earning capacity by deepening and widening it for modern shipping. Since 2005, the government has started privatizing large-scale industrial plants in order to reduce overstaffing and over-regulation, and to encourage both technical improvements and investment. These reforms have to be continued agressively for the country's economic performance to improve.

*An obelisk, covered with hieroglyphs, among the ruins at Luxor (left page). The Red Sea and the Sinai Desert (below left). Cairo and the Nile at dusk (below right).*

| 1882 British troops occupy Egypt | 1922 Britain grants nominal independence | 1948–49 Egypt part of Arab League invasion of Israel after Palestine is partitioned into Arab and Jewish nations; Israel repels invasion | 1956 President Nasser first nationalizes Suez Canal then closes it. Britain, France, and Israel invade to reopen canal—UN intervenes | 1967 Egypt and other Arab nations attack Israel but are defeated in "Six Day War"; Israel occupies the Gaza Strip and Sinai | 1981 President Sadat assassinated and succeeded by Hosni Mubarak | 1992 Cairo damaged in an earthquake which kills more than 500 people | 2005 Despite renewed attacks on Sinai with 88 deaths, a record number of tourists visit Egypt. Unemployment remains an unsolved problem. |
|---|---|---|---|---|---|---|---|
| 1869 Suez Canal completed, allowing quicker access to India and the Pacific | 1914 Egypt made a protectorate of the United Kingdom | 1940–42 German and Italian troops fight battles against Allied forces along the north coast of Egypt and in the Western Desert | 1953 Egypt becomes a republic, King Farouk is exiled | 1960 Construction of the Aswan High Dam on the River Nile begins; it creates Lake Nasser, flooding several ancient sites | 1979 President Sadat ends hostilities with Israel and signs an agreement under which Sinai is returned to Egyptian control | 1990 Egypt opposes Iraq's invasion of oil-rich Kuwait and sides with US and European allies in the Gulf War | 1997 In Upper Egypt Muslim fundamentalists attack tourists and kill 58 people | 2005 President Hosni Mubarak allows opposition candidates to take part in elections to his fifth term in office. |

# Western Africa

Mauritania · · · · · · · · 318
Cape Verde · · · · · · · · 318
Senegal · · · · · · · · · · 319
Gambia · · · · · · · · · · 320
Guinea-Bissau · · · · · · 321
Guinea · · · · · · · · · · 321
Sierra Leone · · · · · · · 322
Liberia · · · · · · · · · · 323
Côte d'Ivoire · · · · · · · 323
Mali · · · · · · · · · · · · 324
Burkina Faso · · · · · · · 325
Ghana · · · · · · · · · · · 325
Togo · · · · · · · · · · · · 326
Benin · · · · · · · · · · · 327
Niger · · · · · · · · · · · 327
Chad · · · · · · · · · · · · 328
Nigeria · · · · · · · · · · 329

# Mauritania

## Fact File

**OFFICIAL NAME** Islamic Republic of Mauritania

**FORM OF GOVERNMENT** Republic with two legislative bodies (Senate and National Assembly)

**CAPITAL** Nouakchott

**AREA** 1,030,700 sq km (397,953 sq miles)

**TIME ZONE** GMT

**POPULATION** 3,365,000

**PROJECTED POPULATION 2015** 3,757,000

**POPULATION DENSITY** 3.3 per sq km (8.5 per sq mile)

**LIFE EXPECTANCY** 53.9

**INFANT MORTALITY (PER 1,000)** 66.7

**OFFICIAL LANGUAGE** Arabic

**OTHER LANGUAGES** Languages from Niger and Congo (including Pulaar, Wolof and Solinka), French

**LITERACY RATE** 51.2 %

**RELIGIONS** Muslim 100 %

**ETHNIC GROUPS** Harratin ("black moors") 40 %, Moors 30 %, black Africans 30 %

**CURRENCY** Ouguiya

**ECONOMY** Services 46 %, industry 29 %, agriculture 25 %

**GNI PER CAPITA** US$ 840

**CLIMATE** Mainly arid, with wet season in far south (May to September)

**HIGHEST POINT** Kediet Ijill 910 m (2,987 ft)

**MAP REFERENCE** Pages 360, 364

Most of Mauritania consists of the wastes of the western Sahara Desert. Islam in the region dates from the Almoravid Empire of the twelfth century. Later, it was conquered by Arab bidan or "white" Moors (*Maure* in French, meaning Moor), nomads who subjugated and enslaved the black Africans of the south, producing a people of mixed Arab and African descent known as *barratin* or "black" Moors. Deep social tensions between the dominant "white" Moors, the "black" Moors, and the subordinate thirty percent of black African farmers in the south lie at the heart of Mauritanian politics. Slavery in Mauritania was not officially abolished until 1970, and it is estimated that tens of thousands of *barratin* still live as slaves. France entered the region early in the nineteenth century and established a protectorate in 1903. Independence finally came in 1960. In 2005, a coup deposed the president and ushered in a military council, which created conditions for genuine democratic institutions and organized elections. Parliamentary elections were held in late 2006/early 2007 and presidential elections in March 2007.

Inland from the low-lying coastal plains of the Atlantic seaboard there are low plateaus—a table-land broken by occasional hills and scarps. The Sahara Desert to the north, which forms 47 percent of Mauritania's total land area, rises to the isolated peak of Kediet Ijill. In the southern third of the country there is just enough rain to support Sahelian thornbush and grasses. After rain, cattle herders drive their herds from the Senegal River through these grasslands and in good years the livestock outnumber the general population five to one. During the 1980s the whole area suffered severely from drought and the nomadic population, which had numbered three-quarters of the national population, fell to less than one-third, many nomads abandoning rural life entirely.

Farmers near the Senegal River grow millet, sorghum, beans, peanuts, and rice, using the late-summer river floods for irrigation. A hydroelectric plant on the river provides water for the irrigated cultivation of rice, cotton, and sugarcane, but drought has also driven many subsistence farmers from the land. Off the coast, cooled by the Canaries current, lie some of the richest fishing grounds in the world. About 100,000 tonnes of fish are landed annually, and the potential catch is estimated at about 600,000 tonnes. In 2001, exploratory oil wells 80 km offshore indicated potential extraction. Mauritania has an estimated 1 billion barrels of reserves. Oil production and exports began in early 2006.

# Cape Verde

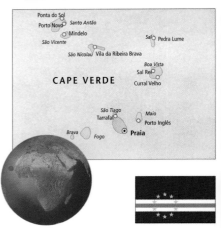

## Fact File

**OFFICIAL NAME** Republic of Cape Verde

**FORM OF GOVERNMENT** Republic with single legislative body (People's National Assembly)

**CAPITAL** Praia

**AREA** 4,033 sq km (1,557 sq miles)

**TIME ZONE** GMT – 1 hour

**POPULATION** 427,000

**PROJECTED POPULATION 2015** 628,000

**POPULATION DENSITY** 105.9 per sq km (274.2 per sq mile)

**LIFE EXPECTANCY** 71.3

**INFANT MORTALITY (PER 1,000)** 42.6

**OFFICIAL LANGUAGE** Portuguese

**OTHER LANGUAGES** Crioulo (blend of Portuguese and West African languages)

**LITERACY RATE** 76.6 %

**RELIGIONS** Roman Catholic and indigenous beliefs, often in combination

**ETHNIC GROUPS** Mixed African-European (Mulatto) 71 %, African 28 %, European 1 %

**CURRENCY** Cape Verdean escudo

**ECONOMY** Services 74 %, industry 16.7 %, agriculture 9.3 %

**GNI PER CAPITA** US$ 2,430

**CLIMATE** Arid, with warm, dry summers

**HIGHEST POINT** Pico do Cano (Fogo) 2,829 m (9,281 ft)

**MAP REFERENCE** Page 360

Cape Verde consists of two small groups of islands 560 km (350 miles) off Dakar, Senegal, on the westernmost part of west Africa. These islands were discovered, uninhabited, by Portuguese navigators in 1456. For several centuries, until 1876, the islands were used by slave traders as a depot for assembling slaves and provisioning ships. As with other places involved in the slave trade, this activity influenced the composition of the population, with 71 percent being today of Afro-Portuguese background. Portuguese colonial administration came to an end with independence in 1975, but

*View of the city of Mindelo and its harbor towards volcanic mountain peaks protruding from the sea, São Vicente, Cape Verde (below). Women removing small fish from a fishing net in Senegal (right).*

because of limited opportunities on the islands more Cape Verdeans now live abroad than at home. Remittances are an important source of domestic income.

The northern group of islands is called the Barlavento or windward group; the southern is called the Sotavento or leeward group. Volcanic, with slopes weathered into unusual shapes by the wind, the land leads steeply up from the sea to mountainous heights. The active volcano of Mt Cano on the island of Fogo in the southern group is the highest point. The most densely populated areas are the coastal plain of São Tiago in the southern group, and Santa Antão and São Vicente in the northern group. A chronic lack of water makes agriculture difficult, and most of the productive farming is done in a small number of irrigated inland valleys. Droughts regularly devastate the crops of maize, beans, and sweet potatoes on which the majority of Cape Verdeans live. The effects of the drought that lasted from 1968 to 1982 were so severe that some 40,000 people emigrated to Portugal.

On the economic front Cape Verde faces a number of severe problems. The natural resource base is limited. The only minerals of any significance are salt and pozzolana, a volcanic rock that is used for making cement. Only two food products are exported—fish and bananas, each representing one-third of total exports. Although almost sixty percent of the population lives in the countryside, the gross national product share of agriculture is only twelve percent, the tuna catch accounting for four percent of that figure. About 82 percent of food is imported and Cape Verde is heavily dependent on foreign aid. The country has been exploring EU membership in recent years.

## Senegal

### Fact File

| | |
|---|---|
| **OFFICIAL NAME** | Republic of Senegal |
| **FORM OF GOVERNMENT** | Republic with single legislative body (National Assembly) |
| **CAPITAL** | Dakar |
| **AREA** | 196,190 sq km (75,749 sq miles) |
| **TIME ZONE** | GMT |
| **POPULATION** | 12,853,000 |
| **PROJECTED POPULATION 2015** | 14,878,000 |
| **POPULATION DENSITY** | 65.5 per sq km (169.7 per sq mile) |
| **LIFE EXPECTANCY** | 57.1 |
| **INFANT MORTALITY (PER 1,000)** | 58.9 |
| **OFFICIAL LANGUAGE** | French |
| **OTHER LANGUAGES** | Wolof, Pulaar, Jola, Mandinka |
| **LITERACY RATE** | 39.3 % |
| **RELIGIONS** | Muslim 94 %, Christian 5 % (mainly Roman Catholic), indigenous beliefs 1 % |
| **ETHNIC GROUPS** | Wolof 43 %, Fula 24 %, Serer 15 %, Diola 4 %, Mandinka 3 %, European and Lebanese 1 %, other 10 % |
| **CURRENCY** | CFA (Communauté Financière Africaine) franc |
| **ECONOMY** | Services 64.4 %, industry 18.9 %, agriculture 16.7 % |
| **GNI PER CAPITA** | US$ 820 |
| **CLIMATE** | Tropical, with wet season June to October |
| **HIGHEST POINT** | Unnamed location in southeast 581 m (1,906 ft) |
| **MAP REFERENCE** | Page 364 |

Dakar, the capital of Senegal, lies on the westernmost point of west Africa and in the seventeenth and eighteenth centuries it was a major slave-trading base. French colonial control of Senegal was established during the suppression of the slave trade in the nineteenth century. As the administrative center of the huge region of French West

Africa

Africa, an effective road network was established in Dakar, plus extensive port facilities and a large civil service.

Independence from France came in 1960. Despite being a de facto one-party state for the next ten years, Senegal avoided military and dictatorial rule, and has recently liberalized its economic and political life. In 1982, Senegal joined with Gambia to form the nominal confederation of Senegambia. However, the envisaged integration of the two countries was never carried out, and the union was dissolved in 1989. Senegal's most serious problem is continuing armed revolt in the oil-rich southern province of Casamance, south of Gambia, a region that differs ethnically, economically, and geographically from the north.

Senegal is split by the near-enclave of Gambia and the Gambia River. To the north the land is drier, with sand dunes along the coast. Inland there are plains, savanna, and semidesert, where Fulani cattle-herders eke out an existence. South of Dakar and Cape Vert it is wetter and more fertile, with coastal mangrove swamps and forest inland. Sorghum is grown in the rainier areas of savanna bushland, while south of Gambia rice is cultivated on the floodplain of the Casamance River—the most fertile part of the country.

Peanuts have long been the foundation of Senegal's economy and are grown on half the cultivated land. Efforts are being made to diversify, and sugarcane, millet, cotton, and rice are now cultivated. Other than the recently developed oil fields in Casamance, with the promise of more offshore, natural resources are few. Though its arrangements are democratic, Senegal's ruling party has been in power since the 1950s, creating a network of patronage through the civil service, the judiciary, and the state-owned industries. Long-overdue reforms are therefore not likely to happen in the foreseeable future. Senegal receives a considerable amount of foreign aid.

*Fishermen at a beach in Gambia fix their boats (below). Market street in Serekunda, Gambia (center).*

# Gambia

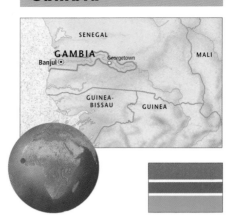

## Fact File

| | |
|---|---|
| **OFFICIAL NAME** | Republic of the Gambia |
| **FORM OF GOVERNMENT** | Republic with single legislative body (House of Representatives) |
| **CAPITAL** | Banjul |
| **AREA** | 11,300 sq km (4,363 sq miles) |
| **TIME ZONE** | GMT |
| **POPULATION** | 1,735,000 |
| **PROJECTED POPULATION 2015** | 2,072,000 |
| **POPULATION DENSITY** | 153.5 per sq km (397.7 per sq mile) |
| **LIFE EXPECTANCY** | 55 |
| **INFANT MORTALITY (PER 1,000)** | 68.7 |
| **OFFICIAL LANGUAGE** | English |
| **OTHER LANGUAGES** | Indigenous languages (including Mandinka, Wolof, Pulaar), Arabic |
| **LITERACY RATE** | 40.1 % |
| **RELIGIONS** | Muslim 90 %, Christian 9 %, indigenous beliefs 1 % |
| **ETHNIC GROUPS** | Indigenous 99 % (including Mandinka 42 %, Fula 18 %, Wolof 16 %, Jola 10 %, Serahuli 9 %), non-Gambian 1 % |
| **CURRENCY** | Dalasi |
| **ECONOMY** | Services 58.5 %, agriculture 32.8 %, industry 8,7 % |
| **GNI PER CAPITA** | US$ 320 |
| **CLIMATE** | Tropical, with wet season June to November |
| **HIGHEST POINT** | Unnamed location 53 m (174 ft) |
| **MAP REFERENCE** | Page 364 |

Surrounded on nearly all sides by Senegal, Gambia is Africa's smallest independent state. Once a part of the Mali Empire, it became a British colony in 1816 and has been independent since 1965. Following independence it was governed for almost thirty years by Sir Dawda Jawara and the People's Progressive Party. A military coup displaced him in 1994. In 1996 a new constitution was adopted and the country returned to civil government. The country has been notably stable since, though resentment of the dominant Mandinka exists among minority tribal groups such as the Fula and Wolof.

A subtropical climate and a sunny dry season has enabled Gambia to expand tourism in recent years but the conflict between tourist life and the main religion, Islam, has made this controversial. In 1982 Gambia joined its neighbor, Senegal, in a union named the Senegambian Federation. This proved unsuccessful and was dissolved in 1989.

The Gambia River and its estuary are navigable for some 200 km (125 miles), allowing ships of up to 3,000 tonnes to reach Georgetown. Consisting of a riverine plain running inland 275 km (170 miles) from the estuary, Gambia's countryside is low and undulating, the land beside the river varying from swamp to savanna. Although rice is grown in the swamps and on the river floodplain, not enough is produced to meet domestic needs. Millet, sorghum, and cassava are grown on higher ground. On the upper river, a dam provides irrigation.

Gambia has unmined deposits of minerals such as ilmenite, rutile, and zircon. The economy has a limited agricultural base, with three-quarters of the population growing crops and raising livestock. Peanuts are the main cash crop, providing more than 75 percent of export earnings, and peanut processing is important industrially. Palm kernels are also exported. Because Banjul is the best harbor on the west African coast, much Senegalese produce passes through Gambia, and re-export forms one-third of economic activity.

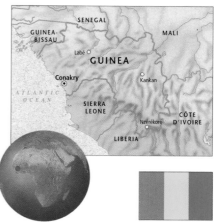

# Guinea

## Guinea-Bissau

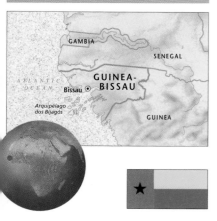

### Fact File

OFFICIAL NAME  Republic of Guinea-Bissau

FORM OF GOVERNMENT  Republic with single legislative body (National People's Assembly)

CAPITAL  Bissau

AREA  36,120 sq km (13,946 sq miles)

TIME ZONE  GMT

POPULATION  1,503,000

PROJECTED POPULATION 2015  2,160,000

POPULATION DENSITY  41.6 per sq km (107.8 per sq mile)

LIFE EXPECTANCY  47.5

INFANT MORTALITY (PER 1,000)  101.6

OFFICIAL LANGUAGE  Portuguese

OTHER LANGUAGES  Crioulo (blend of Portuguese and West African languages), Pulaar, and other indigenous languages

LITERACY RATE  42.4 %

RELIGIONS  Indigenous beliefs 50 %, Muslim 45 %, Christian 5 %

ETHNIC GROUPS  Indigenous 99 % (including Balanta 30 %, Fula 20 %, Manjaca 14 %, Mandinka 13 %, Papel 7 %), European and mixed 1 %

CURRENCY  CFA (Communauté Financière Africaine) franc

ECONOMY  Agriculture 62 %, services 26 %, industry 12 %

GNI PER CAPITA  US$ 200

CLIMATE  Tropical, with wet season June to November

HIGHEST POINT  Unnamed location in northeast 300 m (984 ft)

MAP REFERENCE  Page 364

Guinea-Bissau is a small west African state between Guinea and Senegal. A large part of the country consists of mangrove swamps, estuaries, and islands, and it is both poor and underdeveloped. After the French and British used the area as a slave-trading station in the seventeenth and eighteenth centuries, Portugal named it Portuguese Guinea and claimed it as a colony in 1879. Independence, achieved in 1974, came following twelve years of guerrilla war.

One-party rule plus attempted coups and assassinations marked the next seventeen years. Moves towards multi-party democracy, designed to allow for ethnic divisons and inequalities, began in 1990. After military mutinies and coups, starting in 1998, Guinea-Bissau has seen several interim governments. In 2005, democratic elections were held, and the political situation since appears to be reasonably stable. However, women still face significant disadvantages and female genital mutilation is widespread.

Three main waterways—the Geba, Corubal, and Cacheu Rivers—mark the landscape. These wander across the plains toward broad estuaries and mangrove swamps on the coast. Here, the seasonal rainfall is especially heavy. Rice, the staple food, is grown on the floodplains and in the swamps, as well as on the offshore islands of the Arquipélago dos Bijagós, but not enough is produced to make the country self-sufficient. An area of upland savanna lies toward the border with Guinea in the southeast.

Mineral resources include phosphates, bauxite, and offshore oil but their development has been hampered by political instability, state controls, and (in the case of oil) disputes with Guinea and Senegal. Agriculture and fishing employ ninety percent of the workforce. Cashew nuts, peanuts, and palm kernels are the main exports. Economic reforms featuring monetary stability and private sector growth have been undertaken but progress is being hampered by the burden of high foreign debt and the many cultural and institutional constraints. Guinea-Bissau remains one of the ten poorest countries in the world.

### Fact File

OFFICIAL NAME  Republic of Guinea

FORM OF GOVERNMENT  Republic with single legislative body (People's National Assembly)

CAPITAL  Conakry

AREA  245,857 sq km (94,925 sq miles)

TIME ZONE  GMT

POPULATION  10,211,000

PROJECTED POPULATION 2015  11,449,000

POPULATION DENSITY  41.5 per sq km (107.6 per sq mile)

LIFE EXPECTANCY  49.8

INFANT MORTALITY (PER 1,000)  87.2

OFFICIAL LANGUAGE  French

OTHER LANGUAGES  Malinké languages, Fula and others

LITERACY RATE  29.5 %

RELIGIONS  Muslim 85 %, Christian 8 %, indigenous beliefs 7 %

ETHNIC GROUPS  Fula 40 %, Malinké 30 %, Soussou 20 %, smaller tribes 10 %

CURRENCY  Guinean franc

ECONOMY  Services 40.5 %, industry 37.6 %, agriculture 21.9 %

GNI PER CAPITA  US$ 400

CLIMATE  Tropical, with wet season May to November

HIGHEST POINT  Mt Nimba 1,752 m (5,748 ft)

MAP REFERENCE  Page 364

Guinea is on the African Atlantic coast to the north of Sierra Leone and Liberia. A slave-trading center from the fifteenth century, it became the colony of French Guinea in 1890. After achieving independence in 1958 it was for 25 years a one-party Marxist dictatorship under Ahmed Sékou Touré. A member of the Malinke tribe, he centralized and nationalized, attempted to enforce the use of local languages in place of French, and paid large numbers of state informers to monitor village and family life. Guinea now ranks last or near last on most international social development scales. Women

Africa

*Children from rural Guinea (above). A mother with her child in front of her house in Sierra Leone (right). A traditional village of mud huts with thatched roofs in the Côte d'Ivoire (right page bottom).*

face many disadvantages, including the practice of genital mutilation, which is widespread.

In the past twenty years governmental efforts at reform have led to a number of improvements, and in 1995 Guinea's first multi-party elections took place. The country has had to bear the additional burden of several hundred thousand refugees who have fled from the civil wars in Liberia and Sierra Leone. Many of these people are now returning home.

From mangrove swamps and lagoons along the coast, the land rises through densely forested foothills to the Fouta Djalon Highlands in the east. These highlands—from which the Gambia, Senegal, and Niger Rivers flow north and northeast—form a barrier between the coast and the grassland and savanna woodland of the Upper Niger Plains. Typical wildlife on the savanna includes lion and leopard, while crocodile and hippopotamus are found in the rivers.

The 76 percent of the workforce who live from agriculture are spread fairly evenly through the countryside. Those who live on the wet Atlantic coastal plain, much of which has been cleared for farming, cultivate bananas, palm oil, pineapples, and rice. Cattle are raised by nomadic herders in the interior.

Guinea possesses more than 25 percent of the world's reserves of high-grade bauxite, and three large bauxite mines contribute about eighty percent of the country's export revenue. Since it opened in 1984, the Aredor diamond mine has also been extremely profitable. Good soil and high yields give the country a prospect of self-sufficiency in food but the years of stifling state controls that were imposed by Touré have made market reforms difficult to implement, and what little infrastructure exists is greatly in need of modernizing. Corruption and harassment obstruct business growth. Aside from the bauxite industry, there is little foreign investment.

## Sierra Leone

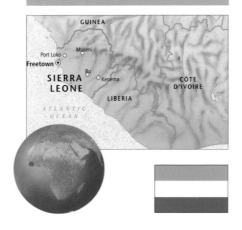

### Fact File

**OFFICIAL NAME** Republic of Sierra Leone

**FORM OF GOVERNMENT** Republic with single legislative body (House of Representatives)

**CAPITAL** Freetown

**AREA** 71,740 sq km (27,699 sq miles)

**TIME ZONE** GMT

**POPULATION** 6,295,000

**PROJECTED POPULATION 2015** 6,929,000

**POPULATION DENSITY** 87.8 per sq km (227.3 per sq mile)

**LIFE EXPECTANCY** 40.9

**INFANT MORTALITY (PER 1,000)** 156.5

**OFFICIAL LANGUAGE** English

**OTHER LANGUAGES** Mande languages (including Malinké, Mende), Temne, Limba, Krio (Creole)

**LITERACY RATE** 35.1 %

**RELIGIONS** Muslim 60 %, indigenous beliefs 30 %, Christian 10 %

**ETHNIC GROUPS** 20 indigenous tribes 90 %, other 10 %

**CURRENCY** Leone

**ECONOMY** Agriculture 49 %, industry 30 %, services 21 %

**GNI PER CAPITA** US$ 260

**CLIMATE** Tropical, with wet season April to November

**HIGHEST POINT** Loma Mansa 1,948 m (6,391 ft)

**MAP REFERENCE** Page 364

Sierra Leone's capital, Freetown, was so named when the British government settled freed slaves there in 1787. Once the freed-slave settlers became a ruling class over the Africans already living in the country, deep social divisions opened. Many settlers, and foreign missionaries, were killed in a war with the indigenous Mende in 1898.

Once a British crown colony, and independent since 1961, Sierra Leone's recent history has been marked by military coups, ethnic factionalism, and violence. Since 1992, civil war has raged in the east and the south, thousands of lives have been lost and thousands of farms in the country's main grain growing areas abandoned. Liberian troops have been involved, and Libyan weapons. Child soldiers have been used by both sides. Following democratic elections in 2002 the government has slowly established its authority. After the withdrawal of UN peacekeeping forces in 2005, and in spite of the tenuous situation in neighboring Liberia, Sierra Leone has remained relatively stable.

Unlike most of west Africa, Sierra Leone is mountainous near the sea. These mountains are volcanic, and run southeast of Freetown on the Atlantic forming a thickly wooded peninsula (the Sierra Leone, or Lion Range). The peninsula interrupts a swampy coastal plain stretching north and south and dominated by mangrove forests. Rolling savanna uplands to the north, known as the Bolilands, were once the scene of government efforts to introduce large-scale mechanized rice cultivation. Rice is also grown in the seasonally flooded riverine grasslands of the southeast and in the swamps near Port Loco. Inland, to the northeast, the land rises to the Loma Mountains and the Tingi Hills. Rainfall on the coast is extremely high. The soils are heavily leached and weathered.

Subsistence farming dominates the agricultural sector, which employs about two-thirds of the population. Rice is the staple food crop and along with palm oil it is produced throughout Sierra Leone, except in the drier north. There, in the savanna, peanuts and cattle herding predominate. The country has substantial mineral resources, and the mining of diamonds, bauxite, and rutile or titanium ore provides essential hard currency. The economy is currently almost at a standstill because infrastructure has collapsed through neglect, and both the mining and agricultural sectors are hampered by social disorder.

# Liberia

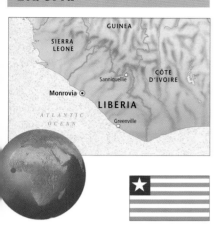

## Fact File

**OFFICIAL NAME** Republic of Liberia

**FORM OF GOVERNMENT** Republic with two legislative bodies (Senate and House of Representatives)

**CAPITAL** Monrovia

**AREA** 111,370 sq km (43,000 sq miles)

**TIME ZONE** GMT

**POPULATION** 3,335,000

**PROJECTED POPULATION 2015** 5,032,000

**POPULATION DENSITY** 29.9 per sq km (77.6 per sq mile)

**LIFE EXPECTANCY** 41.1

**INFANT MORTALITY (PER 1,000)** 143.9

**OFFICIAL LANGUAGE** English

**OTHER LANGUAGES** Indigenous languages

**LITERACY RATE** 57.5 %

**RELIGIONS** Indigenous beliefs 40 %, Christian 40 %, Muslim 20 %

**ETHNIC GROUPS** Indigenous tribes 95 % (including Kpelle, Bassa, Gio, Kru, Grebo, Mano, Krahn, Gola, Gbandi, Loma, Kissi, Vai, Bella), Americo-Liberian and Congo People (descendants of repatriated slaves) 5 %

**CURRENCY** Liberian dollar

**ECONOMY** Agriculture 77 %, services 18 %, industry 5 %

**GNI PER CAPITA** US$ 150

**CLIMATE** Tropical, with wet season May to September

**HIGHEST POINT** Mt Wuteve 1,380 m (4,528 ft)

**MAP REFERENCE** Page 364

Settled by freed slaves after 1822, and a republic since 1847, the west African state of Liberia has always been a socially divided country. The coastal settlements of ex-slaves from the United States formed an élite with a Christian faith and an American colonial lifestyle. They had little in common with the long-established tribal peoples of the interior. During the long rule of the coastal Americo-Liberian élite the country was politically stable. It also made economic progress, the activities of the Firestone Rubber Company turning Liberia into a major rubber producer.

This ended in 1980 with a coup led by Master Sergeant Samuel Doe (a Krahn). When Doe was ousted by forces led by members of the Gio tribe in 1990, civil war began. Massacres and atrocities have marked succeeding years: famine threatens several regions, some 750,000 refugees have fled the country, organized economic life is at a standstill, and the rule of law has ended. In 1997 Charles Taylor was elected president but did not manage to control the rebel factions. Finally, in 2003, he was forced to abdicate. A transitional government of rebel, government, and civil society groups assumed control in October 2003. Democratic elections were held in 2005, but in spite of a strong UN presence the situation remains volatile.

Liberia has three major geographic regions. Like its neighbors, it has a narrow sandy coastal strip of lagoons and mangrove swamps. Inland from the Atlantic Ocean are rolling hills covered in tropical rainforest, which rise to a plateau. This ascends to form a mountainous belt along the Guinean border. Most of the plateau region is grassland or forest—forests cover 39 percent of the land area. Only one percent of the country is arable.

Until the outbreak of civil war Liberia had been a producer and exporter of iron ore, rubber, timber, and coffee. Industries included rubber processing, food processing, construction materials, furniture making, palm oil processing, and diamond mining. Rice was the main staple, but some food was imported. The catch from coastal fisheries was supplemented by inland fish farms.

By the end of the 1990s war had destroyed much of the Liberian economy, especially the infrastructure in and around Monrovia. The business classes fled, and few of them have since returned. With the collapse of the urban commercial part of the economy, many people have reverted to subsistence farming.

# Côte d'Ivoire

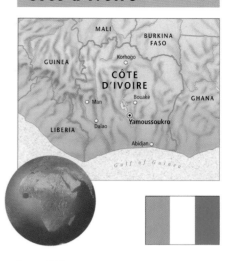

## Fact File

**OFFICIAL NAME** Republic of Côte d'Ivoire

**FORM OF GOVERNMENT** Republic with single legislative body (National Assembly)

**CAPITAL** Yamoussoukro

**AREA** 322,460 sq km (124,502 sq miles)

**TIME ZONE** GMT

**POPULATION** 18,373,000

**PROJECTED POPULATION 2015** 22,343,000

**POPULATION DENSITY** 57 per sq km (147.6 per sq mile)

**LIFE EXPECTANCY** 49.2

**INFANT MORTALITY (PER 1,000)** 85.7

**OFFICIAL LANGUAGE** French

**OTHER LANGUAGES** Baule, Bete, Dioula, Senufo, Gur languages, Mande languages

**LITERACY RATE** 48.7 %

**RELIGIONS** Muslim 35–40 %, indigenous beliefs 25–40 %, Christian 20–30 %

**ETHNIC GROUPS** Akan 42.1 %, Voltaiques or Gur 17.6 %, Northern Mandes 16.5 %, Krous 11 %, Southern Mandes 10 %, other 2.8 %

**CURRENCY** CFA (Communauté Financière Africaine) franc

**ECONOMY** Services 50.3 %, agriculture 27.5 %, industry 22.2 %

**GNI PER CAPITA** US$ 910

**CLIMATE** Tropical, but drier in the north

**HIGHEST POINT** Mt Nimba 1,752 m (5,748 ft)

**MAP REFERENCE** Page 364

Côte d'Ivoire (Ivory Coast) is a west African country on the Gulf of Guinea. In the eighteenth century it was conquered by Akan people from Ghana. In 1893 it became a French colony, achieving independence in 1960. Since then, while retaining a close association with France, Côte d'Ivoire has been a more liberal and commercially oriented society than the socialist states established elsewhere in Africa in the 1960s. This, combined with political stability, has made it relatively prosperous. Under the thirty-year

leadership of Félix Houphouet-Boigny (who died in 1993) investment was secure, and most of this period saw sustained economic growth. In 1999 the first military coup in the country's history overthrew the government. The junta held elections in late 2000, excluding the opposition and rigging the results. Popular protest brought runner-up Laurent Gbagbo into power. Civil unrest continued until early 2003 when rebels were granted ministerial positions in a unity government. Nevertheless, the situation remained volatile until administration and rebels formed a government of national unity in 2007, strongly supported by the UN.

A sandy strip of land some 64 km (40 miles) wide runs along the shore of the Atlantic, broken by sandbars and lagoons around Abidjan. Coastal shipping has always had trouble on the west African coast where there is heavy surf and there are no natural harbors. French construction of the Vridi Canal, giving access between Abidjan and the sea through the sandbars, created a valuable deep-water port. From the coast the land rises gently, and two rainy seasons and an equatorial climate provide a covering of rainforest further inland. There are three major national parks, with wildlife including elephant and pygmy hippopotamus.

Deforestation is a concern as hardwoods such as mahogany and ebony are felled. Growing in the place of native forest is plantation teak. Farther north the landscape changes to savanna grassland. Highlands are found in the northwest.

Côte d'Ivoire has varied mineral resources—petroleum, diamonds, manganese, bauxite, and copper—and is one of the world's main producers of coffee, cocoa beans, and palm oil. 68 percent of the population is engaged in farming, forestry, and raising livestock. Difficulties arise because of fluctuating coffee and cocoa prices, but during the 1990s Côte d'Ivoire prospered due to the discovery of oil and gas along its coast. The per-capita income dropped 15 percent in 1999, however, and only started recovering in 2006.

## Mali

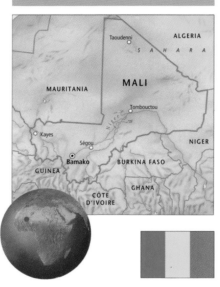

## Fact File

| | |
|---|---|
| **OFFICIAL NAME** | Republic of Mali |
| **FORM OF GOVERNMENT** | Republic with single legislative body (National Assembly) |
| **CAPITAL** | Bamako |
| **AREA** | 1,240,000 sq km (478,764 sq miles) |
| **TIME ZONE** | GMT |
| **POPULATION** | 12,324,000 |
| **PROJECTED POPULATION 2015** | 15,655,000 |
| **POPULATION DENSITY** | 9.9 per sq km (25.7 per sq mile) |
| **LIFE EXPECTANCY** | 49.9 |
| **INFANT MORTALITY (PER 1,000)** | 103.8 |
| **OFFICIAL LANGUAGE** | French |
| **OTHER LANGUAGES** | Bambara, Songhai-Jerma, Mandinka, Soninké, Arabic, Fula |
| **LITERACY RATE** | 46.4 % |
| **RELIGIONS** | Muslim 90 %, indigenous beliefs 9 %, Christian 1 % |
| **ETHNIC GROUPS** | Mande 50 %, Peul 17 %, Voltaic 12 %, Songhai 6 %, Tuareg and Moor 10 %, other 5 % |
| **CURRENCY** | CFA (Communauté Financière Africaine) franc |
| **ECONOMY** | Agriculture 45 %, services 38 %, industry 17 % |
| **GNI PER CAPITA** | US$ 500 |
| **CLIMATE** | Subtropical in south and southwest; arid in north |
| **HIGHEST POINT** | Hombori Tondo 1,155 m (3,789 ft) |
| **MAP REFERENCE** | Pages 361, 364–65 |

Mali is a landlocked west African country, watered by the River Niger in the south and with vast stretches of the Sahara Desert lying to the north. It derives its name from the Malinke or Mandingo people whose empire flourished between the eighth and fourteenth centuries. Later it was a center of trade and Islamic scholarship, based on the city of Timbuktu (now Tombouctou). At the end of the nineteenth century it became a colony of French West Africa, achieving independence in 1960. For the next thirty years the country was ruled by either civilian or military dictators. Demonstrations in 1991 in which about 100 people died were followed by the overthrow of the regime, and free elections were held for the first time in 1992. The political situation has remained quite stable since.

There is a major ethnic division between the black African majority in the south and the minority of Arab Tuareg nomads in the north. Violent Tuareg guerrilla activity in northern Mali ended with a peace pact in 1995.

Mali's flat landscape consists mainly of plains and sandstone plateaus. The need for water is the main concern. The northern and virtually rainless Saharan plains are inhabited almost entirely by Tuareg nomads. The semiarid center—the Sahel—has in recent years suffered from devastating droughts. Such arable land as exists is found in the south, along the Senegal and Niger Rivers, the latter spreading out to form an inland delta before turning southward on its way to the border of Niger. These rivers provide water for stock and for irrigation. Rice is grown on irrigated land; millet, cotton, and peanuts grow elsewhere. Away from the rivers southern Mali is mostly savanna country where mahogany, kapok, and baobab trees grow, these being replaced further north by palms and scrub. Animal life includes lion, antelope, jackal, and hyena.

Some eighty percent of the labor force works in agriculture and fishing—dried fish is exported to Burkina Faso, Côte d'Ivoire, and Ghana. With 65 percent of its land either desert or semidesert, however, and industry limited mainly to a single gold mine, salt production, and small-scale textiles and shoes, Mali is extremely poor. As well as gold there are phosphates, uranium, bauxite, manganese, and copper but development is hampered by poor transport facilities and the fact that the country is landlocked. With expenditures almost double its revenues, Mali is a major recipient of foreign aid.

# Burkina Faso

## Fact File

OFFICIAL NAME  Burkina Faso

FORM OF GOVERNMENT  Republic with single legislative body (Assembly of People's Deputies)

CAPITAL  Ouagadougou

AREA  274,200 sq km (105,869 sq miles)

TIME ZONE  GMT

POPULATION  15,265,000

PROJECTED POPULATION 2015  18,475,000

POPULATION DENSITY  55.7 per sq km (144.2 per sq mile)

LIFE EXPECTANCY  52.6

INFANT MORTALITY (PER 1,000)  86

OFFICIAL LANGUAGE  French

OTHER LANGUAGES  More, Mande languages, Fula, Arabic, English

LITERACY RATE  21.8 %

RELIGIONS  Muslim 50 %, indigenous beliefs 40 %, Christian (mainly Roman Catholic) 10 %

ETHNIC GROUPS  Approximately 160 indigenous tribes: Mossi 40 %, Gurunsi, Senefo, Lobi, Bobo, Mande, Fula, Sanike, Diola, Dagara and others 60 %

CURRENCY  CFA (Communauté Financière Africaine) franc

ECONOMY  Services 50.9 %, agriculture 29.7 %, industry 19.4 %

GNI PER CAPITA  US$ 430

CLIMATE  Tropical, with warm, dry winters and hot, wet summers

HIGHEST POINT  Tena Kourou 749 m (2,457 ft)

MAP REFERENCE  Page 364

**B**urkina Faso (formerly called Upper Volta) is a landlocked African country on the southern edge of the Sahara Desert. It is the size of Italy but has difficulty supporting its people. The desertification of the Sahel—the fringe of the Sahara running from Senegal to Chad—has severely affected large areas, though the parched

*The city of Tombouctou, in Mali, following a dust storm (left page). The large covered market in Kumasi, central Ghana (right).*

savanna of the north and east still supports a nomadic population of cattle-herding Fulani. French colonial control was established between 1895 and 1897 and independence came in 1960. Repeated military coups during the 1970s and 1980s were followed by multiparty elections in the early 1990s. Currently, the country is ruled by Blaise Campaore, who came to power in a military coup in 1987 and has won every election since then.

Near the capital city of Ouagadougou live the Mossi, the traditional rulers and the dominant tribal group, who have been in the region since the twelfth century. They grow sorghum and millet for food, and cultivate cash crops such as peanuts, cotton, and sesame seeds.

In the west and south is a sandstone plateau, while in the southwest are the spectacular Banfora Cliffs. The plateau is cut by the watercourses of the Red, White, and Black Volta Rivers (Volta Rouge, Blanche, and Noir), draining towards Ghana. Although these valleys have more farming potential than the arid north, they cannot yet be developed because of the tsetse and simulium flies that flourish near their rivers. At present the diseases carried by these insects prevent settlement.

Burkina Faso has few natural resources. There is manganese in the far northeast, but to develop it a 350 km (220 mile) extension of the Côte d'Ivoire railway from Abidjan is needed. Industries consist of unprofitable state corporations, a legacy of the country's years as a one-party socialist state. About ten percent of the land area is arable and more than eighty percent of the people work on the land. Drought has caused acute agricultural difficulties and the country depends heavily on foreign aid. Many people have emigrated, sending home their wages earned in other countries. However, political unrest, for example in Côte d'Ivoire, has dried up this much-needed supply. Tourists visit the Parcs Nationaux du W. du Niger, in the east—a reserve shared with Niger and Benin. Gazelles, antilopes, elephants, cape buffalo, and hippopotamus live there.

# Ghana

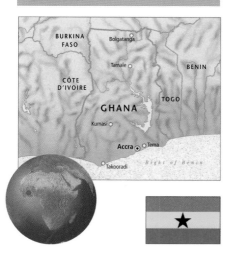

## Fact File

OFFICIAL NAME  Republic of Ghana

FORM OF GOVERNMENT  Republic with single legislative body (Parliament)

CAPITAL  Accra

AREA  239,460 sq km (92,456 sq miles)

TIME ZONE  GMT

POPULATION  23,383,000

PROJECTED POPULATION 2015  27,294,000

POPULATION DENSITY  97.6 per sq km (252.9 per sq mile)

LIFE EXPECTANCY  59.5

INFANT MORTALITY (PER 1,000)  52.3

OFFICIAL LANGUAGE  English

OTHER LANGUAGES  Kwa languages (including Twi, Fanti, Ga, Ewe, Yoruba), Gur languages (including Dagbani, Mossi, Gurma), Fula, Nzima

LITERACY RATE  57.9 %

RELIGIONS  Christian 68.8 %, Muslim 15.9 %, indigenous beliefs 8.5 %, other 0.7 %, none 6.1 %

ETHNIC GROUPS  Indigenous 92.2 % (including Akan 45.3 %, Mole-Dagbon 15.2 %, Ewe 11.7 %, Ga-Dangme 7.3 %), other 7.8 %

CURRENCY  Cedi

ECONOMY  Services 37.5 %, agriculture 37.3 %, industry 25.2 %

GNI PER CAPITA  US$ 590

CLIMATE  Tropical: warm and arid on southeast coast; hot and humid in southwest; hot and arid in north

HIGHEST POINT  Mt Afadjato 880 m (2,887 ft)

MAP REFERENCE  Page 364

**G**hana was once known as the Gold Coast. A well-known source of gold in west Africa for a thousand years, the nation's modern name comes from the Ghana Empire of the eighth to the twelfth centuries. The Ashanti people established themselves in the seventeenth century, selling slaves to Portuguese, British, Dutch and Danish traders. Under British control from 1874, Ghana became the first tropical African colony to win independence in 1956. Soon after this it became a Soviet-style one-party state.

Africa

After 1966, Ghana was wracked by military coups for fifteen years before Flight-Lieutenant Jerry Rawlings took control in 1981. An election in 1996 returned Rawlings to power once more. In 2000 he could not run again since the constitution only allows for two terms. Although government pressure is often brought to bear, vigorous political debate takes place in a relatively free media, and despite economic troubles Ghana still has twice the per capita output of the poorer countries in west Africa.

Geographically, the country is formed by the basin of the Volta Rivers. A large area flooded by the Akosombo Dam is now Lake Volta. This provides hydroelectric power for smelting alumina into aluminum, and for use in the towns, mines, and industries of the Takoradi-Kumasi-Tema triangle. In the north there is savanna country. In earlier days the southern part of the country was covered by dense tropical forest. Much of this has been cleared for agriculture, especially for growing cocoa, which from 1924 until the present day has usually been the leading export.

Like other west African countries, Ghana has few natural harbors. Its coast consists mainly of mangrove swamps, with lagoons toward the mouth of the River Volta. The rivers are home to crocodile, manatee, and hippopotamus. The wildlife of the northern savanna includes lion, leopard, hyena, and antelope.

Ghana is well endowed with natural resources: gold, timber, industrial diamonds, bauxite, manganese, fish, and rubber. In 1995, largely as a result of increased gold, timber, and cocoa production, overall economic growth was about five percent. Although the economy is based on subsistence agriculture, Ghana is not self-sufficient in food. The government's efforts to reverse the statist policies of decades past continue, but face a number of obstacles. Public sector wage increases, and various peace-keeping missions, both internal and external, have strained the budget and led to inflationary deficit financing. Corruption is a continuing obstacle to growth.

# Togo

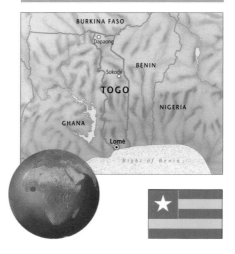

*Traditional houses in Togo (above). A public voodoo ritual in eastern Ghana (below). Children in a canoe paddle through a village of stilt houses, Benin (right page).*

**ECONOMY** Agriculture 40 %, services 35 %, industry 25 %

**GNI PER CAPITA** US$ 360

**CLIMATE** Tropical, with wet seasons March to July and October to November; semiarid in north, with wet season April to July

**HIGHEST POINT** Mont Agou 986 m (3,235 ft)

**MAP REFERENCE** Page 364

## Fact File

**OFFICIAL NAME** Republic of Togo

**FORM OF GOVERNMENT** Republic with single legislative body (National Assembly)

**CAPITAL** Lomé

**AREA** 56,785 sq km (21,925 sq miles)

**TIME ZONE** GMT

**POPULATION** 5,859,000

**PROJECTED POPULATION 2015** 8,045,000

**POPULATION DENSITY** 103.2 per sq km (267.2 per sq mile)

**LIFE EXPECTANCY** 58.3

**INFANT MORTALITY (PER 1,000)** 57.7

**OFFICIAL LANGUAGE** French

**OTHER LANGUAGES** Ewe, Tem, Gur languages, Fula, Yoruba, Hausa

**LITERACY RATE** 60.9 %

**RELIGIONS** Indigenous beliefs 51 %, Christian 29 %, Muslim 20 %

**ETHNIC GROUPS** Indigenous (Ewe, Mina, and Kabye are the largest of 37 tribes) 99 %, European and Syrian-Lebanese 1 %

**CURRENCY** CFA (Communauté Financière Africaine) franc

Togo is a small west African country squeezed between Ghana and Benin. It was colonized by Germany in 1884, later becoming French Togoland. It became independent in 1960. A deep social division exists between the Kabye people in the north and the majority Ewe of the south. The Ewe are generally better educated, and live in the more developed part of the country, but have no say in government. Until his death in 2005, this was run by Africa's longest serving president, General Eyadema, a Kabye who had held this position since a coup in 1967. His son's succession was legitimized by elections in 2006.

Most people live on the coast and the adjacent plains. Inland a mountain chain crosses the country north to south. The far northwest is mainly granite tableland. Roads connect the northern savanna with the railhead of Blitta, and the phosphate mining area with its port of Kpeme. The River Oti crosses in the northwest between Burkina Faso and Ghana, and the River Mono drains south into the Gulf of Guinea. About a quarter of the land is arable. The most fertile land—28 percent of the country—is forested; here slash-and-burn cultivation occurs.

Togo depends on subsistence agriculture. Food crops include yams, cassava, maize, beans, rice, and sorghum. The main export crops are coffee, cocoa, and cotton, which together generate about forty percent of earnings. Cattle, sheep, and pigs are raised in the north. The annual fish catch is about 14,000 tonnes. Togo is almost self-sufficient in food, though drought has recently cut productivity, and the deforestation caused by slash-and-burn agriculture is causing concern. Phosphate mining is the most important industrial activity.

# Benin

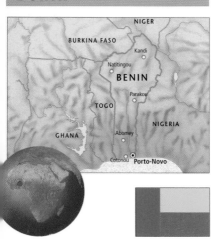

## Fact File

**OFFICIAL NAME** Republic of Benin

**FORM OF GOVERNMENT** Republic with single legislative body (National Assembly)

**CAPITAL** Porto-Novo

**AREA** 112,620 sq km (43,483 sq miles)

**TIME ZONE** GMT + 1 hour

**POPULATION** 8,295,000

**PROJECTED POPULATION 2015** 11,331,000

**POPULATION DENSITY** 73.7 per sq km (190.8 per sq mile)

**LIFE EXPECTANCY** 53.9

**INFANT MORTALITY (PER 1,000)** 76.2

**OFFICIAL LANGUAGE** French

**OTHER LANGUAGES** 60 indigenous languages (including Ewe, Fon, Gun, Yoruba, Mina, Somba, Bariba, Dendi, Hausa, Fula)

**LITERACY RATE** 34.7 %

**RELIGIONS** Christian 42.8 %, Muslim 24.4 %, Vodoun 17.3 %, other 15.5 %

**ETHNIC GROUPS** Indigenous 95.5 %, European and other 1.6 %, unspecified 2.9 %

**CURRENCY** CFA (Communauté Financière Africaine) franc

**ECONOMY** Services 52.3 %, agriculture 33.2 %, industry 14.5 %

**GNI PER CAPITA** US$ 570

**CLIMATE** Tropical; hot and humid in south, drier in north

**HIGHEST POINT** Mt Tanekas 641 m (2,103 ft)

**MAP REFERENCE** Page 365

Benin is a small west African country facing the Gulf of Guinea. It was once part of the Kingdom of Benin, famous for the brass portrait heads made for the Oba and his court in the fifteenth century. By 1625 it was known as Abomey (later Dahomey). Slavery and slave-raiding were endemic, and grew when firearms and external slave markets became available. The town of Ouidah became the shipping point for several million slaves, mostly prisoners captured in raids by the Dahomeyans against their enemies. The captives were sent mainly to Brazil, and most Afro-Brazilian religious cults derive from this area. Under French control from 1850, the country became independent in 1960, eventually falling under the control of General Mathieu Kerekou, who changed its name to Benin. In the 1990s the country slowly moved towards multi-party rule.

The Atakora Range (Chaine de l'Akatora) lies in northwestern Benin. To the northeast are the plains of the Niger, part of the boundary with the state of Niger being formed by the Niger River itself. Further south there are plateaus, and then a fertile plain where the Fon and Yoruba people live as subsistence farmers. Still further south, toward the Bight of Benin, lies a sandy strip with many lagoons. In the country's far north small numbers of Fulani people continue to live as nomads. Also in the north are two wildlife parks—the Parc National de la Pendjan and the Parcs Nationaux du W. du Niger—shared with Burkina Faso and Niger.

Subsistence agriculture, cotton production, and regional trade remain fundamental to Benin's economy. Offshore oilfields promised much when they began producing in 1982, but were soon affected by a fall in petroleum prices. As well as crude oil Benin sells cotton, palm-oil products, cocoa, and peanuts. A 2001 privatization policy continues in telecommunications, water, electricity and agriculture. Benin is hurt, however, by Nigerian trade protection that bans imports from Benin and elsewhere. Consequently, smuggling and criminality in the border region are on the rise.

# Niger

## Fact File

**OFFICIAL NAME** Republic of Niger

**FORM OF GOVERNMENT** Republic with single legislative body (National Assembly)

**CAPITAL** Niamey

**AREA** 1,267,000 sq km (489,189 sq miles)

**TIME ZONE** GMT + 1 hour

**POPULATION** 13,273,000

**PROJECTED POPULATION 2015** 18,754,000

**POPULATION DENSITY** 10.5 per sq km (27.1 per sq mile)

**LIFE EXPECTANCY** 44.3

**INFANT MORTALITY (PER 1,000)** 115.4

**OFFICIAL LANGUAGE** French

**OTHER LANGUAGES** Hausa, Songhai-Djerma, Fulani, Tuareg, Kanouri and others

**LITERACY RATE** 28.7 %

**RELIGIONS** Muslim 80 %, Christian and indigenous beliefs 20 %

**ETHNIC GROUPS** Hausa 55.3 %, Djerma Sonrai 21 %, Tuareg 9.3 %, Peulh 8.5 %, Kanouri Manga 4.7 %, other 1.2 %

**CURRENCY** CFA (Communauté Financière Africaine) franc

**ECONOMY** Services 44 %, agriculture 39 %, industry 17 %

**GNI PER CAPITA** US$ 280

**CLIMATE** Mainly arid; tropical in south, with wet season June to October

**HIGHEST POINT** Mont Bagzane 2,022 m (6,634 ft)

**MAP REFERENCE** Pages 361, 362, 365

Niger is two-thirds desert, which may seem strange for a country that is named after a great river (the name "Niger" comes from the Tuareg word *n'eghirren*, for flowing water), but the River Niger only cuts across the extreme southwest of this large, landlocked country. Elsewhere, there is an arid landscape of stony basins, drifting sands, and a northern highland that forms part of the mountain chain stretching from Algeria to Chad.

The home of the Sokoto Empire of the Fulani in the nineteenth century, the region became part of French West Africa in 1922, and received independence in 1960. Then followed three decades of dictatorial civilian and military rule. Despite the multi-party elections held in 1993, continuing unrest caused by Tuareg rebels in the north and power struggles within the government led to the reimposition of military rule in 1996. With elections in 1999 the country returned to democracy in the so-called Fifth Republic.

Niger's central geographic feature is the Massif de l'Aïr. In these mountains, which rise out of the Saharan plains to jagged peaks up to 1,900 m (6,230 ft) high, there is sometimes sufficient rain for thorny scrub to grow. Formerly nomads grazed their camels, horses, cattle, and goats in this area, but devastating droughts in 1973 and 1983 destroyed their livelihood. To the east and west of the Massif de l'Aïr are the Saharan Desert plains of Ténéré du Tafassasset and the Western Talk. Sand and sandy soil cover most of the desert plains to the north and east, an area which is virtually rainless and, aside from small numbers of people living at the occasional palm-fringed oasis, uninhabited. Plant life includes kapok and baobab trees. Buffalo, antelope, lion, hippopotamus, and crocodiles are found in Niger but their survival today is more a matter of chance than good management.

With its gross domestic product growth barely matching the growth of its population, Niger is one of the most impoverished countries in Africa. Ninety percent of its people earn a living from farming and trading. Where the Niger River crosses the country in the far southwest there are fertile arable soils: crops include yams, cassava, and maize, and rice in areas where the river floods. On the drier land toward Lake Chad (Lac Tchad) millet and sorghum are grown. The drought that has affected extensive areas of the Sahel has reduced Niger from self-sufficiency to being an importer of food. Tin and tungsten are mined, and there are reserves of iron ore, manganese, and molybdenum. During the 1970s, when prices were high, uranium became the main source of revenue, and it continues to be the country's most valuable export. Between 1983 and 1990, however, revenues fell by fifty percent. At present the government of Niger relies on foreign aid for operating expenses and for public investment.

# Chad

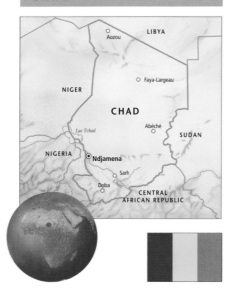

**CURRENCY** CFA (Communauté Financière Africaine) franc

**ECONOMY** Industry 47.8 %, services 30.6 %, agriculture 21.6 %

**GNI PER CAPITA** US$ 540

**CLIMATE** Tropical in south, arid in north

**HIGHEST POINT** Emi Koussi 3,415 m (11,204 ft)

**MAP REFERENCE** Pages 362, 365, 366

## Fact File

**OFFICIAL NAME** Republic of Chad

**FORM OF GOVERNMENT** Republic with two legislative bodies (National Assembly and Senate)

**CAPITAL** Ndjamena

**AREA** 1,284,000 sq km (495,752 sq miles)

**TIME ZONE** GMT + 1 hour

**POPULATION** 10,111,000

**PROJECTED POPULATION 2015** 13,429,000

**POPULATION DENSITY** 7.9 per sq km (20.4 per sq mile)

**LIFE EXPECTANCY** 47.4

**INFANT MORTALITY (PER 1,000)** 100.4

**OFFICIAL LANGUAGES** French, Arabic

**OTHER LANGUAGES** More than 100 indigenous languages (Sara, Baguirmi, Boulala, Tibbu-Gorane and others)

**LITERACY RATE** 25.7 %

**RELIGIONS** Muslim 51 %, Christian 35 %, indigenous beliefs 7 %, others 7 %

**ETHNIC GROUPS** More than 200 indigenous groups: north mainly Arabic, south mainly African

Chad is a landlocked North African country twice the size of France. Much of it is semidesert and thinly populated, and it is one of the poorest and least developed countries in the world. Chad was conquered by the Sudanese warlord Rabah Zobeir late in the nineteenth century, but with 200 distinct ethnic groups in the population a sense of national unity has been slow to emerge. After France established control of the region in 1911 it became part of French Equatorial Africa for fifty years, achieving independence in 1960. Since then there has been almost constant civil war, aggravated by the main ethnic divide—that between the desert-dwelling Muslims in the north and the non-Muslim farmers in the south. In spite of the peace treaties of 2002 and 2003, the situation remains volatile.

The country can be loosely divided into four regions. In the center are broad, arid savanna plains. To the north are deserts with large areas of mobile sand dunes along the southern Sahara. In the northwest are the volcanic mountains of the Tibesti, rising to the 3,415 m (11,204 ft) peak of Emi Koussi. Though surrounded by desert these mountains attract rain, and some farming takes place in the valleys. In the south the valleys of the Chari and Logone Rivers support most of Chad's agriculture, including cotton-growing. Both these rivers drain into Lake Chad (Lac Tchad). But a series of droughts has reduced them to little more than streams, while the shallow Lake Chad itself is steadily shrinking as the desert advances.

Chad's economic difficulties have both political and climatic causes. Civil war in the 1980s disrupted agriculture and spread lasting division, while continuing government corruption and its inability to pay its employees have led to resentment in the civil service. Desertification has had an impoverishing effect, especially among pastoral peoples like the Fula in the Sahel. While oil production from a field discovered at Doba might provide a significant long-term source of revenue, eighty percent of the population is likely to depend on subsistence farming for some time and the country will continue to rely on foreign aid.

# Nigeria

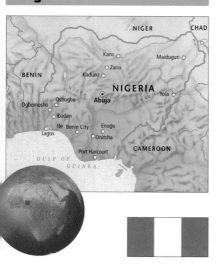

*A nomadic family in Chad outside their home (left page bottom). An antelope in Chad (left page top). Donkeys are used to transport produce in a village in Nigeria (above).*

## Fact File

**OFFICIAL NAME** Federal Republic of Nigeria

**FORM OF GOVERNMENT** Federal republic with two legislative bodies (Senate and House of Representatives)

**CAPITAL** Abuja

**AREA** 923,768 sq km (356,667 sq miles)

**TIME ZONE** GMT + 1 hour

**POPULATION** 138,283,000

**PROJECTED POPULATION 2015** 175,715,000

**POPULATION DENSITY** 149.7 per sq km (387.7 per sq mile)

**LIFE EXPECTANCY** 47.8

**INFANT MORTALITY (PER 1,000)** 93.9

**OFFICIAL LANGUAGE** English

**OTHER LANGUAGES** Mainly Kwa languages (Yoruba, Igbo), Fula Hausa, Edo, Ibibio, Kanuri, Efik, Ijas, Nupe, Tiv, Urhobo and others

**LITERACY RATE** 68 %

**RELIGIONS** Muslim 50 %, Christian 40 %, indigenous beliefs 10 %

**ETHNIC GROUPS** About 250 indigenous groups, the largest of which are Hausa, Fulani, Yoruba, Ibo 68 %; Kanuri, Edo, Tiv, Ibidio, Nupe 25 %; other 7 %

**CURRENCY** Naira

**ECONOMY** Industry 52.7 %, services 29.7 %, agriculture 17.6 %

**GNI PER CAPITA** US$ 930

**CLIMATE** Tropical in south, with wet season April to October; arid in north

**HIGHEST POINT** Chappal Waddi 2,419 m (7,936 ft)

**MAP REFERENCE** Page 365

With the continent's largest population, huge oil revenues, and a territory that is four times the size of the United Kingdom, Nigeria is one of Africa's most important nations. It also ranks as one of the most corrupt countries in the world, and a place where tensions between the main tribal groups are close to breaking point.

Such tensions are not new to the area: regional and ethnic conflict go back to the days of Nigeria's ancient city-states. The life of the Yoruba people centered on the city of Ife, while the Hausa kingdom was in the north. The kingdom of Benin, well known for its portrait bronzes of past rulers, was in the west, and a number of communities of Ibo lived in the southeast. Bringing all these peoples together to form a single nation has proven difficult: since independence, in 1960, there has been a series of military dictatorships. An unsuccessful attempt to secede by the Ibo in 1967 (who set up an independent state named Biafra) failed in 1970, following a bitter civil war in which thousands of people died. A new constitution was adopted in 1999, completing a peaceful transition to civilian government. Further elections were held in 2003 and 2007, and though the latter was considered flawed, it proved to be the first peaceful transition of power from one civilian to another.

## Physical features and land use

Nigeria's coast on the west African Gulf of Guinea consists of long, sandy beaches and mangrove swamps where its rivers flow into the sea. The mouth of the Niger forms an immense delta, threaded with thousands of creeks and lagoons, with Port Harcourt on one of the main channels. Upstream it divides, the Benue (Bénoué) River leading east into Cameroon and the Niger heading northwest toward Benin. These two large rivers provide transport, by boat, for cargo and people. High rainfall on the coast and in the river valleys enables yams, cassava, maize, and vegetables to be grown and on floodland alongside the rivers rice is cultivated.

In the rainy forested belt to the north the hills gradually rise to the semiarid central savanna plateau, and then to the Jos Plateau, reaching 1,780 m (5,840 ft) at Share Hill. Up the Benue (Bénoué) River to the east the land rises to the wooded slopes of the Adamaoua Massif and the Cameroon highlands. From these hill-slope areas come such products as cocoa, rubber, hardwoods, and palm oil. North of the Jos Plateau the savanna becomes dry, in many places degenerating into arid Sahelian scrub, where both herds and herders have difficulty surviving. Around Lake Chad (Lac Tchad) the typical vegetation is hardy acacia and doum palms.

Together, the river systems of the Niger and the Benue (Bénoué) drain sixty percent of Nigeria's total land area. Though much reduced by clearing for cultivation, the Nigerian rainforests still produce mahogany and iriko. Wildlife includes elephant, chimpanzee, and the red river hog.

## People and culture

In addition to the Yoruba, Fulani, Hausa, and Ibo, Nigeria has 245 much smaller ethnic groups. Not only are they divided along lines of ethnicity, language, and regional dialect, there is also a major religious division. The north is largely Islamic (the religion of the Hausa and Fulani) while the south is for the most part Christian, combined with indigenous African beliefs. Outbreaks of communal violence in the north sometimes occur as a result of clashes between Islamic fundamentalists and missionary Christians. Despite widespread Christian proselytizing there is evidence that Islamic influence is gradually growing in the south.

Although seventy percent of the labor force works in agriculture, and many rural people are subsistence farmers, Nigerians have also lived in cities for centuries. This contrasts with many other parts of Africa. Long before European commercial expansion into the region, places such as Benin City, Kano, Ibadan, and Ife were administrative and trading centers with sizeable populations. As in other parts of west Africa, women in the non-Islamic Nigerian cultures play a prominent role in commercial life.

## Economy and resources

Nigeria is rich in natural resources and these are the basis of its economy. They include tin, columbite, iron ore, coal, limestone, lead, zinc, and natural gas. By far the most important, however, is oil: Nigeria is OPEC's fourth largest producer, with oil providing eighty percent of government revenue and ninety percent of export earnings overall. In addition, it has provided a source of independent wealth for the political elite.

Agricultural production has failed to keep pace with population growth, and Nigeria is now a food importer. There are fundamental imbalances in the economy that result in chronic inflation and a steadily depreciating currency. Investors are wary because of political instability and corruption at the highest levels of government. In 2005, an agreement with the IMF was achieved that relieved the country's enormous debt load.

# Central Africa

Cameroon · · · · · · · · · 330

Central African
Republic · · · · · · · 331

Equatorial Guinea · · · · 331

São Tomé
and Príncipe · · · · 332

Gabon · · · · · · · · · 333

Congo · · · · · · · · · 333

Democratic Republic
of the Congo · · · 334

Angola · · · · · · · · · 335

## Cameroon

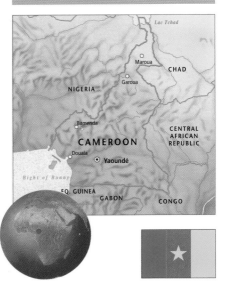

**CURRENCY** CFA (Communauté Financière Africaine) franc

**ECONOMY** Agriculture 43.9 %, services 40.3 %, industry 15.8 %

**GNI PER CAPITA** US$ 1,050

**CLIMATE** Tropical in the south and along coast, semiarid in the north

**HIGHEST POINT** Mt Cameroon 4,095 m (13,435 ft)

**MAP REFERENCE** Page 365

The African state of Cameroon is on the Gulf of Guinea, with Nigeria to the west and Equatorial Guinea, Gabon, and Congo to the south. The Portuguese arrived in 1472, and Cameroon is named after the prawns, *camarãos*, they found here. A German colony from 1884, and later ruled by both British and French, Cameroon became independent in 1960. Although it was a one-party state for thirty years, opposition parties have been allowed since 1991. One of the more prosperous African countries, Cameroon is home to more than 200 distinct tribes and peoples. There is also a broad distinction between the English- and French-speaking parts of the population. In response to the demands of the former in 1996, Cameroon applied for entry and was admitted to the British Commonwealth.

The country can be divided into four regions. First, an area of tropical forest, plateau, and coastal plain extends from the southern frontier to the Sanaga River. Most of the population is concentrated in this southern part. Second, north of this river and Lake Mbakaou (M'Bakaou Reservoir), the land rises to the highlands of the Adamaoua Massif. Third is the mountainous western extension of the Adamaoua Massif which includes Mt Cameroon. Occasionally active, this 4,095 m (13,435 ft) volcanic cone is the highest mountain in west Af-

rica. Fourth is the arid savanna north of the Benue (Bénoué River) and towards Lake Chad (Lac Tchad). This region of savanna supports elephant, lion, and leopard, and a national park—the Parc National de la Bénoué—has been established there.

Cameroon's prosperity was helped by the oil boom between 1970 and 1985. Since then conditions have been more difficult, with prices for coffee, cocoa, and petroleum, the country's major exports, falling. Seventy percent of the population are farmers who, in addition to coffee and cocoa, grow bananas, oilseed, grains, and manioc. Cameroon is self-sufficient in food, but a range of economic difficulties exists. The dismantling of unproductive state industries has been slow to show results, and the swollen ranks of the civil service remain a fiscal burden.

### Fact File

**OFFICIAL NAME** Republic of Cameroon

**FORM OF GOVERNMENT** Republic with single legislative body (National Assembly)

**CAPITAL** Yaoundé

**AREA** 475,440 sq km (183,567 sq miles)

**TIME ZONE** GMT + 1 hour

**POPULATION** 18,468,000

**PROJECTED POPULATION 2015** 21,525,000

**POPULATION DENSITY** 38.8 per sq km (100.6 per sq mile)

**LIFE EXPECTANCY** 53.3

**INFANT MORTALITY (PER 1,000)** 64.6

**OFFICIAL LANGUAGES** French, English

**OTHER LANGUAGES** Fula, Fang, Bamikele, Duala, Gbaya, Weskos and various Bantu languages

**LITERACY RATE** 67.9 %

**RELIGIONS** Indigenous beliefs 40 %, Christian 40 %, Muslim 20 %

**ETHNIC GROUPS** Cameroon Highlanders 31 %, Equatorial Bantu 19 %, Kirdi 11 %, Fulani 10 %, Northwestern Bantu 8 %, Eastern Nigritic 7 %; other African 13 %; non-African 1 %

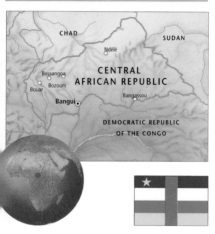

*A small village on Cameroon's arid savanna (left page bottom). Falls on the Kotto River in the Central African Republic (left).*

CURRENCY CFA (Communauté Financière Africaine) franc

ECONOMY Agriculture 55%, services 25%, industry 20%

GNI PER CAPITA US$ 380

CLIMATE Tropical, with hot, dry winters and hot, wet summers

HIGHEST POINT Mt Kayagangir 1,420 m (4,659 ft)

MAP REFERENCE Pages 365, 366

The Central African Republic (CAR) is a landlocked plateau just north of the equator. It is bordered on the west and north by Cameroon and Chad, and on the east and south by Sudan, the Democratic Republic of Congo, and Congo. By the time of European exploration the population of forest-dwelling Pygmies was much reduced, having been largely replaced by Bantu and Azande people. The region was for centuries used as a slave source by African slave-traders from the Sudan. When France took control in 1911 it ended slave-trading. The CAR was run as part of French Equatorial Africa until independence in 1958. After thirty years of political instability and military governments civilian rule was established in 1993. In March 2003 a military coup deposed the civilian government. Civil society groups and the main parties supported the transitional government and in 2005 democratically elected the leader of the coup to be the new president. The government still does not fully control the countryside, where pockets of lawlessness persist.

The average elevation of the CAR plateau is between 2,000 and 2,500 m (6,500 and 8,000 ft). These uplands form a watershed dividing the Congo and Nile river basins. North of the high ground of the Massif des Bongos the land drains towards the interior along water courses into swamps in southern Chad. South of this massif numerous rivers feed into the Ubangi. To the west the Massif du Yadé forms a boundary with Cameroon.

In the south and southeast are forests containing hardwoods such as mahogany and ebony. Dense rainforest in this area provides one of the last homes of the lowland gorilla. Much of the rest of the land is savanna. Plantation forestry undertaken by foreign timber interests has in some places added significantly to natural soil erosion.

The CAR economy is based on subsistence agriculture combined with forestry. Food crops include manioc, yams, millet, maize, and bananas. Cotton, coffee, and tobacco are grown for cash. Industries include sawmills, textiles, footwear, and bicycle assembly. About forty percent of export revenue comes from diamond mining.

The country's economic prospects are constrained by its position, its limited resources, its unskilled workforce, and its poor infrastructure. In addition, AIDS, tuberculosis, leprosy, and sleeping sickness are widespread. These factors are likely to keep the CAR dependent on foreign aid for some time.

# Central African Republic

## Fact File

OFFICIAL NAME Central African Republic

FORM OF GOVERNMENT Republic with single legislative body (National Assembly)

CAPITAL Bangui

AREA 622,984 sq km (240,534 sq miles)

TIME ZONE GMT + 1 hour

POPULATION 4,435,000

PROJECTED POPULATION 2015 5,021,000

POPULATION DENSITY 7.1 per sq km (18.4 per sq mile)

LIFE EXPECTANCY 44

INFANT MORTALITY (PER 1,000) 82.4

OFFICIAL LANGUAGE French

OTHER LANGUAGES Sangho, various Ubangi languages and Fulani

LITERACY RATE 48.6%

RELIGIONS Indigenous beliefs 35%, Protestant 25%, Catholic 25%, Muslim 15%

ETHNIC GROUPS Baya 33%, Banda 27%, Mandjia 13%, Sara 10%, Mboum 7%, M'Baka 4%, Yakoma 4%, other 2%

# Equatorial Guinea

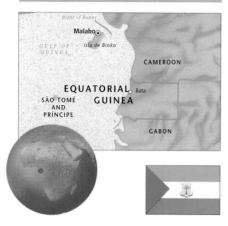

## Fact File

OFFICIAL NAME Republic of Equatorial Guinea

FORM OF GOVERNMENT Republic with single legislative body (House of People's Representatives)

CAPITAL Malabo

AREA 28,051 sq km (10,831 sq miles)

TIME ZONE GMT + 1 hour

POPULATION 616,000

PROJECTED POPULATION 2015 616,000

POPULATION DENSITY 22 per sq km (56.9 per sq mile)

LIFE EXPECTANCY 61.2

INFANT MORTALITY (PER 1,000) 83.8

OFFICIAL LANGUAGES Spanish, French

OTHER LANGUAGES Fang, Bubi, Noowe, creole Portuguese, pidgin English

LITERACY RATE 87%

RELIGIONS Mainly Catholic and some indigenous religions

ETHNIC GROUPS Bubi, Fang

CURRENCY CFA (Communauté Financière Africaine) franc

ECONOMY Industry 92.3%, services 4.8%, agriculture 2.9%

GNI PER CAPITA US$ 12,860

CLIMATE Tropical; wetter on coast

HIGHEST POINT Pico Basile 3,011 m (9,879 ft)

MAP REFERENCE Page 365

Equatorial Guinea consists of five islands in the Gulf of Guinea, plus the small mainland area of Río Muni that lies between Cameroon and Gabon. The largest of the islands, Bioco, was originally Portuguese, and was known for centuries as the slave depot and trans-shipment base of Fernando Po. The Spanish took over in 1778.

After gaining independence from Spain in 1968 Equatorial Guinea fell into the hands of Francisco Macías Nguema. A member of the Mongomo clan of the Fang tribe, his bloody and despotic rule lasted eleven years, after which he was overthrown and later executed. His nephew, also a Fang, continued to govern in much the same way, observers describing the presidential elections of 1996 and 2002 as a political farce. Equatorial Guinea illustrates the problems faced

*Street scene in a provincial town in Equatorial Guinea (left top). This house in São Tomé built in Portuguese colonial style has seen better days (left bottom). Cocoa is dried in Mekome Nkodje, Gabon (right page bottom).*

| | |
|---|---|
| **CURRENCY** | Dobra |
| **ECONOMY** | Services 71.1 %, agriculture 14.9 %, industry 14 % |
| **GNI PER CAPITA** | US$ 870 |
| **CLIMATE** | Tropical, with wet season October to May |
| **HIGHEST POINT** | Pico de São Tomé 2,024 m (6,640 ft) |
| **MAP REFERENCE** | Pages 365, 373 |

São Tomé and Príncipe are two islands lying off the coast of Gabon in the Gulf of Guinea. They were occupied in the 1520s by the Portuguese, who used slaves as laborers on the sugar plantations. The population now consists mainly of the Afro-Portuguese descendants of these first immigrants, plus contract laborers brought from Mozambique and Cape Verde to work on cocoa plantations in the nineteenth century. Following independence in 1975, a one-party Marxist regime was imposed. For a time the islands were allied to the Soviet bloc and Russian and Cuban military advisors were brought in. At a referendum in 1990, however, 72 percent of the people voted in favor of democratic government. Now the main concern of the government is to rebuild the country's relationship with Portugal and to secure beneficial working relationships with the EU and the USA. Nevertheless, the situation has not been stable. The leadership has changed frequently and there were two unsuccessful coup attempts in 1995 and 2003.

An extinct volcano, São Tomé is the largest and most populous of the two main islands, some 440 km (273 miles) off the coast of Gabon. Low lying in the northeast and the southwest, it rises to Pico de São Tomé in the volcanic highlands. The island of Príncipe lies about 150 km (100 miles) to the northeast. As well as the two main islands there are also a number of rocky islets—Caroco, Pedras, Tinhosas, and Rôlas. On both São Tomé and Príncipe, streams drain to the sea from mountainous interiors, up to seventy percent of which are densely forested. The climate is hot and humid, moderated to a certain extent by the cold Benguela current that flows up Africa's western shore.

Following independence in 1975 the cocoa plantations which formed the foundation of the country's economy deteriorated as a result of mismanagement aggravated by drought. By 1987 the production of cocoa had fallen to 3,500 tonnes from an annual output of 9,000 tonnes prior to 1975. While the discovery of oil in the Gulf of Guinea has led to some economic recovery in recent years, São Tomé and Príncipe have serious trade imbalance. During the 1980s agriculture diversified into palm oil, pepper, and coffee but production has faltered since that time. Deforestation and soil erosion are increasing causes for concern. Today, São Tomé imports ninety percent of its food, all its fuel, and most manufactured goods. However, income from the export of oil has a significant positive impact on the country's economy.

by tribal groups trying to adapt to democratic political arrangements.

The island of Bioco is mountainous and volcanic, with fertile soils. It has long supported cocoa on the lowland, and there are coffee plantations on the higher slopes which rise to Pico Basile. Rugged terrain and waterfalls are found in the southern half of the island. On the thinly populated area of mainland, mangrove swamps along the coast lead inland to dense tropical forests. Here, foreign companies have timber concessions, felling okoume and mahogany.

In addition to timber, the country exports cocoa and coffee. In the years before independence, cocoa plantations on Bioco and the mainland provided Equatorial Guinea with the highest per capita income in western Africa. By the end of the Macias era, however, the state was in political and economic ruins and some 100,000 of the population had fled as refugees to neighboring countries. Most of those who remain in the country today are subsistence farmers growing yams, cassava, and bananas.

Equatorial Guinea has a variety of undeveloped mineral resources: titanium, iron ore, manganese, uranium, and alluvial gold. Recently oil exploration has been successful, and an increased production of oil and natural gas has led to the fact that it is believed to have one of the highest per capita incomes in the world, although this wealth is concentrated in very few hands. Aid programs are in limbo since 1993, having been cut off because of corruption and mismanagement.

## São Tomé and Príncipe

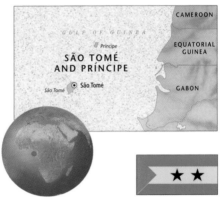

### Fact File

| | |
|---|---|
| **OFFICIAL NAME** | Democratic Republic of São Tomé and Príncipe |
| **FORM OF GOVERNMENT** | Republic with single legislative body (National People's Assembly) |
| **CAPITAL** | São Tomé |
| **AREA** | 1,001 sq km (386 sq miles) |
| **TIME ZONE** | GMT |
| **POPULATION** | 206,000 |
| **PROJECTED POPULATION 2015** | 180,000 |
| **POPULATION DENSITY** | 205.8 per sq km (533.7 per sq mile) |
| **LIFE EXPECTANCY** | 68 |
| **INFANT MORTALITY (PER 1,000)** | 38.4 |
| **OFFICIAL LANGUAGE** | Portuguese |
| **OTHER LANGUAGES** | Crioulo (blend of Portuguese and West African languages) |
| **LITERACY RATE** | 84.9 % |
| **RELIGIONS** | Roman Catholic 70.3 %, Evangelical 3.4 %, New Apostolic 2 %, Adventist 1.8 %, other 3.1 %, none 19.4 % |
| **ETHNIC GROUPS** | Predominantly mixed African-Portuguese, with various African minorities |

# Gabon

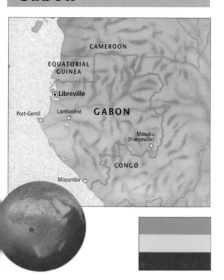

## Fact File

**OFFICIAL NAME** Gabonese Republic

**FORM OF GOVERNMENT** Republic with single legislative body (National Assembly)

**CAPITAL** Libreville

**AREA** 267,667 sq km (103,346 sq miles)

**TIME ZONE** GMT + 1 hour

**POPULATION** 1,486,000

**PROJECTED POPULATION 2015** 1,494,000

**POPULATION DENSITY** 5.6 per sq km (14.4 per sq mile)

**LIFE EXPECTANCY** 53.5

**INFANT MORTALITY (PER 1,000)** 52.7

**OFFICIAL LANGUAGE** French

**OTHER LANGUAGES** Fang, Bantu languages

**LITERACY RATE** 63.2%

**RELIGIONS** Christian 55%–75%, Muslim less than 1%, indigenous beliefs

**ETHNIC GROUPS** Mainly Bantu tribes (including Fang, Eshira, Bapounou, Bateke) 92%, foreign Africans and Europeans 8%

**CURRENCY** CFA (Communauté Financière Africaine) franc

**ECONOMY** Industry 58.2%, services 36%, agriculture 5.8%

**GNI PER CAPITA** US$ 6,670

**CLIMATE** Tropical, with dry season mid-May to mid-September

**HIGHEST POINT** Mt Iboundji 1,575 m (5,167 ft)

**MAP REFERENCE** Page 368

A slave station for the Portuguese after their arrival in 1483, Gabon was administered by France from 1842. After the French navy suppressed the still-continuing local slave trade, it released captives at a place on the coast which it named Libreville (Libertyville). Since Gabon achieved independence in 1966 France has continued to play a role in the country's politics and in its relatively prosperous oil-based economy.

The original inhabitants of this heavily forested equatorial country were probably Pygmies; today the main tribal group is the Fang. However, the more than forty-year rule of President El Hadj Omar Bongo (a Bateke who converted to Islam under Libyan influence in 1973) depended on a coalition that was designed to exclude the Fang from power. Widespread dissatisfaction with this state of affairs led to the introduction of a multi-party system in 1991. Allegations of electoral fraud during various elections since 2002 have exposed the weaknesses of the political structures in Gabon. The country's opposition remains weak, divided, and financially heavily dependent on the current regime. However, the country has in the meantime developed into an island of stability in the region and since 1994 there have not been any complaints concerning human rights questions.

Geographically, a coastal plain marked by sandbars and lagoons is interrupted by the estuary of the Ogooué River. The wooded basin of this large watercourse dominates Gabon, sixty percent of the country's land area being drained by its tributaries. These flow down from the African central plateau and the borders of Equatorial Guinea and Cameroon to the north, and from Congo to the east and south.

Before the development of oil and manganese in the early 1970s, valuable timbers were one of the country's main exports. These included Gabon mahogany, ebony, and walnut. Even today as much as two-thirds of Gabon's total land area consists of untouched rainforest, but the completion in 1986 of the Trans-Gabon Railway from the port of Owendo to the interior town of Massoukou is likely to lead to further exploitation of timber resources.

Gabon has considerable mineral resources. It has about one-quarter of the world's known reserves of manganese, and is the world's fourth biggest manganese producer. France imports most of its uranium from Gabon. Oil currently accounts for fifty percent of gross domestic product. This figure, when combined with Gabon's small population, gives a distorted picture of the country's per capita earnings, disguising the fact that more than half the country's people make their living by subsistence farming. A wide gap separates rural people from the urban élite and the country faces serious fiscal and economic problems.

# Congo

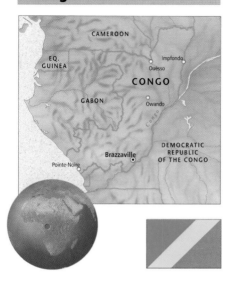

## Fact File

**OFFICIAL NAME** Republic of the Congo

**FORM OF GOVERNMENT** Republic with two legislative bodies (Senate and National Assembly)

**CAPITAL** Brazzaville

**AREA** 342,000 sq km (132,046 sq miles)

**TIME ZONE** GMT + 1 hour

**POPULATION** 3,903,000

**PROJECTED POPULATION 2015** 4,459,000

**POPULATION DENSITY** 11.4 per sq km (29.6 per sq mile)

**LIFE EXPECTANCY** 53.7

**INFANT MORTALITY (PER 1,000)** 81.3

**OFFICIAL LANGUAGE** French

**OTHER LANGUAGES** Lingala, Monoketuba, Kikongo, Téké, Sanga, Ubangi languages

**LITERACY RATE** 83.8%

**RELIGIONS** Christian 50%, indigenous beliefs 48%, Muslim 2%

**ETHNIC GROUPS** About 75 different tribes: Kongo 48%, Sangha 20%, Teke 17%, M'Bochi 12%; other 3%

**CURRENCY** CFA (Communauté Financière Africaine) franc

**ECONOMY** Industry 57.1%, services 37.3%, agriculture 5.6%

**GNI PER CAPITA** US$ 1,540

**CLIMATE** Tropical, with wet season March to June

**HIGHEST POINT** Mt Berongou 903 m (2,963 ft)

**MAP REFERENCE** Page 368

F rom the Atlantic coast, Congo extends 1,000 km (600 miles) inland to the border of the Central African Republic. Its history is obscure, although the first inhabitants may have been Pygmies. Later it was home to the Kongo peoples who supplied slaves for Portuguese traders. In the nineteenth century it was explored by the French-Italian Pierre Savorgnan de Brazza, who gave his name to the capital city, and whose activities led to the region becoming part of French Equatorial Africa in 1891. Congo has been independent since 1960. Ten years after independence, Congo declared itself a People's Republic and Africa's first communist state. Since 1991, however, there have been attempts to introduce the principles of legal opposition and multiparty democracy. In 1997 a brief civil war restored former Marxist President Sassou-Nguesso, but also started a five-year period of ethnic unrest. Finally, in March 2003 southern-based rebel groups agreed to a peace accord, but the truce is tenuous and refugees continue to present a humanitarian crisis.

Road transport within Congo is hampered by tropical rains that make the unpaved roads unuseable but water transport to the interior and the northeast is comparatively easy. Two mighty rivers, the Congo and the Ubangi, provide a commercially navigable highway along virtually the entire eastern frontier.

From a coastal strip on the Atlantic seaboard, the Rivers Kouilou and Niari lead up to the heights of the Massif du Mayombé. This range is crossed by a spectacular French-built railway joining Brazzaville with the port of Pointe-Noire. The Congo below Brazzaville has many cataracts, and the railway was built to carry freight around them. Beyond the massif the land falls away northward to the central plateau, where numerous rivers drain east into the Ubangi and the Congo itself.

Though more than half the Congolese live in towns, subsistence agriculture engages one-third of the workforce, and most of the food produced and consumed is cassava. Rice, maize, and vegetables are also grown, and coffee and cocoa are exported. Some sixty percent of the country is still covered in tropical forest. Timber was once a leading export, but today ninety percent of exports consists of oil. Apart from that, Congo allows other countries such as Gabon or the Central African Republic to use its port and other transport facilities. Manufacture, for example the processing of agricultural products or the production of textiles and shoes in the larger cities, is also an economic enterprise of some importance. Despite its comparative wealth, the government has mortgaged a large part of its oil earnings for expensive development projects.

# Democratic Republic of Congo

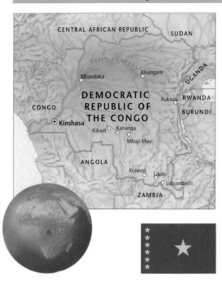

## Fact File

**OFFICIAL NAME**  Democratic Republic of the Congo

**FORM OF GOVERNMENT**  Presidential rule

**CAPITAL**  Kinshasa

**AREA**  2,345,410 sq km (905,563 sq miles)

**TIME ZONE**  GMT + 1/2 hour

**POPULATION**  66,515,000

**PROJECTED POPULATION 2015**  80,569,000

**POPULATION DENSITY**  28.4 per sq km (73.5 per sq mile)

**LIFE EXPECTANCY**  54

**INFANT MORTALITY (PER 1,000)**  83.1

**OFFICIAL LANGUAGE**  French

**OTHER LANGUAGES**  Chiluba, Kikongo, Lingala, Swahili, Luvena, Chokwe, Gbaya, Kituba and others

**LITERACY RATE**  67.2 %

**RELIGIONS**  Roman Catholic 50%, Protestant 20%, Kimbanguist 10%, Muslim 10%, other indigenous beliefs 10%

**ETHNIC GROUPS**  More than 200 indigenous groups, mostly of Bantu origin

**CURRENCY**  New zaire

**ECONOMY**  Agriculture 55%, services 34%, industry 11%

**GNI PER CAPITA**  US$ 140

**CLIMATE**  Tropical; wet season north of equator from April to October, wet season south of equator from November to March

**HIGHEST POINT**  Mt Stanley 5,110 m (16,765 ft)

**MAP REFERENCE**  Pages 368–69

The Democratic Republic of the Congo (DRC), formerly called Zaire, is the centerpiece of central Africa. It is the third-largest country on the continent after Algeria and Sudan and has one of the largest navigable rivers in the world. Historically occupied by the Kongo, Luba, Lunda, and Azande peoples, this enormous region fell into the hands of King Leopold of Belgium in 1885, who exploited it as a private domain. After international condemnation of his brutal rule, in 1908 it became a colony of Belgium. The country won its independence in 1960.

Since that time, 35 years of dictatorial mismanagement and corruption as a one-party state under the control of President Mobutu Sese Seko (who died in 1997) have brought the DRC to the point of collapse. The troubles of its neighbors have added to its own. War and disorder in Sudan, Rwanda, Burundi, and Angola have driven hundreds of thousands of refugees across the borders into the DRC. A military occupation of Kinshasa was successful in bringing the Mobutu regime to an end in 1997. His successor, President Laurent Kabila was assassinated in 2001 and succeeded by his son Joseph. In 2003 the EU dispatched troups to the country to help. In spite of some unrest, elections in 2006 led to a new government and President Kabila was inaugurated in 2007.

Geographically the DRC is dominated by a single feature—the immense basin of the Congo River. The eastern rim of this basin is formed by the Mitumba Mountains (Monts Mitumbe) along the Rift Valley, and the volcanic Ruwenzori Range. In the far southeast Lake Mweru feeds into the Congo's main northward-flowing tributary, the Lualaba. Looping north and west in a great horseshoe, the Congo is joined on the borders of the Central African Republic by the Ubangi. After several cascades below Kinshasa as it descends from the central plateau, the Congo empties into the Atlantic Ocean. The equatorial climate of the main river basin supports one of the world's most extensive rainforests, home to rare animals such as okapi and gorilla. The savanna grasslands of the east and south are home to giraffe, lion, antelope and rhinoceros.

Potentially one of Africa's richest countries, the DRC is currently one of its poorest. Most of its people try to survive the breakdown of civil society by subsistence farming and petty trade. Cash crops such as coffee, sugar, and palm oil continue to be produced, but a severe lack of infrastructure hampers trade. Since 2003, economic stability has improved, but an uncertain legal framework, corruption, and a lack of transparency in government policy continue to hamper growth.

*A village in the Congo highlands (left page bottom).
Dusk on the Congo River in the Democratic Republic of
the Congo (left). Angolan women pounding millet in
the traditional way (below).*

estimated 1.5 million people had lost their lives
in fighting over the past quarter of a century.
The reconstruction of the devastated country and
the reconciliation of the different groups are the
most pressing issues for the current government,
but there is hope that the country finally may
come to rest.

Angola can be divided into two main regions.
There are the relatively narrow coastal plains, and
an extensive tableland that rises from them and
dominates the rest of the country. Divided roughly east to west across the center, this tableland
drains into the Congo Basin to the north, and into
the rivers of the Zambeze Basin to the south and
east. While the tableland is fairly level in the
south, the highlands become mountainous in
central and southwestern Angola. In the province
of Cabinda there are dense tropical rainforests,
and heavy rains can be expected for seven
months of the year. Savanna woodland is found
on much of the tableland, becoming mainly
grassy plains to the south, dotted with acacia and
baobab trees. The cold Benguela current that
flows north from the southern Atlantic Ocean has
a moderating effect on the heat of the coastal
region. Toward Namibia on the southern border
the coastal strip becomes desert.

Angola is rich in petroleum, gold, and diamonds, and has reserves of iron ore, phosphates,
feldspar, bauxite, and uranium. It has large areas
of forest, productive fisheries off the Atlantic
coast, and extensive areas of arable land. While
the country is capable of producing coffee, sisal,
and cotton, the years of civil war have resulted in
economic disarray and the country's output per
capita for many years was one of the lowest in
the world. Subsistence agriculture supports about
85 percent of the people and much of the
nation's food still has to be imported.

# Angola

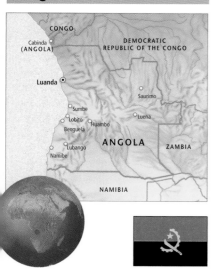

| | |
|---|---|
| LITERACY RATE | 67.4 % |

RELIGIONS  Indigenous beliefs 47 %, Roman
Catholic 38 %, Protestant 15 %

ETHNIC GROUPS  Mainly indigenous, including
Ovimbundu 37 %, Kimbundu 25 %, Bakongo 13 %;
mixed European-African 2 %, European 1 %,
other 22 %

CURRENCY  Kwanza

ECONOMY  Industry 65.8 %, services 24.6 %,
agriculture 9.6 %

GNI PER CAPITA  US$ 2,560

CLIMATE  Mainly tropical with wet season November
to April; semiarid in south and along coast

HIGHEST POINT  Mt Môco 2,620 m (8,596 ft)

MAP REFERENCE  Pages 368, 370

## Fact File

OFFICIAL NAME  Republic of Angola

FORM OF GOVERNMENT  Republic with single
legislative body (National Assembly)

CAPITAL  Luanda

AREA  1,246,700 sq km (481,351 sq miles)

TIME ZONE  GMT + 1 hour

POPULATION  12,531,000

PROJECTED POPULATION 2015  21,231,000

POPULATION DENSITY  10.1 per sq km
(26 per sq mile)

LIFE EXPECTANCY  37.9

INFANT MORTALITY (PER 1,000)  182.3

OFFICIAL LANGUAGE  Portuguese

OTHER LANGUAGES  Bantu, other African languages

A large country on Africa's southwest coast,
Angola is bordered by the states of the
Democratic Republic of the Congo to the north,
Zambia to the east, and Namibia to the south.
The small but resource-rich province of Cabinda
lies separated from the rest of Angola to the north
of the Congo River, wholly surrounded by Congo.

A Portuguese colony since the sixteenth
century, Angola was the source of an estimated
three million slaves who were sent to Brazil and
other places across the Atlantic, largely to work
on sugar plantations. The country received its
independence in 1975 and for the next twenty
years was wracked by civil war. The government,
having established a Marxist one-party state
supported by the USSR and especially Cuba, was
then challenged by the forces of Jonas Savimbi,
who was backed by the USA. The truce mediated
between the two parties by the United Nations,
which came into force in 1994, did not last for
long. A national unity government was installed
in 1997, but serious fighting resumed in late 1998,
rendering hundreds of thousands of people
homeless. After the death of Jonas Savimbi in
2002 both parties stopped fighting after an

Africa

## Eastern Africa

| | |
|---|---|
| Sudan | 336 |
| Eritrea | 336 |
| Ethiopia | 338 |
| Djibouti | 338 |
| Somalia | 339 |
| Uganda | 340 |
| Kenya | 340 |
| Tanzania | 341 |
| Rwanda | 342 |
| Burundi | 343 |

## Sudan

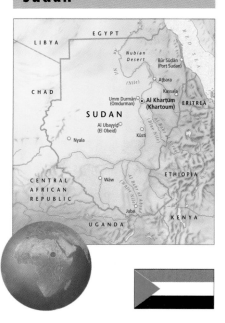

### Fact File

OFFICIAL NAME  Republic of the Sudan

FORM OF GOVERNMENT  Republic, "Government of National Unity"

CAPITAL  Al Kharṭūm (Khartoum)

AREA  2,505,810 sq km (967,493 sq miles)

TIME ZONE  GMT + 2 hours

POPULATION  40,218,000

PROJECTED POPULATION 2015  45,613,000

POPULATION DENSITY  16 per sq km (41.6 per sq mile)

LIFE EXPECTANCY  50.3

INFANT MORTALITY (PER 1,000)  87

OFFICIAL LANGUAGE  Arabic

OTHER LANGUAGES  Mainly Nile-Saharan languages plus Cushitic and Kardofanian languages, English

LITERACY RATE  61.1 %

RELIGIONS  Sunni Muslim 70 %, indigenous beliefs 25 %, Christian 5 %

ETHNIC GROUPS  African 52 %, Arab 39 %, Beja 6 %, other 3 %

CURRENCY  Sudan pound

ECONOMY  Industry 34.4 %, services 33.9 %, agriculture 31.8 %

GNI PER CAPITA  US$ 960

CLIMATE  North mainly arid; south tropical, with wet season April to October

HIGHEST POINT  Mt Kinyeti 3,187 m (10,456 ft)

MAP REFERENCE  Pages 362–63, 366–67

South of Egypt, Sudan is Africa's largest country, and the pathway to the headwaters of the Nile (An Nil). It is also one of Africa's most divided countries. Known in Ancient Egypt as Nubia, its northern region came under Islamic Arab control in the fourteenth century, and Egyptian and British rule in the nineteenth. With some 570 distinct ethnic groups and over 100 languages, it has been difficult for Sudan to form a modern state.

Since achieving independence from Egypt and Britain in 1956 Sudan has seen military rule, coups, and civil conflict for all but ten of the next fifty years. The main cause is the determination of the Muslim north to impose Arab and Islamic values on the varied African, animist, and Christian peoples of the south. Strict sharia (Muslim) law has been proclaimed but is widely ignored. After the government's "war of annihilation" against the 1.5 million Nuba people, supported by opposition groups, it has now also turned against the Muslim, but black, population of the Darfur province. Over half a million people have died in the past twelve years, the miseries of the ethnic Africans being compounded by famine, displacement, rape, and the enslavement of women and children. International attempts to help are obstructed by armed conflict, poor transport infrastructure, and lack of government support. Firthermore, the conflicts started to affect the neighboring Chad and Central African Republic.

In northern Sudan the rocky Sahara Desert stretches westward to become a waste of sand dunes, the land rising to 3,071 m (10,075 ft) at the Darfur Massif toward the border with Chad. In the east the Red Sea Mountains rise 2,000 m (6,500 ft) above a narrow coastal plain. Most people live near the south-north flowing Nile (An Nil), a river that divides into two streams at Khartoum. From here the source of the Blue Nile (Al Bahr al Azraq) can be traced southeast to the Ethiopian border and Lake Tana. The White Nile (Al Bahr al Abyad) runs southwards into the vast marshland of the Sudd (where dense, floating vegetation makes navigation difficult), then further upstream to Uganda and its headwaters in Lake Albert.

About 80 percent of Sudan's workforce are farmers. There is a heavy emphasis on growing cotton, at the expense of food crops, as it accounts for 24 percent of export revenue. Food crops include sorghum (the staple) along with millet, wheat, barley, and peanuts. Declining rainfall and huge displacements of the rural population as a result of war have played havoc with production in recent years. In 2007, a new currency was introduced, the Sudan pound, at an exchange rate of US $2 to 1 pound. Natural resources include copper, chromium ore, zinc, tungsten, mica, silver, gold, and substantial oil reserves.

*Crumbling pyramids in the desert at Meroë in the Sudan witness its long common history with Egypt (right).*

## Eritrea

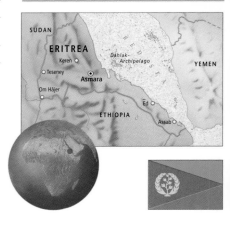

### Fact File

OFFICIAL NAME  State of Eritrea

FORM OF GOVERNMENT  Republic

CAPITAL  Asmara

AREA  121,320 sq km (46,842 sq miles)

TIME ZONE  GMT + 3 hours

POPULATION  5,028,000

PROJECTED POPULATION 2015  6,165,000

POPULATION DENSITY  41.4 per sq km (107.3 per sq mile)

LIFE EXPECTANCY  60.1

INFANT MORTALITY (PER 1,000)  44.2

OFFICIAL LANGUAGES  Tigrinya, Arabic

OTHER LANGUAGES  Tigré, other indigenous languages, English

LITERACY RATE  58.6 %

RELIGIONS  Muslim 50 %, Christian (Coptic Christian, Roman Catholic, Protestant) 50 %

ETHNIC GROUPS  Tigrinya 50 %, Tigré and Kunama 40 %, Afar 4 %, Saho (Red Sea coast dwellers) 3 %, other 3 %

CURRENCY  Nakfa

ECONOMY  Services 55.7 %, industry 22.6 %, agriculture 21.7 %

GNI PER CAPITA  US$ 230

CLIMATE  Hot and arid along coast, cooler and wetter in highlands; wet season June to September

HIGHEST POINT  Soira 3,018 m (9,899 ft)

MAP REFERENCE  Page 367

Eritrea was part of the Aksum Kingdom 2,000 years ago. In the fourth century AD Coptic Christianity was brought to the country, and a member of the Coptic Christian community, Issaias Ifawerki, is now its president. Italian influence in the region began in 1882, and despite the depredations of Mussolini between 1935 and 1941, Eritrea's modernization dates from those years. Italy introduced Western education and industry.

Forced to join Ethiopia in 1962, Eritrea began a thirty-year war of independence, first against the emperor and then against Ethiopia's Soviet-armed and financed Mengistu regime. Fighting from trenches dug from rock in the mountains, and in spite of inferior weapons, the Eritrean troops hung on. Victory and separate nationhood were won in 1993. In 1998 war broke out again for two and a half years, and since 2000 a UN peacekeeping operation has monitored a 25 km- (15.5 mile-) wide temporary security zone on the border with Ethiopia. In November 2006, an international commission set a deadline for Eritrea and Ethiopia to demarcate the border within a year or the demarcation would be based on coordinates.

Consisting of a hot dry desert strip along the Red Sea shore, Eritrea is dominated by rugged mountains in the north, and in the southeast by the arid coastal plain of the Danakil Desert. In and around this desert live the Afar, camel-keeping nomads. The country is bordered on the north by the Sudan, with whom it has uneasy relations, and on the south by Djibouti. Before independence, Eritrea provided Ethiopia's only access to the sea other than through Djibouti. The prospect of being landlocked as a result of Eritrean secession—which is what happened—strengthened Ethiopian resolve during the war.

Poor and war-torn, with its roads and railways destroyed, since 1993 Eritrea has faced the task of reconstruction. Obligatory military service provides labor for public works. During the war trees were cut down by the enemy to deprive Eritrean soldiers of hiding places: these are being replanted by the thousand. In the long term offshore oil deposits may prove important, but the population currently survives by subsistence farming, growing sorghum, lentils, vegetables, and maize. This is supplemented by food aid on which 75 percent of the people rely.

## Causes of famine in Africa

Famine has been a serious problem on the African continent since very early times—there are records of famines in Egypt 6,000 years ago. A good corn harvest in Egypt was essential to the well-being of the region as a whole. A bad harvest affected not only Egypt but also the neighbors with whom it traded. Famine usually occurred because of annual variations in the extent of the flooding of the River Nile, and therefore in the yield of grain for food. Such famines were related to inherent difficulties in the kind of intensive floodplain agriculture that has been practiced over the centuries in the Nile Valley.

Prolonged drought and the spread of deserts in marginal areas are other common causes of famine. Hungry people allow their goats to graze on the sparse vegetation that grows on desert fringes, which frequently results in the plants dying and the desert spreading. This can be seen in the vast sub-Saharan region of the Sahel. A third type of famine is largely the result of human actions. Chronic warfare of the kind that has recently plagued the southern Sudan seriously disrupts agricultural production, displacing such large numbers of people that crops are neither planted nor harvested.

Finally, there is the kind of famine that affected Ethiopia under the Marxist Dergue during 1984–85, which was a direct result of government policies. Huge collectivization programs were initiated in the midst of war and cultivators were forcibly taken from their own land to work on state farms—many of those removed were "resettled" as punishment for their suspected hostility to the regime. This seriously affected the morale of the population and food production throughout the country decreased dramatically. A report prepared by the organization Cultural Survival concluded that the principal reasons for food shortages in Ethiopia at that time were the forcible redistribution of land to people unable or unwilling to work it; the confiscation of grain and livestock; and forced labor

programs and military recruitment, which resulted in a sharp decline in the labor force available for agricultural work.

In Africa as elsewhere, the United Nations World Food Programme (WFP) is the main agency that is active in famine relief. Helping as many as 53 million people worldwide, it operates in virtually all the sub-Saharan African countries. The WFP's Food for Life Program helps people affected by humanitarian crises, such as that in Rwanda and Burundi in 1994. In April 1994 WFP workers provided food for what amounted to a huge city of refugees on the border of Rwanda and Tanzania, where 250,000 people were gathered without food, water, or shelter.

The WFP Food for Growth Program targets needy schoolchildren, mothers who are breast-feeding, and the elderly. In Ethiopia the WFP Food for Work Program, which pays workers with food for their service on development projects, has contributed to the planting of large numbers of trees; in Somalia the same program has been involved in repairing irrigation canals.

*Desert encroaching on an African town (below). Children affected by famine (right).*

Africa

# Ethiopia

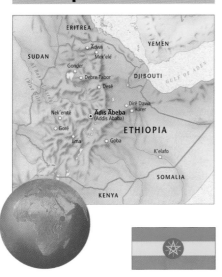

## Fact File

**OFFICIAL NAME** Federal Democratic Republic of Ethiopia

**FORM OF GOVERNMENT** Federal republic with two legislative bodies (Federal Council and Council of People's Representatives)

**CAPITAL** Ādis Ābeba (Addis Ababa)

**AREA** 1,127,127 sq km (435,184 sq miles)

**TIME ZONE** GMT + 3 hours

**POPULATION** 78,254,000

**PROJECTED POPULATION 2015** 100,967,000

**POPULATION DENSITY** 69.4 per sq km (179.8 per sq mile)

**LIFE EXPECTANCY** 49.4

**INFANT MORTALITY (PER 1,000)** 90.2

**OFFICIAL LANGUAGE** Amharic

**OTHER LANGUAGES** Semitic and Kushite (Nubian), English, Italian, French, Arabic

**LITERACY RATE** 42.7 %

**RELIGIONS** Ethiopian Orthodox 50.6 %, Muslim 32.8 %, Protestant 10.2 %, indigenous beliefs 4.6 %, other 1.8 %

**ETHNIC GROUPS** Oromo 32.1 %, Amara 30.1 %, Tigraway 6.2 %, Somalie 5.9 %, Guragie 4.3 %, Sidama 3.5 %, Welaita 2.4 %, other 15.4 %

**CURRENCY** Birr

**ECONOMY** Agriculture 47 %, services 39.8 %, industry 13.2 %

**GNI PER CAPITA** US$ 220

**CLIMATE** Tropical on lowlands, uplands more temperate; wet season April to September

**HIGHEST POINT** Ras Dashen Terara 4,620 m (15,157 ft)

**MAP REFERENCE** Pages 366–67

Ethiopia was known as the land of Punt by the Ancient Egyptians. In the fourth century AD it adopted Coptic Christianity, and despite strong Islamic influences since that time, including a Muslim invasion in 1523, many people remain Christian today. Although Mussolini's Italy occu-pied the country between 1935 and 1941, Ethiopia was never a colony—in fact under Emperor Haile Selassie it had imperial ambitions, and attempted to subjugate both the Somalis and the people of Eritrea. Haile Selassie was deposed in 1974 by a military coup; this triggered a civil war that exacerbated the effects of the famine in 1984. Always poor, Ethiopia is currently destitute—thirty years of war and resulting famine are the legacy of the Marxist dictatorship of Mengistu Haile Mariam. His regime ended in 1991, when he was deposed.

The landscape is dominated by a mountainous volcanic plateau divided in two by the Rift Valley. The western highlands, with an average height of 2,700 m (8,800 ft), are the source of the Blue Nile, which spills out in a cataract from Lake Tana to flow south and west, before finally flowing north into Sudan. East of the western highlands is the Danakil Desert, where a depression falls to 116 m (380 ft) below sea level. This is one of the hottest places on earth. In the highlands, how-ever, the climate is moderate to warm, with frosts at night and occasional falls of snow on the mountains. The eastern highlands below the Rift Valley fall away to the border with Somalia. In the aftermath of Ethiopia's war with its Somali neighbor the southern section of this border is only provisional, and there is an ongoing dispute regarding the Ogadēn region.

More than ninety percent of the country's industry, concerned with food processing, the manufacture of textiles, and chemical and metal production, is owned and managed by the state. Under Ethiopia's land tenure system, the govern-ment owns all land and provides long-term leases to the tenants. This system continues to hinder growth in the industrial sector, as entrepreneurs are unable to use land as collateral for loans.

Drought in the years 1981 to 1985, combined with an unsuccessful attempt to collectivize agri-culture, resulted in a famine in which an estimated 1 million people died. Today, rural production accounts for almost half of gross domestic pro-duct, sixty percent of the exports, and eighty percent of employment. Repair of war-damaged roads and railways continues. Although Ethiopia still needs food aid there is a growing emphasis on aid in the form of credit for infrastructure development.

# Djibouti

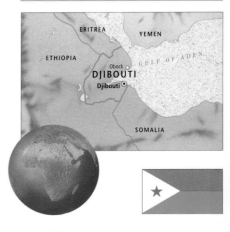

## Fact File

**OFFICIAL NAME** Republic of Djibouti

**FORM OF GOVERNMENT** Republic with single legislative body (Chamber of Deputies)

**CAPITAL** Djibouti

**AREA** 23,000 sq km (8,880 sq miles)

**TIME ZONE** GMT + 3 hours

**POPULATION** 506,000

**PROJECTED POPULATION 2015** 951,000

**POPULATION DENSITY** 22 per sq km (57 per sq mile)

**LIFE EXPECTANCY** 43.3

**INFANT MORTALITY (PER 1,000)** 99.1

**OFFICIAL LANGUAGES** Arabic, French

**OTHER LANGUAGES** Kushite (Nubian) languages plus Afar and Issa

**LITERACY RATE** 67.9 %

**RELIGIONS** Muslim 94 %, Christian 6 %

**ETHNIC GROUPS** Somali 60 %, Afar 35 %, other (including French, Arab, Ethiopian, and Italian) 5 %

**CURRENCY** Djiboutian franc

**ECONOMY** Services 81.9 %, industry 14.9 %, agriculture 3.2 %

**GNI PER CAPITA** US$ 1,090

CLIMATE Semiarid; particularly hot on coast

HIGHEST POINT Mousa Alli (Musa Ālī Terara) 2,028 m (6,654 ft)

MAP REFERENCE Page 367

One of the smallest African countries, Djibouti stands at the entrance to the Red Sea from the Gulf of Aden. This strategic location near the world's busiest shipping lanes has resulted in it being used as a base by European nations for a hundred years. After the construction of the Suez Canal, the British and French took an interest in Djibouti as a way of protecting their investment in the canal route to Europe, the town of Djibouti becoming the capital of French Somaliland in 1892. Although Djibouti won independence in 1977, France continues to play a role in its affairs and maintains a significant military presence in the country.

Since 1977 there has been a continuous political struggle between the majority Issa (who are Somali) and the minority Afar (also known as Danakil). Somalia, across the southeastern border, supports the Issa. Eritrea, to the north, supports the Afar, as does Ethiopia. Thus, both Issa and Afar have numerous external allies watching over their interests and inclined to interfere. The port of Djibouti is also the terminus of rail traffic for the vast landlocked hinterland of Ethiopia, a crucial matter for that state. Unrest among the Afars minority during the 1990s led to multi-party elections in 1999. A peace accord in 2001 ended the final phases of a ten-year uprising by Afar rebels.

Djibouti is one of the hottest places on earth, little rain falls, and water is in high demand. A subterranean river named the Ambouli is one essential source. Two-thirds of the population live in the capital city itself. Those who live elsewhere mostly inhabit the relatively fertile coastal strip along the Gulf of Tadjoura (Golfe de Tadjoura), avoiding the burning interior plateau and its volcanic wastes. Almost ninety percent of the interior terrain is desert, with a vegetation of scrub and desert thorns. Here, nomadic goat and camel herders eke out a living.

Djibouti's economy is that of a free trade zone providing essential services for the region. It has few natural resources (though geothermal energy is being developed, and natural gas has been found), little industry, and agricultural production mainly provides fruit and vegetables for domestic consumption. The services it renders are those of a transit port, of great value to Ethiopia and Somalia, and of an international depot and refueling center. Strongly affected by the civil wars in its neigboring countries, Djibouti suffers from an unemployment rate of more than 60 percent.

# Somalia

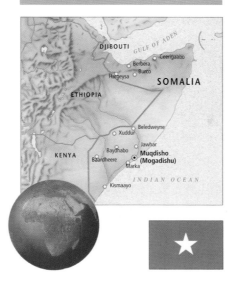

## Fact File

OFFICIAL NAME Somali Democratic Republic

FORM OF GOVERNMENT Republic; no effective central government exists at the present time

CAPITAL Muqdisho (Mogadishu)

AREA 637,657 sq km (246,200 sq miles)

TIME ZONE GMT + 3 hours

POPULATION 9,559,000

PROJECTED POPULATION 2015 10,881,000

POPULATION DENSITY 15 per sq km (38.8 per sq mile)

LIFE EXPECTANCY 49.3

INFANT MORTALITY (PER 1,000) 111

OFFICIAL LANGUAGE Somali

OTHER LANGUAGES Arabic, Italian, other indigenous languages

LITERACY RATE 37.8 %

RELIGIONS Sunni Muslim with tiny Christian minority

ETHNIC GROUPS Somali 85 %, remainder mainly Bantu with small Arab, Asian, and European minorities 15 %

CURRENCY Somali shilling

ECONOMY Agriculture 65 %, services 25 %, industry 10 %

GNI PER CAPITA not available (less than US$ 935)

CLIMATE Mainly hot and arid, with higher rainfall in the south

HIGHEST POINT Mt Shimbiris 2,416 m (7,927 ft)

MAP REFERENCE Page 367

Somalia, a coastal state on the Horn of Africa, is in one respect unlike any other African country. It is the only place where the whole population feels that they are "one people"—Somali—and because of this ethnic homogeneity it has the makings of a nation state. Briefly under the control of Egypt from 1875, the region became a British protectorate in 1885. In 1889 Italy took control of the eastern coast, and from then on the country was divided into British

Traders at the goat and donkey market in Lalibela, in northern Ethiopia (left page). An aerial view of the city of Djibouti, on the Gulf of Aden (below). A group of Somali villagers (above).

Somaliland in the north and Italian Somaliland in the south and east. It has been independent since 1960.

The history of the people of Somalia since independence has been one of repression (under the Soviet-aligned Siyad Barre), military adventure (the invasion of the Ethiopian Ogaden), and civil war. When in 1992 an estimated 2,000 people were dying from war and starvation each day, the United Nations intervened, but its troops were unable to stop the military and civil unrest and withdrew. Anarchy and banditry now prevail and Somalia is riddled by corruption. The power of the interim government ruling since 2000 is only recognized in Muqdisho. Warlords rule the rest of the country. In the absence of any central authority, and without a functioning government in Muqdisho, the northern area once known as British Somaliland seceded and proclaimed itself an independent state. Centered on the city of Hargeysa, it calls itself the Republic of Somaliland. It has not been recognised internationally but has proven politically stable since 1998.

Along the northern shore facing the Gulf of Aden lies the semiarid Guban coastal plain. Behind this is a range of mountains, the Ogo Highlands, running eastward from Ethiopia to the point of the Horn itself. South of the highlands is the Haud Plateau, and beyond this the land slopes down toward the Indian Ocean. Much of Somalia has semidesert thornbush and dry savanna cover. Only in the better watered south is there enough rainfall to support meager forests and grassland. Arable farming takes place between the Rivers Jubba and Shabeelle in the south. Bananas from this area are a major export, mainly to Italy. At the start of the twenty-first century, piracy is also becoming an important source of income. Organized bands of pirates seize ships and their crews, releasing them only in exchange for high ransoms—a method the international community hasn't been able to get under control even with the help of naval forces.

Nomadic pastoralists form much of the population in the north. Searching for grass and water, they wander with their herds across the state boundaries between southern Djibouti, the Ogaden, and northeast Kenya. Livestock accounts for forty percent of gross domestic product and 65 percent of export earnings. A small industrial sector is based on the processing of food products, but the prevailing disorder has caused many facilities to be shut down.

# Uganda

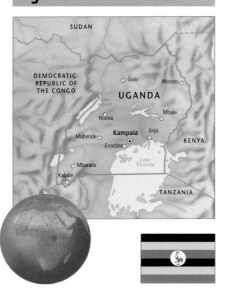

## Fact File

OFFICIAL NAME  Republic of Uganda

FORM OF GOVERNMENT  Republic with single legislative body (National Assembly)

CAPITAL  Kampala

AREA  236,040 sq km (91,135 sq miles)

TIME ZONE  GMT + 3 hours

POPULATION  31.368,000

PROJECTED POPULATION 2015  39,966,000

POPULATION DENSITY  132.9 per sq km (344.2 per sq mile)

LIFE EXPECTANCY  52.3

INFANT MORTALITY (PER 1,000)  66

OFFICIAL LANGUAGE  English

OTHER LANGUAGES  Swahili and other Bantu languages including Buganda, Banyoro, western Nilotic languages, eastern Nilotic languages

LITERACY RATE  66.8 %

RELIGIONS  Protestant 42 %, Roman Catholic 41.9 %, Muslim 12.1 %, other 3.1 %, none 0.9 %

ETHNIC GROUPS  Baganda 16.9 %, Banyakole 9.5 %, Basoga 8.4 %, Bakiga 6.9 %, Iteso 6.4 %, Langi 6.1 %, Acholi 4.7 %, Bagisu 4.6 %, Lugbara 4.2 %, Bunyoro 2.7 %, other 29.6 %

CURRENCY  Ugandan shilling

ECONOMY  Services 45.1 %, agriculture 30.2 %, industry 24.7 %

GNI PER CAPITA  US$ 340

CLIMATE  Tropical, with two wet seasons March to May and September to November; semiarid in northeast

HIGHEST POINT  Mt Stanley 5,110 m (16,765 ft)

MAP REFERENCE  Page 366

Extending north from Africa's largest body of water, Lake Victoria, the east African state of Uganda is a country of lakes and marshland. With a mild climate and varied resources—from fertile soil to freshwater fish to copper—it was once called "the pearl of Africa". After independence in 1962, however, its people suffered two decades of civil war, military coups, atrocities, and massacres, the worst period being the ten years under Idi Amin. It is estimated that between 1966 and Yoweri Museveni's takeover in 1986 more than half a million Ugandan inhabitants were killed.

The Museveni regime has overseen a return to peace and prosperity. Because the tribal basis of the old political parties was a cause of conflict, the government banned overt political activity, while inviting participation in a "one-party/no-party" policy of national unity. Multi-party elections in 1994, 1996, 2001, and 2006 returned Museveni to power.

Uganda's lake system is the source of the Nile. The pattern of lakes originates in the tilting and faulting of the Rift Valley, with the Ruwenzori Range on the western side of the country and the extinct volcano of Mt Elgon to the east. North of the lakes lies a savanna of trees and grassland, where farmers grow millet and sorghum for food, with cotton and tobacco as cash crops. Certain areas where cattle herding is impossible because of tsetse flies have been designated wildlife parks. Desert nomads live in arid Karamoja still further north. Coffee, tea, and sugarcane are grown in the south, which is the most fertile region and has the highest rainfall. This is the most densely settled part of the country, and is where the industrial center of Jinja is located, not far from Kampala, near the large Owen Falls hydroelectric plant.

Agriculture is the basis of the economy, with coffee the main export. Since 1986 the government has been engaged in raising producer prices for export crops, increasing prices for petroleum products (all oil must be imported), and raising civil service wages. Railways are being rebuilt. With the return of public order, Indo-Ugandan entrepreneurs (expelled by the Obote and Amin regimes) are beginning to return from exile. Gold and cobalt mining in the Ruwenzori region is also expected to resume, and since 2003, the Ugandan economy has grown continuously.

# Kenya

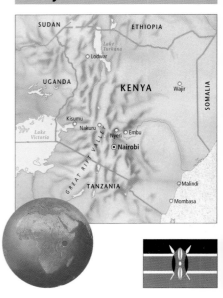

## Fact File

OFFICIAL NAME  Republic of Kenya

FORM OF GOVERNMENT  Republic with single legislative body (National Assembly)

CAPITAL  Nairobi

AREA  582,650 sq km (224,961 sq miles)

TIME ZONE  GMT + 3 hours

POPULATION  37,954,000

PROJECTED POPULATION 2015  46,167,000

POPULATION DENSITY  65.1 per sq km (168.7 per sq mile)

LIFE EXPECTANCY  56.6

INFANT MORTALITY (PER 1,000)  56

OFFICIAL LANGUAGES  English, Swahili

OTHER LANGUAGES  Kikuyu, Luo, Masai and more than 30 others

*The Ruwenzoris in western Uganda, Africa's highest range of mountains (left page). Zebras in the Masai Mara National Reserve in Kenya (top). A Masai woman in traditional dress (above).*

LITERACY RATE 85.1 %

RELIGIONS Protestant 45 %, Roman Catholic 33 %, indigenous beliefs 10 %, Muslim 10 %, other 2 %

ETHNIC GROUPS Kikuyu 22 %, Luhya 14 %, Luo 13 %, Kalenjin 12 %, Kamba 11 %, Kisii 6 %, Meru 6 %, other 16 % (including Asian, European, Arab 1 %)

CURRENCY Kenya shilling

ECONOMY Services 59.5 %, agriculture 23.8 %, industry 16.7 %

GNI PER CAPITA US$ 680

CLIMATE Coastal regions tropical, with wet seasons April to May and October to November; inland plateau cooler and drier

HIGHEST POINT Mt Kenya 5,199 m (17,057 ft)

MAP REFERENCE Pages 368–69

Kenya is where humankind may have originated: remains of humans and pre-humans found in the Olduvai Gorge on the border to Tanzania go back several million years. By the tenth century AD Arabs settled along the coast,

and in the nineteenth century both Britain and Germany became interested in the region. In 1920 Kenya became a British colony. The pleasant climate in the highlands attracted English immigrants who displaced Kikuyu farmers and took their land.

After the Second World War, widespread resentment at this expropriation erupted in the violent Mau Mau rebellion which lasted eight years. Independence came in 1963. Since then, control of the state and its resources has been contested by political parties allied with particular tribes, the domination of the Kikuyu yielding to a trial of multiparty democracy in 1991. Bloody fights broke out after the presidential elections in 2007; they only ended after the president offered the post of prime minister to the opposition leader early in 2008.

The Kenya Highlands consist of a fertile plateau formed by volcanoes and lava flows. The highlands are divided in two by the Rift Valley, the Eastern Highlands falling away toward the densely populated plain near Lake Victoria, and the Western Highlands descending to the valleys of the Tana and Galana Rivers as they cross the Nyika Plain to the north of Mombasa. The populous and fertile coastal belt is fringed by mangrove swamps, coral reefs, and groups of small islands. In the sparsely populated north toward Lake Turkana desert conditions prevail. Kenya's wildlife, consisting of the full range of African fauna, can be seen in the country's several large national parks, and has made it a leading destination for tourists for many years.

By African standards, Kenya has a stable and productive economy. It has a broad and highly successful agricultural base, with cash crops such as coffee and tea. It also has east Africa's largest and most diversified manufacturing sector, producing small-scale consumer goods such as plastics, furniture, batteries, textiles, and soap. While the country had one of the highest rates of population growth (between 1988 and 2000 it experienced an 82 percent increase in population), this number has since dropped to 2.8 % annually.

The continuous increase in the number of its citizens is accompanied by deforestation, lack of drinking water, and infrastructural breakdown. Floods have destroyed roads, bridges, and telecommunications. Crime has caused a steep decline in the number of tourists.

# Tanzania

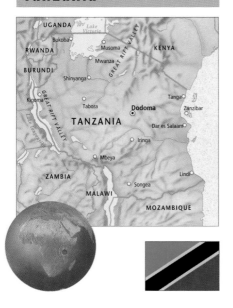

## Fact File

OFFICIAL NAME United Republic of Tanzania

FORM OF GOVERNMENT Republic with single legislative body (National Assembly)

CAPITAL Dodoma

AREA 945,087 sq km (364,898 sq miles)

TIME ZONE GMT + 3 hours

POPULATION 40,213,000

PROJECTED POPULATION 2015 48,999,000

POPULATION DENSITY 42.5 per sq km (110.2 per sq mile)

LIFE EXPECTANCY 51.5

INFANT MORTALITY (PER 1,000) 70.5

OFFICIAL LANGUAGES Swahili, English

OTHER LANGUAGES Bantu and Nilotic languages, Arabic

LITERACY RATE 69.4 %

RELIGIONS Mainland: Muslim 35 %, indigenous beliefs 35 %, Christian 30 %; Zanzibar: Muslim 99 %, other 1 %

ETHNIC GROUPS Indigenous 99 %, other 1 %

CURRENCY Tanzanian shilling

ECONOMY Agriculture 42.8 %, services 38.7 %, industry 18.5 %

GNI PER CAPITA US$ 400

CLIMATE Mainly tropical; hot and humid along coast, drier inland, cooler in mountains

HIGHEST POINT Mt Kilimanjaro 5,895 m (19,340 ft)

MAP REFERENCE Page 369

With Africa's highest mountain (Kilimanjaro) and Serengeti National Park, Tanzania is well known to the outside world. It also the home of some of East Africa's most ancient human remains, those found at Olduvai Gorge on the Kenyan border dating back 2 million years. From the eighth century AD onward, the country's coastal region was subject to Islamic influence from Arab traders who dealt in slaves and ivory. In the nineteenth century British and German settlers arrived.

Africa

341

Tanzania won independence from England in 1961, becoming a de facto one-party state under Julius Nyerere, whose version of African socialism prevailed until he retired in 1985. Opposition parties were allowed in 1992. An uprising by pro-Tanzanian forces violently incorporated the Muslim island of Zanzibar in 1964: unreconciled Islamic interests on the island represent a potential flashpoint. In 1995 the first democratic elections held in the country since the 1970s put an end to the one-party rule. Since then, several elections have been held and won by the ruling party. They were brought about because of Zanzibar's semi-autonomous status and popular opposition and were highly contentious. International observers claimed voting irregularities.

From the coast, Tanzania stretches across a plateau averaging about 1,000 m (3,000 ft) to the Rift Valley lakes of Malawi (Lake Nyasa) and Tanganyika. The eastern Rift Valley, with the alkaline Lake Natron, and Lakes Eyasi and Manyara, divides the Northern Highlands. These are dominated by Mt Kilimanjaro near the Kenyan border. The Southern Highlands overlook Lake Malawi (Lake Nyasa). Semiarid conditions in the north and tsetse flies in the west-central areas mean that people mainly live on the country's margins. Attempts to farm the savanna woodland have failed.

Over eighty percent of the workforce lives off the land, producing cash crops such as coffee, tea, sisal, cotton, and pyrethrum, along with food crops of maize, wheat, cassava, and bananas. Since 1985 there has been some liberalization of the market, along with an effort to boost tourism and a substantial increase in gold production. Recent banking reforms, especially, have helped encourage the growth of the private sector as well as foreign investment. Continued donor assistance and solid macroeconomic policies supported a real GDP growth of nearly seven percent in 2007.

*A crater lake in Volcanoes National Park, Rwanda (above). Mt Kilimanjaro, the highest mountain in Africa, is in Tanzania (below).*

## Rwanda

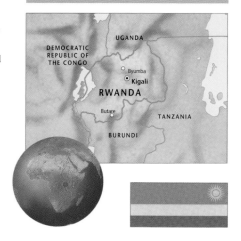

## Fact File

**OFFICIAL NAME** Republic of Rwanda

**FORM OF GOVERNMENT** Republic with two legislative bodies (Senate and Chamber of Deputies)

**CAPITAL** Kigali

**AREA** 26,340 sq km (10,170 sq miles)

**TIME ZONE** GMT + 2 hours

**POPULATION** 10,186,000

**PROJECTED POPULATION 2015** 12,147,000

**POPULATION DENSITY** 386.7 per sq km (1,001.6 per sq mile)

**LIFE EXPECTANCY** 49.8

**INFANT MORTALITY (PER 1,000)** 83.4

**OFFICIAL LANGUAGES** Kinyarwanda, French, English

**OTHER LANGUAGE** Swahili

**LITERACY RATE** 70.4 %

**RELIGIONS** Catholic 56.5 %, Protestant 37.1 %, Muslim 4.6 %, indigenous beliefs 0.1 %, other 1.7 %

**ETHNIC GROUPS** Hutu 84 %, Tutsi 15 %, Twa (Pygmy) 1 %

**CURRENCY** Rwandan franc

**ECONOMY** Agriculture 41.4 %, services 36.9 %, industry 21.7 %

**GNI PER CAPITA** US$ 320

**CLIMATE** Tropical, with two wet seasons (October to December and March to May)

**HIGHEST POINT** Karisimbi 4,519 m (14,826 ft)

**MAP REFERENCE** Page 369

A small landlocked country in central Africa, Rwanda shares much of its social history with Burundi, across its southern border. In the fifteenth and sixteenth centuries a tall cattle-herding people called Tutsi, probably from Sudan, came to the region and formed a small feudal aristocracy that dominated the more numerous Hutu farmers who had settled in the area some time before them. Since then, the Hutu people have endured the situation with

The endangered mountain gorilla still survives in the highlands of Rwanda (above). At the cloth market in Bujumbura, the capital of Burundi (below).

resentment. In recent times, beginning with a Hutu revolt in 1959 (independence from Belgium came in 1962), there have been decades of ethnic strife and intermittent violence, with hundreds of thousands of deaths occurring on both sides. This culminated in the massacre of approximately 800,000 Tutsi (and also some moderate Hutu) by Hutu in 1994, waves of refugees spilling out into the Democratic Republic of Congo, Burundi, Tanzania, and Uganda. It took substantial international assistance and political reforms—including the first local elections in 1999 and the first post-genocide presidential and legislative elections in 2003—for the country to boost investment and agricultural output and to foster reconciliation. Massive population displacements, a Hutu extremist insurgency, and involvement in two wars in the neighboring Democratic Republic of the Congo continue to hinder Rwanda's efforts.

Rwanda is the most densely populated country in Africa. Almost thirty percent of the land is arable, steep slopes are intensively cultivated, and terracing and contour plowing are used in order to keep erosion to a minimum. Lake Kivu and a part of the southward-flowing Ruzizi River form the western boundary of the country. From here the land rises steeply to the mountains, part of the Rift Valley, which constitute the Nile-Congo divide. To the north are the mountains, and several volcanoes, of the Mufumbiro Range. These include one of the last refuges of the mountain gorilla. From the heights of the eastern rim of the Rift Valley a plateau slopes eastward toward the Tanzanian border, the River Kagera marshes, and a number of lakes.

Rwanda's production of coffee and tea provides its main export income. Pyrethrum and sugarcane are other cash crops; cassava, maize, bananas, sorghum, and vegetables being crops grown for food. In keeping with their history as former nomadic herders, the Tutsi people keep cattle. The Hutu generally keep sheep and goats. Arable land is overused and deforestation and soil erosion are widespread. Natural resources include gold, tin, tungsten, and natural gas, but they are undeveloped because of infrastructure and transport difficulties. Even though political and ethnic disorder have affected the economy, it has largely reached pre-1994 levels again, though poverty, especially of women, is more virulent than before. Energy shortages, instability in neighboring states, and lack of adequate transportation to other countries continue to handicap growth.

# Burundi

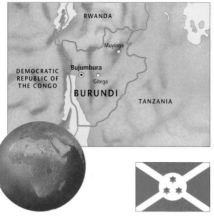

## Fact File

OFFICIAL NAME  Republic of Burundi

FORM OF GOVERNMENT  Republic with single legislative body (National Assembly)

CAPITAL  Bujumbura

AREA  27,830 sq km (10,745 sq miles)

TIME ZONE  GMT + 2 hours

POPULATION  8,691,000

PROJECTED POPULATION 2015  11,223,000

POPULATION DENSITY  312.3 per sq km (808.8 per sq mile)

LIFE EXPECTANCY  51.7

INFANT MORTALITY (PER 1,000)  60.8

OFFICIAL LANGUAGES  Kirundi, French

OTHER LANGUAGES  Swahili

LITERACY RATE  59.3 %

RELIGIONS  Roman Catholic 62 %, indigenous beliefs 23 %, Muslim 10 %, Protestant 5 %

ETHNIC GROUPS  Hutu 85 %, Tutsi 14 %, Twa (Pygmy) 1%

CURRENCY  Burundi franc

ECONOMY  Services 45.4 %, agriculture 33.7 %, industry 20.9 %

GNI PER CAPITA  US$ 110

CLIMATE  Tropical, with wet seasons March to May and September to December

HIGHEST POINT  Mt Heha 2,760 m (9,055 ft)

MAP REFERENCE  Page 369

Burundi is a small, landlocked country in central Africa. Some time in the past a tall cattle-herding people known as the Tutsi (or Watussi) moved into Burundi from the north. Originating on the Upper Nile, the Tutsi established themselves as a ruling class over the much more numerous and physically shorter Bantu farmers called Hutu. This deeply divided social order has been the source of periodic outbreaks of violence, hundreds of thousands of people having been massacred by both sides. The region's original inhabitants were the forest-dwelling Twa (or Pygmy), but few remain. Thanks to an internationally brokered transition process, a new constitution was established and a majority Hutu government elected in 2005. In 2006, a ceasefire was signed with the country's last rebel group, but the government still faces many challenges.

Burundi's topography resembles other lands along the Rift Valley. A narrow strip along the northeastern shore of Lake Tanganyika forms one boundary, which then extends up the valley of the River Ruzizi in the direction of Lake Kivu. From this lowland area an escarpment rises steeply up to the highlands which make up the rest of the country. The mountainous ridge east of Lake Tanganyika forms a watershed between the river systems of the Congo and the Nile. On its eastern slopes the land then falls away into the valley of the Ruvuvu River as it makes its way toward Tanzania and Lake Victoria. Malaria in the lowlands is endemic, a situation the continuing civil disorder makes difficult to change.

About ninety percent of Burundi's people depend on subsistence agriculture, growing corn, sorghum, sweet potatoes, bananas, and manioc. The Tutsi herders produce meat and milk. Export earnings come mainly from coffee and tea, which contribute ninety percent of the GDP. Three factors affect foreign exchange earnings and government revenue: the vagaries of the climate, international coffee and tea prices, and civil unrest. The struggle between Tutsi and Hutu, which has been a continuing feature of Burundi life since 1993, as well as approximately 670,000 refugees from the neighboring Rwanda and Democratic Republic of the Congo have virtually brought cash cropping to a halt. The government has tried to diversify exports, but continuing discord makes it difficult to implement reforms.

Africa

## Southern Africa

Zambia · · · · · · · · · ·  344

Malawi · · · · · · · ·  344

Mozambique · · · · · · ·  345

Zimbabwe · · · · · · · ·  346

Botswana · · · · · · · ·  347

Swaziland · · · · · · · ·  348

Lesotho · · · · · · · ·  349

Namibia · · · · · · · ·  349

South Africa · · · · · ·  350

Comoros · · · · · · · ·  351

Seychelles · · · · · · · ·  352

Madagascar · · · · · · ·  353

Mauritius · · · · · · · ·  353

Dependencies · · · · · ·  354

## Zambia

### Fact File

**OFFICIAL NAME** Republic of Zambia

**FORM OF GOVERNMENT** Republic with single legislative body (National Assembly)

**CAPITAL** Lusaka

**AREA** 752,614 sq km (290,585 sq miles)

**TIME ZONE** GMT + 2 hours

**POPULATION** 11,670,000

**PROJECTED POPULATION 2015** 13,842,000

**POPULATION DENSITY** 15.5 per sq km (40.2 per sq mile)

**LIFE EXPECTANCY** 38.6

**INFANT MORTALITY (PER 1,000)** 101

**OFFICIAL LANGUAGE** English

**OTHER LANGUAGES** Bantu languages (including Bemba, Tonga, Lozi, Lunda, Nyanja, Kaonda)

**LITERACY RATE** 80.6 %

**RELIGIONS** Christian 50–75 %, other (including Muslim, Hindu and indigenous beliefs) 25–50 %

**ETHNIC GROUPS** Indigenous 98.7 %, European 1.1 %, other 0.2 %

**CURRENCY** Kwacha

**ECONOMY** Services 56.5 %, industry 26.2 %, agriculture 17.3 %

**GNI PER CAPITA** US$ 800

**CLIMATE** Tropical, with three seasons: cool and dry May to August, hot and dry August to November, wet December to April

**HIGHEST POINT** Mafinga Hills 2,301 m (7,549 ft)

**MAP REFERENCE** Pages 368–69, 370–71

Zambia is a landlocked country in south-central Africa. It stretches from Victoria Falls in the south to Lake Tanganyika in the north, and is one of the world's major copper producers. Ancestral branches of the Zambian Tonga first entered the area in the eighth century AD, but other African groups now living there are more recent arrivals—the Ngoni and Kololo came as fugitives from Zulu aggression in 1835. Formerly a British colony, and once known as Northern Rhodesia, Zambia became independent in 1964. From that year it was ruled for more than a quarter of a century by President Kaunda, who nationalized commerce and industry and built a one-party socialist state. In 1991, economic decline and political agitation led to Zambia's first free elections. Kaunda was defeated, but even though international observers criticized irregularities in the elections of 1996 and 2002, democracy seems to be prevailing. The elections of 2006, which confirmed the president in power, were considered fair and democratic. Since 2002 a large-scale anti-corruption campaign has been in place.

A wide expanse of high plateau broken by scattered mountains and valleys, Zambia is drained by the Zambeze in the west and south, where the river forms a boundary with Zimbabwe and Namibia. Below Victoria Falls the Zambeze is dammed at the Kariba Gorge to form one of the largest artificial lakes in the world, Lake Kariba. Power from the Lake Kariba hydroelectric station is shared with Zimbabwe. Another major river, the Luangwa, runs southwest from the Malawi border down a broad rift valley to join the Zambeze at the frontier of Mozambique.

Compared with its neighbors, Zambia has a high ratio of urban dwellers who are dependent on the rural sector for food. Commercial farming of maize in the central districts, and other food crops such as sorghum and rice, is proving insufficient to meet their needs. This situation has been aggravated both by drought and the phasing out of agricultural subsidies.

Zambia is dependent on copper production, which accounts for a vast share of its export earnings. While production was down for a long time, the recent large-scale privatization of the industry in conjunction with high copper prices on the world market have led to healthy growth between 2004 and 2006. The same is true for the maize harvests and exports of the last years. However, Zambia still needs to continue its programs to fight its high inflation. In order to make significant steps to relieve widespread poverty, a consistent growth of the GDP between six and seven percent annually is necessary.

## Malawi

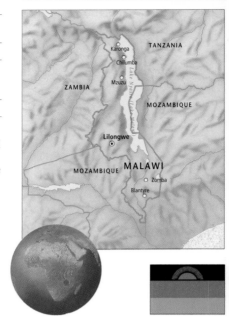

### Fact File

**OFFICIAL NAME** Republic of Malawi

**FORM OF GOVERNMENT** Republic with single legislative body (National Assembly)

**CAPITAL** Lilongwe

**AREA** 118,480 sq km (45,745 sq miles)

**TIME ZONE** GMT + 2 hours

**POPULATION** 13,932,000

**PROJECTED POPULATION 2015** 17,020,000

**POPULATION DENSITY** 117.6 per sq km (304.6 per sq mile)

**LIFE EXPECTANCY** 43.5

**INFANT MORTALITY (PER 1,000)** 90.6

**OFFICIAL LANGUAGES** Chichewa, English

**OTHER LANGUAGES** Indigenous languages

**LITERACY RATE** 62.7 %

**RELIGIONS** Christian 79.9 %, Muslim 12.8 %, other 3 %, none 4.3 %

**ETHNIC GROUPS** Indigenous tribes: Malavi (including Chichewa, Nyanja, Tumbuke, Tonga) 58 %, Lomwe 18 %, Yao 13 %; Ngoni 7 %; Asian and European 4 %

**CURRENCY** Kwacha

**ECONOMY** Services 44.1 %, agriculture 37.8 %, industry 18.1 %

**GNI PER CAPITA** US$ 250

**CLIMATE** Tropical, with wet season November to April

**HIGHEST POINT** Mt Mulanje 3,002 m (9,849 ft)

**MAP REFERENCE** Page 369

Malawi is a hilly and in places mountainous country at the southern end of Africa's Rift Valley, one-fifth of it consisting of Lake Malawi (Lake Nyasa). The lake contains 500 fish species which support a sizeable fishing industry. Most of the country's people are descended from the Bantu who settled the area centuries ago. Arab

slave-trading was suppressed by the incoming British in 1887–89, and in 1907 the country became the British Protectorate of Nyasaland. Independence in 1964 put Dr Hastings Banda in charge and he ruled dictatorially for thirty years. Cumulative difficulties, including drought and crop failures, some 800,000 refugees from Mozambique, and resentment at the apparent assassination of political opponents, led to Banda's removal and Malawi's first multi-party elections in 1994. The country has maintained a relatively stable democratic system since.

At the southern end of Lake Malawi (Lake Nyasa) the Shire River runs through a deep, swampy valley flanked by mountains to the east. Most of the population lives in this southern region, growing maize as the main food crop and cultivating cash crops such as peanuts and sugar-cane. The western central plateau rises northward to the Nyika Uplands, where rainfall is highest. In the Shire Highlands to the south, tea and tobacco are grown on large estates. Savanna grassland in the valleys gives way to open woodland, much of which has been cleared for cultivation. Wildlife is largely confined to reserves.

Agriculture provides a large percentage of exports. Reserves of bauxite and uranium exist, but not in commercially usable quantities. Hydro-electricity supplies only about three percent of total energy use—most needs are met from fuelwood, which is resulting in continued deforestation. The economy depends heavily on foreign aid.

## Mozambique

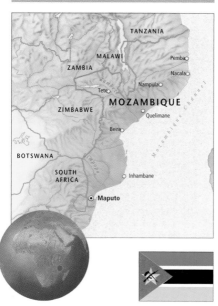

### Fact File

**OFFICIAL NAME** Republic of Mozambique

**FORM OF GOVERNMENT** Republic with single legislative body (Assembly of the Republic)

| | |
|---|---|
| **CAPITAL** | Maputo |
| **AREA** | 801,590 sq km (309,494 sq miles) |
| **TIME ZONE** | GMT + 2 hours |
| **POPULATION** | 21,285,000 |
| **PROJECTED POPULATION 2015** | 24,698,000 |
| **POPULATION DENSITY** | 26.6 per sq km (68.8 per sq mile) |
| **LIFE EXPECTANCY** | 41 |
| **INFANT MORTALITY (PER 1,000)** | 107.8 |
| **OFFICIAL LANGUAGE** | Portuguese |
| **OTHER LANGUAGES** | Swahili, Makua, Nyanja, and other Bantu languages |
| **LITERACY RATE** | 47.8 % |
| **RELIGIONS** | Catholic 23.8 %, Muslim 17.8 %, Zionist Christian 17.5 %, other 17.8 %, none 23.1 % |
| **ETHNIC GROUPS** | Indigenous tribes (including Shangaan, Chokwe, Manyika, Sena, Makua) 99.7 %, other 0.3 % |
| **CURRENCY** | Metical |
| **ECONOMY** | Services 46.8 %, industry 30.1 %, agriculture 23.1 % |
| **GNI PER CAPITA** | US$ 310 |
| **CLIMATE** | Mainly tropical: wet season December to March |
| **HIGHEST POINT** | Monte Binga 2,436 m (7,992 ft) |
| **MAP REFERENCE** | Pages 369, 371 |

Lying on the southeast coast of Africa facing Madagascar, Mozambique is divided in two by the Zambeze River. This division is also found in its social and political life: people in the north support the Renamo party, while south of the river they support Frelimo. Visited by Vasco da Gama in 1498 and colonized by the Portuguese in search of gold, Mozambique remained a slave-trading center until the 1850s.

A long war of liberation against Portugal led to independence in 1975 and brought the Marxist Frelimo (Mozambique liberation front) to power. Frelimo's one-party regime was then challenged by a guerilla movement, Renamo, supported by South Africa. The ensuing civil war, aggravated by famine, led to nearly 1 million deaths. By 1989 Mozambique was world's poorest country. That year Frelimo renounced Marxism. At multi-party elections in 1994 it won by a narrow majority. The country has since established a stable democracy and increasingly sound economic policy.

A considerable amount of rain falls in the north; south of the Zambeze conditions are much drier. North of Maputo, the only natural harbor, is a wide coastal plain where there are coconut, sugar, and sisal plantations. Small landholders grow maize and peanuts. Inland, the terrain rises to the high veld.

Economically, Mozambique has dramatically improved since its democratization in the 1990s. Nevertheless, the majority of the population still lives in poverty and subsistence farming employs more than eighty percent of the workforce. There are substantial agricultural, hydropower, and petroleum resources as well as deposits of coal, copper and bauxite, but these have not yet been fully developed.

*Lake Malawi (Lake Nyasa), near Chilumba, looking toward Mozambique (above). The massive Victoria Falls on the Zambeze River in Zimbabwe (below).*

Africa

# Zimbabwe

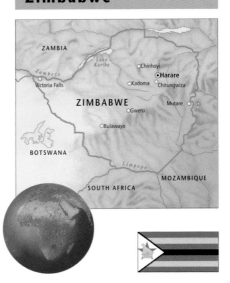

## Fact File

**OFFICIAL NAME** Republic of Zimbabwe

**FORM OF GOVERNMENT** Republic with single legislative body (Parliament)

**CAPITAL** Harare

**AREA** 390,580 sq km (150,803 sq miles)

**TIME ZONE** GMT + 2 hours

**POPULATION** 12,383,000

**PROJECTED POPULATION 2015** 14,508,000

**POPULATION DENSITY** 31.7 per sq km (82.1 per sq mile)

**LIFE EXPECTANCY** 39.7

**INFANT MORTALITY (PER 1,000)** 50.6

**OFFICIAL LANGUAGE** English

**OTHER LANGUAGES** Fanagalo (Creole), Bantu languages (including Shona, Ndebele)

**LITERACY RATE** 90.7 %

**RELIGIONS** Syncretic beliefs 50 %, Christian 25 %, indigenous beliefs 24 %, Muslim and other 1 %

**ETHNIC GROUPS** Indigenous 98 % (Shona 71 %, Ndebele 16 %, other 11 %), European 1 %, other 1 %

**CURRENCY** Zimbabwean dollar

**ECONOMY** Services 59.3 %, industry 22.6 %, agriculture 18.1 %

**GNI PER CAPITA** US$ 340

**CLIMATE** Tropical, moderated by altitude; wet season November to March

**HIGHEST POINT** Inyangani 2,592 m (8,504 ft)

**MAP REFERENCE** Page 371

Zimbabwe is a landlocked country south of Zambia. Zimbabwe means "house of the chief" in the Shona language and refers to what are known as the Great Ruins, built by Bantu peoples in the country's south and thought to date from the ninth century AD. The country's two main tribes today, the minority Ndebele (popularly known as Matabele) and the majority Shona, arrived as nineteenth-century fugitives from the warlike expansion of the Zulus under King Shaka.

British settlement began in the 1890s, and there were 280,000 whites in the country in 1965 when their leader, Ian Smith, declared independence from the UK. African guerrilla action to overthrow Smith led to black majority rule in 1980. Since then the government has been led by Robert Mugabe, a Shona. Though he renounced Marxism-Leninism in 1991, and market reforms are on the agenda, during the 1990s Zimbabwe has edged closer to being a de facto one-party state. After the introduction of more democratic measures Mugabe returned to a more and more dictatorial style of government. In order to strengthen his position in 2000 he forced white farmers from their land and redistributed it to his followers. The elections for parliament in 2001 as well as the presidential elections of 2002 were rigged, ignoring international protest. Opposition and labor groups launched general strikes in 2003 to pressure Mugabe to retire but security forces continued their brutal repression of opponents.

Some 25 percent of the country consists of a broad mountainous ridge known as the High Veld, which crosses the country southwest to northeast. On the northeastern Mozambique border it climbs to the peak of Inyangani. The rolling plateaus of the middle veld fall gently away north and south of this central upland, reaching the riverine low veld regions near the Limpopo River in the south and the Zambeze in the north. On the northern border the Zambeze plunges over Victoria Falls into a number of gorges. The falls, with Lake Kariba further downriver, along with several national parks, are among Zimbabwe's principal tourist attractions. Almost forty percent of electricity needs are met by hydroelectric power, much of it from the Kariba Dam facility shared with Zambia.

Zimbabwe's former near self-sufficiency in food was reversed with the country's involvement in the 1998–2002 war in Congo. Many of its farms are still small-scale subsistence operations, growing maize, cassava, and wheat. Large-scale enterprises produce most of the cash crops, such as tobacco, cotton, and sugarcane. Zimbabwe's mineral resources include coal, chromium, asbestos, gold, nickel, copper, iron, vanadium, lithium, tin, and platinum. Mining employs only five percent of the workforce, but minerals and metals account for about forty percent of exports. The country's biggest problems in recent years, however, have been the suspension of international aid due to the government's arrears on past loans, and hyperinflation since 2004.

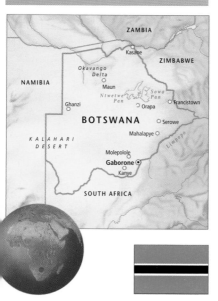

The Round House, one of the Great Ruins in Zimbabwe built by Bantu peoples (left). Zimbabwean dancers in masks and traditional dress (left page bottom left). Lions and vultures around a kill in Chobe National Park in northern Botswana (left page bottom right).

ETHNIC GROUPS Tswana 79 %, Kalanga 11 %, Basarwa 3 %, other 7 %

CURRENCY Pula

ECONOMY Services 51.5 %, industry 46.9 %, agriculture 1.6 %

GNI PER CAPITA US$ 5,840

CLIMATE Semiarid to arid, with warm winters and hot summers

HIGHEST POINT Tsodilo Hill 1,489 m (4,885 ft)

MAP REFERENCE Pages 370–71

A large, dry, landlocked tableland, Botswana is bordered on the south by South Africa, a country with which it has strong historical and economic links. To the west is Namibia (the border touches on Zambia in the north near

Victoria Falls) and to the northeast lies a 600 km (370 mile) frontier with Zimbabwe. Originally peopled by the nomadic San (Bushmen), Botswana's more fertile eastern parts later became settled by Bantu Tswana. In the nineteenth century, after gold had been discovered near the Tati River, the area became the focus of a colonial dispute between the British and the Boers of neighboring Transvaal (now Gauteng) in South Africa. Britain established the Bechuanaland Protectorate in 1885. This name and status within the British Empire was retained until independence in 1966, when Bechuanaland became Botswana.

Geographically a part of the Southern African Plateau, more than half of Botswana consists of the Kalahari Desert. Substantial parts of the remainder of the country consist of saltpans and swamps. There is little surface water except in the north and east, in the basins of the Okavango, Chobe, and Limpopo Rivers. Variations in climate and a limited rainfall enable a certain amount of scrub and thornbush to grow in the Kalahari. The dominant vegetation in Botswana is savanna grassland, which provides sufficient

# Botswana

## Fact File

OFFICIAL NAME Republic of Botswana

FORM OF GOVERNMENT Republic with two legislative bodies (House of Chiefs and National Assembly)

CAPITAL Gaborone

AREA 600,370 sq km (231,803 sq miles)

TIME ZONE GMT + 2 hours

POPULATION 1,842,000

PROJECTED POPULATION 2015 2,062,000

POPULATION DENSITY 3.1 per sq km (7.9 per sq mile)

LIFE EXPECTANCY 50.2

INFANT MORTALITY (PER 1,000) 44

OFFICIAL LANGUAGE English

OTHER LANGUAGES Setswana and other Bantu languages

LITERACY RATE 81.2 %

RELIGIONS Christian 71.6 %, Badimo 6 %, other 1.4 %, unspecified 0.4 %, none 20.6 %

## African wildlife

Nowhere on earth is there anything to equal the variety of African wildlife, much of which can still be seen in a natural setting. There are ninety species of hoofed mammal alone, including a tremendous variety of antelope, from the giant eland to the swift impala. Africa is home to the world's fastest animal, the cheetah, and also the world's largest land animal, the African elephant. In the giraffe it has the tallest animal in the world, while Africa's chimpanzees and gorillas represent families of primates closer to Homo sapiens than any others.

The future welfare of African wildlife is a matter of major international concern. Today, many animals only survive in the many national parks throughout the continent, the oldest and best-known being Kruger National Park in South Africa. Kenya's parks include the 20,000 sq km (8,000 sq mile) expanse of Tsavo, one of the biggest. Tanzania's Serengeti National Park has unrivaled herds of antelope, and the migratory movements of wildebeest amid lions, leopards and other predators—not to mention crocodiles in the rivers—provide a glimpse of life on the grasslands of east Africa as it has been for thousands of years.

Only one large African mammal is known to have become extinct in historical times: this is an antelope called the blaubok. However, there were so few white rhinoceros at the end of the nineteenth century that they were thought to be extinct. Then a few were discovered in the South African province of Natal, and as a result of careful protection in South African national parks their numbers had grown to 6,375 by 1994. Outside South Africa very few white rhinoceros have survived: there may be no more than eighty in Kenya. A number of other animals are endangered, including the critically endangered mountain gorillas found only in small regions in the Democratic Republic of the Congo, Uganda, and Rwanda.

In the early twentieth century professional hunters from Europe and America depleted great numbers of animals such as lion, rhinoceros, and buffalo. Today, the main threat comes from Africans themselves. Pastoral people kill wildlife because antelope compete for grassland with their cattle. Many mountain gorillas died during the civil wars in Rwanda in the 1990s. Most killing in Kenya and Tanzania is done by poachers seeking decorative skins, ivory, and rhino horn. Although the killings are illegal, there is a great demand for these items on the international market and they fetch very high prices, especially when one considers the poverty that reigns in these countries. A 2 kg (4 lb) rhino horn sells for up to US$ 122,000 in Asia, where in powdered form it is valued as an aphrodisiac. It is estimated that in the last two decades 40,000 rhinos have been killed for their horns.

The management of wild animal populations is not easy. After policies designed to ensure the survival of elephants were followed in Tsavo National Park, herds grew until there are now too many elephants for the land to support. This is damaging the habitat of other native species.

Africa

Swaziland is a tiny landlocked kingdom almost surrounded by South Africa. Across its eastern border it is about 130 km (80 miles) from the Indian Ocean and the Mozambique port of Maputo. Enjoying relative stability and prosperity, popular among South African tourists for its wildlife reserves, mountain scenery, and casinos, the kingdom's hereditary Bantu monarchy—one of the oldest on the African continent—is now being pressed to modernize and accept constitutional reforms. In 1977 King Sobhuza II dissolved the parliament and assumed absolute power. His son, King Mswati III since 1986, showed little interest in accepting the reforms demanded by widespread student protests during the 1990s. In 1998 he allowed general elections for 55 representatives who, together with ten members appointed by the king, form the parliament. However, he continues to rule autocratically and only grudgingly admits any democratic reforms.

The country owes its autonomy to events in the mid-nineteenth century. The Swazi were then facing Zulu expansion, as well as pressure from Boer farmers. They sought and received British protection, and from 1906 Swaziland became a British protectorate and was administered by the high commissioner for Basutoland (now Lesotho), Bechuanaland (now Botswana), and Swaziland. Full independence came in 1968.

The landscape descends in three steps from west to east. The high veld in the west is mountainous with a temperate climate, and supports grasslands and plantations of pine and eucalyptus. Mixed farming takes place in the middle veld, the most populous area, where Swazi subsistence farmers grow maize, sorghum, and peanuts. Cash crops such as sugarcane, citrus fruits, and tobacco are produced by often white-run agribusinesses and by Swazi on resettlement schemes. Livestock are raised on the low veld. Overgrazing, soil depletion, drought, and sometimes floods are persistent threats.

Swaziland's economy is relatively diversified and buoyant: during the 1980s it grew at a rate of 4.5 percent a year. Relaxed investment rules have ensured a supply of development capital, and project aid has been forthcoming from a number of donors. Sugar and forestry products are the main earners of hard currency, and are produced by white residents on large plantations. The country has small deposits of gold and diamonds. Mining was once important, but is now in decline. The high-grade iron ore deposits were depleted by 1978 and health concerns have cut the demand for asbestos. Remittances from workers living in South Africa provide up to twenty percent of household income. Though the government encourages foreign investment, the country faces severe economic problems, not least because nearly two-fifths of the adult population has been infected by HIV/AIDS, making Swaziland the country with the highest rate of AIDS infection.

grazing for about 100,000 widely scattered Bantu cattle herders to make a living.

At the time of independence, cattle were almost the country's only export, and Botswana was one of the poorest countries in the world. Since that time the economy has been transformed by the development of mining. Both copper and nickel are exported but the main earner has been diamonds, providing a large share of export revenue. Tourism is also important as the seventeen percent of Botswana's land area that is given over to national parks and game reserves attracts numerous visitors. A large proportion of the population still live as subsistence farmers raising cattle and growing crops such as maize, sorghum, vegetables, and fruit. Difficulties include overgrazing and desertification. Botswana also has the world's second-highest rate of AIDS/HIV infection. Its battle against the disease with the most progressive programs is slowly showing results. The government also managed to reduce the unemployment rate of over forty percent in 2006 to 7.5 percent in 2008.

## Swaziland

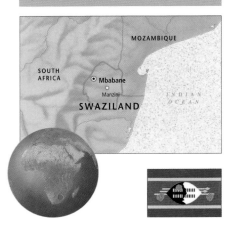

### Fact File

| | |
|---|---|
| OFFICIAL NAME | Kingdom of Swaziland |
| FORM OF GOVERNMENT | Monarchy with two legislative bodies (Senate and House of Assembly) |
| CAPITAL | Mbabane |
| AREA | 17,363 sq km (6,704 sq miles) |
| TIME ZONE | GMT + 2 hours |
| POPULATION | 1,129,000 |
| PROJECTED POPULATION 2015 | 1,189,000 |
| POPULATION DENSITY | 65 per sq km (168.4 per sq mile) |
| LIFE EXPECTANCY | 32 |
| INFANT MORTALITY (PER 1,000) | 69.6 |
| OFFICIAL LANGUAGES | English, Swati |
| OTHER LANGUAGES | Minority languages |
| LITERACY RATE | 81.6 % |
| RELIGIONS | Mixed Christian and indigenous 40 %, Roman Catholic 20 %, Muslim 10 %, other 30 % |
| ETHNIC GROUPS | Indigenous 97 %, European 3 % |
| CURRENCY | Lilangeni |
| ECONOMY | Industry 45.7 %, services 42.5 %, agriculture 11.8 % |
| GNI PER CAPITA | US$ 2,580 |
| CLIMATE | Temperate, with wet season November to March |
| HIGHEST POINT | Emlembe Peak 1,862 m (6,109 ft) |
| MAP REFERENCE | Page 371 |

# Lesotho

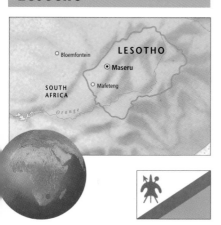

## Fact File

**OFFICIAL NAME** Kingdom of Lesotho

**FORM OF GOVERNMENT** Constitutional monarchy with two legislative houses (Senate and National Assembly)

**CAPITAL** Maseru

**AREA** 30,355 sq km (11,720 sq miles)

**TIME ZONE** GMT + 2 hours

**POPULATION** 2,128,000

**PROJECTED POPULATION 2015** 2,107,000

**POPULATION DENSITY** 70.1 per sq km (181.6 per sq mile)

**LIFE EXPECTANCY** 40.2

**INFANT MORTALITY (PER 1,000)** 78.6

**OFFICIAL LANGUAGES** Sesotho, English

**OTHER LANGUAGES** Zulu, Afrikaans, French, Xhosa

**LITERACY RATE** 84.8 %

**RELIGIONS** Christian 80 %, indigenous beliefs 20 %

**ETHNIC GROUPS** Sotho 99.7 %, European and Asian 0.3 %

**CURRENCY** Loti

**ECONOMY** Industry 45.1 %, services 39.7 %, agriculture 15.2 %

**GNI PER CAPITA** US$ 1,000

**CLIMATE** Temperate, with cool, dry winters and hot, wet summers

**HIGHEST POINT** Thabana-Ntlenyana 3,482 m (11,424 ft)

**MAP REFERENCE** Page 371

Lesotho is a small landlocked country entirely surrounded by South Africa. Formerly the British Protectorate of Basutoland, it is the only country in the world where all the land is higher than 1,000 m (3,300 ft). About two-thirds of the terrain is mountainous, and at higher altitudes it often snows throughout the winter. As the head of a fragile constitutional monarchy, the king of Lesotho has no executive or legislative powers: traditionally, he could be elected or deposed by a majority vote of the College of Chiefs. Proposals to unite Lesotho with post-apartheid South Africa have been resisted by members of the population who feel an independent state will better defend their cultural heritage. In 1998, violent protests and a military mutiny following a contentious election prompted a brief but bloody South African military intervention. Constitutional reforms have since restored political stability; peaceful parliamentary elections were held in 2002.

A high mountainous plateau declining from east to west, Lesotho's highest ridges were formed on basaltic lavas. Treeless, with steep valleys, the wet highlands are soft and boggy in summer and frozen in winter. Numerous river valleys and gorges dissect the plateau, among them the River Orange. To the northwest the border of the country is defined by the Caledon River. This is flanked by a 30 to 65 km (18 to 40 mile) strip of fertile land which supports most of Lesotho's farmers and provides the bulk of its agriculturally useful land. Subsistence crops include maize, sorghum, wheat, and beans. Sheep and goats are kept for wool and mohair on the high plateau.

Lesotho is without important natural resources other than water. Hopes are held for the future of a major hydroelectric facility, the Highlands Water Scheme, which will sell water to South Africa and become a major employer and revenue earner. The scheme will supply all of Lesotho's energy requirements. In scattered hamlets, cottage industry produces woven mohair rugs. Manufacturing based on farm products consists of milling, canning, and the preparation of leather and jute. Roughly 35 percent of Lesotho's male wage earners work across the border in South Africa, most of them as laborers in mines. The wages they send back provide around 45 percent of domestic income.

# Namibia

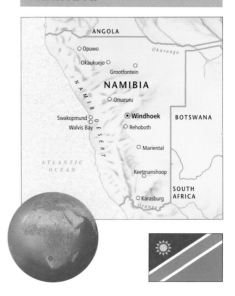

## Fact File

**OFFICIAL NAME** Republic of Namibia

**FORM OF GOVERNMENT** Republic with two legislative bodies (National Council and National Assembly)

**CAPITAL** Windhoek

**AREA** 825,418 sq km (318,694 sq miles)

**TIME ZONE** GMT + 2 hours

**POPULATION** 2,089,000

**PROJECTED POPULATION 2015** 2,288,000

**POPULATION DENSITY** 2.5 per sq km (6.6 per sq mile)

**LIFE EXPECTANCY** 49.9

**INFANT MORTALITY (PER 1,000)** 45.6

**OFFICIAL LANGUAGE** English

**OTHER LANGUAGES** Afrikaans, Bantu and other tribal languages (incl. Wamba, Nama, Herero and Bushman Khoekhoe), German

**LITERACY RATE** 85 %

**RELIGIONS** Christian 80–90 % (at least 50 % Lutheran and 30 % other Christian), indigenous beliefs 10–20 %

**ETHNIC GROUPS** Indigenous tribes 87.5 % (including Ovambo 50 %, Kavangos 9 %, Herero 7 %, Damara 7 %), mixed indigenous-European 7.5 %, European 6 %

**CURRENCY** Namibian dollar

**ECONOMY** Services 55.8 %, industry 33.4 %, agriculture 10.8 %

**GNI PER CAPITA** US$ 3,360

**CLIMATE** Mainly arid, with higher rainfall inland

**HIGHEST POINT** Konigstein 2,606 m (8,550 ft)

**MAP REFERENCE** Page 370

A large, arid country in southwest Africa, Namibia was born of the European scramble for colonies in the nineteenth century. The German connection with the area (formerly South West Africa) began with the arrival of missionaries in the 1840s. Namibia was a German protectorate

Africa

from 1884; the scene of a brutal German punitive action in 1904 in which the Herero were decimated—approximately 60,000 were killed—and scattered; under South African control for many years; and endured 23 years of a bitter anti-colonial war that began in 1966. In 1989 an election gave the guerrilla movement SWAPO (the South West African People's Organization) victory at the polls, and in 1990 came independence.

The virtually uninhabited sand dunes of the Namib Desert fringe the country's south Atlantic coastline. A major escarpment inland separates the desert from a north-south range of mountains that includes the Tsaris Mountains, Aûas Mountains, and Mt Erongo. The interior plateau, which occupies the eastern part of the country, has an average elevation of 1,500 m (5,000 ft) and is covered with the dry scrub grassland typical of the Kalahari Desert. Largely rainless, the coast is often shrouded in fog. Here, welwitschia plants, some of them up to 2,000 years old, live by absorbing moisture from the fog that rolls in from the sea. Namibia's wildlife is typical of southern Africa, with Etosha National Park providing sanctuary for baboon, antelope, elephant, giraffe, zebra, and lion.

Namibia's natural resources include diamonds, copper, uranium (world's fifth largest producer), gold, lead (world's second largest producer), tin, lithium, cadmium, zinc, vanadium, and natural gas, and there are thought to be deposits of oil, coal, and iron ore. Mining accounts for twenty percent of gross domestic product, this sector relying on the expertise of Namibia's small white population. 47 percent of the population work poor soils in an unfavorable climate. Livestock farmers produce beef and mutton, and fishermen try to make do with dwindling catches. About half the country's food is imported.

*High-rise buildings in Pretoria, the South African capital (below). An elephant browsing in Kruger National Park (right page).*

# South Africa

**ETHNIC GROUPS** Indigenous 79 %, European 8.9 %, Indian/Asian 2.5 %, other 9.6 %

**CURRENCY** Rand

**ECONOMY** Services 65.5 %, industry 31.3 %, agriculture 3.2 %

**GNI PER CAPITA** US$ 5,760

**CLIMATE** Mainly semiarid; subtropical on southeast coast

**HIGHEST POINT** Njesuthi 3,408 m (11,181 ft)

**MAP REFERENCE** Pages 370–71

## Fact File

**OFFICIAL NAME** Republic of South Africa

**FORM OF GOVERNMENT** Republic with two legislative bodies (Senate and National Assembly)

**CAPITAL** Pretoria (administrative); Cape Town (legislative); Bloemfontein (judicial)

**AREA** 1,219,912 sq km (471,008 sq miles)

**TIME ZONE** GMT + 2 hours

**POPULATION** 43,786,000

**PROJECTED POPULATION 2015** 50,260,000

**POPULATION DENSITY** 35.9 per sq km (93 per sq mile)

**LIFE EXPECTANCY** 42.4

**INFANT MORTALITY (PER 1,000)** 58.3

**OFFICIAL LANGUAGES** English, Afrikaans, Ndebele, Pedi, Sotho, Swazi, Tsonga, Tswana, Venda, Xhosa, Zulu

**OTHER LANGUAGES** Indigenous and Indian languages

**LITERACY RATE** 86.4 %

**RELIGIONS** Christian 80 %, Muslim 2 %, other or no religion 18 %

Occupying the southernmost tip of the African continent, South Africa comprises a central plateau or veld, bordered to the south and east by the Drakensberg Mountains and to the north by the countries of Namibia, Botswana, Zimbabwe and Mozambique. The Independent State of Lesotho is contained within South Africa's borders. European settlement in the seventeenth century culminated in white minority rule, and a controversial policy of racial segregation was officially implemented in 1948. After fifty years of deepening crisis and international isolation as a result of its racial policies, South Africa changed course in 1990, held democratic elections in 1994, and under a new government rejoined the international community. Always the economic powerhouse of southern Africa, it is now free from sanctions and able to renew normal trading relations. The abandonment of apartheid, and the freeing of long-term political prisoner (and then president)

## Timeline

| | | | | | | |
|---|---|---|---|---|---|---|
| **25,000 BP** Rock paintings on shelters show ceremonial dancers and animals, like antelope, which were hunted for food | **4–500 AD** Bantu people arrive from east Africa to find grazing for sheep and cattle and to plant crops. Displace Khoisan hunter-gatherers | **1100** Different language groups emerge, such as the Xhosa and the Zulu | **1615** British settlement at Table Bay lasts only a few years | **1657** First slaves brought to the Cape from India, Indonesia, and West Africa as agricultural labor and to act as herders | **1795–1802** British occupy Cape, a vital trade route supply post prior to opening of Suez Canal; more British settlers arrive |

| **3 MYA** Cave-dwelling Australopithecines in what is now Cape Province and Gauteng kill animals for meat and eat plants | **120,000 BP** "Modern" humans inhabit cave near Port Elizabeth; they eat shellfish, tortoises, and bird's eggs | **c. 2000 BC** Kalahari San (bushmen) inhabit the Kalahari Desert herding animals | **c. 1000** Urban centers established; bone and ivory crafts; products traded between groups | **1488** First Portuguese vessels arrive at the Cape of Good Hope | **1652** Dutch East India Co. garrison at site of Cape Town supplies Dutch fleet; settlers granted land at Liesbeek River in 1657 | **1713** Khoikhoi pastoralists displaced by "trekboer" settlers in search of grazing land; numerous San people die of smallpox |

Nelson Mandela, have had an uplifting effect on national morale and provided a chance for a fresh start. Problems currently facing the nation include discrepancies between the educational level and skills of blacks and whites; vastly different income levels; increasing unemployment; high urban crime rates; and the ongoing conflict between Zulu groups and the ruling party, the African National Congress.

## Physical features and land use

South Africa has three main geographic regions. First, there is the vast African Plateau of the interior. This slopes gradually north and west to form part of the semiarid and sparsely populated Kalahari basin, while to the east it rises to elevations of 2,000 m (6,500 ft). Second, the Great Escarpment, varying in height, structure, and steepness, forms a rim around the entire plateau from the mountains of the Transvaal Drakensberg in the northeast to Namibia in the northwest. Its highest peaks are in the Drakensberg along the Lesotho border. The third region consists of the narrow, fertile strips of land along the peripheral coastal plains.

Agricultural products include maize (a staple for many African farmers); apples, pears, stone fruit, grapes, and wine from Eastern Cape Province; wheat from Western Cape Province; and sugarcane from coastal KwaZulu-Natal. On the grasslands of the plateau large-scale pastoralism produces wool, mohair, skins, and meat. South Africa is geologically ancient—only a few superficial strata are less than 600 million years old. In the 1880s rocks of the Witwatersrand were found to contain gold and diamonds, and since then gold and diamond mining has been the basis of South Africa's national wealth.

Along the west coast, north of Cape Town, the cold Benguela current inhibits rainfall, producing the desert of the Namib. In the northeast there is dry savanna bushland. On the Mozambique border the best-known of South Africa's eight wildlife reserves, Kruger National Park, contains lions, leopards, giraffes, elephants, and hippopotamuses.

## People and culture

First inhabited by San, or Bushmen, in the fifteenth century Southern Africa was occupied by a wave of cattle-keeping, grain-growing Bantu peoples from the north—their modern descendants being groups such as the Xhosa and the Zulu. Then in 1652 and 1688 two groups of settlers arrived from Europe—the first Dutch, the second French Huguenot, both firmly Protestant in their faith—and established a colony in the south at Cape Town. They became known as Boers (farmers) and later as Afrikaners (after their language, Afrikaans). The British established themselves on the Cape in 1806. Over the years a

population of mixed Afro-European descent emerged who became known as "Cape Coloreds". In the nineteenth century laborers from India were brought in by the British, creating yet another large and distinct ethnic community. There are also a small number of Malays.

After 1948, under the ruling Afrikaners, apartheid (apartness) laws were drafted defining how each community should associate, where each should live, whether they could intermarry, and what work they could do. The entire population was to be organized in a hierarchy of privilege, with whites at the top and blacks at the bottom. Africans were to be confined to a series of internal Black States called "homelands", which were in practice mere labor pools, since the only way people could find employment was by leaving home and traveling to the South African mines. The impracticality, unreality, and injustice of the system aroused widespread international condemnation. The misery it created led to ongoing violent resistance.

## Economy and resources

Although both the Bantu and the first Europeans to colonize South Africa were farming people, and agriculture formed the foundation of the economy for hundreds of years, during the nineteenth century gold and diamonds were the attractions that drew a new wave of settlers. Today, gold and precious stones still make up half the country's total exports, and over the last 100 years almost half the world's gold has come from South African mines. Other important minerals include asbestos, nickel, vanadium, and uranium (which can sometimes be found in old gold mines). In addition, South Africa is the world's largest producer of manganese, platinum, and chromium.

Energy conservation is a vital concern to the country as no petroleum deposits have yet been found. During the long period of South Africa's isolation and of trade boycotts, the state corporation Sasol extracted oil from coal. Though this is a expensive process, extensive deposits of coal make this a feasible supplementary supply. Many white South Africans enjoy a standard of living equal to the highest in the world. The challenge for the government is to provide the conditions in which the fifty percent of people living below the poverty line can have a share of that wealth. Growth has not been strong enough to lower the high unemployment rate, and daunting economic problems remain from the apartheid era.

### PROVINCES

**Eastern Cape • Free State • Gauteng • KwaZulu-Natal • Mpumalanga • Northern Province • Northern Cape • North West • Western Cape**

## Comoros

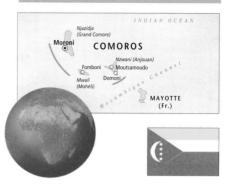

### Fact File

| | |
|---|---|
| OFFICIAL NAME | Federal Islamic Republic of the Comoros |
| FORM OF GOVERNMENT | Federal republic with single legislative body (National Assembly) |
| CAPITAL | Moroni |
| AREA | 2,170 sq km (838 sq miles) |
| TIME ZONE | GMT + 3 hours |
| POPULATION | 732,000 |
| PROJECTED POPULATION 2015 | 1,002,000 |
| POPULATION DENSITY | 337.3 per sq km (873.5 per sq mile) |
| LIFE EXPECTANCY | 63.1 |
| INFANT MORTALITY (PER 1,000) | 68.6 |
| OFFICIAL LANGUAGES | Arabic, French |
| OTHER LANGUAGE | Comoran (blend of Swahili and Arabic) |
| LITERACY RATE | 56.5 % |
| RELIGIONS | Sunni Muslim 98 %, Roman Catholic 2 % |
| ETHNIC GROUPS | Mixture of Malagasy, African, Malay and Arab groups |
| CURRENCY | Comoran franc |
| ECONOMY | Services 56 %, agriculture 40 %, industry 4 % |
| GNI PER CAPITA | US$ 680 |
| CLIMATE | Tropical, with wet season November to May |
| HIGHEST POINT | Kartala 2,360 m (7,743 ft) |
| MAP REFERENCE | Page 372 |

Africa

| | | | | | | | |
|---|---|---|---|---|---|---|---|
| **1800** Zulu nation founded in today's KwaZulu-Natal, forcing Khoshangane clan into Swaziland and Mzilikazi clan into Zimbabwe | **1836–38** 10,000 Boer settlers unhappy with British rule in Cape set out on Great Trek to seek new land in Natal and Orange River areas | **1870** Gold rush in the Kimberley area and discovery of diamonds transform the economic base from agriculture to mining | **1899** Gold-mining industry employs 110,000 workers; almost 100,000 are African laborers | **1912** The African National Congress (ANC) founded by group of black Africans interested in obtaining political rights | **1948** National Party passes law restricting parliamentary representation to whites; "apartheid" official in 1950 | **1962** Nelson Mandela and other leading members of the ANC are imprisoned | **1990** Mandela freed; apartheid abolished (1991); population 37 million (76 % black, 13 % white, 9 % mixed race, 2 % Asian) |
| | **1860** Laborers from India are imported by Natal farmers to work on farms and plantations | **1880–81** British fail to bring Boer republics (Orange Free State, Transvaal) into federation—British defeated in First Boer War | **1899–1902** British defeat the Boers (Afrikaners) in Second Boer War | **1931** South Africa granted independence by Britain as a member of the Commonwealth | **1961** South Africa leaves Commonwealth and becomes a republic, without asking non-whites | **1976** Black African protest over compulsory Afrikaans language lessons results in violence and the loss of 600 lives | **1994** Mandela elected president in first non-racial general election—pronounces the new South Africa a "Rainbow Republic" |

The Comoros are a group of islands in the Mozambique Channel, lying between northern Madagascar and the African coast. Some of the smaller ones are coral islets. The larger islands are volcanic, and three of the four largest constitute the Republic of the Comoros. (Another large island, Mayotte, chose to remain a French dependency but is claimed by the Comoros as indicated by the fourth star on the flag.)

For centuries, Indian and Arab traders have sailed across the Indian Ocean and worked their way along the coast of east Africa, visiting the Comoros as they went. The Comoran population reflects this history. There are large groups with African, Arab, Indonesian, and Madagascan backgrounds, and even a minority with Polynesian ancestors. France controlled the islands after declaring them a colony in 1912. They obtained their independence in 1975.

The island of Njazidja (formerly Grande Comore) consists mainly of a rocky lava plateau, rising at its southern end to the active volcano of Kartala. On the coast is the national capital, Moroni.

Because of the porous volcanic soils, rain quickly drains away, and despite heavy seasonal precipitation rainforests are only found on the mountain's upper slopes. On the island of Nzwani (formerly Anjouan) soils are more fertile, but clearing of land without proper terracing has led to serious erosion. The island of Mwali (formerly Mohéli) is the smallest of the group. It has dense forests and fertile valleys.

Comoros has few natural resources. Subsistence agriculture is the traditional way of life, the main food crops being cassava, mountain rice, and sweet potato. Nevertheless, the islands are not self-sufficient in food, and rice accounts for the vast majority of all imports. Cattle and goats are kept—the latter are another cause of erosion. There are a few small hydroelectric plants; otherwise, fuel must be imported. Revenue-earning exports are vanilla, cloves, perfume oil, and copra.

The government is trying to diversify exports, privatize industrial enterprises, and reduce the high population growth rate, but its authority has been weakened by chronic political instability and several attempted coups. Foreign aid is likely to be needed for some time.

## Seychelles

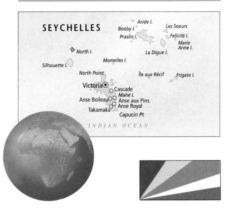

### Fact File

| | |
|---|---|
| **OFFICIAL NAME** | Republic of Seychelles |
| **FORM OF GOVERNMENT** | Republic with single legislative body (People's Assembly) |
| **CAPITAL** | Victoria |
| **AREA** | 455 sq km (176 sq miles) |
| **TIME ZONE** | GMT + 4 hours |
| **POPULATION** | 82,000 |
| **PROJECTED POPULATION 2015** | 89,000 |
| **POPULATION DENSITY** | 180.2 per sq km (465.9 per sq mile) |
| **LIFE EXPECTANCY** | 72.6 |
| **INFANT MORTALITY (PER 1,000)** | 14.4 |
| **OFFICIAL LANGUAGES** | English, French, Creole |
| **LITERACY RATE** | 91.8 % |
| **RELIGIONS** | Roman Catholic 82 %, Anglican 6 %, other Christian 5 %, Hindu 2 %, Muslim 1 %, other 4 % |
| **ETHNIC GROUPS** | Creole (mixture of Asian, African, European) 92 %, British 5 %, other 3 % |
| **CURRENCY** | Seychelles rupee |
| **ECONOMY** | Services 71.9 %, industry 25.7 %, agriculture 2.4 % |
| **GNI PER CAPITA** | US$ 8,960 |
| **CLIMATE** | Tropical, with wet season December to May |
| **HIGHEST POINT** | Morne Seychellois 905 m (2,969 ft) |
| **MAP REFERENCE** | Pages 372, 373 |

The Seychelles are a group of four large and 36 small granite islands, plus a scattering of about 65 coralline islands, in the Indian Ocean northeast of Madagascar. Some 98 percent of the population live on the four main islands, the great majority on tropical and mountainous Mahé. Uninhabited when occupied by the French in 1742, the Seychelles were ceded to the British at the time of the Napoleonic Wars, and became a crown colony in 1903. After independence in 1976 the islands were ruled for fifteen years as a one-party socialist state, and North Korean military advisors were hired to guard against attempted coups. The first open elections were held in 1993 and the previous government party has since stayed in office.

The granite islands consist of a mountainous central spine—sometimes consisting of bare, eroded rock—surrounded by a flat coastal strip with dense tropical vegetation. In the areas cleared for farming vanilla, tobacco, tea, cinnamon and coconuts (for copra) are grown for export, along with food crops such as cassava, sweet potatoes, and bananas. Most food, however, is imported. The outer coralline islands are flat, waterless, and sparsely inhabited, having a total population of only 400. Short droughts periodically occur; though catchments collect some rainwater, there are no natural sources of supply. The Seychelles lie outside the cyclone belt, which is important for an economy depending on tourism.

The island's only natural resources are fish, copra, and cinnamon trees, which in earlier times provided a bare subsistence. Since independence in 1976, however, with the vigorous promotion of the tourist industry, per capita output has increased sevenfold. In recent years foreign investment has been encouraged in order to upgrade hotels and other services. Visitors find many attractions—the unique wildlife includes a rare giant land turtle and the colorful green sea turtle found on the coral reefs. The country's vulnerability in relying so heavily on tourism was shown during the Gulf War, when visitor numbers dropped sharply. The government is moving to reduce over-dependence on this sector by promoting farming, fishing, and small-scale manufacturing, including furniture-making, coconut-fiber rope-making, printing, and the re-export of petroleum products.

# Madagascar

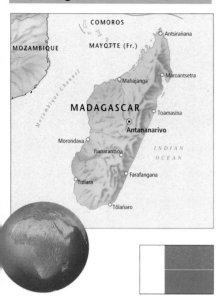

## Fact File

OFFICIAL NAME  Republic of Madagascar

FORM OF GOVERNMENT  Republic with two legislative bodies (Senate and National Assembly)

CAPITAL  Antananarivo

AREA  587,040 sq km (226,656 sq miles)

TIME ZONE  GMT + 3 hours

POPULATION  20,043,000

PROJECTED POPULATION 2015  24,107,000

POPULATION DENSITY  34.1 per sq km (88.4 per sq mile)

LIFE EXPECTANCY  62.5

INFANT MORTALITY (PER 1,000)  55.6

OFFICIAL LANGUAGES  Malagasy, French

LITERACY RATE  68.9 %

RELIGIONS  Indigenous beliefs 52 %, Christian 41 %, Muslim 7 %

ETHNIC GROUPS  Chiefly Malayo-Indonesian inland (including Merina, Betsileo, Betsimisaraka) and mixed African, Arab, Malayo-Indonesian on coasts (including Tsimihety, Sakalava) 99 %; other 1 %

CURRENCY  Malagasy franc

ECONOMY  Services 57.4 %, agriculture 26.8 %, industry 15.8 %

GNI PER CAPITA  US$ 320

CLIMATE  Tropical in coastal regions; temperate inland (wet season November to April); arid in south

HIGHEST POINT  Maromokotro 2,876 m (9,436 ft)

MAP REFERENCE  Page 372

Larger than France, Madagascar is the world's fourth largest island. Located off the southeast coast of Africa, it contrasts sharply with the African mainland in its wildlife, people, culture, language, and history. In the center and the east live the Merina or Hova people who migrated to the island from the islands now known as Indonesia about 2,000 years ago. By the nineteenth century the Merinas, with their capital in Tanarive, ruled much of the country. In 1896 the island became a French colony. It won independence from France in 1960, following a bloody insurrection. From 1975 it was run as a one-party socialist state associated with the Soviet Union. In 1992 riots and mass demonstrations caused by deepening poverty forced the introduction of a multi-party democracy with elections in 1997 and 2002. The latter were contested and challenged legally and decided in court.

To the east the land drops precipitously to the Indian Ocean through forests dissected by rushing streams. Inland lies the mountainous central plateau, accounting for sixty percent of the island's total area, and rising in several places above 2,500 m (8,200 ft). Various geological eras are represented in the island's rugged topography, which features steep faulting, volcanic outcrops, and deep-cut valleys. On the western slopes of the plateau the land falls away more gently to broad and fertile plains. In the central highlands both the landscape and agriculture have a south Asian character, as rice farming is combined with raising cattle and pigs. Land usage is more African in style on the east coast and in the northern highlands, with fallow-farming of food crops such as cassava and maize, and the cultivation of coffee, sugar, and spices for export.

Separated from the African mainland for over 50 million years, Madagascar developed its own distinctive wildlife: three-quarters of the flora and fauna are found nowhere else. The island is known for its 28 species of lemur—dainty, large-eyed primates—and for the tenrec, a small, spiny, insect-eating mammal. Many of the island's 1,000 or so orchid species are endemic, and it is home to half the world's chameleon species.

Among the poorest countries in the world, Madagascar is not self-sufficient in food. The main staples are rice and cassava, but production is failing to keep pace with an annual population growth rate of over three percent. Additional problems derive from past government initiatives. When collective farming was introduced in 1975 it resulted in falling production and widespread resentment. Since 1993 corruption and political instability have accompanied economic confusion and a decay in the infrastructure.

*Looking toward Silhouette Island in the Seychelles (left page top). Antananarivo, the capital of Madagascar (center). A street scene in Toliara, Madagascar (right).*

# Mauritius

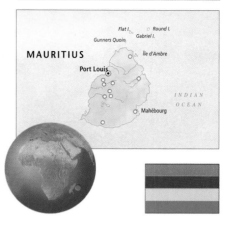

## Fact File

OFFICIAL NAME  Republic of Mauritius

FORM OF GOVERNMENT  Republic with single legislative body (Legislative Assembly)

CAPITAL  Port Louis

AREA  2,040 sq km (788 sq miles)

TIME ZONE  GMT + 4 hours

POPULATION  1,274,000

PROJECTED POPULATION 2015  1,335,000

POPULATION DENSITY  624.5 per sq km (1,616.8 per sq mile)

LIFE EXPECTANCY  73.8

INFANT MORTALITY (PER 1,000)  12.6

OFFICIAL LANGUAGES  English, French

OTHER LANGUAGES  Mauritian (French Creole), Bhojipuri, Tamil, Urdu, Hindi, Telugu, Chinese

LITERACY RATE  84.4 %

RELIGIONS  Hindu 48 %, Christian 32.2 %, (Roman Catholic 23.6 %, Protestant 8.6 %), Muslim 16.6 %, other 2.8 %, none 0.4 %

ETHNIC GROUPS  Indo-Mauritian 68 %, Creole 27 %, Sino-Mauritian 3 %, Franco-Mauritian 2 %

CURRENCY  Mauritian rupee

ECONOMY  Services 70.1 %, industry 25 %, agriculture 4.9 %

GNI PER CAPITA  US$ 5,450

CLIMATE  Tropical, moderated by trade winds

HIGHEST POINT  Piton de la Petite Rivière Noire 828 m (2,717 ft)

MAP REFERENCE  Pages 372, 373

353

Famous as the home of the now-extinct flightless bird, the dodo, the Republic of Mauritius consists of one large and several smaller islands 800 km (500 miles) east of Madagascar. Mauritius was uninhabited when visited by the Portuguese and the Dutch between the fifteenth and seventeenth centuries. It was first settled by the French, after 1715, who brought African slaves for the sugar plantations. In 1810 it was taken over by the British, who brought in numerous indentured laborers from India. These colonial origins produced two distinct communities, one Afro-French Creole (29 percent), the other English-speaking and Indian (68 percent), who compete for influence and power. Independence within the British Commonwealth was granted in 1968 and Mauritius became a republic in 1992. Despite occasional unrest, the country has a record of political stability and economic growth. It attracts considerable foreign investment and has earned one of Africa's highest per capita incomes.

Fringed with coral reefs, the main island rises from coastal plains on its north and east to a plateau surrounded by rugged peaks—the remains of a giant volcano. The climate is tropical, but moderated by rain-bearing winds from the southeast. Sugarcane is grown on ninety percent of the cultivated land, and accounts, with derivatives such as molasses, for 25 percent of export earnings. A by-product of the sugar industry, the cane-waste called bagasse, has been used to fuel power stations. Fast-flowing rivers descending from the plateau are used to produce hydroelectric power.

Industrial diversification (textile and garment manufacture now accounts for about forty percent of export revenue) and the development of a tourist industry (up to half a million visitors per year) have enabled Mauritius to transcend the low-income agricultural economy that existed at the time of independence. Since 1968 annual economic growth most years has been between five and six percent, life expectancy has been increasing and the infrastructure has improved.

*Women agricultural workers walking beside a field of sugarcane in Mauritius (below left). Small town with a view of the Atlantic Ocean, Madeira (below right). The Pico de Teide on the island of Tenerife (right page).*

# Dependencies in Africa

## Mayotte

### Fact File

OFFICIAL NAME Territorial Collectivity of Mayotte

FORM OF GOVERNMENT Territorial collectivity of France

CAPITAL Mamoudzou

AREA 374 sq km (144 sq miles)

TIME ZONE GMT + 3 hours

POPULATION 216,000

LIFE EXPECTANCY 62.5

INFANT MORTALITY (PER 1,000) 57.9

LITERACY RATE Not available

CURRENCY Euro

ECONOMY Mainly agriculture and fishing

CLIMATE Tropical, with wet season November to May

MAP REFERENCE Page 372

Mayotte is a small island at the northern end of the Mozambique Channel, 34 km (21 miles) long, between Madagascar and the mainland. It is the easternmost of the four large islands of the Comoros group (a group first visited by Europeans ships in the sixteenth century) and was the first to be ceded to France in 1841. When, in the 1974 referendum, the other islands chose to become the Republic of the Comoros, Mayotte decided to become a territorial collectivity of France.

Volcanic in origin, Mayotte rises to 660 m (2,165 ft) at its highest point. The people are of African, Arab, and Madagascan descent. Agricultural products include coconuts, cocoa, and spices.

## Réunion

### Fact File

OFFICIAL NAME Department of Réunion

FORM OF GOVERNMENT Overseas department of France

CAPITAL Saint-Denis

AREA 2,517 sq km (972 sq miles)

TIME ZONE GMT + 4 hours

POPULATION 793,000

LIFE EXPECTANCY 72.7

INFANT MORTALITY (PER 1,000) 8.7

LITERACY RATE 79 %

CURRENCY French franc

ECONOMY Services 73 %, industry 16 %, agriculture 8 %

CLIMATE Tropical; cool and dry May to November, hot and rainy November to April

MAP REFERENCE Page 373

Réunion is the largest of the Mascarene Islands which lie southwest of Mauritius and east of Madagascar. After the Portuguese had discovered the uninhabited island in 1513 the French settled them and brought in Africans, Chinese, Malays, and Malabar Indians. A fertile plain surrounds Réunion's rugged and mountainous interior. One of two volcanic peaks, Piton des Neiges rises to 3,069 m (10,069 ft) and is sporadically active. Plentiful rainfall comes with the winter trade winds.

On the intensively cultivated lowlands there are large sugarcane plantations which provide 75 percent of exports and are the island's only significant industry. Vanilla, perfume oils, and tea also produce revenue, while vegetables and maize are grown for local consumption. Tourism is growing, but unemployment is high. The population is divided over continued association with France, which uses Réunion as its main military base in the area.

The small, uninhabited islands of Bassas da India, Europa, Glorieuses, Île Juan de Nova, and Tromelin are associated dependencies.

Africa

# Western Sahara

# St Helena

## Fact File

**OFFICIAL NAME** Western Sahara

**FORM OF GOVERNMENT** Territory disputed by Morocco and Polisario Front independence movement

**CAPITAL** None

**AREA** 266,000 sq km (102,703 sq miles)

**TIME ZONE** GMT

**POPULATION** 394,000

**LIFE EXPECTANCY** 53.9

**INFANT MORTALITY (PER 1,000)** 71.1

**CURRENCY** Moroccan dirham

**ECONOMY** Agriculture not available, industry not available, services 40%

**CLIMATE** Mainly hot and arid

**MAP REFERENCE** Page 360

## Fact File

**OFFICIAL NAME** St Helena

**FORM OF GOVERNMENT** Overseas territory of the United Kingdom

**CAPITAL** Jamestown

**AREA** 410 sq km (158 sq miles)

**TIME ZONE** GMT

**POPULATION** 7,600

**LIFE EXPECTANCY** 78.3

**INFANT MORTALITY (PER 1,000)** 18.3

**LITERACY RATE** 97%

**CURRENCY** St Helenian pound

**ECONOMY** Mainly fishing and agriculture

**CLIMATE** Tropical, moderated by trade winds

**MAP REFERENCE** Page 373

Western Sahara is a former Spanish possession. South of Morocco (and more than half the size of Morocco itself) it consists of the desert country lying between Mauritania and the Atlantic coast. The terrain is largely flat, with large areas of rock and sand, rising to low mountains in the northeast and the south. Possessing the world's largest known deposits of phosphate rock, it is a contested region of uncertain sovereignty, though since 1975 it has been occupied and administered by Morocco. Most of the indigenous people are Sahrawis, a mixture of Berber and Arab. Since 1983 a war has been waged on their behalf by the Polisario Front (Popular Front for the Liberation of the Saguia el Hamra and Rio de Oro) and by 1991 more than 170,000 Sahrawi refugees had fled the country and were living in camps in Algeria. Guerrilla activities continue, despite a United Nations-monitored ceasefire in 1991. Trade and other activities are controlled by the Moroccan government and most food for the urban population must be imported. Western Sahara's standard of living is well below that of Morocco.

The island of St Helena lies about 1,950 km (1,200 miles) off the west coast of Africa. Together with Tristan da Cunha and Ascension Island, it is a British crown colony, and is Britain's main dependency in the South Atlantic. The crater rim of an extinct volcano, St Helena is marked by gorges and valleys, has many freshwater springs, and rises to an elevation of 824 m (2,703 ft).

Discovered by the Portuguese in 1502 and first visited by the English in 1588, St Helena was granted to the British East India Company in 1659. It acquired fame as Napoleon's place of exile from 1815 to 1821, but its importance as a port of call declined after the opening of the Suez Canal in 1869. Today the island's main activities are fishing, livestock raising, and the sale of handicrafts, but it depends on aid from the UK. Tristan da Cunha, 2,000 km (1,243 miles) to the south, has a farming community. Ascension Island, a military base, the site of a US Air Force auxiliary airfield and communications center, has no resident population.

## Autonomous communities

The municipalities of Ceuta and Melilla on the Moroccan coast and the Canary Islands, off southern Morocco, are autonomous communities of Spain. The islands of Madeira, to the north of the Canary Islands, constitute an autonomous region of Portugal.

### Ceuta and Melilla

In 1912 the Sultan of Morocco signed a treaty with France making Morocco a French protectorate. At the same time the French, recognizing Spanish interests in the region, gave Spain several enclaves along the Moroccan coast. Two of these enclaves remain under Spanish administration—Ceuta and Melilla.

The high promontory of Jebel Musa at Ceuta, on the African side of the Strait of Gibraltar, stands opposite Gibraltar on the northern side. Legend has it that Jebel Musa and the Rock of Gibraltar were the two "Pillars of Hercules", set there by Hercules to commemorate his travels and achievements. Today, Ceuta is a military station and seaport with a population of about 76,900.

### Canary Islands

The Canary Islands, grouped off southern Morocco, are an autonomous community of Spain. There are seven large islands and numerous smaller islands, the nearest of which are within 100 km (60 miles) of the African coast. The "inshore" islands of Lanzarote and Fuerteventura are low lying. The more mountainous outer islands of Gran Canaria and Tenerife include the volcanic cone of Pico de Teide (3,718 m; 12,198 ft).

With a subtropical climate and fertile soils, the islands support farming and fruit growing, and such industries as food and fish processing, boat building, and crafts.

Once known as the Fortunate Islands, the Spanish took control of the Canaries in 1479, subjugating the original Guanche and Canario inhabitants. Today, the islands' mild climate makes them a major tourist destination year round. They are divided into two provinces: Las Palmas de Gran Canaria, and Santa Cruz de Tenerife.

### Madeira

Madeira is the largest of a group of volcanic islands forming an autonomous region of Portugal. A tourist destination, they are situated 550 km (340 miles) from the coast of Morocco, and 900 km (560 miles) southwest of Lisbon. The two islands of Madeira and Porto Santo are inhabited, unlike the barren islets of the Desertas and Selvagens. Madeira is 55 km (34 miles) long and 19 km (12 miles) wide, has deep ravines and rugged mountains, contains the group's capital, Funchal, and rises to Pico Ruivo (1,861 m; 6,106 ft) in the middle of the island. It was once heavily forested, but settlers cleared the uplands for plantation use. Produce includes wine (madeira), sugar, and bananas.

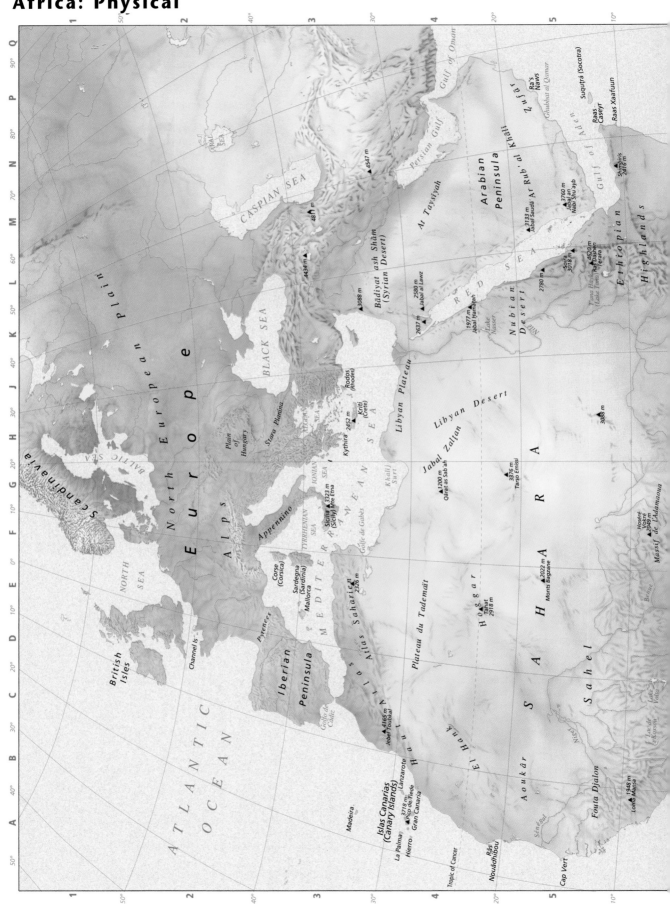

© Random House Australia Pty Ltd

ATLANTIC

OCEAN

INDIAN

OCEAN

Madagascar

Mozambique Channel

Great Rift Valley

Mont Mitumba

Congo Basin

Kalahari Desert

Namib Desert

Drakensberg

Great Karoo

Tropic of Capricorn

Tropic of Capricorn

Sihouette I.
Mahé I.
Platte I.
Coetivy I.
Amirante Isles
Alphonse I.
Providence I.
Farquhar Group
Aldabra Is
Assumption I.

Pemba I.
Mafia I.
Cabo Delgado

Réunion

Tanjona Bobaomby
(Cap d'Ambre)
2876 m
Maromokotro
Helodrano
Antongila
Tanjona Vohimena

Iles de Kerguélen

Heard I.

Prince Edward I.

Iles Crozet

Kilimanjaro
5895 m
Mt Kenya

2960 m

3001 m
Mt Mulanje

Lake Victoria
Lake Nyasa
Lago Niassa
Lake Malawi
Lake Tanganyika
4507 m
Karisimbi
1788 m
Lago de Cabora Bassa
Lake Kariba

Zambezi
Rovuma
Limpopo
Lualaba
Congo
Kasai
Okavango
Cuango
Cunene
Cubango
Orange
Vaal

Ilha do Bazaruto
Cabo de Santa Maria
2436 m
Monte Binga

3482 m
Thabana-
Ntlenyana
2504 m
Kompasberg

Cape of
Good Hope

2573 m
Brandberg

4620 m
Moco

980 m
Mont Iboundji

Walvis Bay
Luderitz Bay

Ponta das
Palmeirinhas
Ponta Albina

Annobón

St Helena

Ascension

Tristan da Cunha

Scale 1:30,000,000     Projection: Azimuthal Equal Area

0    400    800    1200 kilometers

0    200    400    600 miles

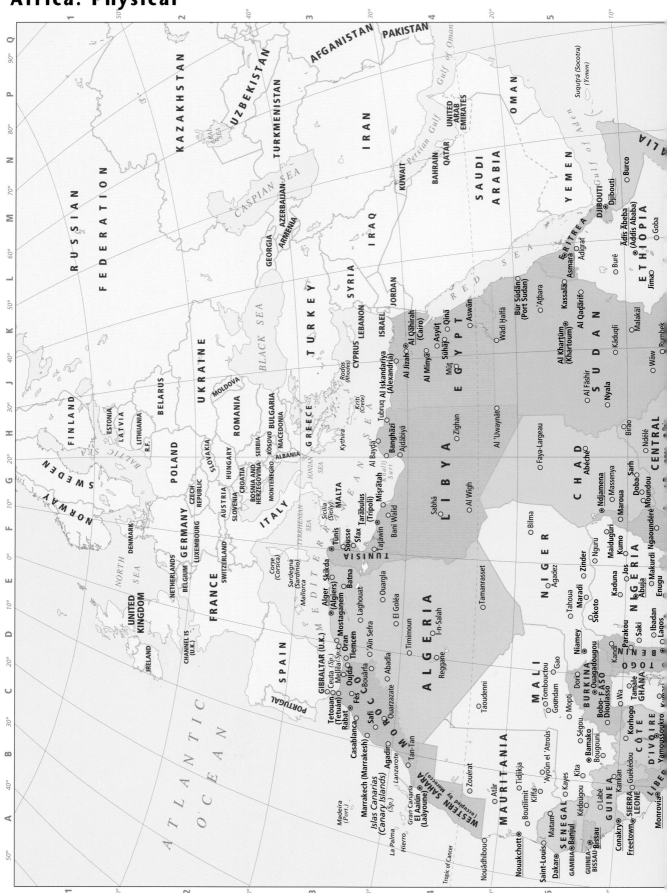

Africa

Africa

ATLANTIC

OCEAN

INDIAN

OCEAN

Mozambique Channel

SEYCHELLES

Victoria
Mahé I.
Sihouette I.
Platte I.
Coetivy I.
Amirante Isles
Alphonse I.
Providence I.
Farquhar Group

MAURITIUS
Port Louis

REUNION (Fr.)
Saint-Denis

Iles de Kerguélen (Fr.)

HEARD AND MACDONALD IS (Aust.)

Tropic of Capricorn

Iles de Crozet (Fr.)

Prince Edward I. (S. Africa)

MADAGASCAR

COMOROS
Moroni

MAYOTTE (Fr.)
Dzaoudzi

Aldabra Is
Assumption I.

Antsirañana
Sambava
Soanierana-Ivongo
Toamasina
Antananarivo
Mahajanga
Antsohihy
Fianarantsoa
Vangaindrano
Tsiroanomandidy
Morondava
Morombe
Toliara
Tôlañaro

MOZAMBIQUE

Kisimayo
Garissa
Nairobi
Mombasa
Moshi
Tanga
Zanzibar
Dar es Salaam
Pemba Island
Mafia I.
Dodoma
Iringa
Songea
Lindi
Mtwara
Nacala
Nampula
Lichinga
Quelimane
Ilha do Bazaruto
Beira
Inhambane
Chokué

TANZANIA
Mwanza
Tabora
Mbeya
Kasama
Mpika
Mansa

RWANDA
Kigali

BURUNDI
Bujumbura

MALAWI
Lilongwe
Blantyre

ZAMBIA
Chingola
Luanshya
Mongu
Lusaka
Kariba
Kabwe

ZIMBABWE
Harare
Gweru
Bulawayo
Chimoio
Chinhoyi

DEMOCRATIC REPUBLIC OF THE CONGO
Goma
Bukavu
Kindu
Kalemie
Kolwezi
Solwezi
Dilolo
Mbuji-Mayi
Kamina
Kananga
Lodja
Saurimo
Luena
Kinshasa

Kenya

Thohoyandou

SWAZILAND
Mbabane

SOUTH AFRICA
Pretoria
Johannesburg
Klerksdorp
Bloemfontein
Durban
East London
Port Elizabeth
Mossel Bay
Beaufort West
De Aar
Upington

LESOTHO
Maseru

BOTSWANA
Francistown
Mahalapye
Gaborone
Maun

NAMIBIA
Rundu
Tsumeb
Otjiwarongo
Windhoek
Keetmanshoop
Swakopmund
Namibe
Oshakati

ANGOLA
Uige
Luanda
Benguela
Huambo
Lubango
Menongue

GABON
Port-Gentil
Moanda
Tchibanga

Brazzaville
Pointe-Noire
Owando

São Tomé

Annobón (Eq. Guinea)

ASCENSION ISLAND (ST HELENA)

ST HELENA (U.K.)

TRISTAN DA CUNHA (St Helena)

Tropic of Capricorn

Cape Town

0    400    800    1200 kilometers
0    200    400    600 miles
Scale 1:30,000,000    Projection: Azimuthal Equal Area

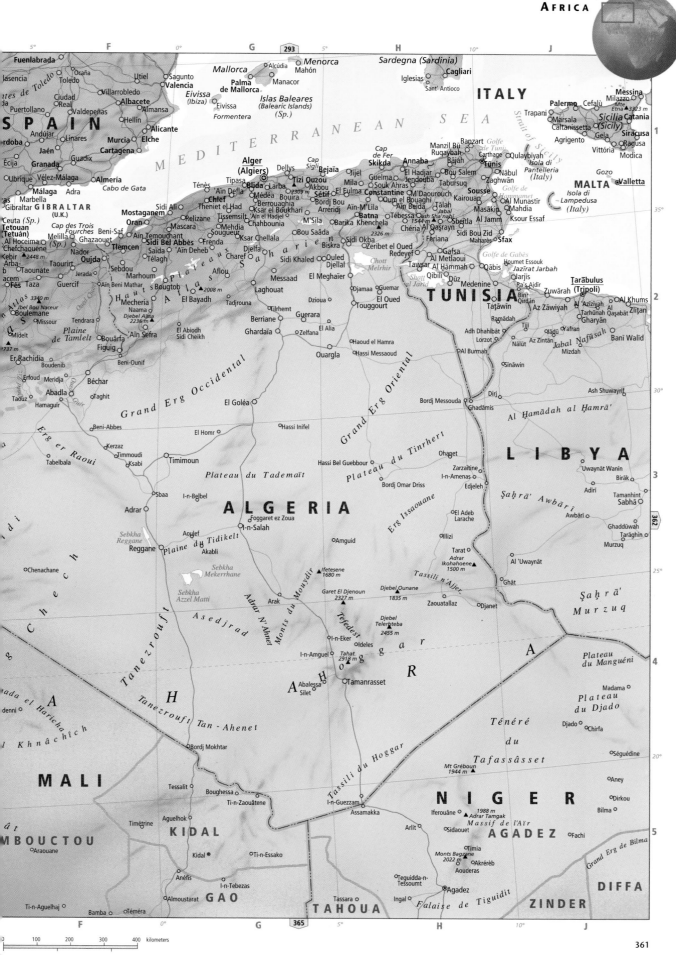

## Map labels

**ITALY**

**SPAIN**

**MEDITERRANEAN SEA**

**TUNISIA**

**ALGERIA**

**LIBYA**

**MALI**

**NIGER**

**MALTA**

Fuenlabrada
Jasencia
Ocaña
Toledo
Montes de Toledo
Utiel
Sagunto
Alcúdia
Menorca
Mallorca
Manacor
Palma de Mallorca
Valencia
Sardegna (Sardinia)
Iglesias
Sant' Antioco
Cagliari
Palermo
Cefalù
Messina
Milazzo
Mte Etna 3323 m
Catania
Trapani
Marsala
Caltanissetta
Sicilia (Sicily)
Siracusa
Gela
Ragusa
Modica
Vittória
Agrigento
Villarrobledo
Ciudad Real
Puertollano
Valdepeñas
Albacete
Almansa
Hellín
Alicante
Eivissa (Ibiza)
Eivissa
Formentera
Islas Baleares (Balearic Islands) (Sp.)
Andújar
Linares
Jaén
Guadix
Murcia
Elche
Cartagena
Granada
Écija
Vélez-Málaga
Almería
Cabo de Gata
Málaga
Adra
Marbella
Gibraltar
GIBRALTAR (U.K.)
Ceuta (Sp.)
Tetouan (Tetuán)
Al Hoceima
Chefchaouene
Melilla (Sp.)
Cap des Trois Fourches
Nador
Oujda
Tlemcen
Sidi Bel Abbès
Oran
Mostaganem
Ghazaouet
Beni-Saf
Aïn Temouchent
Saïda
Aïn Deheb
Frenda
Alger (Algiers)
Tipasa
Blida
Médéa
Tizi Ouzou
Akbou
Bejaïa
Jijel
Skikda
Annaba
Banzart
Tunis
Cap de Fer
Cap Sigli
Dellys
Ténès
Chlef
Larba
Bouira
Berrouaghia
Ksar el Boukhari
Théniet el Had
Aïn Defla
Relizane
Mascara
Tissemsilt
Aïn el Hadjel
M'Sila
Bou Saâda
Barika
Batna
Khenchela
Tébessa
Chéria
Aïn Beïda
Oum el Bouaghi
Aïn M'Lila
Constantine
Mila
El Eulma
Sétif
Bordj Bou Arréridj
M'Daourouch
Guelma
El Hadjar
Souk Ahras
Jendouba
Bou Salem
Bájah
Tabursuq
Zaghwān
Nābul
Qulaybīyah
Carthage
Isola di Pantelleria (Italy)
Golfe de Tunis
Golfe de Hammamet
Sousse
Masākin
Al Munastīr
Mahdia
Kairouan
Tālah
Ash Sha'nabī 1544 m
Sīdī Bū Zīd
Maharès
Al Jamm
Ksour Essaf
Sfax
Isola di Lampedusa (Italy)
Golfe de Gabès
MALTA
Valletta
Gozo
 Feriana
Gafsa
Al Qaşrayn
Sbeitla
Redeyef
Al Metlaoui
Tawzar
Al Hāmmah
Qābis
Houmet Essouk
Jazīrat Jarbah
Jarjis
Medenine
Ra's Ajdīr
Bin Qīrdān
Zuwārah
Tarābulus (Tripoli)
Al 'Azīzīyah
Al Khums
Zlitan
Tarhūnah
Qaşābāt
Gharyān
Bani Walīd
Düz
Qibilī
Matmāta
Taṭāwīn
Ramādah
Nālūt
Jādū
Tiji
Jabal Nafūsah
Az Zāwiyah
Sinäwin
Lorzot
Adh Dhāhibāt
Mizdah
Tāourirt
Jerada
Taourirt
Guercif
Taza
Fès
Boulemane
Missour
Tendrara
Aïn Beni Mathar
Sebdou
Marhoum
Mecheria
Naama
Djebel Aïssa 2236 m
Aïn Sefra
El Bayadh
Tadjrouna
Tilrhemt
Laghouat
Berriane
Ghardaïa
Zelfana
El Alia
Guerara
Messaad
Aflou
Charef
Djelfa
Sidi Khaled
Ouled Djellal
Biskra
Zeribet el Oued
Sidi Okba
El Meghaïer
Djamaa
El Oued
Touggourt
Hassi Messaoud
Ouargla
Haoud el Hamra
Guemar
Dzioua
Chott Melrhir
Shatt al Jarīd
Chahbounia
Bou Saâda
Sougueur
Ksar Chellala
Ksar el Boukhari
Plateaux du Sahara
Hauts Plateaux
Atlas Saharien
Charef
Ber Rechid
Jbel Bou Naceur 3340 m
Aïn Beni Mathar
Haut Atlas
Plaine de Tamlelt
Bouârfa
Figuig
Beni-Ounif
Béchar
Oued Guir
Taghit
Abadla
Hamaguir
Erg er Raoui
Beni-Abbes
Kerzaz
Timmoudi
Ksabi
Tabelbala
Timimoun
Sbaa
I-n-Belbel
Adrar
Reggane
Sebkha Reggane
Plaine du Tidikelt
Akabli
In-Salah
Foggaret ez Zoua
Amguid
Sebkha Mekerrhane
Sebkha Azzel Matti
Chenachane
Araouane
Oued Gir
Grand Erg Occidental
El Goléa
Hassi Inifel
El Homr
Plateau du Tademaït
Hassi Bel Guebbour
Bordj Omar Driss
Ohanet
Zarzaïtine
I-n-Amenas
Edjeleh
Illizi
El Adeb Larache
Grand Erg Oriental
Plateau du Tinrhert
Erg Issaouane
Şahrā' Awbārī
Uwaynāt Wanīn
Birāk
Adīrī
Tamanhint
Sabhā
Awbārī
Ghaddūwah
Tarāghin
Murzuq
Al 'Uwaynāt
Ghāt
Bordj Messouda
Ghadāmis
Dirj
Sināwin
Al Burmah
Ash Shuwayrif
Al Hamādah al Hamrā'
LIBYA
Adrar Ikohahoene 1500 m
Tarat
Tefedest
Djebel Telerhteba 2455 m
Tassili n'Ajjer
Zaouatallaz
Djanet
Şahrā' Murzuq
Aouef
Garet El Djenoun 2327 m
Ifetesene 1680 m
Arak
Tahat 2918 m
I-n-Eker
Oldeles
I-n-Amguel
Abalessa
Silet
Tamanrasset
Hoggar
Ahaggar
Adrar N'Ahnet
Monts du Mouydir
Asedjrad
Tanezrouft
Tanezrouft Tan-Ahenet
Bordj Mokhtar
Tessalit
Boughessa
Ti-n-Zaouâtene
Timétrine
Aguelhok
Kidal
KIDAL
Ti-n-Essako
Anéfis
I-n-Tebezas
Almoustarat
GAO
Ti-n-Aguelhaj
Bamba
Témèra
Tassara
TAHOUA
Ingal
Agadez
Teguidda-n-Tessoumt
Aouderas
Akrèrèb
Timia
Monts Bagzane 2022 m
Massif de l'Aïr
Adrar Tamgak 1988 m
Iferouâne
Sidaouet
Arlit
AGADEZ
Fachi
Dirkou
Aney
Bilma
Grand Erg de Bilma
ZINDER
DIFFA
Mt Gréboun 1944 m
Ténéré du Tafassâsset
Djado
Chirfa
Madama
Plateau du Djado
Plateau du Manguéni
Séguédine
I-n-Guezzam
Assamakka
NIGER
Plateau du Tidikelt
MALI
Tan-Ahenet
Chech

293
362
365
361

Scale 1:9,000,000
Projection: Azimuthal Equal Area
kilometers
miles
0 100 200 300 400
0 100 200

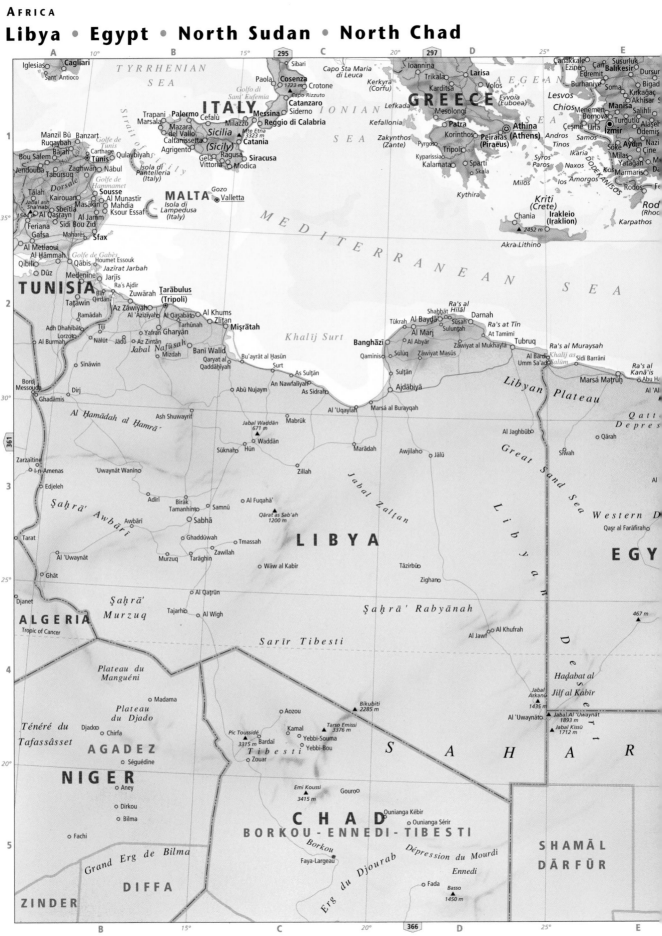

A        B        C        D        E

TYRRHENIAN SEA

Iglesias  Cagliari

Sant' Antioco

Paola  Sibari

Cosenza
1723 m

Capo Sta Maria
di Leuca

Ioannina

GREECE

Larisa

Çanakkale
Ezine  Çan  Balıkesir  Dursur

Trikala  Karditsa  Volos

Burhaniye  Soma  Bornova

AEGEAN

Kerkyra
(Corfu)  Lefkada

Capo Rizzuto

Crotone

Siderno

Catanzaro

Palermo  ITALY

Cefalù  Messina

Milazzo  Reggio di Calabria

IONIAN

Mesolongi

Patra

Korinthos

Kırkağaç  Akhisar

Manisa

Evvoia
(Euboea)

Chios

Lesvos

Menemen

Salihli

Trapani
Marsala

Mazara
del Vallo

Sicilia
(Sicily)

Mte Etna
3323 m

SEA

Zakynthos
(Zante)

Peiraias
(Piraeus)

Athina
(Athens)

Çeşme  Urla

Turgutlu  Alaşel

İzmir

Manzil Bū  Banzart
Ruqaybah

Caltanissetta

Agrigento

Ragusa

Catania

Pyrgos

Tripoli

Andros

Samos

Kyparissia  Sparti

Tinos

Ödemis

Aydın  Nazi

Carthage  Qulaybīyah

Bou Salem  Bājah

Gela

Vittoria

Siracusa

Modica

Kalamata

Skala

Syros
Paros

Naxos

Ikaria

Kos

Milas

Yatağan

DODEKANISOS

Jendouba

Zaghwān  Nābul

Tūnis

Milos

Ios

Amorgos

Marmaris

Kythira

Rod
(Rho

Tālah

Kairouan

Sousse

Al Munastīr

Gozo  Valletta

MALTA

Isola di
Lampedusa
(Italy)

Kriti
(Crete)

Irakleio
(Iraklion)

Karpathos

Jabal ash
Sha'nabi

Masākin  Mahdia

Al Qaşrayn  Al Jamm

Ksour Essaf

Chania

2452 m

Akrá Lithino

Sbeïtla

Feriana  Sidi Bou Zid

Maharès

Gafsa

Sfax

MEDITERRANEAN

SEA

Al Metlaoui

Al Hāmmah

Qibili

Dūz

Qābis

Houmet Essouk

Jazīrat Jarbah

Medenine

Jarjis

Ra's Ajdīr

TUNISIA

Tatawin

Bīr
Qirdan

Zuwārah

Tarābulus
(Tripoli)

Khalīj Surt

Shahbāt  Ra's al
Hilāl

Al Baydā'  Darnah

Ra's at Tīn

Libyan  Plateau

Ra's al Muraysah

Adh Dhahibāt
Lorzota

Ramādah

Az Zāwiyah

Al 'Āzizīyah

Al Qaşabāt

Al Khums

Zlītan

Mişrātah

Tūkrah  Al Bayḍā'

Sulunţah

Susah

At Tamimī

Tubruq

Umm Sa'ad

Al Bardī
Khalīj as
Salūm

Sidi Barrāni

Ra's al
Kanā'is

Ra's al
Kanā'is

Abū Ra

Tīji

Al Burmah

Nālūt  Jādū

Az Zīntān

Yafran  Gharyān

Tarhūnah

Banī Walīd

Banghāzī

Al Abyār

Zāwiyat al Mukhaylī

Marsá Maţrūḥ

Al 'Al

Sīnāwin

Mizdah

Qaryat al
Qaddāḥīyah

Bu'ayrāt al Hasūn

Surt

As Sulţān

Qamīnis

Sulūq

Zāwiyat Masūs

Al Jaghbūb

Bordj
Messouda

Ghadāmis

Dirj

Ash Shuwayrif

Abū Nujaym

An Nawfalīyah

As Sidrah

Sulţān

Ajdābiyā

Siwah

Qāra

Qatt
Depres

Zarzaïtine

I-n-Amenas

Al Ḥamādah al Ḥamrā'

Jabal Waddān
671 m

Mabrūk

Al 'Uqaylah

Marsá al Burayqah

Al Jaghbūb

Great
Sand
Sea

Western D

Edjeleh

Sūknah  Hūn

Waddān

Marādah

Awjilaho

Jālū

L
i
b
y
a
n

Qaşr al Farāfirah

Adīrī

Birāk

Tamanhint

Samnū

Al Fuqahā'

EGY

Tarat

Şaḥrā' Awbārī

Awbārī

Sabhā

Qārat as Sab'ah
1200 m

Jabal  Zalţan

Ghaddūwah

Tmassah

Al 'Uwaynāt

Murzuq

Tarāghin

Zawilah

Wāw al Kabīr

Tāzirbū

LIBYA

467 m

Ghāt

Al Qaţrūn

Zighano

Djanet

Şaḥrā'
Murzuq

Tajarhī

Al Wigh

Şaḥrā' Rabyānah

D

Tropic of Cancer

Sarīr Tibesti

ALGERIA

Plateau du
Manguéni

Ḥaḍabat al
Jilf al Kabīr

Madama

Bikubiti
2285 m

Jabal
Arkanū
1435 m

Jabal Al 'Uwaynāt
1893 m

Al 'Uwaynāto

Jabal Kissū
1712 m

Plateau
du Djado

Aozou

Tarso Emissi
3376 m

Ténéré du
Tafassâsset

Djado

Chirfa

Pic Toussidé
3315 m

Kamal

Bardaï

Yebbi-Souma

Yebbi-Bou

S

A

H

A

R

AGADEZ

Séguédine

Tibesti

Zouar

NIGER

Aney

Emi Koussi
3415 m

Gouro

Ouanianga Kébir

Ouanianga Sérir

SHAMĀL

DĀRFŪR

Dirkou

CHAD

Bilma

BORKOU-ENNEDI-TIBESTI

Borkou

Dépression du Mourdi

Fachi

Faya-Largeau

Ennedi

ZINDER

Grand Erg de Bilma

DIFFA

Erg du Djourab

Fada  Basso
1450 m

A        B        C        D        E

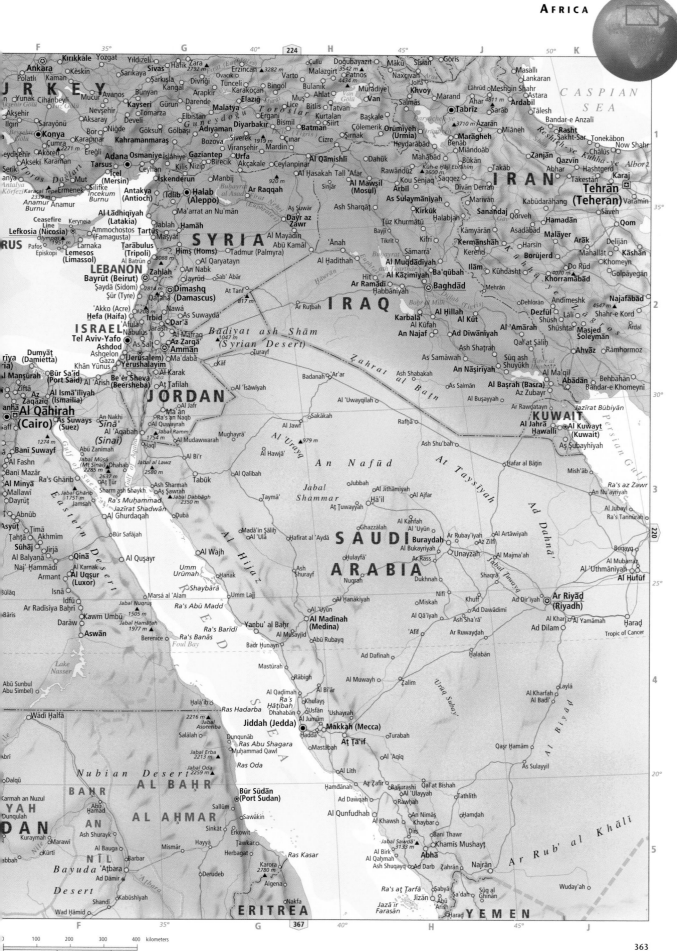

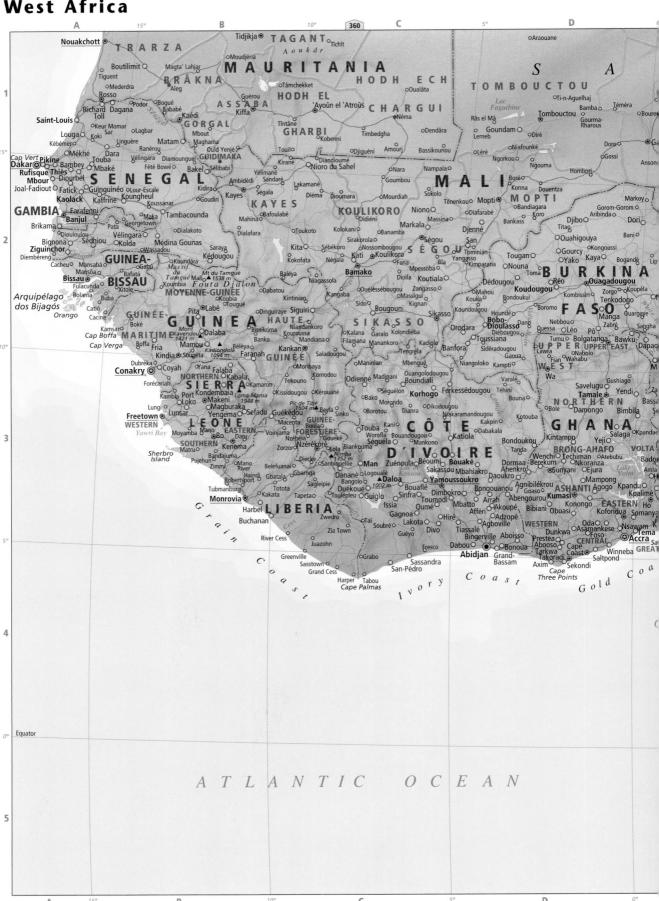

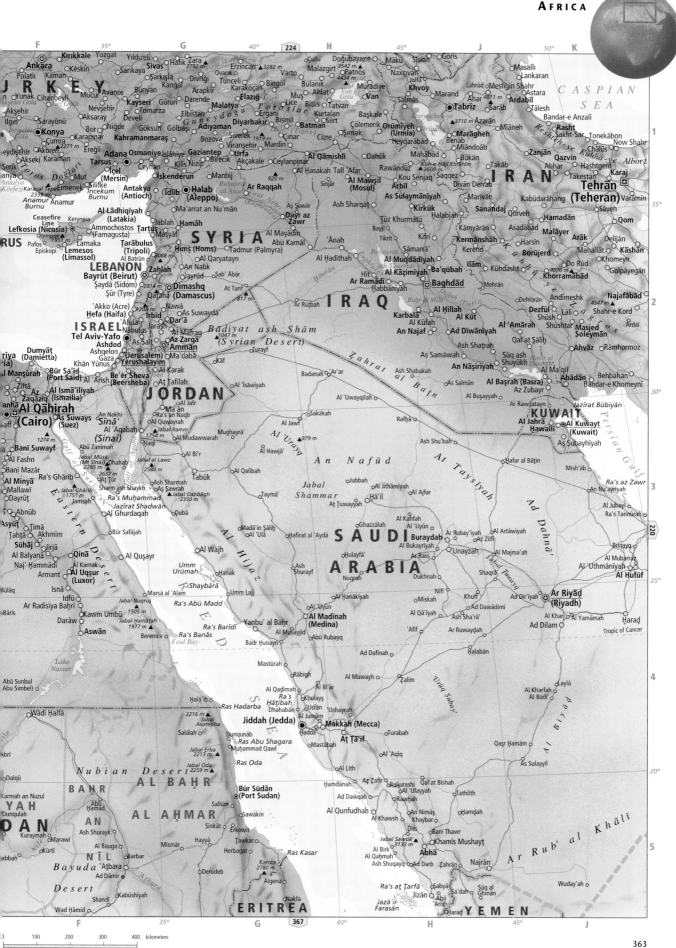

URKEY
Kırıkkale  Yozgat
Ankara  Kėskin
Polatlı  Kaman  Mucur  Avanos  Sarıkaya  Yıldızeli  Sivas  Hafik  Zara  Zara  Erzincan  ▲3282 m  Çullu  Doğubayazıt  Māku  Sīsīan  Göris
Cihanbeyli  İbuğ Gölü  Şarkışla  Divriği  Ovacık  Tunceli  Varto  Malazgirt  3542 m  Patnos  Naxçıvan  Lahrūd  Meshgin Shahr  Masallı  Lankaran
eydişehir  Nevşehir  Kayseri  Gürun  Darende  Arapkir  Karakoçan  Bingöl  Muş  Ahlat  Murādiye  Jolfa  Khvoy  Marand  Āzaran  Astara  CASPIAN
Akşehir  Aksaray  Develi  Tomarza  Elbistan  Malatya  Ergani  Lice  Bitlis  Tatvan  Van  Salmās  ▲4811 m  Tabrīz  Sarāb  Ardabīl  SEA
Ilgın  Bor  Niğde  Göksun  Gölbaşı  Diyarbakır  Siverek  1919 m  Kurtalan  Siirt  Çölemerik  Orūmīyeh  Heydarābād  Marāgheh  Benāb  Miāndoāb  Bandar-e Anzalī  Now Shahr
Konya  Karapınar  Kahramanmaraş  Adıyaman  Viranşehir  Mardin  Cizre  Şırnak  Başkale  (Urmia)  3710 m  Rasht  Sakht-Sar  Tonekābon  Chālūs  Reshteh-ye Alborz  Karaj

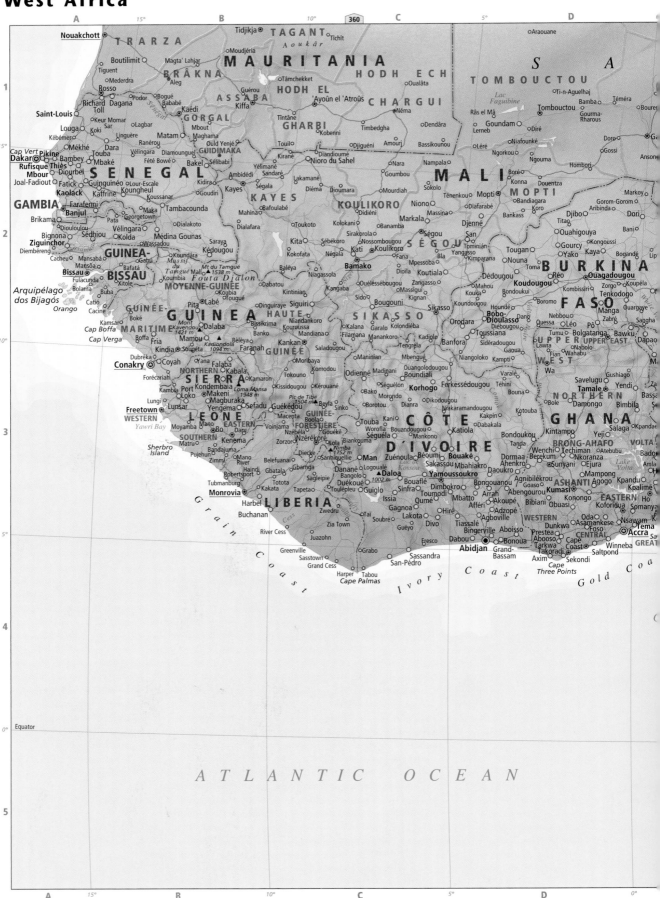

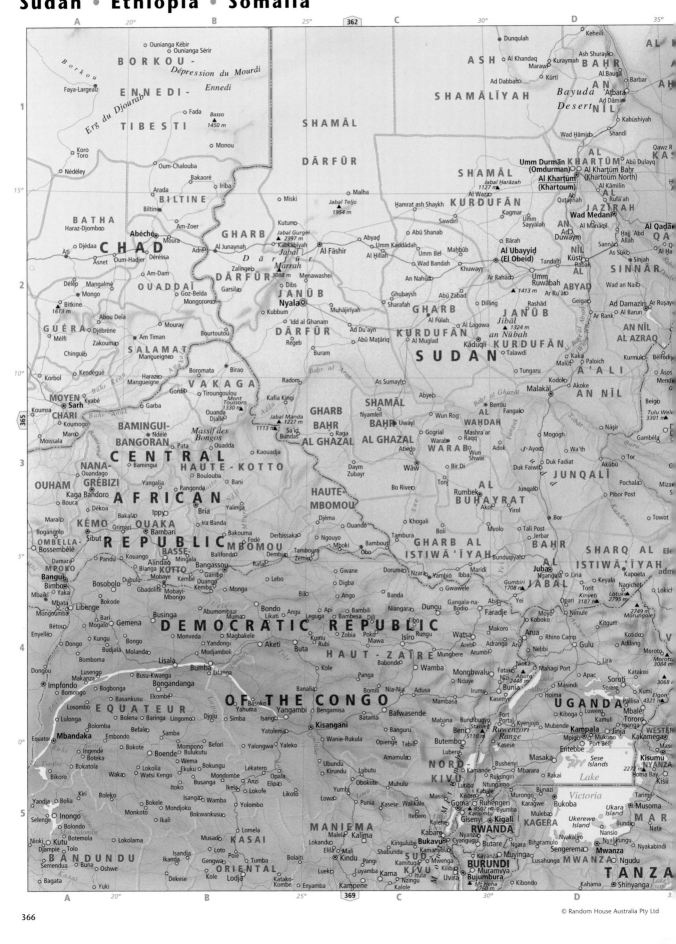

40° **F** 45° 363 **G** 50° **H**

**SAUDI**

Al Qunfudhah○ An Nimāş○ ○Hamdah
Khaybaro
Diis ○Banī Thawr
3133 m▲ Khamīs Mushayṭ○ Al Qa'āmīyāt
Jabal Sawdā'▲ **Abhā**■
Al Birk○ ○Najrān
Al Qaḥmah○ Ad Darb○ Zahrān○ **ARABIA**
Ash Shuqayq○

RED

Ra's Kasar ○Kelamet ○Karora Ra's aṭ Ṭarfā Sabyā○ ○Ṣa'dah Wuday'ah○ ○Sanāw
780 m Algena○ Sabyā○ ○Sū'q Al Ghinān
Nakfa○ Jizān○ Ḥaraḍ○ Khamr○
Keren○ Kelamet Jazā'ir ○Harad Ḥūth○
ordat○ Massawa Farasān Ḥajjah○ ○Raydah
**Asmara**◎ Shibām○ Saywūn○
Dek'emhāre○ Merṣa Fāṭma Az-Zuhrah○ Amrān○ Ma'rib○
Sôira▲3018 m Az Zaydīyah○ **Ṣan'ā'**■
Ādī Ugri○ Adī Keyih○ Jabal an Nabī Shu'ayb▲ Harīb○
Adwa○ Adigrat○ **Al Ḥudaydah**■ 3760 m Manākhah○

**YEMEN** Nuqūb○ ○Ash Shiḥr
Al Mukallā■

SEA

Suquṭrá (Socotra)

**OMAN**

Ṣalālah○

INDIAN OCEAN

**ETHIOPIA**

**SOMALIA**

**Muqdisho (Mogadishu)**■

367

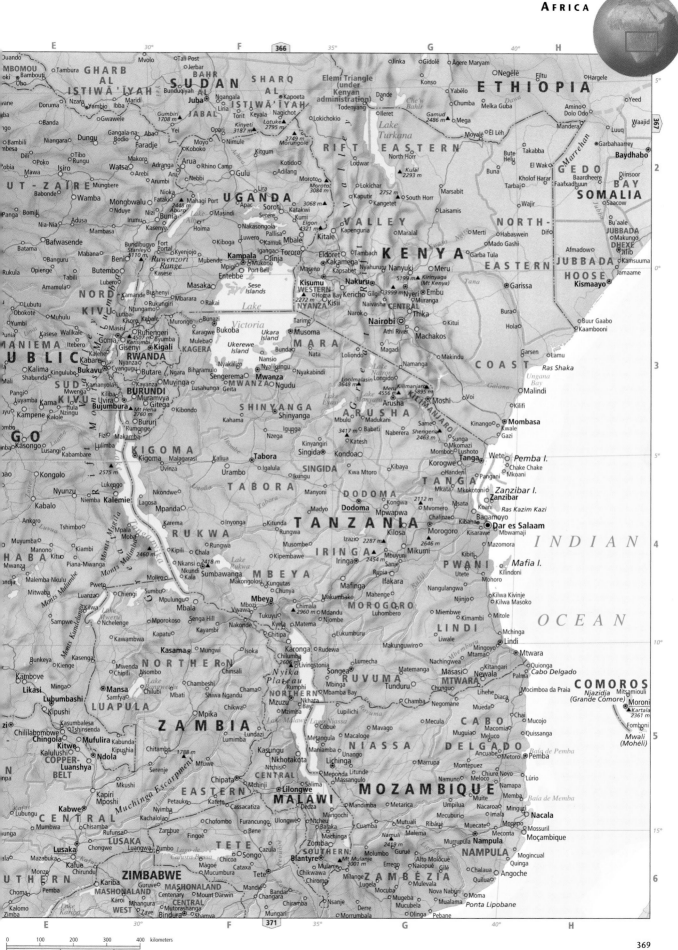

Africa

Scale 1:9,000,000    Projection: Azimuthal Equal Area

0   100   200   300   400 kilometers
0        100        200 miles

## Map labels

**NORTH**
Mumbeji
Jukulu

MOXICO
Cangamba
Sessa
Luanguinga
Luena
Lumbala
N'guimbo
Cangombe
Ninda
Kalabo
Mongu
WESTE

Chongoroi
Cabo de Santa Marta
Lucira
Serra da Neve
Quilengues
Caluquembe
Chicomba
Kuvango
Cuchi
Longa
Menongue
1729 m
Chiume

Bentiaba
Camucuio
Caitou
Lola
Dinde
Bibala
Munhino
Quipungo
HUÍLA
Matala
Dongo
Cassinga
Cuito Cuanavale
Baixo Longa
Mavinga
Neriquinha
Rivungo
Shangombo
Zambezi
Senanga

Lubango

Namibe
Humpata
Virei
Chibia
Chiange
Chibemba
ANGOLA
Cuvelai
Caiundo
CUANDO
Nankova
Calunga
Bambangando
Luiana
Luiana
CAPRI

Ponta Albina
Tombua
Cahama
Quiteve
Nehone
Bondo
CUBANGO
Mavengue
Dirico
Katima
Kongola
Sangwa

Baía dos Tigres
Pediva
Oncócua
CUNENE
Xangongo
Ondjiva
Namacunde
Cuangar
Calai
Bagani
Muhembo

Foz do Cunene
Iona
Humbe
Mucope
Naulila
Nkurenkuru
Rundu
Okavango
Seronga
C

Kunene
Chitado
Ohangwena
Okavango Delta

Cape Fria
Ruacaná
Ombalantu
Oshikango
Ndangwa
OKAVANGO
Gumare
NGAMILAN

Rocky Pt
Ombalantu
Oshakati
OSHANA
Ongandjera
Namutoni
OSHIKOTO
Tsumeb
Tsumkwe
Sehithwa
Nhabe
Maun

Sesfontein
Opuwo
OMUSATI
Okaukuejo
Otavi
Grootfontein
Xhur

KUNENE
Kamanjab
Otjo
OTJOZONDJUPA
Ghanzi
BOTSW

Khorixas
Outjo
Okaputa
GHANZI

Palgrave Pt
Brandberg
2573 m
Kalkfeld
Otjiwarongo
Okakarara
Sehithwa

Namib
Erongo
2350 m
Sukses
NAMIBIA
Hochfeld
Steinhausen

Uis
Omaruru
OMAHEKE
Kalahari

Hentiesbaai
Usakos
Okazize
Okahandja
Buitepos
Xanagas
Tshootsha

Ebony
Karibib
Witvlei
Gobabis
Kang
Tsetseng

Swakopmund
ERONGO
Windhoek
2479 m
Dordabis
Ncojane
KWEN

Walvis Bay
KHOMAS
Gross Ums
Lehututu
Shane
Motokwe
Takatokwane

Walvis Bay
Rehoboth
KGALAGADI
Rokong
SOUTHE

Tropic of Capricorn
Nauchas
Tsumis Park
Hoachanas
Aminuis
Hukuntsi
Jwaneng

Sandwich Bay
Narib
Aranos
Werda

St Francis Bay
HARDAP
Stampriet
Gochas
Desert
Tshabong
Terra Firma
Tosca

Gibeon
Mariental
Morokweng

Dolphin Head
Maltahöhe

Hottentots Bay
Helmeringhausen
Tses
Koës
NOR

Brukkaros
1586 m
Berseba
Bokspits
Tsineng
De Vrybu

Lüderitz Bay
Díaz Pt
Aus
Bethanie
Keetmanshoop
Hotazel
WES

Lüderitz
Aroab
Kuruman
Gakarosa

Elizabeth Bay
Sandverhaar
Seeheim
Schroffenstein
2202 m
Kathu
1855 m
Warren

KARAS
Holoog
Postmasburg

Cape Dernberg
Grünau
Kanus
Karasburg
Upington
Lime
Acres
Kim

Rosh Pinah
Ariamsvlei
Warmbad
Kakamas
Griquatown
Douglas

Oranjemund
Onseepkans
Keimoes
Kenhardt
Koffiefor

Alexander Bay
Steinkopf
Pofadder
Marydale
Prieska
Hope
Jag

Wreck Point
Port Nolloth
Nababiep
NORTHERN CAPE

Kleinsee
Springbok
Granaatboskolk
Van Wyksvlei
Vosburg
Britstown
Cole

Gariës
Brandvlei
De Aar

Bitterfontein
Williston
Victoria West
Richmon

SOUTH AFRICA
Calvinia
Carnarvon
Loxton
Murraysburg
Kompa
250

Vredendal
Vanrhynsdorp
Sutherland
Fraserburg
Graaff-Reinet

Lamberts Bay
Clanwilliam
Beaufort West
Aberdeen

Saint Helena Bay
Citrusdal
Laingsburg
WESTERN CAPE
Willowmore
17

Cape Columbine
Piketberg
2152 m
Prince Albert
Uite

Vredenburg
Porterville
Touws River
Ceres
Calitzdorp
Kwa Nob

Saldanha
Malmesbury
Ladismith
Oudtshoorn
Dysselsdorp
Knysna
Cape
Seal

Atlantis
2252 m
Worcester
George
Jeffrey's Bay

Bellville
Paarl
Stellenbosch
Mossel Bay
Cape George

Cape Town
Nyanga
Strand
Swellendam
Port Beaufort

Cape of Good Hope
False Bay
Hermanus
Bredasdorp

Danger Pt
Quoin Pt
Cape Agulhas

**ATLANTIC OCEAN**

Africa

RN
MBIA
Mkushi
Kapiri Mposhi
EASTERN
Chipata
Mchinji
369
Lilongwe
CENTRAL
Massangulo
Maua
Namuno
Namapa
Baía de
Memba

Lubungu
Kabwe
CENTRAL
Petauke
Katete
Cassacatiza
MALAWI
Mandimba
Metarica
Muite
Umpilua
Nacaroa
Minguri
Monapo
Nacala
Mumbwa
Chisamba
Rufunsa
Nyimba
Kachalola
Chofombo
Furancungo
Ulongwé
Ntcheu
Cuamba
Mutuali
Muecate
Meconta
Mossuril

Lusaka
LUSAKA
Luangwa
Zambué
Zumbo
Lago de
Cahora Bassa
Fingoè
Bene
Balaka
Machinga
Malema
Ribáuè
Mocambique

Mazabuka
Kafue
CENTRAL
Chongwe
Cazula
Songo
Chicoa
SOUTHERN
Zomba
Namuli
2419 m
Gurué
Errego
Gilé
Alto Molócuè
Chalaua
Quinga
Angoche

UTHERN
Monze
Chirundu
TETE
Magoè
Mucumbura
Cataxa
Tete
Chikwawa
Mt Mulanje
3001 m
Mulanje
Milange
Mugeba
Nova Nabúri
Moma

Choma
Kariba
Karoi
Guruve
Centenary
Mandié
Bandar
Changara
Chiramba
Nsanje
Derre
Mocuba
Mucubela
Olinga
Pebane

Kalomo
Mashava
MASHONALAND
WEST
Bindura
Shamva
Mutoko
Mungari
Nhamalàbue
Morrumbala
Namacurra
Quelimane

Gweru
ZIMBABWE
Harare
Chitungwiza
MANICA
Nyanga
Catandica
Maringué
Mopeia

MIDLANDS
Kadoma
Marondera
Rusape
Inyangani
2592 m
Chimoio
Nhamatanda
Chinde
Ponta Timbue

MATABELELAND
NORTH
Bulawayo
Gweru
Shurugwi
Gutu
Cashel
Serra da Gorongosa
1862 m
Gorongosa
Dondo
Beira
Sofala
INDIAN

SOUTHERN CAPE

OCEAN

0   100   200   300   400   kilometers

0   100   200   miles

Scale 1:9,000,000   Projection: Azimuthal Equal Area

# Madagascar

40°　　　　45°　　A　　　　B　　50°　　　　C　　55°　D

○ Kilifi

1 ● Mombasa

Praslin I.

Silhouette I.　　La Digue I.

⊛ Victoria

Mahé I.

5° ● Wete

● Pemba I.

○ Chake Chake

Amirante
Isles

Platte I.

2

● Mafia I.

S E Y C H E L L E S

Alphonse I.

Coetivy I.

St Pierre I.　Providence I.

Aldabra
Is

Cosmoledo
Group

Assumption I.　　　Astove I.

Farquhar
Group

Agalega Is
(Mauritius)

10° TANZANIA

○ Mtwara

○ Quionga

○ Cabo Delgado

○ Palma

CABO DELGADO

○ Mocimboa da Praia

Mitsamiouli

Njazidja　○
(Grande Comore)　Moroni ⊛
▲ Kartala
2361 m

C O M O R O S

Nzwani
(Anjouan)

○ Moutsamoudou

Îles Glorieuses
(Réunion)

Andranovondronina ○

Tanjona Bobaomby
(Cap d'Ambre)

○ Ramena

Ambohitra ⊛ Antsirañana
▲ 1475 m

○ Díaca

○ Mucojo

3 ○ Quissanga

○ Muaguide

Baía de Pemba

⊛ Pemba

○ Fomboni
○ Domoni

Mwali
(Mohéli)

MAYOTTE
(Fr.)

Mamoudzou ⊛ Dzaoudzi

Bobasakoa ○

Aniyorano Avaratra
○ Ampisikinana

Nosy Bé

○ Ambilobe

Iharaña ○

Lúrio

M O Z A M B I Q U E

Lohatanjona Angadoka

ANTSIRANANA
▲ 1785 m

○ Memba

Baía de Memba

Ambanja ○
Maroyáto ○

○ Ampanefena

Maromokotro
▲ 2876 m

○ Doany

○ Sambava

○ Minguri

● Nacala

Bealanana ○

15° ○ Mossuril

● Moçambique

Analalava ○

○ Antsohihy

○ Andapa

○ Ampahana

○ Antalaha

NAMPULA

○ Mogincual

○ Quinga

Lohatanjona Maromony

Befandriana Avaratra ○
○ Leanja

Mahajanga ●
Katsepy ○

○ Ambalakida

○ Boriziny

Maroantsetra ○

○ Mahalevona

○ Ampanavoana

Mandritsara ○

Vinanivao ○

Tanjona Masoala

Tanjona Vilanandro

○ Mitsinjo

Marovoay ○

○ Mampikony

Manarantsandry ○

Mananara
Avaratra ○
▲ 1301 m

I N D I A N

Madirovalo ○

○ Soalala

○ Ambato Boeny

TOAMASINA

Helodrano
Antongila

Tromelin I.
(Réunion)

○ Ambohipaky

○ Sitampiky

○ Tsaratanana

○ Manompana

Besalampy ○

Mahabe ○

Maevatanana ○

○ Soanierana-Ivongo

Île Juan de Nova
(Réunion)

M A H A J A N G A

Ikahavo
▲ 847 m

○ Kandreho

○ Andilamena

○ Tambohorano

○ Ambatomainty

Vatoloha
▲ 1575 m

○ Fenoarivo Atsinanana

○ Amparafaravola

○ Betrandraka

○ Vavatenina

○ Morafenobe

○ Mahavelona

○ Maintirano

○ Beravina

○ Ankazobe

○ Didy

Andilanatoby ○

Ambatondrazaka ○

● Toamasina

O C E A N

○ Reharaka

A N T A N A N A R I V O

○ Antsalova

Tsiroanomandidy ○

○ Ambohidratrimo

○ Maroseranana

○ Fanandrana

○ Masoarivo

Miarinarivo ○

⊛ Antananarivo

○ Moramanga

○ Ampasimanolotra

M A D A G A S C A R

○ Miandrivazo

○ Ambatolampy

○ Anosibe an'Ala

○ Belo Tsiribihina

20° Tanjona Tsiribihina

Tsiribihina

Mania

Antsirabe ○
Ibinty
▲ 2254 m

▲ 2119 m

○ Vatomandry

○ Antanambao
Manampotsy

○ Marolambo

○ Mahanoro

M A U R I T I U S

○ Morondava

○ Malaimbandy

Ambato-
finandrahana ○

Fandriana ○

○ Nosy-Varika

Port Louis ⊛

○ Mahabo

○ Ambositra

○ Vohitrandriana

Curepipe ○
○ Mahébourg

○ Amboromptsy

▲ 2052 m

Saint-
Denis ●

○ Andranopasy

○ Manja

Ikalamavony ○

○ Amboasary
Manankara

○ Amboasary

Amboasary

Amboasary

Amboasary

○ Manakara

Saint
Paul ○

R É U N I O N
(Fr.)

○ Morombe

○ Mandabe

○ Berotoroka

Fianarantsoa ●
FIANARANTSOA

○ Ifanadiana

○ Ampasimanjeva

Saint-
Pierre ○

○ Vohilava

Tanjona
Ankaboa

○ Ambalavao

○ Ikongo

○ Vohipeno

T O L I A R A

○ Zazafotsy
○ Ihosy

Boby
▲ 2658 m

○ Ambohimahasoa
○ Mananjary

○ Manakara

Mascarene Islands

○ Ankazoabo

○ Satrokala

○ Ivohibe

○ Vohipeno

○ Manombo Atsimo

○ Mahaboboka

▲ 1348 m

○ Ranohira

○ Vondrozo

○ Farafangana

Tropic of Capricorn

○ Sakaraha

○ Andranovory

○ Betroka

▲ 1824 m

○ Lopary

Tropic of Capricorn

Toliara ⊛

○ Tongobory
○ Bezaha

○ Benenitra

○ Ranomena

○ Vangaindrano

○ Betioky

○ Belamoty

Ivakoany
▲ 1637 m

○ Midongy Atsimo

○ Soamanonga

○ Fotadrevo

○ Bekily

○ Manankoliva

○ Manambondro

○ Ejeda

○ Berakata

○ Manantenina

○ Ilmanombo

○ Itampolo

○ Tranoroa

25° ○ Beloha

○ Ampanihy

○ Antanimora Atsimo

○ Androka

○ Tsiombe

○ Ambovombe

○ Ambosary

● Tôlañaro

Betanty

Tanjona
Vohimena

○ Tanjona
Vohimena

6

A　　　45°　　B　　　50°　　C　　　55°　　D　　60°

© Random House Australia Pty Ltd

kilometers 0　100　200　300　400

miles 0　100　200

Scale 1:9,000,000　　Projection: Azimuthal Equal Area

# Islands around Africa

## RÉUNION
### (France)
Scale 1:1,500,000

55°30 · 56°

*INDIAN OCEAN*

Pte des Galets
Saint-Denis
Sainte-Marie
Sainte-Suzanne
Le Port
La Possession
Bagatelle
Sainte-André
Saint-Paul
Salazie
Hell-Bourg
Bras-Panon
Pte des Aigrettes
Saint-Gilles-les Bains
Trois Bassins
2401 m ▲
▲ 2632 m
Piton des Neiges
▲ 3069 m
Piton Rouge
Saint-Benoît
Saint-Leu
Cilaos
La Plaine des Cafres
Sainte-Rose
Pte Rouge
Les Makes
Le Riviere
Bois-Blanc
Les Avirons
Piton de la Fournaise
Saint-Louis
Le Tampon
Saint-Pierre
Takamaka
Pte de la Table
Pte du Parc
Saint-Joseph
Langevin
Saint-Philippe

21° · 21°
21°30' · 21°30'
55°30 · 56

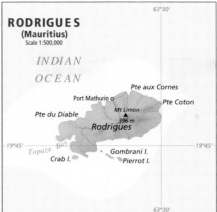

## RODRIGUES
### (Mauritius)
Scale 1:500,000

63°30' · 63°

*INDIAN OCEAN*

Port Mathurin
Pte aux Cornes
Pte du Diable
Mt Limon ▲ 396 m
Pte Coton
*Rodrigues*
*Topaze Bay*
Gombrani I.
Crab I.
Pierrot I.

19°45' · 19°45'
63°30' · 63°

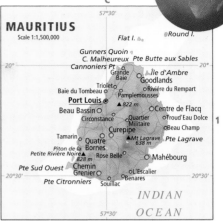

## MAURITIUS
Scale 1:1,500,000

57°30' · 57°

Flat I.
Round I.
Gunners Quoin
C. Malheureux
Pte Butte aux Sables
Cannoniers Pt
Île d'Ambre
Grande Baie
Goodlands
Triolet
Baie du Tombeau
Rivière du Rempart
**Port Louis** ✪
Pamplemousses
▲ 822 m
Beau Bassin
Centre de Flacq
Circonstance
Quartier Militaire
Troud'Eau Dolce
Tamarin
Curepipe
Beau Champ
Quatre Bornes
Mt Lagrave ▲ 638 m
Pte Lagrave
Piton de la Petite Rivière Noire ▲ 828 m
Rose Belle
Mahébourg
Chemin Grenier
L'Escalier
Pte Sud Ouest
Benares
Souillac
Pte Citronniers

20° · 20°
1
20°30' · 20°30'
57°30' · 57°

*INDIAN OCEAN*

## SEYCHELLES
Scale 1:1,500,000

55°30' · 56°

Aride
Curieuse
Les Soeurs
Félicité
Praslin
Marie Anne
La Digue
North I.
Mamelles
Île aux Récifs
Frigate
Mt Dauban ▲ 740 m
Silhouette
North Pt
*Northwest Bay*
Victoria ✪
Cascade
Morne Seychellois ▲ 905 m
Mahé
Anse Boileau
Pte Lazare
Anse Royal
Takamaka
Pte Police
Capucin Pt

4°15' · 4°15'
2
4°45' · 4°45'
55°30' · 56°

*INDIAN OCEAN*

## SOCOTRA
### (Yemen)
Scale 1:4,000,000

53° · 54°

*ARABIAN SEA*

*Ghubbat Qurmah*
Qulansiyah
Hadiboh
Ra's Hūlāf
Ra's Shū'ab
773 m ▲ Qādub
Ar Rak
Hajhir ▲ 1503 m
Ra's Qatānan
*Suqutrā (Socotra)*
'Abd al Kūrī
Samhah
Darsah
Al Ikhwān (The Brothers)

13° · 13°
12° · 12°

*INDIAN OCEAN*

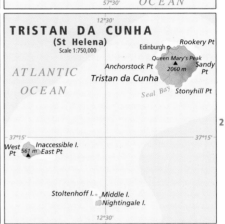

## TRISTAN DA CUNHA
### (St Helena)
Scale 1:750,000

12°30'

*ATLANTIC OCEAN*

Edinburgh
Rookery Pt
Queen Mary's Peak
Anchorstock Pt ▲ 2060 m
Sandy Pt
*Tristan da Cunha*
Stonyhill Pt
*Seal Bay*

West Pt
Inaccessible I. ▲ 561 m
East Pt

37°15' · 37°15'
2
Stoltenhoff I.
Middle I.
Nightingale I.
12°30'

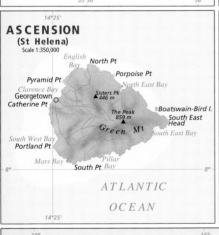

## ASCENSION
### (St Helena)
Scale 1:350,000

14°25'

*English Bay*
North Pt
Pyramid Pt
Porpoise Pt
*North East Bay*
*Clarence Bay*
Sisters Pk ▲ 446 m
Georgetown
Catherine Pt
The Peak ▲ 859 m
Boatswain-Bird I.
South East Head
*Green Mt*
*South East Bay*
*South West Bay*
Portland Pt
Pillar Bay
*Mars Bay*
South Pt

14°25'

*ATLANTIC OCEAN*

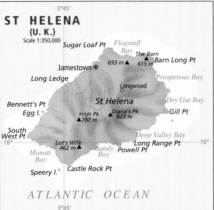

## ST HELENA
### (U.K.)
Scale 1:350,000

5°45'

Sugar Loaf Pt
*Flagstaff Bay*
The Barn
Barn Long Pt
Jamestown ✪
693 m ▲
615 m ▲
Long Ledge
Prosperous Bay
Longwood
Bennett's Pt
*Dry Gut Bay*
Egg I.
*St Helena*
High Pk ▲ 797 m
Diana's Pk ▲ 823 m
Gill Pt
South West Pt
Deep Valley Bay
Lot's Wife ▲ 462 m
Long Range Pt
*Manati Bay*
Powell Pt
*Sandy Bay*
Speery I.
Castle Rock Pt

16° · 16°
5°45'

*ATLANTIC OCEAN*

## MADEIRA
### (Portugal)
Scale 1:2,000,000

17°

Porto Santo ▲ 517 m
Ilhéu de Ferro
Porto Santo
Ilhéu de Baixo
Porto Moniz
São Vicente
Santana
Pto do Pargo
▲ 1862 m
Santa
Calheta
Pico Ruivo de Santana
Pta de São Lourenço
Ribeira Brava
Machico
Madeira
Câmara de Lobos
Santa Cruz
Funchal
Deserta Grande
Ilhas Desertas
Ilhéu do Bugio

33° · 33°
3

*ATLANTIC OCEAN*

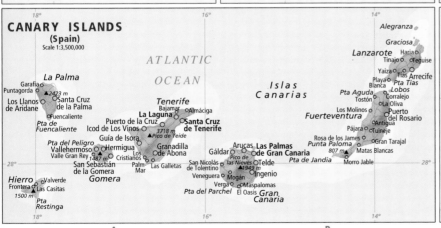

## CANARY ISLANDS
### (Spain)
Scale 1:3,500,000

18° · 16° · 14°

*ATLANTIC OCEAN*

Alegranza
Graciosa
La Palma
Lanzarote
Haria
Teguise
Garafia
Puntagorda
▲ 2423 m
Yaiza
Tinajo
Tías
Arrecife
Los Llanos de Aridane
Santa Cruz de la Palma
Playa Blanca
Pta Tías
*Islas Canarias*
Fuencaliente
Pta Aguda
Lobos
Pta de Fuencaliente
Tenerife
Bajamar
Almáciga
Tostón
Corralejo
La Oliva
Puerto de la Cruz
La Laguna
Los Molinos
Antigua
Icod de Los Vinos
Santa Cruz de Tenerife
Puerto del Rosario
▲ 3718 m
Pico de Teide
*Fuerteventura*
Guía de Isora
Pájara
Tuineje
Pta del Peligro
Arucas
Las Palmas de Gran Canaria
Rosa de los James
Gran Tarajal
Vallehermoso
Hermigua
Granadilla de Abona
Pico de las Nieves ▲ 1949 m
Punta Paloma
▲ 807 m
Matas Blancas
Valle Gran Rey ▲ 1387 m
Los Cristianos
Telde
San Nicolás de Tolentino
Ingenio
Morro Jable
San Sebastián de la Gomera
Palm-Mar
Las Galletas
*Gomera*
Veneguera
Mogán
Verga
Maspalomas
*Gran Canaria*
Hierro
Frontera
Valverde
Las Casitas
Pta del Parchel
El Oasis
1500 m
Pta Restinga

28° · 28°
18° · 16° · 14°

## SÃO TOMÉ AND PRÍNCIPE
Scale 1:3,000,000

7° · 8°

Santo António
Infante Dom Henrique
*Príncipe*

1° · 1°
4

*ATLANTIC OCEAN*

Rio Do Ouro
▲ 2024 m
Pico de São Tomé
São Tomé
Santa Caterina
*São Tomé*
Santa Cruz
Pto Alegre
Ilhéu das Rôlas
Equator
7°

# North America

The continent of North America covers an area of 25.3 million sq km (9.3 million sq miles). It is bounded by the Atlantic Ocean to its east and the Pacific Ocean to its west. Broadest toward the north, it tapers at its southern end, where a narrow isthmus connects it to South America.

The North American continent can be conveniently divided into temperate North America and the more tropical Central America. Central America consists of countries on the mainland and islands in the Caribbean Sea.

Infrastructure, provision of services, and quality-of-life indicators of Central American countries contrast markedly with those of Canada and the United States of America. In addition, a large cultural divide separates mainly English-speaking Canada and the USA from their predominantly Spanish-speaking southern neighbors. For these reasons, Central America is introduced separately.

North America consists of Canada and the United States, plus St Pierre and Miquelon (France) which lie off the east coast of Canada, and Bermuda (UK) which lies off the eastern coast of the USA.

## Physical features

In North America there are both old and young mountains. Young folded mountains (the Cordillera) run along the western part of the continent from Alaska to the Central American isthmus and include a number of active volcanoes. This chain arose following the collision of the American and Pacific plates. In the USA, the Cordillera splits into the Rocky Mountains, which form the eastern arm, and the Sierra Nevada and other ranges, which form the western arm. Several peaks in the Rocky Mountains exceed 4,000 m (13,200 ft). The mountain ranges enclose basins such as the Mojave Desert and Death Valley, and a number of saline lakes. Death Valley lies below sea level at an altitude of -86 m (-282 ft).

The ancient Appalachian Mountains run along the eastern length of the USA; their highest peak, Mt Mitchell, has an altitude of 2,037 m (6,683 ft). An extensive coastal plain lies between this chain and the Atlantic Ocean. Plains and lowlands are found in the continent's interior. Glaciers, which covered much of this area during the ice ages, sculpted the rocky plateaus of Canada and deposited sediments as vast plains that straddle Canada and the USA.

Several important rivers flow through North America, primarily the Missouri, 4,088 km (2,540 miles) long and the Mississippi, 3,766 km (2,340 miles) long. The St Lawrence River links the Great Lakes of Canada and the USA to the Atlantic Ocean. There are several large lakes of which Lake Superior, which covers 82,100 sq km (31,699 sq miles), is the largest. The Rio Grande flows between the USA and Mexico. The Columbia River drains several states in northwestern USA.

## Climate and vegetation

North America contains a broad range of temperate climates from warm temperate along the east coast and Mediterranean in southern California to cooler moist climates in northwest and northeast USA and southern Canada. Most of North America is humid, except for a dry belt across the southwest of the USA and basins within the Rockies. An extensive tornado zone is found in the continental interior of the USA. Tropical cyclones, known in this region as hurricanes, and mostly originating in the Caribbean Sea, often strike the southeastern parts of the USA.

Extensive forests occur in temperate North America, ranging from the predominantly deciduous forests found in eastern parts of the USA to the short-tree boreal forests of the subarctic. Tall trees such as redwoods and firs are found along the Pacific coastline. Other trees include maple, ash, and oak. Deer, brown and grizzly bears, lynx, and beavers are found in these forests. Boreal forests are home to migrating animals such as deer, elk, caribou, and moose.

In southern California, sclerophyllous shrubs thrive in the mild, wet winters and hot, dry summers. Eucalypt trees are an introduced species in this area and are a fire hazard during summer.

Extensive grasslands cover the interior of the continent. Tall-grass prairies occur where rainfall is over 750 mm (30 in), and short-grass prairies where precipitation is around 370 mm (15 in). Large herds of bison once roamed these areas, but they were practically eradicated by hunting.

In Alaska and Canada, north of the boreal forest, there is a belt of tundra where small shrubs, lichens, and grasses grow. Migrating herds of caribou, reindeer and lemmings live in this zone, along with bears, wolves, foxes, and lynx.

## Population

North America had a population of 332.2 million in 2007. High living standards are reflected in the high life expectancies—75.9 years for males and

*New York's Statue of Liberty; below vast cornfields in Colorado (left). Snow seems out of place on this pine in desert Utah (below). The magma core of an ancient volcano in Wyoming (above).*

| Nations | |
|---|---|
| Canada | PAGE 380 |
| United States of America (USA) | PAGE 382 |

| Dependencies | |
|---|---|
| Bermuda | PAGE 387 |
| Greenland | PAGE 388 |
| Jan Mayen | PAGE 389 |
| St Pierre and Miquelon | PAGE 391 |

*The crater of Haleakala Volcano, the world's largest dormant volcano, on Maui, Hawaii (above). Much further north, the beginning of the spring thaw in a town in Canada (right). Bermuda (above right), a tiny island off the USA east coast.*

81 years for females (2007). The low population growth rate of less than one percent also reflects an advanced level of development. Approximately 80.8 percent of the population is urbanized.

### Agriculture, forestry, and fishing

North America is well endowed with water resources, arable land, forests, and fishing areas. These favorable conditions, coupled with scientific farming practices, have enabled the establishment of highly productive agricultural industries. These include grain farming, such as wheat and maize; livestock for meat and dairying; cotton; and intensive farming of fruit and vegetables.

The extensive forests which still remain, following large-scale deforestation in the nineteenth century, are exploited for their valuable timbers. Large areas have been reforested in order to produce a long-term sustainable industry.

There are fishing grounds off both the Atlantic and Pacific coasts, especially along the east coast where the cold Labrador current flows.

### Industrialization

Natural resources, technological innovation, and well-developed infrastructure facilities, including energy supplies, have combined to make North America the world's most important manufacturing region. Continuous innovation in computing, laser technology, optic fibers, and space science have enabled it to withstand strong competition from European and Asian industrial nations.

Manufacturing ranges from chemical industries, metal fabrication, automobiles, aircraft, and high-technology military equipment to books, films, computer software, and recorded music. Tertiary industries, which provide services to a relatively wealthy population, employ millions of people.

North America is well endowed with mineral wealth. Extensive deposits of iron ore and coal have been the cornerstone of the steel industry. However, metals such as chromium and manganese need to be imported. The Cordillera belt contains a large number of metallic ores including copper, zinc, molybdenum, gold, and silver. Nickel and iron ore are extracted from ancient plateau rocks in Canada. Among minerals used for energy supplies, coal, petroleum, and natural gas deposits are widespread. Although a large petroleum producer, the USA must also import large quantities because of heavy consumption.

### Languages

English is the dominant language in North America, except in the Canadian province of Québec, where French is the main language.

Some surviving American Indian languages are spoken by minority groups such as the Pueblo Indians of southwestern USA and the First Nations in western Canada. In southern states of the USA that were once parts of Mexico, such as California, New Mexico and Texas, Spanish is spoken among Hispanics. Considerable Hispanic migration to the USA, particularly from Mexico and Cuba, has made Spanish increasingly important in the USA, particularly in parts of the east coast, such as Florida and New York.

### Boundary disputes and wars

There are no major boundary disputes in the region, nor has the region been directly affected by land war in recent decades. However, the terrorist attacks of 11 September 2001 have left a feeling of vulnerability, especially in the USA.

# Central America

Central America, lying in the tropical zone between North and South America, consists of two distinct parts: a mainland area and a number of islands in the Caribbean Sea.

Mexico, Guatemala, Belize, Honduras, Nicaragua, Costa Rica, El Salvador, and Panama form the mainland. The two largest islands in the Caribbean Sea are Cuba and Hispaniola. The latter is divided into the Dominican Republic and Haiti. There are also several small island nations: Jamaica, Antigua and Barbuda, Dominica, Barbados, Trinidad and Tobago, Grenada, St Kitts and Nevis, St Lucia, St Vincent and the Grenadines, and the Bahamas.

Dependencies include Puerto Rico, the Virgin Islands and Navassa (USA), Aruba and the Netherlands Antilles (Netherlands), Anguilla, Montserrat, the British Virgin Islands, the Cayman Islands and the Turks and Caicos Islands (UK), and Martinique and Guadeloupe (France).

## Physical features

Central America is a region of rugged mountains and volcanic peaks that were produced through the collision of several crustal plates. The Central American isthmus was formed by the interaction of the Caribbean and the Cocos Plates, while the Caribbean islands were the result of the Caribbean Plate moving against the North American Plate. Further north, in Mexico, the Pacific and North American Plates collided.

Volcanic activity is found in several sectors of these ranges, particularly in the area south of Mexico City, which contains volcanoes ranging in height from 3,000 to 4,000 m (10,000 to 14,000 ft). Volcanic eruptions have caused considerable damage through lava flows and ash deposits. Numerous islands in the Caribbean Sea, such as

*Nelson's Harbour in Caribbean Antigua (below) contrasts with Mexican scenes, old and new: an ancient pyramid (right) and a woman washing radishes at the market (top).*

Martinique, with the famous active volcano Mt Pelée, and Antigua are volcanic. In contrast, the Bahamas are an example of coral islands.

## Climate and vegetation

Central America lies within the tropics but because of its mountainous relief, climatic conditions vary with altitude. Such changes are notable in the narrow isthmus where variations in elevation are reflected in differences in vegetation. Low-lying areas, which are limited in extent, may have a hot, humid tropical climate with rainforest vegetation, while in elevated areas such as in the central Mexican Plateau the climate approaches temperate conditions. Mountain slopes facing rain-bearing winds are densely vegetated while, in contrast, northeastern Mexico is semiarid.

In areas of high rainfall there are large tropical evergreen forests, which provide cover for a dense undergrowth made up of smaller plants such as ferns and lianas. Animal life is abundant in these areas, but loss of habitat due to deforestation and hunting have caused several animal species to become endangered.

In drier areas, such as in the Yucatán region of Mexico, shrub vegetation dominates in areas previously farmed during the Mayan civilization.

The region lies within a belt which is affected almost every year by hurricanes. In November 1998 a hurricane devastated the countries lying on the isthmus, particularly Honduras and Nicaragua.

## Population

The population of the mainland is 144.8 million people while the Caribbean has 40.5 million inhabitants (2007). Life expectancies for the mainland are 72.4 years for males and 77.7 years for females, while in the Caribbean they are 68.9 years for males and 74.2 years for females. The mainland's annual population growth rate is 1.3 percent annually; that of the Caribbean is 0.9 percent. Urbanization is high—69.7 percent for the mainland and 64.7 percent for the Caribbean. Increases in urban population, mainly as a result of rural to urban drift, have resulted in overcrowding and slum areas in many places. Mexico City is one of the world's largest cities.

## Agriculture, forestry, and fishing

The economies of Central America are mainly agricultural. Maize, wheat, and rice are the principal cereals. The main livestock on the mainland are cattle, particularly where there are stretches of grassland; in the Caribbean, the main livestock are pigs. Extensive cattle ranches provide beef for export to North America.

Tropical plantation products such as sugarcane, coffee, cocoa, and bananas and other fruit are major export commodities, particularly to North America. Sugar is important in Cuba and Jamaica. Bananas are grown in several countries, such as Guatemala, Honduras, and Belize for export. Coffee is grown in some areas, including Honduras and Nicaragua.

Many of the countries are economically dependent on the USA, which is the principal buyer of their exports. Cuba is the sole exception; since the communist revolution of 1958, Cuba has been selling its sugar to the former Soviet Union (now to Russia). Citrus fruit are also grown in several areas. Coconuts are an important product of the coastal areas around the Caribbean Sea.

## Nations

| | |
|---|---|
| Antigua and Barbuda | PAGE 395 |
| Bahamas | PAGE 392 |
| Barbados | PAGE 398 |
| Belize | PAGE 402 |
| Costa Rica | PAGE 404 |
| Cuba | PAGE 392 |
| Dominica | PAGE 396 |
| Dominican Republic | PAGE 394 |
| El Salvador | PAGE 403 |
| Grenada | PAGE 398 |
| Guatemala | PAGE 401 |
| Haiti | PAGE 394 |
| Honduras | PAGE 402 |
| Jamaica | PAGE 393 |
| Mexico | PAGE 400 |
| Nicaragua | PAGE 404 |
| Panama | PAGE 405 |
| St Kitts and Nevis | PAGE 395 |
| St Lucia | PAGE 397 |
| St Vincent and the Grenadines | PAGE 397 |
| Trinidad and Tobago | PAGE 399 |

## Dependencies & territories

| | |
|---|---|
| Anguilla | PAGE 387 |
| Aruba | PAGE 387 |
| British Virgin Islands | PAGE 388 |
| Cayman Islands | PAGE 388 |
| Guadaloupe | PAGE 389 |
| Martinique | PAGE 390 |
| Montserrat | PAGE 390 |
| Navassa Island | PAGE 390 |
| Netherlands Antilles | PAGE 391 |
| Puerto Rico | PAGE 391 |
| Turks and Caicos Islands | PAGE 391 |
| Virgin Islands of the United States | PAGE 387 |

Coniferous and broad-leaf forests occur on mountain slopes; these have been exploited for timber and firewood. Tropical forests have been logged for valuable hardwoods such as mahogany. Mexico, Cuba, and Guatemala all have forest industries.

Marine resources are abundant around the Caribbean islands, and for many of these nations fishing is a key activity. Belize, for example, relies on lobster and shrimp fishing.

## Industrialization

Several countries have been shifting their economies from agriculture to manufacturing. Mexico is the most industrialized of the Central American countries, producing iron and steel, transport equipment, chemicals, and clothing. Its main export market is the USA. In most countries, manufacturing is either based on locally produced raw materials, such as rum made from sugar or cigars and cigarettes from tobacco in Jamaica, or on other light industry.

Several countries have become tourist destinations, and for some Caribbean countries, with their attractive tropical environments, tourism is a mainstay.

## Languages

Central America was carved up by colonial powers, resulting in the presence of four official languages: Spanish, English, French and Dutch. All the mainland countries, except for Belize, where English is important, are Spanish-speaking.

Cuba, Puerto Rico and the Dominican Republic are Spanish-speaking, although English is also spoken in Puerto Rico. There are several English-speaking Caribbean islands, the largest of which is Jamaica; others are Antigua, the Bahamas, and Barbuda. Martinique is French-speaking, and the tiny Antilles islands are Dutch-speaking.

*A beautifully symmetrical Volcan Concepción appears in the background of this view of Moyogalpa in Nicaragua (above). A stone carving at Tegucigalpa, Honduras (below left), and a lush tropical rainforest in Grenada (below right).*

## Boundary disputes and wars

There have been no major boundary disputes in Central America, except for the Guatemalan claim to the former British Honduras, which is now the independent country of Belize. However, the region has been beset with a variety of insurgencies, often helped by external sources. The USA has several times intervened in the region, invading Grenada in 1983 and Panama in 1989, supporting right-wing opponents of leftist governments in Guatemala and Nicaragua, and imposing economic sanctions on Cuba. The communist revolution in Cuba, and its policy of exporting revolution, had a considerable effect on the region. Cuba received substantial support from the Soviet Union. A leftist guerilla movement succeeded in taking over Nicaragua in 1979 but its government lost office in the 1990 elections. An American Indian revolt took place in 1994 in the Chiapas region of Mexico.

# North America

Canada · · · · · · · · · · 380

United States · · · · · 382
Dependencies · · · · · 387

# Canada

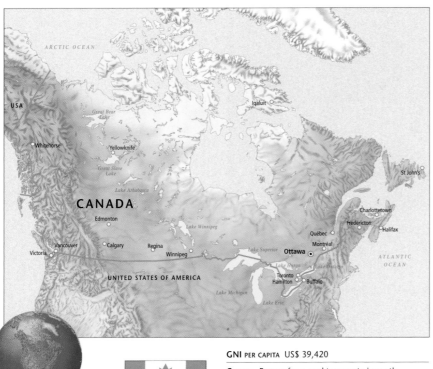

![Flag of Canada]

**GNI PER CAPITA** US$ 39,420

**CLIMATE** Ranges from cool temperate in south to polar in north; long, cold winters; wetter and more temperate on coasts

**HIGHEST POINT** Mt Logan 5,950 m (19,521 ft)

**MAP REFERENCE** Pages 410–11, 412–13, 414–15, 416–17

## Fact File

**OFFICIAL NAME** Canada

**FORM OF GOVERNMENT** Constitutional monarchy with two legislative bodies (Senate and House of Commons)

**CAPITAL** Ottawa

**AREA** 9,984,670 sq km (3,855,085 sq miles)

**TIME ZONE** GMT – 3.5/8 hours

**POPULATION** 33,213,000

**PROJECTED POPULATION 2015** 35,191,000

**POPULATION DENSITY** 3.3 per sq km (8.6 per sq mile)

**LIFE EXPECTANCY** 81.2

**INFANT MORTALITY (PER 1,000)** 5.1

**OFFICIAL LANGUAGES** English, French

**OTHER LANGUAGES** Native American and Eskimo languages

**LITERACY RATE** 99 %

**RELIGIONS** Roman Catholic 42.6 %, Protestant 23.3 %, other Christian 4.4 %, other 13.7 %, none 16 %

**ETHNIC GROUPS** British origin 28 %, French origin 23 %, other European origin 15 %, Native American and Inuit 2 %, other 6 %, mixed background 26 %

**CURRENCY** Canadian dollar

**ECONOMY** Services 69.1 %, industry 28.8 %, agriculture 2.1 %

Canada is the second-largest country in the world, with ninety percent of its population living close to the US border. Its citizens enjoy a standard of living second only to that of the US itself, but the huge scale of Canada's land area, the small, spread out population, and the division between the British and the French have made national unity more difficult to achieve.

Canada was initially populated by Inuit (Eskimo) and First Nation peoples (as indigenous Canadians are called). European settlement began in 1541 after Jacques Cartier's 1534 discovery of the St Lawrence River. Soon, French explorers pushed inland in search of furs and trade. The French were still in a majority when British victory in a war with France, in 1763, gave Britain control of French settlements in Québec. Follow-

ing US independence in 1783, however, many British settlers came north, and this marked the start of the long-resented domination of a French minority by a larger English-speaking population. There have been various Francophone initiatives for the secession of Québec in recent years. A 1995 vote in the province failed by 50.6 to 49.4 percent to settle the matter.

## Physical features and land use

There is much variety among Canada's geographic regions. In the east lie the Atlantic Provinces of New Brunswick, Nova Scotia, Prince Edward Island, and Newfoundland, as well as Québec. The geological foundation of the Atlantic Provinces is ancient worn-down mountains, along with sectors of the still older Canadian Shield. Although farming settlements are common, agriculture in this region has always been marginal (with the exception of such places as the Annapolis Valley in Nova Scotia and Prince Edward Island) and is in decline. Pulp and paper is produced from Québec's coniferous forests and the state is also a major producer of hydropower.

West and south lie the most temperate inland parts of Canada, the St Lawrence-Great Lakes lowlands, including the Ontario Peninsula. This fertile agricultural region reaches west from southern Québec along Lake Ontario and north from Lake Erie. Rural settlement is more dense here than elsewhere and, given the large urban concentrations of Toronto and Montréal, these lowlands are the most heavily populated part of Canada.

The Canadian Shield, or Laurentian Plateau, is an extensive, ancient region floored with some of the world's oldest known rocks. Centered on Hudson Bay, it covers nearly fifty percent of Canadian territory. Except for some low mountains in eastern Québec and Labrador, this is a rolling landscape typified by outcrops of rock and a great amount of surface water in summer. There

| Timeline | 1200 BC Ancestors of today's Inuit spread east and north as far as Arctic Circle | 1497 John Cabot lands near the mouth of the St Lawrence River and claims land for England | 1663 New France made a French colony by Louis XIV; French, English settler rivalry over fur trade; native population c. 200,000 | 1791 British divide Canada into Upper and Lower Canada; French mainly in Lower Canada, along lower St Lawrence |
|---|---|---|---|---|
| 35,000–12,000 BP Humans migrate to North American continent from Asia via land bridge across Bering Strait | 5000 BP Communities in east survive by trapping caribou and bears and fishing; use fur clothing and build wood and skin kayaks | AD 1100 Inuit meet Vikings in Greenland; as a result, more than one-third of Inuit die of such diseases as smallpox and measles | 1534 Jacques Cartier sails up St Lawrence River to site of present-day Montréal | 1670 Hudson's Bay Company established in London |

are hundreds of thousands of water bodies, ranging in size from gigantic to tiny, connected by thousands of rivers and streams. The shield's southern half is covered by boreal forest, whereas the northern half (including the islands of the Canadian Arctic Archipelago) is beyond the tree line and has a cover of rock, ice, and ground-hugging tundra. The Arctic Archipelago islands range from high mountains in the east to low plains in the west.

West of the Canadian Shield lie the central plains. The southern portion of the "Prairie Provinces"—Saskatchewan, Manitoba, and Alberta—has a natural vegetation of prairie grasses. The northern part is forested. In the prairies the mechanization of wheat farming long ago reduced the need for rural labor, and population densities are low.

The Canadian Cordillera, reaching from the northern Yukon to southern British Columbia and southwest Alberta, dominates western Canada, and contains a number of national parks including Yoho, Banff, Jasper, and Kootenay. On the Pacific side the Coast Mountains run south through British Columbia, the coastline deeply embayed by fjords. Off the coast lies Vancouver Island, the peak of another mountain range, now cut off by the sea.

## People and culture

With its major British and French components, its other Europeans who are largely from eastern

and southern Europe, its Asians, and its indigenous First Nations, Métis, and Inuit, Canada is home to many peoples. Most now live in urban settings but this is quite a new development. At confederation in 1867, when Britain granted home rule, eighty percent of the population was rural, and only Montréal had more than 100,000 people. It was not until after the Second World War that rural and urban populations became about equal in size. The war years stimulated the economy, industrialization was rapid, people moved into the cities to work in factories, and Canada emerged from the conflict with a powerful industrial base. It was at this time that British influence began to decline and the USA became of increasing economic and cultural importance in Canadian life.

In the past thirty years Canada's ethnic mix has changed significantly, resulting from a move toward a less restrictive immigration policy that welcomes people with money and skills. Under this policy many Asians have come to settle. The government defines Canada as a "community of communities" within which each ethnic group is encouraged to maintain its own culture. While generally welcomed, these liberalization measures have also produced problems. Since the Supreme Court recognized "aboriginal title", First Nations land claims have been or are being negotiated with the governments concerned where prior treaties did not exist, and in some cases demands are being made for revision of existing treaties. Canada's most intractable political problem, however, remains the unsatisfied demand of many Québécois for autonomy.

## Economy and resources

Canada's resource base includes nickel (Sudbury, Ontario usually provides some twenty percent of the western world's supply), and Canada is also a world leader in the output of zinc, potash, uranium, sulphur, asbestos, aluminum and copper.

*Bow Lake in Banff National Park in the Canadian Rockies (left). Ottawa, on the banks of the Ottawa River (top left). Niagara Falls, from the Canadian side (top right).*

Alberta produces more than 75 percent of the nation's oil and is an important source of natural gas and coal. Hydroelectric power has led to the expansion of pulp and paper industries. Canada is one of the world's leading exporters of wood products.

Agriculture is an important activity, but it only employs around two percent of the labor force. Grain, dairying, fruit, and ranching all flourish. In addition to pigs and sheep, Canadian ranches support about 13 million head of cattle. Fruit-growing is found in British Columbia's irrigated southern plateau and the Fraser River delta. In addition to wheat other export crops include feed grains, oilseeds, apples, potatoes, and maple syrup.

The country's high taxes, regulatory structures, and low productivity have, however, led to on-going problems. Starting the 1990s in recession, Canada's real rates of growth have averaged only one percent through much of the decade. A traditional commitment to high public service and welfare spending is proving hard to maintain. The current account deficit and national debt have led to the slashing of federal transfers to the provinces in the areas of health, education, and welfare. The continuing debate over Québec's future, and the possibility of a split in the confederation, also dampens investor confidence.

### PROVINCES

**Alberta** • Edmonton
**British Columbia** • Victoria
**Manitoba** • Winnipeg
**New Brunswick** • Fredericton
**Newfoundland** • St. John's
**Nova Scotia** • Halifax
**Ontario** • Toronto
**Prince Edward Island** • Charlottetown
**Québec** • Québec
**Saskatchewan** • Regina

### TERRITORIES

**Northwest Territories** • Yellowknife
**Nunavut** • Iqaluit
**Yukon Territory** • Whitehorse

| | | | | | | | |
|---|---|---|---|---|---|---|---|
| **29** Welland nal links Lakes and Ontario, wing ships void gara Falls | **1870** Dominion of Canada acquires the North West Territory from the Hudson's Bay Company | **1905** Saskatchewan and Alberta become provinces; Canada's population grows with European immigrants settling western prairies | **1930s** Depression hits; new national bodies set up including Bank of Canada (1934) and Canadian Wheat Board (1935) | **1945–55** Postwar migration from Europe boosts Canada's population by more than 1 million | **1959** Completion of St Lawrence Seaway creates waterway from Lake Superior to Atlantic of 3,767 km (2,340 miles) | **1960** Demands for French-Canadian rights grow both peacefully and in form of terrorist attacks on public buildings | **1988** Canada and USA sign free trade agreement ending wrangling over foreign investment, banking, and agriculture | **1995** A referendum on the independence of Quebec results in a narrow rejection of secession from Canada (50.6 % to 49.4 %) |
| **7** Britain creates nion of Canada, nging together New Brunswick, Scotia, Ontario, and Québec | **1871** British Columbia becomes sixth province; Prince Edward Island later made the seventh (1873) | **1898** Yukon Territory added to Canada's official land area | **1914** Canada fights alongside Britain and Allies against Germany in First World War | **1939–45** More than 1 million Canadian troops aid Allies on European and Pacific fronts in Second World War | **1949** Newfoundland becomes tenth province; Canada joins North Atlantic Treaty Organization (NATO) | **1982** Constitution Act, signed by Queen Elizabeth II, grants Canada sole power to amend its constitution | **1993** Parliament grants Inuit people (numbering around 30,000) self-governing homeland, Nunavut, effective 1 April 1999 | **1999** Establishment of the Nunavut territory (formerly North West Territory) with its own regional government run by Eskimos |

# United States of America (USA)

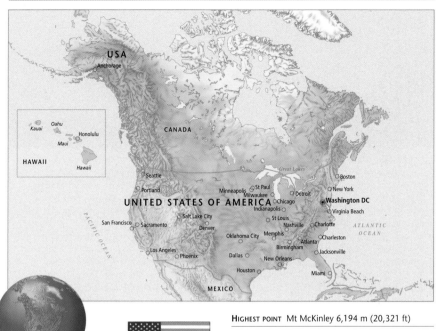

## Fact File

**OFFICIAL NAME** United States of America

**FORM OF GOVERNMENT** Federal republic with two legislative bodies (Senate and House of Representatives)

**CAPITAL** Washington DC

**AREA** 9,631,418 sq km (3,718,694 sq miles)

**TIME ZONE** GMT – 5/11 hours

**POPULATION** 303,825,000

**PROJECTED POPULATION 2015** 329,010,000

**POPULATION DENSITY** 31.5 per sq km (81.7 per sq mile)

**LIFE EXPECTANCY** 78.1

**INFANT MORTALITY (PER 1,000)** 6.3

**OFFICIAL LANGUAGE** English

**OTHER LANGUAGES** Spanish, German, French, Italian, Chinese, indigenous languages

**LITERACY RATE** 99 %

**RELIGIONS** Protestant 52 %, Roman Catholic 24 %, Mormon 2 %, Jewish 1 %, other 10 %, none 10 %

**ETHNIC GROUPS** European 81.7 %, African 12.9 %, Asian 4.2 %, Native American 1.2 %

**CURRENCY** US dollar

**ECONOMY** Services 78.5 %, industry 20.6 %, agriculture 0.9 %

**GNI PER CAPITA** US$ 46,040

**CLIMATE** Varied: eastern states are temperate, with warm summers and snowy winters in north and subtropical conditions in south; southwest is arid and semiarid; west coast is temperate but warmer in California and wetter in the Pacific Northwest; Hawaii is mainly tropical; Alaska is mainly polar but cooler and wetter on south coast

**HIGHEST POINT** Mt McKinley 6,194 m (20,321 ft)

**MAP REFERENCE** Pages 418–19, 420–21, 422–23, 424–25, 426

In the United States of America a variety of peoples, united by a shared belief in social and economic freedom, have built the most prosperous and powerful nation on earth. Abundant resources, a climate and soils ensuring plentiful food supplies, and an open society rewarding individual energy and initiative were all advantages from the beginning. In addition, huge oceans on both eastern and western coasts isolated America from the troubles of Europe and Asia, and its relations with Mexico to the south and Canada to the north were generally benign. Starting with these favorable conditions, and guided by the ideals of democracy and freedom, the United States of America—in this respect unique among nations—successfully invented itself according to its own political and social ideals.

The most serious danger to its existence was self-inflicted. From 1861 to 1865 the US was wracked by a civil war in which the implications of universal human liberty were played out in a struggle between slave-owners in the south of the country and slave-liberators in the north, but the nation survived. Later, in the face of widespread domestic opposition, the US entered the First World War in 1917, its military strength leading to Germany's defeat. Even more decisive was its role in the Second World War between 1941 and 1945, in alliance with Great Britain and the Soviet Union, when its industrial power and military might ensured victory over both Germany and Japan. After 1945, challenged for superpower supremacy by the Soviets, it engaged in a protracted trial of strength known as the Cold War. This ended in 1989 with the collapse of the USSR and its communist allies, leaving the United States politically and economically stronger than ever before.

The economy, already the most powerful, diverse, and technologically advanced in the world, continues to grow. But US prosperity is combined with a variety of problems: drug addiction, crime, long-term unemployment for some sectors of the population, racial tensions, a very low interest in politics and consequently very low voting rates, air and water pollution in some areas from automotive and industrial wastes, traffic congestion approaching "gridlock" in major cities, and rising medical costs. All these side effects appear to be the price of modernity on the American model. It is a price that most other developed countries have been prepared to pay, however, in order to establish high-tech, high-energy industrial societies.

### Physical features and land use

Mainland United States can be divided into three major physical regions. The eastern part consists of the range of the Appalachian Mountains and the coastal plain that runs along the Atlantic Ocean. The broad basin of the Mississippi and Missouri Rivers comprises the central section. The western region is composed of mountain ranges, desert landscapes, and the land along the Pacific coast. In addition, there are two outlying sections of the country—Alaska and Hawaii.

In eastern North America the Appalachians, a band of sedimentary mountains and plateaus which are still widely forested, extend from northern Alabama to the Gulf of St Lawrence. They consist of a number of parallel ranges,

including the Blue Ridge Mountains in Virginia and the Great Smoky Mountains along the North Carolina-Tennessee border. For a long time these ranges constituted a barrier to inland settlement. In New York State the valley of the Mohawk River divides the mountains of the Appalachians from the Adirondacks, which are a southern extension of the ancient granite mass of the Canadian Shield. Traveling up this valley, from east to west, the early settlers were able to find a way through the range that led on to the land bordering the Great Lakes and the Ohio country beyond.

The original vegetation on these mountains was broadleaf deciduous forest of oak, ash, beech, and maple grading into yellow birch, hemlock, and pine towards the north. During the eighteenth and nineteenth centuries much of this forest area was cleared for farming, but declining agriculture in New England and the abandonment of farmland has brought widespread regeneration of tree growth. Flying across eastern America, much of the landscape still gives the impression of continuous woodland.

The coastal plain to the southeast through the Carolinas and Georgia is generally low-lying, and includes many areas of swamp. Nearly 1,700 km (more than 1,000 miles) of barrier islands and sandbars run parallel to the shore and are popular seaside resort areas for the inland population, despite being exposed to occasional hurricanes.

To the west of the Appalachian Range lies the enormous continental drainage basin of the Mississippi-Missouri river system. This basin is about 2,500 km (1,500 miles) wide, extending south from the Canadian border to the Gulf of Mexico. At its northern limit there are the hills along Lake Superior, a vestige of the Canadian Shield. What are called the Central Lowlands of this drainage basin are bounded on the east by the low plateaus of Kentucky and Tennessee. To the west of the Mississippi lie vast areas planted in wheat, and eventually grasslands, as the Great Plains reach 1,500 km (900 miles) across to the foothills of the Rocky Mountains.

Once the home of such tribes as the Mandan, the Omaha, and the Kansa Indians (settled farmers near the Missouri River), and the nomadic Blackfoot, Crow, and Arapaho further west, most of the plains had been taken by incoming ranchers and farmers by the end of the nineteenth century. Former range land was planted in wheat and maize. These crops were hugely productive at first, but overcropping and dry years led to severe soil deterioration in the first decades of the twentieth century. This reached a climax in the disasters of the 1930s, when a large part of the region became a "dustbowl." Although diversification of grain crops, contour plowing, and widespread irrigation have helped to restore agricultural productivity, some areas are still highly sensitive to climatic variation, especially where the original terrain was semidesert. Combined with fluctuations in grain prices, agriculture remains a risky business in a region where much of the land is marginal.

The mountain ranges of the western Cordillera, as it extends south from Canada, are divided by a number of high plateaus and deep valleys. There are two main systems, to the west and the east. The northern and central Rocky Mountains are the eastern arm facing out across the Great Plains, with the Grand Tetons forming spectacular ridges in Wyoming. The southern Rockies of Colorado and New Mexico—the remains of an ancient granite plateau—are also weathered into a series of striking peaks. In Colorado there are more than 1,000 mountains of 3,000 m (10,000 ft) or more. As with the mountains on the east of the continent, the Rockies were a major obstacle for westward-heading settlers. One major route lay through the Wyoming Basin, a rangeland where bison once grazed, and where yesterday's pioneer trails have become interstate highways.

On the lower slopes of the Rockies grow a mixture of piñon pines and juniper scrub, with ponderosa pine, spruce, and fir at higher altitudes. Wildlife includes elk, deer, moose, mountain sheep, bear, and a variety of smaller animals. National parks such as Yellowstone

and Grand Teton provide an opportunity to see these animals in dramatic natural settings, and draw millions of visitors to the region every year.

High plateaus, rocky ranges, and desert basins extend westward across the states of Utah, Arizona, and Nevada, seamed in many places by vast, abrupt canyons, of which the Grand Canyon of the Colorado River is the most spectacular. On the Pacific side of these plateaus is the western branch of the cordillera. This forms a chain of mountains consisting of the Sierra Nevada in the south and the Cascade Range to the north. Stretching from Washington through Oregon to Lassen Peak in California (3,187 m; 10,456 ft), the Cascades include several large volcanoes, including Mt Saint Helens which erupted violently in 1980. The Sierra Nevada faces out over the fertile Central Valley of California, with its fruit and vegetable growing, viticulture, cotton, other crops, and livestock. In the early days long dry summers made farming difficult in the Central Valley. Meltwater from the snows of the Sierra Nevada, much of it diverted in lengthy canals, now provides summer irrigation.

Beyond the Central Valley on its western side rise the comparatively low Coast Ranges, running parallel to the Pacific shore all the way from the Mexican border to Canada. Together, the Coast Ranges, the Cascades, and the Sierra Nevada all serve to keep precipitation away from the interior plateaus and create its arid landscape. East of the Cascade Range in the Pacific Northwest lies the Columbia Basin. Here, the meltwaters of

*A desert landscape in Arches National Park, Utah (left page). Fall colors in northern Maine (left). Juneau, in Alaska, lies on the Inside Passage, a marine waterway that runs through the vast Tongass National Forest (above).*

ancient glaciers have cut deep gorges in the land. In western Washington the most spectacular trees consist of Douglas fir, western hemlock, and Sitka spruce, some almost as tall as the giant redwoods of northern California. The wealth of the United States' Northwest was originally based on timber from the huge conifers that covered the Cascade Range.

The two non-contiguous parts of the United States have very different physical landscapes. The expansive state of Alaska is a mixture of massive glaciated mountains and broad river valleys, with a vegetation cover that varies from dense forest to sparse tundra. For much of the year large areas of Alaska are covered in snow. The Hawaiian islands mostly consist of the tops of prominent volcanoes which protrude above the sea, with a host of distinctive plants nurtured by the tropical climate.

### History and settlement

The first peoples to settle North America probably crossed from Siberia to Alaska during the ice ages between 10,000 and 30,000 years ago. It is thought they became the ancestors of the many Indian tribes living in North America when the first Europeans arrived. Their cultures and languages varied widely, from the Iroquois who lived in bark lodges in the east, to the cliff-dwelling Pueblo peoples of the Southwest, to the salmon-fishing and whale-hunting Indians of Washington State and British Columbia on the Northwest coast who lived in large timber houses. Plains Indians such as the Sioux or the Comanche are sometimes depicted hunting bison on horseback, but this was only possible after horses had been introduced by incoming European traders and settlers from the fifteenth century onward.

The oldest authenticated European settlement in North America was made by Norse Vikings at the northern tip of the island of Newfoundland about AD 1000, but it was occupied for only a short time. The first successful English settlement was at Jamestown, Virginia, in 1607. Not long after this a party of religious dissenters, the so-called Pilgrim Fathers, arrived in 1620 to found the first of the New England colonies at Plymouth. Joined by other migrants later, this became part of the large Massachusetts Bay colony.

A Dutch colony on Manhattan Island that was founded in 1624 was captured by the British in 1664, who changed its name from Nieuw Amsterdam to New York. The Quaker William Penn founded one of the more successful of the early English colonies in 1682. Part of Pennsylvania later split off to become Delaware; North and South Carolina were established in 1663; Georgia, which was originally designed as a philanthropic alternative to a debtor's prison, in 1732. The defeat of the French, which ended the Seven Years War in 1763, brought huge territorial accessions to England: all of France's Canadian territories, the land west of the Mississippi River, plus Louisiana and Florida. The settlers throughout these areas became directly subject to the British Crown, and when London sought to recoup the huge expenses of the war (about £ 101,500,500) by imposing taxes, the cry of "No taxation without representation" was raised in Boston, and resistance to England began. When the American War of Independence broke out in 1776 George Washington commanded the rebel troops, and when it was won and the first elections were held in 1788 he became the inaugural president. In the aftermath, tens of thousands of British "loyalists" decided to leave and moved north to Canada.

The British government had forbidden westward expansion beyond the mountains of the Appalachians. After independence, however, this took place with a rush. Indian tribes were quickly dispossessed from the area and exiled, their land taken for farms, and throughout the nineteenth century there was a series of wars in the region to crush resistance. The last armed Indian defiance was crushed with the Ghost Dance Uprising of 1890.

But by far the most serious crisis for the new nation was the American Civil War of 1861 to 1865. This was both a clash of ideals (liberty versus servitude) and of ways of life (the industrializing, modern north versus the more traditionla, agrarian south). Led by the eloquent commonsense of Abraham Lincoln, the northern forces of the Union defeated the southern armies of the Confederacy, but the legacy of bitterness lasted for many decades and is still palpable at times in the South.

Meanwhile, westward expansion proceeded apace. Pioneers followed trails explored by men such as Meriwether Lewis and William Clark. Railroads spanned the continent, coal and iron were discovered and used, and new cities such as Pittsburgh and Chicago grew up in the interior. European migrants pouring in through the ports of Boston, Philadelphia, and New York substantially changed the nation's ethnic composition. Manufacturing cities, which were big markets in their own right, developed along the shores of the Great Lakes, while the mechanized farming of the Midwestern "corn belt" turned it into the granary of much of the Western world.

The history of California differed from that of the rest of the country in many ways, in that it was a part of Spanish conquest rather than of English settlement. The small, semi-nomadic hunting and seed-gathering Indian cultures of the area were little affected by the northward spread of Spanish forts and missions from New Spain (Mexico) in the 1760s. But by the middle of the nineteenth century pressures from land-hungry pioneers moving in from the eastern states were irresistible: by the end of the century the whole of the Southwest, including Texas, had been either ceded, purchased, or annexed. Since then the Pacific Coast economy has passed through various stages, from gold-prospecting and lumbering, through agriculture and the expansion of the aircraft industry after the Second World War, to the highest of high-tech today in Silicon Valley south of San Francisco Bay.

Once independence was established by the beginning of the nineteenth century, the United

### Timeline

| 3500 BC Native Americans hunt bison; by 2500 BC squash, goosefoot, and sunflowers (seeds used as winter food) cultivated | 300 BC Hohokam, Mogollon, and Anasazi people inhabit the South and Southwest; Anasazi build villages at Chaco, New Mexico | AD 700 Start of Pueblo period in southwest; Native Americans of Hopi, Zuni, and other tribes live in villages built mainly of adobe | 1492 Columbus reaches America while searching for route to Orient; later, French and English establish fur trading posts in Canada | 1584 Sir Walter Raleigh claims Virginia for England, but no permanent settlement created until founding of Jamestown in 1607 |
|---|---|---|---|---|

| 35,000–12,000 BP Modern humans *Homo sapiens sapiens* migrate to North America across Bering Strait land bridge and spread south | 13,000 BP Settlements appear from south of Canadian border to Mexico; stone spearpoints in use in New Mexico | 1000 BC The Adena in eastern North America build ceremonial mounds; agriculture established in Southwest | 200 BC Hopewell culture takes over from Adena; Hopewell become first farmers in eastern North America (until AD 500) | 790 Vikings explore coasts of Europe and North America for the next 100 years, forming settlements in Greenland and Iceland | 1539 Hernando de Soto reaches Florida and travels up the Mississippi; following year Coronado explores Southwest | 1619 First slaves shipped from West Africa to USA |
|---|---|---|---|---|---|---|

States kept Europe at arm's length, and the Monroe Doctrine warned Europe that the representatives of the old empires—Spanish, Portuguese, and British—were not to intervene in the Americas any more. Isolationism was the other side of this doctrine: the US had no wish to be entangled in Europe's troubles. But as the US developed into a major global power this disengagement was no longer possible. In two world wars in the twentieth century American military intervention was decisive, and with the onset of the Cold War, designed to contain the Soviet Union after 1945, it was prepared to intervene wherever it saw the need. However, subsequent action in Korea from 1950 to 1953, and in Vietnam from 1964 to 1975, both with heavy loss of US lives, has made the nation less enthusiastic about overseas military commitments and the risks and casualties of policing trouble-spots (Haiti, Somalia, the Persian Gulf) are often unpopular at home. Generally the American mood is inward-looking, more concerned with domestic than with foreign affairs. This, however, changed dramatically after the terrorist attacks on the World Trade Center in New York City and the Pentagon in Washington D.C. on 11 September 2001. Since then the government has pursued the strategy of actively reshaping the world, especially the Middle East, according to American ideals, interests and security concerns. As

*Rugged country in Great Basin National Park in Nevada (left page). One of California's numerous vineyards (above). The famous Empire State Building in New York City (far right). Undulating farming country in Idaho (below).*

much opposition as this line of politics encountered in the rest of the world, large parts of the US population supported it, at least until after the toppling of Saddam Hussein's regime in Iraq, which was seen as a threat to stability in the Arab world as well as one of the main supporters of terrorist bands.

## People and culture

The United States is a prosperous, industrial, capitalistic democracy, in which anyone with training and skills who is prepared to assimilate can usually find a place. It is the most open multicultural society on earth, which is the main reason why so many people from other countries want to live there. To keep this in

check immense efforts are made to secure the long borders and other entry points into the country such as airports and ports. In addition to tremendous numbers of legal immigrants (the United States still has the highest legal immigration level of any country in the world) illegal entry is estimated to bring in up to 1 million people per year.

The descendants of the original Native American inhabitants are a small but not insignificant element of the population. People arriving from overseas were at first mainly English, and with those of Scottish and Irish descent dominated all other arrivals from the other side of the Atlantic until the middle of the nineteenth

| | | | | | | | |
|---|---|---|---|---|---|---|---|
| **1804** Lewis and Clark explore the Missouri River then cross Rocky Mts and reach the Pacific near mouth of Columbia River | **1848** California gold rush. Within two years 90,000 people from San Francisco, the East, and overseas travel to diggings | **1869** World's first transcontinental railroad is completed when the Union Pacific line and Central Pacific lines link up | **1917** USA enters First World War on the side of the Allies | **1929** Wall Street Crash ruins many investors and affects industry and farming; millions lose jobs in Depression | **1941** USA joins Allies in Second World War after Japan bombs Pearl Harbor; war ends 1945 after USA drops atomic bombs on Japan | **1992** Hurricane Andrew strikes Florida and Louisiana causing $25 billion damage and the loss of more than 50 lives | **2005** Hurricane Katrina causes massive destruction in Louisiana, Mississipi and Alabama and leads to the total evacuation of New Orleans |
| **1776** USA founded, with American colonies adopting Declaration of Independence. Population 3 million | **1805** The Louisiana Purchase acquires a large area of South from France, almost doubling the land area of the USA | **1861–65** Civil War between southern (Confederate) and northern (Union) states; all slaves freed in Confederate states | **1908** Ford launches Model T, a mass market automobile. It transforms US industry and economy; 15.5 million sold in 19 years | **1920** More Americans now living in industrial cities than on the land; women are given the vote in all elections | **1936** Boulder Dam on Colorado River completed impounding Lake Mead; renamed Hoover Dam (1947) | **1969** Apollo 11 mission opens a new chapter in space exploration by landing three astronauts on Moon | **2001** On 11 September Arab terrorists fly three airplanes into the World Trade Center in New York and the Pentagon |

producer of meat, dairy foods, soy beans, maize, oats, wheat, barley, cotton, sugar, and forest products.

Despite twenty years of strong competition from Japan, China and other Asian economies, and increasingly also from India, the giant United States economy remained resurgent throughout the 1990s. One reason for its success may be the greater flexibility of US capitalist enterprise when compared with either Asia or Western Europe. A labor market which is flexible and responsive to changing demands is another factor, and over the last few decades there has been a huge shift in employment from manufacturing to services. The US unemployment rate remains one of the lowest in all the major industrialized states.

But the main reason for the health of the economy is probably its dynamic technological inventiveness. In every field, US firms are at or near the frontier of technological advance. This is especially true in computers, medical equipment, and aerospace. The advantages of this onrush of technology are obvious. But there are major social costs as well. What is called a two-tier labor market has evolved in which those at the bottom lack enough skills and education to compete, failing to get pay rises, health insurance coverage, and other benefits which are strongly tied to full-time employment.

The United States faces a host of unsolved economic problems, which have come to the forefront of national debate in large part due to the massive economic crisis of 2008/2009. These include low rates of savings and inadequate oversight of many aspects of the economy, insufficient investment in infrastructure, soaring health care costs, large budget and trade deficits, as well as the stagnation of income, particularly for the weakest socio-economic groups.

century. During this period the only other major ethnic group to arrive were African slaves imported to work the plantations in the South. After the Civil War, however, mass immigration was encouraged, and a flood of migrants arrived from Italy, Scandinavia, Germany, the Balkans, and various troubled parts of Eastern Europe, including Russia. Many were Jews fleeing poverty and pogroms. In the sixty years between 1860 and 1920, 30 million people arrived, radically changing the ethnic composition of the country. Although there were national concentrations in specific neighborhoods (such as Little Italy in New York City) the ideal of assimilation ensured that by the middle of the twentieth century most of the new arrivals, or their children, had come to share the benefits of other citizens. More recently there has been an influx of Japanese, Chinese, Filipinos, Cubans, Vienamese, Koreans, and large numbers of Mexicans and Central Americans. In some places, Puerto Rican, Cuban, and Mexican groups provide a strongly Hispanic cultural orientation.

One group of long-term residents did not enjoy full participation in American life. These were the African-Americans descended from the slaves, who became increasingly concentrated in the cities. Long after the Civil War, deeply entrenched systematic discrimination barred them from jobs, and from equal access to housing, commercial premises, public facilities, and education—even forcing them to sit at the back of the bus in the old slave states. As a result of agitation and affirmative action, the second half of the twentieth century saw the legal rights of African-Americans secured. What remains, however, are inequalities which law alone seems unable to resolve. Although massive disparities continue to exist, and in urban areas African Americans are often part of a pervasive lower class, the 2008 election of the first black president, Barack Obama, is a cause for hope, not least for social transformation.

## Economy and resources

The US economy is the largest among the industrial nations, possessing an invaluable combination of skilled and unskilled labor and natural resources. Internationally, it is the most powerful, diverse, and scientifically advanced country. With the early application of research and technology, agriculture developed into a highly mechanized industry for food production and processing, with a distinct zonal pattern across the country. Dairy farming predominates in a broad belt from New England to Minnesota. Further west, where the climate is drier, wheat is grown. The corn (maize) belt, highly productive land which was once prairie and forest, consists of the maize-growing eastern and central states from Ohio to Nebraska. Maize is mainly used for feeding to cattle and pigs. In the warmer southern states where cotton and tobacco were once grown on plantations—the old "cotton belt"—a variety of other crops are now cultivated as well, from vegetables to fruit and peanuts. There has been a strong tendency for farming to move from small to large-scale operations and from labor-intensive to mechanized methods. Although agriculture's share of gross domestic product is only one percent, the US remains a leading

## STATES

| | |
|---|---|
| Alabama • Montgomery | Minnesota • St Paul |
| Alaska • Juneau | Mississippi • Jackson |
| Arizona • Phoenix | Missouri • Jefferson City |
| Arkansas • Little Rock | Montana • Helena |
| California • Sacramento | Nebraska • Lincoln |
| Colorado • Denver | Nevada • Carson City |
| Connecticut • Hartford | New Hampshire • Concord |
| Delaware • Dover | New Jersey • Trenton |
| District of Columbia • | New Mexico • Santa Fe |
| Washington DC | New York • Albany |
| Florida • Tallahassee | North Carolina • Raleigh |
| Georgia • Atlanta | North Dakota • Bismarck |
| Hawaii • Honolulu | Ohio • Columbus |
| Idaho • Boise | Oklahoma • Oklahoma City |
| Illinois • Springfield | |
| Indiana • Indianapolis | |
| Iowa • Des Moines | |
| Kansas • Topeka | |
| Kentucky • Frankfort | |
| Louisiana • Baton Rouge | |
| Maine • Augusta | |
| Maryland • Annapolis | |
| Massachusetts • Boston | |
| Michigan • Lansing | |

| |
|---|
| Oregon • Salem |
| Pennsylvania • Harrisburg |
| Rhode Island • Providence |
| South Carolina • Columbia |
| South Dakota • Pierre |
| Tennessee • Nashville |
| Texas • Austin |
| Utah • Salt Lake City |
| Vermont • Montpelier |
| Virginia • Richmond |
| Washington • Olympia |
| West Virginia • Charleston |
| Wisconsin • Madison |
| Wyoming • Cheyenne |

## OVERSEAS TERRITORIES

| | |
|---|---|
| American Samoa | Navassa Island |
| Baker and Howland Islands | Northern Mariana Islands |
| Guam | Palmyra Atoll |
| Jarvis Island | Puerto Rico |
| Johnston Atoll | Virgin Islands of the |
| Kingman Reef | United States |
| Midway Islands | Wake Island |

# Dependencies and territories

## Virgin Islands of the United States

### Fact File

OFFICIAL NAME  Virgin Islands of the United States

FORM OF GOVERNMENT  Unincorporated territory of the United States

CAPITAL  Charlotte Amalie

AREA  352 sq km (136 sq miles)

TIME ZONE  GMT + 7 hours

POPULATION  108,200

LIFE EXPECTANCY  79.3

INFANT MORTALITY (PER 1,000)  7.5

LITERACY RATE  90–95 %

CURRENCY  US dollar

ECONOMY  Services 80 %, industry 19 %, agriculture 1 %

CLIMATE  Subtropical; wet season May to November

MAP REFERENCE  Page 427

The US Virgin Islands consist of 68 hilly volcanic islands east of Puerto Rico in the Caribbean. They are on a key shipping lane and were bought from Denmark by the USA in 1917 to protect the approaches to the Panama Canal. They contain one of the world's largest oil refineries on St Croix, but tourism—with 2.6 million visitors in 2005—is still the main economic activity, accounting for over eighty percent of the island's gross domestic product and eighty percent of employment. Manufacturing includes textiles, pharmaceuticals, electronics, and watch assembly. Business and financial services are also of growing importance. Agriculture is limited, and most food has to be imported. The islands are vulnerable to substantial damage from storms.

*Navajo Indians in Monument Valley, Arizona (left page). Islands of the Great Sound in Bermuda (below).*

## Anguilla

### Fact File

OFFICIAL NAME  Anguilla

FORM OF GOVERNMENT  Overseas territory of the United Kingdom

CAPITAL  The Valley

AREA  102 sq km (39 sq miles)

TIME ZONE  GMT – 4 hours

POPULATION  14,100

LIFE EXPECTANCY  80.5

INFANT MORTALITY (PER 1,000)  3.5

LITERACY RATE  95 %

CURRENCY  East Caribbean dollar

ECONOMY  Services 78 %, industry 18 %, agriculture 4 %

CLIMATE  Tropical, moderated by trade winds

MAP REFERENCE  Page 427

Anguilla's name comes from the Spanish *anguil* meaning "eel". The country is a long, thin, scrub-covered coral atoll in the Caribbean, north of St Kitts and Nevis. First colonized by Britain in 1690, its status as a UK dependent territory was formalized in 1980. While the governor is a crown appointee, a local assembly manages internal matters.

Anguilla has few natural resources and depends heavily on tourism, offshore banking, lobster fishing, and overseas remittances. Drawn by a subtropical climate tempered by trade winds, tourists have multiplied in recent years, reflecting the generally healthy economic conditions in both the USA and the UK. As a result, annual growth has averaged about seven percent, and in 2008 currently stands at ten percent. The offshore finance sector was strengthened by comprehensive legislation enacted in 1994.

## Aruba

### Fact File

OFFICIAL NAME  Aruba

FORM OF GOVERNMENT  Self-governing part of the Kingdom of the Netherlands

CAPITAL  Oranjestad

AREA  193 sq km (74 sq miles)

TIME ZONE  GMT – 4 hours

POPULATION  101,500

LIFE EXPECTANCY  75.1

INFANT MORTALITY (PER 1,000)  14.3

LITERACY RATE  97.3 %

CURRENCY  Aruban florin

ECONOMY  Services 66.3 %, industry 33.3 %, agriculture 0.4 %

CLIMATE  Tropical

MAP REFERENCE  Page 427

Aruba is most unusual among the islands of the Caribbean in that it experiences only a brief low season, and hotel occupancy in 2004 averaged 80 percent, compared to 68 percent throughout the rest of the Caribbean. A flat, limestone island lying off the Venezuelan coast at the mouth of the Gulf of Venezuela, Aruba is barren on its eastern side and more lush on the west. It was once a part of the Netherlands Antilles, but since 1980 has been a separate but autonomous part of the Dutch realm. The population is mainly of African, European, and Asian descent. Closed in 1985, the oil refinery on the island was reopened in 1993. This is a major source of employment and foreign exchange earnings and has greatly spurred economic growth. Tourism is extensive on the western side of the island, which is known as the Turquoise Coast, and its rapid development has led to an expansion of other activities.

## Bermuda

### Fact File

OFFICIAL NAME  Bermuda

FORM OF GOVERNMENT  Overseas territory of the United Kingdom

CAPITAL  Hamilton

AREA  53 sq km (20 sq miles)

North and Central America

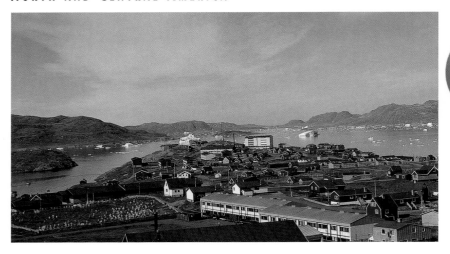

TIME ZONE  GMT – 4 hours

POPULATION  66,500

LIFE EXPECTANCY  78.3

INFANT MORTALITY (PER 1,000)  7.9

LITERACY RATE  98 %

CURRENCY  Bermudian dollar

ECONOMY  Services 89 %, industry 10 %, agriculture 1 %

CLIMATE  Subtropical; windy in winter

**B**ermuda is an island in the Atlantic Ocean 900 km (560 miles) off the coast of South Carolina, USA. It has one of the highest per capita incomes in the world, as its balmy location and lush vegetation draw tourists and its financial services offer tax-haven advantages. Bermuda also has one of the world's biggest flag-of-convenience fleets. The largest of some 360 low-lying coral islands which have grown atop ancient submarine volcanoes, it was discovered by the Spaniard Juan Bermudez in 1503, was later taken over by the British, and has a tradition of self-government going back to its first parliament in 1620. Its people are mainly descendants of former African slaves or British or Portuguese settlers. A move for full independence was rejected by 73 percent of voters in 1995, partly for fear of scaring away foreign business. With ninety percent of tourists coming from the US, links with that country are strong.

## British Virgin Islands

### Fact File

OFFICIAL NAME  British Virgin Islands

FORM OF GOVERNMENT  Overseas territory of the United Kingdom

CAPITAL  Road Town

AREA  153 sq km (59 sq miles)

TIME ZONE  GMT – 4 hours

POPULATION  24,000

LIFE EXPECTANCY  77.1

INFANT MORTALITY (PER 1,000)  15.5

LITERACY RATE  97.8 %

CURRENCY  US dollar

ECONOMY  Services 92 %, industry 6 %, agriculture 2 %

CLIMATE  Subtropical, moderated by trade winds

MAP REFERENCE  Page 427

**E**ast of Puerto Rico in the Caribbean, the British Virgin Islands are the northernmost of the Lesser Antilles. There are four low-lying islands—Tortola, Anegada, Virgin Gorda, and Jost Van Dyke—and 36 coral islets and cays. Most are the peaks of a submerged mountain chain, and they share a subtropical climate moderated by trade winds. With the exception of Anegada, which is flat, the landscape is hilly, with sandy beaches and coral reefs around the coasts. Visited by Columbus in 1493, the British Virgin Islands were for 200 years pirate bases used by the English and the Dutch, until Tortola was annexed by the British in 1672. Today, they are a British dependency enjoying a large measure of self-government, and highly dependent on the tourism which produces some 45 percent of national income. International business makes use of offshore services, incorporation fees generating substantial revenues. Livestock raising is agriculturally important. Soil fertility is low and much food must be imported.

## Cayman Islands

### Fact File

OFFICIAL NAME  Cayman Islands

FORM OF GOVERNMENT  Overseas territory of the United Kingdom

CAPITAL  George Town

AREA  262 sq km (100 sq miles)

TIME ZONE  GMT – 5 hours

POPULATION  47,900

LIFE EXPECTANCY  80.3

INFANT MORTALITY (PER 1,000)  7.1

LITERACY RATE  98 %

CURRENCY  Caymanian dollar

ECONOMY  Services 95.4 %, industry 3.2 %, agriculture 1.4 %

CLIMATE  Tropical, with cool, dry winters and warm, wet summers

MAP REFERENCE  Page 429

**T**he largest of Britain's dependencies in the Caribbean, the Cayman Islands consist of three low-lying coral islands south of Cuba and 300 km (186 miles) west of Jamaica. Until the 1960s the main occupations were farming and fishing. Today the islands are one of the world's biggest offshore financial centers, offering a confidential tax haven to some 70,000 companies and several hundred banks. Tourism is also a mainstay, accounting for seventy percent of gross domestic product and 75 percent of foreign currency earnings. Tourism is aimed at the luxury end of the market and caters mainly to visitors from North America. The Cayman Islands were uninhabited when first discovered by Europeans. Most residents today are of mixed Afro-European descent, while an immigrant Jamaican labor force makes up about one-fifth of the population.

## Greenland

### Fact File

OFFICIAL NAME  Greenland (Kalaallit Nunaat)

FORM OF GOVERNMENT  Self-governing overseas administrative division of Denmark

CAPITAL  Nuuk (Godthab)

AREA  2,166,086 sq km (836,327 sq miles)

TIME ZONE  GMT – 1/4 hours

| | |
|---|---|
| **POPULATION** | 56,300 |
| **LIFE EXPECTANCY** | 70.5 |
| **INFANT MORTALITY (PER 1,000)** | 14.6 |
| **LITERACY RATE** | 100 % |
| **CURRENCY** | Danish krone |
| **ECONOMY** | Fishing |
| **CLIMATE** | Polar, with bitterly cold winters and cool to cold summers |
| **MAP REFERENCE** | Page 411 |

Greenland is nearly fifty times the size of its "mother country", Denmark, yet it has only one percent as much population. It is the biggest island in the world and about 85 percent of its land area is covered by an ice-cap with an average depth of 1,500 m (5,000 ft). There are a few sandy and clay plains in the ice-free areas of the island, but settlement is confined to the rocky coasts.

It was named "Greenland" by the Viking Erik the Red during the tenth century, in the hope that the name would attract other adventurous Norsemen as settlers. The island became a Danish colony in 1721 and part of the Kingdom of Denmark in 1973. Greenland was granted autonomy in 1981, which was further expanded in 2008. Most Greenlanders today are of mixed Inuit and Danish descent, and sometimes live uneasily between these two worlds.

Greenland's economic prospects are somewhat limited in that it is now almost completely dependent on fishing and fish processing. These constitute 95 percent of all exports, and there is the added problem of falling catches of shrimp—in recent years the Arctic fishing industry has contracted. Though it has a certain amount of mineral resources, the last lead and zinc mine was closed in 1990. There is some ship building and also potential for the development of adventure tourism, especially since Greenland Air opened a connection to the east coast of the US in 2007. One problem is the large role of the public sector, which accounts for two-thirds of total employment. About half of government revenue comes from Danish government grants.

## Guadeloupe

### Fact File

| | |
|---|---|
| **OFFICIAL NAME** | Department of Guadeloupe |
| **FORM OF GOVERNMENT** | Overseas department of France |
| **CAPITAL** | Basse-Terre |
| **AREA** | 1,780 sq km (687 sq miles) |
| **TIME ZONE** | GMT – 4 hours |
| **POPULATION** | 453,000 |
| **LIFE EXPECTANCY** | 78.1 |

| | |
|---|---|
| **INFANT MORTALITY (PER 1,000)** | 8.4 |
| **LITERACY RATE** | 90 % |
| **CURRENCY** | Euro |
| **ECONOMY** | Services 68 %, industry 17 %, agriculture 15 % |
| **CLIMATE** | Subtropical, moderated by trade winds |
| **MAP REFERENCE** | Page 427 |

Guadeloupe consists of seven Caribbean islands in the Lesser Antilles, to the southeast of Puerto Rico. The biggest is the high, volcanic Basse-Terre (the active volcano of La Soufrière is the highest point in the Lesser Antilles) lying alongside the slightly smaller flat limestone island of Grande-Terre. A narrow sea channel separates the two. Arawak and Carib Indians were the original inhabitants. The first European settlers to arrive were the French, in 1635. Although there has been considerable agitation for independence, no vote in favor of it has succeeded, and the country is still governed by France—on which it is entirely dependent for subsidies and imported food. Tourism is important, most visitors coming from France. Sugar production is being phased out; bananas now supply about fifty percent of export earnings and the cultivation of other crops such as aubergines and flowers is being encouraged.

## Jan Mayen

### Fact File

| | |
|---|---|
| **OFFICIAL NAME** | Jan Mayen |
| **FORM OF GOVERNMENT** | Territory of Norway |
| **CAPITAL** | None |
| **AREA** | 373 sq km (144 sq miles) |
| **TIME ZONE** | GMT – 1 hour |
| **POPULATION** | No permanent population |
| **ECONOMY** | Radio and meteorological stations |
| **CLIMATE** | Polar; cold, windy, and foggy |
| **MAP REFERENCE** | Page 411 |

The mountainous island of Jan Mayen lies in the Arctic Ocean about 900 km (560 miles)

*Ice floes are visible in the water surrounding the town of Narsaruaq, Greenland (left page top). Chapel of Alto Vista on the eastern coast of Aruba (left page bottom). The former capital of Martinique, Saint-Pierre (above).*

### The colonial legacy

The Caribbean contains many small island states and a significant number of dependencies. This diversity in status is the legacy of centuries of engagement with colonial powers. After Columbus discovered the area at the end of the fifteenth century, Spain took possession of many islands, but Great Britain, France and the Netherlands also claimed, fought over and exploited the Caribbean. From the end of the fifteenth century to the middle of the eighteenth century the indigenous people were nearly wiped out and replaced by a much larger population of Europeans and African slaves, who were forcibly imported to work in the sugar, tobacco, and coffee plantations that dominated the local economies. The Caribbean has long served as an important trading route between North and South Americas and to Europe and the East. In recent years the United States has had a more direct influence on the economic and political developments and activities of some of the Caribbean regions.

The result of the history of the Caribbeans is a diversity of economic, social, and political interests. Some islands have retained their colonial or dependent status (Puerto Rico, for example, formerly a Spanish colony, has associated itself with the US and remains a dependent territory). Others chose independence, such as Cuba, which became independent from Spain in 1898 and severed its political ties to the United States in 1959. The mixture of races (Carib, African, and European) and cultures has created national identities marked by different peoples, languages, customs, and political systems.

Attempts to create larger political or economic entities out of the many small islands were not very successful. Nevertheless, in 1968 many of the islands agreed to the foundation of the Caribbean Free Trade Area. However, there are unifying forces that are responsible for a certain amount of common identity. One of these areas is sports. In cricket, for example, a heritage from British colonial rule, many of the former colonies unite to form one single national team: the team of the "West Indies".

west of Norway. It is volcanic, with the mighty active Beerenberg volcano rising 2,400 m (7,874 ft) straight out of the surf. From its ice-cap some 15 glaciers descend into the sea. Once an important base for Arctic whaling, Jan Mayen's only resources today are rich fishing grounds. These were the subject of a long dispute with Greenland over fishing rights, and possible oil and gas deposits. Mediated by the International Court of Justice, the two parties reached a compromise on this issue in 1993. The island's birdlife is spectacular and includes millions of fulmar, petrel, kittiwake, little auk, guillemot, and puffin.

## Martinique

### Fact File

OFFICIAL NAME  Department of Martinique

FORM OF GOVERNMENT  Overseas department of France

CAPITAL  Fort-de-France

AREA  1,100 sq km (425 sq miles)

TIME ZONE  GMT – 4 hours

POPULATION  401,000

LIFE EXPECTANCY  79.5

INFANT MORTALITY (PER 1,000)  6.6

LITERACY RATE  97.7 %

CURRENCY  Euro

ECONOMY  Services 83 %, industry 11 %, agriculture 6 %

CLIMATE  Tropical, moderated by trade winds; wet season June to October

MAP REFERENCE  Page 427

Christopher Columbus described Martinique as "the most beautiful country in the world"

when he laid eyes on it in 1493. This island in the eastern Caribbean was colonized by France in 1635 and has been French ever since. It consists of three groups of volcanic hills and the intervening lowlands, and is dominated by the dormant volcano Mt Pelée. Mt Pelée is famous for the eruption of 1902, when it killed all the inhabitants of the town of St-Pierre except one prisoner, who was saved by the thickness of his prison cell. The economy is based on sugarcane, bananas, tourism, and light industry, the export of bananas being of growing importance. Most sugarcane is used for making rum. The majority of the workforce is in the service sector and administration, tourism having become more important than agricultural exports as a source of foreign exchange.

## Montserrat

### Fact File

OFFICIAL NAME  Montserrat

FORM OF GOVERNMENT  Overseas territory of the United Kingdom

CAPITAL  Plymouth

AREA  102 sq km (39 sq miles)

TIME ZONE  GMT – 4 hours

POPULATION  9,600 (before a volcanic eruption in 1995 13,000, after the evacuation 4,000)

LIFE EXPECTANCY  79.2

INFANT MORTALITY (PER 1,000)  6.9

LITERACY RATE  97 %

CURRENCY  EC (East Caribbean) dollar

ECONOMY  Services 75.7 %, industry 23.1 %, agriculture 1.2 %

CLIMATE  Tropical

MAP REFERENCE  Page 427

Montserrat is a Caribbean island with seven active volcanoes. In 1995 deep ash from one of them destroyed numerous crops and forced the evacuation of the capital, Plymouth. Montserrat was colonized in 1632 by the British, who at first brought in Irish settlers. (Together with its lush green foliage, this is why it is locally known as "the Emerald Isle".) Later, the island's sugar plantations were worked by African slaves. It has been a self-governing UK dependent territory since 1960. Tourism provides a quarter of the national income, other support coming from the export of electronic components which are assembled on the island, plastic bags, clothing, rum, hot peppers, live plants, and cattle. Data processing facilities and offshore banking are available.

## Navassa

### Fact File

OFFICIAL NAME  Navassa Island

FORM OF GOVERNMENT  Unincorporated territory of the United States

CAPITAL  None

AREA  5.4 sq km (2 sq miles)

TIME ZONE  GMT – 5 hours

POPULATION  No permanent population

CLIMATE  Tropical, moderated by sea breezes

MAP REFERENCE  Page 429

Navassa Island is an uninhabited rocky outcrop in the Caribbean halfway between Cuba and Haiti. It is strategically located for the USA, since it is 160 km (100 miles) south of the Guantanamo Bay (Bahía de Guantánamo) naval base. The island is administered by the US Department of the Interior, which made it a natural reserve in 1999. The surface is mostly exposed rock but it has dense stands of fig-like trees, cacti, and enough grass to support goats. Its principal resource is guano.

*Mud and lava from the 1995 volcanic eruption on Montserrat (left). The oceanfront in old San Juan, Puerto Rico (above).*

# Netherlands Antilles

## Fact File

OFFICIAL NAME  Netherlands Antilles

FORM OF GOVERNMENT  Self-governing part of the Kingdom of the Netherlands

CAPITAL  Willemstad

AREA  960 sq km (371 sq miles)

TIME ZONE  GMT – 4 hours

POPULATION  225,000

LIFE EXPECTANCY  76.5

INFANT MORTALITY (PER 1,000)  9.4

CURRENCY  Netherlands Antillean guilder

ECONOMY  Services 84 %, industry 15 %, agriculture 1 %

CLIMATE  Tropical, moderated by trade winds

MAP REFERENCE  Page 427

The Netherlands Antilles consist of two very different island groups in two parts of the Caribbean. Curaçao and Bonaire are located off the coast of Venezuela, and while they may once have made money from the well-known orange liqueur, today 98 percent of their income comes from petroleum—either processed for products or for transshipment facilities—tourism, and offshore finance. The other group, which lies east of the Virgin Islands, consists of the three islands of Saba, St Eustasius, and part of Sint Maarten (the other half belongs to French Guadeloupe and is called Saint-Martin). The people are largely of African and European descent, the original inhabitants having been killed in the sixteenth century by Spanish settlers. All told, the islands have a high per capita income and a well-developed infrastructure in comparison with others in the region. Nearly all consumer and capital goods are imported from the USA, Mexico and Venezuela. Crops grown include aloes, sorghum, peanuts, vegetables, and tropical fruits; however, poor soils and limited supplies of water for irrigation hamper the further development of agriculture.

# Puerto Rico

## Fact File

OFFICIAL NAME  Commonwealth of Puerto Rico

FORM OF GOVERNMENT  Commonwealth associated with the United States

CAPITAL  San Juan

AREA  9,104 sq km (3,515 sq miles)

TIME ZONE  GMT – 4 hours

POPULATION  3,958,000

LIFE EXPECTANCY  78.6

INFANT MORTALITY (PER 1,000)  8.7

LITERACY RATE  94.1 %

CURRENCY  US dollar

ECONOMY  Services 54 %, industry 45 %, agriculture 1 %

CLIMATE  Tropical, moderated by sea breezes

MAP REFERENCE  Page 427

Puerto Rico is a large Caribbean island east of the Dominican Republic. Ceded by Spain to the USA in 1898, its citizens enjoy a number of privileges: full US citizenship, no federal taxes, and free access to the US. In 1998 the population again voted to continue their self-governing commonwealth status and forgo becoming either the 51st state of the USA or independent. Mountainous, with a narrow coastal plain, the little flat ground available for agriculture is used for growing sugarcane, coffee, bananas, and tobacco. The economy is essentially modern and industrialized. Tax relief and cheap labor have brought many businesses to the island and tourism is growing. Industries include petrochemicals, pharmaceuticals (the island produces over ninety percent of all US tranquillizers), and electronics. The standard of living in Puerto Rico is the highest in Latin America (outside the island tax havens), and is rising.

# St Pierre and Miquelon

## Fact File

OFFICIAL NAME  Territorial collectivity of St Pierre and Miquelon

FORM OF GOVERNMENT  Territorial collectivity of France

CAPITAL  St-Pierre

AREA  242 sq km (93 sq miles)

TIME ZONE  GMT – 4 hours

POPULATION  7,000

LIFE EXPECTANCY  78.9

INFANT MORTALITY (PER 1,000)  7

LITERACY RATE  99 %

CURRENCY  Euro

ECONOMY  Mainly fishing and fish processing

CLIMATE  Cold, wet, and foggy

MAP REFERENCE  Page 417

St Pierre and Miquelon are islands in the North Atlantic Ocean, south of Newfoundland. They are cold and wet and have little vegetation. Surrounded by some of the world's richest fishing grounds, the islands were settled by French fishermen in the seventeenth century. Since then the inhabitants have earned a living from fishing and by servicing the foreign trawler fleets that operate off the coast. A dispute between Canada and France over fishing and mineral rights was settled in 1992. Since the French subsidize the islands, and their economy has been declining, authorities are trying to diversify by developing port facilities, encouraging tourism, and drilling for oil.

# Turks and Caicos Islands

## Fact File

OFFICIAL NAME  Turks and Caicos Islands

FORM OF GOVERNMENT  Overseas territory of the United Kingdom

CAPITAL  Grand Turk (Cockburn Town)

AREA  430 sq km (166 sq miles)

TIME ZONE  GMT – 5 hours

POPULATION  22,300

LIFE EXPECTANCY  75.2

INFANT MORTALITY (PER 1,000)  14.4

LITERACY RATE  98 %

CURRENCY  US dollar

ECONOMY  Mainly fishing and tourism with some subsistence agriculture

CLIMATE  Tropical, moderated by trade winds

MAP REFERENCE  Page 429

The Turks and Caicos Islands are a group of thirty islands, eight of them inhabited, north of Hispaniola. They are composed of low, flat, scrub-covered limestone with areas of marsh and swamp. There is little land for agriculture, though cassava, maize, citrus fruits, and beans are grown on Caicos by subsistence farmers. Today, the islands' economy is mainly based on tourism, fishing, and offshore financial services. Nearly all consumer and capital goods are imported. The islands have been British since 1766, and a crown colony since 1973. Although independence was agreed upon for 1982, the policy was reversed and the islands remain a British overseas territory.

# Caribbean

Bahamas · · · · · · · · · 392
Cuba · · · · · · · · · · 392
Jamaica · · · · · · · · · 393
Haiti · · · · · · · · · · 394
Dominican
        Republic · · · · · · · 394
St Kitts and Nevis · · · 395
Antigua and Barbuda · 395
Dominica · · · · · · · · 396
St Lucia · · · · · · · · · 397
St Vincent and the
        Grenadines · · · · · 397
Barbados · · · · · · · · 398
Grenada · · · · · · · · · 398
Trinidad and Tobago · · 399

# Bahamas

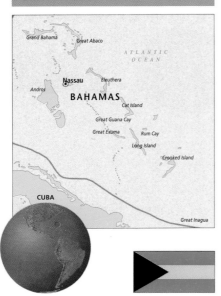

## Fact File

**OFFICIAL NAME** Commonwealth of the Bahamas

**FORM OF GOVERNMENT** Constitutional monarchy with two legislative bodies (Senate and House of Assembly)

**CAPITAL** Nassau

**AREA** 13,940 sq km (5,382 sq miles)

**TIME ZONE** GMT – 5 hours

**POPULATION** 307,000

**PROJECTED POPULATION 2015** 363,000

**POPULATION DENSITY** 22 per sq km (57 per sq mile)

**LIFE EXPECTANCY** 65.7

**INFANT MORTALITY (PER 1,000)** 23.7

**OFFICIAL LANGUAGE** English

**OTHER LANGUAGE** Creole

**LITERACY RATE** 95.6 %

**RELIGIONS** Baptist 35.4 %, Anglican 15.2 %, Roman Catholic 13.5 %, Pentecostal 8.1 %, Methodist 4.8 %, Church of God 4.1 %, other Christian 15.2 %, other 0.8 %, none 2.9 %

**ETHNIC GROUPS** African 85 %, European 12 %, Asian and Hispanic 3 %

**CURRENCY** Bahamian dollar

**ECONOMY** Services 90 %, industry 7 %, agriculture 3 %

**GNI PER CAPITA** not available (more than US$ 11,455)

**CLIMATE** Subtropical, with warm summers and mild winters

**HIGHEST POINT** Mt Alverina 63 m (207 ft)

**MAP REFERENCE** Page 425

Off the southern tip of Florida in the western Atlantic, the Bahamas consists of 700 islands and about 2,400 cays. When Columbus landed here the islands were inhabited by Arawak Indians. The islands were claimed by Britain in 1690, but have had a checkered history since. A pirates' haven in the seventeenth century, they were held for short periods by the USA and Spain before Britain resumed control in 1783. They have been independent since 1983. The 25-year administration of Lynden Pindling ended in 1992 amid allegations of involvement in narcotics trafficking and money laundering. One of the most prosperous of the Caribbean's island states, the Bahamas has attracted many illegal immigrants from Haiti across the water. This influx has placed severe strain on government services. The increase of violent crimes also poses a major problem.

All the islands are fragments of a large coralline limestone shelf. Most are only a few meters above sea level. Their coastlines are fringed with lagoons and coral reefs. Water is scarce. There are no rivers and rainfall disappears into the limestone. Much of the big islands are covered with pine forest. On the smaller islands people work mainly in fishing and agriculture.

Income derived from tourism accounts for about sixty percent of the gross domestic product and it employs about half of the islands' workforce. Tourism in turn has given rise to the manufacture of garments, furniture, jewelry, and perfume. All energy resources must be imported. Offshore banking, insurance, and financial services generate income and provide one of the region's highest standards of living. In addition, the Bahamas has a large open-registry fleet.

# Cuba

## Fact File

**OFFICIAL NAME** Republic of Cuba

**FORM OF GOVERNMENT** Communist state with single legislative body (National Assembly of People's Power)

**CAPITAL** Havana

**AREA** 110,860 sq km (42,803 sq miles)

**TIME ZONE** GMT – 5 hours

**POPULATION** 11,424,000

**PROJECTED POPULATION 2015** 11,250,000

**POPULATION DENSITY** 103 per sq km (266.9 per sq mile)

**LIFE EXPECTANCY** 77.3

**INFANT MORTALITY (PER 1,000)** 5.9

**OFFICIAL LANGUAGE** Spanish

**LITERACY RATE** 99.8 %

**RELIGIONS** Roman Catholic 85%, small minorities of Protestants and African spiritists, none 15 %

**ETHNIC GROUPS** Mixed African-European 51 %, European 37 %, African 11 %, Chinese 1 %

**CURRENCY** Cuban peso

**ECONOMY** Services 69.8 %, industry 25 %, agriculture 5.2 %

**GNI PER CAPITA** not available (US$ 3,706–11,455)

**CLIMATE** Tropical, moderated by trade winds; wet season May to October

**HIGHEST POINT** Pico Turquino 1,974 m (6,476 ft)

**MAP REFERENCE** Pages 428–29

The largest island in the Caribbean, Cuba is the size of all the others combined. Led by Fidel Castro and his brother Raúl, it is the only communist state in the Americas, and despite internal and external pressures it remains politically unchanged after fifty years. Cuba was visited by Columbus in 1492. It was at that time occupied by Arawak and Ciboney Indians. Under Spanish colonial rule sugar plantations worked by African slaves became the foundation of the island's economy—slavery was only abolished, under strong pressure from the Spanish government, in 1878. Gaining independence in 1898 but remaining under American tutelage until 1934, the country was run by a number of corrupt and gangster-ridden regimes until 1958, when Fidel Castro's

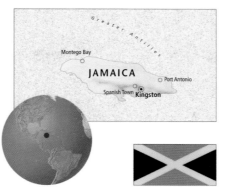

# Jamaica

*Hope Town on Elbow Cay, Abaco Island, Bahamas (left page). An aerial view of Havana, Cuba (above). Port Antonio on the northeast coast of Jamaica (below).*

army captured Havana. In 1976 the de facto monopoly of the Communist Party was formalized, with Castro, supported by his brother, making all decisions. Since the collapse of the Soviet system, on which Cuba had become economically dependent, times have been hard.

Cuba is only 193 km (120 miles) across at its widest point, but it stretches over 1,200 km (745 miles) from the Gulf of Mexico, at its western extremity, to the Windward Passage between Cuba and Haiti in the east. In addition to the main island, the much smaller island of Isla de la Juventud lies off the southwest coast. Less mountainous than the other islands in the Greater Antilles group, Cuba nevertheless has three distinct ranges—the Oriental (Sierra Maestra), the Central, and the Occidental (Sierra de los Oranos). These cover roughly 25 percent of the territory east to west. The remaining 75 percent of Cuba's surface area consists of lowlands and basins. On the more fertile soils sugar plantations, rice fields, coffee plantations, and tobacco fields are found; livestock is run on the central savanna. Cuba's irregular coastline is lined with mangroves, beaches, and coral reefs. Despite deforestation the island still has considerable areas of woodland, ranging from tropical near-jungle to pines growing in upland areas. Cuba has a mostly hot climate and experiences heavy seasonal rainfall and periodic hurricanes.

Sugarcane remains the country's main cash crop, as it has for more than 100 years. Cuba is the world's third-largest sugar producer, and sugar represents almost fifty percent of the country's exports by value. Other crops are tobacco, rice, potatoes, tubers, citrus fruit, and coffee. There are also extensive timber resources, including mahogany and cedar. Cuba has the world's fourth-largest nickel deposits, and production is rising as a result of a joint venture with a Canadian company. In 2006, high metal prices boosted Cuban income from nickel and cobalt production.

Its situation as one of the world's few remaining communist states has left Cuba isolated and with few trading partners. Since late 2000, Venezuela has been providing Cuba oil on preferential terms, payed for in part with the services of Cuban personnel. In addition, because the government has been unwilling to hold multi-party elections, the country has been subject to a severe embargo imposed by the USA. Poor sugar harvests and falling prices for sugar, declining tourism, devastation by cyclones, and mounting deficits are some of the country's difficulties.

## Fact File

**OFFICIAL NAME** Jamaica

**FORM OF GOVERNMENT** Constitutional monarchy with two legislative bodies (Senate and House of Representatives)

**CAPITAL** Kingston

**AREA** 10,991 sq km (4,244 sq miles)

**TIME ZONE** GMT – 5 hours

**POPULATION** 2,804,000

**PROJECTED POPULATION 2015** 2,819,000

**POPULATION DENSITY** 255.1 per sq km (660.7 per sq mile)

**LIFE EXPECTANCY** 73.6

**INFANT MORTALITY (PER 1,000)** 15.6

**OFFICIAL LANGUAGE** English

**OTHER LANGUAGE** Creole

**LITERACY RATE** 87.9 %

**RELIGIONS** Protestant (Seventh-Day Adventist 10.8 %, Pentecostal 9.5 %, other Church of God 8.3 %, Baptist 7.2 %, New Testament Church of God 6.3 %, Church of God in Jamaica 4.8 %, Church of God of Prophecy 4.3 %, Anglican 3.6 %, other 7.7 %) 62.5 %, Roman Catholic 2.6 %, other 14.2 %, none 20.9 %

**ETHNIC GROUPS** African 91.2 %, mixed Afro-European 6.2 %, other or unknown 2.6 %

**CURRENCY** Jamaican dollar

**ECONOMY** Services 62.2 %, industry 32.7 %, agriculture 5.1 %

**GNI PER CAPITA** US$ 3,710

**CLIMATE** Tropical; cooler inland

**HIGHEST POINT** Blue Mountain Peak 2,256 m (7,402 ft)

**MAP REFERENCE** Page 429

The Caribbean island of Jamaica lies 144 km (98 miles) south of Cuba and southwest of Haiti. Mountainous in the interior, it is the most populous of the English-speaking Caribbean islands. Arawak Indians were its first inhabitants. Columbus visited in 1494 and a slave-based sugar producing plantation society was established by the British after they seized the island in 1655. It won independence from Britain in 1962. An important contributor to world music, Jamaica is the home of reggae, a style originating in Kingston's tough urban environment. Also from Jamaica come the Rastafarians, followers of the one-time Emperor of Ethiopia. In September 1988 Jamaica was devastated by the fiercest hurricane to strike the island this century, causing widespread loss of life and leaving twenty percent of the people homeless.

In the northwest of the island is a limestone area of steep ridges and isolated basins, pitted with sink-holes. This "cockpit country" once gave refuge to escaped slaves. In the east the land rises to become the densely forested Blue Mountains. In the west the River Black is navigable upstream for about 30 km (19 miles). Sugar plantations dominate the densely populated and extensively cultivated lowland coastal fringe. Seasonal rains fall most heavily on the northeastern mountain slopes—still covered in the rainforest once found all over the island. In the rainshadow of the mountains, the southern lowlands support only savanna scrub.

Bauxite has been mined since 1952. Most of it is exported as ore, and about one-fifth as alumina, making Jamaica the world's third-largest producer. This accounts for more than fifty percent of exports. Tourism and bauxite production are Jamaica's two main industries, and comprise more than two-thirds of foreign earnings. Other export industries include printing, textiles and food processing, along with rum distilling and sugar production. In agriculture, sugarcane and bananas are the main cash crops, along with coffee, cocoa, and fruit. In recent years the government has removed most price controls and privatized state enterprises. The economy faces serious long-term problems: high but declining interest rates, increased foreign competition, exchange rate instability, a sizable merchandise trade deficit, large-scale unemployment and underemployment, and a high debt burden.

*North and Central America*

# Haiti

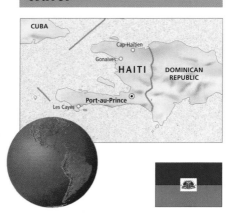

## Fact File

OFFICIAL NAME  Republic of Haiti

FORM OF GOVERNMENT  Republic with two legislative bodies (Senate and Chamber of Deputies)

CAPITAL  Port-au-Prince

AREA  27,750 sq km (10,714 sq miles)

TIME ZONE  GMT – 5 hours

POPULATION  8,925,000

PROJECTED POPULATION 2015  10,830,000

POPULATION DENSITY  321.6 per sq km (833 per sq mile)

LIFE EXPECTANCY  57.6

INFANT MORTALITY (PER 1,000)  62.3

OFFICIAL LANGUAGE  French

OTHER LANGUAGE  French Creole

LITERACY RATE  52.9 %

RELIGIONS  Roman Catholic 80 % (most of whom also practice Voodoo), Protestant 16 % (Baptist 10 %, Pentecostal 4 %, other 2 %), other 1 %, none 3 %

ETHNIC GROUPS  African 95 %, mixed African-European 5 %

CURRENCY  Gourd

ECONOMY  Services 52 %, agriculture 28 %, industry 20 %

GNI PER CAPITA  US$ 560

CLIMATE  Mainly tropical; semiarid in eastern mountains; wet seasons April to June and August to November

HIGHEST POINT  Pic de la Selle 2,680 m (8,792 ft)

MAP REFERENCE  Page 429

Haiti lies in the Caribbean, east of Cuba. It is the western third of the island of Hispaniola, the Dominican Republic occupying the remainder. Visited by Columbus in 1492, it was used by the Spanish for sugarcane cultivation and was ceded to France in 1697. In the aftermath of the French Revolution it was the scene of a slave rebellion which led to the establishment, in 1804, of the world's first black republic. Since then the country has endured two centuries of instability, violence, dictatorship, military rule, and endemic poverty. Today Haiti is the poorest country in the western hemisphere. Under the brutal regime of the Duvalier family, between 1957 and 1986, it became a police state enforced by a private militia called the Tontons Macoute. Recent years have seen faltering steps toward electoral democracy and modest civil service reforms, but political killings were still occurring under a corrupt and ineffective judicial system. Violent unrest and international pressure brought about a change of government in 2004, which was inaugurated in 2006.

Two peninsulas enclose the central plain of the Artibonite River, and the bight of the Golfe de la Gonâve beyond. Some 75 percent of Haiti's terrain is mountainous, the Massif du Nord providing the range which forms the northern peninsula, before extending east into the Dominican Republic where it becomes Hispaniola's Cordillera Central. The southern peninsula contains the Massif de la Hotte at its western end, and the Massif de la Selle in the east. The fertile lowland areas are densely populated, the largest of these being the Plaine du Nord. On the plains the major crop is sugarcane, coffee plantations being found on the higher land. The majority of the population is engaged in subsistence farming, growing cassava, bananas, and corn. Haiti's environmental problems are severe: one-third of its soil is seriously eroded, and extensive deforestation has occurred in the course of charcoal production.

Haiti is without strategic resources and, during a period of economic sanctions imposed to put pressure on the government in 1991, it was forced to find clandestine sources of oil. In addition to sugar refining, light industry includes flour and cement and the manufacture of textiles, shoes, and cooking utensils. Haiti suffers from higher inflation than similar low-income countries, lack of investment, and severe trade deficits. Remittances of Haitians working abroad equal nearly a quarter of the gross domestic product.

# Dominican Republic

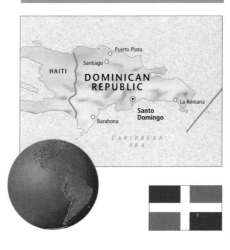

## Fact File

OFFICIAL NAME  Dominican Republic

FORM OF GOVERNMENT  Republic with two legislative bodies (Senate and Chamber of Deputies)

CAPITAL  Santo Domingo

AREA  48,730 sq km (18,815 sq miles)

TIME ZONE  GMT – 4 hours

POPULATION  9,507,000

PROJECTED POPULATION 2015  10,890,000

POPULATION DENSITY  195.1 per sq km (505.3 per sq mile)

LIFE EXPECTANCY  73.4

INFANT MORTALITY (PER 1,000)  26.9

OFFICIAL LANGUAGE  Spanish

OTHER LANGUAGE  French Creole

LITERACY RATE  87 %

RELIGIONS  Roman Catholic 95 %, other 5 %

ETHNIC GROUPS  Mixed African–European 73 %, European 16 %, African 11 %

CURRENCY  Peso

ECONOMY  Services 64.4 %, industry 23.8 %, agriculture 11.8 %

GNI PER CAPITA  US$ 3,550

CLIMATE  Tropical, with wet season May to November

HIGHEST POINT  Pico Duarte 3,175 m (10,416 ft)

MAP REFERENCE  Page 429

The second largest Caribbean nation in both area and population, the Dominican Republic occupies the eastern two-thirds of the island of Hispaniola. The island was visited by Christopher Columbus in 1492 and in 1496 his brother founded the city of Santo Domingo on its southern coast—the oldest Spanish city in the Americas. It was first colonized by Spain but the development of its sugar industry resulted from a period of French control. The country won independence in 1844 and since that time it has been ruled by a series of dictators with only short intervals of democracy. A bitter civil war in 1965 brought the intervention of the USA, which has kept a watch on Dominican affairs since then. Civil unrest continues. In 1996 President Balaguer had to resign after rigging the elections. The elections since 2000, however, were fair.

With a mountainous landscape, including the highest point in the West Indies, Pico Duarte, the Dominican Republic contains three considerable ranges—the Cordillera Septentrional in the north, the massive Cordillera Central, and the southern Sierra de Bahoruco. Between these ranges and to the east lie fertile valleys and lowlands. These include the Cibao Valley in the north, the Vega Real, and the coastal plains where sugar plantations are found. Because of the mountainous terrain there are wide variations in temperature and rainfall. Low-lying areas in the south and east support a dry savanna vegetation suitable for livestock raising. The Dominican Republic also has the lowest point in the West Indies—Lake Enriquillo, 44 m (144 ft) below sea level. The lake bisects the mountains in the southwest.

While still heavily dependent on its traditional agricultural base, in recent years the economy has been supplemented by industrial growth (making use of a vast hydroelectric potential), and a large increase in tourism. The Dominican Republic has good beaches and one of the highest hotel room capacities in the Caribbean. Sugar is still the leading agricultural export, followed by coffee, cocoa, tobacco, and fruit. Nickel and gold mining are increasing in economic importance. Subsistence farming provides most of the rural population with its livelihood, the staple crops being rice and corn. State-owned sugar plantations provide another source of employment. Illegal narcotics also play a part in the economy; the country is a transshipment point for drugs bound for the USA.

## St Kitts and Nevis

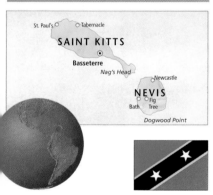

### Fact File

OFFICIAL NAME Federation of St Kitts and Nevis

FORM OF GOVERNMENT Constitutional monarchy with single legislative body (House of Assembly)

CAPITAL Basseterre

AREA 261 sq km (101 sq miles)

TIME ZONE GMT – 4 hours

POPULATION 39,600

PROJECTED POPULATION 2015 56,000

*Bananas are harvested on a plantation on Haiti (left page). Aerial view of the Antigua west coast (right).*

POPULATION DENSITY 151.7 per sq km (392.1 per sq mile)

LIFE EXPECTANCY 72.9

INFANT MORTALITY (PER 1,000) 13.4

OFFICIAL LANGUAGE English

OTHER LANGUAGE English Creole

LITERACY RATE 97.8 %

RELIGIONS Anglican 36.2 %, Methodist 32.1 %, Roman Catholic 10.7 %, Pentecostal 5.5 %, Baptist 3.9 %, followers of the Church of God 3.9 %, other 7.5 %

ETHNIC GROUPS African 94.3 %, mixed African-European 3.3 %, European 0.9 %, other 1.5 %

CURRENCY East Caribbean dollar

ECONOMY Services 70.7 %, industry 25.8 %, agriculture 3.5 %

GNI PER CAPITA US$ 10.130

CLIMATE Tropical, moderated by sea breezes

HIGHEST POINT Mt Liamuiga 1,156 m (3,793 ft)

MAP REFERENCE Page 427

St Kitts and Nevis is a federation of two Caribbean islands in the Leeward Islands group. Each is well-watered and has a mountain of volcanic origin rising to about 1,000 m (3,300 ft). Once inhabited by Carib and Arawak Indians, St Kitts and Nevis were, in 1623 and 1628, the first West Indian islands to be colonized by Britain. Ownership of the islands was disputed with the French until 1783 when it was ceded to the United Kingdom. The islands became an associated state with full internal autonomy in 1967. The island of Anguilla rebelled and was allowed to secede in 1971. In 1983 the country became fully independent from Britain.

As on other Caribbean islands, African slaves were imported as labor for sugar and cotton plantations, this ceasing with the abolition of slavery in 1834. Most islanders today are descended from former slaves. Tourism is currently the most important economic sector, and export-oriented manufacturing is of growing significance, in addition to manufactured products including machinery, food, electronics, clothing, footwear, and beverages. The state-run sugar company, once the economic mainstay, was closed down after the 2005 harvest following decades of losses. To compensate, a program to diversify agriculture and stimulate other sectors was put into place. The main cash crops still are sugarcane on St Kitts and cotton and coconuts on Nevis. Staple foods include rice, yams, vegetables, and bananas, but most food is imported.

Nevis claims it is starved of funds by its partner and is dissatisfied with its place in the federation. In 1996 Nevis announced its intention to seek independence from St Kitts. Nevis has the constitutional right to secede if two-thirds of the elected legislators approve and two-thirds of voters endorse it through a referendum. However, even though parliament decided accordingly to secede in 1998 the necessary popular support could not be mustered in the referendum.

## Antigua and Barbuda

### Fact File

OFFICIAL NAME Antigua and Barbuda

FORM OF GOVERNMENT Democracy with two legislative bodies (Senate and House of Representatives)

CAPITAL St Johns

AREA 443 sq km (170 sq miles)

TIME ZONE GMT – 4 hours

POPULATION 69,800

PROJECTED POPULATION 2015 93,000

POPULATION DENSITY 157.6 per sq km (410.6 per sq mile)

LIFE EXPECTANCY 72.7

INFANT MORTALITY (PER 1,000) 17.7

OFFICIAL LANGUAGE English

OTHER LANGUAGES Indigenous languages (Creole)

LITERACY RATE 85.8 %

RELIGIONS Protestant 81.8 %, Roman Catholic 10.4 %, other 2 %, none or unspecified 5.8 %

ETHNIC GROUPS African 91 %, other 9 %

CURRENCY East Caribbean dollar

ECONOMY Services 74.3 %, industry 22 %, agriculture 3.7 %

GNI PER CAPITA US$ 11,520

CLIMATE Tropical, moderated by sea breezes

HIGHEST POINT Boggy Peak 405 m (1,328 ft)

MAP REFERENCE Page 427

Antigua and Barbuda consists of three islands in the eastern Caribbean. In 1493 the largest of the group was visited by Christopher Columbus on his second voyage, who named it Antigua. It was first settled by the Spanish and the French, but became a British colony in 1667 and in the eighteenth century flourished under a plantation system using African slaves to produce sugar. This ended with the end of slavery in the British Empire in 1834. Originally populated by the Siboney in 2400 BC and later, when the Europeans arrived, by Arawak and Carib Indians, today the islands are peopled by Afro-Caribbean descendants of the plantation days. The islands were run by the Antiguan Labour Party and the Bird family, a combination that has held power almost constantly since 1956. Full independence was obtained in 1981. The elections of 2004, however, brought the former opposition under Baldwin Spencer to power.

Antigua rises to 405 m (1,328 ft) at Boggy Peak, a volcanic prominence in the southwest. Unlike the other Leeward Islands, to which it belongs, Antigua was denuded of forest long ago, and lacks both trees and rivers. In contrast, the flat coral-island game reserve of Barbuda, 40 km (25 miles) to the north, is fairly well wooded. Barbuda's one town is Codrington. The third island, Redonda, is an uninhabited islet southwest of Antigua. The tropical climate and palm-fringed beaches make Antigua and Barbuda an attractive tourist location. There is, however, little fresh water, and the region is hurricane-prone; one in 1995 caused extensive damage.

Since the sugar industry closed in 1971 the islands have relied almost entirely on tourism, with some income from two US military bases on Antigua. Tourism continues to dominate the economy, accounting for more than half of the islands' gross domestic product. Declining numbers of tourists since around 2000 have slowed the economy and pressed the government into a tight fiscal corner.

*The coastal town of Soufrière, Dominica (below). The spires of the Pitons tower above a small village on the southwest coast of St Lucia (above). Kingstown Harbor on the island of St Vincent (right page top).*

# Dominica

## Fact File

| | |
|---|---|
| OFFICIAL NAME | Commonwealth of Dominica |
| FORM OF GOVERNMENT | Parliamentary democracy with single legislative body (House of Assembly) |
| CAPITAL | Roseau |
| AREA | 754 sq km (291 sq miles) |
| TIME ZONE | GMT – 4 hours |
| POPULATION | 72,500 |
| PROJECTED POPULATION 2015 | 67,000 |
| POPULATION DENSITY | 96.2 per sq km (249.1 per sq mile) |
| LIFE EXPECTANCY | 75.3 |
| INFANT MORTALITY (PER 1,000) | 14.1 |
| OFFICIAL LANGUAGE | English |
| OTHER LANGUAGE | French Creole |
| LITERACY RATE | 94 % |
| RELIGIONS | Roman Catholic 61.4 %, Protestant 29.6 %, Rastafarian 1.3 %, other 1.6 %, none 6.1 % |
| ETHNIC GROUPS | African 86.7 %, mixed 8.9 %, indigenous 2.9 %, European 0.8 %, other 0.7 % |
| CURRENCY | East Caribbean dollar |
| ECONOMY | Services 49.5 %, industry 32.8 %, agriculture 17.7 % |
| GNI PER CAPITA | US$ 4,250 |
| CLIMATE | Tropical, moderated by trade winds |

HIGHEST POINT Morne Diablatins 1,447 m (4,747 ft)

MAP REFERENCE Page 427

Fought over for years by the English and the French, the Caribbean island of Dominica was mainly occupied by the British after 1759. Locally it is known as the "nature island" because of its extensive forests and wildlife. It is unusual in still having a community of about 3,000 Carib Indians, whose fierce ancestors, protected by the forests in the interior, held off European colonization for 250 years. In the eighteenth century African slaves were brought to the island as labor and their descendants form the majority of the population today. Independence came to Dominica in 1978. Soon after, it was devastated by a series of hurricanes, while two coup attempts complicated its political life. Today, in free elections, power is contested between three parties in a stable democracy.

The most mountainous of the Lesser Antilles, Dominica is a volcanic island with fertile soils and the second largest boiling lake in the world. A high ridge forms the backbone of the island, from which several rivers flow to an indented coastline. There are many vents and hot springs. The rich volcanic soil supports dense tropical vegetation over 41 percent of Dominica's surface; only nine percent of the land is arable. The climate is warm and humid, with a risk of hurricanes during the rainy season from June to October. During 1995 hurricanes ruined ninety percent of the banana crop. The wildlife to be seen in the Morne Trois Pitons National Park is an important tourist attraction.

Dominica's only mineral resource is pumice and it has to import all its energy. There is hydro-electric potential in the rivers of the interior. Bananas, citrus fruits, and coconuts are the main cash crops—bananas accounting for a large percentage of the exports, as do coconut-based soaps. Other exports include bay oil and vegetables. The country has to import much of its food and is depending on the development of luxury tourism for economic growth. Ecotourism is increasing, with visitors coming to view rare indigenous birds and volcanic sulphur pools. The lack of an airport able to service jetliners makes the country less accessible than its neighbors for mass-market tourism.

# St Lucia

## Fact File

**OFFICIAL NAME** St Lucia

**FORM OF GOVERNMENT** Constitutional monarchy with two legislative bodies (Senate and House of Assembly)

**CAPITAL** Castries

**AREA** 616 sq km (239 sq miles)

**TIME ZONE** GMT – 4 hours

**POPULATION** 173,000

**PROJECTED POPULATION 2015** 180,000

**POPULATION DENSITY** 280.8 per sq km (723.8 per sq mile)

**LIFE EXPECTANCY** 74.3

**INFANT MORTALITY (PER 1,000)** 12.5

**OFFICIAL LANGUAGE** English

**OTHER LANGUAGE** French Creole

**LITERACY RATE** 90.1 %

**RELIGIONS** Roman Catholic 68 %, Seventh Day Adventist 9 %, Pentecostal 5 %, Anglican 2 %, other Christian 7 %, Rastafarian 2 %, other 2 %, none 5 %

**ETHNIC GROUPS** African 82.5 %, mixed 11.9 %, East Indian 2.4 %, other or unspecified 3.2 %

**CURRENCY** East Caribbean dollar

**ECONOMY** Services 80 %, industry 15 %, agriculture 5 %

**GNI PER CAPITA** US$ 5,210

**CLIMATE** Tropical, moderated by trade winds; wet season May to August, dry season January to April

**HIGHEST POINT** Mt Gimie 950 m (3,117 ft)

**MAP REFERENCE** PAGE 427

An island in the Caribbean, St Lucia is one of the prettiest of the Windward Group of the Lesser Antilles. Tropical beaches and typical Caribbean towns like Soufrière have long drawn tourists to the island, who also come to see its varied plant and animal life. Once inhabited by Arawak and Carib Indians, St Lucia was wrangled over between France and Britain before finally being ceded to Britain in 1814. As elsewhere in the Caribbean, African slaves were imported to work sugar plantations until slavery was abolished in 1834. Most of the population are descended from slaves, though some are from South Asia. Internally self-governing from 1967, St Lucia has been fully independent since 1979.

The main features of the island are its forested mountains stretching north to south, cut by river valleys, and rising to Mt Gimie. In the southwest lies the Qualibou, an area with eighteen lava domes and seven craters. In the west, marking the entrance to Jalousie Plantation harbor, are the spectacular twin Pitons, two peaks rising steeply from the sea to a height of about 800 m (2,625 ft). The climate is tropical, with annual rainfall varying from 1,500 mm (59 in) in the lowlands to 3,500 mm (137 in) in mountainous areas.

While not poor, St Lucia still depends heavily on bananas, a crop which is easily ruined by hurricanes and disease. Changes in the EU import preference regime and the increased competition from Latin American bananas have made economic diversification increasingly important in Saint Lucia. Other agricultural exports are coconuts, coconut oil, and cocoa. Clothing is the second largest export, and the free port of Vieux Fort has attracted modern light industry. Grande Cul de Sac Bay in the south is one of the deepest tanker ports in the region and is used for the transshipment of oil.

# St Vincent and the Grenadines

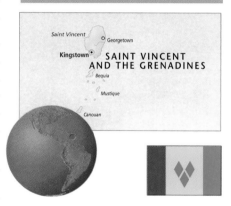

## Fact File

**OFFICIAL NAME** St Vincent and the Grenadines

**FORM OF GOVERNMENT** Constitutional monarchy with single legislative body (House of Assembly)

**CAPITAL** Kingstown

**AREA** 389 sq km (150 sq miles)

**TIME ZONE** GMT – 4 hours

**POPULATION** 118,000

**PROJECTED POPULATION 2015** 124,000

**POPULATION DENSITY** 303.3 per sq km (786.7 per sq mile)

**LIFE EXPECTANCY** 74.3

**INFANT MORTALITY (PER 1,000)** 13.6

**OFFICIAL LANGUAGE** English

**OTHER LANGUAGE** French Creole

**LITERACY RATE** 96 %

**RELIGIONS** Anglican 47 %, Methodist 28 %, Roman Catholic 13 %, other 12 %

**ETHNIC GROUPS** African 66 %, mixed 19 %, Indian 6 %, native American 2 %, other 7 %

**CURRENCY** East Caribbean dollar

**ECONOMY** Services 64 %, industry 26 %, agriculture 10 %

**GNI PER CAPITA** US$ 4,210

**CLIMATE** Tropical, with wet season May to November

**HIGHEST POINT** Mt Soufrière 1,234 m (4,048 ft)

**MAP REFERENCE** Page 427

The mountainous, volcanic Caribbean island of St Vincent has 89 percent of the country's total land area and 95 percent of the population, the rest consisting of the islands of the Northern Grenadines—Bequia, Mustique, Canouan, and Union. St Vincent was visited by Columbus in 1498 but the fierce resistance of the Amerindian Caribs meant that settlement was slow. A long dispute with France (the French often being supported by the Caribs) finally led to it becoming a British colony in 1783. As St Vincent and the Grenadines the country became self-governing in 1969 and independent in 1979.

St Vincent is dominated by a north-south spur of densely forested mountains, cut east to west by numerous short, fast-running rivers and streams. In the north, volcanic Mt Soufrière is still very active. It caused serious damage in 1891 and in 1902 it killed 2,000 people. The 1979 eruption, which was followed by a hurricane the next year, devastated agriculture and caused a major setback in tourism.

The Northern Grenadines are coralline islets, extending south of St Vincent toward Grenada, some of them with picturesque names such as All Awash Island and The Pillories. The tropical climate is moderated by steady trade winds.

Agriculture, led by banana production, is the foundation of the country's economy, most of it small-scale or subsistence farming on the lower mountain slopes or terraces. Other crops exported include arrowroot starch used to make medicines and paper for computer printers. Tourism is of growing importance, with visitors drawn to the clear, clean waters of Mustique and Bequia. Saint Vincent is also home to a small offshore banking sector and has moved to adopt international regulatory standards.

# Barbados

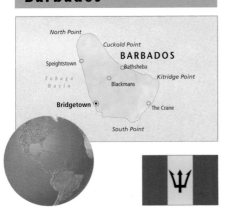

## Fact File

**OFFICIAL NAME** Barbados

**FORM OF GOVERNMENT** Constitutional monarchy, Parliamentary democracy with two legislative bodies (Senate and House of Assembly)

**CAPITAL** Bridgetown

**AREA** 431 sq km (166 sq miles)

**TIME ZONE** GMT – 4 hours

**POPULATION** 282,000

**PROJECTED POPULATION 2015** 300,000

**POPULATION DENSITY** 654.3 per sq km (1,698.8 per sq mile)

**LIFE EXPECTANCY** 73.2

**INFANT MORTALITY (PER 1,000)** 11.1

**OFFICIAL LANGUAGE** English

**OTHER LANGUAGE** English Creole

**LITERACY RATE** 99.7 %

**RELIGIONS** Protestant 67 % (Anglican 40%, Pentecostal 8 %, Methodist 7 %, other 12 %), Roman Catholic 4 %, none 17 %, other 12 %

**ETHNIC GROUPS** African 90 %, European 4 %, other (mixed African-European, East Indian) 6 %

**CURRENCY** Barbadian dollar

**ECONOMY** Services 78 %, industry 16 %, agriculture 6 %

**GNI PER CAPITA** not available (more than US$ 11,455)

**CLIMATE** Tropical, with wet season June to November

**HIGHEST POINT** Mt Hillaby 336 m (1,102 ft)

**MAP REFERENCE** Page 427

Northeast of Trinidad and 435 km (270 miles) off the coast of Venezuela, Barbados is the easternmost of the Caribbean Windward Islands. It is also one of the most orderly and prosperous. After becoming independent from the UK in 1966, power has alternated between two centrist parties, the Democratic Labour Party and the Barbados Labour Party. Both electoral results and freedom of expression are accepted features of Barbados life. Originally inhabited by Arawak Indians and later settled under the British in the seventeenth century, its population is mainly descended from African slaves brought to work on the sugar plantations. The governor-general of Barbados represents the British sovereign and the country has a strong colonial influence. Its neighbors sometimes refer to it as "little England."

The foundation of the island consists of coral deposits formed around a rocky core, and a fringe of coral reef has produced dazzling white beaches. Inland, the rolling terrain rises to hills in the north and center. About fifty percent of the land area is arable, sugar plantations accounting for 85 percent of the cultivated terrain. Barbados is sunnier and drier than many of its neighbors. There is a shortage of water. Surface water is negligible, though when it rains heavily gullies form natural reservoirs.

A small oil industry provides about one-third of the country's needs. Sugar refining is an important source of employment and revenue but has recently been overtaken by the rapid growth in tourism. Facilities are being upgraded to cope with the surge in visitors. Most arrive from Europe and North America and cruise-ship traffic is increasing. Recently, light industrial manufacture has been developed, much of it component assembly for export. The government has promised to build "a modern, technologically dynamic economy."

# Grenada

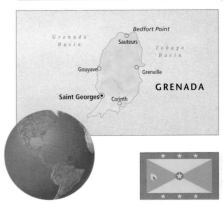

## Fact File

**OFFICIAL NAME** Grenada

**FORM OF GOVERNMENT** Constitutional monarchy with two legislative houses (Senate and House of Representatives)

**CAPITAL** Saint Georges

**AREA** 344 sq km (133 sq miles)

**TIME ZONE** GMT – 4 hours

**POPULATION** 90,300

**PROJECTED POPULATION 2015** 106,000

**POPULATION DENSITY** 262.5 per sq km (678.9 per sq mile)

**LIFE EXPECTANCY** 65.6

**INFANT MORTALITY (PER 1,000)** 13.6

**OFFICIAL LANGUAGE** English

**OTHER LANGUAGE** French patois

**LITERACY RATE** 96 %

**RELIGIONS** Roman Catholic 53 %, Protestant (including Anglican, Seventh Day Adventist, Pentecostal) 33.8 %, other Protestant 13.2 %

**ETHNIC GROUPS** African 82 %, mixed 13 %, East Indian 5 %

**CURRENCY** East Caribbean dollar

**ECONOMY** Services 76.6 %, industry 18 %, agriculture 5.4 %

**GNI PER CAPITA** US$ 4,670

**CLIMATE** Tropical, moderated by trade winds

**HIGHEST POINT** Mt Saint Catherine 840 m (2,756 ft)

**MAP REFERENCE** Page 427

The state of Grenada consists of the island of Grenada, lying off the coast of Venezuela not far from Trinidad, and two small islands of the Southern Grenadines—Carriacou and Petite Martinique. The islands were visited by Columbus in 1498 but the original Carib Indian inhabitants fought off all invaders until French settlers arrived in the 1650s. Grenada then became a typical sugar-producing Caribbean island, with plantations worked by slaves brought from Africa. British since 1762, English is its official language, though some Grenadans still speak a French patois. It won independence in 1974 and in 1979 the country became communist after a bloodless

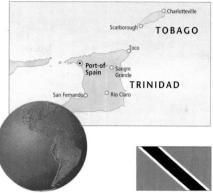

# Trinidad and Tobago

## Fact File

| | |
|---|---|
| **OFFICIAL NAME** | Republic of Trinidad and Tobago |
| **FORM OF GOVERNMENT** | Republic with two legislative bodies (Senate and House of Representatives) |
| **CAPITAL** | Port of Spain |
| **AREA** | 5,128 sq km (1,980 sq miles) |
| **TIME ZONE** | GMT – 4 hours |
| **POPULATION** | 1,047,000 |
| **PROJECTED POPULATION 2015** | 1,374,000 |
| **POPULATION DENSITY** | 204.2 per sq km (528.8 per sq mile) |
| **LIFE EXPECTANCY** | 67 |
| **INFANT MORTALITY (PER 1,000)** | 23.6 |
| **OFFICIAL LANGUAGE** | English |
| **OTHER LANGUAGES** | Hindi, French, Spanish, Chinese, Patois |
| **LITERACY RATE** | 98.6% |
| **RELIGIONS** | Roman Catholic 26%, Hindu 23%, Anglican 8%, other Protestant 24%, Muslim 6%, other 13% |
| **ETHNIC GROUPS** | Indian 40%, African 38%, mixed 21%, other 1% |
| **CURRENCY** | Trinidad and Tobago dollar |
| **ECONOMY** | Industry 61.9%, services 37.5%, agriculture 0.6% |
| **GNI PER CAPITA** | US$ 14,100 |
| **CLIMATE** | Tropical, with wet season June to December |
| **HIGHEST POINT** | El Cerro del Aripo 940 m (3,084 ft) |
| **MAP REFERENCE** | Page 427 |

*A street vendor in Bridgetown, Barbados (left page). Grenada is volcanic in origin and bisected by a mountain ridge; the coastal capital of St Georges, sheltered by hills (above). A view of one of Tobago's many bays (below).*

coup. When the coup leader was murdered by fellow Marxists in 1983, the USA, with support from a number of other Caribbean countries, intervened to restore democratic elections. Since then power has been contested and has alternated between several different political parties, but the country has turned out to be a stable democracy. Economic recovery from the events of 1983, however, has been slow.

The most southerly of the Windward Islands, the main island of Grenada is volcanic in origin and has fertile soils. A forested mountain ridge runs north-south, cut by rivers, and there are a number of lakes, including the Grand Etang at an elevation of 530 m (1,739 ft). The western coastline is precipitous; the southern coastal landscape of beaches is gentler and includes some natural harbors. In recent years the government has become interested in developing eco-tourism but protection of key environmental sites remains a concern. Large resort projects have resulted in serious beach erosion.

Grenada is known in the Caribbean as "the spice island" and is—after Indonesia—the world's leading producer of nutmeg and mace, its main crop. Other exports include cocoa and bananas, but attempts to diversify the economy from an agricultural base have so far been unsuccessful. The farming practised by the rural population is mostly small scale, with the exception of a few cooperatives. The small manufacturing sector is based on food-processing and makes products such as chocolate, sugar, alcoholic beverages, and jam. Garments and furniture are also produced, mainly for export to Trinidad and Tobago. Tourism had largely ceased after the crisis of 1983 but gradually recovered—until the attacks on 11 September 2001 brought a severe decline in the number of visitors. Today, however, Grenada again relies on tourism as its economic mainstay.

Trinidad is a square-shaped Caribbean island at the south end of the Windward Island chain, only 11 km (7 miles) off the coast of Venezuela. Along with Tobago it is the most prosperous island in the West Indies, oil and asphalt forming the basis of its wealth. It was visited by Columbus in 1498 and then held by the Spanish for three centuries before becoming a British possession after it was seized in 1797. The island's sugar plantations were initially worked by African slaves, and then after the abolition of slavery in 1834 East Indian and Chinese labor was imported. Today, in rural districts, some villages are mainly Afro-Trinidadian, some mainly Asian. Since gaining independence in 1962, Trinidad has been vexed by racial and ethnic complications, notably "Black Power" in 1970 and an attempted coup by black Muslim extremists in 1990. In 1995 the first prime minister from the Asian community was sworn in.

Unlike the Caribbean islands to the north, Trinidad is geologically an extension of South America across the Gulf of Paria. It is traversed by three mountain ranges (northern, central and southern) with El Cerro del Aripo in the Northern Range, and is drained by the Caroni, Ortoire and Oropuche Rivers. The Caroni Swamp is notable for the immense variety of its butterflies. The rest of the island is mostly low-lying, fringed with mangrove swamps. Tobago Island is a detached piece of the Northern Range, with volcanic uplands, that lies 34 km (21 miles) to the northeast of Trinidad. Tourism is concentrated on Tobago, which is renowned for its wildlife.

The strength of Trinidad's economy is its oil sector, and its large petroleum reserves. But living standards have fallen since the boom years of 1973 to 1982 and the country's prospects depend largely on the success of efforts towards diversification and on economic reforms. The floating of the exchange rate, capital market liberalization, and the partial privatization of such state operations as the main airline are among recent government initiatives.

## Central America

Mexico · · · · · · · · · · 400
Guatemala · · · · · · · 401
Belize · · · · · · · · · · 402
Honduras · · · · · · · · 402
El Salvador · · · · · · · 403
Nicaragua · · · · · · · · 404
Costa Rica · · · · · · · 404
Panama · · · · · · · · · 405

## Mexico

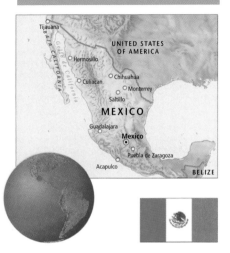

### Fact File

**OFFICIAL NAME** United Mexican States

**FORM OF GOVERNMENT** Federal republic with two legislative chambers (Senate and Chamber of Deputies)

**CAPITAL** Mexico City

**AREA** 1,972,550 sq km (761,602 sq miles)

**TIME ZONE** GMT – 6/8 hours

**POPULATION** 109,955,000

**PROJECTED POPULATION 2015** 115,756,000

**POPULATION DENSITY** 55.7 per sq km (144.4 per sq mile)

**LIFE EXPECTANCY** 75.8

**INFANT MORTALITY (PER 1,000)** 19

**OFFICIAL LANGUAGE** Spanish

**OTHER LANGUAGES** Indigenous languages (Nahuatl [Aztec] and 25 Mayan languages)

**LITERACY RATE** 91 %

**RELIGIONS** Roman Catholic 76.5 %, Protestant 6.3 %, unspecified 13.8 %, other 0.3 %, none 3.1 %

**ETHNIC GROUPS** Mixed indigenous-European (mainly Spanish) 60 %, indigenous 30 %, European 9 %, other 1 %

**CURRENCY** Mexican peso

**ECONOMY** Services 60.5 %, industry 26.6 %, agriculture 3.9 %

**GNI PER CAPITA** US$ 8,340

**CLIMATE** Tropical in south and on coastal lowlands; cooler and drier in central plateau and mountains

**HIGHEST POINT** Vol Citaltepetl (Pico de Orizaba) 5,700 m (18,701 ft)

**MAP REFERENCE** Pages 430–31

The story of Mexico is the story of Central American civilization itself. For thousands of years people have lived in the central valley, and when the Spanish arrived under Cortés in 1519 the population of the Aztec Empire may have numbered 15 million. The pattern of settlement established by Spain in Mexico, with large estates worked by Indians, was followed in many other Central and South American countries. Although most Mexicans are Roman Catholics, relations between Church and state have not always been easy, governments often viewing the Church's power as a challenge to their own. Mexico possesses major petroleum resources, is industrializing rapidly, and includes many traditional Indian cultures among its people from the Tarahumara in the northwest to the Maya of Quintana Roo.

### Physical features and land use

The northern and less populated part of Mexico consists of the basin-and-range country of the Mesa Central. In this region desert scrub is the main plant cover, with grasses, shrubs, and succulents on higher ground. Cattle ranching is notable in this area. The land reaches heights of 2,400 m (7,900 ft) around Mexico City. South of the city three major peaks of the Sierra Volcanica Transversal reach elevations of more than 5,000 m (18,000 ft)—Citlaltepetl, Popocatepetl, and Ixtaccihuatl. An active earthquake zone, this is the most densely settled part of the country.

East of the Mesa Central the land falls steeply from the Sierra Madre Oriental to a broad coastal plain on the Gulf of Mexico fringed with swamps, lagoons, and sandbars. Further south is the isthmus of Tehuantepec, a neck of rainforested land dividing the mountains of the Sierra del Sur from the highlands rising toward the Guatemalan border. The Yucatán Peninsula to the east is a limestone plain lying only a little above sea level, marked by natural wells and sinkholes. Petroleum discoveries in the 1970s in Tabasco and Campeche, in the northwest

Yucatán, have made Mexico one of the world's biggest oil producers.

The Mesa Central ends just as abruptly on its western frontier, falling from the pine-forested heights of the Sierra Madre Occidental to a narrow coastal strip extending north to the Californian border. In the far northwest is the long narrow, dry, mountain-spined peninsula of Baja California.

Contrasts in altitude and latitude produce wide climatic variations from the coasts, where temperatures are uniformly high, to the temperate land which prevails over much of the Mesa Central. Above 2,000 m (6,000 ft) lies what is known as the cold land, *tierra helada*, while on the higher slopes of the snow-capped volcanic cones is the frozen land where temperatures are usually below 10 °C (50 °F).

### People and culture

Most Mexicans are descendants of the Amerindian peoples who lived in the region at the time of the Spanish conquest, and of the Spanish colonists. The Aztecs were one of a number of developed cultures in the region. Their capital, Tenochtitlan, featured monumental architecture in the form of pyramids, and their society was strongly hierarchic, with slaves at the bottom and an emperor at the top. Art, sculpture, and poetry were advanced and they had a form of writing. Aztec religious practices involved the annual sacrifice (and eating) of large numbers of slaves, prisoners, and captives taken in war.

The Maya in Yucatán were another major culture in the region but by the time the Spanish arrived the empire had already collapsed. Only their majestic stone monuments in the jungle remained, with settlements of corn-cultivating Mayan subsistence farmers nearby.

The Spanish brought Christianity and a system of large-scale estates using poorly paid (or unpaid) Amerindian labor. Colonial control was exercised by a form of serfdom under which Amerindians paid either tribute or labor in return for conversion to Christianity. This system was abolished in 1829. In 1810 the independence struggle began: in 1822 Mexico declared itself a republic and in 1836 Spain formally recognized the country's independence. A century of political chaos climaxed with the violent Mexican Revolution of 1910 to 1921.

Since 1929 Mexico has been dominated by one party, the PRI, which has ruled until recently in a corporatist and authoritarian fashion. There was widespread dissatisfaction with the political process and with the unsolved 1994 murders of two high-profile reformers within the ruling party. A peasant revolt in Chiapas in 1994 dramatized the problem of rural poverty and the poor understanding that Mexico's urban élite has of

| Timeline | 2600 BC Beginning of Mayan civilization in Yucatán Peninsula | 300 BC Completion of the Great Pyramid of the Sun Temple at Teotihuacán, in the Valley of Mexico | 1000 Rise of Toltec Empire based in Tula, present-day Hidalgo, to the north of the Valley of Mexico; lasts around 200 years | 1325 Aztecs establish their capital of Teotihuacán, a city housing 100,000–300,000 people | 1629 Floods kill 30,000 people in Mexico City; new drainage systems constructed | 1836 Mexico's independence is formally recognized by Spain | 1847–48 US troops capture Mexico City in Mexican-American War until treaty grants large amounts of territory to USA |
|---|---|---|---|---|---|---|---|
| | 3500 BC Turkeys, corn, beans, and squash are domesticated for food | 1200 BC Rise of Olmec civilization on Mexico's Gulf Coast; it lasts until 300 BC | AD 325 Mayan civilization flourishes during its classic period (which lasts until 925); fine stone buildings with hieroglyphics | 1519 Spanish explorer Cortés expelled by Aztec emperor Montezuma from Tenochtitlan; Cortés destroys city in 1520 | 1521 Spanish rebuild Tenochtitlan and it becomes new Spanish capital, Mexico City | 1810 Hidalgo y Costilla calls for rebellion against Spain; Hidalgo executed in 1811 | 1876 Diaz becomes dictator; expands economy by building railways, developing industries, encouraging foreign investment |

GNI PER CAPITA  US$ 2,440

CLIMATE  Tropical, but cooler in highlands

HIGHEST POINT  Volcan Tajumulco 4,220 m (13,845 ft)

MAP REFERENCE  Page 428

*The Mayan Pyramid of the Magician, Uxmal, Mexico (above).*

the world beyond the cities. The elections held in 2000 for the first time brought a politician from an opposing party into power.

### Economy and resources

Agriculture occupies around a fifth of the population, many farmers living by growing maize, beans, and squash. The main export crops are coffee, cotton, and sugarcane. Some meat is exported from the north, while fish exports include tuna, anchovies, sardines, and shrimp. About one-fifth of Mexico is forested, producing hardwood and chicle, the base for chewing gum.

Mexico is one of the largest oil exporters outside OPEC, most oil coming from the Gulf of Mexico. Petrochemicals provide most of the country's export earnings and are the chief energy source. Mexico is the world's leading producer of silver. Only about twenty percent of the country's mineral reserves have so far been exploited. There are also sizeable deposits of coal and uranium. Hydroelectricity contributes approximately one third of all power used.

Although the economy is diverse, with food-processing, textiles, forestry, and tourism making contributions, it has been through a series of crises beginning with devaluation in 1994. The new administration that took office in December 2006 faces many of the same challenges that the former president tried to tackle, including the need to upgrade infrastructure, modernize the tax system and labor laws, and allow private investment in the energy sector.

| 1917 A new constitution is adopted making the revolution permanent | 1934 Government begins major land reforms; in 1938 all foreign-owned oil company assets taken over by government | 1985 Two earth-quakes occur in south-central Mexico, including Mexico City, killing more than 10,000 people |
| --- | --- | --- |
| 1910–20 Mexican revolution; Madero overthrows Diaz government in 1911 | 1970s Massive oil deposits discovered in the Gulf of Mexico | 1997 Para-military groups in Acteal massacre 45 Indian villagers | 2000 Democratic elections bring to power the first candidate of a party other than the PRI |

# Guatemala

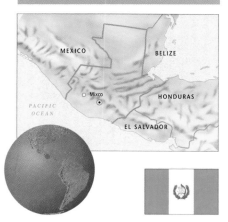

## Fact File

OFFICIAL NAME  Republic of Guatemala

FORM OF GOVERNMENT  Republic with single legislative body (Congress of the Republic)

CAPITAL  Guatemala

AREA  108,890 sq km (42,042 sq miles)

TIME ZONE  GMT – 6 hours

POPULATION  13,002,000

PROJECTED POPULATION 2015  16,227,000

POPULATION DENSITY  119.4 per sq km (309.3 per sq mile)

LIFE EXPECTANCY  70

INFANT MORTALITY (PER 1,000)  28.8

OFFICIAL LANGUAGE  Spanish

OTHER LANGUAGES  23 Maya Quiché languages

LITERACY RATE  69.1 %

RELIGIONS  Roman Catholic 75 %, Protestant 25 %; some traditional Mayan beliefs

ETHNIC GROUPS  Mixed indigenous-European 59.4 %, indigenous 40.5 %, other 0.1 %

CURRENCY  Quetzal

ECONOMY  Services 60.8 %, agriculture 25.9 %, industry 13.2 %

Guatemala lies just south of Mexico, and is the most populous of the Central American states. It was once part of the home of the Mayan civilization which reached its peak about AD 300–900. It has numerous volcanoes, including Tajumulco, the highest peak in Central America. In 1523 the region was overrun by Spanish conquistadors. As elsewhere in Central and South America, the newly arrived Spanish established large agricultural estates worked by Amerindian laborers, setting the social and economic pattern for 300 years. After becoming a republic in 1839, Guatemala has had a history of dictatorship, coups d'état, and guerrilla insurgency. Profound social divisions exist between the Amerindian majority, and an elite of mixed Spanish and Amerindian ancestry (called Ladinos) who run the government. Guatemala has had civilian rule since 1985. In 1996 a United Nations mediated accord was signed by President Alvaro Arzu and the members of the URNG guerrilla movement bringing an end to 36 years of armed struggle.

Two large mountain ranges cross the heart of the country. In the north are the older and more eroded Altos Cuchumatanes. To the south the geologically younger Sierra Madre Range includes 33 volcanoes, of which three are still active. Soil enriched with volcanic ash washed down from the Sierra Madre has created a narrow but fertile plain on the Pacific coast. This has been used for agriculture on a commercial scale only since the 1950s, when malaria was first brought under control and access roads were built. Now cattle and cotton are more important than this region's traditional banana crop. On the lower mountain slopes, up to about 1,500 m (5,000 ft), most of the country's highest quality coffee is grown. In the north of Guatemala the highlands fall away to the large, flat, forested Peten Tableland, where many ancient Mayan ruins are found, and to the plains along the Gulf of Honduras.

Guatemala's economy is largely agricultural. Coffee is the main crop and chief export, other exports being sugar, bananas, cardamom, and beef. From the forests come timber and chicle, the gum used for chewing gum. The country has few mineral or energy reserves, apart from small amounts of petroleum. Industries include sugar refining, furniture, chemicals, metals, rubber, textiles and clothing, and tourism. Tourism, largely comprising visits to the Maya ruins, revived after the military activities of the 1980s. In 2006, the Central American Free Trade Agreement (CAFTA) took effect. The distribution of income remains highly unequal, with 56 percent of the population living below the poverty line. Other ongoing challenges include decreasing revenues, negotiating assistance from international donors, upgrading financial operations, curtailing drug trafficking, and narrowing the trade deficit. Remittances from a large expatriate community are the primary source of foreign income, exceeding the total value of exports and tourism combined.

North and Central America

# Belize

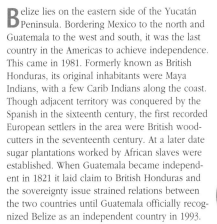

## Fact File

OFFICIAL NAME  Belize

FORM OF GOVERNMENT  Constitutional monarchy with two legislative houses (Senate and House of Representatives)

CAPITAL  Belmopan

AREA  22,966 sq km (8,867 sq miles)

TIME ZONE  GMT – 6 hours

POPULATION  301,000

PROJECTED POPULATION 2015  335,000

POPULATION DENSITY  13.1 per sq km (33.9 per sq mile)

LIFE EXPECTANCY  68.2

INFANT MORTALITY (PER 1,000)  23.7

OFFICIAL LANGUAGE  English

OTHER LANGUAGES  Creole, Spanish, Garifunan, Maya, Ketchi

LITERACY RATE  76.9 %

RELIGIONS  Roman Catholic 49.6 %, Protestant 27 %, other 14 %, none 9.4 %

ETHNIC GROUPS  Mixed indigenous-European 49 %, African 25 %, Maya 11 %, Garifuna 6 %, other 9 %

CURRENCY  Belizean dollar

ECONOMY  Services 65 %, agriculture 21.3 %, industry 13.7 %

GNI PER CAPITA  US$ 3,800

CLIMATE  Tropical, with wet seasons June to July and September to January

HIGHEST POINT  Victoria Peak 1,160 m (3,806 ft)

MAP REFERENCE  Page 428

Belize lies on the eastern side of the Yucatán Peninsula. Bordering Mexico to the north and Guatemala to the west and south, it was the last country in the Americas to achieve independence. This came in 1981. Formerly known as British Honduras, its original inhabitants were Maya Indians, with a few Carib Indians along the coast. Though adjacent territory was conquered by the Spanish in the sixteenth century, the first recorded European settlers in the area were British wood-cutters in the seventeenth century. At a later date sugar plantations worked by African slaves were established. When Guatemala became independent in 1821 it laid claim to British Honduras and the sovereignty issue strained relations between the two countries until Guatemala officially recognized Belize as an independent country in 1993.

The northern part of the country is a swampy plain. In the south the Maya Mountains continue from Guatemala in a northeasterly direction, dividing the coastal plain from the interior. Victoria Peak, on a spur of this range, is flanked by tropical forest, grasslands, and farming regions. Rainforests containing jaguar still cover nearly half the country and in the rivers there are crocodile and manatee. The world's second longest coral reef lies offshore. Belize is much affected by hurricanes. After the 1961 hurricane that destroyed Belize City the capital was moved inland to Belmopan.

Agriculture employs close to a quarter of the labor force, and is the mainstay of the economy. The main domestic staples are maize, rice, kidney beans, and sweet potatoes. Belize enjoyed a boom in the years following independence, citrus fruit processing and tourism helping to reduce the earlier dependence on timber, bananas, and sugar. Sugar still accounts for about thirty percent of export earnings. Timber has lost importance, but the forests still produce valuable rosewood, mahogany, and chicle used for chewing gum. Fisheries specialize in lobsters and shrimp.

# Honduras

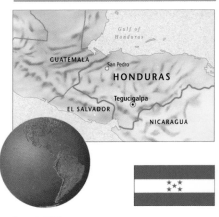

## Fact File

OFFICIAL NAME  Republic of Honduras

FORM OF GOVERNMENT  Republic with single legislative body (National Congress)

CAPITAL  Tegucigalpa

AREA  112,090 sq km (43,278 sq miles)

TIME ZONE  GMT – 6 hours

POPULATION  7,639,000

PROJECTED POPULATION 2015  8,280,000

POPULATION DENSITY  68.2 per sq km (176.5 per sq mile)

LIFE EXPECTANCY  69.4

INFANT MORTALITY (PER 1,000)  24.6

OFFICIAL LANGUAGE  Spanish

OTHER LANGUAGES  Indigenous languages, English

LITERACY RATE  80 %

RELIGIONS  Roman Catholic 97 %, Protestant and other beliefs 3 %

ETHNIC GROUPS  Mixed indigenous-European 90 %, indigenous 7 %, African 2 %, European 1 %

CURRENCY  Lempira

ECONOMY  Services 58.5 %, industry 28.1 %, agriculture 13.4 %

GNI PER CAPITA  US$ 1,600

CLIMATE  Tropical on plains, cooler in mountains

HIGHEST POINT  Cerro Las Minas 2,849 m (9,347 ft)

MAP REFERENCE  Page 428

Honduras is the second largest of the Central American countries. Its mountainous mass lies across the isthmus north of Nicaragua, with Guatemala to the west and El Salvador to the southwest. The Caribbean shoreline runs eastward from the Guatemalan border to the flat and almost uninhabited Mosquito Coast. In the west are the historic ruins of Copan, a site of the ancient Maya civilization which ended long before the Spaniards arrived in 1522. Gold first drew the Spanish to Honduras and when they discovered it in the west they founded Tegucigalpa in 1524. The Honduran mountains are highly metalliferous and silver is still an important export. Independent from Spain since 1821, the country has had decades of military rule with only the occasional elected government.

Caye Caulker, an island off the coast of Belize that is popular with scuba divers (left page top). An aerial view of Tegucigalpa, the capital of Honduras (left page bottom). El Salvador contains about twenty volcanoes, some still active. Izalco Volcano, El Salvador, seen from lush forest (left).

**OFFICIAL LANGUAGE** Spanish

**OTHER LANGUAGES** Indigenous languages (Nahua, Maya)

**LITERACY RATE** 80.2%

**RELIGIONS** Roman Catholic 83%, Protestant and other 17%

**ETHNIC GROUPS** Mixed indigenous-European 90%, indigenous 1%, European 9%

**CURRENCY** US dollar (since 2001)

**ECONOMY** Services 62.7%, industry 27.6%, agriculture 9.7%

**GNI PER CAPITA** US$ 2,850

**CLIMATE** Tropical, with wet season May to October; cooler in mountains

**HIGHEST POINT** Cerro El Pittal 2,730 m (8,957 ft)

**MAP REFERENCE** Page 428

El Salvador is the smallest, most densely populated country in Central America, and the only one without a coast on the Caribbean. It is in a seismic zone and has some twenty volcanoes, several of which are active. Once the home of the Pipil Indians and later a part of the Mexican Empire, the country won full independence in 1841 and established itself as the Republic of El Salvador in 1859. Over 100 years of civil strife and military rule followed.

From the 1880s about 75 percent of the land has been in the hands of 14 families, who farm huge plantations producing coffee, tobacco, and sugar. The potential for conflict between this landed oligarchy and the rural poor has been present since that time and in the 1970s left-wing disillusionment with the electoral process led to the formation of a number of guerrilla groups. Between 1979 and 1991 civil war raged, with the loss of 75,000 lives, and many people emigrated.

Behind El Salvador's narrow Pacific coastal plain rises a volcanic range. Inland is a rich and fertile central plain, occupying 25 percent of the country's total land area. The urban and rural population in this area accounts for sixty percent of the country's total, and produces ninety percent of El Salvador's coffee and tobacco, along with most of its sugar and corn. Further inland still, along the frontier with Honduras, are once forested and unpopulated mountain ranges.

The smallest country in Central America, El Salvador has the third-largest economy. Coffee is a major portion of exports. Manufacturing is based on food and beverage processing, while other industries are textiles, clothing, petroleum products, and cement. To stimulate the sluggish economy, new export markets have been targeted, foreign investment encouraged, and the tax and healthcare systems modernized. The Central America-Dominican Republic Free Trade Agreement (since 2006) strengthened the export trend. Annual remittances equal more than 16 percent of the GDP. The government is pursuing economic diversification—in textile production, international port services, and tourism.

At least 75 percent of Honduras is mountainous. From the central highlands several river valleys run northwest to the coast, where the plains along the Caribbean shore broaden toward the east. The lower valleys have been reclaimed and the forests have been replaced by banana plantations. On the Pacific side there is a short stretch of coast in the Gulf of Fonseca. The adjacent lowlands are used for growing cotton. Rainforest in the northeast provides sanctuary for a great variety of wildlife.

The original "banana republic", Honduras was the world's leading exporter during the 1920s and 1930s. Bananas still account for nearly a quarter of all exports but coffee is now the largest earner. The country depends heavily on the USA for trade: more than half of its exports and about fifty percent of its imports are traded with the USA. Most of the workforce are farmers, many of them at a subsistence level: food staples are corn, beans, and rice. Small-scale manufactures include furniture, textiles, footwear, chemicals, and cement. Subject to an International Monetary Fund (IMF) restructuring program in the 1990s, Honduras has faced difficulties, with its already poor people subject to sharp tax increases. In 1998, Hurricane Mitch killed more than 9,000 people in Central America, devastating crops and leaving thousands homeless. Honduras is currently the second-poorest country in Central America and one of the poorest in the Western Hemisphere. Its hopes lie on expanded trade under the US-Central America Free Trade Agreement (CAFTA), which took effect in 2006.

## El Salvador

### Fact File

**OFFICIAL NAME** Republic of El Salvador

**FORM OF GOVERNMENT** Republic with single legislative body (Legislative Assembly)

**CAPITAL** San Salvador

**AREA** 21,040 sq km (8,123 sq miles)

**TIME ZONE** GMT – 6 hours

**POPULATION** 7,066,000

**PROJECTED POPULATION 2015** 7,602,000

**POPULATION DENSITY** 335.8 per sq km (869.9 per sq mile)

**LIFE EXPECTANCY** 72.1

**INFANT MORTALITY (PER 1,000)** 22.2

# Nicaragua

## Fact File

OFFICIAL NAME  Republic of Nicaragua

FORM OF GOVERNMENT  Republic with single
legislative body (National Assembly)

CAPITAL  Managua

AREA  129,494 sq km (49,998 sq miles)

TIME ZONE  GMT – 6 hours

POPULATION  5,786,000

PROJECTED POPULATION 2015  6,277,000

POPULATION DENSITY  44.7 per sq km
(115.7 per sq mile)

LIFE EXPECTANCY  71.2

INFANT MORTALITY (PER 1,000)  25.9

OFFICIAL LANGUAGE  Spanish

OTHER LANGUAGES  Indigenous languages (among
them Chibcha, Miskito, Sumo), English

LITERACY RATE  67.5 %

RELIGIONS  Roman Catholic 72.9 %, Evangelical 15.1 %,
Moravian 1.5 %, other 2 %, none 8.5 %

ETHNIC GROUPS  Mixed indigenous-European 69 %,
European 17 %, African 9 %, indigenous 5 %

CURRENCY  Córdoba

ECONOMY  Services 57 %, industry 25.9 %,
agriculture 17.1 %

GNI PER CAPITA  US$ 980

CLIMATE  Tropical in lowlands, cooler in highlands;
wet season May to January

HIGHEST POINT  Pico Mogoton 2,107 m (6,913 ft)

MAP REFERENCE  Page 428

The largest republic in the Central American
isthmus, Nicaragua is also the least populated.
The western half, including Lake Nicaragua, the
largest lake in Central America, was settled by the
Spanish in the sixteenth century, and the Caribbean shore was for two centuries the British protectorate of Mosquito Coast (Costa de Miskitos).
Becoming independent from Spain in 1821, Nicaragua then experienced much instability. The 45-
year right-wing rule of the Somoza family ended
in 1979 when they were overthrown by the Marxist Sandinistas. Their left-wing rule provoked a
US-backed insurgency known as the "contras." In
free elections held in 1996 a right-of-center party
defeated the Sandinistas. President Arnoldo
Alemán was excluded from the 2001 elections
due to curruption charges, and was convicted in
2002. The Sandinistas won the 2006 elections.

Nicaragua's broad plain on the Caribbean side
leads to a coastal region of lagoons, beaches, and
river deltas. Rainfall here is heavy and the tropical wildlife includes crocodile and jaguar. Inland,
toward the east, there are mountain ranges brok-
en by basins and fertile valleys. In the west and
south a broad depression containing Lakes
Managua and Nicaragua runs from the Gulf of
Fonseca, on the Pacific coast, to the mouth of the
San Juan del Norte River, on the Caribbean.
Before the Panama Canal was built this was an
important route across the isthmus. This is a
region of cotton growing. Overlooking the lakes
are forty volcanoes, among them the active
Momotombo. An earthquake destroyed most of
Managua in 1972.

Nicaragua is still reorganizing its economy—
at one point under the Sandinistas inflation
reached 3,000 percent. Large-scale confiscation of
estates took place under the Sandinistas but the
peasants to whom land was given have not
always been able to live off their allotments, and
some land has been resold. Coffee and cotton are
the major export crops. Staples grown by the
many subsistence farmers include maize, rice, and
beans. Mineral production is led by silver and
gold followed by tungsten, lead, and zinc. Falling
prices for most of Nicaragua's export commodities, the loss of aid, and the impact of IMF policies reduced the nation's income in 1993 to close
to Haiti's—the poorest in the Americas. Slowly
recovering from the effects of the Sandinista rule
and civil war, the country has progressed towards
macroeconomic stability, but the annual economic growth has been far too slow, forcing it to
rely on international economic aid to meet its
fiscal obligations. In 2005, Nicaragua ratified the
USA-Central America Free Trade Agreement
(CAFTA), which will attract investment, create
jobs, and broaden economic development.

# Costa Rica

## Fact File

OFFICIAL NAME  Republic of Costa Rica

FORM OF GOVERNMENT  Republic with single
legislative body (Legislative Assembly)

CAPITAL  San José

AREA  51,100 sq km (19,730 sq miles)

TIME ZONE  GMT – 6 hours

POPULATION  4,196,000

PROJECTED POPULATION 2015  4,983,000

POPULATION DENSITY  82.1 per sq km (212.7 per sq mile)

LIFE EXPECTANCY  77.4

INFANT MORTALITY (PER 1,000)  9

OFFICIAL LANGUAGE  Spanish

OTHER LANGUAGES  English, Creole

LITERACY RATE  94.9 %

RELIGIONS  Roman Catholic 76.3 %, Evangelical 13.7 %,
other Protestant 2 %, other 4.8 %, none 3.2 %

ETHNIC GROUPS  European and mixed indigenous-
European 94 %, African 3 %, indigenous 1 %,
Chinese 1 %, other 1 %

CURRENCY  Costa Rican colón

ECONOMY  Services 62.1 %, industry 29.4 %,
agriculture 8.5 %

GNI PER CAPITA  US$ 5,560

CLIMATE  Tropical, with wet season May to November

HIGHEST POINT  Cerro Chirripó 3,819 m (12,530 ft)

MAP REFERENCE  Page 428

Costa Rica lies on the Central American isthmus, between Nicaragua and Panama. Its rainforests and wildlife made it popular with tourists beginning in the 1980s. Like a number of other Central American countries, it was historically influenced by the civilizations of the Maya and Aztec, and the earliest human settlements go back 10,000 years. It was named by Christopher Columbus in 1502, *costa rica* meaning "rich coast", and from the 1570s it was a Spanish colony. It gained its independence in 1821 and became a republic in 1848.

Costa Rica is known for its high standards of education, long life expectancy, democratic and stable system of government, a comparatively high per capita income, and a relatively small divide between the rich and the poor. It abolished its national army in 1948. This portrait, however, underestimates the economic role played by US aid in recent times. With that aid now reduced, Costa Rican governments have had to take austerity measures, and this has led to some unrest.

Three ranges form the mountainous skeleton of the country. From the border of Nicaragua, the northern Cordillera de Guanacaste descends to meet the Cordillera Central. Between the Cordillera Central and the southern Cordillera de Talamanca lies the temperate Meseta Central, the valley where San José is situated. The surrounding area is the main coffee-growing region, coffee production supporting a substantial percentage of the population.

The lowlands on the Caribbean and Pacific coasts are heavily forested and rich in wildlife. While the Pacific side is relatively dry, the Caribbean lowlands receive heavy rain. Both coasts have numerous mangrove swamps and white, sandy beaches. There are several volcanoes on the ranges, some of which are active. Cattle are raised in the dry northwest savanna region of Guanacaste.

Costa Rica's basically stable economy depends on tourism, agriculture, and electronics exports. There are sizeable bauxite deposits at Boruca, and aluminum smelting is a major industry. Minerals mined include small quantities of gold, silver, manganese, and mercury. Energy self-sufficiency is being pursued through the development of hydroelectric power. Immigration from Nicaragua has increasingly become a concern. 300,000–500,000 Nicaraguans are estimated to be in Costa Rica, straining the social welfare system.

# Panama

## Fact File

| | |
|---|---|
| OFFICIAL NAME | Republic of Panama |
| FORM OF GOVERNMENT | Republic with single legislative body (Legislative Assembly) |
| CAPITAL | Panama |
| AREA | 78,200 sq km (30,193 sq miles) |
| TIME ZONE | GMT – 5 hours |
| POPULATION | 3,293,000 |
| PROJECTED POPULATION 2015 | 3,774,000 |
| POPULATION DENSITY | 42.1 per sq km (109.1 per sq mile) |
| LIFE EXPECTANCY | 75.2 |
| INFANT MORTALITY (PER 1,000) | 15.6 |
| OFFICIAL LANGUAGE | Spanish |
| OTHER LANGUAGES | Indigenous languages (Guaymi, Chibcha, and others), English |
| LITERACY RATE | 91.9 % |
| RELIGIONS | Roman Catholic 85 %, Protestant 15 % |
| ETHNIC GROUPS | Mixed indigenous-European 70 %, African 14 %, European 10 %, indigenous 6 % |
| CURRENCY | Balboa |
| ECONOMY | Services 77 %, industry 16.4 %, agriculture 6.6 % |
| GNI PER CAPITA | US$ 5,510 |
| CLIMATE | Tropical, with long wet season May to January |

*Nicaraguan children outside their thatched home on the island of Omotepe, with the volcano of Concepción in the background (left page top). The Pacuare River running through rainforest in Costa Rica (center). A cargo ship heading east through the Gatun locks on the Panama Canal (left).*

HIGHEST POINT  Volcán Barú 3,475 m (11,401 ft)

MAP REFERENCE  Page 429

Panama joins two oceans and two continents. With Costa Rica to the west and Colombia to the east, it forms a narrow neck of land connecting Central to South America, while the Panama Canal links the Atlantic Ocean to the Pacific. The Spanish first proposed a canal in the early sixteenth century. Later, at the time of the California Gold Rush, the USA began to press for action. In 1881 work began on a design by de Lesseps, the builder of the Suez Canal, but malaria and yellow fever killed so many workers that it had to be abandoned. Control of these diseases was one of the achievements of the American builders, who eventually completed the canal in 1914. Expansion began in 2007. When finished, by 2013/14, the waterway will be able to handle twice as much traffic as currently.

Part of Colombia until 1903, Panama has been closely linked with the USA since the construction of the canal gave the latter rights over a 16 km (10 mile) wide Canal Zone until the year 2000. A major upheaval took place in Panama during 1989 when the USA invaded and removed the country's "maximum leader" Manuel Noriega in order that he face drug charges in Miami, Florida. Electoral democracy was restored in the country, and Noriega was jailed, but the laundering of large amounts of drug money in association with cartels in Colombia continues to be a problem.

The 3,000 m (9,850 ft) tall mountains of the Serrania de Tabasara (Cordillera Central) run west of the canal along the isthmus, separated from the southern Peninsula de Azuera by a long stretch of plain. East of the canal two more mountain ranges form arcs parallel to the Pacific and Caribbean coasts. Most of the country, however, including 750 offshore islands, lies below 700 m (2,300 ft) and swelters in tropical heat and high humidity. Rainforests are extensive, and those of the Darien National Park, with their abundant wildlife, are among the wildest areas left in the Americas. Most Panamanians live within 20 km (12 miles) of the Canal Zone, a third of them in the capital itself.

Panama's economy is based on a well-developed services sector that accounts for three-fourths of gross domestic product. Services include operating the Panama Canal—which will be enlarged to double its present size by 2014—banking, the Colon Free Zone, insurance, and tourism. The country has the largest open-registry merchant fleet in the world. Panama has one of the highest standards of living in Central America. However, the country's commercial debt is also one of the highest in the world in per capita terms, and during the mid-1990s the country experienced an economic slow-down. When the United States withdrew their forces from Panama at the end of 1999 the effect on the contry's economy was very noticeable in 2000 and 2001, but growth picked up in 2004–06, led by export-oriented services.

North and Central America

# North America: Physical

GREENLAND SEA

Denmark Strait

LABRADOR SEA

Newfoundland

Arctic Circle

Labrador

Île d'Anticosti

ARCTIC OCEAN

WANDEL SEA

Peary Land

Davis Strait

Baffin Bay

Bylot Island

Baffin Island

Prince Charles Island

Southampton I.

Mansel I.

Coats I.

Péninsule d'Ungava

Akimiski Island

CANADIAN SHIELD

Ellesmere Island

Devon Island

Hudson Bay

Belcher Islands

Prince Patrick I.

Bathurst Island

Melville Island

Prince of Wales I.

King William Island

Baker Lake

Victoria Island

Banks Island

Great Bear Lake

CANADIAN

Lake Winnipeg

L. Manitoba

Contwoyto Lake

Dubawnt Lake

Slave

Lake Athabasca

BEAUFORT SEA

CHUKCHI SEA

Ostrov Vrangelya

Bering Strait

Brooks Range

Mackenzie Mountains

ROCKY MO

Lake Claire

Lesser Slave Lake

Peter Pond Lake

Great Slave Lake

Red Deer

North Saskatchewan

South Saskatchewan

G

Columbia Basin

Arctic Circle

Alaska Range

Mt Logan 5959 m

Coast Mountains

Columb

Norton Sound

St. Lawrence Island

Yukon

Mt Foraker 5304 m
Mt McKinley 6194 m

Baranof I.

Prince of Wales I.

Graham Island

Moresby Island

Vancouver Island

BERING SEA

Bristol Bay

Aleutian Range

Kodiak Island

Afognak I.

Gulf of Alaska

Umnak I.

Unalaska I.

Unimak I.

Aleutian Islands

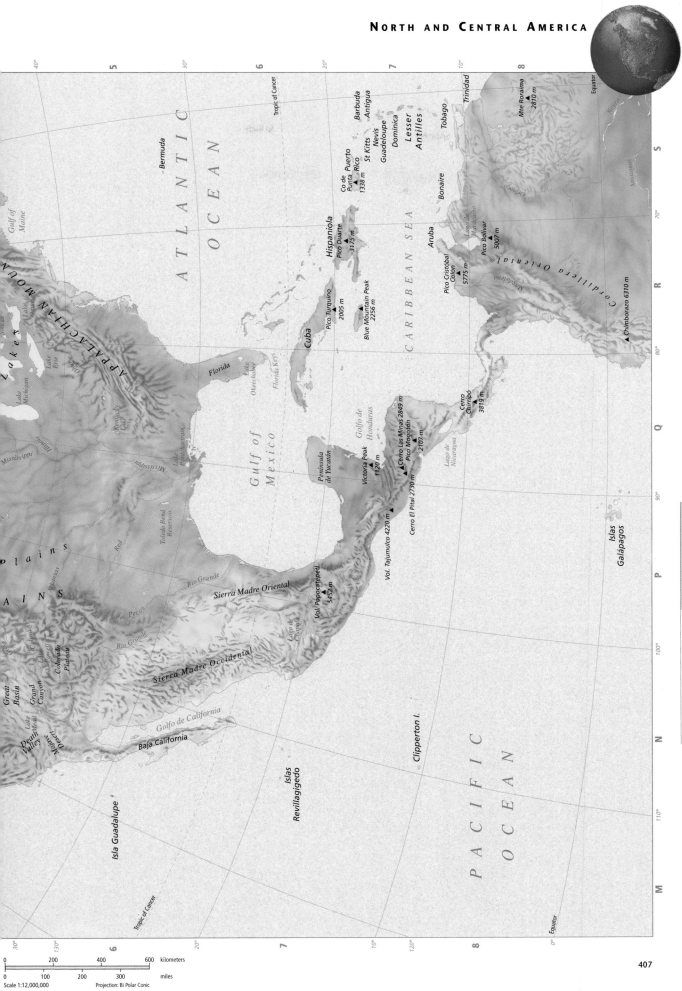

ATLANTIC OCEAN

Gulf of Maine

Bermuda

Tropic of Cancer

Barbuda
Antigua
St Kitts
Nevis
Guadeloupe
Dominica
Lesser Antilles

Co de Puerto
Punta Rico
1338 m

Hispaniola
Pico Duarte
3175 m

Cuba
Pico Turquino
2005 m

Blue Mountain Peak
2256 m

Florida

Lake Okeechobee

Florida Keys

APPALACHIAN MOUN

Lakes

Lake Huron

Lake Erie

Lake Ontario

Lake Michigan

Kentucky Lake

Tennessee

Mississippi

Lake Nipigon

Lake Superior

Mississippi

CARIBBEAN SEA

Aruba
Bonaire

Trinidad

Tobago

Mte Roraima
2810 m

Orinoco

Equator

Lago de Maracaibo
Pico Bolivar
5007 m

Pico Cristóbal Colón
5775 m

Cordillera Oriental

Magdalena

Chimborazo 6310 m

Gulf of Mexico

Golfo de Honduras

Península de Yucatán

Victoria Peak
1120 m

Cerro Las Minas 2849 m
Pico Mogotón
2107 m

Cerro El Pital 2730 m

Vol. Tajumulco 4220 m

Lago de Nicaragua

Cerro Chirripó
3819 m

Islas Galápagos

Sierra Madre Oriental

Vol Popocatépetl
5452 m

Rio Grande

Sierra Madre Occidental

Pecos

Rio Grande

Lago de Chapala

Plains

A I N S

Great Basin

Grand Canyon

Colorado Plateau

Death Valley

Mojave Desert

Lake Mead

Colorado

Powell

Golfo de California

Baja California

Islas Revillagigedo

Clipperton I.

Isla Guadalupe

PACIFIC OCEAN

Tropic of Cancer

Equator

Toledo Bend Reservoir

Arkansas

Red

0    200    400    600   kilometers

0   100   200   300   miles

Scale 1:12,000,000      Projection: Bi Polar Conic

# North America: Political

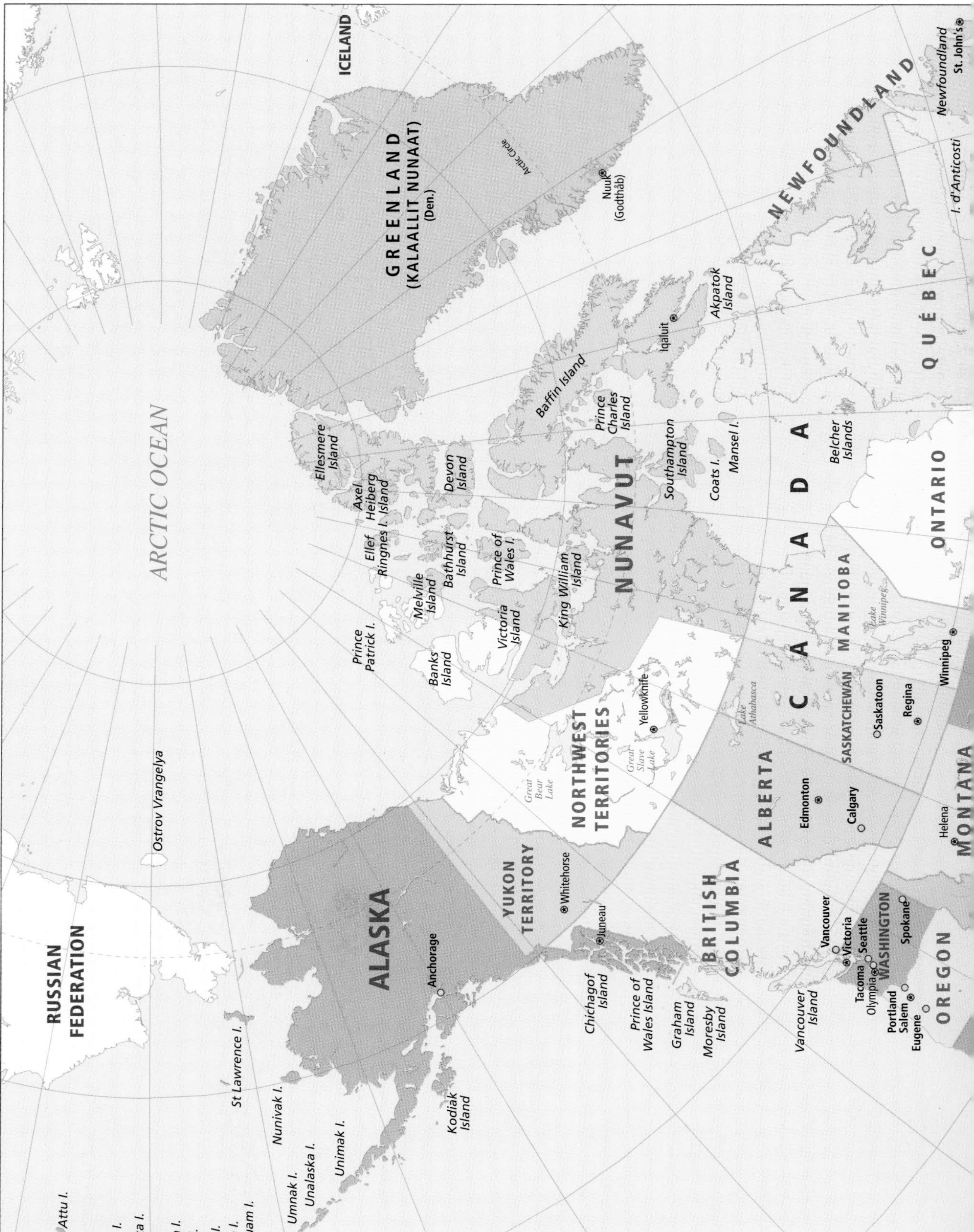

ICELAND

GREENLAND
(KALAALLIT NUNAAT)
(Den.)

*Arctic Circle*

Nuuk
(Godthåb) ◉

NEWFOUNDLAND

*Newfoundland*

St. John's ◉

*I. d'Anticosti*

*Newfoundland*

QUÉBEC

ARCTIC OCEAN

Baffin Island

Iqaluit ◉

Ellesmere Island

*Axel Heiberg Island*

*Ellef Ringnes I.*

*Devon Island*

*Prince Charles Island*

*Southampton Island*

*Coats I.*

*Mansel I.*

*Belcher Islands*

ONTARIO

*Prince Patrick I.*

*Melville Island*

*Bathurst Island*

*Prince of Wales I.*

*King William Island*

NUNAVUT

CANADA

MANITOBA

*Lake Winnipeg*

Winnipeg ◉

*Banks Island*

*Victoria Island*

SASKATCHEWAN

◉ Saskatoon

Regina ◉

*Lake Athabasca*

NORTHWEST TERRITORIES

Yellowknife ◉

*Great Slave Lake*

ALBERTA

Edmonton ◉

Calgary ◯

*Great Bear Lake*

Helena ◉

MONTANA

RUSSIAN FEDERATION

*Ostrov Vrangelya*

ALASKA

Anchorage ◯

YUKON TERRITORY

Whitehorse ◉

Juneau ◉

BRITISH COLUMBIA

Vancouver ◯

Victoria ◉

Seattle ◯

Spokane ◯

WASHINGTON

Tacoma ◯

Olympia ◉

Portland ◯

Salem ◉

Eugene ◯

OREGON

*Chichagof Island*

*Prince of Wales Island*

*Graham Island*

*Moresby Island*

*Vancouver Island*

*St Lawrence I.*

*Nunivak I.*

*Umnak I.*

*Unalaska I.*

*Unimak I.*

*Kodiak Island*

*Attu I.*

*Kiska I.*

*Amchitka I.*

*Kanaga I.*

*Adak I.*

*Atka I.*

*Amlia I.*

*Seguam I.*

GUYANA

BRAZIL

VENEZUELA

COLOMBIA

PERU

ECUADOR

ANGUILLA (U.K.) ANTIGUA AND BARBUDA
GUADELOUPE (Fr.)
DOMINICA
Roseau MARTINIQUE (Fr.)
ST LUCIA Castries BARBADOS
St Johns Basseterre Bridgetown St George's
ST VINCENT AND THE GRENADINES GRENADA Port of Spain
VIRGIN ISLANDS (U.K.) ST KITTS AND NEVIS MONTSERRAT
VIRGIN ISLANDS (U.S.A.)
PUERTO RICO (U.S.A.)
ARUBA (Neth.) NETHERLANDS ANTILLES (Neth.)
TRINIDAD AND TOBAGO

BERMUDA (U.K.)

ATLANTIC OCEAN

Tropic of Cancer

Equator

TURKS AND CAICOS ISLANDS (U.K.)
DOMINICAN REPUBLIC
Santo Domingo
BAHAMAS
HAITI Port-au-Prince
CARIBBEAN SEA

Nassau
Matanzas
CUBA
La Habana (Havana)
Pinar del Rio
Santiago de Cuba
Bayamo
Cienfuegos
CAYMAN ISLANDS (U.K.)
JAMAICA Kingston

NEW HAMPSHIRE
Concord
Montpelier
VERMONT MASSACHUSETTS Boston
NEW YORK Albany Providence
Buffalo Hartford CONNECTICUT RHODE ISLAND
Detroit Hamilton PENNSYLVANIA New York
Toronto OHIO NEW JERSEY
Milwaukee Cleveland Harrisburg Trenton
Madison Lansing Columbus DELAWARE Dover
Chicago INDIANA Annapolis Washington D.C.
Davenport Indianapolis W.VIRGINIA MARYLAND
Springfield Louisville Frankfort Charleston Richmond Virginia Beach
St Louis KENTUCKY VIRGINIA
ILLINOIS Nashville Raleigh NORTH CAROLINA
MISSOURI TENNESSEE Charlotte
Jefferson City Memphis Columbia SOUTH CAROLINA
Little Rock Chattanooga Atlanta Charleston
ARKANSAS Birmingham GEORGIA Savannah
MISSISSIPPI ALABAMA Columbus
Jackson Montgomery Jacksonville
LOUISIANA Mobile Tallahassee
Baton Rouge FLORIDA Orlando
New Orleans St Petersburg Tampa
Fort Lauderdale
Miami

UNITED STATES OF AMERICA

NEBRASKA IOWA
Des Moines
Lincoln
KANSAS Topeka
Denver Pueblo COLORADO
Santa Fe
Albuquerque Amarillo OKLAHOMA Oklahoma City
NEW MEXICO
Lubbock
El Paso
Fort Worth Dallas
TEXAS
Austin Houston
San Antonio Corpus Christi

UTAH
Cheyenne

CALIFORNIA
Bakersfield Las Vegas
Los Angeles ARIZONA
Long Beach Phoenix Mesa
Anaheim Tucson
San Diego Mexicali
Ensenada

Nuevo Laredo
Matamoros
Monterrey
Hermosillo
Chihuahua
San Luis Potosí
MEXICO
Tampico
Mérida
Campeche
Guadalajara León
Querétaro Coatzacoalcos
Morelia México Tuxtla Gutiérrez
Cuernavaca Puebla de Zaragoza
La Paz Acapulco

BELIZE Belmopan
GUATEMALA
Guatemala
San Salvador EL SALVADOR
HONDURAS
Tegucigalpa
NICARAGUA
Managua
COSTA RICA San José
PANAMA
Panamá
Isla de Coiba

Isla Guadalupe (Mex.)

Islas Revillagigedo (Mex.)

Islas Galápagos (Ecu.)

PACIFIC OCEAN

Tropic of Cancer

200 400 600 kilometers
100 200 300 miles
Scale 1:12,000,000    Projection: Bi Polar Conic

# North Canada • Alaska • Greenland

RUSSIAN FEDERATION

Koryakskoye Nagor'ye
Anadyr'
Ugol'nyye Kopi
Mys Navarin
Iul'tin
Ostrov Vrangelya
Ushakovskoye

CHUKCHI SEA

Chukotskiy Poluostrov
Anadyrskiy Zaliv
Mys Chukotskiy
St Lawrence I.

BERING SEA

Bering Strait
C. Lisburne
Point Hope
Wainwright
Pt. Barrow
Barrow
Nuiqsut
Prudhoe
Kaktovik
Herschel

BEAUFORT SEA

C. Prince Alfred
Prince Patrick I.
Passage Point
Banks Island
Sachs Harbour
Prince Albert Peninsula
Holman
Wollaston Peninsula

St Matthew I.
Nunivak I.
Scammon Bay
Kotlik
C. Newenham
Tununak
Bethel
Kuskokwim Bay
Togiak
Dillingham

Seward Peninsula
Kotzebue Sound
Nome
Norton Sound
Kotzebue
Shungnak

Bristol Bay

Alaska Pen.
Aleutian Range
Afognak I.
Kodiak
Kodiak I.
Shelikof Strait
Homer
Seward
Kenai
Anchorage
Palmer
Cordova

Gulf of Alaska

U. S. A.
ALASKA
Kuskokwim Mountains
Kuskokwim
Iliamna
Alaska Range
Mt McKinley 6194 m
Cantwell
Fairbanks
Tanana
Delta Junction
Tok
Glennallen
Chugach Mountains
Yakutat

Brooks Range
Umiat
Sagwon
Chandalar
Arctic Circle
Huslia
Ruby
Koyukuk
Allakaket
Fort Yukon
Chalkyitsik
Sheenjek
Old Crow
Aklavik
Inuvik
Fort McPherson
Tsiigehtchic

BRITISH COLUMBIA

Mackenzie Bay
C. Bathurst
Tuktoyaktuk
Paulatuk

Ogilvie Mountains
YUKON TERRITORY
Dawson
Mayo
Pelly Crossing
Ross River
Keele Peak 2972 m
Selwyn Mountains
Carmacks
Faro
Whitehorse
Haines Junction
Carcross
Skagway
Teslin
Watson Lake
Atlin
Cassiar
Dease Lake
Telegraph Creek

Franklin Mountains
Fort Good Hope
Norman Wells
Tulita
Déline
Great Bear Lake
Colville Lake

NORTHWEST TERRITORIES
Wrigley
Fort Simpson
Rae Lakes
Yellowknife
Edzo
Rae
Lutselk'e
Great Slave Lake
Fort Providence
Kakisa
Hay River
Fort Smith
Fort Fitzgerald
Fort Chipewyan
Lake Athabasca
Stony Rapids

Juneau
Sitka
Petersburg
Wrangell
Ketchikan
Stewart
Prince Rupert
Graham I.
Moresby I.
Queen Charlotte Is.
Alexander Archipelago
C. Knox

COAST MOUNTAINS
Liard River
Fort Liard
Watson Lake
Muncho Lake
Fort Nelson
Fort St John
Dawson Creek
Hudson's Hope
Mackenzie
Chetwynd
Hazelton
New Hazelton
Smithers
Burns Lake
Houston
Vanderhoof
Prince George
McBride
Quesnel
Williams Lake
Bella Coola
Rivers Inlet
Hanceville
Cache Creek

ROCKY MOUNTAINS
ALBERTA
Peace River
Grande Prairie
Slave Lake
Fort McMurray
La Loche
Conklin
Athabasca
Westlock
Whitecourt
Edson
Hinton
Jasper
Edmonton
Leduc
Wetaskiwin
Ponoka
Red Deer
Didsbury
Banff
Golden
Calgary
Drumheller
Hanna
Medicine Hat
Lethbridge
Cardston
Magrath

SASKATCHEWAN
La Ronge
Prince Albert
North Battleford
Biggar
Saskatoon
Rosetown
Kindersley
Melfort
Yorkton
Swift Current
Moose Jaw
Regina

Vancouver Island
Campbell River
Nanaimo
Tofino
C. Scott
Port Hardy
Victoria
Vancouver
Burnaby
Kamloops
Kelowna
Penticton
Cranbrook

WASHINGTON
U. S. A.
C. Flattery
Mt Olympus 2424 m
Olympia
Tacoma
Seattle
C. Disappointment

PACIFIC OCEAN

Scale 1:15,000,000     Projection: Azimuthal Equal Area

# West Canada

**YUKON**

**TERRITORY**

**BRITISH COLUMBIA**

**ALASKA**

**U.S.A.**

St Elias Mts

Mt Hays 2704 m

Mt Fairweather 4663 m

Whitehorse
Robinson
Carcross
Jakes Corner
Johnsons Crossing
Teslin
Skagway
Atlin
Pakina
Mt Murray 2162 m
Watson Lake
Port Liard

Kusawa Lake
Tagish Lake
Atlin Lake
Teslin
Cassiar Mountains
Liard

Trout Lake

Elfin Cove
Hoonah
Hawk Inlet
Juneau
Douglas
Admiralty Island
Chichagof Island

Cassiar
Good Hope Lake
Coal River
Liard River
Muncho Lake
Toad River
Port Nelson

Meszah Peak 2164 m
Dease Lake
King Mtn 2408 m
Mt Roosevelt 2972 m
Summit Lake
Mt Sylvia 2942 m
Port Nelson

Sitka Pt
Sitka
Baranof
Kake
Baranof Island

Stikine Plateau

Telegraph Creek
Iskut
Mt Ratz 3136 m

Mt Will 2515 m

Mt Cushing 2469 m
Ware
Prophet River
Trutch

C

Petersburg
Wrangell

Bob Quinn Lake

2896 m Great Snow Mt
Sikanni Chief
Pink Mountain
Wonowon
Ros

Baranof Island

Prince of Wales Island
Craig
Ketchikan

Stewart

Sustut Peak 2469 m

Williston Lake

Fort St John
Hudson's Hope
Chetwynd
Day

Alexander Archipelago

Dixon Entrance
C. Knox

Hazelton
New Hazelton
Moricetown
755 m Seven Sisters Peaks
Smithers
Telkwa
Houston
Forestdale

Takla Lake

Babine Lake

MacKenzie
Mcleod Lake

R O C K

Masset
Porcher I.
Graham Island
Queen Charlotte Sandspit

Queen Charlotte Mts

Queen Charlotte Islands

Terrace
Prince Rupert
Kitimat

Burns Lake
Fort St James
Fraser Lake
Engen

Summit Lake
Upper Fraser
Sinclair Mills
Mt Sir Ale 3277
Dome C

Pitt I.
Banks I.
Hecate Strait
Lyell I.
Moresby Island
Princess Royal I.
Aristazabel I.
Kunghit I.

Remano

Ootsa Lake
Lily Lake
Vanderhoof
Giscome
Prince George
Red Rock

Hixon
Strathnaver
Crescent Spur
Mc

Eutsuk Lake
François Lake

Fawnie Nose 1926 m

Nazko
Wells
Barkerville
Kersley
Quesnel

Quesnel

Queen Charlotte Sound
Calvert I.

Bella Coola
Mt Saugstad 2908 m

Chilcotin

Redstone
Marguerite
Soda Creek
Williams Lake

Horsefly Lake

C. Scott
Port Hardy
Sointula
Quatsino

Mt Waddlington 4016 m

Mt Tatlow 3065 m

Tatla Lake
Hanceville
Big Creek
Springhouse
Dog Creek
100 Mile House
Lac la Hache

Clearw

C. Cook

Mt Queen Bess 3313 m
Gold Bridge

Pavilion
Cache Creek
Ashcroft
Clinton
Sayona

Port Alice
Kelsey Bay
Sayward
Brem River

Mt Tinniswood 2606 m

Pemberton
Mount Currie
Whistler
Lillooet
Lytton
Spences Bridge
Kamloop
Merritt

Zeballos
Campbell River
Powell River
Brackendale
Squamish

Boston Bar
Yale

Gold River
Comox
Courtenay
Irvines Landing
Sechelt
Mt Garibaldi 2678 m
Britannia Beach

385 m
Princeton
Hope

Nootka I.
Nootka
Estevan Point
Flores I.
Tofino

Vancouver Island

Port Alberni
Nanaimo
Ladysmith

Vancouver
Burnaby
White Rock
Langley
Blaine

Chilliwack
Abbotsford

Harrison Lake

Mt Baker 3285 m
Acme
Pendale

Ucluelet

Duncan
Sidney
Victoria
Sooke

Bellingham
Anacortes
Hamilton
Sedro Woolley
Rockport

Sur

Barkley Sound
C. Beale
Clo-oose
Port Renfrew
C. Flattery
Neah Bay
Sappho
Joyce
Port Angeles
Forks
Oak Harbor
Sequim

Mt Logan 2733 m
Lake Chelan

Ma
Winth
W

PACIFIC OCEAN

412

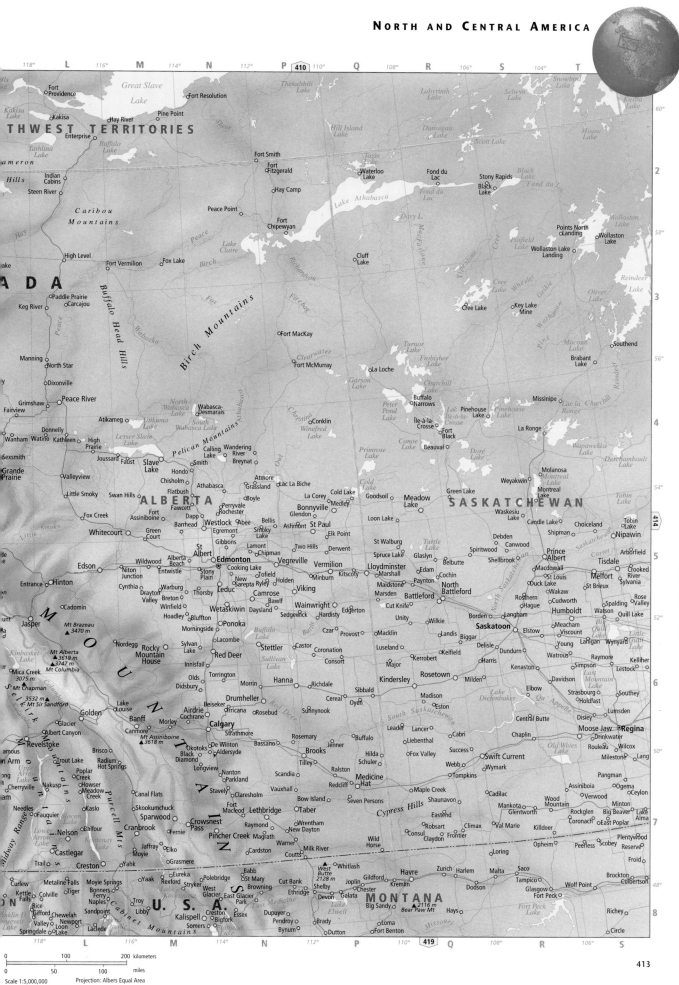

North and Central America

Scale 1:5,000,000      Projection: Albers Equal Area

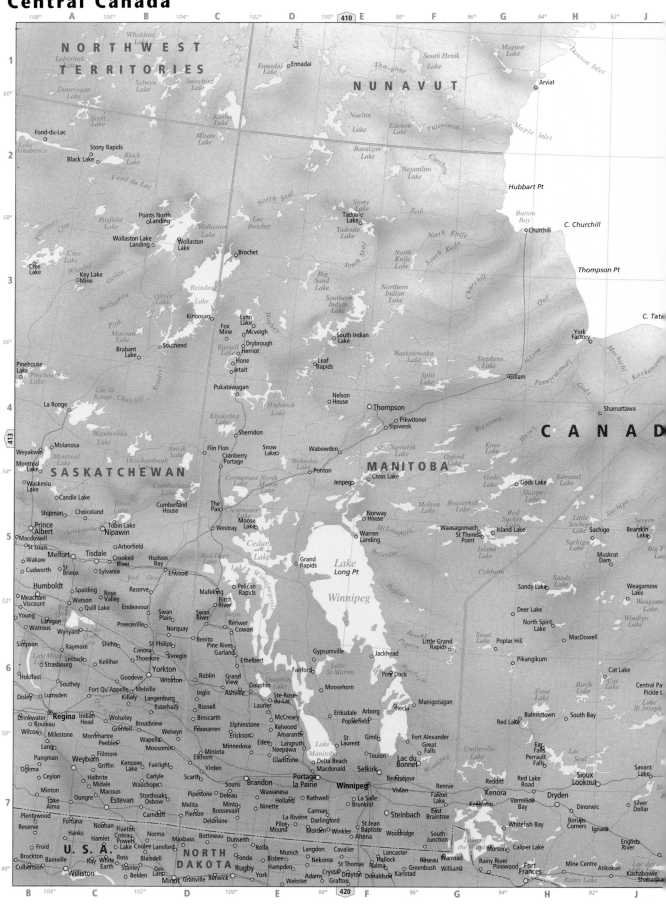

NORTHWEST TERRITORIES

NUNAVUT

CANADA

SASKATCHEWAN

MANITOBA

NORTH DAKOTA

U.S.A.

Lake Winnipeg

Winnipeg

Regina

Péninsule d´Ungava

Hudson

Bay

Mansel I.

Akulivik

Mosquito Bay

Puvirnituq

Rivière de Povungnituk

Povungnituk Bay

Ottawa Is

Inukjuak

Lac Nantais

Lac Payne

Arnaud

Lac La Potherie

Lac Minto

Rivière aux Feuilles

Sleeper Is

King George Islands

Nastapoka Islands

Sanikiluaq

Belcher Is

Sainsbury Pt

Merry I.

Long I.

Lac Burton

Pte Louis-XIV

Nastapoca

Lac Guillaume-Delisle

Lac à l'Eau Claire

Lac d'Iberville

Lac Bienville

Kujjuaraapik

Grande Rivière de la Baleine

Kananupscow

Fort Severn

Winisk

Peawanuck

C. Henrietta Maria

Sutton Ridges

Sutton

Wakwayowkastic

Severn

Shagamu

Shamattawa

Winisk

Réservoir de La Grande Deux

Réservoir de La Grande Trois

Grande Rivière

Radisson

Chisasibi

Lac Duncan

Castor

Lac de la Corvette

Sakami

Lac Sakami

QUÉBEC

James

Bay

North Twin I.

South Twin I.

Nouveau-Comptoir (Wemindji)

Réservoir Opinaca

Eastmain

Kasabonika

Webequie

Attawapiskat

Akimiski I.

C. Duncan

Charlton I.

Eastmain

Ekwan

Witchwood Channel

Missisa Lake

Kopiskau

Fort Albany

Baie de Rupert

Waskaganish

Rivière de Rupert

Lac Mesgouez

Lac Mistassini

Lansdowne House

ONTARIO

Marten Falls

Ogoki

Attawapiskat

Albany

Moosonee

Moose Factory

Hannah Bay

Moose

Nottaway

Harricana

Lac Evans

Mistassini

Ogoki Res.

Ogoki

Kesagami Lake

Chibougamau

Chapais

Caribou Lake

Lake Nipigon

Auden

Aroland

Nakina

Fraserdale

Lac au Goéland

Matagami

Desmaraisville

Miquelon

Bell

Beattyville

Réservoir Gouin

Gerladton

Jellicoe

Longlac

Caramat

Hearst

Mattice

Jogues

Lowther

Opasatika

Kapuskasing

Smooth Rock Falls

Moonbeam

Driftwood

Normétal

Matagami

Lac

Beardmore

Hillsport

Hornepayne

Cochrane

Iroquois Falls

La Sarre

Authier

Villemontel

Ámos

Senneterre

Langlade

Oskélanéo

Nipigon

Red Rock

Terrace Bay

Manitouwadge

Oba

Fire River

Porquis Junction

Matheson

Duparquet

Malartic

Val-d'Or

Forsythé

Parent

St Ignace I.

Marathon

White River

Peterbell

Elsas

Timmins

Ramore

Rouyn-Noranda

Long Lake

Missinaibi

Mattagami

Lake Abitibi

0    100    200 kilometers

0    50    100    miles

Scale 1:5,000,000          Projection: Albers Equal Area

# East Canada

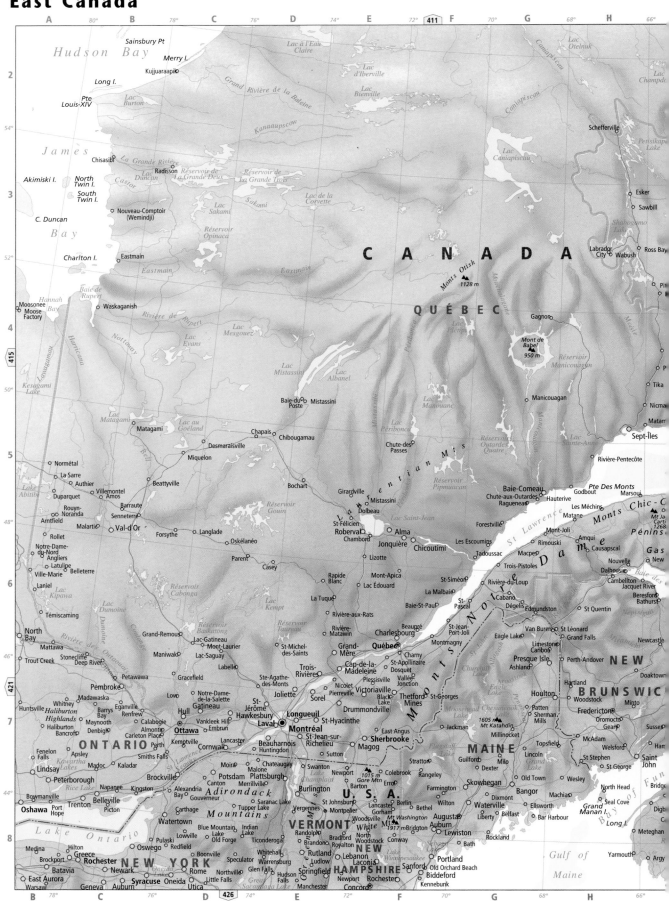

0    100    200 kilometers
0    50    100    miles

Scale 1:5,000,000    Projection: Albers Equal Area

# Northwest United States

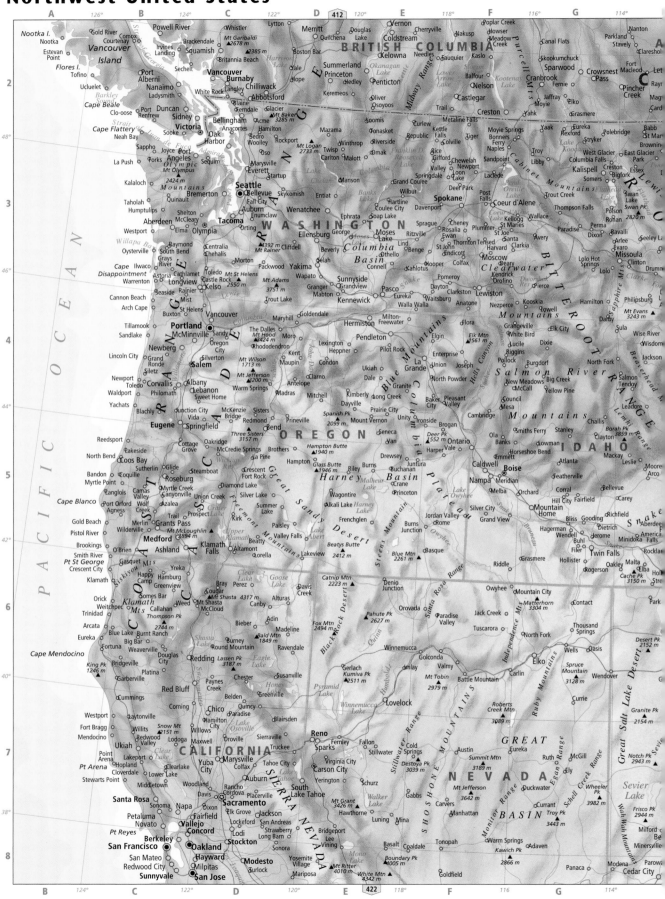

© Random House Australia Pty Ltd

North and Central America

# Central United States

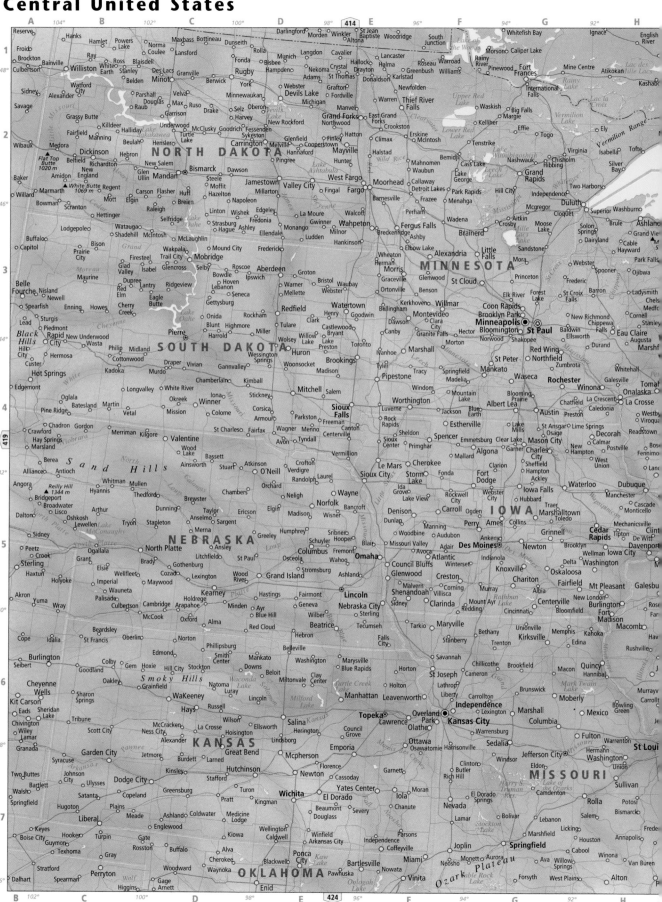

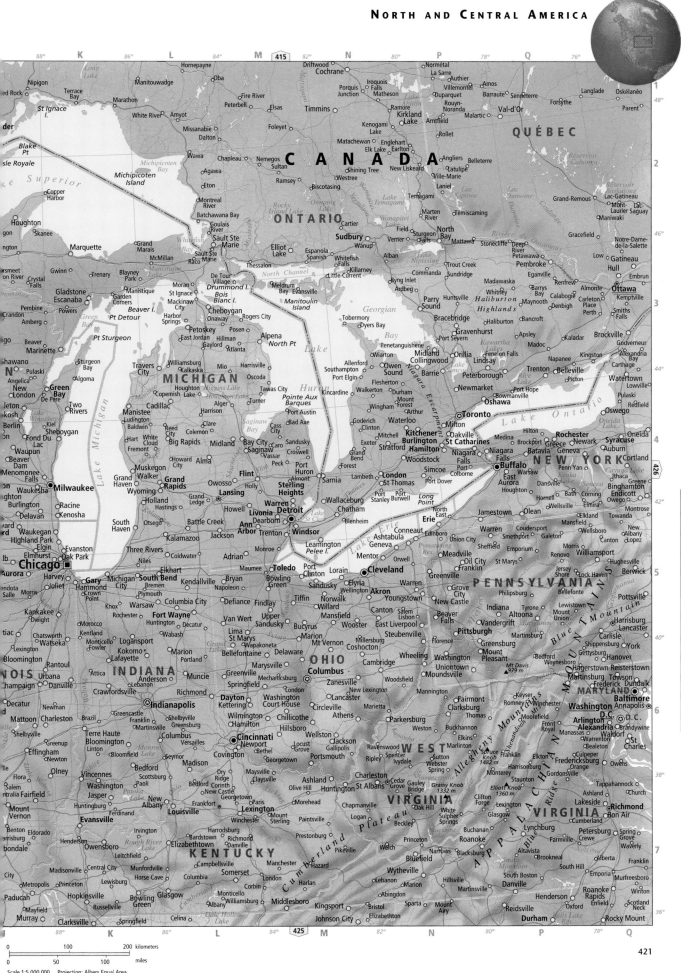

North and Central America

Scale 1:5,000,000   Projection: Albers Equal Area

# Southwest United States

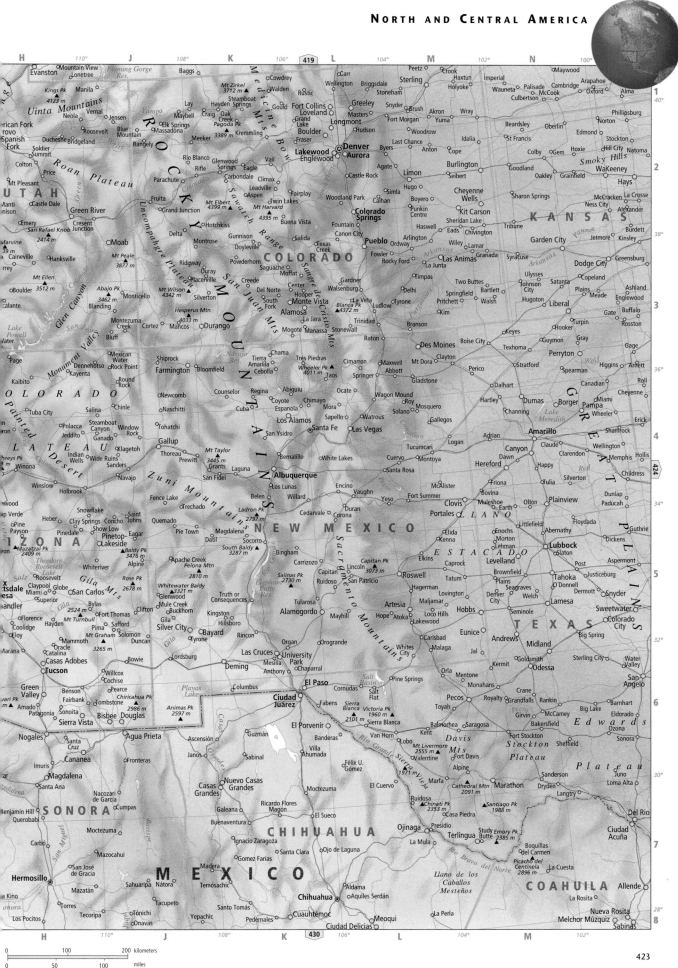

Scale 1:5,000,000   Projection: Albers Equal Area

# Southeast United States

© Random House Australia Pty Ltd

Scale 1:5,000,000   Projection: Albers Equal Area

North and Central America

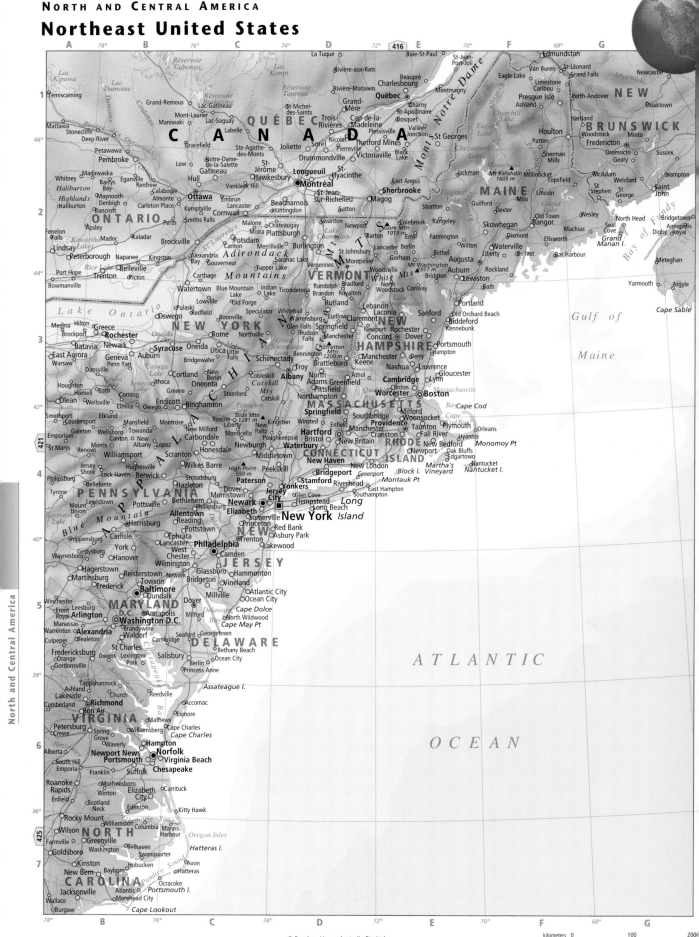

© Random House Australia Pty Ltd

kilometers 0    100    200

miles 0    50    100

Scale 1:5,000,000    Projection: Albers Equal Area

# East Caribbean • North Venezuela

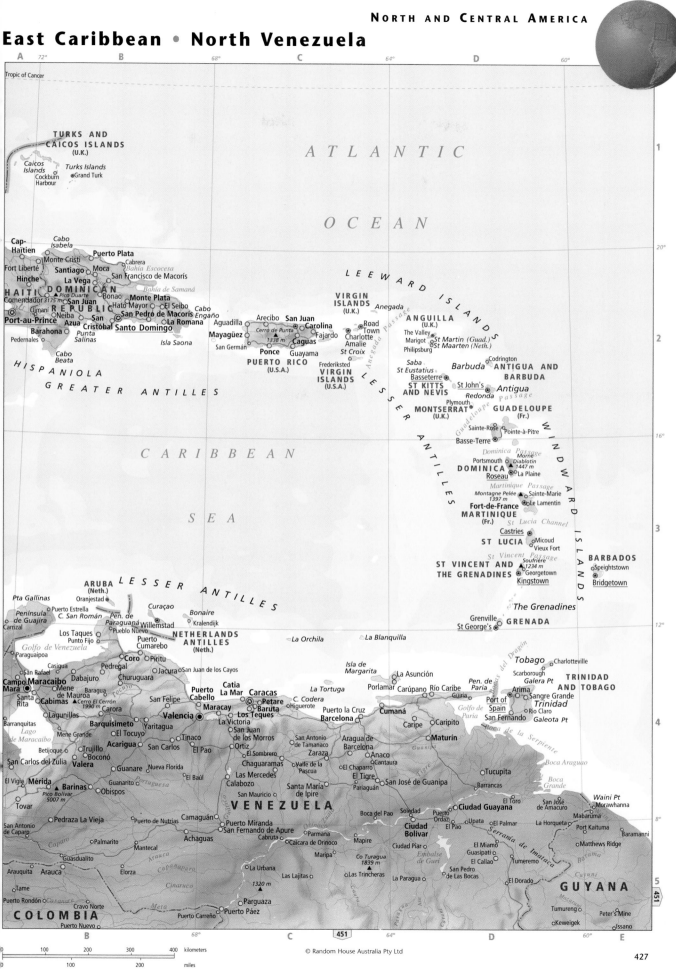

# Central America • West Caribbean

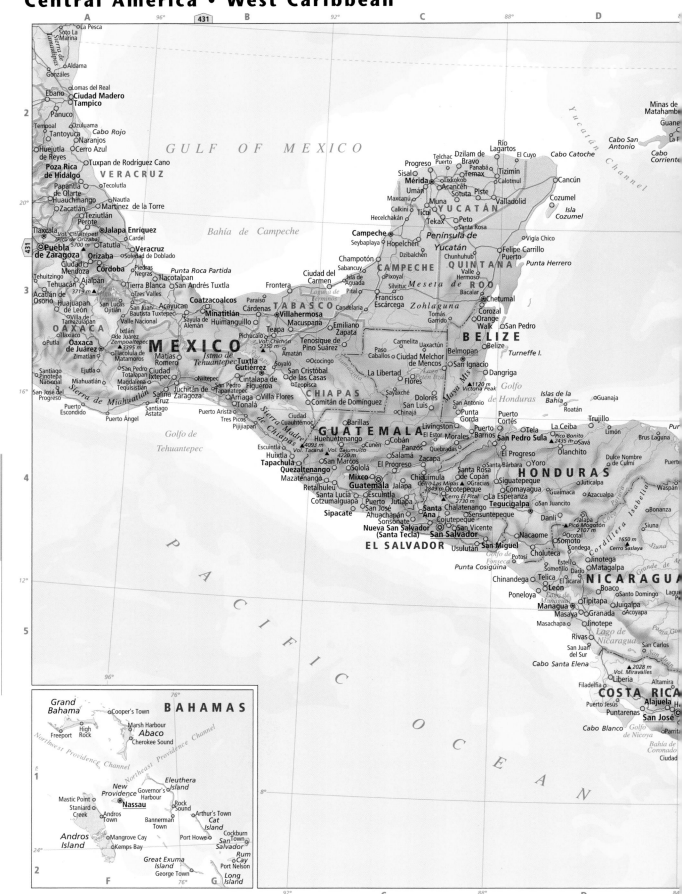

GULF OF MEXICO

VERACRUZ

MEXICO

OAXACA

TABASCO

CHIAPAS

GUATEMALA

BELIZE

HONDURAS

EL SALVADOR

NICARAGUA

COSTA RICA

CAMPECHE

YUCATÁN

QUINTANA ROO

Península de Yucatán

Bahía de Campeche

PACIFIC OCEAN

Golfo de Tehuantepec

Golfo de Honduras

Lago de Nicaragua

BAHAMAS

Grand Bahama

Abaco

New Providence

Nassau

Andros Island

Eleuthera Island

Cat Island

San Salvador

Long Island

2

20°

3

16°

4

12°

427

450

8°

72°

E          80°          F          76°          G          72°          H

**NORTH AND CENTRAL AMERICA**

na
a)  Guanabacoa
Matanzas    Cárdenas
misa   Güines
Batabanó           Colón    Sagua la Grande
Cabo         Jagüey    Santa Clara
abanó        Grande       Caibarién
                Cienfuegos   Sancti    Cabaiguán    Morón
Cayo de los   Canarreros   Spíritus    Ciego de Ávila
Cayo del       Trinidad        Camagüey
Rosario                       Cayos Vertientes   Puerto Padre
        CUBA              Cinco Balas   Las Tunas
                    Cayo           Santa Cruz   Holguín
                Grande    del Sur   Bayamo    Cueto
                        Golfo de       Manzanillo   Palma Soriano   Baracoa
                Sierra    Pico Turquino   Santiago de Cuba
                Maestra    1974 m

Andros
Island       Mangrove Cay
                Kemps Bay
        Great Exuma     Port Howe   Cockburn   San
            Island                    Town   Salvador
    George Town         Rum
                        Cay   Port Nelson
BAHAMAS          Long
                    Island
        Clarence Town
        Mortimers   Crooked
                    Island
        Colonel        Snug
        Hill           Corner   Mayaguana
    Acklins               Island
        Island

TURKS AND
CAICOS ISLANDS
(U.K.)

Tropic of Cancer

Little
Inagua Island   Caicos   Grand Turk
            Northeast   Islands   Cockburn   Turks Islands
            Pt      Matthew   Harbour
                    Town   Great Inagua
                        Island

Cabo Lucrecia
    Banes
Gibara   Moa
Sagua de Tánamo
Cabo        Monte     Puerto
Cristi     Isabela    Plata     Cabrera
Cap-Haïtien   Santiago   Moca   San Francisco de Macorís
Fort         La Vega   Bonao   Bahía Escosesa
Liberté      DOMINICAN   Monte Plata   El Seibo   Cabo
Hinche       Pico Duarte   REPUBLIC   Engaño
Comendador   3175 m   San Juan   San Pedro   Hato Mayor   La Romana
HAITI        Jimaní   Azua   de Macorís   Santo Domingo
Port-au-     Neiba   Punta   Cristóbal
Prince       Barahona   Salinas   Isla
                        Pedernales   Saona

Île de la
Tortue
Monte
Cristi

Golfe de la Gonâve
Saint-Marc
Île de la
Gonâve

NAVASSA   Dame-
ISLAND    Marie   Jérémie
(U.S.A.)       Petit Goâve
        Tiburon   Massif de la Hotte
Port-à-Piment   Les Cayes   Bainet   Jacmel
            Pic de la Selle
            2680 m

GREATER   Grand   Cayman
ANTILLES  Cayman   Brac
            Little
            Cayman
George Town   CAYMAN
            ISLANDS
            (U.K.)

Cayman   Trench

Jamaica Channel
ANTILLES

Montego Bay   Falmouth
South Negril Pt   Ocho Ríos   Port Antonio
Savanna-la-Mar   JAMAICA   Blue Mtn Pk
Mandeville   Black   Spanish   2256 m
River   Town   Kingston
Portland
Pt

HISPANIOLA

CARIBBEAN

Miskitos
ic.)

Providencia
(Col.)

San Andrés
(Col.)

SEA

ARUBA
(Neth.)
Oranjestad   Curaçao
        Pen. de
        Paraguaná
        Willemstad

Pta Gallinas
Cabo de la Vela   Puerto
Península   Estrella   C. San Román
de Guajira   Carrizal   Los Taques   Pueblo
Uribia   Punta Fijo   Nuevo   Puerto
                            Cumarebo
Ríohacha   Maicao       Coro   Jacura
    Carraipía       Golfo de Venezuela   Pedregal   Churuguara
    Paraguaipoa           Dabajuro
Santa Marta   Barrancas   Tule   Casigua   Mene de   Baragua
Barranquilla   Ciénaga   San Rafael   Santa   Mauroa   Carora
Puerto Colombia   Baranoa   P. Cristóbal Colón   Campo   Rita   1990 m   Yaritagua
Soledad   5775 m   Villanueva   Mara   Cabimas   Cerro El Cerrón   Carora
Sabanalarga   Valledupar   Maracaibo   Mene Grande   Barquisimeto
Cartagena   Fundación   Rosario       El Tocuyo
Turbaco   Pivijay   Agustín   Machiques   Lagunillas   Trujillo   Acarigua
Arjona   Calamar   Codazzi   Barranquitas   Betijoque   Boconó   Guanare
El Carmen   Plato   Chiriguaná   La Jagua   Lago   San Carlos del Zulia   Guanarito
de Bolívar   El Difícil   de Ibírico   de Maracaibo   Mérida   Barinas
Sincelejo   Mompós   El Banco   Encontrados   Casigua   Pico Bolívar   Obispos
Lorica   Sincé   Magangué   Tamalameque   El Vigía   5007 m
Cereté   Sahagún   Sucre   La Gloria   Tovar   VENEZUELA   Puerto de Nutrias
Montería   El Banco   Ocaña   La Fría   Pedraza La Vieja   Mantecal
COLOMBIA   Planeta Rica   Sardinata   Cúcuta   San Cristóbal
Turbo   Tierralta   Caucasia   Simití   Chinácota   San Antonio   Palmarito
Garachiné   El Real       Cáceres   Cáchira   Pamplona   de Caparo   Guasdualito
                Zaragoza   Ocaña   Barrancabermeja   Bucaramanga   Arauquita   Arauca
                            Floridablanca   Sierra Nevada   Cubará
            Segovia   Zapatoca   del Cocuy   5493 m   Elorza
Dabeiba   Paramillo   Yarumal   Amalfi   San Gil   Tame   Puerto
3960 m              Antioquia   Socorro   El Cocuy   Rondón   Nuevo
Cupica   Anzá   Cisneros   Puerto   Cravo Norte
Pta Logos   Bello   Berrío   Casanare
        Medellín

Portobelo   Palenque   El Porvenir
Colón   PANAMA   Arch. de San
        Panama Canal   Ailigandi
Golfo de los   Coclé   San Miguelito
Mosquitos   del Norte   Panamá
lcán Barú   Santa   La Chorrera   Chimán   Puerto Obaldía
3475 m   Catalina   Penonomé   La Palma
oque   David   Antón   San Miguel   I. San José
les   Tolé   San Francisco   Aguadulce   del Rey   El Real
Golfo de   Soná   Santiago   Chitré   Garachiné   Yaviza
Chiriquí   Río de Jesús   Atalaya   Las Tablas   Golfo de   Jaqué
Isla   Península   Pedasí   Panamá
de Coiba   de Azuero   Tonosí   Cupica
        Punta   Punta Mala
        Mariato

Golfo
del Darién
Golfo de
Morrosquillo
Golfo de
San Blas
Puerto Rey

E          80°          F          76°          G          72°          H

100   200   300   400   kilometers
100   200   miles
7,000,000   Projection: Lambert Conformal Conic

429

San Diego
Chula Vista
Tijuana
Tecate
Mexicali
El Cajon
Brawley
El Centro
Calexico
Yuma

Ensenada
Cabo Punta Banda
Guadalupe
Santo Tomás
San Vicente
San Telmo
Colonia Vicente Guerrero
San Quintín
El Rosario de Arriba
Punta Baja
Misión de San Fernando
Santa Catarina

BAJA CALIFORNIA

Punta Prieta
Rosarito
Santo Domingo
El Arco
Guerrero Negro
Bahía de los Ángeles

Isla Cedros
Punta Eugenia
Bahía Tortugas
Punta San Hipólito
Bahía Asunción

Isla Ángel de la Guarda
Isla Tiburón

Puerto Peñasco
El Socorro
San Francisco
El Desemboque
Puerto de Lobos
Puerto Libertad
Benjamín Hill
Querobabi

GOLFO DE CALIFORNIA

Sentinel
Dateland
Gila Bend
Casa Grande
Ajo
Why
Sonoyta
Lukeville
Sells

Eloy
Casas Adobes
Mammoth
Florence
Hayden
Coolidge
Pima

ARIZONA
Tucson

Green Valley
Amado
Patagonia
Sonoita
Fairbank
Nogales
Santa Cruz

Benson
Willcox
Cochise
Pearce
Tombstone
Bisbee
Douglas

Caborca
Altar
Imuris
Santa Ana
Magdalena
Cananea
Fronteras

SONORA

Carbó
Moctezuma

Hermosillo
Bahía Kino
San José de Gracia
Mazocahui
Sahuaripa

Torres
Mazatán
Nátora

Los Pocitos
Ortiz
Tecoripa
Tónichi
Yécora
Onavas

Guaymas
Empalme
Cumuripa
Nuri
Rosario

Torín
Esperanza
Quiriego
Chinipas

Ciudad Obregón
Fundición

Navojoa
Álamos
Huatabampo
Masiaca
Punta Rosa
Yavaros

BAJA CALIFORNIA SUR

Volcán Las Tres Vírgenes
Santa Rosalía
San Lucas
Mulegé
Rosarito
Ligui
Loreto
Isla Carmen
Comondú
Ejido Insurgentes
Puerto Adolfo López Mateos
Ciudad Constitución
Cabo San Lázaro
Puerto Cortés
Isla Santa Margarita

Bahía de La Paz
Pichilingue
La Paz
San Pedro
El Triunfo
Todos Santos
Santiago
San José del Cabo
San Lucas
Cabo San Lucas
Punta Arena

Isla San José
Isla Cerralvo
Punta Rosantos

PACIFIC OCEAN

Tropic of Cancer

CHIHUAHUA

Chihuahua

DURANGO

Durango

SINALOA

Culiacán
Los Mochis
Guasave
Guamúchil

Mazatlán
Rosario
Escuinapa
Teacapán
Acaponeta

NAYARIT

Tepic

JALISCO

Guadalajara

Puerto Vallarta
Cabo Corrientes

COLIMA
Colima
Manzanillo
Tecomán

MICHOACÁN

Lázaro Cárdenas
Punta San Telmo

# South America

South America has a land area of 17.6 million sq km (6.9 million sq miles). To its east lies the Atlantic Ocean and to its west is the Pacific. South America is triangular in shape, tapering southward.

The countries that make up the continent had their boundaries determined by the colonial powers that engulfed the entire continent from the sixteenth century onwards. Most of the continent was divided between Spain and Portugal. Portugal established the largest South American colony, Brazil, while Spain claimed most of the remaining area. The Spanish colonies were Venezuela, Colombia, Ecuador, Peru, Bolivia, Chile, Argentina, Uruguay, and Paraguay. In the north, three comparatively small countries were created by Britain, France, and the Netherlands: Guyana, French Guiana, and Suriname respectively.

## Physical features

The Andes Mountains, which arose when the South American and Pacific plates collided, form an elongated zone along the continent's western margin. The range, which is prone to earthquakes and volcanic eruptions, is narrow in the north, broadens out into a high plateau at 4,000 m (13,000 ft) in the center, where Lake Titicaca is situated, and narrows again toward the south.

The basin of the Amazon River, which is 6,570 km (4,080 miles) long, covers 8 million sq km (3 million sq miles) in equatorial South America. It is bordered to the south by the Mato Grosso Plateau and the highlands of Brazil, and to the north by the Guyana Highlands. Angel Falls, which at 979 m (3,212 ft) is the world's highest waterfall, is in Venezuela.

## Climate and vegetation

The continent stretches from the tropics to the sub-polar zones and is climatically diverse. The tropics cover a large area in the north, with the southern part being more temperate.

The broad humid tropical zone is characterized by extensive forests in Brazil, Guyana, and Venezuela, and includes the world's largest remaining rainforest, the Amazon. Vast areas of this zone have been cleared for agriculture—mainly sugarcane plantations and cattle ranches. Currently, the Amazon forests are under threat from logging and from the spread of agriculture and settlement, and are rapidly diminishing in size. The Amazon is rich in wildlife and contains a large number of plant species unique to the area.

In the north of the continent, where wet and dry seasons alternate, the forest trees are deciduous. In areas where there is little rainfall shrubs and thorny vegetation prevail. The subtropical and temperate areas in the south of the continent are marked by extensive grasslands, with dispersed trees, as in the pampas of Argentina and in Patagonia. Toward the west lie desert areas, where vegetation is sparse.

In the central Andes rainfall is concentrated on the eastern slopes, which are forested, though much deforestation has occurred. Along the arid western side, the sparse vegetation is generally thorny shrubs and animal life is limited. The driest region of all is the Atacama Desert in Chile. There are cool temperate rainforests in southern Chile.

South America has abundant wildlife, including llamas, anteaters, armadillos, and iguanas. The giant anteater and giant armadillo are endangered species. Several unique species inhabit the Galapagos Islands, including the giant tortoise and the marine iguana. The seas off the west coast of temperate South America are rich in marine life due to the nutrient-rich cold waters of the Peru Current.

## Population

South America's population is about 373.7 million (2007). Its relatively high living standards are reflected by life expectancies of 69.4 years for males and 76.4 years for females. The current population growth rate is 1.25 percent per year.

The original inhabitants of the continent were Amerindians who, it is believed, migrated from Asia across the Bering Straits. From the seventeenth century, settlers from Portugal and Spain immigrated in considerable numbers, bringing in Africans to work as agricultural labor. In the twentieth century, while migration from Europe was predominant, migrants also came from Asia. People of Italian descent are significant in Argentina, and Japanese people form locally important groups in Brazil and Peru.

The continent is highly urbanized—81.6 percent of the population lives in urban areas. Within the last fifty years, large numbers of people have moved to cities such as São Paulo (population 19.1 million), Buenos Aires (12.4 million), Rio de Janeiro (11.2 million), and Lima (7.5 million). The result is urban congestion and the spread of shanty towns amid modern cities.

## Agriculture

Several agricultural products, including maize, cashews, peanuts, avocadoes, and cacao, were grown in South America before the coming of the Europeans. Rubber-producing plants also grew there. Agriculture was extensively established when the continent was colonized, with crops including introduced species such as rice, wheat, sugarcane, coffee, bananas, and citrus fruits.

The tropical north of the continent produces sugar, bananas, mangoes, and rubber; wheat and temperate fruits are grown in the temperate south. Introduced animals provide the bulk of livestock; cattle are raised in a range of climate areas, and sheep are raised in the temperate grasslands. Among the indigenous animals reared are llamas and alpacas; alpacas are prized for their wool.

*The Moreno Glacier in Argentina (left). An example of the richness of the diminishing Amazon jungle, in Ecuador (above). Tierra del Fuego, Argentina (previous pages).*

## Nations

| | |
|---|---|
| Argentina | PAGE 442 |
| Bolivia | PAGE 441 |
| Brazil | PAGE 439 |
| Chile | PAGE 442 |
| Colombia | PAGE 436 |
| Ecuador | PAGE 438 |
| Guyana | PAGE 437 |
| Paraguay | PAGE 444 |
| Peru | PAGE 440 |
| Suriname | PAGE 438 |
| Uruguay | PAGE 444 |
| Venezuela | PAGE 436 |

## Dependencies & territories

| | |
|---|---|
| Falkland Islands | PAGE 445 |
| French Guiana | PAGE 445 |
| South Georgia and South Sandwich Islands | PAGE 445 |

Irrigation is important in certain regions, particularly in the west—Ecuador, Peru, and Chile. It is also of significance in Argentina.

Much of the forested areas of South America are logged for their timber. This is particularly the case in the Amazon, and conservationists worldwide are voicing their concern about the rate at which the forest is being lost. Tropical hardwoods are exported.

Illegal cultivation of narcotic drugs, particularly in Colombia, is also a matter of world concern.

## Industrialization

South America is endowed with significant mineral deposits, such as tin in Bolivia, iron ore in Brazil, and petroleum in Venezuela. Large quantities of metallic ores are exported, though iron ore is used in Brazil for steel manufacture.

Industrialization has accelerated in South America since the 1950s, as a result of increased electricity generation; much of the continent's hydroelectric potential has been harnessed.

Manufacturing ranges from food processing to metal and chemical industries. Consumer items such as textiles, clothing, and footwear, as well as more expensive items such as automobiles, are manufactured both for the domestic market and for export.

*A view of the Lake District in Chile (above), and fishing boats of the minority Uru people, in Peru (left). The blue-footed booby (below), from the Galapagos Islands, and the statue carving site on Easter Island, off Ecuador (below, right).*

## Languages

The original inhabitants, the Amerindians, belong to various groups and have several languages. Although many no longer speak those languages, in some areas large numbers still do—Guaraní is widespread in Paraguay, for example. The official languages in South America are now those introduced by the colonial powers: Portuguese in Brazil, Spanish in most other countries, English in Guyana, Dutch in Suriname, and French in Guiana. In Guyana and Suriname, South Asian languages—principally Hindi—are also significant. Government, education, and the media predominantly use introduced European languages.

## Boundary disputes and wars

There are currently no major boundary disputes or wars in South America; there was little conflict between the continent's countries during the twentieth century. However, there was considerable civil strife between guerilla groups and governments in several countries—Uruguay, Colombia, and Peru, for example. Armed drug cartels in Colombia also remain a major problem.

In some countries, notably Chile and Argentina, there have been periods of dictatorship during which the military have played a large role in government. During these periods there has been considerable loss of civilian lives.

In 1982 Argentina invaded the United Kingdom-ruled Falkland Islands (Islas Malvinas). After more than 1,000 people lost their lives in the ensuing war, and after international pressure, the islands were returned to United Kingdom rule.

# South America

Colombia · · · · · · · · 436
Venezuela · · · · · · · · 436
Guyana · · · · · · · · 437
Ecuador · · · · · · · · 438
Suriname · · · · · · · · 438
Brazil · · · · · · · · 439
Peru · · · · · · · · 440
Bolivia · · · · · · · · 441
Chile · · · · · · · · 442
Argentina · · · · · · · · 442
Uruguay · · · · · · · · 444
Paraguay · · · · · · · · 444

Dependencies · · · · · · 445

# Colombia

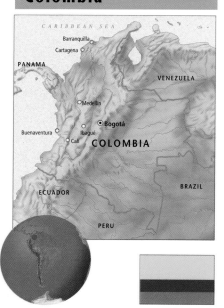

## Fact File

OFFICIAL NAME  Republic of Colombia

FORM OF GOVERNMENT  Republic with two legislative bodies (Senate and House of Representatives)

CAPITAL  Bogotá

AREA  1,138,910 sq km (439,733 sq miles)

TIME ZONE  GMT – 5 hours

POPULATION  45,014,000

PROJECTED POPULATION 2015  50,663,000

POPULATION DENSITY  39.5 per sq km (102.4 per sq mile)

LIFE EXPECTANCY  72.5

INFANT MORTALITY (PER 1,000)  19.5

OFFICIAL LANGUAGE  Spanish

LITERACY RATE  92.8 %

RELIGIONS  Roman Catholic 90 %, Protestant, Jews and other 10 %

ETHNIC GROUPS  Mixed indigenous-European 58 %,

European 20 %, mixed European-African 14 %, African 4 %, mixed indigenous-African 3 %, indigenous 1 %

CURRENCY  Colombian peso

ECONOMY  Services 52.5 %, industry 36 %, agriculture 11.5 %

GNI PER CAPITA  US$ 3,250

CLIMATE  Tropical along coast and on plains, cool to sometimes cold in highlands

HIGHEST POINT  Pico Cristobál Colón 5,775 m (18,947 ft)

MAP REFERENCE  Pages 450–51

Visited by Hojeda and Vespucci in 1499 and named after Columbus, Colombia straddles the South American continent south of the isthmus of Panama. Once the home of the Chibcha Indians, the country came under Spanish control in 1544, after which it became their chief source of gold. Colombia achieved independence in 1819. From that time on the political and economic fortunes of the country have been contested by the anti-clerical free-trading Liberals and the Conservatives, upholders of protectionism and the Church. While Colombia is notorious for its drug cartels and exports of cocaine, it has a diversified and stable economy that has, for thirty years, shown Latin America's most consistent record of growth.

The country can be divided into three regions. The hot, wet Pacific lowlands run south from the Panamanian border; to the north they merge into drier lowlands along the Caribbean. The cities that face the Caribbean—Barranquilla, Santa Marta, and Cartagena—are tourist resorts. Inland, the parallel Andean ranges running north from the Ecuadorian border define the second region, the high valleys of the Cauca and Magdalena Rivers. This is where most people live. The third region comprises the foothills east of the Andes, where the land falls away into the forested basins of the Amazon and Orinoco Rivers. This region amounts to almost two-thirds of Colombia's area but only a few cattle ranchers and Indians live here.

With Latin America's largest proven reserves of coal, Colombia is the region's biggest coal exporter. Some eighty percent of the world's emeralds also come from here. Oil, however, remains the biggest legitimate revenue-earning export. Since 1990 growth in gross domestic product has averaged over four percent annually, led by expanding construction and financial service industries, as well as inflows of foreign capital. Nevertheless, earnings from processed cocaine probably exceed all other sources. Problems include a high poverty index and continuing difficulties related to allegations of drug connections at high levels.

# Venezuela

## Fact File

OFFICIAL NAME  Republic of Venezuela

FORM OF GOVERNMENT  Federal republic with two legislative bodies (Senate and Chamber of Deputies)

CAPITAL  Caracas

AREA  912,050 sq km (352,142 sq miles)

TIME ZONE  GMT – 4 hours

POPULATION  26,415,000

PROJECTED POPULATION 2015  31,294,000

POPULATION DENSITY  29 per sq km (75 per sq mile)

LIFE EXPECTANCY  73.5

INFANT MORTALITY (PER 1,000)  22

OFFICIAL LANGUAGE  Spanish

OTHER LANGUAGES  Indigenous languages (including Goajiro, Guaraúno, Cariña, Pemón)

LITERACY RATE  93 %

RELIGIONS  Roman Catholic 96 %, Protestant 2 %, other 2 %

ETHNIC GROUPS  Mixed indigenous-European 67 %, European 21 %, African 10 %, indigenous 2 %

CURRENCY  Bolívar

ECONOMY  Services 57.8 %, industry 38.4 %, agriculture 3.8 %

GNI PER CAPITA  US$ 7,320

CLIMATE  Tropical, with dry season December to April; cooler in highlands

HIGHEST POINT  Pico Bolívar 5,007 m (16,427 ft)

MAP REFERENCE  Pages 450–51

Venezuela is on the north coast of South America. When the first Spaniards arrived in 1499 they named it "New Venice" because the Indian stilt houses built in the water of Lake Maracaibo reminded them of the Italian city. The liberator Simon Bolivar was a Venezuelan general, the military campaign he led resulting in the country becoming independent in 1821. For the next century Venezuela's economy was largely based on agriculture, but in the 1920s it took a new direction with the development of a petroleum industry. In the last eighty years great wealth (unevenly shared) followed by industrialization have produced one of Latin America's most urbanized societies. Out of every twenty Venezuelans, almost nineteen are city-dwellers, and migration from the countryside left much of the interior depopulated.

Confident that oil revenues would never end, the Venezuelan government expanded the economic role of the state, even buying hotels. Falling oil prices in the early 1980s produced a fiscal crisis, and in 1991 a program of cutbacks and austerity measures triggered street riots in which hundreds died. Two attempted coups took place during 1992. Since that time there has been a concerted effort to achieve economic diversification and to cut back the state sector. In 1999 a new constitution was installed to create more stability, but a short-lived coup in 2002 and fights between government forces and opposition in 2003 shook the country.

The hot lowlands surrounding Lake Maracaibo in the far northwest comprise one of the areas of greatest population density. In this region abundant electricity from oil-fired generators provides power for light industry: food processing, pharmaceuticals, electrical equipment, and machinery. A spur of the northern Andes divides the Maracaibo Basin from the drainage system of the Orinoco to the east. Here are the lowland plains of the Llanos, savanna country used for cattle grazing. Much of the Llanos floods during the summer rains, especially in the west, though it is dry for the rest of the year. To the south is the vast granite plateau of the Guiana Highlands, and the highest waterfall in the world—Angel Falls (979 m; 3,212 ft).

Despite the dangers of fluctuating oil prices, petroleum continues to provide around 90 percent of Venezuela's export earnings and more than half of government revenue. Other minerals exported include iron ore, gold, and diamonds. The main cash crops are coffee, sugarcane, and tobacco; food crops include bananas, sorghum, and maize. Only five percent of arable land is cultivated, and agriculture production does not meet the country's needs. Fueled by high oil prices, record government spending helped boost GDP growth in 2004–2006 to 9–18 percent.

# Guyana

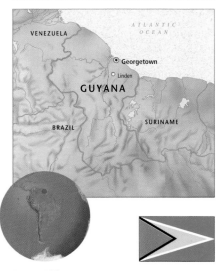

## Fact File

**OFFICIAL NAME** Cooperative Republic of Guyana

**FORM OF GOVERNMENT** Republic with single legislative body (National Assembly)

**CAPITAL** Georgetown

**AREA** 214,970 sq km (83,000 sq miles)

**TIME ZONE** GMT – 3 hours

**POPULATION** 771,000

**PROJECTED POPULATION 2015** 715,000

**POPULATION DENSITY** 3.6 per sq km (9.3 per sq mile)

**LIFE EXPECTANCY** 66.4

**INFANT MORTALITY (PER 1,000)** 30.4

**OFFICIAL LANGUAGE** English

**OTHER LANGUAGES** Amerindian languages, Hindi, Urdu

**LITERACY RATE** 98.8 %

**RELIGIONS** Christian 50 %, Hindu 35 %, Muslim10 %, other 5 %

**ETHNIC GROUPS** Indian 50 %, African 36 %, indigenous 7 %, European, Chinese and mixed 7 %

**CURRENCY** Guyana dollar

**ECONOMY** Industry 47.2 %, agriculture 31.1 %, services 21.7 %

**GNI PER CAPITA** US$ 1,300

**CLIMATE** Tropical with two rainy seasons (May to mid-August, mid-November to mid-January)

**HIGHEST POINT** Mt Roraima 2,810 m (9,219 ft)

**MAP REFERENCE** Page 451

Guyana means "the land of many waters". In 1616 it was settled by the Dutch, who built dikes, reclaimed coastal land, and planted sugarcane. When the indigenous people refused to work in the sugar plantations the Dutch, and later the British, imported slaves from Africa and indentured labor from India. The contrast between the communities descended from these two immigrant groups defines today's Guyanese political life. Beginning in 1953, and sharpened by independence in 1966, a struggle for dominance continues between the Afro-Guyanese and the numerically superior Indo-Guyanese. Until the early 1990s Guyana was ruled mostly by leftist governments. In the country's first free and fair elections in 1992 Cheddi Jagan was elected president. After his death in 1997 he was succeeded by his wife Janet who resigned in 1999 due to poor health. Her successor, Bharrat Jagdeo, was reelected in 2001 and 2006.

Some 95 percent of the people live on the coastal strip, and there is concern about flooding because of poor dike maintenance. The savannas, river valleys, and forested plateaus of the interior are largely unpopulated. There are, however, settlements of two neglected minorities in the forests—blacks descended from escaped slaves; and Carib, Warrau, and Arawak Amerindians.

Numerous rivers, including the country's main river, the Essequibo, flow down from the mountains in the west through tropical forests inhabited by a rich assortment of wildlife including sloth, jaguar, tapir, and capybara. There is diamond dredging in many of the rivers, and in 1995 there was a major cyanide spill at the Omai gold mine near the Essequibo. The effects of mining activities on the wildlife is of major concern to conservationists.

Sugar production and the mining of high-quality bauxite account for the lion's share of exports. Other resources include gold, diamonds, uranium, manganese, oil, copper, and molybdenum. Under successive governments, state ownership and government controls have stunted development and made adaptation to market fluctuations difficult. The bauxite mining sector should benefit in the near future from restructuring and partial privatization. Also in other areas, recent deregulation has shown benefits. Though weak infrastructure hampers tourist development, the spectacular scenery and wildlife of the interior is attracting visitors.

*Riverboats in Puerto Colombia, Colombia (left page top).*
*A view of Caracas, the capital of Venezuela (left).*

# Ecuador

The volcano Cotopaxi in Ecuador (top). Pigs for sale at the market at Otavalo, Ecuador (above).

## Fact File

**OFFICIAL NAME** Republic of Ecuador

**FORM OF GOVERNMENT** Republic with single legislative body (National Congress)

**CAPITAL** Quito

**AREA** 283,560 sq km (109,483 sq miles)

**TIME ZONE** GMT – 5 hours

**POPULATION** 13,928,000

**PROJECTED POPULATION 2015** 14,597,000

**POPULATION DENSITY** 49.1 per sq km (127.2 per sq mile)

**LIFE EXPECTANCY** 76.8

**INFANT MORTALITY (PER 1,000)** 21.4

**OFFICIAL LANGUAGE** Spanish

**OTHER LANGUAGES** Indigenous languages, particularly Quechua and Chibcha

**LITERACY RATE** 91 %

**RELIGIONS** Roman Catholic 95 %, other 5 %

**ETHNIC GROUPS** Indigenous-European 65 %, indigenous 25 %, Spanish and other 7 %, African 3 %

**CURRENCY** US dollar

**ECONOMY** Services 58.2 %, industry 35.1 %, agriculture 6.7 %

**GNI PER CAPITA** US$ 3,080

**CLIMATE** Tropical on coast and plains, cooler in highlands

**HIGHEST POINT** Chimborazo 6,310 m (20,702 ft)

**MAP REFERENCE** Page 450

Ecuador is the smallest of the Andean republics, taking its name from the equator which divides it in half. Quito was briefly an Inca city before being conquered by the Spanish in the 1530s. The city is ringed by volcanoes, including Cotopaxi (5,896 m; 19,344 ft), the world's highest active volcano. The groups of Indians that form 25 percent of the population are pressing for recognition as distinct nationalities within the state.

Ecuador's agriculture is based on the coastal plains where more than half of the arable land can be found. Bananas, coffee, and cocoa are the main crops. Most production is on haciendas—huge estates established during the early years of Spanish occupation. Inland, among the Andes, are valleys where livestock is raised. The eastern slopes of the Andes give way to forested upland and the border with Peru. This region is so little known that hostilities between Peru and Ecuador in 1995 arose partly from uncertainty as to where the frontier should be. This conflict finally was resolved in 1999. Petroleum and natural gas from this area are piped over the Andes to the Pacific port of Esmeraldas.

Ecuador grows more bananas than any other country in the world. Until overtaken by petroleum and natural gas, bananas were its biggest export earner, and access to markets in the United States and the European Union is a continuing concern. The highland Indians survive through subsistence farming, growing maize and potatoes. Recent economic reforms have helped control inflation and increased foreign investment. Growth has been uneven, however, because manufacturing is seriously handicapped by a shortage of electricity.

Ecuador owns the Galapagos Islands, located about 1,000 km (621 miles) off the Pacific coast and home to many unique species of animals such as the giant tortoise, the marine iguana, the flightless cormorant as well as the tree finch. These islands are a popular ecotourism destination, with visitor numbers limited to 40,000 a year so as to protect the fragile ecosystem.

# Suriname

## Fact File

**OFFICIAL NAME** Republic of Suriname

**FORM OF GOVERNMENT** Republic with single legislative body (National Assembly)

**CAPITAL** Paramaribo

**AREA** 163,270 sq km (63,038 sq miles)

**TIME ZONE** GMT – 3 hours

**POPULATION** 476,000

**PROJECTED POPULATION 2015** 475,000

**POPULATION DENSITY** 2.9 per sq km (7.6 per sq mile)

**LIFE EXPECTANCY** 73.5

**INFANT MORTALITY (PER 1,000)** 19.5

**OFFICIAL LANGUAGE** Dutch

**OTHER LANGUAGES** English, Sranang Tongo (Taki-Taki), Hindi, Javanese, Saramaccan

**LITERACY RATE** 89.6 %

**RELIGIONS** Hindu 27.4 %, Protestant 25.2 %, Roman Catholic 22.8 %, Muslim 19.6 %, indigenous 5 %

**ETHNIC GROUPS** Hindustani (East Indian) 37 %, mixed European-African 31 %, Javanese 15 %, African 10 %, Amerindian 3 %, Chinese 2 %, European 1 %, other 1 %

| | |
|---|---|
| **CURRENCY** | Suriname guilder |
| **ECONOMY** | Services 64.8 %, industry 24.4 %, agriculture 10.8 % |
| **GNI PER CAPITA** | US$ 4,730 |
| **CLIMATE** | Tropical: hot and wet year-round |
| **HIGHEST POINT** | Julianatop 1,230 m (4,035 ft) |
| **MAP REFERENCE** | Page 452 |

Formerly known as Dutch Guiana, Suriname is a small country on the northeastern coast of South America. In 1667 two colonial powers exchanged territory: the Dutch gave the British New Amsterdam, which became New York. In return the British gave Suriname to the Dutch. From the Low Countries the new proprietors brought their dike-building skills to reclaim a narrow coastal strip, and soon sugar plantations took the place of marshes and mangrove swamps. At first African slaves were imported to do the work; later labor was brought from India, China, and Java, and these three immigrant groups have determined both the ethnic composition of the country as well as its political fate.

Since 1954 Suriname has had the status of an equal partner in the "Tripartite Kingdom of the Netherlands". This has benefited those who have fled the continual military coups and civil disturbance in Suriname, using their Dutch citizenship to enter the Netherlands in large numbers. As was the case in nearby Guyana, escaped African slaves established isolated settlements in the hinterland. Guerrilla uprisings in both 1986 and 1994 have made the descendants of these people an urban political force.

Inland of the cultivated coastal strip lies a zone of sandy savanna, and south of this a vast area of dense forest begins (92 percent of the nation's total land area). Suriname has the world's highest ratio of forested country and it is still virtually untouched as timber is not among the nation's exports. The forests stretch inland to the Guiana Highlands, which are an extension of the Tumucumaque Mountain Range in northeastern Brazil. Over time, weathered soils have been washed from the uplands down to the alluvial valleys below, providing the foundation of the thriving bauxite industry.

The mining industry, especially bauxite and gold, accounts for over one-third of Suriname's gross domestic product and more than 65 percent of export earnings. Other exports include shrimp, fish, rice, bananas, citrus fruits, and coconuts. For most people rice is the staple food, supplemented by tropical fruits and vegetables.

Both ethnic conflict and economic crises have damaged the country's prospects for some years, although the campaign by guerrillas against the urban political elite seems to have faded for the present. Inflation was running at 600 percent in 1994 but since has dropped considerably and was at 9.5 percent in 2007. The resumption of economic aid by the Netherlands has led to a greater confidence in Suriname's economy. Suriname's economic prospects for the medium term will depend on continued commitment to responsible monetary and fiscal policies and to the introduction of structural reforms to liberalize markets and promote competition.

# Brazil

## Fact File

| | |
|---|---|
| **OFFICIAL NAME** | Federative Republic of Brazil |
| **FORM OF GOVERNMENT** | Federal republic with two legislative bodies (Senate and Chamber of Deputies) |
| **CAPITAL** | Brasília |
| **AREA** | 8,511,965 sq km (3,286,470 sq miles) |
| **TIME ZONE** | GMT – 3/5 hours |
| **POPULATION** | 191,909,000 |
| **PROJECTED POPULATION** 2015 | 210,048,000 |
| **POPULATION DENSITY** | 22.5 per sq km (58.4 per sq mile) |
| **LIFE EXPECTANCY** | 72.5 |
| **INFANT MORTALITY (PER** 1,000) | 26.7 |
| **OFFICIAL LANGUAGE** | Portuguese |
| **OTHER LANGUAGES** | More than 180 indigenous languages (incl. Tupi, Guarani, Gê, Arwak, Carib), Spanish, English, French |
| **LITERACY RATE** | 88.6 % |
| **RELIGIONS** | Roman Catholic 73.6 %, Protestant 15.4 %, other 3.6 %, none 7.4 % |
| **ETHNIC GROUPS** | European 53.7 %, mixed European-African 38.5 %, African 6.2 %, other 1.6 % |
| **CURRENCY** | Real |
| **ECONOMY** | Services 65.8 %, industry 28.7 %, agriculture 5.5 % |
| **GNI PER CAPITA** | US$ 5,910 |
| **CLIMATE** | Mainly tropical, but temperate in south |
| **HIGHEST POINT** | Pico da Neblina 3,014 m (9,888 ft) |
| **MAP REFERENCE** | Pages 450–51, 452–53, 454–55, 456–57 |

Brazil is the fifth largest country in the world and comprises nearly half of South America. Originally the home of numerous Amerindian tribes, Brazil was ruled by the Portuguese after their arrival in 1500. Political independence of a sort came in 1822, but a form of monarchy, sponsored by Portuguese royalty and featuring a self-styled Emperor of Brazil, existed until the first republic was declared in 1889.

Today the well-being of the Amazon Basin is a cause of international concern, yet for most of Brazil's history this huge region was virtually ignored. In the eyes of the first settlers the most valuable land was the fertile coastal strip from Recife to Rio de Janeiro. In the north of this area they established huge sugarcane plantations, brought 4 million African slaves to do the work, and became so dependent on slavery that it was only abolished in 1888. In the south, around São Paulo (now the world's third largest city), a huge coffee-growing industry became established. Ethnically mixed and rich in resources, Brazil has the potential to play a major role internationally and has become the leading power in the region.

## Physical features and land use

Brazil has two major and several minor regions. In the north is the vast tropical area—once an inland sea—drained by the Amazon River and its more than 1,000 tributaries. Occupying the entire northern half of the country, this river system passes through vast regions of rainforest. A greater variety of plant species grows here than in any other habitat in the world and the forest is home to a phenomenal range of animals and birds. More than 1,000 bird species are found here and as many as 3,000 species of fish swim in the rivers, along with other animals such as caiman (alligator), freshwater dolphin, and the endangered manatee—a large herbivorous mammal.

At present it is estimated that the rainforest will be reduced to about fifty percent of its current size by 2020 as a result of logging, mining, ranching, and the resettlement of Brazil's many landless peasants. In early 1998 forest fires raged through the the northern state of Roraima. Ignited partly by traditional Amerindian slash-and-burn horticulture, partly by settlers clearing land, and aggravated by unusually dry conditions, they caused great devastation.

The second main region, the Brazilian Highlands, lies in the center and south of the country. This is an extensive plateau of hard, ancient rock in which weathering has formed deep river valleys. Much of the interior is covered by savanna woodland, thinning to semi-deciduous scrub in the northeast. There are spectacular waterfalls on the Uruguay River on the southern side of the plateau and on the Paraná River west of the coastal highlands.

The interior of the Nordeste (northeast) region is the most undeveloped and drought-stricken corner of Brazil, and it is from here that large numbers of subsistence farmers who can no longer make a living have emigrated to the industrial center of São Paulo, looking for work.

The swampy Pantanal, in the southwest, flooded for seven months of the year, is the largest area of wetland in the world and has a striking diversity of wildlife.

## People and culture

As in the Caribbean countries, the sugar industry's demand for slaves strongly influenced the ethnic composition of Brazil. But to a greater extent than in the slave-owning South of the USA, the result has been both economic and social integration.

*Rio de Janeiro, in Brazil (above). The Igaçu Falls, from the Brazilian side (top). Llamas grazing on the plains at the foot of Mt Sajama, Bolivia (right page bottom).*

While Brazilian society shows extremes of wealth and poverty, the divisions are drawn along socio-economic rather than ethnic lines. Culturally, Brazil is a mixture of elements. This is particularly reflected in its religious life. Most people are Christian, mainly Roman Catholic. But a variety of African popular cults exist, such as candomblé, which are often mixed with Christianity.

Brazil also has the largest population of Japanese outside Japan. Arriving as poor farmers in the 1920s, 2 million of them now live in São Paulo and are prominent in commercial life. In the upper reaches of the Xingu, Araguaia, and Tocantins Rivers small groups of Indians such as the Tapirapé survive in forest refuges. Gold prospectors have driven off or killed Yanomami Indians in Roraima State who stood in their way.

### Economy and resources

Traditional rural activities continue to be important, the rural sector employing 20 percent of the labor force. Brazil is the world's largest producer of coffee, but cocao, sugarcane, cotton, and maize are also major cash crops cultivated on large plantations. Brazilian live-stock numbers are among the world's largest—mainly cattle and pigs—but trends show a steadily falling agricultural contribution to gross domestic product. Industry is increasing in importance, particularly manufacturing, with most of the country's power needs covered by hydroelectricity. The enormous hydroelectric potential of the Amazon and Paraná, however, remains untapped. Despite some development of domestic sources, gasoline is still imported. Brazil started to substitute ethanol made from sugar for gasoline during the 1980s, and ethanol is now offered at almost all gas stations. Even though falling oil and rising sugar prices made this uneconomical in the 1990s, in light of global warming, this model has gained new attention. There are also enormous natural resources: iron ore and manganese, zinc, nickel, gold, and diamonds. The main mining regions can be found in the eastern state of Minas Gerais.

In spite of the advances of the last decades, Brazil must still be considered a developing country as it does not have a fully modern economy. Some difficulties have arisen from heavy state borrowing for unproductive projects; others stem from runaway inflation in the 1980s. Fiscal reforms are difficult to carry through, as many require constitutional amendments. However, these problems are being addressed (consumer prices rose by eight percent in 2005, compared to more than 1,000 percent in 1994) and investor confidence is returning. President Lula da Silva restated his commitment to fiscal responsibility by maintaining the country's primary surplus during the 2006 election.

## Peru

### Fact File

**OFFICIAL NAME** Republic of Peru

**FORM OF GOVERNMENT** Republic with single legislative body (Congress)

**CAPITAL** Lima

**AREA** 1,285,220 sq km (496,223 sq miles)

**TIME ZONE** GMT – 5 hours

**POPULATION** 29,181,000

**PROJECTED POPULATION 2015** 30,768,000

**POPULATION DENSITY** 22.7 per sq km (58.8 per sq mile)

**LIFE EXPECTANCY** 70.4

**INFANT MORTALITY (PER 1,000)** 29.5

**OFFICIAL LANGUAGES** Spanish, Quechua

**OTHER LANGUAGE** Aymara

**LITERACY RATE** 87.7 %

**RELIGIONS** Roman Catholic 81 %, other (including Seventh Day Adventist) 2.7 %, none 16.3 %

**ETHNIC GROUPS** Indigenous 45 %, mixed indigenous-European 37 %, European 15 %; other 3 %

**CURRENCY** Nuevo sol

**ECONOMY** Services 66 %, industry 25.6 %, agriculture 8.4 %

**GNI PER CAPITA** US$ 3,450

**CLIMATE** Tropical in east, arid along coast, cold on high mountains

### Timeline

| | | | | | | | |
|---|---|---|---|---|---|---|---|
| **AD 1500** Portuguese land in Brazil naming it after the *brasa* ("brazil-wood" in Portuguese); the native population is about 2 million | **1530** Portuguese settle on Atlantic coast; establish sugarcane plantations, and grow tobacco and cotton for markets in Europe | **1790** Native peoples used as slaves on plantations; slaves also brought from Africa and elsewhere (slavery abolished 1888) | **1822** John's son Pedro declares independence and is Emperor until 1831; his son Pedro II rules 1841–89 | **1889** Dom Pedro II overthrown and Brazil is proclaimed a republic | **1934** Republic ends; Vargas is President as Depression hits; he becomes dictator (1937) and embarks on major public works | **1942** Brazil joins Allies in Second World War and sends 25,000 troops to fight in Italy | |
| **12,000 BP** Humans inhabit forests, living in small groups, hunting and fishing in rivers, and eating wild fruit and vegetables | **3500 BC** Amerindian people live in Amazon Basin, growing crops of potatoes and maize, and domesticating guinea pigs and llamas | **1690** Prospectors find gold, diamonds in Minas Gerais and Mato Grosso; thousands of Portuguese settle in these regions | **1808** John, ruler of Portugal, flees to Brazil, names Rio de Janeiro capital of Portuguese Empire; returns to Portugal 1821 | **1870** Rubber production soars in Amazon area, attracting migrants from the east and from Europe | **1917** Brazil sides with the Allies in the First World War and declares war on Germany | **1946** New constitution creates democratic system | **1950** Industrialization in southeast results in rural depopulation; by 1960 about 80 % of Brazilians are living near Atlantic coast |

**HIGHEST POINT** Nevado Huascarán 6,768 m (22,204 ft)

**MAP REFERENCE** Pages 450, 454–55

Humans have been living in Peru for about 10,000 years, and by 3,000 years ago Peruvian civilization had emerged, featuring irrigation agriculture, fine pottery, and expertly woven textiles of striking design. The Incas, one of the many tribes that inhabited the highlands of Peru, established a great empire in the thirteenth century that extended from Ecuador south to central Chile. Accomplished engineers, the Incas built an extensive network of roads and bridges, and many fine cities. The most famous of these is Machu Picchu, high above the Urubamba Valley. The Spanish came to Peru in 1532, lured by stories of a "kingdom of gold", and rapidly destroyed Inca civilization.

Before the turn of the century, Peru experienced serious political trouble. Deep social divisions gave rise in 1980 to the movement Sendero Luminoso (Shining Path), a Maoist guerrilla group. By 1990 its activities had resulted in the loss of 23,000 lives—most of them members of its own constituency, the Indians and mixed Spanish-Indians of the Andes—along with damage to the economy in the order of US$ 20 billion. Since 2000, the government has been able to bring about greater stability.

Some forty percent of Peru's population live on its arid coastal plain, which merges in the south with the rainless Atacama Desert of northern Chile. Numerous rivers crossing the plain from the Andes have made fertile valleys where cotton, rice, and sugarcane are grown. Inland, in the valleys of two high ranges of the Andean Sierra, the western and the eastern cordilleras, about fifty percent of the people live, most of them Indians practicing subsistence agriculture. East of the Andes the land falls away into the almost uninhabited region of the Amazon Basin. Here, the Ucayali and Marañón Rivers flow through rainforest to Iquitos, the navigable port farthest inland on the Amazon River.

Peru's economy depends heavily on copper and petroleum exports. Agriculture is limited by the lack of arable land. Fishing for anchovies and sardines has been historically important in the cool Humboldt current offshore, but periodic warming of the ocean from the El Niño effect reduces the catch, as has occurred several times in recent years. In 1992 it fell by thirty percent.

The ruins of Machu Picchu are an incomparable spectacle for tourists. After several years of inconsistent development, the Peruvian economy grew in 2002–06 by more than four percent annually. Despite the strong economic performance, underemployment and poverty are widespread among large sections of the population. Economic growth continues to be driven by exports of minerals, textiles, and agricultural products.

| 1960 Capital moves from Rio de Janeiro to Brasília, a new city built in the highlands of the interior | 1982 Itaipú Dam on Paraná River, one of the world's largest, completed, provides hydroelectric power for growing industries | 1992 Brazil hosts UN summit on global environmental issues, particularly global warming and greenhouse gas emissions |
|---|---|---|
| 3 Trans-Amazon ...ay links ...western the rest country | 1975 Population reaches 108 million (rising from 53 million in 1950) | 1998 Clearing of rainforest in Roraima attracts international attention—attempts are made to halt the process | 2003 The election of Luiz Inácio Lula da Silva is seen as a sign of hope. His government, however, is soon embroiled in corruption scandals |

# Bolivia

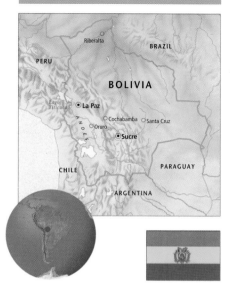

## Fact File

**OFFICIAL NAME** Republic of Bolivia

**FORM OF GOVERNMENT** Republic with two legislative bodies (Senate and Chamber of Deputies)

**CAPITAL** Sucre (official); La Paz (administrative)

**AREA** 1,098,580 sq km (424,161 sq miles)

**TIME ZONE** GMT – 4 hours

**POPULATION** 9,248,000

**PROJECTED POPULATION 2015** 10,854,000

**POPULATION DENSITY** 8.4 per sq km (21.8 per sq mile)

**LIFE EXPECTANCY** 66.5

**INFANT MORTALITY (PER 1,000)** 49.1

**OFFICIAL LANGUAGES** Spanish, Quechua, Aymara

**LITERACY RATE** 86.7 %

**RELIGIONS** Roman Catholic 95 %, other 5 %

**ETHNIC GROUPS** Quechua 30 %, mixed indigenous-European 30 %, Aymara 25 %, European 15 %

**CURRENCY** Boliviano

**ECONOMY** Services 55 %, industry 30.5 %, agriculture 14.5 %

**GNI PER CAPITA** US$ 1,260

**CLIMATE** Tropical north and east; cold, arid west of Andes

**HIGHEST POINT** Nevado Sajama 6,520 m (21,391 ft)

**MAP REFERENCE** Page 455

High on the Altiplano, a plateau nearly 3,600 m (12,000 ft) above sea level, La Paz is the world's loftiest capital city. In the sixteenth century, when the Spanish conquistadores arrived in Bolivia, they found silver and the mine they established at Potosi soon became famous. But the silver boom passed, the prices for the minerals and metals that replaced it (mainly tin) have been volatile, and Bolivia is now South America's poorest nation. It is landlocked, and its rugged terrain makes it doubly inaccessible. Notorious for its political instability (192 coups between 1824 and 1981) and for the hyperinflation that rose to 11,700 percent in 1985, was back down to 4.3 percent in 2007.

Quechua and Aymara Indians together form 55 percent of the population. Subsistence farmers, they grow maize, potatoes, and coca on the Altiplano. This cold, treeless region runs 400 km (250 miles) north to south between two major Andean ranges. At its north, Indians still fish in Lake Titicaca from boats made of reeds. In the south are salt flats. The vegetation of the Altiplano is grassland which changes to scrubland at higher elevations. To the east lies the Oriente, reaching across the foothills and the plains. It includes the semi-arid Chaco of the southeast, the savanna of the center, and the plains of the northern forests whose rivers feed into the Amazon Basin.

The hyperinflation of the 1980s damaged the tin industry, causing the country to fall from first producer in the world to fifth. In the mid-1990s the state airline, railroad, and telephone companies were privatized, as were state mining and oil companies. Metals, natural gas, soybeans, and jewelry are the main exports. In 2005, the government passed a natural gas law that imposed higher taxes on oil and gas companies and required production firms to sign new operating contracts, completed in October 2006, in an effort to keep more of the gas revenues in the country.

South America

# Chile

## Fact File

OFFICIAL NAME  Republic of Chile

FORM OF GOVERNMENT  Republic with two legislative bodies (High Assembly and Chamber of Deputies)

CAPITAL  Santiago

AREA  756,950 sq km (292,258 sq miles)

TIME ZONE  GMT – 4 hours

POPULATION  16,454,000

PROJECTED POPULATION 2015  17,926,000

POPULATION DENSITY  21.7 per sq km (56.3 per sq mile)

LIFE EXPECTANCY  77.2

INFANT MORTALITY (PER 1,000)  7.9

OFFICIAL LANGUAGE  Spanish

LITERACY RATE  95.7 %

RELIGIONS  Roman Catholic 70 %, other 22 %, none 8 %

ETHNIC GROUPS  European and mixed indigenous-European 95 %, indigenous 3 %, other 2 %

CURRENCY  Chilean peso

ECONOMY  Services 63 %, Industry 23.4 %, agriculture 13.6 %

GNI PER CAPITA  US$ 8,350

CLIMATE  Arid in north, cold and wet in far south, temperate elsewhere

HIGHEST POINT  Ojos del Salado 6,880 m (22,572 ft)

MAP REFERENCE  Pages 458, 460

Chile lies between the Andes and the sea. It stretches 4,350 km (2,700 miles) along South America's Pacific coast, yet is never more than

180 km (110 miles) wide. In the fifteenth century, the Incas from Peru tried but failed to subjugate its Araucanian Indian population. This was gradually achieved by the Spanish, against strong resistance, after their arrival in the sixteenth century. The Spanish established mining in the north and huge estates in the Central Valley; by the nineteenth century produce was being exported to California, Australia and elsewhere. Today, fruit and vegetables remain important exports, along with wine.

The Atacama Desert (Desierto de Atacama), in the north, has one of the lowest rainfalls in the world. In the nineteenth century it was the world's main source of nitrate for fertilizer, an export which underwrote Chile's early economic development. Santiago and the port of Valparaíso form an urban cluster midway along the length of the country. Santiago lies in a sheltered, temperate valley between a coastal range of mountains to the west and the high Andes in the interior. This fertile 800 km (500 mile) valley is where Chile's main vineyards are located, and where sixty percent of the population live. It is also where most manufacturing industry is located. Volcanoes, active and inactive, mark the length of the Chilean Andes to the east. In the southern third of the country the coastal range disintegrates into a maze of islands, archipelagoes, and fiords.

In 1970 President Allende nationalized the copper industry and other large enterprises, raised wages, and fixed prices. By 1973 inflation had reached 850 percent. Fearing a Cubanization of Chile, the political right under General Pinochet staged a coup and ruled for the next seventeen years. Devastating for human rights, the coup's effects on the economy were positive. The regime restored economic liberalism and dismantled state controls. Democracy was restored in 1989.

After two decades of political turmoil, Chile is now one of the more economically progressive of South America's democracies. It is the world's leading supplier of copper, and high copper prices remain vital to the nation's economic health. Between 2000 and 2006, annual growth ranged from two to six percent, and Chile maintained a low rate of inflation. The country continues to attract direct foreign investment.

# Argentina

## Fact File

OFFICIAL NAME  Argentine Republic

FORM OF GOVERNMENT  Federal republic with two legislative bodies (Senate and Chamber of Deputies)

CAPITAL  Buenos Aires

AREA  2,766,890 sq km (1,068,296 sq miles)

TIME ZONE  GMT – 3 hours

POPULATION  40,677,000

PROJECTED POPULATION 2015  42,676,000

POPULATION DENSITY  14.7 per sq km (38.1 per sq mile)

LIFE EXPECTANCY  76.5

INFANT MORTALITY (PER 1,000)  13.9

OFFICIAL LANGUAGE  Spanish

OTHER LANGUAGES  English, Italian, German, French, indigenous languages

LITERACY RATE  97.2 %

RELIGIONS  Roman Catholic 92 % (less than 20 % practicing), Protestant 2 %, Jewish 2 %, other 4 %

ETHNIC GROUPS  European 97 %, indigenous, mixed indigenous-European, and other 3 %

## Timeline

AD 600 Northwest settled by communities with complex social organizations—some have 10,000 to 20,000 members

12,000 BP Small human communities live by hunting and fishing in territory now known as Argentina

900 Native populations living in Andes in small-scale communities; culture has total population of 250,000–500,000

CURRENCY Argentine peso

ECONOMY Services 56.5 %, industry 34 %, agriculture 9.5 %

GNI PER CAPITA US$ 6,050

CLIMATE Mainly temperate; subtropical in northern Chaco, cold and arid in Patagonia; snow on Andes

HIGHEST POINT Aconcagua 6,960 m (22,834 ft)

MAP REFERENCE Pages 458–59, 460

With its northern extremity just north of the Tropic of Capricorn, but lying mainly within the temperate zone, Argentina becomes narrower and colder as it tapers south to Tierra del Fuego. The largest Spanish-speaking country of Latin America, it is named for the silver deposits that were sought by early explorers (*Argentina* means "land of silver"). In the nineteenth century many Spanish and Italian immigrants came in search of a better life, and today it contrasts with some of its neighbors in having a population that is mainly middle-class, with cosmopolitan interests, and a strong European background. Most Argentinians are of Spanish and Italian descent, but there are also people of German, Russian, French, and English origin, as well as a Jewish community in Buenos Aires and a Welsh community in Patagonia.

Argentina's politics have been much influenced by the legacy of Colonel Juan Domingo Perón. A major force in Argentine politics from 1946 to 1976, "Perónism" was a mild form of fascism which combined military rule and statist economic policy with progressive labor legislation. After Perón's death in 1974, he was succeeded by his widow. That government was ousted by a military coup in 1976. A three-man junta was then installed. Under this government thousands of people "disappeared" in a violent campaign against left-wing elements. Argentina returned to democracy in 1983.

## Physical features and land use

There are four main regions. In the north lie the subtropical woodlands and swamps of the Gran Chaco, a zone that spills over the northeastern border into Paraguay. Swampy in parts, dry in others and covered with thorny scrub, the Chaco is known as "Green Hell". To the west are the wooded slopes and valleys of the Andes; in the far south is the cold, semiarid Patagonian Plateau. It was the temperate region to the west and south of Buenos Aires that made Argentina famous. Here are the plains of the pampas—moist and fertile near the capital, drier but still productive elsewhere. These grasslands, where the gauchos (part Indian, part Spanish cattleherders) once lived and worked, are the basis of Argentina's cattle industry.

The pampas was largely created by gravel and sand brought down by streams from the Andes. A large native clump-grass called pampas grass, with

coarse gray blades and silvery plumes, provided stock feed when the Spanish settlers arrived. They brought horses and cattle, and began to fence off the more productive land for ranching and cultivation. While beef raising is still important, much of the fertile parts of the pampas are now used for growing wheat, maize, alfalfa, and flax.

Argentina has many lakes on the slopes of the Andes, and the alpine terrain attracts tourists and skiers from elsewhere in South America. The Andes are widely affected by volcanic activity and there are several active volcanoes along the border with Chile, as well as Aconcagua, the highest mountain outside the Himalayas. The huge Paraguay-Paraná-Uruguay river system, the second-largest on the continent, drains south from the Chaco and west from the highlands of Uruguay before emptying into the estuary of the River Plate (Río de la Plata). The three cities located here, two of them national capitals (the ports of Buenos Aires and Montevideo), mark the historic importance of this estuary.

## People and culture

Hunters and fishermen occupied the Argentine region from 12,000 years ago, and in recent times the Yahgan and Ona people made their home in Tierra del Fuego, despite its bitter climate. In the sixteenth century Spanish settlers began moving into Argentina from Peru, Chile, and Paraguay, and in the nineteenth century a ferocious war cleared the pampas of its remaining Indians.

Today, more than one-third of the population is descended from Italian immigrants. Argentinians are overwhelmingly urban: 90.1 percent live in towns and cities, with thirty percent in Buenos Aires itself (an urban agglomeration of around 12.4 million). The European orientation of cultural life is reflected in their art, music, and literature.

*Mountains in the Torres del Paine National Park, Chile (left page bottom). Autumn colors in Tierra del Fuego, Argentina (top). Buenos Aires, Argentina (above).*

## Economy and resources

Although the rural sector remains important, today industry makes a major contribution to the economy. Roughly one-fifth of the workforce is in manufacturing, mainly in industries producing frozen meat, canned meat, tallow, and leather for export. Wheat and fruit are also major exports. Energy available for industry includes nuclear power, hydroelectric power, and petroleum. There are oilfields in Patagonia and in the Mendoza area near the Andes, directly west of Buenos Aires.

Argentina has varied mineral resources—lead, zinc, tin, copper, silver, and uranium. It has a well-educated workforce and a diversified industrial base. Buenos Aires has a thriving computer industry. Episodes of hyperinflation have shaken investor confidence but political stability and reduced inflation in recent years are attracting overseas investment. During the period 2003–06, real GDP growth averaged nine percent, bolstering government revenues and keeping the budget in surplus.

| | | | | | | | | | |
|---|---|---|---|---|---|---|---|---|---|
| **1516** Spanish explorer uan Díaz de Solís, first European to land on what is now Argentine oil; killed by Querandi people | **1573** Towns of Córdoba and Mendoza develop on trade routes between Chile and Argentina | **1816** Argentina declares independence from Spain | **1866** San Roque Dam built on the Primero River providing irrigation and hydroelectric power | **1910** Large numbers of European migrants arrive to farm and work on estates in the southern Pampas region | **1944** Earthquake kills 5,000 people in San Juan province in the Andes | **1955** Perón dismissed in military coup; he flees the country with his first wife, Eva | **1982** Argentina invades Falklands after talks with Britain over sovereignty break down—Britain retakes the islands | **1994** Paraguay and Argentina jointly build Corpus Posados Dam on the Paraná River to create hydroelectric power |
| **1553** Permanent settlements established in northwest by Spanish arriving from Peru in search of gold and silver | **1580** Spanish colonists establish settlement of Buenos Aires on La Plata Estuary | **1830** Argentina lays claim to Islas Malvinas (the Falkland Islands), which are then occupied by Great Britain in 1833 | **1876** Exports of meat and grain to Europe grow rapidly following introduction of refrigerated shipping | **1914** First World War followed by export-led boom in agricultural produce; Argentine population reaches 8 million | **1946** Colonel Juan Perón is elected President and later assumes the powers of a dictator | **1973–74** Perón returns, is re-elected, dies; his third wife, "Isabelita", governs until arrested in 1976 coup in which thousands die | **1990** Full diplomatic relations with Britain are restored | **2002** Argentina, having tried since 1991, gives up trying to stabilise the Peso by allying it to the Dollar. Since then, consolidation of economy |

# Uruguay

## Fact File

OFFICIAL NAME  Eastern Republic of Uruguay

FORM OF GOVERNMENT  Republic with two legislative bodies (Senate and Chamber of Deputies)

CAPITAL  Montevideo

AREA  176,220 sq km (68,038 sq miles)

TIME ZONE  GMT – 3 hours

POPULATION  3,478,000

PROJECTED POPULATION 2015  3,431,000

POPULATION DENSITY  19.7 per sq km (51.1 per sq mile)

LIFE EXPECTANCY  76.1

INFANT MORTALITY (PER 1,000)  11.7

OFFICIAL LANGUAGE  Spanish

LITERACY RATE  98 %

RELIGIONS  Roman Catholic 66 %, Protestant 2 %, Jewish 1 %, unaffiliated 31 %

ETHNIC GROUPS  European 88 %, mixed indigenous-European 8 %, African 4 %

CURRENCY  Uruguayan peso

ECONOMY  Services 57.9 %, industry 32 %, agriculture 10.1 %

GNI PER CAPITA  US$ 6,380

CLIMATE  Temperate, with warm summers and mild winters

HIGHEST POINT  Cerro Catedral 514 m (1,686 ft)

MAP REFERENCE  Page 459

Uruguay, the second-smallest country in South America, lies northeast of Argentina on the estuary of the River Plate (Río de la Plata). Controlled for 150 years alternately by the Portuguese and the Spanish, Uruguay finally gained independence in 1828, after which came forty years of civil war. When peace was secured, waves of immigrants flocked to Uruguay from Spain and Italy, the cattle industry and meat exports expanded, investment poured in, and the country prospered. It may even have prospered too much: many benefits and welfare provisions were introduced in the days of prosperity which in poorer times have proved difficult to pay for. An urban guer-

rilla movement known as the Tupamaros paralyzed the cities during the 1960s, provoking a repressive military crackdown and dictatorship. Democracy was restored in 1984.

Most of Uruguay is temperate and mild: it never snows and frosts are rare, though the pampero, a wind coming off the pampas to the south, can be cold and violent. Most of the country is covered with rich grasslands, a continuation of the Argentine pampas, where cattle and sheep are raised. Although ninety percent of Uruguay's land is suitable for cultivation, only some ten percent is currently used for agriculture, but this is enough to ensure that the country is largely self-sufficient in food. Uruguay's main river is the Negro, flowing east-west across the center of the country. On either side of the Negro the land rises to a plateau that marks the southern limits of the Brazilian Highlands. Water from the uplands feeds down the Negro into a large artificial lake, Lake Rincón del Bonete, which is used for hydro-electric power.

Uruguay's rural economy is based on sheep and cattle raising, and its industries are mainly based on animal products: meat processing, leather, and wool and textile manufacturing. The country is the second largest wool exporter in the world. But Uruguay is not rich in other resources: it has no petroleum or minerals except for agate, amethyst, gold deposits, and small quantities of iron ore. It is entirely dependent on imported oil. The ample supplies of hydroelectricity that are available help to offset this disadvantage, and only governmental regulatory constraints prevent industrial expansion.

Uruguay's prosperous economy is characterized by an export-oriented agricultural sector, a well-educated work force, and high levels of social spending. During a major economic downturn in 1999–2002, largely a spillover of the economic problems of neighboring Argentina and Brazil, the GDP dropped by nearly twenty percent. In 2004, the economy grew again, about 12 percent, as a result of high prices for Uruguayan exports, growth in the region, and low international interest rates, and it continued to grow nearly seven percent annually in 2005 and 2006.

*The Palacio Legislativa in Montevideo, Uruguay (below). The mizzen mast of the Great Britain on the harbor foreshore of Stanley in the Falkland Islands (right page top).*

# Paraguay

## Fact File

OFFICIAL NAME  Republic of Paraguay

FORM OF GOVERNMENT  Republic with two legislative bodies (Senate and Chamber of Deputies)

CAPITAL  Asunción

AREA  406,750 sq km (157,046 sq miles)

TIME ZONE  GMT – 4 hours

POPULATION  6,831,000

PROJECTED POPULATION 2015  7,008,000

POPULATION DENSITY  16.8 per sq km (43.5 per sq mile)

LIFE EXPECTANCY  75.6

INFANT MORTALITY (PER 1,000)  25.6

OFFICIAL LANGUAGE  Spanish, Guaraní

LITERACY RATE  94 %

RELIGIONS  Roman Catholic 89.6 %, Protestant 6.2 %, other Christian 1.1 %, other or unspecified 1.9 %, none 1.1 %

ETHNIC GROUPS  Mixed indigenous-European 95 %; indigenous, European, Asian, and African 5 %

CURRENCY  Guaraní

ECONOMY  Services 60 %, agriculture 22.4 %, industry 17.6 %

# Dependencies in South America

GNI PER CAPITA US$ 1,670

CLIMATE Subtropical; wet in east, semiarid in west

HIGHEST POINT Cerro San Rafael 850 m (2,789 ft)

MAP REFERENCE Pages 455, 458–59

A small landlocked country, Paraguay was originally the home of the Guaraní Indians. It was settled by the Spaniards in 1537 who hoped to use the Guaraní as laborers on their big estates. The strong influence of the Jesuits, however, largely prevented the exploitation of the indigenous people by settlers that occurred elsewhere in South America under Spanish Catholic rule, and a socially benign intermix took place. Today, 95 percent of the population are of combined Indian and Spanish descent.

Fully independent since 1813, Paraguay is best known in modern times for the severe regime imposed by General Stroessner between 1954 and 1989. Assuming power after a period of chronic upheaval—six presidents in six years and revolts that had left thousands dead—he brought economic and political stability, and greatly improved the national infrastructure. This was at the price of considerable repression, and the huge hydroelectric projects that were built on the Paraná River incurred sizeable foreign debts.

Across the plains, south of Asunción, the Paraná River becomes a highway to the sea. Paraguay has some 3,100 km (1,900 miles) of navigable waterways, the most important being the Paraguay River which bisects the country north to south. To the west of Paraguay are the marshy, insect-infested plains of the Gran Chaco, but as the land rises toward the Bolivian border the Chaco changes to semidesert scrub. East of the river the land rises to a plateau forested with tropical hardwoods.

The economy of Paraguay has long been based on agriculture, and large numbers of people still live by means of subsistence farming. Cattle raising and the production of meat products remain the leading agricultural activities but cash crops such as cotton, soybeans, and timber are of increasing importance as a source of export income. Moreover, Paraguay's excess electricity capacity enables it to export power to Brazil.

Paraguay has a market economy marked by a large informal sector. This sector features both re-export of imported consumer goods, such as electronic devices, alcoholic beverages, and perfumes, as well as the activities of thousands of micro-enterprises and urban street vendors. Because of the significance of the informal sector, accurate economic measures are difficult to obtain. While tourism is poorly developed, day-trippers pour in from Brazil and Argentina to buy these goods.

## Falkland Islands

### Fact File

OFFICIAL NAME Colony of the Falkland Islands

FORM OF GOVERNMENT Overseas territory of the UK

CAPITAL Stanley

AREA 12,173 sq km (4,700 sq miles)

TIME ZONE GMT – 4 hours

POPULATION 3,100

CURRENCY Falkland Islands pound

ECONOMY Agriculture 95 %, services and industry 5 %

CLIMATE Cold, wet, and windy

MAP REFERENCE Page 460

The Falkland Islands are in the South Atlantic. They were named for Lord Falkland, a seventeenth-century British Navy official. Lying 772 km (480 miles) northeast of Cape Horn, they consist of a hilly archipelago where rain falls on average 180 days a year. The area is known for the diversity of the bird life. East Falkland and West Falkland are the two main islands and there are about 200 islets. While once most people worked in sheep farming, the main revenue today stems from fishing licenses. In recent years, ecotourism has become a sizeable industry. Sovereignty of the islands is disputed between the United Kingdom and Argentina, which invaded in 1982 to assert its claim. The resulting conflict lasted for three months. In 1995 the UK and Argentina launched a joint oil exploration program.

## French Guiana

### Fact File

OFFICIAL NAME Department of Guiana

FORM OF GOVERNMENT Overseas department of France

CAPITAL Cayenne

AREA 91,000 sq km (35,135 sq miles)

TIME ZONE GMT – 3 hours

POPULATION 209,000

LIFE EXPECTANCY 76.1

INFANT MORTALITY (PER 1,000) 14

LITERACY RATE 83 %

CURRENCY Euro

ECONOMY Services 61 %, industry 21 %, agriculture 18 %

CLIMATE Tropical with two wet seasons (December and June)

MAP REFERENCE Page 452

Located along the northeast coast of South America, French Guiana has a narrow coastal plain and a largely unpopulated, forested hinterland. Brazil lies across its southern and eastern borders. After the French Revolution one of the islands became the French penal colony of Devil's Island (Île du Diable). Now French Guiana is the site of the European Space Agency's rocket base Kourou where the Ariane rockets lift off. Sugarcane plantations influenced its development; today, cash crops such as bananas and sugarcane grow on the coast, and the main exports are fish and fish products. Still, the country is highly dependent on France for its economic viability.

## South Georgia and the South Sandwich Islands

### Fact File

OFFICIAL NAME South Georgia and the South Sandwich Islands

FORM OF GOVERNMENT Overseas territory of the UK

CAPITAL None; Grytviken is a scientific camp

AREA 3,903 sq km (1,507 sq miles)

TIME ZONE GMT – 4 hours

POPULATION No permanent population

ECONOMY Biological station only

CLIMATE Cold, wet, and windy

MAP REFERENCE Pages 461

South Georgia is a barren island in the South Atlantic 1,300 km (800 miles) southeast of the Falklands. Annexed by Captain Cook in 1775, the harbor of Grytviken was long used as a whaling base. Until the 1940s it had a population of up to 800 employed in the whaling industry. Its wildlife is now attracting increasing numbers of ecotourists. In 2001, the small military garrison was replaced by a permanent group of scientists of the British Antarctic Survey, which also has a biological station on Bird Island. The South Sandwich Islands are six uninhabited volcanic cones to the southeast of South Georgia.

# South America: Physical

South America

ATLANTIC OCEAN

Equator

Pta do Calcanhar

Pta do Manguinha

Pta da Baleia

Planalto da Borborema

Serra de Espinhaço

Serra Geral de Goiás

BRAZILIAN HIGHLANDS

Serra dos Gradaús

Rio das Mortes

Planalto do Mato Grosso

Serra do Cachimbo

Juliana top 1230 m

AMAZON BASIN

Selvas

Guiana Highlands

Serra Pacaraima

Mte Roraima 2810 m

Pico da Neblina 3014 m

Ilha de Maracá
C. Norte
Ilha Janaucu
Ilha Mexiana
Baía de Marajó

Rio d'Oyapok

WINDWARD ISLANDS

Barbuda
Antigua

LEEWARD ISLANDS

LESSER ANTILLES

Puerto Rico

Tobago

Trinidad

The Grenadines

I. de Margarita

C. Codera

Aruba  Curaçao  Bonaire

Golfo de Venezuela

Embalse de Guri

Pico Bolívar 5007 m

Llanos

ANDES

Cordillera Oriental

Cordillera Oriental

Cordillera Occidental

Nev. Sajama 6520 m

Lago Titicaca

Lago Poopó

Hispaniola

Cabo Engaño

Pico Duarte 3175 m

Cabo Beata

CARIBBEAN SEA

GREATER ANTILLES

Cuba

Cabo San Antonio

Isla de la Juventud

Pico Turquino 1974 m

Blue Mtn Pk 2256 m

Jamaica

Cabo de la Vela

P. Cristóbal Colón 5775 m

Golfo de Maracaibo

Lago de Maracaibo

Cordillera Occidental

CORDILLERA ORIENTAL

Cauca

Magdalena

Nev. Huascarán 6768 m

Japurá
Negro
Putumayo
Marañón
Ucayali

Pta Salinas ó Lachay

Pen. de Paracas

Bahía San Nicolás

Cordillera Occidental

Chimborazo 6310 m

Cabo Corrientes

Bahía de Buenaventura

Pta Galera

Ensenada de Tumaco

Equator

Bahía de Sta Elena

Golfo de Guayaquil

Bahía de Sechura

Pta Negra

Punta Patuca

Golfo del Darién

Isla del Rey

Golfo de Panamá

Isla de Coiba

Pta Burica

Bahía de Coronado

Lago de Nicaragua

Cerro Chirripó 3819 m

Golfo de los Mosquitos

Bahía de Punta Gorda

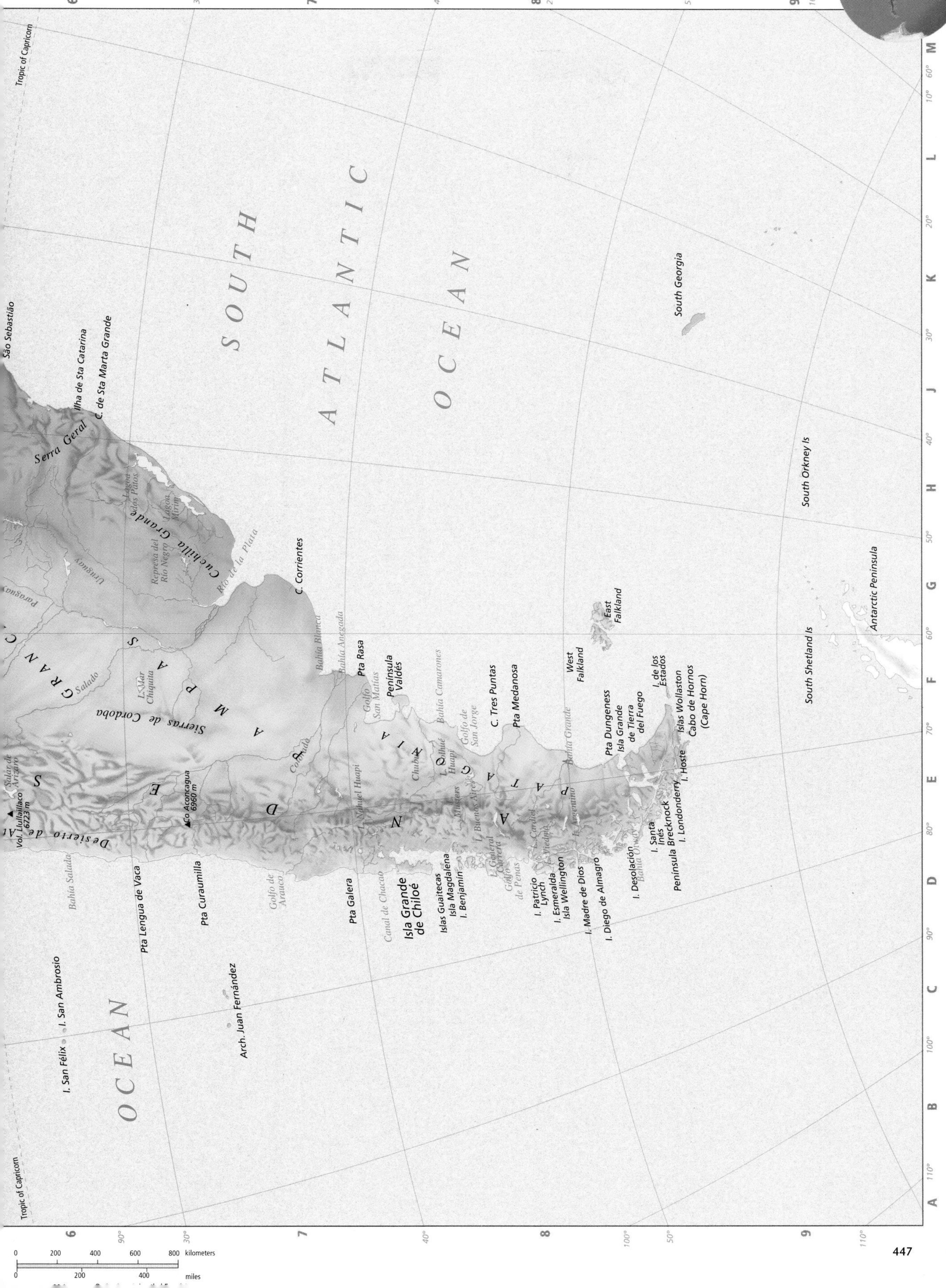
SOUTH ATLANTIC OCEAN
OCEAN
South Georgia
South Orkney Is
South Shetland Is
Antarctic Peninsula
East Falkland
West Falkland
I. de los Estados
Islas Wollaston
Cabo de Hornos (Cape Horn)
I. Hoste
Isla Grande de Tierra del Fuego
Pta Dungeness
Bahía Grande
Pta Medanosa
C. Tres Puntas
Golfo de San Jorge
Bahía Camarones
Península Valdés
Golfo San Matías
Pta Rasa
Bahía Anegada
Bahía Blanca
C. Corrientes
Río de la Plata
Cuchilla Grande
Represa del Río Negro
Lagoa dos Patos
Lagoa Mirim
Uruguay
Paraguay
Serra Geral
Ilha de Sta Catarina
C. de Sta Marta Grande
São Sebastião
Tropic of Capricorn
GRAN CHACO
PAMPAS
L. Mar Chiquita
Salado
Sierras de Córdoba
Colorado
Chubut
PATAGONIA
ANDES
Desierto de Atacama
Salar de Arizaro
Vol. Llullaillaco 6723 m
Co Aconcagua 6960 m
L. Nahuel Huapi
L. Colhué Huapi
L. Musters
L. Buenos Aires
L. General Carrera
L. Cardiel
L. Viedma
L. Argentino
Bahía Salada
Pta Lengua de Vaca
Pta Curaumilla
Golfo de Arauco
Pta Galera
Canal de Chacao
Isla Grande de Chiloé
Islas Guaitecas
Isla Magdalena
I. Benjamín
Golfo de Penas
I. Patricio Lynch
I. Esmeralda
Isla Wellington
I. Madre de Dios
I. Diego de Almagro
I. Desolación
Bahía Otway
I. Santa Inés
Península Brecknock
I. Londonderry
I. San Ambrosio
I. San Félix
Arch. Juan Fernández
0 200 400 600 800 kilometers
0 200 400 miles

South America

# South America: Political

ATLANTIC OCEAN

CARIBBEAN SEA

**BRAZIL**

**VENEZUELA**

**COLOMBIA**

**PERU**

**BOLIVIA**

**ECUADOR**

**GUYANA**

**SURINAME**

**FRENCH GUIANA** (Fr.)

CUBA

HAITI

JAMAICA

DOMINICAN REPUBLIC

CAYMAN ISLANDS (U.K.)

PUERTO RICO (U.S.A.)

VIRGIN ISLANDS (U.K.)

VIRGIN ISLANDS (U.S.A.)

ANGUILLA (U.K.)

ST KITTS AND NEVIS

ANTIGUA AND BARBUDA

GUADELOUPE (Fr.)

MONTSERRAT (U.K.)

DOMINICA

MARTINIQUE (Fr.)

ST LUCIA

ST VINCENT AND THE GRENADINES

The Grenadines

BARBADOS

GRENADA

TRINIDAD AND TOBAGO

NETHERLANDS ANTILLES (Neth.)

ARUBA (Neth.)

HONDURAS

NICARAGUA

COSTA RICA

PANAMA

Natal
João Pessoa
Recife
Maceió
Mossoró
Campina Grande
Caruaru
Garanhuns
Araçiraca
Aracaju
Juazeiro do Norte
Paulo Afonso
Fortaleza
Salvador
Itabuna
Ilhéus
Canavieiras
Parnaíba
Sobral
Senhor do Bonfim
Feira de Santana
Jequié
Vitória da Conquista
Governador Valadares
Juazeiro
Teresina
Picos
Floriano
São Francisco
Grão Mogol
Teófilo Otoni
Barreiras
Bom Jesus da Lapa
Montes Claros
Patos de Minas
Uberaba
Belo Horizonte
São Luís
Caxias
Barra do Corda
Bacabal
Imperatriz
Tocantinópolis
Carolina
Gurupi
Araguaína
Brasília
Anápolis
Goiânia
Araguari
Uberlândia
São José
Ituiutaba
Jataí
Belém
Bragança
Castanhal
Abaetetuba
Cametá
Marabá
São Félix do Xingu
Santa Maria das Barreiras
Araçaços
Catalão
Calçoene
Ilha de Maracá
Ilha Januçu
Ilha Mexiana
Macapá
Pôrto de Moz
Santarém
Altamira
Óbidos
Parintins
Santa Maria
Itaituba
Coxim
Corumbá
Campo Grande
Cuiabá
Cáceres
Rondonópolis
Manaus
Manicoré
Tefé
Boa Vista
Normandía
Georgetown
New Amsterdam
Linden
Paramaribo
Cayenne
St-Laurent du Maroni
São Gabriel da Cachoeira
Leticia
Benjamin Constant
Eirunepé
Lábrea
Humaitá
Bôca do Acre
Xapuri
Brasiléia
Riberalta
Guajará-Mirim
Guayaramerín
Rio Branco
Pôrto Velho
Ariquemes
Pimenta Bueno
Rio Branco
Plácido de Castro
Costa Marques
Trinidad
Cruzeiro do Sul
Pucallpa
Iquitos
Mitú
San José del Guaviare
Puerto Inírida
Puerto Ayacucho
Ciudad Guayana
Ciudad Bolívar
Barcelona
Cumaná
Maturín
La Asunción
Í. de Margarita
Port of Spain
Trinidad
Tucupita
Cabimas
Valencia
Caracas
Coro
Maracaibo
San Fernando de Apure
Barinas
Willemstad
Santa Marta
Barranquilla
Cartagena
Sincelejo
Montería
Valledupar
Cúcuta
San Cristóbal
Bucaramanga
Medellín
Tunja
Yopal
Quibdó
Manizales
Pereira
Bogotá
Armenia
Ibagué
Villavicencio
Cali
Popayán
Florencia
Mocoa
Pasto
Tulcán
Ibarra
Quito
Ambato
Riobamba
Cuenca
Loja
Machala
Guayaquil
Sullana
Piura
Talara
Bayovar
Chiclayo
Trujillo
Chimbote
Cajamarca
Moyobamba
Yurimaguas
Cerro de Pasco
La Oroya
Callao
Lima
Huancayo
Ayacucho
Pisco
Ica
Marcona
Sicuani
Cuzco
Puerto Maldonado
Juliaca
Arequipa
Tacna
Mollendo
Ilo
Arica
La Paz
Cochabamba
Oruro
Sucre
Potosí
Punata
Huanuni
Montero
Santa Cruz
Camiri
Isla del Rey
Isla de Coíba
Tobago

Bahía de São Marcos
B. de Buenaventura
Golfo de Guayaquil

Equator

© Random House Australia Pty Ltd

South America

Tropic of Capricorn

SOUTH ATLANTIC OCEAN

OCEAN

ARGENTINA

URUGUAY

*I. San Félix* | *I. San Ambrosio*

*Arch. Juan Fernández*

Copiapó
La Serena
Coquimbo
Ovalle
Viña del Mar
Valparaíso
Rancagua
Curicó
Talca
Talcahuano
Concepción
Arauco
Los Angeles
Curacautín
Temuco
Valdivia
Osorno
Puerto Montt
Castro
Islas Guaitecas
Isla Magdalena
I. Benjamín
Coihaique
I. Patricio
Lynch
I. Esmeralda
I. Wellington
I. Madre de Dios
I. Diego de Almagro
I. Desolación
Punta Arenas
I. Santa
Inés
I. Londonderry

Salta
Tafí Viejo
San Miguel
de Tucumán
Santiago
del Estero
La Rioja
San Juan
Mendoza
Santiago
San Bernardo
San Rafael
Chillán
San Fernando del
Valle de Catamarca
La Banda
San Francisco
San Luis
Río Cuarto
Mercedes
Villa María
Córdoba
Rafaela
Santa
Fe
Presidencia Roque
Sáenz Peña
Resistencia
Reconquista
Goya
Corrientes
Formosa
Posadas
San
Lorenzo
Asunción
Oberá
Cruz
Alta
Santa
María
Uruguaiana
Rivera
Bagé
Pelotas
Treinta-y-Tres
Las Piedras
Montevideo
Salto
Concordia
Paraná
Rosario
San Nicolás
de los Arroyos
Zárate
Junín
Buenos Aires
La Plata
Olavarría
Tandil
Santa Rosa
Venado
Tuerto
Mar del Plata
Necochea
Tres Arroyos
Punta Alta
Río Colorado
Bahía Blanca
Neuquén
Zapala
San Martín
De Los Andes
San Carlos
de Bariloche
Esquel
Sierra Grande
San Antonio
Oeste
Viedma
Carmen De Patagones
*Golfo*
*San Matías*
Rawson
Trelew
Puerto Madryn
*Golfo de*
*San Jorge*
Comodoro
Rivadavia
Caleta Olivia
Pico Truncado
*Golfo*
*de Penas*
Puerto
Natales
Río Gallegos
*Bahía Grande*
Río Grande
Isla Grande
de Tierra
del Fuego
Río Grande
del Fuego
Ushuaia
I. de los
Estados
*Islas Wollaston*
Curitiba
Itajaí
Joinville
Chapecó
Lajes
Laguna
Caxias do Sul
Passo
Fundo
Porto Alegre
Foz do Iguaçu
Río Grande
*Río de la Plata*
*Bahía Blanca*

FALKLAND
ISLANDS
(U.K.)

Stanley
*East*
*Falkland*
*West*
*Falkland*

*South Shetland*
*Islands (U.K.)*

*Antarctic Peninsula*

*South Orkney*
*Islands (U.K.)*

*South Georgia*

SOUTH GEORGIA AND
SOUTH SANDWICH ISLANDS
(U.K.)

*South Sandwich*
*Islands*

Tropic of Capricorn

0   200   400   600   800  kilometers
0   200   400  miles
Scale 1:21,000,000     Projection: Azimuthal Equal Area

# Colombia • Venezuela • Ecuador • Guyana • Northwest Brazil

A  82°  B  78°  429  C  74°

## 1

Santo Domingo
Juigalpa
Acoyapa
Laguna de Perlas
Bluefields
NICARAGUA
Lago de Nicaragua
Punta Gorda
Bahía de Punta Gorda
San Juan del Norte
San Carlos
Vol. Miravalles ▲ 2028 m
Río Frío
Altamira
Guápiles
Puerto Jesús
Alajuela  Heredia
Puerto Limón
Puntarenas
COSTA RICA
San José  Cartago
Bribri
Parrita
Cerro Chirripó ▲ 3819 m
Dominical
Ciudad Cortés
B. de Coronado
Volcán ▲ 3475 m
Volcán Barú
La Concepción  Boquete
David
Península de Osa
Pta Burica
Puerto Armuelles
San Francisco
Santiago  Aguadulce
Soná  Parita  Chitré
Tolé
Atalaya  Las Tablas
Isla de Coiba
Golfo de Chiriquí
Golfo de los Mosquitos
Santa Catalina
Penonomé
Antón
Coclé
Isla del Rey
La Chorrera
PANAMÁ
Panamá
San Miguelito
Chimán
San Miguel
La Palma
El Real
Yaviza
Garachiné
Jaqué
Cupica
Golfo de Cupica

CARIBBEAN SEA

Portobelo  El Porvenir  Arch. de San Blás
Palenque
Panama Canal
Ailigandi
Gulf del Darién
Golfo del Darién
Acandí
Tierralta
Chigorodó
Paso de las Letras
Riosucio
Dabeiba
3960 m
Paramillo
Ituango
Yarumal
Antioquia
Anzá

Cabo de la Vela
Carrizal
Uribia
Ríohacha
Santa Marta
Barranquilla
Puerto Colombia
Barano  Soledad  Ciénaga
Sabanalarga  P. Cristóbal Colón ▲ 5775 m
Barrancas
Maicao
Carraipía
Campo
Mara
Maracaib
Ca
Villanueva
Cartagena  Turbaco  Pivijay  Valledupar
Arjona  Calamar  Fundación  Augustín Codazzi
El Carmen de Bolívar
El Difícil
Plato
Rosario
Machiques
Ciuda
Barranquitas
Golfo de Morrosquillo  Tolú
Sincelejo  Sincé
Chiriguaná
La Jagua de Ibirico
Encontrados
El Vigi
Lorica  Mompós
Magangué  El Banco  La Gloria  Casigua
Puerto Rey  Cereté  Sahagún  Sucre
Montería  Planeta Rica  El Banco  Ocaña  Sardinata  La Fría  Pedra
Caucasia  Ayapel  Simití  Cáchira  Cúcuta  San C
Cáceres  Zaragoza  Pamplona  Chinácota  San A
Barrancabermeja  Bucaramanga  Cubará
Segovia  Zapatoca  Floridablanca
Amalfi  Puerto Berrío  San Gil  Sierra Nevada del Cocuy ▲ 5493 m
Cisneros  Vélez  Barbosa  Socorro  El Cocuy
Bello  Cocorná  Belén  Paz de Río  Paz
Itagüí  Medellín  Santa Bárbara  Duitama  Sogamoso  Pore
Envigado  Sonsón  Chiquinquirá  Tunja  Yopal
Bolívar  Aguadas  La Dorada  Ubaté
Quibdó  Andes  Salamina  Honda  Zipaquirá  Maní
Nqui  Líbano  Armero  Facatativá
Manizales  Ned. del Ruiz 5399 m  Soacha  Bogotá
Cabo Corrientes  Pereira  Ibagué  Fusagasugá  Villavicencio
Istmina  Cartago  Armenia  4560 m  Puerto López
Bajo Baudó  Tuluá  Sevilla  Saldaña  Cerro Nevado  San Martín  Granada
Pta Charambirá  Buga  Chaparral  Agua de Dios  Pavón
Buenaventura  Yumbo  Natagaima  Colombia
B. de Buenaventura  Cali  Palmira  Baraza  Chafurray
Naya  Puerto Tejada  Aipe  COLOMBIA
Pta Coco  Santander  ▲ 5750 m  Puerto La Concordia
Guapi  Co Munchique  Nev. de Huila  Neiva  San José del Guav
Mosquera  ▲ 3012 m  Popayán  Campoalegre
Volcán Puracé 4646 m  Gigante  San Vicente del Caguán  Calamar
Ensenada de Tumaco  Barbacoas  La Plata  Garzón  de
Tumaco  Sotomayor  La Unión  Altamira  Miraflore
B. de Ancón de Sardinas  El Divíso  Pitalito  Mesa de Iguaje  Macayari
Esmeraldas  San Lorenzo  Sandoná  Florencia
Nev. de Cumbal  Pasto  Cerro Cumare  Macujer
4764 m ▲  Túquerres  Mocoa  720 m
Valdez  Ipiales  Caguán
Punta Galera  Tulcán  Puerto Asís  Tres Esquinas  Santa Rita
Muisné  San Gabriel  Araracuara
Cabo de San Francisco  Otavalo  Ibarra  Lago Agrio  Co Maine Hanari
Rosa Zárate  Cayambe  Volcán Cayambe  Cuyabeno  La Tagua  860 m  La Chorrera
Santo Domingo  Quito  5790 m  Puerto Leguizamo
de los Colorados  5704 m  Hacha
Chone  Vol. Antisana  Puerto Francisco de Orellana  Pantoja
Bahía de Caráquez  Machachi  Baeza  El Encanto
B. de Caráquez  Rocafuerte  Quevedo  Vol. Cotopaxi 5897 m  Tena  Pamar
Manta  Portoviejo  Latacunga  Arica
Montecristi  Santa Ana  ECUADOR  Arica
Jipijapa  Balzar  Ambato  Puyo  Villano  Santa María  El Encanto  Puca Urco
Pajám  Santa Lucía  Zapotal  Chimborazo 6310 m  Riobamba  Vilcabamba  Río Tigre
B. de Sta Elena  Guaranda  Babahoyo  Vol. Sangay  Ayuy  Montalvo
Salinas  Guayaquil  Durán  Alausí  5230 m  Macas  Puerto Tunigrama
Santa Elena  Naranjal  Cañar  Azogues  Morona  Andoas  Santa Clotilde  Arica
Playas  Girón  Cuenca  Gualaceo  Intuto  Pebas
Golfo de Guayaquil  Isla Puná  Machala  Saraguro  Puerto Pardo  Mazán  Francisco de Orellana
Zarumilla  Santa Rosa  Zamora  Borja  Santa María de Nanay  Iquitos
Tumbes  Piñas  Amazonas
Zorritos  Macará  Loja  Omaguas  Tamshiyaco
Canoas  Catacocha  Cariamanga  Orellana  Concordia  Nauta
Máncora  Suyo  PERU  Marañón
Lobitos  Las Lomas  Borja  Requena  Brasil
Talara  Barranca
Pta Pariñas  Sullana  Tambo Grande  Cahuapanas
Negritos  La Huaca  Piura  Chulucanas  Lagunas  Palmeiras do Javari
Paita  San Ignacio
Catacaos  Castilla

## 2

## 3

PACIFIC

OCEAN

## 4

Equator

## 5

450  © Random House Australia Pty Ltd

A  82°  B  78°  C  454  74°  D

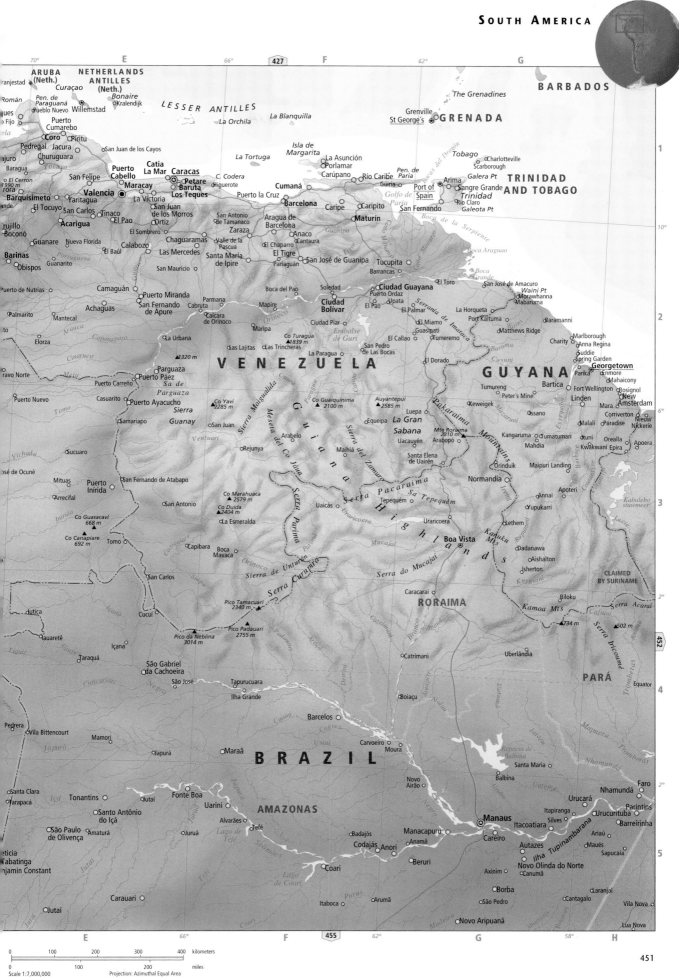

BARBADOS

ARUBA (Neth.)
NETHERLANDS ANTILLES (Neth.)

Oranjestad
Curaçao
Bonaire
Pen. de Paraguaná
Pueblo Nuevo
Willemstad
Kralendijk

Román
LESSER ANTILLES
La Orchila
La Blanquilla
The Grenadines
Grenville
St George's
GRENADA

ajuro
Puerto Cumarebo
La Tortuga
Isla de Margarita
La Asunción
Porlamar
Carúpano
Río Caribe
Pen. de Paria
Güiria
Tobago
Charlotteville
Scarborough
Galera Pt

El Fijo
Coro
Piritu
C. Codera
Higuerote
Cumaná
Arima
Sangre Grande
Trinidad
TRINIDAD AND TOBAGO

la
Pedregal
Jacura
Churuguara
San Juan de los Cayos
Catia La Mar
Caracas
Petare
Baruta
Puerto la Cruz
Barcelona
Caripe
Caripito
Port of Spain
Rio Claro
Galeota Pt

ajuro
Baragua
San Felipe
Puerto Cabello
Maracay
La Victoria
San Juan de los Morros
Aragua de Barcelona
Anaco
Cantaura
Maturín
Golfo de Paria
San Fernando
Boca de la Serpiente

El Cerron 1990 m
Valencia
Yaritagua
La Victoria
El Sombrero
Zaraza
El Chaparro
El Tigre
San José de Guanipa
Tucupita
Boca Araguao

Barquisimeto
El Tocuyo
San Carlos
Tinaco
El Pao
Valle de la Pascua
El Tigre
Pariaguán
Barrancas
Boca Grande

rora
Acarigua
Nueva Florida
Calabozo
Las Mercedes
Santa María de Ipire
San José de Guanipa
El Toro
San José de Amacuro
Waini Pt
Morawhanna
Mabaruma

trujillo
Barinas
Guanare
El Baúl
San Mauricio
Boca del Pao
Soledad
Ciudad Guayana
Port Kaituma
Baramanni

Boconó
Obispos
Guanarito
Camaguán
Puerto Miranda
Parmana
Mapire
Puerto Ordaz
Upata
El Pao
El Palmar
La Horqueta
Matthews Ridge
Marlborough
Anna Regina

Palmarito
Mantecal
Achaguas
San Fernando de Apure
Cabruta
Caicara de Orinoco
Ciudad Bolívar
Ciudad Piar
El Miamo
Guasipati
Tumeremo
Charity
Suddie
Spring Garden

Puerto de Nutrias
Elorza
Camaguán
La Urbana
Maripa
Las Lajitas
Las Trincheras
Co Turagua 1839 m
La Paragua
San Pedro de Las Bocas
El Callao
El Dorado
Parika
Georgetown
Enmore
Mahaicony

ravo Norte
Puerto Carreño
Puerto Páez
Parguaza
320 m
Embalse de Guri
VENEZUELA
GUYANA
Tumureng
Peter's Mine
Bartica
Linden
Fort Wellington
Rosignol
New Amsterdam

Puerto Nuevo
Casuarito
Puerto Ayacucho
Sierra Guanay
Co Yavi 2285 m
Co Guaiquinima 2100 m
Auyantepui 2585 m
Luepa
Kweweigek
Ossano
Mara
Malali
Corriverton
Nieuw Nickerie

Samariapo
San Juan
Arabelo
La Gran Sabana
Equeipa
Uacauyén
Mte Roraima 2810 m
Arabopó
Kangaruma
Mahdia
Tumatumari
Paradise
Apoera

Sucuaro
Rejunya
Maihiá
Santa Elena de Uairén
Orinduik
Maipuri Landing
Kwakwani
Epira
Orealla

Mituas
Arrecifal
Puerto Inírida
San Fernando de Atabapo
San Antonio
Co Marahuaca 2579 m
Co Duida 2404 m
Uaicás
Normandia
Annai
Yupukarri
Apoteri
Lethem

Co Guasacaví 668 m
La Esmeralda
Uraricoera
Uraricuera
Tepequém
Sa Tepequém
Kabalebo stuwmeer

Co Canapiare 692 m
Tomo
Capibara
Boca Mavaca
Mucajaí
Boa Vista
Kaituma
Dadanawa
Aishalton
Isherton

jutica
San Carlos
Orinoco
Sierra de Unturán
Serra Curumuú
Serra do Mucajaí
Caracaraí
RORAIMA
Kamoa Mts
Biloku
Serra Acaraí
CLAIMED BY SURINAME

auareté
Cucuí
Pico Tamacuari 2340 m
Catrimani
734 m
502 m
Serra Iricoumé

Içana
Pico da Neblina 3014 m
Pico Padauari 2755 m
Uberlândia
PARÁ
Equator

Jaraquá
São Gabriel da Cachoeira
São José
Tapurucuara
Ilha Grande
Boiaçu
Catrimani

Pedrera
Vila Bittencourt
Mamori
Maraã
Barcelos
Carvoeiro
Moura
Represa de Balbina
Santa Maria
Nhamundá
Faro

BRAZIL

Santa Clara
Tarapacá
Tonantins
Fonte Boa
Uarini
Novo Airão
Balbina
Urucará
Urucurituba
Parintins

eticia
Tabatinga
njamin Constant
Jutaí
Santo Antônio do Içá
Alvarães
Tefé
AMAZONAS
Itapiranga
Silves
Barreirinha

São Paulo de Olivença
Amaturá
Juruá
Manaus
Itacoatiara
Ariaú
Maués
Sapucaia

Badajós
Codajás
Anori
Anamã
Manacapuru
Careiro
Autazes
Ilha Tupinambarana
Novo Olinda do Norte

Coari
Beruti
Axinim
Canumã

Carauari
Itaboca
Arumã
Borba
Laranjal
Cantagalo
Vila Nova

Jutaí
São Pedro
Novo Aripuanã
Lua Nova

South America

0   100   200   300   400 kilometers
0   100   200 miles
Scale 1:7,000,000
Projection: Azimuthal Equal Area

# Northeast Brazil • Suriname • French Guiana

58°　　　　B　　　　54°　　　　C　　　　50°　　　　D　　　　46°

Georgetown
Parika　Enmore
Mahaicony
Fort Wellington
Rosignol　New Amsterdam
Linden　Mara　Nieuw Nickerie　Paramaribo　Alliance
GUYANA　Corriverton　Wageningen　Nieuw Amsterdam　Mana　Organabo
Malali　Boskamp　Onverwacht　Zanderij　Albina　Iracoubo　Sinnamary　Malmanoury
Paradise　Sabana　　　　St-Laurent　Kourou
Ituni　Corneliskondre　Kwakoegron　Brokopondo　du Maroni　Gare Tigre　Cayenne
Oreallo　Apoera　Njoeng Jacobkondre　　La Forestière　St Elie　Montsinéry　Rémire
Kwakwani　Epira　　　Afobaka　Citron　Délices　　Roura
W J van　　　　Cacao
Blommestein Meer　　　Grand-Santi　Régina　Kaw
Pokigron　　Gramankondre　Aurora　　FRENCH　Bélizon　Guisanbourg
Maipuri　Boslanti　Boto-Pasi　▲ 694 m　GUIANA　St-Georges　Ouanary　Ponta dos Índios
Landing　　Djoemoe　　(Fr.)　Patience　Oiapoque
Apoteri　SURINAME　Cottica　Cormontibo　Mt Bellevue　Clevelândia do Norte
Kabaleba　Mariapasoula　de l'Inini　Saül
stuwmeer　Julianatop　Pontoetoe　De Goeje Gebergte　Camopi　Vila Velha
Meer　1230 m　658 m　851 m　Clément
Oranje Gebergte　Antecume　Bienvenue
Pata　Oscar
Eilerts de Haan　CLAIMED　Mitaraka　Mt Saint-Marcel　Regina　Calçoene
Gebergte　BY SURINAME　690 m　635 m　Lourenço
CLAIMED　Serra Tumucumaque　AMAPÁ　Amapá　Ilha de Maracá
BY SURINAME
Biloku　Serra Acaraí　Tacalé　Cabo Norte
▲ 734 m　▲ 502 m　Yaripo　Merirumã　Serra do Navio　Aporema　Bailique
Serra Iricoumé　Maloca　Azaurio　Ferreira Gomes　Ilha
Pôrto Grande　Curuá
Equator　　Arere　Ilha Janaucu
Ilha
Caviana　Ilha Mexiana
Planalto　Macapá　Afuá　Cabo
Maracanaquará　Mazagão　Pôrto　Chaves　Maguarinho
Santana　Ilha
Itatupá　Anajás　Ilha de Marajó　Soure　Marapanim　Salinópolis
Morro Grande　Barraca da Bôca　Ilha Grande　Anajás　Salvaterra　Curuçá　Maracanã　Bragança
629 m　Bôca do Jari　de Gurupá　Curumu　Cachoeira　Vigia　Igarapé-Açu
Oriximiná　Almeirim　Gurupá　Ilha dos　do Arari　Colares　Capanema　Viseu
Santa Maria　Óbidos　Prainha　Macacos　São Sebastiao　Mosqueiro　Castanhal
Faro　Alenquer　Ilha da Breves　Laguna　da Boa Vista　São Miguel　Ourém　Camiranga
Nhamundá　Juruti　Monte　Mulata　Pôrto de Moz　do Guamá　Irituia
Urucará　Alegre　Melgaço　Belém
Itapiranga　Juruti Velho　Veiros　Portel　Bagre　Curralinho　Abaetetuba
Silves　Parintis　350 m　Santa Cruz　Carvalho　Bom Jardim　Acará
Ariaú　Urucurituba　Santarém　Pacoval　Cametá　São Joaquim
Itacoatiara　Sapucaia　Barreirinha　Belterra　Vitória　Bertinho　Badajós　Canindé
Autazes　Maués　Boimo　Belo Monte　Mocajuba
Novo Olinda do Norte　Aveiro　Baião
Canumã　AMAZONAS　Brasília Legal　Altamira　Pindobal
Cantagalo　Itaituba　Uxituba　Caima　Tucuruí
Laranjal　Vila Nóva　Pôrto Alegre　Itupiranga　Represa de
Lua Nova　Paga Conta　Sem Tripa　Jacundá　Rondon
Entre Rios　Marabá　São João　do Pará
Jacareacanga　São Sebastião　Nazaré　do Araguaia　Imperatriz　Amarante
Cuiaba　Canudos　Manuelzinho　Araraso　BRAZIL　Araguatins　do Maranhão
Campo Grande　Barra de São Manuel　São Félix　Parauapebas　Tocantinópolis　Montes Altos
Recreio　do Xingu　Xinguara　Xambioá　Pôrto Franco
Barracão　Pau d'Arco　Babaçulândia
do Barreto　Conceição　Araguaína　Carolina　Riachão
do Araguaia　Piaçá
Couto　TOCANTINS
Redenção　Magalhães　Itacajá
Aldeia Velha　Tupiratins
Santa Maria　Araguacema　Pedro Afonso
das Barreiras　Miracema
do Tocantins

A　58°　B　54°　C　50°　D

ATLANTIC

OCEAN

Ponta de São Marcos
Ilha de São Luís
Baía de São José

São Luís
Icatu
Axixá
Primeira Cruz
Barreirinhas
Tutóia
Luís Correia
Camocim
Acaraú
Urbano Santos
Araioses
Parnaíba
Granja
São Bernardo
Buriti dos Lopes
Brejo
Luzilândia
Coreaú
Amontada
Paracuru
tapecuru-
Mirim
Pôrto
Massapê
Itapipoca
São Gonçalo do Amarante
Chapadinha
Buriti
Tianguá
Sobral
Cariré
Caucaia
Fortaleza
Peritoró
Miguel Alves
Piracuruca
São Benedito
Maranguape
Aquiraz
Codó
Barras
Piripiri
Ipu
Santa
Quitéria
Canindé
Baturité
Cascavel
eiras
União
Pedro II
Ipueiras
MARANHÃO
Caxias
Campo Maior
Tamboril
Aracati
om Pedro
Timon
Teresina
Altos
Castelo
do Piauí
Crateús
Boa
Viagem
Quixadá
Russas
Areia Branca
São Bento
do Norte
Ponta do
Calcanhar
esidente
utra
Parnarama
Alto Longá
CEARÁ
Quixeramobim
Morada
Nova
Mossoró
Macau
Parazinho
Touros
Buriti Bravo
Novo Parnarama
São Miguel
do Tapuio
Mombaça
Senador Pompeu
Solonópole
Apodi
Açu
Lajes
Cabo de São Roque
Palmeirais
Tauá
RIO GRANDE DO NORTE
Colinas
Acopiara
Jaguaribe
Natal
São João
dos Patos
Amarante
Valença
do Piauí
Iguatu
Icó
Currais Novos
Caicó
Santa Cruz
Cuité
São José de Mipibu
Floriano
Saboeiro
Sousa
Pombal
Acari
Parelhas
Canguaretama
Jerumenha
Oeiras
Picos
Campos Sales
Cajazeiras
Patos
Guarabira
Baía de Traição
ruçuí
PIAUÍ
Jaicós
Boa Esperança
Crato
Juazeiro do Norte
Milagres
Teixeira
PARAÍBA
Santa Rita
Cabedelo
João Pessoa
Bertolínia
Flores do
Piauí
Araripina
Chapada do Araripe
Exu
Conceição
São João
do Cariri
Campina Grande
Timbaúba
Goiana
Eliseu
Martins
Canto do Buriti
Simplício Mendes
Paulistana
Ouricurí
Salgueiro
Serra
Talhada
Flores
Sertânia
Sumé
Limoeiro
Carpina
Paulista
Olinda
Cristino Castro
São João
do Piauí
Afrânio
Parnamirim
Pesqueira
Caruaru
Belo Jardim
Jaboatão
Gravatá
Recife
Cabrobó
Floresta
Ibimirim
Arcoverde
Escada
Caracol
São Raimundo
Nonato
Curaçá
Santa Maria
da Boa Vista
Belém de São Francisco
Chorrochó
Inajá
PERNAMBUCO
Palmares
Barreiros
Petrolina
Juazeiro
Paulo Afonso
Santana
do Ipanema
Garanhuns
União dos Palmares

E    42°    F    38°    G    34°    H

0    100    200    300    400    kilometers
0    100    200    miles
Scale 1:7,000,000    Projection: Azimuthal Equal Area

South America

# Bolivia • Peru • Southwest Brazil • North Paraguay

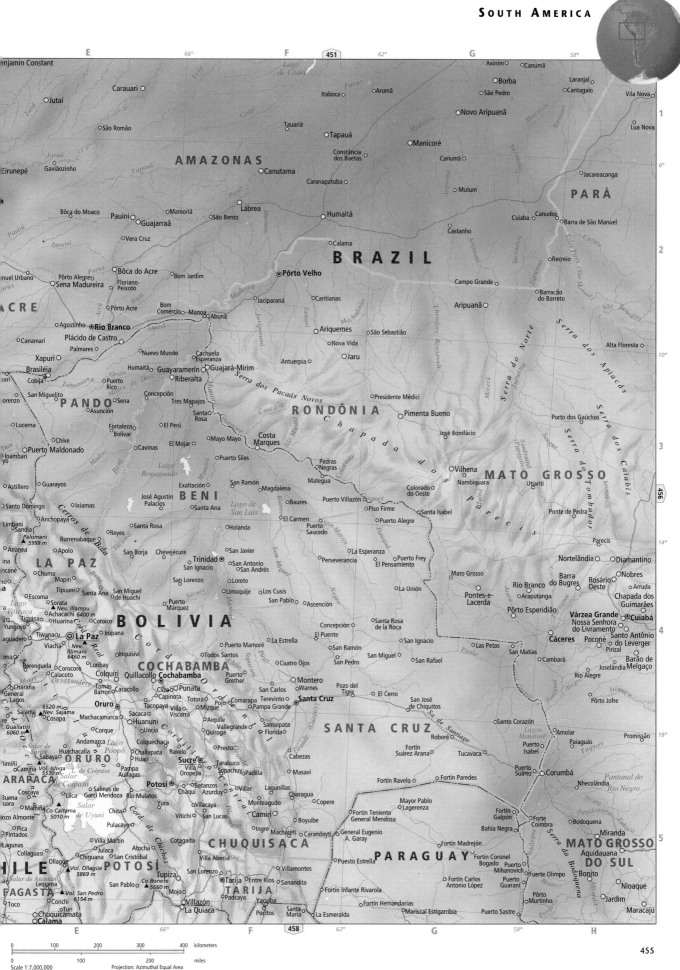

enjamin Constant

**E** 66° **F** 451 62° **G** 58°

Axinim○ ○Canumã

Borba○ Laranjal○ ○Cantagalo
São Pedro○ Vila Nova○

Carauari○ Itaboca○ ○Arumã ○Novo Aripuanã ○Lua Nova 1

Jutaí○

São Romão○ ○Tauariá ○Manicoré Jacareacanga○ 6°

**A M A Z O N A S** ○Canutama ○Tapauá Constância
dos Baetas **P A R Á**

Eirunepé○ Gaviãozinho○ Caranapatuba○ Cuiaba○ ○Canudos
○Mutum Castanho○ ○Barra de São Manuel

Bôca do Moaco○ ○Mamoriá ○Lábrea ○Humaitá **B R A Z I L** Recreio○
Pauini○ ○São Bento Campo Grande○ Barracão○
manuel Urbano○ Pôrto Alegre○ Guajarraã○ Calama○ do Barreto
Sena Madureira○ Vera Cruz○ ●Pôrto Velho

ACRE Bôca do Acre○ ○Bom Jardim Jaciparaná○ ○Caritianas Aripuanã○ Alta Floresta○ 10°
Pôrto Acre○ Bom
Agostinho○ ●Rio Branco Comércio○ ○Manoa Abunã○ ○Ariquemes ○São Sebastião Pôrto dos Gaúchos○
Canamari○ Plácido de Castro○ ○Cachuela ○Nova Vida **S e r r a d o s A p i a c á s**
Palmares○ ○Nuevo Mundo Esperanza ○Jaru Presidente Médici○
Xapuri○ Humaitá○ ○Antuerpia○ **R O N D Ô N I A** Pimenta Bueno○ Porto dos Gaúchos○
Brasiléia○ ○Guayaramerín○Guajará-Mirim **S e r r a d o s P a c a á s N o v o s** José Bonifácio○ **M A T O G R O S S O** 456
Cobija○ Riberalta○ ○Vilhena Utiariti○
San Miguelito○ Puerto○ Concepción○ Costa○ C h a p a d a Nambiquara○ Ponte de Pedra○ 456

**P A N D O** Rico Santao ○Mayo Mayo Marques Pedras○ Colorado○ Parecis○ 14°
Asunción○ Rosa Negras do Oeste Santa Isabel○
Lucerna○ Fortaleza○ ○El Perú Mategua○ Puerto Villazón○ Piso Firme○ Nortelândia○ ○Diamantino
Chive○ Bolívar○ ○Puerto Siles ○San Ramón ○Magdalena Puerto Alegre○ Barra○ ○Nobres
Puerto Maldonado○ Cavinas○ **B E N I** Baures○ Rio Branco○ do Bugres Rosário○
Astillero○ ○Guarayos José Agustín○ ○Santa Ana El Carmen○ La Esperanza○ Pontes-e-○ Araputanga○ ○Arruda
Santo Domingo○ Palacios Holanda○ Puerto○ Perseverancia○ La Unión○ Lacerda Chapada dos Guimarães
Anchopaya○ Ixiamas○ Saucedo Mato Grosso○ Pôrto Esperidião○ ○Cuiabá
Limbani○ Reyes○ ○San Javier La Esperanza○ **Várzea Grande** Santo Antônio
Sandia○ Palomani Rurrenabaque○ Chevejécure○ San Antonio○ El Pensamiento○ Puerto Frey○ Nossa Senhora○ do Leverger
5999 m Apolo○ ●Trinidad San Ignacio○ ○San Andrés ○Loreto do Livramento Pirizal
Ananea○ **L A P A Z** San Borja○ San Lorenzo○ ○Limoquije ○Los Cusis Concepción○ San Ignacio○ **Cáceres** Poconé○ Barão de
Chuma○ Mapiri○ ○San Pablo Santa Rosa○ Las Petas○ Melgaço
Tipuani○ Santa Ana○ Ascención○ de la Roca San Matías○ Joselândia○
Escoma○ Sorata○ Nev. Illampu ○Puerto El Puente○ San Ignacio○ Rio Alegre○
Achacachi 6400 m Márquez ○Concepción ○San Ramón Cambará○ ○Pôrto Jofre
Huarina○ Coroico○ **B O L I V I A** ○San Miguel Santa Rosa○ San Miguel○ Barão de
Tiquina○ Irupana○ de Huachi de la Roca Melgaço

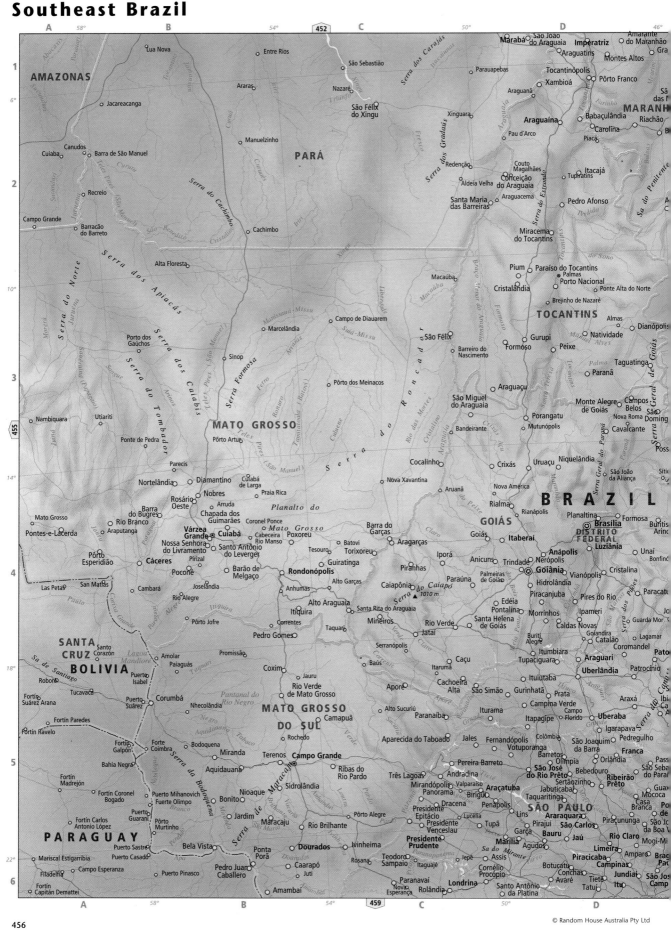

AMAZONAS

Lua Nova

Entre Rios

São Sebastião

Araras

Nazaré

Jacareacanga

São Félix
do Xingu

Xinguara

PARÁ

Canudos

Cuiaba

Barra de São Manuel

Manuelzinho

Recreio

Campo Grande

Barracão
do Barreto

Cachimbo

Alta Floresta

Marcelândia

Campo de Diauarem

Serra dos Carajás

Parauapebas

Araguatins

Marabá
São João
do Araguaia

Imperatriz

Amarante
do Maranhão

Gra

Montes Altos

Tocantinópolis

Xambioá

Pôrto Franco

Sã
das I

Araguaína

Babaçulândia

Carolina

Riachão

MARANH

Pau d'Arco

Piaçã

Redenção

Couto
Magalhães

Itacajá

Conceição
do Araguaia

Tupiratins

Santa Maria
das Barreiras

Aldeia Velha

Araguacema

Pedro Afonso

Macaúba

Miracema
do Tocantins

Pium

Paraíso do Tocantins
Palmas

Cristalândia

Porto Nacional

Ponte Alta do Norte

Brejinho de Nazaré

TOCANTINS

Almas

Dianópolis

São Félix

Barreiro do
Nascimento

Gurupi

Formoso

Peixe

Natividade

Taguatinga

Araguaçu

Paranã

Porto dos
Gaúchos

Sinop

Serra Formosa

Pôrto dos Meinacos

São Miguel
do Araguaia

Araguaçu

Monte Alegre
de Goiás

Campos
Belos

São
Doming

Nambiquara

Utiariti

Porangatu

Nova Roma

Cavalcante

Poss

Ponte de Pedra

Parecis

MATO GROSSO

Pôrto Artu

Cocalinho

Crixás

Uruaçu

Niquelândia

São João
da Aliança

Síti

Nortelândia

Diamantino

Cuiabá
de Larga

Praia Rica

Nova Xavantina

Nova América

Rialma

BRAZIL

Planaltina

Brasília

Formosa

Buritis

Mato Grosso

Rosário
Oeste

Nobres

Arruda

Planalto do

Aruanã

Rianápolis

DISTRITO
FEDERAL

Arinc

Rio Branco

Barra
do Bugres

Chapada dos
Guimarães

Coronel Ponce

Mato Grosso

Barra do
Garças

GOIÁS

Goiás

Itaberaí

Anápolis

Nerópolis

Luziânia

Unaí

Bonfín

Pontes-e-Lacerda

Araputanga

Várzea
Grande

Cuiabá

Cabeceira
Rio Manso

Poxoréu

Aragarças

Iporá

Anicuns

Trindade

Goiânia

Vianópolis

Cristalina

Nossa Senhora
do Livramento

Santo Antônio
do Leverger

Tesouro

Batovi
Torixoreu

Guiratinga

Paraúna

Palmeiras
de Goiás

Hidrolândia

Piracanjuba

Pires do Rio

Paracat

Pôrto
Esperidião

Cáceres

Pirizal

Pocoñé

Barão de
Melgaço

Rondonópolis

Alto Garças

Caiapônia

Serra do Caiapó
1010 m

Edéia

Pontalina

Morrinhos

Ipameri

Guarda Mor

Jo

Las Petas

San Matías

Cambará

Joselândia

Anhumas

Alto Araguaia

Santa Rita do Araguaia

Rio Verde

Santa Helena
de Goiás

Caldas Novas

Goiandira

Lagamar

Rio Alegre

Itiquira

Correntes

Taquari

Mineiros

Jataí

Buriti
Alegre

Itumbiara

Catalão

Coromandel

Pato

Pôrto Jofre

Pedro Gomes

Serranópolis

Caçu

Tupaciguara

Araguari

Patrocínio

SANTA
CRUZ

Santo
Corazón

Amolar

Promissão

Baús

Itarumã

Uberlândia

Araxá

Ibi

BOLIVIA

Paiaguás

Taquari

Coxim

Jauru

Apore

Cachoeira
Alta

Ituiutaba

Campina Verde

Roboré

Sa de
Santiago

Puerto
Isabel

Rio Verde
de Mato Grosso

Alto Sucuriú

São Simão

Gurinhatã

Prata

Itapagipe

Tucavaca

Corumbá

Nhecolândia

Paranaíba

Iturama

Campo
Florido

Uberaba

Fortín
Suárez Arana

Fortín Paredes

Puerto
Suárez

Pantanal do
Rio Negro

MATO GROSSO
DO SUL

Camapuã

Rochedo

Aparecida do Taboado

Colômbia

Igarapava

Fortín Ravelo

Fortín
Galpón

Forte
Coimbra

Bodoquena

Miranda

Terenos

Campo Grande

Jales

Fernandópolis

Votuporanga

São Joaquim
da Barra

Pedregulho

Franca

Bahia Negra

Aquidauana

Ribas do
Rio Pardo

Três Lagoas

Pereira Barreto

Andradina

Barretos

Olímpia

Orlândia

Fortín
Madréjon

Nioaque

Sidrolândia

Mirandópolis

Valparaíso

São José
do Rio Prêto

Bebedouro

Ribeirão
Prêto

Pas

Fortín Coronel
Bogado

Puerto Mihanovich
Fuerte Olimpo

Bonito

Jardim

Maracaju

Pôrto Alegre

Presidente
Epitácio

Panorama

Dracena

Penápolis

Araçatuba

Jabuticabal

Taquaritinga

Sertãozinho

Mococa

Casa
Branca

Guax

Pirajuí

Presidente
Venceslau

Tupã

Lins

LINS

Araraquara

São Carlos

Piraçununga

Rio Claro

pe
da Boa V

Fortín Carlos
Antonio López

Puerto
Guaraní

Pôrto
Murtinho

Bela Vista

Ponta
Porã

Rio Brilhante

Dourados

Ivinheima

Presidente
Prudente

Garça

Marília

Agudos

Bauru

SÃO PAULO

Jaú

Limeira

Mogi-Mi

PARAGUAY

Puerto Sastre

Caarapó

Juti

Rosana

Teodoro
Sampaio

Iepê

Assis

Piracicaba

Amparo

Braç
Pat

Mariscal Estigarribia

Campo Esperanza

Puerto Casado

Puerto Pinasco

Pedro Juan
Caballero

Amambaí

Paranavaí

Nova
Esperança

Londrina

Rolândia

Cornélio
Procópio

Santo Antônio
da Platina

Avaré

Botucatu

Conchas

Tietê

Campinas

Tatuí

Jundiaí

Itu

Camp

Fortín
Capitán Demattei

South America

**BOLIVIA**

*PACIFIC*

*OCEAN*

**ARGENTINA**

Tropic of Capricorn

**POTOSÍ**

**TARIJA**

**JUJUY**

**ANTOFAGASTA**

**SALTA**

**TUCUMÁN**

**CATAMARCA**

**SANTIAGO DEL ESTERO**

**ATACAMA**

**LA RIOJA**

**CÓRDOBA**

**SAN JUAN**

**COQUIMBO**

**SAN LUIS**

**VALPARAÍSO**

**MENDOZA**

**SANTIAGO**

**LIBERTADOR**

**MAULE**

**BÍO BÍO**

**LA PAMPA**

**ARAUCANÍA**

**NEUQUÉN**

**RÍO NEGRO**

Selected place names:
Quillagua, Tocopilla, María Elena, Pedro de Valdivia, Michilla, Calama, Chuquicamata, Ollagüe, San Cristóbal, Chiguana, Tupiza, Villamontes, San Lorenzo, Villazón, La Quiaca, Tartagal, Antofagasta, Mejillones, Baquedano, Sierra Gorda, Carmen Alto, San Pedro de Atacama, Salta, San Salvador de Jujuy, San Pedro, Perico, Tilcara, Humahuaca, Embarcación, Taltal, Altamira, El Salvador, Chañaral, Diego de Almagro, Inca de Oro, Caldera, Copiapó, Tierra Amarilla, Cafayate, Santa María, Tafi Viejo, San Miguel de Tucumán, Bella Vista, Santiago del Estero, La Banda, Andalgalá, Concepción, Aguilares, Termas de Río Hondo, Quimili, Vallenar, Huasco, Freirina, Domeyko, El Tofo, La Serena, Coquimbo, Andacollo, Ovalle, Combarbalá, Illapel, Salamanca, Los Vilos, San Juan, Barreal, Talacasto, Tucunuco, La Rioja, Chamical, Córdoba, Villa María, Villa Dolores, San Luis, Mercedes, Mendoza, Las Heras, Godoy Cruz, Luján, San Rafael, General Alvear, Malargüe, Chillán, Concepción, Talcahuano, Los Angeles, Angol, Temuco, Nueva Imperial, Zapala, Cutral-Có, Neuquén, General Roca, Cipolletti, Río Colorado, Bahía Blanca, Santa Rosa, General Acha

Elevations:
Vol. Ollagüe 5869 m, Vol. San Pedro 6154 m, Vol. Licancábur 5930 m, Co Bonete 5660 m, San Pedro Zapaleri 5655 m, Co del Rincón 5594 m, Nev. de Chani 6200 m, Nev. de Cachi 6720 m, Vol. Llullaillaco 6723 m, Vol. Antofalla 6100 m, Co Galán 6600 m, Sa Nevada 6400 m, Vol. Copiapó 6080 m, Ojos del Salado 6880 m, Co Bonete 6872 m, Co del Toro 6380 m, Famatina 6250 m, Famatina 6375 m, Co Las Tórtolas 6332 m, Co de Olivares 6282 m, Co Mercedario 6770 m, Co Aconcagua 6960 m, Co Juncal 6060 m, Tupungato 6682 m, Vol. San José 5830 m, Vol. Maipú 5290 m, Vol. Tinguiririca 4300 m, Co Sosneado 5189 m, Vol. Descabezado Grande 3830 m, Vol. Peteroa 4090 m, Vol. Longaví 3242 m, Campanario 4020 m, Co Payún 3680 m, Co Nevada 3810 m, Sa Chachahuén 2065 m, Vol. Domuyo 4709 m, Vol. Tromen 3980 m, Vol. Copahue 2969 m, Chihuido Medio 1494 m, Sa de Auca Mahuida 2253 m, Vol. Llaima 3124 m, Río Cuarto 1727 m, Sa del Morro

*Pta Tetas, Pta dos Reyes, Pta Lengua de Vaca, Pta Curaumilla, Pta Topocalma, Pta de Lobos, Pta Lavapié*

*Bahía de Mejillones del Sur, Bahía Salada, Salar de Atacama, Salar de Arizaro, Salar de Ascotán, Salinas Grandes, Golfo de Arauco*

© Random House Australia Pty Ltd

ATLANTIC

OCEAN

0   100   200   300   400   kilometers

0        100        200   miles

Scale 1:7,000,000      Projection: Azimuthal Equal Area

458

**BUENOS AIRES**

**Bahía Blanca**

**ARGENTINA**

**NEUQUÉN**

**RÍO NEGRO**

**CHUBUT**

**SANTA CRUZ**

**MAGALLANES**

**TIERRA DEL FUEGO**

ARAUCANIA

LOS LAGOS

AISÉN

C H I L E

P A T A G O N I A

**SOUTH**

**ATLANTIC**

**OCEAN**

**FALKLAND ISLANDS (U.K.)**

West Falkland

East Falkland

Stanley

Nueva Imperial, Carahue, Puerto Saavedra, Curacautín, Temuco 3124 m, Las Cajas, Cutral-Có, Plaza Huincul, Cipolletti, General Roca, Neuquén, Villa Regina, Chelforó, Colonia Josefa, General Conesa, Villalonga, Stroeder, Coronel Dorrego, Claromecó, Orense, Energía, Tres Arroyos, Punta Alta, Médanos

Pitrufquén, Villarrica, Pucón, Vol. Villarrica 2840 m, Zapala, Picún Leufú, Catan Lil, Cerro Policía, Santa Rosa, La Esperanza, Los Menucos, Sierra Colorada, Valcheta, Aguada Cecilio, San Antonio Oeste, Carmen De Patagones, Viedma

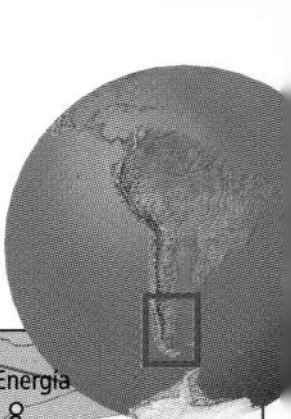

Valdivia, La Unión, Osorno, Purranque, Puerto Varas, Puerto Montt, Maullín, Calbuco, Ancud, Quemchi, Castro, Quellón, Chaitén, Esquel, Gastre, Gan Gan, Telsen, Puerto Madryn, Trelew, Rawson, Gaimán, Dolavón

Coihaique, Balmaceda, Chile Chico, Cochrane, Tortel, Perito Moreno, Las Heras, Caleta Olivia, Comodoro Rivadavia, Puerto Deseado, Puerto San Julián, Río Gallegos, Puerto Natales, El Turbio, Punta Arenas, Porvenir, Río Grande, Ushuaia

Golfo de Penas, Golfo San Jorge, Bahía Grande, Cabo de Hornos (Cape Horn)

© Random House Australia Pty Ltd

kilometers 0 100 200 300 400
miles 0 100 200
Scale 1:7 000 000
Projection: Azimuthal Equal Area

# Islands around South America

## GALÁPAGOS ISLANDS
### (Archipiélago de Colón)
### (Ecuador)
Scale 1: 5,000,000

I. Darwin
(Culpepper)

I. Wolf
(Wenman)

I. Pinta

I.Marchena
Pta Albemarle
C. Berkeley  Vol. Wolf
1707 m       I. Genovesa
Vol. Darwin
1280 m        Equator
905 m
Bahía Banks        I. San Salvador
Vol. La Cumbre
1463 m     I. Pinzón    I. Santa Cruz
I. Fernandina        864 m   C. Norte
Isla            Puerto    896 m
1689 m   Puerto   Ayora
Pta Cristóbal  Villamil   I. Santa Fé  I. San
Pta            I. Tortuga              Cristóbal
Essex   C. Rosa
I. Santa            I. Española
María

PACIFIC
OCEAN

## SAN ANDRÉS
### (Colombia)
Scale 1: 250,000

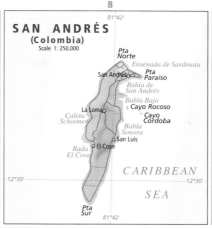

Pta
Norte
Ensenada de Sardinata
Pta
San Andrés   Paraíso
Bahía de
San Andrés
Bahía Baja
La Loma     Cayo Rocoso
Caleta          Cayo
Schooner        Córdoba
Bahía
Sonora
Rada    El Cove   San Luis
El Cove

CARIBBEAN
SEA

Pta
Sur

## EASTER ISLAND
### (Chile)
Scale 1: 350,000

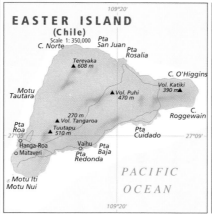

C. Norte   Pta
San Juan
Pta
Rosalia
Terevaka
608 m              C. O'Higgins
Vol. Katiki
390 m
Motu          Vol. Puhi
Tautara        470 m
C.
270 m        Roggewain
Vol. Tangaroa
Pta    510 m   Pta
Roa   Tuutapu   Cuidado
Hanga-Roa   Vaihu     PACIFIC
Mataveri   Pta  Pta     OCEAN
Redonda  Baja
Motu Iti
Motu Nui

## PROVIDENCIA
### (Colombia)
Scale 1: 200,000

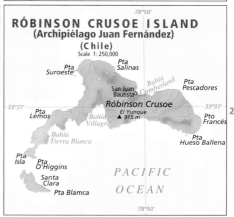

Pta
I. Santa   Bucanera
Catalina
Santa
Isabel
Bahía
Catalina
San      Pueblo
Felipe   Viejo
Aguadulce   Providencia
Bogotá
La Paz
Casabajá    Aguamansa

CARIBBEAN
SEA

## RÓBINSON CRUSOE ISLAND
### (Archipiélago Juan Fernández)
### (Chile)
Scale 1: 250,000

Pta
Suroeste    Pta
Salinas   Bahía
Pta
San Juan   Cumberland   Pescadores
Bautista
Róbinson Crusoe
Pta        El Yunque   Pto
Lemos   Bahía    915 m   Francés
Villagra
Bahía      Pta
Tierra Blanca  Hueso Ballena
Pta
Isla  Pta
O'Higgins
Santa
Clara
Pta Blamca

PACIFIC
OCEAN

## SOUTH GEORGIA
### (U.K.)
Scale 1: 3,000,000

Bird I.
C. Alexandra  Possession Bay
Queen Maud Bay
Cumberland Bay
Mt Paget   Grytviken
2934 m
Annenkov I.   Drygalski
Fjord
ATLANTIC   C. Disappointment
OCEAN

## ARUBA
### (Netherlands)
Scale 1:1,000,000

CARIBBEAN
SEA

Kudarebe
Alto Vista
Noord   71 m
Druif   Paradera
Oranjestad   Santa Cruz
Barcadera   Jamanota
188 m
Savaneta
Sint Nicolaas
Commanders Bay   Seroe Colorado
Pt
Basora

## CURAÇAO
### (Netherlands Antilles)
Scale 1:1,000,000

Nordpunt
Westpunto   St Christoffelberg   CARIBBEAN
372 m
SEA
Santa Cruz   Barber
Santa   Soto
Martabaai
Sint Willebrordus   Bocht Van
Hato
Bullenbaai
Julianadorp   Santa Catharina
Otrabanda   Emmastad
Willemstad
Nieuw Poort   Oostpunt

## BONAIRE
### (Netherlands Antilles)
Scale 1:1,000,000

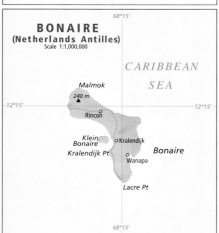

CARIBBEAN
SEA

Malmok
240 m
Rincon

Klein
Bonaire   Kralendijk
Kralendijk Pt   Bonaire
Wanapa

Lacre Pt

## TOBAGO
### (Trinidad and Tobago)
Scale 1:1,000,000

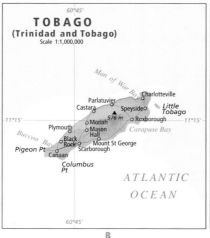

Man of War Bay
Charlotteville
Parlatuvier
Castara   Little
Speyside   Tobago
Plymouth   Roxborough
Moriah   Carapuse Bay
Mason
Buccoo Bay   Hall
Black  Mount St George
Pigeon Pt   Rock  Scarborough
Canaan
Columbus
Pt

ATLANTIC
OCEAN

## TRINIDAD
### (Trinidad and Tobago)
Scale 1: 2,000,000

ATLANTIC
OCEAN

Chupara   Grande
Pta   Riviére   Toco  Galera
Peñas   Corozal  Green   Pt Blanchisseuse   Pt
Pt   Hill   El Cerro del Aripo   Matelot
Macuro   Chaguaramas   940 m   Redhead
Monos   Northern  Arima
Port of Spain  Tunapuna   Salibea   Saline Bay
VENEZUELA   Range
Sangre Grande
Chaguanas   Caroni   Manzanilla
Waterloo   Talparo   Pt
California   Biche   Cocos Bay
Flanagin   Rio
Town  Tabaquite   Claro  Guataro
San   Princes   Pt  Saint Joseph
Fernando   Town
La Brea  St. Marys   New
Golfo   Penal  Grant
de Paria  Guapo Bay   304 m  Guayaguayare
Point Fortino  Siparia   Basse   Trinity Hills  Galeota Pt
Icacos   Bonasse  Terre
Pt   San   Moruga   Mayaro Bay
Fullarton  Francique
Erin
Boca de la Serpiente   10°

VENEZUELA

© Random House Australia Pty Ltd

# Polar Regions

The polar regions lie between 66.5° latitude and the North and South Poles. The continent of Antarctica, which is 14 million sq km (5.5 million sq miles) in area, is almost completely enclosed within the Antarctic Circle (66.5°S) and the South Pole. Antarctica is surrounded by the only continuous seas circling Earth, and during winter the seas freeze around it, making the continent appear larger than it actually is. Various nations have laid claim to certain parts of Antarctica, several of which overlap. Most non-claimant countries—and the United Nations—do not recognize these claims.

The region between the Arctic Circle (66.5°N) and the North Pole includes the Arctic Ocean and the northern fringes of the Eurasian and North American landmasses. The arctic lands are shared by several countries: Canada, the USA, Russia, Finland, Sweden, and Norway.

## Physiography

Eastern Antarctica was once part of the ancient supercontinent of Gondwana, while the Western Peninsula is an island chain related to the geologically younger Andean ranges. Floating ice shelves cover the seas around the land areas, giving the appearance of one large ice-covered continent. Volcanic chains, such as the Scotia Arc, are found

in the Antarctic Peninsula, and there are several active volcanoes. The highest point in Antarctica is Vinson Massif (4,897 m; 16,066 ft), while the average elevation of the continent exceeds 2,440 m (8,000 ft).

The Arctic Circle region encompasses the fringes of the North American, European, and Asian continents which surround the Arctic Ocean. The Arctic Ocean was formed when the Eurasian Plate moved towards the Pacific Plate, while the North American and Eurasian plates separated to form the Atlantic Ocean. The Arctic Ocean, reaching depths of 969 m (3,200 ft), is connected to the Atlantic and Pacific Oceans by several straits through which its cold waters move southward.

## Climate

Very cold climates prevail in the polar regions. Because of Earth's axial tilt, the polar regions receive the Sun's rays obliquely, so although during the summer months there is practically no darkness, there is nevertheless little solar radiation. During the long polar winter "nights", which also last for months, there is no net solar radiation at all to warm the land surface.

Snow reflects a large proportion of solar radiation back to space. This is particularly true of Antarctica, which is covered by extensive ice sheets. Temperatures within the Arctic Circle are higher than those of Antarctica because of the presence of a warming ocean. Within Antarctica, temperatures fall as low as –89.2°C (–128.6°F). In contrast, the lowest recorded temperature on the ice sheet of Greenland is –68°C (–90°F). Temperatures during summer in the Arctic Ocean, when parts of the floating ice melt, are around 0°C (32°F) and during winter, when larger areas are covered by ice, they fall to –34°C (–30°F).

The polar areas are characterized by cold air masses which blow toward warmer, temperate latitudes. In Antarctica, strong, chilly winds blow

over the land surface. Winds blow continuously from west to east (the West Wind Drift) in the seas surrounding Antarctica; the seas are so often stormy that they have prevented explorers reaching the continent until relatively recently.

Winters within the Arctic Circle are windy, cold, and harsh; temperatures in northern Siberia can fall to –50°C (–122°F). During the arctic summer temperatures in the southern margins average around 10°C (50°F), with some short spells up to 30°C (86°F). In Antarctica, only the northern part of the Antarctic Peninsula becomes warm (up to 15°C; 59°F), the temperatures of the interior remaining below freezing.

## Flora and fauna

Marine life thrives in the nutrient-rich waters around Antarctica. Phytoplankton abound, as do the tiny shrimp-like krill, which form part of an elaborate food chain that includes crustaceans, mollusks, fish, whales, porpoises, dolphins, and seals. Most of the fish are unique to the region. The ozone hole above the South Pole could adversely affect the phytoplakton of the Antarctic seas, which would disturb the food chain.

Around the Arctic lies the treeless tundra, south of which is boreal forest where firs, spruce, and larch grow. Lichens and mosses are common in the tundra; low-growing plants sprout in spring and blossom in summer.

There is marked contrast between the natural life of the Arctic Circle in summer and in winter. During summer there are large quantities of fish and whales in the sea, seals on the ice floes, and foxes, wolves, bears, caribou, and reindeer on land. There are also weasels, hares, and lemmings. Birds migrate to the Arctic during the summer in huge numbers; many birds and animals migrate to warmer lands and waters in winter.

## Natural resources

The world's largest deposits of ice are in Antarctica. A large quantity of fresh water is frozen in these, but this water cannot easily be exploited.

| Region | |
|---|---|
| Antarctica | PAGE 468 |

| **Dependencies & territories** | |
|---|---|
| Bouvet Island | PAGE 469 |
| French Southern and Antarctic Lands | PAGE 469 |
| Heard and McDonald Islands | PAGE 469 |
| Peter I Island | PAGE 469 |

*Antarctic scenes: a summer night at Cape Bird (above), a Weddell seal (above right), and penguins galore—a crowd scene (below right), an inquisitive-looking Gentoo penguin (below left), and an Emperor penguin group (left).*

Currently there is concern that global warming could cause the ice sheets to melt, which would raise the levels of the world's oceans. Sea levels have risen in recent times and research indicates that substantial areas of ice shelves have disintegrated since 2002 in response to regional warming.

As a large part of Antarctica was once part of Gondwana, minerals that occur in other parts of Gondwana, such as coal in Australia, might lie beneath the ice sheets. Likewise, because the Antarctic Peninsula can be considered an extension of the Andes, there is a possibility of metallic ore deposits being found in Antarctica, as they have been in the Andes. In addition, the continental shelf around Antarctica could contain petroleum deposits. However, given the current state of technology, mining is not economically feasible in the harsh antarctic conditions.

International agreements which forbid mining and non-peaceful uses of Antarctica have been signed by claimant and non-claimant countries. These aim to ensure the conservation of its environment.

*Polar bears (left) and people fishing under the ice (above left) in Arctic Siberia. An iceberg towers over this group of Adélie penguins in Antarctica (top).*

## Human habitation

Antarctica is uninhabited, except for several scientific research stations. The nearest human habitations lie on the subantarctic islands of Macquarie, Crozet, South Georgia, and Kerguelen. There is now a small amount of tourism developing in the area, mainly in the Antarctic Peninsula; tourists make short, supervized trips ashore from small cruise vessels. There are also tourist flights over the Antarctic.

In contrast, the Arctic region has been inhabited for thousands of years by indigenous groups such as the Inuit (Eskimo) in Canada, the Saami (Lapps) in Scandinavia, and the Nanets and Yakuts of Russia. Relationships have recently been discovered between these now scattered peoples—there is evidence that some of these indigenous groups migrated from Asia to North America, across the Bering Strait.

As the Arctic is not conducive to agriculture, its inhabitants have to gather food, and their ability to succeed in this is determined primarily by environmental conditions. Saami who live in the traditional way herd reindeer, taking their herds to high ground to graze in summer, then moving to woodlands in low mountain territory in winter. Caribou are hunted by the Nanets and Yakuts in the Russian tundra during spring and summer and in the forests during winter; both animals and people need to migrate with the seasons to survive. In Canada, the Inuit hunt seals along the coast during winter and move inland to hunt caribou during summer.

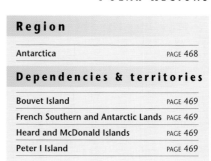

# Polar exploration

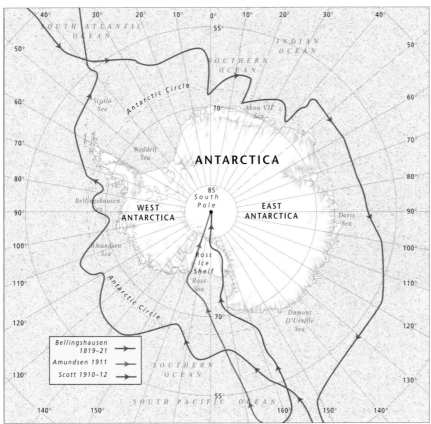

Bellingshausen 1819–21 →
Amundsen 1911 →
Scott 1910–12 →

A number of motives have driven men to explore the frozen wildernesses at the uttermost ends of Earth—commerce, national glory, a personal desire for fame, and scientific discovery are just some of them. The long search for a better route from Europe to Asia through polar seas (either to the northwest or the northeast) combined political and commercial interests. The Norsemen had already discovered Iceland, Greenland, and northeast North America between the ninth and the twelfth centuries.

Then, in the sixteenth century, both English and Dutch seafarers began searching for a way through the Arctic to the riches of China and India. Looking for a Northwest Passage, the English mariner Martin Frobisher discovered and entered Hudson Strait in 1576, marched into the interior, and found a bleak landscape of mosses, juniper bushes, and stunted firs.

Davis Strait between Greenland and Baffin Island was explored by John Davis between 1585 and 1587. The Dutch navigator Willem Barents explored the west coast of Novaya Zemlya and Spitsbergen between 1594 and 1597, while he searched for a Northeast Passage around the top of Russia. He perished in the attempt—his possessions, including his flute, were found intact in a wooden hut 300 years later. With this episode, the search for a sailing route to Asia via the northeast came to an end.

In 1607, Henry Hudson navigated and explored the east coast of Greenland, discovering the island of Jan Mayen on his return. In 1610 he also discovered both the strait and the enormous bay

in Canada which now bear his name. After enduring a freezing winter, however, his crew mutinied. Hudson and his son were abandoned in a little boat and never heard of again.

From Hudson's explorations until the nineteenth century, much pioneering navigation in this region was undertaken by agents of the Hudson's Bay Company, whose main interest was to buy furs. Samuel Hearne navigated the Coppermine River, and Alexander Mackenzie reached the mouth of the river which bears his name. Meanwhile, Russian merchants explored the Siberian coast, and at the direction of Peter the Great, in 1741, the Danish explorer Vitus Bering discovered a strait into the Arctic Ocean between Siberia and Alaska. His grave lies on Bering Island in the Aleutian chain.

Despite disaster, the famous expedition of Sir John Franklin in 1845 found a possible route around the top of North America. Although his party of 129 officers and men disappeared, more was probably learnt about the Arctic Archipelago by the forty relief expeditions that were sent to find him than had been discovered in all the years previously. Among the leaders of these searches, Sir James Ross (who located the position of the north magnetic pole), Captains Penny, Austin, and Ommaney, and Lieutenants M'Clintock, Collinson, and M'Clure all made valuable contributions to the world's knowledge of the Arctic region.

Following this period, the most famous polar explorer was the Norwegian Fridtjof Nansen. In 1893, believing that a polar current flowed beneath the ice from east to west, he forced his small wooden ship *Fram* into the ice on the eastern

side of the Arctic. Three years later it emerged north of Spitsbergen. Previously, in 1888, he had crossed the Greenland ice cap on skis.

The Northwest Passage was first successfully traversed from 1903 to 1906 by the Norwegian explorer Roald Amundsen; the first person to reach the North Pole itself was the American explorer Robert Peary. Accompanied by a few companions, assisted by fifty Inuit, and with sleds pulled by 200 dogs, he reached the pole on 6 April 1909. His success was in part attributable to his use of dogs—an example the British failed to follow two years later in Antarctica. Peary located the North Pole on the frozen surface of a deep ocean with no land nearby. Soundings showed the depth of water below to be 2,743 m (9,000 ft) within only 8 km (5 miles) of the Pole. Research carried out much later has established a maximum depth for the Arctic Ocean of 5,450 m (17,880 ft).

### Finding Antarctica

Unlike the Arctic, Antarctica was unlikely to be a route to anywhere, but the prospect it offered was even more attractive—the possibility of finding a new and humanly habitable continent. The notion of a vast Unknown South Land (*Terra Australis Incognita*) had been around since the time of the ancient Greeks, and was endorsed by the geographer Ptolemy (c. AD 100–160). It was believed to be a continuation of southern Africa, but Vasco da Gama's voyage round the Cape of Good Hope in 1498 showed this belief to be false. Nor could it be an extension of the South American continent: in 1578 Sir Francis Drake found himself blown by gales to latitude 57°S, far below Cape Horn, where he reported that the Atlantic and Pacific Oceans "meete in a most large and free scope".

The British merchant Anthony de la Roche kept hopes alive when he sheltered at South Georgia in 1675, claiming to have seen "High Land" to the south, but this land was probably just the Clerke Rocks. When Captain James Cook circumnavigated Antarctica in the course of his second voyage (1771–75), it finally became clear that the age-old vision of a humanly habitable Great South Land had been only a dream.

During the nineteenth century a number of men from a range of nations expanded our knowledge of the land at the Antarctic perimeter. There were claims and counter claims to being the first to see the mainland (was it one of the Britons—Bransfield or Smith—in 1820, or the Russian Bellingshausen one year later?), and to being the first to step ashore (was it the American Nathanael Palmer in 1820 or the Norwegian Carsten Borchgrevink long after this in 1895?).

Borchgrevink was in fact the explorer to lead the first expedition to winter on the mainland of Antarctica, in 1899, by which time a number of scientific expeditions were being planned for the

region, as well as more ventures to reach the South Pole for its own sake.

These plans led to the epic contest to be first to reach the South Pole, in the years 1910 to 1912, between the Englishman Robert Falcon Scott and the Norwegian Roald Amundsen. It was a clash between amateurism and professionalism, between a Royal Navy man who turned to expeditionary work to pass the time, and an experienced and hardened polar explorer who had spent twenty years preparing himself for the task.

Scott took ponies and mechanical tractors which had not been tried or tested; Amundsen took dog teams and experienced drivers, unsentimentally killing and eating the sled dogs as he went. Amundsen won the race, reaching the South Pole on December 14, 1911. Scott arrived almost a month later, on January 17, 1912. But the death of the British party during their return—exhausted, frozen, and out of food—plus Scott's moving journal of events, later found with his body, have ensured them a permanent place in the annals of polar exploration.

## Polar research

Since the Second World War, the polar regions have very much become the preserve of scientists—mapping Antarctica and conducting oceanographic, geological, glaciological, and biological research programs. Environmental pollutants and global climate change are issues of particular concern. Today some 800 scientists and support staff from around 16 nations are based in Antarctica year-round. Key programs have included:

**1947** US Operation Highjump and Operation Windmill map large parts of the Antarctic coastline and interior.

**1954** Mawson Base (Australian) is set up. Over 25 years its scientists map 3,200 km (2,000 miles) of coastline and 1.3 million sq km (500,000 sq miles) of Antarctic territory.

**1957–58** Scientists from 67 nations conduct research programs in both polar regions.

**1961** The Antarctic Treaty (signed in 1959) comes into force, guaranteeing freedom of access and scientific research in all areas south of 60° S latitude.

**1964–74** International Biological Programme contributes to understanding of Arctic ecology.

**1986** 2,000-m (6,500-ft) ice core recovered at the Russian Vostok Station provide information on climate change from 160,000 years ago.

**1990** International Arctic Sciences Committee is set up to coordinate research programs.

**1991** Arctic Monitoring and Assessment Program is set up by the eight Arctic rim nations and organizations representing indigenous peoples living in the region.

Antarctica: A Russian icebreaker (bottom left); the Cape Evans hut used by both Shackleton and Scott (top left); the inside of Scott's discovery hut (top, far right). Arctic: Remains of an ancient hut on the shore of the Arctic Ocean (bottom, far right).

# Antarctica

## Fact File

| | |
|---|---|
| AREA | 14,000,000 sq km (5,405,400 sq miles) |
| POPULATION | No permanent population |
| ECONOMY | Research stations |
| CLIMATE | Extremely cold and windy |
| MAP REFERENCE | Page 470 |

The fifth largest continent, Antarctica is the coldest and most inhospitable, and differs in important respects from the polar regions of the northern hemisphere. Whereas the Arctic consists of a frozen sea surrounded by land masses, the Antarctic consists of a foundation of continental rock surmounted by a massive ice cap thousands of meters thick, separated from all other major land masses by the wild and stormy waters of the Southern Ocean. Again in contrast to the northern polar region, which was inhabited by hunting peoples within the Arctic Circle, Antarctica had never seen a human being before around 1800. Even today only about 1,000 people, all of them temporary visitors, live there during the long, severe Antarctic winter. Although a number of countries active in the exploration of the continent made territorial claims to parts of it, all such claims were indefinitely deferred after the signing of the Antarctic Treaty in December 1959.

Several factors make the climate uniquely harsh. Although Antarctica receives plenty of sunlight in midsummer, eighty percent of this radiation is reflected back by the permanent cover of snow. Altitude also plays a part: Antarctica has by far the greatest average elevation of any of the continents—2,300 m (7,500 ft)—which helps produce the high winds prevailing over much of the region. Called katabatic (or downflowing) winds, these are gravity-driven, and consist of air pouring down at high speed from the elevated interior toward the coast. At one location the annual mean windspeed recorded was over 70 km/h (44 mph). Although some ninety percent of the world's fresh water is locked up in the ice cap (at places 4,800 m [15,700 ft] thick), Antarctica is also the world's driest continent, the very low temperatures limiting the moisture the air can hold. In fact only 120–150 mm (5–6 in) of water accumulates over the entire continent in the average year. Unique dry valleys, where the rock is exposed and rain has not fallen for about 2 million years, are the driest places in the world. Mummified animal carcases in these valleys have changed little in thousands of years.

The Transantarctic Mountains, which form a boundary between East and West Antarctica, are one of the world's great mountain chains, many peaks exceeding 4,000 m (13,000 ft). Geologically, East Antarctica consists mainly of an ancient continental shield with a history going back 3,000 million years. This was once part of the supercontinent known as Gondwana, from which Africa, South America, India, Australia, and New Zealand broke away. Many Antarctic rocks and fossils match up with those found in other southern continents, showing that the continents were once joined together. Ancient crystalline rocks of

the shield are closely similar to those along the east coast of the Indian peninsula and Sri Lanka. Forming the base of the Transantarctic Mountains, and facing West Antarctica, is a belt of folded sediments 500 to 600 million years old.

It is a sedimentary formation dating from about 280 million years ago, however, that is most revealing. Up to 300 m (1,000 ft) thick, it is found in Australia, India, South Africa, and South America, as well as Antarctica. About 80 million years ago a series of earth movements accompanied extensive volcanic activity and it is thought that eruptions between 20 and 15 million years ago may be linked to the formation of the Transantarctic Mountains.

Plant life on the continent today consists almost entirely of mosses, lichens, and algae. Though soil mites and midges are able to survive, not a single land vertebrate can endure the winter. In contrast, life in the ocean is very rich, with a variety of seals and whales. Antarctica has five species of true or "earless" seals, including the predatory leopard seal, and both orcas and blue whales, the latter an ocean giant growing to a length of 30 m (100 ft). There are 43 species of bird, the best-known being the penguins. The Emperor Penguin, which breeds during the

months of Antarctic darkness, is the only warm-blooded animal to remain on the continent during the bitter winter months. The most numerous birds are the Antarctic petrels, among which are the albatrosses.

The Antarctic Treaty of 1959 provides the legal framework for the management of Antarctica. This treaty superseded and indefinitely deferred the political partition of the continent among a number of separate nations. At present there are 42 treaty member nations, with 26 consultative nations and 16 acceding. Important articles of the treaty include No 1 (that the region is to be used for peaceful purposes only), No 2 (that freedom of scientific investigation and cooperation shall continue), and No 4 (that it does not recognize, dispute, or establish territorial claims, and that no new claims shall be asserted while the treaty is in force). Agreed-to measures adopted at consultative meetings include several conventions on the conservation of Antarctic flora and fauna.

*The French Antarctic research station at Dumont d'Urville, built in 1956 (below). The Gerlache Strait on the western shore of the Antarctic Peninsula; this sheltered spot has allowed some ice to melt (bottom left). New Zealand's Scott Base, Antarctica (bottom right).*

# Dependencies in Antarctica

## Bouvet Island

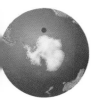

### Fact File

| | |
|---|---|
| OFFICIAL NAME | Bouvet Island |
| FORM OF GOVERNMENT | Dependent territory of Norway |
| CAPITAL | None; administered from Oslo |
| AREA | 59 sq km (23 sq miles) |
| TIME ZONE | GMT |
| POPULATION | No permanent population |
| ECONOMY | Meteorological station |
| CLIMATE | Cold and windy |
| MAP REFERENCE | Page 470 |

Bouvet Island is named for its discoverer, Jean-Baptiste Charles Bouvet de Lozier, who came across it on 1 January 1739. Imagining that he had found a cape of the fabled Great Southern Land, he had in fact stumbled on the loneliest island on earth—the nearest land, in South Africa, being over 1,600 km (1,000 miles) away. Uninhabited except for occasional visiting meteorologists, it rises 935 m (3,068 ft) out of the Southern Ocean, and is largely covered with snow and ice.

## French Southern and Antarctic Lands

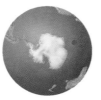

### Fact File

| | |
|---|---|
| OFFICIAL NAME | Territory of the French Southern and Antarctic Lands |
| FORM OF GOVERNMENT | Overseas territory of France |
| CAPITAL | None; administered from Paris |
| AREA | 7,829 sq km (3,023 sq miles) |
| TIME ZONE | GMT + 3.5/6 hours |
| POPULATION | No permanent population |
| ECONOMY | None |
| CLIMATE | Cold and windy |
| MAP REFERENCE | Page 104 |

The French Southern and Antarctic Lands include Île Amsterdam, Île Saint-Paul, and Crozet and Kerguelen Islands in the southern Indian Ocean. Mean annual temperatures range from 4°C to 10°C (39°F to 50°F) and the islands are wet and stormy. The main island of Kerguelen is mountainous (Mt Ross is 1,960 m; 6,430 ft), with an irregular coastline and deep fiords, and there are snowfields in the central area. Vegetation consists of coastal tussock grass and peaty uplands. Breeding colonies of seals and penguins are found in summer. There are no permanent inhabitants; however, the islands are visited by researchers studying the native fauna.

## Heard and McDonald Islands

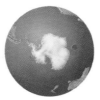

### Fact File

| | |
|---|---|
| OFFICIAL NAME | Territory of Heard and McDonald Islands |
| FORM OF GOVERNMENT | External territory of Australia |
| CAPITAL | None; administered from Canberra |
| AREA | 412 sq km (159 sq miles) |
| TIME ZONE | GMT + 5 hours |
| POPULATION | No permanent population |
| ECONOMY | None |
| CLIMATE | Cold and windy |
| MAP REFERENCE | Page 104 |

*The most inhospitable continent and one of the last regions on Earth to be explored, Antarctica is a long way from everywhere. This sign is at Scott Base, Antarctica (below left). Adélie penguin at Cape Bird, Antarctica (above right).*

Heard and McDonald Islands are two bleak outposts in the Southern Ocean. Heard Island has the distinction of having the highest point in all Australian territory—2,750 m (9,021 ft). Classed as subantarctic islands, their mean annual sea level temperatures are between freezing and 3°C (37°F). They have ice caps, glaciers that descend to sea level, and furious gales. Vegetation consists of tussock grassland and small peaty fields. Seals and penguins breed ashore in summer.

## Peter I Island

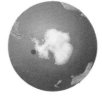

### Fact File

| | |
|---|---|
| OFFICIAL NAME | Peter I Island |
| FORM OF GOVERNMENT | Dependent territory of Norway |
| CAPITAL | None; administered from Oslo |
| AREA | 243 sq km (94 sq miles) |
| TIME ZONE | GMT – 6 hours |
| POPULATION | No permanent population |
| ECONOMY | None |
| CLIMATE | Cold and windy |
| MAP REFERENCE | Page 470 |

One of the Antarctic maritime islands, Peter I Island lies off the continent near the Venable Ice Shelf. It was named by Bellingshausen in honor of the founder of the Russian Navy. Though moderated by the sea, the climate is basically that of the adjacent continent and the temperature rises above freezing only for short periods in summer. In winter the island is entirely surrounded by ice.

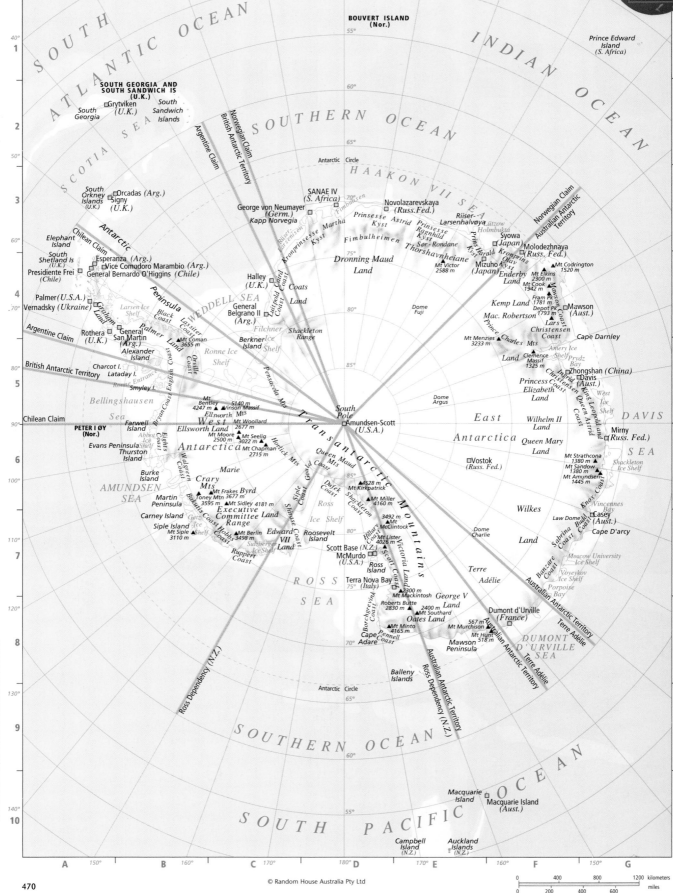

BOUVERT ISLAND
(Nor.)

SOUTH ATLANTIC OCEAN

INDIAN OCEAN

Prince Edward
Island
(S. Africa)

SOUTHERN OCEAN

SOUTH GEORGIA AND
SOUTH SANDWICH IS
(U.K.)

Grytviken
(U.K.)

South
Georgia

South
Sandwich
Islands

SCOTIA SEA

HAAKON VII SEA

Antarctic Circle

Antarctic

South
Orkney
Islands
(U.K.)

Orcadas (Arg.)
Signy
(U.K.)

SANAE IV
(S. Africa)

Novolazarevskaya
(Russ.Fed.)

George von Neumayer
(Germ.)
Kapp Norvegia

Prinsesse Astrid
Kyst

Riiser-
Larsenhalvøya

Prinsesse
Ragnhild
Kyst

Prins Harald
Kyst

Syowa
Japan

Molodezhnaya
Russ. Fed.

Norwegian Claim
Australian Antarctic
Territory

Elephant
Island

Chilean Claim

South
Shetland Is
(U.K.)

Esperanza (Arg.)
Vice Comodoro Marambio (Arg.)
General Bernardo O'Higgins (Chile)

Presidente Frei
(Chile)

Halley
(U.K.)

Prinsesse Martha
Kyst

Fimbulheimen

Dronning Maud
Land

Thorshavnheiane

Mt Victor
2588 m

Mizuho
(Japan)

Olav

Enderby
Land

Mt Codrington
1520 m

Mt Elkins
2300 m

Palmer(U.S.A.)
Vernadsky (Ukraine)

Peninsula

Larsen Ice
Shelf

Coats
Land

Coats
Land

Dome
Fuji

Kemp Land

Mt Cook
1942 m

Fram Pk
1781 m
Depot Pk
1793 m

Mawson
(Aust.)

Graham
Land

Black
Coast

WEDDELL SEA

General
Belgrano II
(Arg.)

Mac. Robertson

Lars
Christensen
Coast

Rothera
(U.K.)

General
San Martin
(Arg.)

Palmer
Land

Luitpold
Coast Coast
Coast

Filchner
Ice
Shelf

Shackleton
Range

Prince
Charles
Mts

Amery Ice
Shelf

Cape Darnley

Argentine Claim

Alexander
Island

Orville
Coast

Berkner
Island

Mt Menzies
3233 m

Clemence
Massif
1325 m

Prydz
Bay

British Antarctic Territory

Charcot I.
Lataday I.

Ronne Ice
Shelf

Mt Coman
3655 m

Zhongshan (China)
Davis
(Aust.)

Smyley I.

Ingrid
Christensen
Coast

King
Leopold and
Queen Astrid
Coast

West
Ice
Shelf

DAVIS

Chilean Claim

Farwell
Island

Bellingshausen
Sea

Mt
Bentley
4247 m
5140 m
Vinson Massif

Pensacola Mts

Princess
Elizabeth
Land

PETER I ØY
(Nor.)

Abbot

Eights
Coast

Evans Peninsula
Thurston
Island

Ellsworth
Mts

Mt Woollard
2677 m

West

South
Pole

Amundsen-Scott
(U.S.A.)

Dome
Argus

Wilhelm II
Land

Mirny
Russ. Fed.

Mt Moore
2500 m

Mt Seelig
3022 m

Transantarctic Mountains

East
Antarctica

Queen Mary
Land

SEA

Shackleton
Ice Shelf

Burke
Island

Antarctica

Mt Chapman
2715 m

Horlick Mts

Queen Maud
Mts

Vostok
(Russ. Fed.)

Mt Strathcona
1380 m
Mt Sandow
1380 m
Mt Amundsen
1445 m

AMUNDSEN
SEA

Marie

Crary
Mts

Mt Frakes Byrd
3595 m
Toney Mtn 3677 m

Siple Coast

Gould Coast

Dufek
Coast

Mt Kirkpatrick

Mt Miller
4160 m

Wilkes

Knox Coast

Vincennes
Bay

Martin
Peninsula

Carney Island

Executive
Committee Land
Range

Mt Sidley 4181 m

Shirase Coast

Ross
Ice
Shelf

Mt
McClintock

Law Dome

Land

Casey
(Aust.)

Siple Island

Mt Siple
3110 m

Mt Berlin
3498 m

Edward
VII
Land

Roosevelt
Island

Hillary Coast

Mt Lister
4026 m

Sabrina Coast

Cape D'arcy

Sulzberger
Ice Shelf

Ruppert
Coast

Scott Base (N.Z.)
McMurdo
(U.S.A.)

Victoria Land

Dome
Charlie

Terre
Adélie

Moscow University
Ice Shelf

Ross
Island

Terra Nova Bay
(Italy)

George V
Land

Voyeykov
Coast

Porpoise
Bay

ROSS
SEA

Mt Mackintosh

2300 m

Mt Minto
4165 m

Roberts Butte
2830 m

Mt Southard
2400 m

Oates Land

Mt Murchison
567 m

Australian Antarctic
Territory

Dumont d'Urville
(France)

Terre Adélie

Cape
Adare

Pennell
Coast

Borchgrevink
Coast

Mawson
Peninsula

Mt Hunt
518 m

DUMONT
D'URVILLE
SEA

Ross Dependency (N.Z.)

Balleny
Islands

Australian Antarctic
Territory

Antarctic Circle

Ross Dependency (N.Z.)

SOUTHERN OCEAN

Macquarie
Island

Macquarie Island
(Aust.)

SOUTH PACIFIC OCEAN

Campbell
Island
(N.Z.)

Auckland
Islands
(N.Z.)

© Random House Australia Pty Ltd

Scale 1:30,000,000     Projection: Polar Azimuthal Equidistant

0   400   800   1200 kilometres
0   200   400   600 miles

# The Artctic

**Polar Regions**

PACIFIC OCEAN

BERING SEA

OKHOTSKOYE MORE (SEA OF OKHOTSK)

Ostrov Sakhalin

Noglik

Nikolayevsk-na-Amure

Okha

Magadan

Klyuchevskaya Sopka 4750 m

Ust'-Kamchatsk

Mys Ozernoy

Ostrov Karaginskiy

Mys Olyutorskiy

Koryakskoye Nagor'ye

Sredinnyy Khrebet

Poluostrov Kamchatka

Mys Tolstoy

Okhotsk

Ayan

Khrebet Dzhugdzhur

Gulf of Alaska

Kodiak I.

Kodiak

Homer

Cordova

Anchorage

Juneau

Skagway

Whitehorse

Watson Lake

Ross River

Yakutat

Mt Logan 5959 m

Tok

Dawson

Pelly

Ogilvie Mountains

Old Crow

Fort Yukon

Allakaket

Shungnak

Brooks Range

Dillingham

Bethel

Tanunak

Nunivak I.

Kotlik

Nome

St Lawrence I.

Mys Chukotskiy

Chukotskiy Poluostrov

Ugol'nyye Kopi

Anadyr'

Gora Belaya 1359 m

1742 m

Gora Volna 1585 m

Sinegor'ye

Omsukchan

Susuman

Khrebet Suntar Khayata

2341 m

Ust'-Nera

Khandyga

Aldan

Yakutsk

Sangar

Khrebet Cherskogo

Bilibino

Cherskiy

Pevek

Arctic Circle

Gora Pobeda 3147 m

Khonuu

Deputatskiy

Zhigansk

Nyurba

Mirnyy

Point Hope

Wainwright

Barrow

Kaktovik

Mt Greenough 2207 m

Ushakovskoye

Ostrov Vrangelya

Mys Kovaskiy

Lyakhovskiye Ostrova

2389 m

Udachnyy

Zhilinda

BEAUFORT SEA

ARCTIC OCEAN

80°

85°

North Pole

Novosibirskiye Ostrova

Tiksi

Siktyakh

Poluostrov Taymyr

Ozero Taymyr

Khatanga

1664 m

Plato Putorana

Noril'sk

Dudinka

Igarka

Urengoy

CANADA

Fort Simpson

Déline

Fort Good Hope

Great Bear Lake

Paulatuk

Kugluktuk

Holman

Victoria Island

Cambridge Bay

Melville I.

King William Island

Prince of Wales Island

Somerset Island

Resolute

Queen Elizabeth Islands

Borden I.

Prince Patrick I.

Banks Island

C. Prince Alfred

Sachs Harbour

C. Parry

C. Bathurst

Mackenzie

Tuktoyaktuk

Ellef Ringnes Island

Amund Ringnes I.

Axel Heiberg Island

Severnaya Zemlya

Zemlya Frantsa-Iosifa

Mys Zhelaniya

Novaya Zemlya

Ostrov Belyy

Poluostrov Yamal

Ostrov Vaygach

Vorkuta

Gorki

Igrim

RUSSIAN FEDERATION

URAL'SKIY KHREBET

Pelly Bay

Repulse Bay

Hall Beach

Pond Inlet

Brodeur Pen.

Devon Island

Eureka

Grise Fiord

Ellesmere Island

2012 m

Alert

Artic Bay

Bylot I.

LINCOLN SEA

1920 m

Kap Bridgman

Kap Eiler Rasmussen

Nord

Nordaustlandet

Barentsøya

Gydanskiy Poluostrov

Gyda

Antipayuta

Yamburg

Novyy Port

Yar-Sale

Nadym

Foxe Basin

Prince Charles I.

Baffin Island

Baffin Bay

Iqaluit

Cumberland Pen.

Hall Pen.

C. Mercy

C. Dyer

Qeqertarsuaq (Disko)

Home Bay

Nuussuaq

Tasiusaq

Upernavik

Kullorsuaq

1234 m

Maarmorilik

Qeqertarsuaq

Kangaatsiaq

Sisimiut

Maniitsoq

Atammik

Nuuk (Godthåb)

Kapisillit

Qeqertarsuatsiaat

Paamiut

Ivittuut

Narsarsuaq

Qaqortoq

Nanortalik

Nunap Isua

Kong Frederik VIII Land

2103 m

1190 m

Knud Rasmussen Land

2935 m

GREENLAND (KALAALLIT NUNAAT) (Den.)

Petermanns Bjerg 2939 m

Kong Christian IX Land

Mont Forel 3360 m

Gunnbjørn Fjeld 3700 m

3147 m

1920 m

Ittoqqortoormiit

Mesters Vig

Traill Ø

Ammassalik

Sermiligaaq

Timmiarmiit

J.A.D. Jensen Nunatakker 1680 m

2680 m

Siorapaluk

Qaanaaq (Thule)

Uummannaq

Savissivik

Kap Parry

C. Baffin

Kap York

C. Adair

Île de France

Kap Marie Valdemar

Store Koldewey

Shannon Ø

Daneborg

Spitsbergen

Longyearbyen

Edgeøya

SVALBARD (Nor.)

BARENTS SEA

Ostrov Kolguyev

Mys Kanin Nos

Shoyna

Oma

Mezen'

Nar'yan Mar

Usinsk

Pechora

Ust'-Tsil'ma

Ukhta

Vuktyl

Yemva

Usogorsk

Syktyvkar

Luza

Vyatka

ATLANTIC OCEAN

GREENLAND SEA

JAN MAYEN (Nor.)

Blönduós

Stykkishólmur

Reykjavik

Seyðisfjörður

Vík

2119 m

Höfn

ICELAND

FAEROE ISLANDS (Den.)

Arctic Circle

70°

60°

NORWAY

Nordkapp

Lakselv

Inari

Tromsø

Harstad

Bodø

Narvik

Kiruna

SWEDEN

FINLAND

Luleå

Skellefteå

Umeå

Oulu

Vaasa

Kuopio

Tampere

Pori

Turku

Murmansk

Polyarnyye Zori

Kandalaksha

Kem'

Medvezh'yegorsk

Petrozavodsk

Arkhangel'sk

Severodvinsk

Onezhskoye Ozero

Kotlas

Vel'sk

Yoshkar-Ola

Cheboksary

Vologda

Nizhniy Novgorod

Kostroma

Yaroslavl'

Poluostrov Rybachiy

Ladozhskoye Ozero

Harstad

Trondheim

Östersund

Sundsvall

Gävle

Uppsala

Helsinki

Tallinn

Sankt-Peterburg (St Petersburg)

Novgorod

Moskva (Moscow)

Pskov

Kaluga

Ålesund

Lillehammer

Bergen

Oslo

Stockholm

Västerås

Örebro

Linköping

Jönköping

Drammen

Stavanger

Kristiansand

Göteborg (Gothenburg)

Helsingborg

Liepāja

Šiauliai

Riga

LATVIA

ESTONIA

LITHUANIA

Vilnius

Kaliningrad

Minsk

BELARUS

Vitsyebsk

Orsha

Bryansk

Kursk

Belgorod

Chernihiv

UKRAINE

Shetland Islands

Orkney Islands

Cape Wrath

Outer Hebrides

Inverness

Fort William

Aberdeen

© Random House Australia Pty Ltd

0 200 400 600 800 1000 kilometers

0 200 400 600 miles

Scale 1:26,000,000

Projection: Polar Azimuthal Equidistant

471

Polar Regions

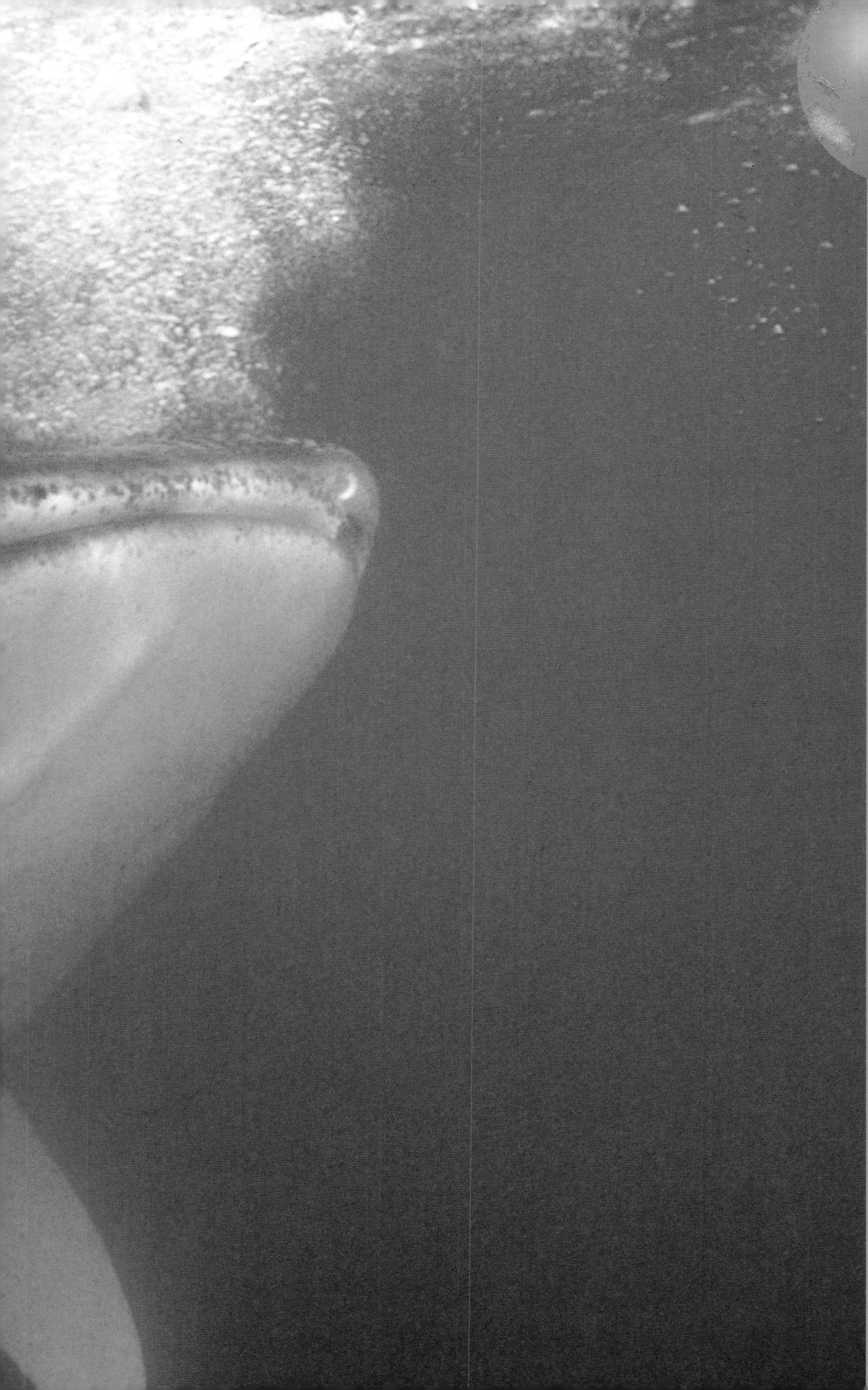

# The Oceans

# The Oceans

Oceans constitute one of Earth's great frontiers. Scientists, environmentalists, governments, industrialists and 'dreamers' all want to understand how oceans function in physical, chemical, ecological and economic terms. The role of oceans in military conflicts and for the security of nations is also still of concern, with many countries spending considerable sums of money on finding ways to exploit oceanic secrets to their advantage.

In stark contrast to all other known planets, oceans constitute approximately seventy percent of Earth. There are five main oceans of the world—the Atlantic, Pacific, Indian, Arctic, and Antarctic (also known as the Southern or South Polar Ocean). The biggest ocean is the Pacific, at about 170 million sq km (66 million sq miles), which occupies almost twice the area of the next biggest, the Atlantic.

Throughout history, these vast oceanic expanses and adjoining seas have challenged humans as to how they should be used. At least some 100,000 years ago, and especially over the last 10,000 years, successful efforts have been made to cross the oceans, allowing human migrations. Trade routes involving various kinds of ships have also developed, growing from local to transoceanic journeys. Today the sea is used, and at times abused, by oceanic craft transporting people and goods to form the connections vital for international commerce.

It is only in the past century or so that humans have really started to make an impact on oceanic environments. These environments have evolved and changed over billions of years. Ecosystems have become established and been modified by changes in atmospheric composition, sea-floor spreading, climatic and current patterns, the discharge of solutes and sediments from rivers, and the development of new life forms. Human interference and exploitation, including the pollution of ocean waters, has quickly altered conditions in many oceanic areas, leading to a decline in fish and mammal stocks, the destruction of habitats and even, potentially, to increased water tempera-

tures. The challenge for the future will be to use our technological knowledge to protect oceanic environments, while allowing increased use of ocean resources by the world's growing population.

## Ocean topography

Oceanographers have greatly expanded our knowledge of the sea floor over the past century. Using first primitive line soundings, then early echo sounders and now sophisticated electronic surveying techniques, it has been possible to build up detailed images of the bottom of the ocean. Submersibles have been used to photograph and document specific features, including remnants of wrecks like the Titanic which lie at great depths.

In recent decades there has been a great acceleration in the exploitation of ocean topography. In particular, the mapping of features such as faults, volcanic ridges and vents, slumps, and canyons, has enabled scientists to reconstruct the history of these features. The theory of plate tectonics has been greatly supported by geological and geophysical studies of the sea floor, especially the identification and interpretation of paleomagnetic strips contained in oceanic basalts. These form as new basalt moves away from mid-ocean spreading centers, and record the magnetic field of the period.

Typically, ocean floors are covered by thin, oozy sediment layers that form abyssal plains separated by ridges, seamounts and plateaus representing past geologic events. Continental margins descend steeply from bordering shelves down steep, often dissented, slopes to plains, the flattest surfaces on Earth. The plain may be as deep as 3,000 to 5,000 m (9840 to 16,400 ft). Beyond these depths there are relatively narrow trenches reaching 10,000 m (32,800 ft) below sea level, such as those found adjacent to the island areas and rising mountain chains of the Pacific.

A broad, rugged and near-continuous mountain range occurs in the centers of the Atlantic, Indian and South Pacific Oceans. This is the mid-oceanic

ridge, now very clearly shown on all topographic maps of the ocean floor. Its crest is characterized by a rift valley which is the source area for new basaltic floors. Oceanographers have described deep gashes or fractures cutting the ocean floor at right angles to the crest of the ridge. These eventually become obscured, away from the ridge, by collections of sediment.

Islands and former islands or seamounts in ocean basins are often related to the oceanic ridge and its fractures. Active and dormant volcanoes provide the rocks that form the foundation of these islands. As oceanic basalt moves away from a volcanic "hot spot", the volcano dies and the island surface erodes and gradually subsides (as in the Emperor Seamounts near Hawaii). Corals colonize the shores of such islands in tropical areas, eventually forming atolls—the legacy of a once active volcanic system.

## Ocean chemistry

The chemical composition of ocean waters is generally constant. Seawater is a solution containing a complex mixture of dissolved solids or solutes. Its evolution over time since the beginning of the Earth is little understood, but it is clearly linked to the development of a protective ozone layer in the atmosphere, to evolving life forms in shallow and deeper waters, to the gasses emitted by volcanoes or deepwater vents, and to run-off from the land. Many different minerals have accumulated in ocean waters, but about one billion years ago the concentration reached a steady-state position. In other words, new dry inputs were balanced by processes that removed the minerals, the most important of which was the deposition of minerals as sediments on continental shelves, slopes, and ocean floors.

The uniformity of ocean chemistry results from continuous mixing—the circulation of waters between oceans and seas—and numerous chemical reactions that take place over a comparatively restricted range of temperatures. Seven dominant elements form the dissolved solids in $H_2O$. They

*The oceans support a vast diversity of marine life: southern right whales (left) live in the cold Antarctic Ocean, while shoals of Mao Mao (above) prefer warm tropical waters.*

are chlorine (as chloride CE-), sodium (as Na+), magnesium (as $Mg_2$+), potassium (as K+), and bromide (as bromide Br-). Gases in a dissolved state, such as carbon dioxide, nitrogen and oxygen, are also present; the availability of oxygen is critical for many life forms. Other minor components of oceanic waters include trace elements, organic particles, and suspended matter.

Salinity is a term used to describe dissolved solids by volume in seawater. It is commonly expressed in parts per thousand (ppt), with the average value for oceanic waters being 35 ppt, varying between 34 and 37 ppt. Rainfall and ice melt tends to dilute the average salinity value; evaporation has the opposite effect, especially under the influence of hot, dry, subtropical high pressure systems.

One property of oceans that can vary quite widely is temperature. In polar regions, vast areas of oceans freeze to form sea ice and ice shelves. Seawater freezes at –2 °C (28.4 °F) at the surface of oceans. At the other end of the scale, tropical waters may have temperatures as high as 30 °C (86 °F). Ocean waters are typically layered, with marked differences in temperature and salinity between mixed surface waters and deeper zones, where temperatures approach freezing.

## Ocean circulation

Differences in temperature and salinity between waters at varying depths, combined with Earth's rotational influence and wind forces, help drive ocean water masses within and between oceanic basins. At depth, the great movements of water are quite slow in comparison with the surface. This results in an upwelling of cold, nutrient-rich currents toward the margins of some continents, such as along the west coast of South America. Surface flows redistribute heat from the tropics to higher latitudes; the Gulf Stream flowing along the east coast of North America towards Europe is a classic example, helping to maintain milder temperatures in countries such as the Republic of Ireland, the United Kingdom and Denmark.

In some parts of oceans, water circulation is somewhat limited. This is the case at the centers of subtropical gyres (circular surface rotations of water), such as the gyre within the North Atlantic

Ocean, where the Sargasso Sea develops salinities up to 30 ppt.

During the Quaternary Period it is hypothesized that significant changes in oceanic circulation occurred. The so-called "conveyor belts" of surface and deeper currents moving masses of water between the basins would have been influenced by the spread of ice on and adjacent to continents. Microscopic organisms buried in sediments on the ocean floor have been used to determine in some detail shifts in temperature and salinity conditions over the past 2 million years.

## Ocean exploration

The exploration of oceans can be described in three phases. First there was the pioneering period of great sea-going nations looking for new lands to exploit and colonize. From Europe the Vikings led the way, followed by the great voyages of the Portuguese, Spanish, Dutch, British and French. These were later joined by other nations, including Germany, Russia and the USA. From Asia and the Middle East came other maritime travellers, crossing the oceans for trade and also to promulgate religious beliefs.

The second phase consolidated the discoveries of the first and led to the establishment of ports and trading routes. Knowledge increased about hazards to shipping, climatic and current conditions, the best use of the sea for naval purposes, and the social and economic conditions of lands bordering the oceans.

The third phase encompasses the scientific exploration of the past five decades, including the use of satellites, permanent recorders, and surface and submerged survey techniques to greatly expand our knowledge of the oceanic realm. This includes an understanding of perhaps the largest mineral deposit on Earth—manganese nodules. It is estimated that about 2 billion tonnes of manganese nodules lie on the floor of our oceans.

Deep-sea drilling has proved invaluable in helping us determine the type of materials found on ocean floors and their age and modes of formation. Increasingly, this new knowledge is alerting scientists and decision-makers to our capacity to adversely affect ocean ecosystems.

### Exploitation and pollution

The pressure to use large tracts of ocean and coastal waters for fishing and the extraction of minerals, including oil, has led in some cases to over-exploitation of our biggest natural resource, the sea. International conventions on rights to ocean use have become a mechanism to resolve disputes and to prevent the loss of endangered species. That differences of opinion still exist between nations—for instance, over whaling rights—indicate that serious issues remain unresolved. Two issues of global significance need to be considered by all countries of the world: water pollution and the impact of the greenhouse effect on ocean levels.

For a long time oceans have been considered a convenient dumping ground for human and chemical waste. It used to be thought that the oceans were big enough either to dilute the waste or at least to carry it conveniently out of sight. This is no longer the case—pollution by radioactive wastes in areas like the Arctic Ocean has proven that our planet is not big enough to absorb such toxic material. Urban industrial societies need to develop informed strategies for waste disposal before it is too late.

### Oceans and the climate

It has been known for some time that oceans moderate the world's climate. Scientists are now able to use computers to model the interaction between oceans and the atmosphere, and are warning governments of potentially serious disturbances to climatic patterns. Phenomena such as El Niño already highlight the variability in ocean-climate patterns and the extreme climatic conditions (floods, droughts, storm surges) that can occur. Ocean warming due to the greenhouse effect also increases the possibility of extreme weather patterns and rising sea levels. These effects are particularly serious for low-lying nations built on coral reefs and coral debris. such as the Maldives.

*Oceanic exploration includes the study of rich plant and marine life (top). Oil is a valuable oceanic resource (center). Lighthouses have ensured safe ocean travel for centuries (right).*

# Indian Ocean

Black Sea

Aral Sea

Caspian Sea

Nile Fan

Mediterranean Sea

**A S I A**

Yellow Sea

Persian Gulf

Tropic of Cancer

East China Sea

Tropic of Cancer

Red Sea

Indus Fan

Arabian Sea

Bay of Bengal

South China Sea

Philippine Trench

**AFRICA**

Owen Fracture Zone

Arabian Basin

Chagos – Laccadive Plateau

Ganges Fan

Andaman Basin

South China Basin

Carlsberg Ridge

Somali Basin

Chagos Trench

Sunda Shelf

Palawan Trough

Celebes Basin

Equator

Borneo

Equator

Mascarene Plateau

Mid-Indian Basin

**INDIAN**

NINETY EAST RIDGE

J A V A   T R E N C H

Sumatera

Investigator Ridge

North Australian Basin

Mozambique Channel

Madagascar

Mascarene Plain

**OCEAN**

Wharton Basin

Exmouth Plateau

Mauritius Trench

MID-INDIAN RIDGE

East Indian Ridge

Tropic of Capricorn

Madagascar Basin

Perth Basin

**AUSTRALIA**

Tropic of Capricorn

Natal Basin

Madagascar Plateau

Broken Ridge

Mozambique Plateau

Mozambique Fracture Zone

SOUTHWEST INDIAN RIDGE

Indomed Fracture Zone

Diamantina Fracture Zone

South Australian Basin

Agulhas Plateau

Fracture Zone

Crozet Basin

SOUTHEAST INDIAN RIDGE

Agulhas Basin

Prince Edward

Crozet Plateau

Kerguelen Plateau

**SOUTHERN   OCEAN**

*ENDERBY PLAIN*

© Random House Australia Pty Ltd

The Oceans

| kilometers | 0 | 1000 | 2000 | 3000 |
|---|---|---|---|---|
| miles | 0 | 500 | 1000 | 1500 |

Scale 1:60,000,000          Projection: Mercator

# Atlantic Ocean

A 90° B 75° C 60° D 45° E 30° F 15° G 0° H 15° J

*Baffin Bay*

Greenland

*Hudson Bay*

Iceland

*Jan Mayen Ridge*

*Faeroe-Iceland Ridge*

NORTH AMERICA

*Imarssuak Seachannel*

*Reykjanes Ridge*

*Maury Seachannel*

*North Sea*

*Baltic Sea*

EUROPE

*Charlie-Gibbs Fracture Zone*

ATLANTIC

*Porcupine Plain*

*Grand Banks of Newfoundland*

OCEAN

*Biscay Plain*

*Laurentian Fan*

*Oceanographer Fracture Zone*

*Azores-Biscay Rise*

*Strait of Gibraltar*

*Mediterranean Sea*

*Mediterranean Ridge*

*Blake Plateau*

*Hatteras Plain*

*Bermuda Rise*

MID-ATLANTIC RIDGE

*Atlantis Fracture Zone*

*Gulf of Mexico*

Tropic of Cancer

*Kane Fracture Zone*

*Cape Verde Basin*

Tropic of Cancer

*Puerto Rico Trench*

*Nares Plain*

AFRICA

*Cayman Trench*

*Ayres Ridge*

*Caribbean Sea*

*Beata Ridge*

*Vema Fracture Zone*

*Gambia Plain*

*Middle America Trench*

*Demerara Plain*

*Doldrums Fracture Zone*

*Amazon Fan*

*Sierra Leone Basin*

*Guinea Basin*

Equator

*Carnegie Ridge*

*Ceara Plain*

*Romanche Fracture Zone*

*Chain Fracture Zone*

Equator

*Pernambuco Plain*

MID-ATLANTIC RIDGE

*Ascension Fracture Zone*

*Nazca Ridge*

SOUTH

*Brazil Basin*

*Angola Basin*

*Peru-Chile Trench*

AMERICA

Tropic of Capricorn

Tropic of Capricorn

PACIFIC

*Rio Grande Rise*

*Walvis Ridge*

OCEAN

*Cape Basin*

ATLANTIC

*Agulhas Basin*

*Humboldt Plain*

*Argentine Plain*

OCEAN

*Falkland Escarpment*

*Falkland Plateau*

*South Georgia Ridge*

*South Sandwich Trench*

ATLANTIC-INDIAN RIDGE

*Drake Passage*

A 90° B 75° C 60° D 45° E 30° F 15° G 0° H 15° J

0  1000  2000  3000 kilometers
0  500  1000  1500 miles

Scale 1:60,000,000     Projection: Mercator

© Random House Australia Pty Ltd

The Oceans

# Pacific Ocean

© Random House Australia Pty Ltd

Gulf of Alaska

Tufts Plain

docino Fracture Zone

Pioneer Fracture Zone

ray Fracture Ridge

Molokai Fracture Zone

Clarion Fracture Zone

OCEAN

Clipperton Fracture Zone

Galapagos Fracture Zone

Marquesas Fracture Zone

Patton Escarpment

Cedros Trench

PACIFIC RISE

Middle America Trench

Easter Fracture Zone

EAST

Challenger Fracture Zone

Agassiz Fracture Zone

Menard Fracture Zone

Eltanin Fracture Zone

uthwest acific Basin

v Fracture Zone

TARCTIC RIDGE

NORTH AMERICA

Gulf of Mexico

Mexico Basin

Cayman Trench

Guatemala Basin

Cocos Ridge

Panama Basin

Carnegie Ridge

Peru Basin

Galapagos Rise

Nazca Ridge

Chile Basin

Chile Rise

Southeast Pacific Basin

Humboldt Plain

Bellingshausen Plain

ATLANTIC OCEAN

Laurentian Fan

Blake Plateau

Hatteras Plain

Bermuda Rise

Puerto Rico Trench

Nares Plain

Beata Ridge

Aves Ridge

Caribbean Sea

SOUTH AMERICA

Peru-Chile Trench

Peru-Chile Trench

Argentine Plain

ATLANTIC OCEAN

Falkland Plateau

Drake Passage

Tropic of Cancer

Tropic of Capricorn

150°  J  135°  K  120°  L  105°  M  90°  N  75°  P  60°  Q

150°  J  135°  K  120°  L  105°  M  90°  N  75°  P  60°  Q

1
45°
2
30°
3
15°
4
0°
5
15°
6
45°
7
8

1000  2000  3000  kilometers
500  1000  1500  miles
ale 1:50,000,000  Projection: Mercator

# Gazetteer

## Abbreviations Used on Maps

**Arch.** Archipelago, Archipel, Archipiélago, Arquipélago
**Arg.** Argentina
**Arm.** Armenia
**Aust.** Australia
**Azer.** Azerbaijan
**B.** Bay, Baía, Baie, Bahía
**B.-H.** Bosnia and Herzegovina
**Belg.** Belgium
**C.A.R.** Central African Republic
**C.** Cape, Cabo, Cap, Capo
**Co** Cerro
**Col.** Colombia
**Cord.** Cordillera
**Croat.** Croatia
**Cuch.** Cuchillo
**Czech Rep.** Czech Republic
**D.C.** District of Columbia
**Dem. Rep. of the Congo** Democratic Republic of the Congo
**Den.** Denmark
**E.** East
**Ecu.** Ecuador
**Emb.** Embalse
**Eq.** Guinea Equatorial Guinea
**Est.** Estrecho
**Fr.** France
**G.** Gora
**G.** Gulf, Golfe, Golfo, Gulfo
**G.** Gunung
**Germ.** Germany
**Harb.** Harbor
**Hung.** Hungary
**I.** Island, Île, Ilha, Isla, Isola
**Is** Islands, Îles, Ilhas, Islas
**Jez.** Jezioro
**K.** Kolpos
**Kep.** Kepulauan
**L.** Lake, Lac, Lacul, Lago, Limni, Loch
**Liech.** Liechtenstein
**Lux.** Luxembourg
**Mace.** Macedonia
**Mex.** Mexico
**Mt** Mount, Mont
**Mte** Monte
**Mti** Monti
**Mtn** Mountain
**Mts** Mountains, Monts
**N.** North
**N.Z.** New Zealand
**Neth.** Netherlands
**Nev.** Nevado
**Nor.** Norway
**P.** Pic, Pico
**P.** Pulau
**P.N.G.** Papua New Guinea
**Peg.** Pegunungan
**Pen.** Peninsula, Péninsula, Péninsule
**Pk** Peak
**Pk** Puncak
**Port.** Portugal
**Pt** Point
**Pta** Ponta, Punta
**Pte** Pointe
**Pto** Porto, Pôrto, Puerto
**R.** River
**Ra.** Range
**Rep.** Republic
**Res.** Reservoir
**Russ. Fed.** Russian Federation
**S.** San
**S.** South
**S.A.** South Africa
**Sa** Serra
**Sd** Sound
**Serr.** Serranía
**Slov.** Slovenia
**Sp.** Spain
**St** Saint
**Sta** Santa
**Ste** Sainte
**Sto** Santo
**Switz.** Switzerland
**Tel.** Teluk
**Tg** Tanjong
**U.** Ujung
**U.A.E.** United Arab Emirates
**U.K.** United Kingdom
**U.S., U.S.A.** United States of America
**Vol.** Volcán
**W.** West

## Foreign Geographical Terms

**Açude** (*Portuguese*) reservoir
**Adası** (*Turkish*) island
**Adrar** (*Berber*) mountains
**Agios** (*Greek*) saint
**Akra** (*Greek*) cape, point
**Alpen** (*German*) Alps
**Alpi** (*Italian*) Alps
**Alta** (*Spanish*) upper
**Altiplanicie** (*Spanish*) high plain, plateau
**-älven** (*Swedish*) river
**Ao** (*Thai*) bay
**Archipel** (*French*) archipelago
**Archipiélago** (*Spanish*) archipelago
**Arquipélago** (*Portuguese*) archipelago
**Avtonomnaya Oblast'** (*Russian*) autonomous region
**Avtonomnyy Okrug** (*Russian*) autonomous area

**Bab** (*Arabic*) strait
**Bælt** (*Danish*) strait
**Bahía** (*Spanish*) bay
**Baḩr, Bahr** (*Arabic*) lake, river, sea
**Baía** (*Portuguese*) bay
**Baie** (*French*) bay
**Barajı** (*Turkish*) dam
**Barragem** (*Portuguese*) reservoir
**Bassin** (*French*) basin
**Beinn, Ben** (*Gaelic*) mountain
**Bjerg** (*Danish*) hill, mountain
**Bôca** (*Portuguese*) river mouth
**Boca** (*Spanish*) river mouth
**Bocht** (*Dutch*) bay
**Bodden** (*German*) bay
**Bogazi** (*Turkish*) strait
**Bögeni** (*Kazakh*) reservoir
**-bre/en** (*Norwegian*) glacier
**Bucht** (*German*) bay
**Bugt, -bugten** (*Danish*) bay
**Buḩayrat** (*Arabic*) lake
**Bukit** (*Malay*) mountain
**-bukten** (*Swedish*) bay
**Burnu, Burun** (*Turkish*) cape, point
**Buuraha** (*Somali*) hill/s, mountain/s

**Cabo** (*Portuguese, Spanish*) cape
**Canal** (*Spanish*) channel
**Cap** (*French*) cape
**Capo** (*Italian*) cape
**Cerro/s** (*Spanish*) hill/s, peak/s
**Chaîne** (*French*) mountain range
**Chapada** (*Portuguese*) hills, upland/s
**Chhâk** (*Cambodian*) bay
**Chott** (*Arabic*) marsh, salt lake
**Cima** (*Italian*) mountain
**Ciudad** (*Spanish*) city
**Co** (*Tibetan*) lake
**Colline** (*Italian*) hill/s
**Cordillera** (*Spanish*) mountain range, mountain chain
**Côte** (*French*) coast, slope
**Cù Lao** (*Vietnamese*) island
**Cuchilla** (*Spanish*) mountain range

**Dag/Dağı** (*Turkish*) mountain
**Dağlar/ı** (*Turkish*) mountains
**-dake** (*Japanese*) peak
**Danau** (*Indonesian*) lake
**Dao** (*Chinese*) island
**Dao** (*Vietnamese*) island
**Daryâcheh** (*Persian*) lake
**Dasht** (*Persian*) desert
**Denizi** (*Turkish*) sea
**Desierto** (*Spanish*) desert
**Détroit** (*French*) strait
**Djebel** (*Arabic*) mountain, mountain range

**-elva** (*Norwegian*) river
**Embalse** (*Spanish*) reservoir
**Ensenada** (*Spanish*) bay
**Erg** (*Arabic*) sand dunes
**Estrecho** (*Spanish*) strait
**Étang** (*French*) lagoon, lake
**ezers** (*Latvian*) lake

**Falaise** (*French*) cliff
**Feng** (*Chinese*) peak
**Fjeld** (*Danish*) mountain
**-fjell** (*Norwegian*) mountain
**-fjord/en** (*Danish, Norwegian, Swedish*) fiord

**Gang** (*Chinese*) harbor
**Gaoyuan** (*Chinese*) plateau
**Garet** (*Arabic*) hill
**Gebergte** (*Dutch*) mountain chain, mountain range
**-gebirge** (*German*) mountain range
**Ghubbat** (*Arabic*) bay
**Gjiri** (*Albanian*) bay
**Golfe** (*French*) gulf
**Golfo** (*Italian, Portuguese*) gulf
**Gölü** (*Turkish*) lake
**Gora** (*Russian*) mountain
**Góry** (*Polish*) mountains
**Gross/er** (*German*) big
**Gryada** (*Russian*) ridge
**Guba** (*Russian*) bay, gulf
**Gulfo** (*Spanish*) gulf
**Gunung** (*Indonesian, Malay*) mountain

**Haixia** (*Chinese*) strait
**-halvøya** (*Norwegian*) peninsula
**Har** (*Hebrew*) mountain
**Haut, Haute** (*French*) high
**Hawr** (*Arabic*) lake
**Hâyk'** (*Amharic*) lake
**Helodrano** (*Malagasy*) bay
**Höhe** (*German*) height
**Hora** (*Belorussian, Czech*) mountain
**-horn** (*German*) peak
**Hory** (*Czech*) mountains
**Hsü** (*Chinese*) island, islet
**Hu** (*Chinese*) lake

**Île/s** (*French*) island/s
**Ilha/s** (*Portuguese*) island/s
**Ilheu** (*Portuguese*) islet
**Isla/s** (*Spanish*) island/s
**Isola, Isole** (*Italian*) island/s

**Jabal** (*Arabic*) mountain, mountain range
**Jarv** (Estonian) lake
**-järvi** (*Finnish*) lake
**Jazirat, Jaza'ir** (*Arabic*) island/s
**Jazireh** (Persian) island
**Jbel** (*Arabic*) mountain
**Jezioro** (*Polish*) lake
**-jima** (*Japanese*) island
**-joki** (*Finnish*) river

**Kalnas** (*Lithuanian*) mountain
**Kangri** (*Tibetan*) mountain
**Kap** (*Danish, German*) cape
**-kapp** (*Norwegian*) cape
**Kepi** (*Albanian*) cape, point
**Kepulauan** (*Indonesian*) islands
**Khalīj** (*Arabic*) bay, gulf
**Khao** (*Thai*) peak
**Khrebet** (*Russian*) mountain range
**Ko** (*Thai*) island
**Köli** (*Kazakh*) lake
**Kolpos** (*Greek*) bay
**Körfezi** (*Turkish*) bay, gulf
**Kray** (*Russian*) territory
**Kryazh** (*Russian*) ridge
**Kūh/hā** (Persian) mountain/s
**-kül** (*Tajik*) lake
**Kyst** (*Danish*) coast
**Kyun** (*Burmese*) island

**Lac** (*French*) lake
**Lacul** (*Romanian*) lake
**Lago** (*Italian, Portuguese, Spanish*) lake
**Lagoa** (*Portuguese*) lagoon, lake
**Laht** (*Estonian*) bay
**Lich** (*Armenian*) lake
**Liedao** (*Chinese*) archipelago, islands
**Limni** (*Greek*) lake
**Ling** (*Chinese*) mountain range
**Loch, Lough** (*Gaelic*) lake
**Lohatanjona** (*Malagasy*) point
**Loi** (*Burmese*) mountain
**Loma** (*Spanish*) hill

**Mae Nam** (*Thai*) river
**-man** (*Korean*) bay
**Mar** (*Spanish*) lake, sea
**Ma'abb** (*Arabic*) river mouth
**Massif** (*French*) mountains, upland
**Meer, -meer** (*Dutch*) lake, sea
**Mesa** (*Spanish*) tableland
**Meseta** (*Spanish*) plateau, tableland
**-misaki** (*Japanese*) cape, point
**Mont/s** (*French*) mountain/s
**Montagne/s** (*French*) mountain/s
**Monte** (*Italian, Portuguese, Spanish*) mountain
**Montes** (*Spanish*) mountain
**Monti** (*Italian*) mountain/s
**More** (*Russian*) sea
**Morne** (*French*) mountain
**Morro** (*Portuguese*) hill
**Munţii** (*Romanian*) mountains
**Mys** (*Russian*) cape, point

**-nada** (*Japanese*) gulf, sea
**Nagor'ye** (*Russian*) upland
**Nevado** (*Spanish*) snow-capped mountain
**Nieuw** (*Dutch*) new
**Nisoi** (*Greek*) islands
**Nizmennost'** (*Russian*) lowland
**Nord** (*French, German*) north
**Norte** (*Portuguese, Spanish*) north
**Nos** (*Bulgarian*) point
**Nosy** (*Malagasy*) island
**Nur, Nuur** (*Mongolian*) lake
**Nuruu** (*Mongolian*) mountain range

**Ø, Øer** (*Danish*) island/s
**-ö, -ön** (*Swedish*) island
**Oblast'** (*Russian*) province
**Odde** (*Danish*) cape, point
**Oros** (*Greek*) mountain
**Ostrov/a** (*Russian*) island/s
**Oued** (*Arabic*) river, watercourse
**-øy, -øya** (*Norwegian*) island
**Ozero** (*Russian*) lake

**Pantanal** (*Portuguese*) marsh, swamp
**Pegunungan** (Indonesian) island
**Pelagos** (*Greek*) sea
**Pendi** (*Chinese*) basin
**Pertuis** (*French*) strait
**Phnum** (*Cambodian*) mountain
**Phou** (*Laotian*) mountain
**Pic** (*French*) peak
**Pico** (*Spanish*) peak
**Pik** (*Russian*) peak
**Piton** (*French*) peak
**Pivostriv** (*Ukrainian*) peninsula
**Piz, pizzo** (*Italian*) peak
**Planalto** (*Portuguese*) plateau
**Planina** (*Bulgarian, Macedonian*) mountains
**Plato** (*Russian*) plateau
**Ploskogor'ye** (*Russian*) plateau, upland
**Pointe** (*French*) point
**Poluostrov** (*Russian*) peninsula
**Ponta** (*Portuguese*) point
**Porthmos** (*Greek*) strait
**Porto, Pôrto** (*Portuguese*) port
**Proliv** (*Russian*) strait
**Puerto** (*Spanish*) port
**Pulau** (*Indonesian, Malay*) island
**Puncak** (*Indonesian*) mountain
**Punta** (*Italian, Spanish*) point

**Qārat** (*Arabic*) hill
**Qooriga** (*Somali*) bay
**Qundao** (*Chinese*) archipelago, islands
**Qurnat** (*Arabic*) peak

**Raas** (*Somali*) cape, point
**Ras, Ra's** (*Arabic*) cape, point
**Ravnina** (*Russian*) plain
**Represa** (*Portuguese, Spanish*) reservoir
**Réservoir** (*French*) reservoir
**Reshteh** (*Persian*) mountain range
**Respublika** (*Russian*) republic
**Respublikasi** (*Uzbek*) republic
**-retto** (*Japanese*) island chain
**Rio, Río** (*Portuguese, Spanish*) river
**Rivière** (*French*) river
**Rubha** (*Gaelic*) cape, point
**Rudohorie** (*Slovak*) mountains

**Sāgar/a** (*Hindi*) lake
**Şaḩrā'** (*Arabic*) desert
**-saki** (*Japanese*) cape, point
**Salar** (*Spanish*) salt-flat, salt-pan
**Salina/s** (*Spanish*) salt-pan/s
**Salto/s** (*Portuguese, Spanish*) waterfall
**-san** (*Japanese*, Korean) mountain
**San, Santa, Santo** (*Spanish*) saint
**-sanchi** (*Japanese*) mountains
**São** (*Portuguese*) saint
**Sarīr** (*Arabic*) desert
**Sebkha, Sebkhet** (*Arabic*) salt-flat
**See, -see** (*German*) lake
**Selat** (*Indonesian*) strait
**Serra** (*Portuguese*) mountain range
**Serranía** (*Spanish*) mountain range
**Shamo** (*Chinese*) desert
**Shan** (*Chinese*) mountain/s
**-shima** (*Japanese*) island
**-shotō** (*Japanese*) islands
**Shuiki** (*Chinese*) reservoir
**Sierra** (*Spanish*) mountain range
**Slieve** (*Gaelic*) mountain
**-spitze** (*German*) peak
**Steno** (*Greek*) strait
**Štít** (*Slovak*) peak
**Stretto** (*Italian*) strait
**Sud** (*French*) south
**Sul** (*Portuguese*) south

**Tanjona** (Malagasy) cape
**Tanjong** (Indonesian, Malay) cape, point
**Tao** (*Chinese*) island
**Tasek** (*Malay*) lake
**Tassili** (*Berber*) plateau
**Taungdan** (*Burmese*) mountain range
**Tekojärvi** (*Finnish*) reservoir
**Teluk** (*Indonesian, Malay*) bay
**Ténéré** (*Berber*) desert
**Tepe** (*Turkish*) peak
**Terara** (*Amharic*) mountain
**Tierra** (*Spanish*) land
**-to** (*Japanese*) island

**Ujung** (*Indonesian*) cape, point
**'Urūq** (*Arabic*) dunes
**Uul** (*Mongolian*) mountain/s

**väin** (*Estonian*) channel, strait
**-vatn** (*Norwegian*) lake
**-vesi** (*Finnish*) lake, water
**Voblasts'** (*Belorussian*) province
**Vodokhranilishche** (*Russian*) reservoir
**Vodoskhovyshche** (*Ukrainian*) reservoir
**Volcán** (*Spanish*) volcano
**Vozvyshennost'** (*Russian*) plateau, upland
**Vozyera** (*Belorussian*) lake
**Vrchovina** (*Czech*) mountains

**Wabē** (*Amharic*) river, stream
**Wādī** (*Arabic*) watercourse
**-wald** (*German*) forest
**Wan** (*Chinese*) bay
**-wan** (*Japanese*) bay

**Yam** (*Hebrew*) lake, sea
**Yang** (*Chinese*) ocean
**Yoma** (*Burmese*) mountain range

**-zaki** (*Japanese*) cape, point
**Zaliv** (*Russian*) bay
**Zangbo** (*Tibetan*) river
**Zatoka** (*Polish*) bay, gulf
**-zee** (*Dutch*) sea
**Zemlya** (*Russian*) land
**Zizhiqu** (*Chinese*) autonomous region

# Gazetteer

- The gazetteer contains the names shown on the continental and detailed regional maps at the end of each section.

- In the code given to locate a place, the bold number refers to the page on which the map is to be found, and the letter-number combination refers to the grid square formed by the lines of latitude and longitude on the map. Inset maps have their own letter-number combination.

- Where a name appears on more than one map, the gazetteer generally lists the largest scale map on which the name appears.

- Names that have a symbol (town or mountain peak) are given an area reference according to the location of the symbol. Names without a symbol are entered in the gazetteer according to the first letter of the name.

- Words in italics describe features in the gazetteer, e.g. island, point and mountain peak; numbers in italics refer to references in the text.

- All entries include the country or area in which the name is located.

- Features composed of a description and a proper name, e. g. Cape Hatteras, are positioned alphabetically by the proper name: Hatteras, Cape.

- Where a name contains a subordinate or alternative name in brackets on the map, the bracketed names are entered in the gazetteer with a cross-reference to the first name, e. g. Peking *see* Beijing, China, **210** G5.

- Words abbreviated on the map, e. g. C. or I., are spelt out in the gazetteer. If the word is English, the description in italics is not included. For example, if I. (standing for island) is abbreviated on the map and spelt out in the gazetteer, island is not added. However, if Island is not in English, e. g. Isla, *island* is added.

- The location (ocean, area of a continent) is included before the area reference when a place is part of a country but not located within the country, e. g. Madeira, Portugal, Atlantic Ocean; and Ceuta, enclave, Spain, N. W. Africa.

---

## A

A Cañiza, Spain, **292** C1
A Coruña, Spain, **292** C1
A Estrada, Spain, **292** C1
A Fonsagrada, Spain, **292** D1
A Guardia, Spain, **292** C2
A Gudiña, Spain, **292** D1
Aachen, Germany, **288** C3
Aalen, Germany, **288** E4
A'ali An Nīl, *state*, Sudan, **366** D2
Aapua, Sweden, **285** L3
Aarau, Switzerland, **291** J3
Aare, *river*, Switzerland, **291** J3, *247*
Aasleagh, Ireland, **309** C4
Aba, China, **215** G2
Aba, Democratic Republic of the Congo, **366** D4
Aba, Nigeria, **368** A1
Abacaxis, *river*, Brazil, **452** A4
Abaco, *island*, Bahamas, **428** F1, *393*
Ābādeh, Iran, **220** F2
Abadla, Algeria, **361** F2
Abaeté, *river*, Brazil, **456** D5
Abaetetuba, Brazil, **452** D3
Abag Qi, China, **210** F4
Abagaytuy, Russian Federation, **210** G2
Abaji, Nigeria, **365** F3
Abajo Peak, *mountain*, U.S.A., **423** J3
Abakaliki, Nigeria, **365** F3
Abakan, *river*, Russian Federation, **223** M2
Abakan, Russian Federation, **223** N2
Abala, Niger, **365** E2
Abala, Congo, **368** C3
Abalak, Niger, **365** E3/F1
Abalessa, Algeria, **361** G4
Abancay, Peru, **454** D3
Abarkūh, Iran, **220** F2
Abashiri, Japan, **209** J2
Abatskiy, Russian Federation, **223** J1
Abau, Papua New Guinea, **140** C5
Abay, Aqmola, Kazakhstan, **212** A2
Abay, Qaraghandy, Kazakhstan, **212** B2
Abaza, Russian Federation, **223** N2
Abba, Central African Republic, **368** C1

Abbeville, Alabama, U.S.A., **425** K4
Abbéville, France, **290** E1
Abbeville, Louisiana, U.S.A., **424** F5
Abbeville, South Carolina, U.S.A., **425** L2
Abbeyfeale, Ireland, **309** C5
Abbeyleix, Ireland, **309** E5
Abborrträsk, Sweden, **284** J4
Abbot Ice Shelf, Antarctica, **470** B6
Abbots Langley, England, U.K., **305** G3
Abbotsbury, England, U.K., **304** E4
Abbotsford, Canada, **412** H7
Abbott, U.S.A., **423** L3
Abbottābād, Pakistan, **218** C2
'Abd al Kūrī, *island*, Suquṭrá (Socotra), Yemen, **373** B2
Abdelcader, Somalia, **367** F2
Abdulino, Russian Federation, **222** E2
Abéché, Chad, **366** B2
Abee, Canada, **413** N4
Abemama, *island*, Kiribati, **139** F4
Abengourou, Côte d'Ivoire, **364** D3
Åbenrå, Denmark, **286** D5
Abeokuta, Nigeria, **365** E3
Aberaeron, Wales, U.K., **304** C2
Aberchirder, Scotland, U.K., **308** G3
Aberdare, Wales, U.K., **304** D3
Aberdaron, Wales, U.K., **304** C2
Aberdeen, Idaho, U.S.A., **418** H5
Aberdeen, Mississippi, U.S.A., **425** H3
Aberdeen, Scotland, U.K., **308** G3, *276*
Aberdeen, South Africa, **370** D5
Aberdeen, South Dakota, U.S.A., **420** D3
Aberdeen, Washington, U.S.A., **418** C3
Aberdeen City, *local authority*, Scotland, U.K., **308** G3
Aberdeenshire, *local authority*, Scotland, U.K., **308** G3

Aberdyfi, Wales, U.K., **304** C2
Aberfeldy, Scotland, U.K., **308** F4
Aberfoyle, Scotland, U.K., **306** D1
Abergavenny, Wales, U.K., **304** E3
Abergele, Wales, U.K., **306** E4
Abernathy, U.S.A., **424** B3
Aberporth, Wales, U.K., **304** C2
Abersoch, Wales, U.K., **304** C2
Abert, Lake, U.S.A., **418** D5
Abertillery, Wales, U.K., **304** D3
Aberystwyth, Wales, U.K., **304** C2
Abhā, Saudi Arabia, **363** H5
Abhar, Iran, **222** D5
Abia, *state*, Nigeria, **365** F3
Abibe, Serranía de, *mountain range*, Colombia, **450** C2
Abide, Turkey, **297** G6
Abidjan, Côte d'Ivoire, **364** D3, *324, 325*
Abilene, U.S.A., **424** C3
Abingdon, England, U.K., **305** F3
Abingdon, U.S.A., **421** N7
Abington, Scotland, U.K., **308** F5
Abiquiu, U.S.A., **423** K3
Abisko, Sweden, **284** J2
Abitibi, Lake, Canada, **415** Q7
Ābīy Ādī, Ethiopia, **367** E2
Abkhazia, *autonomous republic*, Georgia, **222** C4, *190*
Abnūb, Egypt, **363** F3
Abohar, India, **218** C3
Aboisso, Côte d'Ivoire, **364** D3
Abomey, Benin, **365** E3
Abong Mbang, Cameroon, **368** B2
Abongabong, Gunung, *mountain peak*, Indonesia, **200** B1
Abooso, Ghana, **364** D3
Aborlan, Philippines, **204** B4
Abou Deïa, Chad, **366** A2
Aboyne, Scotland, U.K., **308** G3
Abra Pampa, Argentina, **458** D2
Abra, *river*, Philippines, **204** C2

Abrantes, Portugal, **292** C3
Abrī, Sudan, **363** F4
Abriès, France, **291** H4
Abrolhos, Arquipélago dos, *islands*, Brazil, **457** F4
Abrud, Romania, **296** D2
Abruka, *island*, Estonia, **287** L3
Abruzzi, *autonomous region*, Italy, **295** D4, *255*
Absaroka Range, *mountain range*, U.S.A., **419** J4
Absarokee, U.S.A., **419** K4
Abu ad Ḍuhūr, Syria, **225** D2
Abū 'Arīsh, Saudi Arabia, **363** H5
Abu Dhabi *see* Abū Zaby, United Arab Emirates, **221** F4, *176*
Abū Dulayq, Sudan, **366** D1
Abū Durbah, Egypt, **225** B5
Abu Haggag, Egypt, **362** E2
Abū Ḥamad, Sudan, **363** F5
Abū Ḥammād, Egypt, **225** A4
Abū Kamāl, Syria, **363** H2
Abū Maṭāriq, Sudan, **366** C2
Abū Madd, Ra's, *point*, Saudi Arabia, **363** G4
Abū Nujaym, Libya, **362** C2
Ābu Road, India, **218** C4
Abū Rubayq, Saudi Arabia, **363** G4
Abū Rudays, Egypt, **225** B5
Abū Rujmayn, Jabal, *mountain range*, Syria, **225** E2
Abu Shagara, Ras, *point*, Sudan, **363** G4
Abū Shanab, Sudan, **366** C2
Abu Simbel *see* Abū Sunbul, Egypt, **363** F4, *68, 88*
Abū Sunbul (Abu Simbel), Egypt, **363** F4, *68, 88*
Abu 'Ujaylah, Egypt, **225** C4
Abū Zabad, Sudan, **366** C2
Abū Zaby (Abu Dhabi), United Arab Emirates, **221** F4, *176*
Abū Zanīmah, Egypt, **225** B5
Abuja, Nigeria, **365** F3, *329*
Abulog, Philippines, **204** C2
Abumombazi, Democratic Republic of the Congo, **368** D2

Abunã, Brazil, **455** F2
Abunã, *river*, Bolivia/ Brazil, **455** E2
Ābune Yosēf, *mountain peak*, Ethiopia, **367** E2
Aburo, *mountain peak*, Democratic Republic of the Congo, **366** D4
Ābuyē Mēda, *mountain peak*, Ethiopia, **367** E2
Abyad, Al Baḥr al (White Nile), *river*, Sudan, **366** D2, *336*
Abyad, Sudan, **366** C2
Åbybro, Denmark, **286** D4
Abyei, Sudan, **366** C3
Åbyn, Sweden, **284** K4
Açailândia, Brazil, **452** D4
Acámbaro, Mexico, **431** E5
Acancéh, Mexico, **431** H4
Acandí, Colombia, **450** C2
Acaponeta, Mexico, **430** D4
Acapulco, Mexico, **431** F5
Acará, Brazil, **452** D3
Acará, *river*, Brazil, **452** D4
Acará-Mirim, *river*, Brazil, **452** D4
Acaraí, Serra, *mountain range*, Brazil, **452** B3
Acaraú, Brazil, **453** F4
Acaraú, *river*, Brazil, **453** F4
Acaray, Represa de, *reservoir*, Paraguay, **459** F2
Acari, Brazil, **453** G5
Acarigua, Venezuela, **451** E2
Acâş, Romania, **296** D2
Acatlán de Osorio, Mexico, **431** F5
Acayucan, Mexico, **431** G5
Acceglio, Italy, **294** A3
Accomac, U.S.A., **426** C6
Accra, Ghana, **364** D3, *325*
Aceh, *province*, Indonesia, **200** B1
Aceh, *river*, Indonesia, **200** A1
Achacachi, Bolivia, **455** E4
Achaguas, Venezuela, **451** E2
Achahoish, Scotland, U.K., **308** D5
Achalpur, India, **218** D5
Acheng, China, **211** J3
Acheryok, *river*, Russian Federation, **285** U3
Acheux-en-Amiénois, France, **305** K4
Achill Island, Ireland, **309** B4
Achill, Ireland, **309** C4
Achiltibuie, Scotland, U.K., **308** D2

Achinsk, Russian Federation, **300** L4
Achit, Russian Federation, **222** F1
Achnasheen, Scotland, U.K., **308** D3
Achwa, *river*, Uganda, **369** F2
Acigöl, *lake*, Turkey, **297** G7
Acıpayam, Turkey, **297** G7
Acireale, Sicilia, Italy, **295** E7
Ackley, U.S.A., **420** G4
Acklins Island, Bahamas, **429** G2
Acle, England, U.K., **305** J2
Acme, U.S.A., **418** C2
Acomayo, Peru, **454** D3
Aconcagua, Cerro, *mountain peak*, Argentina, **458** B4, *443*
Acopiara, Brazil, **453** F5
Acora, Peru, **455** E4
Acoyapa, Nicaragua, **428** D5
Acquasparta, Italy, **294** D4
Acqui Terme, Italy, **294** B3
Acre, *river*, Brazil, **455** E2
Acre *see* 'Akko, Israel, **225** C3, *173*
Acre, *state*, Brazil, **455** E2
Acri, Italy, **295** F6
Actéon, Groupe, *islands*, French Polynesia, **137** H3
Acton Point, New Zealand, **133** E5
Acton, U.S.A., **419** K4
Actopan, Mexico, **431** F4
Açu, Brazil, **453** G4
Acurenam, Equatorial Guinea, **368** B2
Ad Dabbah, Sudan, **363** F5
Ad Dafinah, Saudi Arabia, **363** H4
Ad Dahnā', *desert*, Saudi Arabia, **363** H3
Ad Dakhla, Western Sahara, **360** C4
Ad Ḍāli, Yemen, **220** D6
Ad Damazīn, Sudan, **366** D2
Ad Dāmir, Sudan, **363** F5
Ad Dammām, Saudi Arabia, **220** F3
Ad Dāmūr, Lebanon, **225** C3
Ad Darb, Saudi Arabia, **363** H5
Ad Dawādimī, Saudi Arabia, **363** H4
Ad Dawḥah (Doha), Qatar, **220** F3, *177, 178*

Ad Dawqah, Saudi Arabia, 363 H5
Ad Dilam, Saudi Arabia, 220 E4
Ad Dirʾīyah, Saudi Arabia, 220 E4
Ad Dīwānīyah, Iraq, 363 H2
Ad Duʾayn, Sudan, 366 C2
Ad Duwaym, Sudan, 366 D2
Ada, Serbia, 296 C3
Ada, U.S.A., 424 D2
Adair, Cape, Canada, 411 M2
Adair, U.S.A., 420 F5
Adaja, river, Spain, 292 E2
Adak, Sweden, 284 J4
Adak Island, Aleutian Islands, U.S.A., 408 F3
Adam, Mount, mountain peak, Falkland Islands, 460 F4
Adamaoua, Massif de l', mountain range, Cameroon, 365 G3, 329, 330
Adamaoua, province, Cameroon, 365 G3
Adamausa, state, Nigeria, 365 G3
Adamawa, state, Nigeria, 365 G3
Adams, Mount, mountain peak, New Zealand, 133 E5
Adams, Mount, mountain peak, U.S.A., 418 D3
Adams, U.S.A., 420 D1
Adams Island, Auckland Islands, New Zealand, 132 J10
Adams Lake, Canada, 413 K6
Adam's Peak, mountain peak, Sri Lanka, 216 E5
Adamstown, Pitcairn Islands, 137 J3, 126
ʿAdan (Aden), Yemen, 220 E6, 175
Adana, province, Turkey, 225 C1
Adana, Turkey, 224 E5, 191
Adang, Teluk, bay, Indonesia, 201 G3
Adapazarı, Turkey, 224 D4
Adare, Cape, Antarctica, 470 D8
Adare, Ireland, 309 D5
Adaut, Indonesia, 199 E5
Adaven, U.S.A., 422 F2
Aday, Kazakhstan, 222 G2
Adda, river, Italy, 294 B2
Adda, river, Sudan, 366 B3
Addis Ababa see Ādīs Ābeba, Ethiopia, 367 E3, 96, 338, 383
Addlestone, England, U.K., 305 G3
Addu Atoll, Maldives, 216 C7
Adel, U.S.A., 425 L4
Adelaide, Australia, 135 H5, 112
Adelaide River, Australia, 134 G1
Adelfia, Italy, 295 F5
Aden, Gulf of, Somalia/Yemen, 220 E6, 175, 339
Aden see ʿAdan, Yemen, 220 E6, 175
Aderbissinat, Niger, 365 F1
Adh Dhahībāt, Tunisia, 362 B2
Ādī Ārkʾay, Ethiopia, 367 E2
Ādī Keyih, Eritrea, 367 E2
Ādī Kwala, Eritrea, 367 E2
Ādī Ugrī, Eritrea, 367 E2
Adi, Pulau, island, Indonesia, 199 F4
Àdige, river, Italy, 294 C3
Àdige, state, Italy, 294 C2
Ādīgrat, Ethiopia, 367 E2
Adıguzel Barajı, dam, Turkey, 297 G6
Ādilābād, India, 216 D2
Adilang, Uganda, 369 F2

Adin, U.S.A., 418 D6
Adirī, Libya, 362 B3
Adirondack Mountains, mountain range, U.S.A., 426 C2, 383
Ādīs Ābeba (Addis Ababa), Ethiopia, 367 E3, 96, 338, 383
Ādīs ʿAlem, Ethiopia, 367 E3
Ādīs Zemen, Ethiopia, 367 E2
Adıyaman, Turkey, 224 E5
Adjud, Romania, 296 F2
Admiralty Gulf, Australia, 134 E1
Admiralty Inlet, U.S.A., 418 C2
Admiralty Island, U.S.A., 412 B3
Admiralty Islands, Lord Howe Island, Australia, 135 U14
Admiralty Islands, Papua New Guinea, 140 B3
Ado-Ekiti, Nigeria, 365 F3
Adok, Sudan, 366 D3
Adonara, Pulau, island, Indonesia, 198 C5
Ādoni, India, 216 D3
Adoumandjali, Central African Republic, 368 C2
Adour, river, France, 290 D5
Adra, Spain, 293 F4
Adranga, Democratic Republic of the Congo, 369 F2
Adrano, Sicilia, Italy, 295 E7
Adrar, administrative region, Mauritania, 360 D4
Adrar, Algeria, 361 F3
Adrar, mountain range, Mauritania, 360 D4
Adré, Chad, 366 B2
Adria, Italy, 294 D3
Adrian, Michigan, U.S.A., 421 L5
Adrian, Texas, U.S.A., 423 M4
Adriatic Sea, Croatia/Italy, 294 D3, 254, 255, 256, 259, 260, 263
Adun Qulu, China, 210 G2
Adusa, Democratic Republic of the Congo, 369 E2
Adutiškis, Lithuania, 287 N5
Ādwa, Ethiopia, 367 E2
Adwāna, India, 218 B5
Adygeya, Respublika, republic, Russian Federation, 298 F4
Adzopé, Côte d'Ivoire, 364 D3
Aegean Sea, Greece/Turkey, 297 E6, 67, 146, 191, 265
Aegviidu, Estonia, 287 M3
Aeron, river, Wales, U.K., 304 C2
Afantou, Greece, 297 G7
Afférì, Côte d'Ivoire, 364 D3
Afghanistan, country, Asia, 196 H6, 22, 49, 73, 83, 144, 146, 168, 173, 183, 184, 187, 188, 272
Afgooye, Somalia, 367 G4
ʿAfif, Saudi Arabia, 363 H4
Afikpo, Nigeria, 368 A1
Āfjord, Norway, 284 E5
Aflao, Ghana, 364 E3
Aflou, Algeria, 361 G2
Afmadow, Somalia, 369 H2
Afobaka, Suriname, 452 B2
Afognak Island, U.S.A., 410 D4
Afrânio, Brazil, 453 F5
Āfrēra Terara, mountain peak, Eritrea, 367 F2
Afrikanda, Russian Federation, 285 R3
ʿAfrīn, river, Syria/Turkey, 225 D1
ʿAfrīn, Syria, 225 D1

Afuá, Brazil, 452 C3
ʿAfula, Israel, 225 C3
Afyon, province, Turkey, 297 G6
Afyon, Turkey, 224 D5
Agadez, department, Niger, 365 F1
Agadez, Niger, 365 F1
Agadir, Morocco, 360 E2
Agalega Islands, Mauritius, 372 D3
Agana, Guam, 138 C3, 122
Agapovka, Russian Federation, 222 F2
Agar, India, 218 C5
Āgaro, Ethiopia, 367 E3
Agartala, India, 219 G5, 169
Agassiz Fracture Zone, tectonic feature, Pacific Ocean, 479 J7
Agate, U.S.A., 423 M2
Agathonisi, island, Dodekanisos, Greece, 297 F7
Agats, Indonesia, 199 G4
Agatti Island, India, 216 C4
Agawa, Canada, 421 L2
Agboville, Côte d'Ivoire, 364 D3
Agbulu, Philippines, 204 C2
Ağdam, Azerbaijan, 222 D5
Agde, Cap d', cape, France, 291 F5
Agde, France, 291 F5
Agen, France, 290 E4
Āgere Maryam, Ethiopia, 369 G1
Agger, Denmark, 286 D4
Aghla Mountain, mountain peak, Ireland, 309 D3
Aghor, Afghanistan, 218 A4
Agia Marina, Dodekanisos, Greece, 297 F7
Agiabampo, Estero de, inlet, Mexico, 430 C3
Agighiol, Romania, 296 G3
Aginskiy Buryatskiy Avtonomnyy Okrug, autonomous area, Russian Federation, 210 F2
Aginskoye, Russian Federation, 210 F2
Agioi Theodoroi, Greece, 297 D7
Agiokampos, Greece, 297 D6
Agios Efstratios, island, Greece, 297 E6
Agios Georgios, island, Greece, 297 E6
Agios Ioannis, Akra, point, Kriti, Greece, 297 E8
Agios Nikolaos, Kriti, Greece, 297 E8
Agios Paraskevi, Greece, 297 F6
Agiou Orous, Kolpos, bay, Greece, 297 D5
Agira, Sicilia, Italy, 295 E7
Aglona, Latvia, 287 N4
Agnantero, Greece, 297 C6
Agness, U.S.A., 418 B5
Agnibilékrou, Côte d'Ivoire, 364 D3
Agnita, Romania, 296 E3
Agno, Philippines, 204 B2
Agnone, Italy, 295 E5
Agogo, Ghana, 364 D3
Agostinho, Brazil, 455 E2
Āgra, India, 218 D4, 47, 93, 168, 169
Agri, river, Italy, 295 F5
Ağri Dağı (Ararat), mountain peak, Turkey, 224 F4, 190, 191
Agrigento, Sicilia, Italy, 295 D7
Agrihan, island, Northern Mariana Islands, 138 C3, 125
Agrinio, Greece, 297 C6
Ağsu, Azerbaijan, 222 D4
Agua de Dios, Colombia, 450 C3
Agua Prieta, Mexico, 430 C2
Aguada Cecilio, Argentina, 460 E1
Aguadas, Colombia, 450 C3
Aguadilla, Puerto Rico, 427 C2

Aguadulce, Panama, 429 E5
Aguadulce, Providencia, Colombia, 461 C1
Aguamansa, Providencia, Colombia, 461 C1
Aguanaval, river, Mexico, 430 E3
Aguanus, river, Canada, 417 K4
Aguapeí, river, Brazil, 456 C5
Aguapey, river, Argentina, 459 F3
Aguaray-guazú, river, Paraguay, 459 E2
Águas Formosas, Brazil, 457 F4
Aguascalientes, Mexico, 430 E4
Aguascalientes, state, Mexico, 430 E4
Aguda, Punta, point, Islas Canarias, Spain, 373 B4
Agudos, Brazil, 459 H2
Águeda, Portugal, 292 C2
Águeda, river, Spain, 292 D2
Aguelhok, Mali, 361 G5
Agüenit, Western Sahara, 360 D4
Aguié, Niger, 365 F2
Aguila, U.S.A., 422 G5
Aguilar, Spain, 292 E4
Aguilar de Campóo, Spain, 292 E1
Aguilares, Argentina, 458 D3
Águilas, Spain, 293 G4
Agul, river, Russian Federation, 223 P1
Āgula'i, Ethiopia, 367 E2
Agulhas, Cape, South Africa, 370 D5
Agulhas Basin, underwater feature, Indian Ocean, 476 A8
Agulhas Negras, mountain peak, Brazil, 457 E6
Agulhas-Plateau, underwater feature, Indian Ocean, 476 A7
Agung, Gunung, mountain peak, Indonesia, 201 F5
Agusan, river, Philippines, 204 D5
Ahar, Iran, 222 D5
Ahaura, New Zealand, 133 C6
Ahaus, Germany, 288 C2
Ahe, island, French Polynesia, 137 G2
Ahipara, New Zealand, 132 D2
Ahipara Bay, New Zealand, 132 D2
Ahititi, New Zealand, 132 E4
Ahlainen, Finland, 287 K2
Ahlat, Turkey, 363 H1
Ahmadābād, India, 218 C5
Ahmadnagar, India, 216 C2
Ahmadpur, India, 216 D2
Ahmadpur East, Pakistan, 218 B3
Ahmar Mountains, Ethiopia, 367 F3
Ahmed al Bāqir, Jabal, mountain peak, Jordan, 225 C5
Ahmetli, Turkey, 297 F6
Ahmovaara, Finland, 285 P5
Ahor, India, 218 C4
Āhtäri, Finland, 287 M1
Ahuachapán, El Salvador, 428 C4
Ahualulco, Mexico, 431 E4
Ahun, France, 290 F3
Ahuriri Point, New Zealand, 132 E5
Ahvāz, Iran, 220 E2
Ahvenanmaa (Åland), island, Finland, 287 J2
Ahvenanmaan Lääni (Åland), province, Finland, 287 J2

Ahvenselkä, Finland, 285 P3
Ai Yin Young, Vietnam, 203 E3
Aiambak, Papua New Guinea, 140 A4
Aiddejavvre, Norway, 285 L2
Aiduna, Indonesia, 199 F4
Aigina, Greece, 297 D7
Aigina, island, Greece, 297 D7
Aiginio, Greece, 297 D5
Aigio, Greece, 297 D6
Aigrettes, Pointe des, point, Réunion, 373 A1
Aiguá, Uruguay, 459 F5
Aiguillon, France, 290 E4
Ailao Shan, mountain range, China, 215 G5
Aileu, East Timor, 198 D5
Ailigandí, Panama, 429 F5
Ailinglapalap, island, Marshall Islands, 139 E4
Ailly-le-Haut-Clocher, France, 305 J4
Ailly-sur-Noye, France, 305 K5
Ailsa Craig, island, Scotland, U.K., 308 D5
Aimogasta, Argentina, 458 C3
Ain, river, France, 291 G3
Aïn Beïda, Algeria, 361 H1
Aïn Ben Tili, Mauritania, 360 E3
Aïn Beni Mathar, Morocco, 361 F2
'Aïn Defla, Algeria, 361 G1
'Aïn Deheb, Algeria, 361 G2
'Aïn el Hadjel, Algeria, 361 G1
Aïn-M'Lila, Algeria, 361 H1
Aïn Oussera, Algeria, 293 J5
'Aïn Sefra, Algeria, 361 F2
'Aïn Temouchent, Algeria, 361 F1
Ainaži, Latvia, 287 M4
Ainsa, Spain, 293 H1
Ainsworth, U.S.A., 420 D4
Aipe, Colombia, 450 C3
Aiquile, Bolivia, 455 F5
Aïr, Massif de l', mountain range, Niger, 365 F1
Airaines, France, 290 E2
Airbangis, Indonesia, 200 B2
Airdrie, Canada, 413 M6
Airdrie, Scotland, U.K., 308 F5
Aire, river, France, 291 G2
Aire-sur-l'Adour, France, 290 D5
Airpanas, Indonesia, 198 D4
Airvault, France, 290 D3
Aisch, river, Germany, 288 E4
Aisén, administrative region, Chile, 460 C3
Aishalton, Guyana, 451 G3
Aisne, river, France, 291 F2
Aïssa, Djebel, mountain peak, Algeria, 361 F2
Aitana, mountain peak, Spain, 293 G3
Aitape, Papua New Guinea, 140 A3
Aitkin, U.S.A., 420 G2
Aitutaki, island, Cook Islands, 137 G2
Aiud, Romania, 296 D2
Aiviekste, river, Latvia, 287 N4
Aix-en-Provence, France, 291 G5
Aix-les-Bains, France, 291 G4
Aizawl, India, 219 H5, 169
Aizenay, France, 290 D3
Aizpute, Latvia, 287 K4
Aizu-Wakamatsu, Japan, 209 G3
Aj Bogd Uul, mountain peak, Mongolia, 213 G3
Ajā, Egypt, 225 A4
Ajaccio, Corse, France, 295 B5
Ajaccio, Golfe d', gulf, Corse, France, 295 B5
Ajaigarh, India, 218 E4

Ajalpán, Mexico, 431 F5
Ajanta, India, 218 C5
Ajanta Range, mountain range, India, 218 C5
Ajaria, autonomous republic, Georgia, 222 C4
Ajaureforsen, Sweden, 284 G4
Ajax, Mount, mountain peak, New Zealand, 133 D6
Ajdābiyā, Libya, 362 D2
Ajdovščina, Slovenia, 294 D3
Ajmah, Jabal al, plateau, Egypt, 225 B5
Ajmer, India, 218 C4
Ajnala, India, 218 C3
Ajo, U.S.A., 422 G5
Ak Dağ, mountain peak, Turkey, 297 F6
Ak Dağlar, mountain range, Turkey, 297 G7
Ak-Dovurak, Russian Federation, 223 N2
Ak-Shyyrak, Kyrgyzstan, 223 K4
Akabira, Japan, 209 H2
Akabli, Algeria, 361 G3
Āk'ak'ī Besek'a, Ethiopia, 367 E3
Akalkot, India, 216 D2
Akanthou, Cyprus, 225 B2
Akaroa, New Zealand, 133 D6
Akaroa Harbour, New Zealand, 133 D6
Akatora, Chaine de l', mountain range, Benin, 364 E2, 327
Akbou, Algeria, 361 G1
Akbulak, Kazakhstan, 223 J3
Akçakale, Turkey, 224 E5
Akçay, Turkey, 297 G7
Akdağ, mountain peak, Turkey, 297 G6
Akelamo, Indonesia, 199 E2
Akeld, England, U.K., 306 F2
Aken, Germany, 288 F3
Åkersberga, Sweden, 287 J3
Akershus, county, Norway, 286 E3
Aketi, Democratic Republic of the Congo, 368 D2
Akhalts'ikhe, Georgia, 222 C4
Akhisar, Turkey, 224 C5
Akhmīm, Egypt, 363 F3
Akhnūr, India, 218 C2
Akhtubinsk, Russian Federation, 222 D3
Aki, Japan, 208 F4
Akiaki, island, French Polynesia, 137 H2
Akiéni, Gabon, 368 B3
Akima, river, Russian Federation, 210 G1
Akima, Russian Federation, 210 F1
Akimiski Island, Canada, 415 P5
Akita, Japan, 209 H3
Akjoujt, Mauritania, 360 D5
Akka, Morocco, 360 E3
Akkajaure, lake, Sweden, 284 H3
Akkavare, mountain peak, Sweden, 284 J3
'Akko (Acre), Israel, 225 C3, 179
Aklampa, Benin, 365 E3
Aklavik, Canada, 410 F3
Aknīste, Latvia, 287 M4
Akodia, India, 218 D5
Akoke, Sudan, 366 D3
Akola, India, 218 D5
Akom II, Cameroon, 368 B2
Akonolinga, Cameroon, 368 B2
Ākordat, Eritrea, 367 E1
Akören, Turkey, 363 F1
Akot, India, 218 D5
Akot, Sudan, 366 D3
Akoupé, Côte d'Ivoire, 364 D3

Akpatok Island, Canada, **411** N3
Akqi, China, **212** C4
Akra Lithino, Greece, **362** D2
Akranes, Iceland, **284** X7
Akrathos, Akra, *point*, Greece, **297** E5
Åkrehamn, Norway, **286** B3
Akrérèb, Niger, **365** F1
Åkrestrømmen, Norway, **286** E2
Akron, Colorado, U.S.A., **423** M1
Akron, Ohio, U.S.A., **421** N5
Akrotiri, Cyprus, **225** B2, *191*
Aksai Chin, *disputed region*, China/India, **218** D2
Aksakal, Turkey, **297** G5
Aksakovo, Bulgaria, **296** F4
Aksaray, Turkey, **224** D5
Aksay, Kazakhstan, **222** E2
Akşehir, Turkey, **224** D5
Akşehir Gölü, *lake*, Turkey, **363** F1
Akseki, Turkey, **363** F1
Aksha, Russian Federation, **210** F2
Aksu, China, **212** D4
Aksu, Kazakhstan, **222** E4
Āksum, Ethiopia, **367** E2, *90*
Aktash, Russian Federation, **223** M2
Aktau *see* Aqtaū, W. Kazakhstan, **222** E4
Aktaz, China, **212** E5
Akto, China, **212** B5
Aktyubinsk *see* Aqtöbe, Kazakhstan, **222** F2
Akūbū, Sudan, **366** D3
Akulivik, Canada, **415** Q1
Akure, Nigeria, **365** F3
Akureyri, Iceland, **284** Y7
Akutikha, Russian Federation, **223** L2
Akwa Ibon, *state*, Nigeria, **365** F4
Akwanga, Nigeria, **365** F3
Akxokesay, China, **213** F5
Akyab *see* Sittwe, Myanmar, **205** B3
Al Abyār, Libya, **362** D2
Al Ajfar, Saudi Arabia, **363** H3
Al Akhḍar, Saudi Arabia, **225** D5
Al 'Alamayn, Egypt, **362** E2
Al 'Amārah, Iraq, **363** J2
Al 'Aqabah, Jordan, **225** C5
Al 'Aqīq, Saudi Arabia, **363** H4
Al 'Arīsh, Egypt, **225** B4
Al Artāwīyah, Saudi Arabia, **363** J3
Al 'Azīzīyah, Libya, **362** B2
Al Bāb, Syria, **225** D1
Al Bad', Saudi Arabia, **225** C5
Al Badī', Saudi Arabia, **363** J4
Al Baḥr Al Aḥmar, *state*, Sudan, **363** F5
Al Balyanā, Egypt, **363** F3
Al Bardī, Libya, **362** E2
Al Barun, Sudan, **366** D2
Al Baṣrah (Basra), Iraq, **363** J2
Al Batrūn, Lebanon, **225** C2
Al Bauga, Sudan, **363** F5
Al Bawīṭī, Egypt, **362** E3
Al Bayḍā', Libya, **362** D2
Al Bayḍā', Yemen, **220** E6
Al Bi'ār, Saudi Arabia, **363** G4
Al Bi'r, Saudi Arabia, **225** D5
Al Birk, Saudi Arabia, **363** H5
Al Biyāḍ, *desert*, Saudi Arabia, **220** E4
Al Buḥayrat, *state*, Sudan, **366** C3
Al Bukayrīyah, Saudi Arabia, **363** H3
Al Burayj, Syria, **225** D2
Al Burmah, Tunisia, **362** A2
Al Buṣayyah, Iraq, **363** J2
Al Fāshir, Sudan, **366** C2
Al Fashn, Egypt, **363** F3
Al Fayyūm, Egypt, **363** F3
Al Fāzah, Yemen, **220** D6
Al Firdān, Egypt, **225** B4
Al Fujayrah, United Arab Emirates, **221** G3, *176*
Al Fūlah, Sudan, **366** C2
Al Fuqahā', Libya, **362** C3
Al Ghayḍah, Yemen, **220** F5
Al Ghurdaqah, Egypt, **363** F3
Al Ḥadīthah, Iraq, **363** H2
Al Ḥadīthah, Saudi Arabia, **225** D4
Al Ḥamdānīyah, Syria, **225** D2
Al Ḥamīdīyah, Syria, **225** C2
Al Ḥāmmah, Tunisia, **362** A2
Al Ḥammām, Egypt, **362** E2
Al Ḥammāmāt, Tunisia, **295** C7
Al Ḥamrāt, Syria, **225** D2
Al Ḥāmūl, Egypt, **225** A4
Al Ḥanākīyah, Saudi Arabia, **363** H4
Al Ḥasā, Jordan, **225** C4
Al Ḥasakah, Syria, **363** H1
Al Ḥawātah, Sudan, **366** D2
Al Ḥawjā', Saudi Arabia, **363** G3
Al Ḥawṭah, Yemen, **220** E5
Al Ḥayz, Egypt, **362** E3
Al Ḥazm, Saudi Arabia, **225** D5
Al Ḥibāk, *desert*, Saudi Arabia, **220** F5
Al Hijaz, *desert*, Saudi Arabia, **363** G3
Al Ḥillah, Iraq, **363** H2
Al Ḥillah, Sudan, **366** C2
Al Hirmil, Lebanon, **225** D2
Al Ḥiṣn, Jordan, **225** C3
Al Hoceima, Morocco, **361** F1
Al Ḥudaydah, Yemen, **220** D6
Al Hufūf, Saudi Arabia, **220** E3
Al Ḥumayḍah, Saudi Arabia, **225** C5
Al Ḥumayshah, Yemen, **220** E6
Al Īsāwīyah, Saudi Arabia, **225** D4
Al Iskandarīya (Alexandria), Egypt, **363** E2, *70, 89, 265, 316, 317*
Al Ismā'īlīyah (Ismailia), Egypt, **225** B4
Al Jafr, Jordan, **225** D4
Al Jaghbūb, Libya, **362** D3
Al Jahrā', Kuwait, **363** J3
Al Jamm, Tunisia, **362** B1
Al Jawf, Libya, **362** D4
Al Jawf, Saudi Arabia, **363** G3
Al Jazīrah, *state*, Sudan, **366** D2
Al Jithāmīyah, Saudi Arabia, **363** H3
Al Jīzah, Egypt, **225** A5, *66*
Al Jubayl, Saudi Arabia, **220** E3
Al Jumūm, Saudi Arabia, **363** G4
Al Junaynah, Sudan, **366** B2
Al Kahfah, Saudi Arabia, **363** H3
Al Kāmil, Oman, **221** G4
Al Kāmilīn, Sudan, **366** D1
Al Karak, Jordan, **225** C4
Al Karīb, Tunisia, **295** B7
Al Karnak, Egypt, **363** F3
Al Kāẓimīyah, Iraq, **363** H2
Al Khābūrah, Oman, **221** G4
Al Khalil (Hebron), West Bank, **225** C4
Al Khandaq, Sudan, **363** F5
Al Khānkah, Egypt, **225** A4
Al Kharfah, Saudi Arabia, **363** J4
Al Khārijah, Egypt, **363** F3
Al Kharj, Saudi Arabia, **220** E4
Al Kharṭūm, *state*, Sudan, **366** D1
Al Kharṭūm (Khartoum), Sudan, **366** D1, *336*
Al Kharṭūm Baḥr (Khartoum North), Sudan, **366** D1
Al Khaṭab, Oman, **221** G3
Al Khawsh, Saudi Arabia, **363** H5
Al Khufrah, Libya, **362** D4
Al Khums, Libya, **362** B2
Al Kidan, *desert*, Saudi Arabia, **221** F4
Al Kiswah, Syria, **225** D3
Al Kūfah, Iraq, **363** H2
Al Kuntillah, Egypt, **225** C5
Al Kūt, Iraq, **363** J2
Al Kuwayt (Kuwait), Kuwait, **363** J3, *177*
Al Lādhiqīyah, *district*, Syria, **225** C2
Al Lādhiqīyah (Latakia), Syria, **225** C2
Al Lagowa, Sudan, **366** C2
Al Līth, Saudi Arabia, **363** H4
Al Madāfi', *plateau*, Saudi Arabia, **225** D5
Al Madīnah (Medina), Saudi Arabia, **363** G4, *73, 90, 174*
Al Mafraq, Jordan, **225** D3
Al Maḥalla al Kubrá, Egypt, **225** A4
Al Mahrah, *mountain range*, Yemen, **220** F5
Al Majma'ah, Saudi Arabia, **363** J3
Al Manāmah, Bahrain, **220** F3, *178*
Al Manāqil, Sudan, **366** D2
Al Manṣūrah, Egypt, **225** A4
Al Manzil, Jordan, **225** D4
Al Manzilah, Egypt, **225** A4
Al Ma'qil, Iraq, **363** J2
Al Marāwi'ah, Yemen, **220** D6
Al Māriyah, Oman, **220** F4
Al Marj, Libya, **362** D2
Al Mawṣil (Mosul), Iraq, **363** H1
Al Mayādīn, Syria, **363** H2
Al Mazār, Jordan, **225** C4
Al Mazra'ah, Jordan, **225** C4
Al Metlaoui, Tunisia, **362** A2
Al Minyā, Egypt, **363** F3
Al Mismīyah, Syria, **225** D3
Al Mubarraz, Saudi Arabia, **220** E3
Al Mudawwarah, Jordan, **225** C5
Al Muglad, Sudan, **366** C2
Al Mukallā, Yemen, **220** E6
Al Mukhā, Yemen, **220** D6
Al Munastīr, Tunisia, **362** B1
Al Muqdādīyah, Iraq, **363** H2
Al Musayjīd, Saudi Arabia, **363** G4
Al Muwayh, Saudi Arabia, **363** H4
Al Qa'ābāt, Libya, **362** B2
Al Qa'āmīyāt, *physical feature*, Saudi Arabia, **367** G1
Al Qa'āmīyāt, *region*, Saudi Arabia, **220** E5
Al Qaḍārif, *state*, Sudan, **366** E2
Al Qaḍārif, Sudan, **366** E2
Al Qadīmah, Saudi Arabia, **363** G4
Al Qadmūs, Syria, **225** D2
Al Qāhirah (Cairo), Egypt, **225** A4, *316, 317*
Al Qaḥmah, Saudi Arabia, **363** H5
Al Qā'īyah, Saudi Arabia, **363** H4
Al Qalībah, Saudi Arabia, **225** D5
Al Qāmishlī, Syria, **363** H1
Al Qanṭarah, Egypt, **225** B4
Al Qaryatayn, Syria, **225** D2
Al Qaṣr, Egypt, **362** E3
Al Qaṣrayn, Tunisia, **362** A1
Al Qaṭrānah, Jordan, **225** D4
Al Qaṭrūn, Libya, **362** B4
Al Qunayṭirah, *district*, Syria, **225** C3
Al Qunayṭirah, Syria, **225** C3
Al Qunfudhah, Saudi Arabia, **363** H5
Al Qurayyāt, Saudi Arabia, **225** D4
Al Quṣayr, Egypt, **363** F3
Al Quṣaymah, Egypt, **225** C4
Al Quṭayfah, Syria, **225** D3
Al Quṭaynah, Sudan, **366** D2
Al Quwayrah, Jordan, **225** C5
Al Ṭawṭah, Yemen, **220** E6
Al Ubayyiḍ (El Obeid), Sudan, **366** D2
Al 'Ulā, Saudi Arabia, **363** G3
Al 'Ulayyah, Saudi Arabia, **363** H5
Al 'Umarī, Jordan, **225** D4
Al 'Uqaylah, Libya, **362** C2
Al Uqṣur (Luxor), Egypt, **363** F3, *317*
Al 'Urayq, *desert*, Saudi Arabia, **363** G3
Al Uthaylī, Saudi Arabia, **225** D5
Al 'Uthmānīyah, Saudi Arabia, **220** E3
Al 'Uwaynāt, E. Libya, **362** D4
Al 'Uwaynāt, W. Libya, **362** B3
Al 'Uwayqīlah, Saudi Arabia, **363** H2
Al 'Uyūn, N. Saudi Arabia, **363** H3
Al 'Uyūn, W. Saudi Arabia, **363** G4
Al Waḥdah, *province*, Sudan, **366** C3
Al Wajh, Saudi Arabia, **363** G3
Al Wāsiṭah, Egypt, **225** A5
Al Waslātīyah, Tunisia, **295** B8
Al Wazz, Sudan, **366** D2
Al Wīgh, Libya, **362** B4
Al Yamāmah, Saudi Arabia, **220** E4
Alabama, *river*, U.S.A., **425** J4
Alabama, *state*, U.S.A., **425** J3, *91, 382, 386*
Alabaster, U.S.A., **425** J3
Alaçam Dağları, *mountain range*, Turkey, **297** G6
Alachua, U.S.A., **425** L5
Aladdin, U.S.A., **419** M4
Alaejos, Spain, **292** E2
Alagoas, *state*, Brazil, **457** G2
Alagoinhas, Brazil, **457** F3
Alahärmä, Finland, **285** L5
Alajärvi, Finland, **285** L5
Alajuela, Costa Rica, **428** D5
Alaköl', *lake*, Kazakhstan, **212** D3
Alakurtti, Russian Federation, **285** Q3
Alalau, *river*, Brazil, **451** G4
Alamagan, *island*, Northern Mariana Islands, **138** C3
Ālamat'ā, Ethiopia, **367** E2
Alamdo, China, **214** E3
Alamo, U.S.A., **422** F3
Alamo Lake, U.S.A., **422** G4
Alamogordo, U.S.A., **423** L5
Alamos, Mexico, **430** C3
Alamosa, U.S.A., **423** L3
Åland *see* Ahvenanmaa, *island*, Finland, **287** J2
Åland *see* Ahvenanmaan Lääni, *province*, Finland, **287** J2
Alantika, Monts, *mountain range*, Cameroon, **365** G3
Alanya (Coracesium), Turkey, **225** A1
Alapaha, U.S.A., **425** L4
Alapayevsk, Russian Federation, **222** G1
Alarcón, Embalse de, *reservoir*, Spain, **293** F3
Alarcón, Spain, **293** F3
Alaşehir, Turkey, **297** G6
Alaska, Gulf of, U.S.A., **410** E4
Alaska, *state*, U.S.A., **410** D3, *30, 45, 60, 87, 95, 376, 382, 384, 386, 466*
Alaska Peninsula, U.S.A., **410** C4
Alaska Range, *mountain range*, U.S.A., **410** D3
Alassio, Italy, **294** B4
Älät, Azerbaijan, **222** D5
Alatri, Italy, **295** D5
Alatyr', Russian Federation, **222** D2
Alausí, Ecuador, **450** B5
Ala-Vuokki, Finland, **285** P4
Alavieska, Finland, **285** M4
Alavus, Finland, **287** L1
'Alawīyīn, Jibāl al, *mountain range*, Syria, **225** D2
Alay kyrka, *mountain range*, Kyrgyzstan/Tajikistan, **212** B5
'Ālayh, Lebanon, **225** C3
Alazeya, *river*, Russian Federation, **301** S2
Alba, Italy, **294** A3
Alba, Mount, *mountain peak*, New Zealand, **133** B7
Alba Iulia, Romania, **296** D3
Albacete, Spain, **293** G3
Ålbæk, Denmark, **286** E4
Alban, Canada, **421** N2
Albanel, Lac, *lake*, Canada, **416** E4
Albania, *country*, Europe, **282** F7, *228, 260, 261, 263, 265*
Albany, Australia, **134** D5
Albany, Kentucky, U.S.A., **425** K4
Albany, New York, U.S.A., **426** D3, *386*
Albany, New Zealand, **132** E3
Albany, Oregon, U.S.A., **418** C4
Albany, *river*, Canada, **415** N6
Albany, Texas, U.S.A., **424** C3
Albarracín, Spain, **293** G2
Albatross Bay, Australia, **135** J1
Albatross Point, Antipodes Islands, New Zealand, **133** P15
Albatross Point, North Island, New Zealand, **132** E4
Albemarle, Punta, *point*, Islas Galápagos (Galapagos Islands), Ecuador, **461** A1
Albemarle Sound, U.S.A., **426** B6
Albenga, Italy, **294** B3
Alberdi, Paraguay, **459** E3
Alberga, *river*, Australia, **135** H4
Albergaria-a-Velha, Portugal, **292** C2
Albert, France, **290** F1
Albert, Lake, Democratic Republic of the Congo/Uganda, **369** F2, *336*
Albert Canyon, Canada, **413** L6
Albert Edward, Mount, *mountain peak*, Papua New Guinea, **140** B5
Albert Lea, U.S.A., **420** G4
Alberta, Mount, *mountain peak*, Canada, **413** L5
Alberta, *province*, Canada, **413** M4, *381*
Alberta, U.S.A., **426** B6
Alberta Beach, Canada, **413** M5
Albertirsa, Hungary, **289** J5
Alberton, Canada, **417** J6
Albertville, France, **291** H4
Albertville, U.S.A., **425** J2
Albeşti, Romania, **296** F2
Albi, France, **290** F5
Albia, U.S.A., **420** G5
Albin, U.S.A., **419** M6
Albina, Ponta, *point*, Angola, **368** B6
Albina, Suriname, **452** B2
Albion, U.S.A., **419** M4
Albocácer, Spain, **293** H2
Alborán, Isla del, *island*, Spain, **293** F5
Ålborg, Denmark, **286** D4
Alborz, Reshteh-ye Kūhhā-ye, *mountain range*, Iran, **222** E5, *146*
Albox, Spain, **293** F4
Albreda, Canada, **413** K5
Albuñol, Spain, **293** F4
Albuquerque, Spain, **292** D3
Albuquerque, U.S.A., **423** K4
Albury, Australia, **135** K6
Alca, Peru, **454** D4
Alcácer do Sal, Portugal, **292** C3
Alcala, Philippines, **204** C2
Alcalá de Guadaira, Spain, **292** E4
Alcalá de Henares, Spain, **293** F2
Alcalà de Xivert, Spain, **293** H2
Alcalá la Real, Spain, **293** F4
Alcamo, Sicilia, Italy, **295** D7
Alcañices, Spain, **292** D2
Alcañiz, Spain, **293** G2
Alcántara, Embalse de, *reservoir*, Spain, **292** D3
Alcántara, Spain, **292** D3
Alcaracejos, Spain, **292** E3
Alcaraz, Spain, **293** F3
Alcaudete, Spain, **292** E4
Alcázar de San Juan, Spain, **293** F3
Alcester, England, U.K., **305** F2
Alchevs'k, Ukraine, **298** E3
Alcobaça, Brazil, **457** F4
Alcolea del Pinar, Spain, **293** F2
Alcora, Spain, **293** G2
Alcorcón, Spain, **293** F2
Alcorisa, Spain, **293** G2
Alcorta, Argentina, **458** E4
Alcoutim, Portugal, **292** D4
Alcova, U.S.A., **419** L5
Alcoy, Spain, **293** G3
Alcubierre, Sierra de, *mountain range*, Spain, **293** G2
Alcúdia, Spain, **293** J3
Aldabra Islands, Seychelles, **372** B2
Aldama, Chihuahua, Mexico, **430** D2
Aldama, Tamaulipas, Mexico, **431** F4
Aldan, *river*, Russian Federation, **301** Q4
Aldan, Russian Federation, **301** P4
Aldanskoye Nagor'ye, *mountain range*, Russian Federation, **301** P4
Alde, *river*, England, U.K., **305** J2
Aldeburgh, England, U.K., **305** J2
Aldeia Velha, Brazil, **452** C5
Alderholt, England, U.K., **305** F4
Aldermen Islands, The, New Zealand, **132** F3
Alderney, *island*, *Guernsey dependency*, English Channel, **290** C2, *279*
Aldershot, England, U.K., **305** G3

Aldersyde, Canada, **413** N6
Aldingham, England, U.K., **306** E3
Aleg, Mauritania, **364** B1
Alegranza, *island*, Islas Canarias, Spain, **373** B4
Alegre, Brazil, **457** F5
Alegre, Monte, *mountain peak*, Brazil, **452** B3
Alegre, *river*, Brazil, **456** B4
Alegrete, Brazil, **459** F3
Alejandro Korn, Argentina, **459** E5
Alekhovshchina, Russian Federation, **299** D2
Aleksandrov, Russian Federation, **299** G4
Aleksandrovac, Serbia, **296** C4
Aleksandrovo, Bulgaria, **296** E4
Aleksandry, Zemlya, *island*, Russian Federation, **300** F1
Alekseevka, Kazakhstan, **212** E2
Aleksin, Russian Federation, **299** F5
Aleksinac, Serbia, **296** C4
Ålem, Sweden, **286** H4
Além Paraíba, Brazil, **457** E5
Alèmbé, Gabon, **368** B3
Ålen, Norway, **284** E5
Alençon, France, **290** E2
Alenquer, Brazil, **452** B3
Alenuihaha Channel, Hawaiian Islands, U.S.A., **422** R9
Aleppo *see* Ḥalab, Syria, **225** D1
Aléria, Corse, France, **295** B4
Alert, Canada, **411** N1
Alert Point, Canada, **411** K1
Alerta, Peru, **454** D3
Alès, France, **291** G4
Aleşd, Romania, **296** D2
Alessandria, Italy, **294** B3
Ålesund, Norway, **286** C1
Aleutian Islands, U.S.A., **301** U4
Aleutian Range, *mountain range*, U.S.A., **410** D4
Aleutian Trench, *underwater feature*, Pacific Ocean, **478** F1
Alexander, Kansas, U.S.A., **420** D6
Alexander, North Dakota, U.S.A., **420** B2
Alexander Archipelago, *islands*, U.S.A., **412** B3
Alexander Bay, South Africa, **370** C4
Alexander City, U.S.A., **425** J3
Alexander Island, Antarctica, **470** B5
Alexandra, Cape, South Georgia, **461** A3
Alexandra, New Zealand, **133** B7
Alexandreia, Greece, **297** D5
Alexandria, Louisiana, U.S.A., **424** F4
Alexandria, Minnesota, U.S.A., **420** F3
Alexandria, Romania, **296** E4
Alexandria, Scotland, U.K., **308** E5
Alexandria *see* Al Iskandarīya, Egypt, **363** E2, *70, 89, 265, 316, 317*
Alexandria, Virginia, U.S.A., **426** B5
Alexandria Bay, U.S.A., **426** C2
Alexandrina, Lake, Australia, **135** H6
Alexandroupoli, Greece, **297** E5
Alexis, *river*, Canada, **417** N3
Alexishafen, Papua New Guinea, **140** B4
Aley, *river*, Russian Federation, **212** D1
Aleysk, Russian Federation, **212** D1
Alfambra, Spain, **293** G2
Alfarràs, Spain, **293** H2
Alfatar, Bulgaria, **296** F4
Alfeld (Leine), Germany, **288** D3
Alfenas, Brazil, **456** E5
Alford, England, U.K., **307** J4
Alfreton, England, U.K., **305** F1
Ålgård, Norway, **286** B3
Algarrobo, Chile, **458** B3
Algarrobo del Aguila, Argentina, **458** C5
Algarve, *region*, Portugal, **292** C2, *250, 251*
Algeciras, Spain, **292** E4
Algena, Eritrea, **220** C5
Alger (Algiers), Algeria, **361** G1, *314*
Alger, U.S.A., **421** L3
Algeria, *country*, Africa, **358** E4, *87, 95, 244, 312, 313, 314, 315, 355*
Alghero, Sardegna, Italy, **295** B5
Algiers *see* Alger, Algeria, **361** G1, *314*
Algoa Bay, South Africa, **371** E5
Algodonales, Spain, **292** E4
Algoma, U.S.A., **421** K3
Algona, U.S.A., **420** F4
Alhama de Granada, Spain, **293** F4
Alhambra, Spain, **293** F3
'Ali Sabieh, Djibouti, **367** F2
Alia, Sicilia, Italy, **295** D7
Aliağa, Turkey, **297** F6
Aliakmonas, Limni, *lake*, Greece, **297** D5
Aliartos, Greece, **297** D6
Alibunar, Serbia, **296** C3
Alicante, Spain, **293** G3
Alice, Punta, *point*, Italy, **295** F6
Alice, U.S.A., **424** C6
Alice Springs, Australia, **134** G3
Aliceville, U.S.A., **425** H3
Alicudi, Isola, *island*, Italy, **295** E6
Alīgarh, India, **218** D4
Alimia, *island*, Dodekanisos, Greece, **297** F7
Alindao, Central African Republic, **368** D1
Alingsås, Sweden, **286** F4
Alīpur, Pakistan, **218** B3
Alīpur Duar, India, **219** G4
Aliseda, Spain, **292** D3
Aliveri, Greece, **297** E6
Aliwal North, South Africa, **371** E5
Aljezur, Portugal, **292** C4
Aljustrel, Portugal, **292** C4
Alkali Lake, U.S.A., **418** E5
Alkamari, Niger, **365** G2
Alkmaar, Netherlands, **288** B2
Allagadda, India, **216** D3
Allagash, *river*, U.S.A., **416** G6
Allahābād, India, **219** E4
Allakaket, U.S.A., **410** D3
Alldays, South Africa, **371** E3
Allegheny, *river*, U.S.A., **421** P5
Allegheny Mountains, *mountain range*, U.S.A., **421** N6
Allen, Lough, *lake*, Ireland, **309** D3
Allen, Mount, *mountain peak*, New Zealand, **133** A8
Allen, Philippines, **204** D3
Allendale, U.S.A., **425** M3
Allendale Town, England, U.K., **306** F3
Allende, Coahuila, Mexico, **431** E2
Allende, Nuevo Léon, Mexico, **431** E3
Allenford, Canada, **421** N3
Allenheads, England, U.K., **306** F3
Allentown, U.S.A., **426** C4
Alleppey, India, **216** D4
Allepuz, Spain, **293** G2
Aller, *river*, Germany, **288** D2
Allgäuer Alpen, *mountain range*, Germany/Austria, **288** E5
Alliance, Suriname, **452** B2
Alliance, U.S.A., **420** B4
Allier, *river*, France, **291** F3
Allihies, Ireland, **309** B6
Allinagaram, India, **216** D4
Allinge-Sandvig, Denmark, **286** G5
Alloa, Scotland, U.K., **308** F4
Alma, Canada, **416** F5
Alma, Georgia, U.S.A., **425** L4
Alma, Michigan, U.S.A., **421** L4
Alma, Nebraska, U.S.A., **420** D5
Almáciga, Islas Canarias, Spain, **373** A4
Almada, Portugal, **292** C3
Almadén, Spain, **292** E3
Almagro, Spain, **293** F3
Almansa, Spain, **293** G3
Almanzor, *mountain peak*, Spain, **292** E2
Almas, Brazil, **456** D3
Almaty, Kazakhstan, **212** C4, *270*
Almaty, *province*, Kazakhstan, **212** C3
Almazán, Spain, **293** F2
Almeirim, Brazil, **452** C3
Almeirim, Portugal, **292** C3
Almenar de Soria, Spain, **293** F2
Almenara, Brazil, **457** F4
Almendra, Embalse de, *reservoir*, Spain, **292** D2
Almendralejo, Spain, **292** D3
Almería, Golfo de, *gulf*, Spain, **293** F4
Almería, Spain, **293** F4
Almese, Italy, **294** A3
Al'met'yevsk, Russian Federation, **222** E2
Älmhult, Sweden, **286** G4
Almina, Punta, *point*, Morocco, **292** E5
Almodôvar, Portugal, **292** C4
Almodóvar del Campo, Spain, **292** E3
Almont, U.S.A., **421** M4
Almonte, Canada, **416** C7
Almora, India, **218** D3
Almoustarat, Mali, **364** E1
Älmsta, Sweden, **287** J3
Almunge, Sweden, **287** J3
Almyros, Greece, **297** D6
Alnön, *island*, Sweden, **287** H1
Alnwick, England, U.K., **307** G2
Alofi, *island*, Wallis and Futuna, **139** G6, *127*
Alofi, Niue, **132** M13, *124*
Alofi Bay, Niue, **132** M13
Aloja, Latvia, **287** M4
Alolya, *river*, Russian Federation, **299** B4
Alongshan, China, **211** H2
Alonnisos, *island*, Voreioi Sporades, Greece, **297** D6
Alor, *island*, Indonesia, **198** D5
Alor, Kepulauan, *islands*, Indonesia, **198** D5
Alor, *mountain peak*, Spain, **292** D3
Alor Setar, Malaysia, **200** C1
Alot, India, **218** C5
Alotau, Papua New Guinea, **140** C5
Alpalhão, Portugal, **292** D3
Alpena, U.S.A., **421** M3
Alpercatas, *river*, Brazil, **452** E5
Alpes, *mountain range*, France, **291** H4
Alpha, Australia, **135** K3
Alphonse Island, Seychelles, **372** C2
Alpine, Arizona, U.S.A., **423** J5
Alpine, Texas, U.S.A., **423** M6
Alps, *mountain range*, Austria/Italy/Switzerland, **280** E6, *20, 23, 24, 89, 100, 228, 239, 245, 247, 248, 249, 255*
Alsace, *administrative region*, France, **291** H2
Alsace, *region*, France, **291** H2, *245*
Alsager, England, U.K., **304** E1
Alsasua, Spain, **293** F1
Alsfeld, Germany, **288** D3
Ålstad, Norway, **284** G3
Alsten, *island*, Norway, **284** F4
Alsterbo, Sweden, **286** G4
Alston, England, U.K., **306** F3
Alsunga, Latvia, **287** K4
Alta, Norway, **285** L2
Alta, *river*, Brazil, **459** F3
Alta Floresta, Brazil, **456** B2
Alta Gracia, Argentina, **458** D4
Altaelva, *river*, Norway, **285** L2
Altamah, *river*, U.S.A., **425** L4
Altamira, Brazil, **452** C4
Altamira, Chile, **458** C2
Altamira, Colombia, **450** C3
Altamira, Costa Rica, **428** D5
Altamont, U.S.A., **418** D5
Altamura, Isla de, *island*, Mexico, **430** C3
Altamura, Italy, **295** F5
Altan, Mongolia, **213** G2
Altanbulag, Mongolia, **213** H2
Altanteel, Mongolia, **213** G3
Altar, Mexico, **430** C2
Altata, Mexico, **430** D4
Altavista, U.S.A., **421** P7
Altay, China, **212** F3
Altay, Dzavhan, Mongolia, **213** H2
Altay, Govĭ-Altay, Mongolia, **213** H3
Altay, *mountain range*, Asia, **212** E2, *185*
Altay, Respublika, *republic*, Russian Federation, **212** E2
Altay, Russian Federation, **300** K5
Altayskiy, Russian Federation, **212** E2
Altayskiy Kray, *territory*, Russian Federation, **212** D1
Altea, Spain, **293** G3
Alteidet, Norway, **285** L1
Altenburg, Germany, **288** F3
Altentreptow, Germany, **288** F2
Alter do Chão, Portugal, **292** D3
Altevatnet, *lake*, Norway, **284** J2
Altınoluk, Turkey, **297** F6
Altınova, Turkey, **297** F6
Altıntaş, Turkey, **297** H6
Altiplano, *plateau*, Bolivia/Peru, **455** E4, *441*
Altkirch, France, **291** H3
Altnaharra, Scotland, U.K., **308** E2
Alto, U.S.A., **424** E4
Alto Araguaia, Brazil, **456** C4
Alto Chicapa, Angola, **368** C5
Alto de Pencoso, Sierra de, *mountain range*, Argentina, **458** C4
Alto Garças, Brazil, **456** C4
Alto Longá, Brazil, **453** E4
Alto Molócuè, Mozambique, **369** G6
Alto Parnaíba, Brazil, **452** E5
Alto Purús, *river*, Peru, **454** D3
Alto Río Senguer, Argentina, **460** C2
Alto Sucuriú, Brazil, **456** C5
Alto Vista, *mountain peak*, Aruba, **461** B3
Alton, England, U.K., **305** G3
Alton, Missouri, U.S.A., **420** H7
Alton, Utah, U.S.A., **422** G3
Altona, Canada, **414** F7
Altoona, U.S.A., **421** P5
Altos, Brazil, **453** E4
Altötting, Germany, **288** F4
Altraga, Mongolia, **213** H2
Altrincham, England, U.K., **306** F4
Altun Shan, *mountain range*, China, **212** E5
Alturas, U.S.A., **418** D6
Altus, U.S.A., **424** C2
Alu *see* Shortland, *island*, Solomon Islands, **141** A1
Alūksne, Latvia, **287** N4
Alūr, India, **216** D3
Alva, U.S.A., **420** D7
Älvängen, Sweden, **286** F4
Alvarães, Brazil, **451** F5
Alvdal, Norway, **286** E1
Älvdalen, Sweden, **286** G2
Alveley, England, U.K., **304** E2
Alvesta, Sweden, **286** G4
Ålvik, Norway, **286** C2
Alvin, U.S.A., **424** E5
Älvkarleby, Sweden, **287** H2
Älvsborg, *county*, Sweden, **286** F4
Älvsbyn, Sweden, **284** K4
Alwar, India, **218** D4
Alxa Zuoqi, China, **210** D5
Alyth, Scotland, U.K., **308** F4
Alytus, Lithuania, **287** M5
Alzamay, Russian Federation, **223** P1
Alzira, Spain, **293** G3
Am-Dam, Chad, **366** B2
Am Timan, Chad, **366** B2
Am-Zoer, Chad, **366** B2
Amada Gaza, Central African Republic, **368** C2
Amadeus, Lake, Australia, **134** G3
Amadjuak Lake, Canada, **411** M3
Amado, U.S.A., **423** H6
Amadora, Portugal, **292** C3
Amagasaki, Japan, **209** F4
Amager, *island*, Denmark, **286** F5
Amahai, Indonesia, **199** E3
Amakusa-shotō, *islands*, Japan, **208** E4
Åmål, Sweden, **286** F3
Amalfi, Colombia, **450** C2
Amalfi, Italy, **295** E5
Amaliada, Greece, **297** C7
Amamapare, Indonesia, **199** G4
Amambaí, Brazil, **459** F2
Amambaí, *river*, Brazil, **459** F2
Amambaí, Serra de, *mountain range*, Brazil/Paraguay, **459** F2
Amamĭshotō, *islands*, Japan, **209** P8
Amamula, Democratic Republic of the Congo, **369** E3
Amanab, Papua New Guinea, **140** A3
Amangeldi, Kazakhstan, **222** H2
Amanqaraghay, Kazakhstan, **222** G2
Amantea, Italy, **295** F6
Amantogay, Kazakhstan, **222** H2
Amanu, *island*, French Polynesia, **137** G2
Amanzimtoti, South Africa, **371** F5
Amapá, Brazil, **452** C2
Amapá, *state*, Brazil, **452** C3
Amapari, *river*, Brazil, **452** C3
Amarante, Brazil, **453** E5
Amarante do Maranhão, Brazil, **452** D4
Amaranth, Canada, **414** E6
Amarapura, Myanmar, **205** C3
Amargosa Valley, U.S.A., **422** E3
Amarillo, U.S.A., **424** B2
Amarkantak, India, **219** E5
Amarnāth, India, **216** C2
Amaro, Monte, *mountain peak*, Italy, **295** E4
Amasya, Turkey, **224** E4
Amatán, Mexico, **431** G5
Amatlán de Cañas, Mexico, **430** D4
Amatrice, Italy, **294** D4
Amaturá, Brazil, **451** E5
Amazon Basin, South America, **446** F4, *439, 441*
Amazon Fan, *underwater feature*, Atlantic Ocean, **477** D5
Amazonas, *river*, Brazil/Peru, **447** G4, *43, 88, 94, 95, 434, 439, 440*
Amazonas, *state*, Brazil, **451** F5
Āmba Ālagē, *mountain peak*, Ethiopia, **367** E2
Amba Farit, *mountain peak*, Ethiopia, **367** E2
Ambāla, India, **218** D3
Ambāla Sadar, India, **218** D3
Ambalakida, Madagascar, **372** B4
Ambalavao, Madagascar, **372** B5
Ambam, Cameroon, **368** B2
Ambanja, Madagascar, **372** B3
Ambarnyy, Russian Federation, **285** R4
Ambato, Ecuador, **450** B4
Ambato Boeny, Madagascar, **372** B4
Ambatofinandrahana, Madagascar, **372** B5
Ambatolampy, Madagascar, **372** B4
Ambatomainty, Madagascar, **372** B4
Ambatondrazaka, Madagascar, **372** B4
Ambazac, France, **290** E4
Amberg, Germany, **288** E4
Amberg, U.S.A., **421** K3
Ambérieu-en-Bugey, France, **291** G3
Amberley, New Zealand, **133** D6
Ambert, France, **291** F4
Ambidédi, Mali, **364** B2
Ambikāpur, India, **219** E5
Ambilobe, Madagascar, **372** B3
Amble, England, U.K., **307** G2
Ambleside, England, U.K., **306** F3
Ambo, Peru, **454** C3
Amboasary, Madagascar, **372** B6
Ambohidratrimo, Madagascar, **372** B4
Ambohimahasoa, Madagascar, **372** B5
Ambohipaky, Madagascar, **372** A4
Ambohitra, *mountain peak*, Madagascar, **372** B3
Amboise, France, **290** E3
Ambon, Indonesia, **199** E3, *76, 93*
Amborompotsy, Madagascar, **372** B5
Ambositra, Madagascar, **372** B5
Ambovombe, Madagascar, **372** B6

Amboy, U.S.A., **422** F4
Ambre, Cap d', *see* Bobaomby, Tanjona, Madagascar, **372** B3
Ambre, Île d', *island*, Mauritius, **373** C1
Ambriz, Angola, **368** B4
Ambrym, *island*, Vanuatu, **141** A2
Ambuaki, Indonesia, **199** F3
Amchitka Island, Aleutian Islands, U.S.A., **408** E3
Amdo, China, **214** D2
Ameca, Mexico, **430** D4
Ameland, *island*, Netherlands, **288** B2
American Falls, U.S.A., **418** H5
American Falls Reservoir, U.S.A., **418** H5
American Fork, U.S.A., **423** H1
American Samoa, *U.S. territory*, Pacific Ocean, **131** H3, *108, 113, 121, 123, 386*
Americana, Brazil, **459** H2
Americus, U.S.A., **425** K3
Amersfoort, Netherlands, **288** B2
Amersham, England, U.K., **305** G3
Amery Ice Shelf, Antarctica, **470** F5
Ames, U.S.A., **420** G4
Amesbury, England, U.K., **305** F3
Amfilochia, Greece, **297** C6
Amfissa, Greece, **297** D6
Amga, *river*, Russian Federation, **301** Q4
Amgalang Bulag, China, **211** G2
Amgu, Russian Federation, **209** G1
Amguid, Algeria, **361** H3
Amgun', *river*, Russian Federation, **211** L2
Amherst, Canada, **417** J7
Amiata, Monte, *mountain peak*, Italy, **294** C4
Amidon, U.S.A., **420** B2
Amiens, France, **290** F2
Amindivi Islands, India, **216** C4
Amino, Ethiopia, **369** H2
Aminuis, Namibia, **370** C3
Amirante Isles, Seychelles, **372** C2
Amisk Lake, Canada, **414** C4
Amite, U.S.A., **424** G4
Amla, India, **218** D5
Amlamé, Togo, **364** E3
Åmli, Norway, **286** D3
Amlia Island, Aleutian Islands, U.S.A., **408** F3
Amlwch, Wales, U.K., **306** D4
'Ammān, Jordan, **225** D4, *180*
Ammanford, Wales, U.K., **304** C3
Ammarnäs, Sweden, **284** H4
Ammassalik, Greenland, **411** R3
Ammersee, *lake*, Germany, **288** E4
Ammochostos (Famagusta), Cyprus, **225** B2, *191*
Ammochostos Bay, Cyprus, **225** C2, *191*
Amnat Charoen, Thailand, **203** E3
Amok, Vanuatu, **141** A2
Amolar, Brazil, **456** B5
Amontada, Brazil, **453** F4
Amorgos, *island*, Kyklades, Greece, **297** E7
Amory, U.S.A., **425** H2
Amos, Canada, **416** B5
Åmot, Norway, **286** D3
Åmot, Sweden, **286** H2
Åmotfors, Sweden, **286** F3
Amourj, Mauritania, **364** C1
Ampahana, Madagascar, **372** C3
Ampanavoana, Madagascar, **372** C4
Ampanefena, Madagascar, **372** B3
Ampanihy, Madagascar, **372** A5
Amparafaravola, Madagascar, **372** B4
Amparai, Sri Lanka, **217** E5
Amparo, Brazil, **459** H2
Ampasimanjeva, Madagascar, **372** B5
Ampasimanolotra, Madagascar, **372** B4
Ampato, Nevado, *mountain peak*, Peru, **454** D4
Ampelonas, Greece, **297** D6
Amper, *river*, Germany, **288** E4
Ampisikinana, Madagascar, **372** B3
Amposta, Spain, **293** H2
Ampthill, England, U.K., **305** G2
Amqui, Canada, **416** H5
'Amrān, Yemen, **220** D5
Amrāvati, India, **218** D5
Amreli, India, **218** B5
Amritsar, India, **218** C3
Åmsele, Sweden, **284** J4
Amstein, Germany, **288** D4
Amsterdam, Île, *island*, French Southern and Antarctic Islands, **104** E12, *469*
Amsterdam, Netherlands, **288** B2, *54, 80, 94, 240, 241*
Amstetten, Austria, **289** G4
Amu Darya, *river*, Turkmenistan/Uzbekistan, **222** G5, *184, 187*
Amund Ringnes Island, Canada, **411** K2
Amundsen, Mount, *mountain peak*, Antarctica, **470** G5
Amundsen Gulf, Canada, **410** G2
Amundsen-Scott, *U.S. research station*, Antarctica, **470** D5
Amundsen Sea, Antarctica, **470** A6
Amuntai, Indonesia, **201** F3
Amur, *river*, Russian Federation, **195** Q5, *145*
Amurang, Teluk, *bay*, Indonesia, **198** C2
Amurrio, Spain, **293** F1
Amursk, Russian Federation, **211** M2
Amurskaya Oblast', *province*, Russian Federation, **211** K1
Amurzet, Russian Federation, **211** K3
Amvrakikos Kolpos, *bay*, Greece, **297** C6
Amyntaio, Greece, **297** C5
Amyot, Canada, **421** L1
Amyūn, Lebanon, **225** C2
An Hai, Vietnam, **203** F3
An Nabatīyah at Taḥtā, Lebanon, **225** C3
An Nabk, Syria, **225** D3
An Nafūd, *desert*, Saudi Arabia, **363** H3, , *174*
An Nahūd, Sudan, **366** C2
An Najaf, Iraq, **363** H2
An Nakhl, Egypt, **225** B5
An Nāqūrah, Lebanon, **225** C3
An Nāṣirīyah, Iraq, **363** J2
An Nawfalīyah, Libya, **362** C2
An Nīl Al Abyaḍ, *state*, Sudan, **366** D2
An Nimāṣ, Saudi Arabia, **363** H5
An Nu'ayrīyah, Saudi Arabia, **220** E3
An Teallach, *mountain peak*, Scotland, U.K., **308** D3
Anaco, Venezuela, **451** F2
Anaconda, U.S.A., **418** H3
Anacortes, U.S.A., **418** C2
Anadarko, U.S.A., **424** C2
Anadyr', Russian Federation, **301** U3
Anadyrskiy Zaliv, *bay*, Russian Federation, **410** A3
Anadyrskoye Ploskogor'ye, *plateau*, Russian Federation, **301** T3
Anafi, *island*, Kyklades, Greece, **297** E7
Anagé, Brazil, **457** F4
'Ānah, Iraq, **363** H2
Anaheim, U.S.A., **422** D5
Anahola, Hawaiian Islands, U.S.A., **422** R9
Anajás, Brazil, **452** D3
Anajás, Ilha, *island*, Brazil, **452** C3
Anakāpalle, India, **217** E2
Analalava, Madagascar, **372** B3
Anamã, Brazil, **451** G5
Anambas, Kepulauan, *islands*, Indonesia, **200** D2
Anambra, *state*, Nigeria, **365** F3
Anamu, *river*, Brazil, **452** B3
Anamur, Turkey, **225** B1
Anamur Burnu, *cape*, Turkey, **363** F1
Anan, Japan, **208** F4
Ānand, India, **218** C5
Ānandpur, India, **219** F5
Ananea, Peru, **455** E4
Anantapur, India, **216** D3
Anantnāg, India, **218** C2
Anan'yiv, Ukraine, **296** H2
Anapa, Russian Federation, **298** E4
Anápolis, Brazil, **456** D4
Anār, Iran, **221** G2
Anār Darreh, Afghanistan, **221** H2
Anārak, Iran, **220** F2
Anare Station, Macquarie Island, **134** R11
Anarjokka, *river*, Norway, **285** M2
Ånäset, Sweden, **284** K4
Anatahan, *island*, Northern Mariana Islands, **138** C3
Anatolia, *region*, Turkey, **194** E6, *70, 87, 88, 91, 146, 191*
Anatoliki Makedonia Kai Thraki, *administrative region*, Greece, **297** E5
Anatom, *island*, Vanuatu, **141** A3
Anatone, U.S.A., **418** F3
Añatuya, Argentina, **458** D3
Anauá, *river*, Brazil, **451** G4
Anbianbu, China, **210** E5
Anbo, China, **211** H5
Ancasti, Sierra de, *mountain range*, Argentina, **458** D3
Anchau, Nigeria, **365** F2
Anchopaya, Bolivia, **455** E4
Anchorage, U.S.A., **410** E3
Anchorstock Point, Tristan da Cunha, **373** C2
Ancón, Peru, **454** C3
Ancón de Sardinas, Bahía de, *bay*, Ecuador, **450** B4
Ancona, Italy, **294** D4
Ancroft, England, U.K., **306** G2
Ancuabe, Mozambique, **369** G5
Ancud, Chile, **460** C1
Ancud, Golfo de, *gulf*, Chile, **460** C2
Anda, China, **211** J3
Andacollo, Chile, **458** B4
Andahuaylas, Peru, **454** D3
Andalgalá, Argentina, **458** C3
Andalucia, *autonomous community*, Spain, **293** F4
Andalusia, U.S.A., **425** J4
Andaman and Nicobar Islands, India, Indian Ocean, **217** G3
Andaman and Nicobar Islands, *union territory*, India, Indian Ocean, **217** H4
Andaman Basin, *underwater feature*, Indian Ocean, **476** F4
Andaman Islands, Andaman and Nicobar Islands, India, **217** H4, *169*
Andaman Sea, Indian Ocean, **202** B3, *155, 157*
Andamarca, Bolivia, **455** E5
Andance, France, **291** G4
Andapa, Madagascar, **372** B3
Andaraí, Brazil, **457** F3
Andenes, Norway, **284** H2
Andéramboukane, Mali, **365** E1
Andermatt, Switzerland, **291** J3
Andernach, Germany, **288** C3
Anderson, Indiana, U.S.A., **421** L5
Anderson, *river*, Canada, **410** G3
Anderson, South Carolina, U.S.A., **425** L2
Andes, Colombia, **450** C3
Andes, *mountain range*, South America, **447** E4, *23, 54, 63, 64, 68, 87, 88, 89, 90, 96, 434, 436, 437, 438, 441, 442, 465*
Andfjorden, *bay*, Norway, **284** H2
Andhra Pradesh, *state*, India, **216** D2, *169*
Andijon, Uzbekistan, **212** B4
Andilamena, Madagascar, **372** B4
Andilanatoby, Madagascar, **372** B4
Andīmeshk, Iran, **220** E2
Andkhvoy, Afghanistan, **218** A1
Andoas, Peru, **450** C5
Andoga, *river*, Russian Federation, **299** F3
Andomskiy Pogost, Russian Federation, **299** F2
Andong, South Korea, **208** E3
Andoom, Australia, **140** A6
Andorra, *country*, Europe, **282** D7, *228, 250, 251, 252*
Andorra la Vella, Andorra, **293** H1, *251*
Andover, England, U.K., **305** F3
Andøya, *island*, Norway, **284** G2
Andradina, Brazil, **456** C5
Andranopasy, Madagascar, **372** A5
Andranovondronina, Madagascar, **372** B3
Andranovory, Madagascar, **372** A5
Andratx, Spain, **293** J3
Andreanof Islands, U.S.A., **301** V4
Andreapol', Russian Federation, **299** D4
Andreas, Cape, Cyprus, **225** C2
Andrelândia, Brazil, **457** E5
Andrews, U.S.A., **423** M5
Andreyevskoye, Russian Federation, **299** F5
Andria, Italy, **295** F5
Andriamena, Madagascar, **372** B4
Androka, Madagascar, **372** A6
Andropov *see* Rybinsk, Russian Federation, **299** G3
Andros, *island*, Kyklades, Greece, **297** E7
Andros Island, Bahamas, **428** F1
Andros Town, Bahamas, **428** F1
Āndrott Island, India, **216** C4
Andselv, Norway, **284** J2
Andujar, Spain, **292** E3
Andulo, Angola, **368** C5
Andun, China, **207** D2
Anéfis, Mali, **364** E1
Anegada, Bahía, *bay*, Argentina, **460** E1
Anegada, *island*, U.K. Virgin Islands, **427** C2, *388*
Anegada Passage, Caribbean Sea, **427** C2
Anécho, Togo, **364** E3
Anelghowhat, Vanuatu, **141** A3
Anepahan, Philippines, **204** B4
Aneto, Pico de, *mountain peak*, Spain, **293** H1
Aney, Niger, **362** B5
Anfu, China, **206** C3
Ang Mo Kio, Singapore, **200** K6
Ang Thong, Thailand, **202** D3
Angadoka, Lohatanjona, *cape*, Madagascar, **372** B3
Angamāli, India, **216** D4
Angara, *river*, Russian Federation, **210** C1
Angara-Débou, Benin, **365** E2
Angarsk, Russian Federation, **210** C1
Angatuba, Brazil, **459** H2
Ånge, Sweden, **286** G1
Ángel de la Guarda, Isla, *island*, Mexico, **430** B2
Angeles, Philippines, **204** C3, *50*
Ängelholm, Sweden, **286** F4
Angelica, U.S.A., **421** J3
Angelina, *river*, U.S.A., **424** E4
Angemuk, Gunung, *mountain peak*, Indonesia, **199** G3
Angermünde, Germany, **289** G2
Ångermanälven, *river*, Sweden, **284** H5
Angers, France, **290** D3
Ängersån, *river*, Sweden, **285** L3
Ängesön, *island*, Sweden, **284** K5
Angical, Brazil, **457** E3
Ângk Tasaôm, Cambodia, **203** E4
Anglem, Mount, *mountain peak*, New Zealand, **133** A8
Anglesey, *island*, Wales, U.K., **306** D4
Angleton, U.S.A., **424** E5
Angliers, Canada, **421** P2
Angmering, England, U.K., **305** G4
Ango, Democratic Republic of the Congo, **369** E2
Angoche, Mozambique, **369** G6
Angohrān, Iran, **221** G3
Angol, Chile, **458** B5
Angola, *country*, Africa, **359** G8, *92, 312, 313, 334, 335*
Angola Basin, *underwater feature*, Atlantic Ocean, **477** H6
Angora, U.S.A., **420** B5
Angoram, Papua New Guinea, **140** B4
Angoulême, France, **290** E4
Angra do Heroísmo, Azores, Portugal, **360** M7
Angu, Democratic Republic of the Congo, **368** D2
Anguang, China, **211** H3
Anguilla, *U.K. dependency*, Caribbean Sea, **427** D2, *276, 378, 387, 395*
Anguille, Cape, Canada, **417** L6
Angus, *local authority*, Scotland, U.K., **308** F4
Anhanduí, *river*, Brazil, **456** B5
Anholt, *island*, Denmark, **286** E4
Anhua, China, **206** B2
Anhui, *province*, China, **206** D1, *161*
Anhumas, Brazil, **456** B4
Anicuns, Brazil, **456** D4
Anie, Pic d', *mountain peak*, France, **293** G1
Anierin, Slieve, *mountain peak*, Ireland, **309** E3
Animas Peak, *mountain peak*, U.S.A., **423** J6
Anina, Romania, **296** C3
Aninīy, Philippines, **204** C4
Aniva, Mys, *cape*, Russian Federation, **301** R5
Aniva Zaliv, *bay*, Russian Federation, **209** H1
Anivorano Avaratra, Madagascar, **372** B3
Anjār, India, **218** B5
Anjiang, China, **206** B3
Anjouan *see* Nzwani, Comoros, **372** A3, *352*
Anju, North Korea, **208** D3
Ankaboa, Tanjona, *cape*, Madagascar, **372** A5
Ankang, China, **206** B1
Ankara, Turkey, **224** D5, *146, 190*
Ankavia, *river*, Madagascar, **372** B4
Ankazoabo, Madagascar, **372** A5
Ankazobe, Madagascar, **372** B4
Ankeny, U.S.A., **420** G5
Anklam, Germany, **288** F2
Ankola, India, **216** C3
Ankoro, Democratic Republic of the Congo, **369** E4
Ankou, China, **215** H2
Ankpa, Nigeria, **365** F3
Anlaby, England, U.K., **307** H4
Anloga, Ghana, **364** E3
Anlong, China, **215** H4
Anlu, China, **206** C2
Ann Arbor, U.S.A., **421** M4
Anna, Lake, U.S.A., **426** B5
Anna Pink, Bahía, *bay*, Chile, **460** B2
Anna Regina, Guyana, **451** G2
Annaba, Algeria, **361** H1
Annaburroo, Australia, **134** G1
Annai, Guyana, **451** G3
Annalee, *river*, Ireland, **309** E3
Annamitique, Chaîne, *mountain range*, Laos/Vietnam, **203** E2, *154*
Annan, Scotland, U.K., **308** F6
Annapolis, Maryland, U.S.A., **426** B5, *386*
Annapolis, Missouri, U.S.A., **420** H7
Annapolis Royal, Canada, **416** J7
Annapurna, *mountain peak*, Nepal, **219** E3
Anndalsvågen, Norway, **284** F4
Annecy, France, **291** H4
Annelund, Sweden, **286** F4
Annemasse, France, **291** H3
Annenkov Island, South Georgia, **461** A3
Annenskiy Most, Russian Federation, **299** F2
Anning, China, **215** G4
Annino, Russian Federation, **299** F3
Anniston, U.S.A., **425** K3
Annobón, *island*, Equatorial Guinea, **365** F5
Annot, France, **291** H5
Ånnsjön, *lake*, Sweden, **284** F5
Ano Viannos, Kriti, Greece, **297** E8
Anori, Brazil, **451** G5
Anosibe an'Ala, Madagascar, **372** B4
Anould, France, **291** H2
Anping, China, **211** H4
Anpu, China, **206** B4
Anpu Gang, *harbor*, China, **203** F1
Anqing, China, **206** D2
Ansai, China, **210** E5

Ansbach, Germany, **288** E4
Anse Boileau, Seychelles, **373** A2
Anse Royal, Seychelles, **373** A2
Anselmo, U.S.A., **420** D5
Anshan, China, **211** H4
Anshun, China, **215** H4
Ansina, Uruguay, **459** F4
Ansley, U.S.A., **420** D5
Anson, U.S.A., **424** C3
Anson Point, Norfolk Island, **135** T13
Ansongo, Mali, **364** E1
Anston, England, U.K., **307** G4
Anstruther, Scotland, U.K., **308** G4
Ansudu, Indonesia, **199** G3
Ant, *river*, England, U.K., **305** J2
Anta, Peru, **454** D3
Antabamba, Peru, **454** D4
Antakya (Antioch), Turkey, **225** D1
Antalaha, Madagascar, **372** C3
Antalya, *province*, Turkey, **297** G7
Antalya, Turkey, **224** D5
Antalya Körfezi, *gulf*, Turkey, **224** D5
Antanambao Manampotsy, Madagascar, **372** B4
Antananarivo, Madagascar, **372** B4, *353*
Antananarivo, *province*, Madagascar, **372** B4
Antanimora Atsimo, Madagascar, **372** B5
Antarctic Peninsula, Antarctica, **470** A3, *464, 465*
Antecume Pata, French Guiana, **452** B2
Antelope, U.S.A., **418** D4
Antequera, Spain, **292** E4
Anthony, U.S.A., **423** K5
Anti Atlas, *mountain range*, Morocco, **360** E3
Anticosti, Île d', *island*, Canada, **417** K5
Antifer, Cap d', *cape*, France, **290** D2
Antigo, U.S.A., **421** J3
Antigua, *island*, Antigua and Barbuda, **427** D2, *378, 395*
Antigua, Islas Canarias, Spain, **373** B4
Antigua and Barbuda, *country*, Caribbean Sea, **427** D2, *378, 395, 396*
Antiguo Morelos, Mexico, **431** F4
Antikyra, Greece, **297** D6
Antikythira, *island*, Greece, **297** D8
Antikythiro, Steno, *strait*, Kriti, Greece, **297** D8
Antioch, U.S.A., **420** B4
Antioch *see* Antakya, Turkey, **22**, D1
Antioche, Pertuis d', *strait*, France, **290** D3
Antioquia, Colombia, **450** C2
Antiparos, *island*, Kyklades, Greece, **297** E7
Antipaxoi, *island*, Ionioi Nisoi, Greece, **297** B6
Antipayuta, Russian Federation, **300** J3
Antipodes Island, Antipodes Islands, New Zealand, **133** P15
Antipodes Islands, New Zealand, **133** P15
Antisana, Volcán, *mountain peak*, Ecuador, **450** B4
Antlers, U.S.A., **424** E2
Antnäs, Sweden, **284** K4
Antofagasta, *administrative region*, Chile, **458** C2
Antofagasta, Chile, **458** B2
Antofagasta de la Sierra, Argentina, **458** C3
Antofalla, Volcán, *mountain peak*, Argentina, **458** C2
Antón, Panama, **429** E5
Anton, U.S.A., **423** M2
Antonio de Biedma, Argentina, **460** D3
Antrain, France, **290** D2
Antrim, *district*, Northern Ireland, U.K., **309** F3
Antrim, Northern Ireland, U.K., **309** F3
Antrim Mountains, *mountain range*, Northern Ireland, U.K., **309** F3
Antsalova, Madagascar, **372** A4
Antsirabe, Madagascar, **372** B4
Antsirañana, Madagascar, **372** B3
Antsirañana, *province*, Madagascar, **372** B3
Antsla, Estonia, **287** N4
Antsohihy, Madagascar, **372** B3
Anttis, Sweden, **285** L3
Antu, China, **211** K4
Antuco, Chile, **458** B5
Antuerpia, Brazil, **455** F3
Antwerp *see* Antwerpen, Belgium, **288** B3, *54, 80, 241, 242*
Antwerpen (Antwerp, Anvers), Belgium, **288** B3, *54, 80, 241, 242*
Antwerpen, *province*, Belgium, **288** B3
Anuanuraro, *island*, French Polynesia, **137** G3
Anuanurunga, *island*, French Polynesia, **137** G3
Anuchino, Russian Federation, **211** L4
Angul, India, **219** F5
Anūpgarh, India, **218** C3
Anuradhapura, Sri Lanka, **216** E4
Anuta, *island*, Solomon Islands, **139** E6
Anvers *see* Antwerp, Belgium, **288** B3, *54, 80, 241, 242*
Anxi, China, **213** G4
Anxiang, China, **206** C2
Anxious Bay, Australia, **134** G5
Anyang, China, **206** C1
A'nyêmaqên Shan, *mountain range*, China, **215** F2
Anykščiai, Lithuania, **287** M5
Anyuan, China, **206** C3
Anyue, China, **215** H3
Anyuy, *river*, Russian Federation, **211** M2
Anzá, Colombia, **450** C2
Anzac Peak, *mountain peak*, Heard and McDonald Islands, **134** S12
Anze, China, **210** F5
Anzhero-Sudzhensk, Russian Federation, **223** M1
Anzi, Democratic Republic of the Congo, **368** D3
Anzio, Italy, **295** D5
Anzob, Tajikistan, **223** H5
Ao Luk, Thailand, **202** C4
Aoba, *island*, Vanuatu, **141** A2
Aoga-shima, *island*, Japan, **138** C1
Aola, Solomon Islands, **141** A1
Aomori, Japan, **209** H2
Aonla, India, **218** D3
Aopo, Samoa, **141** B1
Aôral, Phnum, *mountain peak*, Cambodia, **203** D4
Aosta, Italy, **294** A3
Aotea Island *see* Great Barnier Island, New Zealand, **133** E3
Aotou, Guangdong, China, **207** A1
Aotou, S. Guangdong, China, **207** D3
Aouderas, Niger, **365** F1
Aouk, Bahr, *river*, Central African Republic, **366** A3
Aoukalé, *river*, Chad, **366** B2
Aoukâr, *physical feature*, Mauritania, **360** D5
Aoulef, Algeria, **361** G3
Aozou, Chad, **362** C4
Âp Long Hòa, Vietnam, **203** F4
Âp Luc, Vietnam, **203** E4
Apa, *river*, Brazil/Paraguay, **456** B6
Apac, Uganda, **369** F2
Apache, U.S.A., **424** C2
Apache Creek, U.S.A., **423** J5
Apahida, Romania, **296** D2
Apalachee Bay, U.S.A., **425** K5
Apan, Mexico, **431** F5
Apaporis, *river*, Colombia, **451** E4
Aparecida do Taboado, Brazil, **456** C5
Aparri, Philippines, **204** C2
Apata, New Zealand, **132** E3
Apatin, Serbia, **296** B3
Apatity, Russian Federation, **285** R3
Apatou, French Guiana, **452** B2
Apatzingan, Mexico, **430** E5
Ape, Latvia, **287** N4
Apeldoorn, Netherlands, **288** B2
Api, Democratic Republic of the Congo, **369** E2
Api, Tanjong, *point*, Indonesia, **198** C3
Apia, Samoa, **141** B1, *113*
Apiacás, Serra dos, *mountain range*, Brazil, **456** B2
Aplao, Peru, **454** D4
Apo, Mount, *mountain peak*, Philippines, **204** D5, *149*
Apodi, Brazil, **453** G4
Apoera, Suriname, **452** B2
Apolima Strait, Samoa, **141** B1
Apolo, Bolivia, **455** E4
Aporé, Brazil, **456** C5
Aporé, *river*, Brazil, **456** C5
Aporema, Brazil, **452** C3
Apóstoles, Argentina, **459** F3
Apoteri, Guyana, **451** G3
Appalachian Mountains, *mountain range*, U.S.A., **407** O5, *376, 382, 383, 384*
Appennino, *mountain range*, Italy, **294** B3, *255, 256*
Appennino Abruzzese, *mountain range*, Italy, **295** D4
Appennino Ligure, *mountain range*, Italy, **294** B3
Appennino Lucano, *mountain range*, Italy, **295** E5
Appennino Tosco-Emiliano, *mountain range*, Italy, **294** C3
Appennino Umbro-Marchigiano, *mountain range*, Italy, **294** C4
Appleby-in-Westmorland, England, U.K., **306** F3
Appleby Magna, England, U.K., **305** F2
Applecross, Scotland, U.K., **308** D3
Appledore, Devon, England, U.K., **304** C3
Appledore, Kent, England, U.K., **305** H3
Appleton, U.S.A., **421** J3
Approuague, *river*, French Guiana, **452** C2
Apraksin Bor, Russian Federation, **299** C3
Apricena, Italy, **295** E5
Aprilia, Italy, **295** D5
Apsley, Canada, **416** B7
Apt, France, **291** G5
Apucarana, Brazil, **459** G2
Apucarana, Serra da, *mountain range*, Brazil, **459** G2
Apurímac, *river*, Peru, **454** D4
Aqabah, Gulf of, Red Sea, **225** C5, *179*
Aqadyr, Kazakhstan, **223** J3
Aqal, China, **212** C4
Aqbalyq, Kazakhstan, **212** C3
Āqchah, Afghanistan, **218** A1
'Aqdā, Iran, **220** F2
Aqitag, *mountain peak*, China, **213** F4
Aqköl, Kazakhstan, **223** J4
Aqmola, *province*, Kazakhstan, **212** A2
Aqmola *see* Astana, Kazakhstan, **223** J2, *184*
Aqqikkol Hu, *lake*, China, **212** F5
Aqshataū, Kazakhstan, **212** B3
Aqsorang Biigi, *mountain peak*, Kazakhstan, **212** B2
Aqsū, Aqmola, Kazakhstan, **223** J2
Aqsu, Kazakhstan, **212** C1
Aqsū, Pavlodar, Kazakhstan, **223** K2
Aqsū-Ayuly, Kazakhstan, **212** B2
Aqsūat, Central Shyghys Qazaqstan, Kazakhstan, **212** D3
Aqsūat, E. Shyghys Qazaqstan, Kazakhstan, **212** D2
Aqtasty, Kazakhstan, **223** K2
Aqtaū, E. Kazakhstan, **223** J2
Aqtaū (Aktau), W. Kazakhstan, **222** E4
Aqtöbe (Aktyubinsk), Kazakhstan, **222** F2
Aqtoghay, Pavlodar, Kazakhstan, **223** K2
Aqtoghay, Qaraghandy, Kazakhstan, **212** B2
Aqtoghay, Shyghys Qazaqstan, Kazakhstan, **212** C3
Aquidabán, *river*, Paraguay, **459** F2
Aquidauana, Brazil, **456** B5
Aquidauana, *river*, Brazil, **456** B5
Aquila, Mexico, **430** E5
Aquiles Serdán, Mexico, **430** D2
Aquiraz, Brazil, **453** F4
Aquitaine, *administrative region*, France, **290** D4, *245*
Aqyrap, Kazakhstan, **222** F2
Aqzhar, Kazakhstan, **223** L3
Ar-Asgat, Mongolia, **210** D2
Ar Horqin Qi, China, **211** H4
Ar Radīsīya Baḥrī, Egypt, **363** F4
Ar Rahad, Sudan, **366** D2
Ar Rāk, Suquṭrá (Socotra), Yemen, **373** B2
Ar Ramādī, Iraq, **363** H2
Ar Ramlah, Jordan, **225** D5
Ar Ramthā, Jordan, **225** D3
Ar Rank, Sudan, **366** D2
Ar Raqqa, *district*, Syria, **225** E2
Ar Raqqah, Syria, **363** G1
Ar Rass, Saudi Arabia, **363** H3
Ar Rastan, Syria, **225** D2
Ar Rawḍatayn, Kuwait, **363** J3
Ar Riyāḍ (Riyadh), Saudi Arabia, **220** E4, *174*
Ar Ru'āt, Sudan, **366** D2
Ar Rub' al Khālī, *desert*, Saudi Arabia, **220** E5, *174, 175, 176*
Ar Rubay'īyah, Saudi Arabia, **363** H3
Ar Ruṣayfah, Jordan, **225** D4
Ar Ruṣayriṣ, Sudan, **366** D2
Ar Ruṭbah, Iraq, **363** H2
Ar Ruwayḍah, Saudi Arabia, **220** E4
Ar Ruways, Oman, **220** F4
'Arab, Baḥr al, *river*, Sudan, **366** C2
Arab, U.S.A., **425** J2
'Arab al Mulk, Syria, **225** C2
Arabelo, Venezuela, **451** F3
Arabian Basin, *underwater feature*, Indian Ocean, **476** D3
Arabian Peninsula, Asia, **194** F7, *73, 144, 146, 174, 175*
Arabian Sea, Indian Ocean, **194** H8, *66, 173, 175*
Arabopó, Venezuela, **451** G3
Araçá, *river*, Brazil, **451** F4
Aracaju, Brazil, **457** G3
Aracati, Brazil, **453** G4
Aracatu, Brazil, **457** F4
Araçatuba, Brazil, **456** C5
Aracena, Spain, **292** D4
Aracena, Sierra de, *mountain peak*, Spain, **292** D4
Aracena, Sierra de, *mountain range*, Spain, **292** D4
Aracruz, Brazil, **457** F5
'Arad, Israel, **225** C4
Arad, Romania, **296** C2
Arada, Chad, **366** B2
'Arādah, Oman, **220** F4
Aradan, Russian Federation, **213** G1
Arafura Sea, Australia/Indonesia, **138** B5
Aragarças, Brazil, **456** C4
Aragats Lerr, *mountain peak*, Armenia, **222** C4, *188*
Aragón, *autonomous community*, Spain, **293** G2, *252*
Aragón, *river*, Spain, **293** G1
Aragua de Barcelona, Venezuela, **451** F2
Araguacema, Brazil, **456** D2
Araguaçu, Brazil, **456** D3
Araguaia, *river*, Brazil, **456** D2, *440*
Araguaína, Brazil, **452** D5
Araguao, Boca, *bay*, Venezuela, **451** G2
Araguari, Brazil, **456** D5
Araguari, *river*, Amapá, Brazil, **452** C3
Araguari, *river*, Minas Gerais, Brazil, **456** D5
Araguatins, Brazil, **452** D4
Araioses, Brazil, **453** E4
Arak, Algeria, **361** G3
Arāk, Iran, **220** E2
Arak, Syria, **225** E2
Arakan, *state*, Myanmar, **205** B4
Arakan Yoma, *mountain range*, Myanmar, **205** B3, *157*
Aral, China, **212** D4
Aral Sea, Kazakhstan/Uzbekistan, **222** F3, *185, 187, 188*
Aralköl, Kazakhstan, **222** G2
Aralqi, China, **212** E5
Aral'sk, Kazakhstan, **222** G3
Aralsor Köli, *lake*, Kazakhstan, **222** D3
Aramberri, Mexico, **431** F3
Aramia, *river*, Papua New Guinea, **140** A4
Ārān, Iran, **220** F2
Aran Fawddwy, *mountain peak*, Wales, U.K., **304** D2
Aran Island, Ireland, **309** D2
Aran Islands, Ireland, **309** C4
Aranda de Duero, Spain, **293** F2
Aranèelovac, Serbia, **296** C3
Aranjuez, Spain, **293** F2
Aranos, Namibia, **370** C3
Aranyaprathet, Thailand, **202** D3
Arao, Japan, **208** E4
Araouane, Mali, **361** F5
Arapahoe, U.S.A., **420** D5
Arapey Grande, *river*, Uruguay, **459** F4
Arapiraca, Brazil, **457** G2
Arapis, Akra, *point*, Greece, **297** E5
Arapkir, Turkey, **224** E5
Arapongas, Brazil, **459** G2
Araputanga, Brazil, **455** G4
'Ar'ar, Saudi Arabia, **363** H2
Araracuara, Colombia, **450** D4
Araranguá, Brazil, **459** H3
Araraquara, Brazil, **456** D5
Araras, Brazil, **452** B5
Araras, Serra das, *mountain range*, Brazil, **459** G2
Ararat, Australia, **135** J6
Ararat, Mount *see* Ağri Daği, *mountain peak*, Turkey, **224** F4, *189*
Arari, Brazil, **453** E4
Araria, India, **219** F4
Araripe, Chapada do, *mountain range*, Brazil, **453** F5
Araripina, Brazil, **453** F5
Aras, *river*, Armenia/Azerbaijan/Iran, **363** J1
Arataca, Brazil, **457** F4
Arataua, *mountain peak*, New Zealand, **132** E4
Aratika, *island*, French Polynesia, **137** G2
Aratika, New Zealand, **133** C6
Arauca, Colombia, **451** D2
Arauca, *river*, Venezuela, **451** E2
Araucanía, *administrative region*, Chile, **458** B6
Arauco, Chile, **458** B5
Arauco, Golfo de, *gulf*, Chile, **458** B5
Arauquita, Colombia, **450** D2
Arāvalli Range, *mountain range*, India, **218** C4
Arawa, Papua New Guinea, **140** E2
Araxá, Brazil, **456** D5
Araxos, Akra, *cape*, Greece, **297** C6
Ārba Minch', Ethiopia, **367** E3
Arbīl, Iraq, **363** H1
Arboga, Sweden, **286** G3
Arborfield, Canada, **414** C5
Arborg, Canada, **414** F6
Arbrå, Sweden, **286** H2
Arbroath, Scotland, U.K., **308** G4
Arcachon, Bassin d', *inlet*, France, **290** D4
Arcachon, France, **290** D4
Arcadia, Florida, U.S.A., **425** M6
Arcadia, Louisiana, U.S.A., **424** F3
Arcata, U.S.A., **418** B6
Arcelia, Mexico, **431** E5
Arch Cape, U.S.A., **418** C4
Archer City, U.S.A., **424** C3
Arcidosso, Italy, **294** C4
Arco, U.S.A., **418** H5
Arcos, Brazil, **456** E5
Arcos de la Frontera, Spain, **292** E4
Arcoverde, Brazil, **453** G5
Arctic Bay, Canada, **411** L2
Arctic Ocean, **471** C4, *231, 234, 271, 272, 273, 279, 389, 464, 467, 474, 475*
Arḍ aṣ Ṣawwān, *plain*, Jordan, **225** D4
Ardabīl, Iran, **222** D5
Ardakān, Iran, **221** F2
Ardal, Iran, **363** K2
Årdalstangen, Norway, **286** C2
Ardara, Ireland, **309** D3
Ardatov, Russian Federation, **298** F1
Ardbeg, Canada, **421** N3
Ardee, Ireland, **309** F4

Ardennes, *region*, Belgium/France, **280** E6, *242, 243*
Ardentes, France, **290** E3
Ardgay, Scotland, U.K., **308** E3
Ardglass, Northern Ireland, U.K., **309** G3
Ardino, Bulgaria, **297** E5
Ardlussa, Scotland, U.K., **308** D4
Ardminish, Scotland, U.K., **308** D5
Ardmore, Ireland, **309** E6
Ardmore, U.S.A., **424** D2
Ardnamurchan, Point of, Scotland, U.K., **308** C4
Ardres, France, **305** J4
Ardrishaig, Orkney, Scotland, U.K., **308** D4
Ardrossan, Scotland, U.K., **308** E5
Ards, *district*, Northern Ireland, U.K., **309** G3
Ards Peninsula, Northern Ireland, U.K., **309** G3
Ardud, Romania, **296** D2
Ardvasar, Scotland, U.K., **308** D3
Åre, Sweden, **284** F5
Areavaara, Sweden, **285** L3
Arebi, Democratic Republic of the Congo, **369** E2
Arecibo, Puerto Rico, **427** C2
Areia Branca, Brazil, **453** G4
Arena, Point, U.S.A., **422** A2
Arena, Punta, *point*, Mexico, **430** C4
Arenales, Cerro, *mountain peak*, Chile, **460** C3
Arenas, Punta de, *point*, Argentina, **460** D4
Arenas de San Pedro, Spain, **292** E2
Arendal, Norway, **286** D3
Arendsee, Germany, **288** E2
Areopoli, Greece, **297** D7
Arequipa, Peru, **454** D4
Arere, Brazil, **452** C3
Arès, France, **290** D4
Arévalo, Spain, **292** E2
Arezzo, Italy, **294** C4
Arga, *river*, Spain, **293** G1
Argalasti, Greece, **297** D6
Argan, China, **212** F4, **223** M4
Argatay, Mongolia, **210** D3
Argens, *river*, France, **291** H5
Argenta, Italy, **294** C3
Argentan, France, **290** D2
Argentina, Argentina, **458** D3
Argentina, *country*, South America, **448** F7, *92, 93, 95, 96, 97, 275, 434, 435, 442, 443, 444, 445*
Argentine Plain, *underwater feature*, Atlantic Ocean, **477** D8
Argentino, Lago, *lake*, Argentina, **460** C4
Argentino, *river*, Argentina, **460** C4
Argenton-sur-Creuse, France, **290** E3
Argeş, *river*, Romania, **296** E3
Arghandāb, *river*, Afghanistan, **218** A2
Arghastān, *river*, Afghanistan, **218** A3
Argolikos Kolpos, *bay*, Greece, **297** D7
Argopuro, Gunung, *mountain peak*, Indonesia, **201** F4
Argos Orestiko, Greece, **297** C5
Argos, Greece, **297** D7
Argostoli, Ionioi Nisoi, Greece, **297** C6
Argueil, France, **305** J5
Arguello, Point, U.S.A., **422** C4
Argun', *river*, Russian Federation, **211** H1
Argungu, Nigeria, **365** E2
Argus, Dome, *ice dome*, Antarctica, **470** E5
Arguut, Mongolia, **213** J3
Argyle, Canada, **416** J8
Argyle, Lake, Australia, **134** F2
Argyll, *region*, Scotland, U.K., **308** D4
Argyll and Bute, *local authority*, Scotland, U.K., **308** D4
Arhangay, *province*, Mongolia, **213** J3
Århus, Denmark, **286** E4
Arhust, Mongolia, **210** D3
Ari Atoll, Maldives, **216** C5
Aria, *river*, Papua New Guinea, **140** C4
Ariamsvlei, Namibia, **370** C4
Ariano Irpino, Italy, **295** E5
Arias, Argentina, **458** D4
Ariaú, Brazil, **452** B4
Aribinda, Burkina Faso, **364** D2
Arica, Chile, **455** D5
Arica, Colombia, **450** D5
Arica, Peru, **450** C4
Arichat, Canada, **417** L7
Arid, Cape, Australia, **134** E5
Aride, *island*, Seychelles, **373** A2
Ariguani, *river*, Colombia, **450** C1
Arīḩā (Jericho), West Bank, **225** C4, *182*
Ariki, New Zealand, **133** D5
Arilje, Serbia, **296** C4
Arima, Trinidad, Trinidad and Tobago, **461** C4
Arimo, U.S.A., **419** H5
Arinos, Brazil, **456** D4
Arinos, *river*, Brazil, **456** B3
Ario de Rosales, Mexico, **430** E5
Aripuanã, Brazil, **455** G2
Aripuanã, *river*, Brazil, **455** G2
Ariquemes, Brazil, **455** F2
Arisaig, Scotland, U.K., **308** D4
Arisaig, Sound of, Scotland, U.K., **308** D4
Aristazabel Island, Canada, **412** D5
Aritzo, Sardegna, Italy, **295** B6
Ariza, Spain, **293** F2
Arizaro, Salar de, *salt-pan*, Argentina, **458** C2
Arizona, *state*, U.S.A., **423** H4, *383, 386, 387*
Årjäng, Sweden, **286** F3
Arjeplog, Sweden, **284** H3
Arjona, Colombia, **450** C1
Arkadelphia, U.S.A., **424** F2
Arkansas, *river*, U.S.A., **407** M5
Arkansas, *state*, U.S.A., **424** F2, *63, 386*
Arkansas City, U.S.A., **420** E7
Arkanū, Jabal, *mountain peak*, Libya, **362** D4
Arkatag Shan, *mountain range*, China, **212** F5
Arkhangel'sk, Russian Federation, **300** F3
Arkhangel'skaya Oblast', *province*, Russian Federation, **299** G2
Arkhangel'skoye, Russian Federation, **222** F2
Arkhara, Russian Federation, **211** K2
Arkhipovka, Russian Federation, **299** C5
Arklow, Ireland, **309** F5
Arkona, Kap, *cape*, Germany, **288** F1
Arkonam, India, **216** D3
Arkösund, Sweden, **287** H3
Arlan, *mountain peak*, Turkmenistan, **222** E5
Arlee, U.S.A., **418** G3
Arles, France, **291** G5
Arli, Burkina Faso, **364** E2
Arlington, Colorado, U.S.A., **423** M2
Arlington, Georgia, U.S.A., **425** K4
Arlington, Texas, U.S.A., **424** D3
Arlington, Virginia, U.S.A., **426** B5
Arlit, Niger, **361** H5
Arlon, Belgium, **288** B4
Armagh, *district*, Northern Ireland, U.K., **309** F3
Armagh, Northern Ireland, U.K., **309** F3
Armagnac, *region*, France, **290** E5
Armant, Egypt, **363** F3
Armathia, *island*, Greece, **297** F8
Armavir, Russian Federation, **222** C3
Armenia, Colombia, **450** C3
Armenia, *country*, Asia, **196** F5, *144, 182, 188, 189, 190, 272*
Armero, Colombia, **450** C3
Armidale, Australia, **135** L5
Armour, U.S.A., **420** D4
Armoy, Northern Ireland, U.K., **309** F2
Armstrong, British Columbia, Canada, **413** K6
Armstrong, Ontario, Canada, **415** K6
Armstrong, U.S.A., **424** D6
Armutlu, Turkey, **297** G5
Armutova, Turkey, **297** F6
Arnaia, Greece, **297** D5
Arnaoutis, Cape, Cyprus, **225** A2
Arnaud, *river*, Canada, **415** T2
Arneburg, Germany, **288** F2
Årnes, Norway, **286** E2
Arnett, U.S.A., **424** C1
Arnhem, Cape, Australia, **135** H1
Arnhem, Netherlands, **288** B3
Arnhem Bay, Australia, **135** H1
Arnhem Land, *region*, Australia, **135** G1, *112*
Arnissa, Greece, **297** C5
Arno, *island*, Marshall Islands, **139** F4
Arno, *river*, Italy, **294** C4, *89, 254*
Arnøy, *island*, Norway, **284** K1
Arnstadt, Germany, **288** E3
Arntfield, Canada, **421** P1
Aroab, Namibia, **370** C4
Arohena, New Zealand, **132** E4
Aroland, Canada, **415** L6
Aroma, Sudan, **366** E1
Arona, Italy, **294** B3
Aroostook, *river*, U.S.A., **416** G6
Aropa, Papua New Guinea, **140** E2
Arorae, *island*, Kiribati, **139** F5
Arpela, Finland, **285** M3
Arpino, Italy, **295** D5
Arqalyq, Kazakhstan, **222** H2
Arques, France, **305** K4
Arra Mountains, Ireland, **309** D5
Arrah, Côte d'Ivoire, **364** D3
Arraias, *river*, Brazil, **456** B3
Arraiolos, Portugal, **292** D3
Arran, *island*, Scotland, U.K., **308** D5
Arras, France, **291** F1
Arrats, *river*, France, **290** E5
Arreau, France, **290** E5
Arrecifal, Colombia, **451** E3
Arrecife, Islas Canarias, Spain, **373** B4
Arrecifes, Argentina, **459** E5
Arrée, Montagnes d', *mountain range*, France, **290** C2
Arriaga, Chiapas, Mexico, **431** G5
Arriaga, San Luis Potosí, Mexico, **431** E4
Arrochar, Scotland, U.K., **308** E4
Arroio Grande, Brazil, **459** G4
Arrow, Lough, *lake*, Ireland, **309** D3
Arrowsmith, Mount, *mountain peak*, New Zealand, **133** C6
Arroyo Seco, Mexico, **431** F4
Arruda, Brazil, **456** B4
Års, Denmark, **286** D4
Ars-en-Ré, France, **290** D3
Arsen'yev, Russian Federation, **211** L3
Arsen'yevo, Russian Federation, **299** F6
Arshan, Russian Federation, **213** J2
Arsk, Russian Federation, **222** D1
Årsunda, Sweden, **287** H2
Arta, Greece, **297** C6
Artà, Islas Baleares, Spain, **293** J3
Arteaga, Mexico, **430** E5
Artem, Russian Federation, **211** L4
Artemisa, Cuba, **429** E2
Artemovsk, Russian Federation, **223** N2
Artesia, U.S.A., **423** L5
Arthur, Canada, **421** N4
Arthur, U.S.A., **420** C5
Arthur's Pass, New Zealand, **133** C6
Arthur's Town, Bahamas, **428** G1
Arti, Russian Federation, **222** F1
Artigas, Uruguay, **459** F4
Artsyz, Ukraine, **296** G3
Artux, China, **212** C5
Artvin, Turkey, **224** F4
Artybash, Russian Federation, **212** E2
Aru, Democratic Republic of the Congo, **369** F2
Aru, Kepulauan, *islands*, Indonesia, **199** F4
Aru, Teluk, *bay*, Indonesia, **200** B1
Arua, Uganda, **369** F2
Aruanã, Brazil, **456** C4
Aruba, *Netherlands autonomous region*, Caribbean Sea, **461** B3, *240, 378, 387, 389*
Arucas, Islas Canarias, Spain, **373** B4
Arumã, Brazil, **451** F5
Arumbi, Democratic Republic of the Congo, **369** F2
Arun, *river*, Nepal, **219** F4
Arun Qi, China, **211** H2
Arunachal Pradesh, *state*, India, **219** H3, *169*
Arundel, England, U.K., **305** G4
Aruppukkottai, India, **216** D4
Arus, Tanjong, *point*, Indonesia, **198** C2
Arusha, *administrative region*, Tanzania, **369** G3
Arusha, Tanzania, **369** G3
Arut, *river*, Indonesia, **201** E3
Arvada, U.S.A., **419** L4
Arvagh, Ireland, **309** E4
Arvayheer, Mongolia, **213** J3
Arviat, Canada, **414** G1
Arvidsjaur, Sweden, **284** J4
Arvika, Sweden, **286** F3
Årviksand, Norway, **284** K1
Arwala, Indonesia, **198** D4
Arxan, China, **211** G3
Arys', Kazakhstan, **223** H4
Arys, Solonchak, *lake*, Kazakhstan, **222** H3
Arzamas, Russian Federation, **298** F1
Arzew, Algeria, **293** G5
As Sa'an, Syria, **225** D2
Aş Şafāwī, Jordan, **225** D3
Aş Şaff, Egypt, **225** A5
Aş Şāfī, Jordan, **225** C4
As Safīrah, Syria, **225** D1
Aş Şāliḩiyah, Egypt, **225** A4
As Salmān, Iraq, **363** H2
As Salt, Jordan, **363** G2
As Samāwah, Iraq, **363** J2
As Sawrah, Saudi Arabia, **225** C6
As Sidrah, Libya, **362** C2
As Sinbillāwayn, Egypt, **225** A4
Aş Şubayhīyah, Kuwait, **363** J3
As Sukhnah, Syria, **225** E2
As Sūkī, Sudan, **366** D2
As Sulaymānīyah, Iraq, **363** J1
As Sulayyil, Saudi Arabia, **363** J4
As Sulţān, Libya, **362** C2
As Sumayḩ, Sudan, **366** C3
Aş Şuwār, Syria, **363** H1
As Suwaydā', *district*, Syria, **225** D3
As Suwaydā', Syria, **225** D3
As Suways (Suez), Egypt, **225** B5
Aså, Denmark, **286** E4
Asaba, Nigeria, **365** F3
Asad, Buḩayrat al, *lake*, Syria, **225** E1
Asadābād, Afghanistan, **218** B2
Asadābād, Iran, **220** E2
Asahan, *river*, Indonesia, **200** B2
Asahidake, *mountain peak*, Japan, **209** H2
Asahikawa, Japan, **209** H2
Asamankese, Ghana, **364** D3
Asambi, Indonesia, **198** C4
Āsansol, India, **219** F5
Åsarna, Sweden, **286** G1
Asau, Samoa, **141** B1
Āsbe Teferī, Ethiopia, **367** F3
Asbury Park, U.S.A., **426** C4
Ascea, Italy, **295** E5
Ascención, Bolivia, **455** F4
Ascensión, Mexico, **430** D2
Ascension, *St Helena dependency*, Atlantic Ocean, **373** A3
Ascension Fracture Zone, *tectonic feature*, Atlantic Ocean, **477** F6
Aschaffenburg, Germany, **288** D4
Aschott, New Zealand, **132** F4
Ascoli Piceno, Italy, **294** D4
Ascope, Peru, **454** B2
Ascotán, Salar de, *salt-pan*, Chile, **455** E5
Åse, Norway, **284** G2
Åseda, Sweden, **286** G4
Asedjrad, *mountain range*, Algeria, **361** G4
Āsela, Ethiopia, **367** E3
Åsele, Sweden, **284** H4
Åsen, Sweden, **286** F2
Asenovgrad, Bulgaria, **296** E4
Åseral, Norway, **286** C3
Ash Fork, U.S.A., **422** G4
Ash Sha'rā', Saudi Arabia, **363** H4
Ash Shabakah, Iraq, **363** H2
Ash Shamālīyah, *state*, Sudan, **362** E4
Ash Sharmah, Saudi Arabia, **225** C5
Ash Sharqāţ, Iraq, **363** H1
Ash Shaţrah, Iraq, **363** J2
Ash Shawbak, Jordan, **225** C4
Ash Shaykh 'Uthmān, Yemen, **220** D6
Ash Shiḩr, Yemen, **220** E6
Ash Shu'bah, Saudi Arabia, **363** H3
Ash Shuqayq, Saudi Arabia, **363** H5
Ash Shurayf, Saudi Arabia, **363** G3
Ash Shurayk, Sudan, **363** F5
Ash Shuwayrif, Libya, **362** B3
Ashanti, *administrative region*, Ghana, **364** D3
Ashbourne, England, U.K., **305** F1
Ashbourne, Ireland, **309** F4
Ashburton, New Zealand, **133** C6
Ashburton, *river*, Australia, **134** D3
Ashby, U.S.A., **420** F2
Ashby de la Zouch, England, U.K., **305** F2
Ashchysū, *river*, Kazakhstan, **212** C2
Ashcroft, Canada, **412** J6
Ashdod, Israel, **225** C4
Ashdown, U.S.A., **424** E3
Asheville, U.S.A., **425** L2
Ashford, England, U.K., **305** H3
Ashgabat, Turkmenistan, **222** F5, *187*
Ashibetsu, Japan, **209** H2
Ashikaga, Japan, **209** G3
Ashington, England, U.K., **307** G2
Ashizurimisaki, *point*, Japan, **208** F4
Ashland, Kansas, U.S.A., **420** D7
Ashland, Kentucky, U.S.A., **421** M6
Ashland, Maine, U.S.A., **426** F1
Ashland, Montana, U.S.A., **419** L4
Ashland, Nebraska, U.S.A., **420** E5
Ashland, Oregon, U.S.A., **418** C5
Ashland, Virginia, U.S.A., **426** B6
Ashland, Wisconsin, U.S.A., **420** H2
Ashley, U.S.A., **420** D2
Ashmont, Canada, **413** P4
Ashmore and Cartier Islands, *Australian territory*, Indian Ocean, **134** E1, *112, 121*
Ashmore Reef, *island*, Ashmore and Cartier Islands, **134** P9
Ashmūn, Egypt, **225** A4
Ashmyany, Belarus, **287** M5
Ashoknagar, India, **218** D4
Ashoro, Japan, **209** H2
Ashqelon, Israel, **225** C4
Ashta, India, **218** D5
Ashtabula, Lake, U.S.A., **420** E2
Ashtabula, U.S.A., **421** N5
Ashton, U.S.A., **419** J4
Ashville, Canada, **414** D6
'Āsī, *river*, Lebanon/Syria, **225** D2, *181*
Asi, *river*, Turkey, **225** D1
Asid Gulf, Philippines, **204** C3
Asientos, Mexico, **430** E4
Asifābād, India, **216** D2
Āsika, India, **219** F6
Asilah, Morocco, **361** E1
Asillo, Peru, **455** D4
Asinara, Golfo dell', *gulf*, Sardegna, Italy, **295** B5
Asinara, Isola, *island*, Sardegna, Italy, **295** B5
Asino, Russian Federation, **223** M1
Asipovichy, Belarus, **299** B6
Aska, Finland, **285** N3
Aşkale, Turkey, **224** F5
Askarovo, Russian Federation, **222** F2
Asker, Norway, **286** E3
Askern, England, U.K., **307** G4

Askersund, Sweden, **286** G3
Askim, Norway, **286** E3
Askøy, *island*, Norway, **286** B2
Askvoll, Norway, **286** B2
Asmara, Eritrea, **367** E1, *336*
Asmunti, Finland, **285** N4
Åsnen, *lake*, Sweden, **286** G4
Asnet, Chad, **366** A2
Aso-san, *mountain peak*, Japan, **208** E4
Asola, Italy, **294** C3
Āsop, India, **218** C4
Asopos, Greece, **297** D7
Āsosa, Ethiopia, **366** D2
Asoteriba, Jabal, *mountain peak*, Sudan, **363** G4
Aspang-Markt, Austria, **289** H5
Aspatria, England, U.K., **306** E3
Aspeå, Sweden, **284** H5
Aspen, Canada, **417** K7
Aspen, U.S.A., **423** K2
Aspermont, U.S.A., **424** B3
Aspiring, Mount, *mountain peak*, New Zealand, **133** B7
Aspres-sur-Buëch, France, **291** G4
Assab, Eritrea, **367** F2
Assaba, *administrative region*, Mauritania, **364** B1
Assam, *state*, India, **219** H4, *168*, *169*
Assamakka, Niger, **361** H5
Assateague Island, U.S.A., **426** C6
Assebroek, Belgium, **288** A3
Assen, Netherlands, **288** C2
Assens, Denmark, **286** D5
Assiniboia, Canada, **413** S7
Assiniboine, Mount, *mountain peak*, Canada, **413** M6
Assis, Brazil, **459** G2
Assisi, Italy, **294** D4, *255*
Assumption Island, Seychelles, **372** B2
Assynt, Loch, *inlet*, Scotland, U.K., **308** D2
Åsta, *river*, Norway, **286** E2
Astakida, *island*, Dodekanisos, Greece, **297** F8
Astakos, Greece, **297** C6
Astana (Aqmola), Kazakhstan, **223** J2, *184*
Astara, Iran, **222** D5
Asti, Italy, **294** B3
Astillero, Peru, **455** E3
Asto, Monte, *mountain peak*, Corse, France, **294** B4
Astorga, Spain, **292** D1
Astoria, U.S.A., **418** C3
Astove Island, Seychelles, **372** B3
Astrakhan', Russian Federation, **222** D3
Astrakhanskaya Oblast', *province*, Russian Federation, **222** D3
Åsträsk, Sweden, **284** J4
Astravyets, Belarus, **287** M5
Astrolabe Bay, Papua New Guinea, **140** B4
Astros, Greece, **297** D7
Astrowna, Belarus, **299** B5
Astryna, Belarus, **289** M2
Asturias, *autonomous community*, Spain, **292** D1
Astypalaia, *island*, Kyklades, Greece, **297** E7
Asuisui, Cape, Samoa, **141** B1
Asunción, Bolivia, **455** E3
Asuncion, *island*, Northern Mariana Islands, **138** C3
Asunción, Paraguay, **459** F2
Asvyeya, Belarus, **299** B5
Aswān, Egypt, **363** F4
Asyūţ, Egypt, **363** F3
At-Bashy, Kyrgyzstan, **223** K4
Aţ Ţafīlah, Jordan, **225** C4
Aţ Ţā'if, Saudi Arabia, **363** H4
At Tamīmī, Libya, **362** D2
At Tanf, Syria, **225** E3
At Taysīyah, *desert*, Saudi Arabia, **363** H3
Aţ Ţubayq, *physical feature*, Saudi Arabia, **225** D5
Aţ Ţūr, Egypt, **225** B5
At Turbah, Yemen, **220** D6
Aţ Ţuwayyah, Saudi Arabia, **363** H3
Ata, *island*, Tonga, **141** B4
Ataa, Greenland, **411** P3
Atacama, *administrative district*, Chile, **458** B3
Atacama, Desierto de, *desert*, Chile, **447** E6, *434*, *441*, *442*
Atacama, Salar de, *salt-pan*, Chile, **458** C2
Atafu, *island*, Tokelau, **139** G5
Atakpamé, Togo, **364** E3
Atalaia, Brazil, **457** G2
Atalaia do Norte, Brazil, **451** D5
Atalanti, Greece, **297** D6
Atalaya, Panama, **429** E6
Atalaya, Peru, **454** D3
Atambua, Indonesia, **198** D5
Atammik, Greenland, **411** P3
'Ataq, Yemen, **220** E6
Atāqah, Jabal, *mountain peak*, Egypt, **225** B5
Atâr, Mauritania, **360** D4
Atartīr ad Dahāmī, Jabal, *mountain peak*, Egypt, **225** B5
Atas *see* South Island, Cocos (Keeling) Islands, **134** Q10
Atas Bogd, *mountain peak*, Mongolia, **213** H4
Atasu, Kazakhstan, **223** J3
Atasu, *mountain peak*, Kazakhstan, **223** J3
Atasu, *river*, Kazakhstan, **212** A3
Atata, *island*, Tonga, **141** B4
'Aţbara, *river*, Sudan, **220** B5
'Aţbara, Sudan, **363** F5
Atbasar, Kazakhstan, **223** H2
Atchafalaya Bay, U.S.A., **424** G5
Atebubu, Ghana, **364** D3
Atessa, Italy, **295** E4
Aţfīḩ, Egypt, **225** A5
Ath, Belgium, **288** A3
Ath Thamad, Egypt, **225** C5
Ath Thawrah, Syria, **225** E2
Athabasca, Canada, **413** N4
Athabasca, Lake, Canada, **413** Q2
Athabasca, *river*, Canada, **413** N4
Āthagarh, India, **219** F5
Athboy, Ireland, **309** F4
Athenry, Ireland, **309** D4
Athens, Georgia, U.S.A., **425** L3
Athens, Ohio, U.S.A., **421** M6
Athens *see* Athina, Greece, **297** D7, *67*, *70*, *89*, *264*, *265*
Athens, Tennessee, U.S.A., **425** K2
Athens, Texas, U.S.A., **424** E3
Atherstone, England, U.K., **305** F2
Atherton, Australia, **135** K2
Athi River, Kenya, **369** G3
Athina (Athens), Greece, **297** D7, *67*, *70*, *89*, *264*, *265*
Athleague, Ireland, **309** D4
Athlone, Ireland, **309** E4
Athna, Cyprus, **225** B2
Athol, U.S.A., **426** D3
Athos, *mountain peak*, Greece, **297** E5
Athy, Ireland, **309** F5
Ati, Chad, **366** A2
Atico, Peru, **454** D4
Atiedo, Sudan, **366** C3
Atienza, Spain, **293** F2
Atikameg, Canada, **413** M4
Atikokan, Canada, **420** H1
Atiu, *island*, Cook Islands, **137** F3
Atka Island, Aleutian Islands, U.S.A., **408** F3
Atkarsk, Russian Federation, **222** C2
Atkinson, U.S.A., **420** D4
Atkri, Indonesia, **199** E3
Atlanta, Georgia, U.S.A., **425** K3, *386*
Atlanta, Idaho, U.S.A., **418** G5
Atlanta, Michigan, U.S.A., **421** L3
Atlanta, Texas, U.S.A., **424** E3
Atlantic, Iowa, U.S.A., **420** F5
Atlantic, North Carolina, U.S.A., **426** B7
Atlantic City, U.S.A., **426** C5
Atlantic-Indian Ridge, *underwater feature*, Atlantic Ocean, **477** H9
Atlantic Ocean, **477** E8, *22*, *44*, *45*, *96*, *228*, *230*, *232*, *244*, *245*, *250*, *252*, *253*, *274*, *277*, *278*, *312*, *314*, *318*, *321*, *322*, *323*, *324*, *333*, *334*, *335*, *354*, *355*, *376*, *377*, *381*, *382*, *388*, *391*, *392*, *405*, *434*, *445*, *464*, *466*, *474*, *475*
Atlantis, South Africa, **370** C5
Atlantis Fracture Zone, *tectonic feature*, Atlantic Ocean, **477** D3
Atlas Saharien, *mountain range*, Algeria, **356** F3, *312*, *314*, *315*
Atlin, Canada, **412** C2
Atlin Lake, Canada, **412** C2
Atlixco, Mexico, **431** F5
Atmore, Canada, **413** N4
Atmore, U.S.A., **425** J4
Atnbrua, Norway, **286** E2
Atocha, Bolivia, **455** E5
Atoka, New Mexico, U.S.A., **423** L5
Atoka, Oklahoma, U.S.A., **424** D2
Atori, Solomon Islands, **141** A1
Atouat, Phu, *mountain peak*, Laos/Vietnam, **203** E2
Atoyac de Alvarez, Mexico, **431** E5
Atrak, *river*, Iran/Turkmenistan, **222** F5
Ätran, *river*, Sweden, **286** F4
Ätran, Sweden, **286** F4
Atrato, *river*, Colombia, **450** C2
Atsugi, Japan, **209** G4
Attapu, Laos, **203** E3
Attavyros, *mountain peak*, Dodekanisos, Greece, **297** F7
Attawapiskat, Canada, **415** N5
Attawapiskat, *river*, Canada, **415** L5
Attempt Hill, *mountain peak*, New Zealand, **133** D5
Attica, U.S.A., **421** K5
Attiki, *administrative region*, Greece, **297** D7
Attleborough, England, U.K., **305** J2
Attock, Pakistan, **218** C2
Attu Island, Aleutian Islands, U.S.A., **408** E3
Attūr, India, **216** D4
Atuel, *river*, Argentina, **458** C5
Åtvidaberg, Sweden, **286** H3
Atyraū, Kazakhstan, **222** E3
Auas Mountains, Namibia, **370** C3, *350*
Aubagne, France, **291** G5
Aubenas, France, **291** G4
Aubergenville, France, **290** E2
Aubigney-sur-Nère, France, **290** F3
Aubrac, Monts d', *mountain range*, France, **291** F4
Auburn, Alabama, U.S.A., **425** K3
Auburn, California, U.S.A., **422** C2
Auburn, Illinois, U.S.A., **420** J6
Auburn, Maine, U.S.A., **426** E2
Auburn, New York, U.S.A., **426** B3
Auburn, Washington, U.S.A., **418** C3
Aubusson, France, **290** F4
Auca Mahuida, Sierra de, *mountain peak*, Argentina, **458** C5
Auce, Latvia, **287** L4
Auch, France, **290** E5
Auchenbreck, Scotland, U.K., **308** D5
Auchterarder, Scotland, U.K., **308** F4
Auchtermuchty, Scotland, U.K., **308** F4
Auckland, New Zealand, **132** E3
Auckland Island, Auckland Islands, New Zealand, **132** J10
Auckland Islands, New Zealand, **132** J10
Auden, Canada, **415** K6
Audlem, England, U.K., **304** E2
Audo Range, *mountain range*, Ethiopia, **367** F3
Audresselles, France, **305** J4
Audruicq, France, **290** F1
Audubon, U.S.A., **420** F5
Aue, Germany, **288** F3
Auerbach, Germany, **288** F3
Auffay, France, **305** J5
Augher, Northern Ireland, U.K., **309** E3
Aughnacloy, Northern Ireland, U.K., **309** E3
Aughrim, Ireland, **309** F5
Augsburg, Germany, **288** E4
Augusta, Australia, **134** D5
Augusta, Georgia, U.S.A., **425** L3
Augusta, Golfo di, *gulf*, Sicilia, Italy, **295** E7
Augusta, Maine, U.S.A., **426** F2, *386*
Augusta, Sicilia, Italy, **295** E7
Augusta, Wisconsin, U.S.A., **420** H3
Augusta Victoria, Chile, **458** C2
Augustin Codazzi, Colombia, **450** D1
Augustów, Poland, **289** L2
Augustus, Mount, *mountain peak*, Australia, **134** D3
Auki, Solomon Islands, **141** A1
Aukštadvaris, Lithuania, **287** M5
Auktsjaur, Sweden, **284** J4
Auld, Lake, Australia, **134** E3
Auletta, Italy, **295** E5
Aulnay, France, **290** D3
Ault, France, **290** E1
Aultbea, Scotland, U.K., **308** D3
Aumale, France, **305** J5
Auna, Nigeria, **365** E2
Auneau, France, **290** E2
Auneul, France, **305** K5
Auponhia, Indonesia, **198** D3
Aura, Finland, **287** L2
Auraiya, India, **218** D4
Aurangābād, Bihār, India, **219** F4
Aurangābād, Mahārāshtra, India, **216** C2
Aurdal, Norway, **286** D2
Aure, Norway, **284** D5
Aurillac, France, **290** F4
Aurlandsvangen, Norway, **286** C2
Aurora, Colorado, U.S.A., **423** L2
Aurora, Illinois, U.S.A., **421** J5
Aurora, Missouri, U.S.A., **420** G7
Aurora, Suriname, **452** B2
Aus, Namibia, **370** C4
Ausert, Western Sahara, **360** D4
Auskerry, *island*, Orkney, Scotland, U.K., **308** G1
Aust-Agder, *province*, Norway, **286** C3
Austin, Lake, Australia, **134** D4
Austin, Minnesota, U.S.A., **420** G4
Austin, Nevada, U.S.A., **422** E2
Austin, Texas, U.S.A., **424** D4, *386*
Australes, Îles (Îles Tubuai), *islands*, French Polynesia, **137** F3, *122*
Australia, *country*, Oceania, **130** B4, *23*, *28*, *29*, *39*, *40*, *44*, *45*, *49*, *51*, *54*, *59*, *60*, *61*, *77*, *81*, *83*, *87*, *91*, *92*, *93*, *94*, *95*, *96*, *97*, *100*, *108*, *109*, *110*, *111*, *112*, *113*, *114*, *115*, *116*, *117*, *118*, *120*, *121*, *122*, *123*, *124*, *127*, *228*, *275*, *442*, *465*, *469*
Australian Capital Territory, *territory*, Australia, **135** K6, *112*
Austria, *country*, Europe, **282** F6, *59*, *87*, *95*, *96*, *228*, *238*, *239*, *241*, *245*, *247*, *248*, *249*, *252*, *254*, *255*, *258*, *262*, *267*, *268*
Austvågøy, *island*, Norway, **284** F2
Autazes, Brazil, **451** G5
Authie, *river*, France, **290** E1
Authier, Canada, **416** B5
Autlán de Navarro, Mexico, **430** D5
Autun, France, **291** G3
Auvergne, *administrative region*, France, **291** F4, *245*
Auxerre, France, **291** F3
Auxi-le-Château, France, **305** K4
Auxon, France, **291** F2
Auxonne, France, **291** G3
Auyantepui, *mountain peak*, Venezuela, **451** F3
Auzances, France, **290** F3
Auzangate, Nevado, *mountain peak*, Peru, **454** D3
Ava, U.S.A., **420** G7
Avallon, France, **291** F3
Avalon Peninsula, Canada, **417** Q6
Avalos, *river*, Argentina, **459** E3
Avanos, Turkey, **363** F1
Avaré, Brazil, **459** H2
Avarua, Cook Islands, **137** E3, *121*
Avatele, Niue, **132** M13
Avaviken, Sweden, **284** J4
Avdzaga, Mongolia, **213** J3
Aveiro, Brazil, **452** B4
Aveiro, *district*, Portugal, **292** C2
Aveiro, Portugal, **292** C2
Avellaneda, Argentina, **459** E5
Avellino, Italy, **295** E5
Avenal, U.S.A., **422** C3
Avery, U.S.A., **418** G3
Aves Ridge, *underwater feature*, Caribbean Sea, **479** P3
Avesnes-le-Comte, France, **305** K4
Avesta, Sweden, **286** H2
Aveyron, *river*, France, **290** E4
Avezzano, Italy, **295** D4
Aviá Terai, Argentina, **458** E3
Aviemore, Scotland, U.K., **308** F3
Avigliano, Italy, **295** E5
Avignon, France, **291** G5, *244*
Ávila, Spain, **292** E2
Avilés, Spain, **292** E1
Avinurme, Estonia, **287** N3
Avión, *mountain peak*, Spain, **292** C1
Avlida, Greece, **297** D6
Avoca, Ireland, **309** F5
Avoca, U.S.A., **420** F5
Avola, Canada, **413** K6
Ávola, Sicilia, Italy, **295** E7
Avon, Montana, U.S.A., **418** H3
Avon, North Carolina, U.S.A., **426** C7
Avon, *river*, England, U.K., **305** F3, *276*
Avon, *river*, Midlands, England, U.K., **305** F2
Avon, South Dakota, U.S.A., **420** D4
Avon Park, U.S.A., **425** M6
Avondale, U.S.A., **422** G5
Avradsberg, Sweden, **286** F2
Avraga, Mongolia, **210** E3
Avranches, France, **290** D2
Avrig, Romania, **296** E3
Avu Avu, Solomon Islands, **141** A1
Awakino, New Zealand, **132** E4
Awanui, New Zealand, **132** D2
Āwarē, Ethiopia, **367** F3
Awarua, New Zealand, **132** D2
Āwasa, Ethiopia, **367** E3
Awat, China, **212** D4
Awatere, *river*, New Zealand, **133** D5
Awbārī, Libya, **362** B3
Awbārī, Şaḩrā', *desert*, Libya, **362** B3
Awdheegle, Somalia, **367** F4
Awe, Loch, *lake*, Scotland, U.K., **308** D4
Awin, U.S.A., **425** J4
Awjilah, Libya, **362** D3
Awka, Nigeria, **365** F3
Axel Heiberg Island, Canada, **411** K1
Axim, Ghana, **364** D4
Axinim, Brazil, **451** G5
Axixá, Brazil, **453** E4
Axmar Bruk, Sweden, **287** H2
Axminster, England, U.K., **304** E4
Ayacucho, Argentina, **459** E5
Ayacucho, Peru, **454** C3
Ayagūz, Kazakhstan, **212** D3
Ayagūz, *river*, Kazakhstan, **212** C3
Ayakkuduk, Uzbekistan, **222** H4
Ayakkum Hu, *lake*, China, **212** F5
Ayamonte, Spain, **292** D4
Ayan, Russian Federation, **301** Q4
Ayangba, Nigeria, **365** F3
Ayapata, Peru, **455** D3
Ayapel, Colombia, **450** C2
Ayaviri, Peru, **454** D4
Aydar Kŭli, *lake*, Uzbekistan, **222** H4

Aydin, *province*, Turkey, **297** F7
Aydın, Turkey, **297** F7
Aydın Dağları, *mountain range*, Turkey, **297** F6
Aydıncık, Turkey, **225** B1
Aydingkol Hu, *lake*, China, **212** F4
Āyelu Terara, *mountain peak*, Ethiopia, **367** F2
Ayer Chawan, Pulau, *island*, Singapore, **200** J7
Ayer Hitam, Malaysia, **200** C2
Ayer Merbau, Pulau, *island*, Singapore, **200** J7
Ayerbe, Spain, **293** G1
Ayers Rock *see* Uluru, *mountain peak*, Australia, **128** C4
Ayios Seryios, Cyprus, **225** B2
Āykel, Ethiopia, **367** E2
Aylesbury, England, U.K., **305** G3
Aylesbury, New Zealand, **133** D6
Ayllón, Spain, **293** F2
Aylmer Lake, Canada, **410** J3
Aylsham, England, U.K., **305** J2
'Ayn ad Darāhim, Tunisia, **295** B7
'Ayn 'Īsá, Syria, **225** E1
'Ayn Sukhnah, Egypt, **225** B5
Ayna, Peru, **454** D3
Ayni, Tajikistan, **223** H5
'Ayoûn el 'Atroûs, Mauritania, **364** C1
'Aynūnah, Saudi Arabia, **225** C5
Ayod, Sudan, **366** D3
Ayon, Ostrov, *island*, Russian Federation, **301** T2
Ayora, Spain, **293** G3
Ayorou, Niger, **364** E2
Ayr, Australia, **135** K2
Ayr, *river*, Scotland, U.K., **308** E5
Ayr, Scotland, U.K., **308** E5
Ayr, U.S.A., **420** D5
Ayre, Point of, Isle of Man, **306** D3
Aysary, Kazakhstan, **223** J2
Ayteke Bi, Kazakhstan, **222** G3
Aytos, Bulgaria, **296** F4
Ayuy, Ecuador, **450** C5
Ayvacık, Turkey, **297** F6
Ayvadzh, Tajikistan, **218** B1
Ayvalık, Turkey, **297** F6
Az Zabadānī, Syria, **225** D3
Aẓ Ẓafīr, Saudi Arabia, **363** H5
Aẓ Ẓahrāan (Dhahran), Saudi Arabia, **220** E3
Az Zalaf, Syria, **225** D3
Az Zaqāzīq, Egypt, **225** A4
Az Zarqā', Jordan, **225** D3
Az Zāwiyah, Libya, **362** B2
Az Zaydīyah, Yemen, **220** D5
Az Zilfī, Saudi Arabia, **363** H3
Az Zintān, Libya, **362** B2
Az Zubayr, Iraq, **363** J2
Az Zuhrah, Yemen, **220** D5
Azacualpa, Honduras, **428** D4
Azaila, Spain, **293** G2
Azalea, U.S.A., **418** C5
Āzamgarh, India, **219** E4
Azapa, Chile, **455** D5
Āzarān, Iran, **363** J1
Azare, Nigeria, **365** G2
Azauri, Brazil, **452** B3
A'zāz, Syria, **225** D1
Azazga, Algeria, **293** K4
Azeffâl, *mountain range*, Mauritania/Western Sahara, **360** C4
Azeffoun, Algeria, **293** K4
Azemmour, Morocco, **360** E2
Azerbaijan, *country*, Asia, **196** F6, *144, 145, 183, 188, 189, 190, 272, 273*
Āzezo, Ethiopia, **367** E2
Azogues, Ecuador, **450** B5
Azores, *islands*, Portugal, Atlantic Ocean, **360** M6, *22, 250*
Azores-Biscay Rise, *underwater feature*, Atlantic Ocean, **477** F3
Azov, Sea of, Russian Federation/Ukraine, **298** E3, *268, 269*
Azraq, Al Baḥr al (Blue Nile), *river*, Sudan, **220** B6, *93, 336, 338*
Azraq, Al Baḥr al (Blue Nile), *river*, Ethiopia, **366** E2, *93, 336, 338*
Azraq ash Shīshān, Jordan, **225** D4
Azrou, Morocco, **361** E2
Azua, Dominican Republic, **429** H3
Azuaga, Spain, **292** E3
Azuero, Península de, Panama, **429** E6
Azul, Argentina, **459** E5
Azul, Cerro, *mountain peak*, Argentina, **460** C1
Azul, Cordillera, *mountain range*, Peru, **454** C2
Azurduy, Bolivia, **455** F5
Azyory, Belarus, **289** M2
Azzel Matti, Sebkha, *salt-pan*, Algeria, **361** G3


## B


Ba, Fiji, **141** A4
Ba, *river*, Vietnam, **203** F3
Bá Thước, Vietnam, **215** H5
Baamonde, Spain, **292** D1
Baardheere, Somalia, **369** H2
Baba Burnu, *point*, Turkey, **297** E6
Bababé, Mauritania, **364** B1
Babaçulândia, Brazil, **452** D5
Babadag, Romania, **296** G3
Babadağ, Turkey, **297** G7
Babadurmaz, Turkmenistan, **222** F5
Babaeski, Turkey, **297** F5
Babahoyo, Ecuador, **450** B4
Babanka, Ukraine, **296** H1
Babanki, Cameroon, **365** G3
Babar, Kepulauan, *islands*, Indonesia, **199** E5
Babati, Tanzania, **369** G3
Babayevo, Russian Federation, **299** E3
Babb, U.S.A., **418** H2
Babbacombe Bay, England, U.K., **304** D4
Babel, Mont de, *mountain peak*, Canada, **416** G4
Babelthuap, *island*, Palau, **138** B4, *118*
Babian, *river*, China, **215** G4
Babinavichy, Belarus, **299** C5
Babine Lake, Canada, **412** G4
Babo, Indonesia, **199** F3
Babonde, Democratic Republic of the Congo, **369** E2
Babongo, Cameroon, **365** G3
Baboquivari Peak, *mountain peak*, U.S.A., **423** H6
Baboua, Central African Republic, **368** B1
Babruysk, Belarus, **299** B6
Babushkin, Russian Federation, **210** D2
Babušnica, Serbia, **296** D4
Babuyan Channel, Philippines, **204** C2
Babuyan Islands, Philippines, **204** C2
Bač, Serbia, **296** B3
Bacaadweyn, Somalia, **367** G3
Bacabal, Brazil, **453** E4
Bacajá, *river*, Brazil, **452** C4
Bacalar, Mexico, **431** H5
Bacan, Pulau, *island*, Indonesia, **198** D3
Bacao, Philippines, **204** B4
Bacarra, Philippines, **204** C2
Bacău, Romania, **296** F2
Baccarat, France, **291** H2
Bachu, China, **212** C5
Back, *river*, Canada, **410** J3
Bačka Palanka, Serbia, **296** B3
Bačka Topola, Serbia, **296** B3
Backe, Sweden, **284** H5
Bäckefors, Sweden, **286** F3
Bački Petrovac, Serbia, **296** B3
Baco, Mount, *mountain peak*, Philippines, **204** C3
Bacolod, Philippines, **204** C4
Bacqueville-en-Caux, France, **305** H5
Bacungan, Philippines, **204** B4
Bad Axe, U.S.A., **421** M4
Bad Bevensen, Germany, **288** E2
Bad Freienwalde, Germany, **289** G2
Bad Hersfeld, Germany, **288** D3
Bad Ischl, Austria, **288** F5
Bad Kissingen, Germany, **288** E3
Bad Kreuznach, Germany, **288** C4
Bad Mergentheim, Germany, **288** D4
Bad Neustadt an der Saale, Germany, **288** E3
Bad Oldesloe, Germany, **288** E2
Bad Orb, Germany, **288** D3
Bad Reichenhall, Germany, **288** F5
Bad Segeberg, Germany, **288** E2
Bad Waldsee, Germany, **288** D5
Badagara, India, **216** C4
Badahe, China, **215** H4
Badain Jaran Shamo, *desert*, China, **213** J5
Badajós, Amazonas, Brazil, **451** F5
Badajós, Pará, Brazil, **452** D4
Badajoz, Spain, **292** D3
Badalona, Spain, **293** J2
Badanah, Saudi Arabia, **363** H2
Badanloch, Loch, *lake*, Scotland, U.K., **308** E2
Baddo, *river*, Pakistan, **221** H3
Badéguichéri, Niger, **365** F2
Baden, Austria, **289** H5
Baden-Baden, Germany, **288** D4
Baden-Württemberg, *state*, Germany, **288** D4, *238*
Badger, Canada, **417** N5
Badīn, Pakistan, **218** B4
Badiraguato, Mexico, **430** D3
Badoc, Philippines, **204** C2
Badong, China, **206** B2
Badou, Togo, **364** E3
Badovinci, Serbia, **296** B3
Badr Ḥunayn, Saudi Arabia, **363** G4
Badu Island, Australia, **135** J1
Badulla, Sri Lanka, **217** E5
Baena, Spain, **292** E4
Baeza, Ecuador, **450** C4
Bafang, Cameroon, **368** B1
Bafatá, Guinea-Bissau, **364** B2
Baffa, Pakistan, **218** C2
Baffin, Cape, Canada, **411** M2
Baffin Bay, Canada/Greenland, **411** M2
Baffin Island, Canada, **411** M2, *91, 466*
Bafia, Cameroon, **368** B2
Bafilo, Togo, **364** E3
Bafoulabé, Mali, **364** B2
Bafoussam, Cameroon, **368** B1
Bāfq, Iran, **221** G2
Bafra, Turkey, **224** E4
Bafra Burnu, *cape*, Turkey, **224** E4
Bafwasende, Democratic Republic of the Congo, **369** E2
Bagabag, Philippines, **204** C2
Bagac, Philippines, **204** C3
Bagaha, India, **219** F4
Bāgalkot, India, **216** C2
Bagamoyo, Tanzania, **369** G4
Baganga, Philippines, **204** D5
Bagani, Namibia, **370** D2
Bagansiapiapi, Indonesia, **200** C2
Bağarası, Turkey, **297** F7
Bagaroua, Niger, **365** E2
Bagata, Democratic Republic of the Congo, **368** C3
Bagatelle, Réunion, **373** A1
Bagdad, U.S.A., **422** G4
Bagé, Brazil, **459** F4
Bagenkop, Denmark, **286** E5
Bages et de Sigean, Étang de, *lake*, France, **291** F5
Bāgeshwar, India, **218** D3
Baggs, U.S.A., **423** K1
Baggy Point, England, U.K., **304** C3
Bāgh, India, **218** C5
Baghdād, Iraq, **363** H2, *92, 182*
Bāghīn, Iran, **221** G2
Baghlān, Afghanistan, **218** B1
Bāghrān, Afghanistan, **218** A2
Bagn, Norway, **286** D2
Bagnères-de-Luchon, France, **290** E5
Bagno di Romagna, Italy, **294** C4
Bago, Philippines, **204** C4
Bagrationovsk, Russian Federation, **287** K5
Bagre, Brazil, **452** C3
Bagua Grande, Peru, **454** B1
Bagudo, Nigeria, **365** E2
Baguio, Philippines, **204** C2
Bagzane, Monts, *mountain peak*, Niger, **365** F1, *327*
Bahamas, *country*, Caribbean Sea, **409** R6, *378, 379, 392*
Baharampur, India, **219** G4
Bahāwalpur, Pakistan, **218** B3
Bahía, Islas de la, *islands*, Honduras, **428** D3
Bahia, *state*, Brazil, **457** F3
Bahía Asunción, Mexico, **430** B3
Bahía Blanca, Argentina, **458** D6
Bahía Bustamante, Argentina, **460** D2
Bahía de Caráquez, Ecuador, **450** B4
Bahía de los Ángeles, Mexico, **430** B2
Bahía de los Ángeles, U.S.A., **422** G7
Bahía Kino, Mexico, **430** C2
Bahía Laura, Argentina, **460** D3
Bahía Negra, Paraguay, **455** G5
Bahía Thetis, Argentina, **460** E5
Bahía Tortugas, Mexico, **430** B3
Bahir Dar, Ethiopia, **367** E2
Bahn, *river*, Germany, **288** E4
Baḥr al Jabal, *state*, Sudan, **369** F1
Baḥr an Nīl, *state*, Sudan, **363** F5
Bahraich, India, **219** E4
Bahrain, *country*, Asia, **196** F7, *146, 177, 178*
Bāhū Kalāt, Iran, **221** H3
Bahushewsk, Belarus, **299** C5
Bai, *river*, China, **206** C1
Bai Shan, *mountain peak*, China, **213** G4
Baia, Romania, **296** G3
Baia de Aramă, Romania, **296** D3
Baia de Arieş, Romania, **296** D2
Baía de Traição, Brazil, **453** G5
Baía dos Tigres, Angola, **370** B2
Baía Farta, Angola, **368** B5
Baia Mare, Romania, **296** D2
Baia Sprie, Romania, **296** D2
Baião, Brazil, **452** D4
Baïbokoum, Chad, **365** H3
Baibu, China, **207** D1
Baicheng, Jilin, China, **211** H3
Baicheng, Xinjiang Uygur Zizhiqu, China, **212** D4
Băicoi, Romania, **296** E3
Baie-Comeau, Canada, **416** G5
Baie-du-Poste, Canada, **416** E4
Baie du Tombeau, Mauritius, **373** C1
Baie-Johan-Beetz, Canada, **417** K4
Baie-St-Paul, Canada, **416** F6
Baie Verte, Canada, **417** N5
Baihao, China, **207** B3
Baihe, Hubei, China, **206** B1
Baihe, Jilin, China, **211** K4
Baijiao, China, **207** A4
Baikal, Lake *see* Baykal, Ozero, *lake*, Russian Federation, **210** D1
Bailang, China, **211** H3
Băile Govora, Romania, **296** E3
Băile Herculane, Romania, **296** D3
Băile Tuşnad, Romania, **296** E2
Bailén, Spain, **293** F3
Băileşti, Romania, **296** D3
Bailieborough, Ireland, **309** F4
Bailique, Brazil, **452** C3
Bailleul, France, **305** K4
Bailundo, Angola, **368** C5
Baima, Guangdong, China, **207** B3
Baima, Qinghai, China, **215** G2
Baimuru, Papua New Guinea, **140** B4
Bainang, China, **214** D3
Bainbridge, U.S.A., **425** K4
Bainet, Haiti, **429** G3
Baing, Indonesia, **198** C5
Bainville, U.S.A., **419** M2
Baiona, Spain, **292** C1
Baiquan, China, **211** J3
Bā'ir, Jordan, **225** D4
Bairab Co, *lake*, China, **219** E2
Bairagnia, India, **219** F4
Bairiki, Kiribati, **139** F4, *119*
Bairin Qiao, China, **211** G4
Bairin Youqi, China, **211** G4
Bairin Zuoqi, China, **211** G4
Bairnsdale, Australia, **135** K6
Bais, France, **290** D2
Baisha, China, **215** H3
Baishan, China, **211** J4
Baishui, *river*, China, **215** H2
Baisogala, Lithuania, **287** L5
Baitang, Guangdong, China, **207** C2
Baitang, Qinghai, China, **215** F2
Baitarani, *river*, India, **219** F5
Baixiang, China, **210** F5
Baixo, Ilhéu de, *island*, Madeira, Portugal, **373** C3
Baixo Longa, Angola, **368** C6
Baiyanghe, China, **212** F4
Baiyin, China, **210** D5
Baiyü, China, **215** F3
Baj Baj, India, **219** G5
Baja, Bahía, *bay*, San Andrés, Colombia, **461** B1
Baja, Hungary, **289** J5
Baja, Punta, *point*, Isla de Pascua (Easter Island), Chile, **461** B2
Baja, Punta, *point*, Mexico, **430** A2
Baja California, *peninsula*, Mexico, **430** B2, *400*
Baja California, *state*, Mexico, **430** A2
Baja California Sur, *state*, Mexico, **430** B3
Bājah, Tunisia, **295** B7
Bajamar, Islas Canarias, Spain, **373** A4
Bajestān, Iran, **221** G2
Bājil, Yemen, **220** D6
Bajina Bašta, Serbia, **296** B4
Bajo Baudó, Colombia, **450** C3
Bajo Caracoles, Argentina, **460** C3
Bajoga, Nigeria, **365** G2
Bajovo Polje, Serbia, **296** B4
Bajram Curri, Albania, **296** B4
Bakala, Central African Republic, **366** B3
Bákan, Iran, **363** J1
Bakaoré, Chad, **366** B1
Bakauheni, Indonesia, **200** D4
Bakayan, Gunung, *mountain peak*, Indonesia, **201** G2
Bakchar, Russian Federation, **223** L1
Bakel, Senegal, **364** B2
Baker, California, U.S.A., **422** E4
Baker, *island*, Baker and Howland Islands, **139** G4
Baker, Montana, U.S.A., **419** M3
Baker, Mount, *mountain peak*, U.S.A., **418** D2
Baker and Howland Islands, *U.S. territory*, Pacific Ocean, **131** H1, *121, 386*
Baker City, U.S.A., **418** F4
Baker Lake, Canada, **411** K3
Baker Lake, *lake*, Canada, **411** K3
Bakersfield, California, U.S.A., **422** D4
Bakersfield, Texas, U.S.A., **423** M6
Bakhtiyārpur, India, **219** F4
Bakhty, Kazakhstan, **212** D3
Bakı (Baku), Azerbaijan, **222** D4, *189*
Bakır, *river*, Turkey, **297** F6
Bakkafjörður, Iceland, **284** Z6
Bakkaflói, *bay*, Iceland, **284** Z6
Bakko, Norway, **286** D3
Bakloh, India, **218** C2
Bako, Côte d'Ivoire, **364** C3
Bako, Ethiopia, **367** E3

Bakony, *mountain range*, Hungary, **289** H5
Bakool, *administrative region*, Somalia, **367** F4
Bakop, Papua New Guinea, **140** D4
Bakouma, Central African Republic, **368** D1
Bakoumba, Gabon, **368** B3
Baku *see* Bakı, Azerbaijan, **222** D4, *189*
Bakutis Coast, *region*, Antarctica, **470** B6
Bala, Cerros de, *mountain range*, Bolivia, **455** E3
Bala, Wales, U.K., **304** D2
Balabac, Philippines, **204** B4
Balabac Island, Philippines, **204** B5
Ba'labakk, Lebanon, **225** D2
Balabanovo, Russian Federation, **299** F5
Bālāghāt, India, **218** E5
Bālāghāt Range, *mountain range*, India, **216** C2
Balaguer, Spain, **293** H2
Balaka, Malawi, **369** F5
Balakhta, Russian Federation, **223** N1
Balakovo, Russian Federation, **222** D2
Balambangan, Pulau, *island*, Malaysia, **201** F1
Bălan, Romania, **296** E2
Balanga, Philippines, **204** C3
Balāngīr, India, **219** E5
Balashikha, Russian Federation, **299** F5
Balashov, Russian Federation, **298** F2
Balassagyarmat, Hungary, **289** J4
Balaton, *lake*, Hungary, **289** H5, *262*
Balatonszentgyörgy, Hungary, **289** H5
Balazote, Spain, **293** F3
Balbi, Mount, *mountain peak*, Papua New Guinea, **140** E2
Balbina, Brazil, **451** G4
Balbina, Represa de, *reservoir*, Brazil, **451** G4
Balbriggan, Ireland, **309** F4
Balcarce, Argentina, **459** E5
Balchik, Bulgaria, **296** G4
Balclutha, New Zealand, **133** B8
Balcones Escarpment, U.S.A., **424** C5
Bald Knob, U.S.A., **424** G2
Bald Mountain, *mountain peak*, U.S.A., **422** C1
Balderton, England, U.K., **305** G1
Baldock, England, U.K., **305** G3
Baldone, Latvia, **287** M4
Baldwin, Florida, U.S.A., **425** M4
Baldwin, Michigan, U.S.A., **421** L4
Baldwin, Wisconsin, U.S.A., **420** G3
Baldy Peak, *mountain peak*, U.S.A., **423** J5
Baleares, Islas (Balearic Islands), *islands*, Spain, **293** J3, *253*
Balearic Islands *see* Baleares, Islas, *islands*, Spain, **293** J3, *253*
Baleh, *river*, Malaysia, **201** F2
Baleia, Ponta da, *point*, Brazil, **457** F4
Băleni, Romania, **296** E3
Baler Bay, Philippines, **204** C3
Baler, Philippines, **204** C3
Bāleshwar, India, **219** F5
Baley, Russian Federation, **210** G2
Baléya, Mali, **364** B2
Baléyara, Niger, **365** E2
Balfour, Canada, **413** L7
Balfour, Orkney, Scotland, U.K., **308** G1
Balgazyn, Russian Federation, **213** G2
Balguntay, China, **223** M4
Balḥāf, Yemen, **220** E6
Balho, Djibouti, **367** F2
Bali, *island*, Indonesia, **201** F4, *50, 144, 148*
Bali, *province*, Indonesia, **201** F5
Bali Sea, Indonesia, **201** F4
Baliem, *river*, Indonesia, **199** G3
Balifondo, Central African Republic, **368** D1
Balige, Indonesia, **200** B2
Baliguda, India, **219** E5
Balıkesir, *province*, Turkey, **297** F6
Balıkesir, Turkey, **297** F6
Balıklıçeşme, Turkey, **297** F5
Balikpapan, Indonesia, **201** G3
Balimbing, Indonesia, **200** D4
Balimo, Papua New Guinea, **140** A5
Balingasag, Philippines, **204** D4
Balingen, Germany, **288** D4
Balingoan, Philippines, **204** D4
Balintore, Scotland, U.K., **308** F3
Balj, *river*, Mongolia, **210** E2
Baljurashi, Saudi Arabia, **363** H5
Balkan Peninsula, Europe, **102** C4, *261, 264, 265*
Balkashīno, Kazakhstan, **223** H2
Balkon-Myl'k, Gora, *mountain peak*, Russian Federation, **285** T2
Ballachulish, Scotland, U.K., **308** D4
Balladonia, Australia, **134** E5
Ballaghaderreen, Ireland, **309** D4
Ballālpur, India, **218** D6
Ballangen, Norway, **284** H2
Ballantrae, Scotland, U.K., **308** D5
Ballarat, Australia, **135** J6
Ballard, Lake, Australia, **134** E4
Ballater, Scotland, U.K., **308** F3
Ballenas, Bahía, *bay*, Mexico, **430** B3
Balleny Islands, Antarctica, **470** E8
Ballina, Australia, **135** L4
Ballina, Ireland, **309** C3
Ballinafad, Ireland, **309** D3
Ballinalack, Ireland, **309** E4
Ballinamore, Ireland, **309** E3
Ballinasloe, Ireland, **309** D4
Ballindine, Ireland, **309** D4
Ballinger, U.S.A., **424** C4
Ballinluig, Scotland, U.K., **308** F4
Ballinrobe, Ireland, **309** C4
Ballon, Ireland, **309** F5
Ball's Pyramid, Lord Howe Island, Australia, **135** U14
Ballstad, Norway, **284** F2
Ballybay, Ireland, **309** F3
Ballybofey, Ireland, **309** E3
Ballybunnion, Ireland, **309** C5
Ballycanew, Ireland, **309** F5
Ballycastle, Ireland, **309** C3
Ballycastle, Northern Ireland, U.K., **309** F2
Ballyclare, Northern Ireland, U.K., **309** G3
Ballycroy, Ireland, **309** C3
Ballydesmond, Ireland, **309** C5
Ballyford Head, *point*, Ireland, **309** B4
Ballygar, Ireland, **309** D4
Ballygawley, Northern Ireland, U.K., **309** E3
Ballyhale, Ireland, **309** E5
Ballyheige, Ireland, **309** C5
Ballyheige Bay, Ireland, **309** B5
Ballyhoura Mountains, Ireland, **309** D5
Ballyjamesduff, Ireland, **309** E4
Ballykelly, Northern Ireland, U.K., **309** E2
Ballylynan, Ireland, **309** E5
Ballymacarbry, Ireland, **309** E5
Ballymahon, Ireland, **309** E4
Ballymena, *district*, Northern Ireland, U.K., **309** F3
Ballymena, Northern Ireland, U.K., **309** F3
Ballymoney, *district*, Northern Ireland, U.K., **309** F2
Ballymoney, Northern Ireland, U.K., **309** F2
Ballymote, Ireland, **309** D3
Ballymurphy, Ireland, **309** F5
Ballynahinch, Northern Ireland, U.K., **309** G3
Ballyragget, Ireland, **309** E5
Ballyshannon, Ireland, **309** D3
Ballyteige Bay, Ireland, **309** F5
Ballyvaughan, Ireland, **309** C4
Ballyvourney, Ireland, **309** C6
Balmaceda, Chile, **460** C2
Balmaceda, Sierra, *mountain range*, Argentina, **460** C4
Balmazújvaros, Hungary, **289** K5
Balmertown, Canada, **414** H6
Balmorhea, U.S.A., **423** M6
Balnakeil Bay, Scotland, U.K., **308** E2
Balnapaling, Scotland, U.K., **308** E3
Baloda Bāzār, India, **219** E5
Balombo, Angola, **368** B5
Balonne, *river*, Australia, **135** K4
Bālotra, India, **218** C4
Balqash, Kazakhstan, **212** B3
Balqash Köli, *lake*, Kazakhstan, **212** C3, *185*
Balquhidder, Scotland, U.K., **308** E4
Balranald, Australia, **135** J5
Balş, Romania, **296** E3
Balsas, Brazil, **452** D5
Balsas, Das, *river*, Brazil, **456** D2
Balsas, Mexico, **431** F5
Balsas, *river*, Mexico, **431** F5
Balta, Ukraine, **296** G2
Balta Berilovac, Serbia, **296** D4
Baltasound, Scotland, U.K., **308** L7
Baltic Sea, Europe, **287** J4, *229, 232, 233, 235, 236, 237, 238, 267, 268, 271, 272*
Balṭīm, Egypt, **225** A4
Baltimore, U.S.A., **426** B5
Baltinglass, Ireland, **309** F5
Baltiysk, Russian Federation, **287** J5
Baluchistān, *province*, Pakistan, **218** A3, *175*
Balud, Philippines, **204** C3
Bălūi, Moldova, **296** F2
Bālurghāt, India, **219** G4
Balvatnet, *lake*, Norway, **284** G3
Balvi, Latvia, **287** N4
Balya, Turkey, **297** F6
Balykchy, Kyrgyzstan, **212** C4
Balyktyg-Khem, *river*, Russian Federation, **213** H2
Balyn, Ukraine, **296** F1
Balzar, Ecuador, **450** B4
Bam, Iran, **221** G3
Bama, China, **215** H4
Bamaga, Australia, **135** J1
Bamako, Mali, **364** C2, *324*
Bamba, Mali, **364** D1
Bambama, Congo, **368** B3
Bambamarca, Peru, **454** B2
Bambangando, Angola, **368** D6
Bambari, Central African Republic, **368** D1
Bamberg, Germany, **288** E4
Bamberg, U.S.A., **425** M3
Bambesa, Democratic Republic of the Congo, **369** E2
Bambey, Senegal, **364** A2
Bambili, Democratic Republic of the Congo, **369** E2
Bambio, Central African Republic, **368** C2
Bamboesberg, *mountain peak*, South Africa, **371** E5
Bambouti, Central African Republic, **369** E1
Bambudi, Ethiopia, **366** E2
Bambuí, Brazil, **456** E5
Bamburgh, England, U.K., **307** G2
Bamda, China, **215** F3
Bamenda, Cameroon, **368** B1
Bāmīān, Afghanistan, **218** A2
Bamiancheng, China, **211** H4
Bamingui, Central African Republic, **366** B3
Bamingui, *river*, Central African Republic, **366** A3
Bamingui-Bangoran, Central African Republic, **366** A3
Bâmnák, Cambodia, **203** E3
Bampton, Devon, England, U.K., **304** D4
Bampton, Oxfordshire, England, U.K., **305** F3
Bampūr, Iran, **221** H3
Bampūr, *river*, Iran, **221** G3
Bamy, Turkmenistan, **222** F5
Ban Ban, Laos, **203** D2
Ban Boun Tai, Laos, **202** D1
Ban Don, Ao, *bay*, Thailand, **202** C4
Ban Hangdon, Laos, **203** E3
Ban Hat Lek, Thailand, **203** D4
Ban Huai Yang, Thailand, **202** C4
Ban Khao Sai, Thailand, **202** D2
Ban Khok Kloi, Thailand, **202** C4
Ban Muong, Laos, **203** E2
Ban Na San, Thailand, **202** C4
Ban Nalè, Laos, **202** D2
Ban Nambak, Laos, **203** D1
Ban Napè, Laos, **203** E2
Ban Nongsim, Laos, **203** E3
Ban Pak Pat, Thailand, **202** D2
Ban Phai, Thailand, **203** D2
Ban Phon, Laos, **203** E3
Ban Phônkho, Laos, **203** E2
Ban Phu, Thailand, **202** D2
Ban Rai, Thailand, **202** C3
Ban Thabôk, Laos, **203** D2
Ban Vang-An, Laos, **203** D2
Banaadir, *administrative region*, Somalia, **367** G4
Banaba (Ocean), *island*, Kiribati, **139** F5, *119, 120*
Banagher, Ireland, **309** E4
Banalia, Democratic Republic of the Congo, **369** E2
Banamba, Mali, **364** C2
Bananga, Andaman and Nicobar Islands, India, **217** H5
Banarlı, Turkey, **297** F5
Banās, Ra's, *point*, Egypt, **363** G4
Banās, *river*, India, **218** D4
Banaue, Philippines, **204** C2
Banaz, Turkey, **297** G6
Banbar, China, **215** E3
Banbridge, *district*, Northern Ireland, U.K., **309** F3
Banbridge, Northern Ireland, U.K., **309** F3
Banbury, England, U.K., **305** F2
Banchory, Scotland, U.K., **308** G3
Bancroft, Canada, **416** C7
Bancroft, U.S.A., **420** E5
Banda, Cameroon, **365** G3
Banda, Democratic Republic of the Congo, **369** E2
Bānda, India, **218** E4
Banda Aceh, Indonesia, **200** A1
Banda Elat, Indonesia, **199** F4
Banda Sea, Indonesia, **198** D4
Bandahara, Gunung, *mountain peak*, Indonesia, **200** B2
Bandajuma, Sierra Leone, **364** B3
Bandar, Mozambique, **369** F6
Bandar-e 'Abbās, Iran, **221** G3
Bandar-e Anzalī, Iran, **222** D5
Bandar-e Khomeynī, Iran, **363** J2
Bandar-e Lengeh, Iran, **221** F3
Bandar Seri Begawan, Brunei, **201** F1, *150*
Bandar Sri Aman (Simanggang), Malaysia, **201** E2
Bandar Wanaag, Somalia, **367** F3
Bandarbeyla, Somalia, **367** H3
Bandarlampung, Indonesia, **200** D4
Bandeirante, Brazil, **456** C3
Bandera, Argentina, **458** D3
Bandera, U.S.A., **424** C5
Banderas, Mexico, **430** D2
Bāndhi, Pakistan, **218** B4
Bandiagara, Mali, **364** D2
Bāndīkūi, India, **218** D4
Bandipura, India, **218** C2
Bandırma, Turkey, **297** F5
Bandon, Ireland, **309** D6
Bandon, *river*, Ireland, **309** D6
Bandon, U.S.A., **418** B5
Bandundu, *administrative region*, Democratic Republic of the Congo, **368** C3
Bandundu, Democratic Republic of the Congo, **368** C3
Bandung, Indonesia, **201** D4
Băneasa, Romania, **296** F3
Banes, Cuba, **429** G2
Banff, Canada, **413** M6
Banff, Scotland, U.K., **308** G3
Banfora, Burkina Faso, **364** D2, *325*
Banfu, China, **207** A4
Banga, Democratic Republic of the Congo, **368** D4
Bangalore, India, **216** D3, *169*
Bangangté, Cameroon, **368** B1
Bangassou, Central African Republic, **368** D2
Bangeta, Mount, *mountain peak*, Papua New Guinea, **140** B4
Banggai, Kepulauan, *islands*, Indonesia, **198** C3
Banggi, Pulau, *island*, Malaysia, **201** G1
Banghāzī, Libya, **362** D2
Banghiang, *river*, Laos, **203** E2, *154*
Bangka, Pulau, *island*, Sulawesi Utara, Indonesia, **198** D2
Bangka, Pulau, *island*, Sumatera Selatan, Indonesia, **200** D3
Bangka, Selat, *strait*, Indonesia, **200** D3
Bangkai, Tanjong, *point*, Indonesia, **201** E2
Bangkalan, Indonesia, **201** F4
Bangkaru, Pulau, *island*, Indonesia, **200** B2
Bangkinang, Indonesia, **200** C2
Bangko, Indonesia, **200** C3
Bangkok, Bight of, *bay*, Thailand, **202** D3
Bangkok *see* Krung Thep, Thailand, **202** D3, *155*
Bangladesh, *country*, Asia, **196** K7, *40, 49, 51, 144, 145, 157, 169, 170, 171, 173*
Bangolo, Côte d'Ivoire, **364** C3
Bangor, Northern Ireland, U.K., **309** G3
Bangor, U.S.A., **426** F2
Bangor, Wales, U.K., **304** C1
Bangor Erris, Ireland, **309** C3
Bangs, Mount, *mountain peak*, U.S.A., **422** G3
Bangued, Philippines, **204** C2
Bangui, Central African Republic, **368** C2, *331*
Bangui, Philippines, **204** C2
Bangui-Motaba, Congo, **368** C2
Banguru, Democratic Republic of the Congo, **369** E2
Bangweulu Lake, Zambia, **369** F5
Banhā, Egypt, **225** A4
Bani, Burkina Faso, **364** D2
Bani, Central African Republic, **366** B3
Bani Bangou, Niger, **365** E1
Banī Mazār, Egypt, **363** F3
Banī Suwayf, Egypt, **225** A5
Banī Thawr, Saudi Arabia, **363** H5
Banī Walīd, Libya, **362** B2
Bania, Central African Republic, **368** C2
Baniara, Papua New Guinea, **140** C5
Banija, *mountain range*, Bosnia and Herzegovina, **294** F3
Banikoara, Benin, **365** E2
Bāniyās, Al Qunayṭirah, Syria, **225** C3
Bāniyās, Ṭarṭūs, Syria, **225** C2
Banja Luka, Bosnia and Herzegovina, **294** F3
Banjarmasin, Indonesia, **201** F3
Banjul, Gambia, **364** A2, *320*
Bānka, India, **219** F4
Bankass, Mali, **364** D2
Bankeryd, Sweden, **286** G4
Bankilaré, Niger, **364** E2
Banko, Guinea, **364** B2
Banks, Bahía, *bay*, Islas Galápagos (Galapagos Islands), Ecuador, **461** A1
Banks, U.S.A., **418** F4

Banks Island, British Columbia, Canada, **412** D5
Banks Island, Northwest Territories, Canada, **410** G2
Banks Islands, Vanuatu, **141** A2
Banks Lake, U.S.A., **418** E3
Banks Peninsula, New Zealand, **133** D6
Banksá Bystrica, Slovakia, **289** J4
Bānkura, India, **219** F5
Banli, China, **215** H5
Bann, *river*, Northern Ireland, U.K., **309** F2
Bannerman Town, Bahamas, **428** F1
Banning, U.S.A., **422** E5
Bannockburn, Scotland, U.K., **308** F4, *275*
Bannu, Pakistan, **218** B2
Banovići, Bosnia and Herzegovina, **294** G3
Banqiao, China, **215** H4
Bansko, Bulgaria, **296** D5
Banskobystrický, *administrative region*, Slovakia, **289** J4
Bānswāra, India, **218** C5
Bantayan, Philippines, **204** C4
Bantè, Benin, **365** E3
Banteer, Ireland, **309** D5
Bantry, Ireland, **309** C6
Bantry Bay, Ireland, **309** C6
Bāntva, India, **218** B5
Bantvāl, India, **216** C3
Banyalbufar, Spain, **293** J3
Banyo, Cameroon, **365** G3
Banyoles, Spain, **293** J1
Banyuwangi, Indonesia, **201** F5
Banz, Papua New Guinea, **140** B4
Banzare Coast, *region*, Antarctica, **470** F7
Banzart, Tunisia, **295** B7
Bao Lộc, Vietnam, **203** E4
Baoan, China, **207** B3
Baode, China, **210** E5
Baodi, China, **210** G5
Baoding, China, **210** F5
Baoji, China, **215** H2
Baojing, China, **206** B2
Baolo, Solomon Islands, **141** A1
Baoqing, China, **211** L3
Baoro, Central African Republic, **368** C1
Baoshan, China, **215** F4
Baotou, China, **210** E4
Baoxia, China, **206** B1
Baoyi, China, **206** D1
Baoying, China, **206** D1
Bāp, India, **218** C4
Bapaume, France, **291** F1
Baqanas, Kazakhstan, **212** C3
Baqanas, *river*, Kazakhstan, **212** C3
Ba'qūbah, Iraq, **363** H2
Baquedano, Chile, **458** C2
Bar, Montenegro, **296** B4
Bar Harbor, U.S.A., **426** F2
Bar-le-Duc, France, **291** G2
Bar-sur-Aube, France, **291** G2
Bar-sur-Seine, France, **291** G2
Bara, Indonesia, **198** D3
Bara, Nigeria, **365** G2
Bāra Banki, India, **218** E4
Baraawe, Somalia, **367** F4
Barabinsk, Russian Federation, **223** K1
Barachois, Canada, **417** J5
Baracoa, Cuba, **429** G2
Baradero, Argentina, **459** E4
Baragua, Venezuela, **451** D1
Bārah, Sudan, **366** D2
Barahona, Dominican Republic, **429** H3
Barakaldo, Spain, **293** F1
Barakī, Afghanistan, **218** B2
Bārākot, India, **219** F5
Baralzon Lake, Canada, **414** E2
Baram, *river*, Malaysia, **201** F2
Baram, Tanjong, *point*, Malaysia, **201** F1
Barama, *river*, Guyana, **451** G2
Baramanni, Guyana, **451** G2
Bārāmati, India, **216** C2
Bāramūla, India, **218** C2
Baranavichy, Belarus, **298** C2
Baranoa, Colombia, **450** C1
Baranof, U.S.A., **412** B3
Baranof Island, U.S.A., **412** B3
Barão de Melgaço, Brazil, **456** B4
Baraolt, Romania, **296** E2
Barate, Indonesia, **198** C5
Baraya, Colombia, **450** C3
Barbacena, Brazil, **457** E5
Barbacoas, Colombia, **450** B4
Barbadillo, Spain, **292** E2
Barbados, *country*, Caribbean Sea, **427** E3, *378*, *398*
Barbar, Sudan, **363** F5
Barbas, Cabo, *cape*, Western Sahara, **360** C4
Barbastro, Spain, **293** H1
Barbate de Franco, Spain, **292** D4
Bărbăteşti, Romania, **296** D3
Barber, Curaçao, Netherlands Antilles, **461** C3
Barberton, South Africa, **371** F4
Barbezieux-Saint-Hilaire, France, **290** D4
Barbosa, Colombia, **450** D2
Barbuda, *island*, Antigua and Barbuda, **427** D2, *379*
Bârca, Romania, **296** D4
Barcadera, Aruba, **461** B3
Barcaldine, Australia, **135** K3
Barcarrota, Spain, **292** D3
Barcelona, Spain, **293** J2, *253*
Barcelona, Venezuela, **451** F1
Barcelonnette, France, **291** H4
Barcelos, Brazil, **451** F4
Barciany, Poland, **289** K1
Barcoo, *river*, Australia, **135** J3
Barcs, Hungary, **289** H5
Bärdä, Azerbaijan, **222** D4
Bardaï, Chad, **362** C4
Bardarban, Bangladesh, **219** H5
Bárðarbunga, *mountain peak*, Iceland, **284** Y7
Bardas Blancas, Argentina, **458** C5
Bardawīl, Sabkhat al, *lagoon*, Egypt, **225** B4
Barddhamān, India, **219** F5
Bardejov, Slovakia, **289** K4
Bardney, England, U.K., **305** G1
Bardsey Island, Wales, U.K., **304** C2
Bardsey Sound, Wales, U.K., **304** C2
Bardstown, U.S.A., **421** L7
Bareilly, India, **218** D3
Barentin, France, **290** E2
Barents Sea, Arctic Ocean, **300** E2
Barentsøya, *island*, Svalbard, **300** D2
Barentu, Eritrea, **367** E1
Barfleur, France, **305** F5
Barfleur, Pointe de, *point*, France, **290** D2
Barga, China, **214** B3
Barga, Italy, **294** C3
Bargaal, Somalia, **367** H2
Bargarh, India, **219** F5
Bargrennan, Scotland, U.K., **308** E5
Barham, England, U.K., **305** J3
Bari, *administrative region*, Somalia, **367** G3
Bari, Democratic Republic of the Congo, **368** C2
Bari, Italy, **295** F5, *255*
Bari Sādri, India, **218** C4
Barīdī, Ra's, *point*, Saudi Arabia, **363** G4
Barika, Algeria, **361** H1
Barillas, Guatemala, **428** C4
Barinas, Venezuela, **451** D2
Baring, Cape, Canada, **410** H2
Baringa, Democratic Republic of the Congo, **368** D2
Bārīs, Egypt, **363** F4
Barisāl, Bangladesh, **214** D5
Barisan, Pegunungan, *mountain range*, Indonesia, **200** C3
Barito, *river*, Indonesia, **201** F3
Barkam, China, **215** G3
Barkava, Latvia, **287** N4
Barkerville, Canada, **412** J5
Bārkhān, Pakistan, **218** B3
Barki Saria, India, **219** F4
Barkley Sound, Canada, **412** G7
Barkly East, South Africa, **371** E5
Barkly Homestead Roadhouse, Australia, **135** H2
Barkly Tableland, *plateau*, Australia, **135** H2
Barkly West, South Africa, **370** D4
Barkol, China, **213** G4
Barkol Hu, *lake*, China, **213** G4
Barksdale, U.S.A., **424** B5
Barkway, England, U.K., **305** H3
Bârlad, Romania, **296** F2
Barlee, Lake, Australia, **134** D4
Barletta, Italy, **295** F5
Barley, England, U.K., **305** H2
Barlinek, Poland, **289** G2
Bārmer, India, **218** B4
Barmouth, Wales, U.K., **304** C2
Barmouth Bay, Wales, U.K., **304** C2
Barn, The, *mountain peak*, St. Helena, **373** B3
Barn Long Point, St Helena, **373** B3
Barnagar, India, **218** C5
Barnard Castle, England, U.K., **307** G3
Barnaul, Russian Federation, **223** L2
Barnesville, U.S.A., **420** E2
Barnet, England, U.K., **305** G3
Barneville-Carteret, France, **290** D2
Barney, U.S.A., **425** L4
Barnhart, U.S.A., **424** B4
Barnoldswick, England, U.K., **306** F4
Barnsley, England, U.K., **307** G4
Barnstaple, England, U.K., **304** C3
Barnwell, U.S.A., **425** M3
Baro, *river*, Ethiopia, **366** D3
Baroda, India, **218** D4
Barques, Pointe aux, *point*, U.S.A., **421** M3
Barquisimeto, Venezuela, **451** E1
Barra, Brazil, **457** E3
Barra, *island*, Scotland, U.K., **308** B4
Barra, Ponta da, *island*, Mozambique, **371** G3
Barra, Sound of, Scotland, U.K., **308** B3
Barra de Caratasca, Honduras, **428** E4
Barra de São Manuel, Brazil, **452** A5
Barra do Bugres, Brazil, **456** B4
Barra do Corda, Brazil, **452** E4
Barra do Cuanza, Angola, **368** B4
Barra do Dande, Angola, **368** B4
Barra do Garças, Brazil, **456** C4
Barra do Riacho, Brazil, **457** F5
Barra do Ribeiro, Brazil, **459** G4
Barra Falsa, Ponta da, *island*, Mozambique, **371** G3
Barra Mansa, Brazil, **457** E6
Barraca da Bôca, Brazil, **452** C3
Barracão do Barreto, Brazil, **455** G2
Barranca, N. Peru, **454** C1
Barranca, Peru, **454** C3
Barrancabermeja, Colombia, **450** C2
Barrancas, Colombia, **450** D1
Barrancas, Venezuela, **451** F2
Barrancos, Portugal, **292** D3
Barranqueras, Argentina, **459** E3
Barranquilla, Colombia, **450** C1, *436*
Barranquitas, Venezuela, **450** D2
Barras, Brazil, **453** E4
Barraute, Canada, **416** C5
Barrax, Spain, **293** F3
Barreal, Argentina, **458** C4
Barreiras, Brazil, **457** E3
Barreirinha, Brazil, **452** B4
Barreirinhas, Brazil, **453** E4
Barreiro do Nascimento, Brazil, **456** C3
Barreiros, Brazil, **457** G2
Barretos, Brazil, **456** D5
Barrhead, Canada, **413** M4
Barrhead, Scotland, U.K., **308** E5
Barrie, Canada, **421** P3
Barrier, Cape, New Zealand, **132** E3
Barrington, Mount, *mountain peak*, Australia, **135** L5
Barringun, Australia, **135** K4
Barrocão, Brazil, **457** E4
Barron, U.S.A., **420** H3
Barrow, Point, U.S.A., **410** D2
Barrow, U.S.A., **410** D2
Barrow-in-Furness, England, U.K., **306** E3
Barrow Island, Australia, **134** D3
Barry, Wales, U.K., **304** D3
Barrys Bay, Canada, **416** C7
Bârsana, Romania, **296** E2
Barsanikha, Russian Federation, **299** E3
Barshatas, Kazakhstan, **212** C2
Barshyn, Kazakhstan, **212** A2
Bārsi, India, **216** C2
Barstow, U.S.A., **422** E4
Bārta, Latvia, **287** K4
Bārta, *river*, Latvia/Lithuania, **287** K4
Barth, Germany, **288** F1
Bartica, Guyana, **451** G2
Bartle Frere, *mountain peak*, Australia, **135** K2
Bartlesville, U.S.A., **420** F7
Bartlett, U.S.A., **423** M3
Bartolomeu Dias, Mozambique, **371** G3
Barton, U.S.A., **426** D2
Barton-upon-Humber, England, U.K., **307** H4
Bartoszyce, Poland, **289** K1
Bartow, U.S.A., **425** M6
Baru, Irian Jaya, Indonesia, **199** F3
Baru, Maluku, Indonesia, **198** D2
Barú, Volcán, *mountain peak*, Panama, **429** E5, *405*
Barun, China, **213** H5
Barun-Torey, Ozero, *lake*, Russian Federation, **210** F2
Barung, Indonesia, **201** G2
Barus, Indonesia, **200** B2
Baruta, Venezuela, **451** E1
Baruth, Germany, **288** F2
Baruun-Urt, Mongolia, **210** F3
Baruunharaa, Mongolia, **210** D2
Baruunturuun, Mongolia, **213** G2
Barvas, Scotland, U.K., **308** C2
Barwāni, India, **218** C5
Barwon, *river*, Australia, **135** K4
Baryatino, Russian Federation, **299** E5
Barycz, *river*, Poland, **289** H3
Barysaw, Belarus, **299** B5
Barysh, Russian Federation, **222** D2
Bas-Zaïre, *province*, Democratic Republic of the Congo, **368** B4
Basail, Argentina, **459** E3
Basăk, *river*, Cambodia, **203** E4
Basakan, Gunung, *mountain peak*, Indonesia, **201** G2
Basāl, Pakistan, **218** C2
Basalt, U.S.A., **422** D2
Basalt Island, China, **207** C4
Basankusu, Democratic Republic of the Congo, **368** C2
Basarabeasca, Moldova, **296** G2
Basarabi, Romania, **296** G3
Baschurch, England, U.K., **304** E2
Basco, Philippines, **204** C1
Bascuñán, Cabo, *cape*, Chile, **458** B3
Basel, Switzerland, **291** H3
Bashi Channel, China, **206** E4
Bashkaus, *river*, Russian Federation, **212** F2
Bashkortostan, Respublika, *republic*, Russian Federation, **222** F1
Bāsht, Iran, **220** F2
Basi, India, **221** K3
Basia, India, **219** F5
Basilan Island, Philippines, **204** C5
Basildon, England, U.K., **305** H3
Basile, Pico, *mountain peak*, Equatorial Guinea, **368** A2, *331*, *332*
Basilicata, *autonomous region*, Italy, **295** E5, *255*
Basin, U.S.A., **419** K4
Basingstoke, England, U.K., **305** F3
Basirhat, India, **219** G5
Basīţ, Ra's al, *cape*, Syria, **225** C2
Baška, Croatia, **294** E3
Başkale, Turkey, **224** F5
Baskatong, Réservoir, Canada, **416** D6
Baslow, England, U.K., **305** F1
Basoko, Democratic Republic of the Congo, **368** D2
Basora, Punt, *point*, Aruba, **461** B3
Basque, U.S.A., **418** F5
Basra *see* Al Başrah, Iraq, **363** J2
Bass Strait, Australia, **135** K6
Bassano, Canada, **413** N6
Bassano del Grappa, Italy, **294** C3
Bassar, Togo, **364** E3
Basse-Kotto, *prefecture*, Central African Republic, **366** B3
Basse-Normandie, *administrative region*, France, **290** D2, *245*
Basse-Terre, Guadeloupe, **427** D3, *389*
Basse Terre, Trinidad, Trinidad and Tobago, **461** C4
Bassein, Myanmar, **205** B4
Bassenthwaite Lake, England, U.K., **306** E3
Basseterre, St Kitts and Nevis, **427** D2, *395*
Bassett, U.S.A., **420** D4
Bassikounou, Mauritania, **364** C1
Bassila, Benin, **364** E3
Basso, *mountain peak*, Chad, **362** D5
Bastak, Iran, **221** F3
Bastelica, Corse, France, **295** B4
Bastī, India, **219** E4
Bastia, Corse, France, **294** B4
Bastogne, Belgium, **288** B4
Bastrop, Louisiana, U.S.A., **424** G3
Bastrop, Texas, U.S.A., **424** D4
Bat Khela, Pakistan, **218** B2
Bata, Equatorial Guinea, **368** A2
Batabanó, Cabo, *cape*, Cuba, **429** E2
Batabanó, Cuba, **429** E2
Batabanó, Golfo de, *gulf*, Cuba, **429** E2
Batac, Philippines, **204** C2
Batagol, Russian Federation, **213** J1
Batajnica, Serbia, **296** C3
Batak, Bulgaria, **296** E5
Batakan, Indonesia, **201** F4
Batāla, India, **218** C3
Batalha, Portugal, **292** C3
Batama, Democratic Republic of the Congo, **369** E2
Batan Island, Philippines, **204** D3
Batan Islands, Philippines, **204** C1
Batang, China, **215** F3
Batanga, Gabon, **368** A3
Batangas, Philippines, **204** C3
Batas Island, Philippines, **204** B4
Batavia, U.S.A., **426** A3
Batchawana Bay, Canada, **421** L2
Bătdâmbâng, Cambodia, **203** D3
Batemans Bay, Australia, **135** L6
Batesburg, U.S.A., **425** M3
Batesland, U.S.A., **420** B4
Batesville, Arkansas, U.S.A., **424** G2
Batesville, Mississippi, U.S.A., **424** H2
Batesville, Texas, U.S.A., **424** C5
Batetskiy, Russian Federation, **299** C3
Bath, England, U.K., **304** E3
Bath, Maine, U.S.A., **426** F3
Bath, New York, U.S.A., **426** B3
Bath and North East Somerset, *unitary authority*, England, U.K., **304** E3
Batha, *prefecture*, Chad, **366** A2
Bathgate, Scotland, U.K., **308** F5
Bathurst, Australia, **135** K5
Bathurst, Canada, **416** J6

Bathurst, Cape, Canada, **410** F2
Bathurst Inlet, Canada, **410** J3
Bathurst Island, Australia, **134** F1
Bathurst Island, Canada, **411** J2
Batī, Ethiopia, **367** F2
Batı Menteşe Dağları, *mountain range*, Turkey, **297** F7
Bāţin, Wādī al, *river*, Iraq/Kuwait/Saudi Arabia, **220** E3, *177*
Batkes, Indonesia, **199** E4
Batman, Turkey, **224** F5
Batna, Algeria, **361** H1
Baton Rouge, U.S.A., **424** G4, *386*
Batopilas, Mexico, **430** D3
Batouri, Cameroon, **368** B2
Batovi, Brazil, **456** C4
Batovi, *river*, *see* Tamitatoala, *river*, Brazil, **456** B3
Batrampur, India, **219** E4
Båtsfjord, Norway, **285** P1
Båtsjaur, Sweden, **284** H3
Båtskapp, *cape*, Norway, **285** Q1
Batteau, Canada, **417** P3
Batticaloa, Sri Lanka, **217** E5
Battipaglia, Italy, **295** E5
Battle, England, U.K., **305** H4
Battle, *river*, Canada, **413** P5
Battle Creek, U.S.A., **421** L4
Battle Mountain, U.S.A., **422** E1
Battleford, Canada, **413** Q5
Battonya, Hungary, **289** K5
Batu, Kepulauan, *islands*, Indonesia, **200** B3
Batu, *mountain peak*, Ethiopia, **367** E3
Batu, Tanjong, *point*, Indonesia, **201** G2
Batu Niah, Malaysia, **201** F2
Batu Pahat, Malaysia, **200** C2
Batu Puteh, Gunung, *mountain peak*, Malaysia, **200** C1
Batuberagam, Tanjong, *point*, Indonesia, **200** C4
Batuhitam, Tanjong, *point*, Indonesia, **198** C3
Batui, Indonesia, **198** C3
Batulaki, Philippines, **204** D5
Bat'umi, Georgia, **222** C4
Baturaja, Indonesia, **200** D4
Baturité, Brazil, **453** F4
Baturité, Serra de, *mountain range*, Brazil, **453** F4
Batyrevo, Russian Federation, **222** D1
Batz, Île de, *island*, France, **290** B2
Bau, Malaysia, **201** E2
Bauang, Philippines, **204** C2
Bauchi, Nigeria, **365** F2
Bauchi, *state*, Nigeria, **365** F2
Baudh, India, **219** F5
Baudó, Serranía de, *mountain range*, Colombia, **450** C2
Bauer Bay, Macquarie Island, **134** R11
Baugy, France, **290** F3
Baukau, East Timor, **198** D5
Bauld, Cape, Canada, **417** P4
Baume-les-Dames, France, **291** H3
Baures, Bolivia, **455** F3
Bauru, Brazil, **459** H2
Baús, Brazil, **456** C5
Bauska, Latvia, **287** M4
Bautzen, Germany, **289** G3
Båven, *lake*, Sweden, **287** H3
Bavispe, *river*, Mexico, **430** C2
Bawal, Pulau, *island*, Indonesia, **201** E3
Bawang, Tanjong, *point*, Indonesia, **201** E3
Bawean, Pulau, *island*, Indonesia, **201** E4
Bawku, Ghana, **364** D2
Bawlf, Canada, **413** N5
Bawolung, China, **215** G3
Bawtry, England, U.K., **307** G4
Baxkorgan, China, **212** F5
Baxley, U.S.A., **425** L4
Baxoi, China, **215** F3
Bay, *administrative region*, Somalia, **369** H2
Bay Bulls, Canada, **417** Q6
Bay City, Michigan, U.S.A., **421** M4
Bay City, Texas, U.S.A., **424** E5
Bay Minette, U.S.A., **425** J4
Bay Roberts, Canada, **417** Q6
Bay-Soot, Russian Federation, **213** G2
Bay Springs, U.S.A., **425** H4
Bay View, New Zealand, **132** F4
Bayamo, Cuba, **429** F2
Bāyān, Band-e, *mountain range*, Afghanistan, **218** A2
Bayan, Dornod, Mongolia, **210** F3
Bayan, Dornogovĭ, Mongolia, **210** E3
Bayan, Heilongjiang, China, **211** J3
Bayan, Hentiy, Mongolia, **210** E2
Bayan, Qinghai, China, **215** F2
Bayan Har, China, **210** F4
Bayan Har Shan, *mountain range*, China, **215** F2
Bayan-hushuu, Mongolia, **213** F2
Bayan Mod, China, **210** D4
Bayan Obo, China, **210** E4
Bayan-Ölgiy, *province*, Mongolia, **212** F2
Bayan-Ovoo, Govĭ-Altay, Mongolia, **213** G3
Bayan-Ovoo, Hentiy, Mongolia, **210** E2
Bayan Ovoo, Mongolia, **213** L2
Bayan Qagan, China, **210** F4
Bayan-Ulaan, Mongolia, **213** J3
Bayanauyl, Kazakhstan, **212** B2
Bayanbulag, N. Bayanhongor, Mongolia, **213** H3
Bayanbulag, S. Bayanhongor, Mongolia, **213** H3
Bayanbulak, China, **212** E4
Bayanga, Central African Republic, **368** C2
Bayanga-Didi, Central African Republic, **368** C1
Bayangol, Mongolia, **213** G3
Bayanhongor, Mongolia, **213** J3
Bayanhongor, *province*, Mongolia, **213** H3
Bayanhushuu, Mongolia, **213** H3
Bayansayr, Mongolia, **213** H3
Bayantsagaan, Mongolia, **213** J2
Bayard, U.S.A., **423** J5
Bayasgalant, Sühbaatar, Mongolia, **210** F3
Bayasgalant, Töv, Mongolia, **210** E3
Bayāzīyeh, Iran, **221** G2
Baybay, Philippines, **204** D4
Bayboro, U.S.A., **426** B7
Bayburt, Turkey, **224** F4
Baydhabo, Somalia, **369** H2
Baydrag, *river*, Mongolia, **213** H3
Bayerischer Wald, *mountain range*, Germany, **288** F4
Bayern, *state*, Germany, **288** E4, *238, 239*
Bayès, Cap, *cape*, New Caledonia, **141** A3
Bayeux, France, **290** D2
Bayghanīn, Kazakhstan, **222** F3
Bayḩān al Qiṣāb, Yemen, **220** E6
Bayındır, Turkey, **297** F6
Bayjī, Iraq, **363** H2
Baykal Ozero (Lake Baikal), *lake*, Russian Federation, **210** D1
Baykal'sk, Russian Federation, **210** D2
Baykurt, China, **212** B5
Bayonne, France, **290** D5
Bayovar, Peru, **454** B1
Bayqongyr, Qaraghandy, Kazakhstan, **222** H3
Bayqongyr, Qyzylorda, Kazakhstan, **222** G3
Bayramaly, Turkmenistan, **222** G5
Bayramiç, Turkey, **297** F6
Bayreuth, Germany, **288** E4
Bayrūt (Beirut), Lebanon, **225** C3, *178, 180, 181*
Bayshint, Mongolia, **210** D3
Baystonhill, England, U.K., **304** E2
Bayt al Faqīh, Yemen, **220** D6
Bayt Laḩm (Bethlehem), West Bank, **225** C4, *89*
Baytik Shan, *mountain range*, China/Mongolia, **213** F3
Baytown, U.S.A., **424** E5
Bayuda Desert, Sudan, **363** F5
Bayugan, Philippines, **204** D4
Bayunglincir, Indonesia, **200** C3
Bayyrqum, Kazakhstan, **222** H4
Baza, Spain, **293** F4
Bazardüzü Dağ, *mountain peak*, Azerbaijan, **222** D4, *189*
Bazaruto, Ilha do, *island*, Mozambique, **371** G3
Bazas, France, **290** D4
Bazdār, Pakistan, **218** A4
Bazhong, China, **215** H3
Baziaş, Romania, **296** C3
Bazmān, Iran, **221** H3
Bazmān, Kūh-e, *mountain peak*, Iran, **221** G3
Beachy Head, *point*, England, U.K., **305** H4
Beaconsfield, England, U.K., **305** G3
Beadnell Bay, England, U.K., **307** G2
Beagle Gulf, Australia, **134** F1
Beal, England, U.K., **307** G2
Bealanana, Madagascar, **372** B3
Beale, Cape, Canada, **412** G7
Bealeton, U.S.A., **426** B5
Beaminster, England, U.K., **304** E4
Bear Island, Ireland, **309** B6
Bear Lake, U.S.A., **419** J5
Bear Paw Mountain, *mountain peak*, U.S.A., **419** K2
Beardmore, Canada, **415** L7
Beardsley, U.S.A., **420** C6
Beardstown, U.S.A., **420** H5
Bearskin Lake, Canada, **414** J5
Beas de Segura, Spain, **293** F3
Beata, Cabo, *cape*, Dominican Republic, **429** H3
Beata Ridge, *underwater feature*, Caribbean Sea, **479** P3
Beatrice, U.S.A., **420** E5
Beattock, Scotland, U.K., **308** F5
Beatton, *river*, Canada, **412** J3
Beatty, Nevada, U.S.A., **422** E3
Beatty, Oregon, U.S.A., **418** D5
Beattyville, Canada, **416** C5
Beatys Butte, *mountain peak*, U.S.A., **418** E5
Beau Bassin, Mauritius, **373** C1
Beau Champ, Mauritius, **373** C1
Beaufort, Malaysia, **201** F1
Beaufort, U.S.A., **425** M3
Beaufort Sea, Arctic Ocean, **410** D2
Beaufort West, South Africa, **370** D5
Beaugency, France, **290** E3
Beauharnois, Canada, **416** E7
Beauly, Scotland, U.K., **308** E3
Beaumaris, Wales, U.K., **306** D4
Beaumetz-lès-Loges, France, **305** K4
Beaumont, Kansas, U.S.A., **420** E7
Beaumont, Mississippi, U.S.A., **425** H4
Beaumont, Texas, U.S.A., **424** E4
Beaune, France, **291** G3
Beaupré, Canada, **416** F6
Beaupréau, France, **290** D3
Beauséjour, Canada, **414** F6
Beauvais, France, **290** F2
Beauval, Canada, **413** R4
Beauval, France, **305** K4
Beaver, Utah, U.S.A., **422** G2
Beaver, Wisconsin, U.S.A., **421** J3
Beaver Creek, Canada, **410** E3
Beaver Dam, U.S.A., **421** J4
Beaver Falls, U.S.A., **421** N5
Beaver Island, U.S.A., **421** K3
Beaverhead Mountains, *mountain range*, U.S.A., **418** H4
Beaverhill Lake, Canada, **414** G4
Beaverlodge, Canada, **413** K4
Beāwar, India, **218** C4
Beazley, Argentina, **458** C4
Bebedouro, Brazil, **456** D5
Bebington, England, U.K., **306** E4
Béboto, Chad, **365** H3
Bebrene, Latvia, **287** N4
Beccles, England, U.K., **305** J2
Bečej, Serbia, **296** C3
Becerreá, Spain, **292** D1
Béchar, Algeria, **361** F2
Beckley, U.S.A., **421** N7
Beclean, Romania, **296** E2
Bedale, England, U.K., **307** G3
Bédarieux, France, **291** F5
Beddgelert, Wales, U.K., **304** C1
Bedelē, Ethiopia, **367** E3
Bedēsa, Ethiopia, **367** F3
Bedford, England, U.K., **305** G2
Bedford, Indiana, U.S.A., **421** K6
Bedford, Kentucky, U.S.A., **421** L6
Bedford, Pennsylvania, U.S.A., **421** P6
Bedfordshire, *unitary authority*, England, U.K., **305** G2
Bedi Dat, Pakistan, **218** A4
Bedlington, England, U.K., **307** G2
Bedok, Singapore, **200** K7
Bedok Reservoir, Singapore, **200** K6
Bedourie, Australia, **135** H3
Beenoskee, *mountain peak*, Ireland, **309** B5
Be'ér Menuḥa, Israel, **225** C4
Be'ér Sheva' (Beersheba), Israel, **225** C4, *179*
Beersheba *see* Be'ér Sheva', Israel, **225** C4, *179*
Beeskow, Germany, **289** G2
Beeville, U.S.A., **424** D5
Befale, Democratic Republic of the Congo, **368** D2
Befandriana Avaratra, Madagascar, **372** B4
Befori, Democratic Republic of the Congo, **368** D2
Befotaka, Madagascar, **372** B5
Bega, Australia, **135** K6
Begejski Kanal, *canal*, Serbia, **296** C3
Begunitsy, Russian Federation, **299** B3
Begusarai, India, **219** F4
Beh, *river*, Indonesia, **201** G5
Behbahān, Iran, **220** F2
Behleg, China, **213** F5
Behshahr, Iran, **222** E5
Bei, *river*, China, **206** C3
Bei Shan, *mountain range*, China, **213** G4
Bei'an, China, **211** J2
Beiarn, Norway, **284** G3
Beibu Wan, *bay*, China, **203** F1
Beicheng, China, **215** G4
Beichuan, China, **215** H3
Beida, *river*, China, **213** H4
Beidachi, China, **210** D5
Beidao, China, **215** H2
Beigi, Ethiopia, **366** D3
Beihai, China, **206** B4
Beijian Dao, *island*, China, **207** C5
Beijing (Peking), China, **210** G5, *96, 97, 158, 159, 160, 161, 162*
Beiliu, China, **206** B4
Beilu Heyan, China, **214** E2
Beipiao, China, **211** H4
Beira, Mozambique, **371** F2
Beiru, *river*, China, **206** C1
Beirut *see* Bayrūt, Lebanon, **225** C3, *178, 180, 181*
Beiseker, Canada, **413** N6
Beisfjord, Norway, **284** H2
Beishan, China, **213** H4
Beitbridge, Zimbabwe, **371** F3
Beiuş, Romania, **296** D2
Beixia, China, **207** B1
Beizha, China, **207** B3
Beizhen, China, **208** C2
Beja, *district*, Portugal, **292** C4
Beja, Portugal, **292** D3
Bejaïa, Algeria, **361** H1
Béjar, Spain, **292** E2
Bekdash, Turkmenistan, **222** E4
Békés, Hungary, **289** K5
Békéscsaba, Hungary, **289** K5
Bekily, Madagascar, **372** B5
Bela, India, **219** E4
Bela, Pakistan, **218** A4
Bela Crkva, Serbia, **296** C3
Bela Palanka, Serbia, **296** D4
Bela Vista, Brazil, **456** B6
Bela Vista, Mozambique, **371** F4
Bélabo, Cameroon, **368** B2
Belaghash, Kazakhstan, **212** D2
Belamoty, Madagascar, **372** A5
Belanger, *river*, Canada, **414** F5
Belarus, *country*, Europe, **283** G5, *228, 236, 237, 267, 268, 269, 270, 271*
Belawan, Indonesia, **200** B2
Belaya, Gora, *mountain peak*, Russian Federation, **301** U3
Bélbéji, Niger, **365** F2
Belbutte, Canada, **413** Q5
Belcher Islands, Canada, **415** P3
Belcherāgh, Afghanistan, **218** A2
Belchite, Spain, **293** G2
Belcoo, Northern Ireland, U.K., **309** E3
Belden, California, U.S.A., **422** C1
Belden, North Dakota, U.S.A., **420** B1
Belderg, Ireland, **309** C3
Belebelka, Russian Federation, **299** C4
Belebey, Russian Federation, **222** E2
Beledweyne, Somalia, **367** G4
Belefuanai, Liberia, **364** C3
Belel, Nigeria, **365** G3
Belém, Brazil, **452** D3
Belém de São Francisco, Brazil, **457** F2
Belén, Argentina, **458** C3
Belén, Colombia, **450** D2
Belen, Turkey, **225** B1
Belen, U.S.A., **423** K4
Belene, Bulgaria, **296** E4
Bélep, Île, *islands*, New Caledonia, **141** A3
Belev, Russian Federation, **299** F6
Bèlèya, Guinea, **364** B2
Belfast, *district*, Northern Ireland, U.K., **309** G3
Belfast, Northern Ireland, U.K., **309** G3, *276, 277*
Belfast, U.S.A., **426** F2
Belfast Lough, *inlet*, Northern Ireland, U.K., **309** G3
Belfield, U.S.A., **420** B2
Bēlfodiyo, Ethiopia, **366** D2
Belford, England, U.K., **307** G2
Belfort, France, **291** H3
Belfry, U.S.A., **419** K4
Belgaum, India, **216** C3
Belgium, *country*, Europe, **282** E5, *228, 229, 238, 240, 241, 242, 243, 244, 245, 334, 343*
Belgorod, Russian Federation, **298** E2
Belgorodskaya Oblast', *province*, Russian Federation, **298** E2
Belgrade *see* Beograd, Serbia, **296** C3, *260*
Belgrove, New Zealand, **133** D5
Belhaven, U.S.A., **426** B7
Beli, Nigeria, **365** G3
Beli Manastir, Croatia, **294** G3
Beli Timok, *river*, Serbia, **296** D4
Belice, *river*, Sicilia, Italy, **295** D7
Belidzhi, Russian Federation, **222** D4
Belin-Béliet, France, **290** D4
Bélinga, Gabon, **368** B2
Belinyu, Indonesia, **200** D3
Belitsa, Belarus, **289** M2
Belitsa, Bulgaria, **296** D5
Belitung, Pulau, *island*, Indonesia, **201** D3
Belize, Angola, **368** B3
Belize, Belize, **428** C3, *402*
Belize, *country*, Central America, **409** Q7, *378, 379, 402, 403*
Bélizon, French Guiana, **452** C2

Bell, *river*, Canada, **416** C5
Bell Island, Canada, **417** P4
Bell Rock, *island*, Scotland, U.K., **308** G4
Bell Ville, Argentina, **458** D4
Bella Coola, Canada, **412** F5
Bella Unión, Uruguay, **459** F4
Bella Vista, Corrientes, Argentina, **459** E3
Bella Vista, Santa Cruz, Argentina, **460** C4
Bella Vista, Tucumán, Argentina, **458** D3
Bellac, France, **290** E3
Bellary, India, **216** D3
Belle Fourche, *river*, U.S.A., **419** M4
Belle Fourche, U.S.A., **420** B3
Belle Glade, U.S.A., **425** M6
Belle-Île, *island*, France, **290** C3
Belle Isle, *island*, Canada, **417** P4
Belle Isle, Strait of, Canada, **417** N4
Bellefontaine, U.S.A., **421** M5
Bellefonte, U.S.A., **426** B4
Bellegarde, France, **290** F3
Bellême, France, **290** E2
Bellencombre, France, **305** J5
Belleterre, Canada, **416** B6
Belleville, Canada, **416** C7
Belleville, U.S.A., **420** E6
Bellevue, Idaho, U.S.A., **418** G5
Bellevue, Texas, U.S.A., **424** C3
Bellevue, Washington, U.S.A., **418** C3
Bellevue de l'Inini, Mont, *mountain peak*, French Guiana, **452** C2
Bellingham, England, U.K., **306** F2
Bellingham, Minnesota, U.S.A., **420** E3
Bellingham, Washington, U.S.A., **418** C2
Bellingshausen Sea, Antarctica, **470** A5
Bellingshausen Plain, *underwater feature*, Pacific Ocean, **479** L8
Bellinzona, Switzerland, **291** J3
Bellis, Canada, **413** N4
Bello, Colombia, **450** C2
Bellona, *island*, Solomon Islands, **141** A1, *116*
Bellpat, Pakistan, **218** A3
Belluno, Italy, **294** D2
Bellville, South Africa, **370** C5
Belmont, Scotland, U.K., **308** L7
Belmonte, Brazil, **457** F4
Belmopan, Belize, **428** C3, *402*
Belmullet, Ireland, **309** C3
Belo Horizonte, Brazil, **457** E5
Belo Jardim, Brazil, **457** G2
Belo Monte, Brazil, **452** C4
Belo Tsiribihina, Madagascar, **372** A4
Belogorsk, Russian Federation, **211** K2
Belogradchik, Bulgaria, **296** D4
Beloha, Madagascar, **372** B6
Beloit, Kansas, U.S.A., **420** D6
Beloit, Wisconsin, U.S.A., **421** J4
Belokurikha, Russian Federation, **223** L2
Belomorsk, Russian Federation, **285** S4
Belonia, India, **219** G5
Belorado, Spain, **293** F1
Beloretsk, Russian Federation, **222** F2
Belősovka, Kazakhstan, **212** D2
Belotintsi, Bulgaria, **296** D4
Belovo, Russian Federation, **223** M2
Beloyarskiy, Russian Federation, **300** H3
Beloye, Russian Federation, **299** G3
Beloye More, Russian Federation, **285** R3
Beloye More (White Sea), *sea*, Russian Federation, **285** S4
Beloye Ozero, *lake*, Russian Federation, **299** F2
Belozersk, Russian Federation, **299** F2
Belozerskoye, Russian Federation, **222** H1
Belper, England, U.K., **305** F1
Belsay, England, U.K., **307** G2
Bel'skaya Vozvyshennost', *mountain range*, Russian Federation, **299** D5
Belt, U.S.A., **419** J3
Belterra, Brazil, **452** B4
Belton, U.S.A., **424** D4
Belukha, Gora, *mountain peak*, Kazakhstan/Russian Federation, **212** E2
Belumut, Gunung, *mountain peak*, Malaysia, **200** C2
Belušić, Serbia, **296** C4
Belvedere Marittimo, Italy, **295** E6
Belvès, France, **290** E4
Belyando, *river*, Australia, **135** K3
Belyashi, Russian Federation, **223** M3
Belyayevka, Russian Federation, **222** F2
Belyy, Ostrov, *island*, Russian Federation, **300** J2
Belyy, Russian Federation, **299** D5
Belzig, Germany, **288** F2
Bemarivo, *river*, Madagascar, **372** B3
Bembe, Angola, **368** B4
Bembridge, England, U.K., **305** F4
Bemidji, U.S.A., **420** F2
Bempton, England, U.K., **307** H3
Bemu, Indonesia, **199** E3
Ben Bolt, U.S.A., **424** C6
Bến Giang, Vietnam, **203** E3
Ben Mehidi, Algeria, **295** A7
Ben Slimane, Morocco, **360** E2
Bena Dibele, Democratic Republic of the Congo, **368** D3
Bena-Tshadi, Democratic Republic of the Congo, **368** D3
Benāb, Iran, **222** D5
Benabarre, Spain, **293** H1
Benahmed, Morocco, **360** E2
Benangin, Indonesia, **201** F3
Benares, Mauritus, **373** C1
Benares *see* Vārānasi, India, **219** E4, *54, 89, 169*
Benasque, Spain, **293** H1
Benavente, Spain, **292** E1
Benavides, U.S.A., **424** C6
Benbane Head, *point*, Northern Ireland, U.K., **309** F2
Benbecula, *island*, Scotland, U.K., **308** B3
Bend, U.S.A., **418** D4
Benda, Tanjong, *point*, Indonesia, **201** E4
Bendela, Democratic Republic of the Congo, **368** C3
Bendigo, Australia, **135** J6
Bene, Mozambique, **369** F6
Benedict, Mount, *mountain peak*, Canada, **417** M2
Benenitra, Madagascar, **372** B5
Benevento, Italy, **295** E5
Bengal, Bay of, Indian Ocean, **194** K8, *94, 157, 168, 169, 170, 171*
Bengamisa, Democratic Republic of the Congo, **369** E2
Bengbis, Cameroon, **368** B2
Bengbu, China, **206** D1
Benge, U.S.A., **418** E3
Bengkalis, Pulau, *island*, Indonesia, **200** C2
Bengkulu, Indonesia, **200** C3
Bengkulu, *province*, Indonesia, **200** C4
Bengo, Ponto do, *point*, Angola, **368** B4
Bengo, *province*, Angola, **368** B4
Bengtsfors, Sweden, **286** F3
Benguela, Angola, **368** B5
Benguela, *province*, Angola, **368** B5
Beni, Democratic Republic of the Congo, **369** E2
Beni, *departement*, Bolivia, **455** F3
Beni, *river*, Bolivia, **455** E3
Beni-Abbes, Algeria, **361** F2
Beni Mellal, Morocco, **360** E2
Beni-Ounif, Algeria, **361** F2
Beni-Saf, Algeria, **293** G5
Benicarló, Spain, **293** H2
Benidorm, Spain, **293** G3
Benin City, Nigeria, **365** F3, *329*
Benin, Bight of, West Africa, **365** E3, *327*
Benin, *country*, Africa, **358** F6, *74, 312, 313, 325, 326, 327, 329*
Benisheikh, Nigeria, **365** G2
Benito Juárez, Argentina, **459** E5
Benito, Canada, **414** D6
Benjamín, Isla, *island*, Chile, **460** B2
Benjamin Constant, Brazil, **451** D5
Benjamín Hill, Mexico, **430** C2
Benkovac, Croatia, **294** E3
Benmore, Lake, New Zealand, **133** B6
Benmore, New Zealand, **133** B8
Benna Beola, *mountain peak*, Ireland, **309** C4
Bennan Head, *point*, Scotland, U.K., **308** D5
Bennett, Cape, Auckland Islands, New Zealand, **132** J10
Bennett's Point, St Helena, **373** B3
Bennington, U.S.A., **426** D3
Benom, Gunung, *mountain peak*, Malaysia, **200** C2
Bénoy, Chad, **365** H3
Benson, Arizona, U.S.A., **423** H6
Benson, Minnesota, U.S.A., **420** F3
Benteng, Indonesia, **198** C4
Bentiaba, Angola, **368** B5
Bentinck Island, Australia, **135** H2
Bentiu, Sudan, **366** C3
Bentley, England, U.K., **307** G4
Bentley, Mount, *mountain peak*, Antarctica, **470** C5
Bento Gonçalves, Brazil, **459** G3
Benton, Alabama, U.S.A., **425** J3
Benton, Arkansas, U.S.A., **424** F2
Benton, Illinois, U.S.A., **421** J6
Benue, *river*, Nigeria, **365** F3, *329, 330*
Benue, *state*, Nigeria, **365** F3
Benwee, *mountain peak*, Ireland, **309** C4
Benwee Head, *point*, Ireland, **309** C3
Benwick, England, U.K., **305** G2
Benxi, China, **211** H4
Beo, Indonesia, **198** D1
Beograd (Belgrade), Serbia, **296** C3, *260*
Beohāri, India, **219** E5
Béoumi, Côte d'Ivoire, **364** C3
Beppu, Japan, **208** E4
Beqa, *island*, Fiji, **141** A4
Bequimão, Brazil, **453** E4
Beragh, Northern Ireland, U.K., **309** E3
Beraketa, Madagascar, **372** B5
Bérandjokou, Congo, **368** C2
Beras Basah, Tanjong, *point*, Malaysia, **200** B2
Berat, Albania, **297** B5
Berau, Teluk, *bay*, Indonesia, **199** F3
Beravina, Madagascar, **372** B4
Berbera, Somalia, **367** G2
Berbérati, Central African Republic, **368** C2
Berbice, *river*, Guyana, **451** G3
Berceto, Italy, **294** C3
Berchtesgaden, Germany, **288** F5
Berck, France, **290** E1
Berdyans'k, Ukraine, **298** E3
Berdychiv, Ukraine, **298** C3
Béré, Chad, **365** H3
Bere Alston, England, U.K., **304** C4
Bere Regis, England, U.K., **304** E4
Berea, U.S.A., **420** B4
Berebere, Indonesia, **199** E2
Beregovoye, Russian Federation, **223** L2
Berehomet, Ukraine, **296** E1
Berehove, Ukraine, **296** D1
Bereina, Papua New Guinea, **140** B5
Berekum, Ghana, **364** D3
Berenguela, Bolivia, **455** E4
Berenice, Egypt, **363** G4
Berens, *river*, Canada, **414** F5
Beresford, Canada, **416** J6
Bereşti, Romania, **296** F2
Berettyóújfalu, Hungary, **289** K5
Berezanka, Ukraine, **296** H2
Berezeni, Romania, **296** G2
Berezivka, Ukraine, **296** H2
Berezniki, Russian Federation, **300** G4
Berezovaya, Russian Federation, **223** N2
Berezovskiy, Russian Federation, **223** M1
Berezovyy, Russian Federation, **301** Q4
Berg, Norway, **284** H2
Berga, Spain, **293** H1
Bergama, Turkey, **297** F6
Bergamo, Italy, **294** B3
Bergen, Germany, **288** D2
Bergen, Norway, **286** B2
Bergen op Zoom, Netherlands, **288** B3
Bergerac, France, **290** E4
Bergisch Gladbach, Germany, **288** C3
Bergkvara, Sweden, **286** H4
Berglia, Norway, **284** F4
Bergshamra, Sweden, **287** J3
Bergsstaðir, Iceland, **284** Y7
Bergues, France, **305** K4
Berh, Mongolia, **210** E3
Berhala, Selat, *strait*, Indonesia, **200** D3
Berikat, Tanjong, *point*, Indonesia, **201** D3
Bering Sea, Pacific Ocean, **103** L3, *273*
Bering Strait, Russian Federation/U.S.A., **410** C3, *54, 60, 87, 380, 384, 434, 465, 466*
Beringa, Ostrov, *island*, Russian Federation, **301** T4, *466*
Beritarikap, Tanjong, *point*, Indonesia, **200** B3
Berja, Spain, **293** F4
Berkåk, Norway, **284** E5
Berkeley, Cabo, *cape*, Islas Galápagos (Galapagos Islands), Ecuador, **461** A1
Berkeley, England, U.K., **304** E3
Berkeley, U.S.A., **422** B3
Berkner Island, Antarctica, **470** C5
Berkovitsa, Bulgaria, **296** D4
Berlayar, Tanjong, *point*, Singapore, **200** J7
Berlevåg, Norway, **285** P1
Berlin, Germany, **288** F2, *95, 238, 239*
Berlin, Maine, U.S.A., **426** E2
Berlin, Maryland, U.S.A., **426** C5
Berlin, Mount, *mountain peak*, Antarctica, **470** C7
Berlin, *state*, Germany, **288** F2
Berlin, Wisconsin, U.S.A., **421** J4
Bermeja, Punta, *point*, Argentina, **460** E1
Bermejillo, Mexico, **430** E3
Bermejo, Bolivia, **458** D2
Bermejo, *river*, Chaco/Formosa, Argentina, **458** E2
Bermejo, *river*, San Juan, Argentina, **458** C4
Bermuda, *U.K. dependency*, Atlantic Ocean, **105** R5, *276, 376, 377, 387, 388*
Bermuda Rise, *underwater feature*, Atlantic Ocean, **477** C4
Bern, Switzerland, **291** H3, *83, 246*
Bernagh, Slieve, *mountain range*, Ireland, **309** D5
Bernalillo, U.S.A., **423** K4
Bernardo de Irogoyen, Argentina, **459** G3
Bernasconi, Argentina, **458** D5
Bernaville, France, **305** K4
Bernay, France, **290** E2
Bernburg, Germany, **288** E3
Berndorf, Austria, **289** H5
Berner Alpen, *mountain range*, Switzerland, **291** H3, *246*
Berneray, *island*, Central Western Isles, Scotland, U.K., **308** B3
Berneray, *island*, S. Western Isles, Scotland, U.K., **308** B4
Bernier Island, Australia, **134** C3
Bernina, Piz, *mountain peak*, Switzerland, **291** J3
Beroroha, Madagascar, **372** B5
Berovo, Macedonia, **297** D5
Berre, Étang de, *lake*, France, **291** G5
Berrechid, Morocco, **360** E2
Berri, Australia, **135** J5
Berriane, Algeria, **361** G2
Berriedale, Scotland, U.K., **308** F2
Berrouaghia, Algeria, **293** J4
Berry Springs, Australia, **134** F1
Berryville, U.S.A., **424** F1
Berseba, Namibia, **370** C4
Bershad', Ukraine, **296** G1
Bertinho, Brazil, **452** C4
Bertolínia, Brazil, **453** E5
Bertoua, Cameroon, **368** B2
Bertraghboy Bay, Ireland, **309** B4
Beru, *island*, Kiribati, **139** F5
Beruri, Brazil, **451** G5
Berwick, North Dakota, U.S.A., **420** C1
Berwick, Pennsylvania, U.S.A., **426** B4
Berwick-upon-Tweed, England, U.K., **306** F2
Berwyn, *mountain range*, Wales, U.K., **304** D2
Berzasca, Romania, **296** C3
Besalampy, Madagascar, **372** A4
Besançon, France, **291** H3
Besar, Gunung, *mountain peak*, Indonesia, **201** F3
Beshneh, Iran, **221** F3
Besi, Tanjong, *point*, Indonesia, **198** C5
Beskidy, *mountain range*, Slovakia, **289** J4
Beskol, Kazakhstan, **212** D3
Béssao, Chad, **365** H3
Bessbrook, Northern Ireland, U.K., **309** F3
Bessemer, U.S.A., **425** J3
Besshoqy, Kazakhstan, **222** E4
Bestöbe, Kazakhstan, **223** J2
Bet Guvrin, Israel, **225** C4
Bet She'an, Israel, **225** C3
Betaf, Indonesia, **199** G3
Betanty, Madagascar, **372** B6
Betanzos, Bolivia, **455** F5
Betanzos, Spain, **292** C1
Bétaré Oya, Cameroon, **368** B1
Betarsjön, *lake*, Sweden, **284** H5
Betbulak, Kazakhstan, **223** H3
Beteta, Spain, **293** F2
Bethal, South Africa, **371** E4
Bethanie, Namibia, **370** C4
Bethany, Missouri, U.S.A., **420** G5
Bethany, Oklahoma, U.S.A., **424** D2
Bethany Beach, U.S.A., **426** C5
Bethel, Alaska, U.S.A., **410** C3
Bethel, Maine, U.S.A., **426** E2
Bethel, Ohio, U.S.A., **421** L6
Bethel, Oklahoma, U.S.A., **424** E2
Bethesda, Wales, U.K., **304** C1
Bethlehem *see* Bayt Laḥm, West Bank, **225** C4, *89*
Bethlehem, South Africa, **371** E4
Bethlehem, U.S.A., **426** C4
Béthune, France, **290** F1
Bethune, U.S.A., **425** M2
Betijoque, Venezuela, **451** D2
Betioky, Madagascar, **372** A5
Betlitsa, Russian Federation, **299** D5
Betoota, Australia, **135** J4
Bétou, Congo, **368** C2

Betpaqdala, *desert*, Kazakhstan, **223** H3
Betrandraka, Madagascar, **372** B4
Betroka, Madagascar, **372** B5
Betsiboka, *river*, Madagascar, **372** B4
Bettiah, India, **219** F4
Bettna, Sweden, **287** H3
Bettyhill, Scotland, U.K., **308** E2
Betūl Bāzār, India, **218** D5
Betws-y-coed, Wales, U.K., **304** D1
Beulah, U.S.A., **420** B2
Beverley, England, U.K., **307** H4
Beverly, U.S.A., **418** E3
Beverly Hills, U.S.A., **422** D4
Beverstedt, Germany, **288** D2
Bewdley, England, U.K., **304** E2
Bexhill, England, U.K., **305** H4
Bey Dağı, *mountain peak*, Turkey, **224** E5
Beyağaç, Turkey, **297** G7
Beykoz, Turkey, **297** G5
Beyla, Guinea, **364** C3
Bēylul, Eritrea, **367** F2
Beyneu, Kazakhstan, **222** F3
Beyra, Somalia, **367** G3
Beyşehir Gölü, *lake*, Turkey, **224** D5
Bezaha, Madagascar, **372** A5
Bezhanitsy, Russian Federation, **299** B4
Bezhetsk, Russian Federation, **299** F4
Béziers, France, **291** F5
Bhabua, India, **219** E4
Bhadarwāh, India, **218** C2
Bhadra Reservoir, India, **216** C3
Bhadrak, India, **219** F5
Bhadrapur, Nepal, **219** G4
Bhadrāvati, India, **216** C3
Bhāgalpur, India, **219** F4
Bhairab Bāzār, Bangladesh, **214** D4
Bhairahawa, Nepal, **219** E4
Bhakkar, Pakistan, **218** B3
Bhaktapur, Nepal, **219** F4
Bhamo, Myanmar, **205** C2
Bhandāra, India, **218** D5
Bhānvad, India, **218** B5
Bharatpur, India, **218** D4
Bharūch, India, **218** C5
Bhatinda, India, **218** C3
Bhatkal, India, **216** C3
Bhatpara, India, **219** G5
Bhāvnagar, India, **218** C5
Bhawānipatna, India, **219** E6
Bheigeir, Beinn, *mountain peak*, Scotland, U.K., **308** C5
Bheri, *river*, Nepal, **219** E3
Bhilai, India, **219** E5
Bhīlwāra, India, **218** C4
Bhima, *river*, India, **216** C2
Bhīmavaram, India, **217** E2
Bhind, India, **218** D4
Bhīnmāl, India, **218** C4
Bhiwandi, India, **216** C2
Bhiwāni, India, **218** D3
Bhokardan, India, **218** C5
Bhopāl, India, **218** D5, *169*
Bhopālpatnam, India, **216** E2
Bhor, India, **216** C2
Bhuban, India, **219** F5
Bhubaneshwar, India, **219** F5, *169*
Bhuj, India, **218** B5
Bhumiphon Reservoir, Thailand, **202** C2
Bhusāwal, India, **218** C5
Bhutan, *country*, Asia, **196** L7, *144, 158, 170, 171, 172*
Bia, Phou, *mountain peak*, Laos, **203** D2
Biak, Indonesia, **199** G3
Biak, Pulau, *island*, Indonesia, **199** G3
Biała, *river*, Poland, **289** K4
Biała Piska, Poland, **289** L2
Biała Podlaska, Poland, **289** L2
Białogard, Poland, **289** H2
Białystok, Poland, **289** L2
Bianga, Central African Republic, **368** D2
Biankouma, Côte d'Ivoire, **364** C3
Bianzhuang, China, **206** D1
Biaora, India, **218** D5
Bīārjomand, Iran, **222** F5
Biaro, Pulau, *island*, Indonesia, **198** D2
Biarritz, France, **290** D5
Biasca, Switzerland, **291** J3
Biaza, Russian Federation, **223** K1
Bibā, Egypt, **363** F3
Bibai, Japan, **209** H2
Bibala, Angola, **368** B5
Bibas, Gabon, **368** B2
Bibbiena, Italy, **294** C4
Bibémi, Cameroon, **365** G3
Biberach an der Riß, Germany, **288** D4
Bibiani, Ghana, **364** D3
Bibirevo, Russian Federation, **299** D4
Biblos *see* Jubayl, Lebanon, **225** C2
Bibury, England, U.K., **305** F3
Bicaz, Romania, **296** F2
Bicester, England, U.K., **305** F3
Biche, Trinidad, Trinidad and Tobago, **461** C4
Bichena, Ethiopia, **367** E2
Bichura, Russian Federation, **210** D2
Bickleigh, Central Devon, England, U.K., **304** D4
Bickleigh, W. Devon, England, U.K., **304** C4
Bida, Nigeria, **365** F3
Bīdar, India, **216** D2
Biddeford, U.S.A., **426** E3
Biddle, U.S.A., **419** M4
Biddulph, England, U.K., **304** E1
Bidean nam Bian, *mountain peak*, Scotland, U.K., **308** D4
Bideford, England, U.K., **304** C3
Bidjovagge, Norway, **285** L2
Bidor, Malaysia, **200** C1
Bié, *province*, Angola, **368** C5
Bieber, U.S.A., **418** D6
Biecz, Poland, **289** K4
Biel, Switzerland, **291** H3
Bielefeld, Germany, **288** D3
Bieler See, *lake*, Switzerland, **291** H3
Biella, Italy, **294** B3
Bielsk Podlaski, Poland, **289** L2
Bielsko-Biała, Poland, **289** J4
Biên Hòa, Vietnam, **203** E4
Bienvenue, French Guiana, **452** C2
Bienville, Lac, *lake*, Canada, **416** E2
Biescas, Spain, **293** G1
Bieszczady, *mountain range*, Poland, **289** L4
Biferno, *river*, Italy, **295** E5
Bifoun, Gabon, **368** B3
Big Bar, U.S.A., **422** B1
Big Bay, New Zealand, **133** A7
Big Beaver, Canada, **413** S7
Big Bend, Swaziland, **371** F4
Big Blue, *river*, U.S.A., **420** E5
Big Creek, Canada, **412** H6
Big Creek, U.S.A., **418** G4
Big Falls, U.S.A., **420** G1
Big Lake, U.S.A., **424** B4
Big Piney, U.S.A., **419** J5
Big Quill Lake, Canada, **414** B5
Big Rapids, U.S.A., **421** L4
Big Sand Lake, Canada, **414** E3
Big Sandy, U.S.A., **419** J2
Big Snow Mountain, *mountain peak*, U.S.A., **419** K3
Big South Cape Island (Taukihepa), New Zealand, **133** A8
Big Spring, U.S.A., **424** B3
Big Sur, U.S.A., **422** C3
Big Timber, U.S.A., **419** K4
Big Trout, *river*, Canada, **415** K4
Big Trout Lake, Canada, **414** J5
Big Trout Lake, *lake*, Canada, **414** K5
Big Water, U.S.A., **423** H3
Biga, Turkey, **297** F5
Bigadiç, Turkey, **297** G6
Bigbury Bay, England, U.K., **304** C4
Bigfork, U.S.A., **418** G2
Biggar, Canada, **413** R5
Biggar, Scotland, U.K., **308** F5
Bigge Island, Australia, **134** E1
Biggleswade, England, U.K., **305** G2
Bighorn, *river*, U.S.A., **419** K4
Bighorn Lake, U.S.A., **419** K4
Bighorn Mountains, *mountain range*, U.S.A., **419** L4
Bignona, Senegal, **364** A2
Bigstone, *river*, Canada, **414** G4
Bihać, Bosnia and Herzegovina, **294** E3
Bihār, *state*, India, **219** F4, *169*
Bihār Sharīf, India, **219** F4
Biharamulo, Tanzania, **369** F3
Bijagós, Arquipélago dos, *islands*, Guinea-Bissau, **364** A2, *321*
Bijāpur, India, **216** C2
Bijāwar, India, **218** D4
Bijeljina, Bosnia and Herzegovina, **296** B3
Bijelo Polje, Montenegro, **296** B4
Bijie, China, **215** H4
Bijni, India, **219** G4
Bijnor, India, **218** D3
Bikāner, India, **218** C3
Bikar, *island*, Marshall Islands, **139** F3
Bikin, *river*, Russian Federation, **211** L3
Bikin, Russian Federation, **211** L3
Bikini, *island*, Marshall Islands, **138** E3, *119*
Bikita, Zimbabwe, **371** F3
Bikoro, Democratic Republic of the Congo, **368** C3
Bikubiti, *mountain range*, Libya, **362** C4, *316*
Bílá, Czech Republic, **289** J4
Bila, *river*, Indonesia, **200** B2
Bila Tserkva, Ukraine, **298** D3
Bīlaspur, Himāchal Pradesh, India, **218** D3
Bilāspur, Madhya Pradesh, India, **219** E5
Bilauktaung Range, *mountain range*, Myanmar/Thailand, **202** C3
Bilbao, Spain, **293** F1
Bilbays, Egypt, **225** A4
Bilbor, Romania, **296** E2
Bíldudalur, Iceland, **284** X7
Bílé Karpaty, *mountain range*, Slovakia, **289** H4
Bileća, Bosnia and Herzegovina, **294** G4
Bilecik, *province*, Turkey, **297** G5
Bilecik, Turkey, **297** G5
Biled, Romania, **296** C3
Biłgoraj, Poland, **289** L3
Bilhorod-Dnistrovs'kyy, Ukraine, **296** H2
Bili, Democratic Republic of the Congo, **368** E2
Bilibino, Russian Federation, **301** T3
Bilimora, India, **218** C5
Biliran Island, Philippines, **204** D4
Bilisht, Albania, **297** C5
Bill, U.S.A., **419** M5
Bill of Portland, *point*, England, U.K., **304** E4
Bill Williams, *river*, U.S.A., **422** G4
Billericay, England, U.K., **305** H3
Billingham, England, U.K., **307** G3
Billinghay, England, U.K., **305** G1
Billings, U.S.A., **419** K4
Billingshurst, England, U.K., **305** G3
Billond, Denmark, **286** D5
Billsta, Sweden, **284** J5
Bilma, Niger, **362** B5
Bilo gora, *mountain range*, Croatia, **294** F3
Biloela, Australia, **135** L3
Biloku, Guyana, **451** G4
Biloxi, U.S.A., **425** H4
Bilpa Morea Claypan, *lake*, Australia, **135** J3
Bilqas Qism Awwal, Egypt, **225** A4
Bilston, Scotland, U.K., **308** F5
Biltine, Chad, **366** B2
Biltine, *prefecture*, Chad, **366** B2
Bilto, Norway, **284** K2
Bilton, England, U.K., **307** H4
Bilugyun, *island*, Myanmar, **205** C4
Bilungala, Indonesia, **198** C2
Bilüü, Mongolia, **212** F2
Bilwascarma, Nicaragua, **428** E4
Bilyayivka, Ukraine, **296** H2
Bima, Indonesia, **201** G5
Bimbila, Ghana, **364** E3
Bimbo, Central African Republic, **368** C2
Bimini Islands, Bahamas, **425** N7
Bin Qirdān, Tunisia, **362** B2
Bin Xian, Heilongjiang, China, **211** J3
Bin Xian, Shaanxi, China, **215** J2
Binbrook, England, U.K., **307** H4
Binder, Chad, **365** G3
Bindu, Democratic Republic of the Congo, **368** C4
Bindura, Zimbabwe, **369** F6
Binéfar, Spain, **293** H2
Binga, Monte, *mountain peak*, Mozambique, **371** F2, *345*
Binga, Zimbabwe, **371** E2
Bingerville, Côte d'Ivoire, **364** D3
Bingham, England, U.K., **305** G2
Bingham, U.S.A., **423** K5
Binghamton, U.S.A., **426** C3
Bingley, England, U.K., **307** G4
Bingöl, Turkey, **224** F5
Binhai, China, **206** D1
Binjai, Indonesia, **200** B2
Binna, Raas, *point*, Somalia, **367** H2
Binscarth, Canada, **414** D6
Binser, Mount, *mountain peak*, New Zealand, **133** C6
Bint Jubayl, Lebanon, **225** C3
Bintan, Pulau, *island*, Indonesia, **200** D2
Bintang, Gunung, *mountain peak*, Malaysia, **200** C1
Bintuhan, Indonesia, **200** C4
Bintulu, Malaysia, **201** F2
Bintun, Indonesia, **138** B5
Bintuni, Teluk, *bay*, Indonesia, **199** F3
Binyang, China, **206** B4
Binzhou, China, **211** G5
Bío Bío, *administrative region*, Chile, **458** B5
Bio Bio, *river*, Chile, **458** B5
Bioco, Isla de, *island*, Equatorial Guinea, **368** A2, *331, 332*
Biograd na Moru, Croatia, **294** E4
Biokovo, *mountain peak*, Croatia, **294** E4
Bīr, India, **216** C2
Bir, Ras, *point*, Djibouti, **367** F2
Bir Di, Sudan, **366** C3
Bir Enzarān, Western Sahara, **360** D4
Bir Ghbalou, Algeria, **293** J4
Bi'r Ḥasanah, Egypt, **225** B4
Bi'r Jifjāfah, Egypt, **225** B4
Bîr Mogreïn, Mauritania, **360** D3
Bira, Indonesia, **198** C4
Bira, Russian Federation, **211** L2
Birāk, Libya, **362** B3
Birao, Central African Republic, **366** B2
Birātnagar, Nepal, **219** F4
Birch, *river*, Canada, **413** N2
Birch Lake, Canada, **414** H6
Birch Mountains, *mountain range*, Canada, **413** M3
Birch River, Canada, **414** D5
Bircot, Ethiopia, **367** F3
Bircza, Poland, **289** L4
Bird Island, South Georgia, **461** A3
Birdsville, Australia, **135** H4
Birecik, Turkey, **363** G1
Bireuen, Indonesia, **200** B1
Birigüi, Brazil, **456** C5
Bīrjand, Iran, **221** G2
Birkeland, Norway, **286** D3
Birkenhead, England, U.K., **306** E4
Birlik, north of Töle Bī, Kazakhstan, **212** B3
Birlik, south of Töle Bī, Kazakhstan, **212** B4
Birmingham, England, U.K., **305** F2, *276*
Birmingham, U.S.A., **425** J3
Birnie, *island*, Kiribati, **139** G5
Birnin-Gaouré, Niger, **365** E2
Birnin Gwari, Nigeria, **365** F2
Birnin Kebbi, Nigeria, **365** E2
Birnin Konni, Niger, **365** F2
Birnin Kudu, Nigeria, **365** F2
Birnin-Yauri, Nigeria, **365** E2
Birobidzhan, Russian Federation, **211** L2
Birr, Ireland, **309** E4
Birshoghyr, Kazakhstan, **222** F3
Birsk, Russian Federation, **222** F1
Birstall, England, U.K., **305** F2
Biru, China, **214** E3
Biržai, Lithuania, **287** M4
Birži, Latvia, **287** M4
Bisbee, Arizona, U.S.A., **423** J6
Bisbee, North Dakota, U.S.A., **420** D1
Biscarrosse, France, **290** D4
Biscarrosse et de Parentis, Étang de, *lake*, France, **290** D4
Biscay, Bay of, France, **290** B3, *244, 252*
Biscay Plain, *underwater feature*, Atlantic Ocean, **477** G2
Biscotasing, Canada, **421** M2
Bisert', Russian Federation, **222** F1
Bisertsi, Bulgaria, **296** F4
Biševo, *island*, Croatia, **294** F4
Bishan, Singapore, **200** K6
Bishkek, Kyrgyzstan, **212** B4, *186*
Bishnupur, India, **219** F5
Bisho, South Africa, **371** E5
Bishop, California, U.S.A., **422** D3
Bishop, Texas, U.S.A., **424** D6
Bishop Auckland, England, U.K., **307** G3
Bishop's Cleeve, England, U.K., **304** E3
Bishop's Lydeard, England, U.K., **304** D3
Bishops Stortford, England, U.K., **305** H3
Bishui, China, **211** H1
Biskra, Algeria, **361** H2
Biskupiec, Poland, **289** K2
Bislig, Philippines, **204** D4
Bismarck, Missouri, U.S.A., **420** H7
Bismarck, North Dakota, U.S.A., **420** C2, *386*
Bismarck Archipelago, Papua New Guinea, **140** B3, *61, 87, 88, 115*
Bismarck Sea, Papua New Guinea, **138** C6
Bismark, Germany, **288** E2
Bismark Range, *mountain range*, Papua New Guinea, **140** B4
Bismil, Turkey, **363** H1
Bison, U.S.A., **420** B3
Bissau, Guinea-Bissau, **364** A2, *321*
Bissaula, Nigeria, **365** G3
Bissikrima, Guinea, **364** B2
Bistcho Lake, Canada, **413** K2
Bistriţa, Romania, **296** E2
Biswān, India, **218** E4
Bitam, Gabon, **368** B2
Bitik, Kazakhstan, **222** E2
Bitkine, Chad, **366** A2
Bitlis, Turkey, **363** H1
Bitola, Macedonia, **297** C5
Bitter Creek, U.S.A., **419** K6
Bitterfontein, South Africa, **370** C5
Bitteroot Range, *mountain range*, U.S.A., **418** G3
Bitti, Sardegna, Italy, **295** B5
Biu, Nigeria, **365** G2
Bivolari, Romania, **296** F2
Biwāko, *lake*, Japan, **209** G4
Biya, *river*, Russian Federation, **223** M2
Biyang, China, **206** C1
Biysk, Russian Federation, **223** M2
Bizhou, China, **211** J2
Bjargtangar, *point*, Iceland, **284** W7
Bjästa, Sweden, **284** J5
Bjelovar, Croatia, **294** F3
Bjerringbro, Denmark, **286** D4
Björbo, Sweden, **286** G2

Björköby, Finland, **284** K5
Björksele, Sweden, **284** J4
Björkvattnet, Sweden, **284** F4
Bjørn, Norway, **284** F3
Björna, Sweden, **284** J5
Björneborg, Sweden, **286** G3
Bjørnevatn, Norway, **285** P2
Björnlunda, Sweden, **287** H3
Bjørntoppen, *mountain peak*, Norway, **284** H3
Bjurholm, Sweden, **284** J5
Bjursås, Sweden, **286** G2
Bla, Mali, **364** C2
Blace, Serbia, **296** C4
Blachly, U.S.A., **418** C4
Black, *river*, U.S.A., **424** G2
Black Canyon City, U.S.A., **423** G4
Black Coast, *region*, Antarctica, **470** B4
Black Combe, *mountain peak*, England, U.K., **306** E3
Black Diamond, Canada, **413** M6
Black Head, *point*, England, U.K., **304** B4
Black Hills, U.S.A., **420** B3
Black Isle, *peninsula*, Scotland, U.K., **308** E3
Black Lake, *lake*, Canada, **413** S2
Black Lake, Quebec, Canada, **416** F6
Black Lake, Saskatchewan, Canada, **413** S2
Black Mountain, *mountain range*, Wales, U.K., **304** D3
Black Mountains, *mountain range*, U.S.A., **422** F4
Black Mountains, *mountain range*, Wales, U.K., **304** D3
Black River, Jamaica, **429** F3, *393*
Black Rock, Tobago, Trinidad and Tobago, **461** B4
Black Rock Desert, U.S.A., **418** E6
Black Rock Point, New Zealand, **133** A8
Black Sea, Asia/Europe, **224** B2, *68, 144, 146, 190, 191, 228, 229, 232, 236, 263, 264, 269, 270, 271*
Black Volta, *river*, Côte d'Ivoire/Ghana, **364** D3, *325, 326*
Blackall, Australia, **135** K3
Blackburn, England, U.K., **306** F4
Blackburn with Darwen, England, U.K., **306** F4
Blackfoot, *river*, U.S.A., **419** H5
Blackfoot, U.S.A., **418** H5
Blackfoot Reservoir, U.S.A., **419** J5
Blackpool, England, U.K., **306** E4
Blackpool, *unitary authority*, England, U.K., **306** E4
Blackrock, Ireland, **309** F4
Blacksburg, U.S.A., **421** N7
Blackshear, Lake, U.S.A., **425** K4
Blackshear, U.S.A., **425** L4
Blacksod Bay, Ireland, **309** B3
Blackwater, Australia, **135** K3
Blackwater, Ireland, **309** F5
Blackwater, *river*, Ireland, **309** D5
Blackwell, U.S.A., **420** E7
Blackwood, Cape, Papua New Guinea, **140** B4
Blaenau Ffestiniog, Wales, U.K., **304** D1
Blaenau Gwent, *unitary authority*, Wales, U.K., **304** D3
Blaenavon, Wales, U.K., **304** D3
Blagdon, England, U.K., **304** E3
Blagoevgrad, Bulgaria, **296** D5
Blagoveshchenka, Russian Federation, **223** K2
Blagoveshchensk, Russian Federation, **211** J2
Blain, France, **290** D3
Blaine, U.S.A., **418** C2
Blair, U.S.A., **420** E5
Blair Atholl, Scotland, U.K., **308** F4
Blairgowrie, Scotland, U.K., **308** F4
Blairsden, U.S.A., **422** C2
Blairsville, U.S.A., **425** L2
Blaisdell, U.S.A., **420** B1
Blaj, Romania, **296** D2
Blake Plateau, *underwater feature*, Atlantic Ocean, **477** B3
Blake Point, U.S.A., **421** J1
Blakely, U.S.A., **425** K4
Blakeney, Gloucestershire, England, U.K., **304** E3
Blakeney, Norfolk, England, U.K., **305** J2
Blakeney Point, England, U.K., **305** H1
Blakstad, Norway, **286** D3
Blamca, Punta, *point*, Róbinson Crusoe Island, Archipiélago Juan Fernández, Chile, **461** C2
Blanc, Mont, *mountain peak*, France/Italy, **280** E6, *243, 254*
Blanc-Sablon, Canada, **417** N4
Blanca, Bahía, *bay*, Argentina, **460** F1
Blanca, Sierra, *mountain peak*, U.S.A., **423** L6
Blanca Peak, *mountain peak*, U.S.A., **423** L3
Blanche, Lake, Australia, **135** H4
Blanchisseuse, Trinidad, Trinidad and Tobago, **461** C4
Blanco, Cabo, *cape*, Costa Rica, **428** D5
Blanco, Cape, U.S.A., **418** B5
Blanco, *river*, Argentina, **458** C3
Blanco, *river*, Bolivia, **455** F3
Blanco, U.S.A., **424** C4
Blandford Forum, England, U.K., **304** E4
Blanding, U.S.A., **423** J3
Blangkejeren, Indonesia, **200** B1
Blangy, France, **305** J5
Blankaholm, Sweden, **286** H4
Blankenheim, Germany, **288** C3
Blantyre, Malawi, **369** G6
Blarney, Ireland, **309** D6
Blasket Islands, Ireland, **309** B5
Blattnicksele, Sweden, **284** H4
Blaye, France, **290** D4
Blayney Park, U.S.A., **421** K2
Bleik, Norway, **284** G2
Blekinge, *county*, Sweden, **286** G4
Blenheim, Canada, **421** M4
Blenheim, New Zealand, **133** D5
Blessington, Ireland, **306** B4
Bletchley, England, U.K., **305** G3
Blida, Algeria, **293** J4
Bligh Sound, New Zealand, **133** A7
Bliss, U.S.A., **418** G5
Blitar, Indonesia, **201** F5
Blitta, Togo, **364** E3, *326*
Block Island, U.S.A., **426** E4
Bloemfontein, South Africa, **371** E4, *350*
Bloemhof, South Africa, **371** E4
Blois, France, **290** E3
Blönduós, Iceland, **284** X7
Bloodvein, *river*, Canada, **414** F6
Bloody Foreland, *point*, Ireland, **309** D2
Bloomfield, Indiana, U.S.A., **421** K6
Bloomfield, Iowa, U.S.A., **420** G5
Bloomfield, New Mexico, U.S.A., **423** K3
Blooming Prairie, U.S.A., **420** G4
Bloomington, Illinois, U.S.A., **421** J5
Bloomington, Indiana, U.S.A., **421** K6
Bloomington, Minnesota, U.S.A., **420** G3
Blora, Indonesia, **201** E4
Blountstown, U.S.A., **425** K4
Bloxham, England, U.K., **305** F2
Blue Earth, U.S.A., **420** F4
Blue Hill, U.S.A., **420** D5
Blue Lake, U.S.A., **418** C6
Blue Mountain, *mountain peak*, U.S.A., **418** F5, *393*
Blue Mountain, *mountain range*, U.S.A., **426** B4
Blue Mountain, U.S.A., **423** J1
Blue Mountain Lake, U.S.A., **426** C3
Blue Mountain Peak, Jamaica, **429** F3, *393*
Blue Mountains, *mountain range*, U.S.A., **418** E4
Blue Mud Bay, Australia, **135** H1
Blue Nile *see* Azraq, Al Baḩr al, *river*, Ethiopia, **366** E2, *93, 336, 338*
Blue Nile *see* Azraq, Al Baḩr al, *river*, Sudan, **220** B6, *93, 336, 338*
Blue Rapids, U.S.A., **420** E6
Blue Ridge, *mountain range*, U.S.A., **421** P7, *383*
Blue River, Canada, **413** K5
Blue Stack Mountains, Ireland, **309** D3
Bluefield, U.S.A., **421** N7
Bluefields, Nicaragua, **428** E4
Bluestone Lake, U.S.A., **421** N7
Bluff, New Zealand, **133** B8
Bluff, U.S.A., **423** J3
Bluffton, Canada, **413** M5
Blumenau, Brazil, **459** H3
Blunt, U.S.A., **420** D3
Blyth, Northumberland, England, U.K., **307** G2
Blyth, Nottinghamshire, England, U.K., **307** G4
Blyth Bridge, Scotland, U.K., **308** F5
Blythe, U.S.A., **422** F5
Blytheville, U.S.A., **424** H2
Blyton, England, U.K., **307** H4
Bø, Norway, **286** D3
Bo, Sierra Leone, **364** B3
Bo Hai, *gulf*, China, **208** B3
Bo River, Sudan, **366** C3
Boa Esperança, Brazil, **453** F5
Boa Viagem, Brazil, **453** F4
Boa Vista, Brazil, **451** G3
Boa Vista, *island*, Cape Verde, **360** Q8
Boac, Philippines, **204** C3
Boaco, Nicaragua, **428** D4
Boadilla, Spain, **292** D2
Boali, Central African Republic, **368** C2
Boat of Garten, Scotland, U.K., **308** F3
Boatswain-Bird Island, Ascension, **373** A3
Boayan Island, Philippines, **204** B4
Boaz, U.S.A., **425** J2
Bob Quinn Lake, Canada, **412** D3
Bobai, China, **206** B4
Bobaomby, Tanjona, (Cap d'Ambre), *cape*, Madagascar, **372** B3
Bobasakoa, Madagascar, **372** B3
Bobbio, Italy, **294** B3
Bobia, Pico de, *mountain peak*, Spain, **292** D1
Bobo-Dioulasso, Burkina Faso, **364** D2
Bobolice, Poland, **289** H2
Bobonong, Botswana, **371** E3
Bobota, Romania, **296** D2
Bobovdol, Bulgaria, **296** D4
Bobr, Belarus, **299** B5
Bobr, *river*, Belarus, **299** B5
Bóbr, *river*, Poland, **289** G3
Bobrowniki, Poland, **289** L2
Bobso, China, **215** G2
Boby, *mountain peak*, Madagascar, **372** B5
Boca del Pao, Venezuela, **451** F2
Bôca do Acre, Brazil, **455** E2
Bôca do Jari, Brazil, **452** C3
Bôca do Moaco, Brazil, **455** E2
Boca Mavaca, Venezuela, **451** F3
Boca Raton, U.S.A., **425** M6
Bocaiúva, Brazil, **457** E4
Bocaranga, Central African Republic, **365** H3
Bochart, Canada, **416** E5
Bochnia, Poland, **289** K4
Bocholt, Germany, **288** C3
Bocht Van Hato, *bay*, Curaçao, Netherlands Antilles, **461** C3
Bochum, Germany, **288** C3
Bocoio, Angola, **368** B5
Boconó, Venezuela, **451** D2
Bocşa, Romania, **296** C3
Boda, Central African Republic, **368** C2
Boda, Sweden, **286** G2
Bodaybo, Russian Federation, **301** N4
Bode-Sadu, Nigeria, **365** F3
Boden, Sweden, **284** K4
Bodenham, England, U.K., **304** E2
Bodensee, *lake*, Germany/Switzerland/Austria, **288** D5, *239, 247*
Bodeşti, Romania, **296** F2
Bodmin, England, U.K., **304** C4
Bodmin Moor, *moorland*, England, U.K., **304** C4
Bodø, Norway, **284** G3
Bodoquena, Brazil, **456** B5
Bodoquena, Serra da, *mountain range*, Brazil, **456** B5
Bodrum, Turkey, **297** F7
Bodum, Sweden, **284** H5
Boën, France, **291** G4
Boende, Democratic Republic of the Congo, **368** D3
Boffa, Cap, *cape*, Guinea, **364** A2
Boffa, Guinea, **364** B2
Bog of Allen, *region*, Ireland, **309** E4
Bogale, Myanmar, **205** B4
Bogalusa, U.S.A., **424** H4
Bogandé, Burkina Faso, **364** D2
Bogangolo, Central African Republic, **368** C1
Bogatić, Serbia, **296** B3
Bogbonga, Democratic Republic of the Congo, **368** C2
Bogda Feng, *mountain peak*, China, **212** F4
Bogda Shan, *mountain range*, China, **212** F4
Bogdanci, Macedonia, **297** D5
Bogdïn, *river*, Mongolia, **213** H3
Bogenli, China, **211** J2
Bogense, Denmark, **286** E5
Bögetsay, Kazakhstan, **222** F2
Boggeragh Mountains, *mountain range*, Ireland, **309** D5
Bogia, Papua New Guinea, **140** B4
Bogniebrae, Scotland, U.K., **308** G3
Bognor Regis, England, U.K., **305** G4
Bogo, Cameroon, **365** G2
Bogor, Indonesia, **201** D4
Bogoroditsk, Russian Federation, **299** G6
Bogotá, Colombia, **450** C3, *436*
Bogotá, Providencia, Colombia, **461** C1
Bogotol, Russian Federation, **223** M1
Bogra, Bangladesh, **214** D4
Bogué, Mauritania, **364** B1
Boguslavl', Russian Federation, **299** F3
Bohai, Heilongjiang, China, **211** K3
Bohai, Shandong, China, **211** G5
Bohai Haixia, *strait*, China, **211** H5
Bohai Wan, *bay*, China, **211** G5
Bohicon, Benin, **365** E3
Böhmerwald, Germany, **288** F4
Bohol, *island*, Philippines, **204** D4, *149*
Bohonal, Spain, **292** E3
Böhönye, Hungary, **289** H5
Bohorodchany, Ukraine, **296** E1
Boiaçu, Brazil, **451** G4
Boigu Island, Australia, **140** A5
Boim, Brazil, **452** B4
Bois-Blanc, Réunion, **373** A1
Bois Blanc Island, U.S.A., **421** L3
Boise, U.S.A., **418** F5, *386*
Boise City, U.S.A., **420** B7
Boissevain, Canada, **414** D7
Boizenburg (Elbe), Germany, **288** E2
Bojano, Italy, **295** E5
Bojanowo, Poland, **289** H3
Boji Boji, Nigeria, **365** F3
Bojnūrd, Iran, **222** F5
Bokāro, India, **219** F5
Bokatola, Democratic Republic of the Congo, **368** C3
Bokchito, U.S.A., **424** D2
Boké, Guinea, **364** B2
Bokele, Democratic Republic of the Congo, **368** D3
Boknafjorden, *Fjord*, Norway, **286** B3
Boko, Congo, **368** B3
Boko-Songo, Congo, **368** B3
Bokode, Democratic Republic of the Congo, **368** C2
Bokoro, Chad, **365** H2
Bokote, Democratic Republic of the Congo, **368** D3
Boksitogorsk, Russian Federation, **299** D3
Bokspits, Botswana, **370** D4
Boktor, Russian Federation, **211** M2
Boku, Papua New Guinea, **140** E2
Bokungu, Democratic Republic of the Congo, **368** D3
Bokurdak, Turkmenistan, **222** F5
Bokwankusu, Democratic Republic of the Congo, **368** D3
Bol, Chad, **365** G2
Bolaiti, Democratic Republic of the Congo, **368** D3
Bolama, Guinea-Bissau, **364** A2
Bolān, *river*, Pakistan, **218** A3
Bolaños, Mexico, **430** E4
Bolbec, France, **290** E2
Boldeşti-Scăieni, Romania, **296** F3
Boldu, Romania, **296** F3
Bole, China, **212** D3
Bole, Ghana, **364** D3
Boleko, Democratic Republic of the Congo, **368** C3
Bolena, Democratic Republic of the Congo, **368** C2
Bolesławiec, Poland, **289** G3
Bolgatanga, Ghana, **364** D2
Bolhrad, Ukraine, **296** G3
Boli, China, **211** K3
Boli, Sudan, **366** C3
Bolia, Democratic Republic of the Congo, **368** C3
Boliden, Sweden, **284** K4
Bolinao, Philippines, **204** B2
Bolívar, Bolivia, **455** E3
Bolivar, Colombia, **450** C3
Bolivar, Missouri, U.S.A., **420** G7
Bolívar, Peru, **454** C2
Bolívar, Pico, *mountain peak*, Venezuela, **451** D2, *436*
Bolivar, Tennessee, U.S.A., **425** H2
Bolivia, *country*, South America, **449** F5, *67, 87, 95, 96, 434, 435, 441*
Boljevac, Serbia, **296** C4
Bolkhov, Russian Federation, **299** F6
Bollnäs, Sweden, **286** H2
Bollons Island, Antipodes Islands, New Zealand, **133** P15
Bollstabruk, Sweden, **287** H1
Bollullos par del Condado, Spain, **292** D4
Bolobo, Democratic Republic of the Congo, **368** C3
Bologna, Italy, **294** C3
Bolognesi, Central Peru, **454** C2
Bolognesi, N. Peru, **454** D2
Bologovo, Russian Federation, **299** C4
Bologoye, Russian Federation, **299** E4
Bolomba, Democratic Republic of the Congo, **368** C2
Bolon', Ozero, *lake*, Russian Federation, **211** M2
Bolon', Russian Federation, **211** M2
Bolondo, Democratic Republic of the Congo, **368** C3
Bolong, Philippines, **204** C5
Bolotnoye, Russian Federation, **223** L1
Bolsena, Italy, **294** D4
Bolsena, Lago di, *lake*, Italy, **294** C4
Bol'shakovo, Russian Federation, **287** K5
Bol'shaya Belaya, *river*, Russian Federation, **210** C1

Bol'shaya Glushitsa, Russian Federation, **222** E2
Bol'shaya Kinel', *river*, Russian Federation, **222** E2
Bol'sherech'ye, Russian Federation, **223** J1
Bol'shevik, Ostrov, *island*, Russian Federation, **301** M2
Bol'shoy Begichev, Ostrov, *island*, Russian Federation, **301** N2
Bol'shoy Kavkaz (Caucasus), *mountain range*, Asia/Europe, **222** D4, *189, 190, 273*
Bol'shoy Lyakhovskiy, Ostrov, *island*, Russian Federation, **301** R2
Bol'shoy Uvat, Ozero, *lake*, Russian Federation, **223** H1
Bol'shoy Yenisey, *river*, Russian Federation, **223** P2
Bol'shoye Pole, Russian Federation, **299** B2
Bol'shoye Sorokino, Russian Federation, **223** H1
Bol'shoye Zaborov'ye, Russian Federation, **299** D3
Bolsover, England, U.K., **305** F1
Bolt Head, *point*, England, U.K., **304** D4
Bolton, England, U.K., **306** F4
Bolubolu, Papua New Guinea, **140** C5
Boluntay, China, **213** G5
Boluo, China, **203** G1
Bolva, *river*, Russian Federation, **299** E5
Bolvadin, Turkey, **363** F1
Bolyston, Canada, **417** L7
Bolzano, Italy, **294** C2
Bom Comércio, Brazil, **455** E2
Bom Jardim, Amazonas, Brazil, **455** E2
Bom Jardim, Pará, Brazil, **452** C4
Bom Jesus, Brazil, **459** G3
Bom Jesus da Lapa, Brazil, **457** E3
Bom Retiro, Brazil, **459** H3
Boma, Democratic Republic of the Congo, **368** B4
Bomassa, Congo, **368** C2
Bombala, Australia, **135** K6
Bombay *see* Mumbai, India, **216** C2, *16, 45, 94, 169*
Bombay Beach, U.S.A., **422** F5
Bomboma, Democratic Republic of the Congo, **368** C2
Bomi, China, **215** E3
Bomili, Democratic Republic of the Congo, **369** E2
Bømlo, *island*, Norway, **286** B3
Bomongo, Democratic Republic of the Congo, **368** C2
Bon, Cap, *cape*, Tunisia, **295** C7
Bon Air, U.S.A., **426** B6
Bonaire, *island*, Netherlands Antilles, **461** A4, *391*
Bonanza, Nicaragua, **428** D4
Bonao, Dominican Republic, **429** H3
Bonaparte, *river*, Canada, **412** J6
Bonaparte Archipelago, *islands*, Australia, **134** E1
Bonaparte Lake, Canada, **412** J6
Bonar Bridge, Scotland, U.K., **308** E3
Bonasse, Trinidad, Trinidad and Tobago, **461** C4
Bonaventure, Canada, **416** J5
Bonavista, Canada, **417** Q5
Bonavista Bay, Canada, **417** Q5
Bondo, Angola, **368** C6
Bondo, Democratic Republic of the Congo, **368** D2
Bondoukou, Côte d'Ivoire, **364** D3
Bondoukui, Burkina Faso, **364** D2
Bondowoso, Indonesia, **201** F4
Bondurant, U.S.A., **419** J5
Bone, Teluk, *bay*, Indonesia, **198** C3
Bonerate, Pulau, *island*, Indonesia, **198** C4
Bo'ness, Scotland, U.K., **308** F4
Bonete, Cerro, *mountain peak*, Argentina, **458** C3
Bonete, Cerro, *mountain peak*, Bolivia, **455** E5
Bonete, Spain, **293** G3
Bonfinópolis, Brazil, **456** D4
Bông Lông, Cambodia, **203** E3
Bonga, Ethiopia, **367** E3
Bongabong, Philippines, **204** C3
Bongandanga, Democratic Republic of the Congo, **368** D2
Bongo, Democratic Republic of the Congo, **368** D2
Bongor, Chad, **365** H2
Bongos, Massif des, *mountain range*, Central African Republic, **366** B3
Bongouanou, Côte d'Ivoire, **364** D3
Bonham, U.S.A., **424** D3
Bonifacio, Corse, France, **295** B5
Bonifacio, Strait of, Mediterranean, **280** E7
Bonifay, U.S.A., **425** K4
Bonin Trench, *underwater feature*, Pacific Ocean, **478** D3
Bonito, Brazil, **456** B5
Bonito, Pico, *mountain peak*, Honduras, **428** D4
Bonn, Germany, **288** C3
Bonners Ferry, U.S.A., **418** F2
Bonneville, France, **291** H3
Bonny, Bight of, *gulf*, Nigeria, **368** A2
Bonny, Nigeria, **368** A2
Bonnyrigg, Scotland, U.K., **308** F5
Bonnyville, Canada, **413** P4
Bono, U.S.A., **424** G2
Bonorva, Sardegna, Italy, **295** B5
Bonoua, Côte d'Ivoire, **364** D3
Bontang, Indonesia, **201** G2
Bontoc, Philippines, **204** C2
Bonyhád, Hungary, **289** J5
Boola, Guinea, **364** C3
Booneville, U.S.A., **425** H2
Bööntsagaan Nuur, *lake*, Mongolia, **213** H3
Boonville, U.S.A., **426** C3
Boorama, Somalia, **367** F3
Boosaaso, Somalia, **367** G2
Boothia, Gulf of, Canada, **411** K2
Boothia Peninsula, Canada, **411** K2
Bootle, England, U.K., **306** E4
Booué, Gabon, **368** B3
Boqueirão, Brazil, **459** G4
Boquete, Panama, **429** E5
Boquillas del Carmen, Mexico, **430** E2
Boquirão, Serra do, *mountain range*, Brazil, **459** F3
Bor, Czech Republic, **288** F4
Bor, Russian Federation, **299** E3
Bor, Serbia, **296** D3
Bor, Sudan, **366** D3
Bor, Turkey, **224** D5
Bor-Üdzüür, Mongolia, **213** G3
Bor'a, Romania, **296** E2
Bora Bora, *island*, French Polynesia, **137** F2, *94*
Borah Peak, *mountain peak*, U.S.A., **418** H4
Boran, Kazakhstan, **212** E2
Borang, Tanjong, *point*, Indonesia, **199** F4
Borås, Sweden, **286** F4
Borāzjān, Iran, **220** F3
Borba, Brazil, **451** G5
Borborema, Planalto da, *plateau*, Brazil, **447** J4
Borchgrevink Coast, *region*, Antarctica, **470** D8
Bordeaux, France, **290** D4, *244, 245*
Borden, Canada, **413** R5
Borden Island, Canada, **410** H2
Bordertown, Australia, **135** J6
Bordj Bou Arreridj, Algeria, **361** G1
Bordj Messouda, Algeria, **361** H2
Bordj Mokhtar, Algeria, **361** G4
Bordj Omar Driss, Algeria, **361** H3
Boré, Mali, **364** D1
Boreray, *island*, Scotland, U.K., **308** B3
Borgarfjörður, Iceland, **284** Z7
Borgarnes, Iceland, **284** X7
Borgefjellet, *mountain range*, Norway, **284** F4
Borger, U.S.A., **424** B2
Borgholm, Sweden, **287** H4
Borgo San Dalmazzo, France, **291** H4
Borgo San Lorenzo, Italy, **294** C4
Borgo Valsugara, Italy, **294** C2
Borgomanero, Italy, **294** B3
Borgund, Norway, **286** C2
Borhoyn Tal, Mongolia, **210** E4
Bori, India, **218** D5
Borisoglebsk, Russian Federation, **298** F2
Borisovo-Sudskoye, Russian Federation, **299** F3
Boriziny, Madagascar, **372** B4
Borja, Peru, **450** C5
Borja, Spain, **293** G2
Borken, Germany, **288** C3
Borkou, *physical feature*, Chad, **362** C5
Borkou-Ennedi-Tibesti, *prefecture*, Chad, **362** C5
Borkum, *island*, Germany, **288** C2
Borlänge, Sweden, **286** G2
Bormio, Italy, **294** C2
Borna, Germany, **288** F3
Borneo, *island*, Brunei/Indonesia/Malaysia, **201** F2, *75, 76, 148, 150, 151*
Bornholm, *island*, Denmark, **286** G5
Borno, *state*, Nigeria, **365** G2
Bornova, Turkey, **362** E1
Borodino, Russian Federation, **223** P1
Borodino, Ukraine, **296** G2
Borodinskoye, Russian Federation, **299** B2
Borohoro Shan, *mountain range*, China, **212** D3
Borok, Russian Federation, **299** C3
Boroko, Indonesia, **198** C2
Boromata, Central African Republic, **366** B2
Boromo, Burkina Faso, **364** D2
Borongan, Philippines, **204** D4
Boronów, Poland, **289** J3
Borotou, Côte d'Ivoire, **364** C3
Boroughbridge, England, U.K., **307** G3
Borovichi, Novgorodskaya Oblast', Russian Federation, **299** D3
Borovichi, Pskovskaya Oblast', Russian Federation, **299** B4
Borovoy, Russian Federation, **285** R4
Borovskoy, Kazakhstan, **222** G2
Borre, Denmark, **286** F5
Borrisokane, Ireland, **309** D5
Borrisoleigh, Ireland, **309** E5
Borroloola, Australia, **135** H2
Börrum, Sweden, **287** H3
Borsec, Romania, **296** E2
Børselv, Norway, **285** M1
Borshchiv, Ukraine, **296** F1
Borshchovochnyy Khrebet, *mountain range*, Russian Federation, **211** G1
Borth, Wales, U.K., **304** C2
Börtnan, Sweden, **284** F5
Borūjerd, Iran, **220** E2
Borups Corners, Canada, **414** H7
Borve, Scotland, U.K., **308** C3
Boryslav, Ukraine, **289** L4
Borzya, Russian Federation, **210** G2
Bosa, Sardegna, Italy, **295** B5
Bosagha, Kazakhstan, **212** B3
Bosanska Dubica, Bosnia and Herzegovina, **294** F3
Bosanski Novi, Bosnia and Herzegovina, **294** F3
Bosanski Petrovac, Bosnia and Herzegovina, **294** F3
Bosavi, Mount, *mountain peak*, Papua New Guinea, **140** A4
Boscastle, England, U.K., **304** C4
Boscobel, U.S.A., **420** H4
Bose, China, **215** H5
Boshan, China, **211** G5
Bosherston, Wales, U.K., **304** C3
Bosilegrad, Serbia, **296** D4
Boskamp, Suriname, **452** B2
Boslanti, Suriname, **452** B2
Bosler, U.S.A., **419** M6
Bosna, *river*, Bosnia and Herzegovina, **294** G3
Bosnia and Herzegovina, *country*, Europe, **282** F7, 81, *97, 228, 229, 249, 259, 260, 261*
Bosobolo, Democratic Republic of the Congo, **368** C2
Bosporus *see* Istanbul Boğazı, *strait*, Turkey, **297** G5, *190, 191*
Bossembélé, Central African Republic, **368** C1
Bossentélé, Central African Republic, **368** C1
Bossier City, U.S.A., **424** F3
Bostan, China, **212** E5
Bostān, Pakistan, **218** A3
Bosten Hu, *lake*, China, **212** E4
Boston, England, U.K., **305** G2
Boston, U.S.A., **426** E3, *384, 386*
Boston Bar, Canada, **412** J7
Boston Mountains, *mountain range*, U.S.A., **424** F2
Boston Spa, England, U.K., **307** G4
Bot Makak, Cameroon, **368** B2
Botād, India, **218** B5
Botany Bay, Australia, **135** L5, *94*
Boteå, Sweden, **287** H1
Boteka, Democratic Republic of the Congo, **368** C3
Botemola, Democratic Republic of the Congo, **368** C3
Botevgrad, Bulgaria, **296** D4
Bothel, England, U.K., **306** E3
Bothnia, Gulf of, Finland/Sweden, **287** J2, *232, 235*
Boticas, Portugal, **292** D2
Botna, *river*, Moldova, **296** G2
Botngård, Norway, **284** D5
Boto-Pasi, Suriname, **452** B2
Botolan, Philippines, **204** C3
Botoşani, Romania, **296** F2
Botou, China, **210** G5
Botsmark, Sweden, **284** K4
Botswana, *country*, Africa, **359** H9, *312, 313, 347, 348, 350*
Botte Donato, Monte, *mountain peak*, Italy, **295** F6
Bottenviken Perämeri, *gulf*, Finland/Sweden, **285** L4
Bottineau, U.S.A., **420** C1
Bottrop, Germany, **288** C3
Botucatu, Brazil, **459** H2
Botuporã, Brazil, **457** E3
Bou Ismaïl, Algeria, **293** J4
Bou Izakarn, Morocco, **360** E3
Bou Kadir, Algeria, **293** H4
Bou Naceur, Jbel, *mountain peak*, Morocco, **361** F2
Bou Saâda, Algeria, **293** K5
Bou Salem, Tunisia, **295** B7
Bouaflé, Côte d'Ivoire, **364** C3
Bouaké, Côte d'Ivoire, **364** C3
Bouandougou, Côte d'Ivoire, **364** C3
Bouar, Central African Republic, **368** C1
Bouârfa, Morocco, **361** F2
Bouble, *river*, France, **291** F3
Bouca, Central African Republic, **366** A3
Bouchegouf, Algeria, **295** A7
Boudenib, Morocco, **361** F2
Boudoua, Central African Republic, **368** C2
Bouenza, *administrative region*, Congo, **368** B3
Bougainville Island, Papua New Guinea, **140** E8, *115, 116*
Boughessa, Mali, **361** G5
Bougouni, Mali, **364** C2
Bougtob, Algeria, **361** G2
Bougzoul, Algeria, **293** J5
Bouillon, Belgium, **288** B4
Bouira, Algeria, **293** J4
Boulder, Colorado, U.S.A., **423** L1
Boulder, Montana, U.S.A., **419** H3
Boulder, Utah, U.S.A., **423** H3
Boulder, Wyoming, U.S.A., **419** K5
Boulder City, U.S.A., **422** F4
Boulemane, Morocco, **361** F2
Boulia, Australia, **135** H3
Boulmer, England, U.K., **307** G2
Boulogne-Billancourt, France, **290** F2
Boulogne-sur-Mer, France, **290** E1
Boulouba, Central African Republic, **366** B3
Bouloupari, New Caledonia, **141** A3
Boumango, Gabon, **368** B3
Boumba, *river*, Cameroon, **368** B2
Bouna, Côte d'Ivoire, **364** D3
Boundary Peak, *mountain peak*, U.S.A., **422** D3
Boundiali, Côte d'Ivoire, **364** C3
Boundji, Congo, **368** C3
Bounty Islands, New Zealand, **133** N14
Bounty Trough, *underwater feature*, Pacific Ocean, **478** F7
Bourail, New Caledonia, **141** A3
Bourbourg, France, **305** K4
Bourem, Mali, **364** D1
Bourg-en-Bresse, France, **291** G3
Bourg-Saint-Maurice, France, **291** H4
Bourganeuf, France, **290** E4
Bourges, France, **290** F3
Bourget, Lac du, *lake*, France, **291** G4
Bourgogne, *administrative region*, France, **291** F3, *245, 249, 250*
Bourke, Australia, **135** K5
Bourne, England, U.K., **305** G2
Bournemouth, England, U.K., **305** F4
Bournemouth, England, U.K., **305** F4
Bournemouth, *unitary authority*, England, U.K., **305** F4
Bourtoutou, Chad, **366** B2
Bouse, U.S.A., **422** F5
Boussac, France, **290** F3
Bousso, Chad, **365** H2
Boutilimit, Mauritania, **364** B1
Bouvet Island, *Norwegian dependency*, Atlantic Ocean, **470** D1, *231, 469*
Bouza, Niger, **365** F2
Bova Marina, Sicilia, Italy, **295** E7
Bovalino Marina, Italy, **295** F6
Bovallstrand, Sweden, **286** E3
Bøverdal, Norway, **286** D2
Boves, France, **305** K5
Bovina, U.S.A., **423** M4
Bovril, Argentina, **459** E4
Bow Island, Canada, **413** P7
Bowdle, U.S.A., **420** D3
Bowen, Australia, **135** K3
Bowes, England, U.K., **306** F3
Bowie, Arizona, U.S.A., **423** J5
Bowie, Texas, U.S.A., **424** D3
Bowland, Forest of, England, U.K., **306** F4
Bowling Green, Kentucky, U.S.A., **421** K7
Bowling Green, Missouri, U.S.A., **420** H6
Bowling Green, Ohio, U.S.A., **421** M5
Bowman, U.S.A., **420** B2
Bowmanville, Canada, **416** B8
Bowmore, Scotland, U.K., **308** C5
Bowral, Australia, **135** L5
Bowron, *river*, Canada, **412** J5
Boxing, China, **211** G5
Boyang, China, **206** D2
Boyd, Montana, U.S.A., **419** K4
Boyd, Texas, U.S.A., **424** D3
Boyd Lagoon, *lake*, Australia, **134** F4
Boyero, U.S.A., **423** M2
Boyle, Canada, **413** N4
Boyle, Ireland, **309** D4
Boyne, *river*, Ireland, **309** F4, *275*
Boyuibe, Bolivia, **455** F5
Boz Dağ, *mountain peak*, Turkey, **297** G7
Bozburun, Turkey, **297** G7

Bozcaada, *island*, Turkey, **297** E6
Bozdoğan, Turkey, **297** G7
Bozeman, U.S.A., **419** J4
Bozhou, China, **206** C1
Bozoum, Central African Republic, **365** H3
Bozova, Turkey, **363** G1
Bozovici, Romania, **296** D3
Bozüyük, Turkey, **297** H6
Bozyazı, Turkey, **225** B1
Brabant Lake, Canada, **414** C3
Brabant-Wallon, *province*, Belgium, **288** B3
Brač, *island*, Croatia, **294** F4
Bracadale, Loch, *inlet*, Scotland, U.K., **308** C3
Bracadale, Scotland, U.K., **308** C3
Bracciano, Italy, **295** D4
Bracciano, Lago di, *lake*, Italy, **295** D4
Bracebridge, Canada, **421** P3
Bräcke, Sweden, **286** G1
Brackendale, Canada, **412** H7
Brackettville, U.S.A., **424** B5
Brackley, England, U.K., **305** F2
Bracknell, England, U.K., **305** G3
Bracknell Forest, *unitary authority*, England, U.K., **305** G3
Braço Menor do Araguaia, *river*, Brazil, **456** C3
Brad, Romania, **296** D2
Bradenton, U.S.A., **425** L6
Bradford, England, U.K., **307** G4
Bradford, U.S.A., **426** D3
Bradford on Avon, England, U.K., **304** E3
Bradwell-on-Sea, England, U.K., **305** H3
Brady, Montana, U.S.A., **419** J2
Brady, Nebraska, U.S.A., **420** C5
Brady, Texas, U.S.A., **424** C4
Brae, Shetland, Scotland, U.K., **308** K7
Brædstrup, Denmark, **286** D5
Braemar, Scotland, U.K., **308** F3
Braga, *district*, Portugal, **292** C2
Braga, Portugal, **292** C2
Bragado, Argentina, **458** E5
Bragança, Brazil, **452** D3
Bragança, *district*, Portugal, **292** D2
Bragança, Portugal, **292** D2
Bragança Paulista, Brazil, **459** H2
Brāhmanbāria, Bangladesh, **214** D4
Brāhmani, *river*, India, **219** F5
Brahmapur, India, **217** F2
Brahmaputra, *river*, Asia, **214** E4; *see also* Yarlung Zangbo, *river*, China, **205** B1, *51, 158, 168, 170*
Brăila, Romania, **296** F3
Brailsford, England, U.K., **305** F2
Brainerd, U.S.A., **420** F2
Braintree, England, U.K., **305** H3
Brake (Unterweser), Germany, **288** D2
Brâkna, *administrative region*, Mauritania, **364** B1
Brålanda, Sweden, **286** F3
Brampton, England, U.K., **305** J2
Bramsche, Germany, **288** C2
Bramwell, Australia, **140** A6
Brancaster, England, U.K., **305** H2
Branch, Canada, **417** P6
Branco, *river*, Mato Grosso do Sul, Brazil, **456** B5
Branco, *river*, Roraima, Brazil, **451** G4
Brandberg, *mountain peak*, Namibia, **370** B3
Brandbu, Norway, **286** E2
Brande, Denmark, **286** D5
Brandenburg, *state*, Germany, **288** F2, *238*
Brandenburg an der Havel, Germany, **288** F2
Brandesburton, England, U.K., **307** H4
Brandon, England, U.K., **305** H2
Brandon, Canada, **414** E7
Brandon, U.S.A., **426** D3
Brandon Head, *point*, Ireland, **309** B5
Brandon Hill, Ireland, **309** F5
Brandon Mountain, Ireland, **309** B5
Brandvlei, South Africa, **370** D5
Brandywine, U.S.A., **426** B5
Branford, U.S.A., **425** L5
Brani, Pulau, *island*, Singapore, **200** K7
Braniewo, Poland, **289** J1
Brańsk, Poland, **289** L2
Branson, U.S.A., **423** M3
Brantley, U.S.A., **425** J4
Brantôme, France, **290** E4
Brânzeni, Moldova, **296** F1
Bras d'Or Lake, Canada, **417** L7
Bras-Panon, Réunion, **373** A1
Brasil, Brazil, **450** D5
Brasil, Planalto do, *plateau*, Brazil, **457** E4
Brasiléia, Brazil, **455** E3
Brasília, Brazil, **456** D4, *439, 441*
Brasília de Minas, Brazil, **457** E4
Brasília Legal, Brazil, **452** B4
Braslaw, Belarus, **287** N5
Braşov, Romania, **296** E3
Brasstown Bald, *mountain peak*, U.S.A., **425** L2
Bratca, Romania, **296** D2
Bratislava, Slovakia, **289** H4, *267*
Bratislavský, *administrative region*, Slovakia, **289** H4
Bratsk, Russian Federation, **301** M4
Bratskoye Vodokhranilishche, *reservoir*, Russian Federation, **301** M4
Brattleboro, U.S.A., **426** D3
Brattvåg, Norway, **286** C1
Braunau am Inn, Austria, **288** F4
Braunlage, Germany, **288** E3
Braunschweig, Germany, **288** E2
Braunton, England, U.K., **304** C3
Brava, *island*, Cape Verde, **360** P9
Bravo del Norte, Río, *river*, Mexico, **430** E2
Brawley, U.S.A., **422** F5
Bray, Ireland, **309** F4
Bray, *river*, England, U.K., **304** D3
Bray, U.S.A., **418** D6
Bray-sur-Somme, France, **305** K5
Brazeau, Mount, *mountain peak*, Canada, **413** L5
Brazil, *country*, South America, **448** G5, *30, 43, 76, 79, 87, 92, 93, 95, 96, 97, 327, 335, 434, 435, 439, 440, 441, 445*
Brazil, U.S.A., **421** K6
Brazil Basin, *underwater feature*, Atlantic Ocean, **477** E6
Brasilian Highlands, *mountain range*, Brazil, **446** G5, *439, 444*
Brazos, *river*, U.S.A., **424** D3
Brazzaville, Congo, **368** C3, *333, 334*
Brčko, Bosnia and Herzegovina, **294** G3
Brda, *river*, Poland, **289** H2
Brdów, Poland, **289** J2
Breaksea Island, New Zealand, **133** A7
Bream Bay, New Zealand, **132** E2
Breaza, Romania, **296** E3
Brechfa, Wales, U.K., **304** C3
Brechin, Scotland, U.K., **308** G4
Breckenridge, Minnesota, U.S.A., **420** E2
Breckenridge, Texas, U.S.A., **424** C3
Brecknock, Península, Chile, **460** C5
Břeclav, Czech Republic, **289** H4
Brecon, Wales, U.K., **304** D3
Brecon Beacons, *mountain range*, Wales, U.K., **304** D3
Breda, Netherlands, **288** B3
Bredaryd, Sweden, **286** F4
Bredasdorp, South Africa, **370** D5
Bredbyn, Sweden, **284** J5
Brede, *river*, England, U.K., **305** H4
Bredsel, Sweden, **284** K4
Bredstedt, Germany, **288** D1
Bredy, Russian Federation, **222** G2
Bree, Belgium, **288** B3
Bregalnica, *river*, Macedonia, **296** D5
Bregenz, Austria, **288** D5
Bregovo, Bulgaria, **296** D3
Breiðafjörður, *bay*, Iceland, **284** W7
Breiðdalsvík, Iceland, **284** Z7
Breien, U.S.A., **420** C2
Breivikbotn, Norway, **285** L1
Brejinho de Nazaré, Brazil, **456** D3
Brejo, Brazil, **453** E4
Brekstad, Norway, **284** D5
Brem River, Canada, **412** G6
Bremangerlandet, *island*, Norway, **286** A2
Bremen, Germany, **288** D2
Bremen, *state*, Germany, **288** D2, *238*
Bremen, U.S.A., **421** K5
Bremerhaven, Germany, **288** D2
Bremerton, U.S.A., **418** C3
Bremervörde, Germany, **288** D2
Brenham, U.S.A., **424** D4
Brentwood, England, U.K., **305** H3
Brescia, Italy, **294** C3
Bressanone, Italy, **294** C2
Bressay, *island*, Shetland, Scotland, U.K., **308** K7
Bressuire, France, **290** D3
Brest, Belarus, **298** B2
Brest, France, **290** B2
Brestskaya Voblasts', *province*, Belarus, **289** M2
Bretagne, *administrative region*, France, **290** C2, *229, 244, 245*
Breteuil, France, **305** K5
Breton, Canada, **413** M5
Breton, Pertuis, *strait*, France, **290** D3
Brett, Cape, New Zealand, **132** E2
Bretton, Wales, U.K., **304** E1
Breueh, Pulau, *island*, Indonesia, **200** A1
Breves, Brazil, **452** C3
Brewster, U.S.A., **420** D5
Brewton, U.S.A., **425** J4
Breynat, Canada, **413** N4
Breytovo, Russian Federation, **299** F3
Brežice, Slovenia, **294** E3
Breznik, Bulgaria, **296** D4
Brezno, Slovakia, **289** J4
Brezoi, Romania, **296** E3
Brezolles, France, **290** E2
Bria, Central African Republic, **366** B3
Briançon, France, **291** H4
Briare, France, **290** F3
Bribri, Costa Rica, **429** E5
Briceni, Moldova, **296** F1
Bricquebec, France, **290** D2
Bride, Isle of Man, **306** D3
Bride, *river*, Ireland, **309** D5
Bridge of Orchy, Scotland, U.K., **308** E4
Bridgeland, U.S.A., **423** H1
Bridgend, Islay, Scotland, U.K., **308** C5
Bridgend, Scotland, U.K., **308** F3
Bridgend, *unitary authority*, Wales, U.K., **304** D3
Bridgend, Wales, U.K., **304** D3
Bridgeport, California, U.S.A., **422** D2
Bridgeport, Connecticut, U.S.A., **426** D4
Bridgeport, Nebraska, U.S.A., **420** B5
Bridgeport, Texas, U.S.A., **424** D3
Bridgeton, U.S.A., **426** C5
Bridgetown, Australia, **134** D5
Bridgetown, Barbados, **427** E3, *398*
Bridgetown, Canada, **416** J7
Bridgeville, U.S.A., **422** B1
Bridgewater, Australia, **135** K7
Bridgewater, Canada, **417** J7
Bridgewater, U.S.A., **426** C3
Bridgman, Kap, *cape*, Greenland, **411** S1
Bridgnorth, England, U.K., **304** E2
Bridgton, U.S.A., **426** E2
Bridgwater, England, U.K., **304** D3
Bridgwater Bay, England, U.K., **304** D3
Bridlington, England, U.K., **307** H3
Bridlington Bay, England, U.K., **307** H3
Bridport, England, U.K., **304** E4
Brienz, Switzerland, **291** J3
Brienza, Italy, **295** E5
Brig, Switzerland, **291** H3
Brig Bay, Canada, **417** N4
Brigg, England, U.K., **307** H4
Briggsdale, U.S.A., **423** L1
Brigham City, U.S.A., **419** H6
Brighstone, England, U.K., **305** F4
Brightlingsea, England, U.K., **305** J3
Brighton, England, U.K., **305** G4
Brighton, New Zealand, **133** C7
Brighton, U.S.A., **425** M6
Brighton and Hove, England, U.K., **305** G4
Brignoles, France, **291** G5
Brikama, Gambia, **364** A2
Brilhante, *river*, Brazil, **456** B5
Brilon, Germany, **288** D3
Brindisi, Italy, **295** F5
Brinkley, U.S.A., **424** G2
Brionne, France, **290** E2
Briouze, France, **290** D2
Brisbane, Australia, **135** L4, *112*
Brisco, Canada, **413** L6
Bristol, Alabama, U.S.A., **425** K4
Bristol, Connecticut, U.S.A., **426** D4
Bristol, England, U.K., **304** E3
Bristol, South Dakota, U.S.A., **420** E3
Bristol, Tennessee/Virginia, U.S.A., **421** M7
Bristol Bay, U.S.A., **410** C4
Bristol Channel, England, U.K., **304** C3
Bristol City, *unitary authority*, England, U.K., **304** E3
Bristow Point, Auckland Islands, New Zealand, **132** J10
Britannia Beach, Canada, **412** H7
British Columbia, *province*, Canada, **412** F4, *381, 384*
British Indian Ocean Territory, *U.K. dependency*, Indian Ocean, **104** E9, *193, 276*
Britstown, South Africa, **370** D5
Brittas Bay, Ireland, **304** A2
Brive-la-Gaillarde, France, **290** E4
Brixham, England, U.K., **304** D4
Brno, Czech Republic, **289** H4, *266*
Broad Bay, Scotland, U.K., **308** C2
Broad Haven, *bay*, Ireland, **309** C3
Broad Haven, Wales, U.K., **304** B3
Broad Law, *mountain peak*, Scotland, U.K., **308** F5
Broadford, Ireland, **309** D5
Broadford, Scotland, U.K., **308** D3
Broadmeadows, New Zealand, **133** E5
Broadstairs, England, U.K., **305** J3
Broadus, U.S.A., **419** M4
Broadview, Canada, **414** C6
Broadview, U.S.A., **419** K3
Broadwater, U.S.A., **420** B5
Broadway, England, U.K., **305** F2
Broadwindsor, England, U.K., **304** E4
Brochet, Canada, **414** D3
Brochet, Lac, *lake*, Canada, **414** D2
Brockport, U.S.A., **426** B3
Brockton, U.S.A., **419** M2
Brockville, Canada, **416** D7
Brockway, U.S.A., **419** M3
Brockworth, England, U.K., **304** E3
Brod, Macedonia, **297** C5
Brodeur Peninsula, Canada, **411** L2
Brodick, Scotland, U.K., **308** D5
Brodnica, Poland, **289** J2
Brogan, U.S.A., **418** F4
Broken Arrow, U.S.A., **424** E1
Broken Bow, Nebraska, U.S.A., **419** Q6
Broken Bow, Oklahoma, U.S.A., **424** E2
Broken Bow Lake, U.S.A., **424** E2
Broken Hill, Australia, **135** J5
Broken Ridge, *underwater feature*, Indian Ocean, **476** F7
Brokopondo, Suriname, **452** B2
Bromley, England, U.K., **305** H3
Brömsebro, Sweden, **286** G4
Bromsgrove, England, U.K., **304** E2
Bromyard, England, U.K., **304** E2
Brønderslev, Denmark, **286** D4
Brong-Ahafo, *administrative region*, Ghana, **364** D3
Bronnitsy, Russian Federation, **299** G5
Bronte, Sicilia, Italy, **295** E7
Brooke, England, U.K., **305** J2
Brooke's Point, Philippines, **204** B4
Brookfield, U.S.A., **420** G6
Brookhaven, U.S.A., **424** G4
Brookings, Oregon, U.S.A., **418** B5
Brookings, South Dakota, U.S.A., **420** E3
Brooklyn, U.S.A., **420** G5
Brooklyn Park, U.S.A., **420** G3
Brookneal, U.S.A., **421** P7
Brooks, Canada, **413** P6
Brooks Range, *mountain range*, U.S.A., **410** C3
Brooksville, U.S.A., **425** L5
Broom, Loch, *inlet*, Scotland, U.K., **308** D3
Broome, Australia, **134** E2
Broome, Mount, *mountain peak*, Australia, **134** F2
Broons, France, **290** C2
Brora, *river*, Scotland, U.K., **308** E2
Brora, Scotland, U.K., **308** F2
Broseley, England, U.K., **304** E2
Brøstadbotn, Norway, **284** H2
Broşteni, Romania, **296** E2
Brothers, U.S.A., **418** D5
Brothers, The, *see* Ikhwān, Al, Suquṭrá (Socotra), Yemen, **373** B2
Brou, France, **290** E2
Brough, Cumbria, England, U.K., **306** F3
Brough, East Riding of Yorkshire, England, U.K., **307** H4
Brough Head, *point*, Orkney, Scotland, U.K., **308** F1
Broughshane, Northern Ireland, U.K., **309** F3
Broughton Island, Snares Islands, New Zealand, **132** H9
Brownfield, U.S.A., **423** M5
Brownhills, England, U.K., **305** F2
Browning, U.S.A., **418** H3
Brownsville, Tennessee, U.S.A., **425** H2
Brownsville, Texas, U.S.A., **424** D7
Brownwood, Lake, U.S.A., **424** C4
Brownwood, U.S.A., **424** C4
Brozas, Spain, **292** D3
Bru, Norway, **286** B2
Bruay-en-Artois, France, **290** F1
Bruce, U.S.A., **425** H2
Bruce Bay, New Zealand, **133** B6
Bruce Crossing, U.S.A., **421** J2
Bruck an der Großglocknerstraße, Austria, **288** F5
Bruck an der Mur, Austria, **289** G5
Brue, *river*, England, U.K., **304** E3
Brugge, Belgium, **288** A3, *242*
Bruit, Pulau, *island*, Malaysia, **201** E2
Brukkaros, *mountain peak*, Namibia, **370** C4
Brule, U.S.A., **420** H2
Brumado, Brazil, **457** F4
Brummen, Netherlands, **288** C2
Bruneau, *river*, U.S.A., **418** G5

Brunei, *country*, Asia, **197** N9, *144, 150, 193*
Brunei Bay, Brunei, **201** F1, *150*
Brunflo, Sweden, **284** G5
Brunkild, Canada, **414** F7
Brunswick, Georgia, U.S.A., **425** M4
Brunswick, Missouri, U.S.A., **420** G6
Brunswick, Península de, Chile, **460** C4
Bruntál, Czech Republic, **289** H4
Brus, Serbia, **296** C4
Brus Laguna, Honduras, **428** D4
Brush, U.S.A., **423** M1
Brussels *see* Bruxelles, Belgium, **288** B3, *241, 242*
Brusy, Poland, **289** H2
Bruton, England, U.K., **304** E3
Bruxelles (Brussels), Belgium, **288** B3, *241, 242*
Bruz, France, **290** D2
Bryan, Ohio, U.S.A., **421** L5
Bryan, Texas, U.S.A., **424** D4
Bryan Coast, *region*, Antarctica, **470** B5
Bryansk, Russian Federation, **299** E6
Bryanskaya Oblast', *province*, Russian Federation, **299** D6
Bryant, U.S.A., **420** E3
Brymbo, Wales, U.K., **304** D1
Brynamman, Wales, U.K., **304** D3
Brynderwyn, New Zealand, **132** E3
Bryne, Norway, **286** B3
Brynmawr, Wales, U.K., **304** D3
Bryson City, U.S.A., **425** L2
Brza Palanka, Serbia, **296** D3
Brzeg, Poland, **289** H3
Brzeg Dolny, Poland, **289** H3
Brzoza, Poland, **289** J2
Bu Craa, Western Sahara, **360** D3
Bua Yai, Thailand, **202** D3
Bu'aale, Somalia, **369** H2
Buala, Solomon Islands, **141** A1
Buatan, Indonesia, **200** C2
Bu'ayrāt al Ḩasūn, Libya, **362** C2
Buba, Guinea-Bissau, **364** A2
Bubi, *river*, Zimbabwe, **371** F3
Būbiyān, Jazīrat, *island*, Kuwait, **220** E3, *177*
Bubwith, England, U.K., **307** H4
Buca, Fiji, **141** A4
Buca, Turkey, **297** F6
Bucanera, Punta, *point*, Providencia, Colombia, **461** C1
Bucaramanga, Colombia, **450** D2
Bucas Grande Island, Philippines, **204** D4
Buccoo Bay, Tobago, Trinidad and Tobago, **461** B4
Buchanan, Liberia, **364** B3
Buchanan, Oregon, U.S.A., **418** E5
Buchanan, Virginia, U.S.A., **421** P7
Buchans, Canada, **417** N5
Buchardo, Argentina, **458** D5
Bucharest *see* București, Romania, **296** E3, *263*
Buchloe, Germany, **288** E4
Buchy, France, **305** J5
Buckeye, U.S.A., **422** G5
Buckhannon, U.S.A., **421** N6
Buckhaven, Scotland, U.K., **308** F4
Buckhorn, U.S.A., **423** J5
Buckie, Scotland, U.K., **308** G3
Buckingham, England, U.K., **305** F3
Buckinghamshire, *unitary authority*, England, U.K., **305** F3
Buckles Bay, Macquarie Island, **134** R11
Buco Zau, Angola, **368** B3
Bučovice, Czech Republic, **289** H4
Buctouche, Canada, **417** J6
București (Bucharest), Romania, **296** E3, *263*
Bucyrus, U.S.A., **421** M5
Bud, Norway, **286** C1
Bud Bud, Somalia, **367** G4
Budacu, *mountain peak*, Romania, **296** E2
Budalin, Myanmar, **205** B3
Budapest, Hungary, **289** J5, *262, 263*
Búðardalur, Iceland, **284** X7
Būdarīno, Kazakhstan, **222** E2
Budaun, India, **218** D3
Budd Coast, *region*, Antarctica, **470** G7
Buddi, Ethiopia, **367** F3
Buddusò, Sardegna, Italy, **295** B5
Bude, England, U.K., **304** C4
Bude Bay, England, U.K., **304** C4
Büdelsdorf, Germany, **288** D1
Budești, Romania, **296** F3
Búðir, Iceland, **284** X7
Budjala, Democratic Republic of the Congo, **368** C2
Budleigh Salterton, England, U.K., **304** D4
Budogoshch', Russian Federation, **299** D3
Budrio, Italy, **294** C3
Budva, Montenegro, **296** B4
Buea, Cameroon, **368** A2
Buëch, *river*, France, **291** G4
Buen Pasto, Argentina, **460** D2
Buen Tiempo, Cabo, *cape*, Argentina, **460** D4
Buena Esperanza, Argentina, **458** D5
Buena Vista, U.S.A., **423** K2
Buenaventura, Bahía de, *bay*, Colombia, **450** B3
Buenaventura, Colombia, **450** C3
Buenaventura, Mexico, **430** D2
Buendia, Embalse de, *reservoir*, Spain, **293** F2
Bueno, *river*, Chile, **460** C1
Buenos Aires, Argentina, **459** E5, *93, 434, 442, 443*
Buenos Aires, Lago, *lake*, Argentina, **460** C3
Buenos Aires, *province*, Argentina, **458** E5
Búfalo, Mexico, **430** D3
Buffalo, Canada, **413** P6
Buffalo, New York, U.S.A., **421** P4
Buffalo, Oklahoma, U.S.A., **420** D7
Buffalo, South Dakota, U.S.A., **420** B3
Buffalo, Texas, U.S.A., **424** D4
Buffalo, Wyoming, U.S.A., **419** L4
Buffalo Head Hills, Canada, **413** L2
Buffalo Lake, Alberta, Canada, **413** N5
Buffalo Lake, Northwest Territories, Canada, **413** M1
Buffalo Narrows, Canada, **413** Q4
Buford, U.S.A., **419** M6
Buftea, Romania, **296** E3
Bug, *river*, Belarus/Poland/Ukraine, **289** L2
Buga, Colombia, **450** C3
Buga, Mongolia, **213** G3
Bugana, Nigeria, **365** F3
Bugant, Mongolia, **210** D2
Bugasong, Philippines, **204** C4
Bugdayly, Turkmenistan, **222** E5
Bugel, Tanjong, *point*, Indonesia, **201** E4
Bugio, Ilhéu do, *island*, Madeira, Portugal, **373** C3
Bugøyfjord, Norway, **285** P2
Bugøynes, Norway, **285** P2
Bugsuk Island, Philippines, **204** B4
Bugt, China, **211** H2
Bugul'ma, Russian Federation, **222** E2
Buguruslan, Russian Federation, **222** E2
Buhera, Zimbabwe, **371** F2
Buhl, U.S.A., **418** G5
Buhuși, Romania, **296** F2
Builth Wells, Wales, U.K., **304** D2
Buin, Papua New Guinea, **140** E2
Buitepos, Namibia, **370** C3
Bujanovac, Serbia, **296** C4
Bujaraloz, Spain, **293** G2
Buji, China, **207** C3
Bujoru, Romania, **296** E4
Bujumbura, Burundi, **369** E3, *343*
Buk, Papua New Guinea, **140** A5
Buka Island, Papua New Guinea, **140** E8
Bukaan, Indonesia, **198** C2
Bukalo, Namibia, **370** D2
Bukama, Democratic Republic of the Congo, **369** E4
Būkan, Iran, **363** J1
Bukavu, Democratic Republic of the Congo, **369** E3
Bukhoro, Uzbekistan, **222** G5, *185, 188*
Bukit Batok, Singapore, **200** J6
Bukit Panjang, Singapore, **200** J6
Bukit Timah, Singapore, **200** J6, *150*
Bukittinggi, Indonesia, **200** C3
Bukoba, Tanzania, **369** F3
Bukuru, Nigeria, **365** F3
Bula, Indonesia, **199** E3
Bula, Papua New Guinea, **140** A5
Bulag, Mongolia, **210** E2
Bulagansk, Russian Federation, **210** E1
Bulalacao (San Pedro), Philippines, **204** C3
Bulan, Philippines, **204** C3
Bulangu, Nigeria, **365** G2
Bulanık, Turkey, **363** H1
Būlāq, Egypt, **363** F3
Bulawa, Gunung, *mountain peak*, Indonesia, **198** C2
Bulawayo, Zimbabwe, **371** E3
Buldan, Turkey, **297** G6
Buldāna, India, **218** D5
Buldibuyo, Peru, **454** C2
Bulford, England, U.K., **305** F3
Bulgan, Bayanhongor, Mongolia, **213** H3
Bulgan, Bulgan, Mongolia, **213** J2
Bulgan, Hövsgöl, Mongolia, **213** J2
Bulgan, Ömnögovĭ, Mongolia, **213** J3
Bulgan, *province*, Mongolia, **213** J2
Bulgan, *river*, Mongolia, **213** F3
Bulgaria, *country*, Europe, **282** G7, *228, 245, 260, 261, 263, 264, 265*
Buli, Indonesia, **199** E2
Buli, Teluk, *bay*, Indonesia, **199** E2
Buliluyan, Cape, Philippines, **204** B4
Bulkington, England, U.K., **305** F2
Bull Mountains, *mountain range*, U.S.A., **419** K3
Bullas, Spain, **293** G3
Bullaxaar, Somalia, **367** F2
Bulle, Switzerland, **291** H3
Bullenbaai, *bay*, Curaçao, Netherlands Antilles, **461** C3
Buller, *river*, New Zealand, **133** D5
Bullhead City, U.S.A., **422** F4
Bulloo, *river*, Australia, **135** J4, *112*
Bulls, New Zealand, **132** E5
Bully-les-Minnes, France, **305** K4
Bulolo, Papua New Guinea, **140** B4
Buluan Lake, Philippines, **204** D5
Bulukutu, Democratic Republic of the Congo, **368** D3
Bulungu, Bandundu, Democratic Republic of the Congo, **368** C3
Bulungu, Kasai Occidental, Democratic Republic of the Congo, **368** D4
Bulupulu, Tanjong, *point*, Indonesia, **198** C3
Bumba, Bandundu, Democratic Republic of the Congo, **368** C4
Bumba, Equateur, Democratic Republic of the Congo, **368** D2
Bumbat, Mongolia, **210** D3
Bumbești-Jiu, Romania, **296** D3
Buna, Democratic Republic of the Congo, **368** C3
Buna, Kenya, **369** G2
Bunapas, Papua New Guinea, **140** B4
Bunazi, Tanzania, **369** F3
Bunbeg, Ireland, **309** D2
Bunbury, Australia, **134** D5
Bunclody, Ireland, **309** F5
Buncrana, Ireland, **309** E2
Bunda, Tanzania, **369** F3
Bundaberg, Australia, **135** L3
Būndi, India, **218** C4
Bundibugyo, Uganda, **369** F2
Bundoran, Ireland, **309** D3
Būndu, India, **219** F5
Bunduqīyah, Sudan, **369** F1
Bungalaut, Selat, *strait*, Indonesia, **200** B3
Bungay, England, U.K., **305** J2
Bungo, Angola, **368** C4
Buni, Nigeria, **365** G2
Bunia, Democratic Republic of the Congo, **369** F2
Bunić, Croatia, **294** E3
Bunkeya, Democratic Republic of the Congo, **369** E5
Bunkie, U.S.A., **424** F4
Bunnell, U.S.A., **425** M5
Bunnythorpe, New Zealand, **132** E5
Bunreș, *river*, Romania, **296** F2
Bunta, Indonesia, **198** C3
Bununu Dass, Nigeria, **365** F3
Bünyan, Turkey, **224** E5
Bunza, Nigeria, **365** E2
Buôn Mê Thuột, Vietnam, **203** F3
Buôn Mrông, Vietnam, **203** F3
Buqayq, Saudi Arabia, **220** E3
Buqian, China, **207** D1
Būr Safājah, Egypt, **363** F3
Būr Sa'īd (Port Said), Egypt, **225** B4
Būr Sūdān (Port Sudan), Sudan, **363** G5
Būr Tawfīq, Egypt, **225** B5
Bura, Kenya, **369** G3
Buraan, Somalia, **367** G2
Buram, Sudan, **366** C2
Burāq, Syria, **225** D3
Buraydah, Saudi Arabia, **363** H3
Burbage, England, U.K., **305** F3
Burco, Somalia, **367** G3
Burda, India, **218** D4
Burdekin, *river*, Australia, **135** K2
Burdett, U.S.A., **420** D6
Burdur, *province*, Turkey, **297** G7
Burdur, Turkey, **224** D5
Burdur Gölü, *lake*, Turkey, **297** G7
Burē, Ethiopia, **366** E3
Bure, *river*, England, U.K., **305** J2
Bureå, Sweden, **284** K4
Bureinskiy Khrebet, *mountain range*, Russian Federation, **211** L2
Bürenhayrhan, Mongolia, **213** F3
Bürentsogt, Mongolia, **210** E3
Burevestnik, Russian Federation, **209** J1
Bureya, *river*, Russian Federation, **211** K2
Burfjord, Norway, **285** L2
Burford, England, U.K., **305** F3
Burg bei Magdeburg, Germany, **288** E2
Burgas, *administrative region*, Bulgaria, **296** F4
Burgas, Bulgaria, **296** F4
Burgaw, U.S.A., **425** P2
Burgdorf, Switzerland, **291** H3
Burgdorf, U.S.A., **418** G4
Burgenland, *state*, Austria, **289** H5
Burgeo, Canada, **417** N6
Burgess Hill, England, U.K., **305** G4
Burgh le Marsh, England, U.K., **305** H1
Burghausen, Germany, **288** F4
Burghead, Scotland, U.K., **308** F3
Burgos, Spain, **293** F1, *252*
Burgsvik, Sweden, **287** J4
Burhan Budai Shan, *mountain range*, China, **215** E2
Burhaniye, Turkey, **297** F6
Burhānpur, India, **218** D5
Burhar-Dhanpuri, India, **219** E5
Buri Ram, Thailand, **203** D3
Burias Island, Philippines, **204** C3
Burica, Punta, *point*, Costa Rica/Panama, **429** E6
Buriti, Brazil, **453** E4
Buriti Alegre, Brazil, **456** D5
Buriti Bravo, Brazil, **453** E4
Buriti dos Lopes, Brazil, **453** F4
Buriticupu, *river*, Brazil, **452** D4
Buritirama, Brazil, **457** E3
Buritis, Brazil, **456** D4
Burkburnett, U.S.A., **424** C2
Burke Island, Antarctica, **470** B6
Burketown, Australia, **135** H2
Burkina Faso, *country*, Africa, **358** E5, *324, 325, 326, 327*
Burla, *river*, Russian Federation, **223** K2
Burlington, Canada, **421** P4
Burlington, Colorado, U.S.A., **423** M2
Burlington, Iowa, U.S.A., **420** H5
Burlington, Vermont, U.S.A., **426** D2
Burlington, Wisconsin, U.S.A., **421** J4
Burlit, Russian Federation, **211** L3
Burma *see* Myanmar, *country*, Asia, **197** L7, *73, 89, 144, 155, 157, 158, 159, 170, 171, 184*
Burnaby, Canada, **412** H7
Burnbrae, New Zealand, **133** D6
Burnet, U.S.A., **424** C4
Burney, Monte, *mountain peak*, Chile, **460** C4
Burney, U.S.A., **422** C1
Burnham, England, U.K., **305** G3
Burnham-on-Crouch, England, U.K., **305** H3
Burnham-on-Sea, England, U.K., **304** D3
Burnie, Australia, **135** K7
Burnley, England, U.K., **306** F4
Burns, Oregon, U.S.A., **418** E5
Burns, Wyoming, U.S.A., **419** M6
Burns Junction, U.S.A., **418** F5
Burns Lake, Canada, **412** G4
Burnt Pine, Norfolk Island, **135** T13
Burnt Ranch, U.S.A., **418** C6
Burntisland, Scotland, U.K., **308** F4
Burqin, China, **212** E3
Burqin, *river*, China, **212** E3
Burra, Australia, **135** H5
Burravoe, Shetland, Scotland, U.K., **308** K7
Burray, *island*, Orkney, Scotland, U.K., **308** G2
Burrel, Albania, **297** B5
Burrendong Dam, Australia, **135** K5
Burrow Head, *point*, Scotland, U.K., **308** E6
Burry Port, Wales, U.K., **304** C3
Bursa, *province*, Turkey, **297** G5
Bursa, Turkey, **297** G5
Burtnieks, *lake*, Latvia, **287** M4
Burton, Lac, *lake*, Canada, **415** Q4
Burton Bradstock, England, U.K., **304** E4
Burton Latimer, England, U.K., **305** G2
Burton upon Trent, England, U.K., **305** F2
Burtonport, Ireland, **309** D3
Burträsk, Sweden, **284** K4
Buru, Pulau, *island*, Indonesia, **198** D3
Burundi, *country*, Africa, **359** J7, *313, 334, 337, 342, 343*
Bururi, Burundi, **369** E3
Burwarton, England, U.K., **304** E2
Burwash, England, U.K., **305** H4
Burwash Landing, Canada, **410** F3
Burwell, England, U.K., **305** H2
Bury, England, U.K., **306** F4
Bury St Edmunds, England, U.K., **305** H2
Buryatiya, Respublika, *republic*, Russian Federation, **210** D2
Burylbaytal, Kazakhstan, **212** B3

Busanga, Democratic Republic of the Congo, **368** D3
Busca, Italy, **294** A3
Busha, Ukraine, **296** G1
Būshehr, Iran, **220** F3
Bushenyi, Uganda, **369** F3
Bushmills, Northern Ireland, U.K., **309** F2
Bushnell, U.S.A., **419** N6
Bushtricë, Albania, **296** C5
Businga, Democratic Republic of the Congo, **368** D2
Busira, *river*, Democratic Republic of the Congo, **368** C3
Bus'k, Ukraine, **289** M4
Buskerud, *county*, Norway, **286** D2
Busko-Zdrój, Poland, **289** K3
Buṣrā ash Shām, Syria, **225** D3
Busselton, Australia, **134** D5
Buşteni, Romania, **296** E3
Busto Arsizio, Italy, **294** B3
Busuanga, Philippines, **204** B3
Busu-Kwanga, Democratic Republic of the Congo, **368** D2
Busuanga Island, Philippines, **204** C3
Buta, Democratic Republic of the Congo, **368** D2
Butajīra, Ethiopia, **367** E3
Butare, Rwanda, **369** E3
Butaritari, *island*, Kiribati, **139** F4
Bute, *island*, Scotland, U.K., **308** D5
Bute, Sound of, Scotland, U.K., **308** D5
Bute Helu, Kenya, **369** G2
Butembo, Democratic Republic of the Congo, **369** E2
Butler, Alabama, U.S.A., **425** H3
Butler, Georgia, U.S.A., **425** K3
Butler, Missouri, U.S.A., **420** F6
Butler, Oklahoma, U.S.A., **424** C2
Butlers Bridge, Ireland, **309** E3
Buton, Pulau, *island*, Indonesia, **198** C4
Butte, U.S.A., **418** H3
Butte aux Sables, Pointe, *point*, Mauritius, **373** C1
Buttermere, England, U.K., **306** E3
Butterworth, Malaysia, **200** C1
Butterworth, South Africa, **371** E5
Buttevant, Ireland, **309** D5
Button Bay, Canada, **414** G2
Buttonwillow, U.S.A., **422** D4
Butuan, Philippines, **204** D4
Butuo, China, **215** G4
Butwal, Nepal, **219** E4
Bützow, Germany, **288** E2
Buulobarde, Somalia, **367** G4
Buur Gaabo, Somalia, **369** H3
Buurhakaba, Somalia, **367** F4
Buwārah, Jabal, *mountain peak*, Saudi Arabia, **225** C5
Buxar, India, **219** F4
Buxton, England, U.K., **307** G4
Buxton, U.S.A., **418** C4
Buxy, France, **291** G3
Buy, Russian Federation, **300** F4
Buyanbat, Mongolia, **213** G3
Buyant, Bayan-Ölgiy, Mongolia, **212** F2
Buyant, Bayanhongor, Mongolia, **213** H3
Buyant, Dzavhan, Mongolia, **213** H3
Buyr Nuur, *lake*, Mongolia, **210** G3
Büyükeceli, Turkey, **225** B1
Büyükkarıştıran, Turkey, **297** F5
Buzançais, France, **290** E3
Buzancy, France, **291** G2
Buzău, Romania, **296** F3
Buzi, Mozambique, **371** F2
Buziaş, Romania, **296** C3
Būzūlūk, Kazakhstan, **222** H2
Buzuluk, Russian Federation, **222** E2
Bwagaoia, Papua New Guinea, **135** L1
Byahoml', Belarus, **299** B5
Byala, Ruse, Bulgaria, **296** E4
Byala, Varna, Bulgaria, **296** F4
Byala Slatina, Bulgaria, **296** D4
Byalynichy, Belarus, **299** B6
Byarezina, *river*, Belarus, **299** B6
Byaroza, Belarus, **289** M2
Byarozawka, Belarus, **289** M2
Bychawa, Poland, **289** L3
Bydgoszcz, Poland, **289** J2
Byelaazyorsk, Belarus, **289** M2
Byerazino, Minskaya Voblasts', Belarus, **299** B6
Byerazino, Vitsyebskaya Voblasts', Belarus, **299** B5
Byers, U.S.A., **423** L2
Byeshankovichy, Belarus, **299** B5
Byesyedz', *river*, Russian Federation, **299** D6
Byfield, England, U.K., **305** F2
Bygdeå, Sweden, **284** K4
Bygdin, *lake*, Norway, **286** D2
Bygland, Norway, **286** C3
Bykhaw, Belarus, **299** C6
Bykle, Norway, **286** C3
Bylas, U.S.A., **423** H5
Bylot Island, Canada, **411** M2
Byng Inlet, Canada, **421** N3
Bynum, U.S.A., **418** H3
Byrka, Russian Federation, **211** G2
Byrranga, Gory, *mountain range*, Russian Federation, **300** K2
Byskeälven, *river*, Sweden, **284** K4
Byssa, *river*, Russian Federation, **211** K1
Bytom, Poland, **289** J3
Bytosh', Russian Federation, **299** E6
Bytów, Poland, **289** H1
Byumba, Rwanda, **369** F3
Bzc Cạn, Vietnam, **203** E1
Bzc Liêu, Vietnam, **203** E4
Bzc Ninh, Vietnam, **203** E1
Bzc Quang, Vietnam, **203** E1

## C

C. A. Rosetti, Romania, **296** G3
Cà, *river*, Vietnam, **203** E2
Cà Mau, Mũl, *cape*, Vietnam, **203** E4
Cà Mau, Vietnam, **203** E4
Caacupé, Paraguay, **459** F2
Caaguazú, Cordillera de, *mountain range*, Paraguay, **459** F2
Caaguazú, Paraguay, **459** F2
Caala, Angola, **368** C5
Caarapó, Brazil, **459** F2
Caazapá, Paraguay, **459** F3
Cabaad, Raas, *point*, Somalia, **367** G3
Cabaiguán, Cuba, **429** F2
Caballeria, Cabo de, *cape*, Islas Baleares, Spain, **293** K2
Caballococha, Peru, **450** D5
Caballos Mesteños, Llano de los, *plain*, Mexico, **430** D2
Caban-coch-Reservoir, Wales, U.K., **304** D2
Cabanaconde, Peru, **454** D4
Cabanatuan, Philippines, **204** C3
Cabano, Canada, **416** G6
Čabar, Croatia, **294** E3
Cabauyan Island, Philippines, **204** B2
Cabeceira Rio Manso, Brazil, **456** B4
Cabeço Rainha, *mountain peak*, Portugal, **292** D3
Cabedelo, Brazil, **453** G5
Cabeza de Manzaneda, *mountain peak*, Spain, **292** D1
Cabeza del Buey, Spain, **292** E3
Cabezas, Bolivia, **455** F5
Cabildo, Argentina, **458** E6
Cabimas, Venezuela, **450** D1
Cabinda, Angola, **368** B4, *335*
Cabinda, *province*, Angola, **368** B4
Cabinet Mountains, *mountain range*, U.S.A., **418** F2
Cable, U.S.A., **420** H2
Cabo Blanco, Argentina, **460** E3
Cabo Bojador, Western Sahara, **360** D3
Cabo Delgado, *province*, Mozambique, **369** G5
Cabo Frio, Brazil, **457** E6
Cabo Raso, Argentina, **460** E2
Cabonga, Réservoir, Canada, **416** C6
Cabool, U.S.A., **420** G7
Caboolture, Australia, **135** L4
Caborca, Mexico, **430** B2
Cabot Strait, Canada, **417** L6
Cabrera, Haiti, **429** H3
Cabrera, *island*, Islas Baleares, Spain, **293** J3
Cabrera, Sierra de la, *mountain range*, Spain, **292** D1
Cabri, Canada, **413** Q6
Cabrobó, Brazil, **453** F5
Cabrobó, *river*, Brazil, **457** F2
Cabruta, Venezuela, **451** E2
Cabugao, Philippines, **204** C2
Caçador, Brazil, **459** G3
Čačak, Serbia, **296** C4
Cacao, French Guiana, **452** C2
Caçapava do Sul, Brazil, **459** G4
Caccia, Capo, *cape*, Sardegna, Italy, **295** A5
Cacequi, Brazil, **459** F3
Cáceres, Brazil, **456** B4
Cáceres, Colombia, **450** C2
Cáceres, Spain, **292** D3
Cache Creek, Canada, **412** J6
Cache Peak, *mountain peak*, U.S.A., **418** H5
Cacheu, Guinea-Bissau, **364** A2, *321*
Cachi, Argentina, **458** C2
Cachi, Nevado de, *mountain peak*, Argentina, **458** C2
Cachimbo, Brazil, **456** B2
Cachimbo, Serra do, *mountain range*, Brazil, **447** G4
Cachimo, Angola, **368** D4
Cachingues, Angola, **368** C5
Cáchira, Colombia, **450** D2
Cachoeira, Brazil, **457** F3
Cachoeira Alta, Brazil, **456** C5
Cachoeira do Arari, Brazil, **452** D3
Cachoeira do Itapemirim, Brazil, **457** F5
Cachoeira do Sul, Brazil, **459** G4
Cachuela Esperanza, Bolivia, **455** F3
Čačinci, Croatia, **294** F3
Cacine, Guinea-Bissau, **364** A2
Caçipore, *river*, Brazil, **452** C2
Cacolo, Angola, **368** C5
Cacongo, Angola, **368** B4
Caçu, Brazil, **456** C5
Cacuaco, Angola, **368** B4
Caculé, Brazil, **457** E4
Caddo, U.S.A., **424** D2
Cadereyta, Mexico, **431** F3
Cadillac, Canada, **413** R7
Cadillac, France, **290** D4
Cadillac, U.S.A., **421** L3
Cádiz, Golfo de, *gulf*, Portugal, **292** D4
Cadiz, Philippines, **204** C4
Cádiz, Spain, **292** D4, *253*
Cadiz, U.S.A., **422** F4
Cadomin, Canada, **413** L5
Caen, France, **290** D2
Caerleon, Wales, U.K., **304** E3
Caernarfon, Wales, U.K., **304** C1
Caernarfon Bay, Wales, U.K., **304** C1
Caerphilly, *unitary authority*, Wales, U.K., **304** D3
Caerphilly, Wales, U.K., **304** D3
Caetité, Brazil, **457** E4
Cafayate, Argentina, **458** C3
Cafuini, *river*, Brazil, **452** B3
Cagayan, *river*, Philippines, **204** C2, *149*
Cagayan de Oro, Philippines, **204** D4
Cagli, Italy, **294** D4
Cagliari, Golfo di, *gulf*, Italy, **295** B6
Cagliari, Sardegna, Italy, **295** B6
Caguán, *river*, Colombia, **450** C4
Caguas, Puerto Rico, **427** C2
Caha Mountains, Ireland, **309** C6
Cahama, Angola, **368** B6
Caher, Ireland, **309** E5
Caherdaniel, Ireland, **309** B6
Cahersiveen, Ireland, **309** B6
Cahora Bassa, Lago de, *lake*, Mozambique, **369** F6
Cahore Point, Ireland, **309** F5
Cahors, France, **290** E4
Cahuapanas, Peru, **454** C1
Cahul, Moldova, **296** G3
Cái Nuớc, Vietnam, **203** E4
Caia, Mozambique, **371** G2
Caiabis, Serra dos, *mountain range*, Brazil, **456** B3
Caianda, Angola, **368** D5
Caiapó, Serra do, *mountain range*, Brazil, **456** C4
Caiapônia, Brazil, **456** C4
Caibarién, Cuba, **429** F2
Caicara de Orinoco, Venezuela, **451** E2
Caicó, Brazil, **453** G5
Caicos Islands, Turks and Caicos Islands, **429** G2, *378*
Caijiapo, China, **215** H2
Cailan, *river*, China, **212** E4
Cailloma, Peru, **454** D4
Caima, Brazil, **452** C4
Caineville, U.S.A., **423** H2
Cainnyi, China, **215** G2
Caird Coast, *region*, Antarctica, **470** C4
Cairndow, Scotland, U.K., **308** E4
Cairngorm Mountains, Scotland, U.K., **308** F3
Cairnryan, Scotland, U.K., **308** D6
Cairns, Australia, **135** K2
Cairo, U.S.A., **425** K4
Cairo *see* Al Qāhirah, Egypt, **225** A4, *85, 97, 316, 317*
Cairo Montenotte, Italy, **294** B3
Caister-on-Sea, England, U.K., **305** J2
Caistor, England, U.K., **307** H4
Caitou, Angola, **368** B5
Caiundo, Angola, **368** C6
Cajacay, Peru, **454** C3
Cajamarca, Peru, **454** B2
Cajarc, France, **290** E4
Cajatambo, Peru, **454** C3
Cajàzeiras, Brazil, **453** F5
Čajetina, Serbia, **296** B4
Čajniče, Bosnia and Herzegovina, **296** B4
Caka, China, **213** H5
Caka Yanhu, *lake*, China, **213** H5
Čakovec, Croatia, **294** F2
Çal, Turkey, **297** G6
Cal Madow, Buuraha, *mountain range*, Somalia, **367** G2
Calabar, Nigeria, **368** A2
Calabogie, Canada, **416** C7
Calabozo, Venezuela, **451** E2
Calabria, *autonomous region*, Italy, **295** F6, *255*
Calacoto, Bolivia, **455** E4
Calafat, Romania, **296** D4
Calagua Islands, Philippines, **204** C3
Calahorra, Spain, **293** G1
Calai, Angola, **370** C2
Calais, France, **290** E1
Calalaste, Sierra de, *mountain range*, Argentina, **458** C3
Calama, Brazil, **455** F2
Calama, Chile, **458** C2
Calamar, N. Colombia, **450** C1
Calamar, S. Colombia, **450** D4
Calamba, Philippines, **204** C3
Calamocha, Spain, **293** G2
Calamus, *river*, U.S.A., **420** D4
Călan, Romania, **296** D3
Calanda, Spain, **293** G2
Calandula, Angola, **368** C4
Calang, Indonesia, **200** A1
Calapan, Philippines, **204** C3
Călăraşi, Moldova, **296** G2
Călăraşi, Romania, **296** F3
Calasparra, Spain, **293** G3
Calatagan, Philippines, **204** C3
Calatayud, Spain, **293** G2
Calau, Germany, **289** F3
Calauag, Philippines, **204** C3
Calavite, *cape*, Philippines, **204** B3
Calbayog, Philippines, **204** D3
Calbuco, Chile, **460** C1
Calca, Peru, **454** D3
Calcanhar, Ponta do, *point*, Brazil, **453** G4
Calçoene, Brazil, **452** C2
Calçoene, *river*, Brazil, **452** C2
Calcutta, India, **219** G5, *169*
Caldas da Rainha, Portugal, **292** C3
Caldas Novas, Brazil, **456** D4
Caldera, Chile, **458** B3
Caldew, *river*, England, U.K., **306** E3
Caldey Island, Wales, U.K., **304** C3
Caldicot, Wales, U.K., **304** E3
Caldwell, Idaho, U.S.A., **418** F5
Caldwell, Kansas, U.S.A., **420** E7
Caldwell, Texas, U.S.A., **424** D4
Caledon, *river*, South Africa, **371** E5, *349*
Caledonia, Canada, **416** J7
Caledonia, U.S.A., **420** H4
Caledonia Hills, Canada, **416** J7
Calella, Spain, **293** J2
Caleta Buena, Chile, **455** D5
Caleta Olivia, Argentina, **460** D3
Calexico, U.S.A., **422** F5
Calf, The, *mountain peak*, England, U.K., **306** F3
Calf of Man, *island*, Isle of Man, **306** D3, *279*
Calgary, Canada, **413** M6
Calhan, U.S.A., **423** L2
Calheta, Madeira, Portugal, **373** C3
Calhoun, U.S.A., **425** K2
Cali, Colombia, **450** C3
Calicut *see* Kozhikode, India, **216** C4, *168*
Caliente, California, U.S.A., **422** D4
Caliente, Nevada, U.S.A., **422** F3
California, Golfo de, *gulf*, Mexico, **430** B2
California, *state*, U.S.A., **422** D4, *23, 42, 47, 50, 51, 95, 124, 376, 377, 382, 383, 384, 385, 386, 405, 442*
California, Trinidad, Trinidad and Tobago, **461** C4
Călimăneşti, Romania, **296** E3
Călimani, Munţii, *mountain range*, Romania, **296** E2
Calintaan, Philippines, **204** C3
Calipatria, U.S.A., **422** F5
Caliper Lake, Canada, **414** H7
Calitzdorp, South Africa, **370** D5
Calkini, Mexico, **431** H4
Callac, France, **290** C2
Callahan, U.S.A., **418** C6
Callan, Ireland, **309** E5
Callander, Scotland, U.K., **308** E4
Callao, Peru, **454** C3
Callaway, U.S.A., **420** F2
Calling Lake, Canada, **413** N4
Callington, England, U.K., **304** C4
Calmar, U.S.A., **420** H4
Calne, England, U.K., **304** E3
Calotmul, Mexico, **431** H4
Caloundra, Australia, **135** L4
Caltagirone, Sicilia, Italy, **295** E7
Caltama, Cerro, *mountain peak*, Bolivia, **455** E5
Caltanissetta, Sicilia, Italy, **295** D7
Calucinga, Angola, **368** C5
Călugăreni, Romania, **296** F3
Calulo, Angola, **368** B5
Calunda, Angola, **368** D5
Calunga, Angola, **368** C6
Caluquembe, Angola, **368** B5
Caluula, Raas, *point*, Somalia, **367** H2
Caluula, Somalia, **367** H2
Calvados Chain, The, *islands*, Papua New Guinea, **135** L1

Calvert, *river*, Australia, **135** H2
Calvert Island, Canada, **412** E6
Calvi, Corse, France, **294** B4
Calvillo, Mexico, **430** E4
Calvinia, South Africa, **370** C5
Calw, Germany, **288** D4
Calzada de Calatrava, Spain, **293** F3
Cam, *river*, England, U.K., **305** H2
Cam Lâm (Cam Ranh), Vietnam, **203** F4
Câ'm Phả, Vietnam, **203** E1
Cam Ranh *see* Cam Lâm, Vietnam, **203** F4
Camabatela, Angola, **368** C4
Camaçari, Brazil, **457** F3
Camacho, Mexico, **430** E3
Camacupa, Angola, **368** C5
Camaguán, Venezuela, **451** E2
Camagüey, Cuba, **429** F2
Camah, Gunung, *mountain peak*, Malaysia, **200** C1
Camamu, Brazil, **457** F3
Camaná, Peru, **454** D4
Camanongue, Angola, **368** D5
Camapuã, Brazil, **456** C5
Camaquã, Brazil, **459** G4
Camaquã, *river*, Brazil, **459** G4
Câmara de Lobos, Madeira, Portugal, **373** C3
Camarat, Cap, *cape*, France, **291** H5
Camarès, France, **290** F5
Camaret-sur-Mer, France, **290** B2
Camarones, Argentina, **460** E2
Camarones, Bahía, *bay*, Argentina, **460** E2
Camarones, *river*, Chile, **455** D5
Camas Valley, U.S.A., **418** C5
Cambará, Brazil, **456** B4
Cambellton, Canada, **416** H6
Camberley, England, U.K., **305** G3
Cambo-les-Bains, France, **290** D5
Cambodia, *country*, Asia, **197** M8, *73, 96, 97, 144, 152, 153, 154, 155, 158*
Camborne, England, U.K., **304** B4
Cambrai, France, **291** F1
Cambria, U.S.A., **422** C4
Cambrian Mountains, *mountain range*, Wales, U.K., **304** C3, *276*
Cambridge, England, U.K., **305** H2, *276*
Cambridge, Idaho, U.S.A., **418** F4
Cambridge, Maryland, U.S.A., **426** B5
Cambridge, Massachusetts, U.S.A., **426** E3
Cambridge, Nebraska, U.S.A., **420** C5
Cambridge, New Zealand, **132** E3
Cambridge, Ohio, U.S.A., **421** N5
Cambridge Bay, Canada, **410** J3
Cambridgeshire, *unitary authority*, England, U.K., **305** G2
Cambulo, Angola, **368** D4
Cambundi-Catembo, Angola, **368** C5
Camden, Alabama, U.S.A., **425** J3
Camden, Arkansas, U.S.A., **424** F3
Camden, Australia, **135** L5
Camden, New Jersey, U.S.A., **426** C5
Camden, South Carolina, U.S.A., **425** M2
Camdenton, U.S.A., **420** G6
Cameia, Angola, **368** D5
Camelford, England, U.K., **304** C4
Çameli, Turkey, **297** G7
Camenca, Moldova, **296** G1
Camerino, Italy, **294** D4
Cameron, Arizona, U.S.A., **423** H4
Camerón, Chile, **460** D4
Cameron, Louisiana, U.S.A., **424** F5
Cameron, Missouri, U.S.A., **420** F6
Cameron, Texas, U.S.A., **424** D4
Cameron Hills, Canada, **413** K1
Cameron Mountains, *mountain range*, New Zealand, **133** A8
Cameroon, *country*, Africa, **358** F6, *312, 329, 330, 331, 333*
Cameroon Mountain, Cameroon, **368** A2, *329*
Cametá, Brazil, **452** D4
Camiguin Island, Philippines, **204** D4
Camilla, U.S.A., **425** K4
Camiña, Chile, **455** E5
Camiranga, Brazil, **452** D3
Camiri, Bolivia, **455** F5
Camissombo, Angola, **368** D4
Cammarata, Monte, *mountain peak*, Italy, **295** D7
Camocim, Brazil, **453** F4
Camooweal, Australia, **135** H2
Camopi, French Guiana, **452** C2
Camopi, *river*, French Guiana, **452** C2
Camorta Island, Andaman and Nicobar Islands, India, **217** H4
Camotes Islands, Philippines, **204** C4
Camp Verde, U.S.A., **423** H4
Campagne-lès-Hesdin, France, **305** J4
Campana, Argentina, **459** E5
Campana, Isla, *island*, Chile, **460** B3
Campanario, *mountain peak*, Argentina/Chile, **458** B5
Campania, *autonomous region*, Italy, **295** E5, *255*
Campbell, Cape, New Zealand, **133** E5
Campbell Island, New Zealand, **132** K11
Campbell Plateau, *underwater feature*, Pacific Ocean, **478** F8
Campbell River, Canada, **412** G6
Campbellsville, U.S.A., **421** L7
Campbeltown, Scotland, U.K., **308** D5
Campeche, Bahía de, *bay*, Mexico, **431** G5
Campeche, Mexico, **431** H5
Campeche, *state*, Mexico, **431** H5, *400*
Câmpeni, Romania, **296** D2
Câmpia Turzii, Romania, **296** D2
Campidano, *valley*, Sardegna, Italy, **295** B6
Campillo de Llerena, Spain, **292** D3
Campillos, Spain, **292** E4
Câmpina, Romania, **296** E3
Campina Grande, Brazil, **453** G5
Campina Verde, Brazil, **456** D5
Campinas, Brazil, **459** H2
Campo, Cameroon, **368** A2
Campo Belo, Brazil, **457** E5
Campo Belo do Sul, Brazil, **459** G3
Campo de Diauarem, Brazil, **456** C3
Campo Esperanza, Paraguay, **459** E2
Campo Florido, Brazil, **456** D5
Campo Formoso, Brazil, **457** F3
Campo Gallo, Argentina, **458** D3
Campo Grande, Amazonas, Brazil, **455** G2
Campo Grande, Mato Grosso do Sul, Brazil, **456** B5
Campo Maior, Brazil, **453** E4
Campo Mara, Venezuela, **450** D1
Campo Mourão, Brazil, **459** G2
Campo Novo, Brazil, **459** G3
Campoalegre, Colombia, **450** C3
Campobasso, Italy, **295** E5
Campobello di Licata, Sicilia, Italy, **295** D7
Campos, Brazil, **457** F5
Campos Altos, Brazil, **456** D5
Campos Belos, Brazil, **456** D3
Campos Novos, Brazil, **459** G3
Campos Sales, Brazil, **453** F5
Camprodon, Spain, **293** J1
Câmpulung, Romania, **296** E3
Câmpulung Moldovenesc, Romania, **296** E2
Camrose, Canada, **413** N5
Camrose, Wales, U.K., **304** C3
Camucuio, Angola, **368** B5
Çan, Turkey, **297** F5
Câ'n Tho', Vietnam, **203** E4
Canaan, Tobago, Trinidad and Tobago, **461** B4
Canada, *country*, North America, **408** N3, *31, 44, 81, 94, 100, 162, 275, 376, 377, 380, 381, 382, 383, 384, 391, 464, 465, 469*
Canadian, *river*, U.S.A., **423** L4
Canadian, U.S.A., **424** B2
Canadian Shield, *physical feature*, Canada, **406** M2, *380, 381, 383*
Çanakkale, *province*, Turkey, **297** F6
Çanakkale, Turkey, **297** F5
Canakkale Bogazi, *strait*, Turkey, **297** F5
Canal Flats, Canada, **413** M6
Canala, New Caledonia, **141** A3
Canalejas, Argentina, **458** C5
Canamari, Brazil, **455** E3
Cananea, Mexico, **430** C2
Cananéia, Brazil, **459** H2
Canapiare, Cerro, *mountain peak*, Colombia, **451** E3
Cañar, Ecuador, **450** B5
Canarias, Islas (Canary Islands), Spain, Atlantic Ocean, **373** A4, *253, 355*
Canarreos, Archipélago de los, *islands*, Cuba, **429** E2
Canary Islands, *see* Canarias Islas, *islands*, Spain, Atlantic Ocean, **373** A4, *253, 355*
Canastra, Serra da, *mountain range*, Brazil, **456** D5
Canatlán, Mexico, **430** D3
Canaveral, Cape, U.S.A., **425** M5
Cañaveras, Spain, **293** F2
Canavieiras, Brazil, **457** F4
Canberra, Australia, **135** K6, *111, 112, 121, 124*
Canby, California, U.S.A., **418** D6
Canby, Minnesota, U.S.A., **420** E3
Canche, *river*, France, **305** K4
Canchyuaya, Cerros de, *mountain range*, Peru, **454** C2
Cancún, Mexico, **431** J4
Candarave, Peru, **454** D4
Candé, France, **290** D3
Candelaria, Argentina, **459** F3
Candelaria, Mexico, **431** H5
Candelaro, *river*, Italy, **295** E5
Cândido Mendes, Brazil, **452** E3
Candle Lake, Canada, **413** S5
Candon, Philippines, **204** C2
Canelones, Uruguay, **459** F5
Cañete, Chile, **458** B5
Cangallo, Peru, **454** C3
Cangamba, Angola, **368** C5
Cangandala, Angola, **368** C4
Cangombe, Angola, **368** D5
Cangshan, China, **211** H2
Canguaretama, Brazil, **453** G5
Canguçu, Brazil, **459** G4
Canguçu, Serra do, *mountain range*, Brazil, **459** G4
Cangumbe, Angola, **368** C5
Cangwu, China, **206** B4
Cangxi, China, **215** H3
Cangyuan, China, **215** F5
Cangzhou, China, **210** G5
Caniapiscau, Lac, *lake*, Canada, **416** G2
Caniapiscau, *river*, Canada, **411** N4
Canicatti, Sicilia, Italy, **295** D7
Canigou, Pic du, *mountain peak*, France, **290** F5
Canindé, Ceará, Brazil, **453** F4
Canindé, Pará, Brazil, **452** D4
Canindé, *river*, Brazil, **453** E5
Canisp, *mountain peak*, Scotland, U.K., **308** D2
Cañitas de Felipe Pescador, Mexico, **430** E4
Cañizal, Spain, **292** E2
Canmore, Canada, **413** M6
Canna, *island*, Scotland, U.K., **308** C3
Cannanore, India, **216** C4
Cannanore Islands, India, **216** C4
Cannes, France, **291** H5
Cannington, England, U.K., **304** D3
Cannock, England, U.K., **304** E2
Cannon Beach, U.S.A., **418** C4
Cannoniers Point, Mauritius, **373** C1
Caño Macareo, *river*, Venezuela, **451** G2
Caño Manamo, *river*, Venezuela, **451** F2
Canoas, Brazil, **459** G3
Canoas, Peru, **450** B5
Canoas, *river*, Brazil, **459** G3
Canoe Lake, Canada, **413** Q4
Canoinhas, Brazil, **459** G3
Canon City, U.S.A., **423** L2
Canora, Canada, **414** C6
Canosa di Puglia, Italy, **295** F5
Canso, Canada, **417** L7
Canta, Peru, **454** C3
Cantabria, *autonomous community*, Spain, **293** F1, *253*
Cantábrica, Cordillera, *mountain range*, Spain, **292** D1
Cantagalo, Brazil, **451** G5
Cantalejo, Spain, **293** F2
Cantaura, Venezuela, **451** F2
Canterbury, England, U.K., **305** J3
Canterbury Bight, *bay*, New Zealand, **133** D6
Canterbury Plains, New Zealand, **133** C6
Cantiano, Italy, **294** D4
Cantilan, Philippines, **204** D4
Canto do Buriti, Brazil, **453** E5
Canton, Georgia, U.S.A., **425** K2
Canton, Illinois, U.S.A., **420** H5
Canton, Mississippi, U.S.A., **424** G3
Canton, New York, U.S.A., **426** C2
Canton, Ohio, U.S.A., **421** N5
Canton, Pennsylvania, U.S.A., **426** B4
Canton *see* Guangzhou, China, **207** A2, *75*
Canton, South Dakota, U.S.A., **420** E4
Cantu, *river*, Brazil, **459** G2
Cantwell, U.S.A., **410** E3
Canudos, Brazil, **452** A5
Cañuelas, Argentina, **459** E5
Canumã, N. Amazonas, Brazil, **452** A4
Canumã, S. Amazonas, Brazil, **455** G2
Canutama, Brazil, **455** F2
Canvey Island, England, U.K., **305** H3
Canwood, Canada, **413** R5
Cany-Barville, France, **290** E2
Canyon, U.S.A., **424** B2
Canyon Ferry Lake, U.S.A., **419** J3
Canyonville, U.S.A., **418** C5
Canzar, Angola, **368** D4
Cao Xian, China, **206** C1
Caojian, China, **215** F4
Caombo, Angola, **368** C4
Cap Aracena, Isla, *island*, Chile, **460** C5
Cap aux Meules, Canada, **417** L6
Cap-de-la-Madeleine, Canada, **416** E6
Cap-des-Rosiers, Canada, **417** J5
Cap-Haïtien, Haiti, **429** G3
Cap Sigli, Algeria, **361** G1
Capaccio, Italy, **295** E5
Capaia, Angola, **368** D4
Capanaparo, *river*, Venezuela, **451** E2
Capanema, Pará, Brazil, **452** D3
Capanema, Parana, Brazil, **459** G2
Capão Bonito, Brazil, **459** H2
Caparaó, Serra do, *mountain range*, Brazil, **457** F5
Caparo, *river*, Venezuela, **451** D2
Capas, Philippines, **204** C3
Cape Barren Island, Australia, **135** K7
Cape Basin, *underwater feature*, Atlantic Ocean, **477** H8
Cape Breton Island, Canada, **417** M7
Cape Charles, U.S.A., **426** C6
Cape Coast, Ghana, **364** D3
Cape Cod Bay, U.S.A., **426** E3
Cape Comorin, India, **216** D4, *167*
Cape Dorset, Canada, **411** M3
Cape Girardeau, U.S.A., **421** J7
Cape May Point, U.S.A., **426** C5
Cape North, Canada, **417** K6
Cape Race, Canada, **417** Q6
Cape St George, Canada, **417** M5
Cape Tormentine, Canada, **417** K6
Cape Town, South Africa, **370** C5, *93, 94, 97, 350, 351*
Cape Verde, *country*, Atlantic Ocean, **360** P8, *318, 319, 332*
Cap Verde Basin, *underwater feature*, Atlantic Ocean, **477** F4
Cape York Peninsula, Australia, **135** J1, *112*
Capel Curig, Wales, U.K., **304** D1
Capel St Mary, England, U.K., **305** J2
Capelinha, Brazil, **457** E4
Capenda-Camulemba, Angola, **368** C4
Capibara, Venezuela, **451** E3
Capilla del Monte, Argentina, **458** D4
Capim, *river*, Brazil, **452** D4
Capinota, Bolivia, **455** E4
Capitan, U.S.A., **423** L5
Capitán Bado, Paraguay, **459** F2
Capitan Peak, *mountain peak*, U.S.A., **423** L5
Capitol, U.S.A., **419** M4
Capivari, *river*, Brazil, **457** F3
Čapljina, Bosnia and Herzegovina, **294** F4
Capolo, Angola, **368** B5
Capotoan, Mount, *mountain peak*, Philippines, **204** D3
Cappoquin, Ireland, **309** E5
Capraia, Isola di, *island*, Italy, **294** B4
Capri, Isola di, *island*, Italy, **295** D5
Caprivi, *administrative region*, Namibia, **370** D2
Caprock, U.S.A., **423** M5
Captain Cook, Hawaiian Islands, U.S.A., **422** R10
Capua, Italy, **295** E5
Capucin Point, Seychelles, **373** A2
Caquetá, *river*, Colombia, **450** D4
Car Nicobar Island, Andaman and Nicobar Islands, India, **217** G4
Car, Slieve, *mountain peak*, Ireland, **309** C3
Carabaya, Cordillera de, *mountain range*, Peru, **454** D3
Caracal, Romania, **296** E3
Caracaraí, Brazil, **451** G4
Caracas, Venezuela, **451** E1, *426, 437*
Caracol, Brazil, **457** E2
Caracollo, Bolivia, **455** E4
Caraga, Philippines, **204** D5
Caragh, Lough, *lake*, Ireland, **309** B5
Caraguatatuba, Brazil, **459** J2
Carahue, Chile, **458** B6
Caraí, Brazil, **457** F4
Caraíva, Brazil, **457** F4
Carajás, Serra dos, *mountain range*, Brazil, **452** C5
Caramat, Canada, **415** L7

Caranapatuba, Brazil, **455** F2
Carandaí, Brazil, **457** E5
Carandayti, Bolivia, **455** F5
Carangola, Brazil, **457** E5
Caransebeş, Romania, **296** D3
Carapuse Bay, Tobago, Trinidad and Tobago, **461** B4
Caraquet, Canada, **416** J6
Caráquez, Bahía de, *bay*, Ecuador, **450** B4
Caraşova, Romania, **296** C3
Caratinga, Brazil, **457** E5
Carauari, Brazil, **451** E5
Caravaca de la Cruz, Spain, **293** G3
Caravelas, Brazil, **457** F4
Caraz, Peru, **454** C2
Carazinho, Brazil, **459** G3
Carballo, Spain, **292** C1
Carbó, Mexico, **430** C2
Carbonara, Capo, *cape*, Italy, **295** B6
Carbondale, Colorado, U.S.A., **423** K2
Carbondale, Illinois, U.S.A., **421** J7
Carbondale, Pennsylvania, U.S.A., **426** C4
Carbonear, Canada, **417** Q6
Carboneras, Spain, **293** G4
Carboneras de Cuadazaón, Spain, **293** G3
Carbonia, Sardegna, Italy, **295** B6
Carbonita, Brazil, **457** E4
Carbonne, France, **290** E5
Carcajou, Canada, **413** L3
Carcassonne, France, **290** F5
Carcastillo, Spain, **293** G1
Carcross, Canada, **410** F3
Cardamom Hills, India, **216** D4, *153*
Cardel, Mexico, **431** F5
Cardeña, Spain, **292** E3
Cárdenas, Cuba, **429** E2
Cárdenas, San Luis Potosí, Mexico, **431** F4
Cárdenas, Tabasco, Mexico, **431** G5
Cardiel, Lago, *lake*, Argentina, **460** C3
Cardiff, *unitary authority*, Wales, U.K., **304** D3
Cardiff, Wales, U.K., **304** D3, *276*
Cardigan, Wales, U.K., **304** C2
Cardigan Bay, Wales, U.K., **304** C2
Cardona, Uruguay, **459** F4
Cardoso, Ilha do, *island*, Brazil, **459** H2
Cardrona, Mount, *mountain peak*, New Zealand, **133** B7
Cardston, Canada, **413** N7
Cardwell, Australia, **135** K2
Cardwell, U.S.A., **419** J4
Carei, Romania, **296** D2
Careiro, Brazil, **451** G5
Careme, Gunung, *mountain peak*, Indonesia, **201** E4
Carentan, France, **290** D2
Carey, Lake, Australia, **134** E4
Carey, U.S.A., **418** H5
Cargèse, Corse, France, **295** B4
Carhaix Plouguer, France, **290** C2
Carhué, Argentina, **458** D5
Cariacica, Brazil, **457** F5
Cariamanga, Ecuador, **450** B5
Cariango, Angola, **368** C5
Cariati, Italy, **295** F6
Caribou, *river*, Canada, **414** F2
Caribou, U.S.A., **426** F1
Caribou Lake, Canada, **415** K6
Caribou Mountains, *mountain range*, Canada, **413** L2
Carichic, Mexico, **430** D3
Carigara, Philippines, **204** D4
Cariñena, Spain, **293** G2
Carinhanha, Brazil, **457** E4
Caripe, Venezuela, **451** F1
Caripito, Venezuela, **451** F1
Cariré, Brazil, **453** F4
Caritianas, Brazil, **455** F2
Carleton Place, Canada, **416** C7
Carletonville, South Africa, **371** E4
Cârlibaba, Romania, **296** E2
Carlin, U.S.A., **422** E1
Carlingford, Ireland, **309** F3
Carlingford Lough, *inlet*, Northern Ireland, U.K., **309** F3
Carlinville, U.S.A., **420** J6
Carlisle, England, U.K., **306** F3
Carlisle, U.S.A., **426** B4
Carlos Casares, Argentina, **458** E5
Carlos Chagas, Brazil, **457** F4
Carlow, *county*, Ireland, **309** F5
Carlow, Ireland, **309** F5
Carloway, Scotland, U.K., **308** C2
Carlsbad, California, U.S.A., **422** E5
Carlsbad, New Mexico, U.S.A., **423** L5
Carlsberg Ridge, *underwater feature*, Indian Ocean, **476** C4
Carlton, U.S.A., **418** D2
Carluke, Scotland, U.K., **308** F5
Carlyle, Canada, **414** C7
Carlyle Lake, U.S.A., **421** J6
Carmacks, Canada, **410** F3
Carmagnola, Italy, **294** A3
Carman, Canada, **414** E7
Carmarthen, Wales, U.K., **304** C3
Carmarthen Bay, Wales, U.K., **304** C3
Carmarthenshire, *unitary authority*, Wales, U.K., **304** C3
Carmaux, France, **290** F4
Carmel Head, *point*, Wales, U.K., **306** D4
Carmelita, Guatemala, **428** C3
Carmelo, Uruguay, **459** E4
Carmen, Isla, *island*, Mexico, **430** C3
Carmen Alto, Chile, **458** C2
Carmen De Patagones, Argentina, **460** E1
Carmensa, Argentina, **458** C5
Carmona, Spain, **292** E4
Carmyllie, Scotland, U.K., **308** G4
Carn Eige, *mountain peak*, Scotland, U.K., **308** D3
Carnarvon, Australia, **134** C3
Carnarvon, South Africa, **370** D5
Carndonagh, Ireland, **309** E2
Carnduff, Canada, **414** D7
Carnegie, Lake, Australia, **134** E4
Carnegie Ridge, *underwater feature*, Pacific Ocean, **479** N4
Carnew, Ireland, **309** F5
Carney Island, Antarctica, **470** B7
Carnforth, England, U.K., **306** F3
Carnley Harbour, Auckland Islands, New Zealand, **132** J10
Carnlough, Northern Ireland, U.K., **309** G3
Carnot, Central African Republic, **368** C2
Carnoustie, Scotland, U.K., **308** G4
Carnsore Point, Ireland, **309** F5
Carnwath, Scotland, U.K., **308** F5
Caro, U.S.A., **421** M4
Carol City, U.S.A., **425** M7
Carolina, Brazil, **452** D5
Carolina, Puerto Rico, **427** C2
Caroline Cove, *bay*, Macquarie Island, **134** R11
Caroline Islands, *islands*, Micronesia, **138** C4, *61, 117, 118, 125*
Caroni, *river*, Trinidad, Trinidad and Tobago, **461** C4, *399*
Caroni, *river*, Venezuela, **451** F2
Carora, Venezuela, **451** D1
Carp, U.S.A., **422** F3
Carpathian Mountains, *mountain range*, Europe, **280** G6, *74, 228, 239, 249, 262, 263, 264, 266, 267, 268, 269, 271*
Carpaţii Meridionali, *mountain range*, Romania, **280** G6
Carpentaria, Gulf of, Australia, **135** H1
Carpentras, France, **291** G4
Carpina, Brazil, **453** G5
Carr, U.S.A., **423** L1
Carra, Lough, *lake*, Ireland, **309** C4
Carrabelle, U.S.A., **425** K5
Carradale, Scotland, U.K., **308** D5
Carraipía, Colombia, **450** D1
Carrara, Italy, **294** C3
Carrauntoohil, *mountain peak*, Ireland, **309** C6, *277*
Carrbridge, Scotland, U.K., **308** F3
Carrickfergus, *district*, Northern Ireland, U.K., **309** G3
Carrickfergus, Northern Ireland, U.K., **309** G3
Carrickmacross, Ireland, **309** F4
Carrick-on-Shannon, Ireland, **309** D4
Carrick-on-Suir, Ireland, **309** E5
Carrigallen, Ireland, **309** E4
Carrigan Head, *point*, Ireland, **309** C3
Carrigtohill, Ireland, **309** D6
Carrillo, Mexico, **430** E3
Carrington, U.S.A., **420** D2
Carrizal, Colombia, **450** D1
Carrizal Bajo, Chile, **458** B3
Carrizo Springs, U.S.A., **424** C5
Carrizozo, U.S.A., **423** L5
Carroll, U.S.A., **420** F4
Carrollton, Georgia, U.S.A., **425** K3
Carrollton, Illinois, U.S.A., **420** H6
Carrollton, Missouri, U.S.A., **420** G6
Carrot, *river*, Canada, **414** B5
Carrowkeel, Ireland, **309** E2
Carrowmore Lake, Ireland, **309** C3
Carson, U.S.A., **420** C2
Carson City, U.S.A., **422** D2, *386*
Carstairs, Scotland, U.K., **308** F5
Cartagena, Colombia, **450** C1, *436*
Cartagena, Spain, **293** G4
Cartago, Colombia, **450** C3
Cartago, Costa Rica, **428** E5
Carter, U.S.A., **419** J3
Carterton, England, U.K., **305** F3
Carthage, Mississippi, U.S.A., **425** H3
Carthage, New York, U.S.A., **426** C2
Carthage, Texas, U.S.A., **424** E3
Carthage, Tunisia, **362** B1
Cartier, Canada, **421** N2
Cartier Islet, *island*, Ashmore and Cartier Islands, **134** P9
Cartmel, England, U.K., **306** F3
Cartwright, Canada, **417** N3
Caruaru, Brazil, **453** G5
Carúpano, Venezuela, **451** F1
Caruray, Philippines, **204** B4
Carutapera, Brazil, **452** E3
Carvalho, Brazil, **452** C4
Carvers, U.S.A., **422** E2
Carvoeiro, Brazil, **451** G4
Carvoeiro, Cabo, *cape*, Portugal, **292** C3
Casa Branca, Brazil, **456** D5
Casa Grande, U.S.A., **423** H5
Casa Piedra, U.S.A., **423** L7
Casabaja, Providencia, Colombia, **461** C1
Casablanca, Morocco, **360** E2
Casamance, *river*, Senegal, **364** A2, *320*
Casamassima, Italy, **295** F5
Casamozza, Corse, France, **294** B4
Casanare, *river*, Colombia, **451** D2
Casas Adobes, U.S.A., **423** H5
Casas del Puerto, Spain, **293** G3
Casas Grandes, Mexico, **430** D2
Casas Grandes, *river*, Mexico, **430** D2
Casas Ibáñez, Spain, **293** G3
Casca, Brazil, **459** G3
Cascade, Seychelles, **373** A2
Cascade, U.S.A., **420** H4
Cascade Bay, Norfolk Island, **135** T13
Cascade Point, New Zealand, **133** A6
Cascade Range, *mountain range*, U.S.A., **418** C6, *383, 384*
Cascais, Portugal, **292** C3
Cascavel, Ceará, Brazil, **453** F4
Cascavel, Parana, Brazil, **459** G2
Caserta, Italy, **295** E5
Casey, *Australian research station*, Antarctica, **470** G7
Casey, Canada, **416** D6
Caseyr, Raas, *point*, Somalia, **367** H2
Cashel, Ireland, **309** E5
Cashel, Zimbabwe, **371** F2
Casigua, N. Venezuela, **450** D2
Casigua, W. Venezuela, **451** D1
Casilda, Argentina, **458** E4
Casino, Australia, **135** L4
Casinos, Spain, **293** G3
Casiquiare, *river*, Venezuela, **451** E3
Casma, Peru, **454** B2
Caspe, Spain, **293** G2
Casper, U.S.A., **419** L5, *87*
Caspian Depression *see* Prikaspiyskaya Nizmennost', *lowland*, Kazakhstan/Russian Federation, **222** D3
Caspian Sea, Asia/Europe, **222** E4, *144, 146, 183, 187, 189, 190, 228, 271*
Cass City, U.S.A., **421** M4
Cass Lake, U.S.A., **420** F2
Cassacatiza, Mozambique, **369** F5
Cassai, Angola, **368** D5
Cassamba, Angola, **368** D5
Cassel, France, **305** K4
Cassiar, Canada, **412** E2
Cassiar Mountains, *mountain range*, Canada, **412** D2
Cassinga, Angola, **368** C6
Cassino, Italy, **295** D5
Cassley, *river*, Scotland, U.K., **308** E2
Cassoday, U.S.A., **420** E6
Cassongue, Angola, **368** B5
Castanhal, Brazil, **452** D3
Castanho, Brazil, **455** G2
Castaño, *river*, Argentina, **458** C4
Castaño Viejo, Argentina, **458** C4
Castara, Tobago, Trinidad and Tobago, **461** B4
Castelbuono, Sicilia, Italy, **295** E7
Casteljaloux, France, **290** E4
Castellane, France, **291** H5
Castelli, Buenos Aires, Argentina, **459** F5
Castelli, Chaco, Argentina, **458** E2
Castellnou de Bassella, Spain, **293** H1
Castelló de la Plana, Spain, **293** G2
Castelnau-Magnoac, France, **290** E5
Castelnaudary, France, **290** E5
Castelnovo ne'Monti, Italy, **294** C3
Castelo Branco, *district*, Portugal, **292** D2
Castelo Branco, Portugal, **292** D3
Castelo do Piauí, Brazil, **453** F4
Castelvetrano, Sicilia, Italy, **295** D7
Casterton, Australia, **135** J6
Castets, France, **290** D5
Castilla, Chile, **458** B3
Castilla, Peru, **454** B1
Castilla La Mancha, *autonomous community*, Spain, **293** F3, *253*
Castilla y León, *autonomous community*, Spain, **292** E1, *253*
Castillo, Pampa del, *plain*, Argentina, **460** D3
Castillonnès, France, **290** E4
Castillos, Uruguay, **459** G5
Castle Carrock, England, U.K., **306** F3
Castle Cary, England, U.K., **304** E3
Castle Dale, U.S.A., **423** H2
Castle Dome Peak, *mountain peak*, U.S.A., **422** F5
Castle Donnington, England, U.K., **305** F2
Castle Douglas, Scotland, U.K., **308** F6
Castle Rock, Colorado, U.S.A., **423** L2
Castle Rock, Washington, U.S.A., **418** C3
Castle Rock Point, St Helena, **373** B3
Castlebar, Ireland, **309** C4
Castlebay, Scotland, U.K., **308** B4
Castlebellingham, Ireland, **309** F4
Castleblayney, Ireland, **309** F3
Castlebridge, Ireland, **309** F5
Castlecomer, Ireland, **309** E5
Castleconnell, Ireland, **309** D5
Castlederg, Northern Ireland, U.K., **309** E3
Castledermot, Ireland, **309** F5
Castleford, England, U.K., **307** G4
Castlegar, Canada, **413** L7
Castlegregory, Ireland, **309** B5
Castleisland, Ireland, **309** C5
Castlemaine, Ireland, **309** C5
Castlemartyr, Ireland, **309** D6
Castlepoint, New Zealand, **133** F5
Castlepollard, Ireland, **309** E4
Castlereagh, *district*, Northern Ireland, U.K., **309** G3
Castleton, England, U.K., **307** H3
Castletown, Ireland, **309** E5
Castletown, Isle of Man, **306** D3
Castletown, Scotland, U.K., **308** F2
Castletown Bearhaven, Ireland, **309** C6
Castlewellan, Northern Ireland, U.K., **309** G3
Castlewood, U.S.A., **420** E3
Castor, Canada, **413** P5
Castor, *river*, Canada, **415** Q5
Castor, U.S.A., **424** F3
Castres, France, **290** F5
Castries, St Lucia, **427** D3, *397*
Castro, Brazil, **459** G2
Castro, Chile, **460** C2
Castro, Punta, *point*, Argentina, **460** E2
Castro Marim, Portugal, **292** D4
Castro-Urdiales, Spain, **293** F1
Castro Verde, Portugal, **292** C4
Castrovillari, Italy, **295** F6
Castrovirreyna, Peru, **454** C3
Castuera, Spain, **292** E3
Casuarito, Colombia, **451** E3
Caswell Sound, New Zealand, **133** A7
Cat Island, Bahamas, **428** G1
Cat Lake, Canada, **414** J6
Cat Lake, *lake*, Canada, **414** J6
Catabola, Angola, **368** C5
Catacaos, Peru, **454** B1
Catacocha, Ecuador, **450** B5
Cataguases, Brazil, **457** E5
Catahoula Lake, U.S.A., **424** F4
Catalão, Brazil, **456** D5
Çatalca, Turkey, **297** G5
Catalina, Bahía, *bay*, Providencia, Colombia, **461** C1
Catalina, U.S.A., **423** H5
Cataluña, *autonomous community*, Spain, **293** H2
Catamarca, *province*, Argentina, **458** C3
Catan Lil, Argentina, **460** C1
Catandica, Mozambique, **371** F2
Catanduanes Island, Philippines, **204** D3
Catania, Golfo di, *gulf*, Sicilia, Italy, **295** E7
Catania, Sicilia, Italy, **295** E7, *254*
Catanzaro, Italy, **295** F6
Catarina, Raso da, *mountain range*, Brazil, **457** F2
Catarina, U.S.A., **424** C5
Catarman, Philippines, **204** D3
Catarroja, Spain, **293** G3
Catatumbo, *river*, Venezuela, **450** D2
Cataxa, Mozambique, **369** F6
Catbalogan, Philippines, **204** D4

Catedral, Cerro, *mountain peak*, Uruguay, **459** F5, *444*
Cateel, Philippines, **204** D5
Caterham, England, U.K., **305** G3
Catete, Angola, **368** B4
Cathedral Mountain, *mountain peak*, U.S.A., **423** M6
Catherine Point, Ascension, **373** A3
Cathlamet, U.S.A., **418** C3
Catia La Mar, Venezuela, **451** E1
Catió, Guinea-Bissau, **364** A2
Catnip Mountain, *mountain peak*, U.S.A., **418** E6
Catoche, Cabo, *cape*, Mexico, **431** J4
Catorce, Mexico, **431** E4
Catoute, *mountain peak*, Spain, **292** D1
Catriel, Argentina, **458** C5
Catriló, Argentina, **458** D5
Catrimani, Brazil, **451** G4
Catrimani, *river*, Brazil, **451** F4
Catskill, U.S.A., **426** D3
Catskill Mountains, *mountain range*, U.S.A., **426** C3
Catterick, England, U.K., **307** G3
Catuane, Mozambique, **371** F4
Cauaxi, *river*, Brazil, **452** D4
Cauayan, Luzon Island, Philippines, **204** C2
Cauayan, Negros Island, Philippines, **204** C4
Cauca, *river*, Colombia, **450** C2, *436*
Caucaia, Brazil, **453** F4
Caucasia, Colombia, **450** C2
Caucasus *see* Bol'shoy Kavkaz, *mountain range*, Asia/Europe, **222** D4, *189, 190, 273*
Caucete, Argentina, **458** C4
Caungula, Angola, **368** C4
Cauquenes, Chile, **458** B5
Caura, *river*, Venezuela, **451** F2
Caures, *river*, Brazil, **451** F4
Causapscal, Canada, **416** H5
Căuşeni, Moldova, **296** G2
Caussade, France, **290** E4
Cautário, *river*, Brazil, **455** F3
Cauto, *river*, Cuba, **429** F2
Cavalcante, Brazil, **456** D3
Cavalier, U.S.A., **420** E1
Cavalla, *river*, Liberia, **364** C3
Cavalli Islands, New Zealand, **132** D2
Cavallo, Île, *island*, Corse, France, **295** B5
Cavally, *river*, Côte d'Ivoire, **364** C3
Cavan, *county*, Ireland, **309** E4
Cavan, Ireland, **309** E4
Cavarzere, Italy, **294** D3
Çavdarhisar, Turkey, **297** G6
Cave, New Zealand, **133** C7
Cave City, U.S.A., **424** G2
Cavern Peak, *mountain peak*, Auckland Islands, New Zealand, **132** J10
Caviana, Ilha, *island*, Brazil, **452** C3
Cavinas, Bolivia, **455** E3
Cavnic, Romania, **296** D2
Cawdor, Scotland, U.K., **308** F3
Cawston, England, U.K., **305** J2
Caxias, Brazil, **453** E4
Caxias do Sul, Brazil, **459** G3
Caxito, Angola, **368** B4
Çay, Turkey, **224** D5
Cayambe, Ecuador, **450** B4
Cayambe, Volcán, *mountain peak*, Ecuador, **450** C4
Cayenne, French Guiana, **452** C2, *445*
Cayman Brac, *island*, Cayman Islands, **429** F3
Cayman Islands, *dependency*, Caribbean Sea, **409** Q7, *276, 378, 388*
Cayman Trench, *underwater feature*, Caribbean Sea, **479** N3
Caynabo, Somalia, **367** G3
Cayuga Lake, U.S.A., **426** B3
Cazalla de la Sierra, Spain, **292** E4
Căzăneşti, Romania, **296** F3
Cazaux et de Sanguinet, Étang de, *lake*, France, **290** D4
Čazma, Croatia, **294** F3
Cazombo, Angola, **368** D5
Cazorla, Spain, **293** F4
Cazula, Mozambique, **369** F6
Cea, *river*, Spain, **292** E1
Ceará, *state*, Brazil, **453** F4
Ceara Plain, *underwater feature*, Atlantic Ocean, **477** E6
Cébaco, Isla de, *island*, Panama, **429** E6
Ceballos, Mexico, **430** D3
Cebolla, U.S.A., **423** K3
Cebollati, *river*, Uruguay, **459** F4
Cebu, *island*, Philippines, **204** C4, *149*
Cebu, Philippines, **204** C4
Ceccano, Italy, **295** D5
Cece, Hungary, **289** J5
Cecina, Italy, **294** C4
Cedar, *river*, Iowa, U.S.A., **420** G4
Cedar, *river*, North Dakota, U.S.A., **420** B2
Cedar City, U.S.A., **422** G3
Cedar Grove, U.S.A., **421** N6
Cedar Key, U.S.A., **425** L5
Cedar Lake, Canada, **414** D5
Cedar Rapids, U.S.A., **420** H5
Cedartown, U.S.A., **425** K2
Cedarvale, U.S.A., **423** L4
Cedros, Isla, *island*, Mexico, **430** B2
Cedros Trench, *underwater feature*, Pacific Ocean, **479** L3
Ceduna, Australia, **134** G5
Cedynia, Poland, **289** G2
Cée, Spain, **292** C1
Ceel Gaal, Bari, Somalia, **367** H2
Ceel Gaal, Woqooyi Galbeed, Somalia, **367** F2
Ceelbuur, Somalia, **367** G4
Ceerigaabo, Somalia, **367** G2
Cefalù, Sicilia, Italy, **295** D6
Cega, *river*, Spain, **292** E2
Cegléd, Hungary, **289** J5
Cehegin, Spain, **293** G3
Ceheng, China, **215** H4
Cehu Silvaniei, Romania, **296** D2
Celaya, Mexico, **431** E4
Celbridge, Ireland, **309** F4
Celebes Basin, *underwater feature*, South China Sea, **478** C4
Celebes Sea, Indonesia/Philippines, **198** C2
Celebes *see* Sulawesi, *island*, Indonesia, **198** B3, *148*
Celendín, Peru, **454** C2
Celina, U.S.A., **425** K1
Celje, Slovenia, **294** E2
Celle, Germany, **288** E2
Celny, Russian Federation, **211** M2
Celorico da Beira, Portugal, **292** D2
Celyn, Llyn, *lake*, Wales, U.K., **304** D2
Cenajo, Embalse del, *reservoir*, Spain, **293** G3
Cenderawasih, Teluk, *bay*, Indonesia, **199** F3
Centenary, Zimbabwe, **371** F2
Center, Colorado, U.S.A., **423** L3
Center, Texas, U.S.A., **424** E4
Centerville, Iowa, U.S.A., **420** G5
Centerville, South Dakota, U.S.A., **420** E4
Centinela, Picacho del, *mountain peak*, Mexico, **430** E2
Cento, Italy, **294** C3
Central, *administrative region*, Ghana, **364** D3
Central, *administrative region*, Malawi, **369** F5
Central, Cordillera, *mountain range*, Bolivia, **447** F5
Central, Cordillera, *mountain range*, Panama, **429** E5
Central, *district*, Botswana, **370** D3
Central, *province*, Kenya, **369** G3
Central, *province*, Papua New Guinea, **140** B5
Central, *province*, Zambia, **369** E5
Central African Republic, *country*, Africa, **358** G6, *312, 331, 333, 334*
Central Brāhui Range, *mountain range*, Pakistan, **218** A3
Central Butte, Canada, **413** R6
Central Pacific Basin, *underwater feature*, Pacific Ocean, **478** F4
Central City, U.S.A., **421** K7
Central Makrān Range, *mountain range*, Pakistan, **221** H3
Central Patricia, Canada, **414** J6
Central Range, *mountain range*, Papua New Guinea, **140** A4
Centralia, Illinois, U.S.A., **421** J6
Centralia, Washington, U.S.A., **418** C3
Centre, *administrative region*, France, **290** E3, *245*
Centre, *province*, Cameroon, **368** B2
Centre de Flacq, Mauritius, **373** C1
Centre Group, *islands*, Antipodes Islands, New Zealand, **133** N14
Centre Island, New Zealand, **133** A8
Centreville, U.S.A., **425** J3
Cenxi, China, **206** B4
Čepin, Croatia, **294** G3
Ceram Sea, Indonesia, **199** E3
Cerbère, France, **291** F5
Cercal, Portugal, **292** C4
Cerdedo, Spain, **292** C1
Cereal, Canada, **413** P6
Ceredigion, Wales, U.K., **304** C2
Ceres, Argentina, **458** E3
Ceres, South Africa, **370** C5
Ceresole Reale, Italy, **294** A3
Cereté, Colombia, **450** C2
Cerezo de Abajo, Spain, **293** F2
Cerignola, Italy, **295** E5
Cerizay, France, **290** D3
Çerkezköy, Turkey, **297** G5
Cerknica, Slovenia, **294** E3
Cerna, Romania, **296** G3
Cernavodă, Romania, **296** G3
Cernégula, Spain, **293** F1
Cerralvo, Isla, *island*, Mexico, **430** C3
Cerralvo, Mexico, **431** F3
Cërrik, Albania, **297** B5
Cerritos, Mexico, **431** E4
Cêrro Azul, Brazil, **459** H2
Cerro Azul, Mexico, **431** F4
Cerro de Pasco, Peru, **454** C3
Cerro Policía, Argentina, **460** D1
Cerro Prieto, Mexico, **430** D3
Cerro Sombrero, Chile, **460** D4
Cerros Colorados, Embalse, *reservoir*, Argentina, **458** C6
Cervantes, Philippines, **204** C2
Cervati, Monte, *mountain peak*, Italy, **295** E5
Cervenia, Romania, **296** E4
Cervera, Spain, **293** H2
Cerveteri, Italy, **295** D4
Cervione, Corse, France, **295** B4
César, *river*, Colombia, **450** D1
Cesena, Italy, **294** D3
Cesenatico, Italy, **294** D3
Cēsis, Latvia, **287** M4
Česká Budájovice, Czech Republic, **289** G4
Česká Lípa, Czech Republic, **289** G3
Česká Třebová, Czech Republic, **289** H4
Českomoravská Vrchovina, *mountain range*, Czech Republic, **289** G4
Česma, *river*, Croatia, **294** F3
Çeşme, Turkey, **297** F6
Cess, *river*, Liberia, **364** C3
Cessnock, Australia, **135** L5
Cesvaine, Latvia, **287** N4
Cetate, Romania, **296** D3
Cetinje, Montenegro, **296** B4
Cetraro, Italy, **295** E6
Ceuta, *enclave*, Spain, N.W. Africa, **361** E1, *92, 253, 355*
Cévennes, *mountain range*, France, **291** F4
Ceyhan, Turkey, **363** G1
Ceylanpinar, Turkey, **363** H1
Ceylon, Canada, **419** M2
Cha-am, Thailand, **202** C3
Chābahār, Iran, **221** H3
Chablis, France, **291** F3
Chacabuco, Argentina, **458** E5
Chacao, Canal de, *channel*, Chile, **460** B1
Chacao, Chile, **460** C1
Chachahuén, Sierra, *mountain peak*, Argentina, **458** C5
Chachani, Nevado, *mountain peak*, Peru, **454** D4
Chachapoyas, Peru, **454** C2
Chachevichy, Belarus, **299** B6
Chachora, India, **218** D4
Chaco, *province*, Argentina, **458** E2, *96, 443*
Chad, *country*, Africa, **358** G5, *312, 325, 327, 328, 329, 331, 336*
Chadan, Russian Federation, **213** F2
Chadbourn, U.S.A., **425** N2
Chadi, India, **218** C4
Chadileo, *river*, Argentina, **458** C5
Chador, Russian Federation, **211** H1
Chadron, U.S.A., **420** B4
Chaeryŏng, North Korea, **208** D3, *163*
Chafurray, Colombia, **450** D3
Chaghcharān, Afghanistan, **218** A2
Chagny, France, **291** G3
Chagos Archipelago, *islands*, British Indian Ocean Territory, Indian Ocean, **104** E9, *193*
Chagos-Laccadive Plateau, *underwater feature*, Indian Ocean, **476** D5
Chagos Trench, *underwater feature*, Indian Ocean, **476** D5
Chagoyan, Russian Federation, **211** K1
Chaguanas, Trinidad, Trinidad and Tobago, **461** C4
Chaguaramas, Trinidad, Trinidad and Tobago, **461** C4
Chaguaramas, Venezuela, **451** E2
Chahbounia, Algeria, **361** G1
Chai, Mozambique, **369** H5
Chai Nat, Thailand, **202** D3
Chai Wan, China, **207** C4
Chāībāsa, India, **219** F5
Chain Fracture Zone, *tectonic feature*, Atlantic Ocean, **477** F6
Chaitén, Chile, **460** C2
Chaiyaphum, Thailand, **202** D3
Chajarí, Argentina, **459** F4
Chakari, Zimbabwe, **371** E2
Chake Chake, Tanzania, **369** G4
Chakradharpur, India, **219** F5
Chakrāta, India, **218** D3
Chakwāl, Pakistan, **218** C2
Chala, Peru, **454** C4
Chala, Tanzania, **369** F4
Chalais, France, **290** E4
Chalatenango, El Salvador, **428** C4
Chalaua, Mozambique, **369** G6
Chalaxung, China, **215** F2
Chale, England, U.K., **305** F4
Chaleurs, Baie des, *bay*, Canada, **416** H5
Chalía, *river*, Argentina, **460** C3
Chaling, China, **206** C3
Chalinze, Tanzania, **369** G4
Chalki, *island*, Dodekanisos, Greece, **297** F7
Chalkida, Greece, **297** D6
Chalkyitsik, U.S.A., **410** E3
Challans, France, **290** D3
Challapata, Bolivia, **455** E5
Challenger Fracure Zone, *tectonic feature*, Pacific Ocean, **479** K7
Challis, U.S.A., **418** G4
Chalna, Russian Federation, **299** E2
Chalon-sur-Saône, France, **291** G3
Châlons-en-Champagne, France, **291** G2, *90*
Châlus, France, **290** E4
Chālūs, Iran, **222** E5
Cham, Germany, **288** F4
Chama, U.S.A., **423** K3
Chama, Zambia, **369** F5
Chaman, Pakistan, **218** A3
Chamba, India, **218** D2
Chamba, Tanzania, **369** G5
Chamberlain, U.S.A., **420** D4
Chambers, U.S.A., **420** D4
Chambéry, France, **291** G4
Chambeshi, Zambia, **369** F5
Chambord, Canada, **416** E5
Chamborêt, France, **290** E3
Chamical, Argentina, **458** C4
Chamoli, India, **218** D3
Chamonix-Mont-Blanc, France, **291** H4
Chāmpa, India, **219** E5
Champagne-Ardenne, *administrative region*, France, **291** F2, *245*
Champagnole, France, **291** G3
Champaign, U.S.A., **421** J5
Champaqui, Cerro, *mountain peak*, Argentina, **458** D4
Champdoré, Lac, *lake*, Canada, **416** J2
Champlain, Lake, U.S.A., **426** D2
Champotón, Mexico, **431** H5
Chāmrājnagar, India, **216** D4
Chamzinka, Russian Federation, **222** D2
Chân An, Vietnam, **203** F3
Chañaral, Chile, **458** B3
Chança, *river*, Portugal, **292** D4
Chancani, Argentina, **458** D4
Chanco, Chile, **458** B5
Chandausi, India, **218** D3
Chāndbāli, India, **219** F5
Chandeleur Islands, U.S.A., **425** H5
Chandeleur Sound, U.S.A., **425** H5
Chanderi, India, **218** D4
Chandigarh, India, **218** D3, *169*
Chandler, Canada, **416** J5
Chandler, U.S.A., **423** H5
Chāndpur, Bangladesh, **214** D5
Chandrapur, India, **218** D6
Chang, Ko, *island*, Thailand, **202** D3
Chang, Pakistan, **218** B4
Chang (Yangtze), *river*, China, **206** D2, *30, 51, 64, 65, 70, 144, 158, 159, 160, 161*
Changan, China, **207** B3, *160*
Changane, *river*, Mozambique, **371** F3
Changara, Mozambique, **369** F6
Changbai Shan, *mountain range*, China, **211** J4
Changchun, China, **211** J4, *161*
Changde, China, **206** B2
Changhŭng, South Korea, **208** D4
Chang-hua, Taiwan, **206** E3
Changi, Singapore, **200** K6
Changi Airport, Singapore, **200** K6
Changji, China, **212** E3
Changjiang, China, **203** F2
Changli, China, **211** G5
Changling, China, **211** H3
Changma, China, **213** H5
Changmar, China, **214** A2
Changning, China, **207** C2
Changping, China, **207** B3
Changsha, China, **206** C2, *161*
Changshan, China, **206** D2
Changshantou, China, **210** D5
Changshou, China, **215** H3
Changshu, China, **206** E2
Ch'angsŏng, North Korea, **208** D2
Changting, China, **206** D3
Changtu, China, **211** J4
Changweiliang, China, **213** G5
Changwu, China, **215** H2
Changxing, China, **206** D2
Changyang, China, **206** B2
Changyŏn, North Korea, **208** D3
Changyuan, China, **206** C1
Changzhi, China, **210** F5
Changzhou, China, **206** D2
Chañi, Nevado de, *mountain peak*, Argentina, **458** D2

Chania, Kriti, Greece, **297** E8
Chanion, Kolpos, *bay*, Kriti, Greece, **297** D8
Chankou, China, **215** H2
Channagiri, India, **216** C3
Channapatna, India, **216** D3
Channel Islands, *U.K. dependency*, English Channel, **290** C2, *82, 278, 279*
Channel Islands, U.S.A., **422** D5
Channel-Port aux Basques, Canada, **417** M6
Channing, U.S.A., **423** M4
Chantada, Spain, **292** D1
Chanthaburi, Thailand, **202** D3
Chantonnay, France, **290** D3
Chanute, U.S.A., **420** F7
Chany, Ozero, *lake*, Russian Federation, **223** K2
Chany, Russian Federation, **223** K1
Chao, Peru, **454** B2
Chao Hu, *lake*, China, **206** D2
Chaohu, China, **206** D2
Chaor, China, **211** H2
Chaor, *river*, China, **211** H3
Chaoyang, Guangdong, China, **206** D4
Chaoyang, Liaoning, China, **211** H4
Chaozhou, China, **206** D4
Chapada dos Guimarães, Brazil, **456** B4
Chapadinha, Brazil, **453** E4
Chapaev, Kazakhstan, **222** E2
Chapais, Canada, **416** D5
Chapala, Lago de, *lake*, Mexico, **430** E4
Chapala, Mexico, **430** E4
Chaparral, Colombia, **450** C3
Chaparral, U.S.A., **423** K5
Chapayevsk, Russian Federation, **222** D2
Chapeco, Brazil, **459** G3
Chapecó, *river*, Brazil, **459** G3
Chapel-en-le-Frith, England, U.K., **307** G4
Chapeltown, England, U.K., **307** G4
Chapleau, Canada, **421** M2
Chaplin, Canada, **413** R6
Chapman, Mount, *mountain peak*, Antarctica, **470** C6
Chapman, Mount, *mountain peak*, Canada, **413** K6
Chapmanville, U.S.A., **421** M7
Chapoma, *river*, Russian Federation, **285** U3
Chaqui, Bolivia, **455** F5
Charagua, Bolivia, **455** F5
Charambirá, Punta, *point*, Colombia, **450** B3
Charaña, Bolivia, **455** E4
Charcas, Mexico, **431** E4
Charcot Island, Antarctica, **470** A5
Chard, England, U.K., **304** E4
Chardstock, England, U.K., **304** E4
Charef, Algeria, **361** G2
Charef, Oued, *river*, Morocco, **361** F2
Charente, *river*, France, **290** D4
Chari, *river*, Chad, **366** A3, *328*
Chari-Baguirmi, *prefecture*, Chad, **365** H2
Chārīkār, Afghanistan, **218** B2
Chariton, U.S.A., **420** G5
Charity, Guyana, **451** G2
Chärjew, Turkmenistan, **222** G5
Charkhi Dādri, India, **218** D3
Charleroi, Belgium, **288** B3, *242*
Charles, Cape, U.S.A., **426** C6
Charles City, U.S.A., **420** G4
Charles Fuhr, Argentina, **460** C4
Charlesbourg, Canada, **416** F6
Charleston, Illinois, U.S.A., **421** J6
Charleston, Missouri, U.S.A., **421** J7
Charleston, New Zealand, **133** C5
Charleston, South Carolina, U.S.A., **425** N3
Charleston, West Virginia, U.S.A., **421** N6, *386*
Charleston Peak, *mountain peak*, U.S.A., **422** F3
Charlestown, Ireland, **309** D4
Charlestown of Aberlour, Scotland, U.K., **308** F3
Charleville, Australia, **135** K4
Charleville-Mézières, France, **291** G2
Charlie, Dome, *ice dome*, Antarctica, **470** E7
Charlie-Gibbs Fracture Zone, *tectonic feature*, Atlantic Ocean, **477** E2
Charlotte, U.S.A., **425** M2
Charlotte Amalie, U.S. Virgin Islands, **427** C2, *387*
Charlottetown, Canada, **417** K6, *381*
Charlotteville, Tobago, Trinidad and Tobago, **461** B4
Charlton Island, Canada, **415** P5
Charminster, England, U.K., **304** E4
Charmouth, England, U.K., **304** E4
Charny, Canada, **416** F6
Chārsadda, Pakistan, **218** B2
Charters Towers, Australia, **135** K3
Chartres, France, **290** E2
Chascomús, Argentina, **459** F5
Chashan, China, **207** B2
Chashniki, Belarus, **299** B5
Château-Chinon, France, **291** F3
Château-Gontier, France, **290** D3
Château-Renault, France, **290** E3
Château-Thierry, France, **291** F2
Châteaubriant, France, **290** D3
Châteaudun, France, **290** E2
Chateaugay, U.S.A., **426** C2
Châteaulin, France, **290** B2
Châteauroux, France, **290** E3
Châtellerault, France, **290** E3
Chatfield, U.S.A., **420** G4
Chatham, England, U.K., **305** H3
Chatham, New Brunswick, Canada, **416** J6
Chatham, Ontario, Canada, **421** M4
Chatham Island, New Zealand, **133** Q16, *110*
Chatham Rise, *underwater feature*, Pacific Ocean, **478** F7
Chatham Strait, U.S.A., **412** B4
Châtillon-sur-Seine, France, **291** G3
Chatra, India, **219** F4
Chatrapur, India, **217** F2
Chatsworth, U.S.A., **421** J5
Chattanooga, U.S.A., **425** K2
Chatteris, England, U.K., **305** H2
Chatyr-Tash, Kyrgyzstan, **212** C4
Chatyrtash, Kyrgyzstan, **223** K4
Châu Đốc, Vietnam, **203** E4
Chauk, Myanmar, **205** B3
Chaumont, France, **291** G2
Chauvigny, France, **290** E3
Chavakachcheri, Sri Lanka, **216** E4
Chavan'ga, Russian Federation, **285** T3
Chaves, Brazil, **452** D3
Chaves, Portugal, **292** D2
Chavuma, Zambia, **368** D5
Chavusy, Belarus, **299** C6
Chayevo, Russian Federation, **299** F3
Chaykovskiy, Russian Federation, **222** E1
Chazón, Argentina, **458** D4
Cheb, Czech Republic, **288** F3
Cheboksary, Russian Federation, **222** D1
Cheboygan, U.S.A., **421** L3
Chech, Erg, *desert*, Algeria/Mali, **361** E4
Chechenskaya, Respublika, *republic*, Russian Federation, **222** D4
Chęciny, Poland, **289** K3
Checotah, U.S.A., **424** E2
Cheddar Gorge, England, U.K., **304** E3
Cheduba, *island*, Myanmar, **205** B4
Cheerless Cove, New Zealand, **133** A7
Chefchaouene, Morocco, **361** E1
Chegdomyn, Russian Federation, **301** Q4
Chegga, Mauritania, **361** E3
Chegutu, Zimbabwe, **371** F2
Chehalis, U.S.A., **418** C3
Cheju, South Korea, **208** D4, *164*
Chejudo, *island*, South Korea, **208** D4
Chek Lap Kok, *island*, China, 207 B4
Chekhov, Russian Federation, 299 F5
Chekunda, Russian Federation, 211 L2
Chela, Serra da, *mountain range*, Angola, **368** B6
Chelan, Lake, U.S.A., **418** D2
Cheleken, Turkmenistan, **222** E5
Chelforó, Argentina, **460** D1
Chełm, Poland, **289** L3
Chełmno, Poland, **289** J2
Chelmsford, England, U.K., **305** H3
Chelmuzhi, Russian Federation, **285** S5
Chełmża, Poland, **289** J2
Chelsea, U.S.A., **420** H3
Cheltenham, England, U.K., **304** E3
Cheltenham, New Zealand, **132** E5
Chelu, China, **211** K2
Chelvai, India, **216** E2
Chelyabinsk, Russian Federation, **222** G1
Chelyabinskaya Oblast', *province*, Russian Federation, **222** F2
Chelyuskin, Mys, *cape*, Russian Federation, **301** M2
Chemaïa, Morocco, **360** E2
Chemal, Russian Federation, **223** M2
Chemchâm, Sebkhet, *salt-pan*, Mauritania, **360** D4
Chemin Grenier, Mauritius, **373** C1
Chemnitz, Germany, **288** F3
Chen Barag Qi, China, **211** G2
Chenāb, *river*, Pakistan, **218** B3, *173*
Chenachane, Algeria, **361** F3
Ch'ench'a, Ethiopia, **367** E3
Cheney, U.S.A., **418** F3
Ch'eng-kung, Taiwan, **206** E4
Cheng'an, China, **210** F5
Chengde, China, **211** G4
Chengdu, China, **215** H3, *161*
Chengele, India, **219** J3
Chenghai, China, **206** D4
Chengjiang, China, **207** C2
Chengkou, China, **206** B2
Chengmai, China, **203** F2
Chennai (Madras), India, **216** E3, *93, 94, 169*
Chenxi, China, **206** B3
Chenzhou, China, **206** C3
Chepelare, Bulgaria, **297** E5
Chepén, Peru, **454** B2
Chépénéhé, New Caledonia, **141** A3
Chepes, Argentina, **458** C4
Chepo, Panama, **450** B2
Chepstow, Wales, U.K., **304** E3
Cher, *river*, France, **290** E3
Cheraw, U.S.A., **425** N2
Cherbourg, France, **290** D2, *279*
Cherchell, Algeria, **293** J4
Cherekha, *river*, Russian Federation, **299** B4
Cherepanovo, Russian Federation, **223** L2
Cherepovets, Russian Federation, **299** F3
Chéria, Algeria, **361** H1
Cherkessk, Russian Federation, **222** C4
Chern', Russian Federation, **299** F6
Chernevo, Russian Federation, **299** B3
Chernihiv, Ukraine, **298** D2
Chernivets'ka Oblast', *province*, Ukraine, **296** E1
Chernivtsi, Chernivets'ka Oblast', Ukraine, **296** E1
Chernivtsi, Vinnyts'ka Oblast', Ukraine, **296** G1
Chernyakhovsk, Russian Federation, **287** K5
Chernyshevsk, Russian Federation, **210** G1
Chernyy Yar, Russian Federation, **222** D3
Cherokee, Iowa, U.S.A., **420** F4
Cherokee, Oklahoma, U.S.A., **420** D7
Cherokee Sound, Bahamas, **428** F1
Cherrapunji, India, **219** G4
Cherry Creek, U.S.A., **420** C3
Cherryville, Canada, **413** K6
Cherskiy, Russian Federation, **301** T3
Cherskogo, Khrebet, *mountain range*, Russian Federation, **301** Q3
Cherven Bryag, Bulgaria, **296** E4
Chervonohrad, Ukraine, **289** M3
Chervonoznam'yanka, Ukraine, **296** H2
Chervyen', Belarus, **299** B6
Cherykaw, Belarus, **299** C6
Chesapeake, U.S.A., **426** B6
Chesapeake Bay, U.S.A., **426** B5
Chesham, England, U.K., **305** G3
Cheshire, *unitary authority*, England, U.K., **304** E1
Cheshskaya Guba, *bay*, Russian Federation, **300** F3
Cheshunt, England, U.K., **305** G3
Cheste, Spain, **293** G3
Chester, California, U.S.A., **422** C1
Chester, Canada, **417** J7
Chester, England, U.K., **304** E1
Chester, Illinois, U.S.A., **420** J7
Chester, Montana, U.S.A., **419** J2
Chester, South Carolina, U.S.A., **425** M2
Chester-le-Street, England, U.K., **307** G3
Chesterfield, England, U.K., **305** F1
Chesterfield, Îles, *islands*, New Caledonia, **136** A2
Chesterfield Inlet, Canada, **411** K3
Chestnut, U.S.A., **424** F3
Chesuncook Lake, U.S.A., **426** E1
Chet', *river*, Russian Federation, **223** M1
Chetaibi, Algeria, **295** A7
Cheticamp, Canada, **417** L6
Chetlat Island, India, **216** C4
Chetumal, Mexico, **431** H5
Chetwode Island, New Zealand, **133** E5
Chetwynd, Canada, **412** J4
Cheugda, Russian Federation, **211** K2
Cheung Chau, *island*, China, **207** C4
Chevejécure, Bolivia, **455** E4
Chevilly, France, **290** E2
Cheviot, New Zealand, **133** D6
Cheviot, The, *mountain peak*, England, U.K., **306** F2
Cheviot Hills, England, U.K., **306** F2, *276*
Che'w Bahir, *lake*, Ethiopia, **369** G2
Chew Magna, England, U.K., **304** E3
Chew Valley Lake, England, U.K., **304** E3
Chewelah, U.S.A., **418** F2
Cheyenne, Oklahoma, U.S.A., **424** C2
Cheyenne, *river*, U.S.A., **419** P4
Cheyenne, Wyoming, U.S.A., **419** M6, *386*
Cheyenne Wells, U.S.A., **423** M2
Chhatarpur, India, **218** D4
Chhattīsgarh, *Ebene*, India, **219** E5
Chhindawāra, India, **218** D5
Chhnăng, *river*, Cambodia, **203** E3
Chhota Udepur, India, **218** C5
Chi-lung, Taiwan, **206** E3
Ch'i-shan, Taiwan, **206** E4
Chiāi, Taiwan, **206** E4
Chiang Dao, Doi, *mountain peak*, Thailand, **202** C2
Chiang Kham, Thailand, **202** D2
Chiang Khan, Thailand, **202** D2
Chiang Mai, Thailand, **202** C2, *157*
Chiang Rai, Thailand, **202** C2
Chiange, Angola, **368** B6
Chiapas, *state*, Mexico, **431** G5, *379, 400*
Chiari, Italy, **294** B3
Chiautla de Tapia, Mexico, **431** F5
Chiavenna, Italy, **294** B2
Chiba, Japan, **209** H4
Chibemba, Angola, **368** B6
Chibia, Angola, **368** B6
Chibougamau, Canada, **416** D5
Chic-Chocs, Monts, *mountain range*, Canada, **416** H5
Chicago, U.S.A., **421** K5, *84, 384*
Chicama, Peru, **454** B2
Chicama, *river*, Peru, **454** B2
Chichagof Island, U.S.A., **412** A3
Chichas, Cordillera de, *mountain range*, Bolivia, **455** E5
Chīchāwatni, Pakistan, **218** C3
Chicheng, China, **210** F4
Chichester, England, U.K., **305** G4
Chichi-jima, *island*, Japan, **138** C2
Chichola, India, **218** E5
Chichón, Volcán, *mountain peak*, Mexico, **431** G5
Chickasawhay, *river*, U.S.A., **425** H4
Chickasha, U.S.A., **424** D2
Chickerell, England, U.K., **304** E4
Chiclana de la Frontera, Spain, **292** D4
Chiclayo, Peru, **454** B2
Chico, *river*, Chubut, Argentina, **460** D2
Chico, *river*, Río Negro, Argentina, **460** C2
Chico, *river*, Santa Cruz, Argentina, **460** C3
Chico, *river*, S. Santa Cruz, Argentina, **460** D4
Chico, U.S.A., **422** C2
Chicoa, Mozambique, **369** F6
Chicomba, Angola, **368** B5
Chicotte, Canada, **417** K5
Chicoutimi, Canada, **416** F5
Chicualacuala, Mozambique, **371** F3
Chidambaram, India, **216** D4
Chidenguele, Mozambique, **371** F3
Chidley, Cape, Canada, **411** N3
Chiefland, U.S.A., **425** L5
Chiemsee, *lake*, Germany, **288** F5
Chiengi, Zambia, **369** E4
Chieo Lan Reservoir, Thailand, **202** C4
Chiese, *river*, Italy, **294** C3
Chieti, Italy, **295** E4
Chietla, Mexico, **431** F5
Chifeng, China, **211** G4
Chigorodó, Colombia, **450** C2
Chiguana, Bolivia, **455** E5
Chigubo, Mozambique, **371** F3
Chihuahua, Mexico, **430** D2
Chihuahua, *state*, Mexico, **430** D2
Chihuido Medio, *mountain peak*, Argentina, **458** C6
Chikhachevo, Russian Federation, **299** B4
Chikmagalūr, India, **216** C3
Chikodi, India, **216** C2
Chikoy, *river*, Russian Federation, **210** E2
Chikwa, Zambia, **369** F5
Chikwawa, Malawi, **369** F6
Chila, Angola, **368** B5
Chilakalūrupet, India, **216** E2
Chilapa de Alvarez, Mexico, **431** F5
Chilaw, Sri Lanka, **216** D5
Chilca, Cordillera de, *mountain range*, Peru, **454** D4
Chilcotin, *river*, Canada, **412** G5
Chilcott Island, Coral Sea Islands, **135** K2
Childers, Australia, **135** L4

Childress, U.S.A., 424 B2
Chile, country, South America, 449 E7, 75, 93, 95, 97, 434, 435, 441, 442, 443
Chile Basin, underwater feature, Pacific Ocean, 479 N6
Chile Chico, Argentina, 460 C3
Chile Rise, underwater feature, Pacific Ocean, 479 M7
Chilecito, Argentina, 458 C3
Chilham, England, U.K., 305 H3
Chilia Veche, Romania, 296 G3
Chililabombwe, Zambia, 369 E5
Chilka Lake, India, 219 F6
Chillán, Chile, 458 B5
Chillar, Argentina, 459 E5
Chillicothe, Illinois, U.S.A., 421 J5
Chillicothe, Missouri, U.S.A., 420 G6
Chillicothe, Ohio, U.S.A., 421 M6
Chilliculco, Peru, 455 E4
Chillinji, Pakistan, 218 C1
Chilliwack, Canada, 412 J7
Chilpancingo de los Bravos, Mexico, 431 F5
Chiltal'd, Gora, mountain peak, Russian Federation, 285 Q2
Chilubi, Zambia, 369 E5
Chilumba, Malawi, 369 F5, 345
Chimala, Tanzania, 369 F4
Chimán, Panama, 429 F5
Chimanimani, Zimbabwe, 371 F2
Chimayo, U.S.A., 423 L3
Chimborazo, mountain peak, Ecuador, 450 B4, 438
Chimbote, Peru, 454 B2
Chiméal, Cambodia, 203 D4
Chimoio, Mozambique, 371 F2
Chin, state, Myanmar, 205 B3
China, country, Asia, 196 L6, 27, 30, 35, 40, 42, 45, 47, 49, 51, 54, 56, 59, 60, 63, 64, 65, 66, 69, 70, 73, 74, 75, 76, 86, 87, 88, 89, 89, 90, 91, 93, 95, 96, 97, 144, 145, 154, 157, 158, 159, 160, 161, 162, 163, 164, 165, 169, 172, 173, 186, 188, 193, 251, 271, 272, 273, 439, 446
China, Mexico, 431 F3
Chinácota, Colombia, 450 D2
Chinajá, Guatemala, 428 C3
Chinandega, Nicaragua, 428 D4
Chinati Peak, mountain peak, U.S.A., 423 L7
Chincha Alta, Peru, 454 C3
Chinchaga, river, Canada, 413 K3
Chinchilla, Australia, 135 L4
Chinchilla de Monte Aragón, Spain, 293 G3
Chincholi, India, 216 D2
Chinde, Mozambique, 371 G2
Chindo, island, South Korea, 208 D4
Chindu, China, 215 F2
Chindwin, river, Myanmar, 205 B2
Chingola, Zambia, 369 E5
Chinguar, Angola, 368 C5
Chinguetti, Mauritania, 360 D4
Chinguil, Chad, 366 A2
Chinhae, South Korea, 208 E4
Chinhoyi, Zimbabwe, 371 F2
Chiniot, Pakistan, 218 C3
Chinipas, Mexico, 430 C3
Chinjan, Pakistan, 218 A3
Chinju, South Korea, 208 E4
Chinle, U.S.A., 423 J3
Chinnūr, India, 216 D2
Chinon, France, 290 E3
Chinook Trough, underwater feature, Pacific Ocean, 478 G2
Chinsali, Zambia, 369 F5
Chinsong-ri, North Korea, 208 D2
Chintāmani, India, 216 D3
Chinturu, India, 217 E2
Chioggia, Italy, 294 D3
Chios, Greece, 297 F6
Chios, island, Greece, 297 E6
Chipata, Zambia, 369 F5
Chipili, Zambia, 369 E5
Chipinge, Zimbabwe, 371 F3
Chipman, Canada, 413 N5
Chipoia, Angola, 368 C5
Chippenham, England, U.K., 304 E3
Chippewa, river, U.S.A., 420 H3
Chippewa Falls, U.S.A., 420 H3
Chipping Campden, England, U.K., 305 F2
Chipping Norton, England, U.K., 305 F3
Chipping Ongar, England, U.K., 305 H3
Chipping Sodbury, England, U.K., 304 E3
Chiprovtsi, Bulgaria, 296 D4
Chiquimula, Guatemala, 428 C4
Chiquinata, Bahía, bay, Chile, 454 D5
Chiquinquirá, Colombia, 450 D3
Chiradzulu, Malawi, 371 G2
Chirāla, Cape, India, 217 E3
Chirāla, India, 216 E3
Chiralto, river, Mexico, 431 E5
Chiramba, Mozambique, 369 F6
Chirāwa, India, 218 C3
Chirbury, England, U.K., 304 D2
Chirchiq, Uzbekistan, 223 H4
Chiredzi, Zimbabwe, 371 F3
Chirfa, Niger, 362 B4
Chiricahua Peak, mountain peak, U.S.A., 423 J6
Chiriguaná, Colombia, 450 D2
Chiriquí, Golfo de, gulf, Panama, 429 E6
Chirk, Wales, U.K., 304 D2
Chirmiri, India, 219 E5
Chirnside, Scotland, U.K., 308 G5
Chiromo, Malawi, 369 G6
Chirpan, Bulgaria, 296 E4
Chirripó, Cerro, mountain peak, Costa Rica, 428 E5, 404
Chirundu, Zambia, 369 E6
Chisamba, Zambia, 369 E5
Chisasibi, Canada, 415 Q5
Chishmy, Russian Federation, 222 F2
Chisholm, Canada, 413 M4
Chisholm, U.S.A., 420 G2
Chishui, river, China, 215 H4
Chişinău (Kishinev), Moldova, 296 G2, 270
Chişineu-Chriş, Romania, 296 C2
Chistiān Mandi, Pakistan, 218 C3
Chistopol', Russian Federation, 222 E1
Chīstopol'e, Kazakhstan, 222 H2
Chita, Bolivia, 455 E5
Chita, Russian Federation, 301 N4
Chitado, Angola, 368 B6
Chitambo, Zambia, 369 F5
Chitato, Angola, 368 D4
Chitembo, Angola, 368 C5
Chitinskaya Oblast', province, Russian Federation, 210 F1
Chitipa, Malawi, 369 F4
Chitobe, Mozambique, 371 F3
Chitose, Japan, 209 H2
Chitrāl, Pakistan, 218 B2
Chitré, Panama, 429 E6
Chittagong, Bangladesh, 214 D5, 170
Chittagong, division, Bangladesh, 214 D5
Chittaurgarh, India, 218 C4
Chittoor, India, 216 D3
Chitungwiza, Zimbabwe, 371 F2
Chiume, Angola, 368 D6
Chiure Novo, Mozambique, 369 G5
Chivasso, Italy, 294 A3
Chive, Bolivia, 455 E3
Chivhu, Zimbabwe, 371 F2
Chivington, U.S.A., 423 M2
Chlef, Algeria, 361 G1
Chlef, river, Algeria, 293 H4
Chloride, U.S.A., 422 F4
Chmelevoye, Ukraine, 296 H1
Chmielnik, Poland, 289 K3
Choa Chu Kang, Singapore, 200 J6
Chŏâm Ksant, Cambodia, 203 E3
Choapa, river, Chile, 458 B4, 347
Chobe, district, Botswana, 370 D2, 347
Chocolate Mountains, mountain range, U.S.A., 422 F5
Chocontá, Colombia, 450 D3
Chodavaram, India, 217 E2
Chodzież, Poland, 289 H2
Choele Choel, Argentina, 460 E1
Chofombo, Mozambique, 369 F5
Chograyskoye Vodokhranilishche, reservoir, Russian Federation, 222 C3
Choiceland, Canada, 414 B5
Choiseul, island, Solomon Islands, 141 A1, 116
Choiseul Sound, Falkland Islands, 460 F4
Choix, Mexico, 430 C3
Chojnice, Poland, 289 H2
Choke Canyon Lake, U.S.A., 424 C5
Chókué, Mozambique, 371 F3
Cholame, U.S.A., 422 C4
Cholet, France, 290 D3
Cholila, Argentina, 460 C2
Cholovo, Russian Federation, 299 C3
Choluteca, Honduras, 428 D4
Chom Thong, Thailand, 202 C2
Choma, Zambia, 369 E6
Chŏmch'on, South Korea, 208 E3
Chomutov, Czech Republic, 288 F3
Chon Buri, Thailand, 202 D3
Ch'ŏnan, South Korea, 208 D3
Chone, Ecuador, 450 B4
Ch'ŏngjin, North Korea, 208 E2
Chŏngju, North Korea, 208 D3
Ch'ŏngju, South Korea, 208 D3
Chongming, China, 206 E2
Chongoroi, Angola, 368 B5
Chŏngp'yŏng, North Korea, 208 D3
Chongqing, China, 215 H3, 159
Chongren, China, 206 D3
Chongwe, Zambia, 369 E6
Chŏnju, South Korea, 208 D4
Chonogol, Mongolia, 210 F3
Chonos, Archipiélago de los, islands, Chile, 460 B2
Chop, Ukraine, 289 L4
Chopim, river, Brazil, 459 G2
Chorley, England, U.K., 306 F4
Chorreras, Cerro, mountain peak, Mexico, 430 D3
Chorrochó, Brazil, 457 F2
Chorzele, Poland, 289 K2
Chos Malal, Argentina, 458 B5
Ch'osan, North Korea, 208 D2
Choszczno, Poland, 289 G2
Chota, Peru, 454 B2
Choteau, U.S.A., 419 H3
Chotila, India, 218 B5
Choûm, Mauritania, 360 D4
Choybalsan, Mongolia, 210 F2
Choyr, Mongolia, 210 E3
Christchurch, England, U.K., 305 F4
Christchurch, New Zealand, 133 D6
Christianshåb see Qasigiannguit, Greenland, 411 P3
Christina, Mount, mountain peak, New Zealand, 133 B7
Christina, river, Canada, 413 P4
Christmas Island, Australian territory, Indian Ocean, 104 F9, 108, 112, 127
Christmas Island see Kiritimati, island, Kiribati, 139 J4, 119
Christmas Ridge, underwater feature, Pacific Ocean, 478 G4
Chrudim, Czech Republic, 289 G4
Chrysoupoli, Greece, 297 E5
Chrzanów, Poland, 289 J3
Chu, Laos/Vietnam, 203 E2
Chuanchang, river, China, 206 E1
Chuankou, China, 213 J5
Chuansha, China, 206 E2
Chuanshan, China, 206 B3
Chubalung, China, 215 F3
Chubut, province, Argentina, 460 D2
Chubut, river, Argentina, 460 D2
Chudovo, Russian Federation, 299 C3
Chudskoye Ozero, lake, Russian Federation, 299 A3
Chugach Mountains, mountain range, U.S.A., 410 E3
Chūgoku-sanchi, mountain range, Japan, 208 F4
Chugwater, U.S.A., 419 M6
Chuka, China, 215 F3
Chukchagirskoye, Ozero, lake, Russian Federation, 211 M1
Chukchi Sea, Arctic Ocean, 301 V3
Chukotskiy, Mys, cape, Russian Federation, 301 V3
Chukotskiy Poluostrov, peninsula, Russian Federation, 301 V3
Chukotskoye Nagor'ye, mountain range, Russian Federation, 301 U3
Chula Vista, U.S.A., 422 E5
Chul'man, Russian Federation, 301 P4
Chulmleigh, England, U.K., 304 D4
Chulucanas, Peru, 454 B1
Chulym, river, Russian Federation, 223 M1
Chulym, Russian Federation, 223 L1
Chum Phae, Thailand, 202 D2
Chuma, Bolivia, 455 E4
Chumātang, India, 218 D2
Chumba, Ethiopia, 369 G2
Chumbicha, Argentina, 458 C3
Chumda, China, 215 F2
Chumphon, Thailand, 202 C4
Chumpi, Peru, 454 D4
Chumsaeng, Thailand, 202 D3
Ch'unch'ŏn, South Korea, 208 D3
Chung-yang Shan-mo, mountain range, Taiwan, 206 E4
Chunga, Zambia, 369 E6
Ch'ungju, South Korea, 208 E3
Chungu, Tanzania, 369 G5
Chunhuhub, Mexico, 431 H5
Chūniān, Pakistan, 218 C3
Chunya, Tanzania, 369 F4
Chupa, Russian Federation, 285 R3
Chupara Point, Trinidad, Trinidad and Tobago, 461 C4
Chuquibamba, Peru, 454 D4
Chuquicamata, Chile, 458 C2
Chuquisaca, department, Bolivia, 455 F5
Chur, Switzerland, 291 J3
Church, U.S.A., 426 B6
Church Stretton, England, U.K., 304 E2
Churchill, river, Manitoba, Canada, 414 G3
Churchill, Canada, 414 G2
Churchill, Cape, Canada, 414 H2
Churchill, river, Newfoundland, Canada, 417 K3
Churchill, river, Saskatchewan, Canada, 414 B4
Churchill Falls, Canada, 417 J3
Churchill Lake, Canada, 413 Q3
Churchill Lake, U.S.A., 426 F1
Churilovo, Russian Federation, 299 C5
Chūru, India, 218 C3
Churuguara, Venezuela, 451 E1
Chushal, India, 218 D2
Chute-aux-Outardes, Canada, 416 G5
Chute-des-Passes, Canada, 416 F5
Chuuk Islands, Mikronesia, 138 D4, 118
Chuvashskaya, Respublica, republic, Russian Federation, 222 D1
Chuxiong, China, 215 G4
Chuzhou, China, 206 D1
Ci Xian, China, 210 F5
Ciadâr-Lunga, Moldova, 296 G2
Ciamis, Indonesia, 201 E4
Cianjur, Indonesia, 201 D4
Cianorte, Brazil, 459 G2
Ćićevac, Serbia, 296 C4
Cicia, island, Fiji, 141 A4
Ciechanów, Poland, 289 K2
Ciego de Ávila, Cuba, 429 F2
Ciénaga, Colombia, 450 C1
Cienfuegos, Cuba, 429 E2
Cíes, Illas, islands, Spain, 292 C1
Cieszanów, Poland, 289 L3
Cieszyn, Czech Republic, 289 J4
Cieza, Spain, 293 G3
Cifuentes, Spain, 293 F2
Cigüela, river, Spain, 293 F3
Cihanbeyli, Turkey, 224 D5
Cihuatlán, Mexico, 430 D5
Cikobia, island, Fiji, 141 A4
Cilacap, Indonesia, 201 E4
Cilaos, Réunion, 373 A1
Çıldır Gölü, lake, Turkey, 224 F4
Cili, China, 206 B2
Cilieni, Romania, 296 E4
Cillas, Spain, 293 G2
Cimarron, U.S.A., 423 L3
Cimişlia, Moldova, 296 G2
Çınar, Turkey, 224 F5
Cinaruco, river, Venezuela, 451 E2
Cinca, river, Spain, 293 H2
Cincar, mountain peak, Bosnia and Herzegovina, 294 F4
Cincinnati, Iowa, U.S.A., 420 G5
Cincinnati, Ohio, U.S.A., 421 L6
Cinco Balas, Cayos, islands, Cuba, 429 F2
Cinco Chañares, Argentina, 460 E1
Cinderford, England, U.K., 304 E3
Çine, Turkey, 297 G7
Cintalapa de Figueroa, Mexico, 431 G5
Cinto, Monte, mountain peak, Corse, France, 295 B4
Cinzas, river, Brazil, 459 G2
Ciorani, Romania, 296 F3
Cipolletti, Argentina, 458 C6
Circle, U.S.A., 419 M3
Circleville, Ohio, U.S.A., 421 M6
Circleville, Utah, U.S.A., 422 G2
Circonstance, Mauritius, 373 C1
Cirebon, Indonesia, 201 E4
Cirencester, England, U.K., 305 F3
Ciriè, Italy, 294 A3
Cirò Marina, Italy, 295 F6
Cisco, U.S.A., 424 C3
Cisna, Poland, 289 L4
Cisnădie, Romania, 296 E3
Cisneros, Colombia, 450 C2
Cistierna, Spain, 292 E1
Citaré, river, Brazil, 452 B3
Citlaltepetl, Volcán (Pico de Orizaba), mountain peak, Mexico, 431 F5, 400
Citron, French Guiana, 452 C2
Citronniers, Pointe, point, Mauritius, 373 C1
Citrusdal, South Africa, 370 C5
Città del Vaticano, Vatican City, 295 D5
Città di Castello, Italy, 294 D4
Cittadella, Italy, 294 C3
Cittanova, Italy, 295 F6
Ciucea, Romania, 296 D2
Ciudad Acuña, Mexico, 431 E2
Ciudad Altamirano, Mexico, 431 E5
Ciudad Bolívar, Venezuela, 451 F2
Ciudad Camargo, Mexico, 430 D3
Ciudad Constitución, Mexico, 430 C3
Ciudad Cortés, Costa Rica, 428 E5

Ciudad Cuauhtémoc, Mexico, **431** G6
Ciudad de Loreto, Argentina, **458** D3
Ciudad del Carmen, Mexico, **431** H5
Ciudad del Este, Paraguay, **459** F2
Ciudad Delicias, Mexico, **430** D2
Ciudad Guayana, Venezuela, **451** F2
Ciudad Guerrero, Mexico, **431** F3
Ciudad Guzmán, Mexico, **430** E5
Ciudad Juárez, Mexico, **430** D2
Ciudad Lerdo, Mexico, **430** E3
Ciudad Madero, Mexico, **431** F4
Ciudad Melchor de Mencos, Guatemala, **428** C3
Ciudad Mendoza, Mexico, **431** F5
Ciudad Obregón, Mexico, **430** C3
Ciudad Ojeda, Venezuela, **450** D1
Ciudad Piar, Venezuela, **451** F2
Ciudad Real, Spain, **293** F3
Ciudad Rodrigo, Spain, **292** D2
Ciudad Valles, Mexico, **431** F4
Ciudad Victoria, Mexico, **431** F4
Ciudada Mante, Mexico, **431** F4
Ciudadela, Islas Baleares, Spain, **293** J3
Civita Castellana, Italy, **295** D4
Civitanova Marche, Italy, **294** D4
Civitavecchia, Italy, **295** C4
Çivril, Turkey, **297** G6
Cixi, China, **206** E2
Cizre, Turkey, **224** F5
Clachan, Scotland, U.K., **308** C3
Clackmannan, Scotland, U.K., **308** F4
Clackmannanshire, *local authority*, Scotland, U.K., **308** F4
Clacton-on-Sea, England, U.K., **305** J3
Claerwen Reservoir, Wales, U.K., **304** D2
Claire, Lake, Canada, **413** N2
Clamecy, France, **291** F3
Clane, Ireland, **309** F4
Clanton, U.S.A., **425** J3
Clanwilliam, South Africa, **370** C5
Claonaig, Scotland, U.K., **308** D5
Clapham, England, U.K., **306** F3
Clara, Ireland, **309** E4
Clara City, U.S.A., **420** F3
Clare, *county*, Ireland, **309** C5
Clare, *river*, Ireland, **309** D4
Clare, U.S.A., **421** L4
Clare Island, Ireland, **309** B4
Clarecastle, Ireland, **309** D5
Claremont, U.S.A., **426** D3
Claremore, U.S.A., **424** E1
Claremorris, Ireland, **309** D4
Clarence, Isla, *island*, Chile, **460** C4
Clarence, New Zealand, **133** D6
Clarence, *river*, New Zealand, **133** D6
Clarence Bay, Ascension, **373** A3
Clarence Town, Bahamas, **429** G2
Clarendon, U.S.A., **424** B2
Clarenville, Canada, **417** P5
Claresholm, Canada, **413** N6
Clarinda, U.S.A., **420** F5
Clarion, U.S.A., **420** G4
Clarion Fracture Zone, *tectonic feature*, Pacific Ocean, **479** J3
Clark, U.S.A., **420** E3
Clarke Fork, *river*, U.S.A., **418** G3
Clarkia, U.S.A., **418** F3
Clarks Hill Lake, U.S.A., **425** L3
Clarksburg, U.S.A., **421** N6
Clarksdale, U.S.A., **424** G2
Clarkston, U.S.A., **418** F3
Clarksville, Arkansas, U.S.A., **424** F2
Clarksville, New Zealand, **133** B8
Clarksville, Tennessee, U.S.A., **425** J1
Clarksville, Texas, U.S.A., **424** E3
Clarno, U.S.A., **418** D4
Claro, *river*, N. Goiás, Brazil, **456** C4
Claro, *river*, S. Goiás, Brazil, **456** C5
Claromecó, Argentina, **459** E6
Clashmore, Ireland, **309** E5
Claude, U.S.A., **424** B2
Claudy, Northern Ireland, U.K., **309** E3
Claxton, U.S.A., **425** M3
Clay Center, U.S.A., **420** E6
Clay Cross, England, U.K., **305** F1
Clay Springs, U.S.A., **423** H4
Claydon, Canada, **413** Q7
Claydon, England, U.K., **305** J2
Claypool, U.S.A., **423** H5
Claysville, U.S.A., **421** L6
Clayton, Idaho, U.S.A., **418** G4
Clayton, New Mexico, U.S.A., **423** M3
Clear Island, Ireland, **309** C6
Clear Lake, California, U.S.A., **422** B2
Clear Lake, Iowa, U.S.A., **420** G4
Clear Water Bay, China, **207** C4
Clearlake, U.S.A., **422** B2
Clearwater, Canada, **412** J6
Clearwater, *river*, Canada, **413** P3
Clearwater, *river*, Idaho, U.S.A., **418** F3
Clearwater, *river*, Minnesota, U.S.A., **420** F2
Clearwater, U.S.A., **425** L6
Clearwater Lake, Canada, **414** D5
Clearwater Mountains, *mountain range*, U.S.A., **418** F3
Cleator Moor, England, U.K., **306** E3
Cleburne, U.S.A., **424** D3
Cleethorpes, England, U.K., **307** H4
Clemence Massif, *mountain peak*, Antarctica, **470** F5
Clément, French Guiana, **452** C2
Clementi, Singapore, **200** J7
Clemson, U.S.A., **425** L2
Cleobury Mortimer, England, U.K., **304** E2
Cleopatra Needle, *mountain peak*, Philippines, **204** B4
Cléres, France, **305** J5
Clermont, Australia, **135** K3
Clermont, France, **305** K5
Clermont-Ferrand, France, **291** F4
Clervaux, Luxembourg, **291** H1
Clevedon, England, U.K., **304** E3
Cleveland, Georgia, U.S.A., **425** L2
Cleveland, Mississippi, U.S.A., **424** G3
Cleveland, Ohio, U.S.A., **421** N5
Cleveland, Tennessee, U.S.A., **425** K2
Cleveland, Texas, U.S.A., **424** E4
Cleveland Hills, England, U.K., **307** G3
Clevelândia, Brazil, **459** G3
Clevelândia do Norte, Brazil, **452** C2
Cleveleys, England, U.K., **306** E4
Clew Bay, Ireland, **309** C4
Clewiston, U.S.A., **425** M6
Clifden, Ireland, **309** B4
Cliffdell, U.S.A., **418** D3
Cliffe, England, U.K., **305** H3
Cliffony, Ireland, **309** D3
Clifford Bay, New Zealand, **133** E5
Clifton, U.S.A., **423** J5
Clifton Forge, U.S.A., **421** P7
Climax, Canada, **413** Q7
Climax, Colorado, U.S.A., **423** K2
Climax, Minnesota, U.S.A., **420** E2
Cline, U.S.A., **424** B5
Clinton, British Columbia, Canada, **412** J6
Clinton, Iowa, U.S.A., **420** H5
Clinton, Massachusetts, U.S.A., **426** E3
Clinton, Mississippi, U.S.A., **424** G3
Clinton, Missouri, U.S.A., **420** G6
Clinton, Montana, U.S.A., **418** H3
Clinton, North Carolina, U.S.A., **425** N2
Clinton, Oklahoma, U.S.A., **424** C2
Clinton, Ontario, Canada, **421** N4
Clinton, South Carolina, U.S.A., **425** M2
Clipperton Fracture Zone, *tectonic feature*, Pacific Ocean, **479** J4
Clitheroe, England, U.K., **306** F4
Cliza, Bolivia, **455** F4
Clo-oose, Canada, **412** G7
Clogh, Northern Ireland, U.K., **309** F3
Clogheen, Ireland, **309** D5
Clogher Head, *point*, Ireland, **309** F4
Clonakilty, Ireland, **309** D6
Clonakilty Bay, Ireland, **309** D6
Clonbern, Ireland, **309** D4
Cloncurry, Australia, **135** J3
Clones, Ireland, **309** E3
Clonmel, Ireland, **309** E5
Clonroche, Ireland, **309** F5
Cloonbannin, Ireland, **309** C5
Cloppenburg, Germany, **288** D2
Cloquet, U.S.A., **420** G2
Cloridorme, Canada, **416** J5
Clorinda, Argentina, **459** F2
Cloud Peak, *mountain peak*, U.S.A., **419** L4
Clova, Scotland, U.K., **308** F4
Cloverdale, U.S.A., **422** B2
Clovis, U.S.A., **423** M4
Cluanie, Loch, *lake*, Scotland, U.K., **308** D3
Cluff Lake, Canada, **413** Q2
Cluj-Napoca, Romania, **296** D2
Clun, England, U.K., **304** D2
Cluny, France, **291** G3
Clutha, *river*, New Zealand, **133** B7
Clydach, Wales, U.K., **304** D3
Clyde, *river*, Scotland, U.K., **308** F5, *276*
Clyde Park, U.S.A., **419** J4
Clyde River, Canada, **411** N2
Clydebank, Scotland, U.K., **308** E5
Clydevale, New Zealand, **133** B8
Clyro, Wales, U.K., **304** D2
Cnoc Moy, Scotland, U.K., **308** D5
Coahuila, *state*, Mexico, **430** E3
Coal, *river*, Canada, **412** E1, F2
Coal River, Canada, **412** E1, F2
Coaldale, U.S.A., **422** E2
Coalgate, U.S.A., **424** D2
Coalinga, U.S.A., **422** C3
Coalville, England, U.K., **305** F2
Coari, Brazil, **451** F5
Coari, Lago de, *lake*, Brazil, **451** F5
Coari, *river*, Brazil, **451** F5
Coast, *province*, Kenya, **369** G3
Coast Mountains, *mountain range*, Canada, **412** C2, *381*
Coast Range, *mountain range*, U.S.A., **406** L5
Coatbridge, Scotland, U.K., **308** E5
Coats Island, Canada, **411** L3
Coats Land, *region*, Antarctica, **470** C4
Coatzacoalcos, Mexico, **431** G5
Cobadin, Romania, **296** G3
Cobán, Guatemala, **428** C4
Cobar, Australia, **135** K5
Cobequid Mountains, *mountain range*, Canada, **417** J7
Cobh, Ireland, **309** D6
Cobham, *river*, Canada, **414** G5
Cobija, Bolivia, **455** E3
Cobleskill, U.S.A., **426** C3
Cobourg Peninsula, Australia, **134** G1
Cobram, Australia, **135** K6
Cóbuè, Mozambique, **369** F5
Coburg, Germany, **288** E3
Coburg Island, Canada, **411** M2
Coca, Pizzo di, *mountain peak*, Italy, **294** B2
Cocachacra, Peru, **454** D4
Cocalinho, Brazil, **456** C4
Cochabamba, Bolivia, **455** E4
Cochabamba, *department*, Bolivia, **455** E4
Cochamó, Chile, **460** C1
Cochem, Germany, **288** C3
Cochin, Canada, **413** Q5
Cochin *see* Kochi, India, **216** D4, *77*
Cochise, U.S.A., **423** J5
Cochrane, Alberta, Canada, **413** M6
Cochrane, Chile, **460** C3
Cochrane, Ontario, Canada, **415** P7
Cockburn, Canal, *channel*, Chile, **460** C5
Cockburn, Cape, Australia, **199** F5
Cockburn Harbour, Turks and Caicos Islands, **429** H2
Cockburn Town, Bahamas, **428** G1
Cockburnspath, Scotland, U.K., **308** G5
Cockerham, England, U.K., **306** F4
Cockermouth, England, U.K., **306** E3
Coclé del Norte, Panama, **429** E5
Coco, Punta, *point*, Colombia, **450** B3
Coco, *river*, Honduras/ Nicaragua, **428** D4
Coco Channel, Andaman and Nicobar Islands, India, **217** H3
Cocorná, Colombia, **450** C2
Côcos, Brazil, **457** E4
Cocos Bay, Trinidad, Trinidad and Tobago, **461** C4
Cocos (Keeling) Islands, *Australian territory*, Indian Ocean, **134** Q10, *108, 112, 123, 124*
Cocos Ridge, *underwater feature*, Pacific Ocean, **479** N4
Cocula, Mexico, **430** E4
Cod, Cape, U.S.A., **426** E3
Cod Island, Canada, **411** N4
Codajás, Brazil, **451** F5
Coddington, England, U.K., **305** G1
Codera, Cabo, *cape*, Venezuela, **451** E1
Codfish Island, New Zealand, **133** A8
Codigoro, Italy, **294** D3
Codlea, Romania, **296** E3
Codó, Brazil, **453** E4
Codrington, Antigua and Barbuda, **427** D2, *396*
Codrington, Mount, *mountain peak*, Antarctica, **470** F4
Codsall, England, U.K., **304** E2
Cody, U.S.A., **419** K4
Coe, Glen, *valley*, Scotland, U.K., **308** D4
Coen, Australia, **135** J1
Coeroeni, *river*, Suriname, **452** B2
Coesfeld, Germany, **288** C3
Coetivy Island, Seychelles, **372** D2
Coeur d'Alene, U.S.A., **418** F3
Coeur d'Alene Lake, U.S.A., **418** F3
Coffee Bay, South Africa, **371** E5
Coffeeville, U.S.A., **425** H4
Coffeyville, U.S.A., **420** F7
Coffs Harbour, Australia, **135** L5
Cofrentes, Spain, **293** G3
Cogealac, Romania, **296** G3
Coggeshall, England, U.K., **305** H3
Cognac, France, **290** D4
Cogo, Equatorial Guinea, **368** A2
Cohagen, U.S.A., **419** L3
Coiba, Isla de, *island*, Panama, **429** E6
Coig, *river*, Argentina, **460** C4
Coigeach, Rubha, *point*, Scotland, U.K., **308** D2
Coihaique, Chile, **460** C2
Coimbatore, India, **216** D4
Coimbra, *district*, Portugal, **292** C2
Coimbra, Portugal, **292** C2
Coin, Spain, **292** E4
Coipasa, Lago de, *lake*, Bolivia, **455** E5
Coipasa, Salar de, *salt-pan*, Bolivia, **455** E5
Cojudo Blanco, Cerro, *mountain peak*, Argentina, **460** D3
Cojutepeque, El Salvador, **428** C4
Colac, Australia, **135** J6
Colac Bay, New Zealand, **133** A8
Colares, Brazil, **452** D3
Colatina, Brazil, **457** F5
Colby, U.S.A., **420** C6
Colchester, England, U.K., **305** J3
Cold Lake, Canada, **413** P4
Cold Lake, *lake*, Canada, **413** Q4
Cold Springs, U.S.A., **422** E2
Coldstream, Canada, **413** K6
Coldwater, Kansas, U.S.A., **420** D7
Coldwater, Michigan, U.S.A., **421** L5
Coldwater, Missouri, U.S.A., **420** H7
Colebrook, U.S.A., **426** E2
Coleford, England, U.K., **304** E3
Coleman, U.S.A., **424** C4
Çölemerik, Turkey, **224** F5
Colemon, U.S.A., **421** L4
Coleraine, *district*, Northern Ireland, U.K., **309** F2
Coleraine, Northern Ireland, U.K., **309** F2
Coleridge, Lake, New Zealand, **133** C6
Coles, Punta, *cape*, Peru, **454** D4
Colesberg, South Africa, **370** E5
Colfax, California, U.S.A., **422** C2
Colfax, Louisiana, U.S.A., **424** F4
Colfax, Washington, U.S.A., **418** F3
Colhué Huapi, Lago, *lake*, Argentina, **460** D2
Colico, Italy, **294** B2
Colima, Mexico, **430** E5
Colima, *state*, Mexico, **430** D5
Colinas, Brazil, **453** E5
Coll, *island*, Scotland, U.K., **308** C4
Collaguasi, Chile, **455** E5
College Station, U.S.A., **424** D4
Collie, Australia, **134** D5
Collier Bay, Australia, **134** E2
Collingwood, Canada, **421** N3
Collingwood, New Zealand, **133** D5
Collins, Iowa, U.S.A., **420** G5
Collins, Mississippi, U.S.A., **425** H4
Collipulli, Chile, **458** B5
Collooney, Ireland, **309** D3
Colmar, France, **291** H2
Colmonell, Scotland, U.K., **308** E5
Coln, *river*, England, U.K., **305** F3
Colne, England, U.K., **306** F4
Colne, *river*, England, U.K., **305** H3
Cologne *see* Köln, Germany, **305** C3
Colômbia, Brazil, **456** D5
Colombia, Colombia, **450** C3
Colombia, *country*, South America, **449** E3, *405, 434, 436*
Colombo, Sri Lanka, **216** D5, *166*
Colome, U.S.A., **420** D4
Colomiers, France, **290** E5
Colón, Buenos Aires, Argentina, **458** E4
Colón, Cuba, **429** E2
Colón, Entre Rios, Argentina, **459** E4
Colón, Panama, **429** F5
Colonel Hill, Bahamas, **429** G2
Colonia del Sacramento, Uruguay, **459** F5
Colonia Dora, Argentina, **458** D3
Colonia Josefa, Argentina, **460** E1

Colonia Lavalleja, Uruguay, **459** F4
Colonia Vicente Guerrero, Mexico, **430** A2
Colonsay, *island*, Scotland, U.K., **308** C4
Colorado, *river*, Argentina, **460** E1
Colorado, *river*, Brazil, **455** F3
Colorado, *river*, Mexico/U.S.A., **407** M5, *383, 385*
Colorado, *state*, U.S.A., **423** K2, *376, 383, 386*
Colorado City, Colorado, U.S.A., **422** G3
Colorado City, Texas, U.S.A., **424** B3
Colorado Desert, U.S.A., **422** E5
Colorado do Oeste, Brazil, **455** G3
Colorado Plateau, U.S.A., **423** H3
Colorado Springs, U.S.A., **423** L2
Colotlán, Mexico, **430** E4
Colquechaca, Bolivia, **455** E5
Colquiri, Bolivia, **455** E4
Colquitt, U.S.A., **425** K4
Colsterworth, England, U.K., **305** G2
Colstrip, U.S.A., **419** L4
Coltishall, England, U.K., **305** J2
Colton, U.S.A., **423** H2
Columbia, District of, *district*, U.S.A., **421** Q6
Columbia, Kentucky, U.S.A., **421** L7
Columbia, Louisiana, U.S.A., **424** F3
Columbia, Mississippi, U.S.A., **424** H4
Columbia, Missouri, U.S.A., **420** G6
Columbia, Mount, *mountain peak*, Canada, **413** L5
Columbia, North Carolina, U.S.A., **426** B7
Columbia, *river*, Canada/U.S.A., **406** L4, *376, 385*
Columbia, South Carolina, U.S.A., **425** M3, *386*
Columbia, Tennessee, U.S.A., **425** J2
Columbia Basin, U.S.A., **406** M4, *383*
Columbia City, U.S.A., **421** L5
Columbia Falls, U.S.A., **418** G2
Columbia Mountains, *mountain range*, Canada, **412** J5
Columbia Plateau, U.S.A., **418** E4
Columbiana, U.S.A., **425** J3
Columbine, Cape, South Africa, **370** C5
Columbus, Georgia, U.S.A., **425** K3
Columbus, Indiana, U.S.A., **421** L6
Columbus, Iowa, U.S.A., **421** J4
Columbus, Mississippi, U.S.A., **425** H3
Columbus, Nebraska, U.S.A., **420** E5
Columbus, New Mexico, U.S.A., **423** K6
Columbus, Ohio, U.S.A., **421** M6, *386*
Columbus, Texas, U.S.A., **424** D5
Columbus Point, Tobago, Trinidad and Tobago, **461** B4
Colville, Cape, New Zealand, **132** E3
Colville, *river*, U.S.A., **410** D3
Colville, U.S.A., **418** F2
Colville Lake, Canada, **410** G3
Colwyn Bay, Wales, U.K., **306** E4
Colyford, England, U.K., **304** D4
Comacchio, Italy, **294** D3
Comallo, *river*, Argentina, **460** C1
Coman, Mount, *mountain peak*, Antarctica, **470** B5
Comanche, Oklahoma, U.S.A., **424** D2
Comanche, Texas, U.S.A., **424** C4
Comandante Salas, Argentina, **458** C4
Comănești, Romania, **296** F2
Comarapa, Bolivia, **455** F4
Comarnic, Romania, **296** E3
Comas, Peru, **454** C3
Comayagua, Honduras, **428** D4
Combarbalá, Chile, **458** B4
Combe Martin, England, U.K., **304** C3
Comber, Northern Ireland, U.K., **309** G3
Combermere Bay, Myanmar, **205** B4
Comendador, Dominican Republic, **429** H3
Comeragh Mountains, *mountain range*, Ireland, **309** E5
Comfort, U.S.A., **424** C5
Comfort Bight, Canada, **417** P3
Comino, Capo, *cape*, Sardegna, Italy, **295** B5, *257*
Comitán de Domínguez, Mexico, **431** G5
Commanda, Canada, **421** P3
Commandante Luis Piedrabuena, Argentina, **460** D3
Commanders Bay, Aruba, Netherlands, **461** B3
Commerce, U.S.A., **424** E3
Committee Bay, Canada, **411** L3
Como, Italy, **294** B3
Como, Lago di, *lake*, Italy, **294** B3, *255*
Comodoro Rivadavia, Argentina, **460** D2
Comoé, *river*, Côte d'Ivoire, **364** D3
Comondú, Mexico, **430** C3
Comoros, *country*, Indian Ocean, **359** K8, *351, 352, 354*
Comox, Canada, **412** G7
Compiègne, France, **291** F2
Comprida, Ilha, *island*, Brazil, **459** H2
Comrat, Moldova, **296** G2
Comrie, Scotland, U.K., **308** F4
Côn So'n, Vietnam, **203** E4
Cona, China, **214** D4
Cona Niyeu, Argentina, **460** D1
Conakry, Guinea, **364** B3, *321*
Concarneau, France, **290** C3
Conceição, Brazil, **453** F5
Conceição da Barra, Brazil, **457** F5
Conceição do Araguaia, Brazil, **456** D2
Conceição do Coité, Brazil, **457** F3
Concepción, Argentina, **458** D3
Concepción, Beni, Bolivia, **455** E3
Concepción, Canal, *channel*, Chile, **460** B4
Concepción, Chile, **458** B5
Concepción, Paraguay, **459** F2
Concepción, Santa Cruz, Bolivia, **455** F4
Concepción del Uruguay, Argentina, **459** E4
Conception Bay, Canada, **417** Q6
Concession, Zimbabwe, **371** F2
Conchas, Brazil, **459** H2
Conches-en-Ouche, France, **290** E2
Conchi, Chile, **458** C2
Concho, U.S.A., **423** J4
Conchos, *river*, Mexico, **430** D3
Concord, California, U.S.A., **422** B3
Concord, New Hampshire, U.S.A., **426** E3, *386*
Concord, North Carolina, U.S.A., **425** M2
Concordia, Argentina, **459** E4
Concordia, Peru, **450** C5
Conde, Brazil, **457** G3
Condega, Nicaragua, **428** D4
Condeúba, Brazil, **457** F4
Condom, France, **290** E5
Condon, U.S.A., **418** D4
Cóndor, Cordillera del, *mountain range*, Peru/Ecuador, **450** B5
Conecuh, *river*, U.S.A., **425** J4
Conegliano, Italy, **294** D3
Conejos, Mexico, **430** E3
Confolens, France, **290** E3
Confuso, *river*, Paraguay, **459** E2
Cong, Ireland, **309** C4
Congaz, Moldova, **296** G2
Conghua, China, **207** B1
Congjiang, China, **206** B3
Congleton, England, U.K., **304** E1
Congo, *country*, Africa, **359** G6, *312, 330, 331, 333, 334, 335*
Congo, *river*, Congo, **357** G7, *92, 312, 331, 334, 335, 343*
Congo Basin, Africa, **357** G6, *88, 335*
Congress, U.S.A., **422** G4
Cónico, Cerro, *mountain peak*, Argentina, **460** C2
Coningsby, England, U.K., **307** H4
Coniston, England, U.K., **306** E3
Coniston Water, *lake*, England, U.K., **306** E3
Conklin, Canada, **413** P4
Conlara, Argentina, **458** D4
Conn, Lough, *lake*, Ireland, **309** C3
Connah's Quay, Wales, U.K., **304** D1
Connaught, *province*, Ireland, **309** C4
Conneaut, U.S.A., **421** N5
Connecticut, *river*, U.S.A., **426** D3
Connecticut, *state*, U.S.A., **426** D4, *386*
Connell, U.S.A., **418** E3
Connemara, *region*, Ireland, **309** C4
Conon Bridge, Scotland, U.K., **308** E3
Conroe, Lake, U.S.A., **424** E4
Conroe, U.S.A., **424** E4
Conselheiro Lafaiete, Brazil, **457** E5
Conselheiro Pena, Brazil, **457** F5
Consett, England, U.K., **307** G3
Consort, Canada, **413** P5
Constância dos Baetas, Brazil, **455** F2
Constanța, Romania, **296** G3
Constantine, Algeria, **361** H1
Consuegra, Spain, **293** F3
Consul, Canada, **413** Q7
Contact, U.S.A., **418** G6
Contagem, Brazil, **457** E5
Contamaná, Peru, **454** C2
Contas, de, *river*, Brazil, **457** F3
Contreras, Embalse de, *reservoir*, Spain, **293** G3
Contreras, Isla, *island*, Chile, **460** B4
Contres, France, **290** E3
Contrexéville, France, **291** G2
Contumazá, Peru, **454** B2
Contwoyto Lake, Canada, **410** H3
Conty, France, **305** K5
Conway, Arkansas, U.S.A., **424** F2
Conway, New Hampshire, U.S.A., **426** E3
Conway, South Carolina, U.S.A., **425** N3
Conwy, *unitary authority*, Wales, U.K., **304** D1
Conwy, Wales, U.K., **306** E4
Conwy Bay, Wales, U.K., **306** D4
Coober Pedy, Australia, **135** G4
Cook, Bahía, *bay*, Chile, **460** C5
Cook, Cape, Canada, **412** E6
Cook, Mount, *mountain peak*, Antarctica, **470** F4
Cook, Mount, *mountain peak*, New Zealand, **129** F6
Cook Islands, *New Zealand territory*, Pacific Ocean, **131** J3, *108, 110, 120, 121, 123*
Cook Strait, New Zealand, **133** E5, *110*
Cookeville, U.S.A., **425** K1
Cooking Lake, Canada, **413** N5
Cookstown, *district*, Northern Ireland, U.K., **309** F3
Cookstown, Northern Ireland, U.K., **309** F3
Cooktown, Australia, **135** K2
Coolangatta, Australia, **135** L4
Coolgardie, Australia, **134** E5
Coolidge, U.S.A., **423** H5
Cooma, Australia, **135** K6
Coon Rapids, U.S.A., **420** G3
Coonabarabran, Australia, **135** K5
Coonamble, Australia, **135** K5
Coondapoor, India, **216** C3
Coonoor, India, **216** D4
Cooper, *river*, Australia, **135** H4
Cooper's Town, Bahamas, **428** F1
Cooperstown, U.S.A., **420** D2
Coos Bay, U.S.A., **418** B5
Cootehill, Ireland, **309** E3
Copacabana, Argentina, **458** C3
Copahue, Volcán, *mountain peak*, Chile, **458** B5
Copala, Mexico, **431** F5
Cope, U.S.A., **423** M2
Copeland, U.S.A., **420** C7
Copemish, U.S.A., **421** L3
Copenhagen *see* København, Denmark, **286** F5, *232, 233*
Copere, Bolivia, **455** F5
Copiapó, Chile, **458** B3
Copiapó, *river*, Chile, **458** B3
Copiapó, Volcán, *mountain peak*, Chile, **458** C3
Copixaba, Brazil, **457** E3
Copper Harbor, U.S.A., **421** K2
Copperas Cove, U.S.A., **424** D4
Copperbelt, *province*, Zambia, **369** E5
Copplestone, England, U.K., **304** D4
Coqên, China, **214** C3
Coquille, U.S.A., **418** B5
Coquimbo, *administrative region*, Chile, **458** B4
Coquimbo, Chile, **458** B3
Corabia, Romania, **296** E4
Coração de Jesus, Brazil, **457** E4
Coracesium *see* Alanya, Turkey, **225** A1
Coracora, Peru, **454** D4
Coral, Cape, U.S.A., **425** M6
Coral Bay, Australia, **134** C3
Coral Gables, U.S.A., **425** M7
Coral Harbour, Canada, **411** L3
Coral Sea, Pacific Ocean, **135** K1, *124*
Coral Sea Basin, *underwater feature*, Pacific Ocean, **478** D5
Coral Sea Islands, *Australian territory*, Pacific Ocean, **135** L2, *112, 124*
Corantijn, *river*, Suriname, **452** B2
Corbett, Argentina, **458** E5
Corbie, France, **290** F2
Corbigny, France, **291** F3
Corbin, U.S.A., **421** L7
Corbridge, England, U.K., **306** F3
Corby, England, U.K., **305** G2
Corbyvale, New Zealand, **133** D5
Corcovado, Argentina, **460** C2
Corcovado, Golfo, *gulf*, Chile, **460** C2
Corcovado, Volcán, *mountain peak*, Chile, **460** C2
Cordele, U.S.A., **425** L4
Cordell, U.S.A., **424** C2
Cordes-sur-Ciel, France, **290** E4
Córdoba, Argentina, **458** D4, *443*
Córdoba, Cayo, *island*, San Andrés, Colombia, **461** B1
Córdoba, Durango, Mexico, **430** E3
Córdoba, *province*, Argentina, **458** D4
Córdoba, Sierras de, *mountain range*, Argentina, **447** F7
Córdoba, Spain, **292** E4, *93*
Córdoba, Veracruz, Mexico, **431** F5
Córdova, Peru, **454** C4
Cordova, U.S.A., **410** E3
Coreaú, Brazil, **453** F4
Corfe Castle, England, U.K., **304** E4
Corfu *see* Kerkyra, *island*, Ionioi Nisoi, Greece, **297** B6
Coria, Spain, **292** D2
Corigliano Calabro, Italy, **295** F6
Corinth, Kentucky, U.S.A., **421** L6
Corinth, Mississippi, U.S.A., **425** H2
Corinth *see* Korinthos, Greece, **297** D7, *89*
Corinthian Head, *point*, Heard and McDonald Islands, **134** S12
Corinto, Brazil, **457** E5
Corixa Grande, *river*, Bolivia/Brazil, **455** G4
Cork, *county*, Ireland, **309** C6
Cork, Ireland, **309** D6
Cork Harbour, Ireland, **309** D6
Corleone, Sicilia, Italy, **295** D7
Corleto Perticara, Italy, **295** F5
Çorlu, Turkey, **297** F5
Cormontibo, French Guiana, **452** B2
Cormorant Lake, Canada, **414** D4
Cornélio Procópio, Brazil, **459** G2
Corneliskondre, Suriname, **452** B2
Cornell, U.S.A., **420** H3
Corner Brook, Canada, **417** M5
Cornes, Pointe aux, *point*, Rodrigues, Mauritius, **373** B1
Cornești, Moldova, **296** F2
Corning, California, U.S.A., **422** B2
Corning, Iowa, U.S.A., **420** F5
Corning, New York, U.S.A., **426** B3
Cornudas, U.S.A., **423** L6
Cornwall, Canada, **416** D7
Cornwall, *unitary authority*, England, U.K., **304** C4
Coro, Venezuela, **451** E1
Coroatá, Brazil, **453** E4
Corocoro, Bolivia, **455** E4
Coroico, Bolivia, **455** E4
Coromandel, Brazil, **456** D5
Coromandel Range, *mountain range*, New Zealand, **132** E3
Coron, Philippines, **204** C3
Coron Island, Philippines, **204** C4
Corona, U.S.A., **423** L4
Coronach, Canada, **413** S7
Coronado, Bahía de, *bay*, Costa Rica, **428** D5
Coronation, Canada, **413** P5
Coronation Gulf, Canada, **410** H3
Coronda, Argentina, **458** E4
Coronel Dorrego, Argentina, **458** E6
Coronel Fabriciano, Brazil, **457** E5
Coronel Oviedo, Paraguay, **459** F2
Coronel Ponce, Brazil, **456** B4
Coronel Pringles, Argentina, **458** E5
Coronel Sapucaia, Brazil, **459** F2
Coronel Suárez, Argentina, **458** E5
Coronel Vidal, Argentina, **459** F5
Corongo, Peru, **454** C2
Coropuna, Nevado, *mountain peak*, Peru, **454** D4
Çorovodë, Albania, **297** C5
Corozal, Belize, **428** C3
Corozal Point, Trinidad, Trinidad and Tobago, **461** C4
Corpus Christi, U.S.A., **424** D6
Corque, Bolivia, **455** E5
Corral, U.S.A., **418** G5
Corralejo, Islas Canarias, Spain, **373** B4
Corrales, Spain, **292** E2
Corraun Peninsula, Ireland, **309** B4
Corrente, Brazil, **457** E3
Corrente, *river*, Bahia, Brazil, **457** E3
Corrente, *river*, Goías, Brazil, **456** C5
Correntes, Brazil, **456** B4
Correntina, Brazil, **457** E3
Corrib, Lough, *lake*, Ireland, **309** C4
Corrientes, Argentina, **459** E3
Corrientes, Cabo, *cape*, Argentina, **459** F6
Corrientes, Cabo, *cape*, Colombia, **450** C3
Corrientes, Cabo, *cape*, Cuba, **428** D2
Corrientes, Cabo, *cape*, Mexico, **430** D4
Corrientes, *province*, Argentina, **459** E3

Corrientes, *river*, Argentina, **459** E3
Corrigan, U.S.A., **424** E4
Corrigin, Australia, **134** D5
Corris, Wales, U.K., **304** D2
Corriverton, Guyana, **451** H3
Corrofin, Ireland, **309** C5
Corse, *administrative region*, France, **295** B4
Corse, Cap, *cape*, Corse, France, **294** B4
Corse (Corsica), *island*, France, **295** B4, *244, 245, 254*
Corsham, England, U.K., **304** E3
Corsica *see* Corse, *island*, France, **295** B4, *244, 245, 254*
Corsica, U.S.A., **420** D4
Corsicana, U.S.A., **424** D3
Corte, Corse, France, **295** B4
Cortegana, Spain, **292** D4
Cortez, U.S.A., **423** J3
Cortina d'Ampezzo, Italy, **294** D2
Cortland, U.S.A., **426** B3
Corton, England, U.K., **305** J2
Cortona, Italy, **294** D4
Coruche, Portugal, **292** C3
Çoruh Nehri, *river*, Turkey, **224** F4
Çorum, Turkey, **224** D4
Corumbá, Brazil, **456** B5
Corumbá, *river*, Brazil, **456** D4
Corund, Romania, **296** E2
Coruripe, Brazil, **457** G3
Corvallis, U.S.A., **418** C4
Corvette, Lac de la, *lake*, Canada, **416** D3
Corvo, *island*, Azores, Portugal, **360** L6
Corwen, Wales, U.K., **304** D2
Cosalá, Mexico, **430** D3
Cosapa, Bolivia, **455** E5
Coscaya, Chile, **455** E5
Cosenza, Italy, **295** F6
Coshocton, U.S.A., **421** N5
Cosigüina, Punta, *point*, Nicaragua, **428** C4
Cosmoledo Group, *islands*, Seychelles, **372** B2
Cosne-sur-Loire, France, **291** F3
Cosquín, Argentina, **458** D4
Costa Blanca, *coastal area*, Spain, **293** G3
Costa Brava, *coastal area*, Spain, **293** J2
Costa Daurada, *coastal area*, Spain, **293** H2
Costa de Cantabria, *coastal area*, Spain, **293** F1
Costa de la Luz, *coastal area*, Spain, **292** D4
Costa de Sol, *coastal area*, Spain, **292** E4
Costa del Azahar, *coastal area*, Spain, **293** H3
Costa Marques, Brazil, **455** F3
Costa Rica, *country*, Central America, **409** Q8, *378, 404, 405*
Costa Rica, Mexico, **430** D3
Costa Vasca, *coastal area*, Spain, **293** F1
Costa Verde, *coastal area*, Spain, **292** D1
Costelloe, Ireland, **309** C4
Costeşti, Moldova, **296** F2
Costeşti, Romania, **296** E3
Cotabato, Philippines, **204** D5
Cotagaita, Bolivia, **455** F5
Côte d'Azur, *coastal area*, France, **291** H5
Côte d'Ivoire, *country*, Africa, **358** E6, *312, 322, 323, 324, 325*
Côte d'Or, *region*, France, **291** G3
Coteau, U.S.A., **419** N2
Cotegipe, Brazil, **457** E3
Côtes de Meuse, *mountain range*, France, **291** G2
Coton, Pointe, *point*, Rodrigues, Mauritius, **373** B1
Cotonou, Benin, **365** E3, *327*
Cotopaxi, Volcán, *mountain peak*, Ecuador, **450** B4, *438*
Cotswold Hills, England, U.K., **305** F3, *276*
Cottage Grove, U.S.A., **418** C5
Cottbus, Germany, **289** G3
Cottenham, England, U.K., **305** H2
Cotter, U.S.A., **424** F1
Cottesmore, England, U.K., **305** G2
Cottica, Suriname, **452** B2
Cottonwood, Arizona, U.S.A., **423** G4
Cottonwood, South Dakota, U.S.A., **420** C4
Cotulla, U.S.A., **424** C5
Coubre, Pointe de la, *point*, France, **290** C4
Coudersport, U.S.A., **426** A4
Couëron, France, **290** D3
Cougar, U.S.A., **418** C6
Couiza, France, **290** F5
Coul Point, *point*, Scotland, U.K., **308** C5
Coulee, U.S.A., **420** C1
Coulee City, U.S.A., **418** E3
Coulmier-le-Sec, France, **291** G3
Coulogne, France, **290** E1
Coulonge, *river*, Canada, **416** C6
Council, U.S.A., **418** F4
Council Bluffs, U.S.A., **420** F5
Council Grove, U.S.A., **420** E6
Counselor, U.S.A., **423** K3
Coupar Angus, Scotland, U.K., **308** F4
Courantyne, *river*, Guyana, **451** G3
Courrejolles Point, Campbell Island, New Zealand, **132** K11
Courtenay, Canada, **412** G7
Courtmacsherry, Ireland, **309** D6
Courtown, Ireland, **309** F5
Coutances, France, **290** D2
Couto Magalhães, Brazil, **456** D2
Coutras, France, **290** D4
Coutts, Canada, **413** N7
Covadonga, Spain, **292** E1
Covasna, Romania, **296** F3
Cove Fort, U.S.A., **422** G2
Coventry, England, U.K., **305** F2
Covilhã, Portugal, **292** D2
Covington, Georgia, U.S.A., **425** L3
Covington, Kentucky, U.S.A., **421** L6
Covington, Michigan, U.S.A., **421** J2
Covington, Tennessee, U.S.A., **425** H2
Cowan, Canada, **414** D5
Cowan, Lake, Australia, **134** E5
Cowargarzê, China, **215** F2
Cowbridge, Wales, U.K., **304** D3
Cowdenbeath, Scotland, U.K., **308** F4
Cowdrey, U.S.A., **423** K1
Cowell, Australia, **135** H5
Cowfold, England, U.K., **305** G4
Cowra, Australia, **135** K5
Cox Lake, U.S.A., **424** D4
Coxim, Brazil, **456** B5
Cox's Bāzār, Bangladesh, **219** G5
Coxwold, England, U.K., **307** G3
Coyah, Guinea, **364** B3
Coyote, U.S.A., **423** K3
Coyotitán, Mexico, **430** D4
Cozad, U.S.A., **420** D5
Cozes, France, **290** D4
Cozhê, China, **214** C2
Cozie, Alpi, *mountain range*, Italy, **294** A3
Cozumel, Isla, *island*, Mexico, **431** J4
Cozumel, Mexico, **431** J4
Crab Island, Rodrigues, Mauritius, **373** B1
Cradock, South Africa, **370** E5
Craig, Alaska, U.S.A., **412** C4
Craig, Colorado, U.S.A., **423** K1
Craigavon, *district*, Northern Ireland, U.K., **309** F3
Craigavon, Northern Ireland, U.K., **309** F3
Craignure, Scotland, U.K., **308** D4
Crail, Scotland, U.K., **308** G4
Crailsheim, Germany, **288** E4
Craiova, Romania, **296** D3
Cramlington, England, U.K., **307** G2
Cranberry Portage, Canada, **414** D4
Cranbrook, Canada, **413** M7
Crandon, U.S.A., **421** J3
Crane, Oregon, U.S.A., **418** E5
Crane, Texas, U.S.A., **423** M6
Cranleigh, England, U.K., **305** G3
Cranston, U.S.A., **426** E4
Craon, France, **290** D3
Crary Mountains, *mountain range*, Antarctica, **470** B6
Crasnoe, Moldova, **296** G2
Crater Lake, U.S.A., **418** C5
Crater Point, Papua New Guinea, **140** D4
Crateús, Brazil, **453** F4
Crathorne, England, U.K., **307** G3
Crati, *river*, Italy, **295** F6
Crato, Brazil, **453** F5
Crauford, Cape, Canada, **411** L2
Craven Arms, England, U.K., **304** E2
Cravo Norte, Colombia, **451** D2
Crawford, U.S.A., **420** B4
Crawfordsville, U.S.A., **421** K5
Crawfordville, U.S.A., **425** K4
Crawley, England, U.K., **305** G3
Crécy-en-Ponthieu, France, **305** J4
Credenhill, England, U.K., **304** E2
Crediton, England, U.K., **304** D4
Cree, *river*, Canada, **413** S2
Cree Lake, Canada, **413** R3
Cree Lake, *lake*, Canada, **413** S3
Creede, U.S.A., **423** K3
Creel, Mexico, **430** D3
Creeslough, Ireland, **309** E2
Creil, France, **290** F2
Crema, Italy, **294** B3
Crémieu, France, **291** G4
Cremona, Italy, **294** B3
Crenshaw, U.S.A., **424** G2
Cres, *island*, Croatia, **294** E3
Crescent, U.S.A., **418** D5
Crescent City, U.S.A., **418** B6
Crescent Junction, U.S.A., **423** J2
Crescent Lake, U.S.A., **425** M5
Crescent Spur, Canada, **412** J5
Crespo, Argentina, **459** E4
Crest, France, **291** G4
Creston, Canada, **413** L7
Creston, Iowa, U.S.A., **420** F5
Creston, Montana, U.S.A., **418** G2
Crestview, U.S.A., **425** J4
Creswell, England, U.K., **305** F1
Crete *see* Kriti, *island*, Greece, **297** E8, *67, 88, 265*
Cretin, Cape, Papua New Guinea, **140** B4
Creus, Cabo de, *cape*, Spain, **293** J1
Creuse, *river*, France, **290** E3
Crèvecoeur-le-Grand, France, **305** K5
Crewe, England, U.K., **304** E1
Crewe, U.S.A., **426** A6
Crewkerne, England, U.K., **304** E4
Crianlarich, Scotland, U.K., **308** E4
Criccieth, Wales, U.K., **304** C2
Criciúma, Brazil, **459** H3
Crickhowell, Wales, U.K., **304** D3
Crieff, Scotland, U.K., **308** F4
Criel-sur-Mer, France, **305** J4
Crikvenica, Croatia, **294** E3
Crimean Peninsula *see* Kryms'kyy Pivostriv, *peninsula*, Ukraine, **298** D3, *269*
Criquetot-l'Esneval, France, **305** H5
Cristalândia, Brazil, **456** D3
Cristalina, Brazil, **456** D4
Cristalino, *river*, Mato Grosso, Brazil, **456** C3
Cristalino, *river*, Pará, Brazil, **456** B2
Cristino Castro, Brazil, **457** E2
Cristóbal, Punta, *point*, Islas Galápagos (Galapagos Islands), Ecuador, **461** A2
Cristóbal Colón, Pico, *mountain peak*, Colombia, **450** D1
Cristuru Secuiesc, Romania, **296** E2
Criuleni, Moldova, **296** G2
Crixás, Brazil, **456** D4
Crixás Açu, *river*, Brazil, **456** D3
Crna Gora, *mountain range*, Macedonia/Serbia, **296** C4
Crna Gora (Montenegro), *country*, Europe, **282** F7, *81, 97, 228, 259, 260, 261, 263*
Crni Vrh, *mountain peak*, Serbia, **296** D3
Črnomelj, Slovenia, **294** E3
Croatia, *country*, Europe, **282** F6, *81, 228, 254, 258, 259, 260, 261, 262*
Crockett, U.S.A., **424** E4
Crofton, U.S.A., **420** E4
Croisette, Cap, *cape*, France, **291** G5
Croix, Lac la, *lake*, Canada/U.S.A., **420** H1
Croker Island, Australia, **134** G1
Cromarty, Scotland, U.K., **308** E3
Crombach, Belgium, **288** B3
Cromer, England, U.K., **305** J2
Cromwell, New Zealand, **133** B7
Crook, England, U.K., **307** G3
Crook, U.S.A., **423** M1
Crooked Island, Bahamas, **429** G2
Crooked Island, China, **207** C4
Crooked River, Canada, **414** C5
Crookham, England, U.K., **306** F2
Crookhaven, Ireland, **309** C6
Crookston, U.S.A., **420** E2
Croom, Ireland, **309** D5
Crosby, U.S.A., **420** G2
Cross City, U.S.A., **425** L5
Cross Fell, *mountain peak*, England, U.K., **306** F3
Cross Inn, Wales, U.K., **304** C2
Cross Lake, Canada, **414** F4
Cross River, *state*, Nigeria, **365** F3
Crossett, U.S.A., **424** G3
Crossgar, Northern Ireland, U.K., **309** G3
Crossgates, Wales, U.K., **304** D2
Crosshaven, Ireland, **309** D6
Crossmaglen, Northern Ireland, U.K., **309** F3
Crossville, U.S.A., **425** K2
Croswell, U.S.A., **421** M4
Crotone, Italy, **295** F6
Crouch, *river*, England, U.K., **305** H3
Crow Agency, U.S.A., **419** L4
Crow Head, *point*, Ireland, **309** B6
Crowborough, England, U.K., **305** H3
Crowell, U.S.A., **424** C3
Crowheart, U.S.A., **419** K5
Crowland, England, U.K., **305** G2
Crowle, England, U.K., **307** H4
Crowley, U.S.A., **424** F4
Crowleys Ridge, *mountain range*, U.S.A., **424** G2
Crown Point, U.S.A., **421** K5
Crowsnest Pass, Canada, **413** M7
Croyde, England, U.K., **304** C3
Croydon, Australia, **135** J2
Croydon, England, U.K., **305** G3, *96*
Crozet, Îles, *islands*, French Southern and Antarctic Islands, **104** D13, *465, 469*
Crozet basin, *underwater feature*, Indian Ocean, **476** C7
Crozet Plateau, *underwater feature*, Indian Ocean, **476** C8
Cruachan, Ben, *mountain peak*, Scotland, U.K., **308** D4
Crucero, Peru, **455** D4
Cruillas, Mexico, **431** F3
Crumlin, Northern Ireland, U.K., **309** F3
Crummock Water, *lake*, England, U.K., **306** E3
Crusheen, Ireland, **309** D5
Cruz, Cabo, *cape*, Cuba, **429** F3
Cruz Alta, Brazil, **459** G3
Cruz del Eje, Argentina, **458** D4
Cruzeiro, Brazil, **457** E6
Cruzeiro do Sul, Brazil, **454** D2
Crvenka, Serbia, **296** B3
Crymmych Arms, Wales, U.K., **304** C3
Crystal, U.S.A., **420** E1
Crystal City, U.S.A., **424** C5
Crystal Falls, U.S.A., **421** J2
Csenger, Hungary, **289** L5
Csongrád, Hungary, **289** K5
Csorna, Hungary, **289** H5
Csurgó, Hungary, **289** H5
Cuadrada, Sierra, *mountain range*, Argentina, **460** D2
Cuamba, Mozambique, **369** G5
Cuando, *river*, Angola, **368** D6
Cuando Cubango, *province*, Angola, **368** C6
Cuangar, Angola, **370** C2
Cuango, Angola, **368** C4
Cuanza, *river*, Angola, **368** C4
Cuanza Norte, *province*, Angola, **368** B4
Cuanza Sul, *province*, Angola, **368** B5
Cuarto, *river*, Argentina, **458** D4
Cuatir, *river*, Angola, **368** C6
Cuatro Ciéngas, Mexico, **430** E3
Cuatro Ojos, Bolivia, **455** F4
Cuauhtémoc, Mexico, **430** D2
Cuautla Morelos, Mexico, **431** F5
Cuba, *country*, Caribbean Sea, **409** Q6, *92, 95, 97, 252, 253, 272, 335, 377, 378, 379, 388, 390, 392, 393, 394*
Cuba, U.S.A., **423** K3
Cubal, Angola, **368** B5
Cubango, *river*, Angola, **368** C6
Cubará, Colombia, **450** D2
Cuchi, Angola, **368** C5
Cuchillo-Có, Argentina, **458** D6
Cuckfield, England, U.K., **305** G3
Cucuí, Brazil, **451** E4
Cucumbi, Angola, **368** C5
Cúcuta, Colombia, **450** D2
Cuddalore, India, **216** D4
Cuddapah, India, **216** D3
Cudworth, Canada, **413** S5
Cuebe, *river*, Angola, **368** C6
Cuelei, *river*, Angola, **368** C5
Cuéllar, Spain, **292** E2
Cuemba, Angola, **368** C5
Cuenca, Ecuador, **450** B5
Cuenca, Serrania de, *mountain range*, Spain, **293** G2
Cuenca, Spain, **293** F2
Cuencamé, Mexico, **430** E3
Cuernavaca, Mexico, **431** F5
Cuero, U.S.A., **424** D5
Cuervo, U.S.A., **423** L4
Cueto, Cuba, **429** G2
Cugir, Romania, **296** D3
Cuglieri, Sardegna, Italy, **295** B5
Cuiaba, Brazil, **452** A5
Cuiabá, Brazil, **456** B4
Cuiabá de Larga, Brazil, **456** B4
Cuidado, Punta, *point*, Isla de Pascua (Easter Island), Chile, **461** B2
Cuihengcun, China, **207** A4
Cuilcagh, *mountain peak*, Ireland, **309** E3
Cuillin Hills, Scotland, U.K., **308** C3
Cuillin Sound, Scotland, U.K., **308** C3
Cuilo, Angola, **368** C4
Cuiluan, China, **211** K3
Cuimba, Angola, **368** B4
Cuio, Angola, **368** B5
Cuité, Brazil, **453** G5
Cuito, *river*, Angola, **368** C5
Cuito Cuanavale, Angola, **368** C6
Cuiuni, *river*, Brazil, **451** F4
Cujmir, Romania, **296** D3
Cukai, Malaysia, **200** C1
Cul Mor, *mountain peak*, Scotland, U.K., **308** D2
Culasi, Philippines, **204** C4
Culbertson, Montana, U.S.A., **419** M2

Culbertson, Nebraska, U.S.A., **420** C5
Culebra, Sierra de la, *mountain range*, Spain, **292** D2
Culebras, Peru, **454** B2
Culgoa, *river*, Australia, **135** K4
Culiacán, Mexico, **430** D3
Culiacancito, Mexico, **430** D3
Culion Island, Philippines, **204** B4
Cúllar Baza, Spain, **293** F4
Cullen, Scotland, U.K., **308** G3
Cullera, Spain, **293** G3
Cullivoe, Shetland, Scotland, U.K., **308** K7
Cullman, U.S.A., **425** J2
Cullompton, England, U.K., **304** D4
Çullu, Turkey, **363** H1
Cullybackey, Northern Ireland, U.K., **309** F3
Culmstock, England, U.K., **304** D4
Culpeper, U.S.A., **426** B5
Culpepper *see* Darwin, Isla, *island*, Islas Galápagos (Galapagos Islands), Ecuador, **461** A1
Culuene, *river*, Brazil, **456** C3
Cumaná, Venezuela, **451** F1
Cumare, Cerro, *mountain peak*, Colombia, **450** D4
Cumbal, Nevado de, *mountain peak*, Colombia, **450** C4
Cumberland, Bahía, *bay*, Róbinson Crusoe Island, Archipiélago Juan Fernández, Chile, **461** C2
Cumberland, *river*, U.S.A., **424** K1
Cumberland, U.S.A., **426** A6
Cumberland Bay, South Georgia, **461** A3
Cumberland House, Canada, **414** C5
Cumberland Island, U.S.A., **425** M4
Cumberland Lake, Canada, **414** C4
Cumberland Peninsula, Canada, **411** N3
Cumberland Plateau, U.S.A., **425** J3
Cumberland Sound, Canada, **411** N3
Cumbrian Mountains, *mountain range*, England, U.K., **306** E3, *276*
Cuminapanema, *river*, Brazil, **452** B3
Cummings, U.S.A., **422** B2
Cumpas, Mexico, **430** C2
Çumra, Turkey, **363** F1
Cumuripa, Mexico, **430** C2
Cunén, Guatemala, **428** C4
Cunene, *province*, Angola, **368** C6
Cunene, *river*, Angola, **368** B6
Cuneo, Italy, **294** A3
Cunnamulla, Australia, **135** K4
Cupar, Scotland, U.K., **308** F4
Cupcina, Moldova, **296** F1
Cupica, Colombia, **450** C2
Cupica, Golfo de, *gulf*, Colombia, **450** B2
Ćuprija, Serbia, **296** C4
Curaçá, Brazil, **457** F2
Curaçao, *island*, Netherlands Antilles, **461** C3, *391*
Curacautín, Chile, **458** B6
Curacó, *river*, Argentina, **458** D6
Curaray, *river*, Ecuador/Peru, **450** C4
Curaumilla, Punta, *point*, Chile, **458** B4
Curepipe, Mauritius, **373** C1
Curicó, Chile, **458** B5
Curicuriari, *river*, Brazil, **451** E4
Curieuse, *island*, Seychelles, **373** A2
Curimatá, Brazil, **457** E3
Curimataú, *river*, Brazil, **453** G5
Curitiba, Brazil, **459** H2
Curitibanos, Brazil, **459** G3
Curlew, U.S.A., **418** E2
Curoca, *river*, Angola, **368** B6
Currais Novos, Brazil, **453** G5
Curral Velho, Cape Verde, **360** Q8
Curralinho, Brazil, **452** D3
Currant, U.S.A., **422** F2
Currie, Australia, **135** J6
Currie, U.S.A., **422** F1
Currituck, U.S.A., **426** C6
Curtea de Argeş, Romania, **296** E3
Curtici, Romania, **296** C2
Curtis Island, Australia, **135** L3
Curtis Island, Kermadec Islands, New Zealand, **132** L12
Curuá, Amapá, *river*, Brazil, **452** B3
Curuá, Ilha, *island*, Brazil, **452** C3
Curuá, Pará, *river*, Brazil, **452** B5
Curuá Una, *river*, Brazil, **452** B4
Curuaés, *river*, Brazil, **452** B5
Curuçá, Brazil, **452** D3
Curuçá, *river*, Brazil, **450** D5
Curumu, Brazil, **452** C3
Curupira, Serra, *mountain range*, Brazil/Venezuela, **451** F4
Cururu, Brazil, **456** B2
Cururu, *river*, Brazil, **452** B5
Cururupu, Brazil, **453** E3
Curuzú Cuatiá, Argentina, **459** E3
Curvelo, Brazil, **457** E5
Cushendall, Northern Ireland, U.K., **309** F2
Cushendun, Northern Ireland, U.K., **309** F2
Cushing, Mount, *mountain peak*, Canada, **412** F3
Cushing, U.S.A., **424** D2
Cusseta, U.S.A., **425** K3
Custer, Montana, U.S.A., **419** L3
Custer, South Dakota, U.S.A., **420** B4
Cut Bank, U.S.A., **418** H2
Cut Knife, Canada, **413** Q5
Cutato, *river*, Angola, **368** C5
Cutler Ridge, U.S.A., **425** M7
Cutra, Lough, *lake*, Ireland, **309** D4
Cutral-Có, Argentina, **458** C6
Cuttack, India, **219** F5
Cuvelai, Angola, **368** C6
Cuveşdia, Romania, **296** C3
Cuvette, *administrative region*, Congo, **368** C3
Cuxhaven, Germany, **288** D2
Cuya, Chile, **455** D5
Cuyabeno, Ecuador, **450** C4
Cuyo Islands, Philippines, **204** C4
Cuyuni, *river*, Guyana, **451** G2
Cuza Vodă, Romania, **296** F3
Cuzco, Peru, **454** D3
Čvrsnica, *mountain peak*, Bosnia and Herzegovina, **294** F4
Cwmbran, Wales, U.K., **304** D3
Cyangugu, Rwanda, **369** E3
Cyclades *see* Kyklades, *islands*, Greece, **297** E7
Cynthia, Canada, **413** M5
Cynwyl Elfed, Wales, U.K., **304** C3
Cypress Hills, Canada, **419** J2
Cyprus, *country*, Asia, **196** E6, *97, 146, 147, 191, 192, 229, 245, 265*
Czaplinek, Poland, **289** H2
Czar, Canada, **413** P5
Czarnków, Poland, **289** H2
Czech Republic, *country*, Europe, **282** F6, *81, 228, 229, 238, 245, 248, 249, 266, 267*
Czersk, Poland, **289** H2
Częstochowa, Poland, **289** J3
Człopa, Poland, **289** H2
Człuchów, Poland, **289** H2
Czyżew-Osada, Poland, **289** L2


## D


Đà, *river*, Vietnam, **203** E1, *154*
Da Hinggan Ling, *mountain range*, China, **211** G3
Da Juh, China, **213** G5
Đà Lạt, Vietnam, **203** F4
Đà Nẵng, Vietnam, **203** F2, *153*
Da Qaidam, China, **213** G5
Da Xian, China, **215** H3
Da'an, China, **211** J3
Daanbantayan, Philippines, **204** C4
Daba Shan, *mountain range*, China, **206** B1
Ḑab'ah, Jordan, **225** C4
Dabajuro, Venezuela, **451** D1
Dabakala, Côte d'Ivoire, **364** D3
Dabas, Hungary, **289** J5
Dabat, Ethiopia, **367** E2
Dabatou, Guinea, **364** B2
Dabbāgh, Jabal, *mountain peak*, Saudi Arabia, **225** C6
Dabeiba, Colombia, **450** C2
Daborow, Somalia, **367** G3
Dabou, Côte d'Ivoire, **364** D3
Dabra, India, **218** D4
Dąbrowa Górnicza, Poland, **289** J3
Dăbuleni, Romania, **296** E4
Dacca *see* Dhaka, Bangladesh, **214** D5, *170*
Dachang, China, **215** H4
Dachau, Germany, **288** E4
Dacre, New Zealand, **133** B8
Dadale, Solomon Islands, **141** A1
Dadanawa, Guyana, **451** G3
Dade City, U.S.A., **425** L5
Dādhar, Pakistan, **218** A3
Dadi, Tanjong, *point*, Indonesia, **199** E3
Dadiangas *see* General Santos, Philippines, **204** D5
Dādra and Nagar Haveli, *union territory*, India, **218** C6, *169*
Dādri, *river*, India, **218** D4
Dādu, Pakistan, **218** A4
Dăeni, Romania, **296** G3
Daet, Philippines, **204** C3
Dafang, China, **215** H4
Dafdaf, Jabal, *mountain peak*, Saudi Arabia, **225** C5
Dafeng, China, **206** E1
Dafla Hills, India, **214** E4
Daga Medo, Ethiopia, **367** F3
Dagali, Norway, **286** D2
Dagana, Senegal, **364** A1
Dagang, China, **207** A3
Dagda, Latvia, **287** N4
Dagestan, Respublika, *republic*, Russian Federation, **222** D4
Daglung, China, **214** D3
Dagu, China, **210** G5
Dagua, Papua New Guinea, **140** A3
Daguan, China, **215** G4
Dagupan, Philippines, **204** C2
Dagur, China, **213** G5
Dagzê, China, **214** D3
Dagzhuka, China, **214** D3
Dahlak Archipelago, *islands*, Eritrea, **367** F1
Dahlenburg, Germany, **288** E2
Dahme, Germany, **288** F3
Dāhod, India, **218** C5
Dahongliutan, China, **218** D1
Dahūk, Iraq, **363** H1
Dai Xian, China, **210** F5
Dai Yue Shan (Lantau Island), *island*, China, **207** B4
Dailekh, Nepal, **219** E3
Daimiel, Spain, **293** F3
Dainkog, China, **215** F2
Daiqin Tal, China, **211** H3
Daireaux, Argentina, **458** E5
Dairyland, U.S.A., **420** G2
Daiyun Shan, *mountain range*, China, **206** D3
Dājal, Pakistan, **218** B3
Dajiang, *river*, China, **207** C3
Đak Pé, Vietnam, **203** E3
Dakar, Senegal, **364** A2, *318, 319, 320*
Dakhlet Nouâdhibou, *administrative region*, Mauritania, **360** C4
Daki Takwas, Nigeria, **365** F2
Dakingari, Nigeria, **365** E2
Dako, Gunung, *mountain peak*, Indonesia, **198** C2
Dākor, India, **218** C5
Dakoro, Niger, **365** F2
Đakovica, Kosovo, **296** C4
Đakovo, Croatia, **294** G3
Dala, Angola, **368** D5
Dalaba, Guinea, **364** B2
Dalaguete, Philippines, **204** C4
Dalai Nur, China, **210** G4
Dalakhay, Russian Federation, **213** J2
Ḑalal, Jabal, *mountain peak*, Egypt, **225** B5
Dalaman, Turkey, **297** G7
Dalan, China, **207** D2
Dalandzadgad, Mongolia, **210** D4
Dalang, China, **207** B3
Dalap-Uliga-Darrit, Marshall Islands, **139** F4, *119*
Dalay, Mongolia, **213** J4
Dālbandin, Pakistan, **221** H3
Dalbeattie, Scotland, U.K., **308** F6
Dalby, Australia, **135** L4
Dale, Norway, **286** B2
Dale, U.S.A., **418** E4
Dale Hollow Lake, U.S.A., **425** K1
Dalen, Norway, **286** D3
Daletme, Myanmar, **205** B3
Dalfors, Sweden, **286** G2
Dalhart, U.S.A., **423** M3
Dalhousie, Canada, **416** H5
Dali, China, **205** D2
Dali, Shaanxi, China, **206** B1
Dali, Yunnan, China, **215** G4
Dalian, China, **211** H5
Daliang, China, **213** J5
Dalías, Spain, **293** F4
Dalin, China, **211** H4
Daliuhao, China, **210** F4
Dalkeith, Scotland, U.K., **308** F5
Dallas, U.S.A., **424** D3
Dalmacija, *region*, Croatia, **294** E3
Dalmacio Vélez Sarsfield, Argentina, **458** D4
Dalmally, Scotland, U.K., **308** E4
Dalmellington, Scotland, U.K., **308** E5
Dal'negorsk, Russian Federation, **301** Q5
Dal'nerechensk, Russian Federation, **211** L3
Dal'noye, Kazakhstan, **222** H2
Daloa, Côte d'Ivoire, **364** C3
Dalqū, Sudan, **363** F4
Dalrymple, Lake, Australia, **135** K3
Dalrymple, Scotland, U.K., **308** E5
Dalsbruk, Finland, **287** L2
Dalston, England, U.K., **306** F3
Dāltenganj, India, **214** C4
Dalton, Canada, **421** L1
Dalton, Georgia, U.S.A., **425** K2
Dalton, Nebraska, U.S.A., **420** B5
Dalton-in-Furness, England, U.K., **306** E3
Dalvík, Iceland, **284** Y7
Dalwhinnie, Scotland, U.K., **308** E4
Daly, *river*, Australia, **134** G1
Daly Bay, Canada, **411** L3
Daly Waters, Australia, **134** G2
Dam, *river*, China, **214** E2
Đầm Hà, Vietnam, **203** E1
Damān, India, **218** C5
Daman and Diu, *union territory*, India, **218**, B5, *169*
Damanhūr, Egypt, **363** F2
Damar, Kepulauan, *islands*, Indonesia, **199** E4
Damara, Central African Republic, **368** C2
Damasak, Nigeria, **365** G2
Damascus *see* Dimashq, Syria, **225** D3, *74, 181*
Damaturu, Nigeria, **365** G2
Damāvand, Qolleh-ye, *mountain peak*, Iran, **222** E5
Damba, Angola, **368** C4
Dambatta, Nigeria, **365** F2
Damboa, Nigeria, **365** G2
Dame-Marie, Haiti, **429** G3
Dāmghān, Iran, **222** E5
Dămieneşti, Romania, **296** F2
Damietta *see* Dumyāţ, Egypt, **225** A4
Daming, China, **210** F5
Damoh, India, **218** D5
Damongo, Ghana, **364** D3
Dampelas, Tanjong, *point*, Indonesia, **198** B2
Dampier, Australia, **134** D3
Dampier, Selat, *strait*, Indonesia, **199** E3
Damqawt, Yemen, **220** F5
Damxoi, China, **214** D3
Damxung, China, **214** D3
Dan-Gulbi, Nigeria, **365** F2
Dan Oever, Netherlands, **288** B2
Dan Xian, China, **203** F2
Ḑanā, Jordan, **225** C4
Danakil Depression, Ethiopia, **367** F2
Danakil Desert, Ethiopia, **367** F2, *337, 338*
Danané, Côte d'Ivoire, **364** C3
Dananhu, China, **213** G4
Danao, Philippines, **204** D4
Dānāpur, India, **219** F4
Danba, China, **215** G3
Danby Lake, U.S.A., **422** F4
Dand, Afghanistan, **218** A3
Dande, Ethiopia, **369** G2
Dandeli, India, **216** C3
Dandong, China, **211** J4
Daneborg, Greenland, **411** T2
Daneti, Romania, **296** E4
Danfeng, China, **206** B1
Dang, *river*, China, **213** G5
Dangan Dao, *island*, China, **207** C4
Dangan Liedao, *islands*, China, **207** C4
Dangchang, China, **215** H2
Dange, Angola, **368** C4
Dange, Nigeria, **365** F2
Danger Point, South Africa, **370** C5
Danghe Nanshan, *mountain range*, China, **213** G5
Dangila, Ethiopia, **367** E2
Dângrek, Chuŏr Phnum, *mountain range*, Cambodia/Thailand, **203** D3
Dangriga, Belize, **428** C3
Dangshan, China, **206** D1
Dangtu, China, **206** D2
Dangur, Ethiopia, **366** E2
Daniel, U.S.A., **419** J5
Daniel's Harbour, Canada, **417** N4
Danilovgrad, Montenegro, **296** B4
Daning, China, **210** E5
Danjiangkou, China, **206** B1
Dänkojaure, *lake*, Sweden, **284** G4
Dankov, Russian Federation, **299** G6
Dankova, Pik, *mountain peak*, Kyrgyzstan, **212** C4
Danlí, Honduras, **428** D4
Dannenberg (Elbe), Germany, **288** E2
Dano, Burkina Faso, **364** D2
Dañoso, Cabo, *cape*, Argentina, **460** D3
Danot, Ethiopia, **367** G3
Danshui, China, **207** C3
Dansville, U.S.A., **426** B3
Danube, *river*, Europe, **288** E4; *see also* Donau, *river*, Austria, **289** F4; Donau, *river*, Germany, **288** E4; Duna, *river*, Hungary, **289** J5; Dunărea, *river*, Romania, **296** D4, *64, 228, 259, 261, 262, 263, 264, 267*
Danubyu, Myanmar, **205** B4
Danville, Illinois, U.S.A., **421** J5
Danville, Kentucky, U.S.A., **421** L7
Danville, Virginia, U.S.A., **421** P7
Dao Xian, China, **206** B3
Daojiao, China, **207** B2
Daotanghe, China, **213** J5
Daoukro, Côte d'Ivoire, **364** D3
Daozhen, China, **215** H3
Dapa, Philippines, **204** D4
Dapaong, Togo, **364** E2
Dapitan, Philippines, **204** C4
Dāpoli, India, **216** C2
Dapp, Canada, **413** N4
Daqing, China, **211** J3
Daquan, China, **213** G4
Daquanwan, China, **213** G4
Dar es Salaam, Tanzania, **369** G4,
Dar'ā, *district*, Syria, **225** D3
Dara, Senegal, **364** A1
Dar'ā, Syria, **225** D3
Dārāb, Iran, **221** F3
Darabani, Romania, **296** F1
Darasun, Russian Federation, **210** F2
Đaravica, *mountain peak*, Kosovo, **296** C4, *261*
Darāw, Egypt, **363** F4
Darazo, Nigeria, **365** G2

Darbhanga, India, **219** F4
Darby, U.S.A., **418** G3
D'Arcy, Cape, Antarctica, **470** G7
Darende, Turkey, **224** E5
Darfo Boario Terme, Italy, **291** K4
Dārfūr, *physical feature,* Sudan, **366** B2, *336*
Dargaville, New Zealand, **132** D2
Darhan, Bulgan, Mongolia, **213** J2
Darhan, Selenge, Mongolia, **210** D2
Darhan Muminggan Lianheqi, China, **210** E4
Darién, Golfo del, *gulf,* Colombia, **450** C2
Darién, Serrania del, *mountain range,* Panama, **450** B2
Darien, U.S.A., **425** M4
Darío, Nicaragua, **428** D4
Darīya, Kazakhstan, **223** J3
Darjiling, India, **219** G4
Darlag, China, **215** F2
Darling, *river,* Australia, **135** J5, *112*
Darling Range, *mountain range,* Australia, **128** A4
Darlingford, Canada, **414** E7
Darlington, England, U.K., **307** G3, *275*
Darlington, *unitary authority,* England, U.K., **307** G3
Darłowo, Poland, **289** H1
Dărmăneşti, Romania, **296** F2
Darmstadt, Germany, **288** D4
Darnah, Libya, **362** D2
Darnley, Cape, Antarctica, **470** G4
Daroca, Spain, **293** G2
Darregueira, Argentina, **458** D5
Darsah, *island,* Suquṭrá (Socotra), Yemen, **373** B2
Darsi, India, **216** D3
Dart, *river,* England, U.K., **304** D4
Dartang, China, **214** E3
Dartford, England, U.K., **305** H3
Dartmeet, England, U.K., **304** D4
Dartmoor, *moorland,* England, U.K., **304** C4
Dartmouth, Canada, **417** K7
Dartmouth, England, U.K., **304** D4
Darton, England, U.K., **307** G4
Dartuch, Cabo, *cape,* Islas Baleares, Spain, **293** J3
Daru, Papua New Guinea, **140** A5
Daru, Sierra Leone, **364** B3
Daruvar, Croatia, **294** F3
Darvaza, Turkmenistan, **222** F4
Darvel, Teluk, *bay,* Malaysia, **201** G1
Darvi, Mongolia, **213** G3
Darwāzahgēy, Afghanistan, **218** A3
Darwen, England, U.K., **306** F4
Dārwha, India, **218** D5
Darwin, Australia, **134** G1, *97, 112, 113*
Darwin, Bahía, *bay,* Chile, **460** B2
Darwin, Falkland Islands, **460** F4
Darwin, Isla (Culpepper), *island,* Islas Galápagos (Galapagos Islands), Ecuador, **461** A1
Darwin, Monte, *mountain peak,* Chile, **460** D5
Darwin, Volcán, *mountain peak,* Islas Galápagos (Galapagos Islands), Ecuador, **461** A1
Darya Khān, Pakistan, **218** B3
Dārzīn, Iran, **221** G3
Dasāda, India, **218** B5
Dashbalbar, Mongolia, **210** F2
Dashhowuz, Turkmenistan, **222** F4
Dashi, China, **207** A2
Dashitou, Jilin, China, **211** K4
Dashitou, Xinjiang Uygur Zizhiqu, China, **213** F4
Dashizhai, China, **211** H3
Dasht, *river,* Pakistan, **221** H3
Dashuijing, China, **215** G4
Dashuikeng, China, **207** D3
Dasu, Pakistan, **218** C2
Datang, China, **206** B3
Datça, Turkey, **297** F7
Date, Japan, **209** H2
Dateland, U.S.A., **422** G5
Datia, India, **218** D4
Datian, China, **206** D3
Datil, U.S.A., **423** K4
Datong, Qinghai, China, **213** J5
Datong, *river,* China, **213** J5
Datong, Shanxi, China, **210** F4
Datu, Tanjong, *point,* Malaysia, **201** E2
Datu, Teluk, *bay,* Malaysia, **201** E2
Datuk, Tanjong, *point,* Indonesia, **200** C2
Dauban, Mont, *mountain peak,* Seychelles, **373** A2
Daudnagar, India, **219** F4
Daugai, Lithuania, **287** M5
Daugava, *river,* Latvia, **287** M4
Daugavpils, Latvia, **287** N5
Daule, Indonesia, **198** C4
Daun, Gunung, *mountain peak,* Indonesia, **200** C3
Daund, India, **216** C2
Dauphin, Canada, **414** D6
Dauphin Island, U.S.A., **425** H4
Dauphin Lake, Canada, **414** E6
Daura, Nigeria, **365** F2
Dausa, India, **218** D4
Dava, Scotland, U.K., **308** F3
Dāvangere, India, **216** C3
Davao, Philippines, **204** D5
Davao Gulf, Philippines, **204** D5
Dāvarzan, Iran, **222** F5
Davenport, Iowa, U.S.A., **420** H5
Davenport, Washington, U.S.A., **418** F3
Daventry, England, U.K., **305** F2
David, Panama, **429** E5
Davidson, Canada, **413** R6
Davis, *Australian research station,* Antarctica, **470** G5
Davis, Mount, *mountain peak,* U.S.A., **421** P6
Davis, U.S.A., **422** C2
Davis Creek, U.S.A., **418** D6
Davis Inlet, Canada, **417** L2
Davis Mountains, *mountain range,* U.S.A., **423** M6
Davis Sea, Antarctica, **470** G5
Davis Strait, Canada/Greenland, **411** P3, *466*
Davlekanovo, Russian Federation, **222** F2
Davos, Switzerland, **291** J3
Davy Lake, Canada, **413** Q2
Dawa, *river,* Ethiopia, **369** G2
Dawanshan Dao, *island,* China, **207** B5
Dawei *see* Tavoy, Myanmar, **202** C3
Dawhinava, Belarus, **287** N5
Dawkah, Oman, **221** F5
Dawlish, England, U.K., **304** D4
Dawn, U.S.A., **424** A2
Dawros Head, *point,* Ireland, **309** D3
Dawson, Canada, **410** F3
Dawson, Georgia, U.S.A., **425** K4
Dawson, Minnesota, U.S.A., **420** E3
Dawson, North Dakota, U.S.A., **420** D2
Dawson Creek, Canada, **412** J4
Dawson Falls, New Zealand, **132** E4
Dawson Inlet, Canada, **414** H1
Dawu, China, **205** D1
Dawu, Hubei, China, **206** C2
Dawu, Sichuan, China, **215** G3
Dawusi, China, **213** F5
Dawwah, Oman, **221** G4
Dax, France, **290** D5
Daxatar, China, **210** E4
Daxin, China, **215** H5
Daxing, China, **210** G5
Daxinggou, China, **211** K4
Daxue Shan, *mountain range,* China, **215** G3
Daya Wan, *bay,* China, **207** D3
Dayangshu, China, **211** J2
Dayao, China, **215** G4
Dayi, China, **215** G3
Daym Zubayr, Sudan, **366** C3
Daymán, Cuchilla del, *mountain range,* Uruguay, **459** F4
Dayong, China, **207** A4
Dayr 'Aṭīyah, Syria, **225** D2
Dayr az Zawr, Syria, **363** H1
Dayr Ḥāfir, Syria, **225** D1
Dayrūṭ, Egypt, **363** F3
Daysland, Canada, **413** N5
Dayton, Ohio, U.S.A., **421** L6, *97*
Dayton, Tennessee, U.S.A., **425** K2
Dayton, Washington, U.S.A., **418** F3
Dayton, Wyoming, U.S.A., **419** L4
Daytona Beach, U.S.A., **425** M5
Dayu, China, **206** C3
Dayville, U.S.A., **418** E4
Dazhou, China, **215** H3
De Aar, South Africa, **370** D5
De Funiak Springs, U.S.A., **425** J4
De Goeje Gebergte, *mountain peak,* Suriname, **452** B2
De Jongs, Tanjong, *point,* Indonesia, **199** G4
De Kalb, Illinois, U.S.A., **421** J5
De Kalb, Texas, U.S.A., **424** E3
De Panne, Belgium, **305** K3
De Pere, U.S.A., **421** J3
De Queen, U.S.A., **424** E2
De Tour Village, U.S.A., **421** M3
De Winton, Canada, **413** M6
De Witt, U.S.A., **420** H5
Dead Indian Peak, *mountain peak,* U.S.A., **419** K4
Dead Sea, *lake,* Israel/Jordan, **225** C4, *179, 180*
Deadhorse, U.S.A., **410** E2
Deadman Bay, U.S.A., **425** L5
Deadman Butte, *mountain peak,* U.S.A., **419** L5
Deal, England, U.K., **305** J3
Dealul Bălăneşti, *mountain peak,* Moldova, **296** G2
Deán Funes, Argentina, **458** D4
Dearborn, U.S.A., **421** M4
Dearg, Beinn, *mountain peak,* Highland, Scotland, U.K., **308** E3
Dearg, Beinn, *mountain peak,* Perth and Kinross, Scotland, U.K., **308** F4
Deary, U.S.A., **418** F3
Dease, *river,* Canada, **412** E2
Dease Lake, Canada, **412** E2
Death Valley, U.S.A., **422** E3, *376*
Deba, Spain, **293** F1
Debak, Malaysia, **201** E2
Debar, Macedonia, **297** C5
Debark', Ethiopia, **367** E2
Debden, Canada, **413** R5
Deben, *river,* England, U.K., **305** J2
Debenham, England, U.K., **305** J2
Debesy, Russian Federation, **222** E1
Dębica, Poland, **289** K3
Dęblin, Poland, **289** K3
Dębno, Poland, **289** G2
Debrc, Serbia, **296** B3
Debre Birhan, Ethiopia, **367** E3
Debre Mark'os, Ethiopia, **367** E2
Debre Sīna, Ethiopia, **367** E3
Debre Tabor, Ethiopia, **367** E2
Debre Werk', Ethiopia, **367** E2
Debre Zeyit, Ethiopia, **367** E3
Debrecen, Hungary, **289** K5
Debrzno, Poland, **289** H2
Dečani, Kosovo, **296** C4
Decatur, Alabama, U.S.A., **425** J2
Decatur, Illinois, U.S.A., **421** J6
Decatur, Indiana, U.S.A., **421** L5
Decatur, Texas, U.S.A., **424** D3
Decazeville, France, **290** F4
Deccan, *plateau,* India, **194** J8, *144, 168*
Dechu, India, **218** C4
Decize, France, **291** F3
Decorah, U.S.A., **420** H4
Deddington, England, U.K., **305** F3
Deder, Ethiopia, **367** F3
Dediāpāda, India, **218** C5
Dedo de Deus, *mountain peak,* Brazil, **459** H2
Dédougou, Burkina Faso, **364** D2
Dedovichi, Russian Federation, **299** B4
Dedza, Malawi, **369** F5
Dee, *river,* England, U.K., **306** E4
Dee, *river,* Scotland, U.K., **308** F3
Deel, *river,* Ireland, **309** D5
Deep River, Canada, **416** C6
Deep Valley Bay, St Helena, **373** B3
Deer, *island,* New Caledonia, **136** C3
Deer Lake, Newfoundland, Canada, **417** N5
Deer Lake, Ontario, Canada, **414** G5
Deer Lodge, U.S.A., **418** H3
Deer Park, U.S.A., **418** F3
Deer Peak, *mountain peak,* U.S.A., **418** F4
Defiance, U.S.A., **421** L5
Dêgê, China, **215** F3
Degeberga, Sweden, **286** G5
Degeh Bur, Ethiopia, **367** F3
Degelis, Canada, **416** G6
Degema, Nigeria, **365** F4
Degerfors, Sweden, **286** G3
Deh Bīd, Iran, **220** F2
Deh Shū, Afghanistan, **221** H2
Dehiwala-Mount Lavinia, Sri Lanka, **216** D5
Dehlorān, Iran, **363** J2
Dehra Dūn, India, **218** D3
Dehri, India, **219** F4
Dehua, China, **206** D3
Dehui, China, **211** J3
Dej, Romania, **296** D2
Deje, Sweden, **286** F3
Dejen, Ethiopia, **367** E2
Dejiang, China, **206** B2
Dek'emhāre, Eritrea, **367** E1
Dekese, Democratic Republic of the Congo, **368** D3
Dekina, Nigeria, **365** F3
Dékoa, Central African Republic, **366** A3
Del Norte, U.S.A., **423** K3
Del Rio, U.S.A., **424** B5
Delano, U.S.A., **422** D4
Delano Peak, *mountain peak,* U.S.A., **422** G2
Delārām, Afghanistan, **221** H2
Delareyville, South Africa, **370** E4
Delavan, U.S.A., **421** J4
Delaware, *river,* U.S.A., **426** C4
Delaware, *state,* U.S.A., **426** C5, *384, 386*
Delaware, U.S.A., **421** M5
Delaware Bay, U.S.A., **426** C5
Delčevo, Macedonia, **296** D5
Deleau, Canada, **414** D7
Delémont, Switzerland, **291** H3
Délép, Chad, **366** A2
Delft, Netherlands, **288** B2, *241*
Delfzijl, Netherlands, **288** C2
Delgado, Cabo, *cape,* Mozambique, **369** H5
Delgermörön, Mongolia, **213** H3
Delger Mörön, *river,* Mongolia, **213** H2
Delhi, India, **218** D3, *169*
Delhi, *union territory,* India, **218** D3, *169*
Delhi, U.S.A., **423** M3
Délices, French Guiana, **452** C2
Deliceto, Italy, **295** E5
Delījān, Iran, **220** F2
Déline, Canada, **410** G3
Delingha, China, **213** H5
Delisle, Canada, **413** R6
Delitzsch, Germany, **288** F3
Dellys, Algeria, **361** G1
Delmenhorst, Germany, **288** D2
Delnice, Croatia, **294** E3
Deloraine, Canada, **414** D7
Delray Beach, U.S.A., **425** M6
Delsbo, Sweden, **286** H2
Delta, Colorado, U.S.A., **423** J2
Delta, Iowa, U.S.A., **420** G5
Delta, *state,* Nigeria, **365** F3
Delta, Utah, U.S.A., **422** G2
Delta Beach, Canada, **414** E6
Delta Junction, U.S.A., **410** E3
Deltona, U.S.A., **425** M5
Delvāda, India, **218** B5
Delvin, Ireland, **309** E4
Delvinë, Albania, **297** C6
Delyatyn, Ukraine, **296** E1
Demba, Democratic Republic of the Congo, **368** D4
Dembech'a, Ethiopia, **367** E2
Dembī Dolo, Ethiopia, **366** D3
Dembia, Central African Republic, **368** D1
Demerara Plain, *underwater feature,* Atlantic Ocean, **477** D5
Demidov, Russian Federation, **299** C5
Deming, U.S.A., **423** K5
Demini, *river,* Brazil, **451** F4
Demirci, Turkey, **297** G6
Demirköprü Barajı, *dam,* Turkey, **297** G6
Demirköy, Turkey, **296** F5
Demmin, Germany, **288** F2
Democratic Republic of the Congo, *country,* Africa, **359** G7, *92, 245, 312, 313, 331, 334, 335, 343, 347*
Demopolis, U.S.A., **425** J3
Dempo, Gunung, *mountain peak,* Indonesia, **200** C3
Demta, Indonesia, **199** H3
Demyansk, Russian Federation, **299** D4
Den Chai, Thailand, **202** D2
Den Helder, Netherlands, **288** B2
Denan, Ethiopia, **367** F3
Denbigh, Canada, **416** C7
Denbigh, Wales, U.K., **304** D1
Denbighshire, Wales, U.K., **304** D1
Dendang, Indonesia, **201** D3
Dendâra, Mauritania, **364** C1
Dengfeng, China, **206** C1
Dengi, Nigeria, **365** F3
Dengkou, China, **210** D4
Dêngqên, China, **215** E3
Dengyoufang, China, **210** F4
Dengzhou, China, **206** C1
Denham, Australia, **134** C4
Denia, Spain, **293** H3
Denio Junction, U.S.A., **418** E6
Denison, Iowa, U.S.A., **420** F4
Denison, Texas, U.S.A., **424** D3
Denizli, *province,* Turkey, **297** G7
Denizli, Turkey, **297** G7
Denmark, Australia, **134** D5
Denmark, *country,* Europe, **282** E4, *75, 228, 231, 232, 233, 234, 238, 245, 274, 278, 387, 388, 389, 475*
Denmark, U.S.A., **425** M3
Denmark Strait, Greenland/Iceland, **411** S3
Dennehotso, U.S.A., **423** J3
Denny, Scotland, U.K., **308** F4
Denow, Uzbekistan, **222** H5
Denpasar, Indonesia, **201** F5
Dent Island, Auckland Islands, New Zealand, **132** K11
Denton, U.S.A., **424** D3
d'Entrecasteaux, Point, Australia, **128** A5
D'Entrecasteaux Islands, Papua New Guinea, **140** C5
Denver, U.S.A., **423** L2, *386*
Denver City, U.S.A., **423** M5
Deoghar, India, **219** F4
Deolāli, India, **218** C6
Deoli, India, **218** D5
Deorī Khās, India, **218** D5
Deoria, India, **219** E4
Deosil, India, **219** E5
Dep, *river,* Russian Federation, **211** K1
Depapre, Indonesia, **199** H3

Depot Peak, *mountain peak*, Antarctica, **470** F4
Deputatskiy, Russian Federation, **301** Q3
Dêqên, China, **215** F3
Deqing, Guangdong, China, **206** B4
Deqing, Zhejiang, China, **206** E2
DeQuincy, U.S.A., **424** F4
Der-Chantecoq, Lac du, *lake*, France, **291** G2
Dera Bugti, Pakistan, **218** B3
Dera Ghāzi Khān, Pakistan, **218** B3
Dera Ismāīl Khān, Pakistan, **218** B3
Derbent, Russian Federation, **222** D4
Derbent, Turkey, **297** G6
Derbent, Uzbekistan, **222** H5
Derbissaka, Central African Republic, **368** D1
Derbur, China, **211** H2
Derby, Australia, **134** E2
Derby, England, U.K., **305** F2
Derby City, *unitary authority*, England, U.K., **305** F2
Derbyshire, *unitary authority*, England, U.K., **305** F1, *274, 276*
Déréssa, Chad, **366** B2
Derg, Lough, *lake*, Clare/Galway, Ireland, **309** D5
Derg, Lough, *lake*, Donegal, Ireland, **309** D3
Derg, *river*, Northern Ireland, U.K., **309** E3
Dergachi, Russian Federation, **222** D2
DeRidder, U.S.A., **424** F4
Dermott, U.S.A., **424** B3
Dernberg, Cape, Namibia, **370** B4
Dêrong, China, **215** F3
Déroute, Passage de la, *strait*, Channel Islands/France, **290** C2
Derre, Mozambique, **369** G6
Derri, Somalia, **367** G4
Derry, U.S.A., **426** E3
Derryveagh Mountains, Ireland, **309** D3
Dersingham, England, U.K., **305** H2
Derst, China, **210** F4
Derudeb, Sudan, **363** G5
Derval, France, **290** D3
Derventa, Bosnia and Herzegovina, **294** F3
Derwent, Canada, **413** P5
Derwent, *river*, England, U.K., **307** H4
Derwent Reservoir, England, U.K., **306** F3
Derwent Water, *lake*, England, U.K., **306** E3
Derzhavīnsk, Kazakhstan, **222** H2
Des Lacs, U.S.A., **420** C1
Des Moines, Iowa, U.S.A., **420** G5, *386*
Des Moines, New Mexico, U.S.A., **423** M3
Des Moines, *river*, U.S.A., **420** G5
Des Monts, Pointe, Canada, **416** H5
Desaguadero, Peru, **455** E4
Desaguadero, *river*, Argentina, **458** C4
Desaguadero, *river*, Bolivia, **455** E4
Descabezado Grande, Volcán, *mountain peak*, Chile, **458** B5
Descartes, France, **290** E3
Deschambault Lake, Canada, **414** C4
Deschutes, *river*, U.S.A., **418** D4
Desē, Ethiopia, **367** E2
Deseado, *river*, Argentina, **460** D3
Desengaño, Punta, *point*, Argentina, **460** D3
Desert Center, U.S.A., **422** F5
Desert Peak, *mountain peak*, U.S.A., **422** G1
Deserta Grande, *island*, Madeira, Portugal, **373** C3
Desertas, Ilhas, *islands*, Madeira, Portugal, **373** C3, *355*
Deshnoke, India, **218** C4
Desiderio Tello, Argentina, **458** C4
Deskati, Greece, **297** C6
Desmaraisville, Canada, **416** D5
Desmochado, Paraguay, **459** E3
Desna, *river*, Russian Federation/Ukraine, **298** D2
Desolación, Isla, *island*, Chile, **460** B4
Desolation Point, Philippines, **204** D4
Despotovac, Serbia, **296** C3
Dessau, Germany, **288** F3
Destoya Peak, *mountain peak*, U.S.A., **422** E2
Desvres, France, **305** J4
Deta, Romania, **296** C3
Dete, Zimbabwe, **371** E2
Detmold, Germany, **288** D3
Detour, Point, U.S.A., **421** K3
Detroit, Michigan, U.S.A., **421** M4
Detroit, Texas, U.S.A., **424** E3
Detroit Lakes, U.S.A., **420** F2
Deutsche Bucht, *bay*, Germany, **288** C1
Deva, Romania, **296** D3
Develi, Turkey, **363** G1
Devgarh, India, **218** C4
Devīkot, India, **218** B4
Devil River Peak, *mountain peak*, New Zealand, **133** D5
Devils Lake, *lake*, U.S.A., **420** D2
Devils Lake, U.S.A., **420** D1
Devilsbit Mountain, *mountain peak*, Ireland, **309** E5
Devin, Bulgaria, **297** E5
Devli, India, **218** C4
Devnya, Bulgaria, **296** F4
Devon, *unitary authority*, England, U.K., **304** D4
Devon, U.S.A., **419** J2
Devon Island, Canada, **411** K2
Devonport, Australia, **135** K7
Dewa, Tanjong, *point*, Indonesia, **200** A2
Dewās, India, **218** D5
Dewsbury, England, U.K., **307** G4
Dexter, Maine, U.S.A., **426** F2
Dexter, Missouri, U.S.A., **420** J7
Deyang, China, **215** H3
Deyhūk, Iran, **221** G2
Deyyer, Iran, **220** F3
Dezfūl, Iran, **220** E2
Dezhou, China, **210** G5
Dhahab, Egypt, **225** C5
Dhahabān, Saudi Arabia, **363** G4
Dhahran *see* Az̧ Z̧ahrān, Saudi Arabia, **220** E3
Dhaka (Dacca), Bangladesh, **214** D5, *170*
Dhaka, *division*, Bangladesh, **214** D4
Dhali, Cyprus, **225** B2
Dhamār, Yemen, **220** D6
Dhamtari, India, **219** E5
Dhānāna, India, **218** B4
Dhanbād, India, **219** F5
Dhandhuka, India, **218** B5
Dharampur, India, **218** C5
Dharmjaygarh, India, **219** E5
Dhārwād, India, **216** C3
Dhasa, India, **218** B5
Dhaulagiri, *mountain peak*, Nepal, **219** E3
Dhībān, Jordan, **225** C4
Dhrāngadhra, India, **218** B5
Dhrol, India, **218** B5
Dhubāb, Yemen, **220** D6
Dhuburi, India, **219** G4
Dhule, India, **218** C5
Dhūma, India, **218** D5
Dhuudo, Raas, *point*, Somalia, **367** H3
Dhuudo, Somalia, **367** H3
Dhuusamarreeb, Somalia, **367** G3
Di Linh, Vietnam, **203** F4
Dia, *island*, Greece, **297** E8
Diable, Pointe du, *point*, Rodrigues, Mauritius, **373** B1
Diablo Range, *mountain range*, U.S.A., **422** C3
Diablotin, Morne, *mountain peak*, Dominica, **427** D3, *396*
Diaca, Mozambique, **369** H5
Diafarabé, Mali, **364** C2
Dialafara, Mali, **364** B2
Dialakoto, Senegal, **364** B2
Diamante, Argentina, **458** E4
Diamante, *river*, Argentina, **458** C5
Diamantina, Brazil, **457** E5
Diamantina, Chapada, *mountain range*, Brazil, **457** E3
Diamantina, *river*, Australia, **135** J3
Diamantina Fracture Zone, *tectonic feature*, Indian Ocean, **476** F7
Diamantino, Brazil, **456** B4
Diamond Harbour, India, **219** G5
Diamond Head, *point*, Hawaiian Islands, U.S.A., **422** R9
Diamond Islands, Coral Sea Islands, **135** L2
Diamond Lake, U.S.A., **418** C5
Diamounguel, Senegal, **364** B1
Diana's Peak, *mountain peak*, St Helena, **373** B3
Dianbai, China, **206** B4
Diandioumé, Mali, **364** C1
Dianjiang, China, **215** H3
Dianópolis, Brazil, **456** D3
Dianra, Côte d'Ivoire, **364** C3
Diapaga, Burkina Faso, **365** E2
Diaz Point, Namibia, **370** B4
Dibaya, Democratic Republic of the Congo, **368** D4
Dibaya-Lubwe, Democratic Republic of the Congo, **368** C3
Dibrugarh, India, **219** H4
Dibs, Sudan, **366** B2
Dibsī Faraj, Syria, **225** E2
Dick, Mount, *mountain peak*, New Zealand, **132** J10
Dickens, U.S.A., **424** B3
Dickinson, U.S.A., **420** B2
Dickson, U.S.A., **425** J1
Dicle (Tigris), *river*, Turkey, **224** F5
Didcot, England, U.K., **305** F3
Didiéni, Mali, **364** C2
Didsbury, Canada, **413** M6
Dīdwāna, India, **218** C4
Didy, Madagascar, **372** B4
Didymoteicho, Greece, **297** F5
Die, France, **291** G4
Diébougou, Burkina Faso, **364** D2
Diecke, Guinea, **364** C3
Diefenbaker, Lake, Canada, **413** R6
Diego de Almagro, Chile, **458** B3
Diego de Almagro, Isla, *island*, Chile, **460** B4
Diéma, Mali, **364** C2
Diembéreng, Senegal, **364** A2
Dienvidsusēja, *river*, Latvia, **287** M4
Diepholz, Germany, **288** D2
Dieppe, France, **290** E2
Dietrich, U.S.A., **418** G5
Dieuze, France, **291** H2
Dif, Kenya, **367** F4
Diffa, *department*, Niger, **365** G1
Diffa, Niger, **365** G2
Digba, Democratic Republic of the Congo, **369** E2
Digby, Canada, **416** J7
Digermulen, Norway, **284** G2
Dīglūr, India, **216** D2
Digne-les-Bains, France, **291** H4
Digoin, France, **291** F3
Digos, Philippines, **204** D5
Digri, Pakistan, **218** B4
Digue, La, *island*, Seychelles, **373** A2
Digul, *river*, Indonesia, **199** G4
Diinsoor, Somalia, **369** H2
Dijlah (Tigris), *river*, Iraq, **363** J2
Dijon, France, **291** G3
Dikanäs, Sweden, **284** H4
Dikhil, Djibouti, **367** F2
Dikili, Turkey, **297** F6
Dikimdya, Russian Federation, **301** P4
Dikirnis, Egypt, **225** A4
Dikodougou, Côte d'Ivoire, **364** C3
Diksmuide, Belgium, **288** A3
Dikwa, Nigeria, **365** G2
Dīla, Ethiopia, **367** E3
Dili, Democratic Republic of the Congo, **369** E2
Dili, East Timor, **198** D5, *148, 149*
Dilley, U.S.A., **424** C5
Dilling, Sudan, **366** C2
Dillingen an der Donau, Germany, **288** E4
Dillingham, U.S.A., **410** D4
Dillon, Montana, U.S.A., **418** H4
Dillon, South Carolina, U.S.A., **425** N2
Dilolo, Democratic Republic of the Congo, **368** D5
Dimāpur, India, **219** H4
Dimashq, *district*, Syria, **225** D3
Dimashq (Damascus), Syria, **225** D3, *74, 181*
Dimbelenge, Democratic Republic of the Congo, **368** D4
Dimbokro, Côte d'Ivoire, **364** D3
Dimitrovgrad, Bulgaria, **296** E4
Dimitrovgrad, Russian Federation, **222** D2
Dimitrovgrad, Serbia, **296** D4
Dīmona, Israel, **225** C4
Dinagat Island, Philippines, **204** D4
Dinājpur, Bangladesh, **219** G4
Dinan, France, **290** C2
Dinant, Belgium, **288** B3
Dinar, Turkey, **297** H6
Dinara, *mountain peak*, Croatia, **294** F3, *259*
Dinara, *mountain range*, Croatia, **294** F4
Dinard, France, **290** C2
Dinde, Angola, **368** B5
Dinder, *river*, Ethiopia/Sudan, **366** D2
Dindigul, India, **216** D4
Dindima, Nigeria, **365** G2
Dindori, India, **219** E5
Dinga, Democratic Republic of the Congo, **368** C4
Dinga, N. Pakistan, **218** C2
Dinga, S. Pakistan, **218** A4
Dingalan Bay, Philippines, **204** C3
Dingbian, China, **210** D5
Dinge, Angola, **368** B4
Dinggyê, China, **214** C3
Dingle, Ireland, **309** B5
Dingle Bay, Ireland, **309** B6
Dingnan, China, **206** C3
Dingtao, China, **206** C1
Dinguiraye, Guinea, **364** B2
Dingwall, Scotland, U.K., **308** E3
Dingxi, China, **215** H2
Dingxing, China, **210** F5
Dingyuan, China, **206** D1
Dingzhou, China, **210** F5
Dingzikou, China, **213** G5
Dīnhāta, India, **219** G4
Dinorwic, Canada, **414** H7
Dioïla, Mali, **364** C2
Diou, France, **291** F3
Diouloulou, Senegal, **364** A2
Dioumara, Mali, **364** C2
Dioundiou, Niger, **365** E2
Diourbel, Senegal, **364** A2
Diphu, India, **219** H4
Diplo, Pakistan, **218** B4
Dipolog, Philippines, **204** C4
Dīr, Pakistan, **218** B2
Diré, Mali, **364** D1
Dirē Dawa, Ethiopia, **367** F3
Direction, Cape, Australia, **135** J1
Direction Island, Cocos (Keeling) Islands, **134** Q10
Dirico, Angola, **370** D2
Dirj, Libya, **362** B2
Dirk Hartog Island, Australia, **134** C4
Dirkou, Niger, **362** B5
Dirranbandi, Australia, **135** K4
Ḍirs, Saudi Arabia, **363** H5
Dīsa, India, **218** C4
Disappointment, Cape, South Georgia, **461** A3
Disappointment, Cape, U.S.A., **418** B3
Disappointment, Lake, Australia, **134** E3
Disappointment Island, Auckland Islands, New Zealand, **132** J10
Discovery Bay, Australia, **135** H6
Disko *see* Qeqertarsuaq, *island*, Greenland, **411** P2
Disley, Canada, **413** S6
Dispur, India, **219** G4, *169*
Diss, England, U.K., **305** J2
Distington, England, U.K., **306** E3
Distrito Federal, *federal district*, Brazil, **456** D4
Distrito Federal, *federal district*, Mexico, **431** F5
Ditrău, Romania, **296** E2
Dittaino, *river*, Sicilia, Italy, **295** E7
Diu, India, **218** B5
Diuta Point, Philippines, **204** D4
Dīvān Derrah, Iran, **222** D5
Divénié, Congo, **368** B3
Divielva, *river*, Norway/Sweden, **284** J2
Divinhe, Mozambique, **371** F3
Divinópolis, Brazil, **457** E5
Divnogorsk, Russian Federation, **223** N1
Divo, Côte d'Ivoire, **364** C3
Divriği, Turkey, **363** G1
Dixie, U.S.A., **418** G4
Dixmont, U.S.A., **426** F2
Dixon, California, U.S.A., **422** C2
Dixon, Illinois, U.S.A., **421** J5
Dixon, Montana, U.S.A., **418** G3
Dixon Entrance, *channel*, Canada/U.S.A., **412** C4
Dixons Mills, U.S.A., **425** J3
Dixonville, Canada, **413** L3
Diyarbakır, Turkey, **224** F5
Dja, *river*, Cameroon, **368** B2
Djado, Niger, **362** B4
Djado, Plateau du, *plateau*, Niger, **362** B4
Djamaa, Algeria, **361** H2
Djambala, Congo, **368** B3
Djampie, Democratic Republic of the Congo, **368** C3
Djanet, Algeria, **362** A4
Djébrène, Chad, **366** A2
Djédaa, Chad, **366** A2
Djelfa, Algeria, **361** G2
Djéma, Central African Republic, **369** E1
Djenné, Mali, **364** D2
Djibo, Burkina Faso, **364** D2
Djibouti, *country*, Africa, **196** F8, *337, 338, 339*
Djibouti, Djibouti, **367** F2, *338, 339*
Djiguéni, Mauritania, **364** C1
Djoemoe, Suriname, **452** B2
Djohong, Cameroon, **365** G3
Djolu, Democratic Republic of the Congo, **368** D2
Djougou, Benin, **365** E3
Djoum, Cameroon, **368** B2
Djoumboli, Cameroon, **365** G3
Djourab, Erg du, *desert*, Chad, **362** C5
Djúpivogur, Iceland, **284** Z7
Djupvik, Norway, **284** K2
Djurås, Sweden, **286** G2
Dmitriyevka, Kazakhstan, **222** H2
Dmitriyevskoye, Russian Federation, **299** G4
Dmitrov, Russian Federation, **299** F4
Dnepr, *river*, Russian Federation, **299** C5, *269, 273*
Dnestrovsc, Moldova, **296** G2
Dnipropetrovs'k, Ukraine, **298** E3
Dnistr, *river*, Moldova/Ukraine, **298** C3, *270*
Dnistrovs'kyy Lyman, *lake*, Ukraine, **296** H2
Dno, Russian Federation, **299** C4
Do Gonbardān, Iran, **220** F2
Đô Lương, Vietnam, **203** E2
Do Rūd, Iran, **220** E2
Doaktown, Canada, **416** H6
Đoan Hùng, Vietnam, **203** E1
Doany, Madagascar, **372** B3
Doba, Chad, **365** H3, *328*
Dobbiaco, Italy, **294** D2
Dobbs, Cape, Canada, **411** L3
Dobele, Latvia, **287** L4
Döbeln, Germany, **288** F3
Doberai, Jazirah, *peninsula*, Indonesia, **195** Q10
Döbern, Germany, **289** G3
Dobiegniew, Poland, **289** G2
Dobo, Indonesia, **199** F4
Doboj, Bosnia and Herzegovina, **294** G3
Dobre Miasto, Poland, **289** K2
Dobrich, Bulgaria, **296** F4
Dobro Polje, Bosnia and Herzegovina, **294** G4

Dobrodzień, Poland, **289** J3
Dobrovăţ, Romania, **296** F2
Dobrovelychkivka, Ukraine, **296** H1
Dobrovol'sk, Russian Federation, **287** L5
Dobruchi, Russian Federation, **299** A3
Dobzha, China, **214** D3
Doce, *river*, Brazil, **457** F5
Docking, England, U.K., **305** H2
Doctor Arroyo, Mexico, **431** E4
Doda, India, **218** C2
Dodecanese *see* Dodekanisos, *islands*, Greece, **297** F7
Dodekanisos (Dodecanese), *islands*, Greece, **297** F7
Dodge City, U.S.A., **420** C7
Dodgeville, U.S.A., **420** H4
Dodman Point, England, U.K., **304** C4
Dodoma, *administrative region*, Tanzania, **369** G4
Dodoma, Tanzania, **369** G4, *341*
Dodson, U.S.A., **419** K2
Doetinchem, Netherlands, **288** C3
Dog Creek, Canada, **412** H6
Dog Island, U.S.A., **425** K5
Dog Lake, Canada, **415** K7
Dogai Coring, *lake*, China, **214** D2
Doğanbey, Aydin, Turkey, **297** F7
Doğanbey, İzmir, Turkey, **297** F6
Dōgo, *island*, Japan, **208** F3
Dogondoutchi, Niger, **365** E2
Dogoumbo, Chad, **365** H2
Doğu Menteşe Dağları, *mountain range*, Turkey, **297** G7
Doğubayazıt, Turkey, **224** F5
Do'gyaling, China, **214** D3
Doha *see* Ad Dawḥah, Qatar, **220** F3, *177, 178*
Dohazar, Bangladesh, **219** H5
Doilungdêqên, China, **214** D3
Dokka, Norway, **286** E2
Dokshytsy, Belarus, **287** N5
Dolak, Pulau, *island*, Indonesia, **199** G4
Dolavón, Argentina, **460** E2
Dolbeau, Canada, **416** E5
Dolbenmaen, Wales, U.K., **304** C2
Dolce, Cape, U.S.A., **426** C5
Doldrums Fracture Zone, *tectonic feature*, Atlantic Ocean, **477** D5
Dole, France, **291** G3
Dolgellau, Wales, U.K., **304** D2
Dolianova, Sardegna, Italy, **295** B6
Dolit, Indonesia, **198** D3
Doljevac, Serbia, **296** C4
Dolný Kubín, Slovakia, **289** J4
Dolo Odo, Ethiopia, **369** H2
Dolomiti, *mountain range*, Italy, **294** C2
Doloon, Mongolia, **210** D3
Dolores, Argentina, **459** F5
Dolores, Guatemala, **428** C3
Dolores, Uruguay, **459** E4
Dolphin, Cape, Falkland Islands, **460** F4
Dolphin and Union Strait, Canada, **410** G2
Dolphin Head, *point*, Namibia, **370** B4
Dolyna, Ukraine, **289** L4
Dom, Gunung, *mountain peak*, Indonesia, **199** G3
Dom Pedrito, Brazil, **459** F4
Dom Pedro, Brazil, **453** E4
Domanivka, Ukraine, **296** H2
Domar, China, **214** B2
Domaradz, Poland, **289** L4
Domažlice, Czech Republic, **288** F4
Domba, China, **215** E2
Dombarovskiy, Russian Federation, **222** F2
Dombås, Norway, **286** D1
Dombe, Mozambique, **371** F2
Dombóvár, Hungary, **289** H5
Dome Creek, Canada, **412** J5
Domett, Mount, *mountain peak*, New Zealand, **133** D5
Domeyko, Antofagasta, Chile, **458** C2
Domeyko, Atacama, Chile, **458** B3
Domeyko, Cordillera, *mountain range*, Chile, **458** C2
Domfront, France, **290** D2
Dominica, *country*, Caribbean Sea, **427** D3, *378, 396*
Dominica Passage, Caribbean Sea, **427** D3
Dominical, Costa Rica, **428** E5
Dominican Republic, *country*, Caribbean Sea, **409** R7, *378, 379, 391, 394, 395*
Dominion, Cape, Canada, **411** M3
Dömitz, Germany, **288** E2
Domneşti, Romania, **296** E3
Domo, Ethiopia, **367** G3
Domodedovo, Russian Federation, **299** F5
Domodossola, Italy, **294** B2
Domokos, Greece, **297** D6
Domoni, Comoros, **372** A3
Dompu, Indonesia, **201** G5
Domuyo, Volcán, *mountain peak*, Argentina, **458** B5
Domžale, Slovenia, **294** E2
Don, Mexico, **430** C3
Don, *river*, France, **290** D3
Don, *river*, Russian Federation, **298** F3
Don, *river*, Scotland, U.K., **308** F3
Donaghmore, Northern Ireland, U.K., **306** B3
Donaldson, U.S.A., **420** E1
Donaldsonville, U.S.A., **424** G4
Donard, Slieve, *mountain peak*, Northern Ireland, U.K., **309** G3
Donau (Danube), *river*, Austria, **289** F4
Donau (Danube), *river*, Germany, **288** E4
Donaueschingen, Germany, **288** D5
Donauwörth, Germany, **288** E4
Doncaster, England, U.K., **307** G4
Dondo, Angola, **368** B4
Dondo, Mozambique, **371** F2
Dondra Head, Sri Lanka, **217** E5
Donduşeni, Moldova, **296** F1
Donegal, *county*, Ireland, **309** D3
Donegal, Ireland, **309** D3
Donegal Bay, Ireland, **309** D3
Donegal Point, Ireland, **309** C5
Donets'k, Ukraine, **298** E3
Dong, *river*, N. China, **213** J4
Dong, *river*, S. China, **207** C2
Đông Hà, Vietnam, **203** E2
Đồng Hới, Vietnam, **203** E2
Đông Nai, *river*, Vietnam, **203** E4
Dong Ujimqin Qi, China, **210** G3
Donga, Nigeria, **365** G3
Dong'an, Heilongjiang, China, **211** L3
Dong'an, Hunan, China, **206** B3
Dongarra, Australia, **134** C4
Dongchuan, China, **215** G4
Dongco, China, **214** C2
Dongfang, China, **203** F2
Dongfanghong, China, **211** L3
Dongfeng, Guangdong, China, **207** A3
Dongfeng, Jilin, China, **211** J4
Donggala, Indonesia, **198** B3
Donggou, China, **208** D3
Dongguan, China, **207** B2
Donghai Dao, *island*, China, **203** F1
Dongjiangkou, China, **206** B1
Dongkou, China, **206** B3
Donglan, China, **215** H4
Dongning, China, **211** K3
Dongnyi, China, **215** G3
Dongo, Angola, **368** C5
Dongo, Democratic Republic of the Congo, **368** C2
Dongou, Congo, **368** C2
Dongping, China, **203** G1
Dongping, Guangdong, China, **206** C4
Dongping, Shandong, China, **206** D1
Dongsanjia, China, **211** J3
Dongshan, China, **206** B4
Dongshan Dao, *island*, China, **206** D4
Dongsheng, China, **210** E5
Dongtai, China, **206** E1
Dongting Hu, *lake*, China, **206** C2
Dongyang, China, **206** E2
Dongying, China, **211** G5
Dongzhi, China, **206** D2
Donji Milanovac, Serbia, **296** D3
Donji Mu, Croatia, **294** F4
Donji Srb, Croatia, **294** E3
Dønna, *island*, Norway, **284** E4
Donna, U.S.A., **424** C6
Donnelly, Canada, **413** L4
Donon, *mountain peak*, France, **291** H2
Donostia-San Sebastián, Spain, **293** F1
Donoughmore, Ireland, **309** D6
Donskoy, Russian Federation, **299** G6
Donsol, Philippines, **204** C3
Donxing, China, **208** E1
Dooagh, Ireland, **309** B4
Doon, Loch, *lake*, Scotland, U.K., **308** E5
Doon, *river*, Scotland, U.K., **308** E5
Doonbeg, Ireland, **309** C5
Doonbeg, *river*, Ireland, **309** C5
Dora, Lake, Australia, **134** E3
Dorchester, England, U.K., **304** E4
Dordabis, Namibia, **370** C3
Dordogne, *river*, France, **290** D4, *242*
Dordrecht, Netherlands, **288** B3
Dore, Monts, *mountain range*, France, **290** F4
Doré Lake, Canada, **413** R4
Dores, Scotland, U.K., **308** E3
Dori, Burkina Faso, **364** D2
Dorking, England, U.K., **305** G3
Dormaa Ahenkro, Ghana, **364** D3
Dormans, France, **291** F2
Dornie, Scotland, U.K., **308** D3
Dornoch Firth, *river mouth*, Scotland, U.K., **308** E3
Dornod, *province*, Mongolia, **210** F3
Dornogovĭ, *province*, Mongolia, **210** E3
Doro, Mali, **364** D1
Dorobanţu, Romania, **296** F3
Dorobino, Russian Federation, **299** F6
Dorogobuzh, Russian Federation, **299** D5
Dorohoi, Romania, **296** F2
Dorokhovo, Russian Federation, **299** F5
Dorolemo, Indonesia, **199** E2
Dorotea, Sweden, **284** H4
Dorre Island, Australia, **134** C4
Dorsale, *mountain range*, Tunisia, **362** A1, *315*
Dorset, *unitary authority*, England, U.K., **304** E4
Dortmund, Germany, **288** C3
Dorum, Germany, **288** D2
Doruma, Democratic Republic of the Congo, **369** E2
Dos Bahías, Cabo, *cape*, Argentina, **460** E2
dos Bois, *river*, Brazil, **456** D4
Dos de Mayo, Peru, **454** C2
Dos Pozos, Argentina, **460** E2
Dosi, Indonesia, **199** F4
Dospat, Bulgaria, **297** E5
Dosquet, Canada, **416** F6
Dosso, *department*, Niger, **365** E2
Dosso, Niger, **365** E2
Dossor, Kazakhstan, **222** E3
Dostyq, Kazakhstan, **212** D3
Dothan, U.S.A., **425** K4
Douai, France, **291** F1
Douala, Cameroon, **368** A2
Douarnenez, France, **290** B2
Double Cone, *mountain peak*, New Zealand, **133** B7
Double Mer, *river*, Canada, **417** M2
Doubs, *river*, France, **291** G3
Doubtful Sound, New Zealand, **133** A7
Doubtless Bay, New Zealand, **132** D2
Doudeville, France, **305** H5
Douentza, Mali, **364** D2
Douéoulou, New Caledonia, **141** A3
Doughboy Bay, New Zealand, **133** A8
Douglas, Alaska, U.S.A., **412** B2
Douglas, Arizona, U.S.A., **423** J6
Douglas, Georgia, U.S.A., **425** L4
Douglas, Isle of Man, **306** D3, *279*
Douglas, North Dakota, U.S.A., **420** C2
Douglas, Scotland, U.K., **308** F5
Douglas, South Africa, **370** D4
Douglas, Wyoming, U.S.A., **419** M5
Douglas City, U.S.A., **422** B1
Douglas Lake, Canada, **412** J6
Douglass, U.S.A., **420** E7
Doullens, France, **290** F1
Doumen, China, **207** A4
Dounreay, Scotland, U.K., **308** F2
Dourados, Brazil, **456** B6
Dourados, *river*, Brazil, **456** B6
Dourados, Serra dos, *mountain range*, Brazil, **459** G2
Dourbali, Chad, **365** H2
Douro, *river*, Portugal, **292** D2, *250, 251, 253*
Douze, *river*, France, **290** E5
Dove, *river*, England, U.K., **305** F1
Dover, Delaware, U.S.A., **426** C5, *386*
Dover, England, U.K., **305** J3
Dover, New Hampshire, U.S.A., **426** E3
Dover, New Jersey, U.S.A., **426** C4
Dover, Strait of, France/ U.K., **305** J4
Dovey, *river*, Wales, U.K., **304** D2
Dovre, Norway, **286** D2
Dowi, Tanjong, *point*, Indonesia, **200** B2
Dowlat Yār, Afghanistan, **218** A2
Dowlatābād, Afghanistan, **218** A1
Down, *district*, Northern Ireland, U.K., **309** G3
Downey, U.S.A., **419** H5
Downham Market, England, U.K., **305** H2
Downpatrick, Northern Ireland, U.K., **309** G3
Downpatrick Head, *point*, Ireland, **309** C3
Downs, U.S.A., **420** D6
Downton, England, U.K., **305** F4
Dowshī, Afghanistan, **218** B2
Dowsk, Belarus, **299** C6
Doyleville, U.S.A., **423** K2
Dōzen, *island*, Japan, **208** F3
Drâa, Hamada du, *plateau*, Algeria, **360** E3
Drac, *river*, France, **291** G4
Dracena, Brazil, **456** C5
Dragalina, Romania, **296** F3
Drăgăneşti-Olt, Romania, **296** E3
Drăgăneşti-Vlaşca, Romania, **296** E3
Drăgăşani, Romania, **296** E3
Dragón, Bocas del, *bay*, Trinidad and Tobago, **451** G1
Dragón, Bocas del, *strait*, Trinidad and Tobago/ Venezuela, **427** D4
Dragonada, *island*, Greece, **297** F8
Draguignan, France, **291** H5
Drăguşeni, Romania, **296** F2
Drahichyn, Belarus, **289** M2
Drake, U.S.A., **420** C2
Drake Passage, *strait*, Antarctica, **477** C9
Drakensberg, *mountain range*, South Africa, **357** H10, *350, 351*
Drama, Greece, **297** E5
Drammen, Norway, **286** E3
Drangedal, Norway, **286** D3
Draper, U.S.A., **420** C4
Draperstown, Northern Ireland, U.K., **306** B3
Drava, *river*, Croatia/ Hungary/Slovenia, **294** F2, *258, 259*
Dravograd, Slovenia, **294** E2
Drawa, *river*, Poland, **289** G2
Drawsko, Jezioro, *lake*, Poland, **289** G2
Drayton, U.S.A., **420** E1
Drayton Valley, Canada, **413** M5
Dreikikir, Papua New Guinea, **140** A3
Dremsel, Mount, *mountain peak*, Papua New Guinea, **140** B3
Drenthe, *province*, Netherlands, **288** C2
Drepano, Akra, *point*, Greece, **297** D6
Dresden, Germany, **288** F3
Dretun', Belarus, **299** B5
Dreux, France, **290** E2
Drevsjø, Norway, **286** F2
Drewsey, U.S.A., **418** E5
Dreyers Rock, New Zealand, **133** E5
Driffield, England, U.K., **307** H3
Driftwood, Canada, **415** P7
Driggs, U.S.A., **419** J5
Drimoleague, Ireland, **309** C6
Drin, *river*, Albania, **296** B4, *263*
Drina, *river*, Bosnia and Herzegovina/Serbia, **296** B3
Drinit, Gjiri i, *bay*, Albania, **296** B5
Drinizi, *river*, Albania, **296** C5
Drinkwater, Canada, **413** S6
Driva, *river*, Norway, **286** D1
Drniš, Croatia, **294** F4
Drøbak, Norway, **286** E3
Drobeta-Turnu Severin, Romania, **296** D3
Drobin, Poland, **289** K2
Drocea, *mountain peak*, Romania, **296** D2
Drochia, Moldova, **296** F1
Drogheda, Ireland, **309** F4
Drogobych, Ukraine, **289** L4
Droitwich, England, U.K., **304** E2
Drôme, *river*, France, **291** G4
Dromod, Ireland, **309** E4
Dromore, Northern Ireland, U.K., **309** E3
Dromore West, Ireland, **309** D3
Dronfield, England, U.K., **307** G4
Dronne, *river*, France, **290** E4
Dronning Maud Land, *region*, Antarctica, **470** D4
Dropt, *river*, France, **290** E4
Drosendorf, Austria, **289** G4
Drosh, Pakistan, **218** B2
Druif, Aruba, **461** B3
Druimdrishaig, Scotland, U.K., **308** D5
Drumheller, Canada, **413** N6
Drumkeeran, Ireland, **309** D3
Drummond, U.S.A., **418** H3
Drummond Island, U.S.A., **421** L2
Drummondville, Canada, **416** E7
Drummore, Scotland, U.K., **308** E6
Drumnadrochit, Scotland, U.K., **308** E3
Druskininkai, Lithuania, **289** L1
Drut', *river*, Belarus, **299** B6
Druya, Belarus, **287** N5
Druzhba, Ukraine, **298** D2
Drvar, Bosnia and Herzegovina, **294** F3
Drvenik, Croatia, **294** F4
Dry Gut Bay, St Helena, **373** B3
Dry Ridge, U.S.A., **421** L6
Dryanovo, Bulgaria, **296** E4

Drybrough, Canada, **414** D3
Dryden, Canada, **414** H7
Dryden, U.S.A., **423** M6
Drygalski Fjord, *fiord*, South Georgia, **461** A3
Drygarn Fawr, *mountain peak*, Wales, U.K., **304** D2
Drymen, Scotland, U.K., **308** E4
Drysa, *river*, Belarus, **299** B5
Drysdale, *river*, Australia, **134** F2
Dschang, Cameroon, **368** B1
Du Quoin, U.S.A., **421** J6
Duanshan, China, **215** H4
Duarte, Pico, *mountain peak*, Dominican Republic, **429** H3, *394, 395*
Duau, Mount, *mountain peak*, Papua New Guinea, **140** B4
Dubā, Saudi Arabia, **363** G3
Dubai *see* Dubayy, United Arab Emirates, **221** G3, *146, 147, 176*
Dubăsari Vodokhranilishche, *reservoir*, Moldova, **296** G2
Dubăsari, Moldova, **296** G2
Dubawnt Lake, Canada, **410** J3
Dubayy (Dubai), United Arab Emirates, **221** G3, *146, 147, 176*
Dubbo, Australia, **135** K5
Dubets, Russian Federation, **299** G3
Dubica, Croatia, **294** F3
Dublin, *county*, Ireland, **309** F4, *276, 277*
Dublin, Ireland, **309** F4
Dublin, U.S.A., **425** L3
Dubna, Russian Federation, **299** F4
Dubnica nad Váhom, Slovakia, **289** J4
Dubois, U.S.A., **419** K5
Dubréka, Guinea, **364** B3
Dubrovka, Bryanskaya Oblast', Russian Federation, **299** D6
Dubrovka, Pskovskaya Oblast', Russian Federation, **299** B4
Dubrovnik, Croatia, **294** G4, *259*
Dubrowna, Belarus, **299** C5
Dubulu, Democratic Republic of the Congo, **368** D2
Dubuque, U.S.A., **420** H4
Dubysa, *river*, Lithuania, **287** L5
Duc de Gloucester, Îles du, *islands*, French Polynesia, **137** G3
Duchesne, U.S.A., **423** H1
Ducie Island, Pitcairn Islands, **137** J3, *126*
Duck Lake, Canada, **413** R5
Duckwater, U.S.A., **422** F2
Dudada, India, **216** D2
Duderstadt, Germany, **288** E3
Dudhani, India, **216** D2
Dūdhi, India, **219** E4
Dudinka, Russian Federation, **300** K3
Dudley, England, U.K., **304** E2
Dudorovskiy, Russian Federation, **299** E6
Dudu, India, **218** C4
Duékoué, Côte d'Ivoire, **364** C3
Duero, *river*, Spain, **293** F2
Dufek Coast, *region*, Antarctica, **470** D6
Duff Islands, Solomon Islands, **138** E5
Dufftown, Scotland, U.K., **308** F3
Dugi Otok, *island*, Croatia, **294** E4
Dugui Qarag, China, **210** E5
Duida, Cerro, *mountain peak*, Venezuela, **451** F3
Duisburg, Germany, **288** C3
Duitama, Colombia, **450** D3
Duk Fadiat, Sudan, **366** D3
Duk Faiwil, Sudan, **366** D3
Dukat i Ri, Albania, **297** B5
Dukhān, Qatar, **220** F3
Dukhnah, Saudi Arabia, **363** H3
Dukhovshchina, Russian Federation, **299** D5
Duki, Pakistan, **218** B3
Duki, Russian Federation, **211** L2
Dukla, Poland, **289** K4
Dūkštas, Lithuania, **287** N5
Duku, Nigeria, **365** G2
Dulan, China, **213** H5
Dulansi, China, **213** H5
Dulce, *river*, Argentina, **458** D4
Dulce Nombre de Culmí, Honduras, **428** D4
Dul'durga, Russian Federation, **210** F2
Dŭlgopol, Bulgaria, **296** F4
Duliu, China, **210** G5
Dulnain Bridge, Scotland, U.K., **308** F3
Dulovo, Bulgaria, **296** F4
Duluth, U.S.A., **420** G2
Dulverton, England, U.K., **304** D3
Dūmā, Syria, **225** D3
Dumaguete, Philippines, **204** C4
Dumai, Indonesia, **200** C2
Dumaran Island, Philippines, **204** C4
Dumas, U.S.A., **424** B2
Ḑumayr, Syria, **225** D3
Dumbarton, Scotland, U.K., **308** E5
Dumbea, New Caledonia, **141** A3
Dumbrăveni, Romania, **296** F3
Dumchele, India, **218** D2
Dumfries, Scotland, U.K., **308** F5
Dumfries & Galloway, *local authority*, Scotland, U.K., **308** E5
Dumitra, Romania, **296** E2
Dumka, India, **219** F4
Dumoine, Lac, *lake*, Canada, **416** C6
Dumoine, *river*, Canada, **416** C6
Dumont d'Urville, *French research station*, Antarctica, **470** F8
Dumont d'Urville Sea, Antarctica, **470** F8
Dumyāṭ (Damietta), Egypt, **225** A4
Dumyāṭ, Maṣabb, *river mouth*, Egypt, **225** A4
Dún Laoghaire, Ireland, **309** F4
Dun-sur-Auron, France, **290** F3
Duna (Danube), *river*, Hungary, **289** J5
Dunaff Head, *point*, Ireland, **309** E2
Dunai, Nepal, **219** E3
Dunajská Streda, Slovakia, **289** H5
Dunakeszi, Hungary, **289** J5
Dunărea (Danube), *river*, Romania, **296** D4
Dunaszekcső, Hungary, **289** J5
Dunaújváros, Hungary, **289** J5
Dunav, *river*, Serbia, **296** C3
Dunavtsi, Bulgaria, **296** D4
Dunayivtsi, Ukraine, **296** F1
Dunbar, Scotland, U.K., **308** G4
Dunblane, Scotland, U.K., **308** F4
Dunboyne, Ireland, **309** F4
Duncan, Arizona, U.S.A., **423** J5
Duncan, Canada, **412** H7
Duncan, Cape, Canada, **415** P5
Duncan, Lac, *lake*, Canada, **415** Q5
Duncan, Oklahoma, U.S.A., **424** D2
Duncan Passage, Andaman and Nicobar Islands, India, **217** H4
Duncannon, Ireland, **309** F5
Duncansby Head, Scotland, U.K., **308** F2
Dunchurch, England, U.K., **305** F2
Duncormick, Ireland, **309** F5
Dund-Us, Mongolia, **213** F3
Dundaga, Latvia, **287** L4
Dundalk, Ireland, **309** F3
Dundalk, U.S.A., **426** B5
Dundalk Bay, Ireland, **309** F4
Dundas, Lake, Australia, **134** E5
Dundas, Mount, *mountain peak*, New Zealand, **133** E5
Dundas Strait, Australia, **199** E5
Dundbürd, Mongolia, **210** E3
Dundee, Scotland, U.K., **308** G4
Dundee, South Africa, **371** F4
Dundee City, *local authority*, Scotland, U.K., **308** F4
Dundgovĭ, *province*, Mongolia, **210** D3
Dundonald, Northern Ireland, U.K., **309** G3
Dundrennan, Scotland, U.K., **308** F6
Dundrum, Northern Ireland, U.K., **309** G3
Dundurn, Canada, **413** R6
Dunedin, New Zealand, **133** C7
Dunevegan Lake, Canada, **414** A1
Dunfermline, Scotland, U.K., **308** F4
Dungannon, *district*, Northern Ireland, U.K., **309** F3
Dungannon, Northern Ireland, U.K., **306** B3
Dūngarpur, India, **218** C5
Dungarvan, Ireland, **309** E5
Dungarvan Harbour, Ireland, **309** E5
Dungas, Niger, **365** F2
Dungeness, England, U.K., **305** J4
Dungeness, Punta, *point*, Argentina, **460** D4
Dungiven, Northern Ireland, U.K., **309** F3
Dunglow, Ireland, **309** D3
Dungu, Democratic Republic of the Congo, **369** E2
Dunholme, England, U.K., **307** H4
Dunhua, China, **211** K4
Dunhuang, China, **213** G4
Dunkeld, Scotland, U.K., **308** F4
Dunkerque, France, **290** F1
Dunkery Hill, *mountain peak*, England, U.K., **304** D3
Dunkwa, Ghana, **364** D3
Dunlap, Iowa, U.S.A., **420** F5
Dunlap, Texas, U.S.A., **424** B2
Dunlavin, Ireland, **309** F4
Dunleer, Ireland, **309** F4
Dunlop, Scotland, U.K., **308** E5
Dunmanway, Ireland, **309** C6
Dunmore, Ireland, **309** D4
Dunmore East, Ireland, **309** E5
Dunmurry, Northern Ireland, U.K., **309** F3
Dunn, U.S.A., **425** N2
Dunnellon, U.S.A., **425** L5
Dunnet Head, *cape*, Scotland, U.K., **308** F2
Dunning, U.S.A., **420** C5
Dunoon, Scotland, U.K., **308** E5
Dunquin, Ireland, **309** B5
Dunqulah, Sudan, **363** F5
Dunqunāb, Sudan, **363** G4
Dunrobin, New Zealand, **133** B7
Duns, Scotland, U.K., **308** G5
Dunseith, U.S.A., **420** C1
Dunstable, England, U.K., **305** G3
Dunstan Mountains, *mountain range*, New Zealand, **133** B7
Dunster, Canada, **412** K5
Dunte, Latvia, **287** M4
Dunvant, Wales, U.K., **304** C3
Dunvegan, Loch, *inlet*, Scotland, U.K., **308** C3
Dunvegan, Scotland, U.K., **308** C3
Duolun, China, **210** G4
Duozhu, China, **207** D2
Duparquet, Canada, **416** B5
Dupree, U.S.A., **420** C3
Dupuyer, U.S.A., **418** H2
Duque de Caxias, Brazil, **457** E6
Duque de York, Isla, *island*, Chile, **460** B4
Duquesne, Cape, Australia, **135** H6
Dūrā, West Bank, **225** C4
Durán, Ecuador, **450** B5
Duran, U.S.A., **423** L4
Durance, *river*, France, **291** G5
Durand, U.S.A., **420** H3
Durango, Mexico, **430** D3
Durango, *state*, Mexico, **430** D3
Durango, U.S.A., **423** K3
Durankulak, Bulgaria, **296** G4
Durant, U.S.A., **424** D3
Duraykīsh, Syria, **225** D2
Durazno, Uruguay, **459** F4
Durban, South Africa, **371** F4
Durbe, Latvia, **287** K4
Đurđevac, Croatia, **294** F2
Düre, China, **212** F3
Dureji, Pakistan, **218** A4
Durg, India, **219** E5
Durgārājupatnam, India, **216** E3
Durham, Canada, **421** N3
Durham, England, U.K., **307** G3
Durham, Point, Chatham Islands, New Zealand, **133** Q16
Durham, *unitary authority*, England, U.K., **307** G3
Durham, U.S.A., **421** P7
Duri, Indonesia, **200** C2
Durness, Scotland, U.K., **308** E2
Durnford, Punta, *point*, Western Sahara, **360** C4
Durrës, Albania, **297** B5
Durrington, England, U.K., **305** F3
Durrow, Ireland, **309** E5
Dursey Island, Ireland, **309** B6
Dursley, England, U.K., **304** E3
Dursunbey, Turkey, **297** G6
Durtal, France, **290** D3
Duru, Papua New Guinea, **140** A5
Durukhsi, Somalia, **367** G3
Durusu Gölü, *lake*, Turkey, **297** G5
Durūz, Jabal ad, *mountain peak*, Syria, **225** D3
D'Urville, Tanjong, *point*, Indonesia, **199** G3
D'Urville Island, New Zealand, **133** D5
Dushak, Turkmenistan, **222** G5
Dushan, China, **215** H4
Dushanbe, Tajikistan, **223** H5, *188*
Dushanzi, Gansu, China, **213** G5
Dushanzi, Xinjiang Uygur Zizhiqu, China, **212** E3
Dusky Sound, New Zealand, **133** A7
Düsseldorf, Germany, **288** C3, *56*
Dusunmudo, Indonesia, **200** C3
Dutse, Nigeria, **365** F2
Dutsin-Ma, Nigeria, **365** F2
Duttalūru, India, **216** D3
Dutton, Mount, *mountain peak*, U.S.A., **423** G2
Dutton, U.S.A., **419** J3
Düxanbibazar, China, **212** D5
Duyfken Point, Australia, **135** J1
Duyun, China, **215** H4
Dūz, Tunisia, **362** A2
Dve Mogili, Bulgaria, **296** E4
Dvůr Králové, Czech Republic, **289** G3
Dwārka, India, **218** B5
Dwight, U.S.A., **421** J5
Dworshak Reservoir, U.S.A., **418** G3
Dwyer, U.S.A., **419** M5
Dyat'kovo, Russian Federation, **299** E6
Dyaul Island, Papua New Guinea, **140** C3
Dyce, Scotland, U.K., **308** G3
Dyer, Cape, Canada, **411** N3
Dyers Bay, Canada, **421** N3
Dyersburg, U.S.A., **425** H1
Dyke, Scotland, U.K., **308** F3
Dymchurch, England, U.K., **305** H3
Dymock, England, U.K., **304** E3
Dynapro, *river*, Belarus, **299** C5
Dynów, Poland, **289** L4
Dyrhólaey, *point*, Iceland, **284** Y8
Dyrnes, Norway, **284** C5
Dyrøya, *island*, Norway, **284** H2
Dysselsdorp, South Africa, **370** D5
Dytiki Ellas, *administrative region*, Greece, **297** C6
Dytiki Makedonia, *administrative region*, Greece, **297** C5
Dyurtyuli, Russian Federation, **222** E1
Dyviziya, Ukraine, **296** G3
Dzaanhushuu, Mongolia, **213** J3
Dzadgay, Mongolia, **213** H3
Dzag, Mongolia, **213** H3
Dzalaa, Mongolia, **213** H3
Dzaoudzi, Mayotte, **372** B3
Dzavhan, *province*, Mongolia, **213** G2
Dzavhan, *river*, Mongolia, **213** G2
Dzelter, Mongolia, **210** D2
Dzerzhinsk, Russian Federation, **222** C1
Dzhalinda, Russian Federation, **211** H1
Dzhangala, Kazakhstan, **222** E3
Dzhankel'dy, Uzbekistan, **222** G4
Dzhankoy, Ukraine, **298** D3
Dzhebel, Turkmenistan, **222** E5
Dzhugdzhur, Khrebet, *mountain range*, Russian Federation, **301** Q4
Dzhuryn, Ukraine, **296** G1
Działdowo, Poland, **289** K2
Dzibalchén, Mexico, **431** H5
Dzilam De Bravo, Mexico, **431** H4
Dzioua, Algeria, **361** H2
Dzisna, Belarus, **287** P5
Dzisna, *river*, Belarus/Lithuania, **287** N5
Dzivin, Belarus, **289** M3
Dzöölön, Mongolia, **213** H2
Dzüünbayan, Mongolia, **210** E3
Dzüünbulag, Mongolia, **210** F3
Dzüünharaa, Mongolia, **210** D2
Dzuunmod, Dzavhan, Mongolia, **213** H2
Dzuunmod, Töv, Mongolia, **210** D3
Dzüyl, Mongolia, **213** G3
Dźwierzuty, Poland, **289** K2
Dzyarechyn, Belarus, **289** M2
Dzyarzhynskaya, Hora, *mountain peak*, Belarus, **298** C2, *268*
Dzyatlava, Belarus, **289** M2

## E

Ea H'leo, Vietnam, **203** F3
Eads, U.S.A., **423** M2
Eagar, U.S.A., **423** J4
Eagle, *river*, Canada, **417** M3
Eagle, U.S.A., **423** K2
Eagle Butte, U.S.A., **420** C3
Eagle Lake, California, U.S.A., **422** C1
Eagle Lake, *lake*, U.S.A., **426** F1
Eagle Lake, Maine, U.S.A., **426** F1
Eagle Pass, U.S.A., **424** B5
Eagle River, U.S.A., **421** J3
Ealing, England, U.K., **305** G3
Ear Falls, Canada, **414** H6
Earith, England, U.K., **305** H2
Earl Shilton, England, U.K., **305** F2
Earlton, Canada, **421** P2
Earnslaw, Mount, *mountain peak*, New Zealand, **133** B7
Earth, U.S.A., **423** M4
Easebourne, England, U.K., **305** G4
Easington, England, U.K., **307** J4
Easingwold, England, U.K., **307** G3
Easley, U.S.A., **425** L2
East Angus, Canada, **416** F7
East Antarctica, *region*, Antarctica, **470** E5, *468*
East Aurora, U.S.A., **426** A3
East Ayrshire, *local authority*, Scotland, U.K., **308** E5
East Bay, Papua New Guinea, **140** B4
East Bay, U.S.A., **425** H5
East Braintree, Canada, **414** G7
East Cape, New Zealand, **132** G3
East Caroline Basin, *underwater feature*, Pacific Ocean, **478** D4
East Dereham, England, U.K., **305** H2
East Dunbartonshire, *local authority*, Scotland, U.K., **308** E5
East Falkland, *island*, Falkland Islands, **460** G4, *445*
East Glacier Park, U.S.A., **418** H2
East Grand Forks, U.S.A., **420** E2

East Grinstead, England, U.K., **305** G3
East Hampton, U.S.A., **426** D4
East Harling, England, U.K., **305** H2
East Indian Ridge, *underwater feature*, Indian Ocean, **476** F6
East Islet, *island*, Ashmore and Cartier Islands, **134** P9
East Jordan, U.S.A., **421** L3
East Kilbride, Scotland, U.K., **308** E5
East Linton, Scotland, U.K., **308** G5
East Liverpool, U.S.A., **421** N5
East Loch Tarbert, *inlet*, Scotland, U.K., **308** C3
East London, South Africa, **371** E5
East Lothian, *local authority*, Scotland, U.K., **308** G4
East Malling, England, U.K., **305** H3
East Mariana Basin, *underwater feature*, Pacific Ocean, **478** E4
East New Britain, *province*, Papua New Guinea, **140** D4
East Pacific Rise, *underwater feature*, Pacific Ocean, **479** L7
East Point, Canada, **417** L6
East Point, Lord Howe Island, Australia, **135** U14
East Point, Tristan da Cunha, **373** C2
East Point, U.S.A., **425** K3
East Poplar, Canada, **413** S7
East Renfrewshire, *local authority*, Scotland, U.K., **308** E5
East Riding of Yorkshire, *unitary authority*, England, U.K., **307** H4
East St Louis, U.S.A., **420** H6
East Sepik, *province*, Papua New Guinea, **140** A3
East Sussex, England, U.K., **305** H4, *25*
East Tasman Plateau, *underwater feature*, Pacific Ocean, **478** E7
East Timor, *country*, Asia, **198** D5, *145, 148, 149, 153*
East Wittering, England, U.K., **305** G4
Eastbourne, England, U.K., **305** H4
Eastend, Canada, **413** Q7
Easter Fracture Zone, *tectonic feature*, Pacific Ocean, **479** K6
Easter Island *see* Pascua, Isla de, *island*, Chile, Pacific Ocean, **461** B2, *12, 61, 90, 91, 94, 435*
Eastern, *administrative region*, Ghana, **364** D3
Eastern, *province*, Kenya, **369** G2
Eastern, *province*, Sierra Leone, **364** B3
Eastern, *province*, Zambia, **369** F5
Eastern Cape, *province*, South Africa, **371** E5, *351*
Eastern Desert *see* Sharqīyah, Aṣ Ṣaḥrā' ash, *desert*, Egypt, **225** A5, *317*
Eastern Ghats, *mountain range*, India, **216** D3
Eastern (Lau) Group, *islands*, Bounty Islands, New Zealand, **133** N14
Eastern Group *see* Lau Group, *islands*, Fiji, **141** A4
Eastern Highlands, *province*, Papua New Guinea, **140** B4
Eastland, U.S.A., **424** C3
Eastleigh, England, U.K., **305** F4
Eastmain, Canada, **415** Q5
Eastmain, *river*, Canada, **416** C3
Eastman, U.S.A., **425** L3
Easton, England, U.K., **304** E4
Eastry, England, U.K., **305** J3
Eastwood, England, U.K., **305** F1
Eaton Socon, England, U.K., **305** G2
Eatonton, U.S.A., **425** L3
Eau Claire, Lac à l', *lake*, Canada, **415** S3
Eau Claire, U.S.A., **420** H3
Eauripik, *island*, Micronesia, **138** C4
Eban, Nigeria, **365** E3
Ebano, Mexico, **431** F4
Ebbw Vale, Wales, U.K., **304** D3, *275*
Ebebiyin, Equatorial Guinea, **368** B2
Ebeltoft, Denmark, **286** E4
Eberbach, Germany, **288** D4
Eberswalde-Finow, Germany, **289** F2
Ebetsu, Japan, **209** H2
Ebian, China, **215** G3
Ebino, Japan, **208** E4
Ebinur Hu, *lake*, China, **212** D3
Ebolowa, Cameroon, **368** B2
Ebon, *island*, Marshall Islands, **139** E4
Ebony, Namibia, **370** C3
Ebro, *river*, Spain, **280** D7, *253*
Ebruchorr, Gora, *mountain peak*, Russian Federation, **285** R3
Ecclefechan, Scotland, U.K., **308** F5
Eccleshall, England, U.K., **304** E2
Eceabat, Turkey, **297** F5
Echinos, Greece, **297** E5
Echt, Netherlands, **288** B3
Echuca, Australia, **135** J6
Écija, Spain, **292** E4
Eckenförde, Germany, **288** D1
Eckington, England, U.K., **304** E2
Écommoy, France, **290** E3
Ecuador, *country*, South America, **449** E4, *88, 94, 434, 435, 438, 441*
Écueillé, France, **290** E3
Ēd, Eritrea, **367** F2
Ed, Sweden, **286** E3
Edam, Canada, **413** Q5
Edam, Netherlands, **288** B2
Eday, *island*, Orkney, Scotland, U.K., **308** G1
Eddystone Point, Australia, **135** K7
Ede, Nigeria, **365** E3
Ede Point, Canada, **411** J2
Edéa, Cameroon, **368** A2
Edehon Lake, Canada, **414** F1
Edéia, Brazil, **456** D4
Eden, Australia, **135** K6
Eden, Canada, **414** E6
Eden, *river*, England, U.K., **306** F3, *276*
Eden, Texas, U.S.A., **424** C4
Eden, Wyoming, U.S.A., **419** K5
Edenbridge, England, U.K., **305** H3
Edendale, New Zealand, **133** B8
Edenderry, Ireland, **309** E4
Edenton, U.S.A., **426** B6
Eder, *river*, Germany, **288** D3
Edessa, Greece, **297** D5
Edgartown, U.S.A., **426** E4
Edgeley, U.S.A., **420** D2
Edgemont, U.S.A., **420** B4
Edgeøya, *island*, Svalbard, **300** D2
Edgerton, Canada, **413** P5
Edgeworthstown, Ireland, **309** E4
Edina, U.S.A., **420** G5
Edinboro, U.S.A., **421** N5
Edinburgh, Scotland, U.K., **308** F5, *276*
Edinburgh, Tristan da Cunha, **373** C2
Edinburgh City, Scotland, U.K., **308** F5
Edineŭ, Moldova, **296** F1
Edirne, *province*, Turkey, **297** F5
Edirne, Turkey, **224** C4
Edjeleh, Algeria, **361** H3
Edlingham, England, U.K., **307** G2
Edmond, Kansas, U.S.A., **420** D6
Edmond, Oklahoma, U.S.A., **424** D2
Edmonton, Canada, **413** N5, *381*
Edmund Lake, Canada, **414** H4
Edmundston, Canada, **416** G6
Edna, U.S.A., **424** D5
Edo, *state*, Nigeria, **365** F3
Edolo, Italy, **294** C2
Edremit, Turkey, **297** F6
Edremit Körfezi, *bay*, Turkey, **297** F6
Edsbro, Sweden, **287** J3
Edsbyn, Sweden, **286** G2
Edson, Canada, **413** L5
Eduardo Castex, Argentina, **458** D5
Edward VII Land, *region*, Antarctica, **470** C7
Edwards Plateau, U.S.A., **424** B4
Edzo, Canada, **410** H3
Edzouga, Congo, **368** B3
Efate (Vaté), *island*, Vanuatu, **141** A2
Effie, U.S.A., **420** G2
Effingham, U.S.A., **421** J6
Effon-Alaiye, Nigeria, **365** E3
Eforie, Romania, **296** G3
Eg, Mongolia, **210** E2
Egadi, Isole, *islands*, Sicilia, Italy, **295** D7
Egan Range, *mountain range*, U.S.A., **422** F2
Eganville, Canada, **416** C7
Eger, Hungary, **289** K5
Egeria Point, Christmas Island, **134** N8
Egersund, Norway, **286** C3
Egg Island, St Helena, **373** B3
Eggedal, Norway, **286** D2
Eggenfelden, Germany, **288** F4
Egilsstaðir, Iceland, **284** Z7
Egindibulaq, Kazakhstan, **212** C2
Egiyn, *river*, Mongolia, **213** J2
Égletons, France, **290** F4
Eglinton, Northern Ireland, U.K., **309** E2
Eglwys Fach, Wales, U.K., **304** D2
Egmont, Mount (Mount Taranaki), *mountain peak*, New Zealand, **132** E4
Egremont, Canada, **413** N4
Egremont, England, U.K., **306** E3
Eğrigöz Dağı, *mountain range*, Turkey, **297** G6
Egton, England, U.K., **307** H3
Egtved, Denmark, **286** D5
Egypt, *country*, Africa, **358** H4, *30, 43, 54, 63, 65, 66, 67, 68, 70, 72, 74, 87, 88, 89, 92, 96, 97, 146, 179, 182, 192, 254, 275, 312, 313, 316, 317, 336, 337, 339*
Eiao, *island*, French Polynesia, **137** G1
Eide, Norway, **284** C5
Eidfjord, Norway, **286** C2
Eidsdal, Norway, **286** C1
Eidsvåg, Norway, **286** D1
Eifel, *mountain range*, Germany, **288** C3, *89*
Eigg, *island*, Scotland, U.K., **308** C4
Eight Degree Channel, India/Maldives, **216** C5
Eights Coast, *region*, Antarctica, **470** B6
Eighty Mile Beach, Australia, **134** E2
Eikefjord, Norway, **286** B2
Eiken, Norway, **286** C3
Eilenburg, Germany, **288** F3
Eiler Rasmussen, Kap, *cape*, Greenland, **411** S1
Eilerts de Haan Gebergte, *mountain range*, Suriname, **452** B2
Eilsleben, Germany, **288** E2
Eina, Norway, **286** E2
Einasleigh, Australia, **135** J2
Einasleigh, *river*, Australia, **135** J2
Einbeck, Germany, **288** D3
Eindhoven, Netherlands, **288** B3
Eirunepé, Brazil, **455** E2
Eisenach, Germany, **288** E3
Eisenstadt, Austria, **289** H5
Eisfeld, Germany, **288** E3
Eišiškės, Lithuania, **287** M5
Eitel, Mount, *mountain peak*, Macquarie Island, **134** R11
Eivinvik, Norway, **286** B2
Eivissa (Ibiza), *island*, Islas Baleares, Spain, **293** H3
Eivissa (Ibiza), Islas Baleares, Spain, **293** H3
Ejea de los Caballeros, Spain, **293** G1
Ejeda, Madagascar, **372** A5
Ejido Insurgentes, Mexico, **430** C3
Ejin Horo Qi, China, **210** E5
Ejin Qi, China, **213** J4
Ejura, Ghana, **364** D3
Ejutla, Mexico, **431** F5
Ekalaka, U.S.A., **419** M4
Ekenäs, Sweden, **286** F3
Ekerem, Turkmenistan, **222** E5
Eket, Nigeria, **368** A2
Eketahuna, New Zealand, **132** E5
Ekibastuz, Kazakhstan, **223** K2
Ekombe, Democratic Republic of the Congo, **368** D2
Ekouamou, Congo, **368** C2
Ekshärad, Sweden, **286** F2
Eksjö, Sweden, **286** G4
Ekuku, Democratic Republic of the Congo, **368** D3
Ekwan, *river*, Canada, **415** M5
El Aaiún (Laâyoune), Western Sahara, **360** D3
El Aargub, Western Sahara, **360** C4
El Abiodh Sidi Cheikh, Algeria, **361** G2
El Adeb Larache, Algeria, **361** H3
El Affroun, Algeria, **293** J4
El Alia, Algeria, **361** H2
El Aouinet, Algeria, **295** A8
El Arco, Mexico, **430** B2
El Banco, Colombia, **450** D2
El Barco de Ávila, Spain, **292** E2
El Baúl, Venezuela, **451** E2
El Bayadh, Algeria, **361** G2
El Bolsón, Argentina, **460** C1
El Burgo de Osma, Spain, **293** F2
El Cabaco, Spain, **292** D2
El Caín, Argentina, **460** D1
El Cajon, U.S.A., **422** E5
El Calafate, Argentina, **460** C4
El Callao, Venezuela, **451** G2
El Campo, U.S.A., **424** D5
El Carmen, Bolivia, **455** F3
El Carmen de Bolívar, Colombia, **450** C2
El Centro, U.S.A., **422** F5
El Cerro, Bolivia, **455** G4
El Cerro del Aripo, *mountain peak*, Trinidad, Trinidad and Tobago, **461** C4, *399*
El Cerron, Cerro, *mountain peak*, Venezuela, **451** D1
El Chaparro, Venezuela, **451** F2
El Cocuy, Colombia, **450** D2
El Cove, San Andrés, Colombia, **461** B1
El Cuervo, Mexico, **430** D2
El Cuyo, Mexico, **431** J4
El Desemboque, Mexico, **430** B2
El Difícil, Colombia, **450** C2
El Diviso, Colombia, **450** B4
El Djenoun, Garet, *mountain peak*, Algeria, **361** H4
El Dorado, Arkansas, U.S.A., **424** F3
El Dorado, Kansas, U.S.A., **420** E7
El Dorado, Mexico, **430** D3
El Dorado, Venezuela, **451** G2
El Dorado Springs, U.S.A., **420** G7
El Eglab, *mountain range*, Algeria, **361** E3
El Encanto, Colombia, **450** D4
El Escorial, Spain, **292** E2
El Estor, Guatemala, **428** C4
El Eulma, Algeria, **361** H1
El Fahs, Tunisia, **295** B7
El Fud, Ethiopia, **367** F3
El Fuerte, Mexico, **430** C3
El Goléa, Algeria, **361** G2
El Golfo de Santa Clara, Mexico, **430** B2
El Grado, Spain, **293** H1
El Hadjar, Algeria, **361** H1
El Hank, *mountain range*, Mauritania, **360** E4
El Haouaria, Tunisia, **295** C7
El Harrach, Algeria, **293** J4
El Homr, Algeria, **361** G3
El Jadida, Morocco, **360** E2
El Jaralito, Mexico, **430** D3
El Jicaral, Nicaragua, **428** D4
El Kala, Algeria, **295** B7
El Kef, Tunisia, **295** B7
El Kelaa des Srarhna, Morocco, **360** E2
Ēl Kerē, Ethiopia, **367** F3
Ēl Lēh, Ethiopia, **369** G2
El Limón, Mexico, **431** F4
El Meghaïer, Algeria, **361** H2
El Miamo, Venezuela, **451** G2
El Mojar, Bolivia, **455** F3
El Molinillo, Spain, **292** E3
El Nido, Philippines, **204** B4
El Oasis, Islas Canarias, Spain, **373** B4
El Obeid *see* Al Ubayyiḍ, Sudan, **366** D2
El Oro, Mexico, **430** E3
El Oued, Algeria, **361** H2
El Palmar, Venezuela, **451** G2
El Palmito, Mexico, **430** D3
El Pao, E. Venezuela, **451** F2
El Pao, N. Venezuela, **451** E2
El Paso, U.S.A., **423** K6
El Pensamiento, Bolivia, **455** G4
El Perú, Bolivia, **455** E3
El Portugués, Peru, **454** B2
El Porvenir, Mexico, **430** D2
El Porvenir, Panama, **429** F5
El Potosí, Mexico, **431** E3
El Progreso, Guatemala, **428** C4
El Progreso, Honduras, **428** D4
El Puente, Bolivia, **455** F4
El Puerto de Santa Maria, Spain, **292** D4
El Real, Panama, **429** F5
El Reno, U.S.A., **424** D2
El Rocío, Spain, **292** D4
El Ronquillo, Spain, **292** D4
El Rosario de Arriba, Mexico, **430** B2
El Salado, Argentina, **460** D3
El Salado, Mexico, **431** E3
El Salto, Mexico, **430** D4
El Salvador, Chile, **458** C3
El Salvador, *country*, Central America, **409** P7, *378, 402, 403*
El Salvador, Mexico, **431** E3
El Salvador, Philippines, **204** D4
El Seibo, Dominican Republic, **429** H3
El Soberbio, Argentina, **459** F3
El Socorro, Mexico, **430** B2
El Sombrero, Argentina, **460** D2
El Sombrero, Venezuela, **451** E2
El Sosneado, Argentina, **458** C5
El Sueco, Mexico, **430** D2
El Teleno, *mountain peak*, Spain, **292** D1
El Tigre, Venezuela, **451** F2
El Tocuyo, Venezuela, **451** E2
El Tofo, Chile, **458** B3
El Toro, *mountain peak*, Islas Baleares, Spain, **293** K2
El Toro, Venezuela, **451** G2
El Tránsito, Chile, **458** B3
El Trébol, Argentina, **458** E4
El Triunfo, Mexico, **430** C4
El Turbio, Argentina, **460** C4
El Valle, Colombia, **450** C2
El Vigía, Venezuela, **450** D2
El Wak, Kenya, **369** H2
El Yunque, *mountain peak*, Róbinson Crusoe Island, Archipiélago Juan Fernández, Chile, **461** C2
Ela, Tanjong, *point*, Indonesia, **198** D5
Elafonisos, *island*, Greece, **297** D7
Elafonisou, Steno, *strait*, Greece, **297** D7
Elasa, *island*, Greece, **297** F8
Elassona, Greece, **297** D6
Elat, Israel, **225** C5
Elazığ, Turkey, **224** E5
Elba, Alabama, U.S.A., **425** J4
Elba, Idaho, U.S.A., **418** H5
Elba, Isola d', *island*, Italy, **294** B4
El'ban, Russian Federation, **211** M2
Elbasan, Albania, **297** C5
Elbe, *river*, Germany, **280** F5, *239, 266*
Elbe *see* Labe, *river*, Czech Republic, **289** G3
Elbert, Mount, *mountain peak*, U.S.A., **423** K2
Elberton, U.S.A., **425** L2
Elbeuf, France, **290** E2
Elbistan, Turkey, **224** E5
Elbląg, Poland, **289** J1
Elbow, Canada, **413** R6
Elbow Lake, U.S.A., **420** F3
El'brus, Gora, *mountain peak*, Russian Federation, **222** C4
Elburz Mountains *see* Alborz, Reshteh-ye

Kūhhā-ye, *mountain range*, Iran, **222** E5, *183*
Elche, Spain, **293** G3
Elche de la Sierra, Spain, **293** F3
Elda, Spain, **293** G3
Elder, Mount, *mountain peak*, Macquarie Island, **134** R11
Eldon, U.S.A., **420** G6
Eldorado, Argentina, **459** F3
Eldorado, Illinois, U.S.A., **421** J7
Eldorado, Texas, U.S.A., **424** B4
Eldoret, Kenya, **369** G2
Elea, Cape, Cyprus, **225** C2
Elefsina, Greece, **297** D6
Eleja, Latvia, **287** L4
Elektrostal', Russian Federation, **299** G5
Elemi Triangle, Kenya, **367** D3
Elena, Bulgaria, **296** E4
Elephant Butte Reservoir, U.S.A., **423** K5
Elephant Island, Antarctica, **470** A3
Eleuthera Island, Bahamas, **428** F1
Elfin Cove, U.S.A., **412** A2
Elgå, Norway, **286** E1
Elgin, Illinois, U.S.A., **421** J4
Elgin, Nebraska, U.S.A., **420** D5
Elgin, Nevada, U.S.A., **422** F3
Elgin, North Dakota, U.S.A., **420** C2
Elgin, Oregon, U.S.A., **418** F4
Elgin, Scotland, U.K., **308** F3
Elgin, Texas, U.S.A., **424** D4
Elgol, Scotland, U.K., **308** C3
Elgon, *mountain peak*, Uganda, **369** F2, *340*
Elgoras, Gora, *mountain peak*, Russian Federation, **285** Q2
Eliase, Indonesia, **199** E5
Elida, U.S.A., **423** M5
Elie, Scotland, U.K., **308** G4
Elie de Beaumont, *mountain peak*, New Zealand, **133** C6
Elifaz, Israel, **225** C5
Elila, Democratic Republic of the Congo, **369** E3
Elimäki, Finland, **287** N2
Elin Pelin, Bulgaria, **296** D4
Eling, England, U.K., **305** F4
Elipa, Democratic Republic of the Congo, **368** D3
Eliseu Martins, Brazil, **453** E5
Elista, Russian Federation, **222** C3
Elizabeth, U.S.A., **426** C4
Elizabeth Bay, Namibia, **370** B4
Elizabeth City, U.S.A., **426** B6
Elizabethton, U.S.A., **421** M7
Elizabethtown, Kentucky, U.S.A., **421** L7
Elizabethtown, South Carolina, U.S.A., **425** N2
Elizaveta, Moldova, **296** G2
Ełk, Poland, **289** L2
Elk, *river*, U.S.A., **421** N6
Elk City, Idaho, U.S.A., **418** G4
Elk City, Oklahoma, U.S.A., **424** C2
Elk Grove, U.S.A., **422** C2
Elk Lake, Canada, **421** N2
Elk Mountain, *mountain peak*, U.S.A., **418** F4
Elk Mountain, U.S.A., **419** L6
Elk Point, Canada, **413** P5
Elk River, U.S.A., **420** G3
Elk Springs, U.S.A., **423** J1
Elkhart, U.S.A., **421** L5
Elkhorn, Canada, **414** D7
Elkhovo, Bulgaria, **296** F4
Elkins, Mount, *mountain peak*, Antarctica, **470** F4
Elkins, New Mexico, U.S.A., **423** L5
Elkins, West Virginia, U.S.A., **421** P6
Elkland, U.S.A., **426** B4
Elko, Canada, **413** M7
Elko, U.S.A, **422** F1
Elkton, U.S.A., **421** P6
Ellef Ringnes Island, Canada, **411** J2
Ellen, Mount, *mountain peak*, U.S.A., **423** H3
Ellendale, U.S.A., **420** D2
Ellensburg, U.S.A., **418** D3
Ellesmere, England, U.K., **304** E2
Ellesmere, Lake, New Zealand, **133** D6
Ellesmere Island, Canada, **411** L2
Ellesmere Port, England, U.K., **306** F4
Ellijay, U.S.A., **425** K2
Elliot, South Africa, **371** E5
Elliot Lake, Canada, **421** M2
Elliott, Australia, **134** G2
Elliott Knob, *mountain peak*, U.S.A, **421** P6
Ellisras, South Africa, **371** E3
Elliston, Australia, **135** G5
Ellon, Scotland, U.K., **308** G3
Ellsworth, Iowa, U.S.A., **420** G3
Ellsworth, Kansas, U.S.A., **420** D6
Ellsworth, Maine, U.S.A., **426** F2
Ellsworth Land, *region*, Antarctica, **470** B6
Ellsworth Mountains, *mountain range*, Antarctica, **470** C5
Ellwangen (Jagst), Germany, **288** E4
Elma, U.S.A., **418** C3
Elmalı, Turkey, **297** G7
Elmhurst, U.S.A., **421** K5
Elmira, Canada, **417** K6
Elmira, U.S.A., **426** B3
Elmshorn, Germany, **288** D2
Elorza, Venezuela, **451** E2
Eloy, U.S.A., **423** H5
Elphinstone, Canada, **414** D6
Elsas, Canada, **415** N7
Elsen Nur, *lake*, China, **214** E2
Elsfjord, Norway, **284** F3
Elsie, U.S.A., **420** C5
Elsterwerda, Germany, **288** F3
Elstow, Canada, **413** R6
Eltanin Fracture Zone, *tectonic feature*, Pacific Ocean, **479** J8
Elton, England, U.K., **305** G2
Eluru, India, **217** E2
Elva, Estonia, **287** N3
Elva, Slieve, *mountain peak*, Ireland, **309** C4
Elvanfoot, Scotland, U.K., **308** F5
Elvas, Portugal, **292** D3
Elven, France, **290** C3
Elverum, Norway, **286** E2
Elwell, Lake, U.S.A., **419** J2
Ely, England, U.K., **305** H2
Ely, Minnesota, U.S.A., **420** H2
Ely, Nevada, U.S.A, **422** F2
Elyria, U.S.A., **421** M5
Elze, Germany, **288** D2
Emådalen, Sweden, **286** G2
Emajõgi, *river*, Estonia, **287** N3
Emām, Iran, **222** F5
Emāmshahr, Iran, **222** F5
Emba, Kazakhstan, **222** F3
Embaluh, *river*, Indonesia/Malaysia, **201** F2
Embar, Canada, **416** J3
Embarcación, Argentina, **458** D2
Embleton, England, U.K., **307** G2
Embondo, Democratic Republic of the Congo, **368** C2
Embrun, Canada, **416** D7
Embu, Kenya, **369** G3
Emden, Germany, **288** C2
Emei, China, **215** G3
Emerald, Australia, **135** K3
Emery, U.S.A., **423** H2
Emet, Turkey, **297** G6
Emeti, Papua New Guinea, **140** A4
Emigrant, U.S.A., **419** J4
Emilia Romagna, *autonomous region*, Italy, **294** C3, *255*
Emiliano Zapata, Mexico, **431** H5
Emin, China, **212** D3
Emine, Nos, *point*, Bulgaria, **296** F4
Emissi, Tarso, *mountain peak*, Chad, **362** C4
Emlichheim, Germany, **288** C2
Emmaboda, Sweden, **286** G4
Emmastad, Curaçao, Netherlands Antilles, **461** C3
Emmaste, Estonia, **287** L3
Emmen, Netherlands, **288** C2
Emmetsburg, U.S.A., **420** F4
Emmett, U.S.A., **418** F5
Emmiganūru, India, **216** D3
Emory Peak, *mountain peak*, U.S.A., **423** M7
Empalme, Mexico, **430** C2
Empangeni, South Africa, **371** F4
Empedrado, Argentina, **459** E3
Emperor Seamounts, *underwater feature*, Pacific Ocean, **478** F1, *474*
Emperor Trough, *underwater feature*, Pacific Ocean, **478** F1
Empoli, Italy, **294** C4
Emporia, Kansas, U.S.A., **420** E6
Emporia, Virginia, U.S.A., **426** B6
Emporium, U.S.A., **426** A4
Empress Mine, Zimbabwe, **371** E2
Ems, *river*, Germany, **288** C2
Enånger, Sweden, **287** H2
Enarotali, Indonesia, **199** G3
Encantadas, Serra das, *mountain range*, Brazil, **459** G4
Encarnación, Paraguay, **459** F3
Encinal, U.S.A., **424** C5
Encinitas, U.S.A., **422** E5
Encino, New Mexico, U.S.A., **423** L4
Encino, Texas, U.S.A., **424** C6
Encontrados, Venezuela, **450** D2
Encounter Bay, Australia, **128** C5
Encruzilhada do Sul, Brazil, **459** G4
Encruzilhada, Brazil, **457** F4
Encs, Hungary, **289** K4
Ende, Indonesia, **198** C5
Endeavour, Canada, **414** C5
Enderbury, *island*, Kiribati, **139** G5
Enderby Island, Auckland Islands, New Zealand, **132** J10
Enderby Land, *region*, Antarctica, **470** F4
Enderby Plain, *underwater feature*, Indian Ocean, **476** B8
Endicott, New York, U.S.A., **426** B3
Endicott, Washington, U.S.A., **418** F3
Energía, Argentina, **459** E6
Enewetak, *island*, Marshall Islands, **138** E3, *119*
Enez, Turkey, **297** F5
Enfida, Tunisia, **295** C7
Enfield, Connecticut, U.S.A., **426** D4
Enfield, England, U.K., **305** G3
Enfield, North Carolina, U.S.A., **426** B6
Enga, *province*, Papua New Guinea, **140** A4
Engan, Norway, **284** D5
Engaño, Cabo, *cape*, Dominican Republic, **429** H3
Engaño, Cape, Philippines, **204** C2
Engaru, Japan, **209** H1
Engel's, Russian Federation, **222** D2
Engen, Canada, **412** G4
Enggano, Pulau, *island*, Indonesia, **200** C4
England, *administrative division*, U.K., **304** E2, *46, 54, 59, 74, 77, 78, 79, 80, 88, 90, 91, 92, 93, 93, 94, 96, 110, 243, 244, 245, 252, 274, 275, 276, 279, 315, 342, 380, 384*
Englee, Canada, **417** N4
Englehart, Canada, **421** P2
Englewood, Colorado, U.S.A., **423** L2
Englewood, Kansas, U.S.A., **420** D7
English Bay, Ascension, **373** A3
English Channel, France/U.K., **304** D5, *93, 243, 244, 274, 275, 278, 279*
English Coast, *region*, Antarctica, **470** B5
English River, Canada, **414** J7
Engozero, Ozero, *lake*, Russian Federation, **285** R4
Engozero, Russian Federation, **285** R4
Engure, Latvia, **287** L4
Engures ezers, *lake*, Latvia, **287** L4
Enid, U.S.A., **420** E7
Enköping, Sweden, **287** H3
Enmore, Guyana, **451** H2
Enna, Sicilia, Italy, **295** E7
Ennadai, Canada, **414** D1
Ennadai Lake, Canada, **414** D1
Ennedi, *mountain range*, Chad, **362** D5
Ennell, Lough, *lake*, Ireland, **309** E4
Enning, U.S.A., **420** B3
Ennis, Ireland, **309** D5
Ennis, Montana, U.S.A., **419** J4
Ennis, Texas, U.S.A., **424** D3
Enniscorthy, Ireland, **309** F5
Enniskean, Ireland, **309** D6
Enniskerry, Ireland, **309** F4
Enniskillen, Northern Ireland, U.K., **309** E3
Ennistimon, Ireland, **309** C5
Eno, Finland, **285** Q5
Enochs, U.S.A., **423** M5
Enonkoski, Finland, **287** P1
Enontekiö, Finland, **285** L2
Enping, China, **206** C4
Enschede, Netherlands, **288** C2
Ensenada, Mexico, **430** A2
Enshi, China, **206** B2
Entebbe, Uganda, **369** F2
Entente, *island*, French Polynesia, **137** G2
Enterprise, Alabama, U.S.A., **425** K4
Enterprise, Canada, **413** L1
Enterprise, Oregon, U.S.A., **418** F4
Enterprise, Utah, U.S.A., **422** G3
Entiat, U.S.A., **418** D3
Entrance, Canada, **413** L5
Entre Ríos, Bolivia, **455** F5
Entre Rios, Brazil, **452** B4
Entre Ríos, *province*, Argentina, **459** E4
Entrepeñas, Embalse de, *reservoir*, Spain, **293** F2
Entwistle, Canada, **413** M5
Enugu, Nigeria, **365** F3
Enugu, *state*, Nigeria, **365** F3
Enumclaw, U.S.A., **418** C3
Envermeu, France, **305** J5
Envigado, Colombia, **450** C2
Envira, Brazil, **455** D2
Enyamba, Democratic Republic of the Congo, **368** D3
Enyellé, Congo, **368** C2
Enys, Mount, *mountain peak*, New Zealand, **133** C6
Eolie o Lipari, Isole, *islands*, Italy, **295** E6
Epéna, Congo, **368** C2
Épernay, France, **291** F2
Ephrata, Pennsylvania, U.S.A., **426** B4
Ephrata, Washington, U.S.A., **418** E3
Epi, *island*, Vanuatu, **141** A2
Épinal, France, **291** H2
Epira, Guyana, **451** H3
Episkopi, Cyprus, **225** B2
Episkopi Bay, Cyprus, **225** B2
Epping, England, U.K., **305** H3
Epsom, England, U.K., **305** G3
Epu-pel, Argentina, **458** D5
Epworth, England, U.K., **307** H4
Equateur, *administrative region*, Democratic Republic of the Congo, **368** C2
Equatorial Guinea, *country*, Africa, **359** F6, *330, 331, 332, 333*
Equeipa, Venezuela, **451** F3
Er Rachidia, Morocco, **361** F2
Era, *river*, Papua New Guinea, **140** B4
Erave, Papua New Guinea, **140** A4
Erba, Jabal, *mountain peak*, Sudan, **363** G4
Érd, Hungary, **289** J5
Erdaohezi, China, **211** K3
Erdek, Turkey, **297** F5
Erdemli, Turkey, **225** C1
Erdenet, Bulgan, Mongolia, **213** J2
Erdenet, Hövsgöl, Mongolia, **213** H2
Erdenetsogt, Bayanhongor, Mongolia, **213** J3
Erdenetsogt, Ömnögovĭ, Mongolia, **210** D4
Erding, Germany, **288** E4
Erechim, Brazil, **459** G3
Ereentsav, Mongolia, **210** F2
Ereğli, Turkey, **224** D5
Ereikoussa, *island*, Ionioi Nisoi, Greece, **297** B6
Erenhot, China, **210** E4
Eretria, Greece, **297** D6
Ereymentaū, Kazakhstan, **223** J2
Erezée, Belgium, **288** B3
Erfjord, Norway, **286** C3
Erfoud, Morocco, **361** F2
Erfurt, Germany, **288** E3
Ergani, Turkey, **363** G1
Ergel, Mongolia, **210** E4
Ergene, *river*, Turkey, **297** F5
Ērgli, Latvia, **287** M4
Ergun, *river*, China, **211** H1
Erick, U.S.A., **424** C2
Erickson, Canada, **414** E6
Ericson, U.S.A., **420** D5
Erie, Lake, Canada/U.S.A., **421** N5, *380, 381*
Erie, U.S.A., **421** N4
Erîgât, *desert*, Mali, **361** E4
Eriksdale, Canada, **414** E6
Erillas, *mountain peak*, Spain, **292** E3
Erimo, Japan, **209** H2
Erimo-misaki, *point*, Japan, **209** H2
Erin Point, Trinidad, Trinidad and Tobago, **461** C4
Eringsboda, Sweden, **286** G4
Eriskay, *island*, Scotland, U.K., **308** B3
Eritrea, *country*, Africa, **358** J5, *81, 254, 255, 336, 337, 338, 339*
Erkowit, Sudan, **363** G5
Erlangen, Germany, **288** E4
Erldunda, Australia, **134** G4
Erlongshan, China, **211** L3
Ermelo, South Africa, **371** F4
Ermenek, Turkey, **363** F1
Ermioni, Greece, **297** D7
Ermoupoli, Kyklades, Greece, **297** E7
Erndtebrück, Germany, **288** D3
Ernée, France, **290** D2
Ernei, Romania, **296** E2
Ernstbrunn, Austria, **289** H4
Erode, India, **216** D4
Eromanga, Australia, **135** J4
Erongo, *administrative region*, Namibia, **370** B3
Erongo, *mountain peak*, Namibia, **370** C3, *350*
Errego, Mozambique, **369** G6
Errigal Mountain, *mountain peak*, Ireland, **309** D2
Erris Head, *point*, Ireland, **309** B3
Errol, U.S.A., **426** E2
Erromango, *island*, Vanuatu, **141** A3
Ersekë, Albania, **297** C5
Ershiwuzhan, China, **211** H1
Ershizhan, China, **211** J1
Erskine, U.S.A., **420** E2
Ertai, China, **212** F3
Ertis, Kazakhstan, **223** K2
Ertis, *river*, Kazakhstan, **223** K2
Ertvågøy, *island*, Norway, **284** D5
Eruki, Mount, *mountain peak*, Papua New Guinea, **140** B4
Erval, Brazil, **459** G4
Erwood, Canada, **414** C5
Erythres, Greece, **297** D6
Eryuan, China, **215** F4
Erzgebirge, *mountain range*, Germany, **288** F3
Erzhan, China, **211** J2
Erzin, Russian Federation, **213** G2
Erzincan, Turkey, **224** E5
Erzurum, Turkey, **224** F5
Eržvilkas, Lithuania, **287** L5
Esa'ala, Papua New Guinea, **140** C5
Esashi, N. Hokkaidō, Japan, **209** H1
Esashi, S. Hokkaidō, Japan, **209** H2
Esbjerg, Denmark, **286** D5
Escada, Brazil, **453** G5
Escalada, Spain, **293** F1
Escalante, U.S.A., **423** H3
Escalaplano, Sardegna, Italy, **295** B6
Escalón, Mexico, **430** D3
Escanaba, U.S.A., **421** K3
Eschede, Germany, **288** E2
Escocesa, Bahía, *bay*, Dominican Republic, **429** H3
Escoma, Bolivia, **455** E4
Escondida, Chile, **458** C2
Escondido, U.S.A., **422** E5

Escuinapa, Mexico, **430** D4
Escuintla, Guatemala, **428** C4
Eséka, Cameroon, **368** B2
Eşen, Turkey, **297** G7
Esens, Germany, **288** C2
Eşfahān, Iran, **220** F2, *182*
Esfandak, Iran, **221** H3
Esfarāyen, Iran, **222** F5
Esha Ness, *point*, Shetland, Scotland, U.K., **308** K7
Esigodini, Zimbabwe, **371** E3
Esik, Kazakhstan, **212** C4
Esil, Kazakhstan, **222** H2
Esil, *river*, Kazakhstan, **223** H2
Eskdale, *valley*, Scotland, U.K., **308** G5
Eskdalemuir, Scotland, U.K., **308** F5
Eske, Lough, *lake*, Ireland, **309** D3
Esker, Canada, **416** H3
Eskilstuna, Sweden, **286** H3
Eskişehir, Turkey, **224** D5
Esla, *river*, Spain, **292** E1
Eslöv, Sweden, **286** F5
Eşme, Turkey, **297** G6
Esmeralda, Cuba, **429** F2
Esmeralda, Isla, *island*, Chile, **460** B3
Esmeraldas, Ecuador, **450** B4, *438*
Espakeh, Iran, **221** H3
Espalion, France, **290** F4
Espanola, Canada, **421** N2
Española, Isla, *island*, Islas Galápagos (Galapagos Islands), Ecuador, **461** A2
Espanola, U.S.A., **423** K3
Esperance, Australia, **134** E5
Esperantinópolis, Brazil, **453** E4
Esperanza, *Argentinian research station*, Antarctica, **470** A4
Esperanza, Mexico, **430** C3
Esperanza, Peru, **454** D2
Esperanza, Santa Cruz, Argentina, **460** C4
Esperanza, Santa Fé, Argentina, **458** E4
Espichel, Cabo, *cape*, Portugal, **292** C3
Espiel, Spain, **292** E3
Espigão, Serra do, *mountain range*, Brazil, **459** G3
Espigão Mestre, *mountain range*, Brazil, **456** E3
Espinhaço, Serra do, *mountain range*, Brazil, **447** H6
Espinilho, Serra do, *mountain range*, Brazil, **459** F3
Espinillo, Argentina, **459** E2
Espinosa, Brazil, **457** E4
Espírito Santo, *state*, Brazil, **457** F5
Espíritu Santo, *island*, Vanuatu, **141** A2, *116*
Esplanada, Brazil, **457** G3
Espoo, Finland, **287** M2
Espungabera, Mozambique, **371** F3
Esquel, Argentina, **460** C2
Esquina, Argentina, **459** E4
Esrange, Sweden, **284** K3
Essaouira, Morocco, **360** E2
Essen, Germany, **288** C3
Essequibo, *river*, Guyana, **451** G3, *437*
Essex, California, U.S.A., **422** F4
Essex, Montana, U.S.A., **418** H2
Essex, Punta, *point*, Islas Galápagos (Galapagos Islands), Ecuador, **461** A2
Essex, *unitary authority*, England, U.K., **305** H3
Est, Pointe de l', *point*, Canada, **417** L5
Est, *province*, Cameroon, **368** B2
Estaca de Bares, Punta da, *point*, Spain, **292** D1
Estacado, Llano, *plain*, U.S.A., **423** M4
Estados, Isla de los, *island*, Argentina, **460** E5
Estagel, France, **290** F5
Estaires, France, **305** K4
Estância, Brazil, **457** G3
Estats, Pic d', France/Spain, **293** H1
Estcourt, South Africa, **371** E4
Esteban Rams, Argentina, **458** E3
Estelí, Nicaragua, **428** D4
Estella, Spain, **293** F1
Estepa, Spain, **292** E4
Estépar, Spain, **293** F1
Estepona, Spain, **292** E4
Esterhazy, Canada, **414** C6
Estevan, Canada, **414** C7
Estevan Point, Canada, **412** F7
Estherville, U.S.A., **420** F4
Estill, U.S.A., **425** M3
Estissac, France, **291** F2
Estiva, *river*, Brazil, **453** E5
Eston, Canada, **413** Q6
Estonia, *country*, Europe, **282** G4, *228, 232, 235, 236, 237, 270, 272*
Estrées-St-Denis, France, **305** K5
Estrela, Serra da, *mountain range*, Portugal, **292** C2, *250*
Estremoz, Portugal, **292** D3
Estrondo, Serra do, *mountain range*, Brazil, **452** D5
Estuaire, *province*, Gabon, **368** A2
Esztergom, Hungary, **289** J5
Etah, India, **218** D4
Etampes, France, **290** F2
Étaples, France, **290** E1
Etāwah, India, **218** D4
Etelä-Suomen Lääni, *province*, Finland, **287** M2
Ethelbert, Canada, **414** D6
Ethiopia, *country*, Africa, **358** J6, *90, 96, 97, 254, 255, 312, 313, 336, 337, 338, 339*
Ethiopian Highlands, *mountain range*, Ethiopia, 356 J5
Ethridge, U.S.A., **419** H2
Etive, Loch, *inlet*, Scotland, U.K., **308** D4
Etna, Monte, *mountain peak*, Sicilia, Italy, **295** E7, *254, 255*
Etne, Norway, **286** B3
Eton, Canada, **421** L2
Etoumbi, Congo, **368** B2
Étretat, France, **305** H5
Etropole, Bulgaria, **296** E4
Ettelbruck, Luxembourg, **291** H2
Ettington, England, U.K., **305** F2
Etwall, England, U.K., **305** F2
Etzatlan, Mexico, **430** D4
Eu, France, **305** J4
'Eua, *island*, Tonga, **141** B4
'Eua Iki, *island*, Tonga, **141** B4
Euakafa, *island*, Vava'u Group, Tonga, **141** B3
Euboea *see* Evvoia, *island*, Greece, **297** E6
Eucla, Australia, **134** F5
Euclides da Cunha, Brazil, **457** F3
Eufaula, U.S.A., **425** K4
Eufaula Lake, U.S.A., **424** E2
Eugene, U.S.A., **418** C4
Eugenia, Punta, *point*, Mexico, **430** A3
Eunice, Louisiana, U.S.A., **424** F4
Eunice, New Mexico, U.S.A., **423** M5
Eupen, Belgium, **288** B3
Euphrates, *river*, Asia, **194** F6; *see also* Euphrates, *river*, Iraq, **363** H2; Fırat, *river*, Turkey, **224** E5; Firat Nehri, *river*, Syria, **363** G1, *64, 66, 88, 146, 181, 182*
Eupora, U.S.A., **425** H3
Eura, Finland, **287** L2
Eurajoki, Finland, **287** K2
Eureka, California, U.S.A., **422** A1
Eureka, Canada, **411** L1
Eureka, Montana, U.S.A., **418** G2
Eureka, Nevada, U.S.A, **422** F2
Eureka, Utah, U.S.A., **423** G2
Eureka, Washington, U.S.A., **418** E3
Europa, Île, *island*, Réunion, **371** H3, *354*
Europa, Picos de, *mountain peak*, Spain, **292** E1
Eustis, U.S.A., **425** M5
Eutaw, U.S.A., **425** J3
Eutin, Germany, **288** E1
Eutsuk Lake, Canada, **412** F5
Evanger, Norway, **286** C2
Evans, Lac, *lake*, Canada, **416** C4
Evans, Mount, *mountain peak*, U.S.A., **418** H3
Evans Peninsula, Antarctica, **470** A6
Evans Strait, Canada, **411** L3
Evanston, Illinois, U.S.A., **421** K4
Evanston, Wyoming, U.S.A., **419** J6
Evansville, Canada, **421** M3
Evansville, Illinois, U.S.A., **420** J6
Evansville, Indiana, U.S.A., **421** K7
Evaro, U.S.A., **418** G3
Evaton, South Africa, **371** E4
Evaz, Iran, **220** F3
Everest, Mount, *mountain peak*, China/Nepal, **214** C3, *158, 172*
Everett, U.S.A., **418** C3
Evergreen, U.S.A., **425** J4
Evesham, England, U.K., **305** F2
Evijärvi, Finland, **285** L5
Evijärvi, *lake*, Finland, **285** L5
Evinayong, Equatorial Guinea, **368** B2
Evje, Norway, **286** C3
Évora, *district*, Portugal, **292** D3
Évora, Portugal, **292** D3
Evoron, Ozero, *lake*, Russian Federation, **211** M2
Évreux, France, **290** E2
Évry, France, **290** F2
Evvoia (Euboea), *island*, Greece, **297** E6
Ewan, U.S.A., **418** F3
Ewango, Nigeria, **365** F3
Ewaso Ngiro, *river*, Kenya, **369** G2
Ewe, Loch, *inlet*, Scotland, U.K., **308** D3
Ewo, Congo, **368** B3
Exaltación, Bolivia, **455** F3
Exe, *river*, England, U.K., **304** D4
Executive Committee Range, *mountain range*, Antarctica, **470** C7
Exeter, Canada, **421** N4
Exeter, England, U.K., **304** D4
Exminster, England, U.K., **304** D4
Exmoor, *moorland*, England, U.K., **304** D3
Exmore, U.S.A., **426** C6
Exmouth, Australia, **134** C3
Exmouth, England, U.K., **304** D4
Exmouth Gulf, Australia, **134** C3
Exmouth Plateau, *underwater feature*, Indian Ocean, **476** G6
Extremadura, *district*, Spain, **292** D3, *253*
Extrême-Nord, *province*, Cameroon, **365** G2
Exu, Brazil, **453** F5
Eyasi, Lake, Tanzania, **369** F3, *342*
Eye, Cambridgeshire, England, U.K., **305** G2
Eye, Suffolk, England, U.K., **305** J2
Eye Peninsula, Scotland, U.K., **308** C2
Eyemouth, Scotland, U.K., **308** G5
Eyl, Somalia, **367** G3
Eymet, France, **290** E4
Eynsham, England, U.K., **305** F3
Eyre North, Lake, Australia, **135** H4, *112*
Eyre Peninsula, Australia, **135** H5
Eyre South, Lake, Australia, **135** H4, *112*
Eyreton, New Zealand, **133** D6
Eysturoy, *island*, Faeroe Islands, **302** D1
Eyumojok, Cameroon, **368** A1
Ezequiel Ramos Mexia, Embalse, *reservoir*, Argentina, **460** D1
Ezere, Latvia, **287** L4
Ezernieki, Latvia, **287** N4
Ezhou, China, **206** C2
Ezine, Turkey, **297** F6


## F


Faadhippolhu Atoll, Maldives, **216** C5
Faafxadhuun, Somalia, **369** H2
Faaite, *island*, French Polynesia, **137** G2
Fabens, U.S.A., **423** K6
Fåberg, Norway, **286** E2
Fabiuola, *river*, Spain, **292** D3
Fåborg, Denmark, **286** E5
Fabriano, Italy, **294** D4
Facatativá, Colombia, **450** C3
Fachi, Niger, **365** G1
Facundo, Argentina, **460** C2
Fada, Chad, **362** D5
Fada N'Gourma, Burkina Faso, **364** E2
Faddeyevskiy, Ostrov, *island*, Russian Federation, **301** R2
Faenza, Italy, **294** C3
Faeroe-Iceland Ridge, *underwater feature*, Atlantic Ocean, **477** G1
Faeroe Islands, *Danish territory*, Atlantic Ocean, **302** C2, *228, 234, 278*
Fagamalo, Samoa, **141** B1
Făgăraş, Romania, **296** E3
Fagatogo, American Samoa, **141** B2
Fågelberget, Sweden, **284** G4
Fagernes, Oppland, Norway, **286** D2
Fagernes, Troms, Norway, **284** J2
Fagersta, Sweden, **286** G3
Făget, Romania, **296** D3
Faggo, Nigeria, **365** G2
Fagnano, Lago, *lake*, Argentina, **460** D5
Faguibine, Lac, *lake*, Mali, **364** D1
Fagurhólsmýri, Iceland, **284** Y8
Faial, *island*, Azores, Portugal, **360** M7
Faial, Madeira, Portugal, **373** C3
Fā'id, Egypt, **225** B4
Fair Head, *point*, Northern Ireland, U.K., **309** F2
Fairbank, U.S.A., **423** H6
Fairbanks, U.S.A., **410** E3
Fairfax, U.S.A., **420** D4
Fairfield, California, U.S.A., **422** C2
Fairfield, Idaho, U.S.A., **418** G5
Fairfield, Illinois, U.S.A., **421** J6
Fairfield, Iowa, U.S.A., **420** H5
Fairfield, Montana, U.S.A., **419** J3
Fairfield, North Dakota, U.S.A., **420** B2
Fairfield, Texas, U.S.A., **424** D4
Fairford, Canada, **414** E6
Fairlie, New Zealand, **133** C7
Fairlight, England, U.K., **305** H4
Fairlight, Canada, **414** D7
Fairmont, Nebraska, U.S.A., **420** E5
Fairmont, West Virginia, U.S.A., **421** N6
Fairplay, U.S.A., **423** L2
Fairview, Canada, **413** K3
Fairview, U.S.A., **425** J2
Fairweather, Mount, *mountain peak*, U.S.A., **412** A2
Fais, *island*, Micronesia, **138** C4
Faisalābād, Pakistan, **218** C3
Faither, The, *point*, Shetland, Scotland, U.K., **308** K7
Faizābād, India, **219** E4
Fajaghalia, Solomon Islands, **141** A1
Fajardo, Puerto Rico, **427** C2
Fakahina, *island*, French Polynesia, **137** H2
Fakaofo, *island*, Tokelau, **139** G5
Fakarava, *island*, French Polynesia, **137** G2
Fakenham, England, U.K., **305** H2
Fakfak, Indonesia, **199** F3
Fakiya, Bulgaria, **296** F4
Fakse Bugt, *bay*, Denmark, **286** F5
Faku, China, **211** H4
Falaba, Sierra Leone, **364** B3
Falaise, France, **290** D2
Fălciu, Romania, **296** G2
Falcon Lake, Canada, **414** G7
Falcone, Capo del, *cape*, Sardegna, Italy, **295** A5
Faleasi'u, Samoa, **141** B1
Falelatai, Samoa, **141** B1
Falelima, Samoa, **141** B1
Făleşti, Moldova, **296** F2
Faleula, Samoa, **141** B1
Falfurrias, U.S.A., **424** C6
Falkenberg, Sweden, **286** F4
Falkirk, *local authority*, Scotland, U.K., **308** F5
Falkirk, Scotland, U.K., **308** F5
Falkland, Scotland, U.K., **308** F4
Falkland Escarpment, *underwater feature*, Atlantic Ocean, **477** D9
Falkland Islands, *U.K. dependency*, Atlantic Ocean, **460** F4, *95, 97, 275, 276, 435, 443, 445*
Falkland Plateau, *underwater feature*, Atlantic Ocean, **477** D9
Falkland Sound, Falkland Islands, **460** F4
Falkonera, *island*, Greece, **297** D7
Falköping, Sweden, **286** F3
Fall, *river*, U.S.A., **420** F7
Fall City, U.S.A., **418** D3
Fall River, U.S.A., **426** E4
Fallon, Montana, U.S.A., **419** M3
Fallon, Nevada, U.S.A., **422** D2
Falls City, U.S.A., **420** F5
Falls Lake Reservoir, U.S.A., **421** P7
Fallsville, U.S.A., **424** F2
Falmouth, England, U.K., **304** B4
Falmouth, Jamaica, **429** F3
Falmouth Bay, England, U.K., **304** B4
False Bay, South Africa, **370** C5
False Point, India, **219** F5
Falster, *island*, Denmark, **286** E5
Fălticeni, Romania, **296** F2
Falun, Sweden, **286** G2
Famagusta *see* Ammochostos, Cyprus, **225** B2, *191*
Famatina, Argentina, **458** C3
Famatina, *mountain peak*, Argentina, **458** C3
Famatina, Sierra de, *mountain range*, Argentina, **458** C3
Fan Si Pan, *mountain peak*, Vietnam, **203** D1, *153*
Fana, Mali, **364** C2
Fanad Head, *point*, Ireland, **309** E2
Fanandrana, Madagascar, **372** B4
Fanārah, Egypt, **225** B4
Fanchang, China, **206** D2
Fandriana, Madagascar, **372** B5
Fang, Thailand, **202** C2
Fang-liao, Taiwan, **206** E4
Fang Xian, China, **206** B1
Fangak, *river*, Sudan, **366** D3
Fangak, Sudan, **366** D3
Fangatau, *island*, French Polynesia, **137** G2, H3
Fangcheng, China, **206** C1
Fangzheng, China, **211** K3
Fanjiatun, China, **211** J4
Fanli, China, **206** B1
Fanling, China, **207** C4
Fannich, Loch, *lake*, Scotland, U.K., **308** D3
Fanø, *island*, Denmark, **286** D5
Fano, Italy, **294** D4
Fanshan, China, **206** E3
Fanshi, China, **210** F5
Fara in Sabina, Italy, **295** D4
Faradje, Democratic Republic of the Congo, **369** E2
Farafangana, Madagascar, **372** B5
Farafenni, Gambia, **364** A2
Farāh, Afghanistan, **221** H2
Farallon de Pajaros, *island*, Northern Mariana Islands, **138** C2
Faranah, Guinea, **364** B2
Farasān, Jazā'ir, *islands*, Saudi Arabia, **220** D5
Faraulep, *island*, Micronesia, **138** C4
Fareham, England, U.K., **305** F4
Farewell, Cape, New Zealand, **132** D5
Farewell Spit, New Zealand, **132** D5
Fargo, Georgia, U.S.A., **425** L4
Fargo, North Dakota, U.S.A., **420** E2
Farīdkot, India, **218** C3
Farīdpur, Bangladesh, **219** G5
Färila, Sweden, **286** G2
Faringdon, England, U.K., **305** F3
Farinha, *river*, Brazil, **452** D5
Fāriskūr, Egypt, **225** A4
Farmington, Georgia, U.S.A., **425** L3
Farmington, Illinois, U.S.A., **420** H5

Farmington, Maine, U.S.A., **426** E2
Farmington, New Mexico, U.S.A., **423** J3
Farmville, North Carolina, U.S.A., **426** B7
Farmville, Virginia, U.S.A., **421** P7
Farnborough, England, U.K., **305** G3
Farndon, England, U.K., **304** E1
Farnham, England, U.K., **305** G3
Faro, Brazil, **452** B4
Faro, Canada, **410** F3
Faro, *district*, Portugal, **292** C4
Fårö, *island*, Sweden, **287** J3
Faro, *mountain peak*, Spain, **292** D1
Faro, Portugal, **292** D4
Fårösund, Sweden, **287** J4
Farquhar Group, *islands*, Seychelles, **372** C3
Farrukhābād, India, **218** D4
Farsala, Greece, **297** D6
Farson, U.S.A., **419** K5
Farsund, Norway, **286** C3
Fartak, Ra's, *cape*, Yemen, **220** F5
Fartura, Serra da, *mountain range*, Brazil, **459** G3
Farwell Island, Antarctica, **470** B5
Fasā, Iran, **220** F3
Fasano, Italy, **295** F5
Fáskrúðsfjörður, Iceland, **284** Z7
Fataki, Democratic Republic of the Congo, **369** F2
Fatehābād, India, **218** C3
Fatehpur, India, **218** E4
Fatehpur, Pakistan, **218** B3
Fatick, Senegal, **364** A2
Fátima, Portugal, **292** C3
Fatu Hiva, *island*, French Polynesia, **137** H2
Fatunda, Democratic Republic of the Congo, **368** C3
Fauquembergues, France, **305** K4
Fauquier, Canada, **413** K7
Făurei, Romania, **296** F3
Fauske, Norway, **284** G3
Faust, Canada, **413** M4
Fauville-en-Caux, France, **305** H5
Faversham, England, U.K., **305** H3
Fawcett, Canada, **413** M4
Fawley, England, U.K., **305** F4
Fawnie Nose, *mountain peak*, Canada, **412** G5
Faxaflói, *bay*, Iceland, **284** W7
Faxälven, *river*, Sweden, **284** H5
Faya-Largeau, Chad, **362** C5
Fayaoué, New Caledonia, **141** A3
Fayette, Alabama, U.S.A., **425** J3
Fayette, Mississippi, U.S.A., **424** G4
Fayetteville, Arkansas, U.S.A., **424** E1
Fayetteville, North Carolina, U.S.A., **425** N2
Fayetteville, Tennessee, U.S.A., **425** J2
Fdérik, Mauritania, **360** D4
Feale, *river*, Ireland, **309** C5
Featherville, U.S.A., **418** G5
Fécamp, France, **290** E2
Federación, Argentina, **459** F4
Federal, Argentina, **459** E4
Federal Capital Territory, *state*, Nigeria, **365** F3
Fedje, Norway, **286** B2
Fedorovka, Kazakhstan, **222** G2
Fedyukovo, Russian Federation, **299** E5
Feeagh, Lough, *lake*, Ireland, **309** C4
Fehérgyarmat, Hungary, **289** L5
Fehmarn, *island*, Germany, **288** E1
Fei Xian, China, **208** B4
Feijó, Brazil, **455** D2
Feilding, New Zealand, **132** E5
Feira de Santana, Brazil, **457** F3
Feldbach, Austria, **289** G5
Feldkirch, Austria, **288** D5
Feletoa, Vava'u Group, Tonga, **141** B3
Feliciano, *river*, Argentina, **459** E4
Felicité, *island*, Seychelles, **373** A2
Felidu Atoll, Maldives, **216** C6
Felipe Carrillo Puerto, Mexico, **431** H5
Félix U. Gómez, Mexico, **430** D2
Felixlândia, Brazil, **457** E5
Felixstowe, England, U.K., **305** J3
Feltre, Italy, **294** C2
Femund, *lake*, Norway, **286** E1
Fence Lake, U.S.A., **423** J4
Fenelon Falls, Canada, **416** B7
Fener Burnu, *point*, Turkey, **224** E4
Fenestrelle, Italy, **294** A3
Feng-kang, Taiwan, **206** E4
Feng-lin, Taiwan, **206** E4
Feng-shan, Taiwan, **206** E4
Feng Xian, Shaanxi, China, **215** H2
Feng Xian, Shandong, China, **206** D1
Feng-yüan, Taiwan, **206** E3
Fengari, *mountain peak*, Greece, **297** E5
Fengcheng, Gansu, China, **213** J5
Fengcheng, Jiangxi, China, **206** C2
Fengcheng, Liaoning, China, **211** J4
Fengdu, China, **215** H3
Fenggang, China, **215** H4
Fenghua, China, **206** E2
Fenghuang, Guangdong, China, **206** D4
Fenghuang, Hunan, China, **206** B3
Fengjie, China, **206** B2
Fengning, China, **210** G4
Fengqiu, China, **206** C1
Fengshan, China, **215** F4
Fengshun, China, **206** D4
Fengtai, China, **206** D1
Fengxian, China, **206** E2
Fengxiang, China, **215** H2
Fengxin, China, **206** C2
Fengyang, China, **206** D1
Fengyi, China, **215** H3
Fengzhen, China, **210** F4
Feni, Bangladesh, **219** G5
Feni Islands, Papua New Guinea, **140** D4
Fennimore, U.S.A., **420** H4
Fenoarivo Atsinanana, Madagascar, **372** B4
Fens, The, *region*, England, U.K., **305** G2
Fenyang, China, **210** E5
Feodosiya, Ukraine, **298** E3
Feolin Ferry, Scotland, U.K., **308** C5
Fer, Cap de, *cape*, Algeria, **361** H1
Ferapontovo, Russian Federation, **299** G3
Ferdinand, U.S.A., **421** K6
Ferdows, Iran, **221** G2
Fère-Champenoise, France, **291** F2
Fère-en-Tardenois, France, **291** F2
Feres, Greece, **297** F5
Fergus Falls, U.S.A., **420** E2
Fergusson Island, Papua New Guinea, **140** C5
Feriana, Tunisia, **362** A2
Ferkessédougou, Côte d'Ivoire, **364** C3
Fermanagh, *district*, Northern Ireland, U.K., **309** E3
Fermo, Italy, **294** D4
Fermoselle, Spain, **292** D2
Fermoy, Ireland, **309** D5
Fernández, Argentina, **458** D3
Fernandina, Isla, *island*, Islas Galápagos (Galapagos Islands), Ecuador, **461** A2
Fernandina Beach, U.S.A., **425** M4
Fernandópolis, Brazil, **456** C5
Ferndale, U.S.A., **418** C2
Ferndown, England, U.K., **305** F4
Fernie, Canada, **413** M7
Fernley, U.S.A., **422** D2
Ferns, Ireland, **309** F5
Ferrara, Italy, **294** C3
Ferreira do Alentejo, Portugal, **292** C3
Ferreira Gomes, Brazil, **452** C3
Ferreñafe, Peru, **454** B2
Ferriday, U.S.A., **424** G4
Ferro, Ilhéu de, *island*, Madeira, Portugal, **373** C3
Ferro, *river*, Brazil, **456** B3
Ferrol, Spain, **292** C1
Ferryhill, England, U.K., **307** G3
Ferryland, Canada, **417** Q6
Fès, Morocco, **361** F2, *74*
Feshi, Democratic Republic of the Congo, **368** C4
Fessenden, U.S.A., **420** D2
Festvåg, Norway, **284** G3
Fété Bowé, Senegal, **364** B2
Feteşti, Romania, **296** F3
Fethard, Ireland, **309** E5
Fethiye, Turkey, **297** G7
Fethiye Körfezi, *bay*, Turkey, **297** G7
Fetisovo, Kazakhstan, **222** E4
Fetlar, *island*, Shetland, Scotland, U.K., **308** L7
Fettercairn, Scotland, U.K., **308** G4
Feuilles, Rivière aux, *river*, Canada, **411** M4
Feurs, France, **291** G4
Fevral'sk, Russian Federation, **211** K1
Feyẓābād, Afghanistan, **218** B1
Ffestiniog, Wales, U.K., **304** D2
Fiambalá, Argentina, **458** C3
Fian, Ghana, **364** D2
Fianarantsoa, Madagascar, **372** B5
Fianarantsoa, *province*, Madagascar, **372** B5
Fianga, Chad, **365** H3
Fichē, Ethiopia, **367** E3
Fichtelgebirge, *mountain range*, Germany, **288** E4
Fidenza, Italy, **294** C3
Field, Canada, **421** N2
Fieni, Romania, **296** E3
Fier, Albania, **297** B5
Fierras, *mountain peak*, Sweden, **284** H3
Fife, Scotland, U.K., **308** F4
Fife Ness, *point*, Scotland, U.K., **308** G4
Figari, Capo, *cape*, Sardegna, Italy, **295** B5
Figari, Corse, France, **295** B5
Figeac, France, **290** F4
Figeholm, Sweden, **286** H4
Figueira da Foz, Portugal, **292** C2
Figueres, Spain, **293** J1
Figuig, Morocco, **361** F2
Figuil, Cameroon, **365** G3
Fiji, *country*, Pacific Ocean, **131** G3, *61, 93, 108, 109, 114, 116, 117, 127*
Fiji-Plateau, *underwater feature*, Pacific Ocean, **478** F6
Filabres, Sierra de los, *mountain range*, Spain, **293** F4
Filabusi, Zimbabwe, **371** E3
Filadelfia, Costa Rica, **428** D5
Filadelfia, Paraguay, **459** E2
Fil'akovo, Slovakia, **289** J4
Filamana, Mali, **364** C2
Filchner Ice Shelf, Antarctica, **470** C4
Filer, U.S.A., **418** G5
Filey, England, U.K., **307** H3
Filey Head, *point*, England, U.K., **307** H3
Filiaşi, Romania, **296** D3
Filiates, Greece, **297** C6
Filiatra, Greece, **297** C7
Filicudi, Isola, *island*, Italy, **295** E6
Filingué, Niger, **365** E2
Filippiada, Greece, **297** C6
Filipstad, Sweden, **286** G3
Fillmore, Canada, **414** C7
Fillmore, U.S.A., **422** G2
Filton, England, U.K., **304** E3
Fīltu, Ethiopia, **367** F3
Fimbulheimen, *mountain range*, Antarctica, **470** D3
Fimbulisen, *ice shelf*, Antarctica, **470** D3
Finale Ligure, Italy, **294** B3
Finby, Finland, **287** K2
Findhorn, Scotland, U.K., **308** F3
Findlay, U.S.A., **421** M5
Findon, England, U.K., **305** G4
Fingal, U.S.A., **420** E2
Fingoè, Mozambique, **369** F6
Finke, *river*, Australia, **135** G4, *109*
Finland, *country*, Europe, **282** G3, *94, 228, 231, 232, 234, 235, 245, 271, 273, 464*
Finland, Gulf of, Estonia/Finland/Russian Federation, **287** M3, *235, 236, 271*
Finlay, *river*, Canada, **412** G3
Finley, U.S.A., **420** E2
Finn, *river*, Ireland, **309** D3
Finnmark, *county*, Norway, **285** M1
Finnsnes, Norway, **284** J2
Finnvollheia, *mountain peak*, Norway, **284** E4
Finschhafen, Papua New Guinea, **140** B4
Finsteraarhorn, *mountain peak*, Switzerland, **291** J3
Finsterwalde, Germany, **288** F3
Fintona, Northern Ireland, U.K., **309** E3
Fintown, Ireland, **309** D3
Fionn Loch, *lake*, Scotland, U.K., **308** D3
Fionnphort, Scotland, U.K., **308** C4
Fiora, *river*, Italy, **294** C4
Fırat (Euphrates), *river*, Turkey, **224** E5
Firat Nehri (Euphrates), *river*, Syria, **363** G1, *181, 182*
Fire River, Canada, **415** N7
Firebag, *river*, Canada, **413** P3
Firenze (Florence), Italy, **294** C4, *75, 254, 255*
Firesteel, U.S.A., **420** C3
Firmat, Argentina, **458** E4
Fīrozābād, India, **218** D4
Fīrozpur, India, **218** C3
Firsovo, Russian Federation, **211** G1
Fīrūz Kūh, Iran, **220** F1
Fīrūzābād, Iran, **220** F3
Fisher Strait, Canada, **411** L3
Fishguard, Wales, U.K., **304** C3
Fishguard Bay, Wales, U.K., **304** B2
Fishtoft, England, U.K., **305** H2
Fiskebøl, Norway, **284** G2
Fisterra, Cabo, *cape*, Spain, **292** C1
Fisterra, Spain, **292** C1
Fitful Head, *point*, Scotland, U.K., **308** K8
Fito, Mount, *mountain peak*, Samoa, **141** B1
Fitz Roy, Argentina, **460** D3
Fitz Roy, Monte, *mountain peak*, Argentina, **460** C3
Fitzcarrald, Peru, **454** D3
Fitzgerald, U.S.A., **425** L4
Fitzroy, *river*, Australia, **134** F2
Fitzroy Crossing, Australia, **134** F2
Fiuggi, Italy, **295** D5
Five Sisters, *mountain peak*, Scotland, U.K., **308** D3
Fivemiletown, Northern Ireland, U.K., **309** E3
Fizi, Democratic Republic of the Congo, **369** E3
Fjærland, Norway, **286** C2
Fjällbacka, Sweden, **286** E3
Fjellerup, Denmark, **286** E4
Fjerritslev, Denmark, **286** D4
Flå, Norway, **286** D2
Fladdabister, Shetland, Scotland, U.K., **308** K7
Flagstaff, U.S.A., **423** H4
Flagstaff Bay, St Helena, **373** B3
Flagstaff Lake, U.S.A., **426** E2
Flakstad, Norway, **284** F2
Flamanville, France, **305** F5
Flamborough, England, U.K., **307** H3
Flamborough Head, *point*, England, U.K., **307** H3
Fläming, *mountain range*, Germany, **288** F2
Flaming Gorge Reservoir, U.S.A., **419** K6
Flamingo, U.S.A., **425** M7
Flanagin Town, Trinidad, Trinidad and Tobago, **461** C4
Flannan Isles, *islands*, Scotland, U.K., **308** B2
Flasher, U.S.A., **420** C2
Flåsjön, *lake*, Sweden, **284** G4
Flat Island, Mauritius, **373** C1
Flat Top Butte, *mountain peak*, U.S.A., **420** B2
Flatbush, Canada, **413** M4
Flathead, *river*, U.S.A., **418** H3
Flathead Lake, *lake*, U.S.A., **418** G3
Flattery, Cape, Australia, **135** K1
Flattery, Cape, U.S.A., **418** B2
Flaxton, U.S.A., **419** N2
Fleet, England, U.K., **305** G3
Fleetwood, England, U.K., **306** E4
Flekkefjord, Norway, **286** C3
Flen, Sweden, **286** H3
Flensburg, Germany, **288** D1
Flers, France, **290** D2
Flesberg, Norway, **286** D3
Flesherton, Canada, **421** N3
Fletcher, Mount, *mountain peak*, Macquarie Island, **134** R11
Flevoland, *province*, Netherlands, **288** B2, *240*
Flimby, England, U.K., **306** E3
Flin Flon, Canada, **414** D4
Flinders, *river*, Australia, **135** J2
Flinders Bay, Australia, **134** C6
Flinders Island, Australia, **135** K7
Flinders Ranges, *mountain range*, Australia, **135** H5
Flint, *island*, Kiribati, **139** J6
Flint, *river*, U.S.A., **421** M4
Flint, U.S.A., **421** M4
Flint, Wales, U.K., **304** D1
Flintshire, *unitary authority*, Wales, U.K., **304** D1
Flisa, Norway, **286** F2
Flisa, *river*, Norway, **286** E2
Flixecourt, France, **290** F2
Floby, Sweden, **286** F3
Flora, Illinois, U.S.A., **421** J6
Flora, Oregon, U.S.A., **418** F4
Florac, France, **291** F4
Floral City, U.S.A., **425** L5
Florence, Alabama, U.S.A., **425** J2
Florence, Arizona, U.S.A., **423** H5
Florence, Kansas, U.S.A., **420** E6
Florence, Pennsylvania, U.S.A., **421** N5
Florence *see* Firenze, Italy, **294** C4, *75, 254, 255*
Florence, South Carolina, U.S.A., **425** N2
Florencia, Colombia, **450** C4
Florentino Ameghino, Argentina, **460** E2
Florentino Ameghino, Embalse, *reservoir*, Argentina, **460** D2
Flores, Brazil, **453** G5
Flores, Das, *river*, Brazil, **453** E4
Flores, Guatemala, **428** C3
Flores, *island*, Azores, Portugal, **360** L7
Flores, *island*, Indonesia, **198** C5, *60, 86*
Flores do Piauí, Brazil, **453** E5
Flores Island, Canada, **412** F7
Flores Sea, Indonesia, **198** B4
Floresta, Brazil, **453** F5
Floreşti, Moldova, **296** G2
Floresville, U.S.A., **424** C5
Floriano, Brazil, **453** E5
Floriano Peixoto, Brazil, **455** E2
Florianópolis, Brazil, **459** H3
Florida, Bolivia, **455** F5
Florida, *state*, U.S.A., **425** L5, *51, 92, 377, 384, 385, 386, 392*
Florida, Straits of, Atlantic Ocean/Gulf of Mexico, **425** N7
Florida, Uruguay, **459** F5
Florida Bay, U.S.A., **425** M7
Florida City, U.S.A., **425** M7
Florida Islands, Solomon Islands, **141** A1
Florida Keys, *islands*, U.S.A., **424** M7
Florida Negra, Argentina, **460** D3
Floridablanca, Colombia, **450** D2
Floridia, Sicilia, Italy, **295** E7
Florien, U.S.A., **424** F4
Florina, Greece, **297** C5
Flornes, Norway, **284** E5
Florø, Norway, **286** B2
Flotta, *island*, Orkney, Scotland, U.K., **308** F2
Floydada, U.S.A., **424** B3
Fluk, Indonesia, **198** D3
Fluvià, *river*, Spain, **293** J1
Fly, *river*, Papua New Guinea, **140** A4, *115*
Flying Fish Cove, *bay*, Christmas Island, **134** N8
Foča, Bosnia and Herzegovina, **294** G4
Foça, Turkey, **297** F6
Fochabers, Scotland, U.K., **308** F3
Focşani, Romania, **296** F3

Fodé, Central African Republic, **368** D1
Fofoa, *island*, Vava'u Group, Tonga, **141** B3
Fogang, China, **207** B1
Foggaret ez Zoua, Algeria, **361** G3
Foggia, Italy, **295** E5
Fogo, Canada, **417** P5
Fogo, *island*, Cape Verde, **360** Q9, *319*
Fogo Island, Canada, **417** Q5
Föhr, *island*, Germany, **288** D1
Fóia, *mountain peak*, Portugal, **292** C4
Foinaven, Scotland, U.K., **308** E2
Foix, France, **290** E5
Fokino, Russian Federation, **299** E6
Fokku, Nigeria, **365** E2
Folda, *fiord*, Norway, **284** G3
Folegandros, *island*, Kyklades, Greece, **297** E7
Foley, U.S.A., **425** J4
Foleyet, Canada, **421** M1
Foligno, Italy, **294** D4
Folkestone, England, U.K., **305** J3
Folkingham, England, U.K., **305** G2
Folldal, Norway, **286** E1
Föllinge, Sweden, **284** G5
Follonica, Italy, **294** C4
Fomboni, Comoros, **372** A3
Fond du Lac, Canada, **413** R2
Fond du Lac, *lake*, Canada, **413** R2
Fond du Lac, *river*, Canada, **413** S2
Fond Du Lac, U.S.A., **421** J4
Fonda, Iowa, U.S.A., **420** F4
Fonda, North Dakota, U.S.A., **420** D1
Fondi, Italy, **295** D5
Fonggang, China, **207** C3
Fonseca, Golfo de, *gulf*, Nicaragua, **428** C4, *403*, *404*
Fontaine-le-Dun, France, **305** H5
Fontainebleau, France, **290** F2
Fonte Boa, Brazil, **451** E5
Fontenay-le-Comte, France, **290** D3
Fontur, *point*, Iceland, **284** Z6
Fonuakula, Niue, **132** M13
Fonualei, *island*, Tonga, **136** D2
Fonua'one'one, *island*, Vava'u Group, Tonga, **141** B3
Fonyód, Hungary, **289** H5
Foping, China, **215** H2
Forari, Vanuatu, **141** A2
Forbes, Australia, **135** K5
Forbes, Mount, *mountain peak*, New Zealand, **133** A7
Forbesganj, India, **219** F4
Forchheim, Germany, **288** E4
Ford, Cape, Australia, **134** F1
Førde, Hordaland, Norway, **286** B3
Førde, Sogn og Fjordane, Norway, **286** B2
Fordham, England, U.K., **305** H2
Fordingbridge, England, U.K., **305** F4
Fordon, Poland, **289** J2
Fordville, U.S.A., **420** E1
Fordyce, U.S.A., **424** F3
Forécariah, Guinea, **364** B3
Forel, Mont, *mountain peak*, Greenland, **411** R3
Foreland Point, England, U.K., **304** E4
Forelshogna, *mountain peak*, Norway, **284** E5
Forest, Canada, **421** M4
Forest, U.S.A., **425** H3
Forest Lake, U.S.A., **420** G3
Forestdale, Canada, **412** F4
Forestgrove, U.S.A., **419** K3
Forestville, Canada, **416** G5
Forez, Monts du, *mountain range*, France, **291** F4
Forfar, Scotland, U.K., **308** G4
Forges-les-Eaux, France, **290** E2
Forks, U.S.A., **418** B3
Forli, Italy, **294** D3
Formby, England, U.K., **306** E4
Formentera, *island*, Islas Baleares, Spain, **293** H3
Formentor, Cabo de, *cape*, Islas Baleares, Spain, **293** J3
Formerie, France, **305** J5
Formiga, Brazil, **456** E5
Formosa, Argentina, **459** E3
Formosa, Brazil, **456** D4
Formosa, *province*, Argentina, **459** E2
Formosa do Rio Prêto, Brazil, **456** E3
Formoso, Brazil, **456** D3
Formoso, *river*, Bahia, Brazil, **457** E4
Formoso, *river*, Tocantins, Brazil, **456** D3
Forpost-Kargat, Russian Federation, **223** L1
Forres, Scotland, U.K., **308** F3
Forrest City, U.S.A., **424** G2
Forsayth, Australia, **135** J2
Forshaga, Sweden, **286** F3
Forsinard, Scotland, U.K., **308** F2
Forsnes, Norway, **284** D5
Forssa, Finland, **287** L2
Forst, Germany, **289** G3
Forster, Australia, **135** L5
Forsyth, Georgia, U.S.A., **425** L3
Forsyth, Missouri, U.S.A., **420** G7
Forsyth, Montana, U.S.A., **419** L3
Forsythe, Canada, **416** C5
Fort Abbās, Pakistan, **218** C3
Fort Albany, Canada, **415** P5
Fort Alexander, Canada, **414** F6
Fort Assiniboine, Canada, **413** M4
Fort Augustus, Scotland, U.K., **308** E3
Fort Beaufort, South Africa, **371** E5
Fort Benton, U.S.A., **419** J3
Fort Black, Canada, **413** R4
Fort Bragg, U.S.A., **422** B2
Fort Chipewyan, Canada, **413** P2
Fort Collins, U.S.A., **423** L1
Fort Davis, U.S.A., **423** M6
Fort-de-France, Martinique, **427** D3, *390*
Fort Dodge, U.S.A., **420** F4
Fort Fitzgerald, Canada, **413** P2
Fort Frances, Canada, **414** H7
Fort Good Hope, Canada, **410** G3
Fort Lauderdale, U.S.A., **425** M6
Fort Liard, Canada, **412** H1
Fort Liberté, Haiti, **429** H3
Fort MacKay, Canada, **413** P3
Fort Macleod, Canada, **413** N7
Fort McMurray, Canada, **413** P3
Fort McPherson, Canada, **410** F3
Fort Madison, U.S.A., **420** H5
Fort-Mahon-Plage, France, **305** J4
Fort Morgan, U.S.A., **423** M1
Fort Myers, U.S.A., **425** M6
Fort Nelson, Canada, **412** H2
Fort Nelson, *river*, Canada, **412** H2
Fort Payne, U.S.A., **425** K2
Fort Peck, U.S.A., **419** L2
Fort Peck Lake, U.S.A., **419** L3
Fort Pierce, U.S.A., **425** M6
Fort Portal, Uganda, **369** F2
Fort Providence, Canada, **413** L1
Fort Qu'Appelle, Canada, **414** C6
Fort Resolution, Canada, **413** N1
Fort Rixon, Zimbabwe, **371** E2
Fort Rock, U.S.A., **418** D5
Fort St James, Canada, **412** G4
Fort St John, Canada, **412** J3
Fort Severn, Canada, **415** L3
Fort-Shevchenko, Kazakhstan, **222** E4
Fort Simpson, Canada, **410** G3
Fort Smith, Canada, **413** P1
Fort Smith, U.S.A., **424** E2
Fort Stockton, U.S.A., **423** M6
Fort Summer, U.S.A., **423** L4
Fort Thomas, U.S.A., **423** J5
Fort Valley, U.S.A., **425** L3
Fort Vermilion, Canada, **413** M2
Fort Walton Beach, U.S.A., **425** J4
Fort Wayne, U.S.A., **421** L5
Fort Wellington, Guyana, **451** H2
Fort William, Scotland, U.K., **308** D4
Fort Worth, U.S.A., **424** D3
Fort Yukon, U.S.A., **410** E3
Fortaleza, Bolivia, **455** E3
Fortaleza, Brazil, **453** F4
Forte Coimbra, Brazil, **455** H5
Forteaux, Canada, **417** N4
Fortescue, *river*, Australia, **134** D3
Forth, Firth of, *river mouth*, Scotland, U.K., **308** G4, *79*
Forth, *river*, Scotland, U.K., **308** E4, *276*
Fortín Ávalos Sánchez, Paraguay, **459** E2
Fortín Capitán Demattei, Paraguay, **458** E2
Fortín Capitán Escobar, Paraguay, **458** E2
Fortín Carlos Antonio López, Paraguay, **455** G5
Fortín Coronel Bogado, Paraguay, **455** G5
Fortín Falcón, Paraguay, **459** E2
Fortín Galpón, Paraguay, **455** G5
Fortín Hernandarias, Paraguay, **458** E1
Fortín Infante Rivarola, Paraguay, **455** F5
Fortín Lavalle, Argentina, **459** E2
Fortín Madrejón, Paraguay, **455** G5
Fortín Paredes, Bolivia, **455** G5
Fortín Pilcomayo, Argentina, **458** E2
Fortín Presidente Ayala, Paraguay, **459** E2
Fortín Ravelo, Bolivia, **455** G5
Fortín Suárez Arana, Bolivia, **455** G5
Fortín Teniente General Mendoza, Paraguay, **455** G5
Fortrose, New Zealand, **133** B8
Fortrose, Scotland, U.K., **308** E3
Fortuna, California, U.S.A., **418** B6
Fortuna, North Dakota, U.S.A., **419** N2
Fortuna, Spain, **293** G3
Fortune, Canada, **417** P6
Fortune Bay, Canada, **417** P6
Fortuneswell, England, U.K., **304** E4
Forty Fours, The, *islands*, Chatham Islands, New Zealand, **133** Q16
Forvik, Norway, **284** F4
Foshan, China, **206** C4
Foso, Ghana, **364** D3
Fossano, Italy, **294** A3
Fossbakken, Norway, **284** J2
Fossombrone, Italy, **294** D4
Foster Bugt, *bay*, Greenland, **411** S2
Fotadrevo, Madagascar, **372** A5
Fotokol, Cameroon, **365** G2
Fougamou, Gabon, **368** B3
Fougères, France, **290** D2
Foul Bay, Egypt, **363** G4
Foula, *island*, Shetland, Scotland, U.K., **308** J7
Foulenzem, Gabon, **368** A3
Foulness Point, England, U.K., **305** H3
Foulwind, Cape, New Zealand, **133** C5
Foum Zguid, Morocco, **360** E3
Foumban, Cameroon, **368** B1
Fountain, U.S.A., **423** L2
Four Corners, U.S.A., **419** M4
Fourchu, Canada, **417** L7
Fournaise, Piton de la, *mountain peak*, Réunion, **373** A1
Fournier, Cape, Chatham Islands, New Zealand, **133** Q16
Fournoi, *island*, Dodekanisos, Greece, **297** F7
Fouta Djalon, *mountain range*, Guinea, **364** B2, *322*
Foveaux Strait, New Zealand, **133** A8
Fowler, Colorado, U.S.A., **423** L2
Fowler, Indiana, U.S.A., **421** K5
Fowlers Bay, Australia, **134** G5
Fox, *river*, Canada, **413** N3
Fox Creek, Canada, **413** L4
Fox Glacier, New Zealand, **133** C6
Fox Lake, Canada, **413** M2
Fox Mine, Canada, **414** D3
Fox Mountain, *mountain peak*, U.S.A., **418** E6
Fox Peak, *mountain peak*, New Zealand, **133** C6
Fox Valley, Canada, **413** Q6
Foxdale, Isle of Man, **306** D3
Foxe Basin, Canada, **411** M3
Foxe Channel, Canada, **411** L3
Foxe Peninsula, Canada, **411** M3
Foxen, *lake*, Sweden, **286** E3
Foxford, Ireland, **309** C4
Foxton, New Zealand, **132** E5
Foxwarren, Canada, **414** D6
Foyle, Lough, *inlet*, Northern Ireland, U.K., **309** F2
Foynes, Ireland, **309** C5
Foz do Cunene, Angola, **370** B2
Foz do Iguaçu, Brazil, **459** F2
Foz do Jordão, Brazil, **454** D2
Fraga, Spain, **293** H2
Frailes, Sierra de los, *mountain range*, Mexico, **430** D4
Frakes, Mount, *mountain peak*, Antarctica, **470** C6
Fram Peak, *mountain peak*, Antarctica, **470** F4
Framlingham, England, U.K., **305** J2
Franca, Brazil, **456** D5
Francavilla Fontana, Italy, **295** F5
France, *country*, Europe, **282** D6, *59, 74, 80, 87, 89, 91, 92, 93, 94, 95, 96, 97, 109, 116, 122, 124, 127, 154, 162, 228, 229, 231, 238, 239, 240, 241, 243, 244, 245, 246, 247, 249, 251, 252, 254, 255, 274, 275, 278, 279, 313, 314, 315, 317, 318, 320, 323, 328, 331, 339, 352, 353, 354, 355, 380, 385, 389, 390, 391, 394, 397, 434, 469*
France, Île de, *island*, Greenland, **411** T2
Francés, Puerto, *harbor*, Róbinson Crusoe Island, Archipiélago Juan Fernández, Chile, **461** C2
Franceville, Gabon, **368** B3
Franche-Comtè, *administrative region*, France, **291** G3, *245*
Francisco de Orellana, Peru, **450** D5
Francisco Escárcega, Mexico, **431** H5
Francisco Madero, Mexico, **430** E3
Francisco Sá, Brazil, **457** E4
Francistown, Botswana, **371** E3
Francois Lake, Canada, **412** F5
Frankfort, U.S.A., **421** L6, *386*
Frankfurt (Oder), Germany, **289** G2
Frankfurt am Main, Germany, **288** D3, *239*
Fränkische Alb, *mountain range*, Germany, **288** E4
Franklin, Indiana, U.S.A., **421** K6
Franklin, Mount, *mountain peak*, New Zealand, **133** D6
Franklin, North Carolina, U.S.A., **425** L2
Franklin, Pennsylvania, U.S.A., **421** P5
Franklin, Virginia, U.S.A., **426** B6
Franklin, West Virginia, U.S.A., **421** P6
Franklin D. Roosevelt Lake, U.S.A., **418** E2
Franklin Mountains, *mountain range*, Canada, **410** G3
Frannie, U.S.A., **419** K4
Fränsta, Sweden, **286** H1
Frantsa-Iosifa, Zemlya, *islands*, Russian Federation, **300** F2
Franz Joseph Glacier, New Zealand, **133** C6
Frasca, Capo della, *cape*, Italy, **295** B6
Frascati, Italy, **295** D5
Fraser, *river*, Canada, **406** L3, *381*
Fraser, U.S.A., **423** L2
Fraser Island, Australia, **135** L4
Fraser Lake, Canada, **412** G4
Fraserburg, South Africa, **370** D5
Fraserdale, Canada, **415** P7
Frasertown, New Zealand, **132** F4
Frăteşti, Romania, **296** E4
Fray Bentos, Uruguay, **459** E4
Frazee, U.S.A., **420** F2
Frederic, U.S.A., **420** G3
Fredericia, Denmark, **286** D5
Frederick, Maryland, U.S.A., **426** B5
Frederick, Oklahoma, U.S.A., **424** C2
Frederick, South Dakota, U.S.A., **420** D3
Fredericksburg, Texas, U.S.A., **424** C4
Fredericksburg, Virginia, U.S.A., **426** B5
Fredericktown, U.S.A., **420** H7
Fredericton, Canada, **416** H7, *381*
Frederikshavn, Denmark, **286** E4
Frederiksted, U.S. Virgin Islands, **427** C2
Fredonia, Arizona, U.S.A., **422** G3
Fredonia, North Dakota, U.S.A., **420** D2
Fredrika, Sweden, **284** J4
Fredriksberg, Sweden, **286** G2
Fredrikstad, Norway, **286** E3
Free State, *province*, South Africa, **371** E4, *351*
Freels, Cape, Canada, **417** Q5
Freeman, U.S.A., **420** E4
Freemont Mountains, *mountain range*, U.S.A., **418** D5
Freeport, Bahamas, **428** F1
Freeport, Florida, U.S.A., **425** J4
Freeport, Illinois, U.S.A., **421** J4
Freeport, Texas, U.S.A., **424** E5
Freer, U.S.A., **424** C6
Freetown, Sierra Leone, **364** B3, *322*
Fregenal de la Sierra, Spain, **292** D3
Freiberg, Germany, **288** F3
Freiburg im Breisgau, Germany, **288** C4
Freirina, Chile, **458** B3
Freising, Germany, **288** E4
Freistadt, Austria, **289** G4
Fréjus, France, **291** H5
Fremont, Michigan, U.S.A., **421** L4
Fremont, Nebraska, U.S.A., **420** E5
French Guiana, *French departement*, South America, **452** C2, *245, 434, 445*
French Polynesia, *French territory*, Pacific Ocean, **131** K3, *82, 93, 108, 109, 122, 245*
French Southern and Antarctic Islands, *French territory*, Indian Ocean, **104** C13, *245, 469*
Frenchglen, U.S.A., **418** E5
Frenchpark, Ireland, **309** D4
Frenda, Algeria, **361** G1
Fresco, Côte d'Ivoire, **364** C3
Fresco, *river*, Brazil, **452** C5
Fresnillo, Mexico, **430** E4
Fresno, U.S.A., **422** D3
Fresno Alhándiga, Spain, **292** E2
Fressingfield, England, U.K., **305** J2
Fresvik, Norway, **286** C2
Fréteval, France, **290** E3
Freudenstadt, Germany, **288** D4
Frévent, France, **290** F1
Freycinet Peninsula, Australia, **135** K7
Freyre, Argentina, **458** D4
Freyung, Germany, **288** F4
Fria, Cape, Namibia, **370** B2

Fria, Guinea, **364** B2
Friant, U.S.A., **422** D3
Frías, Argentina, **458** D3
Fribourg, Switzerland, **291** H3
Fridaythorpe, England, U.K., **307** H3
Friedberg, Austria, **289** H5
Friedrichshafen, Germany, **288** D5
Friesach, Austria, **289** G5
Friesland, *province*, Netherlands, **288** B2, *241*
Friesoythe, Germany, **288** C2
Frigate, *island*, Seychelles, **373** A2
Frinton-on-Sea, England, U.K., **305** J3
Frio, *river*, U.S.A., **424** C5
Friockheim, Scotland, U.K., **308** G4
Friona, U.S.A., **423** M4
Frisa, Loch, *lake*, Scotland, U.K., **308** C4
Frisco City, U.S.A., **425** J4
Frisco Peak, *mountain peak*, U.S.A., **422** G2
Fritsla, Sweden, **286** F4
Fritzlar, Germany, **288** D3
Friuli-Venezia Giulia, *autonomous region*, Italy, **294** D2, *255*
Friville-Escarbotin, France, **305** J4
Friza, Proliv, *strait*, Russian Federation, **209** K1
Frobisher Bay, Canada, **411** N3
Frobisher Lake, Canada, **413** Q3
Frohavet, *bay*, Norway, **284** D5
Froid, U.S.A., **419** M2
Froissy, France, **305** K5
Frome, England, U.K., **304** E3
Frome, Lake, Australia, **135** H5
Front Royal, U.S.A., **426** A5
Frontera, Islas Canarias, Spain, **373** A4
Frontera, Mexico, **431** G5
Fronteras, Mexico, **430** C2
Frontier, Canada, **413** Q7
Frosinone, Italy, **295** D5
Frøya, *island*, Norway, **284** D5
Fruges, France, **305** K4
Fruita, U.S.A., **423** J2
Frunzivka, Ukraine, **296** G2
Fruška Gora, *mountain range*, Serbia, **296** B3
Frutigen, Switzerland, **291** H3
Fu Xian, China, **210** E5
Fua'amotu, Tongatapu Group, Tonga, **141** B4
Fu'an, China, **206** D3
Fuding, China, **206** E3
Fuencaliente, Islas Canarias, Spain, **373** A4
Fuencaliente, Punta de, *point*, Islas Canarias, Spain, **373** A4
Fuengirola, Spain, **292** E4
Fuente de Cantos, Spain, **292** D3
Fuente el Fresno, Spain, **293** F3
Fuente Obejuna, Spain, **292** E3
Fuentesaúco, Spain, **292** E2
Fuento-Álamo, Spain, **293** G4
Fuerte Bulnes, Chile, **460** C4
Fuerte Olimpo, Paraguay, **456** B5
Fuerteventura, *island*, Islas Canarias, Spain, **373** B4, *355*
Fuglafjørður, Faeroe Islands, **302** D1
Fugong, China, **215** F4
Fugou, China, **206** C1
Fugu, China, **210** E5
Fuguo, China, **211** G5
Fuhai, China, **212** E3
Fuhe, China, **207** B2
Fuji, Dome, *ice dome*, Antarctica, **470** E4
Fuji, Japan, **209** G4
Fuji-san, *mountain peak*, Japan, **209** G4, *94, 165*
Fujian, *province*, China, **206** D3, *161*
Fujieda, Japan, **209** G4
Fujin, China, **211** L3
Fukagawa, Japan, **209** H2
Fukang, China, **212** E3
Fukave, *island*, Tonga, **141** B4
Fukeshan, China, **211** H1
Fukuchiyama, Japan, **208** F4
Fukui, Japan, **209** G3
Fukuoka, Japan, **208** E4
Fukushima, Japan, **209** H3
Fukuyama, Japan, **208** F4
Fulacunda, Guinea-Bissau, **364** A2
Fulaga, *island*, Fiji, **141** A4
Fulda, Germany, **288** D3
Fulda, *river*, Germany, **288** D3
Fulham, England, U.K., **305** G3
Fuling, China, **215** H3
Fullarton, Trinidad, Trinidad and Tobago, **461** C4
Fulleborn, Papua New Guinea, **140** C4
Fulton, U.S.A., **420** H6
Fulunäs, Sweden, **286** F2
Fumel, France, **290** E4
Funafuti, Tuvalu, **139** F5, *113*
Funan, China, **206** C1
Funäsdalen, Sweden, **286** F1
Funchal, Madeira, Portugal, **373** C3, *355*
Fundación, Colombia, **450** C1
Fundão, Portugal, **292** D2
Fundición, Mexico, **430** C3
Fundulea, Romania, **296** F3
Fundy, Bay of, Canada, **416** H7
Funhalouro, Mozambique, **371** F3
Funing, China, **206** D1
Funtua, Nigeria, **365** F2
Funzie, Scotland, U.K., **308** L7
Fuping, Hebei, China, **210** F5
Fuping, Shaanxi, China, **206** B1
Fuqing, China, **206** D3
Furancungo, Mozambique, **369** F5
Furao, China, **211** K2
Furneaux Group, *islands*, Australia, **135** K6
Furong, *river*, China, **215** H3
Furqlus, Syria, **225** D2
Fürstenau, Germany, **288** C2
Fürstenberg, Germany, **288** F2
Fürth, Germany, **288** E4
Furudal, Sweden, **286** G2
Furukawa, Japan, **209** H3
Fusa, Norway, **286** B2
Fusagasugá, Colombia, **450** C3
Fusha, China, **207** A3
Fushun, Liaoning, China, **211** H4
Fushun, Sichuan, China, **215** H3
Fusong, China, **211** J4
Füssen, Germany, **288** E5
Fusui, China, **215** H5
Futaleufú, Chile, **460** C2
Futian, China, **207** B2
Futog, Serbia, **296** B3
Futuna, *island*, Vanuatu, **141** A3
Futuna, *island*, Wallis and Futuna, **139** G6, *127*
Fuxin, China, **211** H4
Fuxing, China, **215** H3
Fuyang, China, **206** C1
Fuyang, *river*, China, **210** F5
Fuyong, China, **207** B3
Fuyu, Heilongjiang, China, **211** J3
Fuyu, Jilin, China, **211** J3
Fuyuan, Heilongjiang, China, **211** L2
Fuyuan, Yunnan, China, **215** H4
Fuyun, China, **212** F3
Füzesabony, Hungary, **289** K5
Fuzhou, Fujian, China, **206** D3, *161*
Fuzhou, Jiangxi, China, **206** D3
Fyn, *island*, Denmark, **286** E5
Fyne, Loch, *inlet*, Scotland, U.K., **308** D5
Fynshav, Denmark, **286** D5
Fyresdal, Norway, **286** D3
Fyresvatn, *lake*, Norway, **286** C3
Fyteies, Greece, **297** C6


## G


Gaalkacyo, Somalia, **367** G3
Gabbac, Raas, *point*, Somalia, **367** H3
Gabbs, U.S.A., **422** E2
Gabela, Angola, **368** B5
Gabès, Golfe de, *gulf*, Tunisia, **362** B2
Gabon, *country*, Africa, **359** G7, *94, 312, 313, 330, 331, 332, 333, 334*
Gaborone, Botswana, **371** E3, *347*
Gabriel y Galán, Embalse de, *reservoir*, Spain, **292** D2
Gabrovo, Bulgaria, **296** E4
Gabú, Guinea-Bissau, **364** B2
Gacé, France, **290** E2
Gacko, Bosnia and Herzegovina, **294** G4
Gadag-Betgeri, India, **216** C3
Gādarwāra, India, **218** D5
Gäddede, Sweden, **284** G4
Gādra Road, India, **218** B4
Gadsden, U.S.A., **425** K2
Găeşti, Romania, **296** E3
Gaeta, Golfo di, *gulf*, Italy, **295** D5
Gaeta, Italy, **295** D5
Gaferut, *island*, Micronesia, **138** C4
Gaffney, U.S.A., **425** M2
Gafsa, Tunisia, **362** A2
Gagal, Chad, **365** H3
Gagarin, Russian Federation, **299** E5
Gagau, Gunung, *mountain peak*, Malaysia, **200** C1
Gage, U.S.A., **420** D7
Gagnoa, Côte d'Ivoire, **364** C3
Gagnon, Canada, **416** G4
Gahe, China, **213** H5
Gaighāt, Nepal, **219** F4
Gail, *river*, Austria, **288** F5
Gaillac, France, **290** E5
Gaimán, Argentina, **460** E2
Gainesville, Florida, U.S.A., **425** L5
Gainesville, Georgia, U.S.A., **425** L2
Gainesville, Texas, U.S.A., **424** D3
Gainsborough, England, U.K., **307** H4
Gairdner, Lake, Australia, **135** H5
Gairloch, Scotland, U.K., **308** D3
Gaizhou, China, **211** H4
Gaiziņkalns, *mountain peak*, Latvia, **287** M4, *341*
Gakarosa, *mountain peak*, South Africa, **370** D4
Gakem, Nigeria, **365** F3
Gakuch, Pakistan, **218** C1
Gakugsa, Russian Federation, **299** F2
Gal, *river*, Sri Lanka, **217** E5
Gala, China, **219** G3
Galán, Cerro, *mountain peak*, Argentina, **458** C3
Galana, *river*, Kenya, **369** G3, *341*
Galand, Iran, **222** F5
Galang, Pulau, *island*, Indonesia, **200** D2
Galápagos, Islas, (Galapagos Islands), Ecuador, Pacific Ocean, **461** A1, *434, 435, 438*
Galápagos Fracture Zone, *tectonic feature*, Pacific Ocean, **479** J5
Galapagos Islands *see* Galápagos, Islas, Ecuador, Pacific Ocean, **461** A1, *434, 435, 438*
Galápagos Rise, *underwater feature*, Pacific Ocean, **479** M5
Galashiels, Scotland, U.K., **308** G5
Galata, Bulgaria, **296** F4
Galata, U.S.A., **419** J2
Galaţi, Romania, **296** G3
Galatista, Greece, **297** D5
Galatone, Italy, **295** G5
Galbally, Ireland, **309** D5
Gáldar, Islas Canarias, Spain, **373** B4
Galdhøpiggen, *mountain peak*, Norway, **286** D2
Galeana, Mexico, **430** D2
Galena, U.S.A., **420** H4
Galeota Point, Trinidad, Trinidad and Tobago, **461** C4
Galera, Punta, *point*, Chile, **460** B1
Galera, Punta, *point*, Ecuador, **450** B4
Galera, Spain, **293** F4
Galera Point, Trinidad, Trinidad and Tobago, **461** C4
Galéria, Corse, France, **295** B4
Galesburg, U.S.A., **420** H5
Galesville, U.S.A., **420** H3
Galeton, U.S.A., **426** B4
Galets, Pointe des, *point*, Réunion, **373** A1
Galguduud, *administrative region*, Somalia, **367** G3
Galicea Mare, Romania, **296** D3
Galicia, *autonomous region*, Spain, **292** D1, *253*
Galilee, Sea of, *see* Kinneret, Yam, *lake*, Israel, **225** C3, *179, 180*
Gallatin, U.S.A., **425** J1
Gallatin Peak, *mountain peak*, U.S.A., **419** J4
Galle, Sri Lanka, **216** E5
Gállego, *river*, Spain, **293** G1
Gallegos, *river*, Argentina, **460** C4
Gallegos, U.S.A., **423** M4
Galley Head, *point*, Ireland, **309** D6
Gallinas, Punta, *point*, Colombia, **450** D1
Gallipoli, Italy, **295** F5
Gallipoli *see* Gelibolu, Turkey, **297** F5
Gallipolis, U.S.A., **421** M6
Gällivare, Sweden, **284** K3
Gällö, Sweden, **284** G5
Galloway, Mount, *mountain peak*, New Zealand, **133** P15
Galloway, Mull of, *point*, Scotland, U.K., **308** E6, *279*
Gallup, U.S.A., **423** J4
Galmisdale, Scotland, U.K., **308** C4
Galston, Scotland, U.K., **308** E5
Galtström, Sweden, **287** H1
Galtymore, *mountain peak*, Ireland, **309** D5
Galva, U.S.A., **420** H5
Galveston, U.S.A., **424** E5
Galveston Bay, U.S.A., **424** E5
Gálvez, Argentina, **458** E4
Galway, *county*, Ireland, **309** C4
Galway, Ireland, **309** C4
Galway Bay, Ireland, **309** C4
Gâm, *river*, Vietnam, **203** E1
Gamaches, France, **290** E2
Gamba, China, **219** G3
Gamba, Gabon, **368** A3
Gambang, Malaysia, **200** C2
Gambēla, Ethiopia, **366** D3
Gambia, *country*, Africa, **358** D5, *320, 322*
Gambia Plain, *underwater feature*, Atlantic Ocean, **477** F5
Gambier, Îles, *islands*, French Polynesia, **137** H3
Gambo, Canada, **417** P5
Gambo, Central African Republic, **368** D2
Gamboma, Congo, **368** C3
Gamboula, Central African Republic, **368** C2
Gamgadhi, Nepal, **219** E3
Gamleby, Sweden, **286** H4
Gammelstaden, Sweden, **285** L4
Gamph, Slieve, *mountain range*, Ireland, **309** C3
Gamtog, China, **215** F3
Gamud, *mountain peak*, Ethiopia, **369** G2
Gamvik, Norway, **285** P1
Gan, France, **290** D5
Gan, *river*, N. China, **211** J2
Gan, *river*, S. China, **206** C3
Gan Gan, Argentina, **460** D2
Gana, China, **215** G2
Ganado, U.S.A., **423** J4
Gäncä, Azerbaijan, **222** D4
Gancheng, China, **203** F2
Ganda, Angola, **368** B5
Gandadiwata, Gunung, *mountain peak*, Indonesia, **198** B3
Gandajika, Democratic Republic of the Congo, **368** D4
Gandak, *river*, India, **219** F4, *172*
Gandāva, Pakistan, **218** A3
Gander, Canada, **417** P5
Gander Bay, Canada, **417** P5
Gandesa, Spain, **293** H2
Gāndhī Sāgar, *lake*, India, **218** C4
Gāndhīdhām, India, **218** B5
Gāndhīnagar, India, **218** C5, *169*
Gandía, Spain, **293** G3
Gandu, Brazil, **457** F3
Ganga, *river*, India, **219** E4
Gangala-na-Bodio, Democratic Republic of the Congo, **369** E2
Gangānagar, India, **218** C3
Gangāpur, India, **218** D4
Gangara, Niger, **365** F2
Gangaw Taung, *mountain range*, Myanmar, **205** C2
Gangaw, Myanmar, **205** B3
Gangca, China, **213** J5
Gangdisê Shan, *mountain range*, China, **219** E3
Ganges, France, **291** F5
Ganges, Mouths of the, Bangladesh/India, **194** K7
Ganges, *river*, Bangladesh/India, **205** A3, *30, 51, 144, 168, 169, 170, 171, 172*
Ganges Fan, *underwater feature*, Indian Ocean, **476** E4
Gangkou, E. Guangdong, China, **207** D3
Gangkou, W. Guangdong, China, **207** A3
Gangoumen, China, **208** B2
Gangtok, India, **219** G4, *169*
Gangu, China, **215** H2
Ganluo, China, **215** G3
Gannan, China, **211** H3
Gannat, France, **291** F3
Gannvalley, U.S.A., **420** D3
Ganq, China, **213** G5
Ganquan, China, **210** E5
Gänserndorf, Austria, **289** H4
Gansu, *province*, China, **213** J5, *161*
Gantang, Anhui, China, **206** D2
Gantang, Ningxia Huizu Zizhiqu, China, **210** D5
Ganye, Nigeria, **365** G3
Ganyu, China, **206** D1
Ganyushkīno, Kazakhstan, **222** D3
Ganzhou, China, **206** C3
Gao, *administrative region*, Mali, **365** E1
Gao, Mali, **364** D1
Gao Xian, China, **215** H3
Gao'an, China, **206** C2
Gaocheng, China, **210** F5
Gaolan, China, **213** J5
Gaolan Dao, *island*, China, **207** A5
Gaoping, China, **206** C1
Gaoqiao, China, **207** A1
Gaotai, China, **213** H5
Gaotang, China, **210** G5
Gaotouyao, China, **210** E4
Gaoua, Burkina Faso, **364** D2
Gaoyang, China, **210** F5
Gaoyou, China, **206** D1
Gaozhou, China, **206** B4
Gap, France, **291** H4
Gapan, Philippines, **204** C3
Gar, China, **218** E2
Gara, Lough, *lake*, Ireland, **309** D4
Gara Nasa, *mountain peak*, Ethiopia, **366** E3
Garabogazköl Aylagy, *bay*, Turkmenistan, **222** E4
Garacad, Somalia, **367** G3
Garachiné, Panama, **429** F5
Garadag, Somalia, **367** G3
Garafia, Islas Canarias, Spain, **373** A4
Garagum, *desert*, Turkmenistan, **222** F5
Garaina, Papua New Guinea, **140** B5
Garalo, Mali, **364** C2
Garang, China, **213** J5
Garanhuns, Brazil, **457** G2
Garba, Central African Republic, **366** B3
Garba Tula, Kenya, **369** G2
Garbahaarrey, Somalia, **369** H2
Garberville, U.S.A., **422** B1
Garbsen, Germany, **288** D2
Garça, Brazil, **459** H2
Garco, China, **214** D2
Garda, Lago di, *lake*, Italy, **294** C3, *255*
Garde, Cap de, *cape*, Algeria, **295** A7
Gardelegen, Germany, **288** E2
Garden City, U.S.A., **420** C7
Garden Corners, U.S.A., **421** K3
Gardey, Argentina, **459** E5
Gardēz, Afghanistan, **218** B2
Gardiner, U.S.A., **419** J4
Gärdnäs, Sweden, **284** G4
Gardner, Colorado, U.S.A., **423** L3
Gardner, Florida, U.S.A., **425** M6
Gardner Pinnacles, *islands*, Hawaiian Islands, U.S.A., **139** H2
Gardone Val Trompia, Italy, **294** C3

Gare Tigre, French Guiana, **452** C2
Garelochhead, Scotland, U.K., **308** E4
Garforth, England, U.K., **307** G4
Gargždai, Lithuania, **287** K5
Garhchiroli, India, **218** E5
Garibaldi, Brazil, **459** G3
Garibaldi, Mount, *mountain peak*, Canada, **412** H7
Garies, South Africa, **370** C5
Garissa, Kenya, **369** G3
Garland, Canada, **414** D6
Garland, North Carolina, U.S.A., **425** N2
Garland, Texas, U.S.A., **424** D3
Garland, Wyoming, U.S.A., **419** K4
Garliava, Lithuania, **287** L5
Garlin, France, **290** D5
Garmisch-Partenkirchen, Germany, **288** E5
Garmo, Norway, **286** D2
Garmsār, Iran, **220** F1
Garner, U.S.A., **420** G4
Garnett, U.S.A., **420** F6
Garnish, Canada, **417** P6
Garnpung Lake, Australia, **135** J5
Garonne, *river*, France, **290** D4, *244*
Garoowe, Somalia, **367** G3
Garoua Boulaï, Cameroon, **368** B1
Garoua, Cameroon, **365** G3
Garove Island, Papua New Guinea, **140** C4
Garqu Yan, China, **214** E2
Garrison, Montana, U.S.A., **418** H3
Garrison, North Dakota, U.S.A., **420** C2
Garsen, Kenya, **369** H3
Garsila, Sudan, **366** B2
Garson Lake, Canada, **413** Q3
Garstang, England, U.K., **306** F4
Gartempe, *river*, France, **290** E3
Garth, Wales, U.K., **304** D2
Garut, Indonesia, **201** D4
Garut, Tanjong, *point*, Indonesia, **201** D4
Garvagh, Northern Ireland, U.K., **309** F3
Garve, Scotland, U.K., **308** E3
Garwa, India, **219** E4
Garwolin, Poland, **289** K3
Gary, U.S.A., **421** K5
Garyarsa, China, **218** E3
Garzê, China, **215** G3
Garzón, Colombia, **450** C3
Gascogne, *region*, France, **290** D5
Gascoyne, Golfe de, *gulf*, France, **290** C4
Gascoyne, *river*, Australia, **134** D4
Gashua, Nigeria, **365** G2
Gasim, Indonesia, **199** E3
Gasmata, Papua New Guinea, **140** C4
Gaspé, Canada, **417** J5
Gaspé, Péninsule de, Canada, **416** H5
Gaspé, Cap de, *cape*, Canada, **417** J5
Gasquet, U.S.A., **418** C6
Gassol, Nigeria, **365** G3
Gastonia, U.S.A., **425** M2
Gastouni, Greece, **297** C7
Gastre, Argentina, **460** D2
Gata, Cabo de, *cape*, Spain, **293** F4
Gătaia, Romania, **296** C3
Gataivai, Samoa, **141** B1
Gatchina, Russian Federation, **299** C3
Gate, U.S.A., **420** C7
Gatehouse of Fleet, Scotland, U.K., **308** E6
Gateshead, England, U.K., **307** G3
Gatesville, U.S.A., **424** D4
Gatineau, Canada, **416** D7
Gatún, Lago, *reservoir*, Panama, **429** F5
Gau, *island*, Fiji, **141** A4
Gaua *see* Santa Maria, *island*, Vanuatu, **141** A2
Gauja, *river*, Latvia, **287** N4
Gauley Bridge, U.S.A., **421** N6
Gauribidanūr, India, **216** D3
Gausta, *mountain peak*, Norway, **286** D3
Gauteng, *province*, South Africa, **371** E4, *347, 350, 351*
Gāv, *river*, Iran, **220** E1
Gāvbandī, Iran, **220** F3
Gavdopoula, *island*, Greece, **297** D8
Gavdos, *island*, Greece, **297** E8
Gave de Pau, *river*, France, **290** D5
Gaviãozinho, Brazil, **455** E2
Gävle, Sweden, **287** H2
Gävleborg, *county*, Sweden, **286** G2
Gavrilov-Yam, Russian Federation, **299** G4
Gavsele, Sweden, **284** H4
Gāwīlgarh Hills, India, **218** D5
Gawler, Australia, **135** H5
Gaxun Nur, *lake*, China, **213** J4
Gaya, India, **219** F4
Gaya, Nigeria, **365** F2
Gaylord, U.S.A., **421** L3
Gaza, Gaza Strip, **225** C4, *192*
Gaza, *province*, Mozambique, **371** F3
Gaza Strip, *disputed region*, Asia, **225** B4, *147, 179, 182, 192, 317*
Gazanjyk, Turkmenistan, **222** F5
Gazi, Kenya, **369** G3
Gaziantep, Turkey, **224** E5
Gazimur, *river*, Russian Federation, **211** G1
Gazipaşa, Turkey, **225** B1
Gazli, Uzbekistan, **222** G4
Gbadolite, Democratic Republic of the Congo, **368** D2
Gbarnga, Liberia, **364** C3
Gbatala, Liberia, **364** C3
Gboko, Nigeria, **365** F3
Gdańsk, Poland, **289** J1, *268*
Gdańska, Zatoka, *gulf*, Poland, **287** J5
Gdov, Russian Federation, **299** A3
Gdynia, Poland, **289** J1
Geary, Canada, **416** H7
Gebo, U.S.A., **419** K5
Gebre Guracha, Ethiopia, **367** E3
Gech'a, Ethiopia, **366** E3
Geddington, England, U.K., **305** G2
Gediz, *river*, Turkey, **297** F6
Gediz, Turkey, **297** G6
Gedlegubē, Ethiopia, **367** G3
Gedney Drove End, England, U.K., **305** H2
Gedo, *administrative region*, Somalia, **369** H2
Gedser, Denmark, **286** E5
Gedser Odde, *cape*, Denmark, **286** E5
Geelong, Australia, **135** J6
Geesaley, Somalia, **367** H2
Geeveston, Australia, **135** K7
Gê'gyai, China, **218** E2
Geidam, Nigeria, **365** G2
Geigar, Sudan, **366** D2
Geikie, *river*, Canada, **414** B3
Geilo, Norway, **286** D2
Geiranger, Norway, **286** C1
Geisenfeld, Germany, **288** E4
Geita, Tanzania, **369** F3
Gejiu, China, **215** G5
Gela, Golfo di, *gulf*, Italy, **295** D7
Gela, Sicilia, Italy, **295** E7
Geladī, Ethiopia, **367** G3
Gelam, Pulau, *island*, Indonesia, **201** E3
Gelang, Tanjong, *cape*, Malaysia, **200** C2
Gelderland, *province*, Netherlands, **288** B2
Gelibolu (Gallipoli), Turkey, **297** F5
Gelligaer, Wales, U.K., **304** D3
Gelnica, Slovakia, **289** K4
Gelsenkirchen, Germany, **288** C3
Gem, U.S.A., **420** C6
Gembu, Nigeria, **365** G3
Geme, Indonesia, **198** D1
Gemena, Democratic Republic of the Congo, **368** C2
Gemlik, Turkey, **297** G5
Gen, *river*, China, **211** H2
Gençay, France, **290** E3
General Acha, Argentina, **458** D5
General Alvear, Argentina, **458** C5
General Artigas, Paraguay, **459** F3
General Belgrano, Argentina, **459** E5
General Belgrano II, *Argentinian research station*, Antarctica, **470** C4
General Bernardo O'Higgins, *Chilean research station*, Antarctica, **470** A4
General Carrera, Lago, *lake*, Chile, **460** C3
General Cepeda, Mexico, **430** E3
General Conesa, Buenos Aires, Argentina, **459** F5
General Conesa, Río Negro, Argentina, **460** E1
General Eugenio A. Garay, Paraguay, **455** F5
General Guido, Argentina, **459** F5
General José de San Martín, Argentina, **459** E3
General Juan Madariaga, Argentina, **459** F5
General La Madrid, Argentina, **458** E5
General Lagos, Chile, **455** E4
General Lavalle, Argentina, **459** F5
General Levalle, Argentina, **458** D5
General Martín Miguel de Güemes, Argentina, **458** D2
General Pico, Argentina, **458** D5
General Pinedo, Argentina, **458** E3
General Pinto, Argentina, **458** E5
General Roca, Argentina, **460** D1
General San Martin, *Argentinian research station*, Antarctica, **470** B4
General Santos (Dadiangas), Philippines, **204** D5
General-Toshevo, Bulgaria, **296** G4
General Villegas, Argentina, **458** D5
Geneseo, U.S.A., **420** H5
Genet, Ethiopia, **367** E3
Geneva, Nebraska, U.S.A., **420** E5
Geneva, New York, U.S.A., **426** B3
Geneva, Ohio, U.S.A., **421** N5
Geneva *see* Genève, Switzerland, **291** H3, *83, 246, 247*
Genève, Switzerland, **291** H3, *83, 246, 247*
Gengma, China, **215** F5
Gengwa, Democratic Republic of the Congo, **368** D3
Genhe, China, **211** H2
Genil, *river*, Spain, **292** E4
Gennargentu, Monti del, *mountain peak*, Italy, **295** B5
Genoa, *river*, Argentina, **460** C2
Genoa *see* Genova, Italy, **294** B3, *75, 246, 254, 255*
Genova (Genoa), Italy, **294** B3, *75, 246, 254, 255*
Genova, Golfo di, *gulf*, Italy, **294** B4
Genovesa, Isla, *island*, Islas Galápagos (Galapagos Islands), Ecuador, **461** A1
Gent, Belgium, **288** A3
Genteng, Indonesia, **200** D4
Genthin, Germany, **288** F2
Genzano di Lucania, Italy, **295** F5
Geographe Bay, Australia, **134** C5
Georg von Neumayer, *German research station*, Antarctica, **470** D3
Georga, Zemlya, *island*, Russian Federation, **300** F1
George, Cape, Canada, **417** K6
George, Cape, South Africa, **370** D5
George, Lake, U.S.A., **425** M5
George, *river*, Canada, **411** N4
George, South Africa, **370** D5
George, U.S.A., **418** E3
George V Land, *region*, Antarctica, **470** E7
George Sound, New Zealand, **133** A7
George Town, Australia, **135** K7
George Town, Bahamas, **428** G2, *388*
George Town, Cayman Islands, **429** E3
George Town, Malaysia, **200** C1
George West, U.S.A., **424** C5
Georgetown, Ascension, **373** A3
Georgetown, Australia, **135** J2
Georgetown, Delaware, U.S.A., **426** C5
Georgetown, Gambia, **364** B2, *320*
Georgetown, Guyana, **451** G2, *437*
Georgetown, Kentucky, U.S.A., **421** L6
Georgetown, Ohio, U.S.A., **421** M6
Georgetown, St Vincent and the Grenadines, **427** D3
Georgetown, South Carolina, U.S.A., **425** N3
Georgetown, Texas, U.S.A., **424** D4
Georgi Traykov, Bulgaria, **296** F4
Georgia, *country*, Asia, **196** F5, *60, 185, 189, 190, 191, 270, 271, 272, 273*
Georgia, *state*, U.S.A., **425** L3, *91, 383, 384, 386*
Georgia, Strait of, Canada, **412** G7
Georgian Bay, Canada, **421** N3
Georgiana, U.S.A., **425** J4
Georgīevka, Shyghys Qazaqstan, Kazakhstan, **212** D2
Georgīevka, Zhambyl, Kazakhstan, **212** B4
Georgina, *river*, Australia, **135** H3
Gera, Germany, **288** F3
Gerace, Italy, **295** F6
Geraki, Greece, **297** D7
Geral, Serra, *mountain range*, Brazil, **447** G6
Geral de Goiás, Serra, *mountain range*, Brazil, **447** H5
Geral do Paraná, Serra, *mountain range*, Brazil, **456** D4
Geraldine, U.S.A., **419** J3
Geraldton, Australia, **134** C4
Geraldton, Canada, **415** L7
Gerede, Turkey, **224** D4
Gereshk, Afghanistan, **218** A3
Gérgal, Spain, **293** F4
Gering, U.S.A., **419** N6
Gerlach, U.S.A., **422** D1
Gerlachovský Štít, *mountain peak*, Slovakia, **289** K4
Germakolo, Indonesia, **199** F3
Germany, *country*, Europe, **282** E5, *46, 78, 79, 82, 89, 92, 93, 95, 114, 115, 117, 118, 177, 228, 233, 234, 237, 238, 239, 240, 241, 243, 244, 245, 247, 248, 249, 253, 254, 256, 261, 262, 263, 266, 267, 268, 272, 273, 275, 313, 326, 341, 381, 382, 440, 475*
Germencik, Turkey, **297** F7
Germiston, South America, **371** E4
Gero, Japan, **209** G4
Gers, *river*, France, **290** E5
Gêrzê, China, **219** F2
Gestro, Wabē, *river*, Ethiopia, **367** F3
Geta, Finland, **287** J2
Getafe, Spain, **293** F2
Gethsémani, Canada, **417** L4
Gettysburg, Pennsylvania, U.S.A., **426** B5
Gettysburg, South Dakota, U.S.A., **420** D3
Getz Ice Shelf, Antarctica, **470** B7
Geureudong, Gunung, *mountain peak*, Indonesia, **200** B1
Gevgelija, Macedonia, **297** D5
Gevrai, India, **216** C2
Geyikli, Turkey, **297** F6
Geylang, Singapore, **200** K7
Geyser, U.S.A., **419** J3
Geyve, Turkey, **297** H5
Gföhl, Austria, **289** G4
Ghabāghib, Syria, **225** D3
Ghadāmis, Libya, **362** A2
Ghaddūwah, Libya, **362** B3
Ghāghara, *river*, India, **219** E4
Ghāghra, India, **219** F5
Ghaibi Dero, Pakistan, **218** A4
Ghana, *country*, Africa, **358** E6, *74, 91, 93, 312, 323, 324, 325, 326*
Ghanzi, Botswana, **370** D3
Ghanzi, *district*, Botswana, **370** D3
Gharandal, Jordan, **225** C4
Gharb al Istiwā'īyah, *state*, Sudan, **369** E1
Gharb Baḩr al Ghazal, *state*, Sudan, **366** C3
Gharb Dārfūr, *state*, Sudan, **366** B2
Gharb Kurdufān, *state*, Sudan, **366** C2
Ghardaïa, Algeria, **361** G2, *315*
Ghardimaou, Tunisia, **295** B7
Ghārib, Jabal, *mountain peak*, Egypt, **225** B5
Gharo, Pakistan, **218** A4
Gharyān, Libya, **362** B2
Ghāt, Libya, **362** B3
Ghazāl, Baḩr al, *river*, Sudan, **366** C3
Ghazaouet, Algeria, **361** F1
Ghāziābād, India, **218** D3
Ghāzīpur, India, **219** E4
Ghazlānī, Jabal, *mountain peak*, Egypt, **225** C5
Ghazlūna, Pakistan, **218** A3
Ghaznī, Afghanistan, **218** B2
Ghazzālah, Saudi Arabia, **363** H3
Gheorgheni, Romania, **296** E2
Gherla, Romania, **296** D2
Ghijduwon, Uzbekistan, **222** G4
Ghilarza, Sardegna, Italy, **295** B5
Ghlo, Beinn a', *mountain peak*, Scotland, U.K., **308** F4
Ghotāru, India, **218** B4
Ghubaysh, Sudan, **366** C2
Ghunthur, Syria, **225** D2
Ghūrīān, Afghanistan, **221** H2
Ghuzor, Uzbekistan, **222** H5
Gia Rai, Vietnam, **203** E4
Giang, *river*, Vietnam, **203** E2
Giannitsa, Greece, **297** D5
Giant's Causeway, *physical feature*, Northern Ireland, U.K., **309** F2
Gibara, Cuba, **429** F2
Gibbons, Canada, **413** N5
Gibeon, Namibia, **370** C4
Gibostad, Norway, **284** J2
Gibraleón, Spain, **292** D4
Gibraltar, Gibraltar, **292** E4
Gibraltar, Strait of, Morocco/Spain, **292** E5, *252. 278, 355*
Gibraltar, *U.K. dependency*, Europe, **292** E4, *228, 229, 276, 278*
Gibson Desert, Australia, **128** B4
Gīdar, Pakistan, **218** A3
Giddalūr, India, **216** D3
Gideälven, *river*, Sweden, **284** J5
Gīdolē, Ethiopia, **369** G1
Gien, France, **290** F3
Gießen, Germany, **288** D3
Gifford, Scotland, U.K., **308** G5
Gifford, U.S.A., **418** E2
Gifhorn, Germany, **288** E2
Gifu, Japan, **209** G4
Giganta, Cerro, *mountain peak*, Mexico, **430** C3
Gigante, Colombia, **450** C3
Gigha Island, Scotland, U.K., **308** D5
Giglio, Isola del, *island*, Italy, **295** C4
Gignac, France, **291** F5
Gijón, Spain, **292** E1
Gila, *river*, U.S.A., **423** H5
Gila, Tanjong, *point*, Indonesia, **199** E2
Gila, U.S.A., **423** J5
Gila Bend, U.S.A., **422** G5
Gila Mountains, *mountain range*, U.S.A., **423** H5
Gilău, Romania, **296** D2
Gilbert, *river*, Australia, **135** J2
Gilbert Islands, Kiribati, **139** F5, *94, 119*
Gilbués, Brazil, **456** E2
Gildford, U.S.A., **419** J2
Gilé, Mozambique, **369** G6
Gilgandra, Australia, **135** K5
Gilgil, Kenya, **369** G3
Gilgit, Pakistan, **218** C2
Gilgit, *river*, Pakistan, **218** C1
Gill, Lough, *lake*, Ireland, **309** D3
Gill Point, St Helena, **373** B3

Gillam, Canada, **414** G3
Gilleleje, Denmark, **286** F4
Gillette, U.S.A., **419** M4
Gilling West, England, U.K., **307** G3
Gillingham, Dorset, England, U.K., **304** E3
Gillingham, Kent, England, U.K., **305** H3
Gilmer, U.S.A., **424** E3
Gilroy, U.S.A., **422** C3
Gilsland, England, U.K., **306** F3
Giltjaur, Sweden, **284** H4
Giluwe, Mount, *mountain peak*, Papua New Guinea, **140** A4
Gilwern, Wales, U.K., **304** D3
Gīmbī, Ethiopia, **366** E3
Gimli, Canada, **414** F6
Gimo, Sweden, **287** J2
Gimoly, Russian Federation, **285** R5
Gimont, France, **290** E5
Gingoog, Philippines, **204** D4
Gīnīr, Ethiopia, **367** F3
Gioia del Colle, Italy, **295** F5
Gioia Tauro, Italy, **295** E6
Gīr Hills, India, **218** B5
Girard, U.S.A., **420** J6
Girardville, Canada, **416** E5
Girgir, Cape, Papua New Guinea, **140** B3
Girīdīh, India, **219** F4
Girifalco, Italy, **295** F6
Girón, Ecuador, **450** B5
Girona, Spain, **293** J2
Gironde, *river mouth*, France, **290** D4
Girvan, Scotland, U.K., **308** E5
Girvas, Murmanskaya Oblast', Russian Federation, **285** Q3
Girvas, Respublika Kareliya, Russian Federation, **285** R5
Girvin, U.S.A., **423** M6
Gisborne, New Zealand, **132** G4, *111*
Giscome, Canada, **412** H4
Gisenyi, Rwanda, **369** E3
Gislaved, Sweden, **286** F4
Gisors, France, **290** E2
Gitega, Burundi, **369** E3
Giulianova, Italy, **294** D4
Giurgiu, Romania, **296** E4
Givors, France, **291** G4
Giyani, South Africa, **371** F3
Giyon, Ethiopia, **367** E3
Gīzāb, Afghanistan, **218** A2
Gizo, Solomon Islands, **141** A1
Giżycko, Poland, **289** K1
Gjirokastër, Albania, **297** C5, *263*
Gjoa Haven, Canada, **411** K3
Gjøra, Norway, **286** D1
Gjøvik, Norway, **286** E2
Gjuhëzës, Kepi i, *cape*, Albania, **297** B5
Glace Bay, Canada, **417** M6
Glacier, Canada, **413** L6
Glacier, U.S.A., **418** D2
Glad', Russian Federation, **299** D3
Glad Valley, U.S.A., **420** C3
Gladstad, Norway, **284** E4
Gladstone, Canada, **414** E6
Gladstone, Michigan, U.S.A., **421** K3
Gladstone, New Mexico, U.S.A., **423** M3
Gladstone, Queensland, Australia, **135** L3
Gladstone, South Australia, Australia, **135** H5
Gláma, *mountain peak*, Iceland, **284** X7
Glåma, *river*, Norway, **286** E2
Glamis, Scotland, U.K., **308** F4
Glåmos, Norway, **286** E1
Glan, Philippines, **204** D5
Glanaruddery Mountains, Ireland, **309** C5
Glanton, England, U.K., **307** G2
Glarner Alpen, *mountain range*, Switzerland, **291** J3
Glarus, Switzerland, **291** J3
Glasbury, Wales, U.K., **304** D2
Glasgow, Kentucky, U.S.A., **421** L7
Glasgow, Montana, U.S.A., **419** L2
Glasgow, Scotland, U.K., **308** E5, *276*
Glasgow, Virginia, U.S.A., **421** P7
Glasgow City, *local authority*, Scotland, U.K., **308** E5
Glaslyn, Canada, **413** Q5
Glass Butte, *mountain peak*, U.S.A., **418** D5
Glassboro, U.S.A., **426** C5
Glastonbury, England, U.K., **304** E3
Glazov, Russian Federation, **300** G4
Gleisdorf, Austria, **289** G5
Glen Canyon, *gorge*, U.S.A., **423** H3
Glen Cove, U.S.A., **426** D4
Glen Falls, U.S.A., **426** D3
Glen Innes, Australia, **135** L4
Glen Ullin, U.S.A., **419** P3
Glenavy, New Zealand, **133** C7
Glenbarr, Scotland, U.K., **308** D5
Glencross, U.S.A., **420** C3
Glendale, Arizona, U.S.A., **423** G5
Glendale, California, U.S.A., **422** D4
Glendambo, Australia, **135** H5
Glendive, U.S.A., **419** M3
Glendo, U.S.A., **419** M5
Glendon, Canada, **413** P4
Gleneagles, Scotland, U.K., **308** F4
Glenelg, *river*, Australia, **135** J6
Glenfield, U.S.A., **420** D2
Glenfinnan, Scotland, U.K., **308** D4
Glengad Head, *point*, Ireland, **309** E2
Glengarriff, Ireland, **309** C6
Glenluce, Scotland, U.K., **308** E6
Glennallen, U.S.A., **410** E3
Glennamaddy, Ireland, **309** D4
Glennville, U.S.A., **425** M4
Glenorchy, New Zealand, **133** B7
Glenrock, U.S.A., **419** M5
Glenrothes, Scotland, U.K., **308** F4
Glenties, Ireland, **309** D3
Glentworth, Canada, **413** R7
Glenville, U.S.A., **425** K3
Glenwood, Arkansas, U.S.A., **424** F2
Glenwood, Iowa, U.S.A., **420** F5
Glenwood, Minnesota, U.S.A., **420** F3
Glenwood, New Mexico, U.S.A., **423** J5
Glenwood Springs, U.S.A., **423** K2
Glide, U.S.A., **418** C5
Glina, Croatia, **294** F3
Glinojeck, Poland, **289** K2
Glinton, England, U.K., **305** G2
Glittertind, *mountain peak*, Norway, **286** D2, *230*
Gliwice, Poland, **289** J3
Globe, U.S.A., **423** H5
Glodeanu-Sărat, Romania, **296** F3
Glodeni, Moldova, **296** F2
Głogów, Poland, **289** H3
Glomfjord, Norway, **284** F3
Glommersträsk, Sweden, **284** J4
Glonn, *river*, Germany, **288** E4
Glorieuses, Îles, *islands*, Réunion, **372** B3, *354*
Glossop, England, U.K., **307** G4
Gloucester, England, U.K., **304** E3
Gloucester, Papua New Guinea, **140** C4
Gloucester, U.S.A., **426** E3
Gloucestershire, *unitary authority*, England, U.K., **304** E3
Glover Island, Canada, **417** N5
Głubczyce, Poland, **289** H3
Glūbokoe, Kazakhstan, **223** L2
Gmünd, Austria, **289** G4
Gmunden, Austria, **289** F5
Gniew, Poland, **289** J2
Gniewkowo, Poland, **289** J2
Gniezno, Poland, **289** H2
Gnjilane, Kosovo, **296** C4
Goa, *state*, India, **216** C3, *167, 169*
Goālpāra, India, **219** G4
Goaso, Ghana, **364** D3
Goat Fell, *mountain peak*, Scotland, U.K., **308** D5
Goba, Ethiopia, **367** F3
Gobabis, Namibia, **370** C3
Gobernador Duval, Argentina, **460** D1
Gobernador Gregores, Argentina, **460** C3
Gobernador Mayer, Argentina, **460** C4
Gobi, China, **213** H5
Gobi, *desert*, Mongolia, **195** M5, *144, 145, 158, 186*
Gobowen, England, U.K., **304** D2
Gochas, Namibia, **370** C3
Godalming, England, U.K., **305** G3
Godavari, *river*, India, **216** D2
Godbout, Canada, **416** H5
Godda, India, **219** F4
Godē, Ethiopia, **367** F3
Godech, Bulgaria, **296** D4
Godere, Ethiopia, **367** F3
Goderich, Canada, **421** N4
Goderville, France, **305** H5
Godhra, India, **218** C5
Godinlabe, Somalia, **367** G3
Godmanchester, England, U.K., **305** G2
Gödöllő, Hungary, **289** J5
Godoy Cruz, Argentina, **458** C4
Gods, *river*, Canada, **414** H3
Gods Lake, Canada, **414** G4
Gods Lake, *lake*, Canada, **414** G4
Godthåb *see* Nuuk, Greenland, **411** P3, *388*
Goe, Papua New Guinea, **140** A5
Goéland, Lac au, *lake*, Canada, **416** C5
Goes, Netherlands, **288** A3
Goffs, U.S.A., **422** F4
Gogland, Ostrov, *island*, Russian Federation, **287** N2
Gogounou, Benin, **365** E2
Gogrial, Sudan, **366** C3
Gohad, India, **218** D4
Goiana, Brazil, **453** G5
Goiandira, Brazil, **456** D5
Goiânia, Brazil, **456** D4
Goiás, Brazil, **456** C4
Goiás, *state*, Brazil, **456** C4
Goio-Erê, Brazil, **459** G2
Góis, Portugal, **292** C2
Gojra, Pakistan, **218** C3
Gökçeada, *island*, Turkey, **297** E5
Göksun, Turkey, **224** E5
Gokwe, Zimbabwe, **371** E2
Gol, Norway, **286** D2
Gola, India, **218** E3
Golāghāt, India, **219** H4
Golan, *region*, Syria, **225** C3, *179, 182*
Gölbaşı, Turkey, **363** G1
Golbembal, Nigeria, **365** G3
Golconda, U.S.A., **422** E1
Gölcük, Kocaeli, Turkey, **297** G5
Gölcük, Turkey, **297** F6
Gold Beach, U.S.A., **418** B5
Gold Bridge, Canada, **412** H6
Gold Coast, Australia, **135** L4
Gold Coast, *coastal area*, Ghana/Togo, **364** D4
Gold River, Canada, **412** F7
Gołdap, Poland, **289** L1
Golden, Canada, **413** L6
Golden Bay, New Zealand, **132** D5
Golden Meadow, U.S.A., **424** G5
Goldendale, U.S.A., **418** D4
Goldfield, U.S.A., **422** E3
Goldsboro, U.S.A., **425** N2
Goldsmith, U.S.A., **423** M6
Goldthwaite, U.S.A., **424** C4
Goldyrevskiy, Russian Federation, **222** F1
Goleniów, Poland, **289** G2
Goleta, U.S.A., **422** D4
Golets Skalistyy, Gora, *mountain peak*, Russian Federation, **301** Q4
Golfo Aranci, Sardegna, Italy, **295** B5
Gölgeli Dağları, *mountain range*, Turkey, **297** G7
Goliad, U.S.A., **424** D5
Gölmarmara, Turkey, **297** F6
Golmud, China, **213** G5
Golnik, Slovenia, **294** E2
Golo, *river*, Corse, France, **294** B4
Golo Island, Philippines, **204** C3
Golovnino, Russian Federation, **209** J2
Golpāyegān, Iran, **220** F2
Gölpazarı, Turkey, **297** H5
Golspie, Scotland, U.K., **308** F3
Golungo Alto, Angola, **368** B4
Golyam Perelik, *mountain peak*, Bulgaria, **297** E5
Gölyazı, Turkey, **297** G5
Golyshmanovo, Russian Federation, **223** H1
Goma, Democratic Republic of the Congo, **369** E3
Gomati, *river*, India, **219** E4
Gombe, Nigeria, **365** G2
Gombi, Nigeria, **365** G2
Gombrani, *island*, Rodrigues, Mauritius, **373** B1
Gomera, *island*, Islas Canarias, Spain, **373** A4
Gómez Farías, Mexico, **430** D2
Gómez Palacio, Mexico, **430** E3
Gomo, China, **219** F2
Gomorovichi, Russian Federation, **299** E2
Gonaïves, Haiti, **429** G3
Gonâve, Golfe de la, *gulf*, Haiti, **429** G3, *394*
Gonâve, Île de la, *island*, Haiti, **429** G3
Gonbad-e Qābūs, Iran, **222** F5
Gonda, India, **219** E4
Gondal, India, **218** B5
Gonder, Ethiopia, **367** E2
Gondia, India, **218** E5
Gönen, *river*, Turkey, **297** F5
Gönen, Turkey, **297** F5
Gonfreville-L'Orcher, France, **290** E2
Gong Xian, China, **206** C1
Gong'an, China, **206** C2
Gongbo'gyamba, China, **214** E3
Gongcheng, China, **206** B3
Gonggar, China, **214** D3
Gonghe, China, **213** J5
Gonghui, China, **210** F4
Gongliu, China, **223** L4
Gongming, China, **207** B3
Gongpoquan, China, **213** H4
Gongzhuling, China, **211** J4
Goniri, Nigeria, **365** G2
Gonzaga, Philippines, **204** C2
Gonzales, California, U.S.A., **422** C3
Gonzales, Texas, U.S.A., **424** D5
González, Mexico, **431** F4
Goobies, Canada, **417** P6
Good Hope, Cape of, *cape*, South Africa, **370** C5, *76, 92, 350, 351*
Good Hope Lake, Canada, **412** E2
Goodenough Island, Papua New Guinea, **140** C5
Goodeve, Canada, **414** C6
Gooding, U.S.A., **418** G5
Goodland, U.S.A., **420** C6
Goodlands, Mauritius, **373** C1
Goodrich, U.S.A., **420** C2
Goodsoil, Canada, **413** Q4
Goodwick, Wales, U.K., **304** C2
Goodwin, U.S.A., **420** E3
Goole, England, U.K., **307** H4
Goomalling, Australia, **134** D5
Goondiwindi, Australia, **135** L4
Goose Green, Falkland Islands, **460** F4
Goose Lake, U.S.A., **418** D6
Gopalganj, India, **219** F4
Góra, near Płock, Poland, **289** K2
Góra, Poland, **289** H3
Gora, Russian Federation, **299** G2
Gorakhpur, India, **219** E4
Goram, Tanjong, *point*, Indonesia, **198** C4
Goras, India, **218** D4
Goražde, Bosnia and Herzegovina, **294** G4
Gorbitsa, Russian Federation, **211** G1
Gorda, Punta, *point*, Chile, **454** D5
Gördalen, Sweden, **286** F2
Gördes, Turkey, **297** G6
Gordil, Central African Republic, **366** B3
Gordon, Lake, Australia, **135** J7
Gordon, Scotland, U.K., **308** G5
Gordon, U.S.A., **420** B4
Gordondale, Canada, **413** K4
Gordonsville, U.S.A., **426** A5
Goré, Chad, **365** H3
Gorē, Ethiopia, **366** E3
Gore, New Zealand, **133** B8
Gore Mountain, *mountain peak*, U.S.A., **426** E2
Gorebridge, Scotland, U.K., **308** F5
Gorel'de, Turkmenistan, **222** G4
Gorey, Ireland, **309** F5
Gorgal, *administrative region*, Mauritania, **364** B1
Gorge Creek, New Zealand, **133** B7
Gorgona, Isola di, *island*, Italy, **294** B4
Gorgora, Ethiopia, **367** E2
Gorgova, Romania, **296** G3
Gorham, U.S.A., **426** E2
Gorinchem, Netherlands, **288** B3
Goris, Armenia, **363** J1
Goritsy, Russian Federation, **299** F4
Gorizia, Italy, **294** D3
Gorlice, Poland, **289** K4
Görlitz, Germany, **289** G3
Gorlovo, Russian Federation, **299** G6
Gorm, Loch, *lake*, Scotland, U.K., **308** C5
Gorna Oryakhovitsa, Bulgaria, **296** E4
Gornj Dŭbnik, Bulgaria, **296** E4
Gornji Milanovac, Serbia, **296** C3
Gorno Altaysk, Russian Federation, **223** M2
Gornozavodsk, Russian Federation, **209** H1
Gornyak, Russian Federation, **223** L2
Gorodishche, Russian Federation, **299** B3
Gorogoro, Indonesia, **198** D3
Goroka, Papua New Guinea, **140** B4
Gorom-Gorom, Burkina Faso, **364** D2
Gorong, Kepulauan, *islands*, Indonesia, **199** E4
Gorongosa, Mozambique, **371** F2
Gorongosa, Serra da, *mountain range*, Mozambique, **371** F2
Gorontalo, Indonesia, **198** C2
Gort, Ireland, **309** D4
Gortahork, Ireland, **309** D2
Gorumna Island, Ireland, **309** C4
Görvik, Sweden, **284** G5
Goryachegorsk, Russian Federation, **223** M1
Goryachinsk, Russian Federation, **210** E1
Gorzów Wielkopolski, Poland, **289** G2
Gosberton, England, U.K., **305** G2
Gosfield, England, U.K., **305** H3
Gosford, Australia, **135** L5
Gosforth, Cumbria, England, U.K., **306** E3
Gosforth, Tyne and Wear, England, U.K., **307** G2
Goshogawara, Japan, **209** H2
Goslar, Germany, **288** E3
Gospić, Croatia, **294** E3
Gosport, England, U.K., **305** F4
Gossen, *island*, Norway, **286** C1
Gossi, Mali, **364** D1
Gostivar, Macedonia, **296** C5
Gostyń, Poland, **289** H3
Gostynin, Poland, **289** J2
Gota, Ethiopia, **367** F3
Göteborg (Gothenburg), Sweden, **286** E4, *233*
Göteborg Och Bohus, *county*, Sweden, **286** E3
Götene, Sweden, **286** F3
Goth Āmri, Pakistan, **218** A4
Gotha, Germany, **288** E3
Gothem, Sweden, **287** J4
Gothenburg *see* Göteborg, Sweden, **286** E4
Gothenburg, U.S.A., **420** C5
Gothèye, Niger, **365** E2
Gotland, *county*, Sweden, **287** J4
Gotland, *island*, Sweden, **287** J4, *232, 233*
Gotō-rettō, *islands*, Japan, **208** E4
Gotowasi, Indonesia, **199** E2

Gotse Delchev, Bulgaria, 297 D5
Gotska Sandön, *island*, Sweden, 287 J3
Göttingen, Germany, 288 D3
Gouda, Netherlands, 288 B3
Goudiri, Senegal, 364 B2
Goudoumaria, Niger, 365 G2
Gouéké, Guinea, 364 C3
Gouin, Réservoir, Canada, 416 D5
Goulais River, Canada, 421 L2
Goulburn, Australia, 135 K5
Goulburn Islands, Australia, 134 G1
Gould, U.S.A., 423 K1
Gould Coast, *region*, Antarctica, 470 D6
Goulfey, Cameroon, 365 G2
Goumbou, Mali, 364 C2
Goundam, Mali, 364 D1
Goundi, Chad, 365 H3
Gourcy, Burkina Faso, 364 D2
Gourdon, Cape, Papua New Guinea, 140 B4
Gourdon, France, 290 E4
Gouré, Niger, 365 G2
Gourin, France, 290 C2
Gourma-Rharous, Mali, 364 D1
Gournay-en-Bray, France, 305 J5
Gouro, Chad, 362 C5
Gouverneur, U.S.A., 426 C2
Gouzon, France, 290 F3
Governador Valadares, Brazil, 457 E4
Governor's Harbour, Bahamas, 428 F1
Govĭ-Altay, *province*, Mongolia, 213 G3
Govĭ Altayn Nuruu, *mountain range*, Mongolia, 213 H3, 186
Govind Ballabh Pant Sāgar, *reservoir*, India, 219 E4
Gower, Mount, *mountain peak*, Lord Howe Island, Australia, 135 U14
Gowna, Lough, *lake*, Ireland, 309 E4
Gowran, Ireland, 309 E5
Goya, Argentina, 459 E3
Goyoum, Cameroon, 368 B1
Goz-Beïda, Chad, 366 B2
Gozha Co, *lake*, China, 218 D2
Gozo, *island*, Malta, 295 E7, 257
Graaff-Reinet, South Africa, 370 D5
Grabo, Côte d'Ivoire, 364 C4
Grabow, Germany, 288 E2
Gračac, Croatia, 294 E3
Gracefield, Canada, 416 C6
Graceville, U.S.A., 420 E3
Gracias, Honduras, 428 C4
Graciosa, *island*, Azores, Portugal, 360 M7
Graciosa, *island*, Islas Canarias, Spain, 373 B4
Gradačac, Bosnia and Herzegovina, 294 G3
Gradaús, Serra dos, *mountain range*, Brazil, 452 C5
Gradets, Bulgaria, 296 F4
Grady Harbour, Canada, 417 N3
Grafton, Australia, 135 L4
Grafton, U.S.A., 420 E1
Graham, Mount, *mountain peak*, U.S.A., 423 J5
Graham, U.S.A., 424 C3
Graham Island, Canada, 412 D5
Graham Land, *region*, Antarctica, 470 A4
Grahamstown, South Africa, 371 E5

Graie, Alpi, *mountain range*, Italy, 294 A3
Graigue, Ireland, 309 F5
Grain Coast, *coastal area*, Liberia, 364 B3
Grainfield, U.S.A., 420 C6
Grajaú, Brazil, 452 D4
Grajaú, *river*, Brazil, 452 D4
Grajewo, Poland, 289 L2
Gramada, Bulgaria, 296 D4
Gramankondre, Suriname, 452 B2
Gramat, France, 290 E4
Gramatikovo, Bulgaria, 296 F4
Grambling, U.S.A., 424 F3
Grampian Mountains, Scotland, U.K., 308 E4, 276
Gramzow, Germany, 289 G2
Gran, Norway, 286 E2
Gran Altiplanicie Central, *plain*, Argentina, 460 D3
Gran Canaria, *island*, Islas Canarias, Spain, 373 B4, 355
Gran Chaco, *plain*, South America, 447 F6, 95, 443, 445
Gran Pajonal, *mountain range*, Peru, 454 C3
Gran Paradiso, *mountain peak*, Italy, 294 A3
Gran Tarajal, Islas Canarias, Spain, 373 B4
Granaatboskolk, South Africa, 370 C5
Granada, Colombia, 450 D3
Granada, Nicaragua, 428 D5
Granada, Spain, 293 F4, 92, 252
Granada, U.S.A., 423 M2
Granadilla de Abona, Islas Canarias, Spain, 373 A4
Granard, Ireland, 309 E4
Grand, *river*, Missouri, U.S.A., 420 G6
Grand, *river*, South Dakota, U.S.A., 420 C3
Grand Bahama, *island*, Bahamas, 428 F1
Grand Bank, Canada, 417 P6
Grand Banks of Newfoundland, *underwater feature*, Atlantic Ocean, 477 D2
Grand-Bassam, Côte d'Ivoire, 364 C4
Grand Bend, Canada, 421 N4
Grand Canyon, *gorge*, U.S.A., 422 G3, 24, 383
Grand Canyon, U.S.A., 423 G3
Grand Cayman, *island*, Cayman Islands, 429 E3
Grand Cess, Liberia, 364 C4
Grand Coulee, U.S.A., 418 E3
Grand-Entrée, Canada, 417 L6
Grand Erg de Bilma, *desert*, Niger, 365 G1
Grand Erg Occidental, *desert*, Algeria, 361 F2, 315
Grand Erg Oriental, *desert*, Algeria, 361 H3
Grand Falls, Canada, 416 H6
Grand Falls-Windsor, Canada, 417 P5
Grand Forks, U.S.A., 420 E2
Grand Haven, U.S.A., 421 K4
Grand Island, U.S.A., 420 D5
Grand Junction, U.S.A., 423 J2
Grand Lake, Colorado, U.S.A., 423 L1
Grand Lake, Louisiana, U.S.A., 424 F5

Grand Lake, Maine, U.S.A., 426 F2
Grand Lake, Newfoundland, Canada, 417 L3
Grand Lake, Newfoundland Island, Canada, 417 N5
Grand Lake, Ohio, U.S.A., 421 L5
Grand Ledge, U.S.A., 421 L4
Grand-Lieu, Lac de, *lake*, France, 290 D3
Grand Manan Island, Canada, 426 G2
Grand Marais, Michigan, U.S.A., 421 L2
Grand Marais, Minnesota, U.S.A., 420 H2
Grand-Mère, Canada, 416 E6
Grand Prairie, U.S.A., 424 D3
Grand Rapids, Canada, 414 E5
Grand Rapids, Michigan, U.S.A., 421 L4
Grand Rapids, Minnesota, U.S.A., 420 G2
Grand-Remous, Canada, 416 C6
Grand Rivière de la Baleine, *river*, Canada, 416 C2
Grand Ronde, U.S.A., 418 C4
Grand-Santi, French Guiana, 452 B2
Grand Teton, *mountain peak*, U.S.A., 419 J5, 383
Grand Turk, Turks and Caicos Islands, 429 H2, 391
Grand Veymont, Le, *mountain peak*, France, 291 G4
Grand View, Canada, 414 D6
Grand View, Idaho, U.S.A., 418 F5
Grand View, Wisconsin, U.S.A., 420 H2
Grande, Bahía, *gulf*, Argentina, 460 D4
Grande, Boca, *bay*, Venezuela, 451 G2
Grande, Cayo, *island*, Cuba, 429 F2
Grande, Cuchilla, *mountain range*, Uruguay, 447 G7
Grande, Ilha, *island*, Brazil, 457 F6
Grande, Morro, *mountain peak*, Brazil, 452 B3
Grande, Rio, *river*, Mexico/U.S.A., 407 N5
Grande, *river*, Argentina, 458 C5
Grande, *river*, Bahia, Brazil, 457 E3
Grande (Guapay), *river*, Bolivia, 455 F5
Grande, *river*, Minas Gerais, Brazil, 456 C5
Grande, *river*, Peru, 454 C4
Grande Baie, Mauritius, 373 C1
Grande Cache, Canada, 413 K5
Grande Comore *see* Njazidja, Comoros, 372 A3, 352
Grande de Chiloé, Isla, *island*, Chile, 460 B2
Grande de Gurupá, Ilha, *island*, Brazil, 452 C3
Grande de Matagalpa, *river*, Nicaragua, 428 D4
Grande de Santiago, *river*, Mexico, 430 D4
Grande del Durazno, Cuchillo, *mountain range*, Uruguay, 459 F4
Grande Inferior, Cuchillo, *mountain range*, Uruguay, 459 F4
Grande Prairie, Canada, 413 K4
Grande Rivière, Trinidad, Trinidad and Tobago, 461 C4

Grande Tête de l'Obiou, *mountain peak*, France, 291 G4
Grandes, Salinas, *salt-pan*, Argentina, 458 C2
Grandfalls, U.S.A., 423 M6
Grandioznyy, Pik, *mountain peak*, Russian Federation, 223 P2
Grândola, Portugal, 292 C3
Grandtully, Scotland, U.K., 308 F4
Grandview, U.S.A., 418 E3
Grandvilliers, France, 290 E2
Graneros, Chile, 458 B5
Graney, Lough, *lake*, Ireland, 309 D5
Grangemouth, Scotland, U.K., 308 F4
Granger, Washington, U.S.A., 418 D3
Granger, Wyoming, U.S.A., 419 K6
Grangeville, U.S.A., 418 F4
Grăniceşti, Romania, 296 F2
Graninge, Sweden, 287 H1
Granite, Oklahoma, U.S.A., 424 C2
Granite, Oregon, U.S.A., 418 E4
Granite Falls, U.S.A., 420 F3
Granite Peak, *mountain peak*, U.S.A., 422 G1
Granitola, Capo, *cape*, Italy, 295 D7
Granja, Brazil, 453 F4
Grankullavik, Sweden, 287 H4
Granollers, Spain, 293 J2
Granön, Sweden, 284 J4
Gränssjö, Sweden, 284 G4
Grant, Mount, *mountain peak*, U.S.A., 422 D2
Grant, U.S.A., 420 C5
Grantham, England, U.K., 305 G2
Grantown-on-Spey, Scotland, U.K., 308 F3
Grants, U.S.A., 423 K4
Grants Pass, U.S.A., 418 C5
Grantsville, U.S.A., 422 G1
Granville, France, 290 D2
Granville, U.S.A., 420 C1
Granvin, Norway, 286 C2
Grão Mogol, Brazil, 457 E4
Grapevine, U.S.A., 424 D4
Gras, Lac de, *lake*, Canada, 410 H3
Grasbakken, Norway, 285 P1
Grasmere, Canada, 413 M7
Grasmere, England, U.K., 306 E3
Grasmere, U.S.A., 418 G5
Gräsö, *island*, Sweden, 287 J2
Grass Creek, U.S.A., 419 K5
Grasse, France, 291 H5
Grassland, Canada, 413 N4
Grassrange, U.S.A., 419 K3
Grassy Butte, U.S.A., 420 B2
Grassy Knob, *mountain peak*, U.S.A., 421 N6
Grates Cove, Canada, 417 Q5
Gravatá, Brazil, 453 G5
Gravelines, France, 305 K4
Gravenhurst, Canada, 421 P3
Gravesend, England, U.K., 305 H3
Gray, France, 291 G3
Gray, U.S.A., 420 C7
Grays, England, U.K., 305 H3
Grays River, U.S.A., 418 C3
Graz, Austria, 289 G5
Grdelica, Serbia, 296 D4
Great Artesian Basin, Australia, 128 D4, 112
Great Australian Bight, *gulf*, Australia, 128 B5
Great Barrier Island (Aotea Island), New Zealand, 132 E3

Great Barrier Reef, Australia, 128 D3, 112, 124, 127
Great Basin, U.S.A., 422 F2
Great Bear Lake, Canada, 410 G3
Great Bend, U.S.A., 420 D6
Great Bernera, *island*, Scotland, U.K., 308 C2
Great Coco Island, Myanmar, 217 H3
Great Dividing Range, *mountain range*, Australia, 128 D3
Great Dunmow, England, U.K., 305 H3
Great Exhibition Bay, New Zealand, 132 D2
Great Exuma Island, Bahamas, 428 F2
Great Falls, Canada, 414 F6
Great Falls, Montana, U.S.A., 419 J3
Great Falls, South Carolina, U.S.A., 425 M2
Great Gonerby, England, U.K., 305 G2
Great Harwood, England, U.K., 306 F4
Great Inagua Island, Bahamas, 429 G2
Great Island, New Zealand, 132 D2
Great Karoo, *plateau*, South Africa, 357 H10
Great Lake, Australia, 135 K7
Great Lakes, Canada/U.S.A., 406 Q4, 376, 383, 384
Great Linford, England, U.K., 305 G2
Great Malvern, England, U.K., 304 E2
Great Mercury Island, New Zealand, 132 E3
Great Nicobar, *island*, Andaman and Nicobar Islands, 217 H5
Great Oyster Bay, Australia, 128 D6
Great Plain of China, China, 195 N6
Great Rift Valley, E. Africa, 357 H7
Great Sacandaga Lake, U.S.A., 426 C3
Great Salt Lake, U.S.A., 418 H6
Great Salt Lake Desert, U.S.A., 422 G2
Great Sand Sea, *desert*, Egypt/Libya, 362 D3
Great Sandy Desert, Australia, 128 B3
Great Sandy Desert, U.S.A., 418 D5
Great Slave Lake, Canada, 410 H3
Great Smoky Mountains, *mountain range*, U.S.A., 425 L2, 383
Great Snow Mountain, *mountain peak*, Canada, 412 G3
Great Tenasserim, *river*, Myanmar, 202 C3
Great Torrington, England, U.K., 304 C4
Great Waltham, England, U.K., 305 H3
Great Whernside, *mountain peak*, England, U.K., 307 F3
Great Yarmouth, England, U.K., 305 J2
Greater Accra, *administrative region*, Ghana, 364 E3
Greater Antilles, *islands*, Caribbean Sea, 429 E2, 393
Greater London, *unitary authority*, England, U.K., 305 G3
Greater Manchester, *unitary authority*, England, U.K., 306 F4

Greco, Cape, Cyprus, 225 C2
Gredos, Sierra de, *mountain range*, Spain, 292 E2
Greece, *country*, Europe, 282 G8, 29, 65, 70, 71, 89, 147, 192, 228, 245, 255, 260, 261, 263, 264, 265
Greece, U.S.A., 426 B3
Greeley, Colorado, U.S.A., 423 L1
Greeley, Nebraska, U.S.A., 420 D5
Greem-Bell, Ostrov, *island*, Russian Federation, 300 H1
Green, *river*, U.S.A., 423 H2
Green Bay, *bay*, U.S.A., 421 K3
Green Bay, U.S.A., 421 K3
Green Court, Canada, 413 M4
Green Cove Springs, U.S.A., 425 M5
Green Hill, Trinidad, Trinidad and Tobago, 461 C4
Green Islands, Papua New Guinea, 140 E8
Green Lake, Canada, 413 R4
Green Mount, *mountain peak*, Ascension, 373 A3
Green Mountains, *mountain range*, U.S.A., 426 D3
Green River, Papua New Guinea, 140 A3
Green River, Utah, U.S.A., 423 H2
Green River, Wyoming, U.S.A., 419 K6
Green Valley, U.S.A., 423 H6
Greenbrier, *river*, U.S.A., 421 N7
Greenbush, U.S.A., 420 E1
Greencastle, Northern Ireland, U.K., 309 F3
Greencastle, U.S.A., 421 K6
Greene, U.S.A., 426 C3
Greeneville, U.S.A., 425 L1
Greenfield, California, U.S.A., 422 C3
Greenfield, Massachusetts, U.S.A., 426 D3
Greenland (Kalaallit Nunaat), *Danish territory*, Arctic Ocean, 408 U1, 29, 75, 91, 234, 380, 384, 388, 389, 390, 466
Greenland Sea, Arctic Ocean, 411 T3
Greenlaw, Scotland, U.K., 308 G5
Greenock, Scotland, U.K., 308 E5
Greenore, Ireland, 309 F3
Greenough, Mount, *mountain peak*, U.S.A., 410 E3
Greenport, U.S.A., 426 D4
Greensboro, U.S.A., 425 J3
Greensburg, Indiana, U.S.A., 421 L6
Greensburg, Kansas, U.S.A., 420 D7
Greensburg, Pennsylvania, U.S.A., 425 J3
Greenstone Point, Scotland, U.K., 308 D3
Greenup, U.S.A., 421 J6
Greenview, U.S.A., 418 C6
Greenville, Alabama, U.S.A., 425 J4
Greenville, California, U.S.A., 422 C1
Greenville, Florida, U.S.A., 425 L4
Greenville, Illinois, U.S.A., 421 J6
Greenville, Liberia, 364 C3
Greenville, Louisiana, U.S.A., 424 C3
Greenville, North Carolina, U.S.A., 425 P2
Greenville, Ohio, U.S.A., 421 L5

Greenville, Pennsylvania, U.S.A., **421** N5
Greenville, South Carolina, U.S.A., **425** L2
Greenville, Texas, U.S.A., **424** D3
Greenwood, Mississippi, U.S.A., **424** G3
Greenwood, South Carolina, U.S.A., **425** L2
Greers Ferry Lake, U.S.A., **424** F2
Gregório, *river*, Brazil, **454** D2
Gregory, Lake, Australia, **134** F3
Gregory, *river*, Australia, **135** H2
Greifswald, Germany, **288** F1
Greifswalder Bodden, *bay*, Germany, **288** F1
Grein, Austria, **289** G4
Gremč, *physical feature*, Bosnia and Herzegovina, **294** F3
Gremikha, Russian Federation, **285** U2
Gremyachinsk, Russian Federation, **210** E1
Grenå, Denmark, **286** E4
Grenada, *country*, Caribbean Sea, **409** S7, *378, 379, 397, 398, 399*
Grenada, U.S.A., **424** H3
Grenade, France, **290** E5
Grenadines, The, *islands*, St Vincent and the Grenadines, **427** D3, *378, 397, 398*
Grenfell, Canada, **414** C6
Grenivík, Iceland, **284** Y7
Grenoble, France, **291** G4, *245*
Grense Jakobselv, Norway, **285** Q2
Grenville, Cape, Australia, **135** J1
Grenville, Grenada, **427** D3
Gresik, Indonesia, **201** F4
Gretna, U.S.A., **424** G5
Gretna Green, Scotland, U.K., **308** F6
Grevena, Greece, **297** C5
Grevesmühlen, Germany, **288** E2
Grey, *river*, New Zealand, **133** C6
Grey Islands, Canada, **417** P4
Grey Range, *mountain range*, Australia, **135** J4
Greymouth, New Zealand, **133** C6
Greystoke, England, U.K., **306** F3
Greytown, New Zealand, **133** E5
Greytown, South Africa, **371** F4
Gridino, Russian Federation, **285** S4
Griffin, Canada, **414** C7
Griffin, U.S.A., **425** K3
Griffith, Australia, **135** K5
Grigoriopol, Moldova, **296** G2
Grigor'yevka, Russian Federation, **223** N2
Grim, Cape, Australia, **128** D6
Grimari, Central African Republic, **365** J3
Grimma, Germany, **288** F3
Grimmen, Germany, **288** F1
Grimsby, England, U.K., **307** H4
Grimshaw, Canada, **413** L3
Grímsstaðir, Iceland, **284** Y7
Grimstad, Norway, **286** D3
Grindavík, Iceland, **284** X8
Grindsted, Denmark, **286** D5
Grinnell, U.S.A., **420** G5
Grintavec, *mountain peak*, Slovenia, **294** E2
Griquatown, South Africa, **370** D4
Gris Nez, Cap, *cape*, France, **305** J4
Grise Fiord, Canada, **411** L2
Grisslehamn, Sweden, **287** J2
Groais Island, Canada, **417** P4
Grobiöa, Latvia, **287** K4
Grødes, Norway, **286** C2
Grodków, Poland, **289** H3
Groesbeek, Netherlands, **288** B3
Groix, Île de, *island* , France, **290** C3
Grójec, Poland, **289** K3
Grong, Norway, **284** F4
Groningen, Netherlands, **288** C2
Groningen, *province*, Netherlands, **288** C2
Groningen, Suriname, **452** B2
Groote Eylandt, *island*, Australia, **135** H1
Grootfontein, Namibia, **370** C2
Gropniũa, Romania, **296** F2
Grose Morne, *mountain peak*, Canada, **417** N5
Gross Ums, Namibia, **370** C3
Grossa, Punta, *point*, Islas Baleares, Spain, **293** H3
Großer Arber, *mountain peak*, Germany, **288** F4
Grosseto, Italy, **294** C4
Großglockner, *mountain peak*, Austria, **288** F5, *248*
Groswater Bay, Canada, **417** N2
Groton, U.S.A., **420** D3
Grov, Norway, **284** H2
Grove City, U.S.A., **421** N5
Grove Hill, U.S.A., **425** J4
Grover City, U.S.A., **422** C4
Groznyy, Russian Federation, **222** D4
Grua, Norway, **286** E2
Grudovo, Bulgaria, **296** F4
Grudziądz, Poland, **289** J2
Gruinard Bay, Scotland, U.K., **308** D3
Grums, Sweden, **286** F3
Grünau, Namibia, **370** C4
Gruvberget, Sweden, **286** H2
Gruža, Serbia, **296** C4
Gruzdžiai, Lithuania, **287** L4
Gryfice, Poland, **289** G2
Gryllefjord, Norway, **284** H2
Gryt, Sweden, **287** H3
Grytøya, *island*, Norway, **284** H2
Grytviken, South Georgia, **461** A3, *445*
Grytviken, *U.K. research station*, Antarctica, **470** A2
Guacanayabo, Golfo de, *gulf*, Cuba, **429** F2
Guachipas, Argentina, **458** D2
Guaçu, *river*, Brazil, **459** F2
Guadajoz, *river*, Spain, **292** E4
Guadalajara, Mexico, **430** E4
Guadalajara, Spain, **293** F2
Guadalcanal, *island*, Solomon Islands, **141** A1, *116*
Guadalimar, *river*, Spain, **293** F3
Guadalmena, Embalse de, *reservoir*, Murcia, **293** G3
Guadalmena, *river*, Spain, **293** F3
Guadãlmez, *river*, Spain, **292** E3
Guadalope, *river*, Spain, **293** G2
Guadalquivir, *river*, Spain, **292** E4, *253*
Guadalupe, Baja California, Mexico, **430** A1
Guadalupe, Isla, *island*, Mexico, **409** M6
Guadalupe, Nuevo Léon, Mexico, **430** E4
Guadalupe, Spain, **292** E3
Guadalupe Aguilera, Mexico, **430** D3
Guadalupe Victoria, Mexico, **430** D3
Guadarrama, Sierra de, *mountain range*, Spain, **293** F2
Guadeloupe, *French department*, Caribbean Sea, **409** S7, *245, 378, 389*
Guadeloupe Passage, Caribbean Sea, **427** D2
Guadiana, *river*, Portugal/Spain, **280** D4, *253*
Guadix, Spain, **293** F4
Guafo, Boca del, *river mouth*, Chile, **460** B2
Guafo, Isla, *island*, Chile, **460** B2
Guaíba, Brazil, **459** G4
Guaimaca, Honduras, **428** D4
Guáimaro, Cuba, **429** F2
Guaiquinima, Cerro, *mountain peak*, Venezuela, **451** F3
Guaira, Brazil, **459** F2
Guaitecas, Islas, *islands*, Chile, **460** B2
Guajará-Mirim, Brazil, **455** F3
Guajarraã, Brazil, **455** E2
Guajira, Península de, Colombia, **450** D1
Gualaceo, Ecuador, **450** B5
Gualdo Tadino, Italy, **294** D4
Gualeguay, Argentina, **459** E4
Gualeguay, *river*, Argentina, **459** E4
Gualeguaychú, Argentina, **459** E4
Gualicho, Salina, *salt-pan*, Argentina, **460** E1
Gualjaina, Argentina, **460** C2
Guallatiri, Volcán, *mountain peak*, Chile, **455** E5
Guam, *U.S. territory*, Pacific Ocean, **138** C3, *95, 108, 118, 122, 123, 386*
Guamini, Argentina, **458** D5
Guamúchil, Mexico, **430** C3
Guan Xian, China, **215** G3
Guanabacoa, Cuba, **429** E2
Guanaja, Honduras, **428** D3
Guanajuato, Mexico, **431** E4
Guanajuato, *state*, Mexico, **431** E4
Guanambi, Brazil, **457** E4
Guanare, Venezuela, **451** E2
Guanarito, Venezuela, **451** E2
Guanay, Sierra, *mountain range*, Venezuela, **451** E3
Guandacol, Argentina, **458** C3
Guane, Cuba, **428** D2
Guang'an, China, **215** H3
Guangchang, China, **206** D3
Guangde, China, **206** D2
Guangdegong, China, **211** G4
Guangdong, *province*, China, **206** C4, *159, 161*
Guangfeng, China, **206** D2
Guanghai, China, **206** C4
Guangning, China, **206** C4
Guangrao, China, **211** G5
Guangshui, China, **206** C2
Guangxi Zhuangzu Zizhiqu, *autonomous region*, China, **206** B3, *159, 161*
Guangyuan, China, **215** H2
Guangze, China, **206** D3
Guangzhou (Canton), China, **207** A2, *161*
Guanhães, Brazil, **457** E5
Guanhu, China, **206** D1
Guanipa, *river*, Venezuela, **451** F2
Guanlan, China, **207** C3
Guantánamo, Cuba, **429** G2, *390*
Guanting, China, **215** G2
Guanyinge, China, **207** D2
Guanyun, China, **206** D1
Guapay, *river see* Grande, *river*, Bolivia, **455** F5
Guapí, Colombia, **450** C3
Guápiles, Costa Rica, **428** E5
Guapo Bay, Trinidad, Trinidad and Tobago, **461** C4
Guaporé, *river*, Bolivia/Brazil, **455** F3
Guara, Sierra de, *mountain peak*, Spain, **293** G1
Guarabira, Brazil, **453** G5
Guaranda, Ecuador, **450** B4
Guarapari, Brazil, **457** F5
Guarapuava, Brazil, **459** G2
Guaraqueçaba, Brazil, **459** H2
Guaratinguetá, Brazil, **457** E6
Guaratuba, Brazil, **459** H2
Guarayos, Bolivia, **455** E3
Guarda, *district*, Portugal, **292** D2
Guarda, Portugal, **292** D2
Guarda Mor, Brazil, **456** D4
Guárico, *river*, Venezuela, **451** E2
Guarita, *river*, Brazil, **459** G3
Guarujá, Brazil, **459** H2
Guasacaví, Cerro, *mountain peak*, Colombia, **451** E3
Guasave, Mexico, **430** C3
Guasdualito, Venezuela, **451** D2
Guasipati, Venezuela, **451** G2
Guatemala, *country*, Central America, **409** P7, *21, 64, 90, 378, 379, 400, 401, 402*
Guatemala, Guatemala, **428** C4, *401*
Guatemala Basin, *underwater feature*, Pacific Ocean, **479** M4
Guatrache, Argentina, **458** D5
Guatuaro Point, Trinidad, Trinidad and Tobago, **461** C4
Guaviare, *river*, Colombia, **451** D3
Guaxupé, Brazil, **456** D5
Guayabero, *river*, Colombia, **450** D3
Guayaguayare, Trinidad, Trinidad and Tobago, **461** C4
Guayama, Puerto Rico, **427** C2
Guayaquil, Ecuador, **450** B5, *438*
Guayaquil, Golfo de, *gulf*, Ecuador, **450** B5
Guayaramerin, Bolivia, **455** F3
Guaycurú, *river*, Argentina, **459** E3
Guaymas, Mexico, **430** C3
Guayquiraró, *river*, Argentina, **459** E4
Guba, Ethiopia, **366** E2
Guban, *physical feature*, Somalia, **367** F2, *339*
Gubbio, Italy, **294** D4
Guben, Germany, **289** G3
Gubi, Nigeria, **365** F2
Gubin, Poland, **289** G3
Gubio, Nigeria, **365** G2
Gucheng, China, **206** B1
Gudivāda, India, **217** E2
Gudiyattam, India, **216** D3
Gūdūr, India, **216** D3
Gudvangen, Norway, **286** C2
Guékédou, Guinea, **364** B3
Guélengdeng, Chad, **365** H2
Guelma, Algeria, **361** H1
Guelmim, Morocco, **360** D3
Guelta Zemmur, Western Sahara, **360** D3
Guemar, Algeria, **361** H2
Güémez, Mexico, **431** F4
Guéné, Benin, **365** E2
Guer, France, **290** C3
Guéra, *prefecture*, Chad, **366** A2
Guerara, Algeria, **361** G2
Guercif, Morocco, **361** F2
Guéret, France, **290** E3
Guernsey, *island*, Channel Islands, **290** C2, *228, 276, 278*
Guernsey, U.S.A., **419** M5
Guérou, Mauritania, **364** B1
Guerrero, *state*, Mexico, **431** E5
Guerrero Negro, Mexico, **430** B3
Gueugnon, France, **291** G3
Guéyo, Côte d'Ivoire, **364** C3
Gugē, *mountain peak*, Ethiopia, **367** E3
Guguan, *island*, Northern Mariana Islands, **138** C3
Guguang, Gunung, *mountain peak*, Indonesia, **201** G2
Guhāgar, India, **216** C2
Guhakolak, Tanjong, *point*, Indonesia, **200** D4
Gui, *river*, China, **206** B3
Guía de Isora, Islas Canarias, Spain, **373** A4
Guiana Highlands, South America, **447** F3, *435, 437, 439*
Guichi, China, **206** D2
Guichón, Uruguay, **459** F4
Guidari, Chad, **365** H3
Guide, China, **215** G2
Guider, Cameroon, **365** G3
Guidimaka, *administrative region*, Mauritania, **364** B1
Guiding, China, **215** H4
Guigang, China, **206** B4
Guiglo, Côte d'Ivoire, **364** C3
Guijuelo, Spain, **292** E2
Guildford, England, U.K., **305** G3
Guiler, China, **211** H3
Guilford, U.S.A., **426** F2
Guilin, China, **206** B3
Guillaume-Delisle, Lac, *lake*, Canada, **415** S3
Guillestre, France, **291** H4
Guimarães, Brazil, **453** E4
Guimarães, Portugal, **292** C2
Guimbiri, Mont, *mountain peak*, Cameroon, **365** G4
Guinan, China, **215** G2
Guindulman, Philippines, **204** D4
Guinea, *country*, Africa, **358** D5, *312, 313, 321, 322, 323*
Guinea Basin, *underwater feature*, Atlantic Ocean, **477** G5
Guinea-Bissau, *country*, Africa, **358** D5, *312, 313, 321*
Guinée-Forestière, *administrative area*, Guinea, **364** C3
Guinée-Maritime, *administrative region*, Guinea, **364** B2
Güines, Cuba, **429** E2
Guingamp, France, **290** C2
Guinguinéo, Senegal, **364** A2
Guiping, China, **206** B4
Guir, Oued, *river*, Algeria/Morocco, **361** F2
Guiratinga, Brazil, **456** C4
Güiria, Venezuela, **451** F1
Guisanbourg, French Guiana, **452** C2
Guisborough, England, U.K., **307** G3
Guise, France, **291** F2
Guishan Dao, *island*, China, **207** B4
Guist, England, U.K., **305** H2
Guitinguitin, Mount, *mountain peak*, Philippines, **204** C3
Guitiriz, Spain, **292** D1
Guiuan, Philippines, **204** D4
Guixi, China, **206** D2
Guiyang, Guizhou, China, **215** H4, *161*
Guiyang, Hunan, China, **206** C3
Guizhou, China, **207** A3
Guizhou, *province*, China, **215** H4, *159, 161*
Gujarāt, *state*, India, **218** B5, *169*
Gujrānwāla, Pakistan, **218** C2
Gujrāt, Pakistan, **218** C2
Gulang, China, **213** J5
Gulbarga, India, **216** D2
Gulbene, Latvia, **287** N4
Gul'cha, Kyrgyzstan, **223** J4
Gulf, *province*, Papua New Guinea, **140** B5
Gulf Shores, U.S.A., **425** J4
Gulfport, U.S.A., **425** H4
Gulin, China, **215** H4
Guling, China, **206** C2
Guliston, Uzbekistan, **223** H4
Gull Bay, Canada, **415** K7
Gullspång, Sweden, **286** G3
Güllük Körfezi, *bay*, Turkey, **297** F7
Gülnar, Turkey, **225** B1
Gülpınar, Turkey, **297** F6
Gülshat, Kazakhstan, **223** J3
Gulu, Uganda, **369** F2
Gŭlŭbovo, Bulgaria, **296** E4
Gulyantsi, Bulgaria, **296** E4
Gumal, *river*, Pakistan, **218** B2
Gumare, Botswana, **370** D2
Gumarino, Russian Federation, **285** R5
Gumbiri, *mountain peak*, Sudan, **369** F2
Gumdag, Turkmenistan, **222** E5
Gumel, Nigeria, **365** F2
Gumia, India, **219** F5
Gumla, India, **219** F5
Gummi, Nigeria, **365** F2
Gümüşhane, Turkey, **224** E4
Guna, India, **218** D4
Guna Terara, *mountain peak*, Ethiopia, **367** E2
Güncang, China, **214** E3
Gunda, Russian Federation, **210** E1
Güney, Turkey, **297** G6
Güneydoğu Toroslar, *mountain range*, Turkey, **224** E5
Gungu, Democratic Republic of the Congo, **368** C4
Gunja, Croatia, **294** G3
Gunnarn, Sweden, **284** H4
Gunnbjørn Fjeld, *mountain peak*, Greenland, **411** R3
Gunnedah, Australia, **135** L5
Gunners Quoin, *island*, Mauritius, **373** C1
Gunnilbo, Sweden, **286** G3
Gunnison, Colorado, U.S.A., **423** K2
Gunnison, Utah, U.S.A., **423** H2
Guntakal, India, **216** D3
Guntersville Lake, U.S.A., **425** J2
Guntur, India, **216** E2
Gunung, Tanjong, *point*, Indonesia, **201** E2
Gunungsitoli, Indonesia, **200** B2

Gunungsugih, Indonesia, **200** D4
Gunupur, India, **217** E2
Guojiadian, China, **208** D2
Guoyang, China, **206** D1
Gura Galbenei, Moldova, **296** G2
Gura Humorului, Romania, **296** E2
Gurais, India, **218** C2
Gurban Obo, China, **210** F4
Gurbantünggüt Shamo, *desert*, China, **212** E3
Güre, Turkey, **297** G6
Gurgaon, India, **218** D3
Gurgei, Jabal, *mountain peak*, Sudan, **366** B2
Gurguéia, *river*, Brazil, **453** E5
Gurha, India, **218** B4
Guri, Embalse de, *reservoir*, Venezuela, **451** F2
Gurinhatã, Brazil, **456** D5
Gurk, Austria, **289** G5
Guro, Mozambique, **371** F2
Gurskoye, Russian Federation, **211** M2
Gürsu, Turkey, **297** G5
Guru Sikhar, *mountain peak*, India, **218** C4
Gurué, Mozambique, **369** G6
Gürün, Turkey, **224** E5
Gurupá, Brazil, **452** C3
Gurupi, Brazil, **456** D3
Gurupi, *river*, Brazil, **452** D4
Gurupi, Serra do, *mountain range*, Brazil, **452** D4
Guruve, Zimbabwe, **371** F2
Gurvan Sayhan Uul, *mountain range*, Mongolia, **213** J4
Gus'-Khrustal'nyy, Russian Federation, **298** F1
Gusau, Nigeria, **365** F2
Gusev, Russian Federation, **287** L5
Gushan, China, **211** H5
Gushi, China, **206** C1
Gushiago, Ghana, **364** D3
Gusinoozersk, Russian Federation, **210** D2
Guspini, Sardegna, Italy, **295** B6
Gustav Holm, Kap, *cape*, Greenland, **411** R3
Gustavsberg, Sweden, **287** J3
Güstrow, Germany, **288** F2
Gutay, Russian Federation, **210** E2
Guthrie, Oklahoma, U.S.A., **424** D2
Guthrie, Texas, U.S.A., **424** B3
Gutian, China, **206** D3
Gutu, Zimbabwe, **371** F2
Guwāhāti, India, **219** G4
Guyana, *country*, South America, **449** G3, *434, 435, 437, 439*
Guyang, China, **210** E4
Guymon, U.S.A., **420** C7
Guyot, Mount, *mountain peak*, U.S.A., **425** L2
Guyuan, China, **210** D5
Güzelbağ, Turkey, **225** A1
Guzhu, China, **207** D1
Guzmán, Mexico, **430** D2
Gvarv, Norway, **286** D3
Gwa, Myanmar, **205** B4
Gwadabawa, Nigeria, **365** F2
Gwādar, Pakistan, **221** H3
Gwalior, India, **218** D4
Gwanda, Zimbabwe, **371** E3
Gwane, Democratic Republic of the Congo, **369** E2
Gwatar Bay, Iran/Pakistan, **221** H4
Gwawele, Democratic Republic of the Congo, **369** E2
Gwda, *river*, Poland, **289** H2
Gweebarra Bay, Ireland, **309** D3
Gweedore, Ireland, **309** D2
Gweru, Zimbabwe, **371** E2
Gweta, Botswana, **370** E3
Gwinn, U.S.A., **421** K2
Gwinner, U.S.A., **420** E2
Gwoza, Nigeria, **365** G2
Gwynedd, *unitary authority*, Wales, U.K., **304** D2
Gyaca, China, **214** E3
Gyagartang, China, **215** G2
Gyangzê, China, **214** D3
Gyaring, China, **215** F2
Gyaring Co, *lake*, China, **214** D3
Gyaring Hu, *lake*, China, **215** F2
Gyawa, China, **215** G3
Gyda, Russian Federation, **300** J2
Gydanskiy Poluostrov, *peninsula*, Russian Federation, **300** J2
Gyirong, China, **214** C3
Gyitang, China, **215** F3
Gyldenløves Fjord, Greenland, **411** Q3
Gyljen, Sweden, **285** L3
Gympie, Australia, **135** L4
Gyomaendrőd, Hungary, **289** K5
Gyöngyös, Hungary, **289** J5
Győr, Hungary, **289** H5
Gypsumville, Canada, **414** E6
Gytheio, Greece, **297** D7
Gyula, Hungary, **289** K5
Gyumri, Armenia, **222** C4
Gyzylarbat, Turkmenistan, **222** F5, *187*


## H


Hà Đông, Vietnam, **203** E1
Hà Giang, Vietnam, **203** E1
Hà Nam, Vietnam, **203** E1
Hà Nôi (Hanoi), Vietnam, **203** E1, *153, 154*
Hà Tiên, Vietnam, **203** E4
Hş Tĩnh, Vietnam, **203** E2
Häädemeeste, Estonia, **287** M3
Haag in Oberbayern, Germany, **288** F4
Haakon VII Sea, Antarctica, **470** D3
Ha'alaufuli, Vava'u Group, Tonga, **141** B3
Ha'apai Group, *islands*, Tonga, **136** D3, *114*
Haapajärvi, Finland, **285** M5
Haapavesi, Finland, **285** M4
Haapsalu, Estonia, **287** L3
Haarlem, Netherlands, **288** B2, *241*
Haast, New Zealand, **133** B6
Ha'atua, Tongatapu Group, Tonga, **141** B4
Hab, *river*, Pakistan, **218** A4
Habaswein, Kenya, **369** G2
Ḩabbān, Yemen, **220** E6
Ḩabbānīyah, Iraq, **363** H2
Habirag, China, **210** F4
Hacha, Colombia, **450** C4
Hachijō-jima, *island*, Japan, **209** G3
Hachinohe, Japan, **209** H2
Hackås, Sweden, **284** G5
Hackness, England, U.K., **307** H3
Hacufera, Mozambique, **371** F3
Hadagang, China, **211** K3
Hadarba, Ras, *point*, Sudan, **363** G4
Hadat, China, **211** G2
Ḩadbaram, Oman, **221** G5
Ḩadd, Ra's al, *point*, Oman, **221** G4
Ḩaddā', Saudi Arabia, **363** G4
Haddiscoe, England, U.K., **305** J2
Haddunmahti Atoll, Maldives, **216** C6
Hadejia, Nigeria, **365** G2
Ḩadera, Israel, **225** C3
Haderslev, Denmark, **286** D5
Hadgaon, India, **216** D2
Hadīboh, Suquṭrá (Socotra), Yemen, **373** B2
Hadilik, China, **212** E5
Hadleigh, England, U.K., **305** H2
Hadley Bay, Canada, **410** J2
Ḩaḑramawt, *region*, Yemen, **220** E5
Hadseløya, *island*, Norway, **284** F2
Hadsund, Denmark, **286** E4
Hadyach, Ukraine, **298** D2
Haedo, Cuchilla de, *mountain range*, Brazil/Uruguay, **459** F4
Haeju, North Korea, **208** D3
Haenam, South Korea, **208** D4
Ḩafar al Bāṭin, Saudi Arabia, **363** J3
Hafik, Turkey, **363** G1
Ḩafīrat al 'Aydā, Saudi Arabia, **363** G3
Hāfizābād, Pakistan, **218** C2
Hāflong, India, **214** E4
Hafnarfjörður, Iceland, **284** X7
Hafnir, Iceland, **284** X8
Hagen, Germany, **288** C3
Hagenow, Germany, **288** E2
Hāgere Hiywet, Ethiopia, **367** E3
Hagerman, Idaho, U.S.A., **418** G5
Hagerman, New Mexico, U.S.A., **423** L5
Hagerstown, U.S.A., **426** B5
Hagetmau, France, **290** D5
Hagfors, Sweden, **286** F3
Hagi, Japan, **208** E4
Hagi-zaki, *point*, Japan, **208** E4
Hagley, England, U.K., **304** E2
Hags Head, *point*, Ireland, **309** C5
Hague, Canada, **413** R5
Hague, Cap de la, *cape*, France, **290** D2
Hague, The, *see* 's-Gravenhage, Netherlands, **288** B2, *240, 241*
Hague, U.S.A., **420** D2
Haguenau, France, **291** H2
Hagunia, Western Sahara, **360** D3
Haha-jima, *island*, Japan, **138** C2
Hahót, Hungary, **289** H5
Hai Phòng, Vietnam, **203** E1
Hai'an, China, **206** E1
Hai'an Shan, *mountain range*, China, **207** C3
Haicheng, China, **211** H4
Haifa *see* Ḩefa, Israel, **225** C3, *179*
Haifeng, China, **206** C4
Haikang, China, **206** B4
Haikou, China, **203** F1, *161*
Ḩā'il, Saudi Arabia, **363** H3
Hailar, China, **211** G2
Hailar, *river*, China, **211** H2
Hailin, China, **211** K3
Hails, China, **210** D4
Hailsham, England, U.K., **305** H4
Hailun, China, **211** J3
Hailuoto, Finland, **285** M4
Hailuoto, *island*, Finland, **285** M4
Haimen, China, **206** E2
Hainan, *province*, China, **203** F2, *159, 161*
Hainan Dao, *island*, China, **203** F2
Hainaut, *province*, Belgium, **288** A3
Haindi, Liberia, **364** B3
Haines City, U.S.A., **425** M5
Haines Junction, Canada, **410** F3
Haining, China, **206** E2
Haīpur, Pakistan, **218** C2
Haitan Dao, *island*, China, **206** D3
Haiti, *country*, Caribbean Sea, **409** R7, *92, 378, 385, 390, 392, 393, 394, 395*
Haitou, China, **203** F2
Haiyan, China, **206** E2
Haiyang, China, **211** H5
Haiyuan, China, **210** D5
Ḩajar, Al, *mountain range*, Oman, **221** G4, *176*
Hajdúböszörmény, Hungary, **289** K5
Hajdúszoboszló, Hungary, **289** K5
Hajhir, *mountain range*, Suquṭrá (Socotra), Yemen, **373** B2
Ḩājī Ebrāhīm, Kūhe, *mountain peak*, Iran/Iraq, **363** H1, *182*
Hājīpur, India, **214** C4
Ḩajj 'Abd Allāh, Sudan, **366** D2
Ḩajjah, Yemen, **220** D5
Hajnówka, Poland, **289** L2
Haju, China, **213** H4
Hajuu-Ulaan, Mongolia, **210** E3
Hajuu-Us, Mongolia, **210** D3
Haka, Myanmar, **205** B3
Hakkas, Sweden, **284** K3
Hakkstabben, Norway, **285** L1
Hakodate, Japan, **209** H2
Hakupu, Niue, **132** M13
Hāla, Pakistan, **218** B4
Ḩalab (Aleppo), Syria, **225** D1
Ḩalab, *district*, Syria, **225** D1
Ḩalabān, Saudi Arabia, **363** H4
Ḩalabjah, Iraq, **363** J1
Halagigie Point, Niue, **132** M13
Ḩalā'ib, Sudan, **363** G4
Ḩālat 'Ammār, Saudi Arabia, **225** D5
Ḩalbā, Lebanon, **225** D2
Halban, Mongolia, **213** H2
Halberstadt, Germany, **288** E3
Halbrite, Canada, **414** C7
Halcon, Mount, *mountain peak*, Philippines, **204** C3
Haldde, *mountain peak*, Norway, **285** L2
Halden, Norway, **286** E3
Haldwāni, India, **218** D3
Hale, England, U.K., **306** F4
Halesowen, England, U.K., **304** E2
Halesworth, England, U.K., **305** J2
Ḩalfa'al Jadīdah, Sudan, **366** E1
Halfmoon Bay, New Zealand, **133** B8
Haliburton, Canada, **416** B7
Haliburton Highlands, *mountain range*, Canada, **416** B7
Halifax, Canada, **417** K7, *381*
Halifax, England, U.K., **307** G4
Halitpaşa, Turkey, **297** F6
Halkirk, Scotland, U.K., **308** F2
Hall Beach, Canada, **411** L3
Hall Islands, Micronesia, **138** D4
Hall Peninsula, Canada, **411** N3
Halla-san, *mountain peak*, South Korea, **208** D4, *163, 164*
Halland, *county*, Sweden, **286** F4
Halle, Germany, **288** E3
Halle (Westfalen), Germany, **288** D2
Hällefors, Sweden, **286** G3
Hallen, Sweden, **284** G5
Hallencourt, France, **305** J5
Hällestad, Sweden, **286** G3
Hallettsville, U.S.A., **424** D5
Halley, *U.K. research station*, Antarctica, **470** C4
Halliday, U.S.A., **420** B2
Hallingskarvet, *mountain peak*, Norway, **286** C2
Hällnäs, Sweden, **284** J4
Hallock, U.S.A., **420** E1
Halls Creek, Australia, **134** F2
Hallsberg, Sweden, **286** G3
Hallstavik, Sweden, **287** J2
Hallworthy, England, U.K., **304** C4
Halma, U.S.A., **420** E1
Halmahera, Pulau, *island*, Indonesia, **198** D2
Halmahera Sea, Indonesia, **138** A5
Halmeu, Romania, **296** D2
Halmstad, Sweden, **286** F4
Hals, Denmark, **286** E4
Hal'shany, Belarus, **287** N5
Halstad, U.S.A., **420** E2
Halstead, England, U.K., **305** H3
Halsua, Finland, **285** M5
Halswell, New Zealand, **133** D6
Haltang, *river*, China, **213** G5
Halti, *mountain peak*, Finland, **284** K2
Halton, *unitary authority*, England, U.K., **306** F4
Haltwhistle, England, U.K., **306** F3
Halwell, England, U.K., **304** D4
Hàm Yên, Vietnam, **203** E1
Hamada, Japan, **208** F4
Hamadān, Iran, **220** E2
Hamaguir, Algeria, **361** F2
Ḩamāh, *district*, Syria, **225** D2
Ḩamāh, Syria, **225** D2
Hamam, Turkey, **225** D1
Hamamatsu, Japan, **209** G4
Hamar, Norway, **286** E2
Ḩamāṭah, Jabal, *mountain peak*, Egypt, **363** F4
Hamatombetsu, Japan, **209** H1
Hambantota, Sri Lanka, **217** E5
Hamburg, Arkansas, U.S.A., **424** G3
Hamburg, California, U.S.A., **418** C6
Hamburg, Germany, **288** E2, *238, 239*
Hamburg, *state*, Germany, **288** D2
Ḩamḑah, Saudi Arabia, **363** H5
Ḩamdānah, Saudi Arabia, **363** H5
Hamdibey, Turkey, **297** F6
Hämeenkyrö, Finland, **287** L2
Hämeenlinna, Finland, **287** M2
Hameln, Germany, **288** D2
Hamersley Range, *mountain range*, Australia, **128** A4, *111*
Hamhŭng, North Korea, **208** D3
Hami, China, **213** G4
Hamilton, Alabama, U.S.A., **425** J2
Hamilton, Australia, **135** J6
Hamilton, Canada, **421** P4
Hamilton, Montana, U.S.A., **418** G3
Hamilton, Mount, *mountain peak*, Macquarie Island, **134** R11
Hamilton, New Zealand, **132** E3
Hamilton, Ohio, U.S.A., **421** L6
Hamilton, Scotland, U.K., **308** E5
Hamilton, Washington, U.S.A., **418** C2
Hamilton City, U.S.A., **422** C2
Hamilton Inlet, Canada, **417** M3
Hamina, Finland, **287** N2
Hamīrpur, India, **218** D3
Hamlet, North Carolina, U.S.A., **425** N2
Hamlet, North Dakota, U.S.A., **420** B1
Hamm, Germany, **288** C3
Ḩammām, Syria, **225** E2
Hammamet, Golfe de, *gulf*, Tunisia, **362** B1
Ḩammār, Hawr al, *lake*, Iraq, **363** J2
Hammarstrand, Sweden, **284** H5
Hammerdal, Sweden, **284** G5
Hammerfest, Norway, **285** L1
Hammond, Indiana, U.S.A., **421** K5
Hammond, Louisiana, U.S.A., **424** G4
Hammond, Montana, U.S.A., **419** M4
Hammonton, U.S.A., **426** C5
Hampden, Canada, **417** N5
Hampden, New Zealand, **133** C7
Hampden, U.S.A., **420** D1
Hampshire, *unitary authority*, England, U.K., **305** F3
Hampton Butte, *mountain peak*, U.S.A., **418** D5
Hampton, Canada, **416** J7
Hampton, Iowa, U.S.A., **420** G4
Hampton, New Hampshire, U.S.A., **426** E3
Hampton, Oregon, U.S.A., **418** D5
Hampton, South Carolina, U.S.A., **425** M3
Hampton, Virginia, U.S.A., **426** B6
Ḩamrā', Al Ḩamādah al, *plateau*, Libya, **362** B3
Hamrångefjärden, Sweden, **287** H2
Ḩamrat ash Shaykh, Sudan, **366** C2
Hamstreet, England, U.K., **305** H3
Han, *river*, China, **206** B1
Han, *river*, South Korea, **208** D3, *164*
Han Pijesak, Bosnia and Herzegovina, **294** G3
Han Sum, China, **211** G3
Hana, Hawaiian Islands, U.S.A., **422** R9
Hanahan, Papua New Guinea, **140** E2
Ḩanak, Saudi Arabia, **363** G3
Hanalei, Hawaiian Islands, U.S.A., **422** R9
Hanamaki, Japan, **209** H3
Hânceşti, Moldova, **296** G2
Hanceville, Canada, **412** H6
Hancheng, China, **206** B1
Handa Island, Scotland, U.K., **308** D2
Handan, China, **210** F5
Handeni, Tanzania, **369** G4
Handlová, Slovakia, **289** J4
HaNegev, *desert*, Israel, **225** C4, *179*

Hanestad, Norway, **286** E2
Hanford, U.S.A., **422** D3
Hanga-Roa, Isla de Pascua (Easter Island), Chile, **461** B2
Hangay, *province*, Mongolia, **213** J3
Hangayn Nuruu, *mountain range*, Mongolia, **213** H3, *186*
Hanggin Houqi, China, **210** D4
Hanggin Qi, China, **210** E5
Hangu, China, **210** G5
Hangu, Pakistan, **218** B2
Hangzhou, China, **206** E2, *161*
Hanhöhiy Uul, *mountain range*, Mongolia, **213** G2
Ḩanīsh al Kabīr, Jazīrat al, *island*, Yemen, **220** D6
Hankinson, U.S.A., **420** E2
Hanko, Finland, **287** L3
Hanks, U.S.A., **420** B1
Hanksville, U.S.A., **423** H2
Hanle, India, **218** D2
Hanmer Springs, New Zealand, **133** D6
Hanna, Canada, **413** P6
Hannaford, U.S.A., **420** D2
Hannah Bay, Canada, **415** P6
Hannibal, U.S.A., **420** H6
Hannover, Germany, **288** D2, *239*
Hanöbukten, *bay*, Sweden, **286** G5
Hanoi *see* Hà Nôi, Vietnam, **203** E1, *153, 154*
Hanover, U.S.A., **426** B5, *238*
Hanpan, Cape, Papua New Guinea, **140** E2
Hanshou, China, **206** C2
Hānsi, India, **218** C3
Hanson Bay, Chatham Islands, New Zealand, **133** Q16
Hanstholm, Denmark, **286** D4
Hantay, Mongolia, **213** J2
Hanumāngarh, India, **218** C3
Hanuy, *river*, Mongolia, **213** J2
Hanwang, China, **215** H3
Hanyang, China, **206** C2
Hanzhong, China, **215** H2
Hanzhuang, China, **206** D1
Hao, *island*, French Polynesia, **137** G2
Hāora, India, **219** G5
Haoud el Hamra, Algeria, **361** H2
Hapai, Solomon Islands, **141** A1
Haparanda, Sweden, **285** M4
Happisburgh, England, U.K., **305** J2
Happy, U.S.A., **424** B2
Happy Camp, U.S.A., **418** C6
Happy Valley-Goose Bay, Canada, **417** L3
Ḩaql, Saudi Arabia, **225** C5
Har Borog, China, **213** J4
Har Hu, *lake*, China, **213** H5
Har Nuur, *lake*, Mongolia, **213** G2
Har-Us, Mongolia, **213** F2
Har Us Nuur, *lake*, Mongolia, **213** F2
Haraat, Mongolia, **210** D3
Ḩaraḑ, Saudi Arabia, **220** E4
Ḩaraḑ, Yemen, **220** D5
Haradok, Belarus, **299** B5
Harads, Sweden, **284** K3
Haraiki, *island*, French Polynesia, **137** G2
Harappa, Pakistan, **218** C3, *168*
Harare, Zimbabwe, **371** F2, *346*
Harata, Mount, *mountain peak*, New Zealand, **133** C6
Haraz-Djombo, Chad, **366** A2
Ḩarāzah, Jabal, *mountain peak*, Sudan, **366** D1
Haraze Mangueigne, Chad, **366** B3
Harbel, Liberia, **364** B3
Harbin, China, **211** J3, *161*
Harbor Springs, U.S.A., **421** L3
Harbour Breton, Canada, **417** P6
Harbours, Bay of, Falkland Islands, **460** F4
Harda, India, **218** D5
Hardap, *administrative region*, Namibia, **370** C3
Hardeeville, U.S.A., **425** M3
Hardelot-Plage, France, **305** J4
Hardin, U.S.A., **419** L4
Hardisty, Canada, **413** P5
Hardoī, India, **218** E4
Hardy, Península, Chile, **460** D5
Hardy, U.S.A., **424** G1
Hare Bay, Canada, **417** P4
Hārer, Ethiopia, **367** F3
Hargant, China, **211** G2
Hargele, Ethiopia, **367** F3
Hargeysa, Somalia, **367** F3, *339*
Hargla, Estonia, **287** N4
Harhiraa, Mongolia, **213** F2
Harhorin, Mongolia, **213** J3
Hari, *river*, Indonesia, **200** C3
Haria, Islas Canarias, Spain, **373** B4
Harīb, Yemen, **220** E5
Haricha, Hamada el, *Plateau*, Mali, **361** F4
Haridwār, India, **218** D3
Harihar, India, **216** C3
Harihari, New Zealand, **133** C6
Harīrūd, *river*, Afghanistan/Iran, **218** A2
Harisal, India, **218** D5
Harkány, Hungary, **289** J6
Hârlău, Romania, **296** F2
Harlan, U.S.A., **421** M7
Harlech, Wales, U.K., **304** C2
Harlem, U.S.A., **413** Q7
Harleston, England, U.K., **305** J2
Harlingen, Netherlands, **288** B2
Harlingen, U.S.A., **424** D6
Harlow, England, U.K., **305** H3
Harlowton, U.S.A., **419** K3
Harmancık, Turkey, **297** G6
Harmånger, Sweden, **287** H2
Harmod, Mongolia, **213** F2
Harnai, Pakistan, **218** A3
Harney Basin, U.S.A., **418** E5
Harney Lake, *lake*, U.S.A., **418** E5
Härnösand, Sweden, **287** H1
Haroldswick, Scotland, U.K., **308** L7
Harpenden, England, U.K., **305** G3
Harper, Liberia, **364** C4
Harper, Oregon, U.S.A., **418** F5
Harper, Texas, U.S.A., **424** C4
Harqin Qi, China, **211** G4
Harqin Zuoyi, China, **211** G4
Harricana, *river*, Canada, **415** Q6
Harriman, U.S.A., **425** K2
Harris, Canada, **413** R6
Harris, Sound of, Scotland, U.K., **308** B3
Harrisburg, Illinois, U.S.A., **421** J7
Harrisburg, Pennsylvania, U.S.A., **426** B4, *386*
Harrismith, South Africa, **371** E4
Harrison Lake, *lake*, Canada, **412** H7
Harrison, Arkansas, U.S.A., **424** F1
Harrison, Cape, Canada, **417** N2
Harrison, Michigan, U.S.A., **421** L3
Harrison, Nebraska, U.S.A., **419** N5
Harrisonburg, U.S.A., **421** P6
Harrisonville, U.S.A., **420** F6
Harrisville, U.S.A., **421** M3
Harrodsburg, U.S.A., **421** L7
Harrogate, England, U.K., **307** G4
Harrold, U.S.A., **420** D3
Harry S. Truman Reservoir, *reservoir*, U.S.A., **420** G6
Harsīn, Iran, **220** E2
Hârşova, Romania, **296** F3
Harsprånget, Sweden, **284** J3
Harstad, Norway, **284** H2
Harsūd, India, **218** D5
Hart Fell, *mountain peak*, Scotland, U.K., **308** F5
Hart, U.S.A., **421** K4
Hartao, China, **211** H4
Hartberg, Austria, **289** G5
Hårteigen, *mountain peak*, Norway, **286** C2
Hartford, U.S.A., **426** D4, *386*
Hartkjølen, *mountain peak*, Norway, **284** F4
Hartland Point, England, U.K., **304** C3
Hartland, England, U.K., **304** C4
Hartland, Canada, **416** H6
Hartlepool, England, U.K., **307** G3
Hartley, U.S.A., **423** M4
Hartline, U.S.A., **418** E3
Hartola, Finland, **287** M2
Hartshorne, U.S.A., **424** E2
Harun, Gunung, *mountain peak*, Indonesia, **201** G1
Harvard, California, U.S.A., **422** E4
Harvard, Idaho, U.S.A., **418** F3
Harvard, Illinois, U.S.A., **421** J4
Harvard, Mount, *mountain peak*, U.S.A., **423** K2
Harvey, Illinois, U.S.A., **421** K5
Harvey, North Dakota, U.S.A., **420** D2
Harwich, England, U.K., **305** J3
Haryana, *state*, India, **218** C3, *168, 169*
Harz, *mountain range*, Germany, **288** E3, *239*
Hasalbag, China, **212** C5
Hashaat, Mongolia, **210** D3
Hashtgerd, Iran, **220** F1
Ḩāsik, Oman, **221** G5
Hāsilpur, Pakistan, **218** C3
Haskell, U.S.A., **424** C3
Haslemere, England, U.K., **305** G3
Haslev, Denmark, **286** E5
Hassan, India, **216** D3
Hassela, Sweden, **287** H1
Hasselborough Bay, Macquarie Island, **134** R11
Hasselt, Belgium, **288** B3
Haßfurt, Germany, **288** E3
Hassi Bel Guebbour, Algeria, **361** H3
Hassi Inifel, Algeria, **361** G3
Hassi Messaoud, Algeria, **361** H2
Hässleholm, Sweden, **286** F4
Hastings, England, U.K., **305** H4
Hastings, Michigan, U.S.A., **421** L4
Hastings, Nebraska, U.S.A., **420** D5
Hastings, New Zealand, **132** F4, *110*
Hasvik, Norway, **285** L1
Haswell, U.S.A., **423** M2
Hat Yai, Thailand, **202** D4
Hatansuudal, Mongolia, **213** J3
Hatavch, Mongolia, **210** F3
Hatay, *province*, Turkey, **225** D1
Haţeg, Romania, **296** D3
Hatfield, Hertfordshire, England, U.K., **305** G3
Hatfield, S. Yorkshire, England, U.K., **307** G4
Hatgal, Mongolia, **213** J2
Hatherleigh, England, U.K., **304** C4
Hāthras, India, **218** D4
Ḩāţibah, Ra's, *point*, Saudi Arabia, **363** G4
Hatkamba, India, **216** C2
Hatlestrand, Norway, **286** B2
Hato Mayor, Dominican Republic, **429** H3
Hatpaas, Indonesia, **198** D4
Hatta, India, **218** D4
Hatteras, U.S.A., **426** C7
Hatteras Island, U.S.A., **426** C7
Hatteras Plain, *underwater feature*, Atlantic Ocean, **477** C4
Hattfjelldal, Norway, **284** F4
Hattiesburg, U.S.A., **425** H4
Hatton, U.S.A., **420** E2
Hattuselkonen, Finland, **285** Q5
Hattuvaara, Finland, **285** Q5
Hatuma, New Zealand, **132** F5
Hatvan, Hungary, **289** J5
Hau Hoi Wan, *bay*, China, **207** B3
Haud, *region*, Ethiopia, **367** F3, *339*
Haugesund, Norway, **286** B3
Hauho, Finland, **287** M2
Hauhungaroa Range, *mountain range*, New Zealand, **132** E4
Haukeligrend, Norway, **286** C3
Haukipudas, Finland, **285** M4
Haukivesi, *lake*, Finland, **287** N1
Haukivuori, Finland, **287** N1
Haumonia, Argentina, **459** E3
Hauraha, Solomon Islands, **141** A1
Hauraki Gulf, New Zealand, **132** E3
Hausjärvi, Finland, **287** M2
Haut Atlas, *mountain range*, Morocco, **356** E4, *314*
Haut-Ogooué, *province*, Gabon, **368** B3
Hautajärvi, Finland, **285** P3
Haute-Guinée, *administrative region*, Guinea, **364** B2
Haute-Kotto, Central African Republic, **366** B3
Haute-Mbomou, *prefecture*, Central African Republic, **366** C3
Haute-Normandie, *administrative region*, France, **290** E2, *245*
Haute-Zaïre, *administrative region*, Democratic Republic of the Congo, **369** E2
Hautere *see* Solander Island, New Zealand, **133** A8
Hauterive, Canada, **416** G5
Hauts Plateaux, *plateau*, Algeria, **361** F2
Havana *see* La Habana, Cuba, **429** E2, *392, 393*
Havana, U.S.A., **420** H5
Havant, England, U.K., **305** G4
Havel, *river*, Germany, **288** F2
Havelock, New Zealand, **133** D5
Haverfordwest, Wales, U.K., **304** C3
Haverhill, England, U.K., **305** H2
Hāveri, India, **216** C3
Havirga, Mongolia, **210** F3
Havlíčkuv Brod, Czech Republic, **289** G4
Havneby, Denmark, **286** D5
Havøysund, Norway, **285** M1
Havran, Turkey, **297** F6
Havre, U.S.A., **419** K2
Havre-Aubert, Canada, **417** L6
Havre-St-Pierre, Canada, **417** K4
Havsa, Turkey, **297** F5
Havsnäs, Sweden, **284** G4
Hawaii, *island*, Hawaiian Islands, U.S.A., **422** R9
Hawaii, *state*, Hawaiian Islands, U.S.A., **422** R9, *61, 90, 96, 108, 113, 119, 121, 122, 123, 124, 125, 126, 127, 165, 382, 384, 386, 474*
Hawaiian Islands, U.S.A., Pacific Ocean, **422** R9
Hawaiian Ridge, *underwater feature*, Pacific Ocean, **478** G3
Ḩawallī, Kuwait, **363** J3
Hawarden, Wales, U.K., **304** D1
Hawea, Lake, New Zealand, **133** B7
Hawera, New Zealand, **132** E4
Hawes, England, U.K., **306** F3
Haweswater Reservoir, England, U.K., **306** F3
Hawi, Hawaiian Islands, U.S.A., **422** R9
Hawick, Scotland, U.K., **308** G5
Hawk Inlet, U.S.A., **412** B2
Hawke Bay, New Zealand, **132** F4, *110, 111*
Hawkes Bay, Canada, **417** N4
Hawkesbury, Canada, **416** D7
Hawkhurst, England, U.K., **305** H3
Hawkinsville, U.S.A., **425** L3
Hawkswood, New Zealand, **133** D6
Ḩawrān, *river*, Iraq, **363** H2
Hawthorne, U.S.A., **422** D2
Haxby, England, U.K., **307** G3
Haxtun, U.S.A., **423** M1
Hay, Australia, **135** J5
Hay, Mount, *mountain peak*, Canada, **412** A2
Hay, *river*, Canada, **413** K2
Hay, Wales, U.K., **304** D2
Hay Camp, Canada, **413** P2
Hay River, Canada, **413** M1
Hay Springs, U.S.A., **420** B4
Haya, Indonesia, **199** E3
Hayden, Alabama, U.S.A., **425** J3
Hayden, Arizona, U.S.A., **423** H5
Hayden, Colorado, U.S.A., **423** K1
Haydon Bridge, England, U.K., **306** F3
Hayes, *river*, Canada, **414** G4
Hayle, England, U.K., **304** B4
Haymā', Oman, **221** G5
Hayrabolu, Turkey, **297** F5
Ḩays, Yemen, **220** D6
Hays, Kansas, U.S.A., **420** D6
Hays, Montana, U.S.A., **419** K3
Haysyn, Ukraine, **296** G1
Hayvoron, Ukraine, **296** H1
Hayward, California, U.S.A., **422** C3
Hayward, Wisconsin, U.S.A., **420** H2
Haywards Heath, England, U.K., **305** G3
Hayyā, Sudan, **363** G5
Hazār, Kūh-e, *mountain peak*, Iran, **221** G3
Hazard, U.S.A., **421** M7
Hazāreh Toghāy, Afghanistan, **218** A1
Hazārībāg, India, **219** F5
Hazebrouck, France, **290** F1
Hazelton, Canada, **412** F4
Hazelton, North Dakota, U.S.A., **420** C2
Hazleton, Pennsylvania, U.S.A., **426** C4
He Xian, Anhui, China, **206** D2
He Xian, Guangxi Zhuangzu Zizhiqu, China, **206** B3
Heacham, England, U.K., **305** H2
Headcorn, England, U.K., **305** H3
Headford, Ireland, **309** C4
Headland, U.S.A., **425** K4
Heanor, England, U.K., **305** F1
Heard and McDonald Islands, *Australian territory*, Indian Ocean, **134** S12, *112, 469*
Heard Island, Heard and McDonald Islands, **134** S12
Hearne, U.S.A., **424** D4
Hearst, Canada, **415** N7
Heart, *river*, U.S.A., **420** B2
Heasgarnich, Beinn, *mountain peak*, Scotland, U.K., **308** E4
Heathfield, England, U.K., **305** H4
Hebbronville, U.S.A., **424** C6
Hebei, *province*, China, **210** F5, *161*
Hebel, Australia, **135** K4
Heber, U.S.A., **423** H4
Hebi, China, **206** C1
Hebron, Canada, **411** N3
Hebron, Nebraska, U.S.A., **420** E5
Hebron, North Dakota, U.S.A., **420** B2
Hebron *see* Al Khalil, West Bank, **225** C4
Heby, Sweden, **287** H3
Hecate Strait, Canada, **412** D5
Hecelchakán, Mexico, **431** H4
Hechi, China, **206** B3
Hechuan, China, **215** H3
Heckington, England, U.K., **305** G2
Hecla, Canada, **414** F6
Hector, Mount, *mountain peak*, New Zealand, **133** E5
Hector, U.S.A., **420** F3
Hedal, Norway, **286** D2
Hede, Sweden, **286** F1
Hedemora, Sweden, **286** H2
Hedenäset, Sweden, **285** L3
Hedge End, England, U.K., **305** F4
Hedgehope, New Zealand, **133** B8
Hedley, Canada, **412** J7
Hedmark, *county*, Norway, **286** E2
Heerenveen, Netherlands, **288** B2
Ḩefa (Haifa), Israel, **225** C3, *179*
Hefei, China, **206** D2, *161*

Hefeng, China, **206** B2
Hegang, China, **211** K3
Heha, Mount, *mountain peak*, Burundi, **369** E3, *343*
Hei, *river*, China, **213** H5
Heichongtan, China, **213** J5
Heide, Germany, **288** D1
Heidelberg, Germany, **288** D4, *238*
Heidelburg, South Africa, **371** E4
Heidenheim an der Brenz, Germany, **288** E4
Heighington, England, U.K., **305** G1
Heihe, China, **211** J2
Heilbronn, Germany, **288** D4
Heilong, *river*, China, **211** L3
Heilongjiang, *province*, China, **211** J3, *161*
Heimahe, China, **213** H5
Heimdal, Norway, **284** E5
Heinävesi, Finland, **287** P1
Heinola, Finland, **287** N2
Heinze Chaung, *bay*, Myanmar, **202** C3
Heishan, China, **211** H4
Hejian, China, **210** G5
Hejiang, China, **215** H3
Heka, China, **215** F2
Hekla, *mountain peak*, Iceland, **284** Y7
Hekou, China, **213** J5
Helen, *island*, Palau, **138** B4
Helena, U.S.A., **419** H3, *386*
Helensburgh, Scotland, U.K., **308** E4
Helensville, New Zealand, **132** E3
Helgasjön, *lake*, Sweden, **286** G4
Helgoländer Bucht, *bay*, Germany, **288** D1
Heli, China, **211** K3
Heli Shan, *mountain range*, China, **213** J5
Hella, Iceland, **284** X8
Hell-Bourg, Réunion, **373** A1
Helle, Norway, **286** D3
Helleland, Norway, **286** C3
Hellesylt, Norway, **286** C1
Hellín, Spain, **293** G3
Hellissandur, Iceland, **284** X7
Hells Canyon, *gorge*, U.S.A., **418** F4
Helmand, *river*, Afghanistan, **221** H2, *184*
Helmeringhausen, Namibia, **370** C4
Helmond, Netherlands, **288** B3
Helmsdale, *river*, Scotland, U.K., **308** F2
Helmsdale, Scotland, U.K., **308** F2
Helmsley, England, U.K., **307** G3
Helmstedt, Germany, **288** E2
Helodrano Antongila, *bay*, Madagascar, **372** B4
Helong, China, **211** K4
Helotes, U.S.A., **424** C5
Helsingborg, Sweden, **286** F4
Helsingør, Denmark, **286** F4
Helsinki, Finland, **287** M2, *234*
Helska, Mierzeja, *peninsula*, Poland, **289** J1
Helston, England, U.K., **304** B4
Helvellyn, *mountain peak*, England, U.K., **306** E3
Hemel Hempstead, England, U.K., **305** G3
Hemet, U.S.A., **422** E5
Hemling, Sweden, **284** J5
Hemmoor, Germany, **288** D2
Hemnes, Norway, **286** E3
Hempstead, Connecticut, U.S.A., **426** D4
Hempstead, Texas, U.S.A., **424** D4
Hemsby, England, U.K., **305** J2
Hemse, Sweden, **287** J4
Hemsedal, Norway, **286** D2
Hemsö, Sweden, **287** J1
Hen and Chicken Islands, New Zealand, **132** E2
Henan, *province*, China, **206** C1, *161*
Henån, Sweden, **286** E3
Henares, *river*, Spain, **293** F2
Henderson, Argentina, **458** E5
Henderson, Kentucky, U.S.A., **421** K7
Henderson, Nevada, U.S.A., **422** F3
Henderson, North Carolina, U.S.A., **421** P7
Henderson, Tennessee, U.S.A., **425** H2
Henderson, Texas, U.S.A., **424** E3
Henderson Island, Pitcairn Islands, **137** J3, *126*
Hendersonville, North Carolina, U.S.A., **425** L2
Hendersonville, Tennessee, U.S.A., **425** J1
Hendon, England, U.K., **305** G3
Heng-ch'un, Taiwan, **206** E4
Heng Xian, China, **206** B4
Henganofi, Papua New Guinea, **140** B4
Hengduan Shan, *mountain range*, China, **215** F3
Hengelo, Netherlands, **288** C2
Henggang, China, **207** C3
Henghe, China, **207** C2
Hengli, east of Huizhou, Guangdong, China, **207** D2
Hengli, west of Huizhou, Guangdong, China, **207** B2
Hengmen Dao, *island*, China, **207** B3
Hengoed, Wales, U.K., **304** D3
Hengshan, China, **206** C3
Hengshi, China, **207** A1
Hengshui, China, **210** F5
Hengyang, China, **206** C3
Heniches'k, Ukraine, **298** D3
Henley-on-Thames, England, U.K., **305** G3
Hennessey, U.S.A., **424** D1
Henrietta, U.S.A., **424** C3
Henrietta Maria, Cape, Canada, **415** N4
Henry, Illinois, U.S.A., **421** J5
Henry, South Dakota, U.S.A., **420** E3
Henry Kater Peninsula, Canada, **411** N3
Henryetta, U.S.A., **424** E2
Hensler, U.S.A., **420** C2
Henstridge, England, U.K., **304** E4
Hentiesbaai, Namibia, **370** B3
Hentiy, *province*, Mongolia, **210** E3
Hentiyn Nuruu, *mountain range*, Mongolia, **210** D2
Henzada, Myanmar, **205** B4
Heping, China, **206** C3
Heppner, U.S.A., **418** E4
Hepu, China, **206** B4
Herald Islets, *islands*, Kermadec Islands, New Zealand, **132** L12
Herāt, Afghanistan, **221** H2
Herbagat, Sudan, **363** G5
Herbert, Mount, *mountain peak*, New Zealand, **133** D6
Herbertingen, Germany, **288** D4
Herðubreið, *mountain peak*, Iceland, **284** Y7
Heredia, Costa Rica, **428** D5
Hereford, England, U.K., **304** E2
Hereford, U.S.A., **423** M4
Herefordshire, *unitary authority*, England, U.K., **304** E2
Herefoss, Norway, **286** D3
Hereheretue, *island*, French Polynesia, **137** G2
Herekino, New Zealand, **132** D2
Herford, Germany, **288** D2
Herington, U.S.A., **420** E6
Herlen *see* Kerulen, *river*, Mongolia, **210** F3
Herma Ness, *point*, Shetland, Scotland, U.K., **308** K7
Herman, U.S.A., **420** E3
Hermanas, Mexico, **431** E3
Hermann, U.S.A., **420** H6
Hermansverk, Norway, **286** C2
Hermanus, South Africa, **370** C5
Hermigua, Islas Canarias, Spain, **373** A4
Hermiston, U.S.A., **418** E4
Hermitage Bay, Canada, **417** N6
Hermite, Isla, *island*, Chile, **460** D5
Hermosa, U.S.A., **420** B4
Hermosillo, Mexico, **430** C2
Hernandarias, Paraguay, **459** F2
Hernani, Spain, **293** G1
Herne, Germany, **288** C3
Herne Bay, England, U.K., **305** J3
Herning, Denmark, **286** D4
Hérouville-Saint-Clair, France, **290** D2
Herradura, Argentina, **459** E3
Herrera de Pisuerga, Spain, **292** E1
Herrera del Duque, Spain, **292** E3
Herrero, Punta, *point*, Mexico, **431** J5
Herriot, Canada, **414** D3
Herschel Island, Canada, **410** E2
Hertford, England, U.K., **305** G3
Hertfordshire, *unitary authority*, England, U.K., **305** G3
Hervey Bay, Australia, **135** L4
Herzberg, Germany, **288** F3
Hesdin, France, **305** K4
Heshan, China, **206** B4
Hesperus Mountain, *mountain peak*, U.S.A., **423** J3
Hessen, *state*, Germany, **288** D3, *238*
Heswall, England, U.K., **306** E4
Hetauda, Nepal, **219** F4
Hetekylä, Finland, **285** N4
Hettinger, U.S.A., **420** B2
Heuchin, France, **305** K4
Heves, Hungary, **289** K5
Hexham, England, U.K., **306** F3
Hexi, N. Sichuan, China, **215** H2
Hexi, S. Sichuan, China, **215** G4
Hexigten Qi, China, **210** G4
Heydarābād, Iran, **363** J1
Heysham, England, U.K., **306** F3
Heyuan, China, **207** D1
Heze, China, **206** C1
Hezhang, China, **215** H4
Hezuo, China, **215** G2
Hialeah, U.S.A., **425** M7
Hibbing, U.S.A., **420** G2
Hibernia Reef, *island*, Ashmore and Cartier Islands, **134** P9
Hickory, U.S.A., **425** M2
Hico, U.S.A., **424** C4
Hidalgo, Mexico, **431** F3
Hidalgo, *state*, Mexico, **431** F4, *91, 400*
Hidalgo del Parral, Mexico, **430** D3
Hidrolândia, Brazil, **456** D4
Hieflau, Austria, **289** G5
Hienghène, New Caledonia, **141** A3
Hierro, *island*, Islas Canarias, Spain, **373** A4
Hietapera, Finland, **285** P4
Higgins, U.S.A., **424** B1
Higgins Lake, U.S.A., **421** L3
High Hesket, England, U.K., **306** F3
High Island, U.S.A., **424** E5
High Level, Canada, **413** L2
High Peak, *mountain peak*, Philippines, **204** C3
High Peak, *mountain peak*, St Helena, **373** B3
High Point, *mountain peak*, U.S.A., **426** C4
High Point, U.S.A., **425** N2
High Prairie, Canada, **413** L4
High Rock, Bahamas, **428** F1
High Springs, U.S.A., **425** L5
High Wycombe, England, U.K., **305** G3
Higham Ferrers, England, U.K., **305** G2
Highampton, England, U.K., **304** C4
Highclere, England, U.K., **305** F3
Highland, *local authority*, Scotland, U.K., **308** D3, *275*
Highland Park, U.S.A., **421** K4
Highmore, U.S.A., **420** D3
Highrock Lake, Canada, **414** D4
Highworth, England, U.K., **305** F3
Higuera de Zaragoza, Mexico, **430** C3
Higuerote, Venezuela, **451** E1
Hiiraan, *administrative region*, Somalia, **367** F4
Hiiumaa, Estonia, **287** K3
Híjar, Spain, **293** G2
Hikurangi, New Zealand, **132** E2
Hikutavake, Niue, **132** M13
Hilāl, Jabal, *mountain peak*, Egypt, **225** B4
Hilāl, Ra's al, *point*, Libya, **362** D2
Hilda, Canada, **413** P6
Hildesheim, Germany, **288** D2
Hilger, U.S.A., **419** K3
Hill City, Idaho, U.S.A., **418** G5
Hill City, Kansas, U.S.A., **420** D6
Hill City, Minnesota, U.S.A., **420** G2
Hill City, South Dakota, U.S.A., **420** B4
Hill Island Lake, Canada, **413** Q1
Hill of Fearn, Scotland, U.K., **308** F3
Hillary Coast, *region*, Antarctica, **470** D7
Hilleknuten, *mountain peak*, Norway, **286** C3
Hillerød, Denmark, **286** F5
Hillesøy, Norway, **284** J2
Hillman, U.S.A., **421** M3
Hillsboro, New Mexico, U.S.A., **423** K5
Hillsboro, Ohio, U.S.A., **421** M6
Hillsboro, Texas, U.S.A., **424** D3
Hillside, Scotland, U.K., **308** G4
Hillside, Shetland, Scotland, U.K., **308** K7
Hillsport, Canada, **415** M7
Hillston, Australia, **135** K5
Hillsville, U.S.A., **421** N7
Hillswick, Shetland, Scotland, U.K., **308** K7
Hilo, Hawaiian Islands, U.S.A., **422** R10
Hilonghilong, Mount, *mountain peak*, Philippines, **204** D4
Hilongos, Philippines, **204** D4
Hilton, U.S.A., **426** B3
Hilton Head Island, U.S.A., **425** M3
Hilversum, Netherlands, **288** B2
Himāchal Pradesh, *state*, India, **218** D2, *169*
Himalaya, *mountain range*, Asia, **218** D2, *20, 23, 26, 30, 51, 100, 144, 145, 155, 158, 167, 168, 169, 171, 173, 443*
Himanka, Finland, **285** L4
Himarë, Albania, **297** B5
Himatangi, New Zealand, **132** E5
Himatnagar, India, **218** C5
Himeji, Japan, **208** F4
Himi, Japan, **209** G3
Ḥimṣ, *district*, Syria, **225** D2
Ḥimṣ (Homs), Syria, **225** D2, *181*
Hinatuan, Philippines, **204** D4
Hinche, Haiti, **429** G3
Hinchinbrook Island, Australia, **135** K2
Hinckley, England, U.K., **305** F2
Hinda, Congo, **368** B3
Hindaun, India, **218** D4
Hindhead, England, U.K., **305** G3
Hindley, England, U.K., **306** F4
Hinds, New Zealand, **133** C7
Hindu Kush, *mountain range*, Asia, **218** B2, *184*
Hindubāgh, Pakistan, **218** A3
Hindupur, India, **216** D3
Hinganghāt, India, **218** D5
Hingol, *river*, Pakistan, **218** A4
Hinidān, Pakistan, **218** A4
Hinnerjoki, Finland, **287** L2
Hinoba-an, Philippines, **204** C4
Hinton, Canada, **413** L5
Hınzır Burnu, *point*, Turkey, **225** C1
Hippargi, India, **216** D2
Hira, New Zealand, **133** D5
Hirakud Reservoir, India, **219** E5
Hirara, Japan, **209** N8
Hiré, Côte d'Ivoire, **364** C3
Hirekerūr, India, **216** C3
Hiriyūr, India, **216** D3
Hiroo, Japan, **209** H2
Hirosaki, Japan, **209** H2
Hiroshima, Japan, **208** F4, *96, 165*
Hirtshals, Denmark, **286** D4
Hiruharama, New Zealand, **132** G3
Hirwaun, Wales, U.K., **304** D3
Hisār, India, **218** C3
Hisarönü Korfezi, *bay*, Turkey, **297** F7
Ḥismā, Al, *plain*, Saudi Arabia, **225** C5
Hispaniola, *island*, Dominican Republic/ Haiti, **429** G3, *76, 378, 391, 394*
Histon, England, U.K., **305** H2
Ḥisyah, Syria, **225** D2
Hīt, Iraq, **363** H2
Hita, Japan, **208** E4
Hitachi, Japan, **209** H3
Hitchin, England, U.K., **305** G3
Hitoyoshi, Japan, **208** E4
Hitra, *island*, Norway, **284** D5
Hiva Oa, *island*, French Polynesia, **137** H1
Hixon, Canada, **412** H5
Hjälmaren, *lake*, Sweden, **286** G3
Hjellestad, Norway, **286** B2
Hjelmeland, Norway, **286** C3
Hjo, Sweden, **286** G3
Hjørring, Denmark, **286** D4
Hjortkvarn, Sweden, **286** G3
Hkakabo Razi, *mountain peak*, Myanmar, **205** C1
Hkamti, Myanmar, **205** B2
Hlatikulu, Swaziland, **371** F4
Hlohovec, Slovakia, **289** H4
Hlusha, Belarus, **299** B6
Hlyboka, Ukraine, **296** E1
Hlybokaye, Belarus, **287** N5
Hnúšt'a, Slovakia, **289** J4
Ho, Ghana, **364** E3
Hòa Bình, Vietnam, **203** E1
Hoachanas, Namibia, **370** C3
Hoadley, Canada, **413** M5
Hoback Junction, U.S.A., **419** J5
Hobart, Australia, **135** K7, *95, 112*
Hobbs, U.S.A., **423** M5
Hobbs Coast, *region*, Antarctica, **470** C7
Hobe Sound, U.S.A., **425** M6
Hobkirk, Scotland, U.K., **308** G5
Hoboksar, China, **212** E3
Hobro, Denmark, **286** D4
Hobucken, U.S.A., **426** B7
Hobyo, Somalia, **367** G3
Hochalmspitze, *mountain peak*, Austria, **288** F5
Hochfeld, Namibia, **370** C3
Hochschwab, *mountain range*, Austria, **289** G5
Hodda, *mountain peak*, Somalia, **367** H2
Hoddesdon, England, U.K., **305** G3
Hodh ech Chargui, *administrative region*, Mauritania, **360** E5
Hodh el Gharbi, *administrative region*, Mauritania, **364** B1
Hódmezővásárhely, Hungary, **289** J5
Hodnet, England, U.K., **304** E2
Hodonín, Czech Republic, **289** H4
Hödrögö, Mongolia, **213** H2
Hoek van Holland, Netherlands, **288** B3
Hoengsŏng, South Korea, **208** D3
Hoeryŏng, North Korea, **208** E2
Hoeyang, North Korea, **208** D3
Hof, Germany, **288** E3
Höfn, Iceland, **284** Z7
Hofsjökull, *ice cap*, Iceland, **284** Y7
Hofsós, Iceland, **284** Y7
Hōfu, Japan, **208** E4
Hog Harbour, Vanuatu, **141** A2
Höganäs, Sweden, **286** F4
Högby, Sweden, **287** H4
Hoggar, *mountain range*, Algeria, **361** G4

Hoggar, Tassili du, *plateau*, Algeria, **361** H4
Hoghiz, Romania, **296** E3
Höglekardalen, Sweden, **284** F5
Högsäter, Sweden, **286** F3
Høgtuvbreen, *mountain peak*, Norway, **284** F3
Hoh Sai Hu, *lake*, China, **214** E2
Hoh Xil Hu, *lake*, China, **214** D2
Hoh Xil Shan, *mountain range*, China, **214** D2
Hohe Rhön, *mountain range*, Germany, **288** D3
Hohe Tauern, *mountain range*, Austria, **288** F5
Hoher Dachstein, *mountain peak*, Austria, **288** F5
Hohhot, China, **210** E4, *161*
Hohoe, Ghana, **364** E3
Höhöö, Mongolia, **213** J2
Höhtolgoy, Mongolia, **213** F2
Hội An, Vietnam, **203** F3
Hoi Ha, China, **207** C4
Hoima, Uganda, **369** F2
Hoisington, U.S.A., **420** D6
Hokianga Harbour, New Zealand, **132** D2
Hokitika, New Zealand, **133** C6
Hokkaidō, *island*, Japan, **209** H1, *165*
Hokksund, Norway, **286** D3
Hokua, Vanuatu, **141** A2
Hol, Norway, **286** D2
Hola, Kenya, **369** G3
Holalkere, India, **216** D3
Holanda, Bolivia, **455** F4
Holbæk, Denmark, **286** E5
Holbeach, England, U.K., **305** H2
Holboo, Mongolia, **213** G2
Holbrook, Arizona, U.S.A., **423** H4
Holbrook, Idaho, U.S.A., **418** H5
Holden, Canada, **413** N5
Holden, U.S.A., **423** G2
Holdenville, U.S.A., **424** D2
Holderness, *peninsula*, England, U.K., **307** H4
Holdfast, Canada, **413** S6
Holdrege, U.S.A., **420** D5
Holešov, Czech Republic, **289** H4
Holguín, Cuba, **429** F2
Höljes, Sweden, **286** F2
Hollabrunn, Austria, **289** H4
Holland, Canada, **414** E7
Holland, U.S.A., **421** K4
Hollesley, England, U.K., **305** J2
Hollington, England, U.K., **305** H4
Hollis, U.S.A., **424** C2
Hollister, U.S.A., **418** G5
Holly, U.S.A., **421** M4
Holly Ridge, U.S.A., **425** P2
Holly Springs, U.S.A., **425** H2
Hollywood, U.S.A., **425** M6
Holm, Sweden, **287** H1
Holmäjärvi, Sweden, **284** J3
Holman, Canada, **410** H2
Hólmavík, Iceland, **284** X7
Holme upon Spalding Moor, England, U.K., **307** H4
Holmes, Mount, *mountain peak*, U.S.A., **419** J4
Holmfirth, England, U.K., **307** G4
Holmön, Sweden, **284** K5
Holmsund, Sweden, **284** K5
Holoby, Ukraine, **289** M3
Ḥolon, Israel, **225** C3
Holonga, Vava'u Group, Tonga, **141** B3
Holoog, Namibia, **370** C4
Holopaw, U.S.A., **425** M5
Holøydal, Norway, **286** E1
Holstebro, Denmark, **286** D4
Holsted, Denmark, **286** D5
Holsworthy, England, U.K., **304** C4
Holt, England, U.K., **305** J2
Holt Sum, China, **210** G3
Holton, Canada, **417** N2
Holton, U.S.A., **420** F6
Holwerd, Netherlands, **288** B2
Holy Island, England, U.K., **307** G2
Holy Island, Wales, U.K., **306** D4
Holycross, Ireland, **309** E5
Holyhead, Wales, U.K., **306** D4
Holyhead Bay, Wales, U.K., **306** D4
Holyoke, U.S.A., **423** M1
Holywell, Wales, U.K., **306** E4
Holzkirchen, Germany, **288** E5
Homa Bay, Kenya, **369** F3
Homalin, Myanmar, **205** B2
Hombori, Mali, **364** D1, *324*
Home Bay, Canada, **411** N3
Home Island, Cocos (Keeling) Islands, **134** Q10, *123*
Homer, Alaska, U.S.A., **410** D4
Homer, Louisiana, U.S.A., **424** F3
Homersfield, England, U.K., **305** J2
Homerville, U.S.A., **425** L4
Homestead, U.S.A., **425** M7
Hommelstø, Norway, **284** F4
Homnābād, India, **216** D2
Homocea, Romania, **296** F2
Homoine, Mozambique, **371** G3
Homonhon Island, Philippines, **204** D4
Homs *see* Ḥimṣ, Syria, **225** D2
Homyel', Belarus, **298** D2
Hòn Diên, Núi, *mountain peak*, Vietnam, **203** F4
Honaz, Turkey, **297** G7
Honda, Colombia, **450** C3
Honda Bay, Philippines, **204** B4
Hondo, Canada, **413** M4
Hondo, U.S.A., **424** C5
Hondschoote, France, **305** K4
Honduras, *country*, Central America, **409** Q7, *90, 378, 402, 403*
Honduras, Golfo de, *gulf*, Caribbean Sea, **428** D3, *401*
Hone, Canada, **414** D3
Hønefoss, Norway, **286** E2
Honesdale, U.S.A., **426** C4
Honey, Mount, *mountain peak*, Campbell Island, New Zealand, **132** K11
Honey Lake, U.S.A., **422** C1
Honfleur, France, **305** H5
Hông, *river*, Vietnam, **203** E1
Hồng Gai, Vietnam, **203** E1
Hong Kong *see* Xianggang, China, **207** C4, *95, 145, 161*
Hong Kong *see* Xianggang, *special administrative region*, China, **207** C4, *95, 145, 161*
Hong Kong Island, China, **207** C4
Hong'an, China, **206** C2
Hongch'ŏn, South Korea, **208** D3
Honghai Wan, *bay*, China, **206** C4
Honghu, China, **206** C2
Hongjiang, China, **206** B3
Hongor, Dornogovĭ, Mongolia, **210** E3
Hongor, Sühbaatar, Mongolia, **210** F3
Hongqicun, China, **213** G4
Hongshishan, China, **213** H4
Hongshui, *river*, China, **215** H4
Hongtong, China, **210** E5
Honguedo, Détroit d', *strait*, Canada, **416** J5
Hongxing, China, **211** K2
Hongya, China, **215** G3
Hongyuan, China, **215** G2
Hongze, China, **206** D1
Hongze Hu, *lake*, China, **206** D1
Honiara, Solomon Islands, **141** A1, *115*
Honiton, England, U.K., **304** D4
Honkajoki, Finland, **287** L2
Honningsvåg, Norway, **285** N1
Honokaa, Hawaiian Islands, U.S.A., **422** R9
Honolulu, Hawaiian Islands, U.S.A., **422** R9, *386*
Honolulu, *island*, Hawaiian Islands, U.S.A., **139** J2
Honshū, *island*, Japan, **209** G3
Hood, Mount, *mountain peak*, U.S.A., **418** D4
Hoogeveen, Netherlands, **288** C2
Hook, England, U.K., **305** F3
Hook Head, *point*, Ireland, **309** F5
Hooker, Mount, *mountain peak*, New Zealand, **133** B6
Hooker, U.S.A., **420** C7
Hoolt, Mongolia, **213** J3
Hoonah, U.S.A., **412** B2
Hooper, Colorado, U.S.A., **423** L3
Hooper, Nebraska, U.S.A., **420** E5
Hooper, Washington, U.S.A., **418** E3
Hoorn, Netherlands, **288** B2
Höövör, Dornod, Mongolia, **210** F2
Höövör, Hangay, Mongolia, **213** J3
Hope, Arkansas, U.S.A., **424** F3
Hope, Ben, *mountain peak*, Scotland, U.K., **308** E2
Hope, Canada, **412** J7
Hope, Lake, Australia, **134** D5
Hope, Loch, *lake*, Scotland, U.K., **308** E2
Hope, New Mexico, U.S.A., **423** L5
Hope, Wales, U.K., **304** D1
Hopedale, Canada, **417** L2
Hopelchén, Mexico, **431** H5
Hopeman, Scotland, U.K., **308** F3
Hopetoun, Australia, **135** J6
Hopetown, South Africa, **370** D4
Hopin, Myanmar, **205** C2
Hopkins, Lake, Australia, **134** F3
Hopkinsville, U.S.A., **421** K7
Hopland, U.S.A., **422** B2
Hopong, Myanmar, **205** C3
Hopongo, Solomon Islands, **141** A1
Hopseidet, Norway, **285** N1
Horasan, Turkey, **224** F5
Hörby, Sweden, **286** F5
Horcajo de Santiago, Spain, **293** F3
Horda, Norway, **286** C3
Hordaland, *province*, Norway, **286** B2
Horezu, Romania, **296** D3
Horgo, Mongolia, **213** H2
Horgorgoinba, China, **215** F2
Hörh Uul, *mountain peak*, Mongolia, **210** D4
Horia, Romania, **296** G3
Horinger, China, **210** E4
Horiult, Mongolia, **213** J3
Horki, Belarus, **299** C5
Horley, England, U.K., **305** G3
Horlick Mountains, *mountain range*, Antarctica, **470** C6
Hormus, Strait of, Arabian Peninsula/Iran, **221** G3, *175, 176*
Horn, Austria, **289** G4
Horn, Cape *see* Hornos, Cabo de, Chile, **460** D5, *93, 445*
Horn, Norway, **284** F4
Horn Island, U.S.A., **425** H4
Hornavan, *lake*, Sweden, **284** H3
Hornbjarg, *point*, Iceland, **284** X6
Hornburg, Germany, **288** E2
Horncastle, England, U.K., **305** G1
Horndal, Sweden, **286** H2
Horndean, England, U.K., **305** G4
Hörnefors, Sweden, **284** J5
Hornell, U.S.A., **426** B3
Hornepayne, Canada, **415** M7
Hornos, Cabo de (Cape Horn), *cape*, Chile, **460** D5, *93, 445*
Hornoy, France, **305** J5
Hornsea, England, U.K., **307** H4
Horodenka, Ukraine, **296** E1
Horokhiv, Ukraine, **289** M3
Horotiu, New Zealand, **132** E3
Horqin Youyi Zhongqi, China, **211** H3
Horqin Zuoyi Houqi, China, **211** H4
Horqin Zouyi Zhongqi, China, **211** H3
Horqueta, Paraguay, **459** F2
Horrabridge, England, U.K., **304** C4
Horred, Sweden, **286** F4
Horsburgh Island (Luar), Cocos (Keeling) Islands, **134** Q10
Horse Cave, U.S.A., **421** L7
Horse Islands, Canada, **417** P4
Horsefly Lake, Canada, **412** J5
Horsens, Denmark, **286** D5
Horseshoe Bend, U.S.A., **418** F5
Horsforth, England, U.K., **307** G4
Horsham, Australia, **135** J6
Horsham, England, U.K., **305** G3
Horslunde, Denmark, **286** E5
Horsunlu, Turkey, **297** G7
Horta, Azores, Portugal, **360** M7
Horten, Norway, **286** E3
Hortense, U.S.A., **425** M4
Horton, *river*, Canada, **410** G3
Horton, U.S.A., **420** F6
Horwich, England, U.K., **306** F4
Hosa'ina, Ethiopia, **367** E3
Hosdrug, India, **216** C3
Hose, Pegunungan, *mountain range*, Malaysia, **201** F2
Hoséré Vokré, *mountain peak*, Cameroon, **365** G3
Hoshāb, Pakistan, **221** H3
Hoshangābād, India, **218** D5
Hoshiārpur, India, **218** C3
Höshööt, Mongolia, **213** J2
Hoskins, Papua New Guinea, **140** C4
Hösööt, Mongolia, **212** F2
Hospet, India, **216** D3
Hospital, Ireland, **309** D5
Hossa, Finland, **285** P4
Hoste, Isla, *island*, Chile, **460** D5
Hot Springs, Arkansas, U.S.A., **424** F2
Hot Springs, South Dakota, U.S.A., **420** B4
Hotagen, *lake*, Sweden, **284** G5
Hotan, China, **212** C5
Hotan, *river*, China, **212** D5
Hotazel, South Africa, **370** D4
Hotchkiss, U.S.A., **423** K2
Hotham, Cape, Australia, **199** E5
Hotham, Mount, *mountain peak*, Australia, **135** K6
Hoting, Sweden, **284** H4
Hotont, Mongolia, **210** C3
Hottentots Bay, Namibia, **370** B4
Houaïlou, New Caledonia, **141** A3
Houat, Île d', *island*, France, **290** C3
Houdain, France, **305** K4
Houeillès, France, **290** E4
Hougang, Singapore, **200** K6
Houghton, Michigan, U.S.A., **421** J2
Houghton, New York, U.S.A., **426** A3
Houghton Lake, *lake*, U.S.A., **421** L3
Houghton Lake, U.S.A., **421** L3
Houghton-le-Spring, England, U.K., **307** G3
Houghton Regis, England, U.K., **305** G3
Houjie, China, **207** B3
Houlton, U.S.A., **426** G1
Houma, Tongatapu Group, Tonga, **141** B4
Houma, U.S.A., **424** G5
Houmet Essouk, Tunisia, **362** B2
Houndé, Burkina Faso, **364** D2
Houpoto, New Zealand, **132** F3
Hourtin, France, **290** D4
Hourtin et de Carcans, Étang d', *lake*, France, **290** D4
Houston, Canada, **412** F4
Houston, Mississippi, U.S.A., **425** H3
Houston, Missouri, U.S.A., **420** H7
Houston, Texas, U.S.A., **424** E5
Houthalen, Belgium, **288** B3
Houtman Abrolhos, *islands*, Australia, **134** C4
Hov, Norway, **286** E2
Hova, Sweden, **286** G3
Hovd, Mongolia, **213** J3
Hovd, *province*, Mongolia, **213** G3
Hovden, Norway, **286** C3
Hove, England, U.K., **305** G4
Hoven, U.S.A., **420** D3
Hoverla, Hora, *mountain range*, Ukraine, **296** E1
Hoveton, England, U.K., **305** J2
Hovgaard Ø, *island*, Greenland, **411** T2
Hovmantorp, Sweden, **286** G4
Hövsgöl, Mongolia, **210** E4
Hövsgöl, *province*, Mongolia, **213** H2
Hövsgöl Nuur, *lake*, Mongolia, **213** J2
Hövüün, Mongolia, **213** J4
Howard City, U.S.A., **421** L4
Howard Island, Australia, **135** G1
Howden, England, U.K., **307** H4
Howe, Cape, Australia, **135** K6
Howell, U.S.A., **421** M4
Howes, U.S.A., **420** B3
Howick, New Zealand, **132** E3
Howland, *island*, Baker and Howland Islands, **139** G4
Howser, Canada, **413** L6
Howth, Ireland, **309** F4
Hoxie, U.S.A., **420** C6
Höxter, Germany, **288** D3
Hoxtolgay, China, **212** E3
Hoxud, China, **212** E4
Hoy, *island*, Orkney, Scotland, U.K., **308** F2
Høyanger, Norway, **286** C2
Hoyerswerda, Germany, **289** G3
Høylandet, Norway, **284** F4
Höytiäinen, *lake*, Finland, **285** P5
Hradec Králové, Czech Republic, **289** G3
Hranice, Czech Republic, **289** H4
Hrastnik, Slovenia, **294** E2
Hraun, Iceland, **284** X6
Hrodna, Belarus, **298** B2
Hrodzyenskaya Voblasts', *province*, Belarus, **287** M5
Hrubieszów, Poland, **289** L3
Hsi-hseng, Myanmar, **205** C3
Hsin-ch'eng, Taiwan, **206** E3
Hsin-chu, Taiwan, **206** E3
Hu Wan, *bay*, China, **207** B3
Hu Xian, China, **206** B1
Hua Hin, Thailand, **202** C3
Hua-lien, Taiwan, **206** E4
Hua Shan, *mountain peak*, China, **206** B1
Hua Xian, China, **206** C1
Huachacalla, Bolivia, **455** E5
Huacheng, China, **207** A1
Huachi, China, **210** E5
Huacho, Peru, **454** C3
Huacrachuco, Peru, **454** C2
Huade, China, **210** F4
Huadian, China, **211** J4
Huahai, China, **213** H4
Huahaizi, China, **213** G5
Huahine, *island*, French Polynesia, **137** F2
Huai, *river*, China, **206** C1
Huai Yot, Thailand, **202** C5
Huai'an, Hebei, China, **210** F4
Huai'an, Jiangsu, China, **206** D1
Huaibei, China, **206** D1
Huaibin, China, **206** C1
Huaidian, China, **206** C1
Huaihua, China, **206** B3
Huaiji, China, **206** C4
Huailai, China, **210** F4
Huainan, China, **206** D1
Huairen, China, **210** F5
Huaiyang, China, **206** C1
Huaiyin, China, **206** D1
Huaiyu Shan, *mountain range*, China, **206** D2
Huaiyuan, China, **206** D1
Huajuapan de León, Mexico, **431** F5
Hualapai Peak, *mountain peak*, U.S.A., **422** G4
Huallaga, *river*, Peru, **454** C2
Huamachuco, Peru, **454** B2
Huambo, Angola, **368** C5
Huambo, *province*, Angola, **368** C5
Huambos, Peru, **454** B2

Huan, *river*, China, **210** D5
Huan Xian, China, **210** D5
Huanan, China, **211** K3
Huancabamba, Peru, **454** B1
Huancabamba, *river*, Peru, **454** B1
Huancache, Sierra, *mountain range*, Argentina, **460** C2
Huancané, Peru, **455** E4
Huancavelica, Peru, **454** C3
Huancayo, Peru, **454** C3
Huancheng, China, **207** A4
Huang, *river*, Central China, **206** C1
Huang (Yellow), *river*, China, **210** D5, *27, 30, 51, 66, 70, 95, 144, 158, 159, 160, 161*
Huang, *river*, N. China, **210** E4
Huang Xian, China, **211** H5
Huangchuan, China, **206** C1
Huanggangliang, China, **210** G4
Huangge, China, **207** A3
Huanghua, China, **210** G5
Huangjiang, China, **207** B3
Huangling, China, **206** B1
Huangliu, China, **203** F2
Huangnihe, China, **211** K4
Huangpi, China, **206** C2
Huangpu, east of Guangzhou, China, **207** A2
Huangpu, south of Guangzhou, China, **207** A3
Huangquqiao, China, **210** D5
Huangshan, China, **206** D2
Huangshi, China, **206** C2
Huangtang, China, **207** D1
Huangtu Gaoyuan, *plateau*, China, **210** D5
Huanguelén, Argentina, **458** E5
Huangyan, China, **206** E2
Huangyuan, China, **213** J5
Huangzhong, China, **213** J5
Huanren, China, **211** J4
Huanta, Peru, **454** C3
Huánuco, Peru, **454** C2
Huanuni, Bolivia, **455** E5
Huanzo, Cordillera de, *mountain range*, Peru, **454** D4
Huara, Chile, **455** E5
Huaral, Peru, **454** C3
Huaraz, Peru, **454** C2
Huari, Bolivia, **455** E5
Huari, Peru, **454** C2
Huarina, Bolivia, **455** E4
Huarmey, Peru, **454** B3
Huarong, China, **206** C2
Huascarán, Nevado, *mountain peak*, Peru, **454** C2, *441*
Huasco, Chile, **458** B3
Huasco, *river*, Chile, **458** B3
Huashixia, China, **215** F2
Huashuaccasa, Abra, *physical feature*, Peru, **454** D4
Huatabampo, Mexico, **430** C3
Huatong, China, **211** H4
Huauchinanco, Mexico, **431** F4
Huayhuash, Cordillera, *mountain range*, Peru, **454** C3
Huayllay, Peru, **454** C3
Huayuan, China, **206** B2
Huazhou, China, **206** B4
Hubbard, U.S.A., **420** G4
Hubbart Point, Canada, **414** G2
Hubei, *province*, China, **206** B2, *161*
Hubli, India, **216** C3
Huchang, China, **211** J4
Hucknall, England, U.K., **305** F1
Hucqueliers, France, **305** J4
Huddersfield, England, U.K., **307** G4
Huder, China, **211** H2
Hudiksvall, Sweden, **287** H2
Hudson, U.S.A., **423** L1
Hudson, *river*, U.S.A., **426** D3
Hudson, Volcán, *mountain peak*, Chile, **460** C2
Hudson Bay, Canada, **406** Q3, *93, 94, 380*
Hudson Falls, U.S.A., **426** D3
Hudson Strait, Canada, **411** M3, *466*
Hudson's Hope, Canada, **412** J3
Huế, Vietnam, **203** E2
Huebra, *river*, Spain, **292** D2
Huedin, Romania, **296** D2
Huehuetenango, Guatemala, **428** C4
Huejotzingo, Mexico, **431** F5
Huejutla de Reyes, Mexico, **431** F4
Huelva, Spain, **292** D4
Huentelauquén, Chile, **458** B4
Huequi, Volcán, *mountain peak*, Chile, **460** C2
Huércal-Overa, Spain, **293** G4
Huesca, Spain, **293** G1
Huéscar, Spain, **293** F4
Hueso Ballena, Punta, *point*, Róbinson Crusoe Island, Archipiélago Juan Fernández, Chile, **461** C2
Huetamo de Núñes, Mexico, **431** E5
Huff, U.S.A., **420** C2
Huftarøy, *island*, Norway, **286** B2
Hughenden, Australia, **135** J3
Hughes, *river*, Canada, **414** D3
Hughesville, U.S.A., **426** B4
Hugli-Chunchura, India, **214** D5
Hugo, Colorado, U.S.A., **423** M2
Hugo, Oklahoma, U.S.A., **424** E2
Hugoton, U.S.A., **420** C7
Huhora, New Zealand, **132** D2
Hui Xian, Gansu, China, **215** H2
Hui Xian, Henan, China, **206** C1
Hui'an, China, **206** D3
Hui'anbu, China, **210** D5
Huiarau Range, *mountain range*, New Zealand, **132** F4
Hŭich'ŏn, North Korea, **208** D2
Huichuan, China, **215** G2
Huidong, Guangdong, China, **207** D3
Huidong, Sichuan, China, **215** G4
Huihe, China, **211** G2
Huila, Nevado de, *mountain peak*, Colombia, **450** C3
Huíla, *province*, Angola, **368** B5
Huilai, China, **206** D4
Huili, China, **215** G4
Huimanguillo, Mexico, **431** G5
Huimbayoc, Peru, **454** C2
Huimin, China, **210** G5
Huinan, China, **211** J4
Huinca Renancó, Argentina, **458** D5
Huishui, China, **215** H4
Huisne, *river*, France, **290** E2
Huittinen, Finland, **287** L2
Huize, China, **215** G4
Huizhou, China, **207** C2
Hujirt, Hentiy, Mongolia, **210** E3
Hujirt, Töv, Mongolia, **210** D3
Hukeri, India, **216** C2
Hukuntsi, Botswana, **370** D3
Ḥūlāf, Ra's, *point*, Suquṭrá (Socotra), Yemen, **373** B2
Hulan, China, **211** J3
Ḥulayfā', Saudi Arabia, **363** H3
Hulett, U.S.A., **419** M4
Hulin, China, **211** L3
Huliyār, India, **216** D3
Hull, Canada, **416** D7
Hulstay, Mongolia, **210** F2
Hultsfred, Sweden, **286** G4
Hulun Nur, *lake*, China, **210** G2
Ḥulwān, Egypt, **225** A5
Huma, China, **211** J2
Huma, *river*, China, **211** H1
Humahuaca, Argentina, **458** D2
Humaitá, Bolivia, **455** E3
Humaitá, Brazil, **455** F2
Humaitá, Paraguay, **459** E3
Humbe, Angola, **368** B6
Humber, *river*, England, U.K., **307** H4
Humboldt, Canada, **413** S5
Humboldt, Massif du, *mountain peak*, New Caledonia, **141** A3
Humboldt, *river*, U.S.A., **418** E6
Humboldt, U.S.A., **425** H2
Humboldt Plain, *underwater feature*, Pacific Ocean, **479** M8
Hūmedān, Iran, **221** G3
Humen, China, **207** B3
Humenné, Slovakia, **289** K4
Hump, The, *mountain peak*, New Zealand, **133** A8
Humpata, Angola, **368** B6
Humphrey, Idaho, U.S.A., **419** H4
Humphrey, Nebraska, U.S.A., **420** E5
Humphreys Peak, *mountain peak*, U.S.A., **423** H4
Humppila, Finland, **287** L2
Humptulips, U.S.A., **418** C3
Hūn, Libya, **362** C3
Húnaflói, *bay*, Iceland, **284** X7
Hunan, *province*, China, **206** B3, *161*
Hunchun, China, **211** K4
Hundested, Denmark, **286** E5
100 Mile House, Canada, **412** J6
Hunedoara, Romania, **296** D3
Hünfeld, Germany, **288** D3
Hunga, *island*, Vava'u Group, Tonga, **141** B3
Hungary, *country*, Europe, **282** F6, *75, 93, 96, 228, 229, 245, 248, 249, 258, 259, 260, 261, 262, 263, 267, 269*
Hungary, Plain of, Europe, **280** F6, *262*
Hungerford, England, U.K., **305** F3
Hungiy, Mongolia, **213** G2
Hŭngnam, North Korea, **208** D3
Hunish, Rubha, *point*, Scotland, U.K., **308** C3
Hunjiang, China, **211** J4
Hunmanby, England, U.K., **307** H3
Hunsberge, *mountain range*, Namibia, **370** C4
Hunsrück, *mountain range*, Germany, **288** C4, *89*
Hunstanton, England, U.K., **305** H2
Hunstein Range, *mountain range*, Papua New Guinea, **140** A4
Hunt, Mongolia, **213** H3
Hunt, Mount, *mountain peak*, Antarctica, **470** F8
Hunte, *river*, Germany, **288** D2
Hunter, *island*, New Caledonia, **136** C3
Hunter, U.S.A., **420** E2
Hunter Island, Australia, **135** J7
Hunters Hills, The, New Zealand, **133** C7
Huntingburg, U.S.A., **421** K6
Huntingdon, Canada, **416** D7
Huntingdon, England, U.K., **305** G2
Huntington, Indiana, U.S.A., **421** L5
Huntington, West Virginia, U.S.A., **421** M6
Huntington Beach, U.S.A., **422** E5
Huntly, Scotland, U.K., **308** G3
Huntsville, Alabama, U.S.A., **425** J2
Huntsville, Canada, **421** P3
Huntsville, Texas, U.S.A., **424** E4
Hunyuan, China, **210** F5
Hunza, *river*, Pakistan, **218** C1
Huo Xian, China, **210** E5
Huocheng, China, **223** L4
Huolongmen, China, **211** J2
Huolu, China, **206** A2
Huoqiu, China, **206** D1
Huoshan, China, **206** D2
Hurbanovo, Slovakia, **289** J5
Hurd Point, Macquarie Island, **134** R11
Hurdal, Norway, **286** E2
Hurdiyo, Somalia, **367** H2
Hure Qi, China, **211** H4
Hüremt, Mongolia, **213** J2
Hurki, Belarus, **299** B5
Hurler's Cross, Ireland, **309** D5
Huron, Lake, Canada/U.S.A., **421** M3
Huron, U.S.A., **420** D3
Hurricane, U.S.A., **422** G3
Hursley, England, U.K., **305** F3
Hurst Green, England, U.K., **305** H3
Hurstpierpoint, England, U.K., **305** G4
Hurtsboro, U.S.A., **425** K3
Hurunui, *river*, New Zealand, **133** D6
Hurup, Denmark, **286** D4
Husainābād, India, **219** F4
Húsavík, Iceland, **284** Y6
Husbands Bosworth, England, U.K., **305** F2
Huşi, Romania, **296** G2
Huskvarna, Sweden, **286** G4
Huslia, U.S.A., **410** D3
Hustad, Norway, **284** C5
Husum, Germany, **288** D1
Husum, Sweden, **284** J5
Hutag, Mongolia, **213** J2
Hutchinson, U.S.A., **420** D7
Ḥūth, Yemen, **220** D5
Hutovo, Bosnia and Herzegovina, **294** F4
Hutt, Mount, *mountain peak*, New Zealand, **133** C6
Hutton, Mount, *mountain peak*, New Zealand, **133** D5
Huvadu Atoll, Maldives, **216** C6
Huzhen, China, **207** C2
Huzhong, China, **211** H2
Huzhou, China, **206** E2
Hvalpsund, Denmark, **286** D4
Hvammstangi, Iceland, **284** X7
Hvannadalshnúkur, *mountain peak*, Iceland, **284** Y7, *230*
Hvar, Croatia, **294** F4
Hvar, *island*, Croatia, **294** F4
Hvide Sande, Denmark, **286** D5
Hvítá, *river*, Iceland, **284** Y7
Hvizdets', Ukraine, **296** E1
Hvolsvöllur, Iceland, **284** X8
Hwach'ŏn, South Korea, **208** D3
Hwange, Zimbabwe, **371** E2
Hwangju, North Korea, **208** D3
Hyannis, Massachusetts, U.S.A., **426** E4
Hyannis, Nebraska, U.S.A., **420** C5
Hyargus Nuur, *lake*, Mongolia, **213** G2
Hycklinge, Sweden, **286** G4
Hyden, Australia, **134** D5
Hyderābād, India, **216** D2, *169, 173*
Hyderābād, Pakistan, **218** B4
Hyen, Norway, **286** B2
Hyères, France, **291** H5
Hyères, Îles d', *islands*, France, **291** H5
Hyesan, North Korea, **208** E2
Hyrynsalmi, Finland, **285** P4
Hysham, U.S.A., **419** L3
Hythe, Canada, **413** K4
Hythe, Hampshire, England, U.K., **305** F4
Hythe, Kent, England, U.K., **305** J3
Hytölä, Finland, **287** N1
Hyūga, Japan, **208** E4
Hyvinkää, Finland, **287** M2


## I


I-lan, Taiwan, **206** E3
I-n-Amenas, Algeria, **361** H3
I-n-Amguel, Algeria, **361** H4
I-n-Belbel, Algeria, **361** G3
I-n-Eker, Algeria, **361** H4
I-n-Guezzam, Algeria, **361** H5
I-n-Salah, Algeria, **361** G3
I-n-Tebezas, Mali, **365** E1
Iacobeni, Romania, **296** E2
Iaçu, Brazil, **457** F3
Ialomiūa, *river*, Romania, **296** F3
Ialoveni, Moldova, **296** G2
Ianca, Romania, **296** F3
Iargara, Moldova, **296** G2
Iaşi, Romania, **296** F2
Iauaretê, Brazil, **451** E4
Iba, Philippines, **204** B3
Ibadan, Nigeria, **365** E3, *329*
Ibagué, Colombia, **450** C3
Ibar, *river*, Kosovo, **296** C4
Ibarra, Ecuador, **450** B4
Ibarreta, Argentina, **459** E2
Ibb, Yemen, **220** D6
Ibba, Sudan, **369** E2
Iberá, Esteros del, *marshes*, Argentina, **459** E3
Iberia, Peru, **454** C1
Iberian Peninsula, Portugal/Spain, **280** D7, *71, 252, 254*
Iberville, Lac d', *lake*, Canada, **416** E2
Ibestad, Norway, **284** H2
Ibeto, Nigeria, **365** F2
Ibi, Nigeria, **365** F3
Ibiá, Brazil, **456** D5
Ibiapaba, Serra da, *mountain range*, Brazil, **453** F4
Ibicuí, *river*, Brazil, **459** F3
Ibimirim, Brazil, **453** G5
Ibinty, *mountain peak*, Madagascar, **372** C5
Ibiraçu, Brazil, **457** F5
Ibirama, Brazil, **459** H3
Ibirapuita, *river*, Brazil, **459** F4
Ibitiara, Brazil, **457** E3
Ibiza, *mountain peak*, Spain, **292** E2
Ibiza *see* Eivissa, *island*, Islas Baleares, Spain, **293** H3
Ibiza *see* Eivissa, Islas Baleares, Spain, **293** H3
Ibotirama, Brazil, **457** E3
Iboundji, Mont, *mountain peak*, Gabon, **368** B3, *333*
Ibrā', Oman, **221** G4
'Ibrī, Oman, **221** G4
Ibstock, England, U.K., **305** F2
Ica, Peru, **454** C4
Ica, Punta, *point*, Peru, **454** C4
Içá, *river*, Brazil, **451** E5
Icacos Point, Trinidad, Trinidad and Tobago, **461** C4
Içana, Brazil, **451** E4
Içana, *river*, Brazil, **451** E4
Icatu, Brazil, **453** E4
İçel, *province*, Turkey, **225** B1
İçel (Mersin), Turkey, **363** F1
Iceland, *country*, Europe, **282** C3, *22, 75, 80, 228, 230, 233, 234, 278, 384, 466*
Icha, *river*, Russian Federation, **223** K1
Ichalkaranji, India, **216** C2
Ichilo, *river*, Bolivia, **455** F4
Ichinoseki, Japan, **209** H3
Ich'ŏn, South Korea, **208** D3
Icklingham, England, U.K., **305** H2
İçmeler, Turkey, **297** G7
Icó, Brazil, **453** F5
Icod de Los Vinos, Islas Canarias, Spain, **373** A4
Ida Grove, U.S.A., **420** F4
Idabel, U.S.A., **424** E3
Idaburn, New Zealand, **133** B7
Idah, Nigeria, **365** F3
Idaho, *state*, U.S.A., **418** G4, *385, 386*
Idaho Falls, U.S.A., **419** H5
Idalia, U.S.A., **423** M2
Idar-Oberstein, Germany, **288** C4
'Idd al Ghanam, Sudan, **366** B2
Idel', Russian Federation, **285** S4
Ideles, Algeria, **361** H4
Ider, Mongolia, **213** H2
Ider, *river*, Mongolia, **213** H2
Idfū, Egypt, **363** F4
Idiofa, Democratic Republic of the Congo, **368** C4
Idivuoma, Sweden, **285** L2
Idlib, *district*, Syria, **225** D1
Idlib, Syria, **225** D2
Idre, Sweden, **286** F2
Idrija, Slovenia, **294** D3
Idrinskoye, Russian Federation, **223** N2
Iecava, Latvia, **287** M4
Iepê, Brazil, **459** G2
Ieper (Ypres), Belgium, **288** A3
Ierapetra, Kriti, Greece, **297** E8
Ierissou, Kolpos, *bay*, Greece, **297** D5
Iernut, Romania, **296** E2
Ifakara, Tanzania, **369** G4
Ifalik, *island*, Micronesia, **138** C4
Ifanadiana, Madagascar, **372** B5
Ife, Nigeria, **365** E3, *329*
Iferouâne, Niger, **361** H5
Ifetesene, *mountain peak*, Algeria, **361** G3

Ifjord, Norway, **285** N1
Igabi, Nigeria, **365** F2
Igal, Hungary, **289** H5
Igalula, Tanzania, **369** F4
Iganga, Uganda, **369** F2
Igarapava, Brazil, **456** D5
Igarapé-Açu, Brazil, **452** D3
Igarapé Grande, Brazil, **453** E4
Igarka, Russian Federation, **300** K3
Igboho, Nigeria, **365** E3
Iggesund, Sweden, **287** H2
Iglesias, Sardegna, Italy, **295** B6
Igloolik, Canada, **411** L3
Ignace, Canada, **414** J7
Ignacio Zaragoza, Mexico, **430** D2
Ignalina, Lithuania, **287** N5
Ignatovo, Russian Federation, **299** F2
İğneada, Turkey, **296** F5
İğneada Burnu, *cape*, Turkey, **296** G5
Igombe, *river*, Tanzania, **369** F3
Igoumenitsa, Greece, **297** C6
Igra, Russian Federation, **222** E1
Igrim, Russian Federation, **300** H3
Iguaçu, *river*, Brazil, **459** G2
Iguaçu, Saltos do, *water fall*, Argentina/Brazil, **459** F2, *440*
Iguaí, Brazil, **457** F4
Iguaje, Mesa de, *plateau*, Colombia, **450** D4
Iguala, Mexico, **431** F5
Igualada, Spain, **293** H2
Iguape, Brazil, **459** H2
Iguatemi, Brazil, **459** F2
Iguatemi, *river*, Brazil, **459** F2
Iguatu, Brazil, **453** F5
Iguéla, Gabon, **368** A3
Iguidi, Erg, *desert*, Algeria/Mauritania, **360** E3
Igunga, Tanzania, **369** F3
Iharaña, Madagascar, **372** B3
Ihbulag, Mongolia, **210** D4
Ihiala, Nigeria, **365** F3
Ihnāsiyat al Madīnah, Egypt, **225** A5
Ihosy, Madagascar, **372** B5
Ihsuuj, Mongolia, **210** D2
Iida, Japan, **209** G4
Iidaan, Somalia, **367** G3
Iijärvi, *lake*, Finland, **285** N2
Iijoki, *river*, Finland, **285** N4
Iisaku, Estonia, **287** N3
Iisalmi, Finland, **285** N5
Ijebu-Ode, Nigeria, **365** E3
Ijill, Kediet, *mountain peak*, Mauritania, **360** D4
Ijsselmeer, *lake*, Netherlands, **288** B2, *241*
Ijui, Brazil, **459** G3
Ijuí, *river*, Brazil, **459** F3
Ikahavo, *mountain peak*, Madagascar, **372** B4
Ikalamavony, Madagascar, **372** B5
Ikali, Democratic Republic of the Congo, **368** D3
Ikamatua, New Zealand, **133** C6
Ikanda, Democratic Republic of the Congo, **368** D3
Ikare, Nigeria, **365** F3
Ikaria, *island*, Dodekanisos, Greece, **297** F7
Ikawai, New Zealand, **133** C7
Ikeda, Japan, **209** H2
Ikeja, Nigeria, **365** E3
Ikela, Democratic Republic of the Congo, **368** D3
Ikey, Russian Federation, **223** Q2
Ikhtiman, Bulgaria, **296** D4
Ikhwān, Al (The Brothers), *islands*, Suquṭrá (Socotra), Yemen, **373** B2
Ikire, Nigeria, **365** E3
Ikohahoene, Adrar, *mountain peak*, Algeria, **361** H3
Ikom, Nigeria, **365** F3
Ikongo, Madagascar, **372** B5
Ikorodu, Nigeria, **365** E3
Ikot Ekpene, Nigeria, **368** A1
Ikungu, Tanzania, **369** F4
Ila-Orangun, Nigeria, **365** E3
Ilagan, Philippines, **204** C2
Iława, Poland, **289** J2
Ilchester, England, U.K., **304** E4
Ile, *river*, Kazakhstan, **223** K4
Île-à-la-Crosse, Canada, **413** R4
Île-à-la-Crosse, Lac, *lake*, Canada, **413** R4
Île-de-France, *administrative region*, France, **291** F2, *244*, *245*
Ilebo, Democratic Republic of the Congo, **368** D3
Ileksa, *river*, Russian Federation, **285** T5
Ileret, Kenya, **369** G2
Ilesha, Nigeria, **365** E3
Ilfracombe, England, U.K., **304** C3
Ilgaz, Turkey, **224** D4
Ilgın, Turkey, **363** F1
Ilha Grande, Brazil, **451** F4
Ilhéus, Brazil, **457** F4
Ili, *river*, China, **212** D4
Ilia, Romania, **296** D3
Iliamna Lake, U.S.A., **410** D3
Ilidža, Bosnia and Herzegovina, **294** G4
Iligan, Philippines, **204** D4
Iligan Bay, Philippines, **204** C4
Īlīm, Iran, **220** E2
Ilin Island, Philippines, **204** C3
Il'ino, Russian Federation, **299** C5
Il'inskoye, Russian Federation, **299** G4
Ilirska Bistrica, Slovenia, **294** E3
Il'ka, Russian Federation, **210** E2
Ilkeston, England, U.K., **305** F2
Ilkley, England, U.K., **307** G4
Illampu, Nevado de, *mountain peak*, Bolivia, **455** E4
Illapel, Chile, **458** B4
Iller, *river*, Germany, **288** E4
Illichivs'k, Ukraine, **296** H2
Illimani, Nevado, *mountain peak*, Bolivia, **455** E4
Illinois, *river*, U.S.A., **420** H6
Illinois, *state*, U.S.A., **421** J5, *91*, *386*
Illizi, Algeria, **361** H3
Illorsuit, Greenland, **411** P2
Ilulissat, Greenland, **411** P3
Ilmajoki, Finland, **285** L5
Il'men', Ozero, *lake*, Russian Federation, **299** C3
Ilminster, England, U.K., **304** E4
Ilo, Peru, **454** D4
Iloc Island, Philippines, **204** B4
Iloilo, Philippines, **204** C4
Ilomantsi, Finland, **285** Q5
Ilorin, Nigeria, **365** E3
Iłowa, Poland, **289** G3
Ilūkste, Latvia, **287** N5
Ilva Mare, Romania, **296** E2
Ilwaco, U.S.A., **418** C3
Il'ya, Belarus, **287** N5
Imabari, Japan, **208** F4
Imala, Mozambique, **369** G5
Imandra, Ozero, *lake*, Russian Federation, **285** R3
Imanombo, Madagascar, **372** B5
Imari, Japan, **208** E4
Imarssuak Seachannel, *underwater feature*, Atlantic Ocean, **477** E2
Imata, Peru, **454** D4
Imataca, Serranía de, *mountain range*, Venezuela, **451** G2
Imatra, Finland, **287** P2
Imbituba, Punta, *point*, Brazil, **459** H3
Imi-n-Tanoute, Morocco, **360** E2
Imlay, U.S.A., **422** D1
Immingham, England, U.K., **307** H4
Immokalee, U.S.A., **425** M6
Imo, *state*, Nigeria, **365** F3
Imola, Italy, **294** C3
Imonda, Papua New Guinea, **140** A3
Imperatriz, Brazil, **452** D4
Imperia, Italy, **294** B4
Imperial, Peru, **454** C3
Imperial, U.S.A., **420** C5
Impfondo, Congo, **368** C2
Imphāl, India, **214** E4, *169*
Imralı Adası, *island*, Turkey, **297** G5
Imroz, Turkey, **297** E5
Imtān, Syria, **225** D3
Imuris, Mexico, **430** C2
Imuruan Bay, Philippines, **204** B4
Ina, Japan, **209** G4
Inaccessible Island, Tristan da Cunha, **373** C2
Inajá, Brazil, **453** G5
Inambari, Peru, **455** E3
Inambari, *river*, Peru, **455** D3
Inangahua, New Zealand, **133** C5
Inanwatan, Indonesia, **199** F3
Iñapari, Peru, **455** E3
Inari, Finland, **285** N2
Inarijärvi, *lake*, Finland, **285** N2
Inauini, *river*, Brazil, **455** E2
Inca, Spain, **293** J3
Inca de Oro, Chile, **458** C3
İnce Burnu, *point*, Turkey, **297** F5
İncekum Burnu, *point*, Turkey, **225** C1
Inch, Kerry, Ireland, **309** C5
Inch, Wexford, Ireland, **309** F5
Inchard, Loch, *inlet*, Scotland, U.K., **308** D2
Inchiri, *administrative region*, Mauritania, **360** C5
Inch'ŏn, South Korea, **208** D3
Incudine, Monte, *mountain peak*, Corse, France, **295** B5
Inčukalns, Latvia, **287** M4
Inda Silasē, Ethiopia, **367** E2
Indaiá, *river*, Brazil, **456** E5
Indal, Sweden, **287** H1
Indalsälven, *river*, Sweden, **284** G5
Indaw, Myanmar, **205** C3
Indé, Mexico, **430** D3
Independence, Kansas, U.S.A., **420** F7
Independence, Minnesota, U.S.A., **420** G2
Independence, Missouri, U.S.A., **420** F6
Independence Mountains, *mountain range*, U.S.A., **422** E1
Independencia, Bahía de la, *bay*, Peru, **454** C4
Independenūa, near Galati, Romania, **296** F3
Independenūa, Romania, **296** G4
India, Bassas da, *islands*, Réunion, **371** G3
India, *country*, Asia, **196** J8, *23*, *28*, *30*, *47*, *49*, *51*, *54*, *73*, *74*, *75*, *76*, *77*, *79*, *89*, *90*, *91*, *93*, *94*, *95*, *96*, *144*, *145*, *154*, *157*, *158*, *159*, *166*, *167*, *168*, *169*, *170*, *171*, *172*, *173*, *175*, *176*, *185*, *186*, *193*, *244*, *250*, *265*, *275*, *276*, *317*, *350*, *351*, *437*, *439*
Indian Cabins, Canada, **413** L2
Indian Head, Canada, **414** C6
Indian Lake, U.S.A., **426** C3
Indian Ocean, **476** C6, *22*, *45*, *54*, *74*, *75*, *76*, *81*, *95*, *108*, *123*, *127*, *168*, *312*, *339*, *348*, *352*, *353*, *469*, *474*, *475*
Indian Springs, U.S.A., **422** F3
Indian Wells, U.S.A., **423** H4
Indiana, *state*, U.S.A., **421** K5, *386*
Indiana, U.S.A., **421** P5
Indianapolis, U.S.A., **421** K6, *386*
Indianola, Iowa, U.S.A., **420** G5
Indianola, Mississippi, U.S.A., **424** G3
Indigirka, *river*, Russian Federation, **301** R3
Indio, U.S.A., **422** E5
Indo-China Peninsula, Asia, **476** E7, *144*, *153*
Indomed Fracture Zone, *tectonic feature*, Indian Ocean, **476** B7
Indo-Gangetic Plain, India/Pakistan, **194** J7, *168*, *169*
Indonesia, *country*, Asia, **197** N10, *29*, *37*, *42*, *47*, *50*, *51*, *60*, *65*, *73*, *76*, *86*, *92*, *93*, *95*, *108*, *115*, *144*, *145*, *148*, *149*, *240*, *350*, *353*, *399*
Indore, India, **218** C5
Indragiri, *river*, Indonesia, **200** C3
Indramayu, Indonesia, **201** E4
Indravati, *river*, India, **216** E2
Indre, *river*, France, **290** E3
Indre Arna, Norway, **286** B2
Indre Billefjord, Norway, **285** M1
Indura, Belarus, **289** L2
Indus, *river*, Asia, **218** A4, *66*, *70*, *144*, *168*, *173*
Indus Fan, *underwater feature*, Indian Ocean, **476** D3
İnebolu, Turkey, **224** D4
İnegöl, Turkey, **297** G5
Indija, Serbia, **296** C3
Ineu, Romania, **296** C2
Infanta, Philippines, **204** C3
Infante Dom Henrique, São Tomé and Príncipe, **373** C4
Infiernillo, Presa del, *dam*, Mexico, **430** E5
Ingal, Niger, **365** F1
Ingaly, Russian Federation, **223** J1
Ingatestone, England, U.K., **305** H3
Ingende, Democratic Republic of the Congo, **368** C3
Ingeniero Guillermo, N. Juárez, Argentina, **458** E2
Ingeniero Jacobacci, Argentina, **460** D1
Ingenio, Islas Canarias, Spain, **373** B4
Ingettolgoy, Mongolia, **210** D2
Ingham, Australia, **135** K2
Ingleborough, *mountain peak*, England, U.K., **306** F3
Ingleton, England, U.K., **306** F3
Inglewood, U.S.A., **422** D5
Inglis, Canada, **414** D6
Ingoda, *river*, Russian Federation, **210** F2
Ingoldmells, England, U.K., **305** H1
Ingolstadt, Germany, **288** E4
Ingomar, U.S.A., **419** L3
Ingonish, Canada, **417** L6
Ingøya, *island*, Norway, **285** L1
Ingrāj Bāzār, India, **214** D4
Ingre, Bolivia, **455** F5
Ingrid Christensen Coast, *region*, Antarctica, **470** F5
Ingushetiya, Respublika, *republic*, Russian Federation, **222** D4
Inhambane, Mozambique, **371** G3
Inhambane, *province*, Mozambique, **371** F3
Inhambupe, Brazil, **457** F3
Inhaminga, Mozambique, **371** G2
Inharrime, Mozambique, **371** G3
Inhaúmas, Brazil, **457** E3
Inirida, *river*, Colombia, **451** E3
Inishannon, Ireland, **309** D6
Inishbofin, *island*, Ireland, **309** B4
Inisheer, *island*, Ireland, **309** C4
Inishkea North, *island*, Ireland, **309** B3
Inishkea South, *island*, Ireland, **309** B3
Inishmaan, *island*, Ireland, **309** C4
Inishmore, *island*, Ireland, **309** C4
Inishmurray, *island*, Ireland, **309** C3
Inishowen, *peninsula*, Ireland, **309** E2
Inishowen Head, *point*, Ireland, **306** B2
Inishshark, *island*, Ireland, **309** B4
Inishtrahull Island, Ireland, **309** E2
Inishtrahull Sound, Ireland, **309** E2
Inishturk, *island*, Ireland, **309** B4
Injgan Sum, China, **211** G3
Injibara, Ethiopia, **367** E2
Inkom, U.S.A., **418** H5
Inman, U.S.A., **425** L2
Inn, *river*, Germany, **288** F5
Inndyr, Norway, **284** G3
Inner Hebrides, *islands*, Scotland, U.K., **308** C4, *276*
Inner Mongolia *see* Nei Mongol Zizhiqu, *autonomous region*, China, **210** F4, *158*, *161*
Inner Sound, Scotland, U.K., **308** D3
Innerleithen, Scotland, U.K., **308** F5
Innisfail, Australia, **135** K2
Innisfail, Canada, **413** N5
Innokent'yevka, Russian Federation, **211** M2
Innsbruck, Austria, **288** E5
Innset, Sør-Trøndelag, Norway, **284** E5
Innset, Troms, Norway, **284** J2
Innviertel, *region*, Austria, **294** D1
Inongo, Democratic Republic of the Congo, **368** C3
Inowrocław, Poland, **289** J2
Inquisivi, Bolivia, **455** E4
Insch, Scotland, U.K., **308** G3
Insjön, Sweden, **286** G2
Insurăūei, Romania, **296** F3
Inta, Russian Federation, **300** H3
Intendente Alvear, Argentina, **458** D5
İntepe, Turkey, **297** F5
Interlaken, Switzerland, **291** H3
International Falls, U.S.A., **420** G1
Inthanon, Doi, *mountain peak*, Thailand, **202** C2, *155*
Intiyaco, Argentina, **459** E3
Întorsura Buzăului, Romania, **296** F3
Intuto, Peru, **450** C5
Inubō-zaki, *point*, Japan, **209** H4
Inukjuak, Canada, **415** Q2
Inuvik, Canada, **410** F3
Inveraray, Scotland, U.K., **308** D4
Inverbervie, Scotland, U.K., **308** G4
Invercargill, New Zealand, **133** B8
Inverclyde, *local authority*, Scotland, U.K., **308** E5
Inverell, Australia, **135** L4
Invergarry, Scotland, U.K., **308** E3
Invergordon, Scotland, U.K., **308** E3
Invermoriston, Scotland, U.K., **308** E3
Invermory, *river*, Scotland, U.K., **308** E3
Inverness, Canada, **417** L6
Inverness, Scotland, U.K., **308** E3, *276*
Inverurie, Scotland, U.K., **308** G3
Investigator Channel, Myanmar, **202** C4
Investigator Ridge, *underwater feature*, Indian Ocean, **476** F6
Inya, Russian Federation, **212** E2
Inyangani, *mountain peak*, Zimbabwe, **371** F2, *346*
Inyathi, Zimbabwe, **371** E2
Inyokern, U.S.A., **422** E4
Inyonga, Tanzania, **369** F4
Inywa, Myanmar, **205** C3
Inza, Russian Federation, **222** D2
Inzia, *river*, Democratic Republic of the Congo, **368** C4
Iō-jima, *island*, Japan, **138** C2
Ioannina, Greece, **297** C6
Iokanga, *river*, Russian Federation, **285** T3
Iola, U.S.A., **420** F7
Iolotan', Turkmenistan, **222** G5
Ioma, Papua New Guinea, **140** B5
Iona, Angola, **368** B6
Iona, *island*, Scotland, U.K., **308** C4
Iona, U.S.A., **420** D4
Ioneşti, Romania, **296** E3
Ionian Islands *see* Ionioi Nisoi, *administrative region*, Greece, **297** B7
Ionian Sea, Greece/Italy, **297** B6, *265*
Ionioi Nisoi (Ionian Islands), *administrative region*, Greece, **297** B7
Ionioi Nisoi, *islands*, Greece, **280** F8
Ionn-N'yugoayv, Gora, *mountain peak*, Russian Federation, **285** P2
Ios, *island*, Kyklades, Greece, **297** E7
Iowa, *river*, U.S.A., **420** G5

Iowa, *state*, U.S.A., **420** G4, *386*
Iowa City, U.S.A., **420** H5
Iowa Falls, U.S.A., **420** G4
Iowa Park, U.S.A., **424** C3
Ipameri, Brazil, **456** D4
Ipanema, *river*, Brazil, **457** G2
Iparia, Peru, **454** C2
Ipatinga, Brazil, **457** E5
Ipatovo, Russian Federation, **298** F3
Ipeiros, *administrative region*, Greece, **297** C6
Ipel', *river*, Hungary/Slovakia, **289** J4
Ipiales, Colombia, **450** C4
Ipiaú, Brazil, **457** F4
Ipil, Philippines, **204** C5
Ipirá, Brazil, **457** F3
Ipiranga, Brazil, **459** G2
Ipixuna, Amazonas, Brazil, **454** D2
Ipixuna, Maranhão, Brazil, **453** E4
Ipoh, Malaysia, **200** C1
Iporá, Brazil, **456** C4
Ipota, Vanuatu, **141** A3
Ippy, Central African Republic, **366** B3
İpsala, Turkey, **297** F5
Ipswich, Australia, **135** L4
Ipswich, England, U.K., **305** J2
Ipswich, U.S.A., **420** D3
Ipu, Brazil, **453** F4
Ipueiras, Brazil, **453** F4
Ipupiara, Brazil, **457** E3
Iqaluit, Canada, **411** N3, *381*
Iqe, China, **213** G5
Iquipi, Peru, **454** D4
Iquique, Chile, **455** D5
Iquitos, Peru, **450** D5, *441*
Ira Banda, Central African Republic, **368** D1
Iracoubo, French Guiana, **452** C2
Irai, Brazil, **459** G3
Irakleia, Greece, **297** D5
Irakleia, *island*, Kyklades, Greece, **297** E7
Irakleio, Greece, **298** C5
Irakleio (Iraklion), Kriti, Greece, **297** E8
Iraklion *see* Irakleio, Kriti, Greece, **297** E8
Iramaia, Brazil, **457** F3
Iran, *country*, Asia, **196** G6, *22, 83, 146, 147, 172, 173, 177, 178, 182, 183, 184, 187, 189, 271, 336*
Iran, Pegunungan, *mountain range*, Malaysia, **201** F2
Iranian Plateau, Iran, **194** G6
Irapuato, Mexico, **431** E4
Iraq, *country*, Asia, **363** H2, *54, 64, 66, 75, 97, 146, 147, 174, 175, 177, 180, 181, 182, 193, 317, 385*
Irará, Brazil, **457** F3
Iratapuru, *river*, Brazil, **452** C3
Irati, Brazil, **459** G2
Irbes šaurums, *strait*, Estonia/Latvia, **287** K4
Irbid, Jordan, **225** C3
Irbit, Russian Federation, **222** G1
Irecê, Brazil, **457** F3
Ireland, *country*, Europe, **309** D4, *75, 88, 228, 245, 275, 277, 475*
Ireng, *river*, Brazil/Guyana, **451** G3
Iri, South Korea, **208** D4
Irian Jaya, *province*, Indonesia, **199** F3
Iriba, Chad, **366** B1
Iricoumé, Serra, *mountain range*, Brazil, **452** B3
Iriklinskoye Vodokhranilishche, *reservoir*, Russian Federation, **222** F2
Iringa, *administrative region*, Tanzania, **369** F4
Iringa, Tanzania, **369** G4
Īrīnshahr, Iran, **221** H3
Iriomote-jima, *island*, Japan, **209** M8
Iriri, *river*, Brazil, **452** C5
Irish Sea, Ireland/U.K., **306** C4, *274, 276, 277, 279*
Irituia, Brazil, **452** D3
Irkut, *river*, Russian Federation, **210** C2
Irkutsk, Russian Federation, **210** D1
Irkutskaya Oblast', *administrative region*, Russian Federation, **213** J1
Irlir, *mountain peak*, Uzbekistan, **222** G4
Irmãos, Serra Dois, *mountain range*, Brazil, **457** F2
Iroise, Mer d', *sea*, France, **290** B2
Iron Mountains, *mountain range*, Ireland, **309** E3, *277*
Iron River, U.S.A., **421** J2
Ironside, U.S.A., **418** F4
Ironwood, U.S.A., **420** H2
Iroquois Falls, Canada, **415** P7
Irrawaddy, *division*, Myanmar, **205** B4
Irrawaddy, *river*, Myanmar, **205** B3, *157*
Irricana, Canada, **413** N6
Irsina, Italy, **295** F5
Irthing, *river*, England, U.K., **306** F3
Irtysh, *river*, Russian Federation, **194** J4
Irumu, Democratic Republic of the Congo, **369** E2
Irupana, Bolivia, **455** E4
Irurzun, Spain, **293** G1
Irvine, Scotland, U.K., **308** E5
Irvine, U.S.A., **422** E5
Irvines Landing, Canada, **412** G7
Irvinestown, Northern Ireland, U.K., **309** E3
Irving, U.S.A., **424** D3
Irvington, U.S.A., **421** K7
Irwell, New Zealand, **133** D6
Is-sur-Tille, France, **291** G3
Isa, Nigeria, **365** F2
Īsa Khel, Pakistan, **218** B2
Isaba, Spain, **293** G1
Isabel, Bahía, *bay*, Islas Galápagos (Galapagos Islands), Ecuador, **461** A2
Isabel, U.S.A., **420** C3
Isabela, Cabo, *cape*, Dominican Republic, **429** H2
Isabela, Isla, *island*, Islas Galápagos (Galapagos Islands), Ecuador, **461** A2
Isabela, Philippines, **204** C5
Isabelia, Cordillera, *mountain range*, Nicaragua, **428** D4
Isabella, U.S.A., **420** H2
Isabella Lake, U.S.A., **422** D4
Isac, *river*, France, **290** D3
Isaccea, Romania, **296** G3
Ísafjörður, Iceland, **284** X6
Isahaya, Japan, **208** E4
Isakovo, Russian Federation, **299** E5
Işalniţa, Romania, **296** D3
Isandja, Democratic Republic of the Congo, **368** D3
Isanga, Democratic Republic of the Congo, **368** D3
Isangi, Democratic Republic of the Congo, **368** D2
Isanlu, Nigeria, **365** F3
Isar, *river*, Germany, **288** F4
Isbister, Shetland, Scotland, U.K., **308** K7
Ischia, Isola d', *island*, Italy, **295** D5
Ise, Japan, **209** G4
Iseo, Lago d', *lake*, Italy, **294** C3
Isère, *river*, France, **291** G4
Isernia, Italy, **295** E5
Iset', *river*, Russian Federation, **222** G1
Iseyin, Nigeria, **365** E3
Isherton, Guyana, **451** G3
Ishigaki-jima, *island*, Japan, **209** N8
Ishikari-wan, *bay*, Japan, **209** H2
Ishim, *river*, Russian Federation, **223** J1
Ishim, Russian Federation, **223** H1
Ishtamal, *river*, India, **216** C3
Ishtikhon, Uzbekistan, **222** H5
Ishurdi, Bangladesh, **214** D4
Isigny-sur-Mer, France, **290** D2
Işiklar Daği, *mountain range*, Turkey, **297** F5
Isil'kul', Russian Federation, **223** J2
Isinga, Russian Federation, **210** F1
Isipingo, South Africa, **371** F5
Isiro, Democratic Republic of the Congo, **369** E2
Iska, Russian Federation, **222** H1
İskenderun, Turkey, **225** D1
İskūr, *river*, Bulgaria, **296** E4
Iskushuban, Somalia, **367** H2
Iskut, Canada, **412** D3
Iskut, *river*, Canada, **412** D3
Isla de Aguada, Mexico, **431** H5
Isla, Punta, *point*, Róbinson Crusoe Island, Archipiélago Juan Fernández, Chile, **461** C2
İslâhiye, Turkey, **363** G1
Islāmābād, Pakistan, **218** C2, *173*
Islāmkot, Pakistan, **218** B4
Island Bay, Philippines, **204** B4
Island Lake, Canada, **414** G5
Island Lake, *lake*, Canada, **414** G5
Islands, Bay of, New Zealand, **132** E2
Islas Baleares, *autonomous community*, Spain, **293** J3
Islay, *island*, Scotland, U.K., **308** C5
Isle, *river*, France, **290** E4
Isle of Anglesey, *unitary authority*, Wales, U.K., **306** D4
Isle of Man, *U.K. crown dependency*, Europe, **306** D3, *228, 276, 279*
Isle of Walney, *island*, England, U.K., **306** E3
Isle of Wight, *unitary authority*, England, U.K., **305** F4
Isluga, Volcán, *mountain peak*, Chile, **455** E5
Ismail Samani, Pik imeni, *mountain peak*, Tajikistan, **223** J5
Ismailia *see* Al Ismā'īlīyah, Egypt, **225** B4
Isnā, Egypt, **363** F3
Isojoki, Finland, **287** K1
Isoka, Zambia, **369** F5
Isparta, Turkey, **224** D5
Isperikh, Bulgaria, **296** F4
Israel, *country*, Asia, **196** E6, *77, 86, 96, 146, 179, 180, 181, 182, 192, 193, 317*
Issano, Guyana, **451** G3
Issaouane, Erg, *desert*, Algeria, **361** H3
Issia, Côte d'Ivoire, **364** C3
Issoire, France, **291** F4
Issoudun, France, **290** E3
Istállós-kő, *mountain peak*, Hungary, **289** K4
İstanbul, *province*, Turkey, **297** G5
İstanbul, Turkey, **297** G5, *191*
İstanbul Boğazı (Bosporus), *strait*, Turkey, **297** G5, *190, 191*
Istiaia, Greece, **297** D6
Īstīdeh-ye Moqor, Āb-e, *lake*, Afghanistan, **218** A2
Istmina, Colombia, **450** C3
Istok, Kosovo, **296** C4
Istunmäki, Finland, **285** N5
Ita-Suomen Lääni, *province*, Finland, **285** N5
Itabaianinha, Brazil, **457** G3
Itaberaba, Brazil, **457** F3
Itaberaí, Brazil, **456** D4
Itabira, Brazil, **457** E5
Itabirito, Brazil, **457** E5
Itaboca, Brazil, **451** F5
Itabuna, Brazil, **457** F4
Itacaiunas, *river*, Brazil, **452** C4
Itacajá, Brazil, **452** D5
Itacoatiara, Brazil, **451** G5
Itacuaí, *river*, Brazil, **454** D1
Itacurubí del Rosario, Paraguay, **459** F2
Itaetê, Brazil, **457** F3
Itaguaí, Brazil, **457** E6
Itaguajé, Brazil, **459** G2
Itaguari, *river*, Brazil, **457** E4
Itagüí, Colombia, **450** C2
Itaim, *river*, Brazil, **453** F5
Itaituba, Brazil, **452** B4
Itajaí, Brazil, **459** H3
Itajaí-Açu, *river*, Brazil, **459** H3
Itajubá, Brazil, **459** J2
Italy, *country*, Europe, **282** F7, *29, 74, 75, 82, 90, 91, 95, 96, 80, 228, 244, 245, 247, 248, 249, 252, 253, 254, 255, 256, 257, 258, 263, 315, 316, 337, 338, 339, 386, 440, 444*
Itamarandiba, Brazil, **457** E4
Itambacuri, Brazil, **457** F5
Itambé, Pico de, *mountain peak*, Brazil, **457** E5
Itampolo, Madagascar, **372** A5
Itānagar, India, **214** E4, *169*
Itanhaém, São Paulo, Brazil, **459** H2
Itanhém, Bahia, Brazil, **457** F4
Itanhém, *river*, Brazil, **457** F4
Itaobim, Brazil, **457** F4
Itapagipe, Brazil, **456** D5
Itapebi, Brazil, **457** F4
Itapecuru-Mirim, Brazil, **453** E4
Itapemirim, Brazil, **457** F5
Itaperuna, Brazil, **457** F5
Itapetinga, Brazil, **457** F4
Itapetininga, Brazil, **459** H2
Itapeva, Brazil, **459** H2
Itapicuru, *river*, Bahia, Brazil, **457** F3
Itapicuru, *river*, Maranhão, Brazil, **453** E4
Itapicuru, Serra do, *mountain range*, Brazil, **452** E5
Itapipoca, Brazil, **453** F4
Itapiranga, Brazil, **451** G5
Itaqui, Brazil, **459** F3
Itararé, Brazil, **459** H2
Itararé, *river*, Brazil, **459** H2
Itārsi, India, **218** D5
Itarumã, Brazil, **456** C5
Itatupã, Brazil, **452** C3
Ite, Peru, **454** D4
Itea, Greece, **297** D6
Itebero, Democratic Republic of the Congo, **369** E3
Ithaca, U.S.A., **426** B3
Ithaki, Ionioi Nisoi, Greece, **297** C6
Ithaki, *island*, Ionioi Nisoi, Greece, **297** C6
Ithrīyat, Jabal, *mountain range*, Jordan, **225** D4
Itimbiri, *river*, Democratic Republic of the Congo, **368** D2
Itinga, Brazil, **457** F4
Itiquira, Brazil, **456** B4
Itiquira, *river*, Brazil, **456** B4
Itoko, Democratic Republic of the Congo, **368** D3
Ittiri, Sardegna, Italy, **295** B5
Ittoqqortoormiit, Greenland, **411** S2
Itu, Brazil, **459** H2
Ituango, Colombia, **450** C2
Ituí, *river*, Brazil, **454** D1
Ituiutaba, Brazil, **456** D5
Itula, Democratic Republic of the Congo, **369** E3
Itumbiara, Brazil, **456** D5
Ituni, Guyana, **451** G3
Itupiranga, Brazil, **452** D4
Ituporanga, Brazil, **459** H3
Iturama, Brazil, **456** C5
Iturbe, Paraguay, **459** F3
Iturup, *island*, Kuril'skiye Ostrova, Russian Federation, **209** J1
Iturup, Ostrov, *island*, Russian Federation, **301** R5
Ituxi, *river*, Brazil, **455** E2
Ituzaingó, Argentina, **459** F3
Itzehoe, Germany, **288** D2
Iul'tin, Russian Federation, **301** V3
Iutica, Brazil, **451** E4
Iva, Samoa, **141** B1
Ivai, *river*, Brazil, **459** G2
Ivakoany, *mountain peak*, Madagascar, **372** B5
Ivalo, Finland, **285** N2
Ivalojoki, *river*, Finland, **285** N2
Ivanec, Croatia, **294** F2
Ivangorod, Russian Federation, **299** B3
Ivangrad, Montenegro, **296** B4
Ivanhoe, Australia, **135** J5
Ivanhoe, U.S.A., **420** E3
Ivanić Grad, Croatia, **294** F3
Ivanivka, Ukraine, **296** H2
Ivanjica, Serbia, **296** C4
Ivanjska, Bosnia and Herzegovina, **294** F3
Ivankovtsy, Russian Federation, **211** L2
Ivano-Frankivs'k, Ukraine, **298** B3
Ivano-Frankivs'ka Oblast', *province*, Ukraine, **296** D1
Ivanova, Russian Federation, **299** C4
Ivanovka, Russian Federation, **211** G2
Ivanovo, Russian Federation, **300** F4
Ivatsevichy, Belarus, **289** M2
Ivaylovgrad, Bulgaria, **297** F5
Ivdel', Russian Federation, **300** H3
Iveşti, near Bârlad, Romania, **296** F2
Iveşti, Romania, **296** F3
Ivindo, *river*, Gabon, **368** B3
Ivinheima, Brazil, **459** G2
Ivinheima, *river*, Brazil, **456** C6
Ivittuut, Greenland, **411** Q3
Ivohibe, Madagascar, **372** B5
Ivory Coast, *coastal area*, Côte d'Ivoire, Africa, **364** C4
Ivrea, Italy, **294** A3
İvrindi, Turkey, **297** F6
Ivujivik, Canada, **411** M3
Ivyanyets, Belarus, **287** N6
Ivybridge, England, U.K., **304** D4
Ivydale, U.S.A., **421** N6
Iwaki, Japan, **209** H3
Iwakuni, Japan, **208** F4
Iwamizawa, Japan, **209** H2
Iwanai, Japan, **209** H2
Iwo, Nigeria, **365** E3
Iwon, North Korea, **208** E2
Iwye, Belarus, **289** M2
Ixiamas, Bolivia, **455** E3
Ixmiquilpán, Mexico, **431** F4
Ixtlán de Juárez, Mexico, **431** F5
Ixtlán del Río, Mexico, **430** D4
Ixworth, England, U.K., **305** H2
Iyevlevo, Russian Federation, **222** H1
Iza, *river*, Romania, **296** E2
Īzad Khvāst, Iran, **220** F2
Izazi, Tanzania, **369** G4
Izberbash, Russian Federation, **222** D4
Izbica, Poland, **289** H1
Izborsk, Russian Federation, **299** A4
Izhevsk, Russian Federation, **222** E1
Izhma, *river*, Russian Federation, **281** K3
Izmayil, Ukraine, **296** G3
İzmir, *province*, Turkey, **297** F6
İzmir, Turkey, **297** F6
İzmit *see* Kocaeli, Turkey, **297** G5
Iznájar, Embalse de, *reservoir*, Spain, **292** E4
İznik, Turkey, **297** G5
İznik Gölü, *lake*, Turkey, **297** G5
Iznoski, Russian Federation, **299** E5
Izra', Syria, **225** D3
Izsák, Hungary, **289** J5
Izu-Shotō, *islands*, Japan, **209** G4
Izuhara, Japan, **208** E4
Izumi, Japan, **208** E4
Izumo, Japan, **208** F4


## J


J.A.D. Jensen Nunatakker, *mountain peak*, Greenland, 411 Q3
Jaakonvaara, Finland, **285** Q5
Jaala, Finland, **287** N2
Jabalpur, India, **218** D5
Jabbūl, Sabkhat al, *lake*, Syria, **225** D1
Jabiru, Australia, **134** G1
Jablah, Syria, **225** C2
Jablanica, Bosnia and Herzegovina, **294** F4
Jablanica, *mountain range*, Albania/Macedonia, **297** C5
Jabłonowo-Pomorskie, Poland, 289 J2
Jaboatão, Brazil, **453** G5
Jabukovac, Serbia, **296** D3
Jabung, Tanjong, *point*, Indonesia, 200 D3
Jabuticabal, Brazil, **456** D5
Jaca, Spain, **293** G1
Jacaré, *river*, Brazil, **457** F3
Jacareacanga, Brazil, **452** B5
Jacareí, Brazil, **459** J2
Jáchal, *river*, Argentina, **458** C4

Jacinto, Brazil, **457** F4
Jaciparaná, Brazil, **455** F2
Jaciparaná, *river*, Brazil, **455** F2
Jack Creek, U.S.A., **418** F6
Jackhead, Canada, **414** F6
Jackman, U.S.A., **426** E2
Jacksboro, U.S.A., **424** C3
Jackson, Alabama, U.S.A., **425** J4
Jackson, California, U.S.A., **422** C2
Jackson, Cape, New Zealand, **133** E5
Jackson, Michigan, U.S.A., **421** L4
Jackson, Minnesota, U.S.A., **420** F4
Jackson, Mississippi, U.S.A., **424** G3, *386*
Jackson, Montna, U.S.A., **418** H4
Jackson, Ohio, U.S.A., **421** M6
Jackson, Tennessee, U.S.A., **425** H2
Jackson, Wyoming, U.S.A., **419** J5
Jackson Bay, New Zealand, **133** B6
Jackson Lake, U.S.A., **419** J5
Jacksonboro, U.S.A., **425** M3
Jacksons, New Zealand, **133** C6
Jacksonville, Arkansas, U.S.A., **424** F2
Jacksonville, Florida, U.S.A., **425** M4
Jacksonville, Illinois, U.S.A., **420** H6
Jacksonville, North Carolina, U.S.A., **425** P2
Jacksonville, Texas, U.S.A., **424** E4
Jacksonville Beach, U.S.A., **425** M4
Jäckvik, Sweden, **284** H3
Jacmel, Haiti, **429** G3
Jaco, Mexico, **430** E3
Jacobābād, Pakistan, **218** B3
Jacobina, Brazil, **457** F3
Jacquemart Island, Auckland Islands, New Zealand, **132** K11
Jacques-Cartier, Détroit de, *strait*, Canada, **417** J4
Jacquet River, Canada, **416** H6
Jacui, *river*, Brazil, **459** G3
Jacuípe, *river*, Brazil, **457** F3
Jacundá, Brazil, **452** D4
Jacundá, *river*, Brazil, **452** C4
Jacupiranga, Brazil, **459** H2
Jacura, Venezuela, **451** E1
Jadū, Libya, **362** B2
Jaén, Peru, **454** B1
Jaén, Spain, **293** F4
Jaffa, Cape, Australia, **135** H6
Jaffna, Sri Lanka, **216** E4
Jaffray, Canada, **413** M7
Jafr, Qā' al, *salt-pan*, Jordan, **225** D4
Jagdalpur, India, **217** E2
Jagdaqi, China, **211** J2
Jagersfontein, South Africa, **370** E4
Jaggang, China, **214** A2
Jagodina, Serbia, **296** C4
Jagraon, India, **218** C3
Jagtiāl, India, **216** D2
Jaguarão, Brazil, **459** G4
Jaguarão, *river*, Brazil, **459** G4
Jaguari, Brazil, **459** F3
Jaguari, *river*, Brazil, **459** F3
Jaguaribe, Brazil, **453** F4
Jaguaruna, Brazil, **459** H3
Jagüé, Argentina, **458** C3
Jagüey Grande, Cuba, **429** E2
Jahānābād, India, **219** F4
Jahāzpur, India, **218** C4
Jahrom, Iran, **220** F3
Jaicós, Brazil, **453** F5
Jaipur, India, **218** C4, *169*
Jais, India, **219** E4
Jaisalmer, India, **218** B4
Jājapur, India, **219** F5
Jajce, Bosnia and Herzegovina, **294** F3
Jakarta, Indonesia, **201** D4, *93, 148*
Jakarta Raya, *autonomous district*, Indonesia, **200** D4
Jakes Corner, Canada, **412** C1
Jakupica, *mountain range*, Macedonia, **297** C5
Jal, U.S.A., **423** M5
Jalai Nur, China, **210** G2
Jalaid Qi, China, **211** H3
Jalal-Abad, Kyrgyzstan, **212** B4
Jalālah al Baḥrīyah, Jabal al, *mountain range*, Egypt, **225** A5
Jalālah al Qiblīyah, Jabal al, *mountain range*, Egypt, **225** A5
Jalālābād, Afghanistan, **218** B2
Jalapa Enríquez, Mexico, **431** F5
Jalapa, Guatemala, **428** C4
Jalapa, Nicaragua, **428** D4
Jālaun, India, **218** D4
Jales, Brazil, **456** C5
Jaleshwar, India, **219** F5
Jaleswar, Nepal, **219** F4
Jālgaon, India, **218** C5
Jalingo, Nigeria, **365** G3
Jalisco, *state*, Mexico, **430** D4
Jālna, India, **218** C6
Jalor, India, **218** C4
Jalostotitlán, Mexico, **430** E4
Jalpa, Mexico, **430** E4
Jalpāiguri, India, **219** G4
Jalpan, Mexico, **431** F4
Jālū, Libya, **362** D3
Jaluit, *island*, Marshall Islands, **139** F4
Jamaame, Somalia, **369** H3
Jamaica, *country*, Caribbean Sea, **409** R7, *378, 379, 388, 393*
Jamaica Channel, Haiti/ Jamaica, **429** G3
Jamālpur, Bangladesh, **214** D4
Jamanota, *mountain peak*, Aruba, **461** B3
Jamanxin, *river*, Brazil, **452** B5
Jamari, *river*, Brazil, **455** F2
Jambi, Indonesia, **200** C3
Jambi, *province*, Indonesia, **200** C3
Jamboeye, *river*, Indonesia, **200** B1
Jambongan, Pulau, *island*, Malaysia, **201** G1
Jambuair, Tanjong, *point*, Indonesia, **200** B1
James, Isla, *island*, Chile, **460** B2
James, *river*, U.S.A., **420** D2
James Bay, Canada, **415** P5
Jamesābād, Pakistan, **218** B4
Jamestown, New York, U.S.A., **421** P4, *91*
Jamestown, North Dakota, U.S.A., **420** D2
Jamestown, St Helena, **373** B, *355*
Jamkhandi, India, **216** C2
Jammerbugten, *bay*, Denmark, **286** D4
Jammu, India, **218** C2
Jammu and Kashmīr, *state*, India, **218** C2, *145, 169*
Jāmnagar, India, **218** B5
Jāmpur, Pakistan, **218** B3
Jämsä, Finland, **287** M2
Jamsah, Egypt, **363** F3
Jamshedpur, India, **219** F5
Jamtari, Nigeria, **365** G3
Jämtland, *county*, Sweden, **284** F5
Jamūi, India, **219** F4
Jan Mayen, *Norwegian dependency*, Greenland Sea, **471** D8, *231, 389, 390*
Jan Mayen Ridge, *underwater feature*, Atlantic Ocean, **477** G1
Janāb Kurdufān, *state*, Sudan, **366** D2
Janaúba, Brazil, **457** E4
Janaucu, Ilha, *island*, Brazil, **452** C3
Jand, Pakistan, **218** B2
Jandaq, Iran, **221** F2
Jandia, Punta de, *point*, Islas Canarias, Spain, **373** B4
Jane Peak, *mountain peak*, New Zealand, **133** B7
Janesville, U.S.A., **421** J4
Jangeru, Indonesia, **201** G3
Jangipur, India, **219** F4
Janīn, West Bank, **225** C3
Janja, Bosnia and Herzegovina, **296** B3
Janjina, Croatia, **294** F4
Janos, Mexico, **430** C2
Jánoshalma, Hungary, **289** J5
Jánosháza, Hungary, **289** H5
Janów Lubelski, Poland, **289** L3
Janów Podlaski, Poland, **289** L2
Jänsmässholmen, Sweden, **284** F5
Januária, Brazil, **457** E4
Janūb Dārfūr, *state*, Sudan, **366** B2
Janzé, France, **290** D3
Jaorā, India, **218** C5
Japan, *country*, Asia, **197** Q6, *22, 30, 31, 40, 42, 44, 50, 61, 73, 75, 76, 82, 87, 90, 91, 92, 93, 94, 95, 96, 97, 110, 113, 115, 117, 118, 120, 124, 144, 145, 150, 160, 162, 163, 164, 165, 240, 272, 382, 385, 386, 440*
Japan Basin, *underwater feature*, Sea of Japan, **478** C2
Japan Trench, *underwater feature*, Pacific Ocean, **478** D2
Japurá, Brazil, **451** E4
Japura, Indonesia, **200** C3
Japurá, *river*, Brazil, **451** F5
Jaqué, Panama, **429** F6
Jaques Cartier, Mont, *mountain peak*, Canada, **416** J5
Jaraguá do Sul, Brazil, **459** H3
Jaraicejo, Spain, **292** E3
Jarama, *river*, Spain, **293** F2
Jarandilla de la Vera, Spain, **292** E2
Jarash, Jordan, **225** C3
Jarauçu, *river*, Brazil, **452** C4
Jarbah, Jazīrat, *island*, Tunisia, **361** J2
Jardim, Brazil, **456** B5
Jardines de la Reina, Archipélago de los, *islands*, Cuba, **429** F2
Jargalang, China, **211** H4
Jargalant, Arhangay, Mongolia, **213** J3
Jargalant, Govĭ-Altay, Mongolia, **213** H3
Jargalant, Töv, Mongolia, **210** D2
Jargalthaan, Mongolia, **210** E3
Jargeau, France, **290** F3
Jari, *river*, Brazil, **452** C3
Jarīd, Shaṭṭ al, *lake*, Tunisia, **361** H2, *315*
Jarjīs, Tunisia, **362** B2
Järna, Kopparberg, Sweden, **286** G2
Järna, Stockholm, Sweden, **287** H3
Jarny, France, **291** G2
Jarocin, Poland, **289** H3
Jarod, India, **218** D5
Jarosław, Poland, **289** L4
Jarrāhi, *river*, Iran, **220** E2
Jarrell, U.S.A., **424** D4
Jartai, China, **210** D5
Jaru, Brazil, **455** F3
Jarud Qi, China, **211** H3
Järva-Jaani, Estonia, **287** M3
Järvenpää, Finland, **287** M2
Jarvis Island, *U.S. territory*, Pacific Ocean, **131** J2, *122, 123, 386*
Järvsö, Sweden, **286** H2
Jashpurnagar, India, **219** F5
Jašiūnai, Lithuania, **287** M5
Jāsk, Iran, **221** G3
Jasło, Poland, **289** K4
Jasper, Alabama, U.S.A., **425** J3
Jasper, Arkansas, U.S.A., **424** F2
Jasper, Canada, **413** K5
Jasper, Florida, U.S.A., **425** L4
Jasper, Georgia, U.S.A., **425** K2
Jasper, Indiana, U.S.A., **421** K6
Jasper, Texas, U.S.A., **424** F4
Jastrebarsko, Croatia, **294** E3
Jastrowie, Poland, **289** H2
Jastrzebie Zdroj, Poland, **289** J4
Jászárokszállás, Hungary, **289** J5
Jászberény, Hungary, **289** J5
Jataí, Brazil, **456** C4
Jatapu, *river*, Brazil, **451** G4
Jāti, Pakistan, **218** B4
Jatiluhur, Danau, *lake*, Indonesia, **201** D4
Jaú, Brazil, **459** H2
Jáua, Meseta del Cerro, *mountain range*, Venezuela, **451** F3
Jauaperi, *river*, Brazil, **451** G4
Jauja, Peru, **454** C3
Jaunjelgava, Latvia, **287** M4
Jaunpiebalga, Latvia, **287** N4
Jaunpils, Latvia, **287** L4
Jaunpur, India, **219** E4
Jauru, Brazil, **456** B5
Jauru, *river*, Brazil, **456** A4
Java *see* Jawa, *island*, Indonesia, **201** E5, *42, 50, 54, 56, 60, 75, 86, 127, 148, 149, 439*
Java Sea, Indonesia, **201** F4
Java Trench, *underwater feature*, Indian Ocean, **476** F4
Javādi Hills, India, **216** D3
Javalambre, *mountain peak*, Spain, **293** G2
Javarthushuu, Mongolia, **210** F2
Jávea, Spain, **293** H3
Javořice, *mountain peak*, Czech Republic, **289** G4
Jävre, Sweden, **284** K4
Javron, France, **290** D2
Jawa (Java), *island*, Indonesia, **201** E5, *42, 50, 54, 56, 60, 75, 86, 127, 148, 149, 439*
Jawa Barat, *province*, Indonesia, **201** D4
Jawa Tengah, *province*, Indonesia, **201** E4
Jawa Timur, *province*, Indonesia, **201** E5
Jawabarat, *province*, Indonesia, **201** D4
Jawand, Afghanistan, **218** A2
Jawbān Bayk, Syria, **225** D1
Jawhar, Somalia, **367** G4
Jawor, Poland, **289** H3
Jay Em, U.S.A., **419** M5
Jaya, Puncak, *mountain peak*, Indonesia, **199** G4
Jayanca, Peru, **454** B2
Jayapura, Indonesia, **199** H3
Jayawijaya, Pegunungan, *mountain range*, Indonesia, **199** G4
Jaynagar, India, **219** F4
Jaypur, India, **217** E2
Jayrūd, Syria, **225** D3
Jazīreh-ye Forūr, Iran, **221** F3
Jeanerette, U.S.A., **424** G5
Jebba, Nigeria, **365** E3
Jebel, Romania, **296** C3
Jedburgh, Scotland, U.K., **308** G5
Jeddito, U.S.A., **423** H4
Jędrzejów, Poland, **289** K3
Jedwabne, Poland, **289** L2
Jefferson, Mount, *mountain peak*, Nevada, U.S.A., **422** E2
Jefferson, Mount, *mountain peak*, Oregon, U.S.A., **418** D4
Jefferson, U.S.A., **424** E3
Jefferson City, Missouri, U.S.A., **420** G6
Jefferson City, Tennessee, U.S.A., **425** L1, *386*
Jeffrey City, U.S.A., **419** L5
Jeffrey's Bay, South Africa, **370** D5
Jeffryes, Mount, *mountain peak*, Macquarie Island, **134** R11
Jega, Nigeria, **365** E2
Jejuí Guazú, *river*, Paraguay, **459** F2
Jēkabpils, Latvia, **287** M4
Jektvik, Norway, **284** F3
Jeldesa, Ethiopia, **367** F3
Jelenia Góra, Poland, **289** G3
Jelgava, Latvia, **287** L4
Jeli, Malaysia, **200** C1
Jellicoe, Canada, **415** L7
Jemaluang, Malaysia, **200** C2
Jember, Indonesia, **201** F5
Jeminay, China, **212** E3
Jempang, Danau, *lake*, Indonesia, **201** F3
Jena, Germany, **288** E3
Jendouba, Tunisia, **295** B7
Jenner, Canada, **413** P6
Jennings, U.S.A., **424** F4
Jenpeg, Canada, **414** E4
Jensen, U.S.A., **423** J1
Jepara, Indonesia, **201** E4
Jepua, Finland, **285** L5
Jequié, Brazil, **457** F3
Jequitaí, Brazil, **457** E4
Jequitinhonha, Brazil, **457** F4
Jequitinhonha, *river*, Brazil, **457** F4
Jerada, Morocco, **361** F2
Jerbar, Sudan, **369** F1
Jérémie, Haiti, **429** G3
Jeremoabo, Brazil, **457** F3
Jerez de García Salinas, Mexico, **430** E4
Jeréz de la Frontera, Spain, **292** D4
Jergucat, Albania, **297** C6
Jericho *see* Arīḥā, West Bank, **25**, C4, *182*
Jerilderie, Australia, **135** K6
Jerome, U.S.A., **418** G5
Jerramungup, Australia, **134** D5
Jersey, *island*, Channel Islands, **290** C2, *228, 229, 278, 279*
Jersey City, U.S.A., **426** C4
Jersey Shore, U.S.A., **426** B4
Jerseyville, U.S.A., **420** H6
Jerumenha, Brazil, **453** E5
Jerusalem *see* Yerushalayim, Israel, **225** C4, *75, 90, 91, 179, 192, 193*
Jesi, Italy, **294** D4
Jessen, Germany, **288** F3
Jessheim, Norway, **286** E2
Jessore, Bangladesh, **214** D5
Jesup, U.S.A., **425** M4
Jesús María, Argentina, **458** D4
Jesús María, Boca de, *river mouth*, Mexico, **431** F3
Jetait, Canada, **414** D3
Jetmore, U.S.A., **420** D6
Jetpur, India, **218** B5
Jever, Germany, **288** C2
Jeziorak, Jeziora, *lake*, Poland, **289** J2
Jha Jha, India, **219** F4
Jhābua, India, **218** C5
Jhal, Pakistan, **218** A3
Jhang Sadr, Pakistan, **218** C3
Jhānsi, India, **218** D4
Jhārsuguda, India, **219** F5
Jhatpat, Pakistan, **218** B3
Jhelum, Pakistan, **218** C2
Jhelum, *river*, Pakistan, **218** C2, *173*
Jhenida, Bangladesh, **214** D5
Jhumri Tilaiyā, India, **219** F4
Ji Xian, Shanxi, China, **210** E5
Ji Xian, Tianjin Shi, China, **210** G4
Jia Xian, China, **210** E5
Jiaganj-Azimganj, India, **219** G4
Jiahe, Guangdong, China, **207** A2
Jiahe, Hunan, China, **206** C3
Jialing, *river*, China, **215** H3
Jiamusi, China, **211** K3
Ji'an, Jiangxi, China, **206** C3
Ji'an, Jilin, China, **211** J4
Jianchuan, China, **215** F4
Jiande, China, **206** D2
Jiang'an, China, **215** H3
Jiange, China, **215** H2
Jianggao, China, **207** A2
Jianghua, China, **206** B3
Jiangjin, China, **215** H3
Jiangjunmiao, China, **212** F3
Jiangle, China, **206** D3
Jiangling, China, **206** C2
Jiangluo, China, **215** H2
Jiangmen, China, **206** C4
Jiangsu, *province*, China, **206** D1, *161*
Jiangxi, *province*, China, **206** C3, *161*
Jiangxigou, China, **213** J5
Jiangyin, China, **206** E2
Jiangyou, China, **215** H3
Jianhu, China, **206** D1
Jianli, China, **206** C2
Jianning, China, **206** D3
Jian'ou, China, **206** D3
Jianquanzi, China, **213** H4
Jianshi, China, **206** B2
Jianshui, China, **215** G5
Jianyang, Fujian, China, **206** D3
Jianyang, Sichuan, China, **215** H3
Jiaocheng, China, **210** F5
Jiaohe, Hebei, China, **210** G5
Jiaohe, Jilin, China, **211** J4
Jiaojiang, China, **206** E2
Jiaokou, China, **210** E5
Jiaoling, China, **206** D3
Jiaonan, China, **211** G6
Jiaozhou, China, **211** H5
Jiaozuo, China, **206** C1
Jiasa, China, **215** G4
Jiashan, Anhui, China, **206** D1
Jiashan, Zhejiang, China, **206** E2
Jiashi, China, **212** C5
Jiawang, China, **206** D1
Jiaxing, China, **206** E2
Jiayin, China, **211** K2

Jiayuguan, China, **213** H5
Jiazi, China, **206** D4
Jibou, Romania, **296** D2
Jiddah, Saudi Arabia, **363** G4
Jiddat al Ḥarāsīs, *desert*, Oman, **221** G5
Jiddī, Jabal al, *mountain peak*, Egypt, **225** B4
Jiekkevarre, *mountain peak*, Norway, **284** J2
Jieshi Wan, *bay*, China, **206** C4
Jieshou, China, **206** C1
Ješjavrre, *lake*, Norway, **285** M2
Jiexiu, China, **210** E5
Jieyang, China, **206** D4
Jieznas, Lithuania, **287** M5
Jigawa, *state*, Nigeria, **365** F2
Jigzhi, China, **215** G2
Jihlava, Czech Republic, **289** G4
Jihlava, *river*, Czech Republic, **289** G4
Jihoceský, *administrative region*, Czech Republic, **289** F4
Jihomoravský, *administrative region*, Czech Republic, **289** G4
Jijel, Algeria, **361** H1
Jijiga, Ethiopia, **367** F3
Jilf al Kabīr, Haḍabat al, *plain*, Egypt, **362** E4
Jili Hu, *lake*, China, **212** E3
Jilib, Somalia, **369** H2
Jilin, China, **211** J4, *161*
Jilin, *province*, China, **211** J4
Jiloca, *river*, Spain, **293** G2
Jilong, China, **207** D3
Jīma, Ethiopia, **367** E3
Jimaní, Haiti, **429** H3
Jimbolia, Romania, **296** C3
Jimena de la Frontera, Spain, **292** E4
Jiménez, Mexico, **430** D3
Jimenez, Philippines, **204** C4
Jimo, China, **211** H5
Jimsar, China, **212** F3
Jimulco, *mountain peak*, Mexico, **430** E3
Jinan, China, **210** G5, *161*
Jinchai, China, **206** B3
Jinchang, China, **213** J5
Jincheng, China, **206** C1
Jinchuan, China, **215** G3
Jīnd, India, **218** D3
Jindřichuv Hradec, Czech Republic, **289** G4
Jing Xian, Anhui, China, **206** D2
Jing Xian, Hunan, China, **206** B3
Jingbian, China, **210** E5
Jingchuan, China, **215** H2
Jingde, China, **206** D2
Jingdezhen, China, **206** D2
Jinggu, China, **215** G5
Jinghai, Guangdong, China, **206** D4
Jinghai, Tianjin Shi, China, **210** G5
Jinghe, China, **212** D3
Jinghong, China, **215** G5
Jingmen, China, **206** C2
Jingning, China, **215** H2
Jingshan, China, **206** C2
Jingtai, China, **210** D5
Jingxi, China, **215** H5
Jingyu, China, **211** J4
Jingyuan, China, **210** D5
Jingzhi, China, **211** G5
Jinhua, China, **206** D2
Jining, Nei Mongol Zizhiqu, China, **210** F4
Jining, Shandong, China, **206** D1
Jinja, Uganda, **369** F2, *340*
Jinjiang, Fujian, China, **206** D3
Jinjiang, Yunnan, China, **215** G4
Jinjuling, China, **207** B3
Jinka, Ethiopia, **369** G1
Jinkouhe, China, **215** G3
Jinkuang, China, **215** G3
Jinmen Dao, *island*, Taiwan, **206** D3
Jinotega, Nicaragua, **428** D4
Jinotepe, Nicaragua, **428** D5
Jinsha, China, **215** H4
Jinsha (Yangtze), *river*, China, **215** F3, *30, 51, 64, 65, 70, 144, 158, 159, 160, 161*
Jinshantun, China, **211** K3
Jinshi, China, **206** B2
Jinta, China, **213** H5
Jintan, China, **206** D2
Jintang, China, **215** H3
Jinxi, Jiangshi, China, **206** D3
Jinxi, Liaoning, China, **211** H4
Jinxiang, China, **206** D1
Jinzhou, S. Liaoning, China, **211** H5
Jinzhou, W. Liaoning, China, **211** H4
Jipijapa, Ecuador, **450** B4
Jirin Gol, China, **210** G3
Jirjā, Egypt, **363** F3
Jirriiban, Somalia, **367** G3
Jishan, China, **206** B1
Jishou, China, **206** B2
Jisr ash Shughūr, Syria, **225** D2
Jitra, Malaysia, **200** C1
Jiu, *river*, Romania, **296** D3
Jiu'ao Dao, *island*, China, **207** B4
Jiucai Ling, *mountain peak*, China, **206** B3
Jiudengkou, China, **210** D5
Jiufo, China, **207** B2
Jiuhe, China, **207** D2
Jiujiang, China, **206** C2
Jiuling Shan, *mountain range*, China, **206** C2
Jiulong, China, **215** G3
Jiulong (Kowloon), China, **207** C4
Jiuquan, China, **213** H5
Jiutai, China, **211** J3
Jiuyuhang, China, **206** D2
Jiuzhan, Heilongjiang, China, **211** J2
Jiuzhan, Jilin, China, **211** J4
Jiuzhou, China, **215** H4
Jīwani, Pakistan, **221** H3
Jiwen, China, **211** H2
Jixi, Anhui, China, **206** D2
Jixi, Heilongjiang, China, **211** K3
Jixian, China, **211** K3
Jīzān, Saudi Arabia, **363** H5
Jizzakh, Uzbekistan, **222** H4
Joaçaba, Brazil, **459** G3
Joal-Fadiout, Senegal, **364** A2
João Pessoa, Brazil, **453** G5
João Pinheiro, Brazil, **456** D4
Joaquín V. González, Argentina, **458** D2
Jobat, India, **218** C5
Jock, Sweden, **285** L3
Jódar, Spain, **293** F4
Jodhpur, India, **218** C4
Joensuu, Finland, **287** P1
Jōetsu, Japan, **209** G3
Jofane, Mozambique, **371** F3
Jogbani, India, **219** F4
Jogbura, Nepal, **218** E3
Jõgeva, Estonia, **287** N3
Jogues, Canada, **415** N7
Johannesburg, South Africa, **371** E4, *97*
Johannesburg, U.S.A., **422** E4
John Day, *river*, U.S.A., **418** D4
John o'Groats, Scotland, U.K., **308** F2
Johnson, Pico de, *mountain peak*, Mexico, **430** B2
Johnson City, Kansas, U.S.A., **423** N3
Johnson City, Tennessee, U.S.A., **421** M7
Johnsons Crossing, Canada, **412** C1
Johnston, Wales, U.K., **304** B3
Johnston Atoll, *U.S. territory*, Pacific Ocean, **139** H3, *123, 124, 386*
Johnstone, Scotland, U.K., **308** E5
Johnstown, Ireland, **309** E5
Johor, Selat, *strait*, Malaysia/Singapore, **200** J6, *151*
Johor, *state*, Malaysia, **200** C2
Johor Baharu, Malaysia, **200** C2
Jõhvi, Estonia, **287** N3
Joigny, France, **291** F3
Joinville, Brazil, **459** H3
Joinville, France, **291** G2
Jokkmokk, Sweden, **284** J3
Jökulsá á Brú, *river*, Iceland, **284** Z7
Jolfā, Iran, **222** D5
Joliet, U.S.A., **421** J5
Joliette, Canada, **416** E6
Jolo, Philippines, **204** C5
Jolo Island, Philippines, **204** C5
Jombo, *river*, Angola, **368** C5
Jomppala, Finland, **285** N2
Jonava, Lithuania, **287** M5
Jondal, Norway, **286** C2
Jonê, China, **215** G2
Jones, Cape, Canada, **411** K3
Jones Sound, Canada, **411** L2
Jonesboro, Arkansas, U.S.A., **424** G2
Jonesboro, Louisiana, U.S.A., **424** F3
Jonesville, U.S.A., **425** M2
Joniškis, Lithuania, **287** L4
Jönköping, *county*, Sweden, **286** F4
Jönköping, Sweden, **286** G4
Jonquière, Canada, **416** F5
Joplin, Missouri, U.S.A., **420** F7
Joplin, Montana, U.S.A., **419** J2
Jora, India, **218** D4
Jordan, *country*, Asia, **196** E7, *146, 179, 180, 181*
Jordan, *river*, Israel/Jordan, **225** C4, *179, 180, 182, 193*
Jordan, U.S.A., **419** L3
Jordan Valley, U.S.A., **418** F5
Jordão, *river*, Brazil, **459** G2
Jordet, Norway, **286** F2
Jorhāt, India, **219** H4
Jormlien, Sweden, **284** G4
Jörn, Sweden, **284** K4
Joroinen, Finland, **287** N1
Jos, Nigeria, **365** F3, *329*
José Agustín Palacios, Bolivia, **455** E3
José Bonifácio, Brazil, **455** G3
José de San Martin, Argentina, **460** C2
José Pedro Varela, Uruguay, **459** F4
Joselândia, Brazil, **456** B4
Joseni, Romania, **296** E2
Joseph Bonaparte Gulf, Australia, **134** F1
Joseph, Lake, Canada, **416** J3
Joseph, U.S.A., **418** F4
Josephstaal, Papua New Guinea, **140** B4
Josipdol, Croatia, **294** E3
Jössefors, Sweden, **286** F3
Jostedalsbreen, *glacier*, Norway, **286** C2
Jotunheimen, *mountain range*, Norway, **286** D2
Jouberton, South Africa, **371** E4
Joukokylä, Finland, **285** P4
Joussard, Canada, **413** M4
Joutsa, Finland, **287** N2
Joutseno, Finland, **287** P2
Joutsijärvi, Finland, **285** P3
Jowai, India, **219** H4
Joyce, U.S.A., **418** C2
Joyeuse, France, **291** G4
Jreïda, Mauritania, **360** C5
Ju Xian, China, **206** D1
Juan de Fuca, Strait of, Canada/U.S.A., **418** B2
Juan de Nova, Île, *island*, Réunion, **372** A4, *354*
Juan Fernández, Archipiélago, *islands*, Chile, **449** D7
Juanjuí, Peru, **454** C2
Juankoski, Finland, **285** P5
Juárez, Sierra de, *mountain range*, Mexico, **430** A1
Juazeiro, Brazil, **457** F2
Juazeiro do Norte, Brazil, **453** F5
Juazohn, Liberia, **364** C3
Juba, Sudan, **369** F2
Jubayl, Egypt, **225** B5
Jubayl (Biblos), Lebanon, **225** C2
Jubb al Jarrāḥ, Syria, **225** D2
Jubba, *river*, Somalia, **369** H2, *339*
Jubbada Dhexe, *administrative region*, Somalia, **369** H2
Jubbada Hoose, *administrative region*, Somalia, **369** H2
Jubbah, Saudi Arabia, **363** H3
Jubilee Lake, Australia, **134** F4
Júcar, *river*, Spain, **293** G3
Juçara, Brazil, **457** F3
Juchitán de Zaragoza, Mexico, **431** G5
Juchitlán, Mexico, **430** D4
Jucurucu, *river*, Brazil, **457** F4
Judenburg, Austria, **289** G5
Judian, China, **215** F4
Juh, China, **210** E5
Juigalpa, Nicaragua, **428** D4
Juillac, France, **290** E4
Juiná, *river*, Brazil, **455** G3
Juist, *island*, Germany, **288** C2
Juiz de Fora, Brazil, **457** E5
Jujuy, *province*, Argentina, **458** C2
Julaca, Bolivia, **455** E5
Julau, Malaysia, **201** E2
Jule, Norway, **284** F4
Juli, Peru, **455** E4
Julia Creek, Australia, **135** J3
Juliaca, Peru, **455** D4
Julianadorp, Curaçao, Netherlands Antilles, **461** C3
Julianadorp, Netherlands, **288** B2
Julianatop, *mountain peak*, Suriname, **452** B2
Jülich, Germany, **288** C3
Julijske Alpe, *mountain range*, Slovenia, **294** D2
Jullouville, France, **290** D2
Jullundur, India, **218** C3
Julwānia, India, **218** C5
Jumbilla, Peru, **454** C1
Jumilla, Spain, **293** G3
Juminen, Finland, **285** N5
Jun Bulen, China, **211** G3
Jūnāgadh, India, **218** B5
Junāgarh, India, **219** E6
Junan, China, **206** D1
Junaynah, Ra's al, *mountain peak*, Egypt, **225** B5
Juncal, Cerro, *mountain peak*, Chile, **458** B4
Junction, Texas, U.S.A., **424** C4
Junction, Utah, U.S.A., **423** G2
Junction City, U.S.A., **418** C4
Jundiaí, Brazil, **459** H2
Juneau, U.S.A., **412** B2, *383, 386*
Jungfrau, *mountain peak*, Switzerland, **291** H3
Junggar Pendi, *basin*, China, **212** E3, *144, 158*
Juniata, *river*, U.S.A., **426** B4
Junín, Argentina, **458** E5
Junín, Peru, **454** C3
Junín de los Andes, Argentina, **460** C1
Junlian, China, **215** H3
Juno, U.S.A., **424** B4
Junqalī, *state*, Sudan, **366** D3
Junqalī, Sudan, **366** D3
Junsele, Sweden, **284** H5
Juntura, U.S.A., **418** E5
Juntusranta, Finland, **285** P4
Juodkrantė, Lithuania, **287** K5
Juoksenki, Finland, **285** L3
Juorkuna, Finland, **285** N4
Juozapinės kalnas, *mountain peak*, Lithuania, **287** M5, *237*
Juquiá, Brazil, **459** H2
Juquiá, *river*, Brazil, **459** H2
Jura, *island*, Scotland, U.K., **308** D5
Jura, *mountain range*, Switzerland, **291** H3, *239, 245, 247*
Jūra, *river*, Lithuania, **287** L5
Jura, Sound of, Scotland, U.K., **308** D5
Jurací, Brazil, **457** F3
Juradó, Colombia, **450** C2
Jurbarkas, Lithuania, **287** L5
Jurf ad Darāwīsh, Jordan, **225** C4
Jurh, China, **211** H3
Jurilovca, Romania, **296** G3
Jūrmala, Latvia, **287** L4
Jurong, Selat, *strait*, Singapore, **200** J7
Jurong East, Singapore, **200** J6
Jurong Industrial Estate, Singapore, **200** J7
Jurong Town, Singapore, **200** J6
Jurong West, Singapore, **200** J6
Juruá, Brazil, **451** E5
Juruá, *river*, Brazil, **451** F5
Juruá Mirim, *river*, Brazil, **454** D2
Juruena, *river*, Brazil, **452** A5
Juruti, Brazil, **452** B4
Juruti Velho, Brazil, **452** B4
Jurva, Finland, **285** K5
Jus Hua, China, **211** G3
Jussey, France, **291** G3
Justiceburg, U.S.A., **424** B3
Justo Daract, Argentina, **458** D4
Jutaí, Central Amazonas, Brazil, **451** E5
Jutaí, N. Amazonas, Brazil, **451** E5
Jutaí, *river*, Brazil, **451** E5
Jüterbog, Germany, **288** F3
Juti, Brazil, **459** F2
Jutiapa, Guatemala, **428** C4
Juticalpa, Honduras, **428** D4
Juuka, Finland, **285** P5
Juuma, Finland, **285** P3
Juva, Finland, **287** N2
Juventud, Isla de la, *island*, Cuba, **429** E2, *393*
Juye, China, **206** C1
Jūyom, Iran, **221** F3
Juzi, China, **207** C1
Jwaneng, Botswana, **370** D3
Jyderup, Denmark, **286** E5
Jylland, *peninsula*, Denmark, **286** D4
Jyrkkä, Finland, **285** N5
Jyväskylä, Finland, **287** M1


## K


Ka Lae, *point*, Hawaiian Islands, U.S.A., **422** R10
Kaala-Gomén, New Caledonia, **141** A3
Kaamanen, Finland, **285** N2
Kaambooni, Somalia, **367** F5
Kaaresuvanto, Finland, **285** L2
Kaba, *river*, China, **212** E2
Kabaena, Pulau, *island*, Indonesia, **198** C4
Kabala, Sierra Leone, **364** B3
Kabale, Uganda, **369** E3
Kabalebo stuwmeer, *lake*, Suriname, **452** B2
Kabalo, Democratic Republic of the Congo, **369** E4
Kabambare, Democratic Republic of the Congo, **369** E3
Kabanjahe, Indonesia, **200** B2
Kabankalan, Philippines, **204** C4
Kabara, *island*, Fiji, **141** A4
Kabardino-Balkarskaya, Respublika, *republic*, Russian Federation, **222** C4
Kabare, Democratic Republic of the Congo, **369** E3
Kabasalan, Philippines, **204** C5
Kåbdalis, Sweden, **284** J3
Kabelvåg, Norway, **284** G2
Kabin Buri, Thailand, **202** D3
Kabinda, Democratic Republic of the Congo, **368** D4
Kabkābīyah, Sudan, **366** B2
Kābol (Kabul), Afghanistan, **218** B2, *184*
Kabompo, Zambia, **368** D5
Kabongo, Democratic Republic of the Congo, **369** E4
Kabūdarāhang, Iran, **363** J1
Kabul *see* Kābol, Afghanistan, **218** B2, *184*
Kabunda, Democratic Republic of the Congo, **369** E5
Kabūshīyah, Sudan, **363** F5
Kabwe, Zambia, **369** E5
Kačanik, Kosovo, **296** C4
Kachalola, Zambia, **369** F5
Kachchh, Gulf of, India, **218** B5, *169*
Kachia, Nigeria, **365** F3
Kachin State, *state*, Myanmar, **205** C2
Kachiry, Kazakhstan, **223** K2
Kadaiyanallur, India, **216** D4
Kadamatt Island, India, **216** C4
Kadan Kyun (King Island), *island*, Myanmar, **202** C3
Kadarkút, Hungary, **289** H5
Kadavu, *island*, Fiji, **141** A4
Kadavu Passage, *strait*, Fiji, **141** A4
Kadiolo, Mali, **364** C2
Kadiondola, *mountain peak*, Guinea, **364** B2
Kadiri, India, **216** D3
Kadoka, U.S.A., **420** C4
Kadoma, Zimbabwe, **371** E2
Kaduna, Nigeria, **365** F2
Kaduna, *state*, Nigeria, **365** F2
Kāduqlī, Sudan, **366** C2
Kaduy, Russian Federation, **299** F3

Kadwa, *river*, India, **218** C6
Kaédi, Mauritania, **364** B1,
Kaélé, Cameroon, **365** G2
Kaeo, New Zealand, **132** D2
Kaesŏng, North Korea, **208** D3
Kāf, Saudi Arabia, **225** D4
Kafakumba, Democratic Republic of the Congo, **368** D4
Kaffrine, Senegal, **364** A2
Kafia Kingi, Sudan, **366** B3
Kafin Hausa, Nigeria, **365** G2
Kafireas, Akra, *point*, Greece, **297** E6
Kåfjord, Norway, **285** M1
Kafr ash Shaykh, Egypt, **225** A4
Kafr Buhum, Syria, **225** D2
Kafr Sa'd, Egypt, **225** A4
Kafue, *river*, Zambia, **369** E5/E6
Kafue, Zambia, **369** E6
Kaga, Japan, **209** G3
Kaga Bandoro, Central African Republic, **366** A3
Kāgān, Pakistan, **218** C2
Kåge, Sweden, **284** K4
Kågen, *island*, Norway, **284** K2
Kagera, *administrative region*, Tanzania, **369** F3
Kagera, *river*, Rwanda/Tanzania/Uganda, **366** D5, *343*
Kagmar, Sudan, **366** D2
Kagologolo, Indonesia, **200** B3
Kagoshima, Japan, **208** E5
Kahama, Tanzania, **369** F3
Kahān, Pakistan, **218** B3
Kahayan, *river*, Indonesia, **201** F3
Kahemba, Democratic Republic of the Congo, **368** C4
Kaherekoau Mountains, *mountain range*, New Zealand, **133** A7
Kahlotus, U.S.A., **418** E3
Kahnūj, Iran, **221** G3
Kahoe, New Zealand, **132** D2
Kahoka, U.S.A., **420** H5
Kahoolawe, *island*, Hawaiian Islands, U.S.A., **422** R9
Kahperusvaarat, *mountain peak*, Finland, **284** K2
Kahramanmaraş, Turkey, **224** E5
Kahuitara Point, Chatham Islands, New Zealand, **133** Q16
Kahuku, Hawaiian Islands, U.S.A., **422** R9
Kahului, *island*, Hawaiian Islands, U.S.A., **422** R9
Kahuranaki, *mountain peak*, New Zealand, **132** F4
Kai, Kepulauan, *islands*, Indonesia, **199** F4
Kai, Tanjong, *point*, Indonesia, **198** B3
Kai Besar, Pulau, *island*, Indonesia, **199** F4
Kai Iwi, New Zealand, **132** E4
Kai Kecil, Pulau, *island*, Indonesia, **199** F4
Kai Xian, China, **206** B2
Kaiama, Nigeria, **365** E3
Kaiapit, Papua New Guinea, **140** B4
Kaiapoi, New Zealand, **133** D6
Kaibito, U.S.A., **423** H3
Kaifeng, China, **206** C1
Kaikohe, New Zealand, **132** D2
Kaikoura, New Zealand, **133** D6
Kaikoura Peninsula, New Zealand, **133** D6
Kaili, China, **215** H4
Kailu, China, **211** H4
Kailua-Kona, Hawaiian Islands, U.S.A., **422** R10
Kaimana, Indonesia, **199** F3
Kaimar, China, **215** E2
Käina, Estonia, **287** L3
Kainan, Japan, **209** F4
Kainantu, Papua New Guinea, **140** B4
Kainji Reservoir, Nigeria, **365** E2
Kainulasjärvi, Sweden, **285** L3
Kaipara Harbour, New Zealand, **132** D3
Kaiping, China, **206** C4
Kairakau Beach, New Zealand, **132** F4
Kairiru Island, Papua New Guinea, **140** A3
Kaironi, Indonesia, **199** F3
Kairouan, Tunisia, **295** C8
Kairuku, Papua New Guinea, **140** B5
Kaiserslautern, Germany, **288** C4
Kaišiadorys, Lithuania, **287** M5
Kait, Tanjong, *point*, Indonesia, **200** D3
Kaitangata, New Zealand, **133** B8
Kaithal, India, **218** D3
Kaitum, Sweden, **284** K3
Kaitumälven, *river*, Sweden, **284** J3
Kaiwi Channel, Hawaiian Islands, U.S.A., **422** R9
Kaiyuan, Jilin, China, **211** J3
Kaiyuan, Liaoning, China, **211** J4
Kaiyuan, Yunnan, China, **215** G5
Kajaani, Finland, **285** N4
Kajabbi, Australia, **135** J3
Kajuru, Nigeria, **365** F2
Kaka, Sudan, **366** D2
Kaka Point, New Zealand, **133** B8
Kakamas, South Africa, **370** D4
Kakamega, Kenya, **369** F2
Kakana, Andaman and Nicobar Islands, India, **217** H4
Kakaramea, New Zealand, **132** E4
Kakata, Liberia, **364** B3
Kakatahi, New Zealand, **132** E4
Kake, U.S.A., **412** C3
Kakenge, Democratic Republic of the Congo, **368** D3
Kakhovs'ke Vodoskhovyshche, *reservoir*, Ukraine, **298** D3
Kākī, Iran, **220** F3
Kākināda, India, **217** E2
Kakisa, Canada, **413** L1
Kakisa Lake, Canada, **413** K1
Kakogawa, Japan, **208** F4
Kakpin, Côte d'Ivoire, **364** D3
Kaktovik, U.S.A., **410** E3
Kala, *river*, Sri Lanka, **216** E4
Kala, Tanzania, **369** F4
Kalaallit Nunaat *see* Greenland, *Danish territory*, Arctic Ocean, **408** U1, *29, 75, 91, 234, 380, 384, 388, 389, 390, 466*
Kālābāgh, Pakistan, **218** B2
Kalabahi, Indonesia, **198** D5
Kalabakan, Malaysia, **201** G1
Kalabo, Zambia, **368** D5
Kaladar, Canada, **416** C7
Kalahari, *desert*, Botswana, **357** H9, *312, 347, 350, 351*
Kalajoki, *river*, Finland, **285** M5
Kalajoki, Finland, **285** L4
Kalak, Norway, **285** N1
Kalakoski, Finland, **287** L1
Kalalé, Benin, **365** E2
Kalaloch, U.S.A., **418** B3
Kalām, Pakistan, **218** C2
Kalamaria, Greece, **297** D5
Kalamata, Greece, **297** D7
Kalamazoo, *river*, U.S.A., **421** L4
Kalamazoo, U.S.A., **421** L4
Kalamnūr, India, **216** D2
Kalampaka, Greece, **297** C6
Kalampaki, Greece, **297** E5
Kalana, Mali, **364** C2
Kalang, *river*, Singapore, **200** K6
Kalanguy, Russian Federation, **210** G2
Kalānpur, India, **218** C4
Kālānwāli, India, **218** C3
Kalao, Pulau, *island*, Indonesia, **198** C4
Kalaotoa, Pulau, *island*, Indonesia, **198** C4
Kälarne, Sweden, **284** H5
Kalasin, Thailand, **203** D2
Kalāt, Pakistan, **218** A3
Kalatungan Mountain, *mountain peak*, Philippines, **204** D5
Kalau, *island*, Tonga, **141** B4
Kalaupapa, Hawaiian Islands, U.S.A., **422** R9
Kalavryta, Greece, **297** D6
Kalb, Ra's al, *cape*, Yemen, **220** E6
Kalbarri, Australia, **134** C4
Kale, Denizli, Turkey, **297** G7
Kale, Hatay, Turkey, **225** C1
Kalegauk, *island*, Myanmar, **202** C3
Kalehe, Democratic Republic of the Congo, **369** E3
Kalema, Democratic Republic of the Congo, **368** D3
Kalemie, Democratic Republic of the Congo, **369** E4
Kalemyo, Myanmar, **205** B3
Kalevala, Russian Federation, **285** Q4
Kalewa, Myanmar, **205** B3
Kálfafellsstaður, Iceland, **284** Z7
Kalga, Russian Federation, **211** G2
Kalgoorlie-Boulder, Australia, **134** E5
Kaliakra, Nos, *point*, Bulgaria, **298** C4
Kalibo, Philippines, **204** C4
Kalima, Democratic Republic of the Congo, **369** E3
Kalimantan Barat, *province*, Indonesia, **201** E3, *148*
Kalimantan Selatan, *province*, Indonesia, **201** F3
Kalimantan Tengah, *province*, Indonesia, **201** F3
Kalimantan Timur, *province*, Indonesia, **201** F2
Kālimpang, India, **219** G4
Kalinga, India, **219** F5
Kaliningrad, Russian Federation, **298** B2, *237, 271*
Kaliningradskaya Oblast', *province*, Russian Federation, **287** K5
Kālinjra, India, **218** C5
Kalis, Somalia, **367** G3
Kalispell, U.S.A., **418** G2
Kalisz, Poland, **289** J3
Kalisz Pomorski, Poland, **289** G2
Kaliua, Tanzania, **369** F4
Kalix, Sweden, **285** L4
Kalkan, Turkey, **297** G7
Kalkarindji, Australia, **134** G2
Kalkaska, U.S.A., **421** L3
Kalkfeld, Namibia, **370** C3
Kall, Sweden, **284** F5
Kallavesi, *lake*, Finland, **285** N5
Kallislahti, Finland, **287** P2
Kallsjön, *lake*, Sweden, **284** F5
Kalmar, *county*, Sweden, **286** G4
Kalmar, Sweden, **286** H4
Kalmykiya, Respublika, *republic*, Russian Federation, **222** D3
Kálna nad Hronom, Slovakia, **289** J4
Kalnciems, Latvia, **287** L4
Kalocsa, Hungary, **289** J5
Kalole, Democratic Republic of the Congo, **369** E3
Kalomo, Zambia, **369** E6
Kaloniya, Belarus, **289** M2
Kalpa, India, **218** D3
Kalpeni Island, India, **216** C4
Kālpi, India, **218** D4
Kalpin, China, **212** C4
Kaltanėnai, Lithuania, **287** M5
Kālu Khuhar, Pakistan, **218** A4
Kaluga, Russian Federation, **299** F5
Kalulushi, Zambia, **369** E5
Kalumburu, Australia, **134** F1
Kalundborg, Denmark, **286** E5
Kalūr Kot, Pakistan, **218** B2
Kalutara, Sri Lanka, **216** D5
Kaluzhskaya Oblast', *administrative region*, Russian Federation, **299** E5
Kalvarija, Lithuania, **287** L5
Kälviä, Finland, **285** L5
Kalvola, Finland, **287** M2
Kalvträsk, Sweden, **284** J4
Kalwapur, Nepal, **218** E3
Kalyān, India, **216** C2
Kalyāndrug, India, **216** D3
Kalyazin, Russian Federation, **299** F4
Kalymnos, Dodekanisos, Greece, **297** F7
Kalymnos, *island*, Dodekanisos, Greece, **297** F7
Kama, Democratic Republic of the Congo, **369** E3
Kama, Myanmar, **205** B4
Kamaishi, Japan, **209** H3
Kamal, Chad, **362** C4
Kamālia, Pakistan, **218** C3
Kaman, Turkey, **363** F1
Kamande, Democratic Republic of the Congo, **369** E3
Kamanjab, Namibia, **370** B2
Kamanyola, Democratic Republic of the Congo, **369** E3
Kamaron, Sierra Leone, **364** B3
Kamativi, Zimbabwe, **371** E2
Kambalda, Australia, **134** E5
Kambia, Sierra Leone, **364** B3
Kambove, Democratic Republic of the Congo, **369** E5
Kambuno, Gunung, *mountain peak*, Indonesia, **198** B3
Kamchatka, Poluostrov, *peninsula*, Russian Federation, **301** S4, *271, 272, 273*
Kamen, Bulgaria, **296** E4
Kamen'-na-Obi, Russian Federation, **223** L2
Kamena Vourla, Greece, **297** D6
Kamende, Democratic Republic of the Congo, **368** D4
Kamenica, Bosnia and Herzegovina, **294** G3
Kamenka, Kazakhstan, **222** E2
Kamenka, Russian Federation, **298** F2
Kamennogorsk, Russian Federation, **299** B2
Kamennoye, Ozero, *lake*, Russian Federation, **285** Q4
Kameno, Bulgaria, **296** F4
Kamensk-Ural'skiy, Russian Federation, **222** G1
Kamenz, Germany, **289** G3
Kameshnaya, Russian Federation, **299** G2
Kamień Pomorski, Poland, **289** G2
Kamieńsk, Poland, **289** J3
Kamin'-Kashyrs'kyy, Ukraine, **289** M3
Kamina, Democratic Republic of the Congo, **368** D4
Kamina, Togo, **364** E3
Kamloops, Canada, **412** J6
Kamnik, Slovenia, **294** E2
Kamoa Mountains, Guyana, **451** G4
Kampa, Teluk, *bay*, Indonesia, **200** D3
Kampala, Uganda, **369** F2, *340*
Kampar, Malaysia, **200** C1
Kampene, Democratic Republic of the Congo, **369** E3
Kamphaeng, Khao, *mountain peak*, Thailand, **202** C3
Kamphaeng Phet, Thailand, **202** C2
Kâmpóng Cham, Cambodia, **203** E4
Kâmpóng Chhnăng, Cambodia, **203** E3
Kâmpóng Khleăng, Cambodia, **203** E3
Kâmpóng Saôm, Cambodia, **203** D4
Kâmpóng Saôm, Chhâk, *bay*, Cambodia, **203** D4
Kâmpóng Spoe, Cambodia, **203** E4
Kâmpóng Thum, Cambodia, **203** E3
Kâmpôt, Cambodia, **203** E4
Kampti, Burkina Faso, **364** D2
Kampung, *river*, Indonesia, **199** G4
Kamrau, Teluk, *bay*, Indonesia, **199** F3
Kamsar, Guinea, **364** B2
Kamsuuma, Somalia, **369** H2
Kāmthi, India, **218** D5
Kamui-dake, *mountain peak*, Japan, **209** H2
Kamui-misaki, *point*, Japan, **209** H2
Kamuli, Uganda, **369** F2
Kamundan, *river*, Indonesia, **199** F3
Kamyanets, Belarus, **289** L2
Kam"yanets'-Podil's'kyy, Ukraine, **298** C3
Kam"yans'ke, Ukraine, **296** G3
Kamyanyuki, Belarus, **289** L2
Kāmyārān, Iran, **220** E2
Kamyen', Belarus, **299** B5
Kamyshet, Russian Federation, **223** P1
Kamyshin, Russian Federation, **222** D2
Kan, Myanmar, **205** B3
Kana, *river*, Zimbabwe, **371** E2
Kanaaupscow, *river*, Canada, **416** D2
Kanab, U.S.A., **422** G3
Kanaga Island, Aleutian Islands, U.S.A., **408** F3
Kanairiktok, *river*, Canada, **417** K2
Kanā'is, Ra's al, *point*, Egypt, **362** E2
Kanallaki, Greece, **297** C6
Kananga, Democratic Republic of the Congo, **368** D4
Kanāsar, India, **218** B4
Kanash, Russian Federation, **222** D1
Kanazawa, Japan, **209** G3
Kanbalu, Myanmar, **205** B3
Kanchenjunga, *mountain peak*, India, **214** D4, *168, 172*
Kānchipuram, India, **216** D3
Kandalaksha, Russian Federation, **285** R3
Kandalakshskiy Zaliv, *bay*, Russian Federation, **285** R3
Kandi, Benin, **365** E2
Kandi, Tanjong, *point*, Indonesia, **198** C2
Kandila, Greece, **297** C6
Kandıra, Turkey, **297** H5
Kandkhot, Pakistan, **218** B3
Kāndla, India, **218** B5
Kandreho, Madagascar, **372** B4
Kandrian, Papua New Guinea, **140** C4
Kandukūr, India, **216** D3
Kandy, Sri Lanka, **217** E5
Kane Basin, Greenland, **411** N2
Kane Fracture Zone, *tectonic feature*, Atlantic Ocean, **477** D4
Kanem, *prefecture*, Chad, **365** H1
Kaneohe, Hawaiian Islands, U.S.A., **422** R9
Kanepi, Estonia, **287** N4
Kanevka, Russian Federation, **285** U3
Kang, Botswana, **370** D3
Kangaatsiaq, Greenland, **411** P3
Kangaba, Mali, **364** C2
Kangal, Turkey, **363** G1
Kangar, Malaysia, **200** C1
Kangaroo Island, Australia, **135** H6
Kangaruma, Guyana, **451** G3
Kangaslampi, Finland, **287** P1
Kangasniemi, Finland, **287** N2
Kangbao, China, **210** F4
Kangding, China, **215** G3
Kangdong, North Korea, **208** D3
Kangean, Kepulauan, *islands*, Indonesia, **201** F4
Kangeeak Point, Canada, **411** N3
Kangen, *river*, Sudan, **366** D3
Kangeq, *cape*, Greenland, **411** Q3
Kangerlussuaq, *bay*, Greenland, **411** R3
Kangerlussuaq, Greenland, **411** P3
Kangertittivag, *bay*, Greenland, **411** S2
Kangetet, Kenya, **369** G2
Kanggye, North Korea, **208** D2
Kangikajik, *cape*, Greenland, **411** S2
Kangilinnguit, Greenland, **411** Q3
Kangiqsualujjuaq, Canada, **411** N4
Kangiqsujuaq, Canada, **411** M3
Kangirsuk, Canada, **411** M3
Kangiwa, Nigeria, **365** E2
Kangmar, S. Xizang Zizhiqu, China, **214** D3
Kangmar, W. Xizang Zizhiqu, China, **214** C3
Kangnŭng, South Korea, **208** E3
Kango, Gabon, **368** B2
Kangosjärvi, Finland, **285** L3
Kangping, China, **211** H4
Kangra, India, **218** D2

Kangrinboqê Feng, *mountain peak*, China, **218** E3
Kangro, China, **214** C2
Kangtog, China, **214** C2
Kangyidaung, Myanmar, **205** B4
Kani, Côte d'Ivoire, **364** C3
Kani, Myanmar, **205** B3
Kaniama, Democratic Republic of the Congo, **368** D4
Kanibongan, Malaysia, **201** G1
Kaniet Islands, Papua New Guinea, **140** B3
Kanigiri, India, **216** D3
Kanin Nos, Mys, *point*, Russian Federation, **300** F3
Kaniwāra, India, **218** D5
Kanjiža, Serbia, **296** C2
Kankaanpää, Finland, **287** L2
Kankakee, *river*, U.S.A., **421** J5
Kankakee, U.S.A., **421** K5
Kankan, Guinea, **364** C2
Kānker, India, **219** E5
Kankesanturai, Sri Lanka, **216** E4
Kannapolis, U.S.A., **425** M2
Kannauj, India, **218** D4
Kanniyākumāri, India, **216** D4
Kannod, India, **218** D5
Kannus, Finland, **285** L5
Kano, Nigeria, **365** F2, *329*
Kano, *state*, Nigeria, **365** F2
Kanoya, Japan, **208** E5
Kanozero, Ozero, *lake*, Russian Federation, **285** S3
Kanpur, India, **218** E4
Kansas, *river*, U.S.A., **420** E6
Kansas, *state*, U.S.A., **420** D6, *386*
Kansas City, U.S.A., **420** F6
Kansk, Russian Federation, **300** L4
Kantala, Finland, **287** N1
Kantang, Thailand, **202** C5
Kantanos, Kriti, Greece, **297** D8
Kantchari, Burkina Faso, **364** E2
Kanté, Togo, **364** E3
Kantegir, *river*, Russian Federation, **213** F1
Kānthi, India, **219** F5
Kanton, *island*, Kiribati, **139** G5
Kanuku Mountains, *mountain range*, Brazil/Guyana, **451** G3
Kanus, Namibia, **370** C4
Kānwat, India, **218** C4
Kanye, Botswana, **370** E4
Kao, *island*, Tonga, **136** D2, *114*
Kao-hsiung, Taiwan, **206** E4
Kaolack, Senegal, **364** A2
Kaolinovo, Bulgaria, **296** F4
Kaoma, Zambia, **368** D5
Kaouadja, Central African Republic, **366** B3
Kapa, *island*, Vava'u Group, Tonga, **141** B3
Kapaa, Kauai, Hawaiian Islands, U.S.A., **422** R9
Kapaau, Hawaii, Hawaiian Islands, U.S.A., **422** R9
Kapalatmada, Gunung, *mountain peak*, Indonesia, **198** D3
Kapanga, Democratic Republic of the Congo, **368** D4
Kapatu, Zambia, **369** F4
Kapellskär, Sweden, **287** J3
Kapenguria, Kenya, **369** G2
Kapingamarangi Atoll, *island*, Micronesia, **138** D4
Kapiri Mposhi, Zambia, **369** E5
Kapisillit, Greenland, **411** P3
Kapiskau, *river*, Canada, **415** N5
Kapit, Malaysia, **201** F2
Kapiti Island, New Zealand, **133** E5
Kaplice, Czech Republic, **289** G4
Kapoeta, Sudan, **369** F2
Kaposvár, Hungary, **294** F2
Kapp Norvegia, *cape*, Antarctica, **470** C3
Kappelshamn, Sweden, **287** J4
Kapsabet, Kenya, **369** G2
Kapsan, North Korea, **208** E2
Kaptiau, Indonesia, **199** G3
Kaptyrevo, Russian Federation, **223** N2
Kapuas, *river*, Kalimantan Barat, Indonesia, **201** E2
Kapuas, *river*, Kalimantan Tengah, Indonesia, **201** F3
Kapuskasing, *river*, Canada, **415** N7
Kapuskasing, Canada, **415** N7
Kapustnoye, Russian Federation, **285** S3
Kaputir, Kenya, **369** G2
Kapuvár, Hungary, **289** H5
Kara, Togo, **364** E3
Kara-Balta, Kyrgyzstan, **223** J4
Kara-Köl, Kyrgyzstan, **223** J4
Kara K'orē, Ethiopia, **367** E2
Kara-Su, Kyrgyzstan, **223** J4
Karaart, Tajikistan, **223** J5
Karabash, Russian Federation, **222** G1
Karabiğa, Turkey, **297** F5
Karabük, Turkey, **224** D4
Karaburun, Turkey, **297** F6
Karacabey, Turkey, **297** G5
Karacaköy, Turkey, **297** G5
Karaçal Tepe, *mountain peak*, Turkey, **224** D5
Karacasu, Turkey, **297** G7
Karachayevo-Cherkesskaya, Respublika, *republic*, Russian Federation, **222** C4
Karāchi, Pakistan, **218** A4, *173*
Karād, India, **216** C2
Karaganda *see* Qaraghandy, Kazakhstan, **212** B2
Karaginskiy, Ostrov, *island*, Russian Federation, **301** T4
Karagwe, Tanzania, **369** F3
Karahisar, Turkey, **297** G7
Karaidel', Russian Federation, **222** F1
Kāraikkudi, India, **216** D4
Karaj, Iran, **220** F1
Karajül, China, **212** C4
Karak, Malaysia, **200** C2
Karakalpakiya, Uzbekistan, **222** F4
Karakax, *river*, China, **212** C5
Karaki, China, **212** D5
Karakoçan, Turkey, **224** F5
Karakol, Kyrgyzstan, **223** K4
Karakoram Range, *mountain range*, Asia, **212** B5, *26, 75, 144, 168, 173*
Karaköse, Turkey, **224** F5
Karal, Chad, **365** G2
Karaman, *province*, Turkey, **225** B1
Karaman, Turkey, **224** D5
Karamay, China, **212** E3
Karamea, New Zealand, **133** D5
Karamea Bight, *bay*, New Zealand, **133** C5
Karamu, New Zealand, **132** E3
Karamyshevo, Russian Federation, **299** B4
Kāranja, India, **218** D5
Karanji, India, **218** D5
Karanjia, India, **219** F5
Karapelit, Bulgaria, **296** F4
Karapınar, Turkey, **224** D5
Karapürçek, Turkey, **297** G6
Karaqoyyn Köli, *lake*, Kazakhstan, **223** H3
Karas, *administrative region*, Namibia, **370** C4
Karas, Pulau, *island*, Indonesia, **199** F3
Karasay, China, **219** E1
Karasburg, Namibia, **370** C4
Karasjok, Norway, **285** M2
Karašjokka, *river*, Norway, **285** L2
Karasuk, Russian Federation, **223** K2
Karataş, Turkey, **225** C1
Karaterek, Kazakhstan, **223** K2
Karatoprak, Turkey, **297** F7
Karats, *lake*, Sweden, **284** J3
Karats, Sweden, **284** J3
Karatsu, Japan, **208** E4
Karatünggü, China, **212** F3
Karauli, India, **218** D4
Karavastasë, Laguna e, *lagoon*, Albania, **297** B5
Karavostasi, Cyprus, **225** B2
Karawanken, *mountain range*, Austria/Slovenia, **294** E2
Karayulgun, China, **212** D4
Karbalā', Iraq, **363** H2
Kårböle, Sweden, **286** G2
Karcag, Hungary, **289** K5
Karchat, Pakistan, **218** A4
Karditsa, Greece, **297** C6
Kärdla, Estonia, **287** L3
Karelaksha, Russian Federation, **285** R4
Kareli, India, **218** D5
Kareliya, Respublika, *republic*, Russian Federation, **299** D2
Karema, Tanzania, **369** F4
Karen, *state*, Myanmar, **202** C2
Kärendöjärvi, Sweden, **285** L3
Karenga, *river*, Russian Federation, **210** F1
Karera, India, **218** D4
Karere, New Zealand, **132** E5
Kargala, Russian Federation, **223** L1
Kargapol'ye, Russian Federation, **222** G1
Kargasok, Russian Federation, **300** K4
Kargat, Russian Federation, **223** L1
Kargıcak, Turkey, **225** B1
Kargil, India, **218** D2
Kargopol', Russian Federation, **299** G2
Kargowa, Poland, **289** G2
Karguéri, Niger, **365** G2
Karhukangas, Finland, **285** M4
Kari, Nigeria, **365** G2
Kariba, Lake, Zambia/Zimbabwe, **369** E6, *344, 346*
Kariba, Zimbabwe, **369** E6
Karibib, Namibia, **370** C3
Karigasniemi, Finland, **285** M2
Kārikāl, India, **216** D4
Karikari Peninsula, New Zealand, **132** D2
Karimata, Kepulauan, *islands*, Indonesia, **201** D3
Karimata, Selat, *strait*, Indonesia, **201** E3
Karīmnagar, India, **216** D2
Karimunjawa, Kepulauan, *islands*, Indonesia, **201** E4
Karin, Somalia, **367** G2
Karioi, Mount, *mountain peak*, New Zealand, **132** E3
Karisimbi, *mountain peak*, Rwanda, **369** E3, *342*
Karjaa, Finland, **287** L2
Kārkāl, India, **216** C3
Karkar Island, Papua New Guinea, **140** B4
Karkkila, Finland, **287** M2
Karksi-Nuia, Estonia, **287** M3
Karlfell, *mountain peak*, Iceland, **284** Z7
Karlik Shan, *mountain peak*, China, **213** G4
Karlino, Poland, **289** G1
Karlovac, Croatia, **294** E3
Karlovo, Bulgaria, **296** E4
Karlovy Vary, Czech Republic, **288** F3
Karlsborg, Sweden, **286** G3
Karlshamn, Sweden, **286** G4
Karlskoga, Sweden, **286** G3
Karlskrona, Sweden, **286** G4
Karlsruhe, Germany, **288** D4
Karlstad, Sweden, **286** F3
Karlstad, U.S.A., **420** E1
Karma, Niger, **365** E2
Karmah an Nazul, Sudan, **363** F5
Karnāl, India, **218** D3
Karnali, *river*, Nepal, **219** E3, *172*
Karnātaka, *state*, India, **216** C3, *169*
Karnische Alpen, *mountain range*, Austria/Italy, **288** F5
Karnobat, Bulgaria, **296** F4
Kärnten, *state*, Austria, **289** F5
Karoi, Zimbabwe, **369** E6
Karong, India, **214** E4
Karonga, Malawi, **369** F4
Karor, Pakistan, **218** B3
Karora, Sudan, **363** G5
Kärpänkylä, Finland, **285** P4
Karpathos, Dodekanisos, Greece, **297** F8
Karpathos, *island*, Dodekanisos, Greece, **297** F8
Karpathou, Steno, *strait*, Dodekanisos, Greece, **297** F8
Karpenisi, Greece, **297** C6
Karpogory, Russian Federation, **300** F3
Karpuzlu, Aydin, Turkey, **297** F7
Karpuzlu, Edirne, Turkey, **297** F5
Karpysak, Russian Federation, **223** L2
Karratha, Australia, **134** D3
Kars, Turkey, **224** F4
Kärsämäki, Finland, **285** M5
Kārsava, Latvia, **287** N4
Karskoye More, *sea*, Russian Federation, **300** H2
Karstula, Finland, **285** M5
Kartal, Turkey, **297** G5
Kartala, *mountain peak*, Comoros, **372** A3, *351, 352*
Kartaly, Russian Federation, **222** G2
Kartuzy, Poland, **289** J1
Karumba, Australia, **135** J2
Kārūn, *river*, Iran, **220** F2
Karungi, Sweden, **285** L3
Karup, Denmark, **286** D4
Kārvāndar, Iran, **221** H3
Karvia, Finland, **287** L1
Karvio, Finland, **285** P5
Kārwār, India, **216** C3
Karwendelgebirge, *mountain range*, Austria, **288** E5
Karya, Ionioi Nisoi, Greece, **297** C6
Karymskoye, Russian Federation, **210** F2
Karystos, Greece, **297** E7
Kaş, Turkey, **224** C5
Kasaböle, Finland, **287** K2
Kasabonika, Canada, **415** K5
Kasai, Japan, **208** F4
Kasai, *river*, Democratic Republic of the Congo, **368** C3
Kasai Occidental, *administrative region*, Democratic Republic of the Congo, **368** D3
Kasai Oriental, *administrative region*, Democratic Republic of the Congo, **368** D3
Kasaji, Democratic Republic of the Congo, **368** D5
Kasama, Zambia, **369** F5
Kasane, Botswana, **370** E2
Kasar, Ras, *point*, Sudan, **363** G5
Kāsaragod, India, **216** C3
Kasba Lake, Canada, **414** C1
Kasba Tadla, Morocco, **360** E2
Kasempa, Zambia, **369** E5
Kasenga, Democratic Republic of the Congo, **369** E5
Kasenye, Democratic Republic of the Congo, **369** F2
Kasese, Democratic Republic of the Congo, **369** E3
Kasese, Uganda, **369** F2
Kaset Wisai, Thailand, **203** D3
Kāsganj, India, **218** D4
Kashabowie, Canada, **414** J7
Kāshān, Iran, **220** F2
Kashgar *see* Kashi, China, **212** B5
Kashi (Kashgar), China, **212** B5
Kashin, Russian Federation, **299** F4
Kāshīpur, India, **218** D3
Kashira, Russian Federation, **299** G5
Kashiwazaki, Japan, **209** G3
Kashkarantsy, Russian Federation, **285** T3
Kāshmar, Iran, **222** F5
Kasimbar, Indonesia, **198** C3
Kasimov, Russian Federation, **298** F2
Kaskaskia, *river*, U.S.A., **421** J6
Kaskattama, *river*, Canada, **414** J3
Kaskinen, Finland, **287** K1
Kasli, Russian Federation, **222** G1
Kaslo, Canada, **413** L7
Kasongo, Democratic Republic of the Congo, **369** E3
Kasongo-Lunda, Democratic Republic of the Congo, **368** C4
Kasos, *island*, Greece, **297** F8
Kassalā, *state*, Sudan, **366** D1
Kassalā, Sudan, **367** E1
Kassandras, Akra, *point*, Greece, **297** D6
Kassandras, Kolpos, *bay*, Greece, **297** D5
Kassandreia, Greece, **297** D5
Kassel, Germany, **288** D3
Kassiopi, Greece, **297** B6
Kastamonu, Turkey, **224** D4
Kastelli, Kriti, Greece, **297** E8
Kastelli, *strait*, Kriti, Greece, **297** D8
Kastellotizon *see* Megisti, *island*, Greece, **297** G7
Kastoria, Greece, **297** C5
Kastos, *island*, Ionioi Nisoi, Greece, **297** C6
Kastsyanevichy, Belarus, **287** N5
Kasumbalesa, Democratic Republic of the Congo, **369** E5
Kasungu, Malawi, **369** F5
Katahdin, Mount, *mountain peak*, U.S.A., **426** F2
Kataklik, India, **218** D2
Katako-Kombe, Democratic Republic of the Congo, **368** D3
Katakwi, Uganda, **369** F2
Katana, Indonesia, **198** D2
Katanning, Australia, **134** D5
Katastari, Ionioi Nisoi, Greece, **297** C7
Katatjuta (Mount Olga), *mountain peak*, Australia, **134** G4
Katea, Democratic Republic of the Congo, **369** E4
Katen, *river*, Russian Federation, **211** M3
Katenge, Democratic Republic of the Congo, **368** D4
Katerini, Greece, **297** D5
Katesh, Tanzania, **369** G3
Katete, Zambia, **369** F5
Katha, Myanmar, **205** C2
Katherine, Australia, **134** G1
Katherine, *river*, Australia, **134** G1
Kathleen, Canada, **413** L4
Kathmandu, Nepal, **219** F4, *172*
Kathu, South Africa, **370** D4
Kati, Mali, **364** C2
Katiet, Indonesia, **200** B3
Katihār, India, **219** F4
Katiki, Volcán, *mountain peak*, Isla de Pascua (Easter Island), Chile, **461** B2
Katiki Point, New Zealand, **133** C7
Katima Mulilo, Namibia, **370** D2
Katiola, Côte d'Ivoire, **364** C3
Katiu, *island*, French Polynesia, **137** G2
Katlanovo, Macedonia, **296** C5
Kato Achaïa, Greece, **297** C6
Kato Figaleia, Greece, **297** C7
Kato Nevrokopi, Greece, **297** D5
Kato Pyrgos, Cyprus, **225** B2
Kato Tithorea, Greece, **297** D6
Katong, Singapore, **200** K7
Katoomba, Australia, **135** L5
Katoposa, Gunung, *mountain peak*, Indonesia, **198** C3
Katowice, Poland, **289** J3
Kātoya, India, **219** G5
Kātrīnā, Jabal, *mountain peak*, Egypt, **225** B5, *316, 317, 398*
Katrine, Loch, *lake*, Scotland, U.K., **308** E4
Katrineholm, Sweden, **286** H3
Katsepy, Madagascar, **372** B4
Katsina, Nigeria, **365** F2
Katsina, *state*, Nigeria, **365** F2
Katsina-Ala, Nigeria, **365** F3
Kattaqŭrghon, Uzbekistan, **222** H5
Kattavia, Dodekanisos, Greece, **297** F8
Kattegat, *strait*, Denmark/Sweden, **286** E4, *232, 233*

Kattisavan, Sweden, **284** J4
Katui, New Zealand, **132** D2
Katun', *river*, Russian Federation, **212** E2
Kau Sai Chau, *island*, China, **207** C4
Kauai, *island*, Hawaiian Islands, U.S.A., **422** R9
Kauai Channel, Hawaiian Islands, U.S.A., **422** R9
Kauangaroa, New Zealand, **132** E4
Kauehi, *island*, French Polynesia, **137** G2
Kaufbeuren, Germany, **288** E5
Kauhajoki, Finland, **287** L1
Kauhava, Finland, **285** L5
Kaukonen, Finland, **285** M3
Kauksi, Estonia, **287** N3
Kaukura, *island*, French Polynesia, **137** G2
Kaula, *island*, Hawaiian Islands, U.S.A., **422** Q9
Kaulakahi Channel, Hawaiian Islands, U.S.A., **422** Q9
Kauna Point, Hawaiian Islands, U.S.A., **422** R10
Kaunakakai, Hawaiian Islands, U.S.A., **422** R9
Kaunas, Lithuania, **287** L5
Kaup, Papua New Guinea, **140** A3
Kaupokonui, New Zealand, **132** E4
Kaura Namoda, Nigeria, **365** F2
Kaustinen, Finland, **285** L5
Kautokeino, Norway, **285** L2
Kauwhata, New Zealand, **132** E5
Kavadarci, Macedonia, **297** D5
Kavajë, Albania, **297** B5
Kavak, Turkey, **297** F5
Kavaklıdere, Turkey, **297** G7
Kavala, Greece, **297** E5
Kavalas, Kolpos, *bay*, Greece, **297** E5
Kavalerovo, Russian Federation, **211** L3
Kāvali, India, **216** D3
Kavaratti Island, India, **216** C4, *169*
Kavarna, Bulgaria, **296** G4
Kavarskas, Lithuania, **287** M5
Kavendou, Mont, *mountain peak*, Guinea, **364** B2
Kāveri, *river*, India, **216** D3
Kavieng, Papua New Guinea, **140** C3
Kavīr, Dasht-e, *salt-pan*, Iran, **221** F2, *183*
Kaw, French Guiana, **452** C2
Kaw Lake, U.S.A., **420** E7
Kawakawa, New Zealand, **132** E2
Kawambwa, Zambia, **369** E4
Kawardha, India, **219** E5
Kawartha Lakes, *lake*, Canada, **416** B7
Kawasaki, Japan, **209** G4
Kawatiri, New Zealand, **133** D5
Kawau Island, New Zealand, **132** E3
Kaweka, *mountain peak*, New Zealand, **132** F4
Kawhia, New Zealand, **132** E4
Kawhia Harbour, New Zealand, **132** E4
Kawich Peak, *mountain peak*, U.S.A., **422** F3
Kawlin, Myanmar, **205** B3
Kawm Umbū, Egypt, **363** F4
Kaya, Burkina Faso, **364** D2
Kayaapu, Indonesia, **200** C4
Kayah, *state*, Myanmar, **205** C4
Kayambi, Zambia, **369** F4
Kayan, *river*, Indonesia/Malaysia, **201** F2
Kāyankulam, India, **216** D4
Kayanza, Burundi, **369** E3
Kaycee, U.S.A., **419** L5
Kayembe-Mukulu, Democratic Republic of the Congo, **368** D4
Kayenta, U.S.A., **423** H3
Kayes, *administrative region*, Mali, **364** B2
Kayes, Mali, **364** B2
Käylä, Finland, **285** P3
Kayseri, Turkey, **224** E5
Kayuagung, Indonesia, **200** D3
Kayuyu, Democratic Republic of the Congo, **369** E3
Kayyerkan, Russian Federation, **300** K3
Kazakhstan, *country*, Asia, **196** G5, *144, 145, 184, 185, 186, 187, 270, 271, 273*
Kazan', Russian Federation, **222** D1
Kazan-rettō, *islands*, Japan, **138** B2
Kazanlŭk, Bulgaria, **296** E4
Kazanskoye, Russian Federation, **223** H1
Kazarman, Kyrgyzstan, **223** J4
Kazbek, Gora, *mountain peak*, Georgia, **222** C4
Kāzerūn, Iran, **220** F3
Kazhma, Russian Federation, **285** S5
Kazim Kazi, Ras, *point*, Tanzania, **369** G4
Kazincbarcika, Hungary, **289** K4
Kazlū Rūda, Lithuania, **287** L5
Kazon, *river*, Canada, **414** D1
Kaztalovka, Kazakhstan, **222** D3
Kazumba, Democratic Republic of the Congo, **368** D4
Kazungula, Zambia, **371** E2
Kazyr, *river*, Russian Federation, **223** N2
Kcynia, Poland, **289** H2
Ke-hsi Mānsām, Myanmar, **205** C3
Kea, *island*, Kyklades, Greece, **297** E7
Kea, Mauna, *mountain peak*, Hawaiian Islands, U.S.A., **422** R10
Keady, Northern Ireland, U.K., **309** F3
Kearney, U.S.A., **420** D5
Kebang, India, **219** H3
Kebbi, *state*, Nigeria, **365** E2
Kébémer, Senegal, **364** A1
Kebnekaise, *mountain peak*, Sweden, **284** J3, *231*
Kebock Head, *cape*, Scotland, U.K., **308** C2
K'ebrī Dehar, Ethiopia, **367** F3
Kecel, Hungary, **289** J5
K'ech'a Terara, *mountain peak*, Ethiopia, **367** E3
Kechika, *river*, Canada, **412** F2
Kecskemét, Hungary, **289** J5
Kedah, *state*, Malaysia, **200** C1
Kėdainiai, Lithuania, **287** L5
Kédédéssé, Chad, **365** H2
Kediri, Indonesia, **201** F4
Kedong, China, **211** J2
Kédougou, Senegal, **364** B2
Kedrovyy, Russian Federation, **223** K1
Kędzierzyn-Koźle, Poland, **223** K1
Keele Peak, *mountain peak*, Canada, **410** G3
Keeling Islands *see* Cocos (Keeling) Islands, *Australian territory*, Indian Ocean, **134** Q10, *123*
Keen, Mount, *mountain peak*, Scotland, U.K., **308** G4
Keene, U.S.A., **426** D3
Keetmanshoop, Namibia, **370** C4
Keewatin, Canada, **414** G7
Kefallonia, *island*, Ionioi Nisoi, Greece, **297** C6
Kefalos, Dodekanisos, Greece, **297** F7
Kefamenanu, Indonesia, **198** D5
Keffi, Nigeria, **365** F3
Keg River, Canada, **413** L3
Kegaska, Canada, **417** L4
Kegen, Kazakhstan, **223** K4
Kegul'ta, Russian Federation, **222** C3
Kegworth, England, U.K., **305** F2
Keheili, Sudan, **366** D1
Kehra, Estonia, **287** M3
Keighley, England, U.K., **307** G4
Keila, Estonia, **287** M3
Keimoes, South Africa, **370** D4
Ķeipene, Latvia, **287** M4
Kéita, Bahr, *river*, Chad, **366** A3
Keïta, Niger, **365** F2
Keitele, Finland, **285** N5
Keitele, *lake*, Finland, **285** M5
Keith, Australia, **135** J6
Keith, Cape, Australia, **199** E6
Keith, Scotland, U.K., **308** G3
Kejaman, Malaysia, **201** F2
Kekaha, Hawaiian Islands, U.S.A., **422** R9
Kekerengu, New Zealand, **133** E6
Kékes, *mountain peak*, Hungary, **289** K5
Kekri, India, **218** C4
K'elafo, Ethiopia, **367** F3
Kelamet, Eritrea, **367** E1
Kelan, China, **210** E5
Kelang, Malaysia, **200** C2
Kelankylä, Finland, **285** N4
Kelantan, *state*, Malaysia, **200** C1
Keleft, Turkmenistan, **218** A1
Keles, Turkey, **297** G6
Kelfield, Canada, **413** Q6
Kelheim, Germany, **288** E4
Kelimutu, Gunung, *mountain peak*, Indonesia, **198** C5
Keling, Indonesia, **201** E4
Kéllé, Congo, **368** B3
Kelliher, Canada, **414** C6
Kelliher, U.S.A., **420** F2
Kellogg, U.S.A., **418** F3
Kelloselkä, Finland, **285** P3
Kells, Kilkenny, Ireland, **309** E5
Kells, Meath, Ireland, **309** F4
Kelmë, Lithuania, **287** L5
Kel'mentsi, Ukraine, **296** F1
Kélo, Chad, **365** H3
Kelowna, Canada, **413** K7
Kelsey Bay, Canada, **412** G6
Kelso, Scotland, U.K., **308** G5
Kelso, U.S.A., **418** C3
Keluang, Tanjong, *point*, Indonesia, **201** E3
Kelume, Indonesia, **200** D3
Kelvedon, England, U.K., **305** H3
Kelwood, Canada, **414** E6
Kem', *river*, Russian Federation, **285** R4
Kem', Russian Federation, **285** S4
Kemal, Gunung, *mountain peak*, Indonesia, **201** G2
Kemalpa'a, Turkey, **297** F6
Kemano, Canada, **412** F5
Kemba, Central African Republic, **368** D2
Kembangjanggut, Indonesia, **201** G2
Kembé, Central African Republic, **368** D2
Kembolcha, Ethiopia, **220** C6, **367** E2
Kemer, Turkey, **297** G7
Kemer Barajı, *dam*, Turkey, **297** G7
Kemerovo, Russian Federation, **223** M1
Kemerovskaya Oblast', *province*, Russian Federation, **223** M1
Kemi, Finland, **285** M4
Kemihaara, *river*, Finland, **285** P3
Kemijärvi, Finland, **285** N3
Kemijärvi, *lake*, Finland, **285** N3
Kemijoki, *river*, Finland, **285** M3
Keminmaa, Finland, **285** M4
Kemmerer, U.S.A., **419** J6
Kemnath, Germany, **288** E4
Kemnay, Scotland, U.K., **308** G3
Kémo, *prefecture*, Central African Republic, **368** C1
Kemp, Lake, U.S.A., **424** C3
Kemp Land, *region*, Antarctica, **470** F4
Kempele, Finland, **285** M4
Kemps Bay, Bahamas, **428** F1
Kempsey, Australia, **135** L5
Kempsey, England, U.K., **304** E2
Kempston, England, U.K., **305** G2
Kempt, Lac, *lake*, Canada, **416** D6
Kempten (Allgäu), Germany, **288** E5
Kemptville, Canada, **416** D7
Kenai, U.S.A., **410** D3
Kenansville, U.S.A., **425** M6
Kenaston, Canada, **413** R6
Kendal, England, U.K., **306** F3
Kendall, Mount, *mountain peak*, New Zealand, **133** D5
Kendallville, U.S.A., **421** L5
Kendari, Indonesia, **198** C3
Kendawangan, Indonesia, **201** E3
Kendégué, Chad, **366** A2
Kendrāpara, India, **219** F5
Kendrick, U.S.A., **418** F3
Kenedy, U.S.A., **424** D5
Kenema, Sierra Leone, **364** B3
Kenes, Kazakhstan, **223** J4
Keng Hkam, Myanmar, **205** C3
Keng Lon, Myanmar, **205** C3
Keng Tawng, Myanmar, **205** C3
Keng Tung, Myanmar, **205** C3
Kenga, *river*, Russian Federation, **223** L1
Kenge, Democratic Republic of the Congo, **368** C3
Kenhardt, South Africa, **370** D4
Kenilworth, England, U.K., **305** F2
Kénitra, Morocco, **360** E2
Kenmare, *inlet*, Ireland, **309** B6
Kenmare, Ireland, **309** C6
Kenmore, Scotland, U.K., **308** F4
Kenna, U.S.A., **423** M5
Kennebec, *river*, U.S.A., **426** F2
Kennebunk, U.S.A., **426** E3
Kennet, *river*, England, U.K., **305** F3
Kennett, U.S.A., **424** G1
Kennewick, U.S.A., **418** E3
Kenogami Lake, Canada, **421** N1
Kenora, Canada, **414** G7
Kenosee Lake, Canada, **414** C7
Kenosha, U.S.A., **421** K4
Kenozero, Ozero, *lake*, Russian Federation, **299** G1
Kent, *unitary authority*, England, U.K., **305** H3, *275*
Kent, Oregon, U.S.A., **418** D4
Kent, Texas, U.S.A., **423** L6
Kent Peninsula, Canada, **410** J3
Kentland, U.S.A., **421** K5
Kentozero, Russian Federation, **285** Q4
Kentriki Makedonia, *administrative region*, Greece, **297** D5
Kentucky, *state*, U.S.A., **421** L7, *383, 386*
Kentucky, *river*, U.S.A., **421** M7
Kentucky Lake, U.S.A., **425** J1
Kentville, Canada, **417** J7
Kentwood, U.S.A., **424** G4
Kenya, *country*, Africa, **359** J6, *312, 313, 339, 340, 341, 342, 347*
Kenya, Mount *see* Kirinyaga, *mountain peak*, Kenya, **357** J7, *341*
Kenyir, Tasek, *lake*, Malaysia, **200** C1
Keonjhar, India, **219** F5
Kepa, Russian Federation, **285** R4
Kepahiang, Indonesia, **200** C3
Kepanjen, Indonesia, **201** F5
Kępno, Poland, **289** J3
Kepros, Akra, *point*, Greece, **297** E6
Kepsut, Turkey, **297** G6
Kerala, *state*, India, **216** C4, *169*
Keram, *river*, Papua New Guinea, **140** B4
Kerang, Australia, **135** J6
Keratea, Greece, **297** D7
Kerch, Ukraine, **298** E3
Kerema, Papua New Guinea, **140** B4
Keremeos, Canada, **412** K7
Kerempe Burnu, *cape*, Turkey, **224** D4
Keren, Eritrea, **367** E1
Kerend, Iran, **363** J2
Keret', Ozero, *lake*, Russian Federation, **285** R4
Keret', Russian Federation, **285** R3
Kerguélen, Îles de, *islands*, French Southern and Antarctic Islands, **104** E13, *465, 469*
Kerguelen Plateau, *underwater feature*, Indian Ocean, **476** D8
Kericho, Kenya, **369** G3
Kerihun, Gunung, *mountain peak*, Indonesia, **201** F2
Kerikeri, New Zealand, **132** D2
Kerinci, Danau, *lake*, Indonesia, **200** C3
Kerinci, Gunung, *mountain peak*, Indonesia, **200** C3
Kerkhoven, U.S.A., **420** F3
Kerki, Turkmenistan, **222** H5
Kerkinitis, Limni, *lake*, Greece, **297** D5
Kerkyra (Corfu), *island*, Ionioi Nisoi, Greece, **297** B6
Kermadec Islands, New Zealand, **132** L12
Kermadec Trench, *underwater feature*, Pacific Ocean, **478** G7
Kermān, Iran, **221** G2
Kermānshāh, Iran, **220** E2
Kermit, U.S.A., **423** M6
Kern, *river*, U.S.A., **422** D3
Keros, *island*, Kyklades, Greece, **297** E7
Kérou, Benin, **365** E2
Kérouané, Guinea, **364** C3
Kerrobert, Canada, **413** Q6
Kerrville, U.S.A., **424** C4
Kerry, *county*, Ireland, **309** C5
Kerry Head, *point*, Ireland, **309** B5
Kershaw, U.S.A., **425** M2
Kersley, Canada, **412** H5
Kertamulia, Indonesia, **201** E3
Kerulen (Herlen), *river*, Mongolia, **210** F3
Keryneia, Cyprus, **225** B2
Kerzaz, Algeria, **361** F3
Kesagami Lake, Canada, **415** P6
Keşan, Turkey, **297** F5
Kesennuma, Japan, **209** H3
Keshan, China, **211** J2
Keshod, India, **218** B5
Keskikylä, Finland, **285** M4
Keskin, Turkey, **363** F1
Kes'ma, Russian Federation, **299** F3
Kesova Gora, Russian Federation, **299** F4
Kessingland, England, U.K., **305** J2
Kesten'ga, Russian Federation, **285** Q4
Kestilä, Finland, **285** N4
Keswick, England, U.K., **306** E3
Keszthely, Hungary, **289** H5
Ket', *river*, Russian Federation, **300** K4
Keta, Ghana, **364** E3
Ketapang, Jawa Timur, Indonesia, **201** F4
Ketapang, Kalimantan Barat, Indonesia, **201** E3
Ketaun, Indonesia, **200** C3
Ketchikan, U.S.A., **412** D4
Keti Bandar, Pakistan, **218** A4
Kętrzyn, Poland, **289** K1
Ketta, Congo, **368** C2
Kétté, Cameroon, **368** B2
Kettering, England, U.K., **305** G2
Kettering, U.S.A., **421** L6
Kettle, *river*, Canada/U.S.A., **413** K7
Kettle Falls, U.S.A., **418** E2
Keuka Lake, U.S.A., **426** B3
Keur Momar Sar, Senegal, **364** A1
Keuruu, Finland, **287** M1
Keweigek, Guyana, **451** G3
Key, Lough, *lake*, Ireland, **309** D3
Key Lake Mine, Canada, **413** S3
Key Largo, U.S.A., **425** M7
Key West, U.S.A., **425** M7
Keyala, Sudan, **369** F2
Keyes, U.S.A., **420** B7
Keyihe, China, **211** H2
Keymer, England, U.K., **305** G4
Keynsham, England, U.K., **304** E3
Keyser, U.S.A., **421** P6
Kezi, Zimbabwe, **371** E3
Kežmarok, Slovakia, **289** K4
Kgalagadi, *district*, Botswana, **370** D3
Kgatleng, *district*, Botswana, **371** E3
Khabarovsk, Russian Federation, **301** Q5
Khabarovskiy Kray, *territory*, Russian Federation, **211** L2

Khadama, Russian Federation, **223** P2
Khadzhybeys'kyy Lyman, *lake*, Ukraine, **296** H2
Khagaria, India, **219** F4
Khairāgarh, India, **218** E5
Khairpur, Pakistan, **218** B4
Khakasiya, Respublika, *republic*, Russian Federation, **223** M2
Khallikot, India, **219** F6
Khalopyenichy, Belarus, **299** B5
Khalūf, Oman, **221** G4
Kham-Syra, *river*, Russian Federation, **223** P2
Kham Ta Kla, Thailand, **203** D2
Khamar-Daban, Khrebet, *mountain range*, Russian Federation, **213** J2
Khamaria, India, **218** E5
Khambhāliya, India, **218** B5
Khambhāt, Gulf of, India, **218,** B5, *169*
Khambhāt, India, **218** C5
Khāmgaon, India, **218** D5
Khamīs Mushayṭ, Saudi Arabia, **363** H5
Khammam, India, **216** E2
Khamr, Yemen, **220** D5
Khān az Zābīb, Jordan, **225** D4
Khān Shaykhūn, Syria, **225** D2
Khan Tängiri Shyngy, *mountain peak*, Kazakhstan/Kyrgyzstan, **212** D4, *185*
Khān Yūnus, Gaza, **225** B4
Khānābād, Afghanistan, **218** B1
Khanā'ir, Syria, **225** D2
Khandagayty, Russian Federation, **213** F2
Khandāla, India, **218** D6
Khandwa, India, **218** D5
Khandyga, Russian Federation, **301** Q3
Khānewāl, Pakistan, **218** B3
Khanka, Ozero, *lake*, Russian Federation, **211** L3
Khanna, India, **218** D3
Khānpur, Pakistan, **218** B3
Khansiir, Raas, *point*, Somalia, **367** G2
Khantaū, Kazakhstan, **223** J4
Khapalu, Pakistan, **218** D2
Kharabali, Russian Federation, **222** D3
Kharagpur, India, **219** F5
Kharagun, Russian Federation, **210** E2
Khārān, Pakistan, **218** A3
Kharanor, Russian Federation, **210** G2
Kharbara, India, **218** C3
Kharg Island *see* Khārk, Jazīreh-ye, *island*, Iran, **220** E3
Khargon, India, **218** C5
Khāriān, Pakistan, **218** C2
Khariār, India, **219** E5
Kharīm, Jabal, *mountain peak*, Egypt, **225** B4
Khārk, Jazīreh-ye (Kharg Island), *island*, Iran, **220** E3
Kharkiv, Ukraine, **298** E3
Kharlamovskaya, Russian Federation, **299** F3
Kharlovka, *river*, Russian Federation, **285** T2
Kharlovka, Russian Federation, **285** T2
Kharmanli, Bulgaria, **296** E5
Kharovsk, Russian Federation, **299** H3
Khartoum *see* Al Kharṭūm, Sudan, **366** D1, *336*
Khartoum North *see* Al Kharṭūm Baḥr, Sudan, **366** D1
Khasan, Russian Federation, **211** K4
Khasavyurt, Russian Federation, **222** D4
Khāsh, Iran, **221** H3
Khashm al Qirbah, Sudan, **366** E2
Khaskovo, *administrative region*, Bulgaria, **296** E4
Khaskovo, Bulgaria, **296** E5
Khatanga, Russian Federation, **301** M2
Khautavaara, Russian Federation, **299** D2
Khavast, Uzbekistan, **223** H4
Khāvda, India, **218** B5
Khaybar, Saudi Arabia, **363** H5
Khè, Phou, *mountain peak*, Laos, **203** D2
Khela, India, **218** E3
Khemarat, Thailand, **203** E2
Khemis Miliana, Algeria, **293** J4
Khemisset, Morocco, **361** E2
Khenchela, Algeria, **361** H1
Khenifra, Morocco, **361** E2
Khenjān, Afghanistan, **218** B2
Kherālu, India, **218** C5
Khersan, *river*, Iran, **220** E2
Kherson, Ukraine, **298** D3
Kherwāra, India, **218** C5
Kheta, *river*, Russian Federation, **300** L2
Khetolambina, Russian Federation, **285** R3
Khewra, Pakistan, **218** C2
Khilok, Russian Federation, **210** E2
Khimki, Russian Federation, **299** F5
Khipro, Pakistan, **218** B4
Khisarya, Bulgaria, **296** E4
Khislavichi, Russian Federation, **299** D5
Khlong Khlung, Thailand, **202** C2
Khmelita, Russian Federation, **299** D5
Khmel'nyts'kyy, Ukraine, **298** C3
Khnâchîch, El, *mountain range*, Mali, **361** F4
Khogali, Sudan, **366** C3
Khok Samrong, Thailand, **202** D3
Kholm, Russian Federation, **299** C4
Kholm-Zhirkovskiy, Russian Federation, **299** D5
Kholof Harar, Kenya, **369** H2
Khomas, *administrative region*, Namibia, **370** C3
Khomeyn, Iran, **220** F2
Khomeyni-shahr, Iran, **220** F2
Khon Kaen, Thailand, **203** D2
Khonuu, Russian Federation, **301** R3
Khôr 'Angar, Djibouti, **367** F2
Khor, *river*, Russian Federation, **211** M3
Khor, Russian Federation, **211** L3
Khorat *see* Nakhon Ratchasima, Thailand, **202** D3, *144, 155*
Khorinsk, Russian Federation, **210** E1
Khorixas, Namibia, **370** B3
Khorog, Tajikistan, **223** J5
Khorramābād, Iran, **220** E2
Khost, Pakistan, **218** A3
Khouribga, Morocco, **360** E2
Khovu-Aksy, Russian Federation, **213** G2
Khowst, Afghanistan, **218** B2
Khreum, Myanmar, **205** B3
Khuchinarai, Thailand, **203** E2
Khuff, Saudi Arabia, **363** H4
Khujand, Tajikistan, **223** H4
Khŭjayli, Uzbekistan, **222** F4
Khukhan, Thailand, **203** E3
Khulay', Saudi Arabia, **363** G4
Khulna, Bangladesh, **219** G5
Khulna, *division*, Bangladesh, **219** G5
Khunti, India, **219** F5
Khurīyā Murīyā, Jazā'ir (Kuria Muria Islands), *islands*, Oman, **221** G5
Khurja, India, **218** D3
Khushāb, Pakistan, **218** C2
Khust, Ukraine, **296** D1
Khuwayy, Sudan, **366** C2
Khuzdār, Pakistan, **218** A4
Khvalovo, Russian Federation, **299** D3
Khvor, Iran, **221** G2
Khvormūj, Iran, **220** F3
Khvoy, Iran, **363** J1
Khvoynaya, Russian Federation, **299** E3
Khwae Noi, *river*, Thailand, **202** C3
Khyriv, Ukraine, **289** L4
Kia, Solomon Islands, **141** A1
Kiama, Australia, **135** L5
Kiamba, Philippines, **204** D5
Kiambi, Democratic Republic of the Congo, **369** E4
Kiantajärvi, *lake*, Finland, **285** P4
Kibaha, Tanzania, **369** G4
Kibangou, Congo, **368** B3
Kibawe, Philippines, **204** D5
Kibaya, Tanzania, **369** G4
Kibiti, Tanzania, **369** G4
Kiboga, Uganda, **369** F2
Kibombo, Democratic Republic of the Congo, **369** E3
Kibondo, Tanzania, **369** F3
Kibre Mengist, Ethiopia, **367** E3
Kičevo, Macedonia, **297** C5
Kidal, *administrative region*, Mali, **361** G5
Kidal, Mali, **361** G5
Kidapawan, Philippines, **204** D5
Kidderminster, England, U.K., **304** E2
Kidira, Senegal, **364** B2
Kidlington, England, U.K., **305** F3
Kidnappers, Cape, New Zealand, **132** F4
Kidsgrove, England, U.K., **304** E1
Kidurong, Tanjong, *point*, Malaysia, **201** F2
Kidwelly, Wales, U.K., **304** C3
Kiekinkoski, Finland, **285** Q4
Kiel, Germany, **288** E1
Kiel, U.S.A., **421** J4
Kielce, Poland, **289** K3
Kielder Water, *lake*, England, U.K., **306** F2
Kieler Bucht, *bay*, Germany, **288** E1
Kiến ũú'c, Vietnam, **203** E4
Kienge, Democratic Republic of the Congo, **369** E5
Kieta, Papua New Guinea, **140** E8
Kiev *see* Kyyiv, Ukraine, **298** D2, *159, 268, 269, 271, 272*
Kiffa, Mauritania, **364** B1
Kifino Selo, Bosnia and Herzegovina, **294** G4
Kifisia, Greece, **297** D6
Kifisos, *river*, Greece, **297** D6
Kifrī, Iraq, **363** H2
Kigali, Rwanda, **369** F3, *342*
Kignan, Mali, **364** C2
Kigoma, Tanzania, **369** E3
Kigoma, *administrative region*, Tanzania, **369** F3
Kihelkonna, *island*, Estonia, **287** L3
Kihikihi, New Zealand, **132** E4
Kihlanki, Finland, **285** L3
Kihniö, Finland, **287** L1
Kihnu, *island*, Estonia, **287** L3
Kii Landing, Hawaiian Islands, U.S.A., **422** Q9
Kiik, Kazakhstan, **223** J3
Kiiminki, Finland, **285** M4
Kiistala, Finland, **285** M3
Kika, Russian Federation, **210** D1
Kikinda, Serbia, **296** C3
Kikki, Pakistan, **221** H3
Kikondja, Democratic Republic of the Congo, **369** E4
Kikori, Papua New Guinea, **140** B4
Kikori, *river*, Papua New Guinea, **140** A4
Kikwit, Democratic Republic of the Congo, **368** C4
Kil, Sweden, **286** F3
Kilafors, Sweden, **286** H2
Kilauea, Hawaiian Islands, U.S.A., **422** R9
Kilauea Crater, Hawaiian Islands, U.S.A., **422** R10
Kilboghamn, Norway, **284** F3
Kilbotn, Norway, **284** H2
Kilchu, North Korea, **208** E2
Kilcormac, Ireland, **309** E4
Kilcullen, Ireland, **309** F4
Kildare, *county*, Ireland, **309** F4
Kildare, Ireland, **309** F4
Kil'din Ostrov, *island*, Russian Federation, **285** S2
Kil'dinstroy, Russian Federation, **285** R2
Kilembe, Democratic Republic of the Congo, **368** C4
Kilfinan, Scotland, U.K., **308** D5
Kilgore, Nebraska, U.S.A., **420** C4
Kilgore, Texas, U.S.A., **424** E3
Kilham, England, U.K., **306** F2
Kili, *island*, Marshall Islands, **139** E4
Kiliba, Democratic Republic of the Congo, **369** E3
Kilifi, Kenya, **369** G3
Kilimanjaro, *administrative region*, Tanzania, **369** G3
Kilimanjaro, *mountain peak*, Tanzania, **357** J7
Kilindoni, Tanzania, **369** G4
Kilingi-Nõmme, Estonia, **287** M3
Kilis, Turkey, **224** E5
Kiliya, Ukraine, **296** G3
Kilkee, Ireland, **309** C5
Kilkeel, Northern Ireland, U.K., **309** F3
Kilkenny, *county*, Ireland, **309** E5
Kilkenny, Ireland, **309** E5
Kilkhampton, England, U.K., **304** C4
Kilkis, Greece, **297** D5
Killala, Ireland, **309** C3
Killala Bay, Ireland, **309** C3
Killaloe, Ireland, **309** D5
Killaly, Canada, **414** C6
Killarney, Canada, **421** N2
Killarney, Ireland, **309** C5
Killary Harbour, Ireland, **309** B4
Killdeer, Canada, **413** R7
Killdeer, U.S.A., **420** B2
Killeen, U.S.A., **424** D4
Killenaule, Ireland, **309** E5
Killiecrankie, Scotland, U.K., **308** F4
Killimor, Ireland, **309** D4
Killin, Scotland, U.K., **308** E4
Killingi, Sweden, **284** K3
Killinick, Ireland, **309** F5
Killiniq, Canada, **411** N3
Killorglin, Ireland, **309** C5
Killybegs, Ireland, **309** D3
Kilmacrenan, Ireland, **309** E2
Kilmaine, Ireland, **309** C4
Kilmallock, Ireland, **309** D5
Kilmaluag, Scotland, U.K., **308** C3
Kilmarnock, Scotland, U.K., **308** E5
Kilmartin, Scotland, U.K., **308** D4
Kilmelford, Scotland, U.K., **308** D4
Kil'mez', *river*, Russian Federation, **222** E1
Kil'mez', Russian Federation, **222** E1
Kilmore Quay, Ireland, **309** F5
Kilmuckridge, Ireland, **309** F5
Kilosa, Tanzania, **369** G4
Kilrea, Northern Ireland, U.K., **309** F3
Kilrush, Ireland, **309** C5
Kilsyth, Scotland, U.K., **308** E5
Kiltamagh, Ireland, **309** D4
Kilttān Island, India, **216** C4
Kiltullagh, Ireland, **309** D4
Kilvakkala, Finland, **287** L2
Kilwa, Democratic Republic of the Congo, **369** E4
Kilwa Kivinje, Tanzania, **369** G4
Kilwa Masoko, Tanzania, **369** G4
Kilwinning, Scotland, U.K., **308** E5
Kilwo, Indonesia, **199** E3
Kim, Chad, **365** H3
Kim, U.S.A., **423** M3
Kimaan, Indonesia, **199** G4
Kimambi, Tanzania, **369** G4
Kimasozero, Russian Federation, **285** Q4
Kimba, Congo, **368** B3
Kimball, Nebraska, U.S.A., **419** N6
Kimball, South Dakota, U.S.A., **420** D4
Kimbe, Papua New Guinea, **140** C4
Kimberley, South Africa, **370** D4
Kimberly, U.S.A., **418** E4
Kimberley Plateau, Australia, **128** B3, *112*
Kimch'aek, North Korea, **208** E2
Kimch'ŏn, South Korea, **208** E3
Kimito, Finland, **287** L2
Kimje, South Korea, **208** D4
Kimmirut, Canada, **411** N3
Kimolos, *island*, Kyklades, Greece, **297** E7
Kimongo, Congo, **368** B3
Kimovaara, Russian Federation, **285** Q5
Kimovsk, Russian Federation, **299** G6
Kimparana, Mali, **364** D2
Kimpese, Democratic Republic of the Congo, **368** B4
Kimry, Russian Federation, **299** F4
Kimvula, Democratic Republic of the Congo, **368** C4
Kin-u, Myanmar, **205** B3
Kinabalu, Gunung, *mountain peak*, Malaysia, **201** G1, *152*
Kinabatangan, *river*, Malaysia, **201** G1
Kinango, Kenya, **369** G3
Kinaros, *island*, Kyklades, Greece, **297** F7
Kinbasket Lake, Canada, **413** K5
Kinbrace, Scotland, U.K., **308** F2
Kincardine, Canada, **421** N3
Kincraig, Scotland, U.K., **308** F3
Kinda, Democratic Republic of the Congo, **368** E4
Kinder, U.S.A., **424** F4
Kindersley, Canada, **413** Q6
Kindia, Guinea, **364** B2
Kindu, Democratic Republic of the Congo, **369** E3
Kinelakhti, Russian Federation, **299** D2
Kineshma, Russian Federation, **300** F4
King City, U.S.A., **422** C3
King George Bay, Falkland Islands, **460** F4
King George Islands, Canada, **415** Q3
King Island, Australia, **135** J6
King Island *see* Kadan Kyun, *island*, Myanmar, **202** C3
King Leopold and Queen Astrid Coast, *region*, Antarctica, **470** G5
King Leopold Ranges, *mountain range*, Australia, **134** E2
King Mountain, *mountain peak*, Canada, **412** E2
King Peak, *mountain peak*, U.S.A., **422** A1
King Point, Lord Howe Island, Australia, **135** U14
King Sound, Australia, **134** E2
King William Island, Canada, **411** K3
King William's Town, South Africa, **371** E5
Kingaroy, Australia, **135** L4
Kingisepp, Russian Federation, **299** B3
Kingman, Arizona, U.S.A., **422** F4
Kingman, Kansas, U.S.A., **420** D7
Kingman Reef, *U.S. territory*, Pacific Ocean, **139** H4, *123, 386*
King's Lynn, England, U.K., **305** H2
Kings Peak, *mountain peak*, U.S.A., **423** H1
King's Worthy, England, U.K., **305** F3
Kingsbridge, England, U.K., **304** D4
Kingsclere, England, U.K., **305** F3
Kingscote, Australia, **135** H6
Kingscourt, Ireland, **309** F4
Kingsland, U.S.A., **425** M4
Kingsnorth, England, U.K., **305** H3
Kingsport, U.S.A., **421** M7
Kingsteignton, England, U.K., **304** D4
Kingston, Canada, **416** C7
Kingston, Jamaica, **429** F3, *393*
Kingston, New Mexico, U.S.A., **423** K5
Kingston, New York, U.S.A., **426** D4
Kingston, New Zealand, **133** B7
Kingston, Norfolk Island, **135** T13, *125*
Kingston Southeast, Australia, **135** H6
Kingston upon Hull, England, U.K., **307** H4

Kingston upon Hull, *unitary authority*, England, U.K., **307** H4
Kingston upon Thames, England, U.K., **305** G3
Kingstown, St Vincent and the Grenadines, **427** D3, *396, 397*
Kingsville, U.S.A., **424** D6
Kingswood, England, U.K., **304** E3
Kington, England, U.K., **304** D2
Kingulube, Democratic Republic of the Congo, **369** E3
Kingungi, Democratic Republic of the Congo, **368** C4
Kingussie, Scotland, U.K., **308** E3
Kingwood, U.S.A., **424** E4
Kınık, Turkey, **297** F6
Kinkala, Congo, **368** B3
Kinkosi, Democratic Republic of the Congo, **368** C4
Kinloch, New Zealand, **132** E4
Kinloch, Scotland, U.K., **308** C3
Kinloch Rannoch, Scotland, U.K., **308** E4
Kinlochewe, Scotland, U.K., **308** D3
Kinlochleven, Scotland, U.K., **308** E4
Kinloss, Scotland, U.K., **308** F3
Kinna, Sweden, **286** F4
Kinnegad, Ireland, **309** E4
Kinneret, Yam (Sea of Galilee), *lake*, Israel, **225** C3, *179, 180*
Kinniyai, Sri Lanka, **217** E4
Kinnula, Finland, **285** M5
Kinohaku, New Zealand, **132** E4
Kinoosao, Canada, **414** C3
Kinross, Scotland, U.K., **308** F4
Kinsale, Ireland, **309** D6
Kinshasa, *administrative region*, Democratic Republic of the Congo, **368** C3
Kinshasa, Democratic Republic of the Congo, **368** C3, *334*
Kinsley, U.S.A., **420** D7
Kinston, Alabama, U.S.A., **425** J4
Kinston, North Carolina, U.S.A., **426** B7
Kintampo, Ghana, **364** D3
Kintap, Indonesia, **201** F3
Kintinian, Guinea, **364** C2
Kintore, Scotland, U.K., **308** G3
Kintyre, Mull of, *point*, Scotland, U.K., **308** D5
Kintyre, *peninsula*, Scotland, U.K., **308** D5
Kinvarra, Ireland, **309** D4
Kinyangiri, Tanzania, **369** F3
Kinyeti, *mountain peak*, Sudan, **369** F2
Kiowa, U.S.A., **420** D7
Kipawa, Lac, *lake*, Canada, **416** B6
Kipembawe, Tanzania, **369** F4
Kipili, Tanzania, **369** F4
Kipinä, Finland, **285** N4
Kipushi, Democratic Republic of the Congo, **369** E5
Kipushia, Democratic Republic of the Congo, **369** E5
Kır Klar Tepe, *mountain peak*, Turkey, **297** F6
Kirakira, Solomon Islands, **141** A1
Kirandul, India, **217** E2
Kirané, Mali, **364** B1
Kīranūr, India, **216** D4
Kirawsk, Belarus, **299** B6
Kiraz, Turkey, **297** G6
Kirbyville, U.S.A., **424** F4
Kircubbin, Northern Ireland, U.K., **309** G3
Kirensk, Russian Federation, **301** M4
Kirep, *island*, Marshall Islands, **139** F3
Kiri, Democratic Republic of the Congo, **368** C3
Kiribati, *country*, Pacific Ocean, **131** J2, *108, 119, 120*
Kırıkhan, Turkey, **225** D1
Kırıkkale, Turkey, **224** D5
Kirillov, Russian Federation, **299** G3
Kirinyaga (Mount Kenya), *mountain peak*, Kenya, **369** G3, *341*
Kirishi, Russian Federation, **299** C3
Kiritehere, New Zealand, **132** E4
Kiritimati (Christmas Island), *island*, Kiribati, **139** J4, *119*
Kirk, U.S.A., **418** D5
Kirk Michael, Isle of Man, **306** D3
Kırkağaç, Turkey, **297** F6
Kirkby, England, U.K., **306** F4
Kirkby Lonsdale, England, U.K., **306** F3
Kirkby Stephen, England, U.K., **306** F3
Kirkbymoorside, England, U.K., **307** G3
Kirkcaldy, Scotland, U.K., **308** F4
Kirkconnel, Scotland, U.K., **308** E5
Kirkcudbright, Scotland, U.K., **308** E6
Kirkee, India, **216** C2
Kirkenes, Norway, **285** Q2
Kirkham, England, U.K., **306** F4
Kirkintilloch, Scotland, U.K., **308** E5
Kirkkonummi, Finland, **287** M2
Kirkland, U.S.A., **422** G4
Kirkland Lake, Canada, **421** P1
Kirklareli, *province*, Turkey, **296** F5
Kırklareli, Turkey, **297** F5
Kirkmichael, Scotland, U.K., **308** F4
Kirkoswald, England, U.K., **306** F3
Kirkpatrick, Mount, *mountain peak*, Antarctica, **470** D6
Kirkpatrick, Scotland, U.K., **308** F5
Kirksville, U.S.A., **420** G5
Kirkūk, Iraq, **363** H1
Kirkwall, Orkney, Scotland, U.K., **308** G2
Kirkwood, South Africa, **370** E5
Kirov, Russian Federation, **299** E5
Kirovohrad, Ukraine, **298** D3
Kirovohrads'ka Oblast', *province*, Ukraine, **296** H1
Kirovsk, Leningradskaya Oblast', Russian Federation, **299** C3
Kirovsk, Murmanskaya Oblast', Russian Federation, **285** R3
Kīrovskīy, Kazakhstan, **223** K4
Kirriemuir, Scotland, U.K., **308** F4
Kīrthar Range, *mountain range*, Pakistan, **218** A4
Kirton in Lindsey, England, U.K., **307** H4
Kiruna, Sweden, **284** K3
Kirundu, Democratic Republic of the Congo, **369** E3
Kirzhach, Russian Federation, **299** G4
Kisa, Sweden, **286** G4
Kisangani, Democratic Republic of the Congo, **369** E2
Kisantu, Democratic Republic of the Congo, **368** B4
Kisarawe, Tanzania, **369** G4
Kisarazu, Japan, **209** G4
Kisbér, Hungary, **289** J5
Kiselevsk, Russian Federation, **223** M2
Kishanganj, India, **219** F4
Kishangarh, E. Rājasthān, India, **218** C4
Kishangarh, W. Rājasthān, India, **218** B4
Kishi, Nigeria, **365** E3
Kishinev *see* Chişinău, Moldova, **296** G2, *270*
Kishiwada, Japan, **209** F4
Kishorganj, Bangladesh, **219** G4
Kishtwār, India, **218** C2
Kisielnica, Poland, **289** L2
Kisii, Kenya, **369** F3
Kiska Island, Aleutian Islands, U.S.A., **408** E3
Kisko, Finland, **287** L2
Kiskőrös, Hungary, **289** J5
Kiskunfélegyháza, Hungary, **289** J5
Kiskunhalas, Hungary, **289** J5
Kiskunmajsa, Hungary, **289** J5
Kislovodsk, Russian Federation, **222** C4
Kismaayo, Somalia, **369** H3
Kisoro, Uganda, **369** E3
Kissamou, Koplos, *bay*, Kriti, Greece, **297** D8
Kissidougou, Guinea, **364** B3
Kissimmee, U.S.A., **425** M5
Kississing Lake, Canada, **414** D4
Kissū, Jabal, *mountain peak*, Sudan, **362** E4
Kistanje, Croatia, **294** E3
Kisumu, Kenya, **369** F3
Kisvárda, Hungary, **289** L4
Kit Carson, U.S.A., **423** M2
Kita, Mali, **364** C2
Kita-Daitō-shima, *island*, Japan, **138** B2
Kita-Iō-jima, *island*, Japan, **138** C2
Kitakami, Japan, **209** H3
Kitakyūshū, Japan, **208** E4
Kitale, Kenya, **369** G2
Kitami, Japan, **209** H2
Kitami-sanchi, *mountain range*, Japan, **209** H1
Kitangari, Tanzania, **369** G5
Kitchener, Canada, **421** N4
Kitgum, Uganda, **369** F2
Kitimat, Canada, **412** E4
Kitinen, *river*, Finland, **285** N3
Kitkiöjoki, Sweden, **285** L3
Kitmat Ranges, *mountain range*, Canada, **412** F5
Kitona, Democratic Republic of the Congo, **368** B4
Kitros, Greece, **297** D5
Kitsa, *river*, Russian Federation, **285** R2
Kitscoty, Canada, **413** P5
Kitsi, Finland, **285** Q5
Kitsman', Ukraine, **296** E1
Kittelfjäll, Sweden, **284** G4
Kittilä, Finland, **285** M3
Kitty Hawk, U.S.A., **426** C6
Kitu, Democratic Republic of the Congo, **369** E4
Kitui, Kenya, **369** G3
Kitula, Finland, **287** L2
Kitunda, Tanzania, **369** F4
Kitwe, Zambia, **369** E5
Kitzbühel, Austria, **288** F5
Kitzbüheler Alpen, *mountain range*, Austria, **288** F5
Kiu-Lom Reservoir, Thailand, **202** C2
Kiunga, Papua New Guinea, **140** A4
Kiuruvesi, Finland, **285** N5
Kivesjärvi, Finland, **285** N4
Kivijärvi, *lake*, Finland, **285** M5
Kivik, Sweden, **286** G5
Kiviõli, Estonia, **287** N3
Kivu, Lake, Democratic Republic of the Congo/Rwanda, **369** E3, *22, 343*
Kiwai Island, Papua New Guinea, **140** A5
Kīyevka, Kazakhstan, **223** J2
Kıyıköy, Turkey, **297** G5
Kizhinga, Russian Federation, **210** E2
Kizil, *river*, China, **212** B5
Kızılhisar, Turkey, **297** G7
Kızılırmak, Turkey, **224** D5
Kızılot, Turkey, **225** A1
Kizil'skoye, Russian Federation, **222** F2
Kizlyar, Russian Federation, **222** D4
Kjeldebotn, Norway, **284** H2
Kjøllefjord, Norway, **285** N1
Kjøpsvik, Norway, **284** H2
Kladanj, Bosnia and Herzegovina, **294** G3
Kladar, Indonesia, **199** G5
Kladno, Czech Republic, **289** G3
Kladovo, Serbia, **296** D3
Klaeng, Thailand, **202** D3
Klagenfurt, Austria, **289** G5
Klagetoh, U.S.A., **423** J4
Klaipėda, Lithuania, **287** K5
Klaksvík, Faeroe Islands, **302** D1
Klamath, U.S.A., **418** B6
Klamath Falls, U.S.A., **418** D5
Klamath Mountains, *mountain range*, U.S.A., **418** C6
Klappan, *river*, Canada, **412** E3
Klarälven, *river*, Sweden, **286** F2
Klatovy, Czech Republic, **288** F4
Klein Bonaire, *island*, Bonaire, Netherlands Antilles, **461** A4
Kleinsee, South Africa, **370** C4
Klekovača, *mountain peak*, Bosnia and Herzegovina, **294** F3
Klembivka, Ukraine, **296** G1
Klerksdorp, South Africa, **371** E4
Kleszczele, Poland, **289** L2
Kletnya, Russian Federation, **299** D6
Klibreck, Ben, *mountain peak*, Scotland, U.K., **308** E2
Klichaw, Belarus, **299** B6
Klimavichy, Belarus, **299** C6
Klimpfjäll, Sweden, **284** G4
Klin, Russian Federation, **299** F4
Klinsko-Dmitrovskaya Gryada, *mountain range*, Russian Federation, **299** E4
Klintehamn, Sweden, **287** J4
Klippan, Sweden, **286** F4
Klisura, Serbia, **296** D4
Ključ, Bosnia and Herzegovina, **294** F3
Kłodawa, Poland, **289** J2
Kłodzko, Poland, **289** H3
Kløfta, Norway, **286** E2
Klos, Albania, **297** C5
Klötze, Germany, **288** E2
Klövsjö, Sweden, **286** G1
Kluane, Canada, **410** F3
Kluczbork, Poland, **289** J3
Klütz, Germany, **288** E2
Klyuchevskaya Sopka, *mountain peak*, Russian Federation, **301** T4, *272*
Klyuchi, Russian Federation, **223** K2
Knaften, Sweden, **284** J4
Knäred, Sweden, **286** F4
Knaresborough, England, U.K., **307** G3
Knarvik, Norway, **286** B2
Knee Lake, Canada, **414** G4
Knezha, Bulgaria, **296** E4
Knighton, Wales, U.K., **304** D2
Knin, Croatia, **294** F3
Knittelfeld, Austria, **289** G5
Knjaževac, Serbia, **296** D4
Knob Island, U.S.A., **425** L6
Knock, Ireland, **309** D4
Knockalongy, *mountain peak*, Ireland, **309** D3
Knockboy, *mountain peak*, Ireland, **309** C6
Knocklayd, *mountain peak*, Northern Ireland, U.K., **309** F2
Knocktopher, Ireland, **309** E5
Knottingley, England, U.K., **307** G4
Knowle, England, U.K., **305** F2
Knox, Cape, Canada, **412** C4
Knox, U.S.A., **421** K5
Knox Coast, *region*, Antarctica, **470** G6
Knoxville, Iowa, U.S.A., **420** G5
Knoxville, Tennessee, U.S.A., **425** L2
Knoydart, *region*, Scotland, U.K., **308** D3
Knud Rasmussen Land, *region*, Greenland, **411** N2
Knutsford, England, U.K., **306** F4
Knutsholstind, *mountain peak*, Norway, **286** D2
Knysna, South Africa, **370** D5
Ko, Gora, *mountain peak*, Russian Federation, **211** M3
Ko Lanta, Thailand, **202** C5
Koani, Tanzania, **369** G4
Koba, Indonesia, **200** D3
Kobarid, Slovenia, **294** D2
Kobe, Indonesia, **198** D2
Kobe, Japan, **208** F4, *50, 97, 165*
København (Copenhagen), Denmark, **286** F5, *232, 233*
Kobenni, Mauritania, **364** C1
Kobierzyce, Poland, **289** H3
Koblenz, Germany, **288** C3
Kobleve, Ukraine, **296** H2
K'obo, Ethiopia, **367** E2
Koboko, Uganda, **369** F2
Kobona, Russian Federation, **299** C2
Kobozha, Russian Federation, **299** E3
Kobryn, Belarus, **289** M2
Kobuk, *river*, U.S.A., **410** D3
Kocaeli, *province*, Turkey, **297** G5
Kocaeli (İzmit), Turkey, **297** G5
Kočani, Macedonia, **296** D5
Koçarlı, Turkey, **297** F7
Koceljevo, Serbia, **296** B3
Kočevje, Slovenia, **294** E3
Koch Bihār, India, **219** G4
Koch Peak, *mountain peak*, U.S.A., **419** J4
Kocher, *river*, Germany, **288** D4
Kocherinovo, Bulgaria, **296** D4
Kochi (Cochin), India, **216** D4, *77*
Kōchi, Japan, **208** F4
Kochkoma, Russian Federation, **285** S4
Kochubey, Russian Federation, **222** D4
Kock, Poland, **289** L3
Kodarma, India, **219** F4
Kodiak, U.S.A., **410** D4
Kodiak Island, U.S.A., **410** D4
Kodīnar, India, **218** B5
Kodinsk, Russian Federation, **300** L4
Kodok, Sudan, **366** D3
Kodyma, Ukraine, **296** G1
Koës, Namibia, **370** C4
Kofçaz, Turkey, **296** F5
Koffiefontein, South Africa, **370** D4
Köflach, Austria, **289** G5
Koforidua, Ghana, **364** D3
Kōfu, Japan, **209** G4
Kogaluk, *river*, Canada, **415** R2
Kogalym, Russian Federation, **300** J3
Køge, Denmark, **286** F5
Køge Bugt, *bay*, Denmark, **286** F5
Kogi, *state*, Nigeria, **365** F3
Kogon, Uzbekistan, **222** G5
Kohan, Pakistan, **218** A4
Kohāt, Pakistan, **218** B2
Kohila, Estonia, **287** M3
Kohīma, India, **219** H4, *169*
Kohinui, New Zealand, **132** E5
Kohtla-Järve, Estonia, **287** N3
Kohurau, *mountain peak*, New Zealand, **133** C7
Koidern, Canada, **410** E3
Koirakoski, Finland, **285** N5
Koivu, Finland, **285** M3
Kojonup, Australia, **134** D5
Kokas, Indonesia, **199** F3
Kokemäenjoki, *river*, Finland, **287** K2
Kokenau, Indonesia, **199** G4
Koki, Senegal, **364** A1
Kokkola, Finland, **285** L5
Koko, Nigeria, **365** E2
Kokofata, Mali, **364** C2
Kokomo, U.S.A., **421** K5
Kokong, Botswana, **370** D3
Kokonga, New Zealand, **133** C7
Kokopo, Papua New Guinea, **140** D4
Kokoro, Benin, **365** E3
Kökpekti, *river*, Kazakhstan, **212** D2
Kökshetaū, Kazakhstan, **223** H2
Kokstad, South Africa, **371** E5
Koktuma, Kazakhstan, **223** L3
Kokubu, Japan, **208** E5
Kokuy, Russian Federation, **210** G1
Kokyar, China, **212** C5
Kola, Russian Federation, **285** R2
Kolāchi, *river*, Pakistan, **218** A4
Kolaka, Indonesia, **198** C4
Kolār, India, **216** D3
Kolār Gold Fields, India, **216** D3
Kolāras, India, **218** D4
Kolari, Finland, **285** L3
Kolåsen, Sweden, **284** F5
Kolašin, Montenegro, **296** B4
Kolāyat, India, **218** C4
Kolbuszowa, Poland, **289** K3
Kol'chugino, Russian Federation, **299** G4

Kolda, Senegal, **364** B2
Kolding, Denmark, **286** D5
Kole, Haut-Zaïre, Democratic Republic of the Congo, **369** E2
Kole, Kasai Oriental, Democratic Republic of the Congo, **368** D3
Kolerträsk, Sweden, **284** K4
Kolezhma, Russian Federation, **285** S4
Kolga laht, *bay*, Estonia, **287** M3
Kolga-Jaani, Estonia, **287** M3
Kolguyev, Ostrov, *island*, Russian Federation, **300** F3
Kolhāpur, India, **216** C2
Koli, *mountain peak*, Finland, **285** P5
Kolima, *lake*, Finland, **285** M5
Kolín, Czech Republic, **289** G3
K'olīto, Ethiopia, **367** E3
Kolka, Latvia, **287** L4
Kollam (Quilon), India, **216** D4
Kollidam, *river*, India, **216** D4
Kollumúli, *point*, Iceland, **284** Z7
Köln (Cologne), Germany, **288** C3
Kolno, Poland, **289** K2
Koło, Poland, **289** J2
Koloa, *island*, Vava'u Group, Tonga, **141** B3
Kołobrzeg, Poland, **289** G1
Kolokani, Mali, **364** C2
Kolombangara, *island*, Solomon Islands, **141** A1
Kolomna, Russian Federation, **299** G5
Kolomyya, Ukraine, **296** E1
Kolondiéba, Mali, **364** C2
Kolonga, Tongatapu Group, Tonga, **141** B4
Kolono, Indonesia, **198** C4
Kolovai, Tongatapu Group, Tonga, **141** B4
Kolozero, Ozero, *lake*, Russian Federation, **285** R2
Kolp', *river*, Russian Federation, **299** F3
Kolpashevo, Russian Federation, **300** K4
Kolpino, Russian Federation, **299** C3
Kölsillre, Sweden, **286** G1
Kol'skiy Poluostrov, *peninsula*, Russian Federation, **285** R2
Kolsva, Sweden, **286** G3
Kolumadulu Atoll, Maldives, **216** C6
Kolvitsa, Russian Federation, **285** R3
Kolwezi, Democratic Republic of the Congo, **369** E5
Kolyma, *river*, Russian Federation, **301** S3
Kolymskaya Nizmennost', *low land*, Russian Federation, **301** S3
Kolymskoye Nagor'ye, *mountain range*, Russian Federation, **301** S3
Kolyvan', Russian Federation, **223** L1
Komamo, Ukraine, **289** L4
Komandorskiye Ostrova, *islands*, Russian Federation, **301** T4
Komárno, Slovakia, **289** J5
Komatsu, Japan, **209** G3
Kombe, Democratic Republic of the Congo, **369** E3
Kombissiri, Burkina Faso, **364** D2
Komering, *river*, Indonesia, **200** D3
Komi, Respublika, *republic*, Russian Federation, **300** G3
Kominternivs'ke, Ukraine, **296** H2
Komló, Hungary, **289** J5
Komodo, Pulau, *island*, Indonesia, **201** G5
Komodou, Guinea, **364** C3
Komoran, Pulau, *island*, Indonesia, **199** G5
Komotiní, Greece, **297** E5
Kompasberg, *mountain peak*, South Africa, **370** D5
Komsomolets, Ostrov, *island*, Russian Federation, **300** K1
Komsomolets Shyghanaghy, *bay*, Kazakhstan, **222** E3
Komsomol'sk-na-Amure, Russian Federation, **211** M2
Komsomol'skoe, Kazakhstan, **222** G2
Komuniga, Bulgaria, **296** E5
Kon Tum, Vietnam, **203** F3
Konakovo, Russian Federation, **299** F4
Konārak, India, **219** F6
Konawa, U.S.A., **424** D2
Konch, India, **218** D4
Kondagaon, India, **219** E6
Kondembaia, Sierra Leone, **364** B3
Kondoa, Tanzania, **369** G3
Kondopoga, Russian Federation, **285** S5
Kondrovo, Russian Federation, **299** E5
Konduz, Afghanistan, **218** B1
Koné, New Caledonia, **141** A3
Köneürgench, Turkmenistan, **222** F4
Konevo, Russian Federation, **299** G1
Kong, Cameroon, **368** B1
Kong, *river*, Cambodia/Laos, **203** E3
Kong Christian IX Land, *region*, Greenland, **411** R3
Kong Christian X Land, *region*, Greenland, **411** S2
Kong Frederik VI Kyst, *region*, Greenland, **411** Q3
Kong Frederik VIII Land, *region*, Greenland, **411** S2
Kong Frederik IX Land, *region*, Greenland, **411** R3
Kong Karl's Land, *island*, Svalbard, **300** E2
Kong Oscar Fjord, Greenland, **411** S2
Konginkangas, Finland, **287** M1
Kongju, South Korea, **208** D3
Kongola, Namibia, **370** D2
Kongolo, Democratic Republic of the Congo, **369** E4
Kongoussi, Burkina Faso, **364** D2
Kongsberg, Norway, **286** D3
Kongsmoen, Norway, **284** F4
Kongsvinger, Norway, **286** F2
Kongur Shan, *mountain peak*, China, **212** B5
Kongwa, Tanzania, **369** G4
Koni, Poluostrov, *peninsula*, Russian Federation, **301** R4
Konin, Poland, **289** J2
Konini, New Zealand, **132** E5
Konitsa, Greece, **297** C5
Konjic, Bosnia and Herzegovina, **294** G4
Könkämäälven, *river*, Sweden, **284** K2
Konkwesso, Nigeria, **365** E2
Konna, Mali, **364** D2
Könnern, Germany, **288** E3
Konongo, Ghana, **364** D3
Konos, Papua New Guinea, **140** C3
Konosha, Russian Federation, **299** H2
Konotop, Ukraine, **298** D2
Konqi, *river*, China, **212** F4
Końskie, Poland, **289** K3
Konso, Ethiopia, **369** G1
Konstanz, Germany, **288** D5
Konta, India, **217** E2
Kontagora, Nigeria, **365** F2
Kontiolahti, Finland, **285** P5
Kontiomäki, Finland, **285** P4
Konttajärvi, Finland, **285** M3
Konya, Turkey, **224** D5
Koocanusa, Lake, U.S.A., **418** G2
Koor, Indonesia, **199** F3
Kooskia, U.S.A., **418** G3
Kootenay Lake, Canada, **413** L7
Kopaki, New Zealand, **132** E4
Kopaonik, *mountain range*, Serbia, **296** C4
Kopargo, Benin, **364** E3
Kópasker, Iceland, **284** Y6
Kopayhorod, Ukraine, **296** F1
Köpbirlik, Kazakhstan, **223** K3
Köpenick, Germany, **288** F2
Koper, Slovenia, **294** D3, *258*
Kopiago, Papua New Guinea, **140** A4
Köping, Sweden, **286** H3
Koplik, Albania, **296** B4
Kopor'ye, Russian Federation, **299** B3
Koppa, India, **216** C3
Koppang, Norway, **286** E2
Kopparberg, *county*, Sweden, **286** F2
Kopparberg, Sweden, **286** G3
Kopparnäs, Sweden, **284** K4
Kopperå, Norway, **284** E5
Koprivnica, Croatia, **294** F2
Köprübaşı, Turkey, **297** G6
Kop'yevo, Russian Federation, **223** M2
Korab (Maja e Korbit), *mountain peak*, Albania/Macedonia, **296** C5, *260, 263*
K'orahē, Ethiopia, **367** F3
Koramlik, China, **212** E5
Korangal, India, **216** D2
Korba, India, **219** E5
Korba, Tunisia, **295** C7
Korbach, Germany, **288** D3
Korbenichi, Russian Federation, **299** E2
Korbol, Chad, **366** A3
Korçë, Albania, **297** C5
Korčula, *island*, Croatia, **294** F4
Korčulanski Kanal, *channel*, Croatia, **294** F4
Korea Bay, China/North Korea, **208** C3
Korea Strait, Japan/South Korea, **208** E4
Korem, Ethiopia, **367** E2
Koremoa, New Zealand, **132** D3
Korenica, Croatia, **294** E3
Korgas, China, **212** D3
Korgen, Norway, **284** F3
Korhogo, Côte d'Ivoire, **364** C3
Korido, Indonesia, **199** F3
Korim, Indonesia, **199** G3
Korinthiakos Kolpos, *gulf*, Greece, **297** D6
Korinthos (Corinth), Greece, **297** D7, *89*
Kőris-hegy, *mountain peak*, Hungary, **289** H5
Kōriyama, Japan, **209** H3
Korkuteli, Turkey, **224** D5
Korla, China, **212** E4
Kormakitis, *cape*, Cyprus, **225** B2
Körmend, Hungary, **289** H5
Kornat, *island*, Croatia, **294** E4
Kórnik, Poland, **289** H2
Kornsjø, Norway, **286** E3
Koro, *island*, Fiji, **141** A4
Koro, Mali, **364** D2
Koro Toro, Chad, **366** A1
Köroğlu Dağları, *mountain range*, Turkey, **224** D4
Korogwe, Tanzania, **369** G4
Koronadal, Philippines, **204** D5
Koroni, Greece, **297** C7
Koronia, Limni, *lake*, Greece, **297** D5
Koror, Palau, **138** B4, *117*
Körös, *river*, Hungary, **289** K5
Korosten', Ukraine, **298** C2
Korostyn', Russian Federation, **299** C3
Korovou, Fiji, **141** A4
Korpikå, Sweden, **285** L4
Korpilahti, Finland, **287** M1
Korpilombolo, Sweden, **285** L3
Korsberga, Sweden, **286** G4
Korskrogen, Sweden, **286** G2
Korsnäs, Finland, **287** K1
Korsør, Denmark, **286** E5
Kortesjärvi, Finland, **285** L5
Korti Linchang, China, **212** E2
Kortrijk, Belgium, **288** A3
Koryakskoye Nagor'ye, *mountain range*, Russian Federation, **301** T3
Korycin, Poland, **289** L2
Korzybie, Poland, **289** H1
Kos, Dodekanisos, Greece, **297** F7
Kos, *island*, Dodekanisos, Greece, **297** F7
Kosan, North Korea, **211** J5
Kosaya Gora, Russian Federation, **299** F5
Kościan, Poland, **289** H2
Kościerzyna, Poland, **289** J1
Kosciusko, U.S.A., **425** H3
Kosciuszko, Mount, *mountain peak*, Australia, **128** D5, *111*
Kose, Estonia, **287** M3
Kosh-Agach, Russian Federation, **223** M2
Koshikijima-rettō, *islands*, Japan, **208** E5
Košice, Slovakia, **289** K4, *267*
Košický, *administrative region*, Slovakia, **289** K4
Kosiv, Ukraine, **296** E1
Kosjerići, Serbia, **296** B4
Koskenkylä, Finland, **287** M2
Koskenpää, Finland, **287** M1
Koski, Finland, **287** L2
Kosŏng, North Korea, **208** E3
Kosŏng, South Korea, **208** E4
Kosovo, *country*, Europe, **296** C4, *228, 229, 260–263*
Kosovska Mitrovica, Serbia, **296** C4
Kosrae, *island*, Micronesia, **138** E4, *118*
Kossou, Lac de, *lake*, Côte d'Ivoire, **364** C3
Kostajnica, Croatia, **294** F3
Kostenets, Bulgaria, **296** D4
Kostinbrod, Bulgaria, **296** D4
Kostolac, Serbia, **296** C3
Kostomuksha, Russian Federation, **285** Q4
Kostonjärvi, *lake*, Finland, **285** P4
Kostroma, Russian Federation, **300** F4
Kostryzń, Poland, **289** G2
Kostyantynivka, Ukraine, **296** H2
Koszalin, Poland, **289** H1
Koszyce, Poland, **289** K3
Kot Diji, Pakistan, **218** B4
Kot Kapūra, India, **218** C3
Kot Pūtli, India, **218** D4
Kota, India, **218** C4
Kota Baharu, Malaysia, **200** C1
Kota Kinabalu, Malaysia, **201** G1
Kota Tinggi, Malaysia, **200** C2
Kotaagung, Indonesia, **200** D4
Kotabaru, Indonesia, **201** G3
Kotabumi, Indonesia, **200** D4
Kotamobagu, Indonesia, **198** D2
Kotanopan, Indonesia, **200** B2
Kotapinang, Indonesia, **200** C2
Kotare, New Zealand, **132** E4
Kotel, Bulgaria, **296** F4
Kotel'nich, Russian Federation, **300** F4
Kotel'nyy, Ostrov, *island*, Russian Federation, **301** Q2
Kothāpet, India, **216** D2
Köthen, Germany, **288** F3
Kotido, Uganda, **369** F2
Kotila, Finland, **285** P4
Kotka, Finland, **287** N2
Kotlas, Russian Federation, **300** F3
Kotli, India, **218** C2
Kotlik, U.S.A., **410** C3
Kotly, Russian Federation, **299** B3
Koton-Karifi, Nigeria, **365** F3
Kotor, Montenegro, **296** B4
Kotor Varoš, Bosnia and Herzegovina, **294** F3
Kotouba, Côte d'Ivoire, **364** D3
Kotovs'k, Ukraine, **298** C3
Kotri, Pakistan, **218** B4
Kotri, *river*, India, **214** B5
Kottagūdem, India, **216** E2
Kottapatnam, India, **216** E3
Kottayam, India, **216** D4
Kotto, *river*, Central African Republic, **366** B3, *331*
Kotuy, *river*, Russian Federation, **301** M3
Kotzebue, U.S.A., **410** C3
Kotzebue Sound, U.S.A., **410** C3
Kou Senjaq, Iraq, **363** H1
Kouandé, Benin, **365** E2
Kouango, Central African Republic, **368** D1
Koubia, Guinea, **364** B2
Koudougou, Burkina Faso, **364** D2
Koufalia, Greece, **297** D5
Kouilou, *administrative region*, Congo, **368** B3
Kouilou, *river*, Congo, **368** B3, *334*
Kouka, Burkina Faso, **364** D2
Koulamoutou, Gabon, **368** B3
Koulikoro, *administrative region*, Mali, **364** C2
Koulikoro, Mali, **364** C2
Koum, Cameroon, **365** G3
Koumac, New Caledonia, **141** A3
Koumbia, Guinea, **364** B2
Koumogo, Chad, **366** A3
Koumra, Chad, **365** H3
Koundâra, Guinea, **364** B2
Koundougou, Burkina Faso, **364** D2
Koungheul, Senegal, **364** B2
Kountze, U.S.A., **424** E4
Koupéla, Burkina Faso, **364** D2
Kourou, French Guiana, **452** C2, *445*
Kouroussa, Guinea, **364** C2
Koussanar, Senegal, **364** B2
Kousséri, Cameroon, **365** G2
Koussi, Emi, *mountain peak*, Chad, **362** C5
Koutiala, Mali, **364** C2
Koutsochero, Greece, **297** D6
Kouvola, Finland, **287** N2
Kovačica, Serbia, **296** C3
Kovarzino, Russian Federation, **299** G2
Kovaskiy, Mys, *cape*, Russian Federation, **301** S2
Kovda, Russian Federation, **285** R3
Kovdor, Russian Federation, **285** Q3
Kovdozero, Ozero, *lake*, Russian Federation, **285** Q3
Kovel', Ukraine, **289** M3, **298** B2
Kovera, Russian Federation, **299** D2
Kovero, Finland, **287** Q1
Kovzhskoye, Ozero, *lake*, Russian Federation, **299** F2
Kowal, Poland, **289** J2
Kowary, Poland, **289** G3
Kowloon *see* Jiulong, China, **207** C4
Kowon, North Korea, **208** D3
Kowt-e 'Ashrow, Afghanistan, **218** B2
Koxlax, China, **212** D5
Köyceğiz, Turkey, **297** G7
Köyceğiz Gölü, *lake*, Turkey, **297** G7
Koyna Reservoir, India, **216** C2
Koynare, Bulgaria, **296** E4
Koyukuk, *river*, U.S.A., **410** D3
Kozani, Greece, **297** C5
Kozara, *mountain range*, Bosnia and Herzegovina, **294** F3
Kozel'sk, Russian Federation, **299** E5
Kozhikode (Calicut), India, **216** C4, *168*
Kozienice, Poland, **289** K3
Kozloduy, Bulgaria, **296** D4
Kozlovo, Russian Federation, **299** G2
Koz'modem'yansk, Russian Federation, **222** D1
Kpalimé, Togo, **364** E3
Kpandae, Ghana, **364** D3
Kpandu, Ghana, **364** E3
Kra, Isthmus of, Malaysia/Thailand, **202** C4
Kra Buri, Thailand, **202** C4
Krabi, Thailand, **202** C4
Krâchéh, Cambodia, **203** E3
Kräckelbäcken, Sweden, **286** G2
Kragerø, Norway, **286** D3
Kragujevac, Serbia, **296** C3
Krakatau, *mountain peak*, Indonesia, **200** D4, *50, 51, 148*

Kraków, Poland, 289 J3
Kralendijk, Bonaire, Netherlands Antilles, 461 A4
Kralendijk, Netherlands Antilles, 427 B3
Kralendijk Punt, point, Bonaire, Netherlands Antilles, 461 A4
Kraljevica, Croatia, 294 E3
Kraljevo, Serbia, 296 C4
Kralovice, Czech Republic, 288 F4
Kranidi, Greece, 297 D7
Kranj, Slovenia, 294 E2
Kranji Reservoir, Singapore, 200 J6
Krapina, Croatia, 294 E2
Krapkowice, Poland, 289 H3
Kräslava, Latvia, 287 N5
Krasni Okny, Ukraine, 296 G2
Kraśnik, Poland, 289 L3
Krasnoarmeysk, Kazakhstan, 223 H2
Krasnoarmeysk, Russian Federation, 299 G4
Krasnodar, Russian Federation, 222 B3
Krasnodarskiy Kray, territory, Russian Federation, 298 E3
Krasnodarskoye Vodokhranilishche, reservoir, Russian Federation, 298 E3
Krasnodarskoye Vodokhranilishche, Russian Federation, 222 B3
Krasnokamensk, Russian Federation, 211 G2
Krasnomayskiy, Russian Federation, 299 E4
Krasnopollye, Belarus, 299 C6
Krasnoshchel'ye, Russian Federation, 285 T3
Krasnoslobodsk, Russian Federation, 222 C2
Krasnoyarsk, Russian Federation, 223 N1
Krasnoyarskiy Kray, territory, Russian Federation, 223 N2
Krasnoyarskoye Vodokhranilishche, lake, Russian Federation, 223 N2
Krasnoye Selo, Russian Federation, 299 C3
Krasnystaw, Poland, 289 L3
Krasnyy Kholm, Russian Federation, 299 F3
Krasnyy Yar, Russian Federation, 223 J1
Krasukha, Russian Federation, 299 E3
Kratovo, Macedonia, 296 D4
Krau, Indonesia, 199 H3
Kravanh, Chuŏr Phnum, mountain range, Cambodia, 203 D3
Kraynovka, Russian Federation, 222 D4
Krechetovo, Russian Federation, 299 G2
Krefeld, Germany, 288 C3
Kremenchuk, Ukraine, 298 D3
Kremintsi, Ukraine, 296 C1
Kreml', Russian Federation, 285 S4
Kremlin, U.S.A., 419 J2
Kremmling, U.S.A., 423 K1
Krems an der Donau, Austria, 289 G4
Kresna, Bulgaria, 297 D5
Kresstsy, Russian Federation, 299 D3
Krestena, Greece, 297 C7
Kresty, Russian Federation, 299 F5
Kretinga, Lithuania, 287 K5
Kribi, Cameroon, 368 A2
Krieglach, Austria, 289 G5
Krikellos, Greece, 297 C6
Kril'on, Mys, cape, Russian Federation, 209 H1

Krimml, Austria, 288 E5
Krishna, river, India, 216 D2
Krishnadevipeta, India, 217 E2
Krishnagiri, India, 216 D3
Krishnanagar, India, 219 G5
Krishnarāja Sagara, lake, India, 216 C3
Kristiansand, Norway, 286 C3
Kristianstad, county, Sweden, 286 F4
Kristianstad, Sweden, 286 G5
Kristiansund, Norway, 284 C2
Kristiinankaupunki, Finland, 287 K1
Kristineberg, Sweden, 284 J4
Kristinehamn, Sweden, 286 G3
Kriti, administrative region, Greece, 297 E8
Kriti (Crete), island, Greece, 297 E8, 67, 88, 265
Kriva Palanka, Macedonia, 296 D4
Krivoles, Russian Federation, 299 D6
Krivosheino, Russian Federation, 223 L1
Krk, Croatia, 294 E3
Krk, island, Croatia, 294 E3
Krka, river, Croatia, 294 F4
Kroken, Norway, 284 G4
Krokom, Sweden, 284 G5
Krokowa, Poland, 289 J1
Kroksjö, Sweden, 284 H4
Kronach, Germany, 288 E3
Krŏng Kaôh Kŏng, Cambodia, 203 D4
Kronoberg, county, Sweden, 286 F4
Kronoby, Finland, 285 L5
Kronotskiy Zaliv, bay, Russian Federation, 301 T4
Kronprins Olav Kyst, region, Antarctica, 470 F4
Kronprinsesse Martha Kyst, region, Antarctica, 470 C4
Kroonstad, South Africa, 371 E4
Kropotkin, Russian Federation, 298 F3
Krosno, Poland, 289 K4
Krosno Odrzańskie, Poland, 289 G2
Krotoszyn, Poland, 289 H3
Krško, Slovenia, 294 E2
Krugersdorp, South Africa, 371 E4
Kruhlaye, Belarus, 299 B5
Krui, Indonesia, 200 C4
Krujë, Albania, 297 B5
Krumbach (Schwaben), Germany, 288 E4
Krumë, Albania, 296 C4
Krumovgrad, Bulgaria, 297 E5
Krung Thep (Bangkok), Thailand, 202 D3, 155
Krupanj, Serbia, 296 B3
Krupina, Slovakia, 289 J4
Krupki, Belarus, 299 B5
Kruševac, Serbia, 296 C4
Kruševo, Macedonia, 297 C5
Krušné hory, mountain range, Czech Republic, 288 F3
Krutets, Russian Federation, 299 E3
Krutinka, Russian Federation, 223 J1
Krychaw, Belarus, 299 C6
Krymne, Ukraine, 289 M3
Krymskyy PivKryms'kyy Pivostriv (Crimean Peninsula), peninsula, Ukraine, 298 D3
Kryve Ozero, Ukraine, 296 H2

Kryvyy Rih, Ukraine, 298 D3
Ksabi, Algeria, 361 F3
Ksar Chellala, Algeria, 361 G1
Ksar el Boukhari, Algeria, 361 G1
Ksar el Kebir, Morocco, 361 E2
Ksar es Sghir, Morocco, 292 E5
Ksour Essaf, Tunisia, 362 B1
Ktima, Cyprus, 225 B2
K2, mountain peak, China/Pakistan, 218 D2, 173
Kuala Dungun, Malaysia, 200 C1
Kuala Kangsar, Malaysia, 200 C1
Kuala Kerai, Malaysia, 200 C1
Kuala Lipis, Malaysia, 200 C1
Kuala Lumpur, federal territory, Malaysia, 200 C2
Kuala Lumpur, Malaysia, 200 C2, 151
Kuala Penyu, Malaysia, 201 F1
Kuala Selangor, Malaysia, 200 C2
Kuala Terengganu, Malaysia, 200 C1
Kualakurun, Indonesia, 201 F3
Kuan-hsi, Taiwan, 206 E3
Kuan-shan, Taiwan, 206 E4
Kuancheng, China, 211 G4
Kuandian, China, 211 J4
Kuantan, Malaysia, 200 C2
Kuaotunu, New Zealand, 132 E3
Kuban', river, Russian Federation, 298 E3
Kubaybāt, Syria, 225 D2
Kubbum, Sudan, 366 B2
Kubeai, Papua New Guinea, 140 A4
Kubena, river, Russian Federation, 299 H3
Kubenskoye, Ozero, lake, Russian Federation, 299 G3
Kubkain, Papua New Guinea, 140 A4
Kubrat, Bulgaria, 296 F4
Kubukhay, Russian Federation, 210 F2
Kučevo, Serbia, 296 C3
Kuchaiburi, India, 219 F5
Kuchin-Tundra, Gora, mountain peak, Russian Federation, 285 Q2
Kuching, Malaysia, 201 E2
Kuchurhan, river, Ukraine, 296 G2
Kuçovë, Albania, 297 B5
Kudarebe, point, Aruba, 461 B3
Kudat, Malaysia, 201 G1
Kudever', Russian Federation, 299 B4
Kudryavtsivka, Ukraine, 296 H2
Kudus, Indonesia, 201 E4
Kufstein, Austria, 288 F5
Kugluktuk, Canada, 410 H3
Kuha, Finland, 285 N4
Kŭhdasht, Iran, 220 E2
Kuhmalahti, Finland, 287 M2
Kuhmo, Finland, 285 P4
Kuitan, China, 206 C4
Kuito, Angola, 368 C5
Kuivajärvi, Finland, 285 P4
Kuivaniemi, Finland, 285 M4
Kuivastu, Estonia, 287 L3
Kuiyong, China, 207 C3
Kuji, Japan, 209 H2
Kuji, river, Japan, 209 H3
Kujjuaraapik, Canada, 415 R4
Kukawa, Nigeria, 365 G2
Kukës, Albania, 296 C4

Kukmor, Russian Federation, 222 E1
Kula, Bulgaria, 296 D4
Kula, Serbia, 296 B3
Kula, Turkey, 297 G6
Kula Kangri, mountain peak, Bhutan/China, 214 D3, 171
Kulal, mountain peak, Kenya, 369 G2
Kulanak, Kyrgyzstan, 212 B4
Kular, Khrebet, mountain range, Russian Federation, 301 Q3
Kuldīga, Latvia, 287 K4
Kulebaki, Russian Federation, 298 F1
Kulgera, Australia, 134 G4
Kulkuduk, Uzbekistan, 222 G4
Kullaa, Finland, 287 L2
Kullorsuaq, Greenland, 411 P2
Kulmbach, Germany, 288 E3
Kuloharju, Finland, 285 P3
Kulu, India, 218 D3
Kulumadau, Papua New Guinea, 140 D5
Kulunda, Russian Federation, 223 K2
Kumagaya, Japan, 209 G3
Kumai, Indonesia, 201 E3
Kumai, Teluk, bay, Indonesia, 201 E3
Kumamoto, Japan, 208 E4
Kumanovo, Macedonia, 296 C4
Kumara Junction, New Zealand, 133 C6
Kumasi, Ghana, 364 D3, 325, 326
Kumba, Cameroon, 368 A2
Kumbakonam, India, 216 D4
Kumbe, Indonesia, 199 H5
Kumbo, Cameroon, 365 G3
Kŭmch'ŏn, North Korea, 208 D3
Kume-jima, island, Japan, 209 N8
Kumertau, Russian Federation, 222 F2
Kumi, South Korea, 208 E3
Kumi, Uganda, 369 F2
Kumiva Peak, mountain peak, U.S.A., 422 D1
Kumkale, Turkey, 297 F6
Kumkuduk, China, 213 F4
Kumla, Sweden, 286 G3
Kumlinge, Finland, 287 K2
Kummavuopio, Sweden, 284 K2
Kummerower See, lake, Germany, 288 F2
Kumo, Nigeria, 365 G2
Kumon Taungdan, mountain range, Myanmar, 205 C2
Kumphawapi, Thailand, 203 D2
Kumta, India, 216 C3
Kumu, Democratic Republic of the Congo, 369 E2
Kumusi Point, Papua New Guinea, 140 C5
Kümüx, China, 212 F4
Kŭmya, North Korea, 211 J5
Kunágota, Hungary, 289 K5
Kunak, Malaysia, 201 G1
Kunashir, island, Kuril'skiye Ostrova, Russian Federation, 209 J1
Kunda, Estonia, 287 N3
Kunda, India, 219 E4
Kunda-dia-Baze, Angola, 368 C4
Kundelungu, Monts, mountain range, Democratic Republic of the Congo, 369 E4
Kundiawa, Papua New Guinea, 140 B4

Kundla, India, 218 B5
Kundur, Pulau, island, Indonesia, 200 C2
Kunene, administrative region, Namibia, 370 B2
Kunene, river, Namibia, 368 B6
Künes Linchang, China, 212 E4
Künes, river, China, 212 D4
Kungälv, Sweden, 286 E4
Kunghit Island, Canada, 412 D5
Kungsbacka, Sweden, 286 F4
Kungshamn, Sweden, 286 E3
Kungu, Democratic Republic of the Congo, 368 C2
Kungur, Russian Federation, 222 F1
Kungurtug, Russian Federation, 213 H2
Kungutas, Tanzania, 369 F4
Kunhegyes, Hungary, 289 K5
Kunhing, Myanmar, 205 C3
Kunlong, Myanmar, 205 C3
Kunlun Shan, mountain range, China, 212 D5, 144, 158
Kunmadaras, Hungary, 289 K5
Kunming, China, 215 G4, 161
Kunsan, South Korea, 208 D4
Kunshan, China, 206 E2
Kunszentmárton, Hungary, 289 K5
Kunua, Papua New Guinea, 140 E2
Kununurra, Australia, 134 F2
Kun'ya, Russian Federation, 299 C4
Kunyang, China, 215 G4
Kunzulu, Democratic Republic of the Congo, 368 C3
Kuolayarvi, Russian Federation, 285 P3
Kuolio, Finland, 285 P4
Kuolismaa, Russian Federation, 285 Q5
Kuopio, Finland, 285 N5
Kuorpukas, Gora, mountain peak, Russian Federation, 285 Q2
Kuortane, Finland, 287 L1
Kuortti, Finland, 287 N2
Kuouka, Sweden, 284 K3
Kupang, Indonesia, 198 C5
Kupangnunding, Indonesia, 201 F3
Kupiano, Papua New Guinea, 140 C5
Kupingarri, Australia, 134 F2
Kupino, Russian Federation, 223 K2
Kupiškis, Lithuania, 287 M5
Kuqa, China, 212 D4
Kür, river, Azerbaijan, 222 D4, 189
Kur, river, Russian Federation, 211 L2, 190
Kuragino, Russian Federation, 223 N2
Kurashiki, Japan, 208 F4
Kuraymah, Sudan, 363 F5
Kurayoshi, Japan, 208 F4
Kurba, river, Russian Federation, 210 E1
Kürdämir, Azerbaijan, 222 D4
Kurdoğlu Burnu, point, Turkey, 297 G7
Kŭrdzhali, Bulgaria, 297 E5
Kure, island, Hawaiian Islands, U.S.A., 139 G2
Kure, Japan, 208 F4
Küre Dağları, mountain range, Turkey, 224 D4
Kuressaare, Estonia, 287 L3

Kurgal'dzhinskiy, Kazakhstan, 223 J2
Kurgan, Russian Federation, 222 H1
Kurganskaya Oblast', province, Russian Federation, 222 G1
Kurgenitsy, Russian Federation, 299 E1
Kuri, river, Indonesia, 199 F3
Kuria Muria Islands see Khurīyā Murīyā, Jazā'ir, islands, Oman, 221 G5
Kurikka, Finland, 287 L1
Kurilsk, Russian Federation, 301 R5, 273
Kuril Basin, underwater feature, Pacific Ocean, 478 N1
Kuril Islands see Kuril'skiye Ostrova, islands, Russian Federation, 301 R5, 273
Kuril Trench, underwater feature, Pacific Ocean, 478 N2
Kuril'sk, Russian Federation, 209 J1
Kuril'skiye Ostrova (Kuril Islands), islands, Russian Federation, 301 R5, 273
Kurkino, Russian Federation, 299 G6
Kurlek, Russian Federation, 223 L1
Kurleya, Russian Federation, 211 G1
Kurmuk, Sudan, 366 D2
Kurnool, India, 216 D3
Kurovskoye, Russian Federation, 299 G5
Kurow, New Zealand, 133 C7
Kurów, Poland, 289 L3
Kurrayimah, Jordan, 225 C3
Kuršėnai, Lithuania, 287 L4
Kürshim, Kazakhstan, 223 L3
Kurshskiy Zaliv, lagoon, Lithuania/Russian Federation, 287 K5
Kursk, Russian Federation, 298 E2
Kurskaya Oblast', province, Russian Federation, 298 E2
Kursu, Finland, 285 P3
Kuršumlija, Serbia, 296 C4
Kurtak, Russian Federation, 223 N1
Kurtakko, Finland, 285 M3
Kurtalan, Turkey, 224 F5
Kurtamysh, Russian Federation, 222 G2
Kürtī, Sudan, 363 F5
Kuruktag, mountain range, China, 212 E4
Kuruman, South Africa, 370 D4
Kurume, Japan, 208 E4
Kurunegala, Sri Lanka, 216 E5
Kur'ya, Russian Federation, 223 L2
Kuş Gölü, lake, Turkey, 297 F5
Kusa, Russian Federation, 222 F1
Kuşadası, Turkey, 297 F7
Kuşadası Körfezi, bay, Turkey, 297 F7
Kusawa Lake, Canada, 412 A1
Kusha, Russian Federation, 285 T5
Kushalino, Russian Federation, 299 F4
Kushālnagar, India, 216 C3
Kushima, Japan, 208 E5
Kushimoto, Japan, 209 F4
Kushiro, Japan, 209 J2
Kushtagi, India, 216 D3
Kushtia, Bangladesh, 219 G5
Kusite, China, 211 K2
Kuskokwim, river, U.S.A., 410 D3

Kuskokwim Bay, U.S.A., **410** C4
Kuskokwim Mountains, *mountain range*, U.S.A., **410** D3
Kusma, Nepal, **219** E3
Kustanay *see* Qostanay, Kazakhstan, **222** G2
Kūsti, Sudan, **366** D2
Kut, Ko, *island*, Thailand, **202** D4
Kütahya, *province*, Turkey, **297** G6
Kütahya, Turkey, **224** C5
K'ut'aisi, Georgia, **222** C4
Kutarere, New Zealand, **132** F4
Kutina, Croatia, **294** F3
Kutiyāna, India, **218** B5
Kutkai, Myanmar, **205** C3
Kutno, Poland, **289** J2
Kuttura, Finland, **285** N2
Kutu, Democratic Republic of the Congo, **368** C3
Kutum, Sudan, **366** B2
Kúty, Slovakia, **289** H4
Kuujjuaq, Canada, **411** N4
Kuusalu, Estonia, **287** M3
Kuusamo, Finland, **285** P4
Kuusankoski, Finland, **287** N2
Kuusjoki, Finland, **287** L2
Kuvango, Angola, **368** C5
Kuvshinovo, Russian Federation, **299** E4
Kuwait, *country*, Asia, **196** F7, *45, 97, 146, 147, 175, 177, 182, 317*
Kuwait *see* Al Kuwayt, Kuwait, **363** J3, *177*
Kuwalan, *river*, Indonesia, **201** E3
Kuyal'nyts'kyy Lyman, *lake*, Ukraine, **296** H2
Kuybyshev, Russian Federation, **223** K1
Kūybyshevskīy, Kazakhstan, **222** H2
Kuybyshevskoye Vodokhranilishche, *reservoir*, Russian Federation, **298** G2
Kuye, *river*, China, **210** E5
Kuygan, Kazakhstan, **223** J3
Kuytun, China, **212** E3
Kuyucak, Turkey, **297** G7
Kuyuwini, *river*, Guyana, **451** G3
Kuzedeyevo, Russian Federation, **223** M2
Kuzema, *river*, Russian Federation, **285** R4
Kuzema, Russian Federation, **285** S4
Kuznechnoye, Russian Federation, **299** B2
Kuznetsk, Russian Federation, **298** G2
Kuzomen', Russian Federation, **285** T3
Kuzreka, Russian Federation, **285** S3
Kuzumaki, Japan, **209** H2
Kvænangen, *bay*, Norway, **284** K1
Kvænangsbotn, Norway, **285** L2
Kværndrup, Denmark, **286** E5
Kvaløy, *island*, Norway, **284** J2
Kvaløya, *island*, Norway, **285** L1
Kvalsund, Norway, **285** L1
Kvarner, *gulf*, Croatia, **294** E3
Kvarnerič, *bay*, Croatia, **294** E3
Kvenvær, Norway, **284** D5
Kvikkjokk, Sweden, **284** H3
Kvikne, Norway, **286** E1
Kvinesdal, Norway, **286** C3, *230*
Kwa Mashu, South Africa, **371** F4
Kwa Mtoro, Tanzania, **369** G4
Kwa Nobuhle, South Africa, **370** E5
Kwail, North Korea, **208** D3
Kwajalein, *island*, Marshall Islands, **138** E4, *119*
Kwakoegron, Suriname, **452** B2
Kwakwani, Guyana, **451** G3
Kwale, Kenya, **369** G3
Kwale, Nigeria, **365** F3
Kwamouth, Democratic Republic of the Congo, **368** C3
Kwangju, South Korea, **208** D4
Kwara, *state*, Nigeria, **365** E3
Kwatarkwashi, Nigeria, **365** F2
Kwatisore, Indonesia, **199** F3
Kwazulu-Natal, *province*, South Africa, **371** F4, *95, 351*
Kwekwe, Zimbabwe, **371** E2
Kweneng, *district*, Botswana, **370** D3
Kwenge, *river*, Democratic Republic of the Congo, **368** C4
Kwidzyn, Poland, **289** J2
Kwikila, Papua New Guinea, **140** B5
Kwinana, Australia, **134** D5
Kwoka, Gunung, *mountain peak*, Indonesia, **199** F3
Kyabé, Chad, **366** A3
Kyaikkami, Myanmar, **202** C2
Kyaikto, Myanmar, **205** C4
Kyakhta, Russian Federation, **210** D2
Kyancutta, Australia, **135** H5
Kyanda, Russian Federation, **285** U4
Kyangin, Myanmar, **205** B4
Kyaukme, Myanmar, **205** C3
Kyaukpyu, Myanmar, **205** B4
Kyauktaw, Myanmar, **205** B3
Kyeintali, Myanmar, **205** B4
Kyela, Tanzania, **369** F4
Kyenjojo, Uganda, **369** F2
Kyindwe, Myanmar, **205** B3
Kyklades (Cyclades), *islands*, Greece, **297** E7
Kyle of Lochalsh, Scotland, U.K., **308** D3
Kyleakin, Scotland, U.K., **308** D3
Kyll, *river*, Germany, **288** C3
Kyllini Oros, *mountain peak*, Greece, **297** D7
Kylmälä, Finland, **285** N4
Kymi, Greece, **297** E6
Kyŏnggi-man, *bay*, South Korea, **208** D3
Kyŏngju, South Korea, **208** E4
Kyŏngsŏng, North Korea, **208** E2
Kyōto, Japan, **209** F4, *165*
Kyparissia, Greece, **297** C7
Kyparissiakos Kolpos, *bay*, Greece, **297** C7
Kyra, Russian Federation, **210** E2
Kyra Panagia, *island*, Greece, **297** E6
Kyren, Russian Federation, **213** J2
Kyrenia Range, *mountain range*, Cyprus, **225** B2, *191*
Kyrgyz Ala Too, *mountain range*, Kazakhstan/Kyrgyzstan, **212** B4
Kyrgyzstan, *country*, Asia, **196** J5, *144, 185, 186, 187, 188*
Kyritz, Germany, **288** F2
Kyrksæterøra, Norway, **284** D5
Kyrnasivka, Ukraine, **296** G1
Kyrnychky, Ukraine, **296** G3
Kyrönjoki, *river*, Finland, **285** L5
Kyshtovka, Russian Federation, **223** K1
Kythira, Greece, **297** D7
Kythira, *island*, Greece, **297** D7
Kythnos, *island*, Kyklades, Greece, **297** E7
Kythrea, Cyprus, **225** B2
Kyuquot Sound, Canada, **412** F7
Kyushe, Kazakhstan, **222** F3
Kyūshū, *island*, Japan, **208** F4, *165*
Kyushu Palau Ridge, *underwater feature*, Pacific Ocean, **478** D3
Kyustendil, Bulgaria, **296** D4
Kyyiv (Kiev), Ukraine, **298** D2, *159, 268, 269, 271, 272*
Kyyivs'ke, Vodoskhovyshche, *reservoir*, Ukraine, **298** C2
Kyyjärvi, Finland, **285** M5
Kyzyl, Russian Federation, **223** N2
Kyzyl-Kiya, Kyrgyzstan, **223** J4
Kzyl-Orda *see* Qyzylorda, Kazakhstan, **222** H4
Kyzyldangi, Gora, *mountain peak*, Tajikistan, **223** J5
Kyzylkum, Peski, *desert*, Kazakhstan/Uzbekistan, **222** G4, *185*


## L


La Almunia de Doña Godina, Spain, **293** G2
La Asunción, Venezuela, **451** F1
La Banda, Argentina, **458** D3
La Bañeza, Spain, **292** E1
La Barge, U.S.A., **419** J5
La Belle, U.S.A., **425** M6
La Blanquilla, *island*, Venezuela, **451** F1
La Boquilla del Conchos, Mexico, **430** D3
La Brea, Trinidad, Trinidad and Tobago, **461** C4
La Brède, France, **290** D4
La Calera, Chile, **458** B4
La Capelle, France, **291** F2
La Carlota, Argentina, **458** D4
La Carolina, Spain, **293** F3
La Ceiba, Honduras, **428** D4
La Charité-sur-Loire, France, **291** F3
La Châtre, France, **290** E3
La Chorrera, Colombia, **450** D4
La Chorrera, Panama, **429** F5
La Ciudad, Mexico, **430** D4
La Cocha, Argentina, **458** D3
La Concepción, Panama, **429** E5
La Corey, Canada, **413** P4
La Crescent, U.S.A., **420** H4
La Croisière, France, **290** E3
La Crosse, Kansas, U.S.A., **420** D6
La Crosse, Wisconsin, U.S.A., **420** H4
La Cruz, Argentina, **459** F3
La Cruz, Colombia, **450** C4
La Cruz, Mexico, **430** D4
La Cumbre, Volcán, *mountain peak*, Islas Galápagos (Galapagos Islands), Ecuador, **461** A2
La Dorada, Colombia, **450** C3
La Escala, Spain, **293** J1
La Esmeralda, Paraguay, **458** D2
La Esmeralda, Venezuela, **451** F3
La Esperanza, Argentina, **460** D1
La Esperanza, Bolivia, **455** F4
La Esperanza, Honduras, **428** C4
La Estrella, Argentina, **458** D2
La Estrella, Bolivia, **455** F4
La Falda, Argentina, **458** D4
La Fayette, U.S.A., **425** K2
La Fé, Isla de la Juventud, Cuba, **429** E2
La Fé, W. Cuba, **428** D2
La Flèche, France, **290** D3
La Foa, New Caledonia, **141** A3
La Forestière, French Guiana, **452** B2
La Fría, Venezuela, **450** D2
La Galite, *island*, Tunisia, **295** B7
La Giandola, France, **291** H5
La Gloria, Colombia, **450** D2
La Goulette, Tunisia, **295** C7
La Grande, U.S.A., **418** E4
La Grande Deux, Réservoir de, Canada, **416** C3
La Grande Rivière, *river*, Canada, **415** Q5
La Grande Trois, Réservoir de, Canada, **416** D3
La Grange, Georgia, U.S.A., **425** K3
La Grange, Texas, U.S.A., **424** D5
La Grange, Wyoming, U.S.A., **419** M6
La Grave, France, **291** H4
La Guardia, Chile, **458** C3
La Guerche-de-Bretagne, France, **290** D3
La Habana (Havana), Cuba, **429** E2, *392, 393*
La Horqueta, Venezuela, **451** G2
La Huaca, Peru, **454** B1
La Jagua de Ibirico, Colombia, **450** D2
La Jara, U.S.A., **423** L3
La Joya, Mexico, **430** D3
La Joya, Peru, **454** D4
La Junta, U.S.A., **423** M3
La Laguna, Argentina, **458** D4
La Laguna, Islas Canarias, Spain, **373** A4
La Laja, Chile, **458** B5
La Libertad, Guatemala, **428** C3
La Ligua, Chile, **458** B4
La Linea de la Concepción, Spain, **292** E4
La Loberia, Argentina, **460** E1
La Loche, Canada, **413** Q3
La Loma, San Andrés, Colombia, **461** B1
La Maddalena, Sardegna, Italy, **295** B5
La Malbaie, Canada, **416** F6
La Martre, Canada, **411** N5
La Mejorada, Peru, **454** C3
La Merced, Peru, **454** C3
La Moure, U.S.A., **420** D2
La Mula, Mexico, **430** D2
La Mure, France, **291** G4
La Nava de Ricomalillo, Spain, **292** E3
La Negra, Chile, **458** B2
La Noria, Mexico, **430** D4
La Oliva, Islas Canarias, Spain, **373** B4
La Orchila, *island*, Venezuela, **451** E1
La Oroya, Peru, **454** C3
La Paca, Spain, **293** G4
La Palma, *island*, Islas Canarias, Spain, **373** A4
La Palma, Panama, **429** F5
La Paloma, Uruguay, **459** F5
La Pampa, *province*, Argentina, **458** D5
La Paragua, Venezuela, **451** F2
La Paz, Bahía de, *bay*, Mexico, **430** C3
La Paz, Bolivia, **455** E4, *441*
La Paz, *department*, Bolivia, **455** E4
La Paz, Entre Rios, Argentina, **459** E4
La Paz, Mendoza, Argentina, **458** C4
La Paz, Mexico, **430** C3
La Paz, Providencia, Colombia, **461** C1
La Pedrera, Colombia, **451** E4
La Perla, Mexico, **430** D2
La Perouse Strait, Japan/Russian Federation, **209** H1
La Pesca, Mexico, **431** F4
La Piedad Cavadas, Mexico, **430** E4
La Pine, U.S.A., **418** D5
La Plaine, Dominica, **427** D3
La Plaine des Cafres, Réunion, **373** A1
La Plata, Argentina, **459** F5
La Plata, Colombia, **450** C3
La Pobla de Segur, Spain, **293** H1
La Possession, Réunion, **373** A1
La Potherie, Lac, *lake*, Canada, **415** T2
La Pryor, U.S.A., **424** C5
La Push, U.S.A., **418** B3
La Quiaca, Argentina, **458** D2
La Rioja, Argentina, **458** C3
La Rioja, *autonomous community*, Spain, **293** F1, *253*
La Rioja, *province*, Argentina, **458** C3
La Rivière, Canada, **414** E7
La Roca de la Sierra, Spain, **292** D3
La Roche, New Caledonia, **141** A3
La Roche-Chalais, France, **290** D4
La Roche-sur-Yon, France, **290** D3
La Rochelle, France, **290** D3
La Roda, Spain, **293** F3
La Romana, Dominican Republic, **429** H3
La Ronge, Canada, **413** S4
La Rosita, Mexico, **430** E2
La Sábana, Argentina, **459** E3
La Salle, Canada, **414** F7
La Salle, U.S.A., **421** J5
La Sarre, Canada, **416** B5
La Scie, Canada, **417** P5
La Serena, Chile, **458** B3
La Seu d'Urgell, Spain, **293** H1
La Solana, Spain, **293** F3
La Spezia, Italy, **294** B3
La Tagua, Colombia, **450** C4
La Teste, France, **290** D4
La Toma, Argentina, **458** D4
La Tortuga, *island*, Venezuela, **451** F1
La Troya, *river*, Argentina, **458** C3
La Tuque, Canada, **416** E6
La Unión, Bolivia, **455** G4
La Unión, Chile, **460** C1
La Unión, Colombia, **450** C4
La Unión, Mexico, **430** E5
La Unión, Peru, **454** C2
La Urbana, Venezuela, **451** E2
La Vega, Haiti, **429** H3
La Ventana, Mexico, **431** E4
La Vibora, Mexico, **430** E3
La Victoria, Venezuela, **451** E1
La Yarada, Peru, **454** D5
Laage, Germany, **288** F2
Laascaanood, Somalia, **367** G3
Laâyoune *see* El Aaiún, Western Sahara, **360** D3
Labasa, Fiji, **141** A4
Labé, Guinea, **364** B2
Labe (Elbe), *river*, Czech Republic, **289** G3
Labelle, Canada, **416** D6
Labin, Croatia, **294** E3
Labinsk, Russian Federation, **222** C4
Labis, Malaysia, **200** C2
Labo, Mount, *mountain peak*, Philippines, **204** C3
Labo, Philippines, **204** C3
Laboulaye, Argentina, **458** D5
Labrador, *region*, Canada, **411** N4, *91, 380*
Labrador City, Canada, **416** H3
Labrador Sea, Canada/Greenland, **411** P4
Lábrea, Brazil, **455** F2
Labrit, France, **290** D4
Labu, Indonesia, **200** D3
Labuan, *federal territory*, Malaysia, **201** F1
Labudalin, China, **211** H2
Labuha, Indonesia, **198** D3
Labuhanbajo, Indonesia, **198** B5
Labuhanbilik, Indonesia, **200** C2
Labuhanhaji, Indonesia, **200** B2
Labuhanmeringgai, Indonesia, **200** D4
Labuk, Teluk, *bay*, Malaysia, **201** G1
Labyrinth Lake, Canada, **414** A1
Labytnangi, Russian Federation, **300** H3
Laç, Albania, **297** B5
Lac, *prefecture*, Chad, **365** G2
Lac du Bonnet, Canada, **414** F6
Lac-Édouard, Canada, **416** E6
Lac-Gatineau, Canada, **416** D6
Lac La Biche, Canada, **413** P4
Lac la Hache, Canada, **412** J6
Lac-Saguay, Canada, **416** D6
Lacanau, Étang de, *lake*, France, **290** D4
Lacanau, France, **290** D4
Lacaune, France, **290** F5
Laccadive Islands *see* Lakshadweep Islands, *islands*, India, Indian Ocean, **216** B4
Lacha, Ozero, *lake*, Russian Federation, **299** G2
Lachlan, *river*, Australia, **135** K5
Lachung, India, **219** G4
Läckö, Sweden, **286** F3
Laclede, U.S.A., **418** F2
Lacombe, Canada, **413** N5
Laconi, Sardegna, Italy, **295** B6
Laconia, U.S.A., **426** E3
Lacre Punt, *point*, Bonaire, Netherlands Antilles, **461** A4
Lada, *river*, Russian Federation, **299** D3

Ladākh Range, *mountain range*, India, **218** D2, *168*
Ladismith, South Africa, **370** D5
Ladispoli, Italy, **295** D5
Lādnūn, India, **218** C4
Ladozhskoye Ozero, *lake*, Russian Federation, **299** C2
Ladrillero, Golfo, *gulf*, Chile, **460** B3
Ladron Peak, *mountain peak*, U.S.A., **423** K4
Ladushkin, Russian Federation, **287** K5
Ladva, Russian Federation, **299** E2
Ladvozero, Russian Federation, **285** P4
Lady Barron, Australia, **135** K7
Ladybank, Scotland, U.K., **308** F4
Ladysmith, Canada, **412** H7
Ladysmith, South Africa, **371** E4
Ladysmith, U.S.A., **420** H3
Ladyzhyn, Ukraine, **296** G1
Ladyzhynka, Ukraine, **296** H1
Lae, Papua New Guinea, **140** B4
Lærdalsøyri, Norway, **286** C2
Læsø, *island*, Denmark, **286** E4
Lævvajok, Norway, **285** N2
Lafayette, Indiana, U.S.A., **421** K5
Lafayette, Louisiana, U.S.A., **424** G4
Lafia, Nigeria, **365** F3
Lafiagi, Nigeria, **365** F3
Lagamar, Brazil, **456** D5
Lagan', Russian Federation, **222** D3
Lagan, Sweden, **286** F4
Lagarto, Brazil, **457** G3
Lagbar, Senegal, **364** B1
Lågen, *river*, Norway, **286** D2
Lagg, Scotland, U.K., **308** D5
Laggan, Loch, *lake*, Scotland, U.K., **308** E4
Laggan, Scotland, U.K., **308** E3
Laghouat, Algeria, **361** G2
Lagkadas, Greece, **297** D5
Lago Agrio, Ecuador, **450** C4
Lago Ranco, Chile, **460** C1
Lagoa Santa, Brazil, **457** E5
Lagoa Vermelha, Brazil, **459** G3
Lagonegro, Italy, **295** E5
Lagong, Pulau, *island*, Indonesia, **201** E2
Lagonoy, Philippines, **204** C3
Lagonoy Gulf, Philippines, **204** C3
Lagos, Nigeria, **365** E3, *95*
Lagos, Portugal, **292** C4
Lagos, *state*, Nigeria, **365** E3
Lagos de Moreno, Mexico, **430** E4
Lagosa, Tanzania, **369** E4
Lagrange, Australia, **134** E2
Lagrasse, France, **290** F5
Lagrave, Mont, *mountain peak*, Mauritus, **373** C1
Lagrave, Pointe, *point*, Mauritius, **373** C1
Laguiole, France, **290** F4
Laguna, Brazil, **459** H3
Laguna, Ilha da, *island*, Brazil, **452** C3
Laguna, U.S.A., **423** K4
Laguna de Perlas, Nicaragua, **428** E4
Laguna Grande, Argentina, **460** C3
Laguna Madre, *bay*, U.S.A., **424** D6
Lagunas, Chile, **455** E5
Lagunas, Peru, **450** C5
Lagunillas, Bolivia, **455** F5
Lagunillas, Venezuela, **450** D1
Laha, China, **211** J2
Lahad Datu, Malaysia, **201** G1
Lahaina, Hawaiian Islands, U.S.A., **422** R9
Lahat, Indonesia, **200** C3
Lahe, Myanmar, **205** B2
Lahewa, Indonesia, **200** B2
Laḥij, Yemen, **220** D6
Lahn, *river*, Germany, **288** D3
Laholm, Sweden, **286** F4
Laholmsbukten, *bay*, Sweden, **286** F4
Lahore, Pakistan, **218** C3, *173*
Lahr, Germany, **288** C4
Lahri, Pakistan, **218** B3
Lāhrūd, Iran, **222** D5
Lahti, Finland, **287** M2
Laï, Chad, **365** H3
Lai Châu, Vietnam, **203** D1
Lai-hka, Myanmar, **205** C3
Laiagam, Papua New Guinea, **140** A4
Lai'an, China, **206** D1
Laifeng, China, **206** B2
L'Aigle, France, **290** E2
Laihia, Finland, **287** L1
Laingsburg, South Africa, **370** D5
Lainio, Sweden, **285** L3
Lainioälven, *river*, Sweden, **284** K2
Lair, Scotland, U.K., **308** D3
Lairg, Scotland, U.K., **308** E2
Lais, Indonesia, **200** C3
Laisamis, Kenya, **369** G2
Laissac, France, **291** F4
Laisvall, Sweden, **284** H3
Laitila, Finland, **287** K2
Laiwu, China, **210** G5
Laiwui, Indonesia, **198** D3
Laixi, China, **211** H5
Laiyang, China, **211** H5
Laiyuan, China, **210** F5
Laizhou, China, **211** G5
Laizhou Wan, *bay*, China, **211** G5
Laja, Laguna de, *lake*, Chile, **458** B5
Lajeado, Brazil, **459** G3
Lajes, Rio Grande da Norte, Brazil, **453** G4
Lajes, Santa Catarina, Brazil, **459** G3
Lajkovac, Serbia, **296** C3
Lakamané, Mali, **364** C2
Lakatoro, Vanuatu, **141** A2
Lakaträsk, Sweden, **284** K3
Lake, U.S.A., **419** J4
Lake Alma, Canada, **419** M2
Lake Argyle Village, Australia, **134** F2
Lake Cargelligo, Australia, **135** K5
Lake Charles, U.S.A., **424** F4
Lake City, Florida, U.S.A., **425** L4
Lake City, South Carolina, U.S.A., **425** N3
Lake District, *region*, England, U.K., **306** E3, *276*
Lake Elwell, U.S.A., **413** P7
Lake George, U.S.A., **420** F2
Lake Havasu City, U.S.A., **422** F4
Lake Hawea, New Zealand, **133** B7
Lake Jackson, U.S.A., **424** E5
Lake King, Australia, **134** D5
Lake Koocanusa, U.S.A., **413** M7
Lake Louise, Canada, **413** L6
Lake McConaughy, U.S.A., **420** C5
Lake Mills, U.S.A., **420** G4
Lake Preston, U.S.A., **420** E3
Lake Providence, U.S.A., **424** G3
Lake View, U.S.A., **420** F4
Lake Village, U.S.A., **424** G3
Lake Wales, U.S.A., **425** M6
Lakeba, *island*, Fiji, **141** A4
Lakeba Passage, *strait*, Fiji, **141** A4
Lakeland, Australia, **135** J2
Lakeland, Florida, U.S.A., **425** M5
Lakeland, South Carolina, U.S.A., **425** L4
Lakenheath, England, U.K., **305** H2
Lakepa, Niue, **132** M13
Lakeport, U.S.A., **422** B2
Lakes Entrance, Australia, **135** K6
Lakeside, California, U.S.A., **418** B5
Lakeside, Virginia, U.S.A., **426** B6
Laketown, U.S.A., **419** J6
Lakeview, U.S.A., **418** D5
Lakewood, Colorado, U.S.A., **423** L2
Lakewood, New Jersey, U.S.A., **426** C4
Lakewood, New Mexico, U.S.A., **423** L5
Lakhdaria, Algeria, **293** J4
Lakhīmpur, India, **218** E4
Lakhnādon, India, **218** D5
Lakhpat, India, **218** B5
Laki, *mountain peak*, Iceland, **284** Y7
Lakki, Pakistan, **218** B2
Lakonikos Kolpos, *bay*, Greece, **297** D7
Lakota, Côte d'Ivoire, **364** C3
Laksefjorden, *fiord*, Norway, **285** N1
Lakselv, Norway, **285** M1
Lakshadweep, *union territory*, India, **216** C4, *169*
Lakshadweep Islands (Laccadive Islands), *islands*, India, Indian Ocean, **216** B4
Laktaši, Bosnia and Herzegovina, **294** F3
Lakuramau, Papua New Guinea, **140** C3
Lalang, *river*, Indonesia, **200** D3
Lalapansi, Zimbabwe, **371** F2
Lalapaşa, Turkey, **296** F5
Lalara, Gabon, **368** B2
Lālī, Iran, **220** E2
Lāliān, Pakistan, **218** C3
Lalībela, Ethiopia, **367** E2, *339*
Laliki, Indonesia, **198** D4
Lalin, China, **211** J3
Lalín, Spain, **292** C1
Lalinda, Vanuatu, **141** A2
Lalitpur, India, **218** D4
Lalomanu, Samoa, **141** B1
Lālsot, India, **218** D4
Lam Pao Reservoir, Thailand, **203** D2
Lamag, Malaysia, **201** G1
Lamakera, Indonesia, **198** C5
Lamap, Vanuatu, **141** A2
Lamar, Colorado, U.S.A., **423** M2
Lamar, Missouri, U.S.A., **420** F7
Lamarque, Argentina, **460** E1
Lamastre, France, **291** G4
Lamballe, France, **290** C2
Lambaréné, Gabon, **368** B3
Lambay Island, Ireland, **309** G4
Lambayeque, Peru, **454** B2
Lamberts Bay, South Africa, **370** C5
Lambeth, Canada, **421** N4
Lambeth Bluff, *point*, Heard and McDonald Islands, **134** S12
Lambi, Solomon Islands, **141** A1
Lambourn, England, U.K., **305** F3
Lame Deer, U.S.A., **419** L4
Lamego, Portugal, **292** D2
Lamesa, U.S.A., **424** B3
L'Ametlla de Mar, Spain, **293** H2
Lamia, Greece, **297** D6
Lamigan Point, Philippines, **204** D5
Lamitan, Philippines, **204** C5
Lamlash, Scotland, U.K., **308** D5
Lamma Island *see* Pok Liu Chau, *island*, China, **207** C4
Lammermoor Range, *mountain range*, New Zealand, **133** B7
Lammi, Finland, **287** M2
Lamon Bay, Philippines, **204** C3
Lamont, Canada, **413** N5
Lamont, U.S.A., **419** L5
Lamotrek, *island*, Micronesia, **138** C4
Lampang, Thailand, **202** C2
Lampasas, U.S.A., **424** C4
Lampazos de Naranjo, Mexico, **431** E3
Lampedusa, Isola di, *island*, Isole Pelagie, Italy, **295** D8
Lampeter, Wales, U.K., **304** C2
Lamphun, Thailand, **202** C2
Lampung, *province*, Indonesia, **200** D4
Lamu, Kenya, **369** H3
Lan Hsü, *island*, Taiwan, **206** E4
Lanai, *island*, Hawaiian Islands, U.S.A., **422** R9
Lanai City, Hawaiian Islands, U.S.A., **422** R9
Lanao, Lake, Philippines, **204** C5
Lancang (Mekong), *river*, China, **215** F3, *96, 144, 152, 153, 154, 158*
Lancashire, *unitary authority*, England, U.K., **306** F4
Lancaster, California, U.S.A., **422** D4
Lancaster, Canada, **416** D7
Lancaster, England, U.K., **306** F3
Lancaster, Minnesota, U.S.A., **420** E1
Lancaster, New Hampshire, U.S.A., **426** E2
Lancaster, Ohio, U.S.A., **421** M6
Lancaster, Pennsylvania, U.S.A., **426** B4
Lancaster, South Carolina, U.S.A., **425** M2
Lancaster, Wisconsin, U.S.A., **420** H4
Lancaster Sound, Canada, **411** L2
Lance Creek, U.S.A., **419** M5
Lancer, Canada, **413** Q6
Lanciano, Italy, **295** E4
Lanco, Chile, **460** C1
Lancun, China, **211** H5
Landau an der Isar, Germany, **288** F4
Landau in der Pfalz, Germany, **288** D4
Landeck, Austria, **288** E5
Lander, U.S.A., **419** K5
Landes, *region*, France, **290** D4
Landete, Spain, **293** G3
Landfall Island, Andaman and Nicobar Islands, India, **217** H3
Landis, Canada, **413** Q5
Landön, Sweden, **284** G5
Land's End, *point*, England, U.K., **304** B4
Landsberg am Lech, Germany, **288** E4
Landshut, Germany, **294** D1
Landskrona, Sweden, **286** F5
Lanesborough, Ireland, **309** E4
Lang, Canada, **419** M2
Lang Shan, *mountain range*, China, **210** D4
Lạng Sơn, Vietnam, **203** E1
Lang Suan, Thailand, **202** C4
Långå, Sweden, **286** F1
Langar, Afghanistan, **218** C1
Langara, Bahía, *bay*, Argentina, **460** D3
Langavat, Loch, *lake*, Scotland, U.K., **308** C2
Langdon, U.S.A., **420** D1
Langdon Point, Macquarie Island, **134** R11
Langeais, France, **290** E3
Langenburg, Canada, **414** D6
Langenthal, Switzerland, **291** H3
Langeoog, *island*, Germany, **288** C2
Langepas, Russian Federation, **300** J3
Langevin, Réunion, **373** A1
Langfang, China, **210** G5
Langgapayung, Indonesia, **200** B2
Langgar, China, **214** E3
Langham, Canada, **413** R5
Langholm, Scotland, U.K., **308** F5
Langholt, Iceland, **284** Y8
Langjökull, *ice cap*, Iceland, **284** X7
Langkawi, Pulau, *island*, Malaysia, **200** B1
Langkon, Malaysia, **201** G1
Langlade, Canada, **416** D5
Langley, Canada, **412** H7
Langlois, U.S.A., **418** B5
Langon, France, **290** D4
Langøya, *island*, Norway, **284** G2
Langport, England, U.K., **304** E3
Langreo, Spain, **292** E1
Langres, France, **291** G3
Langres, Plateau de, *plateau*, France, **291** G3
Langru, China, **212** C5
Langruth, Canada, **414** E6
Langsa, Indonesia, **200** B1
Långseleån, *river*, Sweden, **284** G4
Langshan, China, **210** D4
Langstrand, Norway, **285** L1
Langtang, Nigeria, **365** F3
Langting, India, **214** E4
Langtoft, England, U.K., **307** H3
Långträsk, Sweden, **284** K4
Langtry, U.S.A., **423** N7
Languedoc, *region*, France, **290** F5
Languedoc-Roussillon, *administrative region*, France, **291** F5, *245*
Långvattnet, Sweden, **284** H4
Langwang, China, **207** A3
Langwathby, England, U.K., **306** F3
Langxi, China, **206** D2
Langzhong, China, **215** H3
Lanhe, China, **207** A3
Laniel, Canada, **421** P2
Łanięta, Poland, **289** J2
Lanigan, Canada, **413** S6
Lanin, Volcán, *mountain peak*, Argentina, **460** C1
Lanivet, England, U.K., **304** C4
Länkäran, Azerbaijan, **222** D5
Länkipohja, Finland, **287** M2
Lanlacuni Bajo, Peru, **454** D3
Lannavaara, Sweden, **285** L2
Lannilis, France, **290** B2
Lannion, France, **290** C2
Lansdowne House, Canada, **415** L5
L'Anse aux Meadows, Canada, **417** P4
Lansford, U.S.A., **420** C1
Lanshan, China, **213** J5
Lansing, U.S.A., **421** L4, *386*
Länsi-Suomen Lääni, *province*, Finland, **285** L5
Lansjärv, Sweden, **285** L3
Lanslebourg-Mont-Cenis, France, **291** H4
Lantang, China, **207** D2
Lantau Island *see* Dai Yue Shan, *island*, China, **207** B4
Lantian, Guangdong, China, **207** C1
Lantian, Shaanxi, China, **206** B1
Lantry, U.S.A., **420** C3
Lanusei, Sardegna, Italy, **295** B6
Lanxi, Anhui, China, **211** J3
Lanxi, Heilongjiang, China, **206** D2
Lanzarote, *island*, Islas Canarias, Spain, **373** B4, *355*
Lanzhou, China, **213** J5, *161*
Laoag, Philippines, **204** C2
Laobie Shan, *mountain range*, China, **215** F5
Laoha, *river*, China, **211** H4
Laoheishan, China, **211** K4
Laohekou, China, **206** B1
Laois, *county*, Ireland, **309** E5
Laon, France, **291** F2
Laos, *country*, Asia, **197** M8, *73, 89, 96, 144, 153, 154, 155, 157, 158*
Lapa, Brazil, **459** H2
Lapachito, Argentina, **459** E3
Lapai, Nigeria, **365** F3
Lapalisse, France, **291** F3
Lapi, Indonesia, **198** D2
Lapinlahti, Finland, **285** N5
Lapithos, Cyprus, **225** B2
Laplace, U.S.A., **424** G4
Lappajärvi, *lake*, Finland, **285** L5
Läppe, Sweden, **286** G3
Lappeenranta, Finland, **287** P2
Lappin Lääni, *province*, Finland, **285** M3
Lappland, *region*, Finland/Russian Federation/Sweden, **284** K3, *235*
Lappohja, Finland, **287** L3
Lappoluobbal, Norway, **285** L2
Lâpseki, Turkey, **297** F5
Laptev Log, Russian Federation, **223** L2
Laptevo, Russian Federation, **299** B4
Laptevykh, More, *sea*, Russian Federation, **301** N2
Lapu, China, **207** B2
Lapu-Lapu, Philippines, **204** C4
Lapua, Finland, **285** L5
Lapväärtti, Finland, **287** K1
L'Aquila, Italy, **295** D4
Lār, Iran, **221** F3
Larache, Morocco, **361** E1
Laramie, U.S.A., **419** M6
Laramie Mountains, *mountain range*, U.S.A., **419** M5
Laranjal, Brazil, **452** B4
Laranjeiras, Brazil, **457** G3
Laranjeiras do Sul, Brazil, **459** G2
Laranjinha, *river*, Brazil, **459** G2
Larantuka, Indonesia, **198** C5
Larba, Algeria, **361** G1
Laredo, U.S.A., **424** C6
Largo, Cayo, *island*, Cuba, **429** E2
Largo, U.S.A., **425** L6

Largs, Scotland, U.K., **308** E5
Larino, Italy, **295** E5
Larionovo, Russian Federation, **299** G3
Larisa, Greece, **297** D6, *265*
Lārkāna, Pakistan, **218** B4
Larkhall, Scotland, U.K., **308** F5
Larmor, France, **290** C3
Larnaka, Cyprus, **225** B2
Larne, *district*, Northern Ireland, U.K., **309** F3
Larne, Northern Ireland, U.K., **309** G3
Larne Lough, *inlet*, Northern Ireland, U.K., **309** G3
Larned, U.S.A., **420** D6
Laro, Cameroon, **365** G3
Larouco, Serra do, *mountain peak*, Portugal, **292** D2
Larrimah, Australia, **134** G2
Lars Christensen Coast, *region*, Antarctica, **470** F4
Larsen Ice Shelf, Antarctica, **470** B4
Larsen Sound, Canada, **411** K2
Laru Mat, Tanjong, *point*, Indonesia, **199** E4
Laruns, France, **290** D5
Larvik, Norway, **286** D3
Las Animas, U.S.A., **423** M2
Las Cañas, Argentina, **458** D3
Las Casitas, Islas Canarias, Spain, **373** A4
Las Catitas, Argentina, **458** C4
Las Cejas, Argentina, **458** D3
Las Cruces, U.S.A., **423** K5
Las Flores, Argentina, **459** E5
Las Galletas, Islas Canarias, Spain, **373** A4
Las Heras, Mendoza, Argentina, **458** C4
Las Heras, Santa Cruz, Argentina, **460** D3
Las Herreras, Mexico, **430** D3
Las Juntas, Chile, **458** C3
Las Lajas, Argentina, **460** C1
Las Lajitas, Venezuela, **451** F2
Las Lomas, Peru, **454** B1
Las Lomitas, Argentina, **458** E2
Las Martinetas, Argentina, **460** D3
Las Mercedes, Venezuela, **451** E2
Las Minas, Cerro, *mountain peak*, Honduras, **428** C4, *402*
Las Negras, Spain, **293** F4
Las Palmas de Gran Canaria, Islas Canarias, Spain, **373** B4, *355*
Las Petas, Bolivia, **455** G4
Las Piedras, Uruguay, **459** F5
Las Plumas, Argentina, **460** D2
Las Tablas, Panama, **429** E6
Las Tres Vírgenes, Volcán, *mountain peak*, Mexico, **430** B3
Las Trincheras, Venezuela, **451** F2
Las Tunas, Cuba, **429** F2
Las Varas, Mexico, **430** D4
Las Varillas, Argentina, **458** D4
Las Vegas, Nevada, U.S.A., **422** F3
Las Vegas, New Mexico, U.S.A., **423** L4
Lasanga Island, Papua New Guinea, **140** B4
Lascano, Uruguay, **459** F4
Lāsh-e Joveyn, Afghanistan, **221** H2
Lashio, Myanmar, **205** C3, **215** F5
Łask, Poland, **289** J3
Lasoni, Tanjong, *point*, Indonesia, **198** C3
Lasqoray, Somalia, **367** G2
Lassen Peak, *mountain peak*, U.S.A., **422** C1, *383*
Lassiter Coast, *region*, Antarctica, **470** B4
Last Chance, U.S.A., **423** M2
Last Mountain Lake, Canada, **413** S6
Lastoursville, Gabon, **368** B3
Lastovo, *island*, Croatia, **294** F4
Lastovski Kanal, *channel*, Croatia, **294** F4
Latacunga, Ecuador, **450** B4
Lataday Island, Antarctica, **470** B5
Latakia *see* Al Lādhiqīyah, Syria, **225** C2
Lätäseno, *river*, Finland/Sweden, **285** L2
Latdalam, Indonesia, **199** E4
Late, *island*, Tonga, **136** D2
Lātehār, India, **219** F5
Laterza, Italy, **295** F5
Latheron, Scotland, U.K., **308** F2
Lathrop, U.S.A., **420** F6
Latikberg, Sweden, **284** H4
Latina, Italy, **295** D5
Latulipe, Canada, **421** P2
Lātūr, India, **216** D2
Latvia, *country*, Europe, **282** G4, *228, 236, 237, 245, 270, 271, 272*
Lau (Eastern) Group, *islands*, Fiji, **141** A4
Laudal, Norway, **286** C3
Lauder, Scotland, U.K., **308** G5
Lauenburg (Elbe), Germany, **288** E2
Lauker, Sweden, **284** J4
Lauksletta, Norway, **284** K1
Laukuva, Lithuania, **287** L5
Lauli'i, Samoa, **141** B1
Launceston, Australia, **135** K7
Launceston, England, U.K., **304** C4
Launggyaung, Myanmar, **205** C2
Lauragh, Ireland, **309** C6
Laurel, Mississippi, U.S.A., **425** H4
Laurel, Montana, U.S.A., **419** K4
Laurel, Nebraska, U.S.A., **420** E4
Laurencekirk, Scotland, U.K., **308** G4
Laurens, U.S.A., **425** L2
Laurens Peninsula, Heard and McDonald Islands, **134** S12
Laurentian Fan, *underwater feature*, Atlantic Ocean, **477** D3
Laurentian Mountains, *mountain range*, Canada, **416** E5, *380*
Lauria, Italy, **295** E5
Laurier, Canada, **414** E6
Laurinburg, U.S.A., **425** N2
Lauriston, New Zealand, **133** C6
Lausanne, Switzerland, **291** H3
Laut, Pulau, *island*, Indonesia, **201** G3
Laut, Selat, *strait*, Indonesia, **201** F4
Lautaporras, Finland, **287** L2
Lautem, East Timor, **198** D5
Lautoka, Fiji, **141** A4
Laval, Canada, **416** E7
Laval, France, **290** D2
Lāvān, Jazīreh-ye, *island*, Iran, **220** F3
Lavanggu, Solomon Islands, **141** A1
Lavapié, Punta, *point*, Chile, **458** A5
Lavassaare, Estonia, **287** M3
Lavenham, England, U.K., **305** H2
Laverton, Australia, **134** E4
Lavia, Finland, **287** L2
Lavik, Norway, **286** B2
Lavina, U.S.A., **419** K3
Lavras, Brazil, **457** E5
Lavras do Sul, Brazil, **459** G4
Lavrio, Greece, **297** E7
Lavumisa, Swaziland, **371** F4
Law, Dome, *ice dome*, Antarctica, **470** F7
Lawa, Myanmar, **205** C2
Lawagamau, *river*, Canada, **415** Q6
Lawdar, Yemen, **220** E6
Lawers, Ben, *mountain peak*, Scotland, U.K., **308** E4
Lawford, England, U.K., **305** J3
Lawit, Gunung, *mountain peak*, Indonesia, **201** F2
Lawit, Gunung, *mountain peak*, Malaysia, **200** C1
Lawksawk, Myanmar, **205** C3
Lawra, Ghana, **364** D2
Lawrence, Kansas, U.S.A., **420** F6
Lawrence, Massachusetts, U.S.A., **426** E3
Lawrence, New Zealand, **133** B7
Lawrenceburg, U.S.A., **425** J2
Lawton, U.S.A., **424** C2
Lawu, Gunung, *mountain peak*, Indonesia, **201** E4
Lawz, Jabal al, *mountain peak*, Saudi Arabia, **225** C5
Laxå, Sweden, **286** G3
Laxey, Isle of Man, **306** D3
Laxford Bridge, Scotland, U.K., **308** D2
Laxo, Shetland, Scotland, U.K., **308** K7
Lay, U.S.A., **423** K1
Layar, Tanjong, *point*, Indonesia, **201** G4
Laylá, Saudi Arabia, **363** J4
Laysan, *island*, Hawaiian Islands, U.S.A., **139** G2
Laytonville, U.S.A., **422** B2
Lazare, Pointe, *point*, Seychelles, **373** A2
Lazarevac, Serbia, **296** C3
Lázaro Cárdenas, Mexico, **430** E5
Lazdijai, Lithuania, **287** L5
Lazio, *autonomous region*, Italy, **295** D5, *255*
Lazo, Russian Federation, **211** L4
Lazu, Romania, **296** F3
Le Blanc, France, **290** E3
Le Caylar, France, **291** F5
Le Conquet, France, **290** B2
Le Creusot, France, **291** G3
Le Croisic, France, **290** C3
Le Crotoy, France, **305** J4
Le Donjon, France, **291** F3
Le Dorat, France, **290** E3
Le Faouët, France, **290** C2
Le Havre, France, **290** E2
Le Lamentin, Martinique, **427** D3
Le Lion-d'Angers, France, **290** D3
Le Lude, France, **290** E3
Le Maire, Estrecho de, *strait*, Argentina, **460** E5
Le Mans, France, **290** E2
Le Mars, U.S.A., **420** E4
Le Mont-Saint-Michel, France, **290** D2
Le Petit-Quevilly, France, **305** J5
Le Port, Réunion, **373** A1
Le Portel, France, **305** J4
Le Puy-en-Velay, France, **291** F4
Le Riviere, Réunion, **373** A1
Le Tampon, Réunion, **373** A1
Le Teil, France, **291** G4
Le Touquet-Paris-Plage, France, **305** J4
Le Tréport, France, **290** E1
Le Verdon-sur-Mer, France, **290** D4
Lead, U.S.A., **420** B3
Leadenham, England, U.K., **305** G1
Leader, Canada, **413** Q6
Leadore, U.S.A., **418** H4
Leadville, U.S.A., **423** K2
Leaf Rapids, Canada, **414** E3
League, Slieve, *mountain peak*, Ireland, **309** D3
Leakey, U.S.A., **424** C5
Leamington, Canada, **421** M4
Leandro N. Alem, Argentina, **459** F3
Leane, Lough, *lake*, Ireland, **309** C5
Leanja, Madagascar, **372** B4
Leap, Ireland, **309** C6
Leasingham, England, U.K., **307** H4
Leatherhead, England, U.K., **305** G3
Leavenworth, U.S.A., **420** F6
Łeba, Poland, **289** H1
Lebak, Philippines, **204** D5
Lébamba, Gabon, **368** B3
Lebane, Serbia, **296** C4
Lebanon, *country*, Asia, **225** C3, *146, 147, 178, 180, 181*
Lebanon, Indiana, U.S.A., **421** K5
Lebanon, Missouri, U.S.A., **420** G7
Lebanon, New Hampshire, U.S.A., **426** D3
Lebanon, Oregon, U.S.A., **418** C4
Lebanon, South Dakota, U.S.A., **420** D3
Lebanon, Tennessee, U.S.A., **425** J1
Lebanon, Virginia, U.S.A., **421** M7
Lebap, Turkmenistan, **222** G4
Lebo, Democratic Republic of the Congo, **368** D2
Lębork, Poland, **289** H1
Lebowakgomo, South Africa, **371** E3
Lebrija, Spain, **292** D4
Łebsko, Jezioro, *lake*, Poland, **289** H1
Lebu, Chile, **458** B5
Lebyazh'e, Kazakhstan, **212** C2
Lecce, Italy, **295** G5
Lecco, Italy, **294** B3
Lechaina, Greece, **297** C7
Lechang, China, **206** C3
Lechinţa, Romania, **296** E2
Lechlade, England, U.K., **305** F3
Lechtaler Alpen, *mountain range*, Austria, **288** E5
Lēči, Latvia, **287** K4
Leck, Germany, **288** D1
Lecompte, U.S.A., **424** F4
Łęczna, Poland, **289** L3
Łęczyca, Poland, **289** J2
Ledang, Gunung, *mountain peak*, Malaysia, **200** C2
Ledbury, England, U.K., **304** E2
Ledesma, Spain, **292** E2
Ledmore, Scotland, U.K., **308** E2
Ledmozero, Russian Federation, **285** R4
Ledu, China, **213** J5
Leduc, Canada, **413** N5
Lee Vining, U.S.A., **422** D3
Leech, *river*, U.S.A., **420** F3
Leech Lake, U.S.A., **420** F2
Leeds, England, U.K., **307** G4
Leeds, U.S.A., **425** J3
Leedstown, England, U.K., **304** B4
Leek, England, U.K., **304** E1
Leeming Bar, England, U.K., **307** G3
Leer, Germany, **288** C2
Leesburg, Florida, U.S.A., **425** M5
Leesburg, Virginia, U.S.A., **426** B5
Leesi, Estonia, **287** M3
Leesville, U.S.A., **424** F4
Leeuwarden, Netherlands, **288** B2
Leeuwin, Cape, Australia, **134** D5
Leeville, U.S.A., **424** G5
Leeward Island, Antipodes Islands, New Zealand, **133** P15
Leeward Islands, Caribbean Sea, **427** C2, *395, 396*
Lefaga, Samoa, **141** B1
Lefka, Cyprus, **225** B2
Lefkada, Ionioi Nisoi, Greece, **297** C6
Lefkada, *island*, Ionioi Nisoi, Greece, **297** C6
Lefkimmi, Ionioi Nisoi, Greece, **297** C6
Lefkoniko, Cyprus, **225** B2
Lefkosia (Nicosia), Cyprus, **225** B2, *191, 192*
Lefroy, Lake, Australia, **134** E5
Leganés, Spain, **293** F2
Legaspi, Philippines, **204** C3
Legé, France, **290** D3
Leggett, U.S.A., **424** E4
Legnica, Poland, **289** H3
Leguga, Democratic Republic of the Congo, **368** E2
Leh, India, **218** D2
Lehliu Gară, Romania, **296** F3
Lehman, U.S.A., **423** M5
Lehrte, Germany, **288** D2
Lehua, *island*, Hawaiian Islands, U.S.A., **422** Q9
Lehututu, Botswana, **370** D3
Lei, *river*, China, **206** C3
Leiah, Pakistan, **218** B3
Leibnitz, Austria, **289** G5
Leicester, England, U.K., **305** F2
Leicester City, *unitary authority*, England, U.K., **305** F2
Leicestershire, *unitary authority*, England, U.K., **305** F2
Leichhardt, *river*, Australia, **135** H2
Leiden, Netherlands, **288** B2, *241*
Leigh, England, U.K., **306** F4
Leigh, New Zealand, **132** E3
Leigh Creek, Australia, **135** H5
Leighlinbridge, Ireland, **309** F5
Leighton Buzzard, England, U.K., **305** G3
Leigong Shan, *mountain peak*, China, **206** B3
Leine, *river*, Germany, **288** D2
Leinster, Mount, Ireland, **309** F5
Leinster, *province*, Ireland, **309** E4
Leipojärvi, Sweden, **284** K3
Leipsoi, *island*, Dodekanisos, Greece, **297** F7
Leipzig, Germany, **288** F3
Leira, Norway, **286** D2
Leirámoen, Norway, **284** G3
Leiranger, Norway, **284** G3
Leiria, *district*, Portugal, **292** C3
Leiria, Portugal, **292** C3
Leirvik, Norway, **286** B3
Leisi, Estonia, **287** L3
Leiston, England, U.K., **305** J2
Leitchfield, U.S.A., **421** K7
Leith, Scotland, U.K., **308** F5
Leitre, Papua New Guinea, **140** A3
Leitrim, *county*, Ireland, **309** D3
Leivonmäki, Finland, **287** N2
Leixlip, Ireland, **309** F4
Leiyang, China, **206** C3
Lejasciems, Latvia, **287** N4
Lejone, Lesotho, **371** E4
Leka, *island*, Norway, **284** E4
Lékana, Congo, **368** B3
Lekatero, Democratic Republic of the Congo, **368** D3
Lékila, Gabon, **368** B3
Leknes, Norway, **284** F2
Lékoni, Gabon, **368** B3
Lékoumou, *administrative region*, Congo, **368** B3
Leksand, Sweden, **286** G2
Lekshmozero, Ozero, *lake*, Russian Federation, **299** G2
Leksozero, Ozero, *lake*, Russian Federation, **285** Q5
Leksvik, Norway, **284** E5
Lelystad, Netherlands, **288** B2
Léman, Lac, *lake*, Switzerland/France, **291** H3, *247*
Lembeye, France, **290** D5
Lembu, Gunung, *mountain peak*, Indonesia, **200** B1
Lemesos (Limassol), Cyprus, **225** B2, *191*
Lemhi Range, *mountain range*, U.S.A., **418** H4
Lemmer, Netherlands, **288** B2
Lemolemo, Indonesia, **198** E3
Lemoore, U.S.A., **422** D3
Lemos, Punta, *point*, Róbinson Crusoe Island, Archipiélago Juan Fernández, Chile, **461** C2
Lempäälä, Finland, **287** L2
Lempdes, France, **291** F4
Lemu, Nigeria, **365** F3
Lemvig, Denmark, **286** D4
Lemyethna, Myanmar, **205** B4
Lena, *river*, Russian Federation, **301** N3, *273*
Lénakel, Vanuatu, **141** A3
Lençóis, Brazil, **457** F3
Lendava, Slovenia, **294** F2
Lendery, Russian Federation, **285** Q5
Lenghu, China, **213** G5
Lengkou, China, **211** G4
Lengshui Jiang, China, **206** B3
Lengshuitan, China, **206** B3
Lengua de Vaca, Punta, *point*, Chile, **458** B4
Lenham, England, U.K., **305** H3
Lenhovda, Sweden, **286** G4
Lenik, *river*, Malaysia, **200** C2
Lenin Atyndagy Choku, *mountain peak*, Kyrgyzstan/Tajikistan, **223** J5
Leningradskaya Oblast', *province*, Russian Federation, **299** C3

Leninogorsk, Kazakhstan, **212** D2
Leninogorsk, Russian Federation, **222** E2
Leninpol', Kyrgyzstan, **212** A4
Leninsk, Kazakhstan, **222** G3
Leninsk-Kuznetskiy, Russian Federation, **223** M2
Leninskīy, Kazakhstan, **212** C1
Leninskoye, Russian Federation, **211** L3
Lenkun Bay, Myanmar, **202** C4
Lennestadt, Germany, **288** D3
Lennox, Isla, *island*, Chile, **460** D5
Lenoir, U.S.A., **425** M2
Lensk, Russian Federation, **301** N3
Lentiira, *lake*, Finland, **285** P4
Lentini, Sicilia, Italy, **295** E7
Lentvaris, Lithuania, **287** M5
Lent'yevo, Russian Federation, **299** F3
Lenya, Myanmar, **202** C4
Léo, Burkina Faso, **364** D2
Leoben, Austria, **289** G5
Leominster, England, U.K., **304** E2
Léon, France, **290** D5
León, Mexico, **430** E4
León, Nicaragua, **428** D4
León, Punta, *point*, Argentina, **460** D4
Leon, *river*, U.S.A., **424** C4
León, Spain, **292** E1
Leonard, U.S.A., **424** D3
Leonarisso, Cyprus, **225** C2
Leone, American Samoa, **141** B2
Leonidi, Greece, **297** D7
Leonora, Australia, **134** E4
Leopoldina, Brazil, **457** E5
Leorda, Romania, **296** F2
Leova, Moldova, **296** G2
Lephepe, Botswana, **371** E3
Leping, China, **206** D2
Lepontine, Alpi, *mountain range*, Italy/Switzerland, **288** D5
Leppävirta, Finland, **287** N1
Lepsi, Kazakhstan, **212** C3
Leptokarya, Greece, **297** D5
Lequena, Chile, **455** E5
Lercara Friddi, Sicilia, Italy, **295** D7
Léré, Chad, **365** G3
Léré, Mali, **364** D1
Lere, Nigeria, **365** F2
Lérida, Colombia, **450** D4
Lerma, Spain, **293** F1
Lermoos, Austria, **288** E5
Lerneb, Mali, **364** D1
Leros, *island*, Dodekanisos, Greece, **297** F7
Lerum, Sweden, **286** F4
Lerwick, Shetland, Scotland, U.K., **308** L7
Les Avirons, Réunion, **373** A1
Les Cayes, Haiti, **429** G3
Les Escoumins, Canada, **416** G5
Les Essarts, France, **290** D3
Les Eyzies-de-Tâyac-Sireuil, France, **290** E4
Les Makes, Réunion, **373** A1
Les Méchins, Canada, **416** H5
Les Riceys, France, **291** G3
Les Sables-d'Olonne, France, **290** D3
Lesbos *see* Lesvos, *island*, Greece, **297** E6
Lesbury, England, U.K., **307** G2
L'Escalier, Mauritius, **373** C1
Leshan, China, **215** G3
Lesina, Italy, **295** E5
Lesina, Lago di, *lake*, Italy, **295** E5
Lesjaskog, Norway, **286** D1
Lesko, Poland, **289** L4
Leskovac, Serbia, **296** C4
Leskovik, Albania, **297** C5
Leslie, Scotland, U.K., **308** F4
Leslie, U.S.A., **418** H5
Leśna, Poland, **289** G3
Lesneven, France, **290** B2
Lesosibirsk, Russian Federation, **300** L4
Lesotho, *country*, Africa, **359** H10, *348, 349, 350, 351*
Lesozavodsk, Russian Federation, **211** L3
L'Esperance Rock, *island*, Kermadec Islands, New Zealand, **132** L12
Lesser Antilles, *islands*, Caribbean Sea, **427** B3, *388, 389, 396, 397*
Lesser Slave Lake, Canada, **413** M4
Lestijärvi, *lake*, Finland, **285** M5
Lestijoki, *river*, Finland, **285** L4
Lestock, Canada, **414** C6
Lesvos (Lesbos), *island*, Greece, **297** E6
Leszno, Poland, **289** H3
Letchworth, England, U.K., **305** G3
Letenye, Hungary, **289** H5
Letha Taung, *mountain range*, Myanmar, **205** B3
Lethbridge, Canada, **413** N7
Lethem, Guyana, **451** G3
Leti, Kepulauan, *islands*, Indonesia, **198** D5
Leticia, Colombia, **451** E5
Letlhakeng, Botswana, **370** E3
Letnerechenskiy, Russian Federation, **285** S4
Letniy Navolok, Russian Federation, **285** T4
Letnyaya Zolotitsa, Russian Federation, **285** T4
Letpadan, Myanmar, **205** B4
Letterkenny, Ireland, **309** E3
Léua, Angola, **368** D5
Leucate, Étang de, *lake*, France, **291** F5
Leuchars, Scotland, U.K., **308** G4
Leuser, Gunung, *mountain peak*, Indonesia, **200** B2
Leusoalii, American Samoa, **141** B2
Leuven, Belgium, **288** B3
Levadeia, Greece, **297** D6
Levan, Albania, **297** B5
Levanger, Norway, **284** E5
Levant, Île du, *island*, France, **291** H5
Levante, Riviera di, *coastal area*, Italy, **294** B3
Levanto, Italy, **294** B3
Levashi, Russian Federation, **222** D4
Levelland, U.S.A., **423** M5
Leven, England, U.K., **307** H4
Leven, Scotland, U.K., **308** F4
Leveque, Cape, Australia, **134** E2
L'Eveque, Cape, Chatham Islands, New Zealand, **133** Q16
Leverkusen, Germany, **288** C3
Levice, Slovakia, **289** J4
Levidi, Greece, **297** D7
Levie, Corse, France, **295** B5
Levitha, *island*, Kyklades, Greece, **297** F7
Levoča, Slovakia, **289** K4
Levroux, France, **290** E3
Levski, Bulgaria, **296** E4
Levuka, Fiji, **141** A4
Lewe, Myanmar, **205** C4
Lewellen, U.S.A., **420** B5
Lewes, England, U.K., **305** H4
Lewin Brzeski, Poland, **289** H3
Lewis, Butt of, *point*, Scotland, U.K., **308** C2
Lewis, Isle of, Scotland, U.K., **308** C2
Lewis, Lake, Australia, **134** G3
Lewis, *river*, U.S.A., **418** C3
Lewis Hills, *mountain peak*, Canada, **417** M5
Lewis Range, *mountain range*, U.S.A., **418** H2
Lewis Smith Lake, U.S.A., **425** J2
Lewisburg, Kentucky, U.S.A., **421** K7
Lewisburg, Tennessee, U.S.A., **425** J2
Lewiston, Idaho, U.S.A., **418** F3
Lewiston, Maine, U.S.A., **426** E2
Lewistown, Montana, U.S.A., **419** K3
Lewistown, Pennsylvania, U.S.A., **426** B4
Lewisville, U.S.A., **424** F3
Lexington, Illinois, U.S.A., **421** J5
Lexington, Kentucky, U.S.A., **421** L6
Lexington, Missouri, U.S.A., **420** G6
Lexington, Nebraska, U.S.A., **420** D5
Lexington, North Carolina, U.S.A., **425** M2
Lexington, Oregon, U.S.A., **418** E4
Lexington, Tennessee, U.S.A., **425** H2
Lexington, Virginia, U.S.A., **421** P7
Lexington Park, U.S.A., **426** B5
Leyburn, England, U.K., **307** G3
Leyland, England, U.K., **306** F4
Leyte, *island*, Philippines, **204** D4, *149*
Leyte Gulf, Philippines, **204** D4
Leżajsk, Poland, **289** L3
Lezhë, Albania, **296** B5
Lezhi, China, **215** H3
L'gov, Russian Federation, **298** E2
Lhabo, China, **215** G3
Lhari, China, **214** E3
Lhasa, China, **214** D3, *159, 161*
Lhazê, China, **214** C3
Lhazhong, China, **214** C3
Lhokkruet, Indonesia, **200** B1
Lhokseumawe, Indonesia, **200** B1
Lhoksukon, Indonesia, **200** B1
Lhorong, China, **215** F3
L'Hospitalet de Llobregat, Spain, **293** J2
Lhozhag, China, **214** D3
Lhünzê, China, **214** E3
Li Xian, Gansu, China, **215** H2
Li Xian, Hunan, China, **206** B2
Lia, Tanjong, *point*, Indonesia, **198** D3
Liang East, Gunung, *mountain peak*, Malaysia, **200** C2
Liancheng, China, **206** D3
Lianga, Philippines, **204** D4
Liangcheng, China, **210** F4
Liangdang, China, **215** H2
Lianghe, China, **215** F4
Lianghekou, Gansu, China, **215** H2
Lianghekou, Sichuan, China, **206** B2
Liangkou, China, **207** B1
Lianglong, China, **207** A2
Liangping, China, **215** H3
Liangpran, Gunung, *mountain peak*, Indonesia, **201** F2
Lianhe, China, **207** A2
Lianhua, China, **206** C3
Lianhua Shan, *mountain range*, China, **207** D2
Lianjiang, Fujian, China, **206** D3
Lianjiang, Guangdong, China, **206** B4
Lianping, China, **206** C3
Lianshan, China, **206** C3
Lianshui, China, **206** D1
Lianyungang, China, **206** D1
Lianzhou, China, **206** C3
Liaobu, China, **207** B3
Liaocheng, China, **210** F5
Liaodong Wan, *bay*, China, **211** H4
Liaohu, China, **215** G4
Liaoning, *province*, China, **211** H4, *161*
Liaoyang, China, **211** H4
Liaoyuan, China, **211** J4
Liaozhong, China, **208** C2
Liard, *river*, Canada, **412** G2
Liard River, Canada, **412** F2
Liāri, Pakistan, **218** A4
Liathach, *mountain peak*, Scotland, U.K., **308** D3
Liatorp, Sweden, **286** G4
Líbano, Colombia, **450** C3
Libby, U.S.A., **418** G2
Libenge, Democratic Republic of the Congo, **368** C2
Liberal, U.S.A., **420** C7
Liberdade, *river*, Brazil, **456** C3
Liberec, Czech Republic, **289** G3
Liberia, Costa Rica, **428** D5
Liberia, *country*, Africa, **358** D6, *312, 321, 322, 323*
Libertador, *administrative region*, Chile, **458** B5
Liberty, Maine, U.S.A., **426** F2
Liberty, Missouri, U.S.A., **420** F6
Liberty, New York, U.S.A., **426** C4
Liberty, Texas, U.S.A., **424** E5
Libo, China, **215** H4
Libourne, France, **290** D4
Librazhd, Albania, **297** C5
Libreville, Gabon, **368** A2, *333*
Libya, *country*, Africa, **358** G4, *146, 312, 313, 316, 317*
Libyan Desert, Egypt/Libya/Sudan, **356** H4, *317*
Libyan Plateau, Libya, **356** H3
Licancábur, Volcán, *mountain peak*, Chile, **458** C2
Licantén, Chile, **458** B5
Licata, Sicilia, Italy, **295** D7
Lice, Turkey, **363** H1
Lichfield, England, U.K., **305** F2
Lichinga, Mozambique, **369** G5
Lichtenburg, South Africa, **371** E4
Lichuan, Hubei, China, **206** B2
Lichuan, Jiangxi, China, **206** D3
Licking, *river*, U.S.A., **421** M6
Licking, U.S.A., **420** H7
Licosa, Punta, *point*, Italy, **295** E5
Lid', *river*, Russian Federation, **299** E3
Lida, Belarus, **289** M2
Lida, U.S.A., **422** E3
Liden, Sweden, **287** H1
Lidgbird, Mount, *mountain peak*, Lord Howe Island, Australia, **135** U14
Lidköping, Sweden, **286** F3
Lido di Ostia, Italy, **295** D5
Lidskaya rawnina, *plain*, Belarus, **289** M2
Lidzbark, Poland, **289** J2
Lidzbark Warmiński, Poland, **289** K1
Liebenthal, Canada, **413** Q6
Liebenwalde, Germany, **288** F2
Lieberose, Germany, **289** G2
Liechtenstein, *country*, Europe, **282** F6, *228, 247, 248*
Liège, Belgium, **288** B3, *242*
Liège, *province*, Belgium, **288** B3
Lieksa, Finland, **285** Q5
Lielupe, *river*, Latvia, **287** L4
Lienz, Austria, **288** F5
Liepāja, Latvia, **287** K4
Liepājas ezers, *lake*, Latvia, **287** K4
Lievestuore, Finland, **287** N1
Liévin, France, **291** F1
Liezen, Austria, **289** G5
Lifanga, Democratic Republic of the Congo, **368** D2
Liffey, *river*, Ireland, **309** F4
Lifford, Ireland, **309** E3
Liffré, France, **290** D2
Lifou, *island*, New Caledonia, **141** A3
Lignières, France, **290** F3
Ligonha, *river*, Mozambique, **369** G6
Ligui, Mexico, **430** C3
Liguria, *autonomous region*, Italy, **294** B3, *255*
Ligurian Sea, Italy, **294** B4
Liha Point, Niue, **132** M13
Lihehe, Tanzania, **369** G5
Lihir Group, *islands*, Papua New Guinea, **140** D3
Lihir Islands, Lihir Group, Papua New Guinea, **140** D3
Lihue, Hawaiian Islands, U.S.A., **422** R9
Lihue, *island*, Hawaiian Islands, U.S.A., **139** J2
Lihula, Estonia, **287** L3
Lijiang, China, **215** G4
Lik, *river*, Laos, **202** D2
Likasi, Democratic Republic of the Congo, **369** E5
Likati, Democratic Republic of the Congo, **368** D2
Likhachevo, Russian Federation, **299** F3
Likhoslavl', Russian Federation, **299** E4
Likiep, *island*, Marshall Islands, **139** E4, *119*
Likoto, Democratic Republic of the Congo, **368** D3
Likouala, *administrative region*, Congo, **368** C2
Liku, Niue, **132** M13
L'Île-Rousse, Corse, France, **294** B4
Lilienthal, Germany, **288** D2
Lilin, China, **207** C3
Liling, China, **206** C3
Lilla Edet, Sweden, **286** F3
Lille, France, **291** F1, *245*
Lillebonne, France, **305** H5
Lillehammer, Norway, **286** E2
Lillers, France, **305** K4
Lillesand, Norway, **286** D3
Lilleshall, England, U.K., **304** E2
Lillestrøm, Norway, **286** E3
Lillhärdal, Sweden, **286** G2
Lillögda, Sweden, **284** H4
Lillooet, Canada, **412** J6
Lilongwe, Malawi, **369** F5, *344*
Liloy, Philippines, **204** C4
Lily Lake, Canada, **412** G5
Lima, Montana, U.S.A., **418** H4
Lima, Ohio, U.S.A., **421** L5
Lima, Peru, **454** C3, *434, 440*
Lima, *river*, Portugal, **292** C2
Lima, Sweden, **286** F2
Liman, Gunung, *mountain peak*, Indonesia, **201** E4
Limanowa, Poland, **289** K4
Limassol *see* Lemesos, Cyprus, **225** B2, *191*
Limavady, *district*, Northern Ireland, U.K., **309** F3
Limavady, Northern Ireland, U.K., **309** F2
Limay, *river*, Argentina, **460** C1
Limay Mahuida, Argentina, **458** C5
Limbani, Peru, **455** E4
Limbaži, Latvia, **287** M4
Limbe, Cameroon, **368** A2
Limboto, Danau, *lake*, Indonesia, **198** C2
Limburg, *province*, Belgium, **288** B3
Limburg, *province*, Netherlands, **288** B3
Limburg an der Lahn, Germany, **288** D3
Lime Acres, South Africa, **370** D4
Lime Springs, U.S.A., **420** G4
Limeira, Brazil, **459** H2
Limerick, *county*, Ireland, **309** D5
Limerick, Ireland, **309** D5
Limestone, U.S.A., **426** G1
Limfjorden, *strait*, Denmark, **286** D4
Liminka, Finland, **285** M4
Limmared, Sweden, **286** F4
Limmen Bight, *bay*, Australia, **135** H1
Limni, Voreioi Sporades, Greece, **297** D6
Limnos, *island*, Greece, **297** E6
Limoeiro, Brazil, **453** G5
Limoges, France, **290** E4
Limón, Honduras, **428** D4
Limon, Mont, *mountain peak*, Rodrigues, Mauritius, **373** B1
Limon, U.S.A., **423** M2
Limoquije, Bolivia, **455** F4
Limousin, *administrative region*, France, **290** E4, *245*
Limpopo, *river*, Southern Africa, **357** H9, *346, 347*
Limufuafua Point, Niue, **132** M13
Linakhamari, Russian Federation, **285** Q2
Lin'an, China, **206** D2
Linao Point, Philippines, **204** C5
Linapacan Island, Philippines, **204** B4
Linard, Piz, *mountain peak*, Switzerland, **291** K3
Linares, Chile, **458** B5
Linares, Mexico, **431** F3
Linares, Spain, **293** F3
Linaria, Greece, **297** E6
Linas, Monte, *mountain peak*, Sardegna, Italy, **295** B6
Lincang, China, **215** G5
Lincoln, Argentina, **458** E5
Lincoln, England, U.K., **305** G1
Lincoln, Illinois, U.S.A., **421** J5
Lincoln, Kansas, U.S.A., **420** D6
Lincoln, Maine, U.S.A., **426** F2

Lincoln, Montana, U.S.A., **418** H3
Lincoln, Nebraska, U.S.A., **420** E5, *386*
Lincoln, New Mexico, U.S.A., **423** L5
Lincoln City, U.S.A., **418** C4
Lincoln Sea, Canada/Greenland, **411** N1
Lincolnshire, *unitary authority*, England, U.K., **307** H4
Lincolnshire Wolds, *region*, England, U.K., **307** H4
Lind, U.S.A., **418** E3
Linden, Guyana, **451** G2
Linden, U.S.A., **425** J3
Lindesberg, Sweden, **286** G3
Lindi, *administrative region*, Tanzania, **369** G4
Lindi, Tanzania, **369** G4
Lindian, China, **211** J3
Lindisfarne, England, U.K., **307** G2
Lindos, Dodekanisos, Greece, **297** G7
Lindozero, Russian Federation, **285** R5
Lindsay, Canada, **416** B7
Lindsay, Montana, U.S.A., **419** M3
Lindsay, Oklahoma, U.S.A., **424** D2
Lindsborg, U.S.A., **420** E6
Line Islands, *islands*, Kiribati, **139** J4, *119*
Linfen, China, **210** E5
Linganamakki Reservoir, India, **216** C3
Lingayen, Philippines, **204** C3
Lingayen Gulf, Philippines, **204** C2, *149*
Lingbao, China, **206** B1
Lingbi, China, **206** D1
Lingen, Germany, **288** C2
Lingfield, England, U.K., **305** G3
Lingga, Kepulauan, *islands*, Indonesia, **200** D3
Lingga, Pulau, *island*, Indonesia, **200** D3
Lingkabau, Malaysia, **201** G1
Lingle, U.S.A., **419** M5
Lingomo, Democratic Republic of the Congo, **368** D2
Lingqiu, China, **210** F5
Lingshan, China, **206** B4
Lingshi, China, **210** E5
Lingshui, China, **203** F2
Lingtai, China, **215** H2
Linguère, Senegal, **364** A1
Lingwu, China, **210** D5
Lingyuan, China, **211** G4
Linhai, Heilongjiang, China, **211** J2
Linhai, Zhejiang, China, **206** E2
Linhares, Brazil, **457** F5
Linhe, China, **210** D4
Linjiang, Gonsu, China, **215** H2
Linjiang, Jilin, China, **211** J4
Linköping, Sweden, **286** G3
Linkou, China, **211** K3
Linkuva, Lithuania, **287** L4
Linnhe, Loch, *inlet*, Scotland, U.K., **308** D4
Linosa, Isola di, *island*, Isole Pelagie, Italy, **295** D8
Linova, Belarus, **289** M2
Linping, China, **206** E2
Linqing, China, **210** F5
Linqu, China, **208** B3
Linquan, China, **206** C1
Lins, Brazil, **456** D5
Linsell, Sweden, **286** F1
Linshu, China, **206** D1
Linshui, China, **215** H3
Linta, *river*, Madagascar, **372** A5
Lintan, China, **215** G2
Lintao, China, **215** G2
Linton, Indiana, U.S.A., **421** K6
Linton, North Dakota, U.S.A., **420** C2
Lintong, China, **206** B1, *159*
Linxi, Hebei, China, **211** G5
Linxi, Nei Mongol Zizhiqu, China, **211** G4
Linxia, China, **215** G2
Linyanti, *river*, Botswana/Namibia, **370** D2
Linyi, N. Shandong, China, **210** G5
Linyi, Shanxi, China, **206** B1
Linyi, S. Shandong, China, **206** D1
Linyou, China, **215** H2
Linz, Austria, **289** G4
Linze, China, **213** J5
Lioboml', Ukraine, **289** M3
Lion, Golfe du, *gulf*, France, **291** F5
Lioua, Chad, **365** G2
Liouesso, Congo, **368** C2
Lipa, Philippines, **204** C3
Lipany, Slovakia, **289** K4
Lipari, Isola, *island*, Italy, **295** E6
Lipari, Italy, **295** E6
Lipcani, Moldova, **296** F1
Liperi, Finland, **285** P5
Lipetsk, Russian Federation, **298** E2
Lipetskaya Oblast', *province*, Russian Federation, **299** G6
Liphook, England, U.K., **305** G3
Lipiany, Poland, **289** G2
Lipin Bor, Russian Federation, **299** F2
Liping, China, **206** B3
Lipki, Russian Federation, **299** F6
Lipljan, Kosovo, **296** C4
Lipnica, Poland, **289** J2
Lipno, Poland, **289** J2
Lipobane, Ponta, *point*, Mozambique, **369** G6
Lipova, Romania, **296** C2
Lippe, *river*, Germany, **288** C3
Lipsk, Poland, **289** L2
Liptougou, Burkina Faso, **364** E2
Liptovský Mikulāš, Slovakia, **289** J4
Lipu, China, **206** B3
Lira, Uganda, **369** F2
Liranga, Congo, **368** C3
Lircay, Peru, **454** C3
Liria, Sudan, **369** F2
Lisala, Democratic Republic of the Congo, **368** D2
Lisbellaw, Northern Ireland, U.K., **309** E3
Lisboa, *district*, Portugal, **292** C3
Lisboa (Lisbon), Portugal, **292** C3, *76, 94, 250, 355*
Lisbon *see* Lisboa, Portugal, **292** C3, *76, 94, 250, 355*
Lisbon, U.S.A., **421** N5
Lisburn, *district*, Northern Ireland, U.K., **309** G3
Lisburn, Northern Ireland, U.K., **309** F3
Lisburne, Cape, U.S.A., **410** C3
Liscannor Bay, Ireland, **309** C5
Lisco, U.S.A., **420** B5
Lisdoonvarna, Ireland, **309** C4
Lishi, China, **210** E5
Lishu, China, **211** J4
Lishui, China, **206** D2
Lisianski, *island*, Hawaiian Islands, U.S.A., **139** G2
Lisieux, France, **290** E2
Liskeard, England, U.K., **304** C4
Liski, Russian Federation, **298** E2
Lismore, Australia, **135** L4
Lismore, Ireland, **309** E5
Lisnaskea, Northern Ireland, U.K., **309** E3
Liss, England, U.K., **305** G3
Lister, Mount, *mountain peak*, Antarctica, **470** D7
Listowel, Ireland, **309** C5
Lit, Sweden, **284** G5
Litang, Guangxi Zhuangzu Zizhiqu, China, **206** B4
Litang, Sichuan, China, **215** G3
Līṭānī, *river*, Lebanon, **225** C3, *181*
Litani, *river*, Suriname, **452** B2
Litchfield, Illinois, U.S.A., **421** J6
Litchfield Nebraska, U.S.A., **420** D5
Lithakia, Ionioi Nisoi, Greece, **297** C7
Lithgow, Australia, **135** L5
Lithino, Akra, *point*, Kriti, Greece, **297** E8
Lithuania, *country*, Europe, **282** G4, *228, 236, 237, 245, 267, 268, 270, 271, 272*
Litovko, Russian Federation, **211** L2
Little Aden, Yemen, **220** D6
Little Andaman, *island*, Andaman and Nicobar Islands, India, **217** H4
Little Cayman, *island*, Cayman Islands, **429** E3
Little Coco Island, Myanmar, **217** H3
Little Colorado, *river*, U.S.A., **423** H4
Little Current, Canada, **421** N3
Little Falls, Minnesota, U.S.A., **420** F3
Little Falls, New York, U.S.A., **426** C3
Little Fort, Canada, **412** J6
Little Grand Rapids, Canada, **414** G5
Little Inagua Island, Bahamas, **429** G2
Little Kanawha, *river*, U.S.A., **421** N6
Little Lake, U.S.A., **422** E4
Little Mecatina, *river*, Canada, **417** L3
Little Minch, The, *strait*, Scotland, U.K., **308** B3
Little Missouri, *river*, U.S.A., **420** B2
Little Nicobar, *island*, Andaman and Nicobar Islands, India, **217** H5
Little Oakley, England, U.K., **305** J3
Little Ouse, *river*, England, U.K., **305** H2
Little Quill Lake, Canada, **414** B6
Little Rock, U.S.A., **424** F2, *386*
Little Sachigo Lake, Canada, **414** H4
Little Sioux, *river*, U.S.A., **420** E4
Little Smoky, Canada, **413** L4
Little Smoky, *river*, Canada, **413** K4
Little Tobago, *island*, Tobago, Trinidad and Tobago, **461** B4
Little Wabash, *river*, U.S.A., **421** J6
Littleborough, England, U.K., **306** F4
Littlefield, Arizona, U.S.A., **422** G3
Littlefield, Texas, U.S.A., **423** M5
Littlehampton, England, U.K., **305** G4
Littlemore, England, U.K., **305** F3
Littleport, England, U.K., **305** H2
Littoral, *province*, Cameroon, **368** A2
Litunde, Mozambique, **369** G5
Liu, *river*, China, **214** E3
Liuba, Gansu, China, **213** J5
Liuba, Shaanxi, China, **215** H2
Liucheng, China, **206** B3
Liuhe, China, **211** J4
Liuhu, China, **211** H3
Liujiang, China, **206** B3
Liulin, China, **210** E5
Liupanshui, China, **215** H4
Liushuquan, China, **213** G4
Liuxi, *river*, China, **207** A2
Liuxihe Reservoir, China, **207** B1
Liuyang, China, **206** C2
Liuyuan, China, **213** G4
Liuzhou, China, **206** B3
Livada, Romania, **296** D2
Livadiya, Russian Federation, **211** L4
Līvāni, Latvia, **287** N4
Livanovka, Kazakhstan, **222** G2
Live Oak, U.S.A., **425** L4
Lively Island, Falkland Islands, **460** F4
Livermore, Mount, *mountain peak*, U.S.A., **423** L6
Liverpool, England, U.K., **306** F4, *276*
Liverpool, Canada, **417** J7
Liverpool Bay, England, U.K., **306** E4
Livingston, Guatemala, **428** C4
Livingston, Lake, U.S.A., **424** E4
Livingston, Montana, U.S.A., **419** J4
Livingston, Texas, U.S.A., **424** E4
Livingstone, Zambia, **371** E2
Livingstonia, Malawi, **369** F5
Livno, Bosnia and Herzegovina, **294** F4
Livo, Finland, **285** N4
Livonia, U.S.A., **421** M4
Livorno, Italy, **294** C4
Livramento do Brumado, Brazil, **457** F3
Liwale, Tanzania, **369** G4
Lixi, China, **215** G4
Lixouri, Ionioi Nisoi, Greece, **297** C6
Liyang, China, **206** D2
Lizard, England, U.K., **304** B5
Lizard Point, England, U.K., **304** B5
Lizotte, Canada, **416** E5
Lizuka, Japan, **208** E4
Ljig, Serbia, **296** C3
Ljubljana, Slovenia, **294** E2, *258*
Ljubovija, Serbia, **296** B3
Ljugarn, Sweden, **287** J4
Ljungan, *river*, Sweden, **287** H1
Ljungby, Sweden, **286** F4
Ljungdalen, Sweden, **284** F5
Ljusdal, Sweden, **286** H2
Ljusnan, *river*, Sweden, **286** G2
Ljustorp, Sweden, **287** H1
Llagostera, Spain, **293** J2
Llaima, Volcán, *mountain peak*, Chile, **458** B6
Llanaelhaearn, Wales, U.K., **304** C2
Llanarth, Wales, U.K., **304** C2
Llanarthney, Wales, U.K., **304** C3
Llanbadarn-fawr, Wales, U.K., **304** C2
Llanbedrog, Wales, U.K., **304** C2
Llanberis, Wales, U.K., **304** C1
Llanbister, Wales, U.K., **304** D2
Llandeilo, Wales, U.K., **304** D3
Llandissilio, Wales, U.K., **304** C3
Llandovery, Wales, U.K., **304** D3
Llandrillo, Wales, U.K., **304** D2
Llandrindod Wells, Wales, U.K., **304** D2
Llandudno, Wales, U.K., **306** E4
Llandwrog, Wales, U.K., **304** C1
Llandysul, Wales, U.K., **304** C2
Llanelli, Wales, U.K., **304** C3
Llanelltyd, Wales, U.K., **304** D2
Llanerchymedd, Wales, U.K., **306** D4
Llanfair Caereinion, Wales, U.K., **304** D2
Llanfair Talhaiarn, Wales, U.K., **304** D1
Llanfair-yn-Neubwll, Wales, U.K., **306** D4
Llanfairfechan, Wales, U.K., **304** D1
Llanfairpwllgwyngyll, Wales, U.K., **304** C1
Llanfihangel-ar-Arth, Wales, U.K., **304** C2
Llanfyllin, Wales, U.K., **304** D2
Llangadfan, Wales, U.K., **304** D2
Llangadog, Wales, U.K., **304** D3
Llangeler, Wales, U.K., **304** C2
Llangelynin, Wales, U.K., **304** C2
Llangfre Head, *point*, Wales, U.K., **306** D4
Llangoed, Wales, U.K., **306** D4
Llangollen, Wales, U.K., **304** D2
Llangurig, Wales, U.K., **304** D2
Llanidloes, Wales, U.K., **304** D2
Llanleigh Head, *point*, Wales, U.K., **304** C2
Llanllyfni, Wales, U.K., **304** C1
Llannor, Wales, U.K., **304** C2
Llano, U.S.A., **424** C4
Llanos, *region*, Colombia/Venezuela, **446** E3, *437*
Llanquihué, Lago, *lake*, Chile, **460** C1
Llanrhystyd, Wales, U.K., **304** C2
Llanrwst, Wales, U.K., **304** D1
Llansannan, Wales, U.K., **304** D1
Llansawel, Wales, U.K., **304** C2
Llantrisant, Wales, U.K., **304** D3
Llantwit Major, Wales, U.K., **304** D3
Llanuwchllyn, Wales, U.K., **304** D2
Llanwenog, Wales, U.K., **304** C2
Llanwnda, Wales, U.K., **304** C1
Llanwnog, Wales, U.K., **304** D2
Llanwrtyd Wells, Wales, U.K., **304** D2
Llata, Peru, **454** C2
Lleida, Spain, **293** H2
Llera de Canales, Mexico, **431** F4
Llerena, Spain, **292** D3
Lleyn Peninsula, Wales, U.K., **304** C2
Llica, Bolivia, **455** E5
Llíria, Spain, **293** G3
Llorente, Philippines, **204** D4
Lloydminster, Canada, **413** Q5
Llullaillaco, Volcán, *mountain peak*, Argentina/Chile, **458** C2
Llyn Alaw, *lake*, Wales, U.K., **306** D4
Lo Wu, China, **207** C3
Loa, *river*, Chile, **458** C2
Loa, U.S.A., **423** H2
Loa Mauna, *mountain peak*, Hawaiian Islands, U.S.A., **422** R10
Loano, Italy, **294** B3
Lobatse, Botswana, **371** E4
Löbau, Germany, **289** G3
Lobaye, *prefecture*, Central African Republic, **368** C2
Loberia, Argentina, **459** E6
Łobez, Poland, **289** G2
Lobito, Angola, **368** B5
Lobitos, Peru, **454** B1
Lobo, Philippines, **204** C3
Lobo, U.S.A., **423** L6
Lobos, Argentina, **459** E5
Lobos, *island*, Islas Canarias, Spain, **373** B4
Lobos, Punta de, *point*, Chile, **458** B5
Lobskoye, Russian Federation, **285** S5
Locarno, Switzerland, **291** J3
Locate, U.S.A., **419** M3
Lochaline, Scotland, U.K., **308** D4
Lochboisdale, Scotland, U.K., **308** B3
Lochcarron, Scotland, U.K., **308** D3
Lochearnhead, Scotland, U.K., **308** E4
Loches, France, **290** E3
Lochgelly, Scotland, U.K., **308** F4
Lochgilphead, Scotland, U.K., **308** D4
Lochgoilhead, Scotland, U.K., **308** E4
Lochinver, Scotland, U.K., **308** D2
Lochmaben, Scotland, U.K., **308** F5
Lochmaddy, Scotland, U.K., **308** B3
Lochnagar, *mountain peak*, Scotland, U.K., **308** F4
Łochów, Poland, **289** K2
Lochranza, Scotland, U.K., **308** D5
Lochy, Loch, *lake*, Scotland, U.K., **308** E3
Lock Haven, U.S.A., **426** B4
Lockeford, U.S.A., **422** C2
Lockeport, Canada, **416** J8
Lockerbie, Scotland, U.K., **308** F5
Lockhart, U.S.A., **424** D5
Loco Hills, U.S.A., **423** M5
Locri, Italy, **295** F6
Locumba, Peru, **454** D4
Locust Grove, U.S.A., **421** M6
Loddon, England, U.K., **305** J2
Lodève, France, **291** F5
Lodeynoye Pole, Russian Federation, **299** D2
Lodge Grass, U.S.A., **419** L4
Lodgepole, U.S.A., **420** B3
Lodhrān, Pakistan, **218** B3
Lodi, Italy, **294** B3
Lodi, U.S.A., **422** C2
Lødingen, Norway, **284** G2
Lodja, Democratic Republic of the Congo, **368** D3
Lodoga, U.S.A., **422** B2
Lodwar, Kenya, **369** G2
Łódź, Poland, **289** J3
Loei, Thailand, **202** D2
Lofoten, *islands*, Norway, **284** F3
Lofsdalen, Sweden, **286** F1
Loftahammar, Sweden, **287** H4
Lofthus, Norway, **286** C2
Loftus, England, U.K., **307** H3

Loga, Niger, **365** E2
Logan, Mount, *mountain peak*, Canada, **410** E3, *380*
Logan, Mount, *mountain peak*, U.S.A., **418** D2
Logan, New Mexico, U.S.A., **423** M4
Logan, Utah, U.S.A., **419** J6
Logan, West Virginia, U.S.A., **421** M7
Logan Mountains, *mountain range*, Canada, **412** E1
Logansport, U.S.A., **421** K5
Loge, *river*, Angola, **368** B4
Logone Birni, Cameroon, **365** H2
Logone, *river*, Chad, **365** H2, *328*
Logone Occidental, *prefecture*, Chad, **365** H3
Logone Oriental, *prefecture*, Chad, **365** H3
Logos, Punta, *point*, Colombia, **450** C2
Logoualé, Côte d'Ivoire, **364** C3
Logroño, Spain, **293** F1
Løgstør, Denmark, **286** D4
Lohārdaga, India, **219** F5
Lohāru, India, **218** C3
Lohāwat, India, **218** C4
Lohéac, France, **290** D3
Lohiniva, Finland, **285** M3
Lohja, Finland, **287** M2
Lohne (Oldenburg), Germany, **288** D2
Loi, Phou, *mountain peak*, Laos, **203** D1
Loi-kaw, Myanmar, **205** C4
Loi-lem, Myanmar, **205** C3
Loimaa, Finland, **287** L2
Loir, *river*, France, **290** E2
Loire, *mountain peak*, France, **291** F3
Loire, *river*, France, **280** D6, *244*
Loitz, Germany, **288** F2
Loja, Ecuador, **450** B5
Loja, Spain, **292** E4
Lokachi, Ukraine, **289** M3
Lokalahti, Finland, **287** K2
Lokan, *river*, Malaysia, **201** G1
Lokan tekojärvi, *lake*, Finland, **285** N3
Lokandu, Democratic Republic of the Congo, **369** E3
Løken, Norway, **286** E3
Lokichar, Kenya, **369** G2
Lokichokio, Kenya, **369** F2
Lokka, Finland, **285** N3
Løkken, Denmark, **286** D4
Løkken, Norway, **284** D5
Loknya, Russian Federation, **299** C4
Lokofe, Democratic Republic of the Congo, **368** D3
Lokoja, Nigeria, **365** F3
Lokolama, Democratic Republic of the Congo, **368** C3
Lokolia, Democratic Republic of the Congo, **368** D3
Lokomo, Cameroon, **368** C2
Lokoro, *river*, Democratic Republic of the Congo, **368** C3
Lokot', Russian Federation, **223** L2
Lola, Angola, **368** B5
Lola, Guinea, **364** C3
Loliondo, Tanzania, **369** G3
Lolland, *island*, Denmark, **286** E5
Lolo, U.S.A., **418** G3
Lolo Hot Springs, U.S.A., **418** G3
Lolobau Island, Papua New Guinea, **140** C4
Lolodorf, Cameroon, **368** B2
Lolowaï, Vanuatu, **141** A2
Loltong, Vanuatu, **141** A2
Lom, Bulgaria, **296** D4
Lom, Norway, **286** D2
Lom Sak, Thailand, **202** D2
Loma, U.S.A., **419** J3
Loma Alta, U.S.A., **424** B5
Lomaloma, Fiji, **141** A4
Lomami, *river*, Democratic Republic of the Congo, **368** D3
Lomas, Peru, **454** C4
Lomas Coloradas, *mountain range*, Argentina, **460** D2, *322*
Lomas de Zamora, Argentina, **459** E5
Lomas del Real, Mexico, **431** F4
Lomawai, Fiji, **141** A4
Lomba, *river*, Angola, **368** C6
Lombadina, Australia, **134** E2
Lombarda, Serra, *mountain range*, Brazil, **452** C2
Lombardia, *autonomous region*, Italy, **294** B3, *255*
Lombez, France, **290** E5
Lombok, *island*, Indonesia, **201** G5, *37*
Lomé, Togo, **364** E3, *326*
Lomela, Democratic Republic of the Congo, **368** D3
Lomen, Norway, **286** D2
Lomié, Cameroon, **368** B2
Lomond, Loch, *lake*, Scotland, U.K., **308** E4
Lomonosov, Russian Federation, **299** B3
Lompobatang, Gunung, *mountain peak*, Indonesia, **198** B4
Lompoc, U.S.A., **422** C4
Łomża, Poland, **289** L2
Loncopué, Argentina, **458** B6
Londinières, France, **305** J5
London, Canada, **421** N4
London, England, U.K., **305** G3, *79, 83, 93, 95, 96, 274, 276, 277, 380, 384*
London, Kentucky, U.S.A., **421** L7
London, Ohio, U.S.A., **421** M6
London, Texas, U.S.A., **424** C4
Londonderry, Cape, Australia, **134** F1
Londonderry, *district*, Northern Ireland, U.K., **309** E3
Londonderry, Isla, *island*, Chile, **460** C5
Londonderry, Northern Ireland, U.K., **309** E3, *277*
Londrina, Brazil, **459** G2
Londuimbali, Angola, **368** C5
Lonetree, U.S.A., **423** H1
Long, Loch, *lake*, Scotland, U.K., **308** D4
Long Ashton, England, U.K., **304** E3
Long Barn, U.S.A., **422** C2
Long Bay, U.S.A., **425** N3
Long Beach, California, U.S.A., **422** D5
Long Beach, New York, U.S.A., **426** D4
Long Beach, North Carolina, U.S.A., **425** N3
Long Bennington, England, U.K., **305** G1
Long Creek, U.S.A., **418** E4
Long Eaton, England, U.K., **305** F2
Long Island, Australia, **135** K3
Long Island, Bahamas, **428** G2
Long Island, New York, U.S.A., **426** D4
Long Island, Nova Scotia, Canada, **416** H7
Long Island, Papua New Guinea, **140** B4
Long Island, Québec, Canada, **415** Q4
Long Lake, Canada, **415** L7
Long Ledge, *point*, St Helena, **373** B3
Long Melford, England, U.K., **305** H2
Long Murum, Malaysia, **201** F2
Long Point, Manitoba, Canada, **414** E5
Long Point, Ontario, Canada, **421** N4
Long Point, Philippines, **204** B4
Long Preston, England, U.K., **306** F3
Long Range Mountains, *mountain range*, Canada, **417** N5
Long Range Point, St Helena, **373** B3
Long Stratton, England, U.K., **305** J2
Long Teru, Malaysia, **201** F2
Long Xian, China, **215** H2
Long Xuyên, Vietnam, **203** E4
Longa, Angola, **368** C5
Longa, Greece, **297** C7
Longa, *river*, Angola, **368** C5
Longaví, *mountain peak*, Chile, **458** B5
Longbawan, Indonesia, **201** F2
Longbridge Deverill, England, U.K., **304** E3
Longchang, China, **215** H3
Longchuan, China, **206** C3
Longde, China, **215** H2
Longfeng, China, **211** J3
Longford, *county*, Ireland, **309** E4
Longford, Ireland, **309** E4
Longframlington, England, U.K., **307** G2
Longgang, China, **207** C3
Longhai, China, **206** D3
Longhorsley, England, U.K., **307** G2
Longhua, Hebei, China, **210** G4
Longhua, north of Huzhen, Guandong, China, **207** C1
Longhua, S. Guangdong, China, **207** C3
Longhua, south of Huzhen, Guangdong, China, **207** C2
Longhui, China, **206** B3
Longido, Tanzania, **369** G3
Longiram, Indonesia, **201** F3
Longjiang, Guangdong, China, **206** D4
Longjiang, Heilongjiang, China, **211** H3
Longkou, China, **211** H5
Longlac, Canada, **415** L7
Longmen, Central Guangdong, China, **206** B4
Longmen, S. Guangdong, China, **207** C1
Longmen Shan, *mountain range*, China, **215** H3
Longmont, U.S.A., **423** L1
Longnan, China, **206** C3
Longnawan, Indonesia, **201** F2
Longonjo, Angola, **368** C5
Longping, China, **215** H4
Longquan, China, **206** D2
Longreach, Australia, **135** J3
Longridge, England, U.K., **306** F4
Longshan, Guangdong, China, **207** A1
Longshan, Hunan, China, **206** B2
Longsheng, China, **206** B3
Longtan, China, **207** A1
Longton, England, U.K., **306** F4
Longtown, England, U.K., **306** F2
Longueuil, Canada, **416** E7
Longueville-sur-Scie, France, **305** J5
Longuyon, France, **291** G2
Longvalley, U.S.A., **420** C4
Longview, Canada, **413** M6
Longview, Texas, U.S.A., **424** E3
Longview, Washington, U.S.A., **418** C3
Longwood, St Helena, **373** B3
Longwu, China, **215** G4
Longxi, China, **215** H2
Longyan, China, **206** D3
Longyandong, China, **207** A2
Longyearbyen, Svalbard, **471** D7, *279*
Longyou, China, **206** D2
Longzhen, China, **211** J2
Longzhou, China, **215** H5
Lonigo, Italy, **294** C3
Lons-le-Saunier, France, **291** G3
Lönsboda, Sweden, **286** G4
Lontra, *river*, Brazil, **456** C5
Looe, England, U.K., **304** C4
Lookout, Cape, U.S.A., **426** B7
Loolmalasin, *mountain peak*, Tanzania, **369** G3
Loomis, U.S.A., **418** E2
Loon Lake, Canada, **413** Q4
Loon Lake, U.S.A., **418** F2
Loop Head, *point*, Ireland, **309** B5
Lop, China, **212** D5
Lop Buri, Thailand, **202** D3
Lop Nur, *lake*, China, **212** F4
Lopary, Madagascar, **372** B5
Lopatino, Russian Federation, **299** D4
Lopatka, Mys, *cape*, Russian Federation, **301** S4
Lopatyn, Ukraine, **289** M3
Lopez, Cap, *cape*, Gabon, **368** A3
Lopez, U.S.A., **426** B4
Lopez Point, U.S.A., **422** B3
Lopori, *river*, Democratic Republic of the Congo, **368** D2
Lopphavet, *channel*, Norway, **284** K1
Loppi, Finland, **287** M2
Lopshen'ga, Russian Federation, **285** T4
Lora del Río, Spain, **292** E4
Lorain, U.S.A., **421** M5
Loralai, Pakistan, **218** B3
Lorca, Spain, **293** G4
Lord Howe Island, Australia, **135** U14
Lord Howe Rise, *underwater feature*, Pacific Ocean, **478** E6
Lordsburg, U.S.A., **423** J5
Lore, East Timor, **198** D5
Lorella, U.S.A., **418** D5
Lorengau, Papua New Guinea, **140** B3
Loreto, Bolivia, **455** F4
Loreto, Brazil, **452** E5
Loreto, Italy, **294** D4
Loreto, Mexico, **430** C3
Loreto, Philippines, **204** D4
Lorica, Colombia, **450** C2
Lorient, France, **290** C3
Loring, U.S.A., **419** L2
Loris, U.S.A., **425** N2
Lorn, Firth of, *river mouth*, Scotland, U.K., **308** D4
Lorraine, *administrative region*, France, **291** G2, *245*
Lorris, France, **290** F3
Lorzot, Tunisia, **361** J2
Los, Sweden, **286** G2
Los Alamos, U.S.A., **423** K4
Los Amores, Argentina, **459** E3
Los Angeles, Chile, **458** B5
Los Angeles, U.S.A., **422** D4, *23, 50*
Los Banos, U.S.A., **422** C3
Los Blancos, Argentina, **458** D2
Los Cristianos, Islas Canarias, Spain, **373** A4
Los Cusis, Bolivia, **455** F4
Los Llanos de Aridane, Islas Canarias, Spain, **373** A4
Los Lunas, U.S.A., **423** K4
Los Menucos, Argentina, **460** D1
Los Mochis, Mexico, **430** C3
Los Molinos, Islas Canarias, Spain, **373** B4
Los Navalmorales, Spain, **292** E3
Los Palacios, Cuba, **428** E2
Los Palos, East Timor, **198** D5
Los Pocitos, Mexico, **430** C2
Los Rosas, Argentina, **458** E4
Los Taques, Venezuela, **451** D1
Los Telares, Argentina, **458** D3
Los Teques, Venezuela, **451** E1
Los Vilos, Chile, **458** B4
Los Yébenes, Spain, **293** F3
Lošinj, *island*, Croatia, **294** E3
Los'mino, Russian Federation, **299** E5
Losombo, Democratic Republic of the Congo, **368** C2
Lossiemouth, Scotland, U.K., **308** F3
Lost Hills, U.S.A., **422** D4
Lostwithiel, England, U.K., **304** C4
Losuia, Papua New Guinea, **140** C5
Lot, *river*, France, **290** E4
Lota, Chile, **458** B5
Løten, Norway, **286** E2
Loto, Democratic Republic of the Congo, **368** D3
Lotofaga, Samoa, **141** B1
Lot's Wife, *mountain peak*, St Helena, **373** B3
Lotta, *river*, Russian Federation, **285** P2
Lotuke, *mountain peak*, Sudan, **369** F2
Louang Namtha, Laos, **202** D1
Louangphrabang, Laos, **202** D2
Loubomo, Congo, **368** B3
Loudéac, France, **290** C2
Loudi, China, **206** B3
Loudima, Congo, **368** B3
Loué, France, **290** D3
Loue, *river*, France, **288** B5
Louga, Senegal, **364** A1
Loughborough, England, U.K., **305** F2
Loughrea, Ireland, **309** D4
Loughton, England, U.K., **305** H3
Louhans, France, **291** G3
Louis-XIV, Pointe, *point*, Canada, **415** Q4
Louis Trichardt, South Africa, **371** E3
Louisburgh, Ireland, **309** C4
Louisiade Archipelago, Papua New Guinea, **140** D5
Louisiana, *state*, U.S.A., **424** F4, *88, 93, 384, 385, 386*
Louisville, Kentucky, U.S.A., **421** L6
Louisville, Mississippi, U.S.A., **425** H3
Louisville Ridge, *underwater feature*, Pacific Ocean, **478** G7
Loukhi, Russian Federation, **285** R3
Loukoléla, Congo, **368** C3
Loukouo, Congo, **368** B3
Loulé, Portugal, **292** C4
Loum, Cameroon, **368** A2
Loup, *river*, U.S.A., **420** D5
Lour-Escale, Senegal, **364** B2
Lourdes, Canada, **417** M5
Lourdes, France, **290** D5
Lourenço, Brazil, **452** C2
Louth, *county*, Ireland, **309** F4
Louth, England, U.K., **307** H4
Loutra Aidipsou, Greece, **297** D6
Loutraki, Greece, **297** D7
Louviers, France, **290** E2
Lövånger, Sweden, **284** K4
Lovat', *river*, Russian Federation, **299** C4
Lövberga, Sweden, **284** G5
Lovech, *administrative region*, Bulgaria, **296** E4
Lovech, Bulgaria, **296** E4
Loveland, U.S.A., **423** L1
Lovell, U.S.A., **419** K4
Lovelock, U.S.A., **422** D1
Lovere, Italy, **294** C3
Loviisa, Finland, **287** N2
Lovington, U.S.A., **423** M5
Lövnäs, Kopperberg, Sweden, **286** F2
Lövnäs, Norbotten, Sweden, **284** H3
Lovozero, Ozero, *lake*, Russian Federation, **285** S3
Lovozero, Russian Federation, **285** S2
Lovrin, Romania, **296** C3
Lövstabruk, Sweden, **287** H2
Lóvua, Lunda Norte, Angola, **368** D4
Lóvua, Moxico, Angola, **368** D5
Low, Canada, **416** D7
Low, Cape, Canada, **411** L3
Lowa, Democratic Republic of the Congo, **369** E3
Lowa, *river*, Democratic Republic of the Congo, **369** E3
Lowell, U.S.A., **418** G3
Löwenberg, Germany, **288** F2
Lower Arrow Lake, Canada, **413** K7
Lower Hutt, New Zealand, **133** E5
Lower Lake, U.S.A., **422** B2
Lower Lough Erne, *lake*, Northern Ireland, U.K., **309** E3
Lower Red Lake, U.S.A., **420** F2
Lower Peirce Reservoir, Singapore, **200** K6
Lowestoft, England, U.K., **305** J2
Łowicz, Poland, **289** J2
Lowman, U.S.A., **418** G4
Lowrah, *river*, Afghanistan, **218** A3
Lowther, Canada, **415** N7
Lowville, U.S.A., **426** C3
Loxton, South Africa, **370** D5
Loxur, China, **215** G2
Loyal, Ben, *mountain peak*, Scotland, U.K., **308** E2
Loyal Valley, U.S.A., **424** C4
Loyalty Islands *see* Loyauté, Îles, *islands*, New Caledonia, **141** A3
Loyauté, Îles (Loyalty Islands), New Caledonia, **141** A3
Loymola, Russian Federation, **299** C2
Loyne, Loch, Scotland, U.K., **308** D3
Lozère, Mont, *mountain peak*, France, **291** F4

Loznica, Serbia, **296** B3
Loznitsa, Bulgaria, **296** F4
Lozoyuela, Spain, **293** F2
Lua Nova, Brazil, **452** B4
Luacano, Angola, **368** D5
Lualuba, *river*, Democratic Republic of the Congo, **369** E2, *334*
Luama, *river*, Democratic Republic of the Congo, **369** E3
Luampa, *river*, Zambia, **368** D5
Luan, China, **210** G4
Lu'an, China, **206** D2
Luan Xian, China, **211** G5
Luanchuan, China, **206** B1
Luanda, Angola, **368** B4, *335*
Luanda, *province*, Angola, **368** B4
Luando, Angola, **368** C5
Luando, *river*, Angola, **368** C5
Luanguinga, *river*, Angola, **368** D5
Luangwa, *river*, Zambia, **369** F5, *344*
Luangwa, Zambia, **371** F2
Luanjing, China, **210** D5
Luanshya, Zambia, **369** E5
Luanza, Democratic Republic of the Congo, **369** E4
Luapula, *province*, Zambia, **369** E5
Luar, Danau, *lake*, Indonesia, **201** F2
Luar *see* Horsburgh Island, Cocos (Keeling) Islands, **134** Q10
Luarca, Spain, **292** D1
Luashi, Democratic Republic of the Congo, **368** D5
Luau, Angola, **368** D5
Luba, Equatorial Guinea, **368** A2
Lubaczów, Poland, **289** L3
Lubalo, Angola, **368** C4
Lubāna, Latvia, **287** N4
Lubang Islands, Philippines, **204** B3
Lubango, Angola, **368** B5
Lubāns, *lake*, Latvia, **287** N4
Lubao, Democratic Republic of the Congo, **369** E4
Lubartów, Poland, **289** L3
Lubawa, Poland, **289** J2
Lübben, Germany, **289** F3
Lubbock, U.S.A., **424** B3
Lübeck, Germany, **288** E2
Lübecker Bucht, *bay*, Germany, **288** E1
Lubefu, Democratic Republic of the Congo, **368** D3
Lubefu, *river*, Democratic Republic of the Congo, **368** D3
Lubero, Democratic Republic of the Congo, **369** E3
Lubin, Poland, **289** H3
Lublin, Poland, **289** L3
Lubliniec, Poland, **289** J3
Lubnān, Jabal, *mountain range*, Lebanon, **225** C3, *181*
Lubny, Ukraine, **298** D3
Lubsko, Poland, **289** G3
Lubuagan, Philippines, **204** C2
Lubudi, Democratic Republic of the Congo, **369** E4
Lubumbashi, Democratic Republic of the Congo, **369** E5
Lubungu, Zambia, **369** E5
Lubutu, Democratic Republic of the Congo, **369** E3
Luby, Poland, **289** J2
Lucala, Angola, **368** C4
Lucan, Ireland, **309** F4
Lücaoshan, China, **213** G5
Lucapa, Angola, **368** D4
Lucca, Italy, **294** C4
Lucélia, Brazil, **456** C5
Lucena, Philippines, **204** C3
Lucena, Spain, **292** E4
Lučenec, Slovakia, **289** J4
Lucera, Italy, **295** E5
Lucerna, Peru, **455** E3
Luchang, China, **215** G4
Lüchow, Germany, **288** E2
Luchuan, China, **206** B4
Lucie, *river*, Suriname, **452** B2
Lucile, U.S.A., **418** F4
Lucira, Angola, **368** B5
Luckau, Germany, **288** F3
Luckeesarai, India, **219** F4
Luckenwalde, Germany, **288** F2
Lucknow, India, **218** E4, *169*
Luçon, France, **290** D3
Lucrecia, Cabo, *cape*, Cuba, **429** G2
Lucusse, Angola, **368** D5
Luda Kamchiya, *river*, Bulgaria, **296** F4
Ludden, U.S.A., **420** D2
Lüderitz, Namibia, **370** C4
Lüderitz Bay, Namibia, **370** B4
Ludhiāna, India, **218** C3
Ludian, China, **215** G4
Ludington, U.S.A., **421** K4
Ludlow, California, U.S.A., **422** E4
Ludlow, Colorado, U.S.A., **423** L3
Ludlow, England, U.K., **304** E2
Ludlow, Vermont, U.S.A., **426** D3
Ludowici, U.S.A., **425** M4
Luduş, Romania, **296** E2
Ludvika, Sweden, **286** G2
Ludwigsburg, Germany, **288** D4
Ludwigshafen am Rhein, Germany, **288** D4
Ludwigslust, Germany, **288** E2
Ludza, Latvia, **287** N4
Luebo, Democratic Republic of the Congo, **368** D4
Lueki, Democratic Republic of the Congo, **369** E3
Luena, Angola, **368** C5
Luepa, Venezuela, **451** G3
Lüeyang, China, **215** H2
Lufeng, China, **206** C4
Lufkin, U.S.A., **424** E4
Luga, *river*, Russian Federation, **299** B3
Luga, Russian Federation, **299** B3
Lugait, Philippines, **204** D4
Lugano, Switzerland, **291** J3
Luganville, Vanuatu, **141** A2
Lugela, Mozambique, **369** G6
Lughaye, Somalia, **367** F2
Lugnaquillia, *mountain peak*, Ireland, **309** F5
Lugo, Italy, **294** C3
Lugo, Spain, **292** D1
Lugoj, Romania, **296** C3
Lūgovoy, Kazakhstan, **223** J4
Lugu, China, **214** C2
Luhačovice, Czech Republic, **289** H4
Luhans'k, Ukraine, **298** E3
Luhombero, Tanzania, **369** G4
Luhuo, China, **215** G3
Lui, Ben, *mountain peak*, Scotland, U.K., **308** E4
Luia, *river*, Mozambique, **369** F6
Luiana, Angola, **370** D2
Luikonlahti, Finland, **285** P5
Luing, *island*, Scotland, U.K., **308** D4
Luís Correia, Brazil, **453** F4
Luitpold Coast, *region*, Antarctica, **470** C4
Luiza, Democratic Republic of the Congo, **368** D4
Luján, Argentina, **458** C4
Lujiang, China, **206** D2
Lukachek, Russian Federation, **211** L1
Lukala, Democratic Republic of the Congo, **368** B4
Lukavac, Bosnia and Herzegovina, **294** G3
Lukengo, Democratic Republic of the Congo, **369** E4
Lukeville, U.S.A., **422** G6
Lukhovitsy, Russian Federation, **299** G5
Lŭki, Bulgaria, **296** E5
Lukolela, Democratic Republic of the Congo, **368** C3
Lukovit, Bulgaria, **296** E4
Lukovnikovo, Russian Federation, **299** E4
Łuków, Poland, **289** L3
Lukula, Democratic Republic of the Congo, **368** B4
Lukulu, Zambia, **368** D5
Lukumburu, Tanzania, **369** G4
Lukunor, *island*, Micronesia, **138** D4
Lukwasa, India, **218** D4
Luleå, Sweden, **285** L4
Luleälven, *river*, Sweden, **284** K4
Lüleburgaz, Turkey, **297** F5
Luliang, China, **215** G4
Lüliang Shan, *mountain range*, China, **210** E5
Lulimba, Democratic Republic of the Congo, **369** E3
Luling, U.S.A., **424** D5
Lulonga, Democratic Republic of the Congo, **368** C2
Lulua, *river*, Democratic Republic of the Congo, **368** D4
Lülung, China, **214** C3
Luma, American Samoa, **141** B2
Lumbala Kaquengue, Angola, **368** D5
Lumbala N'guimbo, Angola, **368** D5
Lumberton, Mississippi, U.S.A., **425** H4
Lumberton, North Carolina, U.S.A., **425** N2
Lumbrales, Spain, **292** D2
Lumbrera, Argentina, **458** D2
Lumbres, France, **305** K4
Lumding, India, **219** H4
Lumecha, Tanzania, **369** G5
Lumimba, Zambia, **369** F5
Lumo, *island*, Micronesia, **138** C4
Lumphăt, Cambodia, **203** E3
Lumsden, Canada, **413** S6
Lumsden, New Zealand, **133** B7
Lumut, Gunung, *mountain peak*, Indonesia, **201** F3, *150*
Lumut, Tanjong, *point*, Indonesia, **200** D3
Lün, Mongolia, **210** D3
Lunan Bay, Scotland, U.K., **308** G4
Lund, Sweden, **286** F5
Lunda Norte, *province*, Angola, **368** C4
Lunda Sul, *province*, Angola, **368** D5
Lundazi, Zambia, **369** F5
Lunde, Sweden, **287** H1
Lundy, *island*, England, U.K., **304** C3
Lune, *river*, England, U.K., **306** F3
Lüneburg, Germany, **288** E2
Lunenburg, Canada, **417** J7
Lunéville, France, **291** H2
Lung Kwu Tan, China, **207** B4
Lungdo, China, **214** B2
Lunggar, China, **214** B3
Lungi, Sierra Leone, **364** B3
Lunglei, India, **219** H5
Lungsang, China, **214** D3
Luning, China, **215** G3
Luning, U.S.A., **422** D2
Lūnkaransar, India, **218** C3
Lunsar, Sierra Leone, **364** B3
Luntai, China, **212** E4
Lunz am See, Austria, **289** G5
Luo, *river*, China, **210** E5
Luobei, China, **211** K3
Luobuzhuang, China, **212** F5
Luochuan, China, **206** B1
Luodian, China, **215** H4
Luoding, China, **206** B4
Luofu Shan, *mountain peak*, China, **207** B2
Luofu Shan, *mountain range*, China, **207** C2
Luogang, China, **207** B2
Luogosanto, Sardegna, Italy, **295** B5
Luohe, China, **206** C1
Luonan, China, **206** B1
Luoning, China, **206** B1
Luoping, China, **215** H4
Luoshan, China, **206** C1
Luotian, China, **206** C2
Luoxiao Shan, *mountain range*, China, **206** C3
Luoyang, China, **206** C1
Luoyuan, China, **206** D3
Luozi, Democratic Republic of the Congo, **368** B3
Lupane, Zimbabwe, **371** E2
Lupeni, Romania, **296** D3
Lupilichi, Mozambique, **369** G5
Luqu, China, **215** G2
Luray, U.S.A., **420** D6
Lure, France, **291** H3
Lure, Montagne de, *mountain peak*, France, **291** G4
Luremo, Angola, **368** C4
Lurgan, Northern Ireland, U.K., **309** F3
Luribay, Bolivia, **455** E4
Lurín, Peru, **454** C3
Lúrio, Mozambique, **369** H5
Lurton, U.S.A., **424** F2
Lusahunga, Tanzania, **369** F3
Lusaka, *province*, Zambia, **369** E6, *344*
Lusaka, Zambia, **369** E6, *344*
Lusambo, Democratic Republic of the Congo, **368** D3
Lusangi, Democratic Republic of the Congo, **369** E3
Luseland, Canada, **413** Q5
Lusengo, Democratic Republic of the Congo, **368** C2
Lushi, China, **206** B1
Lushnjë, Albania, **297** B5
Lushoto, Tanzania, **369** G3
Lushui, China, **215** F4
Lüshun, China, **211** H5
Lusk, U.S.A., **419** M5
Lūt, Dasht-e, *desert*, Iran, **221** G2, *183*
Lūţāk, Iran, **221** H2
Lutembo, Angola, **368** D5
Lutherstadt Eisleben, Germany, **288** E3
Lutherstadt Wittenberg, Germany, **288** F3
Lütian, China, **207** B1
Lutiba, Democratic Republic of the Congo, **369** E3
Lütjenburg, Germany, **288** E1
Lutnes, Norway, **286** F2
Luton, England, U.K., **305** G3
Luton, *unitary authority*, England, U.K., **305** G3
Lutong, Malaysia, **201** F1
Lutselk'e, Canada, **410** H3
Lutshima, Democratic Republic of the Congo, **368** C4
Luts'k, Ukraine, **298** C2
Lutterworth, England, U.K., **305** F2
Lutto, *river*, Finland, **285** P2
Lututów, Poland, **289** J3
Lützow Holmbukta, *bay*, Antarctica, **470** F3
Luumaki, Finland, **287** N2
Luuq, Somalia, **369** H2
Luverne, Alabama, U.S.A., **425** J4
Luverne, Minnesota, U.S.A., **420** E4
Luvozero, Russian Federation, **285** Q4
Luvua, *river*, Democratic Republic of the Congo, **369** E4
Luvuei, Angola, **368** D5
Luwero, Uganda, **369** F2
Luwuk, Indonesia, **198** C3
Luxembourg, *country*, Europe, **282** E6, *228, 238, 240, 243, 244, 245*
Luxembourg, Luxembourg, **291** H2, *243*
Luxembourg, *province*, Belgium, **288** B4
Luxeuil-les-Bains, France, **291** H3
Luxi, E. Yunnan, China, **215** G4
Luxi, Hunan, China, **206** B2
Luxi, W. Yunnan, China, **215** F4
Luxor *see* Al Uqşur, Egypt, **363** F3, *317*
Luyamba, Democratic Republic of the Congo, **369** E3
Luz-Saint-Sauveur, France, **290** D5
Luza, Russian Federation, **300** F3
Luzern, Switzerland, **291** J3
Luzhitsa, Russian Federation, **299** B3
Luzhou, China, **215** H3
Luziânia, Brazil, **456** D4
Luzilândia, Brazil, **453** E4
Luzon, *island*, Philippines, **204** C2, *149*
Luzon Strait, Philippines/Taiwan, **195** N7
Luzy, France, **291** F3
L'viv, Ukraine, **298** B3
L'vivsk'a Oblast', *province*, Ukraine, **289** L4
Lyady, Russian Federation, **299** B3
Lyakhovskiye Ostrova, *islands*, Russian Federation, **301** Q2
Lyall, Mount, *mountain peak*, Campbell Island, New Zealand, **132** K11
Lyall, Mount, *mountain peak*, New Zealand, **133** A7
Lyamtsa, Russian Federation, **285** T4
Lyaskelya, Russian Federation, **299** C2
Lyaskovets, Bulgaria, **296** E4
Lyasnaya, Belarus, **289** M2
Lyavozero, Ozero, *lake*, Russian Federation, **285** S2
Lychkovo, Russian Federation, **299** D4
Lycksele, Sweden, **284** J4
Lydd, England, U.K., **305** H4
Lydford, England, U.K., **304** C4
Lye, Sweden, **287** J4
Lyell Island, Canada, **412** D5
Lyepyel', Belarus, **298** C2
Lygourio, Greece, **297** D7
Lyl'yok, *river*, Russian Federation, **285** U3
Lyman, Ukraine, **296** G3
Lymans'ke, Ukraine, **296** G2
Lyme Bay, England, U.K., **304** D4
Lyme Regis, England, U.K., **304** E4
Lymington, England, U.K., **305** F4
Lynchburg, U.S.A., **421** P7
Lynd, *river*, Australia, **135** J2
Lyndhurst, England, U.K., **305** F4
Lyneham, England, U.K., **305** E3
Lynemouth, England, U.K., **307** G2
Lyness, Orkney, Scotland, U.K., **308** F2
Lyngdal, Norway, **286** C3
Lyngseidet, Norway, **284** K2
Lynmouth, England, U.K., **304** D3
Lynn, U.S.A., **426** E3
Lynn Haven, U.S.A., **425** K4
Lynn Lake, Canada, **414** D3
Lynton, England, U.K., **304** D3
Lyntupy, Belarus, **287** N5
Lyon, France, **291** G4, *245*
Lyon, *river*, Scotland, U.K., **308** E4
Lyons, U.S.A., **425** L3
Lyozna, Belarus, **299** C5
Lysa Hora, Ukraine, **296** H1
Lysøysund, Norway, **284** D5
Lysvik, Sweden, **286** F2
Lysychans'k, Ukraine, **298** E3
Lytham St Anne's, England, U.K., **306** E4
Lyttelton, New Zealand, **133** D6
Lytton, Canada, **412** J6
Lyuban', Russian Federation, **299** C3
Lyubashivka, Ukraine, **296** H2
Lyubertsy, Russian Federation, **299** F5
Lyubytino, Russian Federation, **299** D3
Lyudinovo, Russian Federation, **299** E6
Lyudkovo, Russian Federation, **299** E5
Lyulyakovo, Bulgaria, **296** F4
Lzha, *river*, Latvia/Russian Federation, **299** B4


## M


Mā, *river*, Laos/Vietnam, **203** E1
Ma-kung, Taiwan, **206** D4
Ma-tou, Taiwan, **206** E4
Ma-ubin, Myanmar, **205** B4
Ma Wan Chung, China, **207** B4
Ma'ād, Jordan, **225** C3
Maalahti, Finland, **287** K1
Maamba, Zambia, **371** E2
Ma'an, Cameroon, **368** B2
Ma'ān, Jordan, **225** C4
Maaninkavaara, Finland, **285** P3
Maanīt, Bulgan, Mongolia, **213** J2
Maanīt, Töv, Mongolia, **210** D3
Maanselkä, Finland, **285** P5

Ma'anshan, China, **206** D2
Maarianhamina, Finland, **287** J2
Maarmorilik, Greenland, **411** P2
Ma'arrat an Nu'mān, Syria, **225** D2
Maas, *river*, Netherlands, **288** B3
Maasin, Philippines, **204** D4
Maastricht, Netherlands, **288** B3
Maasupa, Solomon Islands, **141** A1
Maba, Indonesia, **199** E2
Mabalane, Mozambique, **371** F3
Mabana, Democratic Republic of the Congo, **369** E2
Mabaruma, Guyana, **451** G2
Mabein, Myanmar, **205** C3
Mabini, Philippines, **204** D5
Mablethorpe, England, U.K., **307** J4
Mabote, Mozambique, **371** F3
Mabrak, Jabal, *mountain peak*, Jordan, **225** C4
Mabrūk, Libya, **362** C3
Mabton, U.S.A., **418** D3
Mac. Robertson Land, *region*, Antarctica, **470** F4
Macá, Monte, *mountain peak*, Chile, **460** C2
Macachín, Argentina, **458** D5
Macacos, Ilha dos, *island*, Brazil, **452** C3
Macaé, Brazil, **457** F6
Macaloge, Mozambique, **369** G5
Macang, Malaysia, **200** C1
Macao, China, **207** B4, *160, 161, 165*
Macapá, Brazil, **452** C3
Macará, Ecuador, **450** B5
Macarani, Brazil, **457** F4
Macarena, Serranía de la, *mountain range*, Colombia, **450** C3
Macas, Ecuador, **450** B5
Macau, Brazil, **453** G4, *251*
Macaúba, Brazil, **456** C3
Macaúba, *river*, Brazil, **456** C3
Macaúbas, Brazil, **457** E3
Macauley Island, Kermadec Islands, New Zealand, **132** L12
Macayari, Colombia, **450** D4
Macbar, Raas, *point*, Somalia, **367** H3
Macclenny, U.S.A., **425** L4
Macclesfield, England, U.K., **304** E1
Macdonald, Canada, **414** E6
MacDonald, Lake, Australia, **134** F3
MacDonnell Ranges, *mountain range*, Australia, **134** G3, *112*
Macdowall, Canada, **413** R5
MacDowell, Canada, **414** H5
Macduff, Scotland, U.K., **308** G3
Macdui, Ben, *mountain peak*, Scotland, U.K., **308** F3
Macedonia, *country*, Europe, **282** G7, *70, 81, 228, 260, 261, 263, 264, 265*
Maceió, Brazil, **457** G2
Macenta, Guinea, **364** C3
Macerata, Italy, **294** D4
Macfarlane, Lake, Australia, **135** H5
MacFarlane, *river*, Canada, **413** R2
Macgillycuddys Reeks, *mountain range*, Ireland, **309** C6, *277*
Machacamarca, Bolivia, **455** E5
Machachi, Ecuador, **450** B4
Machadinho, *river*, Brazil, **455** F2
Machaila, Mozambique, **371** F3
Machakos, Kenya, **369** G3
Machala, Ecuador, **450** B5
Machang, China, **210** G5
Machanga, Mozambique, **371** F3
Macharetí, Bolivia, **455** F5
Macheng, China, **206** C2
Māchgaon, India, **219** F5
Machhīwāra, India, **218** D3
Machias, U.S.A., **426** G2
Machichaco, Cabo, *cape*, Spain, **293** F1
Machichi, *river*, Canada, **414** J3
Machico, Madeira, Portugal, **373** C3
Machilīpatnam, India, **217** E2
Machinga, Malawi, **369** G6
Machiques, Venezuela, **450** D1
Machrihanish, Scotland, U.K., **308** D5
Machupicchu, Peru, **454** D3, *77, 441*
Machynlleth, Wales, U.K., **304** D2
Macia, Mozambique, **371** F4
Măcin, Romania, **296** G3
Mackay, Australia, **135** K3
Mackay, Lake, *lake*, Australia, **134** F3
Mackay, U.S.A., **418** H5
MacKenzie, Canada, **412** H4
Mackenzie, *river*, Canada, **410** G3
Mackenzie Bay, Canada, **410** F3
Mackenzie King Island, Canada, **410** H2
Mackenzie Mountains, *mountain range*, Canada, **410** F3
Mackinaw City, U.S.A., **421** L3
Mackintosh, Mount, *mountain peak*, Antarctica, **470** E7
Macklin, Canada, **413** Q5
Maclennan, New Zealand, **133** B8
MacLeod, Lake, Australia, **134** C3
Macocola, Angola, **368** C4
Macomb, U.S.A., **420** H5
Macomer, Sardegna, Italy, **295** B5
Macomia, Mozambique, **369** H5
Mâcon, France, **291** G3
Macon, Georgia, U.S.A., **425** L3
Macon, Mississippi, U.S.A., **425** H3
Macon, Missouri, U.S.A., **420** G6
Macondo, Angola, **368** D5
Macoun, Canada, **414** C7
Macoun Lake, Canada, **414** B3
Macpes, Canada, **416** G5
Macquarie, *river*, Australia, **135** K5
Macquarie Harbour, Australia, **135** J7
Macquarie Island, Australian Antarctic Territory, **134** R11, *465*
Macquarie Island, *Australian research station*, Antarctica, **470** F10
Macquarie Ridge, *underwater feature*, Pacific Ocean, **478** E8
MacRitchie Reservoir, Singapore, **200** J6
Macroom, Ireland, **309** D6
Macujer, Colombia, **450** D4
Macuro, Venezuela, **461** C4
Macusani, Peru, **454** D4
Macuspana, Mexico, **431** G5
Ma'dabā, Jordan, **225** C4
Madadeni, South Africa, **371** F4
Madagascar, *country*, Indian Ocean, **359** K9, *63, 93, 312, 313, 345, 352, 353, 354*
Madagascar Basin, *underwater feature*, Indian Ocean, **476** C6
Madagascar Plateau, *underwater feature*, Indian Ocean, **476** B6
Madā'in Şāliḩ, Saudi Arabia, **363** G3
Madalena, Azores, Portugal, **360** M7
Madam, Isle, *island*, Canada, **417** L7
Madama, Niger, **362** B4
Madampe, Sri Lanka, **217** E5
Madan, Bulgaria, **297** E5
Madanapalle, India, **216** D3
Madang, Papua New Guinea, **140** B4
Madang, *province*, Papua New Guinea, **140** B4
Madaoua, Niger, **365** F2
Mādārīpur, Bangladesh, **214** D5
Madau, Turkmenistan, **222** E5
Madawaska, Canada, **416** B7
Maddalena, Isola, *island*, Sardegna, Italy, **295** B5
Madeira, *island*, Portugal, Atlantic Ocean, **373** C3, *251, 354, 355*
Madeira, *river*, Brazil, **451** G5
Madeleine, Îles de la, *islands*, Canada, **417** L6
Madelia, U.S.A., **420** F3
Madeline, U.S.A., **418** D6
Madera, Mexico, **430** C2
Madera, U.S.A., **422** C3
Madhepura, India, **219** F4
Madhubani, India, **219** F4
Madhya Pradesh, *state*, India, **218** D5, *169*
Madidi, *river*, Bolivia, **455** E3
Madimba, Democratic Republic of the Congo, **368** C3
Madinani, Côte d'Ivoire, **364** C3
Madingo-Kayes, Congo, **368** B3
Madingou, Congo, **368** B3
Madingrin, Cameroon, **365** G3
Madirovalo, Madagascar, **372** B4
Madison, Canada, **413** Q6
Madison, Florida, U.S.A., **425** L4
Madison, Georgia, U.S.A., **425** L3
Madison, Indiana, U.S.A., **421** L6
Madison, Iowa, U.S.A., **421** J4
Madison, Nebraska, U.S.A., **420** E5
Madison, *river*, U.S.A., **419** J4
Madison, South Dakota, U.S.A., **420** E3
Madison, Wisconsin, U.S.A., **421** J4, *386*
Madisonville, Kentucky, U.S.A., **421** K7
Madisonville, Texas, U.S.A., **424** E4
Madiun, Indonesia, **201** E4
Madjingo, Gabon, **368** B2
Mado Gashi, Kenya, **369** G2
Madoc, Canada, **416** C7
Madoi, China, **215** F2
Madona, Latvia, **287** N4
Madonie, *mountain range*, Sicilia, Italy, **295** D7
Madra Dağı, *mountain peak*, Turkey, **297** F6
Madrakah, Ra's al, *cape*, Oman, **221** G5
Madras *see* Chennai, India, **216** E3, *93, 94, 169*
Madras, U.S.A., **418** D4
Madre, Laguna, *lagoon*, Mexico, **431** F3
Madre, Sierra, *mountain range*, Philippines, **204** C2
Madre de Chiapas, Sierra, *mountain range*, Mexico, **431** G5
Madre de Dios, Isla, *island*, Chile, **460** B4
Madre de Dios, *river*, Bolivia/Peru, **455** D3
Madre Del Sur, Sierra, *mountain range*, Mexico, **431** E5
Madre Occidental, Sierra, *mountain range*, Mexico, **430** C2, *401*
Madre Oriental, Sierra, *mountain range*, Mexico, **431** E3, *400, 401*
Madrid, *autonomous region*, Spain, **293** F2
Madrid, Spain, **293** F2, *252, 253*
Madridejos, Spain, **293** F3
Maduda, Democratic Republic of the Congo, **368** B3
Madukani, Tanzania, **369** G3
Madura, Australia, **134** F5
Madura, Pulau, *island*, Indonesia, **201** F4
Madura, Selat, *strait*, Indonesia, **201** F4
Madurai, India, **216** D4
Madyo, Tanzania, **369** F4
Mae Hong Son, Thailand, **202** C2
Mae Ramat, Thailand, **202** C2
Mae Sai, Myanmar, **215** F5
Mae Sai, Thailand, **205** C3
Mae Sariang, Thailand, **202** C2
Mae Sot, Thailand, **202** C2
Mae Tho, Doi, *mountain peak*, Thailand, **202** C2
Mae Tub Reservoir, Thailand, **202** C2
Mae Ya, Doi, *mountain peak*, Thailand, **202** C2
Mæl, Norway, **286** D3
Maella, Spain, **293** H2
Maestra, Sierra, *mountain range*, Cuba, **429** F2
Maevatanana, Madagascar, **372** B4
Maewo, *island*, Vanuatu, **141** A2
Mafeking, Canada, **414** D5
Mafeteng, Lesotho, **371** E4
Maffin, Indonesia, **199** G3
Mafia Island, Tanzania, **369** G4
Mafikeng, South Africa, **371** E4
Mafinga, Tanzania, **369** G4, *344*
Mafra, Brazil, **459** H3
Magadan, Russian Federation, **301** S4
Magadi, Kenya, **369** G3
Magallanes, *administrative region*, Chile, **460** C4
Magallanes, Estrecho de, *strait*, Chile, **460** C4
Magangué, Colombia, **450** C2
Mağara, Turkey, **225** B1
Magaria, Niger, **365** F2
Magat, *river*, Philippines, **204** C2
Magbakele, Democratic Republic of the Congo, **368** D2
Magburaka, Sierra Leone, **364** B3
Magdagachi, Russian Federation, **211** J1
Magdalena, Argentina, **459** F5
Magdalena, Bolivia, **455** F3
Magdalena, Isla, *island*, Chile, **460** C2
Magdalena, Mexico, **430** C2
Magdalena, *river*, Colombia, **450** D2, *436*
Magdalena, *river*, Mexico, **430** C2
Magdalena, U.S.A., **423** K4
Magdalena Tequisistlán, Mexico, **431** G5
Magdeburg, Germany, **288** E2
Magdelaine Cays, *islands*, Coral Sea Islands, **135** L2
Magee Island, Northern Ireland, U.K., **309** G3
Magelang, Indonesia, **201** E4
Magerøya, *island*, Norway, **285** M1
Maggiorasca, Monte, *mountain peak*, Italy, **294** B3
Maggiore, Lago, *lake*, Italy, **294** B3, *255*
Maggiore, Monte, *mountain peak*, Italy, **295** E5
Maghāghah, Egypt, **363** F3
Maghama, Mauritania, **364** B1
Magharah, Jabal, *mountain peak*, Egypt, **225** B4
Magherafelt, *district*, Northern Ireland, U.K., **309** F3
Magherafelt, Northern Ireland, U.K., **309** F3
Maghull, England, U.K., **306** F4
Magilligan Point, Northern Ireland, U.K., **309** F2
Mágina, *mountain peak*, Spain, **293** F4
Maglić, *mountain peak*, Bosnia and Herzegovina, **294** G4, *259*
Maglie, Italy, **295** G5
Magma Point, Papua New Guinea, **140** C4
Magna, U.S.A., **423** G1
Magnetic Island, Australia, **135** K2
Magnetity, Russian Federation, **285** R2
Magnitogorsk, Russian Federation, **222** F2
Magnolia, U.S.A., **424** F3
Mago, *island*, Fiji, **141** A4
Màgoé, Mozambique, **369** F6
Magog, Canada, **416** E7
Magpie, Canada, **417** J4
Magpie, Lac, *lake*, Canada, **417** J4
Magrath, Canada, **413** N7
Magta' Lahjar, Mauritania, **364** B1
Maguarinho, Cabo, *cape*, Brazil, **452** D3
Magude, Mozambique, **371** F4
Magumeri, Nigeria, **365** G2
Maguse Lake, Canada, **414** G1
Magwe, *division*, Myanmar, **205** B3
Magwe, Myanmar, **205** B3
Magyichaung, Myanmar, **205** B3
Maha Sarakham, Thailand, **203** D2
Mahābād, Iran, **222** D5
Mahabe, Madagascar, **372** B4
Mahābhārat Lekh, *mountain range*, Nepal, **219** E3
Mahabo, Madagascar, **372** A5
Mahaboboka, Madagascar, **372** A5
Mahadday Weyne, Somalia, **367** G4
Mahagi Port, Democratic Republic of the Congo, **369** F2
Mahaicony, Guyana, **452** B1
Mahājan, India, **218** C3
Mahajanga, Madagascar, **372** B4
Mahajanga, *province*, Madagascar, **372** B4
Mahakam, *river*, Indonesia, **201** F2
Mahalapye, Botswana, **371** E3
Mahalevona, Madagascar, **372** B4
Mahallāt, Iran, **220** F2
Mahānadi, *river*, India, **219** F5
Mahanoro, Madagascar, **372** B4
Mahārājganj, Bihār, India, **219** F4
Mahārājganj, Uttar Pradesh, India, **219** E4
Mahārāshtra, *state*, India, **216** C2, *169*
Maharès, Tunisia, **361** J2
Mahavelona, Madagascar, **372** B4
Maḩbūb, Sudan, **366** C2
Mahbūbnagar, India, **216** D2
Mahdia, Guyana, **451** G3
Mahdia, Tunisia, **362** B1
Mahe, India, **216** C4
Mahé, *island*, Seychelles, **373** A2, *352*
Mahébourg, Mauritius, **373** C1
Mahenge, Tanzania, **369** G4
Maheno, New Zealand, **133** C7
Mahesāna, India, **218** C5
Mahi, *river*, India, **218** C5
Mahia, New Zealand, **132** F4
Mahia Peninsula, New Zealand, **132** F4
Mahilyow, Belarus, **299** C6
Mahilyowskaya Voblasts', *province*, Belarus, **299** C6
Mahina, Mali, **364** B2
Maḩmūd-e Rāqī, Afghanistan, **218** B2
Mahmūdābād, India, **218** E4
Mahmudia, Romania, **296** G3
Mahnomen, U.S.A., **420** F2
Mahoba, India, **218** D4
Mahoenui, New Zealand, **132** E4
Mahón, Islas Baleares, Spain, **293** K3
Mahora, Spain, **293** G3
Mahou, Mali, **364** D2
Mahrāt, Jabal, *mountain range*, Yemen, **220** F5
Mahroni, India, **218** D4
Mahuanggou, China, **213** G5
Mahuva, India, **218** B5
Mahwa, India, **218** D4
Mai-Ndombe, Lac, *lake*, Democratic Republic of the Congo, **368** C3
Maiao, *island*, French Polynesia, **137** F2
Maicao, Colombia, **450** D1
Maîche, France, **291** H3
Maicuru, *river*, Brazil, **452** B3
Maidenhead, England, U.K., **305** G3
Maidi, Indonesia, **198** D2
Maidstone, Canada, **413** Q5
Maidstone, England, U.K., **305** H3
Maiduguri, Nigeria, **365** G2
Maignelay-Montigny, France, **305** K5
Maigualida, Sierra, *mountain range*, Venezuela, **451** F3

Maihar, India, **218** E4
Maihiá, Venezuela, **451** F3
Maikala Range, *mountain range*, India, **218** E5
Mailsi, Pakistan, **218** C3
Main, *river*, Germany, **288** D4
Main-a-Dieu, Canada, **417** M6
Main Brook, Canada, **417** N4
Maine, Gulf of, U.S.A., **426** G3
Maine, *state*, U.S.A., **426** F2, *383, 386*
Maine Hanari, Cerro, *mountain peak*, Colombia, **450** D4
Maïné-Soroa, Niger, **365** G2
Mainit, Lake, Philippines, **204** D4
Mainland, *island*, Orkney, Scotland, U.K., **308** F1
Mainland, *island*, Shetland, Scotland, U.K., **308** K7
Mainpuri, India, **218** D4
Maintirano, Madagascar, **372** A4
Mainz, Germany, **288** D4, *92*
Maio, *island*, Cape Verde, **360** Q8
Maipú, Argentina, **459** F5
Maipú, Volcán, *mountain peak*, Argentina/Chile, **458** C5
Maipuri Landing, Guyana, **451** G3
Maisí, Cuba, **429** G2
Maitencillo, Chile, **458** B4
Maitengwe, Botswana, **371** E3
Maitland, New South Wales, Australia, **135** L5
Maitland, South Australia, Australia, **135** H5
Maizuru, Japan, **209** F4
Maja e Korbit *see* Korab, *mountain peak*, Albania/Macedonia, **296** C5, *260, 263*
Majardah, *river*, Tunisia, **362** A1, *315*
Majardah, Monts de la, *mountain range*, Algeria, **295** A7
Majāz al Bāb, Tunisia, **295** B7
Majdanpek, Serbia, **296** C3
Majene, Indonesia, **198** B3
Majevica, *mountain range*, Bosnia and Herzegovina, **294** G3
Majī, Ethiopia, **366** E3
Majia, *river*, China, **210** G5
Majiagang, China, **211** L3
Majiang, China, **206** B4
Majie, China, **215** H5
Majitang, China, **206** B2
Major, Canada, **413** Q6
Major, Puig, *mountain peak*, Islas Baleares, Spain, **293** J3
Major Buratovich, Argentina, **460** E1
Major Lake, Macquarie Island, **134** R11
Majuro, *island*, Marshall Islands, **139** F4, *119*
Maka, Senegal, **364** B2
Maka, Solomon Islands, **141** A1
Makabana, Congo, **368** B3
Makaha, Hawaiian Islands, U.S.A., **422** R9
Makak, Cameroon, **368** B2
Makale, Indonesia, **198** B3
Makamba, Burundi, **369** E3
Makanza, Democratic Republic of the Congo, **368** C2
Makapu Point, Niue, **132** M13
Makaraka, New Zealand, **132** F4
Makarakomburu, Mount, *mountain peak*, Solomon Islands, **141** A1, *115*
Makarska, Croatia, **294** F4
Makar'yevskaya, Russian Federation, **299** E2
Makassar *see* Ujungpandang, Indonesia, **198** B4
Makassarstraße, *strait*, Indonesia, **198** B3
Makatea, *island*, French Polynesia, **137** G2, *94, 119*
Makaw, Myanmar, **205** C2
Makefu, Niue, **132** M13
Makeni, Sierra Leone, **364** B3
Makhachkala, Russian Federation, **222** D4
Makikihi, New Zealand, **133** C7
Makindu, Kenya, **369** G3
Makīnsk, Kazakhstan, **223** J2
Makira, *island*, Solomon Islands, **141** A1, *116*
Makiyivka, Ukraine, **298** E3
Makkah (Mecca), Saudi Arabia, **363** G4, *73, 74, 174, 185*
Makkola, Finland, **287** P2
Makkovik, Cape, Canada, **417** M2
Makó, Hungary, **289** K5
Makokou, Gabon, **368** B2
Makongolosi, Tanzania, **369** F4
Makoro, Democratic Republic of the Congo, **369** E2
Makotipoko, Congo, **368** C3
Makoua, Congo, **368** C3
Maków Mazowiecki, Poland, **289** K2
Makra, *island*, Kyklades, Greece, **297** E7
Makrakomi, Greece, **297** D6
Makrany, Belarus, **289** M3
Makronisi, *island*, Kyklades, Greece, **297** E7
Maksatikha, Russian Federation, **299** E4
Maksi, India, **218** D5
Maksimikha, Russian Federation, **210** E1
Maksimovka, Russian Federation, **209** G1
Maksudangarh, India, **218** D5
Makthar, Tunisia, **295** B8
Mākū, Iran, **222** C5
Makumbako, Tanzania, **369** F4
Makumbi, Democratic Republic of the Congo, **368** D4
Makungo, Somalia, **369** H2
Makunguwiro, Tanzania, **369** G5
Makurazaki, Japan, **208** E5
Makurdi, Nigeria, **365** F3
Makushino, Russian Federation, **222** H1
Mala, Peru, **454** C3
Mala, Punta, *point*, Panama, **429** F6
Mala, *river*, Peru, **454** C3
Mala Kapela, *mountain range*, Croatia, **294** E3
Mala Vyska, Ukraine, **296** H1
Malå, Sweden, **284** J4
Malabang, Philippines, **204** D5
Malabar, Mount, *mountain peak*, Lord Howe Island, Australia, **135** U14
Malabo, Equatorial Guinea, **368** A2, *331*
Malacca, Strait of, Indonesia/Malaysia, **200** B1, *151*
Malacky, Slovakia, **289** H4
Malad City, U.S.A., **419** H5
Maladzyechna, Belarus, **287** N5
Málaga, Spain, **292** E4
Malaga, U.S.A., **423** L5
Malagarasi, Tanzania, **369** F4
Malahide, Ireland, **309** F4
Malaimbandy, Madagascar, **372** B5
Malaita, *island*, Solomon Islands, **141** A1, *116*
Malakāl, Sudan, **366** D3
Mālākhera, India, **218** D4
Malakula, *island*, Vanuatu, **141** A2
Malalamai, Papua New Guinea, **140** B4
Malali, Guyana, **451** G3
Malam, Papua New Guinea, **140** A5
Malån, *river*, Sweden, **284** J4
Malang, Indonesia, **201** F4
Malanje, Angola, **368** C4
Malanje, *province*, Angola, **368** C4
Malanville, Benin, **365** E2
Malanzán, Argentina, **458** C4
Mälaren, *lake*, Sweden, **287** H3
Malargüe, Argentina, **458** C5
Malartic, Canada, **416** B5
Malaryta, Belarus, **289** M3
Malaso, *river*, Indonesia, **198** B3
Malatayur, Tanjong, *point*, Indonesia, **201** F3
Malatya, Turkey, **224** E5
Malaut, India, **218** C3
Malavalli, India, **216** D3
Malawali, Pulau, *island*, Malaysia, **201** G1
Malawi, *country*, Africa, **359** J8, *40, 312, 313, 344, 345*
Malawi, Lake, Malawi, **369** F5, *342, 344, 345*
Malawiya, Sudan, **366** E1
Malay Peninsula, Malaysia/Thailand, **195** M9, *151, 152, 155*
Malaya Vishera, Russian Federation, **299** D3
Malaybalay, Philippines, **204** D4
Malāyer, Iran, **220** E2
Malayiwan, China, **215** F2
Malaysia, *country*, Asia, **197** N9, *51, 73, 96, 144, 145, 151, 152, 153, 162, 193*
Malazgirt, Turkey, **363** H1
Malbork, Poland, **289** J1
Malden Island, Kiribati, **139** J5
Maldives, *country*, Asia, **196** J9, *40, 144, 167, 193, 475*
Maldon, England, U.K., **305** H3
Maldonado, Uruguay, **459** F5
Malè, Italy, **294** C2
Male, Maldives, **216** C5, *167*
Male Atoll, Maldives, **216** C5
Malé Karpaty, *mountain range*, Slovakia, **289** H4
Malea, Gunung, *mountain peak*, Indonesia, **200** B2
Maleas, Akra, *point*, Greece, **297** D7
Mālegaon, India, **218** C5
Malek Dīn, Afghanistan, **218** B2
Malela, Democratic Republic of the Congo, **369** E3
Malema, Mozambique, **369** G5
Malemba Nkulu, Democratic Republic of the Congo, **369** E4
Malen'ga, Russian Federation, **285** T5
Målerås, Sweden, **286** G4
Maleta, Russian Federation, **210** E2
Malgomaj, *lake*, Sweden, **284** G4
Malha, Sudan, **366** C1
Malheur Lake, U.S.A., **418** E5
Malheureux, Cap, *cape*, Mauritius, **373** C1
Mali, *country*, Africa, **358** E5, *91, 312, 315, 324*
Mali, Democratic Republic of the Congo, **369** E3
Mali, Guinea, **364** B2
Mali Kanal, *canal*, Serbia, **296** B3
Mali Kyun (Tavoy Island), *island*, Myanmar, **202** C3
Maliangping, China, **206** B2
Maliaohe, China, **207** D3
Målilla, Sweden, **286** G4
Malimba, Monts, *mountain range*, Democratic Republic of the Congo, **369** E4
Malin Head, *point*, Ireland, **309** E2
Malin More, Ireland, **309** D3
Malindang, Mount, *mountain peak*, Philippines, **204** C4
Malindi, Kenya, **369** H3
Malinga, Gabon, **368** B3
Malingsbo, Sweden, **286** G3
Malinoa, *island*, Tonga, **141** B4
Malinovka, Russian Federation, **223** M2
Malipo, China, **215** H5
Maliq, Albania, **297** C5
Malita, Philippines, **204** D5
Maljamar, U.S.A., **423** M5
Mālkāngiri, India, **217** E2
Malkāpur, India, **218** D5
Malkara, Turkey, **297** F5
Malkhanskiy Khrebet, *mountain range*, Russian Federation, **210** D2
Mallaig, Scotland, U.K., **308** D3
Mallard, U.S.A., **420** F4
Mallawī, Egypt, **363** F3
Mallorca, *island*, Islas Baleares, Spain, **293** J3
Mallow, Ireland, **309** D5
Mallwyd, Wales, U.K., **304** D2
Malm, Norway, **284** E4
Malmal, Papua New Guinea, **140** C4
Malmanoury, French Guiana, **452** C2
Malmberget, Sweden, **284** K3
Malmédy, Belgium, **288** C3
Malmesbury, England, U.K., **304** E3
Malmesbury, South Africa, **370** C5
Malmköping, Sweden, **287** H3
Malmö, Sweden, **286** F5, *233*
Malmöhus, *county*, Sweden, **286** F5
Malmok, *point*, Bonaire, **461** A4
Malmyzh, Russian Federation, **222** E1
Malnaş, Romania, **296** E2
Maloarkhangel'skoye, Russian Federation, **210** E2
Maloca, Brazil, **452** B3
Maloelap, *island*, Marshall Islands, **139** F4
Malolos, Philippines, **204** C3
Malone, U.S.A., **426** C2
Malonga, Democratic Republic of the Congo, **368** D5
Malosmadulu Atoll, Maldives, **216** C5
Malott, U.S.A., **418** E2
Måløy, Norway, **286** B2
Maloyaroslavets, Russian Federation, **299** F5
Malpas, England, U.K., **304** E1
Malpica, Spain, **292** C1
Mālpura, India, **218** C4
Malta, *country*, Europe, **282** F8, *228, 245, 257*
Malta, Idaho, U.S.A., **418** H5
Malta, Latvia, **287** N4
Malta, Montana, U.S.A., **419** L2
Malta Channel, Italy/Malta, **295** E7
Maltahöhe, Namibia, **370** C3
Maltby, England, U.K., **307** G4
Maltby le Marsh, England, U.K., **307** J4
Malton, England, U.K., **307** H3
Malua, Samoa, **141** B1
Maluku (Moluccas), *islands*, Indonesia, **198** D3, *148*
Maluku, *province*, Indonesia, **199** E4
Malumfashi, Nigeria, **365** F2
Malung, Sweden, **286** F2
Maluso, Philippines, **204** C5
Malūt, Sudan, **366** D2
Maluu, Solomon Islands, **141** A1
Mālvan, India, **216** C2
Malvern, Arkansas, U.S.A., **424** F2
Malvern, Iowa, U.S.A., **420** F5
Malyy Kavkaz, *mountain range*, Asia, **222** C4, *189, 190*
Malyy Kemchug, Russian Federation, **223** N1
Malyy Yenisey, *river*, Russian Federation, **213** H2
Mambasa, Democratic Republic of the Congo, **369** E2
Mamberamo, *river*, Indonesia, **199** G3
Mambéré-Kadéï, *prefecture*, Central African Republic, **368** C2
Mamburao, Philippines, **204** C3
Mamelles, *island*, Seychelles, **373** A2
Mamelodi, South Africa, **371** E4
Mamers, France, **290** E2
Mamfe, Cameroon, **368** A1
Mamiña, Chile, **455** E5
Mamlyutka, Kazakhstan, **223** H1
Mammoth, U.S.A., **423** H5
Mamonovo, Russian Federation, **287** J5
Mamoré, *river*, Bolivia/Brazil, **455** F3
Mamori, Brazil, **451** E4
Mamoriá, Brazil, **455** E2
Mamou, Guinea, **364** B2
Mamoudzou, Mayotte, **372** B3, *354*
Mampikony, Madagascar, **372** B4
Mampodre, *mountain peak*, Spain, **292** E1
Mampong, Ghana, **364** D3
Mamry, Jezioro, *lake*, Poland, **289** K1
Mamuju, Indonesia, **198** B3
Man, Côte d'Ivoire, **364** C3
Man, Isle of, *U.K. dependency*, Europe, **306** D3
Man of War Bay, Tobago, Trinidad and Tobago, **461** B4
Mana, French Guiana, **452** C2
Mana, Hawaiian Islands, U.S.A., **422** R9
Mana, *river*, French Guiana, **452** C2
Manacapuru, Brazil, **451** G5
Manacor, Islas Baleares, Spain, **293** J3
Manado, Indonesia, **198** D2
Managua, Lago de, *lake*, Nicaragua, **428** D4, *404*
Managua, Nicaragua, **428** D4, *404*
Manakara, Madagascar, **372** B5
Manakau, *mountain peak*, New Zealand, **133** D6
Manākhah, Yemen, **220** D5
Manam Island, Papua New Guinea, **140** B4
Manambondro, Madagascar, **372** B5
Mananara Avaratra, Madagascar, **372** B4
Mananjary, Madagascar, **372** B5
Manankoliva, Madagascar, **372** B5
Manankoro, Mali, **364** C2
Manantenina, Madagascar, **372** B5
Manapouri, Lake, New Zealand, **133** A7
Manapouri, New Zealand, **133** A7
Manarantsandry, Madagascar, **372** B4
Manas, *river*, Bhutan/India, **205** A2, *172*
Manas Hu, *lake*, China, **212** E3
Manāsa, India, **218** C4
Manassa, U.S.A., **423** L3
Manassas, U.S.A., **426** B5
Manati Bay, St Helena, **373** B3
Manatuto, East Timor, **198** D5
Manaung, Myanmar, **202** C3
Manaus, Brazil, **451** G5
Manbij, Syria, **225** E1
Manby, England, U.K., **307** J4
Manchester, Connecticut, U.S.A., **426** D4
Manchester, England, U.K., **306** F4, *78, 276*
Manchester, Iowa, U.S.A., **420** H4
Manchester, Missouri, U.S.A., **421** M7
Manchester, New Hampshire, U.S.A., **426** E3
Manchester, Tennessee, U.S.A., **425** J2
Manchester, Vermont, U.S.A., **426** D3
Manchhar Lake, Pakistan, **218** A4
Manciano, Italy, **294** C4
Máncora, Peru, **454** B1
Mancos, U.S.A., **423** J3
Mand, *river*, Iran, **220** F3
Manda, Jabal, *mountain peak*, Sudan, **366** B3
Mandabe, Madagascar, **372** A5
Mandal, Bulgan, Mongolia, **213** J2
Māndal, India, **218** B5
Mandal, Töv, Mongolia, **210** D2
Mandala, Puncak, *mountain peak*, Indonesia, **199** H4
Mandalay, *division*, Myanmar, **205** B3
Mandalay, Myanmar, **205** C3, *157*
Mandalgovĭ, Mongolia, **210** D3
Mandan, U.S.A., **420** C2
Mandaon, Philippines, **204** C3
Mandar, Teluk, *bay*, Indonesia, **198** B3
Mandaue, Philippines, **204** C4
Mandeb, Bab el, *strait*, Red Sea, **367** F2
Mandel, Afghanistan, **221** H2
Mandera, Kenya, **369** H2

Manderfeld, Belgium, **288** C3
Manderson, U.S.A., **419** L4
Mandeville, Jamaica, **429** F3
Mandha, India, **218** B4
Mandheera, Somalia, **367** F3
Mandi, India, **218** D3
Mandi Angin, Gunung, *mountain peak*, Malaysia, **200** C1
Mandi Būrewāla, Pakistan, **218** C3
Mandiana, Guinea, **364** C2
Mandié, Mozambique, **369** F6
Mandimba, Mozambique, **369** G5
Mandioré, Lagoa, *lake*, Bolivia/Brazil, **456** B5
Mandji, Gabon, **368** B3
Mandla, India, **218** E5
Mandø, *island*, Denmark, **286** D5
Mandritsara, Madagascar, **372** B4
Mandsaur, India, **218** C4
Mandul, Pulau, *island*, Indonesia, **201** G2
Mandurah, Australia, **134** D5
Manduria, Italy, **295** F5
Māndvi, E. Gujarāt, India, **218** C5
Māndvi, W. Gujarāt, India, **218** B5
Mandya, India, **216** D3
Manendragarh, India, **219** E5
Manfalūṭ, Egypt, **363** F3
Manfredonia, Golfo di, *gulf*, Italy, **295** F5
Manfredonia, Italy, **295** E5
Manga, Brazil, **457** E4
Manga, Burkina Faso, **364** D2
Manga, Papua New Guinea, **140** D4
Mangai, Democratic Republic of the Congo, **368** C3
Mangai, Papua New Guinea, **140** C3
Mangaia, *island*, Cook Islands, **137** F3
Mangakino, New Zealand, **132** E4
Mangakura, New Zealand, **132** E3
Mangaldai, India, **219** H4
Mangalia, Romania, **296** G4
Mangalmé, Chad, **366** A2
Mangalore, India, **216** C3
Mangamuka, New Zealand, **132** D2
Mangaran, Indonesia, **198** D2
Mangatupoto, New Zealand, **132** E4
Mangaung, South Africa, **371** E4
Mangaweka, *mountain peak*, New Zealand, **132** F4
Mangaweka, New Zealand, **132** E4
Mangawhai, New Zealand, **132** E3
Mangere Island, Chatham Islands, New Zealand, **133** Q16
Manggar, Indonesia, **201** E3
Manggautu, Solomon Islands, **141** A1
Manggo, Solomon Islands, **141** A1
Mangin Taung, *mountain range*, Myanmar, **205** B3
Mangkalihat, Tanjong, *point*, Indonesia, **201** G2
Mangla Reservoir, Pakistan, **218** C2, *173*
Mangnai, China, **213** F5
Mango, Togo, **364** E2
Mangochi, Malawi, **369** G5
Mangoky, *river*, Madagascar, **372** A5
Mangole, Pulau, *island*, Indonesia, **198** D3
Mangonui, New Zealand, **132** D2
Māngrol, India, **218** B5
Mangrove Cay, Bahamas, **428** F1
Mangrūl Pīr, India, **218** D5
Mangueigne, Chad, **366** B2
Mangueirinha, Brazil, **459** G2
Manguéni, Plateau du, *plateau*, Niger, **362** B4
Mangui, China, **211** H1
Manguinho, Ponta do, *point*, Brazil, **457** G3
Mangum, U.S.A., **424** C2
Manhan, Mongolia, **213** J2
Manhattan, Kansas, U.S.A., **420** E6
Manhattan, Nevada, U.S.A., **422** E2
Manhattan, Wyoming, U.S.A., **419** J4
Manhuaçu, Brazil, **457** E5
Manhuaçu, *river*, Brazil, **457** F5
Maní, Colombia, **450** D3
Mania, *river*, Madagascar, **372** B4
Maniago, Italy, **294** D2
Maniamba, Mozambique, **369** F5
Manica, *province*, Mozambique, **371** F2
Manicaland, *province*, Zimbabwe, **371** F2
Manicoré, Brazil, **455** G1
Manicouagan, Canada, **416** G4
Manicouagan, Réservoir, Canada, **416** G4
Manicouagan, *river*, Canada, **416** G4
Maniema, *administrative region*, Democratic Republic of the Congo, **369** E3
Maniganggo, China, **215** F3
Manigotagan, Canada, **414** F6
Manihi, *island*, French Polynesia, **137** G2
Manihiki, *island*, Cook Islands, **139** H6
Maniitsoq, Greenland, **411** P3
Manila, Philippines, **204** C3, *50, 122, 149*
Manila, U.S.A., **423** J1
Manila Bay, Philippines, **204** C3, *149*
Manimbaya, Tanjong, *point*, Indonesia, **198** B3
Maninian, Côte d'Ivoire, **364** C2
Maninita, *island*, Vava'u Group, Tonga, **141** B3
Maninjau, Danau, *lake*, Indonesia, **200** B3
Manipa, Selat, *strait*, Indonesia, **198** D3
Manipur, *state*, India, **219** H4, *169*
Manisa, *province*, Turkey, **297** G6
Manisa, Turkey, **297** F6
Manissauá-Missu, *river*, Brazil, **456** B3
Manistee, *river*, U.S.A., **421** K3
Manistee, U.S.A., **421** K3
Manistique, U.S.A., **421** K3
Manistique Lake, U.S.A., **421** L2
Manitoba, Lake, Canada, **414** E6
Manitoba, *province*, Canada, **414** F4, *381*
Manitoulin Island, Canada, **421** M3
Manitouwadge, Canada, **415** M7
Maniwaki, Canada, **416** D6
Manizales, Colombia, **450** C3
Manja, Madagascar, **372** A5
Manjeri, India, **216** D4
Manjimup, Australia, **134** D5
Manjra, *river*, India, **216** D2
Mankato, Kansas, U.S.A., **420** D6
Mankato, Minnesota, U.S.A., **420** F3
Mankera, Pakistan, **218** B3
Mankim, Cameroon, **368** B1
Mankono, Côte d'Ivoire, **364** C3
Mankota, Canada, **413** R7
Mankulam, Sri Lanka, **216** E4
Manmād, India, **218** C5
Manna, Indonesia, **200** C4
Mannar, Gulf of, India/Sri Lanka, **216** D4
Mannar, Sri Lanka, **216** D4
Mannar Island, Sri Lanka, **216** D4
Mannheim, Germany, **288** D4
Manning, Canada, **413** L3
Manning, Iowa, U.S.A., **420** F5
Manning, North Dakota, U.S.A., **420** B2
Manning, South Carolina, U.S.A., **425** M3
Mannington, U.S.A., **421** N6
Manningtree, England, U.K., **305** J3
Manns Harbor, U.S.A., **426** C7
Mannu, Capo, *cape*, Sardegna, Italy, **295** A5
Mano, Sierra Leone, **364** B3
Mano River, Liberia, **364** B3
Manoa, Bolivia, **455** F2
Manokwari, Indonesia, **199** F3
Manoleasa, Romania, **296** F2
Manombo Atsimo, Madagascar, **372** A5
Manompana, Madagascar, **372** B4
Manono, Democratic Republic of the Congo, **369** E4
Manorbier, Wales, U.K., **304** C3
Manorhamilton, Ireland, **309** D3
Manosque, France, **291** G5
Manouane, Lac, *lake*, Canada, **416** F4
Manp'o, North Korea, **208** D2
Manra, *island*, Kiribati, **139** G5
Manresa, Spain, **293** H2
Mansa, Loma, *mountain peak*, Sierra Leone, **364** B3
Mansa, Zambia, **369** E5
Mansabá, Guinea-Bissau, **364** A2
Mānsehra, Pakistan, **218** C2
Mansel Island, Canada, **411** L3
Mansfeld, Germany, **288** E3
Mansfield, Arkansas, U.S.A., **424** E2
Mansfield, England, U.K., **305** F1
Mansfield, Louisiana, U.S.A., **424** F4
Mansfield, Ohio, U.S.A., **421** M5
Mansfield, Pennsylvania, U.S.A., **426** B4
Mansfield Woodhouse, England, U.K., **305** F1
Mansi, Myanmar, **205** B2
Mansilla de las Mulas, Spain, **292** E1
Mansôa, Guinea-Bissau, **364** A2
Manson, U.S.A., **418** D3
Manston, England, U.K., **304** E4
Manta, Bahía de, *bay*, Ecuador, **450** B4
Manta, Ecuador, **450** B4
Mantadau, Indonesia, **201** G2
Mantalingajan, Mount, *mountain peak*, Philippines, **204** B4
Manteca, U.S.A., **422** C3
Mantecal, Venezuela, **451** E2
Manti, U.S.A., **423** H2
Mantiqueira, Serra da, *mountain range*, Brazil, **456** E6
Mantoudi, Voreioi Sporades, Greece, **297** D6
Mantova, Italy, **294** C3
Mäntsälä, Finland, **287** M2
Mänttyharju, Finland, **287** N2
Mäntyjärvi, Finland, **285** N4
Manú, Peru, **454** D3
Manua Islands, American Samoa, **141** B2
Manuae, Cook Islands, **137** F2
Manuae, *island*, French Polynesia, **137** F2
Manuel Alves, *river*, Brazil, **456** D3
Manuel Rodríguez, Isla, *island*, Chile, **460** B4
Manuel Urbano, Brazil, **455** E2
Manuelzinho, Brazil, **452** B5
Manui, Pulau, *island*, Indonesia, **198** C3
Manūjān, Iran, **221** G3
Manukau, New Zealand, **132** E3
Manukau Harbour, New Zealand, **132** D3
Manundi, Tanjong, *point*, Indonesia, **199** F3
Manunui, New Zealand, **132** E4
Manuoha, *mountain peak*, New Zealand, **132** F4
Manus, *province*, Papua New Guinea, **140** B3
Manus Island, Papua New Guinea, **140** B3, *115*
Manvel, U.S.A., **420** E1
Manville, U.S.A., **419** M5
Manyara, Lake, Tanzania, **369** G3, *342*
Manyas, Turkey, **297** F5
Manych-Gudilo, Ozero, *lake*, Russian Federation, **298** F3
Manyoni, Tanzania, **369** F4
Mānzai, Pakistan, **218** B3
Manzanares, Spain, **293** F3
Manzanilla Point, Trinidad, Trinidad and Tobago, **461** C4
Manzanillo, Cuba, **429** F2
Manzanillo, Mexico, **430** D5
Manẓariyeh, Iran, **220** F2
Manzhouli, China, **210** G2
Manzil Bū Ruqaybah, Tunisia, **362** A1
Manzini, Swaziland, **371** F4
Mao, Chad, **365** H2
Maobosheng, China, **213** J5
Maoke, Pegunungan, *mountain range*, Indonesia, **199** G4
Maomao Shan, *mountain peak*, China, **213** J5
Maoming, China, **206** B4
Maotou Shan, *mountain peak*, China, **215** G4
Mapai, Mozambique, **371** F3
Mapi, Indonesia, **199** G4
Mapi, *river*, Indonesia, **199** G4
Mapinhane, Mozambique, **371** G3
Mapire, Venezuela, **451** F2
Mapiri, Bolivia, **455** E4
Maple Creek, Canada, **413** Q7
Maple Inlet, Canada, **414** G1
Maplesville, U.S.A., **425** J3
Mapmaker Seamounts, *underwater feature*, Pacific Ocean, **478** F3
Maprik, Papua New Guinea, **140** A3
Mapua, New Zealand, **133** D5
Mapuera, *river*, Brazil, **452** B3
Mapulanguene, Mozambique, **371** F3
Maputo, Mozambique, **371** F4, *345, 348*
Maputo, *province*, Mozambique, **371** F4
Maqanshy, Kazakhstan, **212** D3
Maqat, Kazakhstan, **222** E3
Maqên, China, **215** G2
Maqen Gangri, *mountain peak*, China, **215** F2
Maqnā, Saudi Arabia, **225** C5
Maqu, China, **215** G2
Maqueda, Spain, **292** E2
Maquela do Zombo, Angola, **368** C4
Maquinchao, Argentina, **460** D1
Mar Chiquita, Laguna, *lake*, Argentina, **458** D4
Mar del Plata, Argentina, **459** F5
Mar Menor, *lake*, Spain, **293** G4
Mara, *administrative region*, Tanzania, **369** F3
Mara, Guyana, **451** H2
Mara, South Africa, **371** E3
Maraã, Brazil, **451** F4
Marabá, Brazil, **452** D4
Maracá, Ilha de, *island*, Brazil, **452** C2
Maraçacumé, *river*, Brazil, **452** D4
Maracaibo, Lago de, *lake*, Venezuela, **450** D2, *436, 437*
Maracaibo, Venezuela, **450** D1
Maracaju, Brazil, **456** B5
Maracajú, Serra de, *mountain range*, Brazil, **456** B5
Maracanã, Brazil, **452** D3
Maracanaquará, Planalto, *plateau*, Brazil, **452** C3
Maracás, Chapada de, *mountain range*, Brazil, **457** F3
Maracay, Venezuela, **451** E1
Marādah, Libya, **362** C3
Maradi, *department*, Niger, **365** F2
Maradi, Niger, **365** F2
Marāgheh, Iran, **222** D5
Maragogipe, Brazil, **457** F3
Marahuaca, Cerro, *mountain peak*, Venezuela, **451** F3
Marais des Cygnes, *river*, U.S.A., **420** F6
Marajó, Baía de, *bay*, Brazil, **452** D3
Marajó, Ilha de, *island*, Brazil, **452** C3
Maralal, Kenya, **369** G2
Marali, Central African Republic, **366** A3
Maramasike, *island*, Solomon Islands, **141** A1
Maran, Malaysia, **200** C2
Marana, U.S.A., **423** H5
Marand, Iran, **222** D5
Maranguape, Brazil, **453** F4
Maranhão, Barragem de, *reservoir*, Portugal, **292** D3
Maranhão, *river*, Brazil, **456** D4
Maranhão, *state*, Brazil, **453** E4
Maranoa, *river*, Australia, **135** K4
Marañón, *river*, Peru, **450** C5, *441*
Marão, *mountain peak*, Portugal, **292** D2
Marapanim, Brazil, **452** D3
Marapi, Gunung, *mountain peak*, Indonesia, **200** C3
Mărăşeşti, Romania, **296** F3
Marathon, Canada, **415** L7
Marathon, Florida, U.S.A., **425** M7
Marathon, Texas, U.S.A., **423** M6
Marathonas, Greece, **297** E6
Maratua, Pulau, *island*, Indonesia, **201** G2
Maraú, Brazil, **457** F4
Marau Point, New Zealand, **132** G4
Maravari, Solomon Islands, **141** A1
Marawi, Philippines, **204** D4
Marawī, Sudan, **363** F5
Mar'ayt, Yemen, **220** F5
Marbella, Spain, **292** E4
Marble Bar, Australia, **134** D3
Marble Canyon, *gorge*, U.S.A., **423** G3
Marble Falls, U.S.A., **424** C4
Marble Hall, South Africa, **371** E3
Marburg, Germany, **288** D3
Marburg, South Africa, **371** F5
Marcali, Hungary, **289** H5
Marcelândia, Brazil, **456** B3
March, England, U.K., **305** H2
Marche, *autonomous state*, Italy, **294** D4, *255*
Marche-en-Famenne, Belgium, **288** B3
Marchena, Isla, *island*, Islas Galápagos (Galapagos Islands), Ecuador, **461** A1
Marcigny, France, **291** G3
Marcinkonys, Lithuania, **289** M1
Marcona, Peru, **454** C4
Marcos Juárez, Argentina, **458** D4
Mărculeşti, Moldova, **296** G2
Mardan, Pakistan, **218** B2
Mardin, Turkey, **224** F5
Maré, *island*, New Caledonia, **141** A3
Maree, Loch, *lake*, Scotland, U.K., **308** D3
Mareeba, Australia, **135** K2
Maremma, *mountain range*, Italy, **294** C4
Maresfield, England, U.K., **305** H3
Mareyes, Argentina, **458** C4
Marfa, U.S.A., **423** L6
Margaree Forks, Canada, **417** L6
Margaret River, Australia, **134** D5
Margarita, Isla de, *island*, Venezuela, **451** F1
Margate, England, U.K., **305** J3
Margeride, Monts de la, *mountain range*, France, **291** F4
Marghita, Romania, **296** D2
Margie, U.S.A., **420** G1
Margosatubig, Philippines, **204** C5
Mārgow, Dasht-e, *desert*, Afghanistan, **221** H2
Marguerite, Canada, **412** H5
Marhoum, Algeria, **361** F2
Mari, Papua New Guinea, **140** A5

Maria, Îles, *islands*, French Polynesia, **137** F3
Maria, *island*, French Polynesia, **137** H3
Maria Byrd Land, *region*, Antarctica, **470** C6
María Elena, Chile, **458** C2
Maria Grande, Argentina, **459** E4
Maria Island, Australia, **135** H1
Maria van Diemen, Cape, New Zealand, **132** C2
Mariana Trough, *underwater feature*, Pacific Ocean, **478** D4, *22, 97*
Marianao, Cuba, **429** E2
Marianna, Arkansas, U.S.A., **424** G2
Marianna, Florida, U.S.A., **425** K4
Mariannelund, Sweden, **286** G4
Mariano Loza, Argentina, **459** E3
Mariánské Lázně, Czech Republic, **288** F4
Mariato, Punta, *point*, Panama, **429** E6
Mariazell, Austria, **289** G5
Ma'rib, Yemen, **220** E5
Maribor, Slovenia, **294** E2
Maricopa, U.S.A., **422** D4
Marīdī, Sudan, **369** E2
Marie Anne, *island*, Seychelles, **373** A2
Marie Valdemar, Kap, *cape*, Greenland, **411** T2
Mariefred, Sweden, **287** H3
Marielund, Sweden, **284** H4
Mariental, Namibia, **370** C3
Mariestad, Sweden, **286** F3
Marietta, Georgia, U.S.A., **425** K2
Marietta, West Virginia, U.S.A., **421** N6
Marigot, St Martin, Guadeloupe, **427** D2
Mariinsk, Russian Federation, **223** M1
Marijampolė, Lithuania, **287** L5
Marília, Brazil, **459** H2
Marimba, Angola, **368** C4
Marín, Spain, **292** C1
Marina, U.S.A., **422** C3
Marina di Leuca, Italy, **295** G6
Marina di Ragusa, Italy, **295** E7
Marina di Ravenna, Italy, **294** D3
Mar"ina Horka, Belarus, **299** B6
Marinduque Island, Philippines, **204** C3
Marineo, Sicilia, Italy, **295** D7
Marinette, U.S.A., **421** K3
Maringá, Brazil, **459** G2
Maringuè, Mozambique, **371** F2
Marīnovka, Kazakhstan, **223** H2
Marion, Indiana, U.S.A., **421** L5
Marion, Lake, U.S.A., **425** M3
Marion, Ohio, U.S.A., **421** M5
Marion, South Carolina, U.S.A., **425** N2
Marion, Virginia, U.S.A., **421** N7
Maripa, Venezuela, **451** F2
Maripasoula, French Guiana, **452** B2
Mariposa, U.S.A., **422** C3
Marisa, Indonesia, **198** C2
Mariscal Estigarribia, Paraguay, **458** E2
Maritsa, *river*, Bulgaria, **296** E4
Maritsa, *river*, Greece, **297** F5, *265*
Mariupol', Ukraine, **298** E3
Marīvān, Iran, **222** D5
Mariveles, Philippines, **204** C3
Mariy El, Respublika, *republic*, Russian Federation, **222** D1
Märjamaa, Estonia, **287** M3
Mark Twain Lake, U.S.A., **420** G6
Marka, Somalia, **367** F4
Markala, Mali, **364** C2
Markam, China, **215** F3
Mārkāpur, India, **216** D3
Markaryd, Sweden, **286** F4
Marked Tree, U.S.A., **424** G2
Market Deeping, England, U.K., **305** G2
Market Drayton, England, U.K., **304** E2
Market Harborough, England, U.K., **305** G2
Market Rasen, England, U.K., **307** H4
Market Weighton, England, U.K., **307** H4
Markethill, Northern Ireland, U.K., **309** F3
Markit, China, **212** C5
Markopoulo, Greece, **297** D7
Markounda, Central African Republic, **365** H3
Markoy, Burkina Faso, **364** D2
Marksville, U.S.A., **424** F4
Marktredwitz, Germany, **288** F4
Marla, Australia, **134** G4
Marlborough, England, U.K., **305** F3
Marlborough, Guyana, **451** G2
Marlborough Downs, *region*, England, U.K., **305** F3
Marle, France, **291** F2
Marlin, U.S.A., **424** D4
Marlinton, U.S.A., **421** P6
Marlow, England, U.K., **305** G3
Marma, Sweden, **287** H2
Marmagoa, India, **216** C3
Marmande, France, **290** E4
Marmara, Sea of *see* Marmara Denizi, *sea*, Turkey, **297** F5
Marmara, Turkey, **297** F5
Marmara Adası, *island*, Turkey, **297** F5
Marmara Denizi (Sea of Marmara), *sea*, Turkey, **297** F5
Marmaraereğlisi, Turkey, **297** F5
Marmaris, Turkey, **297** G7
Marmarth, U.S.A., **420** B2
Marmion, Lake, Australia, **134** E4
Marmolada, *mountain peak*, Italy, **294** C2
Marnay, France, **291** G3
Marne, *river*, France, **291** G2
Marne-la-Vallée, France, **290** F2
Maro, Chad, **366** A3
Maroantsetra, Madagascar, **372** B4
Maroanui, *mountain peak*, New Zealand, **132** F4
Marofa, *mountain peak*, Portugal, **292** D2
Marokau, *island*, French Polynesia, **137** G2
Marolambo, Madagascar, **372** B5
Maromokotro, *mountain peak*, Madagascar, **372** B3, *353*
Maromony, Lohatanjona, *cape*, Madagascar, **372** B3
Marondera, Zimbabwe, **371** F2
Maroni, *river*, French Guiana, **452** B2
Maroochydore, Australia, **135** L4
Maropiu, New Zealand, **132** D2
Maros, Indonesia, **198** B4
Maroseranana, Madagascar, **372** B4
Marotiri, *island*, French Polynesia, **137** G3
Maroua, Cameroon, **365** G2
Marovato, Madagascar, **372** B3
Marovoay, Madagascar, **372** B4
Marowijne, *river*, Suriname, **452** B2
Marple, England, U.K., **306** F4
Marquesas Fracture Zone, *tectonic feature*, Pacific Ocean, **479** J5
Marquette, U.S.A., **421** K2
Marquise, France, **290** E1
Marquises, Îles, *islands*, French Polynesia, **137** H1, *90, 93, 122*
Marracuene, Mozambique, **371** F4
Marradi, Italy, **294** C3
Marrah, Jabal, *mountain range*, Sudan, **366** B2
Marrakech (Marrakesh), Morocco, **360** E2, *91*
Marrakesh *see* Marrakech, Morocco, **360** E2, *91*
Marree, Australia, **135** H4
Marrehan, *mountain range*, Somalia, **369** H2
Marroqui o de Tarifa, Punta, *point*, Spain, **292** D5
Marrupa, Mozambique, **369** G5
Mars Bay, Ascension, **373** A3
Marsá al 'Alam, Egypt, **363** F3
Marsá al Burayqah, Libya, **362** C2
Marsá Maṭrūḥ, Egypt, **362** E2
Marsabit, Kenya, **369** G2
Marsala, Sicilia, Italy, **295** D7
Marsberg, Germany, **288** D3
Marsden, Canada, **413** Q5
Marseille, France, **291** G5, *244, 245*
Marseille-en-Beauvaisis, France, **305** J5
Marsh Harbour, Bahamas, **428** F1
Marsh Island, U.S.A., **424** F5
Marshall, Arkansas, U.S.A., **424** F2
Marshall, Canada, **413** Q5
Marshall, Minnesota, U.S.A., **420** F3
Marshall, Missouri, U.S.A., **420** G6
Marshall, Texas, U.S.A., **424** E3
Marshall Islands, *country*, Pacific Ocean, **131** G1, *61, 108, 118, 119, 120, 123*
Marshalltown, U.S.A., **420** G4
Marshavitsy, Russian Federation, **299** B4
Marshfield, Missouri, U.S.A., **420** G7
Marshfield, Wisconsin, U.S.A., **420** H3
Marsimang, Tanjong, *point*, Indonesia, **199** E3
Marsland, U.S.A., **420** B4
Marsoui, Canada, **416** H5
Märsta, Sweden, **287** H3
Marstein, Norway, **286** C1
Martaban, Gulf of, Myanmar, **202** C2
Martano, Italy, **295** G5
Martapura, Kalimantan Selatan, Indonesia, **201** F3
Martapura, Sumatera Selatan, Indonesia, **200** D4
Marten Falls, Canada, **415** M6
Marten River, Canada, **421** P2
Martha's Vineyard, *island*, U.S.A., **426** E4
Martigny, Switzerland, **291** H3
Martigues, France, **291** G5
Martin, Lake, U.S.A., **425** K3
Martin, Slovakia, **289** J4
Martin, South Dakota, U.S.A., **420** C4
Martin, Tennessee, U.S.A., **425** H1
Martin Peninsula, Antarctica, **470** B6
Martina, Greece, **297** D6
Martinborough, New Zealand, **133** E5
Martinez de la Torre, Mexico, **431** F4
Martinique, *French department*, Caribbean Sea, **427** D3, *50, 96, 245, 378, 379, 390*
Martinique Passage, Caribbean Sea, **427** D3
Martinsburg, Pennsylvania, U.S.A., **421** P5
Martinsburg, West Virginia, U.S.A., **426** B5
Martinsicuro, Italy, **294** D4
Martinsville, Indiana, U.S.A., **421** K6
Martinsville, Virginia, U.S.A., **421** P7
Martley, England, U.K., **304** E2
Martock, England, U.K., **304** E4
Martos, Spain, **293** F4
Martre, Lac la, *lake*, Canada, **410** G3
Martti, Finland, **285** P3
Marttila, Finland, **287** L2
Mart'yanovo, Russian Federation, **299** C4
Martynovo, Russian Federation, **223** M2
Maruim, Brazil, **457** G3
Marutea, *island*, French Polynesia, **137** H3
Marv Dasht, Iran, **220** F3
Marvine, Mount, *mountain peak*, U.S.A., **423** H2
Mary, Turkmenistan, **222** G5
Maryborough, Australia, **135** L4
Marydale, South Africa, **370** D4
Mar'yevka, Russian Federation, **222** D2
Maryhill, U.S.A., **418** D4
Maryland, *state*, U.S.A., **426** B5, *386*
Marypark, Scotland, U.K., **308** F3
Maryport, England, U.K., **306** E3
Marystown, Canada, **417** P6
Marysvale, U.S.A., **423** G2
Marysville, California, U.S.A., **422** C2
Marysville, Kansas, U.S.A., **420** E6
Marysville, Ohio, U.S.A., **421** M5
Marysville, Washington, U.S.A., **418** C2
Maryville, Missouri, U.S.A., **420** F5
Maryville, Tennessee, U.S.A., **425** K2
Masachapa, Nicaragua, **428** D5
Masaka, Uganda, **369** F3
Masākin, Tunisia, **362** B1
Masalembu, Kepulauan, *islands*, Indonesia, **201** F4
Masallı, Azerbaijan, **222** D5
Masan, South Korea, **208** E4
Masasi, Tanzania, **369** G5
Masavi, Bolivia, **455** F5
Masaya, Nicaragua, **428** D5
Masbate, Philippines, **204** C3
Masbate Island, Philippines, **204** C3
Mascara, Algeria, **361** G1
Mascarane Islands, Mauritius, **372** D5, *354*
Mascarene Plain, *underwater feature*, Indian Ocean, **476** C6
Mascarene Plateau, *underwater feature*, Indian Ocean, **476** C5
Mascasín, Argentina, **458** C4
Masel'gskaya, Russian Federation, **285** S5
Maseno, Kenya, **369** F2
Maseru, Lesotho, **371** E4, *349*
Masham, England, U.K., **307** G3
Mashan, China, **211** K3
Mashava, Zimbabwe, **371** F3
Mashhad, Iran, **222** F5
Mashīz, Iran, **221** G3
Mashonaland Central, *province*, Zimbabwe, **369** F6
Mashonaland East, *province*, Zimbabwe, **371** F2
Mashonaland West, *province*, Zimbabwe, **369** E6
Mashra'ar Raqq, Sudan, **366** C3
Masi, China, **207** C2
Masi, Norway, **285** L2
Masi-Manimba, Democratic Republic of the Congo, **368** C3
Masiaca, Mexico, **430** C3
Masindi, Uganda, **369** F2
Maṣīrah, Jazīrat, *island*, Oman, **221** G4
Maṣīrah, Khalīj, *bay*, Oman, **221** G5
Masisea, Peru, **454** C2
Masisi, Democratic Republic of the Congo, **369** E3
Masjed Soleymān, Iran, **220** E2
Mask, Lough, *lake*, Ireland, **309** C4
Maskanah, Syria, **225** E2
Maslenica, Croatia, **294** E3
Masoala, Tanjona, *cape*, Madagascar, **372** C4
Masoarivo, Madagascar, **372** A4
Mason, U.S.A., **424** C4
Mason City, U.S.A., **420** G4
Mason Hall, Tobago, Trinidad and Tobago, **461** B4
Maspalomas, Islas Canarias, Spain, **373** A4
Masqaṭ (Muscat), Oman, **221** G4, *175*
Massa, Italy, **294** C4
Massachusetts Bay, U.S.A., **426** E3
Massachusetts, *state*, U.S.A., **426** D3, *384, 386*
Massadona, U.S.A., **423** J1
Massafra, Italy, **295** F5
Massaguet, Chad, **365** H2
Massakory, Chad, **365** H2
Massangena, Mozambique, **371** F3
Massango, Angola, **368** C4
Massangulo, Mozambique, **369** G5
Massapê, Brazil, **453** F4
Massassa-Lewémé, Congo, **368** B3
Massawa, Eritrea, **367** E1
Massawa Channel, Eritrea, **367** E1
Massenya, Chad, **365** H2
Masset, Canada, **412** C4
Massif Central, *mountain range*, France, **291** F4, *245*
Massif de la Hotte, Haiti, **429** G3, *394*
Massigui, Mali, **364** C2
Massina, Mali, **364** C2
Massinga, Mozambique, **371** G3
Massingir, Mozambique, **371** F3
Mastābah, Saudi Arabia, **363** G4
Masters, U.S.A., **423** L1
Masterton, New Zealand, **133** E5
Mastic Point, Bahamas, **428** F1
Mastrevik, Norway, **286** B2
Mastūj, Pakistan, **218** C1
Mastūj, *river*, Pakistan, **218** B1
Mastung, Pakistan, **218** A3
Mastūrah, Saudi Arabia, **363** G4
Masty, Belarus, **289** M2
Masuda, Japan, **208** E4
Masugnsbyn, Sweden, **285** L3
Masurai, Gunung, *mountain peak*, Indonesia, **200** C3
Masvingo, *province*, Zimbabwe, **371** F3
Masvingo, Zimbabwe, **371** F3
Maṣyāf, Syria, **225** D2
Mata Utu, Wallis and Futuna, **139** G6, *127*
Matabeleland North, *province*, Zimbabwe, **371** E2
Matabeleland South, *province*, Zimbabwe, **371** E3
Matachewan, Canada, **421** N2
Matadi, Democratic Republic of the Congo, **368** B4
Matagalpa, Nicaragua, **428** D4
Matagami, Canada, **416** C5
Matagami, Lac, *lake*, Canada, **416** B5
Matagorda Island, U.S.A., **424** D5
Matagorda, U.S.A., **424** E5
Mataiva, *island*, French Polynesia, **137** G2
Matakana Island, New Zealand, **132** F3
Matakaoa Point, New Zealand, **132** G3
Matala, Angola, **368** B5
Matam, Senegal, **364** B1
Matamata, New Zealand, **132** E3
Matamec, Canada, **416** J4
Matamey, Niger, **365** F2
Matamoros, Coahuila, Mexico, **430** E3
Matamoros, Tamaulipas, Mexico, **431** F3
Matana, Danau, *lake*, Indonesia, **198** C3
Matane, Canada, **416** H5
Matanzas, Cuba, **429** E2
Mataquito, *river*, Chile, **458** B5
Matara, Sri Lanka, **216** E5
Mataragka, Greece, **297** C6
Mataram, Indonesia, **201** G5
Mataranka, Australia, **134** G1
Matarape, Teluk, *bay*, Indonesia, **198** C3
Mataró, Spain, **293** J2
Matas Blancas, Islas Canarias, Spain, **373** B4
Matata, New Zealand, **132** F3
Mataura, New Zealand, **133** B8
Mataura, *river*, New Zealand, **133** B7
Mataveri, Isla de Pascua (Easter Island), Chile, **461** B2
Matawai, New Zealand, **132** F4

Matay, Kazakhstan, **212** C3
Mategua, Bolivia, **455** F3
Matehuala, Mexico, **431** E4
Matelot, Trinidad, Trinidad and Tobago, **461** C4
Matema, Tanzania, **369** F4
Matemanga, Tanzania, **369** G5
Matemateaonga, *mountain peak*, New Zealand, **132** E4
Matera, Italy, **295** F5
Matese, Monti del, *mountain peak*, Italy, **295** E5
Mátészalka, Hungary, **289** L5
Mateur, Tunisia, **295** B7
Matfors, Sweden, **287** H1
Matha, France, **290** D4
Matheson, Canada, **415** P7
Mathews, U.S.A., **426** B6
Mathis, U.S.A., **424** D5
Mathura, India, **218** D4
Mati, Philippines, **204** D5
Matías Romero, Mexico, **431** G5
Matinha, Brazil, **452** E4
Matīši, Latvia, **287** M4
Matkuli, India, **218** D5
Mātli, Pakistan, **218** B4
Matlock, England, U.K., **305** F1
Matnog, Philippines, **204** D3
Mato Grosso, Brazil, **455** G4, *440*
Mato Grosso, Planalto do, *plateau*, Brazil, **447** G5, *434*
Mato Grosso, *state*, Brazil, **456** B3
Mato Grosso do Sul, *state*, Brazil, **456** B5
Matola, Mozambique, **371** F4
Matomb, Cameroon, **368** B2
Matru, Sierra Leone, **364** B3
Matsiatra, *river*, Madagascar, **372** B5
Matsue, Japan, **208** F4
Matsumae, Japan, **209** H2
Matsumoto, Japan, **209** G3
Matsusaka, Japan, **209** G4
Matsuyama, Japan, **208** F4
Mattagami, *river*, Canada, **415** P7
Mattawa, Canada, **416** B6
Matterhorn, *mountain peak*, Italy/Switzerland, **280** E6, *26, 228*
Matterhorn, *mountain peak*, U.S.A., **418** G6
Matthew Town, Bahamas, **429** G2
Matthews Ridge, Guyana, **451** G2
Mattice, Canada, **415** N7
Mattmar, Sweden, **284** F5
Mattoon, U.S.A., **421** J6
Mattsmyra, Sweden, **286** G2
Matucana, Peru, **454** C3
Matuka, *island*, Fiji, **141** A4
Matumbo, Angola, **368** C5
Maturín, Venezuela, **451** F2
Matutum, Mount, *mountain peak*, Philippines, **204** D5
Mau, India, **219** E4
Mau Rānīpur, India, **218** D4
Maúa, Mozambique, **371** G1
Maubourguet, France, **290** E5
Maud, *river*, Canada, **410** J3
Maudaha, India, **218** E4
Maués, Brazil, **452** B4
Maug, *island*, Northern Mariana Islands, **138** C2
Mauga Silisili, *mountain peak*, Samoa, **141** B1, *113*
Mauganj, India, **219** E4
Maughold Head, *point*, Isle of Man, **306** D3
Maui, *island*, Hawaiian Islands, U.S.A., **422** R9, *377*
Mauke, *island*, Cook Islands, **137** F3
Maule, *administrative region*, Chile, **458** B5
Maule, *river*, Chile, **458** B5
Maullín, Chile, **460** C1
Maulyneill, Ireland, **309** C6
Maumakeogh, *mountain peak*, Ireland, **309** C3
Maumee, U.S.A., **421** M5
Maumere, Indonesia, **198** C5
Maumturk Mountains, Ireland, **309** C4
Maun, Botswana, **370** D2
Maungatua, *mountain peak*, New Zealand, **133** C7
Maunu, Sweden, **285** L2
Maupihaa, *island*, French Polynesia, **137** F2
Maupin, U.S.A., **418** D4
Maupiti, *island*, French Polynesia, **137** F2, *94*
Maures, Massif des, *mountain peak*, France, **291** H5
Mauri, *river*, Bolivia, **455** E4
Mauriac, France, **290** F4
Maurice, Lake, Australia, **134** G4
Maurine, U.S.A., **420** B3
Mauritania, *country*, Africa, **358** D5, *312, 318, 355*
Mauritius, *country*, Indian Ocean, **359** L8, *193, 353, 354*
Mauritius Trench, *underwater feature*, Indian Ocean, **476** C6
Mauron, France, **290** C2
Maury Seachannel, *underwater feature*, Atlantic Ocean, **477** F2
Mauston, U.S.A., **420** H4
Mauterndorf, Austria, **288** F5
Mauzé-sur-le-Mignon, France, **290** D3
Mavago, Mozambique, **369** G5
Mavasjaure, *lake*, Sweden, **284** H3
Mavengue, Angola, **368** C6
Mavinga, Angola, **368** D6
Mawa, Democratic Republic of the Congo, **369** E2
Mawanga, Democratic Republic of the Congo, **368** C4
Mawasangka, Indonesia, **198** C4
Mawei, China, **215** H4
Māwiyah, Yemen, **220** D6
Mawshij, Yemen, **220** D6
Mawson, *Australian research station*, Antarctica, **470** F4
Mawson Coast, *region*, Antarctica, **470** F4
Mawson Peak, *mountain peak*, Heard and McDonald Islands, **134** S12
Mawson Peninsula, Antarctica, **470** E8
Max, U.S.A., **420** C2
Maxaas, Somalia, **367** G4
Maxbass, U.S.A., **414** D7
Maxcanú, Mexico, **431** H4
Maxmo, Finland, **285** L5
Maxwell, California, U.S.A., **422** B2
Maxwell, New Mexico, U.S.A., **423** L3
Maya, China, **215** G2
Maya, *river*, Russian Federation, **301** Q4
Maya, Pulau, *island*, Indonesia, **201** E3
Maya Mountains, *mountain range*, Belize/Guatemala, **428** C3, *402*
Mayaguana Island, Bahamas, **429** G2
Mayagüez, Puerto Rico, **427** C2
Mayahi, Niger, **365** F2
Mayama, Congo, **368** B3
Mayāmey, Iran, **222** F5
Mayaro Bay, Trinidad, Trinidad and Tobago, **461** C4
Maybell, U.S.A., **423** J1
Maybole, Scotland, U.K., **308** E5
Maych'ew, Ethiopia, **367** E2
Maydh, Somalia, **367** G2
Mayenne, France, **290** D2
Mayenne, *river*, France, **290** D2
Mayer, U.S.A., **423** G4
Mayevo, Russian Federation, **299** B4
Mayfield, New Zealand, **133** C6
Mayfield, U.S.A., **421** J7
Mayhan, Mongolia, **213** J3
Mayhill, U.S.A., **423** L5
Maying, China, **215** H2
Maykop, Russian Federation, **222** C4
Mayluu-Suu, Kyrgyzstan, **212** B4
Maymyo, Myanmar, **205** C3
Maynooth, Canada, **416** C7
Mayo, Canada, **410** F3
Mayo, *county*, Ireland, **309** C4
Mayo, *river*, Argentina, **460** C2
Mayo, *river*, Mexico, **430** C3
Mayo, U.S.A., **425** L4
Mayo Alim, Cameroon, **365** G3
Mayo Belwa, Nigeria, **365** G3
Mayo Darlé, Cameroon, **365** G3
Mayo-Kébbi, *prefecture*, Chad, **365** G3
Mayo Mayo, Bolivia, **455** F3
Mayoko, Congo, **368** B3
Mayong, China, **207** B2
Mayor Island (Tuhua), New Zealand, **132** F3
Mayor Pablo Lagerenza, Paraguay, **455** G5
Mayotte, *French territory*, Indian Ocean, **372** B3, *352, 354*
Mayoworth, U.S.A., **419** L5
Mayqayyng, Kazakhstan, **212** B2
Mayraira Point, Philippines, **204** C2
Maysville, Kentucky, U.S.A., **421** M6
Maytiguid Island, Philippines, **204** B4
Mayumba, Gabon, **368** B3
Mayville, North Dakota, U.S.A., **420** E2
Maywood, U.S.A., **420** C5
Maza, Argentina, **458** D5
Mazabuka, Zambia, **369** E6
Mazagão, Brazil, **452** C3
Mazagón, Spain, **292** D4
Mazama, U.S.A., **418** D2
Mazán, Peru, **450** D5
Mazar, China, **212** C5
Mazār-e Sharīf, Afghanistan, **218** A1
Mazara del Vallo, Sicilia, Italy, **295** D7
Mazarredo, Argentina, **460** D3
Mazarrón, Golfo de, *gulf*, Spain, **293** G4
Mazarrón, Spain, **293** G4
Mazaruni, *river*, Guyana, **451** G3
Mazatán, Mexico, **430** C2
Mazatenango, Guatemala, **428** C4
Mazatlán, Mexico, **430** D4
Mazatzal Peak, Berg, U.S.A., **423** H4
Mažeikiai, Lithuania, **287** L4
Mazha, China, **207** C2
Mazı, Turkey, **297** F7
Mazirbe, Latvia, **287** L4
Mazo Cruz, Peru, **455** E4
Mazocahui, Mexico, **430** C2
Mazomora, Tanzania, **369** G4
Mazong Shan, *mountain peak*, China, **213** H4
Mazunga, Zimbabwe, **371** E3
Mazyr, Belarus, **298** C2
Mbabane, Swaziland, **371** F4, *348*
Mbahiakro, Côte d'Ivoire, **364** D3
Mbaïki, Central African Republic, **368** C2
Mbakaou, Lac de, *lake*, Cameroon, **365** G3, *330*
Mbaké, Senegal, **364** A2
Mbala, Zambia, **369** F4
Mbalabala, Zimbabwe, **371** E3
Mbalam, Cameroon, **368** B2
Mbale, Uganda, **369** F2
Mbalmayo, Cameroon, **368** B2
Mbalo, Solomon Islands, **141** A1
Mbamba Bay, Tanzania, **369** F5
Mbandaka, Democratic Republic of the Congo, **368** C2
Mbang, Cameroon, **368** B2
Mbanga, Cameroon, **368** A2
M'banza Congo, Angola, **368** B4
Mbarara, Uganda, **369** F3
Mbari, *river*, Central African Republic, **366** B3
Mbata, Central African Republic, **368** C2
Mbati, Zambia, **369** F5
Mbatto, Côte d'Ivoire, **364** D3
Mbatuna, Solomon Islands, **141** A1
Mbé, Cameroon, **365** G3
Mbemburu, *river*, Tanzania, **369** G5
Mbengué, Côte d'Ivoire, **364** C2
Mbeya, *administrative region*, Tanzania, **369** F4
Mbeya, Tanzania, **369** F4
Mbi, *river*, Central African Republic, **366** A4
Mbigou, Gabon, **368** B3
Mbinda, Congo, **368** B3
Mbinga, Tanzania, **369** G5
Mbizi, Zimbabwe, **371** F3
Mboki, Central African Republic, **369** E1
Mbomo, Congo, **368** B2
Mbomou, *prefecture*, Central African Republic, **368** D1
Mbouda, Cameroon, **368** B1
Mbour, Senegal, **364** A2
Mbout, Mauritania, **364** B1
Mbozi, Tanzania, **369** F4
Mbridge, *river*, Angola, **368** B4
Mbuji-Mayi, Democratic Republic of the Congo, **368** D4
Mbulu, Tanzania, **369** G3
Mburuku, Solomon Islands, **141** A1
Mbuyuni, Tanzania, **369** G4
Mbwamaji, Tanzania, **369** G4
Mc Kean, *island*, Kiribati, **139** G5
McAdam, Canada, **416** H7
McAlester, U.S.A., **424** E2
McAlister, U.S.A., **423** M4
McAllen, U.S.A., **424** C6
McArthur, *river*, Australia, **135** H2
McBride, Canada, **412** J5
McCall, U.S.A., **418** F4
McCamey, U.S.A., **423** M6
McCammon, U.S.A., **419** H5
McCleary, U.S.A., **418** C3
McClintock, Mount, *mountain peak*, Antarctica, **470** D7
McCloud, U.S.A., **418** C6
McClusky, U.S.A., **420** C2
McComb, U.S.A., **424** G4
McCook, U.S.A., **420** C5
McCracken, U.S.A., **420** D6
McCreary, Canada, **414** E6
McCredie Springs, U.S.A., **418** C5
McDonald Islands, Heard and McDonald Islands, **134** S12
McGill, U.S.A., **422** F2
Mcgregor, U.S.A., **420** G2
Mchinga, Tanzania, **369** G4
Mchinji, Malawi, **369** F5
McIntosh, Minnesota, U.S.A., **420** F2
McIntosh, South Dakota, U.S.A., **420** C3
McKenzie, U.S.A., **425** H1
McKenzie Bridge, U.S.A., **418** C4
McKinley, Mount, *mountain peak*, U.S.A., **410** D3, *382*
McKinney, U.S.A., **424** D3
McKittrick, U.S.A., **422** D4
McLaughlin, *river*, Canada, **414** F5
McLaughlin, U.S.A., **420** C3
McLeod Lake, Canada, **412** H4
M'Clintock Channel, Canada, **411** J2
McLoughlin, Mount, *mountain peak*, U.S.A., **418** C5
McLure, Canada, **412** J6
M'Clure Strait, Canada, **410** G2
McMillan, U.S.A., **421** L2
McMinnville, Oregon, U.S.A., **418** C4
McMinnville, Tennessee, U.S.A., **425** K2
McMurdo, *U.S. research station*, Antarctica, **470** D7
Mcpherson, U.S.A., **420** E6
McRae, U.S.A., **425** L3
Mcveigh, Canada, **414** D3
Mdandu, Tanzania, **369** F4
Mdantsane, South Africa, **371** E5
M'Daourouch, Algeria, **361** H1
Meacham, Canada, **413** S5
Mead, Lake, U.S.A., **422** F3, *385*
Meade, U.S.A., **420** C7
Meadow Creek, Canada, **413** L6
Meadow Lake, Canada, **413** Q4
Meadville, U.S.A., **421** N5
Meagaidh, Creag, *mountain peak*, Scotland, U.K., **308** E4
Mealy Mountains, *mountain range*, Canada, **417** M3
Mearim, *river*, Brazil, **452** D5
Measham, England, U.K., **305** F2
Meath, *county*, Ireland, **309** F4
Meaux, France, **291** F2
Mebo, Gunung, *mountain peak*, Indonesia, **199** F3
Mecca *see* Makkah, Saudi Arabia, **363** G4, *73, 74, 174, 185*
Mechanicsburg, Ohio, U.S.A., **421** M5
Mechanicsville, Iowa, U.S.A., **420** H5
Mechelen, Belgium, **288** B3
Mecheria, Algeria, **361** F2
Méchiméré, Chad, **365** H2
Mecklenburg-Vorpommern, *state*, Germany, **288** E2, *238*
Mecklenburger Bucht, *bay*, Germany, **288** E1
Meconta, Mozambique, **369** G5
Mecuburi, Mozambique, **369** G5
Mecula, Mozambique, **369** G5
Medak, Croatia, **294** E3
Medan, Indonesia, **200** B2
Médanos, Argentina, **460** E1
Medanosa, Punta, *point*, Argentina, **460** E3
Medawachchiya, Sri Lanka, **216** E4
Médéa, Algeria, **361** G1
Medellín, Colombia, **450** C2
Medenine, Tunisia, **362** B2
Mederdra, Mauritania, **364** A1
Medford, Oregon, U.S.A., **418** C5
Medford, Wisconsin, U.S.A., **420** H3
Medgidia, Romania, **296** G3
Media Luna, Argentina, **458** C5
Medias, Romania, **296** E2
Medicine Bow, U.S.A., **419** L6
Medicine Bow Mountains, *mountain range*, U.S.A., **419** L6
Medicine Bow Peak, *mountain peak*, U.S.A., **419** L6
Medicine Hat, Canada, **413** P6
Medicine Lodge, U.S.A., **420** D7
Medina *see* Al Madīnah, Saudi Arabia, **363** G4, *73, 90, 174*
Medina, U.S.A., **426** A3
Medina de Rioseco, Spain, **292** E2
Medina del Campo, Spain, **292** E2
Médina Gounas, Senegal, **364** B2
Medina Sidonia, Spain, **292** E4
Medinaceli, Spain, **293** F2
Medininkai, Lithuania, **287** M5
Medinīpur, India, **219** F5
Mediterranean Ridge, *underwater feature*, Mediterranean Sea, **477** J3
Mediterranean Sea, Africa/Asia/Europe, **280** E8, *45, 71, 72, 89, 93, 95, 146, 147, 180, 181, 190, 191, 192, 228, 229, 244, 245, 246, 251, 252, 253, 254, 257, 261, 265, 278, 312, 314, 315, 317*
Medley, Canada, **413** P4
Mednyy, Ostrov, *island*, Russian Federation, **301** T4
Medora, U.S.A., **420** B2
Médouneu, Gabon, **368** B2
Medveditsa, *river*, Russian Federation, **298** F2
Medveđa, Serbia, **296** C4
Medvezh'i, Ostrova, *islands*, Russian Federation, **301** S2
Medvezh'yegorsk, Russian Federation, **285** S5
Medway, *unitary authority*, England, U.K., **305** H3
Medwin Point, Christmas Island, **134** N8
Medyn', Russian Federation, **299** E5
Medzilaborce, Slovakia, **289** K4
Meekatharra, Australia, **134** D4
Meeker, U.S.A., **423** K1
Meelpaeg Lake, Canada, **417** N5

Meerut, India, **218** D3
Meeteetse, U.S.A., **419** K4
Mega, Ethiopia, **369** G2
Mega, Indonesia, **199** E3
Megali Panagia, Greece, **297** D5
Megalo, Ethiopia, **367** F3
Megalopoli, Greece, **297** D7
Meganisi, *island*, Ionioi Nisoi, Greece, **297** C6
Megara, Greece, **297** D6
Meghalaya, *state*, India, **219** G4, *169*
Megisti (Kastellotizon), *island*, Greece, **297** G7
Mehadia, Romania, **296** D3
Mehamn, Norway, **285** N1
Mehar, Pakistan, **218** A4
Meharry, Mount, *mountain peak*, Australia, **134** D3
Mehdia, Algeria, **361** G1
Mehetia, *island*, French Polynesia, **137** G2
Mehr Jān, Iran, **221** G2
Mehrān, Iran, **220** E2
Mehtarlām, Afghanistan, **218** B2
Mei-nung, Taiwan, **206** E4
Meia Ponte, *river*, Brazil, **456** D5
Meicheng, China, **206** D2
Meiganga, Cameroon, **365** G3
Meighen Island, Canada, **411** J1
Meigu, China, **215** G3
Meihekou, China, **211** J4
Meiktila, Myanmar, **205** B3
Meiningen, Germany, **288** E3
Meira, Spain, **292** D1
Meishan, China, **215** G3
Meißen, Germany, **288** F3
Meizhou, China, **206** D3
Meizhou Wan, *bay*, China, **206** D3
Mejicana, *mountain peak*, Argentina, **458** C3
Mejillones, Chile, **458** B2
Mejillones del Sur, Bahía de, *bay*, Chile, **458** B2
Mejit, *island*, Marshall Islands, **139** F3
Mékambo, Gabon, **368** B2
Mek'elē, Ethiopia, **367** E2
Mekerrhane, Sebkha, *salt-pan*, Algeria, **361** G3
Mékhé, Senegal, **364** A1
Mekhtar, Pakistan, **218** B3
Meknès, Morocco, **361** E2
Mekong, *river*, Asia, **195** M8; *see also* Lancang, *river*, China, **215** F3; Mènam Khong, *river*, Laos, **203** E3, *96, 144, 152, 153, 154, 158*
Mekongga, Gunung, *mountain peak*, Indonesia, **198** C3
Mekongga, Pegunungan, *mountain range*, Indonesia, **198** C3
Melaka, Malaysia, **200** C2
Melaka, *state*, Malaysia, **200** C2, *151*
Melanesia, *islands*, Pacific Ocean, **128** E1, *61, 70, 87, 108, 109, 116*
Melanesian Basin, *underwater feature*, Pacific Ocean, **478** E4
Melapalawam, India, **216** D4
Melba, U.S.A., **418** F5
Melbourn, England, U.K., **305** H2
Melbourne, Australia, **135** J6, *112*
Melbourne, U.S.A., **425** M5
Melbu, Norway, **284** G2
Melchhām, Nepal, **219** E3
Melchor, Isla, *island*, Chile, **460** B2
Melchor Múzquiz, Mexico, **431** E3
Melchor Ocampo, Mexico, **430** E3
Meldal, Norway, **284** D5
Meldorf, Germany, **288** D1
Meldrum Bay, Canada, **421** M3
Mele, Vanuatu, **141** A2
Meleuz, Russian Federation, **222** F2
Mélèzes, Rivière aux, *river*, Canada, **411** M4
Mélfi, Chad, **366** A2
Melfi, Italy, **295** E5
Melfjorden, Norway, **284** F3
Melfort, Canada, **414** B5
Melgaço, Brazil, **452** C3
Melgar de Fernamental, Spain, **292** E1
Melham, *river*, England, U.K., **305** H2
Melide, Spain, **292** C1
Meligalas, Greece, **297** C7
Melilla, *enclave*, Spain, N. W. Africa, **361** F1
Melimoyu, Monte, *mountain peak*, Chile, **460** C2
Melintang, Danau, *lake*, Indonesia, **201** F3
Melipilla, Chile, **458** B4
Melita, Canada, **414** D7
Melitopol', Ukraine, **298** E3
Melivoia, Greece, **297** E5
Melk, Austria, **289** G4
Melka Guba, Ethiopia, **369** G2
Melksham, England, U.K., **304** E3
Mellakoski, Finland, **285** M3
Mellerud, Sweden, **286** F3
Mellette, U.S.A., **420** D3
Mellilä, Finland, **287** L2
Mellizo Sur, Cerro, *mountain peak*, Chile, **460** C3
Mělník, Czech Republic, **289** G3
Melo, Uruguay, **459** F4
Meloco, Mozambique, **369** G5
Melong, Cameroon, **368** A1
Melrhir, Chott, *lake*, Algeria, **361** H2
Melrose, Scotland, U.K., **308** G5
Melsisi, Vanuatu, **141** A2
Melstone, U.S.A., **419** L3
Meltaus, Finland, **285** M3
Meltham, England, U.K., **307** G4
Melton, Australia, **135** J6
Melton Mowbray, England, U.K., **305** G2
Meltosjärvi, Finland, **285** M3
Meluco, Mozambique, **369** G5
Melun, France, **290** F2
Melūr, India, **216** D4
Melville, Canada, **414** C6
Melville, Cape, Australia, **135** J1
Melville, Lake, Canada, **417** M3
Melville, U.S.A., **420** D2
Melville Bay, Australia, **135** H1
Melville Island, Australia, **134** G1
Melville Island, Canada, **410** H2
Melville Peninsula, Canada, **411** L3
Melvin, Lough, *lake*, Ireland/Northern Ireland, **309** D3
Memala, Indonesia, **201** F3
Memaliaj, Albania, **297** C5
Memba, Baía de, *bay*, Mozambique, **369** H5
Memba, Mozambique, **369** H5
Membalong, Indonesia, **201** D3
Memmingen, Germany, **288** E5
Memori, Tanjong, *point*, Indonesia, **199** F3
Mempawah, Indonesia, **201** E2
Memphis, Missouri, U.S.A., **420** G5
Memphis, Tennessee, U.S.A., **424** H2
Memphis, Texas, U.S.A., **424** B2
Mena, U.S.A., **424** E2
Menahga, U.S.A., **420** F2
Menai Bridge, Wales, U.K., **304** C1
Ménaka, Mali, **365** E1
Mènam Khong (Mekong), *river*, Asia, **203** E3, *96, 144, 152, 153, 154, 158*
Menanga, Indonesia, **198** D3
Menard, U.S.A., **424** C4
Menard Fracture Zone, *tectonic feature*, Pacific Ocean, **479** K8
Menawashei, Sudan, **366** B2
Mendam, Papua New Guinea, **140** B3
Mendawai, *river*, Indonesia, **201** F3
Mende, France, **291** F4
Mendebo, *mountain range*, Ethiopia, **367** E3
Mendenhall, U.S.A., **424** H4
Méndez, Mexico, **431** F3
Mendī, Ethiopia, **366** E3
Mendi, Papua New Guinea, **140** A4
Mendip Hills, England, U.K., **304** E3
Mendocino, Cape, U.S.A., **422** A1
Mendocino, U.S.A., **422** B2
Mendocino Fracture Zone, *tectonic feature*, Pacific Ocean, **479** H2
Mendol, Pulau, *island*, Indonesia, **200** C2
Mendota, U.S.A., **421** J5
Mendoza, Argentina, **458** C4
Mendoza, *province*, Argentina, **458** C5, *93, 443*
Mene de Mauroa, Venezuela, **451** D1
Mene Grande, Venezuela, **450** D2
Menemen, Turkey, **297** F6
Menesjärvi, Finland, **285** N2
Menfi, Sicilia, Italy, **295** D7
Mengcheng, China, **206** D1
Menggala, Indonesia, **200** D4
Menghai, China, **215** G5
Mengla, China, **215** G5
Mengshan, China, **206** B3
Mengyin, China, **206** D1
Mengzhe, China, **215** G5
Mengzi, China, **215** G5
Menheniot, England, U.K., **304** C4
Menindee, Australia, **135** J5
Menindee Lake, Australia, **135** J5
Mennecy, France, **290** F2
Menno, U.S.A., **420** E4
Menominee, *river*, U.S.A., **421** J3
Menomonee Falls, U.S.A., **421** J4
Menongue, Angola, **368** C5
Menorca, *island*, Islas Baleares, Spain, **293** K2
Mentawai, Selat, *strait*, Indonesia, **200** B3
Mentone, U.S.A., **423** M6
Mentor, U.S.A., **421** N5
Menyapa, Gunung, *mountain peak*, Indonesia, **201** G2
Menyapa, *river*, Indonesia, **201** G2
Menyuan, China, **213** J5
Menza, *river*, Russian Federation, **210** E2
Menza, Russian Federation, **210** E2
Menzel Temime, Tunisia, **295** C7
Menzies, Australia, **134** E4
Menzies, Mount, *mountain peak*, Antarctica, **470** F5
Meoqui, Mexico, **430** D2
Meponda, Mozambique, **369** F5
Meppel, Netherlands, **288** C2
Meppen, Germany, **288** C2
Mequinenza, Embalse de, *reservoir*, Spain, **293** G2
Merak, Indonesia, **200** D4
Merano, Italy, **294** C2
Meratus, Pegunungan, *mountain range*, Indonesia, **201** F3
Merauke, Indonesia, **199** H5
Merced, U.S.A., **422** C3
Mercedario, Cerro, *mountain peak*, Argentina, **458** B4
Mercedes, Corrientes, Argentina, **459** E3
Mercedes, San Luis, Argentina, **458** D4
Mercedes, Uruguay, **459** F4
Mercedes, U.S.A., **424** D6
Mercury Bay, New Zealand, **132** E3
Mercury Islands, New Zealand, **132** E3
Mercy, Cape, Canada, **411** N3
Mere, England, U.K., **304** E3
Mere Lava, *island*, Vanuatu, **141** A2
Meredith, Cape, Falkland Islands, **460** F4
Meredith, Lake, U.S.A., **424** B2
Mereeg, Somalia, **367** G4
Meremere, New Zealand, **132** E3
Méreuch, Cambodia, **203** E3
Mergui, Myanmar, **202** C3
Mergui Archipelago, *islands*, Myanmar, **202** C4
Meriç, Turkey, **297** F5
Mérida, Mexico, **431** H4
Mérida, Spain, **292** D3
Mérida, Venezuela, **450** D2
Meridian, Idaho, U.S.A., **418** F5
Meridian, Mississippi, U.S.A., **425** H3
Meridiano, Argentina, **458** D5
Meridja, Algeria, **361** F2
Mérignac, France, **290** D4
Merijärvi, Finland, **285** M4
Merikarvia, Finland, **287** K2
Merir, *island*, Palau, **138** B4
Merirumã, Brazil, **452** B3
Merke, Kazakhstan, **212** B4
Merkinė, Lithuania, **287** M5
Merlimau, Pulau, *island*, Singapore, **200** J7
Merlin, U.S.A., **418** C5
Merna, U.S.A., **420** D5
Mernye, Hungary, **289** H5
Meron, Har, *mountain peak*, Israel, **225** C3
Merredin, Australia, **134** D5
Merrick, *mountain peak*, Scotland, U.K., **308** E5
Merrill, U.S.A., **421** J3
Merrillville, U.S.A., **426** D2
Merriman, U.S.A., **420** C4
Merriott, England, U.K., **304** E4
Merritt, Canada, **412** J6
Merritt Island, U.S.A., **425** M5
Merry Island, Canada, **415** R4
Mersa Fatma, Eritrea, **367** F2
Mersea Island, England, U.K., **305** H3
Merseburg, Germany, **288** E3
Mersey, *river*, England, U.K., **306** F4
Merseyside, *unitary authority*, England, U.K., **306** E4
Mersin see İçel, Turkey, **363** F1
Mērsrags, Latvia, **287** L4
Merta, India, **218** C4
Merthyr Tydfil, *unitary authority*, Wales, U.K., **304** D3
Merthyr Tydfil, Wales, U.K., **304** D3
Merti, Kenya, **369** G2
Mértola, Portugal, **292** D4
Méru, France, **290** F2
Meru, Kenya, **369** G2
Meru, *mountain peak*, Tanzania, **369** G3
Merville, France, **305** K4
Merzifon, Turkey, **224** E4
Mesa, Arizona, U.S.A., **423** H5
Mesa, Idaho, U.S.A., **418** F4
Meschede, Germany, **288** D3
Mescit Tepe, *mountain range*, Turkey, **224** F4
Mešeišta, Macedonia, **297** C5
Meselefors, Sweden, **284** H4
Mesfinto, Ethiopia, **367** E2
Mesgouez, Lac, *lake*, Canada **416** D4
Meshgīn Shahr, Iran, **222** D5
Mesilla, U.S.A., **423** K5
Mesimeri, Greece, **297** D5
Meskiana, Algeria, **295** A8
Meslay-du-Maine, France, **290** D3
Mesola, Italy, **294** D3
Mesolongi, Greece, **297** C6
Mesquite, Nevada, U.S.A., **422** F3
Mesquite, Texas, U.S.A., **424** D3
Messaad, Algeria, **361** G2
Messina, Sicilia, Italy, **295** E6, *255*
Messina, South Africa, **371** F3
Messina, Stretto di, *strait*, Sicilia, Italy, **295** E7, *254*
Messini, Greece, **297** D7
Messiniakos Kolpos, *bay*, Greece, **297** D7
Mesta, *river*, Bulgaria, **297** D5
Mesters Vig, Greenland, **411** S2
Meston, Akra, *point*, Greece, **297** E6
Mestre, Italy, **294** D3
Mesyagutovo, Russian Federation, **222** F1
Meszah Peak, *mountain peak*, Canada, **412** D2
Meta, *river*, Venezuela, **451** E2
Meta Incognita Peninsula, Canada, **411** N3
Metairie, U.S.A., **424** G4
Metaline Falls, U.S.A., **418** F2
Metallifere, Colline, *mountain range*, Italy, **294** C4
Metán, Argentina, **458** D2
Metangula, Mozambique, **369** F5
Metarica, Mozambique, **369** G5
Meteghan, Canada, **416** H7
Metema, Ethiopia, **367** E2
Meteran, Papua New Guinea, **140** C3
Metheringham, England, U.K., **305** G1
Methoni, Greece, **297** C7
Methven, Scotland, U.K., **308** F4
Methwold, England, U.K., **305** H2
Metković, Croatia, **294** F4
Metoro, Mozambique, **369** G5
Metro, Indonesia, **200** D4
Metropolis, U.S.A., **421** J7
Metsäkylä, Finland, **285** P4
Metsovo, Greece, **297** C6
Mettuppālaiyam, India, **216** D4
Metu, Ethiopia, **366** E3
Metz, France, **291** H2
Meuse, *river*, Belgium/France, **291** G2, *241, 242*
Mevagissey, England, U.K., **304** C4
Mexia, U.S.A., **424** D4
Mexiana, Ilha, *island*, Brazil, **452** D3
Mexicali, Mexico, **430** B1
Mexican Water, U.S.A., **423** J3
Mexico, *country*, Central America, **409** N6, *29, 46, 47, 51, 54, 64, 76, 79, 89, 91, 92, 95, 97, 100, 122, 376, 377, 378, 379, 382, 400, 401, 402*
Mexico, Gulf of, Mexico/U.S.A., **407** P6, *383, 393, 400, 401*
México, Mexico, **431** F5, *79, 91, 378, 400, 401*
México, *state*, Mexico, **431** E5
Mexico, U.S.A., **420** H6
Mexico Basin, *underwater feature*, Gulf of Mexico, **479** M3
Meymaneh, Afghanistan, **218** A2
Meyrueis, France, **291** F4
Mezcalapa, *river*, Mexico, **431** G5
Mezdra, Bulgaria, **296** D4
Mezen', Russian Federation, **300** F3
Mezenc, Mont, *mountain peak*, France, **291** G4
Mezha, *river*, Russian Federation, **299** C5
Mezhdurechensk, Russian Federation, **300** K4
Mezhdusharskiy, Ostrov, *island*, Russian Federation, **300** F2
Mezőkövesd, Hungary, **289** K5
Mezőtúr, Hungary, **289** K5
Mezquital, *river*, Mexico, **430** D4
Mezquitic, Mexico, **430** E4
Mfuwe, Zambia, **369** F5
Mgbidi, Nigeria, **368** A1
Mhangura, Zimbabwe, **371** F2
Mhāsvād, India, **216** C2
Mhlume, Swaziland, **371** F4
Miagao, Philippines, **204** C4
Miahuatlán, Mexico, **431** F5
Miahuatlán, Sierra de, *mountain range*, Mexico, **431** F5
Miajadas, Spain, **292** E3
Miami, Arizona, U.S.A., **423** H5
Miami, Florida, U.S.A., **425** M7, *405*
Miami, Oklahoma, U.S.A., **424** E1
Miami, Texas, U.S.A., **424** B2
Mian Xian, China, **215** H2
Miancaowan, China, **215** F2
Mīāndoāb, Iran, **222** D5
Miandrivazo, Madagascar, **372** B4
Mianduhe, China, **211** H2
Mīāneh, Iran, **222** D5
Mianmian Shan, *mountain range*, China, **215** G4
Mianning, China, **215** G3
Mianowice, Poland, **289** H1
Miānwāli, Pakistan, **218** B2
Mianyang, China, **215** H3
Miao'ergou, China, **212** D3
Miarinarivo, Madagascar, **372** B4

Miass, Russian Federation, **222** G2
Miastko, Poland, **289** H2
Mica Creek, Canada, **413** K5
Michalovce, Slovakia, **289** K4
Michigan, Lake, U.S.A., **421** K4
Michigan, *state*, U.S.A., **421** L3, *386*
Michigan, U.S.A., **420** D1
Michigan City, U.S.A., **421** K5
Michilla, Chile, **458** B2
Michipicoten Bay, Canada, **421** L2
Michipicoten Island, Canada, **421** K2
Michoacán, *state*, Mexico, **430** E5
Michurin, Bulgaria, **296** F4
Michurinsk, Russian Federation, **298** F2
Michurinskoye, Russian Federation, **299** B2
Micomeseng, Equatorial Guinea, **368** B2
Micoud, St Lucia, **427** D3
Micronesia, *country*, Pacific Ocean, **130** E1, *61, 89, 108, 109, 118*
Micronesia, *islands*, Pacific Ocean, **129** F1, *108*
Mid-Atlantic Ridge, *underwater feature*, Atlantic Ocean, **477** D4
Mid Dome, *mountain peak*, New Zealand, **133** B7
Mid-Indian Basin, *underwater feature*, Indian Ocean, **476** E5
Mid-Indian Ridge, *underwater feature*, Indian Ocean, **476** D6
Mid-Pacific Mountains, *underwater feature*, Pacific Ocean, **478** E3
Mid Yell, Shetland, Scotland, U.K., **308** K7
Midai, Pulau, *island*, Indonesia, **201** D2
Midale, Canada, **414** C7
Middelburg, Netherlands, **288** A3
Middelburg, South Africa, **370** E5
Middelkerke, Belgium, **305** K3
Middle America Trench, *underwater feature*, Pacific Ocean, **479** M3
Middle Andaman, *island*, Andaman and Nicobar Islands, India, **217** H3
Middle Island, Tristan da Cunha, **373** C2
Middle Islet, *island*, Ashmore and Cartier Islands, **134** P9
Middle Ridge, *mountain range*, Canada, **417** P6
Middle Wallop, England, U.K., **305** F3
Middleham, England, U.K., **307** G3
Middlemarch, New Zealand, **133** C7
Middlesboro, U.S.A., **421** M7
Middlesbrough, England, U.K., **307** G3
Middlesbrough, *unitary authority*, England, U.K., **307** G3
Middleton, Australia, **135** J3
Middleton, Canada, **416** J7
Middleton, South Africa, **371** E5
Middleton Cheney, England, U.K., **305** F2
Middletown, California, U.S.A., **422** B2
Middletown, New York, U.S.A., **426** C4
Middletown, Northern Ireland, U.K., **309** F3
Middlewich, England, U.K., **304** E1
Midelt, Morocco, **361** F2
Midhurst, England, U.K., **305** G4
Midi, Canal du, *canal*, France, **290** E5
Midi-Pyrénées, *administrative region*, France, **290** E4, *245*
Midland, Canada, **421** P3
Midland, Michigan, U.S.A., **421** L4
Midland, South Dakota, U.S.A., **420** C3
Midland, Texas, U.S.A., **423** M5
Midlands, *province*, Zimbabwe, **371** E2
Midleton, Ireland, **309** D6
Midlothian, *local authority*, Scotland, U.K., **308** F5
Midongy Atsimo, Madagascar, **372** B5
Midouze, *river*, France, **290** D5
Midsayap, Philippines, **204** D5
Midsund, Norway, **286** C1
Midway Islands, *U.S. territory*, Pacific Ocean, **139** G2, *124, 386*
Midway Range, *mountain range*, Canada, **413** K7
Midwest, U.S.A., **419** L5
Midwest City, U.S.A., **424** D2
Midzhur, *mountain peak*, Bulgaria, **296** D4
Miechów, Poland, **289** K3
Międzyrzecz, Poland, **289** G2
Międzyrzec Podlaski, Poland, **289** L3
Miekojärvi, *lake*, Finland, **285** L3
Mielec, Poland, **289** K3
Miembwe, Tanzania, **369** G4
Mier, Mexico, **431** F3
Miercurea-Ciuc, Romania, **296** E2
Mieres, Spain, **292** E1
Mieron, Norway, **285** L2
Mī'ēso, Ethiopia, **367** F3
Migennes, France, **291** F3
Miging, India, **219** H3
Miguel Alemán, Presa, *dam*, Mexico, **431** F5
Miguel Alves, Brazil, **453** E4
Miguel Auza, Mexico, **430** E3
Migyaungye, Myanmar, **205** B4
Mikhaylov, Russian Federation, **299** G5
Mikhaylovka, Russian Federation, **298** F2
Mikhaylovskiy, Russian Federation, **223** K2
Mikhnevo, Russian Federation, **299** F5
Mikkeli, Finland, **287** N2
Mikkelvik, Norway, **284** J1
Mikumi, Tanzania, **369** G4
Mikura-jima, *island*, Japan, **209** G4
Mila, Algeria, **361** H1
Miladummadulu Atoll, Maldives, **216** C5
Milagres, Brazil, **453** F5
Milan *see* Milano, Italy, **294** B3, *254, 255*
Milan, U.S.A., **425** H2
Milange, Mozambique, **369** G6
Milano (Milan), Italy, **294** B3, *254, 255*
Milas, Turkey, **297** F7
Milazzo, Sicilia, Italy, **295** E6
Milden, Canada, **413** R6
Mildenhall, England, U.K., **305** H2
Mildura, Australia, **135** J5
Mile, China, **215** G4
Miles, Australia, **135** L4
Miles City, U.S.A., **419** M3
Milestone, Canada, **419** M2
Milestone, Ireland, **309** D5
Milford, Delaware, U.S.A., **426** C5
Milford, Ireland, **309** E2
Milford, Massachusetts, U.S.A., **426** E3
Milford, Utah, U.S.A., **422** G2
Milford Haven, Wales, U.K., **304** B3
Milford Lake, U.S.A., **420** E6
Milford Sound, *bay*, New Zealand, **133** A7
Milford Sound, New Zealand, **133** A7
Milh, Baḩr al, *lake*, Iraq, **363** H2
Mili, *island*, Marshall Islands, **139** F4
Milicz, Poland, **289** H3
Milk River, Canada, **413** N7
Millárs, *river*, Spain, **293** G2
Millarton, U.S.A., **420** D2
Millas, France, **290** F5
Millau, France, **291** F4
Mille Lacs Lake, U.S.A., **420** G2
Mille Lacs, Lac des, *lake*, Canada, **420** H1
Milledgeville, U.S.A., **425** L3
Millennium, *island*, Kiribati, **137** G2
Miller, Mount, *mountain peak*, Antarctica, **470** D6
Miller, U.S.A., **420** D3
Millerovo, Russian Federation, **298** F3
Millersburg, U.S.A., **421** N5
Millevaches, Plateau de, *plateau*, France, **290** E4
Millicent, Australia, **135** J6
Millington, U.S.A., **424** H2
Millinocket, U.S.A., **426** F2
Millom, England, U.K., **306** E3
Millport, Scotland, U.K., **308** E5
Millport, U.S.A., **425** H3
Mills Lake, Canada, **413** K1
Millstreet, Ireland, **309** C5
Milltown, Canada, **417** P6
Milltown Malbay, Ireland, **309** C5
Millville, U.S.A., **426** C5
Milne Bay, *province*, Papua New Guinea, **140** D5
Milne Land, *island*, Greenland, **411** S2
Milnor, U.S.A., **420** E2
Milnthorpe, England, U.K., **306** F3
Milo, U.S.A., **426** F2
Milolii, Hawaiian Islands, U.S.A., **422** R10
Milos, *island*, Kyklades, Greece, **297** E7
Milpitas, U.S.A., **422** B3
Milton, Canada, **421** P4
Milton, U.S.A., **425** J4
Milton-Freewater, U.S.A., **418** E4
Milton Keynes, England, U.K., **305** G2
Milton Keynes, *unitary authority*, England, U.K., **305** G2
Miltonvale, U.S.A., **420** E6
Milwaukee, U.S.A., **421** K4
Mimbelly, Congo, **365** H4
Mimizan, France, **290** D4
Mimongo, Gabon, **368** B3
Min, *river*, Fujian, China, **206** D3
Min, *river*, Sichuan, China, **215** G3
Min Shan, *mountain range*, China, **215** G2
Min Xian, China, **215** H2
Mina, U.S.A., **422** D2
Mīnāb, Iran, **221** G3
Minami-Iō-jima, *island*, Japan, **138** C2
Minas, Uruguay, **459** F5
Minas de Corrales, Uruguay, **459** F4
Minas de Matahambre, Cuba, **428** E2
Minas Gerais, *state*, Brazil, **457** E5, *93, 440*
Minas Novas, Brazil, **457** E4
Minatitlán, Mexico, **431** G5
Minbu, Myanmar, **205** B3
Minburn, Canada, **413** P5
Minch, The, *strait*, Scotland, U.K., **308** D3
Minchinmávida, *mountain peak*, Chile, **460** C2
Mindanao, *island*, Philippines, **204** D4, *117, 149*
Mindelo, Cape Verde, **360** P8, *319*
Minden, Germany, **288** D2
Minden, Louisiana, U.S.A., **424** F3
Minden, Nebraska, U.S.A., **420** D5
Mindon, Myanmar, **205** B4
Mindoro, *island*, Philippines, **204** C3
Mindouli, Congo, **368** B3
Mine Centre, Canada, **420** G1
Mine Head, *point*, Ireland, **309** E6
Minehead, England, U.K., **304** D3
Mineiros, Brazil, **456** C4
Mineral Wells, U.S.A., **424** C3
Minersville, U.S.A., **422** G2
Minfeng, China, **212** D5
Minga, Democratic Republic of the Congo, **369** E5
Mingala, Central African Republic, **368** D1
Mingãora, Pakistan, **218** C2
Minggang, China, **206** C1
Mingoyo, Tanzania, **369** G5
Mingshui, China, **211** J3
Mingulay, *island*, Scotland, U.K., **308** B4
Minguri, Mozambique, **369** H5
Mingxi, China, **206** D3
Mingyin, China, **215** G4
Mingyuegou, China, **211** K4
Minhang, China, **206** E2
Minhla, Myanmar, **205** B4
Minho, *river*, Portugal/Spain, **292** C1, *250*
Minhou, China, **206** D3
Minicoy Island, India, **216** C4
Minidoka, U.S.A., **418** H5
Minigwal, Lake, Australia, **134** E4
Minilya Roadhouse, Australia, **134** C3
Minimarg, Pakistan, **218** C2
Miñimiñi, Chile, **455** E5
Miniota, Canada, **414** D6
Minle, Gansu, China, **213** J5
Minle, Guangdong, China, **207** B1
Minna, Nigeria, **365** F3
Minneapolis, U.S.A., **420** G3
Minnedosa, Canada, **414** E6
Minnesota, *river*, U.S.A., **420** F3
Minnesota, *state*, U.S.A., **420** F3, *386*
Minnewaukan, U.S.A., **420** D1
Minot, U.S.A., **420** C1
Minqin, China, **213** J5
Minsk, Belarus, **287** N6, *268, 269, 270, 271*
Mińsk Mazowiecki, Poland, **289** K2
Minskaya Voblasts', *province*, Belarus, **299** B5
Minsterley, England, U.K., **304** E2
Minta, Cameroon, **368** B2
Mintlaw, Scotland, U.K., **308** G3
Minto, Lac, *lake*, Canada, **415** S3
Minto, Manitoba, Canada, **414** D7
Minto, Mount, *mountain peak*, Antarctica, **470** D8
Minto, New Brunswick, Canada, **416** H6
Minton, Canada, **419** M2
Minūf, Egypt, **225** A4
Minusinsk, Russian Federation, **223** P2
Minutang, India, **219** J3
Minvoul, Gabon, **368** B2
Min'yar, Russian Federation, **222** F1
Minywa, Myanmar, **205** B3
Minzhong, China, **207** B3
Minzong, India, **219** J4
Mio, U.S.A., **421** L3
Miquelon, Canada, **416** C5
Miquelon, St Pierre and Miquelon, **417** N6, *376*
Mīr Bacheh Kowt, Afghanistan, **218** B2
Mira, Portugal, **292** C2
Mirabela, Brazil, **457** E4
Miracema do Tocantins, Brazil, **456** D2
Miraflores, Chile, **458** B3
Miraflores, Colombia, **450** D4
Miraj, India, **216** C2
Miralta, Brazil, **457** E4
Mīram Shāh, Pakistan, **218** B2
Miramar, Argentina, **459** F6
Mirambeau, France, **290** D4
Miramichi, *river*, Canada, **416** H6
Miran, China, **212** F5
Miranda, Brazil, **456** B5
Miranda, *river*, Brazil, **456** B5
Miranda de Ebro, Spain, **293** F1
Miranda do Douro, Portugal, **292** D2
Mirandela, Portugal, **292** D2
Mirando City, U.S.A., **424** C6
Mirandola, Italy, **294** C3
Mirandópolis, Brazil, **456** C5
Mirante, Serra do, *mountain range*, Brazil, **456** C6
Miras, Albania, **297** C5
Miravalles, *mountain peak*, Spain, **292** D1
Miravalles, Volcán, *mountain peak*, Costa Rica, **428** D5
Mirbāţ, Oman, **221** F5
Mirbāţ, Ra's, *point*, Oman, **221** F5
Mirebeau, France, **290** E3
Mirecourt, France, **291** H2
Mirepoix, France, **290** E5
Miri, Malaysia, **201** F1
Miriam Vale, Australia, **135** L3
Mirim, Lagoa, *lagoon*, Brazil/Uruguay, **459** G4
Miriñay, *river*, Argentina, **459** F3
Mīrjāveh, Iran, **221** H3
Mirny, *Russian Federation research station*, Antarctica, **470** G6
Mirnyy, Russian Federation, **301** N3
Mirobia, Indonesia, **199** F3
Mirosławiec, Poland, **289** H2
Miroslovești, Romania, **296** F2
Mīrpur Khās, Pakistan, **218** B4
Mīrpur Sakro, Pakistan, **218** A4
Mirtoö Pelagos, *sea*, Greece, **297** D7
Mirzāpur, India, **219** E4
Misau, Nigeria, **365** G2
Misaw Lake, Canada, **414** C2
Misawa, Japan, **209** H2
Miscou Island, Canada, **417** J6
Misgār, Pakistan, **218** C1
Misha, Andaman and Nicobar Islands, India, **217** H5
Mish'āb, Saudi Arabia, **220** E3
Mishan, China, **211** K3
Mishino, Russian Federation, **299** E5
Mishkino, Russian Federation, **222** G1
Mishmi Hills, *mountain range*, India, **215** E3
Misi, Finland, **285** N3
Misiki, Papua New Guinea, **140** A4
Misima Island, Papua New Guinea, **140** D5
Misión de San Fernando, Mexico, **430** B2
Misiones, *province*, Argentina, **459** F3
Misiones, Sierra de, *mountain range*, Argentina, **459** F3
Miskah, Saudi Arabia, **363** H4
Miski, Sudan, **366** B2
Miskitos, Cayos, *islands*, Nicaragua, **429** E4
Miskolc, Hungary, **289** K4, *262*
Mismār, Sudan, **363** G5
Misool, Pulau, *island*, Indonesia, **199** E3
Mişrātah, Libya, **362** C2
Missanabie, Canada, **421** L1
Missinipe, Canada, **413** S4
Mission, U.S.A., **420** C4
Missisa Lake, Canada, **415** M5
Mississagi, *river*, Canada, **421** M2
Mississippi, *river*, U.S.A., **407** P5, *30, 78, 88, 91, 92, 93, 376, 382, 383, 384*
Mississippi, *state*, U.S.A., **424** G3, *386*
Missoula, U.S.A., **418** H3
Missour, Morocco, **361** F2
Missouri, *river*, U.S.A., **407** P4, *95, 376, 382, 383, 385*
Missouri, *state*, U.S.A., **420** G6, *386*
Missouri City, U.S.A., **424** E5
Missouri Valley, U.S.A., **420** F5
Mist, U.S.A., **418** C4
Mistassibi, *river*, Canada, **416** E4
Mistassini, Lac, *lake*, Canada, **416** D4
Mistassini, near Lac Mistassini, Canada, **416** E4
Mistassini, near Lac Saint-Jean, Canada, **416** E5
Mistastin Lake, Canada, **417** K2
Mistelbach, Austria, **289** H4
Misti, Volcán, *mountain peak*, Peru, **454** D4
Mīt Ghamr, Egypt, **225** A4
Mita, Punta, *point*, Mexico, **430** D4
Mitaraka, *mountain peak*, Suriname, **452** B2
Mitchell, Australia, **135** K4
Mitchell, Canada, **421** N4
Mitchell, Mount, *mountain peak*, U.S.A., **425** L2, *376*
Mitchell, Oregon, U.S.A., **418** D4
Mitchell, *river*, Australia, **135** J2
Mitchell, South Dakota, U.S.A., **420** D4
Mitchelstown, Ireland, **309** D5
Mithaskot, Pakistan, **218** B3

Mithi, Pakistan, **218** B4
Mitiaro, *island*, Cook Islands, **137** F2
Mitilíni, Turkey, **224** C5
Mito, Japan, **209** H3
Mitole, Tanzania, **369** G4
Mitre, Península, Argentina, **460** D5
Mitsamiouli, Comoros, **372** A3
Mitsinjo, Madagascar, **372** B4
Mittersill, Austria, **288** F5
Mitú, Colombia, **451** D4
Mituas, Colombia, **451** E3
Mitumba, Monts, *mountain range*, Democratic Republic of the Congo, **357** H7, *334*
Mitwaba, Democratic Republic of the Congo, **369** E4
Mitzic, Gabon, **368** B2
Mixco, Guatemala, **428** C4
Miyake-jima, *island*, Japan, **209** G4
Miyako, Japan, **209** H3
Miyako-jima, *island*, Japan, **209** N8
Miyakonojō, Japan, **208** E5
Miyaly, Kazakhstan, **222** E3
Miyazaki, Japan, **208** E5
Miyoshi, Japan, **208** F4
Miyun, China, **210** G4
Mīzan Teferī, Ethiopia, **366** E3
Mizdah, Libya, **362** B2
Mizen Head, *point*, Cork, Ireland, **309** C6
Mizen Head, *point*, Wicklow, Ireland, **309** F5
Mizhhir"ya, Ukraine, **289** L4
Mizhi, China, **210** E5
Mizil, Romania, **296** F3
Miziya, Bulgaria, **296** D4
Mizoram, *state*, India, **219** H5, *169*
Miẓpe Ramon, Israel, **225** C4
Mizque, Bolivia, **455** F4
Mizuho, *Japanese research station*, Antarctica, **470** E4
Mjöbäck, Sweden, **286** F4
Mjölby, Sweden, **286** G3
Mkata, Tanzania, **369** G4
Mkoani, Tanzania, **369** G4
Mkokotoni, Tanzania, **369** G4
Mkomazi, Tanzania, **369** G3
Mkushi, Zambia, **369** E5
Mladá Boleslav, Czech Republic, **289** G3
Mladenovac, Serbia, **296** C3
Mława, Poland, **289** K2
Mlinište, Bosnia and Herzegovina, **294** F3
Mljet, *island*, Croatia, **294** F4
Mljetski Kanal, *channel*, Croatia, **294** F4
Mmabatho, South Africa, **371** E4
Mmadinare, Botswana, **371** E3
Mo, Norway, **286** E2
Mo i Rana, Norway, **284** G3
Moa, Cuba, **429** G2
Moa Island, Australia, **135** J1
Moab, U.S.A., **423** J2
Moabi, Gabon, **368** B3
Moala, *island*, Fiji, **141** A4
Moamba, Mozambique, **371** F4
Moanda, Gabon, **368** B3
Moapa, U.S.A., **422** F3
Moate, Ireland, **309** E4
Moba, Democratic Republic of the Congo, **369** E4
Mobaye, Central African Republic, **368** D2
Mobayi-Mbongo, Democratic Republic of the Congo, **368** D2
Moberly, U.S.A., **420** G6
Mobile, U.S.A., **425** H4
Mobridge, U.S.A., **420** C3
Mộc Châu, Vietnam, **203** E1
Moca, Haiti, **429** H3
Mocajuba, Brazil, **452** D4
Moçambique, Mozambique, **369** H6
Mochudi, Botswana, **371** E3
Mocimboa da Praia, Mozambique, **369** H5
Môco, *mountain peak*, Angola, **368** C5, *335*
Mocoa, Colombia, **450** C4
Mococa, Brazil, **456** D5
Moctezuma, Chihuahua, Mexico, **430** D2
Moctezuma, Sonora, Mexico, **430** C2
Mocuba, Mozambique, **371** G2
Modao Wan, *bay*, China, **207** A4
Modāsa, India, **218** C5
Modbury, England, U.K., **304** D4
Modena, Italy, **294** C3
Modena, U.S.A., **422** G3
Modesto, U.S.A., **422** C3
Modica, Sicilia, Italy, **295** E7
Modjamboli, Democratic Republic of the Congo, **368** D2
Mödling, Austria, **289** H4
Modot, Mongolia, **210** E3
Modriča, Bosnia and Herzegovina, **294** G3
Moe, Australia, **135** K6
Moehau, *mountain peak*, New Zealand, **132** E3
Moelfre, Wales, U.K., **306** D4
Moelv, Norway, **286** E2
Moen, Norway, **284** J2
Moengo, Suriname, **452** B2
Moeraki, Lake, New Zealand, **133** B6
Moers, Germany, **288** C3
Moffat, Scotland, U.K., **308** F5
Moffat, U.S.A., **423** L3
Moffit, U.S.A., **420** C2
Moga, India, **218** C3
Mogadishu *see* Muqdisho, Somalia, **367** G4, *339*
Mogadouro, Portugal, **292** D2
Mogalo, Democratic Republic of the Congo, **368** C2
Mogami, *river*, Japan, **209** G3
Mogán, Islas Canarias, Spain, **373** B4
Mogaung, Myanmar, **205** C2
Mogdy, Russian Federation, **211** L2
Mogi das Cruzes, Brazil, **459** H2
Mogi Guaçu, *river*, Brazil, **456** D5
Mogi-Mirim, Brazil, **459** H2
Mogila, Macedonia, **297** C5
Mogilno, Poland, **289** H2
Mogincual, Mozambique, **369** H6
Mogocha, Russian Federation, **211** G1
Mogogh, Sudan, **366** D3
Mogok, Myanmar, **205** C3
Mogote, U.S.A., **423** K3
Mogotón, Pico, *mountain peak*, Honduras/Nicaragua, **428** D4
Mogroum, Chad, **365** H2
Moguqi, China, **211** H3
Mogzon, Russian Federation, **210** E2
Mohács, Hungary, **289** J6
Mohale's Hoek, Lesotho, **371** E5
Mohammadia, Algeria, **293** H5
Mohammedia, Morocco, **360** E2
Mohana, India, **218** D4
Mohawk, *river*, U.S.A., **426** C3, *383*
Mohe, China, **211** H1
Moheda, Sweden, **286** G4
Mohei, China, **215** G5
Mohéli *see* Mwali, *island*, Comoros, **372** A3, *352*
Mohill, Ireland, **309** E4
Mohnyin, Myanmar, **205** C2
Moho, Peru, **455** E4
Mohoro, Tanzania, **369** G4
Mohurtay, China, **212** E3
Mohyliv-Podol's'kyy, Ukraine, **296** F1
Moi, Norway, **286** C3
Moimenta da Beira, Portugal, **292** D2
Moincêr, China, **214** B3
Moineşti, Romania, **296** F2
Moira, U.S.A., **426** C2
Moirang, India, **219** H4
Moirans, France, **291** G4
Moires, Kriti, Greece, **297** E8
Moisés Ville, Argentina, **458** E4
Moisie, *river*, Canada, **416** H4
Moisiovaara, Finland, **285** P4
Moissac, France, **290** E4
Moissala, Chad, **366** A3
Mojácar, Spain, **293** G4
Mojave, U.S.A., **422** D4
Mojave Desert, U.S.A., **422** E4, *376*
Mojkovac, Montenegro, **296** B4
Mojo, Bolivia, **455** F5
Moju, *river*, Brazil, **452** D4
Mokhotlong, Lesotho, **371** E4
Mokil, *island*, Micronesia, **138** E4
Mokoreta, *mountain peak*, New Zealand, **133** B8
Mokp'o, South Korea, **208** D4,
Moksha, *river*, Russian Federation, **298** F2
Mokwa, Nigeria, **365** F3
Molanda, Democratic Republic of the Congo, **368** D2
Molango, Mexico, **431** F4
Molanosa, Canada, **413** S4
Molaoi, Greece, **297** D7
Molat, *island*, Croatia, **294** E3
Mold, Wales, U.K., **304** D1
Molde, Norway, **286** C1
Moldova, *country*, Europe, **283** G6, *228, 261, 263, 269, 270*
Moldova Nouă, Romania, **296** C3, *263*
Moldoveanu, *mountain peak*, Romania, **296** E3, *263*
Molepolole, Botswana, **371** E3
Moletai, Lithuania, **287** M5
Molfetta, Italy, **295** F5
Molina de Aragón, Spain, **293** G2
Moline, U.S.A., **420** H5
Moliro, Democratic Republic of the Congo, **369** F4
Molise, *autonomous region*, Italy, **295** E5, *255*
Moliterno, Italy, **295** E5
Molkom, Sweden, **286** F3
Möll, *river*, Austria, **288** F5
Mollendo, Peru, **454** D4
Mölndal, Sweden, **286** F4
Molodezhnaya, *Russian Federation research station*, Antarctica **470** F4
Molodezhnyy, Kazakhstan, **212** B2
Mologa, *river*, Russian Federation, **299** E3
Molokai, *island*, Hawaiian Islands, U.S.A., **433** R9
Molokai Fracture Zone, *tectonic feature*, Pacific Ocean, **479** J3
Molos, Greece, **297** D6
Moloskovitsy, Russian Federation, **299** B3
Moloundou, Cameroon, **368** C2
Molson, Lake, Canada, **414** F4
Molteno, South Africa, **371** E5
Molucca Sea, Indonesia, **198**, D3
Moluccas *see* Maluku, *islands*, Indonesia, **198** D3, *148*
Molumbo, Mozambique, **369** G6
Molvotitsy, Russian Federation, **299** D4
Moma, Mozambique, **369** G6
Mombaça, Brazil, **453** F4
Mombasa, Kenya, **369** G3, *74, 341*
Mombetsu, Japan, **209** H1
Mombi New, India, **219** H4
Mombo, Tanzania, **369** G3
Momboré, Cameroon, **365** G3
Momchilgrad, Bulgaria, **297** E5
Mompono, Democratic Republic of the Congo, **368** D2, *404*
Mompós, Colombia, **450** C2
Møn, *island*, Denmark, **286** F5
Mon, *river*, Myanmar, **205** B3
Mon, *state*, Myanmar, **202** C2
Monach, Sound of, Scotland, U.K., **308** B3
Monach Islands, Scotland, U.K., **308** B3
Monaco, Monaco, **291** H5, *246*
Monaco, *country*, Europe, **282** E7, *228, 246*
Monadhliath Mountains, *mountain range*, Scotland, U.K., **308** E3
Monaghan, *county*, Ireland, **309** E3
Monaghan, Ireland, **309** F3
Monahans, U.S.A., **423** M6
Monango, U.S.A., **420** D2
Monapo, Mozambique, **369** H5
Monar, Loch, *lake*, Scotland, U.K., **308** D3
Monarch, U.S.A., **419** J3
Monasterace Marina, Italy, **295** F6
Monasterevin, Ireland, **309** E4
Monastery, Canada, **417** L7
Monastyrshchina, Russian Federation, **299** C5
Monastyrskoye, Ozero, *lake*, Russian Federation, **285** T5
Monatélé, Cameroon, **365** G4
Moncayo, Sierra del, *mountain peak*, Spain, **293** G2
Monchegorsk, Russian Federation, **285** R3
Mönchengladbach, Germany, **288** C3
Moncks Corner, U.S.A., **425** M3
Monclova, Mexico, **431** E3
Moncontour, France, **290** C2
Moncton, Canada, **416** J6
Monday, *river*, Paraguay, **459** F2
Mondego, Cabo, *cape*, Portugal, **292** C2
Mondego, *river*, Portugal, **292** C2
Mondjoku, Democratic Republic of the Congo, **368** D3
Mondo, Chad, **365** H2
Mondombe, Democratic Republic of the Congo, **368** D3
Mondoñedo, Spain, **292** D1
Möndööhöö, Mongolia, **213** G2
Mondovi, Italy, **294** A3
Mondy, Russian Federation, **213** J2
Monemvasia, Greece, **297** D7
Monesterio, Spain, **292** D3
Moneta, U.S.A., **419** L5
Monett, U.S.A., **420** G7
Moneymore, Northern Ireland, U.K., **309** F3
Monforte, Spain, **292** D1
Móng Cái, Vietnam, **203** E1
Möng Hpayak, Myanmar, **205** C3
Möng Küng, Myanmar, **205** C3
Möng Mit, Myanmar, **205** C3
Möng Pawn, Myanmar, **205** C3
Möng Ping, Myanmar, **205** C3
Möng Pu, Myanmar, **205** C3
Möng Yai, Myanmar, **205** C3
Monga, Democratic Republic of the Congo, **368** D2
Mongar, Bhutan, **205** A2
Mongbwalu, Democratic Republic of the Congo, **369** F2
Monghidoro, Italy, **294** C3
Mongo, Chad, **366** A2
Mongol Altayn Nuruu, *mountain range*, Mongolia, **212** F2, *186*
Mongol Els, *physical feature*, Mongolia, **213** G3
Mongolia, *country*, Asia, **197** M5, *94, 144, 145, 271, 272, 273*
Mongoli, Plateau of, Mongolia, **195** M5
Mongomo, Equatorial Guinea, **368** B2
Mongororo, Chad, **366** B2
Mongoumba, Central African Republic, **368** C2
Mongu, Zambia, **368** D6
Monguno, Nigeria, **365** G2
Mönh Hayrhan Uul, *mountain peak*, Mongolia, **213** F3
Moniaive, Scotland, U.K., **308** F5
Monitor Range, *mountain range*, U.S.A., **422** E2
Monivea, Ireland, **309** D4
Monkeyo, Philippines, **204** D5
Mońki, Poland, **289** L2
Monkoto, Democratic Republic of the Congo, **368** D3
Monmouth, Wales, U.K., **304** E3
Monmouthshire, *unitary authority*, Wales, U.K., **304** E3
Mono Island, Solomon Islands, **140** E2
Mono Lake, U.S.A., **422** D3
Monomoy Point, U.S.A., **426** F4
Monongahela, *river*, U.S.A., **421** N6
Monopoli, Italy, **295** F5
Monor, Hungary, **289** J5
Monos, Trinidad, Trinidad and Tobago, **461** C4
Monou, Chad, **366** B1
Monóvar, Spain, **293** G3
Monreal del Campo, Spain, **293** G2
Monreale, Sicilia, Italy, **295** D6
Monroe, Louisiana, U.S.A., **424** F3
Monroe, Michigan, U.S.A., **421** M5
Monroe, North Carolina, U.S.A., **425** M2
Monroe Lake, U.S.A., **421** K6
Monroeville, U.S.A., **425** J4
Monrovia, Liberia, **364** B3, *323*
Monroyo, Spain, **293** G2
Mons, Belgium, **288** A3
Monselice, Italy, **294** C3
Monster, Netherlands, **288** B2
Mont-Apica, Canada, **416** F6
Mont-de-Marsan, France, **290** D5
Mont-Dore, New Caledonia, **141** A3
Mont-Joli, Canada, **416** G5
Mont-Laurier, Canada, **416** D6
Mont-Louis, France, **290** F5
Montague, Canada, **417** K6
Montaigu, France, **290** D3
Montalbán, Spain, **293** G2
Montalcino, Italy, **294** C4
Montalto, *mountain peak*, Italy, **295** E6
Montalvânia, Brazil, **457** E4
Montalvo, Ecuador, **450** C5
Montana, *administrative region*, Bulgaria, **296** D4
Montana, Bulgaria, **296** D4
Montana, *state*, U.S.A., **419** J3, *386*
Montargil, Barragem de, *reservoir*, Portugal, **292** C3
Montargis, France, **290** F3
Montauban, France, **290** E5
Montauban-de-Bretagne, France, **290** C2
Montauk Point, U.S.A., **426** E4
Montbard, France, **291** G3
Montbazon, France, **290** E3
Montblanc, Spain, **293** H2
Montbrison, France, **291** G4
Montdidier, France, **290** F2
Monte Alegre, Brazil, **452** B4
Monte Alegrede Goiás, Brazil, **456** D3
Monte Azul, Brazil, **457** E4
Monte-Carlo, Monaco, **291** H5, *246*
Monte Caseros, Argentina, **459** F4
Monte Comán, Argentina, **458** C5
Monte Creek, Canada, **412** K6
Monte Cristi, Dominican Republic, **429** H3
Monte Dinero, Argentina, **460** D4
Monte Lindo, *river*, Argentina, **459** E2
Monte Lindo, *river*, Paraguay, **459** E2
Monte Plata, Dominican Republic, **429** H3
Monte Quemado, Argentina, **458** D2
Monte Sant'Angelo, Italy, **295** F5
Monte Santo, Brazil, **457** F3
Monte Santu, Capo di, *cape*, Sardegna, Italy, **295** B5
Monte Vista, U.S.A., **423**, K3
Monteagudo, Bolivia, **455** F5
Montebelluna, Italy, **294** D3
Montebourg, France, **305** F5

Montecarlo, Argentina, **459** F3
Montech, France, **290** E5
Montecristi, Ecuador, **450** B4
Montecristo, Isola di, *island*, Italy, **295** C4
Montego Bay, Jamaica, **429** F3
Montélimar, France, **291** G4
Montello, U.S.A., **421** J4
Montemayor, Meseta de, *plateau*, Argentina, **460** D2
Montemor-o-Nova, Portugal, **292** C3
Montemorelos, Mexico, **431** F3
Montemuro, *mountain peak*, Portugal, **292** D2
Montenegro, Brazil, **459** G3
Montenegro *see* Crna Gora, *country*, Europe, **282** F7, *81, 97, 228, 259, 260, 261, 263*
Montepuez, Mozambique, **369** G5
Montepulciano, Italy, **294** C4
Monterey, California, U.S.A., **422** C3
Monterey, Virginia, U.S.A., **421** P6
Monterey Bay, U.S.A., **422** B3
Montería, Colombia, **450** C2
Montero, Bolivia, **455** F4
Monteros, Argentina, **458** D3
Monterotondo, Italy, **295** D4
Monterrey, Mexico, **431** E3
Montes Altos, Brazil, **452** D4
Montes Claros, Brazil, **457** E4
Montevarchi, Italy, **294** C4
Montevideo, Uruguay, **459** F5, *444*
Montevideo, U.S.A., **420** F3
Montezuma Creek, U.S.A., **423** J3
Montgomery, U.S.A., **425** J3, *386*
Montgomery, Wales, U.K., **304** D2
Monti, Sardegna, Italy, **295** B5
Monticello, Arkansas, U.S.A., **424** G3
Monticello, Georgia, U.S.A., **425** L3
Monticello, Indiana, U.S.A., **421** K5
Monticello, Iowa, U.S.A., **420** H4
Monticello, Kentucky, U.S.A., **421** L7
Monticello, Mississippi, U.S.A., **424** G4
Monticello, New York, U.S.A., **426** C4
Monticello, Utah, U.S.A., **423** J3
Monticiano, Italy, **294** C4
Montijo, Golfo de, *gulf*, Panama, **429** E6
Montivilliers, France, **290** E2
Montluçon, France, **290** F3
Montmagny, Canada, **416** F6
Montmarault, France, **291** F3
Montmartre, Canada, **414** C6
Monto, Australia, **135** L3
Montoro, Spain, **292** E3
Montoya, U.S.A., **423** L4
Montpelier, Idaho, U.S.A., **419** J5
Montpelier, Vermont, U.S.A., **426** D2, *386*
Montpellier, France, **291** F5
Montréal, Canada, **416** E7, *83, 93, 380, 381*
Montreal Lake, Canada, **413** S4
Montreal Lake, *lake*, Canada, **413** S4
Montreal River, Canada, **421** L2
Montréjeau, France, **290** E5
Montreuil, France, **305** J4
Montreux, Switzerland, **291** H3
Montrose, Arkansas, U.S.A., **424** G3
Montrose, Colorado, U.S.A., **423** K2
Montrose, Pennsylvania, U.S.A., **426** C4
Montrose, Scotland, U.K., **308** G4
Montserrat, *mountain peak*, Spain, **293** H2
Montserrat, *U.K. dependency*, Caribbean Sea, **409** S7, *276, 378, 390*
Montsinéry, French Guiana, **452** C2
Monument Valley, U.S.A., **423** H3, *387*
Monveda, Democratic Republic of the Congo, **368** D2
Monywa, Myanmar, **205** B3
Monza, Italy, **294** B3
Monze, Zambia, **369** E6
Monzón, Peru, **454** C2
Monzón, Spain, **293** H2
Mookane, Botswana, **371** E3
Moonbeam, Canada, **415** N7
Moora, Australia, **134** D5
Moorbad Lobenstein, Germany, **288** E3
Moorcroft, U.S.A., **419** M4
Moore, Idaho, U.S.A., **418** H5
Moore, Lake, Australia, **134** D5
Moore, Montana, U.S.A., **419** K3
Moore, Mount, *mountain peak*, Antarctica, **470** C6
Moore, Oklahoma, U.S.A., **424** D2
Moorea, *island*, French Polynesia, **137** F2
Moorefield, U.S.A., **421** P6
Moorhead, U.S.A., **420** E2
Moose, *river*, Canada, **415** P6
Moose, U.S.A., **419** J5
Moose Factory, Canada, **415** P6
Moose Jaw, Canada, **413** S6
Moose Lake, Canada, **414** D5
Moose Lake, U.S.A., **420** G2
Moosehead Lake, U.S.A., **426** F2
Moosehorn, Canada, **414** E6
Moosomin, Canada, **414** D6
Moosonee, Canada, **415** P6
Mopeia, Mozambique, **371** G2
Mopti, *administrative region*, Mali, **364** D2
Mopti, Mali, **364** D2
Moqor, Afghanistan, **218** A2
Moquegua, Peru, **454** D4
Mor, Glen, *glen*, Scotland, U.K., **308** E3
Mór, Hungary, **289** J5
Mora, Cameroon, **365** G2
Mora, Minnesota, U.S.A., **420** G3
Mora, New Mexico, U.S.A., **423** L4
Mora, Portugal, **292** C3
Mora, Spain, **293** F3
Mora, Sweden, **286** G2
Mora de Rubielos, Spain, **293** G2
Móra d'Ebre, Spain, **293** H2
Morada Nova, Brazil, **453** F4
Morādābād, India, **218** D3
Morafenobe, Madagascar, **372** A4
Morąg, Poland, **289** J2
Mórahalom, Hungary, **296** B2
Morakovo, Montenegro, **296** B4
Moraleda, Canal, *channel*, Chile, **460** C2
Moraleja, Spain, **292** D2
Morales, Guatemala, **428** C4
Moramanga, Madagascar, **372** B4
Moran, Kansas, U.S.A., **420** F7
Moran, Michigan, U.S.A., **421** L3
Moran, Wyoming, U.S.A., **419** J5
Morane, *island*, French Polynesia, **137** H3
Morar, Loch, *lake*, Scotland, U.K., **308** D4
Morar, Scotland, U.K., **308** D4
Morari, Tso, *lake*, India, **218** D2
Moratalla, Spain, **293** G3
Moratuwa, Sri Lanka, **216** D5
Morava, *river*, Austria/Czech Republic/Slovakia, **289** H4
Moravské Budějovice, Czech Republic, **289** G4
Morawhanna, Guyana, **451** G2
Moray, *local authority*, Scotland, U.K., **308** F3
Moray Firth, *river mouth*, Scotland, U.K., **308** F3
Morbi, India, **218** B5
Morcenx, France, **290** D4
Morden, Canada, **414** E7
Mordoğan, Turkey, **297** F6
Mordoviya, Respublika, *republic*, Russian Federation, **222** C2
More, Ben, *mountain peak*, Scotland, U.K., **308** C4
More Assynt, Ben, Scotland, U.K., **308** E2
Møre og Romsdal, *county*, Norway, **286** C1
Moreau, *river*, U.S.A., **420** B3
Morebattle, Scotland, U.K., **308** G5
Morecambe, England, U.K., **306** F3
Morecambe Bay, England, U.K., **306** E3
Moree, Australia, **135** K4
Morehead, Papua New Guinea, **140** A5
Morehead, U.S.A., **421** M6
Morehead City, U.S.A., **426** B7
Morelia, Mexico, **431** E5
Morella, Spain, **293** G2
Morelos, *state*, Mexico, **431** F5
Morena, India, **218** D4
Morena, Sierra, *mountain range*, Spain, **292** D3, *253*
Moreni, Romania, **296** E3
Morerú, *river*, Brazil, **455** G3
Moresby Island, Canada, **412** C5
Moreton-in-Marsh, England, U.K., **305** F3
Moreton Island, Australia, **135** L4
Moretonhampstead, England, U.K., **304** D4
Moretta, Italy, **294** A3
Moreuil, France, **305** K5
Morgan City, U.S.A., **424** G5
Morgan Hill, U.S.A., **422** C3
Morgan Island, Heard and McDonald Islands, **134** S12
Morganton, U.S.A., **425** L2
Morges, Switzerland, **291** H3
Morghāb, *river*, Afghanistan, **218** A2
Mori, Japan, **209** H2
Moriah, Tobago, Trinidad and Tobago, **461** B4
Moriani-Plage, Corse, France, **295** B4
Moribaya, Guinea, **364** C3
Moricetown, Canada, **412** F4
Morichal, Colombia, **451** D3
Moriki, Nigeria, **365** F2
Morioka, Japan, **209** H3
Morjärv, Sweden, **285** L3
Morlaix, France, **290** C2
Morley, Canada, **413** M6
Morley, England, U.K., **307** G4
Morningside, Canada, **413** N5
Mornington, Isla, *island*, Chile, **460** B3
Mornington Island, Australia, **135** H2
Moro, Pakistan, **218** A4
Moro, U.S.A., **418** D4
Moro Gulf, Philippines, **204** C5
Morobe, Papua New Guinea, **140** B4
Morobe, *province*, Papua New Guinea, **140** B4
Morocco, *country*, Africa, **358** E4, *73, 74, 91, 93, 94, 97, 252, 312, 314, 315, 355*
Morocco, U.S.A., **421** K5
Morococha, Peru, **454** C3
Morogoro, *administrative region*, Tanzania, **369** G4
Morogoro, Tanzania, **369** G4
Morokweng, South Africa, **370** D4
Moroleón, Mexico, **431** E4
Morombe, Madagascar, **372** A5
Morón, Cuba, **429** F2
Mörön, Hentiy, Mongolia, **210** E3
Mörön, Hövsgöl, Mongolia, **213** J2
Morón de la Frontera, Spain, **292** E4
Morona, Ecuador, **450** C5
Morondava, Madagascar, **372** A5
Morondo, Côte d'Ivoire, **364** C3
Moroni, Comoros, **372** A3, *351, 352*
Morotai, Pulau, *island*, Indonesia, **199** E2
Moroto, *mountain peak*, Uganda, **369** F2
Moroto, Uganda, **369** F2
Morozovsk, Russian Federation, **298** F3
Morpará, Brazil, **457** E3
Morpeth, England, U.K., **307** G2
Morphou, Cyprus, **225** B2, *191*
Morphou Bay, Cyprus, **225** B2, *191*
Morrilton, U.S.A., **424** F2
Morrin, Canada, **413** N6
Morrinhos, Brazil, **456** D4
Morrinsville, New Zealand, **132** E3
Morris, Illinois, U.S.A., **421** J5
Morris, Minnesota, U.S.A., **420** F3
Morris, Pennsylvania, U.S.A., **426** B4
Morristown, New Jersey, U.S.A., **426** C4
Morristown, Tennessee, U.S.A., **425** L1
Morro, Sierra del, *mountain peak*, Argentina, **458** D4
Morro Bay, U.S.A., **422** C4
Morro d'Anta, Brazil, **457** F5
Morro do Chapéu, Brazil, **457** F3
Morro Jable, Islas Canarias, Spain, **373** B4
Morrón, *mountain peak*, Spain, **293** F4
Morrosquillo, Golfo de, *gulf*, Colombia, **450** C2
Morrumbala, Mozambique, **371** G2
Morrumbene, Mozambique, **371** G3
Morshansk, Russian Federation, **298** F2
Morshyn, Ukraine, **289** L4
Morson, Canada, **414** G7
Mørsvik, Norway, **284** G3
Mortagne-sur-Sèvre, France, **290** D3
Mortara, Italy, **294** B3
Morte Bay, England, U.K., **304** C3
Morteau, France, **291** H3
Mortehoe, England, U.K., **304** C3
Morteros, Argentina, **458** D4
Mortes, Rio das, *river*, Brazil, **456** C3
Mortimers, Bahamas, **429** G2
Mortlock Islands, Micronesia, **138** D4
Morton, England, U.K., **305** G2
Morton, Minnesota, U.S.A., **420** F3
Morton, Texas, U.S.A., **423** M5
Morton, Washington, U.S.A., **418** C3
Mortyq, Kazakhstan, **222** F2
Moruga, Trinidad, Trinidad and Tobago, **461** C4
Morungole, *mountain peak*, Uganda, **369** F2
Morvan, *region*, France, **291** F3
Morvern, *region*, Scotland, U.K., **308** D4
Morville, England, U.K., **304** E2
Morwell, Australia, **135** K6
Mor'ye, Russian Federation, **299** C2
Mosal'sk, Russian Federation, **299** E5
Mosbach, Germany, **288** D4
Mosborough, England, U.K., **307** G4
Mosby, U.S.A., **419** L3
Moscow *see* Moskva, Russian Federation, **299** F4, *229, 263, 271, 272, 273*
Moscow, U.S.A., **418** F3
Moscow University Ice Shelf, Antarctica, **470** F7
Mosel, *river*, Germany, **288** C4, *239*
Moselle, *river*, France, **291** H2, *243*
Moses Lake, *lake*, U.S.A., **418** E3
Moses Lake, U.S.A., **418** E3
Mosetse, Botswana, **371** E3
Moshchnyy, Ostrov, *island*, Russian Federation, **287** N2
Moshi, Tanzania, **369** G3
Mosina, Poland, **289** H2
Mosjøen, Norway, **284** F4
Moskenesøya, *island*, Norway, **284** E3
Moskosel, Sweden, **284** J4
Moskovskaya Oblast', *province*, Russian Federation, **299** F5
Moskva, *river*, Russian Federation, **299** F5
Moskva (Moscow), Russian Federation, **299** F4, *229, 263, 271, 272, 273*
Mosonmagyaróvár, Hungary, **289** H5
Mosqueiro, Brazil, **452** D3
Mosquera, Colombia, **450** B3
Mosquero, U.S.A., **423** M4
Mosquito Bay, Canada, **415** Q1
Mosquitos, Golfo de los, *gulf*, Panama, **429** E5
Moss, Norway, **286** E3
Mossat, Scotland, U.K., **308** G3
Mossburn, New Zealand, **133** B7
Mossel Bay, South Africa, **370** D5
Mossendjo, Congo, **368** B3
Mossman, Australia, **135** K2
Mossoró, Brazil, **453** G4
Mossuril, Mozambique, **369** H5
Mostaganem, Algeria, **361** G1
Mostar, Bosnia and Herzegovina, **294** F4
Mostardas, Brazil, **459** G4
Mostove, Ukraine, **296** H2
Mostys'ka, Ukraine, **289** L4
Mosul *see* Al Mawṣil, Iraq, **363** H1
Mosŭlp'o, South Korea, **208** D4
Møsvatn, *lake*, Norway, **286** C3
Mot'a, Ethiopia, **367** E2
Mota del Cuervo, Spain, **293** F3
Motala, Sweden, **286** G3
Moth, India, **218** D4
Motherwell, Scotland, U.K., **308** F5
Motilla del Palancar, Spain, **293** G3
Motiti Island, New Zealand, **132** F3
Motokwe, Botswana, **370** D3
Motovskiy Zaliv, *bay*, Russian Federation, **285** R2
Motril, Spain, **293** F4
Motru, Romania, **296** D3
Mott, U.S.A., **420** B2
Mottola, Italy, **295** F5
Motu, *river*, New Zealand, **132** F4
Motu Iti, *island*, Isla de Pascua (Easter Island), Chile, **461** B2
Motu Nui, *island*, Isla de Pascua (Easter Island), Chile, **461** B2
Motu One, *island*, French Polynesia, **137** F2
Motu Tautara, *island*, Isla de Pascua (Easter Island), Chile, **461** B2
Motueka, New Zealand, **133** D5
Motunau Beach, New Zealand, **133** D6
Motunui, New Zealand, **132** E4
Motupena Point, Papua New Guinea, **140** E2
Mou, New Caledonia, **141** A3
Mouali Gbangba, Congo, **368** C2
Mouanko, Cameroon, **368** A2
Mouchalagane, *river*, Canada, **416** G3
Moudjéria, Mauritania, **360** D5
Mouhijärvi, Finland, **287** L2
Mouila, Gabon, **368** B3
Moulins, France, **291** F3
Moulmein, Myanmar, **202** C2
Moultrie, Lake, U.S.A., **425** M3
Moultrie, U.S.A., **425** L4

Mound City, Illinois, U.S.A., **421** J7
Mound City, South Dakota, U.S.A., **420** C3
Moundou, Chad, **365** H3
Moundsville, U.S.A., **421** N6
Moŭng Roessei, Cambodia, **203** D3
Mount Airy, U.S.A., **421** N7
Mount Ayr, U.S.A., **420** F5
Mount Barker, Australia, **134** D5
Mount Bellew, Ireland, **309** D4
Mount Caramel Junction, U.S.A., **422** G3
Mount Carroll, U.S.A., **420** J4
Mount Cook, New Zealand, **133** C6, *110*
Mount Currie, Canada, **412** H6
Mount Darwin, Zimbabwe, **371** F2
Mount Dora, U.S.A., **423** M3
Mount Forest, Canada, **421** N4
Mount Gambier, Australia, **135** J6
Mount Hagen, Papua New Guinea, **140** B4, *115*
Mount Horeb, U.S.A., **420** J4
Mount Hutt, New Zealand, **133** C6
Mount Ida, U.S.A., **424** F2
Mount Isa, Australia, **134** H3
Mount Magnet, Australia, **134** D4
Mount Pearl, Canada, **417** Q6
Mount Pleasant, Iowa, U.S.A., **420** H5
Mount Pleasant, Pennsylvania, U.S.A., **421** P5
Mount Pleasant, South Carolina, U.S.A., **425** N3
Mount Pleasant, Texas, U.S.A., **424** E3
Mount Pleasant, Utah, U.S.A., **423** H2
Mount St George, Tobago, Trinidad and Tobago, **461** B4
Mount Shasta, U.S.A., **418** C6
Mount Sinai *see* Mūsā, Jabal, *mountain peak*, Egypt, **225** B5
Mount Sterling, U.S.A., **421** M6
Mount Union, U.S.A., **421** Q5
Mount Vernon, Alabama, U.S.A., **425** H4
Mount Vernon, Illinois, U.S.A., **421** J6
Mount Vernon, Ohio, U.S.A., **421** M5
Mount Vernon, Oregon, U.S.A., **418** E4
Mountain City, U.S.A., **418** G6
Mountain Home, Arkansas, U.S.A., **424** F1
Mountain Home, Idaho, U.S.A., **418** G5
Mountain Lake, U.S.A., **420** F4
Mountain View, Hawaiian Islands, U.S.A., **422** R10
Mountain View, U.S.A., **423** H1
Mountmellick, Ireland, **309** E4
Mountrath, Ireland, **309** E4
Mount's Bay, England, U.K., **304** B4
Mountshannon, Ireland, **309** D5
Mountsorrel, England, U.K., **305** F2
Moura, Australia, **135** K3
Moura, Brazil, **451** G4
Moura, Chad, **366** B2
Moura, Portugal, **292** D3
Mourão, Portugal, **292** D3
Mouray, Chad, **366** B2
Mourdi, Dépression du, *depression*, Chad, **362** D5
Mourdiah, Mali, **364** C2
Mourea, New Zealand, **132** F4
Mourne Mountains, *mountain range*, Northern Ireland, U.K., **309** F3
Mousehole, England, U.K., **304** B4
Mousgougou, Chad, **365** H2
Moussoro, Chad, **365** H2
Moutamba, Congo, **365** G5
Moûtiers, France, **291** H4
Moutsamoudou, Comoros, **372** A3
Mouy, France, **305** K5
Mouydir, Monts du, *mountain range*, Algeria, **361** G4
Mouzaki, Greece, **297** C6
Mouzarak, Chad, **365** H2
Moville, Ireland, **309** E2
Moxico, *province*, Angola, **368** D5
Moxotó, *river*, Brazil, **457** F2
Moyalē, Ethiopia, **369** G2
Moyamba, Sierra Leone, **364** B3
Moyen Atlas, *mountain range*, Morocco, **361** E2
Moyen Chari, Chad, **366** A3
Moyen-Ogooué, *province*, Gabon, **368** B3
Moyenne-Guinée, *administrative region*, Guinea, **364** B2
Moyie, Canada, **413** M7
Moyie Springs, U.S.A., **418** F2
Moyle, *district*, Northern Ireland, U.K., **309** F2
Moylough, Ireland, **309** D4
Moyo, Uganda, **369** F2
Moyobamba, Peru, **454** C2
Møysalen, *mountain peak*, Norway, **284** G2
Moyto, Chad, **365** H2
Moyu, China, **212** C5
Moyvally, Ireland, **309** F4
Moyynqum, *desert*, Kazakhstan, **223** H4
Moyynty, Kazakhstan, **212** B3
Mozăceni, Romania, **296** E3
Mozambique, *country*, Africa, **359** J9, *312, 332, 344, 345, 346, 348, 350, 351*
Mozambique Channel, East Africa, **371** G3, *352, 354*
Mozambique Fracture Zone, *tectonic feature*, Indian Ocean, **476** B7
Mozambique Plateau, *underwater feature*, Indian Ocean, **476** B7
Mozhaysk, Russian Federation, **299** F5
Mozhga, Russian Federation, **222** E1
Mpala, Democratic Republic of the Congo, **369** E4
Mpanda, Tanzania, **369** F4
Mpandamatenga, Zimbabwe, **371** E2
Mpé, Congo, **368** B3
Mpen, India, **219** J4
Mpen, Myanmar, **205** C2
Mpessoba, Mali, **364** C2
Mpigi, Uganda, **369** F2
Mpika, Zambia, **369** F5
Mporokoso, Zambia, **369** F4
Mpouya, Congo, **368** C3
Mpulungu, Zambia, **369** F4
Mpumalanga, *province*, South Africa, **371** E4, *351*
Mpwapwa, Tanzania, **369** G4
Mrągowo, Poland, **289** K2
Mrakovo, Russian Federation, **222** F2
Mrežičko, Macedonia, **297** C5
Mrkonjić Grad, Bosnia and Herzegovina, **294** F3
Msata, Tanzania, **369** G4
Mshinskaya, Russian Federation, **299** B3
M'Sila, Algeria, **361** G1
Msta, *river*, Russian Federation, **299** D3
Mstsislaw, Belarus, **299** C5
Msuna, Zimbabwe, **371** E2
Mtama, Tanzania, **369** G5
Mtsensk, Russian Federation, **299** F6
Mtwara, *administrative region*, Tanzania, **369** G5
Mtwara, Tanzania, **369** H5
Mú, *mountain peak*, Portugal, **292** C4
Mu, *river*, Myanmar, **205** B3
Mu'a, Tongatapu Group, Tonga, **141** B4
Muaguide, Mozambique, **372** A3
Mualama, Mozambique, **369** G6
Muanda, Democratic Republic of the Congo, **368** B4
Muang Khammouan, Laos, **203** E2
Muang Không, Laos, **203** E3
Muang Khoua, Laos, **202** D1
Muang Nan, Laos, **202** D2
Muang Ngoy, Laos, **203** D1
Muang Pakbeng, Laos, **202** D2
Muang Pakxan, Laos, **203** D2
Muang Pakxong, Laos, **203** E3
Muang Phin, Laos, **203** E2
Muang Phôn-Hông, Laos, **203** D2
Muang Phônsavan, Laos, **203** D2
Muang Xaignabouri, Laos, **202** D2
Muang Xépôn, Laos, **203** E2
Muanzanza, Democratic Republic of the Congo, **368** D4
Muar, Malaysia, **200** C2
Muara, Brunei, **201** F1
Muaraaman, Indonesia, **200** C3
Muarabeliti, Indonesia, **200** C3
Muarabungo, Indonesia, **200** C3
Muaradua, Indonesia, **200** D4
Muaraenim, Indonesia, **200** C3
Muarapayang, Indonesia, **201** F3
Muarasiberut, Indonesia, **200** B3
Mubende, Uganda, **369** F2
Mubi, Nigeria, **365** G2
Mubrani, Indonesia, **199** F3
Mucajaí, *river*, Brazil, **451** F3
Mucajaí, Serra do, *mountain range*, Brazil, **451** F3
Much Wenlock, England, U.K., **304** E2
Muchalls, Scotland, U.K., **308** G3
Muchea, Australia, **134** D5
Muchinga Escarpment, Zambia, **369** E5
Muchuan, China, **215** G3
Muck, *island*, Scotland, U.K., **308** C4
Mucojo, Mozambique, **369** H5
Muconda, Angola, **368** D5
Mucope, Angola, **368** B6
Mucubela, Mozambique, **369** G6
Mucuim, *river*, Brazil, **455** F2
Mucumbura, Mozambique, **369** F6
Mucur, Turkey, **363** F1
Mucuri, Brazil, **457** F4
Mucuri, *river*, Brazil, **457** F4
Muda, *river*, Malaysia/Thailand, **200** C1
Mudanjiang, China, **211** K3
Mudanya, Turkey, **297** G5
Mudaysīsāt, Jabal, *mountain peak*, Jordan, **225** D4
Muddy Gap, U.S.A., **419** L5
Mudhol, India, **216** C2
Mudon, Myanmar, **202** C2
Mudug, *administrative region*, Somalia, **367** G3
Muecate, Mozambique, **369** G5
Mueda, Mozambique, **369** G5
Mufu Shan, *mountain range*, China, **206** C2
Mufulira, Zambia, **369** E5
Mufumbwe, Zambia, **368** E5
Mugang, China, **215** H5
Mugarripug, China, **214** C2
Mugeba, Mozambique, **371** G2
Mughal Sarāi, India, **219** E4
Mughalzhar Tauy, *mountain range*, Kazakhstan, **222** F3
Mūghār, Iran, **220** F2
Mughayrā', Saudi Arabia, **225** D5
Mugila, Monts, *mountain range*, Democratic Republic of the Congo, **369** E4
Muğla, *province*, Turkey, **297** G7
Muğla, Turkey, **297** G7
Muguia, Mozambique, **369** G5
Mugur-Aksy, Russian Federation, **223** N2
Mūḥ, Sabkhat al, *lake*, Syria, **225** E2
Muhājirīyah, Sudan, **366** C2
Muḥammad Qawl, Sudan, **363** G4
Muḥammad, Ra's, *point*, Egypt, **363** F3
Muhar, China, **213** H5
Muhembo, Botswana, **370** D2
Mühlhausen, Germany, **288** E3
Mühlviertel, *region*, Austria, **289** F4
Muhos, Finland, **285** M4
Muhu, *island*, Estonia, **287** L3
Muhulu, Democratic Republic of the Congo, **369** E3
Mui, Ethiopia, **366** E3
Muine Bheag, Ireland, **309** F5
Muirkirk, Scotland, U.K., **308** E5
Muisné, Ecuador, **450** B4
Muite, Mozambique, **369** G5
Mukacheve, Ukraine, **289** L4
Mukah, Malaysia, **201** F2
Mukah, *river*, Malaysia, **201** F2
Mukdahan, Thailand, **203** E2
Mukhino, Russian Federation, **211** J1
Mukhorshibir', Russian Federation, **210** D2
Muko-jima, *island*, Japan, **138** C2
Mukomuko, Indonesia, **200** C3
Mukono, Uganda, **369** F2
Muktsar, India, **218** C3
Mula, China, **215** G3
Mula, La, *mountain peak*, Italy, **295** E6
Mulaku Atoll, Maldives, **216** C6
Mulan, China, **211** K3
Mulanje, Malawi, **369** G6
Mulanje, Mount, *mountain peak*, Malawi, **369** G6, *344*
Mulata, Brazil, **452** C3
Mulbekh, India, **218** D2
Mulberry, U.S.A., **424** F2
Mulchén, Chile, **458** B5
Mule Creek, U.S.A., **423** J5
Muleba, Tanzania, **369** F3
Mulegé, Mexico, **430** C3
Muleshoe, U.S.A., **423** M4
Mulevala, Mozambique, **369** G6
Mulhacén, *mountain peak*, Spain, **293** F4, *252, 253*
Mulhouse, France, **291** H3
Mulifanua, Samoa, **141** B1
Muling, south of Jixi, Heilongjiang, China, **211** K3
Muling, west of Mudanjiang, Heilongjiang, China, **211** K3
Mulitapuili, Cape, Samoa, **141** B1
Mull, *island*, Scotland, U.K., **308** D4
Mull, Sound of, Scotland, U.K., **308** D4
Mullaghareirk Mountains, *mountain range*, Ireland, **309** C5
Mullany's Cross, Ireland, **309** D3
Mullen, U.S.A., **420** C4
Muller, Pegunungan, *mountain range*, Indonesia, **201** F2
Mullet Peninsula, Ireland, **309** B3
Mullewa, Australia, **134** D4
Müllheim, Germany, **288** C5
Mullinavat, Ireland, **309** E5
Mullingar, Ireland, **309** E4
Mullins, U.S.A., **425** N2
Mullion, England, U.K., **304** B4
Mullsjö, Sweden, **286** F4
Mulobezi, Zambia, **368** E6
Mulrany, Ireland, **309** C4
Mulshi Lake, India, **216** C2
Multai, India, **218** D5
Multān, Pakistan, **218** B3
Multia, Finland, **287** M1
Mulu, Gunung, *mountain peak*, Malaysia, **201** F1
Mulumbe, Monts, *mountain range*, Democratic Republic of the Congo, **369** E4
Muma, Democratic Republic of the Congo, **368** D2
Mumbai (Bombay), India, **216** C2, *16, 45, 94, 169*
Mumbeji, Zambia, **368** D5
Mumbles, The, Wales, U.K., **304** C3
Mumbondo, Angola, **368** B5
Mumbwa, Zambia, **369** E5
Mumcular, Turkey, **297** F7
Mumeng, Papua New Guinea, **140** B4
Muna, Mexico, **431** H4
Muna, Pulau, *island*, Indonesia, **198** C4
Muna, *river*, Russian Federation, **301** N3
Munābā, India, **218** B4
Munaðarnes, Iceland, **284** X6
Munai, China, **215** F5
München (Munich), Germany, **288** E4, *239*
Munchique, Cerro, *mountain peak*, Colombia, **450** C3
Muncho Lake, Canada, **412** G2
Munch'ŏn, North Korea, **208** D3
Muncie, U.S.A., **421** L5
Munda, Pakistan, **218** B3
Munda, Solomon Islands, **141** A1
Mundesley, England, U.K., **305** J2
Mundford, England, U.K., **305** H2
Mundo Novo, Brazil, **457** F3
Mundubbera, Australia, **135** L4
Mūndwa, India, **218** C4
Munera, Spain, **293** F3
Munfordville, U.S.A., **421** L7
Mungari, Mozambique, **369** F6
Mungaroa *see* Te Kaukau Point, New Zealand, **133** E5
Mungbere, Democratic Republic of the Congo, **369** E2
Mungeli, India, **219** E5
Munger, India, **219** F4
Mungguresak, Tanjong, *point*, Indonesia, **201** E2
Mungindi, Australia, **135** K4
Mungwi, Zambia, **369** F5
Munhango, Angola, **368** C5
Munhino, Angola, **368** B5
Munich *see* München, Germany, **288** E4, *239*
Munich, U.S.A., **420** D1
Munim, *river*, Brazil, **453** E4
Muniz Freire, Brazil, **457** F5
Munkedal, Sweden, **286** E3
Munkfors, Sweden, **286** F3
Munku-Sardyk, Gora, *mountain peak*, Mongolia/Russian Federation, **213** J2
Munnar, India, **216** D4
Munning, Point, Chatham Islands, New Zealand, **133** Q16
Muñoz Gamero, Península, Chile, **460** C4
Munsfjället, *mountain peak*, Sweden, **284** G4
Munster, Niedersachsen, Germany, **288** E2
Münster, Nordrhein-Westfalen, Germany, **288** C3
Munster, *province*, Ireland, **309** C5
Muntele Mare, *mountain peak*, Romania, **296** D2
Muntinglupa, Philippines, **204** C3
Muntok, Indonesia, **200** D3
Muodoslompolo, Sweden, **285** L3
Muojärvi, *lake*, Finland, **285** P4
Muong Het, Laos, **203** E1
Mu'ò'ng Tè, Vietnam, **203** D1
Muonio, Finland, **285** L3
Muping, China, **211** H5
Muqakoori, Somalia, **367** G4
Muqdisho (Mogadishu), Somalia, **367** G4, *339*
Muradiye, Turkey, **297** F6
Murādnagar, India, **218** D3
Murai Reservoir, Singapore, **200** J6
Murakami, Japan, **209** G3
Murallón, Cerro, *mountain peak*, Chile, **460** C3
Muramvya, Burundi, **369** E3
Muranga, Kenya, **369** G3
Murashi, Russian Federation, **300** F4
Murat, France, **291** F4
Murat, *river*, Turkey, **363** H1

Muratlı, Turkey, 297 F5
Murau, Austria, 289 G5
Muravera, Sardegna, Italy, 295 B6
Muraysah, Ra's al, point, Libya, 362 E2
Murchison, Mount, mountain peak, Antarctica, 470 F8
Murchison, river, Australia, 134 D4
Murcia, autonomous community, Spain, 293 G4, 253
Murcia, Spain, 293 G4
Murdo, U.S.A., 420 C4
Murdochville, Canada, 416 J5
Mureck, Austria, 289 G5
Mureş, river, Romania, 296 D2
Muret, France, 290 E5
Murewa, Zimbabwe, 371 F2
Murfreesboro, North Carolina, U.S.A., 426 B6
Murfreesboro, Tennessee, U.S.A., 425 J2
Murgeni, Romania, 296 G2
Murgha Kibzai, Pakistan, 218 B3
Murghob, Tajikistan, 223 J5
Murgon, Australia, 135 L4
Muria, Gunung, mountain peak, Indonesia, 201 E4
Muriaé, Brazil, 457 E5
Muriege, Angola, 368 D4
Murilo, island, Micronesia, 138 D4
Müritz, lake, Germany, 288 F2
Muriwai, New Zealand, 132 F4
Murjek, Sweden, 284 K3
Murmansk, Russian Federation, 285 R2
Murmanskaya Oblast', province, Russian Federation, 285 Q2
Murmashi, Russian Federation, 285 R2
Murole, Finland, 287 M2
Murom, Russian Federation, 298 F1
Murongo, Tanzania, 369 F3
Muroran, Japan, 209 H2
Muroto, Japan, 208 F4
Muroto-zaki, point, Japan, 208 F4
Murovani Kurylivtsi, Ukraine, 296 F1
Murphy, U.S.A., 425 K2
Murrat al Kubrā, Al Buḥayrat al, lake, Egypt, 225 B4
Murray, Iowa, U.S.A., 420 G5
Murray, Kentucky, U.S.A., 421 J7
Murray, Lake, Papua New Guinea, 140 A4
Murray, Lake, U.S.A., 425 M2
Murray, Mount, mountain peak, Canada, 412 E1
Murray, river, Australia, 135 J6, 112
Murray Bridge, Australia, 135 H6
Murray Fracture Zone, underwater feature, Pacific Ocean, 479 H3
Murray Hill, mountain peak, Christmas Island, 134 N8
Murraysburg, South Africa, 370 D5
Murrayville, U.S.A., 420 H6
Murro di Porco, Capo, cape, Sicilia, Italy, 295 E7
Murroogh, Ireland, 309 C4
Murrupula, Mozambique, 369 G6
Murska Sobota, Slovenia, 294 F2
Murtle Lake, Canada, 412 K5
Murtovaara, Finland, 285 P4
Murud, Gunung, mountain peak, Malaysia, 201 F2
Murud, India, 216 C2
Murupara, New Zealand, 132 F4
Mururoa, island, French Polynesia, 137 H3, 97, 122
Murwāra, India, 218 E5
Murwillumbah, Australia, 135 L4
Murygino, Russian Federation, 299 D5
Murzuq, Libya, 362 B3
Murzuq, Ṣaḥrā', desert, Libya, 362 B4
Mürzzuschlag, Austria, 289 G5
Muş, Turkey, 224 F5
Mūsā, Jabal (Mount Sinai), mountain peak, Egypt, 225 B5, 355
Mūša, river, Lithuania, 287 L4
Musa Ālī Terara, Ethiopia, 220 D6
Musa Ālī Terara, mountain peak, Ethiopia, 367 F2
Mūsa Khel Bāzār, Pakistan, 218 B3
Mūsá Qal'eh, Afghanistan, 218 A2
Musadi, Democratic Republic of the Congo, 368 D3
Musala, mountain peak, Bulgaria, 296 D4, 264
Musala, Pulau, island, Indonesia, 200 B2
Musan, North Korea, 208 E2
Muscat see Masqaṭ, Oman, 221 G4, 175
Musgrave Harbour, Canada, 417 Q5
Musgrave Ranges, mountain range, Australia, 134 G4, 112
Musgravetown, Canada, 417 Q5
Musheramore, mountain peak, Ireland, 309 D5
Mushie, Democratic Republic of the Congo, 368 C3
Mushu, island, Papua New Guinea, 140 A3
Musi, river, Indonesia, 200 D3
Muskeg, river, Canada, 412 H1
Muskegon, river, U.S.A., 421 L4
Muskegon, U.S.A., 421 K4
Muskogee, U.S.A., 424 E2
Muskrat Dam, Canada, 414 J5
Muskwa, river, Canada, 412 H2
Muslimīyah, Syria, 225 D1
Musoma, Tanzania, 369 F3
Musombe, Tanzania, 369 F4
Musquaro, Lac, lake, Canada, 417 L4
Musquodoboit Harbour, Canada, 417 K7
Mussau Island, Papua New Guinea, 140 C3
Musselburgh, Scotland, U.K., 308 F5
Musselshell, U.S.A., 419 K3
Mussende, Angola, 368 C5
Mussidan, France, 290 E4
Musswellbrook, Australia, 135 L5
Mustafakemalpaşa, river, Turkey, 297 G6
Mustafakemalpaşa, Turkey, 297 G6
Mustahīl, Ethiopia, 367 F3
Musters, Lago, lake, Argentina, 460 D2
Mustjala, Estonia, 287 L3
Mustla, Estonia, 287 M3
Mustvee, Estonia, 287 N3
Muszyna, Poland, 289 K4
Mūṭ, Egypt, 362 E3
Mut, Turkey, 225 B1
Mutalau, Niue, 132 M13
Mutare, Zimbabwe, 371 F2
Mutis, Gunung, mountain peak, Indonesia, 198 D5
Mutoko, Zimbabwe, 371 F2
Mutorashanga, Zimbabwe, 369 F6
Mutshatsha, Democratic Republic of the Congo, 368 D5
Mutsu, Japan, 209 H2
Mutton Bay, Canada, 417 M4
Mutton Bird Island, Lord Howe Island, Australia, 135 U14
Muttonbird (Titi) Islands, New Zealand, 133 A8
Muttukūru, India, 216 E3
Mutuali, Mozambique, 369 G5
Mutum, Brazil, 455 G2
Mutum Biyu, Nigeria, 365 G3
Mutunópolis, Brazil, 456 D3
Mutur, Sri Lanka, 217 E4
Muurasjärvi, Finland, 285 M5
Muurola, Finland, 285 M3
Muxaluando, Angola, 368 B4
Muxima, Angola, 368 B4
Muyezerskiy, Russian Federation, 285 R5
Muyinga, Burundi, 369 F3
Muyumba, Democratic Republic of the Congo, 369 E4
Muzaffargarh, Pakistan, 218 B3
Muzaffarnagar, India, 218 D3
Muzaffarpur, India, 219 F4
Muzillac, France, 290 C3
Muztag, China, 219 F1
Muztag, mountain peak, China, 212 E5
Muztagata, mountain peak, China, 212 B5
Mvangan, Cameroon, 368 B2
Mvolo, Sudan, 369 E1
Mvomero, Tanzania, 369 G4
Mvouti, Congo, 368 B3
Mvuma, Zimbabwe, 371 F2
Mwali (Mohéli), island, Comoros, 372 A3, 352
Mwanza, administrative region, Tanzania, 369 F3
Mwanza, Democratic Republic of the Congo, 369 E4
Mwanza, Tanzania, 369 F3
Mweelrea, mountain peak, Ireland, 309 C4
Mweka, Democratic Republic of the Congo, 368 D3
Mwenda, Zambia, 369 E5
Mwene-Ditu, Democratic Republic of the Congo, 368 D4
Mwenezi, Zimbabwe, 371 F3
Mwenga, Democratic Republic of the Congo, 369 E3
Mweru, Lake, Democratic Republic of the Congo/Tanzania, 369 E4, 334
Mwimba, Democratic Republic of the Congo, 368 D4
Mwinilunga, Zambia, 368 D5
Mỹ Tho, Vietnam, 203 E4
Myadzyel, Belarus, 287 N5
Myagostrov, Ostrov, island, Russian Federation, 285 T4
Myājlār, India, 218 B4
Myakka City, U.S.A., 425 L6
Myaksa, Russian Federation, 299 G3
Myanmar (Burma), country, Asia, 197 L7, 73, 89, 144, 157, 158, 170, 171, 184
Myaungmya, Myanmar, 205 B4
Mybster, Scotland, U.K., 308 F2
Myckelgensjö, Sweden, 284 H5
Myingyan, Myanmar, 205 B3
Myinmoletkat Taung, mountain peak, Myanmar, 202 C3
Myitkyinā, Myanmar, 205 C2
Myittha, Myanmar, 205 C3
Mykolayiv, Ukraine, 298 D3
Mykolayivs'ka Oblast', province, Ukraine, 296 H2
Mykonos, island, Kyklades, Greece, 297 E7
Mykonos, Kyklades, Greece, 297 E7
Myla, Russian Federation, 213 J2
Mymensingh, Bangladesh, 214 D4
Mynämäki, Finland, 287 K2
Mynaral, Kazakhstan, 212 B3
Myohaung, Myanmar, 205 B3
Myory, Belarus, 287 N5
Myotha, Myanmar, 205 B3
Mýrdalsjökull, ice cap, Iceland, 284 Y7
Myre, Norway, 284 G2
Myrheden, Sweden, 284 K4
Mýri, Iceland, 284 Y7
Myrina, Greece, 297 E6
Myrtle Beach, U.S.A., 425 N3
Myrtle Creek, U.S.A., 418 C5
Myrtle Point, U.S.A., 418 B5
Myrtou, Cyprus, 225 B2
Myrviken, Sweden, 284 G5
Mysen, Norway, 286 E3
Myshkin, Russian Federation, 299 G4
Myślenice, Poland, 289 J4
Myślibórz, Poland, 289 G2
Mysore, India, 216 D3
Mytilini, Greece, 297 F6
Mytishchi, Russian Federation, 299 F5
Mzimba, Malawi, 369 F5
Mzuzu, Malawi, 369 F5


## N


Nà Hang, Vietnam, 203 E1
Na-lang, Myanmar, 205 C3
Naalehu, Hawaiian Islands, U.S.A., 422 R10
Naama, Algeria, 361 F2
Naantali, Finland, 287 L2
Naarva, Finland, 285 Q5
Naas, Ireland, 309 F4
Naasa, Finland, 284 K5
Nababiep, South Africa, 370 C4
Nabas, Philippines, 204 C4
Naberera, Tanzania, 369 G3
Naberezhnyye Chelny, Russian Federation, 222 E1
Nābha, India, 218 D3
Nabī Shu'ayb, Jabal an, mountain peak, Yemen, 220 D5
Nabileque, river, Brazil, 456 B5
Nabire, Indonesia, 199 F3
Nabolo, Ghana, 364 D2
Nabouwalu, Fiji, 141 A4
Nabq, Egypt, 225 C5
Nabua, Philippines, 204 C3
Nābul, Tunisia, 362 B1
Nābulus, West Bank, 225 C3
Nacala, Mozambique, 372 A3
Nacaome, Honduras, 428 D4
Nacaroa, Mozambique, 369 G5
Nachen, China, 206 B4
Nachingwea, Tanzania, 369 G5
Nāchna, India, 218 B4
Náchod, Czech Republic, 289 H3
Nachuge, Andaman and Nicobar Islands, India, 217 H4
Nacogdoches, U.S.A., 424 E4
Nacozari de García, Mexico, 430 C2
Nadi, Fiji, 141 A4
Nădlac, Romania, 296 C2
Nador, Morocco, 361 F1
Nadporozh'ye, Russian Federation, 299 G3
Nadvirna, Ukraine, 296 E1
Nadvoitsy, Russian Federation, 285 S5
Nadym, Russian Federation, 300 J3
Nærbø, Norway, 286 B3
Næstved, Denmark, 286 E5
Nafpaktos, Greece, 297 C6
Nafplio, Greece, 297 D7
Nafūsah, Jabal, mountain range, Libya, 362 B2
Naga, Philippines, 204 C3
Nagaj, India, 216 C2
Nāgāland, state, India, 219 H4, 169
Nagano, Japan, 209 G3
Nagaoka, Japan, 209 G3
Nagaon, India, 219 H4
Nagar, India, 218 D4
Nagarjuna Sāgar, reservoir, India, 216 D2
Nagasaki, Japan, 208 E4, 96, 165
Nāgaur, India, 218 C4
Nagda, India, 218 C5
Nāgercoil, India, 216 D4
Naggen, Sweden, 286 H1
Nagichot, Sudan, 369 F2
Nagīna, India, 218 D3
Nagles Mountains, Ireland, 309 D5
Nago, Japan, 209 P8
Nāgod, India, 218 E4
Nagorno-Karabakh, autonomous region, Azerbaijan, 222 D5, 189
Nagor'ye, Russian Federation, 299 G4
Nagoya, Japan, 209 G4
Nāgpur, India, 218 D5
Nagqu, China, 214 E3
Nagyatád, Hungary, 289 H5
Nagyhalász, Hungary, 289 K4
Nagykálló, Hungary, 289 K5
Nagykanizsa, Hungary, 289 H5
Nagykáta, Hungary, 289 J5
Nagykőrös, Hungary, 296 B2
Nagza, China, 213 H5
Naha, Japan, 209 N8
Nahariyya, Israel, 225 C3
Nahe, river, Germany, 288 C4
N'Ahnet, Adrar, mountain range, Algeria, 361 G3
Nahrīn, Afghanistan, 218 B1
Nahuel Huapi, Lago, lake, Argentina, 460 C1
Nahuo, China, 206 B4
Naica, Mexico, 430 D3
Naidăş, Romania, 296 C3
Naij Tal, China, 214 E2
Naila, Germany, 288 E3
Nailsworth, England, U.K., 304 E3
Naiman Qi, China, 211 H4
Nain, Canada, 411 N4
Nā'īn, Iran, 220 F2
Nainpur, India, 218 E5
Nainwa, India, 218 C4
Naiopué, Mozambique, 369 G6
Nairai, island, Fiji, 141 A4
Nairn, Scotland, U.K., 308 F3
Nairobi, Kenya, 369 G3, 340, 341
Naissaar, island, Estonia, 287 M3
Naivasha, Kenya, 369 G3
Naj' Ḥammādī, Egypt, 363 F3
Najac, France, 290 F4
Najafābād, Iran, 220 F2
Nájera, Spain, 293 F1
Najībābād, India, 218 D3
Najin, North Korea, 208 E2
N'Ajjer, Tassili, plateau, Algeria, 361 H3
Najrān, Saudi Arabia, 363 H5
Naju, South Korea, 208 D4
Nakasongola, Uganda, 369 F2
Nakatsugawa, Japan, 209 G4
Nakfa, Eritrea, 220 C5
Nakhodka, Russian Federation, 211 L4
Nakhon Nayok, Thailand, 202 D3
Nakhon Phanom, Thailand, 203 E2
Nakhon Ratchasima (Khorat), Thailand, 202 D3, 144, 155
Nakhon Sawan, Thailand, 202 D3
Nakhon Si Thammarat, Thailand, 202 C4
Nakhtarāna, India, 218 B5
Nakina, British Columbia, Canada, 412 C2
Nakina, Ontario, Canada, 415 L6
Nakło nad Notecią, Poland, 289 H2
Nakodar, India, 218 C3
Nakonde, Zambia, 369 F4
Nakskov, Denmark, 286 E5
Näkten, lake, Sweden, 286 G1
Nakuru, Kenya, 369 G3
Nakusp, Canada, 413 L6
Nāl, Pakistan, 218 A4
Nalao, China, 215 H4
Nalayh, Mongolia, 210 D3
Nal'chik, Russian Federation, 222 C4
Naliya, India, 218 B5
Näljänkä, Finland, 285 P4
Nālūt, Libya, 362 B2
Nam Co, lake, China, 214 D3
Nam Định, Vietnam, 203 E1
Nam Ngum Reservoir, Laos, 203 D2
Nam Pawn, river, Myanmar, 205 C4
Nam Phong, Thailand, 203 D2
Namacunde, Angola, 368 C6
Namacurra, Mozambique, 371 G2
Namai, Nepal, 219 E4
Namak, Daryācheh-ye, lake, Iran, 220 F2
Nāmakkal, India, 216 D4
Namanga, Kenya, 369 G3
Namapa, Mozambique, 369 G5
Namatanai, Papua New Guinea, 140 D3
Namber, Indonesia, 199 F3
Nambiquara, Brazil, 455 G3
Nambour, Australia, 135 L4
Nambucca Heads, Australia, 135 L5

Nāmche Bāzār, Nepal, **219** F4
Namdalen, *valley*, Norway, **284** F4
Namib, *desert*, Namibia, **357** G8, *350, 351*
Namibe, Angola, **368** B6
Namibe, *province*, Angola, **368** B6
Namibia, *country*, Africa, **359** G9, *81, 87, 312, 313, 335, 344, 347, 349, 350, 351*
Namidobe, Mozambique, **371** G2
Namlan, Myanmar, **205** C3
Namlea, Indonesia, **198** D3
Namling, China, **214** D3
Namoi, *river*, Australia, **135** K5
Namoluk, *island*, Micronesia, **138** D4
Namonuito, *island*, Micronesia, **138** D4
Namorik, *island*, Marshall Islands, **138** E4
Nampa, U.S.A., **418** F5
Nampala, Mali, **364** C1
Namp'o, North Korea, **208** D3
Nampula, Mozambique, **369** G6
Nampula, *province*, Mozambique, **369** G6
Namsang, Myanmar, **205** C3
Namsen, *river*, Norway, **284** F4
Namsos, Norway, **284** E4
Namsskogan, Norway, **284** F4
Namtu, Myanmar, **205** C3
Namuka-i-lau, *island*, Fiji, **141** A4
Namuli, *mountain peak*, Mozambique, **369** G6
Namuno, Mozambique, **369** G5
Namur, Belgium, **288** B3
Namur, *province*, Belgium, **288** B3
Namutoni, Namibia, **370** C2
Namwala, Zambia, **369** E6
Namwon, South Korea, **208** D4
Namya Ra, Myanmar, **205** C2
Namysłów, Poland, **289** H3
Nan, Mae Nam, *river*, Thailand, **202** D2
Nan, *river*, China, **206** B2, *155*
Nan, Thailand, **202** D2
Nan Xian, China, **206** C2
Nana-Grébizi, Central African Republic, **366** A3
Nana-Mambéré, *prefecture*, Central African Republic, **368** B1
Nanaimo, Canada, **412** H7
Nanam, North Korea, **208** E2
Nan'an, China, **206** D3
Nanao, Japan, **209** G3
Nanbaxian, China, **213** G5
Nanbu, China, **215** H3
Nancha, China, **211** K3
Nanchang, China, **206** C2, *161*
Nancheng, China, **206** D3
Nanchong, China, **215** H3
Nanchuan, China, **215** H3
Nancy, France, **291** H2
Nanda Devi, *mountain peak*, India, **218** D3
Nandan, China, **215** H4
Nānded, India, **216** D2
Nandurbār, India, **218** C5
Nandyāl, India, **216** D3
Nanfen, China, **211** H4
Nanfeng, China, **206** D3
Nang Xian, China, **214** E3
Nanga Eboko, Cameroon, **368** B2
Nanga Parbat, *mountain peak*, Pakistan, **218** C2, *173*
Nangang, China, **207** B2
Nangapinoh, Indonesia, **201** E3
Nangatayap, Indonesia, **201** E3
Nangong, China, **210** F5
Nangqên, China, **215** F2
Nangulangwa, Tanzania, **369** G4
Nanhua, China, **215** G4
Nanhui, China, **206** E2
Nanjangūd, India, **216** D3
Nanjiang, China, **215** H2
Nanjing, China, **206** D1, *95, 159, 161*
Nankang, China, **206** C3
Nankova, Angola, **368** C6
Nanlang, China, **207** B3
Nanle, China, **206** C1
Nanling, China, **206** D2
Nanliu, *river*, China, **206** B4
Nanning, China, **206** B4, *161*
Nanortalik, Greenland, **411** Q3
Nanpiao, China, **211** H4
Nanping, Fujian, China, **206** D3
Nanping, Guangdong, China, **207** A4
Nanping, Sichuan, China, **215** H2
Nanri Dao, *island*, China, **206** D3
Nansei-shotō (Ryukyu Islands), *islands*, Japan, **209** N8, *165*
Nansen Sound, Canada, **411** K1
Nansha, China, **207** B3
Nanshankou, China, **213** G4
Nansio, Tanzania, **369** F3
Nantais, Lac, *lake*, Canada, **415** S1
Nantes, France, **290** D3, *245*
Nanton, Canada, **413** N6
Nantong, south of Rudong, Jiangsu, China, **206** E1
Nantong, southwest of Rudong, Jiangsu, China, **206** E1
Nantou, China, **207** B3
Nantucket, U.S.A., **426** E4
Nantucket Island, U.S.A., **426** E4
Nantwich, England, U.K., **304** E1
Nant-y-moch Reservoir, *reservoir*, Wales, U.K., **304** C2
Nanuku Passage, *strait*, Fiji, **141** A4
Nanumanga, *island*, Tuvalu, **139** F5, *113*
Nanumea, *island*, Tuvalu, **139** F5, *113*
Nanuque, Brazil, **457** F4
Nanutarra Roadhouse, Australia, **134** D3
Nanxi, China, **215** H3
Nanxiong, China, **206** C3
Nanyang, China, **206** C1
Nanyuki, Kenya, **367** E5
Nanzhang, China, **206** B2
Nanzhao, China, **206** C1
Nao, Cabo de la, *cape*, Spain, **293** H3
Naodahan, China, **211** J1
Naogaon, Bangladesh, **214** D4
Naoné, Vanuatu, **141** A2
Napa, U.S.A., **422** B2
Napanee, Canada, **416** C7
Napier, New Zealand, **132** F4, *110*
Napier Broome Bay, Australia, **134** F1
Naples, Florida, U.S.A., **425** M6
Naples, Idaho, U.S.A., **418** F2
Naples *see* Napoli, Italy, **295** E5, *254, 255*
Napo, China, **215** H5
Napo, *river*, Ecuador/Peru, **450** C4
Napoleon, North Dakota, U.S.A., **420** D2
Napoleon, Ohio, U.S.A., **421** L5
Napoli, Golfo di, *gulf*, Italy, **295** E5
Napoli (Naples), Italy, **295** E5, *254, 255*
Napuka, *island*, French Polynesia, **137** G2
Nara, Japan, **209** F4, *165*
Nara, Mali, **364** C1
Narach, Vozyera, *lake*, Belarus, **287** N5
Narach, Belarus, **287** N5
Naracoorte, Australia, **135** J6
Narāinpur, India, **219** E6
Naran Bulag, China, **210** F3
Naranjal, Ecuador, **450** B5
Naranjo, Mexico, **430** C3
Naranjos, Mexico, **431** F4
Narasannapeta, India, **217** F2
Narasapur, India, **217** E2
Narasun, Russian Federation, **210** F2
Narathiwat, Thailand, **202** D5
Narberth, Wales, U.K., **304** C3
Narbonne, France, **291** F5
Narborough, England, U.K., **305** H2
Narbuvollen, Norway, **286** E1
Narcea, *river*, Spain, **292** D1
Naré, Argentina, **458** E4
Nares Land, *island*, Greenland, **411** P1
Nares Plain, *underwater feature*, Atlantic Ocean, **477** C4
Nares Strait, Canada/Greenland, **411** M2
Narew, *river*, Poland, **289** L2
Nargund, India, **216** C3
Narhamcha, Sebkha, *salt-pan*, Mauritania, **360** C5
Nāri, *river*, Pakistan, **218** B3
Narib, Namibia, **370** C3
Narimanov, Russian Federation, **222** D3
Narin, *river*, China, **213** G5
Nariz, Pico, *mountain peak*, Chile, **460** C4
Nārkanda, India, **218** D3
Narkatiāganj, India, **219** F4
Narmada, *river*, India, **218** C5
Narni, Italy, **295** D4
Naro-Fominsk, Russian Federation, **299** F5
Narok, Kenya, **369** G3
Narooma, Australia, **135** L6
Närpes, Finland, **287** K1
Narrabri, Australia, **135** K5
Narrandera, Australia, **135** K5
Narrogin, Australia, **134** D5
Narromine, Australia, **135** K5
Narrows, U.S.A., **421** N7
Narsarsuaq, Greenland, **411** Q3, *389*
Narsimhapur, India, **218** D5
Narsinghdi, Bangladesh, **214** D5
Narsinghgarh, India, **218** D5
Nart, China, **210** F4
Nart, Mongolia, **210** D2
Narva, Estonia, **287** P3
Narva, Russian Federation, **223** N1
Narva Laht, *bay*, Estonia/Russian Federation, **287** N3
Narvacan, Philippines, **204** C2
Narvik, Norway, **284** H2
Nar'yan Mar, Russian Federation, **300** G3
Naryn, Kyrgyzstan, **223** K4
Naryn, *river*, Kyrgyzstan, **212** B4
Naryn, Russian Federation, **213** G2
Naryn Qum, *desert*, Kazakhstan, **222** D3
Narynqol, Kazakhstan, **223** L4
Näsåker, Sweden, **284** H5
Nasau, Fiji, **141** A4
Năsăud, Romania, **296** E2
Nasawa, Vanuatu, **141** A2
Naschitti, U.S.A., **423** J3
Nashoba, U.S.A., **424** E2
Nashua, U.S.A., **426** E3
Nashville, Illinois, U.S.A., **421** J6
Nashville, Tennessee, U.S.A., **425** J1, *386*
Nashwauk, U.S.A., **420** G2
Našice, Croatia, **294** G3
Nāsik, India, **218** C5
Nāṣir, Sudan, **366** D3
Naskaupi, *river*, Canada, **417** K2
Nasondoye, Democratic Republic of the Congo, **368** E5
Nasorolevu, *mountain peak*, Fiji, **141** A4
Nāsriganj, India, **219** F4
Nass, *river*, Canada, **412** E4
Nassarawa, Nigeria, **365** F3
Nassau, Bahamas, **428** F1, *392*
Nassau, Bahía, *bay*, Chile, **460** D5
Nassau, *island*, Cook Islands, **139** H6
Nasser, Lake, Egypt, **363** F4, *317*
Nässjö, Sweden, **286** G4
Nastapoca, *river*, Canada, **415** S3
Nastapoka Islands, Canada, **415** R3
Nasugbu, Philippines, **204** C3
Nasva, Russian Federation, **299** C4
Nata, Botswana, **371** E3
Nata, Tanzania, **369** F3
Natagaima, Colombia, **450** C3
Natal, Brazil, **453** G4
Natal, Indonesia, **200** B2
Natal Basin, *underwater feature*, Indian Ocean, **476** B6
Natalia, U.S.A., **424** C5
Naṭanz, Iran, **220** F2
Natashquan, Canada, **417** K4
Natashquan, *river*, Canada, **417** L4
Natchez, U.S.A., **424** G4
Natchitoches, U.S.A., **424** F4
Natewa Bay, Fiji, **141** A4
National Capital District, *province*, Papua New Guinea, **140** B5
Natitingou, Benin, **364** E2
Natividade, Brazil, **456** D3
Natoma, U.S.A., **420** D6
Nátora, Mexico, **430** C2
Natron, Lake, Tanzania, **369** G3, *342*
Nattam, India, **216** D4
Nattaung, *mountain peak*, Myanmar, **205** C4
Nattavaara, Sweden, **284** K3
Natuna Besar, Pulau, *island*, Indonesia, **201** D1
Naucelle, France, **290** F4
Nauchas, Namibia, **370** C3
Nauen, Germany, **288** F2
Naujan, Lake, Philippines, **204** C3
Naulila, Angola, **368** B6
Naumburg, Germany, **288** E3
Nā'ūr, Jordan, **225** C4
Naurskaya, Russian Federation, **222** D4
Nauru, *country*, Pacific Ocean, **131** F2, *108, 119, 120*
Nauru, *island*, Pacific Ocean, **138** E5, *119*
Nāushahra, India, **218** C2
Naushahro Fīroz, Pakistan, **218** B4
Naustdal, Norway, **286** B2
Nauta, Peru, **450** D5
Nautla, Mexico, **431** F4
Nautsi, Russian Federation, **285** P2
Navahermosa, Spain, **292** E3
Navahrudak, Belarus, **289** M2
Navajo, U.S.A., **423** J4
Navajo Reservoir, U.S.A., **423** K3
Naval, Philippines, **204** D4
Navalmoral de la Mata, Spain, **292** E3
Navalvillar de Pela, Spain, **292** E3
Navan, Ireland, **309** F4
Navapolatsk, Belarus, **299** B5
Navarin, Mys, *cape*, Russian Federation, **410** A3
Navarino, Isla, *island*, Chile, **460** D5
Navarra, *autonomous community*, Spain, **293** G1, *252, 253*
Navasota, *river*, U.S.A., **424** D4
Navassa Island, *U.S. territory*, Caribbean Sea, **429** G3, *378, 386, 390*
Naver, Loch, *lake*, Scotland, U.K., **308** E2
Naver, *river*, Scotland, U.K., **308** E2
Navesti, *river*, Estonia, **287** M3
Navia, *river*, Spain, **292** D1
Navia, Spain, **292** D1
Navidad, Chile, **458** B4
Naviti, *island*, Fiji, **141** A4
Năvodari, Romania, **296** G3
Navojoa, Mexico, **430** C3
Navsāri, India, **218** C5
Navua, Fiji, **141** A4
Nawá, Syria, **225** D3
Nawabganj, Bangladesh, **214** D4
Nawābshāh, Pakistan, **218** B4
Nawāda, India, **219** F4
Nāwah, Afghanistan, **218** A2
Nawalgarh, India, **218** C4
Nawāpāra, India, **219** E5
Nawoiy, Uzbekistan, **222** H4
Naws, Ra's, *cape*, Oman, **221** G5
Naxçıvan, *autonomous state*, Azerbaijan, **222** D5, *189*
Naxçıvan, Azerbaijan, **222** D5
Naxos, *island*, Kyklades, Greece, **297** E7
Naxos, Kyklades, Greece, **297** E7
Nāy Band, E. Iran, **221** G2
Nāy Band, Kūh-e, *mountain peak*, Iran, **221** G2
Nāy Band, S. Iran, **220** F3
Naya, Colombia, **450** C3
Naya Chor, Pakistan, **218** B4
Nayar, Mexico, **430** D4
Nayarit, *state*, Mexico, **430** D4
Nayau, *island*, Fiji, **141** A4
Nayoro, Japan, **209** H1
Nāyudupeta, India, **216** D3
Nazaré, Bahia, Brazil, **457** F3
Nazaré, Pará, Brazil, **452** C5
Nazaré, Portugal, **292** C3
Nazareth *see* Naẕerat, Israel, **225** C3
Nazarovo, Russian Federation, **223** N1
Nazca, Peru, **454** C4
Nazca Ridge, *underwater feature*, Pacific Ocean, **479** N6, *22*
Naze, The, *point*, England, U.K., **305** J3
Naẕerat (Nazareth), Israel, **225** C3
Nazilli, Turkey, **297** G7
Naziya, Russian Federation, **299** C3
Nazko, Canada, **412** H5
Nazko, *river*, Canada, **412** H5
Nazran', Russian Federation, **222** D4
Nazrēt, Ethiopia, **367** E3
Nazyvayevsk, Russian Federation, **223** J1
Nchelenge, Zambia, **369** E4
Ncojane, Botswana, **370** D3
Ncue, Equatorial Guinea, **368** B2
N'dalatando, Angola, **368** B4
Ndali, Benin, **365** E3
Ndélé, Central African Republic, **366** B3
Ndélélé, Cameroon, **368** B2
Ndendé, Gabon, **368** B3
Ndjamena, Chad, **365** H2, *328*
Ndji, *river*, Central African Republic, **366** B3
Ndjolé, Gabon, **368** B3
Ndjounou, Gabon, **368** B3
Ndola, Zambia, **369** E5
Nduye, Democratic Republic of the Congo, **369** E2
Nea Alikarnassos, Kriti, Greece, **297** E8
Nea Anchialos, Greece, **297** D6
Nea Artaki, Greece, **297** D6
Nea Makri, Greece, **297** D6
Nea Moudania, Greece, **297** D5
Nea Zichni, Greece, **297** D5
Neagh, Lough, *lake*, Northern Ireland, U.K., **309** F3
Neah Bay, U.S.A., **418** B2
Neale, Lake, Australia, **134** G3
Neapoli, Kriti, Greece, **297** E8
Neapoli, Peloponnisos, Greece, **297** D7
Near Islands, U.S.A., **301** U4
Neath, *river*, Wales, U.K., **304** D3
Neath, Wales, U.K., **304** D3
Neath Port Talbot, Wales, U.K., **304** D3
Nebbi, Uganda, **369** F2
Nebbou, Burkina Faso, **364** D2
Nebe, Indonesia, **198** C5
Nebitdag, Turkmenistan, **222** E5
Neblina, Pico da, *mountain peak*, Brazil, **451** E4, *439*
Nebolchi, Russian Federation, **299** D3
Nebraska, *state*, U.S.A., **420** D5, *386*
Nebraska City, U.S.A., **420** F5
Nebrodi, Monti, *mountain range*, Sicilia, Italy, **295** E7
Nechi, *river*, Colombia, **450** C2
Necker, *island*, Hawaiian Islands, U.S.A., **139** H2
Necochea, Argentina, **459** E6

Necton, England, U.K., **305** H2
Nedas, *river*, Greece, **297** C7
Nédéley, Chad, **366** A1
Nêdong, China, **214** D3
Nedstrand, Norway, **286** B3
Nedumangād, India, **216** D4
Needham Market, England, U.K., **305** J2
Needles, Canada, **413** K7
Needles, The, *point*, England, U.K., **305** F4
Needles, U.S.A., **422** F4
Neegro, Qooriga, *bay*, Somalia, **367** G3
Neepawa, Canada, **414** E6
Neftçala, Azerbaijan, **222** D5
Neftekamsk, Russian Federation, **222** E1
Nefyn, Wales, U.K., **304** C2
Negage, Angola, **368** C4
Négala, Mali, **364** C2
Negara, Indonesia, **201** F5
Negēlē, Ethiopia, **367** E3
Negeri Sembilan, *state*, Malaysia, **200** C2
Negomane, Mozambique, **369** G5
Negombo, Sri Lanka, **216** D5
Negotin, Serbia, **296** D3
Negra, Cordillera, *mountain range*, Peru, **454** B2
Negra, Punta, *point*, Peru, **454** B1
Negreni, Romania, **296** E3
Negreşti, Romania, **296** F2
Negreşti-Oaş, Romania, **296** D2
Negritos, Peru, **454** B1
Negro, *river*, Amazonas, Brazil, **451** G5
Negro, *river*, Bolivia, **455** F4
Negro, *river*, Choco, Argentina, **459** E3
Negro, *river*, Mato Grosso do Sul, Brazil, **456** B5
Negro, *river*, Paraguay, **459** E2
Negro, *river*, Río Negro, Argentina, **460** D1
Negro, *river*, Uruguay, **459** F4, *444*
Negros, *island*, Philippines, **204** C4, *149*
Negru Vodă, Romania, **296** G4
Neguac, Canada, **416** J6
Nehbandān, Iran, **221** H2
Nehe, China, **211** J2
Nehoiu, Romania, **296** F3
Nehone, Angola, **368** C6
Nei Mongol Gaoyuan, *plateau*, China, **213** J4
Nei Mongol Zizhiqu (Inner Mongolia), *autonomous region*, China, **210** F4, *158, 161*
Neiafu, Vava'u Group, Tonga, **141** B3
Neiba, Dominican Republic, **429** H3
Neiden, Norway, **285** P2
Neiges, Piton des, *mountain peak*, Réunion, **373** A1, *354*
Neihart, U.S.A., **419** J3
Neijiang, China, **215** H3
Neilingding Dao, *island*, China, **207** B4
Neiße, *river*, Germany, **289** G3
Neiva, Colombia, **450** C3
Neixiang, China, **206** B1
Nejanilini Lake, Canada, **414** F2
Nek'emtē, Ethiopia, **367** E3
Nekoma, U.S.A., **420** D1
Neksø, Denmark, **286** G5
Nelidovo, Russian Federation, **299** D4
Neligh, U.S.A., **420** D4
Nellore, India, **216** E3
Nelson, Canada, **413** L7
Nelson, Cape, Papua New Guinea, **140** C5
Nelson, England, U.K., **306** F4
Nelson, Estrecho, *strait*, Chile, **460** B4
Nelson, New Zealand, **133** D5
Nelson, *river*, Canada, **414** G3
Nelson House, Canada, **414** E4
Nelspruit, South Africa, **371** F4
Nelyan Point, Philippines, **204** B4
Néma, Mauritania, **364** C1
Neman, Russian Federation, **287** L5
Nembe, Nigeria, **365** F4
Nembrala, Indonesia, **198** C5
Nemea, Greece, **297** D7
Nemegos, Canada, **421** M2
Nemenùinë, Lithuania, **287** M5
Nemor, *river*, China, **211** J2
Nemunas, *river*, Lithuania, **287** L5
Nemuro, Japan, **209** J2
Nemyriv, Ukraine, **289** L3
Nen, *river*, China, **211** J2
Nenagh, Ireland, **309** D5
Nendo, *island*, Solomon Islands, **138** E6
Nene, *river*, England, U.K., **305** G2
Nenjiang, China, **211** J2
Nenthead, England, U.K., **306** F3
Neo Karlovasi, Dodekanisos, Greece, **297** F7
Neola, U.S.A., **423** H1
Neos Marmaras, Greece, **297** D5
Neosho, *river*, U.S.A., **420** F7
Neosho, U.S.A., **420** F7
Nepal, *country*, Asia, **196** K7, *30, 144, 158, 171, 172*
Nepālganj, Nepal, **219** E3
Nepean Island, Norfolk Island, **135** T13
Nepeña, Peru, **454** B2
Nephi, U.S.A., **423** H2
Nephin, *mountain peak*, Ireland, **309** C3
Nephin Beg Range, *mountain range*, Ireland, **309** C3
Nepisiguit, *river*, Canada, **416** H6
Nepomuk, Czech Republic, **288** F4
Nérac, France, **290** E4
Nerang, Australia, **135** L4
Nerchinsk, Russian Federation, **210** G1
Nereta, Latvia, **287** M4
Nereto, Italy, **294** D4
Neriquinha, Angola, **368** D6
Neris, *river*, Lithuania, **287** M5
Nerja, Spain, **293** F4
Nerl', *river*, Russian Federation, **299** F4
Nerópolis, Brazil, **456** D4
Neryungri, Russian Federation, **301** P4
Nesbyen, Norway, **286** D2
Nesebŭr, Bulgaria, **296** F4
Nesflaten, Norway, **286** C3
Nesjøen, *lake*, Norway, **284** E5
Nesna, Norway, **284** F3
Ness, Loch, *lake*, Scotland, U.K., **308** E3, *276*
Ness City, U.S.A., **420** D6
Nesseby, Norway, **285** P1
Nesterov, Russian Federation, **287** L5
Netanya, Israel, **225** C3
Netherlands, *country*, Europe, **282** E5, *79, 80, 93, 95, 228, 238, 240, 241, 242, 243, 245, 249, 252, 387, 389, 391, 434, 439*
Netherlands Antilles, *Netherlands autonomous region*, Caribbean Sea, **448** F2, *240, 241, 378, 387, 391*
Neto, *river*, Italy, **295** F6
Nettilling Lake, Canada, **411** M3
Neubrandenburg, Germany, **288** F2
Neubukow, Germany, **288** E1
Neuchâtel, Lac de, *lake*, Switzerland, **291** H3, *247*
Neuchâtel, Switzerland, **291** H3
Neuenhagen bei Berlin, Germany, **289** F2
Neufchâteau, France, **291** G2
Neufchâtel-en-Bray, France, **290** E2
Neumünster, Germany, **288** D1
Neung-sur-Beuvron, France, **290** E3
Neunkirchen, Germany, **288** C4
Neuquén, Argentina, **460** D1
Neuquén, *province*, Argentina, **460** C1
Neuquén, *river*, Argentina, **458** C5
Neuruppin, Germany, **288** F2
Neusiedler See, *lake*, Austria, **289** H5
Neuss, Germany, **288** C3
Neustadt am Rübenberge, Germany, **288** D2
Neustadt in Holstein, Germany, **288** E1
Neustrelitz, Germany, **288** F2
Neuville-lès-Dieppe, France, **305** J5
Neuwied, Germany, **288** C3
Nevşehir, Turkey, **363** F1
Neva, *river*, Russian Federation, **299** C3, *273*
Nevada, Cerro, *mountain peak*, Argentina, **458** C5
Nevada, Sierra, *mountain peak*, Argentina, **458** C3, *376*
Nevada, Sierra, *mountain range*, Spain, **293** F4, *253*
Nevada, Sierra, *mountain range*, U.S.A., **422** C2, *383*
Nevada, *state*, U.S.A., **422** E2, *383, 385, 386*
Nevada, U.S.A., **420** F7
Nevada del Cocuy, Sierra, *mountain peak*, Colombia, **450** D2
Nevado, Cerro, *mountain peak*, Colombia, **450** C3
Nevado, Sierra del, *mountain range*, Argentina, **458** C5
Neve, Serra da, *mountain range*, Angola, **368** B5
Nevel', Russian Federation, **299** B4
Nevers, France, **291** F3
Nevesinje, Bosnia and Herzegovina, **294** G4
Nevinnomyssk, Russian Federation, **222** C4
Nevis, Ben, *mountain peak*, Scotland, U.K., **308** E4, *274*
Nev'yansk, Russian Federation, **222** G1
New Albany, Indiana, U.S.A., **421** L6
New Albany, Mississippi, U.S.A., **425** H2
New Albany, Pennsylvania, U.S.A., **426** B4
New Alresford, England, U.K., **305** F3
New Amsterdam, Guyana, **451** H2
New Bedford, U.S.A., **426** E4
New Berlin, U.S.A., **426** C3
New Bern, U.S.A., **426** B7
New Boston, U.S.A., **424** E3
New Braunfels, U.S.A., **424** C5
New Britain, *island*, Papua New Guinea, **140** C4, *115*
New Britain, U.S.A., **426** D4
New Brunswick, *province*, Canada, **416** H6, *380, 381*
New Bussa, Nigeria, **365** E3
New Caledonia, *French territory*, Pacific Ocean, **130** E3, *108, 109, 116, 124, 245*
New Caledonia Basin, *underwater feature*, Pacific Ocean, **478** E6
New Castle, Kentucky, U.S.A., **421** L6
New Castle, Pennsylvania, U.S.A., **421** N5
New Cumnock, Scotland, U.K., **308** E5
New Dayton, Canada, **413** N7
New Deer, Scotland, U.K., **308** G3
New Delhi, India, **218** D3, *167*
New Ellenton, U.S.A., **425** M3
New England, U.S.A., **420** B2
New Galloway, Scotland, U.K., **308** E5
New Georgia, *island*, Solomon Islands, **141** A1, *116*
New Georgia Group, *islands*, Solomon Islands, **141** A1
New Georgia Sound (The Slot), *channel*, Solomon Islands, **141** A1
New Germany, Canada, **417** J7
New Glasgow, Canada, **417** K7
New Grant, Trinidad, Trinidad and Tobago, **461** C4
New Guinea, *island*, Indonesia/Papua New Guinea, **140** A4, *61, 62, 64, 87, 88, 91, 93, 94, 96, 115, 148*
New Hampshire, *state*, U.S.A., **426** E3, *386*
New Hampton, U.S.A., **420** G4
New Hanover, *island*, Papua New Guinea, **140** C3
New Haven, U.S.A., **426** D4
New Hazelton, Canada, **412** F4
New Iberia, U.S.A., **424** G5
New Ireland, *island*, Papua New Guinea, **140** C3, *109, 115*
New Ireland, *province*, Papua New Guinea, **140** D3
New Jersey, *state*, U.S.A., **426** C5, *386*
New Lexington, U.S.A., **421** M6
New Liskeard, Canada, **421** P2
New London, Connecticut, U.S.A., **426** D4
New London, Iowa, U.S.A., **420** H5
New London, Wisconsin, U.S.A., **421** J3
New Meadows, U.S.A., **418** F4
New Mexico, *state*, U.S.A., **423** K4, *87, 89, 377, 383, 386*
New Milford, U.S.A., **426** C4
New Milton, England, U.K., **305** F4
New Mīrpur, India, **218** C2
New Orleans, U.S.A., **424** G5
New Paltz, U.S.A., **426** C4
New Pitsligo, Scotland, U.K., **308** G3
New Plymouth, New Zealand, **132** E4
New Providence, *island*, Bahamas, **428** F1
New Quay, Wales, U.K., **304** C2
New Richmond, Canada, **416** J5
New Richmond, U.S.A., **420** G3
New Rockford, U.S.A., **420** D2
New Romney, England, U.K., **305** H4
New Ross, Ireland, **309** F5
New Salem, U.S.A., **420** C2
New Sarepta, Canada, **413** N5
New Scone, Scotland, U.K., **308** F4
New Smyrna Beach, U.S.A., **425** M5
New South Wales, *state*, Australia, **135** J5, *51, 94, 112*
New Underwood, U.S.A., **420** B3
New Waterford, Canada, **417** L6
New York, *state*, U.S.A., **426** B3, *82, 95, 96, 376, 377, 383, 384, 386*
New York, U.S.A., **426** D4, *384, 385, 386*
New Zealand, *country*, Pacific Ocean, **131** F6, *18, 25, 27, 44, 61, 90, 91, 92, 93, 94, 95, 96, 97, 100, 108, 109, 110, 111, 112, 113, 114, 120, 121, 124, 125, 126, 228*
Newala, Tanzania, **369** G5
Newark, Delaware, U.S.A., **426** C5
Newark, New Jersey, U.S.A., **426** C4
Newark, New York, U.S.A., **426** B3
Newark-on-Trent, England, U.K., **305** G1
Newberg, U.S.A., **418** C4
Newberry, U.S.A., **425** M2
Newbiggin-by-the-sea, England, U.K., **307** G2
Newbridge, Ireland, **309** F4
Newburgh, Scotland, U.K., **308** F4
Newburgh, U.S.A., **426** C4
Newbury, England, U.K., **305** F3
Newby Bridge, England, U.K., **306** F3
Newcastle, Australia, **135** L5
Newcastle, Canada, **416** J6
Newcastle, Northern Ireland, U.K., **309** G3
Newcastle, South Africa, **371** E4
Newcastle, U.S.A., **419** M5
Newcastle Emlyn, Wales, U.K., **304** C2
Newcastle-under-Lyme, England, U.K., **304** E1
Newcastle upon Tyne, England, U.K., **307** G3
Newcastle West, Ireland, **309** C5
Newcastleton, Scotland, U.K., **308** G5
Newcomb, U.S.A., **423** J3
Newell, U.S.A., **420** B3
Newenham, Cape, U.S.A., **410** C4
Newent, England, U.K., **304** E3
Newfolden, U.S.A., **420** E1
Newfoundland, *island*, Canada, **417** N5, *77, 91, 93, 380, 384, 391*
Newfoundland, *province*, Canada, **411** N4, *381*
Newham, England, U.K., **307** G2
Newhaven, England, U.K., **305** H4
Newington, South Africa, **371** F3
Newinn, Ireland, **309** E5
Newman, Australia, **134** D3
Newman, U.S.A., **421** K6
Newmarket, Canada, **421** P3
Newmarket, England, U.K., **305** H2
Newmarket, Ireland, **309** C5
Newmarket on Fergus, Ireland, **309** D5
Newnan, U.S.A., **425** K3
Newnham, England, U.K., **304** E3
Newport, Arkansas, U.S.A., **424** G2
Newport, Essex, England, U.K., **305** H3
Newport, Isle of Wight, England, U.K., **305** F4
Newport, Kentucky, U.S.A., **421** L6
Newport, Mayo, Ireland, **309** C4
Newport, New Hampshire, U.S.A., **426** D3
Newport, Newport, Wales, U.K., **304** E3
Newport, Oregon, U.S.A., **418** B4
Newport, Pembrokeshire, Wales, U.K., **304** C2
Newport, Rhode Island, U.S.A., **426** E4
Newport, Shropshire, England, U.K., **304** E2
Newport, Tennessee, U.S.A., **425** L2
Newport, Tipperary, Ireland, **309** D5
Newport, *unitary authority*, Wales, U.K., **304** D3
Newport, Vermont, U.S.A., **426** D2
Newport, Washington, U.S.A., **418** F2
Newport Bay, Wales, U.K., **304** B2
Newport News, U.S.A., **426** B6
Newport Pagnell, England, U.K., **305** G2
Newquay, England, U.K., **304** B4
Newry, Northern Ireland, U.K., **309** F3
Newry and Mourne, *district*, Northern Ireland, U.K., **309** F3
Newry Canal, Northern Ireland, U.K., **306** B3
Newton, England, U.K., **306** F4
Newton, Illinois, U.S.A., **421** J6
Newton, Iowa, U.S.A., **420** G5
Newton, Kansas, U.S.A., **420** E6
Newton, Mississippi, U.S.A., **425** H3
Newton Abbot, England, U.K., **304** D4
Newton Aycliffe, England, U.K., **307** G3
Newton Stewart, Scotland, U.K., **308** E6
Newtonmore, Scotland, U.K., **308** E3
Newtown, England, U.K., **304** E2
Newtown, Wales, U.K., **304** D2
Newtown Mount Kennedy, Ireland, **309** F4
Newtown St Boswells, Scotland, U.K., **308** G5
Newtownabbey, *district*, Northern Ireland, U.K., **309** F3
Newtownabbey, Northern Ireland, U.K., **309** G3

Newtownards, Northern Ireland, U.K., **309** G3
Newtownbutler, Northern Ireland, U.K., **309** E3
Newtownstewart, Northern Ireland, U.K., **309** E3
Neyland, Wales, U.K., **304** C3
Neyrīz, Iran, **221** F3
Neyshābūr, Iran, **222** F5
Neyva, *river*, Russian Federation, **222** G1
Neyveli, India, **216** D4
Neyyāttinkara, India, **216** D4
Nezperce, U.S.A., **418** F3
Nezvys'ko, Ukraine, **296** E1
Ngabang, Indonesia, **201** E2
Ngabé, Congo, **368** C3
Ngabordamlu, Tanjong, *point*, Indonesia, **199** F4
Ngagahtawng, Myanmar, **205** C2
Ngakawau, New Zealand, **133** C5
Ngala, Nigeria, **365** G2
Ngalipaeng, Indonesia, **198** D2
Ngam, Chad, **365** H2
Ngama, Chad, **365** H2
Ngamiland, *district*, Botswana, **370** D2
Ngamo, Zimbabwe, **371** E2
Ngamring, China, **214** C3
Ngangala, Sudan, **369** F2
Nganglong Kangri, *mountain range*, China, **218** E2
Ngangzê Co, *lake*, China, **214** C3
Ngao, Thailand, **202** D2
Ngaoundal, Cameroon, **365** G3
Ngaoundéré, Cameroon, **365** G3
Ngara, Tanzania, **369** F3
Ngatik, *island*, Micronesia, **138** D4
Ngauruhoe, Mount, *mountain peak*, New Zealand, **132** E4
Ngbala, Congo, **368** B2
Nggatokae, *island*, Solomon Islands, **141** A1
Nghĩa ũşn, Vietnam, **203** E2
Ngo, Congo, **368** C3
Ngoc Linh, *mountain peak*, Vietnam, **203** E3
Ngomedzap, Cameroon, **368** B2
Ngong, Cameroon, **365** G3
Ngoni, Tanjong, *point*, Indonesia, **199** F4
Ngoqumaima, China, **214** C2
Ngoring, China, **215** F2
Ngorkou, Mali, **364** D1
Ngoso, Democratic Republic of the Congo, **368** C3
Ngoto, Central African Republic, **368** C2
Ngouma, Mali, **364** D1
Ngounié, *province*, Gabon, **368** B3
Ngoura, Chad, **365** H2
Ngouri, Chad, **365** H2
Ngourti, Niger, **365** G1
Ngouyo, Central African Republic, **369** E1
Ngudu, Tanzania, **369** F3
Nguia Bouar, Central African Republic, **368** B1
Nguigmi, Niger, **365** G2
Ngulu, *island*, Micronesia, **138** B4
Ngum, *river*, Laos, **203** D2
Ngundu, Zimbabwe, **371** F3
Nguru, Nigeria, **365** G2
Ngwedaung, Myanmar, **205** C4
Ngwezi, *river*, Zambia, **371** E2
Nha Trang, Vietnam, **203** F3, *44*
Nhabe, *river*, Botswana, **370** D3
Nhachengue, Mozambique, **371** G3
Nhamalábue, Mozambique, **371** G2
Nhamatanda, Mozambique, **371** F2
Nhamundá, Brazil, **452** B4
Nhamundá, *river*, Brazil, **452** B3
N'harea, Angola, **368** C5
Nhecolândia, Brazil, **456** B5
Nhill, Australia, **135** J6
Nhulunbuy, Australia, **135** H1
Nia-Nia, Democratic Republic of the Congo, **369** E2
Niafounké, Mali, **364** D1
Niagara Escarpment, Canada, **421** N3
Niagara Falls, Canada/U.S.A., **421** P4, *381*
Niagassola, Guinea, **364** C2
Niakaramandougou, Côte d'Ivoire, **364** C3
Niamey, Niger, **365** E2, *327*
Niandankoro, Guinea, **364** C2
Niangara, Democratic Republic of the Congo, **369** E2
Niangniangba, China, **215** H2
Niangoloko, Burkina Faso, **364** D2
Nianzishan, China, **211** H3
Niari, *administrative region*, Congo, **368** B3, *334*
Nias, Pulau, *island*, Indonesia, **200** B2
Niassa, Lago, *lake*, Mozambique, **369** F5
Niassa, *province*, Mozambique, **369** G5
Nicaragua, *country*, Central America, **409** Q7, *378, 379, 402, 404, 405*
Nicaragua, Lago de, *lake*, Nicaragua, **428** D5, *404*
Nicastro, Italy, **295** F6
Nice, France, **291** H5, *15*
Niceville, U.S.A., **425** J4
Nichinan, Japan, **208** E5
Nickol Bay, Australia, **134** D2
Nicman, Canada, **416** J4
Nikobar Islands, Andaman and Nicobar Islands, India, **217** H4
Nicolae Bălcescu, Romania, **296** G3
Nicolar Bălcescu, Romania, **296** F2
Nicolet, Canada, **416** E6
Nicosia *see* Lefkosia, Cyprus, **225** B2, *191, 192*
Nicosia, Sicilia, Italy, **295** E7
Nicoya, Golfo de, *gulf*, Costa Rica, **428** D5
Niculiuţel, Romania, **296** G3
Nidže Kožuf, *mountain range*, Macedonia, **297** C5
Nidzica, Poland, **289** K2
Niebüll, Germany, **288** D1
Niedere Tauern, *mountain range*, Austria, **289** F5
Niederösterreich, *state*, Austria, **289** G4
Niedersachsen, *state*, Germany, **288** D2
Niedrzwica Duża, Poland, **289** L3
Niefang, Equatorial Guinea, **368** B2
Niem, Central African Republic, **365** H3
Niemba, Democratic Republic of the Congo, **369** E4
Niemegk, Germany, **288** F2
Niemisel, Sweden, **285** L3
Niemodlin, Poland, **289** H3
Nienburg (Weser), Germany, **288** D2
Nieuw Amsterdam, Suriname, **452** B2
Nieuw Nickerie, Suriname, **452** B2
Nieuw Poort, Curaçao, Netherlands Antilles, **461** C3
Nieuwpoort, Belgium, **305** K3
Nieves, Pico de las, *mountain peak*, Islas Canarias, Spain, **373** B4
Nifī, Saudi Arabia, **363** H4
Niğde, Turkey, **363** F1
Niger, *country*, Africa, **358** F5, *74, 91, 93, 94, 312, 315, 324, 325, 327, 328*
Niger, *river*, W. Africa, **356** E5, *89, 312, 322, 324, 327, 328*
Niger, *state*, Nigeria, **365** F2
Nigeria, *country*, Africa, **358** F6, *91, 94, 95, 97, 312, 313, 329, 330*
Nightingale Island, Tristan da Cunha, **373** C2
Nihoa, *island*, Hawaiian Islands, U.S.A., **139** H2
Nihuil, Embalse de, *reservoir*, Argentina, **458** C5
Nii-jima, *island*, Japan, **209** G4
Niigata, Japan, **209** G3
Niihama, Japan, **208** F4
Niihau, *island*, Hawaiian Islands, U.S.A., **422** Q9
Niitsu, Japan, **209** G3
Nijmegen, Netherlands, **288** B3
Nikaia, Greece, **297** D6, *229*
Nikel', Russian Federation, **285** Q2
Nikiforovo, Russian Federation, **299** G2
Nikkaluokta, Sweden, **284** J3
Nikki, Benin, **365** E3
Nikolayevo, Russian Federation, **299** B3
Nikolayevsk-na-Amure, Russian Federation, **301** R4
Nikopol, Bulgaria, **296** E4
Nikopol', Ukraine, **298** D3
Nīkshahr, Iran, **221** H3
Nikšić, Montenegro, **296** B4
Nikumaroro, *island*, Kiribati, **139** G5
Nikunau, *island*, Kiribati, **139** F5
Nilakka, *lake*, Finland, **285** N5
Nilande Atoll, Maldives, **216** C6
Nile, *river*, N. E. Africa, **356** J5, *30, 66, 95, 312, 316, 317, 331, 336, 337, 340, 343*
Nile Fan, *underwater feature*, Mediterranean Sea, **476** A2
Niles, U.S.A., **421** K5
Nilgiri Hills, India, **216** D4
Nilivaara, Sweden, **284** K3
Nilka, China, **212** D4
Nil'maguba, Russian Federation, **287** R4
Niltepec, Mexico, **431** G5
Nīmach, India, **218** C4
Nimba, Côte d'Ivoire, **364** C3, *321, 323*
Nīmbāhera, India, **218** C4
Nimen'ga, Russian Federation, **285** T5
Nîmes, France, **291** G5
Nimule, Sudan, **369** F2
Nin, Croatia, **294** E3
Ninda, Angola, **368** D5
Nine Degree Channel, India, **216** C4
Ninemilehouse, Ireland, **309** E5
Ninette, Canada, **414** E7
Ninety East Ridge, *underwater feature*, Indian Ocean, **476** E6
Ninfas, Punta, *point*, Argentina, **460** E2
Ning Xian, China, **215** J2
Ning'an, China, **211** K3
Ningbo, China, **206** E2
Ningcheng, China, **211** G4
Ningde, China, **206** D3
Ningdu, China, **206** D3
Ningerum, Papua New Guinea, **140** A4
Ningguo, China, **206** D2
Ninghai, China, **206** E2
Ninghua, China, **206** D3
Ningming, China, **215** H5
Ningnan, China, **215** G4
Ningqiang, China, **215** H2
Ningshan, China, **206** B1
Ningxi, China, **207** B2
Ningxia Huizu Zizhiqu, *autonomous region*, China, **210** D5, *161*
Ningxiang, China, **206** C2
Ningyuan, China, **206** B3
Ninh Bình, Vietnam, **203** E1
Ninh Hòa, Vietnam, **203** F3
Ninigo Group, *islands*, Papua New Guinea, **140** A3
Ninohe, Japan, **209** H2
Nioaque, Brazil, **456** B5
Niobrara, *river*, U.S.A., **420** B4
Nioka, Democratic Republic of the Congo, **369** F2
Nioki, Democratic Republic of the Congo, **368** C3
Niono, Mali, **364** C2
Nioro du Sahel, Mali, **364** C1
Niort, France, **290** D3
Nipa, Papua New Guinea, **140** A4
Nipāni, India, **216** C2
Nipawin, Canada, **414** B5
Nipigon, Canada, **415** K7
Nipigon, Lake, Canada, **415** K6
Nipishish Lake, Canada, **417** L2
Nipissing, Lake, Canada, **421** P2
Nipton, U.S.A., **422** F4
Niquelândia, Brazil, **456** D4
Nira, India, **216** C2
Nirmal, India, **216** D2
Nirmāli, India, **219** F4
Niš, Serbia, **296** C4
Niscemi, Sicilia, Italy, **295** E7
Nisko, Poland, **289** L3
Nisland, U.S.A., **420** B3
Nisporeni, Moldova, **296** G2
Nissan, *river*, Sweden, **286** F4
Nissan Island, Papua New Guinea, **140** E2
Nissedal, Norway, **286** D3
Nisser, *lake*, Norway, **286** D3
Nissilä, Finland, **285** N5
Nistru, Moldova, **296** G1
Nisyros, *island*, Dodekanisos, Greece, **297** F7
Nītaure, Latvia, **287** M4
Niterói, Brazil, **457** E6
Nith, *river*, Scotland, U.K., **308** F5
Niton Junction, Canada, **413** M5
Nitra, Slovakia, **289** J4
Nitriansky, *administrative region*, Slovakia, **289** J4
Nitry, France, **291** F3
Niuafo'ou, *island*, Tonga, **136** D2
Niuatoputapu, *island*, Tonga, **136** D2
Niubiziliang, China, **213** G5
Niue, *New Zealand territory*, Pacific Ocean, **131** J3, *108, 110, 124, 125*
Niu'erhe, China, **211** H2
Niulakita, Tuvalu, **139** F5, *113*
Niut, Gunung, *mountain peak*, Indonesia, **201** E2
Niutao, *island*, Tuvalu, **139** F5, *113*
Niutou Dao, *island*, China, **207** B4
Nivala, Finland, **285** M5
Nizām Sāgar, *lake*, India, **216** D2
Nizāmābād, India, **216** D2
Nizgan, *river*, Afghanistan, **218** A2
Nizhegorodskaya Oblast', *province*, Russian Federation, **222** C1
Nizhmozero, Russian Federation, **285** T4
Nizhnaya Tavda, Russian Federation, **222** H1
Nizhnekamsk, Russian Federation, **222** E1
Nizhneudinsk, Russian Federation, **223** P2
Nizhnevartovsk, Russian Federation, **300** J3
Nizhneye Kuyto, Ozero, *lake*, Russian Federation, **285** Q4
Nizhniy Novgorod, Russian Federation, **222** C1
Nizhniy Tagil, Russian Federation, **222** F1
Nizhnyaya Tunguska, *river*, Russian Federation, **300** L3
Nizhyn, Ukraine, **298** D2
Nizi, Democratic Republic of the Congo, **369** F2
Nizip, Turkey, **224** E5
Nízke Tatry, *mountain range*, Slovakia, **289** J4
Nizwá, Oman, **221** G4
Njazidja (Grande Comore), *island*, Comoros, **372** A3, *352*
Njegos, *mountain peak*, Montenegro, **296** B4
Njinjo, Tanzania, **369** G4
Njoeng Jacobkondre, Suriname, **452** B2
Njombe, Tanzania, **369** F4
Njurunda, Sweden, **287** H1
Nkansi, Tanzania, **369** F4
Nkayi, Zimbabwe, **371** E2
Nkhata Bay, Malawi, **369** F5
Nkhotakota, Malawi, **369** F5
Nkondwe, Tanzania, **369** F4
Nkongsamba, Cameroon, **368** A2
Nkoranza, Ghana, **364** D3
Nkoteng, Cameroon, **368** B2
Nkundi, Tanzania, **369** F4
Nkurenkuru, Namibia, **370** C2
Nmai, *river*, Myanmar, **205** C2
Noākhāli, Bangladesh, **214** D5
Noāmundi, India, **219** F5
Noarvaš, *mountain peak*, Norway, **285** M2
Nobber, Ireland, **309** F4
Nobeoka, Japan, **208** E4
Noboribetsu, Japan, **209** H2
Nobres, Brazil, **456** B4
Noccundra, Australia, **135** J4
Nocrich, Romania, **296** E3
Nogales, Mexico, **430** C2
Nogales, U.S.A., **423** H6
Nogara, Italy, **294** C3
Nōgata, Japan, **208** E4
Nogent, France, **291** G2
Nogent-le-Rotrou, France, **290** E2
Nogent-sur-Seine, France, **291** F2
Noginsk, Russian Federation, **299** G5
Nogliki, Russian Federation, **301** R4
Nogoyá, Argentina, **459** E4
Nogoyá, *river*, Argentina, **459** E4
Noguera, Spain, **293** G2
Nohar, India, **218** C3
Nohtā, India, **218** D5
Noia, Spain, **292** C1
Noire, Montagne, *mountain peak*, France, **290** F5
Noirmoutier, Île de, *island*, France, **290** C3
Noirmoutier-en-l'Île, France, **290** C3
Nok Kundi, Pakistan, **221** H3
Nokh, India, **218** C4
Nokha, India, **218** C4
Nokia, Finland, **287** L2
Nokou, Chad, **365** G2
Nokuku, Vanuatu, **141** A2
Nola, Central African Republic, **368** C2
Nom, China, **213** G4
Nome, Alaska, U.S.A., **410** C3
Nome, Texas, U.S.A., **424** E4
Nong Bua, Thailand, **202** D3
Nong Bua Lamphu, Thailand, **203** D2
Nong Khai, Thailand, **203** D2
Nong'an, China, **211** J3
Nonoava, Mexico, **430** D3
Nonouti, *island*, Kiribati, **139** F5
Nonthaburi, Thailand, **202** D3
Nontron, France, **290** E4
Noonan, U.S.A., **419** N2
Noondie, Lake, Australia, **134** D4
Noord, Aruba, **461** B3
Noord-Brabant, *province*, Netherlands, **288** B3
Noord-Holland, *province*, Netherlands, **288** B2, *241*
Noormarkku, Finland, **287** K2
Noosa Heads, Australia, **135** L4
Nootka, Canada, **412** F7
Nootka Island, Canada, **412** F7
Nóqui, Angola, **368** B4
Nora, *river*, Russian Federation, **211** K1
Nora, Sweden, **286** G3
Norala, Philippines, **204** D5
Norcia, Italy, **294** D4
Nord, Greenland, **411** T1
Nord, *province*, Cameroon, **365** G3
Nord-Kivu, *administrative region*, Democratic Republic of the Congo, **369** E3
Nord-Ouest, *province*, Cameroon, **365** G3
Nord-Pas-de-Calais, *administrative region*, France, **290** E1, *245*
Nørd-Trøndelag, *county*, Norway, **284** E4
Nordaustlandet, *island*, Svalbard, **300** C1
Nordberg, Norway, **286** D2
Nordegg, Canada, **413** L5
Norden, Germany, **288** C2
Nordenham, Germany, **288** D2
Nordenshel'da, Arkhipelag, *islands*, Russian Federation, **300** L2
Norderney, *island*, Germany, **288** C2

Nordfjordeid, Norway, **286** C2
Nordfold, Norway, **284** G3
Nordhausen, Germany, **288** E3
Nordhorn, Germany, **288** C2
Nordkapp, *cape*, Norway, **285** M1
Nordkinnhalvøya, *peninsula*, Norway, **285** P1
Nordkjosbotn, Norway, **284** J2
Nordkvaløy, *island*, Norway, **284** J1
Nordland, *county*, Norway, **284** F3
Nordli, Norway, **284** F4
Nördlingen, Germany, **288** E4
Nordmaling, Sweden, **284** J5
Nordmela, Norway, **284** G2
Nordmøre, *island*, Norway, **284** C5
Nordøyane, *island*, Norway, **286** B1
Nordpunt, *point*, Curaçao, Netherlands Antilles, **461** C3
Nordrhein-Westfalen, *state*, Germany, **288** C3, *238*
Nore, Norway, **286** D2
Norèoyar, *islands*, Faeroe Islands, **302** D1
Noresund, Norway, **286** D2
Norfolk, Nebraska, U.S.A., **420** E4
Norfolk, *unitary authority*, England, U.K., **305** H2
Norfolk, Virginia, U.S.A., **426** B6
Norfolk Broads, *region*, England, U.K., **305** J2
Norfolk Island, *Australian territory*, Pacific Ocean, **135** T13, *108, 112, 125, 126*
Norfolk Ridge, *underwater feature*, Pacific Ocean, **478** F6
Noril'sk, Russian Federation, **300** K3
Noring, Gunung, *mountain peak*, Malaysia, **200** C1
Norma, U.S.A., **420** C1
Norman, Lake, *lake*, U.S.A., **425** M2
Norman, *river*, Australia, **135** J2
Norman, U.S.A., **424** D2
Norman Inlet, *bay*, Auckland Islands, New Zealand, **132** J10
Norman Wells, Canada, **410** G3
Normanby Island, Papua New Guinea, **140** C5
Normandia, Brazil, **451** G3
Normanton, Australia, **135** J2
Normétal, Canada, **416** B5
Norquay, Canada, **414** C6
Ñorquinco, Argentina, **460** C1
Norr-dellen, *lake*, Sweden, **286** H2
Norra Bergnäs, Sweden, **284** J3
Norra Storfjället, *mountain peak*, Sweden, **284** G4
Norråker, Sweden, **284** G4
Norrbotten, *county*, Sweden, **284** J3
Nørre Nebel, Denmark, **286** D5
Norrent-Fontès, France, **305** K4
Nørresundby, Denmark, **286** D4
Norris, U.S.A., **419** J4
Norrköping, Sweden, **286** H3
Norrtälje, Sweden, **287** J3
Norseman, Australia, **134** E5
Norsjø, *lake*, Norway, **286** D3
Norsjö, Sweden, **284** J4
Norsk, Russian Federation, **211** K1
Norske Øer, *islands*, Greenland, **411** T2
Norte, Cabo, *cape*, Brazil, **452** D3
Norte, Cabo, *cape*, Isla de Pascua (Easter Island), Chile, **461** B2
Norte, Cabo, *cape*, Islas Galápagos (Galapagos Islands), Ecuador, **461** A2
Norte, Canal do, *channel*, Brazil, **452** C3
Norte, Punta, *point*, Argentina, **460** E1
Norte, Punta, *point*, San Andrés, Colombia, **461** B1
Norte, Serra do, *mountain range*, Brazil, **455** G3
Norte del Cabo San Antonio, Punta, *point*, Argentina, **459** F5
Nortelândia, Brazil, **456** B4
North, Cape, Canada, **417** L6
North, U.S.A., **425** M3
North Adams, U.S.A., **426** D3
North Andaman, *island*, Andaman and Nicobar Islands, India, **217** H3
North Augusta, U.S.A., **425** M3
North Australian Basin, *underwater feature*, Indian Ocean, **476** G5
North Ayrshire, Scotland, U.K., **308** E5
North Battleford, Canada, **413** Q5
North Bay, Canada, **421** P2
North Bend, U.S.A., **418** B5
North Berwick, Scotland, U.K., **308** G4
North Cape, Antipodes Islands, New Zealand, **133** P15
North Cape, Canada, **417** K6
North Cape, New Zealand, **132** D2
North Carolina, *state*, U.S.A., **425** M2, *96, 383, 384, 386*
North Channel, Canada, **421** M2
North Channel, Northern Ireland, U.K., **308** D5
North Dakota, *state*, U.S.A., **420** C2, *386*
North Down, *district*, Northern Ireland, U.K., **309** G3
North Downs, *region*, England, U.K., **305** H3
North East, *district*, Botswana, **371** E3
North East, U.S.A., **421** P4
North East Bay, Ascension, **373** A3
North East Harbour, Campbell Island, New Zealand, **132** K11
North East Island, Snares Islands, New Zealand, **132** H9
North East Lincolnshire, *unitary authority*, England, U.K., **307** H4
North East Point, Christmas Island, **134** N8
North-Eastern, *province*, Kenya, **369** G2
North Esk, *river*, Scotland, U.K., **308** G4
North European Plain, Europe, **280** F5, *239, 268*
North Fiji Basin, *underwater feature*, Pacific Ocean, **478** F5
North Foreland, *cape*, England, U.K., **305** J3
North Fork, Idaho, U.S.A., **418** H4
North Fork, Nevada, U.S.A., **418** G6
North Grimston, England, U.K., **307** H3
North Head, Canada, **426** G2
North Head, *point*, Lord Howe Island, Australia, **135** U14
North Head, *point*, Macquarie Island, **134** R11
North Head, *point*, New Zealand, **132** D3
North Head, U.S.A., **416** H7
North Horr, Kenya, **369** G2
North Hykeham, England, U.K., **305** G1
North Island, New Zealand, **132** D3, *111*
North Island, Seychelles, **373** A2
North Keeling Island, Cocos (Keeling) Islands, **134** Q10
North Knife, *river*, Canada, **414** F2
North Knife Lake, Canada, **414** F2
North Korea, *country*, Asia, **197** P5, *144, 145, 162, 163, 164, 271*
North Lakhimpur, India, **219** H4
North Lanarkshire, *local authority*, Scotland, U.K., **308** F5
North Lincolnshire, *unitary authority*, England, U.K., **307** H4
North Little Rock, U.S.A., **424** F2
North Loup, *river*, U.S.A., **420** C4
North Moose Lake, *lake*, Canada, **414** D4
North Platte, *river*, U.S.A., **419** L5
North Platte, U.S.A., **420** C5
North Point, Ascension, **373** A3
North Point, Seychelles, **373** A2
North Point, U.S.A., **421** M3, **425** L6
North Powder, U.S.A., **418** F4
North Promontory, *point*, Snares Islands, New Zealand, **132** H9
North Rona, *island*, Scotland, U.K., **308** D1
North Ronaldsay, *island*, Orkney, Scotland, U.K., **308** G1
North Saskatchewan, *river*, Canada, **413** R5
North Sea, Europe, **280** E4, *45, 229, 231, 233, 234, 238, 240, 241, 242, 274, 276*
North Seal, *river*, Canada, **414** D2
North Shields, England, U.K., **307** G3
North Solomons, *province*, Papua New Guinea, **140** E2
North Somercotes, England, U.K., **307** J4
North Somerset, *unitary authority*, England, U.K., **304** E3
North Sound, The, Orkney, Scotland, U.K., **308** G1
North Spirit Lake, Canada, **414** H5
North Star, Canada, **413** L3
North Stradbroke Island, Australia, **135** L4
North Sunderland, England, U.K., **307** G2
North Taranaki Bight, *bay*, New Zealand, **132** D4
North Tidworth, England, U.K., **305** F3
North Twin Island, Canada, **415** Q5
North Tyne, *river*, England, U.K., **306** F2
North Uist, *island*, Scotland, U.K., **308** B3
North Wabasca Lake, *lake*, Canada, **413** M3
North Walsham, England, U.K., **305** J2
North West, *province*, South Africa, **370** D4, *351*
North West Cape, Auckland Islands, New Zealand, **132** J10
North West Cape, Australia, **134** C3
North-West Frontier Province, *province*, Pakistan, **218** B2
North West Highlands, *mountain range*, Scotland, U.K., **308** D3, *276*
North West Point, Christmas Island, **134** N8
North-Western, *province*, Zambia, **368** D5
North Wildwood, U.S.A., **426** C5
North Woodstock, U.S.A., **426** E2
North York Moors, *moorland*, England, U.K., **307** H3, *276*
North Yorkshire, *unitary authority*, England, U.K., **307** G3
Northallerton, England, U.K., **307** G3
Northam, Australia, **134** D5
Northampton, Australia, **134** C4
Northampton, England, U.K., **305** G2
Northampton, U.S.A., **426** D3
Northamptonshire, *unitary authority*, England, U.K., **305** F2
Northeast Point, Bahamas, **429** G2
Northeast Providence Channel, Bahamas, **428** F1
Northeim, Germany, **288** D3
Northern, *administrative region*, Ghana, **364** D3
Northern, *administrative region*, Malawi, **369** F5
Northern, *province*, Sierra Leone, **364** B3
Northern, *province*, Zambia, **369** F5
Northern Cape, *province*, South Africa, **370** C4, *351*
Northern Cook Islands, Cook Islands, **139** H5
Northern Indian Lake, Canada, **414** F3
Northern Ireland, *administrative division*, U.K., **309** E3, *275, 276, 277, 279*
Northern Mariana Islands, *U.S. territory*, Pacific Ocean, **138** C3, *108, 109, 125, 127, 386*
Northern Peninsula, Canada, **417** N4
Northern (Oro), *province*, Papua New Guinea, **140** C5
Northern Province, *province*, South Africa, **371** E3, *351*
Northern Range, *mountain range*, Trinidad, Trinidad and Tobago, **461** C4, *399*
Northern Territory, *territory*, Australia, **134** G2, *60, 109, 112*
Northfield, U.S.A., **420** G3
Northton, Scotland, U.K., **308** B3
Northville, U.S.A., **416** D8
Northwest Atlantic Mid-Ocean Canyon, *underwater feature*, Atlantic Ocean, **477** D2
Northwest Bay, Seychelles, **373** A2
Northwest Pacific Basin, *underwater feature*, Pacific Ocean, **478** E2
Northwest Providence Channel, Bahamas, **428** F1
Northwest Territories, *territory*, Canada, **410** G3, *381*
Northwich, England, U.K., **306** F4
Northwood, U.S.A., **420** E2
Norton, England, U.K., **307** H3
Norton, U.S.A., **420** D6
Norton Fitzwarren, England, U.K., **304** D3
Norton Sound, U.S.A., **410** C3
Norwalk, U.S.A., **421** M5
Norway, *country*, Europe, **282** E3, *40, 44, 228, 230, 231, 232, 233, 234, 271, 274, 278, 279, 389, 390, 464, 469*
Norway House, Canada, **414** F5
Norwegian Bay, Canada, **411** K2
Norwegian Sea, Atlantic Ocean, **280** D2, *231*
Norwich, England, U.K., **305** J2
Norwood, U.S.A., **420** G3
Noshiro, Japan, **209** H2
Noṣratābād, Iran, **221** G3
Noss, Isle of, *island*, Scotland, U.K., **308** K7
Nossa Senhora das Dores, Brazil, **457** G3
Nossa Senhora do Livramento, Brazil, **456** B4
Nossebro, Sweden, **286** F3
Nossombougou, Mali, **364** C2
Nosy Bé, *island*, Madagascar, **372** B3
Nosy-Varika, Madagascar, **372** B5
Nota, *river*, Russian Federation, **285** P3
Notch Peak, *mountain peak*, U.S.A., **422** G2
Notio Aigaio, *administrative region*, Greece, **297** E7
Notio Steno Kerkyras, *channel*, Greece, **297** C6
Notodden, Norway, **286** D3
Notre Dame, Monts, *mountain range*, Canada, **416** F7
Notre Dame Bay, Canada, **417** P5
Notre-Dame-de-la-Salette, Canada, **426** C2
Notre-Dame-du-Nord, Canada, **416** B6
Notsé, Togo, **364** E3
Nottaway, *river*, Canada, **416** B4
Nottingham, England, U.K., **305** F2
Nottingham City, *unitary authority*, England, U.K., **305** F2
Nottingham Island, Canada, **411** M3
Nottinghamshire, *unitary authority*, England, U.K., **305** F1
Nottoway, *river*, U.S.A., **426** A6
Nouâdhibou, Mauritania, **360** C4
Nouâdhibou, Râs, *cape*, Western Sahara, **360** C4
Nouakchott, Mauritania, **360** C5, *318*
Nouâmghâr, Mauritania, **360** C5
Nouméa, New Caledonia, **141** A3, *124*
Nouna, Burkina Faso, **364** D2
Noupoort, South Africa, **370** D5
Nouveau-Comptoir (Wemindji), Canada, **415** Q5
Nouvelle, Canada, **416** H5
Nouvelle Calédonie, *island*, New Caledonia, **141** A3
Nova América, Brazil, **456** D4
Nova Caipemba, Angola, **368** B4
Nova Esperança, Brazil, **459** G2
Nova Friburgo, Brazil, **457** E6
Nova Iguaçu, Brazil, **457** E6
Nova Lima, Brazil, **457** E5
Nova Mambone, Mozambique, **371** G3
Nova Nabúri, Mozambique, **369** G6
Nova Roma, Brazil, **456** D3
Nova Scotia, *province*, Canada, **417** J7, *93, 380, 381*
Nova Soure, Brazil, **457** F3
Nova Ushytsya, Ukraine, **296** F1
Nova Varoš, Serbia, **296** B4
Nova Venécia, Brazil, **457** F5
Nova Vida, Brazil, **455** F3
Nova Xavantina, Brazil, **456** C4
Nova Zagora, Bulgaria, **296** F4
Novalukoml', Belarus, **299** B5
Novara, Italy, **294** B3
Novato, U.S.A., **422** B2
Novaya Ladoga, Russian Federation, **299** D2
Novaya Sibir', Ostrov, *island*, Russian Federation, **301** R2
Novaya Zemlya, *island*, Russian Federation, **300** G2, *466*
Nové Zámky, Slovakia, **289** J5
Novelda, Spain, **293** G3
Novgorod, Russian Federation, **299** C3, *271, 273*
Novgorodka, Russian Federation, **299** B4
Novgorodskaya Oblast', *province*, Russian Federation, **299** D3
Novi Bečej, Serbia, **296** C3
Novi Iskŭr, Bulgaria, **296** D4
Novi Ligure, Italy, **294** B3
Novi Pazar, Bulgaria, **296** F4
Novi Pazar, Serbia, **296** C4
Novi Sad, Serbia, **296** B3
Novigrad, Croatia, **294** D3
Novo Airão, Brazil, **451** G5
Novo Aripuanã, Brazil, **455** G1
Novo Hamburgo, Brazil, **459** G3
Novo Mesto, Slovenia, **294** E3
Novo Olinda do Norte, Brazil, **452** A4
Novo Parnarama, Brazil, **453** E4
Novo Selo, Macedonia, **297** D5
Novoarchangel'sk, Ukraine, **296** H1

Novobogatīnskoe, Kazakhstan, **222** E3
Novobureyskiy, Russian Federation, **211** K2
Novocherkassk, Russian Federation, **298** F3
Novodoroninskoye, Russian Federation, **210** F2
Novodugino, Russian Federation, **299** E5
Novogeorgiyevka, Russian Federation, **211** J2
Novokiyevskiy Uval, Russian Federation, **211** K2
Novokruchininskiy, Russian Federation, **210** F2
Novokuybyshevsk, Russian Federation, **222** D2
Novokuznetsk, Russian Federation, **223** M2
Novolazarevskaya, *Russian Federation research station*, Antarctica, **470** D3
Novomoskovsk, Russian Federation, **299** G5
Novonadezhdīnka, Kazakhstan, **222** E2
Novopokrovka, Russian Federation, **211** L3
Novorzhev, Russian Federation, **299** B4
Novoselivka, Ukraine, **296** G2
Novosel'ye, Russian Federation, **299** B3
Novoselytsya, Ukraine, **296** F1
Novosergiyevka, Russian Federation, **222** E2
Novoshakhtinsk, Russian Federation, **222** B3
Novosibirsk, Russian Federation, **223** L2, *273*
Novosibirskaya Oblast', *province*, Russian Federation, **223** K1
Novosibirskiye Ostrova, *islands*, Russian Federation, **301** Q2
Novosibirskoye Vodokhranilishche, *reservoir*, Russian Federation, **223** L2
Novosokol'niki, Russian Federation, **299** C4
Novotroitsk, Russian Federation, **222** F2
Novovolyns'k, Ukraine, **289** M3
Novozavidovskiy, Russian Federation, **299** F4
Novy Pahost, Belarus, **287** N5
Novyy Port, Russian Federation, **300** J3
Novyy Tartas, Russian Federation, **223** K1
Now Shahr, Iran, **222** E5
Now Zād, Afghanistan, **221** H2
Nowa Breźnica, Poland, **289** J3
Nowa Dęba, Poland, **289** K3
Nowa Ruda, Poland, **289** H3
Nowa Sól, Poland, **289** G3
Nowata, U.S.A., **420** F7
Nowe Miasto nad Pilicą, Poland, **289** K3
Nowghāb, Iran, **221** G2
Nowogard, Poland, **289** G2
Nowra, Australia, **135** L5
Nowshāk, *mountain peak*, Afghanistan, **218** B1, *184*
Nowshera, Pakistan, **218** B2
Nowy-Dwór Mazowiecki, Poland, **289** K2
Nowy Sącz, Poland, **289** K4
Nowy Targ, Poland, **289** K4
Noy, *river*, Laos, **203** E2
Noyabr'sk, Russian Federation, **300** J3
Noyon, France, **291** F2
Nozay, France, **290** D3
Nsambi, Democratic Republic of the Congo, **368** C3
Nsanje, Malawi, **369** G6
Nsawam, Ghana, **364** D3
Nsok, Equatorial Guinea, **368** B2
Nsombo, Zambia, **369** E5
Nsukka, Nigeria, **365** F3
Ntandembele, Democratic Republic of the Congo, **368** C3
Ntcheu, Malawi, **369** F5
Ntchisi, Malawi, **369** F5
Ntem, *river*, Cameroon/Equatorial Guinea, **368** B2
Ntoum, Gabon, **368** A2
Ntui, Cameroon, **365** G4
Ntungamo, Uganda, **369** F3
Ntwetwe Pan, *lake*, Botswana, **370** D3
Nu (Salween), *river*, China, **215** F3, *158*
Nu Shan, *mountain range*, China, **215** F4
Nuapapu, *island*, Vava'u Group, Tonga, **141** B3
Nūbah, Jibāl an, *mountain range*, Sudan, **366** D2
Nubian Desert, Sudan, **356** J4
Nüden, Mongolia, **210** E4
Nueces, *river*, U.S.A., **424** C5
Nueltin Lake, Canada, **414** E1
Nueva, Isla, *island*, Chile, **460** D5
Nueva Florida, Venezuela, **451** E2
Nueva Galia, Argentina, **458** D5
Nueva Germania, Paraguay, **459** F2
Nueva Gerona, Cuba, **429** E2
Nueva Imperial, Chile, **458** B6
Nueva Lubecka, Argentina, **460** C2
Nueva Pompeya, Argentina, **458** E2
Nueva Rosita, Mexico, **431** E3
Nueva San Salvador (Santa Tecla), El Salvador, **428** C4
Nueve De Julio, Argentina, **458** E5
Nuevitas, Cuba, **429** F2
Nuevo, Golfo, *gulf*, Argentina, **460** E2
Nuevo Casas Grandes, Mexico, **430** D2
Nuevo Ideal, Mexico, **430** D3
Nuevo Laredo, Mexico, **431** F3
Nuevo Léon, *state*, Mexico, **431** F3
Nuevo Mundo, Bolivia, **455** E3
Nuga, Mongolia, **213** G2
Nugaal, *administrative region*, Somalia, **367** G3
Nuguria Islands, Papua New Guinea, **138** D5
Nūh, India, **218** D3
Nuhaka, New Zealand, **132** F4
Nui, *island*, Tuvalu, **139** F5, *113*
Nuiqsut, U.S.A., **410** D2
Nujiang, China, **215** F3
Nukiki, Solomon Islands, **141** A1
Nuku, Papua New Guinea, **140** A3
Nuku Hiva, *island*, French Polynesia, **137** G1
Nuku'alofa, *island*, Tongatapu Group, Tonga, **141** B4, *114*
Nukufetau, *island*, Tuvalu, **139** F5, *113*
Nukulaelae, *island*, Tuvalu, **139** F5, *113*
Nukumanu Islands, Papua New Guinea, **138** E5
Nukunonu, *island*, Tokelau, **139** G5
Nukuoro, *island*, Micronesia, **138** D4
Nukus, Uzbekistan, **222** F4
Nukutepipi, *island*, French Polynesia, **137** G3
Nullagine, Australia, **134** E3
Nullarbor Plain, Australia, **128** D5
Nulu'erhu Shan, *mountain range*, China, **211** G4
Num, Nepal, **219** F4
Num, Pulau, *island*, Indonesia, **199** F3
Numan, Monts, *mountain peak*, Cameroon, **365** G3
Numan, Nigeria, **365** G3
Nume Tirso, *river*, Sardegna, Italy, **295** B5
Numfor, Pulau, *island*, Indonesia, **199** F3
Nunap Isua, *cape*, Greenland, **411** Q4
Nunavut, *territory*, Canada, **411** J3, *381*
Nuneaton, England, U.K., **305** F2
Nungba, India, **219** H4
Nungnain Sum, China, **211** G3
Nunivak Island, U.S.A., **410** C3
Nunnanen, Finland, **285** M2
Nuoro, Sardegna, Italy, **295** B5
Nuorunen, Gora, *mountain peak*, Russian Federation, **285** Q3
Nuqrah, Saudi Arabia, **363** H3
Nuqruș, Jabal, *mountain peak*, Egypt, **363** F4
Nuqub, Yemen, **220** E6
Nuquí, Colombia, **450** C3
Nur Turu, China, **213** G5
Nura, Kazakhstan, **222** G3
Nura, *river*, Kazakhstan, **212** A2
Nūrābād, Iran, **220** F2
Nurallao, Sardegna, Italy, **295** B6
Nuri, Mexico, **430** C2
Nurmes, Finland, **285** P5
Nurmijärvi, Finland, **285** P5
Nürnberg, Germany, **288** E4
Nurota, Uzbekistan, **222** H4
Nūrpur, India, **218** C2
Nūrpur, Pakistan, **218** B3
Nusa Barung, Pulau, *island*, Indonesia, **201** F5
Nusa Penida, Pulau, *island*, Indonesia, **201** F5
Nusa Tenggara Barat, *province*, Indonesia, **201** G5, *148*
Nusa Tenggara Timur, *province*, Indonesia, **198** C5
Nushki, Pakistan, **218** A3
Nuttal, Pakistan, **218** B3
Nuuk (Godthåb), Greenland, **411** P3, *388*
Nuussuaq, Greenland, **411** P2
Nuvvus, Finland, **285** N2
Nuwaybi' al Muzayyinah, Egypt, **225** C5
Nyagan', Russian Federation, **300** H3
Nyahururu, Kenya, **369** G2
Nyainqêntanglha Feng, *mountain peak*, China, **214** D3
Nyainqêntanglha Shan, *mountain range*, China, **214** D3
Nyakabindi, Tanzania, **369** F3
Nyakaliro, Tanzania, **369** F3
Nyåker, Sweden, **284** J5
Nyala, Sudan, **366** B2
Nyalam, China, **214** C3
Nyalikungu, Tanzania, **369** F3
Nyamandhlovu, Zimbabwe, **371** E2
Nyamlell, Sudan, **366** C3
Nyandoma, Russian Federation, **299** H2
Nyanga, Congo, **368** B3
Nyanga, *province*, Gabon, **368** B3
Nyanga, *river*, Gabon, **368** B3
Nyanga, South Africa, **370** C5
Nyanga, Zimbabwe, **371** F2
Nyanza, *province*, Kenya, **369** F3
Nyanza, Rwanda, **369** E3
Nyaunglebin, Myanmar, **205** C4
Nyazepetrovsk, Russian Federation, **222** F1
Nybergsund, Norway, **286** F2
Nyborg, Denmark, **286** E5
Nybro, Sweden, **286** G4
Nyêmo, China, **214** D3
Nyeri, Kenya, **369** G3
Nyêwo, China, **214** E3
Nyhammar, Sweden, **286** G2
Nyika Plateau, Malawi, **369** F5, *341, 345*
Nyima, China, **214** C3
Nyimba, Zambia, **369** F5
Nyingchi, China, **214** E3
Nyírábrány, Hungary, **289** K5
Nyírbátor, Hungary, **289** L5
Nyíregyháza, Hungary, **289** K5
Nykøbing, Jylland, Denmark, **286** D4
Nykøbing, Sjælland, Denmark, **286** E5
Nyköping, Sweden, **287** H3
Nykroppa, Sweden, **286** G3
Nylstroom, South Africa, **371** E3
Nynäshamn, Sweden, **287** H3
Nyngan, Australia, **135** K5
Nyoman, *river*, Belarus/Poland, **289** L2
Nyon, Switzerland, **291** H3
Nyons, France, **291** G4
Nyrud, Norway, **285** P2
Nysa, Poland, **289** H3
Nysäter, Sweden, **286** F3
Nyūdō-zaki, *point*, Japan, **209** G3
Nyuk, Ozero, *lake*, Russian Federation, **285** R4
Nyukhcha, Russian Federation, **285** T5
Nyunzu, Democratic Republic of the Congo, **369** E4
Nyurang, Indonesia, **201** G2
Nyurba, Russian Federation, **301** N3
Nyvoll, Norway, **285** L1
Nzambi, Congo, **368** B3
Nzara, Sudan, **369** E2
Nzébéla, Guinea, **364** C3
Nzega, Tanzania, **369** F3
Nzérékoré, Guinea, **364** C3
N'zeto, Angola, **368** B4
Nzingu, Democratic Republic of the Congo, **369** E3
Nzwani (Anjouan), *island*, Comoros, **372** A3, *352*


## O


Ō-shima, *island*, Izu-Shotō, Japan, **209** G4
Ō-shima, *island*, Nansei-shotō, Japan, **209** P7
Oa, Mull of, *point*, Scotland, U.K., **308** C5
Oadby, England, U.K., **305** F2
Oahe, Lake, *lake*, U.S.A., **420** C2
Oahu, *island*, Hawaiian Islands, U.S.A., **422** R9, *96*
Oak Bluffs, U.S.A., **426** E4
Oak City, U.S.A., **422** G2
Oak Creek, U.S.A., **423** K1
Oak Harbor, U.S.A., **418** C2
Oak Hill, U.S.A., **421** N7
Oak Park, U.S.A., **421** K5
Oak Ridge, U.S.A., **425** K1
Oakdale, U.S.A., **424** F4
Oakengates, England, U.K., **304** E2
Oakham, England, U.K., **305** G2
Oakhurst, U.S.A., **422** D3
Oakland, U.S.A., **422** B3
Oakley, Idaho, U.S.A., **418** H5
Oakley, Kansas, U.S.A., **420** C6
Oakover, *river*, Australia, **134** E3
Oakridge, U.S.A., **418** C5
Oakura, N. North Island, New Zealand, **132** E2
Oakura, S. North Island, New Zealand, **132** D4
Oakville, Canada, **421** P4
Oamaru, New Zealand, **133** C7
Oasis, U.S.A., **422** F1
Oates Land, *region*, Antarctica, **470** E8
Oaxaca, *state*, Mexico, **431** F5
Oaxaca de Juárez, Mexico, **431** F5
Ob', *river*, Russian Federation, **300** H3
Ob', Russian Federation, **223** L2
Oba, Canada, **421** L1
Obala, Cameroon, **368** B2
Oban, Nigeria, **368** A1
Oban, Scotland, U.K., **308** D4
Obbola, Sweden, **284** K5
Oberá, Argentina, **459** F3
Oberlin, U.S.A., **420** C6
Oberon, U.S.A., **420** D2
Oberösterreich, *state*, Austria, **289** F4
Oberpfälzer Wald, *mountain range*, Germany, **288** F4
Oberstdorf, Germany, **288** E5
Obeslisk, *mountain peak*, New Zealand, **133** B7
Obi, Pulau, *island*, Indonesia, **198** D3
Obi, Selat, *strait*, Indonesia, **198** D3
Óbidos, Brazil, **452** B3
Óbidos, Portugal, **292** C3
Obihiro, Japan, **209** H2
Obispos, Venezuela, **451** D2
Obluch'ye, Russian Federation, **211** K2
Obninsk, Russian Federation, **299** F5
Obo, Central African Republic, **369** E1
Obo, China, **213** J5
Obock, Djibouti, **367** F2
Obokote, Democratic Republic of the Congo, **369** E3
Obol', Belarus, **299** B5
Obol', *river*, Belarus, **299** B5
Oborniki, Poland, **289** H2
Obouya, Congo, **368** C3
Obrenovac, Serbia, **296** C3
O'Brien, U.S.A., **418** C5
Obrochishte, Bulgaria, **296** F4
Obrovac, Croatia, **294** E3
Obskaya Guba, *gulf*, Russian Federation, **300** J3
Obuasi, Ghana, **364** D3
Obytichna Kosa, *physical feature*, Ukraine, **298** E3
Ocala, U.S.A., **425** L5
Ocaña, Andalucía, Spain, **293** F4
Ocaña, Castilla la Mancha, Spain, **293** F3
Ocaña, Colombia, **450** D2
Ocate, U.S.A., **423** L3
Occidental, Cordillera, *mountain range*, Chile/Peru, **447** E5
Occidental, Cordillera, *mountain range*, Colombia, **447** E3
Ocean *see* Banaba, *island*, Kiribati, **139** F5
Ocean Beach, New Zealand, **132** E2
Ocean City, Maryland, U.S.A., **426** C5
Ocean City, New Jersey, U.S.A., **426** C5
Ocean Springs, U.S.A., **425** H4
Oceanographer Fracture Zone, *tectonic feature*, Atlantic Ocean, **477** D3
Oceanside, U.S.A., **422** E5
Ochil Hills, Scotland, U.K., **308** F4
Ocho Rios, Jamaica, **429** F3
Ochopee, U.S.A., **425** M7
Ochthonia, Greece, **297** E6
Ocilla, U.S.A., **425** L4
Ockelbo, Sweden, **287** H2
Ocmulgee, *river*, U.S.A., **425** L3
Ocna Sibiului, Romania, **296** E3
Ocnița, Moldova, **296** F1
Ococingo, Mexico, **431** G5
Oconee, Lake, *lake*, U.S.A., **425** L3
Ocotal, Nicaragua, **428** D4
Ocotepeque, Honduras, **428** C4
Ocotillo Wells, U.S.A., **422** E5
Ocotlán, Mexico, **430** E4
Ocracoke, U.S.A., **426** C7
Ocreza, *river*, Portugal, **292** D3
Octavia, U.S.A., **424** E2
Octeville, France, **305** F5
Oda, Ghana, **364** D3
Oda, Jabal, *mountain peak*, Sudan, **363** G4
Ōda, Japan, **208** F4
Oda, Ras, *point*, Egypt, **363** G4
Ódáðahraun, *lava field*, Iceland, **284** Y7
Ōdate, Japan, **209** H2
Odawara, Japan, **209** G4
Odda, Norway, **286** C2
Odeceixe, Portugal, **292** C4
Odemira, Portugal, **292** C4
Ödemiș, Turkey, **224** C5
Ôdêngk, Cambodia, **203** E4
Odensbacken, Sweden, **286** G3
Odense, Denmark, **286** E5
Oder *see* Odra, *river*, Germany/Poland, **280** F5, *239*
Oderhaff, *lake*, Germany, **289** G2
Odesa (Odessa), Ukraine, **298** D3
Ödeshög, Sweden, **286** G3
Odes'ka Oblast', *province*, Ukraine, **296** G2
Odessa *see* Odesa, Ukraine, **298** D3

Odessa, U.S.A., **423** M6
Odienné, Côte d'Ivoire, **364** C3
Odintsovo, Russian Federation, **299** F5
Odobeşti, Romania, **296** F3
O'Donnell, U.S.A., **424** B3
Odorheiu Secuiesc, Romania, **296** E2
Odoyev, Russian Federation, **299** F6
Odra (Oder), *river*, Germany/Poland, **280** F5, *239*
Odrzywół, Poland, **289** K3
Odžaci, Serbia. **296** B3
Odžak, Bosnia and Herzegovina, **294** G3
Oebisfelde, Germany, **288** E2
Oeiras, Brazil, **453** E5
Oeno Island, Pitcairn Islands, **137** H3, *126*
Ofaqim, Israel, **225** C4
Offa, Nigeria, **365** E3
Offaly, *county*, Ireland, **309** E4
Offenbach am Main, Germany, **288** D3
Offenburg, Germany, **288** C4
Offranville, France, **305** J5
Ofidoussa, *island*, Kyklades, Greece, **297** E7
Ofu, *island*, American Samoa, **141** B2
Ofu, *island*, Vava'u Group, Tonga, **141** B3
Ōfunato, Japan, **209** H3
Ogachi, Japan, **209** H3
Ogaden, *region*, Ethiopia, **367** F3, *338, 339*
Ogallala, U.S.A., **420** C5
Ogan, *river*, Indonesia, **200** D3
Ogasawara-shotō, *islands*, Japan, **138** B2
Ogbomosho, Nigeria, **365** E3
Ogden, U.S.A., **420** F4
Ogeechee, *river*, U.S.A., **425** L3
Ogema, Canada, **419** M2
Ogilvie Mountains, *mountain range*, Canada, **410** F3
Oglala, U.S.A., **420** B4
Ognon, *river*, France, **291** G3
Ogoamas, Gunung, *mountain peak*, Indonesia, **198** C2
Ogoja, Nigeria, **365** F3
Ogoki, Canada, **415** M6
Ogoki Reservoir, Canada, **415** K6
Ogoki, *river*, Canada, **415** L6
Ogooué, *river*, Gabon, **368** A3, *333*
Ogooué-Ivindo, *province*, Gabon, **368** B2
Ogooué-Lolo, *province*, Gabon, **368** B3
Ogooué-Maritime, *province*, Gabon, **368** A3
Ogorelyshi, Russian Federation, **285** S5
Ogre, Latvia, **287** M4
Ogulin, Croatia, **294** E3
Ogun, *state*, Nigeria, **365** E3
Ogurjaly, *island*, Turkmenistan, **222** E5
Ohakune, New Zealand, **132** E4
Ohanet, Algeria, **361** H3
Ohangwena, *administrative region*, Namibia, **370** C2
Ohau, Lake, New Zealand, **133** B7
Ohau, New Zealand, **132** E5
Ohaupo, New Zealand, **132** E3
O'Higgins, Cabo, *cape*, Isla de Pascua (Easter Island), Chile, **461** B2
O'Higgins, Lago, *lake*, Chile, **460** B3
O'Higgins, Punta, *point*, Róbinson Crusoe Island, Archipiélago Juan Fernández, Chile, **461** C2
Ohio, *river*, U.S.A., **407** Q5
Ohio, *state*, U.S.A., **421** M5, *97, 383, 386*
'Ohonua, Tongatapu Group, Tonga, **141** B4
Ohře, *river*, Czech Republic, **289** F3
Ohrid, Lake *see* Ohridsko Jezero, *lake*, Macedonia, **297** C5, *260*
Ohrid, Macedonia, **297** C5, *260*
Ohridsko Jezero (Lake Ohrid), *lake*, Macedonia, **297** C5
Ohura, New Zealand, **132** E4
Oiapoque, Brazil, **452** C2
Oijärvi, Finland, **285** N4
Oil City, U.S.A., **421** P5
Oir, Beinn an, *mountain peak*, Scotland, U.K., **308** C5
Oise, *river*, France, **291** F2
Oisemont, France, **305** J5
Ōita, Japan, **208** E4
Oiti Oros, *mountain peak*, Greece, **297** D6
Öje, Sweden, **286** F2
Ojibwa, U.S.A., **420** H3
Ojinaga, Mexico, **430** D2
Ojo de Laguna, Mexico, **430** D2
Ojos del Salado, *mountain peak*, Argentina/Chile, **458** C3, *442*
Öjung, Sweden, **286** G2
Ok Tedi, Papua New Guinea, **140** A4
Oka, *river*, Russian Federation, **299** F5
Okaba, Indonesia, **199** G5
Okahandja, Namibia, **370** C3
Okaihau, New Zealand, **132** D2
Okak Islands, Canada, **411** N4
Okakarara, Namibia, **370** C3
Okanagan Lake, Canada, **418** E2
Okaputa, Namibia, **370** C3
Okāra, Pakistan, **218** C3
Okarito Lagoon, *bay*, New Zealand, **133** B6
Okaukuejo, Namibia, **370** C2
Okavango, *administrative region*, Namibia, **370** C2
Okavango, *river*, Southern Africa, **357** G8, *347, 348*
Okavango Delta, Botswana, **370** D2
Okawa Point, Chatham Islands, New Zealand, **133** Q16
Okaya, Japan, **209** G3
Okayama, Japan, **208** F4
Okazize, Namibia, **370** C3
Okeechobee, Lake, U.S.A., **425** M6
Okeechobee, U.S.A., **425** M6
Okehampton, England, U.K., **304** C4
Okemah, U.S.A., **424** D2
Okha, Russian Federation, **301** R4
Okhaldhungā, Nepal, **219** F4
Okhotsk, Russian Federation, **301** R4
Okhotsk, Sea of *see* Okhotskoye More, *Sea*, Russian Federation, **301** R4, *271*
Okhotskoye More (Sea of Okhotsk), *Sea*, Russian Federation, **301** R4, *271*
Okhtan-Yarvi, Ozero, *lake*, Russian Federation, **285** Q4
Oki-shotō, *islands*, Japan, **208** F3
Okinawa, Japan, **209** N8, *165*
Okinawa-jima, *island*, Japan, **209** P8
Okinawa-shotō, *islands*, Japan, **209** N8
Okino-Tori-shima, *island*, Japan, **138** B2
Okinoerabu-jima, *island*, Japan, **209** P8
Okiore, New Zealand, **132** F4
Oklahoma, *state*, U.S.A., **424** C2, *91, 386*
Oklahoma City, U.S.A., **424** D2, *386*
Okmulgee, U.S.A., **424** E2
Okondja, Gabon, **368** B3
Okotoks, Canada, **413** M6
Okoyo, Congo, **368** C3
Okpo, Myanmar, **205** B4
Okreek, U.S.A., **420** C4
Oksbøl, Denmark, **286** D5
Øksfjord, Norway, **285** L1
Oktyabr'sk, Kazakhstan, **222** F3
Oktyabr'skiy, Russian Federation, **222** E2
Oktyabr'skoy Revolyutsii, Ostrov, *island*, Russian Federation, **300** L2
Okučani, Croatia, **294** F3
Okulovka, Russian Federation, **299** D3
Okurcalar, Turkey, **225** A1
Okushiri-tō, *island*, Japan, **209** G2
Okuta, Nigeria, **365** E3
Ola, U.S.A., **418** F4
Ólafsfjörður, Iceland, **284** Y6
Olaine, Latvia, **287** L4
Olal, Vanuatu, **141** A2
Olanchito, Honduras, **428** D4
Öland, *island*, Sweden, **287** H4, *232*
Olanga, *river*, Finland/Russian Federation, **285** Q3
Olathe, U.S.A., **420** F6
Olavarría, Argentina, **459** E5
Olbia, Sardegna, Italy, **295** B5
Old Crow, Canada, **410** F3
Old Faithful, U.S.A., **419** J4
Old Forge, U.S.A., **426** C3
Old Head of Kinsale, *point*, Ireland, **309** D6
Old Leake, England, U.K., **305** H1
Old Orchard Beach, U.S.A., **426** E3
Old Town, U.S.A., **426** F2
Old Wives Lake, Canada, **413** R6
Oldcastle, Ireland, **309** E4
Oldenburg in Holstein, Germany, **288** E1
Olderfjord, Norway, **285** M1
Oldervik, Norway, **284** J2
Oldham, England, U.K., **306** F4
Oldmeldrum, Scotland, U.K., **308** G3
Olds, Canada, **413** M6
Öldziyt, Arhangay, Mongolia, **213** J2
Öldziyt, Dorngovĭ, Mongolia, **210** E3
Olean, U.S.A., **426** A3
Olecko, Poland, **289** L1
Olekminsk, Russian Federation, **301** P3
Oleksandriya, Ukraine, **298** D3
Olenegorsk, Russian Federation, **285** R2
Olenek, *river*, Russian Federation, **301** N3
Olenino, Russian Federation, **299** D4
Olenitsa, Russian Federation, **285** S3
Oleniy, Ostrov, *island*, Russian Federation, **285** S4
Olen'ya Rechka, Russian Federation, **213** G1
Oléron, Île d', *island*, France, **290** D4
Oles'ko, Ukraine, **289** M4
Oleśnica, Poland, **289** H3
Olesno, Poland, **289** J3
Ølfjellet, *mountain peak*, Norway, **284** G3
Olga, Mount *see* Katatjuta, *mountain peak*, Australia, **134** G4
Ol'ga, Russian Federation, **211** L4
Ol'ginsk, Russian Federation, **211** L1
Ölgiy, Mongolia, **212** F2
Ølgod, Denmark, **286** D5
Olhava, Finland, **285** M4
Olib, *island*, Croatia, **294** E3
Olímpia, Brazil, **456** D5
Olinalá, Mexico, **431** F5
Olinda, Brazil, **453** G5
Olinga, Mozambique, **369** G6
Olingskog, Sweden, **286** G2
Oliva, Argentina, **458** D4
Oliva, Cordillera de, *mountain range*, Argentina/Chile, **458** C3
Oliva, Spain, **293** G3
Olivares, Cerro de, *mountain peak*, Argentina/Chile, **458** C4
Olivares de Júcar, Spain, **293** F3
Olive, U.S.A., **419** M4
Olive Hill, U.S.A., **421** M6
Oliveira, Brazil, **457** E5
Oliveira dos Brejinhos, Brazil, **457** E3
Olivenza, Spain, **292** D3
Oliver, Canada, **413** K7
Oliver Lake, Canada, **414** C3
Ölkeyek, *river*, Kazakhstan, **222** G3
Ol'khon, Ostrov, *island*, Russian Federation, **210** D1
Olkusz, Poland, **289** J3
Ollagüe, Chile, **455** E5
Ollagüe, Volcán, *mountain peak*, Bolivia/Chile, **455** E5
Ollita, Cordillera de, *mountain range*, Argentina/Chile, **458** B4
Ollombo, Congo, **368** C3
Olmedo, Spain, **292** E2
Olmillos de Sasamon, Spain, **293** F1
Olmos, Peru, **454** B1
Olney, England, U.K., **305** G2
Olney, U.S.A., **421** J6
Olofström, Sweden, **286** G4
Olomane, *river*, Canada, **417** L4
Olomouc, Czech Republic, **289** H4
Olonets, Russian Federation, **299** D2
Olongapo, Philippines, **204** C3
Olonzac, France, **290** F5
Oloron-Sainte-Marie, France, **290** D5
Olosega, *island*, American Samoa, **141** B2
Olot, Spain, **293** J1
Olovo, Bosnia and Herzegovina, **294** G3
Olovyannaya, Russian Federation, **210** F2
Olpe, Germany, **288** C3
Ol'sha, Russian Federation, **299** C5
Olsztyn, Poland, **289** K2
Olsztynek, Poland, **289** K2
Olt, *river*, Romania, **296** E3
Olten, Switzerland, **291** H3
Olteniţa, Romania, **296** F3
Oltina, Romania, **296** F3
Olton, U.S.A., **424** A2
Olutlanga Island, Philippines, **204** C5
Olympia, U.S.A., **418** C3, *386*
Olympic Mountains, *mountain range*, U.S.A., **418** C3
Olympos, *mountain peak*, Cyprus, **225** B2, *191*
Olympos, Oros (Mount Olympus), *mountain peak*, Greece, **280** G7, *265*
Olympus, Mount, *mountain peak*, U.S.A., **418** C3
Olympus, Mount *see* Olympos, Oros, *mountain peak*, Greece, **280** G7, *265*
Olyutorskiy, Mys, *cape*, Russian Federation, **301** U4
Om', *river*, Russian Federation, **223** L1
Om Hājer, Eritrea, **367** E2
Oma, China, **219** E2
Ōma, Japan, **209** H2
Oma, Russian Federation, **300** F3
Ōmagari, Japan, **209** H3
Omagh, *district*, Northern Ireland, U.K., **309** E3
Omagh, Northern Ireland, U.K., **309** E3
Omaguas, Peru, **450** D5
Omaha, U.S.A., **420** F5
Omaheke, *administrative region*, Namibia, **370** C3
Omak, U.S.A., **418** E2
Omakau, New Zealand, **133** B7
Omakere, New Zealand, **132** F5
Oman, *country*, Asia, **196** G8, *146, 175, 176*
Oman, Gulf of, Arabian Peninsula/Iran, **221** G4, *176*
Omarama, New Zealand, **133** B7
Omaruru, Namibia, **370** C3
Omate, Peru, **454** D4
Ombalantu, Namibia, **370** B2
Ombella-Mpoko, *prefecture*, Central African Republic, **368** C1
Ombersley, England, U.K., **304** E2
Ombo, *island*, Norway, **286** B3
Omboué, Gabon, **368** A3
Ombu, China, **214** C3
Omdurman *see* Umm Durmān, Sudan, **366** D1
Ometepec, Mexico, **431** F5
Omineca, *river*, Canada, **412** G4
Omineca Mountains, *mountain range*, Canada, **412** F3
Omiš, Croatia, **294** F4
Ömnögovĭ, *province*, Mongolia, **213** J4
Omo, *river*, Ethiopia, **367** E3
Omoku, Nigeria, **365** F3
Omolon, *river*, Russian Federation, **301** S3
Ömossa, Finland, **287** K1
Omsk, Russian Federation, **223** J2
Omskaya Oblast', *province*, Russian Federation, **223** J1
Omsukchan, Russian Federation, **301** S3
Ōmura, Japan, **208** E4
Omurtag, Bulgaria, **296** F4
Omusati, *administrative region*, Namibia, **370** B2
Ōmuta, Japan, **208** E4
Omutinskiy, Russian Federation, **222** H1
Ona, *river*, Russian Federation, **212** F2
Onalaska, U.S.A., **420** H4
Onaping Lake, U.S.A., **421** N2
Onavas, Mexico, **430** C2
Onaway, U.S.A., **421** L3
Oncativo, Argentina, **458** D4
Onchan, Isle of Man, **306** D3
Oncócua, Angola, **368** B6
Ondangwa, Namibia, **370** C2
Ondava, *river*, Slovakia, **289** K4
Onder, India, **218** D4
Ondjiva, Angola, **368** C6
Ondo, Nigeria, **365** E3
Ondo, *state*, Nigeria, **365** E3
Öndörhaan, Mongolia, **210** E3
Öndörhushuu, Mongolia, **210** F3
Ondozero, Ozero, *lake*, Russian Federation, **285** R5
One and Half Degree Channel, Maldives, **216** C6
100 Mile House, Canada, **412** J6
Onega, *river*, Russian Federation, **281** H3
Oneida, U.S.A., **426** C3
Oneida Lake, U.S.A., **426** B3
O'Neill, U.S.A., **420** D4
Onekotan, Ostrov, *island*, Russian Federation, **301** S5
Oneonta, Alabama, U.S.A., **425** J3
Oneonta, New York, U.S.A., **426** C3
Oneşti, Romania, **296** F2
Onetar, Vanuatu, **141** A2
Onevai, *island*, Tonga, **141** B4
Onezhskaya Guba, *bay*, Russian Federation, **285** S4
Onezhskiy Poluostrov, *peninsula*, Russian Federation, **285** T4
Onezhskoye Ozero, Russian Federation, **299** E2
Onga, Gabon, **368** B3
Ongandjera, Namibia, **370** B2
Onggunoi, Indonesia, **198** D2
Ongi, Mongolia, **213** J3
Ongiyn, *river*, Mongolia, **213** J3
Ongjin, North Korea, **208** D3
Ongniud Qi, China, **211** G4
Ongole, India, **216** E3
Ongon, Mongolia, **213** J3
Onguday, Russian Federation, **212** E2
Onida, U.S.A., **420** C3
Onitsha, Nigeria, **365** F3
Ono, *island*, Fiji, **141** A4
Ōnojō, Japan, **208** E4
Onokhoy, Russian Federation, **210** E2
Onon, *river*, Mongolia, **210** E2
Onor, China, **211** H2
Onotoa, *island*, Kiribati, **139** F5
Ons, Illa de, *island*, Spain, **292** C1
Onseepkans, South Africa, **370** C4
Onslow, Australia, **134** D3
Onslow Bay, U.S.A., **425** P2
Ontario, Lake, Canada/U.S.A., **416** B8, *380, 381*
Ontario, *province*, Canada, **415** K6, *381*
Ontario, U.S.A., **418** F4
Ontonagon, U.S.A., **421** J2
Ontong Java, *island*, Solomon Islands, **138** E5

Ontur, Spain, **293** G3
Onverwacht, Suriname, **452** B2
Onycha, U.S.A., **425** J4
Oodnadatta, Australia, **135** H4
Oodweyne, Somalia, **367** G3
Oologah Lake, U.S.A., **420** F7
Oost-Vlaanderen, *province*, Belgium, **288** A3
Oostende, Belgium, **288** A3
Oostpunt, *point*, Curaçao, Netherlands Antilles, **461** C3
Ootsa Lake, Canada, **412** F5
Opal, U.S.A., **419** J6
Opala, Democratic Republic of the Congo, **368** D3
Opari, Sudan, **369** F2
Opasatika, Canada, **415** N7
Opatija, Croatia, **294** E3
Opatów, Poland, **289** K3
Opava, Czech Republic, **289** H4
Opelika, U.S.A., **425** K3
Opelousas, U.S.A., **424** F4
Opheim, U.S.A., **419** L2
Ophir, Gunung, *mountain peak*, Indonesia, **200** C2
Opienge, Democratic Republic of the Congo, **369** E2
Opinaca, Réservoir, Canada, **416** C3
Opobo, Nigeria, **368** A2
Opochka, Russian Federation, **299** B4
Opoczno, Poland, **289** K3
Opole, Poland, **289** H3
Opole Lubelskie, Poland, **289** K3
Opotiki, New Zealand, **132** F4
Opp, U.S.A., **425** J4
Oppdal, Norway, **286** D1
Oppland, *county*, Norway, **286** D2
Opsa, Belarus, **287** N5
Opua, New Zealand, **132** E2
Opunake, New Zealand, **132** D4
Opuwo, Namibia, **370** B2
Oq-Suu, *river*, Tajikistan, **223** J5
Oracle, U.S.A., **423** H5
Oradea, Romania, **296** C2
Orahov Do, Bosnia and Herzegovina, **294** F4
Orahovac, Serbia, **296** C4
Orahovica, Croatia, **294** F3
Orai, India, **218** D4
Oral, Kazakhstan, **222** E2
Oran, Algeria, **361** F1
Orange, Australia, **135** K5
Orange, Cabo, *cape*, Brazil, **452** C2
Orange, France, **291** G4
Orange, Louisiana, U.S.A., **424** F4
Orange, *river*, Namibia/South Africa, **370** C4, *95, 349, 351*
Orange, Virginia, U.S.A., **426** A5
Orange Walk, Belize, **428** C3
Orangeburg, U.S.A., **425** M3
Orangerie Bay, Papua New Guinea, **140** C5
Orango, *island*, Guinea-Bissau, **364** A2
Oranienburg, Germany, **288** F2
Oranje Gebergte, *mountain range*, Suriname, **452** B2
Oranjemund, Namibia, **370** C4
Oranjestad, Aruba, **461** B3, *387*
Oranmore, Ireland, **309** D4
Oransbari, Indonesia, **199** F3
Orap, Vanuatu, **141** A2
Orapa, Botswana, **371** E3
Orăştie, Romania, **296** D3
Orava, *river*, Slovakia, **289** J4
Oraviţa, Romania, **296** C3
Orawia, New Zealand, **133** A8
Orbec, France, **290** E2
Orbetello, Italy, **295** C4
Órbigo, *river*, Spain, **292** E1
Orbost, Australia, **135** K6
Orcadas, *Argentinian research station*, Antarctica, **470** B3
Orchard, Idaho, U.S.A., **418** G5
Orchard, Nebraska, U.S.A., **420** D4
Orcotuna, Peru, **454** C3
Ord, *river*, Australia, **134** F2
Orderville, U.S.A., **422** G3
Ordes, Spain, **292** C1
Ordu, Turkey, **224** E4
Ordway, U.S.A., **423** M2
Orealla, Guyana, **451** H3
Orebić, Croatia, **294** F4
Örebro, *county*, Sweden, **286** G3
Örebro, Sweden, **286** G3
Oredezh, *river*, Russian Federation, **299** C3
Oredezh, Russian Federation, **299** C3
Oregon, *state*, U.S.A., **418** D4, *383, 386*
Oregon, U.S.A., **421** J4
Oregon City, U.S.A., **418** C4
Oregon Inlet, U.S.A., **426** C7
Orekhovo-Zuyevo, Russian Federation, **299** G5
Orel, Russian Federation, **298** E2
Orellana, N. Peru, **454** B1
Orellana, on Ucayali, *river*, Peru, **454** C2
Ören, Turkey, **297** F7
Orenburg, Russian Federation, **222** F2
Orenburgskaya Oblast', *province*, Russian Federation, **222** E2
Orense, Argentina, **459** E6
Orepuki, New Zealand, **133** A8
Orere, New Zealand, **132** E3
Orestiada, Greece, **297** F5
Oreti, *river*, New Zealand, **133** B7
Orford, England, U.K., **305** J2
Orford Ness, *spit*, England, U.K., **305** J2
Organ, U.S.A., **423** K5
Organabo, French Guiana, **452** C2
Orgaz, Spain, **293** F3
Orgil, Mongolia, **213** H2
Orgiva, Spain, **293** F4
Örgön, Mongolia, **213** J3
Orhaneli, Turkey, **297** G6
Orhei, Moldova, **296** G2
Orhon, *river*, Mongolia, **210** D2
Orhontuul, Mongolia, **210** D2
Orhy, Pic d', *mountain peak*, France/Spain, **293** G1
Orick, U.S.A., **418** B6
Oriental, Cordillera, *mountain range*, Bolivia, **447** F5
Oriental, Cordillera, *mountain range*, Colombia, **447** E3
Oriente, Argentina, **458** E6
Orihuela, Spain, **293** G3
Orillia, Canada, **421** P3
Orimattila, Finland, **287** M2
Orin, U.S.A., **419** M5
Orinduik, Guyana, **451** G3
Orinoco, *river*, Venezuela, **447** F3, *436, 437*
Oriomo, Papua New Guinea, **140** A5
Orissa, *state*, India, **217** E2, *169*
Orissaare, Estonia, **287** L3
Oristano, Golfo di, *gulf*, Italy, **295** A6
Oristano, Sardegna, Italy, **295** B6
Orivesi, *lake*, Finland, **287** P1
Oriximina, Brazil, **452** B3
Orizaba, Mexico, **431** F5
Orizaba, Pico de *see* Citlaltepetl, Volcán, *mountain peak*, Mexico, **431** F5, *400*
Orkanger, Norway, **284** D5
Örkelljunga, Sweden, **286** F4
Orkla, *river*, Norway, **284** D5
Orkney, *local authority*, Scotland, U.K., **308** F1
Orkney Islands, Scotland, U.K., **308** F1, *276*
Orla, U.S.A., **423** M6
Orlândia, Brazil, **456** D5
Orlando, U.S.A., **425** M5
Orléans, France, **290** E3
Orleans, U.S.A., **426** F4
Orlické hory, *mountain range*, Czech Republic, **289** H3
Orlik, Russian Federation, **213** H1
Orlovka, Russian Federation, **223** K1
Orlovskaya Oblast', *province*, Russian Federation, **299** E6
Ormāra, Pakistan, **221** H3
Ormea, Italy, **294** A3
Ormoc, Philippines, **204** D4
Ormond Beach, U.S.A., **425** M5
Ormskirk, England, U.K., **306** F4
Ormylia, Greece, **297** D5
Ørnes, Norway, **284** F3
Orneta, Poland, **289** K1
Ornö, *island*, Sweden, **287** J3
Örnsköldsvik, Sweden, **284** J5
Oro *see* Northern, *province*, Papua New Guinea, **140** C5
Orobie, Alpi, *mountain range*, Italy, **294** B3
Orocué, Colombia, **450** D2
Orodara, Burkina Faso, **364** D2
Orofino, U.S.A., **418** F3
Orog Nuur, *lake*, Mongolia, **213** H3
Orogrande, U.S.A., **423** K5
Oromocto, Canada, **416** H7
Oron, Israel, **225** C4
Oron, Nigeria, **368** A2
Oron, *river*, Jordan, **225** C4
Orona, *island*, Kiribati, **139** G5
Oroquieta, Philippines, **204** C4
Orós, Açude, *reservoir*, Brazil, **453** F5
Orosei, Golfo di, *gulf*, Sardegna, Italy, **295** B5
Orosei, Sardegna, Italy, **295** B5
Orosháza, Hungary, **289** K5
Orovada, U.S.A., **418** F6
Oroville, Lake, U.S.A., **422** C2
Oroville, U.S.A., **422** C2
Orpesa, Spain, **293** H2
Orphir, Orkney, Scotland, U.K., **308** F2
Orqen Zizhiqi, China, **211** H2
Orqohan, China, **211** H2
Orr, Mount, *mountain peak*, New Zealand, **133** C7
Orrin, *river*, Scotland, U.K., **308** E3
Orsa, Sweden, **286** G2
Orsha, Belarus, **299** C5
Örsjö, Sweden, **286** G4
Orsk, Russian Federation, **222** F2
Orşova, Romania, **296** D3
Ørsta, Norway, **286** C1
Ørsted, Denmark, **286** E4
Örsundsbro, Sweden, **287** H3
Orta, Lago d', *lake*, Italy, **294** B3
Orta Nova, Italy, **295** E5
Ortaca, Turkey, **297** G7
Orte, Italy, **295** D4
Ortegal, Cabo, *cape*, Spain, **292** C1
Orthez, France, **290** D5
Ortigueira, Spain, **292** D1
Orting, U.S.A., **418** C3
Ortiz, Mexico, **430** C2
Ortiz, Venezuela, **451** E2
Ortoire, *river*, Trinidad, Trinidad and Tobago, **461** C4, *399*
Orton, England, U.K., **306** F3
Ortón, *river*, Bolivia, **455** E3
Ortona, Italy, **295** E4
Ortonville, U.S.A., **420** E3
Örträsk, Sweden, **284** J4
Orulgan, Khrebet, *mountain range*, Russian Federation, **301** P3
Orūmīyeh, Daryācheh-ye, *lake*, Iran, **363** J1
Orūmīyeh (Urmia), Iran, **363** H1
Oruro, Bolivia, **455** E4
Oruro, *department*, Bolivia, **455** E5
Orust, *island*, Sweden, **286** E3
Orvieto, Italy, **294** C4
Orville Coast, *region*, Antarctica, **470** B5
Orwell, U.S.A., **421** N5
Oryakhovo, Bulgaria, **296** D4
Orynyn, Ukraine, **296** F1
Orzysz, Poland, **289** K2
Os, Norway, **286** E1
Osa, Península de, Costa Rica, **428** E5
Osa, Russian Federation, **222** F1
Osage, U.S.A., **420** G4
Ōsaka, Japan, **209** F4, *150*
Osakarovka, Kazakhstan, **212** B2
Osawatomie, U.S.A., **420** F6
Osby, Sweden, **286** G4
Oscar, French Guiana, **452** C2
Osceola, U.S.A., **420** E5
Oschiri, Sardegna, Italy, **295** B5
Oscoda, U.S.A., **421** M3
Osečina, Serbia, **296** B3
Osen, Norway, **284** E4
Osera, Spain, **293** G2
Osh, Kyrgyzstan, **223** J4, *186, 187*
Oshakati, Namibia, **370** C2
Oshamambe, Japan, **209** H2
Oshana, *administrative region*, Namibia, **370** C2
Oshawa, Canada, **421** P4
Oshikango, Namibia, **370** C2
Oshikoto, *administrative region*, Namibia, **370** C2
Oshkosh, Nebraska, U.S.A., **420** B5
Oshkosh, Wisconsin, U.S.A., **421** J3
Oshogbo, Nigeria, **365** E3
Oshwe, Democratic Republic of the Congo, **368** C3
Osiān, India, **218** C4
Osie, Poland, **289** J2
Osijek, Croatia, **294** G3
Oskaloosa, U.S.A., **420** G5
Oskarshamn, Sweden, **286** H4
Oskarström, Sweden, **286** F4
Oskélanéo, Canada, **416** D5
Öskemen, Kazakhstan, **212** D2
Oslo, *county*, Norway, **286** E3
Oslo, Norway, **286** E3, *230, 469*
Oslofjorden, *fiord*, Norway, **286** E3
Osmānābād, India, **216** D2
Osmaniye, Turkey, **224** E5
Os'mino, Russian Federation, **299** B3
Osnabrück, Germany, **288** D2
Oso, U.S.A., **418** D2
Osogovske Planine, Bulgaria/Macedonia, **296** D4
Osório, Brazil, **459** G3
Osorno, Chile, **460** C1
Osorno, Volcán, *mountain peak*, Chile, **460** C1
Osoyoos, Canada, **413** K7
Ossa, Mount, *mountain peak*, Australia, **135** K7
Ossa, *mountain peak*, Portugal, **292** D3
Ossa de Montiel, Spain, **293** F3
Ossabaw Island, U.S.A., **425** M4
Osse, *river*, France, **290** E5
Ossima, Papua New Guinea, **140** A3
Ossjøen, *lake*, Norway, **286** E2
Östansjö, Sweden, **284** J4
Ostashkov, Russian Federation, **299** D4
Östavall, Sweden, **286** G1
Østby, Norway, **284** E5
Oster, *river*, Russian Federation, **299** D6
Øster Vrå, Denmark, **286** E4
Osterburg, Germany, **288** E2
Österbybruk, Sweden, **287** H2
Österbymo, Sweden, **286** G4
Österdalälven, *river*, Sweden, **286** F2
Østerdalen, *valley*, Norway, **286** E2
Österfärnebo, Sweden, **287** H2
Östergötland, *county*, Sweden, **286** G3
Östersund, Sweden, **284** G5
Østfold, *county*, Norway, **286** E3
Ostfriesische Inseln, Germany, **288** C2
Östhammar, Sweden, **287** J2
Ostiglia, Italy, **294** C3
Ostrava, Czech Republic, **289** J4
Ostróda, Poland, **289** K2
Ostrogozhsk, Russian Federation, **298** E2
Ostrołęka, Poland, **289** K2
Ostrov, Pskovskaya Oblast', Russian Federation, **299** B4
Ostrov, Vologodskaya Oblast', Russian Federation, **299** F3
Ostrów Mazowiecka, Poland, **289** K2
Ostrów Wielkopolski, Poland, **289** H3
Ostrowiec Świętokrzyski, Poland, **289** K3
Ostrzeszów, Poland, **289** J3
Osttirol, *region*, Austria, **288** F5
Ostuni, Italy, **295** F5
Osŭm, *river*, Bulgaria, **296** E4
Ōsumi-shotō, *islands*, Japan, **208** E5
Osun, *state*, Nigeria, **365** E3
Osuna, Spain, **292** E4
Oswego, U.S.A., **426** B3
Oswestry, England, U.K., **304** D2
Oświęcim, Poland, **289** J3
Otago Peninsula, New Zealand, **133** C7, *110*
Otaika, New Zealand, **132** E2
Otaki, New Zealand, **133** E5
Otakiri, New Zealand, **132** F3
Otar, Kazakhstan, **212** B4
Otaru, Japan, **209** H2
Otavalo, Ecuador, **450** B4, *438*
Otavi, Namibia, **370** C2
Otelnuk, Lac, *lake*, Canada, **416** G1
Oţelu Roşu, Romania, **296** D3
Otematata, New Zealand, **133** C7
Otepää, Estonia, **287** N3
Othello, U.S.A., **418** E3
Othonoi, *island*, Ionioi Nisoi, Greece, **297** B6
Oti, *river*, Togo, **364** E2, *326*
Otish, Monts, *mountain range*, Canada, **416** F3
Otjiwarongo, Namibia, **370** C3
Otjozondjupa, *administrative region*, Namibia, **370** C2
Otley, England, U.K., **307** G4
Otnes, Norway, **286** E2
Otog Qi, China, **210** E5
Otog Qianqi, China, **210** D5
Otorohanga, New Zealand, **132** E4
Otorokua Point, New Zealand, **133** B6
Otra, *river*, Norway, **286** C3
Otrabanda, Curaçao, Netherlands Antilles, **461** C3
Otranto, Italy, **295** G5
Otranto, Strait of, Albania/Italy, **280** F7
Otsego, U.S.A., **421** L4
Otta, Norway, **286** D2
Otta, *river*, Norway, **286** C1
Ottawa, Canada, **416** D7, *380, 381*
Ottawa, *river*, Canada, **416** C6, *381*
Ottawa, U.S.A., **420** F6
Ottawa Islands, Canada, **415** P2
Ottenby, Sweden, **286** H4
Otterburn, England, U.K., **306** F2
Otterndorf, Germany, **288** D2
Otterøy, Norway, **284** E4
Otterup, Denmark, **286** E5
Ottery, *river*, England, U.K., **304** C4
Otukpa, Nigeria, **365** F3
Otumpa, Argentina, **458** D3
Oturkpo, Nigeria, **365** F3
Otuzco, Peru, **454** B2
Otway, Bahía, *bay*, Chile, **460** B4
Otway, Cape, Australia, **135** J6
Otyniya, Ukraine, **296** E1
Ötztaler Alpen, *mountain range*, Austria, **288** E5
Ou, *river*, China, **206** E2
Ōu-sanmyaku, *mountain range*, Japan, **209** H2
Ouachita, Lake, U.S.A., **424** F2
Ouachita, *river*, U.S.A., **424** F3
Ouachita Mountains, *mountain range*, U.S.A., **424** E2

Ouadane, Mauritania, **360** D4
Ouadda, Central African Republic, **366** B3
Ouaddaï, *prefecture*, Chad, **366** B2
Ouagadougou, Burkina Faso, **364** D2, *325*
Ouahigouya, Burkina Faso, **364** D2
Ouaka, *prefecture*, Central African Republic, **368** D1
Oualâta, Mauritania, **364** C1
Ouallam, Niger, **365** E2
Ouanary, French Guiana, **452** C2
Ouanda Djallé, Central African Republic, **366** B3
Ouandago, Central African Republic, **366** A3
Ouando, Central African Republic, **369** E1
Ouango, Central African Republic, **368** D2
Ouangolodougou, Côte d'Ivoire, **364** C3
Ouaqui, French Guiana, **452** C2
Ouargaye, Burkina Faso, **364** E2
Ouargla, Algeria, **361** H2
Ouarkziz, Jebel, *mountain range*, Algeria/Morocco, **360** E3
Ouarzazate, Morocco, **360** E2
Oudtshoorn, South Africa, **370** D5
Oued Rhiou, Algeria, **293** H5
Ouégoa, New Caledonia, **141** A3
Ouélésébougou, Mali, **364** C2
Ouessa, Burkina Faso, **364** D2
Ouessant, Île d', *island*, France, **290** B2
Ouésso, Congo, **368** C2
Ouest, *province*, Cameroon, **368** B1
Oughter, Lough, *lake*, Ireland, **309** E3
Oughterard, Ireland, **309** C4
Ouham, *prefecture*, Central African Republic, **365** H3
Ouham-Pendé, *prefecture*, Central African Republic, **365** H3
Ouidah, Benin, **365** E3, *327*
Oujda, Morocco, **361** F2
Oujeft, Mauritania, **360** D5
Oulad Teïma, Morocco, **360** E2
Oulainen, Finland, **285** M4
Ould Yenjé, Mauritania, **364** B1
Ouled Djellal, Algeria, **361** H2
Oulton Broad, England, U.K., **305** J2
Oulu, Finland, **285** M4
Oulujärvi, *lake*, Finland, **285** N4
Oulujoki, *river*, Finland, **285** M4
Oulun Lääni, *province*, Finland, **285** N4
Oulx, Italy, **294** A3
Oum-Chalouba, Chad, **366** B1
Oum el Bouaghi, Algeria, **361** H1
Oum-Hadjer, Chad, **366** A2
Oumm ed Droûs Guebli, Sebkhet, *salt-pan*, Mauritania, **360** D4
Oumm ed Droûs Telli, Sebkhet, *salt-pan*, Mauritania, **360** D4
Ounane, Djebel, *mountain peak*, Algeria, **361** H3
Ounara, Morocco, **360** E2
Ounasjoki, *river*, Finland, **285** M3
Oundle, England, U.K., **305** G2
Oungre, Canada, **414** C7
Ounianga Kébir, Chad, **362** D5
Ounianga Sérir, Chad, **362** D5
Oupu, China, **211** J1
Ouray, U.S.A., **423** K2
Ourém, Brazil, **452** D3
Ourense, Spain, **292** D1
Ouricuri, Brazil, **453** F5
Ouro Prêto, Brazil, **457** E5
Ourville-en-Caux, France, **305** H5
Ouse, *river*, E. Sussex, England, U.K., **305** H4
Ouse, *river*, Yorkshire, England, U.K., **307** H4
Outakoski, Finland, **285** N2
Outaouais, Rivière des, *river*, Canada, **416** B6
Outardes Quatre, Réservoir, Canada, **416** G4
Outer Hebrides, *islands*, Scotland, U.K., **308** B3, *276*
Outjo, Namibia, **370** C3
Outokumpu, Finland, **285** P5
Outram, New Zealand, **133** C7
Ouvéa, *island*, New Caledonia, **141** A3
Ouyen, Australia, **135** J6
Ovacık, Turkey, **363** G1
Ovada, Italy, **294** B3
Ovaka, *island*, Vava'u Group, Tonga, **141** B3
Ovalau, *island*, Fiji, **141** A4
Ovalle, Chile, **458** B4
Ovan, Gabon, **368** B2
Ovando, U.S.A., **418** H3
Ovar, Portugal, **292** C2
Oveng, Cameroon, **368** B2
Overbister, Orkney, Scotland, U.K., **308** G1
Øverbygd, Norway, **284** J2
Overijssel, *province*, Netherlands, **288** C2
Överkalix, Sweden, **285** L3
Overland Park, U.S.A., **420** F6
Overlander Roadhouse, Australia, **134** C4
Overton, U.S.A., **422** F3
Overton, Wales, U.K., **304** E2
Övertorneå, Sweden, **285** L3
Överturingen, Sweden, **286** G1
Överum, Sweden, **286** H4
Övgödiy, Mongolia, **213** H2
Ovidiopol', Ukraine, **296** H2
Ovidiu, Romania, **296** G3
Oviedo, Spain, **292** E1
Ovino, Russian Federation, **299** D3
Oviši, Latvia, **287** K4
Ovoot, Mongolia, **210** F3
Övör-Ereen, Mongolia, **210** F2
Övre Soppero, Sweden, **284** K2
Övt, Mongolia, **213** J3
Owaka, New Zealand, **133** B8
Owando, Congo, **368** C3, *333*
Owase, Japan, **209** G4
Owase-zaki, *point*, Japan, **209** G4
Owego, U.S.A., **426** B3
Owel, Lough, *lake*, Ireland, **309** E4
Owen, Mount, *mountain peak*, New Zealand, **133** D5
Owen Fracture Zone, *tectonic feature*, Indian Ocean, **476** C4
Owen Head, *point*, New Zealand, **133** B8
Owen Sound, Canada, **421** N3
Owen Stanley Range, *mountain range*, Papua New Guinea, **128** D2
Owenga, Chatham Islands, New Zealand, **133** Q16
Owens Lake, U.S.A., **422** E3
Owens, U.S.A., **426** B5
Owensboro, U.S.A., **421** K7
Owerri, Nigeria, **368** A1
Owl, *river*, Alberta, Canada, **413** P4
Owl, *river*, Manitoba, Canada, **414** H3
Owo, Nigeria, **365** F3
Owosso, U.S.A., **421** L4
Owyhee, Lake, U.S.A., **418** F5
Owyhee, *river*, U.S.A., **418** F5
Owyhee, U.S.A., **418** F6
Oxapampa, Peru, **454** C3
Oxbow, Canada, **414** C7
Oxelösund, Sweden, **287** H3
Oxford, Canada, **417** K7
Oxford, England, U.K., **305** F3
Oxford, Mississippi, U.S.A., **425** H2
Oxford, Nebraska, U.S.A., **420** D5
Oxford, New Zealand, **133** D6
Oxford, North Carolina, U.S.A., **421** P7
Oxford Lake, Canada, **414** G4
Oxfordshire, *unitary authority*, England, U.K., **305** F3
Oxnard, U.S.A., **422** D4
Oxted, England, U.K., **305** H3
Oxylithos, Greece, **297** E6
Oyama, Japan, **209** G3
Oyapok, Baie d', *bay*, French Guiana, **452** C2
Oyapok, *river*, French Guiana, **452** C2
Oyat', *river*, Russian Federation, **299** E2
Øye, Norway, **286** D2
Oyem, Gabon, **368** B2
Oyen, Canada, **413** P6
Øyeren, *lake*, Norway, **286** E3
Oykel, *river*, Scotland, U.K., **308** E3
Oykel Bridge, Scotland, U.K., **308** E3
Oyo, Congo, **368** C3
Oyo, Nigeria, **365** E3
Oyo, *state*, Nigeria, **365** E3
Oyón, Peru, **454** C3
Oyster Island, Myanmar, **205** B4
Oysterville, U.S.A., **418** B3
Oytal, Kazakhstan, **223** J4
Oytal, Kyrgyzstan, **223** J4
Oytograk, China, **212** D5
Oyyl, Kazakhstan, **222** E3
Oyyl, *river*, Kazakhstan, **222** E3
Ozamiz, Philippines, **204** C4
Ozark Plateau, U.S.A., **424** E1
Ozarks, Lake of the, U.S.A., **420** G6
Ozbaşı, Turkey, **297** F7
Ózd, Hungary, **289** K4
Özen, Kazakhstan, **222** E4
Ozernoy, Mys, *cape*, Russian Federation, **301** T4
Ozersk, Russian Federation, **287** L5
Ozery, Russian Federation, **299** G5
Özgön, Kyrgyzstan, **223** J4
Ozhukarai, India, **216** D3
Ozieri, Sardegna, Italy, **295** B5
Ozimek, Poland, **289** J3
Ozinki, Russian Federation, **222** D2
Ozizweni, South Africa, **371** F4
Ozona, U.S.A., **424** B4
Ozuluama, Mexico, **431** F4

## P

Pa, *river*, China, **207** A1
Pa-an, Myanmar, **205** C4
Paamiut, Greenland, **411** Q3
Paarl, South Africa, **370** C5
Paavola, Finland, **285** M4
Pabbay, *island*, Central Western Isles, Scotland, U.K., **308** B3
Pabbay, *island*, S. Western Isles, Scotland, U.K., **308** B4
Pabianice, Poland, **289** J3
Pābna, Bangladesh, **214** D5
Pabradė, Lithuania, **287** M5
Pacaás Novos, Serra dos, *mountain range*, Brazil, **455** F3
Pacaraima, Serra, *mountain range*, Brazil/Venezuela, **447** F3
Pacasmayo, Peru, **454** B2
Pacheco, Isla, *island*, Chile, **460** B4
Pachino, Sicilia, Italy, **295** E7
Pachitea, *river*, Peru, **454** C2
Pachmarhi, India, **218** D5
Pachuca, Mexico, **431** F4
Pacific Antarctic Ridge, *underwater feature*, Pacific Ocean, **478** G8
Pacific Ocean, **478** F4, *2, 23, 24, 29, 45, 51, 61, 76, 77, 81, 88, 89, 94, 94, 95, 96, 97, 100, 108, 109, 116, 118, 119, 120, 121, 122, 123, 124, 125, 126, 127, 186, 271, 272, 273, 317, 376, 377, 382, 385, 401, 403, 404, 405, 434, 438, 442, 464, 474*
Pacific Ranges, *mountain range*, Canada, **412** F6
Pacitan, Indonesia, **201** E5
Packwood, U.S.A., **418** D3
Pacov, Czech Republic, **289** G4
Pacoval, Brazil, **452** B4
Pacoval, *river*, Brazil, **452** B4
Padam, India, **218** D2
Padamarang, Pulau, *island*, Indonesia, **198** C4
Padang, Indonesia, **200** C3
Padang, Pulau, *island*, Indonesia, **200** C2
Padangsidempuan, Indonesia, **200** B2
Padangtikar, Pulau, *island*, Indonesia, **201** E3
Padany, Russian Federation, **285** R5
Padasjoki, Finland, **287** M2
Padauari, Pico, *mountain peak*, Brazil, **451** F4
Padauari, *river*, Brazil, **451** F4
Padcaya, Bolivia, **455** F5
Paddle Prairie, Canada, **413** L3
Paderborn, Germany, **288** D3
Padilla, Bolivia, **455** F5
Padina, Romania, **296** F3
Padova, Italy, **294** C3
Padrão, Ponta do, *point*, Angola, **368** B4
Padre Island, U.S.A., **424** D6
Padrón, Spain, **292** C1
Padstow, England, U.K., **304** C4
Padsvillye, Belarus, **287** N5
Paducah, Kentucky, U.S.A., **421** J7
Paducah, Texas, U.S.A., **424** B2
Paektu-san, *mountain peak*, North Korea, **208** F1, *163*
Paeroa, *mountain peak*, New Zealand, **132** F4
Paeroa, New Zealand, **132** E3
Pafos, Cyprus, **225** B2
Pafuri, Mozambique, **371** F3
Pag, Croatia, **294** E3
Pag, *island*, Croatia, **294** E3
Paga, Indonesia, **198** C5
Paga Conta, Brazil, **452** B4
Pagadian, Philippines, **204** C5
Pagai Selatan, Pulau, *island*, Indonesia, **200** B3
Pagai Utara, Pulau, *island*, Indonesia, **200** B3
Pagan, *island*, Northern Mariana Islands, **138** C3, *125*
Pagan, Myanmar, **205** B3, *157*
Pagaralam, Indonesia, **200** C4
Pagasitikos Kolpos, *bay*, Greece, **297** D6
Pagatan, Indonesia, **201** F3
Page, U.S.A., **423** H3
Pagėgiai, Lithuania, **287** K5
Paget, Mount, *mountain peak*, South Georgia, **461** A3
Pago Pago, American Samoa, **141** B2, *121*
Pagoda Peak, *mountain peak*, U.S.A., **423** K1
Pagon, Gunung, *mountain peak*, Brunei, **201** F1
Pagri, China, **214** D4
Pahala, Hawaiian Islands, U.S.A., **422** R10
Pahang, *river*, Malaysia, **200** C2
Pahang, *state*, Malaysia, **200** C2
Pahlāgaon, Andaman and Nicobar Islands, India, **217** H3
Pahoa, Hawaiian Islands, U.S.A., **422** R10
Pahute Peak, *mountain peak*, U.S.A., **418** E6
Paiaguás, Brazil, **456** B5
Paide, Estonia, **287** M3
Paige, U.S.A., **424** D4
Paignton, England, U.K., **304** D4
Paihia, New Zealand, **132** E2
Päijänne, *lake*, Finland, **287** M2
Pail, Pakistan, **218** C2
Pailĭn, Cambodia, **203** D3
Paillaco, Chile, **460** C1
Pailolo Channel, Hawaiian Islands, U.S.A., **422** R9
Paimio, Finland, **287** L2
Paimpol, France, **290** C2
Painan, Indonesia, **200** C3
Paine, Chile, **458** B4
Painswick, England, U.K., **304** E3
Painted Desert, U.S.A., **423** H3
Paintsville, U.S.A., **421** M7
País Vasco, *autonomous community*, Spain, **293** F1
Paisley, Scotland, U.K., **308** E5
Paisley, U.S.A., **418** D5
Paita, Peru, **454** B1
Paitan, China, **207** B2
Paitan, Teluk, *bay*, Malaysia, **201** G1
Paittasjärvi, Sweden, **285** L2
Pajala, Sweden, **285** L3
Paján, Ecuador, **450** B4
Pájara, Islas Canarias, Spain, **373** B4
Pajares, Spain, **292** E1
Pajeú, *river*, Brazil, **453** G5
Pak Khat, Thailand, **203** D2
Pak Tam Chung, China, **207** C4
Pak Thong Chai, Thailand, **202** D3
Pakaraima Mountains, *mountain range*, Guyana, **451** G3
Pakaur, India, **219** F4
Pakch'ŏn, North Korea, **208** D3
Paki, Nigeria, **365** F2
Pakistan, *country*, Asia, **196** H7, *66, 96, 144, 145, 168, 169, 170, 172, 173, 183, 184, 275, 276*
Pakokku, Myanmar, **205** B3
Pakotai, New Zealand, **132** D2
Pakrac, Croatia, **294** F3
Paks, Hungary, **289** J5
Pakuli, Indonesia, **198** B3
Pakuratahi, New Zealand, **133** E5
Pakxé, Laos, **203** E3
Pala, Chad, **365** G3
Pala, U.S.A., **422** E5
Palacios, U.S.A., **424** D5
Palafrugell, Spain, **293** J2
Palaiochora, Kriti, Greece, **297** D8
Palairos, Greece, **297** C6
Palaiseau, France, **290** F2
Pālakollu, India, **217** E2
Palamas, Greece, **297** D6
Palame, Brazil, **457** G3
Palamós, Spain, **293** J2
Palampur, India, **218** D2
Palanan Point, Philippines, **204** C2
Palanga, Lithuania, **287** K5
Palangkaraya, Indonesia, **201** F3
Pālanpur, India, **218** C4
Palapye, Botswana, **371** E3
Palatka, U.S.A., **425** M5
Palau, *country*, Pacific Ocean, **130** C1, *117, 118*
Palau, Sardegna, Italy, **295** B5
Palau Islands, Palau, **138** B4
Palaui Island, Philippines, **204** C2
Palaw, Myanmar, **202** C3
Palawan, *island*, Philippines, **204** B4
Palawan Passage, Philippines, **204** B4
Palawan Trough, *underwater feature*, South China Sea, **478** B4
Palayankottai, India, **216** D4
Paldiski, Estonia, **287** M3
Pale, Bosnia and Herzegovina, **294** G4
Paleleh, Pegunungan, *mountain range*, Indonesia, **198** C2
Palembang, *river*, Indonesia, **200** D3
Palen Lake, U.S.A., **422** F5
Palena, Chile, **460** C2
Palena, Lago, *lake*, Chile, **460** C2
Palencia, Spain, **292** E1
Palenque, Panama, **429** F5
Palermo, Sicilia, Italy, **295** D6
Palestine, Lake, U.S.A., **424** E3
Palestine, U.S.A., **424** E4
Paletwa, Myanmar, **205** B3
Pālghāt, India, **216** D4
Palgrave Point, Namibia, **370** B3
Pāli, India, **218** C4
Paliki, Russian Federation, **299** E6
Palikir, Micronesia, **138** D4, *118, 119*

Palinuro, Italy, **295** E5
Paliouri, Akra, *point*, Greece, **297** D6
Palisade, U.S.A., **420** C5
Pālitāna, India, **218** B5
Pāliyād, India, **218** B5
Palk Strait, India/Sri Lanka, **216** D4
Palkino, Russian Federation, **299** B4
Palkonda, India, **217** E2
Pālkonda Range, *mountain range*, India, **216** D3
Pallas Grean, Ireland, **309** D5
Pallastunturi, *mountain peak*, Finland, **285** M2
Pallës, Bishti i, *point*, Albania, **297** B5
Pallisa, Uganda, **369** F2
Palliser, Cape, New Zealand, **133** E5
Palliser Bay, New Zealand, **133** E5
Pallu, India, **218** C3
Palm Bay, U.S.A., **425** M6
Palm Beach, U.S.A., **425** M6
Palm-Mar, Islas Canarias, Spain, **373** A4
Palm Springs, U.S.A., **422** E5
Palma, Mozambique, **369** H5
Palma, *river*, Brazil, **456** D3
Palma de Mallorca, Spain, **293** J3
Palma del Río, Spain, **292** E4
Palma Soriano, Cuba, **429** F2
Palmaner, India, **216** D3
Palmares, Acre, Brazil, **455** E3
Palmares, Pernambuco, Brazil, **457** G2
Palmares do Sul, Brazil, **459** G4
Palmarito, Venezuela, **451** D2
Palmas, Cape, Liberia, **364** C4
Palmas, Santa Catarina, Brazil, **459** G3
Palmas, Tocantins, Brazil, **456** D3
Palmas de Monte Alto, Brazil, **457** E4
Palmdale, U.S.A., **422** D4
Palmeira, Brazil, **459** H2
Palmeira das Missões, Brazil, **459** G3
Palmeira dos Indios, Brazil, **457** G2
Palmeirais, Brazil, **453** E4
Palmeiras, Brazil, **457** F3
Palmeiras de Goiás, Brazil, **456** D4
Palmeiras do Javari, Brazil, **450** D5
Palmeirinhas, Ponta das, *point*, Angola, **368** B4
Palmer, *U.S. research station*, Antarctica, **470** A4
Palmer, U.S.A., **410** E3
Palmer Land, *region*, Antarctica, **470** B4
Palmerston, Australia, **134** G1
Palmerston, *island*, Cook Islands, **137** E2
Palmerston, New Zealand, **133** C7
Palmerston North, New Zealand, **132** E5
Palmi, Italy, **295** E6
Palmillas, Mexico, **431** F4
Palmira, Colombia, **450** C3
Palmyra *see* Tadmur, Syria, **225** E2
Palmyra Atoll, *U.S. territory*, Pacific Ocean, **131** J1, *126, 386*
Palmyras Point, India, **219** F5
Palo de las Letras, Colombia, **450** C2
Palo Santo, Argentina, **459** E2
Paloh, Indonesia, **201** E2
Paloich, Sudan, **366** D2
Palojärvi, Finland, **285** L2
Palojoensuu, Finland, **285** L2
Paloma, Punta, *point*, Islas Canarias, Spain, **373** B4
Palomani, *mountain peak*, Bolivia/Peru, **455** E4
Palomar Mountain, *mountain peak*, U.S.A., **422** E5
Palopo, Indonesia, **198** C3
Palos, Cabo de, *cape*, Spain, **293** G4
Palpa, Peru, **454** C4
Palpetu, Tanjong, *cape*, Indonesia, **198** D3
Palu, Indonesia, **198** B3
Paluan, Philippines, **204** C3
Paluwat, *island*, Micronesia, **138** C4
Pamanukan, Indonesia, **201** D4
Pamar, Colombia, **450** D4
Pamdai, Indonesia, **199** G3
Pamekasan, Indonesia, **201** F4
Pāmgarh, India, **219** E5
Pamiers, France, **290** E5
Pamirs, *mountain range*, China/Tajikistan, **212** B5, *173, 185, 188*
Pamlico Sound, U.S.A., **426** B7
Pampa, U.S.A., **424** B2
Pampa Aullagas, Bolivia, **455** E5
Pampa de los Guanacos, Argentina, **458** E3
Pampa del Castillo, Argentina, **460** D2
Pampa Grande, Bolivia, **455** F4
Pampachiri, Peru, **454** D4
Pampas, Peru, **454** C3
Pampas, *plain*, Argentina, **447** F7, *443*
Pamplemousses, Mauritius, **373** C1
Pamplona, Colombia, **450** D2
Pamplona, Spain, **293** G1
Pampur, India, **218** C2
Pamukan, Teluk, *bay*, Indonesia, **201** G3
Pamukçu, Turkey, **297** F6
Pan, Phou, *mountain peak*, Laos, **203** E1
Pan Xian, China, **215** H4
Pana, Gabon, **368** B3
Pana, *river*, Russian Federation, **285** S3
Pana, U.S.A., **421** J6
Panabá, Mexico, **431** H4
Panaca, U.S.A., **422** F3
Panagtaran Point, Philippines, **204** B4
Panagyurishte, Bulgaria, **296** E4
Panaitan, Pulau, *island*, Indonesia, **200** D4
Panaji, India, **216** C3, *169*
Panama, *country*, Central America, **409** Q8, *378, 379, 405, 436*
Panamá, Golfo de, *gulf*, Panama, **429** F6
Panamá, Panama, **429** F5
Panama Basin, *underwater feature*, Pacific Ocean, **479** N4
Panama Canal, Panama, **429** E5, *387, 404, 405*
Panama City, U.S.A., **425** K4, *405*
Panamint Range, *mountain range*, U.S.A., **422** E3
Panamint Springs, U.S.A., **422** E3
Panao, Peru, **454** C2
Panarea, Isola, *island*, Italy, **295** E6
Panay, *island*, Philippines, **204** C4
Panay Gulf, Philippines, **204** C4
Pančevo, Serbia, **296** C3
Panciu, Romania, **296** F3
Pâncota, Romania, **296** C2
Panda, Mozambique, **371** F3
Pandan Reservoir, Singapore, **200** J7
Pandanan Island, Philippines, **204** B4
Pandegelang, Indonesia, **200** D4
Pandėlys, Lithuania, **287** M4
Pandharpur, India, **216** C2
Pāndhurna, India, **218** D5
Pando, *department*, Bolivia, **455** E3
Pandu, Democratic Republic of the Congo, **368** C2
Pandu, India, **219** G4
Panevėžys, Lithuania, **287** M5
Pang, Thailand, **202** C2
Pāng-yāng, Myanmar, **205** C3
Panga, Democratic Republic of the Congo, **369** E2
Pangai, Tongatapu Group, Tonga, **141** B4
Pangaimotu, *island*, Vava'u Group, Tonga, **141** B3
Pangani, Tanzania, **369** G4
Panganuran, Philippines, **204** C4
Pangeo, Indonesia, **199** E2
Pangi, Democratic Republic of the Congo, **369** E3
Pangkalanbrandan, Indonesia, **200** B1
Pangkalanbuun, Indonesia, **201** E3
Pangkalpinang, Indonesia, **200** D3
Pangman, Canada, **419** M2
Pangnao, Loi, *mountain peak*, Myanmar, **205** D3
Pangnirtung, Canada, **411** N3
Pangu, China, **211** H1
Panguipulli, Chile, **460** C1
Panguipulli, Lago, *lake*, Chile, **460** C1
Panguitch, U.S.A., **422** G3
Panguna, Papua New Guinea, **140** E2
Paniai, Danau, *lake*, Indonesia, **199** F3
Panié, Mont, *mountain peak*, New Caledonia, **141** A3
Pānīpat, India, **218** D3
Panj, *river*, Afghanistan/Tajikistan, **223** J5
Panjāb, Afghanistan, **218** A2
Panjakent, Tajikistan, **222** H5
Panjang, Pulau, *island*, Indonesia, **201** E2
Panjang *see* West Island, Cocos (Keeling) Islands, **134** Q10
Panjgūr, Pakistan, **221** H3
Panjshīr, *river*, Afghanistan, **218** B2
Pankakoski, Finland, **285** Q5
Pankshin, Nigeria, **365** F3
Panna, India, **218** E4
Pannawonica, Australia, **134** D3
Panngi, Vanuatu, **141** A2
Pano Lefkara, Cyprus, **225** B2
Panorama, Brazil, **456** C5
Panozero, Russian Federation, **285** R4
Panshan, China, **211** H4
Panshi, China, **211** J4
Päntäne, Finland, **287** L1
Pantar, Pulau, *island*, Indonesia, **198** D4
Pantelleria, Isola di, *island*, Sicilia, Italy, **295** D7
Pantemakassar, East Timor, **198** D5
Pantha, Myanmar, **205** B3
Panti, Indonesia, **200** C2
Pantoja, Peru, **450** C4
Pánuco, Mexico, **431** F4
Pánuco, *river*, Mexico, **431** F4
Panychevo, Russian Federation, **223** L1
Panyu (Shiqiao), China, **207** A3
Panzhihua, China, **215** G4
Panzi, Democratic Republic of the Congo, **368** C4
Panzós, Guatemala, **428** C4
Pão de Açúcar, Brazil, **457** G2
Paola, Italy, **295** F6
Paoli, U.S.A., **421** K6
Paoziyan, China, **211** J4
Pápa, Hungary, **289** H5
Papa Playa, Peru, **454** C2
Papa Stour, *island*, Shetland, Scotland, U.K., **308** K7
Papa Westray, *island*, Orkney, Scotland, U.K., **308** G1
Papagaio *see* Sauêruiná, *river*, Brazil, **455** G3
Papakai, New Zealand, **132** E4
Papakura, New Zealand, **132** E3
Papamoa, New Zealand, **132** F3
Papantla de Olarte, Mexico, **431** F4
Paparoa, New Zealand, **132** E3
Papatoetoe, New Zealand, **132** E3
Papeete, French Polynesia, **137** G2, *122*
Papenburg, Germany, **288** C2
Papilys, Lithuania, **287** M4
Papisoi, Tanjong, *point*, Indonesia, **199** F4
Paporotno, Russian Federation, **299** C3
Paposo, Chile, **458** B2
Pāppadāhāndi, India, **217** E2
Paps, The, *mountain peak*, Ireland, **309** C5
Papua, Gulf of, Papua New Guinea, **140** B5
Papua New Guinea, *country*, Pacific Ocean, **130** D2, *39, 40, 50, 97, 108, 109, 112, 115, 116, 119*
Papun, Myanmar, **205** C4
Par, England, U.K., **304** C4
Pará, *river*, Brazil, **452** C3
Pará, *state*, Brazil, **452** C4
Pará de Minas, Brazil, **457** E5
Paraburdoo, Australia, **134** D3
Paracas, Península de, Peru, **454** C3
Paracatu, Brazil, **456** D4
Paracatu, *river*, Brazil, **456** E4
Paracel Islands *see* Xisha Qundao, *sovereignty disputed*, South China Sea, **203** G4, *193*
Parachute, U.S.A., **423** J2
Paraćin, Serbia, **296** C4
Paracuru, Brazil, **453** F4
Paradera, Aruba, **461** B3
Paradise, California, U.S.A., **422** C2
Paradise, Guyana, **451** H3
Paradise, Montana, U.S.A., **418** G3
Paradise Valley, U.S.A., **418** F6
Paradwip, India, **219** F5
Paragould, U.S.A., **424** G1
Paraguá, *river*, Bolivia, **455** G4
Paragua, *river*, Venezuela, **451** F3
Paraguaçu, *river*, Brazil, **457** F3
Paraguai, *river*, Brazil, **456** B4
Paraguaipoa, Venezuela, **450** D1
Paraguaná, Peninsula de, Venezuela, **451** E1
Paraguarí, Paraguay, **459** F2
Paraguay, *country*, South America, **449** F6, *96, 434, 435, 443, 444, 445*
Paraguay, *river*, South America, **447** G6, *443, 445*
Paraiba, *river*, Paraíba, Brazil, **457** G2
Paraíba, *river*, Rio de Janeiro, Brazil, **457** E5
Paraíba, *state*, Brazil, **457** G2
Parainen, Finland, **287** L2
Paraíso, Mexico, **431** G5
Paraiso, Punta, *point*, San Andrés, Colombia, **461** B1
Paraíso do Tocantins, Brazil, **456** D3
Parakou, Benin, **365** E3
Paramaribo, Suriname, **452** B2, *438*
Paramillo, *mountain peak*, Colombia, **450** C2
Paramirim, Brazil, **457** E3
Paramirim, *river*, Brazil, **457** E3
Paramushir, Ostrov, *island*, Russian Federation, **301** S4
Paramythia, Greece, **297** C6
Paraná, Argentina, **458** E4
Paranã, Brazil, **456** D3
Paranã, *river*, Brazil, **456** D4
Paraná, *river*, South America, **447** G6, *439, 440, 441, 443, 445*
Parana, *state*, Brazil, **459** G2
Paranaguá, Brazil, **459** H2
Paranaíba, Brazil, **456** C5
Paranaíba, *river*, Brazil, **456** C5
Paranapanema, *river*, Brazil, **459** G2
Paranapiacaba, Serra, *mountain range*, Brazil, **459** H2
Paranavaí, Brazil, **459** G2
Parang, Philippines, **204** D5
Parangtritis, Indonesia, **201** E5
Parapara Peak, *mountain peak*, New Zealand, **133** D5
Paraso, Solomon Islands, **141** A1
Paraspori, Akra, *point*, Dodekanisos, Greece, **297** F8
Paratwāḍā, India, **218** D5
Parauapebas, Brazil, **452** D5
Parauari, *river*, Brazil, **452** A4
Paraúna, Brazil, **456** C4
Paray-le-Monial, France, **291** G3
Parazinho, Brazil, **453** G4
Parbhani, India, **216** D2
Parbig, *river*, Russian Federation, **223** L1
Parc, Pointe du, *point*, Réunion, **373** A1
Parchel, Punta del, *point*, Islas Canarias, Spain, **373** A4
Parchim, Germany, **288** E2
Parczew, Poland, **289** L3
Parding, China, **214** D2
Pardo, *river*, Bahia, Brazil, **457** F4
Pardo, *river*, Mato Grosso do Sul, Brazil, **456** C5
Pardo, *river*, São Paulo, Brazil, **456** D5
Pardoo Roadhouse, Australia, **134** D3
Pardubice, Czech Republic, **289** G3
Parecis, Brazil, **456** B4
Parecis, Chapada dos, *mountain range*, Brazil, **455** F3
Parelhas, Brazil, **453** G5
Parent, Canada, **416** D6
Pareora, New Zealand, **133** C7
Parepare, Indonesia, **198** B3
Parera, Argentina, **458** D5
Parga, Greece, **297** C6
Pargo, Ponta do, *point*, Madeira, Portugal, **373** C3
Parguaza, Sierra de, *mountain range*, Venezuela, **451** E2
Parguaza, Venezuela, **451** E2
Paria, Golfo de, *gulf*, Trinidad and Tobago/Venezuela, **427** D4, *399*
Paria, Península de, Venezuela, **451** F1
Paria, U.S.A., **423** H3
Pariaguán, Venezuela, **451** F2
Parigi, Indonesia, **198** C3
Parika, Guyana, **451** G2
Parima, *river*, Brazil, **451** F3
Parima, Serra, *mountain range*, Brazil, **451** F3
Pariñas, Punta, *point*, Peru, **454** B1
Parincea, Romania, **296** F2
Parintins, Brazil, **452** B4
Paris, France, **290** F2, *83, 93, 94, 96, 97, 122, 243, 244, 245, 469*
Paris, Kentucky, U.S.A., **421** L6
Paris, Tennessee, U.S.A., **425** H1
Paris, Texas, U.S.A., **424** E3
Parita, Panama, **450** B2
Pārīz, Iran, **221** G3
Park Falls, U.S.A., **420** H3
Park Rapids, U.S.A., **420** F2
Park Valley, U.S.A., **418** H6
Parkano, Finland, **287** L1
Parker, U.S.A., **422** F4
Parkersburg, U.S.A., **421** N6
Parkes, Australia, **135** K5
Parkland, Canada, **413** N6
Parkston, U.S.A., **420** E4
Parlākimidi, India, **217** F2
Parlatuvier, Tobago, Trinidad and Tobago, **461** B4
Parli, India, **216** D2
Parma, Italy, **294** C3
Parmana, Venezuela, **451** F2
Parnaíba, Brazil, **453** F4
Parnaíba, *river*, Brazil, **453** E4
Parnamirim, Brazil, **453** F5
Parnarama, Brazil, **453** E4
Parnassos, *mountain peak*, Greece, **297** D6
Parnon Oros, *mountain range*, Greece, **297** D7
Pärnu, Estonia, **287** M3
Pärnu, *river*, Estonia, **287** M3
Pärnu-Jaagupi, Estonia, **287** M3
Pärnu laht, *bay*, Estonia, **287** M3
Paro, Bhutan, **219** G4
Pārola, India, **218** C5
Paroo, *river*, Australia, **135** J4
Paros, *island*, Kyklades, Greece, **297** E7
Paros, Kyklades, Greece, **297** E7
Parowan, U.S.A., **422** G3

Parpaillon, *mountain range*, France, **291** H4
Parral, Chile, **458** B5
Parras de la Fuente, Mexico, **430** E3
Parrita, Costa Rica, **428** D5
Parrsboro, Canada, **417** J7
Parry, Cape, Canada, **410** G2
Parry, Kap, *cape*, Greenland, **411** M2
Parry Bay, Canada, **411** L3
Parry Islands, Canada, **410** J2
Parry Sound, Canada, **421** N3
Parseierspitze, *mountain peak*, Austria, **288** E5
Parsęta, *river*, Poland, **289** H2
Parshall, U.S.A., **420** B2
Parsons, U.S.A., **420** F7
Partanna, Sicilia, Italy, **295** D7
Pårtefjällen, *mountain peak*, Sweden, **284** H3
Parthenay, France, **290** D3
Partizansk, Russian Federation, **211** L4
Partizánske, Slovakia, **289** J4
Partney, England, U.K., **305** H1
Partry, Ireland, **309** C4
Partry Mountains, *mountain range*, Ireland, **309** C4
Paru, *river*, Brazil, **452** C3
Paru de Este, *river*, Brazil, **452** B3
Paru de Oeste, *river*, Brazil, **452** B3
Parvatsar, India, **218** C4
Paryang, China, **219** E3
Pas-en-Artois, France, **305** K4
Pasadena, California, U.S.A., **422** D4
Pasadena, Texas, U.S.A., **424** E5
Paşalimanı Adası, *island*, Turkey, **297** F5
Pasapuat, Indonesia, **200** C3
Paşayiğit, Turkey, **297** F5
Pascagoula, U.S.A., **425** H4
Paşcani, Romania, **296** F2
Pasco, U.S.A., **418** E3
Pascoal, Monte, *mountain peak*, Brazil, **457** F4
Pascua, Isla de (Easter Island), *island*, Chile, Pacific Ocean, **461** B2, *12, 61, 90, 91, 94, 435*
Pasewalk, Germany, **289** G2
Pasfield Lake, Canada, **414** B2
Pasha, *river*, Russian Federation, **299** D2
Pasha, Russian Federation, **299** D2
Pāsighāt, India, **219** H3
Pasir Panjang, Singapore, **200** J7
Pasir Puteh, Malaysia, **200** C1
Pasir Ris, Singapore, **200** K6
Pasirpengarayan, Indonesia, **200** C2
Påskallavik, Sweden, **286** H4
Pasłęk, Poland, **289** J1
Pasley, Cape, Australia, **128** B5
Pasni, Pakistan, **221** H3
Paso Caballos, Guatemala, **428** C3
Paso de Indios, Argentina, **460** D2
Paso de los Libres, Argentina, **459** F3
Paso de los Toros, Uruguay, **459** F4
Paso de Patria, Paraguay, **459** E3
Paso Socompa, Chile, **458** C2
Pasrūr, Pakistan, **218** C2
Passage Point, Canada, **410** H2
Passau, Germany, **288** F4
Passero, Capo, *cape*, Sicilia, Italy, **295** E7
Passi, Philippines, **204** C4
Passo Fundo, Brazil, **459** G3
Passos, Brazil, **456** D5
Pastavy, Belarus, **287** N5
Pastaza, *river*, Peru, **450** C5
Pasto, Colombia, **450** C4
Pastos Bons, Brazil, **453** E5
Pasu, India, **212** B5
Pasu, Pakistan, **218** C1
Pasuruan, Indonesia, **201** F4
Pasvalys, Lithuania, **287** M4
Pasvikelva, *river*, Norway, **285** P2
Pásztó, Hungary, **289** J5
Pata, Central African Republic, **366** B3
Pata, Senegal, **364** B2
Patagonia, U.S.A., **423** H6
Patah, Gunung, *mountain peak*, Indonesia, **200** C4
Patamea, Samoa, **141** B1
Pātan, Gujarat, India, **218** C5
Pātan, Madhya Pradesh, India, **218** D5
Pātan, Nepal, **219** F4
Patani, Indonesia, **199** E2
Patay, Argentina, **458** D3
Patay, France, **290** E2
Patchway, England, U.K., **304** E3
Patea, New Zealand, **132** E4
Patea, *river*, New Zealand, **132** E4
Pategi, Nigeria, **365** F3
Pateley Bridge, England, U.K., **307** G3
Paterno, Sicilia, Italy, **295** E7
Paterson, U.S.A., **426** C4
Pathfinder Reservoir, U.S.A., **419** L5
Pathiu, Thailand, **202** C4
Patía, *river*, Colombia, **450** B4
Patiāla, India, **218** D3
Patience, French Guiana, **452** C2
Patikul, Philippines, **204** C5
Patmos, *island*, Dodekanisos, Greece, **297** F7
Patna, India, **219** F4, *168, 169*
Patnos, Turkey, **363** H1
Patoka Lake, U.S.A., **421** K6
Patos, Albania, **297** B5
Patos, Brazil, **453** G5
Patos, Lagoa dos, *lagoon*, Brazil, **459** G4
Patos de Minas, Brazil, **456** D5
Patquía, Argentina, **458** C4
Patra, Greece, **297** C6
Patricio Lynch, Isla, *island*, Chile, **460** B3
Patrington, England, U.K., **307** H4
Patrocínio, Brazil, **456** D5
Pattani, Thailand, **202** D5
Pattaya, Thailand, **202** D3
Patten, U.S.A., **426** F1
Patterdale, England, U.K., **306** F3
Patti, Sicilia, Italy, **295** E6
Pattisson, Cape, Chatham Islands, New Zealand, **133** Q16
Pattoki, Pakistan, **218** C3
Patton Escarpment, *underwater feature*, Pacific Ocean, **479** K2
Patuākhāli, Bangladesh, **214** D5
Patuca, Punta, *point*, Honduras, **428** D4
Patuca, *river*, Honduras, **428** D4
Patūr, India, **218** D5
Patzcuaro, Mexico, **430** E5
Pau, France, **290** D5
Paucarbamba, Peru, **454** C3
Paucartambo, Peru, **454** D3
Pauillac, France, **290** D4
Pauini, Brazil, **455** E2
Pauini, *river*, Brazil, **455** E2
Pauk, Myanmar, **205** B3
Pauksa Taung, *mountain peak*, Myanmar, **205** B4
Paulatuk, Canada, **410** G3
Paulden, U.S.A., **422** G4
Paulista, Brazil, **453** G5
Paulistana, Brazil, **457** F2
Paulo, *river*, Bolivia, **455** G4
Paulo Afonso, Brazil, **457** F2
Pauls Valley, U.S.A., **424** D2
Păuneşti, Romania, **296** F2
Paungbyin, Myanmar, **205** B2
Paungde, Myanmar, **205** B4
Paup, Papua New Guinea, **140** A3
Pauri, India, **218** D3
Paurī, India, **218** D4
Pauto, *river*, Colombia, **450** D3
Pauträsk, Sweden, **284** H4
Pāvagada, India, **216** D3
Pavão, Brazil, **457** F4
Pavia, Italy, **294** B3
Pavilion, Canada, **412** J6
Pavilly, France, **305** H5
Pāvilosta, Latvia, **287** K4
Pavlikeni, Bulgaria, **296** E4
Pavlodar, Kazakhstan, **223** K2
Pavlodar, *province*, Kazakhstan, **212** C2
Pavlogradka, Russian Federation, **223** J2
Pavlohrad, Ukraine, **298** E3
Pavlovac, Croatia, **294** F3
Pavlovo, Russian Federation, **298** F1
Pavlovsk, Russian Federation, **223** L2
Pavlovskaya, Russian Federation, **298** E3
Pavón, Colombia, **450** D3
Pavullo nel Frignano, Italy, **294** C3
Pawan, *river*, Indonesia, **201** E3
Pawhuska, U.S.A., **420** E7
Pawnee, *river*, U.S.A., **420** C6
Paximadia, *island*, Greece, **297** E8
Paxoi, *island*, Ionioi Nisoi, Greece, **297** B6
Pay, Russian Federation, **299** E2
Paya Lebar, Singapore, **200** K6
Payagyi, Myanmar, **205** C4
Payakumbuh, Indonesia, **200** C3
Payne, Lac, *lake*, Canada, **415** S2
Paynes Creek, U.S.A., **422** C1
Paynton, Canada, **413** Q5
Payong, Tanjong, *point*, Malaysia, **201** F2
Pays de la Loire, *administrative region*, France, **290** D3, *245*
Paysandú, Uruguay, **459** E4
Payson, U.S.A., **423** H4
Payún, Cerro, *mountain peak*, Argentina, **458** C5
Payung, Indonesia, **200** D3
Paz de Ariporo, Colombia, **450** D3
Paz de Río, Colombia, **450** D2
Pazardzhik, Bulgaria, **296** E4
Pazarlar, Turkey, **297** G6
Pazaryeri, Turkey, **297** G6
Pazin, Croatia, **294** D3
Pea, Tongatapu Group, Tonga, **141** B4
Peace, *river*, Canada, **413** L3
Peace Point, Canada, **413** N2
Peace River, Canada, **413** L3
Peacehaven, England, U.K., **305** G4
Peach Springs, U.S.A., **422** G4
Peak, The, *mountain peak*, Ascension, **373** A3
Peal de Becerro, Spain, **293** F4
Peale, Mount, *mountain peak*, U.S.A., **423** J2
Pearce, U.S.A., **423** J6
Pearl, *river*, U.S.A., **424** G4
Pearl *see* Zhu, *river*, China, **207** B2, *158*
Pearl City, Hawaiian Islands, U.S.A., **422** R9
Pearl Harbor, Hawaiian Islands, U.S.A., **422** R9, *96, 113, 385*
Pearsall, U.S.A., **424** C5
Pearson, U.S.A., **425** L4
Peary Channel, Canada, **411** J2
Peary Land, *region*, Greenland, **411** R1
Peawanuck, Canada, **415** M4
Pebane, Mozambique, **369** G6
Pebas, Peru, **450** D5
Pebble Island, Falkland Islands, **460** F4
Peć, Serbia, **296** C4
Peçanha, Brazil, **457** E5
Peças, Ilha das, *island*, Brazil, **459** H2
Pechenga, *river*, Russian Federation, **285** Q2
Pechenga, Russian Federation, **285** Q2
Pechenicheno, Russian Federation, **299** D5
Pechenizhyn, Ukraine, **296** E1
Pechora, *river*, Russian Federation, **300** G3
Pechora, Russian Federation, **300** G3
Pechory, Russian Federation, **299** A4
Peck, U.S.A., **421** M4
Pecka, Serbia, **296** B3
Pecos, *river*, U.S.A., **423** L4
Pecos, U.S.A., **423** M6
Pécs, Hungary, **289** J5
Pedasí, Panama, **429** E6
Pedder, Lake, Australia, **135** J7
Pededze, *river*, Estonia/Latvia, **287** N4
Pedernales, Dominican Republic, **429** H3
Pedernales, Mexico, **430** D2
Pedhoulas, Cyprus, **225** B2
Pediva, Angola, **368** B6
Pedra Azul, Brazil, **457** F4
Pedra Lume, Cape Verde, **360** Q8
Pedras Negras, Brazil, **455** F3
Pedraza La Vieja, Venezuela, **450** D2
Pedregal, Venezuela, **451** D1
Pedregulho, Brazil, **456** D5
Pedreiras, Brazil, **453** E4
Pedrero, Meseta el, *plateau*, Argentina, **460** D3
Pedriceña, Mexico, **430** E3
Pedro Afonso, Brazil, **456** D2
Pedro Chico, Colombia, **450** D4
Pedro de Valdivia, Chile, **458** C2
Pedro Gomes, Brazil, **456** B4
Pedro Juan Caballero, Paraguay, **459** F2
Pedro Osorio, Brazil, **459** G4
Pedro II, Brazil, **453** F4
Peebles, Canada, **414** C6
Peebles, Scotland, U.K., **308** F5
Peekskill, U.S.A., **426** D4
Peel, Isle of Man, **306** D3, *279*
Peel, *river*, Canada, **410** F3
Peel Sound, Canada, **411** K2
Peene, *river*, Germany, **288** F2
Peenemünde, Germany, **289** G1
Peerless, U.S.A., **413** S7
Peetz, U.S.A., **423** M1
Pegasus Bay, New Zealand, **133** D6
Pegnitz, Germany, **288** E4
Pego, Spain, **293** G3
Pegu, *division*, Myanmar, **205** C4
Pegu, Myanmar, **205** C4
Pegu Yoma, *mountain range*, Myanmar, **205** B4, *157*
Pegwell Bay, England, U.K., **305** J3
Pehlivanköy, Turkey, **297** F5
Pehuajó, Argentina, **458** E5
Peipohja, Finland, **287** L2
Peipsi Järv, *lake*, Estonia, **287** N3
Peiraias (Piraeus), Greece, **297** D7
Peitz, Germany, **289** G3
Peixe, Brazil, **456** D3
Peixe, do, *river*, Brazil, **456** C4
Peixe, *river*, Brazil, **456** C6
Pejirá, Sierra de, *mountain range*, Venezuela, **450** D2
Pekalongan, Indonesia, **201** E4
Pekan, Malaysia, **200** C2
Pekanbaru, Indonesia, **200** C2
Peking *see* Beijing, China, **210** G5, *96, 97, 158, 159, 160, 161, 162*
Peklino, Russian Federation, **299** D6
Peksha, *river*, Russian Federation, **299** G4
Pelabuhanratu, Indonesia, **200** D4
Pelabuhanratu, Teluk, *bay*, Indonesia, **200** D4
Pelagie, Isole, *islands*, Sicilia, Italy, **295** D8
Pelawanbesar, Indonesia, **201** G2
Pelée, Montagne, *mountain peak*, Martinique, **427** D3, *50, 378, 390*
Pelee Island, Canada, **421** M5
Peleng, Pulau, *island*, Indonesia, **198** C3
Peleng, Selat, *strait*, Indonesia, **198** C3
Pelhřimov, Czech Republic, **289** G4
Pelican Mountains, *mountain range*, Canada, **413** M4
Pelican Rapids, Canada, **414** D5
Peligro, Punta del, *point*, Islas Canarias, Spain, **373** A4
Pelkosenniemi, Finland, **285** N3
Pell City, U.S.A., **425** J3
Pellegrini, Lago, *lake*, Argentina, **460** D1
Pello, Finland, **285** M3
Pellworm, *island*, Germany, **288** D1
Pelly Bay, Canada, **411** L3
Pelly Crossing, Canada, **410** F3
Pelly, *river*, Canada, **410** F3
Pelona Mountain, *mountain peak*, U.S.A., **423** J5
Peloponnisos, *administrative region*, Greece, **297** C7, *265*
Peloritani, Monti, *mountain range*, Sicilia, Italy, **295** E7
Pelotas, Brazil, **459** G4
Peltovuoma, Finland, **285** M2
Pemali, Tanjong, *point*, Indonesia, **198** C4
Pemangkat, Indonesia, **201** E2
Pematangsiantar, Indonesia, **200** B2
Pemba, Baía de, *bay*, Mozambique, **369** H5
Pemba, Mozambique, **369** H5
Pemba Island, Tanzania, **369** G4
Pemberton, Canada, **412** H6
Pembine, U.S.A., **421** K3
Pembre, Indonesia, **199** G4
Pembrey, Wales, U.K., **304** C3
Pembroke, Canada, **416** C7
Pembroke, Wales, U.K., **304** C3
Pembroke Dock, Wales, U.K., **304** C3
Pembrokeshire, *unitary authority*, Wales, U.K., **304** B3
Pen-y-ghent, *mountain peak*, England, U.K., **306** F3
Peña de Francia, *mountain peak*, Spain, **292** D2
Peña Nevada, Cerro, *mountain peak*, Mexico, **431** F4
Penafiel, Portugal, **292** C2
Peñafiel, Spain, **292** E2
Penal, Trinidad, Trinidad and Tobago, **461** C4
Penalva, Brazil, **452** E4
Penamacor, Portugal, **292** D2
Penang *see* Pinang, Pulau, *island*, Malaysia, **200** B1, *151*
Penanjung, Teluk, *bay*, Indonesia, **201** E4
Penápolis, Brazil, **456** C5
Peñaranda de Bracamonte, Spain, **292** E2
Peñarroya, *mountain peak*, Spain, **293** G2
Penarth, Wales, U.K., **304** D3
Peñas, Cabo de, *cape*, Spain, **292** E1
Peñas, Cabo, *cape*, Argentina, **460** D4
Penas, Golfo de, *gulf*, Chile, **460** B3
Peñas, Punta, *cape*, Venezuela, **461** C4
Pend Oreille Lake, U.S.A., **418** F2
Pendang, Indonesia, **201** F3
Pendleton, U.S.A., **418** E4
Pendroy, U.S.A., **418** H2
Peneda, *mountain peak*, Portugal, **292** C2
Penetanguishene, Canada, **421** P3
P'eng-hu Lieh-tao (Pescadores), *island*, Taiwan, **206** D4
P'eng-hu Tao, *island*, Taiwan, **206** D4
Peng Xian, China, **215** G3
Penganga, *river*, India, **218** D5
Penge, Democratic Republic of the Congo, **368** D4
Penglai, China, **211** H5

Pengshui, China, **206** B2
Pengxi, China, **215** H3
Peniche, Portugal, **292** C3
Penicuik, Scotland, U.K., **308** F5
Peninga, Russian Federation, **285** R5
Penitente, Serra do, *mountain range*, Brazil, **456** D2
Penkridge, England, U.K., **304** E2
Penmarch, France, **290** B3
Penmarc'h, Pointe de, *point*, France, **290** B3
Penn Yan, U.S.A., **426** B3
Pennell Coast, *region*, Antarctica, **470** D8
Pennine, Alpi, *mountain range*, Italy, **294** A3, *247*
Pennines, *mountain range*, England, U.K., **306** F3, *276*
Pennsylvania, *state*, U.S.A., **426** B4, *384, 386*
Pennycutaway, *river*, Canada, **414** H3
Pennyghael, Scotland, U.K., **308** C4
Peno, Russian Federation, **299** D4
Penobscot, *river*, U.S.A., **426** F1
Penong, Australia, **134** G5
Penonomé, Panama, **429** E5
Penrhyn *see* Tongareva, *island*, Cook Islands, **139** J5
Penrith, England, U.K., **306** F3
Penryn, England, U.K., **304** B4
Pensacola, U.S.A., **425** J4
Pensacola Mountains, *mountain range*, Antarctica, **470** C5
Pentecost, *island*, Vanuatu, **141** A2
Penticton, Canada, **413** K7
Pentire Point, England, U.K., **304** B4
Pentland Firth, *strait*, Orkney, Scotland, U.K., **308** F2
Pentland Hills, Scotland, U.K., **308** F5
Penukonda, India, **216** D3
Penyagolosa, *mountain peak*, Spain, **293** G2
Penybont, Wales, U.K., **304** D2
Penybontfawr, Wales, U.K., **304** D2
Penygadair, *mountain peak*, Wales, U.K., **304** D2
Penza, Russian Federation, **298** G2
Penzance, England, U.K., **304** B4
Penzberg, Germany, **288** E5
Penzenskaya Oblast', *province*, Russian Federation, **298** F2
Peoria, U.S.A., **421** J5
Pepacton Reservoir, U.S.A., **426** C3
Pepe, Pointe, *point*, France, **290** C3
Pepeekeo, Hawaiian Islands, U.S.A., **422** R10
Pepepe, New Zealand, **132** E3
Peperi-Guaçu, *river*, Argentina/Brazil, **459** G3
Pëqin, Albania, **297** B5
Pér, Hungary, **289** H5
Perä-Posio, Finland, **285** N3
Perabumulih, Indonesia, **200** D3
Perak, *river*, Malaysia, **200** C1
Perak, *state*, Malaysia, **200** C1
Perama, Kriti, Greece, **297** E8
Perambalūr, India, **216** D4
Peranka, Finland, **285** P4
Percé, Canada, **417** J5
Percival Lakes, Australia, **134** F3
Perdida, *river*, Brazil, **456** D2
Perdido, Monte, *mountain peak*, Spain, **293** H1
Perdido, *river*, Argentina, **460** D2
Perdido, *river*, Brazil, **456** B5
Perdika, Greece, **297** C6
Perechyn, Ukraine, **289** L4
Perehins'ke, Ukraine, **289** M4
Pereira, Colombia, **450** C3
Pereira Barreto, Brazil, **456** C5
Peremyshl', Russian Federation, **299** F5
Perené, Peru, **454** C3
Pereslavl' Zalesskiy, Russian Federation, **299** G4
Pereyaslavka, Russian Federation, **211** L3
Perez, U.S.A., **418** D6
Pergamino, Argentina, **458** E4
Pergola, Italy, **294** D4
Perham, U.S.A., **420** F2
Perho, Finland, **285** M5
Perhonjoki, *river*, Finland, **285** L5
Péribonca, Lac, *lake*, Canada, **416** F4
Péribonca, *river*, Canada, **416** F4
Perico, Argentina, **458** D2
Perico, U.S.A., **423** M3
Pericos, Mexico, **430** D3
Périers, France, **290** D2
Perigoso, Canal, *channel*, Brazil, **452** D3
Périgueux, France, **290** E4
Peristera, *island*, Greece, **297** E6
Perito Moreno, Argentina, **460** C3
Peritoró, Brazil, **453** E4
Perleberg, Germany, **288** E2
Perlis, *state*, Malaysia, **200** B1
Perm', Russian Federation, **300** G4
Perma, U.S.A., **418** G3
Përmet, Albania, **297** C5
Permskaya Oblast', *province*, Russian Federation, **222** F1
Pernambuco, *state*, Brazil, **457** G2, *93*
Pernambuco Plain, *underwater feature*, Atlantic Ocean, **477** F6
Pernik, Bulgaria, **296** D4
Perniö, Finland, **287** L2
Péronne, France, **291** F2
Perote, Mexico, **431** F5
Perpignan, France, **291** F5
Perranporth, England, U.K., **304** B4
Perrault Falls, Canada, **414** H6
Perros-Guirec, France, **290** C2
Perry, Florida, U.S.A., **425** L4
Perry, Georgia, U.S.A., **425** L3
Perry, Iowa, U.S.A., **420** F5
Perry, Oklahoma, U.S.A., **424** D1
Perryton, U.S.A., **420** C7
Perryvale, Canada, **413** N4
Perryville, U.S.A., **420** J7
Persåsen, Sweden, **286** G1
Perseverance Harbour, Campbell Island, New Zealand, **132** K11
Perseverancia, Bolivia, **455** F4
Pershore, England, U.K., **304** E2
Persian Gulf, Asia, **220** E3, *45, 64, 146, 159, 176, 177, 178, 182, 183, 254, 385*
Pertandangan, Tanjong, *point*, Indonesia, **200** C2
Perth, Australia, **134** D5, *112*
Perth, Canada, **416** C7
Perth, Scotland, U.K., **308** F4
Perth and Kinross, *local authority*, Scotland, U.K., **308** F4
Perth-Andover, Canada, **416** H6
Perth Basin, *underwater feature*, Indian Ocean, **476** G6
Pertusato, Cap, *cape*, Corse, France, **295** B5
Peru, *country*, South America, **449** E4, *29, 54, 67, 76, 77, 85, 87, 88, 89, 90, 92, 93, 94, 95, 97, 126, 434, 435, 438, 440, 441, 442, 443*
Peru Basin, *underwater feature*, Pacific Ocean, **479** M5
Peru-Chile Trench, *underwater feature*, Pacific Ocean, **479** N5
Perugia, Italy, **294** D4
Perugorria, Argentina, **459** E3
Peruíbe, Brazil, **459** H2
Perušić, Croatia, **294** E3
Pervomays'k, Ukraine, **296** H1
Pervomayskiy, Russian Federation, **210** F2
Pervomayskoye, Russian Federation, **299** B2
Pervoural'sk, Russian Federation, **222** F1
Pesagi, Gunung, *mountain peak*, Indonesia, **200** D4
Pesaro, Italy, **294** D4
Pescadores, Punta, *point*, Róbinson Crusoe Island, Archipiélago Juan Fernández, Chile, **461** C2
Pescadores *see* P'eng-hu Lieh-tao, *island*, Taiwan, **206** D4
Pescara, Italy, **295** E4
Peschanoye, Russian Federation, **285** S5
Peschici, Italy, **295** F5
Pesek, Pulau, *island*, Singapore, **200** J7
Pesek Kechil, Pulau, *island*, Singapore, **200** J7
Peshāwar, Pakistan, **218** B2
Peshkopi, Albania, **297** C5
Peshtera, Bulgaria, **296** E4
Pesochnya, Russian Federation, **299** D6
Pesqueira, Brazil, **453** G5
Pessac, France, **290** D4
Pestovo, Russian Federation, **299** E3
Petacalco, Bahía de, *bay*, Mexico, **430** E5
Petäiskylä, Finland, **285** P5
Petäjävesi, Finland, **287** M1
Petalidi, Greece, **297** C7
Petaluma, U.S.A., **422** B2
Pétange, Luxembourg, **291** G2
Petare, Venezuela, **451** E1
Petatlan, Mexico, **431** E5
Petauke, Zambia, **369** F5
Petawawa, Canada, **416** C7
Petén Itzá, Lago, *lake*, Guatemala, **428** C3
Petenwell Lake, U.S.A., **420** H3
Peter I Øy, *Norwegian dependency*, Antarctica, **470** A6, *469*
Peter Pond Lake, Canada, **413** Q4
Peterbell, Canada, **415** N7
Peterborough, Australia, **135** H5
Peterborough, Canada, **416** B7
Peterborough, England, U.K., **305** G2
Peterborough, *unitary authority*, England, U.K., **305** G2
Peterculter, Scotland, U.K., **308** G3
Peterlee, England, U.K., **307** G3
Petermanns Bjerg, *mountain peak*, Greenland, **411** S2
Peteroa, Volcán, *mountain peak*, Chile, **458** B5
Peter's Mine, Guyana, **451** G2
Petersburg, U.S.A., **426** B6
Petersfield, England, U.K., **305** G3
Petisikapau Lake, Canada, **416** H2
Petit Goâve, Haiti, **429** G3
Petite Rivière Noire, Piton de la, *mountain peak*, Mauritius, **373** C1, *353*
Petitot, *river*, Canada, **412** J2
Petkula, Finland, **285** N3
Peto, Mexico, **431** H4
Petolahti, Finland, **287** K1
Petoskey, U.S.A., **421** L3
Petre Bay, Chatham Islands, New Zealand, **133** Q16
Petrich, Bulgaria, **297** D5
Petrila, Romania, **296** D3
Petrivka, Ukraine, **296** H2
Petrodvorets, Russian Federation, **299** B3
Petrolina, Brazil, **457** F2
Petropavl, Kazakhstan, **223** H2
Petropavlovka, Russian Federation, **210** D2
Petropavlovsk-Kamchatskiy, Russian Federation, **301** S4
Petrópolis, Brazil, **457** E6
Petroşani, Romania, **296** D3
Petrovichi, Russian Federation, **299** D6
Petrovka, Russian Federation, **223** L2
Petrovo, Russian Federation, **299** E3
Petrovsk Zabaykal'skiy, Russian Federation, **210** E2
Petrovskoye, Russian Federation, **299** G4
Petrozavodsk, Russian Federation, **299** E2
Petruşeni, Moldova, **296** F2
Pettigo, Northern Ireland, U.K., **309** E3
Petukhovo, Russian Federation, **222** H1
Petushki, Russian Federation, **299** G5
Petworth, England, U.K., **305** G4
Peureulak, Indonesia, **200** B1
Pevek, Russian Federation, **301** U3
Pewsey, England, U.K., **305** F3
Pézenas, France, **291** F5
Pezinok, Slovakia, **289** H4
Pezu, Pakistan, **218** B2
Pfaffenhofen an der Ilm, Germany, **288** E4
Pforzheim, Germany, **288** D4
Phalaborwa, South Africa, **371** F3
Phālia, Pakistan, **218** C2
Phalodi, India, **218** C4
Phalsund, India, **218** B4
Phan Rang, Vietnam, **203** F4
Phan Thiết, Vietnam, **203** F4
Phang Khon, Thailand, **203** D2
Phangan, Ko, *island*, Thailand, **202** D4
Phangnga, Thailand, **202** C4
Pharr, U.S.A., **424** C6
Phayao, Thailand, **202** C2
Phenix City, U.S.A., **425** K3
Phet Buri Reservoir, Thailand, **202** C3
Phetchabun, Thailand, **202** D2
Phetchaburi, Thailand, **202** C3
Phiamay, Phou, *mountain peak*, Laos, **203** E3
Phichit, Thailand, **202** D2
Phidim, Nepal, **219** F4
Philadelphia, Mississippi, U.S.A., **425** H3
Philadelphia, Pennsylvania, U.S.A., **426** C4, *384*
Philip, U.S.A., **420** C3
Philip Island, Norfolk Island, **135** T13
Philippeville, Belgium, **288** B3
Philippine Sea, Philippines, **204** D2
Philippine Trench, *underwater feature*, Pacific Ocean, **478** C3
Philippines, *country*, Asia, **197** P8, *50, 51, 61, 76, 88, 95, 97, 108, 125, 144, 145, 149, 152, 193, 252, 253*
Philipsburg, Montana, U.S.A., **418** H3
Philipsburg, Pennsylvania, U.S.A., **421** P5
Philipsburg, St Maarten, Netherlands Antilles, **427** D2
Philipstown, South Africa, **370** D5
Phillip Island, Australia, **135** J6
Phillips, U.S.A., **420** H3
Phillipsburg, Kansas, U.S.A., **420** D6
Phillipsburg, Pennsylvania, U.S.A., **426** C4
Philomath, U.S.A., **418** C4
Philpots Island, Canada, **411** M2
Phimai, Thailand, **203** D3
Phitsanulok, Thailand, **202** D2
Phnom Penh *see* Phnum Pénh, Cambodia, **203** E4, *152, 153*
Phnum Pénh (Phnom Penh), Cambodia, **203** E4, *152, 153*
Phoenix *see* Rawaki, *island*, Kiribati, **139** G5
Phoenix, U.S.A., **423** G5, *386*
Phoenix Islands, Kiribati, **139** G5, *119*
Phon, Thailand, **203** D3
Phôngsali, Laos, **202** D1
Photharam, Thailand, **202** C3
Phra Nakhon Si Ayutthaya, Thailand, **202** D3
Phra Thong, Ko, *island*, Thailand, **202** C4
Phrae, Thailand, **202** D2
Phsar Réam, Cambodia, **203** D4
Phú Nhơn, Vietnam, **203** F3
Phú Quốc, Đao, *island*, Vietnam, **203** D4
Phú Thọ, Vietnam, **203** E1
Phuket, Ko, *island*, Thailand, **202** C4
Phuket, Thailand, **202** C5
Phulabāni, India, **219** F5
Phumĭ Banam, Cambodia, **203** E4
Phumĭ Bântéay Chhmar, Cambodia, **203** D3
Phumĭ Chrăng Khpós, Cambodia, **203** D4
Phumĭ Krêk, Cambodia, **203** E4
Phumĭ Mlu Prey, Cambodia, **203** E3
Phumĭ Moŭng, Cambodia, **203** D3
Phumĭ Phsa Rôméas, Cambodia, **203** E3
Phumĭ Prâmaôy, Cambodia, **203** D3
Phumĭ Prêk Preăh, Cambodia, **203** E3
Phumĭ Prey Chruk, Cambodia, **203** D3
Phumĭ Sâmraông, E. Cambodia, **203** E3
Phumĭ Sâmraông, W. Cambodia, **203** D3
Phumĭ Véal Rénh, Cambodia, **203** D4
Phuthaditjhaba, South Africa, **371** E4
Pi Xian, Jiangsu, China, **206** D1
Pi Xian, Sichuan, China, **215** G3
Piacá, Brazil, **452** D5
Piacenza, Italy, **294** B3
Piadena, Italy, **294** C3
Piana-Mwanga, Democratic Republic of the Congo, **369** E4
Pianguan, China, **210** E5
Pianosa, Isola, Adriatic Sea, *island*, Italy, **295** E4
Pianosa, Isola, Tyrrhenian Sea, *island*, Italy, **294** C4
Piaski, Poland, **289** L3
Piatra, near Bals, Romania, **296** E3
Piatra, Romania, **296** E4
Piatra Neamţ, Romania, **296** F2
Piauí, *river*, Brazil, **457** E2
Piauí, *state*, Brazil, **453** E5
Piave, *river*, Italy, **294** D2
Piazza Armerina, Sicilia, Italy, **295** E7
Pibor Post, Sudan, **366** D3
Pica, Chile, **455** E5
Picardie, *administrative region*, France, **290** E2, *245*
Picayune, U.S.A., **425** H4
Picentini, Monti, *mountain peak*, Italy, **295** E5
Picháchic, Mexico, **430** D2
Pichanal, Argentina, **458** D2
Pichhor, India, **218** D4
Pichi Mahuida, Argentina, **460** E1
Pichilemu, Chile, **458** B5
Pichilingue, Mexico, **430** C3
Pichucalo, Mexico, **431** G5
Pickering, England, U.K., **307** H3
Pickle Lake, Canada, **414** J6
Pico, *island*, Azores, Portugal, **360** M7
Pico de Salamanca, Argentina, **460** D2
Pico Truncado, Argentina, **460** D3
Picos, Brazil, **453** F5
Picota, Peru, **454** C2
Picton, Canada, **416** C8
Picton, Isla, *island*, Chile, **460** D5
Picton, New Zealand, **133** D5
Picton, U.S.A., **426** B2
Picún Leufú, Argentina, **460** D1
Picún Leufú, *river*, Argentina, **460** C1
Pidārak, Pakistan, **221** H3
Pidi, Democratic Republic of the Congo, **369** E4
Pidurutalagala, *mountain peak*, Sri Lanka, **217** E5, *166*
Pie Town, U.S.A., **423** J4
Piedmont, Alabama, U.S.A., **425** K3
Piedmont, South Dakota, U.S.A., **420** B3
Piedrabuena, Spain, **292** E3
Piedrahita, Spain, **292** E2
Piedras, de las, *river*, Peru, **454** D3
Piedras Negras, Coahuila, Mexico, **431** E2
Piedras Negras, Veracruz, Mexico, **431** F5

Pieksämäki, Finland, **287** N1
Pielavesi, Finland, **285** N5
Pielinen, *lake,* Finland, **285** P5
Piemonte, *autonomous region,* Italy, **294** A3, *255*
Pieniężno, Poland, **289** K1
Pierce, U.S.A., **418** G3
Pierceland, Canada, **410** J4
Pierowall, Orkney, Scotland, U.K., **308** F1
Pierre, U.S.A., **420** C3, *386*
Pierrelatte, France, **291** G4
Pierreville, Canada, **416** E6
Pierrot Island, Rodrigues, Mauritius, **373** B1
Pierson, Canada, **414** D7
Piet Retief, South Africa, **371** F4
Pietarsaari, Finland, **285** L5
Pietermaritzburg, South Africa, **371** F4
Pietersburg, South Africa, **371** E3
Pieve di Cadore, Italy, **294** D2
Pigeon, *river,* Canada, **414** F5
Pigeon Point, Tobago, Trinidad and Tobago, **461** B4
Pigüé, Argentina, **458** D5
Pihāni, India, **218** E4
Pihlajavesi, Finland, **287** M1
Pihtipudas, Finland, **285** M5
Piippola, Finland, **285** N4
Pijijiapan, Mexico, **431** G6
Pikalevo, Russian Federation, **299** E3
Pikangikum, Canada, **414** H6
Piketberg, South Africa, **370** C5
Pikeville, U.S.A., **421** M7
Pikine, Senegal, **364** A2
Pikit, Philippines, **204** D5
Pikou, China, **211** H5
Pikounda, Congo, **368** C2
Pikwitonei, Canada, **414** F4
Pila, Argentina, **459** E5
Piła, Poland, **289** H2
Pilagá, *river,* Argentina, **459** E2
Pilão Arcado, Brazil, **457** E2
Pilar, Argentina, **459** E5
Pilar, Cabo, *cape,* Chile, **460** B4
Pilar, Paraguay, **459** E3
Pilaya, *river,* Bolivia, **455** F5
Pilbara, *region,* Australia, **134** D3
Pilcaniyeu, Argentina, **460** C1
Pilcomayo, *river,* Argentina/Bolivia/Paraguay, **455** F5
Pīleru, India, **216** D3
Pili, Philippines, **204** C3
Pīlībhīt, India, **218** D3
Pilica, *river,* Poland, **289** K3
Pillar Bay, Ascension, **373** A3
Pillcopata, Peru, **454** D3
Pilões, Serra dos, *mountain range,* Brazil, **456** D4
Pilón, Cuba, **429** F3
Pilot Mound, Canada, **414** E7
Pilot Rock, U.S.A., **418** E4
Pilsen *see* Plzeň, Czech Republic, **288** F4
Pilzno, Poland, **289** K4
Pima, U.S.A., **423** J5
Pimenta Bueno, Brazil, **455** G3
Pimperne, England, U.K., **304** E4
Pimpri-Chinchwad, India, **216** C2
Pináculo, Cerro, *mountain peak,* Argentina, **460** C4
Pinamalayan, Philippines, **204** C3
Pinang (Penang), Pulau, *island,* Malaysia, **200** B1
Pinang, *state,* Malaysia, **200** B1, *151*
Pinangah, Malaysia, **201** G1
Pinar del Río, Cuba, **428** E2
Pınarhisar, Turkey, **297** F5
Piñas, Ecuador, **450** B5
Pinatubo, Mount, *mountain peak,* Philippines, **204** C3, *50, 51, 97*
Pinchbeck, England, U.K., **305** G2
Pincher Creek, Canada, **413** N7
Pindaré, *river,* Brazil, **452** D4
Pindaré-Mirim, Brazil, **452** E4
Pindi Gheb, Pakistan, **218** C2
Pindobal, Brazil, **452** D4
Pindos Oros (Pindus Mountains), *mountain range,* Albania, **297** C5, *265*
Pindushi, Russian Federation, **285** S5
Pindwāra, India, **218** C4
Pine, Cape, Canada, **417** Q6
Pine, U.S.A., **423** H4
Pine Bluff, U.S.A., **424** F2
Pine Creek, Australia, **134** G1
Pine Dock, Canada, **414** F6
Pine Hills, U.S.A., **425** M5
Pine Point, Canada, **413** M1
Pine Ridge, U.S.A., **420** B4
Pine River, Canada, **414** D6
Pine Springs, U.S.A., **423** L6
Pinedale, Arizona, U.S.A., **423** H4
Pinedale, Wyoming, U.S.A., **419** K5
Pinehouse Lake, Canada, **413** R4
Pinehouse Lake, *lake,* Canada, **413** R4
Pineimuta, *river,* Canada, **415** K5
Pineios, *river,* Greece, **297** D6
Pinerolo, Italy, **294** A3
Pines, Isle of *see* Pins, Île des, *island,* New Caledonia, **141** A3
Pinetop-Lakeside, U.S.A., **423** J4
Pineville, U.S.A., **424** F4
Pinewood, Canada, **414** G7
Piney, France, **291** G2
Ping, Mae Nam, *river,* Thailand, **202** C2, *155*
P'ing-tung, Taiwan, **206** E4
Ping'an, China, **207** C2
Pingchang, China, **215** H3
Pingdi, China, **207** C3
Pingdingshan, China, **206** C1
Pingdu, China, **211** G5
Pingelap, *island,* Micronesia, **138** E4
Pingguo, China, **215** H5
Pinghai, China, **207** D3
Pinghe, China, **206** D3
Pinghu, Guangdong, China, **207** C3
Pinghu, Zhejiang, China, **206** E2
Pingjiang, China, **206** C2
Pingle, China, **206** B3
Pingli, China, **206** B1
Pingliang, China, **215** H2
Pingling, China, **207** C1
Pingluo, China, **210** D5
Pingquan, China, **211** G4
Pingree, U.S.A., **420** D2
Pingsha, China, **206** C4
Pingshan, China, **207** C3
Pingtan, Fujian, China, **206** D3
Pingtan, Guangdong, China, **207** D2
Pingwu, China, **215** H2
Pingxiang, Guangxi Zhuangzu Zizhiqu, China, **215** H5
Pingxiang, Jiangxi, China, **206** C3
Pingxiang, Vietnam, **203** E1
Pingyang, China, **206** E3
Pingyao, China, **210** F5
Pingyi, China, **206** D1
Pingyin, China, **210** G5
Pingyuanjie, China, **215** G5
Pingzhuang, China, **211** G4
Pinheiro, Brazil, **452** E4
Pinheiro Machado, Brazil, **459** G4
Pinhel, Portugal, **292** D2
Pinhoe, England, U.K., **304** D4
Pini, Pulau, *island,* Indonesia, **200** B2
Pinjarra, Australia, **134** D5
Pink, *river,* Canada, **414** B3
Pink Mountain, Canada, **412** H3
Pinlebu, Myanmar, **205** B2
Pinnacle, *mountain peak,* New Zealand, **133** D5
Pinnes, Akra, *point,* Greece, **297** E5
Pinoso, Spain, **293** G3
Pins, Île des (Isle of Pines), *island,* New Caledonia, **141** A3
Pinsk, Belarus, **298** C2
Pinta, Isla, *island,* Islas Galápagos (Galapagos Islands), Ecuador, **461** A1
Pintados, Chile, **455** E5
Pintamo, Finland, **285** N4
Pintatu, Indonesia, **198** D2
Pinto, Argentina, **458** D3
Pintuyan, Philippines, **204** D4
Pınzón, Isla, *island,* Islas Galápagos (Galapagos Islands), Ecuador, **461** A2
Piombino, Italy, **294** C4
Pioneer Fracture Zone, *tectonic feature,* Pacific Ocean, **479** H2
Pioner, Ostrov, *island,* Russian Federation, **300** K2
Pionerskiy, Russian Federation, **287** K5
Piopio, New Zealand, **132** E4
Piotrków Trybunalski, Poland, **289** J3
Piperi, *island,* Greece, **297** E6
Pipestone, Canada, **414** D7
Pipestone, *river,* Canada, **413** R3
Pipestone, U.S.A., **420** E3
Pipili, India, **219** F5
Pipiriki, New Zealand, **132** E4
Pipmuacan, Réservoir, Canada, **416** F5
Pipri, India, **219** E4
Piquiri, *river,* Brazil, **459** G2
Pīr Panjāl Range, *mountain range,* India, **218** C2
Piracanjuba, Brazil, **456** D4
Piracicaba, Brazil, **459** H2
Piracicaba, *river,* Brazil, **459** H2
Piraçununga, Brazil, **456** D5
Piracuruca, Brazil, **453** F4
Piraeus *see* Peiraias, Greece, **297** D7
Piraí do Sul, Brazil, **459** H2
Pirajuí, Brazil, **456** D5
Pirané, Argentina, **459** E2
Piranhas, Brazil, **456** C4
Piranhas, *river,* Brazil, **453** G5
Pirapó, *river,* Brazil, **459** G2
Pirapora, Brazil, **457** E4
Piratini, Brazil, **459** G4
Piratini, *river,* Brazil, **459** G4
Piray, *river,* Bolivia, **455** F4
Piray Guazu, *river,* Argentina, **459** F3
Pires do Rio, Brazil, **456** D4
Piripiri, Brazil, **453** F4
Piripiri, New Zealand, **132** F5
Píritu, Venezuela, **451** E1
Pirizal, Brazil, **456** B4
Pirmasens, Germany, **288** C4
Pirna, Germany, **289** F3
Pirnmill, Scotland, U.K., **308** D5
Pirón, *river,* Spain, **292** E2
Pirongia Mountain, *mountain peak,* New Zealand, **132** E3
Pirot, Serbia, **296** D4
Pirovac, Croatia, **294** E4
Pirttikoski, Finland, **285** N3
Pirttikylä, Finland, **287** K1
Piru, Indonesia, **199** E3
Pisa, Italy, **294** C4, *254, 255*
Pisa, Mount, *mountain peak,* New Zealand, **133** B7
Pisagua, Chile, **455** D5
Pisco, Peru, **454** C3
Pisco, *river,* Peru, **454** C3
Písek, Czech Republic, **289** G4
Pisgah, Mount, *mountain peak,* New Zealand, **133** C7
Pishchanka, Ukraine, **296** G1
Pising, Indonesia, **198** C4
Piso Firme, Bolivia, **455** G3
Pissos, France, **290** D4
Pistayarvi, Ozero, *lake,* Russian Federation, **285** Q4
Piste, Mexico, **431** H4
Pisticci, Italy, **295** F5
Pistoia, Italy, **294** C4
Pistol River, U.S.A., **418** B5
Pisuerga, *river,* Spain, **292** E1
Pisz, Poland, **289** K2
Pita, Guinea, **364** B2
Pitaga, Canada, **416** J3
Pital, Cerro El, *mountain peak,* El Salvador, **428** C4
Pital, Mexico, **431** H5
Pitalito, Colombia, **450** C4
Pitanga, Brazil, **459** G2
Pitangui, Brazil, **457** E5
Pitcairn Island, Pitcairn Islands, **137** J3, *125*
Pitcairn Islands, *U.K. dependency,* Pacific Ocean, **137** J3, *91, 108, 125, 126, 276*
Piteå, Sweden, **284** K4
Piteälven, *river,* Sweden, **284** J4
Pitești, Romania, **296** E3
Pithiviers, France, **290** F2
Pitkyaranta, Russian Federation, **299** C2
Pitlochry, Scotland, U.K., **308** F4
Pitoa, Cameroon, **365** G3
Pitomača, Croatia, **294** F3
Pitrufquén, Chile, **460** C1
Pitscottie, Scotland, U.K., **308** G4
Pitt Island, Canada, **412** D5
Pitt Island, Chatham Islands, New Zealand, **133** Q16
Pitt Strait, Chatham Islands, New Zealand, **133** Q16
Pittentrail, Scotland, U.K., **308** E3
Pittsburgh, U.S.A., **421** N5, *384*
Pittsfield, U.S.A., **426** D3
Pium, Brazil, **456** D3
Piura, Peru, **454** B1
Pivijay, Colombia, **450** C1
Pivka, Slovenia, **294** E3
Pixa, China, **212** C5
Pixoyal, Mexico, **431** H5
Pizacoma, Peru, **455** E4
Pizhi, Nigeria, **365** F3
Pizzo, Italy, **295** F6
Placentia, Canada, **417** Q6
Placentia Bay, Canada, **417** P6
Placer, Philippines, **204** C4
Placerville, California, U.S.A., **422** C2
Placerville, Colorado, U.S.A., **423** J2
Plácido de Castro, Brazil, **455** E3
Plačkovica, *mountain peak,* Macedonia, **297** D5
Plains, Kansas, U.S.A., **420** C7
Plains, Texas, U.S.A., **423** M5
Plainview, U.S.A., **424** B2
Plakoti, Cape, Cyprus, **225** B2
Plampang, Indonesia, **201** G5
Plana, Bosnia and Herzegovina, **294** G4
Planaltina, Brazil, **456** D4
Planeta Rica, Colombia, **450** C2
Plano, U.S.A., **424** D3
Plantation, U.S.A., **425** M6
Plaquemine, U.S.A., **424** G4
Plasencia, Spain, **292** D2
Plastun, Russian Federation, **209** G1
Plata, Río de la, *estuary,* Argentina/Uruguay, **447** G7, *443, 444*
Platanos, Greece, **297** C7
Plateau, *state,* Nigeria, **365** F3
Plateaux, *administrative region,* Congo, **368** B3
Platičevo, Serbia, **296** B3
Platina, U.S.A., **422** B1
Plato, Colombia, **450** C2
Platte, *river,* U.S.A., **420** D5
Platte Island, Seychelles, **372** D2
Platteville, U.S.A., **420** H4
Plattsburgh, U.S.A., **426** D2
Plau, Germany, **288** F2
Plauen, Germany, **288** F3
Plauer See, Germany, **288** F2
Plav, Montenegro, **296** B4
Plava, *river,* Russian Federation, **299** F6
Pļaviņas, Latvia, **287** M4
Plavsk, Russian Federation, **299** F6
Plây Cu (Pleiku), Vietnam, **203** F3
Playa Blanca, Islas Canarias, Spain, **373** B4
Playas, Ecuador, **450** B5
Playas Lake, U.S.A., **423** J6
Plaza Huincul, Argentina, **460** D1
Pld'ma, Russian Federation, **299** E2
Pleasant Plains, U.S.A., **424** G2
Pleasant Valley, U.S.A., **418** F4
Pleasanton, U.S.A., **424** C5
Plechý, *mountain peak,* Czech Republic, **289** F4
Plei Câ'n, Vietnam, **203** E3
Pleiku *see* Plây Cu, Vietnam, **203** F3
Plenty, Bay of, New Zealand, **132** F3
Plentywood, U.S.A., **419** M2
Plessisville, Canada, **416** F6
Pleszew, Poland, **289** H3
Plétipi, Lac, *lake,* Canada, **416** F4
Pleven, Bulgaria, **296** E4
Plevna, U.S.A., **419** M3
Plitvice, Croatia, **294** E3
Pljevlja, Montenegro, **296** B4
Ploaghe, Sardegna, Italy, **295** B5
Płock, Poland, **289** J2
Ploërmel, France, **290** C3
Ploiești, Romania, **296** F3
Plomari, Greece, **297** F6
Plomb du Cantal, *mountain peak,* France, **290** F4
Plön, Germany, **288** E1
Płońsk, Poland, **289** K2
Plopeni, Romania, **296** E3
Ploskosh', Russian Federation, **299** C4
Ploskoye, Russian Federation, **299** E5
Plotava, Russian Federation, **223** L2
Plotnikovo, Russian Federation, **223** L1
Płoty, Poland, **289** G2
Plouaret, France, **290** C2
Ploudalmézeau, France, **290** B2
Plovdiv, *administrative region,* Bulgaria, **296** E4
Plovdiv, Bulgaria, **296** E4
Plummer, U.S.A., **418** F3
Plumpton, England, U.K., **306** F3
Plumtree, Zimbabwe, **371** E3
Plungė, Lithuania, **287** K5
Plyeshchanitsy, Belarus, **287** N5
Plymouth, England, U.K., **304** C4
Plymouth, Indiana, U.S.A., **421** K5
Plymouth, Massachusetts, U.S.A., **426** E4, *384*
Plymouth, Montserrat, **427** D2, *390*
Plymouth, Tobago, Trinidad and Tobago, **461** B4
Plympton, England, U.K., **304** C4
Plynlimon Fawr, *mountain peak,* Wales, U.K., **304** D2
Plyussa, *river,* Russian Federation, **299** B3
Plyussa, Russian Federation, **299** B3
Plzeň (Pilsen), Czech Republic, **288** F4
Pnevno, Ukraine, **289** M3
Pniewy, Poland, **289** H2
Pô, Burkina Faso, **364** D2
Po, *river,* Italy, **280** E6, *255*
Po, Tanjong, *point,* Malaysia, **201** E2
Po Toi, *island,* China, **207** C4
Pobeda, Gora, *mountain peak,* Russian Federation, **301** R3
Pobedy, Pik, *mountain peak,* China, **212** D4, *186, 187*
Pobuz'ke, Ukraine, **296** H1
Pocahontas, U.S.A., **424** G1
Pocatello, U.S.A., **418** H5
Pochala, Sudan, **366** D3
Pochinok, Russian Federation, **299** D5
Pocitos, Argentina, **458** D2
Pocklington, England, U.K., **307** H4
Poções, Brazil, **457** F4
Poconé, Brazil, **456** B4
Poços de Caldas, Brazil, **456** D5
Podberez'ye, Novgorodskaya Oblast', Russian Federation, **299** C3
Podberez'ye, Pskovskaya Oblast', Russian Federation, **299** C4
Podbořany, Czech Republic, **288** F3
Podborov'ye, Russian Federation, **299** B4

Poddor'ye, Russian Federation, **299** C4
Podgorac, Serbia, **296** C4
Podgorica, Montenegro, **296** B4
Podol'sk, Russian Federation, **299** F5
Podor, Senegal, **364** B1
Podporozh'ye, Russian Federation, **299** E2
Podujevo, Kosovo, **296** C4
Pofadder, South Africa, **370** C4
Poggibonsi, Italy, **294** C4
Pogoanele, Romania, **296** F3
Pogradec, Albania, **297** C5
Pogranichnyy, Russian Federation, **211** K3
P'ohang, South Korea, **208** E3
Pohjaslahti, Finland, **287** M1
Pohjois-Ii, Finland, **285** M4
Pohnpei, *island*, Micronesia, **138** D4, *118*
Pohořelice, Czech Republic, **289** H4
Poiana Mare, Romania, **296** D4
Poiana Stampei, Romania, **296** E2
Poie, Democratic Republic of the Congo, **366** B5
Point Arena, U.S.A., **422** B2
Point Fortin, Trinidad, Trinidad and Tobago, **461** C4
Point Hope, U.S.A., **410** C3
Point of Rocks, U.S.A., **419** K6
Pointblank, U.S.A., **424** E4
Pointe-à-Pitre, Guadeloupe, **427** D2
Pointe-Noire, Congo, **368** B3, *334*
Pointe-Parent, Canada, **417** L4
Points North Landing, Canada, **414** B2
Poitiers, France, **290** E3
Poitou-Charentes, *administrative region*, France, **290** D3, *245*
Poix, France, **305** J5
Pojo, Bolivia, **455** F4
Pok Liu Chau (Lamma Island), *island*, China, **207** C4
Pokaran, India, **218** B4
Pokeno, New Zealand, **132** E3
Pokhara, Nepal, **219** E3
Pokigron, Suriname, **452** B2
Pokka, Finland, **285** M2
Poko, Democratic Republic of the Congo, **369** E2
Pokrovka, Novosibirskaya Oblast', Russian Federation, **223** K1
Pokrovka, Primorskiy Kray, Russian Federation, **211** K4
Pokrovsk, Russian Federation, **223** P2
Pol-e 'Alam, Afghanistan, **218** B2
Pola, *river*, Russian Federation, **299** C4
Pola, Russian Federation, **299** C4
Polacca, U.S.A., **423** H4
Polān, Iran, **221** H3
Poland, *country*, Europe, **282** F5, *96, 228, 229, 232, 236, 237, 238, 239, 245, 266, 267, 268, 269, 271, 272*
Polanów, Poland, **289** H1
Polatlı, Turkey, **224** D5
Polatsk, Belarus, **298** C1
Polebridge, U.S.A., **418** G2
Polegate, England, U.K., **305** H4
Polevskoye, Russian Federation, **222** G1
Polewali, Indonesia, **198** B3
Polewali, New Zealand, **132** E3
Polga, Russian Federation, **285** S5
Polgárdi, Hungary, **289** J5
Poli, Cameroon, **365** G3
Poli, China, **206** D1
Poliçan, Albania, **297** C5
Policastro, Golfo di, *gulf*, Italy, **295** E6
Police, Pointe, *point*, Seychelles, **373** A2
Police, Poland, **289** G2
Polichnitos, Greece, **297** F6
Poligny, France, **291** G3
Polillo Islands, Philippines, **204** C3
Polinik, *mountain peak*, Austria, **288** F5
Polis, Cyprus, **225** B2
Polist', *river*, Russian Federation, **299** C4
Pollāchi, India, **216** D4
Pollença, Spain, **293** J3
Pollock, New Zealand, **132** E3
Pollock, U.S.A., **418** F4
Polo, Solomon Islands, **141** A1
Polovragi, Romania, **296** D3
Polperro, England, U.K., **304** C4
Polski Trŭmbesh, Bulgaria, **296** E4
Polson, U.S.A., **418** G3
Poltava, Ukraine, **298** D3
Põltsamaa, Estonia, **287** M3
Põlva, Estonia, **287** N3
Polyaigos, *island*, Kyklades, Greece, **297** E7
Polyarnyy, Russian Federation, **285** R2
Polyarnyye Zori, Russian Federation, **285** R3
Polygyros, Greece, **297** D5
Polykastro, Greece, **297** D5
Polynesia, *islands*, Pacific Ocean, **129** J3, *61, 108, 109*
Pomabamba, Peru, **454** C2
Pomarance, Italy, **294** C4
Pomarkku, Finland, **287** K2
Pomas, Cape, Papua New Guinea, **140** D4
Pombal, Brazil, **453** G5
Pombal, Portugal, **292** C3
Pomeroy, Northern Ireland, U.K., **309** F3
Pomeroy, U.S.A., **418** F3
Pomichna, Ukraine, **296** H1
Pomio, Papua New Guinea, **140** C4
Pomorie, Bulgaria, **296** F4
Pomorska, Zatoka, *bay*, Germany/Poland, **289** G1
Pomovaara, *mountain peak*, Finland, **285** N3
Pompeu, Brazil, **457** E5
Pompeyevka, Russian Federation, **211** K2
Ponca City, U.S.A., **420** E7
Ponce, Puerto Rico, **427** C2
Pond Inlet, Canada, **411** M2
Pondicherry, India, **216** D4, *169*
Pondicherry, *union territory*, India, **216** D3, *169*
Poneloya, Nicaragua, **428** D4
Ponente, Riviera di, *coastal area*, Italy, **294** A4
Ponérihouen, New Caledonia, **141** A3
Ponferrada, Spain, **292** D1
Ponizov'ye, Russian Federation, **299** C5
Ponnāni, India, **216** C4
Ponoka, Canada, **413** N5
Ponomarëvka, Novosibirskaya Oblast', Russian Federation, **223** L1
Ponomarevka, Orenburgskaya Oblast', Russian Federation, **222** E2
Ponorogo, Indonesia, **201** E4
Ponoy, *river*, Russian Federation, **285** S3
Pons, France, **290** D4
Pont-à-Mousson, France, **291** H2
Pont-Saint-Esprit, France, **291** G4
Ponta de Pedras, Brazil, **452** D3
Ponta Delgada, Azores, Portugal, **360** M7
Ponta do Sol, Cape Verde, **360** P8
Ponta dos Índios, Brazil, **452** C2
Ponta Grossa, Brazil, **459** G2
Ponta Porã, Brazil, **456** B6
Pontal, *river*, Brazil, **457** F2
Pontalina, Brazil, **456** D4
Pontão, Portugal, **292** C3
Pontardawe, Wales, U.K., **304** D3
Pontarlier, France, **291** H3
Pontaumur, France, **290** F4
Pontchartrain, Lake, U.S.A., **424** G4
Pontchâteau, France, **290** C3
Ponte Alta do Norte, Brazil, **456** D3
Ponte da Barca, Portugal, **292** C2
Ponte de Pedra, Brazil, **456** B3
Pontedera, Italy, **294** C4
Pontedeume, Spain, **292** C1
Pontefract, England, U.K., **307** G4
Ponteland, England, U.K., **307** G2
Pontes-e-Lacerda, Brazil, **455** G4
Pontevedra, Spain, **292** C1
Pontiac, U.S.A., **421** J5
Pontian Kecil, Malaysia, **200** C2
Pontianak, Indonesia, **201** E3
Pontivy, France, **290** C2
Pontoetoe, Suriname, **452** B2
Pontoise, France, **290** F2
Ponton, Canada, **414** E4
Pontoon, Ireland, **309** C4
Pontotoc, U.S.A., **425** H2
Pontremoli, Italy, **294** B3
Pontrhydfendigaid, Wales, U.K., **304** D2
Pontrilas, England, U.K., **304** E3
Ponts, Spain, **293** H2
Pontyberem, Wales, U.K., **304** C3
Pontypridd, Wales, U.K., **304** D3
Ponui Island, New Zealand, **132** E3
Ponya, *river*, Belarus, **287** N5
Ponza, Isola di, *island*, Italy, **295** D5
Pool, *administrative region*, Congo, **368** B3
Poole, England, U.K., **305** E4
Poole, *unitary authority*, England, U.K., **304** E4
Poole Bay, England, U.K., **305** F4
Poolewe, Scotland, U.K., **308** D3
Pooley Bridge, England, U.K., **306** F3
Poopó, Lago, *lake*, Bolivia, **455** E5
Poor Knights Islands, New Zealand, **132** E2
Popa, Mount, *mountain peak*, Myanmar, **205** B3
Popayán, Colombia, **450** C3
Pope, Latvia, **287** K4
Poperinge, Belgium, **305** K4
Poplar, *river*, Canada, **414** F5
Poplar Bluff, U.S.A., **420** H7
Poplar Creek, Canada, **413** L6
Poplar Hill, Canada, **414** G5
Poplarfield, Canada, **414** F6
Poplarville, U.S.A., **425** H4
Popocatépetl, Volcán, *mountain peak*, Mexico, **431** F5, *400*
Popokabaka, Democratic Republic of the Congo, **368** C4
Popoli, Italy, **295** D4
Popondetta, Papua New Guinea, **140** C5
Popov Porog, Russian Federation, **285** R5
Popovo, Bulgaria, **296** F4
Poprad, Slovakia, **289** K4
Porangahau, New Zealand, **132** F5
Porangatu, Brazil, **456** D3
Porazava, Belarus, **289** M2
Porbandar, India, **218** B5
Porcher Island, Canada, **412** D5
Porcuna, Spain, **292** E4
Porcupine, Cape, Canada, **417** N3
Porcupine, *river*, Canada/U.S.A., **406** J2
Porcupine Plain, *underwater feature*, Atlantic Ocean, **477** F2
Pordenone, Italy, **294** D3
Pore, Colombia, **450** D3
Poreč, Croatia, **294** D3
Porech'ye, Moskovskaya Oblast', Russian Federation, **299** E5
Porech'ye, Tverskaya Oblast', Russian Federation, **299** F3
Poretskoye, Russian Federation, **298** G1
Pórfido, Punta, *point*, Argentina, **460** E1
Porgera, Papua New Guinea, **140** A4
Pori, Finland, **287** K2
Porirua, New Zealand, **133** E5
Porjus, Sweden, **284** J3
Porkhov, Russian Federation, **299** B4
Porlamar, Venezuela, **451** F1
Porlock, England, U.K., **304** D3
Pormpuraaw, Australia, **135** J1
Pornic, France, **290** C3
Poronaysk, Russian Federation, **301** R5
Poros, Greece, **297** D7
Porosozero, Russian Federation, **285** R5
Porpoise Bay, Antarctica, **470** F7
Porpoise Point, Ascension, **373** A3
Porquerolles, Île de, *island*, France, **291** H5
Porquis Junction, Canada, **415** P7
Porsangen, *bay*, Norway, **285** M1
Porsgrunn, Norway, **286** D3
Port-à-Piment, Haiti, **429** G3
Port Alberni, Canada, **412** G7
Port Alfred, South Africa, **371** E5
Port Alice, Canada, **412** F6
Port Angeles, U.S.A., **418** C2
Port Antonio, Jamaica, **429** F3, *393*
Port Arthur, Australia, **135** K7, *95*
Port Arthur, U.S.A., **424** F5
Port Askaig, Scotland, U.K., **308** C5
Port-au-Prince, Haiti, **429** G3, *394*
Port Augusta, Australia, **135** H5
Port Austin, U.S.A., **421** M4
Port aux Choix, Canada, **417** N4
Port Barre, U.S.A., **424** G4
Port Beaufort, South Africa, **370** D5
Port Bell, Uganda, **369** F2
Port Blair, Andaman and Nicobar Islands, India, **217** H4, *169*
Port Burwell, Canada, **421** N4
Port Canning, India, **219** G5
Port Chalmers, New Zealand, **133** C7
Port Charlotte, U.S.A., **425** L6
Port Clinton, U.S.A., **421** M5
Port Colborne, Canada, **421** P4
Port-de-Paix, Haiti, **429** G3
Port Dickson, Malaysia, **200** C2
Port Dover, Canada, **421** N4
Port Elgin, Canada, **421** N3
Port Elizabeth, South Africa, **370** E5, *350*
Port Ellen, Scotland, U.K., **308** C5
Port Erin, Isle of Man, **306** D3
Port Fitzroy, New Zealand, **132** E3
Port-Gentil, Gabon, **368** A3
Port Gibson, U.S.A., **424** G4
Port Glasgow, Scotland, U.K., **308** E5
Port Harcourt, Nigeria, **368** A2, *329*
Port Hardy, Canada, **412** F6
Port Hawkesbury, Canada, **417** L7
Port Hedland, Australia, **134** D3
Port Hood, Canada, **417** L6
Port Hope, Canada, **416** B8
Port Hope, U.S.A., **426** A3
Port Hope Simpson, Canada, **417** N3
Port Howe, Bahamas, **428** G1
Port Huron, U.S.A., **421** M4
Port Isaac Bay, England, U.K., **304** B4
Port Isabel, U.S.A., **424** D6
Port Kaituma, Guyana, **451** G2
Port Laoise, Ireland, **309** E4
Port Lavaca, U.S.A., **424** D5
Port Lincoln, Australia, **135** H5
Port Logan, Scotland, U.K., **308** E6
Port Loko, Sierra Leone, **364** B3, *322*
Port Louis, Mauritius, **373** C1, *353*
Port Macquarie, Australia, **135** L5
Port Mathurin, Rodrigues, Mauritius, **373** B1
Port-Menier, Canada, **417** J5
Port Moresby, Papua New Guinea, **140** B5, *115*
Port Nelson, Bahamas, **428** G2
Port Nolloth, South Africa, **370** C4
Port O'Connor, U.S.A., **424** D5
Port of Ness, Scotland, U.K., **308** C2
Port of Spain, Trinidad, Trinidad and Tobago, **461** C4
Port Orford, U.S.A., **418** B5
Port Pegasus, *bay*, New Zealand, **133** A8
Port Phillip Bay, Australia, **135** J6
Port Pirie, Australia, **135** H5
Port Puponga, New Zealand, **132** D5
Port Renfrew, Canada, **412** G7
Port Ross, *bay*, Auckland Islands, New Zealand, **132** J10
Port Said *see* Būr Sa'īd, Egypt, **225** B4
Port St Joe, U.S.A., **425** K5
Port St Johns, South Africa, **371** E5
Port St Mary, Isle of Man, **306** D3
Port Severn, Canada, **421** P3
Port Shepstone, South Africa, **371** F5
Port Stanley, Canada, **421** N4
Port Stephens, Falkland Islands, **460** F4
Port Sudan *see* Būr Sūdān, Sudan, **363** G5
Port Sulphur, U.S.A., **425** H5
Port Talbot, Wales, U.K., **304** D3
Port-Vendres, France, **291** F5
Port-Vila, Vanuatu, **141** A2, *116, 117*
Port-Vladimir, Russian Federation, **285** R2
Port Waikato, New Zealand, **132** E3
Port Wakefield, Australia, **135** H5
Port William, Scotland, U.K., **308** E6
Portadown, Northern Ireland, U.K., **309** F3
Portaferry, Northern Ireland, U.K., **309** G3
Portage, U.S.A., **421** J4
Portage la Prairie, Canada, **414** E7
Portalegre, *district*, Portugal, **292** D3
Portalegre, Portugal, **292** D3
Portales, U.S.A., **423** M4
Portarlington, Ireland, **309** E4
Portavogie, Northern Ireland, U.K., **309** G3
Portchester, England, U.K., **305** F4
Porteirinha, Brazil, **457** E4
Portel, Brazil, **452** C3
Portel, Portugal, **292** D3
Porteño, *river*, Argentina, **459** E2
Porterville, South Africa, **370** C5
Porterville, U.S.A., **422** D3
Porth, Wales, U.K., **304** D3
Porthcawl, Wales, U.K., **304** D3
Porthleven, England, U.K., **304** B4
Porthmadog, Wales, U.K., **304** C2
Portimão, Portugal, **292** C4
Portimo, Finland, **285** N3
Portishead, England, U.K., **304** E3
Portknockie, Scotland, U.K., **308** G3
Portland, Australia, **135** J6
Portland, Indiana, U.S.A., **421** L5
Portland, Maine, U.S.A., **426** E3
Portland, Oregon, U.S.A., **418** C4
Portland Island, New Zealand, **132** F4

Portland Point, Ascension, **373** A3
Portland Point, Jamaica, **429** F3
Portland Roads, Australia, **135** J1
Portlaw, Ireland, **309** E5
Portlethen, Scotland, U.K., **308** G3
Portmagee, Ireland, **309** B6
Portnacroish, Scotland, U.K., **308** D4
Portnaguran, Scotland, U.K., **308** C2
Portnahaven, Scotland, U.K., **308** C5
Pôrto, Brazil, **453** E4
Porto, *district*, Portugal, **292** C2
Porto, Golfe de, *gulf*, Corse, France, **295** B4
Porto, Portugal, **292** C2, *251*
Pôrto Acre, Brazil, **455** E2
Pôrto Alegre, Amazonas, Brazil, **455** E2
Pôrto Alegre, Mato Grosso do Sul, Brazil, **456** C5
Pôrto Alegre, Pará, Brazil, **452** C4
Porto Alegre, Rio Grande do Sul, Brazil, **459** G4
Porto Alegre, São Tomé and Príncipe, **373** C4
Porto Amboim, Angola, **368** B5
Pôrto Artur, Brazil, **456** B3
Pôrto Belo, Brazil, **459** H3
Porto Botté, Sardegna, Italy, **295** B6
Porto Cristo, Islas Baleares, Spain, **293** J3
Pôrto de Moz, Brazil, **452** C3
Porto dos Gaúchos, Brazil, **456** B3
Pôrto dos Meinacos, Brazil, **456** C3
Porto Empedocle, Sicilia, Italy, **295** D7
Pôrto Esperidião, Brazil, **455** G4
Pôrto Franco, Brazil, **452** D5
Pôrto Grande, Brazil, **452** C3
Porto Inglês, Cape Verde, **360** Q8
Pôrto Jofre, Brazil, **456** B4
Porto Moniz, Madeira, Portugal, **373** C3
Pôrto Murtinho, Brazil, **456** B5
Porto Nacional, Brazil, **456** D3
Porto-Novo, Benin, **365** E3, *327*
Porto Novo, Cape Verde, **360** P8
Porto Recanati, Italy, **294** D4
Pôrto Santana, Brazil, **452** C3
Porto Santo, *island*, Madeira, Portugal, **373** C3, *355*
Porto Santo, Madeira, Portugal, **373** C3
Pôrto Seguro, Brazil, **457** F4
Porto Tolle, Italy, **294** D3
Porto Torres, Sardegna, Italy, **295** B5
Porto-Vecchio, Corse, France, **295** B5
Pôrto Velho, Brazil, **455** F2
Porto Walter, Brazil, **454** D2
Portobelo, Panama, **429** F5
Portoferraio, Italy, **294** C4
Portofino, Italy, **294** B3
Portogruaro, Italy, **294** D3
Portoviejo, Ecuador, **450** B4
Portpatrick, Scotland, U.K., **308** D6
Portreath, England, U.K., **304** B4
Portree, Scotland, U.K., **308** C3
Portrush, Northern Ireland, U.K., **309** F2
Portsalon, Ireland, **309** E2
Portsmouth, Dominica, **427** D3
Portsmouth, England, U.K., **305** F4
Portsmouth, New Hampshire, U.S.A., **426** E3
Portsmouth, Ohio, U.S.A., **421** M6
Portsmouth, Virginia, U.S.A., **426** B6
Portsmouth City, England, U.K., **305** F4
Portsmouth Island, U.S.A., **426** B7
Portsoy, Scotland, U.K., **308** G3
Portstewart, Northern Ireland, U.K., **309** F2
Porttipahdan tekojärvi, *lake*, Finland, **285** M2
Portugal, *country*, Europe, **282** D8, *80, 92, 95, 228, 245, 250, 251, 252, 313, 319, 321, 332, 345, 355, 434, 440*
Portuguesa, *river*, Venezuela, **451** E2
Portumna, Ireland, **309** D4
Porvenir, Chile, **460** C4
Porvoo, Finland, **287** M2
Por'ya Guba, Russian Federation, **285** R3
Porzuna, Spain, **292** E3
Posadas, Argentina, **459** F3
Posarae, Solomon Islands, **141** A1
Posen, U.S.A., **421** M3
Posevnaya, Russian Federation, **223** L2
Poshekhon'ye, Russian Federation, **299** G3
Posht-e Bādām, Iran, **221** G2
Posio, Finland, **285** P3
Poso, Danau, *lake*, Indonesia, **198** C3
Poso, Indonesia, **198** C3
Poso, Teluk, *bay*, Indonesia, **198** C3
Posŏng, South Korea, **208** D4
Pospelikha, Russian Federation, **223** L2
Posse, Brazil, **456** D4
Possession Bay, South Georgia, **461** A3
Post, U.S.A., **424** B3
Post Falls, U.S.A., **418** F3
Postmasburg, South Africa, **370** D4
Postojna, Slovenia, **294** E3
Postville, U.S.A., **420** H4
Posušje, Croatia, **294** F4
Poteau, U.S.A., **424** E2
Poteet, U.S.A., **424** C5
Potenza, Italy, **295** E5
Poth, U.S.A., **424** C5
P'ot'i, Georgia, **222** C4
Potiskum, Nigeria, **365** G2
Potok, Croatia, **294** F3
Potomac, *river*, U.S.A., **426** B5
Potosí, Bolivia, **455** F5, *441*
Potosí, *department*, Bolivia, **455** E5
Potosí, Nicaragua, **428** D4
Potosi, U.S.A., **420** H7
Potro, Cerro de, *mountain peak*, Chile, **458** C3
Potsdam, Germany, **288** F2
Potsdam, U.S.A., **426** C2
Potters Bar, England, U.K., **305** G3
Pottstown, U.S.A., **426** C4
Pottsville, U.S.A., **426** B4
Pottuvil, Sri Lanka, **217** E5
Potwar Plateau, Pakistan, **218** C2
Pouce Coupe, Canada, **412** J4
Pouch Cove, Canada, **417** Q6
Pouembout, New Caledonia, **141** A3
Poughkeepsie, U.S.A., **426** D4
Poukawa, New Zealand, **132** F4
Poulton-le-Fylde, England, U.K., **306** F4
Poum, New Caledonia, **141** A3
Pouso Alegre, Brazil, **456** E6
Poutasi, Samoa, **141** B1
Poŭthĭsăt, Cambodia, **203** D3
Povenets, Russian Federation, **285** S5
Povenetskiy Zaliv, *bay*, Russian Federation, **285** S5
Poverty Bay, New Zealand, **132** F4
Póvoa de Varzim, Portugal, **292** C2
Povoação, Azores, Portugal, **360** M7
Povorot, Russian Federation, **210** D2
Povungnituk, Rivière de, *river*, Canada, **415** R1
Povungnituk Bay, Canada, **415** Q2
Powder, *river*, U.S.A., **419** L5
Powder River, U.S.A., **419** L5
Powderhorn, U.S.A., **423** K2
Powell, Lake, U.S.A., **423** H3
Powell, U.S.A., **419** K4
Powell Point, St Helena, **373** B3
Powell River, Canada, **412** G7
Power, U.S.A., **419** J3
Powers, U.S.A., **421** K3
Powers Lake, U.S.A., **420** B1
Powick, England, U.K., **304** E2
Powo, China, **215** F2
Powys, Wales, U.K., **304** D2
Poxoreu, Brazil, **456** B4
Poya, New Caledonia, **141** A3
Poyan Reservoir, Singapore, **200** J6
Poyang Hu, *lake*, China, **206** D2
Poza Rica de Hidalgo, Mexico, **431** F4
Požarevac, Serbia, **296** C3
Požega, Serbia, **296** C4
Pozharskoye, Russian Federation, **211** L3
Pozhnya, Russian Federation, **299** C4
Poznań, Poland, **289** H2
Pozo Alcón, Spain, **293** F4
Pozo Almonte, Chile, **455** E5
Pozo-Cañada, Spain, **293** G3
Pozo Colorado, Paraguay, **459** E2
Pozo del Tigre, Bolivia, **455** G4
Pozo Hondo, Argentina, **458** D3
Prabuty, Poland, **289** J2
Prachatice, Czech Republic, **289** G4
Prachin Buri, Thailand, **202** D3
Prachuap Khiri Khan, Thailand, **202** C4
Praděd, *mountain peak*, Czech Republic, **289** H3
Pradelles, France, **291** F4
Prades, France, **290** F5
Prado, Brazil, **457** F4
Præstø, Denmark, **286** F5
Prague *see* Praha, Czech Republic, **289** G3, *266*
Praha (Prague), Czech Republic, **289** G3, *266*
Praia, Cape Verde, **360** Q9, *318*
Praia da Vitória, Azores, Portugal, **360** M7
Praia Rica, Brazil, **456** B4
Prainha, Brazil, **452** C3
Prairie City, Oregon, U.S.A., **418** E4
Prairie City, South Dakota, U.S.A., **420** B3
Prakhon Chai, Thailand, **203** D3
Pramanta, Greece, **297** C6
Pran Buri Reservoir, Thailand, **202** C3
Prapat, Indonesia, **200** B2
Prasat, Thailand, **203** D3
Praslin, *island*, Seychelles, **373** A2
Prastos, Greece, **297** D7
Praszka, Poland, **289** J3
Prat, Isla, *island*, Chile, **460** B3
Prata, Brazil, **456** D5
Pratāpgarh, India, **218** C5
Prato, Italy, **294** C4
Pratt, U.S.A., **420** D7
Prattville, U.S.A., **425** J3
Prawle Point, England, U.K., **304** D4
Praya, Indonesia, **201** G5
Prazaroki, Belarus, **299** B5
Prechistoye, Russian Federation, **299** D5
Predazzo, Italy, **294** C2
Predlitz, Austria, **289** F5
Preeceville, Canada, **414** C6
Pregarten, Austria, **289** G4
Pregolya, *river*, Russian Federation, **287** K5
Preila, Lithuania, **287** K5
Preiüi, Latvia, **287** N4
Prejmer, Romania, **296** E3
Premio, Canada, **416** J4
Premuda, *island*, Croatia, **294** E3
Prenj, *mountain peak*, Bosnia and Herzegovina, **294** F4
Prenzlau, Germany, **289** F2
Preobrazheniye, Russian Federation, **211** L4
Preparis Island, Myanmar, **217** H3
Preparis North Channel, Myanmar, **217** H3
Preparis South Channel, Myanmar, **217** H3
Přerov, Czech Republic, **289** H4
Presanella, Cima, *mountain peak*, Italy, **294** C2
Prescott, U.S.A., **422** G4
Preservation Inlet, *bay*, New Zealand, **133** A8
Preševo, Serbia, **296** C4
Presidencia de la Plaza, Argentina, **459** E3
Presidencia Roque Sáenz Peña, Argentina, **458** E3
Presidente Dutra, Brazil, **453** E4
Presidente Epitácio, Brazil, **456** C5
Presidente Frei, *Chilean research station*, Antarctica, **470** A4
Presidente Médici, Brazil, **455** G3
Presidente Prudente, Brazil, **459** G2
Presidente Ríos, Lago, *lake*, Chile, **460** B3
Presidente Venceslau, Brazil, **456** C5
Presidio, U.S.A., **423** L7
Presnovka, Kazakhstan, **222** H2
Prešov, Slovakia, **289** K4
Prešovský, *administrative region*, Slovakia, **289** K4
Prespa, Lake *see* Prespansko Jezero, *lake*, Macedonia, **297** C5
Prespansko Jezero (Lake Prespa), *lake*, Macedonia, **297** C5
Presque Isle, U.S.A., **426** F1
Prestatyn, Wales, U.K., **306** E4
Prestea, Ghana, **364** D3
Presteigne, Wales, U.K., **304** D2
Presto, Bolivia, **455** F5
Preston, Dorset, England, U.K., **304** E4
Preston, Lancashire, England, U.K., **306** F4
Preston, U.S.A., **420** G4
Prestonburg, U.S.A., **421** M7
Prestwick, Scotland, U.K., **308** E5
Prêto, *river*, Brazil, **457** E3
Pretoria, South Africa, **371** E4, *350*
Preuilly-sur-Claise, France, **290** E3
Preveza, Greece, **297** C6
Prewitt, U.S.A., **423** J4
Priargunsk, Russian Federation, **211** G2
Priboj, Serbia, **296** B4
Příbram, Czech Republic, **289** G4
Price, Cape, Andaman and Nicobar Islands, India, **217** H3
Price, U.S.A., **423** H2
Prienai, Lithuania, **287** L5
Prieska, South Africa, **370** D4
Prieta, Peña, *mountain peak*, Spain, **292** E1
Prievidza, Slovakia, **289** J4
Prijedor, Bosnia and Herzegovina, **294** F3
Prijepolje, Serbia and Montenegro, **296** B4
Prikaspiyskaya Nizmennost', Kazakhstan/Russian Federation, **222** D3
Prilenskoye Plato, *plateau*, Russian Federation, **301** N3
Prilep, Macedonia, **297** C5
Primeira Cruz, Brazil, **453** E4
Primero, *river*, Argentina, **458** D4, *443*
Primghar, U.S.A., **420** F4
Primolano, Italy, **294** C3
Primorsk, Russian Federation, **299** B2
Primorskiy Khrebet, *mountain range*, Russian Federation, **210** D1
Primorskiy Kray, *territory*, Russian Federation, **211** L3
Primorsko, Bulgaria, **296** F4
Primošten, Croatia, **294** E4
Primrose Lake, Canada, **413** Q4
Prince Albert, Canada, **413** S5
Prince Albert, South Africa, **370** D5
Prince Albert Peninsula, Canada, **410** H2
Prince Alfred, Cape, Canada, **410** F2
Prince Charles Island, Canada, **411** M3
Prince Charles Mountains, *mountain range*, Antarctica, **470** F4
Prince Edward Fracture Zone, *tectonic feature*, Indian Ocean, **476** B8
Prince Edward Island, *province*, Canada, **417** K6, *380, 381*
Prince Edward Island, South Africa, Indian Ocean, **359** J11
Prince George, Canada, **412** H5
Prince of Wales Island, Australia, **135** J1
Prince of Wales Island, Canada, **411** J2
Prince of Wales Island, U.S.A., **412** C4
Prince Patrick Island, Canada, **410** G2
Prince Regent Inlet, Canada, **411** K2
Prince Rupert, Canada, **412** D4
Princes Risborough, England, U.K., **305** G3
Princes Town, Trinidad, Trinidad and Tobago, **461** C4
Princess Anne, U.S.A., **426** C5
Princess Charlotte Bay, Australia, **135** J1
Princess Elizabeth Land, *region*, Antarctica, **470** F5
Princess Royal Island, Canada, **412** E5
Princeton, Canada, **412** J7
Princeton, Illinois, U.S.A., **421** J5
Princeton, Kentucky, U.S.A., **421** K7
Princeton, Minnesota, U.S.A., **420** G3
Princeton, New Jersey, U.S.A., **426** C4
Princeton, Oregon, U.S.A., **418** E5
Princeton, West Virginia, U.S.A., **421** N7
Príncipe, *island*, São Tomé and Príncipe, **373** C4, *332*
Prineville, U.S.A., **418** D4
Prins Harald Kyst, *region*, Antarctica, **470** E3
Prinsesse Astrid Kyst, *region*, Antarctica, **470** D3
Prinsesse Ragnhild Kyst, *region*, Antarctica, **470** E3
Prinzapolka, Nicaragua, **428** E4
Prion Lake, Macquarie Island, **134** R11
Prior, Cabo, *cape*, Spain, **292** C1
Priozersk, Russian Federation, **299** C2
Prirechnyy, Russian Federation, **285** Q2
Prissac, France, **290** E3
Priština, Kosovo, **296** C4
Pritchett, U.S.A., **423** M3
Pritzwalk, Germany, **288** F2
Privas, France, **291** G4
Priverno, Italy, **295** D5
Privolzhskaya Vozvyshennost', *mountain range*, Russian Federation, **298** F3
Priyutnoye, Russian Federation, **298** F3
Prizren, Serbia, **296** C4
Prnjavor, Bosnia and Herzegovina, **294** F3
Probolinggo, Indonesia, **201** F4
Probus, England, U.K., **304** C4
Proddatūr, India, **216** D3
Progreso, Mexico, **431** H4
Progresso, Brazil, **454** D2
Prokhladnyy, Russian Federation, **222** C4
Prokletije, *mountain range*, Albania, **296** B4
Prokop'yevsk, Russian Federation, **223** M2
Prokuplje, Serbia, **296** C4
Proletariy, Russian Federation, **299** C3
Proletarka, Russian Federation, **285** S5

Prome *see* Pyè, Myanmar, **205** B4
Promissão, Brazil, **456** B5
Pronya, *river*, Belarus, **299** C5
Prophet River, Canada, **412** H2
Propriá, Brazil, **457** G3
Propriano, Corse, France, **295** B5
Prorva, Kazakhstan, **222** E3
Proserpine, Australia, **135** K3
Prosna, *river*, Poland, **289** H2
Prospect, U.S.A., **418** C5
Prosperous Bay, St Helena, **373** B3
Prostějov, Czech Republic, **289** H4
Protva, *river*, Russian Federation, **299** F5
Provadiya, Bulgaria, **296** F4
Provence-Alpes-Côte-D'Azur, *administrative region*, France, **291** G5, *245*
Providence, Cape, New Zealand, **133** A8
Providence, U.S.A., **426** E4, *386*
Providence Island, Seychelles, **372** C2
Providencia, *island*, Colombia, Caribbean Sea, **461** C1
Provost, Canada, **413** P5
Prozor, Bosnia and Herzegovina, **294** F4
Prudentópolis, Brazil, **459** G2
Prudnik, Poland, **289** H3
Prundeni, Romania, **296** E3
Prundu, Romania, **296** F3
Prut, *river*, Ukraine, **296** E1, *270*
Pruzhany, Belarus, **289** M2
Pryazha, Russian Federation, **299** D2
Prydz Bay, Antarctica, **470** F5
Pryluky, Ukraine, **298** D2
Prymors'ke, Ukraine, **296** G3
Prypyats', *river*, Belarus, **298** C2
Przasnysz, Poland, **289** K2
Przedbórz, Poland, **289** J3
Przemyśl, Poland, **289** L4
Przeworsk, Poland, **289** L3
Psachna, Greece, **297** D6
Psara, *island*, Greece, **297** E6
Pskov, Russian Federation, **299** B4
Pskovskaya Oblast', *province*, Russian Federation, **299** B4
Pskovskiy, Kazakhstan, **222** G2
Pskovskoye Ozero, *lake*, Russian Federation, **299** A3
Ptolemaïda, Greece, **297** C5
Ptuj, Slovenia, **294** E2
Pu, *river*, China, **210** D5
Pu-li, Taiwan, **206** E4
Pu Xian, China, **210** E5
Puán, Argentina, **458** D5
Pu'an, China, **215** H4
Pu'apu'a, Samoa, **141** B1
Puava, Cape, Samoa, **141** B1
Puca Urco, Peru, **450** D5
Pucallpa, Peru, **454** C2
Pucará, Peru, **454** D4
Pucará, *river*, Peru, **455** D4
Pucheng, Fujian, China, **206** D3
Pucheng, Shaanxi, China, **206** B1
Pucio Point, Philippines, **204** C4
Pucioasa, Romania, **296** E3
Pucón, Chile, **460** C1
Pudasjärvi, Finland, **285** N4
Puddletown, England, U.K., **304** E4
Pudozh, Russian Federation, **299** F2
Pudsey, England, U.K., **307** G4
Pudukkottai, India, **216** D4
Puebla, *state*, Mexico, **431** F5
Puebla de Don Fadrique, Spain, **293** F4
Puebla de Guzmán, Spain, **292** D4
Puebla de Sanabria, Spain, **292** D1
Puebla de Trives, Spain, **292** D1
Puebla de Zaragoza, Mexico, **431** F5
Pueblo, U.S.A., **423** L2
Pueblo Nuevo, Venezuela, **451** E1
Pueblo Viejo, Providencia, Colombia, **461** C1
Puelches, Argentina, **458** D6
Puelén, Argentina, **458** C5
Puente-Genil, Spain, **292** E4
Pu'er, China, **215** G5
Puertecitos, Mexico, **430** B2
Puerto Adela, Paraguay, **459** F2
Puerto Adolfo López Mateos, Mexico, **430** B3
Puerto Aisen, Chile, **460** C2
Puerto Alegre, Bolivia, **455** G3
Puerto Ángel, Mexico, **431** F6
Puerto Antequera, Paraguay, **459** F2
Puerto Arista, Mexico, **431** G6
Puerto Armuelles, Panama, **429** E5
Puerto Asís, Colombia, **450** C4
Puerto Ayacucho, Venezuela, **451** E3
Puerto Ayora, Islas Galápagos (Galapagos Islands), Ecuador, **461** A2
Puerto Barrios, Guatemala, **428** C4
Puerto Bermejo, Argentina, **459** E3
Puerto Bermúdez, Peru, **454** C3
Puerto Berrío, Colombia, **450** C2
Puerto Caballas, Peru, **454** C4
Puerto Cabello, Venezuela, **451** E1
Puerto Cabezas, Nicaragua, **428** E4
Puerto Carreño, Colombia, **451** E2
Puerto Casado, Paraguay, **459** E2
Puerto Cisnes, Chile, **460** C2
Puerto Coig, Argentina, **460** D4
Puerto Colombia, Colombia, **450** C1, *437*
Puerto Cooper, Paraguay, **459** F2
Puerto Cortés, Honduras, **428** D4
Puerto Cortés, Mexico, **430** C3
Puerto Cumarebo, Venezuela, **451** E1
Puerto de la Cruz, Islas Canarias, Spain, **373** A4
Puerto de Lobos, Mexico, **430** B2
Puerto de Nutrias, Venezuela, **451** E2
Puerto del Rosario, Islas Canarias, Spain, **373** B4
Puerto Deseado, Argentina, **460** E3
Puerto Escondido, Mexico, **431** F6
Puerto Estrella, Colombia, **450** D1
Puerto Francisco de Orellana, Ecuador, **450** C4
Puerto Frey, Bolivia, **455** G4
Puerto Grether, Bolivia, **455** F4
Puerto Guaraní, Paraguay, **455** H5
Puerto Harborton, Argentina, **460** D5
Puerto Inírida, Colombia, **451** E3
Puerto Irigoyen, Argentina, **458** E2
Puerto Isabel, Bolivia, **455** H5
Puerto Jesús, Costa Rica, **428** D5
Puerto La Concordia, Colombia, **450** D3
Puerto la Cruz, Venezuela, **451** F1
Puerto Leguízamo, Colombia, **450** C4
Puerto Lempira, Honduras, **428** E4
Puerto Libertad, Mexico, **430** B2
Puerto Limón, Costa Rica, **429** E5
Puerto Lobos, Argentina, **460** E2
Puerto López, Colombia, **450** D3
Puerto Lumbreras, Spain, **293** G4
Puerto Madryn, Argentina, **460** E2
Puerto Maldonado, Peru, **455** E3
Puerto Mamoré, Bolivia, **455** F4
Puerto Márquez, Bolivia, **455** E4
Puerto Mihanovich, Paraguay, **455** H5
Puerto Miraña, Colombia, **451** D4
Puerto Miranda, Venezuela, **451** E2
Puerto Montt, Chile, **460** C1
Puerto Morin, Peru, **454** B2
Puerto Natales, Chile, **460** C4
Puerto Nuevo, Colombia, **451** E3
Puerto Obaldía, Panama, **429** F5
Puerto Ocopa, Peru, **454** C3
Puerto Ordaz, Venezuela, **451** F2
Puerto Padre, Cuba, **429** F2
Puerto Páez, Venezuela, **451** E2
Puerto Pardo, Peru, **450** C5
Puerto Peñasco, Mexico, **430** B2
Puerto Pinasco, Paraguay, **459** F2
Puerto Piràmides, Argentina, **460** E2
Puerto Plata, Dominican Republic, **429** H3
Puerto Portillo, Peru, **454** D2
Puerto Princesa, Philippines, **204** B4
Puerto Rey, Colombia, **450** C2
Puerto Rico, Argentina, **459** F3
Puerto Rico, Bolivia, **455** E3
Puerto Rico, *U.S. territory*, Caribbean Sea, **427** C2, *95, 252, 253, 378, 379, 386, 387, 388, 389, 390, 391*
Puerto Rico Trench, *underwater feature*, Caribbean Sea, **479** P3
Puerto Rondón, Colombia, **450** D2
Puerto Saavedra, Chile, **460** C1
Puerto San Jose, Guatemala, **428** C4
Puerto San Julián, Argentina, **460** D3
Puerto Santa Cruz, Argentina, **460** D4
Puerto Sastre, Paraguay, **456** A5
Puerto Saucedo, Bolivia, **455** F3
Puerto Siles, Bolivia, **455** F3
Puerto Suárez, Bolivia, **455** H5
Puerto Supe, Peru, **454** C3
Puerto Tahuantinsuyo, Peru, **455** D3
Puerto Tejada, Colombia, **450** C3
Puerto Tunigrama, Peru, **450** C5
Puerto Vallarta, Mexico, **430** D4
Puerto Varas, Chile, **460** C1
Puerto Victoria, Peru, **454** C2
Puerto Villamil, Islas Galápagos (Galapagos Islands), Ecuador, **461** A2
Puerto Villazón, Bolivia, **455** G3
Puerto Visser, Argentina, **460** D2
Puerto Williams, Chile, **460** D5
Puertollano, Spain, **292** E3
Puesto Estrella, Paraguay, **455** F5
Pugachev, Russian Federation, **222** D2
Puge, China, **215** G4
Puget Sound, U.S.A., **418** C3
Puglia, *autonomous region*, Italy, **295** F5, *255*
Puhi, Volcán, *mountain peak*, Isla de Pascua (Easter Island), Chile, **461** B2
Puhos, Finland, **285** N4
Pui O Wan, *bay*, China, **207** B4
Puigcerdà, Spain, **293** H1
Puig-reig, Spain, **293** H1
Pujehun, Sierra Leone, **364** B3
Pukaki, Lake, New Zealand, **133** B6
Pukapuka, *island*, Cook Islands, **139** H6
Pukapuka, *island*, French Polynesia, **137** H2
Pukarua, *island*, French Polynesia, **137** H2
Pukatawagan, Canada, **414** D4
Pukch'ŏng, North Korea, **208** E2
Pukë, Albania, **296** B4
Pukekura, New Zealand, **133** C6
Pukeuri, New Zealand, **133** C7
Pukhnovo, Russian Federation, **299** C5
Pukuatu, Tanjong, *point*, Indonesia, **198** C5
Pula, Croatia, **294** D3
Pula, Sardegna, Italy, **295** B6
Pulacayo, Bolivia, **455** E5
Pulai, Indonesia, **201** G2
Pulanduta Point, Philippines, **204** C4
Pulangpisau, Indonesia, **201** F3
Pular, Cerro, *mountain peak*, Chile, **458** C2
Pulaski, New York, U.S.A., **426** B3
Pulaski, Tennessee, U.S.A., **425** J2
Pulaski, Wisconsin, U.S.A., **421** J3
Pulau, *river*, Indonesia, **199** G4
Puławy, Poland, **289** K3
Pulborough, England, U.K., **305** G4
Pulicat Lake, India, **216** E3
Pulkkila, Finland, **285** M4
Pulo Anna, *island*, Palau, **138** B4
Pulo Pandang, *island*, Cocos (Keeling) Islands, **134** Q10
Pulog, Mount, *mountain peak*, Philippines, **204** C2
Pulozero, Russian Federation, **285** R2
Pulsujärvi, Sweden, **284** K2
Pułtusk, Poland, **289** K2
Pulu, China, **212** D5
Pulusuk, *island*, Micronesia, **138** C4
Pumasillo, Cerro, *mountain peak*, Peru, **454** D3
Pummanki, Russian Federation, **285** Q2
Pumpënai, Lithuania, **287** M5
Pumpsaint, Wales, U.K., **304** D2
Puná, Isla, *island*, Ecuador, **450** B5
Punakaiki, New Zealand, **133** C6
Punākha, Bhutan, **214** D4
Punalur, India, **216** D4
Punata, Bolivia, **455** F4
Pūndri, India, **218** D3
Pune, India, **216** C2
Pungeşti, Romania, **296** F2
Punggol, *river*, Singapore, **200** K6
Punggol, Singapore, **200** K6
Punggol, Tanjong, *point*, Singapore, **200** K6
P'ungsan, North Korea, **208** E2
Punia, Democratic Republic of the Congo, **369** E3
Punitaqui, Chile, **458** B4
Punjab, *province*, Pakistan, **218** B3
Punjab, *state*, India, **218** C3, *168, 169*
Punkaharju, Finland, **287** P2
Punkalaidun, Finland, **287** L2
Punkin Centre, U.S.A., **423** M2
Puno, Peru, **455** D4
Punta, Cerro de, *mountain peak*, Puerto Rico, **427** C2
Punta Alta, Argentina, **460** E1
Punta Arenas, Chile, **460** C4
Punta Banda, Cabo, *cape*, Mexico, **430** A2
Punta Delgada, Argentina, **460** E2
Punta Delgada, Chile, **460** D4
Punta Gorda, Bahía de, *bay*, Costa Rica, **428** E5
Punta Gorda, Belize, **428** C3
Punta Gorda, Nicaragua, **428** E5
Punta Gorda, *river*, Nicaragua, **428** D5
Punta Norte, Argentina, **460** E2
Punta Prieta, Mexico, **430** B2
Puntagorda, Islas Canarias, Spain, **373** A4
Puntarenas, Costa Rica, **428** D5
Punto Fijo, Venezuela, **451** D1
Puokio, Finland, **285** N4
Puolanka, Finland, **285** N4
Puoltikasvaara, Sweden, **284** K3
Puottaure, Sweden, **284** K3
Puqi, China, **206** C2
Puquio, Peru, **454** C4
Puquios, Chile, **458** C3
Puracé, Volcán, *mountain peak*, Colombia, **450** C3
Pūranpur, India, **218** E3
Purari, *river*, Papua New Guinea, **140** B4
Purcell, U.S.A., **424** D2
Purcell Mountains, *mountain range*, Canada, **413** L6
Purekkari neem, *point*, Estonia, **287** M3
Purén, Chile, **458** B6
Purgatoire, *river*, U.S.A., **423** M3
Puri, India, **219** F6
Purificación, Mexico, **430** D5
Purna, India, **218** D6
Purnach, *river*, Russian Federation, **285** U3
Pūrnia, India, **219** F4
Purranque, Chile, **460** C1
Puruarán, Mexico, **431** E5
Purukcahu, Indonesia, **201** F3
Puruliya, India, **219** F5
Purus, *river*, Brazil, **451** F5
Puruvesi, *lake*, Finland, **287** P1
Pŭrvomay, Bulgaria, **296** E4
Purwakarta, Indonesia, **201** D4
Purwokerto, Indonesia, **201** E4
Pusad, India, **218** D6
Pusan, South Korea, **208** E4
Pushkin, Russian Federation, **299** C3
Pushlakhta, Russian Federation, **285** T4
Pushnoy, Russian Federation, **285** S4
Püspökladány, Hungary, **289** K5
Pustaya Guba, Russian Federation, **285** R3
Pustoshka, Russian Federation, **299** B4
Pu'tai, Taiwan, **206** E4
Putao, Myanmar, **205** C2
Putaruru, New Zealand, **132** E4
Putia, Indonesia, **198** D3
Putian, China, **206** D3
Putina, Peru, **455** E4
Puting, Tanjong, *point*, Indonesia, **201** E3
Putla, Mexico, **431** F5
Putlitz, Germany, **288** F2
Putnam, U.S.A., **424** C2
Putorana, Plato, *mountain range*, Russian Federation, **300** L3
Putorino, New Zealand, **132** F4
Putre, Chile, **455** E5
Puttalam, Sri Lanka, **216** D4
Puttalam Lagoon, Sri Lanka, **216** D4
Puttgarden, Germany, **288** E1
Puttūr, India, **216** C3
Putumayo, *river*, Colombia/Peru, **450** C4
Putus, Tanjong, *point*, Indonesia, **201** E3
Putussibau, Indonesia, **201** F2
Putyla, Ukraine, **296** E2
Puukkokumpu, Finland, **285** M4
Puula, *lake*, Finland, **287** N2
Puumala, Finland, **287** P2
Puuwai, Hawaiian Islands, U.S.A., **422** Q9
Puvirnituq, Canada, **415** R1
Puyang, China, **206** C1
Puyehue, Chile, **460** C1
Puyo, Ecuador, **450** C4
Puysegur Point, New Zealand, **133** A8
Pwani, *administrative region*, Tanzania, **369** G4

Pweto, Democratic Republic of the Congo, **369** E4
Pwllheli, Wales, U.K., **304** C2
Pyal'ma, Russian Federation, **285** S5
Pyamalaw, *river,* Myanmar, **205** B4
Pyaozero, Ozero, *lake,* Russian Federation, **285** Q3
Pyapon, Myanmar, **205** B4
Pyasinskiy Zaliv, *bay,* Russian Federation, **300** J2
Pyatigorsk, Russian Federation, **222** C4
Pyawbwe, Myanmar, **205** C3
Pyazhelka, Russian Federation, **299** E2
Pyè (Prome), Myanmar, **205** B4
Pyhäjärvi, Finland, **285** N5
Pyhäjoki, Finland, **285** M4
Pyhäjoki, *river,* Finland, **285** M4
Pyhältö, Finland, **287** N2
Pyhäntä, Finland, **285** N4
Pyhäranta, Finland, **287** K2
Pyhäselkä, Finland, **287** Q1
Pyhäselkä, *lake,* Finland, **287** P1
Pyhätunturi, *mountain peak,* Finland, **285** N3
Pyinmana, Myanmar, **205** C4
Pyle, Wales, U.K., **304** D3
Pylkönmäki, Finland, **285** M5
Pylos, Greece, **297** C7
Pymatuning Reservoir, U.S.A., **421** N5
P'yŏnggang, North Korea, **208** D3
P'yŏngsŏng, North Korea, **208** D3
P'yŏngt'aek, South Korea, **208** D3
P'yŏngyang, North Korea, **208** D3, *163*
Pyramid Island, Chatham Islands, New Zealand, **133** Q16
Pyramid Lake, U.S.A., **422** D1
Pyramid Point, Ascension, **373** A3
Pyrenees, *mountain range,* Andorra/France/Spain, **280** D7, *244, 245, 251, 252, 253*
Pyrgetos, Greece, **297** D6
Pyrgi, Greece, **297** E6
Pyrgos, Greece, **297** C7
Pyrzyce, Poland, **289** G2
Pyshna, Belarus, **299** B5
Pyttegga, *mountain peak,* Norway, **286** C1
Pyu, Myanmar, **205** C4
Pyuntaza, Myanmar, **205** C4
Pyzdry, Poland, **289** H2


## Q


Qaanaag (Thule), Greenland, **411** N2
Qabanbay, Kazakhstan, **212** D3
Qabātiyah, West Bank, **225** C3
Qābis, Tunisia, **362** B2
Qādub, Suquṭrá (Socotra), Yemen, **373** B2
Qagan, China, **211** G2
Qagan Nur, China, **210** F4
Qagan Nur, *lake,* China, **210** F4
Qagan Teg, China, **210** F4
Qagca, China, **215** F2
Qaidam Pendi, *basin,* China, **213** G5
Qakar, China, **212** D5
Qala'an Naḥl, Sudan, **366** D2
Qalāt, Afghanistan, **218** A2
Qal'at al Ḥiṣn, Syria, **225** D2
Qal'at Bīshah, Saudi Arabia, **363** H5
Qal'at Ṣāliḥ, Iraq, **363** J2
Qalba Zhotasy, *mountain range,* Kazakhstan, **212** D2
Qal'eh Shahr, Afghanistan, **218** A2
Qal'eh-ye Now, Afghanistan, **221** H2
Qal'eh-ye Sarkārī, Afghanistan, **218** A2
Qallābāt, Sudan, **366** E2
Qalyūb, Egypt, **225** A4
Qamalung, China, **215** F2
Qamar, Ghubbat al, *bay,* Oman/Yemen, **220** F5
Qambar, Pakistan, **218** A4
Qamdo, China, **215** F3
Qamīnis, Libya, **362** C2
Qandahār, Afghanistan, **218** A3
Qandala, Somalia, **367** G2
Qanshenggel, Kazakhstan, **212** B3
Qapqal, China, **212** D4
Qapshaghay, Kazakhstan, **212** C4
Qapshaghay Bögeni, *reservoir,* Kazakhstan, **212** C3
Qaqortoq, Greenland, **411** Q3
Qarabas, Kazakhstan, **212** B2
Qaraböget, Kazakhstan, **212** A3
Qarabulaq, Almaty, Kazakhstan, **212** C3
Qarabulaq, Shyghys Qazaqstan, Kazakhstan, **212** E3
Qarabulaq, Yuzhnyy Qazaqstan, Kazakhstan, **223** H4
Qarabutaq, Kazakhstan, **222** G3
Qaraghandy, *province,* Kazakhstan, **212** B2
Qaraghandy (Karaganda), Kazakhstan, **212** B2
Qaraghayly, Kazakhstan, **212** B2
Qārah, Egypt, **362** E3
Qarak, China, **212** C5
Qarakŭl, *lake,* Tajikistan, **212** B5
Qaraqamys, Kazakhstan, **222** E3
Qarasor Köli, Kazakhstan, **212** B2
Qaratal, *river,* Kazakhstan, **212** C3
Qaratöbe, Kazakhstan, **222** E3
Qaraūyl, Kazakhstan, **212** C2
Qarazhal, Kazakhstan, **212** A2
Qardho, Somalia, **367** G3
Qarqan, *river,* China, **212** E5
Qarqaraly, Kazakhstan, **212** B2
Qarqi, Central Xinjiang Uygur Zizhiqu, China, **212** E4
Qarqi, W. Xinjiang Uygur Zizhiqu, China, **212** D4
Qarsan, China, **211** H3
Qarshi, Uzbekistan, **222** H5
Qarṭabā, Lebanon, **225** C2
Qaryat al Qaddāḥīyah, Libya, **362** C2
Qāṣen, Iran, **221** G2
Qasigiannguit (Christianshåb), Greenland, **411** P3
Qaskeleng, Kazakhstan, **212** C4
Qaṣr al Farāfirah, Egypt, **362** E3
Qaṣr Ḥamām, Saudi Arabia, **363** J4
Qaṭanā, Syria, **225** D3
Qaṭānan, Ra's, *point,* Suquṭrá (Socotra), Yemen, **373** B2
Qatar, *country,* Asia, **196** F7, *146, 176, 177, 178*
Qaṭmah, Syria, **225** D1
Qaṭrūyeh, Iran, **221** F3
Qattara Depression, Egypt, **362** E2, *317*
Qawz Rajab, Sudan, **366** E1
Qaynar, Kazakhstan, **212** C2
Qaysar, Kuh-e, *mountain peak,* Afghanistan, **218** A2
Qayü, China, **214** E3
Qazimämmäd, Azerbaijan, **222** D5
Qazvīn, Iran, **222** D5
Qeh, China, **213** J4
Qeqertarsuaq, Greenland, **411** P3
Qeqertarsuaq (Disko), *island,* Greenland, **411** P2
Qeqertarsuatsiaat, Greenland, **411** P3
Qeqertarsuup Tunua, *bay,* Greenland, **411** P3
Qeshm, Jazīreh-ye, *island,* Iran, **221** G3
Qeyṣār, Afghanistan, **218** A2
Qêyi, China, **215** G3
Qeẓi'ot, Israel, **225** C4
Qi Xian, Henan, China, **206** C1
Qi Xian, Shaanxi, China, **210** F5
Qian Shan, *mountain range,* China, **211** H4
Qian Xian, China, **206** B1
Qian'an, China, **211** J3
Qianjiang, Hubei, China, **206** C2
Qianjiang, Sichuan, China, **206** B2
Qianning, China, **215** G3
Qianshan, China, **207** B4
Qiansuo, China, **215** G4
Qianwei, China, **215** G3
Qianxi, China, **215** H4
Qianyang, China, **215** H2
Qi'ao, China, **207** B4
Qi'ao Dao, *island,* China, **207** B4
Qiaotou, China, **207** C2
Qiaowan, China, **213** H4
Qiaozhen, China, **210** E5
Qibilī, Tunisia, **362** A2
Qichun, China, **206** C2
Qidaogou, China, **211** J4
Qidong, Hunan, China, **206** C3
Qidong, Jiangsu, China, **206** E2
Qidukou, China, **215** E2
Qiemo, China, **212** E5
Qigan, China, **207** A1
Qihregt, China, **210** F4
Qijiang, China, **215** H3
Qijiaojing, China, **213** F4
Qijing, China, **207** B1
Qila Abdullāh, Pakistan, **218** A3
Qila Saifullāh, Pakistan, **218** B3
Qilian, China, **213** J5
Qilian Shan, *mountain range,* China, **213** H5, *158*
Qiman, China, **212** D4
Qimen, China, **206** D2
Qin, *river,* China, **206** C1
Qin Ling, *mountain range,* China, **195** M6
Qin Xian, China, **210** F5
Qinā, Egypt, **363** F3
Qin'an, China, **215** H2
Qing'an, China, **211** J3
Qingchengzi, China, **211** H4
Qingdao, China, **211** H5
Qinggang, China, **211** J3
Qinghai, *province,* China, **215** E2, *161*
Qinghai Hu, *lake,* China, **213** H5
Qinghe, China, **212** F3
Qinghemen, China, **211** H4
Qingjian, China, **210** E5
Qingshui, China, **213** H5
Qingshuihe, Nei Mongol Zizhiqu, China, **210** E5
Qingshuihe, Qinghai, China, **215** F2
Qingtian, China, **206** E2
Qingtongxia, China, **210** D5
Qingxi, China, **207** C3
Qingxu, China, **210** F5
Qingyang, China, **210** D5
Qingyuan, Guangdong, China, **206** C4
Qingyuan, Liaoning, China, **211** J4
Qingyuan, Zhejiang, China, **206** D3
Qingzang Gaoyuan (Plateau of Tibet), *plateau,* China, **214** C2, *144, 158*
Qingzhou, China, **208** B3
Qinhuangdao, China, **211** G5
Qinyang, China, **206** C1
Qinyuan, China, **210** F5
Qinzhou, China, **206** B4
Qinzhou Wan, *bay,* China, **203** F1
Qionghai, China, **203** F2
Qionglai, China, **215** G3
Qiongzhou Haixia, *strait,* China, **203** F1
Qiqian, China, **211** H1
Qiqihar, China, **211** H3
Qīr, Iran, **220** F3
Qiryat Gat, Israel, **225** C4
Qishi, China, **207** C2
Qitai, China, **212** F3
Qitaihe, China, **211** K3
Qiubei, China, **215** H4
Qixia, China, **211** H5
Qiyahe, China, **211** H1
Qiyang, China, **206** B3
Qizhan, China, **211** J2
Qom, Iran, **220** F2
Qomo, China, **214** E3
Qomsheh, Iran, **220** F2
Qongj, China, **210** E4
Qoraqalpoghiston, Respublika, *autonomous republic,* Uzbekistan, **222** F4
Qorveh, Iran, **363** J1
Qosköl, Kazakhstan, **222** H3
Qostanay (Kustanay), Kazakhstan, **222** G2
Qotanqaraghay, Kazakhstan, **212** E2
Qu Xian, China, **215** H3
Quabbin Reservoir, U.S.A., **426** D3
Quang Ngãi, Vietnam, **203** F3
Quanzhou, Fujian, China, **206** D3
Quanzhou, Guangxi Zhuangzu Zizhiqu, China, **206** B3
Qu'Appelle, *river,* Canada, **414** C6
Quaqtaq, Canada, **411** N3
Quaraí, Brazil, **459** F4
Quarai, *river,* Brazil/Uruguay, **459** F4
Quarles, Pegunungan, *mountain range,* Indonesia, **198** B3
Quarry Hills, New Zealand, **133** B8
Quartier Militaire, Mauritius, **373** C1
Quartu Sant'Elena, Sardegna, Italy, **295** B6
Quartzite Mountain, *mountain peak,* U.S.A., **422** E3
Quartzsite, U.S.A., **422** F5
Quatre Bornes, Mauritius, **373** C1
Quatsino, Canada, **412** F6
Quba, Azerbaijan, **222** D4
Qūchān, Iran, **222** F5
Queanbeyan, Australia, **135** K6
Québec, Canada, **416** F6, *93, 381*
Québec, *province,* Canada, **416** F4, *377, 380, 381*
Quebracho Coto, Argentina, **458** D3
Quebradas, Guatemala, **428** C4
Qued Zem, Morocco, **360** E2
Quedal, Cabo, *cape,* Chile, **460** B1
Quedlinburg, Germany, **288** E3
Queen Bess, Mount, *mountain peak,* Canada, **412** G6
Queen Charlotte, Canada, **412** D5
Queen Charlotte Bay, Falkland Islands, **460** E4
Queen Charlotte Islands, Canada, **412** C5
Queen Charlotte Mountains, *mountain range,* Canada, **412** C5
Queen Charlotte Sound, Canada, **412** E6
Queen Elizabeth Islands, Canada, **411** J2
Queen Mary Land, *region,* Antarctica, **470** F6
Queen Mary's Peak, *mountain peak,* Tristan da Cunha, **373** C2
Queen Maud Bay, South Georgia, **461** A3
Queen Maud Gulf, Canada, **411** J3
Queen Maud Mountains, *mountain range,* Antarctica, **470** D6
Queenborough, England, U.K., **305** H3
Queensbury, New Zealand, **133** B7
Queensland, *state,* Australia, **135** J3, *112*
Queenstown, Australia, **135** K7
Queenstown, New Zealand, **133** B7
Queenstown, South Africa, **371** E5
Queguay Grande, *river,* Uruguay, **459** F4
Quehué, Argentina, **458** D5
Queilén, Chile, **460** C2
Queimadas, Brazil, **457** F3
Quela, Angola, **368** C4
Quelimane, Mozambique, **371** G2
Quellón, Chile, **460** C2
Quemado, U.S.A., **423** J4
Quembo, *river,* Angola, **368** C5
Quemchi, Chile, **460** C2
Quemú-Quemú, Argentina, **458** D5
Quequén, Argentina, **459** E6
Quequén Grande, *river,* Argentina, **459** E5
Querétaro, Mexico, **431** E4
Querétaro, *state,* Mexico, **431** E4
Querfurt, Germany, **288** E3
Querobabi, Mexico, **430** C2
Quesnel, Canada, **412** H5
Quesnel Lake, Canada, **412** J5
Quetta, Pakistan, **218** A3, *172*
Queule, Chile, **460** C1
Quevedo, Ecuador, **450** B4
Quezaltenango, Guatemala, **428** C4
Quezon, Philippines, **204** B4
Quezon City, Philippines, **204** C3
Qufu, China, **206** D1
Qui Nhơn, Vietnam, **203** F3
Quibaxe, Angola, **368** B4
Quibdó, Colombia, **450** C3
Quiberon, France, **290** C3
Quiculungo, Angola, **368** C4
Quiindy, Paraguay, **459** F2
Quilán, Cabo, *cape,* Chile, **460** B2
Quilchena, Canada, **412** J6
Quilengues, Angola, **368** B5
Quilino, Argentina, **458** D4
Quill Lake, Canada, **414** B5
Quillabamba, Peru, **454** D3
Quillacollo, Bolivia, **455** E4
Quillagua, Chile, **455** E5
Quillan, France, **290** F5
Quillota, Chile, **458** B4
Quilmes, Argentina, **459** E5
Quilon *see* Kollam, India, **216** D4
Quilpie, Australia, **135** J4
Quilpue, Chile, **458** B4
Quilua, Mozambique, **369** G6
Quimbele, Angola, **368** C4
Quimilí, Argentina, **458** D3
Quimper, France, **290** B3
Quimperlé, France, **290** C3
Quinault, U.S.A., **418** C3
Quince Mil, Peru, **454** D3
Quincy, California, U.S.A., **422** C2
Quincy, Florida, U.S.A., **425** K4
Quincy, Missouri, U.S.A., **420** H6
Quines, Argentina, **458** D4
Quinga, Mozambique, **369** H6
Quingyun Shan, *mountain range,* China, **207** B1
Quinn, *river,* U.S.A., **418** E6
Quintana Roo, *state,* Mexico, **431** H5, *400*
Quintanar de la Orden, Spain, **293** F3
Quinzau, Angola, **368** B4
Quionga, Mozambique, **369** H5
Quipungo, Angola, **368** B5
Quiriego, Mexico, **430** C3
Quirihue, Chile, **458** B5
Quirima, Angola, **368** C5
Quiroga, Argentina, **458** E5
Quiroga, Bolivia, **455** F5
Quiroga, Spain, **292** D1
Quissanga, Mozambique, **369** H5
Quissico, Mozambique, **371** F3
Quitapa, Angola, **368** C5
Quiteve, Angola, **368** C6
Quitman, Georgia, U.S.A., **425** L4
Quitman, Mississippi, U.S.A., **425** H3
Quito, Ecuador, **450** B4, *438*
Quixadá, Brazil, **453** F4
Quixeramobim, Brazil, **453** F4
Qujing, China, **215** G4
Qulanötpes, *river,* Kazakhstan, **212** A2
Qulansiyah, Suquṭrá (Socotra), Yemen, **373** B2
Qulaybīyah, Tunisia, **362** B1
Qulsary, Kazakhstan, **222** E3
Qumar, *river,* China, **214** E2
Qumar Heyan, China, **214** E2
Qumarlêb, China, **215** E2
Qumarrabdün, China, **215** E2
Qumé, Côte d'Ivoire, **364** C3
Qumigxung, China, **214** C3
Qŭnghirot, Uzbekistan, **222** F4
Qungtag, China, **214** C3
Qu'nyido, China, **215** F3

Quoich, Loch, *lake*, Scotland, U.K., **308** D3
Quoin Point, South Africa, **370** C5
Quorn, Australia, **135** H5
Qŭqon, Uzbekistan, **223** J4
Qurmah, Ghubbat, *bay*, Suquṭrá (Socotra), Yemen, **373** B2
Qurunbāliyah, Tunisia, **295** C7
Quryq, Kazakhstan, **222** E4
Qusaq, *river*, Kazakhstan, **212** B3
Qusmuryn, Kazakhstan, **222** G2
Qusmuryn Köli, *lake*, Kazakhstan, **222** G2
Quthing, Lesotho, **371** E5
Quwo, China, **206** B1
Quzhou, Hebei, China, **210** F5
Quzhou, Zhejiang, China, **206** D2
Quzi, China, **210** D5
Qyzylorda (Kzyl-Orda), Kazakhstan, **222** H4
Qyzyltū, Kazakhstan, **223** J2
Qyzylzhar, Kazakhstan, **212** A2

## R

Raab, *river*, Austria, **289** G5
Raahe, Finland, **285** M4
Raanujärvi, Finland, **285** M3
Raasay, *island*, Scotland, U.K., **308** C3
Raasay, Sound of, Scotland, U.K., **308** C3
Raattama, Finland, **285** M2
Rab, *island*, Croatia, **294** E3
Rab, Croatia, **294** E3
Raba, *river*, Poland, **289** K4
Rába, *river*, Hungary, **289** H5
Raba, Indonesia, **201** G5
Rabak, Sudan, **366** D2
Rabat, Morocco, **360** E2, *314*
Rabaul, Papua New Guinea, **140** D4
Rabi, *island*, Fiji, **141** A4
Rabia, Indonesia, **199** E3
Rābigh, Saudi Arabia, **363** G4
Rabka, Poland, **289** J4
Râbniţa, Moldova, **296** G2
Rabocheostrovsk, Russian Federation, **285** S4
Rabrovo, Serbia, **296** C3
Rabyānah, Ṣaḥrā', *desert*, Libya, **362** D4
Rạch Giá, Vietnam, **203** E4
Rạch Giá, Vinh, *bay*, Vietnam, **203** E4
Rachal, U.S.A., **424** C6
Racibórz, Poland, **289** J3
Racine, U.S.A., **421** K4
Raco, U.S.A., **421** L2
Rada El Cove, *bay*, San Andrés, Colombia, **461** B1
Radashkovichy, Belarus, **287** N5
Rădăuţi, Romania, **296** E2
Råde, Norway, **286** E3
Radeberg, Germany, **289** F3
Radekhiv, Ukraine, **289** M3
Rădeşti, Romania, **296** E3
Rādhanpur, India, **218** B5
Radisson, Canada, **415** R5
Radium Hot Springs, Canada, **413** L6
Radnevo, Bulgaria, **296** E4
Radom, Poland, **289** K3
Radom, Sudan, **366** B3
Radomir, Bulgaria, **296** D4
Radomsko, Poland, **289** J3
Radovets, Bulgaria, **296** F5
Radoviš, Macedonia, **297** D5
Radøy, *island*, Norway, **286** B2
Radstadt, Austria, **288** F5
Radstock, England, U.K., **304** E3
Răducăneni, Romania, **296** F2
Radun', Belarus, **289** M1
Radviliškis, Lithuania, **287** L5
Radziejów, Poland, **289** J2
Radzyń Podlaski, Poland, **289** L3
Rae, Canada, **410** H3
Rāe Bareli, India, **219** E4
Rae Lakes, Canada, **410** H3
Raeford, U.S.A., **425** N2
Raes Junction, New Zealand, **133** B7
Raetea, *mountain peak*, New Zealand, **132** D2
Raetihi, New Zealand, **132** E4
Rafaela, Argentina, **458** E4
Rafaḥ, Gaza, **225** C4
Rafaï, Central African Republic, **368** D2
Rafford, Scotland, U.K., **308** F3
Rafḥā, Saudi Arabia, **363** H3
Rafsanjān, Iran, **221** G2
Raga, Sudan, **366** C3
Raglan, New Zealand, **132** E3
Raglan, Wales, U.K., **304** E3
Raglitsy, Russian Federation, **299** C3
Ragueneau, Canada, **416** G5
Ragusa, Sicilia, Italy, **295** E7
Ra'gyagoinba, China, **215** G2
Raha, Indonesia, **198** C4
Rahad, *river*, Sudan, **366** D2
Rahama, Nigeria, **365** F2
Rāhatgarh, India, **218** D5
Rahīm Ki Bāzār, Pakistan, **218** B4
Rahīmyār Khān, Pakistan, **218** B3
Råholt, Norway, **286** E2
Rahon, India, **218** D3
Rahouia, Algeria, **293** H5
Raiatea, *island*, French Polynesia, **137** F2
Rāichūr, India, **216** D2
Raiganj, India, **219** G4
Raigarh, India, **219** E5
Rainbow Lake, Canada, **413** K2
Rainer, Mount, *mountain peak*, U.S.A., **418** D3
Rainier, U.S.A., **418** C3
Rainy Lake, Canada/U.S.A., **420** G1
Rainy River, Canada, **414** G7
Raippaluoto (Vallgrund), *island*, Finland, **284** K5
Raipur, India, **219** E5
Raisen, India, **218** D5
Raisio, Finland, **287** L2
Raith, Canada, **414** K7
Raivavae, *island*, French Polynesia, **137** G3
Rāj-Nāndgaon, India, **219** E5
Raja-Jooseppi, Finland, **285** P2
Rajagangapur, India, **219** F5
Rājahmundry, India, **217** E2
Rajala, Finland, **285** N3
Rajang, *river*, Malaysia, **201** F2
Rājanpur, Pakistan, **218** B3
Rājapālaiyam, India, **216** D4
Rājapur, India, **216** C2
Rājasthān, *state*, India, **218** C4, *93*, *169*
Rajauli, India, **219** F4
Rājgarh, E. Central Rājasthān, India, **218** D4
Rājgarh, N. Rājasthān, India, **218** C3
Rājkot, India, **218** B5
Rājpīpla, India, **218** C5
Rājpur, India, **218** D5
Rājsamand, India, **218** C4
Rajshahi, Bangladesh, **214** D4
Rajshahi, *division*, Bangladesh, **214** D4
Raka, China, **214** C3
Rakahanga, *island*, Cook Islands, **139** H5
Rakai, Uganda, **369** F3
Rakaia, New Zealand, **133** D6
Rakaw, Belarus, **287** N6
Rakhiv, Ukraine, **296** E1
Rakhmet, Kazakhstan, **222** H3
Rakhni, Pakistan, **218** B3
Rakhyūt, Oman, **220** F5
Rakiraki, Fiji, **141** A4
Rakkestad, Norway, **286** E3
Rakovník, Czech Republic, **288** F4
Rakovski, Bulgaria, **296** E4
Rakvere, Estonia, **287** N3
Raleigh, North Carolina, U.S.A., **425** N2, *386*
Raleigh, North Dakota, U.S.A., **420** C2
Ralston, Canada, **413** P6
Ralston, U.S.A., **419** K4
Ramādah, Tunisia, **362** B2
Ramalho, Serra do, *mountain range*, Brazil, **457** E4
Rāmanāthapuram, India, **216** D4
Rāmānuj Ganj, India, **219** E5
Rambouillet, France, **290** E2
Rāmdevra, India, **218** B4
Rāmechhāp, Nepal, **219** F4
Ramena, Madagascar, **372** B3
Rameshki, Russian Federation, **299** F4
Ramgarh, Bihār, India, **219** F5
Rāmgarh, Rājasthān, India, **218** B4
Rāmhormoz, Iran, **363** J2
Ramírez, Isla, *island*, Chile, **460** B4
Ramla, Israel, **225** C4
Ramlu, *mountain peak*, Eritrea/Ethiopia, **367** F2
Ramm, Jabal, *mountain peak*, Jordan, **225** C5, *180*
Ramm, Jordan, **225** C5
Rāmnagar, India, **218** D3
Ramnäs, Sweden, **286** H3
Ramni, Belarus, **299** C5
Râmnicu Sărat, Romania, **296** F3
Râmnicu Vâlcea, Romania, **296** E3
Ramor, Lough, *lake*, Ireland, **309** F4
Ramore, Canada, **415** P7
Ramotswa, Botswana, **371** E3
Rampside, England, U.K., **306** E3
Rāmpur, Gujarat, India, **218** B5
Rāmpur, Himāchal Pradesh, India, **218** D3
Rampūr, Orissa, India, **217** F1
Rāmpur, Uttar Pradesh, India, **218** D3
Rāmpur Hāt, India, **219** F4
Rāmpura, India, **218** C4
Ramree, *island*, Myanmar, **205** B4
Ramsele, Sweden, **284** H5
Ramsey, Canada, **421** M2
Ramsey, England, U.K., **305** G2
Ramsey, Isle of Man, **306** D3
Ramsey Bay, Isle of Man, **306** D3
Ramsey Island, Wales, U.K., **304** B3
Ramsgate, England, U.K., **305** J3
Ramsjö, Sweden, **286** G1
Ramu, Bangladesh, **214** E5
Ramu, *river*, Papua New Guinea, **140** B4
Ramundberget, Sweden, **284** F5
Ramvik, Sweden, **287** H1
Ramygala, Lithuania, **287** M5
Rana Pratap Sāgar, *lake*, India, **218** C4
Ranakah, Gunung, *mountain peak*, Indonesia, **198** C5
Ranau, Danau, *lake*, Indonesia, **200** C4
Rānāvāv, India, **218** B5
Ranbausawa, Tanjong, *point*, Indonesia, **199** F3
Rancagua, Chile, **458** B5
Ranchester, U.S.A., **419** L4
Rānchī, India, **219** F5
Rancho Cordova, U.S.A., **422** C2
Ranco, Lago, *lake*, Chile, **460** C1
Randado, U.S.A., **424** C6
Randalstown, Northern Ireland, U.K., **309** F3
Randazzo, Sicilia, Italy, **295** E7
Rånddalen, Sweden, **286** F1
Randers, Denmark, **286** E4
Randijaure, *lake*, Sweden, **284** J3
Randolph, Nebraska, U.S.A., **420** E4
Randolph, Vermont, U.S.A., **426** D3
Råneå, Sweden, **285** L4
Ranérou, Senegal, **364** B1
Ranfurly, New Zealand, **133** C7
Rangae, Thailand, **202** D5
Rangamati, Bangladesh, **214** E5
Rangatira Island, Chatham Islands, New Zealand, **133** Q16
Rangaunu Bay, New Zealand, **132** D2
Rangeley, U.S.A., **426** E2
Rangely, U.S.A., **423** J1
Rangia, India, **219** G4
Rangipo, New Zealand, **132** E4
Rangiriri, New Zealand, **132** E3
Rangiroa, *island*, French Polynesia, **137** G2
Rangitaiki, *river*, New Zealand, **132** F4
Rangitata, New Zealand, **133** C7
Rangiuru, New Zealand, **132** F3
Rangoon *see* Yangon, Myanmar, **205** C4, *157*
Rangpur, Bangladesh, **214** D4
Rangsang, Pulau, *island*, Indonesia, **200** C2
Rānībennur, India, **216** C3
Raniganj, India, **219** F5
Rānīpur, Pakistan, **218** B4
Rankin, U.S.A., **423** N6
Rankin Inlet, Canada, **411** K3
Rannoch, Loch, *lake*, Scotland, U.K., **308** E4
Rannoch Moor, *moorland*, Scotland, U.K., **308** E4
Rano, Nigeria, **365** F2
Ranobe, *river*, Madagascar, **372** A4
Ranohira, Madagascar, **372** B5
Ranomena, Madagascar, **372** B5
Ranong, Thailand, **202** C4
Ransarn, *lake*, Sweden, **284** G4
Ransiki, Indonesia, **199** F3
Rantajärvi, Sweden, **285** L3
Rantasalmi, Finland, **287** P1
Rantau, Indonesia, **201** F3
Rantekombola, Gunung, *mountain peak*, Indonesia, **198** C3
Rantepao, Indonesia, **198** B3
Rantoul, U.S.A., **421** J5
Rantsila, Finland, **285** M4
Ranua, Finland, **285** N4
Raoping, China, **206** D4
Raoui, Erg er, *desert*, Algeria, **361** F3
Raoul Island, Kermadec Islands, New Zealand, **132** L12
Rapa, *island*, French Polynesia, **137** G3
Rapahoe, New Zealand, **133** C6
Rapallo, Italy, **294** B3
Rāpar, India, **218** B5
Rapel, *river*, Chile, **458** B4
Raper, Cabo, *cape*, Chile, **460** B3
Raper, Cape, Canada, **411** N3
Raphoe, Ireland, **309** E3
Rapid City, U.S.A., **420** B3
Rapide Blanc, Canada, **416** E6
Räpina, Estonia, **287** N3
Rapla, Estonia, **287** M3
Rappahannock, *river*, U.S.A., **426** B5
Rapu Rapu Island, Philippines, **204** D3
Raroia, *island*, French Polynesia, **137** G2
Rarotonga, *island*, Cook Islands, **137** F3
Ra's Ajdīr, Tunisia, **362** B2
Ra's an Naqb, Jordan, **225** C5
Ra's at Tin, Libya, **224** B6
Ras Dashen Terara, *mountain peak*, Ethiopia, **367** E2, *338*
Râs el Mâ, Mali, **364** D1
Ra's Ghārib, Egypt, **363** F3
Ra's Matārimah, Egypt, **225** B5
Ra's Sudr, Egypt, **225** B5
Ra's Tannūrah, Saudi Arabia, **220** E3
Raša, Croatia, **294** E3
Rasa, Punta, *point*, Argentina, **460** E1
Rasa Island, Philippines, **204** B4
Râşcani, Moldova, **296** F2
Raseiniai, Lithuania, **287** L5
Rashaant, Bayan-Ölgiy, Mongolia, **213** F3
Rashaant, Dundgovĭ, Mongolia, **210** D3
Rashād, Sudan, **366** D2
Rashm, Iran, **221** F1
Rasht, Iran, **222** D5
Rasi Salai, Thailand, **203** E3
Rāsk, Iran, **221** H3
Raška, Serbia, **296** C4
Råsken, *river*, Norway, **286** C2
Râşnov, Romania, **296** E3
Raso, Cabo, *cape*, Argentina, **460** E2
Rastede, Germany, **288** D2
Rastegai'sa, *mountain peak*, Norway, **285** N2
Råstojaure, *lake*, Sweden, **284** K2
Rasu, Monte, *mountain peak*, Sardegna, Italy, **295** B5
Rasūl, Pakistan, **218** C2
Rat Islands, U.S.A., **301** U4
Rata, New Zealand, **132** E5
Rata, Tanjong, *point*, Indonesia, **200** D4
Rätan, Sweden, **286** G1
Ratanpur, India, **219** E5
Ratchaburi, Thailand, **202** C3
Rāth, India, **218** D4
Rath Luirc, Ireland, **309** D5
Rathangan, Ireland, **309** E4
Rathbun Lake, U.S.A., **420** G5
Rathdowney, Ireland, **309** E5
Rathdrum, Ireland, **309** F5
Rathenow, Germany, **288** F2
Rathfriland, Northern Ireland, U.K., **309** F3
Rathkeale, Ireland, **309** D5
Rathlin Island, Northern Ireland, U.K., **309** F2
Rathvilly, Ireland, **309** F5
Rathwell, Canada, **414** E7
Rätische Alpen, *mountain range*, Switzerland, **291** J3
Ratlām, India, **218** C5
Ratnāgiri, India, **216** C2
Ratne, Ukraine, **289** M3
Ratodero, Pakistan, **218** B4
Raton, U.S.A., **423** L3
Rättvik, Sweden, **286** G2
Ratz, Mount, *mountain peak*, Canada, **412** C3
Raub, Malaysia, **200** C2
Raub, U.S.A., **420** B2
Rauch, Argentina, **459** E5
Raufarhöfn, Iceland, **284** Z6
Raukumara Range, *mountain range*, New Zealand, **132** F4
Rauland, Norway, **286** D3
Rauma, Finland, **287** K2
Rauma, *river*, Norway, **286** D1
Raunds, England, U.K., **305** G2
Raung, Gunung, *mountain peak*, Indonesia, **201** F5
Raurkela, India, **219** F5
Răut, *river*, Moldova, **296** G2
Rautavaara, Finland, **285** P5
Rautjärvi, Finland, **287** P2
Rava-Rus'ka, Ukraine, **289** L3
Ravalli, U.S.A., **418** G3
Rāvar, Iran, **221** G2
Ravelo, Bolivia, **455** F5
Ravendale, U.S.A., **422** C1
Ravenglass, England, U.K., **306** E3
Ravenna, Italy, **294** D3
Ravensburg, Germany, **288** D5
Ravenshoe, Australia, **135** K2
Ravensthorpe, Australia, **134** E5
Ravenswood, U.S.A., **421** N6
Rāvi, *river*, India/Pakistan, **218** C3, *173*
Rawa Mazowiecka, Poland, **289** K3
Rawaki (Phoenix), *island*, Kiribati, **139** G5
Rāwalpindi, Pakistan, **218** C2
Rawāndūz, Iraq, **363** H1
Rawarra, *river*, Indonesia, **199** F3
Rawas, Indonesia, **199** F3
Rāwatsār, India, **218** C3
Rawḥah, Saudi Arabia, **363** H5
Rawicz, Poland, **289** H3
Rawlins, U.S.A., **419** L6
Rawson, Argentina, **460** E2
Rawtenstall, England, U.K., **306** F4
Rawu, China, **215** F3
Ray, Cape, Canada, **417** M6
Ray, U.S.A., **420** B1
Raya, Gunung, *mountain peak*, Indonesia, **201** F3

Raya, Tanjong, *point*, Aceh, Indonesia, **200** B2
Raya, Tanjong, *point*, Sumatera Selatan, Indonesia, **200** D3
Raychikhinsk, Russian Federation, **211** K2
Raydah, Yemen, **220** D5
Rayleigh, England, U.K., **305** H3
Raymond, Canada, **413** N7
Raymond, U.S.A., **418** C3
Raymondville, U.S.A., **424** D6
Raymore, Canada, **414** B6
Raynesford, U.S.A., **419** J3
Rayong, Thailand, **202** D3
Raystown Lake, U.S.A., **426** A4
Raz, Pointe du, *point*, France, **290** B3
Ražanj, Serbia, **296** C4
Razelm, Lacul, *lake*, Romania, **296** G3
Razgrad, Bulgaria, **296** F4
Razim, Lacul, *lagoon*, Romania, **298** C4
Razlog, Bulgaria, **296** D5
Razmak, Pakistan, **218** B2
Ré, Île de, *island*, France, **290** D3
Reading, England, U.K., **305** G3
Reading, U.S.A., **426** C4
Reading, *unitary authority*, England, U.K., **305** G3
Readstown, U.S.A., **420** H4
Real, Cordillera, *mountain range*, Bolivia, **455** E4
Realicó, Argentina, **458** D5
Reao, *island*, French Polynesia, **137** H2
Rebbenesøy, *island*, Norway, **284** H1
Rebecca, Lake, Australia, **134** E5
Reboly, Russian Federation, **285** Q5
Rebordelo, Portugal, **292** D2
Rebun-tō, *island*, Japan, **209** H1
Recess, Ireland, **309** C4
Rechane, Russian Federation, **299** C4
Recherche, Archipelago of, *islands*, Australia, **134** E5
Recife, Brazil, **453** G5, *439*
Recife, Cape, South Africa, **371** E5
Récifs, Île aux, *island*, Seychelles, **373** A2
Recinto, Chile, **458** B5
Recklinghausen, Germany, **288** C3
Reconquista, Argentina, **459** E3
Recreio, Brazil, **455** G2
Recreo, Argentina, **458** D3
Red, *river*, Minnesota, U.S.A., **420** E2
Red, *river*, Oklahoma, U.S.A., **424** C2
Red Bank, New Jersey, U.S.A., **426** C4
Red Bank, Tennessee, U.S.A., **425** K2
Red Bay, Canada, **417** N4
Red Bluff, U.S.A., **422** B1
Red Cloud, U.S.A., **420** D5
Red Deer, Canada, **413** N5
Red Deer, *river*, Alberta, Canada, **413** N6
Red Deer, *river*, Saskatchewan, Canada, **414** C5
Red Deer Lake, Canada, **414** D5
Red Elm, U.S.A., **420** C3
Red Indian Lake, Canada, **417** N5
Red Lake, Canada, **414** H6
Red Lake Road, Canada, **414** H7
Red Lodge, U.S.A., **419** K4
Red Rock, British Columbia, Canada, **412** H5
Red Rock, Ontario, Canada, **421** J1
Red Sea, Africa/Asia, **220** C4, *22, 74, 144, 159, 174, 175, 179, 312, 317, 337, 339*
Red Sucker Lake, Canada, **414** G4
Red Wing, U.S.A., **420** G3
Redang, Pulau, *island*, Malaysia, **200** C1
Redbird, U.S.A., **419** M5
Redcar, England, U.K., **307** G3
Redcar and Cleveland, England, U.K., **307** G3
Redcliff, Canada, **413** P6
Redcliff, Zimbabwe, **371** E2
Redding, California, U.S.A., **422** B1
Redding, Iowa, U.S.A., **420** F5
Redditch, England, U.K., **305** F2
Redditt, Canada, **414** G7
Rede, *river*, England, U.K., **306** F2
Redenção de Gurguéia, Brazil, **457** E2
Redenção, Brazil, **452** C5
Redeyef, Tunisia, **361** H2
Redfield, New York, U.S.A., **426** C3
Redfield, South Dakota, U.S.A., **420** D3
Redhead, Trinidad, Trinidad and Tobago, **461** C4
Redhill, England, U.K., **305** G3
Rédics, Hungary, **289** H5
Redkino, Russian Federation, **299** F4
Redland, Orkney, Scotland, U.K., **308** F1
Redlynch, England, U.K., **305** F4
Redmond, U.S.A., **418** D4
Redon, France, **290** C3
Redonda, *island*, Antigua and Barbuda, **427** D2, *396*
Redonda, Punta, *point*, Isla de Pascua (Easter Island), Chile, **461** B2
Redondo, Portugal, **292** D3
Redruth, England, U.K., **304** B4
Redstone, Canada, **412** H5
Redwood City, U.S.A., **422** B3
Redwood Valley, U.S.A., **422** B2
Red'ya, *river*, Russian Federation, **299** C4
Ree, Lough, *lake*, Ireland, **309** E4
Reed City, U.S.A., **421** L4
Reedpoint, U.S.A., **419** K4
Reedsburg, U.S.A., **420** H4
Reedsport, U.S.A., **418** B5
Reedville, U.S.A., **426** B6
Reefton, New Zealand, **133** C6
Reform, U.S.A., **425** J3
Regeb, Sudan, **366** B2
Regen, Germany, **288** F4
Regen, *river*, Germany, **288** F4
Regensburg, Germany, **288** F4
Regent, U.S.A., **420** B2
Reggane, Algeria, **361** G3
Reggane, Sebkha, *lake*, Algeria, **361** F3
Reggio di Calabria, Italy, **295** E6
Reggio nell'Emilia, Italy, **294** C3
Reghin, Romania, **296** E2
Regina, Brazil, **452** C2
Regina, Canada, **414** B6, *381*
Régina, French Guiana, **452** C2
Regina, U.S.A., **423** K3
Regna, Sweden, **286** G3
Reharaka, Madagascar, **372** A4
Rehli, India, **218** D5
Rehoboth, Namibia, **370** C3
Reḥovot, Israel, **225** C4
Reichenau, Switzerland, **291** J3
Reichenbach, Germany, **288** F3
Reidsville, U.S.A., **421** P7
Reigate, England, U.K., **305** G3
Reigh, Rubha, *point*, Scotland, U.K., **308** C3
Reilly Hill, U.S.A., **420** B5
Reims, France, **291** G2
Reina Adelaida, Archipiélago de la, *islands*, Chile, **460** B4
Reinbek, Germany, **288** E2
Reindeer, *river*, Canada, **414** C4
Reindeer Lake, Canada, **414** C3
Reinga, Cape, New Zealand, **132** D2
Reinosa, Spain, **292** E1
Reinøy, *island*, Norway, **284** J2
Reinsfjell, *mountain peak*, Norway, **284** E5
Reisaelva, *river*, Norway, **284** K2
Reisjärvi, Finland, **285** M5
Reisseck, *mountain peak*, Austria, **294** D2
Reisterstown, U.S.A., **426** B5
Reitoru, *island*, French Polynesia, **137** G2
Rejunya, Venezuela, **451** F3
Rekovac, Serbia, **296** C4
Relizane, Algeria, **361** G1
Rémalard, France, **290** E2
Remanso, Brazil, **457** E2
Rembang, Indonesia, **201** E4
Remennikovo, Russian Federation, **299** B4
Rémire, French Guiana, **452** C2
Remiremont, France, **291** H2
Remo, *mountain peak*, Italy, **295** D4
Rempang, Pulau, *island*, Indonesia, **200** C2
Remscheid, Germany, **288** C3
Rena, Norway, **286** E2
Renam, Myanmar, **205** C2
Rencēni, Latvia, **287** M4
Rend Lake, U.S.A., **421** J6
Renda, Latvia, **287** L4
Rendova, *island*, Solomon Islands, **141** A1
Rendsburg, Germany, **288** D1
Renfrew, Canada, **416** C7
Renfrewshire, *local authority*, Scotland, U.K., **308** E5
Rengat, Indonesia, **200** C3
Rengo, Chile, **458** B5
Renhua, China, **206** C3
Reni, Ukraine, **296** G3
Renmark, Australia, **135** J5
Rennebu, Norway, **286** D1
Rennell, *island*, Solomon Islands, **141** A1
Rennes, France, **290** D2
Rennie, Canada, **414** G7
Reno, U.S.A., **422** D2
Renovo, U.S.A., **426** B4
Renqiu, China, **210** G5
Renshan, China, **207** D3
Renshou, China, **215** H3
Rensjön, Sweden, **284** J2
Renwer, Canada, **414** D5
Réo, Burkina Faso, **364** D2
Reo, Indonesia, **198** C5
Répcelak, Hungary, **289** H5
Repetek, Turkmenistan, **222** G5
Republic, U.S.A., **418** E2
Repulse Bay, Canada, **411** L3
Repvåg, Norway, **285** M1
Requena, Peru, **454** D1
Requena, Spain, **293** G3
Réquista, France, **290** F4
Rere, Solomon Islands, **141** A1
Resang, Tanjong, *point*, Malaysia, **200** C2
Resen, Macedonia, **297** C5
Reserva, Brazil, **459** G2
Reserve, Canada, **414** C5
Reserve, U.S.A., **419** M2
Resistencia, Argentina, **459** E3
Reşiūa, Romania, **296** C3
Resko, Poland, **289** G2
Resolute, Canada, **411** K2
Resolution Island, Canada, **411** N4
Resolution Island, New Zealand, **133** A7
Resseta, *river*, Russian Federation, **299** E6
Restigouche, *river*, Canada, **416** H6
Restinga, Punta, *point*, Islas Canarias, Spain, **373** A4
Retalhuleu, Guatemala, **428** C4
Reteag, Romania, **296** E2
Retén Llico, Chile, **458** B5
Retford, England, U.K., **307** H4
Rethel, France, **291** G2
Rethymno, Kriti, Greece, **297** E8
Retz, Austria, **289** G4
Réunion, *French department*, Indian Ocean, **373** A1, *245, 354*
Reus, Spain, **293** H2
Reutlingen, Germany, **288** D4
Revda, Russian Federation, **285** S3
Revelstoke, Canada, **413** K6
Reventazón, Peru, **454** B2
Revermont, *region*, France, **291** G3
Revillagigedo, Islas, *islands*, Mexico, **409** M7
Revivim, Israel, **225** C4
Revúboè, *river*, Mozambique, **369** F6
Revúca, Slovakia, **289** K4
Rewa, India, **219** E4
Rewāri, India, **218** D3
Rexburg, U.S.A., **419** J5
Rexford, U.S.A., **418** G2
Rey, Isla del, *island*, Panama, **429** F5
Rey Bouba, Cameroon, **365** G3
Reyes, Bolivia, **455** E4
Reyes, Point, U.S.A., **422** B3
Reyes, Punta dos, *point*, Chile, **458** B2
Reyhanlı, Turkey, **225** D1
Reykhólar, Iceland, **284** X7
Reykjanes Ridge, *underwater feature*, Atlantic Ocean, **477** E2
Reykjavík, Iceland, **284** X7, *230*
Reynosa, Mexico, **431** F3
Rēzekne, Latvia, **287** N4
Rezina, Moldova, **296** G2
Rgotina, Serbia, **296** D3
Rhayader, Wales, U.K., **304** D2
Rhein, *river*, Austria, **291** J3
Rhein, *river*, Germany, **288** C3
Rhein, *river*, Switzerland, **291** J3
Rheine, Germany, **288** C2
Rheinland-Pfalz, *state*, Germany, **288** C3, *238*
Rheinwaldhorn, *mountain peak*, Switzerland, **291** J3
Rhiconich, Scotland, U.K., **308** E2
Rhin, *river*, France, **291** H3
Rhine, *river*, Europe, **288** C3; *see also* Rhein, *river*, Austria, **291** J3; Rhein, *river*, Switzerland, **291** J3; Rhin, *river*, France, **291** H3, , *89, 228, 239, 241, 247, 248*
Rhinelander, U.S.A., **421** J3
Rhino Camp, Uganda, **369** F2
Rhinow, Germany, **288** F2
Rhir, Cap, *cape*, Morocco, **360** D2
Rho, Italy, **294** B3
Rhode Island, *state*, U.S.A., **426** E4, *386*
Rhodes see Rodos, *island*, Dodekanisos, Greece, **297** G7, *265*
Rhododendron, U.S.A., **418** D4
Rhondda, Wales, U.K., **304** D3
Rhondda Cynon Taff, Wales, U.K., **304** D3
Rhône, *river*, France/Switzerland, **280** E7, *228, 244*
Rhône-Alpes, *administrative region*, France, **291** G4, *245*
Rhosllanerchrugog, Wales, U.K., **304** D1
Rhossili, Wales, U.K., **304** C3
Rhum, *island*, Scotland, U.K., **308** C4
Rhyl, Wales, U.K., **306** E4
Riaba, Equatorial Guinea, **368** A2
Riachão, Brazil, **452** D5
Riachão das Neves, Brazil, **457** E3
Riachão do Jacuípe, Brazil, **457** F3
Riacho de Santana, Brazil, **457** E3
Rialma, Brazil, **456** D4
Rianápolis, Brazil, **456** D4
Riang, India, **219** H4
Riaño, Spain, **292** E1
Riánsares, *river*, Spain, **293** F3
Riau, Kepulauan, *islands*, Indonesia, **200** D2
Riau, *province*, Indonesia, **200** C2
Ribadeo, Spain, **292** D1
Ribadesella, Spain, **292** E1
Ribas do Rio Pardo, Brazil, **456** C5
Ribáuè, Mozambique, **369** G5
Ribe, Denmark, **286** D5
Ribeira, *river*, Brazil, **459** H2
Ribeira Brava, Madeira, Portugal, **373** C3
Ribeirão Prêto, Brazil, **456** D5
Ribera, Sicilia, Italy, **295** D7
Ribérac, France, **290** E4
Riberalta, Bolivia, **455** E3
Ribnica, Slovenia, **294** E3
Ribnitz-Damgarten, Germany, **288** F1
Ricardo Flores Magón, Mexico, **430** D2
Rice, California, U.S.A., **422** F4
Rice, Washington, U.S.A., **418** E2
Rice Lake, Canada, **416** B7
Riceboro, U.S.A., **425** M4
Rich Hill, U.S.A., **420** F6
Richard Toll, Senegal, **364** A1
Richards Bay, South Africa, **371** F4
Richardson, *river*, Canada, **413** P2
Richardton, U.S.A., **420** B2
Richdale, Canada, **413** P6
Richey, U.S.A., **419** M3
Richfield, Idaho, U.S.A., **418** G5
Richfield, Utah, U.S.A., **423** G2
Richibucto, Canada, **416** J6
Richland Center, U.S.A., **420** H4
Richland Springs, U.S.A., **424** C4
Richmond, Australia, **135** J3
Richmond, England, U.K., **307** G3
Richmond, Indiana, U.S.A., **421** L6
Richmond, Kentucky, U.S.A., **421** L7
Richmond, Mount, *mountain peak*, New Zealand, **133** D5
Richmond, New Zealand, **133** D5
Richmond, South Africa, **370** D5
Richmond, Virginia, U.S.A., **426** B6, *386*
Richmond Hill, U.S.A., **425** M4
Richmond Range, *mountain range*, New Zealand, **133** D5
Ricobayo, Embalse de, *reservoir*, Spain, **292** E2
Riddle, U.S.A., **418** F5
Ridgecrest, U.S.A., **422** E4
Ridgeview, U.S.A., **420** C3
Ridgeway, U.S.A., **423** K2
Riedenburg, Germany, **288** E4
Riedlingen, Germany, **288** D4
Riepentjåkkå, *mountain peak*, Sweden, **284** H3
Riesa, Germany, **288** F3
Riesco, Isla, *island*, Chile, **460** C4
Rietavas, Lithuania, **287** K5
Rieti, Italy, **295** D4
Riez, France, **291** H5
Rifle, U.S.A., **423** K2
Rifstangi, *point*, Iceland, **284** Y6
Rift Valley, *province*, Kenya, **369** G2, *91, 312, 334, 338, 340, 341, 343, 344*
Rig-Rig, Chad, **365** G2
Riga, Gulf of, Estonia/Latvia, **287** L4, *237*
Rīga, Latvia, **287** M4, *236*
Rigby, U.S.A., **419** J5
Rīgestān, *region*, Afghanistan, **218** A3
Riggins, U.S.A., **418** F4
Riguldi, Estonia, **287** L3
Riihimäki, Finland, **287** M2
Riiser-Larsenhalvøya, *peninsula*, Antarctica, **470** E3
Riisipere, Estonia, **287** M3
Rijau, Nigeria, **365** F2
Rijeka, Croatia, **294** E3
Riksgränsen, Sweden, **284** J2
Riley, U.S.A., **418** E5
Rimatara, *island*, French Polynesia, **137** F3
Rimavská Sobota, Slovakia, **289** K4
Rimbo, Sweden, **287** J3
Rimforsa, Sweden, **286** G3
Rimini, Italy, **294** D3, *256*
Rimouski, Canada, **416** G5
Rinbung, China, **214** D3
Rinca, Pulau, *island*, Indonesia, **198** B5
Rincon, Bonaire, Netherlands Antilles, **461** A4
Rincón, Cerro del, *mountain peak*, Argentina/Chile, **458** C2
Rincon, U.S.A., **423** K5
Rinda, China, **215** G3
Rindal, Norway, **284** D5
Rindü, China, **214** D3
Rineia, *island*, Kyklades, Greece, **297** E7
Ringarum, Sweden, **286** H3
Rīngas, India, **218** C4
Ringdove, Vanuatu, **141** A2
Ringgi, Solomon Islands, **141** A1
Ringim, Nigeria, **365** F2
Ringkøbing, Denmark, **286** D4

Ringling, U.S.A., **419** J3
Ringsted, Denmark, **286** E5
Ringvassøy, *island*, Norway, **284** J2
Ringwood, England, U.K., **305** F4
Riñihue, Chile, **460** C1
Rinjani, Gunung, *mountain peak*, Indonesia, **201** G5
Rintala, Russian Federation, **299** B2
Rinteln, Germany, **288** D2
Rio, Greece, **297** C6
Rio Alegre, Brazil, **456** B4
Rio Blanco, U.S.A., **423** K2
Rio Branco, Acre, Brazil, **455** E2
Rio Branco, Mato Grosso, Brazil, **455** G4
Rio Branco do Sul, Brazil, **459** H2
Río Bravo, Mexico, **431** F3
Rio Brilhante, Brazil, **456** B5
Río Bueno, Chile, **460** C1
Río Caribe, Venezuela, **451** F1
Río Ceballos, Argentina, **458** D4
Rio Claro, Brazil, **459** H2
Rio Claro, Trinidad, Trinidad and Tobago, **461** C4
Río Colorado, Argentina, **460** E1
Río Cuarto, Argentina, **458** D4
Rio de Janeiro, Brazil, **457** E6, *85, 95, 97, 434, 439, 441, 441*
Rio de Janeiro, *state*, Brazil, **457** E5
Río de Jesús, Panama, **429** E6
Rio Do Ouro, São Tomé and Príncipe, **373** C4
Rio Do Sul, Brazil, **459** H3
Río Frío, Costa Rica, **428** E5
Río Gallegos, Argentina, **460** D4
Río Grande, Argentina, **460** D4
Rio Grande, Brazil, **459** G4
Río Grande, Mexico, **430** E4, *376*
Rio Grande City, U.S.A., **424** C6
Rio Grande do Norte, *state*, Brazil, **453** G4
Rio Grande do Sul, *state*, Brazil, **459** G3
Rio Grande Rise, *underwater feature*, Atlantic Ocean, **477** E8
Río Lagartos, Mexico, **431** H4
Rio Largo, Brazil, **457** G2
Rio Maior, Portugal, **292** C3
Río Mayo, Argentina, **460** C2
Río Mulatos, Bolivia, **455** E5
Rio Negro, Brazil, **459** H3
Rio Negro, Pantanal do, *swamp*, Brazil, **456** B5
Río Negro, *province*, Argentina, **460** D1
Río Negro, Represa del, *reservoir*, Uruguay, **459** F4
Rio Pardo, Brazil, **459** G4
Rio Pardo de Minas, Brazil, **457** E4
Río Primero, Argentina, **458** D4
Río Tigre, Ecuador, **450** C5
Rio Tuba, Philippines, **204** B4
Rio Verde, Brazil, **456** C4
Río Verde, Chile, **460** C4
Río Verde, Mexico, **431** F4
Rio Verde de Mato Grosso, Brazil, **456** B5
Riobamba, Ecuador, **450** B4
Ríohacha, Colombia, **450** D1
Rioja, Peru, **454** C2
Riom, France, **291** F4
Ríosucio, Colombia, **450** C2
Ripanj, Serbia, **296** C3
Ripley, England, U.K., **307** G3
Ripley, Tennessee, U.S.A., **425** H2
Ripley, West Virginia, U.S.A., **421** N6
Ripoll, Spain, **293** J1
Ripon, England, U.K., **307** G3
Ripon, U.S.A., **421** J4
Risan, Montenegro, **296** B4
Risbäck, Sweden, **284** G4
Risca, Wales, U.K., **304** D3
Riscle, France, **290** D5
Rishīkesh, India, **218** D3
Rishiri-tō, *island*, Japan, **209** H1
Rishon LeẔiyyon, Israel, **225** C4
Risør, Norway, **286** D3
Risøyhamn, Norway, **284** G2
Rissa, Norway, **284** E5
Risti, Estonia, **287** M3
Ristiina, Finland, **287** N2
Ristijärvi, Finland, **285** P4
Ristna, Estonia, **287** L3
Ritter, Mount, *mountain peak*, U.S.A., **422** D3
Ritzville, U.S.A., **418** E3
Riva del Garda, Italy, **294** C3
Rivadavia, Buenos Aires, Argentina, **458** D5
Rivadavia, Chile, **458** B3
Rivadavia, Mendoza, Argentina, **458** C4
Rivadavia, Salta, Argentina, **458** D2
Rivarolo Canavese, Italy, **294** A3
Rivas, Nicaragua, **428** D5
River Cess, Liberia, **364** C3
Rivera, Argentina, **458** D5
Rivera, Uruguay, **459** F4
Rivergaro, Italy, **294** B3
Riverhead, U.S.A., **426** D4
Rivers, *state*, Nigeria, **365** F4
Rivers Inlet, Canada, **410** G4
Riversdale, North Island, New Zealand, **133** F5
Riversdale, South Island, New Zealand, **133** B7
Riverside, California, U.S.A., **422** E5
Riverside, Washington, U.S.A., **418** E2
Riverton, New Zealand, **133** B8
Riverton, U.S.A., **419** K5
Riviera, U.S.A., **424** D6
Rivière-aux-Rats, Canada, **416** E6
Rivière-du-Loup, Canada, **416** G6
Rivière du Rempart, Mauritius, **373** C1
Rivière-Matawin, Canada, **416** E6
Rivière-Pentecôte, Canada, **416** H5
Rivière-St-Jean, Canada, **417** J4
Rivière-St-Paul, Canada, **417** N4
Rivne, Ukraine, **298** C2
Rivoli, Italy, **294** A3
Rivungo, Angola, **368** D6
Riyadh *see* Ar Riyāḑ, Saudi Arabia, **220** E4, *174*
Rizhao, China, **206** D1
Rizokarpaso, Cyprus, **225** C2
Rizzuto, Capo, *cape*, Italy, **295** F6
Rjukan, Norway, **286** D3
Roa, Punta, *point*, Isla de Pascua (Easter Island), Chile, **461** B2
Road Town, U.K. Virgin Islands, **427** C2, *388*
Roade, England, U.K., **305** G2
Roag, Loch, *inlet*, Scotland, U.K., **308** B2
Roan Plateau, U.S.A., **423** H2
Roanne, France, **291** G3
Roanoke, Alabama, U.S.A., **425** K3
Roanoke, Virginia, U.S.A., **421** P7
Roanoke Rapids, U.S.A., **426** B6
Roaringwater Bay, Ireland, **309** C6
Roatán, Honduras, **428** D3
Robbins Island, Australia, **135** K7
Robē, Ethiopia, **367** E3
Röbel, Germany, **288** F2
Roberta, U.S.A., **425** K3
Roberts Butte, *mountain peak*, Antarctica, **470** E8
Roberts Creek Mountain, *mountain peak*, U.S.A., **422** E1
Robertsfors, Sweden, **284** K4
Robertsganj, India, **219** E4
Robertsport, Liberia, **364** B3
Roberval, Canada, **416** E5
Robin Hood's Bay, England, U.K., **307** H3
Robinson, Canada, **412** B1
Róbinson Crusoe, *island*, Archipiélago Juan Fernández, Chile, Pacific Ocean, **461** C2
Robinvale, Australia, **135** J5
Roblin, Canada, **414** D6
Robooksibia, Indonesia, **199** F3
Roboré, Bolivia, **455** G5
Robsart, Canada, **413** Q7
Robson, Mount, *mountain peak*, Canada, **413** K5
Robstown, U.S.A., **424** D6
Roca Partida, Punta, *point*, Mexico, **431** G5
Rocafuerte, Ecuador, **450** B4
Rocha, Uruguay, **459** F5
Rochdale, England, U.K., **306** F4
Rochechouart, France, **290** E4
Rochedo, Brazil, **456** B5
Rochefort, France, **290** D4
Rochegda, Russian Federation, **300** F3
Rochelle, U.S.A., **425** L4
Rochester, Canada, **413** N4
Rochester, England, U.K., **305** H3
Rochester, Indiana, U.S.A., **421** K5
Rochester, Minnesota, U.S.A., **420** G3
Rochester, New Hampshire, U.S.A., **426** E3
Rochester, New York, U.S.A., **426** B3
Rochford, England, U.K., **305** H3
Rock Hill, U.S.A., **425** M2
Rock Point, U.S.A., **423** J3
Rock Rapids, U.S.A., **420** E4
Rock River, U.S.A., **419** M6
Rock Sound, Bahamas, **428** G1
Rock Springs, Montana, U.S.A., **419** L3
Rock Springs, Wyoming, U.S.A., **419** K6
Rockall, *island*, U.K., **282** C4
Rockford, U.S.A., **421** J4
Rockglen, Canada, **413** S7
Rockham, U.S.A., **420** D3
Rockhampton, Australia, **135** L3
Rockingham, Australia, **134** D5
Rockingham, England, U.K., **305** G2
Rockingham, U.S.A., **425** N2
Rockingham Forest, England, U.K., **305** G2
Rockland, Idaho, U.S.A., **418** H5
Rockland, Maine, U.S.A., **426** F2
Rockport, Texas, U.S.A., **424** D5
Rockport, Washington, U.S.A., **418** D2
Rocksprings, U.S.A., **424** B5
Rockwell City, U.S.A., **420** F4
Rocky Ford, U.S.A., **423** M2
Rocky Harbour, Canada, **417** N5
Rocky Island Lake, Canada, **421** M2
Rocky Mount, U.S.A., **426** B7
Rocky Mountain House, Canada, **413** M5
Rocky Mountains, *mountain range*, Canada/U.S.A., **406** M3, *94, 95, 376, 383, 385*
Rocky Point, Namibia, **370** B2
Rockypoint, U.S.A., **419** M4
Rocoso, Cayo, *island*, San Andrés, Colombia, **461** B1
Rødby, Denmark, **286** E5
Rødding, Denmark, **286** D5
Rodel, Scotland, U.K., **308** C3
Roden, *river*, England, U.K., **304** E2
Rodeo, Argentina, **458** C4
Rodeo, Mexico, **430** D3
Rodez, France, **290** F4
Roding, Germany, **288** F4
Rodino, Russian Federation, **223** L2
Rodna, Romania, **296** E2
Rodnya, Belarus, **299** D6
Rodolivos, Greece, **297** D5
Rodonit, Kepi i, *cape*, Albania, **297** B5
Rodopi Planina, *mountain range*, Bulgaria, **296** E4
Rodos, Greece, **297** G7
Rodos (Rhodes), *island*, Dodekanisos, Greece, **297** G7, *265*
Rodrigues, *island*, Mauritius, **373** B1
Rødvig, Denmark, **286** F5
Roebourne, Australia, **134** D3
Roebuck Bay, Australia, **134** E2
Roeselare, Belgium, **288** A3
Rogaguado, Lago, *lake*, Bolivia, **455** E3
Rogaland, *county*, Norway, **286** B3
Rogatica, Bosnia and Herzegovina, **294** G4
Rogen, *lake*, Sweden, **286** F1
Rogers, U.S.A., **424** E1
Rogers City, U.S.A., **421** M3
Rogerson, U.S.A., **418** G5
Roggewain, Cabo, *cape*, Isla de Pascua (Easter Island), Chile, **461** B2
Rogliano, Corse, France, **294** B4
Rogliano, Italy, **295** F6
Rognan, Norway, **284** G3
Rogne, Norway, **286** D2
Rohat, India, **218** C4
Rohatyn, Ukraine, **289** M4
Rohri, Pakistan, **218** B4
Rohtak, India, **218** D3
Rohuküla, Estonia, **287** L3
Roi Et, Thailand, **203** D2
Roing, India, **219** H3
Roja, Latvia, **287** L4
Rojas, Argentina, **458** E5
Rojhān, Pakistan, **218** B3
Rojo, Cabo, *cape*, Mexico, **431** F4
Rokan, *river*, Indonesia, **200** C2
Rokhmoyva, Gora, *mountain peak*, Russian Federation, **285** P3
Rokiškis, Lithuania, **287** M5
Rokkasho, Japan, **209** H2
Rola Co, *lake*, China, **214** D2
Rolândia, Brazil, **459** G2
Rôlas, Ilhéu das, *island*, São Tomé and Príncipe, **373** C4, *332*
Røldal, Norway, **286** C3
Roll, U.S.A., **424** C2
Rolla, Missouri, U.S.A., **420** H7
Rolla, North Dakota, U.S.A., **420** D1
Rollag, Norway, **286** D2
Rolleston, Mount, *mountain peak*, New Zealand, **133** C6
Rollet, Canada, **416** B6
Rolvsøya, *island*, Norway, **285** L1
Roma, Australia, **135** K4
Roma, Lesotho, **371** E4
Roma (Rome), Italy, **295** D5, *70, 71, 74, 83, 89, 96, 244, 254, 255, 257, 316*
Roma, Sweden, **287** J4
Roma, U.S.A., **424** C6
Romaine, *river*, Canada, **417** K4
Roman, Romania, **296** F2
Roman-Kosh, Hora, *mountain peak*, Ukraine, **298** D4
Romanche Fracture Zone, *tectonic feature*, Atlantic Ocean, **477** E5
Romania, *country*, Europe, **282** G6, *228, 245, 260, 261, 262, 263, 264, 269, 270, 272*
Romano, Cape, U.S.A., **425** L7
Romano, Cayo, *island*, Cuba, **429** F2
Romanovka, Russian Federation, **210** F1
Rombebai, Danau, *lake*, Indonesia, **199** G3
Romblon, Philippines, **204** C3
Rome, Alabama, U.S.A., **425** J4
Rome, New York, U.S.A., **426** C3
Rome, Oregon, U.S.A., **418** F5
Rome *see* Roma, Italy, **295** D5, *70, 71, 74, 83, 89, 96, 244, 254, 255, 257, 316*
Romney, U.S.A., **421** P6
Romny, Russian Federation, **211** K2
Romny, Ukraine, **298** D2
Rømø, *island*, Denmark, **286** D5
Rompin, *river*, Malaysia, **200** C2
Romsey, England, U.K., **305** F3
Romuli, Romania, **296** E2
Ron Phibun, Thailand, **202** C4
Ronan, U.S.A., **418** G3
Ronas Hill, Shetland, Scotland, U.K., **308** K7
Roncador, Serra do, *mountain range*, Brazil, **456** C4
Ronda, Serrania de, *mountain range*, Spain, **292** E4
Ronda, Spain, **292** E4
Rønde, Denmark, **286** E4
Rondon do Pará, Brazil, **452** D4
Rondônia, *state*, Brazil, **455** F3
Rondonópolis, Brazil, **456** B4
Rondslottet, *mountain peak*, Norway, **286** D2
Rông, Kaôh, *island*, Cambodia, **202** D4
Rong, *river*, China, **206** B3
Rong Xian, China, **206** B4
Rong'an, China, **206** B3
Rongbaca, China, **215** F3
Rongcheng, China, **211** H5
Ronge, Lac la, *lake*, Canada, **413** S4
Rongelap, *island*, Marshall Islands, **138** E3
Rongjiang, China, **206** B3
Rongklang, *mountain range*, Myanmar, **205** B3
Rongqi, China, **207** A3
Rongxar, China, **214** C3
Rønne, Denmark, **286** G5
Ronne Entrance, *strait*, Antarctica, **470** B5
Ronne Ice Shelf, Antarctica, **470** C5
Ronneby, Sweden, **286** G4
Rønnede, Denmark, **286** F5
Rönnöfors, Sweden, **284** F5
Ronuro, *river*, Brazil, **456** B3
Rookery Point, Tristan da Cunha, **373** C2
Roorkee, India, **218** D3
Roosendaal, Netherlands, **288** B3
Roosevelt, Arizona, U.S.A., **423** H5
Roosevelt, Mount, *mountain peak*, Canada, **412** G2
Roosevelt, Utah, U.S.A., **423** J1
Roosevelt Island, Antarctica, **470** D7
Ropeid, Norway, **286** C3
Roper, *river*, Australia, **134** G1
Roper Bar, Australia, **135** G1
Ropi, *mountain peak*, Finland, **284** K2
Roquefort, France, **290** D4
Roraima, Monte, *mountain peak*, Guyana, **451** G3, *437*
Roraima, *state*, Brazil, **451** G4, *439, 441*
Røros, Norway, **286** E1
Rørvik, Norway, **284** E4
Ros', Belarus, **289** M2
Rosa, Cabo, *cape*, Islas Galápagos (Galapagos Islands), Ecuador, **461** A2
Rosa, Monte, *mountain peak*, Italy, **294** A3
Rosa, Punta, *point*, Mexico, **430** C3
Rosa de los James, Islas Canarias, Spain, **373** B4
Rosa Zárate, Ecuador, **450** B4
Rosal de la Frontera, Spain, **292** D4
Rosalia, Punta, *point*, Isla de Pascua (Easter Island), Chile, **461** B2
Rosalia, U.S.A., **418** F3
Rosana, Brazil, **459** G2
Rosantos, Punta, *point*, Mexico, **430** C3
Rosario, Argentina, **458** E4
Rosário, Brazil, **453** E4
Rosario, Cayo del, *island*, Cuba, **429** E2
Rosario, Paraguay, **459** F2
Rosario, Sinaloa, Mexico, **430** D4
Rosario, Sonora, Mexico, **430** C3
Rosario, Venezuela, **450** D1
Rosario de la Frontera, Argentina, **458** D2
Rosario de Lerma, Argentina, **458** D2
Rosario del Tala, Argentina, **459** E4

Rosário do Sul, Brazil, 459 F4
Rosário Oeste, Brazil, 456 B4
Rosarito, Baja California Sur, Mexico, 430 C3
Rosarito, Baja California, Mexico, 430 B2
Roscoe, New York, U.S.A., 426 C4
Roscoe, South Dakota, U.S.A., 420 D3
Roscoff, France, 290 C2
Roscommon, county, Ireland, 309 D4
Roscommon, Ireland, 309 D4
Roscrea, Ireland, 309 E5
Rose, island, American Samoa, 139 H6
Rose, U.S.A., 424 E1
Rose Belle, Mauritius, 373 C1
Rose Blanche, Canada, 417 M6
Rose Peak, mountain peak, U.S.A., 423 J5
Rose Prairie, Canada, 412 J3
Rose Valley, Canada, 414 C5
Roseau, Dominica, 427 D3, 396
Roseau, U.S.A., 420 F1
Rosebud, Canada, 413 N6
Roseburg, U.S.A., 418 C5
Rosedale Abbey, England, U.K., 307 H3
Rosehearty, Scotland, U.K., 308 G3
Rosemarkie, Scotland, U.K., 308 E3
Rosemary, Canada, 413 N6
Rosenberg, U.S.A., 424 E5
Rosendal, Norway, 286 C3
Rosenheim, Germany, 288 F5
Roses, Golfo de, gulf, Spain, 293 J1
Roseto degli Abruzzi, Italy, 294 D4
Rosetown, Canada, 413 Q6
Roseville, U.S.A., 420 H5
Rosh Pinah, Namibia, 370 C4
Rosières-en-Santerre, France, 305 K5
Rosignol, Guyana, 451 H2
Roşiorii de Vede, Romania, 296 E3
Rositsa, Bulgaria, 296 F4
Roskilde, Denmark, 286 F5
Roslavl', Russian Federation, 299 D6
Ross, Mount, mountain peak, New Zealand, 133 E5, 469
Ross, New Zealand, 133 C6
Ross, Point, Norfolk Island, 135 T13
Ross, U.S.A., 420 B1
Ross Bay Junction, Canada, 416 H3
Ross Carbery, Ireland, 309 C6
Ross Hill, mountain peak, Christmas Island, 134 N8
Ross Ice Shelf, Antarctica, 470 D6
Ross Island, Antarctica, 470 D7
Ross-on-Wye, England, U.K., 304 E3
Ross River, Canada, 410 F3
Ross Sea, Antarctica, 470 C7, 37
Rossan Point, Ireland, 309 C3
Rossano, Italy, 295 F6
Rossel Island, Papua New Guinea, 140 D5
Rossignol, Lake, Canada, 416 J7
Rossington, England, U.K., 307 G4
Rosslare, Ireland, 309 F5
Rosslare Harbour, Ireland, 309 F5
Rosso, Mauritania, 364 A1
Rossosh', Russian Federation, 298 E2
Rosston, U.S.A., 420 D7
Røssvatnet, lake, Norway, 284 F4
Rostāq, Afghanistan, 218 B1
Rosthern, Canada, 413 R5
Rostock, Germany, 288 F1
Rostov, Russian Federation, 299 G4
Rostov-na-Donu, Russian Federation, 222 B3
Rostovskaya Oblast', province, Russian Federation, 222 B3
Røsvik, Norway, 284 G3
Roswell, Georgia, U.S.A., 425 K2
Roswell, New Mexico, U.S.A., 423 L5
Rota, island, Northern Mariana Islands, 138 C3, 125
Rotenburg (Wümme), Germany, 288 D2
Rothbury, England, U.K., 307 G2
Rothbury Forest, England, U.K., 307 G2
Rothenburg ob der Tauber, Germany, 288 E4
Rothera, U.K. research station, Antarctica, 470 A4
Rotherham, England, U.K., 307 G4
Rothes, Scotland, U.K., 308 F3
Rothesay, Scotland, U.K., 308 D5
Rothwell, England, U.K., 305 G2
Roti, island, Indonesia, 198 C5
Roti, Selat, strait, Indonesia, 198 C5
Rotokohu, New Zealand, 133 C5
Rotomanu, New Zealand, 133 C6
Rotondella, Italy, 295 F5
Rotondo, Monte, mountain peak, Corse, France, 295 B4
Rotorua, Lake, New Zealand, 132 F3
Rotorua, New Zealand, 132 F4
Rott, river, Germany, 288 F4
Rotterdam, Netherlands, 288 B3, 241
Rottweil, Germany, 288 D4
Rotuma, island, Fiji, 139 F6
Roubaix, France, 291 F1
Rouen, France, 290 E2
Rouge, Le Piton, mountain peak, Réunion, 373 A1
Rouge, Pointe, point, Réunion, 373 A1
Rough River Lake, U.S.A., 421 K7
Rouleau, Canada, 413 S6
Round Island, Mauritius, 373 C1
Round Mountain, mountain peak, Australia, 135 L5
Round Mountain, U.S.A., 422 C1
Round Rock, Arizona, U.S.A., 423 J3
Round Rock, Texas, U.S.A., 424 D4
Roundup, U.S.A., 419 K3
Roura, French Guiana, 452 C2
Rous, Península, Chile, 460 D5
Rousay, island, Orkney, Scotland, U.K., 308 F1
Rouyn-Noranda, Canada, 416 B5
Rovaniemi, Finland, 285 M3
Rovereto, Italy, 294 C3
Roverud, Norway, 286 F2
Rovigo, Italy, 294 C3
Rovinari, Romania, 296 D3
Rovinj, Croatia, 294 D3
Rovkuly, Russian Federation, 285 Q4
Rovuma, river, Mozambique/Tanzania, 369 G5
Roxas, Palawan Island, Philippines, 204 B4
Roxas, Panay Island, Philippines, 204 C4
Roxborough, Tobago, Trinidad and Tobago, 461 B4
Roxby Downs, Australia, 135 H5
Roy, Montana, U.S.A., 419 K3
Roy, New Mexico, U.S.A., 423 L4
Royal Leamington Spa, England, U.K., 305 F2
Royal Tunbridge Wells, England, U.K., 305 H3
Royale, Isle, island, U.S.A., 421 J2
Royalton, U.S.A., 426 D3
Royalty, U.S.A., 423 M6
Royan, France, 290 D4
Roybridge, Scotland, U.K., 308 E4
Roye, France, 291 F2
Royston, England, U.K., 305 G2
Royston, U.S.A., 425 L2
Rožaj, Montenegro, 296 C4
Różan, Poland, 289 K2
Rozdil'na, Ukraine, 296 H2
Rozhniv, Ukraine, 296 E1
Rožňava, Slovakia, 289 K4
Roznov, Romania, 296 F2
Rrëshen, Albania, 296 B5
Rtishchevo, Russian Federation, 222 C2
Ruabon, Wales, U.K., 304 D2
Ruacana, Namibia, 370 B2
Ruahine, New Zealand, 132 E4
Ruahine Range, mountain range, New Zealand, 132 F5
Ruakaka, New Zealand, 132 E2
Ruapehu, Mount, mountain peak, New Zealand, 129 G5
Ruapuke Island, New Zealand, 133 B8
Ruatahuna, New Zealand, 132 F4
Ruawai, New Zealand, 132 E3
Ruba, Belarus, 299 C5
Rubi, Democratic Republic of the Congo, 369 E2
Rubio, mountain peak, Spain, 293 F2
Rubtsovsk, Russian Federation, 223 L2
Ruby, U.S.A., 410 D3
Ruby Mountains, mountain range, U.S.A., 422 F1
Rucăr, Romania, 296 E3
Rucava, Latvia, 287 K4
Rucheng, China, 206 C3
Rūdbār, Afghanistan, 221 H2
Rudewa, Tanzania, 369 F5
Rudkøbing, Denmark, 286 E5
Rudky, Ukraine, 289 L4
Rudna Glava, Serbia, 296 D3
Rudnaya Pristan', Russian Federation, 209 F1
Rudnya, Russian Federation, 299 C5
Rudnytsya, Ukraine, 296 G1
Rūdnyy, Kazakhstan, 222 G2
Rudo, Bosnia and Herzegovina, 296 B4
Rudong, China, 206 E1
Rue, France, 305 J4
Rufā'ah, Sudan, 366 D2
Ruffec, France, 290 E3
Rufiji, river, Tanzania, 369 G4
Rufino, Argentina, 458 D5
Rufisque, Senegal, 364 A2
Rufrufua, Indonesia, 199 F3
Rufunsa, Zambia, 369 E6
Rugāji, Latvia, 287 N4
Rugao, China, 206 E1
Rugby, England, U.K., 305 F2
Rugby, U.S.A., 420 D1
Rugeley, England, U.K., 305 F2
Rugozero, Russian Federation, 285 R4
Ruguy, Russian Federation, 299 D3
Ruhengeri, Rwanda, 369 E3
Ruhnu, island, Estonia, 287 L4
Ruhu, China, 207 C2
Rui'an, China, 206 E3
Ruichang, China, 206 C2
Ruidosa, U.S.A., 423 L7
Ruidoso, U.S.A., 423 L5
Ruijin, China, 206 D3
Ruili, China, 215 F4
Ruivo de Santana, Pico, mountain peak, Madeira, Portugal, 373 C3
Ruiz, Mexico, 430 D4
Ruiz, Nevado del, mountain peak, Colombia, 450 C3
Rūjiena, Latvia, 287 M4
Ruka, Finland, 285 P3
Ruki, river, Democratic Republic of the Congo, 368 C3
Rukungiri, Uganda, 369 E3
Rukwa, administrative region, Tanzania, 369 F4
Rukwa, Lake, Tanzania, 369 F4
Rum Cay, island, Bahamas, 428 G2
Ruma, Serbia, 296 B3
Rumah Kulit, Malaysia, 201 F2
Rumbek, Sudan, 366 C3
Rumberpon, Pulau, island, Indonesia, 199 F3
Rumginae, Papua New Guinea, 140 A4
Rumney, Wales, U.K., 304 D3
Rumoi, Japan, 209 H2
Rumonge, Burundi, 369 E3
Rumphi, Malawi, 369 F5
Runan, China, 206 C1
Runaway, Cape, New Zealand, 132 F3
Runcorn, England, U.K., 306 F4
Rundu, Namibia, 370 C2
Rungu, Democratic Republic of the Congo, 369 E2
Rungwa, Tanzania, 369 F4
Ru'nying, China, 215 G2
Ruo, river, China, 213 H4
Ruokolahti, Finland, 287 P2
Ruokto, Sweden, 284 J3
Ruoqiang, China, 212 F5
Ruovesi, Finland, 287 M1
Rupanco, Lago, lake, Chile, 460 C1
Rupat, Pulau, island, Indonesia, 200 C2
Rupea, Romania, 296 E2
Rupert, Baie de, bay, Canada, 415 Q6
Rupert, Rivière de, river, Canada, 416 C4
Rupia, Tanzania, 369 G4
Ruppert Coast, region, Antarctica, 470 C7
Rupununi, river, Guyana, 451 G3
Rurrenabaque, Bolivia, 455 E4
Rurutu, island, French Polynesia, 137 F3
Rusape, Zimbabwe, 371 F2
Ruscova, Romania, 296 E2
Ruse, administrative region, Bulgaria, 296 F4
Ruse, Bulgaria, 296 F4
Rusele, Sweden, 284 J4
Rush, Ireland, 309 F4
Rushan, China, 211 H5
Rushden, England, U.K., 305 G2
Rushville, U.S.A., 420 H5
Ruskeala, Russian Federation, 299 C2
Ruskträsk, Sweden, 284 J4
Rusnë, Lithuania, 287 K5
Ruso, U.S.A., 420 C2
Rusokastro, Bulgaria, 296 F4
Russas, Brazil, 453 G4
Russell, Canada, 414 D6
Russell, U.S.A., 420 D6
Russell Islands, Solomon Islands, 141 A1
Russell Lake, lake, Canada, 414 D3
Russellville, Alabama, U.S.A., 425 J2
Russellville, Arkansas, U.S.A., 424 F2
Russellville, Kentucky, U.S.A., 421 K7
Russian Federation, country, Asia/Europe, 196 J3, 86, 88, 90, 92, 94, 96, 100, 145, 164, 184, 186, 189, 190, 228, 229, 231, 232, 234, 235, 237, 261, 267, 268, 269, 270, 271, 272, 273, 378, 386, 464, 465, 475
Rustefjelbma, Norway, 285 P1
Rustenburg, South Africa, 371 E4
Rustic, U.S.A., 423 L1
Ruston, U.S.A., 424 F3
Ruten, mountain peak, Norway, 286 D2
Ruteng, Indonesia, 198 C5
Ruth, U.S.A., 422 F2
Rutherfordton, U.S.A., 425 M2
Ruthin, Wales, U.K., 304 D1
Rutland, unitary authority, England, U.K., 305 G2
Rutland, U.S.A., 426 D3
Rutland Island, Andaman and Nicobar Islands, India, 217 H4
Ruukki, Finland, 285 M4
Ruvuma, administrative region, Tanzania, 369 G5
Ruwāq, Jabal ar, mountain range, Syria, 225 D3
Ruwenzori Range, mountain range, Uganda, 369 F2, 334, 340, 341
Ruza, river, Russian Federation, 299 E5
Ruza, Russian Federation, 299 F5
Ruzayevka, Russian Federation, 222 C2
Ruzhany, Belarus, 289 M2
Ruzizi, river, Burundi/Rwanda/Democratic Republic of the Congo, 369 E3, 343
Ružomberok, Slovakia, 289 J4
Rwanda, country, Africa, 359 J7, 97, 313, 334, 337, 342, 343, 347
Ry, Denmark, 286 D4
Ryall, Mount, mountain peak, New Zealand, 133 C6
Ryanzanskaya Oblast', province, Russian Federation, 222 C2
Ryasnopil', Ukraine, 296 H2
Ryazan', Russian Federation, 298 E2, 272
Ryazanskaya Oblast', province, Russian Federation, 298 E2
Rybachiy, Poluostrov, peninsula, Russian Federation, 285 R2
Rybinsk (Andropov), Russian Federation, 299 G3
Rybinskoye Vodokhranilishche, reservoir, Russian Federation, 299 G3
Rybnik, Poland, 289 J3
Rybreka, Russian Federation, 299 E2
Rychwał, Poland, 289 J2
Rycroft, Canada, 413 K4
Ryd, Sweden, 286 G4
Ryde, England, U.K., 305 F4
Rye, Australia, 135 J6
Rye, England, U.K., 305 H4
Rye, river, England, U.K., 307 G3
Rye Bay, England, U.K., 305 H4
Ryegate, U.S.A., 419 K3
Rykhta, Ukraine, 296 F1
Ryki, Poland, 289 K3
Ryley, Canada, 413 N5
Rynda, river, Russian Federation, 285 T2
Rynda, Russian Federation, 285 T2
Ryōtsu, Japan, 209 G3
Rypin, Poland, 289 J2
Rysy, mountain peak, Slovakia, 289 J4, 267
Rytinki, Finland, 285 N4
Ryukyu Islands see Nansei-shotō, islands, Japan, 209 N8, 165
Ryukyu Trench, underwater feature, Pacific Ocean, 478 C3
Rzeczenica, Poland, 289 H2
Rzepin, Poland, 289 G2
Rzeszów, Poland, 289 L3
Rzhev, Russian Federation, 299 E4

## S

's-Gravenhage (The Hague), Netherlands, 288 B2, , 240, 241
's-Hertogenbosch, Netherlands, 288 B3
Sa Đéc, Vietnam, 203 E4
Sa Dragonera, island, Islas Baleares, Spain, 293 J3
Sa Kaeo, Thailand, 202 D3
Saacow, Somalia, 369 H2
Sa'ādatābād, Iran, 221 G3
Saale, river, Germany, 288 E3
Saalfeld, Germany, 288 E3
Saâne, river, France, 305 H5
Saarbrücken, Germany, 288 C4
Sääre, Estonia, 287 L4
Saaremaa, island, Estonia, 287 K3
Saarijärvi, Finland, 287 M1
Saariselkä, Finland, 285 N2
Saarland, state, Germany, 288 C4, 238
Saarlouis, Germany, 288 C4
Saasaai, Samoa, 141 B1
Saavedra, Argentina, 458 D5
Sab' Ābār, Syria, 225 D3
Saba, island, Netherlands Antilles, 427 D2, 391
Šabac, Serbia, 296 B3
Sabadell, Spain, 293 J2
Sabae, Japan, 209 G4
Sab'ah, Qārat as, mountain peak, Libya, 362 C3
Sabah, state, Malaysia, 201 G1, 151, 152

Sabalgarh, India, **218** D4
Sabana, La Gran, *grassland*, Venezuela, **451** F3
Sabana, Suriname, **452** B2
Sabanalarga, Colombia, **450** C1
Sabang, Indonesia, **200** A1
Săbăoani, Romania, **296** F2
Sabará, Brazil, **457** E5
Sabasṭīyah, West Bank, **225** C3
Sab'atayn, Ramlat as, *desert*, Yemen, **220** E5
Sabaya, Bolivia, **455** E5
Sabhā, Libya, **362** B3
Sabinal, Cayo, *island*, Cuba, **429** F2
Sabinal, Mexico, **430** D2
Sabinal, U.S.A., **424** C5
Sabinas, Mexico, **431** E3
Sabinas Hidalgo, Mexico, **431** E3
Sabini, Monti, *mountain range*, Italy, **295** D4
Sablayan, Philippines, **204** C3
Sable, Cape, Canada, **416** J8
Sablé-sur-Sarthe, France, **290** D3
Saboeiro, Brazil, **453** F5
Sabonkafi, Niger, **365** F2
Sabra, Tanjong, *point*, Indonesia, **199** E3
Sabres, France, **290** D4
Sabrina Coast, *region*, Antarctica, **470** F7
Sabsevār, Iran, **222** F5
Ṣabyā, Saudi Arabia, **363** H5
Sabzevārān, Iran, **221** G3
Sacaca, Bolivia, **455** E5
Sacedón, Spain, **293** F2
Săcel, Romania, **296** E2
Săcele, N. Romania, **296** E3
Săcele, S. E. Romania, **296** G3
Sachigo, Canada, **414** H5
Sachigo, *river*, Canada, **415** K4
Sachigo Lake, Canada, **414** H5
Sachs Harbour, Canada, **410** G2
Sachsen, *state*, Germany, **288** F3, *238*
Sachsen-Anhalt, *state*, Germany, **288** E2, *238*
Sackville, Canada, **417** J7
Saco, U.S.A., **419** L2
Sacol Island, Philippines, **204** C5
Sacramento, *river*, U.S.A., **418** C6
Sacramento, U.S.A., **422** C2, *386*
Sacramento Mountains, *mountain range*, U.S.A., **423** L5
Săcueni, Romania, **296** D2
Sada, South Africa, **371** E5
Ṣadad, Syria, **225** D2
Ṣa'dah, Yemen, **220** D5
Sadāseopet, India, **216** D2
Saddle Peak, *mountain peak*, Andaman and Nicobar Islands, India, **217** H3
Sadêng, China, **214** E3
Ṣadḥ, Oman, **221** G5
Sadi, Ethiopia, **366** E3
Sadīch, Iran, **221** G3
Sado, *river*, Portugal, **292** C3
Sado-shima, *island*, Japan, **209** G3
Sadot, Egypt, **225** C4
Sadovoye, Russian Federation, **298** F3
Sadri, India, **218** C4
Sädvajaure, *lake*, Sweden, **284** G3
Sæby, Denmark, **286** E4
Ṣaf, Rāshīn, Egypt, **225** A5
Safata Bay, Samoa, **141** B1
Säffle, Sweden, **286** F3
Safford, U.S.A., **423** J5
Saffron Walden, England, U.K., **305** H2
Safi, Morocco, **360** E2
Safid Khers, *mountain range*, Afghanistan, **223** J5
Sāfītā, Syria, **225** D2
Safonovo, Russian Federation, **299** D5
Safotu, Samoa, **141** B1
Safune, Samoa, **141** B1
Sag Sag, Papua New Guinea, **140** C4
Saga, China, **214** C3
Saga, Japan, **208** E4
Sagaing, *division*, Myanmar, **205** B3
Sagaing, Myanmar, **205** B3
Sagami-wan, *bay*, Japan, **209** G4
Sāgar, India, **218** D5
Sagauli, India, **219** F4
Saggi, Har, *mountain peak*, Israel, **225** C4
Sāghand, Iran, **221** G2
Saghyz, Kazakhstan, **222** E3
Saginaw, U.S.A., **421** M4
Saginaw Bay, U.S.A., **421** M4
Sagleipie, Liberia, **364** C3
Sagone, Golfe de, *gulf*, Corse, France, **295** B4
Sagone, Samoa, **141** B1
Sagra, *mountain peak*, Spain, **293** F4
Sagres, Ponta de, *point*, Portugal, **292** C4
Sagres, Portugal, **292** C4
Sagu, Myanmar, **205** B3
Sagua de Tánamo, Cuba, **429** G2
Sagua la Grande, Cuba, **429** E2
Saguache, U.S.A., **423** K2
Sagunto, Spain, **293** G3
Sagwon, U.S.A., **410** E3
Sa'gya, China, **214** C3
Saḥāb, Jordan, **225** D4
Sahagán, Colombia, **450** C2
Sahagún, Spain, **292** E1
Sahara, *desert*, N. Africa, **356** E5, *28, 49, 74, 86, 87, 88, 91, 100, 312, 313, 315, 316, 318, 324, 325, 328, 336*
Sahāranpur, India, **218** D3
Saharsa, India, **219** F4
Sahel, Africa, *region*, **356** E5, *312, 313, 324, 325, 328, 337*
Sāhibganj, India, **219** F4
Sah'īrah, Jabal, *mountain peak*, Egypt, **225** C5
Sāhīwāl, N. Punjab, Pakistan, **218** C3
Sāhīwāl, S. Punjab, Pakistan, **218** C3
Sahlābād, Iran, **221** G2
Ṣaḥrā', Jabal, *mountain peak*, Egypt, **225** C6
Sahuaripa, Mexico, **430** C2
Sahuayo, Mexico, **430** E4
Sai, *river*, Indonesia, **201** E2
Sai Kung, China, **207** C4
Saibai, Australia, **140** A5
Saibai Island, Australia, **140** A5
Sa'id Bundas, Sudan, **366** B3
Saïda, Algeria, **361** G2
Saidor, Papua New Guinea, **140** B4
Saidpur, Bangladesh, **214** D4
Saigon *see* Thanh Phố Hồ Chí Minh, Vietnam, **203** E4, *97, 153*
Saihan Toroi, China, **213** J4
Saija, Finland, **285** P3
Saiki, Japan, **208** E4
Saimaa, *lake*, Finland, **287** N2
Saindak, Pakistan, **221** H3
Sainsbury Point, Canada, **415** Q4
St Abb's Head, *point*, Scotland, U.K., **308** G5
St Agnes, England, U.K., **304** B4
St Alban's, Canada, **417** P6
St Albans, England, U.K., **305** G3
St Albans, U.S.A., **421** N6
St Alban's Head, *point*, England, U.K., **304** E4
St Albert, Canada, **413** N5
Saint-Amand-en-Puisaye, France, **291** F3
Saint-Amand-Montrond, France, **290** F3
St Andrä, Austria, **289** G5
Saint-André, Réunion, **373** A1
St Andrews, Scotland, U.K., **308** G4
St Anne, Channel Islands, **304** E5
St Ansgar, U.S.A., **420** G4
St Anthony, Canada, **417** P4
St-Apollinaire, Canada, **416** F6
Saint Arnaud, New Zealand, **133** D5
St Arvans, Wales, U.K., **304** E3
St Asaph, Wales, U.K., **304** D1
St-Augustin, Canada, **417** M4
St-Augustin, *river*, Canada, **417** M4
St Augustine, U.S.A., **425** M5
St Austell, England, U.K., **304** C4
Saint-Avold, France, **291** H2
Saint-Barthélemy, Pic de, *mountain peak*, France, **290** E5
St Bees, England, U.K., **306** E3
Saint-Benoît, Réunion, **373** A1
St Brides Bay, Wales, U.K., **304** B3
Saint-Brieuc, France, **290** C2
St Brieux, Canada, **413** S5
Saint-Calais, France, **290** E3
St Catharines, Canada, **421** P4
St Catherines Island, U.S.A., **424** M4
St Catherine's Point, England, U.K., **305** F4
St Charles, Maryland, U.S.A., **426** B5
St Charles, South Dakota, U.S.A., **420** D4
Saint-Chély-d'Apcher, France, **291** F4
St Christoffelberg, *mountain peak*, Curaçao, Netherlands Antilles, **461** C3
St Clair, Lake, Canada, **421** M4
Saint-Claude, France, **291** G3
St Clears, Wales, U.K., **304** C3
St Cloud, U.S.A., **420** F3
St Columb Major, England, U.K., **304** C4
St Croix, *island*, U.S. Virgin Islands, **427** C2
St Croix, *river*, U.S.A., **420** G3
St Croix Falls, U.S.A., **420** G3
St David's, Wales, U.K., **304** B3
St David's Head, *point*, Wales, U.K., **304** B3
Saint-Denis, Réunion, **373** A1, *354*
Saint-Dié, France, **291** H2
Saint-Dizier, France, **291** G2
St Elias Mountains, *mountain range*, Canada, **412** A2
St Elie, French Guiana, **452** C2
St Endellion, England, U.K., **304** C4
Saint-Étienne, France, **291** G4
Saint-Étienne-du-Rouvray, France, **305** J5
St Eustatius, *island*, Netherlands Antilles, **427** D2, *391*
St-Félicien, Canada, **416** E5
St Finan's Bay, Ireland, **309** B6
Saint-Florent, Corse, France, **294** B4
Saint-Flour, France, **291** F4
St Francis, U.S.A., **420** C6
St Francis Bay, Namibia, **370** B4
St George, Australia, **135** K4
St George, Canada, **416** H7
St George, Cape, Papua New Guinea, **140** D4
St George, Point, U.S.A., **418** B6
St George, South Carolina, U.S.A., **425** M3
St George, Utah, U.S.A., **422** G3
St George Island, U.S.A., **425** K5
St-Georges, Canada, **416** F6
St-Georges, French Guiana, **452** C2
St George's, Grenada, **427** D3, *398*
St George's Bay, Canada, **417** M5
St George's Channel, Ireland/Wales, **304** A3
St Germans, England, U.K., **304** C4
Saint-Gilles-les Bains, Réunion, **373** A1
Saint-Girons, France, **290** E5
St Govan's Head, *point*, Wales, U.K., **304** C3
St Gregory, Mount, *mountain peak*, Canada, **417** M5
St Helena, *island*, Atlantic Ocean, **373** B3, *244*
St Helena, *U.K. dependency*, Atlantic Ocean, **359** E8, *276, 355*
Saint Helena Bay, South Africa, **370** C5
St Helens, Australia, **135** K7
St Helens, England, U.K., **306** F4
St Helens, Mount, *mountain peak*, U.S.A., **418** C3, *383*
St Helens, U.S.A., **418** C4
St Helier, Jersey, Channel Islands, **290** C2, *279*
St Hilary, England, U.K., **304** B4
St-Hyacinthe, Canada, **416** E7
St Ignace, U.S.A., **421** L3
St Ignace Island, Canada, **415** K7
St Ishmael, Wales, U.K., **304** C3
St Ive, England, U.K., **304** C4
St Ives, Cambridgeshire, England, U.K., **305** G2
St Ives, Cornwall, England, U.K., **304** B4
St Ives Bay, England, U.K., **304** B4
Saint-Jean, Lac, *lake*, Canada, **416** F5
St Jean Baptiste, Canada, **414** F7
Saint-Jean-d'Angély, France, **290** D4
Saint-Jean-de-Maurienne, France, **291** H4
Saint-Jean-de-Monts, France, **290** C3
Saint-Jean-Pied-de-Port, France, **290** D5
St-Jean-Port-Joli, Canada, **416** F6
St-Jean-sur-Richelieu, Canada, **416** E7
St-Jérôme, Canada, **416** D7
St Joe, U.S.A., **418** F3
Saint John, Canada, **416** H7
St John, Cape, Canada, **417** P4
St John, *river*, U.S.A., **426** F1
St John, U.S.A., **418** F3
St John Island, Canada, **417** N4
St John's, Antigua and Barbuda, **427** D2, *395*
St John's, Canada, **417** Q6, *381*
Saint Johns, U.S.A., **423** J4
St John's Chapel, England, U.K., **306** F3
St John's Point, Ireland, **309** D3
St Johnsbury, U.S.A., **426** D2
St Joseph, Lake, Canada, **414** J6
Saint-Joseph, New Caledonia, **141** A3
Saint-Joseph, Réunion, **373** A1
Saint Joseph, Trinidad, Trinidad and Tobago, **461** C4
St Joseph, U.S.A., **420** F6
St Joseph Point, U.S.A., **425** K5
Saint-Junien, France, **290** E4
St Just, England, U.K., **304** B4
Saint-Just-en-Chaussée, France, **305** K5
St Keverne, England, U.K., **304** B4
St Kitts und Nevis, *country*, Caribbean Sea, **409** S7, *378, 387, 395*
St Laurent, Canada, **414** F6
St-Laurent du Maroni, French Guiana, **452** C2
St Lawrence, Canada, **417** P6
St Lawrence, Gulf of, Canada, **417** K5, *382*
St Lawrence, *river*, Canada/U.S.A., **426** C2, *93, 376, 380*
St Lawrence Island, U.S.A., **410** B3
St Lawrence Seaway, *river*, Canada/U.S.A., **416** D7
St Léonard, Canada, **416** H6
Saint-Leu, Réunion, **373** A1
St Lewis, *river*, Canada, **417** N3
Saint-Lô, France, **290** D2
St Louis, Canada, **413** S5
Saint-Louis, Réunion, **373** A1
Saint-Louis, Senegal, **364** A1
St Louis, U.S.A., **420** H6
St Lucia, *country*, Caribbean Sea, **409** S7, *378, 396, 397*
St Lucia, Lake, South Africa, **371** F4
St Lucia Channel, Caribbean Sea, **427** D3
St Maarten, *island*, Netherlands Antilles, **427** D2
St Magnus Bay, Shetland, Scotland, U.K., **308** K7
Saint-Malo, France, **290** D1
Saint-Malo, Golfe de, *Golf*, France, **290** C2
Saint-Marc, Haiti, **429** G3
Saint-Marcel, Mont, *mountain peak*, French Guiana, **452** C2
Saint-Marcellin, France, **291** G4
St Margaret's Hope, Orkney, Scotland, U.K., **308** G2
St Maries, U.S.A., **418** F3
Saint Marks, U.S.A., **425** K4
St Martin, Channel Islands, **304** E5
St Martin, *island*, Guadeloupe, **427** D2, *391*
St Martin, Lake, Canada, **414** E6
Saint-Martory, France, **290** E5
St Mary, Mount, *mountain peak*, New Zealand, **133** B7
St Mary, U.S.A., **418** H2
St Mary Peak, *mountain peak*, Australia, **135** H5
St Mary's, Cape, Canada, **417** P6
St Marys, Ohio, U.S.A., **421** L5
St Mary's, Orkney, Scotland, U.K., **308** G2
St Marys, Pennsylvania, U.S.A., **421** P5
St Marys, *river*, Canada, **417** K7
St Marys, Trinidad, Trinidad and Tobago, **461** C4
St Mary's Bay, Canada, **417** Q6
Saint-Mathieu, Pointe de, *point*, France, **290** B2
St Matthew Island, U.S.A., **410** B3
St Matthias Group, *islands*, Papua New Guinea, **140** C3
St Mawes, England, U.K., **304** B4
St-Michel-des-Saints, Canada, **416** E6
Saint-Mihiel, France, **291** G2
Saint Moritz, Switzerland, **291** J3
Saint-Nazaire, France, **290** C3
Saint-Nectaire, France, **291** F4
St Neots, England, U.K., **305** G2
Saint-Nicolas d'Aliermont, France, **305** J5
Saint-Niklaas, Belgium, **288** B3
Saint-Omer, France, **290** F1
St Osyth, England, U.K., **305** J3
Saint-Palais, France, **290** D5
St-Pascal, Canada, **416** G6
St Paul, Arkansas, U.S.A., **424** F2
St Paul, Canada, **413** P5
Saint Paul, Cape, Ghana, **364** E3
St Paul, Minnesota, U.S.A., **420** G3, *386*
St Paul, Nebraska, U.S.A., **420** D5
Saint-Paul, Réunion, **373** A1
St-Paul, *river*, Canada, **417** M3
Saint-Péray, France, **291** G4
St Peter, U.S.A., **420** G3
St Peter in the Wood, Channel Islands, **304** E5
St Peter Port, Guernsey, Channel Islands, **290** C2, *278, 279*
St Peters, Canada, **417** K6
St Petersburg *see* Sankt-Peterburg, Russian Federation, **299** C3, *271, 272, 273*
St Petersburg, U.S.A., **425** L6
Saint-Philippe, Réunion, **373** A1
St Philips, Canada, **414** D6
Saint-Pierre, Réunion, **373** A1
St Pierre, St Pierre and Miquelon, **417** N6, *376, 391*

St Pierre and Miquelon, *French territorial collectivity*, Atlantic Ocean, **409** T4, *245*, *391*
Saint-Pierre-Église, France, **305** F5
Saint-Pierre-en-Port, France, **305** H5
St Pierre Island, Seychelles, **372** C2
Saint-Pol-sur-Mer, France, **305** K3
Saint-Pol-sur-Ternoise, France, **305** K4
St Pölten, Austria, **289** G4
Saint-Pons-de-Thomières, France, **290** F5
Saint-Pourçain-sur-Sioule, France, **291** F3
St Quentin, Canada, **416** H6
Saint-Quentin, France, **291** F2
Saint-Riquier, France, **305** J4
Saint-Saëns, France, **305** J5
St Sampson, Channel Islands, **304** E5
Saint-Sauveur-sur-Tinée, France, **291** H4
St-Siméon, Canada, **416** G6
St Simons Island, U.S.A., **425** M4
St Stephen, Canada, **416** H7
St Stephen, U.S.A., **425** N3
St Theresa Point, Canada, **414** G5
St Thomas, Canada, **421** N4
St Thomas, U.S.A., **420** E1
Saint-Tropez, France, **291** H5
Saint-Vaast-la-Hougue, France, **290** D2
Saint-Valéry-en-Caux, France, **290** E2
Saint-Valéry-sur-Somme, France, **290** E1
Saint-Vallier, France, **291** G3
St Vincent, Gulf, Australia, **135** H5
St Vincent and the Grenadines, *country*, Caribbean Sea, **409** S7, *378*, *396*, *397*
St Vincent Passage, Caribbean Sea, **427** D3
Saint-Vivien-de-Médoc, France, **290** D4
St Walburg, Canada, **413** Q5
St Xavier, U.S.A., **419** L4
Saint-Yrieix-la-Perche, France, **290** E4
Sainte-Adresse, France, **305** H5
Sainte-Anne, Lac, *lake*, Canada, **416** H4
Ste-Agathe-des-Monts, Canada, **416** D6
Sainte-Énimie, France, **291** F4
Sainte-Marie, Martinique, **427** D3
Sainte-Marie, Réunion, **373** A1
Sainte-Mère-Église, France, **305** F5
Sainte-Rose, Guadeloupe, **427** D2
Sainte-Rose, Réunion, **373** A1
Ste-Rose-du-Lac, Canada, **414** E6
Sainte-Suzanne, Réunion, **373** A1
Saintes, France, **290** D4
Saintes-Maries-de-la-Mer, France, **291** G5
Saintfield, Northern Ireland, U.K., **309** G3
Sāipal, *mountain peak*, Nepal, **219** E3
Saipan, *island*, Northern Mariana Islands, **138** C3, *125*
Sajam, Indonesia, **199** F3
Sajama, Bolivia, **455** E5
Sajama, Nevado, *mountain peak*, Bolivia, **455** E5, *440*, *441*
Sājir, Ra's, *cape*, Oman, **220** F5
Sājūr, *river*, Syria/Turkey, **225** D1
Saka, Ethiopia, **367** E3
Sakākah, Saudi Arabia, **363** H3
Sakakawea, Lake, U.S.A., **420** C2
Sakami, Lac, Canada, **416** C3
Sakami, *river*, Canada, **416** D3
Sakaraha, Madagascar, **372** A5
Sakassou, Côte d'Ivoire, **364** C3
Sakata, Japan, **209** G3
Saketa, Indonesia, **198** D3
Sakété, Benin, **365** E3
Sakha, Respublika, *republic*, Russian Federation, **301** P3
Sakhalin, Ostrov, *island*, Russian Federation, **301** R4
Sakht-Sar, Iran, **222** E5
Şäki, Azerbaijan, **222** D4
Saki, Nigeria, **365** E3
Šakiai, Lithuania, **287** L5
Sakishima-shotō, *islands*, Japan, **209** M8
Sakleshpur, India, **216** C3
Sakmara, *river*, Russian Federation, **222** F2
Sakon Nakhon, Thailand, **203** E2
Sakra, Pulau, *island*, Singapore, **200** J7
Sakrivier, South Africa, **370** D5
Sakura, Japan, **209** H4
Säkylä, Finland, **287** L2
Sal, *island*, Cape Verde, **360** Q8
Sal Rei, Cape Verde, **360** Q8
Šal'a, Slovakia, **289** H4
Sala, Sweden, **286** H3
Sala y Gómez, *Chilean dependency*, Pacific Ocean, **105** P11
Salacgrīva, Latvia, **287** M4
Salada, Bahía, *bay*, Chile, **458** B3
Saladas, Argentina, **459** E3
Saladillo, Argentina, **459** E5
Saladillo, *river*, Córdoba, Argentina, **458** D4
Saladillo, *river*, Santa Fé, Argentina, **459** E4
Saladillo, *river*, Santiago del Estero, Argentina, **458** D3
Salado, *river*, Buenos Aires, Argentina, **459** E5
Salado, *river*, Formosa, Argentina, **459** E2
Salado, *river*, Mexico, **431** E3
Salado, *river*, Rio Nego, Argentina, **460** E1
Salado, *river*, Santiago del Estero, Argentina, **458** D3
Saladougou, Guinea, **364** C2
Salaga, Ghana, **364** D3
Sala'ilua, Samoa, **141** B1
Salal, Chad, **365** H2
Şalālah, Oman, **221** F5
Salālah, Sudan, **363** G4
Salamá, Guatemala, **428** C4
Salamanca, Chile, **458** B4
Salamanca, Mexico, **431** E4
Salamanca, Spain, **292** E2
Salamat, *prefecture*, Chad, **366** B2
Salamaua, Papua New Guinea, **140** B4
Salamina, Colombia, **450** C3
Salamīyah, Syria, **225** D2
Salamo, Papua New Guinea, **140** C5
Salani, Samoa, **141** B1
Salantai, Lithuania, **287** K4
Salas, Spain, **292** D1
Salas de los Infantes, Spain, **293** F1
Salatiga, Indonesia, **201** E4
Sălătrucu, Romania, **296** E3
Salau, France, **290** E5
Salavat, Russian Federation, **222** F2
Salawati, Pulau, *island*, Indonesia, **199** E3
Salāya, India, **218** B5
Salazar, Argentina, **458** D5
Salazie, Réunion, **373** A1
Salbris, France, **290** F3
Salcea, Romania, **296** F2
Šalčininkai, Lithuania, **287** M5
Salcombe, England, U.K., **304** D4
Sălcuţa, Romania, **296** D3
Salda Gölü, *lake*, Turkey, **297** G7
Saldaña, Colombia, **450** C3
Saldanha, South Africa, **370** C5
Saldungaray, Argentina, **458** E6
Saldus, Latvia, **287** L4
Sale, Australia, **135** K6
Sale, England, U.K., **306** F4
Salehurst, England, U.K., **305** H4
Salekhard, Russian Federation, **300** H3
Salelologa, Samoa, **141** B1
Salem, Illinois, U.S.A., **421** J6
Salem, India, **216** D4
Salem, Missouri, U.S.A., **420** H7
Salem, Ohio, U.S.A., **421** N5
Salem, Oregon, U.S.A., **418** C4, *386*
Salem, South Dakota, U.S.A., **420** E4
Salemi, Sicilia, Italy, **295** D7
Salen, Scotland, U.K., **308** D4
Sälen, Sweden, **286** F2
Salernes, France, **291** H5
Salerno, Golfo di, *gulf*, Italy, **295** E5
Salerno, Italy, **295** E5
Salford, England, U.K., **306** F4
Salgado, *river*, Brazil, **453** F5
Salgótarján, Hungary, **289** J4
Salgueiro, Brazil, **453** F5
Salibea, Trinidad, Trinidad and Tobago, **461** C4
Salida, U.S.A., **423** L2
Salihli, Turkey, **297** G6
Salihorsk, Belarus, **298** C2
Salima, Malawi, **369** F5
Salina, Arizona, U.S.A., **423** J3
Salina, Isola, *island*, Italy, **295** E6
Salina, Kansas, U.S.A., **420** E6
Salina, Utah, U.S.A., **423** H2
Salina Cruz, Mexico, **431** G5
Salinas, Brazil, **457** E4
Salinas, Cabo de, *cape*, Islas Baleares, Spain, **293** J3
Salinas, Ecuador, **450** B5
Salinas, Pampa de la, *plain*, Argentina, **458** C4
Salinas, Punta, *point*, Dominican Republic, **429** H3
Salinas, Punta, *point*, Róbinson Crusoe Island, Archipiélago Juan Fernández, Chile, **461** C2
Salinas, U.S.A., **422** C3
Salinas de Garci Mendoza, Bolivia, **455** E5
Salinas de Hidalgo, Mexico, **430** E4
Salinas ó Lachay, Punta, *point*, Peru, **454** B3
Salinas Peak, *mountain peak*, U.S.A., **423** K5
Saline Bay, Trinidad, Trinidad and Tobago, **461** C4
Saline Lake, U.S.A., **424** F4
Salinitas, Chile, **458** B2
Salinópolis, Brazil, **452** D3
Salisbury, England, U.K., **305** F3
Salisbury, Maryland, U.S.A., **426** C5
Salisbury, North Carolina, U.S.A., **425** M2
Salisbury Island, Canada, **411** M3
Salisbury Plain, England, U.K., **305** E3
Sălişte, Romania, **296** D3
Salitre, *river*, Brazil, **457** F3
Şalkhad, Syria, **225** D3
Salla, Finland, **285** P3
Salliqueló, Argentina, **458** D5
Sallisaw, U.S.A., **424** E2
Salluit, Canada, **411** M3
Sallūm, Sudan, **363** G5
Sally's Cove, Canada, **417** N5
Salmās, Iran, **224** F5
Salmi, Russian Federation, **299** C2
Salmi, Sweden, **284** K2
Salmon, *river*, U.S.A., **418** F4
Salmon, U.S.A., **418** H4
Salmon Arm, Canada, **413** K6
Salmon Peak, *mountain peak*, U.S.A., **424** B5
Salmon River Mountains, *mountain range*, U.S.A., **418** F4
Salo, Finland, **287** L2
Saloinen, Finland, **285** M4
Salonica *see* Thessaloniki, Greece, **297** D5, *265*
Salonta, Romania, **296** C2
Salor, *river*, Spain, **292** D3
Salsacate, Argentina, **458** D4
Sal'sk, Russian Federation, **298** F3
Salso, *river*, Sicilia, Italy, **295** D7
Salsomaggiore Terme, Italy, **294** B3
Salt, *river*, U.S.A., **423** H5
Salt Basin, U.S.A., **423** L6
Salt Flat, U.S.A., **423** L6
Salt Lake City, U.S.A., **423** H1, *386*
Salta, Argentina, **458** D2
Salta, *province*, Argentina, **458** D2
Saltash, England, U.K., **304** C4
Saltburn-by-the-Sea, England, U.K., **307** H3
Saltcoats, Scotland, U.K., **308** E5
Saltee Islands, Ireland, **309** F5
Saltillo, Mexico, **431** E3
Salto, Argentina, **459** E5
Salto, *river*, Italy, **295** D4
Salto, Uruguay, **459** F4
Salto da Divisa, Brazil, **457** F4
Salto del Guairá, Paraguay, **459** F2
Salto Santiago, Represa de, *reservoir*, Brazil, **459** G2
Salton Sea, *lake*, U.S.A., **422** E5
Saltpond, Ghana, **364** D3
Saltvik, Finland, **287** K2
Saluafata, Samoa, **141** B1
Saluda, U.S.A., **425** M3
Salūm, Khalīj as, *gulf*, Egypt/Libya, **362** E2
Sālūmbar, India, **218** C4
Saluzzo, Italy, **294** A3
Salvacion, Philippines, **204** D4
Salvador, Brazil, **457** F3
Salvaterra, Brazil, **452** D3
Salvatierra, Mexico, **431** E4
Salviac, France, **290** E4
Salween, *river*, Asia, **195** L7; *see also* Nu, *river*, China, **215** F3; Thanlwin, *river*, Myanmar, **205** C4, *158*
Salyan, Azerbaijan, **222** D5
Salzburg, Austria, **288** F5, *249*
Salzburg, *state*, Austria, **288** F5
Salzgitter, Germany, **288** E2
Salzkammergut, *region*, Austria, **289** F5
Salzwedel, Germany, **288** E2
Sām, India, **218** B4
Sam A Tsuen, China, **207** C3
Sam Rayburn Reservoir, U.S.A., **424** E4
Sâm Sơn, Vietnam, **203** E2
Samagaltay, Russian Federation, **223** N2
Samaipata, Bolivia, **455** F5
Samal Island, Philippines, **204** D5
Samalaeulu, Samoa, **141** B1
Samālūţ, Egypt, **363** F3
Samaná, Bahía de, *bay*, Dominican Republic, **429** H3
Samandağı, Turkey, **225** C1
Samangān, Afghanistan, **218** B2
Samar, *island*, Philippines, **204** D4
Samara, Russian Federation, **222** E2
Samarai, Papua New Guinea, **140** C5
Samariapo, Venezuela, **451** E3
Samarinda, Indonesia, **201** G3
Samarqand, Uzbekistan, **222** H5, *91*, *185*, *188*
Sāmarrā', Iraq, **363** H2, *182*
Samarskaya Oblast', *province*, Russian Federation, **222** D2
Samasodu, Solomon Islands, **141** A1
Samastīpur, India, **219** F4
Samataitai, Samoa, **141** B1
Samatau, Samoa, **141** B1
Samba Cajú, Angola, **368** C4
Samba, Democratic Republic of the Congo, **369** E3
Sambaliung, Pegunungan, *mountain range*, Indonesia, **201** G2
Sambalpur, India, **219** F5
Sambar, Tanjong, *point*, Indonesia, **201** E3
Sambas, Indonesia, **201** E2
Sambau, Indonesia, **200** D3
Sambava, Madagascar, **372** C3
Sāmbhar, India, **218** C4
Sambir, Ukraine, **289** L4
Sambito, *river*, Brazil, **453** F5
Sambo, Angola, **368** C5
Samborombón, Bahía, *bay*, Argentina, **459** F5
Sambre, *river*, France, **291** F1, *242*
Sambro, Canada, **417** K7
Samch'ŏk, South Korea, **208** E3
Samdari, India, **218** C4
Same, Tanzania, **369** G3
Samer, France, **305** J4
Samfya, Zambia, **369** E5
Samḩah, *island*, Suquṭrá (Socotra), Yemen, **373** B2
Sami, India, **218** B5
Samia, Tanjong, *point*, Indonesia, **198** C2
Samijiyŏn, North Korea, **211** K4
Samka, Myanmar, **205** C3
Samnū, Libya, **362** B3
Samoa, *country*, Pacific Ocean, **131** H3, *94*, *108*, *113*, *114*, *126*, *127*
Samobor, Croatia, **294** E3
Samokov, Bulgaria, **296** D4
Šamorín, Slovakia, **289** H4
Samos, Dodekanisos, Greece, **297** F7
Samos, *island*, Dodekanisos, Greece, **297** F7
Samosir, Pulau, *island*, Indonesia, **200** B2
Samothraki, *island*, Greece, **297** E5
Sampit, Indonesia, **201** F3
Sampit, *river*, Indonesia, **201** F3
Sampit, Teluk, *bay*, Indonesia, **201** F3
Sampun, Papua New Guinea, **140** D4
Sampwe, Democratic Republic of the Congo, **369** E4
Samsang, China, **214** B3
Samsø Bælt, *strait*, Denmark, **286** E5
Samsu, North Korea, **208** E2
Samsun, Turkey, **224** E4
Samucumbi, Angola, **368** C5
Samui, Ko, *island*, Thailand, **202** D4
Samut Prakan, Thailand, **202** D3
Samut Sakhon, Thailand, **202** D3
Samut Songkhram, Thailand, **202** D3
San, Mali, **364** D2
San, *river*, Cambodia, **203** E3
San Agustín, Argentina, **459** E5
San Agustín de Valle Fértil, Argentina, **458** C4
San Ambrosio, Isla, *island*, Chile, **449** E6
San Andreas, U.S.A., **422** C2
San Andrés, Bahía de, *bay*, San Andrés, Colombia, **461** B1
San Andrés, Bolivia, **455** F4
San Andrés, *island*, Colombia, Caribbean Sea, **461** B1
San Andres, Philippines, **204** C3
San Andrés, San Andrés, Colombia, **461** B1
San Andrés Tuxtla, Mexico, **431** G5
San Angelo, U.S.A., **424** B4
San Antonio, Belize, **428** C3
San Antonio, Bolivia, **455** F4
San Antonio, Cabo, *cape*, Cuba, **428** D2
San Antonio, Catamarca, Argentina, **458** D3
San Antonio, Chile, **458** B4
San Antonio, Mount, *mountain peak*, U.S.A., **422** E4
San Antonio, San Luis, Argentina, **458** C4
San Antonio, U.S.A., **424** C5
San Antonio, Venezuela, **451** E3
San Antonio Abad, Islas Baleares, Spain, **293** H3
San Antonio Bay, Philippines, **204** B4
San Antonio de Caparo, Venezuela, **450** D2
San Antonio de los Cobres, Argentina, **458** C2
San Antonio de Tamanaco, Venezuela, **451** E2

San Antonio Oeste, Argentina, **460** E1
San Ardo, U.S.A., **422** C3
San Augustin, Cape, Philippines, **204** D5
San Bartolo, Mexico, **431** E4
San Bartolomeo in Galdo, Italy, **295** E5
San Benedetto del Tronto, Italy, **294** D4
San Bernando, Argentina, **458** E3
San Bernardino, U.S.A., **422** E4
San Bernardino Mountains, *mountain range*, U.S.A., **422** E4
San Bernardo, Chile, **458** B4
San Bernardo, Mexico, **430** D3
San Blás, Archipiélago, *islands*, Panama, **429** F5
San Blas, Nayarit, Mexico, **430** D4
San Blas, Sinaloa, Mexico, **430** C3
San Borja, Bolivia, **455** E4
San Buenaventura, Mexico, **430** E3
San Camilo, Argentina, **458** E2
San Carlos, Argentina, **458** C4
San Carlos, Bolivia, **455** F4
San Carlos, Chile, **458** B5
San Carlos, Luzon Island, Philippines, **204** C3
San Carlos, Mexico, **431** F3
San Carlos, N. Venezuela, **451** E2
San Carlos, Negros Island, Philippines, **204** C4
San Carlos, Nicaragua, **428** D5
San Carlos, *river*, Paraguay, **459** E2
San Carlos, S. Venezuela, **451** E4
San Carlos, Uruguay, **459** F5
San Carlos, U.S.A., **423** H5
San Carlos Centro, Argentina, **458** E4
San Carlos de Bariloche, Argentina, **460** C1
San Carlos de Bolívar, Argentina, **458** E5
San Carlos del Zulia, Venezuela, **450** D2
San Ciro de Acosta, Mexico, **431** F4
San Clemente, Chile, **458** B5
San Clemente, *island*, U.S.A., **422** D5
San Clemente, Spain, **293** F3
San Clemente, U.S.A., **422** E5
San Cristóbal, Argentina, **458** E4
San Cristóbal, Bolivia, **455** E5
San Cristóbal, Dominican Republic, **429** H3
San Cristóbal, Isla, *island*, Islas Galápagos (Galapagos Islands), Ecuador, **461** A2, *116*
San Cristóbal, Venezuela, **450** D2
San Cristóbal de las Casas, Mexico, **431** G5
San Diego, California, U.S.A., **422** E5
San Diego, Texas, U.S.A., **424** C6
San Dimas, Mexico, **430** D3
San Donà di Piave, Italy, **294** D3
San Estanislao, Paraguay, **459** F2
San Esteban de Gormaz, Spain, **293** F2
San Felipe, Baja California, Mexico, **430** B2
San Felipe, Chile, **458** B4
San Felipe, Guanajuato, Mexico, **431** E4
San Felipe, Providencia, Colombia, **461** C1
San Felipe, Venezuela, **451** E1
San Felipe de Jesús, Mexico, **430** D3
San Feliu de Guíxols, Spain, **293** J2
San Félix, Isla, *island*, Chile, **449** D6
San Fernando, Argentina, **459** E5
San Fernando, Central Luzon Island, Philippines, **204** C3
San Fernando, Chile, **458** B5
San Fernando, Mexico, **431** F3
San Fernando, N. Luzon Island, Philippines, **204** C2
San Fernando, Spain, **292** D4
San Fernando, Trinidad, Trinidad and Tobago, **461** C4
San Fernando de Apure, Venezuela, **451** E2
San Fernando de Atabapo, Venezuela, **451** E3
San Fernando del Valle de Catamarca, Argentina, **458** D3
San Fidel, U.S.A., **423** K4
San Francique, Trinidad, Trinidad and Tobago, **461** C4
San Francisco, Argentina, **458** D4
San Francisco, Cabo de, *cape*, Ecuador, **450** B4
San Francisco, Mexico, **430** B2
San Francisco, Panama, **429** E5
San Francisco, Philippines, **204** C3
San Francisco, U.S.A., **422** B3, *23, 50, 82, 96, 385*
San Francisco de Macorís, Dominican Republic, **429** H3
San Francisco de Paula, Cabo, *cape*, Argentina, **460** D3
San Francisco del Chañar, Argentina, **458** D3
San Francisco del Oro, Mexico, **430** D3
San Gabriel, Ecuador, **450** C4
San Germán, Puerto Rico, **427** C2
San Gil, Colombia, **450** D2
San Hipólito, Punta, *point*, Mexico, **430** B3
San Ignacio, Belize, **428** C3
San Ignacio, Beni, Bolivia, **455** F4
San Ignacio, Paraguay, **459** F3
San Ignacio, Peru, **454** B1
San Ignacio, Santa Cruz, Bolivia, **455** G4
San Ildefonso, Cape, Philippines, **204** C2
San Javier, Bolivia, **455** F4
San Javier, Chile, **458** B5
San Javier, Misiones, Argentina, **459** F3
San Javier, Santa Fé, Argentina, **459** E4
San Javier, Spain, **293** G4
San Jerónimo, Serranía de, *mountain range*, Colombia, **450** C2
San Joaquin, *river*, U.S.A., **422** C3
San Joaquin Valley, U.S.A., **422** C3
San Jorge, Argentina, **458** E4
San Jorge, Golfo de, *gulf*, Argentina, **460** D3
San Jorge, Golfo de, *gulf*, Spain, **293** H2
San Jorge, *river*, Colombia, **450** C2
San José, Costa Rica, **428** D5, *404, 405*
San José, Golfo, *gulf*, Argentina, **460** E2
San José, Isla, *island*, Mexico, **430** C3
San José, Isla, *island*, Panama, **429** F5
San Jose, Luzon Island, Philippines, **204** C3
San Jose, Mindoro Island, Philippines, **204** C3
San Jose, Panay Island, Philippines, **204** C4
San José, Spain, **293** F4
San Jose, U.S.A., **422** C3
San José, Volcán, *mountain peak*, Chile, **458** B4
San José de Amacuro, Venezuela, **451** G2
San José de Chiquitos, Bolivia, **455** G4
San José de Dimas, Mexico, **430** C2
San José de Feliciano, Argentina, **459** E4
San José de Gracia, Baja California Sur, Mexico, **430** B3
San José de Gracia, Sinaloa, Mexico, **430** D3
San José de Guanipa, Venezuela, **451** F2
San José de Jáchal, Argentina, **458** C4
San José de la Dormida, Argentina, **458** D4
San José de la Mariquina, Chile, **460** C1
San José de Mayo, Uruguay, **459** F5
San José de Ocuné, Colombia, **451** D3
San José de Quero, Peru, **454** C3
San José de Raíces, Mexico, **431** E3
San Jose del Boqueron, Argentina, **458** D3
San José del Cabo, Mexico, **430** C4
San José del Guaviare, Colombia, **450** D3
San José del Progreso, Mexico, **431** F5
San Jose Island, U.S.A., **424** D6
San Juan, Argentina, **458** C4
San Juan, Cabo, *cape*, Equatorial Guinea, **368** A2
San Juan, Cabo, *cape*, Argentina, **460** E5
San Juan, Dominican Republic, **429** H3
San Juan, Peru, **454** C4
San Juan, Pico, *mountain peak*, Cuba, **429** E2
San Juan, *province*, Argentina, **458** C4, *443*
San Juan, Puerto Rico, **427** C2, *390, 391*
San Juan, Punta, *point*, Isla de Pascua (Easter Island), Chile, **461** B2
San Juan, *river*, Costa Rica/ Nicaragua, **428** D5
San Juan, U.S.A., **423** H3
San Juan, Venezuela, **451** F3
San Juan Bautista, Islas Baleares, Spain, **293** H3
San Juan Bautista, Paraguay, **459** F3
San Juan Bautista, Róbinson Crusoe Island, Archipiélago Juan Fernández, Chile, **461** C2
San Juan Bautista Tuxtepec, Mexico, **431** F5
San Juan de Guadalupe, Mexico, **430** E3
San Juan de los Cayos, Venezuela, **451** E1
San Juan de los Morros, Venezuela, **451** E2
San Juan de Salvamento, Argentina, **460** E5
San Juan del Norte, Nicaragua, **428** E5, *404*
San Juan del Río, Durango, Mexico, **430** D3
San Juan del Río, Queretaro, Mexico, **431** F4
San Juan del Sur, Nicaragua, **428** D5
San Juan Mountains, *mountain range*, U.S.A., **423** K3
San Juancito, Honduras, **428** D4
San Juanico, Punta, *point*, Mexico, **430** B3
San Justo, Argentina, **458** E4
San Lázaro, Cabo, *cape*, Mexico, **430** B3
San Lorenzo, Argentina, **458** E4
San Lorenzo, Beni, Bolivia, **455** F4
San Lorenzo, Ecuador, **450** B4
San Lorenzo, Monte, *mountain peak*, Chile, **460** C3
San Lorenzo, *mountain peak*, Spain, **293** F1
San Lorenzo, Paraguay, **459** F2
San Lorenzo, Peru, **455** E3
San Lorenzo, Tarija, Bolivia, **455** F5
San Lucas, Baja California Sur, Mexico, **430** B3
San Lucas, Bolivia, **455** F5
San Lucas, Cabo, *cape*, Mexico, **430** C4
San Lucas, S. Baja California Sur, Mexico, **430** C4
San Lucas Ojitlán, Mexico, **431** F5
San Luis, Argentina, **458** C4
San Luis, Guatemala, **428** C3
San Luis, Lago de, *lake*, Bolivia, **455** F3
San Luis, Mexico, **430** D3
San Luis, *province*, Argentina, **458** C4
San Luís, San Andrés, Colombia, **461** B1
San Luis, Sierra de, *mountain range*, Argentina, **458** D4
San Luis de la Paz, Mexico, **431** E4
San Luis del Palmar, Argentina, **459** E3
San Luis Obispo, U.S.A., **422** C4
San Luis Potosí, Mexico, **431** E4
San Luis Potosí, *state*, Mexico, **431** E4
San Luis Río Colorado, Mexico, **430** B1
San Luisito, Mexico, **430** B2
San Marco, Capo, *cape*, Italy, **295** D7
San Marcos, Guatemala, **428** C4
San Marcos, Mexico, **431** F5
San Marcos, U.S.A., **424** D5
San Marino, *country*, Europe, **282** F7, *228, 256*
San Marino, San Marino, **294** D4, *256*
San Martín, Argentina, **458** D3
San Martin, Cape, U.S.A., **422** B4
San Martín, Colombia, **450** D3
San Martin, Lago, *lake*, Argentina, **460** C3
San Martín, *river*, Bolivia, **455** F4
San Martín De Los Andes, Argentina, **460** C1
San Martín de Valdeiglesias, Spain, **292** E2
San Mateo, U.S.A., **422** B3
San Matías, Bolivia, **455** G4
San Matías, Golfo, *gulf*, Argentina, **460** E1
San Mauricio, Venezuela, **451** E2
San Miguel, Bolivia, **455** G4
San Miguel, El Salvador, **428** C4
San Miguel, *island*, U.S.A., **422** C4
San Miguel, Panama, **429** F5
San Miguel, Peru, **454** D3
San Miguel, *river*, Bolivia, **455** F4
San Miguel, *river*, Colombia/Ecuador, **450** C4
San Miguel, *river*, Mexico, **430** C2
San Miguel Bay, Philippines, **204** C3
San Miguel de Huachi, Bolivia, **455** E4
San Miguel de Tucumán, Argentina, **458** D3
San Miguel del Monte, Argentina, **459** E5
San Miguelito, Bolivia, **455** E3
San Miguelito, Panama, **429** F5
San Millán, *mountain peak*, Spain, **293** F1
San Nicolás, Bahía, *bay*, Peru, **454** C4
San Nicolas, *island*, U.S.A., **422** C5
San Nicolás de los Arroyos, Argentina, **459** E4
San Nicolás de Tolentino, Islas Canarias, Spain, **373** B4
San Pablo, Beni, Bolivia, **455** F4
San Pablo, Philippines, **204** C3
San Pablo, Potosí, Bolivia, **455** E5
San Patricio, U.S.A., **423** L5
San Pedro, Belize, **428** D3
San Pedro, Bolivia, **455** F4
San Pedro, Buenos Aires, Argentina, **459** E4
San-Pédro, Côte d'Ivoire, **364** C4
San Pedro, Jujuy, Argentina, **458** D2
San Pedro, Mexico, **430** C4
San Pedro, Misiones, Argentina, **459** F3
San Pedro, Paraguay, **459** F2
San Pedro, *river*, Cuba, **429** F2
San Pedro *see* Bulalacao, Philippines, **204** C3
San Pedro, Sierra de, *mountain range*, Spain, **292** D3
San Pedro, Volcán, *mountain peak*, Chile, **458** C1
San Pedro de Arimena, Colombia, **450** D3
San Pedro de Atacama, Chile, **458** C2
San Pedro de Las Bocas, Venezuela, **451** F2
San Pedro de las Colonias, Mexico, **430** E3
San Pedro de Macorís, Dominican Republic, **429** H3
San Pedro Sula, Honduras, **428** D4
San Pedro Tapanatepec, Mexico, **431** G5
San Pedro Totalapan, Mexico, **431** F5
San Pietro, Isola di, *island*, Italy, **295** A6
San Quintín, Mexico, **430** B2
San Rafael, Argentina, **458** C5
San Rafael, Bolivia, **455** G4
San Rafael, Cerro, *mountain peak*, Paraguay, **459** F3, *445*
San Rafael, Venezuela, **450** D1
San Rafael Knob, *mountain peak*, U.S.A., **423** H2
San Ramón, Beni, Bolivia, **455** F3
San Ramón, Santa Cruz, Bolivia, **455** F4
San Ramón de la Nueva Orán, Argentina, **458** D2
San Remigio, Philippines, **204** C4
San Remo, Italy, **294** A4
San Román, Cabo, *cape*, Venezuela, **451** D1
San Roque, Argentina, **459** E3
San Saba, U.S.A., **424** C4
San Salvador, Argentina, **459** E4
San Salvador, El Salvador, **428** C4, *403*
San Salvador, Isla, *island*, Islas Galápagos (Galapagos Islands), Ecuador, **461** A1
San Salvador, *island*, Bahamas, **428** G2
San Salvador de Jujuy, Argentina, **458** D2
San Sebastián, Argentina, **460** D4
San Sebastián, Bahía, *gulf*, Argentina, **460** D4
San Sebastián de la Gomera, Islas Canarias, Spain, **373** A4
San Severo, Italy, **295** E5
San Telmo, Mexico, **430** A2
San Telmo, Punta, *point*, Mexico, **430** D5
San Tin, China, **207** C4
San Valentín, Monte, *mountain peak*, Chile, **460** C3
San Vicente, El Salvador, **428** C4
San Vicente, Mexico, **430** A2
San Vicente de Cañete, Peru, **454** C3
San Vicente de Toranzo, Spain, **293** F1
San Vicente del Caguán, Colombia, **450** C3
San Vincenzo, Italy, **294** C4
San Vito, Capo, *cape*, Sicilia, Italy, **295** D6
San Ysidro, U.S.A., **423** K4
Ṣan'ā', Yemen, **220** D5, *175*
Sanaag, *administrative region*, Somalia, **367** G2
SANAE IV, *South African research station*, Antarctica, **470** D3
Sanaga, *river*, Cameroon, **368** B2, *330*
Sanaigmore, Scotland, U.K., **308** C5
Sanana, Pulau, *island*, Indonesia, **198** D3
Sanandaj, Iran, **222** D5
Sanandita, Bolivia, **455** F5
Sanāw, Yemen, **220** F5
Sanchahe, China, **211** J3
Sanchakou, China, **212** C5
Sanchidrián, Spain, **292** E2
Sānchor, India, **218** B4
Sanchursk, Russian Federation, **222** D1
Sanco Point, Philippines, **204** D4
Sancti Spiritus, Cuba, **429** F2
Sand, Hedmark, Norway, **286** E2
Sand, Rogaland, Norway, **286** C3

Sand Hill, *river*, Canada, **417** N3
Sand Hills, U.S.A., **420** B4
Sand Springs, Montana, U.S.A., **419** L3
Sand Springs, Oklahoma, U.S.A., **424** D1
Sandai, Indonesia, **201** E3
Sandakan, Malaysia, **201** G1
Sândăn, Cambodia, **203** E3
Sandane, Norway, **286** C2
Sandanski, Bulgaria, **297** D5
Sandaré, Mali, **364** B2
Sandarne, Sweden, **287** H2
Sanday, *island*, Orkney, Scotland, U.K., **308** G1
Sanday Sound, Orkney, Scotland, U.K., **308** G1
Sandbach, England, U.K., **304** E1
Sandbukta, Norway, **284** K2
Sanddøla, *river*, Norway, **284** F4
Sande, Sogn og Fjordane, Norway, **286** B2
Sande, Vestfold, Norway, **286** E3
Sandefjord, Norway, **286** E3
Sandell Bay, Macquarie Island, **134** R11
Sanders, U.S.A., **423** J4
Sanderson, U.S.A., **423** M6
Sandfire Roadhouse, Australia, **134** E2
Sandgerði, Iceland, **284** X7
Sandhead, Scotland, U.K., **308** E6
Sandhurst, England, U.K., **305** G3
Sandia, Peru, **455** E4
Sandıklı, Turkey, **297** H6
Sandīla, India, **218** E4
Sanding, Pulau, *island*, Indonesia, **200** C3
Sandlake, U.S.A., **418** C4
Sandnäset, Sweden, **284** H5
Sandnes, Norway, **286** B3
Sandness, Shetland, Scotland, U.K., **308** K7
Sandnessjøen, Norway, **284** F4
Sandoa, Democratic Republic of the Congo, **368** D4
Sandomierz, Poland, **289** K3
Sândominic, Romania, **296** E2
Sandön, *island*, Sweden, **285** L4
Sandoná, Colombia, **450** C4
Sandovo, Russian Federation, **299** F3
Sandow, Mount, *mountain peak*, Antarctica, **470** G5
Sandown, England, U.K., **305** F4
Sandoy, *island*, Faeroe Islands, **302** D2
Sandplace, England, U.K., **304** C4
Sandpoint, U.S.A., **418** F2
Sandray, *island*, Scotland, U.K., **308** B4
Sandsend, England, U.K., **307** H3
Sandspit, Canada, **412** D5
Sandstone, U.S.A., **420** G2
Sandu, China, **206** C3
Sandusky, *river*, U.S.A., **421** M5
Sandusky, Michigan, U.S.A., **421** M4
Sandusky, Ohio, U.S.A., **421** M5
Sandverhaar, Namibia, **370** C4
Sandvik, Sweden, **287** H4
Sandvika, Norway, **284** F5
Sandviken, Sweden, **287** H2
Sandwich, England, U.K., **305** J3
Sandwich Bay, Canada, **417** N3
Sandwich Bay, Namibia, **370** B3
Sandwick, Scotland, U.K., **308** K7
Sandy, England, U.K., **305** G2
Sandy, U.S.A., **418** C4
Sandy Bay, Macquarie Island, **134** R11
Sandy Bay, St Helena, **373** B3
Sandy Cape, Australia, **135** L3
Sandy Lake, Australia, **134** E2
Sandy Lake, *lake*, Canada, **414** H5
Sandy Lake, Newfoundland, Canada, **417** N5
Sandy Lake, Ontario, Canada, **414** H5
Sandy Point, Tristan da Cunha, **373** C2
Sandykgachy, Turkmenistan, **222** G5
Sanford, Florida, U.S.A., **425** M5
Sanford, Maine, U.S.A., **426** E3
Sanford, North Carolina, U.S.A., **425** N2
Sang, Loi, *mountain peak*, Myanmar, **205** C3
Sangān, Kūh-e, *mountain peak*, Afghanistan, **221** H2
Sangar, Russian Federation, **301** P3
Sangay, Volcán, *mountain peak*, Ecuador, **450** B4
Sângeorgiu de Pădure, Romania, **296** E2
Sângeorz-Băi, Romania, **296** E2
Sanger, U.S.A., **422** D3
Sângerei, Moldova, **296** G2
Sangerhausen, Germany, **288** E3
Sanggarpar, China, **215** G2
Sanggau, Indonesia, **201** E2
Sangha, *administrative region*, Congo, **368** C2
Sangha, Burkina Faso, **364** E2
Sangha-Mbaéré, *prefecture*, Central African Republic, **368** C2
Sānghar, Pakistan, **218** B4
Sangihe, Pulau, *island*, Indonesia, **198** D2
Sanginkylä, Finland, **285** N4
Sangis, Sweden, **285** L4
Sangiyn Dalay, Mongolia, **213** H3
Sangkha, Thailand, **203** D3
Sāngli, India, **216** C2
Sangmélima, Cameroon, **368** B2
Sango, Zimbabwe, **371** F3
Sāngola, India, **216** C2
Sangonera, *river*, Spain, **293** G4
Sangre de Cristo Mountains, *mountain range*, U.S.A., **423** L2
Sangre Grande, Trinidad, Trinidad and Tobago, **461** C4
Sangri, China, **214** D3
Sangruma, China, **215** F2
Sangrūr, India, **218** C3
Sangsang, China, **214** C3
Sangue, *river*, Brazil, **455** H3
Sangwali, Namibia, **370** D2
Sangzhi, China, **206** B2
Sanibel Island, U.S.A., **425** L6
Sanikiluaq, Canada, **415** Q3
Sanje, Tanzania, **369** G4
Sanjiachang, China, **215** G4
Sanjiao, China, **207** A3
Sanjō, Japan, **209** G3
Sankarankovil, India, **216** D4
Sankt Gallen, Switzerland, **291** J3
Sankt Peter-Ording, Germany, **288** D1
Sankt-Peterburg (St Petersburg), Russian Federation, **299** C3, *271, 272, 273*
Sanlúcar de Barrameda, Spain, **292** D4
Sanluri, Sardegna, Italy, **295** B6
Sanmen Dao, *island*, China, **207** D4
Sanmen Wan, *bay*, China, **206** E2
Sanmenxia, China, **206** B1
Sanming, China, **206** D3
Sänna, Sweden, **286** G3
Sannār, Sudan, **366** D2
Sânnicolau Mare, Romania, **296** C2
Sanniki, Poland, **289** J2
Sanniquellie, Liberia, **364** C3
Sanok, Poland, **289** L4
Sanquhar, Scotland, U.K., **308** F5
Sansepolcro, Italy, **294** D4
Sansha Wan, *bay*, China, **206** D3
Sanski Most, Bosnia and Herzegovina, **294** F3
Sansui, China, **206** B3
Sansuri, *mountain peak*, North Korea, **211** H4
Sant' Antioco, Isola di, *island*, Sardegna, Italy, **295** B6
Sant' Antioco, Sardegna, Italy, **295** B6
Sant' Arcangelo, Italy, **295** F5
Sant Carles de la Ràpita, Spain, **293** H2
Sant' Eufemia, Golfo di, *gulf*, Italy, **295** E6
Sant Mateu, Spain, **293** H2
Santa Ana, Beni, Bolivia, **455** F3
Santa Ana, Ecuador, **450** B4
Santa Ana, El Salvador, **428** C4
Santa Ana, La Paz, Bolivia, **455** E4
Santa Ana, Mexico, **430** C2
Santa Ana, U.S.A., **422** D5
Santa Anna, U.S.A., **424** C4
Santa Bárbara, Colombia, **450** C3
Santa Bárbara, Honduras, **428** C4
Santa Bárbara, Mexico, **430** D3
Santa Barbara, *mountain peak*, Spain, **293** F4
Santa Barbara, U.S.A., **422** D4
Santa Catalina, Isla, *island*, Providencia, Colombia, **461** C1
Santa Catalina, *island*, U.S.A., **422** D5
Santa Catalina, Panama, **429** E5
Santa Catalina, Philippines, **204** C4
Santa Catarina, Baja California, Mexico, **430** B2
Santa Catarina, Ilha de, *island*, Brazil, **459** H3
Santa Catarina, Nuevo Leon, Mexico, **431** E3
Santa Catarina, *state*, Brazil, **459** G3
Santa Caterina, São Tomé and Príncipe, **373** C4
Santa Catharina, Curaçao, Netherlands Antilles, **461** C3
Santa Clara, Colombia, **451** E5
Santa Clara, Cuba, **429** F2
Santa Clara, *island*, Róbinson Crusoe Island, Archipiélago Juan Fernández, Chile, **461** C2
Santa Clara, Mexico, **430** D2
Santa Clarita, U.S.A., **422** D4
Santa Clotilde, Peru, **450** D5
Santa Coloma de Gramanet, Spain, **293** J2
Santa Cristina, Italy, **294** C2
Santa Croce Camerina, Sicilia, Italy, **295** E7
Santa Cruz, Aruba, **461** B3
Santa Cruz, Bolivia, **455** F4
Santa Cruz, Chile, **458** B5
Santa Cruz, Curaçao, Netherlands Antilles, **461** C3
Santa Cruz, *department*, Bolivia, **455** F5
Santa Cruz, Isla, *island*, Islas Galápagos (Galapagos Islands), Ecuador, **461** A2, *116*
Santa Cruz, *island*, U.S.A., **422** C4
Santa Cruz, Luzon Island, Philippines, **204** C3
Santa Cruz, Madeira, Portugal, **373** C3
Santa Cruz, Marinduque Island, Philippines, **204** C3
Santa Cruz, Mexico, **430** C2
Santa Cruz, Pará, Brazil, **452** C4
Santa Cruz, *province*, Argentina, **460** C3
Santa Cruz, Rio Grande do Norte, Brazil, **453** G5
Santa Cruz, *river*, Argentina, **460** D4
Santa Cruz, São Tomé and Príncipe, **373** C4
Santa Cruz, U.S.A., **422** B3
Santa Cruz Cabrália, Brazil, **457** F4
Santa Cruz de la Palma, Islas Canarias, Spain, **373** A4
Santa Cruz de Moya, Spain, **293** G3
Santa Cruz de Mudela, Spain, **293** F3
Santa Cruz de Tenerife, Islas Canarias, Spain, **373** A4, *355*
Santa Cruz del Sur, Cuba, **429** F2
Santa Cruz do Sul, Brazil, **459** G3
Santa Cruz Islands, Solomon Islands, **138** E6
Santa da Boa Vista, Brazil, **459** G4
Santa Elena, Argentina, **459** E4
Santa Elena, Bahía de, *bay*, Ecuador, **450** B4
Santa Elena, Cabo, *cape*, Costa Rica, **428** D5
Santa Elena, Ecuador, **450** B5
Santa Elena de Uairén, Venezuela, **451** G3
Santa Eufemia, Spain, **292** E3
Santa Eugenia, Spain, **292** C1
Santa Fe, Argentina, **458** E4
Santa Fé, Isla, *island*, Islas Galápagos (Galapagos Islands), Ecuador, **461** A2
Santa Fé, *province*, Argentina, **458** E3
Santa Fe, U.S.A., **423** L4, *386*
Santa Helena, Brazil, **452** E4
Santa Helena de Goiás, Brazil, **456** C4
Santa Inés, Isla, *island*, Chile, **460** B4
Santa Isabel, Argentina, **458** C5
Santa Isabel, Brazil, **455** G3
Santa Isabel, *island*, Solomon Islands, **141** A1, *116*
Santa Isabel, Providencia, Colombia, **461** C1
Santa Lucia, Argentina, **459** E3
Santa Lucía, Ecuador, **450** B4
Santa Lucia Cotzumalguapa, Guatemala, **428** C4
Santa Lucia Range, *mountain range*, U.S.A., **422** C3
Santa Luzia, Brazil, **452** E4
Santa Luzia, Portugal, **292** C4
Santa Mare, Romania, **296** F2
Santa Margarita, Isla, *island*, Mexico, **430** B3
Santa Maria, Amazonas, Brazil, **452** A3
Santa María, Bahía de, *bay*, Mexico, **430** C3
Santa Maria, Cabo de, *cape*, Mozambique, **371** F4
Santa Maria, Cabo de, *cape*, Portugal, **292** D4
Santa María, Catamarca, Argentina, **458** C3
Santa María, Isla, *island*, Islas Galápagos (Galapagos Islands), Ecuador, **461** A2
Santa Maria, *island*, Azores, Portugal, **360** M7
Santa Maria (Gaua), *island*, Vanuatu, **141** A2
Santa María, Peru, **450** C4
Santa Maria, Rio Grande do Sul, Brazil, **459** G3
Santa Maria, *river*, Mato Grosso do Sul, Brazil, **456** B5
Santa Maria, *river*, Rio Grande do Sul, Brazil, **459** F4
Santa María, Salta, Argentina, **458** D2
Santa Maria, U.S.A., **422** C4
Santa Maria da Boa Vista, Brazil, **453** F5
Santa Maria da Vitória, Brazil, **457** E3
Santa Maria das Barreiras, Brazil, **452** D5
Santa María de Ipire, Venezuela, **451** F2
Santa María de Nanay, Peru, **450** D5
Santa Maria del Río, Mexico, **431** E4
Santa Maria di Leuca, Capo, *cape*, Italy, **295** G6
Santa Marta, Cabo de, *point*, Angola, **368** B5
Santa Marta, Colombia, **450** C1, *436*
Santa Marta, Spain, **292** D3
Santa Marta Grande, Cabo de, *cape*, Brazil, **459** H3
Santa Martabaai, *bay*, Curaçao, Netherlands Antilles, **461** C3
Santa Monica, U.S.A., **422** D5
Santa Paula, U.S.A., **422** D4
Santa Quitéria, Brazil, **453** F4
Santa Rita, Brazil, **453** G5
Santa Rita, Colombia, **450** D4
Santa Rita, Venezuela, **450** D1
Santa Rita de Cássia, Brazil, **457** E3
Santa Rita de Sihuas, Peru, **454** D4
Santa Rita do Araguaia, Brazil, **456** C4
Santa Rosa, Acre, Brazil, **454** D2
Santa Rosa, Argentina, **460** D1
Santa Rosa, California, U.S.A., **422** B2
Santa Rosa, Ecuador, **450** B5
Santa Rosa, *island*, U.S.A., **422** C5
Santa Rosa, Mexico, **431** H5
Santa Rosa, N. Beni, Bolivia, **455** F3
Santa Rosa, New Mexico, U.S.A., **423** L4
Santa Rosa, Peru, **454** D4
Santa Rosa, Rio Grande do Sul, Brazil, **459** F3
Santa Rosa, S. Beni, Bolivia, **455** E4
Santa Rosa de Copán, Honduras, **428** C4
Santa Rosa de la Roca, Bolivia, **455** G4
Santa Rosa Range, *mountain range*, U.S.A., **418** F6
Santa Rosalía, Mexico, **430** B3
Santa Sylvina, Argentina, **458** E3
Santa Tecla *see* Nueva San Salvador, El Salvador, **428** C4
Santa Teresa, *river*, Brazil, **456** D3
Santa Teresa Gallura, Sardegna, Italy, **295** B5
Santa Victoria, Sierra, *mountain range*, Argentina, **458** D2
Santa Vitória do Palmar, Brazil, **459** G4
Santa, *river*, Peru, **454** B2
Santa, Peru, **454** B2
Santa, U.S.A., **418** F3
Santai, Sichuan, China, **215** H3
Santai, Xinjiang Uygur Zizhiqu, China, **212** D3
Santalpur, India, **218** B5
Santana, Brazil, **457** E3
Santana, Coxilha de, *mountain range*, Brazil/Uruguay, **459** F4
Santana, Madeira, Portugal, **373** C3
Santana do Ipanema, Brazil, **457** G2
Santander, Colombia, **450** C3
Santander, Philippines, **204** C4
Santander, Spain, **293** F1
Santander Jiménez, Mexico, **431** F3
Santanghu, China, **213** G3
Santanyí, Islas Baleares, Spain, **293** J3
Santarém, Brazil, **452** B4
Santarém, *district*, Portugal, **292** C3
Santarém, Portugal, **292** C3
Santee, *river*, U.S.A., **425** N3
Santiago, *administrative region*, Chile, **458** B4
Santiago, Brazil, **459** F3
Santiago, Cabo, *cape*, Chile, **460** B4
Santiago, Chile, **458** B4, *442*
Santiago, Dominican Republic, **429** H3
Santiago, Mexico, **430** C4
Santiago, Panama, **429** E5
Santiago, Philippines, **204** C2
Santiago, *river*, Peru, **450** C5
Santiago, Sierra de, *mountain range*, Bolivia, **455** G4
Santiago Astata, Mexico, **431** G6
Santiago de Cao, Peru, **454** B2
Santiago de Chocorvos, Peru, **454** C3
Santiago de Chuco, Peru, **454** B2
Santiago de Compostela, Spain, **292** C1

Santiago de Cuba, Cuba, **429** G2
Santiago del Estero, Argentina, **458** D3
Santiago del Estero, *province*, Argentina, **458** D3
Santiago do Cacém, Portugal, **292** C3
Santiago Ixcuintla, Mexico, **430** D4
Santiago Papasquiaro, Mexico, **430** D3
Santiago Peak, *mountain peak*, U.S.A., **423** M7
Santiago Pinotepa Nacional, Mexico, **431** F5
Santigi, Tanjong, *point*, Indonesia, **198** C3
Säntis, *mountain peak*, Switzerland, **291** J3
Santo Amaro, Brazil, **457** F3
Santo André, Brazil, **459** H2
Santo Angelo, Brazil, **459** F3
Santo Antão, *island*, Cape Verde, **360** Q8, *318*
Santo António, São Tomé and Príncipe, **373** C4
Santo Antônio da Platina, Brazil, **459** G2
Santo Antônio de Jesus, Brazil, **457** F3
Santo Antônio do Içá, Brazil, **451** E5
Santo Antônio do Leverger, Brazil, **456** B4
Santo Corazón, Bolivia, **455** G4
Santo Domingo, Baja California, Mexico, **430** B2
Santo Domingo, Baja California Sur, Mexico, **430** B3
Santo Domingo, Dominican Republic, **429** H3, *394*
Santo Domingo, Nicaragua, **428** D4
Santo Domingo, Peru, **455** E3
Santo Domingo de los Colorados, Ecuador, **450** B4
Santo Estêvão, *river*, Portugal, **292** C3
Santo Inácio, Brazil, **457** E3
Santo Stefano di Camastra, Sicilia, Italy, **295** E6
Santo Tomás, Baja California, Mexico, **430** A2
Santo Tomás, Chihuahua, Mexico, **430** D2
Santo Tomás, Peru, **454** D4
Santo Tomé, Argentina, **459** E3
Santorini *see* Thira, *island*, Kyklades, Greece, **297** E7
Santos, Brazil, **459** H2
Santos Dumont, Brazil, **457** E5
Sanxiang, China, **207** A4
Sanya, China, **203** F2
Sanyati, *river*, Zimbabwe, **371** E2
Sanying, China, **210** D5
Sanyuan, China, **206** B1
Sanza Pombo, Angola, **368** C4
Sanzao Dao, *island*, China, **207** A4
Sanzao, China, **207** A4
Sanzhan, China, **211** J2
São Benedito, Brazil, **453** F4
São Benedito, *river*, Brazil, **456** B2
São Bento, Amazonas, Brazil, **455** F2
São Bento, Maranhão, Brazil, **453** E4
São Bento do Norte, Brazil, **453** G4
São Bernardo do Campo, Brazil, **459** H2
São Bernardo, Brazil, **453** E4
São Borja, Brazil, **459** F3
Sao Carlos, Santa Catarina, Brazil, **459** G3
São Carlos, São Paulo, Brazil, **459** H2
São Desidério, Brazil, **457** E3
São Domingos, Brazil, **456** D3
São Domingos, Serra, *mountain range*, Brazil, **456** D4
São Félix, Brazil, **456** C3
São Félix do Xingu, Brazil, **452** C5
São Fidélis, Brazil, **457** F5
São Francisco, Brazil, **457** E4
São Francisco, *river*, Brazil, **457** F2
São Francisco de Assis, Brazil, **459** F3
Sao Francisco de Paula, Brazil, **459** G3
São Francisco do Sul, Brazil, **459** H3
São Gabriel, Brazil, **459** F4
São Gabriel da Cachoeira, Brazil, **451** E4
São Gonçalo, Brazil, **457** E6
São Gonçalo do Amarante, Brazil, **453** F4
São Gotardo, Brazil, **456** D5
São João da Aliança, Brazil, **456** D4
São João da Barra, Brazil, **457** F5
São João da Boa Vista, Brazil, **456** D5
São João da Madeira, Portugal, **292** C2
São João do Araguaia, Brazil, **452** D4
São João do Cariri, Brazil, **453** G5
São João do Paraíso, Brazil, **457** E4
São João do Piauí, Brazil, **453** E5
São João dos Patos, Brazil, **453** E5
São Joaquim, Pará, Brazil, **452** D4
São Joaquim, Santa Catarina, Brazil, **459** G3
São Joaquim da Barra, Brazil, **456** D5
São Jorge, *island*, Azores, Portugal, **360** M7
São José, Amazonas, Brazil, **451** E4
São José, Baía de, *bay*, Brazil, **453** E4
São José, Santa Catarina, Brazil, **459** H3
São José de Mipibu, Brazil, **453** G5
São José do Norte, Brazil, **459** G4
São José do Rio Prêto, Brazil, **456** D5
São Jose dos Campos, Brazil, **456** E6
São José dos Pinhais, Brazil, **459** H2
São Leopoldo, Brazil, **459** G3
São Lourenço, Brazil, **457** E6
São Lourenço, Ponta de, *point*, Madeira, Portugal, **373** C3
São Lourenço do Sul, Brazil, **459** G4
São Luís, Brazil, **453** E4
São Luís, Ilha de, *island*, Brazil, **453** E4
São Luis Gonzaga, Brazil, **459** F3
São Mamede, *mountain peak*, Portugal, **292** D3
São Manuel *see* Teles Pires, *river*, Brazil, **452** B5
São Marcos, Baía de, *bay*, Brazil, **453** E4
São Marcos, *river*, Brazil, **456** D4
São Mateus, Brazil, **457** F5
São Miguel, *island*, Azores, Portugal, **360** M7
São Miguel, *river*, Brazil, **455** F3
São Miguel do Araguaia, Brazil, **456** C3
São Miguel do Guamá, Brazil, **452** D3
São Miguel do Tapuio, Brazil, **453** F4
São Miguel dos Campos, Brazil, **457** G2
São Nicolau, *island*, Cape Verde, **360** P8
São Paulo, Brazil, **459** H2, *434, 439*
São Paulo, *state*, Brazil, **459** H2
São Paulo de Olivença, Brazil, **451** E5
São Pedro, Brazil, **451** G5
São Pedro, *river*, Brazil, **453** F5
São Pedro do Sul, Portugal, **292** C2
São Raimundo das Mangabeiras, Brazil, **452** E5
São Raimundo Nonato, Brazil, **457** E2
São Romão, Amazonas, Brazil, **455** E1
São Romão, Minas Gerais, Brazil, **457** E4
São Roque, Cabo de, *cape*, Brazil, **453** G4
São Sebastião, Ilha de, *island*, Brazil, **459** J2
São Sebastião, Pará, Brazil, **452** C4
São Sebastião, Rondônia, Brazil, **455** G2
São Sebastiao da Boa Vista, Brazil, **452** D3
São Sebastião do Paraíso, Brazil, **456** D5
São Sepé, Brazil, **459** G4
São Simão, Brazil, **456** C5
São Tiago, *island*, Cape Verde, **360** Q8, *319*
São Tomé, Cabo de, *cape*, Brazil, **457** F5
São Tomé, *island*, São Tomé and Príncipe, **373** C4
São Tomé, Pico de, *mountain peak*, São Tomé and Príncipe, **373** C4, *332*
São Tomé, São Tomé and Príncipe, **373** C4, *332*
São Tomé and Príncipe, *country*, Atlantic Ocean, **359** F6, *332*
São Vicente, Brazil, **459** H2
São Vicente, Cabo de, *cape*, Portugal, **292** C4
São Vicente, *island*, Cape Verde, **360** P8, *319*
São Vicente, Madeira, Portugal, **373** C3
Saona, Isla, *island*, Dominican Republic, **429** H3
Saône, *river*, France, **291** G3, *245*
Sapanca, Turkey, **297** H5
Sapanda, Papua New Guinea, **140** B4
Sapele, Nigeria, **365** F3
Sapello, U.S.A., **423** L4
Sapelo Island, U.S.A., **425** M4
Sapernoye, Russian Federation, **299** C2
Sapes, Greece, **297** E5
Saposoa, Peru, **454** C2
Sapphire Mountains, *mountain range*, U.S.A., **418** G3
Sappho, U.S.A., **418** B2
Sapporo, Japan, **209** H2
Sapri, Italy, **295** E5
Sapucaia, Brazil, **452** B4
Sapulpa, U.S.A., **424** D1
Sapulut, Malaysia, **201** G1
Saqqez, Iran, **222** D5
Sar Bīsheh, Iran, **221** G2
Šar Planina, *mountain range*, Macedonia/Serbia, **296** C4
Sara, Philippines, **204** C4
Sarāb, Iran, **363** J1
Saraburi, Thailand, **202** D3
Saraby, Norway, **285** L1
Saragosa, U.S.A., **423** M6
Saraguro, Ecuador, **450** B5
Saraipāli, India, **219** E5
Säräisniemi, Finland, **285** N4
Sarajärvi, Finland, **285** N4
Sarajevo, Bosnia and Herzegovina, **294** G4, *249, 259, 261*
Saraktash, Russian Federation, **222** F2
Saramati, *mountain peak*, Myanmar, **205** B2
Saran, Gunung, *mountain peak*, Indonesia, **201** E3
Saranac Lake, U.S.A., **426** C2
Sarandë, Albania, **297** C6
Sarandi, Brazil, **459** G3
Sarandí del Yí, Uruguay, **459** F4
Sarandi Grande, Uruguay, **459** F4
Sarangani Islands, Philippines, **204** D5
Sārangarh, India, **219** E5
Sārangpur, India, **218** D5
Saransk, Russian Federation, **298** G2
Sarapul, Russian Federation, **222** E1
Sarasota, U.S.A., **425** L6
Sarata, Ukraine, **296** G2
Saratoga, U.S.A., **419** L6
Saratok, Malaysia, **201** E2
Saratov, Russian Federation, **222** D2
Saratovskaya Oblast', *province*, Russian Federation, **222** D2
Sarāvān, Iran, **221** H3
Saravan, Laos, **203** E3
Sarawak, *state*, Malaysia, **201** F2, *150, 151, 152*
Saray, Turkey, **297** F5
Saraya, Senegal, **364** B2
Sarāyā, Syria, **225** C2
Sarayakpınar, Turkey, **296** F5
Sarayköy, Turkey, **297** G7
Sarayönü, Turkey, **224** D5
Sarbāz, Iran, **221** H3
Sárbogárd, Hungary, **289** J5
Sarco, Chile, **458** B3
Sardārpur, India, **218** C5
Sardārshahr, India, **218** C3
Sardegna, *autonomous region*, Italy, **295** B5, *255*
Sardegna (Sardinia), *island*, Italy, **295** C5, *89, 95, 246, 254, 255*
Sardinata, Colombia, **450** D2
Sardinata, Ensenada de, *bay*, San Andrés, Colombia, **461** B1
Sardinia *see* Sardegna, *island*, Italy, **295** C5, *89, 95, 246, 254, 255*
Sardis Lake, U.S.A., **425** H2
Sar-e Pol, Afghanistan, **218** A1
Sargent, U.S.A., **420** D5
Sargodha, Pakistan, **218** C2
Sarh, Chad, **366** A3
Sarhro, Jebel, *mountain range*, Morocco, **360** E2
Sārī, Iran, **222** E5
Saria, *island*, Dodekanisos, Greece, **297** F8
Sarichioi, Romania, **296** G3
Sarigan, *island*, Northern Mariana Islands, **138** C3
Sarıgöl, Turkey, **297** G6
Sarıkaya, Turkey, **363** G1
Sarikei, Malaysia, **201** E2
Sarıkemer, Turkey, **297** F7
Sarıköy, Turkey, **297** F5
Sarimbun Reservoir, Singapore, **200** J6
Sarina, Australia, **135** K3
Sariñena, Spain, **293** G2
Sariwon, North Korea, **208** D3
Sarıyer, Turkey, **297** G5
Sark, *Guernsey dependency*, English Channel, **290** C2, *279*
Sarkāri Tala, India, **218** B4
Särkijärvi, Finland, **285** L3
Särkisalmi, Finland, **287** P2
Şarkışla, Turkey, **363** G1
Şarköy, Turkey, **297** F5
Sărmaşu, Romania, **296** E2
Sarmi, Indonesia, **199** G3
Sarmiento, Argentina, **460** D2
Särna, Sweden, **286** F2
Sarnen, Switzerland, **291** J3
Sarnia, Canada, **421** M4
Sarny, Ukraine, **298** C2
Särö, Sweden, **286** E4
Saros Körfezi, *bay*, Turkey, **297** F5
Sárospatak, Hungary, **289** K4
Sarowbī, Afghanistan, **218** B2
Sarpsborg, Norway, **286** E3
Sarqan, Kazakhstan, **212** C3
Sarre, England, U.K., **305** J3
Sarrebourg, France, **291** H2
Sarriá, Spain, **292** D1
Sarroch, Sardegna, Italy, **295** B6
Sartène, Corse, France, **295** B5
Sarthe, *river*, France, **290** D3
Saru, *river*, Japan, **209** H2
Saruhanlı, Turkey, **297** F6
Sárvár, Hungary, **289** H5
Sarvestān, Iran, **220** F3
Sárvíz, *river*, Hungary, **294** G2
Särvsjö, Sweden, **286** F1
Sary-Tash, Kyrgyzstan, **212** B5
Saryesik-Atyrau-Qumy, *desert*, Kazakhstan, **212** B3
Saryg-Sep, Russian Federation, **213** G2
Saryözek, Kazakhstan, **212** C3
Saryqopa Köli, *lake*, Kazakhstan, **222** G2
Saryshagan, Kazakhstan, **212** B3
Sarysu, *river*, Kazakhstan, **212** A2
Sarzhal, Kazakhstan, **212** C2
Sasak, Indonesia, **200** B3
Sasamungga, Solomon Islands, **141** A1
Sasar, Tanjong, *point*, Indonesia, **198** C5
Sasarām, India, **219** E4
Sasebo, Japan, **208** E4
Saser Kangri, *mountain peak*, India, **218** D2
Saskatchewan, *province*, Canada, **413** R4, *381*
Saskatchewan, *river*, Canada, **413** S5
Saskatoon, Canada, **413** R5
Saslaya, Cerro, *mountain peak*, Nicaragua, **428** D4
Sasolburg, South Africa, **371** E4
Sasovo, Russian Federation, **298** F2
Sassandra, Côte d'Ivoire, **364** C4
Sassari, Sardegna, Italy, **295** B5
Sassnitz, Germany, **288** F1
Sasstown, Liberia, **364** C4
Sasyk, Ozero, *lake*, Ukraine, **296** G3
Sasyqköl, *lake*, Kazakhstan, **212** D3
Sata-misaki, *point*, Japan, **208** E5
Satāna, India, **218** C5
Satanta, U.S.A., **420** C7
Satapuala, Samoa, **141** B1
Sātāra, India, **216** C2
Sataua, Samoa, **141** B1
Satawal, *island*, Micronesia, **138** C4
Sätbaev, Kazakhstan, **222** H3
Säter, Sweden, **286** G2
Satipo, Peru, **454** C3
Sātmala Hills, India, **218** C5
Satna, India, **218** E4
Sátoraljaújhely, Hungary, **289** K4
Sātpura Range, *mountain range*, India, **218** C5
Satrokala, Madagascar, **372** B5
Satti, India, **218** D2
Sattūr, India, **216** D4
Satu Mare, Romania, **296** D2
Satun, Thailand, **202** D5
Satupa'itea, Samoa, **141** B1
Sauce, Argentina, **459** E4
Saucillo, Mexico, **430** D2
Sauda, Norway, **286** C3
Saūdakent, Kazakhstan, **223** H4
Saudi Arabia, *country*, Asia, **196** F7, *146, 147, 174, 175, 176, 177, 178, 180*
Sauêruiná (Papagaio), *river*, Brazil, **455** G3
Saugstad, Mount, *mountain peak*, Canada, **412** F5
Saül, French Guiana, **452** C2
Sauldre, *river*, France, **290** E3
Saulgau, Germany, **288** D4
Saulieu, France, **291** G3
Saulkrasti, Latvia, **287** M4
Sault Ste Marie, Canada, **421** L2
Sault Ste Marie, U.S.A., **421** L2
Saumlaki, Indonesia, **199** E4
Saumur, France, **290** D3
Saunders, Cape, Australia, **129** G6
Saundersfoot, Wales, U.K., **304** C3
Saurimo, Angola, **368** D4
Sauvo, Finland, **287** L2
Sauzé-Vaussais, France, **290** E3
Savá, Honduras, **428** D4
Sava, *river*, Europe, **280** F6, *259, 261*
Savage, U.S.A., **419** M3
Savageton, U.S.A., **419** M5
Savai'i, *island*, Samoa, **141** B1, *113, 114*
Savalou, Benin, **365** E3
Savaneta, Aruba, **461** B3
Savanna-la-Mar, Jamaica, **429** F3
Savannah, Georgia, U.S.A., **425** M3
Savannah, Missouri, U.S.A., **420** F6
Savannah, *river*, U.S.A., **425** M3
Savannah, Tennessee, U.S.A., **425** H2
Savannakhét, Laos, **203** E2
Savant Lake, Canada, **414** J6
Sāvantvādi, India, **216** C3
Sävar, Sweden, **284** K5
Savaştepe, Turkey, **297** F6
Savè, Benin, **365** E3
Save, *river*, Mozambique, **371** F3
Sāveh, Iran, **220** F2
Savelugu, Ghana, **364** D3
Savenay, France, **290** D3
Săveni, Romania, **296** F2
Saverdun, France, **290** E5
Savikylä, Finland, **285** P5

Savissivik, Denmark, **411** N2
Savitaipale, Finland, **287** N2
Šavnik, Montenegro, **296** B4
Savona, Canada, **412** J6
Savona, Italy, **294** B3
Savonlinna, Finland, **287** P2, *235*
Savonranta, Finland, **287** P1
Savran', Ukraine, **296** H1
Sävsjö, Sweden, **286** G4
Savu Sea, Indonesia, **198** C5
Savukoski, Finland, **285** P3
Savusavu, Fiji, **141** A4
Savuti, Botswana, **370** D2
Saw, Myanmar, **205** B3
Sawākin, Sudan, **363** G5
Sawan, Myanmar, **205** C2
Sawankhalok, Thailand, **202** C2
Sawatch Range, *mountain range*, U.S.A., **423** K2
Sawbill, Canada, **416** H3
Sawdā', Jabal, *mountain peak*, Saudi Arabia, **363** H5, *174*
Sawdā', Qurnat as, *mountain peak*, Lebanon, **225** D2, *180*
Sawdirī, Sudan, **366** C2
Sawel Mountain, *mountain peak*, Northern Ireland, U.K., **306** A3
Sawi, Ao, *bay*, Thailand, **202** C4
Ṣawqirah, Ghubbat, *bay*, Oman, **221** G5
Sawston, England, U.K., **305** H2
Sawtell, Australia, **135** L5
Sawu, *island*, Indonesia, **134** E1
Sawu, Pulau, *island*, Indonesia, **198** C5
Saxilby, England, U.K., **305** G1
Saxmundham, England, U.K., **305** J2
Saxnäs, Sweden, **284** G4
Say, Niger, **365** E2
Sayán, Peru, **454** C3
Sayaq, Kazakhstan, **212** C3
Sayaxché, Guatemala, **428** C3
Ṣaydā (Sidon), Lebanon, **225** C3
Sayghān, Afghanistan, **218** A2
Sayḥūt, Yemen, **220** F5
Sāylac, Somalia, **367** F2
Säyneinen, Finland, **285** P5
Saynshand, Dornogovĭ, Mongolia, **210** E3
Saynshand, Ömnögovĭ, Mongolia, **213** J4
Sayn-Ust, Mongolia, **213** G3
Sayötesh, Kazakhstan, **222** E4
Sayqal, Baḥr, *lake*, Syria, **225** D3
Sayram Hu, *lake*, China, **212** D3
Sayre, U.S.A., **424** C2
Sayula, Mexico, **430** E5
Sayula de Alemán, Mexico, **431** G5
Sayward, Canada, **412** G6
Saywūn, Yemen, **220** E5
Sazan, *island*, Albania, **297** B5
Sazonovo, Russian Federation, **299** E3
Sbaa, Algeria, **361** F3
Sbega, Russian Federation, **211** G1
Sbeïtla, Tunisia, **362** A1
Scafell Pike, *mountain peak*, England, U.K., **306** E3
Scalasaig, Scotland, U.K., **308** C4
Scalby, England, U.K., **307** H3
Scalloway, Shetland, Scotland, U.K., **308** K7
Scalp, *mountain peak*, Ireland, **309** D5
Scalpay, *island*, Scotland, U.K., **308** C3
Scammon Bay, U.S.A., **410** C3
Scandia, Canada, **413** N6
Scandinavia, *region*, Europe, **280** F3, *75, 88, 231, 234*
Scansano, Italy, **294** C4
Scanzano, Italy, **295** F5
Scapa Flow, *bay*, Orkney, Scotland, U.K., **308** F2
Scarba, *island*, Scotland, U.K., **308** D4
Scarborough, England, U.K., **307** H3
Scarborough, Tobago, Trinidad and Tobago, **461** B4
Scargill, New Zealand, **133** D6
Scarp, *island*, Scotland, U.K., **308** B2
Scarth, Canada, **414** D7
Schaffhausen, Switzerland, **291** J3
Schärding, Austria, **294** D1
Schefferville, Canada, **416** H2
Scheibbs, Austria, **289** G5
Schelde, *river*, Belgium, **288** A3, *241*
Schell Creek Range, *mountain range*, U.S.A., **422** F2
Schenectady, U.S.A., **426** C3
Scheveningen, Netherlands, **288** B2
Schiermonnikoog, Netherlands, **288** C2
Schitu Duca, Romania, **296** F2
Schleiden, Germany, **288** C3
Schleswig, Germany, **288** D1
Schleswig-Holstein, *state*, Germany, **288** D1, *238*
Schongau, Germany, **288** E5
Schooner, Caleta, *bay*, San Andrés, Colombia, **461** B1
Schouten Islands, Papua New Guinea, **140** B3
Schrader, Mount, *mountain peak*, Papua New Guinea, **140** B4
Schroffenstein, *mountain peak*, Namibia, **370** C4
Schulenburg, U.S.A., **424** D5
Schuler, Canada, **413** P6
Schurz, U.S.A., **422** D2
Schuyler, U.S.A., **420** E5
Schwabach, Germany, **288** E4
Schwäbisch Hall, Germany, **288** D4
Schwäbische Alb, *mountain range*, Germany, **288** D4
Schwaner, Pegunungan, *mountain range*, Indonesia, **201** E3
Schwarzwald, *mountain range*, Germany, **280** E6, *228, 239*
Schwaz, Austria, **288** E5
Schwedt, Germany, **289** G2
Schweinfurt, Germany, **288** E3
Schwerin, Germany, **288** E2
Schweriner See, *lake*, Germany, **288** E2
Schwyz, Switzerland, **291** J3
Sciacca, Sicilia, Italy, **295** D7
Scilly, Isles of, England, U.K., **304** A5
Scioto, *river*, U.S.A., **421** M5
Scobey, U.S.A., **419** M2
Scole, England, U.K., **305** J2
Scotch Corner, England, U.K., **307** G3
Scotland, *administrative division*, U.K., **308** D3, *75, 93, 94, 95, 274, 275, 276, 278, 279*
Scotland Neck, U.S.A., **426** B6
Scott, Cape, Canada, **412** E6
Scott Base, *New Zealand research station*, Antarctica, **470** D7, *469*
Scott City, U.S.A., **420** C6
Scott Coast, *region*, Antarctica, **470** D7
Scott Lake, Canada, **413** S2
Scottburgh, South Africa, **371** F5
Scottish Borders, *local authority*, Scotland, U.K., **308** F5
Scottsbluff, U.S.A., **419** N6
Scottsboro, U.S.A., **425** J2
Scottsburg, U.S.A., **421** L6
Scottsdale, Australia, **135** K7
Scottsdale, U.S.A., **423** H5
Scourie, Scotland, U.K., **308** D2
Scousburgh, Scotland, U.K., **308** K8
Scrabster, Scotland, U.K., **308** F2
Scranton, North Dakota, U.S.A., **420** B2
Scranton, Pennsylvania, U.S.A., **426** C4
Scunthorpe, England, U.K., **307** H4
Seaford, England, U.K., **305** H4
Seaford, U.S.A., **426** C5
Seagraves, U.S.A., **423** M5
Seal, Cape, South Africa, **370** D5
Seal, *river*, Canada, **414** F2
Seal Bay, Tristan da Cunha, **373** C2
Seal Cove, Canada, **426** G2
Seal Cove, U.S.A., **416** H7
Seamer, England, U.K., **307** H3
Searchlight, U.S.A., **422** F4
Searcy, U.S.A., **424** G2
Seascale, England, U.K., **306** E3
Seaside, U.S.A., **418** C4
Seaton, England, U.K., **304** D4
Seattle, U.S.A., **418** C3
Seaward Kaikoura Range, *mountain range*, New Zealand, **133** D6
Sebago Lake, U.S.A., **426** E3
Sebakor, Teluk, *bay*, Indonesia, **199** F3
Sebangka, Pulau, *island*, Indonesia, **200** D2
Sebastían Vizcaíno, Bahía, *bay*, Mexico, **430** B2
Sebatik, Pulau, *island*, Indonesia/Malaysia, **201** G1
Sebayan, Gunung, *mountain peak*, Indonesia, **201** E3
Sebba, Burkina Faso, **364** E2
Sebdou, Algeria, **361** F2
Sébékoro, Mali, **364** C2
Seberida, Indonesia, **200** C3
Sebeş, Romania, **296** D3
Sebezh, Russian Federation, **299** B4
Sebina, Botswana, **371** E3
Sebiş, Romania, **296** D2
Sebring, U.S.A., **425** M6
Sebuku, Pulau, *island*, Indonesia, **201** G3
Sechelt, Canada, **412** H7
Sechura, Bahía de, *bay*, Peru, **454** B1
Sechura, Desierto de, *desert*, Peru, **454** B2
Sechura, Peru, **454** B1
Secondigny, France, **290** D3
Secretary Island, New Zealand, **133** A7
Secunderābād, India, **216** D2
Sécure, *river*, Bolivia, **455** F4
Seda, Lithuania, **287** L4
Seda, *river*, Latvia, **287** M4
Seda, *river*, Portugal, **292** D3
Sedalia, U.S.A., **420** G6
Sedan, France, **291** G2
Sedaung Taung, *mountain peak*, Myanmar, **202** C3
Sedbergh, England, U.K., **306** F3
Seddon, Kap, *cape*, Greenland, **411** N2
Seddon, New Zealand, **133** E5
Sede Boqer, Israel, **225** C4
Sedeh, Iran, **221** G2
Sedel'nikovo, Russian Federation, **223** K1
Sederot, Israel, **225** C4
Sedgewick, Canada, **413** P5
Sédhiou, Senegal, **364** A2
Sedoa, Indonesia, **198** C3
Sedom, Israel, **225** C4
Sedrata, Algeria, **295** A7
Sedro Woolley, U.S.A., **418** C2
Sędziszów Małopolski, Poland, **289** K3
Seeheim, Namibia, **370** C4
Seeley Lake, U.S.A., **418** H3
Seelig, Mount, *mountain peak*, Antarctica, **470** C6
Seelow, Germany, **289** G2
Seely, U.S.A., **419** M4
Sées, France, **290** E2
Seesen, Germany, **288** E3
Sefadu, Sierra Leone, **364** B3
Seferihisar, Turkey, **297** F6
Sefophe, Botswana, **371** E3
Ségala, Mali, **364** B2
Segamat, Malaysia, **200** C2
Segarcea, Romania, **296** D3
Ségbana, Benin, **365** E2
Seget, Indonesia, **199** E3
Segezha, Russian Federation, **285** S5
Seglvik, Norway, **284** K1
Segorbe, Spain, **293** G3
Ségou, *administrative region*, Mali, **364** C2
Ségou, Mali, **364** C2
Segovia, Colombia, **450** C2
Segovia, Spain, **292** E2
Segozero, Ozero, *lake*, Russian Federation, **285** R5
Segre, *river*, Spain, **293** H2
Seguam Island, Aleutian Islands, U.S.A., **408** F3
Séguédine, Niger, **362** B4
Séguéla, Côte d'Ivoire, **364** C3
Séguélon, Côte d'Ivoire, **364** C3
Seguin, U.S.A., **424** D5
Segundo, *river*, Argentina, **458** D4
Segura, Portugal, **292** D3
Segura, *river*, Spain, **293** F3
Sehithwa, Botswana, **370** D3
Sehore, India, **218** D5
Sehulea, Papua New Guinea, **140** C5
Sehwān, Pakistan, **218** A4
Seibert, U.S.A., **423** M2
Seiland, *island*, Norway, **285** L1
Seiling, U.S.A., **424** C1
Seille, *river*, France, **291** G3
Seinäjoki, Finland, **287** L1
Seine, Baie de la, *bay*, France, **290** D2
Seine, *river*, France, **280** E6, *244*
Seini, Romania, **296** D2
Sejny, Poland, **289** L1
Sekayu, Indonesia, **200** C3
Sekondi, Ghana, **364** D4
Sekseüil, Kazakhstan, **222** G3
Sela Dingay, Ethiopia, **367** E3
Selah, U.S.A., **418** D3
Selangor, *state*, Malaysia, **200** C2
Selaphum, Thailand, **203** D2
Selatan, Tanjong, *point*, Indonesia, **201** F4
Selattyn, England, U.K., **304** D2
Selayar, Pulau, *island*, Indonesia, **198** B4
Selayar, Selat, *strait*, Indonesia, **198** B4
Selbekken, Norway, **284** D5
Selbu, Norway, **284** E5
Selby, England, U.K., **307** G4
Selby, U.S.A., **420** C3
Selçuk, Turkey, **297** F7
Sele, *river*, Italy, **295** E5
Selebi Phikwe, Botswana, **371** E3
Selemdzha, *river*, Russian Federation, **301** Q4
Selendi, Turkey, **297** G6
Selenduma, Russian Federation, **210** D2
Selenge, Democratic Republic of the Congo, **368** C3
Selenge, Mongolia, **213** J2
Selenge, *province*, Mongolia, **210** D2
Selenge, *river*, Mongolia, **210** D2
Selenginsk, Russian Federation, **210** D1
Selenicë, Albania, **297** B5
Sélestat, France, **291** H2
Seletar, Pulau, *island*, Singapore, **200** K6
Seletar Reservoir, Singapore, **200** J6
Selfridge, U.S.A., **420** C2
Sel'ga, Russian Federation, **285** R5
Sel'gon, Russian Federation, **211** L2
Sélibabi, Mauritania, **364** B1
Seliger, Ozero, *lake*, Russian Federation, **299** D4
Seligman, U.S.A., **422** G4
Selimiye, Turkey, **297** F7
Selizharovo, Russian Federation, **299** D4
Selkirk, Canada, **414** F6
Selkirk, Scotland, U.K., **308** G5
Selkirk Mountains, *mountain range*, Canada, **413** K6
Selle, Pic de la, *mountain peak*, Haiti, **429** G3, *394*
Selles-sur-Cher, France, **290** E3
Sellindge, England, U.K., **305** J3
Sells, U.S.A., **423** H6
Selma, Alabama, U.S.A., **425** J3
Selma, California, U.S.A., **422** D3
Selmer, U.S.A., **425** H2
Selo, Russian Federation, **299** G2
Selong, Indonesia, **201** G5
Selsey, England, U.K., **305** G4
Sel'tso, Russian Federation, **299** E6
Selty, Russian Federation, **222** E1
Selvas, *region*, Brazil, **446** F4
Selwyn Lake, Canada, **414** B1
Selwyn Mountains, *mountain range*, Canada, **410** F3
Selyatyn, Ukraine, **296** E2
Selz, U.S.A., **420** D2
Sem, Norway, **286** E3
Sem Tripa, Brazil, **452** C4
Semara, Western Sahara, **360** D3
Semarang, Indonesia, **201** E4
Semaras, Indonesia, **201** G3
Sematan, Malaysia, **201** E2
Semayang, Danau, *lake*, Indonesia, **201** G3
Sembawang, Singapore, **200** J6
Sembé, Congo, **368** B2
Sembulu, Danau, *lake*, Indonesia, **201** F3
Semendua, Democratic Republic of the Congo, **368** C3
Semeru, Gunung, *mountain peak*, Indonesia, **201** F5
Semey, Kazakhstan, **212** D2
Seminoe Reservoir, U.S.A., **419** L5
Seminole, U.S.A., **423** M5
Semiozer'ye, Russian Federation, **210** E2
Semirara Islands, Philippines, **204** C4
Semlevo, Russian Federation, **299** E5
Semnān, Iran, **220** F1
Semois, Belgium, **288** B4
Semois, *river*, Belgium, **291** G2
Semporna, Malaysia, **201** G1
Semuda, Indonesia, **201** F3
Sên, *river*, Cambodia, **203** E3
Sena, Bolivia, **455** E3
Seňa, Slovakia, **289** K4
Sena Madureira, Brazil, **455** E2
Senador Pompeu, Brazil, **453** F4
Senanayake Samudra, *lake*, Sri Lanka, **217** E5
Senanga, Zambia, **368** D6
Sendai, Honshū, Japan, **209** H3
Sendai, Kyūshū, Japan, **208** E5
Senebui, Tanjong, *point*, Indonesia, **200** C2
Senec, Slovakia, **289** H4
Seneca, Oregon, U.S.A., **418** E4
Seneca, South Dakota, U.S.A., **420** D3
Seneca Lake, U.S.A., **426** B3
Senegal, *country*, Africa, **358** D5, *91, 93, 94, 313, 319, 320, 321, 325*
Sénégal, *river*, Senegal, **364** B1, *318, 322, 324*
Senftenberg, Germany, **289** G3
Senga Hill, Zambia, **369** F4
Sengerema, Tanzania, **369** F3
Senguerr, *river*, Argentina, **460** C2
Senhor do Bonfim, Brazil, **457** F3
Senigallia, Italy, **294** D4
Senirkent, Turkey, **363** F1
Senj, Croatia, **294** E3
Senj, Mongolia, **210** E3
Senja, *island*, Norway, **284** H2
Senjitu, China, **210** G4
Senlin Shan, *mountain peak*, China, **211** K4
Senlis, France, **290** F2
Sennen, England, U.K., **304** B4
Senneterre, Canada, **416** C5
Sennybridge, Wales, U.K., **304** D3

Senoia, U.S.A., **425** K3
Senokos, Bulgaria, **296** G4
Senorbì, Sardegna, Italy, **295** B6
Sens, France, **291** F2
Sensuntepeque, El Salvador, **428** C4
Senta, Serbia, **296** C3
Sentani, Danau, *lake*, Indonesia, **199** H3
Sentarum, Danau, *lake*, Indonesia, **201** E2
Sentinel, U.S.A., **422** G5
Sento Sé, Brazil, **457** F2
Sentosa, *island*, Singapore, **200** J7
Senyavin Islands, Micronesia, **138** D4
Seoni, India, **218** D5
Seoul *see* Sŏul, South Korea, **208** D3, *163, 164*
Separation Point, Canada, **417** N3
Separation Point, New Zealand, **133** D5
Sepasu, Indonesia, **201** G2
Sepi, Solomon Islands, **141** A1
Sepik, *river*, Papua New Guinea, **140** A4
Sept-Îles, Canada, **416** H4
Septemvri, Bulgaria, **296** E4
Sequim, U.S.A., **418** C2
Seram, India, **216** D2
Seram, Pulau, *island*, Indonesia, **199** E3
Serang, Indonesia, **200** D4
Serangoon, Pulau, *island*, Singapore, **200** K6
Serangoon, *river*, Singapore, **200** K6
Serangoon, Singapore, **200** K6
Serangoon Harbour, Singapore, **200** K6
Serasan, Pulau, *island*, Indonesia, **201** E2
Serasan, Selat, *strait*, Indonesia/Malaysia, **201** E2
Seraya, Pulau, *island*, Singapore, **200** J7
Şerbăneşti, Romania, **296** E3
Serbia, *country*, Europe, **282** F7, *81, 97, 228, 259, 260, 261, 262, 263, 264*
Sêrca, China, **215** E3
Serdo, Ethiopia, **367** F2
Serebryansk, Kazakhstan, **212** D2
Serebryanyye Prudy, Russian Federation, **299** G5
Sered', Slovakia, **289** H4
Seredka, Russian Federation, **299** B3
Seredžius, Lithuania, **287** L5
Seremban, Malaysia, **200** C2
Serempaka, Gunung, *mountain peak*, Indonesia, **201** F3
Serenje, Zambia, **369** F5
Serere, Uganda, **369** F2
Sergelen, Dornod, Mongolia, **210** F2
Sergelen, Sühbaatar, Mongolia, **210** E3
Sergeyevka, Russian Federation, **211** L4
Sergipe, *state*, Brazil, **457** G3
Sergiyev Posad, Russian Federation, **299** G4
Sergiyevo, Russian Federation, **285** T5
Sergozero, Ozero, *lake*, Russian Federation, **285** T3
Serh, China, **213** H5
Sérifontaine, France, **305** J5
Serifos, *island*, Kyklades, Greece, **297** E7
Serik, Turkey, **363** F1
Sermata, Kepulauan, *islands*, Indonesia, **199** E5
Sermiligaaq, Greenland, **411** R3
Seroe Colorado, Aruba, **461** B3
Seronga, Botswana, **370** D2
Serov, Russian Federation, **300** H4
Serowe, Botswana, **371** E3
Serpa, Portugal, **292** D4
Serpiente, Boca de la, *strait*, Trinidad and Tobago/Venezuela, **461** C4
Serpukhov, Russian Federation, **299** F5
Serra, Brazil, **457** F5
Serra do Navio, Brazil, **452** C3
Serra Formosa, Brazil, **456** B3
Serra San Bruno, Italy, **295** F6
Serra Talhada, Brazil, **453** F5
Serrano, Isla, *island*, Chile, **460** B3
Serranópolis, Brazil, **456** C5
Serre, *river*, France, **291** F2
Serres, France, **291** G4
Serres, Greece, **297** D5
Serrezuela, Argentina, **458** D4
Serrinha, Brazil, **457** F3
Sêrro, Brazil, **457** E5
Serrota, *mountain peak*, Spain, **292** E2
Sertânia, Brazil, **453** G5
Sertãozinho, Brazil, **456** D5
Sêrtar, China, **215** G2
Sertung, Pulau, *island*, Indonesia, **200** D4
Serui, Indonesia, **199** G3
Serule, Botswana, **371** E3
Seruyan, *river*, Indonesia, **201** F3
Servia, Greece, **297** D5
Seryshevo, Russian Federation, **211** K2
Sesayap, Indonesia, **201** G2
Sese Islands, Uganda, **369** F3
Sesepe, Indonesia, **198** D3
Sesfontein, Namibia, **370** B2
Sesheke, Zambia, **370** D2
Seskarö, *island*, Sweden, **285** L4
Sessa, Angola, **368** D5
Sessa Aurunca, Italy, **295** D5
Sestri Levante, Italy, **294** B3
Šeta, Lithuania, **287** M5
Sète, France, **291** F5
Sete Lagoas, Brazil, **457** E5
Setermoen, Norway, **284** J2
Setesdal, *valley*, Norway, **286** C3
Sétif, Algeria, **361** H1
Settat, Morocco, **360** E2
Setté Cama, Gabon, **368** A3
Settle, England, U.K., **306** F3
Setúbal, Baía de, *bay*, Portugal, **292** C3
Setúbal, *district*, Portugal, **292** C3
Setúbal, Portugal, **292** C3
Seui, Sardegna, Italy, **295** B6
Seul, Lac, *lake*, Canada, **414** H6
Sevana Lich, *lake*, Armenia, **222** D4, *189*
Sevastopol', Ukraine, **298** D4
Seven Persons, Canada, **413** P7
Seven Sisters Peaks, *mountain peak*, Canada, **412** E4, *25*
Sevenoaks, England, U.K., **305** H3
Severn, *river*, Canada, **415** K4
Severn, *river*, Wales, U.K., **304** D2, *276*
Severn Lake, Canada, **414** J4
Severnaya Osetiya-Alaniya, Respublika, *republic*, Russian Federation, **222** C4
Severnaya Zemlya, *islands*, Russian Federation, **301** M1
Severnoye, Novosibirskaya Oblast', Russian Federation, **223** K1
Severnoye, Orenburgskaya Oblast', Russian Federation, **222** E2
Severnyye Uvaly, *mountain range*, Russian Federation, **300** F4
Severobaykal'sk, Russian Federation, **301** M4
Severočeský, *administrative region*, Czech Republic, **289** F3
Severodvinsk, Russian Federation, **300** F3
Severomoravský, *administrative region*, Czech Republic, **289** H4
Severomorsk, Russian Federation, **285** R2
Severo-Sibirskaya Nizmennost', Russian Federation, **300** K2
Severo-Yeniseyskiy, Russian Federation, **300** L3
Severo-Zadonsk, Russian Federation, **299** G5
Severy, U.S.A., **420** E7
Sevettijärvi, Finland, **285** P2
Sevi, Russian Federation, **213** G1
Sevier, *river*, U.S.A., **422** G2
Sevier Desert, U.S.A., **422** G2
Sevier Lake, U.S.A., **422** G2
Sevilla, Colombia, **450** C3
Sevilla, Spain, **292** E4
Sevlievo, Bulgaria, **296** E4
Sevnica, Slovenia, **294** E2
Sèvre Niortaise, *river*, France, **290** D3
Sevryukovo, Russian Federation, **299** F5
Seward, U.S.A., **410** E3
Seward Peninsula, Canada, **413** C3
Sexsmith, Canada, **413** K4
Seybaplaya, Mexico, **431** H5
Seychelles, *country*, Indian Ocean, **359** L7, *352, 353*
Seychellois, Morne, *mountain peak*, Seychelles, **373** A2, *352*
Seydişehir, Turkey, **363** F1
Seyðisfjörður, Iceland, **284** Z7
Seymor, U.S.A., **421** L6
Seymour, Australia, **135** K6
Seymour, U.S.A., **424** C3
Seyssel, France, **291** G4
Sežana, Slovenia, **294** D3
Sézanne, France, **291** F2
Sezze, Italy, **295** D5
Sfakia, Kriti, Greece, **297** E8
Sfântu Gheorghe, Central Romania, **296** E3
Sfântu Gheorghe, E. Romania, **296** G3
Sfax, Tunisia, **362** B2
Sgurr Mor, *mountain peak*, Scotland, U.K., **308** D3
Sha, *river*, China, **206** D3
Sha Tau Kok *see* Shatoujiao, China, **207** C3
Sha Tin, China, **207** C4
Sha Xian, China, **206** D3
Shaanxi, *province*, China, **210** E5, *161*
Shaba, *administrative region*, Democratic Republic of the Congo, **369** E4
Shabaqua Corners, Canada, **414** K7
Shabeellaha Dhexe, *administrative region*, Somalia, **367** G4
Shabeellaha Hoose, *administrative region*, Somalia, **367** F4
Shabeelle, *river*, Somalia, **367** F4, *339*
Shabelē, Wabē, *river*, Ethiopia, **367** F3
Shabla, Bulgaria, **296** G4
Shabla, Nos, *point*, Bulgaria, **296** G4
Shabogamo Lake, *lake*, Canada, **416** H3
Shabunda, Democratic Republic of the Congo, **369** E3
Shache, China, **212** C5
Shackleton Coast, *region*, Antarctica, **470** D6
Shackleton Ice Shelf, Antarctica, **470** G6
Shackleton Range, *mountain range*, Antarctica, **470** C4
Shadehill, U.S.A., **420** B3
Shadrinsk, Russian Federation, **222** G1
Shadwān, Jazīrat, *island*, Egypt, **363** F3
Shaftesbury, England, U.K., **304** E3
Shag Point, New Zealand, **133** C7
Shagamu, *river*, Canada, **415** L4
Shagari, Nigeria, **365** F2
Shaghan, Kazakhstan, **212** C2
Shaghan, *river*, Kazakhstan, **212** C2
Shāh, *river*, Iran, **222** D5
Shah Alam, Malaysia, **200** C2
Shāhāda, India, **218** C5
Shahany, Ozero, *lake*, Ukraine, **296** H3
Shahbā', Syria, **225** D3
Shāhbandar, Pakistan, **218** A4
Shahdol, India, **219** E5
Shahe, Guangdong, China, **207** A2
Shahe, Hebei, China, **210** F5
Shāhganj, India, **219** E4
Shaḥḥāt, Libya, **362** D2
Shāhjahānpur, India, **218** D4
Shāhpur, India, **216** D2
Shāhpur Chākar, Pakistan, **218** B4
Shāhpura, Madhya Pradesh, India, **218** E5
Shāhpura, N. Rājasthān, India, **218** C4
Shāhpura, S. Rājasthān, India, **218** C4
Shahrak, Afghanistan, **218** A2
Shahr-e Kord, Iran, **220** F2
Shajing, nordeast of Yonghan, Guangdong, China, **207** C1
Shajing, southeast of Taiping, Guangdong, China, **207** B3
Shaka, Ras, *point*, Kenya, **369** H3
Shakhovskaya, Russian Federation, **299** E4
Shakhtīnsk, Kazakhstan, **212** B2
Shakhty, Russian Federation, **298** F3
Shakhun'ya, Russian Federation, **300** F4
Shakopee, U.S.A., **420** G3
Shalday, Kazakhstan, **212** C2
Shallotte, U.S.A., **425** N3
Shalqar, Kazakhstan, **222** F3
Shal'skiy, Russian Federation, **299** E2
Shaluli Shan, *mountain range*, China, **215** F3
Shalya, Russian Federation, **222** F1
Shām, Bādiyat ash (Syrian Desert), Asia, **225** D3, *180, 181, 182*
Shām, Jabal ash, *mountain peak*, Oman, **221** G4
Sham Tseng, China, **207** C4
Shamāl Baḥr al Ghazal, *state*, Sudan, **366** C3
Shamāl Dārfūr, *state*, Sudan, **362** E5
Shamāl Kurdufān, *state*, Sudan, **366** C1
Shamattawa, Canada, **414** H4
Shamattawa, *river*, Canada, **415** M4
Shambu, Ethiopia, **367** E3
Shāmkūh, Iran, **222** F5
Shāmli, India, **218** D3
Shammar, Jabal, *mountain range*, Saudi Arabia, **363** G3
Shāmpur, India, **218** D4
Shamrock, U.S.A., **424** B2
Shamsābād, India, **218** D5
Shamva, Zimbabwe, **369** F6
Shan, *state*, Myanmar, **215** F5
Shan State, *state*, Myanmar, **205** C3
Shan Xian, China, **206** C1
Sha'nabī, Jabal ash, *mountain peak*, Tunisia, **362** A1
Shandan, China, **213** J5
Shandī, Sudan, **363** F5
Shandon, U.S.A., **422** C4
Shandong, *province*, China, **211** G5, *161*
Shangcai, China, **206** C1
Shangcheng, China, **206** C2
Shangchuan Dao, *island*, China, **206** C4
Shangdu, China, **210** F4
Shanggao, China, **206** C2
Shanghai, China, **206** E2, *161*
Shanghang, China, **206** D3
Shanghe, China, **210** G5
Shangkuli, China, **211** H2
Shangnan, China, **206** B1
Shangombo, Zambia, **368** D6
Shangqiu, China, **206** C1
Shangrao, China, **206** D2
Shangyu, China, **206** E2
Shangyun, China, **215** F5
Shangzhi, China, **211** J3
Shangzhou, China, **206** B1
Shanhaiguan, China, **211** H4, *161*
Shanhetun, China, **211** J3
Shani, Nigeria, **365** G2
Shanklin, England, U.K., **305** F4
Shankou, China, **213** G4
Shanlaragh, Ireland, **309** C6
Shannon, Mouth of the, *river mouth*, Ireland, **309** B5
Shannon, North Island, New Zealand, **132** E5
Shannon, *river*, Ireland, **309** D4, *277*
Shannon, South Island, New Zealand, **133** C7
Shannon Ø, *island*, Greenland, **411** T2
Shanshan, China, **212** F4
Shantarskiye Ostrova, *islands*, Russian Federation, **301** Q4
Shantou, China, **206** D4
Shanwei, China, **206** C4
Shanxi, *province*, China, **215** J2, *161*
Shanya, *river*, Russian Federation, **299** E5
Shanyang, China, **206** B1
Shanyin, China, **210** F5
Shaodong, China, **206** B3
Shaoguan, China, **206** C3
Shaowu, China, **206** D3
Shaoxing, China, **206** E2
Shaoyang, China, **206** B3
Shap, England, U.K., **306** F3
Shapa, China, **206** B4
Shapinsay, *island*, Orkney, Scotland, U.K., **308** G1
Shapki, Russian Federation, **299** C3
Shaqrā', Saudi Arabia, **363** J3
Shaqrā', Yemen, **220** E6
Shaquanzi, China, **212** D3
Shar, Kazakhstan, **212** D2
Shar, *river*, Kazakhstan, **212** D2
Sharafah, Sudan, **366** C2
Sharashova, Belarus, **289** M2
Sharbaqty, Kazakhstan, **223** K2
Sharbulag, Mongolia, **213** G2
Share, Nigeria, **365** E3
Sharga, Bulgan, Mongolia, **213** J2
Sharga, Govĭ-Altay, Mongolia, **213** G3
Sharga, Hövsgöl, Mongolia, **213** H2
Sharhorod, Ukraine, **296** G1
Sharhulsan, Mongolia, **210** D3
Shari, Japan, **209** J2
Shark Bay, Australia, **134** C4, *34*
Sharkawshchyna, Belarus, **287** N5
Sharlyk, Russian Federation, **222** E2
Sharm ash Shaykh, Egypt, **225** C6
Sharon Springs, U.S.A., **420** C6
Sharpe Lake, Canada, **414** H4
Sharq al Istiwā'īyah, *state*, Sudan, **369** E1
Sharqī, Jabal ash, *mountain range*, Lebanon/Syria, **225** D3, *181*
Sharqīyah, Aş-Şahrā' ash, Egypt, **225** A5, *317*
Shar'ya, Russian Federation, **300** F4
Sharyn, *river*, Kazakhstan, **212** C4
Sharypovo, Russian Federation, **223** M1
Shashamenē, Ethiopia, **367** E3
Shashe, *river*, Botswana/Zimbabwe, **371** E3
Shashi, China, **206** C2
Shasta, Mount, *mountain peak*, U.S.A., **418** C6
Shasta Lake, U.S.A., **422** B1
Shatou, China, **207** A3
Shatoujiao (Sha Tau Kok), China, **207** C3
Shatsk, Russian Federation, **298** F2
Shats'k, Ukraine, **289** L3
Shatura, Russian Federation, **299** G5
Shaunavon, Canada, **413** Q7
Shawan, Guangdong, China, **207** A3
Shawan, Sichuan, China, **215** G3
Shawano, U.S.A., **421** J3
Shawmarīyah, Jabal ash, *mountain range*, Syria, **225** D2
Shawmut, U.S.A., **419** K3

Shawnee, U.S.A., **424** D2
Shaxi, China, **207** A3
Shayang, China, **206** C2
Shaybārā, *island*, Saudi Arabia, **363** G3
Shaykh, Jabal ash, *mountain peak*, Syria, **225** C3
Shaykh Miskīn, Syria, **225** D3
Shchelkovo, Russian Federation, **299** G5
Shchūchīnsk, Kazakhstan, **223** J2
Shchuch'ye, Russian Federation, **222** G1
Shchuchyn, Belarus, **289** M2
She Xian, China, **206** D2
Shebalino, Russian Federation, **223** M2
Sheberghān, Afghanistan, **218** A1
Sheboygan, U.S.A., **421** K4
Shebunino, Russian Federation, **209** H1
Shediac, Canada, **417** J6
Sheelin, Lough, *lake*, Ireland, **309** E4
Sheenjek, *river*, U.S.A., **410** E3
Sheep Haven, *bay*, Ireland, **309** D2
Sheerness, England, U.K., **305** H3
Sheet Harbour, Canada, **417** K7
Shefar'am, Israel, **225** C3
Sheffield, Alabama, U.S.A., **425** J2
Sheffield, England, U.K., **307** G4
Sheffield, Iowa, U.S.A., **420** G4
Sheffield, Pennsylvania, U.S.A., **421** P5
Sheffield, Texas, U.S.A., **423** N6
Sheho, Canada, **414** C6
Shehong, China, **215** H3
Shek Kong, China, **207** C4
Shek Pik, China, **207** B4
Shek Uk Shan, *mountain peak*, China, **207** C4
Shekhūpura, Pakistan, **218** C3
Shekou, China, **207** B4
Sheksna, Russian Federation, **299** G3
Shelagskiy, Mys, *cape*, Russian Federation, **301** U2
Shelburne, Canada, **416** J8
Shelburne Bay, Australia, **135** J1
Shelby, U.S.A., **419** J2
Shelbyville, Illinois, U.S.A., **421** J6
Shelbyville, Indiana, U.S.A., **421** L6
Shelbyville, Lake, U.S.A., **421** J6
Shelbyville, Tennessee, U.S.A., **425** J2
Sheldon, U.S.A., **420** F4
Sheldrake, Canada, **416** J4
Shelek, Kazakhstan, **212** C4
Shelek, *river*, Kazakhstan, **212** C4
Shelekhov, Russian Federation, **210** D1
Shelikhova, Zaliv, *gulf*, Russian Federation, **301** S3
Shelikof Strait, U.S.A., **410** D4
Shell, U.S.A., **419** L4
Shellbrook, Canada, **413** R5
Shelley, U.S.A., **419** H5
Shelokhovskaya, Russian Federation, **299** G2
Shelton, U.S.A., **418** C3
Shemonaīkha, Kazakhstan, **212** D2
Shenandoah, U.S.A., **420** F5
Shenandoah Mountains, *mountain range*, U.S.A., **421** P6
Shendam, Nigeria, **365** F3
Sheng Xian, China, **206** E2
Shengang, China, **207** B2
Shengena, *mountain peak*, Tanzania, **369** G3
Shëngjin, Albania, **296** B5
Shengze, China, **206** E2
Shenjingzi, China, **211** J3
Shenkursk, Russian Federation, **300** F3
Shenmu, China, **210** E5
Shenshu, China, **211** K3
Shenwan, China, **207** A4
Shenyang, China, **211** H4, *161*
Shenzhen, China, **207** C3
Sheopur, India, **218** D4
Shepetivka, Ukraine, **298** C2
Shepparton, Australia, **135** K6
Sheppey, Isle of, England, U.K., **305** H3
Shepton Mallet, England, U.K., **304** E3
Sherard, Cape, Canada, **411** M2
Sherborne, England, U.K., **304** E4
Sherbro Island, Sierra Leone, **364** B3
Sherbrooke, Canada, **416** F7
Shercock, Ireland, **309** F4
Shergarh, India, **218** C4
Sherghāti, India, **214** C4, **219** F4
Sheridan, Arkansas, U.S.A., **424** F2
Sheridan, Montana, U.S.A., **419** H4
Sheridan, Wyoming, U.S.A., **419** L4
Sheridan Lake, U.S.A., **423** M2
Sheringham, England, U.K., **305** J2
Sherlovaya Gora, Russian Federation, **210** G2
Sherman, U.S.A., **424** D3
Sherman Mills, U.S.A., **426** F2
Sherpur, Bangladesh, **214** D4
Sherridon, Canada, **414** D4
Sherston, England, U.K., **304** E3
Sheshma, *river*, Russian Federation, **222** E2
Shetland, *local authority*, Scotland, U.K., **308** J7
Shetland Islands, Scotland, U.K., **308** J7, *276*
Shetpe, Kazakhstan, **222** E4
Sheung Shui, China, **207** C4
Shewa Gīmīra, Ethiopia, **366** E3
Sheyang, China, **206** E1
Sheyenne, *river*, U.S.A., **420** E2
Shiant Islands, Scotland, U.K., **308** C3
Shiashkotan, Ostrov, *island*, Russian Federation, **301** S5
Shiawassee, *river*, U.S.A., **421** L4
Shibām, Yemen, **220** E5
Shibaocheng, China, **213** H5
Shibata, Japan, **209** G3
Shibazhan, China, **211** J1
Shibecha, Japan, **209** J2
Shibetsu, Japan, **209** H1
Shibīn al Kawm, Egypt, **225** A4
Shidao, China, **211** H5
Shiderti, Kazakhstan, **212** B2
Shiel, Glen, *valley*, Scotland, U.K., **308** D3
Shiel, Loch, *lake*, Scotland, U.K., **308** D4
Shield, Cape, Australia, **135** H1
Shieldaig, Scotland, U.K., **308** D3
Shifā, Jabal ash, *physical feature*, Saudi Arabia, **225** D5
Shifnal, England, U.K., **304** E2
Shigu, China, **215** G4
Shiguaigou, China, **210** E4
Shiguan, China, **207** B2
Shīḩān, *mountain peak*, Jordan, **225** C4
Shihezi, China, **212** E3
Shihoro, Japan, **209** H2
Shiiba, Japan, **208** E4
Shijak, Albania, **297** B5
Shijiazhuang, China, **210** F5, *161*
Shikārpur, Pakistan, **218** B4
Shikohābād, India, **218** D4
Shikoku, *island*, Japan, **208** F4, *165*
Shikoku-sanchi, *mountain range*, Japan, **208** F4
Shikotan, *island*, Kuril'skiye Ostrova, Russian Federation, **209** J2
Shil'da, Russian Federation, **222** F2
Shildon, England, U.K., **307** G3
Shiliguri, India, **219** G4
Shilka, *river*, Russian Federation, **211** G1
Shilka, Russian Federation, **210** G2
Shillelagh, Ireland, **309** F5
Shillong, India, **219** G4, *169*
Shilong, Guangdong, China, **207** B2
Shilong, Guangxi Zhuangzu Zizhiqu, China, **206** B4
Shilou, China, **207** A3
Shilovo, Russian Federation, **298** F2
Shimanovsk, Russian Federation, **211** J1
Shimbiris, *mountain peak*, Somalia, **367** G2, *339*
Shimla, India, **218** D3
Shimoda, Japan, **209** G4
Shimoga, India, **216** C3
Shimonoseki, Japan, **208** E4
Shimshāl, India, **212** B5
Shimshāl, Pakistan, **218** C1
Shimsk, Russian Federation, **299** C3
Shin, Loch, *lake*, Scotland, U.K., **308** E2
Shīndand, Afghanistan, **221** H2
Shiner, U.S.A., **424** D5
Shinfield, England, U.K., **305** G3
Shingbwiyang, Myanmar, **205** C2
Shingle Peak, *mountain peak*, New Zealand, **133** D5
Shining Tree, Canada, **421** N2
Shinjō, Japan, **209** H3
Shinshār, Syria, **225** D2
Shinyanga, *administrative region*, Tanzania, **369** F3
Shinyanga, Tanzania, **369** F3
Shiojiri, Japan, **209** G3
Shiono-misaki, *point*, Japan, **209** F4
Shioya-saki, *point*, Japan, **209** H3
Shipai, China, **207** A2
Shiping, China, **215** G5
Shipley, England, U.K., **307** G4
Shipman, Canada, **413** S5
Shippegan, Canada, **417** J6
Shippensburg, U.S.A., **426** B4
Shiprock, U.S.A., **423** J3
Shipston on Stour, England, U.K., **305** F2
Shipton, England, U.K., **304** E2
Shipu, China, **206** E2
Shipunovo, Russian Federation, **223** L2
Shiqiao *see* Panyu, China, **207** A3
Shiqiao, China, **215** H3
Shiquan, China, **206** B1
Shīr Kūh, *mountain peak*, Iran, **221** F2
Shira, Russian Federation, **223** M2
Shirakawa, Japan, **209** H3
Shirase Coast, *region*, Antarctica, **470** C6
Shīrāz, Iran, **220** F3
Shirbīn, Egypt, **225** A4
Shiree, Mongolia, **213** H3
Shireet, Mongolia, **210** F3
Shiren, China, **211** J4
Shiretoko-misaki, *point*, Japan, **209** J1
Shiriya-zaki, *point*, Japan, **209** H2
Shirley Basin, U.S.A., **419** L5
Shirpur, India, **218** C5
Shisanjianfang, China, **213** F4
Shisanzhan, China, **211** J2
Shishhid, *river*, Mongolia, **213** H2
Shishou, China, **206** C2
Shisizhan, China, **211** J2
Shitan, east of Guangzhou, Guangdong, China, **207** B2
Shitan, north of Guangzhou, Guangdong, China, **206** C3
Shiv, India, **218** B4
Shivpurī, India, **218** D4
Shiwa Ngandu, Zambia, **369** F5
Shiwei, China, **211** H2
Shixian, China, **211** K4
Shiyan, Guangdong, China, **207** B3
Shiyan, Hubei, China, **206** B1
Shiyizhan, China, **211** J2
Shizhan, China, **211** J2
Shizong, China, **215** G4
Shizuishan, China, **210** D5
Shizuoka, Japan, **209** G4
Shklow, Belarus, **299** C5
Shkodër, Albania, **296** B4
Shkumbin, *river*, Albania, **297** B5
Shlissel'burg, Russian Federation, **299** C3
Shoksha, Russian Federation, **299** E2
Sholaqqorghan, Kazakhstan, **223** H4
Shombozero, Russian Federation, **285** R4
Shonzhy, Kazakhstan, **212** C4
Shoqpar, Kazakhstan, **212** B4
Shoranūr, India, **216** D4
Shoreham-by-Sea, England, U.K., **305** G4
Shortland (Alu), *island*, Solomon Islands, **141** A1
Shoshone Mountains, *mountain range*, U.S.A., **422** E2
Shoshong, Botswana, **371** E3
Shoshoni, U.S.A., **419** K5
Shouchang, China, **206** D2
Shouguang, China, **208** B3
Shouwangfen, China, **211** G4
Shouxian, China, **206** D1
Shouyang, China, **210** F5
Shouzhou, China, **210** F5
Show Low, U.S.A., **423** H4
Shoyna, Russian Federation, **300** F3
Shreveport, U.S.A., **424** F3
Shrewsbury, England, U.K., **304** E2
Shri Mohangarh, India, **218** B4
Shrivenham, England, U.K., **305** F3
Shropshire, *unitary authority*, England, U.K., **304** E2
Shū, Kazakhstan, **212** B4
Shu, *river*, China, **206** D1
Shū, *river*, Kazakhstan, **223** H4
Shu'ab, Ra's, *point*, Suquṭrá (Socotra), Yemen, **373** B2
Shuajingsi, China, **215** G3
Shuangcheng, China, **211** J3
Shuangfeng, China, **206** C3
Shuangjiang, China, **215** F5
Shuangliao, China, **211** H4
Shuangliao, South Korea, **211** H4
Shuangyashan, China, **211** K3
Shubarqudyq, Kazakhstan, **222** F3
Shubrā al Khaymah, Egypt, **225** A4
Shucheng, China, **206** D2
Shuitou, China, **207** B1
Shujālpur, India, **218** D5
Shūl, *river*, Iran, **220** F2
Shulan, China, **211** J3
Shule, China, **212** C5
Shule, *river*, China, **213** H5
Shule Nanshan, *mountain range*, China, **213** H5
Shūlgareh, Afghanistan, **218** A1
Shulu, China, **210** F5
Shumen, Bulgaria, **296** F4
Shumerlya, Russian Federation, **222** D1
Shumikha, Russian Federation, **222** G1
Shumilina, Belarus, **299** B5
Shunchang, China, **206** D3
Shunde, China, **206** C4
Shun'ga, Russian Federation, **285** S5
Shungnak, U.S.A., **410** D3
Shūr-e Gaz, Iran, **221** G3
Shūrāb, Iran, **221** G2
Shurugwi, Zimbabwe, **371** E2
Shūsf, Iran, **221** H2
Shūsh, Iran, **220** E2
Shūshtar, Iran, **220** E2
Shuswap Lake, Canada, **413** K6
Shuwak, Sudan, **366** E2
Shuya, *river*, Russian Federation, **299** D2
Shuya, Russian Federation, **299** E2
Shuyang, China, **206** D1
Shuyeretskoye, Russian Federation, **285** S4
Shwebo, Myanmar, **205** B3
Shyghanaq, Kazakhstan, **212** B3
Shyghys Qazaqstan, *province*, Kazakhstan, **212** D2
Shymkent, Kazakhstan, **223** H4
Shyngghyrlaū, *river*, Kazakhstan, **222** E2
Shyok, India, **218** D2
Shyryayeve, Ukraine, **296** H2
Si Sa Ket, Thailand, **203** E3
Si Xian, China, **206** D1
Siāhān Range, *mountain range*, Pakistan, **221** H3
Siālkot, Pakistan, **218** C2
Sialum, Papua New Guinea, **140** B4
Sianów, Poland, **289** H1
Siapa, *river*, Venezuela, **451** E4
Siargao Island, Philippines, **204** D4
Siasi, Philippines, **204** C5
Siassi, Papua New Guinea, **140** B4
Siatista, Greece, **297** C5
Siatlai, Myanmar, **205** B3
Siaton, Philippines, **204** C4
Siau, Pulau, *island*, Indonesia, **198** D2
Šiaulėnai, Lithuania, **287** L5
Šiauliai, Lithuania, **287** L5
Sibari, Italy, **295** F6
Sibati, China, **212** F3
Sibayak, Gunung, *mountain peak*, Indonesia, **200** B2
Sibbald, Canada, **413** P6
Šibenik, Croatia, **294** E4
Siberia *see* Siber', *region*, Russian Federation, **195** N3, *87, 100, 144, 272, 273, 384, 464, 465*
Siber' (Siberia), *region*, Russian Federation, **195** N3, *87, 100, 144, 272, 273, 384, 464, 465*
Siberimanua, Indonesia, **200** B3
Siberut, Pulau, *island*, Indonesia, **200** B3
Siberut, Selat, *strait*, Indonesia, **200** B3
Sibi, Pakistan, **218** A3
Sibiti, Congo, **368** B3
Sibiu, Romania, **296** E3
Sible Hedingham, England, U.K., **305** H3
Sibolga, Indonesia, **200** B2
Siborongborong, Indonesia, **200** B2
Sibsāgar, India, **219** H4
Sibsey, England, U.K., **307** J4
Sibu, Malaysia, **201** E2
Sibuco, Philippines, **204** C5
Sibut, Central African Republic, **368** C1
Sibutu Group, *islands*, Philippines, **204** B5
Sibutu Island, Philippines, **204** B5
Sibuyan Island, Philippines, **204** C3
Sicamous, Canada, **413** K6
Sicapoo, Mount, *mountain peak*, Philippines, **204** C2
Sichuan, *province*, China, **215** G3, *56, 86, 159, 160, 161*
Sichuan Pendi, *basin*, China, **215** H3
Sicié, Cap, *cape*, France, **291** G5
Sicilia, *autonomous region*, Italy, **295** D7, *255*
Sicilia (Sicily), *island*, Italy, **295** E7, *71, 89, 254, 255, 257, 315*
Sicily *see* Sicilia, *island*, Italy, **295** E7, *71, 89, 254, 255, 257, 315*
Sicily, Strait of, Italy, **295** C7
Sicuani, Peru, **454** D4
Šid, Serbia, **296** B3
Sidaouet, Niger, **365** F1
Sidbury, England, U.K., **304** D4
Siddhapur, India, **218** C5
Siddipet, India, **216** D2
Sidéradougou, Burkina Faso, **364** D2
Siderno, Italy, **295** F6
Sideros, Akra, *point*, Kriti, Greece, **297** F8
Sidhi, India, **219** E4
Sidi Ali, Algeria, **361** G1
Sīdī Barrānī, Egypt, **362** E2
Sidi Bel Abbès, Algeria, **361** F1
Sidi Bou Zid, Tunisia, **362** A2
Sidi el Hani, Sebkhet de, *salt-pan*, Tunisia, **295** C8
Sidi Ifni, Morocco, **360** D3
Sidi Kacem, Morocco, **361** E2
Sidi Khaled, Algeria, **361** G2
Sidi Lakhdar, Algeria, **293** H4
Sidi Okba, Algeria, **361** H2
Sīdī Sālim, Egypt, **225** A4
Sidikalang, Indonesia, **200** B2
Sidirokastra, Greece, **297** D5
Sidlaw Hills, Scotland, U.K., **308** F4
Sidley, Mount, *mountain peak*, Antarctica, **470** C6
Sidmouth, England, U.K., **304** D4
Sidney, Canada, **412** H7

Sidney, Iowa, U.S.A., **420** F5
Sidney, Montana, U.S.A., **419** M3
Sidney, Nebraska, U.S.A., **420** B5
Sidney Lanier, Lake, U.S.A., **425** L2
Sido, Mali, **364** C2
Sidon *see* Şaydā, Lebanon, **225** C3
Sidorovo, Russian Federation, **299** G4
Sidrolândia, Brazil, **456** B5
Siedlce, Poland, **289** L2
Siegen, Germany, **288** D3
Sielkentjahke, *mountain peak*, Sweden, **284** G4
Siembra, Indonesia, **199** F3
Siemens, Cape, Papua New Guinea, **140** C3
Siemiatycze, Poland, **289** L2
Siĕmréab, Cambodia, **203** D3
Siena, Italy, **294** C4
Sieppijärvi, Finland, **285** M3
Sieradz, Poland, **289** J3
Sierpc, Poland, **289** J2
Sierra, Punta, *point*, Argentina, **460** E1
Sierra Blanca, U.S.A., **423** L6
Sierra Colorada, Argentina, **460** D1
Sierra Gorda, Chile, **458** C2
Sierra Grande, Argentina, **460** E1
Sierra Leone, *country*, Africa, **358** D6, *94, 312, 321, 322*
Sierra Leone Basin, *underwater feature*, Atlantic Ocean, **477** F5
Sierra Mojada, Mexico, **430** E3
Sierra Vista, U.S.A., **423** H6
Sierraville, U.S.A., **422** C2
Sierre, Switzerland, **291** H3
Şieu, Romania, **296** E2
Sievi, Finland, **285** M5
Sifnos, *island*, Kyklades, Greece, **297** E7
Sig, Algeria, **293** G5
Sig, Russian Federation, **285** S4
Sigatoka, Fiji, **141** A4
Sigean, France, **291** F5
Sigenti, Indonesia, **198** C2
Sigep, Tanjong, *point*, Indonesia, **200** B3
Sighetu Marmaţiei, Romania, **296** D2
Sighişoara, Romania, **296** E2
Sigli, Indonesia, **200** B1
Siglufjörður, Iceland, **284** Y6
Signal de Botrange, *mountain peak*, Belgium, **288** C3
Signy, *U.K. research station*, Antarctica, **470** A3
Sigri, Greece, **297** E6
Siguatepeque, Honduras, **428** D4
Sigüenza, Spain, **293** F2
Sigüés, Spain, **293** G1
Siguiri, Guinea, **364** C2
Sigulda, Latvia, **287** M4
Sihong, China, **206** D1
Sihora, India, **218** E5
Sihuas, Peru, **454** C2
Sihui, China, **206** C4
Siikainen, Finland, **287** K2
Siikajoki, *river*, Finland, **285** M4
Siilinjärvi, Finland, **285** N5
Siirt, Turkey, **224** F5
Siivikko, Finland, **285** N4
Sikaiana, *island*, Solomon Islands, **141** A1
Sikanni Chief, Canada, **412** H3
Sīkar, India, **218** C4
Sikasso, *administrative region*, Mali, **364** C2
Sikasso, Mali, **364** C2
Sikaw, Myanmar, **205** C3
Sikea, Greece, **297** D5
Sikes, U.S.A., **424** F3
Sikeston, U.S.A., **421** J7
Sikhote-Alin', *mountain range*, Russian Federation, **211** L3
Sikinos, *island*, Kyklades, Greece, **297** E7
Sikkim, *state*, India, **219** G4, *169*
Siktyakh, Russian Federation, **301** P3
Sil, *river*, Spain, **292** D1
Sila, La, *mountain range*, Italy, **295** F6
Silandro Schlanders, Italy, **294** C2
Silay, Philippines, **204** C4
Silba, *island*, Croatia, **294** E3
Silchar, India, **219** H4
Silet, Algeria, **361** G4
Siletz, U.S.A., **418** C4
Silhouette, *island*, Seychelles, **373** A2, *353*
Silifke, Turkey, **225** B1
Silin, China, **215** H5
Siling Co, *lake*, China, **214** D3
Silíqua, Sardegna, Italy, **295** B6
Silistră, Bulgaria, **298** C4
Silivri, Turkey, **297** G5
Siljan, *lake*, Sweden, **286** G2
Silkeborg, Denmark, **286** D4
Sillamäe, Estonia, **287** N3
Sillé-le-Guillaume, France, **290** D2
Sillon de Talbert, *point*, France, **290** C2
Silloth, England, U.K., **306** E3
Silsbee, U.S.A., **424** E4
Siluko, Nigeria, **365** F3
Šilutė, Lithuania, **287** K5
Silvassa, India, **218** C5, *169*
Silver Bay, U.S.A., **420** H2
Silver City, Idaho, U.S.A., **418** F5
Silver City, New Mexico, U.S.A., **423** J5
Silver Dollar, Canada, **414** J7
Silver Lake, U.S.A., **418** D5
Silverdale, New Zealand, **132** E3
Silverstone, England, U.K., **305** F2
Silverton, Colorado, U.S.A., **423** K3
Silverton, England, U.K., **304** D4
Silverton, Oregon, U.S.A., **418** C4
Silverton, Texas, U.S.A., **424** B2
Silves, Brazil, **451** G5
Silvituc, Mexico, **431** H5
Silvrettagruppe, *mountain range*, Switzerland/Austria, **291** J3
Sima, China, **207** C3
Simanggang *see* Bandar Sri Aman, Malaysia, **201** E2
Simao, China, **215** G5
Simão Dias, Brazil, **457** G3
Simara, Nepal, **219** F4
Simaria Ghāt, India, **219** F4
Simav, Turkey, **297** G6
Simav Dağları, *mountain range*, Turkey, **297** G6
Simba, Democratic Republic of the Congo, **368** D2
Simbai, Papua New Guinea, **140** B4
Simbu, *province*, Papua New Guinea, **140** B4
Simcoe, Canada, **421** N4
Simcoe, Lake, Canada, **421** P3
Simdega, India, **219** F5
Simēn, *mountain range*, Ethiopia, **367** E2
Simeria, Romania, **296** D3
Simeulue, Pulau, *island*, Indonesia, **200** B2
Simferopol', Ukraine, **298** D4
Simga, India, **219** E5
Simi Valley, U.S.A., **422** D4
Simití, Colombia, **450** D2
Simla, U.S.A., **423** L2
Simleu Silvaniei, Romania, **296** D2
Simms, U.S.A., **419** J3
Simnas, Lithuania, **287** L5
Simo, Finland, **285** M4
Simojärvi, *lake*, Finland, **285** N3
Simojoki, *river*, Finland, **285** M4
Simplício Mendes, Brazil, **453** F5
Simpson, Canada, **413** S6
Simpson, Mount, *mountain peak*, Papua New Guinea, **140** C5
Simpson Desert, Australia, **128** C4
Simrishamn, Sweden, **286** G5
Simushir, Ostrov, *island*, Russian Federation, **301** S5
Sīnā' (Sinai), *peninsula*, Egypt, **225** B4, *182, 317*
Sina Dhaqa, Somalia, **367** G3
Sinabang, Indonesia, **200** B2
Sinai, Mount *see* Mūsā, Jabal, *mountain peak*, Egypt, **225** B5, *355*
Sinai *see* Sīnā', *peninsula*, Egypt, **225** B4, *182, 317*
Sinaia, Romania, **296** E3
Sinaloa, *state*, Mexico, **430** C3
Sinalunga, Italy, **294** C4
Sinarades, Greece, **297** B6
Sīnāwin, Libya, **362** B2
Sinbaungwe, Myanmar, **205** B4
Sinbo, Myanmar, **205** C2
Sinbyugyun, Myanmar, **205** B3
Şinca Nouă, Romania, **296** E3
Sincé, Colombia, **450** C2
Sincelejo, Colombia, **450** C2
Sinch'ŏn, North Korea, **208** D3
Sinclair, Lake, U.S.A., **425** L3
Sinclair, U.S.A., **419** L6
Sinclair Mills, Canada, **412** J4
Sinclair's Bay, Scotland, U.K., **308** F2
Sind, *river*, India, **218** D4
Sindangan, Philippines, **204** C4
Sindangbarang, Indonesia, **201** D4
Sindara, Gabon, **368** B3
Sindari, India, **218** B4
Sindh, *province*, Pakistan, **218** B4
Sindhnūr, India, **216** D3
Sindi, Estonia, **287** M3
Sındırgı, Turkey, **297** G6
Sindri, India, **219** F5
Sinegor'ye, Russian Federation, **301** S3
Sinendé, Benin, **365** E2
Sines, Portugal, **292** C4
Sinewit, Mount, *mountain peak*, Papua New Guinea, **140** D4
Sinfra, Côte d'Ivoire, **364** C3
Sing Buri, Thailand, **202** D3
Singapore, *country*, Asia, **197** M9, *45, 46, 51, 79, 144, 145, 150, 151*
Singapore, Singapore, **200** K7, *150*
Singapore, Straits of, Indonesia/Singapore, **200** K7, *151*
Singaraja, Indonesia, **201** F5
Singarāyakonda, India, **216** E3
Singida, *administrative region*, Tanzania, **369** F4
Singida, Tanzania, **369** F3
Singkang, Indonesia, **198** C4
Singkarak, Danau, *lake*, Indonesia, **200** B3
Singkawang, Indonesia, **201** E2
Singkep, Pulau, *island*, Indonesia, **200** D3
Singleton, Australia, **135** L5
Singoli, India, **218** C4
Singsås, Norway, **284** E5
Siniscola, Sardegna, Italy, **295** B5
Sinj, Croatia, **294** F4
Sinjah, Sudan, **366** D2
Sinjai, Indonesia, **198** C4
Sinjār, Iraq, **363** H1
Sinkan, Myanmar, **205** C2
Sinkāt, Sudan, **363** G5
Sinko, Guinea, **364** C3
Sinn Bishr, Jabal, *mountain peak*, Egypt, **225** B5
Sinnamary, French Guiana, **452** C2
Sinnār, *state*, Sudan, **366** D2
Sinni, *river*, Italy, **295** F5
Sinoie, Lacul, *lake*, Romania, **296** G3
Sinop, Brazil, **456** B3
Sinop, Turkey, **224** E4
Sinp'o, North Korea, **208** E2
Sint Nicolaas, Aruba, **461** B3
Sint Willebrordus, Curaçao, Netherlands Antilles, **461** C3
Sintang, Indonesia, **201** E2
Sinton, U.S.A., **424** D5
Sintra, Portugal, **292** C3
Sinú, *river*, Colombia, **450** C2
Sinŭiju, North Korea, **208** D2
Sinujiif, Somalia, **367** G3
Sinyaya, *river*, Latvia/Russian Federation, **299** B4
Siocon, Philippines, **204** C5
Siófok, Hungary, **289** J5
Sion, Switzerland, **291** H3
Sion Mills, Northern Ireland, U.K., **309** E3
Siorapaluk, Greenland, **411** M2
Sioux Center, U.S.A., **420** E4
Sioux City, U.S.A., **420** E4
Sioux Falls, U.S.A., **420** E4
Sioux Lookout, Canada, **414** J6
Sipacate, Guatemala, **428** C4
Sipalay, Philippines, **204** C4
Sipang, Tanjong, *point*, Malaysia, **201** E2
Siparia, Trinidad, Trinidad and Tobago, **461** C4
Siping, China, **211** J4
Sipiwesk, Canada, **414** F4
Sipiwesk Lake, Canada, **414** F4
Siple, Mount, *mountain peak*, Antarctica, **470** B7
Siple Coast, *region*, Antarctica, **470** C6
Siple Island, Antarctica, **470** B7
Sipocot, Philippines, **204** C3
Sipura, Pulau, *island*, Indonesia, **200** B3
Siquijor Island, Philippines, **204** C4
Sir Alexander, Mount, *mountain peak*, Canada, **412** J5
Sir Edward Pellew Group, *islands*, Australia, **135** H2
Sir Sandford, Mount, *mountain peak*, Canada, **413** L6
Sir Wilfrid Laurier, Mount, *mountain peak*, Canada, **413** K5
Sira, India, **216** D3
Sira, Norway, **286** C3
Sira, *river*, Norway, **286** C3
Siracusa, Sicilia, Italy, **295** E7
Sirājganj, Bangladesh, **205** A2
Sirakorola, Mali, **364** C2
Siret, Romania, **296** F2
Sirevåg, Norway, **286** B3
Sirḩān, Wādī as, *physical feature*, Saudi Arabia, **225** D4
Siri, Cape, Papua New Guinea, **140** D5
Sirik, Tanjong, *point*, Malaysia, **201** E2
Sirikit Reservoir, Thailand, **202** D2
Sirinthornb Reservoir, Thailand, **203** E3
Sīrjān, Iran, **221** G3
Sirkka, Finland, **285** M3
Şirnak, Turkey, **224** F5
Sirohi, India, **218** C4
Široki Brijeg, Bosnia and Herzegovina, **294** F4
Sirombu, Indonesia, **200** B2
Sironj, India, **218** D4
Sirrī, Jazīreh-ye, *island*, Iran, **220** F3
Sirsa, India, **218** C3
Sirsi, India, **216** C3
Sirsilla, India, **216** D2
Širvintos, Lithuania, **287** M5
Sisa, Mount, *mountain peak*, Papua New Guinea, **140** A4
Sisak, Croatia, **294** F3
Sisal, Mexico, **431** H4
Sisante, Spain, **293** F3
Sishilipu, China, **215** H2
Sisian, Armenia, **363** J1
Sisimiut, Greenland, **411** P3
Siskiyou Mountains, *mountain range*, U.S.A., **418** C6
Sisŏphŏn, Cambodia, **203** D3
Sissano, Papua New Guinea, **140** A3
Sisteron, France, **291** G4
Sisters, The, *islands*, Chatham Islands, New Zealand, **133** Q16
Sisters, U.S.A., **418** D4
Sisters Peak, *mountain peak*, Ascension, **373** A3
Sitampiky, Madagascar, **372** B4
Sītāpur, India, **218** E4
Sitasjaure, *lake*, Sweden, **284** H3
Siteia, Kriti, Greece, **297** F8
Siteki, Swaziland, **371** F4
Sitian, China, **213** G4
Sítio da Abadia, Brazil, **456** D4
Sitio do Mato, Brazil, **457** E3
Sitka, U.S.A., **412** B3
Sitka Point, U.S.A., **412** A3
Sittang, *river*, Myanmar, **205** C4
Sittingbourne, England, U.K., **305** H3
Sittwe (Akyab), Myanmar, **205** B3
Situbondo, Indonesia, **201** F4
Siufago, American Samoa, **141** B2
Siumu, Samoa, **141** B1
Siuna, Nicaragua, **428** D4
Siuna, *river*, Nicaragua, **428** D4
Siuntio, Finland, **287** M2
Siuri, India, **219** F5
Siuruanjoki, *river*, Finland, **285** N4
Sivaganga, India, **216** D4
Sivaki, Russian Federation, **211** J1
Sīvand, Iran, **220** F2
Sivas, Turkey, **224** E5
Sivaslı, Turkey, **297** G6
Siverek, Turkey, **224** E5
Sivrihisar, Turkey, **224** D5
Siwa, Indonesia, **198** C3
Sīwah, Egypt, **362** E3
Siwālik Range, *mountain range*, India/Nepal, **218** D3, *172*
Siwān, India, **219** F4
Sixin, China, **213** H5
Siyabuswa, South Africa, **371** E4
Siyang, China, **206** D1
Siyitang, China, **210** E4
Siz'ma, Russian Federation, **299** G3
Sjælland, *island*, Denmark, **286** E5, *233*
Sjenica, Serbia, **296** B4
Sjøåsen, Norway, **284** E4
Sjöbo, Sweden, **286** F5
Sjøholt, Norway, **286** C1
Sjötorp, Sweden, **286** F3
Sjoutnäset, Sweden, **284** G4
Sjøvegan, Norway, **284** H2
Skadarsko Jezero (Ligeni i Shkodrës), *lake*, Montenegro, **296** B4
Skærbæk, Denmark, **286** D5
Skagen, Denmark, **286** E4
Skagerrak, *strait*, Denmark/Norway, **286** C4, *231, 233*
Skagway, U.S.A., **412** B2
Skaill, Orkney, Scotland, U.K., **308** G2
Skala, Greece, **297** D7
Skala-Podil's'ka, Ukraine, **296** F1
Skanderborg, Denmark, **286** D4
Skanee, U.S.A., **421** J2
Skånevik, Norway, **286** B3
Skansnäs, Sweden, **284** H4
Skantzoura, *island*, Greece, **297** E6
Skara, Sweden, **286** F3
Skarabord, *county*, Sweden, **286** F3
Skarberget, Norway, **284** H2
Skārdu, Pakistan, **218** C2
Skare, Norway, **286** C3
Skarnes, Norway, **286** E2
Skärplinge, Sweden, **287** H2
Skarvsjö, Sweden, **284** H4
Skarżysko-Kamienna, Poland, **289** K3
Skaudvilė, Lithuania, **287** L5
Skaulo, Sweden, **284** K3
Skeena, *river*, Canada, **412** F4
Skeena Mountains, *mountain range*, Canada, **412** E3
Skegness, England, U.K., **305** H1
Skei, Møre og Romsdal, Norway, **284** D5
Skei, Sogn og Fjordane, Norway, **286** C2
Skellefteå, Sweden, **284** K4
Skelmersdale, England, U.K., **306** F4
Skenfrith, Wales, U.K., **304** E3
Skępe, Poland, **289** J2
Skerries, Ireland, **309** F4
Ski, Norway, **286** E3
Skiathos, *island*, Voreioi Sporades, Greece, **297** D6
Skiathos, Voreioi Sporades, Greece, **297** D6
Skibbereen, Ireland, **309** C6
Skibotn, Norway, **284** K2

Skiddaw, *mountain peak*, England, U.K., **306** E3
Skien, Norway, **286** D3
Skikda, Algeria, **361** H1
Skillingaryd, Sweden, **286** G4
Skillinge, Sweden, **286** G5
Skipsea, England, U.K., **307** H4
Skipskjølen, *mountain peak*, Norway, **285** P1
Skipton, England, U.K., **306** F4
Skive, Denmark, **286** D4
Skjånes, Norway, **285** P1
Skjern, Denmark, **286** D5
Skjervøy, Norway, **284** K1
Skjolden, Norway, **286** C2
Sklithro, Greece, **297** D6
Skoczów, Poland, **289** J4
Skog, Sweden, **287** H2
Skoganvarre, Norway, **285** M2
Skógar, Iceland, **284** Y8
Skokholm Island, Wales, U.K., **304** B3
Skole, Ukraine, **289** L4
Skomer Island, Wales, U.K., **304** B3
Skón, Cambodia, **203** E3
Skookumchuck, Canada, **413** M7
Skopelos, *island*, Voreioi Sporades, Greece, **297** D6
Skopelos, Voreioi Sporades, Greece, **297** D6
Skopje, Macedonia, **296** C5, *260*
Skorovatn, Norway, **284** F4
Skorped, Sweden, **284** H5
Skotterud, Norway, **286** F3
Skövde, Sweden, **286** F3
Skovorodino, Russian Federation, **301** P4
Skowhegan, U.S.A., **426** F2
Skrad, Croatia, **294** E3
Skreia, Norway, **286** E2
Skrimfjella, *mountain peak*, Norway, **286** D3
Skrīveri, Latvia, **287** M4
Skrunda, Latvia, **287** L4
Skudeneshavn, Norway, **286** B3
Skulgam, Norway, **284** J2
Skull, Ireland, **309** C6
Skuodas, Lithuania, **287** K4
Skurup, Sweden, **286** F5
Skutvik, Norway, **284** G2
Skwierzyna, Poland, **289** G2
Skye, *island*, Scotland, U.K., **308** C3
Skykomish, U.S.A., **418** D3
Skyropoula, *island*, Greece, **297** E6
Skyros, Greece, **297** E6
Skyros, *island*, Greece, **297** E6
Skyttmon, Sweden, **284** G5
Slagelse, Denmark, **286** E5
Slamet, Gunung, *mountain peak*, Indonesia, **201** E4
Slane, Ireland, **309** F4
Slaney, *river*, Ireland, **309** F5
Slantsy, Russian Federation, **299** B3
Slaný, Czech Republic, **289** G3
Slater, U.S.A., **419** M6
Slatina, Romania, **296** E3
Slaton, U.S.A., **424** B3
Slave, *river*, Canada, **413** N1
Slave Coast, *coastal area*, Benin/Nigeria, **365** E3
Slave Lake, Canada, **413** M4
Slavgorod, Russian Federation, **223** K2
Slavkovichi, Russian Federation, **299** B4
Slavnoye, Russian Federation, **209** K1
Slavonija, *region*, Croatia, **294** F3
Slavonska Požega, Croatia, **294** F3
Slavonski Brod, Croatia, **294** G3
Slavs'ke, Ukraine, **296** D1
Slavskoye, Ukraine, **289** L4
Slavyanka, Russian Federation, **211** K4
Slavyanovo, Bulgaria, **296** E4
Slawharad, Belarus, **299** C6
Sławno, Poland, **289** H1
Slea Head, *point*, Ireland, **309** B5
Sleaford, England, U.K., **305** G1
Sleat, Sound of, Scotland, U.K., **308** D4
Sleeper Islands, Canada, **415** Q3
Sleights, England, U.K., **307** H3
Ślesin, Poland, **289** J2
Slide Mountain, *mountain peak*, U.S.A., **426** C4
Slidell, U.S.A., **424** H4
Slieve Aughty Mountains, Ireland, **309** D4
Slievecallan, *mountain peak*, Ireland, **309** C5
Slievefelim Mountains, Ireland, **309** D5
Slievemore, *mountain peak*, Ireland, **309** B3
Slievenamon, *mountain peak*, Ireland, **309** E5
Sligachan, Scotland, U.K., **308** C3
Sligo, *county*, Ireland, **309** D3
Sligo, Ireland, **309** D3
Sligo Bay, Ireland, **309** D3
Slite, Sweden, **287** J4
Sliven, Bulgaria, **296** F4
Slivo Pole, Bulgaria, **296** F4
Sljeme, *mountain peak*, Croatia, **294** E3
Slobidka, Ukraine, **296** G2
Slobozia, Moldova, **296** G2
Slobozia, Romania, **296** F3
Slocan Lake, Canada, **413** L7
Slogen, *mountain peak*, Norway, **286** C1
Słomniki, Poland, **289** K3
Slonim, Belarus, **289** M2
Slot, The *see* New Georgia Sound, *channel*, Solomon Islands, **141** A1
Slough, England, U.K., **305** G3
Slough, *unitary authority*, England, U.K., **305** G3
Slovakia, *country*, Europe, **282** F6, *81, 228, 245, 248, 249, 262, 266, 267, 269*
Slovenia, *country*, Europe, **282** F6, *81, 228, 245, 248, 254, 258, 259, 261, 262*
Slovenska Bistrica, Slovenia, **294** E2
Slovenske gorice, *mountain range*, Slovenia, **294** E2, *258*
Slovenske Rudohorie, *mountain range*, Slovakia, **289** K4
Słubice, Poland, **289** G2
Slunj, Croatia, **294** E3
Słupca, Poland, **289** H2
Słupsk, Poland, **289** H1
Slussfors, Sweden, **284** H4
Slyne Head, *point*, Ireland, **309** B4
Slyudyanka, Russian Federation, **210** C2
Smallwood Reservoir, Canada, **417** J2
Smalyavichy, Belarus, **299** B5
Smarhon, Belarus, **287** N5
Smederevo, Serbia, **296** C3
Smederevska Palanka, Serbia, **296** C3
Smeeni, Romania, **296** F3
Smerdel', *river*, Russian Federation, **299** C4
Smerwick Harbour, Ireland, **309** B5
Smethport, U.S.A., **426** A4
Smidovich, Russian Federation, **211** L2
Smilavichy, Belarus, **299** B6
Smiltene, Latvia, **287** M4
Smith, Canada, **413** M4
Smith, *river*, U.S.A., **419** J3
Smith Bay, Canada, **411** M2
Smith Center, U.S.A., **420** D6
Smith Island, U.S.A., **425** P3
Smith Mountain Lake, U.S.A., **421** P7
Smith River, U.S.A., **418** B6
Smithers, Canada, **412** F4
Smithfield, North Carolina, U.S.A., **425** N2
Smithfield, Utah, U.S.A., **419** J6
Smiths Falls, Canada, **416** D7
Smiths Ferry, U.S.A., **418** F4
Smithson Bight, *bay*, Christmas Island, **134** N8
Smithton, Australia, **135** K7
Smokvica, Macedonia, **297** D5
Smoky, *river*, Canada, **413** K4
Smoky Hills, U.S.A., **420** C6
Smoky Lake, Canada, **413** N4
Smøla, *island*, Norway, **284** C5
Smolensk, Russian Federation, **299** C5
Smolenskaya Oblast', *province*, Russian Federation, **299** D5
Smolensko-Moskovskaya Vozvyshennost', *mountain range*, Russian Federation, **299** D5
Smolikas, *mountain peak*, Greece, **297** C5
Smolyan, Bulgaria, **297** E5
Smooth Rock Falls, Canada, **415** P7
Smyadovo, Bulgaria, **296** F4
Smyley Island, Antarctica, **470** B5
Smyrna, U.S.A., **425** K3
Smyth, Canal, *channel*, Chile, **460** B4
Snaefell, *mountain peak*, Isle of Man, **306** D3
Snag, Canada, **410** E3
Snaght, Slieve, *mountain peak*, Ireland, **309** E2
Snaith, England, U.K., **307** G4
Snake, *river*, U.S.A., **406** M4
Snake River Plain, U.S.A., **418** H5
Snares Islands, New Zealand, **132** H9
Snåsa, Norway, **284** F4
Snåsavatnet, *lake*, Norway, **284** E4
Sneek, Netherlands, **288** B2
Sneem, Ireland, **309** C6
Snegamook Lake, Canada, **417** L2
Snettisham, England, U.K., **305** H2
Śniardwy, Jezioro, *lake*, Poland, **289** K2
Sniežka, Czech Republic, **289** G3
Snina, Slovakia, **289** L4
Snizort, Loch, *lake*, Scotland, U.K., **308** C3
Snøhetta, *mountain peak*, Norway, **286** D1
Snønuten, *mountain peak*, Norway, **286** C3
Snota, *mountain peak*, Norway, **284** D5
Snow Lake, Canada, **414** D4
Snow Mountain, *mountain peak*, U.S.A., **422** B2
Snowbird Lake, Canada, **414** C1
Snowdon, *mountain peak*, Wales, U.K., **304** C1, *276*
Snowflake, U.S.A., **423** H4
Snowtown, Australia, **135** H5
Snowy Mountains, *mountain range*, Australia, **135** K6, *113*
Snug Corner, Bahamas, **429** G2
Snyatyn, Ukraine, **296** E1
Snyder, Colorado, U.S.A., **423** M1
Snyder, Oklahoma, U.S.A., **424** C2
Snyder, Texas, U.S.A., **424** B3
Soacha, Colombia, **450** C3
Soai Dao, Phu, *mountain peak*, Laos, **202** D2
Soalala, Madagascar, **372** B4
Soamanonga, Madagascar, **372** A5
Soanierana-Ivongo, Madagascar, **372** B4
Soap Lake, U.S.A., **418** E3
Sobāt, *river*, Sudan, **366** D3
Soběslav, Czech Republic, **289** G4
Sobradinho, Represa de, *reservoir*, Brazil, **457** E3
Sobral, Brazil, **453** F4
Sobrance, Slovakia, **289** L4
Sóc Trăng, Vietnam, **203** E4
Sočanica, Serbia, **296** C4
Sochaczew, Poland, **289** K2
Sochi, Russian Federation, **224** E4
Sochos, Greece, **297** D5
Société, Archipel de la, French Polynesia, **137** F2, *122, 123*
Socorro, Colombia, **450** D2
Socorro, U.S.A., **423** K4
Socotra *see* Suquṭrá, *island*, Yemen, **373** B2
Soda Creek, Canada, **412** H5
Soda Springs, U.S.A., **419** J5
Sodankylä, Finland, **285** N3
Söderhamn, Sweden, **287** H2
Söderköping, Sweden, **286** H3
Sodermanland, *county*, Sweden, **287** H3
Södertälje, Sweden, **287** H3
Sodo, Ethiopia, **367** E3
Södra Kvarken, *strait*, Finland/Sweden, **287** J2
Södra Vallgrund, Finland, **284** K5
Soe, Indonesia, **198** D5
Soekmekaar, South Africa, **371** E3
Soela väin, *strait*, Estonia, **287** L3
Soest, Germany, **288** D3
Soeurs, Les, *islands*, Seychelles, **373** A2
Sofades, Greece, **297** D6
Sofala, Mozambique, **371** F3, *74*
Sofala, *province*, Mozambique, **371** F2
Sofia *see* Sofiya, Bulgaria, **296** D4, *264*
Sofiko, Greece, **297** D7
Sofiya, *administrative region*, Bulgaria, **296** D4
Sofiya (Sofia), Bulgaria, **296** D4, *264*
Sofiysk, E. Khabarovskiy Kray, Russian Federation, **211** M2
Sofiysk, *river*, Russian Federation, **211** L1
Sofiysk, W. Khabarovskiy Kray, Russian Federation, **211** L1
Sofporog, Russian Federation, **285** Q4
Sōfu-gan, *island*, Japan, **138** C2
Sog Xian, China, **214** E3
Sogamoso, Colombia, **450** D3
Sogda, Russian Federation, **211** L2
Sogn og Fjordane, *county*, Norway, **286** C2
Søgne, Norway, **286** C3
Sognefjorden, *fiord*, Norway, **286** B2
Sogo Nur, *lake*, China, **213** J4
Sogod, Philippines, **204** D4
Sŏgwip'o, South Korea, **208** D4
Soham, England, U.K., **305** H2
Sohano, Papua New Guinea, **140** E2
Sohela, India, **219** E5
Soi Dao Tai, Khao, *mountain peak*, Thailand, **202** D3
Soignies, Belgium, **288** B3
Soila, China, **215** F3
Soini, Finland, **285** M5
Sointula, Canada, **412** F6
Soira, *mountain peak*, Eritrea, **367** E2, *337*
Soissons, France, **291** F2
Sojat, India, **218** C4
Sokal', Ukraine, **289** M3
Sokch'o, South Korea, **208** E3
Söke, Turkey, **297** F7
Sokhondo, Gora, *mountain peak*, Russian Federation, **210** E2
Sokhumi, Georgia, **222** C4
Sokna, Norway, **286** D2
Soko Banja, Serbia, **296** C4
Sokodé, Togo, **364** E3
Sokolac, Bosnia and Herzegovina, **294** G4
Sokółka, Poland, **289** L2
Sokolo, Mali, **364** C2
Sokołów-Podlaski, Poland, **289** L2
Sokoły, Poland, **289** L2
Sokosti, *mountain peak*, Finland, **285** P2
Sokoto, Nigeria, **365** F2
Sokoto, *state*, Nigeria, **365** F2
Sokyryany, Ukraine, **296** F1
Sol'-Iletsk, Russian Federation, **222** F2
Sola, Vanuatu, **141** A2
Solan, India, **218** D3
Solander Island (Hautere), New Zealand, **133** A8
Solano, Bahía, *bay*, Argentina, **460** D2
Solano, U.S.A., **423** L4
Solāpur, India, **216** C2
Solberg, Sweden, **284** H5
Solca, Romania, **296** E2
Soldăneşti, Moldova, **296** G2
Soldier Summit, U.S.A., **423** H2
Soledad, Colombia, **450** C1
Soledad, U.S.A., **422** C3
Soledad, Venezuela, **451** F2
Soledad de Doblado, Mexico, **431** F5
Soledade, Brazil, **459** G3
Solenzara, Corse, France, **295** B5
Solheim, Norway, **286** B2
Solihull, England, U.K., **305** F2
Solikamsk, Russian Federation, **300** G4
Solimões, *river*, Brazil, **451** F5
Solingen, Germany, **288** C3
Solitary, Mount, *mountain peak*, New Zealand, **133** A7
Sollefteå, Sweden, **284** H5
Sollentuna, Sweden, **287** H3
Sóller, Spain, **293** J3
Solnechnogorsk, Russian Federation, **299** F4
Solo, *river*, Indonesia, **201** E4
Solo *see* Surakarta, Indonesia, **201** E4
Solok, Indonesia, **200** C3
Sololá, Guatemala, **428** C4
Solomon, *river*, U.S.A., **420** D6
Solomon, U.S.A., **423** J5
Solomon Islands, *country*, Pacific Ocean, **131** F2, *61, 87, 93, 108, 109, 115, 116, 117*
Salomon Sea, Papua New Guinea/Solomon Islands, **128** E2
Solon, China, **211** H3
Solon Springs, U.S.A., **420** H2
Soloneshnoye, Russian Federation, **223** L2
Solonópole, Brazil, **453** F4
Solor, Kepulauan, *islands*, Indonesia, **198** C5
Solothurn, Switzerland, **291** H3
Solotvyn, Ukraine, **296** E1
Solovetskiye Ostrova, *island*, Russian Federation, **285** S4
Solsem, Norway, **284** E4
Solsona, Spain, **293** H2
Solt, Hungary, **289** J5
Šolta, *island*, Croatia, **294** F4
Soltau, Germany, **288** D2
Sol'tsy, Russian Federation, **299** C3
Solvacion, Bahía, *bay*, Chile, **460** B4
Sölvesborg, Sweden, **286** G4
Solway Firth, *river mouth*, Scotland, U.K., **308** F6
Solwezi, Zambia, **369** E5
Soma, Turkey, **297** F6
Somali Basin, *underwater feature*, Indian Ocean, **476** C4
Somalia, *country*, Africa, **358** K6, *254, 312, 313, 337, 338, 339, 385*
Somanya, Ghana, **364** D3
Sombo, Angola, **368** D4
Sombor, Serbia, **296** B3
Sombrerete, Mexico, **430** E4
Sombrero Channel, Andaman and Nicobar Islands, India, **217** H5
Şomcuta Mare, Romania, **296** D2
Somers, U.S.A., **418** G2
Somerset, *unitary authority*, England, U.K., **304** E3
Somerset, U.S.A., **421** L7
Somerset East, South Africa, **370** E5
Somerset Island, Canada, **411** K2
Somerton, England, U.K., **304** E3
Somerville, New Jersey, U.S.A., **426** C4
Somerville, Texas, U.S.A., **424** D4
Somes Bar, U.S.A., **418** C6
Somino, Russian Federation, **299** E3
Somme, *river*, France, **290** E1
Sommen, *lake*, Sweden, **286** G4
Sommières, France, **291** G5
Sømna, *island*, Norway, **284** E4
Somotillo, Nicaragua, **428** D4

Somoto, Nicaragua, **428** D4
Sompeta, India, **217** F2
Somuncurá, Meseta de, *plateau*, Argentina, **460** D1
Sơn, Cù Lao, *island*, Vietnam, **203** E4
Son, *river*, India, **219** E4
Sơn Hş, Vietnam, **203** F3
Sơn La, Vietnam, **203** D1
Sơn Tây, Vietnam, **203** E1
Soná, Panama, **429** E5
Sŏnch'ŏn, North Korea, **208** D3
Sønderborg, Denmark, **286** D5
Sondrio, Italy, **294** B2
Sonepur, India, **219** E5
Song, Malaysia, **201** F2
Sông ũốc, Vietnam, **203** E4
Song Xian, China, **206** B1
Songbai, China, **206** C3
Songe, Norway, **286** D3
Songea, Tanzania, **369** G5
Songeons, France, **305** J5
Songgang, China, **207** B3
Songhua, *river*, China, **211** K3
Songjiang, China, **206** E2
Songkhla, Thailand, **202** D5
Songling, China, **211** H2
Songming, China, **215** G4
Songmushan, China, **207** B3
Songnim, North Korea, **208** D3
Songo, Angola, **368** B4
Songo, Mozambique, **369** F6
Songpan, China, **215** G2
Songsak, India, **219** G4
Songxi, China, **206** D3
Songzi, China, **206** B2
Sonid Youqi, China, **210** F4
Sonid Zuoqi, China, **210** F4
Sonīpat, India, **218** D3
Sonkajärvi, Finland, **285** N5
Sonkovo, Russian Federation, **299** F4
Sonmiāni, Pakistan, **218** A4
Sonmiāni Bay, Pakistan, **218** A4
Sono, do, *river*, Brazil, **456** D3
Sonoita, U.S.A., **423** H6
Sonoma, U.S.A., **422** B2
Sonora, Bahía, *bay*, San Andrés, Colombia, **461** B1
Sonora, California, U.S.A., **422** C3
Sonora, *river*, Mexico, **430** C2
Sonora, *state*, Mexico, **430** B2
Sonora, Texas, U.S.A., **424** B4
Sonoran Desert, U.S.A., **422** F5
Sonostrov, Russian Federation, **285** S3
Sonoyta, Mexico, **430** B2
Sonskiy, Russian Federation, **223** N2
Sonsón, Colombia, **450** C3
Sonsonate, El Salvador, **428** C4
Sonsorol, *island*, Palau, **138** B4
Sooke, Canada, **412** H7
Sop Huai, Thailand, **202** C2
Sopachuy, Bolivia, **455** F5
Sopki, Russian Federation, **299** C4
Sopokha, Russian Federation, **285** S5
Sopot, Bulgaria, **296** E4
Sopot, Poland, **289** J1
Sopot, Serbia, **296** C3
Sopron, Hungary, **289** H5
Sor, *river*, Portugal, **292** C3
Sör-dellen, *lake*, Sweden, **287** H2
Sør-Flatanger, Norway, **284** E4
Sør-Rondane, *mountain range*, Antarctica, **470** E3
Sør-Trøndelag, *county*, Norway, **284** E5
Sora, Italy, **295** D5
Sorāh, Pakistan, **218** B4
Söråker, Sweden, **287** H1
Sorang, Kazakhstan, **212** B2
Sorata, Bolivia, **455** E4
Sorbe, *river*, Spain, **293** F2
Sørbøvåg, Norway, **286** B2
Sörbygden, Sweden, **286** H1
Sorel, Canada, **416** E6
Sorell, Australia, **135** K7
Sorgono, Sardegna, Italy, **295** B5
Soria, Spain, **293** F2
Sørli, Norway, **284** F4
Soro, India, **219** F5
Soro, Pakistan, **218** A3
Soroca, Moldova, **296** G1
Sorocaba, Brazil, **459** H2
Sorochinsk, Russian Federation, **222** E2
Sorok, Russian Federation, **213** J1
Sorokino, Russian Federation, **299** B4
Sorol, *island*, Micronesia, **138** C4
Sorong, Indonesia, **199** E3
Sorot', *river*, Russian Federation, **299** B4
Soroti, Uganda, **369** F2
Sørøya, *island*, Norway, **285** L1
Sørøysundet, *Kanal*, Norway, **285** L1
Sørreisa, Norway, **284** J2
Sorrento, Italy, **295** E5
Sorsatunturi, *mountain peak*, Finland, **285** P3
Sorsele, Sweden, **284** H4
Sorsogon, Philippines, **204** D3
Sortavala, Russian Federation, **299** C2
Sortland, Norway, **284** G2
Sørvågen, Norway, **284** F3
Sørvika, Norway, **286** E1
Sosanpal, India, **217** E2
Sösdala, Sweden, **286** F4
Sösjöfjällen, *mountain peak*, Sweden, **284** F5
Sosneado, Cerro, *mountain peak*, Argentina, **458** C5
Sosnovets, Russian Federation, **285** S4
Sosnovyy, Russian Federation, **285** R3
Sosnovyy Bor, Russian Federation, **299** B3
Sosnowiec, Poland, **289** J3
Sospel, France, **291** H5
Sotkamo, Finland, **285** P4
Soto, Curaçao, Netherlands Antilles, **461** C3
Soto La Marina, Mexico, **431** F4
Sotomayor, Colombia, **450** C4
Sotra, *island*, Norway, **286** B2
Sotteville-lès-Rouen, France, **305** J5
Sotuf, Adrar, *mountain range*, Western Sahara, **360** C4
Sotuta, Mexico, **431** H4
Souanké, Congo, **368** B2
Soubré, Côte d'Ivoire, **364** C3
Souda, Kriti, Greece, **297** E8
Soufli, Greece, **297** F5
Soufrière, *mountain peak*, St Vincent and the Grenadines, **427** D3, *397*
Sougéta, Guinea, **364** B2
Sougueur, Algeria, **361** G1
Souillac, France, **290** E4
Souillac, Mauritius, **373** C1
Souk Ahras, Algeria, **361** H1
Souk-el-Arba-du-Rharb, Morocco, **361** E2
Sŏul (Seoul), South Korea, **208** D3, *163, 164*
Sour el Ghozlane, Algeria, **293** J4
Soure, Brazil, **452** D3
Souris, Canada, **414** D7
Sousa, Brazil, **453** F5
Sousse, Tunisia, **362** B1
South Africa, *country*, **359** H9, *24, 42, 56, 59, 77, 81, 86, 90, 91, 94, 95, 96, 97, 228, 312, 313, 345, 347, 348, 349, 350, 351, 469*
South Andaman, *island*, Andaman and Nicobar Islands, India, **217** H4
South Australia, *state*, Australia, **134** G4, *112*
South Australian Basin, *underwater feature*, Indian Ocean, **476** H7
South Ayrshire, Scotland, U.K., **308** E5
South Baldy, *mountain peak*, U.S.A., **423** K5
South Bay, Canada, **414** H6
South Bend, Indiana, U.S.A., **421** K5
South Bend, Washington, U.S.A., **418** C3
South Boston, U.S.A., **421** P7
South Bruny Island, Australia, **135** K7
South Cape, New Zealand, **133** A8
South Carolina, *state*, U.S.A., **424** M2, *384, 386, 388*
South Cave, England, U.K., **307** H4
South China Basin, *underwater feature*, South China Sea, **478** B3
South China Sea, China/ Philippines/Vietnam, **195** N8, *145, 154, 193*
South Dakota, *state*, U.S.A., **420** C3, *386*
South Downs, *region*, England, U.K., **305** G4
South East, *district*, Botswana, **371** E3
South East Bay, Ascension, **373** A3
South East Cape, Australia, **135** K7
South East Harbour, Campbell Island, New Zealand, **132** K11
South East Head, *point*, Ascension, **373** A3
South Elmsall, England, U.K., **307** G4
South Fork, U.S.A., **423** K3
South Georgia, *island*, South Georgia and South Sandwich Islands, **449** J9, *465*
South Georgia and South Sandwich Islands, *U.K. dependency*, Atlantic Ocean, **449** J9, *276, 445, 467*
South Georgia Ridge, *underwater feature*, Atlantic Ocean, **477** D9
South Gloucestershire, *unitary authority*, England, U.K., **304** E3
South Harris, *island*, Scotland, U.K., **308** B3
South Harting, England, U.K., **305** G4
South Haven, U.S.A., **421** K4
South Henik Lake, Canada, **414** F1
South Hill, U.S.A., **426** A6
South Horr, Kenya, **369** G2
South Indian Lake, Canada, **414** E3
South Island (Atas), Cocos (Keeling) Islands, **134** Q10
South Island, New Zealand, **133** D6, *110, 111*
South Junction, Canada, **414** G7
South Keeling Islands, Cocos (Keeling) Islands, **134** Q10
South Knife, *river*, Canada, **414** F2
South Korea, *country*, Asia, **197** P6, *46, 97, 113, 144, 145, 150, 163, 164*
South Lake Tahoe, U.S.A., **422** C2
South Lanarkshire, Scotland, U.K., **308** E5
South Miami, U.S.A., **425** M7
South Molton, England, U.K., **304** D3
South Nahanni, *river*, Canada, **410** G3
South Negril Point, Jamaica, **429** F3
South Orkney Islands, Antarctica, **470** A3
South Ossetia, *former autonomous republic*, Georgia, **222** C4, *190*
South Pacific Ocean, **129** J5, *29, 44, 77, 97, 108, 116, 121, 122, 125*
South Pass City, U.S.A., **419** K5
South Petherton, England, U.K., **304** E4
South Platte, *river*, U.S.A., **420** C5
South Platte, U.S.A., **419** M7
South Point, Ascension, **373** A3
South Point, Christmas Island, **134** N8
South Promontory, *point*, Snares Islands, New Zealand, **132** H9
South Ronaldsay, *island*, Orkney, Scotland, U.K., **308** G2
South Sandwich Islands, South Georgia and South Sandwich Islands, **449** K9
South Sandwich Trench, *underwater feature*, Atlantic Ocean, **477** E9
South Saskatchewan, *river*, Canada, **413** Q6
South Seal, *river*, Canada, **414** E2
South Shetland Islands, Antarctica, **470** A4
South Shields, England, U.K., **307** G3
South Taranaki Bight, *gulf*, New Zealand, **132** D4
South Twin Island, Canada, **415** Q5
South Tyne, *river*, England, U.K., **306** F3
South Uist, *island*, Scotland, U.K., **308** B3
South Wabasca Lake, Canada, **413** N4
South West Bay, Ascension, **373** A3
South West Cape, Auckland Islands, New Zealand, **132** J10
South West Point, Macquarie Island, **134** R11
South West Point, St Helena, **373** B3
South Wootton, England, U.K., **305** H2
South Yorkshire, *unitary authority*, England, U.K., **307** G4
Southam, England, U.K., **305** F2
Southampton, Canada, **421** N3
Southampton, England, U.K., **305** F4
Southampton, U.S.A., **426** D4
Southampton City, *unitary authority*, England, U.K., **305** F4
Southampton Island, Canada, **411** L3
Southard, Mount, *mountain peak*, Antarctica, **470** E8
Southaven, U.S.A., **424** H2
Southbridge, U.S.A., **426** E3
Southeast Indian Ridge, *underwater feature*, Indian Ocean, **476** E7
Southeast Pacific Basin, *underwater feature*, Pacific Ocean, **479** M7
Southend, Canada, **414** C3
Southend, Scotland, U.K., **308** D5
Southend-on-Sea, England, U.K., **305** H3
Southend-on-Sea, *unitary authority*, England, U.K., **305** H3
Southern, *administrative region*, Malawi, **369** F6
Southern, *district*, Botswana, **370** D3
Southern, *province*, Sierra Leone, **364** B3
Southern, *province*, Zambia, **369** E6
Southern Alps, *mountain range*, New Zealand, **129** F6, *110*
Southern Cook Islands, Cook Islands, **137** F2
Southern Cross, Australia, **128** A6
Southern Highlands, *province*, Papua New Guinea, **140** A4
Southern Indian Lake, Canada, **414** E3
Southern Ocean, **104** D 14, *469, 474*
Southern Uplands, *mountain range*, Scotland, U.K., **308** E5, *275, 276*
Southery, England, U.K., **305** H2
Southey, Canada, **414** B6
Southminster, England, U.K., **305** H3
Southport, Australia, **135** K7
Southport, England, U.K., **306** E4
Southport, U.S.A., **425** N3
Southwell, England, U.K., **305** G1
Southwest Indian Ridge, *underwater feature*, Indian Ocean, **476** B7
Southwest Pacific Basin, *underwater feature*, Pacific Ocean, **479** H7
Southwest Point, Papua New Guinea, **140** B3
Southwold, England, U.K., **305** J2
Sovata, Romania, **296** E2
Sovdozero, Russian Federation, **285** R5
Sovetsk, Russian Federation, **287** K5
Sovetskiy, Russian Federation, **299** B2
Sowa Pan, *lake*, Botswana, **371** E3
Soweto, South Africa, **371** E4
Soyaló, Mexico, **431** G5
Soyda, *river*, Russian Federation, **299** F2
Soyo, Angola, **368** B4
Sozaq, Kazakhstan, **223** H4
Sozh, *river*, Belarus, **299** C6
Sozopol, Bulgaria, **296** F4
Spain, *country*, Europe, **282** D8, *56, 73, 74, 80, 84, 87, 89, 91, 92, 93, 94, 95, 117, 118, 122, 228, 229, 240, 245, 249, 251, 252, 253, 254, 257, 278, 313, 314, 355, 389, 391, 400, 402, 404, 434, 443, 444*
Spalding, Canada, **414** B5
Spalding, England, U.K., **305** G2
Spanish, Canada, **421** M2
Spanish Fork, U.S.A., **423** H1
Spanish Peak, *mountain peak*, U.S.A., **418** E4
Spanish Town, Jamaica, **429** F3
Sparks, U.S.A., **422** D2
Sparta, U.S.A., **425** K2
Sparta *see* Sparti, Greece, **297** D7, *67, 70, 89*
Spartanburg, U.S.A., **425** M2
Spartel, Cap, *cape*, Morocco, **292** D5
Sparti (Sparta), Greece, **297** D7, *67, 70, 89*
Spartivento, Capo, *cape*, Italy, **295** F7
Sparwood, Canada, **413** M7
Spas-Demensk, Russian Federation, **299** D5
Spassk, Russian Federation, **223** M2
Spasskaya Guba, Russian Federation, **285** R5
Spassk-Dal'niy, Russian Federation, **211** L3
Spatha, Akra, *point*, Kriti, Greece, **297** D8
Spean Bridge, Scotland, U.K., **308** E4
Spearfish, U.S.A., **420** B3
Spearman, U.S.A., **420** C7
Speculator, U.S.A., **426** C3
Speery Island, St Helena, **373** B3
Speightstown, Barbados, **427** E3
Spencer, Idaho, U.S.A., **419** H4
Spencer, Iowa, U.S.A., **420** F4
Spencer, West Virginia, U.S.A., **421** N6
Spencer Gulf, Australia, **135** H6
Spencerville, New Zealand, **133** D6
Spences Bridge, Canada, **412** J6
Spennymoor, England, U.K., **307** G3
Sperrin Mountains, *mountain range*, Northern Ireland, U.K., **309** E3
Spetses, Greece, **297** D7
Spetses, *island*, Greece, **297** D7
Speyer, Germany, **288** D4
Speyside, Tobago, Trinidad and Tobago, **461** B4
Spiekeroog, *island*, Germany, **288** C2
Spili, Kriti, Greece, **297** E8
Spilsby, England, U.K., **305** H1
Spīn Būldak, Afghanistan, **218** A3
Spinazzola, Italy, **295** F5
Spirit River, Canada, **413** K4
Spirits Bay, New Zealand, **132** D2
Spiritwood, Canada, **413** R5
Spit Point, Heard and McDonald Islands, **134** S12
Spitsbergen, *island*, Svalbard, **300** C2, *466*
Spittal an der Drau, Austria, **288** F5
Spittal of Glenshee, Scotland, U.K., **308** F4
Split, Croatia, **294** F4
Split Lake, Canada, **414** F3
Spofford, U.S.A., **424** B5
Spofforth, England, U.K., **307** G4
Špoģi, Latvia, **287** N4
Spokane, U.S.A., **418** F3
Spoleto, Italy, **294** D4
Spondigna, Italy, **294** C2
Spooner, U.S.A., **420** H3
Spotted Horse, U.S.A., **419** M4

Sprague, U.S.A., **418** F3
Spratly Islands, *sovereignty disputed*, South China Sea, **203** G4, *145, 193*
Spreča, *river*, Bosnia and Herzegovina, **294** G3
Spring Garden, Guyana, **451** G2
Spring Grove, U.S.A., **426** B6
Spring Hill, U.S.A., **425** L5
Springbok, South Africa, **370** C4
Springdale, Arkansas, U.S.A., **424** E1
Springdale, Canada, **417** N5
Springdale, Washington, U.S.A., **418** F2
Springe, Germany, **288** D2
Springer, U.S.A., **423** L3
Springfield, Colorado, U.S.A., **423** M3
Springfield, Illinois, U.S.A., **421** J6, *386*
Springfield, Massachusetts, U.S.A., **426** D3
Springfield, Minnesota, U.S.A., **420** F3
Springfield, Missouri, U.S.A., **420** G7
Springfield, Ohio, U.S.A., **421** M6
Springfield, Oregon, U.S.A., **418** C4
Springfield, Tennessee, U.S.A., **425** J1
Springfield, Vermont, U.S.A., **426** D3
Springfontein, South Africa, **371** E5
Springhill, U.S.A., **424** F3
Springhouse, Canada, **412** H6
Springs Junction, New Zealand, **133** D6
Springsure, Australia, **135** K3
Sprova, Norway, **284** E4
Sprowston, England, U.K., **305** J2
Spruce Knob, *mountain peak*, U.S.A., **421** P6
Spruce Lake, Canada, **413** Q5
Spruce Mountain, *mountain peak*, U.S.A., **422** F1
Spurn Head, *point*, England, U.K., **307** J4
Spyglass Point, New Zealand, **133** D6
Squamish, Canada, **412** H7
Square Islands, Canada, **417** P3
Squillace, Golfo di, *gulf*, Italy, **295** F6
Squinzano, Italy, **295** G5
Srbija (Serbia) *country*, Europe, **282** F7, *81, 97, 228, 259, 260, 261, 262, 263, 264*
Srbobran, Serbia, **296** B3
Srê Âmbĕl, Cambodia, **203** D4
Sredinnyy Khrebet, *mountain range*, Russian Federation, **301** T4
Sredishte, Bulgaria, **296** F4
Sredne-Russkaya Vozvyshennost', *mountain range*, Russian Federation, **298** E2
Sredne-Sibirskoye Ploskogor'ye, *mountain range*, Russian Federation, **300** L3
Sredneye Kuyto, Ozero, *lake*, Russian Federation, **285** Q4
Srednogarie, Bulgaria, **296** E4
Śrem, Poland, **289** H2
Sremska Mitrovica, Serbia, **296** B3
Srêpôk, *river*, Cambodia, **203** E3
Sretensk, Russian Federation, **210** G1
Sri Jayawardanapura-Kotte, Sri Lanka, **216** D5, *166*
Sri Lanka, *country*, Asia, **196** K9, *73, 89, 123, 144, 166, 167*
Sribner, U.S.A., **420** E5
Srīkākulam, India, **217** E2
Srīnagar, Jammu and Kashmīr, India, **218** C2, *169*
Srīnagar, Uttar Pradesh, India, **218** D3
Srinakarin Reservoir, Thailand, **202** C3
Srostki, Russian Federation, **223** M2
Srpska Crnja, Serbia, **296** C3
Stack Skerry, *island*, Scotland, U.K., **308** E1
Stade, Germany, **288** D2
Stadlandet, *cape*, Norway, **286** B1
Stafford, England, U.K., **304** E2
Stafford, U.S.A., **420** D7
Staffordshire, *unitary authority*, England, U.K., **304** E2
Staindrop, England, U.K., **307** G3
Staines, England, U.K., **305** G3
Stainz, Austria, **289** G5
Stalbridge, England, U.K., **304** E4
Stalham, England, U.K., **305** J2
Stalingrad *see* Volgograd, Russian Federation, **298** F3, *273*
Stalowa Wola, Poland, **289** L3
Stamford, Connecticut, U.S.A., **426** D4
Stamford, England, U.K., **305** G2
Stamford, Lake, U.S.A., **424** C3
Stamford, New York, U.S.A., **426** C3
Stamford, Texas, U.S.A., **424** C3
Stamford Bridge, England, U.K., **307** H4
Stamfordham, England, U.K., **307** G2
Stampriet, Namibia, **370** C3
Stanberry, U.S.A., **420** F5
Standerton, South Africa, **371** E4
Stanford, U.S.A., **419** J3
Stange, Norway, **286** E2
Stangenestind, *mountain peak*, Norway, **285** P1
Stanger, South Africa, **371** F4
Stanhope, England, U.K., **306** F3
Staniard Creek, Bahamas, **428** F1
Stănileşti, Romania, **296** G2
Stanilovo, Russian Federation, **299** F3
Stanišić, Serbia, **296** B3
Stanke Dimitrov, Bulgaria, **296** D4
Stanley, England, U.K., **307** G3
Stanley, Falkland Islands, **460** G4, *444, 445*
Stanley, Idaho, U.S.A., **418** G4
Stanley, Iowa, U.S.A., **420** H3
Stanley, *mountain peak*, Democratic Republic of the Congo, **369** E2, *334, 340*
Stanley, North Dakota, U.S.A., **420** B1
Stanovoy Khrebet, *mountain range*, Russian Federation, **301** P4
Stanovoye Nagor'ye, *mountain range*, Russian Federation, **301** N4
Stanthorpe, Australia, **135** L4
Stanton, England, U.K., **305** H2
Stantsiya Sumerichi, Russian Federation, **285** S5
Stapleton, U.S.A., **420** C5
Stará L'ubovňa, Slovakia, **289** K4
Stara Pazova, Serbia, **296** C3
Stara Planina, *mountain range*, Bulgaria, **296** D4
Stara Ushytsya, Ukraine, **296** F1
Stara Vyzhivka, Ukraine, **289** M3
Stara Zagora, Bulgaria, **296** E4
Starachowice, Poland, **289** K3
Staraya Russa, Russian Federation, **299** C3
Staraya Toropa, Russian Federation, **299** C4
Starbuck Island, Kiribati, **139** J5
Starchiojd, Romania, **296** F3
Starcross, England, U.K., **304** D4
Stargard-Szczeciński, Poland, **289** G2
Staritsa, Russian Federation, **299** E4
Starke, U.S.A., **425** L5
Starkville, U.S.A., **425** H3
Starnberger See, *lake*, Germany, **288** E5
Staro Oryakhovo, Bulgaria, **296** F4
Starosel'ye, Russian Federation, **299** F6
Start Bay, England, U.K., **304** D4
Start Point, England, U.K., **304** D4
Startup, U.S.A., **418** D3
Staryy Oskol, Russian Federation, **298** E2
Staryy Sambir, Ukraine, **289** L4
Staryya Darohi, Belarus, **299** B6
Staszów, Poland, **289** K3
Statesboro, U.S.A., **425** M3
Statesville, U.S.A., **425** M2
Staunton, U.S.A., **421** P6
Stavanger, Norway, **286** B3
Stavaträsk, Sweden, **284** K4
Staveley, England, U.K., **305** F1
Staveley, New Zealand, **133** C6
Stavely, Canada, **413** N6
Stavropol', Russian Federation, **298** F3
Stavropol'skiy Kray, *territory*, Russian Federation, **298** F3
Stavros, Greece, **297** D5
Stawell, Australia, **135** J6
Stawiski, Poland, **289** L2
Stawiszyn, Poland, **289** J3
Steamboat, U.S.A., **418** C5
Steamboat Canyon, U.S.A., **423** J4
Steamboat Mountain, *mountain peak*, U.S.A., **419** K6
Steamboat Springs, U.S.A., **423** K1
Steele, U.S.A., **420** C2
Steels Point, Norfolk Island, **135** T13
Steen River, Canada, **413** L2
Steens Mountain, *mountain range*, U.S.A., **418** E5
Steenvoorde, France, **305** K4
Steenwijk, Netherlands, **288** C2
Steep Point, Australia, **134** C4
Ştefan Vodă, Moldova, **296** G2
Stefansson Island, Canada, **410** J2
Steffen, Cerro, *mountain peak*, Argentina, **460** C2
Stege, Denmark, **286** F5
Steiermark, *state*, Austria, **289** G5
Steinbach, Canada, **414** F7
Steine, Norway, **284** G2
Steinfort, Luxembourg, **291** G2
Steinhatchee, U.S.A., **425** L5
Steinhausen, Namibia, **370** C3
Steinkjer, Norway, **284** E5
Steinkopf, South Africa, **370** C4
Stellarton, Canada, **417** K7
Stellenbosch, South Africa, **370** C5
Stenay, France, **291** G2
Stendal, Germany, **288** E2
Stende, Latvia, **287** L4
Steneby, Sweden, **286** F3
Stenness, Loch of, *lake*, Orkney, Scotland, U.K., **308** F1
Stenstorp, Sweden, **286** F3
Stenudden, Sweden, **284** H3
Stenungsund, Sweden, **286** E3
Stephens Lake, Canada, **414** G3
Stephens, Cape, New Zealand, **133** D5
Stephenville, Canada, **417** M5
Stephenville, U.S.A., **424** C3
Stepojevac, Serbia, **296** C3
Sterea Ellas, *administrative region*, Greece, **297** E6
Sterling, Colorado, U.S.A., **423** M1
Sterling, Illinois, U.S.A., **420** J5
Sterling, Nebraska, U.S.A., **420** E5
Sterling City, U.S.A., **424** B4
Sterling Heights, U.S.A., **421** M4
Sterlitamak, Russian Federation, **222** F2
Sternes, Kriti, Greece, **297** E8
Stettler, Canada, **413** N5
Steubenville, U.S.A., **421** N5
Stevenage, England, U.K., **305** G3
Stevens Point, U.S.A., **421** J3
Stevenson, Mount, *mountain peak*, New Zealand, **133** C6
Stevenson, U.S.A., **425** K2
Stewart, Canada, **412** E4
Stewart, Isla, *island*, Chile, **460** C5
Stewart Island, New Zealand, **133** B8
Stewarts Point, U.S.A., **422** B2
Steyr, Austria, **289** G4
Stibb Cross, England, U.K., **304** C4
Stickney, U.S.A., **420** D4
Stikine, *river*, Canada, **412** D3
Stikine Plateau, Canada, **412** D2
Stillington, England, U.K., **307** G3
Stillwater, Nevada, U.S.A., **422** D2
Stillwater, New Zealand, **133** C6
Stillwater, Oklahoma, U.S.A., **424** D1
Stillwater Range, *mountain range*, U.S.A., **422** D2
Stilo, Italy, **295** F6
Stilton, England, U.K., **305** G2
Štimlje, Kosovo, **296** C4
Stintino, Sardegna, Italy, **295** B5
Štip, Macedonia, **297** D5
Stirling, *local authority*, Scotland, U.K., **308** E4
Stirling, Scotland, U.K., **308** F4
Stjernøya, *island*, Norway, **285** L1
Stjørdalshalsen, Norway, **284** E5
Stockerau, Austria, **289** H4
Stockholm, *county*, Sweden, **287** H3
Stockholm, Sweden, **287** J3, *85, 231, 232, 235*
Stockport, England, U.K., **306** F4
Stockton, California, U.S.A., **422** C3
Stockton, Kansas, U.S.A., **420** D6
Stockton Lake, U.S.A., **420** G7
Stockton Plateau, U.S.A., **423** M6
Stockton-on-Tees, England, U.K., **307** G3, *275*
Stockton-on-Tees, *unitary authority*, England, U.K., **307** G3
Stoczek Łukowski, Poland, **289** K3
Stod, Czech Republic, **288** F4
Stöde, Sweden, **286** H1
Stødi, Norway, **284** G3
Stœng Trông, Cambodia, **203** E3
Stoer, Point of, Scotland, U.K., **308** D2
Stoke-on-Trent, England, U.K., **304** E1
Stoke-on-Trent, *unitary authority*, England, U.K., **304** E1
Stokes, Bahía, *bay*, Chile, **460** C5
Stokes, Mount, *mountain peak*, New Zealand, **133** E5
Stokesay, England, U.K., **304** E2
Stokesley, England, U.K., **307** G3
Stokksnes, *point*, Iceland, **284** Z7
Stolac, Bosnia and Herzegovina, **294** G4
Stoltenhoff Island, Tristan da Cunha, **373** C2
Ston, Croatia, **294** F4
Stone, Gloucestershire, England, U.K., **304** E3
Stone, Staffordshire, England, U.K., **304** E2
Stonecliffe, Canada, **416** C6
Stoneham, U.S.A., **423** M1
Stonehaven, Scotland, U.K., **308** G4
Stonewall, U.S.A., **423** L3
Stony Lake, Canada, **414** E2
Stony Plain, Canada, **413** M5
Stony Rapids, Canada, **413** S2
Stonyhill Point, Tristan da Cunha, **373** C2
Stör, *river*, Germany, **288** D2
Stora Blåsjön, Sweden, **284** G4
Stora Lulevatten, *lake*, Sweden, **284** J3
Stora Sjöfallet, *lake*, Sweden, **284** H3
Storå, Sweden, **286** G3
Storavan, *lake*, Sweden, **284** J4
Storby, Finland, **287** J2
Stord, *island*, Norway, **286** B3
Stordal, Norway, **284** E5
Store Bælt, *strait*, Denmark, **286** E5
Store Koldewey, *island*, Greenland, **411** T2
Store Sølnkletten, *mountain peak*, Norway, **286** E2
Støren, Norway, **284** E5
Storfjordbotn, Norway, **285** N1
Storfors, Sweden, **286** G3
Storforshei, Norway, **284** G3
Storjord, Norway, **284** G3
Storkow, Germany, **289** F2
Storlien, Sweden, **284** F5
Storm Lake, U.S.A., **420** F4
Stornoway, Scotland, U.K., **308** C2
Storozhynets', Ukraine, **296** E1
Storr, The, *mountain peak*, Scotland, U.K., **308** C3
Storsätern, Sweden, **286** F1
Storsjön, *lake*, by Östersund, Sweden, **284** G5
Storsjön, *lake*, near Ljungdalen, Sweden, **284** F5
Storsteinfjellet, *mountain peak*, Norway, **284** H2
Storthoaks, Canada, **414** D7
Storuman, *lake*, Sweden, **284** H4
Storuman, Sweden, **284** H4
Storvätteshågna, *mountain peak*, Sweden, **286** F1
Storvik, Sweden, **286** H2
Story, U.S.A., **419** L4
Stoughton, U.S.A., **421** J4
Stour, *river*, England, U.K., **305** F2
Stourbridge, England, U.K., **304** E2
Stourport-on-Severn, England, U.K., **304** E2
Stout Lake, Canada, **414** G5
Støvring, Denmark, **286** D4
Stow, Scotland, U.K., **308** G5
Stowmarket, England, U.K., **305** H2
Stow-on-the-Wold, England, U.K., **305** F3
Stoyba, Russian Federation, **211** K1
Strabane, *district*, Northern Ireland, U.K., **309** E3
Strabane, Northern Ireland, U.K., **309** E3
Stradbally, Ireland, **309** E4
Stradbroke, England, U.K., **305** J2
Stradella, Italy, **294** B3
Stradishall, England, U.K., **305** H2
Stradsett, England, U.K., **305** H2
Strahan, Australia, **135** K7
Strakonice, Czech Republic, **289** F4
Straldzha, Bulgaria, **296** F4
Stralki, Belarus, **287** P5
Stralsund, Germany, **288** F1
Strand, South Africa, **370** C5
Stranda, Norway, **286** C1
Strangford, Northern Ireland, U.K., **309** G3
Strangford Lough, *lake*, Northern Ireland, U.K., **309** G3
Strängnäs, Sweden, **287** H3
Stranorlar, Ireland, **309** E3
Stranraer, Scotland, U.K., **308** D6
Strasbourg, Canada, **413** S6
Strasbourg, France, **291** H2, *245*
Strasburg, U.S.A., **420** C2
Străşeni, Moldova, **296** G2
Straßwalchen, Austria, **288** F5
Stratford, Canada, **421** N4

Stratford, New Zealand, **132** E4
Stratford, U.S.A., **423** M3
Stratford-upon-Avon, England, U.K., **305** F2
Strathaven, Scotland, U.K., **308** E5
Strathcona, Mount, *mountain peak*, Antarctica, **470** G5
Strathdon, Scotland, U.K., **308** F3
Strathmore, Canada, **413** N6
Strathnaver, Canada, **412** H5
Strathspey, *valley*, Scotland, U.K., **308** F3
Strathy, Scotland, U.K., **308** E2
Strathy Point, Scotland, U.K., **308** E2
Strathyre, Scotland, U.K., **308** E4
Stratton, England, U.K., **304** C4
Stratton, U.S.A., **426** E2
Stratton Mountain, *mountain peak*, U.S.A., **426** D3
Straubing, Germany, **288** F4
Straumen, Norway, **284** E5
Straumnes, *point*, Iceland, **284** W6
Strawberry, U.S.A., **422** C2
Streaky Bay, Australia, **134** G5
Streatley, England, U.K., **305** F3
Středočeský, *administrative region*, Czech Republic, **289** G4
Street, England, U.K., **304** E3
Strehaia, Romania, **296** D3
Strel'na, *river*, Russian Federation, **285** T3
Strel'na, Russian Federation, **285** U3
Strenči, Latvia, **287** M4
Stretham, England, U.K., **305** H2
Strevell, U.S.A., **418** H5
Streymoy, Insel, Faeroe Islands, **302** D1
Stříbo, Czech Republic, **291** L4
Stříbro, Czech Republic, **288** F4
Strichen, Scotland, U.K., **308** G3
Strickland, *river*, Papua New Guinea, **140** A4
Strimonikos Kolpos, *bay*, Greece, **297** D5
Stroeder, Argentina, **460** E1
Strofades, *island*, Ionioi Nisoi, Greece, **297** C7
Strokestown, Ireland, **309** D4
Stromboli, Isola, *island*, Italy, **295** E6
Stromeferry, Scotland, U.K., **308** D3
Stromness, Orkney, Scotland, U.K., **308** F2
Strömsbruk, Sweden, **287** H2
Stromsburg, U.S.A., **420** E5
Strömsnäsbruk, Sweden, **286** F4
Strömstad, Sweden, **286** E3
Strömsund, Sweden, **284** G5
Strong, Mount, *mountain peak*, Papua New Guinea, **140** B4
Stronsay, *island*, Orkney, Scotland, U.K., **308** G1
Stronsay Firth, *channel*, Orkney, Scotland, U.K., **308** G1
Strontian, Scotland, U.K., **308** D4
Stroud, England, U.K., **304** E3
Stroudsburg, U.S.A., **426** C4
Struer, Denmark, **286** D4
Struga, Macedonia, **297** C5
Strumble Head, *point*, Wales, U.K., **304** B2
Strumica, Macedonia, **297** D5
Stryker, U.S.A., **418** G2
Stryukove, Ukraine, **296** H2
Stryy, Ukraine, **289** L4
Strzegom, Poland, **289** H3
Strzelce Opolskie, Poland, **289** J3
Strzelecki Desert, Australia, **135** H4
Strzelin, Poland, **289** H3
Strzelno, Poland, **289** J2
Stuart, Florida, U.S.A., **425** M6
Stuart, Nebraska, U.S.A., **420** D4
Stubaier Alpen, *mountain range*, Austria, **288** E5
Stubbington, England, U.K., **305** F4
Stuben, Austria, **288** E5
Studley, England, U.K., **305** F2
Study Butte, U.S.A., **423** M7
Stugudal, Norway, **284** E5
Stugun, Sweden, **284** G5
Stupino, Russian Federation, **299** G5
Sturgeon, Point, U.S.A., **421** K3
Sturgeon Bay, U.S.A., **421** K3
Sturgeon Falls, Canada, **421** P2
Sturgeon Lake, Canada, **414** J6
Sturgis, U.S.A., **420** B3
Sturminster Newton, England, U.K., **304** E4
Štúrovo, Slovakia, **289** J5
Sturt, *river*, Australia, **134** F2
Stutterheim, South Africa, **371** E5
Stuttgart, Germany, **288** D4, *239*
Stuttgart, U.S.A., **424** G2
Stykkishólmur, Iceland, **284** X7
Stylida, Greece, **297** D6
Suaçuí Grande, *river*, Brazil, **457** E5
Suai, East Timor, **198** D5
Suana, Democratic Republic of the Congo, **368** D4
Su'ao, Taiwan, **206** E3
Subang, Indonesia, **201** D4
Subay', 'Urūq, *desert*, Saudi Arabia, **363** H4
Subei, China, **213** G5
Subi, Pulau, *island*, Indonesia, **201** E2
Subi Besar, Pulau, *island*, Indonesia, **201** E2
Subiaco, Italy, **295** D5
Subotica, Serbia, **296** B2
Subrag, China, **211** G3
Success, Canada, **413** Q6
Suceava, Romania, **296** F2
Sučevići, Croatia, **294** F3
Sucevița, Romania, **296** E2
Suchary, Belarus, **299** C6
Suchorze, Poland, **289** H1
Suchowola, Poland, **289** L2
Suck, *river*, Ireland, **309** D4
Sucre, Bolivia, **455** F5, *441*
Sucre, Colombia, **450** C2
Sucuaro, Colombia, **451** E3
Sucunduri, *river*, Brazil, **455** G1
Sucuriú, *river*, Brazil, **456** C5
Sud, *province*, Cameroon, **365** G4
Sud-Kivu, *administrative region*, Democratic Republic of the Congo, **369** E3
Sud Ouest, Pointe, *point*, Mauritius, **373** C1
Sud-Ouest, *province*, Cameroon, **368** A2
Suda, *river*, Russian Federation, **299** F3
Sudan, *country*, Africa, **358** H5, *82, 89, 97, 146, 312, 313, 317, 331, 334, 336, 337, 338, 342*
Sudbury, Canada, **421** N2, *381*
Sudbury, England, U.K., **305** H2
Suddie, Guyana, **451** G2
Sudety, *mountain range*, Czech Republic/Poland, **289** G3, *267*
Sudimir, Russian Federation, **299** E6
Sudok, Sweden, **284** K3
Suđureyri, Iceland, **284** X6
Suđuroy, *island*, Faeroe Islands, **302** D2
Sue, *river*, Sudan, **366** C3
Suez, Gulf of, Egypt, **225** B5, *317*
Suez Canal *see* Suways, Qanāt as, Egypt, **225** B4, *94, 95, 97, 144, 151, 275, 312, 317, 339, 350, 355, 405*
Suez *see* As Suways, Egypt, **225** B5
Suffolk, *unitary authority*, England, U.K., **305** J2
Suffolk, U.S.A., **426** B6
Sug-Aksy, Russian Federation, **223** N2
Sugar Loaf Point, St Helena, **373** B3
Sugarloaf, The, *mountain peak*, Papua New Guinea, **140** A4
Sugarloaf Passage, *channel*, Lord Howe Island, Australia, **135** U14
Sugehe, China, **211** H2
Sugun, China, **212** C5
Suhait, China, **210** D5
Sūhāj, Egypt, **363** F3
Şuḩār, Oman, **221** G4
Sühbaatar, Mongolia, **210** D2
Sühbaatar, *province*, Mongolia, **210** F3
Suheli Island, India, **216** C4
Suhl, Germany, **288** E3
Sūi, Pakistan, **218** B3
Sui, *river*, China, **206** C4
Sui Xian, China, **206** C1
Suiá-Missu, *river*, Brazil, **456** C3
Šuica, Bosnia and Herzegovina, **294** F4
Suichang, China, **206** D2
Suichuan, China, **206** C3
Suide, China, **210** E5
Suihua, China, **211** J3
Suijiang, China, **215** G3
Suileng, China, **211** J3
Suining, Hunan, China, **206** B3
Suining, Jiangsu, China, **206** D1
Suining, Sichuan, China, **215** H3
Suippes, France, **291** G2
Suir, *river*, Ireland, **309** E5
Suixi, Anhui, China, **206** D1
Suixi, Guangdong, China, **206** B4
Suiyang, Guizhou, China, **215** H4
Suiyang, Heilongjiang, China, **211** K3
Suizhong, China, **211** H4
Suizhou, China, **206** C2
Sūjāngarh, India, **218** C4
Sujāwal, Pakistan, **218** B4
Sukabumi, Indonesia, **200** D4
Sukadana, Indonesia, **201** E3
Sukadana, Teluk, *bay*, Indonesia, **201** E3
Sukagawa, Japan, **209** H3
Sukaraja, Indonesia, **201** E3
Sukau, Malaysia, **201** G1
Sukeva, Finland, **285** N5
Sukhinichi, Russian Federation, **299** E5
Sukhodol, Russian Federation, **222** E2
Sukhona, *river*, Russian Federation, **281** J3
Sukhothai, Thailand, **202** C2
Sukkozero, Russian Federation, **285** R5
Sukkur, Pakistan, **218** B4
Sukma, India, **217** E2
Sūknah, Libya, **362** C3
Sukses, Namibia, **370** C3
Sukumo, Japan, **208** F4
Sul, Canal do, *channel*, Brazil, **452** D3
Sula, *island*, Norway, **286** B2
Sula, Ozero, *lake*, Russian Federation, **285** Q5
Sula, U.S.A., **418** H4
Sula Sgeir, *island*, Scotland, U.K., **308** C1
Sulaimān Range, *mountain range*, Pakistan, **218** B3
Sulawesi (Celebes), *island*, Indonesia, **198** B3, *148*
Sulawesi Selatan, *province*, Indonesia, **198** B3
Sulawesi Tengah, *province*, Indonesia, **198** C3
Sulawesi Tenggara, *province*, Indonesia, **198** C4
Sulawesi Utara, *province*, Indonesia, **198** C2
Sulby, Isle of Man, **306** D3
Sule Skerry, *island*, Scotland, U.K., **308** E1
Sulechów, Poland, **289** G2
Sulęcin, Poland, **289** G2
Suleja, Nigeria, **365** F3
Sulejów, Poland, **289** J3
Sulina, Romania, **296** G3
Sulingen, Germany, **288** D2
Sulitjelma, Norway, **284** H3
Sulkava, Finland, **287** P2
Sullana, Peru, **454** B1
Sulligent, U.S.A., **425** H3
Sullivan, U.S.A., **420** H6
Sullivan Lake, Canada, **413** N5
Sully, Wales, U.K., **304** D3
Sully-sur-Loire, France, **290** F3
Sulmona, Italy, **295** D4
Sulofoloa, Solomon Islands, **141** A1
Süloğlu, Turkey, **297** F5
Sulphur, Louisiana, U.S.A., **424** F4
Sulphur, Oklahoma, U.S.A., **424** D2
Sulphur Springs, U.S.A., **424** E3
Sultan, Canada, **421** M2
Sulṭān, Libya, **362** D2
Sultaniça, Turkey, **297** F5
Sultānpur, India, **219** E4
Sulu Archipelago, *islands*, Philippines, **204** C5, *149*
Sulu Sea, Malaysia/Philippines, **204** B4
Suluca, Turkey, **297** F5
Suluntah, Libya, **362** D2
Sulūq, Libya, **362** D2
Sulzbach-Rosenberg, Germany, **288** E4
Sulzberger Ice Shelf, Antarctica, **470** C7
Sumatera (Sumatra), *island*, Indonesia, **200** C2, *51, 75, 148*
Sumatera Barat, *province*, Indonesia, **200** B3
Sumatera Selatan, *province*, Indonesia, **200** D3
Sumatera Utara, *province*, Indonesia, **200** B2
Sumatra *see* Sumatera, *island*, Indonesia, **200** C2, *51, 75, 148*
Šumava, *mountain range*, Czech Republic, **288** F4
Sumba, Angola, **368** B4
Sumba, *island*, Indonesia, **198** B5
Sumbawa, *island*, Indonesia, **201** G5
Sumbawa Besar, Indonesia, **201** G5
Sumbawanga, Tanzania, **369** F4
Sumbay, Peru, **454** D4
Sumbe, Angola, **368** B5
Sumbu, Zambia, **369** F4
Sumburgh, Scotland, U.K., **308** K8
Sumburgh Head, *point*, Shetland, Scotland, U.K., **308** K8
Sumdo, China, **215** G3
Sumé, Brazil, **453** G5
Sümiyn Bulag, Mongolia, **210** F2
Summer Beaver, Canada, **414** K5
Summer Isles, *islands*, Scotland, U.K., **308** D3
Summer Lake, U.S.A., **418** D5
Summerland, Canada, **412** K7
Summerside, Canada, **417** K6
Summersville Lake, U.S.A., **421** N6
Summerville, Canada, **417** Q5
Summerville, U.S.A., **425** M3
Summit Lake, Central British Columbia, Canada, **412** H4
Summit Lake, N. British Columbia, Canada, **412** G2
Summit Mountain, *mountain peak*, U.S.A., **422** E2
Sumner, Lake, New Zealand, **133** D6
Sumner, New Zealand, **133** D6
Sumozero, Ozero, *lake*, Russian Federation, **299** F2
Šumperk, Czech Republic, **289** H4
Sumprabum, Myanmar, **205** C2
Sumqayıt, Azerbaijan, **222** D4
Sumskiy Posad, Russian Federation, **285** S4
Sumter, U.S.A., **425** M3
Sumy, Ukraine, **298** D2
Sumzom, China, **215** F3
Sun City, South Africa, **371** E4
Sun City, U.S.A., **422** E5
Sun Kosi, *river*, Nepal, **219** F4
Sunagawa, Japan, **209** H2
Sunan, North Korea, **208** D3
Sunbury, Australia, **135** J6
Sunchales, Argentina, **458** E4
Sunch'ŏn, South Korea, **208** D4
Sunda, Selat, *strait*, Indonesia, **200** D4
Sunda Shelf, *underwater feature*, South China Sea, **478** B4, *148*
Sundance, U.S.A., **419** M4
Sundargarh, India, **219** F5
Sunde, Agder, Norway, **286** D3
Sunde, Hordland, Norway, **286** B3
Sunderland, England, U.K., **307** G3
Sundridge, Canada, **421** P3
Sundsvall, Sweden, **287** H1
Sundumbili, South Africa, **371** F4
Sunga, Tanzania, **369** G3
Sungai Petani, Malaysia, **200** C1
Sungaidareh, Indonesia, **200** C3
Sungaipenuh, Indonesia, **200** C3
Sungei Seletar Reservoir, Singapore, **200** K6
Sungu, Democratic Republic of the Congo, **368** C3
Sungurlare, Bulgaria, **296** F4
Sunne, Sweden, **286** F3
Sunnersta, Sweden, **287** H3
Sunniland, U.S.A., **425** M6
Sunnynook, Canada, **413** P6
Sunnyside, U.S.A., **418** E3
Sunnyvale, U.S.A., **422** B3
Suntar Khayata, Khrebet, *mountain range*, Russian Federation, **301** Q3
Sunwu, China, **211** J2
Sunyani, Ghana, **364** D3
Suō-nada, *gulf*, Japan, **208** E4
Suomussalmi, Finland, **285** P4
Suonenjoki, Finland, **287** N1
Suŏng, Cambodia, **203** E4
Šuošjavrre, Norway, **285** M2
Suoyarvi, Russian Federation, **299** D1
Supai, U.S.A., **422** G3
Supaul, India, **219** F4
Superior, Arizona, U.S.A., **423** H5
Superior, Lake, Canada/U.S.A., **421** J2, *376, 381, 383*
Superior, Wisconsin, U.S.A., **420** G2
Supiori, Pulau, *island*, Indonesia, **199** F3
Sūq al Ghinān, Yemen, **220** D5
Sūq ash Shuyūkh, Iraq, **363** J2
Suqian, China, **206** D1
Suquṭrá (Socotra), *island*, Yemen, **373** B2
Şūr (Tyre), Lebanon, **225** C3, *180, 181*
Şūr, Oman, **221** G4
Sur, Punta, *point*, San Andrés, Colombia, **461** B1
Sur del Cabo San Antonio, Punta, *point*, Argentina, **459** F5
Sura, *river*, Russian Federation, **222** D2
Sūrāb, Pakistan, **218** A3
Surabaya, Indonesia, **201** F4
Surakarta (Solo), Indonesia, **201** E4
Surallah, Philippines, **204** D5
Şūrān, Syria, **225** D2
Surat, India, **218** C5
Surat Thani, Thailand, **202** C4
Sūratgarh, India, **218** C3
Surazh, Belarus, **299** C5
Surduc, Romania, **296** D2
Surdulica, Serbia, **296** D4
Surendranagar, India, **218** B5
Sûrétiméat, Mount, *mountain peak*, Vanuatu, **141** A2
Surgères, France, **290** D3
Surgut, Russian Federation, **300** J3
Suriāpet, India, **216** D2
Surigao, Philippines, **204** D4
Surin, Thailand, **203** D3
Suriname, *country*, South America, **449** G3, *80, 240, 434, 435, 438, 439*
Surire, Salar de, *salt-pan*, Chile, **455** E5
Surkovo, Russian Federation, **299** G3
Surna, *river*, Norway, **284** D5
Suroeste, Punta, *point*, Róbinson Crusoe Island,

Archipiélago Juan Fernández, Chile, **461** C2
Surrency, U.S.A., **425** L4
Surrey, *unitary authority,* England, U.K., **305** G3
Surt, Khalīj, *gulf,* Libya, **362** C2
Surt, Libya, **362** C2
Surtanāhu, Pakistan, **218** B4
Surubiú, *river,* Brazil, **452** D4
Surud, Raas, *point,* Somalia, **367** G2
Surulangun, Indonesia, **200** C3
Susa, Italy, **294** A3
Sušac, *island,* Croatia, **294** F4
Sūsah, Libya, **362** D2
Susak, *island,* Croatia, **294** E3
Susaki, Japan, **208** F4
Susanville, U.S.A., **422** C1
Susimu-jima, *island,* Japan, **138** C1
Susquehanna, *river,* U.S.A., **426** B4
Susques, Argentina, **458** C2
Sussex, Canada, **416** J7
Sussex, U.S.A., **419** L5
Sustut Peak, *mountain peak,* Canada, **412** F3
Susuka, Solomon Islands, **141** A1
Susuman, Russian Federation, **301** R3
Susurluk, Turkey, **297** G6
Šušvė, *river,* Lithuania, **287** L5
Şuţeşti, Romania, **296** F3
Sutherland, South Africa, **370** D5
Sutherlin, U.S.A., **418** C5
Sutlej, *river,* India/Pakistan, **218** B3, *173*
Sutterton, England, U.K., **305** G2
Sutton, Canada, **416** E7
Sutton, England, U.K., **305** H2
Sutton, *river,* Canada, **415** M4
Sutton, U.S.A., **421** N6
Sutton Bridge, England, U.K., **305** H2
Sutton Coldfield, England, U.K., **305** F2
Sutton in Ashfield, England, U.K., **305** F1
Sutton on Sea, England, U.K., **307** J4
Sutton Ridges, *mountain range,* Canada, **415** M4
Suttons Corner, U.S.A., **425** K4
Suu, Solomon Islands, **141** A1
Suugant, Mongolia, **210** D3
Süüj, Mongolia, **210** D3
Suur Munamägi, *mountain peak,* Estonia, **287** N4
Suva, Fiji, **141** A4, *117*
Suvasvesi, *lake,* Finland, **285** P5
Suvorov, Russian Federation, **299** F5
Suvorove, Moldova, **296** G3
Suvorovo, Bulgaria, **296** F4
Suwa, Japan, **209** G3
Suwałki, Poland, **289** L1
Suwannaphum, Thailand, **203** D3
Suwarrow, *island,* Cook Islands, **139** H6
Ṣuwayliḥ, Jordan, **225** C3
Suways, Qanāt as (Suez Canal), Egypt, **225** B4, *94, 95, 97, 144, 151, 275, 312, 317, 339, 350, 355, 405*
Suwon, South Korea, **208** D3
Suxik, China, **213** G5
Suyo, Peru, **454** B1
Suzaka, Japan, **209** G3
Suzhou, Anhui, China, **206** D1
Suzhou, Jiangsu, China, **206** E2
Suzu, Japan, **209** G3
Suzzara, Italy, **294** C3
Sværholthalvøya, *peninsula,* Norway, **285** M1
Svågan, *river,* Sweden, **286** H1
Svalbard, *Norwegian territory,* Arctic Ocean, **300** C2, *228, 279*
Svalyava, Ukraine, **289** L4
Svanøy, *island,* Norway, **286** B2
Svanvik, Norway, **285** P2
Svappavaara, Sweden, **284** K3
Svärdsjö, Sweden, **286** G2
Svartå, Sweden, **286** G3
Svartlå, Sweden, **284** K3
Svay Riĕng, Cambodia, **203** E4
Svėdasai, Lithuania, **287** M5
Sveg, Sweden, **286** G1
Švėkšna, Lithuania, **287** K5
Svelgen, Norway, **286** B2
Švenčionys, Lithuania, **287** N5
Svendborg, Denmark, **286** E5
Svenes, Norway, **286** D3
Svenljunga, Sweden, **286** F4
Svensby, Norway, **284** J2
Svenstavik, Sweden, **286** G1
Šventoji, Lithuania, **287** K4
Sverdlovskaya Oblast', *province,* Russian Federation, **222** G1
Sveti Nikole, Macedonia, **296** C5
Svetlaya, Russian Federation, **211** M3
Svetlograd, Russian Federation, **298** F3
Svetlyy, Russian Federation, **287** K5
Svetlyy Yar, Russian Federation, **298** F3
Svetogorsk, Russian Federation, **299** B2
Svíanúkar, *mountain peak,* Iceland, **284** Y7
Svidník, Slovakia, **289** K4
Svilengrad, Bulgaria, **297** F5
Svir, Belarus, **287** N5
Svir', *river,* Russian Federation, **299** D2
Svirsk, Russian Federation, **210** C1
Svishtov, Bulgaria, **296** E4
Svislach, Belarus, **289** M2
Svislach, *river,* Belarus, **299** B6
Svitavy, Czech Republic, **289** H4
Svity, Russian Federation, **299** D5
Svobodnyy, Russian Federation, **211** K2
Svoge, Bulgaria, **296** D4
Svolvær, Norway, **284** G2
Svrljig, Serbia, **296** D4
Svullrya, Norway, **286** F2
Svyatoy Nos, Mys, *cape,* Russian Federation, **285** U2
Swābi, Pakistan, **218** C2
Swadlincote, England, U.K., **305** F2
Swaffham, England, U.K., **305** H2
Swains, *island,* American Samoa, **139** G6
Swainsboro, U.S.A., **425** L3
Swakopmund, Namibia, **370** B3
Swan Hill, Australia, **135** J6
Swan Hills, Canada, **413** M4
Swan Lake, Canada, **414** D5
Swan Lake, U.S.A., **418** H3
Swan Peak, *mountain peak,* U.S.A., **418** H3
Swan Plain, Canada, **414** C5
Swan River, Canada, **414** D5
Swanage, England, U.K., **305** F4
Swanquarter, U.S.A., **426** B7
Swansea, Australia, **135** K7
Swansea, *unitary authority,* Wales, U.K., **304** C3
Swansea, Wales, U.K., **304** D3
Swansea Bay, Wales, U.K., **304** D3
Swanton, U.S.A., **426** D2
Swarzędz, Poland, **289** H2
Swaziland, *country,* Africa, **359** J9, *95, 348, 351*
Sweden, *country,* Europe, **282** F3, *93, 94, 228, 231, 231, 232, 233, 234, 235, 245, 272, 464*
Sweet Home, U.S.A., **418** C4
Sweetwater, Tennessee, U.S.A., **425** K2
Sweetwater, Texas, U.S.A., **424** B3
Sweetwater Station, U.S.A., **419** K5
Swellendam, South Africa, **370** D5
Świdnica, Poland, **289** H3
Świdnik, Poland, **289** L3
Świdwin, Poland, **289** G2
Swiebodzin, Poland, **289** G2
Świętokrzyskie, Góry, *mountain range,* Poland, **289** K3
Swift Current, Canada, **413** R6
Swifton, U.S.A., **424** G2
Swindon, England, U.K., **305** F3
Swindon, *unitary authority,* England, U.K., **305** F3
Swineshead, England, U.K., **305** G2
Swinford, Ireland, **309** D4
Świnoujâcie, Poland, **289** G2
Switzerland, *country,* Europe, **291** H3, *79, 82, 95, 97, 228, 229, 238, 239, 244, 245, 246, 247, 248, 254, 255*
Swords, Ireland, **309** F4
Syanno, Belarus, **299** B5
Syarednenemanskaya nizina, *plain,* Belarus/Lithuania, **289** M2
Syas', *river,* Russian Federation, **299** D3
Syas'stroy, Russian Federation, **299** D2
Sybil Point, Ireland, **309** B5
Sychevka, Russian Federation, **299** E5
Syców, Poland, **289** H3
Sydney, Australia, **135** L5, *96, 110, 111, 112*
Sydney, Canada, **417** L6
Sydney Bay, Norfolk Island, **135** T13
Sykeston, U.S.A., **420** D2
Sykkylven, Norway, **286** C1
Sykouri, Greece, **297** D6
Syktyvkar, Russian Federation, **300** G3
Sylacauga, U.S.A., **425** J3
Sylhet, Bangladesh, **214** D4
Sylsjön, *lake,* Sweden, **284** F5
Sylt, *island,* Germany, **286** D5
Sylvan Lake, Canada, **413** M5
Sylvania, Canada, **414** B5
Sylvania, U.S.A., **425** M3
Sylvester, U.S.A., **425** L4
Sylvia, Mount, *mountain peak,* Canada, **412** G2
Symi, *island,* Dodekanisos, Greece, **297** F7
Synnfjell, *mountain peak,* Norway, **286** D2
Synod Inn, Wales, U.K., **304** C2
Syowa, *Japanese research station,* Antarctica, **470** F3
Syracuse, Kansas, U.S.A., **423** N3
Syracuse, New York, U.S.A., **426** B3
Syrdar'ya, *river,* Kazakhstan, **222** G3, *185, 188*
Syria, *country,* Asia, **196** E6, *54, 71, 74, 146, 147, 180, 181, 182, 316*
Syriam, Myanmar, **205** C4
Syrian Desert *see* Shām, Bādiyat ash, Asia, **225** D3, *180, 181, 182*
Syrna, *island,* Kyklades, Greece, **297** F7
Syros, *island,* Kyklades, Greece, **297** E7
Sysmä, Finland, **287** M2
Sysslebäck, Sweden, **286** F2
Syston, England, U.K., **305** F2
Systyg-Khem, Russian Federation, **223** P2
Syt'kovo, Russian Federation, **299** D4
Syväri, *lake,* Finland, **285** P5
Syzran', Russian Federation, **222** D2
Szamotuły, Poland, **289** H2
Szarvas, Hungary, **289** K5
Szczecin, Poland, **289** G2
Szczecinek, Poland, **289** H2
Szczeciński, Zalew, *bay,* Poland, **289** G2
Szczekociny, Poland, **289** J3
Szczuczyn, Poland, **289** L2
Szczytno, Poland, **289** K2
Szeged, Hungary, **289** K5
Szeghalom, Hungary, **289** K5
Székesfehérvár, Hungary, **289** J5
Szekszárd, Hungary, **289** J5
Szentes, Hungary, **289** K5
Szentlőrinc, Hungary, **289** H5
Szerencs, Hungary, **289** K4
Szigetvár, Hungary, **289** H5
Szolnok, Hungary, **289** K5
Szombathely, Hungary, **289** H5
Szprotawa, Poland, **289** G3
Szubin, Poland, **289** H2

## T

Ta-Kaw, Myanmar, **205** C3
Ta-wu, Taiwan, **206** E4
Taal, Lake, Philippines, **204** C3
Tabaco, Philippines, **204** C3
Tabaco, *river,* Brazil, **456** B5
Taban Han, *river,* China, **210** E4
Tabaquite, Trinidad, Trinidad and Tobago, **461** C4
Tabar Islands, Papua New Guinea, **140** D3
Tabarka, Tunisia, **295** B7
Ṭabas, Iran, **221** G2
Tabasco, *state,* Mexico, **431** G5, *400*
Tabāsīn, Iran, **221** G2
Tabatinga, Brazil, **451** E5
Tabatinga, Serra da, *mountain range,* Brazil, **457** E3
Tabelbala, Algeria, **361** F3
Taber, Canada, **413** N7
Taberg, Sweden, **286** G4
Tabernas, Spain, **293** F4
Tabibuga, Papua New Guinea, **140** B4
Tabili, Democratic Republic of the Congo, **369** E2
Tabiteuea, *island,* Kiribati, **139** F5
Tablas Island, Philippines, **204** C3
Table, Pointe de la, *point,* Réunion, **373** A1
Table Head, *point,* Canada, **417** P3
Table Rock Lake, U.S.A., **420** G7
Tabletop, Mount, *mountain peak,* Papua New Guinea, **140** B4
Tabligbo, Togo, **364** E3
Tábor, Czech Republic, **289** G4
Tabora, *administrative region,* Tanzania, **369** F4
Tabora, *river,* Tanzania, **369** F4
Tabora, Tanzania, **369** F3
Tabou, Côte d'Ivoire, **364** C4
Tabrīz, Iran, **222** D5, *92*
Tabuaeran, *island,* Kiribati, **139** J4
Tabuan, Pulau, *island,* Indonesia, **200** D4
Tabubil, Papua New Guinea, **140** A4
Tabuk, Philippines, **204** C2
Tabūk, Saudi Arabia, **363** G3
Tabulga, Russian Federation, **223** K2
Tabursuq, Tunisia, **362** A1
Tabwemasana, Mount, *mountain peak,* Vanuatu, **141** A2, *116*
Täby, Sweden, **287** J3
Tacalé, Brazil, **452** B3
Tacaná, Volcán, *mountain peak,* Guatemala/Mexico, **428** B4
Tacheng, China, **212** D3
Tacloban, Philippines, **204** D4
Tacna, Peru, **455** D5
Taco Pozo, Argentina, **458** D2
Tacoma, U.S.A., **418** C3
Tacopaya, Bolivia, **455** E4
Tacora, Volcán, *mountain peak,* Chile, **455** E4
Tacuarembó, Uruguay, **459** F4
Tacupeto, Mexico, **430** C2
Tacurong, Philippines, **204** D5
Tadcaster, England, U.K., **307** G4
Tademaït, Plateau du, *plateau,* Algeria, **361** G3
Tādepallegūdem, India, **217** E2
Tadine, New Caledonia, **141** A3
Tadjoura, Djibouti, **367** F2
Tadjoura, Golfe de, *gulf,* Djibouti, **367** F2, *339*
Tadjrouna, Algeria, **361** G2
Tadley, England, U.K., **305** F3
Tadmur (Palmyra), Syria, **225** E2
Tadoule Lake, Canada, **414** E2
Tadoule Lake, *lake,* Canada, **414** E2
Tadoussac, Canada, **416** G5
Tadpatri, India, **216** D3
Taech'on, South Korea, **208** D3
Taegu, South Korea, **208** E4
Taejŏn, South Korea, **208** D3
Taf, *river,* Wales, U.K., **304** C3
Tafalla, Spain, **293** G1
Tafassâsset, Ténéré du, *desert,* Niger, **361** H4
Tafermaar, Indonesia, **199** F4
Tafi Viejo, Argentina, **458** D3
Tafraoute, Morocco, **360** E3
Taft, Iran, **221** F2
Taft, Philippines, **204** D4
Taft, U.S.A., **422** D4
Taftān, Kūh-e, *mountain peak,* Iran, **221** H3
Tafua, Samoa, **141** B1
Ţaga, Romania, **296** E2
Taga, Samoa, **141** B1
Taganrog, Russian Federation, **222** B3
Tagant, *administrative region,* Mauritania, **360** D5
Tagawa, Japan, **208** E4
Tagbilaran, Philippines, **204** C4
Taghit, Algeria, **361** F2
Taghmon, Ireland, **309** F5
Tagish Lake, Canada, **412** B2
Tagtabazar, Turkmenistan, **222** G5
Taguatinga, Brazil, **456** D3
Tagula, Papua New Guinea, **140** D5
Tagula Island, Papua New Guinea, **140** D5
Tagum, Philippines, **204** D5
Tahan, Gunung, *mountain peak,* Malaysia, **200** C1
Taharoa, New Zealand, **136** C4
Tahat, *mountain peak,* Algeria, **361** H4, *314*
Tahawai, New Zealand, **132** E3
Tahe, China, **211** J1
Tahilt, Mongolia, **213** H3
Tahiti, *island,* French Polynesia, **137** G2, *76, 94, 109, 122*
Tahlequah, U.S.A., **424** E2
Tahoe, Lake, U.S.A., **422** C2
Tahoe City, U.S.A., **422** C2
Tahoka, U.S.A., **424** B3
Taholah, U.S.A., **418** B3
Tahora, New Zealand, **132** E4
Tahoua, *department,* Niger, **365** E1
Tahoua, Niger, **365** F2
Ṭahṭā, Egypt, **363** F3
Tahuamanu, *river,* Bolivia/Peru, **455** E3
Tahuatu, *island,* French Polynesia, **137** G2
Tahulandang, Pulau, *island,* Indonesia, **198** D2
Tahuna, Indonesia, **198** D2
Tahuna, New Zealand, **132** E3
Taï, Côte d'Ivoire, **364** C3
T'ai-chung, Taiwan, **206** E3
Tai Hu, *lake,* China, **206** E2
Tai Long, China, **207** C4
Tai Long Wan, *bay,* China, **207** C4
Tai Mo Shan, *mountain peak,* China, **207** C4
T'ai-nan, Taiwan, **206** E4
Tai O, China, **207** B4
Tai Pang Wan, *bay,* China, **207** C3
T'ai-pei, Taiwan, **206** E3, *162, 163*
Tai Po, China, **207** C4
Tai Po Tsai, China, **207** C4
T'ai-tung, Taiwan, **206** E4
Tai'an, China, **210** G5
Taibai, China, **210** E5
Taibai Shan, *mountain peak,* China, **215** H2
Taibus Qi, China, **210** F4
Taieri, *river,* New Zealand, **133** C7
Taigu, China, **210** F5

Taihang Shan, *mountain range*, China, **210** F5
Taihape, New Zealand, **132** E4
Taihe, Anhui, China, **206** C1
Taihe, Guangdong, China, **207** A2
Taihe, Jiangxi, China, **206** C3
Taihu, China, **206** D2
Taikang, China, **206** C1
Taikkyi, Myanmar, **205** B4
Tailai, China, **211** H3
Tailem Bend, Australia, **135** H6
Taimei, China, **207** C2
Tain, Scotland, U.K., **308** E3
Tainaro, Akra, *point*, Greece, **297** D7
Taining, China, **206** D3
Taiping, Guangdong, China, **207** B3
Taiping, Guangxi Zhuangzu Zizhiqu, China, **215** H5
Taiping, Malaysia, **200** C1
Taipingchang, China, **207** A2
Tairua, New Zealand, **132** E3
Tais, Indonesia, **200** C4
Taishan, China, **206** C4
Taissy, France, **291** G2
Taitao, Península de, Chile, **460** B3
Taivalkoski, Finland, **285** P4
Taivassalo, Finland, **287** K2
Taiwan, *country*, Asia, **197** P7, *46, 79, 82, 93, 95, 113, 144, 145, 150, 160, 162, 165, 193*
Taiwan Strait, China/Taiwan, **206** D4
Taiyanggou, China, **211** J2
Taiyuan, China, **210** F5, *161*
Taizhou, China, **206** D1
Ta'izz, Yemen, **220** D6
Tajarhī, Libya, **362** B4
Tajikistan, *country*, Asia, **196** J6, *30, 144, 184, 186, 188, 189*
Tajitos, Mexico, **430** B2
Tajo, *river*, Spain, **280** D8, *250, 253*
Tajumulco, Volcán, *mountain peak*, Guatemala, **428** C4, *401*
Tajuña, *river*, Spain, **293** F2
Tak, Thailand, **202** C2
Takāb, Iran, **222** D5
Takabba, Kenya, **369** H2
Takaka, New Zealand, **133** D5
Takamaka, Réunion, **373** A1
Takamaka, Seychelles, **373** A2
Takamatsu, Japan, **208** F4
Takanabe, Japan, **208** E4
Takaoka, Japan, **209** G3
Takapuna, New Zealand, **132** E3
Takaroa, *island*, French Polynesia, **137** G2
Takasaki, Japan, **209** G3
Takatokwane, Botswana, **370** D3
Takayama, Japan, **209** G3
Takefu, Japan, **209** G4
Takengon, Indonesia, **200** B1
Tākestān, Iran, **222** D5
Takêv, Cambodia, **203** E4
Takhteh Pol, Afghanistan, **218** A3
Takikawa, Japan, **209** H2
Takis, Papua New Guinea, **140** C4
Takla Lake, Canada, **412** G4
Taklimakan Shamo, *desert*, China, **212** D5, *158*
Takoradi, Ghana, **364** D4, *325, 326*
Taksimo, Russian Federation, **301** N4
Takua Pa, Thailand, **202** C4
Takum, Nigeria, **365** F3
Takutea, *island*, Cook Islands, **137** F2
Tala, Uruguay, **459** F5
Talacasto, Argentina, **458** C4
Talachyn, Belarus, **299** B5
Talagang, Pakistan, **218** C2
Tālah, Tunisia, **362** A1
Talaimannar, Sri Lanka, **216** D4
Talakan, Russian Federation, **211** L2
Talangbatu, Indonesia, **200** D4
Talara, Peru, **454** B1
Talarrubias, Spain, **292** E3
Talas, Kyrgyzstan, **212** B4
Talasea, Papua New Guinea, **140** C4
Talaud, Kepulauan, *islands*, Indonesia, **198** D1
Talavera de la Reina, Spain, **292** E3
Talawdī, Sudan, **366** D2
Talaya, Russian Federation, **223** P1
Talca, Chile, **458** B5
Talcahuano, Chile, **458** B5
Tālcher, India, **219** F5
Taldom, Russian Federation, **299** F4
Taldykorgan *see* Taldyqorghan, Kazakhstan, **212** C3
Taldyqorghan (Taldykorgan), Kazakhstan, **212** C3
Tālesh, Iran, **222** D5
Talgarth, Wales, U.K., **304** D3
Talghar, Kazakhstan, **212** C4
Talhār, Pakistan, **218** B4
Tali Post, Sudan, **369** F1
Taliabu, Pulau, *island*, Indonesia, **198** D3
Tālīkota, India, **216** D2
Talitsa, Russian Federation, **222** G1
Taljāpur, India, **216** D2
Tall 'Afar, Iraq, **363** H1
Talladega, U.S.A., **425** J3
Tallahassee, U.S.A., **425** K4, *386*
Tallinn, Estonia, **287** M3, *235, 236*
Tallow, Ireland, **309** E5
Tallsjö, Sweden, **284** J4
Tallulah, U.S.A., **424** G3
Talluskylä, Finland, **285** N5
Tălmaciu, Romania, **296** E3
Tal'menka, Russian Federation, **223** L2
Talo, *mountain peak*, Ethiopia, **367** E2
Taloda, India, **218** C5
Tāloqān, Afghanistan, **218** B1
Talparo, Trinidad, Trinidad and Tobago, **461** C4
Talshand, Mongolia, **213** H3
Talsi, Latvia, **287** L4
Taltal, Chile, **458** B2
Taluk, Indonesia, **200** C3
Talvikyulya, Russian Federation, **285** P2
Tam Kỳ, Vietnam, **203** F3
Tamacuarí, Pico, *mountain peak*, Brazil/Venezuela, **451** F4
Tamakautoga, Niue, **132** M13
Tamalameque, Colombia, **450** D2
Tamale, Ghana, **364** D3
Tamana, *island*, Kiribati, **139** F5
Tamanhint, Libya, **362** B3
Tamanrasset, Algeria, **361** H4
Tamanthi, Myanmar, **205** B2
Tamar, *river*, England, U.K., **304** C4
Tamarin, Mauritius, **373** C1
Tamási, Hungary, **289** J5
Tamaulipas, Sierra de, *mountain range*, Mexico, **431** F4
Tamaulipas, *state*, Mexico, **431** F3
Tamazula, Mexico, **430** D3
Tambach, Kenya, **369** G2
Tambacounda, Senegal, **364** B2
Tambey, Russian Federation, **300** J2
Tambo, *river*, Peru, **454** D4
Tambo Grande, Peru, **454** B1
Tambohorano, Madagascar, **372** A4
Tambora, Gunung, *mountain peak*, Indonesia, **201** G5, *95*
Tamboril, Brazil, **453** F4
Tamboura, Central African Republic, **369** E1
Tambov, Russian Federation, **298** F2
Tambovskaya Oblast', *province*, Russian Federation, **222** C2
Tambre, *river*, Spain, **292** C1
Tambura, Sudan, **369** E1
Tâmchekket, Mauritania, **364** B1
Tame, Colombia, **450** D2
Tamgak, Adrar, *mountain peak*, Niger, **361** H5
Tamgué, Massif du, *mountain range*, Guinea, **364** B2
Tamgué, Mont du, *mountain peak*, Guinea, **364** B2
Tamiang, Ujung, *point*, Indonesia, **200** B1
Tamil Nādu, *state*, India, **216** D3, *169*
Tamiš, *river*, Serbia, **296** C3
Tamitatoala (Batovi), *river*, Brazil, **456** B3
Tamitsa, Russian Federation, **285** U4
Ţāmiyah, Egypt, **225** A5
Tamlelt, Plaine de, *plain*, Morocco, **361** F2
Tammisaari, Finland, **287** L3
Tampa, U.S.A., **425** L5
Tampa Bay, U.S.A., **425** L6
Tampere, Finland, **287** L2
Tampico, Mexico, **431** F4
Tampico, U.S.A., **419** L2
Tampines, Singapore, **200** K6
Tampo, Indonesia, **198** C4
Tampoc, *river*, French Guiana, **452** C2
Tamsalu, Estonia, **287** N3
Tamshiyacu, Peru, **450** D5
Tamuín, Mexico, **431** F4
Tamulol, Indonesia, **199** E3
Tamworth, Australia, **135** L5
Tamworth, England, U.K., **305** F2
Tân An, on Song Vam Co Tay, Vietnam, **203** E4
Tân An, Vietnam, **203** E4
Tan-shui, Taiwan, **206** E3
Tan-Tan, Morocco, **360** D3
Tana, Lake *see* T'ana Hāyk', *lake*, Ethiopia, **367** E2, *93, 336, 338*
Tana, Norway, **285** P1
Tana, *river*, Kenya, **369** G3, *341*
T'ana Hāyk' (Lake Tana), Ethiopia, **367** E2, *93, 336, 338*
Tanabe, Japan, **209** F4
Tanahbala, Pulau, *island*, Indonesia, **200** B3
Tanahgrogot, Indonesia, **201** G3
Tanahjampea, Pulau, *island*, Indonesia, **198** B4
Tanahmasa, Pulau, *island*, Indonesia, **200** B3
Tanahmerah, Indonesia, **199** H4
Tanami Desert, Australia, **128** C3
Tanana, *river*, U.S.A., **410** E3
Tanana, U.S.A., **410** D3
Tanat, *river*, Wales, U.K., **304** D2
Tanbei, China, **207** A3
Tanch'ŏn, North Korea, **208** E2
Tanda, Côte d'Ivoire, **364** D3
Tanda, India, **219** E4
Tandag, Philippines, **204** D4
Tandaltī, Sudan, **366** D2
Tăndărei, Romania, **296** F3
Tandil, Argentina, **459** E5
Tandil, Sierra del, *mountain range*, Argentina, **459** E5
Tandjilé, *prefecture*, Chad, **365** H3
Tandjungpinang, Indonesia, **200** D2
Tando Ādam, Pakistan, **218** B4
Tando Allāhyār, Pakistan, **218** B4
Tando Bāgo, Pakistan, **218** B4
Tanen Taunggyi, *mountain range*, Thailand, **202** C2
Tanezrouft, *mountain range*, Algeria, **361** F4
Tanezrouft Tan-Ahenet, *mountain range*, Algeria, **361** F4
Tang, *river*, China, **206** C1
Tanga, *administrative region*, Tanzania, **369** G4
Tanga, Tanzania, **369** G4
Tanga Islands, Papua New Guinea, **140** D3
Tangail, Bangladesh, **214** D4
Tanganyika, Lake, E. Africa, **357** J7, *342, 343, 344*
Tangaroa, Volcán, *mountain peak*, Isla de Pascua (Easter Island), Chile, **461** B2
Tangen, Norway, **286** E2
Tanger (Tangier), Morocco, **361** E1
Tangermünde, Germany, **288** E2
Tanggo, China, **214** E3
Tanggor, China, **215** G2
Tanggula Shan, *mountain range*, China, **214** D2
Tanggulashan, China, **214** E2
Tanghe, China, **206** C1
Tangier *see* Tanger, Morocco, **361** E1
Tangjia, China, **207** B4
Tangjiang, China, **206** C3
Tangmai, China, **215** E3
Tangnag, China, **215** G2
Tangoio, New Zealand, **132** F4
Tangra Yumco, *lake*, China, **214** C3
Tangse, Indonesia, **200** A1
Tangshan, China, **211** G5, *97*
Tangtang, China, **207** B1
Tangtouxia, China, **207** C3
Tangu, Papua New Guinea, **140** B4
Tangung, Indonesia, **201** G2
Tangxia, China, **207** B2
Tangyin, China, **206** C1
Tangyuan, China, **211** K3
Tanhua, Finland, **285** N3
Tanimbar, Kepulauan, *islands*, Indonesia, **199** E4
Tanisapata, Indonesia, **199** F3
Tanjungbalai, Indonesia, **200** B2
Tanjungpandan, Indonesia, **201** D3
Tanjungredeb, Indonesia, **201** G2
Tanjungselor, Indonesia, **201** G2
Tānk, Pakistan, **218** B2
Tankhoy, Russian Federation, **210** D2
Tankse, India, **218** D2
Tanna, *island*, Vanuatu, **141** A3
Tannadice, Scotland, U.K., **308** G4
Tännäs, Sweden, **286** F1
Tannila, Finland, **285** M4
Tannūrah, Ra's, *cape*, Saudi Arabia, **220** F3
Tanout, Niger, **365** F2
Tanque al Revés, Mexico, **430** E3
Ţanţā, Egypt, **225** A4
Tantoyuca, Mexico, **431** F4
Tanuanella, Sardegna, Italy, **295** B5
Tanumshede, Sweden, **286** E3
Tanunak, U.S.A., **410** C3
Tanzania, *country*, Africa, **359** J7, *37, 56, 58, 86, 93, 176, 312, 337, 341, 342, 343*
Tanzhou, north of Zhongshan, Guangdong, China, **207** A3
Tanzhou, south of Zhongshan, Guangdong, China, **207** A4
Tao, Ko, *island*, Thailand, **202** D4
Tao, *river*, Central China, **215** G2
Tao, *river*, N. China, **206** C3
Tao'er, *river*, China, **211** H3
Taojiang, China, **206** C2
Taonan, China, **211** H3
Taongi, *island*, Marshall Islands, **139** E3
Taormina, Sicilia, Italy, **295** E7
Taos, U.S.A., **423** L3
Taoudenni, Mali, **361** F4
Taounate, Morocco, **361** F2
Taourirt, Morocco, **361** F2
Taouz, Morocco, **361** F2
T'ao-yüan, Taiwan, **206** E3
Taoyuan, China, **206** B2
Tap Mun Chau, *island*, China, **207** C4
Tapa, Estonia, **287** M3
Tapajós, *river*, Brazil, **452** B4
Tapaktuan, Indonesia, **200** B2
Tapalqué, Argentina, **459** E5
Tapan, Indonesia, **200** C3
Tapanahoni, *river*, Suriname, **452** B2
Tapanui, New Zealand, **133** B7
Tapanuli, Teluk, *bay*, Indonesia, **200** B2
Tapará, Serra do, *mountain range*, Brazil, **452** C4
Tapauá, Brazil, **455** F1
Tapauá, *river*, Brazil, **455** E2
Tapaulama, Tanjong, *point*, Indonesia, **198** C3
Tapera, Brazil, **459** G3
Tapes, Brazil, **459** G4
Tapeta, Liberia, **364** C3
Tapi, *river*, India, **218** C5
Tapis, Gunung, *mountain peak*, Malaysia, **200** C2
Tapolca, Hungary, **289** H5
Tappahannock, U.S.A., **426** B6
Tapuae-o-Uenuku, *mountain peak*, New Zealand, **133** D5
Tapul Group, *islands*, Philippines, **204** B5
Tapul Island, Philippines, **204** C5
Tapurucuara, Brazil, **451** F4
Taqab, Sudan, **363** F5
Taquari, Brazil, **456** C4
Taquari, *river*, Mato Grosso do Sul, Brazil, **456** B5
Taquari, *river*, Rio Grande do Sul, Brazil, **459** G3
Taquaritinga, Brazil, **456** D5
Tara, *river*, Russian Federation, **223** K1
Tara, Russian Federation, **223** J1
Taraba, *state*, Nigeria, **365** G3
Tarabuco, Bolivia, **455** F5
Ţarābulus (Tripoli), Lebanon, **225** C2
Ţarābulus (Tripolis), Libya, **362** B2, *316*
Taraclia, Moldova, **296** G3
Taradale, New Zealand, **132** F4
Tarāghin, Libya, **362** B3
Taraka, Mount, *mountain peak*, Papua New Guinea, **140** E2
Tarakan, Indonesia, **201** G2
Taranaki, Mount, *see* Egmont, Mount, *mountain peak*, New Zealand, **133** E4, *111*
Tarancón, Spain, **293** F2
Taranto, Golfo di, *gulf*, Italy, **295** F5
Taranto, Italy, **295** F5, *255*
Tarapaca, *administrative region*, Chile, **455** E5
Tarapacá, Colombia, 451 E5
Taraponui, *mountain peak*, New Zealand, **132** F4
Tarapoto, Peru, **454** C2
Taraquá, Brazil, **451** E4
Tarare, France, **291** G4
Tararua Range, *mountain range*, New Zealand, **133** E5
Tarasa Dwip Island, Andaman and Nicobar Islands, India, **217** H4
Tarascon-sur-Ariège, France, **290** E5
Tarat, Algeria, **361** H3
Tarata, Peru, **455** D4
Tarauacá, Brazil, **454** D2
Tarauacá, *river*, Brazil, **455** D2
Tarawa, *island*, Kiribati, **139** F4, *120*
Tarawera, Mount, *mountain peak*, New Zealand, **132** F4
Tarawera, New Zealand, **132** F4
Tarawere, Lake, New Zealand, **132** F4
Taraz, Kazakhstan, **212** A4
Tarazona, Spain, **293** G2
Tarbagatay, Khrebet, *mountain range*, Kazakhstan, **212** D3
Tarbaj, Kenya, **369** H2
Tarbat Ness, *point*, Scotland, U.K., **308** F3
Tarbela Reservoir, Pakistan, **218** C2, *173*
Tarbert, Argyll and Bute, Scotland, U.K., **308** D5
Tarbert, Harris, Scotland, U.K., **308** C3
Tarbert, Ireland, **309** C5
Tarbes, France, **290** E5
Tarcento, Italy, **294** D2
Tarčin, Bosnia and Herzegovina, **294** G4
Tarcoola, Australia, **135** G5
Tardoki-Yani, Gora, *mountain peak*, Russian Federation, **211** M2
Taree, Australia, **135** L5
Tärendö, Sweden, **285** L3

Ţarfā, Ra's aţ, *point*, Saudi Arabia, **363** H5
Tarfaya, Morocco, **360** D3
Târgovişte, Romania, **296** E3
Târgu Bujor, Romania, **296** F3
Târgu Cărbuneşti, Romania, **296** D3
Târgu Frumos, Romania, **296** F2
Târgu Jiu, Romania, **296** D3
Târgu Lapuş, Romania, **296** D2
Târgu Mureş, Romania, **296** E2
Târgu Neamţ, Romania, **296** F2
Târgu Ocna, Romania, **296** F2
Târgu Secuiesc, Romania, **296** F3
Tarhu, China, **210** D4
Tarhūnah, Libya, **362** B2
Tari, Papua New Guinea, **140** A4
Tarifa, Spain, **292** E4
Tarigtig Point, Philippines, **204** C2
Tarija, Bolivia, **455** F5
Tarija, *department*, Bolivia, **455** F5
Tarija, *river*, Bolivia, **458** D2
Tariku, *river*, Indonesia, **199** G3
Tarim, *river*, China, **212** D4
Tarim Pendi, *basin*, China, **212** D5, *144, 158*
Tarime, Tanzania, **369** F3
Tarīn Kowt, Afghanistan, **218** A2
Taripa, Indonesia, **198** C3
Taritatu, *river*, Indonesia, **199** G3
Tarjannevesi, *lake*, Finland, **287** L1
Tarkio, U.S.A., **420** F5
Tarkwa, Ghana, **364** D3
Tarlac, Philippines, **204** C3
Tarleton, England, U.K., **306** F4
Tarma, Peru, **454** C3
Tarn, *river*, France, **290** E5
Târnăveni, Romania, **296** E2
Tarnobrzeg, Poland, **289** K3
Tarnogród, Poland, **289** L3
Tarnów, Poland, **289** K3
Tärnsjö, Sweden, **287** H2
Târnvik, Norway, **284** G3
Taroudannt, Morocco, **360** E2
Tarquinia, Italy, **295** C4
Tarrabool Lake, Australia, **135** H4
Tarrafal, Cape Verde, **360** Q8
Tarragona, Spain, **293** H2
Tårrajaur, Sweden, **284** J3
Tàrrega, Spain, **293** H2
Tarsumdo, China, **215** G2
Tarsus, Turkey, **363** F1
Tart, China, **213** G5
Tarta, Turkmenistan, **222** E5
Tartagal, Salta, Argentina, **458** D2
Tartagal, Santa Fé, Argentina, **459** E3
Tartas, France, **290** D5
Tartu, Estonia, **287** N3
Ţarţūs, *district*, Syria, **225** C2
Ţarţūs, Syria, **225** C2
Tarumirim, Brazil, **457** E5
Tarusa, Russian Federation, **299** F5
Tarutung, Indonesia, **200** B2
Tarutyne, Ukraine, **296** G2
Tarvisio, Italy, **294** D2
Tasaôm, Cambodia, **203** E4
Tasböget, Kazakhstan, **222** H4
Tash-Kömür, Kyrgyzstan, **212** B4

Tashanta, Russian Federation, **223** M3
Tashigang, Bhutan, **205** A2
Tashkent *see* Toshkent, Uzbekistan, **223** H4, *185*
Tashkepri, Turkmenistan, **222** G5
Tashtagol, Russian Federation, **223** M2
Tashtyp, Russian Federation, **223** M2
Tasikmalaya, Indonesia, **201** E4
Tasiusaq, Greenland, **411** P2
Tåsjö, Sweden, **284** G4
Tasker, Niger, **365** G1
Taskesken, Kazakhstan, **212** D1
Taskul, Papua New Guinea, **140** C3
Tasman Basin, *underwater feature*, Pacific Ocean, **478** E7
Tasman Bay, New Zealand, **133** D5
Tasman Plain, *underwater feature*, Pacific Ocean, **478** E7
Tasman Sea, Pacific Ocean, **128** E5
Tasmania, *state*, Australia, **135** J7, *87, 93, 95, 108, 112*
Tasmat, Vanuatu, **141** A2
Tăşnad, Romania, **296** D2
Tassara, Niger, **365** F1
Tasso Fragoso, Brazil, **452** E5
Tasu, Turkey, **225** B1
Tata, Hungary, **289** J5
Tata, Morocco, **360** E3
Tata Mailau, Gunung, *mountain peak*, East Timor, **198** D5, *148*
Tatabánya, Hungary, **289** J5
Tatakoto, *island*, French Polynesia, **137** H2
Tatam, Indonesia, **199** E2
Tatamagouche, Canada, **417** K7
Tatarbunary, Ukraine, **296** G2
Tatarka, Belarus, **299** B6
Tatarsk, Russian Federation, **223** K1
Tatarskiy Proliv, *strait*, Russian Federation, **301** R4
Tatarstan, Respublika, *republic*, Russian Federation, **222** D1
Tatau, Malaysia, **201** F2
Taţāwīn, Tunisia, **362** B2
Tateyama, Japan, **209** G4
Tathlina Lake, Canada, **413** L1
Tathlīth, Saudi Arabia, **363** H5
Tatla Lake, Canada, **412** G6
Tatlow, Mount, *mountain peak*, Canada, **412** H6
Tatnam, Cape, Canada, **414** J3
Tatrang, China, **212** E5
Tatuí, Brazil, **459** H2
Tatum, U.S.A., **423** M5
Tatvan, Turkey, **224** F5
Tau, *island*, American Samoa, **141** B2
Tau, Norway, **286** B3
Tauá, Brazil, **453** F4
Tauariá, Brazil, **455** F1
Taubaté, Brazil, **456** E6
Taukihepa *see* Big South Cape Island, New Zealand, **133** A8
Taula, *island*, Vava'u Group, Tonga, **141** B3
Taunga, *island*, Vava'u Group, Tonga, **141** B3
Taungdwingyi, Myanmar, **205** B3
Taunggyi, Myanmar, **205** C3
Taungtha, Myanmar, **205** B3
Taungup, Myanmar, **205** B4

Taunton, England, U.K., **304** D3
Taunton, U.S.A., **426** E4
Taunus, *mountain range*, Germany, **288** D3
Taupeka Point, Chatham Islands, New Zealand, **133** Q16
Taupiri, New Zealand, **132** E3
Taupo, Lake, New Zealand, **132** F4, *110*
Taupo, New Zealand, **132** F4
Taūqum, *desert*, Kazakhstan, **212** B3
Tauragë, Lithuania, **287** L5
Tauranga, New Zealand, **132** F3
Taureau, Réservoir, Canada, **416** E6
Tauri, *river*, Papua New Guinea, **140** B4
Tauroa Peninsula, New Zealand, **132** D2
Taurus Mountains *see* Toros Dağları, *mountain range*, Turkey, **224** D5, *146, 191*
Taūshyq, Kazakhstan, **222** E4
Tauu Islands, Papua New Guinea, **138** D5
Tavan Bogd Uul, *mountain peak*, Mongolia, **212** F2, *186*
Tavanbulag, Mongolia, **213** J3
Tavas, Turkey, **297** G7
Tavda, Russian Federation, **222** H1
Tavelsjö, Sweden, **284** K4
Taverham, England, U.K., **305** J2
Taveuni, *island*, Fiji, **141** A4
Tavin, Dundgovĭ, Mongolia, **210** D3
Tavin, Selenge, Mongolia, **210** D2
Tavira, Portugal, **292** D4
Tavistock, England, U.K., **304** C4
Tavolara, Isola, *island*, Sardegna, Italy, **295** B5
Tavoy (Dawei), Myanmar, **202** C3
Tavoy Island *see* Mali Kyun, *island*, Myanmar, **202** C3
Tavoy Point, Myanmar, **202** C3
Tavrichanka, Russian Federation, **211** K4
Tavricheskoye, Russian Federation, **223** J2
Tavşanlı, Turkey, **297** G6
Tavy, *river*, England, U.K., **304** C4
Taw, *river*, England, U.K., **304** D4
Tawa Reservoir, India, **218** D5
Tawaeli, Indonesia, **198** B3
Tawakoni, Lake, U.S.A., **424** E3
Tawas City, U.S.A., **421** M3
Tawau, Malaysia, **201** G1
Tawhiuau, *mountain peak*, New Zealand, **132** F4
Tawitawi Island, *island*, Philippines, **204** B5
Tawkar, Sudan, **363** G5
Tawsar, Tunisia, **361** H2
Taxco de Alarcón, Mexico, **431** F5
Taxkorgan, China, **212** B5
Tay, *river*, Scotland, U.K., **308** F4, *276*
Tây Ninh, Vietnam, **203** E4
Tayabas Bay, Philippines, **204** C3
Taybola, Russian Federation, **285** R2
Tayeeglow, Somalia, **367** F4
Tayga, Russian Federation, **223** M1
Taygan, Mongolia, **213** H3

Tayinloan, Scotland, U.K., **308** D5
Taylor, Canada, **412** J3
Taylor, Mount, *mountain peak*, U.S.A., **423** K4
Taylor, Nebraska, U.S.A., **420** D5
Taylor, Texas, U.S.A., **424** E4
Taylors, U.S.A., **425** L2
Taymā', Saudi Arabia, **363** G3
Taymyr, Ozero, *lake*, Russian Federation, **301** M2
Taymyr, Poluostrov, *peninsula*, Russian Federation, **300** K2
Taynuilt, Scotland, U.K., **308** D4
Taypaq, Kazakhstan, **222** E3
Tayport, Scotland, U.K., **308** G4
Tayshet, Russian Federation, **300** L4
Taytay, Philippines, **204** B4
Tayuan, China, **211** J2
Ţayyebāt, Iran, **221** H2
Ţayyib al Ism, Saudi Arabia, **225** C5
Taz, *river*, Russian Federation, **300** K3
Taza, Morocco, **361** F2
Tazin Lake, Canada, **413** Q2
Tāzirbū, Libya, **362** D3
Tazlău, Romania, **296** F2
Tazungdām, Myanmar, **205** C1
T'bilisi, Georgia, **222** C4, *190*
Tchad, Lac, *lake*, Chad, **365** G2, *328, 329, 330*
Tchamba, Togo, **364** E3
Tchaourou, Benin, **365** E3
Tchibanga, Gabon, **368** B3
Tchin-Tabaradene, Niger, **365** F1
Tchindjenge, Angola, **368** B5
Tcholliré, Cameroon, **365** G3
Tczew, Poland, **289** J1
Té, *river*, Cambodia, **203** E3
Teacapán, Mexico, **430** D4

Teapa, Mexico, **431** G5
Teare, Mount, *mountain peak*, Canada, **412** J5
Teba, Indonesia, **199** G3
Tebay, England, U.K., **306** F3
Tébessa, Algeria, **361** H1
Tebicuary, *river*, Paraguay, **459** F3
Tebingtinggi, Indonesia, **200** B2
Tebingtinggi, Pulau, *island*, Indonesia, **200** C2
Tecate, Mexico, **430** A1
Techiman, Ghana, **364** D3
Techirghiol, Romania, **296** G3
Techniti Limni Kremaston, *reservoir*, Greece, **297** C6
Tecka, Argentina, **460** C2
Tecka, *river*, Argentina, **460** C2
Tecolutla, Mexico, **431** F4
Tecomán, Mexico, **430** E5
Tecoripa, Mexico, **430** C2
Tecpán de Galeana, Mexico, **431** E5
Tecuci, Romania, **296** F3
Tecumseh, U.S.A., **420** E5
Ted Ceidaar Dabole, Somalia, **367** F4
Teel, Mongolia, **213** J2
Teeli, Russian Federation, **223** N2
Tees Bay, England, U.K., **307** G3
Teesdale, *region*, England, U.K., **306** F3
Tefé, Brazil, **451** F5
Tefé, Lago de, *lake*, Brazil, **451** F5
Tefé, *river*, Brazil, **451** F5
Tefedest, *mountain range*, Algeria, **361** H4
Tefenni, Turkey, **297** G7
Tegal, Indonesia, **201** E4
Tegernsee, Germany, **288** E5
Tegid, Llyn, *lake*, Wales, U.K., **304** D2
Tegina, Nigeria, **365** F2
Tegucigalpa, Honduras, **428** D4, *379, 402, 403*
Teguelda-n-Tessoumt, Niger, **365** F1
Teguise, Islas Canarias, Spain, **373** B4
Teheran *see* Tehrān, Iran, **220** F1, *146, 183*
Téhini, Côte d'Ivoire, **364** D3
Tehrān (Teheran), Iran, **220** F1, *146, 183*
Tehri, India, **218** D3
Tehuacán, Mexico, **431** F5
Tehuantepec, Golfo de, *gulf*, Mexico, **431** G6, *400*
Tehuantepec, Istmo de, *isthmus*, Mexico, **431** G5
Tehuitzingo, Mexico, **431** F5
Tehumardi, Estonia, **287** L3
Teide, Pico de, *mountain peak*, Islas Canarias, Spain, **373** A4, *354, 355*
Teifi, *river*, Wales, U.K., **304** C2
Teignmouth, England, U.K., **304** D4
Teisko, Finland, **287** L2
Teiuş, Romania, **296** D2
Teixeira, Brazil, **453** G5
Tejen, Turkmenistan, **222** G5
Tejo, *river*, Portugal, **292** C3
Tekapo, Lake, New Zealand, **133** C6
Tekapo, New Zealand, **133** C7
Tekax, Mexico, **431** H4
Tekeli, Kazakhstan, **212** C3
Tekes, China, **212** D4
Tekes, *river*, China/Kazakhstan, **212** D4
Tekirdağ, *province*, Turkey, **297** F5
Tekirdağ, Turkey, **297** F5

Teku, Indonesia, **198** C3
Tel Aviv-Yafo, Israel, **225** C3
Tela, Honduras, **428** D4
Télagh, Algeria, **361** F2
Télataï, Mali, **365** E1
Telč, Czech Republic, **289** G4
Telchac Puerto, Mexico, **431** H4
Telciu, Romania, **296** E2
Telde, Islas Canarias, Spain, **373** B4
Tele, *river*, Democratic Republic of the Congo, **368** D2
Telefomin, Papua New Guinea, **140** A4
Telegraph Creek, Canada, **412** D3
Telêmaco Borba, Brazil, **459** G2
Telemark, *county*, Norway, **286** C2
Telemba, Russian Federation, **210** F1
Télemsès, Niger, **365** E1
Teleneşti, Moldova, **296** G2
Teleorman, *river*, Romania, **296** E3
Telerhteba, Djebel, *mountain peak*, Algeria, **361** H4
Teles Pires (São Manuel), *river*, Brazil, **452** B5
Telescope Peak, *mountain peak*, U.S.A., **422** E3
Telford, England, U.K., **304** E2
Telford and Wrekin, *unitary authority*, England, U.K., **304** E2
Telica, Nicaragua, **428** D4
Teljo, Jabal, *mountain peak*, Sudan, **366** C2
Telkwa, Canada, **412** F4
Telmen Nuur, *lake*, Mongolia, **213** H2
Telok Blangah, Singapore, **200** J7
Teloloapan, Mexico, **431** F5
Telsen, Argentina, **460** D2
Telšiai, Lithuania, **287** L5
Telukbatang, Indonesia, **201** E3
Telukdalam, Indonesia, **200** B2
Telupid, Malaysia, **201** G1
Tema, Ghana, **364** E3, *326*
Temagami, Canada, **421** P2
Temagami, Lake, Canada, **421** N2
Tematangi, *island*, French Polynesia, **137** G3
Temax, Mexico, **431** H4
Tembagapura, Indonesia, **199** G3
Tembesi, *river*, Indonesia, **200** C3
Tembhurni, India, **216** C2
Tembilahan, Indonesia, **200** C3
Tembisa, South Africa, **371** E4
Tembito, Indonesia, **198** C2
Tembleque, Spain, **293** F3
Tembo, Democratic Republic of the Congo, **368** C4
Tembo Aluma, Angola, **368** C4
Temecula, U.S.A., **422** E5
Téméra, Mali, **364** D1
Temerin, Serbia, **296** B3
Temerloh, Malaysia, **200** C2
Temirtaū, Kazakhstan, **212** B2
Témiscaming, Canada, **416** B6
Temoe, *island*, French Polynesia, **137** H3
Temora, Australia, **135** K5

Temósachic, Mexico, 430 D2
Tempe, Danau, lake, Indonesia, 198 B4
Tempe, U.S.A., 423 H5
Tempio Pausania, Sardegna, Italy, 295 B5
Temple, U.S.A., 424 D4
Temple Bar, Wales, U.K., 304 C2
Temple Ewell, England, U.K., 305 J3
Temple Sowerby, England, U.K., 306 F3
Templemore, Ireland, 309 E5
Templeton, Wales, U.K., 304 C3
Templetouhy, Ireland, 309 E5
Templin, Germany, 288 F2
Tempoal, Mexico, 431 F4
Tempué, Angola, 368 C5
Temska, Serbia, 296 D4
Temuco, Chile, 460 C1
Temuka, New Zealand, 133 C7
Ten Degree Channel, Andaman and Nicobar Islands, India, 217 G4
Ten Sleep, U.S.A., 419 L4
Ten Thousand Islands, U.S.A., 425 M7
Tena, Ecuador, 450 C4
Tenāli, India, 216 E2
Tenamatua, Gunung, mountain peak, Indonesia, 198 C3
Tenasserim, division, Myanmar, 202 C3
Tenbury Wells, England, U.K., 304 E2
Tenby, Wales, U.K., 304 C3
Tendaho, Ethiopia, 367 F2
Tende, France, 291 H4
Tendō, Japan, 209 H3
Tendoy, U.S.A., 418 H4
Tendrara, Morocco, 361 F2
Ténenkou, Mali, 364 C2
Tenerife, island, Islas Canarias, Spain, 373 A4, 355
Ténès, Algeria, 361 G1
Teng Xian, China, 206 B4
Tengchong, China, 215 F4
Tengeh Reservoir, Singapore, 200 J6
Tengiz Köli, lake, Kazakhstan, 223 H2
Tengréla, Côte d'Ivoire, 364 C2
Tenhola, Finland, 287 L2
Tenja, Croatia, 294 G3
Tenke, Democratic Republic of the Congo, 369 E5
Tenkiller Ferry Lake, U.S.A., 424 E2
Tenkodogo, Burkina Faso, 364 D2
Tenmarou, Vanuatu, 141 A2
Tenna, river, Italy, 294 D4
Tennant Creek, Australia, 134 G2
Tennessee, river, U.S.A., 425 H2
Tennessee, state, U.S.A., 425 J2, 383, 386
Tennevoll, Norway, 284 H2
Tenniöjoki, river, Finland/Russian Federation, 285 P3
Tenojoki, river, Finland, 285 N2
Tenosique de Pino Suárez, Mexico, 431 H5
Tenryū, river, Japan, 209 G4
Tensed, U.S.A., 418 F3
Tenstrike, U.S.A., 420 F2
Tenterden, England, U.K., 305 H3
Tenterfield, Australia, 135 L4
Tentolomatinan, Gunung, mountain peak, Indonesia, 198 C2
Tentudia, mountain peak, Spain, 292 D3
Teodoro Sampaio, Brazil, 459 G2
Teófilo Otoni, Brazil, 457 F4
Teopisca, Mexico, 431 G5
Tepa, Indonesia, 199 E4
Tepa Point, Niue, 132 M13
Tepasto, Finland, 285 M3
Tepatitlán, Mexico, 430 E4
Tepehuanes, Mexico, 430 D3
Tepelenë, Albania, 297 B5
Tepequém, Brazil, 451 G3
Tepequém, Serra, mountain range, Brazil, 451 G3
Tepic, Mexico, 430 D4
Teploye, Russian Federation, 299 F6
Tepoto, island, French Polynesia, 137 G2
Tepsa, Finland, 285 M3
Téra, Niger, 364 E2
Tera, river, Spain, 292 D1
Tera Nova Bay, Italian research station, Antarctica, 470 D7
Teraina, island, Kiribati, 139 H4
Teramo, Italy, 294 D4
Teratyn, Poland, 289 L3
Terceira, island, Azores, Portugal, 360 M7
Teregova, Romania, 296 D3
Terengganu, state, Malaysia, 200 C1
Terenos, Brazil, 456 B5
Teresina, Brazil, 453 E4
Teresópolis, Brazil, 457 E6
Terespol, Poland, 289 L2
Terevaka, mountain peak, Isla de Pascua (Easter Island), Chile, 461 B2
Terevinto, Bolivia, 455 F4
Tergun Daba Shan, mountain range, China, 213 G5
Teriberka, river, Russian Federation, 285 S2
Teriberka, Russian Federation, 285 S2
Teriberskiy, Mys, cape, Russian Federation, 285 S2
Terlingua, U.S.A., 423 M7
Termas de Río Hondo, Argentina, 458 D3
Terminillo, Monte, mountain peak, Italy, 295 D4
Términos, Laguna de, lagoon, Mexico, 431 H5
Termit-Kaoboul, Niger, 365 G1
Termiz, Uzbekistan, 218 A1
Termoli, Italy, 295 E5
Tern, island, Hawaiian Islands, U.S.A., 139 H2
Ternate, Indonesia, 198 D2, 76
Terneuzen, Netherlands, 288 A3
Terney, Russian Federation, 209 G1
Terni, Italy, 295 D4
Ternivka, Ukraine, 296 G1
Ternopil', Ukraine, 298 C3
Terpeniya, Mys, cape, Russian Federation, 301 R5
Terra Firma, South Africa, 370 D4
Terrace, Canada, 412 E4
Terrace Bay, Canada, 415 L7
Terracina, Italy, 295 D5
Terråk, Norway, 284 F4
Terralba, Sardegna, Italy, 295 B6
Terrassa, Spain, 293 H2
Terre Adélie, region, Antarctica, 470 E7
Terre Haute, U.S.A., 421 K6
Terrebonne Bay, U.S.A., 424 G5
Terreton, U.S.A., 418 H5
Terrington St Clement, England, U.K., 305 H2
Terry, Mississippi, U.S.A., 424 G3
Terry, Montana, U.S.A., 419 M3
Terschelling, island, Netherlands, 288 B2
Tertenia, Sardegna, Italy, 295 B6
Teruel, Spain, 293 G2
Tervel, Bulgaria, 296 F4
Tērvete, Latvia, 287 L4
Tervo, Finland, 285 N5
Tervola, Finland, 285 M3
Tešanj, Bosnia and Herzegovina, 294 F3
Teseney, Eritrea, 367 E1
Teshig, Mongolia, 213 J2
Teshikaga, Japan, 209 J2
Teshio, river, Japan, 209 H1
Teskey Ala-Too, mountain range, Kyrgyzstan, 212 C4
Teslin, Canada, 412 C1
Teslin Lake, Canada, 412 C1
Tesouro, Brazil, 456 C4
Tesovo Netyl'skiy, Russian Federation, 299 C3
Tessalit, Mali, 361 G4
Tessaoua, Niger, 365 F2
Tessin, Germany, 288 F1
Test, river, England, U.K., 305 F3
Tét, Hungary, 289 H5
Tetas, Punta, point, Chile, 458 B2
Tetbury, England, U.K., 304 E3
Tete, Mozambique, 369 F6
Tete, province, Mozambique, 369 F6
Tête Jaune Cache, Canada, 413 K5
Tetepare, island, Solomon Islands, 141 A1
Tetere, Solomon Islands, 141 A1
Teteven, Bulgaria, 296 E4
Tetiaroa, island, French Polynesia, 137 G2
Tetney, England, U.K., 307 H4
Teton, U.S.A., 419 J5
Tetonia, U.S.A., 419 J5
Tetouan (Tetuán), Morocco, 361 E1
Tetovo, Macedonia, 296 C4
Tetrino, Russian Federation, 285 U3
Tetuán see Tetouan, Morocco, 361 E1
Teuco, river, Argentina, 458 E2
Teulada, Capo, cape, Italy, 295 B6
Teulada, Sardegna, Italy, 295 B6
Teulon, Canada, 414 F6
Teutoburger Wald, mountain range, Germany, 288 C2
Teuva, Finland, 287 K1
Teverya, Israel, 225 C3
Teviotdale, valley, Scotland, U.K., 308 G5
Tevriz, Russian Federation, 223 J1
Tewkesbury, England, U.K., 304 E3
Têwo, China, 215 G2
Texarkana, U.S.A., 424 E3
Texas, Australia, 135 L4
Texas, state, U.S.A., 423 M5, 94, 377, 384, 386
Texas City, U.S.A., 424 E5
Texas Creek, U.S.A., 423 L2
Texel, island, Netherlands, 288 B2
Texhoma, U.S.A., 420 C7
Texoma, Lake, U.S.A., 424 D2
Teyateyaneng, Lesotho, 371 E4
Teziutlan, Mexico, 431 F5
Tezpur, India, 219 H4
Tha-anne, river, Canada, 414 E1
Tha Song Yang, Thailand, 202 C2
Tha Tum, Thailand, 203 D3
Thabana-Ntlenyana, mountain peak, Lesotho, 371 E4, 349
Thabazimbi, South Africa, 371 E3
Thabong, South Africa, 371 E4
Thabt, Jabal ath, mountain peak, Egypt, 225 C5
Thagaya, Myanmar, 205 C4
Thái Nguyên, Vietnam, 203 E1
Thailand, country, Asia, 197 L8, 47, 73, 79, 89, 96, 144, 145, 151, 152, 154, 155, 157, 158
Thailand, Gulf of, South East Asia, 202 D4
Thal, Pakistan, 218 B2
Thale, Germany, 288 E3
Thamarīt, Oman, 367 H1
Thame, England, U.K., 305 G3
Thames, Firth of, bay, New Zealand, 132 E3
Thames, New Zealand, 132 E3
Thames, river, Canada, 421 N4
Thames, river, England, U.K., 305 H3, 276
Than Kyun, island, Myanmar, 202 C4
Thāna Ghāzi, India, 218 D4
Thāne, India, 216 C2
Thānesar, India, 218 D3
Thanh Hóa, Vietnam, 203 E2
Thánh Lang Xã, Vietnam, 203 E2
Thanh Phố Hồ Chí Minh (Saigon), Vietnam, 203 E4, 97, 153
Thanjāvur, India, 216 D4
Thanlwin (Salween), river, Myanmar, 205 C1
Thāno Būla Khān, Pakistan, 218 A4
Thap Sakae, Thailand, 202 C4
Thar Desert, India/Pakistan, 218 B4, 28, 168, 169
Thargomindah, Australia, 135 J4
Tharthār, Buḥayrat ath, lake, Iraq, 363 H2
Tharwānīyah, Oman, 221 F4
Thasos, Greece, 297 E5
Thasos, island, Greece, 297 E5
Thatcham, England, U.K., 305 F3
Thaton, Myanmar, 205 C4
Thatta, Pakistan, 218 A4
Thau, Bassin de, lake, France, 291 F5
Thaxted, England, U.K., 305 H3
The Dalles, U.S.A., 418 D4
The Forks, New Zealand, 133 C6
The Hague see 's-Gravenhage, Netherlands, 288 B2
The Pas, Canada, 414 D5
The Valley, Anguilla, 427 D2, 387
Thedford, U.S.A., 420 C5
Theinkun, Myanmar, 202 C4
Thekulthili Lake, Canada, 413 P1
Thelon, river, Canada, 410 J3
Theniet el Had, Algeria, 361 G1
Thenon, France, 290 E4
Theodore, Canada, 414 C6
Theodore Roosevelt, river, Brazil, 455 G2
Theodore Roosevelt Lake, U.S.A., 423 H5
Thermaïkos Kolpos, bay, Greece, 297 D5
Thermo, Greece, 297 C6
Thermopolis, U.S.A., 419 K5
Thesiger Bay, Canada, 410 G2
Thessalia, administrative region, Greece, 297 D6
Thessalon, Canada, 421 M2
Thessaloniki (Salonica), Greece, 297 D5, 265
Thet, river, England, U.K., 305 H2
Thetford Mines, Canada, 416 F6
Thetford, England, U.K., 305 H2
Thibodaux, U.S.A., 424 G5
Thief River Falls, U.S.A., 420 E1
Thiene, Italy, 294 C3
Thiers, France, 291 F4
Thiès, Senegal, 364 A2
Thika, Kenya, 369 G3
Thimphu, Bhutan, 205 A2, 171
Thio, New Caledonia, 141 A3
Thionville, France, 291 H2
Thira (Santorini), island, Kyklades, Greece, 297 E7
Thirsk, England, U.K., 307 G3
Thiruvananthapuram (Trivandrum), India, 216 D4, 169
Thiruvattiyur, India, 216 E3
Thisted, Denmark, 286 D4
Thisvi, Greece, 297 D6
Thiva, Greece, 297 D6
Thiviers, France, 290 E4
Thlewiaza, river, Canada, 414 F1
Thohoyandou, South Africa, 371 F3
Thới Bình, Vietnam, 203 E4
Thomas, U.S.A., 421 P6
Thomaston, Alabama, U.S.A., 425 J3
Thomaston, Georgia, U.S.A., 425 K3
Thomastown, Ireland, 309 E5
Thomasville, Alabama, U.S.A., 425 J4
Thomasville, Georgia, U.S.A., 425 K4
Thompson, Canada, 414 F4
Thompson Falls, U.S.A., 418 G3
Thompson Peak, mountain peak, U.S.A., 418 C6
Thompson Point, Canada, 414 H2
Thomson, river, Australia, 135 J3
Thomson, U.S.A., 425 L3
Thoreau, U.S.A., 423 J4
Thornaby on Tees, England, U.K., 307 G3
Thornbury, England, U.K., 304 E3
Thorne, England, U.K., 307 H4
Thornhill, Scotland, U.K., 308 F5
Thornton, England, U.K., 306 F4
Thornton, U.S.A., 418 F3
Thorsby, Canada, 413 M5
Thorshavnheiane, mountain range, Antarctica, 470 E3
Thouars, France, 290 D3
Thouet, river, France, 290 D3
Thousand Springs, U.S.A., 418 G6
Thrakiko Pelagos, sea, Greece, 297 E5
Thrapston, England, U.K., 305 G2
Three Forks, U.S.A., 419 J4
Three King Islands, New Zealand, 132 D2
Three Points, Cape, Ghana, 364 D4
Three Rivers, Michigan, U.S.A., 421 L5
Three Rivers, Texas, U.S.A., 424 C5
Three Sisters, mountain peak, U.S.A., 418 D4
Throckmorton, U.S.A., 424 C3
Thu, Cù Lao, island, Vietnam, 203 F4
Thủ Dầu Một, Vietnam, 203 E4
Thul, Pakistan, 218 B3
Thule see Qaanaag, Greenland, 411 N2
Thun, Switzerland, 291 H3
Thunder Bay, Canada, 421 J1
Thuner See, lake, Switzerland, 291 H3
Thung Chang, Thailand, 202 D2
Thung Song, Thailand, 202 C4
Thüringen, state, Germany, 288 E3, 238
Thüringer Wald, mountain range, Germany, 288 E3
Thurles, Ireland, 309 E5
Thurrock, unitary authority, England, U.K., 305 H3
Thursby, England, U.K., 306 E3
Thursday Island, Australia, 140 A5
Thurso, river, Scotland, U.K., 308 F2
Thurso, Scotland, U.K., 308 F2
Thurston Island, Antarctica, 470 B6
Thwaite, England, U.K., 306 F3
Thyborøn, Denmark, 286 D4
Ti-n-Aguelhaj, Mali, 364 D1
Ti-n-Bessaïs, Sebkhet, salt-pan, Mauritania, 360 E4
Ti-n-Essako, Mali, 361 G5
Ti-n-Zaouâtene, Mali, 361 G5
Ti-Tree, Australia, 134 G3
Tian Shan, mountain range, China/Kyrgyzstan, 212 C4, 186, 187
Tiancang, China, 213 H4
Tianchang, China, 206 D1
Tiancheng, China, 213 H5
Tiandeng, China, 215 H5
Tian'e, China, 215 H4
Tianguá, Brazil, 453 F4
Tianjin, China, 210 G5, 161
Tianjun, China, 213 H5
Tianlin, China, 215 H4
Tianmen, China, 206 C2
Tianqiaoling, China, 211 K4
Tianquan, China, 215 G3
Tianshui, China, 215 H2
Tianshuibu, China, 210 D5
Tianshuihai, China, 218 D2
Tianshuijing, China, 213 G4
Tiantai, China, 206 E2
Tiantangwei, China, 207 C3
Tianxin, China, 207 A4
Tianyang, China, 215 H5
Tianzhu, China, 206 B3
Tianzhuangtai, China, 211 H4
Tiaret, Algeria, 293 H5
Tías, Islas Canarias, Spain, 373 B4
Tias, Punta, point, Islas Canarias, Spain, 373 B4
Tiassalé, Côte d'Ivoire, 364 D3

Ti'avea, Samoa, **141** B1
Tibaji, *river*, Brazil, **459** G2
Ţibana, Romania, **296** F2
Tibati, Cameroon, **365** G3
Tibba, Pakistan, **218** B3
Tibé, Pic de, *mountain peak*, Guinea, **364** C3
Tibesti, *mountain range*, Chad, **362** C4, *316, 328*
Tibesti, Sarīr, *desert*, Libya, **362** C4
Tibet, Plateau of *see* Qingzang Gaoyuan, *plateau*, China, **214** C2, *144, 158*
Tibet *see* Xizang Zizhiqu, *autonomous region*, China, **214** C2, *23, 73, 97, 144, 160, 161, 170, 171, 172, 173*
Tibiao, Philippines, **204** C4
Tibo, Democratic Republic of the Congo, **369** E2
Tibooburra, Australia, **135** J4
Tibro, Sweden, **286** G3
Tiburon, Haiti, **429** G3
Tiburón, Isla, *island*, Mexico, **430** B2
Ticao Island, Philippines, **204** C3
Ticehurst, England, U.K., **305** H3
Tîchît, Mauritania, **360** E5
Tichla, Western Sahara, **360** D4
Ticonderoga, U.S.A., **426** D3
Ticul, Mexico, **431** H4
Tidaholm, Sweden, **286** G3
Tidarméné, Mali, **365** E1
Tiddim, Myanmar, **205** B3
Tidikelt, Plaine du, *plain*, Algeria, **361** G3
Tidjikja, Mauritania, **360** D5
Tiechang, Guangdong, China, **207** B2
Tiechang, Jilin, China, **211** J4
Tiedra, Spain, **292** E2
Tiefa, China, **211** H4
Tiefencastel, Switzerland, **291** J3
Tieli, China, **211** K3
Tieling, China, **211** H4
Tielongtan, China, **218** D2
Tienen, Belgium, **288** B3
Tierp, Sweden, **287** H2
Tierra Amarilla, Chile, **458** B3
Tierra Amarilla, U.S.A., **423** K3
Tierra Blanca, Bahía, *bay*, Róbinson Crusoe Island, Archipiélago Juan Fernández, Chile, **461** C2
Tierra Blanca, Mexico, **431** F5
Tierra Colorada, Mexico, **431** F5
Tierra de Campos, *region*, Spain, **292** E2
Tierra del Fuego, Isla Grande de, *island*, Chile/Argentina, **460** C4, *87, 434, 443*
Tierra del Fuego, *province*, Argentina, **460** D4
Tierralta, Colombia, **450** C2
Tiétar, *river*, Spain, **292** E2
Tietê, Brazil, **459** H2
Tieté, *river*, Brazil, **456** C5
Tifariti, Western Sahara, **360** D3
Tiffin, U.S.A., **421** M5
Tifton, U.S.A., **425** L4
Tifu, Indonesia, **198** D3
Tiger, U.S.A., **418** F2
Tigharry, Scotland, U.K., **308** B3
Tighina, Moldova, **296** G2
Tighnabruaich, Scotland, U.K., **308** D5
Tignère, Cameroon, **365** G3
Tignish, Canada, **417** J6
Tigre, Cerro del, *mountain peak*, Mexico, **431** F4
Tigre, *river*, Peru, **450** C5
Tigre, *river*, Venezuela, **451** F2
Tigris, *river*, Asia, **194** F6; *see also* Dicle, *river*, Turkey, **224** F5; Dijlah, *river*, Iraq, **363** J2, *64, 66, 88, 146, 182*
Tiguent, Mauritania, **364** A1
Tiguidit, Falaise de, *escarpment*, Niger, **365** F1
Tihoi, New Zealand, **132** E4
Tiistenjoki, Finland, **287** L1
Tijāra, India, **218** D4
Tījī, Libya, **362** B2
Tijola, Spain, **293** F4
Tijuana, Mexico, **430** A1
Tijuco, *river*, Brazil, **456** D5
Tika, Canada, **416** J4
Tikanlik, China, **212** E4
Tikehau, *island*, French Polynesia, **137** G2
Tikei, *island*, French Polynesia, **137** G2
Tikem, Chad, **365** H3
Tikhvin, Russian Federation, **299** D3
Tikhvinskaya Gryada, *mountain range*, Russian Federation, **299** D3
Tikitiki, New Zealand, **132** G3
Tikokino, New Zealand, **132** F4
Tikopia, *island*, Solomon Islands, **139** E6
Tikota, India, **216** C2
Tikrīt, Iraq, **363** H2
Tiksha, Russian Federation, **285** R4
Tiksheozero, Ozero *lake*, Russian Federation, **285** R3
Tiksi, Russian Federation, **301** P2
Tiladummati Atoll, Maldives, **216** C5
Tilburg, Netherlands, **288** B3
Tilbury, England, U.K., **305** H3
Tilcara, Argentina, **458** D2
Tilehurst, England, U.K., **305** F3
Till, *river*, England, U.K., **306** F2
Tillabéri, *department*, Niger, **364** E2
Tillabéri, Niger, **365** E2
Tillamook, U.S.A., **418** C4
Tilley, Canada, **413** P6
Tillia, Niger, **365** E1
Tillman, U.S.A., **425** M3
Tillyfourie, Scotland, U.K., **308** G3
Tiloa, Niger, **365** E1
Tilomonte, Chile, **458** C2
Tilos, *island*, Dodekanisos, Greece, **297** F7
Tilrhemt, Algeria, **361** G2
Ţimā, Egypt, **363** F3
Timah, Bukit, *mountain peak*, Singapore, **200** J6
Timanskiy Kryazh, *mountain range*, Russian Federation, **300** G3
Timaru, New Zealand, **133** C7
Timashevsk, Russian Federation, **298** E3
Timbaúba, Brazil, **453** G5
Timbedgha, Mauritania, **364** C1
Timber Creek, Australia, **134** G2
Timbue, Ponta, *cape*, Mozambique, **371** G2
Timbun Mata, Pulau, *island*, Malaysia, **201** G1
Timétrine, Mali, **361** F5
Timia, Niger, **361** H5
Timimoun, Algeria, **361** G3
Timirist, Râs, *cape*, Mauritania, **360** C5
Timiş, *river*, Romania, **296** D3
Timişoara, Romania, **296** C3
Timmiarmiut, Greenland, **411** Q3
Timmins, Canada, **421** N1
Timmoudi, Algeria, **361** F3
Timms Hill, *mountain peak*, U.S.A., **420** H3
Timoforo, *river*, Indonesia, **199** F3
Timokhino, Russian Federation, **299** F3
Timolin, Ireland, **309** F5
Timon, Brazil, **453** E4
Timor, *island*, Indonesia/East Timor, **198** D5, *148*
Timor Sea, Australia/Indonesia, **128** A3
Timor Timur, *province*, Indonesia, **198** D5
Timoshino, Russian Federation, **299** F2
Timote, Argentina, **458** D5
Timpas, U.S.A., **423** M3
Timrå, Sweden, **287** H1
Timūrni, India, **218** D5
Tīn, Ra's at, *point*, Libya, **362** D2
Tinabogan, Indonesia, **198** C2
Tinaco, Venezuela, **451** E2
Ţīnah, Khalīj aţ, *bay*, Egypt, **225** B4
Tinaja, Punta, *point*, Peru, **454** C4
Tinajo, Islas Canarias, Spain, **373** B4
Tinambac, Philippines, **204** C3
Tinchebray, France, **290** D2
Tindouf, Algeria, **360** E3
Tinfouchy, Algeria, **361** E3
Ting, *river*, China, **206** D3
Tinggoa, Solomon Islands, **141** A1
Tingo María, Peru, **454** C2
Tingri, China, **214** C3
Tingstäde, Sweden, **287** J4
Tinguiririca, Volcán, *mountain peak*, Chile, **458** B5
Tingvoll, Norway, **284** D5
Tinian, *island*, Northern Mariana Islands, **138** C, *125*
Tinjar, *river*, Malaysia, **201** F2
Tinniswood, Mount, *mountain peak*, Canada, **412** H6
Tinnoset, Norway, **286** D3
Tinogasta, Argentina, **458** C3
Tinombo, Indonesia, **198** C2
Tinos, *island*, Kyklades, Greece, **297** E7
Tinos, Kyklades, Greece, **297** E7
Tinrhert, Plateau du, *mountain range*, Algeria, **361** H3
Tinsukia, India, **219** H4
Tintagel, England, U.K., **304** C4
Tîntâne, Mauritania, **364** B1
Tintang, Indonesia, **201** G2
Tintina, Argentina, **458** D3
Tioman, Pulau, *island*, Malaysia, **200** D2
Tiong Bahru, Singapore, **200** J7
Tipasa, Algeria, **361** G1
Tipitapa, Nicaragua, **428** D4
Tipperary, *county*, Ireland, **309** D5
Tipperary, Ireland, **309** D5
Tipton, Mount, *mountain peak*, U.S.A., **422** F4
Tipton, U.S.A., **420** H5
Tiptree, England, U.K., **305** H3
Tiptūr, India, **216** D3
Tipuani, Bolivia, **455** E4
Tiquicheo, Mexico, **431** E5
Tiquié, *river*, Brazil, **451** E4
Tiquina, Bolivia, **455** E4
Tiracambu, Serra do, *mountain range*, Brazil, **452** D4
Tīrān, Jazīrat, *island*, Saudi Arabia, **225** C6
Tirana *see* Tiranë, Albania, **297** B5, *263*
Tiranë (Tirana), Albania, **297** B5, *263*
Tirano, Italy, **294** C2
Tiraspol, Moldova, **296** G2
Tiraumea, New Zealand, **132** F5
Tirebolu, Turkey, **224** E4
Tiree, *island*, Scotland, U.K., **308** B4
Tirga Mór, *mountain peak*, Scotland, U.K., **308** C3
Tiris Zemmour, *administrative region*, Mauritania, **360** D4
Tirol, *state*, Austria, **288** E5
Tiroungoulou, Central African Republic, **366** B3
Tirstrup, Denmark, **286** E4
Tirua Point, New Zealand, **132** E4
Tiruchchirāppalli, India, **216** D4
Tirunelveli, India, **216** D4
Tiruntán, Peru, **454** C2
Tirupati, India, **216** D3
Tiruppur, India, **216** D4
Tiruvannāmalai, India, **216** D3
Tisaiyānvilai, India, **216** D4
Tisbury, England, U.K., **304** E3
Tisdale, Canada, **414** B5
Tisgui-Remz, Morocco, **360** E3
Tishomingo, U.S.A., **424** D2
Ţīsīyah, Syria, **225** D3
Tiškovka, Ukraine, **296** H1
Tissemsilt, Algeria, **361** G1
Tisza, *river*, Europe, **280** G6, *261, 262*
Tiszaföldvár, Hungary, **289** K5
Tiszafüred, Hungary, **289** K5
Tiszaújváros, Hungary, **289** K5
Tiszavasvári, Hungary, **289** K5
Titaguas, Spain, **293** G3
Titao, Burkina Faso, **364** D2
Titel, Serbia, **296** C3
Titi Islands *see* Muttonbird Islands, New Zealand, **133** A8
Titicaca, Lago, *lake*, Bolivia/Peru, **455** E4, *434, 441*
Titlāgarh, India, **219** E5
Titlis, *mountain peak*, Switzerland, **291** J3
Titran, Norway, **284** D5
Tittmoning, Germany, **288** F4
Titu, Romania, **296** E3
Titusville, U.S.A., **425** M5
Tivari, India, **218** C4
Tivat, Montenegro, **296** B4
Tiverton, England, U.K., **304** D4
Tivoli, Italy, **295** D5
Tivoli, U.S.A., **424** D5
Tiwanacu, Bolivia, **455** E4
Tixkokob, Mexico, **431** H4
Tixtla, Mexico, **431** F5
Tiyās, Syria, **225** D2
Tizi Ouzou, Algeria, **361** G1
Tizimín, Mexico, **431** H4
Tiznit, Morocco, **360** E3
Tjaktjajaure, *lake*, Sweden, **284** H3
Tjåmotis, Sweden, **284** J3
Tjeggelvas, *lake*, Sweden, **284** H3
Tjentište, Bosnia and Herzegovina, **294** G4
Tjörn, *island*, Sweden, **286** E4
Þjórsá, *river*, Iceland, **284** Y7
Tjøtta, Norway, **284** F4
Tlacolula de Matamoros, Mexico, **431** F5
Tlacotalpan, Mexico, **431** G5
Tlalnepantla, Mexico, **431** F5
Tlaltenango, Mexico, **430** E4
Tlapa de Comonfort, Mexico, **431** F5
Tlaxcala, Mexico, **431** F5
Tlaxcala, *state*, Mexico, **431** F5
Tlaxiaco, Mexico, **431** F5
Tlemcen, Algeria, **361** F2
Tlokweng, Botswana, **371** E3
Tlumach, Ukraine, **296** E1
Tmassah, Libya, **362** C3
Tmeïmîchât, Mauritania, **360** D4
Toa Payoh, Singapore, **200** K6
Toad River, Canada, **412** G2
Toamasina, Madagascar, **372** B4
Toamasina, *province*, Madagascar, **372** B4
Toay, Argentina, **458** D5
Toba, China, **215** F3
Toba, *mountain peak*, China, **215** E3
Toba Danau, *lake*, Indonesia, **200** B2, *148*
Toba Kākar Range, *mountain range*, Pakistan, **218** A3
Toba Tek Singh, Pakistan, **218** C3
Tobago, *island*, Trinidad and Tobago, **461** B4, *399*
Tobarra, Spain, **293** G3
Tobelo, Indonesia, **198** D2
Tobercurry, Ireland, **309** D3
Tobermory, Canada, **421** N3
Tobermory, Scotland, U.K., **308** C4
Tobi, *island*, Palau, **138** B4
Tobin, Mount, *mountain peak*, U.S.A., **422** E1
Tobin Lake, Canada, **414** C5
Tobin Lake, *lake*, Canada, **414** C5
Toboali, Indonesia, **200** D3
Toboli, Indonesia, **198** C3
Tobol'sk, Russian Federation, **223** H1
Tobyl, Kazakhstan, **222** G2
Tocantinópolis, Brazil, **452** D5
Tocantins, *river*, E. Pará, Brazil, **452** D4, *440*
Tocantins, *river*, W. Pará, Brazil, **452** B4, *440*
Tocantins, *state*, Brazil, **456** D3
Töcksfors, Sweden, **286** E3
Toco, Chile, **458** C2
Toco, Trinidad, Trinidad and Tobago, **461** C4
Toconao, Chile, **458** C2
Tocopilla, Chile, **458** B2
Tocuyo, *river*, Venezuela, **451** E1
Toda Rāisingh, India, **218** C4
Todal, Norway, **286** D1
Toddington, England, U.K., **305** F3
Todenyang, Kenya, **366** E4
Todi, Italy, **294** D4
Todos Santos, Bolivia, **455** F4
Todos Santos, Mexico, **430** C4
Toe Head, *point*, Ireland, **309** C6
Toetoes Bay, New Zealand, **133** B8
Tofield, Canada, **413** N5
Tofino, Canada, **412** G7
Toft, Shetland, Scotland, U.K., **308** K7
Tofte, U.S.A., **420** H2
Toftlund, Denmark, **286** D5
Tofua, *island*, Tonga, **136** D2, *114*
Togdheer, *administrative region*, Somalia, **367** G3
Togiak, U.S.A., **410** C4
Togian, Kepulauan, *islands*, Indonesia, **198** C3
Togo, *country*, Africa, **358** F6, *312, 326*
Togo, U.S.A., **420** G2
Tögöl, Mongolia, **213** H2
Tögrög, Govĭ-Altay, Mongolia, **213** G3
Tögrög, Hovd, Mongolia, **213** G3
Togtoh, China, **210** E4
Toguchin, Russian Federation, **223** L1
Tohatchi, U.S.A., **423** J4
Toholampi, Finland, **285** M5
Töhöm, Mongolia, **210** E3
Toivala, Finland, **285** N5
Tok, *river*, Russian Federation, **222** E2
Tok, U.S.A., **410** E3
Tokaj, Hungary, **289** K4
Tōkamachi, Japan, **209** G3
Tokara-rettō, *islands*, Japan, **208** E5
Tokarahi, New Zealand, **133** C7
Tokari, Russian Federation, **299** E2
Tokat, Turkey, **224** E4
Tokelau, *New Zealand territory*, Pacific Ocean, **131** H2, *110, 126, 127*
Tokirima, New Zealand, **132** E4
Tokmak, Kyrgyzstan, **212** B4
Tokomaru Bay, New Zealand, **132** G4
Tokoroa, New Zealand, **132** E4
Tokouno, Guinea, **364** C3
Toksovo, Russian Federation, **299** C2
Toksun, China, **212** F4
Toktogul, Kyrgyzstan, **212** B4
Toktomush, Tajikistan, **223** J5
Toku, *island*, Tonga, **136** D2
Tokuno-shima, *island*, Japan, **209** P8
Tokushima, Japan, **208** F4
Tokuyama, Japan, **208** E4
Tōkyō, Japan, **209** G4, *82, 83, 150, 164*
Tokzār, Afghanistan, **218** A2
Tolaga Bay, New Zealand, **132** G4
Tôlañaro, Madagascar, **372** B6
Tolbo, Mongolia, **212** F2
Tolé, Panama, **429** E5
Töle Bī, Kazakhstan, **212** B4
Toledo, Brazil, **459** G2
Toledo, Iowa, U.S.A., **420** G5
Toledo, Montes de, *mountain range*, Spain, **292** E3
Toledo, Ohio, U.S.A., **421** M5
Toledo, Oregon, U.S.A., **418** C4
Toledo, Philippines, **204** C4
Toledo, Spain, **292** E3
Toledo, Washington, U.S.A., **418** C3
Toledo Bend Reservoir, U.S.A., **424** E4

Tolga, Norway, 286 E1
Toli, China, 212 D3
Toliara, Madagascar, 372 A5, *353*
Toliara, *province*, Madagascar, 372 A5
Tolitoli, Indonesia, 198 C2
Tolkmicko, Poland, 289 J1
Tollesbury, England, U.K., 305 H3
Tolmachevo, Russian Federation, 299 B3
Tolmezzo, Italy, 294 D2
Tolmin, Slovenia, 294 D2
Tolna, Hungary, 289 J5
Tolo, Democratic Republic of the Congo, 368 C3
Tolo, Teluk, *bay*, Indonesia, 198 C3
Tolong Bay, Philippines, 204 C4
Tolsta Head, *cape*, Scotland, U.K., 308 C2
Tolstoy, Mys, *cape*, Russian Federation, 301 S4
Tolú, Colombia, 450 C2
Toluca, Mexico, 431 F5
Tolvayarvi, Russian Federation, 285 Q5
Tolvuya, Russian Federation, 285 S5
Tol'yatti, Russian Federation, 222 D2
Tom Burke, South Africa, 371 E3
Tom Price, Australia, 134 D3
Tom Price, Mount, *mountain peak*, Australia, 134 D3
Toma, Burkina Faso, 364 D2
Tomah, U.S.A., 420 H4
Tomakomai, Japan, 209 H2
Tomanivi, *mountain peak*, Fiji, 141 A4
Tomar, Kazakhstan, 212 B3
Tomar, Portugal, 292 C3
Tomarza, Turkey, 363 G1
Tomás Barron, Bolivia, 455 E4
Tomás Garrido, Mexico, 431 H5
Tomás Gomensoro, Uruguay, 459 F4
Tomaszów Lubelski, Poland, 289 L3
Tomaszów Mazowiecki, Poland, 289 K3
Tomatin, Scotland, U.K., 308 F3
Tomatlán, Mexico, 430 D5
Tombador, Serra do, *mountain range*, Brazil, 456 B3
Tombigbee, *river*, U.S.A., 425 H4
Tomboco, Angola, 368 B4
Tombos, Brazil, 457 E5
Tombouctou, *administrative region*, Mali, 364 D1
Tombouctou, Mali, 364 D1, *92, 324, 325*
Tombstone, U.S.A., 423 J6
Tombua, Angola, 368 B6
Tome, Chile, 458 B5
Tomelilla, Sweden, 286 F5
Tomelloso, Spain, 293 F3
Tomini, Teluk, *bay*, Indonesia, 198 C3
Tominián, Mali, 364 D2
Tomintoul, Scotland, U.K., 308 F3
Tomislavgrad, Bosnia and Herzegovina, 294 F4
Tomma, *island*, Norway, 284 F3
Tømmervåg, Norway, 284 C5
Tomo, Colombia, 451 E3
Tomo, *river*, Colombia, 451 E3
Tompkins, Canada, 413 Q6
Tomsk, Russian Federation, 223 L1
Tomskaya Oblast', *province*, Russian Federation, 223 K1
Tomu, Indonesia, 199 F3
Tonalá, Mexico, 431 G5
Tonantins, Brazil, 451 E5
Tonasket, U.S.A., 418 E2
Tonate, French Guiana, 452 C2
Tonbridge, England, U.K., 305 H3
Tondano, Indonesia, 198 D2
Tønder, Denmark, 286 D5
Tondi, India, 216 D4
Tonekābon, Iran, 222 E5
Toney Mountain, *mountain peak*, Antarctica, 470 B6
Tong O, China, 207 C4
Tonga, *country*, Pacific Ocean, 131 H3, *93, 108, 113, 114, 125*
Tonga Trench, *underwater feature*, Pacific Ocean, 478 G6
Tong'an, Fujian, China, 206 D3
Tong'an, Sichuan, China, 215 G4
Tongareva (Penrhyn), *island*, Cook Islands, 139 J5
Tongariro, Mount, *mountain peak*, New Zealand, 132 E4
Tongatapu, *island*, Tonga, 141 B4, *93, 114*
Tongatapu Group, *islands*, Tonga, 141 B4
Tongbai, China, 206 C1
Tongbei, China, 211 J3
Tongcheng, China, 206 D2
T'ongch'ŏn, North Korea, 208 E3
Tongchuan, China, 206 B1
Tongdao, China, 206 B3
Tongerai, Tanjong, *point*, Indonesia, 199 E3
Tonggu, China, 206 C2
Tongguan, Hunan, China, 206 C2
Tongguan, Shaanxi, China, 206 B1
Tongguzbasti, China, 212 D5
Tonghai, China, 215 G4
Tonghe, China, 211 K3
Tonghua, China, 211 J4
Tongjiang, Heilongjiang, China, 211 L3
Tongjiang, Sichuan, China, 215 H3
Tongken, *river*, China, 211 J3
Tonglau, Myanmar, 205 C3
Tongliao, China, 211 H4
Tongling, China, 206 D2
Tongobory, Madagascar, 372 A5
Tongren, Guizhou, China, 206 B3
Tongren, Qinghai, China, 215 G2
Tongshi, China, 203 F2
Tongue, Kyle of, *inlet*, Scotland, U.K., 308 E2
Tongue, *river*, U.S.A., 419 L4
Tongue, Scotland, U.K., 308 E2
Tongwei, China, 215 H2
Tongxin, China, 210 D5
Tongxing, China, 210 G4
Tongyu, China, 211 H3
Tongzhou, China, 210 G5
Tongzi, China, 215 H3
Tónichi, Mexico, 430 C2
Tonj, Sudan, 366 C3
Tonk, India, 218 C4
Tonkin, Gulf of, China/Vietnam, 203 E1, *159*
Tônlé Sab, *lake*, Cambodia, 203 E3, *152*
Tonnerre, France, 291 F3
Tonopah, U.S.A., 422 E2
Tonosí, Panama, 429 E6
Tønsberg, Norway, 286 E3
Tonstad, Norway, 286 C3
Tooele, U.S.A., 422 G1
Toora-Khem, Russian Federation, 223 P2
Tooromt, Mongolia, 213 G2
Toowoomba, Australia, 135 L4
Tooxin, Somalia, 367 H2
Top Springs, Australia, 134 G2
Topalki, Russian Federation, 299 F3
Topaze Bay, Rodrigues, Mauritius, 373 B1
Topcliffe, England, U.K., 307 G3
Topeka, U.S.A., 420 F6, *386*
Topia, Mexico, 430 D3
Topliŭa, Romania, 296 E2
Topocalma, Punta, *point*, Chile, 458 B5
Topock, U.S.A., 422 F4
Topola, Serbia, 296 C3
Topol'čani, Macedonia, 297 C5
Topol'čany, Slovakia, 289 J4
Topolobampo, Mexico, 430 C3
Topolog, Romania, 296 G3
Topoloveni, Romania, 296 E3
Topolovgrad, Bulgaria, 296 F4
Topozero, Ozero, *lake*, Russian Federation, 285 Q4
Topsfield, U.S.A., 426 G2
Topsham, England, U.K., 304 D4
Topuni, New Zealand, 132 E3
Toqyraūyn, *river*, Kazakhstan, 212 B2
Tor, Ethiopia, 366 D3
Tor Bay, Canada, 417 L7
Torbalı, Turkey, 297 F6
Torbat-e Ḩeydarīyeh, Iran, 222 F5
Torbay, *unitary authority*, England, U.K., 304 D4
Tørberget, Norway, 286 F2
Tordesillas, Spain, 292 E2, *92*
Töre, Sweden, 285 L4
Töreboda, Sweden, 286 G3
Torekov, Sweden, 286 F4
Torelló, Spain, 293 J1
Torfaen, *unitary authority*, Wales, U.K., 304 D3
Torgau, Germany, 288 F3
Torgelow, Germany, 289 G2
Torghay, *river*, Kazakhstan, 222 G3
Torghay, Central Kazakhstan, 222 G3
Torghay, E. Kazakhstan, 223 J2
Tori-shima, *island*, Japan, 138 C1
Torilla Peninsula, Australia, 135 L3
Torín, Mexico, 430 C3
Torino (Turin), Italy, 294 A3, *255*
Torit, Sudan, 369 F2
Torixoreu, Brazil, 456 C4
Torkestān, Selseleh-ye Band-e, *mountain range*, Afghanistan, 218 A2
Þorlákshöfn, Iceland, 284 X8
Törmänen, Finland, 285 N2
Tormes, *river*, Spain, 292 E2
Tornaľa, Slovakia, 289 K4
Torneälven, *river*, Sweden, 284 K2
Torneträsk, Sweden, 284 J2
Torneträsk, *lake*, Sweden, 284 J2
Torngat Mountains, *mountain range*, Canada, 411 N3
Tornio, Finland, 285 M4
Tornionjoki, *river*, Finland, 285 L3
Tornquist, Argentina, 458 D6
Toro, Cerro del, *mountain peak*, Argentina/Chile, 458 C3
Toro, Nigeria, 365 F2
Toro, Spain, 292 E2
Torodi, Niger, 365 E2
Torokina, Papua New Guinea, 140 E2
Törökszentmiklós, Hungary, 289 K5
Toronto, Canada, 421 P4, *380, 381*
Toronto, U.S.A., 420 E3
Toropets, Russian Federation, 299 C4
Tororo, Uganda, 369 F2
Toros Dağları, *mountain range*, Turkey, 224 D5, *146, 191*
Torphins, Scotland, U.K., 308 G3
Torpo, Norway, 286 D2
Torpoint, England, U.K., 304 C4
Torquay, Australia, 135 J6
Torquay, England, U.K., 304 D4
Torrance, U.S.A., 422 D5
Torrão, Portugal, 292 C3
Torre de la Higuera, Spain, 292 D4
Torre de Moncorvo, Portugal, 292 D2
Torre del Grecco, Italy, 295 E5
Torrebaja, Spain, 293 G2
Torreblanca, Spain, 293 H2
Torrecilla en Cameros, Spain, 293 F1
Torrelaguna, Spain, 293 F2
Torrelavega, Spain, 292 E1
Torrens, Lake, Australia, 135 H5
Torreón, Mexico, 430 E3
Tôrres, Brazil, 459 H3
Torres, Mexico, 430 C2
Torres Islands, Vanuatu, 141 A2
Torres Novas, Portugal, 292 C3
Torres Strait, Australia/Papua New Guinea, 140 A5
Torres Vedras, Portugal, 292 C3
Torrevieja, Spain, 293 G4
Torrey, U.S.A., 423 H2
Torricelli Mountains, *mountain range*, Papua New Guinea, 140 A3
Torridge, *river*, England, U.K., 304 C4
Torridon, Scotland, U.K., 308 D3
Torriglia, Italy, 294 B3
Torrington, Canada, 413 N6
Torrington, U.S.A., 419 M5
Torröjen, *lake*, Sweden, 284 F5
Torsås, Sweden, 286 G4
Torsby, Sweden, 286 F2
Tórshavn, Faeroe Islands, 302 D1
Tortel, Chile, 460 C3
Tórtolas, Cerro Las, *mountain peak*, Chile, 458 C3
Tórtoles de Esgueva, Spain, 292 E2
Tortoli, Sardegna, Italy, 295 B6
Tortona, Italy, 294 B3
Tortosa, Cabo de, *cape*, Spain, 293 H2
Tortosa, Spain, 293 H2
Tortue, Île de la, *island*, Haiti, 429 G2
Tortuga, Isla, *island*, Islas Galápagos (Galapagos Islands), Ecuador, 461 A2
Ţorūd, Iran, 222 F5
Toruń, Poland, 289 J2
Torup, Sweden, 286 F4
Tõrva, Estonia, 287 M4
Tory, Russian Federation, 213 J2
Tory Island, Ireland, 309 D2
Tory Sound, Ireland, 309 D2
Torzhkovskaya Gryada, *mountain range*, Russian Federation, 299 E4
Torzhok, Russian Federation, 299 E4
Tosa-wan, *bay*, Japan, 208 F4
Tosashimizu, Japan, 208 F4
Tosbotn, Norway, 284 F4
Tosca, South Africa, 370 D4
Toscana, *autonomous region*, Italy, 294 C4, *255*
Toshkent (Tashkent), Uzbekistan, 223 H4, *185*
Tosno, Russian Federation, 299 C3
Tosontsengel, Mongolia, 213 H2
Tossa de Mar, Spain, 293 J2
Tost, China, 210 D4
Tostado, Argentina, 458 E3
Tõstamaa, Estonia, 287 L3
Tostedt, Germany, 288 D2
Tostón, Islas Canarias, Spain, 373 B4
Toston, U.S.A., 419 J3
Totana, Spain, 293 G4
Tôtes, France, 305 J5
Tótkomlós, Hungary, 289 K5
Totnes, England, U.K., 304 D4
Totness, Suriname, 452 B2
Totora, Bolivia, 455 F4
Totoral, Chile, 458 B3
Totota, Liberia, 364 C3
Totoya, *island*, Fiji, 141 A4
Totton, England, U.K., 305 F4
Tottori, Japan, 208 F4
Touba, Côte d'Ivoire, 364 C3
Touba, Senegal, 364 A2
Toubkal, Jebel, *mountain peak*, Morocco, 360 E2, *314*
Touboro, Cameroon, 365 H3
Toucy, France, 291 F3
Tougan, Burkina Faso, 364 D2
Touggourt, Algeria, 361 H2
Tougué, Guinea, 364 B2
Touho, New Caledonia, 141 A3
Touil, Mauritania, 364 B1
Toukoto, Mali, 364 C2
Toul, Cairn, *mountain peak*, Scotland, U.K., 308 F3
Toul, France, 291 G2
Toulépleu, Côte d'Ivoire, 364 C3
Toulon, France, 291 G5
Toulouse, France, 290 E5, *91, 245*
Toumodi, Côte d'Ivoire, 364 C3
Toungo, Nigeria, 365 G3
Toungoo, Myanmar, 205 C4
Tourba, Chad, 365 H2
Touriñán, Cabo, *cape*, Spain, 292 C1
Tourlaville, France, 290 D2
Tournai, Belgium, 288 A3
Tournavista, Peru, 454 C2
Touros, Brazil, 453 G4
Tourouvre, France, 290 E2
Tours, France, 290 E3
Toury, France, 290 E2
Tous, Embalse de, *reservoir*, Spain, 293 G3
Toussiana, Burkina Faso, 364 D2
Toussidé, Pic, *mountain peak*, Chad, 362 C4
Toussoro, Mont, *mountain peak*, Central African Republic, 366 B3
Touws River, South Africa, 370 D5
Töv, *province*, Mongolia, 210 D3
Tovar, Venezuela, 450 D2
Tovarkovskiy, Russian Federation, 299 G6
Towada, Japan, 209 H2
Towanda, U.S.A., 426 B4
Towcester, England, U.K., 305 G2
Townsville, Australia, 135 K2
Towot, Sudan, 366 D3
Towrzī, Afghanistan, 218 A3
Towson, U.S.A., 426 B5
Towuti, Danau, *lake*, Indonesia, 198 C3
Toxkan, *river*, China, 212 C4
Toyah, U.S.A., 423 M6
Toyama, Japan, 209 G3
Toyama-wan, *bay*, Japan, 209 G3
Toyohashi, Japan, 209 G4
Toyo'oka, Japan, 208 F4
Toyota, Japan, 209 G4
Töysä, Finland, 287 L1
Trà Vinh, Vietnam, 203 E4
Trabanca, Spain, 292 D2
Trabzon, Turkey, 224 E4
Tracadie, Canada, 416 J6
Tracy, U.S.A., 420 F3
Traer, U.S.A., 420 G4
Traiguén, Chile, 458 B6
Trail, Canada, 413 L7
Trail, U.S.A., 418 C5
Trail City, U.S.A., 420 C3
Traill Ø, *island*, Greenland, 411 S2
Traisen, Austria, 289 G4
Tralee, Ireland, 309 C5
Tramore, Ireland, 309 E5
Tranås, Sweden, 286 G3
Trancas, Argentina, 458 D3
Trang, Thailand, 202 C5
Tranomaro, Madagascar, 372 B5
Tranoroa, Madagascar, 372 B5
Tranøy, Norway, 284 G2
Tranqueras, Uruguay, 459 F4
Transantarctic Mountains, *mountain range*, Antarctica, 470 D5
Transtrand, Sweden, 286 F2
Trapani, Sicilia, Italy, 295 D6
Trarza, *administrative region*, Mauritania, 360 C5
Trasimeno, Lago, *lake*, Italy, 294 C4
Trat, Thailand, 203 D3
Traunsee, Austria, 289 F5
Travemünde, Germany, 288 E2
Travers City, U.S.A., 421 L3
Travnik, Bosnia and Herzegovina, 294 F3
Trawsfynydd, Llyn, *reservoir*, Wales, U.K., 304 C2
Trawsfynydd, Wales, U.K., 304 D2
Treasury Islands, Solomon Islands, 141 A1
Třebíč, Czech Republic, 289 G4
Trebinje, Bosnia and Herzegovina, 294 G4
Trebisacce, Italy, 295 F6
Trebišov, Slovakia, 289 K4
Treble Mountain, *mountain peak*, New Zealand, 133 A7
Trebnje, Slovenia, 294 E3
Trechado, U.S.A., 423 J4
Tredegar, Wales, U.K., 304 D3
Tregaron, Wales, U.K., 304 D2
Tregony, England, U.K., 304 C4

Treig, Loch, *lake*, Scotland, U.K., **308** E4
Treinta-y-Tres, Uruguay, **459** F4
Trelew, Argentina, **460** E2
Trelleborg, Sweden, **286** F5
Trelleck, Wales, U.K., **304** E3
Tremadoc Bay, Wales, U.K., **304** C2
Tremiti, Isole, *islands*, Italy, **295** E4
Tremp, Spain, **293** H1
Trenary, U.S.A., **421** K2
Trenčianský, *administrative region*, Slovakia, **289** H4
Trenčín, Slovakia, **289** J4, *266*
Trenque Lauquen, Argentina, **458** D5
Trent, *river*, England, U.K., **307** H4
Trentino-Alto Adige, *autonomous region*, Italy, **294** C2, *255*
Trento, Italy, **294** C2
Trenton, Canada, **416** C7
Trenton, Michigan, U.S.A., **421** M4
Trenton, Missouri, U.S.A., **420** G5
Trenton, New Jersey, U.S.A., **426** C4, *386*
Trepassey, Canada, **417** Q6
Tres Arroyos, Argentina, **459** E6
Tres Cerros, Argentina, **460** D3
Três Corações, Brazil, **457** E5
Tres Esquinas, Colombia, **450** C4
Tres Isletas, Argentina, **458** E3
Três Lagoas, Brazil, **456** C5
Tres Lagos, Argentina, **460** C3
Tres Lomas, Argentina, **458** D5
Tres Mapajos, Bolivia, **455** F3
Tres Marías, Islas, *islands*, Mexico, **430** D4
Três Marias, Represa, *reservoir*, Brazil, **457** E5
Tres Montes, Península, Chile, **460** B3
Tres Picos, Cerro, *mountain peak*, Argentina, **458** E6
Tres Picos, Mexico, **431** G6
Tres Piedras, U.S.A., **423** L3
Três Pontas, Brazil, **456** E5
Tres Puntas, Cabo, *cape*, Argentina, **460** E3
Três Rios, Brazil, **457** E6
Tres Valles, Mexico, **431** F5
Tresfjord, Norway, **286** C1
Tretten, Norway, **286** E2
Treviglio, Italy, **294** B3
Treviso, Italy, **294** D3
Trevose Head, *point*, England, U.K., **304** B4
Trévoux, France, **291** G4
Trgovište, Serbia, **296** D4
Tria Nisia, *island*, Kyklades, Greece, **297** F7
Tribal Areas, *province*, Pakistan, **218** B2
Tribune, U.S.A., **420** C6
Tricase, Italy, **295** G6
Trichonida, Limni, *lake*, Greece, **297** C6
Trichūr, India, **216** D4
Trier, Germany, **288** C4
Trieste, Golfo di, *gulf*, Italy, **294** D3
Trieste, Italy, **294** D3
Triglav, *mountain peak*, Slovenia, **294** D2, *258*
Trigno, *river*, Italy, **295** E5
Trikala, Greece, **297** C6
Trikomo, Cyprus, **225** B2
Trikora, Puncak, *mountain peak*, Indonesia, **199** G4
Trilj, Croatia, **294** F4
Trim, Ireland, **309** F4
Trimdon, England, U.K., **307** G3
Trincomalee, Sri Lanka, **217** E4
Trindade, Brazil, **456** D4
Trindade, *island*, Brazil, Atlantic Ocean, **105** T10
Tring, England, U.K., **305** G3
Trinidad, Bolivia, **455** F4
Trinidad, California, U.S.A., **418** B6
Trinidad, Colombia, **450** D3
Trinidad, Colorado, U.S.A., **423** L3
Trinidad, Cuba, **429** F2
Trinidad, Golfo, *gulf*, Chile, **460** B3
Trinidad, *island*, Trinidad and Tobago, **461** C4, *398*
Trinidad, Uruguay, **459** F4
Trinidad and Tobago, *country*, Caribbean Sea, **409** S7, *378, 399*
Trinity, *river*, U.S.A., **424** E4
Trinity Bay, Canada, **417** Q6
Trinity Hills, *mountain peak*, Trinidad, Trinidad and Tobago, **461** C4
Trino, Italy, **294** B3
Triolet, Mauritius, **373** C1
Tripa, *river*, Indonesia, **200** B1
Tripoli, Greece, **297** D7
Tripoli *see* Ṭarābulus, Lebanon, **225** C2
Tripolis *see* Ṭarābulus, Libya, **362** B2, *316*
Tripura, *state*, India, **219** G5, *169*
Tristan da Cunha, *island*, St Helena, **373** C2, *355*
Tristan da Cunha, *St Helena dependency*, Atlantic Ocean, **359** D10
Triunfo, *river*, Brazil, **452** C5
Trivandrum *see* Thiruvananthapuram, India, **216** D4, *169*
Trivento, Italy, **295** E5
Trnava, Slovakia, **289** H4
Trnavský, *administrative region*, Slovakia, **289** H4
Trobriand Islands, Papua New Guinea, **140** C5
Troebratskīy, Kazakhstan, **222** H2
Trofors, Norway, **284** F4
Trogir, Croatia, **294** F4
Troglav, *mountain peak*, Bosnia and Herzegovina, **294** F4
Troia, Italy, **295** E5
Trois Bassins, Réunion, **373** A1
Trois Fourches, Cap des, *cape*, Morocco, **293** F5
Trois-Pistoles, Canada, **416** G5
Trois-Rivières, Canada, **416** E6
Troisdorf, Germany, **288** C3
Troitsk, Russian Federation, **222** G2
Troitskoye, Russian Federation, **211** M2
Trollhättan, Sweden, **286** F3
Trombetas, *river*, Brazil, **452** B3
Tromelin Île, *island*, Réunion, **372** C4, *354*
Tromen, Volcán, *mountain peak*, Argentina, **458** B5
Troms, *county*, Norway, **284** J2
Tromsø, Norway, **284** J2
Tromvik, Norway, **284** J2
Tron, *mountain peak*, Norway, **286** E1
Tronador, Cerro, *mountain peak*, Chile, **460** C1
Trondheim, Norway, **284** E5
Trönninge, Sweden, **286** F4
Troodos, Cyprus, **225** B2, *191*
Troodos Mountains, *mountain range*, Cyprus, **225** B2
Troon, Scotland, U.K., **308** E5
Tropaia, Greece, **297** C7
Tropeiros, Serra dos, *mountain range*, Brazil, **457** E4
Trostan, *mountain peak*, Northern Ireland, U.K., **309** F2
Trou d'Eau Dolce, Mauritius, **373** C1
Trout Creek, Canada, **416** B7
Trout Creek, U.S.A., **418** G3
Trout Lake, Canada, **413** L6
Trout Lake, *lake*, Northwest Territories, Canada, **412** J1
Trout Lake, *lake*, Ontario, Canada, **414** H6
Trout Lake, U.S.A., **418** D4
Trouville-sur-Mer, France, **290** E2
Trowbridge, England, U.K., **304** E3
Troy, Alabama, U.S.A., **425** K4
Troy, Montana, U.S.A., **418** G2
Troy, New York, U.S.A., **426** D3
Troy Peak, *mountain peak*, U.S.A., **422** F2
Troyan, Bulgaria, **296** E4
Troyanka, Ukraine, **296** H1
Troyes, France, **291** G2
Troyits'ke, Ukraine, **296** H2
Trstenik, Serbia, **296** C4
Trsteno, Croatia, **294** F4
Truckee, U.S.A., **422** C2
Trujillo, Honduras, **428** D4
Trujillo, Peru, **454** B2
Trujillo, Spain, **292** E3
Trujillo, Venezuela, **451** D2
Trumann, U.S.A., **424** G2
Trumbull, Mount, *mountain peak*, U.S.A., **422** G3
Trŭn, Bulgaria, **296** D4
Truro, England, U.K., **304** B4
Truro, Canada, **417** K7
Trus Madi, Gunung, *mountain peak*, Malaysia, **201** G1
Truşeşti, Romania, **296** F2
Truskmore, *mountain peak*, Ireland, **309** D3
Trutch, Canada, **412** H3
Truth or Consequences, U.S.A., **423** K5
Trutnov, Czech Republic, **289** G3
Truyère, *river*, France, **290** F4
Trwyn Cilan, *point*, Wales, U.K., **304** C2
Tryavna, Bulgaria, **296** E4
Tryon, U.S.A., **420** C5
Trysilelva, *river*, Norway, **286** E2
Tryškiai, Lithuania, **287** L4
Tržac, Bosnia and Herzegovina, **294** E3
Trzcianka, Poland, **289** H2
Trzciel, Poland, **289** G2
Trzebnica, Poland, **289** H3
Tsagaan-Olom, Mongolia, **213** H3
Tsagaan Ovoo, Mongolia, **213** J3
Tsagaanchuluut, Mongolia, **213** H3
Tsagaandörvölj, Mongolia, **210** E3
Tsagaannuur, Bayan-Ölgiy, Mongolia, **212** F2
Tsagaannuur, Dornod, Mongolia, **211** G3
Tsagan Aman, Russian Federation, **222** D3
Tsakir, Russian Federation, **213** J2
Tsåktso, *mountain peak*, Sweden, **284** K2
Tsaratanana, Madagascar, **372** B4
Tsaris Mountains, Namibia, **370** C3, *350*
Tsebrykove, Ukraine, **296** H2
Tseel, Mongolia, **213** G3
Tsengel, Mongolia, **213** J2
Tsentral'nyy, Russian Federation, **223** M1
Tses, Namibia, **370** C4
Tsetseng, Botswana, **370** D3
Tsetserleg, Mongolia, **213** J3
Tsévié, Togo, **364** E3
Tshabong, Botswana, **370** D4
Tshane, Botswana, **370** D3
Tshela, Democratic Republic of the Congo, **368** B3
Tshibala, Democratic Republic of the Congo, **368** D4
Tshibwika, Democratic Republic of the Congo, **368** D4
Tshikapa, Democratic Republic of the Congo, **368** D4
Tshilenge, Democratic Republic of the Congo, **368** D4
Tshimbalanga, Democratic Republic of the Congo, **368** D4
Tshimbo, Democratic Republic of the Congo, **369** E4
Tshimbulu, Democratic Republic of the Congo, **368** D4
Tshinsenda, Democratic Republic of the Congo, **369** E5
Tshokwane, South Africa, **371** F3
Tshootsha, Botswana, **370** D3
Tsiigehtchic, Canada, **410** F3
Tsimlyanskoye Vodokhranilishche, *reservoir*, Russian Federation, **222** C3
Tsineng, South Africa, **370** D4
Tsiombe, Madagascar, **372** B6
Tsiribihina, *river*, Madagascar, **372** A4
Tsiribihina, Tanjona, *cape*, Madagascar, **372** A4
Tsiroanomandidy, Madagascar, **372** B4
Tsivil'sk, Russian Federation, **222** D1
Tsolo, South Africa, **371** E5
Tsoohor, Mongolia, **210** D4
Tsuchiura, Japan, **209** H3
Tsuen Wan, China, **207** C4
Tsumeb, Namibia, **370** C2
Tsumis Park, Namibia, **370** C3
Tsumkwe, Namibia, **370** D2
Tsuruga, Japan, **209** G4
Tsuruoka, Japan, **209** G3
Tsushima, *island*, Japan, **208** E4
Tsuyama, Japan, **208** F4
Tu, *river*, Myanmar, **205** C3
Tuai, New Zealand, **132** F4
Tuakau, New Zealand, **132** E3
Tuam, Ireland, **309** D4
Tuamarina, New Zealand, **133** D5
Tuamotu, Archipel des, *islands*, French Polynesia, **137** G2, *122*
Tuan, Tanjong, *cape*, Malaysia, **200** C2
Tuần Giáo, Vietnam, **203** D1
Tu'anuku, Vava'u Group, Tonga, **141** B3
Tuangku, Pulau, Insel, Indonesia, **200** B2
Tuao, Philippines, **204** C2
Tuaran, Malaysia, **201** C1
Tuas, Singapore, **200** J7
Tuba City, U.S.A., **423** H3
Tuban, Indonesia, **201** F4
Tubarão, Brazil, **459** H3
Ṭubarjal, Saudi Arabia, **225** E4
Ṭūbās, West Bank, **225** C3
Tübingen, Germany, **288** D4
Tubmanburg, Liberia, **364** B3
Tubou, Fiji, **141** A4
Tubruq, Libya, **362** D2
Tubuai, Îles *see* Australes, Îles, *islands*, French Polynesia, **137** F3, *122*
Tubuai, *island*, French Polynesia, **137** G3
Tucano, Brazil, **457** F3
Tucavaca, Bolivia, **455** G5
Tuchan, France, **290** F5
Tuchola, Poland, **289** H2
Tucson, U.S.A., **423** H5
Tucumán, *province*, Argentina, **458** D3
Tucumcari, U.S.A., **423** M4
Tucunuco, Argentina, **458** C4
Tucupita, Venezuela, **451** F2
Tucuruí, Brazil, **452** D4
Tucuruí, Represa de, *reservoir*, Brazil, **452** D4
Tudela, Spain, **293** G1
Tudor Vladimirescu, Romania, **296** F3
Tudu, Estonia, **287** N3
Tudun Wada, Nigeria, **365** F2
Tuekta, Russian Federation, **223** M2
Tuen Mun, China, **207** B4
Tueré, *river*, Brazil, **452** C4
Tufi, Papua New Guinea, **140** C5
Tufts Plai, *underwater feature*, Pacific Ocean, **479** J1
Tugozvonovo, Russian Federation, **223** L2
Tuguegarao, Philippines, **204** C2
Tugulym, Russian Federation, **222** G1
Tugutuy, Russian Federation, **210** D1
Tuhkakylä, Finland, **285** P4
Tuhua, *mountain peak*, New Zealand, **132** E4
Tuhua, New Zealand, **132** E4
Tuhua *see* Mayor Island, New Zealand, **133** F3
Tui, Spain, **292** C1
Tuiguang, China, **207** A2
Tuineje, Islas Canarias, Spain, **373** B4
Tuira, *river*, Panama, **429** F5
Tuirc, Beinn an, *mountain peak*, Scotland, U.K., **308** D5
Tukangbesi, Kepulauan, *islands*, Indonesia, **198** D4
Tukayel, Ethiopia, **367** G3
Tukhkala, Russian Federation, **285** Q4
Tukosmera, Mont, *mountain peak*, Vanuatu, **141** A3
Tūkrah, Libya, **362** D2
Tuktoyaktuk, Canada, **410** F3
Tukums, Latvia, **287** L4
Tukuyu, Tanzania, **369** F4
Tula, American Samoa, **141** B2
Tula, Mexico, **431** F4
Tula, Russian Federation, **299** F5
Tulaghi, Solomon Islands, **141** A1
Tulangbawang, *river*, Indonesia, **200** D4
Tulare, U.S.A., **420** D3
Tularosa, U.S.A., **423** K5
Tulcán, Ecuador, **450** C4
Tulcea, Romania, **296** G3
Tul'chyn, Ukraine, **296** G1
Tule, Venezuela, **450** D1
Tulghes, Romania, **296** E2
Tuli, Zimbabwe, **371** E3
Tulia, U.S.A., **424** B2
Tulihe, China, **211** H2
Tulita, Canada, **410** G3
Ṭūlkarm, West Bank, **225** C3
Tulla, Ireland, **309** D5
Tullahoma, U.S.A., **425** J2
Tullamore, Ireland, **309** E4
Tulle, France, **290** E4
Tulln, Austria, **289** H4
Tullos, U.S.A., **424** F4
Tullow, Ireland, **309** F5
Tully, Australia, **135** K2
Tulnici, Romania, **296** F3
Tuloma, *river*, Russian Federation, **285** R2
Tulos, Ozero, *lake*, Russian Federation, **285** Q5
Tulos, Russian Federation, **285** Q5
Tulppio, Finland, **285** P3
Tulsa, U.S.A., **424** E1
Tul'skaya Oblast', *province*, Russian Federation, **299** F6
Tuluá, Colombia, **450** C3
Tuluceşti, Romania, **296** G3
Tuma, Russian Federation, **298** F1
Tumaco, Colombia, **450** B4
Tumaco, Ensenada de, *bay*, Colombia, **450** B4
Tumannyy, Russian Federation, **285** S2
Tumatumari, Guyana, **451** G3
Tumba, Democratic Republic of the Congo, **368** D3
Tumba, Lac, *lake*, Democratic Republic of the Congo, **368** C3
Tumba, Sweden, **287** H3
Tumbangsamba, Indonesia, **201** F3
Tumbes, Peru, **450** B5
Tumby Bay, Australia, **135** H5
Tumcha, *river*, Russian Federation, **285** Q3
Tumd Youqi, China, **210** E4
Tumd Zuoqi, China, **210** E4
Tumen, China, **208** E2
Tumen, *river*, China/North Korea, **211** K4
Tumeremo, Venezuela, **451** G2
Tumkūr, India, **216** D3
Tumpu, Gunung, *mountain peak*, Indonesia, **198** C3
Tumu, Ghana, **364** D2
Tumucumaque Serra, *mountain range*, Brazil, **452** B2, *439*
Tumureng, Guyana, **451** G2
Tuna, India, **218** B5
Tunapuna, Trinidad, Trinidad and Tobago, **461** C4
Tunceli, Turkey, **363** G1
Tunchang, China, **203** F2
Tunduru, Tanzania, **369** G5

Tundzha, river, Bulgaria, 296 E4
Tunga, Nigeria, 365 F3
Tungabhadra Reservoir, India, 216 C3
Tungaru, Sudan, 366 D2
Tungawan, Philippines, 204 C5
Tungokochen, Russian Federation, 210 F1
Tungozero, Russian Federation, 285 Q4
Tünhel, Mongolia, 210 D2
Tuni, India, 217 E2
Tunis, Golfe de, gulf, Tunisia, 362 B1
Tūnis, Tunisia, 362 B1, 315
Tunisia, country, Africa, 358 F3, 97, 312, 315
Tunja, Colombia, 450 D3
Tunnsjøen, lake, Norway, 284 F4
Tunstall, East Riding of Yorkshire, England, U.K., 307 H4
Tunstall, Suffolk, England, U.K., 305 J2
Tuntsa, Finland, 285 P3
Tunuk, Kyrgyzstan, 212 B4
Tunungayualok Island, Canada, 417 L1
Tunupo, mountain peak, New Zealand, 132 F4
Tunuyán, Argentina, 458 C4
Tunuyán, river, Argentina, 458 C4
Tuohikotti, Finland, 287 N2
Tuole, China, 213 H5
Tuotuo, river, China, 214 D2
Tupã, Brazil, 456 C5
Tupaciguara, Brazil, 456 D5
Tupai, island, French Polynesia, 137 F2
Tupanciretã, Brazil, 459 G3
Tupelo, U.S.A., 425 H2
Tupinambarana, Ilha, island, Brazil, 451 G5
Tupiratins, Brazil, 456 D2
Tupiza, Bolivia, 455 F5
Tupper Lake, U.S.A., 426 C2
Tüpqaraghan, Müyis, point, Kazakhstan, 222 D4
Tupungato, Argentina, 458 C4
Tupungato, mountain peak, Argentina/Chile, 458 C4
Tuquan, China, 211 H3
Túquerres, Colombia, 450 C4
Tura, China, 212 E5
Tura, India, 219 G4
Tura, Russian Federation, 301 M3
Turabah, Saudi Arabia, 363 H4
Turagua, Cerro, mountain peak, Venezuela, 451 F2
Turaiyūr, India, 216 D4
Turakina, New Zealand, 132 E5
Turakirae Head, point, New Zealand, 133 E5
Turama, river, Papua New Guinea, 140 A4
Turan, Russian Federation, 223 N2
Turana, Khrebet, mountain range, Russian Federation, 211 K2
Turangi, New Zealand, 132 E4
Turanskaya Nizmennost', lowland, Asia, 222 G4
Ţurayf, Saudi Arabia, 225 E4
Turbaco, Colombia, 450 C1
Turbat, Pakistan, 221 H3
Turbo, Colombia, 450 C2
Turda, Romania, 296 D2
Turégano, Spain, 292 E2
Tureia, island, French Polynesia, 137 H3
Turek, Poland, 289 J3
Tŭrgovishte, Bulgaria, 296 F4
Turgutlu, Turkey, 297 F6
Turhal, Turkey, 224 E4
Turi, Chile, 458 C2
Türi, Estonia, 287 M3
Turia, river, Spain, 293 G2
Turiaçu, Brazil, 452 E3
Turiaçu, river, Brazil, 452 D4
Turin see Torino, Italy, 294 A3, 255
Turinsk, Russian Federation, 222 G1
Turiya, river, Ukraine, 289 M3
Turiys'k, Ukraine, 289 M3
Turka, river, Russian Federation, 210 E1
Turka, Ukraine, 289 L4
Turkana, Lake, Kenya, 369 G2, 56, 341
Turkey, country, Asia/Europe, 196 E6, 54, 87, 146, 147, 177, 181, 182, 183, 187, 188, 189, 190, 191, 192, 239, 264, 265, 171
Türkistan, Kazakhstan, 223 H4
Türkmenbashi, Turkmenistan, 222 E4
Turkmenistan, country, Asia, 196 D6, 94, 144, 184, 185, 186, 187
Turks and Caicos Islands, U.K. dependency, Caribbean Sea, 409 K6, 276, 378, 391
Turks Island Passage, Turks and Caicos Islands, 429 H2
Turks Islands, Turks and Caicos Islands, 429 H2
Turku, Finland, 287 L2
Turley, Cape, Canada, 417 N2
Turlock, U.S.A., 422 C3
Turnagain, Cape, New Zealand, 132 F5
Turnberry, Scotland, U.K., 308 E5
Turnbull, Mount, mountain peak, U.S.A., 423 H5
Turneffe Island, Belize, 428 D3
Turner, U.S.A., 421 M3
Turnhout, Belgium, 288 B2
Turnor Lake, Canada, 413 Q3
Turnov, Czech Republic, 289 G3
Turnu Măgurele, Romania, 296 E4
Turochak, Russian Federation, 223 M2
Turon, U.S.A., 420 D7
Turpan, China, 212 F4
Turpan Pendi, depression, China, 212 F4, 144, 158
Turpin, U.S.A., 420 C7
Turquino, Pico, mountain peak, Cuba, 429 F3
Turriff, Scotland, U.K., 308 G3
Turt, Mongolia, 213 J2
Tŭrtkŭl, Uzbekistan, 222 G4
Turtle Creek Lake, U.S.A., 420 E6
Turtle Lake, Canada, 413 Q5
Turtle Lake, U.S.A., 420 C2
Turvo, Brazil, 459 H3
Turvo, river, N. São Paulo, Brazil, 456 D5
Turvo, river, Rio Grande do Sol, Brazil, 459 G3
Turvo, river, S. São Paulo, Brazil, 456 D6
Tuscaloosa, U.S.A., 425 J3
Tuscarora, U.S.A., 418 F6
Tuscola, U.S.A., 424 C3
Tustna, island, Norway, 284 C5
Tutaekuri, river, New Zealand, 132 F4
Tutamoe, mountain peak, N. North Island, New Zealand, 132 D2
Tutamoe, mountain peak, E. North Island, New Zealand, 132 F4
Tutayev, Russian Federation, 299 G4
Tutbury, England, U.K., 305 F2
Tuticorin, India, 216 D4
Tutóia, Brazil, 453 E4
Tutoko, Mount, mountain peak, New Zealand, 133 B7
Tutrakan, Bulgaria, 296 F3
Tuttlingen, Germany, 288 D5
Tutuala, East Timor, 198 D5
Tutuila, island, American Samoa, 141 B2
Tutume, Botswana, 371 E3
Tuturumuri, New Zealand, 133 E5
Tuul, river, Mongolia, 210 D3
Tuusniemi, Finland, 285 P5
Tuusula, Finland, 287 M2
Tuutapu, mountain peak, Isla de Pascua (Easter Island), Chile, 461 B2
Tuvalu, country, Pacific Ocean, 131 G2, 108, 113
Tuvuca, island, Fiji, 141 A4
Ţuwayq, Jabal, mountain range, Saudi Arabia, 363 J3
Tuxpan, Jalisco, Mexico, 430 E5
Tuxpan, Nayarit, Mexico, 430 D4
Tuxpan de Rodríguez Cano, Mexico, 431 F4
Tuxtla Gutiérrez, Mexico, 431 G5
Tuy, river, Russian Federation, 223 J1
Tuy Hòa, Vietnam, 203 F3
Tuz Gölü, lake, Turkey, 224 D5
Ţūz Khurmātū, Iraq, 363 H2
Tuzi, Montenegro, 296 B4
Tuzla, Bosnia and Herzegovina, 294 G3
Tuzla, Romania, 296 G4
Tuzla, Turkey, 225 C1
Tvedestrand, Norway, 286 D3
Tveitsund, Norway, 286 D3
Tver', Russian Federation, 299 E4
Tverskaya Oblast', province, Russian Federation, 299 E4
Tvøroyri, Faeroe Islands, 302 D2
Tvrdošín, Slovakia, 289 J4
Tvŭrdista, Bulgaria, 296 E4
Twatt, Orkney, Scotland, U.K., 308 F1
Tweed, river, Scotland, U.K., 308 G5, 276
Tweedmouth, England, U.K., 306 F2
Twentynine Palms, U.S.A., 422 F4
Twilight Cove, Australia, 134 F5
Twin Bridges, U.S.A., 418 H4
Twin City, U.S.A., 425 L3
Twin Falls, Canada, 417 J3
Twin Falls, U.S.A., 418 G5
Twin Lakes, U.S.A., 423 K2
Twisp, U.S.A., 418 D2
Twizel, New Zealand, 133 C7
Two Buttes, U.S.A., 423 M3
Two Harbors, U.S.A., 420 H2
Two Hills, Canada, 413 P5
Two Medicine, river, U.S.A., 418 H2
Two Rivers, U.S.A., 421 K3
Twodot, U.S.A., 419 J3
Twyford, Berkshire, England, U.K., 305 G3
Twyford, Hampshire, England, U.K., 305 F3
Tychy, Poland, 289 J3
Tyfors, Sweden, 286 G2
Tygda, river, Russian Federation, 211 J1
Tygda, Russian Federation, 211 J1
Tyler, Minnesota, U.S.A., 420 E3
Tyler, Texas, U.S.A., 424 E3
Tylertown, U.S.A., 424 G4
Tylihul, river, Ukraine, 296 H2
Tym, river, Russian Federation, 300 K3
Tympaki, Kriti, Greece, 297 E8
Tynda, Russian Federation, 301 P4
Tyndall, U.S.A., 420 E4
Tyndrum, Scotland, U.K., 308 E4
Tyne & Wear, unitary authority, England, U.K., 307 G3
Tynemouth, England, U.K., 307 G2
Tyngsjö, Sweden, 286 F2
Tynset, Norway, 286 E1
Tyrävaara, Finland, 285 P4
Tyre see Şūr, Lebanon, 225 C3, 180, 181
Tyrifjorden, lake, Norway, 286 E2
Tyrma, river, Russian Federation, 211 K2
Tyrma, Russian Federation, 211 L2
Tyrnavos, Greece, 297 D6
Tyrone, Colorado, U.S.A., 423 L3
Tyrone, New Mexico, U.S.A., 423 J5
Tyrone, Pennsylvania, U.S.A., 421 P5
Tyrrhenian Sea, Italy, 295 C5, 254
Tysse, Norway, 286 B2
Tytuvėnai, Lithuania, 287 L5
Tyugël'say, Kyrgyzstan, 212 B4
Tyukalinsk, Russian Federation, 223 J1
Tyul'gan, Russian Federation, 222 F2
Tyumen', Russian Federation, 222 H1
Tyumenskaya Oblast', province, Russian Federation, 222 H1
Tyungur, Russian Federation, 223 M2
Tyva, Respublika, republic, Russian Federation, 223 P2
Tywi, river, Wales, U.K., 304 D2
Tywyn, Wales, U.K., 304 C2
Tzaneen, South Africa, 371 F3

## U

Ua Huka, island, French Polynesia, 137 H1
Ua Pu, island, French Polynesia, 137 G1
Uacauyén, Venezuela, 451 G3
Uafato, Samoa, 141 B1
Uaicás, Brazil, 451 F3
Uarandab, Ethiopia, 367 F3
Uarini, Brazil, 451 F5
Uatumã, river, Brazil, 451 G5
Uauá, Brazil, 457 F2
Uaupés, river, Brazil, 451 E4
Uaxactún, Guatemala, 428 C3
Ub, Serbia, 296 C3
Ubá, Brazil, 457 E5
Uba, Nigeria, 365 G2
Ubaí, Brazil, 457 E4
Ubaitaba, Brazil, 457 F4
Ubangi, river, Democratic Republic of the Congo, 368 C2, 331, 334
Ubate, Colombia, 450 D3
Ubauro, Pakistan, 218 B3
Ube, Japan, 208 E4
Úbeda, Spain, 293 F3
Uberaba, Brazil, 456 D5
Uberlândia, Minas Gerais, Brazil, 456 D5
Uberlândia, Roraima, Brazil, 451 G4
Ubia, Gunung, mountain peak, Indonesia, 199 G3
Ubin, Pulau, island, Singapore, 200 K6
Ubiña, Peña, mountain peak, Spain, 292 E1
Ubinskoye, Ozero, lake, Russian Federation, 223 K1
Ubolratna Reservoir, Thailand, 203 D2
Ubombo, South Africa, 371 F4
Ubon Ratchathani, Thailand, 203 E3
Ubrique, Spain, 292 E4
Ubuna, Solomon Islands, 141 A1
Ubundu, Democratic Republic of the Congo, 369 E3
Ucayali, river, Peru, 454 C2, 441
Uch, Pakistan, 218 B3
Uchami, Russian Federation, 300 L3
Uchiza, Peru, 454 C2
Uchquduq, Uzbekistan, 222 G4
Uchte, Germany, 288 D2
Uckfield, England, U.K., 305 H4
Ucluelet, Canada, 412 G7
Uda, river, Russian Federation, 301 Q4
Udachnyy, Russian Federation, 301 N3
Udagamandalam, India, 216 D4
Udaipur, N. Rājasthān, India, 218 C4
Udaipur, S. Rājasthān, India, 218 C4
Udbina, Croatia, 294 E3
Udbyhøj, Denmark, 286 E4
Uddevalla, Sweden, 286 E3
Uddheden, Sweden, 286 F3
Uddjaure, lake, Sweden, 284 H4
Udgīr, India, 216 D2
Udine, Italy, 294 D2
Udintsev Fracture Zone, tectonic feature, Pacific Ocean, 479 H8
Udipi, India, 216 C3
Udmurtskaya Respublika, republic, Russian Federation, 222 E1
Udomlya, Russian Federation, 299 E4
Udon Thani, Thailand, 203 D2
Udu Point, Fiji, 141 A4
Uecker, river, Germany, 289 F2
Ueda, Japan, 209 G3
Uekuli, Indonesia, 198 C3
Uele, river, Democratic Republic of the Congo, 368 D2
Uelzen, Germany, 288 E2
Ufa, Russian Federation, 222 F2
Uftyuga, river, Russian Federation, 299 G2
Ugāle, Latvia, 287 L4
Ugalla, river, Tanzania, 369 F4
Uganda, country, Africa, 359 J6, 30, 92, 312, 336, 340, 341, 343, 347
Ugento, Italy, 295 G6
Ughelli, Nigeria, 365 F3
Ugíjar, Spain, 293 F4
Ugine, France, 291 H4
Uglekamensk, Russian Federation, 211 L4
Uglich, Russian Federation, 299 G4
Ugljan, island, Croatia, 294 E4
Uglovka, Russian Federation, 299 D3
Uglovoye, Russian Federation, 211 L4
Ugol'nyye Kopi, Russian Federation, 301 U3
Ŭgovoy, Kazakhstan, 212 B4
Ugra, Russian Federation, 299 E5
Ugŭrchin, Bulgaria, 296 E4
Uherské Hradiště, Czech Republic, 289 H4
Uig, Scotland, U.K., 308 C3
Uíge, Angola, 368 B4
Uíge, province, Angola, 368 C4
Ŭijŏnbu, South Korea, 208 D3
Uimaharju, Finland, 285 Q5
Uinta Mountains, mountain range, U.S.A., 423 H1
Uis, Namibia, 370 B3
Ŭisŏng, South Korea, 208 E3
Uitenhage, South Africa, 370 E5
Ujae, island, Marshall Islands, 138 E4
Ujelang, island, Marshall Islands, 138 E4
Újfehértó, Hungary, 289 K5
Ujjain, India, 218 C5
Ujong Tanjong, point, Cocos (Keeling) Islands, 134 Q10
Ujungpandang (Makassar), Indonesia, 198 B4
Ukara Island, Tanzania, 369 F3
Ukata, Nigeria, 365 F2
Ukerewe Island, Tanzania, 369 F3
Ukhra, river, Russian Federation, 299 G3
Ukhta, Russian Federation, 300 G3
Ukiah, U.S.A., 422 B2
Ukmergė, Lithuania, 287 M5
Ukraine, country, Europe, 283 G6, 88, 97, 228, 229, 236, 247, 259, 262, 263, 267, 268, 269, 270, 271, 272, 273
Uku, Angola, 368 B5
Ula, Turkey, 297 G7
Ula', Turkey, 297 F5
Ulaan-Ereg, Mongolia, 210 E3
Ulaan-Uul, Mongolia, 210 E3
Ulaanbaatar (Ulan Bator), Mongolia, 210 D3, 186
Ulaandel, Mongolia, 210 F3
Ulaangom, Mongolia, 213 G2
Ulaanjirem, Mongolia, 210 D3
Ulaantolgoy, Mongolia, 213 G3
Ulan Bator see Ulaanbaatar, Mongolia, 210 D3, 186
Ulan-Burgasy Khrebet, mountain range, Russian Federation, 210 D1

Ulan Had Sum, China, **210** F4
Ulan Hua, China, **210** E4
Ulan-Khol, Russian Federation, **222** D3
Ulan-Ude, Russian Federation, **210** D2
Ulan Ul Hu, *lake*, China, **214** D2
Ulanbel, Kazakhstan, **223** J4
Ulanhot, China, **211** H3
Ulantolgoy, Mongolia, **223** N3
Ulawa, *island*, Solomon Islands, **141** A1
Ulawun, Mount, *mountain peak*, Papua New Guinea, **140** C4
Ulbanep, Mount, *mountain peak*, Papua New Guinea, **140** A3
Ulbster, Scotland, U.K., **308** F2
Ulchin, South Korea, **208** E3
Ulcinj, Montenegro, **296** B5
Uldz, Mongolia, **210** E2
Uldz, *river*, Mongolia, **210** F2
Ulety, Russian Federation, **210** F2
Ulfborg, Denmark, **286** D4
Ulhāsnagar, India, **216** C2
Uliastay, Mongolia, **213** H3
Ulithi, *island*, Micronesia, **138** B3
Ülken Borsyq Qumy, *desert*, Kazakhstan, **222** F3
Ülken Vladīmīrovka, Kazakhstan, **212** C2
Ülkennaryn, Kazakhstan, **212** E2
Ulla, Belarus, **299** B5
Ulla, *river*, Spain, **292** C1
Ullånger, Sweden, **287** J1
Ullapool, Scotland, U.K., **308** D3
Ullared, Sweden, **286** F4
Ullatti, Sweden, **284** K3
Ullava, Finland, **285** L5
Ullfors, Sweden, **287** H2
Ullswater, *lake*, England, U.K., **306** F3
Ullŭngdo, *island*, South Korea, **208** E3
Ulm, Germany, **288** D4
Ul'ma, *river*, Russian Federation, **211** K2
Ulmeni, near Baia Mare, Romania, **296** D2
Ulmeni, Romania, **296** F3
Ulog, Bosnia and Herzegovina, **294** G4
Ulongwé, Mozambique, **369** F5
Ulricehamn, Sweden, **286** F4
Ulsan, South Korea, **208** E4
Ulsberg, Norway, **286** D1
Ulsta, Shetland, Scotland, U.K., **308** K7
Ulu, Indonesia, **198** D2
Ulubat Gölü, *lake*, Turkey, **297** G5
Uluçınar, Turkey, **225** C1
Ulugan Bay, Philippines, **204** B4
Ulugqat, China, **212** B5
Ulundi, South Africa, **371** F4
Ulungur, *river*, China, **212** E3
Ulungur Hu, *lake*, China, **212** E3
Uluriyskiy Golets, Gora, *mountain peak*, Russian Federation, **210** E2
Uluru (Ayers Rock), *mountain peak*, Australia, **128** C4
Ulva, *island*, Scotland, U.K., **308** C4
Ulverston, England, U.K., **306** E3
Ulvik, Norway, **286** C2
Ul'yanovka, Ukraine, **296** H1
Ul'yanovsk, Russian Federation, **222** D2
Ul'yanovskaya Oblast', *province*, Russian Federation, **222** D2
Ūl'yanovskīy, Kazakhstan, **212** B2
Ulysses, U.S.A., **420** C7
Umag, Croatia, **294** D3
Umán, Mexico, **431** H4
Uman', Ukraine, **298** D3
Umaria, India, **218** E5
Umarkot, India, **219** E6
Umarkot, Pakistan, **218** B4
Umba, *river*, Russian Federation, **285** S3
Umba, Russian Federation, **285** S3
Umboi Island, Papua New Guinea, **140** B4
Umbozero, Ozero, *lake*, Russian Federation, **285** S3
Umbria, *autonomous state*, Italy, **294** D4, *255*
Umbukul, Papua New Guinea, **140** C3
Umbulan Gayohpecoh, Indonesia, **200** D3
Umeå, Sweden, **284** K5
Umeälven, *river*, Sweden, **284** J4
Umfreville Lake, Canada, **414** G6
Umiat, U.S.A., **410** D3
Umlazi, South Africa, **371** F4
Umm ad Daraj, Jabal, *mountain peak*, Jordan, **225** C3
Umm Bel, Sudan, **366** C2
Umm Durmān (Omdurman), Sudan, **366** D1
Umm Kaddādah, Sudan, **366** C2
Umm Lajj, Saudi Arabia, **363** G3
Umm Ruwābah, Sudan, **366** D2
Umm Sa'ad, Libya, **362** E2
Umm Ṣawwānah, Jabal, *mountain peak*, Jordan, **225** C4
Umm Sayyālah, Sudan, **366** D2
Umm Shawmar, Jabal, *mountain peak*, Egypt, **225** B5
Umm 'Umayd, Ra's, *mountain peak*, Egypt, **225** B6
Umm Urūmah, *island*, Saudi Arabia, **363** G3
Umnak Island, Aleutian Islands, U.S.A., **408** G3
Umpilua, Mozambique, **369** G5
Umpulo, Angola, **368** C5
Umred, India, **218** D5
Umtata, South Africa, **371** E5
Umuahia, Nigeria, **368** A1
Umuarama, Brazil, **459** G2
Umuna, *island*, Vava'u Group, Tonga, **141** B3
Umurbey, Turkey, **297** F5
Umzinto, South Africa, **371** F5
Una, Brazil, **457** F4
Una, India, **218** B5
Una, Mount, *mountain peak*, New Zealand, **133** D6
Una, *river*, Bosnia and Herzegovina, **294** F3
Una, Russian Federation, **285** U4
Unaðsdalur, Iceland, **284** X6
Unaí, Brazil, **456** D4
Unaja, Finland, **287** K2
Unalaska Island, Aleutian Islands, U.S.A., **408** G3
Unango, Mozambique, **369** G5
Unapool, Scotland, U.K., **308** D2
Unari, Finland, **285** M3
Unari, *lake*, Finland, **285** M3
'Unayzah, Jordan, **225** C4
'Unayzah, Saudi Arabia, **363** H3
Uncia, Bolivia, **455** E5
Uncompahgre Plateau, U.S.A., **423** J2
Undersåker, Sweden, **284** F5
Underwood, U.S.A., **420** C2
Unduksa, Russian Federation, **285** S4
Unea Island, Papua New Guinea, **140** C4
Unecha, Russian Federation, **298** D2
Unezhma, Russian Federation, **285** T5
Ungana Bay, Kenya, **369** H3
Ungava, Péninsule d', *peninsula*, Canada, **411** M3
Ungheni, Moldova, **296** F2
União, Brazil, **453** E4
União da Vitória, Brazil, **459** G3
União dos Palmares, Brazil, **457** G2
Unichowo, Poland, **289** H1
Unije, *island*, Croatia, **294** E3
Unini, Peru, **454** C3
Unini, *river*, Brazil, **451** F4
Unión, Bahía, *bay*, Argentina, **460** E1
Union, Missouri, U.S.A., **420** H6
Union, Oregon, U.S.A., **418** F4
Unión, Paraguay, **459** F2
Union City, Pennsylvania, U.S.A., **421** P5
Union City, Tennessee, U.S.A., **425** H1
Union Creek, U.S.A., **418** C5
Union Springs, U.S.A., **425** K3
Uniontown, U.S.A., **421** P6
Unionville, U.S.A., **420** G5
United Arab Emirates, *country*, Asia, **196** G7, *146, 147, 176, 177*
United Kingdom, *country*, Europe, **282** C4, *25, 45, 73, 78, 79, 80, 84, 88, 89, 91, 94, 95, 96, 97, 120, 126, 147, 176, 177, 182, 192, 193, 228, 245, 251, 257, 274, 275, 276, 277, 278, 317, 346, 382, 387, 388, 389, 390, 391, 398, 399, 435, 443, 445, 475*
United States of America, *country*, North America, **409** M5, *U.S.A. 23, 24, 27, 29, 30, 31, 40, 44, 46, 47, 51, 73, 77, 79, 78, 82, 84, 87, 91, 94, 95, 96, 97, 110, 113, 114, 117, 118, 119, 121, 122, 123, 124, 125, 126, 147, 149, 150, 153, 154, 162, 163, 165, 176, 177, 179, 182, 183, 185, 192, 193, 236, 239, 245, 247, 253, 261, 271, 272, 275, 277, 317, 332, 335, 376, 377, 379, 381, 382, 383, 384, 385, 386, 387, 388, 389, 390, 391, 392, 393, 394, 396, 397, 400, 403, 404, 405, 438, 440, 441, 464, 475*
Unitsa, Russian Federation, **285** S5
Unity, Canada, **413** Q5
Unity, U.S.A., **418** E4
University Park, U.S.A., **423** K5
Unnão, India, **218** E4
Unpongkor, Vanuatu, **141** A3
Unquera, Spain, **292** E1
Unst, *island*, Shetland, Scotland, U.K., **308** L7
Unturán, Sierra de, *mountain range*, Venezuela, **451** F3
Unuli Horog, China, **214** D2
Upata, Venezuela, **451** F2
Upavon, England, U.K., **305** F3
Upernavik, Greenland, **411** P2
Upía, *river*, Colombia, **450** D3
Upington, South Africa, **370** D4
Upleta, India, **218** B5
Uplyme, England, U.K., **304** E4
Upoloksha, Russian Federation, **285** Q3
Upolu, *island*, Samoa, **141** B1, *113, 114*
Upper Arrow Lake, Canada, **413** K6
Upper East, *administrative region*, Ghana, **364** D2
Upper Fraser, Canada, **412** H4
Upper Hutt, New Zealand, **133** E5
Upper Klamath Lake, U.S.A., **418** D5
Upper Lough Erne, *lake*, Northern Ireland, U.K., **309** E3
Upper Peirce Reservoir, Singapore, **200** J6
Upper Red Lake, U.S.A., **420** F1
Upper Sandusky, U.S.A., **421** M5
Upper West, *administrative region*, Ghana, **364** D2
Uppingham, England, U.K., **305** G2
Upplands-Väsby, Sweden, **287** H3
Uppsala, *county*, Sweden, **287** H3
Uppsala, Sweden, **287** H3
Upsala, Canada, **414** J7
Upshi, India, **218** D2
Upton, U.S.A., **419** M4
Upton upon Severn, England, U.K., **304** E2
'Uqayribāt, Syria, **225** D2
Urabá, Golfo de, *gulf*, Colombia, **450** C2
Urad Houqi, China, **210** D4
Urad Qianqi, China, **210** E4
Urad Zhongqi, China, **210** E4
Urakawa, Japan, **209** H2
Ural, *river*, Russian Federation, **222** E2, *144, 228*
Ural Mountains *see* Ural'skiy Khrebet, *mountain range*, Russian Federation, **194** G4, *144, 228, 272, 273*
Ural'skiy Khrebet (Ural Mountains), *mountain range*, Russian Federation, **194** G4, *144, 228, 272, 273*
Urambo, Tanzania, **369** F4
Urandi, Brazil, **457** E4
Uraricoera, Brazil, **451** G3
Uraricoera, *river*, Brazil, **451** F3
Urawa, Japan, **209** G4
'Urayf an Nāqah, Jabal, *mountain peak*, Egypt, **225** C4
Urbana, U.S.A., **421** J5
Urbano Santos, Brazil, **453** E4
Urbino, Italy, **294** D4
Urbión, Sierra de, *mountain peak*, Spain, **293** F1
Urçay, France, **290** F3
Urcel, France, **291** F2
Urcos, Peru, **454** D3
Urdgol, Mongolia, **213** G3
Urdos, France, **290** D5
Urdzhar, Kazakhstan, **223** L3
Ure, *river*, England, U.K., **307** G3
Urengoy, Russian Federation, **300** J3
'Urf, Jabal al, *mountain peak*, Egypt, **225** B6
Urfa, Turkey, **224** E5
Urganch, Uzbekistan, **222** G4
Urho, China, **212** E3
Uriah, Mount, *mountain peak*, New Zealand, **133** C6
Uribia, Colombia, **450** D1
Urie, *river*, Scotland, U.K., **308** G3
Uril, Russian Federation, **211** K2
Ūrītskīy, Kazakhstan, **222** H2
Urjala, Finland, **287** L2
Urla, Turkey, **297** F6
Urlingford, Ireland, **309** E5
Ūrmā aṣ Ṣughrā, Syria, **225** D1
Urmi, *river*, Russian Federation, **211** L2
Urmia *see* Orūmīyeh, Iran, **363** H1
Uromi, Nigeria, **365** F3
Uroševac, Kosovo, **296** C4
Urosozero, Russian Federation, **285** S5
Ūroteppa, Tajikistan, **223** H5
Urov, *river*, Russian Federation, **211** H1
Urt, Mongolia, **213** J4
Urt Moron, China, **213** G5
Uruáchic, Mexico, **430** C3
Uruaçu, Brazil, **456** D4
Uruapan, Mexico, **430** E5
Uruará, *river*, Brazil, **452** C4
Urubamba, Cordillera, *mountain range*, Peru, **454** D3
Urubamba, *river*, Peru, **454** D3, *441*
Urubu, *river*, Brazil, **451** G5
Urucará, Brazil, **451** H5
Uruçui Prêto, *river*, Brazil, **453** E5
Uruçuí, Brazil, **453** E5
Uruçui, Serra do, *mountain range*, Brazil, **453** E5
Urucuia, *river*, Brazil, **456** E4
Urucurituba, Brazil, **451** H5
Uruguai, *river*, Brazil, **459** G3
Uruguaiana, Brazil, **459** F3
Uruguay, *country*, South America, **449** G7, *96, 434, 435, 443, 444*
Uruguay, *river*, South America, **447** G6, *439, 443*
Ürümqi, China, **212** E4, *161*
Urung, Indonesia, **199** E3
Urup, *island*, Kuril'skiye Ostrova, Russian Federation, **209** K1
Urup, Ostrov, *island*, Russian Federation, **301** S5
Uryumkan, *river*, Russian Federation, **211** G2
Urziceni, Romania, **296** F3
Us, *river*, Russian Federation, **213** G2
Usa, Japan, **208** E4
Usa, *river*, Russian Federation, **300** G3
Usadishche, Russian Federation, **299** D3
Uşak, *province*, Turkey, **297** G6
Uşak, Turkey, **297** G6
Usakos, Namibia, **370** C3
Usborne, Mount, *mountain peak*, Falkland Islands, **460** F4
Ušće, Serbia, **296** C4
Usedom, Germany, **289** F2
'Usfān, Saudi Arabia, **363** G4
Usha, *river*, Belarus, **299** B6
Ushachy, Belarus, **299** B5
Ushakovskoye, Russian Federation, **301** V2
'Ushayrah, Saudi Arabia, **363** H4
Üshtöbe, Kazakhstan, **223** K3
Ushuaia, Argentina, **460** D5
Ushumun, Russian Federation, **211** J1
Usino, Papua New Guinea, **140** B4
Usinsk, Russian Federation, **300** G3
Usk, *river*, Wales, U.K., **304** D3
Usk, Wales, U.K., **304** E3
Uslar, Germany, **288** D3
Usmas ezers, *lake*, Latvia, **287** K4
Usogorsk, Russian Federation, **300** F3
Usol'ye-Sibirskoye, Russian Federation, **301** M4
Ussel, France, **290** F4
Ussuriysk, Russian Federation, **211** K4
Ust'-Barguzin, Russian Federation, **210** E1
Ust'-Chorna, Ukraine, **296** D1
Ust'-Dolyssy, Russian Federation, **299** B4
Ust'-Ilim'sk, Russian Federation, **301** M4
Ust'-Ishim, Russian Federation, **223** J1
Ust'-Kamchatsk, Russian Federation, **301** T4
Ust'-Kan, Russian Federation, **212** E2
Ust'-Koksa, Russian Federation, **212** E2
Ust'-Kut, Russian Federation, **301** M4
Ust'-Luga, Russian Federation, **299** B3
Ust'-Nera, Russian Federation, **301** R3
Ust'-Ordynskiy Buryatskiy Avtonomnyy Okrug, *autonomous area*, Russian Federation, **210** D1
Ust'-Ordynskiy, Russian Federation, **210** D1
Ust'-Reka, Russian Federation, **299** F2
Ust'-Tsil'ma, Russian Federation, **300** G3
Ust'-Tygda, Russian Federation, **211** J1
Ust'-Umal'ta, Russian Federation, **211** L2
Ust'-Undurga, Russian Federation, **211** G1
Ústí nad Labem, Czech Republic, **289** G3
Ustica, Isola di, *island*, Sicilia, Italy, **295** D6
Ustka, Poland, **289** H1
Ustrem, Bulgaria, **296** F4
Ustronie Morskie, Poland, **289** G1
Ustrzyki Dolne, Poland, **289** L4
Ust'ye, *river*, Russian Federation, **299** G4
Ust'ye, Russian Federation, **299** G3
Ustyurt, Plato, *plateau*, Kazakhstan/Uzbekistan, **222** F4, *185*
Ustyuzhna, Russian Federation, **299** F3
Usu, China, **212** E3
Usulután, El Salvador, **428** C4

Usumacinta, Mexico, **431** H5
Usvyaty, Russian Federation, **299** C5
Uta, Indonesia, **199** G4
'Uta Vava'u, *island*, Vava'u Group, Tonga, **141** B3
Utah, *state*, U.S.A., **423** H2, *376, 383, 386*
Utah Lake, U.S.A., **423** G1
Utajärvi, Finland, **285** N4
Utembo, *river*, Angola, **368** D6
Utena, Lithuania, **287** M5
Utete, Tanzania, **369** G4
Uthai Thani, Thailand, **202** D3
Uthal, Pakistan, **218** A4
Utiariti, Brazil, **455** G3
Utica, Montana, U.S.A., **419** J3
Utica, New York, U.S.A., **426** C3
Utiel, Spain, **293** G3
Utikuma Lake, Canada, **413** M4
Utirik, *island*, Marshall Islands, **139** F3
Utorgosh, Russian Federation, **299** C3
Utraula, India, **219** E4
Utrecht, Netherlands, **288** B2, *241*
Utrecht, *province*, Netherlands, **288** B2
Utrera, Spain, **292** E4
Utsjoki, Finland, **285** N2
Utsunomiya, Japan, **209** G3
Utta, Russian Federation, **222** D3
Uttar Pradesh, *state*, India, **218** E4, *168, 169*
Uttaradit, Thailand, **202** D2
Uttarkāshi, India, **218** D3
Uttoxeter, England, U.K., **305** F2
Utubulak, China, **212** E3
Utupua, *island*, Solomon Islands, **138** E6
Uturoa, French Polynesia, **137** F2
Uubulan, Mongolia, **213** J2
Uummannaq, Greenland, **411** P2
Uurainen, Finland, **287** M1
Üüreg Nuur, *lake*, Mongolia, **213** F2
Uusikaupunki, Finland, **287** K2
Uvac, *river*, Serbia, **296** B4
Uvalde, U.S.A., **424** C5
Uvarovka, Russian Federation, **299** E5
Uvdal, Norway, **286** D2
Uvea *see* Wallis, *island*, Wallis and Futuna, **139** G6, *127*
Uvinza, Tanzania, **369** F4
Uvira, Democratic Republic of the Congo, **369** E3
Uvol, Papua New Guinea, **140** C4
Uvongo, South Africa, **371** F5
Uvs, *province*, Mongolia, **213** G2
Uvs Nuur, *lake*, Mongolia, **213** G2
Uwajima, Japan, **208** F4
Uwayl, Sudan, **366** C3
'Uwaynāt, Jabal Al, *mountain peak*, Sudan, **362** E4
Uwaynāt Wanīn, Libya, **362** B3
Uxbridge, England, U.K., **305** G3
Uxin Ju, China, **210** E5
Uxin Qi, China, **210** E5
Uxituba, Brazil, **452** B4
Uxxaktal, China, **212** E4
Üydzin, Mongolia, **210** D3
Uyo, Nigeria, **368** A1
Uyuni, Salar de, *salt-pan*, Bolivia, **455** E5
Užava, Latvia, **287** K4
Uzbekistan, *country*, Asia, **196** H5, *144, 184, 185, 186, 187, 188*
Uzerche, France, **290** E4
Uzès, France, **291** G4
Uzh, *river*, Ukraine, **289** L4
Uzhhorod, Ukraine, **289** L4
Uzhur, Russian Federation, **223** M1
Užice, Serbia, **296** B4
Uzunköprü, Turkey, **297** F5
Uzunkuyu, Turkey, **297** F6
Užventis, Lithuania, **287** L5
Uzynaghash, Kazakhstan, **223** K4


## V


Vaal, *river*, South Africa, **370** D4
Vaala, Finland, **285** N4
Vaalajärvi, Finland, **285** N3
Vaals, Netherlands, **288** B3
Vaaraslahti, Finland, **285** N5
Vaasa, Finland, **287** K1
Vabalninkas, Lithuania, **287** M5
Vác, Hungary, **289** J5
Vacaria, Brazil, **459** G3
Vacaria, *river*, Brazil, **456** B5
Vaccarès, Étang de, *lake*, France, **291** G5
Vacha, Germany, **288** E3
Vacha, Russian Federation, **285** R5
Vadheim, Norway, **286** B2
Vadodara, India, **218** C5
Vadsø, Norway, **285** P1
Vadstena, Sweden, **286** G3
Vaduz, Liechtenstein, **291** J3, *248*
Vågaholmen, Norway, **284** F3
Vågåmo, Norway, **286** D2
Vágar, *island*, Faeroe Islands, **302** D1
Vagay, *river*, Russian Federation, **223** H1
Vagay, Russian Federation, **223** H1
Vägsele, Sweden, **284** J4
Vågsfjorden, *bay*, Norway, **284** H2
Vägsjöfors, Sweden, **286** F2
Váh, *river*, Slovakia, **289** J4
Vähäkyrö, Finland, **285** L5
Vahitahi, *island*, French Polynesia, **137** H2
Vaihu, Isla de Pascua (Easter Island), Chile, **461** B2
Vail, U.S.A., **423** K2
Vailoa, Samoa, **141** B1
Vaini, Tongatapu Group, Tonga, **141** B4
Vaitogi, American Samoa, **141** B2
Vaitupu, *island*, Tuvalu, **139** F5, *113*
Vakaga, *prefecture*, Central African Republic, **366** B3
Vakīlābād, Iran, **221** G3
Vaksdal, Norway, **286** B2
Val-de-Reuil, France, **290** E2
Val-d'Or, Canada, **416** C5
Val Marie, Canada, **413** R7
Valaam, Ostrov, *island*, Russian Federation, **299** C2
Vålådalen, Sweden, **284** F5
Valandovo, Macedonia, **297** D5
Valaxa, *island*, Greece, **297** E6
Valbo, Sweden, **287** H2
Valcheta, Argentina, **460** D1
Valday, Novgorodskaya Oblast', Russian Federation, **299** D4
Valday, Respublika Kareliya, Russian Federation, **285** S5
Valdayskaya Vozvyshennost', *mountain range*, Russian Federation, **299** D4, *247*
Valdenoceda, Spain, **293** F1
Valdepeñas, Spain, **293** F3
Valderaduey, *river*, Spain, **292** E2
Valdés, Peninsula, Argentina, **460** E2
Valdez, Ecuador, **450** B4
Valdivia, Chile, **460** C1
Valdosta, U.S.A., **425** L4
Valdres, *region*, Norway, **286** D2
Vale, Channel Islands, **304** E5
Vale, U.S.A., **418** F5
Vale of Glamorgan, *unitary authority*, Wales, U.K., **304** D3
Valea lui Mihai, Romania, **296** D2
Valemount, Canada, **413** K5
Valença, Brazil, **457** F3
Valença do Piauí, Brazil, **453** F5
Valençay, France, **290** E3
Valence, France, **291** G4
Valencia, *autonomous community*, Spain, **293** G3, *253*
Valencia, Golfo de, *gulf*, Spain, **293** H3
Valencia, Philippines, **204** D5
Valencia, Spain, **293** G3
Valencia, Venezuela, **451** E1
Valencia de Alcántara, Spain, **292** D3
Valencia Island, Ireland, **309** B6
Valenciennes, France, **291** F1
Vălenii de Munte, Romania, **296** F3
Valentin, Russian Federation, **211** L4
Valentine, Arizona, U.S.A., **422** G4
Valentine, Nebraska, U.S.A., **420** C4
Valentine, Texas, U.S.A., **423** L6
Valenza, Italy, **294** B3
Valera, Venezuela, **451** D2
Valesdir, Vanuatu, **141** A2
Valga, Estonia, **287** N4
Valjevo, Serbia, **296** B3
Valjok, Norway, **285** M2
Valka, Latvia, **287** M4
Valkeakoski, Finland, **287** L2
Vall de Uxó, Spain, **293** G3
Valladolid, Mexico, **431** H4
Valladolid, Spain, **292** E2
Vallata, Italy, **295** E5
Valle, Norway, **286** C3
Valle D'Aosta, *autonomous region*, Italy, **294** A3, *255*
Valle de la Pascua, Venezuela, **451** E2
Valle Fértil, Sierra del, *mountain range*, Argentina, **458** C4
Valle Gran Rey, Islas Canarias, Spain, **373** A4
Valle Hermoso, Mexico, **431** F3
Valle Nacional, Mexico, **431** F5
Valledupar, Colombia, **450** D1
Vallée-Jonction, Canada, **416** F6
Vallegrande, Bolivia, **455** F5
Vallehermoso, Islas Canarias, Spain, **373** A4
Vallejo, U.S.A., **422** B2
Vallen, Sweden, **284** K4
Vallenar, Chile, **458** B3
Valletta, Malta, **362** B1, *257*
Valley, U.S.A., **418** F2
Valley City, U.S.A., **420** D2
Valley Falls, U.S.A., **418** D5
Valleyview, Canada, **413** L4
Vallgrund *see* Raippaluoto, *island*, Finland, **284** K5
Vallo della Lucania, Italy, **295** E5
Vallorbe, Switzerland, **291** H3
Valls, Spain, **293** H2
Valmiera, Latvia, **287** M4
Valmont, France, **305** H5
Valmy, U.S.A., **422** E1
Valognes, France, **290** D2
Valøya, Norway, **284** E4
Valozhyn, Belarus, **287** N5
Valpaços, Portugal, **292** D2
Vālpārai, India, **216** D4
Valparaíso, *administrative region*, Chile, **458** B4
Valparaíso, Brazil, **456** C5
Valparaíso, Chile, **458** B4, *442*
Valparaíso, Mexico, **430** E4
Valparaiso, U.S.A., **425** J4
Valpovo, Croatia, **294** G3
Vals, Tanjong, *point*, Indonesia, **199** G5
Valsād, India, **218** C5
Valset, Norway, **284** D5
Valsjöbyn, Sweden, **284** G4
Valtimo, Finland, **285** P5
Valuyki, Russian Federation, **298** E2
Valverde, Islas Canarias, Spain, **373** A4
Valverde del Camino, Spain, **292** D4
Vammala, Finland, **287** L2
Vamvakas, Akra, *point*, Greece, **297** F6
Van, Turkey, **224** F5
Van, U.S.A., **418** E4
Van Buren, Arkansas, U.S.A., **424** E2
Van Buren, Maine, U.S.A., **426** G1
Van Buren, Missouri, U.S.A., **420** H7
Vân Canh, Vietnam, **203** F3
Van Diemen Gulf, Australia, **134** G1
Van Gölü, *lake*, Turkey, **224** F5
Van Horn, U.S.A., **423** L6
Van Rees, Pegunungan, *mountain range*, Indonesia, **199** G3
Van Tassell, U.S.A., **419** M5
Van Wert, U.S.A., **421** L5
Van Wyksvlei, South Africa, **370** D5
Vananda, U.S.A., **419** L3
Vanavana, *island*, French Polynesia, **137** H3
Vancouver, Canada, **412** H7
Vancouver, U.S.A., **418** C4
Vancouver Island, Canada, **412** G7, *380*
Vancouver Rock, *island*, Snares Islands, New Zealand, **132** H9
Vandalia, U.S.A., **421** J6
Vanderbijlpark, South Africa, **371** E4
Vandergrift, U.S.A., **421** P5
Vanderhoof, Canada, **412** H5
Vanderlin Island, Australia, **135** H2
Vändra, Estonia, **287** M3
Vänern, *lake*, Sweden, **286** F3
Vänersborg, Sweden, **286** F3
Vang, Norway, **286** D2
Vangaindrano, Madagascar, **372** B5
Vangunu, *island*, Solomon Islands, **141** A1
Vanikoro, *island*, Solomon Islands, **138** E6
Vanimo, Papua New Guinea, **140** A3
Vanino, Russian Federation, **301** Q5
Vânju Mare, Romania, **296** D3
Vankleek Hill, Canada, **416** D7
Vanna, *island*, Norway, **284** J1
Vannareid, Norway, **284** J1
Vännäsby, Sweden, **284** J5
Vannes, France, **290** C3
Vannvikan, Norway, **284** E5
Vanrhynsdorp, South Africa, **370** C5
Vānsada, India, **218** C5
Vansbro, Sweden, **286** G2
Vantaa, Finland, **287** M2
Vanua Balavu, *island*, Fiji, **141** A4
Vanua Lava, *island*, Vanuatu, **141** A2
Vanua Levu, *island*, Fiji, **141** A4, *117*
Vanuatu, *country*, Pacific Ocean, **131** F3, *61, 108, 109, 116*
Vao, New Caledonia, **141** A3
Vara, Sweden, **286** F3
Varades, France, **290** D3
Varalé, Côte d'Ivoire, **364** D3
Varāmīn, Iran, **363** K1
Vārānasi (Benares), India, **219** E4, *54, 89, 169*
Varangerbotn, Norway, **285** P1
Varangerfjorden, *fiord*, Norway, **285** P1
Varangerhalvøya, *peninsula*, Norway, **285** P1
Varano, Lago di, *lake*, Italy, **295** E5
Varapayeva, Belarus, **287** N5
Varaždin, Croatia, **294** F2
Varberg, Sweden, **286** F4
Varda, Greece, **297** C6
Vardar, *river*, Macedonia, **297** C6
Varde, Denmark, **286** D5
Vardø, Norway, **285** Q1
Varejoki, Finland, **285** M3
Varel, Germany, **288** D2
Varëna, Lithuania, **287** M5
Varengeville-sur-Mer, France, **305** H5
Vareš, Bosnia and Herzegovina, **294** G3
Varese, Italy, **294** B3
Varfolomeyevka, Russian Federation, **211** L3
Varginha, Brazil, **457** E5
Varhaug, Norway, **286** B3
Varillas, Chile, **458** B2
Varkaus, Finland, **287** N1
Varkiza, Greece, **297** D7
Värmeln, *lake*, Sweden, **286** F3
Värmland, *county*, Sweden, **286** F3
Värmlandsnäs, *peninsula*, Sweden, **286** F3
Varna, *administrative region*, Bulgaria, **296** F4
Varna, Bulgaria, **298** C4
Värnamo, Sweden, **286** G4
Varniai, Lithuania, **287** L5
Varnja, Estonia, **287** N3
Varnyany, Belarus, **287** M5
Varosha, Cyprus, **225** C2
Várpalota, Hungary, **289** J5
Varto, Turkey, **363** H1
Várzea, *river*, Brazil, **459** G3
Várzea da Palma, Brazil, **457** E4
Várzea Grande, Brazil, **456** B4
Varzi, Italy, **294** B3
Varzino, Russian Federation, **285** U2
Varzuga, *river*, Russian Federation, **285** T3
Varzuga, Russian Federation, **285** T3
Vasa Barris, *river*, Brazil, **457** F3
Vásárosnamény, Hungary, **289** L4
Vașcău, Romania, **296** D2
Vasikkaselkä, *lake*, Finland, **285** N2
Vasilika, Greece, **297** D5
Vaškai, Lithuania, **287** M4
Vaskelovo, Russian Federation, **299** C2
Vaskojoki, *river*, Finland, **285** M2
Vaslui, Romania, **296** F2
Vassar, U.S.A., **421** M4
Västansjö, Sweden, **284** G4
Västbäcka, Sweden, **286** G2
Vastenjaure, *lake*, Sweden, **284** H3
Västerås, Sweden, **286** H3
Västerbotton, *county*, Sweden, **284** H4
Västerdalälven, *river*, Sweden, **286** F2
Västergarn, Sweden, **287** J4
Västerhaninge, Sweden, **287** J3
Västernorrland, *county*, Sweden, **287** H1
Västervik, Sweden, **287** H4
Västmanland, *county*, Sweden, **286** G3
Vasto, Italy, **295** E4
Västra Silen, *lake*, Sweden, **286** F3
Vasvár, Hungary, **289** H5
Vatan, France, **290** E3
Vaté *see* Efate, *island*, Vanuatu, **141** A2
Vatersay, *island*, Scotland, U.K., **308** B4
Vatican City, *country*, Europe, **282** F7, *228, 246, 256, 257*
Vaticano, Capo, *cape*, Italy, **295** E6
Vatnajökull, *ice cap*, Iceland, **284** Y7
Vatneyri, Iceland, **284** X7
Vatoa, *island*, Fiji, **141** A4
Vatoloha, *mountain peak*, Madagascar, **372** B4
Vatomandry, Madagascar, **372** B4
Vatra Dornei, Romania, **296** E2
Vatra Moldoviței, Romania, **296** E2
Vättern, *lake*, Sweden, **286** G3
Vattholma, Sweden, **287** H2
Vatulele, *island*, Fiji, **141** A4
Vaucouleurs, France, **291** G2
Vaughn, Montana, U.S.A., **419** J3
Vaughn, New Mexico, U.S.A., **423** L4
Vaupés, *river*, Colombia, **450** D4
Vauxhall, Canada, **413** N6
Vavatenina, Madagascar, **372** B4
Vava'u Group, *islands*, Tonga, **141** B3, *114*
Vavenby, Canada, **412** K6
Vavuniya, Sri Lanka, **216** E4
Vawkavysk, Belarus, **289** M2
Vawkavyskaye wzvyshsha, *mountain range*, Belarus, **289** M2
Växjö, Sweden, **286** G4
Vaygach, Ostrov, *island*, Russian Federation, **300** H2
Vechta, Germany, **288** D2
Vecinos, Spain, **292** E2
Vecpiebalga, Latvia, **287** M4
Veddige, Sweden, **286** F4
Vedea, *river*, Romania, **296** E3

Vedea, Romania, **296** E4
Vedel, Kap, *cape*, Greenland, **411** S3
Vedevåg, Sweden, **286** G3
Vedia, Argentina, **458** E5
Veeate, *island*, Vava'u Group, Tonga, **141** B3
Veendam, Netherlands, **288** C2
Vega, *island*, Norway, **284** E4
Vegadeo, Spain, **292** D1
Veglie, Italy, **295** F5
Vegreville, Canada, **413** N5
Veidnes, Norway, **285** N1
Veinticinco de Mayo, Argentina, **459** E5
Veiros, Brazil, **452** C4
Vejen, Denmark, **286** D5
Vejer de la Frontera, Spain, **292** E4
Vejle, Denmark, **286** D5
Vekshino, Russian Federation, **299** C4
Vela, Cabo de la, *cape*, Colombia, **450** D1
Velasco, Sierra de, *mountain range*, Argentina, **458** C3
Velay, Monts du, *mountain range*, France, **291** F4
Velebit, *mountain range*, Croatia, **294** E3
Velenje, Slovenia, **294** E2
Veles, Macedonia, **297** C5
Vélez, Colombia, **450** D2
Vélez-Málaga, Spain, **292** E4
Vélez Rubio, Spain, **293** F4
Velhas, das, *river*, Brazil, **457** E5
Velika Gorica, Croatia, **294** F3
Velika Hlusha, Ukraine, **289** M3
Velika Kapela, *mountain range*, Croatia, **294** E3
Velika Kladuša, Bosnia and Herzegovina, **294** E3
Velika Kruša, Serbia, **296** C4
Velika Plana, Serbia, **296** C3
Velikaya, *river*, Russian Federation, **299** B4
Velikaya Guba, Russian Federation, **285** S5
Velikaya Kema, Russian Federation, **209** G1
Veliki Kanal, *canal*, Serbia, **296** B3
Velikiye Luki, Russian Federation, **299** C4
Veliko Tŭrnovo, Bulgaria, **296** E4
Vélingara, N. Senegal, **364** B2
Vélingara, S. Senegal, **364** B2
Velingrad, Bulgaria, **296** D4
Velizh, Russian Federation, **299** C5
Velká Bíteš, Czech Republic, **289** H4
Vel'ké Kapusany, Slovakia, **289** L4
Velké Meziříčí, Czech Republic, **289** G4
Vel'ký Meder, Slovakia, **289** H5
Vella Lavella, *island*, Solomon Islands, **141** A2
Velletri, Italy, **295** D5
Vellinge, Sweden, **286** F5
Vellore, India, **216** D3
Velopoula, *island*, Greece, **297** D7
Vel'sk, Russian Federation, **300** F3
Velva, U.S.A., **420** C1
Velyka Mykhaylivka, Ukraine, **296** G2
Velyki Mosty, Ukraine, **289** M3
Velykodolyns'ke, Ukraine, **296** H2
Vema Fracture Zone, *tectonic feature*, Atlantic Ocean, **477** D4
Vemb, Denmark, **286** D4
Vemhån, Sweden, **286** G1
Vena, Sweden, **286** H4
Venaco, Corse, France, **295** B4
Venado Tuerto, Argentina, **458** D4
Venceslau Bras, Brazil, **459** H2
Vendas Novas, Portugal, **292** C3
Vendinga, Russian Federation, **300** F3
Vendôme, France, **290** E3
Veneguera, Islas Canarias, Spain, **373** B4
Veneto, *autonomous region*, Italy, **294** C3, *255*
Venev, Russian Federation, **299** G5
Venezia, Golfo di, *gulf*, Italy, **294** D3
Venezia (Venice), Italy, **294** D3, *54, 75, 80, 90, 254*
Venezuela, *country*, South America, **449** F3, *92, 387, 391, 398, 399, 434, 435, 436, 437*
Venezuela, Golfo de, *gulf*, Venezuela, **450** D1, *387*
Vengurla, India, **216** C3
Venice, Florida, U.S.A., **425** L6
Venice, Louisiana, U.S.A., **425** H5
Venice *see* Venezia, Italy, **294** D3, *54, 75, 80, 90, 254*
Venjan, Sweden, **286** F2
Venkatāpuram, India, **216** E2
Venlo, Netherlands, **288** C3
Venta, *river*, Latvia/Lithuania, **287** K4
Venta de Baños, Spain, **292** E2
Ventana, Sierra de la, *mountain range*, Argentina, **458** D5
Ventisquero, *mountain peak*, Argentina, **460** C1
Ventnor, England, U.K., **305** F4
Ventotene, Isola, *island*, Italy, **295** D5
Ventoux, Mont, *mountain peak*, France, **291** G4
Ventspils, Latvia, **287** K4
Ventuari, *river*, Venezuela, **451** E3
Ventura, U.S.A., **422** D4
Vepsovskaya Vozvyshennost', *mountain range*, Russian Federation, **299** E2
Vera, Argentina, **459** E3
Vera, Spain, **293** G4
Vera Cruz, Brazil, **455** E2
Veracruz, Mexico, **431** F5
Veracruz, *state*, Mexico, **431** F4
Verāval, India, **218** B5
Vercelli, Italy, **294** B3
Verdalsøra, Norway, **284** E5
Verde, Peninsula, Argentina, **460** F1
Verde, *river*, Argentina, **460** E1
Verde, *river*, Goiás, Brazil, **456** C4
Verde, *river*, Mato Grosso do Sul, Brazil, **456** C5
Verde, *river*, Paraguay, **459** E2
Verde, *river*, U.S.A., **423** H4
Verde Grande, *river*, Brazil, **457** E4
Verden (Aller), Germany, **288** D2
Verdigre, U.S.A., **420** D4
Verdun, France, **291** G2
Vereeniging, South Africa, **371** E4
Veregin, Canada, **414** C6
Verga, Cap, *cape*, Guinea, **364** A2
Verga, Islas Canarias, Spain, **373** B4
Vergara, Uruguay, **459** G4
Vergennes, U.S.A., **426** D2
Vergt, France, **290** E4
Verín, Spain, **292** D2
Verkhnetulomskiy, Russian Federation, **285** Q2
Verkhnetulomskoye Vodokhranilishche, *lake*, Russian Federation, **285** P2
Verkhneye Kuyto, Ozero, *lake*, Russian Federation, **285** Q4
Verkhniy Kuzhebar, Russian Federation, **223** N2
Verkhniy Ufaley, Russian Federation, **222** G1
Verkhoyansk, Russian Federation, **301** Q3
Verkhoyanskiy Khrebet, *mountain range*, Russian Federation, **301** P3
Vermilion, Canada, **413** P5
Vermilion, *river*, Canada, **421** N2
Vermilion Bay, Canada, **414** H7
Vermilion Lake, U.S.A., **420** G1
Vermilion Range, *mountain range*, U.S.A., **420** H2
Vermillion, U.S.A., **420** E4
Vermont, *state*, U.S.A., **426** D2, *386*
Vernadsky, *Ukrainian research station*, Antarctica, **470** A4
Vernal, U.S.A., **423** J1
Vernantes, France, **290** E3
Vernár, Slovakia, **289** K4
Verner, Canada, **421** N2
Vernon, Alabama, U.S.A., **425** H3
Vernon, Canada, **413** K6
Vernon, France, **290** E2
Vernon, Texas, U.S.A., **424** C2
Vernon, Utah, U.S.A., **422** G1
Vero Beach, U.S.A., **425** M6
Veroia, Greece, **297** D5
Verona, Italy, **294** C3
Verónica, Argentina, **459** F5
Versailles, U.S.A., **421** L6
Vert, Cap, *cape*, Senegal, **364** A2
Vertientes, Cuba, **429** F2
Vertou, France, **290** D3
Vervins, France, **291** F2
Verwood, Canada, **413** S7
Vesanto, Finland, **285** N5
Veselovskoye, Russian Federation, **223** K2
Vesle, *river*, France, **291** F2
Vesoul, France, **291** H3
Vest-Agder, *county*, Norway, **286** C3
Vestbygd, Norway, **286** C3
Vesterålen, *islands*, Norway, **284** G2
Vesterø Havn, Denmark, **286** E4
Vestfjorden, *fiord*, Norway, **284** F3
Vestfold, *county*, Norway, **286** D3
Vestre Gausdal, Norway, **286** E2
Vestvågøy, *island*, Norway, **284** F2
Vesuvio, *mountain peak*, Italy, **295** E5, *50, 90, 254*
Ves'yegorsk, Russian Federation, **299** F3
Veszprém, Hungary, **289** H5
Vetal, U.S.A., **420** C4
Veteli, Finland, **285** L5
Vetlanda, Sweden, **286** G4
Vetovo, Bulgaria, **296** F4
Vetralla, Italy, **295** D4
Vetrenyy Poyas, Kryazh, *mountain range*, Russian Federation, **285** S5
Vetsikko, Finland, **285** N2
Veurne, Belgium, **290** F1
Vézère, *river*, France, **290** E4
Vị Thanh, Vietnam, **203** E4
Viacha, Bolivia, **455** E4
Viana, Angola, **368** B4
Viana, Brazil, **453** E4
Viana do Castelo, *district*, Portugal, **292** C2
Viana do Castelo, Portugal, **292** C2
Viangchan (Vientiane), Laos, **203** D2, *154*
Viangphoukha, Laos, **202** D1
Vianópolis, Brazil, **456** D4
Viareggio, Italy, **294** C4
Vibo Valentia, Italy, **295** F6
Viborg, Denmark, **286** D4
Vic, Spain, **293** J2
Vice Comodoro Marambio, *Argentinian research station*, Antarctica, **470** A4
Vicenza, Italy, **294** C3
Vichada, *river*, Colombia, **451** E3
Vichy, France, **291** F3, *244*
Vici, U.S.A., **424** C1
Vicksburg, U.S.A., **424** G3
Viçosa, Brazil, **457** E5
Victor, Mount, *mountain peak*, Antarctica, **470** E4
Victor, U.S.A., **419** J5
Victor Harbor, Australia, **135** H6
Victoria, Argentina, **459** E4
Victoria, Chile, **458** B6
Victoria, Canada, **412** H7, *381*
Victoria, Isla, *island*, Chile, **460** B2
Victoria, Lake, Tanzania/Uganda, **369** F3, *317, 340, 341, 343*
Victoria, Malaysia, **201** F1
Victoria, Mount, *mountain peak*, Myanmar, **205** B3
Victoria, Mount, *mountain peak*, New Zealand, **133** D6
Victoria, Mount, *mountain peak*, Papua New Guinea, **140** B5
Victoria, *river*, Australia, **134** G2
Victoria, Romania, **296** E3
Victoria, Seychelles, **373** A2, *352*
Victoria, Sierra de la, *mountain range*, Argentina, **459** F2
Victoria, *state*, Australia, **135** J6, *112*
Victoria, U.S.A., **424** D5
Victoria Falls, Zimbabwe, **371** E2, *344, 345, 346, 347*
Victoria Island, Canada, **410** H2
Victoria Lake, Canada, **417** N5
Victoria Land, *region*, Antarctica, **470** E7
Victoria Peak, *mountain peak*, Belize, **428** C3, *402*
Victoria Peak, *mountain peak*, Philippines, **204** B4
Victoria Peak, *mountain peak*, U.S.A., **423** L6
Victoria Point, Macquarie Island, **134** R11
Victoria River Wayside Inn, Australia, **134** G2
Victoria West, South Africa, **370** D5
Victoriaville, Canada, **416** F6
Victorica, Argentina, **458** D5
Victorville, U.S.A., **422** E4
Victory, Mount, *mountain peak*, Papua New Guinea, **140** C5
Vicuña Mackenna, Argentina, **458** D4
Vida, U.S.A., **418** C4
Vidal, U.S.A., **422** F4
Vidalia, U.S.A., **425** L3
Vidamlya, Belarus, **289** L2
Videbæk, Denmark, **286** D4
Videle, Romania, **296** E3
Vidigueira, Portugal, **292** D3
Vidin, Bulgaria, **296** D4
Vidio, Cabo, *cape*, Spain, **292** D1
Vidlin, Shetland, Scotland, U.K., **308** K7
Vidlitsa, Russian Federation, **299** D2
Vidsel, Sweden, **284** K4
Viduklė, Lithuania, **287** L5
Viduša, *mountain range*, Bosnia and Herzegovina, **294** G4
Vidzy, Belarus, **287** N5
Viedma, Argentina, **460** E1
Viedma, Lago, *lake*, Argentina, **460** C3
Vieja, Sierra, *mountain range*, U.S.A., **423** L6
Viekšniai, Lithuania, **287** L4
Vienna *see* Wien, Austria, **289** H4, *83, 191, 248, 249*
Vienne, France, **291** G4
Vienne, *river*, France, **290** E3
Vientiane *see* Viangchan, Laos, **203** D2, *154*
Viento, Cordillera del, *mountain range*, Argentina, **458** B5
Vieremä, Finland, **285** N5
Vierwaldstätter See, *lake*, Switzerland, **291** J3
Vierzon, France, **290** F3
Viesīte, Latvia, **287** M4
Vieste, Italy, **295** F5
Việt Tri, Vietnam, **203** E1
Vietas, Sweden, **284** J3
Vietnam, *country*, Asia, **197** M8, *28, 44, 93, 94, 96, 97, 144, 153, 154, 158, 162, 193, 385*
Vieux Fort, St Lucia, **427** D3, *397*
Vif, France, **291** G4
Viga, Philippines, **204** D3
Vigan, Philippines, **204** C2
Vigia, Brazil, **452** D3
Vigía Chico, Mexico, **431** J5
Vignacourt, France, **305** K4
Vignemale, *mountain peak*, France/Spain, **293** G1
Vignola, Italy, **294** C3
Vigo, Spain, **292** C1
Vihanti, Finland, **285** M4
Vihāri, Pakistan, **218** C3
Vihiers, France, **290** D3
Vihtari, Finland, **287** P1
Vihti, Finland, **287** M2
Viiala, Finland, **287** L2
Viipustunturit, *mountain peak*, Finland, **285** M2
Viitasaari, Finland, **285** M5
Viitna, Estonia, **287** N3
Vijāpur, India, **218** C5
Vijayawāda, India, **216** E2
Vík, Iceland, **284** Y8
Vik, Norway, **284** F4
Vika, Sweden, **286** G2
Vikajärvi, Finland, **285** N3
Vikanes, Norway, **286** B2
Vikārābād, India, **216** D2
Vikeke, East Timor, **198** D5
Vikersund, Norway, **286** E3
Vikhren, *mountain peak*, Macedonia, **297** D5
Viking, Canada, **413** P5
Vikna, *island*, Norway, **284** E4
Vikran, Norway, **284** J2
Viksjö, Sweden, **287** H1
Viksøyri, Norway, **286** C2
Vila Bittencourt, Brazil, **451** E4
Vila da Ribeira Brava, Cape Verde, **360** Q8
Vila de Sena, Mozambique, **371** G2
Vila do Bispo, Portugal, **292** C4
Vila Franca de Xira, Portugal, **292** C3
Vila Nova, Brazil, **452** B4
Vila Real, *district*, Portugal, **292** D2
Vila Real, Portugal, **292** D2
Vila Velha, Amapá, Brazil, **452** C2
Vila Velha, Espíritu Santo, Brazil, **457** F5
Vilacaya, Bolivia, **455** F5
Vilaine, *river*, France, **290** D2
Viļaka, Latvia, **287** N4
Vilakalaka, Vanuatu, **141** A2
Vilaller, Spain, **293** H1
Vilanandro, Tanjona, *cape*, Madagascar, **372** A4
Vilanculos, Mozambique, **371** G3
Viļāni, Latvia, **287** N4
Vilanova i la Geltrú, Spain, **293** H2
Vilar Formoso, Portugal, **292** D2
Vilātikkulam, India, **216** D4
Vilcabamba, Cordillera, *mountain range*, Peru, **454** D3
Vilhelmina, Sweden, **284** H4
Vilhena, Brazil, **455** G3
Viliya, *river*, Belarus, **298** C2
Viljandi, Estonia, **287** M3
Vilkaviškis, Lithuania, **287** L5
Vilkija, Lithuania, **287** L5
Villa Abecia, Bolivia, **455** F5
Villa Ahumada, Mexico, **430** D2
Villa Ángela, Argentina, **458** E3
Villa Berthet, Argentina, **458** E3
Villa Constitución, Argentina, **458** E4
Villa de Alvarez, Mexico, **430** E5
Villa de Cos, Mexico, **430** E4
Villa de Tamazulapan, Mexico, **431** F5
Villa del Rosario, Argentina, **458** D4
Villa Dolores, Argentina, **458** D4
Villa Flores, Mexico, **431** G5
Villa Florida, Paraguay, **459** F3
Villa Gesell, Argentina, **459** F5
Villa Hayes, Paraguay, **459** F2
Villa Huidobro, Argentina, **458** D5
Villa Iris, Argentina, **458** D6
Villa Juárez, Mexico, **431** E3
Villa María, Argentina, **458** D4
Villa Martín, Bolivia, **455** E5
Villa Mazán, Argentina, **458** C3
Villa Nueva, Argentina, **458** C4
Villa Ocampo, Argentina, **459** E3
Villa Ocampo, Mexico, **430** D3
Villa Ojo de Agua, Argentina, **458** D3
Villa Oropeza, Bolivia, **455** F5

Villa Regina, Argentina, **460** D1
Villa San José, Argentina, **459** E4
Villa Tehuelche, Chile, **460** C4
Villa Unión, Argentina, **458** C3
Villa Unión, Durango, Mexico, **430** D4
Villa Unión, Sinaloa, Mexico, **430** D4
Villa Valeria, Argentina, **458** D5
Villa Viscarra, Bolivia, **455** F4
Villablino, Spain, **292** D1
Villacarrillo, Spain, **293** F3
Villacastin, Spain, **292** E2
Villach, Austria, **289** F5
Villada, Spain, **292** E1
Villagarcía de Arousa, Spain, **292** C1
Villagra, Bahía, *bay*, Róbinson Crusoe Island, Archipiélago Juan Fernández, Chile, **461** C2
Villagrán, Mexico, **431** F3
Villaguay, Argentina, **459** E4
Villahermosa, Mexico, **431** G5
Villahermosa, Spain, **293** F3
Villahoz, Spain, **293** F1
Villajoyosa, Spain, **293** G3
Villalba, Spain, **292** D1
Villaldama, Mexico, **431** E3
Villalonga, Argentina, **460** E1
Villalpando, Spain, **292** E2
Villamalea, Spain, **293** G3
Villamartín, Spain, **292** E4
Villamontes, Bolivia, **455** F5
Villandraut, France, **290** D4
Villano, Ecuador, **450** C4
Villanueva, Colombia, **450** D1
Villanueva, Mexico, **430** E4
Villanueva de Córdoba, Spain, **292** E3
Villanueva de la Serena, Spain, **292** E3
Villanueva del Fresno, Spain, **292** D3
Villány, Hungary, **289** J6
Villapalacios, Spain, **293** F3
Villar, Bolivia, **455** F5
Villarrica, Chile, **460** C1
Villarrica, Lago, *lake*, Chile, **460** C1
Villarrica, Paraguay, **459** F2
Villarrica, Volcán, *mountain peak*, Chile, **460** C1
Villarrobledo, Spain, **293** F3
Villasis, Philippines, **204** C3
Villavicencio, Colombia, **450** D3
Villazón, Bolivia, **455** F6
Ville-Marie, Canada, **416** B6
Villedieu-les-Poêles, France, **290** D2
Villefranche-de-Rouergue, France, **290** F4
Villefranche-sur-Saône, France, **291** G3
Villemontel, Canada, **416** B5
Villena, Spain, **293** G3
Villeneuve-sur-Lot, France, **290** E4
Villers-Bocage, France, **290** D2
Villers-Bretonneux, France, **305** K5
Villeurbanne, France, **291** G4
Villingen-Schwenningen, Germany, **288** D4
Villisca, U.S.A., **420** F5
Vilnius, Lithuania, **287** M5, *237*
Vilppula, Finland, **287** M2
Vils, *river*, Germany, **288** E4
Vilsbiburg, Germany, **288** F4
Vilshofen, Germany, **288** F4
Vilusi, Montenegro, **294** G4
Vilyeyka, Belarus, **287** N5
Vilyuy, Russian Federation, **301** P3
Vimianzo, Spain, **292** C1
Vimieiro, Portugal, **292** D3
Vimmerby, Sweden, **286** G4
Vimoutiers, France, **290** E2
Viña del Mar, Chile, **458** B4
Vinanivao, Madagascar, **372** C4
Vinaròs, Spain, **293** H2
Vincennes, U.S.A., **421** K6
Vincennes Bay, Antarctica, **470** G6
Vindelälven, *river*, Sweden, **284** H3
Vindeln, Sweden, **284** J4
Vindhya Range, *mountain range*, India, **194** J7, *169*
Vineland, U.S.A., **426** C5
Vinga, Romania, **296** C2
Vingåker, Sweden, **286** G3
Vinh, Vietnam, **203** E2
Vĩnh Long, Vietnam, **203** E4
Vinica, Macedonia, **296** D5
Vinita, U.S.A., **420** F7
Vinje, Norway, **286** C2
Vinkovci, Croatia, **294** G3
Vinnitsy, Russian Federation, **299** E2
Vinnyts'ka Oblast', *province*, Ukraine, **296** G1
Vinnytsya, Ukraine, **298** C3
Vinson Massif, *mountain peak*, Antarctica, **470** C5, *464*
Vinstra, Norway, **286** D2
Vinsulla, Canada, **412** J6
Vinza, Congo, **368** B3
Vinzili, Russian Federation, **222** H1
Vipiteno, Italy, **294** C2
Virac, Philippines, **204** D3
Viramgām, India, **218** C5
Viranşehir, Turkey, **224** E5
Virandozero, Russian Federation, **285** S4
Virden, Canada, **414** D7
Vire, France, **290** D2
Virei, Angola, **368** B6
Vireši, Latvia, **287** N4
Virgem da Lapa, Brazil, **457** E4
Virgin Islands, *U.K. dependency*, Caribbean Sea, **409** S7, *276, 378, 388*
Virgin Islands, *U.S. territory*, Caribbean Sea, **409** S7, *378, 386, 387, 388, 391*
Virginia, Ireland, **309** E4
Virginia, South Africa, **371** E4
Virginia, *state*, U.S.A., **421** P7, *77, 93, 383, 386*
Virginia, U.S.A., **420** G2
Virginia Beach, U.S.A., **426** B6
Virginia City, U.S.A., **422** D2
Virihaure, *lake*, Sweden, **284** H3
Virma, Russian Federation, **285** S4
Virolanti, Finland, **287** N2
Viroqua, U.S.A., **420** H4
Virovitica, Croatia, **294** F3
Virserum, Sweden, **286** G4
Virtaniemi, Finland, **285** P2
Virtsu, Estonia, **287** L3
Virttaa, Finland, **287** L2
Virú, Peru, **454** B2
Vis, *island*, Croatia, **294** F4
Visaginas, Lithuania, **287** N5
Visale, Solomon Islands, **141** A1
Visalia, U.S.A., **422** D3
Visayan Sea, Philippines, **204** C4
Visby, Sweden, **287** J4
Viscount, Canada, **413** S6
Viscount Melville Sound, Canada, **410** H2
Višegrad, Bosnia and Herzegovina, **296** B4
Viseu, Brazil, **452** D3
Viseu, *district*, Portugal, **292** D2
Viseu, Portugal, **292** D2
Vişeu de Sus, Romania, **296** E2
Vishākhapatnam, India, **217** E2
Vishnevaya, Russian Federation, **299** F5
Vīshnevka, Kazakhstan, **223** J2
Vislanda, Sweden, **286** G4
Visoko, Bosnia and Herzegovina, **294** G4
Vissefjärda, Sweden, **286** G4
Visso, Italy, **294** D4
Vit, *river*, Bulgaria, **296** E4
Viterbo, Italy, **295** D4
Viti Levu, *island*, Fiji, **141** A4, *117*
Vitichi, Bolivia, **455** F5
Vitigudino, Spain, **292** D2
Vitina, Bosnia and Herzegovina, **294** F4
Vitis, Austria, **289** G4
Vítor, Peru, **454** D4
Vitória, Espírito Santo, Brazil, **457** F5
Vitória, Pará, Brazil, **452** C4
Vitória da Conquista, Brazil, **457** F4
Vitória do Mearim, Brazil, **453** E4
Vitoria-Gasteiz, Spain, **293** F1
Vitorog, *mountain peak*, Bosnia and Herzegovina, **294** F3
Vitré, France, **290** D2
Vitry-le-François, France, **291** G2
Vitsyebsk, Belarus, **299** C5
Vitsyebskaya Voblasts', *province*, Belarus, **287** N5
Vittangi, Sweden, **284** K3
Vitteaux, France, **291** G3
Vittoria, Sicilia, Italy, **295** E7
Vityaz Trench, *underwater feature*, Pacific Ocean, **478** F5
Vivarais, Monts du, *mountain range*, France, **291** G4
Viveiro, Spain, **292** D1
Vivian, Canada, **414** F7
Vivian, U.S.A., **420** C4
Viviers, France, **291** G4
Vivigani, Papua New Guinea, **140** C5
Vivo, South Africa, **371** E3
Vivonne, France, **290** E3
Vizcaíno, Sierra, *mountain range*, Mexico, **430** B3
Vize, Turkey, **297** F5
Vizianagaram, India, **217** E2
Vižinada, Croatia, **294** D3
Viziru, Romania, **296** F3
Vizzini, Sicilia, Italy, **295** E7
Vjosë, *river*, Albania, **297** B5
Vlaams Brabant, *province*, Belgium, **288** B3
Vlădeasa, *mountain peak*, Romania, **296** D2
Vladičin Han, Serbia, **296** C4
Vladikavkaz, Russian Federation, **222** C4
Vladimir, Russian Federation, **298** F1
Vladimirci, Serbia, **296** B3
Vladimirovo, Bulgaria, **296** D4
Vladimirskaya Oblast', *province*, Russian Federation, **299** G4
Vladivostok, Russian Federation, **211** K4, *273*
Vladychnoye, Russian Federation, **299** G3
Vlasenica, Bosnia and Herzegovina, **294** G3
Vlašić, *mountain peak*, Bosnia and Herzegovina, **294** F3
Vlasotince, Serbia, **296** D4
Vlieland, *island*, Netherlands, **288** B2
Vlissingen, Netherlands, **288** A3
Vlorë, Albania, **297** B5
Vltava, *river*, Czech Republic, **289** G4, *266*
Voćin, Croatia, **294** F3
Vöcklabruck, Austria, **288** F4
Vodla, *river*, Russian Federation, **299** F2
Vodlozero, Ozero, *lake*, Russian Federation, **285** T5
Vogel, Cape, Papua New Guinea, **140** C5
Vogelsberg, *mountain peak*, Germany, **288** D3
Voghera, Italy, **294** B3
Voh, New Caledonia, **141** A3
Vohilava, Madagascar, **372** B5
Vohimena, Tanjona, *cape*, Madagascar, **372** A6
Vohipeno, Madagascar, **372** B5
Vohitrandriana, Madagascar, **372** B5
Võhma, Estonia, **287** M3
Võhma, Saaremaa Island, Estonia, **287** L3
Voi, Kenya, **369** G3
Void-Vacon, France, **291** G2
Voineasa, Romania, **296** D3
Voinjama, Liberia, **364** C3
Voiron, France, **291** G4
Voitila, Finland, **287** M2
Vojakkala, Finland, **287** M2
Vojmån, Sweden, **284** H4
Vojmsjön, *lake*, Sweden, **284** G4
Vojnić, Croatia, **294** E3
Vojvodina, *province*, Serbia, **296** B3, *261*
Voknavolok, Russian Federation, **285** Q4
Voko, Cameroon, **365** G3
Volary, Czech Republic, **289** F4
Volborg, U.S.A., **419** M4
Volcán, Panama, **429** E5
Volchikha, Russian Federation, **223** L2
Volch'ya, *river*, Russian Federation, **299** B2
Volda, Norway, **286** C1
Volendam, Netherlands, **288** B2
Volga, *river*, Russian Federation, **281** H4, *228, 271, 273*
Volga, Russian Federation, **222** D1
Volga-Baltiyskiy Kanal, *canal*, Russian Federation, **299** F2
Volgino, Russian Federation, **299** D3
Volgodonsk, Russian Federation, **298** F3
Volgograd (Stalingrad), Russian Federation, **298** F3, *273*
Volgogradskaya Oblast', *province*, Russian Federation, **298** F3, *235, 262, 272*
Volgogradskoye Vodokhranilishche, *reservoir*, Russian Federation, **298** G3
Völkermarkt, Austria, **289** G5
Volkhov, *river*, Russian Federation, **299** C3
Volkhov, Russian Federation, **299** D3
Volksrust, South Africa, **371** E4
Volna, Gora, *mountain peak*, Russian Federation, **301** S3
Voloddymr-Volyns'kyy, Ukraine, **289** M3
Volodino, Russian Federation, **223** L1
Vologda, Russian Federation, **299** G3
Vologodskaya Oblast', *province*, Russian Federation, **299** F2
Volokolamsk, Russian Federation, **299** E4
Voloma, Russian Federation, **285** Q5
Volos, Greece, **297** D6
Volosovo, Russian Federation, **299** B3
Volot, Russian Federation, **299** C4
Volovets', Ukraine, **289** L4
Volovo, Russian Federation, **299** F6
Volta, *administrative region*, Ghana, **364** E3
Volta Noire, *river*, Burkina Faso, **364** D2, *325, 326*
Volta, Lake, Ghana, **364** D3, *326*
Volta Redonda, Brazil, **457** E6
Volterra, Italy, **294** C4
Volturino, Monte, *mountain peak*, Italy, **295** E5
Volturno, *river*, Italy, **295** E5
Volvi, Limni, *lake*, Greece, **297** D5
Volyns'ka Oblast', *province*, Ukraine, **289** M3
Volzhskiy, Russian Federation, **298** F3
Vondrozo, Madagascar, **372** B5
Von'ga, Russian Federation, **285** S4
Vonitsa, Greece, **297** C6
Võnnu, Estonia, **287** N3
Vop', *river*, Russian Federation, **299** D5
Vopnafjörður, Iceland, **284** Z7
Voranava, Belarus, **287** M5
Vorarlberg, *state*, Austria, **288** D5
Vordingborg, Denmark, **286** E5
Voreio Aigaio, *administrative region*, Greece, **297** E6
Voreioi Sporades, *islands*, Greece, **297** D6
Voreios Evvoikos Kolpos, *bay*, Greece, **297** D6
Vorenzha, Russian Federation, **285** S5
Vorga, Russian Federation, **299** D6
Vorkuta, Russian Federation, **300** H3
Vormsi, *island*, Estonia, **287** L3
Vorob'yevo, Russian Federation, **223** K1
Vorokhta, Ukraine, **296** E1
Voronezh, Russian Federation, **298** E2
Voronezhskaya Oblast', *province*, Russian Federation, **222** B2
Voronovo, Belarus, **289** M1
Voron'ya, *river*, Russian Federation, **285** S2
Vorozhgora, Russian Federation, **285** S5
Võrtsjärv, *lake*, Estonia, **287** M3
Võru, Estonia, **287** N4
Vorzogory, Russian Federation, **285** T5
Vosburg, South Africa, **370** D5
Vosges, *mountain range*, France, **291** H3, *245*
Voskresensk, Russian Federation, **299** G5
Voss, Norway, **286** C2
Vostochnaya Litsa, Russian Federation, **285** T2
Vostochno-Sibirskoye More, *sea*, Russian Federation, **301** S2
Vostochnyy Sayan, *mountain range*, Russian Federation, **223** N2
Vostok, *island*, Kiribati, **139** J6
Vostok, *Russian Federation research station*, Antarctica, **470** E6
Votkinsk, Russian Federation, **222** E1
Votuporanga, Brazil, **456** D5
Vouxa, Akra, *point*, Kriti, Greece, **297** D8
Vouziers, France, **291** G2
Voves, France, **290** E2
Voxna, Sweden, **286** G2
Voyeykov Ice Shelf, Antarctica, **470** F7
Voynitsa, Russian Federation, **285** Q4
Vozhe, Ozero, *lake*, Russian Federation, **299** G2
Vozhega, Russian Federation, **299** H2
Voznesens'k, Ukraine, **296** H2
Voznesen'ye, Russian Federation, **299** E2
Vrå, Sweden, **286** F4
Vrådal, Norway, **286** D3
Vradiyivka, Ukraine, **296** H2
Vrangelya, Ostrov, *island*, Russian Federation, **301** U2
Vranica, *mountain peak*, Bosnia and Herzegovina, **294** F4
Vranino, Bulgaria, **296** G4
Vranje, Serbia, **296** C4
Vranjska Banja, Serbia, **296** D4
Vranov nad Topľou, Slovakia, **289** K4
Vratsa, Bulgaria, **296** D4
Vrbas, *river*, Bosnia and Herzegovina, **294** F3
Vrbas, Serbia, **296** B3
Vrbovec, Croatia, **294** F3
Vrbovsko, Croatia, **294** E3
Vredenburg, South Africa, **370** C5
Vredendal, South Africa, **370** C5
Vrgorac, Croatia, **294** F4
Vrhnika, Slovenia, **294** E2
Vrigstad, Sweden, **286** G4
Vrnjačka Banja, Serbia, **296** C4
Vršac, Serbia, **296** C3
Vrtoče, Bosnia and Herzegovina, **294** F3
Vryburg, South Africa, **370** D4
Vryheid, South Africa, **371** F4
Vsetín, Czech Republic, **289** J4
Vsevolozhsk, Russian Federation, **299** C2
Vučitrn, Kosovo, **296** C4
Vukovar, Croatia, **294** G3
Vuktyl, Russian Federation, **300** G3
Vulcan, Romania, **296** D3
Vulcăneşti, Moldova, **296** G3
Vulcano, Isola, *island*, Italy, **295** E6
Vŭlchedrŭm, Bulgaria, **296** D4
Vulture, Monte, *mountain peak*, Italy, **295** E5

Vūng T'u, Vietnam, **203** E4
Vunindawa, Fiji, **141** A4
Vunisea, Fiji, **141** A4
Vuohijarvi, *lake*, Finland, **287** N2
Vuohtomäki, Finland, **285** N5
Vuokatti, Finland, **285** P4
Vuoksa, Ozero, *lake*, Russian Federation, **299** B2
Vuolijoki, Finland, **285** N4
Vuollerim, Sweden, **284** K3
Vuolvojaure, *lake*, Sweden, **284** J3
Vuoriyarvi, Russian Federation, **285** Q3
Vuotso, Finland, **285** N2
Vuottas, Sweden, **284** K3
Vuva, *river*, Russian Federation, **285** Q2
Vwawa, Tanzania, **369** F4
Vyalozero, Ozero, *lake*, Russian Federation, **285** S3
Vyāra, India, **218** C5
Vyatka, Russian Federation, **300** F4
Vyazemskiy, Russian Federation, **211** L3
Vyaz'ma, Russian Federation, **299** E5
Vybor, Russian Federation, **299** B4
Vyborg, Russian Federation, **299** B2
Vychegda, *river*, Russian Federation, **281** J3
Východočeský, *administrative region*, Czech Republic, **289** G3
Vydropuzhsk, Russian Federation, **299** E4
Vyerkhnyadzvinsk, Belarus, **287** N5
Vyetryna, Belarus, **299** B5
Vygozero, Ozero, *lake*, Russian Federation, **285** S5
Vykhcha, *river*, Russian Federation, **285** T3
Vylkove, Romania, **296** G3
Vylok, Ukraine, **296** D1
Vym', *river*, Russian Federation, **281** K3
Vyra, Russian Federation, **299** B3
Vyritsa, Russian Federation, **299** C3
Vyrnwy, Lake, Wales, U.K., **304** D2
Vyshniy Volochek, Russian Federation, **299** E4
Vyškov, Czech Republic, **289** H4
Vysokaye, Belarus, **289** L2
Vysokogornyy, Russian Federation, **211** M2
Vysokoye, Russian Federation, **299** E4
Vytegra, Russian Federation, **299** F2
Vyyezzhiy Log, Russian Federation, **223** N2

W

W J van Blommestein Meer, *lake*, Suriname, **452** B2
Wa, Ghana, **364** D3
Waajid, Somalia, **369** H2
Waal, *river*, Netherlands, **288** B3
Waar, Pulau, *island*, Indonesia, **199** F3
Waarlangier, Tanjong, *point*, Indonesia, **199** F4
Waasagomach, Canada, **414** G5
Wabag, Papua New Guinea, **140** A4
Wabasca-Desmarais, Canada, **413** N4

Wabash, *river*, U.S.A., **421** K6
Wabash, U.S.A., **421** L5
Wabaska, *river*, Canada, **413** M3
Wabowden, Canada, **414** E4
Wabush, Canada, **416** H3
Waccamaw, Lake, U.S.A., **425** N2
Waccasassa Bay, U.S.A., **425** L5
Waco, Canada, **416** J4
Waco, U.S.A., **424** D4
Waconda Lake, U.S.A., **420** D6
Wad, Pakistan, **218** A4
Wad an Nail, Sudan, **366** D2
Wad Bandah, Sudan, **366** C2
Wad Ḥāmid, Sudan, **363** F5
Wad Medanī, Sudan, **366** D2
Waddān, Jabal, *mountain peak*, Libya, **362** C3
Waddān, Libya, **362** C3
Waddeneilanden, *islands*, Netherlands, **288** B2
Waddenzee, *bay*, Netherlands, **288** B2, *241*
Waddington, England, U.K., **305** G1
Waddington, New Zealand, **133** D6
Waddlington, Mount, *mountain peak*, Canada, **412** G6
Wadebridge, England, U.K., **304** C4
Wadena, U.S.A., **420** F2
Wadhurst, England, U.K., **305** H3
Wādī as Sīr, Jordan, **225** C4
Wādī Ḥalfā, Sudan, **363** F4
Wādī Mūsá, Jordan, **225** C4
Wadley, U.S.A., **425** L3
Wadowice, Poland, **289** J4
Wafangdian, China, **211** H5
Wagaru, Myanmar, **202** C3
Wageningen, Suriname, **452** B2
Wagga Wagga, Australia, **135** K6
Wagin, Australia, **134** D5
Wagner, U.S.A., **420** D4
Wagon Mound, U.S.A., **423** L3
Wagontire, U.S.A., **418** E5
Wągrowiec, Poland, **289** H2
Wāh, Pakistan, **218** C2
Wah Wah Mountains, *mountain range*, U.S.A., **422** G2
Wahabu, Ghana, **364** D2
Wahai, Indonesia, **199** E3
Wahala, Togo, **364** E3
Waharoa, New Zealand, **132** E3
Wahiawa, Hawaiian Islands, U.S.A., **422** R9
Wahoo, U.S.A., **420** E5
Wahpeton, U.S.A., **420** E2
Waialua, Hawaiian Islands, U.S.A., **422** R9
Waianae, Hawaiian Islands, U.S.A., **422** R9
Waiau, New Zealand, **133** D6
Waiau, *river*, N. South Island, New Zealand, **133** D6
Waiau, *river*, S. South Island, New Zealand, **133** A7
Waigeo, Pulau, *island*, Indonesia, **199** E2
Waiharara, New Zealand, **132** D2
Waihau Bay, New Zealand, **132** G4
Waiheke Island, New Zealand, **132** E3
Waihi, New Zealand, **132** E3
Waihirere, New Zealand, **132** F4

Waihola, New Zealand, **133** C8
Waiinu Beach, New Zealand, **132** E4
Waikabubak, Indonesia, **198** B5
Waikanae, New Zealand, **133** E5
Waikari, New Zealand, **133** D6
Waikato, *river*, New Zealand, **132** E3
Waikouaiti, New Zealand, **133** C7
Wailea, Hawaiian Islands, U.S.A., **422** R9
Wailingding Dao, *island*, China, **207** C4
Wailuku, Hawaiian Islands, U.S.A., **422** R9
Waimate, New Zealand, **133** C7
Waimea, Hawaiian Islands, U.S.A., **422** R9
Wainfleet All Saints, England, U.K., **305** H1
Waingapu, Indonesia, **198** C5
Waini, *river*, Guyana, **451** G2
Waini Point, *point*, Guyana, **451** G2
Wainuiuru, New Zealand, **133** E5
Wainwright, Canada, **413** P5
Wainwright, U.S.A., **410** C2
Waiohau, New Zealand, **132** F4
Waiotama, New Zealand, **132** E2
Waiotapu, New Zealand, **132** F4
Waiouru, New Zealand, **132** E4
Waipahi, New Zealand, **133** B8
Waipara, New Zealand, **133** D6
Waipawa, New Zealand, **132** F4
Waipiro Bay, New Zealand, **132** G4
Waipu, New Zealand, **132** E2
Wairarapa, Lake, New Zealand, **133** E5
Wairau, *river*, New Zealand, **133** D5
Wairau Valley, New Zealand, **133** D5
Wairoa, *river*, New Zealand, **132** F4
Wairoa, New Zealand, **132** F4
Waitahanui, New Zealand, **132** F4
Waitakaruru, New Zealand, **132** E3
Waitakere, New Zealand, **132** E3
Waitaki, *river*, New Zealand, **133** C7
Waitangi, Chatham Islands, New Zealand, **133** Q16
Waitara, *river*, New Zealand, **132** E4
Waitati, New Zealand, **133** C7
Waite, Mount, *mountain peak*, Macquarie Island, **134** R11
Waitotara, New Zealand, **132** E4
Waitsburg, U.S.A., **418** E3
Waiuku, New Zealand, **132** E3
Waiwera, New Zealand, **132** E3
Waiyevo, Fiji, **141** A4
Wajima, Japan, **209** G3
Wajir, Kenya, **369** H2
Waka, Central Equateur, Democratic Republic of the Congo, **368** D2
Waka, S. Equateur, Democratic Republic of the Congo, **368** D3
Waka, Tanjong, *point*, Indonesia, **198** D3

Wakatipu, Lake, New Zealand, **133** B7
Wakaw, Canada, **413** S5
Wakayama, Japan, **208** F4
Wake, *U.S. territory*, Pacific Ocean, **138** E2, *126, 127, 386*
WaKeeney, U.S.A., **420** D6
Wakefield, England, U.K., **307** G4
Wakefield, U.S.A., **424** G4
Wakkanai, Japan, **209** H1
Wakpala, U.S.A., **420** C3
Waku-Kungo, Angola, **368** C5
Wakunai, Papua New Guinea, **140** E2
Wan'an, China, **206** C3
Wanapa, Bonaire, Netherlands Antilles, **461** A4
Wanapiri, Indonesia, **199** F4
Wanapitei Lake, Canada, **421** N2
Wanapitei, *river*, Canada, **421** N2
Wanda Shan, *mountain range*, China, **211** K3
Wandai, Indonesia, **199** G3
Wandel Sea, Greenland, **411** T1
Wandering River, Canada, **413** N4
Wanding, China, **215** F4
Wandsworth, England, U.K., **305** G3
Walgett, Australia, **135** K4
Walgreen Coast, *region*, Antarctica, **470** B6
Walikale, Democratic Republic of the Congo, **369** E3
Walker, U.S.A., **421** L4
Walker Lake, U.S.A., **422** D2
Walkerton, Canada, **421** N3
Walla Walla, U.S.A., **418** E3
Wallace, Idaho, U.S.A., **418** G3
Wallace, North Carolina, U.S.A., **425** P2
Wallaceburg, Canada, **421** M4
Wallaroo, Australia, **135** H5
Wallasey, England, U.K., **306** E4
Walldürn, Germany, **288** D4
Waller, U.S.A., **424** E5
Wallingford, England, U.K., **305** F3
Wallingford, New Zealand, **132** F5
Wallis (Uvea), *island*, Wallis and Futuna, **139** G6, *127*
Wallis and Futuna, *French territory*, Pacific Ocean, **131** G3, *127, 245*
Walliser Alpen, *mountain range*, Switzerland, **291** H3
Walls, Shetland, Scotland, U.K., **308** K7
Walmer, England, U.K., **305** J3
Walnut, U.S.A., **421** J5
Walpole, Australia, **134** D5
Walpole, *island*, New Caledonia, **141** A3
Walsall, England, U.K., **305** E2
Walsenburg, U.S.A., **423** L3
Walsh, U.S.A., **423** M3
Waltair, India, **217** E2
Walter F. George Reservoir, U.S.A., **425** K4
Walterboro, U.S.A., **425** M3
Walters, U.S.A., **424** C2
Waltham on the Wolds, England, U.K., **305** G2
Waltman, U.S.A., **419** L5
Walton on the Naze, England, U.K., **305** J3
Walvis Bay, Namibia, **370** B3
Walvis Ridge, *underwater feature*, Atlantic Ocean, **477** G8

Wamal, Indonesia, **199** G5
Wamba, Equateur, Democratic Republic of the Congo, **368** D3
Wamba, Haute-Zaire, Democratic Republic of the Congo, **369** E2
Wamena, Indonesia, **199** G3
Wamsutter, U.S.A., **419** L6
Wan Xian, China, **206** B2
Wanaka, Lake, New Zealand, **133** B7
Wanaka, New Zealand, **133** B7
Wang, Mae Nam, *river*, Thailand, **202** C2, *155*
Wang Gaxun, China, **213** H5
Wang Nua, Thailand, **202** C2
Wang Saphung, Thailand, **202** D2
Wanganui, New Zealand, **132** E4
Wangaratta, Australia, **135** K6
Wangdian, China, **215** H4
Wangen im Allgäu, Germany, **288** D5
Wangerooge, *island*, Germany, **288** D2
Wanggamet, Gunung, *mountain peak*, Indonesia, **198** C5
Wanggao, China, **206** B3
Wanggar, *river*, Indonesia, **199** F3
Wangkui, China, **211** J3
Wangmo, China, **215** H4
Wangniudun, China, **207** B2
Wangou, China, **211** J4
Wangqi, China, **211** J4
Wangqing, China, **211** K4
Wanham, Canada, **413** K4
Wanie-Rukula, Democratic Republic of the Congo, **369** E2
Wanlaweyn, Somalia, **367** F4
Wanning, China, **203** F2
Wanpan Yang, *bay*, China, **206** E2
Wanqingsha, China, **207** B3
Wanshan Qundao, *islands*, China, **207** B5
Wantage, England, U.K., **305** F3
Wanup, Canada, **421** N2
Wanyuan, China, **206** A1
Wanzai, Guangdong, China, **207** B4
Wanzai, Jiangxi, China, **206** C2
Wanzleben, Germany, **288** E2
Wapakoneta, U.S.A., **421** L5
Wapato, U.S.A., **418** D3
Wapawekka Lake, Canada, **413** S4
Wapekeka, Canada, **415** K5
Wapella, Canada, **414** D6
Wapoga, *river*, Indonesia, **199** G3
Wapsipinicon, *river*, U.S.A., **420** H4

Warab, *state*, Sudan, **366** C3
Warab, Sudan, **366** C3
Warangal, India, **216** D2
Wararisbari, Tanjong, *point*, Indonesia, **199** G3
Warboys, England, U.K., **305** G2
Warburg, Canada, **413** M5
Warburg, Germany, **288** D3
Warburton, *river*, Australia, **135** H4
Ward Hunt, Cape, Papua New Guinea, **140** C5
Wardha, India, **218** D5
Ware, Canada, **412** G3
Wareham, England, U.K., **304** E4
Warialda, Australia, **135** L4
Warizhên, China, **215** G3
Wark, England, U.K., **306** F2
Warka, Poland, **289** K3
Warkworth, England, U.K., **307** G2
Warkworth, New Zealand, **132** E3
Warlingham, England, U.K., **305** G3
Warm Springs, Nevada, U.S.A., **422** E2
Warm Springs, Oregon, U.S.A., **418** D4
Warmandi, Indonesia, **199** F3
Warmbad, Namibia, **370** C4
Warmbad, South Africa, **371** E3
Warmington, England, U.K., **305** F2
Warminster, England, U.K., **304** E3
Warnemünde, Germany, **288** F2
Warner, Canada, **413** N7
Warner, U.S.A., **420** D3
Warner Robins, U.S.A., **425** L3
Warnes, Bolivia, **455** F4
Waropen, Teluk, *bay*, Indonesia, **199** G3
Warora, India, **218** D5
Warracknabeal, Australia, **135** J6
Warrego, *river*, Australia, **135** K4
Warren, Arkansas, U.S.A., **424** F3
Warren, Michigan, U.S.A., **421** M4
Warren, Minnesota, U.S.A., **420** E1
Warren, Montana, U.S.A., **419** K4
Warren, Ohio, U.S.A., **421** N5
Warren, Pennsylvania, U.S.A., **421** P5
Warren Landing, Canada, **414** F5
Warrensburg, Missouri, U.S.A., **420** G6
Warrensburg, New York, U.S.A., **426** D3
Warrenton, Oregon, U.S.A., **418** C3
Warrenton, South Africa, **370** D4
Warrenton, Virginia, U.S.A., **426** B5
Warri, Nigeria, **365** F3
Warrington, England, U.K., **306** F4
Warrington, *unitary authority*, England, U.K., **306** F4
Warrington, U.S.A., **425** J4
Warrnambool, Australia, **135** J6
Warroad, U.S.A., **420** F1
Warsaw, Indiana, U.S.A., **421** L5
Warsaw, New York, U.S.A., **421** P4
Warsaw *see* Warszawa, Poland, **289** K2, *267, 268*
Warshiikh, Somalia, **367** G4

Warslow, England, U.K., **305** F1
Warsop, England, U.K., **305** F1
Warszawa (Warsaw), Poland, **289** K2, *267, 268*
Warta, *river*, Poland, **280** F5
Warud, India, **218** D5
Waruta, *river*, Indonesia, **199** G3
Warwick, Australia, **135** L4
Warwick, England, U.K., **305** F2
Warwickshire, *unitary authority*, England, U.K., **305** F2
Warzhong, China, **215** G3
Wasatch Range, *mountain range*, U.S.A., **423** H2
Wasby, Lake, Australia, **135** J4
Waseca, U.S.A., **420** G3
Wash, The, *bay*, England, U.K., **305** H2
Washakie Needles, *mountain peak*, U.S.A., **419** K5
Washburn, U.S.A., **420** H2
Wāshīm, India, **218** D5
Washington, D. C., U.S.A., **426** B5, *121, 122, 123, 124, 126, 382, 385, 386*
Washington, England, U.K., **307** G3
Washington, Indiana, U.S.A., **421** K6
Washington, Iowa, U.S.A., **420** H5
Washington, Kansas, U.S.A., **420** E6
Washington, Missouri, U.S.A., **420** H6
Washington, Mount, *mountain peak*, U.S.A., **426** E2
Washington, North Carolina, U.S.A., **426** B7
Washington, Pennsylvania, U.S.A., **421** N5
Washington, *state*, U.S.A., **418** D3, *83, 97, 383, 384, 386*
Washington, Utah, U.S.A., **422** G3
Washington Court House, U.S.A., **421** M6
Washita, *river*, U.S.A., **424** C2
Wasile, Indonesia, **198** D2
Waskaganish, Canada, **415** Q6
Waskaiowaka Lake, Canada, **414** F3
Waskesiu Lake, Canada, **413** R5
Waskish, U.S.A., **420** F1
Waspán, Nicaragua, **428** D4
Wassadou, Senegal, **364** B2
Wasserkuppe, *mountain peak*, Germany, **288** D3
Wast Water, *lake*, England, U.K., **306** E3
Wasta, U.S.A., **420** B3
Wasu, Papua New Guinea, **140** B4
Wasua, Papua New Guinea, **140** A5
Watam, Indonesia, **199** E2
Watam, Papua New Guinea, **140** B3
Watampone, Indonesia, **198** C4
Watauga, U.S.A., **420** C3
Watchet, England, U.K., **304** D3
Water Valley, U.S.A., **424** B4
Waterbury, U.S.A., **426** D4
Waterford, *county*, Ireland, **309** E5
Waterford, Ireland, **309** E5
Waterford Harbour, Ireland, **309** E6
Watergate Bay, England, U.K., **304** B4
Watergrasshill, Ireland, **309** D5
Waterloo, Belgium, **288** B3, *95, 244*
Waterloo, Canada, **421** N4
Waterloo, Trinidad, Trinidad and Tobago, **461** C4
Waterloo, U.S.A., **420** G4
Waterloo Lake, Canada, **413** Q2
Waterlooville, England, U.K., **305** F4
Watersmeet, U.S.A., **421** J2
Watertown, New York, U.S.A., **426** C3
Watertown, South Dakota, U.S.A., **420** E3
Waterville, U.S.A., **426** F2
Watford, England, U.K., **305** G3
Watford City, U.S.A., **420** B2
Wa'th, Sudan, **366** D3
Wathaman, *river*, Canada, **414** B3
Watino, Canada, **413** L4
Watlington, England, U.K., **305** F3
Watmuri, Indonesia, **199** E4
Watonga, U.S.A., **424** C2
Watrous, Canada, **413** S6
Watrous, U.S.A., **423** L4
Watsa, Democratic Republic of the Congo, **369** E2
Watseka, U.S.A., **421** K5
Watsi Kengo, Democratic Republic of the Congo, **368** D3
Watson, Canada, **414** B5
Watson Lake, Canada, **412** E1
Watsonville, U.S.A., **422** C3
Watten, Loch, *lake*, Scotland, U.K., **308** F2
Watten, Scotland, U.K., **308** F2
Watton, England, U.K., **305** H2
Watts Bar Lake, U.S.A., **425** K2
Wattwil, Switzerland, **291** J3
Watubela, Kepulauan, *islands*, Indonesia, **199** E4
Watunea, Indonesia, **198** C4
Watzmann, *mountain peak*, Germany, **288** F5
Wau, Papua New Guinea, **140** B4
Waubay, U.S.A., **420** E3
Waubun, U.S.A., **420** F2
Wauchope, Canada, **414** D7
Wauchula, U.S.A., **425** M6
Waukegan, U.S.A., **421** K4
Waukesha, U.S.A., **421** J4
Wauneta, U.S.A., **420** C5
Waupaca, U.S.A., **421** J3
Waupun, U.S.A., **421** J4
Waurika, U.S.A., **424** D2
Wausau, U.S.A., **421** J3
Wautoma, U.S.A., **421** J3
Waverly, Tennessee, U.S.A., **425** J1
Waverly, Virginia, U.S.A., **426** B6
Wavre, Belgium, **288** B3
Wāw, Sudan, **366** C3
Wāw al Kabīr, Libya, **362** C3
Wawa, Canada, **421** L2
Wawa, Nigeria, **365** E3
Wawanesa, Canada, **414** E7
Wawoi, *river*, Papua New Guinea, **140** A4
Waxahachie, U.S.A., **424** D3
Waya, *island*, Fiji, **141** A4
Wayabula, Indonesia, **199** E2
Waycross, U.S.A., **425** L4
Wayne, U.S.A., **420** E4
Waynesboro, Alabama, U.S.A., **425** H4
Waynesboro, Georgia, U.S.A., **425** L3
Waynesboro, Pennsylvania, U.S.A., **426** B5
Waynesboro, Tennessee, U.S.A., **425** J2
Waynoka, U.S.A., **420** D7
Waza, Cameroon, **365** G2
Wazīrābād, Pakistan, **218** C2
Wda, *river*, Poland, **289** J2
Wdzydze, Jezioro, *lake*, Poland, **289** H1
Wé, New Caledonia, **141** A3
We, Pulau, *island*, Indonesia, **200** A1
Weagamow Lake, Canada, **414** J5
Weagamow Lake, *lake*, Canada, **414** J5
Weald, The, *region*, England, U.K., **305** H3
Weatherford, Oklahoma, U.S.A., **424** C2
Weatherford, Texas, U.S.A., **424** D3
Weaverham, England, U.K., **304** E1
Weaverville, U.S.A., **422** B1
Webb, Canada, **413** Q6
Webequie, Canada, **415** L5
Webster, Iowa, U.S.A., **420** G3
Webster, North Dakota, U.S.A., **420** D1
Webster, South Dakota, U.S.A., **420** E3
Webster City, U.S.A., **420** G4
Webster Spring, U.S.A., **421** N6
Weda, Teluk, *bay*, Indonesia, **199** E2
Wedau, Papua New Guinea, **140** C5
Weddell Island, Falkland Islands, **460** E4
Weddell Sea, Antarctica, **470** B4
Wedmore, England, U.K., **304** E3
Weduar, Tanjong, *point*, Indonesia, **199** F4
Wedza, Zimbabwe, **371** F2
Wee Waa, Australia, **135** K5
Weed, U.S.A., **418** C6
Weedon Bec, England, U.K., **305** F2
Węgorzewo, Poland, **289** K1
Węgrów, Poland, **289** K2
Wei, *river*, Henan, China, **210** F5
Wei, *river*, Shaanxi, China, **206** B1
Weichang, China, **210** G4
Weiden in der Oberpfalz, Germany, **288** F4
Weifang, China, **211** G5
Weihai, China, **211** H5
Weihe, China, **211** K3
Weimar, Germany, **288** E3
Weinan, China, **206** B1
Weining, China, **215** H4
Weipa, Australia, **135** J1
Weishan, China, **215** G4
Weishi, China, **206** C1
Weiss Lake, U.S.A., **425** K2
Weißenburg in Bayern, Germany, **288** E4
Weitchpec, U.S.A., **418** C6
Weitra, Austria, **289** G4
Weixi, China, **215** F4
Weiya, China, **213** G4
Weizhou Dao, *island*, China, **203** F1
Wejherowo, Poland, **289** J1
Wekakura Point, New Zealand, **133** C5
Wekusko Lake, Canada, **414** E4
Welch, Texas, U.S.A., **423** M5
Welch, West Virginia, U.S.A., **421** N7
Weldiya, Ethiopia, **367** E2
Weldon, U.S.A., **422** D4
Welel, Tulu, *mountain peak*, Ethiopia, **366** D3
Welk'īt'ē, Ethiopia, **367** E3
Welkom, South Africa, **371** E4
Welland, *river*, England, U.K., **305** G2, *381*
Wellawaya, Sri Lanka, **217** E5
Wellesbourne, England, U.K., **305** F2
Wellesley Islands, Australia, **135** H2
Wellfleet, U.S.A., **420** C5
Wellingborough, England, U.K., **305** G2
Wellington, Colorado, U.S.A., **423** L1
Wellington, England, U.K., **304** E2
Wellington, Isla, *island*, Chile, **460** B3
Wellington, Kansas, U.S.A., **420** E7
Wellington, New Zealand, **133** E5, *110*
Wellington, Ohio, U.S.A., **421** M5
Wellington, Texas, U.S.A., **424** B2
Wellington Bridge, Ireland, **309** F5
Wellman, U.S.A., **420** H5
Wells, England, U.K., **304** E3
Wells, Canada, **412** J5
Wells, Lake, Australia, **134** E4
Wells, U.S.A., **422** F1
Wells next the Sea, England, U.K., **305** H2
Wellsboro, U.S.A., **426** B4
Wellsford, New Zealand, **132** E3
Wellston, U.S.A., **421** M6
Wellsville, U.S.A., **426** B3
Wels, Austria, **289** G4
Welsford, Canada, **416** H7
Welshpool, Wales, U.K., **304** D2
Welwyn, Canada, **414** D6
Welwyn Garden City, England, U.K., **305** G3
Wem, England, U.K., **304** E2
Wema, Democratic Republic of the Congo, **368** D3
Wembley, Canada, **413** K4
Wemindji *see* Nouveau-Comptoir, Canada, **416,** B3
Wen Xian, China, **215** H2
Wenatchee, U.S.A., **418** D3
Wenchang, China, **203** F2
Wencheng, China, **206** E3
Wenchi, Ghana, **364** D3
Wenchuan, China, **215** G3
Wendell, U.S.A., **418** G5
Wenden, U.S.A., **422** G5
Wendeng, China, **211** H5
Wendens Ambo, England, U.K., **305** H3
Wendover, England, U.K., **305** G3
Wendover, U.S.A., **422** F1
Wenfengzhen, China, **215** H2
Wenjiang, China, **215** G3
Wenling, China, **206** E2
Wenman *see* Wolf, Isla, *island*, Islas Galápagos (Galapagos Islands), Ecuador, **461** A1
Wenquan, Guangdong, China, **207** B1
Wenquan, Qinghai, China, **214** D2
Wenquan, Xinjiang Uygur Zizhiqu, China, **212** D3
Wenshan, China, **215** H5
Wensum, *river*, England, U.K., **305** H2
Wentworth, Australia, **135** J5
Wenxi, China, **206** B1
Wenzhou, China, **206** E2
Werda, Botswana, **370** D4
Werdēr, Ethiopia, **367** G3
Werfen, Austria, **288** F5
Werota, Ethiopia, **367** E2
Werta, *river*, Germany, **288** E4
Wertheim, Germany, **288** D4
Wesel, Germany, **288** C3
Weser, *river*, Germany, **288** D2
Wesley, U.S.A., **426** G2
Wesleyville, Canada, **417** Q5
Wessel, Cape, Australia, **135** H1
Wessel Islands, Australia, **135** H1
Wessington Springs, U.S.A., **420** D3
Wesson, U.S.A., **424** G4
West Antarctica, *region*, Antarctica, **470** B5, *468*
West Bank, *disputed region*, Asia, **225** C3, *179, 180, 182, 192, 193*
West Bay, *bay*, U.S.A., **425** H5
West Bay, Heard and McDonald Islands, **134** S12
West Bay, U.S.A., **425** K4
West Bengal, *state*, India, **219** F5, *169*
West Berkshire, *unitary authority*, England, U.K., **305** F3
West Bridgford, England, U.K., **305** F2
West Bromwich, England, U.K., **305** F2
West Burra, *island*, Shetland, Scotland, U.K., **308** K7
West Butte, *mountain peak*, U.S.A., **419** J2
West Caroline Basin, *underwater feature*, Pacific Ocean, **478** C4
West Chester, U.S.A., **426** C5
West Dunbartonshire, *local authority*, Scotland, U.K., **308** E5
West Falkland, *island*, Falkland Islands, **460** F4, *445*
West Fargo, U.S.A., **420** E2
West Glacier, U.S.A., **418** G2
West Haddon, England, U.K., **305** F2
West Ice Shelf, Antarctica, **470** G5
West Island (Panjang), Cocos (Keeling) Islands, **134** Q10, *123*
West Islet, *island*, Ashmore and Cartier Islands, **134** P9
West Linton, Scotland, U.K., **308** F5
West Lothian, *local authority*, Scotland, U.K., **308** F5
West Midlands, *unitary authority*, England, U.K., **304** E2
West New Britain, *province*, Papua New Guinea, **140** C4
West Nicholson, Zimbabwe, **371** E3
West Palm Beach, U.S.A., **425** M6
West Plains, U.S.A., **420** H7
West Point, Australia, **135** G6
West Point, Tristan da Cunha, **373** C2
West Point, U.S.A., **425** H3
West Sepik, *province*, Papua New Guinea, **140** A3
West Sussex, *unitary authority*, England, U.K., **305** G4
West Union, U.S.A., **420** H4
West Virginia, *state*, U.S.A., **421** N6, *386*
West-Vlaanderen, *province*, Belgium, **288** A3
West Wyalong, Australia, **135** K5
West Yorkshire, *unitary authority*, England, U.K., **307** G4
Westbury, England, U.K., **304** E3
Westby, U.S.A., **420** H4
Westerland, Germany, **286** D5
Western, *administrative region*, Ghana, **364** D3
Western, *province*, Kenya, **369** F3
Western, *province*, Papua New Guinea, **140** A4
Western, *province*, Sierra Leone, **364** B3
Western, *province*, Zambia, **368** D6
Western Australia, *state*, Australia, **134** D4, *112*
Western Cape, *province*, South Africa, **370** D5, *351*
Western Chain, *islands*, Snares Islands, New Zealand, **132** H9
Western Desert, Egypt, **362** E3, *317*
Western Ghats, *mountain range*, India, **216** C2, *169*
Western Group, *islands*, Antipodes Islands, New Zealand, **133** N14
Western Highlands, *province*, Papua New Guinea, **140** B4
Western Isles, *islands*, Scotland, U.K., **308** B2
Western Isles, *local authority*, Scotland, U.K., **308** B3
Western Sahara, *country*, Africa, **358** D4, *312, 314, 355*
Westerstede, Germany, **288** C2
Westerwald, *mountain range*, Germany, **288** C3
Westhill, Scotland, U.K., **308** G3
Westleton, England, U.K., **305** J2
Westlock, Canada, **413** N4
Westmeath, *county*, Ireland, **309** E4
Weston, U.S.A., **421** N6
Weston-super-Mare, England, U.K., **304** E3
Westport, California, U.S.A., **422** B2
Westport, Canada, **417** N5
Westport, Ireland, **309** C4
Westport, New Zealand, **133** C5
Westport, Washington, U.S.A., **418** B3
Westpunt, Curaçao, Netherlands Antilles, **461** C3
Westray, Canada, **414** D5
Westray, *island*, Orkney, Scotland, U.K., **308** F1
Westray Firth, *strait*, Orkney, Scotland, U.K., **308** F1
Westree, Canada, **421** N2
Westvleteren, Belgium, **305** K4
Westward Ho, England, U.K., **304** C3
Wetar, Pulau, *island*, Indonesia, **198** D4
Wetar, Selat, *strait*, Indonesia/East Timor, **198** D5
Wetaskiwin, Canada, **413** N5
Wete, Tanzania, **369** G4
Wetherby, England, U.K., **307** G4
Weto, Nigeria, **365** F3
Wewahitchka, U.S.A., **425** K4
Wewak, Papua New Guinea, **140** A3
Wexford, *county*, Ireland, **309** F5

Wexford, Ireland, **309** F5
Wexford Bay, Ireland, **309** F5
Weyakwin, Canada, **413** S4
Weybridge, England, U.K., **305** G3
Weyburn, Canada, **414** C7
Weyer Markt, Austria, **289** G5
Weyhe, Germany, **288** D2
Weymouth, England, U.K., **304** E4
Whakaari *see* White Island, New Zealand, **132** F3
Whakamaru, New Zealand, **132** E4
Whakapara, New Zealand, **132** E2
Whakapunake, *mountain peak*, New Zealand, **132** F4
Whakatane, New Zealand, **132**, F3
Whakatu, New Zealand, **132** F4
Whale Cove, Canada, **411** K3
Whalsay, *island*, Shetland, Scotland, U.K., **308** L7
Whangaehu, *river*, New Zealand, **132** E4
Whangamata, New Zealand, **132** E3
Whangamomona, New Zealand, **132** E4
Whanganui, *river*, New Zealand, **132** E4
Whanganui Inlet, *bay*, New Zealand, **132** D5
Whangaparaoa, New Zealand, **132** F3
Whangara, New Zealand, **132** G4
Whangarei, New Zealand, **132** E2
Wharfe, *river*, England, U.K., **307** G4
Wharram le Street, England, U.K., **307** H3
Wharton, Península, Chile, **460** B3
Wharton Basin, *underwater feature*, Indian Ocean, **476** F6
Whatawhata, New Zealand, **132** E3
Wheatland, U.S.A., **419** M5
Wheaton, U.S.A., **420** E3
Wheddon Cross, England, U.K., **304** D3
Wheeler, *river*, Canada, **414** B3
Wheeler, U.S.A., **424** B2
Wheeler Peak, *mountain peak*, Nevada, U.S.A., **422** F2
Wheeler Peak, *mountain peak*, New Mexico, U.S.A., **423** L3
Wheeling, U.S.A., **421** N5
Whenuakite, New Zealand, **132** E3
Whernside, *mountain peak*, England, U.K., **306** F3
Wherwell, England, U.K., **305** F3
Whiddon Down, England, U.K., **304** D4
Whirinaki, New Zealand, **132** D2
Whistler, Canada, **412** H6
Whitby, England, U.K., **307** H3
Whitchurch, England, U.K., **304** E2
Whitchurch, Wales, U.K., **304** D3
Whitcombe, Mount, *mountain peak*, New Zealand, **133** C6
White, Lake, Australia, **134** F3
White, *river*, Arkansas, U.S.A., **424** F1
White, *river*, Indiana, U.S.A., **421** K6
White, *river*, Nevada, U.S.A., **422** F3
White, *river*, South Dakota, U.S.A., **420** B4
White, *river*, Utah, U.S.A., **423** J1
White Bay, Canada, **417** N5
White Bird, U.S.A., **418** F4
White Butte, *mountain peak*, U.S.A., **420** B2
White Cloud, U.S.A., **421** L4
White Earth, U.S.A., **420** B1
White Island (Whakaari), New Zealand, **132** F3
White Lake, U.S.A., **424** F5
White Lakes, U.S.A., **423** L4
White Mountain, *mountain peak*, U.S.A., **422** D3
White Mountains, *mountain range*, U.S.A., **426** E2
White Nile *see* Abyaḍ, Al Baḥr al, *river*, Sudan, **366** D2, *336*
White River, Canada, **415** M7
White River, U.S.A., **420** C4
White Rock, Canada, **412** H7
White Sea *see* Beloye More, Russian Federation, **285** S4
White Sulphur Springs, Montana, U.S.A., **419** J3
White Sulphur Springs, West Virginia, U.S.A., **421** N7
White Volta, *river*, Burkina Faso, **364** E2, *325, 326*
Whitecourt, Canada, **413** M4
Whiteface, *river*, U.S.A., **420** G2
Whitefish Bay, Canada, **414** G7
Whitefish Bay, U.S.A., **421** L2
Whitefish Falls, Canada, **421** N2
Whitehall, Iowa, U.S.A., **420** H3
Whitehall, Montana, U.S.A., **419** H4
Whitehall, New York, U.S.A., **426** D3
Whitehall, Orkney, Scotland, U.K., **308** G1
Whitehaven, England, U.K., **306** E3
Whitehead, Northern Ireland, U.K., **309** G3
Whitehill, England, U.K., **305** G3
Whitehorse, Canada, **410** F3, *381*
Whiteriver, U.S.A., **423** J5
Whites City, U.S.A., **423** L5
Whiteville, U.S.A., **425** N2
Whitewater Baldy, *mountain peak*, U.S.A., **423** J5
Whithorn, Scotland, U.K., **308** E6
Whitianga, New Zealand, **136** C4
Whitland, Wales, U.K., **304** C3
Whitlash, U.S.A., **419** J2
Whitley Bay, England, U.K., **307** G2
Whitman, U.S.A., **420** C4
Whitmire, U.S.A., **425** M2
Whitney, Canada, **416** B7
Whitney, Mount, *mountain peak*, U.S.A., **422** D3
Whitsand Bay, England, U.K., **304** C4
Whitstable, England, U.K., **305** H3
Whitsunday Group, *islands*, Australia, **135** K3
Whittington, England, U.K., **304** D2
Whittlesey, England, U.K., **305** G2
Whittlesey, Mount, *mountain peak*, U.S.A., **420** H2
Wholdaia Lake, Canada, **414** B1
Why, U.S.A., **422** G5
Whyalla, Australia, **135** H5
Whycocomagh, Canada, **417** L7
Wiang Pa Pao, Thailand, **202** C2
Wiarton, Canada, **421** N3
Wibaux, U.S.A., **419** M3
Wichita, U.S.A., **420** E7
Wichita Falls, U.S.A., **424** C3
Wick, Scotland, U.K., **308** F2
Wickenburg, U.S.A., **422** G5
Wickham Market, England, U.K., **305** J2
Wickiup Reservoir, U.S.A., **418** C5
Wicklow, *county*, Ireland, **309** F5
Wicklow, Ireland, **309** F5
Wicklow Head, *point*, Ireland, **309** G5
Wicklow Mountains, *mountain range*, Ireland, **309** F5, *277*
Wide Ruins, U.S.A., **423** J4
Widecombe in the Moor, England, U.K., **304** D4
Widnes, England, U.K., **306** F4
Wielbark, Poland, **289** K2
Wieleń, Poland, **289** H2
Wieliczka, Poland, **289** K3
Wieluń, Poland, **289** J3
Wien (Vienna), Austria, **289** H4, *83, 191, 248, 249*
Wien, *state*, Austria, **289** H4
Wiener Neustadt, Austria, **289** H5
Wieprz, *river*, Poland, **289** L3
Wieren, Germany, **288** E2
Wies, Austria, **289** G5
Wiesbaden, Germany, **288** D3
Wiesmoor, Germany, **288** C2
Wietze, Germany, **288** D2
Wigan, England, U.K., **306** F4
Wiggen, Switzerland, **291** H3
Wiggins, U.S.A., **425** H4
Wight, Isle of, England, U.K., **305** F4
Wigmore, England, U.K., **304** E2
Wigston, England, U.K., **305** F2
Wigton, England, U.K., **306** E3
Wigtown, Scotland, U.K., **308** E6
Wigtown Bay, Scotland, U.K., **308** E6
Wik'ro, Ethiopia, **367** E2
Wilber, U.S.A., **420** E5
Wilbur, U.S.A., **418** E3
Wilburton, U.S.A., **424** E2
Wilcannia, Australia, **135** J5
Wilcox, Canada, **414** B6
Wilczęta, Poland, **289** J1
Wild Horse, Canada, **413** P7
Wild Rice, *river*, U.S.A., **420** E2
Wilderville, U.S.A., **418** C5
Wildhorn, *mountain peak*, Switzerland, **291** H3
Wildon, Austria, **289** G5
Wildspitze, *mountain peak*, Austria, **288** E5
Wildwood, Canada, **413** M5
Wiley, U.S.A., **423** M2
Wilhelm, Mount, *mountain peak*, Papua New Guinea, **140** B4, *115*
Wilhelm II Land, *region*, Antarctica, **470** F5
Wilhelmshaven, Germany, **288** C2
Wilkes Barre, U.S.A., **426** C4
Wilkes Land, *region*, Antarctica, **470** F6
Wilkie, Canada, **413** Q5
Will, Mount, *mountain peak*, Canada, **412** E3
Willamette, *river*, U.S.A., **418** C4
Willand, England, U.K., **304** D4
Willapa Bay, U.S.A., **418** B3
Willard, Montana, U.S.A., **419** M3
Willard, New Mexico, U.S.A., **423** K4
Willard, Ohio, U.S.A., **421** M5
Willcox, U.S.A., **423** J5
Willemstad, Curaçao, Netherlands Antilles, **461** C3, *391*
William, Mount, *mountain peak*, Australia, **135** J6
Williams, Arizona, U.S.A., **423** G4
Williams, Minnesota, U.S.A., **420** F1
Williams Lake, Canada, **412** H5
Williamsburg, Kentucky, U.S.A., **421** L7
Williamsburg, Michigan, U.S.A., **421** L3
Williamsburg, Virginia, U.S.A., **426** B6
Williamsport, Canada, **417** N4
Williamsport, U.S.A., **426** B4
Williamston, U.S.A., **426** B7
Willis Group, *islands*, Coral Sea Islands, **135** L2, *124*
Williston, Florida, U.S.A., **425** L5
Williston, North Dakota, U.S.A., **420** B1
Williston, South Africa, **370** D5
Williston Lake, Canada, **412** H3
Williton, England, U.K., **304** D3
Willits, U.S.A., **422** B2
Willmar, U.S.A., **420** F3
Willow, *river*, Canada, **412** H5
Willow Lake, U.S.A., **420** E3
Willow Springs, U.S.A., **420** G7
Willowmore, South Africa, **370** D5
Willows, U.S.A., **422** B2
Wilmington, Delaware, U.S.A., **426** C5
Wilmington, North Carolina, U.S.A., **425** N2
Wilmington, Ohio, U.S.A., **421** M6
Wilmslow, England, U.K., **306** F4
Wilsall, U.S.A., **419** J4
Wilson, Cape, Canada, **411** L3
Wilson, Kansas, U.S.A., **420** D6
Wilson, Mount, *mountain peak*, Colorado, U.S.A., **423** J3
Wilson, Mount, *mountain peak*, Oregon, U.S.A., **418** D4
Wilson, North Carolina, U.S.A., **425** P2
Wilsons Promontory, Australia, **135** K6
Wilton, Maine, U.S.A., **426** E2
Wilton, North Dakota, U.S.A., **419** P3
Wiltshire, England, U.K., **304** F3
Wiluna, Australia, **134** E4
Wimbleball Lake, England, U.K., **304** D3
Wimbledon, New Zealand, **132** F5
Wimbourne Minster, England, U.K., **305** E4
Wimereux, France, **305** J4
Winburg, South Africa, **371** E4
Wincanton, England, U.K., **304** E3
Winchelsea, England, U.K., **305** H4
Winchester, England, U.K., **305** F3
Winchester, Kentucky, U.S.A., **421** L6
Winchester, Tennessee, U.S.A., **425** J2
Winchester, Virginia, U.S.A., **421** P6
Winchester, Wyoming, U.S.A., **419** K5
Wind, *river*, U.S.A., **419** K5
Wind River Range, *mountain range*, U.S.A., **419** J5
Winder, U.S.A., **425** L3
Windermere, England, U.K., **306** F3
Windermere, *lake*, England, U.K., **306** F3
Windhoek, Namibia, **370** C3, *349*
Windigo Lake, Canada, **414** J5
Windom, U.S.A., **420** F4
Windorah, Australia, **135** J4
Window Rock, U.S.A., **423** J4
Windsor, Canada, **417** J7
Windsor, England, U.K., **305** G3
Windsor, U.S.A., **420** G6
Windsor and Maidenhead, *unitary authority*, England, U.K., **305** G3
Windward Islands, Antipodes Islands, New Zealand, **133** P15
Windward Islands, Caribbean Sea, **427** D2, *397, 398, 399*
Windward Passage, Cuba/Haiti, **429** G3, *393*
Winefred Lake, Canada, **413** P4
Winfield, Alabama, U.S.A., **425** J3
Winfield, Canada, **413** M5
Winfield, Kansas, U.S.A., **420** E7
Wingham, Canada, **421** N4
Winifred, U.S.A., **419** K3
Winisk, Canada, **415** M4
Winisk, *river*, Canada, **415** L4
Winiskisis Channel, *river*, Canada, **415** L5
Winkleigh, England, U.K., **304** D4
Winkler, Canada, **414** F7
Winneba, Ghana, **364** D3
Winnebago, Lake, U.S.A., **421** J3
Winnemucca, U.S.A., **422** E1
Winnemucca Lake, U.S.A., **422** D1
Winner, U.S.A., **420** D4
Winnfield, U.S.A., **424** F4
Winnibigoshish, Lake, U.S.A., **420** G2
Winnipeg, Canada, **414** F7, *381*
Winnipeg, Lake, Canada, **414** E5
Winnipeg, *river*, Canada, **414** G6
Winnipegoshish, Lake, Canada, **414** D5
Winnipesaukee, Lake, U.S.A., **426** E3
Winnsboro, U.S.A., **424** G3
Winona, Arizona, U.S.A., **423** H4
Winona, Minnesota, U.S.A., **420** H3
Winona, Mississippi, U.S.A., **424** H3
Winona, Missouri, U.S.A., **420** H7
Winschoten, Netherlands, **288** C2
Winsen (Luhe), Germany, **288** E2
Winsford, England, U.K., **304** E1
Winslow, Arizona, U.S.A., **423** H4
Winslow, Arkansas, U.S.A., **424** E2
Winslow, England, U.K., **305** G3
Winsted, U.S.A., **426** D4
Winters, U.S.A., **424** C4
Winterset, U.S.A., **420** F5
Winterthur, Switzerland, **291** J3
Winterton, England, U.K., **307** H4
Winthrop, U.S.A., **418** D2
Winton, Australia, **135** J3
Winton, New Zealand, **133** B8
Winton, U.S.A., **426** B6
Wintua, Vanuatu, **141** A2
Winwick, England, U.K., **305** G2
Wirksworth, England, U.K., **305** F1
Wisbech, England, U.K., **305** H2
Wisconsin, *river*, U.S.A., **420** J3
Wisconsin, *state*, U.S.A., **420** H3, *386*
Wisconsin Dells, U.S.A., **420** H4
Wisconsin Rapids, U.S.A., **420** H3
Wisdom, U.S.A., **418** H4
Wise River, U.S.A., **418** H4
Wishaw, Scotland, U.K., **308** F5
Wishek, U.S.A., **420** D2
Wisła, Poland, **289** J4
Wisła, *river*, Poland, **280** G5
Wismar, Germany, **288** E2
Wisner, U.S.A., **420** E5
Wissant, France, **305** J4
Wisznice, Poland, **289** L3
Witham, England, U.K., **305** H3
Witheridge, England, U.K., **304** D4
Withernsea, England, U.K., **307** J4
Witley, England, U.K., **305** G3
Witney, England, U.K., **305** F3
Witnica, Poland, **289** G2
Wittenberge, Germany, **288** E2
Wittenburg, Germany, **288** E2
Wittenoom, Australia, **134** D3
Wittingen, Germany, **288** E2
Wittstock, Germany, **288** F2
Witu Islands, Papua New Guinea, **140** C4
Witvlei, Namibia, **370** C3
Wiveliscombe, England, U.K., **304** D3
Wivenhoe, England, U.K., **305** H3
Władysławowo, Poland, **287** J5
Włocławek, Poland, **289** J2
Włodawa, Poland, **289** L3
Włoszczowa, Poland, **289** J3
Woburn, England, U.K., **305** G3
Wodonga, Australia, **135** K6
Wodzisław, Poland, **289** K3
Wodzisłow Śląski, Poland, **289** J4
Woken, China, **211** K3
Woken, *river*, China, **211** K3
Woking, England, U.K., **305** G3

Wokingham, England, U.K., **305** G3
Wokingham, *unitary authority*, England, U.K., **305** G3
Woldegk, Germany, **288** F2
Woleai, *island*, Micronesia, **138** C4
Woleu-Ntem, *province*, Gabon, **368** B2
Wolf, Isla (Wenman), *island*, Islas Galápagos (Galapagos Islands), Ecuador, **461** A1
Wolf, *river*, U.S.A., **420** C7
Wolf, Volcán, *mountain peak*, Islas Galápagos (Galapagos Islands), Ecuador, **461** A1
Wolf Creek, California, U.S.A., **418** C5
Wolf Creek, Montana, U.S.A., **419** H3
Wolf Point, U.S.A., **419** M2
Wolfen, Germany, **288** F3
Wolfsberg, Austria, **289** G5
Wolfsburg, Germany, **288** E2
Wolfville, Canada, **417** J7
Wolin, Poland, **289** G2
Wollaston, Islas, *islands*, Chile, **460** D5
Wollaston Lake, Canada, **414** C2
Wollaston Lake, *lake*, Canada, **414** C2
Wollaston Lake Landing, Canada, **414** C3
Wollaston Peninsula, Canada, **410** H3
Wollogorang, Australia, **135** H2
Wollongong, Australia, **135** L5
Wolmaransstad, South Africa, **371** E4
Wołów, Poland, **289** H3
Wolseley, Canada, **414** C6
Wolsey, U.S.A., **420** D3
Wolsingham, England, U.K., **307** G3
Wolsztyn, Poland, **289** H2
Wolverhampton, England, U.K., **304** E2
Wong Chuk Hang, China, **207** C4, *172*
Wongan Hills, Australia, **134** D5
Wonju, South Korea, **208** D3
Wonosobo, Indonesia, **201** E4
Wonowon, Canada, **412** J3
Wonsan, North Korea, **208** D3
Wonthaggi, Australia, **135** K6
Wood, Mount, *mountain peak*, U.S.A., **419** K4
Wood Lake, U.S.A., **420** C4
Wood Mountain, Canada, **413** R7
Wood River, U.S.A., **420** D5
Woodbine, Georgia, U.S.A., **425** M4
Woodbine, Iowa, U.S.A., **420** F5
Woodbridge, England, U.K., **305** J2
Woodcote, England, U.K., **305** F3
Woodend, New Zealand, **133** D6
Woodhall Spa, England, U.K., **305** G1
Woodland, U.S.A., **422** C2
Woodland Park, U.S.A., **423** L2
Woodlands, Singapore, **200** J6
Woodlark Island, Papua New Guinea, **140** D5
Woodley, England, U.K., **305** G3
Woodridge, Canada, **414** F7
Woodroffe, Mount, *mountain peak*, Australia, **134** G4
Woodrow, U.S.A., **423** M2
Woodruff, Utah, U.S.A., **419** J6
Woodruff, Wisconsin, U.S.A., **420** J3
Woods, Lake of the, Canada/U.S.A., **414** G7
Woodsfield, U.S.A., **421** N6
Woodstock, England, U.K., **305** F3
Woodstock, New Brunswick, Canada, **416** H6
Woodstock, New Zealand, **133** D5
Woodstock, Ontario, Canada, **421** N4
Woodstock, U.S.A., **425** J3
Woodsville, U.S.A., **416** F7
Woodville, New Zealand, **132** E5
Woodville, U.S.A., **424** E4
Woodward, U.S.A., **424** C1
Woollard, Mount, *mountain peak*, Antarctica, **470** C6
Woomera, Australia, **135** H5
Woonsocket, Rhode Island, U.S.A., **426** E4
Woonsocket, South Dakota, U.S.A., **420** D3
Wooster, U.S.A., **421** N5
Wootton Bassett, England, U.K., **305** F3
Woqooyi Galbeed, *administrative region*, Somalia, **367** F2
Worcester, England, U.K., **304** E2
Worcester, South Africa, **370** C5
Worcester, U.S.A., **426** E3
Worcestershire, *unitary authority*, England, U.K., **304** E2
Workington, England, U.K., **306** E3
Worksop, England, U.K., **307** G4
Worland, U.S.A., **419** L5
Wormhout, France, **305** K4
Worms, Germany, **288** D4
Worms Head, *point*, Wales, U.K., **304** C3
Worofla, Côte d'Ivoire, **364** C3
Worsley, Canada, **413** K3
Worthing, England, U.K., **305** G4
Worthington, U.S.A., **420** F4
Wotho, *island*, Marshall Islands, **138** E3
Wotje, *island*, Marshall Islands, **139** F4
Wotu, Indonesia, **198** C3
Wowoni, Pulau, *island*, Indonesia, **198** C4
Wragby, England, U.K., **307** H4
Wrangell, U.S.A., **412** C3
Wrangle, England, U.K., **305** H1
Wrath, Cape, Scotland, U.K., **308** D2
Wray, U.S.A., **423** M1
Wreck Island, Cocos (Keeling) Islands, **134** Q10
Wreck Point, South Africa, **370** C4
Wrelton, England, U.K., **307** H3
Wrens, U.S.A., **425** L3
Wrentham, Canada, **413** N7
Wrexham, *unitary authority*, Wales, U.K., **304** E1
Wrexham, Wales, U.K., **304** E1
Wright, U.S.A., **419** M5
Wright Patman Lake, *lake*, U.S.A., **424** E3
Wrigley, Canada, **410** G3
Wrocław, Poland, **289** H3
Wronki, Poland, **289** H2
Wroxton, Canada, **414** D6
Września, Poland, **289** H2
Wschowa, Poland, **289** H3
Wu, *river*, China, **215** H4
Wu Shan, *mountain range*, China, **206** B2
Wu'an, China, **210** F5
Wubin, Australia, **134** D5
Wuchagou, China, **211** H3
Wuchang, China, **211** J3
Wuchuan, Guangdong, China, **206** B4
Wuchuan, Guizhou, China, **215** H3
Wuchuan, Nei Mongol Zizhiqu, China, **210** E4
Wuda, China, **210** D5
Wudaoliang, China, **214** E2
Wuday'ah, Saudi Arabia, **220** E5
Wudi, China, **210** G5
Wudil, Nigeria, **365** F2
Wuding, China, **215** G4
Wudu, China, **215** H2
Wufeng, China, **206** B2
Wugang, China, **206** B3
Wugong, China, **206** B1
Wuhai, China, **210** D5
Wuhan, China, **206** C2, *159, 161*
Wuhe, China, **206** D1
Wuhu, China, **206** D2
Wuhua, China, **206** C4
Wüjang, China, **214** A2
Wukari, Nigeria, **365** F3
Wulang, China, **215** E3
Wuli, China, **214** E2
Wuliang Shan, *mountain range*, China, **215** G5
Wuling Shan, *mountain range*, China, **206** B2
Wum, Cameroon, **365** G3
Wumai, *river*, China, **205** B1
Wumeng Shan, *mountain range*, China, **215** G4
Wuming, China, **206** B4
Wun Rog, Sudan, **366** C3
Wun Shwai, Sudan, **366** C3
Wunnummin Lake, Canada, **406** Q3
Wuping, China, **206** D3
Wuppertal, Germany, **288** C3
Wuqia, China, **212** B5
Wurno, Nigeria, **365** F2
Würzburg, Germany, **288** D4
Wurzen, Germany, **288** F3
Wushan, China, **206** B2
Wushi, Guangdong, China, **206** C3
Wushi, Xinjiang Uygur Zizhiqu, China, **212** C4
Wusi, Vanuatu, **141** A2
Wusuli, *river*, China/Russian Federation, **211** L3
Wuwei, Anhui, China, **206** D2
Wuwei, Gansu, China, **213** J5
Wuxi, Jiangsu, China, **206** E2
Wuxi, Sichuan, China, **206** B2
Wuxu, China, **206** B4
Wuxuan, China, **206** B4
Wuyi Shan, *mountain range*, China, **206** D3
Wuyiling, China, **211** K2
Wuyishan, China, **206** D3
Wuyuan, Jiangxi, China, **206** D2
Wuyuan, Nei Mongol Zizhiqu, China, **210** E4
Wuyur, *river*, China, **211** J3
Wuzhai, China, **210** E5
Wuzhan, China, **211** J2
Wuzhong, China, **210** D5
Wuzhou, China, **206** B4
Wye, England, U.K., **305** H3
Wye, *river*, England, U.K., **304** E3
Wye, *river*, Wales, U.K., **304** D2
Wymark, Canada, **413** R6
Wymondham, England, U.K., **305** J2
Wyndham, Australia, **134** F2
Wynne, U.S.A., **424** G2
Wynyard, Canada, **414** B6
Wyoming, *state*, U.S.A., **419** K5, *87, 376, 383, 386*
Wyoming, U.S.A., **421** L4
Wyoming Range, *mountain range*, U.S.A., **419** J5
Wyszków, Poland, **289** K2
Wyszogród, Poland, **289** K2
Wytheville, U.S.A., **421** N7
Wyvis, Ben, *mountain peak*, Scotland, U.K., **308** E3
Wyżyna Lubelska, *region*, Poland, **289** L3
Wyżyna Matopolska, *region*, Poland, **289** J3


## X


Xá-Muteba, Angola, **368** C4
Xaafuun, Raas, *point*, Somalia, **367** H2
Xaafuun, Somalia, **367** H2
Xabyai, China, **215** F3
Xagquka, China, **214** E3
Xai Lai Leng, Phu, *mountain peak*, Laos/Vietnam, **203** E2
Xai-Xai, Mozambique, **371** F4
Xaidulla, China, **218** D1
Xainza, China, **214** D3
Xaitongmoin, China, **214** C3
Xam Nua, Laos, **203** E1
Xambioá, Brazil, **452** D5
Xanagas, Botswana, **370** D3
Xangongo, Angola, **368** B6
Xankändi', Azerbaijian, **222** D5
Xanthi, Greece, **297** E5
Xanxerê, Brazil, **459** G3
Xapuri, Brazil, **455** E3
Xar Burd, China, **210** D4
Xarag, China, **213** H5
Xarardheere, Somalia, **367** G4
Xar'oi, China, **215** G2
Xátiva, Spain, **293** G3
Xayar, China, **212** D4
Xêgar, China, **219** F3
Xénô, Laos, **203** E2
Xert, Spain, **293** H2
Xerta, Spain, **293** H2
Xhumo, Botswana, **370** D3
Xi Ujimqin Qi, China, **210** G3
Xi Xian, Henan, China, **206** C1
Xi Xian, Shanxi, China, **210** E5
Xiamaya, China, **213** G4
Xiamen, China, **206** D3
Xi'an, China, **206** B1, *160, 161*
Xiancun, China, **207** B2
Xianfeng, China, **206** B2
Xiang, *river*, China, **206** B3
Xiangcheng, China, **215** F3
Xiangfan, China, **206** C1
Xianggang (Hong Kong), China, **207** C4, *95, 145, 161*
Xianggang (Hong Kong), *special administrative region*, China, **207** C4, *95, 145, 161*
Xiangkhoang, Laos, **203** D2
Xiangkhoang, Plateau de, Laos, **202** D1, *154*
Xiangning, China, **215** J2
Xiangride, China, **215** F2
Xiangshan, China, **206** E2
Xiangshui, Guangdong, China, **207** C2
Xiangshui, Jiangsu, China, **206** D1
Xiangtan, China, **206** C3
Xiangtang, China, **206** C2
Xianju, China, **206** E2
Xianning, China, **206** C2
Xiantao, China, **206** C2
Xianyang, China, **206** B1
Xianyou, China, **206** D3
Xiao Hinggan Ling, *mountain range*, China, **211** J2
Xiao Xian, China, **206** D1
Xiaochuan, China, **215** H2
Xiao'ergou, China, **211** H2
Xiaogan, China, **206** C2
Xiaoguai, China, **212** E3
Xiaojia, China, **207** A4
Xiaojin, China, **215** G3
Xiaolin, China, **207** A4
Xiaolou, China, **207** B2
Xiaoyi, China, **210** E5
Xiapu, China, **206** E3
Xiayong, China, **207** D3
Xiazha, China, **207** B4
Xichang, China, **215** G4
Xifei, *river*, China, **206** D1
Xifeng, Gansu, China, **215** H2
Xifeng, Guizhou, China, **215** H4
Xifeng, Heilongjiang, China, **211** L3
Xifeng, Liaoning, China, **211** J4
Xigazê, China, **214** D3
Xiheying, China, **210** F5
Xiis, Somalia, **367** G2
Xiji, China, **211** J3
Xil, China, **210** F4
Xiliao, *river*, China, **211** H4
Xilin Hot, China, **210** G4
Ximakou, China, **206** C2
Ximiao, China, **213** J4
Xin Barag Youqi, China, **210** G2
Xin Barag Zouqi, China, **211** G2
Xin'an, east of Huizhou, Guangdong, China, **207** E2
Xin'an, southwest of Huizhou, Guangdong, China, **207** B3
Xinbin, China, **211** J4
Xinbo, China, **210** G4
Xincheng, Heilongjiang, China, **211** K3
Xincheng, Ningxia Huizu Zizhiqu, China, **210** D5
Xinchepaizi, China, **212** E3
Xindu, Guangxi Zhuangzu Zizhiqu, China, **206** B3
Xindu, Sichuan, China, **215** H3
Xinfengjiang Shuiku, *reservoir*, China, **207** C1
Xing Xian, China, **210** E5
Xing'an, China, **206** B3
Xingan, China, **206** C3
Xingcheng, China, **211** H4
Xingguo, China, **206** C3
Xinghai, China, **215** F2
Xinghe, China, **210** F4
Xinghua, China, **206** D1
Xinghua Wan, *bay*, China, **206** D3
Xingkai Hu, *lake*, China, **211** L3
Xinglong, China, **210** G4
Xinglongzhen, China, **211** J3
Xingning, China, **206** C3
Xingrenbu, China, **210** D5
Xingshan, China, **206** B2
Xingtai, China, **210** F5
Xingtang, China, **210** F5
Xingu, *river*, Brazil, **452** C4, *440*
Xinguara, Brazil, **452** D5
Xingwen, China, **215** H3
Xingxingxia, China, **213** G4
Xingyi, China, **215** H4
Xinhe, China, **212** D4
Xinhuacun, China, **213** J5
Xinhuang, China, **206** B3
Xinhui, China, **206** C4
Xining, China, **213** J5, *161*
Xiniuwei, China, **207** C1
Xinjiang, China, **206** B1, *161*
Xinjiang Uygur Zizhiqu, *autonomous region*, China, **212** E4, *158*
Xinjie, Nei Mongol Zizhiqu, China, **210** E5
Xinjie, Qinghai, China, **215** G2
Xinjin, Liaoning, China, **211** H5
Xinjin, Sichuan, China, **215** G3
Xinlincun, China, **211** L3
Xinlitun, China, **211** H4
Xinlong, China, **215** G3
Xinmin, China, **211** H4
Xinpu, China, **206** D1
Xinqing, China, **211** K2
Xinshao, China, **206** B3
Xintai, China, **206** D1
Xintang, China, **207** B2
Xinxiang, China, **206** C1
Xinxing, China, **206** C4
Xinxu, China, **207** C3
Xinyang, China, **206** C1
Xinying, China, **203** F2
Xinyu, China, **206** C3
Xinyuan, China, **212** D4
Xinzao, China, **207** A2
Xinzhan, China, **211** J4
Xinzhangfang, China, **211** H2
Xinzheng, China, **206** C1
Xinzhou, China, **210** F5
Xinzuotang, China, **207** C2
Xiongyuecheng, China, **211** H4
Xiping, China, **206** C1
Xiqing Shan, *mountain range*, China, **215** G2
Xique-Xique, Brazil, **457** E3
Xisha Qundao (Paracel Islands), *sovereignty disputed*, South China Sea, **203** G2, *193*
Xishui, Guizhou, China, **215** H3
Xishui, Jiangxi, China, **206** C2
Xistral, *mountain peak*, Spain, **292** D1
Xitieshan, China, **213** G5
Xitole, Guinea-Bissau, **364** B2
Xiuning, China, **206** D2
Xiushan, China, **206** B2
Xiushui, China, **206** C2
Xiuwu, China, **206** C1
Xiuyan, China, **211** H4
Xiuying, China, **203** F2
Xixia, China, **206** B1
Xixiang, China, **215** H2
Xiyang, China, **211** J4
Xizang Zizhiqu (Tibet), *autonomous region*, China, **214** C2, *23, 73, 97, 144, 160, 161, 170, 171, 172, 173*
Xizhi, *river*, China, **207** D2
Xoka, China, **214** E3
Xorkol, China, **213** F5
Xuancheng, China, **206** D2
Xuan'en, China, **206** B2
Xuanhua, China, **210** F4
Xuanwei, China, **215** H4
Xuchang, China, **206** C1
Xuddur, Somalia, **367** F4
Xudun, Somalia, **367** G3
Xuecheng, China, **206** D1
Xuefeng Shan, *mountain range*, China, **206** B3
Xugui, China, **215** E2
Xümatang, China, **215** F2
Xun, *river*, China, **211** J2
Xunhe, China, **211** K2
Xunhua, China, **215** G2
Xunwu, China, **206** C3
Xunyang, China, **206** B1
Xunyi, China, **206** B1
Xupu, China, **206** B3
Xur, China, **215** E2
Xuwen, China, **206** B4
Xuyi, China, **206** D1
Xuyong, China, **215** H3
Xuzhou, China, **206** D1
Xylokastro, Greece, **297** D6

## Y


Yaak, U.S.A., 418 G2
Ya'an, China, 215 G3
Yabassi, Cameroon, 368 A2
Yabēlo, Ethiopia, 369 G2
Yablanitsa, Bulgaria, 296 E4
Yablonovyy Khrebet, mountain range, Russian Federation, 210 E2
Yabluniv, Ukraine, 296 E1
Yabo, Nigeria, 365 F2
Yabrai Shan, mountain range, China, 213 J5
Yabrūd, Syria, 225 D3
Yabuli, China, 211 K3
Yachats, U.S.A., 418 B4
Yacheng, China, 203 F2
Yacuiba, Bolivia, 455 F5
Yacuma, river, Bolivia, 455 E4
Yadé, Massif du, mountain range, Central African Republic, 365 G3
Yādgīr, India, 216 D2
Yadong, China, 211 H2
Yadua, island, Fiji, 141 A4
Yafran, Libya, 362 B2
Yağcılar, Turkey, 297 G6
Yagoua, Cameroon, 365 H2
Yagra, China, 214 B3
Yaguarón, river, Uruguay, 459 G4
Yaguas, Peru, 451 D5
Yahk, Canada, 413 L7
Yahuma, Democratic Republic of the Congo, 368 D2
Yai, Khao, mountain peak, Myanmar/Thailand, 202 C3
Yaiza, Islas Canarias, Spain, 373 B4
Yaizu, Japan, 209 G4
Yajiang, China, 215 G3
Yaka, Central African Republic, 368 C2
Yakamul, Papua New Guinea, 140 A3
Yakeshi, China, 211 H2
Yakhchāl, Afghanistan, 218 A3
Yakima, U.S.A., 418 D3
Yako, Burkina Faso, 364 D2
Yakoruda, Bulgaria, 296 D4
Yakumo, Japan, 209 H2
Yakutat, U.S.A., 410 F4
Yakutsk, Russian Federation, 301 P3
Yala, Thailand, 202 D5
Yale, Canada, 412 J7
Yaleko, Democratic Republic of the Congo, 368 D2
Yalıkavak, Turkey, 297 F7
Yalinga, Central African Republic, 366 B3
Yaloké, Central African Republic, 368 C1
Yalong, river, China, 215 G3
Yalongwa, Democratic Republic of the Congo, 368 D3
Yalova, Turkey, 297 G5
Yalpuh, Ozero, lake, Ukraine, 296 G3
Yalta, Ukraine, 298 D4, 268
Yalu, river, China, 211 J4, 163
Yalutorovsk, Russian Federation, 222 H1
Yamagata, Japan, 209 H3
Yamaguchi, Japan, 208 E4
Yamal, Poluostrov, peninsula, Russian Federation, 300 H3
Yamarovka, Russian Federation, 210 E2
Yambi, Mesa de, plateau, Colombia, 450 D4
Yambio, Sudan, 369 E2
Yambol, Bulgaria, 296 F4
Yamburg, Russian Federation, 300 J3
Yamdena, Pulau, island, Indonesia, 199 E4
Yamin, Puncak, mountain peak, Indonesia, 199 G4
Yamm, Russian Federation, 299 B3
Yamma Yamma, Lake, lake, Australia, 135 J4
Yamoussoukro, Côte d'Ivoire, 364 C3, 323
Yampa, river, U.S.A., 423 J1
Yampil', Ukraine, 296 G1
Yamuna, river, India, 218 E4
Yamur, Danau, lake, Indonesia, 199 F3
Yamzho Yumco, lake, China, 214 D3
Yan Shan, China, 210 G4
Yan Shan, mountain range, China, 211 G4
Yana, river, Russian Federation, 301 Q3
Yana, Sierra Leone, 364 B3
Yanam, India, 217 E2
Yan'an, China, 210 E5
Yanaoca, Peru, 454 D4
Yanbu' al Baḥr, Saudi Arabia, 363 G4
Yanchang, China, 210 E5
Yancheng, China, 206 E1
Yanchiwan, China, 213 H5
Yanchuan, China, 210 E5
Yandaxkak, China, 212 F5
Yandja, Democratic Republic of the Congo, 368 C3
Yandongi, Democratic Republic of the Congo, 368 D2
Yandun, China, 213 G4
Yang, river, China, 210 F4
Yang Xian, China, 215 H2
Yangalia, Central African Republic, 366 B3
Yangambi, Democratic Republic of the Congo, 368 D2
Ya'ngamdo, China, 214 E3
Yangasso, Mali, 364 C2
Yangbajain, China, 214 D3
Yangbi, China, 215 F4
Yangcheng, China, 206 C1
Yangchun, China, 206 B4
Yangcun, China, 207 C2
Yanggang, China, 211 L3
Yanggao, China, 210 F4
Yanggu, China, 210 F5
Yanggu, South Korea, 208 D3
Yangiyŭl, Uzbekistan, 223 H4
Yangjiang, China, 206 B4
Yangkang, China, 213 H5
Yanglin, China, 215 G4
Yangon, division, Myanmar, 205 C4
Yangon (Rangoon), Myanmar, 205 C4, 157
Yangquan, China, 210 F5
Yangshan, China, 206 C3
Yangshuo, China, 206 B3, 159
Yangtze, river, China, 195 M7; see also Chang Jiang, river, China, 206 D2; Jinsha, river, China, 205 C1, 30, 51, 64, 65, 70, 144, 158, 159, 160, 161
Yangwu, China, 215 G5
Yangxin, China, 206 C2
Yangyang, South Korea, 208 E3
Yangyuan, China, 210 F4
Yangzhou, China, 206 D1
Yanhe, China, 206 B2
Yanhu, China, 214 B2
Yanishēvo, Russian Federation, 299 F2
Yanis"yarvi, Ozero, lake, Russian Federation, 299 C1
Yanji, China, 211 K4
Yanjing, E. Sichuan, China, 215 H3
Yanjing, W. Sichuan, China, 215 G4
Yanjing, Xizang Zizhiqu, China, 215 F3
Yanmen, China, 215 F4
Yano-Indigirskaya Nizmennost', Russian Federation, 301 Q2
Yanqi, China, 212 E4
Yanqing, China, 210 F4
Yanshan, Guangxi Zuangzu Zizhiqu, China, 206 B3
Yanshan, Hebei, China, 210 G5
Yanshan, Jiangxi, China, 206 D2
Yanshan, Yunnan, China, 215 H5
Yanskiy Zaliv, bay, Russian Federation, 301 Q2
Yantai, China, 211 H5
Yantarnyy, Russian Federation, 287 J5
Yantian, China, 207 C3
Yantou, China, 206 E2
Yanweigang, China, 206 D1
Yanzhou, China, 206 D1
Yao Xian, China, 206 B1
Yao'an, China, 215 G4
Yaoundé, Cameroon, 365 G4, 330
Yap, island, Micronesia, 138 B4, 118
Yapacani, river, Bolivia, 455 F4
Yapen, Pulau, island, Indonesia, 199 F3
Yapen, Selat, strait, Indonesia, 199 F3
Yaqui, river, Mexico, 430 C2
Yar-Sale, Russian Federation, 300 J3
Yaradzhi, Turkmenistan, 222 F5
Yare, river, England, U.K., 305 J2
Yaremcha, Ukraine, 296 E1
Yaren, Nauru, 138 E5, 120
Yargatti, India, 216 C3
Yarí, river, Colombia, 450 D4
Yarīm, Yemen, 220 D6
Yaripo, Brazil, 452 B3
Yaritagua, Venezuela, 451 E1
Yarkant, river, China, 212 C5
Yarlung Zangbo (Brahmaputra), river, China, 205 B1, 51, 158, 168, 170
Yarm, England, U.K., 307 G3
Yarmouth, Canada, 416 H8
Yarmouth, England, U.K., 305 F4
Yarnell, U.S.A., 422 G4
Yaroslavl', Russian Federation, 299 G4
Yaroslavskaya Oblast', province, Russian Federation, 299 G4
Yartsevo, Russian Federation, 299 D5
Yarumal, Colombia, 450 C2
Yasa, Democratic Republic of the Congo, 368 C3
Yasawa Group, islands, Fiji, 141 A4
Yasenkovo, Bulgaria, 296 F4
Yashevo, river, Russian Federation, 300 K3
Yashi, Nigeria, 365 F2
Yashikera, Nigeria, 365 E3
Yashkino, Russian Federation, 211 L1
Yashkul', Russian Federation, 222 D3
Yasinya, Ukraine, 296 E1
Yasnogorsk, Russian Federation, 299 F5
Yasnoye, Russian Federation, 287 K5
Yasnyy, Russian Federation, 222 F2
Yasothon, Thailand, 203 E3
Yāsūj, Iran, 220 F2
Yasun Burnu, point, Turkey, 224 E4
Yatağan, Turkey, 297 G7
Yate, England, U.K., 304 E3
Yaté, New Caledonia, 141 A3
Yates Center, U.S.A., 420 F7
Yathkyed Lake, Canada, 411 K3
Yatolema, Democratic Republic of the Congo, 368 D2
Yatsushiro, Japan, 208 E4
Yaṭṭah, West Bank, 225 C4
Yatton, England, U.K., 304 E3
Yauca, Peru, 454 C4
Yauli, Peru, 454 C3
Yauna Moloca, Colombia, 451 D4
Yauri, Peru, 454 D4
Yauyos, Peru, 454 C3
Yavari, river, Brazil/Peru, 454 D1
Yavaros, Mexico, 430 C3
Yavatmāl, India, 218 D5
Yavi, Cerro, mountain peak, Venezuela, 451 F3
Yaviza, Panama, 429 F5
Yavlenka, Kazakhstan, 223 H2
Yavoriv, Ukraine, 296 E1
Yaw, river, Myanmar, 205 B3
Yawatahama, Japan, 208 F4
Yawatongguzlangar, China, 212 D5
Yawri Bay, Sierra Leone, 364 B3
Yayao, China, 207 B2
Yayladağı, Turkey, 225 D2
Yazd, Iran, 221 F2
Yazhelbitsy, Russian Federation, 299 D3
Yazmān, Pakistan, 218 B3
Yazoo City, U.S.A., 424 G3
Yazulu, Russian Federation, 223 M2
Yazykovo, Russian Federation, 298 G2
Ybbsitz, Austria, 289 G5
Yding Skovhøj, mountain peak, Denmark, 286 D5, 233
Ydra, Greece, 297 D7
Ydra, island, Greece, 297 D7
Ye, Myanmar, 202 C3
Ye-u, Myanmar, 205 B3
Ye Xian, China, 206 C1
Yealmpton, England, U.K., 304 D4
Yebbi-Bou, Chad, 362 C4
Yebbi-Souma, Chad, 362 C4
Yecheng, China, 212 C5
Yecla, Spain, 293 G3
Yécora, Mexico, 430 C2
Yeed, Somalia, 369 H2
Yeehaw Junction, U.S.A., 425 M6
Yefimovskiy, Russian Federation, 299 E3
Yefremov, Russian Federation, 299 G6
Yegor'yevsk, Russian Federation, 299 G5
Yégué, Togo, 364 E3
Yegyi, Myanmar, 205 B4
Yei, river, Sudan, 369 F1
Yei, Sudan, 369 F2
Yeji, Ghana, 364 D3
Yekaterinburg, Russian Federation, 222 G1, 273
Yekimovichi, Russian Federation, 299 D5
Yelanka, Russian Federation, 223 K1
Yelets, Russian Federation, 298 E2
Yélimané, Mali, 364 B1
Yelizavety, Mys, cape, Russian Federation, 301 R4
Yelizovo, Russian Federation, 301 S4
Yell, island, Shetland, Scotland, U.K., 308 K7
Yellow see Huang, river, China, 195 M6, 27, 30, 51, 66, 70, 95, 144, 158, 159, 160, 161
Yellow Pine, U.S.A., 418 G4
Yellowknife, Canada, 410 H3, 381
Yellowstone, river, U.S.A., 419 K3
Yellowstone Lake, U.S.A., 419 J4
Yel'nya, Russian Federation, 299 D5
Yelovo, Russian Federation, 222 F1
Yel'tsy, Russian Federation, 299 D4
Yelwa, Nigeria, 365 E2
Yematan, China, 215 F2
Yemel'yanovka, Russian Federation, 285 Q5
Yemen, country, Asia, 196 F8, 146, 175, 176
Yemişli, Turkey, 225 C1
Yemva, Russian Federation, 300 G3
Yên Bái, Vietnam, 203 E1
Yên Châu, Vietnam, 203 E1
Yena, river, Russian Federation, 285 Q3
Yena, Russian Federation, 285 Q3
Yendi, Ghana, 364 D3
Yénéganou, Congo, 368 B3
Yengema, Sierra Leone, 364 B3
Yengisar, Central Xinjiang Uygur Zizhiqu, China, 212 E4
Yengisar, W. Xinjiang Uygur Zizhiqu, China, 212 C5
Yengo, Congo, 368 C2
Yenice, Turkey, 297 G6
Yenihisar, Turkey, 297 F7
Yenisey, river, Russian Federation, 223 N2, 273
Yeniseyskiy Kryazh, mountain range, Russian Federation, 300 L3
Yenozero, Ozero, lake, Russian Federation, 285 T2
Yenyukovo, Russian Federation, 299 F3
Yeovil, England, U.K., 304 E4
Yepachic, Mexico, 430 C2
Yeppoon, Australia, 135 L3
Yerbent, Turkmenistan, 222 F5
Yerevan, Armenia, 222 C4, 188, 189
Yerington, U.S.A., 422 D2
Yermala, India, 216 C2
Yeroêam, Israel, 225 C4
Yershi, Russian Federation, 299 E5
Yershov, Russian Federation, 222 D2
Yerupaja, Cerro, mountain peak, Peru, 454 C3
Yerushalayim (Jerusalem), Israel, 225 C4, 75, 90, 91, 179, 192, 193
Yerville, France, 305 H5
Yes Tor, mountain peak, England, U.K., 304 C4
Yesagyo, Myanmar, 205 B3
Yesan, South Korea, 208 D3
Yeşilova, Turkey, 297 G7
Yeso, U.S.A., 423 L4
Yeste, Spain, 293 F3
Yeu, Île d', island, France, 290 C3
Yevgora, Russian Federation, 285 R5
Yevpatoriya, Ukraine, 298 D3
Yevreyskaya Avtonomnaya Oblast', autonomous region, Russian Federation, 211 K2
Yeysk, Russian Federation, 298 E3
Yeyungou, China, 212 E4
Ygrande, France, 291 F3
Yi, river, Uruguay, 459 F4
Yi Xian, China, 211 H4
Yialousa, Cyprus, 225 C2
Yi'an, China, 211 J3
Yibin, China, 215 H3
Yibir, Jabal, mountain peak, United Arab Emirates, 221 G3, 176
Yichang, China, 206 B2
Yicheng, Hubei, China, 206 C2
Yicheng, Shanxi, China, 210 E6
Yichuan, China, 215 J1
Yichun, Heilongjiang, China, 211 K3
Yichun, Jiangxi, China, 206 C3
Yidun, China, 215 F3
Yifeng, China, 206 C2
Yijun, China, 206 B1
Yilaha, China, 211 J2
Yilan, China, 211 K3
Yıldızeli, Turkey, 363 G1
Yilehuli Shan, mountain range, China, 211 J2
Yiliang, Central Yunnan, China, 215 G4
Yiliang, N. Yunnan, China, 215 G4
Yiliekede, China, 211 H2
Yiliping, China, 213 G5
Yima, China, 206 B1
Yimen, China, 215 G4
Yimianpo, China, 211 K3
Yimuhe, China, 211 H1
Yinan, China, 206 D1
Yinchuan, China, 210 D5, 161
Ying Xian, China, 210 F5
Yingcheng, China, 206 C2
Yingde, China, 206 C3
Yingjiang, China, 215 F4
Yingjing, China, 215 G3
Yingkou, China, 211 H4
Yingshan, Hubei, China, 206 C2
Yingshan, Sichuan, China, 215 H3
Yingshang, China, 206 D1
Yingtan, China, 206 D2
Yining, China, 212 D4
Yinjiang, China, 206 B2
Yi'ong, China, 215 E3
Yi'ong, river, China, 214 E3
Yipinglang, China, 215 G4
Yiquan, China, 215 H4
Yirga 'Alem, Ethiopia, 367 E3
Yirga Ch'efē, Ethiopia, 367 E3
Yirol, Sudan, 366 D3
Yirshi, China, 211 G3
Yishan, China, 206 B3
Yishui, China, 206 D1
Yishun, Singapore, 200 K6
Yitong, river, China, 211 J3
Yitulihe, China, 211 H2
Yiwu, Xinjiang Uygur Zizhiqu, China, 213 G4
Yiwu, Zhejiang, China, 206 E2
Yixiken, China, 211 J1
Yixing, China, 206 D2
Yiyang, Hunan, China, 206 C2
Yiyang, Jiangxi, China, 206 D2
Yiyuan, China, 211 G5
Yizhang, China, 206 C3
Yizheng, China, 206 D1
Ylakiai, Lithuania, 287 K4
Ylämaa, Finland, 287 N2
Yli-Kärppä, Finland, 285 M4
Yli-li, Finland, 285 M4
Ylikiiminki, Finland, 285 N4
Ylistaro, Finland, 285 L5
Ylitornio, Finland, 285 L3
Ylivieska, Finland, 285 M4
Yläsjärvi, Finland, 285 M3
Ylöjärvi, Finland, 287 L2
Yoakum, U.S.A., 424 D5
Yobe, state, Nigeria, 365 G2
Yoboki, Djibouti, 367 F2

Yody, Belarus, **287** N5
Yog Point, Philippines, **204** D3
Yogyakarta, *autonomous district*, Indonesia, **201** E5
Yogyakarta, Indonesia, **201** E4
Yokadouma, Cameroon, **368** C2
Yokkaichi, Japan, **209** G4
Yoko, Cameroon, **368** B1
Yokohama, Japan, **209** G4, *165*
Yokote, Japan, **209** H3
Yola, Nigeria, **365** G3
Yolombo, Democratic Republic of the Congo, **368** D3
Yom, Mae Nam, *river*, Thailand, **202** C2, *156*
Yŏmju, North Korea, **208** D3
Yonago, Japan, **208** F4
Yonaguni-jima, *island*, Japan, **209** M8
Yonezawa, Japan, **209** G3
Yong'an, China, **206** D3
Yongchang, China, **213** J5
Yongcheng, China, **206** D1
Yongchuan, China, **215** H3
Yongdeng, China, **213** J5
Yŏngdong, South Korea, **208** D3
Yongfeng, China, **206** C3
Yongfu, China, **206** B3
Yonghan, China, **207** B1
Yonghe, China, **207** B2
Yŏnghŭng, North Korea, **208** D3
Yongjing, China, **215** G2
Yŭngju, South Korea, **208** E3
Yongkang, China, **206** E2
Yongning, China, **210** D5
Yongping, China, **215** F4
Yongren, China, **215** G4
Yongshan, China, **215** G3
Yongsheng, China, **215** G4
Yongshun, China, **206** B2
Yongtai, China, **206** D3
Yongxin, China, **206** C3
Yongxing, China, **206** C3
Yongxiu, China, **206** C2
Yongzhou, China, **206** B3
Yonkers, U.S.A., **426** D4
Yonne, *river*, France, **291** F2
Yopal, Colombia, **450** D3
Yopurga, China, **212** C5
York, Australia, **134** D5
York, Cape, Australia, **135** J1
York, England, U.K., **307** G4
York, Kap, *cape*, Greenland, **411** N2
York, North Dakota, U.S.A., **420** D1
York, Pennsylvania, U.S.A., **426** B5
York City, *unitary authority*, England, U.K., **307** G4
York Factory, Canada, **414** H3
Yorke Peninsula, Australia, **135** H5
Yorketown, Australia, **135** H5
Yorkshire Wolds, *region*, England, U.K., **307** H3
Yorkton, Canada, **414** C6
Yoro, Honduras, **428** D4
Yosemite Village, U.S.A., **422** D3
Yoshkar-Ola, Russian Federation, **222** D1
Yŏsu, South Korea, **208** D4
Yotvata, Israel, **225** C5
You, *river*, China, **215** H5
You Xian, China, **206** C3
Youghal, Ireland, **309** E6
Youghal Bay, Ireland, **309** E6
Youhao, China, **211** K3
Young, Australia, **135** K5
Young, Canada, **413** S6
Young, Cape, Chatham Islands, New Zealand, **133** Q16
Young, Uruguay, **459** F4
Youngstown, U.S.A., **421** N5
Youshashan, China, **213** F5
Youssoufia, Morocco, **360** E2
Youyang, China, **206** B2
Yozgat, Turkey, **224** D5
Ypané, *river*, Paraguay, **459** F2
Ypé-Jhú, Paraguay, **459** F2
Yport, France, **305** H5
Ypres *see* Ieper, Belgium, **288** A3
Yreka, U.S.A., **418** C6
Yrghyz, Kazakhstan, **222** G3
Yser, *river*, France, **305** K4
Ystad, Sweden, **286** F5
Ystalyfera, Wales, U.K., **304** D3
Ystwyth, *river*, Wales, U.K., **304** D2
Ysyk-Köl, *lake*, Kyrgyzstan, **212** C4, *187*
Ythan, *river*, Scotland, U.K., **308** G3
Ytteresse, Finland, **285** L5
Ytterhogdal, Sweden, **286** G1
Yttermalung, Sweden, **286** F2
Yü-li, Taiwan, **206** E4
Yu Shan, *mountain peak*, Taiwan, **206** E4, *162*
Yu Xian, China, **210** F5
Yu'alliq, Jabal, *mountain peak*, Egypt, **225** B4
Yuan, *river*, Hunan, China, **206** B2
Yuan, *river*, Jiangxi, China, **206** C3
Yuan, *river*, Yunnan, China, **215** G5
Yüan-lin, Taiwan, **206** E4
Yuanjiang, China, **215** G5
Yuanling, China, **206** B2
Yuanmou, China, **215** G4
Yuanping, China, **210** F5
Yuanqu, China, **206** B1
Yuat, *river*, Papua New Guinea, **140** A4
Yuba City, U.S.A., **422** C2
Yucatán, Península, Mexico, **431** H5, *400, 402*
Yucatán, *state*, Mexico, **431** H4, *88, 90, 378*
Yucatán Channel, Cuba/Mexico, **428** D2
Yuci, China, **210** F5
Yudaokou, China, **210** G4
Yudi Shan, *mountain peak*, China, **211** H1
Yuduba, China, **215** H2
Yuechi, China, **215** H3
Yuen Long, China, **207** C4
Yuendumu, Australia, **134** G3
Yueqing, China, **206** E2
Yueqing Wan, *bay*, China, **206** E2
Yuexi, Anhui, China, **206** D2
Yuexi, Sichuan, China, **215** G3
Yueyang, China, **206** C2
Yugan, China, **206** D2
Yuhebu, China, **210** E5
Yujiang, China, **206** D2
Yukhavichy, Belarus, **299** B5
Yukhnov, Russian Federation, **299** E5
Yuki, Democratic Republic of the Congo, **368** C3
Yukon, *river*, Canada/U.S.A., **410** C3
Yukon Territory, *territoriy*, Canada, **410** F3, *381*
Yulara, Australia, **134** G4
Yulee, U.S.A., **425** M4
Yuli, China, **212** E4
Yulin, Guangxi Zhuangzu Zizhiqu, China, **206** B4
Yulin, Shaanxi, China, **210** E5
Yuma, Arizona, U.S.A., **422** F5
Yuma, Colorado, U.S.A., **423** M1
Yuma, Russian Federation, **285** R4
Yumbi, Equateur, Democratic Republic of the Congo, **368** C3
Yumbi, Maniema, Democratic Republic of the Congo, **369** E3
Yumbo, Colombia, **450** C3
Yumen, China, **213** H5
Yumenguan, China, **213** G4
Yumenzhen, China, **213** H4
Yumin, China, **212** D3
Yumurtalık, Turkey, **225** C1
Yun Gui Gaoyuan, *plateau*, China, **215** G4
Yun Ling, *mountain range*, China, **215** F4
Yun Xian, Hubei, China, **206** B1
Yun Xian, Yunnan, China, **215** G4
Yuna, *river*, Dominican Republic, **429** H3
Yunak, Turkey, **363** F1
Yunan, China, **206** B4
Yun'anzhen, China, **206** B2
Yuncheng, Shandong, China, **206** C1
Yuncheng, Shanxi, China, **206** B1
Yunfu, China, **206** C4
Yunguyo, Peru, **455** E4
Yunkai Dashan, *mountain range*, China, **206** B4
Yunmeng, China, **206** C2
Yunnan, *province*, China, **215** G4, *161*
Yunwu Shan, *mountain peak*, China, **210** G4
Yunxi, China, **206** B1
Yunxiao, China, **206** D4
Yunyang, China, **206** B2
Yuping, China, **206** B3
Yupukarri, Guyana, **451** G3
Yuqing, China, **215** H4
Yura, Bolivia, **455** E5
Yuratsishki, Belarus, **287** M5
Yurimaguas, Peru, **454** C1
Yurkino, Russian Federation, **299** G4
Yur'yev-Pol'skiy, Russian Federation, **299** G4
Yushan, China, **206** D2
Yushkozero, Russian Federation, **285** R4
Yushu, Jilin, China, **211** J3
Yushu, Qinghai, China, **215** F2
Yushutun, China, **211** H3
Yusta, Russian Federation, **222** D3
Yustozero, Russian Federation, **285** R5
Yutian, China, **212** D5
Yuty, Paraguay, **459** F3
Yuwang, China, **210** D5
Yuwotou, China, **207** A3
Yuxi, China, **215** G4
Yuxia, China, **215** H4
Yuyao, China, **206** E2
Yuzhno-Kuril'sk, Russian Federation, **209** J1
Yuzhno-Sakhalinsk, Russian Federation, **301** R5
Yuzhnoural'sk, Russian Federation, **222** G2
Yuzhnoye, Russian Federation, **209** H1
Yuzhou, China, **206** C1
Yvetot, France, **290** E2
Ywathitke, Myanmar, **205** B3

## Z

Zaandam, Netherlands, **288** B2
Zabīd, Yemen, **220** D6
Zabłudów, Poland, **289** L2
Zabok, Croatia, **294** E2
Zābol, Iran, **221** H2
Zabolot'ye, Russian Federation, **299** D5
Zabor'ye, Russian Federation, **299** C5
Zabré, Burkina Faso, **364** D2
Zabrze, Poland, **289** J3
Zabzugu, Togo, **364** E3
Zacapa, Guatemala, **428** C4
Zacapu, Mexico, **430** E5
Zacatecas, Mexico, **430** E4
Zacatecas, *state*, Mexico, **430** E4
Zacatlán, Mexico, **431** F5
Zacharo, Greece, **297** C7
Zadar, Croatia, **294** E3
Zadoi, China, **215** E2
Za'farāna, Egypt, **225** B5
Zafra, Spain, **292** D3
Żagań, Poland, **289** G3
Zaghwān, Tunisia, **362** B1
Zagora, Greece, **297** D6
Zagora, Morocco, **361** E2
Zagreb, Croatia, **294** E3, *258, 259*
Zāgros, Kūhhā-ye (Zagros Mountains), *mountain range*, Iran, **220** E2, *146, 182, 183*
Zagros Mountains *see* Zāgros, Kūhhā-ye, *mountain range*, Iran, **220** E2, *146, 182, 183*
Žagubica, Serbia, **296** C3
Zagustay, Russian Federation, **210** E2
Za'gya, *river*, China, **214** D2
Zāhedān, Iran, **221** H3
Zahirābād, India, **216** D2
Zaḩlah, Lebanon, **225** C3
Ẓahrān, Saudi Arabia, **363** H5
Ẓahrat al Baṭn, *physical feature*, Iraq, **363** H2
Zainsk, Russian Federation, **222** E1
Zaire, *province*, Angola, **368** B4
Zaïre, *river*, Democratic Republic of the Congo, **357** H6, *334*
Zaječar, Serbia, **296** D4
Zaka, Zimbabwe, **371** F3
Zakamensk, Russian Federation, **213** J2
Zakarpats'ka Oblast', *province*, Ukraine, **289** L4
Zakopane, Poland, **289** J4
Zakouma, Chad, **366** A2
Zakros, Kriti, Greece, **297** F8
Zakynthos, Ionioi Nisoi, Greece, **297** C7
Zakynthos (Zante), *island*, Ionioi Nisoi, Greece, **297** C7
Zakynthos, Porthmos, *strait*, Greece, **297** C7
Zalaegerszeg, Hungary, **289** H5
Zalanga, Nigeria, **365** G2
Zalantun, China, **211** H3
Zalău, Romania, **296** D2
Zalesovo, Russian Federation, **223** L2
Ẓalim, Saudi Arabia, **363** H4
Zalingei, Sudan, **366** B2
Zalischyki, Ukraine, **296** E1
Zalṭan, Jabal, *mountain range*, Libya, **362** C3
Zaluch'ye, Russian Federation, **299** C4
Zama Lake, Canada, **413** K2
Zambeze, *river*, Mozambique, **357** J8, *95, 312, 344, 345*
Zambezi, Zambia, **368** D5, *346*
Zambézia, *province*, Mozambique, **369** G6
Zambia, *country*, Africa, **359** H8, *312, 313, 335, 344, 346, 347*
Zamboanga, Philippines, **204** C5
Zambrów, Poland, **289** L2
Zambue, Mozambique, **369** F6
Zamora, Ecuador, **450** B5
Zamora, *river*, Ecuador, **450** B5
Zamora, Spain, **292** E2
Zamora de Hidalgo, Mexico, **430** E5
Zamość, Poland, **289** L3
Zamuro, Sierra del, *mountain range*, Venezuela, **451** F3
Zanaga, Congo, **368** B3
Zanda, China, **218** D3
Zanderij, Suriname, **452** B2
Zanesville, U.S.A., **421** M6
Zangasso, Mali, **364** C2
Zangla, India, **218** D2
Zanjān, Iran, **222** D5
Zante *see* Zakynthos, *island*, Ionioi Nisoi, Greece, **297** C7
Zanzibar, Tanzania, **369** G4, *75, 176*
Zanzibar Island, Tanzania, **369** G4, *342*
Zaokskiy, Russian Federation, **299** F5
Zaouatallaz, Algeria, **361** H4
Zaoyang, China, **206** C1
Zaozhuang, China, **206** D1
Zapadna Morova, *river*, Serbia, **296** C4
Zapadnaya Dvina, Russian Federation, **299** D4
Zapadno Sibirskaya Ravnina, *plain*, Russian Federation, **300** J3
Zapadno-Karel'skaya Vozvyshennost', *mountain range*, Russian Federation, **285** Q4
Zapadnyy Sayan, *mountain range*, Russian Federation, **213** F2
Západočeský, *administrative region*, Czech Republic, **288** F4
Zapala, Argentina, **460** C1
Zapaleri, Cerro, *mountain peak*, Chile, **458** C2
Zapata, U.S.A., **424** C6
Zapatoca, Colombia, **450** D2
Zapolyarnyy, Russian Federation, **285** Q2
Zapol'ye, Russian Federation, **299** B3
Zapopan, Mexico, **430** E4
Zaporizhzhya, Ukraine, **298** E3
Zapotal, Ecuador, **450** B4
Zaqatala, Azerbaijan, **222** D4
Zaqên, China, **214** E2
Zara, Turkey, **363** G1
Zarafshon, Uzbekistan, **222** G4
Zaragoza, Colombia, **450** C2
Zaragoza, Spain, **293** G2
Zarand, Iran, **221** G2
Zaranj, Afghanistan, **221** H2
Zarasai, Lithuania, **287** N5
Zárate, Argentina, **459** E5
Zaraysk, Russian Federation, **299** G5
Zaraza, Venezuela, **451** F2
Zarechensk, Russian Federation, **285** Q3
Zareh Sharan, Afghanistan, **218** B2
Zarghūn Shahr, Afghanistan, **218** B2
Zaria, Nigeria, **365** F2
Zarinsk, Russian Federation, **223** L2
Zărneşti, Romania, **296** E3
Žarnovica, Slovakia, **289** J4
Zarubikha, Russian Federation, **285** S2
Zarubino, Russian Federation, **211** K4
Zarumilla, Peru, **450** B5
Żary, Poland, **289** G3
Zarzaïtine, Algeria, **361** H3
Zasheyek, by Ozero Imandra, Russian Federation, **285** R3
Zasheyek, by Ozero Umbozero, Russian Federation, **285** S3
Zasheyek, Respublika Kareliya, Russian Federation, **285** Q3
Zaslawye, Belarus, **287** N5
Zāskār Mountains, *mountain range*, India, **218** D2
Zāskār, *river*, India, **218** D2
Žatec, Czech Republic, **288** F3
Zatoka, Ukraine, **296** H2
Zatyshshya, Ukraine, **296** G2
Zaunguzskiye Garagum, *desert*, Turkmenistan, **222** F4
Zave, Zimbabwe, **369** F6
Zavitinsk, Russian Federation, **211** K2
Zavodoukovsk, Russian Federation, **222** H1
Zawiercie, Poland, **289** J3
Zawīlah, Libya, **362** C3
Zāwiyat al Mukhaylá, Libya, **362** D2
Zāwiyat Masūs, Libya, **362** D2
Zawr, Ra's az, *cape*, Saudi Arabia, **220** E3
Zaysan Köli, *lake*, Kazakhstan, **212** E2
Zaysan, Kazakhstan, **223** L3
Zayü, China, **215** F3
Zazafotsy, Madagascar, **372** B5
Zban, Kazakhstan, **222** G3
Zban, *river*, Kazakhstan, **222** G3
Zblewo, Poland, **289** J2
Zd'ár nad Sázavou, Czech Republic, **289** G4
Zdvinsk, Russian Federation, **223** K2
Zeballos, Canada, **412** F7
Zeeland, *province*, Netherlands, **288** A3
Ẓe'elim, Israel, **225** C4
Ẓefat, Israel, **225** C3
Zehdenick, Germany, **288** F2
Zeitz, Germany, **288** F3
Zelenoborskiy, Russian Federation, **285** R3
Zelenogorsk, Russian Federation, **299** B2
Zelenogradsk, Russian Federation, **287** K5
Zelfana, Algeria, **361** G2
Želiezovce, Slovakia, **289** J4
Zelina, Croatia, **294** F2
Zelinggou, China, **213** H5
Zeltiöi, Latvia, **287** N4
Zèl'va, Belarus, **289** M2
Zemen, Bulgaria, **296** D4
Zémio, Central African Republic, **369** E1
Zempoaltepec, *mountain peak*, Mexico, **431** G5
Zênda, China, **215** F2
Zeng, *river*, China, **207** B2
Zengcheng, China, **207** B2
Zenica, Bosnia and Herzegovina, **294** F3
Zennor, England, U.K., **304** B4
Zenzach, Algeria, **293** J5
Žepče, Bosnia and Herzegovina, **294** F3

# GAZETTEER

Zepu, China, **212** C5
Zeravshan, *river*,
Tajikistan/Uzbekistan,
**223** H5
Zerbst, Germany, **288** F3
Zerendi, Kazakhstan, **223**
H2
Zeribet el Oued, Algeria,
**361** H2
Zermatt, Switzerland, **291**
H3
Zeven, Germany, **288** D2
Zeya, *river*, Russian
Federation, **301** P4
Zeya, Russian Federation,
**301** P4
Zeyskoye
Vodokhranilishche,
*reservoir*, Russian
Federation, **301** P4
Zeytindağ, Turkey, **297** F6
Zêzere, *river*, Portugal, **292**
D2
Zghartā, Lebanon, **225** C2
Zgierz, Poland, **289** J3
Zgorzelec, Poland, **289** G3
Zguriţa, Moldova, **296** F1
Zhabinka, Belarus, **289** M2
Zhalghyztobe, Kazakhstan,
**223** L3
Zhalpaqtal, Kazakhstan,
**222** D3
Zhaltyr, Kazakhstan, **223**
H2
Zhaludok, Belarus, **289** M2
Zhambay, Kazakhstan, **222**
E3
Zhambyl, Kazakhstan, **223**
J3
Zhambyl, *province*,
Kazakhstan, **212** A3
Zhanang, China, **214** D3
Zhanatas, Kazakhstan, **223**
H4
Zhang, *river*, China, **206** B2
Zhangaortalyq,
Kazakhstan, **223** K3
Zhangaözen, Kazakhstan,
**222** E4
Zhangaqala, Kazakhstan,
**222** D3
Zhangaqorghan,
Kazakhstan, **222** H4
Zhangbei, China, **210** F4
Zhangdiyingzi, China, **211**
J2
Zhangguangcai Ling,
*mountain range*, China,
**211** K4
Zhanghuang, China, **206**
B4
Zhangjiabian, China, **207**
A3
Zhangjiajie, China, **206** B2
Zhangjiakou, China, **210**
F4
Zhangmutou, China, **207**
C3
Zhangping, China, **206** D3
Zhangpu, China, **206** D3
Zhangshu, China, **206** C2
Zhangwu, China, **211** H4
Zhangye, China, **213** J5
Zhangzhou, China, **206** D3

Zhangzi, China, **206** C1
Zhanhe, China, **211** J2
Zhanjiang, China, **206** B4
Zhansügirov, Kazakhstan,
**212** C3
Zhanyi, China, **215** G4
Zhanyu, China, **211** H3
Zhao Xian, China, **210** F5
Zhao'an, China, **206** D4
Zhaodong, China, **211** J3
Zhaojiapu, China, **210**
G5
Zhaojue, China, **215** G4
Zhaoping, China, **206** B3
Zhaoqing, China, **206** C4
Zhaosu, China, **212** D4
Zhaotong, China, **215** G4
Zhaoyuan, China, **211** J3
Zhaozhou, China, **211** J3
Zhaqsy, Kazakhstan, **222**
H2
Zhari Namco, *lake*, China,
**219** F3
Zharkent, Kazakhstan, **223**
K4
Zharma, Kazakhstan, **223**
L3
Zharqamys, Kazakhstan,
**222** F3
Zharyq, Kazakhstan, **223** J3
Zhashui, China, **206** B1
Zhaslyk, Uzbekistan, **222**
F4
Zhaxigang, China, **218** D2
Zhaxizê, China, **215** F3
Zhayyq, *river*, Kazakhstan,
**222** E3
Zhdeneve, Ukraine, **296** D1
Zhejiang, *province*, China,
**206** D2, *161*
Zhelaniya, Mys, *cape*,
Russian Federation, **300**
H2
Zhelcha, *river*, Russian
Federation, **299** A3
Zhem, *river*, Kazakhstan,
**300** G5
Zhen'an, China, **206** B1
Zhenba, China, **215** H2
Zhengguo, China, **207** B2
Zhenghe, China, **206** D3
Zhengxiangbai Qi, China,
**210** F4
Zhengzhou, China, **206**
C1, *161*
Zhenhai, China, **206** E2
Zhenjiang, China, **206** D1
Zhenlai, China, **211** H3
Zhenlong, China, **207** C3
Zhenning, China, **215** H4
Zhenping, China, **206** B1
Zhenxiong, China, **215** H4
Zhenyuan, China, **206** B3
Zhesang, China, **215** H5
Zhetibay, Kazakhstan, **222**
E4
Zhetiqara, Kazakhstan, **222**
G2
Zhezqazghan, Kazakhstan,
**222** H3
Zhicheng, China, **206** B2
Zhichitsy, Russian
Federation, **299** C5
Zhidan, China, **215** J1

Zhigansk, Russian
Federation, **301** P3
Zhigung, China, **214** D3
Zhijiang, China, **206** B3
Zhijin, China, **215** H4
Zhilinda, Russian
Federation, **301** N2
Zhiwan Dao, *island*,
China, **207** C4
Zhizdra, *river*, Russian
Federation, **299** E5
Zhizdra, Russian
Federation, **299** E6
Zhlobin, Belarus, **298** D2
Zhob, Pakistan, **218** B3
Zhob, *river*, Pakistan, **218**
B3
Zhodzina, Belarus, **299** B5
Zhong Xian, China, **206** B2
Zhongba, China, **214** C3
Zhongdian, China, **215** F4
Zhongghar Alataū Zhotasy,
*physical feature*, China/
Kazakhstan, **212** C3
Zhongluotan, China, **207**
A2
Zhongning, China, **210** D5
Zhongshan, China, **207** A3
Zhongshan, *Chinese
research station*,
Antarctica, **470** F5
Zhongtang, China, **207** B2
Zhongwei, China, **210** D5
Zhongxiang, China, **206**
C2
Zhongxin, China, **207** B2
Zhosaly, Kazakhstan, **222**
G3
Zhoucun, China, **210** G5
Zhoukou, China, **206** C1
Zhoushan, China, **206** E2
Zhovkva, Ukraine, **289** M3
Zhovten', Ukraine, **296** H2
Zhu (Pearl), *river*, China,
**207** B2, *158*
Zhuanghe, China, **211** H5
Zhubgyügoin, China, **215**
F2
Zhucheng, China, **211** G5
Zhucun, China, **207** B2
Zhugqu, China, **215** H2
Zhuhai, China, **207** B4
Zhuji, China, **206** E2
Zhujiang Kou, *gulf*, China,
**207** B4
Zhukovka, Russian
Federation, **299** D6
Zhukovo, Russian
Federation, **299** F3
Zhuliao, China, **207** A2
Zhumadian, China, **206** C1
Zhuolu, China, **210** F4
Zhuozi, China, **210** F4
Zhuozi Shan, *mountain
peak*, China, **210** D5
Zhuryn, Kazakhstan, **222**
F3
Zhushan, China, **206** B1
Zhuxi, China, **206** B1
Zhuzhou, China, **206** C3
Zhydachiv, Ukraine, **289**
M4
Zhympīty, Kazakhstan,
**222** E2

Zhytomyr, Ukraine, **298** C2
Zi, *river*, China, **206** B2
Zia Town, Liberia, **364** C3
Žiar nad Hronom,
Slovakia, **289** J4
Zībāk, Afghanistan, **218** B1
Zibo, China, **211** G5
Zicavo, Corse, France, **295**
B5
Zichang, China, **215**
Ziębice, Poland, **289** H3
Zielona Góra, Poland, **289**
G3
Zierikzee, Netherlands,
**288** A3
Ziftâ, Egypt, **225** A4
Zighan, Libya, **362** D3
Zigon, Myanmar, **205** A3
Zigong, China, **215** H3
Ziguéy, Chad, **365** H2
Zigui, China, **206** B2
Ziguinchor, Senegal, **364**
A2
Zihag, China, **215** G3
Zihuatanejo, Mexico, **430**
C4
Zijin, China, **206** C4
Zikhron Ya'aqov, Israel,
**225** C3
Žilina, Slovakia, **289** J4
Žilinský, *administrative
region*, Slovakia, **289** J4
Zillah, Libya, **362** C3
Zillertaler Alpen, *moun-
tain range*, Austria, **288**
E5
Zilupe, Latvia, **287** N4
Zima, Russian Federation,
**301** M4
Zimatlán, Mexico, **431** F5
Zimba, Zambia, **369** E6
Zimbabwe, *country*, Africa,
**359** H8, *49, 59, 91, 95,
312, 313, 344, 345, 346,
347, 350, 351*
Zimmi, Sierra Leone, **364**
B3
Zimnicea, Romania, **296**
E4
Zinder, *department*, Niger,
**365** F2
Zinder, Niger, **365** F2
Zinjibār, Yemen, **220** E6
Zipaquirá, Colombia, **450**
D3
Ziqudukou, China, **215** E2
Zirc, Hungary, **289** H5
Zirkel, Mount, *mountain
peak*, U.S.A., **423** K1
Zitácuaro, Mexico, **431** E5
Zitong, China, **215** H3
Zittau, Germany, **289** G3
Živinice, Bosnia and
Herzegovina, **294** G3
Zixing, China, **206** C3
Ziyang, China, **206** B1
Ziyuan, China, **206** B3
Ziz, Oued, *river*, Morocco,
**361** F2
Zizhong, China, **215** H3
Zizhou, China, **210** E5
Zlatna, Romania, **296** D2

Zlatograd, Bulgaria, **297** E5
Zlatoust, Russian
Federation, **222** F1
Zlín, Czech Republic, **289**
H4
Zliţan, Libya, **362** B2
Złoczew, Poland, **289** J3
Złotoryja, Poland, **289**
G3
Złotów, Poland, **289** H2
Zmeinogorsk, Russian
Federation, **223** L2
Żmigród, Poland, **289** H3
Znamenka, Kazakhstan,
**212** C2
Znamenka, Respublika
Khasiya, Russian
Federation, **223** N2
Znamenka, Smolenskaya
Oblast', Russian
Federation, **299** E5
Znamenskoye, Omskaya
Oblast', Russian
Federation, **223** J1
Znamenskoye, Orlovskaya
Oblast', Russian
Federation, **299** E6
Żnin, Poland, **289** H2
Znojmo, Czech Republic,
**289** H4
Zobia, Democratic
Republic of the Congo,
**369** E2
Zoetermeer, Netherlands,
**288** B2
Zogang, China, **215** F3
Zogqên, China, **215** F2
Zohlaguna, Meseta de,
*mountain range*, Mexico,
**431** H5
Zoigê, China, **215** G2
Zolochiv, Ukraine, **289** M4
Zomba, Malawi, **369** G6
Zongga, China, **219** F3
Zongjiafangzi, China, **213**
H5
Zonguldak, Turkey, **224**
D4
Zorgo, Burkina Faso, **364**
D2
Zorita, Spain, **292** E3
Zornitsa, Bulgaria, **296** F4
Zorritos, Peru, **450** B5
Żory, Poland, **289** J3
Zorzor, Liberia, **364** C3
Zossen, Germany, **288** F2
Zouar, Chad, **362** C4
Zouérat, Mauritania, **360**
D4
Zoushi, China, **206** B2
Zovka, Russian Federation,
**299** B3
Zrenjanin, Serbia ,
**296** C3
Zschopau, Germany, **288**
F3
Zubova Polyana, Russian
Federation, **298** F2
Zubovo, Kaluzhskaya
Oblast', Russian
Federation, **299** E5
Zubovo, Vologodskaya
Oblast', Russian
Federation, **299** F2

Zubtsov, Russian
Federation, **299** E4
Zuénoula, Côte d'Ivoire,
**364** C3
Zufār, *region*, Oman, **220**
F5, *176*
Zug, Switzerland, **291** J3
Zug, Western Sahara, **360**
D4
Zuger See, *lake*,
Switzerland, **291** J3
Zugspitze, *mountain peak*,
Germany, **288** E5, *238*
Zuid-Holland, *province*,
Netherlands, **288** B3
Zújar, *river*, Spain, **292** E3
Zülpich, Germany, **288** C3
Zumbo, Mozambique, **369**
F6
Zumbrota, U.S.A., **420** G3
Zumpango, Mexico, **431**
F5
Zun-Torey, Ozero, *lake*,
Russian Federation, **210**
G2
Zungeru, Nigeria, **365** F3
Zunhua, China, **211** G4
Zuni Mountains, *mountain
range*, U.S.A., **423** H4
Zunyi, China, **215** H4
Zuo, *river*, China/Vietnam,
**215** H5
Zuoquan, China, **210** F5
Zuotan, China, **207** C1
Zuoyun, China, **210** F5
Županja, Croatia, **294** G3
Žur, Serbia,
**296** C4
Zürich, Switzerland, **291**
J3, *246*
Zurich, U.S.A., **419** K2
Zürich See, *lake*,
Switzerland, **291** J3
Zuru, Nigeria, **365** F2
Zutiua, *river*, Brazil, **452**
E4
Zuwārah, Libya, **362** B2
Zuwarah, Libya, **362** B2
Zvezdets, Bulgaria, **296** F4
Zvishavane, Zimbabwe,
**371** F3
Zvolen, Slovakia, **289** J4
Zvornik, Bosnia and
Herzegovina, **294** G3
Zwedru, Liberia, **364** C3
Zwelitsha, South Africa,
**371** E5
Zwettl, Austria, **289** G4
Zwickau, Germany, **288** F3
Zwierzyniec, Poland, **289**
L3
Zwoleń, Poland, **289** K3
Zwolle, Netherlands, **288**
C2
Zyembin, Belarus, **299** B5
Żyrardów, Poland, **289** K2
Zyryanovsk, Kazakhstan,
**212** E2
Zyryanskoye, Russian
Federation, **223** M1
Żywiec, Poland, **289** J4